Scholarships 2012

RELATED TITLES FOR COLLEGE-BOUND STUDENTS

College Admissions and Financial Aid

From Here to Freshman Year: College Admissions Strategies for All Four Years of High School

Get Paid to Play: Every Student Athlete's Guide to Over $1 Million in College Scholarships

Paying for College: Making the Cost of a College Education Affordable

You're Accepted: A Stress-Free and Proven Approach to Getting Into College

Test Preparation

ACT Premier with CD-ROM

ACT: Strategies, Practice, and Review

SAT Premier with CD-ROM

SAT: Strategies, Practice, and Review

12 Practice Tests for the SAT

Essay Writing for High School Students

Scholarships
2012

by Gail Schlachter, R. David Weber,
and the Staff of Reference Service Press

Introduction by Douglas Bucher

New York

Published by Kaplan Publishing, a division of Kaplan, Inc.
395 Hudson Street
New York, NY 10014

Printed in the United States of America

10 9 8 7 6 5 4 3 2 1

ISBN 13: 978-1-60978-115-6

CONTENTS

About the Authors vii

Reference Service Press viii

Preface xi

PART ONE: GETTING STARTED

Searching for Scholarships 1

A Special Note for International Students. 13

PART TWO: SCHOLARSHIP LISTINGS

Unrestricted by Subject Area 15

Humanities. 217

Sciences. 307

Social Sciences 453

INDEXES

Subject Index 531

Residency Index. 541

Tenability Index. 544

Sponsoring Organization Index. 548

Calendar Index 564

Lots of books list scholarships. What makes this book different?

1. The funding opportunities described here can be used at any number of schools.
Look through other scholarship books, and you'll see that most of them contain large numbers of scholarships that can be used only at a particular college or university. So even if you're lucky, only a handful of these school-specific scholarships will be for the schools you're considering. And even this handful of scholarship listings is of little value because the schools you apply to (or are considering applying to) will gladly send you information about all their scholarship programs free of charge.

But, not one of the scholarships listed in this book is limited to only one particular school. The result: more listings in this book have the potential to be of use to you.

2. Only the biggest and the best funding programs are covered in this book.
Most of the other scholarship books are bulked up with awards that may be worth only a few hundred dollars. While any free money you can get your hands on for college is good, you will have to be careful that you don't waste your time and money chasing scholarships that will hardly put a dent in your overall college cost burden.

The scholarships in this book all offer students the chance to receive at least $1,000 per year. So more of the scholarships in this book will really be worth the investment of your time.

3. Not one dollar of the programs listed in this book needs to be repaid.
Most scholarship books list awards that are really loans. We're not against loans, especially college loans with reduced interest rates or delayed repayment. *But of the funding opportunities covered in this book, not one dollar has to be repaid, provided stated requirements are met.* Accepting one of these scholarships need not add to the debt burden you'll face when you finish school.

In fact, we're so convinced this book contains the most helpful and most accurate scholarship information on the market that we offer satisfaction guaranteed or your money back (details on the inside front cover).

About the Authors

PART ONE

Douglas Bucher

Douglas Bucher is the Director of Financial Aid Operations at New York University (NYU), the largest private university in the United States. He also formerly served as president of the Eastern Association of Student Financial Aid Administrators and is a member of the New York Association of Student Financial Aid Administrators. He teaches seminars for the U.S. Department of Education and has conducted a variety of sessions on financial aid at many professional con- ferences. He also teaches a graduate seminar course in NYU's School of Education and acts as a consultant for public, private, and proprietary two- and four-year schools.

PART TWO

Gail Schlachter

Dr. Gail Schlachter is president of Reference Service Press, a publishing company specializing in the development of electronic and print directories of financial aid. Dr. Schlachter has taught library-related courses on the graduate-school level and has presented dozens of workshops and lectures in the field. Dr. Schlachter has served on the councils of the American Library Association (ALA) and the California Library Association, is a past president of the ALA's Reference and User Services Association, and has served as editor-in-chief of *Reference and User Services Quarterly*, the official journal of ALA's Reference and User Services Association. In recognition of her outstanding contributions to the field of reference librarianship, Dr. Schlachter has been a recipient of both the Isadore Gilbert Mudge Award and the Louis Shores–Oryx Press Award and was named the "Outstanding Alumna" by the University of Wisconsin's School of Library and Information Studies. In addition, her financial aid print resources have won numerous awards, including the Choice "Outstanding Reference Book" award, *Library Journal*'s "Best Reference Book of the Year" award, the National Education and Information Center Advisory Committee "Best of the Best" award, and the Knowledge Industry Publications "Award for Library Literature."

R. David Weber

Dr. R. David Weber has served as Reference Service Press's (RSP's) chief editor since 1988. In that capacity, he has been involved in building, refining, and maintaining RSP's award-winning financial aid database. In addition, Dr. Weber has taught at East Los Angeles College, where he was named "Teacher of the Year" on several occasions, and Harbor College. Besides his work in the area of financial aid, Dr. Weber has written a number of critically acclaimed reference books, including *Dissertations in Urban History* and the three-volume *Energy Information Guide.*

Reference Service Press

Reference Service Press (RSP) began in 1977 with a single financial aid publication, *Directory of Financial Aids for Women,* and now specializes in the development of financial aid resources in multiple formats, including books, large-print books, discs, CD-ROMs, print-on-demand reports, electronic databases, and online sources. RSP is committed to collecting, organizing, and disseminating—in both print and electronic format—the most current and accurate information available on scholarships, fellowships, loans, grants, awards, internships, and other types of funding opportunities. The company has compiled one of the largest financial aid databases currently available—with up-to-date information on more than 45,000 portable programs (not restricted to any one school) that are open to high school students, high school graduates, undergraduates, graduate students, professionals, and post doctorates. The database identifies billions of dollars in funding opportunities that will be awarded to millions of recipients each year. Using that information, RSP publishes a number of award-winning financial aid directories aimed at specific groups.

After you've mined the resources described in this book, you might be interested in continuing your funding search by looking through other RSP books. You may be able to find these titles in your local public or academic library. Or, contact RSP to order your own copy:

Reference Service Press
5000 Windplay Drive, Suite 4
El Dorado Hills, CA 95762-9319
Phone: (916) 939-9620; Fax: (916) 939-9626
Email: info@rspfunding.com
Website: www.rspfunding.com

Specialized Financial Aid Directories from Reference Service Press

College Student's Guide to Merit and Other No-Need Funding
Named "best of the best" by *Choice.* The focus here is on 1,300 merit scholarships and other no-need funding programs open specifically to students currently in or returning to college. 502 pages. ISBN 1-58841-212-1. $32.50, plus $7 shipping.

Directory of Financial Aids for Women
Published since 1977, this is the only comprehensive and current source of information on 1,500 scholarships, fellowships, grants, internships, and awards designed primarily or exclusively for women. *School Library Journal* calls this "the cream of the crop." 556 pages. ISBN 1-58841-216-4. $45, plus $7 shipping.

Financial Aid for African Americans
Selected as the "Editor's Choice" by *Reference Books Bulletin,* this unique directory describes 1,300 scholarships, fellowships, grants, awards, and internships for African Americans. 542 pages. ISBN 1-58841-217-2. $42.50, plus $7 shipping.

Financial Aid for Asian Americans
Use this award-winning source to find funding for Americans of Chinese, Japanese, Korean, Vietnamese, Filipino, or other Asian origin. Nearly 1,100 opportunities described. 348 pages. ISBN 1-58841-218-0. $40, plus $7 shipping.

Financial Aid for Hispanic Americans
Called a "landmark resource" by *Reference Books Bulletin*, this directory describes nearly 1,300 funding programs open to Americans of Mexican, Puerto Rican, Central American, or other Latin American heritage. 484 pages. ISBN 1-58841-219-9. $42.50, plus $7 shipping.

Financial Aid for Native Americans
Detailed information is provided in this award-winning directory on more than 1,300 funding opportunities open to American Indians, Native Alaskans, and Native Hawaiians. 518 pages. ISBN 1-58841-220-2. $45, plus $7 shipping.

Financial Aid for Research and Creative Activities Abroad
Nearly 1,100 funding programs (scholarships, fellowships, grants, etc.) available to support research, professional, or creative activities abroad are described here. 422 pages. ISBN 1-58841-206-7. $45, plus $7 shipping.

Financial Aid for Study and Training Abroad
Called "the best available reference source" by *Guide to Reference*, this directory covers more than 1,000 financial aid opportunities available to support structured or independent study abroad. 362 pages. ISBN 1-58841-205-9. $40, plus $7 shipping.

Financial Aid for the Disabled and Their Families
Chosen one of the "Best Reference Books of the Year" by *Library Journal*, this directory describes in detail more than 1,300 funding opportunities for these groups. 530 pages. ISBN 1-58841-204-0. $40, plus $7 shipping.

Financial Aid for Veterans, Military Personnel, and Their Dependents
According to *Reference Book Review*, this directory, with its 1,200 entries, is "the most comprehensive guide available on the subject." 482 pages. ISBN 1-58841-209-1. $40, plus $7 shipping.

High School Senior's Guide to Merit and Other No-Need Funding
Here's your guide to 1,100 merit awards and other no-need funding programs that never look at income when awarding money to high school seniors for college. 424 pages. ISBN 1-58841-210-5. $29.95, plus $7 shipping.

How to Pay for Your Degree in Business & Related Fields
Described here are more than 800 scholarships, fellowships, grants, and awards available to support undergraduate and graduate students working on a degree in business or a related field. 302 pages. ISBN 1-58841-214-8. $30, plus $7 shipping.

How to Pay for Your Degree in Education & Related Fields
Use this directory to identify 1,000 funding opportunities to support undergraduate and graduate students preparing for a career in teaching, guidance, etc. 298 pages. ISBN 1-58841-221-0. $30, plus $7 shipping.

How to Pay for Your Degree in Engineering
Check here for the 900+ biggest and best scholarships, fellowships, awards, grants, and other funding opportunities available to support undergraduate or graduate studies in all types of engineering. 324 pages. ISBN 1-58841-222-9. $30, plus $7 shipping.

How to Pay for Your Degree in Nursing
More than 800 scholarships, fellowships, and loans that support study or research for nurses or nursing students (both undergraduate and graduate) are described in this directory—more than twice the number of programs listed in any other nursing-related directory. 250 pages. ISBN 1-58841-207-5. $30, plus $7 shipping.

How to Pay for Your Law Degree
Here's information on more than 625 fellowships, loans, grants, awards, internships, and bar exam stipends available to law students working on a J.D., LL.M., or other law-related degree. There's no other guide like this one. 262 pages. ISBN 1-58841-208-3. $30, plus $7 shipping.

Money for Christian College Students
This is the only directory to describe more than 800 funding opportunities available to support Christian students working on an undergraduate or graduate degree (secular or religious). 275 pages. ISBN 1-58841-196-6. $30, plus $7 shipping.

Money for Graduate Students in the Arts & Humanities
This directory identifies nearly 1,100 funding opportunities available to support graduate study, training, research, and creative activities in the humanities. "Highly recommended" by *Choice.* 292 pages. ISBN 1-58841-197-4. $42.50, plus $7 shipping.

Money for Graduate Students in the Biological Sciences
This unique directory focuses specifically on funding for graduate study and research in the biological sciences. More than 800+ funding opportunities are described. 248 pages. ISBN 1-58841-198-2. $37.50, plus $7 shipping.

Money for Graduate Students in the Health Sciences
Described here are the 1,000 fellowships, grants, awards, and traineeships set aside just for students interested in working on a graduate degree in dentistry, genetics, medicine, nutrition, pharmacology, etc. 304 pages. ISBN 1-58841-199-0. $42.50, plus $7 shipping.

Money for Graduate Students in the Physical & Earth Sciences
Nearly 900 funding opportunities for graduate study or research in the physical and earth sciences are described in detail and accessed through five indexes. 276 pages. ISBN 1-58841-200-8. $40, plus $7 shipping.

Money for Graduate Students in the Social & Behavioral Sciences
This directory covers 1,100 funding opportunities for graduate study and research in the social sciences that are indexed by title, sponsor, subject, geographic coverage, and deadline. 316 pages. ISBN 1-58841-201-6. $42.50, plus $7 shipping.

Preface

While getting a college degree may be the best investment you will ever make, paying for it is another matter. Going to college is expensive. It can cost $100,000 or more just to complete a bachelor's degree. That's more than most students can afford to pay on their own, especially in these tough economic times. So what can you do?

Fortunately, money is available. According to the College Board, there is more than $125 billion in financial aid available to undergraduates each year. Of this, at least $62 billion comes from federal loans and grants, $24 billion from the colleges, $6 billion from tuition tax credits, $8 billion from the states, and $8 billion from employer grants and private scholarships.

How can you find out about financial aid that might be available to you? For some sources of funding, it's not difficult at all. To learn about federal resources, call 800-4-FEDAID or visit the U.S. Department of Education's website at www.ed.gov. To find out what your state is offering, go to www.rspfunding.com/finaidinfo_stateaid.html to link to your state higher education agency. Similarly, you can write to the colleges of your choice or check with your employer to learn about funding from those sources.

Information on private sources of funding is much more elusive. That's where this book can help. Here, in one place, you'll find detailed information on more than 3,000 of the biggest and best scholarships available to fund education after high school. These programs are open to high school seniors, high school graduates, currently enrolled college students, and those returning to college after a break. They can be used to support study in any area, in junior and community colleges, vocational and technical institutes, four-year colleges, and universities. No other source can match the scope, currency, and detail provided in this book. That's why we have a satisfaction guaranteed or your money back offer (see details on the inside front cover).

What's Unique about This Book?

All scholarship directories identify funding opportunities. But this directory is unique in several ways:

- **This directory covers only programs open to support college studies.** Most other directories mix together programs for a number of groups—high school students, college students, and even graduate students or post doctorates. Here, you won't spend your time sifting through programs that aren't aimed at you.

- **Only free money is identified.** If a program requires repayment or charges interest, it's not listed. Here's your chance to find out about billions of dollars in aid, knowing that not one dollar will ever need to be repaid, provided stated requirements are met.

- **Not every funding opportunity is based on need or on academics.** Many sources award money based on career plans, writing ability, research skills, religious or ethnic background, military or organizational activities, athletic success, personal characteristics, and even pure luck in random drawings.

- **The money awarded by these scholarships can be taken to any number of schools.** Unlike other financial aid directories that often list large numbers of scholarships available only to students enrolled at one specific school, all of the entries in this book are "portable."

- **Only the biggest and best funding programs are covered.** To be listed here, a program has to offer at least $1,000 per year. Many go way beyond that, paying $20,000 or more each year, or covering the full cost of college attendance. Other scholarship books are often bulked up with awards that may be worth only a few hundred dollars. While any free money you can get your hands on for college is good, you will have to be careful that you don't waste your time and energy chasing scholarships that will hardly put a dent in your overall college cost burden.

- **Searching for scholarships couldn't be easier.** You can identify funding programs by discipline, specific subject, sponsoring organization, where you live, where you want to go to school, and when you want to apply. Plus, you'll find all the information you need to decide if a program is right for you: eligibility requirements, financial data, duration, number awarded, and application date. You even get fax numbers, toll-free numbers, email addresses, and website locations (when available), along with complete contact information.

What's Not Covered?

While this book is intended to be the most current and comprehensive source of free money available to college students in the United States, there are some things we have specifically excluded:

- **Funding not aimed at incoming, currently enrolled, or returning college students.** If a program is open only to graduate school students, for instance, or to adults of any age interested in photography, it is not covered. If a scholarship is not specifically for college students, it has not been included.

- **Individual school-based programs.** Financial aid given by individual schools solely for the benefit of their own students is not covered. Instead, the directory identifies "portable" programs—ones that can be used at any number of schools.

- **Money for study outside the United States.** Only funding that supports study in the United States is covered. For information on sources of funding to go abroad, see the titles listed in the Reference Service Press section in this directory.

- **Very restrictive programs.** In general, programs are excluded if they are open only to a limited geographic area (students in specific cities or counties), are available only to members of a union, social organization, or professional association, or offer only limited financial support (less than $1,000 per year).

- **Programs that did not respond to our research inquiries.** Despite our best efforts—up to four letters and three follow-up phone calls—some organizations did not supply information. Consequently, their programs have not been included.

How to Use This Book

We've divided this book into three sections: introductory materials; a detailed list of free money available for college, organized by discipline; and a set of indexes to help you pinpoint appropriate funding programs.

Getting Started

The first section of the directory, written by Douglas Bucher, the former Director of Financial Aid Operations at Drexel University, offers tips on searching for scholarships, applying for aid, and avoiding scholarship search scams.

Scholarship Listings

The main section (part two) of the directory, prepared by Gail Schlachter, R. David Weber, and the staff of Reference Service Press, describes more than 3,000 scholarships, competitions, and awards that provide free money for college. The programs listed are sponsored by federal and state gov- errment agencies, professional organizations, foundations, educational associations, and military/ veterans organizations. All areas of the sciences, social sciences, and humanities are covered.

To help you tailor your search, the entries in this section are grouped into four main categories:

1. **Unrestricted by Subject Area.** Described here are funding opportunities that can be used to support study in any subject area (though the programs may be restricted in other ways).

2. **Humanities.** Described here are programs that 1) reward outstanding artistic and creative work by students, or 2) support college studies in the humanities, including architecture, art, creative writing, design, history, journalism, languages, literature, music, and religion.

3. **Sciences.** Described here are sources of free money that 1) reward student speeches, essays, inventions, organizational involvement, and other activities in the sciences, or 2) support college studies in a number of scientific fields, including agricultural sciences, chemistry, computer science, engineering, environmental sciences, food science, horticulture, mathematics, marine sciences, nursing, nutrition, pharmacology, and technology.

4. **Social Sciences.** Described here are programs that 1) reward outstanding speeches, essays, organizational involvement, and other activities in the social sciences, or 2) support college studies in various social science fields, including accounting, business administration, criminology, economics, education, geography, home economics, international relations, labor relations, political science, sales and marketing, sociology, social services, sports and recreation, and tourism.

Each program entry in part two has been prepared to give you a concise but clear picture of the available funding. Information, as available, is provided on organizational points of contact, program, eligibility, money awarded, duration, number of awards, and application deadline.

Indexes

To help you find the aid you need, we have included five indexes; these will let you access the listings by specific subject, residency, tenability (where you want to study), sponsoring organization, and deadline date. These indexes use a word-by-word alphabetical arrangement. Note: Numbers in the index refer to *entry* numbers, not to page numbers.

1. **Subject Index.** Use this index when you want to identify funding programs by specific subject.

2. **Residency Index.** Some programs listed in this book are restricted to residents of a particular state, region, or other geographic location. Others are open to students wherever they live. This index helps you identify programs available only to residents in your area, as well as programs that have no residency restrictions.

3. **Tenability Index.** Some programs described in this book are restricted to persons attending schools in specific cities, counties, states, or regions. This index will help you locate funding specifically for the geographic area where you attend or plan to attend school.

4. **Sponsoring Organization Index.** This index makes it easy to identify agencies that offer free money for college. Sponsoring organizations are listed alphabetically, word by word. In addition, we've used a code to help you identify which programs sponsored by these organizations fall within your general area of interest (Unrestricted by Subject Area, Humanities, Sciences, or Social Sciences).

5. **Calendar Index.** Because most financial aid programs have specific deadline dates, some may have already closed by the time you begin to look for funding. You can use the Calendar Index to identify which programs are still open.

How to Get the Most Out of This Book

To Locate Financial Aid by Discipline. If you want to get an overall picture of the funding available for any area of college study, turn to the first category, Unrestricted by Subject Area. You'll find more than 1,100 general programs that support study in any area (though they may be restricted in other ways). If you've decided on your area of specialization, turn next to the appropriate chapter (Humanities, Sciences, or Social Sciences) and browse through the listings there.

To Find Information on a Particular Financial Aid Program. If you know the name and disciplinary focus of a particular financial aid program, you can go directly to the appropriate category in part two, where you'll find program profiles grouped by discipline and arranged alphabetically by title.

To Browse Quickly Through the Listings. Turn to the section in part two that interests you (Unrestricted by Subject Area, Humanities, Sciences, Social Sciences) and read the "Summary" field in each entry. In seconds, you'll know if this is an opportunity that might apply to you. If it is, be sure to read the entire entry to make sure you meet all of the requirements. Don't apply if you don't qualify!

To Locate Financial Aid for Studies in a Particular Subject Area. Turn to the subject index first if you are interested in identifying funding by specific subject area. Be sure also to check the listings under the "General Programs" heading; these programs support studies in any area (though they may be restricted in other ways).

To Locate Financial Aid Based on Where You Live. Use the Residency Index to identify funding that supports applicants in your area. The index is subdivided by broad subject area. When using this index, be sure also to check the listings under the term "United States," because the programs indexed there have no geographic restrictions and can be used in any area.

To Locate Financial Aid Based on Where You Want to Study. Use the Tenability Index to identify funding that supports study in a particular geographic location. The index is subdivided by broad subject area. When using this index, be sure also to check the listings under the term "United States," because the programs indexed there have no geographic restrictions and can be used in any area.

To Locate Financial Aid Programs Sponsored by a Particular Organization. The Sponsoring Organization Index makes it easy to determine which groups are providing free money for college and to identify specific financial aid programs offered by a particular sponsor. Each entry number in the index is coded to indicate broad subject coverage, to help you target appropriate entries.

Let Us Hear from You

We'd like to hear from you. Send your comments, suggestions, questions, problems, or success stories to: Gail Schlachter, Kaplan Scholarships Editor, 5000 Windplay Drive, Suite 4, El Dorado Hills, CA 95762, or email her at GailSchlachter@rspfunding.com.

SAMPLE ENTRY

① ② **541 KAPLAN/NEWSWEEK "MY TURN" ESSAY COMPETITION**

③ Kaplan, Inc.
Attn: Pre-College
1440 Broadway, Eighth Floor
New York, NY 10018
Phone: (212) 997-5886; 800 KAP-TEST
Web: www.kaptest.com/essay

④ **Summary:** To recognize and reward, with college scholarships, high school students who write outstanding essays on topics related to their personal development and growth.

⑤ **Eligibility:** Open to U.S. high school students planning to attend college after graduation. Applicants must write an essay of 500 to 1,000 words on a topic of their choice in which they share an opinion, experience, or personal feeling. Judges look for direct personal experiences and observations with a fresh, original, engaging, moving, and thought-provoking point of view that appeals to a national readership. Selection is based on 1) effectiveness, insightfulness, creativity, and completeness (33%); 2) organization and development of the ideas expressed, with clear and appropriate examples to support them (33%); and 3) consistency in the use of language, variety in sentence structure and range of vocabulary, and use of proper grammar, spelling, and punctuation (33%).

⑥ **Financial data:** First prize is $5,000, second $2,000, and third $1,000. All funds are to be used for future educational needs.

⑦ **Duration:** The competition is held annually.

⑧ **Number awarded:** 10 each year: 1 first-prize winner, 1 second-prize winner, and 8 third-prize winners.

⑨ **Deadline:** January of each year.

Definitions

① **Entry number:** Consecutive number assigned to the references and used to index the entry.

② **Program title:** Title of scholarship, competition, or award.

③ **Sponsoring organization:** Name, address, telephone number, toll-free number, fax number, email address, and website location (when information was supplied) for the organization sponsoring the program.

④ **Summary:** Identifies the major program requirements; read the rest of the entry for additional detail.

⑤ **Eligibility:** Qualifications required of applicants and factors considered in the selection process.

⑥ **Financial data:** Financial details of the program, including fixed sum, average amount, or range of funds offered, expenses for which funds may and may not be applied, and cash-related benefits supplied (e.g., room and board).

⑦ **Duration:** Time period for which support is provided; renewal prospects.

⑧ **Number awarded:** Total number of recipients each year or other specified period.

⑨ **Deadline:** The month by which applications must be submitted. When the sponsor has not specified a deadline date for a program, this field is not included in our entry description.

Note: The information provided for the funding opportunities covered in this book was verified when the entries were prepared. Since then, it is possible that some changes may have occurred (for example, in the address or website URL). If you have any questions about the information provided in a specific entry, send an email to GailSchlachter@rspfunding.com. Be sure to include the name of the program and its entry number as part of your query.

PART ONE

GETTING STARTED

by Douglas Bucher

Searching for Scholarships

If you are reading this book, it's a good bet that you're looking for money to help you achieve your higher-education goals. As you will see, the key to success in this area is motivated, energetic research—a process that you have already started by reading these very words. There are numerous sources of aid available; many of these are listed in this volume. In addition, this book includes other strategies for finding resources, locally and globally, using both technology, such as computers and the Internet, and old-fashioned methods, such as talking to people who may be able to help.

All of the information we will discuss is available to you in books or other easily obtainable sources that will cost you little or nothing to use. Any company that says you have to pay them to research the same data you could research on your own is not worthy of your dollars. Ignore all of the promises. In most cases, the companies will provide no more information than you could have gleaned yourself.

Scholarship Scams

For years, in fact, students' desire to finance their educations has been fodder for those who would take advantage of people with trusting natures. Financial aid personnel at colleges and universities have been aware of such unethical approaches for some time now, and recently the Federal Trade Commission (FTC) issued a warning about these "scholarship scams." Among the telltale signs you should look for—and then stay far away from—are the following:

"*We guarantee you'll get a scholarship or your money back.*" In reality, almost every financial aid applicant is eligible for something. A guarantee like this is, therefore, worth nothing.

"*You can't get this information anywhere else.*" Nonsense. We live in an information-rich society. Any legitimate source of financial aid will make information widely available through a number of means and media. Don't pay a premium for what is free or readily available in an inexpensive format—like this book!

"*Credit card or bank account number required to hold scholarship.*" Don't even think about it. Legitimate scholarship providers do not require this information as a condition for you to receive funds.

"*We'll do all the work.*" Okay, this one is tempting. We are all very busy people with a million things to do who feel that we can't possibly find the time to do this kind of research. But there is only one person who is going to benefit from the kind of work that this entails, and that is you. A pitch like this appeals to the lazy instincts in all of us, but there is no one you can expect to be more motivated to do the research than yourself.

"*The scholarship will cost you some money.*" This one hardly deserves comment. There is a strong preconception in this country that, as a general rule, you need to spend money to make money. While this may be true on Wall Street, it doesn't apply here. The investment you are making is in your education, and the best resource you can invest is your time.

"*You are a finalist*" or "*You have been selected*" in a contest you never entered. The absurdity of this is clear once you think about it for a moment. It is very flattering to think that some organization pored through the records of every person in the country to find that you are the most qualified to receive its generous award—and you didn't even apply! Remember, if it seems too good to be true, it is.

In other words, *caveat emptor!*

Setting a Timetable for Your Search

If there is one piece of advice that can be a key to a successful search for scholarship funding, it is to start early. In fact, keep in mind that each step described in this book requires a good deal of time. Furthermore, many small sources of funding have deadlines some 9 to 12 months before the beginning of the term for which you will be applying.

When should you start? The answer depends on your personal pace. If you have the time and energy to research a subject extensively for a short period of time, you could start some 14 months before the beginning of school. If, on the other hand, you wish to make this a more leisurely process, give yourself a good 18 months. In any case, the bottom line is that you can never begin too early. When you are done reading this, sit down with a calendar and make a plan. When can you start? How much time can you devote each week?

Here is a summary timetable to help you plan:

- *24–18 months before money is needed:* Perform the extensive searches discussed in this chapter.
- *18–12 months before money is needed:* Write for applications; follow up if necessary.
- *–9 months before money is needed:* Mail all applications with required documentation.
- *9–6 months before money is needed:* Follow up with any organization from which you have not heard a decision (if deadline has passed).
- *Summer before school*: Notify the financial aid office of any scholarships you have been awarded. Be sure to ask what effect this will have on earlier awards and your options.
- *Late summer right before school:* Write thank-you notes to organizations.
- *Fall:* Begin the process again for renewing scholarships and finding new sources of aid.

Types of Scholarships

The types of scholarships you may receive for your education can be broken down into three general categories: individual scholarships, state scholarships, and loans.

Individual Scholarships

While going through your college search, be sure to ask admissions officers about scholarships. Each school has different rules for scholarship consideration. Be sure to find out about all scholarships available, what must be done to be considered, and—very important—the deadline by which to apply. More and more schools are offering scholarships for reasons other than athletic or academic achievement. Some scholarships are reserved for very specific types of students. See if any of these exist at the colleges to which you are applying. Much of this information might be on their home page, so you can research on your own.

Become familiar with your college's financial aid office, which might be able to provide additional information on scholarship sources. At some schools, the financial aid officers are more familiar with scholarship sources than the admissions officers.

Another great source of scholarship information might be the academic departments with which you are affiliated. Many of the faculty members know about scholarships specifically for your major. Some departments have their own scholarships that other offices on campus might not even know about. Professors also have many contacts outside of the college that might be sources of scholarship information.

State Scholarships

Some state education authorities and other state agencies offer assistance above and beyond the usual tuition-assistance programs. Some states offer aid for particular fields of study to residents of the state who remain in-state to complete their studies. You should contact your state's higher-education agency to investigate opportunities.

Loans and Forgivable Loans

There is another form of aid that predominates in certain fields, particularly those with a shortage of qualified professionals. Often called *forgivable loans,* these arrangements provide funding for school and a guaranteed job after graduation.

Sometimes offered by private employers, sometimes by government agencies, forgivable loans work in the following way: An organization provides funding for a student's academic expenses in the form of a loan. In return, the student agrees to work for the organization (under terms usually outlined in a contract) for a given period of time. If the student keeps up his or her part of the bargain, the loan will be forgiven or reduced. If the student chooses not to work for the organization, he or she is given a repayment schedule and must pay back the entire balance with interest. Depending on the field, the jobs provided are usually competitively paid, though more often than not, they are located in areas that are underserved or understaffed.

Some organizations offer regular loans as well as scholarships. Some philanthropic agencies even offer interest-free loans to students. These can be very good opportunities to save money on interest you would otherwise pay on federal or private loans. Again, consider carefully the terms of any loan agreement you sign.

Getting On with the Search

There are a number of sources of aid to consider and several strategies for finding them. Some sources may be obscure, while others may be quite obvious to you. Who might have money to give? Unions, professional organizations, high schools, clubs, lodges, foundations, and local and state governments might have resources to share with you. At the very least, they are worth exploring.

A parent can easily check with his or her union or professional organization regarding available opportunities. A teacher, guidance counselor, or professor might know of opportunities with a variety of organizations.

Many high school guidance offices have a list of scholarships that have been secured by former students. These scholarships often are provided by local agencies that lack the resources to publicize them in other ways. Contacting guidance offices at local high schools is an effective way to canvass the entire community. While the local scholarships might be small, they can add up to larger sums of money.

You might even consider contacting civic, fraternal, religious, and business organizations in your community. Many of them have scholarships that are not well publicized. These awards are also usually small, but they add up quickly. These organizations enjoy supporting the future of their communities through education and make themselves visible in the yellow pages or on lists at local chambers of commerce. Even if you don't know anyone at a given organization, you should still contact it about the possibility of a scholarship.

I have met students in my career who actually talked some of these organizations into creating scholarships. A few hundred dollars may not be much to an organization, but it can really help an individual recipient. Soliciting these organizations might make you that lucky recipient. They might like your tenacity and award you a scholarship for this. Don't be pushy, but do be aggressive.

Employers represent another major local source of scholarships. You might be working part-time or full-time for a company that offers scholarships to its employees. If it is a national chain, your boss might not even know if a scholarship exists. Ask your boss to check with the central office. If you are planning to attend school locally and keep your job, you might want to check out tuition remission scholarships from your employer.

Many parents or relatives have employers that offer scholarships to dependents. Have your parents check with their benefits/personnel office to see if any programs exist. Don't assume you have to be a high school student or live at home to qualify; you'll find out if such restrictions exist when you ask. Many of these scholarships can be awarded to dependents other than just sons or daughters. Ask all your family members to check out the possibilities.

Graduate Funding

A graduate student is one who is pursuing an advanced degree beyond the bachelor's. When an individual has not yet received a bachelor's degree, he or she is referred to as an undergraduate student. While some aid resources are specifically geared toward undergraduate students, others are earmarked solely for graduate students involved in advanced study of a given field. Knowing this will help you avoid wasting your time on resources for which you are not eligible. Concentrate only on scholarships available to you.

Books

There are many places to search for scholarships. This book contains extensive lists of scholarships, but no book can be totally inclusive. Therefore, as with any research project, you should not depend on only one source. Multiple sources will yield the most extensive data and thus the most scholarship dollars.

There is usually a scholarship section in the reference room of any public library. Many of these books focus exclusively on particular types of scholarships for majors, grade levels, etc., saving you time you would otherwise spend reading fruitlessly. Of course, there is always the chance that human error may enter into the picture, and you may overlook a valuable source. Having family members look through the same books you're reading will allow you to compare lists and eliminate duplicates. Many people also do group searches with friends. The possibility of your friends applying for the same scholarships should not deter you, because most scholarships offer more than one award, and having more eyes search the same books will reduce the chance of overlooking resources.

Online Resources

Students are increasingly turning to the Internet for scholarship searches, many of which allow you to access data free of charge. The great advantage of using the Internet is that it is less labor-intensive than using books; the computer can match details about yourself with criteria in the database faster than you can, saving valuable time. Another advantage is that most of these sites are up-to-date and have the most current information. Criteria for scholarships change, and using the Internet will allow you to search for the most current criteria. In addition, many schools list their own scholarships with these services, so you may discover special scholarships at schools you might attend. In some cases, you can apply online for scholarships.

There's a good deal of overlap among these databases, but you'll find exclusive listings in each one. Try, then, to search a number of databases; eliminate duplicates by checking the application information on the listings. If you get duplicates, use the application information from the most recently updated scholarship listing.

It's important to have a good basic knowledge about financial aid before searching for scholarships. The Kaplan website at www.kaptest.com is a good place to begin.

Another excellent reference is the "Parents and Students" page on the National Association of Student Financial Aid Administrators (NASFAA) website at www.nasfaa.org. This organization is the professional association for financial aid administrators, and it has links to extensive resources for financial aid.

Many colleges now have websites that contain important information about aid. You may be able to get information about scholarships offered through the college and how to apply. Many of these sites also have links to other financial aid information or scholarship search databases. Check the sites of all colleges you are considering.

Some other sites that might be helpful in your research include the following:

- U.S. Department of Education; www.ed.gov/students
- U.S. Department of Education: Federal Student Aid; www.studentaid.ed.gov
- FastWeb—Scholarship Search; www.fastweb.com
- Scholarship Resource Network Express; www.srnexpress.com
- Scholarships.com; www.scholarships.com
- Reference Service Press Funding; www.rspfunding.com
- Sallie Mae College Answer: www.collegeanswer.com

Many high schools, colleges, and libraries have purchased scholarship databases that you can use to broaden your search. They may not be as up-to-date as the Internet sources, but they should not be overlooked.

How to Apply

As previously mentioned, early planning is important to a successful scholarship search. Once you have your list of addresses of possible donors, you must contact them. Be sure to check the application deadlines for the scholarships you have discovered. Eliminate any for which the deadline has passed or will soon pass (usually within six to eight weeks). This way, you will not waste the donor's or your time. Scholarships that you eliminate now could be resources for following years. Remember, the college experience lasts more than one year; your scholarship research should extend for the number of years you need to complete your degree.

Writing the First Letter

Your first letter to a scholarship provider should be a very simple letter of introduction. Some providers require the initial processing to be done online through a scholarship database. If you must write a letter, it probably will not be read by the actual committee that will choose the scholarship recipient, so there is no need to go into great detail about yourself or why you are applying. Keep it simple so the request moves quickly. Use a regular business letter format, similar to the sample letter below.

Sample Letter of Introduction

Today's Date

AAA Foundation
999 7th Avenue
New York, NY 10000

Attn: Talent Scholarship Office

Dear AAA Foundation,

I am a high school student at ABC High School and am applying to attend XYZ College for fall 2011.

I would like to receive application forms for the Talent Scholarship that I read about in Kaplan's *Scholarships 2011.*

Also, I would like to receive any other scholarship or fellowship program information that is available through your organization. Enclosed is a self-addressed, stamped envelope for your convenience. I have also provided a phone number and email address if you would like to contact me.

Thank you in advance for your assistance and information.

Sincerely,

Suzy Student
123 High Street
Philadelphia, PA 19100
(555) 444-4444
suzys@xxx.com

Try to address the letter to a specific individual. If you have a phone number, call to make sure the letter is going directly to the right office. If there is no phone number or specific office, send your letter to the attention of the scholarship's name. Someone in the organization will know which office should receive your request.

Be sure to date your letter so you remember when it was sent. Include your return address so that the organization can easily send you the application. Keep your letter brief; its purpose is simply to request an application. It will not be used to make any recipient decisions; that is the purpose of the application.

The text should mention the specific scholarships for which you are applying. Some agencies administer more than one scholarship, so this will help ensure that they send you the correct application. If an organization administers more than one scholarship, and you are applying for more than one of them, you should use a separate letter for each scholarship. Mail these letters in separate envelopes.

The letter should briefly describe how you will use the scholarship money (e.g., to attend a certain college, to conduct research, etc.) and it should also mention how you found out about the scholarship. Many agencies like to know how their information is disseminated. They want to make sure it is going to the correct "market" and to a diverse population. They will appreciate this data as they plan future cycles. You should also tell them when you intend to use the money so that they send you information for the right year, and ask them to send any other scholarship applications that they administer that might be appropriate for you. Include a phone number and/or an email address in case the organization wants to contact you.

There is no need to send the letter by certified mail, but be sure to include a self-addressed, stamped envelope with the letter. Many of these organizations are nonprofit and will appreciate the help to reduce postage costs. A self-addressed envelope will also get you an earlier response, because the organization won't have to type an envelope. Remember, time is critical!

The Follow-up Letter

Once the initial letters have been mailed, carefully keep track of responses. Be sure to note the application deadline (if known) of each scholarship for your records. Obviously, those due the soonest should be watched very carefully.

If you still have not received anything after six to eight weeks, it is appropriate to send a second letter. You should send your original letter (with a new date) again as if it had never been sent to the organization. It is not wise to send a different letter that says something about the organization not getting or not answering your first request. That could be perceived as being too pushy. You don't want to turn off any possible donors.

If you send a second letter and still receive no response, you might not want to send another letter. Even if the organization's listing contains the most up-to-date information, there's a chance the organization is no longer offering scholarships. You might want to call to ask if the organization has your application and will mail it soon, or if the organization is no longer offering the scholarship. If you don't have a contact number, use directory assistance.

When you call, remember to be polite. You might want to begin your conversation by asking general questions about the scholarship. This way, you can discreetly find out if it is still being offered. If it isn't being offered, ask if the organization has any new scholarship programs for which you qualify. If so, have them send you an application. If the scholarship is still being offered, tell them you have sent a request and want to make sure that they have received it (remember, don't be too aggressive). You might find that it is not easy to confirm that they have the request. If this is the case, ask if you can fax a copy of the letter. Some agencies will be able to tell you if they have the letter, in which case you should ask when you can expect to receive the application. Be sure to confirm the deadline for submission.

Be sure to keep good records on the progress of each individual search. Record notes and conversations on the file copy of the letter so you can easily check the status of the search. Organizations that drop out along the way should be considered when you begin your search again the following year.

The Application

Once you have secured the applications, it's time to begin the process of completing them. You should approach this step as if you are applying for a job. Initial impressions on paper are very important, so you want your application to stand out from all the others. Neatness is very important. You should type your application but first make several photocopies so you can go through some drafts before the final edition. Use all personal resources to review your various drafts. The application should be your own, but seeking input from others can improve it.

Be sure to read the entire application and any accompanying instructions before completing it, because failing to answer as instructed might eliminate you from consideration. For most scholarships, there are many more applicants than recipients. It is easy to eliminate the applicants who did not provide all requested information. Don't lose out because of a mistake that could have been avoided with proper planning.

Many applications require supplemental information from other sources. If such information is needed, be sure to plan your time to secure what is requested. Some items, such as academic transcripts and letters of reference, might take some time to obtain. Don't wait until the last minute; it might be too late to send in a complete application. The importance of planning cannot be overemphasized.

If letters of recommendation are needed, seek people who will provide the most positive influence on your application. You might need recommendations for many of the applications. If this is the case, it is best to have these recommendations tailored to the specific application, because general recommendations do not make as much of an impact. Find out if the recommendations are to be sealed and included with the application or if they are to be sent in separately by the recommendation writers. If the recommendations must be separate, tell the writers not to send them until the day you expect your application to reach the organization, because it is easier for the scholarship provider to match up documents if the application arrives first. If any of the documents are misplaced, you could be eliminated from consideration.

If the instructions say nothing about enclosing other documents, consider including a cover letter with your application. This letter should be short and precise, highlighting the reasons why you would make an excellent recipient of the scholarship. A letter with bullet points often is most effective. You might also want to include a statement of your academic and career objectives and how the donor's scholarship would influence these. A cover letter might help differentiate your application from the others, but don't overdo it. A quick summary is all that is needed.

In mailing your application, there are different techniques that can be used to ensure that it is received. A simple approach is to send the application via certified mail so that you can be sure the envelope gets to the organization. Another approach is to send a response form for the organization with a self-addressed, stamped envelope. This could be a check-off letter to acknowledge that all necessary documents have been received. This approach is particularly helpful if documents are being sent under separate cover. If you send the application via first-class mail, you might want to call the scholarship office (if you have the phone number) a few weeks later to make sure it was received.

When You Get Your Scholarship(s)

Congratulations! You've done the hard work and are now receiving aid from one or a number of organizations. What should you do next?

Thank-You Letters

If you are awarded a scholarship by an organization, foundation, or individual, an important final step is the thank-you letter. After all, many of these organizations award scholarships for purely philanthropic reasons, and the only immediate reward they can expect is sincere thanks. Thank-you letters are an effective method to communicate gratitude, lay groundwork for future renewal, and encourage the continuation of these programs for future recipients.

The letter itself need not be a terribly complicated affair. Short, simple, sincere, and to the point will do just fine (see the sample letter below). You do not need to, nor should you, copy this version verbatim. Your thank-you letter should, like your initial letters and application, let your own personality shine through. If you have nice penmanship, a handwritten version may help achieve the desired personal effect. Remember, you are receiving an award because you deserve it and because someone is willing to grant it. Don't be afraid to let your happiness show!

Sample Thank-You Letter

Today's Date

AAA Foundation
999 7th Avenue
New York, NY 10000

To Whom It May Concern (or, if you have a contact name, by all means use it!),

I am taking this occasion to express my deep appreciation for the opportunity that your generous (grant, loan, etc.) has given me. I know that it will allow me to achieve my goals, and I hope that the results will justify your faith in me.

Thank you for your time and attention.

Sincerely,

Your name

Notifying the School

You must tell your school about any outside scholarships you receive. Most financial aid packages need to be adjusted in order to "make room" for outside sources of aid. This is because most packages contain federal aid and therefore have to follow federal guidelines as to how much aid a student who receives other forms of aid can receive. The internal policies of various schools might also require changes to your package. Most financial aid offices will reduce the least desirable forms of aid first (e.g., loans with higher interest rates, work-study).

If your school guarantees its own scholarship over your academic period and the outside award does not, or it is explicitly one-time-only, it may make more financial sense to turn down the outside offer in order to keep the money your school is offering.

Depending on the kind of outside aid you are receiving, you might also have to make arrangements with the business or bursar's office of your college. Depending on the documentation you have, your school might extend credit to you based upon a certain expectation of funds.

Finally, remember that the aid you are receiving may be contingent on certain aspects of your enrollment; you may have to register for a certain number of credits or a certain major, for example. Keep any requirements for the award in mind as you enroll in school.

Renewing Scholarships for Subsequent Years

Renewal procedures vary depending on the kind of award you receive. Some groups offer one-time-only forms of aid, while others automatically renew previous recipients as long as they are enrolled in an eligible program. More commonly, scholarship programs require new applications each year from all interested parties. Remember that you've done it before; use your knowledge of the process to your advantage. Start early in gathering applications, recommendations, and other supporting materials to reapply for your hard-won award. At this time, you should also consider using the research you have already done to reapply for aid for which you may not have been eligible the previous year. There is no reason to limit your options and waste your hard work from the year before.

Once you are in school, there are usually many announcements of large-scale scholarship competitions. Most schools have specific offices that coordinate these prestigious awards. Sometimes this coordination is done at the financial aid office, but not always. Begin at the aid office; if they don't coordinate or know about these awards, check with the academic dean. Academic deans administer applications for the many awards that are associated with strong academic performance.

Summary

If you remember nothing else from this chapter, be sure to recall the following key points:

Start Early

Give yourself plenty of time to find what you are looking for and apply for it. Missed deadlines are nobody's fault but your own, and even the most benevolent organization will usually not make exceptions to its deadline rules.

Use All Resources and Strategies Available to You

Don't hobble your search by ignoring possibilities you don't know much about. Investigate everything, because you never know when an unlikely source of funding may decide to grant you a scholarship. Look everywhere you can, using every tool available to you. Be sure to use the power of the Internet. Anything else would be cheating yourself.

Know What You Are Looking For

On the other hand, when it becomes clear that a particular source is not appropriate for you, move on. If you are going to be an undergraduate student and you find a listing for graduate aid, it is probably pointless to follow that path any farther.

Follow All Steps and Instructions

You would be surprised at how many people ignore this simple advice. Remember, you are asking for assistance with your education. The least you can do is precisely follow the instructions given to you. One of the qualities these organizations might be looking for is an ability to read and understand instructions and deadlines.

Be Confident and Self-Assured but Polite and Respectful

You need to have a good self-image, a high level of confidence in your abilities, and pride in your past achievements. But remember, nobody owes you anything, and if you treat people with anything less than polite respect, you are almost automatically proving yourself to be unworthy of their assistance. Just show folks the same respect and courtesy that you expect to be shown yourself.

Remember to Thank Those Who Have Helped

Remember, the most that many of these organizations and individuals receive in return for their generosity is the occasional thank you (and maybe a tax deduction!). An expression of gratitude will confirm that they have made the right choice, and it will lay the groundwork for possible renewals.

Don't Pay Anyone to Do This Work for You

No need to dwell on this any further. You have been warned, but if you want to learn more about this subject, the FTC in 1996 inaugurated "Project $cholar$cam," an educational campaign to alert students and parents about fraudulent scholarship companies. These warnings can be found on its website at www.ftc.gov/bcp/conline/edcams/scholarship.

With that, good luck in your search for financial aid and, more importantly, best wishes in all of your academic endeavors.

A Special Note for International Students

In our quickly shrinking world, cross-border education has become an ever more important feature of American colleges. Large and small schools alike are sending students abroad in increasing numbers and have opened at least part of their U.S. enrollment to students from around the world.

If you are a non-U.S. student who is considering coming here to study, you probably already know that while American colleges and universities are highly regarded around the world, the American custom of actually paying for an education is truly a foreign notion. Many countries provide free or heavily subsidized higher education for their citizens. Study in the United States, in contrast, requires careful financial planning—especially for international students, who are cut off from most need-based U.S. government aid programs.

While some students who come here receive funding from their college or university—or from the U.S. government—and others are supported by their home government, the vast majority are here without support other than their savings and family back home. The rules governing those residing in the United States on a student visa largely prohibit or limit the ability to work. The result is that for all but the wealthiest families, study in the United States requires a great deal of sacrifice, and for many it is not even in the realm of possibility.

Fortunately, many of the resources discussed in this book are not necessarily limited to U.S. students. Most of the advice within these pages applies to the international student just as much as to the domestic student. In fact, the one piece of advice that this book hopes to drive home more than any other—start early!—applies to international students even more. Despite the Internet revolution (a technology that you should certainly take advantage of), much business continues to be transacted through the mail. As you may know, international post brings a whole new meaning to the term *snail mail.*

Of course, a key part of your research should be to look for financial assistance at the school you plan to attend. The admissions and financial aid offices may have information on both institutional and external sources of assistance. Many schools also have offices that specialize in assisting international students in all facets of the enrollment process, including finding or facilitating sources of funding. Check your college's website for a guide to services it offers.

There are other sources of information particularly designed for international students, as well:

In addition to administering the Fulbright program, the Institute of International Education (IIE) is a particularly rich source of information on all aspects of international education in the United States:

Institute of International Education
809 United Nations Plaza
New York, NY 10017-3580 USA
Phone: (212) 984-5400
Fax: (212) 984-5452
Website: www.iie.org

Another source of information for international students is NAFSA: Association of International Educators. This is the professional association of those who administer the college international student offices mentioned above.

NAFSA: Association of International Educators
1307 New York Avenue, N.W., 8th Floor
Washington, DC 20005-4701 USA
Phone: (202) 737-3699
Fax: (202) 737-3657
Website: www.nafsa.org

You may also visit the Financial Aid Information Page (FinAid) at www.edupass.org for more general information about financing a U.S. education.

While financial resources for international students are by no means plentiful, opportunities do exist. As international education becomes an ever more important feature of American higher education, you can be sure that more sources of funding will become available. Some schools have begun to work with banks to develop financing tools for this key population. More developments are sure to follow.

Unrestricted

1 AARP WOMEN'S SCHOLARSHIP PROGRAM

American Association of Retired Persons
Attn: AARP Foundation
601 E Street, N.W.
Washington, DC 20049
Phone: (202) 434-3525; (888) OUR-AARP; TDD: (877) 434-7598
Web: www.aarp.org/womensscholarship

Summary: To provide financial assistance to mature women (40 years of age and older) who are interested in returning to college.

Eligibility: Open to women who are at least 40 years of age. Priority is given to women who 1) are raising the children of another family member; 2) are in low-paying jobs and lacking a retirement benefit and/or health insurance; or 3) have been out of the work force for more than 5 years. Applicants must be planning to enroll as an undergraduate at a community college, 4-year university, or technical school. Selection is based on personal circumstances and achievements, educational goals, financial need, and the likely impact of the scholarship on the applicants' lives, families, and communities.

Financial data: Stipends range from $500 to $5,000, depending on the need of the recipient and the cost of the education or training program. Funds are paid directly to the institution to be used for payment of tuition, fees, and books.

Duration: 1 year; may be renewed.

Number awarded: Varies each year; recently, more than 200 of these scholarships, worth more than $450,000, were awarded.

Deadline: March of each year.

2 ACADEMIC COMPETITIVENESS GRANTS

Department of Education
Attn: Federal Student Aid Information Center
P.O. Box 84
Washington, DC 20044-0084
Phone: (319) 337-5665; (800) 4-FED-AID; TDD: (800) 730-8913
Web: www.FederalStudentAid.ed.gov

Summary: To provide financial assistance for undergraduate education to students who can demonstrate financial need and completion of a rigorous high school program.

Eligibility: Open to U.S. citizens who are high school seniors and first-year undergraduate students. Applicants must demonstrate financial need and qualify for a federal Pell Grant. They must also have completed a high school program as determined by their state or local education agency and recognized by the U.S. Department of Education.

Financial data: Grants are $750 for the first year of undergraduate study or $1,300 for the second year. Funding is in addition to that provided by the Pell Grant. Recipients must earn a GPA of 3.0 or higher in their first year of college to qualify for the second year of support.

Duration: Up to 2 years.

Number awarded: Varies each year.

Deadline: Deadline not specified.

3 ACCESS MISSOURI FINANCIAL ASSISTANCE PROGRAM

Missouri Department of Higher Education
Attn: Student Financial Assistance
3515 Amazonas Drive
Jefferson City, MO 65109-5717
Phone: (573) 751-2361; (800) 473-6757; Fax: (573) 751-6635
Email: info@dhe.mo.gov
Web: www.dhe.mo.gov/accessmo.html

Summary: To provide financial assistance to college students in Missouri who demonstrate financial need.

Eligibility: Open to residents of Missouri who are full-time students working on their first baccalaureate degree at a participating postsecondary school in the state. Applicants must have an expected family contribution (EFC) of $12,000 or less. Students working on a degree or certificate in theology or divinity are not eligible. U.S. citizenship or permanent resident status is required.

Financial data: At public 2-year colleges, stipends range from $300 to $1,000; at public 4-year colleges and universities, stipends range from $1,000 to $2,150; at private institutions, stipends range from $2,000 to $4,600.

Duration: 1 year; may be renewed, provided the recipient maintains a GPA of 2.5 or higher and meets the financial need limitation.

Number awarded: Varies each year; recently, 38,958 of these scholarships, worth more than $72 million, were awarded.

Deadline: March of each year.

4 ADULT SKILLS EDUCATION PROGRAM

Career College Association
Attn: Imagine America Foundation
1101 Connecticut Avenue, N.W., Suite 901
Washington, DC 20036
Phone: (202) 336-6719; Fax: (202) 408-8102
Email: torianb@imagine-america.org
Web: www.imagine-america.org/scholarship/02-about-ASEP.asp

Summary: To provide financial assistance to adults (over 21 years of age) interested in attending a career college.

Eligibility: Open to adults over 21 years of age who have a high school diploma, have a GED, or can pass an Ability to Benefit test. Applicants must be interested in attending 1 of the more than 500 career colleges that participate in the program. They must complete a student assessment provided by the National Center for Competency Testing (NCCT). All applications are submitted to the college that the student wishes to attend. Selection is based on the results of the NCCT assessment. U.S. citizenship or permanent resident status is required.

Financial data: The stipend is $1,000. Funds must be used for payment of tuition at a participating career college.

Duration: 1 year; nonrenewable.

Number awarded: Varies each year; each participating career college determines how many scholarships it wishes to award.

Deadline: June of each year.

5 AER STATESIDE SPOUSE EDUCATION ASSISTANCE PROGRAM

Army Emergency Relief
200 Stovall Street
Alexandria, VA 22332-0600
Phone: (703) 428-0000; (866) 878-6378; Fax: (703) 325-7183
Email: aer@aerhq.org
Web: www.aerhq.org/education_spouseeducation_StateSide.asp

Summary: To provide financial assistance for college to the dependent spouses of Army personnel living in the United States.

Eligibility: Open to spouses of Army soldiers on active duty, widow(er)s of soldiers who died while on active duty, spouses of retired soldiers, and widow(er)s of soldiers who died while in a retired status. Applicants must be residing in the United States. They must be enrolled or accepted for enrollment as a full-time student at an approved postsecondary or vocational institution. Study for a second undergraduate or graduate degree is not supported. Financial need is considered in the selection process.

Financial data: The maximum stipend is $2,800 per academic year.

Duration: 1 year; may be renewed up to 3 additional years.

Number awarded: Varies each year. Recently, 546 spouses received $1,517,400 in support.

Deadline: February of each year.

6 AFRICAN AMERICAN FUTURE ACHIEVERS SCHOLARSHIP PROGRAM

Ronald McDonald House Charities
Attn: U.S. Scholarship Program
One Kroc Drive
Oak Brook, IL 60523
Phone: (630) 623-7048; Fax: (630) 623-7488
Email: info@rmhc.org
Web: rmhc.org/what-we-do/rmhc-u-s-scholarships

Summary: To provide financial assistance for college to African American high school seniors in specified geographic areas.

Eligibility: Open to high school seniors in designated McDonald's market areas who are legal residents of the United States and have at least 1 parent of African American or Black Caribbean heritage. Applicants must be planning to enroll full-time at an accredited 2- or 4-year college, university, or vocational/technical school. They must have a GPA of 2.7 or higher. Along with their application, they must submit a personal statement, up to 2 pages in length, on their African American or Black Caribbean background, career goals, and desire to contribute to their community; information about unique, personal, or financial circumstances may be added. Selection is based on that statement, high school transcripts, a letter of recommendation, and financial need.

Financial data: Most awards are $1,000 per year. Funds are paid directly to the recipient's school.
Duration: 1 year; nonrenewable.
Number awarded: Varies each year; since RMHC began this program, it has awarded more than $37 million in scholarships.
Deadline: February of each year.

7 AIR FORCE ROTC GENERAL MILITARY COURSE INCENTIVE

U.S. Air Force
Attn: Headquarters AFROTC/RRUC
551 East Maxwell Boulevard
Maxwell AFB, AL 36112-5917
Phone: (334) 953-2091; (866) 4-AFROTC; Fax: (334) 953-6167
Email: afrotc1@maxwell.af.mil
Web: afrotc.com/learn-about/programs-and-scholarships
Summary: To provide financial assistance to college sophomores interested in joining Air Force ROTC and serving as Air Force officers following completion of their bachelor's degree.
Eligibility: Open to U.S. citizens who are entering the spring semester of their sophomore year in the general military course at a college or university with an Air Force ROTC unit on campus or a college with a cross-enrollment agreement with such a school. Applicants must be full-time students, have a GPA of 2.0 or higher both cumulatively and during the prior term, be enrolled in both the Aerospace Studies 200 class and the Leadership Laboratory, pass the Air Force Officer Qualifying Test, meet Air Force physical fitness and weight requirements, and be able to be commissioned before they become 31 years of age. They must agree to serve for at least 4 years as active-duty Air Force officers following graduation from college.
Financial data: Selected cadets receive up to $1,500 for tuition and a stipend of $250 per month.
Duration: 1 semester (the spring semester of junior year); nonrenewable.
Deadline: Deadline not specified.

8 AIR FORCE ROTC HIGH SCHOOL SCHOLARSHIPS

U.S. Air Force
Attn: Headquarters AFROTC/RRUC
551 East Maxwell Boulevard
Maxwell AFB, AL 36112-5917
Phone: (334) 953-2091; (866) 4-AFROTC; Fax: (334) 953-6167
Email: afrotc1@maxwell.af.mil
Web: afrotc.com/scholarships/high-school
Summary: To provide financial assistance to high school seniors or graduates who are interested in joining Air Force ROTC in college and are willing to serve as Air Force officers following completion of their bachelor's degree.
Eligibility: Open to high school seniors who are U.S. citizens at least 17 years of age and have been accepted at a college or university with an Air Force ROTC unit on campus or a college with a cross-enrollment agreement with such a college. Applicants must have a cumulative GPA of 3.0 or higher, a class rank in the top 40%, and an ACT composite score of 24 or higher or an SAT score of 1100 or higher (mathematics and critical reading portion only). At the time of their commissioning in the Air Force, they must be no more than 31 years of age. They must agree to serve for at least 4 years as active-duty Air Force officers following graduation from college. Recently, scholarships were offered to students planning to major (in order or priority) in 1) the science and technical fields of architecture, chemistry, computer science, engineering (aeronautical, aerospace, astronautical, architectural, civil, computer, electrical, environmental, or mechanical), mathematics, meteorology and atmospheric sciences, operations research, or physics; 2) foreign languages (Arabic, Azeri, Bengali, Cambodian, Chinese, Hausa, Hindi, Indonesian, Japanese, Kazakh, Kurdish, Malay, Pashto, Persian-Iranian, Persian-Afghan, Russian, Serbo-Croatian, Swahili, Thai, Turkish, Uighar, Urdu/Punjabi, Uzbek, or Vietnamese); 3) all other fields.
Financial data: Type 1 scholarships provide payment of full tuition and most laboratory fees, as well as $900 per year for books. Type 2 scholarships pay the same benefits except tuition is capped at $18,000 per year; students who attend an institution where tuition exceeds $18,000 must pay the difference. Type 7 scholarships pay full tuition and most laboratory fees, but students must attend a public college or university where they qualify for the in-state tuition rate or a college or university where the tuition is less than the in-state rate; they may not attend an institution with higher tuition and pay the difference. Approximately 5% of scholarship offers are for Type 1, approximately 20% are for Type 2, and approximately 75% are for Type 7. All recipients are also awarded a tax-free subsistence allowance for 10 months of each year that is $300 per month as a freshman, $350 per month as a sophomore, $450 per month as a junior, and $500 per month as a senior.
Duration: 4 years.
Number awarded: Approximately 2,000 each year.
Deadline: November of each year.

9 AIR FORCE ROTC IN-COLLEGE SCHOLARSHIP PROGRAM

U.S. Air Force
Attn: Headquarters AFROTC/RRUC
551 East Maxwell Boulevard
Maxwell AFB, AL 36112-5917
Phone: (334) 953-2091; (866) 4-AFROTC; Fax: (334) 953-6167
Email: afrotc1@maxwell.af.mil
Web: afrotc.com/scholarships/in-college/programs
Summary: To provide financial assistance to undergraduate students who are willing to join Air Force ROTC in college and serve as Air Force officers following completion of their bachelor's degree.
Eligibility: Open to U.S. citizens enrolled as freshmen or sophomores at 1 of the 144 colleges and universities that have an Air Force ROTC unit on campus. Applicants must have a cumulative GPA of 2.5 or higher and be able to pass the Air Force Officer Qualifying Test and the Air Force ROTC Physical Fitness Test. At the time of commissioning, they may be no more than 31 years of age. They must agree to serve for at least 4 years as active-duty Air Force officers following graduation from college. Phase 1 is open to students enrolled in the Air Force ROTC program who do not currently have a scholarship but now wish to apply. Phase 2 is open to Phase 1 nonselects and students not enrolled in Air Force ROTC. Phase 3 is open only to Phase 2 nonselects.
Financial data: Cadets selected in Phase 1 are awarded type 2 AFROTC scholarships that provide for payment of tuition and fees, to a maximum of $18,000 per year. A limited number of cadets selected in Phase 2 are also awarded type 2 AFROTC scholarships, but most are awarded type 3 AFROTC scholarships with tuition capped at $9,000 per year. Cadets selected in Phase 3 are awarded type 6 AFROTC scholarships with tuition capped at $3,000 per year. All recipients are also awarded a book allowance of $900 per year and a tax-free subsistence allowance for 10 months of each year that is $350 per month during the sophomore year, $450 during the junior year, and $500 during the senior year.
Duration: 3 years for students selected as freshmen or 2 years for students selected as sophomores.
Number awarded: Varies each year.
Deadline: February of each year.

10 AIR FORCE ROTC PROFESSIONAL OFFICER CORPS INCENTIVE

U.S. Air Force
Attn: Headquarters AFROTC/RRUC
551 East Maxwell Boulevard
Maxwell AFB, AL 36112-5917
Phone: (334) 953-2091; (866) 4-AFROTC; Fax: (334) 953-6167
Email: afrotc1@maxwell.af.mil
Web: afrotc.com/learn-about/programs-and-scholarships
Summary: To provide financial assistance for undergraduate and graduate studies to individuals who have completed 2 years of college and who are willing to join Air Force ROTC and serve as Air Force officers following completion of their degree.
Eligibility: Open to U.S. citizens who have completed 2 years of the general military course at a college or university with an Air Force ROTC unit on campus or a college with a cross-enrollment agreement with such a college. They must be full-time students, have a GPA of 2.0 or higher both cumulatively and for the prior term, be enrolled in both Aerospace Studies class and Leadership Laboratory, pass the Air Force Officer Qualifying Test, meet Air Force physical fitness and weight requirements, and be able to be commissioned before they become 31 years of age. They must agree to serve for at least 4 years as active-duty Air Force officers following graduation from college with either a bachelor's or graduate degree.
Financial data: This scholarship provides $3,000 per year for tuition and a monthly subsistence allowance of $450 as a junior or $500 as a senior.
Duration: Until completion of a graduate degree.
Number awarded: Varies each year.
Deadline: Deadline not specified.

11 AIR RIFLE NATIONAL CHAMPIONSHIP SCHOLARSHIPS

American Legion
Attn: Americanism and Children & Youth Division
700 North Pennsylvania Street
P.O. Box 1055

Indianapolis, IN 46206-1055
Phone: (317) 630-1249; Fax: (317) 630-1223;
Email: acy@legion.org
Web: www.legion.org/programs/youthprograms/shooting
Summary: To provide college scholarships to the top competitors in the American Legion Junior Position Air Rifle Tournament.
Eligibility: Open to students between the ages of 14 and 20 who compete in air rifle tournaments sponsored by local posts of the American Legion. Based on posted scores in the precision and sporter categories, the top 30 competitors and state and regional champions compete in a qualification round and a postal tournament. The top 15 shooters then participate in a shoulder-to-shoulder match in August at the Olympic Training Center, Colorado Springs, Colorado.
Financial data: The awards are $2,500 college scholarships.
Duration: The awards are presented annually.
Number awarded: 2 each year: 1 in the precision category and 1 in the sporter category.
Deadline: Deadline not specified.

12 AIRMEN MEMORIAL FOUNDATION SCHOLARSHIP PROGRAM

Air Force Sergeants Association
Attn: Scholastic Program Coordinator
5211 Auth Road
Suitland, MD 20746
Phone: (301) 899-3500, ext. 230; (800) 638-0594, ext. 230; Fax: (301) 899-8136;
Email: staff@hqafsa.org
Web: www.hqafsa.org
Summary: To provide financial assistance for college to the dependent children of enlisted Air Force personnel.
Eligibility: Open to the unmarried children (including stepchildren and legally adopted children) of active-duty, retired, or veteran members of the U.S. Air Force, Air National Guard, or Air Force Reserves. Applicants must be attending or planning to attend an accredited academic institution. They must have an unweighted GPA of 3.5 or higher. Along with their application, they must submit 1) a paragraph on their life objectives and what they plan to do with the education they receive; and 2) an essay on the most urgent problem facing society today. High school seniors must also submit a transcript of all high school grades and a record of their SAT or ACT scores. Selection is based on academic record, character, leadership skills, writing ability, versatility, and potential for success. Financial need is not a consideration.
Financial data: Stipends are $3,000, $2,000, $1,500, or $1,000; funds may be used for tuition, room and board, fees, books, supplies, and transportation.
Duration: 1 year; may be renewed if the recipient maintains full-time enrollment.
Number awarded: Varies each year. Recently, 21 of these scholarships were awarded: 2 at $3,000 (designated the Richard Howard Scholarship and the Julene Howard Scholarship), 2 at $2,000 (designated the Sharon Piccoli Memorial Scholarship and the Sgt. James R. Seal Memorial Scholarship), 1 at $1,500, and 16 at $1,000 (including the Audrey Andrews Memorial Scholarship plus 3 sponsored by the United Services Automobile Association (USAA) Insurance Corporation). Since this program began, it has awarded more than $400,000 in financial aid.
Deadline: March of each year.

13 AKASH KURUVILLA MEMORIAL SCHOLARSHIPS

Akash Kuruvilla Memorial Scholarship Fund
P.O. Box 140900
Gainesville, FL 32614-0900
Email: info@akmsf.com
Web: www.akmsf.com
Summary: To provide financial assistance to entering or continuing undergraduates who demonstrate qualities of leadership, diversity, integrity, and academia.
Eligibility: Open to graduating high school seniors who have a GPA of 3.5 or higher and continuing full-time undergraduates who have a GPA of 3.0 or higher. Applicants must be able to demonstrate the qualities of the young man after whom this program is named: leadership, diversity, integrity, and academia. Along with their application, they must submit 1) a 750-word essay on what the phrase "The American Dream" means to them, and 2) a 500-word personal statement about themselves. Other factors considered in the selection process include financial need, character, and the applicants' potential to make an impact on their peers and community. Male and female applicants are considered separately.
Financial data: The stipend is $1,000.
Duration: 1 year.
Number awarded: 2 each year: 1 to a male and 1 to a female.
Deadline: May of each year.

14 ALABAMA G.I. DEPENDENTS' SCHOLARSHIP PROGRAM

Alabama Department of Veterans Affairs
770 Washington Avenue, Suite 530
Montgomery, AL 36102-1509
Phone: (334) 242-5077; Fax: (334) 242-5102;
Email: willie.moore@va.state.al.us
Web: www.va.state.al.us/scholarship.htm
Summary: To provide educational benefits to the dependents of disabled, deceased, and other Alabama veterans.
Eligibility: Open to spouses, children, stepchildren, and unremarried widow(er)s of veterans who served honorably for 90 days or more and 1) are currently rated as 20% or more service-connected disabled or were so rated at time of death; 2) were a former prisoner of war; 3) have been declared missing in action; 4) died as the result of a service-connected disability; or 5) died while on active military duty in the line of duty. The veteran must have been a permanent civilian resident of Alabama for at least 1 year prior to entering active military service; veterans who were not Alabama residents at the time of entering active military service may also qualify if they have a 100% disability and were permanent residents of Alabama for at least 5 years prior to filing the application for this program or prior to death, if deceased. Children and stepchildren must be under the age of 26, but spouses and unremarried widow(er)s may be of any age.
Financial data: Eligible dependents may attend any state-supported Alabama institution of higher learning or enroll in a prescribed course of study at any Alabama state-supported trade school without payment of any tuition, book fees, or laboratory charges.
Duration: This is an entitlement program for 4 years of full-time undergraduate or graduate study or part-time equivalent. Spouses and unremarried widow(er)s whose veteran spouse is rated between 20% and 90% disabled, or 100% disabled but not permanently so, may attend only 2 standard academic years.
Number awarded: Varies each year.
Deadline: Applications may be submitted at any time.

15 ALABAMA POLICE OFFICER'S AND FIREFIGHTER'S SURVIVOR'S EDUCATIONAL ASSISTANCE PROGRAM

Alabama Commission on Higher Education
Attn: Grants Coordinator
100 North Union Street
P.O. Box 302000
Montgomery, AL 36130-2000
Phone: (334) 242-2273; Fax: (334) 242-0268;
Email: cheryl.newton@ache.alabama.gov
Web: www.ache.alabama.gov/StudentAsst/Programs.htm
Summary: To provide financial assistance to the spouses and dependents of deceased police officers and fire fighters in Alabama interested in attending college in the state.
Eligibility: Open to the unremarried spouses and children of police officers and fire fighters killed in the line of duty in Alabama. Applicants may be high school seniors or currently-enrolled undergraduates in Alabama.
Financial data: Grants are offered to cover tuition, fees, books, and supplies. There is no limit on the amount awarded to recipients.
Duration: 1 year; may be renewed.
Number awarded: Varies each year.
Deadline: Deadline not specified.

16 ALABAMA STUDENT ASSISTANCE PROGRAM

Alabama Commission on Higher Education
Attn: Grants Coordinator
100 North Union Street
P.O. Box 302000
Montgomery, AL 36130-2000
Phone: (334) 242-2273; Fax: (334) 242-0268;
Email: cheryl.newton@ache.alabama.gov
Web: www.ache.alabama.gov/StudentAsst/Programs.htm
Summary: To provide financial assistance to undergraduate students who are residents of Alabama and interested in attending college in the state.
Eligibility: Open to residents of Alabama who are attending or planning to attend eligible Alabama institutions (nearly 80 schools participate in this

program). Applicants must be able to demonstrate financial need. Eligible students are required to submit the Free Application for Federal Student Aid (FAFSA).

Financial data: Stipends range from $300 to $2,500 per academic year.

Duration: 1 year; may be renewed.

Deadline: Deadline not specified.

17 ALABAMA STUDENT GRANT PROGRAM

Alabama Commission on Higher Education
Attn: Grants Coordinator
100 North Union Street
P.O. Box 302000
Montgomery, AL 36130-2000
Phone: (334) 242-2273; Fax: (334) 242-0268;
Email: cheryl.newton@ache.alabama.gov
Web: www.ache.alabama.gov/StudentAsst/Programs.htm

Summary: To provide financial assistance to undergraduates at private colleges or universities in Alabama.

Eligibility: Open to undergraduate students who are attending 1 of 14 designated private colleges or universities in Alabama on at least a half-time basis. Alabama residency is required, but financial need is not considered.

Financial data: Stipends up to $1,200 per year are available.

Number awarded: Varies each year.

Deadline: Each participating institution sets its own deadline date.

18 ALABAMA TWO-YEAR COLLEGE ACADEMIC SCHOLARSHIP PROGRAM

Alabama Commission on Higher Education
Attn: Grants Coordinator
100 North Union Street
P.O. Box 302000
Montgomery, AL 36130-2000
Phone: (334) 242-2273; Fax: (334) 242-0268;
Email: cheryl.newton@ache.alabama.gov
Web: www.ache.alabama.gov/StudentAsst/Programs.htm

Summary: To provide financial assistance to entering junior college students in Alabama.

Eligibility: Open to students who have been accepted for enrollment at an Alabama public 2-year postsecondary educational institution. Selection is based on academic merit. Preference is given to Alabama residents.

Financial data: Scholarships are available to cover the cost of in-state tuition and books.

Duration: 1 year; may be renewed if the recipient maintains a high level of academic achievement.

Number awarded: Varies each year.

Deadline: Deadline not specified.

19 ALASKA FREE TUITION FOR SPOUSE AND DEPENDENT OF ARMED SERVICES MEMBER

Department of Military and Veterans Affairs
Attn: Office of Veterans Affairs
P.O. Box 5800
Fort Richardson, AK 99505-5800
Phone: (907) 428-6016; Fax: (907) 428-6019;
Email: jerry_beale@ak-prepared.com
Web: veterans.alaska.gov/state_benefits.htm

Summary: To provide financial assistance for college to dependents and spouses in Alaska of servicemembers who died or were declared prisoners of war or missing in action.

Eligibility: Open to the spouses and dependent children of Alaska residents who died in the line of duty, died of injuries sustained in the line of duty, or were listed by the Department of Defense as a prisoner of war or missing in action. Applicants must be in good standing at a state-supported educational institution in Alaska.

Financial data: Those eligible may attend any state-supported educational institution in Alaska without payment of tuition or fees.

Duration: 1 year; may be renewed.

Number awarded: Varies each year.

Deadline: Deadline not specified.

20 ALASKA HOUSING FINANCE CORPORATION SCHOLARSHIPS

Alaska Housing Finance Corporation
Attn: Public Housing Division
4300 Boniface Parkway
P.O. Box 101020
Anchorage, AK 99510-1020
Phone: (907) 330-8415; (800) 478-AHFC (within AK); Fax: (907) 338-1683
Email: tsteele@ahfc.state.ak.us
Web: www.ahfc.state.ak.us/grants/scholarships.cfm

Summary: To provide financial assistance to residents of subsidized housing in Alaska who plan to attend college in the state.

Eligibility: Open to high school seniors who plan to enroll at a postsecondary education program and to adults who wish to attend a vocational, trade, or academic school. The school must be located in Alaska. Applicants must reside in a subsidized rental unit owned by the Alaska Housing Finance Corporation (AHFC) or receive assistance through the Housing Choice Voucher program. Along with their application, they must submit an essay of 350 to 500 words that includes how the rental housing they receive through AHFC has influenced their life, their career goal and why they made that decision, the ways they contribute to their family's or their community's well being, and how this scholarship will help them reach their goal. Selection is based on that essay (50 points), 2 letters of reference (20 points), and overall quality of the application (5 points).

Financial data: The stipend is $1,000 per year.

Duration: 1 year; may be renewed 1 additional year and for a third year after a break of at least 1 year.

Number awarded: Up to 10 each year.

Deadline: April of each year.

21 ALASKA LEGION AUXILIARY SCHOLARSHIP

American Legion Auxiliary
Department of Alaska
Attn: Secretary/Treasurer
1392 Sixth Avenue
Fairbanks, AK 99701
Phone: (907) 455-4420; Fax: (907) 474-3040
Email: akaladep@ptialaska.net
Web: www.alaskalegion.org/Auxiliary.htm

Summary: To provide financial assistance to veterans' children in Alaska who plan to attend college in any state.

Eligibility: Open to the children of veterans who served during eligibility dates for membership in the American Legion. Applicants must be between 17 and 24 years of age, high school seniors or graduates who have not yet attended an institution of higher learning, and residents of Alaska. They must be planning to attend a college or university in any state.

Financial data: The stipend is $1,500, half of which is payable each semester toward tuition, matriculation, laboratory, or similar fees.

Duration: 1 year.

Number awarded: 1 each year.

Deadline: March of each year.

22 ALASKA SEA SERVICES SCHOLARSHIPS

Navy League of the United States
Attn: Scholarships
2300 Wilson Boulevard, Suite 200
Arlington, VA 22201-5424
Phone: (703) 528-1775; (800) 356-5760; Fax: (703) 528-2333
Email: scholarships@navyleague.org
Web: www.navyleague.org/scholarship

Summary: To provide financial assistance to spouses and dependent children of naval personnel in Alaska who are interested in attending college in any state.

Eligibility: Open to the spouses and dependent children of active-duty, inactive-duty, and retired (with or without pay) members of the regular and Reserve Navy, Marine Corps, or Coast Guard who are residents of Alaska. Applicants must be enrolled or planning to enroll full-time at an accredited 4-year college or university in any state to work on an undergraduate degree. Selection is based on academic proficiency, character, leadership ability, community involvement, and financial need.

Financial data: The stipend is $1,000 per year; funds are paid directly to the academic institution for tuition, books, and fees.

Duration: 1 year; may be renewed 1 additional year.

Number awarded: Up to 4 each year.

Deadline: February of each year.

23 ALBERT YANNI SCHOLARSHIP PROGRAM

West Virginia Department of Education
Attn: Division of Technical and Adult Education Services
1900 Kanawha Boulevard, East
Building 6, Room 243
Charleston, WV 25305
Phone: (304) 558-3897; Fax: (304) 558-0048
Email: gcoulson@access.k12.wv.us
Web: careertech.k12.wv.su

Summary: To provide financial assistance to high school seniors in West Virginia who plan to enroll in a postsecondary technical program in any state.

Eligibility: Open to seniors graduating from public high schools in West Virginia who have completed at least 4 units in a single technical concentration. Applicants must be planning to attend an accredited postsecondary institution or technical center in any state to work on a certificate or degree in a career field related to their high school technical concentration. They must rank in the top 25% of their class and have a GPA of 3.0 or higher with no grades below a "C." Along with their application, they must submit a 500-word essay on how their participation in high school career and technical education relates to the course of study they will be pursuing in postsecondary school, their career goal, their plan for achieving their career goal, and any paid or unpaid work experience they have and how those experiences have influenced their career plans. Selection is based on the essay (50 points for content and 50 points for form); recommendations from an academic teacher (25 points), a technical teacher (25 points), and a peer (10 points); awards, honors, and school and community involvement (40 points); and bonus points for following all directions in the preparation and submission of the application (10 points).

Financial data: The stipend is $2,000.

Duration: 1 year.

Number awarded: 20 each year.

Deadline: March of each year.

24 ALL NATIVE AMERICAN HIGH SCHOOL ACADEMIC TEAM SCHOLARSHIPS

American Indian Graduate Center
Attn: Executive Director
4520 Montgomery Boulevard, N.E., Suite 1-B
Albuquerque, NM 87109-1291
Phone: (505) 881-4584; (800) 628-1920; Fax: (505) 884-0427
Email: aigc@aigc.com
Web: www.aigc.com/02scholarships/allnative/highschool.htm

Summary: To provide financial assistance for college to Native American high school students.

Eligibility: Open to enrolled members of U.S. federally-recognized American Indian tribes and Alaska Native groups who can provide a Certificate of Indian Blood (CIB). A teacher or community member must nominate students. Nominees must be high school seniors planning to enroll full-time at an accredited college or university. They must be able to demonstrate academic excellence, leadership, and community service. Along with their application, they must submit a 1,000-word essay on their most outstanding intellectual endeavor. Selection is based on the student's academic, artistic, or leadership endeavor. Financial need is not considered in the selection process.

Financial data: A stipend is awarded (amount not specified).

Duration: 1 year.

Number awarded: 10 each year.

Deadline: April of each year.

25 ALLAN JEROME BURRY SCHOLARSHIP

United Methodist Church
Attn: General Board of Higher Education and Ministry
Office of Loans and Scholarships
1001 19th Avenue South
P.O. Box 340007
Nashville, TN 37203-0007
Phone: (615) 340-7344; Fax: (615) 340-7367
Email: umscholar@gbhem.org
Web: www.gbhem.org/loansandscholarships

Summary: To provide financial assistance to undergraduate students attending schools affiliated with the United Methodist Church.

Eligibility: Open to U.S. citizens and permanent residents who have been active, full members of a United Methodist Church for at least 3 years prior to applying. Applicants must be enrolled full-time at a college or university related to the United Methodist Church and be nominated by their campus ministry unit or college chaplain. They must have a GPA of "B+" or higher and be able to document financial need. Selection is based on academic performance, leadership skills, and participation in the activities of the Methodist campus ministry or chaplaincy program at their institution.

Financial data: The stipend ranges from $500 to $1,200.

Duration: 1 year.

Number awarded: 1 each year.

Deadline: January of each year.

26 ALL-INK COLLEGE SCHOLARSHIPS

All-Ink.com
1460 North Main Street, Suite 2
Spanish Fork, UT 84660
Phone: (801) 794-0123; (888) 567-6511; Fax: (801) 794-0124
Email: CSP@all-ink.com
Web: www.all-ink.com/scholarship.aspx

Summary: To provide financial assistance for college or graduate school to students who submit a scholarship application online.

Eligibility: Open to U.S. citizens and permanent residents who are enrolled or planning to enroll at an accredited college or university at any academic level from freshman through graduate student. Applicants must have a GPA of 2.5 or higher. They must submit, through an online process, an essay of 50 to 200 words on a person who has had the greatest impact on their life and another essay of the same length on what they hope to achieve in their personal and professional life after graduation. Applications are not accepted through the mail.

Financial data: The stipend is $1,000.

Duration: 1 year.

Number awarded: Varies each year; recently 5 of these scholarships were awarded.

Deadline: December of each year.

27 ALLOGAN SLAGLE MEMORIAL SCHOLARSHIP

Association on American Indian Affairs, Inc.
Attn: Director of Scholarship Programs
966 Hungerford Drive, Suite 12-B
Rockville, MD 20850
Phone: (240) 314-7155; Fax: (240) 314-7159
Email: lw.aaia@verizon.net
Web: www.indian-affairs.org/scholarships/allogan_slagle.htm

Summary: To provide financial assistance for college to Native American students whose tribe is not federally-recognized.

Eligibility: Open to American Indian and Native Alaskan full-time undergraduate students. Applicants must be members of tribes that are either state-recognized or that are not federally-recognized but are seeking federal recognition. Along with their application, they must submit documentation of financial need, a Certificate of Indian Blood showing at least one-quarter Indian blood (if available) or other verification of tribal involvement, an essay on their educational goals, 2 letters of recommendation, and their most recent transcript. Selection is based on need.

Financial data: The stipend is $1,500.

Duration: 1 year; recipients may reapply.

Number awarded: Varies each year; recently, 4 of these scholarships were awarded.

Deadline: June of each year.

28 ALPHA OMICRON ARIZONA ENDOWMENT SCHOLARSHIP

Epsilon Sigma Alpha International
Attn: ESA Foundation
P.O. Box 270517
Fort Collins, CO 80527
Phone: (970) 223-2824; Fax: (970) 223-4456
Email: esainfo@esaintl.com
Web: www.esaintl.com/esaf

Summary: To provide financial assistance to residents of Arizona who plan to attend college in any state.

Eligibility: Open to residents of Arizona who are 1) graduating high school seniors with a GPA of 3.0 or higher or with minimum scores of 22 on the ACT or 1030 on the combined critical reading and mathematics SAT; 2) enrolled in college with a GPA of 3.0 or higher; 3) enrolled at a technical school or returning to school after an absence for retraining of job skills or obtaining a degree; or 4) engaged in online study through an accredited college, university, or vocational school. Applicants may be attending or planning to attend school in any state and major in any field. Selection is based on character (10%), leadership (10%), service (5%), financial need (25%), and scholastic ability (50%).

Financial data: The stipend is $1,000.

Duration: 1 year; may be renewed.

Number awarded: 1 each year.

Deadline: January of each year.

29 ALPHONSE A. MIELE SCHOLARSHIP

UNICO National
Attn: UNICO Foundation, Inc.
271 U.S. Highway 46 West, Suite A-108
Fairfield, NJ 07004
Phone: (973) 808-0035; (800) 877-1492; Fax: (973) 808-0043
Email: unico.national@verizon.net
Web: www.unico.org/foundation.asp

Summary: To provide financial assistance for college to high school seniors who may be of any nationality but are recommended by an Italian American service organization.

Eligibility: Open to high school seniors of any race, creed, or national origin who are planning to attend an accredited college or university. Applicants must have a GPA of 3.0 or higher and be able to demonstrate financial need, participation in extracurricular and community activities, character, and personality. Along with their application, they must submit SAT or ACT test scores and a letter of recommendation from a UNICO chapter in the city or town where they live.

Financial data: The stipend is $1,500 per year.

Duration: 4 years.

Number awarded: 1 each year.

Deadline: April of each year.

30 AL'S FORMAL WEAR SALUTE TO EDUCATION SCHOLARSHIPS

Formal Specialists, Ltd.
Attn: Kim Jordan
7807 Main Street
Houston, TX 77030
Phone: (713) 791-1888; (877) 730-4TUX
Email: info@alsformalwear.com
Web: www.alsformalwear.com/scholarships.asp

Summary: To provide financial assistance to high school seniors in designated states who submit outstanding essays and who plan to attend college in any state.

Eligibility: Open to seniors graduating from high schools in Arkansas, Colorado, Louisiana, Mississippi, Oklahoma, Texas, or Wyoming. Applicants must be planning to attend a college or university in any state. Along with their application, they must submit 2 letters of recommendation, a transcript, a list of athletic or scholastic achievements and/or community activities in which they have participated, information on their financial situation, and a 500-word essay describing their educational goals and explaining why the sponsor should help them achieve those goals by investing in their education.

Financial data: The stipend is $1,000. Funds are paid directly to the accredited college, university, or other institution of higher learned designated by the winner.

Duration: 1 year.

Number awarded: 2 each year.

Deadline: May of each year.

31 AMELIA KEMP MEMORIAL SCHOLARSHIP

Women of the Evangelical Lutheran Church in America
Attn: Scholarships
8765 West Higgins Road
Chicago, IL 60631-4101
Phone: (773) 380-2736; (800) 638-3522, ext. 2736; Fax: (773) 380-2419
Email: emily.hansen@elca.org
Web: www.elca.org/Growing-In-Faith/Ministry/Women-of-the-ELCA.aspx

Summary: To provide financial assistance to lay women of color who are members of Evangelical Lutheran Church of America (ELCA) congregations and who wish to study on the undergraduate, graduate, professional, or vocational school level.

Eligibility: Open to ELCA lay women of color who are at least 21 years of age and have experienced an interruption of at least 2 years in their education since high school. Applicants must have been admitted to an educational institution to prepare for a career in other than a church-certified profession. U.S. citizenship is required.

Financial data: The maximum stipend is $1,000.

Duration: Up to 2 years.

Number awarded: Varies each year, depending upon the funds available.

Deadline: February of each year.

32 AMERICAN INDIAN SCHOLARSHIPS

Daughters of the American Revolution–National Society
Attn: Committee Services Office, Scholarships
1776 D Street, N.W.
Washington, DC 20006-5303
Phone: (202) 628-1776
Web: www.dar.org/natsociety/edout_scholar.cfm

Summary: To provide supplementary financial assistance to Native American students who are interested in working on an undergraduate or graduate degree.

Eligibility: Open to Native Americans of any age, any tribe, in any state who are enrolled or planning to enroll in a college, university, or vocational school. Applicants must have a GPA of 2.75 or higher. Graduate students are eligible, but undergraduate students receive preference. Selection is based on academic achievement and financial need.

Financial data: The stipend is $1,000. The funds are paid directly to the recipient's college.

Duration: This is a 1-time award.

Number awarded: 1 each year.

Deadline: March of each year.

33 AMERICAN LEGION BASEBALL SCHOLARSHIPS

American Legion Baseball
700 North Pennsylvania Street
Indianapolis, IN 46204
Phone: (317) 630-1249; Fax: (317) 630-1369
Email: acy@legion.org
Web: www.baseball.legion.org

Summary: To provide financial assistance to participants in the American Legion baseball program who plan to attend college.

Eligibility: Open to participants in the American Legion baseball program who are high school graduates or college freshmen; students still in high school are not eligible. In each American Legion department, candidates may be nominated by a team manager or head coach. The department baseball committee selects a player who demonstrates outstanding leadership, citizenship, character, scholarship, and financial need.

Financial data: The stipend ranges from $600 to $750. Funds are disbursed jointly to the winner and the school.

Duration: Students have 8 years to utilize the scholarship funds from the date of the award, excluding any time spent on active military duty.

Number awarded: Up to 51 each year: 1 in each state and Puerto Rico. Recently, $22,000 in scholarships was awarded by this program.

Deadline: July of each year.

34 AMERICAN LEGION LEGACY SCHOLARSHIPS

American Legion
Attn: Americanism and Children & Youth Division
700 North Pennsylvania Street
P.O. Box 1055
Indianapolis, IN 46206-1055
Phone: (317) 630-1202; Fax: (317) 630-1223
Email: acy@legion.org
Web: www.legion.org/programs/resources/scholarships

Summary: To provide financial assistance for college to children of U.S. military personnel killed on active duty on or after September 11, 2001.

Eligibility: Open to the children (including adopted children and stepchildren) of active-duty U.S. military personnel (including federalized National Guard and Reserve members) who died on active duty on or after September 11, 2001. Applicants must be high school seniors or graduates planning to enroll full-time at an accredited institution of higher education in the United States. Selection is based on academic achievement, school and community activities, leadership skills, and financial need.

Financial data: The stipend depends on the availability of funds.

Duration: 1 year; may be renewed.

Number awarded: Varies each year.

Deadline: April of each year.

35 AMERICAN PATRIOT SCHOLARSHIPS

Military Officers Association of America
Attn: Educational Assistance Program
201 North Washington Street
Alexandria, VA 22314-2539
Phone: (703) 549-2311; (800) 234-MOAA; Fax: (703) 838-5819
Email: edassist@moaa.org
Web: www.moaa.org/about_scholarship_aboutfund/index.htm

Summary: To provide financial assistance for undergraduate education to children of members of the uniformed services who have died.

Eligibility: Open to children under 24 years of age of active, Reserve, and National Guard uniformed service personnel (Army, Navy, Air Force, Marines, Coast Guard, Public Health Service, or National Oceanographic and Atmospheric Administration) whose parent has died on active service. Applicants must be working on an undergraduate degree. They must have a GPA of 3.0 or higher. Selection is based on academic ability, activities, and financial need.

Financial data: The stipend is at least $2,500 per year.

Duration: 1 year; may be renewed up to 4 additional years.

Number awarded: Varies each year; recently, 60 students were receiving support from this program.

Deadline: February of each year.

36 AMERICORPS NATIONAL CIVILIAN COMMUNITY CORPS

Corporation for National and Community Service
1201 New York Avenue, N.W.
Washington, DC 20525
Phone: (202) 606-5000, ext. 144; (800) 942-2677; Fax: (202) 565-2791; TDD: (800) 833-3722
Email: questions@americorps.org
Web: www.americorps.org/for_individuals/choose/nccc.asp

Summary: To enable young Americans to receive experience and training by participating in a residential national service program while earning funds for higher education.

Eligibility: Open to U.S. citizens or permanent residents between the ages of 18 and 24. Members work in teams of 10 to 12 people on a variety of projects in 6 different areas: environment, education, public safety, unmet needs, homeland security, and disaster relief. Selection is based on an application, personal references, and a telephone interview.

Financial data: Corps members receive a living allowance of approximately $4,000, housing, meals, limited medical insurance, up to $400 per month for child care (if necessary), member uniforms, and an education award of $4,725 for future education costs or repayment of student loans.

Duration: Members serve 10 months and complete 1,700 hours of community service, including 80 hours of independent service.

Number awarded: Varies each year.

Deadline: March of each year for the fall cycle; July of each year for the winter cycle.

37 AMERICORPS STATE AND NATIONAL PROGRAM

Corporation for National and Community Service
1201 New York Avenue, N.W.
Washington, DC 20525
Phone: (202) 606-5000; (800) 942-2677; Fax: (202) 565-2784; TDD: (800) 833-3722
Email: questions@americorps.org
Web: www.americorps.org/for_individuals/choose/state_national.asp

Summary: To enable Americans to earn money for college or graduate school while serving as volunteers for public or nonprofit organizations that work to meet the nation's education, public safety, human, or environmental needs.

Eligibility: Open to applicants who are at least 17 years old, are U.S. citizens or permanent residents, and have completed at least their high school diploma or agree to obtain the diploma before using the education award. They must be interested in working on community projects in 1 of 4 areas: education, public safety, health, and the environment. Additional qualifications are set by participating agencies.

Financial data: Full-time participants (at least 1,700 service hours) receive a modest living allowance of approximately $9,300, limited health care, and a post-service education award of $4,725 to pay for college, graduate school, or repayment of student loans. Half-time members (900 service hours) receive a post-service education award of $2,362 per term. Other education awards are $1,800 for reduced half time (675 service hours), $1,250 for quarter time (450 service hours), or $1,000 for minimum time (300 service hours). In lieu of the education award, participants may elect to receive an end-of-service stipend of $1,200.

Duration: The length of the term is established by each participating agency but ranges from 9 to 12 months.

Number awarded: Varies each year; recently, approximately 44,000 members served in this program.

Deadline: Each participating organization sets its own deadline.

38 AMERICORPS VISTA

Corporation for National and Community Service
1201 New York Avenue, N.W.
Washington, DC 20525
Phone: (202) 606-5000; (800) 942-2677; Fax: (202) 565-2784; TDD: (800) 833-3722
Email: questions@americorps.org
Web: www.americorps.org/for_individuals/choose/vista.asp

Summary: To enable Americans to earn money for higher education or other purposes while working as volunteers for public or nonprofit organizations that serve low-income communities.

Eligibility: Open to U.S. citizens or permanent residents 18 years of age or older who either have a baccalaureate degree or at least 3 years of related volunteer/job experience and skills. Participants serve at approved public or nonprofit sponsoring organizations in low-income communities located in the United States, Virgin Islands, or Puerto Rico. Assignments may include working to fight illiteracy, improve health services, create businesses, increase housing opportunities, or bridge the digital divide. Sponsors may also establish particular skill, education, or experience requirements; Spanish language skills are desirable for some assignments.

Financial data: Participants receive a monthly living allowance for housing, food, and incidentals; the allowance does not affect Social Security, veterans', or public assistance benefits but is subject to taxation. Health insurance is also provided for participants, but not for family members. Upon completion of service, participants also receive a stipend of $100 per month or an educational award of $4,725 per year of service that may be used to pay for educational expenses, repay student loans, or pay the expenses of participating in a school-to-work program. Up to $9,450 in educational benefits may be earned.

Duration: Full-time service of at least 1 year is required to earn educational benefits; up to 2 years of service may be performed.

Number awarded: Varies each year; recently, approximately 6,000 volunteers served in this program.

Deadline: March of each year for first consideration; October of each year for fall replacements.

39 AMLN SCHOLARSHIP FOR ARAB AMERICAN STUDENTS

American Mideast Leadership Network
Attn: Scholarship Selection Committee
P.O. Box 2156
Long Island City, NY 11102
Phone: (347) 924-9674; Fax: (917) 591-2177
Email: info@amln.org
Web: www.amln.org/amln_new/scholarships.html

Summary: To provide financial assistance for undergraduate or graduate study at colleges in Connecticut, New Jersey, and New York to students of Arab heritage.

Eligibility: Open to U.S. citizens, permanent residents, and holders of passports stamped I-551 who are of Arab heritage. Applicants must be high school seniors, undergraduates, or graduate students enrolled full-time in a degree-seeking program at an accredited college, university, or community college in the Tri-State area of Connecticut, New Jersey, and New York. They must have a GPA of 3.0 or higher and a record of active involvement in their local Arab American community. Along with their application, they must submit 3 essays of 500 words each on 1) how their Arab heritage, family upbringing, and/or role models have influenced their academic and personal long-term goals; 2) how they contribute to their community and what they have learned from their experiences; and 3) how they intend to give back to the Arab American community after completing their degree. Financial need is not considered in the selection process.

Financial data: Stipends range from $1,000 to $3,000 per year.

Duration: 1 year; may be renewed, provided the recipient maintains a GPA of 3.0 or higher.

Number awarded: 1 or more each year.

Deadline: December.

40 ANDRE SOBEL AWARD

Andre Sobel River of Life Foundation
Attn: Awards
8899 Beverly Boulevard, Suite 111
Los Angeles, CA 90048
Phone: (310) 276-7111; Fax: (310) 276-0244
Email: info@andreriveroflife.org
Web: www.andreriveroflife.org/participate/award

Summary: To recognize and reward young cancer survivors who submit outstanding essays on their illness.

Eligibility: Open to cancer survivors between 12 and 21 years of age. Applicants are allowed to define themselves as a survivor; no medical definition or certain amount of time is required. They must submit an essay, up to 1,500 words in length, on a topic that changes annually but relates to their illness. Recently, applicants were invited to write on their experience facing illness and how it has changed them.

Financial data: First prize is $5,000. Other cash prizes are awarded to second- and third-place winners.

Duration: The competition is held annually.

Number awarded: 3 cash prizes are awarded each year.

Deadline: March of each year.

41 ANGIE M. HOUTZ MEMORIAL FUND SCHOLARSHIP

Angie M. Houtz Memorial Fund
P.O. Box 634
Olney, MD 20830-0634
Email: angiefund@yahoo.com
Web: www.angiemhoutzmemorialfund.com

Summary: To provide financial assistance to students enrolled at public colleges and universities in Maryland.

Eligibility: Open to graduating high school seniors or current college students from any state who are attending or planning to attend a public 2- or 4-year college or university in Maryland. Applicants must have a GPA of 3.0 or higher and a record of at least 200 hours in community service activities during the past 5 years. Along with their application, they must submit an essay of 1 to 2 pages on how they plan to make community service part of their life in the next year and why. Financial need is not considered in the selection process.

Financial data: The stipend is $3,000.

Duration: 1 year.

Number awarded: 1 or 2 each year.

Deadline: April of each year.

42 ANNE AND MATT HARBISON SCHOLARSHIP

P. Buckley Moss Society
20 Stoneridge Drive, Suite 102
Waynesboro, VA 22980
Phone: (540) 943-5678; Fax: (540) 949-8408
Email: society@mosssociety.org
Web: www.mosssociety.org/page.php?id=30

Summary: To provide financial assistance for college to high school seniors with language-related learning disabilities.

Eligibility: Open to high school seniors with language-related learning disabilities. They must be nominated by a member of the P. Buckley Moss Society. The nomination packet must include verification of a language-related learning disability from a counselor or case manager, a high school transcript, 2 letters of recommendation, and 4 essays by the nominees (on themselves; their learning disability and its effect on their lives; their extracurricular, community, work, and church accomplishments; and their plans for next year).

Financial data: The stipend is $1,500. Funds are paid to the recipient's college or university.

Duration: 1 year; may be renewed for up to 3 additional years.

Number awarded: 1 each year.

Deadline: March of each year.

43 ANSWERS.COM SCHOLARSHIP PROGRAM

Answers Corporation
c/o Center for Scholarship Administration, Inc.
4320 Wade Hampton Boulevard, Suite G
P.O. Box 1465
Taylors, SC 29687-0031
Phone: (864) 268-3363; Fax: (864) 268-7160
Email: allisonlee@bellsouth.net
Web: www.scholarshipprograms.org/wiki/index.htm

Summary: To recognize and reward, with college scholarships, students who answer questions on the Answers.com website.

Eligibility: Open to high school seniors and current college undergraduates who are citizens of the United States, Australia, Canada, India, Ireland, New Zealand, or the United Kingdom. Applicants must be attending or planning to attend a college or university in their country. They must have answered at least 50 questions on the Answers.com website. Selection is based solely on the quality of the answers.

Financial data: Awards, in the form of scholarships for undergraduate study, are $5,000, $2,500, or $1,000. Funds may be used for expenses that relate directly to school expenditures, such as tuition, fees, books, materials, and other expenses that relate directly to a degree program (but not room and board).

Duration: The competition is held annually.

Number awarded: 13 each year: 1 at $5,000, 2 at $2,500, and 10 at $1,000.

Deadline: March of each year.

44 APCA SCHOLARSHIPS

Asian Pacific Islanders for Professional and Community Advancement
c/o Suwathin Phiansunthon, Scholarship Committee
P.O. Box 2694
San Ramon, CA 94583
Phone: (732) 420-7339
Email: info@apca-att.org
Web: www.apca-att.org/scholarship.html

Summary: To provide financial assistance to high school seniors from selected states who are interested in attending college in any state.

Eligibility: Open to seniors graduating from high schools in Arizona, California, Colorado, Georgia, Michigan, New Jersey, Texas, and Washington, D.C. Applicants must be planning to continue their education at an accredited 2- or 4-year college or university or vocational school in any state. They must have a GPA of 2.75 or higher. Along with their application, they must submit a 750-word essay on making a difference in their community. Financial need is not considered in the selection process. Students of all ethnic backgrounds are eligible, but a goal of the sponsoring organization is to promote growth and influence on issues that impact Asian Pacific Islanders.

Financial data: The stipend is $1,500.

Duration: 1 year; nonrenewable.

Number awarded: Varies each year; recently, 7 of these scholarships were awarded.

Deadline: April of each year.

45 ARCF/ARKANSAS SERVICE MEMORIAL FUND

Arkansas Community Foundation
1400 West Markham, Suite 206
Little Rock, AR 72201
Phone: (501) 372-1116; (800) 220-ARCF; Fax: (501) 372-1166
Email: arcf@arcf.org
Web: www.arcf.org/page12787.cfm

Summary: To provide financial assistance for college to children of deceased veterans or other government officials in Arkansas.

Eligibility: Open to seniors graduating from high schools in Arkansas whose parent died in service to the community, state, or nation. Applicants must be planning to attend an accredited 2- or 4-year college in Arkansas on a full-time basis. Selection is based on such factors as academics, school activities, community service, future goals, faculty and adviser recommendations, and financial need.

Financial data: Stipends range from $500 to $5,000 per year.

Duration: 1 year; may be renewed as long as the recipient is making satisfactory progress toward a degree.

Number awarded: Varies each year; since this program was established, it has awarded 124 scholarships worth $485,000.

Deadline: April of each year.

46 ARIZONA COLLEGE ACCESS AID PROGRAM

Arizona Commission for Postsecondary Education
2020 North Central Avenue, Suite 550
Phoenix, AZ 85004-4503
Phone: (602) 258-2435; Fax: (602) 258-2483
Email: acpe@azhighered.gov
Web: www.azhighered.gov/ACAAP_Grant.html

Summary: To provide financial assistance to students at Arizona colleges and universities who can demonstrate substantial financial need.

Eligibility: Open to sophomores, juniors, and seniors at accredited postsecondary institutions in Arizona who have been residents of the state for at least the past 12 months. Applicants must be able to demonstrate substantial financial need. They must be U.S. citizens or eligible noncitizens. Funds are awarded on a first-come, first-served basis.

Financial data: The maximum stipend is $2,000 per year for full-time students.

Duration: 1 year; recipients may reapply.

Number awarded: Varies each year.

Deadline: Deadline not specified.

47 ARIZONA EARLY GRADUATION SCHOLARSHIP GRANTS

Arizona Commission for Postsecondary Education
2020 North Central Avenue, Suite 550
Phoenix, AZ 85004-4503
Phone: (602) 258-2435; Fax: (602) 258-2483
Email: acpe@azhighered.gov
Web: www.azhighered.gov/EGSG_Grant.html

Summary: To provide financial assistance to students in Arizona high schools who graduate early and attend college in the state.

Eligibility: Open to high school students who have been residents of Arizona for at least the past 12 months. Applicants must graduate from a charter school or public high school at least 1 semester earlier than their cohort class and enroll at an accredited postsecondary institution or vocational program in the state on at least a half-time basis. They must have achieved passing scores on all required components of the Arizona Instrument to Measure Standards (AIMS). Financial need is not considered in the selection process.

Financial data: The stipend is up to $2,000 for students who graduate at least 1 year early or up to $1,500 for students who graduate at least 1 semester early.

Duration: 1 year; may be renewed 1 additional year, provided the recipients meet the satisfactory academic progress requirements set by their institution.

Number awarded: Varies each year.

Deadline: Deadline not specified.

48 ARIZONA LEVERAGING EDUCATIONAL ASSISTANCE PARTNERSHIP GRANTS

Arizona Commission for Postsecondary Education
2020 North Central Avenue, Suite 650
Phoenix, AZ 85004-4503
Phone: (602) 258-2435; Fax: (602) 258-2483
Email: acpe@azhighered.gov
Web: www.azhighered.gov/LEAP_Grant.html

Summary: To provide financial assistance to undergraduate and graduate students in Arizona who can demonstrate financial need.

Eligibility: Open to Arizona residents who are attending or planning to attend a participating Arizona postsecondary educational institution as either a full-time or part-time undergraduate or graduate student. Applicants must be able to demonstrate financial need.

Financial data: Awards range from $100 to $2,500 per year.

Duration: 1 year; may be renewed.

Number awarded: Varies each year; recently, approximately $3.4 million in these grants were awarded.

Deadline: Each participating institution in Arizona sets its own deadline.

49 ARIZONA POSTSECONDARY EDUCATION GRANTS

Arizona Commission for Postsecondary Education
2020 North Central Avenue, Suite 550
Phoenix, AZ 85004-4503
Phone: (602) 258-2435; Fax: (602) 258-2483
Email: acpe@azhighered.gov
Web: www.azhighered.gov/PEG_Grant.html

Summary: To provide financial assistance to graduates of Arizona high schools who wish to attend a private postsecondary institution in the state.

Eligibility: Open to graduates of Arizona high schools who have been residents of the state for at least the past 12 months. Applicants must be attending or planning to attend an accredited private baccalaureate degree-granting institution in Arizona as a full-time student. U.S. citizenship or legal resident status is required. Financial need is not considered in the selection process. Priority is given to students who have received this funding previously; awards are made to initial applicants on a first-come, first-served basis.

Financial data: The award is $2,000 per year. Participants must agree when they accept the award to repay the full amount if they do not graduate with their bachelor's degree within 5 years of the initial receipt of the award.

Duration: 1 year; may be renewed up to 3 additional years.

Number awarded: Varies each year.

Deadline: Applications are accepted throughout the year to accommodate the various enrollment periods for the different private postsecondary institutions.

50 ARIZONA PRIVATE POSTSECONDARY EDUCATION STUDENT FINANCIAL ASSISTANCE PROGRAM FOR COMMUNITY COLLEGE STUDENTS

Arizona Commission for Postsecondary Education
2020 North Central Avenue, Suite 550
Phoenix, AZ 85004-4503
Phone: (602) 258-2435; Fax: (602) 258-2483
Email: acpe@azhighered.gov
Web: www.azhighered.gov/PFAP_Grant.html

Summary: To provide financial assistance to graduates of Arizona community colleges who wish to attend a private postsecondary institution in the state.

Eligibility: Open to students who have graduated or are about to graduate from a public community college in Arizona with an associate degree. Applicants must be planning to attend a private baccalaureate degree-granting institution in Arizona and be enrolled in a bachelor's degree program on a full-time basis. They must be able to demonstrate financial need.

Financial data: The award is $2,000 per year. Participants must agree when they accept the award to repay the full amount if they do not graduate with their bachelor's degree within 3 years of the initial receipt of the award.

Duration: 2 years.

Number awarded: Varies; grants are awarded on a priority of receipt basis.

Deadline: Applications are accepted throughout the year to accommodate the various enrollment periods for the different private postsecondary institutions.

51 ARIZONA PRIVATE SCHOOL ASSOCIATION SCHOLARSHIP

Arizona Private School Association
7776 South Pointe Parkway West, Suite 110
Phoenix, AZ 85044
Phone: (602) 254-5199; Fax: (602) 254-5073
Email: apsa@arizonapsa.org
Web: www.arizonapsa.org/scholarships.htm

Summary: To provide financial assistance to high school seniors in Arizona who are interested in attending a career college to prepare for jobs.

Eligibility: Open to high school seniors in Arizona who are interested in attending a career college in the state. The sponsor provides 2 scholarships to each high school in the state. Recipients are then selected by the scholarship directors or counselors at their high school.

Financial data: The stipend is a $1,000 award certificate to be used to pay for tuition at a career college in Arizona.

Duration: 1 year.

Number awarded: 2 each year at each high school in Arizona.

Deadline: Deadline not specified.

52 ARIZONA PTA SCHOLARSHIP PROGRAM

Arizona PTA
Attn: Scholarship Chair
2721 North Seventh Avenue
Phoenix, AZ 85007-1102
Phone: (602) 279-1811; (800) 992-0112 (within AZ); Fax: (602) 279-1814
Email: az_office@pta.org
Web: www.azpta.org

Summary: To provide financial assistance to high school seniors and current college students in Arizona who are interested in attending college in the state.

Eligibility: Open to Arizona residents who are high school seniors or college students and have earned a GPA of 3.0 or higher. Applicants must be attending or planning to attend a community college or university in Arizona. Along with their application, they must submit a personal essay that includes their educational background and goals; personal and career goals and why; any obstacles they have had to overcome; how their academic choices, clubs, activities, volunteer work, and/or internships support their goals; and why they deserve this scholarship. Selection is based primarily on financial need.

Financial data: The stipend is $500 per semester, up to a lifetime total of $4,000. Funds are paid directly to the recipient's school.

Duration: 1 semester; may be renewed each semester for up to a total of 4 years, provided the recipient attends school full-time and maintains a GPA of 2.65 or higher.
Number awarded: Varies each year.
Deadline: February of each year.

53 ARKANSAS ACADEMIC CHALLENGE SCHOLARSHIP

Arkansas Department of Higher Education
Attn: Financial Aid Division
114 East Capitol Avenue
Little Rock, AR 72201-3818
Phone: (501) 371-2050; (800) 54-STUDY; Fax: (501) 371-2001;
Email: finaid@adhe.edu
Web: www.adhe.edu/divisions/financialaid/Pages/fa_programs.aspx

Summary: To provide financial assistance to residents of Arkansas who are traditional or nontraditional students and interested in attending college in the state.
Eligibility: Open to Arkansas residents who are either traditional or nontraditional students. Traditional students must be graduating high school seniors, have completed the Smart Core curriculum requirements, have a GPA of 2.5 or higher, have an ACT score of at least 19 or an equivalent SAT score, and be planning to enroll full-time in an associate or baccalaureate degree program at an approved institution in the state. Nontraditional students must 1) have graduated from an Arkansas high school with a GPA of 2.5 or higher and an ACT score of at least 19 or an equivalent SAT score; 2) have completed at least 12 semester hours of credit at an approved institution of higher education with a postsecondary GPA of 2.5 or higher; or 3) have graduated from a private, out-of-state, or home school high school and have an ACT score of at least 19 or an equivalent SAT score; they must be enrolled or planning to enroll full- or part-time in an associate or baccalaureate degree program at an approved institution in the state. All applicants must be U.S. citizens or permanent residents and have a family income less than $65,000, plus $5,000 additional per child.
Financial data: The maximum stipend is $2,500 for freshmen, $2,750 for sophomores, $3,000 for juniors, or $3,500 for seniors.
Duration: 1 year; may be renewed up to 3 additional years if the recipient maintains full-time enrollment and a GPA of 2.75 or higher.
Number awarded: Up to 5,000 each year.
Deadline: May of each year.

54 ARKANSAS GOVERNOR'S COMMISSION ON PEOPLE WITH DISABILITIES SCHOLARSHIPS

Arkansas Governor's Commission on People with Disabilities
Attn: Scholarship Committee
525 West Capitol Avenue
P.O. Box 3781
Little Rock, AR 72203
Phone: (501) 296-1637; Fax: (501) 296-1883; TDD: (501) 296-1637
Web: www.arsinfo.org/default.aspx?id=31

Summary: To provide financial assistance to Arkansas students with disabilities who are interested in attending college or graduate school in any state.
Eligibility: Open to high school seniors, high school graduates, undergraduates, and graduate students who have a disability and are residents of Arkansas. Applicants must be attending or planning to attend a college or university in any state. Selection is based on a description of their disability (20 points), present and past school involvement (10 points), a brief statement on their career goals (15 points), community and volunteer activities (10 points), a brief essay on the positive or negative effects their disability has had on their life thus far (20 points), 3 letters of recommendation (10 points), and financial need (10 points).
Financial data: The stipend varies, up to $1,000 per year.
Duration: 1 year; recipients may reapply.
Number awarded: Several each year.
Deadline: February of each year.

55 ARKANSAS GOVERNOR'S DISTINGUISHED SCHOLARS PROGRAM

Arkansas Department of Higher Education
Attn: Financial Aid Division
114 East Capitol Avenue
Little Rock, AR 72201-3818
Phone: (501) 371-2050; (800) 54-STUDY; Fax: (501) 371-2001
Email: finaid@adhe.edu
Web: www.adhe.edu/divisions/financialaid/Pages/fa_govscholars.aspx

Summary: To provide financial assistance to exceptional high school seniors in Arkansas.
Eligibility: Open to high school seniors who are U.S. citizens or permanent residents, are residents of Arkansas, can demonstrate leadership, and are planning to enroll in a college or university in Arkansas. Applicants must have an SAT combined critical reading and mathematics score of 1410 or higher, have an ACT score of 32 or higher, be a National Merit Finalist or a National Achievement Scholar, or have a GPA of 3.5 or higher in academic classes. Selection is based on high school GPA (35%), class rank (10%), ACT or SAT score (45%), and school and community leadership (10%).
Financial data: Stipends up to $10,000 per year are provided.
Duration: 1 year; may be renewed for up to 3 additional years, provided the recipient maintains a cumulative GPA of 3.25 or higher and completes at least 30 semester hours each year.
Number awarded: Up to 300 each year.
Deadline: January of each year.

56 ARKANSAS GOVERNOR'S SCHOLARS PROGRAM

Arkansas Department of Higher Education
Attn: Financial Aid Division
114 East Capitol Avenue
Little Rock, AR 72201-3818
Phone: (501) 371-2050; (800) 54-STUDY; Fax: (501) 371-2001
Email: finaid@adhe.edu
Web: www.adhe.edu/divisions/financialaid/Pages/fa_govscholars.aspx

Summary: To provide financial assistance to outstanding high school seniors in Arkansas.
Eligibility: Open to high school seniors who are U.S. citizens or permanent residents, are residents of Arkansas, can demonstrate leadership, and are planning to enroll in a college or university in the state. Applicants must have an SAT combined critical reading and mathematics score of 1220 or higher, an ACT score of 27 or higher, or a GPA of 3.5 or higher in academic classes. Selection is based on high school GPA (35%), class rank (10%), ACT or SAT score (45%), and school and community leadership (10%).
Financial data: The stipend is $4,000 per year.
Duration: 1 year; may be renewed for up to 3 additional years, provided the recipient maintains a 3.0 cumulative GPA and completes at least 30 semester hours each year.
Number awarded: Up to 75 each year (1 in each Arkansas county).
Deadline: January of each year.

57 ARKANSAS HIGHER EDUCATION OPPORTUNITIES GRANT

Arkansas Department of Higher Education
Attn: Financial Aid Division
114 East Capitol Avenue
Little Rock, AR 72201-3818
Phone: (501) 371-2050; (800) 54-STUDY; Fax: (501) 371-2001
Email: finaid@adhe.edu
Web: www.adhe.edu/divisions/financialaid/Pages/fa_gogrant.aspx

Summary: To provide financial assistance to high school seniors in Arkansas who come from a low-income family and plan to attend college in the state.
Eligibility: Open to high school seniors in Arkansas who have been residents of the state for at least 1 year and plan to attend an eligible Arkansas institution. Applicants must come from a family with an annual income of less than $25,000 per year for a 1-member family, rising by $5,000 for each additional family member to a maximum of $75,000. They must be U.S. citizens or permanent residents.
Financial data: The stipend is $1,000 per year for full-time students or $500 per year for part-time students.
Duration: 1 year; may be renewed up to 3 additional years, provided the recipient maintains a GPA of 2.0 or higher and continues to demonstrate financial need.
Number awarded: 10 each year.
Deadline: August of each year.

58 ARKANSAS LAW ENFORCEMENT OFFICERS' DEPENDENTS' SCHOLARSHIPS

Arkansas Department of Higher Education
Attn: Financial Aid Division
114 East Capitol Avenue
Little Rock, AR 72201-3818

Phone: (501) 371-2050; (800) 54-STUDY; Fax: (501) 371-2001
Email: finaid@adhe.edu
Web: www.adhe.edu/divisions/financialaid/Pages/fa_leod.aspx

Summary: To provide financial assistance for undergraduate education to the dependents of deceased or disabled Arkansas law enforcement officers, fire fighters, or other designated public employees.

Eligibility: Open to the spouses and/or children (natural, adopted, or step) of Arkansas residents who were killed or permanently disabled in the line of duty as law enforcement officers, municipal and/or college or university police officers, sheriffs and deputy sheriffs, constables, state correction employees, game wardens, state park employees who are commissioned law enforcement officers or emergency response employees, full-time or volunteer fire fighters, state forestry employees engaged in fighting forest fires, certain Arkansas Highway and Transportation Department employees, emergency medical technicians, or Department of Community Punishment employees. Children must be less than 23 years of age. Spouses may not have remarried. All applicants must have been Arkansas residents for at least 6 months.

Financial data: The scholarship covers tuition, on-campus room charges, and fees (but not books, school supplies, food, materials, or dues for extracurricular activities) at any state-supported college or university in Arkansas.

Duration: Up to 8 semesters, as long as the student is working on a baccalaureate or associate degree.

Number awarded: Varies each year.

Deadline: July of each year for fall term, November of each year for spring or winter term, April of each year for first summer session, or June of each year for second summer session.

59 ARKANSAS MILITARY DEPENDENTS' SCHOLARSHIP PROGRAM

Arkansas Department of Higher Education
Attn: Financial Aid Division
114 East Capitol Avenue
Little Rock, AR 72201-3818
Phone: (501) 371-2050; (800) 54-STUDY; Fax: (501) 371-2001
Email: finaid@adhe.edu
Web: www.adhe.edu/divisions/financialaid/Pages/fa_mds.aspx

Summary: To provide financial assistance for educational purposes to dependents of certain categories of Arkansas veterans.

Eligibility: Open to the natural children, adopted children, stepchildren, and spouses of Arkansas residents who have been declared to be a prisoner of war, killed in action, missing in action, killed on ordnance delivery, or 100% totally and permanently disabled during, or as a result of, active military service. Applicants and their parent or spouse must be residents of Arkansas. They must be working on, or planning to work on, a bachelor's degree or certificate of completion at a public college, university, or technical school in Arkansas.

Financial data: The program pays for tuition, general registration fees, special course fees, activity fees, room and board (if provided in campus facilities), and other charges associated with earning a degree or certificate.

Duration: 1 year; undergraduates may obtain renewal as long as they make satisfactory progress toward a baccalaureate degree; graduate students may obtain renewal as long as they maintain a minimum GPA of 2.0 and make satisfactory progress toward a degree.

Number awarded: Varies each year; recently, 4 of these scholarships were awarded.

Deadline: July of each year for fall term, November of each year for spring or winter term, April of each year for first summer session, or June of each year for second summer session.

60 ARKANSAS SECOND EFFORT SCHOLARSHIP

Arkansas Department of Higher Education
Attn: Financial Aid Division
114 East Capitol Avenue
Little Rock, AR 72201-3818
Phone: (501) 371-2050; (800) 54-STUDY; Fax: (501) 371-2001
Email: finaid@adhe.edu
Web: www.adhe.edu/divisions/financialaid/Pages/fa_ses.aspx

Summary: To provide financial assistance for undergraduate study to students in Arkansas who have earned a General Educational Development (GED) certificate.

Eligibility: Open to Arkansas residents who did not graduate from high school but completed their GED certificate in the previous year. Applicants must be attending or planning to attend an approved Arkansas 2- or 4-year public or private postsecondary institution. They must be at least 18 years of age or a former member of a high school class that has graduated. The students who received the highest GED scores are awarded this scholarship. Financial need is not considered. Students do not apply for this award; eligible candidates are contacted directly by the Arkansas Department of Higher Education if they achieve the highest scores.

Financial data: The stipend is $1,000 per year or the cost of tuition, whichever is less.

Duration: 1 year; may be renewed for an additional 3 years (or equivalent for part-time students) or until completion of a baccalaureate degree, provided the recipient maintains a GPA of 2.5 or higher.

Number awarded: 10 each year.

Deadline: Deadline not specified.

61 ARKANSAS WORKFORCE IMPROVEMENT GRANTS

Arkansas Department of Higher Education
Attn: Financial Aid Division
114 East Capitol Avenue
Little Rock, AR 72201-3818
Phone: (501) 371-2050; (800) 54-STUDY; Fax: (501) 371-2001
Email: finaid@adhe.edu
Web: www.adhe.edu/divisions/financialaid/Pages/fa_wig.aspx

Summary: To provide financial assistance to nontraditional students in Arkansas.

Eligibility: Open to Arkansas residents who are 24 years of age and older and who are returning to college. Applicants should be students who are able to demonstrate financial need but might not be eligible for assistance from traditional state and federal programs. They must submit a Free Application for Federal Student Aid (FAFSA) to an Arkansas college or university and are automatically considered for these awards in accordance with that school's established procedures. U.S. citizenship or permanent resident status is required.

Financial data: The maximum stipend is $2,000 for full-time study. Grants for part-time study are prorated. The actual amount depends on unmet financial need after receipt of a Pell Grant.

Duration: 1 year; may be renewed.

Number awarded: Varies each year.

Deadline: Each Arkansas institution sets its own deadline.

62 ARMED SERVICES YMCA ANNUAL ESSAY CONTEST

Armed Services YMCA
Attn: Essay Contest
6359 Walker Lane, Suite 200
Alexandria, VA 22310
Phone: (703) 313-9600, ext. 106; (800) 597-1260; Fax: (703) 313-9668
Email: tharper@asymca.org
Web: www.asymca.org/Programs.aspx?pgmID=27&mid=27

Summary: To recognize and reward outstanding essays by children of armed service personnel.

Eligibility: Open to children of active-duty and retired military personnel in the Army, Navy, Marines, Air Force, Coast Guard, and National Guard/Reserve. Applicants must submit an essay on a topic that changes annually; recently, students were asked to write on "My Military Hero." Essays by students in grades 1–8 must be from 100 to 300 words and essays by students in grades 9–12 must be from 300 to 500 words.

Financial data: For preschool through grade 8, first prize is a $500 savings bond and second prize is a $100 savings bond. For grades 9–12, first prize is a $1,000 savings bond, second prize is a $200 savings bond, and honorable mention is a $100 savings bond.

Duration: The contest is held annually.

Number awarded: A total of 14 prizes are awarded each year. A first prize and a second prize are awarded for 6 categories: first and second grade, third and fourth grade, fifth and sixth grade, seventh and eighth grade, ninth and tenth grade, and eleventh and twelfth grade. An additional 2 honorable mentions are awarded at the high school level.

Deadline: March of each year.

63 ARMENIAN STUDENTS' ASSOCIATION SCHOLARSHIPS

Armenian Students' Association
Attn: Scholarship Committee
333 Atlantic Avenue
Warwick, RI 02888
Phone: (401) 461-6114; Fax: (401) 461-6112
Email: headasa@aol.com
Web: www.asainc.org/national/scholarships.shtml

Summary: To provide financial assistance for undergraduate and graduate education to students of Armenian ancestry.
Eligibility: Open to undergraduate and graduate students of Armenian descent who have completed at least the first year of college (including graduate, medical, and law school). Applicants must be enrolled full-time at a 4-year college or university or a 2-year college and planning to transfer to a 4-year institution in the following fall. They must be a U.S. citizen or have appropriate visa status to study in the United States. Along with their application, they must submit a 300-word essay about themselves, including their future plans. Financial need is considered in the selection process.
Financial data: The stipends range from $500 to $2,500.
Duration: 1 year.
Number awarded: Varies each year, recently, 19 of these scholarships were awarded.
Deadline: March of each year.

64 ARMY AND AIR FORCE MUTUAL AID ASSOCIATION SCHOLARSHIPS

U.S. Army
ROTC Cadet Command
Attn: ATCC-OP-I-S
55 Patch Road, Building 56
Fort Monroe, VA 23651-1052
Phone: (757) 788-3473; (800) USA-ROTC; Fax: (757) 788-4643
Email: atccps@usacc.army.mil
Web: www.goarmy.com/rotc/college_students.jsp
Summary: To provide additional financial assistance to Army ROTC scholarship and non-scholarship cadets.
Eligibility: Open to students who are entering their senior year of the Army ROTC program. Applicants may be either scholarship or non-scholarship cadets, but they must meet scholarship eligibility requirements (GPA of 2.5 or higher, ACT score of 19 or higher or combined mathematics and critical reading SAT score of 920 or higher, physical fitness score of 180 or higher with at least 60 points in each individual APFT event).
Financial data: The stipend is $1,000.
Duration: 1 year.
Number awarded: 3 each year: 1 in the ROTC eastern region, 1 in the ROTC western region, and 1 awarded nationally.
Deadline: June of each year.

65 ARMY COLLEGE FUND

U.S. Army
Human Resources Command
AHRC-PDE-EI
Attn: Education Incentives and Counseling Branch
200 Stovall Street, Suite 3N17
Alexandria, VA 22332-0472
Phone: (703) 325-0285; (800) 872-8272; Fax: (703) 325-6599
Email: pdeei@hoffman.army.mil
Web: www.goarmy.com/benefits/education_money.jsp
Summary: To provide financial assistance for college to Army enlistees after they have completed their service obligation.
Eligibility: Open to high school seniors or graduates who enlist in an approved military occupational specialty (MOS) for at least 2 years, score 50 or above on the Armed Forces Qualification Test (AFQT), enroll in the Montgomery GI Bill, and attend a Department of Veterans Affairs–approved postsecondary educational institution on a full-time basis after completion of their service obligation.
Financial data: The Army College Fund (ACF) provides money for college in addition to that which the enlistee receives under the Montgomery GI Bill. The maximum benefit, depending on MOS, is $44,028 for a 2-year enlistment, $63,756 for a 3-year enlistment, $70,956 for a 4-year enlistment, $78,156 for a 5-year enlistment, or $81,756 for a 6-year enlistment.
Duration: 36 months; funds must be utilized within 10 years of leaving the Army.
Number awarded: Varies each year.
Deadline: Applications may be submitted at any time.

66 ARMY ROTC 4-YEAR SCHOLARSHIPS

U.S. Army
ROTC Cadet Command
Attn: ATCC-OP-I-S
55 Patch Road, Building 56
Fort Monroe, VA 23651-1052
Phone: (757) 788-4559; (800) USA-ROTC; Fax: (757) 788-4643;
Email: atccps@usacc.army.mil
Web: www.goarmy.com/rotc/high_school_students.jsp
Summary: To provide financial assistance to high school seniors or graduates who are interested in enrolling in Army ROTC in college.
Eligibility: Open to applicants who 1) are U.S. citizens; 2) are at least 17 years of age by October of the year in which they are seeking a scholarship; 3) are able to complete a college degree and receive their commission before their 31st birthday; 4) score at least 920 on the combined mathematics and critical reading SAT or 19 on the ACT; 5) have a high school GPA of 2.5 or higher; and 6) meet medical and other regulatory requirements. Current college or university students may apply if their school considers them beginning freshmen with 4 academic years remaining for a bachelor's degree.
Financial data: This scholarship provides financial assistance of up to $20,000 per year for college tuition and educational fees or for room and board, whichever the student selects. In addition, a flat rate of $1,200 per year is provided for the purchase of textbooks, classroom supplies, and equipment. Recipients are also awarded a stipend for up to 10 months of each year that is $300 per month during their freshman year, $350 per month during their sophomore year, $450 per month during their junior year, and $500 per month during their senior year.
Duration: 4 years, until completion of a baccalaureate degree.
Number awarded: Approximately 1,500 each year.
Deadline: November of each year.

67 ARMY ROTC ADVANCED COURSE

U.S. Army
ROTC Cadet Command
Attn: ATCC-OP-I-S
55 Patch Road, Building 56
Fort Monroe, VA 23651-1052
Phone: (757) 788-4559; (800) USA-ROTC; Fax: (757) 788-4643
Email: atccps@usacc.army.mil
Web: www.goarmy.com/rotc/ar_advanced_course.jsp
Summary: To provide financial assistance to non-scholarship participants in the Army ROTC Program who have qualified for the Advanced Course.
Eligibility: Open to non-scholarship cadets in the ROTC Program. They must have qualified for the ROTC Advanced Course. The Advanced Course is usually taken during the final 2 years of college.
Financial data: Participants receive a stipend of $450 per month during their junior year and $500 per month during their senior year, as well as pay for attending the 6-week advanced camp during the summer between the junior and senior years of college.
Duration: 2 years.
Number awarded: Varies each year.
Deadline: Deadline not specified.

68 ARMY ROTC COLLEGE SCHOLARSHIP PROGRAM

U.S. Army
ROTC Cadet Command
Attn: ATCC-OP-I-S
55 Patch Road, Building 56
Fort Monroe, VA 23651-1052
Phone: (757) 788-4559; (800) USA-ROTC; Fax: (757) 788-4643
Email: atccps@usacc.army.mil
Web: www.goarmy.com/rotc/college_students.jsp
Summary: To provide financial assistance to students who are or will be enrolled in Army ROTC.
Eligibility: Open to U.S. citizens between 17 and 27 years of age who have already completed 1 or 2 years in a college or university with an Army ROTC unit on campus or in a college with a cross-enrollment agreement with a college with an Army ROTC unit on campus. Applicants must have 2 or 3 years remaining for their bachelor's degree (or 4 years of a 5-year bachelor's program) and must be able to complete that degree before their 31st birthday. They must have a GPA of 2.5 or higher in their previous college study and scores of at least 920 on the combined mathematics and critical reading SAT or 19 on the ACT.
Financial data: These scholarships provide financial assistance for college tuition and educational fees, up to an annual amount of $20,000. In addition, a flat rate of $1,200 is provided for the purchase of textbooks, classroom supplies, and equipment. Recipients are also awarded a stipend for up to 10 months of each year that is $350 per month during their sophomore year, $450 per month during their junior year, and $500 per month during their senior year.
Duration: 2 or 3 years, until the recipient completes the bachelor's degree.

Number awarded: Varies each year; a recent allocation provided for 700 4-year scholarships, 1,800 3-year scholarships, and 2,800 2-year scholarships.
Deadline: December of each year.

69 ARRIVE ALIVE SCHOLARSHIP PROGRAM

Carter Mario Injury Lawyers
Attn: Marketing Director
158 Cherry Street
Milford, CT 06460
Phone: (203) 876-2711; Fax: (203) 877-9509
Web: www.cartermario.com/arrive-program09.php
Summary: To provide financial assistance to high school seniors in Connecticut who plan to attend college in any state and submit outstanding essays on the dangers of drinking and driving.
Eligibility: Open to seniors graduating from high schools in Connecticut who plan to enroll at a 4-year college or university in any state. Applicants must submit an essay on a topic that changes annually but relates to the dangers of driving while intoxicated. Selection is based on that essay, academic achievement, and community service.
Financial data: The stipend is $1,000.
Duration: 1 year.
Number awarded: 10 each year.
Deadline: March of each year.

70 ARRL GENERAL FUND SCHOLARSHIPS

American Radio Relay League
Attn: ARRL Foundation
225 Main Street
Newington, CT 06111
Phone: (860) 594-0397; Fax: (860) 594-0259
Email: foundation@arrl.org
Web: www.arrlf.org/programs/scholarships
Summary: To provide financial assistance to licensed radio amateurs who are interested in working on an undergraduate or graduate degree in any field.
Eligibility: Open to undergraduate or graduate students at accredited institutions in any subject area who are licensed radio amateurs (any class). Applicants must submit an essay on the role amateur radio has played in their lives and provide documentation of financial need.
Financial data: The stipend is $2,000.
Duration: 1 year.
Number awarded: Varies each year; recently, 2 of these scholarships were awarded.
Deadline: January of each year.

71 ASHLEY MARIE EASTERBROOK INTERNET SCHOLARSHIP FUND

Foundation for Ashley's Dream
675 East Big Beaver Road, Suite 101
Troy, MI 48083
Phone: (248) 720-0245; Fax: (248) 524-9803
Email: webform@ashleysdream.org
Web: www.ashleysdream.org
Summary: To provide financial assistance to high school seniors who have been involved in community activities, especially those related to the prevention of drunken driving.
Eligibility: Open to high school seniors whose GPA is between 3.5 and 3.74 and who plan to attend an accredited 4-year college or university. Along with their application, they must submit an essay of 500 words on either preventing teenage binge drinking or preventing drunk driving. Preference is given to students who have 1) paid or volunteer work experience, or 2) involvement in organized programs or activities that are designed to help other students improve the quality of their life. Financial need is not considered in the selection process.
Financial data: The stipend is $1,000.
Duration: 1 year.
Number awarded: 1 each year.
Deadline: March of each year.

72 ASIAN STUDENTS INCREASING ACHIEVEMENT (ASIA) SCHOLARSHIP PROGRAM

Ronald McDonald House Charities
Attn: U.S. Scholarship Program
One Kroc Drive
Oak Brook, IL 60523
Phone: (630) 623-7048; Fax: (630) 623-7488
Email: info@rmhc.org
Web: rmhc.org/what-we-do/rmhc-u-s-scholarships
Summary: To provide financial assistance for college to Asian Pacific high school seniors in specified geographic areas.
Eligibility: Open to high school seniors in designated McDonald's market areas who are legal residents of the United States and have at least 1 parent of Asian Pacific heritage. Applicants must be planning to enroll full time at an accredited 2- or 4-year college, university, or vocational/technical school. They must have a GPA of 2.7 or higher. Along with their application, they must submit a personal statement, up to 2 pages in length, on their Asian Pacific background, career goals, and desire to contribute to their community; information about unique, personal, or financial circumstances may be added. Selection is based on that statement, high school transcripts, a letter of recommendation, and financial need.
Financial data: Most awards are $1,000 per year. Funds are paid directly to the recipient's school.
Duration: 1 year; nonrenewable.
Number awarded: Varies each year; since RMHC began this program, it has awarded more than $37 million in scholarships.
Deadline: February of each year.

73 ASSOCIATION FOR COMPENSATORY EDUCATORS OF TEXAS STUDENT SCHOLARSHIPS

Association for Compensatory Educators of Texas
Attn: Scholarship Chair
P.O. Box 3516
Humble, TX 77347
Phone: (832) 644-5020; Fax: (832) 644-8520
Email: sjensen@aisd.net
Web: www.acetx.org/content/scholarships
Summary: To provide financial assistance to high school seniors in Texas who have participated in a compensatory education program and plan to attend college in any state.
Eligibility: Open to seniors graduating from high schools in Texas and planning to attend a college, university, or other postsecondary institution in any state. Applicants must have participated for at least 2 years, at some time in their school career, in a federal- or state-funded compensatory education program (e.g., bilingual/ESL, homeless, migrant, pregnant or parenting). Along with their application, they must submit a brief essay on the problems they have faced in grades preK–12 and how the school programs helped them to be successful. The highest-scoring applicant receives the Wade and Sandy Burroughs Scholarship.
Financial data: The stipend is $1,000. The winner of the Wade and Sandy Burroughs Scholarship receives an additional $500.
Duration: 1 year.
Number awarded: 20 each year.
Deadline: January of each year.

74 ASSOCIATION OF BLIND CITIZENS SCHOLARSHIPS

Association of Blind Citizens
P.O. Box 246
Holbrook, MA 02343
Phone: (781) 961-1023; Fax: (781) 961-0004
Email: scholarship@blindcitizens.org
Web: www.blindcitizens.org/abc_scholarship.htm
Summary: To provide financial assistance for college to individuals who are blind or visually impaired.
Eligibility: Open to high school seniors, high school graduates, and currently-enrolled college students who are blind or visually impaired. Applicants must be interested in working on a college degree. Along with their application, they must submit an autobiography, indicating how the scholarship award would help them achieve their goal of attending college or a recognized vocational program; a high school or college transcript; a certificate of legal blindness or a letter from their ophthalmologist; and 2 letters of reference. The highest ranked applicant receives the Reggie Johnson Memorial Scholarship.
Financial data: Stipends are $2,000 or $1,000. Funds may be used to pay for tuition, living expenses, or related expenses resulting from vision impairment.
Duration: 1 year.
Number awarded: 8 each year: 1 at $2,000 (the Reggie Johnson Memorial Scholarship) and 7 at $1,000.
Deadline: April of each year.

75 ASSOCIATION ON AMERICAN INDIAN AFFAIRS/ADOLPH VAN PELT SCHOLARSHIPS

Association on American Indian Affairs, Inc.
Attn: Director of Scholarship Programs
966 Hungerford Drive, Suite 12-B
Rockville, MD 20850
Phone: (240) 314-7155; Fax: (240) 314-7159
Email: lw.aaia@verizon.net
Web: www.indian-affairs.org/scholarships/adolph_van_pelt.htm

Summary: To provide financial assistance to Native American undergraduate students.

Eligibility: Open to Native American students interested in working on an undergraduate degree on a full-time basis. Applicants must submit documentation of financial need, a Certificate of Indian Blood showing at least one-quarter Indian blood, proof of tribal enrollment, an essay on their educational goals, 2 letters of recommendation, and their most recent transcript. Selection is based on merit and need.

Financial data: The stipend is $1,500.

Duration: 1 year; recipients may reapply.

Number awarded: Varies each year; recently, 4 new and 2 renewal scholarships were awarded.

Deadline: June of each year.

76 ATSUHIKO TATEUCHI MEMORIAL SCHOLARSHIP

Seattle Foundation
Attn: Scholarship Administrator
1200 Fifth Avenue, Suite 1300
Seattle, WA 98101-3151
Phone: (206) 622-2294; Fax: (206) 622-7673
Email: scholarships@seattlefoundation.org
Web: www.seattlefoundation.org/page10004940.cfm

Summary: To provide financial assistance to residents of Pacific Rim states, especially students of Japanese or other Asian ancestry, who are interested in working on an undergraduate degree at a college in any state.

Eligibility: Open to residents of Alaska, California, Hawaii, Oregon, and Washington who are graduating high school seniors or undergraduates. Applicants must be attending or planning to attend a public or private community college, 4-year college or university, or trade/vocational school in any state. They must have a GPA of 3.0 or higher and be able to demonstrate financial need. Preference is given to students of Japanese or other Asian ancestry. Along with their application, they must submit a 500-word essay on the most interesting book they have read and how it influenced them.

Financial data: The stipend is $5,000.

Duration: 1 year; nonrenewable.

Number awarded: At least 1 each year.

Deadline: February of each year.

77 AXA ACHIEVEMENT SCHOLARSHIPS

Scholarship America
Attn: Scholarship Management Services
One Scholarship Way
P.O. Box 297
St. Peter, MN 56082
Phone: (507) 931-1682; (800) 537-4180; Fax: (507) 931-9168
Email: axaachievement@scholarshipamerica.org
Web: www.axa-achievement.com

Summary: To provide financial assistance for college to high school seniors who demonstrate outstanding achievement.

Eligibility: Open to graduating high school seniors who plan to enroll full-time in an accredited 2- or 4-year college or university in the United States. Applicants must demonstrate ambition and achievement in school and community activities or work experience. In the selection process, primary consideration is given to a demonstrated achievement in a non-academic area as reported by the applicant and supported by an appraisal completed by an adult professional who is not a relative. Other factors considered include extracurricular activities in school and community, work experience, and academic record. From among the recipients, students whose achievements are especially noteworthy are designated as national AXA Achievers.

Financial data: The stipend is $10,000. Funds may be used only for undergraduate educational expenses. Students selected as national AXA Achievers receive an additional stipend of $15,000, a computer, and the offer of an internship.

Duration: 1 year. Awards are not renewable, but recipients may arrange to receive payment in installments over multiple years as long as they continue to meet eligibility requirements.

Number awarded: 52 each year: 1 from each state, the District of Columbia, and Puerto Rico. Of those 52, 10 are designated as national AXA Achievers.

Deadline: December of each year.

78 "BABE" SLATTERY SCHOLARSHIPS

Western Athletic Scholarship Association
Attn: Scholarship Coordinator
13730 Loumont Street
Whittier, CA 90601

Summary: To provide financial assistance for college to outstanding softball players.

Eligibility: Open to graduating high school seniors who have played an active role in amateur softball. Applicants must be planning to attend an accredited 2- or 4-year college or university. They need not have played on a high school team and are not required to play softball in college. Selection is based on academic achievement, community service, participation in softball, and financial need.

Financial data: The stipend is $2,000 per year.

Duration: 1 year; may be renewed.

Number awarded: Up to 10 each year.

Deadline: February of each year.

79 BANK OF AMERICA ACHIEVEMENT AWARDS

Bank of America Foundation
Attn: Achievement Awards Program
CA5-704-08-03
315 Montgomery Street, Eighth Floor
San Francisco, CA 94104-1866
Phone: (800) 537-4180
Web: www.bankofamerica.com/foundation/index.cfm?template=fd_ca

Summary: To recognize and reward high school seniors in California who excel in various subject areas and plan to attend college in any state.

Eligibility: Open to high school seniors in California who are chosen by faculty committees in their schools. The committees select students to receive certificates in specific study areas (agriculture, art, business, communications, computer studies, drama, English, English as a Second Language, foreign language, history, home economics, mathematics, music, religious studies, science, social science, and trades and industrial studies). Small high schools (those with 199 or fewer students in grades 10–12) may award a total of 7 certificates and large high schools (those with 200 or more students) present a total of 14 certificates. In addition, the faculty committees select graduating seniors to receive plaques in 4 general study areas (applied arts/trade, fine arts, liberal arts, and science and mathematics); certificate winners may not also receive plaques. The number of plaques awarded by each high school depends on the size of the school (2 plaques with enrollment of 1 to 199 students in grades 10–12, 3 plaques with 200 to 599 students, and 4 plaques for schools with more than 600 students). Winners of plaques are then eligible to enter the Achievement Awards competition. Of all plaque winners statewide, 320 finalists (8 in each of 10 regions in each of the 4 general study areas) are selected to enter competitions involving 1) an essay judged on written expression, logical progression, ability to focus on topic, and creative interpretation, and 2) a group discussion judged on cooperation, sound and logical thinking, oral communication and command of English, and originality of thought.

Financial data: The cash awards are $2,000 for first-place winners, $1,500 for second-place winners, $1,000 for third-place winners, and $500 for other participating finalists.

Duration: Prizes are awarded annually.

Number awarded: All 320 finalists receive cash awards; the top 40 finalists (1 in each general study area in each region) receive first-place awards and other finalists receive awards depending on their scores in the competition.

Deadline: Schools must select their plaque recipients before the end of January of each year.

80 BARKING FOUNDATION SCHOLARSHIPS

Barking Foundation
Attn: Executive Director
49 Florida Avenue
P.O. Box 855
Bangor, ME 04402-0885
Phone: (207) 990-2910; Fax: (207) 990-2975
Email: info@barkingfoundation.org
Web: www.barkingfoundation.org

Summary: To provide financial assistance to residents of Maine for education at the undergraduate level.

Eligibility: Open to students who have been residents of Maine for at least 4 years and are interested in working on an undergraduate degree at a college or university in any state. Applicants must submit an essay, up to 500 words in length, on what they consider a pressing issue facing the state of Maine. Selection is based on that essay, academics, extracurricular service and work, references, and financial need.
Financial data: The stipend is $3,000 per year.
Duration: 1 year; may be renewed, provided the recipient maintains a GPA of 3.0 or higher.
Number awarded: Approximately 50 each year.
Deadline: February of each year.

81 BEN SELLING SCHOLARSHIP

Oregon Student Assistance Commission
Attn: Grants and Scholarships Division
1500 Valley River Drive, Suite 100
Eugene, OR 97401-2146
Phone: (541) 687-7395; (800) 452-8807, ext. 7395; Fax: (541) 687-7414; TDD: (800) 735-2900
Email: awardinfo@osac.state.or.us
Web: www.osac.state.or.us/osac_programs.html
Summary: To provide financial assistance to residents of Oregon who are attending college in any state.
Eligibility: Open to residents of Oregon who are entering their sophomore or higher years at a college or university in any state. Applicants must have a cumulative GPA of 3.5 or higher.
Financial data: Stipends are at least $1,000.
Duration: 1 year.
Number awarded: Varies each year; recently, 25 of these scholarships were awarded.
Deadline: February of each year.

82 BENJAMIN BANNEKER CHAPTER BLACKS IN GOVERNMENT SCHOLARSHIP

Blacks in Government-Benjamin Banneker Chapter
Attn: Scholarship Awards Committee
P.O. Box 15652
Arlington, VA 22215-5652
Web: bbcgsa.org/Educational_Scholarships.aspx
Summary: To provide financial assistance to high school seniors and GED recipients in the Washington, D.C. metropolitan area who plan to attend college in any state.
Eligibility: Open to residents of the Washington, D.C. metropolitan area who either are graduating high school seniors or have a GED diploma. Applicants must have a GPA of 2.5 higher and be planning to attend an accredited institution of higher learning in any state. Along with their application, they must submit an essay on applying the teaching of Benjamin Banneker to today's life issues. Selection is based on that essay, academic achievement, extracurricular activities, community and public service, SAT scores, and a statement of educational and career goals.
Financial data: A stipend is awarded (amount not specified).
Duration: 1 year.
Number awarded: 1 or more each year.
Deadline: January of each year.

83 BERNIE VARNADORE SCHOLARSHIPS

Dixie Boys Baseball, Inc.
P.O. Box 1778
Marshall, TX 75671
Phone: (903) 927-1845; Fax: (903) 927-1846
Email: boys@dixie.org
Web: baseball.dixie.org/scholarships99bf.htm
Summary: To provide financial assistance for college to high school senior males who have participated in a Dixie Boys or Dixie Majors franchised baseball program.
Eligibility: Open to high school senior males who played baseball in a Dixie Boys (for boys 13 and 14 years of age), Dixie Pre-Majors (for boys 15 or 16 years of age), or Dixie Majors (for boys from 15 through 19 years of age) franchised program. Applicants must submit a 150-word essay on their career objectives, how college relates to those, and how they expect to contribute to society. While it is a basic requirement that the applicants have participated in the baseball program, ability is not a factor. Selection is based on high school grades and testing, school and community leadership, and financial need.
Financial data: The stipend is $1,250.
Duration: 1 year.
Number awarded: 11 each year.
Deadline: March of each year.

84 BESSIE COLEMAN SCHOLARSHIP AWARD

The Weekly
Attn: Coleman Scholarship
P.O. Box 151789
Dallas, TX 75315
Phone: (214) 428-8958; Fax: (214) 428-2807
Email: theweeklysks@earthlink.net
Summary: To provide financial assistance to high school seniors planning to attend an historically African American college or university.
Eligibility: Open to high school seniors who are interested in attending an historically African American college or university. As part of the application process, students must write an essay (700 to 1,500 words) comparing themselves to Bessie Coleman (the first African American to receive an international pilots license) and indicating how they plan to "make a name" for themselves in their chosen profession. Males and females compete separately. Neither income nor GPA is considered in the selection process.
Financial data: The stipend is $5,000.
Duration: 1 year.
Number awarded: 2 each year: 1 is set aside for a female and 1 for a male.
Deadline: December of each year.

85 BEST BUY@15 SCHOLARSHIP PROGRAM

Scholarship America
Attn: Scholarship Management Services
One Scholarship Way
P.O. Box 297
St. Peter, MN 56082
Phone: (507) 931-1682; (800) 537-4180; Fax: (507) 931-9168
Email: bestbuy@scholarshipamerica.org
Web: bestbuy.scholarshipamerica.org/index.php
Summary: To provide financial assistance for college to high school students who demonstrate outstanding volunteer community service.
Eligibility: Open to high school students in grades 9–12 who plan to enroll full-time at an accredited 2- or 4-year college or university or vocational/technical school in the United States after graduation. Applicants must be able to demonstrate "solid academic performance and exemplary community service." Consideration may also be given to participation in school activities and work experience, but financial need is not considered. Applications are only available at Best Buy stores throughout the country.
Financial data: The stipend is $1,500.
Duration: 1 year; nonrenewable.
Number awarded: 1,000 each year.
Deadline: February of each year.

86 BETA ZETA OKC/ROBERT GLENN RAPP FOUNDATION ENDOWMENT SCHOLARSHIP

Epsilon Sigma Alpha International
Attn: ESA Foundation
P.O. Box 270517
Fort Collins, CO 80527
Phone: (970) 223-2824; Fax: (970) 223-4456
Email: esainfo@esaintl.com
Web: www.esaintl.com/esaf
Summary: To provide financial assistance to residents of Oklahoma who plan to attend college in the state.
Eligibility: Open to residents of Oklahoma who are 1) graduating high school seniors with a GPA of 3.0 or higher or with minimum scores of 22 on the ACT or 1030 on the combined critical reading and mathematics SAT; 2) enrolled in college with a GPA of 3.0 or higher; 3) enrolled at a technical school or returning to school after an absence for retraining of job skills or obtaining a degree; or 4) engaged in online study through an accredited college, university, or vocational school. Applicants must be attending or planning to attend school in Oklahoma. They may major in any field. Selection is based on character (10%), leadership (10%), service (5%), financial need (50%), and scholastic ability (25%).

Financial data: The stipend is $1,000.
Duration: 1 year; may be renewed.
Number awarded: 4 each year.
Deadline: January of each year.

87 BETTER BUSINESS BUREAU OF DELAWARE EDUCATION FOUNDATION SCHOLARSHIP

Better Business Bureau of Delaware
Attn: Education Foundation
Scholarship Committee
60 Reads Way
New Castle, DE 19720
Phone: (302) 230-0108; Fax: (302) 230-0116
Email: info@delaware.bbb.org
Web: Delaware.bbb.org/scholarship

Summary: To provide financial assistance to high school seniors in Delaware who personify high ethics and plan to attend college in any state.
Eligibility: Open to seniors graduating from high schools in Delaware who plan to attend an accredited college or university in any state. Applicants must have a GPA of 3.0 or higher and a record of high ethics as demonstrated through leadership, community service, overall personal integrity, and academic history. Along with their application, they must submit a 500-word essay on what business ethics mean to them and how they have seen it demonstrated. Financial need is not considered in the selection process.
Financial data: The stipend is $2,500.
Duration: 1 year.
Number awarded: 1 each year.
Deadline: January of each year.

88 BILLY WELU SCHOLARSHIP

Professional Bowlers Association
Attn: Billy Welu Bowling Scholarship
719 Second Avenue, Suite 701
Seattle, WA 98104
Phone: (206) 332-9688; Fax: (206) 654-6030
Web: www.pba.com/corporate/scholarships.asp

Summary: To provide financial assistance to college students who are active bowlers.
Eligibility: Open to currently-enrolled college students who compete in the sport of bowling. Applicants must submit a 500-word essay describing how the scholarship will positively affect their bowling, academic, and personal goals. They must have a GPA of 2.5 or higher. Financial need is not considered in the selection process.
Financial data: The stipend is $1,000.
Duration: 1 year.
Number awarded: 1 each year.
Deadline: May of each year.

89 BLACK MESA SCHOLARSHIP FUND

Oklahoma City Community Foundation
Attn: Scholarship Administrator
1000 North Broadway
P.O. Box 1146
Oklahoma City, OK 73101
Phone: (405) 235-5603; Fax: (405) 235-5612
Email: a.rose@occf.org
Web: www.occf.org/scholarships/1bmfsf.html

Summary: To provide financial assistance to high school seniors in Oklahoma who are planning to attend college in any state.
Eligibility: Open to seniors graduating from high schools in Oklahoma who are planning to attend a college or university in any state. Applicants must submit a 500-word essay on a business or industry they find interesting and 100-word essays on each of the following topics: 1) aspects of high school they have found to be the most useful; 2) any areas on which they wish they had spent more time; 3) the universities to which they are applying and how they created that list; 4) where they want to be after they complete their undergraduate studies; and 5) the aspect of this scholarship that interests them the most. Financial need is not considered in the selection process.
Financial data: The stipend is $1,000 per year.
Duration: 1 year; may be renewed up to 3 additional years.
Number awarded: 1 each year.
Deadline: February of each year.

90 BLOGGING SCHOLARSHIP

College Scholarships Foundation
5506 Red Robin Road
Raleigh, NC 27613
Phone: (919) 630-4895; (888) 501-9050
Email: info@collegescholarships.org
Web: www.collegescholarships.org/our-scholarships/blogging.htm

Summary: To recognize and reward, with college scholarships, students who maintain a weblog.
Eligibility: Open to U.S. citizens and permanent residents currently enrolled full-time at a postsecondary institution in the United States. Applicants must be maintaining a weblog while they are in school. Selection is based on a 300-word essay they submit online. The essay should cover such questions as the most interesting or inspiring blog post they have ever read, why they found it inspiring, how they have used blogging to help themselves or others, the most powerful social change they have seen come out of blogging, why they started blogging, what blogging means to them, and why blogging is important to them.
Financial data: The prize is a $10,000 scholarship.
Duration: The prize is awarded annually.
Number awarded: 1 each year.
Deadline: October of each year.

91 BMW SCHOLARSHIP OF HOPE

Epsilon Sigma Alpha International
Attn: ESA Foundation
P.O. Box 270517
Fort Collins, CO 80527
Phone: (970) 223-2824; Fax: (970) 223-4456
Email: esainfo@esaintl.com
Web: www.esaintl.com/esaf

Summary: To provide financial assistance for college to students who have epilepsy.
Eligibility: Open to students who have epilepsy. Applicants must be 1) graduating high school seniors with a GPA of 3.0 or higher or with minimum scores of 22 on the ACT or 1030 on the combined critical reading and mathematics SAT; 2) enrolled in college with a GPA of 3.0 or higher; 3) enrolled at a technical school or returning to school after an absence for retraining of job skills or obtaining a degree; or 4) engaged in online study through an accredited college, university, or vocational school. They may be attending or planning to attend an accredited school anywhere in the United States and major in any field. Selection is based on character (10%), leadership (10%), service (35%), financial need (35%), and scholastic ability (10%).
Financial data: The stipend is $1,000.
Duration: 1 year; may be renewed.
Number awarded: 1 each year.
Deadline: January of each year.

92 BOEING COMPANY SCHOLARSHIP

Independent Colleges of Washington
600 Stewart Street, Suite 600
Seattle, WA 98101
Phone: (206) 623-4494; Fax: (206) 625-9621
Email: info@icwashington.org
Web: www.icwashington.org/scholarships/index.html

Summary: To provide financial assistance to students enrolled at colleges and universities that are members of the Independent Colleges of Washington (ICW).
Eligibility: Open to students enrolled at ICW-member colleges and universities who have a GPA of 3.25 or higher. Applicants must submit a 1-page essay on how their education at an independent college will impact their role in the future of Washington. Selection is based on merit.
Financial data: The stipend is $2,500.
Duration: 1 year; nonrenewable.
Number awarded: 1 each year.
Deadline: March of each year.

93 BOETTCHER FOUNDATION SCHOLARSHIPS

Boettcher Foundation
Attn: Directory, Scholars Program
600 17th Street, Suite 2210 South
Denver, CO 80202-5422

Phone: (303) 534-1937; (800) 323-9640
Email: scholarships@boettcherfoundation.org
Web: www.boettcherfoundation.org/scholarships/index.html

Summary: To provide merit scholarships to Colorado high school seniors who are interested in attending a college or university in the state.

Eligibility: Open to seniors graduating from high schools in Colorado who are in the upper 5% of their graduating class (or 1 of the top 2 students in classes smaller than 40). Applicants must have scores of at least 27 on the ACT or 1200 on the SAT critical reading and mathematics sections combined. They must be planning to enroll full time at a designated college or university in Colorado. U.S. citizenship or permanent resident status is required. Selection is based on scholastic ability, leadership and involvement, service to community and school, and character. Financial need is not considered.

Financial data: These scholarships provide full tuition and fees at a participating accredited 4-year undergraduate institution in Colorado, a stipend of $2,800 per year to help cover living expenses, and a book allowance. Funds are paid directly to the recipient's institution. Supplemental support includes 1) community enrichment programming, through which each college or university that receives a scholar is eligible for funding to support the scholars' activities for a variety of programs that are academically enriching and help prepare the scholars for graduate school; 2) educational enrichment grants, through which scholars may apply for up to $3,000 for projects or programs in the 4 categories of academic/professional development, internships, research, and/or special classes/field sessions; and 3) international education grants, through which scholars may choose to exchange half of 1 year's scholarship for a $5,500 grant towards an international education experience or to exchange 1 year's scholarship for an $8,600 grant for such an experience. In addition, scholars may nominate a counselor, principal, superintendent, or teacher who has been especially dedicated to providing the youth of Colorado with an outstanding education; those nominees receive a Teacher Recognition Award of $1,000 that they may use toward an educational program or project to benefit students at their schools.

Duration: These are 4-year scholarships, but they are not renewed annually if the recipient fails to maintain a GPA of 3.0 or higher.

Number awarded: 40 each year.

Deadline: October of each year.

94 BOOMER ESIASON FOUNDATION SCHOLARSHIP PROGRAM

Boomer Esiason Foundation
c/o Jerry Cahill
483 Tenth Avenue, Suite 300
New York, NY 10018
Phone: (646) 292-7930; Fax: (646) 292-7945
Email: jcahillbef@aol.com
Web: www.cfscholarships.com/BEFScholarships/index.htm

Summary: To provide financial assistance to undergraduate and graduate students who have cystic fibrosis (CF).

Eligibility: Open to CF patients who are working on an undergraduate or graduate degree. Applicants must submit a letter from their doctor confirming the diagnosis of CF and a list of daily medications, information on financial need, a detailed breakdown of tuition costs from their academic institution, transcripts, and a 2-page essay on 1) their post-graduation goals and 2) the importance of compliance with CF therapies and what they practice on a daily basis to stay healthy. Selection is based on academic ability, character, leadership potential, service to the community, and financial need. Finalists are interviewed by telephone.

Financial data: Stipends range from $500 to $2,000. Funds are paid directly to the academic institution to assist in covering the cost of tuition and fees.

Duration: 1 year; nonrenewable.

Number awarded: 10 to 15 each year.

Deadline: March, June, September, or December of each year.

95 BOWFIN MEMORIAL SCHOLARSHIPS

Pearl Harbor Submarine Officers' Wives' Club
c/o Lana Vargas
Pearl Harbor Submarine Memorial Association
11 Arizona Memorial Drive
Honolulu, HI 96818
Phone: (808) 423-1341; Fax: (808) 422-5201
Email: submariescholarships@ymail.com
Web: www.phsowc.org/PHSOWC/Scholarships.html

Summary: To provide financial assistance to the children of submarine force personnel who live in Hawaii and plan to attend college in any state.

Eligibility: Open to the children of submarine force personnel (active duty, retired, or deceased) who are under 23 years of age. Applicants may attend school anywhere in the United States, but their submarine sponsor or surviving parent must live in Hawaii. Selection is based on academic achievement, extracurricular activities, community involvement, motivation and goals, and financial need.

Financial data: Stipends range from $250 to $5,000 per year.

Duration: 1 year; may be renewed upon annual reapplication.

Number awarded: Varies each year; recently, 11 of these scholarships were awarded.

Deadline: February of each year.

96 BRIGHT HORIZONS SCHOLARSHIP

Connecticut Sun Foundation
Attn: Bright Horizons Scholarship
One Mohegan Sun Boulevard
Uncasville, CT 06382
Phone: (860) 862-4000; Fax: (860) 862-4010
Email: dpride@connecticutsun.com
Web: www.wnba.com/sun/community/ctsunfoundation.html

Summary: To provide financial assistance to high school seniors in Connecticut who plan to attend college in the state.

Eligibility: Open to seniors graduating from high schools in Connecticut who plan to attend an accredited 4-year college or university in the state. Applicants must have minimum scores of 1300 on the SAT or 28 on the ACT. They must have a GPA of 3.25 or higher and be able to demonstrate financial need. Along with their application, they must submit a 500-word essay describing the greatest challenge in their community and how they hope to make a positive change. Selection is based on that essay, academic accomplishments, extracurricular activities, letters of recommendation, and financial need. Finalists are invited to a required interview.

Financial data: The stipend is $2,500 per year.

Duration: 4 years.

Number awarded: 1 each year.

Deadline: May of each year.

97 BRIGHT LIGHTS SCHOLARSHIPS

Governor's Coalition for Youth with Disabilities
P.O. Box 2485
Hartford, CT 06146-2485
Phone: (860) 263-6018
Email: info@gcyd.org
Web: www.gcyd.org/scholarship.html

Summary: To provide financial assistance for college to Connecticut residents who have a disability.

Eligibility: Open to seniors graduating from high schools in Connecticut who have a disability. Applicants must be planning to attend 1) a college or university in Connecticut or any other state; 2) any of the 4 campuses of the Connecticut State University System; or 3) any of the 12 Connecticut community colleges. Along with their application, they must submit an essay of 500 to 600 words describing the nature of their disability, its limitations, and how they have overcome the challenges it has presented. Selection is based on 1) the manner in which applicants have overcome the obstacles created by their disability; 2) the degree to which they have contributed to their school and community through service, leadership, and being a positive role model; and 3) their promise for a successful career.

Financial data: For students at colleges and universities nationwide, the stipend ranges from $500 to $5,000. For students at Connecticut State Universities, the stipend is $500 per semester. For students at Connecticut community colleges, the award provides full payment of tuition and fees.

Duration: 1 year. National scholarships are nonrenewable, Connecticut State University scholarships may be renewed for a total of 8 semesters, and Connecticut community college scholarships may be renewed for a total of 3 years.

Number awarded: At least 5 national scholarships (1 from each U.S. Congressional district in Connecticut), 4 Connecticut State University scholarships (1 at each campus), and 12 community college scholarships (1 at each college) are awarded each year. Since the program began, it has awarded more then 200 scholarships worth more than $600,000.

Deadline: February of each year.

98 BRL SCHOLARSHIP PROGRAM

Babe Ruth League, Inc.
1770 Brunswick Pike
P.O. Box 5000
Trenton, NJ 08638

Phone: (609) 695-1434; Fax: (609) 695-2505
Email: scholarships@baberuthleague.org
Web: www.baberuthleague.org/side-indexes/scholarships.html

Summary: To provide financial assistance for college to high school seniors who played Babe Ruth League (BRL) baseball or softball.

Eligibility: Open to graduating high school seniors who played BRL baseball or softball previously. Applicants must be planning to attend college. Along with their application, they must submit a 100-word essay on how playing BRL baseball or softball has affected their life. Financial need is not considered in the selection process.

Financial data: The stipend is $1,000.

Duration: 1 year.

Number awarded: Varies each year, recently, 10 of these scholarships were awarded.

Deadline: June of each year.

99 BUDDY PELLETIER SURFING FOUNDATION SCHOLARSHIP

Buddy Pelletier Surfing Foundation
5121 Chalk Street
Morehead City, NC 28557
Phone: (252) 727-7917; Fax: (252) 727-7965
Email: lynne.pelletier@bbandt.com
Web: buddy.pelletier.com

Summary: To provide financial assistance to members of the East coast surfing community who are interested in attending college in any state.

Eligibility: Open to residents of east coast states who are of any age and high school seniors, continuing college students, or returning college students. Applicants must have participated in activities of the surfing community. Along with their application, they must submit a brief summary of their surfing history, organizations, and volunteer activities; a brief history of their community involvement outside of the surfing community; a 500-word essay on their plans for the future and how their education will benefit the surfing community and the community at large; and information on their financial need.

Financial data: The stipend is $1,000.

Duration: 1 year.

Number awarded: 1 each year.

Deadline: May of each year.

100 BURGER KING SCHOLARS PROGRAM

Burger King Corporation
c/o International Scholarship and Tuition Services, Inc.
200 Crutchfield Avenue
Nashville, TN 37210
Phone: (615) 320-3149; (866) 851-4275; Fax: (615) 320-3151;
Email: contactus@applyists.com
Web: www.bk.com/companyinfo/community/BKS.aspx

Summary: To provide financial assistance for college to high school seniors in the United States, Canada, and Puerto Rico who work part-time.

Eligibility: Open to high school seniors in the United States, Canada, and Puerto Rico who are working part-time (an average of at least 15 hours per week) for 40 weeks per year. Applicants must be able to demonstrate financial need, participation in community service and/or co-curricular activities, good conduct and attitude in school and on the job, and a cumulative GPA of 2.5 or higher.

Financial data: The stipend is $1,000 per year.

Duration: 1 year; nonrenewable.

Number awarded: Varies each year; recently, 320 of these scholarships were awarded.

Deadline: January of each year.

101 C. RAYMOND AND DELSIA R. COLLINS FUND SCHOLARSHIP

Greater Kanawha Valley Foundation
Attn: Scholarship Coordinator
1600 Huntington Square
900 Lee Street, East
P.O. Box 3041
Charleston, WV 25331-3041
Phone: (304) 346-3620; (800) 467-5909; Fax: (304) 346-3640
Email: shoover@tgkvf.org
Web: www.tgkvf.org/scholar.htm

Summary: To provide financial assistance for college to residents of West Virginia.

Eligibility: Open to residents of West Virginia who are attending or planning to attend a college or university anywhere in the country. Applicants must have an ACT score of 20 or higher; be able to demonstrate good moral character, academic excellence, and financial need; and have a GPA of 2.5 or higher.

Financial data: The stipend is $1,000 per year.

Duration: 1 year; may be renewed.

Number awarded: 1 or more each year.

Deadline: January of each year.

102 CALIFORNIA ALARM ASSOCIATION SCHOLARSHIPS

California Alarm Association
333 Washington Boulevard, Suite 433
Marina del Rey, CA 90292
Phone: (800) 437-7658; Fax: (800) 490-9682
Email: info@caaonline.org
Web: caaonline.org

Summary: To provide financial assistance to high school seniors in California who are the children of active-duty law enforcement and fire service personnel and interested in attending college in any state.

Eligibility: Open to seniors graduating from high schools in California who have been accepted at an accredited college or university in any state. Applicants must have a father, mother, or legal guardian who is a full-time active employee (not on disability) of the police or sheriff's department or a paid employee or volunteer of a fire department in California. Along with their application, they must submit an essay of 500 to 750 words on what it means to them to have their parent or guardian involved in securing our community. Selection is based on that essay (25 points), grade average (25 points), SAT scores (30 points), and extracurricular activities (20 points); financial need is not considered. First, regional winners (northern and southern California) are selected; from those, state winners are selected.

Financial data: Regional winners receive $1,000 for first place and $1,000 for second place. State winners receive an additional $1,500 for first place and $1,000 for second place.

Duration: 1 year; nonrenewable.

Number awarded: 4 regional winners are selected each year; of those, 2 are selected as state winners.

Deadline: April of each year.

103 CALIFORNIA FEE WAIVER PROGRAM FOR DEPENDENTS OF TOTALLY DISABLED VETERANS

California Department of Veterans Affairs
Attn: Division of Veterans Services
1227 O Street, Room 105
Sacramento, CA 95814
Phone: (916) 503-8397; (800) 952-LOAN (within CA); Fax: (916) 653-2563
TDD: (800) 324-5966;
Email: ruckergl@cdva.ca.gov
Web: www.cdva.ca.gov/VetService/Waivers.aspx

Summary: To provide financial assistance for college to dependents of disabled and other California veterans.

Eligibility: Open to spouses (including registered domestic partners), children, and unremarried widow(er)s of veterans who are currently totally service-connected disabled (or are being compensated for a service-connected disability at a rate of 100%) or who died of a service-connected cause or disability. The veteran parent must have served during a qualifying war period and must have been discharged or released from military service under honorable conditions. The child cannot be over 27 years of age (extended to 30 if the student was in the military); there are no age limitations for spouses or surviving spouses. This program does not have an income limit. Dependents in college are not eligible if they are qualified to receive educational benefits from the U.S. Department of Veterans Affairs. Applicants must be attending or planning to attend a community college, branch of the California State University system, or campus of the University of California.

Financial data: Full-time college students receive a waiver of tuition and registration fees at any publicly-supported community or state college or university in California.

Duration: Children of eligible veterans may receive postsecondary benefits until the needed training is completed or until the dependent reaches 27 years of age (extended to 30 if the dependent serves in the armed forces). Widow(er)s and spouses are limited to a maximum of 48 months' full-time training or the equivalent in part-time training.

Number awarded: Varies each year.

Deadline: Deadline not specified.

104 CALIFORNIA FEE WAIVER PROGRAM FOR RECIPIENTS OF THE MEDAL OF HONOR AND THEIR CHILDREN

California Department of Veterans Affairs
Attn: Division of Veterans Services
1227 O Street, Room 101
Sacramento, CA 95814
Phone: (916) 503-8397; (800) 952-LOAN (within CA); Fax: (916) 653-2563; TDD: (800) 324-5966
Email: ruckergl@cdva.ca.gov
Web: www.cdva.ca.gov/VetService/Waivers.aspx

Summary: To provide financial assistance for college to veterans in California who received the Medal of Honor and their children.

Eligibility: Open to recipients of the Medal of Honor and their children younger than 27 years of age who are residents of California. Applicants must be attending or planning to attend a community college, branch of the California State University system, or campus of the University of California.

Financial data: Full-time college students receive a waiver of tuition and registration fees at any publicly-supported community or state college or university in California.

Duration: 1 year; may be renewed.

Number awarded: Varies each year.

Deadline: Deadline not specified.

105 CALIFORNIA FOUNDATION FOR GIFTED EDUCATION COLLEGE SCHOLARSHIP

California Association for the Gifted
Attn: California Foundation for Gifted Education
9278 Madison Avenue
Orangevale, CA 95662
Phone: (916) 988-3999; Fax: (916) 988-5999
Email: judithr11@aol.com
Web: www.cagifted.org/displaycommon.cfm?an=15

Summary: To provide financial assistance to high school students in California who have participated in gifted and talented programs and plan to attend college in any state.

Eligibility: Open to seniors graduating from high schools in California and juniors at those schools who expect to participate in an early entrance program at a participating college or university. Applicants must be planning to enter a recognized institution of higher education in any state. They must be able to demonstrate outstanding achievement in a chosen area of talent or giftedness and be nominated by a teacher, mentor, or member of a gifted association. Along with their application, they must submit 1) an essay of 1 to 3 pages on their intellectual or artistic passion; 2) a sample of demonstrated excellence in an area of gift or talent (e.g., portfolio, school or sample projects, honors awarded); 3) 2 letters of reference; and 4) a transcript. Financial need is not considered in the selection process.

Financial data: The stipend is $1,000.

Duration: 1 year.

Number awarded: Varies each year; recently, 3 of these scholarships were awarded.

Deadline: February of each year.

106 CALIFORNIA LEGION AUXILIARY EDUCATIONAL ASSISTANCE

American Legion Auxiliary
Department of California
Veterans War Memorial Building
401 Van Ness Avenue, Room 113
San Francisco, CA 94102-4586
Phone: (415) 861-5092; Fax: (415) 861-8365
Email: calegionaux@calegionaux.org
Web: www.calegionaux.org/scholarships.htm

Summary: To provide financial assistance to high school seniors in California who are the children of veterans or military personnel and require assistance to continue their education.

Eligibility: Open to seniors graduating from high schools in California who are the children of active-duty military personnel or veterans who served during war time. Applicants must be planning to continue their education at a college, university, or business/trade school in California. Financial need is considered in the selection process. Each high school in California may nominate only 1 student for these scholarships; the faculty selects the nominee if more than 1 student wishes to apply. Financial need is considered in the selection process.

Financial data: Stipends are $1,000 or $500 per year.

Duration: 1 year; 1 of the scholarships may be renewed 1 additional year.

Number awarded: 8 each year: 1 at $1,000 that may be renewed, 4 at $1,000 that are nonrenewable, and 3 at $500 that are nonrenewable.

Deadline: March of each year.

107 CALIFORNIA LEGION AUXILIARY SCHOLARSHIPS FOR CONTINUING AND/OR REENTRY STUDENTS

American Legion Auxiliary
Department of California
Veterans War Memorial Building
401 Van Ness Avenue, Room 113
San Francisco, CA 94102-4586
Phone: (415) 861-5092; Fax: (415) 861-8365
Email: calegionaux@calegionaux.org
Web: www.calegionaux.org/scholarships.htm

Summary: To provide financial assistance to California residents who are active-duty military personnel, veterans, or children of veterans and require assistance to continue their education.

Eligibility: Open to California residents who are 1) active-duty military personnel; 2) veterans of World War I, World War II, Korea, Vietnam, Grenada/Lebanon, Panama, or Desert Shield/Desert Storm; and 3) children of veterans who served during those periods of war. Applicants must be continuing or reentry students at a college, university, or business/trade school in California. Financial need is considered in the selection process.

Financial data: The stipend is $1,000 or $500.

Duration: 1 year.

Number awarded: 5 each year: 3 at $1,000 and 2 at $500.

Deadline: March of each year.

108 CALIFORNIA STATE FAIR ACADEMIC ACHIEVERS SCHOLARSHIPS

California State Fair
Attn: Friends of the Fair Scholarship Program
1600 Exposition Boulevard
P.O. Box 15649
Sacramento, CA 95852
Phone: (916) 263-3149
Email: entryoffice@calexpo.com
Web: www.bigfun.org/competition-youth.php

Summary: To provide financial assistance to high school seniors in California who rank in the top 10% of their class and plan to attend college in the state.

Eligibility: Open to seniors graduating from high schools in California who rank in the top 10% of their class for academic performance. Applicants must be planning to attend an accredited 4-year college or university in the state. Along with their application, they must submit a 500-word essay on a topic that changes annually; recently, applicants were invited to present their ideas on how Americans could reduce their carbon footprint. Selection is based on personal commitment, goals established for their chosen field, leadership potential, and civic accomplishments.

Financial data: Stipends are $1,500 or $750.

Duration: 1 year.

Number awarded: 2 each year: 1 at $1,500 and 1 at $750.

Deadline: March of each year.

109 CALIFORNIA WINE GRAPE GROWERS FOUNDATION SCHOLARSHIPS

California Association of Winegrape Growers
Attn: California Wine Grape Growers Foundation
1325 J Street, Suite 1560
Sacramento, CA 95814
Phone: (916) 379-8995; (800) 241-1800; Fax: (916) 924-5374
Email: info@cawg.org
Web: www.cwggf.org/index.php?page_id=293

Summary: To provide financial assistance for college to high school seniors in California whose parent(s) work in the grape wine vineyards.

Eligibility: Open to high school seniors in California who plan to attend a branch of the University of California, a branch of the California State University system, or a community college in the state. Applicants must have a parent or legal guardian who was employed as a vineyard worker by a winegrape grower during either or both of the 2 preceding seasons. Along with their application, they must submit a high school transcript, a copy of their SAT or ACT scores (if they are planning to attend a 4-year university), a letter of recommendation from a school official, and a 2-page essay on themselves and their career goals. Applications are available in both English and Spanish. Selection is based on financial need, demonstrated academic ability, community involvement and leadership and/or work history, and determination to succeed.

Financial data: The stipend is $1,000 per year at a 4-year university or $500 per year at a community college.

Duration: 4 years at branches of the University of California or California State University system; 2 years at community colleges.

Number awarded: 6 each year: 2 at 4-year universities and 4 at community colleges.

Deadline: March of each year.

110 CALIFORNIA-HAWAII ELKS ASSOCIATION VOCATIONAL GRANTS

California-Hawaii Elks Association
Attn: Scholarship Committee
5450 East Lamona Avenue
Fresno, CA 93727-2224
Phone: (559) 255-4531; Fax: (559) 456-2659
Web: www.chea-elks.org/vocationalgrant.html

Summary: To provide financial assistance for vocational school to residents of California and Hawaii.

Eligibility: Open to residents of California or Hawaii who are high school seniors or older. Applicants must be enrolled or planning to enroll in a vocational/technical program of 2 years or less that leads to a terminal associate degree, diploma, or certificate, but less than a bachelor's degree. Students planning to transfer to a 4-year school to work on a bachelor's degree are not eligible. Selection is based on motivation, financial need, aptitude toward chosen vocation, grades, and completeness and neatness of the application brochure. Applications are available from an Elks Lodge in California or Hawaii; they must be endorsed by the lodge. U.S. citizenship is required.

Financial data: The stipend is $1,000 per year. Funds may be used for tuition and fees, room and board (if living on campus), and books and supplies. They may not be used for general living expenses or child care costs.

Duration: 1 year; may be renewed for 1 additional year.

Number awarded: 58 each year: 55 to residents of California and 3 to residents of Hawaii.

Deadline: Applications may be submitted at any time.

111 CALIFORNIA-HAWAII ELKS MAJOR PROJECT UNDERGRADUATE SCHOLARSHIP PROGRAM FOR STUDENTS WITH DISABILITIES

California-Hawaii Elks Association
Attn: Scholarship Committee
5450 East Lamona Avenue
Fresno, CA 93727-2224
Phone: (559) 255-4531; Fax: (559) 456-2659
Web: www.chea-elks.org/scholarshipmenu.html

Summary: To provide financial assistance to residents of California and Hawaii who have a disability and are interested in attending college in any state.

Eligibility: Open to residents of California or Hawaii who have a physical impairment, neurological impairment, visual impairment, hearing impairment, and/or speech/language disorder. Applicants must be a senior in high school, be a high school graduate, or have passed the GED test. They must be planning to attend a college, university, community college, or vocational school in any state. U.S. citizenship is required. Selection is based on financial need, GPA, severity of disability, seriousness of purpose, and depth of character. Applications are available from an Elks Lodge in California or Hawaii; students must first request an interview with the lodge's scholarship chairman, secretary, or Exalted Ruler.

Financial data: The stipend is $2,000 per year for 4-year colleges or universities or $1,000 for community colleges and vocational schools.

Duration: 1 year; may be renewed for up to 3 additional years or until completion of an undergraduate degree, whichever occurs first.

Number awarded: 20 to 30 each year.

Deadline: March of each year.

112 CALVARY FOUNDATION SCHOLARSHIPS

Calvary United Methodist Church
Attn: Calvary Foundation
P.O. Box 2504
Arlington, VA 22202
Phone: (703) 892-5185
Email: calmeth@erols.com
Web: www.calmeth.org

Summary: To provide financial assistance to residents of Virginia, Maryland, and the District of Columbia and students attending college in those states.

Eligibility: Open to 1) residents of Virginia, Maryland, and the District of Columbia attending or planning to attend college or graduate school in any state; and 2) undergraduate and graduate students from any state who are attending, or planning to attend, a college or university in Virginia, Maryland, or the District of Columbia. Applicants must submit 2-page statements on 1) their academic strengths, challenges, work experience, and/or volunteer experience; 2) their reasons for applying for the scholarship, proposed field of study, future career plans, and reasons for choosing their preferred study institution; 3) their principal interests and activities; and 4) their choice of an assigned list of topics. High school seniors must also submit a copy of their SAT or ACT scores and official transcripts. Students already enrolled in college must also submit transcripts. Financial need is considered in the selection process.

Financial data: A stipend is awarded (amount not specified).

Duration: 1 year.

Number awarded: 1 or more each year.

Deadline: April of each year.

113 CAMPUS DISCOVERY "VALUE OF COLLEGE" SCHOLARSHIP

CampusDiscovery.com
c/o WiseChoiceBrands
1229 King Street, Third Floor
P.O. Box 25457
Alexandria, VA 22313
Email: info@campusdiscovery.com
Web: www.campusdiscovery.com

Summary: To recognize and reward college students and recent graduates who complete an online evaluation of their college.

Eligibility: Open to students currently enrolled at an accredited 2- or 4-year college or university and to recent graduates of those institutions. Applicants must complete an online survey about their college and also submit a 200-word essay on what they have gotten out of their college experience and why it has been valuable to attend. Selection is based on writing ability (25%), wisdom (25%), originality (25%), and overall excellence (25%). U.S. citizenship or permanent resident status is required.

Financial data: The award is $5,000. If the recipient is still attending college, funds are disbursed directly to the institution. If the recipient has already graduated, funds are paid directly to the individual.

Duration: The award is presented annually.

Number awarded: 1 each year.

Deadline: January of each year.

114 CANDY HOWARTH SCHOLARSHIP

American Legion Auxiliary
Department of New Jersey
c/o Lucille M. Miller, Secretary/Treasurer
1540 Kuser Road, Suite A-8
Hamilton, NJ 08619
Phone: (609) 581-9580; Fax: (609) 581-8429
Email: newjerseyala@juno.com
Web: www.alanj.org

Summary: To provide financial assistance to New Jersey residents who are the descendants of veterans and planning to attend college in any state.

Eligibility: Open to the children, grandchildren, and great-grandchildren of veterans who served in the U.S. armed forces during specified periods of war time. Applicants must be graduating high school seniors who have been residents of New Jersey for at least 2 years. They must be planning to attend a college or university in any state. Along with their application, they must submit a 1,000-word essay on a topic that changes annually; recently, students were asked to write on the topic, "Honoring Our Promise Everyday-How I Can Serve My Country and Our Veterans." Selection is based on academic achievement (40%), character (15%), leadership (15%), Americanism (15%), and financial need (15%).

Financial data: Stipends range from $1,000 to $2,500.

Duration: 1 year; nonrenewable.

Number awarded: 1 each year.

Deadline: April of each year.

115 CAPED GENERAL EXCELLENCE SCHOLARSHIP

California Association for Postsecondary Education and Disability
Attn: Executive Assistant
71423 Biskra Road
Rancho Mirage, CA 92270
Phone: (760) 346-8206; Fax: (760) 340-5275; TDD: (760) 341-4084
Email: caped2000@aol.com
Web: www.caped.net/scholarships.html

Summary: To provide financial assistance to undergraduate and graduate students in California who have a disability and can demonstrate academic achievement and involvement in community and campus activities.

Eligibility: Open to students at public and private colleges and universities in California who have a disability. Undergraduates must have completed at least 6 semester credits and have a GPA of 2.5 or higher. Graduate students must have completed at least 3 semester units and have a GPA of 3.0 or higher. Applicants must submit a 1-page personal letter that demonstrates their writing skills, progress towards meeting their educational and vocational goals, management of their disability, and involvement in community activities. They must also submit a letter of recommendation from a faculty member, verification of disability, official transcripts, proof of current enrollment, and documentation of financial need. This award is presented to the applicant who demonstrates the highest level of academic achievement and involvement in community and campus life.

Financial data: The stipend is $1,500.

Duration: 1 year.

Number awarded: 1 each year.

Deadline: September of each year.

116 CAPEX.COM "A GPA ISN'T EVERYTHING" SCHOLARSHIP

Cappex.com, LLC
600 Laurel Avenue
Highland Park, IL 60035
Web: www.cappex.com/scholarships/GPAisntEverythingScholarship.jsp

Summary: To provide financial assistance for college to high school seniors who complete a profile for Cappex.com but whose GPA is not outstanding.

Eligibility: Open to high school seniors who complete an online profile for Cappex.com that will enable colleges and universities to contact them for recruiting purposes. They must be U.S. citizens or permanent residents planning to attend an accredited college or university in the United States. In completing their profile, they must describe their extracurricular, leadership, and volunteer activities. This scholarship is reserved for high school seniors who want to "get some cash for getting an A in street smarts."

Financial data: The stipend is $1,000.

Duration: 1 year.

Number awarded: 1 each year.

Deadline: July of each year.

117 CAPITOL SCHOLARSHIP PROGRAM

Connecticut Department of Higher Education
Attn: Office of Student Financial Aid
61 Woodland Street
Hartford, CT 06105-2326
Phone: (860) 947-1855; Fax: (860) 947-1313
Email: csp@ctdhe.org
Web: www.ctdhe.org/SFA/default.htm

Summary: To provide financial assistance for undergraduate education to high school seniors or graduates in Connecticut.

Eligibility: Open to residents of Connecticut who are U.S. citizens or nationals and high school seniors or graduates. They must be in the top 20% of their graduating class or have scores of 1800 or higher on the SAT or 27 or higher on the ACT, and they must be planning to attend a college in Connecticut or in a state that has a reciprocity agreement with Connecticut. Financial need is considered in the selection process.

Financial data: Stipends range from $2,000 to $3,000 at Connecticut 4-year degree and 2-year proprietary colleges or from $500 to $1,000 at Connecticut 2-year public colleges. Students attending approved out-of-state colleges receive grants of $500 per year.

Duration: 1 year.

Number awarded: Varies each year.

Deadline: February of each year.

118 CAPSTONE CORPORATION SCHOLARSHIP AWARD

National Naval Officers Association-Washington, D.C. Chapter
Attn: Scholarship Program
2701 Park Center Drive, A1108
Alexandria, VA 22302
Phone: (703) 566-3840; Fax: (703) 566-3813
Email: Stephen.Williams@Navy.mil
Web: dcnnoa.memberlodge.com/Default.aspx?pageId=309002

Summary: To provide financial assistance to minority high school seniors from the Washington, D.C. area who plan to attend college in any state.

Eligibility: Open to minority seniors graduating from high schools in the Washington, D.C. metropolitan area who plan to enroll full-time at an accredited 2- or 4-year college or university in any state. Applicants must have a GPA of 3.0 or higher. U.S. citizenship or permanent resident status is required. Selection is based on academic achievement, community involvement, and financial need.

Financial data: The stipend is $1,000.

Duration: 1 year; nonrenewable.

Number awarded: 1 each year.

Deadline: March of each year.

119 CAREER AID FOR TECHNICAL STUDENTS PROGRAM

New Hampshire Charitable Foundation
37 Pleasant Street
Concord, NH 03301-4005
Phone: (603) 225-6641; (800) 464-6641; Fax: (603) 225-1700
Email: info@nhcf.org
Web: www.nhcf.org/page16960.cfm

Summary: To provide financial assistance to New Hampshire residents preparing for a vocational or technical career.

Eligibility: Open to residents of New Hampshire entering a 2- or 3-year degree program or a shorter-term technical degree training program that leads to an associate degree, a trade license, or certification. Applicants must be dependent students younger than 24 years of age and planning to enroll at least half-time at a community college, vocational school, trade school, or other short-term training program. They must be able to demonstrate financial need. Although academic excellence is not considered in the selection process, applicants should be able to demonstrate reasonable achievement and a commitment to their chosen field of study.

Financial data: Stipends range from $100 to $3,500, depending on the need of the recipient. A total of $250,000 is distributed annually.

Duration: 1 year.

Number awarded: Varies each year.

Deadline: June of each year.

120 CAREER COLLEGES & SCHOOLS OF TEXAS SCHOLARSHIP

Career Colleges & Schools of Texas
823 Congress Avenue, Suite 230
Austin, TX 78701
Phone: (512) 479-0425; Fax: (512) 495-9031
Email: ccst@assnmgmt.com
Web: www.careercholarships.org

Summary: To provide financial assistance to high school seniors in Texas who are interested in attending a career college in the state.

Eligibility: Open to high school seniors in Texas who are interested in attending a career college in the state. The sponsor provides 4 scholarships to each of the 1,500 high schools in the state. Recipients are then selected by the scholarship directors or counselors at their high school. Selection criteria vary by school but usually include academic excellence, financial need, and/or student leadership.

Financial data: The stipend is a $1,000 award certificate to be used to pay for tuition at any of the participating career colleges in Texas.

Duration: 1 year.

Number awarded: 6,000 each year (4 at each of the 1,500 high schools in the state).

Deadline: Deadline not specified.

121 CARVER SCHOLARS PROGRAM

Roy J. Carver Charitable Trust
202 Iowa Avenue
Muscatine, IA 52761-3733

Phone: (563) 263-4010; Fax: (563) 263-1547
Email: info@carvertrust.org
Web: www.carvertrust.org

Summary: To provide financial assistance for college to students in Iowa who have overcome significant obstacles to attend college.

Eligibility: Open to students attending the 3 public universities in Iowa, the 23 participating private 4-year colleges and universities in the state, or a community college in Iowa and planning to transfer to 1 of those 4-year institutions. Applicants must be sophomores seeking support for their junior year. They must present evidence of unusual social and/or other barriers to attending college full-time; examples include, but are not limited to, students who 1) are from 1-parent families; 2) are attending college while working full-time; 3) have social, mental, or physical disabilities; or 4) have families to support. They must have graduated from a high school in Iowa or have been residents of the state for at least 5 consecutive years immediately prior to applying, be full-time students, have at least a 2.8 GPA, be U.S. citizens, and submit a financial profile indicating insufficient personal, family, and institutional resources to pay full-time college tuition. A particular goal of the program is to assist students "who fall between the cracks of other financial aid programs." Applications must be submitted to the financial aid office at the Iowa college or university the applicant attends.

Financial data: Stipends generally average $5,200 at public universities or $7,600 at private colleges in Iowa.

Duration: 1 year; may be renewed 1 additional year.

Number awarded: Varies each year; since the program's establishment, it has awarded more than 1,750 scholarships worth nearly $14 million.

Deadline: March of each year.

122 CELEBRATION OF EXCELLENCE SCHOLARSHIP

Georgia Association of Homes and Services for Children
Attn: Celebration of Excellence
34 Peachtree Street, N.W., Suite 2230
Atlanta, GA 30303
Phone: (404) 572-6178; Fax: (404) 572-6171
Email: susan@catalystforcare.org
Web: www.celebrationofexcellence.org

Summary: To provide financial assistance to residents of Georgia who have been in foster care and plan to attend college or graduate school in any state.

Eligibility: Open to Georgia residents who were in the custody of the Georgia Department of Family and Children Services (DFCS) or placed at a licensed private residential program at the time of their 16th birthday. Students who were emancipated at the age of 16 or older are also eligible. Applicants must be attending or planning to attend an approved college, university, vocational program, or graduate school in any state. They must submit an essay of 3 to 5 pages that discusses their educational and career goals, their extracurricular activities and community involvement, and why they think this scholarship will help them reach their goals. Selection is based on that essay, transcripts, SAT/ACT or GRE/LSAT/GMAT scores, 2 letters of reference, and financial need.

Financial data: The stipend is $1,500 per year for graduate students or $1,000 per year for undergraduates.

Duration: 1 year; may be renewed for 1 additional year of graduate study or 3 additional years of undergraduate study.

Number awarded: 1 or more each year.

Deadline: April of each year.

123 CENTER FOR EDUCATION SOLUTIONS/A. PATRICK CHARNON SCHOLARSHIP

Center for Education Solutions
P.O. Box 208
San Francisco, CA 94104-0208
Phone: (925) 934-7304
Email: scholarship@cesresources.org
Web: www.cesresources.org/charnon.html

Summary: To provide financial assistance to entering or continuing undergraduate students who demonstrate a commitment to their community.

Eligibility: Open to students who are admitted or enrolled in a full-time undergraduate program of study at an accredited 4-year college or university. They must demonstrate dedication and commitment to their communities. Along with their application, they must submit a 2- to 4-page essay on how community service experiences have shaped their lives and how they will use their college education to build communities in a manner consistent with values of compassion, tolerance, generosity, and respect. The selection committee looks for candidates whose values reflect the goals of the program and who have demonstrated their commitment to those values by their actions.

Financial data: The stipend is $1,500 per year.

Duration: 1 year; may be renewed up to 3 additional years.

Number awarded: 1 each year.

Deadline: March of each year.

124 CHAIRSCHOLARS FOUNDATION NATIONAL SCHOLARSHIPS

ChairScholars Foundation, Inc.
16101 Carencia Lane
Odessa, FL 33556-3278
Phone: (813) 926-0544; (888) 926-0544; Fax: (813) 920-7661
Email: chairscholars@tampabay.rr.com
Web: www.chairscholars.org/national.html

Summary: To provide financial assistance for college to physically challenged students.

Eligibility: Open to high school seniors and college freshmen who have a significant physical challenge, although they are not required to be in a wheelchair. Applicants should be able to demonstrate financial need, have a GPA of 3.0 or higher, and show some form of community service or social contribution in the past. Along with their application, they must submit an essay of 300 to 500 words on how they became physically challenged, how their situation has affected them and their family, and their goals and aspirations for the future. Graduate students and all students over 21 years of age are not eligible.

Financial data: Stipends range from $1,000 to $5,000 per year. Funds are to be used for tuition and school expenses.

Duration: Up to 4 years for high school seniors; up to 3 years for college freshmen. The maximum total award is $20,000.

Number awarded: 15 to 20 each year.

Deadline: February of each year.

125 CHAPEL OF FOUR CHAPLAINS NATIONAL ESSAY SCHOLARSHIP CONTEST

Chapel of Four Chaplains
Naval Business Center, Building 649
1201 Constitution Avenue
Philadelphia, PA 19112-1307
Phone: (215) 218-1943; (866) 400-0975; Fax: (215) 218-1949
Email: chapel@fourchaplains.org
Web: www.fourchaplains.org/programs.html

Summary: To recognize and reward, with college scholarships, high school seniors who submit outstanding essays on a topic related to public service.

Eligibility: Open to public and private high school seniors, except for the children of members of the Chapel of Four Chaplains, youth committee, board of directors, or board of trustees. The topic of the essay changes annually; recently, students were invited to identify a compelling problem, need, or unresolved conflict (e.g., racial discrimination, religious intolerance, community injustice, public indifference, civic discord, societal ignorance) that, through caring intervention, can be transformed and corrected. Essays must be typed, double spaced, and no more than 450 words. Selection is based on imaginative creativity, correct grammar and spelling, clarity, relevance, and logical presentation.

Financial data: Prizes are scholarships of $1,000 for first, $750 for second, $500 for third, $400 for fourth, and $300 for fifth.

Duration: The competition is held annually.

Number awarded: 5 each year.

Deadline: November of each year.

126 CHARLES AND MELVA T. OWEN MEMORIAL SCHOLARSHIPS

National Federation of the Blind
Attn: Scholarship Committee
1800 Johnson Street
Baltimore, MD 21230
Phone: (410) 659-9314, ext. 2415; Fax: (410) 685-5653
Email: scholarships@nfb.org
Web: www.nfb.org/nfb/scholarship_program.asp

Summary: To provide financial assistance to blind entering or continuing undergraduate or graduate students.

Eligibility: Open to legally blind students who are working on or planning to work full-time on an undergraduate or graduate degree. Scholarships, however, are not awarded for the study of religion or solely to further general or cultural education; the academic program should be directed towards attaining financial independence. Along with their application, they must submit transcripts, standardized test scores, proof of legal blindness, 2 letters of recommendation, and a letter of endorsement from their National Federation of the Blind state

president or designee. Selection is based on academic excellence, service to the community, and financial need.
Financial data: Stipends are $10,000 or $3,000.
Duration: 1 year; recipients may resubmit applications up to 2 additional years.
Number awarded: 2 each year: 1 at $10,000 and 1 at $3,000.
Deadline: March of each year.

127 CHARLES B. WASHINGTON SCHOLARSHIPS

Urban League of Nebraska, Inc.
Attn: Scholarships
3040 Lake Street
Omaha, NE 68111
Phone: (402) 451-1066
Web: www.urbanleagueneb.org/education_connection/scholarships.shtml
Summary: To provide financial assistance to residents of Nebraska who plan to attend college in any state.
Eligibility: Open to Nebraska residents who are seniors in high school or students currently enrolled in college. Applicants must be attending or planning to attend a college or university in any state. They must have a GPA of 2.5 or higher and be able to document financial need and at least 5 to 10 hours of community involvement. Along with their application, they must submit a 500-word essay on their goals and ambitions and the reasons they should receive this scholarship.
Financial data: A stipend is awarded (amount not specified).
Duration: 1 year.
Number awarded: Varies each year; recently, 6 of these scholarships were awarded.
Deadline: March of each year.

128 CHARLEY WOOTAN GRANT PROGRAM

Texas Guaranteed Student Loan Corporation
c/o Scholarship Management Services
One Scholarship Way
P.O. Box 297
St. Peter, MN 56082
Phone: (507) 931-1682; (800) 537-4180; Fax: (507) 931-9168
Email: Wootan@ScholarshipAmerica.org
Web: www.tgslc.org/wootan
Summary: To provide financial assistance for college to residents of the United States and its territories who demonstrate financial need.
Eligibility: Open to U.S. citizens and permanent residents of the United States, District of Columbia, Puerto Rico, Guam, the U.S. Virgin Islands, or other U.S. territory or commonwealth. Applicants must be high school seniors or graduates (including GED recipients who plan to enroll or undergraduates who are already enrolled at least half-time at an approved 2- or 4-year college or university or vocational/technical school. Selection is based entirely on financial need.
Financial data: Stipends range from $1,000 to $4,245, depending on the need of the recipient.
Duration: 1 year; recipients may reapply.
Number awarded: Varies each year; a total of $2 million is available through this program annually, of which $1 million is provided to students in Texas and $1 million to students in other states, the District of Columbia, or U.S. territories. It is administered by Scholarship Management Services, a division of Scholarship America.
Deadline: May of each year.

129 CHARLIE BURKART SCHOLARSHIP

Iowa Section PGA of America
3182 Highway 22
Riverside, IA 52327
Phone: (319) 648-0026
Web: www.iowapga.com/junior-programs/burkart-scholarship
Summary: To provide financial assistance to high school seniors from Iowa and western Illinois who have an affiliation with golf and plan to attend college in any state.
Eligibility: Open to seniors graduating from high schools in Iowa and those portions of western Illinois that are part of the Iowa Section PGA (including the cities of Monmouth, Macomb, Galesburg, Moline, Rock Island, Kewanee, and Galena, but not the cities of Freeport, Springfield, or Quincy). Applicants must be planning to enroll full-time at a college or university in any state. Along with their application, they must submit a statement on their interest in golf, other activities and awards, educational and vocational plans, and financial need. Selection is based first on interest and activity in golf and the potential for future contributions, then on academic ability and financial need.
Financial data: The stipend is $1,000 per year.
Duration: 4 years.
Number awarded: 1 each year.
Deadline: June of each year.

130 CHATEAU STE. MICHELLE SCHOLARSHIP FUND

College Success Foundation
1605 N.W. Sammamish Road, Suite 200
Issaquah, WA 98027
Phone: (425) 416-2000; (877) 655-4097; Fax: (425) 416-2001
Email: info@collegesuccessfoundation.org
Web: www.collegesuccessfoundation.org/Chateau
Summary: To provide financial assistance to underrepresented minority residents of Washington, especially those whose families work in agriculture, who are attending or planning to attend college in the state.
Eligibility: Open to residents of Washington who are high school seniors or college freshmen or sophomores. Applicants must be enrolled or planning to enroll full-time at a 4-year college or university in the state. They must have a GPA of 2.75 or higher and be able to demonstrate financial need (family income of $39,000 or less for a family of 1, rising to $94,000 or less for a family of 7). Preference is given to members of underrepresented groups whose parents work in the agricultural sector.
Financial data: The stipend is $5,000 per year.
Duration: 1 year; may be renewed up to 3 additional years.
Number awarded: Varies each year; since the program was established, it has awarded more than 140 scholarships.
Deadline: May of each year.

131 CHICAGO LIGHTHOUSE SCHOLARSHIPS

Chicago Lighthouse for People Who Are Blind or Visually Impaired
Attn: Scholarship Program Coordinator
1850 West Roosevelt Road
Chicago, IL 60608-1298
Phone: (312) 666-1331; Fax: (312) 243-8539; TDD: (312) 666-8874
Email: scholarships@chicagolighthouse.org
Web: www.thechicagolighthouse.org
Summary: To provide financial assistance to blind or visually impaired college and graduate students from any state.
Eligibility: Open to residents of any state who are blind or visually impaired. Applicants must be attending or planning to attend an accredited college, university, or community college as an undergraduate or graduate student. Along with their application, they must submit an essay about their visual impairment, background, educational and career goals, and how this scholarship will help achieve those goals.
Financial data: Stipends range up to $5,000.
Duration: 1 year.
Number awarded: Varies each year; recently, 14 of these scholarships were awarded.
Deadline: April of each year.

132 CHICK AND SOPHIE MAJOR MEMORIAL DUCK CALLING CONTEST

Stuttgart Chamber of Commerce
507 South Main Street
P.O. Box 1500
Stuttgart, AR 72160
Phone: (870) 673-1602; Fax: (870) 673-1604
Email: stuttgartchamber@centurytel.net
Web: stuttgartarkansas.org/index.php?fuseaction=p0004.&mod=45
Summary: To recognize and reward, with college scholarships, high school seniors who are outstanding duck callers.
Eligibility: Open to high school seniors. Contestants are allowed 90 seconds in which to present 1) hail or long distance call; 2) mating or lonesome duck call; 3) feed or clatter call; and 4) comeback call.
Financial data: The prizes are a $2,000 scholarship for the winner, a $1,000 scholarship for second place, a $750 scholarship for third place, and a $500 scholarship for fourth place. Funds must be applied toward higher education.
Duration: The competition is held annually.
Number awarded: 4 prizes are presented each year.

Deadline: The competition is held annually on the Friday and Saturday following Thanksgiving.

133 CHICK EVANS CADDIE SCHOLARSHIPS

Western Golf Association
Attn: Evans Scholars Foundation
1 Briar Road
Golf, IL 60029-0301
Phone: (847) 724-4600; Fax: (847) 724-7133
Email: evansscholars@wgaesf.com
Web: www.evansscholarsfoundation.com

Summary: To provide financial assistance for college to students who have worked as golf caddies.

Eligibility: Open to students who have completed their junior year in high school, rank in the upper quarter of their graduating class, have a GPA of 3.0 or higher, have taken the SAT or ACT test, are able to demonstrate financial need, and have been a full-time caddie on a regular basis for at least 2 years. Applicants from 12 states (Colorado, Illinois, Indiana, Michigan, Minnesota, Missouri, Ohio, Oregon, Pennsylvania, Virginia, Washington, and Wisconsin) must attend designated universities; applicants from other states must attend their state university, as approved by the scholarship committee. Selection is based on character, integrity, leadership, and financial need.

Financial data: The awards cover tuition and housing at universities approved by the scholarship committee.

Duration: 1 year; may be renewed for up to 3 additional years.

Number awarded: Varies each year; recently, 865 caddies were receiving support from this program.

Deadline: September of each year.

134 CHIEF MASTER SERGEANTS OF THE AIR FORCE SCHOLARSHIPS

Air Force Sergeants Association
Attn: Scholarship Coordinator
P.O. Box 50
Temple Hills, MD 20757
Phone: (301) 899-3500, ext. 237; (800) 638-0594; Fax: (301) 899-8136
Email: staff@hqafsa.org
Web: www.hqafsa.org

Summary: To provide financial assistance for college to the dependent children of enlisted Air Force personnel.

Eligibility: Open to the unmarried children (including stepchildren and legally adopted children) of active-duty, retired, or veteran members of the U.S. Air Force, Air National Guard, or Air Force Reserves. Applicants must be attending or planning to attend an accredited academic institution. They must have an unweighted GPA of 3.5 or higher. Along with their application, they must submit 1) a paragraph on their life objectives and what they plan to do with the education they receive; and 2) an essay on the most urgent problem facing society today. High school seniors must also submit a transcript of all high school grades and a record of their SAT or ACT scores. Selection is based on academic record, character, leadership skills, writing ability, versatility, and potential for success. Financial need is not a consideration. A unique aspect of these scholarships is that applicants may supply additional information regarding circumstances that entitle them to special consideration; examples of such circumstances include student disabilities, financial hardships, parent disabled and unable to work, parent missing in action/killed in action/prisoner of war, or other unusual extenuating circumstances.

Financial data: Stipends are $3,000, $2,000, or $1,000; funds may be used for tuition, room and board, fees, books, supplies, and transportation.

Duration: 1 year; may be renewed if the recipient maintains full-time enrollment.

Number awarded: 12 each year: 1 at $3,000, 1 at $2,000, and 10 at $1,000. Since this program began, it has awarded more than $250,000 in scholarships.

Deadline: March of each year.

135 CHINESE AMERICAN CITIZENS ALLIANCE FOUNDATION ESSAY CONTEST

Chinese American Citizens Alliance
1044 Stockton Street
San Francisco, CA 94108
Phone: (415) 434-2222
Email: info@cacanational.org
Web: www.cacanational.org/Essay-Contest

Summary: To recognize and reward high school students of Chinese descent who write outstanding essays on a topic related to Asian Americans.

Eligibility: Open to high school students of Chinese descent. Candidates apply through their local lodge of the Chinese American Citizens Alliance and meet at a site arranged by that lodge, usually on the first Saturday in March. They are given a topic and devote the next 2 hours to writing a 500-word essay, in English, on that topic. Recently, the topic related to the census and why so many Chinese Americans do not comply with the law and participate in the census. Selection is based on originality, clarity of thought and expression, and correctness of grammar and spelling.

Financial data: Prizes are $1,000 for first place, $700 for second place, $500 for third place, and $100 for merit awards.

Duration: The competition is held annually.

Number awarded: Varies each year; recently, prizes included 1 first place, 1 second place, 1 third place, and 10 merit awards.

Deadline: February of each year.

136 CHITTENDEN BANK SCHOLARSHIP

Vermont Student Assistance Corporation
Attn: Scholarship Programs
10 East Allen Street
P.O. Box 2000
Winooski, VT 05404-2601
Phone: (802) 654-3798; (888) 253-4819; Fax: (802) 654-3765; TDD: (800) 281-3341 (within VT)
Email: info@vsac.org
Web: services.vsac.org/wps/wcm/connect/vsac/VSAC

Summary: To provide financial assistance to high school seniors in Vermont who plan to attend college in any state.

Eligibility: Open to residents of Vermont who are graduating from a high school in the state. Applicants must be planning to attend an accredited 2- or 4-year college or university in any state. They must have a GPA of 3.0 or higher and a record of school and community involvement. Along with their application, they must submit 1) a 100-word essay on the school, church, and community activities in which they have participated; 2) a 250-word essay on their short- and long-term academic, educational, career, vocational, and/or employment goals; and 3) a 250-word essay on what they believe distinguishes their application from others that may be submitted. Selection is based on those essays, academic achievement, letters of recommendation, and financial need.

Financial data: The stipend is $2,500 per year.

Duration: 1 year; may be renewed up to 3 additional years.

Number awarded: 2 each year.

Deadline: March of each year.

137 CHRISTIAN COLLEGE LEADERS SCHOLARSHIPS

Foundation for College Christian Leaders
2658 Del Mar Heights Road
PMB 266
Del Mar, CA 92014
Phone: (858) 481-0848
Email: LMHays@aol.com
Web: www.collegechristianleader.com

Summary: To provide financial assistance for college to Christian students from California, Oregon, and Washington.

Eligibility: Open to entering or continuing undergraduate students who reside or attend college in California, Oregon, or Washington. Applicants must have a GPA of 3.0 or higher, be able to document financial need (parents must have a combined income of less than $60,000), and be able to demonstrate Christian testimony and Christian leadership. Selection is based on identified leadership history, academic achievement, financial need, and demonstrated academic, vocational, and ministry training to further the Kingdom of Jesus Christ. Special consideration is given to minority students.

Financial data: A stipend is awarded (amount not specified).

Duration: 1 year; may be renewed.

Deadline: May of each year.

138 CIF/FARMERS SCHOLAR-ATHLETE OF THE YEAR

California Interscholastic Federation
Attn: State Office
4658 Duckhorn Drive
Sacramento, CA 95834

Phone: (916) 239-4477; Fax: (510) 521-4449
Email: info@cifstate.org
Web: www.cifstate.org
Summary: To provide financial assistance to high school seniors in California who have participated in athletics and plan to attend college in any state.
Eligibility: Open to high school seniors in California who have an unweighted cumulative GPA of 3.5 or higher and have demonstrated superior athletic ability in at least 2 years of varsity play within California. Students must submit an application to their principal or counselor and an essay, up to 500 words, on how they display character in their athletic and academic efforts. They may include examples of meaningful behavior in their high school experience, lessons learned about the importance of character in their life, and opportunities that coaches, cheerleaders, athletes, and fans have to promote character in interscholastic athletics. Based on those essays, school officials nominate students for these scholarships. Males and females are judged separately.
Financial data: The stipend is $5,000 for state winners and $2,000 for section winners.
Duration: 1 year; nonrenewable.
Number awarded: 22 each year: 1 female and 1 male are selected as state winners and 10 females and 10 males (1 per section) are selected as section winners.
Deadline: Students must submit their application and essay to their counselor or principal by mid-February of each year. School officials forward the packets to the state office by the end of March.

139 CINDY KOLB MEMORIAL SCHOLARSHIP

California Association for Postsecondary Education and Disability
Attn: Executive Assistant
71423 Biskra Road
Rancho Mirage, CA 92270
Phone: (760) 346-8206; Fax: (760) 340-5275; TDD: (760) 341-4084
Email: caped2000@aol.com
Web: www.caped.net/scholarships.html
Summary: To provide financial assistance to students enrolled at 4-year college and universities in California who have a disability.
Eligibility: Open to students at 4-year colleges and universities in California who have a disability. Applicants must have completed at least 6 semester credits with a GPA of 2.5 or higher. Along with their application, they must submit a 1-page personal letter that demonstrates their writing skills, progress towards meeting their educational and vocational goals, management of their disability, and involvement in community activities. They must also submit a letter of recommendation from a faculty member, verification of disability, official transcripts, proof of current enrollment, and documentation of financial need.
Financial data: The stipend is $1,000.
Duration: 1 year.
Number awarded: 1 each year.
Deadline: September of each year.

140 CIVILIAN MARKSMANSHIP PROGRAM UNDERGRADUATE ROTC SCHOLARSHIPS

Corporation for the Promotion of Rifle Practice and Firearms Safety, Inc.
Attn: Civilian Marksmanship Program
Camp Perry Training Site, Building 3
P.O. Box 576
Port Clinton, OH 43452
Phone: (419) 635-2141, ext. 1109; Fax: (419) 635-2573
Email: programs@odcmp.com
Web: www.odcmp.com/Programs/Scholarship.htm
Summary: To provide financial assistance to rifle shooters who are high school seniors involved in a JROTC program or college undergraduates enrolled in an ROTC program.
Eligibility: Open to 1) high school seniors involved in Army, Marine Corps, Navy, or Air Force JROTC who will attend a 4-year college or university and enroll in an ROTC program; and 2) undergraduates enrolled in an Army, Air Force, or Navy ROTC or Marine Corps Platoon Leaders Course at a 4-year college or university. Applicants must be able to demonstrate excellence in rifle team programs at their high school or college, good moral character, academic achievement (GPA of 2.5 or higher), financial need, and motivation to complete a college education and serve as an officer of the armed services of the United States. U.S. citizenship is required.
Financial data: The stipend is $1,000 per year.
Duration: 1 year; may be renewed up to 3 additional years, provided the recipient remains enrolled in ROTC, maintains a GPA of 2.5 or higher, continues to participate in ROTC or college rifle team activities, and continues to meet the moral character standards for eligibility.
Number awarded: 100 each year.
Deadline: March of each year.

141 CLAIRE OLIPHANT MEMORIAL SCHOLARSHIP

American Legion Auxiliary
Department of New Jersey
c/o Lucille M. Miller, Secretary/Treasurer
1540 Kuser Road, Suite A-8
Hamilton, NJ 08619
Phone: (609) 581-9580; Fax: (609) 581-8429
Email: newjerseyala@juno.com
Web: www.alanj.org
Summary: To provide financial assistance to New Jersey residents who are the descendants of veterans and planning to attend college in any state.
Eligibility: Open to the children, grandchildren, and great-grandchildren of veterans who served in the U.S. armed forces during specified periods of war time. Applicants must be graduating high school seniors who have been residents of New Jersey for at least 2 years. They must be planning to attend a college or university in any state. Along with their application, they must submit a 1,000-word essay on a topic that changes annually; recently, students were asked to write on the topic, "Honoring Our Promise Everyday-How I Can Serve My Country and Our Veterans." Selection is based on academic achievement (40%), character (15%), leadership (15%), Americanism (15%), and financial need (15%).
Financial data: The stipend is $1,800.
Duration: 1 year.
Number awarded: 1 each year.
Deadline: April each year.

142 CLARKE SINCLAIR MEMORIAL ARCHERY COLLEGE SCHOLARSHIPS

Clarke Sinclair Memorial Archery Scholarship Corporation
c/o Lorretta Sinclair
P.O. Box 1827
Ridgecrest, CA 93555
Phone: (760) 384-8875
Email: lzsinclair@yahoo.com
Web: www.clarkesinclair.org/Scholarships.htm
Summary: To provide financial assistance to undergraduate students who have participated in archery-related activities.
Eligibility: Open to students currently enrolled in college who have at least 1 year remaining until graduation. Applicants must have a record of participation in archery-related activities and be a member of an archery team. They must have a GPA of 3.0 or higher. Along with their application, they must submit a short essay on 1) growing a college club and their participation, 2) things archery has taught them, or 3) the most important thing about a competition. Financial need is not considered in the selection process.
Financial data: Stipends are $1,000 or $500.
Duration: 1 year.
Number awarded: 3 each year: 1 at $1,000 and 2 at $500.
Deadline: April of each year.

143 CLYDE RUSSELL SCHOLARSHIPS

Clyde Russell Scholarship Fund
P.O. Box 2457
Augusta, ME 04338
Email: info@ClydeRussellScholarshipFund.org
Web: www.ClydeRussellScholarshipFund.org
Summary: To provide financial assistance to high school seniors in Maine interested in attending a 4-year college in any state or a community college in Maine.
Eligibility: Open to residents of Maine in 2 categories: 1) graduating high school seniors who will attend a 4-year college in any state; and 2) graduating seniors who will attend a Maine community college. Applicants must submit a letter of intent that explains their goals and objectives, 4 letters of recommendation, documentation of financial need, and a copy of their most recent transcripts. Finalists are interviewed.
Financial data: For high school seniors entering a 4-year college in any state, the stipend is $5,000. For high school seniors entering a community college, the stipend is $2,000. Runners-up in both categories receive $500. All funds are paid directly to the student.
Duration: 1 year; nonrenewable.

Number awarded: Varies each year.
Deadline: January of each year.

144 COAGULIFE EDUCATION SCHOLARSHIPS

CoaguLife
Attn: Scholarship Selection Committee
8690 Eagle Creek Parkway
Savage, MN 55378
Phone: (952) 886-9200; (866) 858-9200, ext. 102; Fax: (952) 487-2829
Email: info@coagulife.com
Web: www.coagulife.com

Summary: To provide financial assistance for college to students who have an inherited bleeding disorder.

Eligibility: Open to college-bound graduating high school seniors or students already enrolled full-time at an accredited college, university, or trade school. Applicants must have hemophilia, von Willebrand Disease, or a similar inherited bleeding disorder. Along with their application, they must submit an essay on 1 of 3 assigned topics. Selection is based on the essay, GPA, difficulty of course work, letters of recommendation, community service, and a statement regarding personal, academic, and career goals.

Financial data: The maximum stipend is $5,000 per year. Awards may not exceed the total yearly cost of tuition, books, fees, room, and board. Funds are paid directly to the institution.

Duration: 1 year; may be renewed as long as the recipient maintains a GPA of 3.0 or higher.

Number awarded: 1 or more each year.

Deadline: May of each year.

145 COAST GUARD EXCHANGE SYSTEM SCHOLARSHIP PROGRAM

Coast Guard Exchange System
Attn: Scholarship Committee
870 Greenbrier Circle, Tower II, Suite 502
Chesapeake, VA 23320-2681
Phone: (757) 420-2480, ext. 3019; Fax: (757) 420-7185
Email: JSias@cg-exchange.com
Web: www.uscg.mil/mwr/hqrec/CGESScholarshipProgram.asp

Summary: To provide financial assistance for college to high school seniors whose parent is affiliated with the Coast Guard.

Eligibility: Open to graduating high school seniors and students in the final year of home schooling who are planning to enroll full-time at an accredited college or university. Applicants must be the dependent children of active and Reserve Coast Guard members, retired Coast Guard members, civilian employees of the Coast Guard, or members of the Coast Guard Auxiliary. Along with their application, they must submit a 1-page essay explaining what they hope to achieve in their college career, including their educational, professional, and personal goals. Selection is based on that essay, SAT and/or ACT scores, GPA, class ranking, participation in school-oriented and other activities, demonstrated leadership qualities, personal accomplishments and interests, and letters of recommendation.

Financial data: Stipends are $1,500 or $500.

Duration: 1 year.

Number awarded: 3 each year: 1 at $1,500 and 2 at $500.

Deadline: February of each year.

146 COAST GUARD FOUNDATION COLLEGE SCHOLARSHIPS

Coast Guard Foundation
Commandant (G-1112)
Attn: Scholarship Program Manager
2100 Second Street, S.W., Jemal 9-0733
Washington, DC 20593-0001
Phone: (202) 475-5159; (800) 872-4957
Email: yvette.d.wright@uscg.mil
Web: coastguardfoundation.org/pages/Scholarship-Guide.html

Summary: To provide financial assistance for college to the dependent children of Coast Guard enlisted personnel.

Eligibility: Open to the dependent children of enlisted members of the U.S. Coast Guard on active duty, retired, or deceased and of enlisted personnel in the Coast Guard Reserve currently on extended active duty 180 days or more. Applicants must be attending or planning to attend a college, university, or vocational school as a full-time undergraduate student. Along with their application, they must submit their SAT or ACT scores, a letter of recommendation, transcripts, and a financial information statement.

Financial data: The stipend is $2,500.

Duration: 1 year.

Number awarded: 1 each year.

Deadline: March of each year.

147 COAST GUARD FOUNDATION SCHOLARSHIPS

Coast Guard Foundation
Commandant (G-1112)
Attn: Scholarship Program Manager
2100 Second Street, S.W., Jemal 9-0733
Washington, DC 20593-0001
Phone: (202) 475-5159; (800) 872-4957
Email: yvette.d.wright@uscg.mil
Web: coastguardfoundation.org/pages/Scholarship-Guide.html

Summary: To provide financial assistance for college to the dependent children of Coast Guard enlisted personnel.

Eligibility: Open to the dependent children of enlisted members of the U.S. Coast Guard on active duty, retired, or deceased, and of enlisted personnel in the Coast Guard Reserve currently on extended active duty 180 days or more. Applicants must be attending or planning to attend a college, university, or vocational school as a full-time undergraduate student. Along with their application, they must submit their SAT or ACT scores, a letter of recommendation, transcripts, and a financial information statement.

Financial data: The stipend is $5,000 per year.

Duration: 1 year; may be renewed up to 3 additional years.

Number awarded: Varies each year; recently, 14 of these scholarships were awarded.

Deadline: March of each year.

148 COAST GUARD HEADQUARTERS BLACKS IN GOVERNMENT SCHOLARSHIP

Blacks in Government-Coast Guard Headquarters Chapter
Attn: Scholarship Program
3005 Georgia Avenue, N.W.
Washington, DC 20001-5015
Phone: (202) 475-5057
Email: Gail.M.McGee@uscg.mil
Web: www.bignet.org/regional/CGHC/whatsnew.htm

Summary: To provide financial assistance for college to high school seniors in the Washington, D.C. metropolitan area.

Eligibility: Open to seniors graduating from high schools in the Washington, D.C. metropolitan area with a GPA of 2.0 or higher. Applicants must be planning to attend an accredited institution of higher learning. Along with their application, they must submit an essay of 350 to 500 words on 1 of the following topics: their chosen field of study and why; how their community, church, or family has influenced them; or why it is important for them to attend college. Finalists are interviewed.

Financial data: A stipend is awarded (amount not specified).

Duration: 1 year.

Number awarded: Up to 3 each year.

Deadline: March of each year.

149 COCA-COLA ALL-STATE COMMUNITY COLLEGE ACADEMIC TEAM

Phi Theta Kappa
Attn: Scholarship Programs Director
1625 Eastover Drive
P.O. Box 13729
Jackson, MS 39236-3729
Phone: (601) 984-3539; Fax: (601) 984-3546
Email: scholarship.programs@ptk.org
Web: www.ptk.org/schol/aaat/cocacola.htm

Summary: To recognize and reward the outstanding achievements of community college students.

Eligibility: Open to students who have completed at least 36 hours at a community college in the United States (including 30 hours completed within the past 5 years) and are on track to earn an associate or bachelor's degree. Candidates must be nominated by a designated official at their college. Nominees must have a cumulative GPA of at least 3.5 for all college course work completed in the last 5 years, regardless of institution attended. They must submit a 2-page essay describing their most significant endeavor since attending community college in which they applied their academic or intellectual skills from their community college education to benefit their school, community, or society. Selection is based on information in the essay; awards, honors, and recognition for academic achievement; academic rigor and GPA; participation in honors programs; and service to the college and the community.

Financial data: Gold Awards are $1,500, Silver Awards are $1,250, Bronze Awards are $1,000, and other finalist awards are $1,000.

Duration: The competition is held annually.

Number awarded: 300 each year: 50 Gold Awards (1 from each state), 50 Silver Awards (1 from each state), 50 Bronze Awards (1 from each state), and 150 other finalist awards (selected from multiple states).

Deadline: November of each year.

150 COCA-COLA FIRST GENERATION NORTH CAROLINA SCHOLARSHIPS

North Carolina Independent Colleges and Universities
Attn: Independent College Fund of North Carolina
530 North Blount Street
Raleigh, NC 27604
Phone: (919) 832-5817; Fax: (919) 829-7358
Email: info@ncicu.org
Web: www.ncicu.org/ICFNC.html

Summary: To provide financial assistance to students who are attending or planning to attend an independent college or university in North Carolina and are the first member of their family to do so.

Eligibility: Open to residents of any state who are enrolled or planning to enroll full time at 1 of the 36 private colleges and universities in North Carolina. Applicants must be the first member of their immediate family to attend college. They must have a GPA of 3.0 or higher and be able to demonstrate financial need.

Financial data: The stipend is $5,000 per year.

Duration: 1 year; may be renewed.

Number awarded: 36 each year: 1 at each of the private colleges and universities in North Carolina.

Deadline: Deadline not specified.

151 COCA-COLA SCHOLARSHIPS

Coca-Cola Scholars Foundation, Inc.
P.O. Box 442
Atlanta, GA 30301-0442
Phone: (800) 306-COKE; Fax: (404) 733-5439
Email: scholars@na.ko.com
Web: www.coca-colascholars.org/cokeWeb/page.jsp?navigation=15

Summary: To provide financial assistance for college to meritorious students.

Eligibility: Open to high school and home-school seniors who are planning to attend an accredited U.S. college or university. Applicants must have a GPA of 3.0 or higher at the end of their junior year in high school. They must be a U.S. citizen, national, permanent resident, refugee, asylee, Cuban-Haitian entrant, or humanitarian parolee. Selection is based on demonstrated leadership in academics, school, community, and civic activities, as well as personal character and the motivation to serve and succeed.

Financial data: The stipend is $5,000 per year (for National Scholars) or $2,500 per year (for Regional Scholars).

Duration: All scholarships are for 4 years.

Number awarded: 250 each year: 50 National Scholars and 200 Regional Scholars.

Deadline: October of each year; approximately 2,200 semifinalists are chosen and they submit an additional application, including detailed biographical data, an essay, secondary school report, and recommendations, by the end of January.

152 COCHRAN/GREENE SCHOLARSHIP

National Naval Officers Association-Washington, D.C. Chapter
Attn: Scholarship Program
2701 Park Center Drive, A1108
Alexandria, VA 22302
Phone: (703) 566-3840; Fax: (703) 566-3813
Email: Stephen.Williams@Navy.mil
Web: dcnnoa.memberlodge.com/Default.aspx?pageId=309002

Summary: To provide financial assistance to female minority high school seniors from the Washington, D.C. area who are interested in attending college in any state.

Eligibility: Open to female minority seniors graduating from high schools in the Washington, D.C. metropolitan area who plan to enroll full-time at an accredited 2- or 4-year college or university in any state. Applicants must have a GPA of 2.5 or higher. Selection is based on academic achievement, community involvement, and financial need.

Financial data: The stipend is $1,500.

Duration: 1 year; nonrenewable.

Number awarded: 1 each year.

Deadline: March of each year.

153 COLIN HIGGINS FOUNDATION YOUTH COURAGE AWARDS

Colin Higgins Foundation
Attn: Youth Courage Awards
c/o Tides Foundation New York Office
55 Exchange Place, Suite 402
New York, NY 10005
Phone: (212) 509-4975; Fax: (212) 509-1059
Email: info@colinhiggins.org
Web: www.colinhiggins.org/courageawards/index.cfm

Summary: To recognize and reward young people who have shown courage in the face of adversity related to discrimination against members of the lesbian, gay, bisexual, transgender, and questioning (LGBTQ) communities.

Eligibility: Open to candidates under 24 years of age who are 1) LGBTQ youth who have "bravely stood up to hostility and intolerance based on their sexual orientation and triumphed over bigotry"; or 2) allies who are working to end homophobia and discrimination against LGBTQ communities. Applicants must be nominated; letters of nomination must include 350-word essays describing why the nominee represents the ideals of this award. Self-nominations are not accepted.

Financial data: The award is a $10,000 grant.

Duration: The awards are presented annually.

Number awarded: 2 or 3 each year.

Deadline: February of each year.

154 COLLEGE SCHOLARSHIP PROGRAM OF THE HISPANIC SCHOLARSHIP FUND

Hispanic Scholarship Fund
Attn: Selection Committee
55 Second Street, Suite 1500
San Francisco, CA 94105
Phone: (415) 808-2365; (877) HSF-INFO; Fax: (415) 808-2302
Email: scholar1@hsf.net
Web: www.hsf.net/Scholarships.aspx?id=460

Summary: To provide financial assistance for college or graduate school to Hispanic American students.

Eligibility: Open to U.S. citizens, permanent residents, and visitors with a passport stamped I-551. Applicants must be of Hispanic heritage and enrolled full-time in a degree program at an accredited community college, 4-year university, or graduate school in the United States, Puerto Rico, Guam, or the U.S. Virgin Islands. They must have a GPA of 3.0 or higher and have applied for federal financial aid. Selection is based on academic achievement, personal strengths, leadership, and financial need.

Financial data: Stipends normally range from $1,000 to $5,000 per year.

Duration: 1 year; recipients may reapply.

Number awarded: More than 4,000 each year.

Deadline: February of each year.

155 COLLEGE SCHOLARSHIPS FOUNDATION MINORITY STUDENT SCHOLARSHIP

College Scholarships Foundation
5506 Red Robin Road
Raleigh, NC 27613
Phone: (919) 630-4895; (888) 501-9050
Email: info@collegescholarships.org
Web: www.collegescholarships.org/our-scholarships/minority.htm

Summary: To provide financial assistance to undergraduate and graduate students who are members of minority groups.

Eligibility: Open to full-time undergraduate and graduate students who are Black, Hispanic, Native American, or Pacific Islander. Applicants must have a GPA of 3.0 or higher. Along with their application, they must submit a 300-word essay on how being a minority affected their pre-college education, how being a minority has positively affected their character, and where they see themselves in 10 years. U.S. citizenship is required.

Financial data: The stipend is $1,000.
Duration: 1 year.
Number awarded: 1 each year.
Deadline: December of each year.

156 COLLEGE SCHOLARSHIPS FOUNDATION TWITTER SCHOLARSHIP

College Scholarships Foundation
5506 Red Robin Road
Raleigh, NC 27613
Phone: (919) 630-4895; (888) 501-9050
Email: info@collegescholarships.org
Web: www.collegescholarships.org/our-scholarships/140.htm

Summary: To recognize and reward, with scholarships for continued study, college students who submit outstanding Tweets.
Eligibility: Open to students currently enrolled full-time at a postsecondary institution. Applicants must use Twitter to send a Tweet of 140 characters or less on how we can use Twitter to improve the world. They must submit the Tweet online.
Financial data: Scholarship awards are $1,400 for the winner, $140 for the first runner-up, and $140 for the second runner-up.
Duration: The competition is held annually.
Number awarded: 3 each year.
Deadline: October of each year.

157 COLLEGE SCHOLARSHIPS FOUNDATION WOMEN'S SCHOLARSHIP

College Scholarships Foundation
5506 Red Robin Road
Raleigh, NC 27613
Phone: (919) 630-4895; (888) 501-9050
Email: info@collegescholarships.org
Web: www.collegescholarships.org/our-scholarships/women.htm

Summary: To provide financial assistance to women working on an undergraduate or graduate degree.
Eligibility: Open to women who are working full-time on an undergraduate or graduate degree. Applicants must have a GPA of 3.0 or higher. Along with their application, they must submit a 300-word essay on how their education plans have affected their plans of starting a family, what trends they foresee occurring for women in the workforce, and where they see themselves in 10 years. U.S. citizenship is required.
Financial data: The stipend is $1,000.
Duration: 1 year.
Number awarded: 1 each year.
Deadline: December of each year.

158 COLLEGE STUDENT PRE-COMMISSIONING INITIATIVE

U.S. Coast Guard
Attn: Recruiting Command
2300 Wilson Boulevard, Suite 500
Arlington, VA 22201
Phone: (703) 235-1775; (877) NOW-USCG; Fax: (703) 235-1881
Email: Margaret.A.Jackson@uscg.mil
Web: www.gocoastguard.com/find-your-fit/officer-opportunities

Summary: To provide financial assistance to college students at minority institutions willing to serve in the Coast Guard following graduation.
Eligibility: Open to students entering their junior or senior year at a college or university designated as an Historically Black College or University (HBCU), Hispanic Serving Institution (HSI), Tribal College or University (TCU), or an institution located in Guam, Puerto Rico, or the U.S. Virgin Islands. Applicants must be U.S. citizens; have a GPA of 2.5 or higher; have scores of 1100 or higher on the critical reading and mathematics SAT, 23 or higher on the ACT, or 109 or higher on the ASVAB GT; be between 19 and 27 years of age; have no more than 2 dependents; and meet all physical requirements for a Coast Guard commission. They must agree to attend the Coast Guard Officer Candidate School following graduation and serve on active duty as an officer for at least 3 years.
Financial data: Those selected to participate receive full payment of tuition, books, and fees; monthly housing and food allowances; medical and life insurance; special training in leadership, management, law enforcement, navigation, and marine science; 30 days of paid vacation per year; and a monthly salary of up to $2,200.
Duration: Up to 2 years.
Number awarded: Varies each year.
Deadline: February of each year.

159 COLLEGE SUCCESS FOUNDATION DC LEADERSHIP 1000 SCHOLARSHIP

College Success Foundation
1220 12th Street, S.E., Suite 110
Washington, DC 20003-3718
Phone: (202) 207-1800; (866) 240-3567; Fax: (202) 207-1801
Web: www.collegesuccessfoundation.org/Page.aspx?pid=509

Summary: To provide financial assistance to residents of Washington, D.C. who demonstrate financial need and are attending or planning to attend a 4-year college in any state.
Eligibility: Open to residents of Washington, D.C. who are high school seniors or college freshmen or sophomores. Applicants must be enrolled or planning to enroll full-time at a 4-year college or university in any state. They must have a GPA of 2.75 or higher and be able to demonstrate financial need by qualifying for the federal Pell Grant program.
Financial data: The stipend is $5,000 per year.
Duration: 1 year; may be renewed up to 3 additional years.
Number awarded: Varies each year.
Deadline: Deadline not specified.

160 COLLEGEBOUNDFUND ACADEMIC PROMISE SCHOLARSHIP

Rhode Island Higher Education Assistance Authority
Attn: Scholarship and Grant Division
560 Jefferson Boulevard, Suite 100
Warwick, RI 02886-1304
Phone: (401) 736-1170; (800) 922-9855; Fax: (401) 732-3541; TDD: (401) 734-9481
Email: scholarships@riheaa.org
Web: www.riheaa.org/borrowers/scholarships

Summary: To provide financial assistance to high school seniors in Rhode Island who can demonstrate academic promise and plan to attend college in any state.
Eligibility: Open to U.S. citizens and permanent residents who have been residents of Rhode Island since the beginning of the year prior to the academic year in which they enroll in college. Applicants must be high school seniors accepted for full-time enrollment in a program that leads to a certificate or degree, not owe a refund on a federal Title IV grant, not be in default on a Title IV loan, and not already possess a bachelor's degree. They must file a Free Application for Federal Student Aid (FAFSA) and take the SAT or ACT test. Selection is based on those test scores and high school GPA.
Financial data: The stipend is $2,500 per year.
Duration: 1 year; may be renewed for up to 3 additional years, provided the recipient maintains a cumulative GPA of 3.0 or minimum GPAs of 2.50 for the first year, 2.62 for the second year, or 2.75 for the third year.
Number awarded: Varies each year; recently, 155 of these scholarships were awarded.
Deadline: February of each year.

161 COLLEGEINVEST OPPORTUNITY SCHOLARSHIPS

CollegeInvest
1560 Broadway, Suite 1700
Denver, CO 80202
Phone: (800) 448-2424; Fax: (303) 296-4811
Email: info@collegeinvest.org
Web: www.collegeinvest.org/default.aspx?pageID=3

Summary: To provide financial assistance to residents of Colorado who attend college in the state and can demonstrate financial need.
Eligibility: Open to residents of Colorado who are attending or planning to attend a 2- or 4-year college, university, or vocational school in the state as a full-time undergraduate student. Applicants must complete the Free Application for Federal Student Aid (FAFSA) and have an Expected Family Contribution (EFC) of $15,000 or less. Recipients are selected in a random drawing. U.S. citizenship or legal resident status is required.
Financial data: The stipend is $1,000.
Duration: 1 year; nonrenewable.
Number awarded: 38 each year.
Deadline: March of each year.

162 COLLEGEINVEST SERVICE SCHOLARSHIPS

CollegeInvest
1560 Broadway, Suite 1700
Denver, CO 80202
Phone: (800) 448-2424; Fax: (303) 296-4811
Email: info@collegeinvest.org
Web: www.collegeinvest.org/default.aspx?pageID=3

Summary: To provide financial assistance for college in the state to residents of Colorado who can demonstrate financial need and agree to provide volunteer service.

Eligibility: Open to residents of Colorado who are attending or planning to attend a 2- or 4-year college, university, or vocational school in the state as a full-time undergraduate student. Applicants must complete the Free Application for Federal Student Aid (FAFSA) and have an Expected Family Contribution (EFC) of $15,000 or less. They must commit to perform at least 40 hours per year for 2 years in a service-to-children volunteer program; the volunteer work may take place at their college or with a qualified community partner of the sponsoring organization. Recipients are selected in a random drawing. U.S. citizenship or legal resident status is required.

Financial data: The stipend is $3,000 per year.

Duration: 2 years.

Number awarded: 27 each year.

Deadline: March of each year.

163 COLLEGENET SCHOLARSHIP

CollegeNET
Attn: Heidi Peterson
805 S.W. Broadway, Suite 1600
Portland, OR 97205-3356
Phone: (503) 973-5200; Fax: (503) 973-5252
Email: help@collegenet.com
Web: www.collegenet.com

Summary: To provide financial assistance to students who are enrolled or planning to enroll in college and who participate in online discussions on the CollegeNET website.

Eligibility: Open to students who 1) sign up for an account with CollegeNET; 2) create a personal profile about their personality and accomplishments; and 3) explore the discussion forums, find a topic that interests them or create their own topic, and take part in the discussions by posting messages to them. Visitors to the site vote for scholarship recipients on the basis of the messages.

Financial data: The stipend is $5,000. Students who are not selected as the winner may still receive a $1,000 scholarship to the college of their choice if they are the top vote-getter among students applying to that college.

Duration: 1 year.

Number awarded: 1 scholarship is awarded in each competition cycle, which lasts approximately 1 week.

Deadline: Deadline not specified.

164 COLLEGE-SPONSORED ACHIEVEMENT SCHOLARSHIP AWARDS

National Merit Scholarship Corporation
Attn: National Achievement Scholarship Program
1560 Sherman Avenue, Suite 200
Evanston, IL 60201-4897
Phone: (847) 866-5100; Fax: (847) 866-5113
Web: www.nationalmerit.org/nasp.php

Summary: To provide financial assistance from participating colleges to African American high school seniors who achieve high scores on the National Achievement Scholarship Program but who are not named as semifinalists.

Eligibility: Open to African American high school seniors who apply for the National Achievement Scholarship Program and are among the top scorers but are not named semifinalists. Their names are circulated to about 1,500 4-year colleges and universities in the United States. College officials select the award winners.

Financial data: College officials calculate each winner's stipend (based on financial information reported directly to the college), which ranges from $500 to $2,000 per year. Some colleges use a method known as "packaging aid" to meet the financial need of their award winners; in such instances, a College-Sponsored Achievement Scholarship may be supplemented with loans, employment, and grants. However, unless all of the winner's need is met with gift aid, the stipend must represent at least half of the student's need, up to a maximum annual stipend of $2,000.

Duration: 1 year; renewable for up to 3 additional years.

Number awarded: Approximately 200 each year.

Deadline: Applicants must take the PSAT/NMSQT no later than October of their junior year.

165 COLLEGE-SPONSORED MERIT SCHOLARSHIP AWARDS

National Merit Scholarship Corporation
Attn: Department of Educational Services and Selection
1560 Sherman Avenue, Suite 200
Evanston, IL 60201-4897
Phone: (847) 866-5100; Fax: (847) 866-5113
Web: www.nationalmerit.org/nmsp.php

Summary: To provide financial assistance from participating colleges to finalists for the National Merit Scholarship Program but who are not awarded Merit Scholarships.

Eligibility: Open to high school seniors who are high scorers in the National Merit Scholarship Program but who are not awarded scholarships. After recipients of National Merit Scholarships and Corporate-Sponsored Merit Scholarships have been chosen, the remaining National Merit finalists are contacted and asked to report their current college choice. Those who reply that a sponsor college or university is their first choice are referred to officials of that institution as candidates for the College-Sponsored Merit Scholarship Program. College officials select the award winners.

Financial data: College officials determine each winner's stipend within a range of $500 to $2,000 per year. The college may meet part of a winner's financial need with loans, employment, and grants; however, unless the student's total need (as calculated by the college) is met with gift aid, the Merit Scholarship must represent at least half the winner's need, up to an annual maximum stipend of $2,000.

Duration: 1 year; renewable for up to 3 additional years.

Number awarded: Approximately 4,600 each year.

Deadline: To qualify for the National Merit Scholarship Program, applicants must take the PSAT/NMSQT no later than October of their junior year.

166 COLORADO CENTENNIAL SCHOLARS PROGRAM

Colorado Commission on Higher Education
1560 Broadway, Suite 1600
Denver, CO 80202
Phone: (303) 866-2723; Fax: (303) 866-4266
Email: cche@state.co.us
Web: highered.colorado.gov

Summary: To provide merit-based financial assistance to residents of Colorado who are interested in attending college in the state.

Eligibility: Open to residents of Colorado who are high school seniors or recent graduates already enrolled at least half-time at a college or university in the state. Applicants must have a GPA of 3.75 or higher. They must be U.S. citizens, nationals, or permanent residents. Financial need is not considered in the selection process.

Financial data: The amount of assistance varies, up to the actual cost of tuition and fees.

Duration: 1 year; renewable if the recipient maintains a GPA of 3.5 or higher.

Number awarded: Varies each year.

Deadline: Each participating institution sets its own deadlines.

167 COLORADO COLLEGE OPPORTUNITY FUND

College in Colorado
Attn: College Opportunity Fund
1560 Broadway, Suite 1700
Denver, CO 80202
Phone: (720) 264-8550; (800) 777-2757 (within CO)
Email: askCOF@college-assist.org
Web: cof.college-assist.org/COFApp/COFApp/Default.aspx

Summary: To provide financial assistance to Colorado residents who have significant financial need and are planning to enter or continue at a college or university in the state.

Eligibility: Open to residents of Colorado who are enrolled or planning to enroll at an eligible college or university in the state. Applicants must be able to demonstrate financial need. They must be U.S. citizens or permanent residents or otherwise lawfully present in the United States.

Financial data: The stipend varies annually. Recently the rate was $68 per semester hour at public colleges and universities or $34 per semester hour at private institutions, so a student who makes normal academic progress of 30 semester hours per academic year receives $2,040 at public institutions or $1,020 at private colleges and universities in the state. Funds are paid directly to the recipient's institution as partial payment of in-state tuition.

Duration: 1 year; may be renewed for a total of 145 undergraduate credit hours.
Number awarded: Varies each year.
Deadline: Deadline not specified.

168 COLORADO DEPENDENTS TUITION ASSISTANCE PROGRAM

Colorado Commission on Higher Education
1560 Broadway, Suite 1600
Denver, CO 80202
Phone: (303) 866-2723; Fax: (303) 866-4266
Email: cche@state.co.us
Web: highered.colorado.gov

Summary: To provide financial assistance for college to the dependents of disabled or deceased Colorado National Guardsmen, law enforcement officers, and fire fighters.
Eligibility: Open to dependents of Colorado law enforcement officers, fire fighters, and National Guardsmen disabled or killed in the line of duty, as well as dependents of prisoners of war or service personnel listed as missing in action. Students must be Colorado residents under 22 years of age enrolled at 1) a state-supported 2- or 4-year Colorado college or university; 2) a private college, university, or vocational school in Colorado approved by the commission; or 3) an out-of-state 4-year college. Financial need is considered in the selection process.
Financial data: Eligible students receive free tuition at Colorado public institutions of higher education. If the recipient wishes to attend a private college, university, or proprietary school, the award is limited to the amount of tuition at a comparable state-supported institution. Students who have applied to live in a dormitory, but have not been accepted because there is not enough space, may be provided supplemental assistance. Students who choose to live off-campus are not eligible for room reimbursement or a meal plan. Students who attend a nonresidential Colorado institution and do not live at home are eligible for a grant of $1,000 per semester to assist with living expenses. Students who attend an out-of-state institution are eligible for the amount of tuition equivalent to that at a comparable Colorado public institution, but they are not eligible for room and board.
Duration: Up to 6 years or until completion of a bachelor's degree, provided the recipient maintains a GPA of 2.5 or higher.
Number awarded: Varies each year; recently, nearly $365,000 was allocated to this program.
Deadline: Deadline not specified.

169 COLORADO LEGION AUXILIARY DEPARTMENT PRESIDENT'S SCHOLARSHIPS

American Legion Auxiliary
Department of Colorado
7465 East First Avenue, Suite D
Denver, CO 80230
Phone: (303) 367-5388; Fax: (303) 367-5388
Email: ala@impactmail.net
Web: www.freewebs.com/ala-colorado

Summary: To provide financial assistance to children and grandchildren of veterans in Colorado who plan to attend college in the state.
Eligibility: Open to children and grandchildren of veterans who served in the armed forces during wartime eligibility dates for membership in the American Legion. Applicants must be residents of Colorado who are high school seniors planning to attend a college in the state. Along with their application, they must submit a 1,000-word essay on the topic, "My Obligations as an American." Selection is based on character (15%), Americanism (15%), leadership (15%), scholarship (15%), and financial need (40%).
Financial data: Stipends are $1,000 or $500.
Duration: 1 year.
Number awarded: 3 each year: 1 at 1,000 and 2 at $500.
Deadline: March of each year.

170 COLORADO LEVERAGING EDUCATIONAL ASSISTANCE PARTNERSHIP (CLEAP)

Colorado Commission on Higher Education
1560 Broadway, Suite 1600
Denver, CO 80202
Phone: (303) 866-2723; Fax: (303) 866-4266
Email: cche@state.co.us
Web: highered.colorado.gov

Summary: To provide financial assistance for undergraduate education to residents of Colorado who can demonstrate financial need.
Eligibility: Open to residents of Colorado who are enrolled or accepted for enrollment in eligible postsecondary institutions in Colorado. Applicants must be able to demonstrate substantial financial need.
Financial data: The amount of assistance varies, to a maximum of $5,000 per year.
Duration: 1 year; renewable.
Number awarded: Varies each year.
Deadline: Each participating institution sets its own deadlines.

171 COLORADO SECTION COLLEGE SCHOLARSHIP FOR JEWISH WOMEN

National Council of Jewish Women-Colorado Section
Attn: Scholarship Program
1642 South Parker Road, Suite 105
P.O. Box 371647
Denver, CO 80237
Phone: (303) 696-8086

Summary: To provide financial assistance to Jewish women from Colorado who are interested in attending college or graduate school in any state.
Eligibility: Open to Jewish residents of Colorado who are women at least 16 years of age. Applicants must be attending, be accepted at, or have applied to an accredited college, university, junior college, community college, technical school, or graduate school in any state. Along with their application, they must submit a 1-page essay about their personal and educational goals and why they feel they deserve this scholarship, information about their academic record, documentation of their involvement in the community, and documentation of financial need.
Financial data: The stipend is at least $2,000.
Duration: 1 year.
Number awarded: At least 3 each year.
Deadline: March of each year.

172 COLORADO STUDENT GRANTS

Colorado Commission on Higher Education
1560 Broadway, Suite 1600
Denver, CO 80202
Phone: (303) 866-2723; Fax: (303) 866-4266
Email: cche@state.co.us
Web: highered.colorado.gov

Summary: To provide financial assistance for undergraduate education to residents of Colorado who can demonstrate financial need.
Eligibility: Open to residents of Colorado who are enrolled or accepted for enrollment in participating postsecondary institutions in Colorado. Selection is based on financial need, as indicated by the student's expected family contribution (EFC) from their Free Application for Federal Student Aid (FAFSA). Students whose EFC is between zero and $6,926 are in level 1, students whose EFC is between $6,926 and 200% of that required for the minimum Pell Grant (or $9,234) are in level 2, and all other students who demonstrate financial need are in level 3.
Financial data: The amount of assistance varies. Students in level 1 receive from $850 to the maximum amount of unmet need, up to $5,000; students in level 2 receive from $600 to $2,500 or the maximum amount of unmet need, whichever is less; students in level 3 receive from $300 to $500.
Duration: 1 year; renewable.
Number awarded: Varies each year.
Deadline: Each participating institution sets its own deadlines.

173 COLORADO STUDENT OF INTEGRITY SCHOLARSHIP

Better Business Bureau Serving Denver/Boulder
Attn: Torch Awards for Marketplace Trust
1020 Cherokee Street
Denver, CO 80204
Phone: (303) 996-3965; Fax: (303) 577-8111
Email: scholarship@denver.bbb.org
Web: denver.bbb.org/scholarship

Summary: To provide financial assistance to high school seniors in Colorado who plan to attend college in the state and can demonstrate character, leadership, and ethical values.

Eligibility: Open to seniors graduating from high schools in Colorado who plan to attend an accredited institution of higher education in the state. Applicants must have a GPA of 3.0 or higher and be able to demonstrate financial need. They must be able to document involvement in volunteer activities outside of school and leadership in extracurricular and school-related activities. Along with their application, they must submit a 400-word essay on why they consider themselves a passionate character-builder and how they propose to motivate and help others to join them as passionate character-builders.
Financial data: The stipend is $2,500 per year.
Duration: 4 years.
Number awarded: 1 each year.
Deadline: September of each year.

174 COMMANDER WILLIAM S. STUHR SCHOLARSHIPS

Commander William S. Stuhr Scholarship Fund
Attn: Executive Director
P.O. Box 1138
Kitty Hawk, NC 27949-1138
Phone: (252) 255-3013; Fax: (252) 255-3014
Email: stuhrstudents@earthlink.net
Summary: To provide financial assistance for college to the dependent children of retired or active-duty military personnel.
Eligibility: Open to the dependent children of military personnel who are serving on active duty or retired with pay after 20 years' service (not merely separated from service). Applicants must be high school seniors who rank in the top 10% of their class and have an SAT score of at least 1250 or an ACT score of at least 27. They must plan to attend a 4-year accredited college. Selection is based on academic performance, extracurricular activities, demonstrated leadership potential, and financial need.
Financial data: The stipend is $1,200 per year.
Duration: 4 years, provided the recipient makes the dean's list at their college at least once during their first 2 years.
Number awarded: 6 each year: 1 for a child of a military servicemember from each of the 6 branches (Air Force, Army, Coast Guard, Marine Corps, Navy, and Reserves/National Guard).
Deadline: February of each year.

175 COMMUNITY COLLEGE TRANSFER SCHOLARS FUND OF THE INDEPENDENT COLLEGE FUND OF MARYLAND

Independent College Fund of Maryland
Attn: Director of Programs and Scholarships
3225 Ellerslie Avenue, Suite C160
Baltimore, MD 21218-3519
Phone: (443) 997-5703; Fax: (443) 997-2740
Email: LSubot@jhmi.edu
Web: www.i-fundinfo.org
Summary: To provide financial assistance to students graduating from community colleges in Maryland and planning to transfer to member institutions of the Independent College Fund of Maryland.
Eligibility: Open to students who have an associate degree from an accredited Maryland community college. Applicants must have been admitted as a full-time student at a member institution. They must have a GPA of 3.0 or higher and be able to demonstrate financial need. U.S. citizenship is required.
Financial data: A stipend is awarded (amount not specified).
Duration: 1 year.
Number awarded: 1 or more each year.
Deadline: Deadline not specified.

176 CONGRESSIONAL MEDAL OF HONOR SOCIETY SCHOLARSHIPS

Congressional Medal of Honor Society
40 Patriots Point Road
Mt. Pleasant, SC 29464
Phone: (843) 884-8862; Fax: (843) 884-1471
Email: medalhq@earthlink.net
Web: www.cmohs.org
Summary: To provide financial assistance to dependents of Congressional Medal of Honor winners who are interested in pursuing postsecondary education.
Eligibility: Open to the sons and daughters of Congressional Medal of Honor recipients. They must be high school seniors or graduates and have been accepted by an accredited college or university.
Financial data: The stipend is $2,000 per year.
Duration: 1 year; may be renewed for up to 3 additional years.
Number awarded: Varies; approximately 15 each year.
Deadline: August or December of each year.

177 CONNECTICUT AID FOR PUBLIC COLLEGE STUDENTS

Connecticut Department of Higher Education
Attn: Office of Student Financial Aid
61 Woodland Street
Hartford, CT 06105-2326
Phone: (860) 947-1855; Fax: (860) 947-1311
Email: sfa@ctdhe.org
Web: www.ctdhe.org/SFA/default.htm
Summary: To provide financial assistance to Connecticut residents attending public colleges in the state.
Eligibility: Open to residents of Connecticut who are attending a public college in the state. Selection is based on financial need.
Financial data: Awards up to the amount of unmet financial need are provided.
Duration: 1 year.
Number awarded: Varies each year.
Deadline: Deadline not specified.

178 CONNECTICUT ALARM & SYSTEMS INTEGRATORS ASSOCIATION SCHOLARSHIP AWARDS

Connecticut Alarm & Systems Integrators Association
Attn: Scholarship Committee
P.O. Box 7230
Wilton, CT 06897
Phone: (203) 762-2444; (800) 762-3099; Fax: (203) 762-9211
Email: premes@casiact.org
Web: www.casiact.org/youthscholorship.html
Summary: To provide financial assistance to high school seniors in Connecticut who are the children of active-duty law enforcement and fire service personnel and interested in attending college in any state.
Eligibility: Open to seniors graduating from high schools in Connecticut who have been accepted at an accredited college or university in any state. Applicants must have a father, mother, or legal guardian who is a full-time active employee (not on disability) of the police or sheriff's department or a paid employee or volunteer of a fire department in Connecticut. Along with their application, they must submit an essay of 500 to 750 words on what it means to them to have their parent or guardian involved in securing our community. Selection is based on that essay (25 points), grade average (25 points), SAT scores (30 points), and academic prizes, awards, school and outside extracurricular activities, and hobbies (20 points); financial need is not considered.
Financial data: The first-place winner receives a $1,000 scholarship and the second-place winner receives a $500 scholarship.
Duration: The awards are presented annually.
Number awarded: 2 each year.
Deadline: March of each year.

179 CONNECTICUT INDEPENDENT COLLEGE STUDENT GRANTS

Connecticut Department of Higher Education
Attn: Office of Student Financial Aid
61 Woodland Street
Hartford, CT 06105-2326
Phone: (860) 947-1855; Fax: (860) 947-1311
Email: sfa@ctdhe.org
Web: www.ctdhe.org/SFA/default.htm
Summary: To provide financial assistance for undergraduate education to students attending independent colleges in Connecticut.
Eligibility: Open to residents of Connecticut who are attending an independent college in the state. Selection is based on financial need.
Financial data: Grants up to $8,341 per year are provided.
Duration: 1 year.
Number awarded: Varies each year.
Deadline: Deadline not specified.

180 CONNECTICUT JUNIOR SOCCER ASSOCIATION SCHOLARSHIPS

Connecticut Junior Soccer Association
Attn: Scholarship Committee
11 Executive Drive
Farmington, CT 06032
Phone: (860) 676-1161; Fax: (860) 676-1162
Email: office@cjsa.net
Web: www.cjsa.net

Summary: To provide financial assistance to high school seniors in Connecticut who have been involved in soccer and plan to attend college in any state.

Eligibility: Open to seniors graduating from high schools in Connecticut who have played soccer with a club affiliated with the Connecticut Junior Soccer Association. Applicants must have a "C+" average or higher and plans to attend a school of higher education in any state. Along with their application, they must submit a 250-word essay on "What Soccer Means to Me."

Financial data: The stipend is $1,000.

Duration: 1 year.

Number awarded: 4 each year.

Deadline: March of each year.

181 CONNECTICUT NATIONAL GUARD FOUNDATION SCHOLARSHIPS

Connecticut National Guard Foundation, Inc.
Attn: Scholarship Committee
360 Broad Street
Hartford, CT 06105-3795
Phone: (860) 241-1550; Fax: (860) 293-2929
Email: ctngfi@sbcglobal.net
Web: www.ctngfoundation.org/Scholarship.asp

Summary: To provide financial assistance for college to members of the Connecticut National Guard and their families.

Eligibility: Open to members of the Connecticut Army National Guard and Organized Militia, their children, and their spouses. Applicants must be enrolled or planning to enroll in an accredited college or technical program. Along with their application, they must submit a letter of recommendation, a list of extracurricular activities, high school or college transcripts, and a 200-word statement on their educational and future goals. Selection is based on achievement and citizenship.

Financial data: Stipends are $2,000 or $1,000.

Duration: 1 year.

Number awarded: 5 each year: 2 at $2,000 and 3 at $1,000.

Deadline: March of each year.

182 CONNECTICUT TUITION WAIVER FOR VETERANS

Connecticut Department of Higher Education
Attn: Education and Employment Information Center
61 Woodland Street
Hartford, CT 06105-2326
Phone: (860) 947-1816; (800) 842-0229 (within CT); Fax: (860) 947-1310
Email: veterans@ctdhe.org
Web: www.ctdhe.org/SFA/default.htm

Summary: To provide financial assistance for college to certain Connecticut veterans and military personnel and their dependents.

Eligibility: Open to 1) honorably-discharged Connecticut veterans who served at least 90 days during specified periods of wartime; 2) active members of the Connecticut Army and Air National Guard; 3) Connecticut residents who are a dependent child or surviving spouse of a member of the armed forces killed in action on or after September 11, 2001 who was also a Connecticut resident; and 4) Connecticut residents who are dependent children of a person officially declared missing in action or a prisoner of war while serving in the armed forces after January 1, 1960. Applicants must be attending or planning to attend a public college or university in the state.

Financial data: The program provides a waiver of 100% of tuition for general fund courses at Connecticut public colleges or universities, 50% of tuition for extension and summer courses at campuses of Connecticut State University, and 50% of part-time fees at *OnlineCSU.*

Duration: Up to 4 years.

Number awarded: Varies each year.

Deadline: Deadline not specified.

183 CORPORATE-SPONSORED ACHIEVEMENT SCHOLARSHIPS

National Merit Scholarship Corporation
Attn: National Achievement Scholarship Program
1560 Sherman Avenue, Suite 200
Evanston, IL 60201-4897
Phone: (847) 866-5100; Fax: (847) 866-5113
Web: www.nationalmerit.org/nasp.php

Summary: To provide financial assistance from corporate sponsors to finalists for the National Achievement Scholarship Program but who are not awarded Achievement Scholarships.

Eligibility: Open to African American high school seniors who are high scorers in the National Achievement Scholarship Program but who are not awarded scholarships. Because winners of these scholarships must meet preferential criteria specified by sponsors, not all finalists for the National Achievement Scholarship Program are considered for this award, and the awards are not subject to regional allocation. Further, corporate sponsors frequently offer their awards to finalists who are children of their employees or residents of an area where a plant or office is located. Some companies offer scholarships to students who plan to pursue particular college majors or careers. Finalists who have qualifications that especially interest a sponsor are identified and winners are selected from among eligible candidates. Financial need is considered for some of the awards.

Financial data: Most of these scholarships provide stipends that are individually determined, taking into account college costs and family financial circumstances. Variable stipend awards of this type range from at least $500 to $2,000 per year, although some have a higher annual minimum and a few range as high as $10,000 per year. Some renewable awards provide a fixed annual stipend (between $1,000 and $5,000) that is the same for every recipient of the sponsor's awards. Other corporate-sponsored scholarships are nonrenewable and provide a single payment (from $2,500 to $5,000) for the recipient's first year of college study.

Duration: 1 year; most awards are renewable up to 3 additional years.

Number awarded: Approximately 100 each year.

Deadline: Applicants must take the PSAT/NMSQT no later than October of their junior year.

184 CORPORATE-SPONSORED MERIT AND SPECIAL SCHOLARSHIPS

National Merit Scholarship Corporation
Attn: Department of Educational Services and Selection
1560 Sherman Avenue, Suite 200
Evanston, IL 60201-4897
Phone: (847) 866-5100; Fax: (847) 866-5113
Web: www.nationalmerit.org/nmsp.php

Summary: To provide financial assistance from corporate sponsors to finalists for the National Merit Scholarship Program but who are not awarded Merit Scholarships.

Eligibility: Open to high school seniors who are high scorers in the National Merit Scholarship Program but who are not awarded scholarships. Those who are named as finalists receive these Merit Scholarships, awarded by corporate sponsors to students who fulfill preferential criteria specified by the award sponsor; usually, the criteria require that the recipient be the child of an employee of the sponsoring corporation, although some are offered to residents of a service area or community where a business has plants or offices or to students with career plans the sponsor wishes to encourage. Some corporate sponsors also offer Special Scholarships; those are offered to students who did not qualify as finalists in the National Merit Scholarship Program but may receive these awards because the corporate sponsor wishes to award scholarships to the specified groups, even though not all have achieved status as Merit Scholars. Some of the Corporate and Special Scholarships are merit-based; others consider financial need.

Financial data: Most of these scholarships provide stipends that are individually determined, taking into account college costs and family financial circumstances. Variable stipend awards of this type range from at least $500 to $2,000 per year, although some have a higher annual minimum and a few range as high as $10,000 per year. Some renewable awards provide a fixed annual stipend (between $1,000 and $5,000) that is the same for every recipient of the sponsor's awards. Other corporate-sponsored scholarships are nonrenewable and provide a single payment (from $2,500 to $5,000) for the recipient's first year of college study.

Duration: 1 year; many may be renewed up to 3 additional years.

Number awarded: Approximately 1,000 Corporate-Sponsored Merit Scholarships and 1,300 Corporate-Sponsored Special Scholarships are awarded each year.

Deadline: To qualify for the National Merit Scholarship Program, applicants must take the PSAT/NMSQT no later than October of their junior year.

185 COSA GENERAL SCHOLARSHIPS

Confederation of Oregon School Administrators
Attn: Youth Development Program
707 13th Street, S.E., Suite 100
Salem, OR 97301-4035
Phone: (503) 581-3141; Fax: (503) 581-9840
Web: www.cosa.k12.or.us

Summary: To provide financial assistance to high school seniors in Oregon who are interested in attending a community college, college, or university in the state.

Eligibility: Open to graduating high school seniors in Oregon. Applicants must be interested in attending a community college, college, or university in the state. They must have been active in community and school affairs, have at least a 3.5 GPA, and be able to enroll in the fall term after graduating from high school. Along with their application, they must submit a 1-page autobiography (that includes their personal goals), the name of the school they plan to attend, and the endorsement of a member of the Confederation of Oregon School Administrators (COSA). Financial need is not considered in the selection process.

Financial data: The stipend is $1,000. Funds are paid directly to the recipient.

Duration: 1 year; nonrenewable.

Number awarded: 3 each year.

Deadline: February of each year.

186 COSTCO WHOLESALE SCHOLARSHIPS

Independent Colleges of Washington
600 Stewart Street, Suite 600
Seattle, WA 98101
Phone: (206) 623-4494; Fax: (206) 625-9621
Email: info@icwashington.org
Web: www.icwashington.org/scholarships/index.html

Summary: To provide financial assistance to underrepresented minority students enrolled at participating colleges and universities that are members of the Independent Colleges of Washington (ICW).

Eligibility: Open to students enrolled at ICW-member colleges and universities. Applicants must be members of underrepresented minority populations and able to demonstrate financial need. No application is required; each ICW institution makes a selection from all of its students.

Financial data: The stipend varies at each institution.

Duration: 1 year; nonrenewable.

Number awarded: Varies each year; recently, 18 of these scholarships were awarded.

Deadline: Each institution sets its own deadline.

187 COURAGE CENTER SCHOLARSHIP FOR PEOPLE WITH DISABILITIES

Courage Center
Attn: Vocational Services Department
3915 Golden Valley Road
Minneapolis, MN 55422
Phone: (763) 520-0553; (888) 8-INTAKE; Fax: (763) 520-0392; TDD: (763) 520-0245
Email: vocationalservices@couragecenter.org
Web: www.couragecenter.org/ContentPages/disabilities_scholarship.aspx

Summary: To provide financial assistance to Minnesota residents who have a disability and are interested in attending college in any state.

Eligibility: Open to U.S. citizens who are residents of Minnesota or have received Courage Center services. Applicants must have a sensory impairment or physical disability and a desire to gain technical expertise beyond high school. They must be attending or planning to attend a college or technical school in any state. Along with their application, they must submit a concise essay that reflects their educational aspirations, career goals, and how a scholarship will help meet their needs. Selection is based on that essay, employment history, honors and awards, leadership experience, and financial need. Graduation ranking is not considered.

Financial data: The stipend is $1,000.

Duration: 1 year.

Number awarded: 1 or more each year.

Deadline: May of each year.

188 CREDIT UNION FOUNDATION COLLEGE SCHOLARSHIP AWARDS PROGRAM

Credit Union Foundation of Maryland and the District of Columbia
Attn: Scholarship Committee
8975 Guilford Road, Suite 190
Columbia, MD 21046
Phone: (443) 325-0771; (800) 492-4206; Fax: (410) 290-7832
Email: essay@cufmddc.org
Web: www.cufmddc.org/scholarship.htm

Summary: To recognize and reward, with college scholarships, members of credit unions in Maryland and the District of Columbia who submit outstanding essays or videos on topics related to credit unions.

Eligibility: Open to members of credit unions in Maryland and the District of Columbia who are high school seniors or students already enrolled at colleges or universities in any state. Applicants must submit either a 750-word essay or a short video on a topic related to credit unions. Recently, students who submitted an essay were asked to visualize a credit union run by people under 30 years of age and then to explain what their credit union looks like, where it is located, the products and services they emphasize, and the unique aspects that make their credit union stand out. Students who submitted a video were asked to demonstrate how credit unions and banks differ.

Financial data: Awards, in the form of college scholarships, are $1,000.

Duration: The competition is held annually.

Number awarded: 11 each year: 10 for essays and 1 for a video.

Deadline: March of each year.

189 CRIB TO COLLEGE SCHOLARSHIP PROGRAM

Crumley Roberts Attorneys at Law
Attn: Director of Community Relations
2400 Freeman Mill Road, Suite 200
Greensboro, NC 27406
Phone: (336) 333-0044; (866) 336-4547; Fax: (336) 333-9894
Email: scholarship@cribtocollege.org
Web: cribtocollege.org

Summary: To provide financial assistance for college study in any state to high school seniors in North and South Carolina and to community college students from North Carolina.

Eligibility: Open to 1) seniors graduating from high schools in North Carolina; 2) seniors graduating from high school in South Carolina; and 3) community college transfer students from North Carolina. Applicants must be planning to attend an accredited college, university, or technical school in any state. They must have a GPA of 3.0 or higher. Selection is based on academic merit, community involvement, extracurricular activities, and a written essay.

Financial data: Awards include a $1,000 scholarship and a laptop computer.

Duration: 1 year; nonrenewable.

Number awarded: 13 each year: 5 to North Carolina high school seniors, 3 to South Carolina high school seniors, and 5 to North Carolina community college transfer students.

Deadline: March of each year.

190 CVS/ALL KIDS CAN SCHOLARS PROGRAM

Autism Society of America
Attn: Awards and Scholarships
4340 East-West Highway, Suite 350
Bethesda, MD 20814-4579
Phone: (301) 657-0881; (800) 3-AUTISM; Fax: (301) 657-0869
Email: info@autism-society.org
Web: www.autism-society.org/site/PageServer?pagename=asa_awards

Summary: To provide financial assistance for college to students with autism.

Eligibility: Open to persons with autism who have successfully met all the requirements for admission to a college, university, trade school, or other postsecondary institution. Applicants must submit a personal statement of less than 500 words describing their qualifications and proposed plan of study, secondary school transcripts, documentation of status as an individual with autism, and 2 letters of recommendation.

Financial data: The stipend is $1,000.

Duration: 1 year.

Number awarded: 5 each year.

Deadline: March of each year.

191 CVS CAREMARK/ERIC DELSON MEMORIAL SCHOLARSHIP

CVS Caremark
Attn: Research Team
P.O. Box 832407
Richardson, TX 75083
Phone: (866) 792-2731
Web: www.caremark.com/wps/portal/HEALTH_RESOURCES?topic=prchemophilia

Summary: To provide financial assistance for high school, college, or graduate school to students with a bleeding disorder.

Eligibility: Open to students diagnosed with a bleeding disorder who are 1) high school seniors, high school graduates or equivalent (GED), college students, or graduate students currently enrolled or planning to enroll full-time at an accredited 2- or 4-year college, university, or vocational/technical school; or 2) students entering grades 7–12 at a private secondary school in the United States. Selection is based on academic record, demonstrated leadership and participation in school and community activities, work experience, a statement of educational and career goals, unusual personal or family circumstances, and an outside appraisal.

Financial data: The stipend is $2,500 for college students or $1,500 for high school students. Funds are paid in 2 equal installments directly to the recipient.

Duration: 1 year; may be renewed for up to 3 additional years, provided the recipient maintains a GPA of 2.5 or higher for the freshman year and 3.0 or higher for subsequent years.

Number awarded: 4 each year: 3 for college students and 1 for a high school student.

Deadline: June of each year.

192 CYSTIC FIBROSIS SCHOLARSHIPS

Cystic Fibrosis Scholarship Foundation
1555 Sherman Avenue, Suite 116
Evanston, IL 60201
Phone: (847) 328-0127; Fax: (847) 328-0127
Email: MKBCFSF@aol.com
Web: www.cfscholarship.org

Summary: To provide financial assistance to undergraduate students who have cystic fibrosis (CF).

Eligibility: Open to students enrolled or planning to enroll in college (either a 2- or 4-year program) or vocational school. Applicants must have CF. Along with their application, they must submit a 500-word essay about their favorite book from the 20th century and why. Selection is based on academic achievement, leadership, and financial need.

Financial data: The stipend is $1,000 per year. Funds are sent directly to the student's institution to be used for tuition, books, room, and board.

Duration: 1 year; recipients may reapply.

Number awarded: Varies each year; recently, 63 of these scholarships were awarded.

Deadline: March of each year.

193 DALE E. FRIDELL MEMORIAL SCHOLARSHIPS

StraightForward Media
508 Seventh Street, Suite 202
Rapid City, SD 57701
Phone: (605) 348-3042; Fax: (605) 348-3043
Email: info@straightforwardmedia.com
Web: www.straightforwardmedia.com/fridell

Summary: To provide financial assistance for college to students who submit essays on why they deserve the award.

Eligibility: Open to all students who are attending or planning to attend a university, college, trade school, technical institute, vocational training, or other postsecondary education program. Applicants may not have already been receiving or awarded a full tuition scholarship or waiver from another source. International students are welcome to apply. There is no application form. Students must submit online essays (no minimum or maximum word limit) on 1) why the completion of a postsecondary education is important to them and what they hope to achieve once they get a degree; and 2) how this scholarship will help them meet their educational and professional goals. Financial need is not considered in the selection process.

Financial data: The stipend is $1,000. Funds are paid directly to the student.

Duration: 1 year.

Number awarded: 4 each year: 1 for each award cycle.

Deadline: January, April, July, or October of each year.

194 DALE SCHROEDER SCHOLARSHIP PROGRAM

Dale Schroeder Charitable Trust
301 ACT Drive
P.O. Box 4030
Iowa City, IA 52243-4030
Phone: (319) 337-1647; (866) 228-8142
Web: www.act.org/daleschroeder

Summary: To provide financial assistance to high school seniors in small towns in Iowa who plan to attend a public university in the state.

Eligibility: Open to seniors graduating from high schools in Iowa communities that have a population of 10,000 or less. Applicants must have a GPA of 2.5 or higher and be planning to work full-time on a bachelor's degree at a public university in the state. Selection is based on academic achievement and potential, leadership ability, school activities, character, volunteerism and community service, employment history, and financial need.

Financial data: Stipends range up to $15,000 per year.

Duration: 1 year; may be renewed up to 3 additional years, provided the recipient maintains a GPA of 2.5 or higher.

Number awarded: 1 or more each year.

Deadline: April of each year.

195 DAN AND LUCILLE WOOD ATHLETIC SCHOLARSHIPS

New Mexico Activities Association
Attn: Associate Director
6600 Palomas Avenue, N.E.
Albuquerque, NM 87109
Phone: (505) 923-3275; (888) 820-NMAA; Fax: (505) 923-3114
Email: mmartinez@nmact.org
Web: www.nmact.org/scholarship_information_forms

Summary: To provide financial assistance to high school seniors in New Mexico who have participated in sports and plan to attend college in any state.

Eligibility: Open to seniors graduating from high schools in New Mexico with a GPA of 3.0 or higher. Applicants must have participated in at least 1 sport sanctioned by the New Mexico Activities Association (NMAA) during their sophomore and junior year and at least 2 sports during their senior year. They must be planning to attend a college or university in any state. Along with their application, they must submit a personal statement on how involvement in athletics impacted their high school career. Financial need is not considered in the selection process.

Financial data: The stipend is $1,000. From among all its scholarship recipients, the NMAA selects the 2 most outstanding and awards them a stipend of $2,500.

Duration: 1 year.

Number awarded: 2 each year. The NMAA also awards 2 additional at-large scholarships to applicants for all its programs.

Deadline: February of each year.

196 DANIEL E. LAMBERT MEMORIAL SCHOLARSHIP

American Legion
Department of Maine
P.O. Box 900
Waterville, ME 04903-0900
Phone: (207) 873-3229; Fax: (207) 872-0501
Email: legionme@mainelegion.org
Web: www.mainelegion.org/pages/programs/scholarships.php

Summary: To provide financial assistance to the children of veterans in Maine who plan to attend college in any state.

Eligibility: Open to residents of Maine who are the child or grandchild of a veteran. Applicants must be attending or planning to attend an accredited college or vocational/technical school in any state. They must have demonstrated, by their past behavior, that they believe in the American way of life. U.S. citizenship is required. Financial need is considered in the selection process.

Financial data: The stipend is $1,000.

Duration: 1 year.

Number awarded: 1 each year.

Deadline: April of each year.

197 DANIELS SCHOLARSHIP PROGRAM

Daniels Fund
Attn: Scholarship Program
101 Monroe Street
Denver, CO 80206

Phone: (720) 941-4453; (877) 791-4726; Fax: (720) 941-4208
Email: scholars@danielsfund.org
Web: www.danielsfund.org/Scholarships_NEW/About.asp

Summary: To provide financial assistance to high school students in Colorado, Utah, Wyoming, and New Mexico who can demonstrate financial need and plan to attend college in any state.

Eligibility: Open to seniors graduating from high schools in Colorado, Utah, Wyoming, and New Mexico. Applicants must be planning to attend an accredited 2- or 4-year college or university in any state, but they must intend to complete a bachelor's degree. They must have a composite ACT score of 17 or higher or a combined critical reading and mathematics SAT score of 810 or higher. Selection is based primarily on financial need, although strength of character, academic performance or promise, leadership potential, potential to contribute to the community, and a well-rounded personality are also considered. Students may not apply directly for these scholarships; they must be nominated by a designated referral agency, which may be a youth service agency in their home community or their high school. They must have U.S. citizenship or status as a permanent resident, refugee, or asylum-holder. Semifinalists are interviewed.

Financial data: Stipends cover the recipient's unmet financial need, but pay for tuition and fees, room and board, books and supplies, and miscellaneous educational expenses.

Duration: 1 year; may be renewed up to 3 additional years, provided the recipient makes satisfactory academic progress and holds a job that entails at least 125 hours per academic year for the first year and 250 hours per academic year for the remaining 3 years.

Number awarded: 250 each year.

Deadline: December of each year.

198 DARLENE HOOLEY SCHOLARSHIP FOR OREGON VETERANS

Oregon Student Assistance Commission
Attn: Grants and Scholarships Division
1500 Valley River Drive, Suite 100
Eugene, OR 97401-2146
Phone: (541) 6877395; (800) 452-8807, ext. 7395; Fax: (541) 687-7414; TDD: (800) 735-2900
Email: awardinfo@osac.state.or.us
Web: www.osac.state.or.us/osac_programs.html

Summary: To provide financial assistance to veterans in Oregon who served during the Global War on Terror and are interested in working on an undergraduate or graduate degree at a college in the state.

Eligibility: Open to Oregon veterans who served during the Global War on Terror; there is no minimum length of service requirement. Applicants must be enrolled or planning to enroll at least half-time as an undergraduate or graduate student at a college or university in Oregon.

Financial data: A stipend is awarded (amount not specified).

Duration: 1 year; recipients may reapply.

Number awarded: Varies each year.

Deadline: February of each year.

199 DAUGHTERS OF THE CINCINNATI SCHOLARSHIP PROGRAM

Daughters of the Cincinnati
Attn: Scholarship Administrator
20 West 44th Street, Suite 508
New York, NY 10036
Phone: (212) 991-9945
Email: scholarships@daughters1894.org
Web: www.daughters1894.org

Summary: To provide financial assistance for college to high school seniors who are the daughters of active-duty, deceased, or retired military officers.

Eligibility: Open to high school seniors who are the daughters of career commissioned officers of the regular Army, Navy, Air Force, Coast Guard, or Marine Corps on active duty, deceased, or retired. Applicants must be planning to enroll at a college or university in any state. Along with their application, they must submit an official school transcript, SAT or ACT scores, a letter of recommendation, and documentation of financial need.

Financial data: Scholarship amounts have recently averaged $4,000 per year. Funds are paid directly to the college of the student's choice.

Duration: 1 year; may be renewed up to 3 additional years, provided the recipient remains in good academic standing.

Number awarded: Approximately 12 each year.

Deadline: March of each year.

200 DAVIDSON FELLOWS AWARDS

Davidson Institute for Talent Development
Attn: Davidson Fellows Program
9665 Gateway Drive, Suite B
Reno, NV 89521
Phone: (775) 852-3483, ext. 435; Fax: (775) 852-2184
Email: DavidsonFellows@davidsongifted.org
Web: www.davidsongifted.org/fellows

Summary: To recognize and reward, with college scholarships, young people who complete significant pieces of work in designated areas.

Eligibility: Open to U.S. citizens and permanent residents under 18 years of age. Applicants must have completed a "significant piece of work" in 1 of the following submission categories: 1) philosophy: a portfolio presenting analyses of fundamental assumptions or beliefs relating to human thought or culture; 2) music: a portfolio demonstrating the applicant's talent as a composer, vocalist, classical instrumentalist, or other instrumentalist; 3) literature: a portfolio displaying a number of literary styles and genres; 4) science: a project in a specific area or science, such as biology, chemistry, earth science, engineering, environmental science, medicine, physics, or space science; 5) mathematics: a project in a specific area of mathematics, such as calculus, fractals, or number theory; 6) technology: a project in a specific area of technology, such as computer programming or artificial intelligence; or 7) "outside the box": university graduate level or comparable work completed with the supervision of an expert or experts. Selection is based on the quality and scope of the entry (50 points), the level of significance of the work (30 points), and the applicant's depth of knowledge and understanding of the work and the related domain area (20 points).

Financial data: Awards are $50,000, $25,000, or $10,000. Funds must be used for tuition and related expenses at an accredited college or university. Scholarship money is available for 10 years after the date of the award.

Duration: The awards are presented annually.

Number awarded: Varies each year; recently, 20 of these awards were presented: 3 at $50,000, 9 at $25,000, and 8 at $10,000.

Deadline: A screening form for the "outside the box" category is due in late January. Preliminary submissions for all other categories are due in mid-February. Completed applications for all categories are due in early March of each year.

201 DAVIS-PUTTER SCHOLARSHIPS

Davis-Putter Scholarship Fund
P.O. Box 7307
New York, NY 10116-7307
Email: information@davisputter.org
Web: www.davisputter.org

Summary: To provide financial assistance to undergraduate and graduate student activists.

Eligibility: Open to undergraduate and graduate students who are involved in "struggles for civil rights, economic justice, international solidarity or other progressive issues." While U.S. citizenship is not required, applicants must be living in the United States and planning to enroll in school here. They must submit a completed application, a personal statement, financial need reports, recommendation letters, transcripts, and a photograph.

Financial data: Grants range up to $8,000, depending upon need.

Duration: 1 year.

Number awarded: Varies each year; recently, a total of 27 of these scholarships were awarded.

Deadline: March of each year.

202 DEBORAH HUMPHREY SCHOLARSHIP

Epsilon Sigma Alpha International
Attn: ESA Foundation
P.O. Box 270517
Fort Collins, CO 80527
Phone: (970) 223-2824; Fax: (970) 223-4456
Email: esainfo@esaintl.com
Web: www.esaintl.com/esaf

Summary: To provide financial assistance to residents of New Mexico planning to attend college in the state.

Eligibility: Open to residents of New Mexico who are 1) graduating high school seniors with a GPA of 3.0 or higher or with minimum scores of 22 on the ACT or 1030 on the combined critical reading and mathematics SAT; 2) enrolled in college with a GPA of 3.0 or higher; 3) enrolled at a technical school or returning to school after an absence for retraining of job skills or obtaining a degree; or 4) engaged in online study through an accredited college, university, or vocational school. Applicants must be attending or planning to attend school in New Mexico. They may major in any field. Selection is based on character (10%), leadership (10%), service (5%), financial need (50%), and scholastic ability (25%).

Financial data: The stipend is $1,000.

Duration: 1 year; may be renewed.

Number awarded: 1 each year.

Deadline: January of each year.

203 DELAWARE EDUCATIONAL BENEFITS FOR CHILDREN OF DECEASED VETERANS AND OTHERS

Delaware Higher Education Commission
Carvel State Office Building, Fifth Floor
820 North French Street
Wilmington, DE 19801-3509
Phone: (302) 577-5240; (800) 292-7935; Fax: (302) 577-6765
Email: dhec@doe.k12.de.us
Web: www.doe.k12.de.us/infosuites/students_family/dhec/default.shtml

Summary: To provide financial assistance for undergraduate education to dependents of deceased Delaware veterans, state police officers, and Department of Transportation employees and members of the armed forces declared prisoners of war or missing in action.

Eligibility: Open to applicants who have been Delaware residents for at least 3 consecutive years and are the children, between 16 and 24 years of age, of members of the armed forces 1) whose cause of death was service-related, 2) who are being held or were held as a prisoner of war, or 3) who are officially declared missing in action. The parent must have been a resident of Delaware at the time of death or declaration of missing in action or prisoner of war status. Also eligible are children of Delaware state police officers whose cause of death was service-related and employees of the state Department of Transportation routinely employed in job-related activities upon the state highway system whose cause of death was job related. U.S. citizenship or eligible noncitizen status is required.

Financial data: Eligible students receive full tuition at any state-supported institution in Delaware or, if the desired educational program is not available at a state-supported school, at any private institution in Delaware. If the desired educational program is not offered at either a public or private institution in Delaware, this program pays the full cost of tuition at the out-of-state school the recipient attends. Students who wish to attend a private or out-of-state school even though their program is offered at a Delaware public institution receive the equivalent of the average tuition and fees at the state school, recently set at $6,980 per year.

Duration: 1 year; may be renewed for 3 additional years.

Number awarded: Varies each year.

Deadline: Applications may be submitted at any time, but they must be received at least 4 weeks before the beginning of classes.

204 DELAWARE GOVERNOR'S EDUCATION GRANTS FOR UNEMPLOYED WORKERS

Delaware Higher Education Commission
Carvel State Office Building, Fifth Floor
820 North French Street
Wilmington, DE 19801-3509
Phone: (302) 577-5240; (800) 292-7935; Fax: (302) 577-6765
Email: dhec@doe.k12.de.us
Web: www.doe.k12.de.us/infosuites/students_family/dhec/default.shtml

Summary: To provide financial assistance to Delaware residents who are unemployed and wish to receive additional training.

Eligibility: Open to residents of Delaware who are high school graduates or GED recipients. Applicants must have lost their jobs due to the current economic climate, have been unsuccessful in obtaining employment within their current career field, have been actively seeking employment for at least 90 days, be registered with the Department of Labor's Division of Employment and Training (DET), be recommended by a DET career counselor, and be ineligible for the Department of Labor's Dislocated Worker Training Program. They must be enrolled as a part-time undergraduate at a participating Delaware college or adult education center. U.S. citizenship or eligible noncitizen status is required.

Financial data: Grants cover 80% of tuition and fees, to a maximum of $2,000 per year. The participating institution agrees to provide 10% of tuition and fees and the student is expected to pay the remaining 10%.

Duration: 1 year; renewable.

Number awarded: Varies each year.

Deadline: Applications may be submitted at any time, but they must be received by the end of the drop/add date at the participating college.

205 DELAWARE GOVERNOR'S EDUCATION GRANTS FOR WORKING ADULTS

Delaware Higher Education Commission
Carvel State Office Building, Fifth Floor
820 North French Street
Wilmington, DE 19801-3509
Phone: (302) 577-5240; (800) 292-7935; Fax: (302) 577-6765
Email: dhec@doe.k12.de.us
Web: www.doe.k12.de.us/infosuites/students_family/dhec/default.shtml

Summary: To provide financial assistance for part-time education to Delaware working adults with financial need.

Eligibility: Open to residents of Delaware who are at least 18 years of age and high school graduates or GED recipients. Applicants must be employed by a company in Delaware; if employed full-time, they must work for an eligible small business with 100 or fewer employees. They must be enrolled as a part-time undergraduate at a participating Delaware college or adult education center. Their income may not exceed $31,200 for a single individual or $42,000 for a family of 2, rising to $117,600 for a family of 9. U.S. citizenship or eligible noncitizen status is required.

Financial data: Grants cover 65% of tuition and fees, to a maximum of $2,000 per year. The participating institution agrees to provide 10% of tuition and fees and the student or employer is expected to pay the remaining 25%.

Duration: 1 year; renewable.

Number awarded: Varies each year.

Deadline: Applications may be submitted at any time, but they must be received by the end of the drop/add date at the participating college.

206 DELAWARE SCHOLARSHIP INCENTIVE PROGRAM

Delaware Higher Education Commission
Carvel State Office Building, Fifth Floor
820 North French Street
Wilmington, DE 19801-3509
Phone: (302) 577-5240; (800) 292-7935; Fax: (302) 577-6765
Email: dhec@doe.k12.de.us
Web: www.doe.k12.de.us/infosuites/students_family/dhec/default.shtml

Summary: To provide financial assistance for undergraduate or graduate study to Delaware residents with financial need.

Eligibility: Open to Delaware residents who are 1) enrolled full-time in an undergraduate degree program at a Delaware or Pennsylvania college or university; or 2) enrolled full-time in a graduate degree program at an accredited out-of-state institution or at a private institution in Delaware if their major is not offered at the University of Delaware, Delaware State University, or Delaware Technical and Community College. Applicants must be able to demonstrate financial need and have a GPA of 2.5 or higher. U.S. citizenship or eligible noncitizen status is required.

Financial data: The amount awarded depends on the need of the recipient but does not exceed the cost of tuition, fees, and books. Currently, the maximum for undergraduates ranges from $700 to $2,200 per year, depending on GPA; the maximum for graduate students is $1,000 per year.

Duration: 1 year; nonrenewable.

Number awarded: Approximately 1,500 each year.

Deadline: April of each year.

207 DELAWARE WOMEN TRAILBLAZER SCHOLARSHIPS

Delaware Higher Education Commission
Carvel State Office Building, Fifth Floor
820 North French Street
Wilmington, DE 19801-3509
Phone: (302) 577-5240; (800) 292-7935; Fax: (302) 577-6765
Email: dhec@doe.k12.de.us
Web: www.doe.k12.de.us/infosuites/students_family/dhec/default.shtml

Summary: To provide financial assistance to women who are residents of Delaware and interested in working on an undergraduate degree at a college in the state.

Eligibility: Open to women who are Delaware residents planning to enroll in a public or private nonprofit college in the state as an undergraduate student. Applicants must have a cumulative GPA of 2.5 or higher. They must be U.S. citizens or eligible noncitizens. Selection is based on financial need (50%) and community and school activities, vision, participation, and leadership (50%).

Financial data: The stipend is $2,500 per year.

Duration: 1 year; recipients may reapply.

Number awarded: 10 each year.

Deadline: April of each year.

208 DEMOLAY AND PINE TREE YOUTH FOUNDATION SCHOLARSHIPS

DeMolay and Pine Tree Youth Foundation
c/o Edward L. King
P.O. Box 816
Bangor, ME 04402-0816
Web: www.pinetreeyouth.org/scholarships.htm

Summary: To provide financial assistance to high school seniors in Maine who plan to attend college in any state.

Eligibility: Open to high school seniors in Maine. Certain scholarships are limited to graduates of particular schools, but most are given based on an open competition. Scholarships are awarded without regard to race, religion, age, gender, national origin, or "Masonic Family" relationships. Applicants must submit their high school transcript, a summary of their honors and extracurricular activities, and a narrative describing themselves, their background, and their future plans. Financial need is considered in the selection process.

Financial data: Stipends range from $500 to $1,500.

Duration: 1 year.

Number awarded: Varies each year; recently, 17 of these scholarships were awarded.

Deadline: March of each year.

209 DHS CHILDREN, ADULT, AND FAMILY SERVICES SCHOLARSHIP

Oregon Student Assistance Commission
Attn: Grants and Scholarships Division
1500 Valley River Drive, Suite 100
Eugene, OR 97401-2146
Phone: (541) 687-7395; (800) 452-8807, ext. 7395; Fax: (541) 687-7414; TDD: (800) 735-2900
Email: awardinfo@osac.state.or.us
Web: www.osac.state.or.us/osac_programs.html

Summary: To provide financial assistance for college to residents of Oregon who are or were in foster care or related programs.

Eligibility: Open to residents of Oregon who are either 1) graduating high school seniors currently in foster care or participating in the Independent Living Program (ILP); and 2) GED recipients and continuing college students formerly in foster care. Applicants must be attending or planning to attend a public college or university in Oregon.

Financial data: Stipends range from $500 to $5,000.

Duration: 1 year.

Number awarded: Varies each year.

Deadline: February of each year.

210 DIAMOND STATE SCHOLARSHIPS

Delaware Higher Education Commission
Carvel State Office Building, Fifth Floor
820 North French Street
Wilmington, DE 19801-3509
Phone: (302) 577-5240; (800) 292-7935; Fax: (302) 577-6765
Email: dhec@doe.k12.de.us
Web: www.doe.k12.de.us/infosuites/students_family/dhec/default.shtml

Summary: To provide financial assistance to Delaware high school seniors who have outstanding academic records and plan to attend college in any state.

Eligibility: Open to graduating high school seniors who are Delaware residents who have a combined score of 1800 on the SAT and who rank in the upper quarter of their class. Applicants must be planning to enroll in an accredited college or university on a full-time basis. U.S. citizenship or permanent resident status is required.

Financial data: The stipend is $1,250 per year.

Duration: 1 year; may be renewed up to 3 additional years, provided the recipient maintains a GPA of 3.0 or higher.

Number awarded: Approximately 50 each year.

Deadline: March of each year.

211 DINAH SHORE SCHOLARSHIP

Ladies Professional Golf Association
Attn: LPGA Foundation
100 International Golf Drive
Daytona Beach, FL 32124-1082
Phone: (386) 274-6200; Fax: (386) 274-1099
Email: foundation.scholarships@lpga.com
Web: www.lpgafoundation.org/Scholarships/dshore.aspx

Summary: To provide financial assistance for college to female graduating high school seniors who played golf in high school.

Eligibility: Open to female high school seniors who have a GPA of 3.2 or higher. Applicants must have played in at least 50% of their high school golf team's scheduled events or have played golf "regularly" for the past 2 years. They must be planning to enroll full-time at a college or university in the United States, but they must not be planning to play collegiate golf. Along with their application, they must submit a letter that describes how golf has been an integral part of their lives and includes their personal, academic, and professional goals; chosen discipline of study; and how this scholarship will be of assistance. Financial need is not considered in the selection process.

Financial data: The stipend is $5,000.

Duration: 1 year.

Number awarded: 1 each year.

Deadline: May of each year.

212 DISABLED WORKERS COMMITTEE SCHOLARSHIP

Disabled Workers Committee
Attn: Matthew Shafner, Scholarship Committee Chair
2 Union Plaza, Suite 200
New London, CT 06320
Phone: (860) 442-4416

Summary: To provide financial assistance to children of people with disabilities in Connecticut who are interested in attending college in any state.

Eligibility: Open to seniors graduating from high schools in Connecticut whose parent is totally and permanently disabled as the result of an injury. The injury must arise out of the workplace. Applicants must be interested in attending a college or university in any state. Selection is based on academic achievement and financial need.

Financial data: The stipend is $5,000.

Duration: 1 year.

Number awarded: 2 each year.

Deadline: April of each year.

213 DIVISION I DEGREE-COMPLETION AWARD PROGRAM

National Collegiate Athletic Association
Attn: Leadership Advisory Board
700 West Washington Avenue
P.O. Box 6222
Indianapolis, IN 46206-6222
Phone: (317) 917-6307; Fax: (317) 917-6364
Email: kcooper@ncaa.org
Web: www.ncaa.org/wps/ncaa?ContentID=1086

Summary: To provide financial assistance to student-athletes at Division I colleges and universities who have exhausted their eligibility for aid from the institutions they attend.

Eligibility: Open to student-athletes who have exhausted their 5 years of eligibility for institutional aid at a Division I member institution of the National Collegiate Athletic Association (NCAA). Applicants must be entering at least their sixth year of college and be within 30 semester hours of their degree requirements. They must submit documentation of financial need.

Financial data: Awards provide payment of the actual cost of tuition and fees plus a book allowance ($400 per semester for full-time students or an equivalent amount for part-time students).

Duration: 1 academic term; may be renewed if the recipient earns a GPA of 2.0 or higher.

Number awarded: Varies each year.

Deadline: May of each year.

214 DIVISION II DEGREE-COMPLETION AWARD PROGRAM

National Collegiate Athletic Association
Attn: Leadership Advisory Board
700 West Washington Avenue
P.O. Box 6222
Indianapolis, IN 46206-6222
Phone: (317) 917-6222; Fax: (317) 917-6364
Email: esummers@ncaa.org
Web: www.ncaa.org/wps/ncaa?ContentID=468

Summary: To provide financial assistance to student-athletes at Division II colleges and universities who have exhausted their eligibility for aid from the institutions they attend.
Eligibility: Open to student-athletes who have exhausted their eligibility for institutional aid at a Division II member institution of the National Collegiate Athletic Association (NCAA). Applicants must be within their first 10 semesters or 15 quarters of full-time college attendance. They must have a GPA of 2.5 or higher and be within 32 semester hours of their first undergraduate degree. Selection is based on financial circumstances, athletic achievement, and involvement in campus and community activities.
Financial data: The award is the lesser of 1) the recipient's athletics aid for the final year of eligibility; 2) tuition for the remaining credits toward completing an undergraduate degree; or 3) $6,000.
Duration: Until completion of an undergraduate degree.
Number awarded: Varies each year; recently, 86 of these awards were granted.
Deadline: April of each year.

215 DIXIE SOFTBALL SCHOLARSHIPS

Dixie Softball, Inc.
Attn: President
1101 Skelton Drive
Birmingham, AL 35224
Phone: (205) 785-2255; Fax: (205) 785-2258
Email: softball@dixie.org
Web: softball.dixie.org/scholarships9876.htm
Summary: To provide financial assistance for college to high school senior women who have participated in the Dixie Softball program.
Eligibility: Open to high school senior women who played in the Dixie Softball program for at least 2 seasons. Applicants must submit a transcript of grades, a letter of recommendation from a high school principal or other school official, verification from a Dixie Softball local official of the number of years the applicant participated in the program, and documentation of financial need. Ability as an athlete is not considered in the selection process.
Financial data: The stipend is $1,500.
Duration: 1 year.
Number awarded: 6 each year.
Deadline: February of each year.

216 DIXIE YOUTH BASEBALL SCHOLARSHIPS

Dixie Youth Baseball, Inc.
Attn: Scholarship Committee
P.O. Box 877
Marshall, TX 75671-0877
Phone: (903) 927-2255; Fax: (903) 927-1846
Email: dyb@dixie.org
Web: youth.dixie.org/scholarships1c78.htm
Summary: To provide financial assistance for college to high school senior males who have participated in a Dixie Youth Baseball franchised league.
Eligibility: Open to high school senior males who played in a Dixie Youth Baseball franchised league when they were 12 years of age or younger. Applicants must submit a transcript of grades, a letter of recommendation from a high school principal or other school official, verification from a Dixie Youth local official of participation in a franchised league, and documentation of financial need. Ability as an athlete is not considered in the selection process.
Financial data: The stipend is $2,000.
Duration: 1 year.
Number awarded: Varies each year; recently, 70 of these scholarships were awarded.
Deadline: February of each year.

217 DKF VETERANS ASSISTANCE FOUNDATION SCHOLARSHIPS

DKF Veterans Assistance Foundation
P.O. Box 7166
San Carlos, CA 94070
Phone: (650) 595-3896
Email: admin@dkfveterans.com
Web: www.dkfveterans.com
Summary: To provide financial assistance for college to California residents who are veterans of Operation Enduring Freedom (OEF) in Afghanistan or Operation Iraqi Freedom (OIF) or the dependents of deceased or disabled veterans of those actions.
Eligibility: Open to 1) veterans of the U.S. armed forces (including the Coast Guard) who served in support of OEF or OIF within the central command area of responsibility; and 2) dependents of those veterans who were killed in action or incurred disabilities rated as 75% or more. Applicants must be residents of California enrolled or planning to enroll full-time at a college, university, community college, or trade institution in any state. Along with their application, they must submit a cover letter introducing themselves and their educational goals.
Financial data: The stipend is $5,000 per year for students at universities and state colleges or $1,500 per year for students at community colleges and trade institutions.
Duration: 1 year; may be renewed up to 3 additional years, provided the recipient maintains a GPA of 3.0 or higher.
Number awarded: A limited number of these scholarships are awarded each year.
Deadline: Deadline not specified.

218 DOLLARS FOR SCHOLARS PROGRAM

United Methodist Higher Education Foundation
Attn: Scholarships Administrator
1001 19th Avenue South
P.O. Box 340005
Nashville, TN 37203-0005
Phone: (615) 340-7385; (800) 811-8110; Fax: (615) 340-7330
Email: umhefscholarships@gbhem.org
Web: www.umhef.org/receive.php?id=dollars_for_scholars
Summary: To provide financial assistance to students at Methodist colleges, universities, and seminaries whose home churches agree to contribute to their support.
Eligibility: Open to students attending or planning to attend a United Methodist–related college, university, or seminary as a full-time student. Applicants must have been an active, full member of a United Methodist Church for at least 1 year prior to applying. Their home church must nominate them and agree to contribute to their support. Many of the United Methodist colleges and universities have also agreed to contribute matching funds for a Triple Your Dollars for Scholars Program, and a few United Methodist conference foundations have agreed to contribute additional matching funds for a Quadruple Your Dollars for Scholars Program. Awards are granted on a first-come, first-served basis. Some of the awards are designated for Hispanic, Asian, and Native American (HANA) students funded by the General Board of Higher Education and Ministry.
Financial data: The sponsoring church contributes $1,000 and the United Methodist Higher Education Foundation (UMHEF) contributes a matching $1,000. Students who attend a participating United Methodist college or university receive an additional $1,000 for the Triple Your Dollars for Scholars Program, and those from a participating conference receive a fourth $1,000 increment for the Quadruple Your Dollars for Scholars Program.
Duration: 1 year; may be renewed as long as the recipients maintain satisfactory academic progress as defined by their institution.
Number awarded: 350 each year, including 25 designated for HANA students.
Deadline: Local churches must submit applications in March of each year for senior colleges and universities and seminaries or May of each year for 2-year colleges.

219 DON ARMSTRONG COLLEGE SCHOLARSHIP

Rhode Island High School Hockey Coaches Association
c/o Bill Russo, Scholarship Committee
36 Cameron Court
Warwick, RI 02886
Email: coach@rihockey.net
Web: www.rihshl.goalline.ca/page.php?page_id=13569
Summary: To provide financial assistance to high school seniors in Rhode Island who have played hockey and plan to attend college in any state.
Eligibility: Open to graduating seniors who have played hockey in programs of the Rhode Island Interscholastic League. Applicants must be planning to attend college in any state. Along with their application, they must submit an essay of 200 to 250 words on how they plan to pay for their college education and why this scholarship is important to them. Selection is based on academic record, character, community service, and activities. Boys and girls are considered separately and awards are distributed among them on the percentage breakdown of players in the league.
Financial data: A stipend is awarded (amount not specified).
Duration: 1 year.

Number awarded: Varies each year; recently, 5 boys and 2 girls were awarded these scholarships.
Deadline: February of each year.

220 DONALD LEE PATTON SCHOLARSHIP

Community Foundation of Muncie and Delaware County, Inc.
201 East Jackson Street
P.O. Box 807
Muncie, IN 47308
Phone: (765) 747-7181; Fax: (765) 289-7770
Email: info@cfmdin.org
Web: www.cfmdin.org/main/community-foundation-scholarships
Summary: To provide financial assistance to high school seniors in Indiana who have played on the wrestling team and are planning to attend college in any state.
Eligibility: Open to seniors who are graduating from high schools in Indiana and planning to attend an accredited college or university in any state. Applicants must have been members of their high school's wrestling team for at least 2 years. Along with their application, they must submit a personal note on what wrestling has meant to their life. Selection is based on academic achievement, participation in school organizations, awards and honors attained, participation in community service activities, and financial need.
Financial data: A stipend is awarded (amount not specified).
Duration: 1 year.
Number awarded: 1 each year.
Deadline: March of each year.

221 DONALDSON D. FRIZZELL MEMORIAL SCHOLARSHIPS

First Command Educational Foundation
Attn: Scholarship Programs Manager
1 FirstComm Plaza
Fort Worth, TX 76109-4999
Phone: (817) 569-2634; (877) 872-8289; Fax: (817) 569-2970
Email: Scholarships@fcef.com
Web: www.fcef.com/direct-apply-scholarship.php
Summary: To provide financial assistance to students, especially those with ties to the military, entering or attending college.
Eligibility: Open to 2 categories of applicants: 1) traditional students, including high school seniors and students already enrolled at a college, university, or accredited trade school; and 2) nontraditional students, including those defined by their institution as nontraditional and adult students planning to return to a college, university, or accredited trade school. Traditional students must have a GPA of 3.0 or higher. Applicants must submit 1-page essays on 1) their active involvement in community service programs; 2) the impact of financial literacy on their future; and 3) why they need this scholarship. Selection is based primarily on the essays, academic merit, and financial need.
Financial data: Stipends are $5,000 or $2,500. Funds are disbursed directly to the recipient's college, university, or trade school.
Duration: 1 year.
Number awarded: 6 each year: 2 at $5,000 and 4 at $2,500. Awards are split evenly between the 2 categories.
Deadline: The online application process begins in February of each year and continues until 200 applications have been received in each category.

222 DOROTHY CAMPBELL MEMORIAL SCHOLARSHIP

Oregon Student Assistance Commission
Attn: Grants and Scholarships Division
1500 Valley River Drive, Suite 100
Eugene, OR 97401-2146
Phone: (541) 687-7395; (800) 452-8807, ext. 7395; Fax: (541) 687-7414; TDD: (800) 735-2900
Email: awardinfo@osac.state.or.us
Web: www.osac.state.or.us/osac_programs.html
Summary: To provide financial assistance to women in Oregon who are interested in golf and planning to attend college in the state.
Eligibility: Open to residents of Oregon who are U.S. citizens or permanent residents. Applicants must be female high school seniors or graduates with a cumulative GPA of 2.75 or higher and a strong continuing interest in golf. They must be enrolled or planning to enroll full-time at an Oregon 4-year college. Along with their application, they must submit a 1-page essay on the contribution that golf has made to their development. Financial need is considered in the selection process.
Financial data: The stipend is at least $1,500.
Duration: 1 year; may be renewed up to 3 additional years.
Number awarded: Varies each year; recently, 2 of these scholarships were awarded.
Deadline: February of each year.

223 DOROTHY KELLERMAN SCHOLARSHIP

American Legion Auxiliary
Department of New Jersey
c/o Lucille M. Miller, Secretary/Treasurer
1540 Kuser Road, Suite A-8
Hamilton, NJ 08619
Phone: (609) 581-9580; Fax: (609) 581-8429
Email: newjerseyala@juno.com
Web: www.alanj.org
Summary: To provide financial assistance to New Jersey residents who are the descendants of veterans and planning to attend college in any state.
Eligibility: Open to the children, grandchildren, and great-grandchildren of veterans who served in the U.S. armed forces during specified periods of war time. Applicants must be graduating high school seniors who have been residents of New Jersey for at least 2 years. They must be planning to attend a college or university in any state. Along with their application, they must submit a 1,000-word essay on a topic that changes annually; recently, students were asked to write on the topic, "Honoring Our Promise Everyday-How I Can Serve My Country and Our Veterans." Selection is based on academic achievement (40%), character (15%), leadership (15%), Americanism (15%), and financial need (15%).
Financial data: Stipends range from $1,000 to $2,500.
Duration: 1 year; nonrenewable.
Number awarded: 1 each year.
Deadline: April of each year.

224 DOROTHY YOTHERS VOCATIONAL GRANTS

Washington State Elks Association
4512 South Pine Street
P.O. Box 110760
Tacoma, WA 98411-0760
Phone: (253) 472-6223; (800) 825-ELKS; Fax: (253) 472-6217
Web: www.wselks.com/scholarships.htm
Summary: To provide financial assistance to high school seniors in Washington state who are interested in pursuing vocational training or a 2-year associate degree.
Eligibility: Open to graduating high school students and GED students who are residents of Washington. Applicants must be U.S. citizens and planning to work on an associate degree, diploma, certificate, or other course of vocational training that does not exceed 2 years in length. Students seeking education that requires a 4-year degree are ineligible. Along with their application, they must submit 1) a 250-word statement of their activities, accomplishments, needs, and objectives that they believe qualify them for this grant; and 2) a 200-word statement from a parent or guardian describing the family's obligations and resources. Selection is based on motivation, skills, completeness and neatness of the application, and financial need.
Financial data: Stipends range from $500 to $1,500.
Duration: 1 year.
Number awarded: The Washington State Elks Association awards 60 scholarships each year.
Deadline: February of each year.

225 DORTHEA AND ROLAND BOHDE SCHOLASTIC ACHIEVEMENT SCHOLARSHIP

American Council of the Blind
Attn: Coordinator, Scholarship Program
2200 Wilson Boulevard, Suite 650
Arlington, VA 22201
Phone: (202) 467-5081; (800) 424-8666; Fax: (703) 465-5085
Email: info@acb.org
Web: www.acb.org
Summary: To provide financial assistance to outstanding blind students.
Eligibility: Open to legally blind students enrolling or continuing in an undergraduate program. Applicants must submit verification of legal blindness in both eyes; SAT or ACT scores; information on extracurricular activities (including membership in the American Council of the Blind); employment

record; and an autobiographical sketch that includes their personal goals, strengths, weaknesses, hobbies, honors, achievements, and reasons for choice of field or courses of study. A cumulative GPA of 3.3 or higher is generally required. Financial need is not considered in the selection process.

Financial data: A stipend is awarded (amount not specified). In addition, the winner receives a Kurzweil-1000 Reading System.

Duration: 1 year.

Number awarded: 1 each year.

Deadline: February of each year.

226 DR. NICHOLAS S. DICAPRIO SCHOLARSHIP

American Council of the Blind
Attn: Coordinator, Scholarship Program
2200 Wilson Boulevard, Suite 650
Arlington, VA 22201
Phone: (202) 467-5081; (800) 424-8666; Fax: (703) 465-5085
Email: info@acb.org
Web: www.acb.org

Summary: To provide financial assistance to outstanding blind undergraduates.

Eligibility: Open to legally blind undergraduate students. Applicants must submit verification of legal blindness in both eyes; SAT or ACT scores; information on extracurricular activities (including membership in the American Council of the Blind); employment record; and an autobiographical sketch that includes their personal goals, strengths, weaknesses, hobbies, honors, achievements, and reasons for choice of field or courses of study. A cumulative GPA of 3.3 or higher is generally required. Financial need is not considered in the selection process.

Financial data: The stipend is $2,500. In addition, the winner receives a Kurzweil-1000 Reading System.

Duration: 1 year.

Number awarded: 1 each year.

Deadline: February of each year.

227 DREAMS2 SCHOLARSHIP

Community Foundation for Greater Atlanta, Inc.
50 Hurt Plaza, Suite 449
Atlanta, GA 30303
Phone: (404) 688-5525; Fax: (404) 688-3060
Email: scholarships@cfgreateratlanta.org
Web: www.cfgreateratlanta.org/Grants-Support/Scholarships.aspx

Summary: To provide financial assistance to high school seniors and current undergraduates from any state who have financial need but only average grades.

Eligibility: Open to residents of any state who are graduating high school seniors or current undergraduates and are enrolled or accepted for enrollment as a full-time student at an accredited 2- or 4-year college, university, or technical school. Applicants must have a GPA between 2.0 and 3.0. They must be able to demonstrate financial need.

Financial data: The stipend is $2,000 per year.

Duration: 1 year; recipients may reapply if they have maintained a GPA of their school's required minimum or a 2.0, but renewal is not guaranteed.

Number awarded: 6 each year.

Deadline: March of each year.

228 DUANE BUCKLEY MEMORIAL SCHOLARSHIP

American Council of the Blind
Attn: Coordinator, Scholarship Program
2200 Wilson Boulevard, Suite 650
Arlington, VA 22201
Phone: (202) 467-5081; (800) 424-8666; Fax: (703) 465-5085
Email: info@acb.org
Web: www.acb.org

Summary: To provide financial assistance for college to blind high school seniors.

Eligibility: Open to graduating high school seniors who are legally blind in both eyes. Applicants must submit verification of legal blindness in both eyes; SAT or ACT scores; information on extracurricular activities (including membership in the American Council of the Blind); employment record; and an autobiographical sketch that includes their personal goals, strengths, weaknesses, hobbies, honors, achievements, and reasons for choice of field or courses of study. A cumulative GPA of 3.3 or higher is generally required. Financial need is not considered in the selection process.

Financial data: The stipend is $1,000. In addition, the winner receives a Kurzweil-1000 Reading System.

Duration: 1 year.

Number awarded: 1 each year.

Deadline: February of each year.

229 DUNKIN' DONUTS SCHOLARSHIPS

Scholarship America
Attn: Scholarship Management Services
One Scholarship Way
P.O. Box 297
St. Peter, MN 56082
Phone: (507) 931-1682; (800) 537-4180; Fax: (507) 931-9168
Web: www.dunkindonuts.com/scholarship

Summary: To provide financial assistance to residents of Connecticut, Rhode Island, and parts of Massachusetts who are attending or planning to attend college in any state.

Eligibility: Open to 1) seniors graduating from high schools in Connecticut, Rhode Island, and the Massachusetts counties of Bristol, Hampden, Hampshire, and Franklin; and 2) recent graduates of those high schools already enrolled at a college or university in any state. Applicants must be able to demonstrate a positive academic record, demonstrated leadership, commitment to school and community activities, and experience in a work environment.

Financial data: The stipend is $1,000.

Duration: 1 year.

Number awarded: 75 each year.

Deadline: March of each year.

230 DWIGHT MOSLEY SCHOLARSHIPS

United States Tennis Association
Attn: USTA Serves
70 West Red Oak Lane
White Plains, NY 10604
Phone: (914) 696-7223
Email: eliezer@usta.com
Web: www.usta.com/USTA/Home/AboutUs/USTAServes.aspx

Summary: To provide financial assistance for college to high school seniors from diverse ethnic backgrounds who have participated in an organized community tennis program.

Eligibility: Open to high school seniors from diverse ethnic backgrounds who have excelled academically, demonstrated achievements in leadership, and participated extensively in an organized community tennis program. Applicants must be planning to enroll as a full-time undergraduate student at a 4-year college or university. They must have a GPA of 3.0 or higher and be able to demonstrate financial need and sportsmanship. Along with their application, they must submit 1) an essay about themselves and how their participation in a tennis program has influenced their life; and 2) documentation of a state and/or section ranking of the United States Tennis Association. Males and females are considered separately.

Financial data: The stipend is $2,500 per year. Funds are paid directly to the recipient's college or university.

Duration: 4 years.

Number awarded: 2 each year: 1 male and 1 female.

Deadline: February of each year.

231 E. CRAIG BRANDENBURG SCHOLARSHIP

United Methodist Church
Attn: General Board of Higher Education and Ministry
Office of Loans and Scholarships
1001 19th Avenue South
P.O. Box 340007
Nashville, TN 37203-0007
Phone: (615) 340-7344; Fax: (615) 340-7367
Email: umscholar@gbhem.org
Web: www.gbhem.org/loansandscholarships

Summary: To provide financial assistance to mature Methodist students who are working on an undergraduate or graduate degree to change their profession or continue study after interruption.

Eligibility: Open to full-time undergraduate and graduate students who are 35 years of age or older. Applicants must have been active, full members of a United Methodist Church for at least 1 year prior to applying. They must 1) be able to demonstrate special need because of a change of profession or vocation,

interruption of study, or resumption of education; 2) have a GPA of 2.5 or higher; and 3) be U.S. citizens or permanent residents. Preference is given to applicants attending United Methodist colleges, universities, or seminaries.
Financial data: Stipends range from $500 to $2,000.
Duration: 1 year; recipients may reapply.
Number awarded: Varies each year.
Deadline: February of each year.

232 E. WAYNE COOLEY SCHOLARSHIP AWARD

Iowa Girls High School Athletic Union
Attn: Scholarships
2900 Grand Avenue
P.O. Box 10348
Des Moines, IA 50306-0348
Phone: (515) 288-9741; Fax: (515) 284-1969
Email: jasoneslinger@ighsau.org
Web: www.ighsau.org/aspx/cooley_award.aspx

Summary: To provide financial assistance to female high school seniors in Iowa who have participated in athletics and plan to attend college in the state.
Eligibility: Open to women graduating from high schools in Iowa who have a GPA of 3.75 or higher and an ACT score of 23 or higher. Applicants must have earned a varsity letter in at least 2 different sports and have participated in at least 2 sports each year of high school. They must be planning to attend a college or university in Iowa. Each high school in the state may nominate 1 student. Selection is based on academic achievements, athletic accomplishments, nonsports extracurricular activities, and community involvement.
Financial data: The winner's stipend is $3,750 per year. Finalists receive a $1,000 scholarship.
Duration: 4 years for the winner, provided she maintains at least a 2.5 GPA while enrolled in college. The scholarships for finalists are for 1 year.
Number awarded: 6 each year: 1 winner and 5 finalists.
Deadline: December of each year.

233 EASTER SEALS SOUTH CAROLINA EDUCATIONAL SCHOLARSHIPS

Easter Seals South Carolina
Attn: Scholarship Program
3020 Farrow Road
P.O. Box 5715
Columbia, SC 29250
Phone: (803) 429-8474; Fax: (803) 738-1934
Email: TAdger@sc.easterseals.com
Web: sc.easterseals.com

Summary: To provide financial assistance for college or graduate school to South Carolina students who have a disability.
Eligibility: Open to South Carolina residents and students attending a college or university in the state who have a significant and medically certified mobility impairment. Applicants must be enrolled or planning to enroll in an undergraduate or graduate program. They must be able to demonstrate financial need. Preference is given to students carrying at least 9 credit hours and making satisfactory academic progress toward graduation.
Financial data: The maximum stipend is $1,000.
Duration: 1 year; may be renewed.
Number awarded: 1 or more each year.
Deadline: June of each year.

234 EDITH, LOUIS AND MAX S. MILLEN MEMORIAL EDUCATION GRANT

Jewish War Veterans of the U.S.A.
1811 R Street, N.W.
Washington, DC 20009-1659
Phone: (202) 265-6280; Fax: (202) 234-5662
Email: jwv@jvw.org
Web: www.jwv.org/programs/service/awards/olympiad_memorial_award

Summary: To recognize and reward outstanding high school athletes.
Eligibility: Open to outstanding senior high school athletes. Applicants must show evidence of accomplishments within the Olympic spirit, including excellence in all endeavors, sportsmanship, and friendship, with an emphasis on achievements in sports. The award is presented on a non-sectarian basis. Selection is based on athletic accomplishment (60%), academic achievement (20%), community service (10%), and leadership and citizenship (10%).
Financial data: The award is $1,000 for the winner and $300 and $200 for the runners-up.
Duration: The awards are presented annually.
Number awarded: 3 each year.
Deadline: Applications must be submitted to the commander at a date especially by each department; that may be as early as March of each year.

235 EDUCATION ADVANTAGE UNIVERSITY SCHOLARSHIP

Baxter Healthcare Corporation
Attn: Education Advantage Program
One Baxter Parkway
Deerfield, IL 60015-4625
Phone: (847) 948-2000; (800) 423-2090; Fax: (800) 568-5020
Email: baxter@scholarshipamerica.org
Web: www.myeducationadvantage.com/education/scholarship

Summary: To provide financial assistance to people who have hemophilia A and are interested in working on a bachelor's degree.
Eligibility: Open to people who have hemophilia A or hemophilia with inhibitors and are enrolled or planning to enroll full-time at a 4-year college or university. Applicants must submit a personal statement that focuses on their unique experiences that make them stand out from other students (e.g., their experiences of living with hemophilia, how it impacts their education or career goals, noteworthy volunteer activities within the hemophilia community). Both merit-based and need-based scholarships are available. U.S. citizenship or permanent resident status is required.
Financial data: The stipend is $15,000 per year.
Duration: 1 year; may be renewed up to 3 additional years, provided the recipient remains enrolled full-time, maintains a GPA of 2.0 or higher, provides evidence of participation in annual comprehensive clinic and routine dental care, performs 20 hours of community service, and submits a 250-word essay on their academic progress, career goals and developments, and the value of funding assistance.
Number awarded: 1 or more each year.
Deadline: April of each year.

236 EDWARD WILMOT BLYDEN GRANT

Virgin Islands Board of Education
Dronningen Gade 60B, 61, and 62
P.O. Box 11900
St. Thomas, VI 00801
Phone: (340) 774-4546; Fax: (340) 774-3384
Email: stt@myviboe.com
Web: myviboe.com

Summary: To provide financial assistance to residents of the Virgin Islands who wish to attend a college in the territory or on the mainland.
Eligibility: Open to residents of the Virgin Islands who are seniors or graduates of high schools in the territory. Applicants must have a GPA of 2.0 or higher and be attending or accepted for enrollment at an accredited institution of higher learning in the territory or on the mainland. They may be planning to major in any field. Financial need is considered in the selection process.
Financial data: The stipend is $1,000 per year.
Duration: 1 year; may be renewed up to 3 additional years.
Number awarded: 1 each year.
Deadline: April of each year.

237 EDWIN GARDNER WEED RUGE EDUCATIONAL FUND SCHOLARSHIP

Center for Scholarship Administration, Inc.
Attn: Wachovia Accounts
4320 Wade Hampton Boulevard, Suite G
Taylors, SC 29687
Phone: (866) 608-0001
Email: wachoviascholars@bellsouth.net
Web: www.wachoviascholars.com/ferb/index.php

Summary: To provide financial assistance to high school seniors and graduates from Florida who plan to attend college in the state.
Eligibility: Open to residents of Florida who are high school seniors or recent graduates. Applicants must be enrolled or planning to enroll full-time at an accredited 2- or 4-year college or university in Florida. They must have a GPA of 2.0 or higher. Preference is given to residents of Apalachicola. Selection is based on academic ability, personal character, leadership, and financial need.
Financial data: A stipend is awarded (amount not specified).

Duration: 1 year; may be renewed up to 3 additional years or until completion of a bachelor's degree (whichever comes first.

Number awarded: 1 or more each year.

Deadline: March of each year.

238 EL RICHARDS/FRANCIS WALSH SPIRIT SCHOLARSHIPS

New Mexico Activities Association
Attn: Associate Director
6600 Palomas Avenue, N.E.
Albuquerque, NM 87109
Phone: (505) 923-3275; (888) 820-NMAA; Fax: (505) 923-3114
Email: mmartinez@nmact.org
Web: www.nmact.org/scholarship_information_forms

Summary: To provide financial assistance to high school seniors in New Mexico who have participated in spirit activities and plan to attend college in any state.

Eligibility: Open to seniors graduating from high schools in New Mexico with a GPA of 3.0 or higher. Applicants must have participated actively in a cheer or dance/drill program at a school that is a member of the New Mexico Activities Association (NMAA) for at least 3 years in grades 8–12. They must be planning to attend a college or university in any state. Along with their application, they must submit a personal statement on how involvement in spirit impacted their high school career. Financial need is not considered in the selection process.

Financial data: The stipend is $1,000. From among all its scholarship recipients, the NMAA selects the 2 most outstanding and awards them a stipend of $2,500.

Duration: 1 year.

Number awarded: 2 each year. The NMAA also awards 2 additional at-large scholarships to applicants for all its programs.

Deadline: February of each year.

239 ELECTRONIC SECURITY ASSOCIATION OF INDIANA YOUTH SCHOLARSHIP PROGRAM

Electronic Security Association of Indiana
Attn: Youth Scholarship Program
2602 East 55th Street
Indianapolis, IN 46220
Phone: (317) 334-1906
Web: www.ibfaa.org

Summary: To provide financial assistance to high school seniors in Indiana who are the children of active-duty law enforcement and fire service personnel and interested in attending college in any state.

Eligibility: Open to seniors graduating from high schools in Indiana who have been accepted at an accredited college or university in any state. Applicants must have a father, mother, or legal guardian who is a full-time active employee (not on disability) of the police or sheriff's department or a paid employee or volunteer of a fire department in Indiana. Along with their application, they must submit an essay of 500 to 1,000 words on what it means to them to have their parent or guardian involved in securing our community. Selection is based on that essay (20 points), grade average (35 points), SAT or ACT scores (30 points), and academic prizes, awards, school and outside extracurricular activities, and hobbies (15 points); financial need is not considered.

Financial data: The first-place winner receives a $1,000 scholarship, second a $750 scholarship, and third a $500 scholarship.

Duration: The awards are presented annually.

Number awarded: 3 each year.

Deadline: March of each year.

240 ELECTRONIC SECURITY ASSOCIATION YOUTH SCHOLARSHIP PROGRAM

Electronic Security Association
Attn: Youth Scholarship Program
2300 Valley View Lane, Suite 230
Irving, TX 75062
Phone: (214) 260-5970; (888) 447-1689; Fax: (214) 260-5979
Email: jasons@alarm.org
Web: www.alarm.org/pubsafety/ysp

Summary: To provide financial assistance for college to high school seniors whose parents are active-duty law enforcement or fire service personnel.

Eligibility: Open to seniors graduating from high school who are the children of full-time active-duty (not on disability) law enforcement and fire service personnel. Applicants must submit an essay on what it means to them to have their parent or guardian involved in securing our community. Selection is based on that essay, academic achievement, national test scores, and extracurricular participation. State chapters of the sponsor in 14 states hold their own competitions; each awards its own prizes, but each state winner is automatically nominated for this program. Students in other states may apply directly to the national organization; those applications will be judged, and 1 of those will be entered with the 14 state winners to compete for the national awards.

Financial data: Stipends are $7,500 or $2,500. The student residing in a state without a chapter or in a non-participating state who is selected to compete with the 14 state winners receives an award of $1,000.

Duration: 1 year.

Number awarded: 2 each year: 1 at $7,500 and 1 at $2,500.

Deadline: Deadline not specified.

241 ELIZABETH NASH FOUNDATION SCHOLARSHIP PROGRAM

Elizabeth Nash Foundation
P.O. Box 1260
Los Gatos, CA 95031-1260
Email: scholarships@elizabethnashfoundation.org
Web: www.elizabethnashfoundation.org/scholarshipprogram.html

Summary: To provide financial assistance for college or graduate school to individuals with cystic fibrosis (CF).

Eligibility: Open to undergraduate and graduate students who have CF. Applicants must be able to demonstrate clear academic goals and a commitment to participate in activities outside the classroom. U.S. citizenship is required. Selection is based on academic record, character, demonstrated leadership, service to CF-related causes and the broader community, and financial need.

Financial data: Stipends range from $1,000 to $2,500. Funds are paid directly to the academic institution to be applied to tuition and fees.

Duration: 1 year; recipients may reapply.

Number awarded: Varies each year; recently, 12 of these scholarships were awarded.

Deadline: April of each year.

242 ELSIE BAILEY SCHOLARSHIP

American Legion Auxiliary
Department of New Jersey
c/o Lucille M. Miller, Secretary/Treasurer
1540 Kuser Road, Suite A-8
Hamilton, NJ 08619
Phone: (609) 581-9580; Fax: (609) 581-8429
Email: newjerseyala@juno.com
Web: www.alanj.org

Summary: To provide financial assistance to New Jersey residents who are the descendants of veterans and planning to attend college in any state.

Eligibility: Open to the children, grandchildren, and great-grandchildren of veterans who served in the U.S. armed forces during specified periods of war time. Applicants must be graduating high school seniors who have been residents of New Jersey for at least 2 years. They must be planning to attend a college or university in any state. Along with their application, they must submit a 1,000-word essay on a topic that changes annually; recently, students were asked to write on the topic, "Honoring Our Promise Everyday-How I Can Serve My Country and Our Veterans." Selection is based on academic achievement (40%), character (15%), leadership (15%), Americanism (15%), and financial need (15%).

Financial data: Stipends range from $1,000 to $2,500.

Duration: 1 year; nonrenewable.

Number awarded: 1 each year.

Deadline: April of each year.

243 EMILY LESTER SCHOLARSHIP

Vermont Student Assistance Corporation
Attn: Scholarship Programs
10 East Allen Street
P.O. Box 2000
Winooski, VT 05404-2601
Phone: (802) 654-3798; (888) 253-4819; Fax: (802) 654-3765; TDD: (800) 281-3341 (within VT)
Email: info@vsac.org
Web: services.vsac.org/wps/wcm/connect/vsac/VSAC

Summary: To provide financial assistance to residents of Vermont who are or have been under the custody of the Department for Children and Families (DCF) and wish to attend college in any state.
Eligibility: Open to residents of Vermont who are 1) currently under the custody of the DCF, or 2) between 18 and 24 years of age and have been under the custody of the DCF for at least 6 months when they were between 16 and 18 years of age. Applicants must be attending or planning to attend college in any state. They must be able to demonstrate financial need.
Financial data: Stipends may range up to $3,000, but most range from $1,000 to $2,000.
Duration: 1 year.
Number awarded: Varies each year.
Deadline: March of each year.

244 ENHANCED AIR FORCE ROTC HISPANIC SERVING INSTITUTION SCHOLARSHIP PROGRAM

U.S. Air Force
Attn: Headquarters AFROTC/RRUC
551 East Maxwell Boulevard
Maxwell AFB, AL 36112-5917
Phone: (334) 953-2091; (866) 4-AFROTC; Fax: (334) 953-6167
Email: afrotc1@maxwell.af.mil
Web: afrotc.com/scholarships/in-college/minority-school-scholarships
Summary: To provide financial assistance to students at designated Hispanic Serving Institutions (HSIs) who are willing to join Air Force ROTC in college and serve as Air Force officers following completion of their bachelor's degree.
Eligibility: Open to U.S. citizens who are at least 17 years of age and currently enrolled at 1 of 5 designated HSIs that have an Air Force ROTC unit on campus. Applicants do not need to be Hispanic, as long as they are enrolled at the university and have a cumulative GPA of 2.5 or higher. At the time of commissioning, they may be no more than 31 years of age. They must be able to pass the Air Force Officer Qualifying Test (AFOQT) and the Air Force ROTC Physical Fitness Test. Currently, the program is accepting applications from students with any major.
Financial data: Awards are type 2 AFROTC scholarships that provide for payment of tuition and fees, to a maximum of $18,000 per year, plus an annual book allowance of $900. Recipients are also awarded a tax-free subsistence allowance for 10 months of each year that is $350 per month during the sophomore year, $450 during the junior year, and $500 during the senior year.
Duration: Up to 3 and a half years (beginning as early as the spring semester of the freshman year).
Number awarded: Up to 75 each year: 15 at each of the participating AFROTC units.
Deadline: Applications may be submitted at any time.

245 ENHANCED AIR FORCE ROTC HISTORICALLY BLACK COLLEGES AND UNIVERSITIES SCHOLARSHIP PROGRAM

U.S. Air Force
Attn: Headquarters AFROTC/RRUC
551 East Maxwell Boulevard
Maxwell AFB, AL 36112-5917
Phone: (334) 953-2091; (866) 4-AFROTC; Fax: (334) 953-6167
Email: afrotc1@maxwell.af.mil
Web: afrotc.com/scholarships/in-college/minority-school-scholarships
Summary: To provide financial assistance to students at designated Historically Black Colleges and Universities (HBCUs) who are willing to join Air Force ROTC and serve as Air Force officers following completion of their bachelor's degree.
Eligibility: Open to U.S. citizens at least 17 years of age who are currently enrolled as freshmen at 1 of the 7 HBCUs that have an Air Force ROTC unit on campus. Applicants do not need to be African American, as long as they are attending an HBCU and have a cumulative GPA of 2.5 or higher. At the time of commissioning, they may be no more than 31 years of age. They must be able to pass the Air Force Officer Qualifying Test (AFOQT) and the Air Force ROTC Physical Fitness Test. Currently, the program is accepting applications from students with any major.
Financial data: Awards are type 2 AFROTC scholarships that provide for payment of tuition and fees, to a maximum of $18,000 per year, plus an annual book allowance of $900. Recipients are also awarded a tax-free subsistence allowance for 10 months of each year that is $350 per month during the sophomore year, $450 during the junior year, and $500 during the senior year.
Duration: Up to 3 and a half years (beginning as early as the spring semester of the freshman year).
Number awarded: Up to 105 each year: 15 at each of the participating AFROTC units.
Deadline: Applications may be submitted at any time.

246 EPPS SCHOLARSHIP FUND

Greater Kansas City Community Foundation
Attn: Scholarship Coordinator
1055 Broadway, Suite 130
Kansas City, MO 64105-1595
Phone: (816) 842-7444; Fax: (816) 842-8079
Email: scholarships@gkccf.org
Web: www.gkccf.org/scholarship.aspx?id=1788
Summary: To provide financial assistance to high school seniors in Missouri who plan to attend a 4-year college or university in any state, major in any field, and then continue on to law school.
Eligibility: Open to seniors graduating from high schools in Missouri who have a GPA of 3.0 or higher. Applicants must be planning to attend a 4-year college or university in any state and then an accredited law school. Along with their application, they must submit a 250-word personal statement that includes their leadership experience and group contributions, knowledge of lawyers and the legal profession, and ways in which they have dealt with adversity. Selection is based on academic achievement, interest in preparing for a legal career, community service, and financial need.
Financial data: The stipend is $2,000.
Duration: 1 year; nonrenewable.
Number awarded: 1 or more each year.
Deadline: June of each year.

247 ERCA COMMUNITY CONTRIBUTION SCHOLARSHIP

Educational Research Center of America, Inc.
Attn: Scholarship Committee
777 Sunrise Highway
P.O. Box 9012
Lynbrook, NY 11563
Phone: (202) 393-7799
Email: info@studentresearch.org
Web: www.studentresearch.org/public/application.html
Summary: To provide financial assistance for college to high school seniors who have provided outstanding service to their community.
Eligibility: Open to college-bound high school seniors. Applicants must have recognized a need or problem in their community, have determined a way to address that need or solve that problem, have developed an action plan, and have worked to put the plan in place so as to address the need or solve the problem. Selection is based on that description, honors or awards received, GPA, and a letter of reference.
Financial data: The stipend is $1,000.
Duration: 1 year.
Number awarded: 25 each year.
Deadline: July of each year.

248 ERIC C. MARDER SCHOLARSHIP PROGRAM

Immune Deficiency Foundation
Attn: Scholarship/Medical Programs
40 West Chesapeake Avenue, Suite 308
Towson, MD 21204-4803
Phone: (410) 321-6647; (800) 296-4433; Fax: (410) 321-9165
Email: idf@primaryimmune.org
Web: www.primaryimmune.org/patients_families/scholarship.htm
Summary: To provide financial assistance to undergraduates with a primary immune deficiency disease.
Eligibility: Open to undergraduates entering or attending college or technical training school who have a primary immune deficiency disease. Applicants must submit an autobiographical essay, 2 letters of recommendation, a family financial statement, and a letter of verification from their immunologist. Financial need is the main factor considered in selecting the recipients and the size of the award.
Financial data: Stipends range from $750 to $2,000, depending on the recipient's financial need.
Duration: 1 year; may be renewed.
Number awarded: Varies each year.
Deadline: Deadline not specified.

249 ERIC DOSTIE MEMORIAL COLLEGE SCHOLARSHIP

NuFACTOR Specialty Pharmacy
Attn: Scholarship Administrator
41093 Country Center Drive, Suite B
Temecula, CA 92591
Phone: (951) 296-2516; (800) 323-6832, ext. 1300; Fax: (877) 432-6258
Email: info@kelleycom.com
Web: www.nufactor.com/pages/eric_dostie.html

Summary: To provide financial assistance for college to students with hemophilia or members of their families.

Eligibility: Open to 1) students with hemophilia or a related bleeding disorder; or 2) members of their families. Applicants must be U.S. citizens and enrolled or planning to enroll full-time at an accredited 2- or 4-year college program. They must have a GPA of 2.5 or higher. Along with their application, they must submit a 400-word essay that explains what motivates them to pursue a higher education, what subjects they plan to study, what major forces or obstacles in their life has led to that path of study, what they plan to do with their education after school, and how that may be of benefit to humankind. Financial need is also considered in the selection process.

Financial data: The stipend is $1,000.

Duration: 1 year.

Number awarded: 10 each year.

Deadline: February of each year.

250 ERIN MARIE EMERINE MEMORIAL SCHOLARSHIP

Columbus Foundation
Attn: Scholarship Administrator
1234 East Broad Street
Columbus, OH 43205-1453
Phone: (614) 251-4000; Fax: (614) 251-4009
Email: dhigginb@columbusfoundation.org
Web: www.edonorcentral.com

Summary: To provide financial assistance to women from any state working on an undergraduate or graduate degree at a college or university in Ohio.

Eligibility: Open to women currently attending an accredited 4-year college or university in Ohio. Applicants may be residents of any state, although preference may be given to Ohio residents. They must meet 1 of the following stipulations: 1) returned to college as an undergraduate or graduate student after an extended absence of at least 2 years; 2) 23 years of age or older and in college for the first time or applying for graduate school for the first time with a GPA of 3.0 or higher; or 3) has completed the freshman year with a GPA of 3.0 or higher. Along with their application, they must submit their most recent transcript, 2 letters of recommendation, a list of volunteer activities, a list of extracurricular activities, a personal essay on how volunteering has impacted their life, and information on financial need.

Financial data: The stipend is $1,500.

Duration: 1 year.

Number awarded: 1 or more each year.

Deadline: April of each year.

251 ESA FOUNDATION GENERAL SCHOLARSHIPS

Epsilon Sigma Alpha International
Attn: ESA Foundation
P.O. Box 270517
Fort Collins, CO 80527
Phone: (970) 223-2824; Fax: (970) 223-4456
Email: esainfo@esaintl.com
Web: www.esaintl.com/esaf

Summary: To provide financial assistance to students from any state interested in majoring in any field in college.

Eligibility: Open to students who are 1) graduating high school seniors with a GPA of 2.0 or higher or with minimum scores of 22 on the ACT or 1030 on the combined critical reading and mathematics SAT; 2) enrolled in college with a GPA of 2.0 or higher; 3) enrolled at a technical school or returning to school after an absence for retraining of job skills or obtaining a degree; or 4) engaged in online study through an accredited college, university, or vocational school. Applicants may be attending or planning to attend an accredited school anywhere in the United States and major in any field. Selection is based on character (20%), leadership (20%), service (20%), financial need (20%), and scholastic ability (20%).

Financial data: The stipend is $1,000.

Duration: 1 year; may be renewed.

Number awarded: Varies each year, depending on the availability of funds. Recently, 10 of these scholarships were awarded.

Deadline: January of each year.

252 ESERA TUALOLO ATHLETIC SCHOLARSHIP

Parents, Families and Friends of Lesbians and Gays
Attn: Safe Schools Coordinator
1726 M Street, N.W., Suite 400
Washington, DC 20036-4521
Phone: (202) 467-8180, ext. 219; Fax: (202) 467-8194
Email: scholarships@pflag.org
Web: community.pflag.org/Page.aspx?pid=374

Summary: To provide financial assistance for college to high school seniors and recent graduates who have been involved in the gay, lesbian, bisexual, or transgender (GLBT) community and also in athletics.

Eligibility: Open to high school seniors and prior-year graduates who have not attended college. Applicants must have applied to an accredited postsecondary institution to work on 1) an associate degree leading to transfer to complete a bachelor's degree; or 2) a bachelor's degree at a 4-year college or university. They must self-identify either as a GLBT person or as a supporter of GLBT people. Along with their application, they must submit a high school transcript showing a GPA of 3.0 or higher, 2 letters of recommendation, and a 2-page essay discussing either their life as an GLBT student or how they have been involved with and supported the GLBT community. Financial need is also considered in the selection process. This scholarship is presented to the applicant who demonstrates outstanding athletic achievement.

Financial data: The stipend is $1,000.

Duration: 1 year; nonrenewable.

Number awarded: 1 each year.

Deadline: March of each year.

253 ESSAY COMPETITION FOR CHILDREN OF PUBLIC EMPLOYEES

Civil Service Employees Insurance Group
Attn: Scholarship Contest
P.O. Box 8041
Walnut Creek, CA 94596-8041
Phone: (800) 282-6848
Web: www.cse-insurance.com/scholarship.htm

Summary: To recognize and reward, with college scholarships, the best essays written on teenage automobile safety by the children of full-time public employees (including military personnel) in selected states.

Eligibility: Open to high school seniors in 3 geographic regions: southern California, northern California, and Arizona/Nevada. Applicants must have been accepted as a full-time student at an accredited 4-year college, university, or trade school in the United States. Applicants must have a cumulative GPA of 3.0 or higher. Their parent or legal guardian must be currently employed full-time (or if retired or deceased, must have been employed full-time) by a government entity, including, but not limited to, peace officers, fire fighters, educators, postal employees, military personnel, or federal, state, and local government workers. Qualified students are invited to write an essay (up to 500 words) that discusses the ways the teenage automobile accident rate can be reduced. Essays are evaluated on the basis of originality, creativity, and writing proficiency. Also required in the application process are an official transcript and letters of recommendation.

Financial data: Prizes in each region are $1,500 scholarships for first place, $1,000 scholarships for second place, and $500 scholarships each for third through fifth places.

Duration: The prizes are awarded annually.

Number awarded: 15 each year: 5 in each region.

Deadline: April of each year.

254 E.U. PARKER SCHOLARSHIP

National Federation of the Blind
Attn: Scholarship Committee
1800 Johnson Street
Baltimore, MD 21230
Phone: (410) 659-9314, ext. 2415; Fax: (410) 685-5653
Email: scholarships@nfb.org
Web: www.nfb.org/nfb/scholarship_program.asp

Summary: To provide financial assistance to entering and continuing undergraduate and graduate students who are blind.

Eligibility: Open to legally blind students who are working on or planning to work full-time on an undergraduate or graduate degree. Along with their application, they must submit transcripts, standardized test scores, proof of legal blindness, 2 letters of recommendation, and a letter of endorsement from their National Federation of the Blind state president or designee. Selection is based on academic excellence, service to the community, and financial need.
Financial data: The stipend is $3,000.
Duration: 1 year; recipients may resubmit applications up to 2 additional years.
Number awarded: 1 each year.
Deadline: March of each year.

255 EUNICE RIGGINS MEMORIAL SCHOLARSHIP

Alpha Delta Kappa–North Carolina Chapter
c/o Rebecca R. Meyst, President
351 North Peace Haven Road
Winston-Salem, NC 27104-2536
Summary: To provide financial assistance to female high school seniors in North Carolina who plan to attend college in the state.
Eligibility: Open to women graduating from high schools in North Carolina and planning to enroll at a 4-year college or university in the state. Applicants must rank in the top 10% of their class and have scores of at least 1344 on the SAT or 20 on the ACT. Along with their application, they must submit a letter on their plans, career goals, and reasons for wanting this scholarship. Selection is based on character and participation in extracurricular activities; financial need is not considered.
Financial data: The stipend is $2,000.
Duration: 1 year; nonrenewable.
Number awarded: 1 each year.
Deadline: January of each year.

256 EVANS MEMORIAL FUND SCHOLARSHIPS

Greater Kanawha Valley Foundation
Attn: Scholarship Coordinator
1600 Huntington Square
900 Lee Street, East
P.O. Box 3041
Charleston, WV 25331-3041
Phone: (304) 346-3620; (800) 467-5909; Fax: (304) 346-3640
Email: shoover@tgkvf.org
Web: www.tgkvf.org/scholar.htm
Summary: To provide financial assistance to residents of West Virginia who are interested in attending college in the state.
Eligibility: Open to residents of West Virginia who are attending or planning to attend a college or university in the state. Applicants must have an ACT score of 20 or higher; be able to demonstrate good moral character, academic excellence, and financial need; and have a GPA of 2.5 or higher.
Financial data: Stipends average $1,000 per year.
Duration: 1 year; may be renewed.
Number awarded: Varies each year; recently, 32 of these scholarships were awarded.
Deadline: January of each year.

257 EVE KRAFT EDUCATION AND COLLEGE SCHOLARSHIPS

United States Tennis Association
Attn: USTA Serves
70 West Red Oak Lane
White Plains, NY 10604
Phone: (914) 696-7223
Email: eliezer@usta.com
Web: www.usta.com/USTA/Home/AboutUs/USTAServes.aspx
Summary: To provide financial assistance for college to high school seniors who have participated in an organized community tennis program.
Eligibility: Open to high school seniors who have excelled academically, demonstrated achievements in leadership, and participated extensively in an organized community tennis program. Applicants must be planning to enroll as a full-time undergraduate student at a 4-year college or university. They must be able to demonstrate financial need. Along with their application, they must submit an essay about themselves and how their participation in a tennis program has influenced their life. Males and females are considered separately.
Financial data: The stipend is $2,500. Funds are paid directly to the recipient's college or university.
Duration: 1 year; nonrenewable.
Number awarded: 2 each year: 1 male and 1 female.
Deadline: February of each year.

258 EVERLY SCHOLARSHIP

Everly Scholarship Fund, Inc.
c/o Sherman Silverstein Kohl et al.
Fairway Corporate Center
4300 Haddonfield Road, Suite 311
Pennsauken, NJ 08109
Phone: (856) 661-2094; Fax: (856) 662-0165
Email: jlolio@ssskrplaw.com
Summary: To provide financial assistance to high school seniors in New Jersey who plan to attend college in any state.
Eligibility: Open to seniors graduating from high schools in New Jersey in the top 20% of their class. Applicants must have a GPA of 3.0 or higher and a combined SAT mathematics and critical reading score of 1100 or higher. They must be planning to enroll full-time at an accredited college or university in any state. Along with their application, they must submit 2 essays: 1) the events or people that have shaped their thinking and why; and 2) the career they will be pursuing and how it will contribute to society. Semifinalists are interviewed. Financial need is considered in the selection process.
Financial data: Stipends range up to $2,500 per year. Funds are paid to the student in equal installments each semester upon receipt of the term bill and verification of payment (cancelled check or receipt).
Duration: 1 year; may be renewed until graduation as long as the recipient maintains full-time enrollment and a GPA of 2.75 or higher the first year and 3.0 or higher in subsequent years.
Number awarded: Varies each year. Recently, 16 of these scholarships were awarded.
Deadline: April of each year.

259 EVERYDAY HERO WRITING SCHOLARSHIPS

The RARE Foundation
Attn: Program Director
27500 Cosgrove
Warren, MI 48092
Phone: (248) 526-7273; Fax: (248) 458-1371
Web: www.rarefoundation.org/writingSCHOLARSHIPS.html
Summary: To recognize and reward, with scholarships to attend college in the state, high school seniors in Michigan who submit outstanding essays on "everyday heroes."
Eligibility: Open to seniors graduating from high schools in Michigan who plan to attend a college, university, or other postsecondary school in the state. Applicants must submit an essay, of 500 to 1,000 words, about a person in their community whom they consider an "everyday hero" because through their life's work, they are making a difference for others, now and for the future. Special consideration is given to students who focus on individuals in their communities who do more than what is required of them and go above and beyond in making a difference in the world around them. Selection is based on organization of the essay, strength of the idea, depth of research, specificity of examples supporting the theme, and creativity of the work.
Financial data: The award is a $2,500 scholarship, paid directly to the Michigan institution where the winner enrolls.
Duration: The competition is held annually.
Number awarded: 4 each year.
Deadline: February of each year.

260 EXCEPTIONAL CIRCUMSTANCES SCHOLARSHIPS

Workforce Safety & Insurance
1600 East Century Avenue, Suite 1
P.O. Box 5585
Bismarck, ND 58506-5585
Phone: (701) 328-3828; (800) 440-3796; Fax: (701) 328-3820; TDD: (800) 366-6888
Email: ndwsi@nd.gov
Web: www.workforcesafety.com/workers/typesofbenefits.asp
Summary: To provide financial assistance for college to injured workers in North Dakota.
Eligibility: Open to injured workers in North Dakota who can demonstrate that a program of higher or technical education would be beneficial and appropriate because of exceptional circumstances. Applicants must have completed

a rehabilitation process with Workforce Safety & Insurance (WSI) and have no outstanding litigation on any rehabilitation plan.

Financial data: The maximum stipend is $10,000 per year.

Duration: 1 year; may be renewed up to 4 additional years, provided the recipient reapplies and maintains a satisfactory GPA.

Number awarded: Varies each year.

Deadline: Deadline not specified.

261 EXECUTIVE WOMEN INTERNATIONAL SCHOLARSHIP PROGRAM

Executive Women International
Attn: Scholarship Coordinator
515 South 700 East, Suite 2A
Salt Lake City, UT 84102
Phone: (801) 355-2800; (877) 4EWI-NOW; Fax: (801) 355-2852
Email: ewi@ewiconnect.com
Web: www.ewiconnect.com/Script/Content/community/comm_ewisp.cfm

Summary: To provide financial assistance for college to high school juniors with outstanding business and leadership potential.

Eligibility: Open to high school juniors attending public, private, and parochial schools located in Executive Women International (EWI) chapter cities. Applicants must be planning to attend college in the United States or Canada to prepare for a career in a business or professional field of study. Along with their application, they must submit a 750-word essay on who or what inspires them. Selection is based on academic achievement; leadership in school, civic, and other extracurricular activities; and motivation to serve and succeed in all endeavors.

Financial data: Stipends are $10,000 for the first-place winner, $6,000 for the second-place winner, $4,000 for the third-place winner, and $2,000 for finalists. These funds are paid to the winners' colleges. Chapter scholarships are $4,000 for first place, $2,500 for second place, and $1,000 for runners-up. Winners also receive scholarships (generally under $2,000). A total of $200,000 is distributed through this program each year.

Duration: The scholarship funds are disbursed over a period of no more than 5 years.

Number awarded: 8 national winners are selected each year: 1 first place, 1 second place, 1 third place, and 5 other finalists.

Deadline: Applications must be received by local chapters by the end of March so they can select their winners by mid-April.

262 EXEMPTION FOR DEPENDENTS OF TEXAS VETERANS

Texas Higher Education Coordinating Board
Attn: Grants and Special Programs
1200 East Anderson Lane
P.O. Box 12788, Capitol Station
Austin, TX 78711-2788
Phone: (512) 427-6340; (800) 242-3062; Fax: (512) 427-6127
Email: grantinfo@thecb.state.tx.us
Web: www.collegeforalltexans.com/apps/financialaid/tofa2.cfm?ID=500

Summary: To exempt children of disabled or deceased veterans of the U.S. military from payment of tuition at public universities in Texas.

Eligibility: Open to residents of Texas whose parent was a resident of the state at the time of entry into the U.S. military and who died or became totally disabled as a result of service-related injury or illness. Applicants may not be in default on a loan made or guaranteed by the state of Texas or in default on a federal education loan if that default affects their eligibility for GI education benefits. They must be attending or planning to attend a public college or university in the state.

Financial data: Eligible students are exempt from payment of tuition, dues, fees, and charges at state-supported colleges and universities in Texas.

Duration: 1 year; may be renewed.

Number awarded: Varies each year; recently, 9 of these awards were granted.

Deadline: Deadline not specified.

263 EXEMPTION FOR ORPHANS OF TEXAS MEMBERS OF THE U.S. ARMED FORCES OR NATIONAL GUARD

Texas Higher Education Coordinating Board
Attn: Grants and Special Programs
1200 East Anderson Lane
P.O. Box 12788, Capitol Station
Austin, TX 78711-2788
Phone: (512) 427-6340; (800) 242-3062; Fax: (512) 427-6127
Email: grantinfo@thecb.state.tx.us
Web: www.collegeforalltexans.com/apps/financialaid/tofa2.cfm?ID=507

Summary: To exempt residents of Texas whose parent died in service to the U.S. military or National Guard from payment of tuition at public universities in the state.

Eligibility: Open to residents of Texas who are the dependent children of a parent who died as a result of injury or illness directly related to service in the U.S. military or the National Guard. Applicants must have used up all federal education benefits for which they are eligible. They must be attending or planning to attend a public college or university in the state.

Financial data: Eligible students are exempt from payment of tuition, dues, fees, and charges at state-supported colleges and universities in Texas.

Duration: 1 year; may be renewed.

Number awarded: Varies each year.

Deadline: Deadline not specified.

264 EXEMPTION FOR TEXAS VETERANS

Texas Higher Education Coordinating Board
Attn: Grants and Special Programs
1200 East Anderson Lane
P.O. Box 12788, Capitol Station
Austin, TX 78711-2788
Phone: (512) 427-6340; (800) 242-3062; Fax: (512) 427-6127
Email: grantinfo@thecb.state.tx.us
Web: www.collegeforalltexans.com/apps/financialaid/tofa2.cfm?ID=500

Summary: To exempt Texas veterans from payment of tuition for undergraduate or graduate study at public universities in the state.

Eligibility: Open to veterans who were legal residents of Texas at the time they entered the U.S. armed forces and served for at least 181 days of active military duty, excluding basic training, during specified periods of war time. Applicants must have received an honorable discharge or separation or a general discharge under honorable conditions. They must be enrolled at a public college or university in Texas and all their other federal veterans education benefits (not including Pell and SEOG grants) may not exceed the value of this exemption. If they are in default on a student loan made or guaranteed by the state of Texas or on a federal education loan that affects their eligibility for GI education benefits, they are not eligible.

Financial data: Veterans who are eligible for this benefit are entitled to free tuition and fees at state-supported colleges and universities in Texas.

Duration: Exemptions may be claimed up to a cumulative total of 150 credit hours, including undergraduate and graduate study.

Number awarded: Varies each year; recently, 8,885 of these awards were granted.

Deadline: Deadline not specified.

265 EXEMPTION FROM TUITION FEES FOR DEPENDENTS OF KENTUCKY VETERANS

Kentucky Department of Veterans Affairs
Attn: Division of Field Operations
321 West Main Street, Room 390
Louisville, KY 40202
Phone: (502) 595-4447; (800) 928-4012 (within KY); Fax: (502) 595-4448
Email: Pamela.Cypert@ky.gov
Web: www.veterans.ky.gov/benefits/tuitionwaiver.htm

Summary: To provide financial assistance for undergraduate or graduate studies to the children or unremarried widow(er)s of deceased Kentucky veterans.

Eligibility: Open to the children, stepchildren, adopted children, and unremarried widow(er)s of veterans who were residents of Kentucky when they entered military service or joined the Kentucky National Guard. The qualifying veteran must have been killed in action during a wartime period or died as a result of a service-connected disability incurred during a wartime period. Applicants must be attending or planning to attend a state-supported college or university in Kentucky to work on an undergraduate or graduate degree.

Financial data: Eligible dependents and survivors are exempt from tuition and matriculation fees at any state-supported institution of higher education in Kentucky.

Duration: There are no age or time limits on the waiver.

Number awarded: Varies each year.

Deadline: Deadline not specified.

266 EXERCISE FOR LIFE SCHOLARSHIPS

Boomer Esiason Foundation
c/o Jerry Cahill
483 Tenth Avenue, Suite 300
New York, NY 10018
Phone: (646) 292-7930; Fax: (646) 292-7945
Email: jcahillbef@aol.com
Web: www.cfscholarships.com/ExerciseForLife/index.htm

Summary: To provide financial assistance for college to high school seniors who have been involved in athletics and who have cystic fibrosis (CF).

Eligibility: Open to CF patients who are college-bound high school seniors. Applicants must have been involved in athletics. They should be jogging on a regular basis and training for a 1.5 mile run. Along with their application, they must submit a letter from their doctor confirming the diagnosis of CF and a list of daily medications, information on financial need, a detailed breakdown of tuition costs from their academic institution, transcripts, and a 2-page essay on 1) their post-graduation goals; and 2) the importance of compliance with CF therapies and what they practice on a daily basis to stay healthy. Selection is based on academic ability, athletic ability, character, leadership potential, service to the community, financial need, and daily compliance to CF therapy. Male and female students compete separately.

Financial data: The stipend is $10,000. Funds are paid directly to the academic institution to assist in covering the cost of tuition and fees.

Duration: 1 year; nonrenewable.

Number awarded: 2 each year: 1 to a male and 1 to a female.

Deadline: June of each year.

267 EXPLOSIVE ORDNANCE DISPOSAL (EOD) MEMORIAL SCHOLARSHIPS

Explosive Ordnance Disposal Memorial
Attn: Executive Director
7040 CR 772
Webster, FL 33597
Phone: (813) 389-0351
Email: scholarship@eodmemorial.org
Web: www.eodmemorial.org/scholarship.html

Summary: To provide financial assistance for college to spouses and other family members of technicians or military officers who have worked in explosive ordnance disposal.

Eligibility: Open to children, stepchildren, spouses, grandchildren, and other recognized dependents of graduates of Naval School Explosive Ordnance Disposal (NAVSCOLEOD) who served or are serving in the Army, Navy, Air Force, or Marine Corps. Active-duty personnel and NAVSCOLEOD graduates are not eligible. Selection is based on GPA, community involvement and volunteerism, extracurricular activities, awards, paid employment, an essay, future goals, letters of recommendation, and overall impression.

Financial data: A stipend is awarded (amount not specified). Funds are paid directly to the academic institution for the student's tuition, books, fees, and on-campus housing.

Duration: 1 year; may be renewed up to 3 additional years.

Number awarded: Varies each year.

Deadline: March of each year.

268 FANNIE WILDER EDUCATIONAL FUND SCHOLARSHIP

Center for Scholarship Administration, Inc.
Attn: Wachovia Accounts
4320 Wade Hampton Boulevard, Suite G
Taylors, SC 29687
Phone: (866) 608-0001
Email: wachoviascholars@bellsouth.net
Web: www.wachoviascholars.com/wilder/index.php

Summary: To provide financial assistance to women from Georgia who plan to attend college in any state.

Eligibility: Open to female residents of Georgia who have a cumulative GPA of 2.5 or higher. Applicants must be attending or planning to attend an accredited 4-year college or university in any state. Selection is based on academic ability, educational goals, career ambitions, and financial need.

Financial data: A stipend is awarded (amount not specified).

Duration: 1 year; may be renewed up to 3 additional years or until completion of a bachelor's degree (whichever comes first).

Number awarded: 1 or more each year.

Deadline: April of each year.

269 FASFEPA SCHOLARSHIPS

Florida Association of State and Federal Educational Program Administrators
c/o Maria I. Pouncey, Scholarship Committee
Panhandle Area Educational Consortium
315 North Key Street
Quincy, FL 32351
Phone: (850) 875-3806
Email: pounceym@paec.org
Web: fasfepa.org

Summary: To provide financial assistance to high school seniors in Florida who plan to attend college in any state.

Eligibility: Open to seniors graduating from high schools in Florida and planning to enroll full-time at a college or university in any state. Applicants may be planning to major in any field of the arts and sciences. They must have a GPA of 3.0 or higher. Along with their application, they must submit a 200-word essay on how this scholarship would enhance their ability to continue their education. Selection is based on GPA (40 points), participation in school and community activities (10 points), letters of recommendation (10 points), and financial need (40 points).

Financial data: The stipend is $1,000. Funds are paid directly to the student, $500 upon verification of enrollment for the first semester and $500 upon verification of completion of the first semester with a GPA of 2.0 or better and enrollment for the second semester.

Duration: 1 year.

Number awarded: 5 each year: 1 in each district of Florida.

Deadline: February of each year.

270 FEDERAL EMPLOYEE EDUCATION AND ASSISTANCE FUND SCHOLARSHIPS

Federal Employee Education and Assistance Fund
Attn: Scholarship Program
3333 South Wadsworth Boulevard, Suite 300
Lakewood, CO 80227
Phone: (303) 933-7580; (800) 323-4140; Fax: (303) 933-7587
Email: admin@feea.org
Web: www.feea.org

Summary: To provide financial assistance for college or graduate school to civilian federal and postal employees and their families.

Eligibility: Open to civilian federal and postal employees and their dependent children and spouses who are entering or enrolled in an accredited 2- or 4-year undergraduate, graduate, or postgraduate program. Dependents must be full-time students; federal employees may be part-time students. Active-duty military members and their dependents are eligible only through a sponsoring civilian employee spouse. Military retirees and dependents are eligible if the retiree is a current civilian federal employee. Applicants or their sponsoring federal employee must have at least 3 years of civilian federal service. Along with their application, they must submit a 2-page essay on a topic related to a career in public service with the federal government, a letter of recommendation, a transcript with a GPA of 3.0 or higher, and a copy of their federal "Notice of Personnel Action"; high school seniors must also submit a copy of their ACT, SAT, or other examination scores. Financial need is not considered in the selection process. The judging committees in each of the sponsor's 26 regions nominate their top 2 winners for the Federal Employee Education and Assistance Fund-National Treasury Employees Union (FEEA-NTEU) Scholarships and for the David O. "Doc" and Marion M. Cooke Memorial Scholarship.

Financial data: Stipends range from $250 to $2,500. The winners of the FEEA-NTEU Scholarships receive an additional $5,000 and the winner of the David O. "Doc" and Marion M. Cooke Memorial Scholarship receives an additional stipend of up to $3,000.

Duration: 1 year; recipients may reapply.

Number awarded: More than 400 each year. Of those, 6 receive FEEA-NTEU Scholarships and 1 receives the David O. "Doc" and Marion M. Cooke Memorial Scholarship. Since the program was established, it has made 7,748 awards worth approximately $9.5 million.

Deadline: March of each year.

271 FEDERAL PELL GRANTS

Department of Education
Attn: Federal Student Aid Information Center
P.O. Box 84
Washington, DC 20044-0084
Phone: (319) 337-5665; (800) 4-FED-AID; TDD: (800) 730-8913
Web: www.FederalStudentAid.ed.gov

Summary: To provide financial assistance for undergraduate education to students with financial need.

Eligibility: Open to students who have not yet earned a bachelor's or professional degree. They are eligible for these grants if they meet specified financial need qualifications and are U.S. citizens or eligible noncitizens working toward a degree in an eligible program. They must have a valid Social Security number and have completed registration with the Selective Service if required.

Financial data: The amount of the grant is based on the cost of attendance at the recipient's college or university, minus the expected family contribution, up to a specified maximum, which depends on annual program funding. Recently, grants ranged from $400 to $5,350 per year.

Duration: Up to 5 years of undergraduate study.

Number awarded: Varies each year; under this program, the federal government guarantees that each participating school will receive enough money to pay the Pell grants of its eligible students. Recently, 5.5 million grants, worth more than $14.6 billion, were awarded.

Deadline: Students may submit applications between January of the current year through June of the following year.

272 FEDERAL SUPPLEMENTAL EDUCATIONAL OPPORTUNITY GRANTS

Department of Education
Attn: Federal Student Aid Information Center
P.O. Box 84
Washington, DC 20044-0084
Phone: (319) 337-5665; (800) 4-FED-AID; TDD: (800) 730-8913
Web: www.FederalStudentAid.ed.gov

Summary: To provide financial assistance for undergraduate education to students with exceptional financial need.

Eligibility: Open to students who have not yet earned a bachelor's or professional degree. They are eligible for these grants if they meet specified financial need qualifications and are U.S. citizens or eligible noncitizens working toward a degree in an eligible program. They must have a valid Social Security number and have completed registration with the Selective Service if required. Applicants for federal Pell Grants who demonstrate the greatest financial need qualify for these grants.

Financial data: The amount of the award is based on the cost of attendance at the recipient's college or university, minus the expected family contribution. Grants range between $100 and $4,000 per year.

Duration: Up to 5 years of undergraduate study.

Number awarded: Varies each year, depending on the availability of funds; under this program, the federal government does not guarantee that each participating school will receive enough money to pay the FSEOG grants of all of its eligible students. Recently, nearly 1,500,000 grants, worth more than $1 billion, were awarded by this program.

Deadline: Each participating school sets its own deadline.

273 FIRST CAVALRY DIVISION ASSOCIATION SCHOLARSHIPS

First Cavalry Division Association
Attn: Foundation
302 North Main Street
Copperas Cove, TX 76522-1703
Phone: (254) 547-6537; Fax: (254) 547-8853
Email: firstcav@1cda.org
Web: www.1cda.org

Summary: To provide financial assistance for undergraduate education to soldiers currently or formerly assigned to the First Cavalry Division and their families.

Eligibility: Open to children of soldiers who died or have been declared totally and permanently disabled from injuries incurred while serving with the First Cavalry Division during any armed conflict; children of soldiers who died while serving in the First Cavalry Division during peacetime; and active-duty soldiers currently assigned or attached to the First Cavalry Division and their spouses and children.

Financial data: The stipend is $1,200 per year. The checks are made out jointly to the student and the school and may be used for whatever the student needs, including tuition, books, and clothing.

Duration: 1 year; may be renewed up to 3 additional years.

Number awarded: Varies each year; since the program was established, it has awarded more than $640,500 to 444 children of disabled and deceased Cavalry members and more than $184,500 to 224 current members of the Division and their families.

Deadline: June of each year.

274 FIRST COMMAND EDUCATIONAL FOUNDATION ROTC SCHOLARSHIPS

U.S. Army
ROTC Cadet Command
Attn: ATCC-OP-I-S
55 Patch Road, Building 56
Fort Monroe, VA 23651-1052
Phone: (757) 788-3473; (800) USA-ROTC; Fax: (757) 788-4643
Email: atccps@usacc.army.mil
Web: www.goarmy.com/rotc/college_students.jsp

Summary: To provide additional financial assistance to Army ROTC scholarship and non-scholarship cadets.

Eligibility: Open to students who are entering their senior year of the Army ROTC program. Applicants may be either scholarship or non-scholarship cadets, but they must meet scholarship eligibility requirements (GPA of 2.5 or higher, ACT score of 19 or higher or combined mathematics and critical reading SAT score of 920 or higher, physical fitness score of 180 or higher with at least 60 points in each individual APFT event).

Financial data: The stipend is $1,000.

Duration: 1 year.

Number awarded: 5 each year: 1 in the ROTC eastern region, 1 in the ROTC western region, and 3 awarded nationally.

Deadline: June of each year.

275 FIRST MARINE DIVISION ASSOCIATION SCHOLARSHIPS

First Marine Division Association
410 Pier View Way
Oceanside, CA 92054
Phone: (760) 967-8561; (877) 967-8561; Fax: (760) 967-8567
Email: oldbreed@sbcglobal.net
Web: www.1stmarinedivisionassociation.org/scholarships.php

Summary: To provide financial assistance for college to dependents of deceased or disabled veterans of the First Marine Division.

Eligibility: Open to dependents of veterans who served in the First Marine Division or in a unit attached to that Division, are honorably discharged, and now are either totally and permanently disabled or deceased from any cause. Applicants must be attending or planning to attend an accredited college, university, or trade school as a full-time undergraduate student. Graduate students and students still in high school or prep school are not eligible.

Financial data: The stipend is $1,750 per year.

Duration: 1 year; may be renewed up to 3 additional years.

Number awarded: Varies each year; since the program began, more than 520 students have received more than $1.5 million in tuition assistance.

Deadline: Deadline not specified.

276 FIRST SERGEANT DOUGLAS AND CHARLOTTE DEHORSE SCHOLARSHIP

Catching the Dream
8200 Mountain Road, N.E., Suite 203
Albuquerque, NM 87110-7835
Phone: (505) 262-2351; Fax: (505) 262-0534
Email: NScholarsh@aol.com
Web: www.catchingthedream.org/First_Sergeant_Douglas_Scholarship.htm

Summary: To provide financial assistance to American Indians who have ties to the military and are working on an undergraduate or graduate degree.

Eligibility: Open to American Indians who 1) have completed 1 year of an Army, Navy, or Air Force Junior Reserve Officer Training (JROTC) program; 2) are enrolled in an Army, Navy, or Air Force Reserve Officer Training (ROTC) program; or 3) are a veteran of the U.S. Army, Navy, Air Force, Marines, Merchant Marine, or Coast Guard. Applicants must be enrolled in an undergraduate or graduate program of study. Along with their application, they must submit a personal essay, high school transcripts, and letters of recommendation.

Financial data: A stipend is awarded (amount not specified).

Duration: 1 year.

Number awarded: 1 or more each year.

Deadline: April of each year for fall semester or quarter; September of each year for spring semester or winter quarter.

277 FIRST STATE MANUFACTURED HOUSING ASSOCIATION SCHOLARSHIP

Delaware Higher Education Commission
Carvel State Office Building, Fifth Floor
820 North French Street
Wilmington, DE 19801-3509
Phone: (302) 577-5240; (800) 292-7935; Fax: (302) 577-6765
Email: dhec@doe.k12.de.us
Web: www.doe.k12.de.us/infosuites/students_family/dhec/default.shtml

Summary: To provide financial assistance to Delaware residents who have lived in a manufactured home and plan to attend college in any state.

Eligibility: Open to Delaware residents who have lived in a manufactured home for at least 1 year. Applicants may be planning to pursue any type of accredited training, licensing, or certification program or any accredited degree program at a school in any state. Selection is based on academic record, an essay, recommendations, and financial need.

Financial data: The maximum stipend is $2,000 per year.

Duration: 1 year.

Number awarded: 2 each year (usually 1 for a traditional student and 1 for a nontraditional student).

Deadline: April of each year.

278 FLETCHER "BUSTER" BRUSH MEMORIAL SCHOLARSHIPS

Fletcher "Buster" Brush Memorial Scholarship Fund
P.O. Box 45
Middlebury, VT 05753
Phone: (802) 388-7917
Email: info@brushscholarship.org
Web: www.brushscholarship.org

Summary: To provide financial assistance to high school seniors in New Hampshire and Vermont who plan to attend college in any state.

Eligibility: Open to seniors graduating from high schools in New Hampshire and Vermont who plan to attend a college or university in any state. Applicants must submit 100-word essays on 1) a community activity that has been most meaningful to them and why; 2) the extracurricular activity at school that is most important to them and why; and 3) the attributes of the adult who has influenced them the most during their high school years. Financial need is not considered in the selection process.

Financial data: The stipend is $1,000 per year.

Duration: 1 year; may be renewed up to 3 additional years.

Number awarded: 2 each year: 1 to a New Hampshire resident and 1 to a Vermont resident.

Deadline: April.

279 FLICKER OF HOPE SCHOLARSHIPS

Flicker of Hope Foundation
Attn: Scholarship Committee
8624 Janet Lane
Vienna, VA 22180
Phone: (703) 698-1626; Fax: (703) 698-6225
Email: info@flickerofhope.org
Web: www.flickerofhope.org/whatwedo.htm

Summary: To provide financial assistance for college to burn survivors.

Eligibility: Open to high school seniors and graduates who are burn survivors and enrolled or planning to enroll in college. Applicants must submit a 500-word essay describing the circumstances of how they were burned, how that injury has affected their life, and the benefits to be derived from their planned course of study. Selection is based on severity of burn injury, academic performance, community service, and financial need.

Financial data: A stipend is awarded (amount not specified). Funds are paid directly to the postsecondary institution.

Duration: 1 year.

Number awarded: Varies each year; recently, 14 of these scholarships were awarded.

Deadline: May of each year.

280 FLORA BURNS/VIRGINIA STATE COUNCIL ENDOWMENT SCHOLARSHIP

Epsilon Sigma Alpha International
Attn: ESA Foundation
P.O. Box 270517
Fort Collins, CO 80527
Phone: (970) 223-2824; Fax: (970) 223-4456
Email: esainfo@esaintl.com
Web: www.esaintl.com/esaf

Summary: To provide financial assistance to students of Virginia studying any field at a college in any state.

Eligibility: Open to residents of Virginia who are 1) graduating high school seniors with a GPA of 3.0 or higher or with minimum scores of 22 on the ACT or 1030 on the combined critical reading and mathematics SAT; 2) enrolled in college with a GPA of 3.0 or higher; 3) enrolled at a technical school or returning to school after an absence for retraining of job skills or obtaining a degree; or 4) engaged in online study through an accredited college, university, or vocational school. Applicants may be majoring in any field at a school in any state. Selection is based on character (10%), leadership (10%), service (5%), financial need (50%), and scholastic ability (25%).

Financial data: The stipend is $2,000.

Duration: 1 year; may be renewed.

Number awarded: 2 each year.

Deadline: January of each year.

281 FLORIDA ACADEMIC SCHOLARS AWARD PROGRAM

Florida Department of Education
Attn: Office of Student Financial Assistance
325 West Gaines Street
Tallahassee, FL 32399-0400
Phone: (850) 410-5160; (888) 827-2004; Fax: (850) 487-1809
Email: osfa@fldoe.org
Web: www.floridastudentfinancialaid.org/SSFAD/factsheets/BF.htm

Summary: To provide financial assistance for college to outstanding high school seniors in Florida.

Eligibility: Open to seniors in Florida public and private high schools who have been Florida residents for at least 1 year and will attend eligible Florida institutions of higher education. Applicants must have 1) earned a GPA of 3.5 or higher in a specified high school academic curriculum; 2) achieved scores of at least 1270 combined mathematics and critical reading on the SAT or 28 on the ACT; and 3) completed at least 75 hours of community service. Also eligible are National Merit and Achievement scholars and finalists, National Hispanic Scholars, IB Diploma recipients, and home-schooled students and GED recipients who achieve the same minimum SAT or ACT scores. U.S. citizenship or permanent resident status is required.

Financial data: Stipends are $126 per semester hour for students at 4-year institutions, $78 per semester hour for students at 2-year institutions, $87 per semester hour for students enrolled in community college baccalaureate programs, or $64 per semester hour for students at career and technical centers.

Duration: Recipients may use this award 1) for up to 132 credit hours required to complete a standard undergraduate degree at their institution; 2) for up to 7 years from high school graduation (if initially funded within 3 years after high school graduation); or 3) until completion of their first baccalaureate degree program, whichever comes first. Renewal requires a GPA of 3.0 or higher.

Number awarded: Varies each year; recently, this program awarded 10,579 new and 25,150 renewal awards.

Deadline: March of each year.

282 FLORIDA ACADEMIC TOP SCHOLARS AWARD PROGRAM

Florida Department of Education
Attn: Office of Student Financial Assistance
325 West Gaines Street
Tallahassee, FL 32399-0400
Phone: (850) 410-5160; (888) 827-2004; Fax: (850) 487-1809
Email: osfa@fldoe.org
Web: www.floridastudentfinancialaid.org/SSFAD/factsheets/BF.htm

Summary: To provide financial assistance for college to the top high school seniors in Florida.

Eligibility: Open to seniors in Florida public and private high schools who have been Florida residents for at least 1 year and will attend eligible Florida institutions of higher education. They must have completed a specified curriculum while in high school. U.S. citizenship or permanent resident status is required. The Academic Top Scholars Award is presented to the student with the highest academic ranking in each county, based on GPA and SAT/ACT test scores.

Financial data: The Academic Top Scholars awardees receive an annual stipend of $54 per semester hour in addition to their Academic Scholars Award.

Duration: Recipients may use this award 1) for up to 132 credit hours required to complete a standard undergraduate degree at their institution; 2) for up to 7 years from high school graduation (if initially funded within 3 years after high

school graduation); or 3) until completion of their first baccalaureate degree program, whichever comes first. Renewal requires a GPA of 3.0 or higher.
Number awarded: Varies each year. Recently, this program awarded 64 new and 184 renewal scholarships.
Deadline: March of each year.

283 FLORIDA ASSOCIATION FOR MEDIA IN EDUCATION INTELLECTUAL FREEDOM STUDENT SCHOLARSHIP

Florida Association for Media in Education
Attn: Intellectual Freedom Committee
1876-B Eider Court
Tallahassee, FL 32308
Phone: (850) 531-8351; Fax: (850) 531-8344
Email: info@floridamedia.org
Web: www.floridamedia.org/displaycommon.cfm?an=1&subarticlenbr=51

Summary: To recognize and reward, with scholarships for college study in any state, high school seniors in Florida who submit outstanding essays on intellectual freedom.
Eligibility: Open to seniors graduating from high schools in Florida whose library media specialist is a member of the Florida Association for Media in Education (FAME). Applicants must submit an essay, up to 1,000 words in length, on the importance of intellectual freedom. Selection is based on originality, ability to select and analyze an important issue related to intellectual freedom, and ability to organize ideas logically and express them effectively.
Financial data: The award is $1,000. Funds must be used to defray the cost of tuition and other school-related expenses at a college or university in any state.
Duration: 1 year.
Number awarded: 1 or more each year.
Deadline: March of each year.

284 FLORIDA GOLD SEAL VOCATIONAL SCHOLARS AWARDS

Florida Department of Education
Attn: Office of Student Financial Assistance
325 West Gaines Street
Tallahassee, FL 32399-0400
Phone: (850) 410-5160; (888) 827-2004; Fax: (850) 487-1809
Email: osfa@fldoe.org
Web: www.floridastudentfinancialaid.org/SSFAD/factsheets/BF.htm

Summary: To provide financial assistance for vocational education to outstanding high school seniors in Florida.
Eligibility: Open to graduating high school seniors in Florida who plan to attend a vocational, technical, trade, or business school in the state. Applicants must have earned a GPA of 3.0 or higher in their required academic program and 3.5 or higher in their vocational classes in high school. They must also have achieved the following minimum scores: 1) on the CPT, 83 in reading, 83 in sentence skills, and 72 in algebra; 2) on the SAT, 440 in critical reading and 440 in mathematics; or 3) on the ACT, 17 in English, 18 in reading, and 19 in mathematics. U.S. citizenship or permanent resident status is required.
Financial data: Stipends are $95 per semester hour for students at 4-year institutions, $59 per semester hour for students at 2-year institutions, $65 per semester hour for students enrolled in community college baccalaureate programs, or $48 per semester hour for students at career and technical centers.
Duration: Recipients may use this award 1) for up to 90 semester hours; 2) for up to 7 years from high school graduation (if initially funded within 3 years after high school graduation); or 3) until completion of their first baccalaureate degree program, whichever comes first. Renewal requires a GPA of 2.75 or higher.
Number awarded: Varies each year; recently, this program awarded 1,557 new and 79 renewal scholarships.
Deadline: March of each year.

285 FLORIDA LEGION AUXILIARY DEPARTMENT SCHOLARSHIP

American Legion Auxiliary
Department of Florida
1912A Lee Road
P.O. Box 547917
Orlando, FL 32854-7917
Phone: (407) 293-7411; Fax: (407) 299-6522
Email: contact@alafl.org
Web: alafl.org

Summary: To provide financial assistance to the children of Florida veterans who are interested in attending college in the state.
Eligibility: Open to children and stepchildren of honorably-discharged veterans who are Florida residents. Applicants must be attending or planning to attend a postsecondary school in the state on a full-time basis. Financial need is considered in the selection process.
Financial data: The stipends are up to $2,000 for a 4-year university or up to $1,000 for a community college or vocational/technical school. All funds are paid directly to the institution.
Duration: 1 year; may be renewed if the recipient needs further financial assistance and has maintained a GPA of 2.5 or higher.
Number awarded: Varies each year, depending on the availability of funds.
Deadline: January of each year.

286 FLORIDA MEDALLION SCHOLARS AWARDS

Florida Department of Education
Attn: Office of Student Financial Assistance
325 West Gaines Street
Tallahassee, FL 32399-0400
Phone: (850) 410-5160; (888) 827-2004; Fax: (850) 487-1809
Email: osfa@fldoe.org
Web: www.floridastudentfinancialaid.org/SSFAD/factsheets/BF.htm

Summary: To provide financial assistance for college to outstanding high school seniors in Florida.
Eligibility: Open to seniors in Florida public and private high schools who have been Florida residents for at least 1 year and who plan to attend eligible Florida institutions of higher education. Applicants must have 1) earned a GPA of 3.0 or higher in a specified high school academic curriculum; and 2) achieved combined mathematics and critical reading scores of at least 970 on the SAT or 20 on the ACT. Also eligible are National Medallion and Achievement scholars and finalists who complete 75 hours of community service, National Hispanic Scholars who complete 75 hours of community service, home-schooled students who achieve scores of at least 1070 combined mathematics and critical reading on the SAT or 23 on the ACT, and GED recipients who achieve test scores of at least 970 combined mathematics and critical reading on the SAT or 20 on the ACT and a GPA of 3.0 or higher.
Financial data: Stipends are $95 per semester hour for students at 4-year institutions, $59 per semester hour for students at 2-year institutions, $65 per semester hour for students enrolled in community college baccalaureate programs, or $48 per semester hour for students at career and technical centers.
Duration: Recipients may use this award 1) for up to 132 semester hours; 2) for up to 7 years from high school graduation (if initially funded within 3 years after high school graduation); or 3) until completion of their first baccalaureate degree program, whichever comes first. Renewal requires a GPA of 2.75 or higher.
Number awarded: Varies each year; recently, this program awarded 40,361 new and 91,640 renewal scholarships.
Deadline: March of each year.

287 FLORIDA PUBLIC POSTSECONDARY CAREER EDUCATION STUDENT ASSISTANCE GRANTS

Florida Department of Education
Attn: Office of Student Financial Assistance
325 West Gaines Street
Tallahassee, FL 32399-0400
Phone: (850) 410-5160; (888) 827-2004; Fax: (850) 487-1809
Email: osfa@fldoe.org
Web: www.floridastudentfinancialaid.org/SSFAD/factsheets/FSAG-CE.htm

Summary: To provide financial assistance to Florida residents enrolled at a community college or career center in the state.
Eligibility: Open to Florida residents enrolled in certificate programs of at least 450 clock hours at community colleges and career centers operated by district school boards. Applicants must be U.S. citizens or eligible noncitizens. A minimum of 1 year of Florida residency is required. Financial need must be documented; applicants must submit the Free Application for Federal Student Aid (FAFSA) and demonstrate substantial financial need. Priority is given to students who rank in the top 20% of their high school class and plan to attend 1 of the 11 state universities.
Financial data: Stipends range from $200 to a maximum that varies each year but recently was $2,069 per year.
Duration: Grants may be received until completion of 110% of the number of clock hours required to complete a program.

Number awarded: Varies each year; recently, this program awarded 3,262 new and 456 renewal scholarships.
Deadline: Each participating institution sets its own deadline.

288 FLORIDA ROAD-TO-INDEPENDENCE SCHOLARSHIPS

Florida Department of Education
Attn: Office of Student Financial Assistance
325 West Gaines Street
Tallahassee, FL 32399-0400
Phone: (850) 410-5160; (888) 827-2004; Fax: (850) 487-1809
Email: osfa@fldoe.org
Web: www.floridastudentfinancialaid.org

Summary: To provide financial assistance for college or vocational training to Florida residents who have been in foster care.
Eligibility: Open to Florida residents between 18 and 23 years of age who have spent at least 6 months living in foster care prior to their 18th birthday. Applicants must be enrolled full-time at a Florida public state university, public community college or career center, or eligible Florida private college, university, technical school, high school, or GED program.
Financial data: The amount of the award is based on the living and educational needs of the recipients and may be up to the amount they should have earned if they had worked 40 hours per week at a federal minimum wage job. Recently, grants averaged $7,876 per year.
Duration: 1 year; may be renewed.
Number awarded: Varies each year; recently, this program funded 1,083 new and 1,816 renewal scholarships.
Deadline: Deadline not specified.

289 FLORIDA SCHOLARSHIPS FOR CHILDREN AND SPOUSES OF DECEASED OR DISABLED VETERANS

Florida Department of Education
Attn: Office of Student Financial Assistance
325 West Gaines Street
Tallahassee, FL 32399-0400
Phone: (850) 410-5160; (888) 827-2004; Fax: (850) 487-1809
Email: osfa@fldoe.org
Web: www.floridastudentfinancialaid.org/SSFAD/factsheets/CDDV.htm

Summary: To provide financial assistance for college to the children and spouses of Florida veterans who are disabled, deceased, or officially classified as prisoners of war (POW) or missing in action (MIA).
Eligibility: Open to residents of Florida who are the dependent children or spouses of veterans or service members who 1) died as a result of service-connected injuries, diseases, or disabilities sustained while on active duty during a period of war; 2) have a service-connected 100% total and permanent disability; or 3) were classified as POW or MIA by the U.S. armed forces or as civilian personnel captured while serving with the consent or authorization of the U.S. government during wartime service. The veteran or service member must have been a resident of Florida for at least 1 year before death, disability, or POW/MIA status. Children must be between 16 and 22 years of age. Spouses of deceased veterans or service members must be unremarried and must apply within 5 years of their spouse's death. Spouses of disabled veterans must have been married for at least 1 year.
Financial data: Stipends are $126 per semester hour for students at 4-year institutions, $78 per semester hour for students at 2-year institutions, $87 per semester hour for students enrolled in community college baccalaureate programs, or $64 per semester hour for students at career and technical centers.
Duration: 1 quarter or semester; may be renewed for up to 110% of the required credit hours of an initial baccalaureate or certificate program, provided the student maintains a GPA of 2.0 or higher.
Number awarded: Varies each year; recently, 295 new and 331 renewal scholarships were awarded.
Deadline: March of each year.

290 FLORIDA STATE ELKS ASSOCIATION HOPE SCHOLARSHIP PROGRAM

Florida State Elks Association
P.O. Box 49
Umatilla, FL 32784-0049
Phone: (352) 669-2241; Fax: (352) 669-1236
Email: fsea@mpinet.net
Web: www.floridaelks.org/HOPE/index.html

Summary: To provide financial assistance to high school seniors in Florida who plan to attend college in any state.
Eligibility: Open to seniors graduating from high schools in Florida and planning to attend a college or university in any state. Applicants must submit an essay of 250 to 300 words on the area of study where the scholarship would be applied, why they selected that area, and how their education will benefit society. Selection is based on that essay, academic achievement, work experience, leadership and extracurricular activities, community service, honors and awards, and financial need. U.S. citizenship is required.
Financial data: A stipend is awarded (amount not specified).
Duration: 1 year.
Number awarded: Varies each year; a total of $30,000 is available for this program annually.
Deadline: November of each year.

291 FLORIDA STUDENT ASSISTANCE GRANTS

Florida Department of Education
Attn: Office of Student Financial Assistance
325 West Gaines Street
Tallahassee, FL 32399-0400
Phone: (850) 410-5160; (888) 827-2004; Fax: (850) 487-1809
Email: osfa@fldoe.org
Web: www.floridastudentfinancialaid.org/SSFAD/factsheets/FSAG.htm

Summary: To provide financial assistance for undergraduate studies to needy Florida residents.
Eligibility: Open to 1) undergraduate students who are enrolled full- or part-time at public Florida universities and community colleges; 2) full-time students at eligible private, nonprofit 4-year colleges and universities; and 3) full-time students at other postsecondary degree-granting private colleges and universities not eligible under the private institution program. Applicants must be U.S. citizens or eligible noncitizens who have at least 1 year of Florida residency. They must submit the Free Application for Federal Student Aid (FAFSA) and demonstrate substantial financial need. Priority is given to students who rank in the top 20% of their high school class and plan to attend 1 of the 11 state universities.
Financial data: Stipends range from $200 to a maximum that varies each year but recently was $2,069 per year.
Duration: Grants may be received for up to 9 semesters or 14 quarters or until receipt of a bachelor's degree, whichever comes first. Renewal requires that the student earn a GPA of 2.0 or higher each semester.
Number awarded: Varies each year; recently, this program supported 83,572 students at public institutions (41,278 new and 42,294 renewal), 12,106 students at private institutions (5,077 new and 7,029 renewal), and 13,010 students at other postsecondary institutions (8,216 new and 4,794 renewal), for a total of 108,688 (54,571 new and 54,117 renewal).
Deadline: Each participating institution sets its own deadline.

292 FLOYD QUALLS MEMORIAL SCHOLARSHIPS

American Council of the Blind
Attn: Coordinator, Scholarship Program
2200 Wilson Boulevard, Suite 650
Arlington, VA 22201
Phone: (202) 467-5081; (800) 424-8666; Fax: (703) 465-5085
Email: info@acb.org
Web: www.acb.org

Summary: To provide financial assistance to entering and continuing undergraduate and graduate students who are blind.
Eligibility: Open to legally blind students in 4 categories: entering freshmen in academic programs, undergraduates (sophomores, juniors, and seniors) in academic programs, graduate students in academic programs, and vocational school students or students working on an associate's degree from a community college. Applicants must submit verification of legal blindness in both eyes; SAT, ACT, GRE, or similar scores; information on extracurricular activities (including membership in the American Council of the Blind); employment record; and an autobiographical sketch that includes their personal goals, strengths, weaknesses, hobbies, honors, achievements, and reasons for choice of field or courses of study. A cumulative GPA of 3.3 or higher is generally required. Financial need is not considered in the selection process.
Financial data: The stipend is $2,500. In addition, the winners receive a Kurzweil-1000 Reading System.
Duration: 1 year.
Number awarded: 4 each year: 1 in each of the 4 categories.
Deadline: February of each year.

293 FORD MOTOR COMPANY SCHOLARSHIP PROGRAM OF THE HISPANIC SCHOLARSHIP FUND

Hispanic Scholarship Fund
Attn: Selection Committee
55 Second Street, Suite 1500
San Francisco, CA 94105
Phone: (415) 808-2376; (877) HSF-INFO; Fax: (415) 808-2302
Email: highschool@hsf.net
Web: www.hsf.net/scholarships.aspx?id=482

Summary: To provide financial assistance to Hispanic American high school seniors who are interested in attending college.

Eligibility: Open to U.S. citizens, permanent residents, and visitors with a passport stamped I-551. Applicants must be high school seniors of Hispanic heritage and have applied for federal financial aid. They must have a GPA of 3.0 or higher and definite plans to enroll full-time at an accredited 4-year college or university in the United States, Puerto Rico, Guam, or the U.S. Virgin Islands for the following fall. Selection is based on academic achievement, personal strengths, leadership, and financial need.

Financial data: The stipend is $2,500.

Duration: 1 year; nonrenewable.

Number awarded: Varies each year.

Deadline: February of each year.

294 FORD OPPORTUNITY PROGRAM SCHOLARSHIP

Oregon Student Assistance Commission
Attn: Ford Family Foundation Scholarship Office
440 East Broadway, Suite 200
Eugene, OR 97401
Phone: (541) 485-6211; (877) 864-2872; TDD: (800) 735-2900
Email: fordscholarships@tfff.org
Web: www.osac.state.or.us/ford.html

Summary: To provide financial assistance to residents of Oregon and Siskiyou County, California who are single parents working on a college degree at a school in Oregon or California.

Eligibility: Open to residents of Oregon and Siskiyou County, California who are U.S. citizens or permanent residents. Applicants must be single heads of household with custody of a dependent child or children. They must have a cumulative high school or college GPA of 3.0 or higher or a comparable GED score, and they must be planning to earn a bachelor's degree. Students from Oregon must attend a college or university in the state; students from Siskiyou County, California must attend a college or university in California. Selection is based on leadership ability through participation in school and community activities, concern for others and contribution of time and energy to volunteer projects and/or service organizations, motivation and desire to contribute to personal success through paid work experience, ability to succeed in college, and ability to communicate personal strengths and goals clearly.

Financial data: This program provides up to 90% of a recipient's unmet financial need, to a maximum of $25,000 per year.

Duration: 1 year; may be renewed for up to 3 additional years.

Number awarded: 55 each year: 50 from Oregon and 5 from Siskiyou County.

Deadline: February of each year.

295 FORD SCHOLARS PROGRAM

Oregon Student Assistance Commission
Attn: Ford Family Foundation Scholarship Office
440 East Broadway, Suite 200
Eugene, OR 97401
Phone: (541) 485-6211; (877) 864-2872; TDD: (800) 735-2900
Email: fordscholarships@tfff.org
Web: www.osac.state.or.us/ford_scholars.html

Summary: To provide financial assistance to residents of Oregon and Siskiyou County, California who are seeking a college degree.

Eligibility: Open to U.S. citizens and permanent residents who are residents of Oregon or of Siskiyou County, California. Applicants must be 1) graduating high school seniors; 2) high school graduates who have not yet been full-time undergraduates; or 3) students who have completed 2 years at a community college and are entering their junior year at a 4-year college. They must have a cumulative high school or college GPA of 3.0 or higher and be planning to complete a 4-year degree. Students from Oregon must attend a college or university in the state; students from Siskiyou County, California must attend a college or university in California. Selection is based on leadership ability through participation in school and community activities, concern for others and contribution of time and energy to volunteer projects and/or service organizations, motivation and desire to contribute to personal success through paid work experience, ability to succeed in college, and ability to communicate personal strengths and goals clearly.

Financial data: This program provides up to 90% of a recipient's unmet financial need, to a maximum of $25,000 per year.

Duration: 1 year; may be renewed for up to 3 additional years.

Number awarded: 120 each year: 100 from Oregon and 20 from Siskiyou County, California.

Deadline: February of each year.

296 FORD SCHOLARSHIPS

National Center for Learning Disabilities
Attn: Scholarship
381 Park Avenue South, Suite 1401
New York, NY 10016-8806
Phone: (212) 545-7510; (888) 575-7373; Fax: (212) 545-9665
Email: AFScholarship@ncld.org
Web: www.ncld.org

Summary: To provide financial assistance for college to high school seniors with learning disabilities.

Eligibility: Open to high school seniors with learning disabilities who plan to work on a 4-year university degree. Applicants must have a GPA of 3.0 or higher and be able to demonstrate financial need. Along with their application, they must submit an essay (750 to 1,000 words in length) describing their frustrations and triumphs in dealing with their specific learning disability; their essay should also include the characteristics they possess that make them an ideal candidate for this scholarship and should make specific mention of how they believe a college education will enhance their lives. If they prefer, they may submit a video or audio tape (up to 15 minutes in length) with accompanying script or outline that presents the same information as the essay. Other required submissions include high school transcripts, 3 letters of recommendation, a financial statement, standardized test (SAT, ACT) scores, and current documentation of a learning disability that includes evaluation reports, I.E.P., and/or 504 plan. U.S. citizenship is required.

Financial data: The stipend is $2,500 per year for winners. Runners-up receive a 1-time cash award (amount not specified). Winners and runners-up also receive Kurzweil 3000 Scan/Read software.

Duration: 4 years for winners, provided the recipients submit annual reports (written or in video format) detailing their progress in school and describing their insights about their personal growth.

Number awarded: 2 winners and 2 runners-up are selected each year.

Deadline: December of each year.

297 FORWARD FACE SCHOLARSHIPS

Forward Face
Attn: Scholarship Committee
317 East 34th Street, Suite 901A
New York, NY 10016
Phone: (212) 684-5860; Fax: (212) 684-5864
Email: info@forwardface.org
Web: www.forwardface.org/services/scholarships.html

Summary: To provide financial assistance for educational purposes to students with craniofacial conditions.

Eligibility: Open to students who are 13 years of age or older and have a craniofacial condition. Applicants must write essays on how a particular teacher or faculty member has made a positive impact on them, the impact of their craniofacial condition on their educational experiences, the personal qualities and abilities that make them the best candidate for the scholarship, a description of themselves that enables the readers to get to know them as persons, and where they see themselves in 10 years. Selection is based on personal qualities, goals, and recommendations. Financial need is not a consideration.

Financial data: The scholarship is $1,000. Funds must be used for educational purposes.

Duration: 1 year; nonrenewable.

Number awarded: Up to 3 each year.

Deadline: January of each year.

298 FOUNDATION FOR AMATEUR RADIO UNDERGRADUATE SCHOLARSHIPS

Foundation for Amateur Radio, Inc.
Attn: Scholarship Committee
P.O. Box 911
Columbia, MD 21044-0911

Phone: (410) 552-2652; Fax: (410) 981-5146
Email: dave.prestel@gmail.com
Web: www.farweb.org/scholarships

Summary: To provide funding to licensed radio amateurs who are interested in working on an undergraduate or graduate degree in any field.

Eligibility: Open to licensed radio amateurs who are working on an associate, bachelor's, or graduate degree in any field. Applicants must be interested in working full-time on a bachelor's degree in any field at a college or university in any state. Financial need is considered in the selection process.

Financial data: Stipends range from $1,000 to $5,000.

Duration: 1 year.

Number awarded: 10 or more each year.

Deadline: March of each year.

299 FOUNDATION FOR RURAL SERVICE COLLEGE SCHOLARSHIP PROGRAM

Foundation for Rural Service
Attn: Selection Committee
4121 Wilson Boulevard, Tenth Floor
Arlington, VA 22203
Phone: (703) 351-2026; Fax: (703) 351-2027
Email: foundation@frs.org
Web: www.frs.org

Summary: To provide financial assistance for college to high school seniors who live in rural areas of the United States.

Eligibility: Open to graduating high school seniors who receive local telecommunications service from a current member of the National Telecommunications Cooperative Association (NTCA) that serves as a sponsor; associate NTCA members (businesses that provide goods and services to the telecommunications industry) may also sponsor a student. Applicants must live in a rural area and be interested in returning to rural America following graduation. They must have a GPA of 2.0 or higher and have been accepted by an accredited 2- or 4-year college, university, or vocational/technical school. Along with their application, they must submit transcripts, letters of recommendation, an endorsement by their sponsor, and a 300-word essay on an assigned topic. Financial need is not considered in the selection process.

Financial data: The stipend is $2,500 (of which $500 is provided by the sponsoring NTCA member cooperative).

Duration: 1 year; nonrenewable.

Number awarded: 30 each year.

Deadline: February of each year.

300 FRANCIS OUIMET SCHOLARSHIPS

Francis Ouimet Scholarship Fund
c/o William F. Connell Golf House and Museum
300 Arnold Palmer Boulevard
Norton, MA 02766
Phone: (774) 430-9090; Fax: (774) 430-9091
Email: marionm@ouimet.org
Web: www.ouimet.org

Summary: To provide financial assistance to residents of Massachusetts who have worked at a golf course and are interested in attending college in any state.

Eligibility: Open to students entering or attending college or technical school in any state. Applicants must have worked for at least 2 years at a public, private, semi-private, resort, or municipal golf club in Massachusetts as caddies, helpers in pro shop operations (including bag room, range, cart storage, and starter's area), or workers in course superintendent operations. Ineligible students include those who have worked at a golf course but in a position not in direct service to golf (e.g., workers in the dining room, office, kitchen, banquet area) and those who have worked in a job related to golf but not actually at a golf course (e.g., driving range, off-course golf stores, miniature golf course). Selection is based on academic achievement and potential, leadership (including school and community activities), interviews, essays, motivation, character, integrity, service to golf, and recommendations. In addition, awards may be either financial need-based or "Honorary," with need not considered.

Financial data: Stipends range from $1,500 to $7,500 per year.

Duration: 1 year; may be renewed for 3 additional years.

Number awarded: Varies each year; recently, 270 financial need scholarships, worth $1.5 million, and 68 honorary scholarships were awarded.

Deadline: November of each year.

301 FRANK O'BANNON GRANT PROGRAM

State Student Assistance Commission of Indiana
Attn: Grant Division
150 West Market Street, Suite 500
Indianapolis, IN 46204-2811
Phone: (317) 232-2350; (888) 528-4719 (within IN); Fax: (317) 232-3260
Email: grants@ssaci.state.in.us
Web: www.in.gov/ssaci/2346.htm

Summary: To provide financial assistance to Indiana residents who are working full-time on an undergraduate degree.

Eligibility: Open to Indiana residents who are high school seniors, high school graduates, or GED certificate recipients. Applicants must be attending or planning to attend an eligible Indiana postsecondary institution as a full-time undergraduate student working on an associate or first bachelor's degree. They must be able to demonstrate financial need for tuition assistance. U.S. citizenship or eligible noncitizen status is required.

Financial data: This program offers tuition assistance from $200 to several thousand dollars per year, depending on the level of appropriations, the number of eligible students making application, the calculation of student's financial need, and the cost of tuition and fees at the schools of choice.

Duration: 1 year.

Number awarded: Varies each year.

Deadline: March of each year.

302 FRANK O'NEILL MEMORIAL SCHOLARSHIP

American Student Financial Aid
2780 South Jones Boulevard, Suite 3416
Las Vegas, NV 89146
Email: questions@easyaid.com
Web: www.easyaid.com/scholarship_form.html

Summary: To provide financial assistance to students entering or attending college who submit an online essay.

Eligibility: Open to anyone attending or planning to attend a university, college, trade school, technical institute, vocational training, or other postsecondary educational program. Applicants may not have been receiving or awarded a full-tuition scholarship or waiver from another source. They must submit an essay, up to 750 words in length, on a topic that changes annually but relates to a current issue; recently, students were asked if they think the recent economic stimulus package will solve the depression the United States is experiencing. Selection is based entirely on the essay; there is no other application form.

Financial data: The stipend is $1,000.

Duration: 1 year.

Number awarded: 1 or 2 each year.

Deadline: December of each year.

303 FRED SCHEIGERT SCHOLARSHIPS

Council of Citizens with Low Vision International
c/o American Council of the Blind
2200 Wilson Boulevard, Suite 650
Arlington, VA 22201
Phone: (202) 467-5081; (800) 733-2258; Fax: (703) 465-5085
Email: scholarship@cclvi.org
Web: www.cclvi.org/scholars.htm

Summary: To provide financial assistance to entering and continuing undergraduate and graduate students with low vision.

Eligibility: Open to full-time undergraduate and graduate students who have been certified by an ophthalmologist as having low vision (acuity of 20/70 or worse in the better seeing eye with best correction or side vision with a maximum diameter of no greater than 30 degrees). Applicants may be part-time or full-time entering freshmen, undergraduates, or graduate students. They must have a GPA of 3.2 or higher.

Financial data: The stipend is $3,000.

Duration: 1 year.

Number awarded: 3 each year.

Deadline: February of each year.

304 FREDERICK B. ABRAMSON MEMORIAL SCHOLARSHIP AWARDS

Abramson Scholarship Foundation
Attn: Scholarship Committee
2040 S Street, N.W.

Washington, DC 20009
Phone: (202) 683-4816; Fax: (202) 328-2003
Email: info@abramsonfoundation.org
Web: www.abramsonfoundation.org/scholarship/index.shtml

Summary: To provide financial assistance for college to high school seniors in the District of Columbia.

Eligibility: Open to seniors graduating from high schools in Washington, D.C. who have been accepted to an accredited 4-year college or university in the United States. Applicants must be able to demonstrate commitment to community service and social change, financial need (family income less than $70,000), and academic excellence (GPA of 2.75 or higher, SAT critical reading and mathematics scores of 1000 or higher, and SAT writing score of 3 or above). Along with their application, they must submit an essay of 300 to 500 words explaining why they should be selected to receive this scholarship.

Financial data: Stipends range up to $10,000.

Duration: 1 year.

Number awarded: Varies each year; recently, 9 of these scholarships were awarded.

Deadline: April of each year.

305 FREE TUITION FOR DEPENDENTS OF DISABLED OR DECEASED SOUTH DAKOTA NATIONAL GUARD MEMBERS

South Dakota Board of Regents
Attn: Scholarship Committee
306 East Capitol Avenue, Suite 200
Pierre, SD 57501-2545
Phone: (605) 773-3455; Fax: (605) 773-2422
Email: info@sdbor.edu
Web: www.sdbor.edu/student/prospective/Military.htm

Summary: To provide financial assistance for college to the dependents of disabled and deceased members of the South Dakota National Guard.

Eligibility: Open to the spouses and children of members of the South Dakota Army or Air National Guard who died or sustained a total and permanent disability while on state active duty, federal active duty, or any authorized duty training. Applicants must be younger than 25 years of age and proposing to work on an undergraduate degree at a public institution of higher education in South Dakota.

Financial data: Qualifying applicants are eligible to attend a state-supported postsecondary institution in South Dakota without payment of tuition.

Duration: 8 semesters or 12 quarters of either full- or part-time study.

Number awarded: Varies each year.

Deadline: Deadline not specified.

306 FREEDOM ALLIANCE SCHOLARSHIPS

Freedom Alliance
Attn: Scholarship Fund
22570 Markey Court, Suite 240
Dulles, VA 20166-6915
Phone: (703) 444-7940; (800) 475-6620; Fax: (703) 444-9893
Web: www.freedomalliance.org

Summary: To provide financial assistance for college to the children of deceased and disabled military personnel.

Eligibility: Open to high school seniors, high school graduates, and undergraduate students under 26 years of age who are dependent children of military personnel (soldier, sailor, airman, Marine, or Guardsman). The military parent must 1) have been killed or permanently disabled as a result of an operational mission or training accident; or 2) be currently classified as a POW or MIA. For disabled parents, the disability must be permanent, service-connected, and rated at 100% by the U.S. Department of Veterans Affairs. Applicants must submit a 500-word essay on what their parent's service means to them.

Financial data: A stipend is awarded (amount not specified).

Duration: 1 year; may be renewed up to 3 additional years, provided the recipient remains enrolled full-time with a GPA of 2.0 or higher.

Number awarded: Varies each year; recently, 167 of these scholarships were awarded.

Deadline: August of each year.

307 FREEDOM IN ACADEMIA ESSAY CONTEST

Foundation for Individual Rights in Education
601 Walnut Street, Suite 510
Philadelphia, PA 19106
Phone: (215) 717-FIRE; Fax: (215) 717-3440
Email: fire@thefire.org
Web: www.thefire.org/takeaction/students/essaycontest

Summary: To recognize and reward, with college scholarships, high school seniors who submit outstanding essays on individual rights in colleges and universities.

Eligibility: Open to graduating high school seniors who plan to attend a college or university. Applicants are invited to view 2 online videos describing incidents in which the sponsoring organization defended free speech on particular campuses. Based on those videos, they write an essay of 700 to 1,200 words in which they discuss the issues involved and explain how the universities violated constitutional rights of free expression. The essay should focus on why such practices are incompatible with higher education and why free speech is important in our nation's colleges and universities.

Financial data: Prizes, all in the form of college scholarships, are $5,000 for first place, $2,500 for second place, or $1,000 for runners-up.

Duration: The contest is held annually.

Number awarded: 8 each year: 1 first place, 2 second places, and 5 runners-up.

Deadline: November of each year.

308 GAMEWARDENS OF VIETNAM ASSOCIATION SCHOLARSHIP

Gamewardens of Vietnam Association, Inc.
c/o David Ajax, Scholarship Program
6630 Perry Court
Arvada, CO 80003
Email: dpajax@hotmail.com
Web: www.tf116.org/scholarship.html

Summary: To provide financial assistance for college to the children or grandchildren of veterans who served in Vietnam as part of the Navy's "Operation Gamewarden."

Eligibility: Open to the children and grandchildren of living or deceased members of the U.S. Navy River Patrol Force (TF-116) who served in Vietnam in "Operation Gamewarden" during any period from 1966 through 1971. High school students (under 21 years of age) planning to enter college as full-time students and students already enrolled in college (under 23 years of age) are eligible. Selection is based on academic merit, grades, recommendations, and financial need. Special consideration is given to applicants whose parent sponsors are members of the Gamewardens of Vietnam Association, Inc.

Financial data: Stipends are $2,000. Awards are paid directly to the college the student is attending.

Duration: 1 year.

Number awarded: 1 to 4 each year.

Deadline: April of each year.

309 GARRY L. BRIESE ENDOWED SCHOLARSHIP FUND AWARD

International Association of Fire Chiefs
Attn: IAFC Foundation
4025 Fair Ridge Drive
Fairfax, VA 22033-2868
Phone: (703) 273-0911; Fax: (703) 273-9363
Email: foundation@iafc.org
Web: www.iafcf.org./Scholarship.htm

Summary: To provide financial assistance to fire fighters, especially company officers, who wish to further their academic education.

Eligibility: Open to active members of state, county, provincial, municipal, community, industrial, or federal fire departments in the United States or Canada who have demonstrated proficiency as members for at least 2 years of paid service or 3 years of volunteer service. Dependents of members are not eligible. Applicants must be planning to attend a recognized institution of higher education. Along with their application, they must submit a 250-word essay that includes a brief description of the course work, how the course work will benefit their fire service career and department and improve the fire service, and their financial need. Preference is given to members of the International Association of Fire Chiefs (IAFC) and to company officers, especially driver/engineers and/or lieutenants, working on an associate or bachelor's degree.

Financial data: A stipend is awarded (amount not specified).

Number awarded: 1 each year.

Deadline: May of each year.

310 GATES MILLENNIUM UNDERGRADUATE SCHOLARS PROGRAM

Bill and Melinda Gates Foundation
P.O. Box 10500
Fairfax, VA 22031-8044
Phone: (877) 690-GMSP; Fax: (703) 205-2079
Web: www.gmsp.org

Summary: To provide financial assistance to outstanding low-income minority students, particularly those interested in majoring in specific fields in college.

Eligibility: Open to African Americans, Alaska Natives, American Indians, Hispanic Americans, and Asian Pacific Islander Americans who are graduating high school seniors with a GPA of 3.3 or higher. Principals, teachers, guidance counselors, tribal higher education representatives, and other professional educators are invited to nominate students with outstanding academic qualifications, particularly those likely to succeed in the fields of computer science, education, engineering, library science, mathematics, public health, or science. Nominees should have significant financial need and have demonstrated leadership abilities through participation in community service, extracurricular, or other activities. U.S. citizenship or permanent resident status is required. Nominees must be planning to enter an accredited college or university as a full-time, degree-seeking freshman in the following fall.

Financial data: The program covers the cost of tuition, fees, books, and living expenses not paid for by grants and scholarships already committed as part of the recipient's financial aid package.

Duration: 4 years or the completion of the undergraduate degree, if the recipient maintains at least a 3.0 GPA.

Number awarded: Under the Gates Millennium Scholars Program, a total of 4,000 students receive support each year.

Deadline: January of each year.

311 GEN AND KELLY TANABE SCHOLARSHIP

Gen and Kelly Tanabe
3286 Oak Court
Belmont, CA 94002
Phone: (650) 618-2221
Email: tanabe@gmail.com
Web: www.genkellyscholarship.com

Summary: To provide financial assistance for undergraduate or graduate study to U.S. citizens and permanent residents.

Eligibility: Open to U.S. citizens and permanent residents who are high school students (grades 9–12), college undergraduates, or graduate students. Applicants must submit an essay, up to 250 words, on a topic of their choice. Selection is based primarily on that essay.

Financial data: The stipend is $1,000.

Duration: 1 year.

Number awarded: 1 each year.

Deadline: July of each year.

312 GENE RABBITT SCHOLARSHIP

USA Boxing, Inc.
Attn: Foundation
One Olympic Plaza
Colorado Springs, CO 80909
Phone: (719) 866-2315
Email: dsprowls@usaboxing.org
Web: www.usaboxing.org/content/index/4752

Summary: To provide financial assistance for college to female athletes registered with USA Boxing.

Eligibility: Open to women currently enrolled and making satisfactory academic progress at 2- and 4-year colleges and universities or at technical or vocational schools. Applicants must have been registered USA Boxing athletes for at least 3 consecutive years with at least 2 bouts at sanctioned events each year. They must be recommended by the chair of the Local Boxing Committee (LBC). Selection is based on information in the application (including financial need), not on boxing achievement.

Financial data: The stipend is at least $1,000.

Duration: 1 year; may be renewed.

Number awarded: 1 each year.

Deadline: July of each year.

313 GENERAL CREIGHTON W. ABRAMS SCHOLARSHIPS

U.S. Army
ROTC Cadet Command
Attn: ATCC-OP-I-S
55 Patch Road, Building 56
Fort Monroe, VA 23651-1052
Phone: (757) 788-3473; (800) USA-ROTC; Fax: (757) 788-4643
Email: atccps@usacc.army.mil
Web: www.goarmy.com/rotc/college_students.jsp

Summary: To provide financial assistance to Army ROTC non-scholarship cadets.

Eligibility: Open to students who are entering their senior year of the Army ROTC program. Applicants must be non-scholarship cadets.

Financial data: The national stipend is $1,500; regional stipends are $1,000.

Duration: 1 year.

Number awarded: 7 each year: 3 in the ROTC eastern region, 3 in the ROTC western region, and 1 awarded nationally.

Deadline: June of each year.

314 GENERAL EDWARD W. WALDON SCHOLARSHIP PROGRAM

Grand Lodge of Minnesota, A.F. & A.M.
Attn: Grand Secretary
11501 Masonic Home Drive
Bloomington, MN 55437-3699
Phone: (952) 948-6700; (800) 245-6050 (within MN); Fax: (952) 948-6710
Email: grandlodge@qwest.net
Web: www.mn-masons.org/page931.aspx

Summary: To provide financial assistance to members of the National Guard and Reserve units in Minnesota who have deployed to combat zones since September 11, 2001 and plan to attend college in any state.

Eligibility: Open to members of the Minnesota National Guard and Minnesota Reserve units who have deployed in combat zones since September 11, 2001. Applicants must be interested in attending college in any state and be seeking funding either to help pay for tuition or to assist with the administrative fee for the Montgomery GI Bill. Awards are not based on grades or past results as a student. If there are more applicants than available scholarships, recipients are selected in a random drawing.

Financial data: The stipend is $1,000.

Duration: 1 year.

Number awarded: 100 each year.

Deadline: September of each year.

315 GENERAL HENRY H. ARNOLD EDUCATION GRANT PROGRAM

Air Force Aid Society
Attn: Education Assistance Department
241 18th Street South, Suite 202
Arlington, VA 22202-3409
Phone: (703) 607-3072, ext. 51; (800) 429-9475; Fax: (703) 607-3022
Web: www.afas.org/Education/ArnoldEdGrant.cfm

Summary: To provide financial assistance for college to dependents of active-duty, retired, disabled, or deceased Air Force personnel.

Eligibility: Open to 1) dependent children of Air Force personnel who are active duty, Reservists on extended active duty, retired due to length of active-duty service or disability, or deceased while on active duty or in retired status; 2) spouses of active-duty Air Force members and Reservists on extended active duty; and 3) surviving spouses of Air Force members who died while on active duty or in retired status. Applicants must be enrolled or planning to enroll as full-time undergraduate students in an accredited college, university, or vocational/trade school. Spouses must be attending school within the 48 contiguous states. Selection is based on family income and education costs.

Financial data: The stipend is $2,000.

Duration: 1 year; may be renewed if the recipient maintains a GPA of 2.0 or higher.

Number awarded: Varies each year.

Deadline: March of each year.

316 GENERAL MELVIN ZAIS SCHOLARSHIPS

U.S. Army
ROTC Cadet Command

Attn: ATCC-OP-I-S
55 Patch Road, Building 56
Fort Monroe, VA 23651-1052
Phone: (757) 788-3473; (800) USA-ROTC; Fax: (757) 788-4643
Email: atccps@usacc.army.mil
Web: www.goarmy.com/rotc/college_students.jsp

Summary: To provide financial assistance to Army ROTC non-scholarship cadets.

Eligibility: Open to students who are entering their senior year of the Army ROTC program. Applicants must be non-scholarship cadets.

Financial data: The stipend is $1,000.

Duration: 1 year.

Number awarded: 3 each year: 1 in the ROTC eastern region, 1 in the ROTC western region, and 1 awarded nationally.

Deadline: June of each year.

317 GENERAL WILLIAM E. DEPUY MEMORIAL SCHOLARSHIP PROGRAM

Society of the First Infantry Division
Attn: 1st Infantry Division Foundation
1933 Morris Road
Blue Bell, PA 19422-1422
Phone: (888) 324-4733; Fax: (215) 661-1934
Email: Fdn1ID@aol.com
Web: www.bigredone.org/foundation/scholarships.cfm

Summary: To provide financial assistance for college to the children of certain deceased members of the First Infantry Division.

Eligibility: Open to the children of soldiers who served in the First Infantry Division and were killed while serving in combat with the Division or in peacetime training accidents. This is an entitlement program. All eligible applicants receive an award.

Financial data: The stipend is $2,500 per year.

Duration: 1 year; may be renewed up to 3 additional years.

Number awarded: Varies each year.

Deadline: Deadline not specified.

318 GEOFFREY FOUNDATION SCHOLARSHIPS

Geoffrey Foundation
Ocean Avenue
P.O. Box 1112
Kennebunkport, ME 04046
Phone: (207) 967-5798

Summary: To provide financial assistance to deaf students who attend school with hearing students and communicate using spoken language.

Eligibility: Open to U.S. citizens who are hearing impaired (severe to profound hearing loss greater than 80 dB) and are utilizing an auditory-verbal approach to communication. Applicants must be currently enrolled or planning to attend a preschool, elementary school, junior high or high school, or college for hearing students on a full-time basis in the forthcoming year. They must submit a current audiogram plus 3 letters of recommendation.

Financial data: The amount awarded varies, depending upon the needs of the recipient.

Duration: 1 year or longer.

Number awarded: Varies each year. The foundation awards grants in excess of $30,000 each year to children and college students.

Deadline: March of each year.

319 GEORGE BARTOL MEMORIAL SCHOLARSHIPS

George Bartol Memorial Scholarship Fund
c/o Kari Bartol Romano
4616 Edgewater Drive
Orlando, FL 32804
Phone: (407) 718-7601
Email: livebait3@aol.com
Web: www.mindsmatterusa.org/Scholarship.html

Summary: To provide financial assistance for college to children of brain tumor patients.

Eligibility: Open to students enrolled full-time at an accredited 2- or 4-year college or university who have a GPA of 2.5 or higher. Applicants must have a parent battling a primary brain tumor or a parent who has passed away as a result of a primary brain tumor. They must be between 18 and 23 years of age. Along with their application, they must submit 5 essays on the following topics: 1) their parent who has lost their battle to a primary brain tumor or who is currently battling a primary brain tumor; 2) their academic and professional goals; 3) the advice they would give to another child whose parent was just diagnosed with brain cancer; 4) their current financial status and how their parent's medical condition has increased their financial need for this scholarship; and 5) how their parent's medical condition has changed their outlook on life. Selection is based on the essays, grades, letters of recommendation, and financial need. Children of Vietnam veterans who have not been awarded VA Chapter 35 benefits are strongly encouraged to apply.

Financial data: The stipend is $1,000 per semester ($3,000 per year, including summer semester). Students at schools on the quarter system may receive $750 per quarter ($3,000 per year, including summer quarter). Funds are paid directly to the financial aid office at the school the recipient is attending.

Duration: 1 semester or quarter; may be renewed if the recipient maintains a GPA of 2.5 or higher.

Number awarded: Varies each year; recently, 3 of these scholarships were awarded.

Deadline: September of each year.

320 GEORGE COLEMAN SCHOLARSHIP

New England Association of Collegiate Registrars and Admissions Officers
c/o Patrick Sullivan, Scholarship Committee
University of Massachusetts at Amherst
140 Hicks Way OFC 1
Amherst, MA 01003-9333
Phone: (413) 545-5295; Fax: (413) 577-0386
Email: psulliva@grad.umass.edu
Web: www.neacrao.org/scholarship_info.html

Summary: To provide financial assistance to high school seniors in New England who plan to attend a college or university that is a member of the New England Association of Collegiate Registrars and Admissions Officers (NEACRAO).

Eligibility: Open to seniors graduating from high schools in New England who are recommended by their guidance counselor. Applicants must be planning to attend a NEACRAO member institution. They must have a GPA of 3.0 or higher. Along with their application, they must submit a 250-word essay on their career goals. Selection is based on academic record and potential of the applicant to succeed in a postsecondary academic environment.

Financial data: The stipend is $1,500.

Duration: 1 year.

Number awarded: 3 each year.

Deadline: March of each year.

321 GEORGE "SLATS" O'BRIEN SCHOLARSHIPS

Western Athletic Scholarship Association
Attn: Scholarship Coordinator
13730 Loumont Street
Whittier, CA 90601

Summary: To provide financial assistance for college to outstanding volleyball players.

Eligibility: Open to graduating high school seniors who have played an active role in amateur volleyball. Applicants must be planning to attend an accredited 2- or 4-year college or university. They need not have played on a high school team and are not required to play volleyball in college. Selection is based on academic achievement, community service, participation in volleyball, and financial need.

Financial data: The stipend is $2,000 per year.

Duration: 1 year; may be renewed.

Number awarded: Up to 10 each year.

Deadline: February of each year.

322 GEORGE WASHINGTON FOUNDATION SCHOLARSHIPS

George Washington Foundation
c/o James R. Sharples, Secretary
2581 Mapleway Road
Yakima, WA 98908
Email: gwfoundation@compwrx.com

Summary: To provide financial assistance to high school seniors in Washington who plan to attend college in the state.

Eligibility: Open to seniors graduating from high schools in Washington and planning to attend college in the state. Applicants must rank in the top 20% of their graduating class, although that requirement may be waived in case of

financial difficulty at home. Selection is based on financial need and potential for future use and benefit to society.
Financial data: The stipend is $1,050 per year.
Duration: 1 year; may be renewed for 1 additional year.
Number awarded: Varies each year.
Deadline: February of each year.

323 GEORGIA ACCEL PROGRAM

Georgia Student Finance Commission
Attn: Scholarships and Grants Division
2082 East Exchange Place, Suite 200
Tucker, GA 30084-5305
Phone: (770) 724-9000; (800) 505-GSFC; Fax: (770) 724-9089
Email: gsfcinfo@gsfc.org
Web: www.gacollege411.org
Summary: To provide financial assistance to high school students in Georgia who are enrolled concurrently in college-level courses.
Eligibility: Open to Georgia residents who are enrolled simultaneously as a junior or senior at an eligible public or private high school in the state and at an eligible Georgia public or private postsecondary institution. Applicants must be taking college degree–level courses in English language arts, mathematics, social studies, science, or foreign language. U.S. citizenship or permanent resident status is required.
Financial data: Accel Scholars who attend public colleges or universities receive full tuition and payment of mandatory fees plus a book allowance of $300 per academic year. The stipend for Accel Scholarships at private colleges and universities is $3,500 per year; funds may be used only for tuition and mandatory fees.
Duration: 1 year; may be renewed for 1 additional year.
Number awarded: Varies each year.
Deadline: Applications must be submitted on or before the last day of the academic term.

324 GEORGIA ELECTRONIC LIFE SAFETY & SYSTEMS ASSOCIATION SCHOLARSHIP PROGRAM

Georgia Electronic Life Safety & Systems Association
Attn: Scholarship Committee Chair
P.O. Box 1438
Jonesboro, GA 30237
Phone: (800) 948-9531, ext. 108; Fax: (770) 692-2892
Email: karen@paragonsystem.com
Web: www.gelssa.com/plaintext/scholarships/forms.aspx
Summary: To provide financial assistance to high school seniors in Georgia who are the children of active-duty law enforcement and fire service personnel and interested in attending college in any state.
Eligibility: Open to seniors graduating from high schools in Georgia who have been accepted at an accredited college or university in any state. Applicants must have a father, mother, or legal guardian who is a full-time active employee (not on disability and not an administrative staff member) of the police or sheriff's department or a paid employee or volunteer of a fire department in Georgia. Along with their application, they must submit an essay of 500 to 1,000 words on what it means to them to have their parent or guardian involved in securing our community. Selection is based on that essay (25 points), grade average (25 points), SAT or ACT scores (30 points), and academic prizes, awards, school and outside extracurricular activities, and hobbies (20 points); financial need is not considered.
Financial data: The stipend is $1,500.
Duration: 1 year.
Number awarded: 1 each year.
Deadline: April of each year.

325 GEORGIA LAW ENFORCEMENT PERSONNEL DEPENDENTS GRANT

Georgia Student Finance Commission
Attn: Scholarships and Grants Division
2082 East Exchange Place, Suite 200
Tucker, GA 30084-5305
Phone: (770) 724-9000; (800) 505-GSFC; Fax: (770) 724-9089
Email: gsfcinfo@gsfc.org
Web: www.gacollege411.org
Summary: To provide financial assistance for college to children of disabled or deceased Georgia law enforcement personnel.
Eligibility: Open to dependent children of law enforcement officers, fire fighters, and prison guards in Georgia who have been permanently disabled or killed in the line of duty. Applicants must be enrolled as full-time undergraduate students in a Georgia private or public college, university, or technical institution. U.S. citizenship or permanent resident status and compliance with the Georgia Drug-Free Postsecondary Education Act are required. Financial need is not considered in the selection process.
Financial data: The grant is $2,000 per academic year, not to exceed $8,000 during an entire program of study.
Duration: 1 year; may be renewed (if satisfactory progress is maintained) for up to 3 additional years.
Number awarded: Varies each year; recently, 20 of these grants were awarded.
Deadline: Applications must be submitted on or before the last day of the academic term.

326 GEORGIA LEAP GRANT PROGRAM

Georgia Student Finance Commission
Attn: Scholarships and Grants Division
2082 East Exchange Place, Suite 200
Tucker, GA 30084-5305
Phone: (770) 724-9000; (800) 505-GSFC; Fax: (770) 724-9089
Email: gsfcinfo@gsfc.org
Web: www.gacollege411.org
Summary: To provide financial assistance for college to residents of Georgia who demonstrate financial need.
Eligibility: Open to Georgia residents who are enrolled as regular undergraduate students in an eligible Georgia public or private college, university, or technical college. Applicants must be able to demonstrate substantial financial need and must be eligible for a federal Pell Grant. They must be at least a half-time student maintaining satisfactory academic progress. U.S. citizenship or permanent resident status and compliance with the Georgia Drug-Free Postsecondary Education Act are required.
Financial data: Grants range from $300 to $2,000 per academic year.
Duration: 1 year; may be renewed (if satisfactory progress is maintained) for up to 3 additional years.
Number awarded: Varies each year; recently, 3,008 of these grants were awarded.
Deadline: Deadline not specified.

327 GEORGIA LEGION AUXILIARY PAST DEPARTMENT PRESIDENTS SCHOLARSHIP

American Legion Auxiliary
Department of Georgia
3035 Mt. Zion Road
Stockbridge, GA 30281-4101
Phone: (678) 289-8446; Fax: (678) 289-9496
Email: amlegaux@bellsouth.net
Web: www.galegion.org/auxiliary.htm
Summary: To provide financial assistance to the children of Georgia veterans who plan to attend college in any state.
Eligibility: Open to residents of Georgia who are high school seniors and children of veterans. Preference is given to children of deceased veterans. Applicants must be sponsored by a local unit of the American Legion Auxiliary in Georgia. Selection is based on a statement explaining why they want to further their education and their need for a scholarship.
Financial data: The stipend is $1,000.
Duration: 1 year.
Number awarded: 2 each year.
Deadline: May of each year.

328 GEORGIA PUBLIC SAFETY MEMORIAL GRANT

Georgia Student Finance Commission
Attn: Scholarships and Grants Division
2082 East Exchange Place, Suite 200
Tucker, GA 30084-5305
Phone: (770) 724-9000; (800) 505-GSFC; Fax: (770) 724-9089
Email: gsfcinfo@gsfc.org
Web: www.gacollege411.org
Summary: To provide financial assistance for college to the children of Georgia public safety officers who have been permanently disabled or killed in the line of duty.

Eligibility: Open to dependent children of Georgia law enforcement officers, fire fighters, EMT, correction officers, or prison guards who have been permanently disabled or killed in the line of duty. Applicants must be enrolled or accepted as full-time undergraduate students in a Georgia public college, university, or technical institution and be in compliance with the Georgia Drug-Free Postsecondary Education Act. U.S. citizenship or permanent resident status is required. Financial need is not considered in the selection process.
Financial data: The award covers the cost of attendance at a public postsecondary school in Georgia, minus any other aid received.
Duration: 1 year; may be renewed (if satisfactory progress is maintained) for up to 3 additional years.
Number awarded: Varies each year; recently, 18 of these grants were awarded.
Deadline: July of each year.

329 GEORGIA'S HERO SCHOLARSHIP PROGRAM

Georgia Student Finance Commission
Attn: Scholarships and Grants Division
2082 East Exchange Place, Suite 200
Tucker, GA 30084-5305
Phone: (770) 724-9000; (800) 505-GSFC; Fax: (770) 724-9089
Email: gsfcinfo@gsfc.org
Web: www.gacollege411.org
Summary: To provide financial assistance for college to members of the National Guard or Reserves in Georgia and the children and spouses of deceased or disabled Guard or Reserve members.
Eligibility: Open to Georgia residents who are active members of the Georgia National Guard or U.S. Military Reserves, were deployed outside the United States for active-duty service on or after February 1, 2003 to a location designated as a combat zone, and served in that combat zone for at least 181 consecutive days. Also eligible are 1) the children, younger than 25 years of age, of Guard and Reserve members who completed at least 1 term of service (of 181 days each) overseas on or after February 1, 2003; 2) the children, younger than 25 years of age, of Guard and Reserve members who were killed or totally disabled during service overseas on or after February 1, 2003, regardless of their length of service; and 3) the spouses of Guard and Reserve members who were killed in a combat zone, died as a result of injuries, or became 100% disabled as a result of injuries received in a combat zone during service overseas on or after February 1, 2003, regardless of their length of service. Applicants must be interested in attending a unit of the University System of Georgia, a unit of the Georgia Department of Technical and Adult Education, or an eligible private college or university in Georgia.
Financial data: The stipend is $2,000 per academic year, not to exceed $8,000 during an entire program of study.
Duration: 1 year; may be renewed (if satisfactory progress is maintained) for up to 3 additional years.
Number awarded: Varies each year.
Deadline: June of each year.

330 GILBERT MATCHING STUDENT GRANT PROGRAM

Massachusetts Office of Student Financial Assistance
454 Broadway, Suite 200
Revere, MA 02151
Phone: (617) 727-9420; Fax: (617) 727-0667
Email: osfa@osfa.mass.edu
Web: www.osfa.mass.edu/default.asp?page=gilbert
Summary: To provide financial assistance for college to Massachusetts residents who are attending accredited independent institutions.
Eligibility: Open to students who have been permanent legal residents of Massachusetts for at least 1 year and are working full-time on an associate or bachelor's degree at an independent, regionally accredited college or university in the state. U.S. citizenship or permanent resident status is required. Selection is based on financial need.
Financial data: Awards range from $200 to $2,500 per year, depending on the need of the recipient.
Duration: 1 year; may be renewed.
Number awarded: Varies each year.
Deadline: Deadlines are established by the school the student attends.

331 GIRLS GOING PLACES ENTREPRENEURSHIP AWARDS

Guardian Life Insurance Company of America
Attn: Girls Going Places
7 Hanover Square, H26-J
New York, NY 10004-2616
Phone: (212) 598-7881; (888) 600-4667; Fax: (212) 919-2586
Email: guardianwomenschannel@glic.com
Web: www.girlsgoingplaces.com/home
Summary: To recognize and reward outstanding girls between 12 and 18 years of age who demonstrate "budding entrepreneurship."
Eligibility: Open to girls between the ages of 12 and 18 who are U.S. citizens or legal residents and enrolled in middle school, high school, or a home school program; students enrolled at a college or university are ineligible. They must be nominated; nominators must submit a 750-word recommendation letter in which they explain how their nominee makes a difference in her school, her community, or people's lives; how she has demonstrated budding entrepreneurship or financial acumen; and how she has taken the first steps toward financial independence. Nominees must submit 250-word personal statements on such topics as entrepreneurship, business leadership, financial independence, or making a difference in the community through entrepreneurship. Selection is based on the nominee's demonstration of budding entrepreneurship; significance of nominee's steps toward financial independence; nominee's ability to make a difference in her school and community; and nominee's initiative to start a new business or service.
Financial data: First prize is $10,000, second $5,000, and third $3,000; 12 other finalists receive $1,000. Winners may use the funds to further their entrepreneurial pursuits or save for college.
Duration: The competition is held annually.
Number awarded: 15 each year.
Deadline: February of each year.

332 GLAD EMPLOYEE NETWORK LGBT SCHOLARSHIP

Parents, Families and Friends of Lesbians and Gays
Attn: Safe Schools Coordinator
1726 M Street, N.W., Suite 400
Washington, DC 20036-4521
Phone: (202) 467-8180, ext. 219; Fax: (202) 467-8194
Email: scholarships@pflag.org
Web: community.pflag.org/Page.aspx?pid=374
Summary: To provide financial assistance for college to high school seniors and recent graduates who have been involved in the lesbian, gay, bisexual, or transgender (LGBT) community.
Eligibility: Open to high school seniors and prior-year graduates who have not attended college. Applicants must have applied to an accredited higher education institution to work on; 1) an associate degree leading to transfer to complete a bachelor's degree; or 2) a bachelor's degree at a 4-year college or university. They must self-identify either as LGBT person or as a supporter of LGBT people. Along with their application, they must submit a high school transcript showing a GPA of 3.0 or higher, 2 letters of recommendation, and a 2-page essay discussing either their life as an LGBT student or how they have been involved with and supported the LGBT community. Financial need is also considered in the selection process.
Financial data: The stipend is $2,500.
Duration: 1 year; nonrenewable.
Number awarded: 1 each year.
Deadline: March of each year.

333 GOLD STAR SCHOLARSHIP PROGRAM FOR SURVIVING CHILDREN OF NAVAL PERSONNEL DECEASED AFTER RETIREMENT

Navy-Marine Corps Relief Society
Attn: Education Division
875 North Randolph Street, Suite 225
Arlington, VA 22203-1757
Phone: (703) 696-4960; Fax: (703) 696-0144
Email: education@nmcrs.org
Web: www.nmcrs.org/goldstar.html
Summary: To provide financial assistance for college to the children of Navy or Marine Corps personnel who died as a result of disabilities or length of service.
Eligibility: Open to the unmarried, dependent children, stepchildren, or legally adopted children under the age of 23 of members of the Navy or Marine Corps who died after retirement due to disability or length of service. Applicants must be enrolled or planning to enroll full-time at a college, university, or vocational/technical school. They must have a GPA of 2.0 or higher and be able to demonstrate financial need.
Financial data: Stipends range from $500 to $2,500 per year. Funds are disbursed directly to the financial institution.
Duration: 1 year; may be renewed up to 3 additional years.

Number awarded: Varies each year.
Deadline: February of each year.

334 GOLD STAR SCHOLARSHIP PROGRAM FOR SURVIVING CHILDREN OF NAVAL PERSONNEL DECEASED WHILE ON ACTIVE DUTY

Navy-Marine Corps Relief Society
Attn: Education Division
875 North Randolph Street, Suite 225
Arlington, VA 22203-1757
Phone: (703) 696-4960; Fax: (703) 696-0144
Email: education@nmcrs.org
Web: www.nmcrs.org/goldstar.html

Summary: To provide financial assistance for college to the children of Navy or Marine Corps personnel who died while on active duty.
Eligibility: Open to the unmarried, dependent children, stepchildren, or legally adopted children under the age of 23 of members of the Navy or Marine Corps who died while on active duty but not in a hostile fire zone. Applicants must be enrolled or planning to enroll full-time at a college, university, or vocational/technical school. They must have a GPA of 2.0 or higher and be able to demonstrate financial need.
Financial data: Stipends range from $500 to $2,500 per year. Funds are disbursed directly to the financial institution.
Duration: 1 year; may be renewed up to 3 additional years.
Number awarded: Varies each year.
Deadline: February of each year.

335 GRAEME CLARK SCHOLARSHIPS

Cochlear Americas
Attn: Scholarships
13059 East Peakview Avenue
Centennial, CO 80111
Phone: (303) 790-9010; (800) 523-5798; Fax: (303) 790-1157
Email: Recipients@Cochlear.com
Web: www.cochlearamericas.com/support/168.asp

Summary: To provide financial assistance for college to students who have received a cochlear nucleus implant.
Eligibility: Open to graduating high school seniors, current university students, and mature aged students who have been accepted into a university course. Applicants must have received a cochlear nucleus implant. Along with their application, they must submit a 1,000-word personal statement on their academic aspirations and other interests, including why they chose their proposed area of study, their post-graduate aspirations, their definition of success, and why they wish to receive this scholarship. Selection is based on academic achievement and demonstrated commitment to the ideals of leadership and humanity.
Financial data: The stipend is $2,000 per year.
Duration: 1 year; may be renewed up to 3 additional years.
Number awarded: Varies each year; recently, 5 of these scholarships were awarded.
Deadline: July of each year.

336 GRAND LODGE OF IOWA MASONIC SCHOLARSHIP

Grand Lodge of Iowa, A.F. & A.M.
Attn: Scholarship Selection Committee
813 First Avenue S.E.
P.O. Box 279
Cedar Rapids, IA 52406-0279
Phone: (319) 365-1438; Fax: (319) 365-1439
Email: scholarships@gl-iowa.org
Web: www.gl-iowa.org/Scholarship.html

Summary: To provide financial assistance to high school seniors in Iowa who plan to attend college in any state.
Eligibility: Open to seniors graduating from public high schools in Iowa. Applicants must be planning to attend a 2- or 4-year college or university in any state. They need not have a Masonic connection. Finalists are interviewed. Selection is based on service to school and community (with special emphasis on leadership roles in those areas), academic record, communication skills, and financial need.
Financial data: The stipend is $2,000. Funds may be used for tuition, fees, and books.
Duration: 1 year.
Number awarded: Approximately 60 each year.
Deadline: January of each year.

337 GRAND LODGE OF OHIO SCHOLARSHIPS

Grand Lodge of Ohio, Free & Accepted Masons
Attn: Scholarship Foundation
634 High Street
P.O. Box 629
Worthington, OH 43085
Phone: (800) 292-6092; Fax: (614) 885-5319
Email: mwatson@freemason.com
Web: www.freemason.com/scholarship-foundation.html

Summary: To provide financial assistance to residents of Ohio who are enrolled or planning to enroll at a college in any state.
Eligibility: Open to residents of Ohio who are attending or planning to attend a college or university in any state. Applicants must submit a brief essay explaining why they believe they should be selected to receive this scholarship. Selection is based on that essay, GPA, involvement in school and non-school activities, community service or volunteer work, and financial need.
Financial data: The stipend is $2,000. Funds are paid directly to the student.
Duration: 1 year.
Number awarded: 25 each year: 1 in each Masonic District in Ohio.
Deadline: Applications must be submitted to the District Scholarship Committee by February of each year.

338 GROUP PHOTOGRAPHERS ASSOCIATION NATIONAL SCHOLARSHIP PROGRAM

Group Photographers Association
Attn: Scholarship Program
10220 East Sprague Avenue, Main Floor
Spokane Valley, WA 99206
Phone: (800) 558-5010; Fax: (800) 247-5121
Email: info@groupphotographers.com
Web: www.groupphotographers.com

Summary: To provide financial assistance for college to high school seniors who have participated in youth sports.
Eligibility: Open to seniors graduating from high school who have been accepted at a 4-year college or university. Applicants must submit a 250-word essay explaining why participation in youth sports has enhanced them as a person and student. Their essay should include the name of the college or university they plan to attend, their intended major, sports played, favorite youth program, and favorite coach's name. Financial need is not considered in the selection process.
Financial data: Stipends are $3,000 or $1,000.
Duration: 1 year.
Number awarded: 11 each year: 1 national winner at $3,000 and 10 regional winners at $1,000 each.
Deadline: March of each year.

339 GUARDIAN SCHOLARSHIPS

Workforce Safety & Insurance
1600 East Century Avenue, Suite 1
P.O. Box 5585
Bismarck, ND 58506-5585
Phone: (701) 328-3828; (800) 440-3796; Fax: (701) 328-3820; TDD: (800) 366-6888
Email: ndwsi@nd.gov
Web: www.workforcesafety.com/workers/typesofbenefits.asp

Summary: To provide financial assistance for college to children and spouses of workers who died in work-related accidents in North Dakota.
Eligibility: Open to spouses and dependent children of workers who lost their lives in work-related accidents in North Dakota. Applicants must be attending or planning to attend an accredited college, university, or technical school.
Financial data: The maximum stipend is $4,000 per year.
Duration: 1 year; may be renewed up to 4 additional years.
Number awarded: Varies each year; recently, 32 of these scholarships were awarded.
Deadline: Deadline not specified.

340 GUIDE DOGS FOR THE BLIND DOROTHEA AND ROLAND BOHDE LEADERSHIP SCHOLARSHIP

National Federation of the Blind
Attn: Scholarship Committee
1800 Johnson Street
Baltimore, MD 21230
Phone: (410) 659-9314, ext. 2415; Fax: (410) 685-5653
Email: scholarships@nfb.org
Web: www.nfb.org/nfb/scholarship_program.asp

Summary: To provide financial assistance to blind undergraduate and graduate students, especially those who use a guide dog.

Eligibility: Open to legally blind students who are working on or planning to work full-time on an undergraduate or graduate degree. Preference is given to applicants who have chosen to use a guide dog as their primary travel aid. Along with their application, they must submit transcripts, standardized test scores, proof of legal blindness, 2 letters of recommendation, and a letter of endorsement from their National Federation of the Blind state president or designee. Selection is based on academic excellence, service to the community, and financial need.

Financial data: The stipend is $3,000.

Duration: 1 year; recipients may resubmit applications up to 2 additional years.

Number awarded: 1 each year.

Deadline: March of each year.

341 GUILDSCHOLAR PROGRAM

Jewish Guild for the Blind
Attn: GuildScholar Program
15 West 65th Street
New York, NY 10023
Phone: (212) 769-7801; (800) 284-4422; Fax: (212) 769-6266
Email: guildscholar@jgb.org
Web: www.jgb.org/guildscholar.asp?GS=TRue

Summary: To provide financial assistance for college to blind high school seniors.

Eligibility: Open to college-bound high school seniors who can document legal blindness. Applicants must submit copies of school transcripts and SAT or ACT scores, proof of U.S. citizenship, 3 letters of recommendation, proof of legal blindness, a 500-word personal statement describing their educational and personal goals, a 500-word essay describing the influence of an outstanding teacher on their education, and documentation of financial need (if they wish that to be considered in the selection process).

Financial data: The stipend ranges up to $15,000.

Duration: 1 year.

Number awarded: 12 to 15 each year.

Deadline: June of each year (the end of the junior year of high school).

342 GWOT ASSISTANCE FUND

Navy-Marine Corps Relief Society
Attn: Education Division
875 North Randolph Street, Suite 225
Arlington, VA 22203-1757
Phone: (703) 696-4960; Fax: (703) 696-0144
Email: education@nmcrs.org
Web: www.nmcrs.org/goldstar.html

Summary: To provide financial assistance for college to the spouses of deceased Navy and Marine Corps military personnel who became disabled or died during the Global War on Terrorism (GWOT).

Eligibility: Open to the spouses of disabled or deceased sailors and Marines who were injured or died while on active duty under hostile fire in a theater of combat operations during the GWOT. Applicants must be enrolled or planning to enroll full- or part-time at a college, university, or vocational/technical school. They must have a GPA of 2.0 or higher and be able to demonstrate financial need.

Financial data: Stipends range from $500 to $2,500 per year. Funds are disbursed directly to the financial institution.

Duration: 1 year; may be renewed up to 3 additional years.

Number awarded: Varies each year.

Deadline: February of each year.

343 HAGOP, AROUSIAG, AND ARPY KASHMANIAN FUND SCHOLARSHIPS

New York Community Trust
Attn: Armenian Scholarship Administrator
909 Third Avenue
New York, NY 10022
Phone: (212) 686-0010, ext. 535; Fax: (212) 532-8528
Email: jh@nyct-cfi.org
Web: www.nycommunitytrust.org

Summary: To provide financial assistance to full-time undergraduates of Armenian descent from selected eastern states.

Eligibility: Open to full-time undergraduate students of Armenian descent. Applicants must have at least a 3.2 GPA, a record of involvement in the Armenian community, and documented financial need. They must reside in New York, New Jersey, or Connecticut.

Financial data: Stipends range from $1,000 to $6,000.

Duration: 1 year; may be renewed up to 3 additional years.

Number awarded: Several each year.

Deadline: April of each year.

344 HANA SCHOLARSHIPS

United Methodist Church
Attn: General Board of Higher Education and Ministry
Office of Loans and Scholarships
1001 19th Avenue South
P.O. Box 340007
Nashville, TN 37203-0007
Phone: (615) 340-7344; Fax: (615) 340-7367
Email: umscholar@gbhem.org
Web: www.gbhem.org/loansandscholarships

Summary: To provide financial assistance to upper-division and graduate Methodist students who are of Hispanic, Asian, Native American, Alaska Native, or Pacific Islander ancestry.

Eligibility: Open to full-time juniors, seniors, and graduate students at accredited colleges and universities in the United States who have been active, full members of a United Methodist Church (UMC) for at least 1 year prior to applying. Applicants must have at least 1 parent who is Hispanic, Asian, Native American, Alaska Native, or Pacific Islander. They must be able to demonstrate involvement in their Hispanic, Asian, or Native American (HANA) community in the UMC. Selection is based on that involvement, academic ability (GPA of at least 2.85 for undergraduates or 3.0 for graduate students), and financial need. U.S. citizenship or permanent resident status is required.

Financial data: The maximum stipend is $3,000 for undergraduates or $5,000 for graduate students.

Duration: 1 year; recipients may reapply.

Number awarded: 50 each year.

Deadline: March of each year.

345 HANK LEBONNE SCHOLARSHIP

National Federation of the Blind
Attn: Scholarship Committee
1800 Johnson Street
Baltimore, MD 21230
Phone: (410) 659-9314, ext. 2415; Fax: (410) 685-5653
Email: scholarships@nfb.org
Web: www.nfb.org/nfb/scholarship_program.asp

Summary: To provide financial assistance to legally blind students working on or planning to work on an undergraduate or graduate degree.

Eligibility: Open to legally blind students who are working on or planning to work full-time on an undergraduate or graduate degree. Along with their application, they must submit transcripts, standardized test scores, proof of legal blindness, 2 letters of recommendation, and a letter of endorsement from their National Federation of the Blind state president or designee. Selection is based on academic excellence, service to the community, and financial need.

Financial data: The stipend is $5,000.

Duration: 1 year; recipients may resubmit applications up to 2 additional years.

Number awarded: 1 each year.

Deadline: March of each year.

346 HAROLD DWIGHT HARRAH SCHOLARSHIPS

Vietnam Veterans of America–Chapter 522
P.O. Box 551
Indian Rocks Beach, FL 33785-0551
Phone: (727) 278-4111
Web: www.vva522.org/scholarship.html

Summary: To provide financial assistance to high school seniors in Florida who are related to a veteran and interested in attending college in any state.

Eligibility: Open to seniors graduating from public or private high schools in Florida and planning to attend college in any state. Applicants must be U.S. citizens and related to a veteran. They must have a GPA of 3.25 and be able to document financial need and volunteer work or community service activities within the past 12 months. Along with their application, they must submit a 1,000-word essay on how this scholarship will support their educational goals.

Financial data: The stipend is $1,000. Funds are disbursed directly to the recipient's college or university.

Duration: 1 year.

Number awarded: 3 each year.

Deadline: March of each year.

347 HAROLD HAYDEN MEMORIAL SCHOLARSHIP

National Organization of Black County Officials
1090 Vermont Avenue, N.W., Suite 1290
Washington, DC 20005
Phone: (202) 350-6696; Fax: (202) 350-6699
Email: nobco@nocboinc.org
Web: www.nobcoinc.org/scholarship.html

Summary: To provide financial assistance for college to high school and currently-enrolled college students nominated by members of the National Association of Black County Officials (NABCO).

Eligibility: Open to high school seniors and currently-enrolled college students. Applicants must submit an endorsement from a NABCO member and a brief (up to 3 pages) autobiographical essay. Selection is based on academic record, leadership record, character and personality, personal achievement, interest in government and politics, and commitment to human and civil rights. Financial need is not considered in the selection process.

Financial data: A stipend is awarded (amount not specified).

Duration: 1 year.

Number awarded: Varies each year; recently, 5 of these scholarships were awarded.

Deadline: June of each year.

348 HARTFORD WHALERS BOOSTER CLUB SCHOLARSHIPS

Hartford Whalers Booster Club
Attn: Scholarship Coordinator
P.O. Box 273
Hartford, CT 06141
Phone: (860) 643-0842
Email: HartfordWhalersBoosterClub@hotmail.com
Web: www.whalerwatch.com/hartford_whalers_booster_club_sc.htm

Summary: To provide financial assistance to high school seniors from Connecticut who are interested in playing hockey in college.

Eligibility: Open to Connecticut residents who are graduating high school seniors. Applicants must be interested in attending a 4-year college or university with a hockey program. Selection is based on academic achievement, financial need, and hockey ability.

Financial data: A stipend up to $1,000 per year is provided.

Duration: 1 year.

Number awarded: 1 each year.

Deadline: February of each year.

349 HATTIE TEDROW MEMORIAL FUND SCHOLARSHIP

American Legion
Department of North Dakota
405 West Main Street, Suite 4A
P.O. Box 5057
West Fargo, ND 58078
Phone: (701) 293-3120; Fax: (701) 293-9951
Email: Programs@ndlegion.org
Web: www.ndlegion.org/Americanism_Programs/Children&Youth.htm

Summary: To provide financial assistance to high school seniors in North Dakota who are direct descendants of veterans and interested in attending college in any state.

Eligibility: Open to seniors graduating from high schools in North Dakota and planning to attend a college, university, trade school, or technical school in any state. Applicants must be the children, grandchildren, or great-grandchildren of veterans who served honorably in the U.S. armed forces. Along with their application, they must submit a 500-word essay on why they should receive this scholarship. Selection is based on the essay and academic performance; financial need is not considered.

Financial data: The stipend is $2,000.

Duration: 1 year; nonrenewable.

Number awarded: 1 each year.

Deadline: April of each year.

350 HAWAIIAN CIVIC CLUB OF HONOLULU SCHOLARSHIP

Hawaiian Civic Club of Honolulu
Attn: Scholarship Committee
P.O. Box 1513
Honolulu, HI 96806
Email: newmail@hotbot.com
Web: www.hcchonolulu.org/scholarship

Summary: To provide financial assistance for undergraduate or graduate studies to persons of Hawaiian descent.

Eligibility: Open to applicants of Hawaiian descent (descendants of the aboriginal inhabitants of the Hawaiian Islands prior to 1778) who are residents of Hawaii, able to demonstrate academic achievement, and enrolled or planning to enroll full-time in an accredited 2-year college, 4-year college, or graduate school. Graduating seniors and current undergraduate students must have a GPA of 2.5 or higher; graduate students must have at least a 3.0 GPA. Along with their application, they must submit a 2-page essay on a topic that changes annually but relates to issues of concern to the Hawaiian community; a recent topic related to the leadership, cultural and governmental, of the Hawaiian community. Selection is based on the quality of the essay, academic standing, financial need, and the completeness of the application package.

Financial data: The amount of the stipend varies. Scholarship checks are made payable to the recipient and the institution and are mailed to the college or university financial aid office. Funds may be used for tuition, fees, books, and other educational expenses.

Duration: 1 year.

Number awarded: Varies each year; recently, 50 of these scholarships, worth $72,000, were awarded.

Deadline: May of each year.

351 HAZ LA U SCHOLARSHIP PROGRAM OF THE HISPANIC SCHOLARSHIP FUND

Hispanic Scholarship Fund
Attn: Selection Committee
55 Second Street, Suite 1500
San Francisco, CA 94105
Phone: (415) 808-2376; (877) HSF-INFO; Fax: (415) 808-2302
Email: highschool@hsf.net
Web: www.hsf.net/Haz_La_U_Scholarship.aspx

Summary: To provide financial assistance to Hispanic American high school seniors who are interested in working on their first undergraduate degree.

Eligibility: Open to U.S. citizens and permanent residents (must have a permanent resident card or a passport stamped I-551) of Hispanic heritage. Applicants must be high school seniors planning to enroll full-time at an accredited institution in the United States, Puerto Rico, Guam, or the U.S. Virgin Islands as a freshman at a 4-year college or university or a first-year student at a 2-year college. They must have a GPA of 3.0 or higher. Selection is based on academic achievement, personal strengths, leadership, and financial need.

Financial data: The stipend is $15,000 or $2,500.

Duration: 1 year; nonrenewable.

Number awarded: 11 each year: 1 at $15,000 and 10 at $2,500.

Deadline: December of each year.

352 HAZAROS TABAKOGLU FUND SCHOLARSHIPS

New York Community Trust
Attn: Armenian Scholarship Administrator
909 Third Avenue
New York, NY 10022

Phone: (212) 686-0010, ext. 535; Fax: (212) 532-8528
Email: jh@nyct-cfi.org
Web: www.nycommunitytrust.org

Summary: To provide financial assistance to full-time undergraduates of Armenian descent from selected eastern states.

Eligibility: Open to full-time undergraduate students of Armenian descent. Applicants must have at least a 3.2 GPA, a record of involvement in the Armenian community, and documented financial need. They must reside in New York, New Jersey, or Connecticut.

Financial data: Stipends range from $1,000 to $6,000.

Duration: 1 year; may be renewed up to 3 additional years.

Number awarded: Several each year.

Deadline: April of each year.

353 HAZEL KNAPP ENDOWMENT SCHOLARSHIP

Epsilon Sigma Alpha International
Attn: ESA Foundation
P.O. Box 270517
Fort Collins, CO 80527
Phone: (970) 223-2824; Fax: (970) 223-4456
Email: esainfo@esaintl.com
Web: www.esaintl.com/esaf

Summary: To provide financial assistance to residents of Oregon planning to attend college in any state.

Eligibility: Open to residents of Oregon who are 1) graduating high school seniors with a GPA of 3.0 or higher or with minimum scores of 22 on the ACT or 1030 on the combined critical reading and mathematics SAT; 2) enrolled in college with a GPA of 3.0 or higher; 3) enrolled at a technical school or returning to school after an absence for retraining of job skills or obtaining a degree; or 4) engaged in online study through an accredited college, university, or vocational school. Applicants may be attending or planning to attend a school in any state and major in any field. Selection is based on character (20%), leadership (20%), service (20%), financial need (20%), and scholastic ability (20%).

Financial data: The stipend is $1,000.

Duration: 1 year; may be renewed.

Number awarded: 1 each year.

Deadline: January of each year.

354 HEALTHY LIFESTYLES SCHOLARSHIP

Stay Fit
6393 Penn Avenue
Pittsburgh, PA 15206
Phone: (412) 943-7113
Email: stayfit@fitnessexercises.tv
Web: www.fitnessexercises.tv/scholarships.php

Summary: To recognize and reward, with college scholarships, high school seniors and college freshmen who submit outstanding essays on a healthy lifestyle.

Eligibility: Open to high school seniors and first-year college students who are residents of the United States or Canada. Applicants must be younger than 25 years of age. They must submit 1) a 1,000-word essay on why a healthy lifestyle is important in school; and 2) a 500-word description of their career plans, goals, and personal ambitions. Selection is based entirely on those essays.

Financial data: The prize is a $5,000 scholarship.

Duration: The scholarship is presented annually.

Number awarded: 1 each year.

Deadline: December of each year.

355 HEATHER WESTPHAL MEMORIAL SCHOLARSHIP AWARD

International Association of Fire Chiefs
Attn: IAFC Foundation
4025 Fair Ridge Drive
Fairfax, VA 22033-2868
Phone: (703) 273-0911; Fax: (703) 273-9363
Email: foundation@iafc.org
Web: www.iafcf.org./Scholarship.htm

Summary: To provide financial assistance to female fire fighters who wish to further their academic education.

Eligibility: Open to women who are active members of state, county, provincial, municipal, community, industrial, or federal fire departments in the United States or Canada and have demonstrated proficiency as members for at least 2 years of paid or 3 years of volunteer service. Dependents of members are not eligible. Applicants must be planning to attend a recognized institution of higher education. Along with their application, they must submit a 250-word essay that includes a brief description of the course work, how the course work will benefit their fire service career and department and improve the fire service, and their financial need. Preference is given to members of the International Association of Fire Chiefs (IAFC).

Financial data: A stipend is awarded (amount not specified).

Number awarded: 1 each year.

Deadline: May of each year.

356 HELEN ABBOTT COMMUNITY SERVICE AWARDS

Arab American Institute Foundation
Attn: Executive Director
1600 K Street, N.W., Suite 601
Washington, DC 20006
Phone: (202) 429-9210; Fax: (202) 429-9214
Email: aaif@aaiusa.org
Web: www.aaiusa.org/foundation/154/student-resource-center

Summary: To recognize and reward Arab American college and high school students who can demonstrate a strong record of community service.

Eligibility: Open to U.S. citizens and permanent residents of Arab descent who are currently enrolled as either high school students or college/university students. Applicants must have a GPA of 3.0 or higher. Along with their application, they must submit 1) a resume that indicates a strong interest and commitment to community service; and 2) a 500-word essay on how their field of study is a springboard for a life of community service.

Financial data: Awards are $1,000 for college/university students or $500 for high school students.

Duration: The awards are granted annually.

Number awarded: 3 each year: 2 to college/university students and 1 to a high school student.

Deadline: March of each year.

357 HELEN KLIMEK STUDENT SCHOLARSHIP

American Legion Auxiliary
Department of New York
112 State Street, Suite 1310
Albany, NY 12207
Phone: (518) 463-1162; (800) 421-6348; Fax: (518) 449-5406
Email: alanyterry@nycap.rr.com
Web: www.deptny.org/Scholarships.htm

Summary: To provide financial assistance to New York residents who are the descendants of veterans and interested in attending college in any state.

Eligibility: Open to residents of New York who are high school seniors or graduates and attending or planning to attend an accredited college or university in any state. Applicants must be the children, grandchildren, or great-grandchildren of veterans who served during specified periods of war time. Along with their application they must submit a 700-word statement on the significance or value of volunteerism as a resource towards the positive development of their personal and professional future. Selection is based on character (20%), Americanism (15%), volunteer involvement (20%), leadership (15%), scholarship (15%), and financial need (15%). U.S. citizenship is required.

Financial data: The stipend is $1,000. Funds are paid directly to the recipient's school.

Duration: 1 year.

Number awarded: 1 each year.

Deadline: February of each year.

358 HELEN L. AND DOUGLAS ELIASON SCHOLARSHIPS

Delaware Community Foundation
Attn: Executive Vice President
100 West 10th Street, Suite 115
P.O. Box 1636
Wilmington, DE 19899
Phone: (302) 571-8004; Fax: (302) 571-1553
Email: rgentsch@delcf.org
Web: www.delcf.org/scholarships_guidelines.html

Summary: To provide financial assistance to working adults and low-income high school seniors in Delaware who are interested in pursuing additional education at a school in any state.

Eligibility: Open to residents of Delaware whose total family income is limited. Preference is given to working adults who want to improve their employment potential through continuing education, although low- and moderate-income high school students are also eligible. Applicants must be able to demonstrate that they possess the ability and motivation to achieve their academic goal. Along with their applications, they must include brief essays on their immediate educational goals, how achieving those goals will improve their lives, their need for assistance (including any special circumstances or expenses), and the least amount of assistance that will enable them to start with their educational plans. Aid is available for credit courses or, in special circumstances, non-credit courses.

Financial data: Stipends depend on the need of the recipient.

Duration: 1 year; may be renewed if the recipient continues to make good academic progress toward their goal.

Number awarded: Varies each year.

Deadline: March of each year.

359 HELEN LEE SCHOLARSHIP

Philip Jaisohn Memorial Foundation
Attn: Education and Scholarship Committee
6705 Old York Road
Philadelphia, PA 19126
Phone: (215) 224-2000; Fax: (215) 224-9164
Email: jaisohnhouse@gmail.com or jaisohnfoundation@gmail.com
Web: http://www.jaisohn.org/

Summary: To provide financial assistance to Korean American undergraduate and graduate students who demonstrate significant financial need.

Eligibility: Open to Korean American undergraduate and graduate students who are currently enrolled at a college or university in the United States. Applicants must be able to demonstrate academic excellence, leadership and service to their school and community, and financial need. Along with their application, they must submit an essay on either "Who is Dr. Jaisohn to Me," or "The Significance of Dr. Jaisohn's Ideal to Korean Americans." They must also submit a brief statement on how they can contribute to and be involved in the activities of the Philip Jaisohn Memorial Foundation. Selection is based primarily on financial need.

Financial data: The stipend is $3,000.

Duration: 1 year.

Number awarded: 1 each year.

Deadline: November of each year.

360 HELLENIC PROFESSIONAL SOCIETY OF ILLINOIS SCHOLARSHIPS

Hellenic Professional Society of Illinois
c/o George Logothetis
2326 Indian Ridge Drive
Glenview, IL 60026-1028
Phone: (847) 924-3505
Email: george.p.logothetis@accenture.com
Web: www.hpsi.org/scholar.htm

Summary: To provide financial assistance to Hellenic residents of Illinois interested in attending college or graduate school in any state.

Eligibility: Open to Illinois residents of Hellenic descent who are high school seniors, full-time undergraduates, or full- or part-time graduate students. Applicants must submit an essay describing their Hellenic family background, what being a member of the Hellenic community means to them, and how they plan to contribute to their Hellenic heritage as a professional. Selection is based on that statement, academic performance, and involvement in activities.

Financial data: Stipends are $1,000 or $500.

Duration: 1 year; nonrenewable.

Number awarded: 3 each year: 1 at $1,000 and 2 at $500.

Deadline: May of each year.

361 HELLENIC PROFESSIONAL SOCIETY OF TEXAS SCHOLARSHIPS

Hellenic Professional Society of Texas
Attn: Scholarship Committee Chair
P.O. Box 66616
Houston, TX 77266-6616
Email: petro_y@yahoo.com
Web: www.hpst.org/pages/scholarship.html

Summary: To provide financial assistance to students of Hellenic origin who are attending or planning to attend a college or graduate school in Texas.

Eligibility: Open to undergraduate and graduate students of Hellenic heritage who are attending or planning to attend a college or university in Texas. Students of non-Greek descent may be eligible if they can demonstrate clear, strong, and sustained excellence in academic studies related to Greek letters or affairs. High school seniors must have a GPA of 3.0 or higher and a combined critical reading and mathematics SAT score of 1100 or higher; current undergraduates must have a GPA of 3.2 or higher; current graduate students must have a GPA of 3.5 or higher. Applicants must submit a statement of their future professional plans and a brief description of special projects or other relevant activities they may have undertaken that demonstrate special skills.

Financial data: A stipend is awarded (amount not specified).

Duration: 1 year.

Number awarded: Varies each year; recently, 8 of these scholarships were awarded.

Deadline: December of each year.

362 HELM LEADERSHIP FELLOWS

Christian Church (Disciples of Christ)
Attn: Higher Education and Leadership Ministries
11477 Olde Cabin Road, Suite 310
St. Louis, MO 6314-7130
Phone: (314) 991-3000; Fax: (314) 991-2957
Email: helm@helmdisciples.org
Web: www.helmdisciples.org/aid/undergrad.htm

Summary: To provide financial assistance for college to members of the Christian Church (Disciples of Christ) who are interested in taking a leadership role in the church.

Eligibility: Open to high school seniors and transfers from community college who plan to be a full-time student at a 4-year college or university in the United States or Canada. Applicants must be a participating member of a congregation of the Christian Church (Disciples of Christ) who express a commitment to serve the church as a clergy or lay leader. Some preference is given to students attending colleges and universities related to the Christian Church (Disciples of Christ).

Financial data: The stipend is $2,000 per year.

Duration: 1 year; may be renewed up to 3 additional years, provided the recipient has a GPA of 2.5 or higher after the first semester of undergraduate work, 2.8 or higher after 3 semesters, and 3.0 or higher after 5 semesters.

Number awarded: Approximately 7 each year.

Deadline: March of each year.

363 HELPING HANDS BOOK SCHOLARSHIP PROGRAM

Helping Hands Foundation
Attn: Scholarship Director
4480-H South Cobb Drive
PMB 435
Smyrna, GA 30080

Summary: To provide high school seniors, undergraduates, and graduate students with funds to purchase textbooks and other study materials.

Eligibility: Open to students who are 16 years of age or older and who are planning to attend or are currently attending a 2- or 4-year college, university, or vocational/technical institute. Applicants must be enrolled as a high school, college, or graduate student in the United States, Canada, or Mexico. Along with their application, they must submit a 500-word essay describing their educational plans as they relate to their career objectives and why they feel this scholarship will help them achieve those goals. Selection is based on academic record and career potential.

Financial data: Stipends range from $100 to $1,000 per semester. Funds are intended to be used to purchase textbooks and study materials. Checks are sent directly to the recipient.

Duration: These are 1-time nonrenewable awards.

Number awarded: Up to 50 each year.

Deadline: July of each year for fall semester; December of each year for spring semester.

364 HEMOPHILIA FEDERATION OF AMERICA EDUCATIONAL SCHOLARSHIPS

Hemophilia Federation of America
Attn: Scholarship Committee
210 Seventh Street, S.E., Suite 200B
Washington, DC 20003
Phone: (202) 675-6984; (800) 230-9797; Fax: (202) 675-6983
Email: info@hemophiliafed.org
Web: hemophiliafed.org/programs-and-services/educational-scholarships

Summary: To provide financial assistance for college to students who have a blood clotting disorder.
Eligibility: Open to high school seniors and current college students who have a blood clotting disorder. Applicants must be attending or planning to attend an accredited 2- or 4-year college, university, or trade school in the United States. Along with their application, they must submit a 1-page essay on their goals and aspirations and how the blood clotting community has played a part in their lives. Financial need is also considered in the selection process.
Financial data: The stipend is $1,500 per year.
Duration: 1 year; may be renewed.
Number awarded: 6 each year.
Deadline: April of each year.

365 HERBERT FULLAM SCHOLARSHIP

Vermont Student Assistance Corporation
Attn: Scholarship Programs
10 East Allen Street
P.O. Box 2000
Winooski, VT 05404-2601
Phone: (802) 654-3798; (888) 253-4819; Fax: (802) 654-3765; TDD: (800) 281-3341 (within VT)
Email: info@vsac.org
Web: services.vsac.org/wps/wcm/connect/vsac/VSAC
Summary: To provide financial assistance to high school seniors in Vermont who plan to attend college in any state and whose parent is a police officer in the state.
Eligibility: Open to high school seniors in Vermont who are planning to enroll in a degree program at a 2- or 4-year college or university in any state. Applicants must be the child of a Vermont police officer. Along with their application, they must submit 1) a 100-word essay on their interest in and commitment to pursuing their chosen career or vocation; 2) a 100-word essay on any significant barriers that limit their access to education; and 3) a 250-word essay on their short- and long-term academic, educational, career, vocational, and/or employment goals. Selection is based on those essays and financial need.
Financial data: The stipend is $1,000.
Duration: 1 year.
Number awarded: 1 each year.
Deadline: March of each year.

366 HERBERT LEHMAN EDUCATION FUND

NAACP Legal Defense and Educational Fund
Attn: Director of Scholarship Programs
99 Hudson Street, Suite 1600
New York, NY 10013-2897
Phone: (212) 965-2265; Fax: (212) 219-1595
Email: scholarships@naacpldf.org
Web: www.naacpldf.org/scholarships
Summary: To provide financial assistance for college to high school seniors and recent graduates, especially African Americans.
Eligibility: Open to high school seniors, high school graduates, and college freshmen attending or planning to attend 4-year colleges and universities. Applicants must be dedicated to advancing the cause of civil rights, excel academically, show exceptional leadership potential, and have made an impact on their communities through service to others. They must also be able to demonstrate financial need.
Financial data: The stipend is $2,000 per year.
Duration: 1 year; may be renewed for up to 3 additional years if the student remains enrolled full-time, maintains good academic standing, and fulfills all program requirements.
Number awarded: Varies each year; recently, a total of 79 new and renewal scholarships were awarded.
Deadline: March of each year.

367 HERMIONE GRANT CALHOUN SCHOLARSHIP

National Federation of the Blind
Attn: Scholarship Committee
1800 Johnson Street
Baltimore, MD 21230
Phone: (410) 659-9314, ext. 2415; Fax: (410) 685-5653
Email: scholarships@nfb.org
Web: www.nfb.org/nfb/scholarship_program.asp
Summary: To provide financial assistance to female blind students interested in working on an undergraduate or graduate degree.
Eligibility: Open to legally blind women who are working on or planning to work full-time on an undergraduate or graduate degree. Along with their application, they must submit transcripts, standardized test scores, proof of legal blindness, 2 letters of recommendation, and a letter of endorsement from their National Federation of the Blind state president or designee. Selection is based on academic excellence, service to the community, and financial need.
Financial data: The stipend is $3,000.
Duration: 1 year; recipients may resubmit applications up to 2 additional years.
Number awarded: 1 each year.
Deadline: March of each year.

368 HEROES TRIBUTE SCHOLARSHIPS

Marine Corps Scholarship Foundation, Inc.
P.O. Box 3008
Princeton, NJ 08543-3008
Phone: (609) 921-3534; (800) 292-7777; Fax: (609) 452-2259
Email: mcsfnj@marine-scholars.org
Web: www.mcsf.com
Summary: To provide financial assistance for college to the children of Marines and Navy Corpsmen serving with the Marines who were killed on September 11, 2001 or in combat since that date.
Eligibility: Open to the children of 1) Marines and former Marines killed in the terrorist attacks on September 11, 2001; and 2) Marines and U.S. Navy Corpsmen serving with the Marines who were killed in combat since September 11, 2001. Applicants must be high school seniors, high school graduates, or current undergraduates in an accredited college, university, or postsecondary vocational/technical school. They must submit academic transcripts, documentation of their parent's service, and a 500-word essay on a topic that changes periodically. Only undergraduate study is supported. There is no maximum family income limitation. All qualified applicants receive scholarships.
Financial data: The stipend is $7,500 per year.
Duration: 4 years.
Number awarded: Varies each year; recently, 4 of these scholarships were awarded.
Deadline: March of each year.

369 HISPANIC AMERICAN COMMITMENT TO EDUCATIONAL RESOURCES (HACER) SCHOLARSHIP PROGRAM

Ronald McDonald House Charities
Attn: U.S. Scholarship Program
One Kroc Drive
Oak Brook, IL 60523
Phone: (630) 623-7048; Fax: (630) 623-7488
Email: info@rmhc.org
Web: rmhc.org/what-we-do/rmhc-u-s-scholarships
Summary: To provide financial assistance for college to Hispanic high school seniors in specified geographic areas.
Eligibility: Open to high school seniors in designated McDonald's market areas who are legal residents of the United States and have at least 1 parent of Hispanic heritage. Applicants must be planning to enroll full-time at an accredited 2- or 4-year college, university, or vocational/technical school. They must have a GPA of 2.7 or higher. Along with their application, they must submit a personal statement, up to 2 pages in length, on their Hispanic background, career goals, and desire to contribute to their community; information about unique, personal, or financial circumstances may be added. Selection is based on that statement, high school transcripts, a letter of recommendation, and financial need.
Financial data: Most awards are $1,000 per year. Funds are paid directly to the recipient's school.
Duration: 1 year; nonrenewable.
Number awarded: Varies each year; since RMHC began this program, it has awarded more than $37 million in scholarships.
Deadline: February of each year.

370 HISPANIC COLLEGE FUND SCHOLARSHIPS

Hispanic College Fund
Attn: Scholarship Processing
1301 K Street, N.W., Suite 450-A West
Washington, DC 20005
Phone: (202) 296-5400; (800) 644-4223; Fax: (202) 296-3774
Email: hcf-info@hispanicfund.org

Web: scholarships.hispanicfund.org/applications
Summary: To provide financial assistance to Hispanic American undergraduate students.
Eligibility: Open to U.S. citizens and permanent residents of Hispanic background (at least 1 grandparent must be 100% Hispanic) who are enrolled or planning to enroll at an accredited college or university in the 50 states or Puerto Rico as a full-time student. Applicants must have a GPA of 3.0 or higher and be able to demonstrate financial need.
Financial data: Stipends range from $500 to $5,000, depending on the need of the recipient. Funds are paid directly to the recipient's college or university to help cover tuition and fees.
Duration: 1 year; recipients may reapply.
Number awarded: Varies each year; recently, a total of $1 million was available for these scholarships.
Deadline: March of each year.

371 H-MART LEADERSHIP SCHOLARSHIP

Philip Jaisohn Memorial Foundation
Attn: Education and Scholarship Committee
6705 Old York Road
Philadelphia, PA 19126
Phone: (215) 224-2000
Web: www.jaisohn.org/zeroboard/view/php?id=Announcements&no=34
Summary: To provide financial assistance to Korean American undergraduate and graduate students who demonstrate involvement in extracurricular, athletic, and community activities.
Eligibility: Open to Korean American undergraduate and graduate students who are currently enrolled at a college or university in the United States. Applicants must be able to demonstrate academic excellence, leadership and service to their school and community, and financial need. Along with their application, they must submit an essay on either "Who is Dr. Jaisohn to Me," or "The Significance of Dr. Jaisohn's Ideal to Korean Americans." They must also submit a brief statement on how they can contribute to and be involved in the activities of the Philip Jaisohn Memorial Foundation. Selection is based primarily on leadership in extracurricular activities, varsity sports, or community activities.
Financial data: The stipend is $3,000.
Duration: 1 year.
Number awarded: 1 each year.
Deadline: November of each year.

372 HOOD GOOD SPORT SCHOLARSHIP

HP Hood LLC
Attn: Good Sport Scholarship
Six Kimball Lane
Lynnfield, MA 01940
Phone: (800) 662-4468
Web: www.hood.com/promo/goodsportfinal
Summary: To provide financial assistance to high school seniors in New England who have participated in a varsity sport and plan to attend college in any state.
Eligibility: Open to seniors graduating from high schools in the New England states who have participated in at least 1 varsity sport. Applicants must be planning to attend an accredited 2- or 4-year college or university in any state. They must have a GPA of 3.0 or higher and a record of volunteer work in their community. Along with their application, they must submit a 250-word essay on why they are a "good sport" on and off the field. Entries are posted online and the public votes for the outstanding students. The 15 students in each state who receive the most votes are then interviewed to select the winners. Financial need is not considered.
Financial data: The stipend is $5,000.
Duration: 1 year.
Number awarded: 18 each year: 3 in each of the New England states.
Deadline: March.

373 HOPE GRANTS FOR CERTIFICATE AND DIPLOMA PROGRAMS

Georgia Student Finance Commission
Attn: Scholarships and Grants Division
2082 East Exchange Place, Suite 200
Tucker, GA 30084-5305
Phone: (770) 724-9000; (800) 505-GSFC; Fax: (770) 724-9089
Email: gsfcinfo@gsfc.org
Web: www.gacollege411.org
Summary: To provide financial assistance to residents of Georgia who are interested in earning a certificate or diploma at a public technical institute in the state.
Eligibility: Open to Georgia residents who are working on a certificate or diploma in a non-degree program of study at a public institution in the state. The certificate or degree program must be approved by the Georgia Department of Technical and Adult education or be a comparable program approved by the Board of Regents. Continuing education programs are not eligible.
Financial data: These grants pay tuition and mandatory fees at public technical institutes in Georgia, along with a book allowance of up to $300 per year.
Duration: This assistance may be used for a total of 63 semester hours of study.
Number awarded: Varies each year; recently, 108,387 of these grants were awarded.
Deadline: Applications must be submitted on or before the last day of the academic term.

374 HOPE SCHOLARSHIPS FOR DEGREE-SEEKING STUDENTS

Georgia Student Finance Commission
Attn: Scholarships and Grants Division
2082 East Exchange Place, Suite 200
Tucker, GA 30084-5305
Phone: (770) 724-9000; (800) 505-GSFC; Fax: (770) 724-9089
Email: gsfcinfo@gsfc.org
Web: www.gacollege411.org
Summary: To provide financial assistance to outstanding students who are attending or planning to attend a college or university in Georgia.
Eligibility: Open to Georgia residents who are enrolled or planning to enroll full-time at a college or university within the state. Students who are applying as seniors at eligible high schools must have at least a 3.0 cumulative GPA if they earned a college preparatory diploma or a 3.2 cumulative GPA for another diploma type. Students who complete an eligible home study program are eligible if they have a GPA of 3.0 or higher. Students who graduate from an ineligible high school or home study program may also be eligible if they 1) score in the national composite 85th percentile or higher on the SAT or ACT tests; or 2) complete the first year of college with a GPA of 3.0 or higher. Students who are applying for the first time as college students must have earned a GPA of 3.0 or higher in college regardless of their high school GPA. U.S. citizenship or permanent resident status is required.
Financial data: HOPE Scholars who attend public colleges or universities receive full tuition and mandatory fees plus a book allowance of $300 per academic year. The stipend for HOPE Scholarships at private colleges and universities is $3,500 per year; funds may be used only for tuition and mandatory fees.
Duration: 1 year; may be renewed for up to 3 additional years if the recipient maintains a cumulative GPA of 3.0 or higher in college.
Number awarded: Varies each year; recently, 106,187 of these scholarships (90,604 at public institutions and 15,583 at private institutions) were awarded.
Deadline: Applications must be submitted on or before the last day of the academic term.

375 HORATIO ALGER NATIONAL SCHOLARSHIP PROGRAM

Horatio Alger Association of Distinguished Americans, Inc.
99 Canal Center Plaza
Alexandria, VA 22314
Phone: (703) 684-9444; Fax: (703) 548-3822
Email: horatioaa@aol.com
Web: www.horatioalger.com/scholarships/program_national.cfm
Summary: To provide financial assistance for college to high school seniors who can demonstrate integrity and perseverance in overcoming adversity.
Eligibility: Open to seniors at high schools in all 50 states, the District of Columbia, and Puerto Rico. Applicants must be planning to enroll at a college in any state to work on a bachelor's degree (they may begin at a 2-year college and then transfer to a 4-year institution). They must be U.S. citizens, be able to demonstrate critical financial need ($50,000 or less adjusted gross income per family), have a GPA of 2.0 or higher, and have a record of involvement in co-curricular and community activities. Along with their application, they must submit 1) an essay of 250 to 350 words on their career goals and the importance of a college education in attaining those goals; 2) an essay of 150 to 200 words on the life of a member of the Horatio Alger Association and how they have applied the virtues exemplified in the member's life story in their own life; and 3) information on the adversities they have encountered. Examples of adversity include having been in foster care or a ward of the state; having been homeless; experiencing the death, incarceration, or abandonment of a parent or guardian; living

in a household where alcohol or drugs are or were abused; having a physical or mental disability or serious illness; or suffering from physical or mental abuse.
Financial data: The stipend is $5,000 per year.
Duration: 4 years.
Number awarded: 104 each year: 2 in each state, the District of Columbia, and Puerto Rico.
Deadline: October of each year.

376 HOWARD P. RAWLINGS EDUCATIONAL ASSISTANCE GRANTS

Maryland Higher Education Commission
Attn: Office of Student Financial Assistance
839 Bestgate Road, Suite 400
Annapolis, MD 21401-3013
Phone: (410) 260-4565; (800) 974-1024, ext. 4565; Fax: (410) 260-3200; TDD: (800) 735-2258
Email: osfamail@mhec.state.md.us
Web: www.mhec.state.md.us/financialAid/ProgramDescriptions/prog_ea.asp
Summary: To provide financial assistance to undergraduate students in Maryland.
Eligibility: Open to Maryland residents who are enrolled or planning to enroll full-time as an undergraduate student at a Maryland 2- or 4-year college or university. Financial need must be documented.
Financial data: At 4-year institutions, the amount of the grant equals 40% of the financial need as calculated by the Office of Students Financial Assistance (OSFA); at community colleges, the amount of the grant equals 60% of the financial need. Awards are limited to a minimum of $400 and a maximum of $3,000 per year. The total amount of all state awards may not exceed the cost of attendance as determined by the school's financial aid office or $19,000, whichever is less.
Duration: 1 year; recipients may reapply for up to 3 additional years if they maintain satisfactory academic progress and continue to demonstrate financial need.
Number awarded: Varies each year.
Deadline: February of each year.

377 HOWARD P. RAWLINGS GUARANTEED ACCESS GRANTS

Maryland Higher Education Commission
Attn: Office of Student Financial Assistance
839 Bestgate Road, Suite 400
Annapolis, MD 21401-3013
Phone: (410) 260-4555; (800) 974-1024, ext. 4555; Fax: (410) 260-3200; TDD: (800) 735-2258
Email: tlowe@mhec.state.md.us
Web: www.mhec.state.md.us/financialAid/ProgramDescriptions/prog_ga.asp
Summary: To provide financial assistance to needy undergraduate students in Maryland.
Eligibility: Open to seniors graduating from high schools in Maryland and planning to enroll as full-time undergraduate students in a program leading to a degree, diploma, or certificate at a 2- or 4-year college or university in the state. Applicants must have a high school GPA of 2.5 or higher and be able to demonstrate financial need. Currently, the maximum allowable total income is $14,079 for a family of 1, rising to $48,113 for a family of 8 plus $4,862 for each additional family member.
Financial data: Awards equal 100% of financial need, ranging from $400 to $13,700 per year. The total amount of all state awards may not exceed the cost of attendance as determined by the school's financial aid office or $19,000, whichever is less.
Duration: 1 year; recipients may reapply for up to 3 additional years if they maintain satisfactory academic progress and continue to demonstrate financial need.
Number awarded: Varies each year.
Deadline: February of each year.

378 HOWARD STILES NUCHOLS SCHOLARSHIP

United Daughters of the Confederacy–Virginia Division
c/o Janice Busic, Education Committee Chair
P.O. Box 356
Honaker, VA 24260
Email: 2vp@vaudc.org
Web: vaudc.org/gift.html
Summary: To provide financial assistance for college to Confederate descendants from Virginia.
Eligibility: Open to residents of Virginia who are 1) lineal descendants of Confederates, or 2) collateral descendants and also members of the Children of the Confederacy or the United Daughters of the Confederacy (UDC). Applicants must submit proof of the Confederate military record of at least 1 ancestor, with the company and regiment in which he served. They must also submit a personal letter pledging to make the best possible use of the scholarship; describing their health, social, family, religious, and fraternal connections within the community; and reflecting on what a Southern heritage means to them (using the term "War Between the States" in lieu of "Civil War"). They must have a GPA of 3.0 or higher and be able to demonstrate financial need. Preference is given to applicants who are current or former members of the Virginia division of the Children of the Confederacy.
Financial data: The amount of the stipend depends on the availability of funds. Payment is made directly to the college or university the recipient attends.
Duration: 1 year; may be renewed up to 3 additional years if the recipient maintains a GPA of 3.0 or higher.
Number awarded: This scholarship is offered whenever a prior recipient graduates or is no longer eligible.
Deadline: April of the years in which the scholarship is available.

379 H.S. AND ANGELINE LEWIS SCHOLARSHIPS

American Legion Auxiliary
Department of Wisconsin
Attn: Education Chair
2930 American Legion Drive
P.O. Box 140
Portage, WI 53901-0140
Phone: (608) 745-0124; (866) 664-3863; Fax: (608) 745-1947
Email: alawi@amlegionauxwi.org
Web: www.amlegionauxwi.org/Scholarships.htm
Summary: To provide financial assistance to Wisconsin residents who are related to veterans or members of the American Legion Auxiliary and interested in working on an undergraduate or graduate degree at a school in any state.
Eligibility: Open to the children, wives, and widows of veterans who are high school seniors or graduates and have a GPA of 3.5 or higher. Grandchildren and great-grandchildren of members of the American Legion Auxiliary are also eligible. Applicants must be residents of Wisconsin and interested in working on an undergraduate or graduate degree at a school in any state. Along with their application, they must submit a 300-word essay on "Education–An Investment in the Future." Financial need is considered in the selection process.
Financial data: The stipend is $1,000.
Duration: 1 year; nonrenewable.
Number awarded: 6 each year: 1 to a graduate student and 5 to undergraduates.
Deadline: March of each year.

380 H.W. ALMEN-WEST OKC ROTARY SCHOLARSHIP

Oklahoma City Community Foundation
Attn: Scholarship Administrator
1000 North Broadway
P.O. Box 1146
Oklahoma City, OK 73101
Phone: (405) 235-5603; Fax: (405) 235-5612
Email: a.rose@occf.org
Web: www.occf.org/scholarships/almen.html
Summary: To provide financial assistance to high school seniors in Oklahoma who plan to attend college in any state.
Eligibility: Open to seniors graduating from high schools in Oklahoma with a GPA of 2.75 or higher. Applicants must be planning to attend a college, university, community college, or technology center as a full-time student. Along with their application, they must submit a 500-word essay on the object of Rotary in their community. Their family income may not exceed $100,000 per year. Selection is based on the essay (50%), academic achievement (20%), academic plan (10%), and community service (20%).
Financial data: Stipends are $4,000 for students at colleges and universities or $2,000 for students at community colleges or technology centers.
Duration: 1 year; nonrenewable.
Number awarded: Approximately 20 each year.
Deadline: February of each year.

381 IBE/CCC SCHOLARSHIP PROGRAM

Indiana Black Expo, Inc.
Attn: Scholarship Program
3145 North Meridian
Indianapolis, IN 46208
Phone: (317) 925-2702; Fax: (317) 925-6624
Email: communications@indianablackexpo.com
Web: www.indianablackexpo.com/programs-youth.asp

Summary: To provide financial assistance to high school seniors in Indiana who are planning to enroll at a college or university in any state, especially at an Historically Black College or University (HBCU).

Eligibility: Open to seniors graduating from high schools in Indiana and planning to enroll full-time at a college or university in any state. Applicants must have a GPA of 2.5 or higher and a family income of $30,000 per year or less. Special consideration is given to students who 1) are the first in their family to attend college; or 2) plan to attend an HBCU. Along with their application, they must submit a 1-page essay on how this scholarship will help them achieve their educational goals and benefit their community. Selection is based on academic achievement, extracurricular activities, and financial need.

Financial data: Stipends are $1,000 for undergraduates or $1,500 for graduate students.

Duration: 1 year.

Number awarded: Varies each year; recently, 58 of these scholarships were awarded. At least 2 scholarships are reserved for students attending an HBCU. Since its establishment, this program has awarded nearly $2 million in scholarships.

Deadline: April of each year.

382 ICW UPS FOUNDATION SCHOLARSHIPS

Independent Colleges of Washington
600 Stewart Street, Suite 600
Seattle, WA 98101
Phone: (206) 623-4494; Fax: (206) 625-9621
Email: info@icwashington.org
Web: www.icwashington.org/scholarships/index.html

Summary: To provide financial assistance to residents of any state enrolled at colleges and universities that are members of the Independent Colleges of Washington (ICW).

Eligibility: Open to residents of any state enrolled at ICW-member colleges and universities. Selection is based on merit as determined by the institution. No application is required; each ICW institution makes a selection from all of its students.

Financial data: Stipends range from $2,500 to $3,500.

Duration: 1 year; nonrenewable.

Number awarded: 10 each year: 1 at each of the 10 ICW colleges and universities.

Deadline: Each institution sets its own deadline.

383 IDAHO FREEDOM SCHOLARSHIPS

Idaho State Board of Education
Len B. Jordan Office Building
650 West State Street, Room 307
P.O. Box 83720
Boise, ID 83720-0037
Phone: (208) 332-1574; Fax: (208) 334-2632
Email: scholarshiphelp@osbe.idaho.gov
Web: www.boardofed.idaho.gov/scholarships/freedom.asp

Summary: To provide financial assistance for college to dependent children of Idaho veterans who are deceased or listed as prisoners of war or missing in action.

Eligibility: Open to dependent children of Idaho veterans who have been determined by the federal government to have been 1) killed in action or died of injuries or wounds sustained in action; 2) prisoners of war (POW); or 3) missing in action (MIA) in southeast Asia (including Korea) or any area of armed conflict in which the United States is a party.

Financial data: Each scholarship provides a full waiver of tuition and fees at public institutions of higher education or public vocational schools within Idaho, an allowance of $500 per semester for books, and on-campus housing and subsistence.

Duration: Benefits are available for a maximum of 36 months.

Number awarded: Varies each year.

Deadline: Deadline not specified.

384 IDAHO GOVERNOR'S CUP SCHOLARSHIP

Idaho State Board of Education
Len B. Jordan Office Building
650 West State Street, Room 307
P.O. Box 83720
Boise, ID 83720-0037
Phone: (208) 332-1574; Fax: (208) 334-2632
Email: scholarshiphelp@osbe.idaho.gov
Web: www.boardofed.idaho.gov/scholarships/challenge.asp

Summary: To provide financial assistance to outstanding high school seniors in Idaho who wish to attend a postsecondary institution in the state.

Eligibility: Open to graduating high school seniors who are U.S. citizens, Idaho residents, and planning to enroll full-time at an eligible postsecondary educational institution in the state. Applicants must have maintained a GPA of 2.8 or better, must take the ACT or SAT examinations, and should have demonstrated a commitment to public service.

Financial data: The stipend is $3,000 per year.

Duration: 1 year; may be renewed for up to 3 additional years.

Number awarded: Varies each year; recently, 19 of these scholarships were awarded.

Deadline: January of each year.

385 IDAHO LEVERAGING EDUCATIONAL ASSISTANCE STATE PARTNERSHIP PROGRAM

Idaho State Board of Education
Len B. Jordan Office Building
650 West State Street, Room 307
P.O. Box 83720
Boise, ID 83720-0037
Phone: (208) 332-1574; Fax: (208) 334-2632
Email: scholarshiphelp@osbe.idaho.gov
Web: www.boardofed.idaho.gov/scholarships/leap.asp

Summary: To provide financial assistance to students from any state attending a college or university in Idaho.

Eligibility: Open to students from any state attending a designated public or private college or university within Idaho. Applicants must have financial need; they may be enrolled part-time.

Financial data: Awards range up to $5,000 per year for full-time students.

Number awarded: Varies each year; recently, approximately 1,800 students received these grants.

Deadline: Deadline not specified.

386 IDAHO MINORITY AND "AT RISK" STUDENT SCHOLARSHIP

Idaho State Board of Education
Len B. Jordan Office Building
650 West State Street, Room 307
P.O. Box 83720
Boise, ID 83720-0037
Phone: (208) 332-1574; Fax: (208) 334-2632
Email: scholarshiphelp@osbe.idaho.gov
Web: www.boardofed.idaho.gov/scholarships/minority.asp

Summary: To provide financial assistance to "at risk" high school seniors in Idaho who plan to attend college in the state.

Eligibility: Open to residents of Idaho who are graduates of high schools in the state. Applicants must meet at least 3 of the following 5 requirements: 1) have a disability; 2) be a member of an ethnic minority group historically underrepresented in higher education in Idaho; 3) have substantial financial need; 4) be a first-generation college student; 5) be a migrant farm worker or a dependent of a farm worker. U.S. citizenship is required.

Financial data: The maximum stipend is $3,000 per year.

Duration: 1 year; may be renewed for up to 3 additional years.

Number awarded: Approximately 40 each year.

Deadline: Deadline not specified.

387 IDAHO OPPORTUNITY SCHOLARSHIP

Idaho State Board of Education
Len B. Jordan Office Building
650 West State Street, Room 307
P.O. Box 83720
Boise, ID 83720-0037

Phone: (208) 332-1574; Fax: (208) 334-2632
Email: scholarshiphelp@osbe.idaho.gov
Web: www.boardofed.idaho.gov/scholarships/challenge.asp
Summary: To provide financial assistance to high school seniors in Idaho who have significant financial need and wish to attend a postsecondary institution in the state.
Eligibility: Open to seniors graduating from high schools in Idaho and recipients of GED certification in the state. Applicants must be planning to enroll full-time at an eligible postsecondary educational institution in Idaho. They must have applied for federal financial aid but still demonstrate need for further assistance.
Financial data: A stipend is awarded (amount not specified). This program is designed to be a "last dollar" mechanism, so it provides support only after students have been awarded federal financial aid and have contributed their own or their families' funding.
Duration: 1 year; may be renewed, provided the recipient maintains satisfactory academic progress.
Number awarded: Varies each year.
Deadline: February of each year.

388 IDAHO PUBLIC SAFETY OFFICER DEPENDENT SCHOLARSHIP

Idaho State Board of Education
Len B. Jordan Office Building
650 West State Street, Room 307
P.O. Box 83720
Boise, ID 83720-0037
Phone: (208) 332-1574; Fax: (208) 334-2632
Email: scholarshiphelp@osbe.idaho.gov
Web: www.boardofed.idaho.gov/scholarships/freedom.asp
Summary: To provide financial assistance for college to dependents of disabled or deceased Idaho public safety officers.
Eligibility: Open to dependents of full-time Idaho public safety officers employed in the state who were killed or disabled in the line of duty.
Financial data: Each scholarship provides a full waiver of tuition and fees at public institutions of higher education or public vocational schools within Idaho, an allowance of $500 per semester for books, on-campus housing, and a campus meal plan.
Duration: Benefits are available for a maximum of 36 months.
Number awarded: Varies each year; recently, 4 of these scholarships were awarded.
Deadline: Deadline not specified.

389 ILLINOIS FALLEN HEROES SCHOLARSHIP

Office of the State Treasurer
Attn: Bright Start Account Representative
400 West Monroe Street, Suite 401
Springfield, IL 62704
Phone: (217) 782-6540; Fax: (217) 524-3822
Email: fallenheroes@treasurer.state.il.us
Web: www.treasurer.il.gov/programs/scholarships/fallen-heroes.aspx
Summary: To provide financial assistance for college to the children of Illinois service members killed in Iraq.
Eligibility: Open to the children of fallen Illinois service members who served in Operation Iraqi Freedom or Operation Enduring Freedom. Applicants must be U.S. citizens of any age under 30 years. They may be planning to attend an accredited college or university anywhere in the United States or at selected institutions abroad. Children of all Illinois active and Reserve servicemen and women are eligible.
Financial data: The stipend is $2,500. Funds are deposited into an age-based Bright Start portfolio (the Illinois 529 program) and are available when the student reaches college age. The older the child, the more conservative the investment becomes. Funds may be used only for tuition, fees, room, and board, and must be spent before the child reaches 30 years of age.
Duration: 1 year.
Number awarded: Varies each year.
Deadline: May of each year.

390 ILLINOIS GENERAL ASSEMBLY LEGISLATIVE SCHOLARSHIPS

Illinois State Board of Education
Attn: Governmental Relations
100 North First Street
Springfield, IL 62777-0001
Phone: (217) 782-4321; (866) 262-6663; Fax: (217) 524-4928; TDD: (217) 782-1900
Web: www.isbe.state.il.us/gov_relations/html/scholarships.htm
Summary: To provide financial assistance for college to high school seniors in Illinois who are sponsored by members of the state legislature.
Eligibility: Open to high school seniors in Illinois. Each year, Illinois law provides for each state legislator to award scholarships to state-supported universities. High school seniors in Illinois can apply for these scholarships, but they must be a resident within the legislative district of the awarding legislator and contact their state senator or state representative for information on the application process.
Financial data: A stipend is awarded (amount not specified).
Duration: 1 year, 2 years, or 4 years.
Number awarded: Each state legislator awards 1 4-year scholarship, 2 2-year scholarships, or 4 1-year scholarships.
Deadline: Deadline not specified.

391 ILLINOIS GRANT PROGRAM FOR DEPENDENTS OF CORRECTIONAL OFFICERS

Illinois Student Assistance Commission
Attn: Scholarship and Grant Services
1755 Lake Cook Road
Deerfield, IL 60015-5209
Phone: (847) 948-8550; (800) 899-ISAC; Fax: (847) 831-8549; TDD: (800) 526-0844
Email: collegezone@isac.org
Web: www.collegezone.com/studentzone/407_635.htm
Summary: To provide financial assistance to the children or spouses of disabled or deceased Illinois correctional workers who plan to attend college in the state.
Eligibility: Open to the spouses and children of Illinois correctional officers who were at least 90% disabled or killed in the line of duty. Applicants must be enrolled on at least a half-time basis as an undergraduate at an approved Illinois public or private 2- or 4-year college or university. They need not be Illinois residents at the time of application. U.S. citizenship or eligible noncitizen status is required.
Financial data: The grants provide full payment of tuition and mandatory fees at approved public colleges in Illinois or an equivalent amount at private colleges.
Duration: Up to 8 academic semesters or 12 academic quarters of study.
Number awarded: Varies each year.
Deadline: September of each year for the academic year; February of each year for spring semester or winter or spring quarter; June of each year for summer term.

392 ILLINOIS GRANT PROGRAM FOR DEPENDENTS OF POLICE OR FIRE OFFICERS

Illinois Student Assistance Commission
Attn: Scholarship and Grant Services
1755 Lake Cook Road
Deerfield, IL 60015-5209
Phone: (847) 948-8550; (800) 899-ISAC; Fax: (847) 831-8549; TDD: (800) 526-0844
Email: collegezone@isac.org
Web: www.collegezone.com/studentzone/407_633.htm
Summary: To provide financial assistance to the children or spouses of disabled or deceased Illinois police or fire officers who plan to attend college or graduate school in the state.
Eligibility: Open to the spouses and children of Illinois police and fire officers who were at least 90% disabled or killed in the line of duty. Applicants must be enrolled on at least a half-time basis in either undergraduate or graduate study at an approved Illinois public or private 2- or 4-year college, university, or hospital school. They need not be Illinois residents at the time of application. U.S. citizenship or eligible noncitizen status is required.
Financial data: The grants provide full payment of tuition and mandatory fees at approved public colleges in Illinois or an equivalent amount at private colleges.
Duration: Up to 8 academic semesters or 12 academic quarters of study.
Number awarded: Varies each year.
Deadline: September of each year for the academic year; February of each year for spring semester or winter or spring quarter; June of each year for summer term.

393 ILLINOIS MIA/POW SCHOLARSHIP

Illinois Department of Veterans' Affairs
833 South Spring Street
P.O. Box 19432
Springfield, IL 62794-9432
Phone: (217) 782-6641; (800) 437-9824 (within IL); Fax: (217) 524-0344; TDD: (217) 524-4645
Email: webmail@dva.state.il.us
Web: www.veterans.illinois.gov/benefits/education.htm

Summary: To provide financial assistance for 1) the undergraduate education of Illinois dependents of disabled or deceased veterans or those listed as prisoners of war or missing in action; and 2) the rehabilitation or education of disabled dependents of those veterans.

Eligibility: Open to the spouses, natural children, legally adopted children, or stepchildren of a veteran or servicemember who 1) has been declared by the U.S. Department of Defense or the U.S. Department of Veterans Affairs to be permanently disabled from service-connected causes with 100% disability, deceased as the result of a service-connected disability, a prisoner of war, or missing in action; and 2) at the time of entering service was an Illinois resident or was an Illinois resident within 6 months of entering such service. Special support is available for dependents who are disabled.

Financial data: An eligible dependent is entitled to full payment of tuition and certain fees at any Illinois state-supported college, university, or community college. In lieu of that benefit, an eligible dependent who has a physical, mental, or developmental disability is entitled to receive a grant to be used to cover the cost of treating the disability at 1 or more appropriate therapeutic, rehabilitative, or educational facilities. For all recipients, the total benefit cannot exceed the cost equivalent of 4 calendar years of full-time enrollment, including summer terms, at the University of Illinois.

Duration: This scholarship may be used for a period equivalent to 4 calendar years, including summer terms. Dependents have 12 years from the initial term of study to complete the equivalent of 4 calendar years. Disabled dependents who elect to use the grant for rehabilitative purposes may do so as long as the total benefit does not exceed the cost equivalent of 4 calendar years of full-time enrollment at the University of Illinois.

Number awarded: Varies each year.

Deadline: Deadline not specified.

394 ILLINOIS MONETARY AWARD PROGRAM

Illinois Student Assistance Commission
Attn: Scholarship and Grant Services
1755 Lake Cook Road
Deerfield, IL 60015-5209
Phone: (847) 948-8550; (800) 899-ISAC; Fax: (847) 831-8549; TDD: (800) 526-0844
Email: collegezone@isac.org
Web: www.collegezone.com/studentzone/407_445.htm

Summary: To provide financial assistance to undergraduate students in Illinois.

Eligibility: Open to Illinois residents who are enrolled for at least 3 credit hours per term as an undergraduate student at an approved institution of higher education in the state. Applicants must be able to demonstrate financial need. High school grades and test scores are not considered in the selection process. U.S. citizenship or eligible noncitizenship status is required.

Financial data: The actual dollar amount of the award depends on financial need and the cost of the recipient's schooling; in no case does the award exceed the actual cost of tuition and fees or $4,968 per year, whichever is less. The funds may be used only for tuition and mandatory fees; funds cannot be spent on books, travel, or housing. All awards are paid directly to the recipient's school.

Duration: 1 year; may be renewed until completion of 135 credit hours.

Number awarded: Varies each year.

Deadline: Funding for this program is limited. To increase your chances of receiving funding, apply as soon after the beginning of January as possible.

395 ILLINOIS SHERIFFS' ASSOCIATION COLLEGE SCHOLARSHIP PROGRAM

Illinois Sheriffs' Association
401 East Washington, Suite 1000
Springfield, IL 62701
Phone: (217) 753-2372; Fax: (217) 753-2405
Email: ContactUs@ilsheriff.org
Web: www.ilsheriff.org/youth_programs_0.aspx

Summary: To provide financial assistance for college to students in Illinois.

Eligibility: Open to residents of Illinois who are attending or planning to attend an accredited college or university in the state as a full-time undergraduate student. Immediate family members of county sheriffs in Illinois are ineligible, but families of sheriff's department employees may apply. Applicants must submit 1) transcripts from high school and/or college; 2) a letter of recommendation from a principal, counselor, or department head; 3) a personal letter explaining their reasons for applying and plans for the future; and 4) an essay, up to 350 words, on a topic that changes annually but recently required students to describe the biggest problem affecting the youth in their county and their suggestions to their sheriff for dealing with the problem. Selection is based on academic honors and awards, extracurricular activities, letters of recommendation, and financial need.

Financial data: The stipend ranges from $500 to $1,000. Funds are paid directly to the recipient's college or university.

Duration: 1 year; may be renewed.

Number awarded: At least 102 each year. Awards are distributed so that each county with an associate membership in the Illinois Sheriffs' Association is allotted 1 scholarship and 1 additional scholarship is awarded for every 500 total associated members.

Deadline: March of each year.

396 ILLINOIS VETERAN GRANT PROGRAM

Illinois Student Assistance Commission
Attn: Scholarship and Grant Services
1755 Lake Cook Road
Deerfield, IL 60015-5209
Phone: (847) 948-8550; (800) 899-ISAC; Fax: (847) 831-8549; TDD: (800) 526-0844
Email: collegezone@isac.org
Web: www.collegezone.com/studentzone/407_629.htm

Summary: To provide financial assistance to Illinois veterans Guard who are interested in attending college or graduate school in the state.

Eligibility: Open to Illinois residents who served in the U.S. armed forces (including members of the Reserves and the Illinois National Guard) for at least 1 year on active duty and have been honorably discharged. The 1-year service requirement does not apply to veterans who 1) served in a foreign country in a time of hostilities in that country; 2) were medically discharged for service-related reasons; or 3) were discharged prior to August 11, 1967. Applicants must have been Illinois residents for at least 6 months before entering service and they must have returned to Illinois within 6 months after separation from service. Current members of the Reserve Officer Training Corps are not eligible.

Financial data: This program pays all tuition and certain fees at all Illinois public colleges, universities, and community colleges.

Duration: This scholarship may be used for the equivalent of up to 4 years of full-time enrollment, provided the recipient maintains the minimum GPA required by their college or university.

Number awarded: Varies each year.

Deadline: Applications may be submitted at any time.

397 IMAGINE AMERICA SCHOLARSHIPS

Career College Association
Attn: Imagine America Foundation
1101 Connecticut Avenue, N.W., Suite 901
Washington, DC 20036
Phone: (202) 336-6719; Fax: (202) 408-8102
Email: torianb@imagine-america.org
Web: www.imagine-america.org/scholarship/01-about-scholarship.asp

Summary: To provide financial assistance to high school seniors interested in attending a career college.

Eligibility: Open to seniors graduating from high schools that are enrolled in the Imagine America program. Applicants must be interested in attending 1 of the more than 500 career colleges that participate in the program. They must have a GPA of 2.5 or higher. All applications are submitted online to the college that the student wishes to attend. Selection is based on likelihood of successful completion of postsecondary education, demonstrated voluntary community service during senior year of high school, and financial need.

Financial data: The stipend is $1,000. Funds must be used for payment of tuition at a participating career college.

Duration: 1 year.

Number awarded: Varies each year; up to 3 students at each enrolled high school may receive a scholarship.

Deadline: December of each year.

398 INA BRUDNICK SCHOLARSHIP AWARD

Great Comebacks Award Program
c/o ConvaTec Customer Interaction Center
100 Headquarters Park Drive
Skillman, NJ 08558
Phone: (800) 422-8811
Email: info@greatcomebacks.com
Web: www.greatcomebacks.com/us/programs/index.shtml

Summary: To provide financial assistance to college students with an inflammatory bowel disease (IBD) or other related physical conditions.

Eligibility: Open to people between 17 and 24 years of age who have undergone an ostomy and/or have an IBD (Crohn's disease or ulcerative colitis). Applicants must be able to demonstrate financial need. Along with their application, they must submit statements on how their life has been changed or affected by their medical condition and their ostomy, how their comeback has positively affected their life and those around them, and what advice they would give to others struggling with similar medical conditions or facing ostomy surgery.

Financial data: The stipend is $1,000.

Duration: 1 year.

Number awarded: 4 each year: 1 from each region of the country.

Deadline: July of each year.

399 INDEPENDENT COLLEGE FUND OF MARYLAND LEADERSHIP SCHOLARSHIPS

Independent College Fund of Maryland
Attn: Director of Programs and Scholarships
3225 Ellerslie Avenue, Suite C160
Baltimore, MD 21218-3519
Phone: (443) 997-5703; Fax: (443) 997-2740
Email: LSubot@jhmi.edu
Web: www.i-fundinfo.org/scholarships/business-scholarships.html

Summary: To provide financial assistance to students from any state at member institutions of the Independent College Fund of Maryland who have demonstrated outstanding leadership on campus or in the community.

Eligibility: Open to students from any state currently enrolled at member institutions. Applicants must have demonstrated outstanding leadership qualities on campus and/or in the community. They must have a GPA of 3.2 or higher and be able to demonstrate financial need.

Financial data: The stipend is $5,000.

Duration: 1 year.

Number awarded: 10 each year: 1 at each member institution.

Deadline: Deadline not specified.

400 INDIANA CHILD OF VETERAN AND PUBLIC SAFETY OFFICER SUPPLEMENTAL GRANT PROGRAM

State Student Assistance Commission of Indiana
Attn: Grant Division
150 West Market Street, Suite 500
Indianapolis, IN 46204-2811
Phone: (317) 232-2350; (888) 528-4719 (within IN); Fax: (317) 232-3260
Email: grants@ssaci.state.in.us
Web: www.in.gov/ssaci/2338.htm

Summary: To provide financial assistance to residents of Indiana who are the children or spouses of specified categories of deceased or disabled veterans or public safety officers and interested in attending college or graduate school in the state.

Eligibility: Open to 1) children of disabled Indiana veterans; 2) children and spouses of members of the Indiana National Guard killed while serving on state active duty; and 3) children and spouses of Indiana public safety officers killed in the line of duty. The veterans portion is open to Indiana residents who are the natural or adopted children of veterans who served in the active-duty U.S. armed forces during a period of wartime. Applicants may be of any age; parents must have lived in Indiana for at least 3 years during their lifetime. The veteran parent must also 1) have a service-connected disability as determined by the U.S. Department of Veterans Affairs or the Department of Defense; 2) have received a Purple Heart Medal; or 3) have been a resident of Indiana at the time of entry into the service and declared a POW or MIA after January 1, 1960. Students at the Indiana Soldiers' and Sailors' Children's Home are also eligible. The National Guard portion of this program is open to children and spouses of members of the Indiana National Guard who suffered a service-connected death while serving on state active duty. The public safety officer portion of this program is open to 1) the children and spouses of regular law enforcement officers, regular fire fighters, volunteer fire fighters, county police reserve officers, city police reserve officers, paramedics, emergency medical technicians, and advanced emergency medical technicians killed in the line of duty; and 2) the children and spouses of Indiana state police troopers permanently and totally disabled in the line of duty. Children must be younger than 23 years of age and enrolled full-time in an undergraduate or graduate degree program at a public college or university in Indiana. Spouses must be enrolled in an undergraduate program and must have been married to the covered public safety officer at the time of death or disability.

Financial data: Qualified applicants receive a 100% remission of tuition and all mandatory fees for undergraduate or graduate work at state-supported postsecondary schools and universities in Indiana. Support is not provided for such fees as room and board.

Duration: Up to 124 semester hours of study.

Number awarded: Varies each year.

Deadline: Applications must be submitted at least 30 days before the start of the college term.

401 INDIANA PART-TIME GRANT PROGRAM

State Student Assistance Commission of Indiana
Attn: Grant Division
150 West Market Street, Suite 500
Indianapolis, IN 46204-2811
Phone: (317) 232-2350; (888) 528-4719 (within IN); Fax: (317) 232-3260
Email: grants@ssaci.state.in.us
Web: www.in.gov/ssaci/2362.htm

Summary: To provide financial assistance to Indiana residents who are working part-time on an undergraduate degree at a school in the state.

Eligibility: Open to Indiana residents who are high school seniors, high school graduates, or GED certificate recipients. Applicants must be attending or planning to attend an eligible Indiana postsecondary institution as a part-time undergraduate student working on an associate or first bachelor's degree. They must be able to demonstrate financial need for tuition assistance.

Financial data: The amount of the award depends on the availability of funds and the number of credit hours taken.

Duration: 1 term (quarter or semester); may be renewed.

Number awarded: Varies each year.

Deadline: Deadline not specified.

402 INTER-TRIBAL COUNCIL OF AT&T EMPLOYEES SCHOLARSHIP PROGRAM

Inter-Tribal Council of AT&T Employees
c/o Carolyn Free
2528 Center West Parkway, Suite B
Augusta, GA 30909
Phone: (706) 729-5473
Email: cf2735@att.com

Summary: To provide financial assistance for college to Native American students.

Eligibility: Open to Native Americans who are graduating high school seniors or undergraduates already enrolled full-time at an accredited college or university. Applicants must submit a 300-word essay on a topic that changes annually but relates to issues of concern to Native Americans; recently, students were invited to write on their feelings, as a Native American, about legalized gambling on reservations. Selection is based on scholastic discipline, personal achievement, and community involvement. U.S. citizenship or permanent resident status is required.

Financial data: The stipend is $1,000.

Duration: 1 year; recipients may reapply.

Number awarded: 1 or more each year.

Deadline: April or September of each year.

403 IOWA MOTOR CARRIERS FOUNDATION SCHOLARSHIPS

Iowa Motor Truck Association
Attn: Iowa Motor Carriers Foundation
717 East Court Avenue
Des Moines, IA 50309
Phone: (515) 244-5193; Fax: (515) 244-2204
Email: imta@iowamotortruck.com
Web: www.iowamotortruck.com/Scholarships/Foundation.asp

Summary: To provide financial assistance to residents of Iowa majoring in any field of study at a college or university in the state.

Eligibility: Open to Iowa residents attending or planning to attend a college, university, trade school, or community college in the state. Applicants must

submit a brief letter describing why they are applying for this scholarship, their intended career goal, its estimated cost, and their choices of educational institutions. Selection is based on academic record, outside activities that pertain to school and community citizenship, and financial need.
Financial data: The stipend is $1,000.
Duration: 1 year.
Number awarded: 4 each year.
Deadline: March of each year.

404 IOWA UNCOMMON STUDENT AWARDS

Hoover Presidential Library Association, Inc.
Attn: Manager of Academic Programs
302 Parkside Drive
P.O. Box 696
West Branch, IA 52358-0696
Phone: (319) 643-5327; (800) 828-0475; Fax: (319) 643-2391
Email: scholarship@hooverassociation.org
Web: www.hooverassociation.org/uncommonstudentpage.html
Summary: To provide financial assistance to high school students in Iowa who complete a project during the summer prior to their senior year and plan to attend college in any state.
Eligibility: Open to Iowa residents. They may apply for these awards during their junior year in high school or a home school program. Applicants must submit a project proposal and 2 letters of recommendation. Based on those proposals, finalists are selected to visit the Hoover Presidential Library and Museum in West Branch for a summer weekend, and then complete the project during the remainder of the summer. In the fall, they return to the Library and Museum to present their completed projects to the committee that selects the scholarship winners on the basis of that work. Students may be planning to attend a 2- or 4-year college or university in any state. Grades, test scores, and financial need are not considered in the selection process.
Financial data: Each of the finalists receives a $1,000 award. The winners receive $5,000 scholarships, $2,500 paid to the accredited college or university of their choice for their freshman year and $2,500 for their sophomore year.
Duration: The competition is held annually. The scholarships are for 2 years.
Number awarded: 15 finalists are selected each year. Of those, 3 are chosen to receive scholarships.
Deadline: Project proposals must be submitted by March of each year.

405 IRMA GESCHE SCHOLARSHIP

Rebekah Assembly of Texas
Attn: Scholarship Committee
16400 KC Road 4060
Scurry, TX 75158
Summary: To provide financial assistance to high school seniors in Texas planning to attend college in the state.
Eligibility: Open to seniors graduating from high schools in Texas who are interested in attending a 2- or 4-year college or university in the state. Applicants must submit a completed application along with a high school transcript, a letter describing their educational goals, and 3 letters of recommendation. Selection is based on academic ability, community service, personal development, and financial need.
Financial data: The stipend is $1,000.
Duration: 1 year.
Number awarded: 1 each year.
Deadline: December of each year.

406 IVA MCCANTS SCHOLARSHIP

National Association of Federal Education Program Administrators
c/o Rick Carder, President
125 David Drive
Sutter Creek, CA 95685
Phone: (916) 669-5102; Fax: (888) 487-6441
Email: rickc@sia-us.com
Web: www.nafepa.org
Summary: To provide financial assistance to high school seniors and college freshmen who are interested in working on a degree in any field.
Eligibility: Open to graduating high school seniors and graduates already enrolled in the first year of college. Applicants must be working on or planning to work on a degree in education or another field of their choice. They must be nominated by their state affiliate of the sponsoring organization. Along with their application, they must submit a 300-word personal narrative explaining why they are applying for this scholarship, including their awards, interests, leadership activities within the community, and future goals. Selection is based on that essay (20 points), a high school or college transcript from the current semester (20 points), extracurricular and leadership activities within the community or church (20 points), 3 letters of recommendation (20 points), and financial need (20 points).
Financial data: The stipend is $2,500.
Duration: 1 year.
Number awarded: 1 each year.
Deadline: Each state affiliate sets its own deadline; for a list of those, contact the sponsor.

407 J & J SCHOLARSHIP

Northern Indiana Community Foundation
Attn: Program Scholarship Coordinator
715 Main Street
P.O. Box 807
Rochester, IN 46975
Phone: (574) 223-2227; (877) 432-6423; Fax: (574) 224-3709
Email: corinne@nicf.org
Web: www.nicf.org
Summary: To provide financial assistance for college to high school seniors and nontraditional students from Indiana.
Eligibility: Open to seniors and previous graduates who have attended high school in Indiana for at least 4 years. Applicants must be planning to attend a college, university, or trade school. They must have a GPA of 2.0 or higher. Along with their application, they must submit a 3-paragraph essay on "These Are My Aspirations." Selection is based on the essay, citizenship, desire to advance their education, academic record, and financial need.
Financial data: A stipend is awarded (amount not specified).
Duration: 1 year; may be renewed until completion of an undergraduate degree.
Number awarded: Varies each year; recently, 34 of these scholarships were awarded.
Deadline: March of each year.

408 JACK AND JILL SCHOLARSHIPS

Jack and Jill Foundation of America
1930 17th Street, N.W.
Washington, DC 20009
Phone: (202) 232-5290; Fax: (202) 232-1747
Web: www.jackandjillfoundation.org/scholarships
Summary: To provide financial assistance to African American high school seniors who plan to attend college in any state.
Eligibility: Open to African American seniors graduating from high schools in any state with a GPA of 3.0 or higher. Applicants must be planning to enroll full-time at an accredited 4-year college or university. Dependents of members of Jack and Jill of America are not eligible.
Financial data: Stipends range from $1,500 to $2,500. Funds may be used for tuition or room and board.
Duration: 1 year.
Number awarded: Varies each year.
Deadline: March of each year.

409 JACK KENT COOKE UNDERGRADUATE TRANSFER SCHOLARSHIPS

Jack Kent Cooke Foundation
44325 Woodridge Parkway
Lansdowne, VA 20176-5199
Phone: (703) 723-8000; (800) 498-6478; Fax: (703) 723-8030
Web: www.jkcf.org/scholarships/undergraduate-transfer-scholarships
Summary: To provide financial assistance to students at 2-year colleges planning to transfer to a 4-year college or university in the United States or abroad.
Eligibility: Open to students who are currently enrolled as sophomores at accredited U.S. community or 2-year colleges (or who graduated from such a college within the past 5 years). Candidates must be interested in transferring to a full-time baccalaureate program at an accredited college or university in the United States or abroad. They must be nominated by their college and have a GPA of 3.5 or higher. Selection is based on academic ability and achievement, critical thinking ability, unmet financial need, will to succeed, leadership and public service, and appreciation for and participation in the arts and humanities.

Financial data: Stipends up to $30,000 per year are provided. Funds are paid directly to the institution.

Duration: 1 year; may be renewed until completion of an undergraduate degree, as long as the fellow continues to meet the eligibility requirements.

Number awarded: Approximately 50 each year.

Deadline: Campus faculty representatives must submit applications by January of each year.

410 JAIME HORN MEMORIAL SOFTBALL SCHOLARSHIP

Babe Ruth League, Inc.
1770 Brunswick Pike
P.O. Box 5000
Trenton, NJ 08638
Phone: (609) 695-1434; Fax: (609) 695-2505
Email: scholarships@baberuthleague.org
Web: www.baberuthleague.org/side-indexes/scholarships.html

Summary: To provide financial assistance for college to high school senior girls who played Babe Ruth League softball.

Eligibility: Open to graduating high school senior girls who played Babe Ruth League softball previously. Applicants must be planning to attend college. Along with their application, they must submit brief statements on why they played softball, what they enjoyed most as a participant, the benefits they gained by playing Babe Ruth softball, and how they feel having played Babe Ruth softball will help them to be successful in college and in life after graduation. Financial need is considered in the selection process.

Financial data: The stipend is $1,000.

Duration: 1 year.

Number awarded: 1 each year.

Deadline: August of each year.

411 JAMES B. MORRIS SCHOLARSHIP

James B. Morris Scholarship Fund
Attn: Scholarship Selection Committee
525 S.W. Fifth Street, Suite A
Des Moines, IA 50309-4501
Phone: (515) 282-8192; Fax: (515) 282-9117
Email: morris@assoc-mgmt.com
Web: www.morrisscholarship.org

Summary: To provide financial assistance to minority undergraduate, graduate, and law students in Iowa.

Eligibility: Open to minority students (African Americans, Asian/Pacific Islanders, Hispanics, or Native Americans) who are interested in studying at a college, graduate school, or law school. Applicants must be either Iowa residents and high school graduates who are attending a college or university anywhere in the United States or non-Iowa residents who are attending a college or university in Iowa; preference is given to native Iowans who are attending an Iowa college or university. Along with their application, they must submit an essay of 250 to 500 words on why they are applying for this scholarship, activities or organizations in which they are involved, and their future plans. Selection is based on the essay, academic achievement (GPA of 2.5 or higher), community service, and financial need. U.S. citizenship is required.

Financial data: The stipend is $2,300 per year.

Duration: 1 year; may be renewed.

Number awarded: Varies each year; recently, 24 of these scholarships were awarded.

Deadline: March of each year.

412 JAMES F. BYRNES FOUNDATION SCHOLARSHIPS

James F. Byrnes Foundation
P.O. Box 6781
Columbia, SC 29260-6781
Phone: (803) 254-9325; Fax: (803) 254-9354
Email: info@byrnesscholars.org
Web: www.byrnesscholars.org/foundation/eligible.php

Summary: To provide financial assistance for college to South Carolina residents who have lost 1 or both parents by death.

Eligibility: Open to residents of South Carolina who have lost 1 or both parents by death. Applicants must be planning to work on a bachelor's degree at an accredited 4-year college or university. They must be able to demonstrate financial need, a satisfactory scholastic record, and the characteristics of character, ability, and enterprise. Both high school seniors and college students who have completed no more than 1 year are eligible, but preference is given to high school applicants. College students must have a GPA of 2.5 or higher. Semifinalists are interviewed.

Financial data: The stipend is $3,250 per year.

Duration: Up to 4 years.

Number awarded: Varies; currently, approximately 40 scholars are supported at any particular time.

Deadline: February of each year.

413 JAMES LEE LOVE SCHOLARSHIPS

North Carolina State Education Assistance Authority
Attn: Grants, Training, and Outreach Department
10 Alexander Drive
P.O. Box 13663
Research Triangle Park, NC 27709-3663
Phone: (919) 549-8614; (800) 700-1775; Fax: (919) 248-4687
Email: information@ncseaa.edu
Web: www.ncseaa.edu

Summary: To provide financial assistance to residents of North Carolina who are attending or planning to attend a public university in the state.

Eligibility: Open to residents of North Carolina who are entering or attending a public university in the state. Applicants must be enrolled or planning to enroll full-time and able to demonstrate financial need. Current high school seniors must rank in the top 25% of their graduating class; current university students must have a GPA of 3.0 or higher.

Financial data: The stipend depends on the availability of funds; recently, they averaged approximately $4,600.

Duration: 1 year; nonrenewable.

Number awarded: Up to 16 each year: 1 at each constituent institution of the University of North Carolina system.

Deadline: February of each year.

414 JAMES MCPHERSON MEMORIAL ENDOWMENT SCHOLARSHIP

Epsilon Sigma Alpha International
Attn: ESA Foundation
P.O. Box 270517
Fort Collins, CO 80527
Phone: (970) 223-2824; Fax: (970) 223-4456
Email: esainfo@esaintl.com
Web: www.esaintl.com/esaf

Summary: To provide financial assistance to residents of Virginia who plan to attend college in any state.

Eligibility: Open to residents of Virginia who are 1) graduating high school seniors with a GPA of 3.0 or higher or with minimum scores of 22 on the ACT or 1030 on the combined critical reading and mathematics SAT; 2) enrolled in college with a GPA of 3.0 or higher; 3) enrolled at a technical school or returning to school after an absence for retraining of job skills or obtaining a degree; or 4) engaged in online study through an accredited college, university, or vocational school. Applicants may be attending or planning to attend a school in any state and major in any field. Selection is based on character (20%), leadership (20%), service (20%), financial need (20%), and scholastic ability (20%).

Financial data: The stipend is $1,000.

Duration: 1 year; may be renewed.

Number awarded: 1 each year.

Deadline: January of each year.

415 JAMES R. OLSEN MEMORIAL SCHOLARSHIP

American Council of the Blind
Attn: Coordinator, Scholarship Program
2200 Wilson Boulevard, Suite 650
Arlington, VA 22201
Phone: (202) 467-5081; (800) 424-8666; Fax: (703) 465-5085
Email: info@acb.org
Web: www.acb.org

Summary: To provide financial assistance to outstanding blind students.

Eligibility: Open to legally blind students enrolling or continuing in an undergraduate program. Applicants must submit verification of legal blindness in both eyes; SAT or ACT scores; information on extracurricular activities (including membership in the American Council of the Blind); employment record; and an autobiographical sketch that includes their personal goals, strengths, weaknesses, hobbies, honors, achievements, and reasons for choice

of field or courses of study. A cumulative GPA of 3.3 or higher is generally required. Financial need is not considered in the selection process.
Financial data: A stipend is awarded (amount not specified). In addition, the winner receives a Kurzweil-1000 Reading System.
Duration: 1 year.
Number awarded: 1 each year.
Deadline: February of each year.

416 JARMAN FAMILY SCHOLARSHIP

Community Foundation of Gaston County
Attn: Program Communications Coordinator
1201 East Garrison Boulevard
P.O. Box 123
Gastonia, NC 28053
Phone: (704) 864-0927; Fax: (704) 869-0222
Email: info@cfgaston.org
Web: www.cfgaston.org/grantseekers/scholarships.aspx
Summary: To provide financial assistance to children of religious ministers in North and South Carolina who are working on an undergraduate or graduate degree at a school in any state.
Eligibility: Open to residents of North and South Carolina who are the children of full-time religious ministers. Applicants must be attending or planning to attend a college or university in any state. Selection is based on character, academic achievement, and financial need.
Financial data: The stipend is $5,000 per year. Funds are paid directly to the recipient's college or university.
Duration: 1 year; recipients may reapply.
Number awarded: 1 each year.
Deadline: February of each year.

417 JEANINE WILLIS MEMORIAL SCHOLARSHIPS

New Jersey Youth Soccer
Attn: Paul Hausser Memorial Fund
569 Abbington Drive, Suite 5
East Windsor, NU 08520
Phone: (609) 490-0725; Fax: (609) 490-0731
Email: office@NJYouthsoccer.com
Web: www.njyouthsoccer.com/awards/willis.htm
Summary: To provide financial assistance to high school seniors in New Jersey who have been involved in soccer and are interested in attending college in any state.
Eligibility: Open to seniors graduating from high schools in New Jersey who have played for an affiliated New Jersey Youth Soccer club and participated in the State Cup program for at least 2 years. Applicants must be interested in enrolling at a college, university, or technical school in any state. Along with their application, they must submit their school record and an essay on why they believe they deserve the scholarship. Financial need is not considered in the selection process.
Financial data: The stipend is $1,000.
Duration: 1 year.
Number awarded: Up to 2 each year.
Deadline: December of each year.

418 JEANNE MANFORD MEMORIAL SCHOLARSHIP

Parents, Families and Friends of Lesbians and Gays
Attn: Safe Schools Coordinator
1726 M Street, N.W., Suite 400
Washington, DC 20036-4521
Phone: (202) 467-8180, ext. 219; Fax: (202) 467-8194
Email: scholarships@pflag.org
Web: community.pflag.org/Page.aspx?pid=374
Summary: To provide financial assistance for college to high school seniors and recent graduates who can demonstrate leadership in the gay, lesbian, bisexual, or transgender (GLBT) community.
Eligibility: Open to high school seniors and prior-year graduates who have not attended college. Applicants must have applied to an accredited higher education institution to work on 1) an associate degree leading to transfer to complete a bachelor's degree; or 2) a bachelor's degree at a 4-year college or university. They must self-identify either as a GLBT person or as a supporter of GLBT people. Along with their application, they must submit a high school transcript showing a GPA of 3.0 or higher, 2 letters of recommendation, and a 2-page essay discussing either their life as a GLBT student or how they have been involved with and supported the GLBT community. Financial need is also considered in the selection process. This scholarship is presented to the applicant who demonstrates outstanding leadership in the GLBT community.
Financial data: The stipend is $5,000.
Duration: 1 year; nonrenewable.
Number awarded: 1 each year.
Deadline: March of each year.

419 JEANNETTE C. EYERLY MEMORIAL SCHOLARSHIP

National Federation of the Blind
Attn: Scholarship Committee
1800 Johnson Street
Baltimore, MD 21230
Phone: (410) 659-9314, ext. 2415; Fax: (410) 685-5653
Email: scholarships@nfb.org
Web: www.nfb.org/nfb/scholarship_program.asp
Summary: To provide financial assistance to legally blind students working on or planning to work on an undergraduate or graduate degree.
Eligibility: Open to legally blind students who are working on or planning to work full-time on an undergraduate or graduate degree. Along with their application, they must submit transcripts, standardized test scores, proof of legal blindness, 2 letters of recommendation, and a letter of endorsement from their National Federation of the Blind state president or designee. Selection is based on academic excellence, service to the community, and financial need.
Financial data: The stipend is $3,000.
Duration: 1 year; recipients may resubmit applications up to 2 additional years.
Number awarded: 1 each year.
Deadline: March of each year.

420 JEFF KROSNOFF SCHOLARSHIP

Jeff Krosnoff Scholarship Fund
P.O. Box 8585
La Crescenta, CA 91224-0585
Email: jtheisinger@gmail.com
Web: www.krosnoffscholarship.com/Scholarship.htm
Summary: To provide financial assistance to high school seniors in California who submit outstanding essays and plan to attend college in any state.
Eligibility: Open to seniors graduating from high schools in California who plan to attend a 4-year college or university in any state. Applicants must be able to demonstrate excellent academic credentials, a breadth of interests, a driving desire to succeed in their chosen endeavors, outstanding community citizenship, and the ability to share their experiences through the written word. They must have a GPA of 3.0 or higher. Selection is based on an essay on a topic that changes annually; recently, applicants were asked to select something that inspires them and to explain why. Financial need is not considered.
Financial data: The stipend is $10,000.
Duration: 1 year.
Number awarded: 1 each year.
Deadline: January of each year.

421 JERRY HARVEY ENDOWMENT SCHOLARSHIP

Epsilon Sigma Alpha International
Attn: ESA Foundation
P.O. Box 270517
Fort Collins, CO 80527
Phone: (970) 223-2824; Fax: (970) 223-4456
Email: esainfo@esaintl.com
Web: www.esaintl.com/esaf
Summary: To provide financial assistance to residents of Texas who plan to attend college in any state.
Eligibility: Open to residents of Texas who are 1) graduating high school seniors with a GPA of 3.0 or higher or with minimum scores of 22 on the ACT or 1030 on the combined critical reading and mathematics SAT; 2) enrolled in college with a GPA of 3.0 or higher; 3) enrolled at a technical school or returning to school after an absence for retraining of job skills or obtaining a degree; or 4) engaged in online study through an accredited college, university, or vocational school. Applicants may be attending or planning to attend a school in any state and major in any field. Selection is based on character (10%), leadership (20%), service (10%), financial need (30%), and scholastic ability (30%).
Financial data: The stipend is $1,400.

Duration: 1 year; may be renewed.
Number awarded: 1 each year.
Deadline: January of each year.

422 JESSE BROWN MEMORIAL YOUTH SCHOLARSHIP PROGRAM

Disabled American Veterans
Attn: Voluntary Services Department
P.O. Box 14301
Cincinnati, OH 45250-0301
Phone: (859) 441-7300; (877) 426-2838; Fax: (859) 441-1416
Web: www.dav.org/volunteers/Scholarship.aspx

Summary: To provide financial assistance to college students who demonstrate outstanding volunteer service to hospitalized disabled veterans.

Eligibility: Open to students who are 21 years of age or younger and have volunteered at least 100 hours for the Department of Veterans Affairs Voluntary Service (VAVS) programs to assist disabled veterans. They may be attending an accredited college, university, community college, or vocational school. Nominations must be submitted by Chiefs of Voluntary Services at VA medical centers. Self-nominations are also accepted if the student includes a 750-word essay on what volunteering at a VA medical center means to them.

Financial data: Stipends range up to $15,000.

Duration: Funds must be used before the recipient's 25th birthday.

Number awarded: Varies each year; recently, 12 of these scholarships were awarded: 1 at $15,000, 1 at $10,000, 2 at $7,500, and 8 at $5,000.

Deadline: February of each year.

423 JEWELL HILTON BONNER SCHOLARSHIP

Navy League of the United States
Attn: Scholarships
2300 Wilson Boulevard, Suite 200
Arlington, VA 22201-5424
Phone: (703) 528-1775; (800) 356-5760; Fax: (703) 528-2333
Email: scholarships@navyleague.org
Web: www.navyleague.org/scholarship

Summary: To provide financial assistance for college to dependent children of sea service personnel, especially Native Americans.

Eligibility: Open to U.S. citizens who are 1) dependents or direct descendants of an active, Reserve, retired, or honorably discharged member of the U.S. sea service (including the Navy, Marine Corps, Coast Guard, or Merchant Marines); or 2) current active members of the Naval Sea Cadet Corps. Applicants must be entering their freshman year at an accredited college or university. They must have a GPA of 3.0 or higher. Along with their application, they must submit transcripts, 2 letters of recommendation, SAT/ACT scores, documentation of financial need, proof of qualifying sea service duty, and a 1-page personal statement on why they should be considered for this scholarship. Preference is given to applicants of Native American heritage.

Financial data: The stipend is $2,500 per year.

Duration: 4 years, provided the recipient maintains a GPA of 3.0 or higher.

Number awarded: 1 each year.

Deadline: February of each year.

424 JEWISH SOCIAL SERVICE AGENCY OF METROPOLITAN WASHINGTON COLLEGE SCHOLARSHIP PROGRAM

Jewish Social Service Agency of Metropolitan Washington
200 Wood Hill Road
Rockville, MD 20850
Phone: (301) 610-8353
Email: dbecker@jssa.org
Web: www.jssa.org/services/community/scholarships

Summary: To provide financial assistance to Jewish residents of the Washington, D.C. area who plan to attend college or graduate school in any state.

Eligibility: Open to Jewish residents of the metropolitan Washington area who are younger than 30 years of age and enrolled or accepted for enrollment as full-time students in accredited 4-year undergraduate or graduate degree programs. Applicants must be U.S. citizens or working toward citizenship. Along with their application, they must submit brief essays on 1) their likely field of study or, if already enrolled, their current or intended major; 2) why they chose the particular school that they are attending or planning to attend; and 3) their educational expectations, goals, and future plans. Students in community colleges, Israeli schools, or year-abroad programs are not eligible. Selection is based primarily on financial need.

Financial data: Stipends range from $1,000 to $2,500 per year.

Duration: 1 year; may be renewed up to 3 additional years.

Number awarded: A number of named scholarships are awarded each year.

Deadline: March of each year.

425 J.F. SCHIRMER SCHOLARSHIP

American Mensa Education and Research Foundation
1229 Corporate Drive West
Arlington, TX 76006-6103
Phone: (817) 607-5577; (800) 66-MENSA; Fax: (817) 649-5232
Email: info@mensafoundation.org
Web: www.mensafoundation.org/AM/Template.cfm?Section=Scholarships1

Summary: To provide financial assistance for undergraduate or graduate study to qualified students.

Eligibility: Open to any student who is enrolled or will enroll in a degree program at an accredited American institution of postsecondary education. Membership in Mensa is not required, but applicants must be U.S. citizens or permanent residents. There are no restrictions as to age, race, gender, level of postsecondary education, GPA, or financial need. Selection is based on a 550-word essay that describes the applicant's career, vocational, or academic goals.

Financial data: The stipend is $1,000.

Duration: 1 year; may be renewed for up to 3 additional years if the recipient remains in school and achieves satisfactory grades.

Number awarded: 4 each year.

Deadline: January of each year.

426 JOHN A. PFAFF SCHOLARSHIP

National Association of Federal Education Program Administrators
c/o Rick Carder, President
125 David Drive
Sutter Creek, CA 95685
Phone: (916) 669-5102; Fax: (888) 487-6441
Email: rickc@sia-us.com
Web: www.nafepa.org

Summary: To provide financial assistance to high school seniors and college freshmen who are interested in working on a degree in any field other than education.

Eligibility: Open to graduating high school seniors and graduates already enrolled in the first year of college. Applicants must be working on or planning to work on a degree in any field other than education. They must be nominated by their state affiliate of the sponsoring organization. Along with their application, they must submit a 300-word personal narrative explaining why they are applying for this scholarship, including their awards, interests, leadership activities within the community, and future goals. Selection is based on that essay (20 points), a high school or college transcript from the current semester (20 points), extracurricular and leadership activities within the community or church (20 points), 3 letters of recommendation (20 points), and financial need (20 points).

Financial data: The stipend is $2,500.

Duration: 1 year.

Number awarded: 1 each year.

Deadline: Each state affiliate sets its own deadline; for a list of those, contact the sponsor.

427 JOHN AND ABIGAIL ADAMS SCHOLARSHIP PROGRAM

Massachusetts Office of Student Financial Assistance
454 Broadway, Suite 200
Revere, MA 02151
Phone: (617) 727-9420; Fax: (617) 727-0667
Email: osfa@osfa.mass.edu
Web: www.osfa.mass.edu/default.asp?page=adamsScholarship

Summary: To provide financial assistance for college to Massachusetts residents who earn high scores on the MCAS tests.

Eligibility: Open to permanent Massachusetts residents who are U.S. citizens or permanent residents. Applicants must score "Advanced" in either the mathematics or the English language section of the grade 10 MCAS and score either "Advanced" or "Proficient" in the other of those 2 sections. They must also have a combined MCAS score on those assessments that ranks in the top 25% in their school district and be planning to enroll full-time at a Massachusetts public college or university. Financial need is not considered.

Financial data: Recipients of these scholarships are eligible for an award of a non-need-based tuition waiver for state-supported undergraduate courses in Massachusetts.
Duration: Up to 4 academic years, provided the student maintains a college GPA of 3.0 or higher.
Number awarded: Varies each year.
Deadline: April of each year.

428 JOHN CORNELIUS/MAX ENGLISH MEMORIAL SCHOLARSHIP AWARD

Marine Corps Tankers Association
P.O. Box 20761
El Cajon, CA 92021
Web: www.usmarinetankers.org/scholarship-program
Summary: To provide financial assistance for college or graduate school to children and grandchildren of Marines who served in a tank unit.
Eligibility: Open to high school seniors and graduates who are children, grandchildren, or under the guardianship of an active, Reserve, retired, or honorably discharged Marine who served in a tank unit. Marine or Navy Corpsmen currently assigned to tank units are also eligible. Applicants must be enrolled or planning to enroll full-time at a college or graduate school. Their sponsor must be a member of the Marine Corps Tankers Association or, if not a member, must join if the application is accepted. Along with their application, they must submit an essay on their educational goals, future aspirations, and concern for the future of our society and for the peoples of the world. Selection is based on that essay, academic record, school activities, leadership potential, and community service.
Financial data: The stipend is at least $2,000 per year.
Duration: 1 year; recipients may reapply.
Number awarded: 8 to 12 each year.
Deadline: March of each year.

429 JOHN EDGAR THOMSON FOUNDATION AID

John Edgar Thomson Foundation
Attn: Director
201 South 18th Street, Suite 318
Philadelphia, PA 19103
Phone: (215) 545-6083; (800) 888-1278; Fax: (215) 545-5102
Email: sjethomson@aol.com
Summary: To provide financial assistance for education or maintenance to daughters of railroad employees who died while employed by a railroad in the United States.
Eligibility: Open to women whose parent died in the active employ of a railroad in the United States, although the cause of death need not be work related. Applicants must live in the home of the surviving parent or guardian (unless attending college full-time and living on campus), be in good health, and receive satisfactory academic grades. Eligibility of the daughter is also dependent upon the parent's remaining unmarried. Consideration is given to other factors as well, including the financial status of the family.
Financial data: Payments are made on a monthly basis to assist with the education or maintenance of eligible daughters. The payment is available from infancy to age 18 or, under certain circumstances, to age 22 (for pursuit of higher education). This supplement to family income is to be used in its entirety for the benefit of the recipient. The grant may be terminated at any time if the financial need ceases or the daughter or surviving parent is either unable or fails to meet the eligibility requirements.
Duration: Monthly payments may be made up to 22 years.
Number awarded: Varies; generally, 100 or more each year.
Deadline: Deadline not specified.

430 JOHN GYLES EDUCATION AWARDS

John Gyles Education Center
Attn: Secretary
259-103 Brunswick Street
P.O. Box 4808, Station A
Fredericton, NB E3B 5G4
Canada
Phone: (506) 459-7460
Web: www.johngyleseducationcenter.com
Summary: To provide financial assistance for college to American and Canadian residents.
Eligibility: Open to full-time students who are citizens of the United States or Canada. Applicants must have a GPA of 2.7 or higher. They may be studying any subject at a college or university. Along with their application, they must submit an essay on their career plans, goals, and personal ambitions. Selection is based on academic ability, financial need, and other criteria.
Financial data: Stipends up to $3,000 are provided.
Duration: 1 year.
Number awarded: Varies each year.
Deadline: May of each year.

431 JOHN I. HAAS SCHOLARSHIP

John I. Haas, Inc.
1112 North 16th Avenue
P.O. Box 1441
Yakima, WA 98907
Phone: (509) 248-4187
Summary: To provide financial assistance for college to the children of farmers engaged in growing hops.
Eligibility: Open to graduating high school seniors who are the sons or daughters of families that operate a hop farm in any part of the United States. Applicants must submit an essay of 750 to 1,000 words on their long-term goals and what they have done and plan to do to achieve their goals. Selection is based on academic achievement (GPA of 2.5 or higher), community and extracurricular activities, and the essay.
Financial data: The stipend is $5,000. Funds are prorated over the academic year (by quarter or semester) and paid to the winner or directly to the winner's school.
Duration: 1 year (the first year of college).
Number awarded: 1 each year.
Deadline: March of each year.

432 JOHN, KARL, ELIZABETH WURFFEL MEMORIAL FUND

Synod of the Northeast
Attn: Student Loan/Scholarship Programs
5811 Heritage Landing Drive
East Syracuse, NY 13057-9360
Phone: (315) 446-5990, ext. 215; (800) 585-5881, ext. 215; Fax: (315) 446-3708
Email: SynodOffice@Synodne.org
Web: www.synodne.org
Summary: To provide financial assistance to Presbyterians in the Synod of the Northeast who are interested in attending college or graduate school in any state.
Eligibility: Open to members of Presbyterian churches in the Synod of the Northeast (Connecticut, Maine, Massachusetts, New Hampshire, New Jersey, New York, Rhode Island, and Vermont) who are entering into a program in any state leading to 1) a 4-year baccalaureate degree; 2) a 3-year master of divinity degree; or 3) a 2-year Christian education degree. Applicants must submit an essay of 400 to 500 words on why they should be considered for this assistance, their reasons for wanting to pursue a college or seminary education, their extracurricular activities and interests (school, church, and community), and the role their faith will take in fulfilling their academic goals. Selection is based on financial need, academic potential, church and campus ministry involvement, community and mission involvement, and continued academic improvement.
Financial data: The stipend is $2,000 per year.
Duration: 1 year; may be renewed up to 3 additional years.
Number awarded: 3 each year.
Deadline: March of each year.

433 JOHN M. AZARIAN MEMORIAL ARMENIAN YOUTH SCHOLARSHIP

Azarian Group, LLC
6 Prospect Street, Suite 1B
Midland Park, NJ 07432
Phone: (201) 444-7111; Fax: (201) 444-6655
Email: info@azariangroup.com
Web: www.azariangroup.com/scholarship.html
Summary: To provide financial assistance for college to students of Armenian descent.
Eligibility: Open to U.S. citizens and permanent residents of Armenian descent who are enrolled full time at an accredited college or university. Applicants must submit a current resume, copies of any work they have published, 2 letters of recommendation, and documentation of financial need. Selection is based

on character, intellectual ability, promise of growth, personal characteristics, financial need, and involvement in the Armenian community.

Financial data: Stipends range from $1,000 to $3,000.

Duration: 1 year.

Number awarded: Varies each year; recently, 9 of these scholarships were awarded. Since the program was established, it has awarded more than $400,000 in scholarships.

Deadline: June of each year.

434 JOHN P. BURKE MEMORIAL FUND SCHOLARSHIPS

Rhode Island Golf Association
Attn: John P. Burke Memorial Fund
One Button Hole Drive, Suite 2
Providence, RI 02909-5750
Phone: (401) 272-1350; Fax: (401) 331-3627
Email: burkefund@rigalinks.org
Web: burkefund.org/scholarships.html

Summary: To provide financial assistance to residents of Rhode Island who have worked at a golf course and plan to attend college in any state.

Eligibility: Open to residents of Rhode Island who are graduating high school seniors or current college students. Applicants must have at least 2 years of successful employment as a caddie, golf shop operations worker, cart or bag room employee, practice range work, golf course maintenance staff member, or clubhouse staff employee at a member club of the Rhode Island Golf Association (RIGA). They must be attending or planning to attend an accredited college or university. Along with their application, they must submit a high school or college transcript; 4 letters of recommendation (from a high school principal or guidance counselor, an officer or board member of the sponsoring club, a member of the sponsoring club who knows the student, and the golf professional of the sponsoring club); a list of school activities (e.g., academic and athletic interscholastic contests, editorships, officer of student organizations, responsible positions in school functions); and documentation of financial need.

Financial data: A stipend is awarded (amount not specified); funds may be used only for tuition, room, board, and other costs billed by postsecondary schools.

Duration: 1 year; may be renewed for up to 3 additional years if the recipient maintains a GPA of 2.0 or higher.

Number awarded: Varies each year; recently, 22 of these scholarships were awarded.

Deadline: April of each year.

435 JON C. LADDA MEMORIAL FOUNDATION SCHOLARSHIP

Jon C. Ladda Memorial Foundation
P.O. Box 55
Unionville, CT 06085
Email: info@jonladda.org
Web: www.jonladda.org

Summary: To provide financial assistance for college to children of deceased and disabled U.S. Naval Academy graduates and members of the Navy submarine service.

Eligibility: Open to children of U.S. Naval Academy graduates and members of the U.S. Navy submarine service. The parent must have died on active duty or been medically retired with a 100% disability. Applicants must be enrolled or accepted at a 4-year college or university, including any of the service academies. Along with their application, they must submit an essay on a topic that changes annually. Selection is based on academic achievement, financial need, and merit.

Financial data: A stipend is awarded (amount not specified). Funds are disbursed directly to the recipient's institution.

Duration: 1 year; may be renewed.

Number awarded: 1 or more each year.

Deadline: March of each year.

436 JORDAN SCHOLARSHIP FUND

International Council of Community Churches
21116 Washington Parkway
Frankfort, IL 60423-3112
Phone: (815) 464-5690; Fax: (815) 464-5692
Email: iccc60423@sbcglobal.net
Web: www.iccusa.com

Summary: To provide financial assistance for college to students affiliated with a Community Church in good standing with the International Council of Community Churches.

Eligibility: Open to high school seniors and older adults seeking to further their education who are in need of financial assistance. Applicants must be affiliated with a Community Church in good standing with the International Council of Community Churches. They must submit an application form, proof of financial need, 2 letters of recommendation (1 must be from a pastor of their church), grade transcripts, and a statement of education and career goals.

Financial data: The maximum stipend is $1,000.

Duration: 1 year.

Number awarded: Several each year.

Deadline: Deadline not specified.

437 JOSEPH DARIMONT VOCATIONAL AWARDS

Washington State Elks Association
4512 South Pine Street
P.O. Box 110760
Tacoma, WA 98411-0760
Phone: (253) 472-6223; (800) 825-ELKS; Fax: (253) 472-6217
Web: www.wselks.com/scholarships.htm

Summary: To provide financial assistance to adults in Washington state who are interested in pursuing vocational training or a 2-year associate degree.

Eligibility: Open to residents of Washington who are between 21 and 50 years of age. Applicants must be U.S. citizens and planning to work on an associate degree, diploma, certificate, or other course of vocational training that does not exceed 2 years in length. Students seeking education that requires a 4-year degree are ineligible. Along with their application, they must submit a 250-word statement of their activities, accomplishments, needs, and objectives that they believe qualify them for this grant. Selection is based on motivation, skills, completeness and neatness of the application, and financial need.

Financial data: The stipend is $1,000.

Duration: 1 year.

Number awarded: The Washington State Elks Association awards 60 scholarships each year.

Deadline: February of each year.

438 JOSHUA DAVID GARDNER MEMORIAL SCHOLARSHIP

Joshua David Gardner Memorial Scholarship Endowment, Inc.
7033 Cobblecreek Drive
Colorado Springs, CO 80922
Phone: (719) 597-1320
Email: gardner@joshgardnerendowment.org
Web: www.joshgardnerendowment.org

Summary: To provide financial assistance to undergraduates enrolled or planning to enroll at an Historically Black College or University (HBCU).

Eligibility: Open to U.S. citizens between 17 and 25 years of age who are enrolled or planning to enroll at an accredited 4-year HBCU. Applicants must have a GPA of 2.8 or higher and scores of at least 900 on the critical reading and mathematics SAT or 19 on the ACT. Along with their application, they must submit a 500-word essay on the importance of personal integrity for leaders. Financial need is considered in the selection process.

Financial data: The stipend is $2,000.

Duration: 1 year; nonrenewable.

Number awarded: At least 2 each year.

Deadline: April of each year.

439 JUNE NELSON MEMORIAL SCHOLARSHIP

Association of Alaska School Boards
1111 West Ninth Street
Juneau, AK 99801
Phone: (907) 586-1083; Fax: (907) 586-2995
Email: aasb@aasb.org
Web: aasb.org

Summary: To provide financial assistance to high school seniors in Alaska who plan to attend college in any state.

Eligibility: Open to seniors graduating from high schools in Alaska who have been accepted as a full-time student at a business, trade, or collegiate institution in any state. Applicants must submit an essay, up to 750 words, on a topic that changes annually but relates to education; recently, students were asked to write on what communities, parents, and students can do to decrease Alaska's dropout rate, which is double the national average. Selection is based on the essay; involvement in community service, cultural activities, student leadership, and student activities; high school transcripts; SAT or ACT score; and 2 letters of recommendation. Financial need is not considered.

Financial data: The stipend is $1,000, including $500 paid at high school graduation and $500 paid after the recipient completes 1 semester of college with a GPA of 2.5 or higher.
Duration: 1 year; nonrenewable.
Number awarded: 10 each year.
Deadline: March of each year.

440 JUNIOR AND COMMUNITY COLLEGE ATHLETIC SCHOLARSHIPS

Alabama Commission on Higher Education
Attn: Grants Coordinator
100 North Union Street
P.O. Box 302000
Montgomery, AL 36130-2000
Phone: (334) 242-2273; Fax: (334) 242-0268
Email: cheryl.newton@ache.alabama.gov
Web: www.ache.alabama.gov/StudentAsst/Programs.htm
Summary: To provide financial assistance to athletes in Alabama interested in attending a junior or community college in the state.
Eligibility: Open to full-time students enrolled in public junior and community colleges in Alabama. Selection is based on athletic ability as determined through try-outs.
Financial data: Awards cover the cost of tuition and books.
Duration: Scholarships are available as long as the recipient continues to participate in the designated sport or activity.
Number awarded: Varies each year.
Deadline: Deadline not specified.

441 JUST ENTERPRISES (JUDI AND STEVE YORK) ENDOWMENT SCHOLARSHIP

Epsilon Sigma Alpha International
Attn: ESA Foundation
P.O. Box 270517
Fort Collins, CO 80527
Phone: (970) 223-2824; Fax: (970) 223-4456
Email: esainfo@esaintl.com
Web: www.esaintl.com/esaf
Summary: To provide financial assistance to residents of Oklahoma planning to attend college in any state.
Eligibility: Open to residents of Oklahoma who are 1) graduating high school seniors with a GPA of 3.0 or higher or with minimum scores of 22 on the ACT or 1030 on the combined critical reading and mathematics SAT; 2) enrolled in college with a GPA of 3.0 or higher; 3) enrolled at a technical school or returning to school after an absence for retraining of job skills or obtaining a degree; or 4) engaged in online study through an accredited college, university, or vocational school. Applicants may be attending or planning to attend a school in any state and major in any field. Selection is based on character (10%), leadership (20%), service (10%), financial need (30%), and scholastic ability (30%).
Financial data: The stipend is $1,000.
Duration: 1 year; may be renewed.
Number awarded: 1 each year.
Deadline: January of each year.

442 K2TEO MARTIN J. GREEN, SR. MEMORIAL SCHOLARSHIP

American Radio Relay League
Attn: ARRL Foundation
225 Main Street
Newington, CT 06111
Phone: (860) 594-0397; Fax: (860) 594-0259
Email: foundation@arrl.org
Web: www.arrlf.org/programs/scholarships
Summary: To provide financial assistance to licensed radio amateurs who are interested in working on an undergraduate or graduate degree in any field.
Eligibility: Open to undergraduate or graduate students in any field who are enrolled at accredited institutions and are licensed radio amateurs of general class. Applicants must submit an essay on the role amateur radio has played in their lives and provide documentation of financial need. Preference is given to students whose parents, grandparents, siblings, or other relatives are also ham radio operators.
Financial data: The stipend is $1,000.
Duration: 1 year.
Number awarded: 1 each year.
Deadline: January of each year.

443 KAE SUMNER EINFELDT SCHOLARSHIP

Tall Clubs International
Attn: Scholarship Committee
P.O. Box 441
Portland, OR 97207
Phone: (888) I-M-TALL-2
Email: tallwindmills@sbcglobal.net
Web: www.tall.org/scholarships.cfm?CFID=998394&CFTOKEN=81538320
Summary: To provide financial assistance for college to high school seniors and current college students who meet the minimum height requirements of the Tall Clubs International (TCI).
Eligibility: Open to 1) graduating high school seniors who will be attending a 2- or 4-year college or university; and 2) students currently attending a 2- or 4-year institution of higher learning who are younger than 21 years of age. Applicants must live within a geographic area served by a participating TCI and must meet the minimum TCI height requirements: 5'10" for females and 6'2" for males. Applications must be submitted to the local TCI club, which nominates the most outstanding applicant for the national competition. Selection is based on academic record and achievements, involvement in school clubs and activities, personal achievements, involvement in clubs and activities outside the school community, and an essay on "What being tall means to me."
Financial data: The stipend is $1,000.
Duration: 1 year.
Number awarded: 2 or 3 each year.
Deadline: Local clubs must submit their nominations by May of each year.

444 KANSAS COMPREHENSIVE GRANTS

Kansas Board of Regents
Attn: Student Financial Assistance
1000 S.W. Jackson Street, Suite 520
Topeka, KS 66612-1368
Phone: (785) 296-3517; Fax: (785) 296-0983
Email: dlindeman@ksbor.org
Web: www.kansasregents.org/financial_aid/awards.html
Summary: To provide need-based grants to Kansas residents who are attending college in the state.
Eligibility: Open to residents of Kansas who are enrolled full-time at 1) the 18 private colleges and universities located in the state; 2) the 6 public universities; or 3) Washburn University. Financial need must be demonstrated.
Financial data: Stipends range from $200 to $3,000 per year at the private institutions and from $100 to $1,100 at the public institutions.
Duration: 1 year; may be renewed as long as the recipient remains in academic "good standing" and is able to demonstrate financial need.
Number awarded: Varies; generally, 7,000 or more each year. The funding level allows about 1 in 3 eligible students to be assisted.
Deadline: March of each year.

445 KANSAS ETHNIC MINORITY SCHOLARSHIP PROGRAM

Kansas Board of Regents
Attn: Student Financial Assistance
1000 S.W. Jackson Street, Suite 520
Topeka, KS 66612-1368
Phone: (785) 296-3517; Fax: (785) 296-0983
Email: dlindeman@ksbor.org
Web: www.kansasregents.org/financial_aid/minority.html
Summary: To provide financial assistance to minority students in Kansas who are interested in attending college in the state.
Eligibility: Open to Kansas residents who fall into 1 of these minority groups: American Indian, Alaskan Native, African American, Asian, Pacific Islander, or Hispanic. Applicants may be current college students (enrolled in community colleges, colleges, or universities in Kansas), but high school seniors graduating in the current year receive priority consideration. Minimum academic requirements include 1 of the following: 1) ACT score of 21 or higher or combined mathematics and critical reading SAT score of 990 or higher; 2) cumulative GPA of 3.0 or higher; 3) high school rank in upper 33%; 4) completion of the Kansas Scholars Curriculum (4 years of English, 3 years of mathematics, 3 years of science, 3 years of social studies, and 2 years of foreign language); 5) selection by the National Merit Corporation in any category; or 6) selection by the College Board as a Hispanic Scholar. Selection is based primarily on financial need.
Financial data: A stipend of up to $1,850 is provided, depending on financial need and availability of state funds.
Duration: 1 year; may be renewed for up to 3 additional years (4 additional years for designated 5-year programs) if the recipient maintains a 2.0 cumulative GPA and has financial need.

Number awarded: Approximately 200 each year.
Deadline: April of each year.

446 KANSAS FOSTER AND ADOPTIVE CHILDREN SCHOLARSHIP FUND

Greater Kansas City Community Foundation
Attn: Scholarship Coordinator
1055 Broadway, Suite 130
Kansas City, MO 64105-1595
Phone: (816) 842-7444; Fax: (816) 842-8079
Email: scholarships@gkccf.org
Web: www.gkccf.org/scholarship.aspx?id=584

Summary: To provide financial assistance to residents of Kansas who are current or former foster children and planning to attend college in any state.

Eligibility: Open to residents of Kansas who are or have been foster children, including those who have been adopted. Applicants must be attending or planning to attend a college, university, junior college, vocational/technical school, or other trade school in any state. Along with their application, they must submit brief statements on their intended field of study, what they hope to do with their education, the school and community organizations with which they have been involved, and which of those has been most important to them.

Financial data: A stipend is awarded (amount not specified).

Duration: 1 year.

Number awarded: 1 or more each year.

Deadline: Applications may be submitted at any time, but awards are made in June and November of each year.

447 KANSAS FOSTER CHILD EDUCATION ASSISTANCE PROGRAM

Kansas Board of Regents
Attn: Student Financial Assistance
1000 S.W. Jackson Street, Suite 520
Topeka, KS 66612-1368
Phone: (785) 296-3517; Fax: (785) 296-0983
Email: dlindeman@ksbor.org
Web: www.kansasregents.org/financial_aid/awards.html

Summary: To provide financial assistance for college to residents of Kansas who have been in foster care.

Eligibility: Open to residents of Kansas who were 1) foster care children in the custody of the Department of Social and Rehabilitation Services at age 18; 2) in foster care placement while graduating from high school or completing their GED requirements prior to their 18th birthday; 3) adopted from foster care after 16 years of age; or 4) left a foster care placement subject to a guardianship after 16 years of age. Applicants must be enrolled or planning to enroll full-time at educational institutions in Kansas, including area vocational/technical schools and colleges, community colleges, regents universities, and Washburn University. Enrollment must begin within 2 years following graduation from high school or completion of GED requirements.

Financial data: Qualifying students are permitted to enroll at an approved Kansas institution without payment of tuition or fees. They are responsible for other costs, such as books, room, and board.

Duration: 1 year; may be renewed as long as the recipient remains enrolled as a full-time undergraduate and employed an average of at least 10 hours per week.

Number awarded: Varies each year; no institution is required to honor more than 5 waivers in any academic year.

Deadline: Deadline not specified.

448 KANSAS MILITARY SERVICE SCHOLARSHIPS

Kansas Board of Regents
Attn: Student Financial Assistance
1000 S.W. Jackson Street, Suite 520
Topeka, KS 66612-1368
Phone: (785) 296-3517; Fax: (785) 296-0983
Email: dlindeman@ksbor.org
Web: www.kansasregents.org/financial_aid/awards.html

Summary: To provide financial assistance for college to residents of Kansas who have served or are still serving in the military.

Eligibility: Open to students who graduated from high school in Kansas or received a GED credential and have been a resident of the state for at least 2 years. Applicants must have served in the U.S. armed forces in Iraq or Afghanistan, or in international waters or on foreign soil in support of military operations in Iraq or Afghanistan, for at least 90 days after September 11, 2001 or for less than 90 days because of injuries received during such service. They must still be in military service or have received an honorable discharge with orders that indicate they served after September 11, 2001 in Operations Enduring Freedom, Nobel Eagle, and/or Iraqi Freedom. Qualified veterans and military personnel may enroll at a public postsecondary institution in Kansas, including area vocational schools, area vocational/technical schools, community colleges, the municipal university, state educational institutions, or technical colleges. They are not required to demonstrate financial need.

Financial data: Qualifying students are permitted to enroll at an approved Kansas institution without payment of tuition or fees. If they receive any federal military tuition assistance, that money must be applied to their tuition and fees and they are eligible only for the remaining balance in scholarship assistance.

Duration: 1 year; may be renewed for a total of 10 semesters as long as the recipient remains in good academic standing.

Number awarded: Varies each year.

Deadline: April of each year.

449 KANSAS STATE COUNCIL ENDOWMENT SCHOLARSHIP

Epsilon Sigma Alpha International
Attn: ESA Foundation
P.O. Box 270517
Fort Collins, CO 80527
Phone: (970) 223-2824; Fax: (970) 223-4456
Email: esainfo@esaintl.com
Web: www.esaintl.com/esaf

Summary: To provide financial assistance to residents of Kansas planning to attend college in any state.

Eligibility: Open to residents of Kansas who are 1) graduating high school seniors with a GPA of 3.0 or higher or with minimum scores of 22 on the ACT or 1030 on the combined critical reading and mathematics SAT; 2) enrolled in college with a GPA of 3.0 or higher; 3) enrolled at a technical school or returning to school after an absence for retraining of job skills or obtaining a degree; or 4) engaged in online study through an accredited college, university, or vocational school. Applicants may be attending or planning to attend a school in any state and major in any field. Selection is based on character (10%), leadership (20%), service (10%), financial need (30%), and scholastic ability (30%).

Financial data: The stipend is $1,100.

Duration: 1 year; may be renewed.

Number awarded: 1 each year.

Deadline: January of each year.

450 KANSAS STATE SCHOLARSHIPS

Kansas Board of Regents
Attn: Student Financial Assistance
1000 S.W. Jackson Street, Suite 520
Topeka, KS 66612-1368
Phone: (785) 296-3517; Fax: (785) 296-0983
Email: dlindeman@ksbor.org
Web: www.kansasregents.org/financial_aid/state.html

Summary: To provide need-based assistance to students who are in the top of their high school class in Kansas and planning to attend college.

Eligibility: Open to high school seniors in Kansas who are designated as State Scholars. Selection for this program is based on ACT Assessment scores (recently, the average score of designees was 29), completion of the Kansas Scholars Curriculum (4 years of English, 4 years of mathematics, 3 years of science, 3 years of social studies, 2 years of foreign language, and 1 year of computer technology), and academic record (recently, the average GPA of designees was 3.90). State Scholars who demonstrate financial need are eligible for these scholarships.

Financial data: The stipend ranges up to $1,000 per year, depending upon the recipient's financial need.

Duration: Up to 4 academic years (unless enrolled in a designated 5-year program) as long as the recipient maintains a 3.0 GPA and financial need.

Number awarded: Varies; generally, at least 1,200 each year. Generally, between 20 and 40% of high school seniors who complete the Kansas Scholars Curriculum are designated as Kansas State Scholars.

Deadline: April of each year.

451 KANSAS TUITION WAIVER FOR DEPENDENTS AND SPOUSES OF DECEASED MILITARY PERSONNEL

Kansas Board of Regents
Attn: Student Financial Assistance

1000 S.W. Jackson Street, Suite 520
Topeka, KS 66612-1368
Phone: (785) 296-3517; Fax: (785) 296-0983
Email: dlindeman@ksbor.org
Web: www.kansasregents.org/financial_aid/awards.html

Summary: To provide financial assistance for college to residents of Kansas whose parent or spouse died on active military service after September 11, 2001.

Eligibility: Open to residents of Kansas who are the dependent children or spouses of members of the U.S. armed forces who died on or after September 11, 2001 while, and as a result of, serving on active military duty. The deceased military member must have been a resident of Kansas at the time of death. Applicants must be enrolled or planning to enroll at a public educational institution in Kansas, including area vocational/technical schools and colleges, community colleges, the state universities, and Washburn University.

Financial data: Qualifying students are permitted to enroll at an approved Kansas institution without payment of tuition or fees. They are responsible for other costs, such as books, room, and board.

Duration: 1 year; may be renewed for a total of 10 semesters of undergraduate study.

Number awarded: Varies each year.

Deadline: Deadline not specified.

452 KANSAS TUITION WAIVER FOR DEPENDENTS AND SPOUSES OF DECEASED PUBLIC SAFETY OFFICERS

Kansas Board of Regents
Attn: Student Financial Assistance
1000 S.W. Jackson Street, Suite 520
Topeka, KS 66612-1368
Phone: (785) 296-3517; Fax: (785) 296-0983
Email: dlindeman@ksbor.org
Web: www.kansasregents.org/scholarships_and_grants

Summary: To provide financial assistance for college to residents of Kansas whose parent or spouse died in the line of duty as a public safety officer.

Eligibility: Open to residents of Kansas who are the dependent children or spouses of public safety officers (law enforcement officers, fire fighters, and emergency medical services attendants) who died as the result of injuries sustained in the line of duty. Applicants must be enrolled or planning to enroll at a public educational institution in Kansas, including area vocational/technical schools and colleges, community colleges, the state universities, and Washburn University.

Financial data: Qualifying students are permitted to enroll at an approved Kansas institution without payment of tuition or fees. They are responsible for other costs, such as books, room, and board.

Duration: 1 year; may be renewed for a total of 10 semesters of undergraduate study.

Number awarded: Varies each year.

Deadline: Deadline not specified.

453 KANSAS TUITION WAIVER FOR PRISONERS OF WAR

Kansas Board of Regents
Attn: Student Financial Assistance
1000 S.W. Jackson Street, Suite 520
Topeka, KS 66612-1368
Phone: (785) 296-3517; Fax: (785) 296-0983
Email: dlindeman@ksbor.org
Web: www.kansasregents.org/financial_aid/awards.html

Summary: To provide financial assistance for college to residents of Kansas who have been a prisoner of war.

Eligibility: Open to current residents of Kansas who entered active service in the U.S. armed forces as a resident of the state. Applicants must have been declared a prisoner of war after January 1, 1960 while serving in the armed forces. They must be enrolled or planning to enroll at a public educational institution in Kansas, including area vocational/technical schools and colleges, community colleges, the state universities, and Washburn University.

Financial data: Qualifying students are permitted to enroll at an approved Kansas institution without payment of tuition or fees. They are responsible for other costs, such as books, room, and board.

Duration: 1 year; may be renewed for a total of 10 semesters of undergraduate study.

Number awarded: Varies each year.

Deadline: Deadline not specified.

454 KAPPA SCHOLARSHIP ENDOWMENT FUND AWARDS

Kappa Alpha Psi Fraternity-Washington (DC) Alumni Chapter
Attn: Kappa Scholarship Endowment Fund, Inc.
P.O. Box 29331
Washington, DC 20017-0331
Phone: (202) 829-8367; Fax: (202) 829-8367
Web: www.ksef-inc.com/students.html

Summary: To provide financial assistance to high school seniors in Washington, D.C. who plan to attend college in any state.

Eligibility: Open to seniors graduating from public or charter high schools in Washington, D.C. with a GPA of 2.5 or higher. Applicants must be planning to enroll full-time at an accredited 4-year institution of higher learning in any state. They must be able to demonstrate involvement in school and community activities and financial need.

Financial data: Stipend amounts vary; recently, they averaged $4,000.

Duration: 1 year.

Number awarded: Varies each year; recently, 29 of these scholarships, with a total value of $116,000, were awarded.

Deadline: March of each year.

455 KATHERN F. GRUBER SCHOLARSHIPS

Blinded Veterans Association
477 H Street, N.W.
Washington, DC 20001-2694
Phone: (202) 371-8880; (800) 669-7079; Fax: (202) 371-8258
Email: bva@bva.org
Web: www.bva.org/services.html

Summary: To provide financial assistance for undergraduate or graduate study to spouses and children of blinded veterans.

Eligibility: Open to dependent children and spouses of blinded veterans of the U.S. armed forces. The veteran need not be a member of the Blinded Veterans Association. The veteran's blindness may be either service connected or nonservice connected, but it must meet the following definition: central visual acuity of 20/200 or less in the better eye with corrective glasses, or central visual acuity of more than 20/200 if there is a field defect in which the peripheral field has contracted to such an extent that the widest diameter of visual field subtends an angular distance no greater than 20 degrees in the better eye. Applicants must have been accepted or be currently enrolled as a full-time student in an undergraduate or graduate program at an accredited institution of higher learning. Along with their application, they must submit a 300-word essay on their career goals and aspirations. Financial need is not considered in the selection process.

Financial data: The stipend is $2,000; funds are intended to be used to cover the student's expenses, including tuition, other academic fees, books, dormitory fees, and cafeteria fees. Funds are paid directly to the recipient's school.

Duration: 1 year; recipients may reapply.

Number awarded: 6 each year.

Deadline: April of each year.

456 KEN YAMADA SCHOLARSHIP ENDOWMENT

United Methodist Higher Education Foundation
Attn: Scholarships Administrator
1001 19th Avenue South
P.O. Box 340005
Nashville, TN 37203-0005
Phone: (615) 340-7385; (800) 811-8110; Fax: (615) 340-7330
Email: umhefscholarships@gbhem.org
Web: www.umhef.org/receive.php?id=endowed_funds

Summary: To provide financial assistance to Methodist students who are entering freshmen at Methodist-related colleges and universities.

Eligibility: Open to students enrolling as full-time freshmen at United Methodist–related colleges and universities. Applicants must have been active, full members of a United Methodist Church for at least 1 year prior to applying. They must have a GPA of 3.0 or higher and be able to demonstrate financial need. Along with their application, they must submit a 200-word essay on their involvement and/or leadership responsibilities in their church, school, and community within the last 3 years. U.S. citizenship or permanent resident status is required.

Financial data: The stipend is at least $1,000 per year.

Duration: 1 year; nonrenewable.

Number awarded: Varies each year; recently, 2 of these scholarships were awarded.

Deadline: May of each year.

457 KENNETH JERNIGAN SCHOLARSHIP

National Federation of the Blind
Attn: Scholarship Committee
1800 Johnson Street
Baltimore, MD 21230
Phone: (410) 659-9314, ext. 2415; Fax: (410) 685-5653
Email: scholarships@nfb.org
Web: www.nfb.org/nfb/scholarship_program.asp

Summary: To provide financial assistance to entering or continuing undergraduate and graduate blind students.

Eligibility: Open to legally blind students who are working on or planning to work full-time on an undergraduate or graduate degree. Along with their application, they must submit transcripts, standardized test scores, proof of legal blindness, 2 letters of recommendation, and a letter of endorsement from their National Federation of the Blind state president or designee. Selection is based on academic excellence, service to the community, and financial need.

Financial data: The stipend is $12,000.

Duration: 1 year; recipients may resubmit applications up to 2 additional years.

Number awarded: 1 each year.

Deadline: March of each year.

458 KENTUCKY ASSOCIATION FOR PUPIL TRANSPORTATION EDUCATION SCHOLARSHIP

Kentucky Association for Pupil Transportation
c/o Wayne Wright, Vice President
1621 Southtown Boulevard
Owensboro, KY 42301
Phone: (270) 887-7109
Email: wayne.wright@christian.kyschool.us
Web: www.thekapt.com

Summary: To provide financial assistance to high school seniors in Kentucky whose parent is employed in the public school pupil transportation field and who plan to attend college in any state.

Eligibility: Open to seniors graduating from public high schools in Kentucky who have a GPA of 3.0 or higher. Applicants must be planning to attend a college, university, or technical school in any state. Their parent or guardian must be employed in the public school pupil transportation field and have a gross family income of less than $55,000 per year. Along with their application, they must submit a 250-word essay on why they have applied for the scholarship and how they would use it. Selection is based on that essay, academic achievement, leadership, citizenship, and service to school and community.

Financial data: The stipend is $1,000.

Duration: 1 year.

Number awarded: 4 each year.

Deadline: February of each year.

459 KENTUCKY BURGLAR & FIRE ALARM ASSOCIATION YOUTH SCHOLARSHIP PROGRAM

Kentucky Burglar & Fire Alarm Association
Attn: Scholarship Committee Chair
P.O. Box 991721
Louisville, KY 40269-1721
Phone: (502) 558-8866; Fax: (502) 415-7334
Email: execdir@kbfaa.org
Web: www.kfbaa.org

Summary: To provide financial assistance to high school seniors in Kentucky who are the children of active-duty law enforcement and fire service personnel and interested in attending college in any state.

Eligibility: Open to seniors graduating from high schools in Kentucky who have been accepted at an accredited college or university in any state. Applicants must have a father, mother, or legal guardian who is a full-time active employee (not on disability) of the police or sheriff's department or a paid employee or volunteer of a fire department in Kentucky. Along with their application, they must submit an essay of 500 to 1,000 words on what it means to them to have their parent or guardian involved in securing our community. Selection is based on that essay (25 points), grade average (25 points), SAT or ACT scores (30 points), and academic prizes, awards, school and outside extracurricular activities, and hobbies (20 points); financial need is not considered.

Financial data: The stipend is $1,000.

Duration: 1 year.

Number awarded: 1 each year.

Deadline: March of each year.

460 KENTUCKY DECEASED OR DISABLED LAW ENFORCEMENT OFFICER AND FIRE FIGHTER DEPENDENT TUITION WAIVER

Kentucky Fire Commission
Attn: Executive Director
300 North Main Street
Versailles, KY 40383
Phone: (859) 256-3478; (800) 782-6823; Fax: (859) 256-3125
Email: ronnie.day@kctcs.net
Web: www.kctcs.edu/kyfirecommission

Summary: To provide financial assistance for college to the children and spouses of Kentucky police officers or fire fighters deceased or disabled in the line of duty.

Eligibility: Open to spouses, widow(er)s, and children of Kentucky residents who became a law enforcement officer, fire fighter, or volunteer fire fighter and who 1) were killed while in active service or training for active service; 2) died as a result of a service-connected disability; or 3) became permanently and totally disabled as a result of active service or training for active service. Children must be younger than 23 years of age; spouses and widow(er)s may be of any age.

Financial data: Recipients are entitled to a waiver of tuition at state-supported universities, community colleges, and technical training institutions in Kentucky.

Duration: 1 year; may be renewed up to a maximum total of 36 months.

Number awarded: Varies each year; all qualified applicants are entitled to this aid.

Deadline: Deadline not specified.

461 KENTUCKY STATE COUNCIL ENDOWMENT SCHOLARSHIP

Epsilon Sigma Alpha International
Attn: ESA Foundation
P.O. Box 270517
Fort Collins, CO 80527
Phone: (970) 223-2824; Fax: (970) 223-4456
Email: esainfo@esaintl.com
Web: www.esaintl.com/esaf

Summary: To provide financial assistance to residents of Kentucky who plan to attend college in any state.

Eligibility: Open to residents of Kentucky who are 1) graduating high school seniors with a GPA of 3.0 or higher or with minimum scores of 22 on the ACT or 1030 on the combined critical reading and mathematics SAT; 2) enrolled in college with a GPA of 3.0 or higher; 3) enrolled at a technical school or returning to school after an absence for retraining of job skills or obtaining a degree; or 4) engaged in online study through an accredited college, university, or vocational school. Applicants may be attending or planning to attend a school in any state and major in any field. Selection is based on character (10%), leadership (10%), service (5%), financial need (50%), and scholastic ability (25%).

Financial data: The stipend is $1,000.

Duration: 1 year; may be renewed.

Number awarded: 1 each year.

Deadline: January of each year.

462 KENTUCKY VETERANS TUITION WAIVER PROGRAM

Kentucky Department of Veterans Affairs
Attn: Division of Field Operations
321 West Main Street, Room 390
Louisville, KY 40202
Phone: (502) 595-4447; (800) 928-4012 (within KY); Fax: (502) 595-4448
Email: Pamela.Cypert@ky.gov
Web: www.veterans.ky.gov/benefits/tuitionwaiver.htm

Summary: To provide financial assistance for college to the children, spouses, or unremarried widow(er)s of disabled or deceased Kentucky veterans.

Eligibility: Open to the children, stepchildren, spouses, and unremarried widow(er)s of veterans who are residents of Kentucky (or were residents at the time of their death). The qualifying veteran must meet 1 of the following conditions: 1) died on active duty (regardless of wartime service); 2) died as a result of a service-connected disability (regardless of wartime service); 3) has a 100% service-connected disability; 4) is totally disabled (non-service connected) with wartime service; or 5) is deceased and served during wartime. The military service may have been as a member of the U.S. armed forces, the Kentucky National Guard, or a Reserve component; service in the Guard or Reserves must have been on state active duty, active duty for training, inactive duty training, or active duty with the U.S. armed forces. Children of veterans must be under 23 years of age; no age limit applies to spouses or unremarried widow(er)s. All applicants must be attending or planning to attend a 2-year, 4-year, or vocational technical school operated and funded by the Kentucky Department of Education.

Financial data: Eligible dependents and survivors are exempt from tuition and matriculation fees at any state-supported institution of higher education in Kentucky.

Duration: Tuition is waived until the recipient completes 45 months of training, receives a college degree, or (in the case of children of veterans) reaches 26 years of age, whichever comes first. Spouses and unremarried widow(er)s are not subject to the age limitation.

Number awarded: Varies each year.

Deadline: Deadline not specified.

463 KERMIT B. NASH ACADEMIC SCHOLARSHIP

Sickle Cell Disease Association of America
Attn: Scholarship Committee
231 East Baltimore Street, Suite 900
Baltimore, MD 21202
Phone: (410) 528-1555; (800) 421-8453; Fax: (410) 528-1495
Email: scdaa@sicklecelldisease.org
Web: www.sicklecelldisease.org/programs/nash_scholarship.phtml

Summary: To provide financial assistance for college to graduating high school seniors who have sickle cell disease.

Eligibility: Open to graduating high school seniors who have sickle cell disease (not the trait). Applicants must have a GPA of 3.0 or higher and be U.S. citizens or permanent residents planning to attend an accredited 4-year college or university as a full-time student. They must submit a personal essay, up to 1,000 words, on an aspect of the impact of the disease on their lives or on society. Selection is based on GPA, general academic achievement and promise, SAT scores, leadership and community service, severity of academic challenges and obstacles posed by sickle cell disease, and the quality of their essay.

Financial data: The stipend is $5,000 per year.

Duration: Up to 4 years.

Number awarded: 1 each year.

Deadline: May of each year.

464 KEVIN CHILD SCHOLARSHIP

National Hemophilia Foundation
Attn: Information Resource Center
116 West 32nd Street, 11th Floor
New York, NY 10001-3212
Phone: (212) 328-3750; (800) 42-HANDI, ext. 3750; Fax: (212) 328-3777
Email: handi@hemophilia.org
Web: www.hemophilia.org

Summary: To provide financial assistance for college to students with hemophilia.

Eligibility: Open to high school seniors entering their first year of undergraduate study as well as those currently enrolled in college. Applicants must have hemophilia A or B. Along with their application, they must submit a 1-page essay on their occupational objectives and goals in life and how the educational program they have planned will meet those objectives. Selection is based on that essay, academic performance, and participation in school and community activities.

Financial data: The stipend is $1,000.

Duration: 1 year.

Number awarded: 1 each year.

Deadline: May of each year.

465 KEYES FIBRE CORPORATION SCHOLARSHIP

Washington Apple Education Foundation
Attn: Scholarship Committee
2900 Euclid Avenue
Wenatchee, WA 98801
Phone: (509) 663-7713; Fax: (509) 663-7469
Email: waef@waef.org
Web: www.waef.org/index.php?page_id=238

Summary: To provide financial assistance to residents of Washington whose parents are employed in the tree fruit or grape industry and who are interested in attending college in any state.

Eligibility: Open to Washington residents who are high school seniors or students already enrolled at a college or university in any state. Applicants themselves or their parents or guardians must be employed in an entry-level labor or management position in the tree fruit or grape industries. Along with their application, they must submit an official transcript, their SAT or ACT scores, 2 letters of reference, and an essay on an assigned topic. Financial need is also considered in the selection process.

Financial data: The stipend is $1,000. The money may be used to pay for tuition, room, board, books, educational supplies, and miscellaneous institutional fees.

Duration: 1 year.

Number awarded: 1 each year.

Deadline: February of each year.

466 KFC COLONEL'S SCHOLARS

KFC Corporation
Attn: Kentucky Fried Chicken Foundation
P.O. Box 725489
Atlanta, GA 31139
Phone: (866) KFC-7240
Email: scholars@kfc.com
Web: www.kfcscholars.org/scholarships

Summary: To provide financial assistance to high school seniors who plan to attend a college or university in their state.

Eligibility: Open to graduating high school seniors planning to attend a public college or university in their home state to work on a bachelor's degree. They must have a GPA of 2.75 or higher and be able to demonstrate financial need. U.S. citizenship or permanent resident status is required.

Financial data: The stipend is $5,000 per year.

Duration: 1 year; may be renewed up to 3 additional years, provided the recipients remain enrolled full-time with a GPA of 2.75 or higher.

Number awarded: 75 each year.

Deadline: February of each year.

467 KIDNEY & UROLOGY FOUNDATION OF AMERICA SCHOLARSHIP AWARDS

Kidney & Urology Foundation of America
Attn: Program Associate
152 Madison Avenue, Suite 201
New York, NY 10016
Phone: (212) 629-9770; (800) 633-6628; Fax: (212) 629-5652
Email: HReel@kidneyurology.org
Web: www.kidneyurology.org/Patient_Resources/scholarships.php

Summary: To provide financial assistance for college to patients who have been diagnosed with kidney or urologic disease.

Eligibility: Open to young adults between 17 and 25 years of age who are attending or planning to attend college. Applicants must have been diagnosed with kidney or urologic disease. Along with their application, they must submit an essay of 1 to 2 pages on questions related to their disease, their educational background and goals, and their contributions to the renal, urologic, or transplant community. Selection is based on achievements, commitment to working on a college degree, and financial need. Priority is given to applicants from the sponsoring organization's participating partner centers.

Financial data: The stipend is $2,000 per year. Funds are paid directly to the recipient's institution.

Duration: 1 year; may be renewed up to 3 additional years.

Number awarded: Varies each year; recently, 7 new and 20 renewal scholarships were awarded.

Deadline: May of each year.

468 KIDS' CHANCE OF INDIANA SCHOLARSHIP PROGRAM

Kids' Chance of Indiana, Inc.
Attn: Scholarship Committee
721 East Broadway
Fortville, IN 46040
Phone: (317) 485-0043, ext. 123; Fax: (317) 485-4299
Email: office@kidschancein.org
Web: www.kidschancein.org/scholarship.html

Summary: To provide financial assistance to Indiana residents whose parent was killed or permanently disabled in a work-related accident and who are interested in attending college or graduate school in any state.

Eligibility: Open to Indiana residents between 16 and 25 years of age who are the children of workers fatally or catastrophically injured as a result of a work-related accident or occupational disease. The death or injury must be compensable by the Workers' Compensation Board of the state of Indiana and must have resulted in a substantial decline in the family's income that is likely to impede the student's pursuit of his or her educational objectives. Applicants must be attending or planning to attend a trade/vocational school, junior/community college, 4-year college or university, or graduate school in any state. Financial need is considered in the selection process.

Financial data: Stipends range up to $3,000 per year. Funds may be used for tuition and fees, books, room and board, and utilities.

Duration: 1 year; may be renewed.

Number awarded: Varies each year.

Deadline: Deadline not specified.

469 KIDS' CHANCE OF WEST VIRGINIA SCHOLARSHIPS

Greater Kanawha Valley Foundation
Attn: Scholarship Coordinator
1600 Huntington Square
900 Lee Street, East
P.O. Box 3041
Charleston, WV 25331-3041
Phone: (304) 346-3620; (800) 467-5909; Fax: (304) 346-3640
Email: shoover@tgkvf.org
Web: www.tgkvf.org/scholar.htm

Summary: To provide financial assistance for college to students whose parent was injured or killed in a West Virginia work-related accident.

Eligibility: Open to children between 16 and 25 years of age whose parent 1) was fatally injured in a West Virginia work-related accident; or 2) is currently receiving permanent total disability benefits from the West Virginia Workers' Compensation Division. Applicants may reside in any state and be pursuing any field of study at an accredited trade or vocational school, college, or university. They must have at least a 2.5 GPA and demonstrate good moral character. Preference is given to applicants who can demonstrate financial need, academic excellence, leadership abilities, and contributions to school and community.

Financial data: The stipend is $1,000 per year.

Duration: 1 year; may be renewed.

Number awarded: Varies each year; recently, 8 of these scholarships were awarded.

Deadline: January of each year.

470 KIT FARAGHER SCHOLARSHIP

Kit Faragher Foundation
1525 Josephine Street
Denver, CO 80206
Web: www.kitfaragherfoundation.org/Scholarship.html

Summary: To provide financial assistance to high school seniors in Colorado who plan to attend college in any state.

Eligibility: Open to seniors graduating from high schools in Colorado who plan to attend an accredited 2- or 4-year college, university, or technical school in any state. Applicants must have a GPA of 2.5 or higher and be able to demonstrate financial need, a positive attitude, strong commitment, and a drive toward accomplishment. Along with their application, they must submit an essay of 500 to 700 words that captures a sense of the style of person they are and describes their short- and long-term educational and personal goals.

Financial data: The stipend is $2,500 per year. Funds are sent directly to the recipient's institution to be used for tuition, books, laboratory fees, or other costs directly related to the degree program.

Duration: 1 year; may be renewed 1 additional year, provided the recipient maintains a GPA of 2.5 or higher.

Number awarded: 1 each year.

Deadline: May of each year.

471 KITTIE M. FAIREY EDUCATIONAL FUND SCHOLARSHIP PROGRAM

Center for Scholarship Administration, Inc.
Attn: Wachovia Accounts
4320 Wade Hampton Boulevard, Suite G
Taylors, SC 29687
Phone: (866) 608-0001
Email: wachoviascholars@bellsouth.net
Web: www.wachoviascholars.com/kmfr/index.php

Summary: To provide financial assistance to high school seniors in South Carolina who are interested in attending college in the state.

Eligibility: Open to seniors graduating from high schools in South Carolina and planning to enroll full-time at an accredited 4-year college or university in the state. Applicants must have a GPA of 3.0 or higher, have a combined SAT score of 1800 or higher or a composite ACT score of 26 or higher, and come from a family whose adjusted gross income is not more than $40,000. Selection is based on academic ability, educational goals, career ambitions, and financial need.

Financial data: Awards are limited to up to half of the standard fees of the institutions for room, board, and tuition for students living on campus. Students living off campus are eligible for up to half of tuition costs. Payment is made directly to the college or university.

Duration: 1 year; may be renewed up to 3 additional years.

Number awarded: 1 or more each year.

Deadline: January of each year.

472 KNIGHTS OF PYTHIAS OF INDIANA EDUCATIONAL ASSISTANCE

Knights of Pythias of Indiana
c/o Dennis O. Adams, Chair
P.O. Box 365
New Castle, IN 47362-0365
Phone: (765) 533-4287
Email: dennyvoiceofandersonspeedway@msn.com
Web: www.knightsofpythiasofnewcastle.com

Summary: To provide financial assistance to high school seniors in Indiana who plan to attend college in any state.

Eligibility: Open to seniors graduating from high schools or home school programs in Indiana. Applicants must be planning to attend an accredited college or university in any state. They must have a GPA of 3.0 or higher. Along with their application, they must submit essays up to 600 words each on 1) their goals after graduating from college; and 2) their financial need.

Financial data: The stipend is $1,000 per year. Funds are paid directly to the recipient's college.

Duration: 1 year; may be renewed up to 3 additional years.

Number awarded: 1 or more each year.

Deadline: January of each year.

473 KOHL'S KIDS WHO CARE SCHOLARSHIPS

Kohl's Department Stores, Inc.
Attn: Community Relations Department
N56 W17000 Ridgewood Drive
Menomonee Falls, WI 53051
Phone: (262) 703-7000; Fax: (262) 703-7115
Email: community.relations@kohls.com
Web: www.kohlscorporation.com/CommunityRelations/scholarship/index.asp

Summary: To recognize and reward kids who volunteer in their communities.

Eligibility: Open to kids who volunteer and have made a difference in their communities within the past 12 months. Nominations may be submitted in 1 of 2 age groups: kids between the ages of 6 and 12, and kids between the ages of 13 and 18. Awards are presented on the individual store level, on the regional level, and on the national level. Selection is based on creativity, initiative, generosity, leadership, and project reach.

Financial data: Awards are presented in each of the 2 age groups. Store-level winners receive a $50 Kohl's gift card and a certificate. Regional winners receive a $1,000 college scholarship, a certificate, and appearance on an in-store poster. National winners receive a $5,000 college scholarship, a plaque, a feature in a national back-to-school ad, appearance on an in-store poster, and a $1,000 grant to the charity of their choice.

Duration: The competition is held annually.

Number awarded: Each year, more than 2,000 awards are presented on the store level, 194 on the regional level, and 10 (5 in each age category) on the national level.

Deadline: March of each year.

474 KUCHLER-KILLIAN MEMORIAL SCHOLARSHIP

National Federation of the Blind
Attn: Scholarship Committee
1800 Johnson Street
Baltimore, MD 21230
Phone: (410) 659-9314, ext. 2415; Fax: (410) 685-5653
Email: scholarships@nfb.org
Web: www.nfb.org/nfb/scholarship_program.asp

Summary: To provide financial assistance to blind students working on an undergraduate or graduate degree in any field.

Eligibility: Open to legally blind students who are working on or planning to work full-time on an undergraduate or graduate degree in any field. Along with their application, they must submit transcripts, standardized test scores, proof of legal blindness, 2 letters of recommendation, and a letter of endorsement from their National Federation of the Blind state president or designee. Selection is based on academic excellence, service to the community, and financial need.

Financial data: The stipend is $3,000.

Duration: 1 year; recipients may resubmit applications up to 2 additional years.

Number awarded: 1 each year.

Deadline: March of each year.

475 KYLE LEE FOUNDATION SCHOLARSHIP

Kyle Lee Foundation, Inc.
3843 South Bristol Street, Number 293
Santa Ana, CA 92704
Phone: (714) 433-3204
Email: foundation@kylelee28.com
Web: www.kylelee28.com

Summary: To provide financial assistance for college to cancer survivors.

Eligibility: Open to high school seniors and current college students who have had cancer, especially Ewing's sarcoma. Applicants must submit a letter from their doctor confirming their cancer diagnosis, copies of academic transcripts, 2 letters of recommendation, and a 700-word essay outlining their goals in college and how their fight with cancer has affected their life and goals.

Financial data: Stipends are $1,000 or $500.

Duration: 1 year.

Number awarded: Varies each year; recently, 5 of these scholarships were awarded.

Deadline: May of each year.

476 LA FRA NATIONAL PRESIDENT'S SCHOLARSHIP

Ladies Auxiliary of the Fleet Reserve Association
Attn: Administrator
P.O. Box 490678
Everett, MA 02149-0012
Phone: (617) 548-1191
Email: msakathy@live.com
Web: www.la-fra.org/scholarship.html

Summary: To provide financial assistance for college to the children and grandchildren of naval personnel.

Eligibility: Open to the children and grandchildren of Navy, Marine, Coast Guard, active Fleet Reserve, Fleet Marine Corps Reserve, and Coast Guard Reserve personnel on active duty, retired with pay, or deceased while on active duty or retired with pay. Applicants must submit an essay on their life experiences, career objectives, and what motivated them to select those objectives. Selection is based on academic record, financial need, extracurricular activities, leadership skills, and participation in community activities. U.S. citizenship is required.

Financial data: The stipend is $2,500.

Duration: 1 year; may be renewed.

Number awarded: 1 each year.

Deadline: April of each year.

477 LA FRA SCHOLARSHIP

Ladies Auxiliary of the Fleet Reserve Association
Attn: Administrator
P.O. Box 490678
Everett, MA 02149-0012
Phone: (617) 548-1191
Email: msakathy@live.com
Web: www.la-fra.org/scholarship.html

Summary: To provide financial assistance for college to the daughters and granddaughters of naval personnel.

Eligibility: Open to the daughters and granddaughters of Navy, Marine, Coast Guard, active Fleet Reserve, Fleet Marine Corps Reserve, and Coast Guard Reserve personnel on active duty, retired with pay, or deceased while on active duty or retired with pay. Applicants must submit an essay on their life experiences, career objectives, and what motivated them to select those objectives. Selection is based on academic record, financial need, extracurricular activities, leadership skills, and participation in community activities. U.S. citizenship is required.

Financial data: The stipend is $2,500.

Duration: 1 year; may be renewed.

Number awarded: 1 each year.

Deadline: April of each year.

478 LADIES OF IMANI SCHOLARSHIP FOR EXCELLENCE

Ladies of Imani
P.O. Box 91943
Washington, DC 20090
Phone: (202) 466-1624
Email: ladiesofimani@ladiesofimani.org
Web: www.ladiesofimani.org

Summary: To provide financial assistance to high school seniors from the Washington, D.C. metropolitan areas who plan to attend college in any state.

Eligibility: Open to seniors graduating from high schools in Baltimore, northern Virginia, and the metropolitan Washington, D.C. area who are planning to attend a college or university in any state. Applicants must have a GPA of 3.0 or higher. Along with their application, they must submit a 100-word essay on the person, living or dead, they would most like to engage in conversation and the question they would most want to ask. Based on the essay and other information on the application, 10 finalists are invited to an oral competition in which they answer questions on current events, community service, and their future plans. Awards are presented to the students with the most outstanding answers to those questions.

Financial data: The stipend is $1,000.

Duration: 1 year.

Number awarded: At least 3 each year.

Deadline: March of each year.

479 LAMEY-WELLEHAN MAINE DIFFERENCE SCHOLARSHIP

Lamey-Wellehan Shoes
Attn: President
940 Turner Street
Auburn, ME 04210
Phone: (207) 784-6595; (800) 370-6900; Fax: (207) 784-9650
Email: jim@lwshoes.com
Web: www.lwshoes.com

Summary: To provide financial assistance to residents of Maine who are interested in attending college in the state.

Eligibility: Open to Maine residents who are high school seniors or students already attending a college in the state. Applicants must submit brief essays on 1) their interest in the economics and ecology of Maine, including how they plan to apply those interests to their studies and career; and 2) what they want Maine to be like in 30 years and how they would personally want to be involved in shaping it. Financial need is considered in the selection process, but the primary consideration is the applicant's ability to contribute to the economy and the environment of Maine.

Financial data: The stipend is $1,000 per year.

Duration: 1 year; may be renewed.

Number awarded: 1 each year.

Deadline: May of each year.

480 LANFORD FAMILY HIGHWAY WORKER MEMORIAL SCHOLARSHIP PROGRAM

American Road and Transportation Builders Association
Attn: Transportation Development Foundation
1219 28th Street, N.W.
Washington, DC 20007-3389
Phone: (202) 289-4434, ext. 411; Fax: (202) 289-4435
Email: hbolton@artba.org
Web: www.artba.org

Summary: To provide financial assistance for college to children of highway workers killed or disabled on the job.

Eligibility: Open to the sons, daughters, and legally adopted children of highway workers who have died or become permanently disabled in roadway construction zone accidents. Applicants must be attending or planning to attend an accredited 4-year college or university, 2-year college, or vocational/technical school. Their parent must have been employed by a transportation construction firm or a transportation public agency at the time of death or disabling injury. Selection is based on academic performance (GPA of 2.5 or higher), a 200-word statement from the applicant on reasons for wanting to continue education, letters of recommendation, and financial need.

Financial data: The stipend is $2,000. Funds are paid directly to the recipient's institution to be used for tuition, books, or required fees, but not for room and board.

Duration: 1 year.

Number awarded: Varies each year; recently, 7 of these scholarships were awarded.

Deadline: March of each year.

481 LAURA BLACKBURN MEMORIAL SCHOLARSHIP

American Legion Auxiliary
Department of Kentucky
c/o Artie Eakins, Education Committee
3649 Rockhouse Road
Robards, KY 42452
Phone: (270) 521-7183
Email: arties@bellsouth.net
Web: www.kyamlegionaux.org

Summary: To provide financial assistance to descendants of veterans in Kentucky who plan to attend college in any state.

Eligibility: Open to the children, grandchildren, and great-grandchildren of veterans who served in the armed forces during eligibility dates for membership in the American Legion. Applicants must be Kentucky residents enrolled in their senior year at an accredited high school. They must be planning to attend a college or university in any state. Selection is based on academic achievement (40%), character (20%), leadership (20%), and Americanism (20%).

Financial data: The stipend is $1,000.

Duration: 1 year.

Number awarded: 1 each year.

Deadline: March of each year.

482 LAWRENCE C. YEARDLEY FUND SCHOLARSHIP

Greater Kanawha Valley Foundation
Attn: Scholarship Coordinator
1600 Huntington Square
900 Lee Street, East
P.O. Box 3041
Charleston, WV 25331-3041
Phone: (304) 346-3620; (800) 467-5909; Fax: (304) 346-3640
Email: shoover@tgkvf.org
Web: www.tgkvf.org/scholar.htm

Summary: To provide financial assistance to residents of West Virginia who are interested in attending college in any state.

Eligibility: Open to residents of West Virginia who are attending or planning to attend a college or university anywhere in the country. Applicants must have an ACT score of 20 or higher; be able to demonstrate good moral character, academic excellence, and extreme financial need; and have a GPA of 2.5 or higher.

Financial data: The stipend is $1,000 per year.

Duration: 1 year; may be renewed.

Number awarded: 1 or 2 each year.

Deadline: January of each year.

483 LAWRENCE MADEIROS SCHOLARSHIP

Adirondack Spintacular
Attn: Scholarship Panel
P.O. Box 11
Mayfield, NY 12117
Phone: (518) 863-8998; Fax: (518) 863-8998
Email: carol@adirondackspintacular.com
Web: www.adirondackspintacular.com/pages2/scholarship.html

Summary: To provide financial assistance for college to high school seniors who have a chronic disorder.

Eligibility: Open to seniors graduating from high school who have been accepted at an accredited college or university. Applicants must be diagnosed with a chronic disorder. Along with their application, they must submit brief essays on 1) how living with or around a chronic disorder has impacted their life; 2) their goals and aspirations in life; and 3) their passion. Financial need may also be considered.

Financial data: The stipend is $1,000.

Duration: 1 year.

Number awarded: Varies each year; recently, 6 of these scholarships were awarded.

Deadline: May of each year.

484 L.B. CEBIK, W4RNL, AND JEAN CEBIK, N4TZP, MEMORIAL SCHOLARSHIP

American Radio Relay League
Attn: ARRL Foundation
225 Main Street
Newington, CT 06111
Phone: (860) 594-0397; Fax: (860) 594-0259
Email: foundation@arrl.org
Web: www.arrlf.org/programs/scholarships

Summary: To provide financial assistance to licensed radio amateurs who are interested in working on an undergraduate degree in any area.

Eligibility: Open to undergraduate students at 4-year colleges and universities who have an amateur radio license of technician class or higher. Applicants must submit an essay on the role amateur radio has played in their lives and provide documentation of financial need. They may be studying any academic area.

Financial data: The stipend is $1,000.

Duration: 1 year.

Number awarded: 1 each year.

Deadline: January of each year.

485 LEADERSHIP 1000 SCHOLARSHIP PROGRAM

College Success Foundation
1605 N.W. Sammamish Road, Suite 200
Issaquah, WA 98027
Phone: (425) 416-2000; (877) 655-4097; Fax: (425) 416-2001
Email: info@collegesuccessfoundation.org
Web: www.collegesuccessfoundation.org/Page.aspx?pid=418

Summary: To provide financial assistance to residents of Washington who are attending or planning to attend college in the state.

Eligibility: Open to residents of Washington who are high school seniors or college freshmen or sophomores. Applicants must be enrolled or planning to enroll full-time at a 4-year college or university in the state. They must have a GPA of 2.75 or higher and be able to demonstrate financial need (family income of $39,000 or less for a family of 1, rising to $94,000 or less for a family of 7).

Financial data: The stipend is $5,000 per year.

Duration: 1 year; may be renewed up to 3 additional years.

Number awarded: Varies each year.

Deadline: May of each year.

486 LEAGUE AT AT&T FOUNDATION ACADEMIC SCHOLARSHIPS

Lesbian, Bisexual, Gay and Transgendered United Employees (LEAGUE) at AT&T Foundation
Attn: LEAGUE Foundation
c/o Charles Eader, Executive Director
One AT&T Way, Room 4B214J
Bedminster, NJ 07921-2694
Phone: (571) 354-4525; TDD: (800) 855-2880
Email: info@leaguefoundation.org
Web: www.leaguefoundation.org/scholarships/apply.cfm

Summary: To provide financial assistance for college to high school seniors who identify with the gay, lesbian, bisexual, or transgender communities.

Eligibility: Open to high school seniors who have been accepted for full-time study at an accredited 2- or 4-year college or university. Applicants must identify as a gay, lesbian, bisexual, or transgendered person. They must have at least a 3.0 GPA and a record of active involvement in community service. Along with their application, they must submit 250-word essays on 1) their academic, career, and personal goals and plans for service to the community, especially on how they plan to increase respect for the individual and aid inclusion of human differences; and 2) how being a lesbian, gay, bisexual, or transgendered person has affected their personal life. Selection is based on academic record, personal plans, community service, leadership, and concern for others.

Financial data: Stipends are $2,500 (for the Matthew Shepard Memorial Scholarship and the Laurel Hester Memorial Scholarship) or $1,500.

Duration: 1 year.

Number awarded: Varies each year; recently, 7 of these scholarships were awarded: 1 Matthew Shepard Memorial Scholarship, 1 Laurel Hester Memorial Scholarship, and 5 others.

Deadline: April of each year.

487 LEBANESE AMERICAN HERITAGE CLUB SCHOLARSHIPS

Lebanese American Heritage Club
Attn: Arab American Scholarship Foundation
4337 Maple Road
Dearborn, MI 48126
Phone: (313) 846-8480; Fax: (313) 846-2710
Email: lahc@lahc.org

Web: www.lahc.org/scholarship1
Summary: To provide financial assistance to Americans of Arab descent who reside in Michigan and are interested in attending college or graduate school in any state.
Eligibility: Open to Michigan residents of Arab descent who are enrolled or planning to enroll full-time at a college or graduate school in any state. Applicants must be U.S. citizens or permanent residents and able to demonstrate financial need. They must have a GPA of 3.0 or higher if they are high school seniors or undergraduates or 3.5 or higher if they are graduate students. Along with their application, they must submit a 500-word essay on how they can contribute to the well being of their community after they complete their education. Preference is given to students who are working on a degree in mass communications or political science.
Financial data: The stipend is $1,000. Funds are paid directly to the recipient's institution.
Duration: 1 year; recipients may reapply.
Number awarded: More than 70 each year.
Deadline: April of each year.

488 LEGACY OF LEARNING SCHOLARSHIPS

Workers Compensation Fund
392 East 6400 South
Murray, UT 84107
Phone: (801) 288-8051; (800) 446-2667; Fax: (801) 288-8372
Web: www.wcfgroup.com/legacy-learning
Summary: To provide financial assistance to children and spouses of workers who died in work-related accidents in Utah and are interested in attending college or graduate school in any state.
Eligibility: Open to Utah residents who are the children and spouses of workers who died in accidents that occurred on job sites covered by the sponsoring company. Applicants must be attending or planning to attend an accredited college or university in any state to work on an undergraduate or graduate degree. Selection is based on GPA, SAT/ACT scores, general character, community involvement, and financial need.
Financial data: The stipend is $1,500 per year.
Duration: 1 year; may be renewed as long as the recipient remains in college.
Number awarded: Varies each year; since this program was established, it has awarded more than 965 scholarships valued in excess of $1.2 million.
Deadline: Deadline not specified.

489 LEGISLATIVE INCENTIVE FOR FUTURE EXCELLENCE (LIFE) SCHOLARSHIP PROGRAM

South Carolina Commission on Higher Education
Attn: LIFE Scholarship Program Manager
1333 Main Street, Suite 200
Columbia, SC 29201
Phone: (803) 737-2260; (877) 349-7183; Fax: (803) 737-2297
Email: tmassie@che.sc.gov
Web: www.che.sc.gov/New_Web/GoingToCollege/LIFE_Hm.htm
Summary: To provide financial assistance for college to residents of South Carolina.
Eligibility: Open to residents of South Carolina who graduate from high school or complete a home school program and attend an eligible South Carolina public or private college or university. As an entering freshman at a 4-year college or university, they must meet any 2 of the following requirements: 1) have earned a GPA of 3.0 or higher in high school; 2) score at least 1100 on the mathematics and critical reading sections of the SAT or 24 on the ACT; and/or 3) graduate in the top 30% of their high school class. Students entering a 2-year or technical institution must have a high school GPA of 3.0 or higher. Continuing college students must have completed an average of 30 credit hours for each academic year and maintained a GPA of 3.0 or higher. Students transferring must have completed 30 credit hours for a second-year transfer, 60 for a third-year transfer, or 90 for a fourth-year transfer; their cumulative GPA must be 3.0 or higher. U.S. citizenship or permanent resident status is required. Applicants may not have been convicted of any felonies or alcohol- or drug-related charges. Students at 4-year institutions who complete at least 14 credit hours of mathematics and science (including at least 6 hours in mathematics and 6 hours in life and physical sciences) qualify for an enhanced mathematics and sciences award.
Financial data: The stipend is $4,700 per year, plus a $300 book allowance, at 4-year colleges or universities. Students at public and private 2-year colleges receive a stipend of the cost of tuition at a regional campus of the University of South Carolina plus a $300 book allowance. Technical school students receive the cost of tuition plus a $300 book allowance. Students who qualify for the enhanced mathematics and sciences award receive an additional stipend of $2,500 per year beginning with their sophomore year. Funds may be applied only toward the cost of attendance at an eligible South Carolina institution.
Duration: 1 year; may be renewed up to a total of 10 semesters for a 5-year program, 8 semesters for a 4-year program, 4 semesters for a 2-year program, or 2 semesters for a 1-year certificate or diploma program.
Number awarded: Varies each year; recently, 29,182 of these scholarships, worth nearly $75.3 million, were awarded.
Deadline: Deadline not specified.

490 LETENDRE EDUCATION FUND SCHOLARSHIPS

National Association for the Education of Homeless Children and Youth
Attn: LeTendre Education Fund
9176 Harvey Hollow Drive
Mechanicsville, VA 23116
Phone: (757) 221-7776; Fax: (757) 221-5300
Email: pxpopp@wm.edu
Web: www.naehcy.org/letendre_ab.html
Summary: To provide financial assistance for college to high school students and recent graduates who are currently or formerly homeless.
Eligibility: Open to high school seniors, students enrolled in GED or other alternative education programs, or students who recently obtained their diploma or GED certificate (under 21 years of age). Applicants must be homeless or have been homeless during their school attendance. This includes students who live in shelters, cars, campgrounds, or other places "not meant for human habitation." Also eligible are students who are living with friends or relatives temporarily because they lack permanent housing. Along with their application, they must submit an essay of 500 to 1,000 words on the impact of homelessness on their lives and their desire to attend college. Selection is based on the essay, demonstrated commitment to education during the experience of homelessness, academic achievement and accomplishments, and potential impact of the scholarship on the student's educational career.
Financial data: The stipend is $1,500. Funds must be used for tuition, application fees, books, preparation courses, visits to prospective colleges, or other educationally-related expenses.
Duration: 1 year; nonrenewable.
Number awarded: At least 2 each year.
Deadline: September of each year.

491 LEW MUCKLE GRANT

Virgin Islands Board of Education
Dronningen Gade 60B, 61, and 62
P.O. Box 11900
St. Thomas, VI 00801
Phone: (340) 774-4546; Fax: (340) 774-3384
Email: stt@myviboe.com
Web: myviboe.com
Summary: To provide financial assistance to residents of the Virgin Islands who wish to attend a college in the territory or on the mainland.
Eligibility: Open to residents of the Virgin Islands who are seniors or graduates of high schools in the territory. Applicants must have a GPA of 2.0 or higher and be attending or accepted for enrollment at an accredited institution of higher learning in the territory or on the mainland. They may be planning to major in any field. Financial need is considered in the selection process.
Financial data: The stipend is $3,000 per year.
Duration: 1 year; may be renewed up to 3 additional years.
Number awarded: 1 each year.
Deadline: April of each year.

492 LIEUTENANT GENERAL CLARENCE L. HUEBNER SCHOLARSHIPS

Society of the First Infantry Division
Attn: 1st Infantry Division Foundation
1933 Morris Road
Blue Bell, PA 19422-1422
Phone: (888) 324-4733; Fax: (215) 661-1934
Email: Fdn1ID@aol.com
Web: www.bigredone.org/foundation/scholarships.cfm
Summary: To provide financial support for college to the children or grandchildren of members of the First Infantry Division.
Eligibility: Open to high school seniors who are the children or grandchildren of soldiers who served in the First Infantry Division of the U.S. Army. Applicants must submit academic transcripts, letters of recommendation,

and a 200-word essay on a major problem facing the country today and their recommendations for the solution of the problem. Selection is based on academic achievement, extracurricular activities, community service, and work experience.

Financial data: The stipend is $1,000 per year, payable to the recipient's school annually.

Duration: 4 years.

Number awarded: Varies each year; recently, 3 of these scholarships were awarded.

Deadline: May of each year.

493 LINDA LAEL MILLER SCHOLARSHIPS FOR WOMEN

Linda Lael Miller Scholarships
c/o Nancy Berland Public Relations, Inc.
2816 N.W. 57th Street, Suite 101
Oklahoma City, OK 73112
Phone: (800) 308-3169
Email: NBPR@nancyberland.com
Web: www.lindalaelmiller.com/scholarships/scholarships.asp

Summary: To provide financial assistance for college to mature women.

Eligibility: Open to women who are 25 years of age or older and legal residents of the United States or Canada. Applicants must be enrolled or planning to enroll at a college, university, or other postsecondary institution. Along with their application, they must submit a 500-word essay on why they are applying for this scholarship, how achieving their educational goals will enhance their and their family's future, the specific purpose for which they would use the funds, and the dollar amount they are requesting. Selection is based on the essay's readability, demonstration of commitment to education and/or career, and the possible impact of the scholarship on the life of the recipient, her family, and/or her community.

Financial data: Stipend amounts vary; recently, they averaged $1,500. Funds are disbursed to the registrar of the recipient's college for payment of tuition, and/or the college bookstore for purchase of books and other supplies, and/or the accredited child care facility that the recipient's children will attend.

Duration: 1 year.

Number awarded: Varies each year; recently, 10 of these scholarships were awarded.

Deadline: August of each year.

494 LITTLE PEOPLE OF AMERICA SCHOLARSHIPS

Little People of America, Inc.
Attn: Vice President of Programs
250 El Camino Real, Suite 201
Tustin, CA 92780
Phone: (714) 368-3689; (888) LPA-2001; Fax: (714) 368-3367
Email: info@lpaonline.org
Web: www.lpaonline.org/mc/page.do?sitePageID=85959&orgID=lpa

Summary: To provide financial assistance for college to members and nonmembers of the Little People of America (LPA).

Eligibility: Open to members of LPA (limited to people who, for medical reasons, are 4 feet 10 inches or under in height). Applicants must be high school seniors or students attending college or trade school. Along with their application, they must submit a 500-word personal statement that explains their reasons for applying for a scholarship, their plans for the future, how they intend to be of service to LPA after graduation, and any other relevant information about themselves, their family, their background, and their educational achievements. Financial need is also considered in the selection process. If sufficient funds are available after all LPA members have been served, scholarships may also be given, first, to immediate family members of dwarfs who are also paid members of LPA, and, second, to people with dwarfism who are not members of LPA.

Financial data: Stipends range from $250 to $1,000.

Duration: 1 year; may be renewed.

Number awarded: Varies; generally between 5 and 10 each year.

Deadline: April of each year.

495 LOUIS B. RUSSELL, JR. MEMORIAL SCHOLARSHIP

Indiana State Teachers Association
Attn: Scholarships
150 West Market Street, Suite 900
Indianapolis, IN 46204-2875
Phone: (317) 263-3400; (800) 382-4037; Fax: (317) 655-3700;
Email: mshoup@ista-in.org
Web: www.ista-in.org/dynamic.aspx?id=1038

Summary: To provide financial assistance to ethnic minority high school seniors in Indiana who are interested in attending vocational school in any state.

Eligibility: Open to ethnic minority high school seniors in Indiana who are interested in continuing their education in the area of industrial arts, vocational education, or technical preparation at an accredited postsecondary institution in any state. Selection is based on academic achievement, leadership ability as expressed through co-curricular activities and community involvement, recommendations, and a 300-word essay on their educational goals and how they plan to use this scholarship.

Financial data: The stipend is $1,000.

Duration: 1 year; may be renewed for 1 additional year, provided the recipient maintains a GPA of "C+" or higher.

Number awarded: 1 each year.

Deadline: February of each year.

496 LOUIS J. AND ELMER M. ROSENBAUM MEMORIAL SCHOLARSHIP

Greater Cedar Rapids Community Foundation
Attn: Scholarship Office
200 First Street, S.W.
Cedar Rapids, IA 52404
Phone: (319) 366-2862; Fax: (319) 366-2912
Email: info@gcrcf.org
Web: www.gcrcf.org/page22850.cfm

Summary: To provide financial assistance to high school seniors and college students from any state who have lost 1 or both parents.

Eligibility: Open to graduating high school seniors and current college students from any state. Applicants must have lost, through death or other tragic circumstance, 1 or both parents. Along with their application, they must submit a 250-word statement of their educational, career, and employment goals and how their future education will help them achieve those goals; their statement may also reflect on the challenges they have faced of a personal, cultural, or financial nature that they have overcome or still face and how those challenges prevented them from participating in community and/or school activities. Financial need is considered in the selection process.

Financial data: The stipend is $5,000 per year.

Duration: 1 year; may be renewed.

Number awarded: 1 or more each year.

Deadline: March of each year.

497 LOUISE TUMARKIN ZAZOVE SCHOLARSHIPS

Louise Tumarkin Zazove Foundation
6858 North Kenneth Avenue
Chicago, IL 60712-4705
Email: earl@ltzfoundation.org
Web: www.ltzfoundation.org/scholarships.php

Summary: To provide financial assistance for college (and possibly for high school or graduate school) to people with hearing loss.

Eligibility: Open to U.S. citizens and permanent residents who have a significant bilateral hearing loss. Strong preference is given to undergraduate students, but support may be provided for graduate school or high school tuition in certain situations. Applicants must submit a transcript of high school and/or college grades, 3 letters of recommendation, documentation of the severity of the hearing loss, information on any special circumstances by or about the family, and documentation of financial need.

Financial data: A stipend is awarded (amount not specified). Funds are paid directly to schools.

Duration: 1 year; may be renewed up to 3 additional years, provided the recipient continues to do well in school and demonstrate financial need.

Number awarded: Varies each year; since the program was established, it has awarded 14 scholarships.

Deadline: May of each year.

498 LOUISIANA EDUCATIONAL BENEFITS FOR CHILDREN, SPOUSES, AND SURVIVING SPOUSES OF VETERANS

Louisiana Department of Veterans Affairs
Attn: Education Program
1885 Wooddale Boulevard, Room 1013
P.O. Box 94095, Capitol Station
Baton Rouge, LA 70804-9095
Phone: (225) 922-0500, ext. 206; (877) GEAUXVA; Fax: (225) 922-0511
Email: Bill.Dixon@vetaffairs.la.gov
Web: vetaffairs.la.gov/education

Summary: To provide financial assistance to children, spouses, and surviving spouses of certain disabled or deceased Louisiana veterans who plan to attend college in the state.

Eligibility: Open to children (between 16 and 25 years of age), spouses, or surviving spouses of veterans who served during specified periods of war time and 1) were killed in action or died in active service; 2) died of a service-connected disability; 3) are missing in action (MIA) or a prisoner of war (POW); 4) sustained a disability rated as 90% or more by the U.S. Department of Veterans Affairs; or 5) have been determined to be unemployable as a result of a service-connected disability. Deceased, MIA, and POW veterans must have resided in Louisiana for at least 12 months prior to entry into service. Living disabled veterans must have resided in Louisiana for at least 24 months prior to the child's admission into the program.

Financial data: Eligible persons accepted as full-time students at Louisiana state-supported colleges, universities, trade schools, or vocational/technical schools are admitted free and are exempt from payment of all tuition, laboratory, athletic, medical, and other special fees. Free registration does not cover books, supplies, room and board, or fees assessed by the student body on themselves (such as yearbooks and weekly papers).

Duration: Support is provided for a maximum of 4 school years, to be completed in not more than 5 years from date of original entry.

Number awarded: Varies each year.

Deadline: Applications must be received no later than 3 months prior to the beginning of a semester.

499 LOUISIANA GO GRANT PROGRAM

Louisiana Office of Student Financial Assistance
1885 Wooddale Boulevard
P.O. Box 91202
Baton Rouge, LA 70821-9202
Phone: (225) 922-1012; (800) 259-LOAN, ext. 1012; Fax: (225) 922-0790
Email: custserv@osfa.state.la.us
Web: www.osfa.state.la.us

Summary: To provide financial assistance to residents of Louisiana who are enrolled or planning to enroll at a college in the state and are eligible for a federal Pell grant or other need-based assistance.

Eligibility: Open to residents of Louisiana who are entering or attending a public or private college or university in the state. Applicants must be eligible for a federal Pell grant or other need-based assistance when they enter college or become eligible after they have already enrolled. Students over 25 years of age are also eligible for this program if they qualify for a Pell grant.

Financial data: The stipend is $2,000 per year for full-time students, $1,000 per year for half-time students, or $500 per year for students enrolled less than half time.

Duration: 1 year; may be renewed for up to 4 additional years or a maximum of $10,000 in funds from this program, provided the recipient remains eligible for a Pell grant.

Number awarded: Varies each year.

Deadline: Deadline not specified.

500 LOUISIANA LEVERAGING EDUCATIONAL ASSISTANCE PARTNERSHIP

Louisiana Office of Student Financial Assistance
1885 Wooddale Boulevard
P.O. Box 91202
Baton Rouge, LA 70821-9202
Phone: (225) 922-1012; (800) 259-LOAN, ext. 1012; Fax: (225) 922-0790
Email: custserv@osfa.state.la.us
Web: www.osfa.state.la.us

Summary: To provide need-based funds to academically qualified high school seniors and graduates in Louisiana who are planning to attend college.

Eligibility: Open to Louisiana residents (for at least 1 year) who have financial need of at least $199. They must be enrolled as a full-time undergraduate student, be a U.S. citizen or eligible noncitizen; have earned at least a 2.0 GPA in high school, a minimum average score of 45 on the GED, or a composite score of at least 20 on the ACT; have applied for federal aid; not owe a refund on federal aid; and not be in default on federal aid. The Louisiana Office of Student Financial Assistance allocates award funds to Louisiana postsecondary schools based on prior fall enrollment. Students are selected for the award by the financial aid officers at their participating schools.

Financial data: Individual grants range from $200 to $2,000 per year; the average award recently was $369; a total of approximately $1.5 million is distributed each year. Funds may be used for educational expenses, including tuition, fees, supplies, and living expenses (e.g., room and board, transportation).

Duration: 1 year; may be renewed if the recipient continues to meet all eligibility requirements and maintains a GPA of 2.0 or higher.

Number awarded: Approximately 4,000 each year.

Deadline: Deadline not specified.

501 LOUISIANA LIFE SAFETY & SECURITY ASSOCIATION YOUTH SCHOLARSHIP PROGRAM

Louisiana Life Safety & Security Association
Attn: Youth Scholarship Program
100 Beauvais Avenue, Suite A-2
Lafayette, LA 70507
Phone: (337) 886-7282; Fax: (337) 886-7284
Email: llssa@llssa.org
Web: www.llssa.org/content/view/45/87

Summary: To provide financial assistance to high school seniors in Louisiana who are the children of active-duty law enforcement and fire service personnel and interested in attending college in any state.

Eligibility: Open to seniors graduating from high schools in Louisiana who have been accepted at an accredited college or university in any state. Applicants must have a father, mother, or legal guardian who is a full-time active employee (not on disability) of the police or sheriff's department or a paid employee or volunteer of a fire department in Louisiana. Along with their application, they must submit an essay of 500 to 1,000 words on what it means to them to have their parent or guardian involved in securing our community. Selection is based on that essay (25 points), grade average (25 points), SAT or ACT scores (30 points), and academic prizes, awards, school and outside extracurricular activities, and hobbies (20 points); financial need is not considered.

Financial data: The first-place winner receives a $1,000 scholarship and second a $500 scholarship.

Duration: The awards are presented annually.

Number awarded: 2 each year.

Deadline: March of each year.

502 LOUISIANA TOPS OPPORTUNITY AWARD

Louisiana Office of Student Financial Assistance
1885 Wooddale Boulevard
P.O. Box 91202
Baton Rouge, LA 70821-9202
Phone: (225) 922-1012; (800) 259-LOAN, ext. 1012; Fax: (225) 922-0790
Email: custserv@osfa.state.la.us
Web: www.osfa.state.la.us

Summary: To provide financial assistance to graduating high school seniors in Louisiana who plan to attend college in the state.

Eligibility: Open to graduating seniors at high schools in Louisiana who have completed a core curriculum of 17.5 units and have filed a Free Application for Federal Student Aid (FAFSA). Applicants must be registered with Selective Service (if required), have no criminal convictions, be a U.S. citizen or permanent resident, and enter an eligible postsecondary institution in Louisiana as a first-time freshman by the first semester following the first anniversary of their high school graduation (unless entering into military service). Independent students or at least 1 parent or legal guardian of dependent students must have been a Louisiana resident for at least 24 months prior to the date of high school graduation. For the Opportunity component, students must have at least a 2.5 GPA and a minimum score of 20 on the ACT (or an ACT score of 22 or higher for home-schooled students).

Financial data: This program provides tuition reimbursement to students who attend public colleges or universities in Louisiana or provides the equivalent of the average public tuition charged in Louisiana to students attending independent colleges or universities in the state.

Duration: 1 year; may be renewed for up to 3 additional years if the recipient continues to attend a Louisiana public or independent college or university as a full-time undergraduate student and maintains at least a 2.3 GPA at the end of the first academic year and 2.5 at the end of all other academic years.

Number awarded: Varies each year.

Deadline: June of each year.

503 LOUISIANA TOPS TECH AWARD

Louisiana Office of Student Financial Assistance
1885 Wooddale Boulevard
P.O. Box 91202
Baton Rouge, LA 70821-9202
Phone: (225) 922-1012; (800) 259-LOAN, ext. 1012; Fax: (225) 922-0790
Email: custserv@osfa.state.la.us

Web: www.osfa.state.la.us/TOPS_T.htm

Summary: To provide financial assistance to graduating high school seniors in Louisiana who are interested in pursuing a technical or vocational education in the state.

Eligibility: Open to seniors graduating from high schools in Louisiana who have completed a core curriculum of 13 units plus either 1) an option of 4 additional units in fine arts, foreign language, or computer education; or 2) an option of 6 additional units in career education, technical courses, and base computer courses. Applicants must have a GPA of 2.5 or higher and an ACT score of at least 17 (or an ACT score of 19 or higher for home-schooled students). They must be registered with Selective Service (if required), have no criminal convictions, be a U.S. citizen or permanent resident, and enter an eligible postsecondary institution as a first-time freshman by the first semester following the first anniversary of their high school graduation (unless entering into military service). Independent students or at least 1 parent or legal guardian of dependent students must have been a Louisiana resident for at least 24 months prior to the date of high school graduation. Applicants must plan to attend a campus of the Louisiana Technical College, Louisiana community college, accredited 2- or 4-year public college or university, or a private college or university that is a member of the Louisiana Association of Independent Colleges and Universities (LAICA) that offers a vocational or technical education certificate, diploma, or non-academic degree program. Students who plan to pursue an academic program or degree are not eligible.

Financial data: At public postsecondary institutions that do not offer baccalaureate degrees, this program provides full payment of tuition for skill or occupational training. At public postsecondary institutions that do offer baccalaureate degrees and at private institutions, the program provides payment of the average of awards paid to students at public schools that do not offer baccalaureate degrees.

Duration: 1 year; may be renewed for 1 additional year if the recipient earns at least 24 credits per academic year and maintains a GPA of 2.5 or higher at the end of each spring semester.

Number awarded: Varies each year.

Deadline: June of each year.

504 LYNN M. SMITH MEMORIAL SCHOLARSHIP

California Association for Postsecondary Education and Disability
Attn: Executive Assistant
71423 Biskra Road
Rancho Mirage, CA 92270
Phone: (760) 346-8206; Fax: (760) 340-5275; TDD: (760) 341-4084
Email: caped2000@aol.com
Web: www.caped.net/scholarships.html

Summary: To provide financial assistance to community college students in California who have a disability.

Eligibility: Open to students at community colleges in California who have a disability. Applicants must be preparing for a vocational career and have completed at least 6 semester credits with a GPA of 2.5 or higher. Along with their application, they must submit a 1-page personal letter that demonstrates their writing skills, progress towards meeting their educational and vocational goals, management of their disability, and involvement in community activities. They must also submit a letter of recommendation from a faculty member, verification of disability, official transcripts, proof of current enrollment, and documentation of financial need.

Financial data: The stipend is $1,000.

Duration: 1 year.

Number awarded: 1 each year.

Deadline: September of each year.

505 MAASFEP GENERAL SCHOLARSHIPS

Minnesota Association of Administrators of State and Federal Education Programs
c/o Matthew Mohs, Treasurer
2140 Timmy Street
St. Paul, MN 55120
Phone: (651) 632-3787
Email: matthew.mohs@spps.org
Web: www.maasfep.org/scholarships.shtml

Summary: To provide financial assistance to high school seniors in Minnesota who have participated in a Title I program and plan to attend college in any state.

Eligibility: Open to seniors graduating from high schools in Minnesota who have participated in a Title I program while in high school. Applicants must be planning to attend a 4-year college or university or 2-year college or vocational/technical school in any state. They must have a GPA of 2.5 or higher for their junior and senior years of high school. Along with their application, they must submit 1) a 100-word essay on how the Title I program helped them with their education; 2) a 100-word essay on their plans for the future; and 3) a 250-word essay on a challenging experience they have had in their life and how they overcame it. Selection is based on those essays, desire for education beyond high school, study habits, positive attitude, and interest in school, community, and/or work-related activities.

Financial data: The stipend is $2,000.

Duration: 1 year.

Number awarded: 2 each year: 1 to a student attending a 4-year college or university and 1 to a student attending a 2-year college or vocational/technical school.

Deadline: January of each year.

506 MADISON/KALATHAS/DAVIS SCHOLARSHIP AWARD

National Naval Officers Association–Washington, D.C. Chapter
Attn: Scholarship Program
2701 Park Center Drive, A1108
Alexandria, VA 22302
Phone: (703) 566-3840; Fax: (703) 566-3813
Email: Stephen.Williams@Navy.mil
Web: dcnnoa.memberlodge.com/Default.aspx?pageId=309002

Summary: To provide financial assistance to minority high school seniors from the Washington, D.C. area who plan to attend college in any state.

Eligibility: Open to minority seniors graduating from high schools in the Washington, D.C. metropolitan area who plan to enroll full-time at an accredited 2- or 4-year college or university in any state. Applicants must be U.S. citizens or permanent residents and have a GPA of 3.0 or higher. Selection is based on academic achievement, community involvement, and financial need.

Financial data: The stipend is $1,500.

Duration: 1 year; nonrenewable.

Number awarded: 1 each year.

Deadline: March of each year.

507 MAINE LEGISLATURE MEMORIAL SCHOLARSHIP FUND

Maine Education Services
Attn: MES Foundation
131 Presumpscot Street
Portland, ME 04103
Phone: (207) 791-3600; (800) 922-6352; Fax: (207) 791-3616
Email: info@mesfoundation.com
Web: www.mesfoundation.com

Summary: To provide financial assistance to residents of Maine planning to attend or currently attending a college or university in the state.

Eligibility: Open to residents of Maine who are either seniors graduating from high schools in the state or already in college. Applicants must be planning to enroll or be currently enrolled in an accredited 2- or 4-year degree-granting Maine college, university, or technical school as an undergraduate or graduate student. Selection is based on academic excellence as demonstrated by transcripts and GPA, contributions to community and employment, letters of recommendation, a 300-word essay on educational goals and intentions, and financial need.

Financial data: The stipend is $1,000.

Duration: 1 year.

Number awarded: 16 each year: 1 from each county in Maine.

Deadline: April of each year.

508 MAINE STATE CHAMBER OF COMMERCE SCHOLARSHIPS

Maine Education Services
Attn: MES Foundation
One City Center, 11th Floor
Portland, ME 04101
Phone: (207) 791-3600; (800) 922-6352; Fax: (207) 791-3616
Email: info@mesfoundation.com
Web: www.mesfoundation.com/scholarships/scholarships_mes_chamber.asp

Summary: To provide financial assistance for a college-level technical, education, or business program to residents of Maine.

Eligibility: Open to residents of Maine who are 1) high school seniors planning to work on a technical associate degree at a 2-year college; 2) high school seniors planning to work on a business-related bachelor's degree at a 4-year college or

university; and 3) adult learners planning to attend a 2-year college to work on a degree in a business- or education-related field (those applicants must meet federal financial aid criteria for independent student status, i.e., be 24 years of age or older, or be married, or have legal dependents other than a spouse, or be an orphan or ward of the court, or be a veteran of the U.S. armed forces). Preference is given to applicants planning to attend college in Maine. Selection is based on academic achievement, employment and community activities, a letter of recommendation from a high school or community official, an essay describing challenges that businesses face in Maine, and financial need.
Financial data: The stipend is $1,500.
Duration: 1 year.
Number awarded: 3 each year: 1 to a high school senior pursuing a technical degree at a 2-year college, 1 to a high school senior pursuing a business degree at a 4-year institution, and 1 to an adult learner working on a 2-year degree in business or education.
Deadline: April of each year.

509 MAINE STATE GOLF ASSOCIATION SCHOLARSHIP

Maine State Golf Association
Attn: Scholarship Fund
58 Val Halla Road
Cumberland, ME 04021
Phone: (207) 829-3549; Fax: (207) 829-3584
Email: msga@mesga.org
Web: www.mesga.org
Summary: To provide financial assistance to high school seniors and graduates in Maine who have participated in golf and plan to attend college in any state.
Eligibility: Open to graduates and prospective graduates of accredited Maine secondary schools who plan to attend college in any state. Applicants must have shown an active interest in golf by participating as a player, serving as a caddie, and/or working at a golf shop or course. They must demonstrate outstanding character, integrity, and leadership through participation in extracurricular, civic, and/or community activities. Financial need is also considered.
Financial data: The stipend is $1,100 per year.
Duration: 1 year; may be renewed until completion of a baccalaureate degree, provided the recipient maintains a GPA of 1.8 or higher for the first year, 2.0 or higher for the second year, or 2.5 or higher for the third and fourth years.
Number awarded: Varies each year; recently, 13 of these scholarships were awarded.
Deadline: March of each year.

510 MAINE TUITION WAIVER PROGRAM FOR ADOPTED CHILDREN

Finance Authority of Maine
Attn: Education Finance Programs
5 Community Drive
P.O. Box 949
Augusta, ME 04332-0949
Phone: (207) 623-3263; (800) 228-3734; Fax: (207) 623-0095; TDD: (207) 626-2717
Email: education@famemaine.com
Web: www.famemaine.com/Education_Home.aspx
Summary: To provide financial assistance to residents of Maine who have been adopted and are interested in attending college in the state.
Eligibility: Open to any adopted child or minor ward of a permanency guardian who receives a subsidy from the Maine Department of Health and Human Services. They must be enrolled in or accepted for enrollment in a branch of the University of Maine system, the Maine Community College System, or the Maine Maritime Academy. Awards are granted on a first-come, first-served basis.
Financial data: Eligible students receive waivers of tuition and fees.
Duration: 1 year; may be renewed up to 3 additional years.
Number awarded: A total of 30 slots are available for the tuition waiver programs for foster and adopted children.
Deadline: Applications may be submitted at any time.

511 MAINE TUITION WAIVER PROGRAM FOR CHILDREN AND SPOUSES OF FIRE FIGHTERS, LAW ENFORCEMENT OFFICERS, AND EMERGENCY MEDICAL SERVICES PERSONNEL KILLED IN THE LINE OF DUTY

Finance Authority of Maine
Attn: Education Finance Programs
5 Community Drive
P.O. Box 949
Augusta, ME 04332-0949
Phone: (207) 623-3263; (800) 228-3734; Fax: (207) 623-0095; TDD: (207) 626-2717
Email: education@famemaine.com
Web: www.famemaine.com/Education_Home.aspx
Summary: To provide financial assistance to children and spouses of deceased law enforcement officers, fire fighters, and emergency medical services personnel in Maine who are interested in attending college in the state.
Eligibility: Open to children and spouses of fire fighters, law enforcement officers, and emergency medical services personnel who have been killed in the line of duty or died as a result of injuries received during the performance of their duties. Applicants must be enrolled in or accepted for enrollment in a branch of the University of Maine system, the Maine Community College System, or the Maine Maritime Academy. Awards are granted on a first-come, first-served basis.
Financial data: Eligible students receive waivers of tuition and fees.
Duration: 1 year; may be renewed up to 3 additional years.
Number awarded: Varies each year.
Deadline: Applications may be submitted at any time.

512 MAINE TUITION WAIVER PROGRAM FOR FOSTER CHILDREN

Finance Authority of Maine
Attn: Education Finance Programs
5 Community Drive
P.O. Box 949
Augusta, ME 04332-0949
Phone: (207) 623-3263; (800) 228-3734; Fax: (207) 623-0095; TDD: (207) 626-2717
Email: education@famemaine.com
Web: www.famemaine.com/Education_Home.aspx
Summary: To provide financial assistance to foster children in Maine who are interested in attending college in the state.
Eligibility: Open to foster children who were under the custody of the Maine Department of Health and Human Services when they graduated from high school. They must be enrolled in or accepted for enrollment in a branch of the University of Maine system, the Maine Community College System, or the Maine Maritime Academy. Awards are granted on a first-come, first-served basis.
Financial data: Eligible students receive waivers of tuition and fees.
Duration: 1 year; may be renewed up to 3 additional years.
Number awarded: A total of 30 slots are available for the tuition waiver programs for foster and adopted children.
Deadline: Applications may be submitted at any time.

513 MAINE VETERANS DEPENDENTS EDUCATIONAL BENEFITS

Bureau of Veterans' Services
117 State House Station
Augusta, ME 04333-0117
Phone: (207) 626-4464; (800) 345-0116 (within ME); Fax: (207) 626-4471
Email: mainebvs@maine.gov
Web: www.maine.gov/dvem/bvs/educational_benefits.htm
Summary: To provide financial assistance for undergraduate or graduate education to dependents of disabled and other Maine veterans.
Eligibility: Open to children (high school seniors or graduates under 22 years of age), non-divorced spouses, or unremarried widow(er)s of veterans who meet 1 or more of the following requirements: 1) living and determined to have a total permanent disability resulting from a service-connected cause; 2) killed in action; 3) died from a service-connected disability; 4) died while totally and permanently disabled due to a service-connected disability but whose death was not related to the service-connected disability; or 5) a member of the armed forces on active duty who has been listed for more than 90 days as missing in action, captured, forcibly detained, or interned in the line of duty by a foreign government or power. The veteran parent must have been a resident of Maine at the time of entry into service or a resident of Maine for 5 years preceding application for these benefits. Children may be working on an associate or bachelor's degree. Spouses, widows, and widowers may work on an associate, bachelor's, or master's degree.
Financial data: Recipients are entitled to free tuition at institutions of higher education supported by the state of Maine.

Duration: Children may receive up to 8 semesters of support; they have 6 years from the date of first entrance to complete those 8 semesters. Continuation in the program is based on their earning a GPA of 2.0 or higher each semester. Spouses are entitled to receive up to 120 credit hours of educational benefits and have 10 years from the date of first entrance to complete their program.
Number awarded: Varies each year.
Deadline: Deadline not specified.

514 MAINE VIETNAM VETERANS SCHOLARSHIP FUND

Maine Community Foundation
Attn: Program Director
245 Main Street
Ellsworth, ME 04605
Phone: (207) 667-9735; (877) 700-6800; Fax: (207) 667-0447
Email: info@mainecf.org
Web: www.mainecf.org/statewidescholars.aspx
Summary: To provide financial assistance for college or graduate school to Vietnam veterans or the dependents of Vietnam or other veterans in Maine.
Eligibility: Open to residents of Maine who are Vietnam veterans or the descendants of veterans who served in the Vietnam Theater. As a second priority, children of veterans from other time periods are also considered. Graduating high school seniors, nontraditional students, undergraduates, and graduate students are eligible to apply. Selection is based on financial need, extracurricular activities, work experience, academic achievement, and a personal statement of career goals and how the applicant's educational plans relate to them.
Financial data: The stipend is $1,000 per year.
Duration: 1 year.
Number awarded: 3 to 6 each year.
Deadline: April of each year.

515 MAINELY CHARACTER SCHOLARSHIP

Mainely Character
P.O. Box 11131
Portland, ME 04103
Email: info@mainelycharacter.org
Web: www.mainelycharacter.org
Summary: To provide financial assistance to Maine residents who demonstrate principles of character and plan to attend college in any state.
Eligibility: Open to residents of Maine who are high school seniors or have received a high school diploma and are entering the first year of postsecondary education at a school in any state. Selection is based on character, determined by an assessment process that includes a written essay demonstrating the principles of courage, integrity, responsibility, and concern. A personal interview is also required.
Financial data: The stipend is $5,000 or $2,500.
Duration: 1 year; nonrenewable.
Number awarded: 2 each year: 1 at $5,000 and 1 at $2,500.
Deadline: February of each year.

516 MAJOR DON S. GENTILE SCHOLARSHIP

UNICO National
Attn: UNICO Foundation, Inc.
271 U.S. Highway 46 West, Suite A-108
Fairfield, NJ 07004
Phone: (973) 808-0035; (800) 877-1492; Fax: (973) 808-0043
Email: unico.national@verizon.net
Web: www.unico.org/foundation.asp
Summary: To provide financial assistance for college to Italian American high school seniors.
Eligibility: Open to high school seniors of Italian origin (i.e., at least 1 parent or grandparent of Italian origin) who are planning to attend an accredited college or university. Applicants must have a GPA of 3.0 or higher and be able to demonstrate financial need, participation in extracurricular and community activities, character, and personality. Along with their application, they must submit SAT or ACT test scores and a letter of recommendation from a UNICO chapter in the city or town where they live.
Financial data: The stipend is $1,500 per year.
Duration: 4 years.
Number awarded: 1 each year.
Deadline: April of each year.

517 MARGARET "PEGGY" RADAR MEMORIAL ENDOWMENT SCHOLARSHIP

Epsilon Sigma Alpha International
Attn: ESA Foundation
P.O. Box 270517
Fort Collins, CO 80527
Phone: (970) 223-2824; Fax: (970) 223-4456
Email: esainfo@esaintl.com
Web: www.esaintl.com/esaf
Summary: To provide financial assistance to residents of Washington who plan to attend college in any state.
Eligibility: Open to residents of Washington who are 1) graduating high school seniors with a GPA of 3.0 or higher or with minimum scores of 22 on the ACT or 1030 on the combined critical reading and mathematics SAT; 2) enrolled in college with a GPA of 3.0 or higher; 3) enrolled at a technical school or returning to school after an absence for retraining of job skills or obtaining a degree; or 4) engaged in online study through an accredited college, university, or vocational school. Applicants may be attending or planning to attend a school in any state and major in any field. Selection is based on character (20%), leadership (20%), service (20%), financial need (20%), and scholastic ability (20%).
Financial data: The stipend is $2,500.
Duration: 1 year; may be renewed.
Number awarded: 3 each year.
Deadline: January of each year.

518 MARGUERITE ROSS BARNETT MEMORIAL SCHOLARSHIP

Missouri Department of Higher Education
Attn: Student Financial Assistance
3515 Amazonas Drive
Jefferson City, MO 65109-5717
Phone: (573) 751-2361; (800) 473-6757; Fax: (573) 751-6635
Email: info@dhe.mo.gov
Web: www.dhe.mo.gov/rossbarnett.html
Summary: To provide financial assistance for college to students in Missouri who are employed while attending school part-time.
Eligibility: Open to residents of Missouri who are enrolled at least half-time but less than full-time at participating Missouri postsecondary institutions. Applicants must be able to demonstrate financial need and must be employed at least 20 hours per week. Students working on a degree or certificate in theology or divinity are not eligible. U.S. citizenship or permanent resident status is required.
Financial data: The maximum annual award is the least of 1) the actual tuition charged at the school the recipient is attending part-time; 2) the amount of tuition charged to a Missouri undergraduate resident enrolled part-time in the same class level at the University of Missouri; or 3) the recipient's demonstrated financial need.
Duration: 1 semester; may be renewed until the recipient has obtained a baccalaureate degree or has completed 150 semester credit hours, whichever comes first. A GPA of 2.5 or higher is required for renewal.
Number awarded: Varies each year; recently, 184 of these scholarships, worth $420,580, were awarded.
Deadline: March of each year.

519 MARIA C. JACKSON/GENERAL GEORGE A. WHITE SCHOLARSHIP

Oregon Student Assistance Commission
Attn: Grants and Scholarships Division
1500 Valley River Drive, Suite 100
Eugene, OR 97401-2146
Phone: (541) 687-7395; (800) 452-8807, ext. 7395; Fax: (541) 687-7414; TDD: (800) 735-2900
Email: awardinfo@osac.state.or.us
Web: www.osac.state.or.us/osac_programs.html

Summary: To provide financial assistance to veterans and children of veterans and military personnel in Oregon who are interested in attending college or graduate school in the state.

Eligibility: Open to residents of Oregon who served, or whose parents are serving or have served, in the U.S. armed forces. Applicants or their parents must have resided in Oregon at the time of enlistment. They must be enrolled or planning to enroll at a college or graduate school in the state. College and university undergraduates must have a GPA of 3.75 or higher, but there is no minimum GPA requirement for graduate students or those attending a technical school. Selection is based on scholastic ability and financial need.

Financial data: A stipend is awarded (amount not specified).

Number awarded: Varies each year.

Deadline: February of each year.

520 MARIAN WOOD BAIRD SCHOLARSHIP

United States Tennis Association
Attn: USTA Serves
70 West Red Oak Lane
White Plains, NY 10604
Phone: (914) 696-7223
Email: eliezer@usta.com
Web: www.usta.com/USTA/Home/AboutUs/USTAServes.aspx

Summary: To provide financial assistance for college to high school seniors who have participated in an organized community tennis program.

Eligibility: Open to high school seniors who have excelled academically, demonstrated achievements in leadership, and participated extensively in an organized community tennis program. Applicants must be planning to enroll as a full-time undergraduate student at a 4-year college or university. They must have a GPA of 3.0 or higher and be able to demonstrate financial need and sportsmanship. Along with their application, they must submit an essay about themselves and how their participation in a tennis program has influenced their life.

Financial data: The stipend is $3,750 per year. Funds are paid directly to the recipient's college or university.

Duration: 4 years.

Number awarded: 1 each year.

Deadline: February of each year.

521 MARILYNN SMITH SCHOLARSHIP

Ladies Professional Golf Association
Attn: LPGA Foundation
100 International Golf Drive
Daytona Beach, FL 32124-1082
Phone: (386) 274-6200; Fax: (386) 274-1099
Email: foundation.scholarships@lpga.com
Web: www.lpgafoundation.org/Scholarships/msmith.aspx

Summary: To provide financial assistance to female graduating high school seniors who played golf in high school and plan to continue playing in college.

Eligibility: Open to female high school seniors who have a GPA of 3.2 or higher. Applicants must have played in at least 50% of their high school golf team's scheduled events or have played golf "regularly" for the past 2 years. They must be planning to enroll full-time at a college or university in the United States and play competitive golf. Along with their application, they must submit a letter that describes how golf has been an integral part of their lives and includes their personal, academic, and professional goals; their chosen discipline of study; and how this scholarship will be of assistance. Financial need is not considered in the selection process.

Financial data: The stipend is $3,000.

Duration: 1 year.

Number awarded: 2 each year.

Deadline: May of each year.

522 MARINE CORPS LEAGUE SCHOLARSHIPS

Marine Corps League
Attn: National Executive Director
P.O. Box 3070
Merrifield, VA 22116-3070
Phone: (703) 207-9588; (800) MCL-1775; Fax: (703) 207-0047
Email: mcl@mcleague.org
Web: www.mcleague.org

Summary: To provide college aid to students whose parents served in the Marines and, also, to members of the Marine Corps League or Marine Corps League Auxiliary.

Eligibility: Open to 1) children of Marines who lost their lives in the line of duty; 2) spouses, children, grandchildren, great-grandchildren, and stepchildren of active Marine Corps League and/or Auxiliary members; and 3) members of the Marine Corps League and/or Marine Corps League Auxiliary who are honorably discharged and in need of rehabilitation training not provided by government programs. Applicants must be seeking further education and training as a full-time student and be recommended by the commandant of an active chartered detachment of the Marine Corps League or the president of an active chartered unit of the Auxiliary. They must have a GPA of 3.0 or higher. Financial need is not considered in the selection process.

Financial data: A stipend is awarded (amount not specified). Funds are paid directly to the recipient.

Duration: 1 year; may be renewed up to 3 additional years (all renewals must complete an application and attach a transcript from the college or university).

Number awarded: Varies, depending upon the amount of funds available each year.

Deadline: June of each year.

523 MARINE CORPS SCHOLARSHIPS

Marine Corps Scholarship Foundation, Inc.
P.O. Box 3008
Princeton, NJ 08543-3008
Phone: (609) 921-3534; (800) 292-7777; Fax: (609) 452-2259
Email: mcsfnj@marine-scholars.org
Web: www.mcsf.com

Summary: To provide financial assistance for college to the children of present or former members of the U.S. Marine Corps.

Eligibility: Open to the children of 1) Marines on active duty or in the Reserves; 2) former Marines and Marine Reservists who served at least 90 days and received an honorable discharge, received a medical discharge, or were killed while serving in the U.S. Marines; 3) active-duty, Reserve, and former U.S. Navy Corpsmen who are serving or have served with the U.S. Marine Corps; and 4) U.S. Navy Corpsmen who have served with the U.S. Marine Corps, have received an honorable discharge or medical discharge, or were killed while serving in the U.S. Navy. Applicants must be high school seniors, high school graduates, or current undergraduates in an accredited college, university, or postsecondary vocational/technical school. They must submit academic transcripts; a written statement of service from their parent's commanding officer or a copy of their parent's honorable discharge; and a 500-word essay on a topic that changes periodically. Only undergraduate study is supported. The family income of applicants must be less than $82,000 per year.

Financial data: The stipends of most scholarships range from $500 to $2,500 per year, depending upon the recipient's financial needs and educational requirements. The Toyota Scholars Program, established in 2004 by Toyota Motor Sales, U.S.A., Inc., provides stipends of $5,000 per year. Certain named scholarships (including the Dr. Jack C. Berger and Virginia Butts Berger Memorial Cornerstone Scholarship, the General and Mrs. Graves B. Erskine Memorial Cornerstone Scholarship, the Frederick L. Swindal Cornerstone Scholarship, the Davenport Family Foundation Cornerstone Scholarship, the Captain E. Phillips Hathaway USMCR (Ret.) Memorial Cornerstone Scholarship, and the Ralph M. Parsons Foundation Cornerstone Scholarship) are for $10,000 per year.

Duration: 1 year; may be renewed upon reapplication.

Number awarded: Varies each year; recently, 1,405 of these scholarships, with a total value of more than $3.5 million, were awarded.

Deadline: March of each year.

524 MARINE GUNNERY SERGEANT JOHN DAVID FRY SCHOLARSHIP

Department of Veterans Affairs
Attn: Veterans Benefits Administration
810 Vermont Avenue, N.W.
Washington, DC 20420

Phone: (202) 418-4343; (888) GI-BILL1
Web: www.gibill.va.gov

Summary: To provide financial assistance to children of military personnel who died in the line of duty on or after September 11, 2001.

Eligibility: Open to the children of active-duty members of the Armed Forces who have died in the line of duty on or after September 11, 2001. Applicants must be planning to enroll as undergraduates at a college or university. They must be at least 18 years of age, even if they have completed high school.

Financial data: Eligible students receive payment of tuition and fees, up to the level of tuition and fees at the most expensive public institution of higher learning in their state of residence; the actual amount depends on the state of residence. A monthly living stipend based on the military housing allowance for the zip code where the school is located and an annual book allowance of $1,000 are also provided.

Duration: Participants receive up to 36 months of entitlement. They have 15 years in which to utilize the benefit.

Number awarded: Varies each year.

Deadline: Deadline not specified.

525 MARION HUBER LEARNING THROUGH LISTENING AWARDS

Recording for the Blind and Dyslexic
Attn: Strategic Communications Department
Anne T. Macdonald Center
20 Roszel Road
Princeton, NJ 08540
Phone: (609) 243-7051; (866) RFBD-585
Email: dnagy@rfbd.org
Web: www.rfbd.org/applications_awards.htm

Summary: To provide financial assistance to outstanding high school students with learning disabilities who plan to continue their education.

Eligibility: Open to seniors graduating from public or private high schools in the United States or its territories who have a specific learning disability (visual impairment alone does not satisfy this requirement). Applicants must be planning to continue their education at a 2- or 4-year college or vocational school. They must be registered Recording for the Blind and Dyslexic borrowers and have earned a GPA of 3.0 or higher in grades 10–12. Selection is based on outstanding scholastic achievement, leadership, enterprise, and service to others.

Financial data: Stipends are $6,000 or $2,000.

Duration: 1 year.

Number awarded: 6 each year: 3 at $6,000 and 3 at $2,000.

Deadline: April of each year.

526 MARION J. BAGLEY SCHOLARSHIP

American Legion Auxiliary
Department of New Hampshire
State House Annex
25 Capitol Street, Room 432
Concord, NH 03301-6312
Phone: (603) 271-2212; (800) 778-3816; Fax: (603) 271-5352
Email: nhalasec@amlegion.state.nh.us
Web: www.nhlegion.org/Auxiliary%20Scholarships/INDEX%20PAGE.htm

Summary: To provide financial assistance to New Hampshire residents who plan to attend college in any state.

Eligibility: Open to New Hampshire residents who are graduating high school seniors, graduates of a high school or equivalent, or students currently attending an institution of higher learning in any state. Applicants must submit 3 letters of recommendation; a list of school, church, and community activities or organizations in which they have participated; transcripts; and a 1,000-word essay on "My Obligations as an American." Financial need is considered in the selection process.

Financial data: The stipend is $1,000.

Duration: 1 year.

Number awarded: 1 each year.

Deadline: April of each year.

527 MARJORIE RUSHFORD ENDOWMENT SCHOLARSHIPS

Epsilon Sigma Alpha International
Attn: ESA Foundation
P.O. Box 270517
Fort Collins, CO 80527
Phone: (970) 223-2824; Fax: (970) 223-4456
Email: esainfo@esaintl.com
Web: www.esaintl.com/esaf

Summary: To provide financial assistance to residents of South Carolina and Virginia who plan to attend college in any state.

Eligibility: Open to residents of South Carolina and Virginia who are enrolled at a college or university in any state and have a GPA of 3.0 or higher. Applicants may be majoring in any field. Selection is based on character (10%), leadership (10%), service (5%), financial need (50%), and scholastic ability (25%).

Financial data: The stipend is $1,000.

Duration: 1 year; may be renewed.

Number awarded: 2 each year: 1 to a student who graduated from high school in South Carolina and 1 who graduated from high school in Virginia.

Deadline: January of each year.

528 MARLIN R. SCARBOROUGH MEMORIAL SCHOLARSHIP

South Dakota Board of Regents
Attn: Scholarship Committee
306 East Capitol Avenue, Suite 200
Pierre, SD 57501-2545
Phone: (605) 773-3455; Fax: (605) 773-5320
Email: info@sdbor.edu
Web: www.sdbor.edu/administration/academics/Scholarships.htm

Summary: To provide financial assistance to students at public universities in South Dakota who are entering their junior year.

Eligibility: Open to students entering their junior year at public universities in South Dakota. Applicants must have a GPA of 3.5 or higher. They must be nominated by their university. Along with their application, they must submit an essay explaining their leadership and academic qualities, career plans, and educational interests.

Financial data: The stipend is $1,000; funds are allocated to the institution for distribution to the student.

Duration: 1 year; nonrenewable.

Number awarded: 1 each year.

Deadline: Deadline not specified.

529 MARTIN LUTHER KING, JR. SCHOLARSHIP

North Carolina Association of Educators, Inc.
Attn: Minority Affairs Commission
700 South Salisbury Street
P.O. Box 27347
Raleigh, NC 27611-7347
Phone: (919) 832-3000, ext. 205; (800) 662-7924, ext. 205; Fax: (919) 839-8229
Web: www.ncae.org/cms/Martin+Luther+King+Jr+Scholarship/228.html

Summary: To provide financial assistance to minority and other high school seniors in North Carolina who plan to attend college in any state.

Eligibility: Open to seniors graduating from high schools in North Carolina who plan to attend a college or university in any state. They must have a GPA of 2.5 or higher. Applications are considered and judged by members of the association's Minority Affairs Commission. Selection is based on character, personality, and scholastic achievement.

Financial data: A stipend is awarded (amount not specified).

Duration: 1 year.

Number awarded: 1 or more each year.

Deadline: January of each year.

530 MARVIN JOHNSON SCHOLARSHIP

Heritage Fund–The Community Foundation for Bartholomew County
Attn: Educational Scholarships
538 Franklin Street
P.O. Box 1547
Columbus, IN 47202-1547
Phone: (812) 376-7772; Fax: (812) 376-0051
Email: info@heritagefundbc.org
Web: www.heritagefundbc.org/scholarships

Summary: To provide financial assistance to dependents of employees in the trucking industry who plan to attend college in selected states.

Eligibility: Open to high school seniors and graduates who are the child or spouse of a trucking company employee or of an independent contractor affiliated with a trucking company. Applicants must be planning to attend an accredited 4-year college or university in Indiana, Ohio, Michigan, Illinois, or Kentucky. Along with their application, they must submit a 1-page essay on how

they have been influenced by an individual or an event and how they believe it will shape their future. Financial need is also considered in the selection process.
Financial data: The stipend is $1,000.
Duration: 1 year.
Number awarded: 1 or more each year.
Deadline: February of each year.

531 MARY BARRETT MARSHALL SCHOLARSHIP

American Legion Auxiliary
Department of Kentucky
c/o Lois Smith, Student Loan Fund Committee
812 Madison Street
Rockport, IN 47635-1241
Phone: (812) 649-2163
Web: www.kyamlegionaux.org
Summary: To provide financial assistance to female dependents of veterans in Kentucky who plan to attend college in the state.
Eligibility: Open to the daughters, wives, sisters, widows, granddaughters, or great-granddaughters of veterans eligible for membership in the American Legion who are high school seniors or graduates and 5-year residents of Kentucky. Applicants must be planning to attend a college or university in Kentucky.
Financial data: The stipend is $1,000. The funds may be used for tuition, registration fees, laboratory fees, and books, but not for room and board.
Duration: 1 year.
Number awarded: 1 each year.
Deadline: March of each year.

532 MARY C. RAWLINS SCHOLARSHIP

Connecticut Association of Affirmative Action Professionals
c/o Patricia Alston, Scholarship Committee Chair
300 Corporate Place
Rocky Hill, CT 06067
Phone: (860) 258-5800; Fax: (860) 258-5858
Email: patricia.alston@po.state.ct.us
Summary: To provide financial assistance to high school seniors in Connecticut who plan to attend college in any state.
Eligibility: Open to seniors graduating from high schools in Connecticut and planning to attend a 2- or 4-year college or university in any state. Applicants must have a GPA of 2.5 or higher.
Financial data: Stipends range from $500 to $1,000.
Duration: 1 year.
Number awarded: 1 or 2 each year.
Deadline: March of each year.

533 MARY KARELE MILLIGAN SCHOLARSHIP

Czech Center Museum Houston
Attn: Scholarship Coordinator
4920 San Jacinto Street
Houston, TX 77004
Phone: (713) 528-2060; Fax: (713) 528-2017
Email: czech@czechcenter.org
Web: www.czechcenter.org/scholarships/scholarships.asp
Summary: To provide financial assistance for college to students of Czech descent.
Eligibility: Open to full-time undergraduate students currently enrolled at a 4-year college or university. Applicants must be born of Czech parentage (at least 1 parent), be able to identify and communicate with the Czech community, be U.S. citizens, and be able to demonstrate financial need. Preference is given to residents of Texas, but applications are accepted from residents of other states who are the child of a member of the Czech Center Museum Houston.
Financial data: The stipend is $1,000 per year.
Duration: 1 year; may be renewed up to 3 additional years.
Number awarded: 3 each year.
Deadline: March of each year.

534 MARY LOU MANZIE MEMORIAL SCHOLARSHIPS

National Leased Housing Association
Attn: NLHA Education Fund
1900 L Street, N.W., Suite 300
Washington, DC 20036
Phone: (202) 785-8888; Fax: (202) 785-2008
Email: info@hudnlha.com
Web: www.hudnlha.com/education_fund/index.asp
Summary: To provide financial assistance to nontraditional students who are residents of federally-assisted rental housing properties or members of families receiving rental subsidy through federal housing programs.
Eligibility: Open to U.S. citizens and permanent residents who reside in a federally-assisted rental housing property or whose families receive rental subsidy through a recognized federal housing program (e.g., Section 8, Rent Supplement, Rental Assistance Payments, Low Income Housing Tax Credit). Applicants must be nontraditional students enrolling in a program of higher education or certified training of at least 10 class hours per week. They must be able to demonstrate financial need, a commitment to achieving an education or training that promotes marketability in the community workforce, and a goal of achieving full-time employment within the next 5 years. Along with their application, they must submit a 1-page narrative on their goals with respect to their educational or training program.
Financial data: A stipend is awarded (amount not specified). Funds are disbursed directly to the recipient's school to be used for partial payment of tuition, books, or other expenses directly related to the student's education.
Duration: 1 year.
Number awarded: Varies each year; recently, 8 of these scholarships were awarded.
Deadline: February of each year.

535 MARY MACON MCGUIRE SCHOLARSHIP

General Federation of Women's Clubs of Virginia
Attn: Scholarship Committee
513 Forest Avenue
P.O. Box 8750
Richmond, VA 23226
Phone: (804) 288-3724; (800) 699-8392; Fax: (804) 288-0341
Email: headquarters@gfwcvirginia.org
Web: www.gfwcvirginia.org/forms/scholarships.htm
Summary: To provide financial assistance to women heads of households in Virginia who have returned to school.
Eligibility: Open to women residents of Virginia who are heads of households. Applicants must be currently enrolled in a course of study (vocational or academic) at an accredited Virginia school. They must have returned to school to upgrade their education and employment skills in order to better provide for their families. Selection is based on 3 letters of recommendation (1 of a general nature, 2 from recent professors, teachers, counselors, or advisers); a resume of educational and employment history, financial circumstances, and community activities; and an essay up to 2,000 words that outlines the financial need for the grant as well as the reasons for entering the field of study selected.
Financial data: The stipend is $2,500. Funds are paid directly to the recipient's college or university.
Duration: 1 year.
Number awarded: 2 each year.
Deadline: March of each year.

536 MARY P. OENSLAGER SCHOLASTIC ACHIEVEMENT AWARDS

Recording for the Blind and Dyslexic
Attn: Strategic Communications Department
Anne T. Macdonald Center
20 Roszel Road
Princeton, NJ 08540
Phone: (609) 243-7051; (866) RFBD-585
Email: dnagy@rfbd.org
Web: www.rfbd.org/applications_awards.htm
Summary: To recognize and reward the outstanding academic achievements of blind college seniors and graduate students.
Eligibility: Open to candidates who 1) are legally blind; 2) have received, or will receive, a bachelor's, master's, or doctoral degree from a 4-year accredited college or university in the United States or its territories during the year the award is given; 3) have an overall academic average of 3.0 or higher; and 4) have been registered borrowers from Recording for the Blind and Dyslexic for at least 1 year. Selection is based on evidence of leadership, enterprise, and service to others.
Financial data: Top winners receive $6,000 each, special honors winners $3,000 each, and honors winners $1,000 each.
Duration: The awards are presented annually.

Number awarded: 9 each year: 3 top winners, 3 special honors winners, and 3 honors winners.
Deadline: April of each year.

537 MARY ROSE MILLS–LINDA RANKIN MEMORIAL SCHOLARSHIP

Alpha Delta Kappa–North Carolina Chapter
c/o Rebecca R. Meyst, President
351 North Peace Haven Road
Winston-Salem, NC 27104-2536

Summary: To provide financial assistance to high school seniors in North Carolina who plan to attend college in any state.
Eligibility: Open to seniors graduating from high schools in North Carolina and planning to enroll at a 4-year college or university in any state. Applicants must rank in the top 10% of their class and have scores of at least 1488 on the SAT or 22 on the ACT. Along with their application, they must submit a letter on their plans, career goals, and reasons for wanting this scholarship. Selection is based on character and participation in extracurricular activities; financial need is not considered.
Financial data: The stipend is $2,000.
Duration: 1 year; nonrenewable.
Number awarded: 1 each year.
Deadline: January of each year.

538 MARYANN K. MURTHA MEMORIAL SCHOLARSHIP

American Legion Auxiliary
Department of New York
112 State Street, Suite 1310
Albany, NY 12207
Phone: (518) 463-1162; (800) 421-6348; Fax: (518) 449-5406
Email: alanyterry@nycap.rr.com
Web: www.deptny.org/Scholarships.htm

Summary: To provide financial assistance to New York residents who are the descendants of veterans and interested in attending college in any state.
Eligibility: Open to residents of New York who are high school seniors or graduates and attending or planning to attend an accredited college or university in any state. Applicants must be the children, grandchildren, or great-grandchildren of veterans who served during specified periods of war time. Along with their application, they must submit a 700-word article describing their plans and goals for the future and how they hope to use their talent and education to help others. Selection is based on character (20%), Americanism (15%), community involvement (15%), leadership (15%), scholarship (20%), and financial need (15%). U.S. citizenship is required.
Financial data: The stipend is $1,000. Funds are paid directly to the recipient's school.
Duration: 1 year.
Number awarded: 1 each year.
Deadline: February of each year.

539 MARYLAND, DELAWARE, AND DISTRICT OF COLUMBIA ELKS ASSOCIATION VOCATIONAL SCHOLARSHIPS

Maryland, Delaware, and District of Columbia Elks Association
c/o Joseph John Pallozzi, Scholarship Chair
15 Briarwood Road
Baltimore, MD 21228-2002
Phone: (410) 747-0581
Email: jpallozzi@juno.com
Web: www.mddedcelksassn.org

Summary: To provide financial assistance to residents of Delaware, Maryland, and the District of Columbia who are interested in enrolling in a vocational education program in any state.
Eligibility: Open to residents of Delaware, Maryland, and the District of Columbia who are high school seniors, high school graduates, or GED recipients. Applicants must be enrolled or planning to enroll full-time at a vocational/technical school or other 2-year educational institution in any state to work on a degree or certificate other than a bachelor's degree. Their application must be endorsed by an official of their local Elks Lodge. Along with their application, they must submit 1) a 200-word statement of their activities, accomplishments, needs, and objectives that they believe qualify them for this grant; and 2) a 150-word letter from a parent or other knowledgeable family member describing the family financial situation. Selection is based on grades, motivation, skills, completeness and neatness of the application, and financial need. U.S. citizenship is required.
Financial data: The stipend is $1,000. Funds are disbursed directly to the educational institution to be used for tuition and fees, books and supplies, or room and board (only if the student lives on campus).
Duration: 1 or 2 years; nonrenewable.
Number awarded: 10 each year.
Deadline: March of each year.

540 MARYLAND DELEGATE SCHOLARSHIP PROGRAM

Maryland Higher Education Commission
Attn: Office of Student Financial Assistance
839 Bestgate Road, Suite 400
Annapolis, MD 21401-3013
Phone: (410) 260-4565; (800) 974-1024, ext 4565; Fax: (410) 260-3200; TDD: (800) 735-2258
Email: osfamail@mhec.state.md.us
Web: www.mhec.state.md.us

Summary: To provide financial assistance to vocational, undergraduate, and graduate students in Maryland.
Eligibility: Open to students enrolled or planning to enroll either part-time or full-time in a vocational, undergraduate, or graduate program in Maryland. Applicants and their parents must be Maryland residents. Awards are made by state delegates to students in their district. Financial need must be demonstrated if the Office of Student Financial Assistance makes the award for the delegate.
Financial data: The minimum annual award is $200. The total amount of all state awards may not exceed the cost of attendance as determined by the school's financial aid office or $19,000, whichever is less.
Duration: 1 year; may be renewed for up to 3 additional years if the recipient maintains satisfactory academic progress.
Number awarded: Varies each year.
Deadline: February of each year.

541 MARYLAND DISTINGUISHED SCHOLAR AWARDS

Maryland Higher Education Commission
Attn: Office of Student Financial Assistance
839 Bestgate Road, Suite 400
Annapolis, MD 21401-3013
Phone: (410) 260-4546; (800) 974-1024, ext. 454; Fax: (410) 260-3200; TDD: (800) 735-2258
Email: tmckelvi@mhec.state.md.us
Web: www.mhec.state.md.us/financialAid/ProgramDescriptions/prog_ds.asp

Summary: To provide financial assistance to high school juniors in Maryland who plan to attend college in the state.
Eligibility: Open to high school juniors in Maryland who intend to enroll full-time at an accredited college, university, or private career school in the state. Students may qualify in 1 of 3 ways: 1) superior academic achievement, in which finalists are selected on the basis of GPA (minimum 3.7) and scores on PSAT, SAT, or ACT exams; 2) National Achievement Scholarship and National Merit Scholarship programs, in which finalists automatically receive these scholarships if they enroll in eligible Maryland institutions; and 3) superior talent in the arts, in which finalists are selected in statewide auditions or portfolio evaluations in visual art, instrumental music, vocal music, dance, or drama. Financial need is not considered.
Financial data: The stipend is $3,000 per year. The total amount of all state awards may not exceed the cost of attendance as determined by the school's financial aid office or $19,000, whichever is less.
Duration: 1 year; may be renewed up to 3 additional years if the recipient maintains at least a 3.0 GPA and remains enrolled full-time at an eligible Maryland institution.
Number awarded: 350 each year.
Deadline: Applications in the academic achievement category must be submitted in February of each year; nominations in the talent category must be submitted in April of each year.

542 MARYLAND DISTINGUISHED SCHOLAR COMMUNITY COLLEGE TRANSFER PROGRAM

Maryland Higher Education Commission
Attn: Office of Student Financial Assistance
839 Bestgate Road, Suite 400
Annapolis, MD 21401-3013
Phone: (410) 260-4545; (800) 974-1024, ext. 4545; Fax: (410) 260-3200; TDD: (800) 735-2258
Email: grogers@mhec.state.md.us

Web: www.mhec.state.md.us

Summary: To provide financial assistance to Maryland residents transferring from a community college to a 4-year institution in the state.

Eligibility: Open to residents of Maryland who have completed at least 60 credit hours or an associate degree program at a community college in the state with a GPA of 3.0 or higher. Applicants must be planning to transfer to a 4-year institution of higher education in Maryland and enroll as a full-time undergraduate student. Selection is based on cumulative GPA; financial need is not considered.

Financial data: The stipend is $3,000 per year. The total amount of all state awards may not exceed the cost of attendance as determined by the school's financial aid office or $19,000, whichever is less.

Duration: 1 year; may be renewed 1 additional year if the recipient maintains at least a 3.0 GPA and remains enrolled full-time at an eligible Maryland institution.

Number awarded: Varies each year.

Deadline: February of each year.

543 MARYLAND PART-TIME GRANTS

Maryland Higher Education Commission
Attn: Office of Student Financial Assistance
839 Bestgate Road, Suite 400
Annapolis, MD 21401-3013
Phone: (410) 260-4565; (800) 974-1024, ext. 4565; Fax: (410) 260-3200; TDD: (800) 735-2258
Email: osfamail@mhec.state.md.us
Web: www.mhec.state.md.us

Summary: To provide financial assistance to students in Maryland who are attending college on a part-time basis.

Eligibility: Open to students at Maryland colleges who are enrolled for at least 6 but no more than 11 credits each semester. Applicants must be able to demonstrate financial need. Both they and their parents must be Maryland residents.

Financial data: Grants range from $200 to $2,000 per year.

Duration: 1 year; may be renewed for up to 7 additional years.

Number awarded: Varies each year.

Deadline: February of each year.

544 MARYLAND SCHOLARSHIPS FOR VETERANS OF THE AFGHANISTAN AND IRAQ CONFLICTS

Maryland Higher Education Commission
Attn: Office of Student Financial Assistance
839 Bestgate Road, Suite 400
Annapolis, MD 21401-3013
Phone: (410) 260-4563; (800) 974-1024, ext. 4563; Fax: (410) 260-3200; TDD: (800) 735-2258
Email: lasplin@mhec.state.md.us
Web: www.mhec.state.md.us

Summary: To provide financial assistance for college to residents of Maryland who served in the armed forces in Afghanistan or Iraq and their children and spouses.

Eligibility: Open to Maryland residents who are 1) a veteran who served at least 60 days in Afghanistan on or after October 24, 2001 or in Iraq on or after March 19, 2003; 2) an active-duty member of the armed forces who served at least 60 days in Afghanistan or Iraq on or after those dates; 3) a member of a Reserve component of the armed forces or the Maryland National Guard who was activated as a result of the Afghanistan or Iraq conflicts and served at least 60 days; and 4) the children and spouses of such veterans, active-duty armed forces personnel, or members of Reserve forces or Maryland National Guard. Applicants must be enrolled or accepted for enrollment in a regular undergraduate program at an eligible Maryland institution. In the selection process, veterans are given priority over dependent children and spouses.

Financial data: The stipend is equal to 50% of the annual tuition, mandatory fees, and room and board of a resident undergraduate at a 4-year public institution within the University System of Maryland, currently capped at $9,026 per year. The total amount of all state awards may not exceed the cost of attendance as determined by the school's financial aid office or $19,000, whichever is less.

Duration: 1 year; may be renewed for an additional 4 years of full-time study or 7 years of part-time study, provided the recipient remains enrolled in an eligible program with a GPA of 2.5 or higher.

Number awarded: Varies each year.

Deadline: February of each year.

545 MARYLAND SENATORIAL SCHOLARSHIPS

Maryland Higher Education Commission
Attn: Office of Student Financial Assistance
839 Bestgate Road, Suite 400
Annapolis, MD 21401-3013
Phone: (410) 260-4565; (800) 974-1024, ext. 4565; Fax: (410) 260-3200; TDD: (800) 735-2258
Email: osfamail@mhec.state.md.us
Web: www.mhec.state.md.us

Summary: To provide financial assistance to vocational, undergraduate, and graduate students in Maryland.

Eligibility: Open to students enrolled either part-time or full-time in a vocational, undergraduate, or graduate program in Maryland. Applicants and their parents must be Maryland residents and able to demonstrate financial need. Awards are made by state senators to students in their districts. Some senators ask the Office of Student Financial Assistance to make awards for them; those awards are made on the basis of financial need.

Financial data: Stipends range from $400 to $9,000 per year, depending on the need of the recipient. The total amount of all state awards may not exceed the cost of attendance as determined by the school's financial aid office or $19,000, whichever is less.

Duration: 1 year; may be renewed for up to 3 additional years of full-time study or 7 additional years of part-time study, provided the recipient maintains satisfactory academic progress.

Number awarded: Varies each year.

Deadline: February of each year.

546 MARYLAND TUITION WAIVER FOR FOSTER CARE RECIPIENTS

Maryland Higher Education Commission
Attn: Office of Student Financial Assistance
839 Bestgate Road, Suite 400
Annapolis, MD 21401-3013
Phone: (410) 260-4565; (800) 974-1024, ext. 4565; Fax: (410) 260-3200; TDD: (800) 735-2258
Email: osfamail@mhec.state.md.us
Web: www.mhec.state.md.us

Summary: To provide financial assistance to residents of Maryland who have lived in foster care and plan to attend college in the state.

Eligibility: Open to Maryland residents under 21 years of age who either 1) resided in a foster care home in the state at the time they graduated from high school or completed a GED examination; or 2) resided in a foster care home in the state on their 14th birthday and were then adopted. Applicants must be planning to enroll as a degree candidate at a public 2- or 4-year higher educational institution in Maryland.

Financial data: Recipients are exempt from paying tuition and mandatory fees at public colleges and universities in Maryland.

Duration: 1 year; may be renewed for an additional 4 years or until completion of a bachelor's degree, whichever comes first, provided the recipient maintains satisfactory academic progress.

Number awarded: Varies each year.

Deadline: February of each year.

547 MAS/FPS SCHOLARSHIPS

Michigan Association of State and Federal Program Specialists
c/o Sara L. Shriver, Executive Secretary
11630 West Cannonsville Road
Trufant, MI 49347
Phone: (989) 620-5899
Email: masfps@gmail.com
Web: www.masfps.org

Summary: To provide financial assistance to high school seniors in Michigan who are planning to attend college in any state.

Eligibility: Open to seniors graduating from high schools in Michigan and planning to enroll at a college or university in any state. Applicants may be intending to major in any field. Along with their application, they must submit a 300-word personal narrative explaining why they are applying for this scholarship, including their awards, interests, leadership activities within the community, and future goals. Selection is based on that essay (20 points), a high school or college transcript from the current semester (20 points), extracurricular and leadership activities within the community or church (20 points), 3 letters of recommendation (20 points), and financial need (20 points).

Financial data: Stipends are $1,000, $500, or $250.

Duration: 1 year.
Number awarded: 3 each year: 1 each at $1,000, $500, and $250.
Deadline: January.

548 MASSACHUSETTS AUXILIARY PLUMBING-HEATING-COOLING CONTRACTORS ASSOCIATION SCHOLARSHIP

Plumbing-Heating-Cooling Contractors–National Association
Attn: PHCC Educational Foundation
180 South Washington Street
P.O. Box 6808
Falls Church, VA 22040
Phone: (703) 237-8100; (800) 533-7694; Fax: (703) 237-7442
Email: scholarships@naphcc.org
Web: www.foundation.phccweb.org/Scholarships/MAScholarship.htm
Summary: To provide financial assistance to high school seniors in Massachusetts who plan to attend college in any state and are recommended by a member of the Plumbing-Heating-Cooling Contractors (PHCC) Auxiliary.
Eligibility: Open to seniors graduating from high schools in Massachusetts who plan to enroll full-time at a 4-year college or university in any state. Applicants must be U.S. citizens and have a GPA of 2.0 or higher. They must be recommended by a member of the PHCC Association National Auxiliary who has maintained active status for at least the 2 previous years and who is a resident of Massachusetts. Along with their application, they must submit 1) an essay on why they are applying for a scholarship; 2) a statement about their career goals and how they anticipate using their education in the future; 3) a list of extracurricular and community service activities; 4) transcripts; 5) a letter of recommendation from a high school principal or counselor; and 6) ACT and/or SAT scores. Financial need is not considered in the selection process.
Financial data: The stipend is $1,500.
Duration: 1 year; nonrenewable.
Number awarded: 1 each year.
Deadline: April of each year.

549 MASSACHUSETTS CASH GRANT PROGRAM

Massachusetts Office of Student Financial Assistance
454 Broadway, Suite 200
Revere, MA 02151
Phone: (617) 727-9420; Fax: (617) 727-0667
Email: osfa@osfa.mass.edu
Web: www.osfa.mass.edu/default.asp?page=cashGrant
Summary: To provide financial assistance to Massachusetts residents who are attending state-supported colleges and universities.
Eligibility: Open to permanent legal residents of Massachusetts (for at least 1 year) who are enrolled as an undergraduate at a state-supported college or university. U.S. citizenship or permanent resident status is required. Financial need must be demonstrated.
Financial data: These awards provide assistance in meeting institutionally-held charges, such as mandatory fees and non-state-supported tuition. The amount of the award depends on the need of the recipient.
Duration: 1 year; may be renewed.
Number awarded: Varies each year.
Deadline: Deadlines are established by the financial aid office of each participating Massachusetts institution.

550 MASSACHUSETTS DSS ADOPTED CHILDREN TUITION WAIVER

Massachusetts Office of Student Financial Assistance
454 Broadway, Suite 200
Revere, MA 02151
Phone: (617) 727-9420; Fax: (617) 727-0667
Email: osfa@osfa.mass.edu
Web: www.osfa.mass.edu/default.asp?page=adoptedChildWaiver
Summary: To provide financial assistance for college to students adopted through the Massachusetts Department of Social Services (DSS).
Eligibility: Open to students 24 years of age or younger who were adopted through DSS by state employees or eligible Massachusetts residents, regardless of the date of adoption. Applicants must be U.S. citizens or permanent residents attending or planning to attend a Massachusetts public institution of higher education as an undergraduate student.
Financial data: All tuition for state-supported courses is waived.
Duration: Up to 4 academic years.
Number awarded: Varies each year.
Deadline: April of each year.

551 MASSACHUSETTS DSS TUITION WAIVER FOR FOSTER CARE CHILDREN

Massachusetts Office of Student Financial Assistance
454 Broadway, Suite 200
Revere, MA 02151
Phone: (617) 727-9420; Fax: (617) 727-0667
Email: osfa@osfa.mass.edu
Web: www.osfa.mass.edu/default.asp?page=fosterChildWaiver
Summary: To provide financial assistance for college to foster children in the custody of the Massachusetts Department of Social Services (DSS).
Eligibility: Open to students 24 years of age or younger who have been in the custody of the DSS for at least 12 consecutive months. Applicants may not have been adopted or returned home. They must be U.S. citizens or permanent residents attending or planning to attend a college or university in Massachusetts as a full-time undergraduate student.
Financial data: All tuition for state-supported courses is waived.
Duration: Up to 4 academic years.
Number awarded: Varies each year.
Deadline: April of each year.

552 MASSACHUSETTS EDUCATIONAL REWARDS GRANT PROGRAM

Massachusetts Office of Student Financial Assistance
454 Broadway, Suite 200
Revere, MA 02151
Phone: (617) 727-9420; Fax: (617) 727-0667
Email: osfa@osfa.mass.edu
Web: www.osfa.mass.edu/default.asp?page=educationalRewardsGrant
Summary: To provide financial assistance for college to Massachusetts residents who are working in low-income jobs and interested in obtaining additional training to transition to employment in targeted high-demand occupations.
Eligibility: Open to 1) dislocated workers; and 2) incumbent workers whose income is at or below 200% of the federal poverty level (currently, $21,660 for a family of 1, rising to $74,020 for a family of 8). Applicants must have been residents of Massachusetts for at least 1 year and be able to demonstrate financial need. They must be enrolled full- or part-time in a certificate or degree program in Massachusetts that will provide training in a high-demand occupational field. U.S. citizenship or permanent resident status is required.
Financial data: Awards range from $200 to $3,000 per year, depending on the need of the recipient. The award may include up to 30% of the student's calculated cost of living.
Duration: 1 year; may be renewed.
Number awarded: Varies each year.
Deadline: September of each year.

553 MASSACHUSETTS ELKS ASSOCIATION VOCATIONAL GRANTS

Massachusetts Elks Association
c/o Dennis Solomon, Vocational Scholarship Committee Chair
6 York Terrace
Beverly, MA 01913
Phone: (978) 969-1166
Web: www.masselks.org
Summary: To provide financial assistance to residents of Massachusetts interested in enrolling in a vocational educational program in any state.
Eligibility: Open to Massachusetts residents interested in enrolling full-time in a vocational technical course at a school or college leading to a terminal associate degree, a certificate, or a diploma, but not a bachelor's degree. Applicants are not required to have a high school diploma or GED certificate and they may be of any age. U.S. citizenship is required.
Financial data: The stipend is $1,000.
Duration: 1 year; recipients may reapply for a second year.
Number awarded: Varies each year; recently, 36 of these grants were awarded.
Deadline: February of each year.

554 MASSACHUSETTS ELKS SCHOLARSHIPS

Massachusetts Elks Association
Attn: Massachusetts Elks Scholarship, Inc.
63 Bay State Road
Lynnfield, MA 01940

Phone: (617) 246-5900; Fax: (617) 245-1228
Email: m.esi9@verizon.net
Web: www.masselks.org
Summary: To provide financial assistance to high school seniors in Massachusetts who plan to attend college in any state.
Eligibility: Open to seniors graduating from high schools in Massachusetts and planning to enroll at a 4-year college or university in any state. Applicants must be planning to work on a bachelor's degree. Selection is based on academic achievement, leadership, and financial need.
Financial data: Stipends range from $500 to $1,500 per year.
Duration: 1 year; may be renewed.
Number awarded: Varies each year; a total of $450,000 is available for this program annually.
Deadline: January of each year.

555 MASSACHUSETTS FOSTER CHILD GRANT PROGRAM

Massachusetts Office of Student Financial Assistance
454 Broadway, Suite 200
Revere, MA 02151
Phone: (617) 727-9420; Fax: (617) 727-0667
Email: osfa@osfa.mass.edu
Web: www.osfa.mass.edu/default.asp?page=fosterChild
Summary: To provide financial assistance for college to foster children in the custody of the Massachusetts Department of Social Services (DSS).
Eligibility: Open to students 24 years of age or younger who are current or former foster children placed in the custody of the DSS through a care and protection petition. Applicants must have signed a voluntary agreement with DSS establishing terms and conditions for receiving this aid. They must be U.S. citizens or permanent residents attending or planning to attend a college or university in the continental United States as a full-time undergraduate student.
Financial data: The stipend is $6,000 per year.
Duration: Up to 5 academic years.
Number awarded: Varies each year.
Deadline: April of each year.

556 MASSACHUSETTS JOINT ADMISSIONS TUITION ADVANTAGE WAIVER PROGRAM

Massachusetts Office of Student Financial Assistance
454 Broadway, Suite 200
Revere, MA 02151
Phone: (617) 727-9420; Fax: (617) 727-0667
Email: osfa@osfa.mass.edu
Web: www.osfa.mass.edu/default.asp?page=jointAdmissionsWaiver
Summary: To provide financial assistance to Massachusetts students who transfer from a community college to a public 4-year institution in the state.
Eligibility: Open to students who completed an associate degree at a public community college in Massachusetts within the prior calendar year as a participant in a Joint Admissions Program. Applicants must have earned a GPA of 3.0 or higher and be transferring to a state college or participating university.
Financial data: Eligible students receive a waiver of tuition equal to 33% of the resident tuition rate at the college or university they attend.
Duration: Up to 2 academic years, provided the recipient maintains a cumulative GPA of 3.0 or higher.
Number awarded: Varies each year.
Deadline: April of each year.

557 MASSACHUSETTS NEED BASED TUITION WAIVER PROGRAM

Massachusetts Office of Student Financial Assistance
454 Broadway, Suite 200
Revere, MA 02151
Phone: (617) 727-9420; Fax: (617) 727-0667
Email: osfa@osfa.mass.edu
Web: www.osfa.mass.edu/default.asp?page=needBasedWaiver
Summary: To provide financial assistance for college to Massachusetts residents who demonstrate financial need.
Eligibility: Open to permanent legal residents of Massachusetts (for at least 1 year) who are U.S. citizens or permanent residents, in compliance with Selective Service registration, current on all federal student loans, enrolled for at least 3 undergraduate units in an eligible program at a Massachusetts institution of higher learning, and able to document financial need.
Financial data: Eligible students are exempt from any tuition payments for an undergraduate degree or certificate program at public colleges or universities in Massachusetts. These awards, in combination with other resources in the student's financial aid package, may not exceed the student's demonstrated financial need.
Duration: Up to 4 academic years, for a total of 130 semester hours.
Number awarded: Varies each year.
Deadline: April of each year.

558 MASSACHUSETTS PART-TIME GRANT PROGRAM

Massachusetts Office of Student Financial Assistance
454 Broadway, Suite 200
Revere, MA 02151
Phone: (617) 727-9420; Fax: (617) 727-0667
Email: osfa@osfa.mass.edu
Web: www.osfa.mass.edu/default.asp?page=partTimeGrant
Summary: To provide financial assistance to Massachusetts residents who are attending colleges and universities on a part-time basis.
Eligibility: Open to permanent legal residents of Massachusetts (for at least 1 year) who are enrolled part-time at a public, private, independent, for profit, or nonprofit institution in Massachusetts. U.S. citizenship or permanent resident status is required. Financial need must be demonstrated.
Financial data: Awards range from $200 to a maximum that depends on the type of institution the student attends.
Duration: 1 year; may be renewed.
Number awarded: Varies each year.
Deadline: Deadlines are established by the financial aid office of each participating Massachusetts institution.

559 MASSACHUSETTS PUBLIC SERVICE GRANT PROGRAM

Massachusetts Office of Student Financial Assistance
454 Broadway, Suite 200
Revere, MA 02151
Phone: (617) 727-9420; Fax: (617) 727-0667
Email: osfa@osfa.mass.edu
Web: www.osfa.mass.edu/default.asp?page=publicServiceGrant
Summary: To provide financial assistance for college to children or widow(er)s of deceased public service officers and others in Massachusetts.
Eligibility: Open to Massachusetts residents only. They must be 1) the children or spouses of fire fighters, police officers, or corrections officers who were killed or died from injuries incurred in the line of duty; 2) children of prisoners of war or military service personnel missing in action in southeast Asia whose wartime service was credited to Massachusetts and whose service was between February 1, 1955 and the termination of the Vietnam campaign; or 3) children of veterans whose service was credited to Massachusetts and who were killed in action or died as a result of their service.
Financial data: Scholarships provide up to the cost of tuition at a state-supported college or university in Massachusetts; if the recipient attends a private Massachusetts college or university, the scholarship is equivalent to tuition at a public institution, up to $2,500.
Duration: 1 year; renewable.
Number awarded: Varies each year.
Deadline: April of each year.

560 MASSACHUSETTS VALEDICTORIAN TUITION WAIVER PROGRAM

Massachusetts Office of Student Financial Assistance
454 Broadway, Suite 200
Revere, MA 02151
Phone: (617) 727-9420; Fax: (617) 727-0667
Email: osfa@osfa.mass.edu
Web: www.osfa.mass.edu/default.asp?page=valedictorianWaiver
Summary: To provide financial assistance for college to Massachusetts residents who have been designated as valedictorians at their high school.
Eligibility: Open to seniors designated by a public or private high school in Massachusetts as a valedictorian. Applicants must have been permanent legal residents of Massachusetts for at least 1 year and be planning to enroll at a public higher education institution in the state. They must be in compliance with Selective Service registration and may not be in default on any federal student loan.

Financial data: Eligible students are exempt from any tuition payments for an undergraduate degree or certificate program at public colleges or universities in Massachusetts.
Duration: Up to 4 academic years, for a total of 130 semester hours.
Number awarded: Varies each year.
Deadline: Deadline not specified.

561 MASSACHUSETTS VETERANS TUITION WAIVER PROGRAM

Massachusetts Office of Student Financial Assistance
454 Broadway, Suite 200
Revere, MA 02151
Phone: (617) 727-9420; Fax: (617) 727-0667
Email: osfa@osfa.mass.edu
Web: www.osfa.mass.edu/default.asp?page=categoricalwaiver
Summary: To provide financial assistance for college to Massachusetts residents who are veterans.
Eligibility: Open to permanent legal residents of Massachusetts (for at least 1 year). They must be veterans who served actively during the Spanish-American War, World War I, World War II, Korea, Vietnam, the Lebanese peace keeping force, the Grenada rescue mission, the Panamanian intervention force, the Persian Gulf, or Operation Restore Hope in Somalia. They may not be in default on any federal student loan.
Financial data: Eligible veterans are exempt from any tuition payments for an undergraduate degree or certificate program at public colleges or universities in Massachusetts.
Duration: Up to 4 academic years, for a total of 130 semester hours.
Number awarded: Varies each year.
Deadline: Deadline not specified.

562 MASSGRANT PROGRAM

Massachusetts Office of Student Financial Assistance
454 Broadway, Suite 200
Revere, MA 02151
Phone: (617) 727-9420; Fax: (617) 727-0667
Email: osfa@osfa.mass.edu
Web: www.osfa.mass.edu/default.asp?page=massGrant
Summary: To provide financial assistance to Massachusetts residents who are attending college in designated states.
Eligibility: Open to students enrolled in a certificate, associate, or bachelor's degree program. Applicants must have been permanent legal residents of Massachusetts for at least 1 year and attending state-approved postsecondary schools (public, private, independent, for profit, or nonprofit) as full-time undergraduate students in Connecticut, Maine, Massachusetts, New Hampshire, Pennsylvania, Rhode Island, Vermont, or Washington, D.C. U.S. citizenship or permanent resident status is required. Selection is based on financial need, with an expected family contribution between zero and $4,617.
Financial data: Award amounts vary, depending on the type of institution.
Duration: 1 year; may be renewed for up to 4 additional years.
Number awarded: Varies each year.
Deadline: April of each year.

563 MCCA SCHOLARSHIPS

Missouri Cheerleading Coaches Association
Attn: Scholarship Director
802 South 18th Street
Unionville, MO 63565
Email: barbhodges@missouricheercoaches.org
Web: www.missouricheercoaches.org
Summary: To provide financial assistance to cheerleaders in Missouri whose coach is a member of the Missouri Cheerleading Coaches Association (MCCA) and who plan to attend college in any state.
Eligibility: Open to seniors graduating from high schools in Missouri with a GPA of 3.0 or higher and planning to attend a college or university in any state. Applicants must be cheerleaders whose coach is a MCCA member. Along with their application, they must submit a short essay on what cheerleading means to them. Selection is based on that essay, 3 letters of recommendation, transcripts, and community service; financial need is not considered.
Financial data: Stipends are $1,000 or $500. Funds are paid directly to the recipient's college or university.
Duration: 1 year; nonrenewable.
Number awarded: 14 each year: 6 at $1,000 and 8 at $500.
Deadline: January of each year.

564 MEDAL OF HONOR AFCEA ROTC SCHOLARSHIPS

Armed Forces Communications and Electronics Association
Attn: AFCEA Educational Foundation
4400 Fair Lakes Court
Fairfax, VA 22033-3899
Phone: (703) 631-6149; (800) 336-4583, ext. 6149; Fax: (703) 631-4693
Email: scholarship@afcea.org
Web: www.afcea.org/education/scholarships/rotc/MedalofHonor.asp
Summary: To provide financial assistance to ROTC cadets who demonstrate outstanding leadership performance and potential.
Eligibility: Open to ROTC cadets enrolled full-time at an accredited degree-granting 4-year college or university in the United States. Applicants must be sophomores or juniors at the time of application and have a GPA of 3.0 or higher with a major in an academic discipline. They must be U.S. citizens. Selection is based on demonstrated leadership performance and potential and strong commitment to serve in the U.S. armed forces.
Financial data: The stipend is $4,000.
Duration: 1 year.
Number awarded: 4 each year: 1 each for Army, Navy, Marine Corps, and Air Force ROTC students.
Deadline: February of each year.

565 MEDALLION FUND

New Hampshire Charitable Foundation
37 Pleasant Street
Concord, NH 03301-4005
Phone: (603) 225-6641; (800) 464-6641; Fax: (603) 225-1700
Email: info@nhcf.org
Web: www.nhcf.org/page16960.cfm
Summary: To provide financial assistance to New Hampshire residents preparing for a vocational or technical career.
Eligibility: Open to residents of New Hampshire of any age who are enrolling in an accredited vocational or technical program that does not lead to a 4-year baccalaureate degree. Applicants must be planning to attend a community college, vocational school, trade school, apprenticeship, or other short-term training program. They must be able to demonstrate financial need. Applicants should be able to demonstrate competence and a commitment to their chosen field of study. Preference is given to applicants 1) whose fields are in the traditional manufacturing trade sector (e.g., plumbing, electrical, constructing, machining); 2) who have a clear vision for how their education will help them achieve or improve their employment goals; 3) who have had little or no other educational or training opportunities; and 4) who have made a commitment to their educational program both financially and otherwise.
Financial data: Stipends are provided (amount not specified).
Duration: 1 year.
Number awarded: Varies each year.
Deadline: Applications may be submitted at any time.

566 METHODIST SEPTEMBER 11 MEMORIAL SCHOLARSHIPS

United Methodist Higher Education Foundation
Attn: Scholarships Administrator
1001 19th Avenue South
P.O. Box 340005
Nashville, TN 37203-0005
Phone: (615) 340-7385; (800) 811-8110; Fax: (615) 340-7330
Email: umhefscholarships@gbhem.org
Web: www.umhef.org/receive.php?id=sept_11_scholarship
Summary: To provide financial assistance to undergraduate and graduate students at Methodist institutions and Methodist students whose parent or guardian was disabled or killed in the terrorist attacks on September 11, 2001.
Eligibility: Open to 1) students attending a United Methodist–related college or university in the United States, and 2) United Methodist students attending a higher education institution in the United States. Applicants must have lost a parent or guardian or had a parent or guardian disabled as a result of the September 11, 2001 terrorist attacks. They must be enrolled as full-time undergraduate or graduate students. U.S. citizenship or permanent resident status is required.
Financial data: The stipend depends on the number of applicants.

Duration: 1 year; may be renewed as long as the recipients maintain satisfactory academic progress as defined by their institution.
Number awarded: Varies each year; a total of $30,000 is available for this program.
Deadline: Applications may be submitted at any time.

567 MG JAMES URSANO SCHOLARSHIP FUND

Army Emergency Relief
200 Stovall Street
Alexandria, VA 22332-0600
Phone: (703) 428-0000; (866) 878-6378; Fax: (703) 325-7183
Email: Education@aerhq.org
Web: www.aerhq.org/education_dependentchildren.asp

Summary: To provide financial assistance for college to the dependent children of Army personnel.
Eligibility: Open to dependent children under 23 years of age (including stepchildren and legally adopted children) of soldiers on active duty, retired, or deceased while on active duty or after retirement. Applicants must be unmarried and enrolled, accepted, or pending acceptance as full-time students at accredited postsecondary educational institutions. Selection is based primarily on financial need, but academic achievements and individual accomplishments are also considered.
Financial data: The amount varies, depending on the needs of the recipient, but ranges from $1,000 to $5,200 per academic year. Recently, awards averaged more than $3,000.
Duration: 1 year; may be renewed for up to 3 additional years, provided the recipient maintains a GPA of 2.0 or higher.
Number awarded: Varies each year; recently, 3,310 of these scholarships, with a value of $9,961,826, were awarded.
Deadline: February of each year.

568 MICHAEL AND DEBORAH WEINBERG SCHOLARSHIP

Vermont Student Assistance Corporation
Attn: Scholarship Programs
10 East Allen Street
P.O. Box 2000
Winooski, VT 05404-2601
Phone: (802) 654-3798; (888) 253-4819; Fax: (802) 654-3765; TDD: (800) 281-3341 (within VT)
Email: info@vsac.org
Web: services.vsac.org/wps/wcm/connect/vsac/VSAC

Summary: To provide financial assistance to residents of Vermont whose parents have volunteered with a rescue squad or fire department and who plan to attend college in any state.
Eligibility: Open to residents of Vermont who are attending or planning to attend a college or university in any state. Applicants' parents must have volunteered with a Vermont community rescue squad and/or fire department for at least 5 years. Along with their application, they must submit 1) a 250-word essay on their beliefs related to the value of community service; and 2) a 250-word essay on what they believe distinguishes their application from others that may be submitted. Selection is based on those essays, academic achievement, and financial need.
Financial data: The stipend is $2,000.
Duration: 1 year.
Number awarded: 1 each year.
Deadline: March of each year.

569 MICHAEL C. FERGUSON ACHIEVEMENT AWARDS

Delaware Higher Education Commission
Carvel State Office Building, Fifth Floor
820 North French Street
Wilmington, DE 19801-3509
Phone: (302) 577-5240; (800) 292-7935; Fax: (302) 577-6765
Email: dhec@doe.k12.de.us
Web: www.doe.k12.de.us/infosuites/students_family/dhec/default.shtml

Summary: To recognize and reward, with scholarships for college in any state, Delaware students in eighth and tenth grades who achieve high scores on the Delaware Student Testing Program.
Eligibility: Open to Delaware students in the eighth and tenth grades who have demonstrated superior performance on the Delaware Student Testing Program in reading, writing, and mathematics. Half of the awards in each class are reserved for students who participate in the free and reduced lunch program.
Financial data: The awards are $1,000 college scholarships. Students who achieve high scores in more than 1 program area (reading, writing, and mathematics) and in both eighth and tenth grades may receive multiple awards.
Duration: The awards are presented annually.
Number awarded: Up to 150 eighth graders and 150 tenth graders receive these awards each year. For each grade, 75 of the awards are reserved for students who participate in the free and reduced lunch program and 75 are presented to other students. Within each grade category, 25 awards are presented to top scorers in reading, 25 in writing, and 25 in mathematics.
Deadline: Deadline not specified.

570 MICHAEL "PUGSTER" SILOVICH SCHOLARSHIPS

Western Athletic Scholarship Association
Attn: Scholarship Coordinator
13730 Loumont Street
Whittier, CA 90601

Summary: To provide financial assistance for college to outstanding baseball players.
Eligibility: Open to graduating high school seniors who have played an active role in amateur baseball. Applicants must be planning to attend an accredited 2- or 4-year college or university. They need not have played on a high school team and are not required to play baseball in college. Selection is based on academic achievement, community service, participation in baseball, and financial need.
Financial data: The stipend is $2,000 per year.
Duration: 1 year; may be renewed.
Number awarded: Up to 10 each year.
Deadline: February of each year.

571 MICHIGAN CHILDREN OF VETERANS TUITION GRANTS

Michigan Department of Treasury
Michigan Higher Education Assistance Authority
Attn: Office of Scholarships and Grants
P.O. Box 30462
Lansing, MI 48909-7962
Phone: (517) 373-0457; (888) 4-GRANTS; Fax: (517) 335-6851
Email: osg@michigan.gov
Web: www.michigan.gov/mistudentaid

Summary: To provide financial assistance for college to the children of Michigan veterans who are totally disabled or deceased as a result of service-connected causes.
Eligibility: Open to children of Michigan veterans who have been totally and permanently disabled as a result of a service-connected illness or injury prior to death and has now died, have died or become totally and permanently disabled as a result of a service-connected illness or injury, have been killed in action or died from another cause while serving in a war or war condition, or are listed as missing in action in a foreign country. Applicants must be between 16 and 26 years of age and must have lived in Michigan at least 12 months prior to the date of application. They must be enrolled or planning to enroll at least half-time at a public institution of higher education in Michigan. U.S. citizenship or permanent resident status is required.
Financial data: Recipients are exempt from payment of the first $2,800 per year of tuition or any other fee that takes the place of tuition.
Duration: 1 year; may be renewed for up to 3 additional years if the recipient maintains full-time enrollment and a GPA of 2.25 or higher.
Number awarded: Varies each year; recently, 400 of these grants were awarded.
Deadline: Deadline not specified.

572 MICHIGAN COMPETITIVE SCHOLARSHIP PROGRAM

Michigan Department of Treasury
Michigan Higher Education Assistance Authority
Attn: Office of Scholarships and Grants
P.O. Box 30462
Lansing, MI 48909-7962
Phone: (517) 373-3394; (888) 4-GRANTS; Fax: (517) 335-5984
Email: osg@michigan.gov
Web: www.michigan.gov/mistudentaid

Summary: To provide financial assistance for college to residents of Michigan.
Eligibility: Open to Michigan residents who are attending or planning to attend an eligible Michigan college at least half-time. Applicants must demonstrate financial need, achieve a qualifying score on the ACT test (recently, the qualifying score was 23 or higher), and be a U.S. citizen, permanent resident,

or approved refugee. Students working on a degree in theology, divinity, or religious education are ineligible.

Financial data: Awards are restricted to tuition and fees, recently to a maximum of $1,300 per academic year at public universities or $2,100 at independent colleges and universities.

Duration: 1 year; the award may be renewed until 1 of the following circumstances is reached: 1) 10 years following high school graduation; 2) completion of an undergraduate degree; or 3) receipt of 10 semesters or 15 quarters of undergraduate aid. Renewals are granted only if the student maintains a GPA of 2.0 or higher and meets the institution's satisfactory academic progress policy.

Number awarded: Varies each year; recently, 27,885 students received these scholarships.

Deadline: Priority is given to students who apply by February of each year.

573 MICHIGAN ELKS ASSOCIATION GOLD KEY SCHOLARSHIP PROGRAM

Michigan Elks Association
c/o Brad P. Saegesser, Scholarship Committee Chair
2405 Townline Road
Tawas City, MI 48763
Phone: (989) 820-7171
Email: brad@idealwifi.net
Web: www.mielks.org/program/gold.html

Summary: To provide financial assistance to "special needs" students in Michigan who plan to attend college in any state.

Eligibility: Open to "special needs" students who are Michigan residents. For the purposes of this program, "special needs" students are defined as those who are physically or mentally challenged. Applicants must be high school seniors and planning to attend an accredited college, university, trade school, or vocational school in any state. They must submit a statement on the nature and degree of their "special needs"; the school they have chosen to attend and why; their educational and career goals; how they anticipate financing school; the special equipment, devices, and/or supportive services they require; and their extracurricular activities, interests, and/or hobbies. Other required submissions include high school transcripts, a 200-word letter from their parent describing the family financial situation and the student's need for assistance, 3 letters of recommendation, and verification of "special needs" from a doctor. Sponsorship by a local Elks lodge is required.

Financial data: The stipend is $2,000 per year.

Duration: 1 year; may be renewed up to 3 additional years.

Number awarded: Varies each year; recently, 8 first-year, 8 second-year, 10 third-year, and 9 fourth-year scholarships were awarded.

Deadline: The sponsoring lodge must forward the application to the district commissioner by November of each year.

574 MICHIGAN LEGION AUXILIARY NATIONAL PRESIDENT'S SCHOLARSHIP

American Legion Auxiliary
Department of Michigan
212 North Verlinden Avenue
Lansing, MI 48915
Phone: (517) 267-8809; Fax: (517) 371-3698
Email: scholarships@michalaux.org
Web: www.michalaux.org/scholarships.htm

Summary: To provide financial assistance to children of veterans in Michigan who plan to attend college in any state.

Eligibility: Open to Michigan residents who are the children of veterans who served during designated periods of war time. Applicants must be in their senior year or graduates of an accredited high school and may not yet have attended an institution of higher learning. They must have completed 50 hours of community service during their high school years. Selection is based on scholarship, character, leadership, Americanism, and financial need. The winner competes for the American Legion National President's Scholarship. If the Michigan winners are not awarded the national scholarship, then they receive this departmental scholarship.

Financial data: The stipend ranges from $1,000 to $2,500.

Duration: 1 year.

Number awarded: 1 each year.

Deadline: February of each year.

575 MICHIGAN POLICE OFFICER AND FIRE FIGHTERS SURVIVOR TUITION

Michigan Commission on Law Enforcement Standards
c/o Michigan Department of State Police
106 West Allegan, Suite 600
Lansing, MI 48909
Phone: (517) 322-3968; Fax: (517) 322-5611
Email: email@mcoles.org
Web: www.michigan.gov/mcoles/0,1607,7-229—147664—,00.html

Summary: To provide financial assistance to children and spouses of deceased Michigan police officers and fire fighters who plan to attend college in the state.

Eligibility: Open to children and spouses of Michigan police officers (including sheriffs, deputy sheriffs, village or township marshals, police officers of any city or other local jurisdiction, or officer of the state police) or fire fighter (including a member, volunteer or paid, of a fire department or other organization who was directly involved in fire suppression) killed in the line of duty. Children must have been younger than 21 at the time of death of the police officer or fire fighter and must apply for this assistance before the age of 21. Applicants must have been residents of Michigan for 12 consecutive months prior to applying. Their family income must be less than 400% of the federal poverty level.

Financial data: This program provides waiver of tuition at Michigan public colleges, universities, and community colleges.

Duration: Until completion of 124 credit hours or 9 semesters of study.

Number awarded: Varies each year.

Deadline: April of each year.

576 MICHIGAN SCHOOL SAFETY PATROL SCHOLARSHIPS

AAA Michigan
Attn: Community Safety Services
1 Auto Club Drive
Dearborn, MI 48126
Phone: (313) 336-1414; (800) 646-4222
Email: CommunitySafety@AAAMichigan.com
Web: www.autoclubgroup.com/Michigan/about_us/SchoolSafetyPatrol.asp

Summary: To provide financial assistance to high school seniors in Michigan who have served on their school safety patrol and plan to attend college in any state.

Eligibility: Open to seniors graduating from public or parochial high schools or private preparatory schools in Michigan. Applicants must have served on their AAA school safety patrol and have a strong record of participation in other community and extracurricular activities, a GPA of 3.0 or higher, and scores of 21 or better on the ACT or 950 or better on the combined mathematics and critical reading SAT. They must be planning to attend a college or university in any state. Along with their application, they must submit a letter that describes their community participation, extracurricular activities, and what being a safety patroller meant to them. Financial need is not considered in the selection process.

Financial data: The stipend is $1,000.

Duration: 1 year.

Number awarded: 2 each year.

Deadline: Students must submit their applications to their school guidance office by March of each year.

577 MICHIGAN STATE TROOPERS ASSISTANCE FUND SCHOLARSHIP PROGRAM

Michigan State Troopers Assistance Fund
c/o Scholarship Committee
1715 Abbey Road, Suite B
East Lansing, MI 48823
Phone: (517) 336-7782; Fax: (517) 336-8997
Web: www.mspta.net/MSTAF.htm

Summary: To provide financial assistance to high school seniors in Michigan who plan to attend college in any state.

Eligibility: Open to seniors graduating from high schools in Michigan who plan to attend an accredited college or vocational school in any state. Applicants must submit an essay describing the community events in which they have participated and how the experience has affected them. Selection is based on GPA (3.25 or higher), extracurricular and leadership service activities, and financial need.

Financial data: The stipend is $1,000.

Duration: 1 year.

Number awarded: 20 each year.
Deadline: March of each year.

578 MICHIGAN STATE YOUTH SOCCER ASSOCIATION COLLEGE SCHOLARSHIPS

Michigan State Youth Soccer Association
9401 General Drive, Suite 120
Plymouth, MI 48170
Phone: (734) 459-6220; Fax: (734) 459-6242
Web: www.michiganyouthsoccer.org/programs/scholarship.html
Summary: To provide financial assistance for college to high school seniors in Michigan who have played soccer.
Eligibility: Open to high school seniors who have played on an affiliate team of the Michigan State Youth Soccer Association for at least 6 seasons (3 years). Applicants must have a GPA of 2.75 or higher and be planning to attend an accredited college, university, or community college. Along with their application, they must submit 1) an official high school transcript, including ACT and/or SAT scores; 2) a 1-page personal biography that includes their athletic achievements, honorary or special interest organizations, community involvement, high school major, course of study they plan to pursue, awards or scholarships they have received, and a description of any way they have given back to soccer; and 3) an essay about how they feel soccer has helped them as an individual.
Financial data: The stipend is $1,000.
Duration: 1 year.
Number awarded: 5 each year.
Deadline: January of each year.

579 MICHIGAN TUITION GRANT PROGRAM

Michigan Department of Treasury
Michigan Higher Education Assistance Authority
Attn: Office of Scholarships and Grants
P.O. Box 30462
Lansing, MI 48909-7962
Phone: (517) 373-3394; (888) 4-GRANTS; Fax: (517) 335-5984
Email: osg@michigan.gov
Web: www.michigan.gov/mistudentaid
Summary: To provide financial assistance to residents of Michigan who plan to work on an undergraduate or graduate degree at a private college in the state.
Eligibility: Open to Michigan residents who are attending or planning to attend an independent, private, nonprofit degree-granting Michigan college or university at least half-time as an undergraduate or graduate student. Applicants must demonstrate financial need and be a U.S. citizen, permanent resident, or approved refugee. Students working on a degree in theology, divinity, or religious education are ineligible.
Financial data: Awards are limited to tuition and fees, to a maximum of $2,100 per academic year.
Duration: 1 year; the award may be renewed for a total of 10 semesters or 15 quarters of undergraduate aid or 6 semesters or 9 quarters of graduate aid.
Number awarded: Varies each year; recently, 35,518 of these grants were awarded.
Deadline: Priority is given to students who apply by February of each year.

580 MICHIGAN TUITION INCENTIVE PROGRAM

Michigan Department of Treasury
Michigan Higher Education Assistance Authority
Attn: Office of Scholarships and Grants
P.O. Box 30462
Lansing, MI 48909-7962
Phone: (517) 373-0457; (888) 4-GRANTS; Fax: (517) 335-6851
Email: osg@michigan.gov
Web: www.michigan.gov/mistudentaid
Summary: To provide financial assistance to high school seniors in Michigan who have been covered by Medicaid.
Eligibility: Open to Michigan residents who have (or have had) Medicaid coverage for 24 months within a 36 consecutive month period as identified by the Michigan Department of Human Services (DHS), formerly the Family Independence Agency (FIA). That financial eligibility can be established as early as sixth grade. Students who meet the financial eligibility guidelines are then eligible for this assistance if they graduate from high school or complete a GED prior to becoming 20 years of age. All applicants must be U.S. citizens or permanent residents. Phase I is for students who enroll in a program leading to an associate degree or certificate. Phase II is for students who enroll at least half-time at a Michigan degree-granting college or university in a 4-year program other than theology or divinity. Participants must have earned at least 56 transferable semester credits or an associate degree or certificate in Phase I before admission to Phase II.
Financial data: Phase I provides payment of tuition and mandatory fees. Phase II pays tuition and mandatory fees up to $500 per semester to a lifetime maximum of $2,000.
Duration: Students may participate in Phase I for up to 80 semester credits. Course work for Phase II must be completed within 30 months of completion of Phase I requirements.
Number awarded: Varies each year; recently, 11,710 of these awards were granted.
Deadline: Deadline not specified.

581 MIDWEST AREA REGIONAL COUNCIL (MARC) ENDOWMENT SCHOLARSHIP

Epsilon Sigma Alpha International
Attn: ESA Foundation
P.O. Box 270517
Fort Collins, CO 80527
Phone: (970) 223-2824; Fax: (970) 223-4456
Email: esainfo@esaintl.com
Web: www.esaintl.com/esaf
Summary: To provide financial assistance to residents of designated midwestern states who plan to attend college in any state.
Eligibility: Open to residents of Illinois, Indiana, Iowa, Michigan, Minnesota, Missouri, Nebraska, Ohio, South Dakota, or Wisconsin who are 1) graduating high school seniors with a GPA of 3.0 or higher or with minimum scores of 22 on the ACT or 1030 on the combined critical reading and mathematics SAT; 2) enrolled in college with a GPA of 3.0 or higher; 3) enrolled at a technical school or returning to school after an absence for retraining of job skills or obtaining a degree; or 4) engaged in online study through an accredited college, university, or vocational school. Applicants may be attending or planning to attend a school in any state and major in any field. Selection is based on character (10%), leadership (20%), service (10%), financial need (30%), and scholastic ability (30%).
Financial data: The stipend is $1,000.
Duration: 1 year; may be renewed.
Number awarded: 1 each year.
Deadline: January of each year.

582 MIDWEST STUDENT EXCHANGE PROGRAM

Midwestern Higher Education Commission
Attn: Midwest Student Exchange Program
1300 South Second Street, Suite 130
Minneapolis, MN 55454-1079
Phone: (612) 626-1602; Fax: (612) 626-8290
Email: jenniferd@mhec.org
Web: www.mhec.org/index.asp?pageID=1
Summary: To provide a tuition discount to undergraduate and graduate students from selected midwestern states who are attending schools affiliated with the Midwest Student Exchange Program.
Eligibility: Open to undergraduate and graduate students from states in the Midwest that participate in the Midwest Student Exchange Program, which is an interstate initiative established to increase interstate educational opportunities for students in Indiana, Kansas, Michigan, Minnesota, Missouri, Nebraska, North Dakota, and Wisconsin. Residents of these states may enroll in programs in the other participating states, but only at the level at which their home state admits students. All of the enrollment and eligibility decisions for the program are made by the institution.
Financial data: Participants in this program pay no more than 150% of the regular resident tuition, plus any required fees, at public colleges and universities in the state where they are enrolled. Students attending designated independent colleges and universities participating in the program receive at least a 10% reduction in their tuition. Savings typically range from $500 to $3,000 per year.
Duration: Students receive these benefits as long as they are enrolled in the program to which they were originally admitted and are making satisfactory progress towards a degree.
Number awarded: Varies each year; recently, 3,261 students were participating in this program.
Deadline: Deadline not specified.

583 MIGRANT STUDENT LEADERSHIP AND ACADEMIC SCHOLARSHIP

Washington Apple Education Foundation
Attn: Scholarship Committee
2900 Euclid Avenue
Wenatchee, WA 98801
Phone: (509) 663-7713; Fax: (509) 663-7469
Email: waef@waef.org
Web: www.waef.org/index.php?page_id=238

Summary: To provide financial assistance to residents of Washington whose families have worked as migrant laborers and who are interested in attending college in any state.

Eligibility: Open to residents of Washington who are current or former high school seniors or students already enrolled at a 2- or 4-year college, university, or trade/technical school in any state. Applicants must have moved across school boundaries for family employment in agriculture or fishing seasonal work, meeting federal eligibility criteria of the Title 1 Migrant Education Program. They must be able to demonstrate a high degree of community service involvement or ability to be a positive role model for migrant youth. Along with their application, they must submit an official transcript, their SAT or ACT scores, 2 letters of reference, and an essay on an assigned topic. Financial need is also considered in the selection process.

Financial data: The stipend is $1,000.

Duration: 1 year.

Number awarded: 2 each year.

Deadline: February of each year.

584 MIKE HYLTON AND RON NiEDERMAN SCHOLARSHIPS

Factor Support Network Pharmacy
Attn: Scholarship Committee
900 Avenida Acaso, Suite A
Camarillo, CA 93012-8749
Phone: (805) 388-9336; (877) FSN-4-YOU; Fax: (805) 482-6324
Email: Scholarships@FactorSupport.com
Web: www.factorsupport.com/scholarships.htm

Summary: To provide financial assistance for college to men with hemophilia and their immediate families.

Eligibility: Open to men with bleeding disorders and their immediate family members. Applicants must be entering or attending a college, university, juniors college, or vocational school. They must submit 3 short essays: 1) their career goals; 2) how hemophilia or von Willebrand Disease has affected their life; and 3) their efforts to be involved in the bleeding disorder community and what they can do to educate their peers and others outside their family about bleeding disorders. Selection is based on academic goals, volunteer work, school activities, other pertinent experience and achievements, and financial need.

Financial data: The stipend is $1,000. Funds are paid directly to the recipient.

Duration: 1 year.

Number awarded: 10 each year.

Deadline: April of each year.

585 MILDRED R. KNOLES SCHOLARSHIPS

American Legion Auxiliary
Department of Illinois
2720 East Lincoln Street
P.O. Box 1426
Bloomington, IL 61702-1426
Phone: (309) 663-9366; Fax: (309) 663-5827
Email: staff@ilala.org
Web: illegion.org/auxiliary/scholar.html

Summary: To provide financial assistance to Illinois veterans and their descendants who are attending college in any state.

Eligibility: Open to veterans who served during designated periods of war time and their children, grandchildren, and great-grandchildren. Applicants must be currently enrolled at a college or university in any state and studying any field except nursing. They must be residents of Illinois or members of the American Legion Family, Department of Illinois. Along with their application, they must submit a 1,000-word essay on "What my education will do for me." Selection is based on that essay (25%) character and leadership (25%), scholarship (25%), and financial need (25%).

Financial data: Stipends are $1,200 or $800.

Duration: 1 year.

Number awarded: Varies; each year 1 scholarship at $1,200 and several at $800 are awarded.

Deadline: March of each year.

586 MILITARY EDUCATION SCHOLARSHIP PROGRAM

VA Mortgage Center.com
2101 Chapel Plaza Court, Suite 107
Columbia, MO 65203
Phone: (573) 876-2729; (800) 405-6682
Web: www.vamortgagecenter.com/scholarships.html

Summary: To provide financial assistance for college to students who have ties to the military.

Eligibility: Open to 1) current and prospective ROTC program students; 2) active-duty military personnel with plans to attend college; 3) honorably-discharged veterans of the U.S. military; and 4) children of veterans or active-duty military. Applicants must be attending or planning to attend college. Selection is based primarily on an essay.

Financial data: The stipend is $1,500.

Duration: 1 year.

Number awarded: 10 each year: 5 each term.

Deadline: April or October of each year.

587 MILITARY FAMILY SUPPORT TRUST SCHOLARSHIPS

Military Family Support Trust
1010 American Eagle Boulevard
P.O. Box 301
Sun City Center, FL 33573
Phone: (813) 634-4675; Fax: (813) 633-2412
Email: president@mobc-online.org
Web: www.mobc-online.org

Summary: To provide financial assistance for college to children and grandchildren of retired and deceased officers who served in the military or designated public service agencies.

Eligibility: Open to graduating high school seniors who have a GPA of 3.0 and a minimum score of 21 on the ACT, 900 on the 2-part SAT, or 1350 on the 3-part SAT. Applicants must have a parent, guardian, or grandparent who is 1) a retired active-duty, National Guard, or Reserve officer or former officer of the U.S. Army, Navy, Marine Corps, Air Force, Coast Guard, Public Health Service, or National Oceanic and Atmospheric Administration, at the rank of O-1 through O-10, WO-1 through WO-5, or E-5 through E-9; 2) an officer who died while on active duty in service to the country; 3) a recipient of the Purple Heart, regardless of pay grade or length of service; 4) a World War II combat veteran of the Merchant Marine; 5) a federal employee at the grade of GS-7 or higher; 6) a Foreign Service Officer at the grade of FSO-8 or lower; or 7) an honorably discharged or retired foreign military officer of friendly nations meeting the service and disability retirement criteria of the respective country and living in the United States. Applicants must have been accepted to an accredited program at a college or university. Selection is based on leadership (40%), scholarship (30%), and financial need (30%).

Financial data: Stipends are $3,000, $2,000, $1,500, or $500 per year.

Duration: 4 years, provided the recipient maintains a GPA of 3.0 or higher.

Number awarded: 12 each year: 2 at $3,000 per year, 4 at $2,000 per year, 2 at $1,500 per year, and 4 at $500 per year.

Deadline: February of each year.

588 MILITARY NONRESIDENT TUITION WAIVER AFTER ASSIGNMENT IN TEXAS

Texas Higher Education Coordinating Board
Attn: Grants and Special Programs
1200 East Anderson Lane
P.O. Box 12788, Capitol Station
Austin, TX 78711-2788
Phone: (512) 427-6340; (800) 242-3062; Fax: (512) 427-6127
Email: grantinfo@thecb.state.tx.us
Web: www.collegeforalltexans.com/apps/financialaid/tofa2.cfm?ID=463

Summary: To provide educational assistance to the spouses and children of Texas military personnel assigned elsewhere.

Eligibility: Open to the spouses and dependent children of members of the U.S. armed forces or commissioned officers of the Public Health Service who remain in Texas when the member is reassigned to duty outside of the state. The spouse or dependent child must reside continuously in Texas. Applicants must be attending or planning to attend a Texas public college or university.

Financial data: Eligible students are entitled to pay tuition and fees at the resident rate at publicly-supported colleges and universities in Texas.

Duration: The waiver remains in effect for the duration of the member's first assignment outside of Texas.

Number awarded: Varies each year.

Deadline: Deadline not specified.

589 MILITARY NONRESIDENT TUITION WAIVER FOR MEMBERS, SPOUSES OR CHILDREN ASSIGNED TO DUTY IN TEXAS

Texas Higher Education Coordinating Board
Attn: Grants and Special Programs
1200 East Anderson Lane
P.O. Box 12788, Capitol Station
Austin, TX 78711-2788
Phone: (512) 427-6340; (800) 242-3062; Fax: (512) 427-6127
Email: grantinfo@thecb.state.tx.us
Web: www.collegeforalltexans.com/apps/financialaid/tofa2.cfm?ID=452

Summary: To exempt military personnel stationed in Texas and their dependents from the payment of nonresident tuition at public institutions of higher education in the state.

Eligibility: Open to members of the U.S. armed forces and commissioned officers of the Public Health Service from states other than Texas, their spouses, and dependent children. Applicants must be assigned to Texas and attending or planning to attend a public college or university in the state.

Financial data: Although persons eligible under this program are classified as nonresidents, they are entitled to pay the resident tuition at Texas institutions of higher education, regardless of their length of residence in Texas.

Duration: 1 year; may be renewed.

Number awarded: Varies each year; recently, 11,600 students received these waivers.

Deadline: Deadline not specified.

590 MILITARY NONRESIDENT TUITION WAIVER FOR MEMBERS, SPOUSES OR CHILDREN WHO REMAIN CONTINUOUSLY ENROLLED IN HIGHER EDUCATION IN TEXAS

Texas Higher Education Coordinating Board
Attn: Grants and Special Programs
1200 East Anderson Lane
P.O. Box 12788, Capitol Station
Austin, TX 78711-2788
Phone: (512) 427-6340; (800) 242-3062; Fax: (512) 427-6127
Email: grantinfo@thecb.state.tx.us
Web: www.collegeforalltexans.com/apps/financialaid/tofa2.cfm?ID=436

Summary: To waive nonresident tuition at Texas public colleges and universities for members of the armed forces and their families who are no longer in the military.

Eligibility: Open to members of the U.S. armed forces, commissioned officers of the Public Health Service (PHS), their spouses, and their children. Applicants must have previously been eligible to pay tuition at the resident rate while enrolled in a degree or certificate program at a Texas public college or university because they were a member, spouse, or child of a member of the armed forces or PHS. This waiver is available after the servicemember, spouse, or parent is no longer a member of the armed forces or a commissioned officer of the PHS. The student must remain continuously enrolled in the same degree or certificate program in subsequent terms or semesters.

Financial data: The student's eligibility to pay tuition and fees at the rate provided for Texas students does not terminate because the member, spouse, or parent is no longer in the service.

Duration: 1 year.

Number awarded: Varies each year.

Deadline: Deadline not specified.

591 MILITARY SPOUSE SCHOLARSHIPS FOR ALL MILITARY SPOUSES

National Military Family Association, Inc.
Attn: Spouse Scholarship Program
2500 North Van Dorn Street, Suite 102
Alexandria, VA 22302-1601
Phone: (703) 931-NMFA; (800) 260-0218; Fax: (703) 931-4600
Email: scholarships@militaryfamily.org
Web: www.militaryfamily.org/our-programs/military-spouse-scholarships

Summary: To provide financial assistance for postsecondary study to spouses of active and retired military personnel.

Eligibility: Open to the spouses of military personnel (active, retired, Reserve, Guard, or survivor). Applicants must be attending or planning to attend an accredited postsecondary institution to work on an undergraduate or graduate degree, professional certification, vocational training, GED or ESL, or other postsecondary training. They may enroll part- or full-time and in-class or online. Along with their application, they must submit an essay on a question that changes annually; recently, applicants were asked to write about what they like most about the health care they are receiving as a military family member, what they like the least, and what they would recommend to change it. Selection is based on that essay, community involvement, and academic achievement.

Financial data: The stipend is $1,000. Funds are paid directly to the educational institution to be used for tuition, fees, and school room and board. Support is not provided for books, rent, or previous education loans.

Duration: 1 year; recipients may reapply.

Number awarded: Varies each year; recently, the program awarded a total of 293 scholarships.

Deadline: January of each year.

592 MILITARY SPOUSE SCHOLARSHIPS FOR SPOUSES OF THE FALLEN

National Military Family Association, Inc.
Attn: Spouse Scholarship Program
2500 North Van Dorn Street, Suite 102
Alexandria, VA 22302-1601
Phone: (703) 931-NMFA; (800) 260-0218; Fax: (703) 931-4600
Email: scholarships@militaryfamily.org
Web: www.militaryfamily.org/our-programs/military-spouse-scholarships

Summary: To provide financial assistance for postsecondary study to spouses of military personnel who have been killed as a result of service since September 11, 2001.

Eligibility: Open to the spouses of military personnel who have been killed as a result of active-duty service since September 11, 2001. Applicants must be able to verify that the death was a result of service in support of the Global War on Terror. They must be attending or planning to attend an accredited postsecondary institution to work on an undergraduate or graduate degree, professional certification, vocational training, GED or ESL, or other postsecondary training. They may enroll part- or full-time and in-class or online. Along with their application, they must submit an essay on a question that changes annually; recently, applicants were asked to write about what they like most about the health care they are receiving as a military family member, what they like the least, and what they would recommend to change it. Selection is based on that essay, community involvement, and academic achievement.

Financial data: The stipend is $1,000. Funds are paid directly to the educational institution to be used for tuition, fees, and school room and board. Support is not provided for books, rent, or previous education loans.

Duration: 1 year; recipients may reapply.

Number awarded: Varies each year; recently, the program awarded a total of 293 scholarships.

Deadline: January of each year.

593 MILITARY SPOUSE SCHOLARSHIPS FOR SPOUSES OF THE WOUNDED

National Military Family Association, Inc.
Attn: Spouse Scholarship Program
2500 North Van Dorn Street, Suite 102
Alexandria, VA 22302-1601
Phone: (703) 931-NMFA; (800) 260-0218; Fax: (703) 931-4600
Email: scholarships@militaryfamily.org
Web: www.militaryfamily.org/our-programs/military-spouse-scholarships

Summary: To provide financial assistance for postsecondary study to spouses of military personnel who have been wounded as a result of service since September 11, 2001.

Eligibility: Open to the spouses of military personnel who have been wounded as a result of active-duty service since September 11, 2001. Applicants must be able to verify that the wound or injury was a result of service in support of the Global War on Terror. They must be attending or planning to attend an accredited postsecondary institution to work on an undergraduate or graduate degree, professional certification, vocational training, GED or ESL, or other postsecondary training. They may enroll part- or full-time and in-class or online. Along with their application, they must submit an essay on a question that changes annually; recently, applicants were asked to write about what they like most about the health care they are receiving as a military family member, what they like the least, and what they would recommend to change it. Selection is based on that essay, community involvement, and academic achievement.

Financial data: The stipend is $1,000. Funds are paid directly to the educational institution to be used for tuition, fees, and school room and board. Support is not provided for books, rent, or previous education loans.

Duration: 1 year; recipients may reapply.

Number awarded: Varies each year; recently, the program awarded a total of 293 scholarships.
Deadline: January of each year.

594 MILLIE BROTHER SCHOLARSHIPS

Children of Deaf Adults Inc.
c/o Jennie E. Pyers, Scholarship Committee
Wellesley College
106 Central Street, SCI480
Wellesley, MA 02842
Phone: (781) 283-3736; Fax: (781) 283-3730
Email: coda.scholarship@gmail.com
Web: coda-international.org/blog/scholarship

Summary: To provide financial assistance for college to the children of deaf parents.
Eligibility: Open to the hearing children of deaf parents who are high school seniors or graduates attending or planning to attend college. Applicants must submit a 2-page essay on 1) how their experience as the child of deaf parents has shaped their life and goals; and 2) their future career aspirations; essays are judged on organization, content, and creativity. In addition to the essay, selection is based on a high school and/or college transcript and 2 letters of recommendation.
Financial data: The stipend is $3,000.
Duration: 1 year; recipients may reapply.
Number awarded: 2 each year.
Deadline: March of each year.

595 MILLIE GONZALEZ MEMORIAL SCHOLARSHIPS

Factor Support Network Pharmacy
Attn: Scholarship Committee
900 Avenida Acaso, Suite A
Camarillo, CA 93012-8749
Phone: (805) 388-9336; (877) FSN-4-YOU; Fax: (805) 482-6324
Email: Scholarships@FactorSupport.com
Web: www.factorsupport.com/scholarships.htm

Summary: To provide financial assistance to women with a bleeding disorder.
Eligibility: Open to women with hemophilia or von Willebrand Disease who are entering or attending a college, university, juniors college, or vocational school. Applicants must submit 3 short essays: 1) their career goals; 2) how hemophilia or von Willebrand Disease has affected their life; and 3) their efforts to be involved in the bleeding disorder community and what they can do to educate their peers and others outside their family about bleeding disorders. Selection is based on academic goals, volunteer work, school activities, other pertinent experience and achievements, and financial need.
Financial data: The stipend is $1,000. Funds are paid directly to the recipient.
Duration: 1 year.
Number awarded: 5 each year.
Deadline: April of each year.

596 MILTON FISHER SCHOLARSHIP FOR INNOVATION AND CREATIVITY

Community Foundation for Greater New Haven
Attn: Associate Philanthropic Officer
70 Audubon Street
New Haven, CT 06510-9755
Phone: (203) 777-7079; Fax: (203) 777-6584
Email: bwatkins@cfgnh.org
Web: www.cfgnh.org

Summary: To provide financial assistance to residents of Connecticut and New York City who demonstrate outstanding innovation and creativity and plan to attend college in any state.
Eligibility: Open to residents of Connecticut and New York City who are high school juniors or seniors, recent high school graduates entering college in any state for the first time, or first-year students at colleges in any state. Students from other states attending or planning to attend a college, university, vocational school, or technical school in Connecticut or New York City are also eligible. Applicants must have demonstrated innovation and creativity, as in 1) solving artistic, scientific, or technical problems in new or unusual ways; 2) coming up with a distinctive solution to problems faced by their school, community, or family; or 3) creating a new group, organization, or institution that serves an important need. Along with their application, they must submit 1) a 400-word essay on their college plans and long-term goals, including what they hope to accomplish, how their goals build on what they have already accomplished, and special circumstances or obstacles in their lives; and 2) an 800-word essay on their innovative and creative activities. Selection is based primarily on those activities. Financial need is not considered, but it is used to determine the amount of the stipend.
Financial data: Stipends range up to $5,000 per year, depending on the need of the recipient.
Duration: 4 years.
Number awarded: Varies each year; recently, 8 of these scholarships were awarded.
Deadline: April of each year.

597 MINNESOTA ACADEMIC EXCELLENCE SCHOLARSHIP

Minnesota Office of Higher Education
Attn: Manager of State Financial Aid Programs
1450 Energy Park Drive, Suite 350
St. Paul, MN 55108-5227
Phone: (651) 642-0567; (800) 657-3866; Fax: (651) 642-0675; TDD: (800) 627-3529
Email: Ginny.Dodds@state.mn.us
Web: www.ohe.state.mn.us

Summary: To provide financial assistance to outstanding high school seniors or graduates in Minnesota who plan to attend college in the state.
Eligibility: Open to Minnesota residents who have demonstrated outstanding ability, achievement, and potential in English, creative writing, fine arts, foreign language, mathematics, science, or social science. Applicants must have been admitted as full-time students at a branch of the University of Minnesota, a Minnesota state university, or a private, baccalaureate degree-granting college or university in Minnesota.
Financial data: Scholarships at public institutions cover the full price of tuition and fees; scholarships at private institutions cover an amount equal to the lesser of the actual tuition and fees charged by the institution or the tuition and fees in comparable public institutions.
Duration: 1 year; may be renewed up to 3 additional years.
Number awarded: Varies each year.
Deadline: Deadline not specified.

598 MINNESOTA ACHIEVE SCHOLARSHIP PROGRAM

Minnesota Office of Higher Education
Attn: Manager of State Financial Aid Programs
1450 Energy Park Drive, Suite 350
St. Paul, MN 55108-5227
Phone: (651) 642-0567; (800) 657-3866; Fax: (651) 642-0675; TDD: (800) 627-3529
Email: Ginny.Dodds@state.mn.us
Web: www.ohe.state.mn.us

Summary: To provide financial assistance for college to high school seniors in Minnesota who complete a college-preparatory program.
Eligibility: Open to seniors graduating from high schools or home school programs in Minnesota who are planning to attend a public or private postsecondary institution in the state. Applicants must have completed 1 of the following programs of study while in high school or a home school setting: 1) a set of courses similar to the State Scholars Initiative, including 4 years of English, 3 years of science, 3 years of mathematics, 3 years of social studies, and 1 year of foreign language; 2) Advanced Placement (AP) or International Baccalaureate (IB) courses, including at least 2 courses and passing scores of 3 or higher on the AP examinations or 4 or higher on the IB examinations; 3) Minnesota Coursework requirements, including 4 years of language arts, 3 years of science (including 1 year each of a biological and physical science), 3 years of mathematics, and 2 years of a single foreign language; or 4) the Minnesota Dual Credit Program, with a grade of "B" or higher in both a mathematics course and a science course through the Post Secondary Options Enrollment program or the Concurrent Enrollment Program, worth at least 6 college credits. They must come from a low- to middle-income family (income less than $75,000 per year). U.S. citizenship or permanent resident status is required.
Financial data: The stipend ranges from $1,200 to $4,000, depending on need of the recipient.
Duration: 1 year; nonrenewable.
Number awarded: Varies each year.
Deadline: Deadline not specified.

599 MINNESOTA ASSOCIATION OF TOWNSHIPS SCHOLARSHIP PROGRAM

Minnesota Association of Townships
Attn: Scholarship Program
P.O. Box 267
St. Michael, MN 55376
Phone: (763) 497-2330; (800) 228-0296; Fax: (763) 497-3361
Email: info@mntownships.org
Web: www.mntownships.org

Summary: To provide financial assistance to high school juniors in Minnesota who plan to attend college in any state.

Eligibility: Open to students currently enrolled as juniors at public, private, and parochial high schools and home study programs in Minnesota. Applicants must be planning to attend a college, university, or vocational school in any state following graduation from high school. They must submit an essay, from 450 to 500 words, on a topic that changes annually but relates to the township form of government in Minnesota, its place and purpose in local government, and the involvement of citizens in grassroots government. Along with their application and essay, they must submit a current high school transcript and a letter of recommendation from a high school teacher or counselor. Financial need is not considered in the selection process.

Financial data: The stipend is $1,000.

Duration: 1 year.

Number awarded: Up to 4 each year.

Deadline: April of each year.

600 MINNESOTA CHILD CARE GRANT PROGRAM

Minnesota Office of Higher Education
Attn: Manager of State Financial Aid Programs
1450 Energy Park Drive, Suite 350
St. Paul, MN 55108-5227
Phone: (651) 642-0567; (800) 657-3866; Fax: (651) 642-0675; TDD: (800) 627-3529
Email: Ginny.Dodds@state.mn.us
Web: www.ohe.state.mn.us

Summary: To provide financial assistance for child care to students in Minnesota who are not receiving Minnesota Family Investment Program (MFIP) benefits.

Eligibility: Open to Minnesota residents who are working on an undergraduate degree or vocational certificate in the state and who have children age 12 and under (14 and under if disabled). U.S. citizenship or eligible noncitizen status is required. This assistance is available to help eligible residents pay child care expenses. Recipients must demonstrate financial need but must not be receiving MFIP benefits.

Financial data: The amount of the assistance depends on the income of applicant and spouse, number of day care hours necessary to cover education and work obligations, student's enrollment status, and number of eligible children in applicant's family. The maximum available is $2,600 per eligible child per academic year.

Duration: 1 year; may be renewed as long as the recipient remains enrolled on at least a half-time basis in an undergraduate program.

Number awarded: Varies each year; recently, a total of $1.1 million was provided for this program.

Deadline: Deadline not specified.

601 MINNESOTA EDUCATION AND TRAINING VOUCHERS FOR FORMER YOUTH IN CARE

Minnesota Department of Human Services
Attn: Social Services Program Consultant
444 Lafayette Road, Third Floor South
St. Paul, MN 55155-3832
Phone: (651) 431-4663
Email: DHS_ETVcoordinator@state.mn.us
Web: www.dhs.state.mn.us

Summary: To provide financial assistance for college to Minnesota residents who have been foster children.

Eligibility: Open to Minnesota residents who are younger than 21 years of age and meet at least 1 of the following conditions: were in foster care on or after their 16th birthday and remained in foster care up to or beyond their 18th birthday; were in foster care on or after their 16th birthday when a relative accepted a transfer of permanent and physical custody through a juvenile court order; are or were under state guardianship; or were adopted from foster care at age 16 or older. Applicants must have been accepted into an accredited postsecondary program that they began or will begin when they are between 18 and 21 years of age. They must attach a copy of their Free Application for Federal Student Aid (FAFSA), apply for other sources of financial aid, and submit 2 letters of recommendation.

Financial data: Stipends depend on the need of the recipient, to a maximum of $5,000 per year.

Duration: 1 year; may be renewed provided the recipient maintains a GPA of 2.0 or higher and remains younger than 23 years of age.

Number awarded: Varies each year; recently, a total of 42 students had received support through this program.

Deadline: June of each year.

602 MINNESOTA G.I. BILL PROGRAM

Minnesota Office of Higher Education
Attn: Manager of State Financial Aid Programs
1450 Energy Park Drive, Suite 350
St. Paul, MN 55108-5227
Phone: (651) 642-0567; (800) 657-3866; Fax: (651) 642-0675; TDD: (800) 627-3529
Email: Ginny.Dodds@state.mn.us
Web: www.ohe.state.mn.us

Summary: To provide financial assistance for college or graduate school in the state to residents of Minnesota who served in the military after September 11, 2001 and the families of deceased or disabled military personnel.

Eligibility: Open to residents of Minnesota enrolled at colleges and universities in the state as undergraduate or graduate students. Applicants must be 1) a veteran who is serving or has served honorably in a branch of the U.S. armed forces at any time on or after September 11, 2001; 2) a non-veteran who has served honorably for a total of 5 years or more cumulatively as a member of the Minnesota National Guard or other active or Reserve component of the U.S. armed forces, and any part of that service occurred on or after September 11, 2001; or 3) a surviving child or spouse of a person who has served in the military at any time on or after September 11, 2001 and who has died or has a total and permanent disability as a result of that military service. Financial need is also considered in the selection process.

Financial data: The stipend is $1,000 per semester for full-time study or $500 per semester for part-time study.

Duration: 1 year; may be renewed up to 4 additional years, provided the recipient continues to make satisfactory academic progress.

Number awarded: Varies each year.

Deadline: Deadline not specified.

603 MINNESOTA LEGION AUXILIARY DEPARTMENT SCHOLARSHIPS

American Legion Auxiliary
Department of Minnesota
State Veterans Service Building
20 West 12th Street, Room 314
St. Paul, MN 55155-2069
Phone: (651) 224-7634; (888) 217-9598; Fax: (651) 224-5243
Email: deptoffice@mnala.org
Web: www.mnala.org/ala/scholarship.asp

Summary: To provide financial assistance to the children and grandchildren of Minnesota veterans who are interested in attending college in the state.

Eligibility: Open to the children and grandchildren of veterans who served during designated periods of war time. Applicants must be a resident of Minnesota or a member of an American Legion post, American Legion Auxiliary unit, or Sons of the American Legion detachment in the Department of Minnesota. They must be high school seniors or graduates, have a GPA of 2.0 or higher, be able to demonstrate financial need, and be planning to attend a vocational or business school, college, or university in Minnesota. Along with their application, they must submit a brief essay, telling of their plans for college, career goals, and extracurricular and community activities.

Financial data: The stipend is $1,000. Funds are to be used to pay for tuition or books and are sent directly to the recipient's school.

Duration: 1 year.

Number awarded: 7 each year.

Deadline: March of each year.

604 MINNESOTA MASONIC CHARITIES SIGNATURE SCHOLARSHIPS

Minnesota Masonic Charities
Attn: Scholarships

11501 Masonic Home Drive
Bloomington, MN 55437
Phone: (952) 948-6004; Fax: (952) 948-6210
Email: comments@mnmasonic.org
Web: mnmasoniccharities.org/content/signature-scholarships

Summary: To provide financial assistance to high school seniors in Minnesota who plan to attend college in any state or abroad.

Eligibility: Open to seniors graduating from high schools in Minnesota who have a GPA of 3.0 or higher. Applicants must be planning to attend a college or university in any geographic location, including outside of the United States. Along with their application, they must submit brief essays on 1) their accomplishments in classroom or extracurricular activities in which they took pride; 2) why they should receive this scholarship; and 3) the person after whom these scholarships are named with whom they most identify and why. They must also submit a long essay on the values of Masonry and the relationship of those to their own lives. In the selection process, no consideration is given to Masonic ties, age, gender, religion, national origin, or financial need.

Financial data: The stipend is $5,000 per year.

Duration: 1 year; may be renewed up to 3 additional years.

Number awarded: 5 each year.

Deadline: February of each year.

605 MINNESOTA MASONIC MATCHING FUNDS SCHOLARSHIP PROGRAM

Grand Lodge of Minnesota, A.F. & A.M.
Attn: Grand Secretary
11501 Masonic Home Drive
Bloomington, MN 55437-3699
Phone: (952) 948-6700; (800) 245-6050 (within MN); Fax: (952) 948-6710
Email: grandlodge@qwest.net
Web: www.mn-masons.org/page931.aspx

Summary: To provide financial assistance to high school seniors in Minnesota who plan to attend college in any state.

Eligibility: Open to seniors graduating from high schools in Minnesota and planning to attend college in any state. Students must submit their applications to local Masonic lodges in Minnesota (for a list, contact the Grand Lodge). Each lodge selects the students.

Financial data: This program provides up to $1,500 to individual lodges, but they determine the amounts paid to students. This program dispenses $150,000 per year to lodges, but the total paid to students is more than $300,000 per year.

Duration: 1 year.

Number awarded: Approximately 450 students receive support from Masonic lodges in Minnesota each year. Since this program began, it has awarded more than $2,750,000 in funds.

Deadline: Each lodge sets its own application deadline.

606 MINNESOTA PUBLIC SAFETY OFFICERS' SURVIVOR GRANT

Minnesota Office of Higher Education
Attn: Manager of State Financial Aid Programs
1450 Energy Park Drive, Suite 350
St. Paul, MN 55108-5227
Phone: (651) 642-0567; (800) 657-3866; Fax: (651) 642-0675; TDD: (800) 627-3529
Email: Ginny.Dodds@state.mn.us
Web: www.ohe.state.mn.us

Summary: To provide financial assistance for college to survivors of deceased Minnesota public safety officers.

Eligibility: Open to dependent children (under 23 years of age) and surviving spouses of public safety officers killed in the line of duty on or after January 1, 1973. Applicants must be Minnesota residents who are enrolled at least half-time in an undergraduate degree or certificate program at a Minnesota public postsecondary institution or at a private, residential, 2- or 4-year, liberal arts, degree-granting college or university in Minnesota.

Financial data: Scholarships cover tuition and fees at state-supported institutions or provide an equivalent amount at private colleges and universities. Recently, the maximum grant was $10,488 at 4-year colleges or universities or $5,808 at 2-year colleges.

Duration: 1 year; may be renewed for a maximum of 8 semesters or 12 quarters.

Number awarded: Varies each year. Recently, a total of $40,000 was available for this program.

Deadline: Deadline not specified.

607 MINNESOTA SECTION PGA FOUNDATION JUNIOR GOLF SCHOLARSHIP

Minnesota PGA Junior Golf Association
Attn: Minnesota Section PGA Foundation
12800 Bunker Prairie Road
Coon Rapids, MN 55448
Phone: (763) 754-6641
Email: info@minnesotajuniorgolf.com
Web: www.minnesotajuniorgolf.com

Summary: To provide financial assistance to high school seniors in Minnesota who have been involved in golf and are interested in attending college in any state.

Eligibility: Open to seniors graduating from high schools in Minnesota who 1) are members of the Minnesota Section PGA Junior Golf Association; or 2) participate in a junior golf program where a Minnesota Section PGA Professional is employed. Applicants must be planning to enroll full-time at an accredited college or university in the United States. They must have a GPA of 3.0 or higher. Along with their application, they must submit a 1-page essay on why they feel they deserve a scholarship. Selection is based on that essay, high school grades, class rank, ACT/SAT scores, and extracurricular activities.

Financial data: The stipend is $4,000.

Duration: 1 year.

Number awarded: 4 each year.

Deadline: March of each year.

608 MINNESOTA STATE GRANT PROGRAM

Minnesota Office of Higher Education
Attn: Manager of State Financial Aid Programs
1450 Energy Park Drive, Suite 350
St. Paul, MN 55108-5227
Phone: (651) 642-0567; (800) 657-3866; Fax: (651) 642-0675; TDD: (800) 627-3529
Email: Ginny.Dodds@state.mn.us
Web: www.ohe.state.mn.us

Summary: To provide financial assistance to undergraduate students in Minnesota who demonstrate financial need.

Eligibility: Open to Minnesota residents who are enrolled for at least 3 credits as undergraduate students at 1 of more than 130 eligible schools in the state. They must be 1) an independent student who has resided in Minnesota for purposes other than postsecondary education for at least 12 months; 2) a dependent student whose parent or legal guardian resides in Minnesota; 3) a student who graduated from a Minnesota high school, if the student was a resident of the state during high school; or 4) a student who, after residing in Minnesota for a minimum of 1 year, earned a high school equivalency certificate in Minnesota. Students in default on a student loan or more than 30 days behind for child support owed to a public agency are not eligible.

Financial data: Applicants are required to contribute at least 46% of their cost of attendance (tuition and fees plus allowances for room and board, books and supplies, and miscellaneous expenses) from savings, earnings, loans, or other assistance from school or private sources. The other 54% is to be contributed by parents (for dependent students) or by independent students, along with a federal Pell Grant and these State Grants. Recently, maximum grants ranged from $6,309 at public technical colleges to $9,444 at private 4-year colleges; the average was approximately $1,785.

Duration: Assistance continues until the student has completed a baccalaureate degree or full-time enrollment of 8 semesters or 12 quarters, whichever comes first.

Number awarded: Varies each year. Recently, approximately 72,000 undergraduate students received $155 million in support through this program. Approximately 44% of grant funds was awarded to students with family incomes below $20,000, 39% to students with family incomes from $20,000 to $50,000, and 17% to students with family incomes over $50,000.

Deadline: June of each year.

609 MINNESOTA STATE MEMORIAL ENDOWMENT SCHOLARSHIP

Epsilon Sigma Alpha International
Attn: ESA Foundation
P.O. Box 270517
Fort Collins, CO 80527
Phone: (970) 223-2824; Fax: (970) 223-4456
Email: esainfo@esaintl.com
Web: www.esaintl.com/esaf

Summary: To provide financial assistance to residents of Minnesota who plan to attend college in any state.
Eligibility: Open to residents of Minnesota who are 1) graduating high school seniors with a GPA of 3.0 or higher or with minimum scores of 22 on the ACT or 1030 on the combined critical reading and mathematics SAT; 2) enrolled in college with a GPA of 3.0 or higher; 3) enrolled at a technical school or returning to school after an absence for retraining of job skills or obtaining a degree; or 4) engaged in online study through an accredited college, university, or vocational school. Applicants may be attending or planning to attend a school in any state and major in any field. Selection is based on character (10%), leadership (20%), service (10%), financial need (30%), and scholastic ability (30%).
Financial data: The stipend is $2,500.
Duration: 1 year; may be renewed.
Number awarded: 4 each year.
Deadline: January of each year.

610 MINNESOTA VETERANS' DEPENDENTS ASSISTANCE PROGRAM

Minnesota Office of Higher Education
Attn: Manager of State Financial Aid Programs
1450 Energy Park Drive, Suite 350
St. Paul, MN 55108-5227
Phone: (651) 642-0567; (800) 657-3866; Fax: (651) 642-0675; TDD: (800) 627-3529
Email: Ginny.Dodds@state.mn.us
Web: www.ohe.state.mn.us
Summary: To provide financial assistance for college to the dependents of Minnesota veterans and military personnel listed as POWs or MIAs.
Eligibility: Open to 1) spouses of a prisoner of war or person missing in action; or 2) children born before or during the period of time the parent served as a POW or was declared MIA; or 3) children legally adopted or in the legal custody of a parent prior to and during the time the parent served as a POW or was declared to be MIA. Veteran parents must have been residents of Minnesota at the time of entry into service or at the time declared to be a POW or MIA, which must have occurred after August 1, 1958.
Financial data: Students who attend private postsecondary institutions receive up to $250 per year for tuition and fees. Students who attend a Minnesota public postsecondary institution are exempt from all tuition charges.
Duration: Assistance continues until the student completes a bachelor's degree or receives a certificate of completion.
Number awarded: Varies each year.
Deadline: Deadline not specified.

611 MINNIE PEARL SCHOLARSHIP PROGRAM

Hearing Bridges
Attn: Scholarship Program
415 Fourth Avenue South, Suite A
Nashville, TN 37201
Phone: (615) 248-8828; (866) 385-6524; TDD: (615) 248-8828
Email: info@hearingbridges.org
Web: www.hearingbridges.org/scholarships
Summary: To provide financial assistance to hearing impaired high school seniors who want to attend college.
Eligibility: Open to high school seniors who have severe to profound bilateral hearing loss and a GPA of 3.0 or higher. Applicants must be planning to enroll full-time at a college, university, junior college, or technical school. Along with their application, they must submit brief essays on what a college education means to them, their goals after graduating from college, why they are a good candidate for this scholarship, and a difficult situation in their life and how they handled it. Selection is based on those essays, academic performance, extracurricular activities, an audiology report, and letters of recommendation. U.S. citizenship is required.
Financial data: The stipend is $2,500 per year. Payment is made directly to the college, university, or school at the rate of $1,000 per semester; a bonus of $500 is paid directly to students who achieve a GPA of 3.5 or higher.
Duration: 1 year; may be renewed up to 3 additional years if the recipient maintains a GPA of 3.0 or higher.
Number awarded: 1 each year.
Deadline: March of each year.

612 MISS AMERICA COMPETITION AWARDS

Miss America Pageant
Attn: Scholarship Department
222 New Road, Suite 700
Linwood, NJ 08221
Phone: (609) 653-8700, ext. 127; Fax: (609) 653-8740
Email: info@missamerica.org
Web: www.missamerica.org/scholarships
Summary: To provide educational scholarships to participants in the Miss America Pageant on local, state, and national levels.
Eligibility: Open to candidates who meet certain basic requirements and agree to abide by all the rules of the local, state, and national Miss America Pageants. Among the qualifications required are that the applicant be female, between the ages of 17 and 24, a resident of the town or state in which they first compete, in good health, of good moral character, and a citizen of the United States. A complete list of all eligibility requirements is available from each local and state pageant. Separate scholarships are awarded to the winners of the talent competition and the lifestyle and fitness in swimsuit competition. In addition, the Charles and Theresa Brown Scholarships are awarded to Miss America, the top 4 runners-up, Miss Alaska, Miss Hawaii, Miss Illinois, Miss Ohio, and 1 other state representative.
Financial data: More than $45 million in cash and tuition assistance is awarded annually at the local, state, and national Miss America Pageants. At the national level, nearly $500,000 is awarded: Miss America receives $50,000 in scholarship money, the first runner-up $25,000, second runner-up $20,000, third runner-up $15,000, fourth runner-up $10,000, the top finalist $8,000, 4 other finalists $6,000 each, the top 2 semifinalists $5,000 each, 3 other semifinalists $4,000 each, and other national contestants $3,000 each. Other awards include those for the 3 preliminary talent winners at $2,000 each, the 3 preliminary lifestyle and fitness in swimsuit winners at $1,000 each, and the 5 non-finalist talent winners at $1,000 each. The Charles and Theresa Brown Scholarships are $2,500 each.
Duration: The pageants are held every year.
Number awarded: At the national level, 52 contestants (1 from each state, the District of Columbia, and the Virgin Islands) share the awards.
Deadline: Varies, depending upon the date of local pageants leading to the state and national finals.

613 MISS AMERICA SCHOLAR AWARDS

Miss America Pageant
Attn: Scholarship Department
222 New Road, Suite 700
Linwood, NJ 08221
Phone: (609) 653-8700, ext. 127; Fax: (609) 653-8740
Email: info@missamerica.org
Web: www.missamerica.org/scholarships/missstate.aspx
Summary: To recognize and reward, with college scholarships, women who participate in the Miss America Pageant at the state level and demonstrate academic excellence.
Eligibility: Open to women who compete at the state level of the Miss America Pageant. Selection is based on academic excellence (grades, course content, and academic standing of the institution).
Financial data: The stipend is $1,000.
Duration: 1 year.
Number awarded: Up to 52 each year: 1 for each of the states, the District of Columbia, and the Virgin Islands.
Deadline: Varies, depending upon the date of local pageants leading to the state finals.

614 MISS DEAF AMERICA AMBASSADOR PROGRAM

National Association of the Deaf
8630 Fenton Street, Suite 820
Silver Spring, MD 20910-3819
Phone: (301) 587-1788; Fax: (301) 587-1791; TDD: (301) 587-1789
Email: nadinfo@nad.org
Web: www.nad.org/youth-leadership-programs
Summary: To recognize and reward outstanding young deaf women.
Eligibility: Open to young deaf women between the ages of 18 and 30. They compete first on the state level; winners then take part in the national pageant. Winners are selected on the basis of artistic expression, community service, academics, current events, deaf culture, and more.
Financial data: The national winner receives an educational scholarship (amount not specified).
Duration: The competition is held biennially during the summer of even-numbered years, in conjunction with the National Association of the Deaf conventions.

Deadline: The deadline dates of the state competitions vary; check with the sponsor in your area.

615 MISSISSIPPI EDUCATIONAL ASSISTANCE FOR MIA/POW DEPENDENTS

Mississippi State Veterans Affairs Board
3460 Highway 80 East
P.O. Box 5947
Pearl, MS 39288-5947
Phone: (601) 576-4850; Fax: (601) 576-4868
Email: grice@vab.state.ms.us
Web: www.vab.state.ms.us/booklet.htm

Summary: To provide financial assistance for college to the children of Mississippi residents who are POWs or MIAs.

Eligibility: Open to the children of members of the armed services whose official home of record and residence is in Mississippi and who are officially reported as being either a prisoner of a foreign government or missing in action. Applicants must be attending or planning to attend a state-supported college or university in Mississippi.

Financial data: This is an entitlement program; assistance covers all costs of college attendance.

Duration: Up to 8 semesters.

Number awarded: Varies each year.

Deadline: Deadline not specified.

616 MISSISSIPPI EMINENT SCHOLARS GRANTS

Mississippi Office of Student Financial Aid
3825 Ridgewood Road
Jackson, MS 39211-6453
Phone: (601) 432-6997; (800) 327-2980 (within MS); Fax: (601) 432-6527
Email: sfa@ihl.state.ms.us
Web: www.mississippi.edu/riseupms/financialaid-state.php

Summary: To provide financial assistance to residents of Mississippi who have exceptional academic records and plan to attend college in the state.

Eligibility: Open to seniors graduating from high schools in Mississippi, home-schooled students in the state with less than 12 college hours, and college students who graduated from high school or completed a home school program within the past 3 years and have completed 12 or more college hours. Applicants must have been residents of Mississippi for at least 1 year prior to enrolling in college and have a high school or college GPA of 3.5 or higher and a score of 29 or higher on the ACT or 1280 or higher on the SAT; if they qualified as a semifinalist or finalist in the National Merit Scholarship Competition or the National Achievement Scholarship Competition, they are not required to have the minimum ACT score. They must be enrolled or planning to enroll as a full-time student at an approved college or university in the state.

Financial data: The stipend is $2,500 per year, not to exceed tuition and required fees.

Duration: 1 year; may be renewed for up to 4 additional years or completion of an undergraduate degree, as long as the recipient maintains continuous full-time enrollment and a cumulative GPA of 3.5 or higher.

Number awarded: Varies each year.

Deadline: September of each year.

617 MISSISSIPPI HIGHER EDUCATION LEGISLATIVE PLAN FOR NEEDY STUDENTS

Mississippi Office of Student Financial Aid
3825 Ridgewood Road
Jackson, MS 39211-6453
Phone: (601) 432-6997; (800) 327-2980 (within MS); Fax: (601) 432-6527
Email: sfa@ihl.state.ms.us
Web: www.mississippi.edu/riseupms/financialaid-state.php

Summary: To provide financial assistance for college to residents of Mississippi who demonstrate financial need.

Eligibility: Open to residents of Mississippi (for at least 2 years) who have graduated from high school within the immediate past 2 years. They must be enrolled or planning to enroll full-time at a college or university in the state. High school seniors entering their freshman year in college must have a cumulative high school GPA of 2.5 or higher and have completed specific high school core curriculum requirements. College freshmen entering their sophomore year must have achieved a cumulative GPA of 2.5 or higher on all college course work previously completed. All applicants must have scored 20 or higher on the ACT and be able to demonstrate financial need with an average family adjusted gross income of $41,500 or less over the prior 2 years (rising by $5,000 for each sibling in the family under 21 years of age).

Financial data: Students in this program receive a full waiver of tuition at eligible Mississippi public institutions of higher learning or eligible Mississippi public community/junior colleges. Students attending private institutions receive an award amount equal to the award of a student attending the nearest comparable public institution.

Duration: 1 year; may be renewed up to 4 additional years, provided the recipient continues to meet all program requirement and maintains a GPA of 2.5 or higher.

Number awarded: Varies each year, depending on the availability of funds; awards are granted on a first-come, first-served basis.

Deadline: March of each year.

618 MISSISSIPPI LAW ENFORCEMENT OFFICERS AND FIREMEN SCHOLARSHIP PROGRAM

Mississippi Office of Student Financial Aid
3825 Ridgewood Road
Jackson, MS 39211-6453
Phone: (601) 432-6997; (800) 327-2980 (within MS); Fax: (601) 432-6527
Email: sfa@ihl.state.ms.us
Web: www.mississippi.edu/riseupms/financialaid-state.php

Summary: To provide financial assistance to the spouses and children of disabled or deceased Mississippi law enforcement officers and fire fighters who are interested in attending college in the state.

Eligibility: Open to children and spouses of law enforcement officers, full-time fire fighters, and volunteer fire fighters who became permanently and totally disabled or who died in the line of duty and were Mississippi residents at the time of death or injury. Applicants must be high school seniors or graduates interested in attending a state-supported postsecondary institution in Mississippi on a full-time basis. Children may be natural, adopted, or stepchildren up to 23 years of age; spouses may be of any age.

Financial data: Students in this program receive full payment of tuition fees, the average cost of campus housing, required fees, and applicable course fees at state-supported colleges and universities in Mississippi. Funds may not be used to pay for books, food, school supplies, materials, dues, or fees for extracurricular activities.

Duration: Up to 8 semesters.

Number awarded: Varies each year.

Deadline: September of each year.

619 MISSISSIPPI TUITION ASSISTANCE GRANTS

Mississippi Office of Student Financial Aid
3825 Ridgewood Road
Jackson, MS 39211-6453
Phone: (601) 432-6997; (800) 327-2980 (within MS); Fax: (601) 432-6527
Email: sfa@ihl.state.ms.us
Web: www.mississippi.edu/riseupms/financialaid-state.php

Summary: To provide financial assistance to Mississippi residents who demonstrate significant financial need and are interested in attending college in the state.

Eligibility: Open to students entering their freshman, sophomore, junior, or senior year as a full-time student at an eligible Mississippi college or university. Applicants must have been Mississippi residents for at least 1 year and be receiving less than the full federal Pell Grant for college. High school seniors must have a GPA of 2.5 or higher and an ACT score of 15 or higher. Home-schooled students must submit a transcript showing the course work corresponding to that of a high school graduate for grades 9–12 and an ACT score of 15 or higher. Students already enrolled in college must have a cumulative GPA of 2.5 or higher. All applicants must be attending or planning to attend a 2- or 4-year public or private accredited college or university in Mississippi.

Financial data: Awards depend on the availability of funds and the need of the recipient; the maximum award for a freshman or sophomore is $500 per year; the maximum award for a junior or senior is $1,000 per year.

Duration: 1 year; may be renewed for up to 4 additional years or completion of an undergraduate degree, as long as the recipient maintains continuous full-time enrollment and a GPA of 2.5 or higher.

Number awarded: Varies each year.

Deadline: September of each year.

620 MISSOURI AMERICAN LEGION COMMANDER'S SCHOLARSHIPS

American Legion
Department of Missouri
P.O. Box 179
Jefferson City, MO 65102-0179
Phone: (573) 893-2353; (800) 846-9023; Fax: (573) 893-2980
Email: info@missourilegion.org
Web: www.missourilegion.org/programs/scholarships/index.htm

Summary: To provide financial assistance to veterans in Missouri who are interested in attending college in the state.

Eligibility: Open to residents of Missouri who served at least 90 days in the U.S. armed forces and received an honorable discharge. Applicants must be enrolled or planning to enroll full-time at an accredited vocational/technical school, college, or university in Missouri.

Financial data: The stipend is $1,000.

Duration: 1 year.

Number awarded: 2 each year.

Deadline: April of each year.

621 MISSOURI GENERAL BPW SCHOLARSHIPS

Missouri Business and Professional Women's Foundation, Inc.
P.O. Box 28243
Kansas City, MO 64188
Phone: (816) 333-6959; Fax: (816) 333-6959
Email: jo.mofedbpw@gmail.com
Web: www.mofedbpw.org/files/index.php?id=14

Summary: To provide financial assistance to women in Missouri who plan to attend college in any state.

Eligibility: Open to women in Missouri who have been accepted into an accredited program or course of study in any state to upgrade their skills and/or complete education for career advancement. Along with their application, they must submit brief statements on the following: their achievements and/or specific recognitions in their field of endeavor; professional and/or civic affiliations; present and long-range career goals; how they plan to participate in and contribute to their community upon completion of their program of study; why they feel they would make a good recipient; and any special circumstances that may have influenced their ability to continue or complete their education. They must also demonstrate financial need and U.S. citizenship.

Financial data: A stipend is awarded (amount not specified).

Duration: 1 year.

Number awarded: Varies each year; recently, 3 of these scholarships were awarded.

Deadline: December of each year.

622 MISSOURI HIGHER EDUCATION ACADEMIC "BRIGHT FLIGHT" SCHOLARSHIP PROGRAM

Missouri Department of Higher Education
Attn: Student Financial Assistance
3515 Amazonas Drive
Jefferson City, MO 65109-5717
Phone: (573) 751-2361; (800) 473-6757; Fax: (573) 751-6635
Email: info@dhe.mo.gov
Web: www.dhe.mo.gov/brightflight.html

Summary: To provide financial assistance to high school seniors in Missouri who achieve high scores on standardized tests and plan to attend college in the state.

Eligibility: Open to seniors graduating from high schools in Missouri who plan to enroll full-time at a participating college or university in the state. Applicants with SAT scores of 800 or higher in critical reading and 790 or higher in mathematics or composite ACT scores of 31 or higher qualify for the highest level of awards. Applicants with SAT scores of 770 to 799 in critical reading and 780 to 789 in mathematics or composite ACT scores of 30 qualify for the second level of awards. Students working on a degree or certificate in theology or divinity are not eligible. U.S. citizenship or permanent resident status is required.

Financial data: The stipend for students in the highest level of SAT or ACT scores is $3,000 per year. The stipend for students in the second level of SAT or ACT scores is $1,000 per year.

Duration: 1 year; may be renewed for up to 4 additional years or until completion of a baccalaureate degree, provided the recipient maintains full-time status and satisfactory academic progress.

Number awarded: Varies each year; recently, 8,823 of these scholarships, worth more than $16 million, were awarded.

Deadline: July of each year.

623 MISSOURI PUBLIC SERVICE OFFICER OR EMPLOYEE'S CHILD SURVIVOR GRANT PROGRAM

Missouri Department of Higher Education
Attn: Student Financial Assistance
3515 Amazonas Drive
Jefferson City, MO 65109-5717
Phone: (573) 751-2361; (800) 473-6757; Fax: (573) 751-6635
Email: info@dhe.mo.gov
Web: www.dhe.mo.gov/publicserviceofficer.html

Summary: To provide financial assistance for college to spouses and children of disabled and deceased Missouri public employees and public safety officers.

Eligibility: Open to residents of Missouri who are 1) public safety officers who were permanently disabled in the line of duty; 2) spouses of public safety officers who were permanently and totally disabled in the line of duty; or 3) children of Missouri public safety officers or Department of Transportation employees who were killed or permanently disabled while engaged in the construction or maintenance of highways, roads, and bridges. Applicants must be Missouri residents enrolled or accepted for enrollment as a full-time undergraduate student at a participating Missouri college or university; children must be younger than 24 years of age. Students working on a degree or certificate in theology or divinity are not eligible. U.S. citizenship or permanent resident status is required.

Financial data: The maximum annual grant is the lesser of 1) the actual tuition charged at the school where the recipient is enrolled; or 2) the amount of tuition charged to a Missouri undergraduate resident enrolled full-time in the same class level and in the same academic major as an applicant at the University of Missouri at Columbia.

Duration: 1 year; may be renewed.

Number awarded: Varies each year; recently, 11 students received $47,045 in support from this program.

Deadline: There is no application deadline, but early submission of the completed application is encouraged.

624 MISSOURI STATE COUNCIL ENDOWMENT SCHOLARSHIP

Epsilon Sigma Alpha International
Attn: ESA Foundation
P.O. Box 270517
Fort Collins, CO 80527
Phone: (970) 223-2824; Fax: (970) 223-4456
Email: esainfo@esaintl.com
Web: www.esaintl.com/esaf

Summary: To provide financial assistance to residents of Missouri who plan to attend college in any state.

Eligibility: Open to residents of Missouri who are 1) graduating high school seniors with a GPA of 3.0 or higher or with minimum scores of 22 on the ACT or 1030 on the combined critical reading and mathematics SAT; 2) enrolled in college with a GPA of 3.0 or higher; 3) enrolled at a technical school or returning to school after an absence for retraining of job skills or obtaining a degree; or 4) engaged in online study through an accredited college, university, or vocational school. Applicants may be attending or planning to attend a school in any state and major in any field. Selection is based on character (10%), leadership (20%), service (10%), financial need (30%), and scholastic ability (30%).

Financial data: The stipend is $1,000.

Duration: 1 year; may be renewed.

Number awarded: 1 each year.

Deadline: January of each year.

625 MISSOURI VIETNAM VETERAN SURVIVOR GRANT PROGRAM

Missouri Department of Higher Education
Attn: Student Financial Assistance
3515 Amazonas Drive
Jefferson City, MO 65109-5717
Phone: (573) 751-2361; (800) 473-6757; Fax: (573) 751-6635
Email: info@dhe.mo.gov
Web: www.dhe.mo.gov/vietnamveterans.html

Summary: To provide financial assistance to survivors of certain deceased Missouri Vietnam veterans who plan to attend college in the state.

Eligibility: Open to surviving spouses and children of veterans who served in the military in Vietnam or the war zone in southeast Asia, who were residents of Missouri when first entering military service and at the time of death, whose death was attributed to or caused by exposure to toxic chemicals during the Vietnam conflict, and who served in the Vietnam Theater between 1961 and 1972. Applicants must be Missouri residents enrolled in a program leading to a certificate, associate degree, or baccalaureate degree at an approved postsecondary institution in the state. Students working on a degree or certificate in theology or divinity are not eligible. U.S. citizenship or permanent resident status is required.

Financial data: The maximum annual grant is the lesser of 1) the actual tuition charged at the school where the recipient is enrolled; or 2) the amount of tuition charged to a Missouri undergraduate resident enrolled full-time in the same class level and in the same academic major as an applicant at the Missouri public 4-year regional institutions.

Duration: 1 semester; may be renewed until the recipient has obtained a baccalaureate degree or has completed 150 semester credit hours, whichever comes first.

Number awarded: Up to 12 each year.

Deadline: There is no application deadline, but early submission of the completed application is encouraged.

626 MISSOURI WARTIME VETERAN'S SURVIVOR GRANT PROGRAM

Missouri Department of Higher Education
Attn: Student Financial Assistance
3515 Amazonas Drive
Jefferson City, MO 65109-5717
Phone: (573) 751-2361; (800) 473-6757; Fax: (573) 751-6635
Email: info@dhe.mo.gov
Web: www.dhe.mo.gov/wartimevetsurvivor.html

Summary: To provide financial assistance to survivors of deceased or disabled Missouri post-September 11, 2001 veterans who plan to attend college or graduate school in the state.

Eligibility: Open to spouses and children of veterans whose deaths or injuries were a result of combat action or were attributed to an illness that was contracted while serving in combat action, or who became 80% disabled as a result of injuries or accidents sustained in combat action since September 11, 2001. The veteran must have been a Missouri resident when first entering military service or at the time of death or injury. The spouse or child must be a U.S. citizen or permanent resident or otherwise lawfully present in the United States; children of veterans must be younger than 25 years of age. All applicants must be enrolled or accepted for enrollment at least half-time at an approved public college or university in Missouri and working on an associate, baccalaureate, master's, or doctoral degree.

Financial data: The maximum annual grant is the lesser of 1) the actual tuition charged at the school where the recipient is enrolled; or 2) the amount of tuition charged to a Missouri resident enrolled in the same number of hours at the University of Missouri Columbia. Additional allowances provide up to $2,000 per semester for room and board and the lesser of the actual cost for books or $500.

Duration: 1 year. May be renewed, provided the recipient maintains a GPA of 2.5 or higher and makes satisfactory academic progress; children of veterans are eligible until they turn 25 years of age or receive their first bachelor's degree, whichever occurs first.

Number awarded: Up to 25 each year.

Deadline: There is no application deadline, but early submission of the completed application is encouraged.

627 MISSOURI'S A+ SCHOOLS FINANCIAL INCENTIVE PROGRAM

Missouri Department of Elementary and Secondary Education
Attn: Division of School Improvement
205 Jefferson Street
P.O. Box 480
Jefferson City, MO 65102-0480
Phone: (573) 751-9094; Fax: (573) 522-8455
Email: webreplyimpraplus@dese.mo.gov
Web: dese.mo.gov/divimprove/aplus/index.html

Summary: To provide financial assistance to high school seniors who graduate from a designated "A+ School" in Missouri and are interested in attending a community college or vocational institute in the state.

Eligibility: Open to students who graduate from a designated "A+ School" in Missouri. Applicants must meet the following requirements: have attended a designated A+ School for 3 consecutive years prior to graduation, have a GPA of at least 2.5, have at least a 95% attendance record, perform at least 50 hours of unpaid tutoring or mentoring, maintain a record of good citizenship and avoid the unlawful use of drugs or alcohol, and be planning to attend a community college or postsecondary vocational/technical school on a full-time basis in Missouri.

Financial data: Recipients are offered state-paid assistance (full tuition and books) to attend any public community college or technical school in the state.

Duration: 1 year; may be renewed if the recipient maintains a GPA of 2.5 or higher.

Number awarded: Since the tuition program began in 1997, more than 106,500 students have qualified for this assistance and more than 44,100 have utilized at least 1 semester of the financial incentive.

Deadline: Deadline not specified.

628 MOMENI FOUNDATION FINANCIAL ASSISTANCE SCHOLARSHIPS

Momeni Foundation
12720 S.W. Allen Boulevard
Beaverton, OR 97005
Phone: (503) 349-4939; Fax: (503) 626-5719
Email: momenifoundation@aol.com
Web: momenifoundation.org/fas_doc.html

Summary: To provide financial assistance for college or graduate school in the United States or Iran to students of Iranian descent.

Eligibility: Open to graduating high school seniors, undergraduates, and graduate students who are enrolled or planning to enroll full-time at an accredited college. Applicants may be citizens or residents of any country, but they must be of Iranian descent. They must have a GPA of 3.0 or higher. Along with their application, they must submit 1) a short narrative, in English or Persian, describing their goals and plans and what has motivated them to follow those goals and plans; and 2) a resume of extracurricular activities, community leadership or volunteerism, membership in clubs or organizations, and any other evidence of outstanding achievement. Students planning to attend or attending universities in Iran are especially encouraged to apply. Financial need is considered in the selection process.

Financial data: The stipend ranges from $500 to $1,000.

Duration: 1 year.

Number awarded: At least 10 each year.

Deadline: June of each year.

629 MONTANA COMMUNITY COLLEGE HONOR SCHOLARSHIPS

Montana Guaranteed Student Loan Program
2500 Broadway
P.O. Box 203101
Helena, MT 59620-3101
Phone: (406) 444-0638; (800) 537-7508; Fax: (406) 444-1869
Email: scholarships@mgslp.state.mt.us
Web: www.mgslp.state.mt.us/Content/Paying_for_College/Scholarships

Summary: To provide financial assistance to outstanding community college students in Montana planning to transfer to a university in the state.

Eligibility: Open to residents of Montana who are graduating from a community college in the state and planning to transfer to a branch of the Montana University System. Their college must verify that they are one of the highest ranking members of their class desiring to attend a Montana University System unit.

Financial data: Students eligible for this benefit are entitled to attend any unit of the Montana University System without payment of undergraduate registration or incidental fees.

Duration: 1 year; nonrenewable.

Number awarded: The number of scholarships awarded at each community college is based on the size of the graduating class.

Deadline: Deadline not specified.

630 MONTANA GEAR UP ACHIEVEMENT GRANTS

Office of the Commissioner of Higher Education
Attn: Montana GEAR UP Program
P.O. Box 203201
Helena, MT 59620-3201
Phone: (406) 444-0350; Fax: (406) 444-0425
Email: cchenoweth@montana.edu
Web: www.gearup.montana.edu/scholarships_grants.htm

Summary: To provide financial assistance for college to juniors at high schools in Montana that are participating in the Gaining Early Awareness and Readiness for Undergraduate Programs (GEAR UP) federal program.

Eligibility: Open to high school juniors who have been enrolled in the college preparatory curriculum for at least 2 years at a Montana high school that is participating in the GEAR UP program. Applicants must have a cumulative GPA

of 2.0 or higher at the end of the fourth semester of high school and upon high school graduation. They must enroll in a Montana postsecondary institution within 18 months of high school graduation.
Financial data: The stipend is $1,500.
Duration: 1 year.
Number awarded: Varies each year; recently, 262 students received these grants.
Deadline: November of each year.

631 MONTANA GOVERNOR'S "BEST AND BRIGHTEST" MERIT AT-LARGE SCHOLARSHIPS

Montana Guaranteed Student Loan Program
2500 Broadway
P.O. Box 203101
Helena, MT 59620-3101
Phone: (406) 444-0638; (800) 537-7508; Fax: (406) 444-1869
Email: scholarships@mgslp.state.mt.us
Web: www.mgslp.state.mt.us/Content/Paying_for_College/Scholarships
Summary: To provide financial assistance to Montana residents who are attending or planning to attend designated institutions in the state and can demonstrate academic merit.
Eligibility: Open to residents of Montana who have been accepted or are enrolled as a full-time student at components of the Montana University System, community colleges, Indian colleges, or designated private institutions in the state. Applicants must have a GPA of 3.0 or higher and a score of at least 20 on the ACT or 1440 on the SAT. Nontraditional and home-schooled students are encouraged to apply.
Financial data: The stipend is $2,000 per year.
Duration: 1 year; may be renewed 1 additional year for students at community colleges or 3 additional years for students at 4-year campuses. Renewal requires satisfactory academic progress and full-time enrollment.
Number awarded: Varies each year; recently, this program awarded 121 new and 119 renewal scholarships.
Deadline: February of each year.

632 MONTANA GOVERNOR'S "BEST AND BRIGHTEST" MERIT SCHOLARSHIPS

Montana Guaranteed Student Loan Program
2500 Broadway
P.O. Box 203101
Helena, MT 59620-3101
Phone: (406) 444-0638; (800) 537-7508; Fax: (406) 444-1869
Email: scholarships@mgslp.state.mt.us
Web: www.mgslp.state.mt.us/Content/Paying_for_College/Scholarships
Summary: To provide financial assistance to high school seniors in Montana who are planning to attend designated institutions in the state and can demonstrate academic merit.
Eligibility: Open to graduating high school seniors in Montana who have been accepted as a full-time student at components of the Montana University System, community colleges, Indian colleges, or designated private institutions in the state. Applicants must have a GPA of 3.0 or higher and a score of at least 20 on the ACT or 1440 on the SAT. They must be nominated by officials at their high school.
Financial data: The stipend is $2,000 per year.
Duration: 1 year; may be renewed 1 additional year for students at community colleges or 3 additional years for students at 4-year campuses. Renewal requires satisfactory academic progress and full-time enrollment.
Number awarded: Varies each year; recently, this program awarded 166 new and 271 renewal scholarships.
Deadline: February of each year.

633 MONTANA GOVERNOR'S "BEST AND BRIGHTEST" NEED-BASED SCHOLARSHIPS

Montana Guaranteed Student Loan Program
2500 Broadway
P.O. Box 203101
Helena, MT 59620-3101
Phone: (406) 444-0638; (800) 537-7508; Fax: (406) 444-1869
Email: scholarships@mgslp.state.mt.us
Web: www.mgslp.state.mt.us/Content/Paying_for_College/Scholarships
Summary: To provide financial assistance to Montana residents who are attending or planning to attend designated institutions in the state and can demonstrate financial need.
Eligibility: Open to residents of Montana who have been accepted or are enrolled as a full-time student at components of the Montana University System, community colleges, Indian colleges, or designated private institutions in the state. Each institution is allocated a specific number of general, health science, technology, or trade/green scholarships. Selection is based only on financial need.
Financial data: The stipend is $1,000 per year.
Duration: 1 year; may be renewed 1 additional year provided the recipient maintains satisfactory academic progress and continues to demonstrate financial need.
Number awarded: Varies each year; recently, this program awarded 553 new and 764 renewal scholarships.
Deadline: February of each year.

634 MONTANA HONOR SCHOLARSHIPS FOR NATIONAL MERIT SCHOLARSHIP SEMIFINALISTS

Montana Guaranteed Student Loan Program
2500 Broadway
P.O. Box 203101
Helena, MT 59620-3101
Phone: (406) 444-0638; (800) 537-7508; Fax: (406) 444-1869
Email: scholarships@mgslp.state.mt.us
Web: www.mgslp.state.mt.us/Content/Paying_for_College/Scholarships
Summary: To provide financial assistance for undergraduate education to National Merit Scholarship semifinalists in Montana.
Eligibility: Open to residents of Montana who are National Merit Scholarship semifinalists. Students must enroll at a campus of the Montana University System or community college in the state within 9 months of high school graduation.
Financial data: Students eligible for this benefit are entitled to attend any unit of the Montana University System without payment of undergraduate registration or incidental fees.
Duration: The waiver is valid through the completion of the first academic year of enrollment.
Number awarded: Varies each year.
Deadline: Deadline not specified.

635 MONTANA HONORABLY DISCHARGED VETERAN WAIVER

Montana Guaranteed Student Loan Program
2500 Broadway
P.O. Box 203101
Helena, MT 59620-3101
Phone: (406) 444-0638; (800) 537-7508; Fax: (406) 444-1869
Email: scholarships@mgslp.state.mt.us
Web: www.mgslp.state.mt.us
Summary: To provide financial assistance for undergraduate or graduate studies to selected Montana veterans.
Eligibility: Open to honorably-discharged veterans who served with the U.S. armed forces and who are residents of Montana. Only veterans who at some time qualified for U.S. Department of Veterans Affairs (VA) educational benefits, but who are no longer eligible or have exhausted their benefits, are entitled to this waiver. Veterans who served any time prior to May 8, 1975 are eligible to work on undergraduate or graduate degrees. Veterans whose service began after May 7, 1975 are eligible only to work on their first undergraduate degree. They must have received an Armed Forces Expeditionary Medal for service in Lebanon, Grenada, or Panama; served in a combat theater in the Persian Gulf between August 2, 1990 and April 11, 1991 and received the Southwest Asia Service Medal; were awarded the Kosovo Campaign Medal; or served in a combat theater in Afghanistan or Iraq after September 11, 2001 and received the Global War on Terrorism Expeditionary Medal, the Afghanistan Campaign Medal, or the Iraq Campaign Medal. Financial need must be demonstrated.
Financial data: Veterans eligible for this benefit are entitled to attend any unit of the Montana University System without payment of registration or incidental fees.
Duration: Students are eligible for continued fee waiver as long as they make reasonable academic progress as full-time students.
Number awarded: Varies each year.
Deadline: Deadline not specified.

636 MONTANA NATIONAL GUARD SCHOLARSHIPS

Montana National Guard
Attn: Education Service Officer
P.O. Box 4789
Fort Harrison, MT 59636-4789
Phone: (406) 324-3238
Web: www.montanaguard.com/rrwebsite/ed_mtscholarship.htm

Summary: To provide financial assistance for college to members of the Montana National Guard.

Eligibility: Open to members of the Montana National Guard who are enrolled or accepted for enrollment at a college, university, vocational/technical college, or other VA-approved training program in the state. Applicants must be in pay grades E-1 through E-7, W-1 through W-3, or O-1 through O-2; have completed Initial Active Duty for Training; have a high school diploma or GED; be eligible for Montgomery GI Bill Selected Reserve Benefits or be under a 6-year obligation to the Montana National Guard; and not have completed more than 16 years of military service. Funds are awarded on a first-come, first-served basis until exhausted.

Financial data: Support is provided at the rate of $100 per credit, up to $1,000 per semester, to assist with tuition and books.

Duration: 1 year; may be renewed.

Number awarded: Varies each year.

Deadline: Deadline not specified.

637 MONTANA STATE ESA COUNCIL ENDOWMENT SCHOLARSHIP

Epsilon Sigma Alpha International
Attn: ESA Foundation
P.O. Box 270517
Fort Collins, CO 80527
Phone: (970) 223-2824; Fax: (970) 223-4456
Email: esainfo@esaintl.com
Web: www.esaintl.com/esaf

Summary: To provide financial assistance to residents of Montana interested in attending college in the state.

Eligibility: Open to residents of Montana who are 1) graduating high school seniors with a GPA of 3.0 or higher or with minimum scores of 22 on the ACT or 1030 on the combined critical reading and mathematics SAT; 2) enrolled in college with a GPA of 3.0 or higher; 3) enrolled at a technical school or returning to school after an absence for retraining of job skills or obtaining a degree; or 4) engaged in online study through an accredited college, university, or vocational school. Applicants must be attending or planning to attend a school in Montana and major in any field. Selection is based on character (10%), leadership (20%), service (10%), financial need (30%), and scholastic ability (30%).

Financial data: The stipend is $1,000.

Duration: 1 year; may be renewed.

Number awarded: 1 each year.

Deadline: January of each year.

638 MONTANA TUITION ASSISTANCE PROGRAM BAKER GRANTS

Montana Guaranteed Student Loan Program
2500 Broadway
P.O. Box 203101
Helena, MT 59620-3101
Phone: (406) 444-0638; (800) 537-7508; Fax: (406) 444-1869
Email: scholarships@mgslp.state.mt.us
Web: www.mgslp.state.mt.us/Content/Paying_for_College/Grants

Summary: To provide financial assistance to Montana residents who are attending college in the state and working to support themselves.

Eligibility: Open to residents of Montana who are attending units of the Montana University System, community colleges, Indian colleges, or designated private institutions in the state full-time. Applicants must be working and have at least $3,275 in earned income during the prior calendar year. (That amount is based on the minimum wage multiplied by 500 hours; if the minimum wage is increased, the amount a student must earn is increased accordingly.) They must be making satisfactory academic progress toward their first undergraduate degree and have an expected family contribution from the results of their Free Application for Federal Student Aid (FAFSA) of $7,850 or less.

Financial data: The grant is intended to offset any federal Pell Grant dollars the student may have lost due to earned wages. Recently, grants ranged from $100 to $1,000.

Duration: 1 year.

Number awarded: Varies each year; recently, 2,400 students received more than $2.0 million in grants through this program.

Deadline: Deadline not specified.

639 MONTANA UNIVERSITY SYSTEM HONOR SCHOLARSHIPS

Montana Guaranteed Student Loan Program
2500 Broadway
P.O. Box 203101
Helena, MT 59620-3101
Phone: (406) 444-0638; (800) 537-7508; Fax: (406) 444-1869
Email: scholarships@mgslp.state.mt.us
Web: www.mgslp.state.mt.us/Content/Paying_for_College/Scholarships

Summary: To provide financial assistance to high school students in Montana who have outstanding academic records and plan to attend college in the state.

Eligibility: Open to residents of Montana who are graduating from high school and planning to attend a branch of the Montana University System or a community college in the state. Applicants must have been enrolled at an accredited high school for at least 3 years prior to graduation, meet the college preparatory requirements, submit ACT or SAT scores to their high school, and have a GPA of 3.4 or higher. They must be nominated by their high school. Selection is based on class rank and ACT or SAT score.

Financial data: Students eligible for this benefit are entitled to attend any unit of the Montana University System or any community college in the state without payment of tuition or registration fees.

Duration: 1 year; may be renewed for up to 3 additional years if the recipient maintains full-time enrollment and a GPA of 3.4 or higher.

Number awarded: Up to 200 each year.

Deadline: Applications must be submitted to high school officials by February of each year.

640 MONTANA WAR ORPHANS WAIVER

Montana Guaranteed Student Loan Program
2500 Broadway
P.O. Box 203101
Helena, MT 59620-3101
Phone: (406) 444-0638; (800) 537-7508; Fax: (406) 444-1869
Email: scholarships@mgslp.state.mt.us
Web: www.mgslp.state.mt.us

Summary: To provide financial assistance for undergraduate education to the children of Montana veterans who died in the line of duty or as a result of service-connected disabilities.

Eligibility: Open to children of members of the U.S. armed forces who served on active duty during World War II, the Korean Conflict, the Vietnam Conflict the Afghanistan Conflict, or the Iraq Conflict; were legal residents of Montana at the time of entry into service; and were killed in action or died as a result of injury, disease, or other disability while in the service. Applicants must be no older than 25 years of age. Financial need is considered in the selection process.

Financial data: Students eligible for this benefit are entitled to attend any unit of the Montana University System without payment of undergraduate registration or incidental fees.

Duration: Undergraduate students are eligible for continued fee waiver as long as they maintain reasonable academic progress as full-time students.

Number awarded: Varies each year.

Deadline: Deadline not specified.

641 MONTGOMERY GI BILL (ACTIVE DUTY)

Department of Veterans Affairs
Attn: Veterans Benefits Administration
810 Vermont Avenue, N.W.
Washington, DC 20420
Phone: (202) 418-4343; (888) GI-BILL1
Web: www.gibill.va.gov/GI_Bill_Info/benefits.htm

Summary: To provide financial assistance for college, graduate school, and other types of postsecondary schools to new enlistees in any of the armed forces after they have completed their service obligation.

Eligibility: Open to veterans who received an honorable discharge and have a high school diploma, a GED, or, in some cases, up to 12 hours of college credit; veterans who already have a bachelor's degree are eligible to work on a master's degree or higher. Applicants must also meet the requirements of 1 of the following categories: 1) entered active duty for the first time after June 30, 1985, had military pay reduced by $100 per month for the first 12 months, and continuously served for 3 years, or 2 years if that was their original enlistment, or 2 years if they entered Selected Reserve within a year of leaving active duty and served

4 years (the 2 by 4 program); 2) entered active duty before January 1, 1977, had remaining entitlement under the Vietnam Era GI Bill on December 31, 1989, served at least 1 day between October 19, 1984 and June 30, 1985, and stayed on active duty through June 30, 1988 (or June 30, 1987 if they entered Selected Reserve within 1 year of leaving active duty and served 4 years); 3) on active duty on September 30, 1990 and separated involuntarily after February 2, 1991, involuntarily separated on or after November 30, 1993, or voluntarily separated under either the Voluntary Separation Incentive (VSI) or Special Separation Benefit (SSB) program, and before separation had military pay reduced by $1,200; or 4) on active duty on October 9, 1996, had money remaining in an account from the Veterans Educational Assistance Program (VEAP), elected Montgomery GI Bill (MGIB) by October 9, 1997, and paid $1,200. Certain National Guard members may also qualify under category 4 if they served on full-time active duty between July 1, 1985 and November 28, 1989, elected MGIB between October 9, 1996 and July 8, 1997, and paid $1,200. Following completion of their service obligation, participants may enroll in colleges or universities for associate, bachelor, or graduate degrees; in courses leading to a certificate or diploma from business, technical, or vocational schools; for apprenticeships or on-the-job training programs; in correspondence courses; in flight training; for preparatory courses necessary for admission to a college or graduate school; for licensing and certification tests approved for veterans; or in state-approved teacher certification programs. Veterans who wish to enroll in certain high-cost technology programs (life science, physical science, engineering, mathematics, engineering and science technology, computer specialties, and engineering, science, and computer management) may be eligible for an accelerated payment.

Financial data: For veterans in categories 1, 3, and 4 who served on active duty for 3 years or more, the current monthly stipend for college or university work is $1,368 for full-time study, $1,026 for three-quarter time study, $684 for half-time study, or $342 for quarter-time study or less; for apprenticeship and on-the-job training, the monthly stipend is $1,026 for the first 6 months, $752.40 for the second 6 months, and $478.80 for the remainder of the program. For enlistees whose initial active-duty obligation was less than 3 years, the current monthly stipend for college or university work is $1,111 for full-time study, $833.25 for three-quarter time study, $550.50 for half-time study, or $275.75 for quarter-time study or less; for apprenticeship and on-the-job training, the monthly stipend is $833.25 for the first 6 months, $611.05 for the second 6 months, and $388.85 for the remainder of the program. For veterans in category 2 with remaining eligibility, the current monthly stipend for institutional study full-time is $1,556 for no dependents, $1,592 with 1 dependent, $1,623 with 2 dependents, and $16 for each additional dependent; for three-quarter time study, the monthly stipend is $1,167.50 for no dependents, $1,194 with 1 dependent, $1,217.50 with 2 dependents, and $12 for each additional dependent; for half-time study, the monthly stipend is $778 for no dependents, $796 with 1 dependent, $811.50 with 2 dependents, and $8.50 for each additional dependent. For those veterans pursuing an apprenticeship or on-the-job training, the current monthly stipend for the first 6 months is $1,128.75 for no dependents, $1,141.13 with 1 dependent, $1,152 with 2 dependents, and $5.25 for each additional dependent; for the second 6 months, the current monthly stipend is $808.78 for no dependents, $818.13 with 1 dependent, $825.83 with 2 dependents, and $3.85 for each additional dependent; for the third 6 months, the current monthly stipend is $502.60 for no dependents, $508.73 with 1 dependent, $513.45 with 2 dependents, and $2.45 for each additional dependent; for the remainder of the training period, the current monthly stipend is $490.70 for no dependents, $496.48 with 1 dependent, $501.73 with 2 dependents, and $2.45 for each additional dependent. Other rates apply for less than half-time study, cooperative education, correspondence courses, and flight training. Veterans who qualify for the accelerated payment and whose entitlement does not cover 60% of tuition and fees receive an additional lump sum payment to make up the difference between their entitlement and 60% of tuition and fees.

Duration: 36 months; active-duty servicemembers must utilize the funds within 10 years of leaving the armed services; Reservists may draw on their funds while still serving.

Number awarded: Varies each year.

Deadline: Deadline not specified.

642 MONTGOMERY GI BILL (SELECTED RESERVE)

Department of Veterans Affairs
Attn: Veterans Benefits Administration
810 Vermont Avenue, N.W.
Washington, DC 20420
Phone: (202) 418-4343; (888) GI-BILL1
Web: www.gibill.va.gov/GI_Bill_Info/benefits.htm

Summary: To provide financial assistance for college or graduate school to members of the Reserves or National Guard.

Eligibility: Open to members of the Reserve elements of the Army, Navy, Air Force, Marine Corps, and Coast Guard, as well as the Army National Guard and the Air National Guard. To be eligible, a Reservist must 1) have a 6-year obligation to serve in the Selected Reserves signed after June 30, 1985 (or, if an officer, to agree to serve 6 years in addition to the original obligation); 2) complete Initial Active Duty for Training (IADT); 3) meet the requirements for a high school diploma or equivalent certificate before completing IADT; and 4) remain in good standing in a drilling Selected Reserve unit. Reservists who enlisted after June 30, 1985 can receive benefits for undergraduate degrees, graduate training, or technical courses leading to certificates at colleges and universities. Reservists whose 6-year commitment began after September 30, 1990 may also use these benefits for a certificate or diploma from business, technical, or vocational schools; cooperative training; apprenticeship or on-the-job training; correspondence courses; independent study programs; tutorial assistance; remedial, deficiency, or refresher training; flight training; or state-approved alternative teacher certification programs.

Financial data: The current monthly rate is $333 for full-time study, $249 for three-quarter time study, $169 for half-time study, or $83.25 for less than half-time study. For apprenticeship and on-the-job training, the monthly stipend is $249.75 for the first 6 months, $183.15 for the second 6 months, and $116.55 for the remainder of the program. Other rates apply for cooperative education, correspondence courses, and flight training.

Duration: Up to 36 months for full-time study, 48 months for three-quarter study, 72 months for half-time study, or 144 months for less than half-time study.

Number awarded: Varies each year.

Deadline: Applications may be submitted at any time.

643 MONTGOMERY GI BILL TUITION ASSISTANCE TOP-UP

Department of Veterans Affairs
Attn: Veterans Benefits Administration
810 Vermont Avenue, N.W.
Washington, DC 20420
Phone: (202) 418-4343; (888) GI-BILL1
Web: www.gibill.va.gov/GI_Bill_Info/benefits.htm

Summary: To supplement the tuition assistance provided by the military services to their members.

Eligibility: Open to military personnel who have served at least 2 full years on active duty and are approved for tuition assistance by their military service. Applicants must be participating in the Montgomery GI Bill (MGIB) Active Duty program and be eligible for MGIB benefits. This assistance is available to servicemembers whose military service does not pay 100% of tuition and fees.

Financial data: This program pays the difference between what the military services pay for tuition assistance and the full amount of tuition and fees, to a maximum of $1,075 per month.

Duration: Up to 36 months of payments are available.

Number awarded: Varies each year.

Deadline: Deadline not specified.

644 MOOSE YOUTH AWARENESS PROGRAM

Moose International, Inc.
Attn: Department of Fraternal Programs
155 South International Drive
Mooseheart, IL 60539-1183
Phone: (630) 966-2224; Fax: (630) 966-2225
Web: www.mooseintl.org/public/ComScv/YouthAware.asp

Summary: To recognize and reward, with college scholarships, high school students who deliver talks to children about current issues.

Eligibility: Open to high school students who develop brief talks to deliver to groups of children 4 to 9 years of age whom they identify in their community. The talks must deal with such current issues as drug and alcohol abuse, child abuse, "stranger danger," bullying and peer pressure, and healthy habits and nutrition. Students must make at least 3 talks in their community and submit written reports on their presentations. School officials select 2 participating students to attend a local student congress; selection is based on academic ability and leadership qualities. At those congresses, participants present their talks to fellow students, and 60 of them are selected by their peers to attend the International Student Congress. At that Congress, participating students vote to select the winners of the scholarships.

Financial data: First prize is a $12,000 scholarship, second an $8,000 scholarship, third a $5,000 scholarship, fourth a $3,000 scholarship, and fifth a $2,000 scholarship. All expenses to attend the International Student Congress are paid by local Moose Lodges.

Duration: The competition is held annually.

Number awarded: 5 each year.

Deadline: Local student congresses are held in October and November of each year.

645 MORTON A. GIBSON MEMORIAL SCHOLARSHIP

Jewish Social Service Agency of Metropolitan Washington
200 Wood Hill Road
Rockville, MD 20850
Phone: (301) 610-8353
Email: dbecker@jssa.org
Web: www.jssa.org/services/community/scholarships

Summary: To provide financial assistance to Jewish students from the Washington, D.C. area who have completed volunteer service activities and plan to attend college in any state.

Eligibility: Open to high school seniors who have performed significant volunteer service in the Jewish community or under the auspices of Jewish organizations in the Washington, D.C. area. Applicants must have been admitted as full-time students to an accredited 4-year undergraduate program in the United States. They must be U.S. citizens or working toward citizenship. Along with their application, they must submit a 500-word essay describing their volunteer service. Students in community colleges, Israeli schools, or year-abroad programs are not eligible. Selection is based on volunteer service, financial need, and academic achievement.

Financial data: The stipend is $2,500.

Duration: 1 year.

Number awarded: 1 or 2 each year.

Deadline: March of each year.

646 MOTHER ELNORA JOHNSON VISIONARY AWARD

David and Dovetta Wilson Scholarship Fund, Inc.
115-67 237th Street
Elmont, NY 11003-3926
Phone: (516) 285-4573
Email: DDWSF4@aol.com
Web: www.wilsonfund.org/ElnoraJohnson.html

Summary: To provide financial assistance to high school seniors who are interested in going to college and demonstrate a commitment to the values and vision of Mother Elnora Johnson.

Eligibility: Open to graduating high school seniors who have actively participated in community and religious projects and can demonstrate financial need. Applicants must be U.S. citizens or permanent residents and have a GPA of 3.0 or higher. Along with their application, they must submit 3 letters of recommendation, high school transcripts, and an essay (up to 250 words) on "How My College Education Will Help Me Make a Positive Impact on My Community." This award is presented to applicants who demonstrate that the values of Mother Elnora Johnson, a "love of God, hard work, and education," are the means to a successful life.

Financial data: The stipend is $1,000.

Duration: 1 year.

Number awarded: 1 or more each year.

Deadline: March of each year.

647 MOUNT OLIVET FOUNDATION GRANTS

Mount Olivet United Methodist Church
Attn: Mount Olivet Foundation
1500 North Glebe Road
Arlington, VA 22207-2199
Phone: (703) 527-3934; Fax: (703) 524-8613
Email: scutshaw@mtolivet-umc.org
Web: www.mountolivetfoundation.org

Summary: To provide financial assistance to undergraduate and graduate students, particularly Methodists.

Eligibility: Open to undergraduate and graduate students, especially those already enrolled in a degree program. In the selection process, first preference is given to individuals connected to Mount Olivet United Methodist Church, second to members of a United Methodist Church in any state, third to residents of Arlington and northern Virginia, fourth to residents of the Washington, D.C. metropolitan area, and finally to residents of other areas. Financial need is considered in the selection process.

Financial data: Stipends range from $500 to $1,500.

Duration: 1 year.

Number awarded: A limited number are awarded each year.

Deadline: March, June, September, or December of each year.

648 MOUSE HOLE SCHOLARSHIPS

Blind Mice Mart
16810 Pinemoor Way
Houston, TX 77058
Phone: (713) 883-7277
Email: blindmicemart@att.net
Web: www.blindmicemart.com/assets/product_images/Scholarship.htm

Summary: To provide financial assistance for college to blind students and the children of blind parents.

Eligibility: Open to visually impaired students and to sighted students who have visually impaired parents. Applicants must be high school seniors or graduates who have never been enrolled in college. Along with their application, they must submit an essay, between 3 and 15 pages in length, on a topic that changes annually; recently, students were asked to speculate on what will be happening to them in the following 10 years. Essays are judged on originality, creativity, grammar, spelling, and the judge's overall impression of the applicant.

Financial data: The maximum stipend is $1,250.

Duration: 1 year.

Number awarded: Varies each year; the program attempts to award 2 scholarships at $1,250 and others depending on the availability of funds. Recently, a total of $4,250 in scholarships were awarded.

Deadline: May of each year.

649 MR. AND MRS. GUS T. JONES MEMORIAL SCHOLARSHIP

San Antonio Area Foundation
Attn: Scholarship Funds Program Officer
110 Broadway, Suite 230
San Antonio, TX 78205
Phone: (210) 228-3759; Fax: (210) 225-1980
Email: buresti@ssafdn.org
Web: www.saafdn.org/NetCommunity/Page.aspx?pid=257

Summary: To provide financial assistance to high school seniors in Texas who plan to attend college in any state.

Eligibility: Open to seniors graduating from high schools in Texas. Applicants must be planning to attend college in any state and major in any field. Selection is based on academic achievement and financial need.

Financial data: Stipends vary; recently, they averaged $1,800.

Duration: 1 year; may be renewed.

Number awarded: Varies each year; recently, 6 of these scholarships were awarded.

Deadline: March of each year.

650 MR. AND MRS. MOICHI OKAZAKI SCHOLARSHIP

Club 100 Veterans
Attn: Scholarship Committee
520 Kamoku Street
Honolulu, HI 96826-5120
Phone: (808) 946-0272
Email: daisyy@hgea.net

Summary: To provide financial assistance to high school seniors and college students from Hawaii who are attending or planning to attend a college or university on the mainland.

Eligibility: Open to 1) high school seniors from Hawaii who are planning to attend an institution of higher learning on the mainland; and 2) full-time undergraduate students at community colleges, vocational/trade schools, 4-year colleges and universities on the mainland who graduated from a high school in Hawaii. Applicants must have a GPA of 2.5 or higher and be able to demonstrate civic responsibility and community service. Along with their application, they must submit an essay on how the pre- and postwar lives and roles of Asian American women who are married to a veteran of the 100th Infantry Battalion have changed. They must also conduct and transcribe a 60-minute interview with at least 1 of the wives of 100th Infantry Battalion Infantry veterans. Selection is based on that essay and the applicant's promotion of the legacy of the 100th Infantry Battalion and its motto of "For Continuing Service." Financial need is not considered.

Financial data: The stipend is $1,000.

Duration: 1 year; nonrenewable.

Number awarded: 1 each year.

Deadline: April of each year.

651 MSSDAR SCHOLARSHIP

Daughters of the American Revolution–Missouri State Society
Attn: State Scholarship Chair
821 Main Street
Boonville, MO 65233-1657
Phone: (660) 882-5320
Email: hyhope@sbcglobal.net
Web: www.mssdar.org

Summary: To provide financial assistance to high school seniors in Missouri who plan to attend college in the state.

Eligibility: Open to seniors graduating from high schools in Missouri in the top 10% of their class. Applicants must be planning to attend an accredited college or university in Missouri. They must be sponsored by a chapter of the Daughters of the American Revolution (DAR) in Missouri and able to demonstrate financial need. U.S. citizenship is required.

Financial data: A stipend is awarded (amount not specified).

Duration: 1 year.

Number awarded: 1 or more each year.

Deadline: January of each year.

652 N. JOYCE PAYNE/MILLER BREWING COMPANY SCHOLARSHIP

Thurgood Marshall College Fund
Attn: Scholarship Manager
80 Maiden Lane, Suite 2204
New York, NY 10038
Phone: (212) 573-8487; (877) 690-8673; Fax: (212) 573-8497
Email: srogers@tmcfund.org
Web: www.thurgoodmarshallfund.net

Summary: To provide financial assistance to African American males enrolled at colleges and universities that are members of the Thurgood Marshall College Fund (TMCF).

Eligibility: Open to African American males currently enrolled full-time at 1 of the 47 colleges and universities that are TMCF members. Applicants must have a GPA of 3.0 or higher and be able to demonstrate financial need. U.S. citizenship is required.

Financial data: The stipend is $4,400.

Duration: 1 year.

Number awarded: 1 each year.

Deadline: July of each year.

653 NA HOALOHA O KAMEHAMEHA CLASS OF '52 SCHOLARSHIP

Ke Ali'i Pauahi Foundation
Attn: Financial Aid & Scholarship Services
567 South King Street, Suite 160
Honolulu, HI 96813
Phone: (808) 534-3966; (800) 842-4682, ext. 43966; Fax: (808) 534-3890
Email: scholarships@pauahi.org
Web: www.pauahi.org/scholarships

Summary: To provide financial assistance to undergraduate students at schools in any state, especially those of Hawaiian descent.

Eligibility: Open to students who are working on or planning to work on a certificate or degree from an accredited vocational or business school or a 2- or 4-year college or university in any state. Applicants must have a GPA of 2.0 or higher and be able to demonstrate financial need. Residency in Hawaii is not required, but preference is given to Native Hawaiians (descendants of the aboriginal inhabitants of the Hawaiian Islands prior to 1778).

Financial data: The stipend is $1,000.

Duration: 1 year.

Number awarded: 2 each year.

Deadline: March of each year.

654 NACA REGIONAL COUNCIL STUDENT LEADER SCHOLARSHIPS

National Association for Campus Activities
Attn: NACA Foundation
13 Harbison Way
Columbia, SC 29212-3401
Phone: (803) 732-6222; Fax: (803) 749-1047
Email: scholarships@naca.org
Web: www.naca.org/Scholarships/Pages/default.aspx

Summary: To provide financial assistance to outstanding college student leaders.

Eligibility: Open to full-time undergraduate students who have made significant contributions to their campus communities, have played leadership roles in campus activities, and have demonstrated leadership skills and abilities. Financial need is not considered in the selection process. U.S. citizenship is required.

Financial data: The amounts of the awards vary each year; scholarships are to be used for educational expenses, including tuition, books, fees, or other related expenses.

Number awarded: 7 each year: 1 in each of the association's regions.

Deadline: April of each year.

655 NANCY PENN LYONS SCHOLARSHIP FUND

Community Foundation for Greater Atlanta, Inc.
50 Hurt Plaza, Suite 449
Atlanta, GA 30303
Phone: (404) 688-5525; Fax: (404) 688-3060
Email: scholarships@cfgreateratlanta.org
Web: www.cfgreateratlanta.org/Grants-Support/Scholarships.aspx

Summary: To provide financial assistance to seniors at high schools in Georgia planning to attend a "prestigious" or out-of-state university.

Eligibility: Open to seniors graduating from high schools in Georgia who have been residents of the state for at least 1 year. Applicants must have a cumulative high school GPA of 3.0 or higher and a combined SAT critical reading and mathematics score of 1000 or higher or an ACT composite score of 22 or higher. They must be able to demonstrate financial need and commitment to community service. Preference is given to students attending selective private and/or out-of-state universities; students attending public colleges or universities in Georgia are not eligible.

Financial data: The stipend is $5,000 per year.

Duration: 1 year; may be renewed up to 3 additional years.

Number awarded: 5 each year.

Deadline: April of each year.

656 NANOR KRIKORIAN HIGH SCHOOL STUDENT SCHOLARSHIPS

Armenian Youth Federation
104 North Belmont Street, Suite 206
Glendale, CA 91206
Phone: (818) 507-1933; Fax: (818) 240-3442
Email: ayf@ayfwest.org
Web: www.ayfwest.org/programs/scholarship

Summary: To provide financial assistance for college to high school seniors of Armenian descent.

Eligibility: Open to college-bound high school seniors of Armenian descent. Applicants must be able to demonstrate involvement in community service activities, clubs and organizations on campus, and athletics. Along with their application, they must submit a 1,000-word essay on how their major and/or future plans will benefit the Armenian community. Financial need is not considered in the selection process.

Financial data: Stipends are $1,000, $500, or $250.

Duration: 1 year.

Number awarded: 4 each year: 1 at $1,000, 1 at $500, and 2 at $250.

Deadline: March of each year.

657 NATIONAL ACHIEVEMENT SCHOLARSHIP PROGRAM

National Merit Scholarship Corporation
Attn: National Achievement Scholarship Program
1560 Sherman Avenue, Suite 200
Evanston, IL 60201-4897
Phone: (847) 866-5100; Fax: (847) 866-5113
Web: www.nationalmerit.org/nasp.php

Summary: To provide financial assistance for college to Black American high school seniors with exceptional scores on standardized examinations.

Eligibility: Open to Black American seniors who are enrolled full-time in a secondary school and progressing normally toward graduation or completion of high school requirements. Applicants must be U.S. citizens (or intend to become a citizen as soon as qualified) and be planning to attend an accredited college or university in the United States. They must take the PSAT/NMSQT at the proper time in high school (no later than the 11th grade) and mark section 14 on the PSAT/NMSQT answer sheet, which identifies them as a Black American who is requesting consideration in the Achievement Program. Final selection is based on the student's academic record, a self-description, PSAT/NMSQT and SAT scores, and a recommendation written by the principal or another official. Financial information is not considered, nor are college choice, course of study, or career plans.

Financial data: The stipend is $2,500.

Duration: 1 year.

Number awarded: Approximately 700 each year.

Deadline: Applicants must take the PSAT/NMSQT no later than October of their junior year.

658 NATIONAL ASSOCIATION OF NEGRO BUSINESS AND PROFESSIONAL WOMEN'S CLUBS NATIONAL SCHOLARSHIPS

National Association of Negro Business and Professional Women's Clubs
Attn: Scholarship Committee
1806 New Hampshire Avenue, N.W.
Washington, DC 20009-3206
Phone: (202) 483-4206; Fax: (202) 462-7253
Email: education@nanbpwc.org
Web: www.nanbpwc.org/ScholarshipApplications.asp

Summary: To provide financial assistance for college to African American high school seniors.

Eligibility: Open to African American high school seniors planning to enroll in an accredited college or university. Applicants must have a GPA of 3.0 or higher. Along with their application, they must submit an essay (at least 300 words) on "Why Education is Important to Me." Financial need is not considered in the selection process.

Financial data: The stipend is $1,000.

Duration: 1 year.

Number awarded: 10 each year.

Deadline: February of each year.

659 NATIONAL COLLEGIATE CANCER FOUNDATION SCHOLARSHIP

National Collegiate Cancer Foundation
Attn: Scholarship Committee
P.O. Box 5950
Bethesda, MD 20824
Phone: (240) 515-6262
Email: info@collegiatecancer.org
Web: www.collegiatecancer.org/scholarships.html

Summary: To provide financial assistance for college or graduate school to cancer survivors.

Eligibility: Open to students between 18 and 35 years of age who are cancer survivors or currently undergoing treatment for cancer. Applicants must be enrolled or planning to enroll at a college or university to work on a certificate or an associate, bachelor's, master's, or doctoral degree. Along with their application, they must submit a 1,000-word essay on 1 of 4 assigned topics related to their experiences with cancer and college. Selection is based on the essay, letters of recommendation, displaying a "Will Win" attitude, overall story of cancer survivorship, commitment to education, and financial need.

Financial data: The stipend is $1,000.

Duration: 1 year.

Number awarded: 1 or more each year.

Deadline: May of each year.

660 NATIONAL FEDERATION OF THE BLIND SCHOLARSHIPS

National Federation of the Blind
Attn: Scholarship Committee
1800 Johnson Street
Baltimore, MD 21230
Phone: (410) 659-9314, ext. 2415; Fax: (410) 685-5653
Email: scholarships@nfb.org
Web: www.nfb.org/nfb/scholarship_program.asp

Summary: To provide financial assistance for college or graduate school to blind students.

Eligibility: Open to legally blind students who are working on or planning to work on an undergraduate or graduate degree. In general, full-time enrollment is required, although 1 scholarship may be awarded to a part-time student who is working full-time. Along with their application, they must submit transcripts, standardized test scores, proof of legal blindness, 2 letters of recommendation, and a letter of endorsement from their National Federation of the Blind state president or designee. Selection is based on academic excellence, service to the community, and financial need.

Financial data: Stipends are $7,000, $5,000, or $3,000.

Duration: 1 year; recipients may resubmit applications up to 2 additional years.

Number awarded: 18 each year: 2 at $7,000, 3 at $5,000, and 13 at $3,000.

Deadline: March of each year.

661 NATIONAL INDEPENDENT AUTOMOBILE DEALERS ASSOCIATION SCHOLARSHIP

National Independent Automobile Dealers Association
Attn: NIADA Foundation
2521 Brown Boulevard, Suite 100
Arlington, TX 76006-5203
Phone: (817) 640-3838, ext. 21; (800) 682-3837; Fax: (817) 649-5866
Email: georgia@niada.com
Web: www.niadafoundation.org/Scholarships/SCHOLARSHIPS.html

Summary: To provide financial assistance to high school seniors who have an association with the automobile industry.

Eligibility: Open to high school seniors who plan to attend college in any state. Applicants must indicate their experience or family association with the automobile industry. They must have excellent high school records and must demonstrate an aptitude for college work. Along with their application, they must submit an official high school transcript, copies of their SAT or ACT scores, an essay on their educational and professional goals, an essay on how the scholarship funds will help them and why they feel they should receive a scholarship, and letters of recommendation. Financial need is not considered in the selection process.

Financial data: The stipend is $3,500.

Duration: 1 year.

Number awarded: 4 each year: 1 in each region.

Deadline: March of each year.

662 NATIONAL ITALIAN AMERICAN FOUNDATION GENERAL CATEGORY I SCHOLARSHIPS

National Italian American Foundation
Attn: Education Director
1860 19th Street, N.W.
Washington, DC 20009
Phone: (202) 387-0600; Fax: (202) 387-0800
Email: scholarships@niaf.org
Web: www.niaf.org/scholarships/about.asp

Summary: To provide financial assistance to Italian American college and graduate students.

Eligibility: Open to Italian Americans (defined as having at least 1 ancestor who has immigrated from Italy) who are U.S. citizens or permanent residents. Applicants must be currently enrolled at or entering an accredited college or university in the United States and have a GPA of 3.5 or higher. They may be high school seniors, undergraduates, graduate students, or doctoral candidates. Selection is based on academic performance, field of study, career objectives, and the potential, commitment, and abilities applicants have demonstrated that would enable them to make significant contributions to their chosen field of study. Some scholarships also require financial need, but most do not.

Financial data: Stipends range from $2,000 to $12,000.

Duration: 1 year. Recipients are encouraged to reapply.

Number awarded: Varies each year.

Deadline: March of each year.

663 NATIONAL MARITIME INTELLIGENCE CENTER BLACKS IN GOVERNMENT SCHOLARSHIP

Blacks in Government–National Maritime Intelligence Center Chapter
c/o Jeanelle Jones
P.O. Box 1034
Suitland, MD 20752-1034
Phone: (301) 669-3693
Email: jjones@nmic.navy.mil

Summary: To provide financial assistance to high school seniors in the Washington, D.C. metropolitan area who plan to attend college in any state.
Eligibility: Open to seniors graduating from high schools within a 200-mile radius of Washington, D.C. Applicants must have a GPA of 2.5 higher and be planning to attend an accredited institution of higher learning in any state. Along with their application, they must submit an essay of 450 to 600 words on 1 of the following topics: their intended degree and how it might impact their life and/or community; who has influenced and/or shaped their life and how; how they plan to impact and elevate their community; and what education means to them. Finalists are interviewed. Financial need is not considered in the selection process.
Financial data: A stipend is awarded (amount not specified).
Duration: 1 year.
Number awarded: 1 or more each year.
Deadline: March of each year.

664 NATIONAL MERIT SCHOLARSHIP PROGRAM

National Merit Scholarship Corporation
Attn: Department of Educational Services and Selection
1560 Sherman Avenue, Suite 200
Evanston, IL 60201-4897
Phone: (847) 866-5100; Fax: (847) 866-5113
Web: www.nationalmerit.org/nmsp.php
Summary: To provide financial assistance for college to high school seniors who achieve outstanding scores on standardized tests.
Eligibility: Open to students who are enrolled full-time in a secondary school, progressing normally toward graduation or completion of high school, and planning to enter college in the fall following high school graduation. Applicants must be a U.S. citizen or a permanent resident in the process of becoming a U.S. citizen and be taking the PSAT/NMSQT at the proper time in the high school program and no later than the third year in grades 9 through 12, regardless of grade classification or educational pattern. On the basis of the PSAT/NMSQT results, approximately 16,000 of the highest scorers are designated as semifinalists; they are apportioned among states based on the number of graduating seniors in each state, to ensure equitable geographical representation. Finalists for National Merit Scholarships must be graduating seniors who are selected from among the semifinalists on the basis of SAT scores, academic performance in all of grades 9–12, and recommendations by high school principals.
Financial data: The award is $2,500.
Duration: 1 year.
Number awarded: Up to 2,500 each year.
Deadline: Applicants must take the PSAT/NMSQT no later than October of their junior year.

665 NATIONAL MS SOCIETY SCHOLARSHIP PROGRAM

National Multiple Sclerosis Society
Attn: Scholarship Fund
900 South Broadway, Suite 200
Denver, CO 80209
Phone: (303) 698-6100, ext. 15102
Email: susan.goldsmith@nmss.org
Web: www.nationalMSsociety.org/scholarship
Summary: To provide financial assistance for college to students who have Multiple Sclerosis (MS) or are the children of people with MS.
Eligibility: Open to 1) high school seniors who have MS and will be attending an accredited postsecondary school for the first time; 2) high school seniors who are the children of parents with MS and will be attending an accredited postsecondary school for the first time; 3) high school (or GED) graduates of any age who have MS and will be attending an accredited postsecondary school for the first time; and 4) high school (or GED) graduates of any age who have a parent with MS and will be attending an accredited postgraduate school for the first time. Applicants must be U.S. citizens or permanent residents who plan to enroll in an undergraduate course of study at an accredited 2- or 4-year college, university, or vocational/technical school in the United States to work on a degree, license, or certificate. Along with their application, they must submit a 1-page personal statement on the impact MS has had on their life. Selection is based on that statement, academic record, leadership and participation in school or community activities, work experience, goals and aspirations, an outside appraisal, special circumstances, and financial need. The 2 highest-ranked applicants are designated as the National MS Society Presidential Scholar and the National MS Society Mike Dugan Scholar.
Financial data: Stipends range from $1,000 to $3,000 per year.
Duration: 1 year; may be renewed.
Number awarded: Varies each year; recently, 510 of these scholarships (332 new awards and 178 renewals) with a value of $1,021,600 were awarded.
Deadline: January of each year.

666 NATIONAL ORGANIZATION OF ITALIAN AMERICAN WOMEN SCHOLARSHIPS

National Organization of Italian American Women
25 West 43rd Street, Suite 1005
New York, NY 10036
Phone: (212) 642-2003; Fax: (212) 642-2006
Email: noiaw@noiaw.org
Web: www.noiaw.org/pages/scholarships/scholarships.php
Summary: To provide financial assistance for college, graduate school, or law school to women of Italian descent.
Eligibility: Open to women who have at least 1 parent of Italian American descent and are working on an associate, bachelor's, master's, or law degree. Applicants must be enrolled full-time and have a GPA of 3.5 or higher. Along with their application, they must submit a 1-page autobiography, transcript, and resume. Financial need is considered in the selection process. The program includes the Hon. Geraldine A. Ferraro Endowed Scholarship for students working on a law degree.
Financial data: The stipend is $2,000.
Duration: 1 year; nonrenewable.
Number awarded: 5 each year, including the Hon. Geraldine A. Ferraro Endowed Scholarship for an Italian American woman working on an advanced degree in law and 4 scholarships for undergraduate and graduate students in any field.
Deadline: February of each year.

667 NATIONAL PRESBYTERIAN COLLEGE SCHOLARSHIP

Presbyterian Church (USA)
Attn: Office of Financial Aid for Studies
100 Witherspoon Street, Room M-052
Louisville, KY 40202-1396
Phone: (502) 569-5224; (888) 728-7228, ext. 5224; Fax: (502) 569-8766
Email: finaid@pcusa.org
Web: www.pcusa.org/financialaid/programs/natpresbycollege.htm
Summary: To provide financial assistance to high school seniors planning to attend a Presbyterian college.
Eligibility: Open to be high school seniors preparing to enroll as full-time incoming freshmen at a participating college related to the Presbyterian Church (USA). Applicants must be members of the PCUSA, have a GPA of 3.0 or higher, be U.S. citizens or permanent residents, and be able to demonstrate financial need. They must submit an essay (up to 500 words) on their career choice and the influence that informed their choice. Selection is based on that essay; personal qualities of character and leadership as reflected in contributions to church, school, and community; academic achievements; and recommendations from school and church officials.
Financial data: Stipends range from $250 to $1,400 per year, depending upon the financial need of the recipient.
Duration: 1 year; may be renewed up to 3 additional years, provided the recipient maintains of GPA of 3.0 or higher.
Number awarded: Approximately 100 each year.
Deadline: January of each year.

668 NATIONAL PRESIDENT'S SCHOLARSHIP

American Legion Auxiliary
8945 North Meridian Street
Indianapolis, IN 46260
Phone: (317) 569-4500; Fax: (317) 569-4502
Email: alahq@legion-aux.org
Web: www.legion-aux.org/Scholarships/NationalPresident/index.aspx
Summary: To provide financial assistance for college to the children of war veterans.
Eligibility: Open to children of veterans who served during war time. Applicants must be high school seniors who have completed at least 50 hours of volunteer service within the community. Each Department (state) organization of the American Legion Auxiliary nominates 1 candidate for the National President's Scholarship annually. Nominees must submit a 1,000-word essay on a topic that changes annually; recently, students were asked to write on

"Answering the Call to Serve My Community and Our Veterans." Selection is based on the essay (20%), character and leadership (20%), scholarship, (40%), and financial need (20%).

Financial data: Stipends are $2,500, $2,000, or $1,500. Funds are paid directly to the recipient's school.

Duration: 1 year; recipients may not reapply.

Number awarded: 15 each year: in each of the 5 divisions of the Auxiliary, 1 scholarship at $2,500, 1 at $2,000, and 1 at $1,500 are awarded.

Deadline: February of each year.

669 NATIONAL TEMPERANCE SCHOLARSHIP

United Methodist Higher Education Foundation
Attn: Scholarships Administrator
1001 19th Avenue South
P.O. Box 340005
Nashville, TN 37203-0005
Phone: (615) 340-7385; (800) 811-8110; Fax: (615) 340-7330
Email: umhefscholarships@gbhem.org
Web: www.umhef.org/receive.php?id=endowed_funds

Summary: To provide financial assistance to undergraduate and graduate Methodist students at Methodist-related colleges and universities.

Eligibility: Open to full-time undergraduate and graduate students at United Methodist–related colleges and universities. Applicants must have been active, full members of a United Methodist Church for at least 1 year prior to applying. They must have a GPA of 3.0 or higher and be able to demonstrate financial need. Along with their application, they must submit a 200-word essay on their involvement and/or leadership responsibilities in their church, school, and community within the last 3 years. U.S. citizenship or permanent resident status is required.

Financial data: The stipend is at least $1,000 per year.

Duration: 1 year; recipients may reapply.

Number awarded: 1 each year.

Deadline: May of each year.

670 NATIVE AMERICAN EDUCATION GRANTS

Presbyterian Church (USA)
Attn: Office of Financial Aid for Studies
100 Witherspoon Street, Room M-052
Louisville, KY 40202-1396
Phone: (502) 569-5776; (888) 728-7228, ext. 5776; Fax: (502) 569-8766
Email: finaid@pcusa.org
Web: www.pcusa.org/financialaid/programs/nativeamericanedugrant.htm

Summary: To provide financial assistance to Native American students, especially members of the Presbyterian Church (USA), interested in continuing their college education.

Eligibility: Open to Alaska Native and Native American students who have completed at least 2 years of full-time study at an accredited institution in the United States and have a GPA of 2.5 or higher. Applicants must be making satisfactory progress toward a degree, able to provide proof of tribal membership, U.S. citizens or permanent residents, recommended by their church pastor, and able to demonstrate financial need. Students from all faith traditions are encouraged to apply, but preference is given to members of the PCUSA.

Financial data: Stipends range from $500 to $1,500 per year, depending upon the recipient's financial need.

Duration: 1 year; may be renewed.

Number awarded: Varies each year.

Deadline: June of each year.

671 NATIVE AMERICAN WOMEN'S HEALTH EDUCATION RESOURCE CENTER SCHOLARSHIPS

Native American Women's Health Education Resource Center
P.O. Box 572
Lake Andes, SD 57356-0572
Phone: (605) 487-7072; Fax: (605) 487-7964
Web: www.nativeshop.org/nawherc.html

Summary: To provide financial assistance to American Indian women currently enrolled in college.

Eligibility: Open to American Indian women who are currently enrolled in college and need financial assistance.

Financial data: The stipend is either $300 or $500 per semester (up to $1,000 per year).

Duration: The stipends are offered each semester.

Number awarded: 2 per semester.

Deadline: March of each year.

672 NATIVE VISION SCHOLARSHIPS

Native Vision
c/o Johns Hopkins University
Center for American Indian Health
621 North Washington Street
Baltimore, MD 21205
Phone: (410) 955-6931; Fax: (410) 955-2010
Email: mhammen@jhsph.edu
Web: www.nativevision.org

Summary: To provide financial assistance for college to American Indian high school seniors who have participated in a sports camp.

Eligibility: Open to graduating high school seniors who are enrolled members of a federally-recognized tribe. Applicants must have been admitted to an accredited community college or 4-year undergraduate program. They must be able to demonstrate a sustained involvement in the community, an applied interest in American Indian concerns and initiatives, a GPA of 3.0 or higher, and involvement in extracurricular and/or athletic activities. Along with their application, they must submit a high school transcript, 2 letters of recommendation, and a 200-word essay on their goals for the future and how this scholarship will help them achieve their dreams; their essay should emphasize how their goals relate to their continued involvement in American Indian communities. The program is intended for students who also participate in the sponsor's summer Sports and Life Skills camp.

Financial data: The stipend is $5,000.

Duration: 1 year.

Number awarded: 2 or 3 each year.

Deadline: May of each year.

673 NAVAL HELICOPTER ASSOCIATION UNDERGRADUATE SCHOLARSHIPS

Naval Helicopter Association
Attn: Scholarship Fund
P.O. Box 180578
Coronado, CA 92178-0578
Phone: (619) 435-7139; Fax: (619) 435-7354
Email: info@nhascholarship.org
Web: www.nhascholarship.org/nhascholarshipfund/index.html

Summary: To provide financial assistance for college to students who have an affiliation with the rotary wing activities of the sea services.

Eligibility: Open to high school seniors and current undergraduates who are 1) children, grandchildren, or spouses of current or former Navy, Marine Corps, or Coast Guard rotary wing aviators or aircrewmen; 2) individuals who are serving or have served in maintenance or support billets in rotary wing squadrons or wings and their spouses and children. Applicants must provide information on their rotary wing affiliation and a personal statement on their educational plans and future goals. Selection is based on that statement, academic proficiency, scholastic achievements and awards, extracurricular activities, employment history, and letters of recommendation.

Financial data: Stipends are $3,000, $2,500, or $2,000.

Duration: 1 year.

Number awarded: Varies each year; recently, 9 of these scholarships were awarded: 3 at $3,000, 1 at $2,500, and 5 at $2,000.

Deadline: January of each year.

674 NAVAL SPECIAL WARFARE SCHOLARSHIPS FOR DEPENDENT CHILDREN AND SPOUSES

Naval Special Warfare Foundation
Attn: Scholarship Committee
P.O. Box 5965
Virginia Beach, VA 23471
Phone: (757) 363-7490; Fax: (757) 363-7491
Email: info@nswfoundation.org
Web: www.nswfoundation.org/education.htm

Summary: To provide financial assistance for college to dependents of military personnel serving on active duty in Naval Special Warfare (NSW) commands.

Eligibility: Open to the dependent spouses and children of active-duty SEALs or Special Warfare Combatant crewmen (SWCC) and other active-duty

military personnel serving in NSW commands. Family members of a SEAL or SWCC who died in service to the country are also eligible. Applicants must be entering or continuing in college with the goal of working on an associate or bachelor's degree. Selection is based on merit and academic potential, judged by scholastic achievement and a written essay.
Financial data: A stipend is awarded (amount not specified).
Duration: 1 year; may be renewed.
Number awarded: 1 or more each year.
Deadline: March of each year.

675 NAVY COLLEGE FUND

U.S. Navy
Attn: Navy Personnel Command (PERS-675)
5720 Integrity Drive
Millington, TN 38055-6040
Phone: (901) 874-4258; (866) U-ASK-NPC; Fax: (901) 874-2052
Email: MILL_MGIB@navy.mil
Web: www.navyjobs.com/benefits/education/earnmoney
Summary: To provide financial assistance for college to Navy enlistees during and after they have completed their service obligation.
Eligibility: Open to high school seniors and graduates between 17 and 35 years of age who enlist in the Navy for 3 to 4 years of active duty. They must score 50 or above on the ASVAB and also enroll in the Montgomery GI Bill. Sailors currently on active duty in selected Navy ratings with critical personnel shortages are also eligible. Applicants must be interested in attending a Department of Veterans Affairs–approved postsecondary educational institution on a full-time basis after completion of their service obligation.
Financial data: The Navy College Fund provides, in addition to the Montgomery GI Bill, up to $15,000 for college tuition and expenses.
Duration: Enlistees may begin using this educational benefit on a part-time basis after 2 years of continuous active duty. Funds must be utilized within 10 years of leaving the Navy.
Number awarded: Varies each year.
Deadline: Applications may be submitted at any time.

676 NAVY LEAGUE FOUNDATION SCHOLARSHIPS

Navy League of the United States
Attn: Scholarships
2300 Wilson Boulevard, Suite 200
Arlington, VA 22201-5424
Phone: (703) 528-1775; (800) 356-5760; Fax: (703) 528-2333
Email: scholarships@navyleague.org
Web: www.navyleague.org/scholarship
Summary: To provide financial assistance for college to dependent children of sea service personnel.
Eligibility: Open to U.S. citizens who are 1) dependents or direct descendants of an active, Reserve, retired, or honorably discharged member of the U.S. sea service (including the Navy, Marine Corps, Coast Guard, or Merchant Marine), or 2) currently an active member of the Naval Sea Cadet Corps. Applicants must be entering their freshman year at an accredited college or university. They must have a GPA of 3.0 or higher. Along with their application, they must submit transcripts, 2 letters of recommendation, SAT/ACT scores, documentation of financial need, proof of qualifying sea service duty, and a 1-page personal statement on why they should be considered for this scholarship.
Financial data: The stipend is $2,500 per year.
Duration: 4 years, provided the recipient maintains a GPA of 3.0 or higher.
Number awarded: Approximately 5 each year.
Deadline: February of each year.

677 NAVY/MARINE CORPS/COAST GUARD ENLISTED DEPENDENT SPOUSE SCHOLARSHIP

Navy Wives Clubs of America
P.O. Box 54022
Millington, TN 38053-6022
Phone: (866) 511-NWCA
Email: nwca@navywivesclubsofamerica.org
Web: www.navywivesclubsofamerica.org/scholarinfo.htm
Summary: To provide financial assistance for undergraduate or graduate study to spouses of naval personnel.
Eligibility: Open to the spouses of active-duty Navy, Marine Corps, or Coast Guard members who can demonstrate financial need. Applicants must be 1) a high school graduate or senior planning to attend college full-time next year; 2) currently enrolled in an undergraduate program and planning to continue as a full-time undergraduate; 3) a college graduate or senior planning to be a full-time graduate student next year; or 4) a high school graduate or GED recipient planning to attend vocational or business school next year. Along with their application, they must submit a brief statement on why they feel they should be awarded this scholarship and any special circumstances (financial or other) they wish to have considered. Financial need is also considered in the selection process.
Financial data: The stipends range from $500 to $1,000 each year (depending upon the donations from chapters of the Navy Wives Clubs of America).
Duration: 1 year.
Number awarded: 1 or more each year.
Deadline: May of each year.

678 NAVY/MARINE CORPS JROTC SCHOLARSHIP

National Naval Officers Association–Washington, D.C. Chapter
Attn: Scholarship Program
2701 Park Center Drive, A1108
Alexandria, VA 22302
Phone: (703) 566-3840; Fax: (703) 566-3813
Email: Stephen.Williams@Navy.mil
Web: dcnnoa.memberlodge.com/Default.aspx?pageId=309002
Summary: To provide financial assistance to minority high school seniors from the Washington, D.C. area who have participated in Navy or Marine Corps Junior Reserve Officers Training Corps (JROTC) and are planning to attend college in any state.
Eligibility: Open to minority seniors graduating from high schools in the Washington, D.C. metropolitan area who have participated in Navy or Marine Corps JROTC. Applicants must be planning to enroll full-time at an accredited 2- or 4-year college or university in any state. They must have a GPA of 2.5 or higher. Selection is based on academic achievement, community involvement, and financial need.
Financial data: The stipend is $1,000.
Duration: 1 year; nonrenewable.
Number awarded: 1 each year.
Deadline: March of each year.

679 NAVY SUPPLY CORPS FOUNDATION MEMORIAL SCHOLARSHIPS

Navy Supply Corps Foundation
c/o CDR Jack Evans (ret), Chief Staff Officer
1425 Prince Avenue
Athens, GA 30606-2205
Phone: (706) 354-4111; Fax: (706) 354-0334
Email: foundation@usnscf.com
Web: www.usnscf.com/programs/scholarships.aspx
Summary: To provide financial assistance for college to children of Navy Supply Corps personnel who died on active duty.
Eligibility: Open to children of Navy Supply Corps personnel who died on active duty after 2001. The program applies to Active Duty Supply Corps Officers as well as Reserve Supply Corps Officers in the following categories: Mobilization, Active Duty for Special Work (ADSW), Active Duty for Training (ADT), Annual Training (AT), and Inactive Duty for Training (IDT). Applicants must be attending or planning to attend a 2- or 4-year accredited college on a full-time basis and have a GPA of 2.5 or higher in high school and/or college. Selection is based on character, leadership, academic achievement, extracurricular activities, and financial need.
Financial data: The stipend is $2,500 per year.
Duration: 4 years.
Number awarded: Varies each year; recently, 1 of these scholarships was awarded.
Deadline: March of each year.

680 NAVY SUPPLY CORPS FOUNDATION SCHOLARSHIPS

Navy Supply Corps Foundation
c/o CDR Jack Evans (ret), Chief Staff Officer
1425 Prince Avenue
Athens, GA 30606-2205
Phone: (706) 354-4111; Fax: (706) 354-0334
Email: foundation@usnscf.com
Web: www.usnscf.com/programs/scholarships.aspx

Summary: To provide financial assistance for college to relatives of current or former Navy Supply Corps personnel.
Eligibility: Open to dependents (child, grandchild, or spouse) of a living or deceased regular, retired, Reserve, or prior Navy Supply Corps officer, warrant officer, or enlisted personnel. Enlisted ratings that apply are AK (Aviation Storekeeper), SK (Storekeeper), MS (Mess Specialist), DK (Disbursing Clerk), SH (Ship Serviceman), LI (Lithographer), and PC (Postal Clerk). Applicants must be attending or planning to attend a 2- or 4-year accredited college on a full-time basis and have a GPA of 2.5 or higher in high school and/or college. Selection is based on character, leadership, academic achievement, extracurricular activities, and financial need.
Financial data: Stipends range from $1,000 to $5,000.
Duration: 1 year.
Number awarded: Varies each year; recently, the foundation awarded 95 scholarships: 17 at $5,000, 47 at $2,500, and 31 at $1,000. Since the program was established, it has awarded 1,786 scholarships with a total value of more than $3,562,000.
Deadline: March of each year.

681 NAVY WIVES CLUBS OF AMERICA NATIONAL SCHOLARSHIPS

Navy Wives Clubs of America
P.O. Box 54022
Millington, TN 38053-6022
Phone: (866) 511-NWCA
Email: nwca@navywivesclubsofamerica.org
Web: www.navywivesclubsofamerica.org/scholarinfo.htm
Summary: To provide financial assistance for college or graduate school to the children of naval personnel.
Eligibility: Open to the children (natural born, legally adopted, or stepchildren) of enlisted members of the Navy, Marine Corps, or Coast Guard on active duty, retired with pay, or deceased. Applicants must be attending or planning to attend an accredited college or university as a full-time undergraduate or graduate student. They must have a GPA of 2.5 or higher. Along with their application, they must submit an essay on their career objectives and the reasons they chose those objectives. Selection is based on academic standing, moral character, and financial need. Some scholarships are reserved for students majoring in special education, medical students, and children of members of Navy Wives Clubs of America (NWCA).
Financial data: The stipend is $1,500.
Duration: 1 year; may be renewed up to 3 additional years.
Number awarded: 30 each year, including at least 4 to freshmen, 4 to current undergraduates applying for the first time, 2 to medical students, 1 to a student majoring in special education, and 4 to children of NWCA members.
Deadline: May of each year.

682 NAVY-MARINE CORPS ROTC 2-YEAR SCHOLARSHIPS

U.S. Navy
Attn: Naval Education and Training Command
NSTC OD2
250 Dallas Street, Suite A
Pensacola, FL 32508-5268
Phone: (850) 452-4941, ext. 25166; (800) NAV-ROTC, ext. 25166
Fax: (850) 452-2486;
Email: PNSC_NROTC.scholarship@navy.mil
Web: www.nrotc.navy.mil/scholarships.aspx
Summary: To provide financial assistance to upper-division students who are interested in joining Navy ROTC in college.
Eligibility: Open to students who have completed at least 2 years of college (or 3 years if enrolled in a 5-year program) with a GPA of 2.5 or higher overall and 2.0 or higher in calculus and physics. Preference is given to students at colleges with a Navy ROTC unit on campus or at colleges with a cross-enrollment agreement with a college with an NROTC unit. Applicants must be U.S. citizens between the ages of 17 and 21 who plan to pursue an approved course of study in college and complete their degree before they reach the age of 27. Former and current enlisted military personnel are also eligible if they will complete the program by the age of 30.
Financial data: These scholarships provide payment of full tuition and required educational fees, as well as a specified amount for textbooks, supplies, and equipment. The program also provides a stipend for 10 months of the year that is $350 per month as a junior and $400 per month as a senior.
Duration: 2 years, until the recipient completes the bachelor's degree.
Number awarded: Approximately 800 each year.
Deadline: March of each year.

683 NAVY-MARINE CORPS ROTC 4-YEAR SCHOLARSHIPS

U.S. Navy
Attn: Naval Education and Training Command
NSTC OD2
250 Dallas Street, Suite A
Pensacola, FL 32508-5268
Phone: (850) 452-4941, ext. 25166; (800) NAV-ROTC, ext. 25166; Fax: (850) 452-2486
Email: PNSC_NROTC.scholarship@navy.mil
Web: www.nrotc.navy.mil/scholarships.aspx
Summary: To provide financial assistance to graduating high school seniors who are interested in joining Navy ROTC in college.
Eligibility: Open to graduating high school seniors who have been accepted at a college with a Navy ROTC unit on campus or a college with a cross-enrollment agreement with such a college. Applicants must be U.S. citizens between 17 and 23 years of age who are willing to serve for 4 years as active-duty Navy officers following graduation from college. They must not have reached their 27th birthday by the time of college graduation and commissioning; applicants who have prior active-duty military service may be eligible for age adjustments for the amount of time equal to their prior service, up to a maximum of 36 months. The qualifying scores for the Navy option are 530 critical reading and 520 mathematics on the SAT or 22 on both English and mathematics on the ACT; for the Marine Corps option they are 1000 composite on the SAT or 22 composite on the ACT. Currently enlisted and former military personnel are also eligible if they will complete the program by the age of 30.
Financial data: These scholarships provide payment of full tuition and required educational fees, as well as a specified amount for textbooks, supplies, and equipment. The program also provides a stipend for 10 months of the year that is $250 per month as a freshman, $300 per month as a sophomore, $350 per month as a junior, and $400 per month as a senior.
Duration: 4 years.
Number awarded: Approximately 2,200 each year.
Deadline: January of each year.

684 NAVY-MARINE CORPS ROTC COLLEGE PROGRAM

U.S. Navy
Attn: Naval Education and Training Command
NSTC OD2
250 Dallas Street, Suite A
Pensacola, FL 32508-5268
Phone: (850) 452-4941, ext. 25166; (800) NAV-ROTC, ext. 25166; Fax: (850) 452-2486
Email: PNSC_NROTC.scholarship@navy.mil
Web: www.nrotc.navy.mil/scholarships.aspx
Summary: To provide financial assistance to lower-division students who are interested in joining Navy ROTC in college.
Eligibility: Open to U.S. citizens between the ages of 17 and 21 who are already enrolled as non-scholarship students in naval science courses at a college or university with a Navy ROTC program on campus. They must apply before the spring of their sophomore year. All applications must be submitted through the professors of naval science at the college or university attended.
Financial data: Participants in this program receive free naval science textbooks, all required uniforms, and a stipend for 10 months of the year that is $350 per month as a junior and $400 per month as a senior.
Duration: 2 or 4 years.
Deadline: March of each year.

685 NAZARETH ASSOCIATION SCHOLARSHIPS

Nazareth Association
Attn: Scholarships
P.O. Box 224
Nazareth, MI 49074-0224
Phone: (269) 342-1191
Email: office@nazarethassociation.org
Web: www.nazarethassociation.org/11.html
Summary: To provide financial assistance to residents of Michigan attending a Catholic college in any state.
Eligibility: Open to residents of Michigan currently enrolled full-time as juniors or seniors at a Catholic college or university in any state. Applicants must have a GPA of 3.0 or higher. Along with their application, they must submit a 500-word essay on their educational, career, and personal goals as related to the mission and philosophy of the sponsoring organization. Selection is based on the essay, GPA, academic major, extracurricular and community service activities, and relationship to the sponsoring organization.

Financial data: The stipend is $1,000 per year.
Duration: 1 year; may be renewed 1 additional year.
Number awarded: 8 each year.
Deadline: March of each year.

686 NC REACH SCHOLARSHIPS

NC Reach
c/o Orphan Foundation of America
21351 Gentry Drive, Suite 130
Sterling, VA 20166
Phone: (571) 203-0270; (800) 585-6112; Fax: (866) 283-0223
Email: ncreach@orphan.org
Web: www.NCReach.org

Summary: To provide financial assistance to North Carolina residents who have been in the foster care system of the Department of Social Services (DSS) and are interested in attending college in the state.

Eligibility: Open to residents of North Carolina who either 1) aged out of the DSS foster care system after the age of 18; or 2) were adopted from the foster care system through DSS after the age of 12. Applicants must be younger than 26 years of age and enrolled or planning to enroll at least half-time at 1 of the 74 public colleges, universities, or community colleges in North Carolina.

Financial data: The stipend depends on the annual Cost of Attendance (COA) as calculated by the school. The program funds up to the full COA, after all other financial aid available to the student (e.g., Pell Grant, ETV funds, scholarships) has been considered.

Duration: 1 year; may be renewed as long as the recipient remains younger than 26 and maintains satisfactory progress toward completion of an undergraduate degree, diploma, or certificate.

Number awarded: Varies each year.

Deadline: Deadline not specified.

687 NCAIAW SCHOLARSHIP

North Carolina Alliance for Athletics, Health, Physical Education, Recreation and Dance
Attn: Executive Director
727 West Hargett Street, Suite 111
P.O. Box 27751
Raleigh, NC 27611
Phone: (919) 833-1219; (888) 840-6500; Fax: (919) 833-7700
Email: ncaahperd@ncaahperd.org
Web: www.ncaahperd.org/awards/ncaahperd_scholarships.html

Summary: To provide financial assistance to women who are college seniors involved in sports at an institution that is a member of the former North Carolina Association of Intercollegiate Athletics for Women (NCAIAW).

Eligibility: Open to women who have been a participant on 1 or more varsity athletic teams either as a player or in the support role of manager, trainer, etc. Applicants must be attending 1 of the following former NCAIAW colleges or universities in North Carolina: Appalachian State, Belmont Abbey, Bennett, Campbell, Davidson, Duke, East Carolina, Gardner-Webb, High Point, Mars Hill, Meredith, North Carolina A&T, North Carolina State, Pembroke State, Salem, University of North Carolina at Ashville, University of North Carolina at Chapel Hill, University of North Carolina at Charlotte, University of North Carolina at Wilmington, Wake Forest, or Western Carolina. They must be college seniors at the time of application, be able to demonstrate high standards of scholarship, and show evidence of leadership potential (as indicated by participation in school and community activities).

Financial data: The stipend is $1,000. Funds are sent to the recipient's school.

Duration: 1 year.

Number awarded: 1 each year.

Deadline: June of each year.

688 NCCE SCHOLARSHIPS

National Commission for Cooperative Education
360 Huntington Avenue, 384 CP
Boston, MA 02115-5096
Phone: (617) 373-3770; Fax: (617) 373-3463
Email: ncce@co-op.edu
Web: www.co-op.edu/scholarships.htm

Summary: To provide financial assistance to students participating or planning to participate in cooperative education projects at designated colleges and universities.

Eligibility: Open to high school seniors and community college transfer students entering 1 of the 10 partner colleges and universities. Applicants must be planning to participate in college cooperative education. They must have a GPA of 3.5 or higher. Along with their application, they must submit a 1-page essay describing why they have chosen to enter a college cooperative education program. Applications are especially encouraged from minorities, women, and students interested in science, mathematics, engineering, and technology. Selection is based on merit; financial need is not considered.

Financial data: The stipend is $6,000 per year.

Duration: 1 year; may be renewed up to 3 additional years or (for some programs) up to 4 additional years.

Number awarded: Varies each year; recently, 200 of these scholarships were awarded: 30 at Drexel, 30 at Johnson & Wales, 20 at Kettering, 10 at C.W. Post Campus of LIU, 20 at Northeastern, 15 at Pace, 15 at Rochester Tech, 15 at Cincinnati, 15 at Toledo, and 30 at Wentworth Tech.

Deadline: February of each year.

689 NCDXF SCHOLARSHIP

American Radio Relay League
Attn: ARRL Foundation
225 Main Street
Newington, CT 06111
Phone: (860) 594-0397; Fax: (860) 594-0259
Email: foundation@arrl.org
Web: www.arrlf.org/programs/scholarships

Summary: To provide financial assistance for college study of any field to licensed radio amateurs.

Eligibility: Open to licensed radio amateurs who plan to seek a degree at a junior college, 4-year college or university, or trade school in the United States. There is no restriction on the field of study. Applicants must have at least a technician class license; preference is given to students indicating an interest and activity in DXing. Along with their application, they must submit an essay on the role amateur radio has played in their lives and provide documentation of financial need.

Financial data: The stipend is $1,500.

Duration: 1 year.

Number awarded: Up to 2 each year.

Deadline: January of each year.

690 NEBRASKA ELKS ASSOCIATION VOCATIONAL SCHOLARSHIP GRANTS

Nebraska Elks Association
c/o Melvin Nespor, Scholarship Committee
P.O. Box 14
Endicott, NE 68350-0014
Email: mnespor@beatricene.com
Web: webpages.charter.net/neelks/elk_scholarships.htm

Summary: To provide financial assistance to high school seniors in Nebraska who plan to attend a vocational school in the state.

Eligibility: Open to seniors graduating from high schools in Nebraska. Applicants must be planning to attend a 2-year or less vocational/technical program for an associate degree, diploma, or certificate. Selection is based on motivation (general worthiness, desire); aptitude toward chosen vocation; grades and test scores; completeness, neatness, and accuracy in following instructions when filling out the application; and financial need. Each Nebraska Elks Lodge can submit 1 application from a girl and 1 from a boy.

Financial data: Stipends depend on the need of the recipient, to a maximum of $1,000.

Duration: 1 year.

Number awarded: 6 each year.

Deadline: January of each year.

691 NEBRASKA WAIVER OF TUITION FOR VETERANS' DEPENDENTS

Department of Veterans' Affairs
State Office Building
301 Centennial Mall South, Sixth Floor
P.O. Box 95083
Lincoln, NE 68509-5083
Phone: (402) 471-2458; Fax: (402) 471-2491
Email: john.hilgert@nebraska.gov
Web: www.vets.state.ne.us/index_html?page=content/benefits.html

Summary: To provide financial assistance for college to dependents of deceased and disabled veterans and military personnel in Nebraska.

Eligibility: Open to spouses, widow(er)s, and children who are residents of Nebraska and whose parent, stepparent, or spouse was a member of the U.S. armed forces and 1) died of a service-connected disability; 2) died subsequent to discharge as a result of injury or illness sustained while in service; 3) is permanently and totally disabled as a result of military service; or 4) is classified as missing in action or as a prisoner of war during armed hostilities after August 4, 1964. Applicants must be attending or planning to attend a branch of the University of Nebraska, a state college, or a community college in Nebraska.

Financial data: Tuition is waived at public institutions in Nebraska.

Duration: The waiver is valid for 1 degree, diploma, or certificate from a community college and 1 baccalaureate degree.

Number awarded: Varies each year; recently, 311 of these grants were awarded.

Deadline: Deadline not specified.

692 NED MCWHERTER SCHOLARS PROGRAM

Tennessee Student Assistance Corporation
Parkway Towers
404 James Robertson Parkway, Suite 1510
Nashville, TN 37243-0820
Phone: (615) 741-1346; (800) 342-1663; Fax: (615) 741-6101
Email: TSAC.Aidinfo@tn.gov
Web: www.tn.gov/collegepays/mon_college/ned_mc_shcolar.htm

Summary: To provide financial assistance to outstanding Tennessee high school seniors who plan to attend college in the state.

Eligibility: Open to seniors graduating from high schools in Tennessee who have scores of at least 29 on the ACT or 1280 on the mathematics and critical reading SAT and a GPA of 3.5 or higher. Applicants must be planning to enroll full-time at an eligible college or university in Tennessee. The selection process includes consideration of difficulty of courses and leadership positions held while in high school, but financial need is not considered. U.S. citizenship or permanent resident status is required.

Financial data: Stipends up to $6,000 per year are provided.

Duration: 1 year; may be renewed for up to 3 additional years if the recipient remains a full-time student and maintains a minimum GPA of 3.2.

Number awarded: Approximately 50 each year.

Deadline: February of each year.

693 NEIL CHURCHILL MEMORIAL SCHOLARSHIPS

National Leased Housing Association
Attn: NLHA Education Fund
1900 L Street, N.W., Suite 300
Washington, DC 20036
Phone: (202) 785-8888; Fax: (202) 785-2008
Email: info@hudnlha.com
Web: www.hudnlha.com/education_fund/index.asp

Summary: To provide financial assistance for college to residents of federally-assisted rental housing properties and members of families receiving rental subsidy through federal housing programs.

Eligibility: Open to U.S. citizens and permanent residents who reside in a federally-assisted rental housing property or whose families receive rental subsidy through a recognized federal housing program (e.g., Section 8, Rent Supplement, Rental Assistance Payments, Low Income Housing Tax Credit). Applicants must be graduating high school seniors, current undergraduates, or GED recipients entering an accredited undergraduate program. They must have a GPA of 2.5 or higher and be able to demonstrate financial need and community leadership through volunteer work at school or in the community. Along with their application, they must submit a 1-page essay on what education means to their future.

Financial data: A stipend is awarded (amount not specified). Funds are disbursed directly to the recipient's institution of higher learning for partial payment of tuition, books, room and board, or other activities directly related to the student's education.

Duration: 1 year.

Number awarded: Varies each year; recently, 8 of these scholarships were awarded.

Deadline: February of each year.

694 NEVADA STATE ELKS ASSOCIATION VOCATIONAL GRANT PROGRAM

Nevada State Elks Association
c/o John Vore
1830 West Irons Avenue
Pahrump, NV 89048
Phone: (775) 751-2059
Email: jtel@pahrump.net
Web: www.nsea-elks.org

Summary: To provide financial assistance to residents of Nevada who are interested in enrolling in a vocational education program in any state.

Eligibility: Open to residents of Nevada who are high school seniors, high school graduates, or GED recipients. Applicants must be enrolled or planning to enroll full-time at a vocational/technical school or other 2-year educational institution in any state to work on a degree or certificate other than a bachelor's degree. Their application must be endorsed by an official of their local Elks Lodge. Along with their application, they must submit 1) a 200-word statement of their activities, accomplishments, needs, and objectives that they believe qualify them for this grant; and 2) a 150-word letter from a parent or other knowledgeable family member describing the family financial situation. Selection is based on grades, motivation, skills, completeness and neatness of the application, and financial need. U.S. citizenship is required.

Financial data: The stipend is $1,000. Funds are disbursed directly to the educational institution to be used for tuition and fees, books and supplies, or room and board (only if the student lives on campus).

Duration: 1 or 2 years; nonrenewable.

Number awarded: 1 or more each year.

Deadline: February.

695 NEW CENTURY SCHOLARS PROGRAM

Phi Theta Kappa
Attn: Scholarship Programs Director
1625 Eastover Drive
P.O. Box 13729
Jackson, MS 39236-3729
Phone: (601) 984-3539; Fax: (601) 984-3546
Email: scholarship.programs@ptk.org
Web: www.ptk.org/schol/aaat/newcent.htm

Summary: To recognize and reward the outstanding achievements of community college students.

Eligibility: Open to students who have completed at least 36 hours at a community college in the United States, Alberta (Canada), or the 7 nations and U.S. territories where Phi Theta Kappa has a chapter. Candidates must be nominated by a designated official at their college. Students at colleges in the United States are not required to be members of Phi Theta Kappa, but membership is required for students at colleges outside the country. Nominees must have a cumulative GPA of at least 3.5 for all college course work completed in the last 5 years, regardless of institution attended, and be on track to earn an associate or bachelor's degree. They must submit a 2-page essay describing their most significant endeavor since attending community college in which they applied their academic or intellectual skills from their community college education to benefit their school, community, or society. Selection is based on information in the essay; awards, honors, and recognition for academic achievement; academic rigor and GPA; participation in honors programs; and service to the college and the community.

Financial data: The award is $2,000.

Duration: The competition is held annually.

Number awarded: 52 each year: 1 from each state, 1 from Alberta, Canada, and 1 from outside Canada and the United States.

Deadline: November of each year.

696 NEW DAY EDUCATION AND REHABILITATION AWARDS

Kidney & Urology Foundation of America
Attn: Program Associate
152 Madison Avenue, Suite 201
New York, NY 10016
Phone: (212) 629-9770; (800) 633-6628; Fax: (212) 629-5652
Email: HReel@kidneyurology.org
Web: www.kidneyurology.org/Patient_Resources/scholarships.php

Summary: To provide financial assistance to adults who have been diagnosed with kidney or urologic disease and are interested in returning to college.

Eligibility: Open to adults older than 25 years of age who have been diagnosed with kidney or urologic disease. Applicants must be interested in completing a degree, learning a new job skill, changing careers, or engaging in physical rehabilitation. Along with their application, they must submit an essay of 1 to 2 pages on questions related to their disease, their educational background and goals, and their contributions to the renal, urologic, or transplant community. Selection is based on evidence of prior achievements, motivation to accomplish

stated goals, and financial need. Priority is given to applicants from the sponsoring organization's participating partner centers.
Financial data: The stipend is $1,500 per year. Funds are paid directly to the recipient's institution.
Duration: 1 year; may be renewed up to 3 additional years.
Number awarded: Varies each year; recently, 4 of these awards were presented.
Deadline: May of each year.

697 NEW ENGLAND FEMARA SCHOLARSHIPS

American Radio Relay League
Attn: ARRL Foundation
225 Main Street
Newington, CT 06111
Phone: (860) 594-0397; Fax: (860) 594-0259
Email: foundation@arrl.org
Web: www.arrlf.org/programs/scholarships
Summary: To provide financial assistance to licensed radio amateurs, especially those from the New England states, who are interested in working on an undergraduate or graduate degree in any field.
Eligibility: Open to undergraduate or graduate students in any subject area who are enrolled at accredited institutions in any state and are licensed radio amateurs of technician class or higher. Applicants must submit an essay on the role amateur radio has played in their lives and provide documentation of financial need. Preference is given to residents of the New England states.
Financial data: The stipend is $1,000.
Duration: 1 year.
Number awarded: Varies, depending upon the availability of funds; recently, 3 of these scholarships were awarded.
Deadline: January of each year.

698 NEW HAMPSHIRE CHARITABLE FOUNDATION ADULT STUDENT AID PROGRAM

New Hampshire Charitable Foundation
37 Pleasant Street
Concord, NH 03301-4005
Phone: (603) 225-6641; (800) 464-6641; Fax: (603) 225-1700
Email: info@nhcf.org
Web: www.nhcf.org/page16960.cfm
Summary: To provide funding for undergraduate study to adults in New Hampshire who are returning to school in the state.
Eligibility: Open to New Hampshire residents who are 24 years of age or older. Applicants should 1) have had little or no education beyond high school; and 2) be now returning to school to upgrade skills for employment or career advancement, to qualify for a degree program, or to make a career change. They must demonstrate that they have secured all available financial aid and still have a remaining unmet need. Preference for funding is given in the following order: 1) students who have previously received funding through this program and have successfully completed prior work; 2) students with the least amount of higher education or training; and 3) single parents. Only undergraduate students are eligible.
Financial data: The maximum award is $500 per term, or a total of $1,500 per recipient. Most awards are in the form of grants, although interest-free loans may also be provided.
Duration: 1 academic term; may be renewed up to 2 additional terms.
Number awarded: Varies each year.
Deadline: May, August, or December of each year.

699 NEW HAMPSHIRE CHARITABLE FOUNDATION STATEWIDE STUDENT AID PROGRAM

New Hampshire Charitable Foundation
37 Pleasant Street
Concord, NH 03301-4005
Phone: (603) 225-6641; (800) 464-6641; Fax: (603) 225-1700
Email: info@nhcf.org
Web: www.nhcf.org/page16960.cfm
Summary: To provide scholarships or loans for undergraduate or graduate study in any state to New Hampshire residents.
Eligibility: Open to New Hampshire residents who are graduating high school seniors planning to enter a 4-year college or university, undergraduate students between 17 and 23 years of age working on a 4-year degree, or graduate students of any age. Applicants must be enrolled on at least a half-time basis at a school in New Hampshire or another state. Selection is based on financial need, academic merit, community service, school activities, and work experience. Priority is given to students with the fewest financial resources.
Financial data: Awards range from $500 to $3,500 and average $1,800. Most are made in the form of grants (recently, 82% of all awards) or no-interest or low-interest loans.
Duration: 1 year; approximately one-third of the awards are renewable.
Number awarded: Varies each year; approximately $700,000 is awarded annually.
Deadline: April of each year.

700 NEW HAMPSHIRE INCENTIVE PROGRAM

New Hampshire Postsecondary Education Commission
Attn: Financial Aid Programs Coordinator
3 Barrell Court, Suite 300
Concord, NH 03301-8543
Phone: (603) 271-2555, ext. 360; Fax: (603) 271-2696; TDD: (800) 735-2964
Email: cynthia.capodestria@pec.state.nh.us
Web: www.nh.gov/postsecondary/financial/nhip.html
Summary: To provide financial assistance to New Hampshire residents who are interested in attending college in New England.
Eligibility: Open to residents of New Hampshire. They must be U.S. citizens or permanent residents, accepted at or enrolled part- or full-time in an eligible postsecondary institution in 1 of the 6 New England states, and able to demonstrate both academic ability and financial need. Upperclassmen must have a GPA of 2.0 or higher.
Financial data: The stipends range from $125 to $1,000 per year; recently, they averaged $641.
Duration: 1 year.
Number awarded: Varies each year; recently, 4,967 of these awards were granted.
Deadline: April of each year.

701 NEW HAMPSHIRE LEGION DEPARTMENT SCHOLARSHIP

American Legion
Department of New Hampshire
State House Annex
25 Capitol Street, Room 431
Concord, NH 03301-6312
Phone: (603) 271-2211; (800) 778-3816; Fax: (603) 271-5352
Email: adjutantnh@amlegion.state.nh.us
Web: www.nhlegion.org/Legion%20Scholarships/Index%20Page.htm
Summary: To provide financial assistance to residents of New Hampshire entering a college or university in any state.
Eligibility: Open to seniors graduating from high schools in New Hampshire who have been residents of the state for at least 3 years. Applicants must be entering their first year at a 4-year college or university. They must have a GPA of 3.0 or higher for their junior and senior years of high school. Financial need is considered in the selection process.
Financial data: The stipend is $1,000.
Duration: 1 year.
Number awarded: 2 each year.
Deadline: April of each year.

702 NEW HAMPSHIRE LEGION DEPARTMENT VOCATIONAL EDUCATION SCHOLARSHIP

American Legion
Department of New Hampshire
State House Annex
25 Capitol Street, Room 431
Concord, NH 03301-6312
Phone: (603) 271-2211; (800) 778-3816; Fax: (603) 271-5352
Email: adjutantnh@amlegion.state.nh.us
Web: www.nhlegion.org/Legion%20Scholarships/Index%20Page.htm
Summary: To provide financial assistance to residents of New Hampshire entering a vocational training program at a school in any state.
Eligibility: Open to seniors graduating from high schools in New Hampshire who have been residents of the state for at least 3 years. Applicants must be entering their first year of vocational training at a school in any state to work on an associate degree. They must have a GPA of 3.0 or higher for their junior and senior years of high school. Financial need is also considered in the selection process.
Financial data: The stipend is $1,000.

Duration: 1 year.
Number awarded: 1 each year.
Deadline: April of each year.

703 NEW HAMPSHIRE LEVERAGED INCENTIVE GRANT PROGRAM

New Hampshire Postsecondary Education Commission
Attn: Financial Aid Programs Coordinator
3 Barrell Court, Suite 300
Concord, NH 03301-8543
Phone: (603) 271-2555, ext. 352; Fax: (603) 271-2696; TDD: (800) 735-2964
Email: jknapp@pec.state.nh.us
Web: www.nh.gov/postsecondary/financial/lev_inc_grnt.html

Summary: To provide financial assistance to New Hampshire residents who are attending college in the state and can demonstrate financial need.
Eligibility: Open to residents of New Hampshire who are currently enrolled as sophomores, juniors, or seniors at accredited colleges and universities in the state. Selection is based on financial need (as determined by federal formulas) and academic merit (as determined by the institution.
Financial data: Grants range from $146 to $10,000 per year; recently, they averaged $1,566.
Duration: 1 year; may be renewed.
Number awarded: Varies each year; recently, 357 of these grants were awarded.
Deadline: Deadline not specified.

704 NEW HAMPSHIRE SCHOLARSHIPS FOR ORPHANS OF VETERANS

New Hampshire Postsecondary Education Commission
Attn: Financial Aid Programs Coordinator
3 Barrell Court, Suite 300
Concord, NH 03301-8543
Phone: (603) 271-2555, ext. 352; Fax: (603) 271-2696; TDD: (800) 735-2964
Email: jknapp@pec.state.nh.us
Web: www.nh.gov/postsecondary/financial/war_orphans.html

Summary: To provide financial assistance to the children of New Hampshire veterans who died of service-connected causes and plan to attend college in the state.
Eligibility: Open to New Hampshire residents between 16 and 25 years of age whose parent(s) died while on active duty or as a result of a service-related disability incurred during World War II, the Korean Conflict, the southeast Asian Conflict (Vietnam), or the Gulf Wars. Parents must have been residents of New Hampshire at the time of death. Applicants must be enrolled at least half-time as undergraduate students at a public college or university in New Hampshire. Financial need is not considered in the selection process.
Financial data: The stipend is $2,500 per year, to be used for the payment of room, board, books, and supplies. Recipients are also eligible to receive a tuition waiver from the institution.
Duration: 1 year; may be renewed for up to 3 additional years.
Number awarded: Varies each year; recently, 2 of these scholarships were awarded.
Deadline: Deadline not specified.

705 NEW JERSEY ASSOCIATION FOR COLLEGE ADMISSION COUNSELING SCHOLARSHIPS

New Jersey Association for College Admission Counseling
c/o Maryann Stickney, Scholarship Committee
P.O. Box 206
Manasquan, NJ 08736
Email: scholarship@njacac.org
Web: www.njacac.org/index.php?page=scholarship.php

Summary: To provide financial assistance to residents of New Jersey whose high school or community college counselor is a member of the New Jersey Association for College Admission Counseling (NJACAC) and who plan to attend college in any state.
Eligibility: Open to residents of New Jersey who are either high school seniors planning to enroll full-time at an accredited 2- or 4-year college or university in any state or community college sophomores planning to transfer to an accredited 4-year college or university in any state. Applicant's high school counselor or community college representative must be an NJACAC member. Along with their application, they must submit a 400-word essay on the depth and breadth of their involvement in community service, leadership activities, or employment experience. Financial need is not considered in the selection process. U.S. citizenship is required.
Financial data: The stipend is $1,000.
Duration: 1 year.
Number awarded: 6 each year.
Deadline: February of each year.

706 NEW JERSEY BANKERS EDUCATION FOUNDATION SCHOLARSHIPS

New Jersey Bankers Association
Attn: New Jersey Bankers Education Foundation, Inc.
411 North Avenue East
Cranford, NJ 07016-2436
Phone: (908) 272-8500, ext. 614; Fax: (908) 272-6626
Email: j.meredith@njbankers.com
Web: www.njbankers.com

Summary: To provide financial assistance to dependents of deceased and disabled military personnel who have a connection to New Jersey and are interested in attending college in any state.
Eligibility: Open to the spouses, children, stepchildren, and grandchildren of members of the armed services who died or became disabled while on active duty; it is not required that the military person died in combat. Applicants must have a high school or equivalency diploma and be attending college in any state. Adult dependents who wish to obtain a high school equivalency diploma are also eligible. Either the dependent or the servicemember must have a connection to New Jersey; the applicant's permanent address must be in New Jersey or the servicemember's last permanent address or military base must have been in the state. Financial need is considered in the selection process.
Financial data: A stipend is awarded (amount not specified).
Duration: 1 year; may be renewed if the recipient maintains a "C" average.
Number awarded: 1 or more each year.
Deadline: June of each year.

707 NEW JERSEY BURGLAR & FIRE ALARM ASSOCIATION YOUTH SCHOLARSHIP PROGRAM

New Jersey Burglar & Fire Alarm Association
Attn: Scholarship Committee Chair
202 West State Street
Trenton, NJ 08608
Phone: (609) 695-4444; (800) 613-6523; Fax: (609) 695-3333
Email: membership@njbfaa.org
Web: www.njbfaa.org/scholarship.html

Summary: To provide financial assistance to high school seniors in New Jersey who are the children of police and fire personnel and interested in attending college in any state.
Eligibility: Open to seniors who are graduating from high schools in New Jersey and are the children of active-duty police and fire personnel. Children of federal law enforcement officers, reserve officers, part-time employees, or retired, disabled, or deceased fire and policy personnel are not eligible. Applicants must be planning to enroll at an accredited college or university in any state. Along with their application, they must submit an essay of 500 to 1,000 words on what it means to them to have their parent or guardian employed in securing our community. Selection is based on that essay (25%), grade average (25%), SAT or ACT scores (30 points), and academic prizes, awards, hobbies, and school and outside extracurricular activities.
Financial data: Stipends are $1,500 or $1,000.
Duration: 1 year.
Number awarded: 2 each year: 1 at $1,500 and 1 at $1,000.
Deadline: March of each year.

708 NEW JERSEY LEGION AUXILIARY DEPARTMENT SCHOLARSHIPS

American Legion Auxiliary
Department of New Jersey
c/o Lucille M. Miller, Secretary/Treasurer
1540 Kuser Road, Suite A-8
Hamilton, NJ 08619
Phone: (609) 581-9580; Fax: (609) 581-8429
Email: newjerseyala@juno.com
Web: www.alanj.org

Summary: To provide financial assistance to New Jersey residents who are the descendants of veterans and planning to attend college in any state.
Eligibility: Open to the children, grandchildren, and great-grandchildren of veterans who served in the U.S. armed forces during specified periods of war time. Applicants must be graduating high school seniors who have been residents of New Jersey for at least 2 years. They must be planning to attend a college or university in any state. Along with their application, they must submit a 1,000-word essay on a topic that changes annually; recently, students were asked to write on the topic, "Honoring Our Promise Everyday—How I Can Serve My Country and Our Veterans." Selection is based on academic achievement (40%), character (15%), leadership (15%), Americanism (15%), and financial need (15%).
Financial data: Stipends range from $1,000 to $2,500.
Duration: 1 year.
Number awarded: 3 each year: 1 in North Jersey, 1 in Central Jersey, and 1 in South Jersey.
Deadline: April of each year.

709 NEW JERSEY NETS AND DEVILS SCHOLARSHIP

New Jersey Nets and Devils Foundation
Attn: Program and Grants Manager
390 Murray Hill Parkway
East Rutherford, NJ 07073
Phone: (201) 635-3140; Fax: (201) 935-1088
Web: www.nba.com/nets/foundation/Nets_Devils_Foundation-80248-64.html
Summary: To provide financial assistance to students enrolled at selected colleges in New Jersey who have demonstrated a commitment to community leadership and a desire to make a difference.
Eligibility: Open to students who have graduated from a New Jersey high school in the last 2 years, demonstrate an ongoing history of community service, have documented financial need, and have demonstrated the ability to do college-level academic work. Applicants must be enrolled at 1 of the following colleges or universities: Bloomfield College, Essex County College, Hudson Community College, New Jersey City University, New Jersey Institute of Technology, Passaic Community College, Rider University, Rutgers University Newark, Rutgers University Camden, Seton Hall University, or William Patterson University. Applicants first submit an application to their college representative that details their grades, awards, extracurricular activities, and community service and a 250-word essay that outlines the candidate's interest in the scholarship program. The college representatives from the 11 participating universities then submit the applications of their top 6 candidates to the foundation for final selection. Finalists are selected based on financial need, history of community service or volunteerism, and academic standing.
Financial data: The stipend is $1,000 per year and is matched dollar for dollar by the recipient's college, making the total $2,000 per year.
Duration: 4 years.
Number awarded: Approximately 42 each year.
Deadline: Deadline not specified.

710 NEW JERSEY POW/MIA TUITION BENEFIT PROGRAM

New Jersey Department of Military and Veterans Affairs
Attn: Division of Veterans Programs
101 Eggert Crossing Road
P.O. Box 340
Trenton, NJ 08625-0340
Phone: (609) 530-7045; (800) 624-0508 (within NJ); Fax: (609) 530-7075
Web: www.state.nj.us/military/veterans/programs.html
Summary: To provide financial assistance for college to the children of New Jersey military personnel reported as missing in action or prisoners of war during the southeast Asian conflict.
Eligibility: Open to New Jersey residents attending or accepted at a New Jersey public or independent postsecondary institution whose parents were military service personnel officially declared prisoners of war or missing in action after January 1, 1960.
Financial data: This program entitles recipients to full undergraduate tuition at any public or independent postsecondary educational institution in New Jersey.
Duration: Assistance continues until completion of a bachelor's degree.
Number awarded: Varies each year.
Deadline: February of each year for the spring term and September for the fall and spring terms.

711 NEW JERSEY STATE ELKS SPECIAL CHILDREN'S SCHOLARSHIP

New Jersey State Elks
Attn: Special Children's Committee
665 Rahway Avenue
P.O. Box 1596
Woodbridge, NJ 07095-1596
Phone: (732) 326-1300
Email: info@njelks.org
Web: www.njelks.org
Summary: To provide financial assistance to high school seniors in New Jersey who have a disability and plan to attend college in any state.
Eligibility: Open to seniors graduating from high schools in New Jersey who have a disability. Applicants must be planning to attend a college or university in any state. Selection is based on academic standing, general worthiness, and financial need. Boys and girls are judged separately.
Financial data: The stipend is $2,500 per year. Funds are paid directly to the recipient's college or university.
Duration: 4 years.
Number awarded: 2 each year: 1 to a boy and 1 to a girl.
Deadline: April of each year.

712 NEW JERSEY UTILITIES ASSOCIATION EQUAL EMPLOYMENT OPPORTUNITY SCHOLARSHIPS

New Jersey Utilities Association
50 West State Street, Suite 1117
Trenton, NJ 08608
Phone: (609) 392-1000; Fax: (609) 396-4231
Web: www.njua.org/html/njua_eeo_scholarship.cfm
Summary: To provide financial assistance to minority, female, and disabled high school seniors in New Jersey interested in attending college in any state.
Eligibility: Open to seniors graduating from high schools in New Jersey who are women, minorities (Black or African American, Hispanic or Latino, American Indian or Alaska Native, Asian, Native Hawaiian or Pacific Islander, or 2 or more races), and persons with disabilities. Applicants must be planning to work on a bachelor's degree at a college or university in any state. They must be able to demonstrate financial need. Children of employees of any New Jersey Utilities Association-member company are ineligible. Selection is based on overall academic excellence and demonstrated financial need. U.S. citizenship or permanent resident status is required.
Financial data: The stipend is $1,500 per year.
Duration: 4 years.
Number awarded: 2 each year.
Deadline: March of each year.

713 NEW JERSEY VIETNAM VETERANS' MEMORIAL SCHOLARSHIPS

New Jersey Vietnam Veterans' Memorial
Attn: Scholarship Committee
1 Memorial Lane
P.O. Box 648
Holmdel, NJ 07733
Phone: (732) 335-0033; Fax: (732) 335-1107
Web: www.njvvmf.org
Summary: To recognize and reward, with scholarships for college in any state, New Jersey high school seniors who have visited the New Jersey Vietnam Veterans' Memorial and written an essay about the experience.
Eligibility: Open to seniors graduating from high schools in New Jersey who have visited the New Jersey Vietnam Veterans' Memorial. Applicants must submit an essay in which they reflect upon their visit. They must submit proof of acceptance to a college or trade school in any state, but letters of recommendation and transcripts are not required.
Financial data: The award is a $2,500 scholarship.
Duration: The awards are granted annually.
Number awarded: 2 each year.
Deadline: April of each year.

714 NEW MEXICO ACTIVITIES ASSOCIATION ACTIVITIES SCHOLARSHIPS

New Mexico Activities Association
Attn: Associate Director
6600 Palomas Avenue, N.E.
Albuquerque, NM 87109
Phone: (505) 923-3275; (888) 820-NMAA; Fax: (505) 923-3114
Email: mmartinez@nmact.org
Web: www.nmact.org/scholarship_information_forms

Summary: To provide financial assistance to high school seniors in New Mexico who have participated in sanctioned extracurricular activities and plan to attend college in any state.

Eligibility: Open to seniors graduating from high schools in New Mexico with a GPA of 3.0 or higher. Applicants must have participated in at least 1 extracurricular activity sanctioned by the New Mexico Activities Association (NMAA) during their sophomore and junior years and at least 2 activities during their senior year. They must be planning to attend a college or university in any state. Along with their application, they must submit a personal statement on how involvement in extracurricular activities impacted their high school career. Financial need is not considered in the selection process.

Financial data: The stipend is $1,000. From among all its scholarship recipients, the NMAA selects the 2 most outstanding and awards them a stipend of $2,500.

Duration: 1 year.

Number awarded: 2 each year. The NMAA also awards 2 additional at-large scholarships to applicants for all its programs.

Deadline: February of each year.

715 NEW MEXICO ACTIVITIES ASSOCIATION EXTRAORDINARY PARTICIPATION SCHOLARSHIPS

New Mexico Activities Association
Attn: Associate Director
6600 Palomas Avenue, N.E.
Albuquerque, NM 87109
Phone: (505) 923-3275; (888) 820-NMAA; Fax: (505) 923-3114
Email: mmartinez@nmact.org
Web: www.nmact.org/scholarship_information_forms

Summary: To provide financial assistance to high school seniors in New Mexico who have participated in sanctioned sports and extracurricular activities and plan to attend college in any state.

Eligibility: Open to seniors graduating from high schools in New Mexico with a GPA of 3.0 or higher. Applicants must have participated in at least 1 sport and at least 1 extracurricular activity sanctioned by the New Mexico Activities Association (NMAA) throughout their high school career. They must be planning to attend a college or university in any state. Along with their application, they must submit a personal statement on how involvement in athletics and extracurricular activities impacted their high school career. Financial need is not considered in the selection process.

Financial data: The stipend is $1,000. From among all its scholarship recipients, the NMAA selects the 2 most outstanding and awards them a stipend of $2,500.

Duration: 1 year.

Number awarded: 2 each year. The NMAA also awards 2 additional at-large scholarships to applicants for all its programs.

Deadline: February of each year.

716 NEW MEXICO CHILDREN OF DECEASED MILITARY AND STATE POLICE PERSONNEL SCHOLARSHIPS

New Mexico Department of Veterans' Services
Attn: Benefits Division
407 Galisteo Street, Room 142
Santa Fe, NM 87504
Phone: (505) 827-6374; (866) 433-VETS; Fax: (505) 827-6372
Email: alan.martinez@state.nm.us
Web: www.dvs.state.nm.us/benefits.html

Summary: To provide financial assistance for college or graduate school to the children of deceased military and state police personnel in New Mexico.

Eligibility: Open to the children of 1) military personnel killed in action or as a result of such action during a period of armed conflict; 2) members of the New Mexico National Guard killed while on active duty; and 3) New Mexico State Police killed on active duty. Applicants must be between the ages of 16 and 26 and enrolled in a state-supported school in New Mexico. Children of deceased veterans must be nominated by the New Mexico Veterans' Service Commission; children of National Guard members must be nominated by the adjutant general of the state; children of state police must be nominated by the New Mexico State Police Board. Selection is based on merit and financial need.

Financial data: The scholarships provide full waiver of tuition at state-funded postsecondary schools in New Mexico. A stipend of $150 per semester ($300 per year) provides assistance with books and fees.

Duration: 1 year; may be renewed.

Deadline: Deadline not specified.

717 NEW MEXICO COMPETITIVE SCHOLARSHIPS

New Mexico Higher Education Department
Attn: Financial Aid Division
2048 Galisteo Street
Santa Fe, NM 87505-2100
Phone: (505) 476-8411; (800) 279-9777; Fax: (505) 476-8454
Email: Theresa.acker@state.nm.us
Web: hed.state.nm.us

Summary: To provide financial assistance to residents of other states who wish to attend a college or university in New Mexico.

Eligibility: Open to students who are not residents of New Mexico but who wish to enroll full-time at public 4-year institutions of higher education in the state. Applicants to the University of New Mexico and New Mexico State University must have either 1) a high school GPA of 3.5 or higher and an ACT score of 23 or higher; or 2) a high school GPA of 3.0 or higher and an ACT score of 26 or higher. Applicants to other public 4-year institutions in the state must have either 1) a high school GPA of 3.5 or higher and an ACT score of 20 or higher; or 2) a high school GPA of 3.0 or higher and an ACT score of 23 or higher. Equivalent SAT scores may be used in lieu of ACT scores.

Financial data: For recipients, the out-of-state portion of tuition is waived and a stipend of at least $100 is paid.

Duration: 1 year; may be renewed up to 3 additional years.

Number awarded: Varies each year, depending on the availability of funds.

Deadline: Deadlines are established by the participating institutions.

718 NEW MEXICO ELKS ASSOCIATION CHARITABLE AND BENEVOLENT TRUST SCHOLARSHIPS

New Mexico Elks Association
Attn: Charitable and Benevolent Trust Commission
c/o Michael Stewart, Scholarship Committee
199 Old El Paso Highway
Alamagordo, NM 87123
Fax: (575) 921-5597
Email: michaelstewart.per@Live.com
Web: www.nmelks.org/scholarships.htm

Summary: To provide financial assistance for college to high school seniors in New Mexico.

Eligibility: Open to seniors graduating from a high school in New Mexico. They must have exhibited outstanding scholastic and leadership ability, including extracurricular and civic activities. High school class rank, GPA, and standardized test scores must be validated by a school official. An endorsement from the local Elks Lodge is required. Financial need is also considered in the selection process. Some awards are designated for females and some for males.

Financial data: Stipends are either $2,000 or $1,000 per year.

Duration: 1 or 4 years.

Number awarded: Varies each year; recently, 26 of these scholarships were awarded: 1 at $2,000 per year for 4 years to the top female applicant, 1 at $2,000 per year for 4 years to the top male applicant, 12 at $2,000 for 1 year (6 for females and 6 for males), and 12 at $1,000 for 1 year (6 for females and 6 for males).

Deadline: Applications must be submitted to local Elks Lodges by March of each year.

719 NEW MEXICO LEGISLATIVE ENDOWMENT SCHOLARSHIPS

New Mexico Higher Education Department
Attn: Financial Aid Division
2048 Galisteo Street
Santa Fe, NM 87505-2100
Phone: (505) 476-8411; (800) 279-9777; Fax: (505) 476-8454
Email: Theresa.acker@state.nm.us
Web: hed.state.nm.us

Summary: To provide financial assistance to needy residents of New Mexico who plan to attend a public college or university in the state.

Eligibility: Open to residents of New Mexico enrolled or planning to enroll at least half-time at a public institution of higher education in the state. Applicants must be able to demonstrate substantial financial need. Preference is given to 1) students transferring from New Mexico 2-year public postsecondary institutions to 4-year institutions; and 2) returning adult students at 2- and 4-year public institutions.
Financial data: Full-time students receive up to $2,500 per year at 4-year institutions or up to $1,000 per year at 2-year institutions. Part-time students are eligible for prorated awards.
Duration: 1 year; may be renewed.
Number awarded: Varies each year.
Deadline: Deadlines are established by the participating institutions.

720 NEW MEXICO LEGISLATIVE LOTTERY SCHOLARSHIPS

New Mexico Higher Education Department
Attn: Financial Aid Division
2048 Galisteo Street
Santa Fe, NM 87505-2100
Phone: (505) 476-8411; (800) 279-9777; Fax: (505) 476-8454
Email: Theresa.acker@state.nm.us
Web: hed.state.nm.us
Summary: To provide financial assistance to residents of New Mexico who plan to attend a public college or university in the state.
Eligibility: Open to full-time students at New Mexico public colleges and universities who graduated from a public or private high school in New Mexico or obtained a New Mexico GED. Applicants who earn at least a 2.5 GPA during their first college semester are eligible to begin receiving the award for their second semester of full-time enrollment.
Financial data: Scholarships are equal to 100% of tuition at the New Mexico public postsecondary institution where the student is enrolled.
Duration: Up to 8 consecutive semesters.
Number awarded: Varies each year, depending on the availability of funds.
Deadline: Deadlines are established by the participating institutions.

721 NEW MEXICO SCHOLARS PROGRAM

New Mexico Higher Education Department
Attn: Financial Aid Division
2048 Galisteo Street
Santa Fe, NM 87505-2100
Phone: (505) 476-8411; (800) 279-9777; Fax: (505) 476-8454
Email: Theresa.acker@state.nm.us
Web: hed.state.nm.us
Summary: To provide financial assistance to graduating high school seniors in New Mexico who plan to attend a public college or university or designated private college in the state.
Eligibility: Open to graduating high school seniors in New Mexico who plan to enroll full-time at a public institution of higher education or selected private college in the state. Applicants must be in the top 5% of their high school graduating class or have an ACT score of at least 25. If 1 member of a family is enrolled in college, the family income may be no greater than $30,000 a year; if 2 or more members of the family are enrolled in college, the family income may be no greater than $40,000.
Financial data: This program provides recipients with tuition, fees, and books at a participating college or university in New Mexico.
Duration: 1 year; may be renewed.
Number awarded: Varies each year, depending on the availability of funds.
Deadline: Deadlines are established by the participating institutions.

722 NEW MEXICO STATE COUNCIL ROADRUNNER ENDOWMENT SCHOLARSHIP

Epsilon Sigma Alpha International
Attn: ESA Foundation
P.O. Box 270517
Fort Collins, CO 80527
Phone: (970) 223-2824; Fax: (970) 223-4456
Email: esainfo@esaintl.com
Web: www.esaintl.com/esaf
Summary: To provide financial assistance to residents of New Mexico or neighboring cities who plan to attend college in any state.
Eligibility: Open to residents of New Mexico who are 1) graduating high school seniors with a GPA of 3.0 or higher or with minimum scores of 22 on the ACT or 1030 on the combined critical reading and mathematics SAT; 2) enrolled in college with a GPA of 3.0 or higher; 3) enrolled at a technical school or returning to school after an absence for retraining of job skills or obtaining a degree; or 4) engaged in online study through an accredited college, university, or vocational school. Applicants may be attending or planning to attend a school in any state and major in any field. Residents of El Paso and Farwell, Texas are also eligible. Selection is based on character (10%), leadership (10%), service (35%), financial need (35%), and scholastic ability (10%).
Financial data: The stipend is $1,000.
Duration: 1 year; may be renewed.
Number awarded: 1 each year.
Deadline: January of each year.

723 NEW MEXICO STUDENT INCENTIVE GRANTS

New Mexico Higher Education Department
Attn: Financial Aid Division
2048 Galisteo Street
Santa Fe, NM 87505-2100
Phone: (505) 476-8411; (800) 279-9777; Fax: (505) 476-8454
Email: Theresa.acker@state.nm.us
Web: hed.state.nm.us
Summary: To provide financial assistance to needy residents of New Mexico attending public or private nonprofit colleges in the state.
Eligibility: Open to full-time and half-time undergraduate students at public or private nonprofit colleges and universities in New Mexico who can demonstrate substantial financial need. Applicants must be U.S. citizens and New Mexico residents.
Financial data: The amount of the award is set by the participating college or university; generally, the awards range from $200 to $2,500 per year.
Duration: 1 year; may be renewed.
Number awarded: Varies each year, depending on the availability of funds.
Deadline: Deadlines are established by the participating institutions.

724 NEW MEXICO VIETNAM VETERAN SCHOLARSHIPS

New Mexico Department of Veterans' Services
Attn: Benefits Division
407 Galisteo Street, Room 142
Santa Fe, NM 87504
Phone: (505) 827-6374; (866) 433-VETS; Fax: (505) 827-6372
Email: alan.martinez@state.nm.us
Web: www.dvs.state.nm.us/benefits.html
Summary: To provide financial assistance to Vietnam veterans in New Mexico who are interested in working on an undergraduate or master's degree at a public college in the state.
Eligibility: Open to Vietnam veterans who have been residents of New Mexico for at least 10 years. Applicants must have been honorably discharged and have been awarded the Vietnam Service Medal or the Vietnam Campaign Medal. They must be planning to attend a state-supported college, university, or community college in New Mexico to work on an undergraduate or master's degree. Awards are granted on a first-come, first-served basis.
Financial data: The scholarships provide full payment of tuition and purchase of required books at any state-funded postsecondary institution in New Mexico.
Duration: 1 year.
Deadline: Deadline not specified.

725 NEW YORK APTS PROGRAM

New York State Higher Education Services Corporation
Attn: Student Information
99 Washington Avenue
Albany, NY 12255
Phone: (518) 473-1574; (888) NYS-HESC; Fax: (518) 473-3749; TDD: (800) 445-5234
Email: webmail@hesc.com
Web: www.hesc.com/content.nsf/SFC/0/Aid_for_PartTime_Study
Summary: To provide financial assistance to students who are attending college on a part-time basis in New York.
Eligibility: Open to students who are enrolled part-time (at least 3 but less than 12 hours per semester) in an undergraduate degree program in New York; meet the income limits established for this program (students whose parents could not claim them as dependents may earn no more than $34,250 per year; the total family income if parents do claim the student as a dependent may not exceed $50,550 per year); be a New York resident and a U.S. citizen or eligible

noncitizen; have a tuition bill of at least $100 per year; not have used up their Tuition Assistance Program (TAP) eligibility; and not be in default on a student loan.

Financial data: Stipends range up to $2,000 per year; awards may not exceed actual tuition charges.

Duration: 1 year; recipients may reapply for up to 8 years of part-time study if they maintain a GPA of at least 2.0.

Number awarded: Varies each year; recently, more than 20,000 students received more than $12 million in assistance through this program.

Deadline: Deadline not specified.

726 NEW YORK LEGION AUXILIARY DEPARTMENT SCHOLARSHIP

American Legion Auxiliary
Department of New York
112 State Street, Suite 1310
Albany, NY 12207
Phone: (518) 463-1162; (800) 421-6348; Fax: (518) 449-5406
Email: alanyterry@nycap.rr.com
Web: www.deptny.org/Scholarships.htm

Summary: To provide financial assistance to New York residents who are the descendants of veterans and interested in attending college in any state.

Eligibility: Open to residents of New York who are high school seniors or graduates and attending or planning to attend an accredited college or university in any state. Applicants must be the children, grandchildren, or great-grandchildren of veterans who served during specified periods of war time. Along with their application, they must submit a 500-word essay on a subject of their choice. Selection is based on character (20%), Americanism (20%), leadership (20%), scholarship (15%), and financial need (25%). U.S. citizenship is required.

Financial data: The stipend is $1,000. Funds are paid directly to the recipient's school.

Duration: 1 year.

Number awarded: 1 each year.

Deadline: February of each year.

727 NEW YORK MEMORIAL SCHOLARSHIPS

New York State Higher Education Services Corporation
Attn: Student Information
99 Washington Avenue
Albany, NY 12255
Phone: (518) 473-1574; (888) NYS-HESC; Fax: (518) 473-3749; TDD: (800) 445-5234
Email: webmail@hesc.com
Web: www.hesc.com/content.nsf/SFC/0/NYS_Memorial_Scholarships

Summary: To provide financial aid for college in the state to the children or spouses of public service officers in New York state who died as the result of injuries sustained in the line of duty.

Eligibility: Open to New York State residents whose parent or spouse was a police officer, peace officer (including corrections officer), fire fighter, volunteer fire fighter, or emergency medical service worker in New York and died as the result of injuries sustained in the line of duty. Applicants must be accepted or enrolled as a full-time undergraduate at a public college or university or private institution in New York.

Financial data: At public colleges and universities, this program provides payment of actual tuition and mandatory educational fees; actual room and board charged to students living on campus or an allowance for room and board for commuter students; and allowances for books, supplies, and transportation. At private institutions, the award is equal to the amount charged at the State University of New York (SUNY) for 4-year tuition and average mandatory fees (or the student's actual tuition and fees, whichever is less) plus allowances for room, board, books, supplies, and transportation.

Duration: This program is available for 4 years of full-time undergraduate study (or 5 years in an approved 5-year bachelor's degree program).

Number awarded: Varies each year; recently, more than 60 students received $558,000 in assistance through this program.

Deadline: April of each year.

728 NEW YORK METROPOLITAN CHAPTER SCHOLARSHIP FUND

Finlandia Foundation–New York Metropolitan Chapter
Attn: Scholarships
P.O. Box 165, Bowling Green Station
New York, NY 10274-0165
Email: scholarships@finlandiafoundationny.org
Web: www.finlandiafoundationny.org/scholarships.html

Summary: To provide financial assistance for study or research to students at colleges and universities in the United States, especially those of Finnish heritage.

Eligibility: Open to students at colleges and universities in the United States. Applicants must submit information on their language proficiency, work experience, memberships (academic, professional, and social), fellowships and scholarships, awards, publications, exhibitions, performances, and future goals and ambitions. Financial need is not considered in the selection process. Preference is given to applicants of Finnish heritage.

Financial data: Stipends range from $500 to $5,000 per year.

Duration: 1 year.

Number awarded: 1 or more each year.

Deadline: February of each year.

729 NEW YORK PART-TIME TAP PROGRAM

New York State Higher Education Services Corporation
Attn: Student Information
99 Washington Avenue
Albany, NY 12255
Phone: (518) 473-1574; (888) NYS-HESC; Fax: (518) 473-3749; TDD: (800) 445-5234
Email: webmail@hesc.com
Web: www.hesc.com/content.nsf/SFC/0/PartTime_TAP_Program

Summary: To provide financial assistance to residents of New York who are enrolled part-time at a college in the state.

Eligibility: Open to residents of New York who are enrolled part-time (at least 6 but less than 12 hours per semester) in an undergraduate degree program in the state. Applicants must be charged at least $200 in tuition per year. They must meet the net taxable income limits established for the New York Tuition Assistance Program (TAP); currently, those are $80,000 per year for dependent students or those who are married or have tax dependents, or $10,000 per year for single independent students with no dependents. U.S. citizenship or eligible noncitizenship status is required.

Financial data: The stipend depends on the number of units the recipient is taking, ranging from 50% of full TAP awards for those taking 6 semester hours to 91.67% of full TAP awards for those taking 11 semester hours. For dependent students or those who are married or have tax dependents, full TAP awards range from $500 to $5,000. For single independent students with no dependents, full TAP awards range from $500 to $3,025.

Duration: 1 year; recipients may reapply for up to 8 years of part-time study if they maintain a GPA of at least 2.0.

Number awarded: Varies each year.

Deadline: Deadline not specified.

730 NEW YORK STATE LEADERS OF TOMORROW SCHOLARSHIPS

New York Lottery
Attn: LOT Scholarship
University at Albany–East Campus
Five University Place-A409
Rensselaer, NY 12144
Phone: (518) 512-5198, ext. 225; Fax: (518) 512-5226
Email: jlefkovits@uamail.albany.edu
Web: www.nylottery.org

Summary: To provide financial assistance to high school seniors in New York who plan to attend college in the state.

Eligibility: Open to seniors graduating from high schools in New York who have a GPA of 3.0 or higher. Applicants must be planning to attend an accredited college, university, trade school, or community college in the state that participates in the Tuition Assistance Program. They must be U.S. citizens or qualifying noncitizens. Selection is based on academic performance, participation in extracurricular activities, and commitment to community service.

Financial data: The stipend is $1,250 per year.

Duration: Up to 4 years, provided the recipient remains enrolled at an accredited New York State institution with a GPA of 3.0 or higher. The college program must be completed within 5 years of high school graduation.

Number awarded: Up to 1 from each participating public and private high school in New York State; recently, 1,209 of these scholarships were awarded.

Deadline: April each year.

731 NEW YORK STATE MILITARY SERVICE RECOGNITION SCHOLARSHIPS

New York State Higher Education Services Corporation
Attn: Student Information
99 Washington Avenue
Albany, NY 12255
Phone: (518) 473-1574; (888) NYS-HESC; Fax: (518) 473-3749; TDD: (800) 445-5234
Email: webmail@hesc.com
Web: www.hesc.com

Summary: To provide financial assistance to disabled veterans and the family members of deceased or disabled veterans who are residents of New York and interested in attending college in the state.

Eligibility: Open to New York residents who served in the armed forces of the United States or state organized militia at any time on or after August 2, 1990 and became severely and permanently disabled as a result of injury or illness suffered or incurred in a combat theater or combat zone or during military training operations in preparation for duty in a combat theater or combat zone of operations. Also eligible are the children, spouses, or financial dependents of members of the armed forces of the United States or state organized militia who at any time after August 2, 1990 1) died, became severely and permanently disabled as a result of injury or illness suffered or incurred, or are classified as missing in action in a combat theater or combat zone of operations; 2) died as a result of injuries incurred in those designated areas; or 3) died or became severely and permanently disabled as a result of injury or illness suffered or incurred during military training operations in preparation for duty in a combat theater or combat zone of operations. Applicants must be attending or accepted at an approved program of study as full-time undergraduates at a public college or university or private institution in New York.

Financial data: At public colleges and universities, this program provides payment of actual tuition and mandatory educational fees; actual room and board charged to students living on campus or an allowance for room and board for commuter students; and allowances for books, supplies, and transportation. At private institutions, the award is equal to the amount charged at the State University of New York (SUNY) for 4-year tuition and average mandatory fees (or the student's actual tuition and fees, whichever is less) plus allowances for room, board, books, supplies, and transportation.

Duration: This program is available for 4 years of full-time undergraduate study (or 5 years in an approved 5-year bachelor's degree program).

Number awarded: Varies each year.

Deadline: April of each year.

732 NEW YORK STATE SCHOLARSHIPS FOR ACADEMIC EXCELLENCE

New York State Higher Education Services Corporation
Attn: Student Information
99 Washington Avenue
Albany, NY 12255
Phone: (518) 473-1574; (888) NYS-HESC; Fax: (518) 473-3749; TDD: (800) 445-5234
Email: webmail@hesc.com
Web: www.hesc.com

Summary: To provide financial assistance to high school seniors in New York who have a record of academic excellence and plan to attend a college or university in the state.

Eligibility: Open to seniors graduating from high schools in New York who plan to enroll full-time in an approved undergraduate program in the state. U.S. citizenship or qualifying noncitizenship status is required. Selection is based on student grades in certain Regents examinations. The top graduating scholar at each registered high school in New York receives 1 of these awards, and the others are distributed to other outstanding high school graduates in the same ratio of total students graduating from each high school in the state as compared to the total number of students who graduated during the prior school year.

Financial data: Stipends are $1,500 or $500. Recipients can accept other non-loan student aid, but the total of that assistance and this scholarship cannot exceed the cost of attendance.

Duration: This program is available for 4 years of full-time undergraduate study (or 5 years in an approved 5-year bachelor's degree program).

Number awarded: 8,000 each year: 2,000 at $1,500 and 6,000 at $500.

Deadline: April of each year.

733 NEW YORK TUITION ASSISTANCE PROGRAM (TAP)

New York State Higher Education Services Corporation
Attn: Student Information
99 Washington Avenue
Albany, NY 12255
Phone: (518) 473-1574; (888) NYS-HESC; Fax: (518) 473-3749; TDD: (800) 445-5234
Email: webmail@hesc.com
Web: www.hesc.com/content.nsf/SFC/0/About_TAP

Summary: To provide financial assistance to New York State residents enrolled as undergraduate or graduate students at postsecondary institutions in the state.

Eligibility: Open to residents of New York who are U.S. citizens or eligible noncitizens. Applicants' income may not exceed the limitations for this program: for undergraduate students who are dependents or are married or have tax dependents, the limit is $80,000 net taxable family income; for graduate students who are dependents or are married or have tax dependents, the limit is $20,000 net taxable family income; for single independent undergraduate students with no dependents, the limit is $10,000 net taxable income; for single independent graduate students with no dependents, the limit is $5,666 net taxable income. Applicants must be enrolled in school full-time in New York (at least 12 credits per semester); have tuition charges of at least $200 per year; and not be in default on a federal or state loan.

Financial data: TAP awards are based on net taxable income, tuition charges, and type of institution attended. For undergraduate students at degree-granting and not-for-profit institutions, the award range is $500 to $5,000 for dependent students or independent students who are married or have tax dependents, or $500 to $3,025 for independent students who are single with no dependents. For students at proprietary registered non-degree private business schools, the award range is $100 to $800 for dependent students or independent students who are married or have tax dependents, or $100 to $640 for independent students who are single with no dependents. For all graduate students, awards range from $75 to $550.

Duration: Up to 4 years for undergraduate students (or 5 years in approved 5-year baccalaureate programs); up to 4 years for graduate or professional students. The combined undergraduate-graduate total cannot exceed 8 years.

Number awarded: Varies each year; recently, nearly 342,000 students received approximately $636 million in assistance through this program.

Deadline: April of each year.

734 NEW YORK VETERANS TUITION AWARDS

New York State Higher Education Services Corporation
Attn: Student Information
99 Washington Avenue
Albany, NY 12255
Phone: (518) 473-1574; (888) NYS-HESC; Fax: (518) 473-3749; TDD: (800) 445-5234
Email: webmail@hesc.com
Web: www.hesc.com/content.nsf/SFC/0/Veterans_Tuition_Awards

Summary: To provide tuition assistance to eligible veterans enrolled in an undergraduate or graduate program in New York.

Eligibility: Open to veterans who served in the U.S. armed forces in 1) Indochina between February 28, 1961 and May 7, 1975; 2) hostilities that occurred after February 28, 1961 as evidenced by receipt of an Armed Forces Expeditionary Medal, Navy Expeditionary Medal, or Marine Corps Expeditionary Medal; 3) the Persian Gulf on or after August 2, 1990; or 4) Afghanistan on or after September 11, 2001. Applicants must have been discharged from the service under honorable conditions, must be a New York resident, must be a U.S. citizen or eligible noncitizen, must be enrolled full- or part-time at an undergraduate or graduate degree-granting institution in New York State or in an approved vocational training program in the state, must be charged at least $200 tuition per year, and must apply for a New York Tuition Assistance Program (TAP) award.

Financial data: For full-time study, the maximum stipend is 98% of tuition or $4,895.10, whichever is less. For part-time study, the stipend is based on the number of credits certified and the student's actual part-time tuition.

Duration: For undergraduate study, up to 8 semesters, or up to 10 semesters for a program requiring 5 years for completion; for graduate study, up to 6 semesters; for vocational programs, up to 4 semesters. Award limits are based on full-time study or equivalent part-time study.

Number awarded: Varies each year.

Deadline: April of each year.

735 NEXTGEN ACCESS SCHOLARSHIP PROGRAM

Finance Authority of Maine
Attn: NextGen Program
5 Community Drive
P.O. Box 949
Augusta, ME 04332-0949

Phone: (207) 623-3263; (800) 228-3734; Fax: (207) 623-0095; TDD: (207) 626-2717
Email: nextgen@famemaine.com
Web: www.famemaine.com/NextGen_Home.aspx

Summary: To provide financial assistance to Maine residents who are interested in working on a college degree but do not qualify for a Maine State Grant.

Eligibility: Open to residents of Maine who are enrolled in the first year of college or university. Applicants may not be eligible for a Maine State Grant and must have an estimated family contribution of $1,500 or less. They must be enrolled at an institution in Maine or in a state that has a reciprocity agreement with Maine (Connecticut, Massachusetts, New Hampshire, Pennsylvania, Rhode Island, Vermont, or Washington, D.C.).

Financial data: The maximum annual stipend is $1,000 at institutions in Maine or $500 at institutions outside of Maine.

Duration: 1 year; may be renewed up to 4 additional years if the recipient remains a Maine resident and maintains satisfactory academic progress.

Deadline: April of each year.

736 NEXTGEN STUDENT GRANT PROGRAM

Finance Authority of Maine
Attn: NextGen Program
5 Community Drive
P.O. Box 949
Augusta, ME 04332-0949
Phone: (207) 623-3263; (800) 228-3734; Fax: (207) 623-0095; TDD: (207) 626-2717
Email: nextgen@famemaine.com
Web: www.famemaine.com/NextGen_Home.aspx

Summary: To provide financial assistance to Maine residents who can demonstrate financial need and plan to attend college in designated states.

Eligibility: Open to residents of Maine who are enrolled full-time at a college or university in Maine, Connecticut, Massachusetts, New Hampshire, Pennsylvania, Vermont, or Washington, D.C. Applicants' families must exhibit financial need, even though their expected family contribution exceeds the maximum Pell Grant eligibility.

Financial data: Stipends range from $400 to $1,000 per year, depending on the need of the recipient.

Duration: 1 year; may be renewed up to 4 additional years if the recipient remains a Maine resident and maintains satisfactory academic progress.

Deadline: April of each year.

737 NISSAN MISSISSIPPI SCHOLARSHIPS

Mississippi Office of Student Financial Aid
3825 Ridgewood Road
Jackson, MS 39211-6453
Phone: (601) 432-6997; (800) 327-2980 (within MS); Fax: (601) 432-6527
Email: sfa@ihl.state.ms.us
Web: www.mississippi.edu/riseupms/financialaid-state.php

Summary: To provide financial assistance for college to high school seniors in Mississippi who plan to attend a public college in the state.

Eligibility: Open to residents of Mississippi who are graduating seniors at high schools in the state. Applicants must have been accepted for enrollment at a public 2- or 4-year college or university in the state. They must have a GPA of 2.5 or higher after 7 semesters of high school and minimum scores of 20 on the ACT or 940 on the combined critical reading and mathematics SAT. Along with their application, they must submit a 200-word essay on the topic, "How do my plans for the future and my college major support the automotive industry in Mississippi?" Selection is based on the essay (15%); academic achievement (50%); extracurricular activities, work, leadership, and community involvement (15%); and demonstrated financial need (20%).

Financial data: Students in this program receive full payment of tuition and required fees plus an allowance for books.

Duration: 1 year; may be renewed 1 additional year for students at 2-year public colleges (followed by up to 3 years of support if the recipient transfers to a 4-year college or university) or up to 4 additional years for students at 4-year public colleges and universities. Renewal requires that the recipient reapplies each year; maintains a GPA of 2.5 or higher; displays leadership skills through participation in community service, extracurricular, or other activities; demonstrates full-time enrollment and satisfactory academic progress toward completion of a degree; maintains Mississippi residency; and maintains good standing at the college or university.

Number awarded: 1 or more each year.

Deadline: February of each year.

738 NISSAN NORTH AMERICA SCHOLARSHIP

American Indian College Fund
Attn: Scholarship Department
8333 Greenwood Boulevard
Denver, CO 80221
Phone: (303) 426-8900; (800) 776-FUND; Fax: (303) 426-1200
Email: scholarships@collegefund.org
Web: www.collegefund.org/scholarships/schol_mainstream.html

Summary: To provide financial assistance to Native American students enrolling in a bachelor's degree program at a mainstream college.

Eligibility: Open to American Indians and Alaska Natives who can document proof of enrollment or descendancy. Applicants must be enrolled or planning to enroll full-time in a bachelor's degree program at a mainstream institution. They must have a GPA of 2.5 GPA or higher and be able to demonstrate leadership and commitment to an American Indian community. Applications are available only online and include required essays on specified topics. Selection is based on exceptional academic achievement.

Financial data: The stipend is $5,000 per year.

Duration: 1 year; may be renewed.

Number awarded: 20 each year.

Deadline: May of each year.

739 NJCDCA SCHOLARSHIPS

New Jersey Cheerleading & Dance Coaches Association
c/o Carol Stevens, Scholarship Director
A19 Carver Place
Lawrenceville, NJ 08648-1417
Phone: (609) 895-0985
Email: carol.stevens@njcdca.com
Web: njcdca.com/scholar_info.htm

Summary: To provide financial assistance to high school cheerleaders whose school is a member of the New Jersey Cheerleading & Dance Coaches Association (NJCDCA) and who plan to attend college in any state.

Eligibility: Open to seniors graduating from high schools in New Jersey that are members of the NJCDCA. Applicants must be planning to attend a college or university in any state. Along with their application, they must submit a 200-word essay on the impact that cheerleading has had in their lives and their greatest challenge as a cheerleader. Financial need is considered in the selection process.

Financial data: A stipend is awarded (amount not specified).

Duration: 1 year.

Number awarded: Varies each year; recently, 18 of these scholarships were awarded.

Deadline: March of each year.

740 NMASBO SCHOLARSHIPS

New Mexico Association of School Business Officials
Attn: Executive Director
P.O. Box 7535
Albuquerque, NM 87194-7535
Phone: (505) 923-3283; Fax: (505) 923-3114
Email: jmontano110@comcast.net
Web: www.nmasbo.org/about/scholarships_and_awards

Summary: To provide financial assistance to high school seniors in New Mexico who plan to enroll at a college in the state.

Eligibility: Open to seniors graduating from high schools in New Mexico with a GPA of 3.0 or higher. Applicants must be planning to enroll full-time at a college or university in the state to work on a degree in any field. Along with their application, they must submit a 1-page essay on their plans for attending college and how this scholarship will help them achieve their educational goals. Financial need is not considered in the selection process.

Financial data: The stipend is $1,500.

Duration: 1 year.

Number awarded: 6 to 10 each year.

Deadline: March of each year.

741 NONRESIDENT TUITION WAIVERS FOR VETERANS AND THEIR DEPENDENTS WHO MOVE TO TEXAS

Texas Higher Education Coordinating Board
Attn: Grants and Special Programs
1200 East Anderson Lane

P.O. Box 12788, Capitol Station
Austin, TX 78711-2788
Phone: (512) 427-6340; (800) 242-3062; Fax: (512) 427-6127
Email: grantinfo@thecb.state.tx.us
Web: www.collegeforalltexans.com/apps/financialaid/tofa2.cfm?ID=502

Summary: To exempt veterans who move to Texas and their dependents from the payment of nonresident tuition at public institutions of higher education in the state.

Eligibility: Open to former members of the U.S. armed forces and commissioned officers of the Public Health Service who are retired or have been honorably discharged, their spouses, and dependent children. Applicants must have moved to Texas upon separation from the service and be attending or planning to attend a public college or university in the state. They must have indicated their intent to become a Texas resident by registering to vote and doing 1 of the following: owning real property in Texas, registering an automobile in Texas, or executing a will indicating that they are a resident of the state.

Financial data: Although persons eligible under this program are still classified as nonresidents, they are entitled to pay the resident tuition at Texas institutions of higher education on an immediate basis.

Duration: 1 year.

Number awarded: Varies each year.

Deadline: Deadline not specified.

742 NORA STONE SMITH SCHOLARSHIP

Seattle Foundation
Attn: African American Scholarship Program
1200 Fifth Avenue, Suite 1300
Seattle, WA 98101-3151
Phone: (206) 622-2294; Fax: (206) 622-7673
Email: scholarships@seattlefoundation.org
Web: www.seattlefoundation.org/page10004940.cfm

Summary: To provide financial assistance for college to high school seniors who have been enrolled in English as a Second Language/English Language Learners (ESL/ELL) programs.

Eligibility: Open to seniors graduating from high schools who are current or former ESL/ELL students. Applicants must be planning to enroll full-time at a 2- or 4-year college, university, or vocational/trade school. Along with their application, they must submit a 250-word essay about themselves, where they are from, how they came to be here, their educational achievements, and their future goals. Financial need is considered in the selection process.

Financial data: The maximum stipend is $2,000 per year.

Duration: 1 year; may be renewed up to 3 additional years.

Number awarded: 1 or more each year.

Deadline: March or October of each year.

743 NORMAN AND RUTH GOOD EDUCATIONAL ENDOWMENT AWARDS

Lincoln Community Foundation
215 Centennial Mall South, Suite 100
Lincoln, NE 68508
Phone: (402) 474-2345; (888) 448-4668; Fax: (402) 476-8532
Email: lcf@lcf.org
Web: www.lcf.org/page29412.cfm

Summary: To provide financial assistance to upper-division students attending private colleges in Nebraska.

Eligibility: Open to juniors or seniors attending a private college in Nebraska. Applicants must have at least a 3.5 GPA and be working on a degree program, not special studies. Selection is based on academic achievement; financial need is not considered.

Financial data: The amount awarded varies, up to one half of the recipient's educational expenses.

Duration: 1 year; recipients may reapply.

Number awarded: Varies each year; recently, 14 of these awards were presented.

Deadline: April of each year.

744 NORTH CAROLINA ALPHA DELTA KAPPA STUDENT ACHIEVEMENT SCHOLARSHIP

North Carolina Community Foundation
Attn: Program Associate
4601 Six Forks Road, Suite 524
Raleigh, NC 27609
Phone: (919) 828-4387; (800) 201-9533; Fax: (919) 828-5495
Email: sltaylor@nccommunityfoundation.org
Web: www.nccommunityfoundation.org

Summary: To provide financial assistance to high school seniors in North Carolina who are not in the highest academic rank and are interested in attending college in any state.

Eligibility: Open to seniors graduating from high schools in North Carolina who have a weighted GPA between 2.5 and 3.5 and either an SAT score between 1344 and 1560 or an ACT score between 20 and 24. Applicants must be interested in attending a college or university in any state. Selection is based on integrity, leadership potential and service to school, community, and church; financial need is not considered.

Financial data: A stipend is awarded (amount not specified).

Duration: 1 year.

Number awarded: 1 or more each year.

Deadline: January of each year.

745 NORTH CAROLINA ASSOCIATION OF EDUCATIONAL OFFICE PROFESSIONALS STUDENT SCHOLARSHIPS

North Carolina Association of Educational Office Professionals, Inc.
c/o Janet McGrant, State Student Scholarship Chair
428 West Boulevard
Charlotte, NC 28532
Web: www.ncaeop.org/scholarships.html

Summary: To provide financial assistance to residents of North Carolina who are high school seniors or college freshmen and attending or planning to attend college in any state.

Eligibility: Open to residents of North Carolina who are either 1) graduating high school seniors planning to enroll full-time at a college or university in any state; or 2) freshmen already enrolled. Applicants may be planning to major in any field. Along with their application, they must submit a 1-page biographical sketch on why they are choosing to further their education (including a statement of financial need); an official high school transcript; and verification of acceptance or enrollment from their college. U.S. citizenship is required. Selection is based on academic achievement (35 points); character, extracurricular activities, and employment (35 points); and financial need (30 points).

Financial data: Stipends range from $200 to $1,200.

Duration: 1 year.

Number awarded: 14 each year: 1 at $1,200, 1 at $1,000, 2 at $800, 1 at $600, 1 at $500, 1 at $400, and 7 at $200.

Deadline: Districts must submit applications to the state chair by November of each year.

746 NORTH CAROLINA EDUCATION AND TRAINING VOUCHER SCHOLARSHIPS

North Carolina Education and Training Voucher Program
c/o Orphan Foundation of America
21351 Gentry Drive, Suite 130
Sterling, VA 20166
Phone: (571) 203-0270; (800) 585-6118; Fax: (866) 283-0223
Email: nc@statevoucher.org
Web: www.statevoucher.org/state/shtml?state=NC

Summary: To provide financial assistance to North Carolina residents who are or have been in the foster care system of the Department of Social Services (DSS) and are interested in attending college in any state.

Eligibility: Open to residents of North Carolina who either 1) were in DSS foster care on or after their 17th birthday; or 2) were adopted from the foster care system through DSS after the age of 16. Applicants must be 18, 19, or 20 years of age when they first apply. They must be enrolled or planning to enroll at an accredited college, university, or vocational/technical training program in any state. Along with their application, they must submit an essay of 250 to 500 words on their goals for furthering their education. They must be U.S. citizens or eligible noncitizens and have personal assets worth less than $10,000.

Financial data: The stipend ranges up to $5,000 per year.

Duration: 1 year; may be renewed as long as the recipient maintains satisfactory progress toward completion of an undergraduate degree, diploma, or certificate.

Number awarded: Varies each year.

Deadline: Deadline not specified.

747 NORTH CAROLINA EDUCATION LOTTERY SCHOLARSHIP

North Carolina State Education Assistance Authority
Attn: Nurse Scholars Program
10 T.W. Alexander Drive
P.O. Box 13663
Research Triangle Park, NC 27709-3663
Phone: (919) 549-8614; (800) 700-1775; Fax: (919) 248-4687
Email: information@ncseaa.edu
Web: www.ncseaa.edu

Summary: To provide financial assistance to residents of North Carolina who can demonstrate financial need and are interested in attending college in the state.

Eligibility: Open to North Carolina residents who are enrolled or planning to enroll in at least 6 credit hours per semester at a community college, campus of the University of North Carolina system, or eligible private college or university in the state. Applicants must be able to demonstrate financial need using the same criteria as for federal Pell Grants (with the exception that students ineligible for a Pell Grant with an estimated family contribution of $5,000 or less are eligible for this program).

Financial data: Stipends depend on the need of the recipient, ranging from $100 to $2,500 per year.

Duration: 1 year; may be renewed as long as the recipient continues to make satisfactory academic progress.

Number awarded: Varies each year; recently, a total of 29,492 students were receiving $35,133,991 through this program.

Deadline: Deadline not specified.

748 NORTH CAROLINA ELECTRONIC SECURITY ASSOCIATION YOUTH SCHOLARSHIP PROGRAM

North Carolina Electronic Security Association
Attn: Executive Director
P.O. Box 41368
Raleigh, NC 27629
Phone: (919) 713-0885; (800) 762-0866; Fax: (919) 878-7413
Email: elaine@execman.net
Web: www.ncbfaa.net

Summary: To provide financial assistance to high school seniors in North Carolina who are the children of active-duty law enforcement and fire service personnel and interested in attending college in any state.

Eligibility: Open to seniors graduating from high schools in North Carolina who have been accepted at an accredited college or university in any state. Applicants must have a father, mother, or legal guardian who is a full-time active employee (not on disability) of the police or sheriff's department or a paid employee or volunteer of a fire department in North Carolina. Along with their application, they must submit an essay of 500 to 750 words on what it means to them to have their parent or guardian involved in securing our community. Selection is based on that essay (20 points), grade average (35 points), SAT or ACT scores (30 points), and academic prizes, awards, school and outside extracurricular activities, and hobbies (15 points); financial need is not considered.

Financial data: The first-place winner receives a $1,000 scholarship and second a $500 scholarship.

Duration: The awards are presented annually.

Number awarded: 2 each year.

Deadline: March of each year.

749 NORTH CAROLINA LEGISLATIVE TUITION GRANTS

North Carolina State Education Assistance Authority
Attn: Grants, Training, and Outreach Department
10 T.W. Alexander Drive
P.O. Box 13663
Research Triangle Park, NC 27709-3663
Phone: (919) 549-8614; (800) 700-1775; Fax: (919) 248-4687
Email: information@ncseaa.edu
Web: www.ncseaa.edu/NCLTG.htm

Summary: To provide financial assistance to students enrolled in private colleges in North Carolina.

Eligibility: Open to North Carolina residents attending a legislatively-designated private college in the state on a full-time basis. Financial need is not considered in the selection process. Students of theology, divinity, religious education, or any other course of study designed primarily for career preparation in a religious vocation are not eligible.

Financial data: The stipend is $1,950 per year. Funds are paid to the institution on behalf of the recipient.

Duration: 1 year; may be renewed.

Number awarded: Varies each year; recently, a total of 33,509 students were receiving $56,339,992 through this program.

Deadline: Deadline not specified.

750 NORTH CAROLINA SCHOLARSHIPS FOR CHILDREN OF WAR VETERANS

Division of Veterans Affairs
Albemarle Building
325 North Salisbury Street, Suite 1065
Raleigh, NC 27603-5941
Phone: (919) 733-3851; Fax: (919) 733-2834
Email: ncdva.aso@ncmail.net
Web: www.doa.state.nc.us/vets/benefits-scholarships.htm

Summary: To provide financial assistance to the children of disabled and other classes of North Carolina veterans who plan to attend college in the state.

Eligibility: Open to applicants from 5 categories: Class I-A: the veteran parent died in wartime service or as a result of a service-connected condition incurred in wartime service; Class I-B: the veteran parent is rated by the U.S. Department of Veterans Affairs (VA) as 100% disabled as a result of wartime service and currently or at the time of death drawing compensation for such disability; Class II: the veteran parent is rated by the VA as much as 20% but less than 100% disabled due to wartime service, or was awarded a Purple Heart medal for wounds received, and currently or at the time of death drawing compensation for such disability; Class III: the veteran parent is currently or was at the time of death receiving a VA pension for total and permanent disability, or the veteran parent is deceased but does not qualify under any other provisions, or the veteran parent served in a combat zone or waters adjacent to a combat zone and received a campaign badge or medal but does not qualify under any other provisions; Class IV: the veteran parent was a prisoner of war or missing in action. For all classes, applicants must 1) be under 25 years of age and have a veteran parent who was a resident of North Carolina at the time of entrance into the armed forces; or 2) be the natural child, or adopted child prior to age 15, who was born in North Carolina, has been a resident of the state continuously since birth, and is the child of a veteran whose disabilities occurred during a period of war.

Financial data: Students in Classes I-A, II, III, and IV receive $4,500 per academic year if they attend a private college or junior college; if attending a public postsecondary institution, they receive free tuition, a room allowance, a board allowance, and exemption from certain mandatory fees. Students in Class I-B receive $1,500 per academic year if they attend a private college or junior college; if attending a public postsecondary institution, they receive free tuition and exemption from certain mandatory fees.

Duration: 4 academic years.

Number awarded: An unlimited number of awards are made under Classes I-A, I-B, and IV. Classes II and III are limited to 100 awards each year in each class.

Deadline: Applications for Classes I-A, I-B, and IV may be submitted at any time; applications for Classes II and III must be submitted by February of each year.

751 NORTH CAROLINA STATE CONTRACTUAL SCHOLARSHIP FUND PROGRAM

North Carolina State Education Assistance Authority
Attn: Grants, Training, and Outreach Department
10 T.W. Alexander Drive
P.O. Box 13663
Research Triangle Park, NC 27709-3663
Phone: (919) 549-8614; (800) 700-1775; Fax: (919) 248-4687
Email: information@ncseaa.edu
Web: www.ncseaa.edu/SCSF.htm

Summary: To provide financial assistance to residents of North Carolina enrolled at private colleges and universities in the state.

Eligibility: Open to North Carolina residents who are enrolled full- or part-time at approved North Carolina private colleges and universities. Applicants must normally be undergraduates, although they may have a bachelor's degree if they are enrolled in a licensure program for teachers or nurses. Students enrolled in a program of study in theology, divinity, religious education, or any other program of study designed primarily for career preparation in a religious vocation are not eligible. Financial need is considered in the selection process.

Financial data: Stipends depend on the need of the recipient and the availability of funds. Recently, they averaged more than $2,600 per year.

Duration: 1 year.

Number awarded: Varies each year; recently, a total of 16,137 students received $42,992,813 through this program.

Deadline: Deadline not specified.

752 NORTH DAKOTA ACADEMIC SCHOLARSHIP

North Dakota Department of Public Instruction
600 East Boulevard Avenue, Department 201
Bismarck, ND 58505-0440
Phone: (701) 328-2755; Fax: (701) 328-4770
Email: ckudrna@nd.gov
Web: www.dpi.state.nd.us/resource/act/act.shtm

Summary: To provide financial assistance to high school seniors in North Dakota who complete a prescribed curriculum and plan to attend college in the state.

Eligibility: Open to seniors graduating from high schools in North Dakota who complete 1 unit of algebra II, 1 unit of mathematics for which algebra II is a prerequisite, 2 units of the same foreign language or Native American language, 1 unit of fine arts or CTE, and 1 additional unit of fine arts, CTE, or foreign language. Applicants must have a cumulative GPA of 3.0 or higher with no grade lower than a "C" in any unit, a score of 24 or higher on the ACT, and a completed AP course. They must be planning to attend a public or private college or university in North Dakota. Financial need is not considered in the selection process.

Financial data: The stipend is $1,500 per year.

Duration: 1 year; may be renewed up to 3 additional years, provided the recipient maintains a GPA of 2.75 or higher.

Number awarded: Varies each year.

Deadline: June of each year.

753 NORTH DAKOTA CAREER AND TECHNICAL EDUCATION SCHOLARSHIP

North Dakota Department of Public Instruction
600 East Boulevard Avenue, Department 201
Bismarck, ND 58505-0440
Phone: (701) 328-2755; Fax: (701) 328-4770
Email: ckudrna@nd.gov
Web: www.dpi.state.nd.us/resource/act/act.shtm

Summary: To provide financial assistance to high school seniors in North Dakota who complete a prescribed curriculum and plan to attend vocational school in the state.

Eligibility: Open to seniors graduating from high schools in North Dakota who complete 1 unit of algebra II, 2 units of a CTE coordinated plan of study, 2 additional units of CTE, and 1 additional elective unit. Applicants must have a cumulative GPA of 3.0 or higher with no grade lower than a "C" in any unit and a score of 24 or higher on the ACT or 3 scores of 5 on the WorkKeys tests. They must be planning to attend a vocational or technical school in North Dakota. Financial need is not considered in the selection process.

Financial data: The stipend is $1,500 per year.

Duration: 1 year; may be renewed up to 3 additional years, provided the recipient maintains a GPA of 2.75 or higher.

Number awarded: Varies each year.

Deadline: June of each year.

754 NORTH DAKOTA EDUCATIONAL ASSISTANCE FOR DEPENDENTS OF VETERANS

Department of Veterans Affairs
4201 38th Street, S.W., Suite 104
P.O. Box 9003
Fargo, ND 58106-9003
Phone: (701) 239-7165; (866) 634-8387; Fax: (701) 239-7166
Web: www.nd.gov/veterans/benefits/waiver.html

Summary: To provide financial assistance for college to the spouses, widow(er)s, and children of disabled and other North Dakota veterans and military personnel.

Eligibility: Open to the spouses, widow(er)s, and dependent children of veterans who are totally disabled as a result of service-connected causes, or who were killed in action, or who have died as a result of wounds or service-connected disabilities, or who were identified as prisoners of war or missing in action. Veteran parents must have been born in and lived in North Dakota until entrance into the armed forces (or must have resided in the state for at least 6 months prior to entrance into military service) and must have served during wartime.

Financial data: Eligible dependents receive free tuition and are exempt from fees at any state-supported institution of higher education, technical school, or vocational school in North Dakota.

Duration: Up to 45 months or 10 academic semesters.

Number awarded: Varies each year.

Deadline: Deadline not specified.

755 NORTH DAKOTA FEE WAIVER FOR SURVIVORS OF DECEASED PUBLIC SERVICE OFFICIALS

North Dakota University System
Attn: Director of Financial Aid
State Capitol, Tenth Floor
600 East Boulevard Avenue, Department 215
Bismarck, ND 58505-0230
Phone: (701) 328-4114; Fax: (701) 328-2961
Email: ndus.office@ndus.nodak.edu
Web: www.ndus.nodak.edu/policies/sbhe-policies/policy.asp?ref=2282

Summary: To waive tuition and fees for survivors of deceased fire fighters, emergency medical services personnel, and peace officers at public institutions in North Dakota.

Eligibility: Open to residents of North Dakota who are the survivors of fire fighters, emergency medical services personnel, and peace officers who died as a direct result of injuries received in the performance of official duties. Applicants must be attending or planning to attend a public college or university in North Dakota.

Financial data: Qualified students are entitled to a waiver of all tuition and fees (except fees charged to retire outstanding bonds).

Duration: 1 academic year; renewable.

Number awarded: Varies each year.

Deadline: Deadline not specified.

756 NORTH DAKOTA SCHOLARS PROGRAM

North Dakota University System
Attn: Director of Financial Aid
State Capitol, Tenth Floor
600 East Boulevard Avenue, Department 215
Bismarck, ND 58505-0230
Phone: (701) 328-4114; Fax: (701) 328-2961
Email: ndus.office@ndus.nodak.edu
Web: www.ndus.nodak.edu/students/financial-aid/details.asp?id=110

Summary: To provide financial assistance to outstanding high school seniors in North Dakota who are interested in attending college in the state.

Eligibility: Open to seniors at high schools in North Dakota who took the ACT test in their junior year and scored in the upper 5th percentile of all North Dakota ACT test takers. Applicants must be interested in attending a college or university in North Dakota.

Financial data: Students who attend a public or tribal college receive full payment of tuition. Students who attend a private institution in North Dakota receive a stipend equivalent to tuition at North Dakota State University or the University of North Dakota.

Duration: 1 academic year; renewable up to 3 additional years, if the recipient maintains a cumulative GPA of 3.5 or higher.

Number awarded: 45 to 50 each year.

Deadline: Deadline not specified.

757 NORTH DAKOTA STATE STUDENT INCENTIVE GRANT PROGRAM

North Dakota University System
Attn: Director of Financial Aid
State Capitol, Tenth Floor
600 East Boulevard Avenue, Department 215
Bismarck, ND 58505-0230
Phone: (701) 328-4114; Fax: (701) 328-2961
Email: ndus.office@ndus.nodak.edu
Web: www.ndus.nodak.edu/students/financial-aid/details.asp?id=108

Summary: To provide financial assistance to residents of North Dakota who need additional funding to attend a college or university in the state.

Eligibility: Open to residents of North Dakota who are high school graduates (or have a GED) and are eligible for admission as a full-time student at a public, private, or tribal college in the state. Applicants must be U.S. citizens or permanent residents and able to demonstrate financial need.

Financial data: Stipends range from $800 to $1,000 per year.

Duration: 1 academic year; renewable.

Number awarded: From 7,900 to 8,500 each year.

Deadline: March of each year.

758 NORTH DAKOTA VETERANS DEPENDENTS FEE WAIVER

North Dakota University System
Attn: Director of Financial Aid
State Capitol, Tenth Floor
600 East Boulevard Avenue, Department 215
Bismarck, ND 58505-0230
Phone: (701) 328-4114; Fax: (701) 328-2961
Email: ndus.office@ndus.nodak.edu
Web: www.ndus.nodak.edu/policies/sbhe-policies/policy.asp?ref=2282

Summary: To waive tuition and fees for dependents of deceased or other veterans at public institutions in North Dakota.

Eligibility: Open to the dependents of veterans who were North Dakota residents when they entered the armed forces and died of service-related causes, were killed in action, were prisoners of war, or were declared missing in action. Applicants must be attending or planning to attend a public college or university in North Dakota.

Financial data: Qualified students are entitled to a waiver of all tuition and fees (except fees charged to retire outstanding bonds) at public institutions in North Dakota.

Duration: 1 academic year; renewable.

Number awarded: Varies each year.

Deadline: Deadline not specified.

759 NORTHWEST FARM CREDIT SERVICES SCHOLARSHIPS

Washington Apple Education Foundation
Attn: Scholarship Committee
2900 Euclid Avenue
Wenatchee, WA 98801
Phone: (509) 663-7713; Fax: (509) 663-7469
Email: waef@waef.org
Web: www.waef.org/index.php?page_id=238

Summary: To provide financial assistance to residents of Washington whose parents are employed in the tree fruit industry and who are interested in attending college in any state.

Eligibility: Open to Washington residents who are high school seniors or students already enrolled at a college or university in any state. The parents or guardians of applicants must be employed in an entry-level laborer or entry-level management position by a commercial grower or packer in Washington's tree fruit industry. Along with their application, they must submit an official transcript, their SAT or ACT scores, 2 letters of reference, and an essay on an assigned topic. Financial need is also considered in the selection process.

Financial data: The stipend is $1,250. The money may be used to pay for tuition, room, board, books, educational supplies, and miscellaneous institutional fees.

Duration: 1 year.

Number awarded: 2 each year.

Deadline: February of each year.

760 NORTHWESTERN VERMONT VIETNAM VETERANS OF AMERICA COLLEGE SCHOLARSHIPS

Northwestern Vermont Vietnam Veterans of America
Attn: Scholarship Committee
P.O. Box 965
St. Albans, VT 05478
Email: wemchogisle@comcast.net

Summary: To recognize and reward, with college scholarships, high school seniors in Vermont who are relatives of current or former military personnel and submit outstanding essays.

Eligibility: Open to seniors graduating from high schools in Vermont who are relatives of a U.S. military servicemember currently serving on active duty or who has been honorably discharged or an active-duty or honorably-discharged member of the Vermont National Guard. The relative must also be a resident of Vermont. Applicants must submit an essay on a topic that changes annually.

Financial data: The award is a $1,500 scholarship for use at a college or university in any state.

Duration: The competition is held annually.

Number awarded: 2 each year.

Deadline: March of each year.

761 NOVO NORDISK DONNELLY AWARDS

World Team Tennis, Inc.
Attn: Billie Jean King WTT Charities
1776 Broadway, Suite 600
New York, NY 10019
Phone: (212) 586-3444, ext. 20; Fax: (212) 586-6277
Email: dstone@wtt.com
Web: www.wtt.com/page.aspx?article_id=1429

Summary: To recognize and reward young tennis players who have diabetes.

Eligibility: Open to scholar/athletes between 12 and 21 years of age who play tennis competitively either on a school team or as a ranked tournament player and have type I diabetes. Applicants must submit a 500-word essay on the significance of diabetes in their lives. Selection is based on values, commitment, sportsmanship, community involvement, and financial need.

Financial data: Awards are $5,000 for winners or $2,500 for regional finalists; funds may be used for education, tennis development, and/or medical care.

Duration: The nonrenewable awards are presented annually.

Number awarded: 4 each year: 2 winners and 2 regional finalists.

Deadline: April of each year.

762 NOVOTNI COLLEGE SCHOLARSHIP FUND

American Deficit Disorder Association
P.O. Box 7557
Wilmington, DE 19803-9997
Phone: (800) 939-1019; Fax: (800) 939-1019
Email: adda@jmoadmin.com
Web: www.add.org/mc/page.do?sitPageID=92513

Summary: To provide financial assistance for college to students who have attention deficit/hyperactivity disorder (AD/HD).

Eligibility: Open to students who have been diagnosed with AD/HD by a licensed physician or mental health professional. Applicants must be enrolled or planning to enroll at an approved college or university as an undergraduate student. Along with their application, they must submit a 500-word essay on why they would like to be considered for this scholarship, the ways in which AD/HD has been a challenge for them in the educational setting, and the strategies they have used to meet the challenge.

Financial data: Stipends are $5,000, $3,000, or $1,000. Funds are paid directly to the recipient's college.

Duration: 1 year; recipients may reapply.

Number awarded: 1 or more each year.

Deadline: March of each year.

763 NWTF XTREME JAKES SCHOLARSHIPS

National Wild Turkey Federation
Attn: JAKES Program
770 Augusta Road
P.O. Box 530
Edgefield, SC 29824-0530
Phone: (803) 637-3106; (800) THE-NWTF
Email: kmorris@nwtf.net
Web: www.nwtf.org/jakes/xtreme/scholarships.html

Summary: To provide financial assistance to high school seniors who are interested in hunting and planning to attend college to major in any subject area.

Eligibility: Open to seniors graduating from high school with a GPA of 3.0 or higher and planning to work on a degree in any subject area at an accredited college, university, community college, or technical college. Applicants must support the preservation of the hunting tradition and actively participate in hunting sports, be involved in school activities (e.g., FFA, ecology club, science club, student council), demonstrate ability as a leader among their peers, demonstrate community involvement (e.g., Scouting, 4-H, civic group or club, volunteer work), and be members of the National Wild Turkey Federation (NWTF) Xtreme JAKES (Juniors Acquiring Knowledge, Ethics, and Sportsmanship) Program. Along with their application, they must submit an essay on why hunting is important to them and/or their family, including their dedication to the conservation and preservation of our hunting heritage. Financial need is not considered in the selection process. Students first apply to their local NWTF chapter; winners at that level are entered in their state/provincial competition. Those winners are considered for selection as the national scholarship winner.

Financial data: Chapter scholarships are at least $250; state/provincial scholarships are at least $1,000; the national scholarship winner receives $10,000. All funds are paid directly to the recipient's institution to be used for tuition, books, fees, and housing.

Duration: 1 year; nonrenewable.

Number awarded: The number of local and state/provincial scholarships varies each year; 1 national scholarship winner is selected annually.

Deadline: Applications must be submitted to local chapters by December of each year.

764 OHIO BURGLAR & FIRE ALARM ASSOCIATION YOUTH SCHOLARSHIP PROGRAM

Ohio Burglar & Fire Alarm Association
Attn: Youth Scholarship Program
1145 Slade Avenue
Columbus, OH 43235-4052
Phone: (800) 746-2322; Fax: (614) 457-1748
Email: info@secureohio.org
Web: www.secureohio.org

Summary: To provide financial assistance to high school seniors in Ohio who are the children of active-duty law enforcement and fire service personnel and interested in attending college in any state.

Eligibility: Open to seniors graduating from high schools in Ohio who have been accepted at an accredited college or university in any state. Applicants must have a father, mother, or legal guardian who is a full-time active employee (not on disability) of the police or sheriff's department or a paid employee or volunteer of a fire department in Ohio. Along with their application, they must submit an essay of 500 to 750 words on what it means to them to have their parent or guardian involved in securing our community. Selection is based on that essay (20 points), grade average (35 points), SAT or ACT scores (30 points), and academic prizes, awards, school and outside extracurricular activities, and hobbies (15 points); financial need is not considered.

Financial data: The stipend is $1,000.

Duration: 1 year.

Number awarded: 1 each year.

Deadline: March of each year.

765 OHIO COLLEGE OPPORTUNITY GRANT PROGRAM

Ohio Board of Regents
Attn: State Grants and Scholarships
30 East Broad Street, 36th Floor
Columbus, OH 43215-3414
Phone: (614) 728-8862; (888) 833-1133; Fax: (614) 466-5866
Email: tbraswell@regents.state.oh.us
Web: regents.ohio.gov/sgs/ocog

Summary: To provide financial assistance for college to students in Ohio who demonstrate financial need.

Eligibility: Open to Ohio residents who are attending or planning to attend public and private colleges and universities in the state. Applicants must be able to demonstrate financial need, with an expected family contribution up to $2,190 and a family income of $75,000 or less.

Financial data: Maximum stipends for full-time enrollment are $1,008 per year for students at public institutions or $2,256 for students at private institutions. Part-time stipends are prorated appropriately.

Duration: 1 year; may be renewed up to 4 additional years or until degree completion, whichever comes first.

Number awarded: Varies each year.

Deadline: September of each year.

766 OHIO ELKS ASSOCIATION EDUCATION GRANTS

Ohio Elks Association
c/o David Sunderland, Educational Fund Board
2020 Morning Glory Drive
Elida, OH 45807
Phone: (419) 339-2701
Email: djs5134@wcoil.com
Web: web-ster.net/ohioelks

Summary: To provide financial assistance to Ohio residents interested in attending a career or technology institution in any state.

Eligibility: Open to high school seniors and graduates who reside within the jurisdiction of a B.P.O. Elks Lodge belonging to the Ohio Elks Association and who are enrolled or planning to enroll at a career or technology institution in any state. Bachelor's or graduate degree programs do not qualify. Applicants must be U.S. citizens. Along with their application, they must submit a 200-word letter explaining their reasons for wishing to pursue this educational goal, information on financial need, transcripts, and documentation of participation in scholarship, leadership, athletics, dramatics, community service, or other career-oriented activities. Selection is based on motivation (400 points), academics (200 points), and financial need (400 points).

Financial data: The stipend is $1,000 per year. Funds are sent to the recipient's institution upon verification of enrollment. Funds must be used for tuition, fees, room, and board; it may not be used for general living expenses (e.g., apartment rent, mortgage payments, automobile expenses, child care).

Duration: 1 year; recipients may apply for 1 more year of support. No student will be awarded more than 2 annual grants.

Number awarded: Varies each year; recently, 48 of these grants were awarded.

Deadline: January of each year.

767 OHIO LEGION AUXILIARY DEPARTMENT PRESIDENT'S SCHOLARSHIP

American Legion Auxiliary
Department of Ohio
1100 Brandywine Boulevard, Building D
P.O. Box 2760
Zanesville, OH 43702-2760
Phone: (740) 452-8245; Fax: (740) 452-2620
Email: ala_katie@rrohio.com

Summary: To provide financial assistance to the descendants of veterans in Ohio who are interested in attending college in any state.

Eligibility: Open to the children, grandchildren, and great-grandchildren of living or deceased veterans who served during designated periods of war time. Applicants must be residents of Ohio, seniors at an accredited high school, and sponsored by an American Legion Auxiliary Unit. Along with their application, they must submit an original article (up to 500 words) written by the applicant on "What the American Flag Represents to Me." Selection is based on character, Americanism, leadership, scholarship, and financial need.

Financial data: Stipends are $1,500 or $1,000. Funds are paid to the recipient's school.

Duration: 1 year.

Number awarded: 2 each year: 1 at $1,500 and 1 at $1,000.

Deadline: February of each year.

768 OHIO LEGION SCHOLARSHIPS

American Legion
Department of Ohio
60 Big Run Road
P.O. Box 8007
Delaware, OH 43015
Phone: (740) 362-7478; Fax: (740) 362-1429
Email: legion@ohiolegion.com
Web: www.ohiolegion.com/scholarships/info.htm

Summary: To provide financial assistance to residents of Ohio who are members of the American Legion, their families, or dependents of deceased military personnel and interested in attending college in any state.

Eligibility: Open to residents of Ohio who are Legionnaires, direct descendants of living or deceased Legionnaires, or surviving spouses or children of deceased U.S. military personnel who died on active duty or of injuries received on active duty. Applicants must be attending or planning to attend colleges, universities, or other approved postsecondary schools in any state with a vocational objective. Selection is based on academic achievement as measured by course grades, scholastic test scores, difficulty of curriculum, participation in outside activities, and the judging committee's general impression.

Financial data: Stipends are at least $2,000.

Duration: 1 year.

Number awarded: Varies each year; recently, 14 of these scholarships were awarded.

Deadline: April of each year.

769 OHIO SAFETY OFFICERS COLLEGE MEMORIAL FUND

Ohio Board of Regents
Attn: State Grants and Scholarships
30 East Broad Street, 36th Floor
Columbus, OH 43215-3414
Phone: (614) 466-7420; (888) 833-1133; Fax: (614) 466-5866
Email: osom_admin@regents.state.oh.us
Web: regents.ohio.gov/sgs/oso

Summary: To provide financial assistance to Ohio residents who are interested in attending college in the state and whose parent or spouse was killed in the line of duty as a safety officer or member of the armed forces.

Eligibility: Open to Ohio residents whose parent or spouse was 1) a peace officer, fire fighter, or other safety officer killed in the line of duty anywhere in the United States; or 2) a member of the U.S. armed forces killed in the line of duty during Operation Enduring Freedom, Operation Iraqi Freedom, or other designated combat zone. Applicants must be interested in attending a participating Ohio college or university. Children and spouses of military personnel are eligible for this program only if they do not qualify for the Ohio War Orphans Scholarship.

Financial data: At Ohio public colleges and universities, the program provides full payment of tuition. At Ohio private colleges and universities, the stipend is equivalent to the average amounts paid to students attending public institutions, currently $3,990 per year.

Duration: 1 year; may be renewed up to 3 additional years.

Number awarded: Varies each year; recently, 54 students received benefits from this program.

Deadline: Application deadlines are established by each participating college and university.

770 OHIO WAR ORPHANS SCHOLARSHIP

Ohio Board of Regents
Attn: State Grants and Scholarships
30 East Broad Street, 36th Floor
Columbus, OH 43215-3414
Phone: (614) 752-9528; (888) 833-1133; Fax: (614) 466-5866
Email: jabdullah-simmons@regents.state.oh.us
Web: regents.ohio.gov/sgs/war_orphans

Summary: To provide financial assistance to the children of deceased or disabled Ohio veterans who plan to attend college in the state.

Eligibility: Open to residents of Ohio who are under 25 years of age and interested in enrolling full-time at an eligible college or university in the state. Applicants must be the child of a veteran who 1) was a member of the U.S. armed forces, including the organized Reserves and Ohio National Guard, for a period of 90 days or more (or discharged because of a disability incurred after less than 90 days of service); 2) served during World War I, World War II, the Korean Conflict, the Vietnam era, or the Persian Gulf War; 3) entered service as a resident of Ohio; and 4) as a result of that service, either was killed or became at least 60% service-connected disabled. Also eligible are children of veterans who have a permanent and total non-service connected disability and are receiving disability benefits from the U.S. Department of Veterans Affairs. If the veteran parent served only in the organized Reserves or Ohio National Guard, the parent must have been killed or became permanently and totally disabled while at a scheduled training assembly, field training period (of any duration or length), or active duty for training, pursuant to bona fide orders issued by a competent authority. Financial need is considered in the selection process.

Financial data: At Ohio public colleges and universities, the program provides payment of 80% of tuition and fees. At Ohio private colleges and universities, the stipend is $4,400 per year (or 80% of the average amount paid to students attending public institutions).

Duration: 1 year; may be renewed up to 4 additional years, provided the recipient maintains a GPA of 2.0 or higher.

Number awarded: Varies, depending upon the funds available. If sufficient funds are available, all eligible applicants are given a scholarship. Recently, 861 students received benefits from this program.

Deadline: June of each year.

771 OKLAHOMA COUNCIL DISTRICT IV SCHOLARSHIP

Epsilon Sigma Alpha International
Attn: ESA Foundation
P.O. Box 270517
Fort Collins, CO 80527
Phone: (970) 223-2824; Fax: (970) 223-4456
Email: esainfo@esaintl.com
Web: www.esaintl.com/esaf

Summary: To provide financial assistance to residents of Oklahoma who plan to attend college in the state.

Eligibility: Open to residents of Oklahoma who are 1) graduating high school seniors with a GPA of 3.0 or higher or with minimum scores of 22 on the ACT or 1030 on the combined critical reading and mathematics SAT; 2) enrolled in college with a GPA of 3.0 or higher; 3) enrolled at a technical school or returning to school after an absence for retraining of job skills or obtaining a degree; or 4) engaged in online study through an accredited college, university, or vocational school. Applicants may be attending or planning to attend a school in Oklahoma and major in any field. Selection is based on character (10%), leadership (10%), service (5%), financial need (50%), and scholastic ability (25%).

Financial data: The stipend is $1,000.

Duration: 1 year; may be renewed.

Number awarded: 1 each year.

Deadline: January of each year.

772 OKLAHOMA FOUNDATION FOR EXCELLENCE ACADEMIC ALL-STATE SCHOLARSHIPS

Oklahoma Foundation for Excellence
120 North Robinson, Suite 1420-W
Oklahoma City, OK 73102-7400
Phone: (405) 236-0006; Fax: (405) 236-8590
Email: info@ofe.org
Web: www.ofe.org/awards/index.htm

Summary: To provide financial assistance for college to seniors at public high schools in Oklahoma who demonstrate academic excellence.

Eligibility: Open to seniors at public high schools in Oklahoma who are nominated by their principal or superintendent. Nominees must meet at least 1 of the following criteria: ACT score of 30 or higher, combined critical reading and mathematics SAT score of 1340 or higher, National Merit Scholarship Program semifinalist, National Achievement Scholarship Program semifinalist, or National Hispanic Scholar Awards Program semifinalist. In addition to those minimum criteria, selection is based on leadership ability, motivation, academic achievement, and character. Contributions to the improvement of school and community are also considered.

Financial data: The stipend is $1,000.

Duration: 1 year.

Number awarded: 100 each year.

Deadline: November of each year.

773 OKLAHOMA HIGHER LEARNING ACCESS PROGRAM

Oklahoma State Regents for Higher Education
Attn: Director of Scholarship and Grant Programs
655 Research Parkway, Suite 200
P.O. Box 108850
Oklahoma City, OK 73101-8850
Phone: (405) 225-9152; (800) 858-1840; Fax: (405) 225-9230
Email: okpromise@osrhe.edu
Web: www.okhighered.org/okpromise

Summary: To provide financial assistance to Oklahoma residents who complete a specified high school curriculum.

Eligibility: Open to students who sign up in their 8th, 9th, or 10th grade year at an Oklahoma high school. If they complete a specified college preparatory curriculum and demonstrate a commitment to academic success, they receive assistance when they attend college. Applicants must 1) demonstrate financial need (currently defined as a family income less than $50,000 at the time of application and less than $100,000 at the time of entering college); 2) achieve a GPA of 2.5 or higher both cumulatively and in the required curriculum; 3) fulfill an agreement to attend school, do homework regularly, refrain from substance abuse and criminal or delinquent acts, and have school work and records reviewed by school officials; and 4) be admitted as a regular entering freshman at an Oklahoma college, university, or area vocational technical school. Home-schooled students are eligible if they achieve a composite ACT score of 22 or higher. U.S. citizenship or permanent resident status is required.

Financial data: Students enrolled at an institution in the Oklahoma State System of Higher Education receive resident tuition, paid to the institution on their behalf. Students enrolled at an accredited private institution have tuition paid at an amount equivalent to the resident tuition at a comparable institution of the state system. Students enrolled in eligible vocational/technical programs have their tuition paid. No provision is made for other educational expenses, such as books, supplies, room, board, or other special fees.

Duration: Up to 5 years or until completion of a bachelor's degree, whichever occurs first. The award must be taken up within 3 years of high school graduation. Renewal requires that the student achieves a GPA of 2.0 or higher during the sophomore year of college and 2.5 or higher during the junior and senior years.

Number awarded: Varies each year; recently, approximately 19,000 students received $54 million in support from this program.

Deadline: Applications must be submitted by June following completion of the student's 8th, 9th, or 10th grade year.

774 OKLAHOMA INDEPENDENT LIVING ACT TUITION WAIVERS

Oklahoma State Regents for Higher Education
Attn: Director of Scholarship and Grant Programs
655 Research Parkway, Suite 200
P.O. Box 108850
Oklahoma City, OK 73101-8850
Phone: (405) 225-9239; (800) 858-1840; Fax: (405) 225-9230
Email: studentinfo@osrhe.edu

Web: www.okhighered.org/student-center/financial-aid/dhs.shtml

Summary: To provide financial assistance to residents in Oklahoma who have been in a foster care program of the Department of Human Services (DHS) and are interested in attending college in the state.

Eligibility: Open to residents of Oklahoma who graduated within the previous 3 years from an accredited high school in the state or from a high school bordering Oklahoma as approved by the State Board of Education, or who have completed the GED requirements. Applicants must be younger than 21 years of age and have been in DHS custody for at least 9 months between 16 and 18 years of age. They must currently be enrolled at an Oklahoma public college or university or in certain programs at technology centers.

Financial data: Under this program, all resident tuition fees are waived.

Duration: 1 year; may be renewed until the student reaches 26 years of age or completes a baccalaureate degree or program certificate, whichever comes first.

Number awarded: Varies each year.

Deadline: Deadline not specified.

775 OKLAHOMA STATE REGENTS ACADEMIC SCHOLARS PROGRAM

Oklahoma State Regents for Higher Education
Attn: Director of Scholarship and Grant Programs
655 Research Parkway, Suite 200
P.O. Box 108850
Oklahoma City, OK 73101-8850
Phone: (405) 225-9131; (800) 858-1840; Fax: (405) 225-9230
Email: llangston@osrhe.edu
Web: www.okhighered.org/academic-scholars

Summary: To provide financial assistance to outstanding high school seniors and recent graduates who wish to attend a college or university in Oklahoma.

Eligibility: Open to high school seniors who have 5 ways to qualify: 1) residents of Oklahoma whose ACT or SAT score is at least at the 99.5 percentile level (currently, scores totaling at least 133 in all ACT skill areas or 1580 on the mathematics and critical reading SAT) and whose GPA and/or class rank are considered exceptional; 2) residents of any state designated as a National Merit Scholar; 3) residents of any state designated as a National Merit Scholar Finalist; 4) residents of any state designated as a Presidential Scholar; or 5) institutional nominees, from Oklahoma's comprehensive universities (University of Oklahoma, University of Tulsa, Oklahoma State University) who have either an ACT of at least 32 (or SAT equivalent) or a GPA of 3.9 or higher and a ranking in the top 2% of their class, from Oklahoma's regional universities who have either an ACT of at least 30 (or SAT equivalent) or a GPA of 3.8 or higher and a ranking in the top 4% of their class, or from Oklahoma's 2-year colleges who have either an ACT of at least 29 (or SAT equivalent) or a GPA of 3.7 or higher and a ranking in the top 5% of their class.

Financial data: The program provides funding for tuition, fees, room and board, and textbooks. The exact amount of funding awarded varies each year; for "automatic qualifiers" (the first 4 ways to qualify), it is currently $5,500 per year for students at the 3 comprehensive universities, $4,000 per year for students at other 4-year public or private colleges or universities in Oklahoma, or $3,500 per year for students at Oklahoma 2-year colleges. For institutional nominees, the current rate is $2,800 per year at the 3 comprehensive universities, $2,000 per year at other 4-year institutions, or $1,800 at 2-year colleges. Students who enroll at public universities and colleges are also eligible for a tuition waiver.

Duration: Up to 4 years of undergraduate study, as long as the recipient remains a full-time student with a GPA of 3.25 or higher.

Number awarded: Varies each year; recently, 649 entering freshmen received this support (including 413 "automatic qualifiers" and 236 institutional nominees). A total of 2,136 students were enrolled in the program.

Deadline: September of each year.

776 OKLAHOMA TUITION AID GRANT PROGRAM

Oklahoma State Regents for Higher Education
Attn: Director of Scholarship and Grant Programs
655 Research Parkway, Suite 200
P.O. Box 108850
Oklahoma City, OK 73101-8850
Phone: (405) 225-9456; (877) 662-6231; Fax: (405) 225-9476
Email: otaginfo@otag.org
Web: www.okhighered.org/student-center/financial-aid/otag.shtml

Summary: To provide financial assistance to Oklahoma residents who demonstrate financial need and plan to attend college in the state.

Eligibility: Open to residents of Oklahoma who are attending or planning to attend public or private institutions in Oklahoma. Applicants must complete the Free Application for Federal Student Aid and demonstrate financial need with an expected family contribution of $1,700 or lower. Undocumented immigrants are eligible if they 1) have graduated from a public or private high school in Oklahoma or have successfully completed the GED in Oklahoma; and 2) will have resided in Oklahoma with a parent or guardian for at least 2 years prior to graduation from high school or successful completion of the GED in Oklahoma.

Financial data: At public colleges, universities, and technology centers, the annual stipend is $1,000 or 75% of enrollment costs, whichever is less. At private colleges and universities, the annual stipend is $1,300 or 75% of enrollment costs, whichever is less.

Duration: 1 year; renewable.

Number awarded: Varies each year.

Deadline: Applications are accepted through June of each year, but students should apply as early after the beginning of January as possible and by the end of April for best consideration.

777 OKLAHOMA TUITION EQUALIZATION GRANT PROGRAM

Oklahoma State Regents for Higher Education
Attn: Director of Scholarship and Grant Programs
655 Research Parkway, Suite 200
P.O. Box 108850
Oklahoma City, OK 73101-8850
Phone: (405) 225-9456; (877) 662-6231; Fax: (405) 225-9230
Email: studentinfo@osrhe.edu
Web: www.okhighered.org/student-center/financial-aid/oteg.shtml

Summary: To provide financial assistance to Oklahoma residents who meet financial need requirements and are entering a private college in the state as first-time freshmen.

Eligibility: Open to residents of Oklahoma entering a nonprofit private or independent institution of higher education in the state as a full-time undergraduate for the first time. Applicants must have a family income of $50,000 or less.

Financial data: The stipend is $2,000 per year.

Duration: 1 year; may be renewed up to 4 additional years.

Number awarded: Varies each year.

Deadline: Deadline not specified.

778 OKLAHOMA TUITION WAIVER FOR DEPENDENTS OF PEACE OFFICERS AND FIRE FIGHTERS

Oklahoma State Regents for Higher Education
Attn: Director of Scholarship and Grant Programs
655 Research Parkway, Suite 200
P.O. Box 108850
Oklahoma City, OK 73101-8850
Phone: (405) 225-9239; (800) 858-1840; Fax: (405) 225-9230
Email: studentinfo@osrhe.edu
Web: www.okhighered.org/student-center/financial-aid/grants.shtml

Summary: To provide financial assistance for college to the children of deceased Oklahoma peace officers and fire fighters.

Eligibility: Open to the children of Oklahoma peace officers or fire fighters who lost their lives in the line of duty. Selection is based on financial need, academic aptitude and achievement, student activity participation, academic level, and academic discipline or field of study.

Financial data: Eligible applicants are entitled to receive free tuition at any Oklahoma state-supported postsecondary educational, technical, or vocational school.

Duration: Assistance continues for 5 years or until receipt of a bachelor's degree, whichever occurs first.

Number awarded: Varies each year.

Deadline: Deadline not specified.

779 OKLAHOMA TUITION WAIVER FOR PRISONERS OF WAR, PERSONS MISSING IN ACTION, AND DEPENDENTS

Oklahoma State Regents for Higher Education
Attn: Director of Scholarship and Grant Programs
655 Research Parkway, Suite 200
P.O. Box 108850
Oklahoma City, OK 73101-8850
Phone: (405) 225-9239; (800) 858-1840; Fax: (405) 225-9230
Email: studentinfo@osrhe.edu
Web: www.okhighered.org/student-center/financial-aid/grants.shtml

Summary: To provide financial assistance for college to Oklahoma residents (or their dependents) who were declared prisoners of war or missing in action.

Eligibility: Open to veterans who were declared prisoners of war or missing in action after January 1, 1960 and were residents of Oklahoma at the time of entrance into the armed forces or when declared POW/MIA. Dependent children of those veterans are also eligible as long as they are under 24 years of age. Selection is based on financial need, academic aptitude and achievement, student activity participation, academic level, and academic discipline or field of study.

Financial data: Eligible applicants are entitled to receive free tuition at any Oklahoma state-supported postsecondary educational, technical, or vocational school.

Duration: Assistance continues for 5 years or until receipt of a bachelor's degree, whichever occurs first.

Number awarded: Varies each year.

Deadline: Deadline not specified.

780 OKLAHOMA YOUTH WITH PROMISE SCHOLARSHIP PROGRAM

Oklahoma City Community Foundation
Attn: Scholarship Administrator
1000 North Broadway
P.O. Box 1146
Oklahoma City, OK 73101
Phone: (405) 235-5603; Fax: (405) 235-5612
Email: a.rose@occf.org
Web: www.occf.org/scholarships/oywpn.html

Summary: To provide financial assistance to residents of Oklahoma who graduate from high school while in foster care or other licensed placement.

Eligibility: Open to graduates of high schools in Oklahoma who are attending or planning to attend a college or university in any state. Applicants must have been in custody of the Oklahoma Department of Human Services in foster care or other licensed placement when they graduated from high school. They must have a GPA of 2.0 or higher and be able to demonstrate financial need.

Financial data: The stipend is $800 per year for freshmen or $1,200 per year for upper classmen.

Duration: 1 year; may be renewed.

Number awarded: Varies each year.

Deadline: May of each year.

781 ONE FAMILY SCHOLARS PROGRAM

One Family, Inc.
Attn: Field Services Director
186 South Street, Fourth Floor
Boston, MA 02111
Phone: (617) 423-0504, ext. 226
Email: ypere@onefamilyinc.org
Web: www.onefamilyinc.org/scholars

Summary: To provide financial assistance for college to women in Massachusetts who are homeless or formerly homeless.

Eligibility: Open to women in Massachusetts who are homeless or have been homeless. Applicants must be attempting to enter or reenter college to work on an associate or bachelor's degree. They must apply through 1 of 5 participating social service organizations at sites in Massachusetts. Along with their application, they must submit a personal essay and 3 letters of reference. They must also apply for financial aid and participate in an interview. Selection is based on financial need (family earnings below 200% of the federal poverty level), clear and realistic academic and career goals, potential for success in chosen academic program, and desire to participate actively in all aspects of the program.

Financial data: Scholars receive grants up to $11,000 per year. They are also reimbursed for reasonable childcare, transportation, and lost wages incurred to participate in mandatory activities.

Duration: 1 year; may be renewed until completion of a degree, provided the scholar successfully completes 6 to 9 credits per semester; participates in mandatory leadership development retreats, seminars, and activities; maintains a GPA of 3.0 or higher, remains a Massachusetts resident; and maintains contact with site coordinators.

Number awarded: Varies each year; recently, 125 scholars received support from this program.

Deadline: March of each year.

782 ONE PUKA PUKA ACHIEVEMENT SCHOLARSHIP

Club 100 Veterans
Attn: Scholarship Committee
520 Kamoku Street
Honolulu, HI 96826-5120
Phone: (808) 946-0272
Email: daisyy@hgea.net

Summary: To provide financial assistance for college to family members of veterans who served in the 100th Infantry Battalion of World War II.

Eligibility: Open to direct family members and descendants of 100th Infantry Battalion World War II veterans. Applicants must be high school seniors planning to attend an institution of higher learning or full-time undergraduate students at community colleges, vocational/trade schools, 4-year colleges, and universities. Along with their application, they must submit an essay on a topic that changes annually but relates to the experience of the Nisei men who fought in the racially-segregated 100th Infantry Battalion during World War II. Selection is based on that essay, academic achievement, extracurricular activities, and community service. Financial need is not considered.

Financial data: The stipend is $3,000.

Duration: 1 year; nonrenewable.

Number awarded: 1 each year.

Deadline: April of each year.

783 OPERATION ENDURING FREEDOM AND OPERATION IRAQI FREEDOM SCHOLARSHIP

Vermont Student Assistance Corporation
Attn: Scholarship Programs
10 East Allen Street
P.O. Box 2000
Winooski, VT 05404-2601
Phone: (802) 654-3798; (888) 253-4819; Fax: (802) 654-3765; TDD: (800) 281-3341 (within VT)
Email: info@vsac.org
Web: services.vsac.org/wps/wcm/connect/vsac/VSAC

Summary: To provide financial assistance to residents of Vermont whose parent has served or is serving in Operating Enduring Freedom in Afghanistan or Operation Iraqi Freedom.

Eligibility: Open to residents of Vermont who are children of a member of any branch of the armed forces or National Guard whose residence or home of record is in Vermont. Applicants must plan to enroll full-time in a certificate, associate degree, or bachelor's degree program at an accredited postsecondary school in any state. The parent must have served or currently be serving in Operation Enduring Freedom or Operation Iraqi Freedom. Preference is given to applicants whose parent was killed, wounded, or became permanently disabled as a result of their service. Along with their application, they must submit 1) a 100-word essay on any significant barriers that limit their access to education; and 2) a 250-word essay on their short- and long-term academic, educational, career, vocational, and/or employment goals. Selection is based on those essays, a letter of recommendation, and financial need.

Financial data: The stipend ranges from $3,500 to $7,000 per year.

Duration: 1 year; may be renewed up to 3 additional years.

Number awarded: Varies each year; recently, 14 of these scholarships were awarded.

Deadline: March of each year.

784 OPPORTUNITY SCHOLARSHIPS

National Leased Housing Association
Attn: NLHA Education Fund
1900 L Street, N.W., Suite 300
Washington, DC 20036
Phone: (202) 785-8888; Fax: (202) 785-2008
Email: info@hudnlha.com
Web: www.hudnlha.com/education_fund/index.asp

Summary: To provide financial assistance for college to residents of federally-assisted rental housing properties and members of families receiving rental subsidies through federal housing programs.

Eligibility: Open to U.S. citizens and permanent residents who reside in a federally-assisted rental housing property or whose families receive rental subsidy through a recognized federal housing program (e.g., Section 8, Rent Supplement, Rental Assistance Payments, Low Income Housing Tax Credit). Applicants must be graduating high school seniors, current undergraduates, or GED recipients entering an accredited undergraduate program. They must have a GPA of 2.5 or higher and be able to demonstrate financial need and community leadership through volunteer work at school or in the community. Along with their application, they must submit a 1-page essay on what education means to their future.

Financial data: A stipend is awarded (amount not specified). Funds are disbursed directly to the recipient's institution of higher learning for partial payment of tuition, books, room and board, or other activities directly related to the student's education.

Duration: 1 year.

Number awarded: 1 or more each year.

Deadline: February of each year.

785 OPTIMIST INTERNATIONAL COMMUNICATION CONTEST FOR THE DEAF AND HARD OF HEARING

Optimist International
Attn: Programs Department
4494 Lindell Boulevard
St. Louis, MO 63108
Phone: (314) 371-6000; (800) 500-8130, ext. 235; Fax: (314) 371-6006
Email: programs@optimist.org
Web: www.optimist.org/e/member/scholarships2.cfm

Summary: To recognize and reward, with college scholarships, outstanding presentations made by hearing impaired high school students.

Eligibility: Open to young people up to and including grade 12 in the United States and Canada, to CEGEP in Quebec, and to grade 13 in the Caribbean. Applicants must be identified by a qualified audiologist as deaf or hard of hearing with a hearing loss of 40 decibels or more. They are invited to make a presentation (using oral communication, sign language, or a combination of both) from 4 to 5 minutes on a topic that changes annually; a recent topic was "Cyber Communication: Progress or Problem?" Competition is first conducted at the level of individual clubs, with winners advancing to zone and then district competitions. Selection is based on material organization (40 points), delivery and presentation (30 points), and overall effectiveness (30 points).

Financial data: Each district winner receives a $2,500 college scholarship, payable to an educational institution of the recipient's choice, subject to the approval of Optimist International.

Duration: The competition is held annually.

Number awarded: Nearly 300 Optimist International clubs participate in this program each year. Each participating district offers 1 scholarship; some districts may offer a second award with separate competitions for signing and oral competitors, or for male and female entrants.

Deadline: Each club sets its own deadline. Districts must submit materials to the national office by June of each year.

786 OPTIMIST INTERNATIONAL ESSAY CONTEST

Optimist International
Attn: Programs Department
4494 Lindell Boulevard
St. Louis, MO 63108
Phone: (314) 371-6000; (800) 500-8130, ext. 235; Fax: (314) 371-6009
Email: programs@optimist.org
Web: www.optimist.org/e/member/scholarships3.cfm

Summary: To recognize and reward, with college scholarships, outstanding essays by high school students on a topic that changes annually.

Eligibility: Open to high school students in the United States, the Caribbean, or Canada who are younger than 19 years of age. Applicants are invited to write an essay of 400 to 500 words on a topic that changes each year; a recent topic was "The Internet: Today's Evolution or Tomorrow's Menace?" They compete on the local club, district, and national/international levels. Essays may be written in the official language of the area where the club is located (English, Spanish, or French). Selection is based on material organization (40 points); vocabulary and style (30 points); grammar, punctuation, and spelling (20 points); neatness (5 points); and adherence to contest rules (5 points).

Financial data: The international first-place winner receives $6,000, second $3,750, and third $2,250. Funds are to be used to pay college costs. District winners are awarded a $2,500 college scholarship.

Duration: The competition is held annually.

Number awarded: 3 international winners are selected each year. A total of $44,000 in scholarships is awarded annually.

Deadline: Clubs must submit their winning essay to the district chair by the end of February of each year. Districts must submit their winner's information to the national office in April.

787 OPTIMIST INTERNATIONAL ORATORICAL CONTEST

Optimist International
Attn: Programs Department
4494 Lindell Boulevard
St. Louis, MO 63108
Phone: (314) 371-6000; (800) 500-8130, ext. 235; Fax: (314) 371-6009
Email: programs@optimist.org
Web: www.optimist.org/e/member/scholarships4.cfm

Summary: To recognize and reward, with college scholarships, outstanding orators at the high school or younger level.

Eligibility: Open to all students in public, private, or parochial elementary, junior high, and senior high schools in the United States, Canada, or the Caribbean who are under 16 years of age. All contestants must prepare their own orations of 4 to 5 minutes, but they may receive advice and make minor changes or improvements in the oration at any time. Each year a different subject is selected for the orations; a recent topic was "Cyber Communication: Progress or Problem?" The orations may be delivered in a language other than English if that language is an official language of the country in which the sponsoring club is located. Selection is based on poise (20 points), content of speech (35 points), delivery and presentation (35 points), and overall effectiveness (10 points). Competition is first conducted at the level of individual clubs, with winners advancing to zone and then district competitions. At the discretion of the district, boys may compete against boys and girls against girls in separate contests.

Financial data: Each district awards either 2 scholarships of $2,500 (1 for a boy and 1 for a girl) or (if the district chooses to have a combined gender contest) a first-place scholarship of $2,500, a second-place scholarship of $1,500, and a third-place scholarship of $1,000.

Duration: The competition is held annually.

Number awarded: Each year, more than $150,000 is awarded in scholarships.

Deadline: Each local club sets its own deadline. The district deadline is the end of June.

788 OREGON ASSOCIATION OF STUDENT COUNCILS SCHOLARSHIPS

Confederation of Oregon School Administrators
Attn: COSA Foundation
707 13th Street, S.E., Suite 100
Salem, OR 97301-4035
Phone: (503) 581-3141; Fax: (503) 581-9840
Email: nancy@oasc.org
Web: www.cosa.k12.or.us/member/scholarships.html

Summary: To provide financial assistance to high school seniors in Oregon who are interested in attending a community college, college, or university in the state.

Eligibility: Open to graduating high school seniors in Oregon. Applicants must be interested in attending a community college, college, or university in the state. They must have been active in community and school affairs, have at least a 3.5 GPA, and be able to enroll in the fall term after graduating from high school. Preference is given to students who have been involved in leadership and service. Along with their application, they must submit a 1-page autobiography (that includes their personal goals), the name of the school they plan to attend, and the endorsement of a member of the Confederation of Oregon School Administrators (COSA). Financial need is not considered in the selection process.

Financial data: The stipend is $1,000. Funds are paid directly to the recipient.

Duration: 1 year; nonrenewable.

Number awarded: 2 each year.

Deadline: February of each year.

789 OREGON CHAFEE EDUCATION AND TRAINING SCHOLARSHIPS

Oregon Student Assistance Commission
Attn: Chafee Program
1500 Valley River Drive, Suite 100
Eugene, OR 97401-2146
Phone: (541) 687-7443; (800) 452-8807, ext. 7443; Fax: (541) 687-7414; TDD: (800) 735-2900
Email: awardinfo@osac.state.or.us
Web: www.osac.state.or.us/chafeetv.html

Summary: To provide financial assistance for college to Oregon residents who are or have been in foster care.

Eligibility: Open to residents of Oregon who 1) currently are in a foster care placement with Oregon's Department of Human Services (DHS) or 1 of the 9

federally-recognized tribes in the state; 2) have been in foster care for at least 180 days after their 14th birthday; or 3) were adopted from the DHS foster care system after age 16. Applicants must be younger than 21 years of age. Along with their application, they must submit essays of 250 to 350 words on 1) their most significant challenge or accomplishment and its value to their life; and 2) their long-range goals and what they need to achieve them.
Financial data: The stipend is $4,000.
Duration: 1 year; may be renewed until recipient reaches 23 years of age.
Number awarded: 1 or more each year.
Deadline: February of each year.

790 OREGON DAIRY WOMEN COLLEGE SCHOLARSHIPS

Oregon Dairy Women
c/o Ida Ruby
37955 Fir Ridge Road
Scio, OR 97374-9704
Phone: (503) 394-2686
Summary: To provide financial assistance to children of Oregon dairy farmers who are attending a 4-year college or university in any state.
Eligibility: Open to the children of Oregon dairy farmers who have lived on a dairy for at least 5 years and have a GPA of 2.7 or higher. Applicants must be enrolled full-time as a junior or higher at a 4-year college or university in any state. Selection is based on academic achievement, letters of recommendation, and an autobiography.
Financial data: The stipend is $1,500.
Duration: 1 year.
Number awarded: 2 each year.
Deadline: March of each year.

791 OREGON DECEASED OR DISABLED PUBLIC SAFETY OFFICER GRANT PROGRAM

Oregon Student Assistance Commission
Attn: Grants and Scholarships Division
1500 Valley River Drive, Suite 100
Eugene, OR 97401-2130
Phone: (541) 687-7466; (800) 452-8807, ext. 7466; Fax: (541) 687-7414; TDD: (800) 735-2900
Email: awardinfo@osac.state.or.us
Web: www.getcollegefunds.org
Summary: To provide financial assistance for college or graduate school in the state to the children of disabled or deceased Oregon public safety officers.
Eligibility: Open to the natural, adopted, or stepchildren of Oregon public safety officers (fire fighters, state fire marshals, chief deputy fire marshals, deputy state fire marshals, police chiefs, police officers, sheriffs, deputy sheriffs, county adult parole and probation officers, correction officers, and investigators of the Criminal Justice Division of the Department of Justice) who, in the line of duty, were killed or disabled. Applicants must be enrolled or planning to enroll as a full-time undergraduate student at a public or private college or university in Oregon. Children of deceased officers are also eligible for graduate study. Financial need must be demonstrated.
Financial data: At a public 2- or 4-year college or university, the amount of the award is equal to the cost of tuition and fees. At an eligible private college, the award amount is equal to the cost of tuition and fees at the University of Oregon.
Duration: 1 year; may be renewed for up to 3 additional years of undergraduate study, if the student maintains satisfactory academic progress and demonstrates continued financial need. Children of deceased public safety officers may receive support for 12 quarters of graduate study.
Number awarded: Varies each year.
Deadline: Deadline not specified.

792 OREGON EDUCATIONAL AID FOR VETERANS

Oregon Department of Veterans' Affairs
Attn: Educational Aid Program
700 Summer Street, N.E., Suite 150
Salem, OR 97301-1285
Phone: (503) 373-2085; (800) 692-9666 (within OR); Fax: (503) 373-2362; TDD: (503) 373-2217
Email: orvetsbenefits@odva.state.or.us
Web: www.oregon.gov/ODVA/BENEFITS/OregonEducationBenefit.shtml
Summary: To provide financial assistance for college to certain Oregon veterans.
Eligibility: Open to veterans who served on active duty in the U.S. armed forces for not less than 90 days during the Korean War or subsequent to June 30, 1958. Applicants must be residents of Oregon released from military service under honorable conditions. They must be enrolled or planning to enroll in classroom instruction, home study courses, or vocational training from an accredited educational institution. U.S. citizenship is required.
Financial data: Full-time students are entitled to receive up to $150 per month and part-time students up to $100 per month.
Duration: Benefits are paid for as many months as the veteran spent in active service, up to a maximum of 36 months. One month of entitlement will be charged for each month paid, regardless of the amount paid.
Number awarded: Varies each year.
Deadline: Applications must be submitted at the time of enrollment.

793 OREGON LEGION AUXILIARY DEPARTMENT SCHOLARSHIPS

American Legion Auxiliary
Department of Oregon
30450 S.W. Parkway Avenue
P.O. Box 1730
Wilsonville, OR 97070-1730
Phone: (503) 682-3162; Fax: (503) 685-5008
Email: alaor@pcez.com
Summary: To provide financial assistance to the dependents of Oregon veterans who are interested in attending college in any state.
Eligibility: Open to Oregon residents who are children or wives of disabled veterans or widows of veterans. Applicants must be interested in obtaining education beyond the high school level at a college, university, business school, vocational school, or any other accredited postsecondary school in the state of Oregon. Selection is based on ability, aptitude, character, seriousness of purpose, and financial need.
Financial data: The stipend is $1,000.
Duration: 1 year; nonrenewable.
Number awarded: 3 each year; 1 of these is to be used for vocational or business school.
Deadline: March of each year.

794 OREGON LEGION AUXILIARY NATIONAL PRESIDENT'S SCHOLARSHIP

American Legion Auxiliary
Department of Oregon
30450 S.W. Parkway Avenue
P.O. Box 1730
Wilsonville, OR 97070-1730
Phone: (503) 682-3162; Fax: (503) 685-5008
Email: alaor@pcez.com
Summary: To provide financial assistance to the children of war veterans in Oregon who plan to attend college in any state.
Eligibility: Open to Oregon residents who are the children of veterans who served during specified periods of war time. Applicants must be high school seniors or graduates who have not yet attended an institution of higher learning. They must be planning to attend a college or university in any state. Selection is based on character, Americanism, leadership, scholarship, and financial need. The winner then competes for the American Legion Auxiliary National President's Scholarship. If the Oregon winner is not awarded a national scholarship, then he or she receives the first-place award and the second winner receives the second-place award; if the Oregon winner is also a national winner, then the second-place winner in Oregon receives the first-place award and the alternate receives the second-place award.
Financial data: The first-place award is $2,000 and the second-place award is $1,500.
Duration: 1 year; nonrenewable.
Number awarded: 2 each year.
Deadline: February of each year.

795 OREGON OCCUPATIONAL SAFETY AND HEALTH DIVISION WORKERS MEMORIAL SCHOLARSHIPS

Oregon Student Assistance Commission
Attn: Grants and Scholarships Division

1500 Valley River Drive, Suite 100
Eugene, OR 97401-2146
Phone: (541) 687-7395; (800) 452-8807, ext. 7395; Fax: (541) 687-7414; TDD: (800) 735-2900
Email: awardinfo@osac.state.or.us
Web: www.osac.state.or.us/osac_programs.html

Summary: To provide financial assistance to the children and spouses of disabled or deceased workers in Oregon who are interested in attending college or graduate school in any state.

Eligibility: Open to residents of Oregon who are U.S. citizens or permanent residents. Applicants must be high school seniors or graduates who 1) are dependents or spouses of an Oregon worker who has suffered permanent total disability on the job; or 2) are receiving, or have received, fatality benefits as dependents or spouses of a worker fatally injured in Oregon. They may be attending a college or graduate school in any state. Along with their application, they must submit an essay of up to 500 words on how the injury or death of their parent or spouse has affected or influenced their decision to further their education. Financial need is not required, but it is considered in the selection process.

Financial data: Stipend amounts vary; recently, they were at least $4,786.

Duration: 1 year.

Number awarded: 1 or more each year.

Deadline: February of each year.

796 OREGON OPPORTUNITY GRANTS

Oregon Student Assistance Commission
1500 Valley River Drive, Suite 100
Eugene, OR 97401-2130
Phone: (541) 687-7400; (800) 452-8807; Fax: (541) 687-7414; TDD: (800) 735-2900
Email: awardinfo@osac.state.or.us
Web: www.getcollegefunds.org/ong.html

Summary: To provide financial assistance for college to residents of Oregon who have financial need.

Eligibility: Open to residents of Oregon who are attending or planning to attend a nonprofit college or university in Oregon as a full-time student. Applicants must have an annual family income below specified levels; for dependent students, that is 55% of the Oregon median family income (MFI); for independent students, the maximum family income is 50% of the Oregon MFI if married or 30% if single. They must be U.S. citizens or eligible noncitizens. Students who are working on a degree in theology, divinity, or religious education are not eligible.

Financial data: Awards depend on the need of the recipient. Recently, the maximum stipend for a student at a community college was $2,600 or for a student at a public 4-year college or university it was $3,200. Specific award amounts are established for each eligible private college or university within Oregon. Contact the sponsor for the amount of the supplemental awards available at private institutions.

Duration: 1 year; may be renewed for up to 3 additional years, if the student maintains satisfactory academic progress and demonstrates continued financial need.

Number awarded: Varies each year; recently, more than 38,000 of these grants were awarded.

Deadline: The priority deadline is in August of each year.

797 OREGON STATE COUNCIL ENDOWMENT SCHOLARSHIPS

Epsilon Sigma Alpha International
Attn: ESA Foundation
P.O. Box 270517
Fort Collins, CO 80527
Phone: (970) 223-2824; Fax: (970) 223-4456
Email: esainfo@esaintl.com
Web: www.esaintl.com/esaf

Summary: To provide financial assistance to residents of Oregon who plan to attend college in any state.

Eligibility: Open to residents of Oregon who are 1) graduating high school seniors with a GPA of 3.0 or higher or with minimum scores of 22 on the ACT or 1030 on the combined critical reading and mathematics SAT; 2) enrolled in college with a GPA of 3.0 or higher; 3) enrolled at a technical school or returning to school after an absence for retraining of job skills or obtaining a degree; or 4) engaged in online study through an accredited college, university, or vocational school. Applicants may be attending or planning to attend a school in any state and major in any field. Selection is based on character (20%), leadership (20%), service (20%), financial need (20%), and scholastic ability (20%).

Financial data: The stipend is $1,000.

Duration: 1 year; may be renewed.

Number awarded: 1 each year.

Deadline: January of each year.

798 OREGON STATE ELKS ASSOCIATION VOCATIONAL GRANTS

Oregon State Elks Association
c/o Hugh Kerwin, Scholarship Chair
P.O. Box 2205
Gearhart, OR 97138-2205
Phone: (503) 738-5266
Email: hugh@seasurf.net
Web: www.oregonelks.org

Summary: To provide financial assistance to residents of Oregon who are interested in enrolling in a vocational education program in any state.

Eligibility: Open to residents of Oregon who are enrolled or planning to enroll full-time at a vocational/technical school or other 2-year educational institution in any state to work on a degree or certificate other than a bachelor's degree. Applicants are not required to have a high school diploma or GED certificate. Their application must be endorsed by an official of their local Elks Lodge. Along with their application, they must submit 1) a 200-word statement of their activities, accomplishments, needs, and objectives that they believe qualify them for this grant; and 2) a 150-word letter from a parent or other knowledgeable family member describing the family financial situation. Selection is based on grades, motivation and responsibility, skills and abilities, completeness and neatness of the application, and financial need. U.S. citizenship is required.

Financial data: The stipend is $1,000. Funds are disbursed directly to the educational institution to be used for tuition, fees, books, and supplies.

Duration: 1 year; recipients may reapply for 1 additional year.

Number awarded: 1 or more each year.

Deadline: March of each year.

799 OSCAR AND MILDRED LARSON AWARD

Vasa Order of America
Attn: Vice Grand Master
1456 Kennebec Road
Grand Blanc, MI 48439
Phone: (810) 695-3248
Email: wmlund1@aol.com
Web: www.vasaorder.com/benefits.htm

Summary: To provide financial assistance for college or graduate school to students of Swedish heritage.

Eligibility: Open to residents of the United States, Canada, and Sweden who are enrolled or accepted as full-time undergraduate or graduate students at an accredited 4-year college or university in the United States. Applicants must be Swedish born or of Swedish ancestry. Membership in Vasa Order of America is not required. Selection is based on a grade transcript, letters of recommendation from school and local Vasa lodge officials, and an essay of up to 1,000 words on a topic related to Vasa.

Financial data: The stipend is $3,000 per year.

Duration: 1 year; may be renewed up to 3 additional years for a total award of $12,000.

Number awarded: 1 each year.

Deadline: February of each year.

800 PALMETTO FELLOWS SCHOLARSHIPS

South Carolina Commission on Higher Education
Attn: Director of Student Services
1333 Main Street, Suite 200
Columbia, SC 29201
Phone: (803) 737-2244; (877) 349-7183; Fax: (803) 737-2297
Email: kwoodfaulk@che.sc.gov
Web: www.che.sc.gov/New_Web/GoingToCollege/PF_Hm.htm

Summary: To provide financial assistance for college to high school seniors in South Carolina who have achieved a high score on a college entrance examination.

Eligibility: Open to residents of South Carolina who are enrolled in a public or private high school or an approved home school program. Applicants must be planning to attend a 4-year public or private college or university in South Carolina during the fall immediately following graduation. They must either 1) score at least 1200 on the mathematics and critical reading sections of the SAT or 27 on the ACT, have a GPA of 3.5 or higher, and rank in the top 6% of their class; or 2) score at least 1400 on the mathematics and critical reading sections of the SAT or 32 on the ACT and have a GPA of 4.0. Early awards are based on test scores, GPA, and class rank at the end of the junior year; final awards are based on test scores, GPA, and class rank at the end of the senior year. U.S. citizenship or permanent resident status is required. Students who complete at least 14 credit hours of mathematics and science (including at least 6 hours in mathematics and 6 hours in life and physical sciences) qualify for an enhanced mathematics and sciences award. Financial need is not considered in the selection process.

Financial data: The stipend is $6,700 for the freshman year and $7,500 per year for sophomore and later years. Students who qualify for the enhanced mathematics and sciences award receive an additional $2,500 per year beginning with their sophomore year.

Duration: 1 year; may be renewed for 3 additional years, provided the recipient maintains full-time enrollment and a GPA of 3.0 or higher.

Number awarded: Varies each year; recently, 5,506 of these scholarships, worth more than $22 million, were awarded.

Deadline: December of each year for early awards; June of each year for final awards.

801 PAPA JOHN'S SCHOLARSHIPS

Papa John's International, Inc.
Attn: Scholarship Administrator
4005 Briar Ridge Road
LaGrange, KY 40031
Phone: (502) 261-7272; (800) 865-9373
Email: info@papajohnsscholars.com
Web: www.papajohnsscholars.com

Summary: To provide financial assistance for college to high school seniors at selected U.S. high schools.

Eligibility: Open to graduating high school seniors who have a GPA of 2.5 or higher. Applicants must attend a high school located near a participating Papa John's restaurant. Selection is based on creative ability, community involvement, academic achievement, quality of character, demonstrated leadership, life goals and interests, athletic achievement, and meaningful obstacles overcome.

Financial data: The stipend is $1,000.

Duration: 1 year.

Number awarded: Varies each year; recently, 1,185 of these scholarships were awarded.

Deadline: Deadlines are established by guidance offices of schools located near a participating Papa John's restaurant.

802 PARR FAMILY MEMORIAL ENDOWMENT SCHOLARSHIP

Epsilon Sigma Alpha International
Attn: ESA Foundation
P.O. Box 270517
Fort Collins, CO 80527
Phone: (970) 223-2824; Fax: (970) 223-4456
Email: esainfo@esaintl.com
Web: www.esaintl.com/esaf

Summary: To provide financial assistance for college to students from designated states whose grades are in the "C" range.

Eligibility: Open to residents of Illinois, Indiana, Iowa, Michigan, Minnesota, Missouri, Nebraska, Ohio, South Dakota, or Wisconsin. Applicants may be 1) graduating high school seniors with a GPA of 2.5 to 3.0; 2) enrolled in college with a GPA of 2.5 to 3.0; 3) enrolled at a technical school or returning to school after an absence for retraining of job skills or obtaining a degree; or 4) engaged in online study through an accredited college, university, or vocational school. They may be attending or planning to attend a school in any state and major in any field. Selection is based on character (20%), leadership (20%), service (20%), financial need (20%), and scholastic ability (20%).

Financial data: The stipend is $2,000.

Duration: 1 year; may be renewed.

Number awarded: 2 each year.

Deadline: January of each year.

803 PARTNERSHIP FOR ACCESS TO HIGHER EDUCATION (PATH) GRANTS

Pennsylvania Higher Education Assistance Agency
Attn: State Grant and Special Programs
1200 North Seventh Street
P.O. Box 8114
Harrisburg, PA 17105-8114
Phone: (717) 720-2800; (800) 692-7392; TDD: (800) 654-5988
Web: www.pheaa.org/specialprograms/index.shtml

Summary: To provide additional financial assistance to residents of Pennsylvania who have received a scholarship from a local organization that is part of the Partnership for Access to Higher Education (PATH) program.

Eligibility: Open to residents of Pennsylvania who are enrolled at least half-time at an approved State Grant institution. Applicants must have received a State Grant from the Pennsylvania Higher Education Assistance Agency (PHEAA) and a scholarship from a participating PATH organization. They must be nominated by the PATH organization. Financial need is considered in the selection process.

Financial data: The maximum additional grant is $3,500 per academic year.

Duration: 1 year; may be renewed.

Number awarded: Varies each year.

Deadline: Deadline not specified.

804 PATRICIA CREED SCHOLARSHIP

Connecticut Women's Golf Association
c/o Judy Gamble, Scholarship Committee
27 Cold Spring Circle
Shelton, CT 06484
Phone: (203) 929-0435
Email: scholarships@cwga.org
Web: www.cwga.org/CWGA/index.php?section=16

Summary: To provide financial assistance to women high school seniors from Connecticut who are golfers and planning to attend college in any state.

Eligibility: Open to female high school seniors who are residents of Connecticut planning to attend a public college or university in any state. Applicants must be active golfers with a handicap. Along with their application, they must submit a 200-word essay on how golf has made an impact on their life. Selection is based on character, academic achievement, interest in golf, and financial need.

Financial data: A stipend is awarded (amount not specified).

Duration: 1 year.

Number awarded: 1 or 2 each year.

Deadline: April of each year.

805 PATSY TAKEMOTO MINK EDUCATION FOUNDATION EDUCATION SUPPORT AWARD

Patsy Takemoto Mink Education Foundation for Low-Income Women and Children
P.O. Box 769
Granby, MA 01033
Email: admin@ptmfoundation.net
Web: www.patsyminkfoundation.org/edsupport.html

Summary: To provide financial assistance for college or graduate school to low-income women.

Eligibility: Open to women who are at least 17 years of age and are from a low-income family (less than $17,500 annually for a family of 2, $22,000 for a family of 3, or $26,500 for a family of 4). Applicants must be mothers with minor children. They must be 1) enrolled in a skills training, ESL, or GED program; or 2) working on an associate, bachelor's, master's, professional, or doctoral degree. Along with their application, they must submit brief essays on what this award will help them accomplish, the program in which they are or will be enrolled, how they decided on that educational pursuit, their educational goals, their educational experience, and their personal and educational history.

Financial data: The stipend is $2,000.

Duration: 1 year.

Number awarded: 5 each year.

Deadline: June of each year.

806 PATTY AND MELVIN ALPERIN FIRST GENERATION SCHOLARSHIP

Rhode Island Foundation
Attn: Funds Administrator
One Union Station
Providence, RI 02903
Phone: (401) 427-4017; Fax: (401) 331-8085
Email: lmonahan@rifoundation.org

Web: www.rifoundation.org
Summary: To provide financial assistance to high school seniors in Rhode Island whose parents did not attend college and who plan to attend college in any state.
Eligibility: Open to seniors graduating from high schools in Rhode Island whose parents did not have the benefit of attending college. Applicants must be planning to enroll at an accredited 2- or 4-year college or university in any state. Along with their application, they must submit an essay (up to 300 words) on what it means to them to be of the first generation in their family to work on a college degree. Selection is based on academic excellence, character, and financial need.
Financial data: The stipend ranges up to $1,000.
Duration: 1 year; may be renewed for up to 3 additional years if the recipient maintains good academic standing.
Number awarded: Varies each year.
Deadline: May of each year.

807 PAUL TSONGAS SCHOLARSHIP PROGRAM

Massachusetts Office of Student Financial Assistance
454 Broadway, Suite 200
Revere, MA 02151
Phone: (617) 727-9420; Fax: (617) 727-0667
Email: osfa@osfa.mass.edu
Web: www.osfa.mass.edu/default.asp?page=tsongasScholarship
Summary: To provide financial assistance to Massachusetts students who attend 1 of the state colleges in Massachusetts.
Eligibility: Open to residents of Massachusetts who have graduated from high school within 5 years and are attending or planning to attend a state college in Massachusetts. Applicants must be U.S. citizens or permanent residents and have a GPA of 3.75 or higher and SAT score of 1200 or higher.
Financial data: Eligible students receive a waiver of tuition and mandatory fees.
Duration: Up to 4 academic years, if the recipient maintains a GPA of 3.3 or higher in college.
Number awarded: 45 each year: 5 at each state college in Massachusetts.
Deadline: April of each year.

808 PEGGY WORTHY TOWNES ENDOWED SCHOLARSHIP

United Methodist Higher Education Foundation
Attn: Scholarships Administrator
1001 19th Avenue South
P.O. Box 340005
Nashville, TN 37203-0005
Phone: (615) 340-7385; (800) 811-8110; Fax: (615) 340-7330
Email: umhefscholarships@gbhem.org
Web: www.umhef.org/receive.php?id=endowed_funds
Summary: To provide financial assistance to Methodist students who are entering freshmen at Methodist-related colleges and universities.
Eligibility: Open to students enrolling as full-time freshmen at United Methodist-related colleges and universities. Applicants must have been active, full members of a United Methodist Church for at least 1 year prior to applying. They must have a GPA of 3.0 or higher and be able to demonstrate financial need. Along with their application, they must submit a 200-word essay on their involvement and/or leadership responsibilities in their church, school, and community within the last 3 years. U.S. citizenship or permanent resident status is required.
Financial data: The stipend is at least $1,000.
Duration: 1 year; nonrenewable.
Number awarded: 1 each year.
Deadline: May of each year.

809 PENNSYLVANIA BURGLAR & FIRE ALARM ASSOCIATION YOUTH SCHOLARSHIP PROGRAM

Pennsylvania Burglar & Fire Alarm Association
Attn: Youth Scholarship Program
3718 West Lake Road
Erie, PA 16505
Phone: (814) 838-3093; (800) 458-8512 (within PA); Fax: (814) 838-5127
Email: info@pbfaa.com
Web: www.pbfaa.com/Default.aspx?pageId=566892
Summary: To provide financial assistance to high school seniors in Pennsylvania who are the children of active-duty law enforcement and fire service personnel and interested in attending college in any state.
Eligibility: Open to seniors graduating from high schools in Pennsylvania who have been accepted at an accredited college or university in any state. Applicants must have a father, mother, or legal guardian who is a full-time active employee (not on disability) of the police or sheriff's department or a paid employee or volunteer of a fire department in Pennsylvania. Along with their application, they must submit an essay of 500 to 700 words on what it means to them to have their parent or guardian involved in securing our community. Selection is based on that essay (20 points), grade average (35 points), SAT scores (30 points), and academic prizes, awards, school and outside extracurricular activities, and hobbies (15 points); financial need is not considered. Children of law enforcement personnel and children of fire service personnel compete in separate categories.
Financial data: The stipend is $1,000.
Duration: 1 year.
Number awarded: 2 each year: 1 for the law enforcement category and 1 for the fire service category.
Deadline: March of each year.

810 PENNSYLVANIA CHAFEE EDUCATION AND TRAINING GRANT PROGRAM

Pennsylvania Higher Education Assistance Agency
Attn: State Grant and Special Programs
1200 North Seventh Street
P.O. Box 8114
Harrisburg, PA 17105-8114
Phone: (717) 720-2800; (800) 692-7392; TDD: (800) 654-5988
Email: paetg@pheaa.org
Web: www.pheaa.org/specialprograms/pa_chafee_grant_program.shtml
Summary: To provide financial assistance to residents of Pennsylvania who have been in foster care and plan to attend college in the state.
Eligibility: Open to residents of Pennsylvania who are eligible for services under the Commonwealth's Chafee Foster Care Independence Program, were adopted from foster care after their 16th birthday, or were participating in this program on their 21st birthday (until they turn 23 years of age). Applicants must be enrolled in an approved college or career school in Pennsylvania on at least a half-time basis.
Financial data: The maximum stipend is $5,000 per year. Awards may not exceed the actual cost of attendance, minus other financial aid the student receives.
Duration: 1 year; may be renewed if the recipient remains enrolled at least half-time and makes satisfactory academic progress.
Number awarded: Varies each year.
Deadline: April of each year.

811 PENNSYLVANIA EDUCATIONAL GRATUITY FOR VETERANS' DEPENDENTS

Office of the Deputy Adjutant General for Veterans Affairs
Building S-0-47, FTIG
Annville, PA 17003-5002
Phone: (717) 865-8910; (800) 54 PA VET (within PA); Fax: (717) 861-8589
Email: jamebutler@state.pa.us
Web: www.milvet.state.pa.us/DMVA/201.htm
Summary: To provide financial assistance for college to the children of disabled or deceased Pennsylvania veterans.
Eligibility: Open to children (between 16 and 23 years of age) of honorably-discharged veterans who are rated totally and permanently disabled as a result of wartime service or who have died of such a disability. Applicants must have lived in Pennsylvania for at least 5 years immediately preceding the date of application, be able to demonstrate financial need, and have been accepted or be currently enrolled in a Pennsylvania state or state-aided secondary or post-secondary educational institution.
Financial data: The stipend is $500 per semester ($1,000 per year). The money is paid directly to the recipient's school and is to be applied to the costs of tuition, board, room, books, supplies, and/or matriculation fees.
Duration: The allowance is paid for up to 4 academic years or for the duration of the course of study, whichever is less.
Number awarded: Varies each year.
Deadline: Deadline not specified.

812 PENNSYLVANIA FEDERATION OF DEMOCRATIC WOMEN MEMORIAL SCHOLARSHIP

Pennsylvania Federation of Democratic Women
c/o Bonita Hannis, Scholarship Chair
36 Betts Lane
Lock Haven, PA 17745
Phone: (570) 769-7175
Email: behannis@kcnet.org
Web: www.pfdw.org/ScholarshipAwards/tabid/101/Default.aspx

Summary: To provide financial assistance to women from Pennsylvania who are registered Democrats and attending college in any state.

Eligibility: Open to women who are residents of Pennsylvania and currently enrolled as juniors at an accredited college or university in any state. Applicants must be registered Democrats and an active participant in the Democratic Party with a Democratic Party family background. Along with their application, they must submit a 1-page essay describing their need for this scholarship, their professional goals, their Democratic Party activities, and their family Democratic Party involvement.

Financial data: The stipend is $5,000.

Duration: 1 year (the senior year of college).

Number awarded: Varies each year; recently, 4 of these scholarships were awarded.

Deadline: April of each year.

813 PENNSYLVANIA GRANTS FOR CHILDREN OF SOLDIERS DECLARED POW/MIA

Pennsylvania Higher Education Assistance Agency
Attn: State Grant and Special Programs
1200 North Seventh Street
P.O. Box 8114
Harrisburg, PA 17105-8114
Phone: (717) 720-2800; (800) 692-7392; TDD: (717) 720-2366
Web: www.pheaa.org

Summary: To provide financial assistance for college to the children of POWs/MIAs from Pennsylvania.

Eligibility: Open to dependent children of members or former members of the U.S. armed services who served on active duty after January 31, 1955, who are or have been prisoners of war or are or have been listed as missing in action, and who were residents of Pennsylvania for at least 12 months preceding service on active duty. Eligible children must be enrolled in a program of at least 1 year in duration on at least a half-time basis at an approved school and must demonstrate financial need.

Financial data: The amount of the award depends on the financial need of the recipient, up to a maximum of $3,500 at a Pennsylvania school or $800 at a school outside of Pennsylvania that is approved for participation in the program.

Duration: 1 year; may be renewed for 3 additional years.

Number awarded: Varies each year.

Deadline: March of each year.

814 PENNSYLVANIA GRANTS FOR VETERANS

Pennsylvania Higher Education Assistance Agency
Attn: State Grant and Special Programs
1200 North Seventh Street
P.O. Box 8114
Harrisburg, PA 17105-8114
Phone: (717) 720-2800; (800) 692-7392; TDD: (800) 654-5988
Email: info@pheaa.org
Web: www.pheaa.org/specialprograms/index.shtml

Summary: To provide financial assistance to Pennsylvania veterans who are interested in attending college in any state.

Eligibility: Open to veterans who served on active duty with the U.S. armed services (or were a cadet or midshipman at a service academy); were released or discharged under conditions other than dishonorable, bad conduct, uncharacterized, or other than honorable; have resided in Pennsylvania for at least 12 months immediately preceding the date of application; graduated from high school; and are enrolled on at least a half-time basis in an approved program of study that is at least 2 academic years in length. First priority is given to veterans who have separated from active duty after January 1 of the current year. All veterans are considered without regard to the financial status of their parents.

Financial data: The amount of the award depends on the financial need of the recipient, up to a maximum of $3,500 at a Pennsylvania school or $800 at a school outside of Pennsylvania that is approved for participation in the program.

Duration: 1 year; may be renewed for 3 additional years.

Number awarded: Varies each year.

Deadline: April of each year for renewal applicants and any nonrenewals who will enroll in a baccalaureate degree program; July of each year for nonrenewals who will enroll in a 2-year or 3-year terminal program.

815 PENNSYLVANIA HOUSE OF REPRESENTATIVES SCHOLARSHIP

The Foundation for Enhancing Communities
Attn: Program Officer
200 North Third Street
P.O. Box 678
Harrisburg, PA 17108-0678
Phone: (717) 236-5040; Fax: (717) 231-4463
Email: dawn@tfec.org
Web: www.tfec.org/index.cfm?act=scholarship_eligibility

Summary: To provide financial assistance to high school seniors in Pennsylvania who plan to attend a college or university in the state.

Eligibility: Open to seniors graduating from high schools in Pennsylvania with a GPA of 3.0 or higher. Applicants must be planning to enroll full-time at a college, university, or career school in Pennsylvania. Selection is based on academic achievement, commitment to community, demonstrated leadership qualities, extracurricular activities, a 500-word personal essay, and financial need.

Financial data: The program provides full payment of tuition at member institutions of the State System of Higher Education. Students who attend other Pennsylvania colleges and universities receive an equivalent amount (approximately $2,500 per year) paid jointly to them and their institution.

Duration: 4 years, provided the recipient maintains a GPA of 2.5 in the first year of college and 3.0 or higher in each subsequent year.

Number awarded: 2 each year.

Deadline: March of each year.

816 PENNSYLVANIA POSTSECONDARY EDUCATIONAL GRATUITY PROGRAM

Pennsylvania Higher Education Assistance Agency
Attn: State Grant and Special Programs
1200 North Seventh Street
P.O. Box 8114
Harrisburg, PA 17105-8114
Phone: (717) 720-2800; (800) 692-7392; TDD: (800) 654-5988
Email: info@pheaa.org
Web: www.pheaa.org

Summary: To provide financial assistance for college to the children of Pennsylvania public service personnel who died in the line of service.

Eligibility: Open to residents of Pennsylvania who are the children of 1) Pennsylvania police officers, fire fighters, rescue and ambulance squad members, corrections facility employees, or National Guard members who died in the line of duty after January 1, 1976; or 2) Pennsylvania sheriffs, deputy sheriffs, National Guard members, and certain other individuals on federal or state active military duty who died after September 11, 2001 as a direct result of performing their official duties. Applicants must be 25 years of age or younger and enrolled or accepted at a Pennsylvania community college, state-owned institution, or state-related institution as a full-time student working on an associate or baccalaureate degree. They must have already applied for other scholarships, including state and federal grants and financial aid from the postsecondary institution to which they are applying.

Financial data: Grants cover tuition, fees, room, and board charged by the institution, less awarded scholarships and federal and state grants.

Duration: Up to 5 years.

Number awarded: Varies each year.

Deadline: March of each year.

817 PENNSYLVANIA STATE GRANTS

Pennsylvania Higher Education Assistance Agency
Attn: State Grant and Special Programs
1200 North Seventh Street
P.O. Box 8141
Harrisburg, PA 17102-8141

Phone: (717) 720-2800; (800) 692-7392; TDD: (800) 654-5988
Email: info@pheaa.org
Web: www.pheaa.org/stategrants/index.shtml

Summary: To provide financial assistance to high school seniors in Pennsylvania who have financial need and are interested in attending college in Pennsylvania or most other states.

Eligibility: Open to seniors graduating from high schools in Pennsylvania who plan to attend a postsecondary school in Pennsylvania on at least a half-time basis. Applicants may also attend accredited colleges in other states, except those states that border Pennsylvania and do not allow their grant recipients to attend Pennsylvania schools (i.e., Maryland, New Jersey, and New York). They must be able to demonstrate financial need.

Financial data: Grants depend on financial need and the type of school attended. Recently, annual grants at Pennsylvania institutions ranged from $1,350 to $4,000 at 4-year private schools, from $1,050 to $3,404 at state system schools, from $1,600 to $3,660 at state-related schools, from $1,100 to $3,600 at junior colleges, from $350 to $1,200 at community colleges, from $700 to $3,350 at nursing schools, and from $1,100 to $3,550 at business, trade, and technical schools. For students at out-of-state institutions, the maximum grant was $400, or $600 if enrolled in a state that permits their students to carry their state grants to Pennsylvania, or $800 for veterans.

Duration: 1 year; may be renewed for 3 additional years.

Number awarded: Varies each year.

Deadline: April of each year for renewal applicants, new applicants who plan to enroll in a baccalaureate degree program, and students in college transfer programs at 2-year public or junior colleges; July of each year for first-time applicants for business, trade, or technical schools, hospital schools of nursing, or 2-year terminal programs at community, junior, or 4-year colleges.

818 PENNSYLVANIA WRESTLING COACHES ASSOCIATION SCHOLARSHIPS

Pennsylvania Wrestling Coaches Association
c/o Bob Greenly
1016 Shakespeare Avenue
Milton, PA 17847
Phone: (570) 742-3277; Fax: (570) 742-5300
Email: bgreenly@acfindustries.com
Web: www.pawrsl.com/pa/index_pwca.htm

Summary: To provide financial assistance to high school seniors in Pennsylvania who have been involved in wrestling and plan to attend college in any state.

Eligibility: Open to wrestlers in their senior year at a public or accredited private school in Pennsylvania. Applicants must be planning to enroll at an accredited institution of higher education or a technical school in any state. They must have a GPA of 2.0 or higher. Along with their application, they must submit an essay on how the sport of wrestling can be improved. They may choose to have their application judged on the essay only, or they can choose to have it count 50% along with 25% for academic achievement and 25% for athletic achievement. Financial need is not considered.

Financial data: Stipends are $1,000 for students judged on the complete application or $500 for students judged only on the essay. Funds are sent directly to the recipient's financial aid office.

Duration: 1 year.

Number awarded: 6 each year: 2 at $1,000 for the complete application and $500 for the essay.

Deadline: March of each year.

819 PENTAGON ASSISTANCE FUND

Navy-Marine Corps Relief Society
Attn: Education Division
875 North Randolph Street, Suite 225
Arlington, VA 22203-1757
Phone: (703) 696-4960; Fax: (703) 696-0144
Email: education@hq.nmcrs.org
Web: www.nmcrs.org/goldstar.html

Summary: To provide financial assistance for college to the children and spouses of deceased military personnel who died at the Pentagon on September 11, 2001.

Eligibility: Open to the children and spouses of deceased military personnel who died at the Pentagon as a result of the terrorist attack of September 11, 2001. Applicants must be enrolled or planning to enroll full-time (spouses may enroll part-time) at a college, university, or vocational/technical school. They must have a GPA of 2.0 or higher and be able to demonstrate financial need. Children must be 23 years of age or younger. Spouses may be eligible if the service member became disabled as a result of the attack.

Financial data: Stipends range from $500 to $2,500 per year. Funds are disbursed directly to the financial institution.

Duration: 1 year; may be renewed up to 3 additional years.

Number awarded: Varies each year.

Deadline: Children must apply by February of each year. Spouses must apply at least 2 months prior to the start of their studies.

820 PETER CONNACHER MEMORIAL AMERICAN EX-PRISONER OF WAR SCHOLARSHIPS

Oregon Student Assistance Commission
Attn: Grants and Scholarships Division
1500 Valley River Drive, Suite 100
Eugene, OR 97401-2146
Phone: (541) 687-7395; (800) 452-8807, ext. 7395; Fax: (541) 687-7414; TDD: (800) 735-2900
Email: awardinfo@osac.state.or.us
Web: www.osac.state.or.us/osac_programs.html

Summary: To provide financial assistance for college or graduate school to ex-prisoners of war and their descendants.

Eligibility: Open to U.S. citizens who 1) were military or civilian prisoners of war; or 2) are the descendants of ex-prisoners of war. They may be undergraduate or graduate students. A copy of the ex-prisoner of war's discharge papers from the U.S. armed forces must accompany the application. In addition, written proof of POW status must be submitted, along with a statement of the relationship between the applicant and the ex-prisoner of war (father, grandfather, etc.). Selection is based on academic record and financial need. Preference is given to Oregon residents or their dependents.

Financial data: The stipend amount varies; recently, it was at least $1,150.

Duration: 1 year; may be renewed for up to 3 additional years for undergraduate students or 2 additional years for graduate students. Renewal is dependent on evidence of continued financial need and satisfactory academic progress.

Number awarded: Varies each year; recently, 4 of these scholarships were awarded.

Deadline: February of each year.

821 PFIZER EPILEPSY SCHOLARSHIP AWARD

Pfizer Inc.
c/o Adelphi Eden Health Communications
30 Irving Place, 10th Floor
New York, NY 10003
Phone: (800) AWARD-PF;
Email: info@epilepsy-scholarship.com
Web: www.epilepsy-scholarship.com

Summary: To provide financial assistance for college or graduate school to individuals with epilepsy.

Eligibility: Open to students who are under a physician's care for epilepsy (taking prescribed medication) and submit an application with 2 letters of recommendation (1 from the physician) plus verification of academic status. They must be high school seniors entering college in the fall; college freshmen, sophomores, or juniors continuing in the fall; or college seniors planning to enter graduate school in the fall. Along with their application, they must submit a 250-word essay on something they have dealt with as a person with epilepsy; they may choose to write on 1) how they have overcome the challenges of epilepsy; 2) what living with epilepsy means to them; 3) someone who has been helpful to them in their success; or 4) an achievement of which they are proud. Selection is based on success in overcoming the challenges of epilepsy, success in school, participation in extracurricular or community activities, and desire to make the most out of college or graduate school; financial need is not considered.

Financial data: The stipend is $2,000.

Duration: 1 year; nonrenewable.

Number awarded: 40 each year.

Deadline: June of each year.

822 PHIL THETA KAPPA ALL-USA COMMUNITY COLLEGE ACADEMIC TEAM

Phi Theta Kappa
Attn: Scholarship Programs Director
1625 Eastover Drive
P.O. Box 13729
Jackson, MS 39236-3729

Phone: (601) 984-3539; Fax: (601) 984-3546
Email: scholarship.programs@ptk.org
Web: www.ptk.org/schol/aaat/all_usa.htm

Summary: To recognize and reward the outstanding achievements of community college students.

Eligibility: Open to students who have completed at least 36 hours at a community college in the United States (including 30 hours completed within the past 5 years) and are on track to earn an associate or bachelor's degree. Candidates must be nominated by a designated official at their college. Nominees must have a cumulative GPA of at least 3.5 for all college course work completed in the last 5 years, regardless of institution attended. They must submit a 2-page essay describing their most significant endeavor since attending community college in which they applied their academic or intellectual skills from their community college education to benefit their school, community, or society. Selection is based on information in the essay; awards, honors, and recognition for academic achievement; academic rigor and GPA; participation in honors programs; and service to the college and the community.

Financial data: The award is $2,500.

Duration: The competition is held annually.

Number awarded: 20 each year.

Deadline: November of each year.

823 PHIPPS MEMORIAL SCHOLARSHIP

General Federation of Women's Clubs of Connecticut
c/o JoAnn Calnen, President
74 Spruceland Road
Enfield, CT 06082-2359
Email: gfwcct@yahoo.com
Web: www.gfwcct.org

Summary: To provide financial assistance to women in Connecticut who are working on an undergraduate or graduate degree.

Eligibility: Open to female residents of Connecticut who have completed at least 2 years of college. Applicants must have a GPA of 3.0 or higher as nd be working on a bachelor's or master's degree. Selection is based on academic ability, future promise, and financial need.

Financial data: The stipend is $1,000.

Duration: 1 year.

Number awarded: 1 each year.

Deadline: February of each year.

824 PHYLLIS G. MEEKINS SCHOLARSHIP

Ladies Professional Golf Association
Attn: LPGA Foundation
100 International Golf Drive
Daytona Beach, FL 32124-1082
Phone: (386) 274-6200; Fax: (386) 274-1099
Email: foundation.scholarships@lpga.com
Web: www.lpgafoundation.org/Scholarships/pmeekins.aspx

Summary: To provide financial assistance to minority female graduating high school seniors who played golf in high school and plan to continue to play in college.

Eligibility: Open to female high school seniors who are members of a recognized minority group. Applicants must have a GPA of 3.0 or higher and a background in golf. They must be planning to enroll full-time at a college or university in the United States and play competitive golf. Along with their application, they must submit a letter that describes how golf has been an integral part of their lives and includes their personal, academic, and professional goals; their chosen discipline of study; and how this scholarship will be of assistance. Financial need is considered in the selection process. U.S. citizenship or legal resident status is required.

Financial data: The stipend is $1,250.

Duration: 1 year.

Number awarded: 1 each year.

Deadline: May of each year.

825 PHYLLIS J. JONES MEMORIAL SCHOLARSHIPS FOR HEAD START GRADUATES

National Head Start Association
Attn: Scholarships and Awards
1651 Prince Street
Alexandria, VA 22314
Phone: (703) 739-0875; Fax: (703) 739-0878
Email: yvinci@nhsa.org
Web: www.nhsa.org/services/programs/awards_and_scholarships

Summary: To provide financial assistance for college to students who were in the Head Start program.

Eligibility: Open to former Head Start students who are enrolled or planning to enroll at a 4-year college or university, 2-year community college, or vocational/technical school. Applicants must be an individual member of the National Head Start Association (NHSA) or their local program must be an NHSA member. Along with their application, they must submit a 300-word statement on their goals and aspirations for furthering their education and the role Head Start has played in their education. Selection is based on that statement (40 points), financial need (30 points), and 3 letters of reference or recommendation (30 points). Students submit their applications to their local program, which forwards 2 to the state association. Each state association forwards 2 applications to the regional association, which selects 2 for nomination to the national headquarters.

Financial data: The stipend is $1,500.

Duration: 1 year.

Number awarded: 2 each year.

Deadline: January of each year.

826 PHYLLIS LAWSON SCHOLARSHIP FOR HIGH SCHOOL SENIORS

Washington Association of Vocational Administrators
c/o Linda Hupka, Scholarship Chair
Bremerton High School
1500 13th Street
Bremerton, WA 98337
Phone: (360) 473-0800; Fax: (360) 473-0820
Web: www.wavanet.org

Summary: To provide financial assistance to high school seniors in Washington who have an outstanding record in career and technical education classes and plan to attend college in any state.

Eligibility: Open to seniors graduating from high schools in Washington who have an outstanding record in the field of career and technical education (CTE). Applicants must be planning to attend college in any state. Along with their application, they must submit 1) information on their involvement in CTE student activities, involvement in other activities that demonstrate initiative and provide a positive contribution to school or community, and occupational work experience; and 2) a 300-word statement explaining what CTE has meant to them. Selection is based on the information on their involvement in CTE and related activities (40%), their statement on what CTE has meant to them (40%), and a letter of reference from their CTE program instructor (20%).

Financial data: The stipend is $1,000.

Duration: 1 year.

Number awarded: 1 each year.

Deadline: April of each year.

827 PINKROSE BREAST CANCER SCHOLARSHIP

PinkRose Foundation, Inc.
P.O. Box 4025
Dedham, MA 02027
Email: info@pinkrose.org
Web: www.pinkrose.org/scholarship.htm

Summary: To provide financial assistance for college to high school graduates who have lost a parent to breast cancer.

Eligibility: Open to legal residents of the United States who are younger than 25 years of age and have lost a parent or legal guardian to breast cancer. Applicants must have a high school diploma or equivalent and be planning to enroll in a postsecondary education or certificate training program. Along with their application, they must submit a 2-page statement that includes 1) autobiographical information describing the significant impact of breast cancer on their life and how it altered their academic motivation and interests, professional and volunteer experience, and career objectives; and 2) their interest in this scholarship, especially how obtaining a postsecondary degree or certificate will benefit their future by helping to fulfill their goals and dreams. Financial need is not considered in the selection process.

Financial data: A stipend is awarded (amount not specified).

Duration: 1 year.

Number awarded: Varies each year.

Deadline: August of each year.

828 PNC/KHSAA SWEET 16 SCHOLARSHIPS

Kentucky High School Athletic Association
Attn: Assistant Commissioner
2280 Executive Drive
Lexington, KY 40505
Phone: (859) 299-5472; Fax: (859) 293-5999
Email: bcope@khsaa.org
Web: www.khsaa.org

Summary: To provide financial assistance for college to student-athletes in Kentucky high schools.

Eligibility: Open to high school seniors in Kentucky who have participated in athletics or cheerleading. The awards are presented in conjunction with the state basketball tournament, but all student-athletes, not just basketball players, are eligible. Students must be nominated by a school representative. Letters of nomination must explain why the student is an exemplary leader and should receive the scholarship. Selection is based on academic achievement, leadership, citizenship, and sportsmanship. Men and women are judged separately.

Financial data: The stipend is $1,000.

Duration: 1 year; nonrenewable.

Number awarded: 32 each year: 1 female and 1 male in each of 16 regions in Kentucky.

Deadline: February of each year.

829 POLICE FAMILY SURVIVORS FUND SCHOLARSHIPS

American Federation of Police and Concerned Citizens
c/o American Police Hall of Fame
6350 Horizon Drive
Titusville, FL 32780
Phone: (321) 264-0911; Fax: (321) 264-0033
Email: policeinfo@aphf.org
Web: www.aphf.org/programs.html

Summary: To provide financial assistance for college to children of police officers killed in the line of duty.

Eligibility: Open to children of police officers who were killed in the line of duty. Applicants must be attending or planning to attend a traditional 4-year college, university, technical school, or vocational institution. Students currently enrolled in college must submit a copy of their most recent transcript; students entering college for the first time must submit a high school transcript, ACT/SAT scores, and a copy of the acceptance letter from the institution they plan to attend. Financial need is not considered in the selection process.

Financial data: The stipend is $1,500 per year.

Duration: 1 year; may be renewed up to 3 additional years, provided the recipient maintains a GPA of 3.0 or higher.

Number awarded: Varies each year.

Deadline: Deadline not specified.

830 POLISH ROMAN CATHOLIC UNION OF AMERICA EDUCATION FUND SCHOLARSHIPS

Polish Roman Catholic Union of America
Attn: Education Fund Scholarship Program
984 North Milwaukee Avenue
Chicago, IL 60622-4101
Phone: (773) 782-2600; (800) 772-8632; Fax: (773) 278-4595
Email: info@prcua.org
Web: www.prcua.org/benefits/educationfundscholarship.htm

Summary: To provide financial assistance to undergraduate and graduate students of Polish heritage.

Eligibility: Open to students enrolled full-time as sophomores, juniors, and seniors in an undergraduate program or full- or part-time as a graduate or professional school students. Along with their application, they must submit brief statements on 1) the Polonian organization(s) that benefited from their membership and how; 2) the organized or other group(s) the benefited from their membership or service and how; and 3) how this scholarship will help them in working on their degree. Selection is based on academic achievement, Polonia involvement, and community service.

Financial data: A stipend is awarded (amount not specified). Funds are paid directly to the institution.

Duration: 1 year.

Number awarded: 1 or more each year.

Deadline: May of each year.

831 POLONIA FOUNDATION OF OHIO STUDENT GRANT

Polonia Foundation of Ohio, Inc.
6966 Broadway Avenue
Cleveland, OH 44105

Summary: To provide financial assistance to Ohio residents who are of Polish descent and interested in attending college, graduate school, or law school in any state.

Eligibility: Open to residents of Ohio who are of Polish descent. Applicants must be attending or planning to attend college, graduate school, or law school in any state. Along with their application, they must submit an essay of 250 to 500 words about themselves, including their familiarity with their Polish heritage, accomplishments, aspirations, future plans, and ultimate goals in life. Financial need, academic achievement, and involvement in Polish groups are considered in the selection process. U.S. citizenship or permanent resident status is required.

Financial data: The stipend ranges from $750 to $1,500.

Duration: 1 year; law students may apply for renewal, but other awards are nonrenewable.

Number awarded: Varies each year.

Deadline: May of each year.

832 PORTLAND WOMEN'S CLUB SCHOLARSHIP

Oregon Student Assistance Commission
Attn: Grants and Scholarships Division
1500 Valley River Drive, Suite 100
Eugene, OR 97401-2146
Phone: (541) 687-7395; (800) 452-8807, ext. 7395; Fax: (541) 687-7414; TDD: (800) 735-2900
Email: awardinfo@osac.state.or.us
Web: www.osac.state.or.us/osac_programs.html

Summary: To provide financial assistance for college to high school seniors and recent graduates, especially women, from Oregon who plan to attend college in any state.

Eligibility: Open to graduating seniors and recent graduates from high schools in Oregon who had a cumulative high school GPA of 3.0 or higher. Preference is given to women. Applicants must be attending or planning to attend a college or university in any state. Along with their application, they must submit an essay of 250 to 350 words on how their struggle with a life challenge has influenced their commitment to community involvement.

Financial data: The stipend is at least $1,500 per year.

Duration: 1 year; may be renewed if the recipient shows satisfactory academic progress and continued financial need.

Number awarded: Varies each year; recently, 5 of these scholarships were awarded.

Deadline: February of each year.

833 POSSIBLE WOMAN FOUNDATION INTERNATIONAL SCHOLARSHIP

Possible Woman Foundation International
1054 Redwood Drive
Norcross, GA 30093
Fax: (770) 381-9616
Email: info@possiblewomanfoundation
Web: www.possiblewomanfoundation.org/scholarships.html

Summary: To provide financial assistance for college or graduate school to women who are returning to school.

Eligibility: Open to women who are returning to school after a hiatus, changing careers, seeking advancement in their career or work life, or stay-at-home mothers entering the workplace and in need of additional education or training. Applicants must be at least 25 years of age and may be at any level of education (high school graduate, some college, 4-year college graduate, graduate school, doctoral). Along with their application, they must submit a 2-page essay on the topic, "How Having the Opportunity for Beginning or Continuing My Academic Education Will Positively Impact My Life." Selection is based on the essay, career and life goals, leadership and participation in community activities, honors and awards received, and financial need. U.S. citizenship or permanent resident status is required and study must be conducted in the United States.

Financial data: The stipend ranges from $2,000 to $5,000. Funds are paid directly to the recipient's institution.

Duration: 1 year; nonrenewable.

Number awarded: Varies each year; recently, 6 of these scholarships were awarded.

Deadline: January of each year.

834 POST-9/11 GI BILL

Department of Veterans Affairs
Attn: Veterans Benefits Administration
810 Vermont Avenue, N.W.
Washington, DC 20420
Phone: (202) 418-4343; (888) GI-BILL1
Web: www.gibill.va.gov/gi_bill_info/CH33/Benefit_Comparison_Chart.htm

Summary: To provide financial assistance to veterans or military personnel who entered service on or after September 11, 2001.

Eligibility: Open to current and former military who served on active duty for at least 90 aggregate days after September 11, 2001. Applicants must be planning to enroll at an accredited college or university as an undergraduate or graduate student; study in a certificate program, on-the-job training, apprenticeship program, flight training, and non-college degree study do not qualify for support.

Financial data: Active-duty personnel receive payment of tuition and fees, up to the level of tuition and fees at the most expensive public institution of higher learning in their state of residence; the actual amount depends on the state of residence and the length of service completed. Veterans also receive a monthly housing allowance based on the Basic Allowance for Housing (BAH) for an E-5 with dependents at the location of the school they are attending (or $1,333 per month at schools in foreign countries); an annual book allowance of $1,000; and (for participants who live in a rural county remote from an educational institution) a rural benefit payment of $500 per year.

Duration: Most participants receive up to 36 months of entitlement under this program.

Number awarded: Varies each year.

Deadline: Deadline not specified.

835 PRINCIPAL'S LEADERSHIP AWARDS

National Association of Secondary School Principals
Attn: Department of Student Activities
1904 Association Drive
Reston, VA 20191-1537
Phone: (703) 860-7252; (800) 253-7746, ext. 252; Fax: (703) 476-5432
Email: recognition@principals.org
Web: www.principals.org/AwardsandRecognition/StudentAwards.aspx

Summary: To recognize and reward, with college scholarships, high school seniors who demonstrate outstanding leadership.

Eligibility: Open to high school seniors. Each principal of a public, private, or parochial high school in the United States or Puerto Rico may nominate 1 student leader from the top 20% of the senior class. Nominees must also submit an original essay. Selection is based primarily on leadership qualities, as judged by participation in service organizations and clubs, achievements in the arts and sciences, employment experience, and academic record. U.S. citizenship is not required.

Financial data: Stipends range from $1,000 to $12,000.

Duration: The awards are presented annually.

Number awarded: 100 each year: the national winner at $12,000, the national finalist at $8,500, the national semi-finalist at $5,000, 5 regional winners at $1,500 each, and 92 other winners at $1,000 each.

Deadline: Principals must submit their nomination by December of each year.

836 PRISCILLA MAXWELL ENDICOTT SCHOLARSHIPS

Connecticut Women's Golf Association
c/o Judy Gamble, Scholarship Committee
27 Cold Spring Circle
Shelton, CT 06484
Phone: (203) 929-0435
Email: scholarships@cwga.org
Web: www.cwga.org/CWGA/index.php?section=16

Summary: To provide financial assistance to women golfers from Connecticut who are interested in attending college in any state.

Eligibility: Open to high school seniors and college students who are residents of Connecticut attending or planning to attend a 4-year college or university in any state. Applicants must be active women golfers with a handicap. Along with their application, they must submit a 200-word essay on how golf has made an impact on their life. Selection is based on participation in golf programs, academic achievement, and financial need.

Financial data: The maximum stipend is $3,000 per year.

Duration: Up to 4 years.

Number awarded: Varies each year; recently, 5 of these scholarships were awarded.

Deadline: April of each year.

837 PRISCILLA R. MORTON SCHOLARSHIPS

United Methodist Higher Education Foundation
Attn: Scholarships Administrator
1001 19th Avenue South
P.O. Box 340005
Nashville, TN 37203-0005
Phone: (615) 340-7385; (800) 811-8110; Fax: (615) 340-7330
Email: umhefscholarships@gbhem.org
Web: www.umhef.org/receive.php?id=endowed_funds

Summary: To provide financial assistance to members of the United Methodist Church who are interested in working on an undergraduate, graduate, or professional degree.

Eligibility: Open to undergraduate, graduate, and professional students who have been active, full members of a United Methodist Church for at least 1 year prior to applying. Applicants must have a GPA of 3.5 or higher and be able to demonstrate financial need. Along with their application, they must submit a 200-word essay on their involvement and/or leadership responsibilities in their church, school, and community within the last 3 years. U.S. citizenship or permanent resident status is required. Preference is given to students enrolled or planning to enroll full-time at a United Methodist–related college, university, seminary, or theological school.

Financial data: The stipend is at least $1,000 per year.

Duration: 1 year; recipients may reapply.

Number awarded: Varies each year; recently, 21 of these scholarships were awarded.

Deadline: May of each year.

838 PROFESSOR ULLA HEDNER SCHOLARSHIPS

Novo Nordisk Inc.
Attn: Customer Care
100 College Road West
Princeton, NJ 08540
Phone: (609) 987-5800; (877) NOVO-777; Fax: (800) 826-6993
Web: www.changingpossibilities-us.com/SupportPrograms/Education.aspx

Summary: To provide financial assistance to high school seniors and current college students who have a bleeding disorder.

Eligibility: Open to high school seniors and students under 23 years of age currently enrolled in college or vocational school. Applicants must have hemophilia with an inhibitor or factor VII deficiency. Along with their application, they must submit a 500-word essay on 1 of the following topics: 1) how has having hemophilia with inhibitors, congenital factor VII deficiency, or acquired hemophilia affected their life; 2) how has having hemophilia with inhibitors, congenital factor VII deficiency, or acquired hemophilia affected their educational goals; or 3) how will they use their education to achieve their life goals.

Financial data: Stipends range from $2,000 to $7,000 per year.

Duration: 1 year; recipients may reapply.

Number awarded: Varies each year.

Deadline: April of each year.

839 PROJECT RED FLAG ACADEMIC SCHOLARSHIP FOR WOMEN WITH BLEEDING DISORDERS

National Hemophilia Foundation
Attn: Manager of Education
P.O. Box 971483
Ypsilanti, MI 48197
Phone: (734) 890-2504
Email: pflax@hemophilia.org
Web: www.projectredflag.org/scholarship.htm

Summary: To provide financial assistance for college or graduate school to women who have hemophilia, von Willebrand Disease, or a clotting factor deficiency.

Eligibility: Open to women who are entering or already enrolled in an undergraduate or graduate program at a university, college, or accredited vocational school. Applicants must have von Willebrand Disease, hemophilia or other clotting factor deficiency, or carrier status. Along with their application, they must submit a 250-word essay that describes how their education and future career plans will benefit others in the bleeding disorders community. Financial need is not considered in the selection process.

Financial data: The stipend is $2,500.

Duration: 1 year.

Number awarded: 2 each year.

Deadline: May of each year.

840 PRUDENTIAL SPIRIT OF COMMUNITY AWARDS

National Association of Secondary School Principals
Attn: Department of Student Activities
1904 Association Drive
Reston, VA 20191-1537
Phone: (703) 860-7308; (800) 253-7746, ext. 308; Fax: (703) 476-5432
Email: spirit@principals.org
Web: www.principals.org/AwardsandRecognition/StudentAwards.aspx

Summary: To recognize and reward middle level and high school students who demonstrate exemplary community service.

Eligibility: Open to students in grades 5–12 at public and private schools in the United States. Students must submit 500-word essays on 1) what motivated them to do their volunteer work; 2) the effort required to do their volunteer work; 3) what their volunteer activity accomplished; and 4) what they got out of their volunteer work. Each school may select 1 honoree for every 1,000 students. At the local level, honorees are chosen on the basis of their individual community service activity or significant leadership in a group activity that has taken place during the previous year. Local honorees are then certified by their school principal, Girl Scout council executive director, county 4-H agent, American Red Cross chapter official, YMCA representative, or HandsOn Network of the Points of Light Institute to compete at the state level. As a result of that judging, 1 high school and 1 middle level student in each state and the District of Columbia are named state honorees. The state honorees then compete for national awards.

Financial data: Each state honoree receives $1,000, a silver medallion, and an all-expense paid trip to Washington, D.C. to compete at the national level. National honorees receive an additional $5,000, a gold medallion, a crystal trophy for their school or organization, and a $5,000 grant for the nonprofit, charitable organization of their choice.

Duration: The competition is held annually.

Number awarded: 102 state honorees are chosen each year: 1 middle level student and 1 high school student from each state and the District of Columbia; 10 of those (5 middle level students and 5 high school students) are named national honorees.

Deadline: Students must submit applications to their principal, Girl Scout council, county 4-H agent, American Red Cross chapter, YMCA, or HandsOn Network by October of each year.

841 PUBLIC EDUCATION AND CITIZENSHIP STATEWIDE ESSAY CONTEST

Grand Lodge of Free & Accepted Masons of the State of Florida
Attn: Public Education and Citizenship Committee
220 North Ocean Street
P.O. Box 1020
Jacksonville, FL 32201-1020
Phone: (800) 375-2339; Fax: (904) 632-3865
Email: scholarship@floridamason.org
Web: www.glflamason.org/masoniceducation/scholarship.html

Summary: To recognize and reward, with college scholarships, outstanding essays written by high school seniors in Florida on the importance of education.

Eligibility: Open to all graduating high school seniors in Florida who will be attending a state-supported school in Florida during the following semester/quarter. State-supported schools include any community college, university, or division of higher learning governed by the State Board of Regents. Students are invited to submit a 1,000-word essay on "Why Education Is Important." All work must be original. Essays are judged on merit, without regard to sex, race, creed, or religion.

Financial data: The award is $1,000. Funds are paid to the recipient's school.

Duration: The competition is held annually.

Number awarded: 10 each year.

Deadline: February of each year.

842 PURSUING VICTORY WITH HONOR SCHOLARSHIPS

New Mexico Activities Association
Attn: Associate Director
6600 Palomas Avenue, N.E.
Albuquerque, NM 87109
Phone: (505) 923-3275; (888) 820-NMAA; Fax: (505) 923-3114
Email: mmartinez@nmact.org
Web: www.nmact.org/scholarship_information_forms

Summary: To provide financial assistance to high school seniors in New Mexico who have demonstrated outstanding sportsmanship through participation in sanctioned sports and extracurricular activities and plan to attend college in any state.

Eligibility: Open to seniors graduating from high schools in New Mexico who have participated in sports and/or extracurricular activities sanctioned by the New Mexico Activities Association (NMAA) throughout their high school career. They must be planning to attend a college or university in any state. Along with their application, they must submit a 1-page personal statement on the importance of sportsmanship and its relevance in interscholastic activities and life. Awards are presented to students who have exhibited true sportsmanship by pursuing victory with honor. Financial need is not considered.

Financial data: The stipend is $1,000. From among all its scholarship recipients, the NMAA selects the 2 most outstanding and awards them a stipend of $2,500.

Duration: 1 year.

Number awarded: 6 each year. The NMAA also awards 2 additional at large scholarships to applicants for all its programs.

Deadline: February of each year.

843 QUALITY OF LIFE AWARDS

Miss America Pageant
Attn: Scholarship Department
222 New Road, Suite 700
Linwood, NJ 08221
Phone: (609) 653-8700, ext. 127; Fax: (609) 653-8740
Email: info@missamerica.org
Web: www.missamerica.org/scholarships/quality.aspx

Summary: To recognize and reward, with college scholarships, women who participate in the Miss America Pageant at the national level and demonstrate outstanding community service.

Eligibility: Open to women who compete at the national level of the Miss America Pageant and demonstrate a commitment to enhancing the quality of life for others through volunteerism and community service. Applicants must demonstrate that they have fulfilled a legitimate need in their community through the creation, development, and/or participation in a community service project. Selection is based on the depth of service, creativity of the project, and effects on the lives of others.

Financial data: The awards are college scholarships of $6,000 for the winner, $4,000 for the first runner-up, and $2,000 for the second runner-up.

Duration: The awards are presented annually.

Number awarded: 3 each year.

Deadline: Deadline not specified.

844 QUANDEL GROUP "GOOD CITIZEN" SCHOLARSHIPS

Association of Independent Colleges and Universities of Pennsylvania
101 North Front Street
Harrisburg, PA 17101-1405
Phone: (717) 232-8649; Fax: (717) 233-8574
Email: info@aicup.org
Web: www.aicup.org

Summary: To provide financial assistance to students from any state who are enrolled at member institutions of the Association of Independent Colleges and Universities of Pennsylvania (AICUP) and have demonstrated outstanding commitment to community service.

Eligibility: Open to undergraduate students from any state enrolled full-time at AICUP colleges and universities. Applicants must have shown an extraordinary commitment to community service and have demonstrated creativity in shaping their volunteer activities. Along with their application, they must submit a 2-page essay on their volunteer or extracurricular activities on and off campus, how those activities relate to their major, their career and academic goals after graduation, and how they will remain involved in their community after graduation. Selection is based on the extent of their volunteer and community service activities (30%), leadership activities and taking initiative (30%), evidence of commitment to community service (30%), and additional material, such as reference letters (10%). There is no minimum GPA requirement; grades are considered only in the event of a tie. Applications must be submitted to the financial aid office at the AICUP college or university that the student attends.

Financial data: The stipend is $1,000.

Duration: 1 year.

Number awarded: Varies each year; recently, 8 of these scholarships were awarded.

Deadline: April of each year.

845 QUE LLUEVA CAFE SCHOLARSHIPS

Chicano Organizing & Research in Education
P.O. Box 160144

Sacramento, CA 95816
Email: information@ca-core.org
Web: www.ca-core.org/scholarships

Summary: To provide financial assistance to undocumented Latino students who are interested in attending college.

Eligibility: Open to undocumented Latino students in the United States and Puerto Rico. Applicants must be high school or GED graduates planning to enroll for the first time at an accredited college or university in the United States or Puerto Rico.

Financial data: A stipend is awarded (amount not specified).

Duration: 1 year.

Number awarded: Varies each year.

Deadline: February of each year.

846 R. PRESTON WOODRUFF, JR. SCHOLARSHIPS

Arkansas Student Loan Authority
3801 Woodland Heights, Suite 200
Little Rock, AR 72212
Phone: (501) 682-2952; (800) 443-6030
Web: www.asla.info/collegeplanning/woodruffscholarship.htm

Summary: To provide financial assistance to residents of Arkansas or students attending a postsecondary institution in the state.

Eligibility: Open to 1) residents of Arkansas, who may be attending a postsecondary institution in or out of the state; and 2) residents of other states attending a postsecondary institution in Arkansas. Postsecondary educational institutions include 2-year colleges, 4-year colleges and universities, and technical and trade schools. Applicants may enter online or by submitting a postcard with their name, address, telephone number, and name of their educational institution. Winners are selected at random. Once selected, students must submit a 500-word essay on an assigned topic. The author of the essay judged to be most outstanding receives a renewable scholarship.

Financial data: The stipend is $1,000. Funds are mailed to the financial aid office at the designated school.

Duration: 1 year; of the scholarships awarded each year, 1 may be renewed up to 3 additional years but the others are nonrenewable.

Number awarded: 25 each year.

Deadline: March of each year.

847 RALPH AND RUTH STROTHER SCHOLARSHIP

Epsilon Sigma Alpha International
Attn: ESA Foundation
P.O. Box 270517
Fort Collins, CO 80527
Phone: (970) 223-2824; Fax: (970) 223-4456
Email: esainfo@esaintl.com
Web: www.esaintl.com/esaf

Summary: To provide financial assistance to residents of New Mexico planning to attend college in the state.

Eligibility: Open to residents of New Mexico who are 1) graduating high school seniors with a GPA of 3.0 or higher or with minimum scores of 22 on the ACT or 1030 on the combined critical reading and mathematics SAT; 2) enrolled in college with a GPA of 3.0 or higher; 3) enrolled at a technical school or returning to school after an absence for retraining of job skills or obtaining a degree; or 4) engaged in online study through an accredited college, university, or vocational school. Applicants must be attending or planning to attend a school in New Mexico and major in any field. Selection is based on character (10%), leadership (10%), service (5%), financial need (25%), and scholastic ability (50%).

Financial data: The stipend is $1,000.

Duration: 1 year; may be renewed.

Number awarded: 1 each year.

Deadline: January of each year.

848 RAY PELLEGRINI "REACH FOR THE STARS" SCHOLARSHIP

Vermont Principals' Association
Attn: Associate Executive Director
2 Prospect Street, Suite 3
Montpelier, VT 05602
Phone: (802) 229-0547
Email: wscott@vaponline.org
Web: www.vpaonline.org/pellegrini_scholarship.asp

Summary: To provide financial assistance to high school seniors in Vermont who are entering a college in the state and the first generation in their family to attend college.

Eligibility: Open to seniors graduating from high schools in Vermont who plan to attend college in the state and remain in Vermont after graduation. Applicants must be the first generation in their family to attend college. In the selection process, strong consideration is given to community service and/or volunteer work; financial need is not a factor.

Financial data: The stipend is $1,000. Funds are disbursed after completion of the first semester at a college or university in Vermont.

Duration: 1 year.

Number awarded: 1 each year.

Deadline: April of each year.

849 RAYMOND T. WELLINGTON, JR. MEMORIAL SCHOLARSHIP

American Legion Auxiliary
Department of New York
112 State Street, Suite 1310
Albany, NY 12207
Phone: (518) 463-1162; (800) 421-6348; Fax: (518) 449-5406
Email: alanyterry@nycap.rr.com
Web: www.deptny.org/Scholarships.htm

Summary: To provide financial assistance to New York residents who are the descendants of veterans and interested in attending college in any state.

Eligibility: Open to residents of New York who are high school seniors or graduates and attending or planning to attend an accredited college or university in any state. Applicants must be the children, grandchildren, or great-grandchildren of veterans who served during specified periods of war time. Along with their application, they must submit a 700-word autobiography that includes their interests, experiences, long-range plans, and goals. Selection is based on character (15%), Americanism (15%), community involvement (15%), leadership (15%), scholarship (20%), and financial need (20%). U.S. citizenship is required.

Financial data: The stipend is $1,000. Funds are paid directly to the recipient's school.

Duration: 1 year.

Number awarded: 1 each year.

Deadline: February of each year.

850 REAM'S FOOD STORES SCHOLARSHIPS

Utah Sports Hall of Fame Foundation
c/o Berdean Jarman, Scholarship Chair
873 West 1200 North
Orem, UT 84057
Phone: (801) 225-3352
Web: www.utahsportshalloffame.org/AboutUs.html

Summary: To recognize and reward outstanding high school seniors in Utah who have been involved in athletics and are interested in attending college in the state.

Eligibility: Open to high school seniors. Each high school in Utah may nominate 1 boy and 1 girl who are graduating this year. Nominees must be planning to attend college in the state. Selection is based on academic record, personal character, financial need, leadership qualities, and involvement in athletic activities, including football, basketball, cross country, volleyball, tennis, track and field, soccer, rodeo, baseball, swimming, wrestling, officiating, community recreation, or intramural sports.

Financial data: The stipend is $2,000. Funds are paid to the recipient's institution.

Duration: 1 year; nonrenewable.

Number awarded: 6 each year: 3 to boys and 3 to girls.

Deadline: March of each year.

851 REGIONAL GATORADE AWARDS OF AMERICAN LEGION BASEBALL

American Legion Baseball
700 North Pennsylvania Street
Indianapolis, IN 46204
Phone: (317) 630-1249; Fax: (317) 630-1369
Email: acy@legion.org
Web: www.baseball.legion.org

Summary: To recognize and reward, with college scholarships, participants in the American Legion baseball program who demonstrate outstanding leadership.
Eligibility: Open to participants in the American Legion baseball regional tournaments and the American Legion World Series. Candidates must be high school seniors or graduates who will be entering college as a freshman in the fall; students still in high school are not eligible. Selection is based on integrity, mental attitude, cooperation, citizenship, sportsmanship, scholastic aptitude, and general good conduct. Winners are named in each of 8 regions, and then 1 of them receives additional funding as the George W. Rulon American Legion Player of the Year.
Financial data: Each regional winner receives a $1,000 scholarship. The winner selected as the George W. Rulon American Legion Player of the Year receives an additional $2,500 in scholarships.
Duration: The awards are presented annually.
Number awarded: 1 each year.
Deadline: Deadline not specified.

852 REGIONAL UNIVERSITY BACCALAUREATE SCHOLARSHIP PROGRAM

Oklahoma State Regents for Higher Education
Attn: Director of Scholarship and Grant Programs
655 Research Parkway, Suite 200
P.O. Box 108850
Oklahoma City, OK 73101-8850
Phone: (405) 225-9239; (800) 858-1840; Fax: (405) 225-9230
Email: studentinfo@osrhe.edu
Web: www.okhighered.org/student-center/financial-aid/rubs.shtml
Summary: To provide financial assistance to Oklahoma residents who are attending designated publicly-supported regional universities in the state.
Eligibility: Open to residents of Oklahoma who are attending 1 of 11 designated regional public institutions in the state and working on an undergraduate degree. Applicants must 1) be designated a National Merit Semifinalist or Commended Student; or 2) have an ACT score of at least 30 and have an exceptional GPA and class ranking as determined by the collegiate institution. Selection is based on academic promise.
Financial data: The stipend is $3,000 per year. Awardees also receive a resident tuition waiver from the institution.
Duration: Up to 4 years if the recipient maintains a cumulative GPA of 3.25 or higher and full-time enrollment.
Number awarded: Up to 165 each year: 15 at each of the 11 participating regional universities.
Deadline: Deadline not specified.

853 REGULAR AIR FORCE ROTC HISPANIC SERVING INSTITUTION SCHOLARSHIP PROGRAM

U.S. Air Force
Attn: Headquarters AFROTC/RRUC
551 East Maxwell Boulevard
Maxwell AFB, AL 36112-5917
Phone: (334) 953-2091; (866) 4-AFROTC; Fax: (334) 953-6167
Email: afrotc1@maxwell.af.mil
Web: afrotc.com/scholarships/in-college/minority-school-scholarships
Summary: To provide financial assistance to students at Hispanic Serving Institutions (HSIs) who are willing to join Air Force ROTC in college and serve as Air Force officers following completion of their bachelor's degree.
Eligibility: Open to U.S. citizens at least 17 years of age who are currently enrolled at an HSI that has an Air Force ROTC unit on campus or that has a cross-enrollment agreement with another school that hosts a unit. Applicants do not need to be Hispanic, as long as they are attending an HSI and have a cumulative GPA of 2.5 or higher. At the time of commissioning, they may be no more than 31 years of age. They must be able to pass the Air Force Officer Qualifying Test (AFOQT) and the Air Force ROTC Physical Fitness Test. Currently, the program is accepting applications from students with any major.
Financial data: Awards are type 2 AFROTC scholarships that provide for payment of tuition and fees, to a maximum of $18,000 per year, plus an annual book allowance of $900. Recipients are also awarded a tax-free subsistence allowance for 10 months of each year that is $350 per month during the sophomore year, $450 during the junior year, and $500 during the senior year.
Duration: 2 to 3 years, beginning during the current term.
Number awarded: Varies each year; AFROTC units at every HSI may nominate an unlimited number of cadets to receive these scholarships.
Deadline: Applications may be submitted at any time.

854 REGULAR AIR FORCE ROTC HISTORICALLY BLACK COLLEGES AND UNIVERSITIES SCHOLARSHIP PROGRAM

U.S. Air Force
Attn: Headquarters AFROTC/RRUC
551 East Maxwell Boulevard
Maxwell AFB, AL 36112-5917
Phone: (334) 953-2091; (866) 4-AFROTC; Fax: (334) 953-6167
Email: afrotc1@maxwell.af.mil
Web: afrotc.com/scholarships/in-college/minority-school-scholarships
Summary: To provide financial assistance to students at Historically Black Colleges and Universities (HBCUs) who are willing to serve as Air Force officers following completion of their bachelor's degree.
Eligibility: Open to U.S. citizens at least 17 years of age who are currently enrolled at an HBCU that has an Air Force ROTC unit on campus or that has a cross-enrollment agreement with another school that hosts a unit. Applicants do not need to be African American, as long as they are attending an HBCU and have a cumulative GPA of 2.5 or higher. At the time of commissioning, they may be no more than 31 years of age. They must be able to pass the Air Force Officer Qualifying Test (AFOQT) and the Air Force ROTC Physical Fitness Test. Currently, the program is accepting applications from students with any major.
Financial data: Awards are type 2; AFROTC scholarships that provide for payment of tuition and fees, to a maximum of $18,000 per year, plus an annual book allowance of $900. Recipients are also awarded a tax-free subsistence allowance for 10 months of each year that is $350 per month during the sophomore year, $450 during the junior year, and $500 during the senior year.
Duration: 2 to 3 years, beginning during the current term.
Number awarded: Varies each year; AFROTC units at every HBCU may nominate an unlimited number of cadets to receive these scholarships.
Deadline: Applications may be submitted at any time.

855 REHABGYM SCHOLARSHIP

Vermont Student Assistance Corporation
Attn: Scholarship Programs
10 East Allen Street
P.O. Box 2000
Winooski, VT 05404-2601
Phone: (802) 654-3798; (888) 253-4819; Fax: (802) 654-3765; TDD: (800) 281-3341 (within VT)
Email: info@vsac.org
Web: services.vsac.org/wps/wcm/connect/vsac/VSAC
Summary: To provide financial assistance to residents of Vermont who have undergone a significant physical challenge and plan to attend college in any state.
Eligibility: Open to residents of Vermont who are attending or planning to attend a college or university in any state. Applicants must be able to demonstrate that they have undergone a significant physical challenge or illness and have met the challenge with courage and perseverance. Along with their application, they must submit 1) a 100-word essay on any significant barriers that limit their access to education; and 2) a 250-word essay on what they believe distinguishes their application from others that may be submitted. Selection is based on those essays and financial need.
Financial data: The stipend is $1,000.
Duration: 1 year.
Number awarded: 1 or more each year.
Deadline: March of each year.

856 RENEE FELDMAN SCHOLARSHIPS

Blinded Veterans Association Auxiliary
c/o Barbara Stocking, Scholarship Chair
3801 Coco Grove Avenue
Miami, FL 33133
Phone: (305) 446-8008
Summary: To provide financial assistance for college to spouses and children of blinded veterans.
Eligibility: Open to children and spouses of blinded veterans who are attending or planning to attend a college, university, community college, or vocational school. The veteran is not required to be a member of the Blinded Veterans Association. Applicants must submit a 300-word essay on their career goals and aspirations. Selection is based on that essay, academic achievement, and letters of reference.
Financial data: Stipends are $2,000 or $1,000. Funds are paid directly to the recipient's school to be applied to tuition, books, and general fees.
Duration: 1 year.
Number awarded: 5 each year: 3 at $2,000 and 2 at $1,000.
Deadline: April of each year.

857 RESERVE EDUCATIONAL ASSISTANCE PROGRAM

Department of Veterans Affairs
Attn: Veterans Benefits Administration
810 Vermont Avenue, N.W.
Washington, DC 20420
Phone: (202) 418-4343; (888) GI-BILL1
Web: www.gibill.va.gov/GI_Bill_Info/benefits.htm

Summary: To provide financial assistance for college or graduate school to members of the Reserves or National Guard who are called to active duty during a period of national emergency.

Eligibility: Open to members of the Reserve elements of the Army, Navy, Air Force, Marine Corps, and Coast Guard, as well as the Army National Guard and the Air National Guard. To be eligible, a Reservist must 1) have a 6-year obligation to serve in the Selected Reserves signed after June 30, 1985 (or, if an officer, agree to serve 6 years in addition to the original obligation); 2) complete Initial Active Duty for Training (IADT); 3) meet the requirements for a high school diploma or equivalent certificate before completing IADT; and 4) remain in good standing in a drilling Selected Reserve unit. Reservists who enlisted after June 30, 1985 can receive benefits for undergraduate degrees, graduate training, or technical courses leading to certificates at colleges and universities. Reservists whose 6-year commitment began after September 30, 1990 may also use these benefits for a certificate or diploma from business, technical, or vocational schools; cooperative training; apprenticeship or on-the-job training; correspondence courses; independent study programs; tutorial assistance; remedial, deficiency, or refresher training; flight training; or state-approved alternative teacher certification programs.

Financial data: For full-time study at a college or university, the current monthly rate is $528.40 for personnel with consecutive service of 90 days but less than 1 year, $792.60 for personnel with consecutive service of more than 1 year but less than 2 years, or $1,056.80 for those with consecutive service of 2 years or more. Reduced rates apply for part-time college or university study, apprenticeship and on-the-job training, licensing and certification training, cooperative education, correspondence courses, and flight training.

Duration: Up to 36 months for full-time study, 48 months for three-quarter study, 72 months for half-time study, or 144 months for less than half-time study.

Number awarded: Varies each year.

Deadline: Applications may be submitted at any time.

858 REV. DR. KAREN LAYMAN GIFT OF HOPE: 21ST CENTURY SCHOLARS PROGRAM

United Methodist Church
Attn: General Board of Higher Education and Ministry
Office of Loans and Scholarships
1001 19th Avenue South
P.O. Box 340007
Nashville, TN 37203-0007
Phone: (615) 340-7344; Fax: (615) 340-7367
Email: umscholar@gbhem.org
Web: www.gbhem.org/loansandscholarships

Summary: To provide financial assistance to undergraduate Methodist students who can demonstrate leadership in the church.

Eligibility: Open to full-time undergraduate students at United Methodist institutions who have been active, full members of a United Methodist Church for at least 3 years prior to applying. Applicants must have a GPA of 3.0 or higher and be able to show evidence of leadership and participation in religious activities during college either through their campus ministry or through local United Methodist Churches in the city where their college is located. They must also show how their education will provide leadership for the church and society and improve the quality of life for others. U.S. citizenship, permanent resident status, or membership in the Central Conferences of the United Methodist Church is required. Financial need is considered in the selection process.

Financial data: The stipend is $1,000.

Duration: 1 year; recipients may reapply.

Number awarded: Varies each year; recently, 1,000 of these scholarships were awarded.

Deadline: April of each year.

859 RHODE ISLAND ASSOCIATION OF FORMER LEGISLATORS SCHOLARSHIP

Rhode Island Foundation
Attn: Funds Administrator
One Union Station
Providence, RI 02903
Phone: (401) 427-4017; Fax: (401) 331-8085
Email: lmonahan@rifoundation.org
Web: www.rifoundation.org

Summary: To provide financial assistance to graduating high school seniors in Rhode Island who have been involved in community service activities and plan to attend college in any state.

Eligibility: Open to seniors graduating from high schools in Rhode Island who plan to attend a college or university in any state. Applicants must have distinguished themselves by their outstanding involvement in community service and be able to demonstrate financial need. Along with their application, they must submit an essay (up to 300 words) explaining the nature of their community service participation, the work's influence on them, and how they plan to continue their public service work into the future.

Financial data: The stipend is $1,500.

Duration: 1 year; nonrenewable.

Number awarded: 5 each year.

Deadline: May of each year.

860 RHODE ISLAND EDUCATIONAL BENEFITS FOR DISABLED AMERICAN VETERANS

Division of Veterans Affairs
480 Metacom Avenue
Bristol, RI 02809-0689
Phone: (401) 254-8350; Fax: (401) 254-2320; TDD: (401) 254-1345
Email: devangelista@dhs.ri.gov
Web: www.dhs.ri.gov/VeteransServices/tabid/307/Default.aspx

Summary: To provide assistance to disabled veterans in Rhode Island who wish to pursue higher education at a public institution in the state.

Eligibility: Open to permanent residents of Rhode Island who have been verified by the Department of Veterans Affairs (DVA) as having a disability of at least 10% resulting from military service.

Financial data: Eligible veterans are entitled to take courses at any public institution of higher education in Rhode Island without the payment of tuition, exclusive of other fees and charges.

Number awarded: Varies each year.

Deadline: Deadline not specified.

861 RICHARD T. NUSKE MEMORIAL SCHOLARSHIPS

Vietnam Veterans of America–Wisconsin State Council
c/o Virginia Nuske, Scholarship Committee Chair
N5448 Broder Road
Shawano, WI 54166
Phone: (715) 524-2487
Web: www.vva.org/vva-wisconsin.html

Summary: To recognize and reward high school seniors in Wisconsin who submit outstanding essays based on an interview of a Vietnam veteran, especially if the veteran is a relative.

Eligibility: Open to seniors graduating from high schools in Wisconsin who plan to attend an accredited institution of higher education in any state. Applicants must submit an essay, from 3 to 5 pages in length, based on an interview of a veteran of any branch who served on active duty anywhere in the world during the Vietnam War (from January 1, 1959 to May 7, 1975). Essays are judged on originality, appearance, and elements of grammar; up to 30 points may be awarded, depending on the quality of the essay. An additional 15 points are awarded if the student is the child or grandchild of the veteran; an additional 5 points are awarded if the student is another relative (niece, cousin) of the veteran.

Financial data: The award is a $1,500 scholarship that may be used at a college or university in any state.

Duration: The awards are presented annually.

Number awarded: 4 each year.

Deadline: January of each year.

862 RICHARD W. BENDICKSEN MEMORIAL SCHOLARSHIP

American Radio Relay League
Attn: ARRL Foundation
225 Main Street
Newington, CT 06111
Phone: (860) 594-0397; Fax: (860) 594-0259
Email: foundation@arrl.org
Web: www.arrlf.org/programs/scholarships

Summary: To provide financial assistance to licensed radio amateurs who are interested in working on an undergraduate degree in any field.

Eligibility: Open to undergraduate students at 4-year colleges and universities who have an active amateur radio license (any class). Applicants must submit an essay on the role amateur radio has played in their lives and provide documentation of financial need. They may be studying any academic area.

Financial data: The stipend is $1,000.

Duration: 1 year.

Number awarded: 1 each year.

Deadline: January of each year.

863 ROBERT AND ALTA VAN TRIES MASONIC LEGACY SCHOLARSHIP

Minnesota Masonic Charities
Attn: Scholarships
11501 Masonic Home Drive
Bloomington, MN 55437
Phone: (952) 948-6004; Fax: (952) 948-6210
Email: comments@mnmasonic.org
Web: mnmasoniccharities.org/content/signature-scholarships

Summary: To provide financial assistance to high school seniors in Minnesota who plan to attend college in any state or abroad.

Eligibility: Open to seniors graduating from high schools in Minnesota who have a GPA of 3.0 or higher. Applicants must be planning to attend a college or university in any geographic location, including outside of the United States. Along with their application, they must submit brief essays on 1) their accomplishments in classroom or extracurricular activities in which they took pride; 2) why they should receive this scholarship; and 3) the person after whom these scholarships are named with whom they most identify and why. They must also submit a long essay on the values of Masonry and the relationship of those to their own lives. In the selection process, no consideration is given to Masonic ties, age, gender, religion, national origin, or financial need.

Financial data: The stipend is $4,000 per year.

Duration: 1 year; may be renewed up to 3 additional years.

Number awarded: 1 each year.

Deadline: February of each year.

864 ROBERT C. BYRD HONORS SCHOLARSHIP PROGRAM

Department of Education
Attn: Office of Postsecondary Education
Institutional Development and Undergraduate Education Service
1990 K Street, N.W., Room 6051
Washington, DC 20006-8500
Phone: (202) 502-7657; Fax: (202) 502-7861
Email: darryl.davis@ed.gov
Web: www.ed.gov/programs/iduesbyrd/index.html

Summary: To provide financial assistance for college to outstanding high school seniors.

Eligibility: Open to U.S. citizens or eligible noncitizens who are graduating from a public or private high school (home-schooled students are also eligible) and planning to attend an accredited college, university, postsecondary vocational school, or proprietary institution of higher education as a full-time student. These awards are administered by an officially designated state educational agency (SEA) in each state that establishes the exact requirements for that state; typically, states require students to rank in the upper quarter of their high school class and have a minimum score of 1200 on the SAT or 27 on the ACT.

Financial data: The stipend is $1,500 per year.

Duration: 1 year; may be renewed up to 3 additional years as long as recipients maintain full-time enrollment and meet the satisfactory academic progress requirements of their school.

Number awarded: Varies each year; each state is allocated a number of these scholarships proportional to its population. Recently, a total of 26,855 new and renewal scholarships were granted.

Deadline: March of each year.

865 ROBERT D. BLUE SCHOLARSHIP

Treasurer of State
State Capitol Building
Des Moines, IA 50319-0005
Phone: (515) 281-3067; Fax: (515) 281-7562
Email: treasurer@tos.state.ia.us
Web: www.rdblue.org

Summary: To provide financial assistance to Iowa residents who are currently attending or planning to attend a college or university in the state.

Eligibility: Open to graduating high school seniors and students currently attending a college or university as an undergraduate or graduate student. Applicants must have spent the majority of their lives in Iowa and be attending or planning to attend a college or university in the state. They must submit a completed application form, an official transcript, 3 letters of recommendation, a statement of expenses and awards from their college financial aid office, and a 500-word essay on an individual from their community who has demonstrated the responsibilities of being a citizen in that community. Selection is based on that essay (25%), financial need (45%), academic performance (20%), and recommendations (10%).

Financial data: Stipends range from $500 to $1,000.

Duration: 1 year.

Number awarded: Varies each year; recently, 20 of these scholarships (all at $1,000) were awarded.

Deadline: May of each year.

866 ROBERT GUTHRIE PKU SCHOLARSHIP

National PKU News
6869 Woodlawn Avenue, N.E., Suite 116
Seattle, WA 98115-5469
Phone: (206) 525-8140; Fax: (206) 525-5023
Email: schuett@pkunews.org
Web: www.pkunews.org/guthrie/guthrie.htm

Summary: To provide financial assistance for college to students with phenylketonuria (PKU).

Eligibility: Open to college-age people from any country who have PKU and are on the required diet. Applicants must be accepted as an undergraduate at an accredited college or technical school before the scholarship is awarded, but they may apply before acceptance is confirmed. Along with their application, they must submit a statement that includes why they are applying for the scholarship, their educational objectives and career plans, extracurricular activities, honors and awards, their current diet and how they cope with it on a daily basis, their overall experience with PKU, their attitudes toward the PKU diet now and in the past, and the influence PKU has had on their life. Selection is based on that statement, academic record, educational and career goals, extracurricular activities, volunteer work, and letters of recommendation. Financial need is considered but is not required; students can be awarded a scholarship without having significant financial need.

Financial data: Stipends vary but recently have been $2,000.

Duration: 1 year.

Number awarded: Varies each year; recently, 4 of these scholarships were awarded.

Deadline: October of each year.

867 ROBERT R. LEE PROMISE CATEGORY A SCHOLARSHIP

Idaho State Board of Education
Len B. Jordan Office Building
650 West State Street, Room 307
P.O. Box 83720
Boise, ID 83720-0037
Phone: (208) 332-1574; Fax: (208) 334-2632
Email: scholarshiphelp@osbe.idaho.gov
Web: www.boardofed.idaho.gov/scholarships/promisea.asp

Summary: To provide financial assistance for college or professional/technical school to outstanding high school seniors in Idaho.

Eligibility: Open to graduating high school seniors who are Idaho residents planning to enroll full-time in academic or professional/technical programs in public or private institutions in the state. Academic applicants must also be in the top 10% of their class and have a cumulative GPA of 3.5 or higher and an ACT score of 28 or higher. Professional/technical applicants must have a cumulative GPA of 2.8 or higher and must take the COMPASS test (reading, writing, and algebra scores are required). U.S. citizenship is also required.

Financial data: The stipend is $3,000 per year.

Duration: 1 year. Academic scholarships may be renewed for up to 3 additional years and professional/technical scholarships may be renewed for up to 2 additional years; renewal is granted only if the recipient remains enrolled full-time with a rank in the top 50% of the students in the class and a GPA of 3.0 or higher.
Number awarded: Approximately 25 each year; academic students receive 75% of the awards and professional/technical students receive 25%.
Deadline: January of each year.

868 ROBERT S. SHUMAKE FAMILY FOUNDATION SCHOLARSHIP

Thurgood Marshall College Fund
Attn: Scholarship Manager
80 Maiden Lane, Suite 2204
New York, NY 10038
Phone: (212) 573-8487; (877) 690-8673; Fax: (212) 573-8497
Email: srogers@tmcfund.org
Web: www.thurgoodmarshallfund.net
Summary: To provide financial assistance to high school seniors whose school participated in the Robert S. Shumake Scholarship Relays and who plan to attend a college or university in any state.
Eligibility: Open to seniors graduating from high schools in Illinois, Indiana, Michigan, and Ohio that have participated in the Robert S. Shumake Scholarship Relays. Applicants must be U.S. citizens planning to attend an accredited 4-year college or university in any state. They must have a GPA of 2.5 or higher. Along with their application, they must submit a 250-word essay on the importance of education, homeownership, and entrepreneurship. Financial need is not considered in the selection process.
Financial data: The stipend is $2,500.
Duration: 1 year; nonrenewable.
Number awarded: 4 each year.
Deadline: March of each year.

869 ROBERT SMILEY SCHOLARSHIP

Iowa Girls High School Athletic Union
Attn: Scholarships
2900 Grand Avenue
P.O. Box 10348
Des Moines, IA 50306-0348
Phone: (515) 288-9741; Fax: (515) 284-1969
Email: lisa@ighsau.org
Web: www.ighsau.org
Summary: To provide financial assistance to female high school seniors in Iowa who have participated in athletics and plan to attend college in the state.
Eligibility: Open to women graduating from high schools in Iowa who have lettered in 1 varsity sport sponsored by the Iowa Girls High School Athletic Union (IGHSAU) each year of high school and have a GPA of 2.5 or higher. Applicants must be planning to attend a college or university in Iowa. Each high school in the state may nominate 1 student. Selection is based on academic achievements, athletic accomplishments, non-sports extracurricular activities, and community involvement.
Financial data: The stipend is $1,000.
Duration: 1 year.
Number awarded: 1 each year.
Deadline: March of each year.

870 RONALD MCDONALD HOUSE CHARITIES SCHOLARS PROGRAM

Ronald McDonald House Charities
Attn: U.S. Scholarship Program
One Kroc Drive
Oak Brook, IL 60523
Phone: (630) 623-7048; Fax: (630) 623-7488
Email: info@rmhc.org
Web: rmhc.org/what-we-do/rmhc-u-s-scholarships
Summary: To provide financial assistance for college to high school seniors in specified geographic areas.
Eligibility: Open to high school seniors in designated McDonald's market areas who are legal residents of the United States. Applicants must be planning to enroll full-time at an accredited 2- or 4-year college, university, or vocational/technical school. They must have a GPA of 2.7 or higher. Along with their application, they must submit a personal statement, up to 2 pages in length, on their career goals and desire to contribute to their community; information about unique, personal, or financial circumstances may be added. Selection is based on that statement, high school transcripts, a letter of recommendation, and financial need.
Financial data: Most awards are $1,000 per year. Funds are paid directly to the recipient's school.
Duration: 1 year; nonrenewable.
Number awarded: Varies each year; since RMHC began this program, it has awarded more than $37 million in scholarships.
Deadline: February of each year.

871 RONALD REAGAN COLLEGE LEADERS SCHOLARSHIP PROGRAM

Phillips Foundation
1 Massachusetts Avenue, N.W., Suite 620
Washington, DC 20001
Phone: (202) 250-3887, ext. 628
Email: jhollingsworth@thephillipsfoundation.org
Web: www.thephillipsfoundation.org/index.php?q=node/3
Summary: To provide financial assistance to college students who "demonstrate leadership on behalf of the cause of freedom, American values, and constitutional principles."
Eligibility: Open to U.S. citizens enrolled as full-time students at accredited 4-year degree-granting institutions in the United States or its possessions who are applying during their sophomore or junior year. Applicants must submit an essay of 500 to 750 words describing their personal background, career objectives, and scope of participation in activities that promote the cause of freedom, American values, and constitutional principles and addressing the ideological climate at their school. Selection is based on merit.
Financial data: Stipends currently are $5,000, $2,500, or $1,000 per year.
Duration: 1 year. Recipients who apply as sophomores use the scholarship during their junior year and may apply for renewal for their senior year. Recipients who apply as juniors use the scholarship during their senior year.
Number awarded: Varies each year; recently, this program awarded 40 new scholarships (6 at $5,000, 21 at $2,500, and 13 at $1,000) and 26 renewal scholarships (6 at $5,000, 12 at $2,500, and 8 at $1,000).
Deadline: January of each year.

872 ROOTHBERT FUND SCHOLARSHIPS AND GRANTS

Roothbert Fund, Inc.
475 Riverside Drive, Room 1830
New York, NY 10115
Phone: (212) 870-3116
Email: mail@roothbertfund.org
Web: www.roothbertfund.org/scholarships.php
Summary: To provide financial assistance for college or graduate school to residents of designated eastern states who are primarily motivated by spiritual values.
Eligibility: Open to undergraduate and graduate students who are current residents of or planning to move to the following states: Connecticut, Delaware, District of Columbia, Maine, Maryland, Massachusetts, New Hampshire, New Jersey, New York, North Carolina, Ohio, Pennsylvania, Rhode Island, Vermont, Virginia, or West Virginia. Applicants are not required to be adherents of any particular form of religious practice or worship, but they must be motivated by spiritual values. They may be studying any field at a college or university in the United States. Preference is given to applicants with outstanding academic records who are considering teaching as a vocation. Finalists are invited to New York, New Haven, Philadelphia, or Washington, D.C. for an interview; applicants must affirm their willingness to attend the interview if invited. The fund does not pay transportation expenses for those asked to interview. Being invited for an interview does not guarantee a scholarship, but no grants are awarded without an interview.
Financial data: Grants range from $2,000 to $3,000 per year.
Duration: 1 year; may be renewed.
Number awarded: Approximately 20 each year.
Deadline: January of each year.

873 ROSA L. PARKS SCHOLARSHIPS

Rosa L. Parks Scholarship Foundation
P.O. Box 950
Detroit, MI 48231
Phone: (313) 222-2538
Email: rpscholarship@dnps.com

Web: www.rosaparksscholarshipfoundation.org

Summary: To provide financial assistance for college to high school seniors in Michigan.

Eligibility: Open to seniors graduating from public and private high schools in Michigan. Applicants must have a GPA of 2.5 or higher. Along with their application, they must submit an essay, high school transcript, and ACT or SAT scores. Selection is based on academic achievement, community service and leadership, financial need, and commitment to the principles embraced by Rosa Parks and the civil rights movement.

Financial data: The stipend is $2,000.

Duration: 1 year; nonrenewable.

Number awarded: Approximately 40 each year; since this program was established, more then 800 high school seniors have received scholarships.

Deadline: February of each year.

874 ROSAMOND P. HAEBERLE MEMORIAL SCHOLARSHIP

Daughters of the American Revolution–Michigan State Society
c/o Toni Barger, Memorial Scholarship Committee
130 Lake Region Circle
Winter Haven, FL 33881-9535
Phone: (863) 326-1687
Email: tonibarger@aol.com
Web: www.michigandar.org/scholarships.htm

Summary: To provide financial assistance to Michigan veterans and military personnel interested in attending college in the state.

Eligibility: Open to residents of Michigan who have served on active duty in the U.S. armed forces (including Reserves and National Guard) for at least 6 continuous months and are either currently serving in the armed forces or have received a separation from active duty under honorable conditions. Applicants must be currently accepted to and/or enrolled at a 2- or 4-year accredited college, university, or technical/trade school in Michigan. They must be enrolled at least half-time and have a cumulative high school or undergraduate GPA of 2.5 or higher. Along with their application, they must submit a 1-page essay on what serving their country has meant to them and how it has influenced their future goals and priorities. Selection is based on academic performance, extracurricular activities, community service, potential to succeed in an academic environment, financial need, and military service record.

Financial data: The stipend is $1,500.

Duration: 1 year.

Number awarded: 1 each year.

Deadline: March of each year.

875 ROSE SCHOLARSHIP

Zonta International District 10 Foundation
c/o Janis Wood
3 Surrey Lane
McLoud, OK 74851
Phone: (405) 273-3918
Email: janis@zontadistrict10.org
Web: www.zontadistrict10.org/RoseScholarship.htm

Summary: To provide financial assistance to nontraditional college students in designated states.

Eligibility: Open to nontraditional students who live in Arkansas, Louisiana, New Mexico, Oklahoma, or Texas. Applicants must be attending an accredited educational institution to obtain postsecondary training or certification in a program that does not require a baccalaureate degree. They must be able to document financial need, but other factors considered in the selection process include good citizenship, character, reputation, and moral and ethical standing. U.S. citizenship is required.

Financial data: The stipend is $1,000. Funds are paid directly to the institution providing the certification or training.

Duration: 1 year.

Number awarded: 1 each year.

Deadline: March of each year.

876 RURAL AMERICAN SCHOLARSHIP

Rural American Scholarship Fund
P.O. Box 2674
Oak Harbor, WA 98277-2674
Phone: (360) 679-1979; Fax: (360) 679-1979
Email: Therasf@comcast.net
Web: www.ruralasf.org

Summary: To provide financial assistance to older students from rural areas who are attending a college or university in the Northwest.

Eligibility: Open to students who currently reside in or hail from a rural community. Applicants must be at least 23 years of age, have completed at least 90 college credits or an associate degree, have a cumulative GPA of 2.8 or higher, and be enrolled full-time at 1 of 8 designated colleges in the Northwest. Along with their application, they must submit a brief autobiography describing how their experiences have shaped who they are, their hopes and dreams for the future, their proposed field of study, how they plan to use the knowledge and skills they acquire through their education, what it means to be from rural America, and why they believe they qualify for this scholarship. As part of the selection process, an interview will be used to assess need, motivation, commitment, and performance. Awards are granted in the following priority order: 1) first-time degree seekers; 2) prior recipients who need a fifth year to complete their degree; and 3) master's degree candidates. Financial need is considered.

Financial data: Stipends range from $1,500 to $5,000.

Duration: 1 year; recipients may reapply.

Number awarded: Varies each year; recently, 70 of these scholarships were awarded.

Deadline: February of each year.

877 RUTH ANN JOHNSON FUND SCHOLARSHIPS

Greater Kanawha Valley Foundation
Attn: Scholarship Coordinator
1600 Huntington Square
900 Lee Street, East
P.O. Box 3041
Charleston, WV 25331-3041
Phone: (304) 346-3620; (800) 467-5909; Fax: (304) 346-3640
Email: shoover@tgkvf.org
Web: www.tgkvf.org/scholar.htm

Summary: To provide financial assistance to residents of West Virginia who are interested in attending college in any state.

Eligibility: Open to residents of West Virginia who are attending or planning to attend a college or university anywhere in the country. Applicants must have an ACT score of 20 or higher; be able to demonstrate good moral character, academic excellence, and extreme financial need; and have a GPA of 2.5 or higher.

Financial data: The stipend is $1,000 per year.

Duration: 1 year; may be renewed.

Number awarded: Varies each year; recently, 55 of these scholarships were awarded.

Deadline: January of each year.

878 RYAN MULLALY SECOND CHANCE SCHOLARSHIPS

Ryan Mullaly Second Chance Fund
26 Meadow Lane
Pennington, NJ 08534
Phone: (609) 737-1800
Email: The2dChanceFund@aol.com
Web: www.ryans2dchancefund.org

Summary: To provide financial assistance for college to students who have cancer.

Eligibility: Open to U.S. citizens and permanent residents who were diagnosed with cancer or a recurrence of cancer between age 13 and graduation from high school. Applicants must have a treatment history that includes chemotherapy and/or radiation and must be able to demonstrate that their high school years were substantially impacted by treatment and/or side effects of treatment. They must be 22 years of age or younger and currently 1) working on an associate or bachelor's degree at an accredited 2- or 4-year college or university; or 2) enrolled in an accredited postsecondary vocational or trade program that will culminate in certification. Priority is given to students still undergoing treatment, those with permanent effects from treatment, and those at the beginning of their postsecondary education.

Financial data: The stipend is $1,000.

Duration: 1 year; nonrenewable.

Number awarded: Up to 15 each year.

Deadline: May of each year.

879 SALLIE MAE FUND FIRST IN MY FAMILY SCHOLARSHIP PROGRAM

Hispanic College Fund
Attn: Scholarship Processing

1301 K Street, N.W., Suite 450-A West
Washington, DC 20005
Phone: (202) 296-5400; (800) 644-4223; Fax: (202) 296-3774
Email: hcf-info@hispanicfund.org
Web: scholarships.hispanicfund.org/applications

Summary: To provide financial assistance to Hispanic American undergraduate students who are the first in their family to attend college.

Eligibility: Open to U.S. citizens and permanent residents of Hispanic background (at least 1 grandparent must be 100% Hispanic) who are entering their freshman, sophomore, junior, or senior year of college and are the first member of their family to attend college. Applicants must be residing in the United States and planning to enroll full-time at an accredited college or university in the 50 states or Puerto Rico. They must have a GPA of 3.0 or higher and be able to demonstrate financial need.

Financial data: Stipends range from $500 to $5,000, depending on the need of the recipient. Funds are paid directly to the recipient's college or university to help cover tuition and fees.

Duration: 1 year; recipients may reapply.

Number awarded: Varies each year; recently, 155 students received scholarships worth a total of approximately $500,000.

Deadline: April of each year.

880 SALVATORE TADDONIO FAMILY FOUNDATION SCHOLARSHIP

Salvatore Taddonio Family Foundation
c/o Sandra Taddonio Madsen
5139 Arbutus Street
Arvada, CO 80002-1719
Email: sandymadsen@comcast.net

Summary: To provide financial assistance to residents of Colorado who are interested in attending college in the state.

Eligibility: Open to Colorado residents who are enrolled or planning to enroll full-time at a college in the state and whose parents are Colorado residents. High school seniors must have a GPA of 3.0 or higher. Applicants must have been born in the United States. Selection is based on merit, including extracurricular activities, community service activities, and an essay on how they plan to use their educational experience at college to better the community in which they live.

Financial data: The stipend is based on the cost of in-state tuition, fees, and books at the University of Colorado at Denver.

Duration: 1 year; may be renewed if recipient maintains a GPA of 3.0 or higher.

Number awarded: Several each year.

Deadline: July of each year.

881 SAM WALTON COMMUNITY SCHOLARSHIPS

Wal-Mart Foundation
Scholarship Programs Director
702 S.W. Eighth Street
Bentonville, AR 72716-8071
Phone: (501) 277-1905; (800) 530-9925; Fax: (501) 273-6850
Web: www.walmartstores.com/CommunityGiving/8732.aspx

Summary: To provide financial assistance for college to high school seniors, home school graduates, and GED recipients.

Eligibility: Open to U.S. citizens and permanent residents who graduate from high school, receive a home school diploma, or complete a GED equivalency certificate during the current year and plan to enroll full-time at an accredited U.S. 2- or 4-year college or university. Applicants must have a cumulative GPA of 2.5 or higher and be able to demonstrate financial need. They must have taken the ACT and/or SAT examination. Selection is based on academic achievements and records, school and community activities and leadership, and financial need.

Financial data: The stipend is $3,000. Funds may be used for tuition, fees, books, and on-campus board and room at an accredited U.S. institution.

Duration: 1 year; nonrenewable.

Number awarded: More than 2,500 each year.

Deadline: January of each year.

882 SAMMY AWARDS

Milk Processor Education Program
Attn: Scholar Athlete Milk Mustache of the Year (SAMMY)
1250 H Street, N.W., Suite 950
Washington, DC 20005
Phone: (202) 737-0153; (800) WHY-MILK; Fax: (202) 737-0156
Web: www.sammyapplication.com

Summary: To provide financial assistance for college to outstanding high school scholar-athletes.

Eligibility: Open to residents of the 48 contiguous United States and the District of Columbia who are currently high school seniors and who participate in a high school or club sport. Applicants must have a GPA of 3.2 or higher. They must submit a 250-word essay on how they refuel with milk while excelling in academics, athletics, community service, and leadership. The country is divided into 25 geographic regions and 3 finalists are selected from each region. From those, 1 winner from each region is chosen. Selection is based on academic achievement (35%), athletic excellence (35%), leadership (15%), citizenship/community service (10%), and a 75-word essay on how drinking milk is part of their life and training regimen (5%).

Financial data: College scholarships of $7,500 each are awarded. In addition, each winner plus 2 guests are invited to attend the winners' ceremony at Disney World in Orlando, Florida.

Duration: The awards are presented annually.

Number awarded: 25 each year (1 from each of 25 geographic districts).

Deadline: March of each year.

883 SAMSUNG AMERICAN LEGION SCHOLARSHIPS

American Legion
Attn: Americanism and Children & Youth Division
700 North Pennsylvania Street
P.O. Box 1055
Indianapolis, IN 46206-1055
Phone: (317) 630-1202; Fax: (317) 630-1223
Email: acy@legion.org
Web: www.legion.org/programs/resources/scholarships

Summary: To provide financial assistance for college to descendants of veterans who participate in Girls State or Boys State.

Eligibility: Open to students entering their senior year of high school who are selected to participate in Girls State or Boys State, sponsored by the American Legion Auxiliary or American Legion in their state. Applicants must be the child, grandchild, or great-grandchild of a veteran who saw active-duty service during specified periods of war time. Finalists are chosen at each participating Girls and Boys State, and they are then nominated for the national awards. Selection is based on academic record, community service, involvement in school and community activities, and financial need. Special consideration is given to descendants of U.S. veterans of the Korean War.

Financial data: Stipends are $20,000 or $1,000.

Duration: 4 years.

Number awarded: Varies each year; recently, 10 scholarships at $20,000 and 88 at $1,000 were awarded.

Deadline: Deadline not specified.

884 SAMUEL SMITH STEWART MASONIC SCHOLARSHIP

Grand Lodge of Missouri, A.F. & A.M.
Attn: Masonic Scholarship Fund of Missouri
6033 Masonic Drive, Suite B
Columbia, MO 65202-6535
Phone: (573) 474-8561
Web: www.momason.org/programs.asp

Summary: To provide financial assistance for college to high school seniors and current college students in Missouri.

Eligibility: Open to 1) seniors graduating from public high schools, private high schools, or accredited home school programs in Missouri; 2) residents of Missouri who are completing a 2-year program and transferring to a 4-year college or university; and 3) residents of Missouri at a certified technological or trade school planning to transfer. Applicants must be attending or planning to attend an accredited college or university in the United States as a full-time student. They must have a GPA of 3.0 or higher and be able to demonstrate financial need. Along with their application, they must submit an essay of 300 to 500 words on why they are applying for this scholarship.

Financial data: The stipend is $5,000.

Duration: 1 year; may be renewed if the recipient remains enrolled full-time with a GPA of 3.0 or higher.

Number awarded: 1 or more each year.

Deadline: March of each year.

885 SANDY WEISENBERGER ENDOWMENT SCHOLARSHIP

Epsilon Sigma Alpha International
Attn: ESA Foundation
P.O. Box 270517
Fort Collins, CO 80527
Phone: (970) 223-2824; Fax: (970) 223-4456
Email: esainfo@esaintl.com
Web: www.esaintl.com/esaf

Summary: To provide financial assistance to residents of Minnesota who plan to attend college in any state.

Eligibility: Open to residents of Minnesota who are 1) graduating high school seniors with a GPA of 3.0 or higher or with minimum scores of 22 on the ACT or 1030 on the combined critical reading and mathematics SAT; 2) enrolled in college with a GPA of 3.0 or higher; 3) enrolled at a technical school or returning to school after an absence for retraining of job skills or obtaining a degree; or 4) engaged in online study through an accredited college, university, or vocational school. Applicants may be attending or planning to attend a school in any state and major in any field. Selection is based on character (20%), leadership (20%), service (20%), financial need (20%), and scholastic ability (20%).

Financial data: The stipend is $1,000.

Duration: 1 year; may be renewed.

Number awarded: 1 each year.

Deadline: January of each year.

886 SARBANES SCHOLARSHIP PROGRAM

National Fallen Firefighters Foundation
Attn: Scholarship Committee
P.O. Drawer 498
Emmitsburg, MD 21727
Phone: (301) 447-1365; Fax: (301) 447-1645
Email: firehero@erols.com
Web: www.firehero.org/resources/families/scholarships/sarbanes.htm

Summary: To provide financial assistance for college or graduate school to the spouses and children of deceased fire fighters.

Eligibility: Open to the spouses, life partners, children, and stepchildren of fallen fire fighters honored at the National Fallen Firefighters Memorial in Emmitsburg, Maryland. Children must currently be under 30 years of age and have been under 22 years of age at the time of their fire fighter's death; there is no age cutoff for spouses or partners. Applicants must have a high school diploma or the equivalent; be pursuing or planning to pursue undergraduate, graduate, or job skills training at an accredited university, college, community college, or technical school; and be able to demonstrate academic and personal potential. Along with their application, they must submit a personal statement, up to 400 words, explaining why they want the scholarship; their personal, educational, and career goals; their extracurricular, community, and/or volunteer activities; any special circumstances (such as financial hardship or family responsibilities); and any other information they want the scholarship committee to know about them. Selection is based on academic standing (GPA of 2.0 or higher); involvement in extracurricular activities, including community and volunteer activities; the personal statement; and 2 letters of recommendation, at least 1 of which should be from a member of the fire service.

Financial data: Stipends average more than $1,500.

Duration: 1 year; may be renewed.

Number awarded: Varies each year; recently, 92 of these scholarships (41 new and 51 renewal) worth more than $150,000 were awarded. Since the program was established, it has awarded 562 scholarships worth more than $1,338,000.

Deadline: March of each year.

887 SCHERING-PLOUGH "WILL TO WIN" SCHOLARSHIPS

Schering-Plough Corporation
Attn: "Will to Win" Scholarship Program
P.O. Box 6503
Carlstadt, NJ 07072
Phone: (800) SCHERING
Email: requests@schering-ploughwilltowin.com
Web: www.schering-ploughwilltowin.com

Summary: To provide financial assistance for college to high school seniors with outstanding abilities in community service, athletics, art, or science who have asthma.

Eligibility: Open to high school seniors with asthma who have achieved excellence in 1 of the following 5 categories: performing arts (dance, music, theater), visual arts (painting, drawing, sculpture, photography, film), community service, athletics, or science. Applicants must have a GPA of 3.5 or higher and a record of achievement in their entry category, including at least 1 award. They must be U.S. citizens planning to attend an accredited college or university in the United States in the following fall.

Financial data: The stipend is $5,000. Funds are paid directly to the student's college.

Duration: 1 year; nonrenewable.

Number awarded: 10 each year: 2 in each of the 5 categories.

Deadline: April of each year.

888 SCHOLARSHIP HONORING SENATOR BARRY GOLDWATER, K7UGA

American Radio Relay League
Attn: ARRL Foundation
225 Main Street
Newington, CT 06111
Phone: (860) 594-0397; Fax: (860) 594-0259
Email: foundation@arrl.org
Web: www.arrlf.org/programs/scholarships

Summary: To provide financial assistance to licensed radio amateurs who are interested in working on an undergraduate or graduate degree in any field.

Eligibility: Open to undergraduate or graduate students at accredited institutions who are licensed radio amateurs at the novice class or higher. Applicants may be working on a degree in any academic discipline. Along with their application, they must submit an essay on the role amateur radio has played in their lives and provide documentation of financial need.

Financial data: The stipend is $5,000.

Duration: 1 year.

Number awarded: 1 each year.

Deadline: January of each year.

889 SCHOLARSHIPS FOR ELCA SERVICE ABROAD

Women of the Evangelical Lutheran Church in America
Attn: Scholarships
8765 West Higgins Road
Chicago, IL 60631-4101
Phone: (773) 380-2736; (800) 638-3522, ext. 2736; Fax: (773) 380-2419
Email: emily.hansen@elca.org
Web: www.elca.org/Growing-In-Faith/Ministry/Women-of-the-ELCA.aspx

Summary: To provide financial assistance to lay women who are affiliated with the Evangelical Lutheran Church of America (ELCA) congregations and who wish to pursue postsecondary education to prepare for service abroad, either in general or in health fields.

Eligibility: Open to ELCA lay women who are at least 21 years of age and have experienced an interruption of at least 2 years in their education since high school. Applicants must have been admitted to an academic institution to prepare for a career other than the ordained ministry. This program is available only to women studying for ELCA service abroad, either in general or in health professions associated with ELCA projects abroad. U.S. citizenship is required.

Financial data: The stipend ranges from $800 to $1,000 per year.

Duration: Up to 2 years.

Number awarded: Varies each year, depending upon the funds available.

Deadline: February of each year.

890 SCHOLARSHIPS FOR MILITARY CHILDREN

Defense Commissary Agency
Attn: SSP
1300 E Avenue
Fort Lee, VA 23801-1800
Phone: (804) 734-8410
Email: info@militaryscholar.org
Web: www.militaryscholar.org

Summary: To provide financial assistance for college to the children of veterans and military personnel.

Eligibility: Open to sons and daughters of U.S. military servicemembers (including active duty, retirees, Guard/Reserves, and survivors of deceased members) who are enrolled or accepted for enrollment at a college or university. Applicants must be younger than 23 years of age and enrolled in the Defense Enrollment Eligibility Reporting System (DEERS). They must have a GPA of 3.0 or higher. Along with their application, they must submit a 500-word essay on a topic that changes annually; recently, students were asked to write on "You can travel back in time, however, you cannot change events. What point in history would you visit and why." Selection is based on merit.

Financial data: The stipend is $1,500.

Duration: 1 year; recipients may reapply.

Number awarded: At least 1 scholarship is allocated for each of the commissaries worldwide operated by the Defense Commissary Agency (DeCA).

Deadline: February of each year.

891 SCHOLARSHIPS FOR USPHS COMMISSIONED CORPS DEPENDENTS

Commissioned Officers Association of the USPHS Inc.
Attn: PHS Commissioned Officers Foundation for the Advancement of Public Health
8201 Corporate Drive, Suite 200
Landover, MD 20785
Phone: (301) 731-9080; Fax: (301) 731-9084
Email: info@phscof.org
Web: www.phscof.org/education.html

Summary: To provide financial assistance for college to dependents of officers of the United States Public Health Service (USPHS) Commissioned Corps.

Eligibility: Open to dependent children and dependent spouses of active-duty, retired, or deceased officers of the USPHS Commissioned Corps. Applicants must be entering or continuing students at a college or vocational school. They must have a GPA of 3.0 or higher. Financial need is not considered in the selection process.

Financial data: Stipends range up to $1,000.

Duration: 1 year.

Number awarded: Varies each year; recently, 13 of these scholarships were awarded.

Deadline: May of each year.

892 SCHWALLIE FAMILY SCHOLARSHIPS

Organization for Autism Research
Attn: Scholarship
2000 North 14th Street, Suite 710
Arlington, VA 22201
Phone: (703) 243-9710
Web: www.researchautism.org/news/otherevents/scholarship.asp

Summary: To provide financial assistance for college to individuals with autism or Asperger's Syndrome.

Eligibility: Open to individuals with an established autism or Asperger's Syndrome diagnosis who are attending or planning to attend an accredited institution of higher education. Applicants must be enrolled at least part-time and be working toward certification or accreditation in a particular field. Along with their application, they must submit a 1,000-word autobiographical essay that includes their reasons for applying for this scholarship. Selection is based on originality of content, previous challenges overcome, future aspirations, and financial need.

Financial data: The stipend is $3,000.

Duration: 1 year; nonrenewable.

Number awarded: 7 each year: 4 to students at 4-year colleges or universities, 2 to students at 2-year colleges, and 1 to a student at a vocational/technical school.

Deadline: April of each year.

893 SCLEOF SCHOLARSHIP AWARDS

South Carolina Law Enforcement Officers' Association
7339 Broad River Road
P.O. Box 210709
Columbia, SC 29221-0709
Phone: (803) 781-5913; (800) 922-0038; Fax: (803) 781-9208
Email: scleoaagm@aol.com
Web: www.scleoa.org/Scholarship.htm

Summary: To provide financial assistance to high school seniors in South Carolina who are interested in law enforcement and plan to attend college in the state.

Eligibility: Open to seniors graduating from high schools in South Carolina whose parents or legal guardians have been South Carolina residents for at least 1 year. Applicants must be planning to attend an accredited college, university, or technical school in South Carolina and major in any field. Along with their application, they must submit an essay up to 1,000 words on a topic that changes annually but relates to law enforcement. Recently, students were invited to write on the reasons why South Carolina has the highest violent crime rate of any state in the country. The program includes 1 award reserved for the child of a member of the South Carolina Law Enforcement Officers' Association (SCLEOA). Semifinalists are interviewed. Financial need is not considered in the selection process.

Financial data: Awards are $5,000, $2,000, or $1,000.

Duration: 1 year.

Number awarded: 4 each year: 1 at $5,000, 2 at $2,000 (including 1 reserved for the child of an SCLEOA member), and 1 at $1,000.

Deadline: February of each year.

894 SCOTT MECHAM BBB STUDENT OF INTEGRITY AWARDS

Better Business Bureau of Nebraska, South Dakota, and Southwest Iowa
Attn: Communications Director
11811 P Street
Omaha, NE 68137
Phone: (402) 898-8526; (800) 649-6814, ext. 8526
Email: mriekes@bbbnebraska.org
Web: nebraska.bbb.org/studentaward

Summary: To provide financial assistance to high school students who live in the service area of the Better Business Bureau (BBB) of Nebraska, South Dakota, and Southwest Iowa and plan to attend college in any state.

Eligibility: Open to juniors and seniors at high schools in 1) the Omaha metropolitan area and southwest Iowa; 2) the Lincoln metropolitan area and the remainder of Nebraska; or 3) South Dakota. Applicants must be planning to attend a college or university in any state. They must be nominated by an official of their high school or religious institution. Along with their application, they must submit information on their school-related extracurricular activities; information on any work experience, community activities, and/or organizations in which they have participated; 2 letters of recommendation; a description of their postsecondary education plans; a transcript and/or ACT/SAT scores; and a 500-word essay on the importance of integrity. Selection is based on that essay (35%), recommendations and nominations (20%), community service (20%), leadership (20%), and academics (5%). Students who apply as juniors but are not chosen may apply again as seniors.

Financial data: The stipend is $2,000. Funds are disbursed directly to the recipient's college or university to be applied toward tuition and/or room and board.

Duration: 1 year.

Number awarded: 3 each year: 1 in each of the 3 geographic areas served by this BBB.

Deadline: March of each year.

895 SCOTTISH RITE FOUNDATION OF WASHINGTON UNDERGRADUATE SCHOLARSHIPS

Scottish Rite Foundation of Washington
c/o Seattle Scottish Rite Masonic Center
1207 North 152nd Street
Shoreline, Washington 98133
Phone: (206) 324-3330; Fax: (206) 324-3332
Email: Esoterika316@gmail.com
Web: www.wascottishrite.org/index.htm

Summary: To provide financial assistance to upper-division students from Washington working on an undergraduate degree at a college or university in the state.

Eligibility: Open to residents of Washington enrolled full-time as an entering junior, senior, or fifth-year undergraduate at a 4-year college or university in the state. Applicants must have a GPA of 3.0 or higher. Along with their application, they must submit a 100-word statement on their education and career goals. Selection is based on that statement, academic achievement, awards received, and participation in school, church, community, and/or other activities. Financial need is not considered. U.S. citizenship is required, but affiliation with a Masonic body is not.

Financial data: Stipend amounts vary each year; recently, the 2 highest-ranked applicants received the Barr and the Rinderhagen Scholarships of $5,000 per year and the highest-ranked renewal applicant received a scholarship of $3,000. Other stipends were $2,500.

Duration: 1 year; may be renewed 1 additional year if the recipient maintains a GPA of 3.0 or higher.

Number awarded: Varies each year; recently, the foundation awarded 43 first-time scholarships and 44 renewal scholarships.

Deadline: March of each year.

896 SDATAT SCHOLARSHIP

South Dakota Association of Towns and Townships
Attn: Scholarship Program
351 Wisconsin, S.W., Suite 101
P.O. Box 903
Huron, SD 57350-0903
Phone: (605) 353-1439; Fax: (605) 352-5322
Email: sdtstaff@santel.net
Web: sdtownships.com/7.html

Summary: To provide financial assistance to high school seniors in South Dakota who plan to attend college in the state.

Eligibility: Open to seniors graduating from high schools in South Dakota or who are home schooled. Applicants must be planning to attend a university, college, or vocational school in South Dakota. Along with their application, they must submit a 500-word essay on a topic that changes annually but relates to government; recently, students were asked to explain if they plan to vote, what the privilege of voting means to them, and what qualities are important to them in a candidate. The application may be accompanied by up to 2 letters of support; financial need is not considered in the selection process.

Financial data: The stipend is $1,000.

Duration: 1 year.

Number awarded: 1 each year.

Deadline: March of each year.

897 SEABEE MEMORIAL SCHOLARSHIP ASSOCIATION PROGRAM

Seabee Memorial Scholarship Association
P.O. Box 6574
Silver Spring, MD 20916
Phone: (301) 570-2850; Fax: (301) 570-2873
Email: smsa@erols.com
Web: www.seabee.org/scholarships.shtml

Summary: To provide financial assistance for college to the children or grandchildren of active or deceased members of the Naval Construction Battalion (Seabees) or Navy Civil Engineering Corps.

Eligibility: Open to the children, stepchildren, and grandchildren of regular, Reserve, retired, or deceased officers and enlisted members who are now serving in or have been honorably discharged from the Naval Construction Force (Seabees) or Navy Civil Engineering Corps. Applicants may be high school seniors, high school graduates, or students currently enrolled full-time at a 4-year college or university. Selection is based on financial need, character, good citizenship, leadership, and scholastic record.

Financial data: The stipend is $1,900 per year.

Duration: 1 year; may be renewed for 3 additional years.

Number awarded: Varies each year; recently, 30 new scholarships were awarded through this program.

Deadline: April of each year.

898 SEAN SILVER MEMORIAL SCHOLARSHIP

Ulman Cancer Fund for Young Adults
Attn: Scholarship Program Coordinator
10440 Little Patuxent Parkway, Suite 1G
Columbia, MD 21044
Phone: (410) 964-0202, ext. 106; (888) 393-FUND
Email: scholarship@ulmanfund.org
Web: www.ulmanfund.org/Services/tabid/53/Default.aspx

Summary: To provide financial assistance for college or graduate school to young adults who have cancer.

Eligibility: Open to students who are younger than 30 years of age and currently undergoing active treatment for cancer. Applicants must be attending or planning to attend a 4-year college or university to work on an undergraduate or graduate degree. They must be U.S. citizens or permanent residents. Along with their application, they must submit an essay of at least 1,000 words on what they have discovered about themselves while attending school as a young adult receiving treatment for or living with cancer. Selection is based on demonstrated dedication to community service, commitment to educational and professional goals, use of their cancer experience to impact the lives of other young adults affected by cancer, medical hardship, and financial need.

Financial data: The stipend is $2,500. Funds are paid directly to the educational institution.

Duration: 1 year.

Number awarded: 1 each year.

Deadline: April of each year.

899 SECOND CHANCE ENDOWMENT SCHOLARSHIP

Epsilon Sigma Alpha International
Attn: ESA Foundation
P.O. Box 270517
Fort Collins, CO 80527
Phone: (970) 223-2824; Fax: (970) 223-4456
Email: esainfo@esaintl.com
Web: www.esaintl.com/esaf

Summary: To provide financial assistance for continuing education to nontraditional students from Illinois.

Eligibility: Open to Illinois residents who are nontraditional students over 25 years of age. Applicants must be interested in pursuing continuing education to acquire new job skills or update present skills. They may be attending or planning to attend school in any state and major in any field. Selection is based on character (10%), leadership (10%), service (5%), financial need (50%), and scholastic ability (25%).

Financial data: The stipend is $1,000.

Duration: 1 year; nonrenewable.

Number awarded: 1 each year.

Deadline: January of each year.

900 SENATOR GEORGE J. MITCHELL SCHOLARSHIPS

The Mitchell Institute
22 Monument Square, Suite 200
Portland, ME 04101
Phone: (207) 773-7700; (888) 220-7209 (within ME); Fax: (207) 773-1133
Email: info@mitchellinstitute.org
Web: www.mitchellinstitute.org/scholarships.html

Summary: To provide financial assistance to high school seniors in Maine who plan to attend college in any state.

Eligibility: Open to seniors graduating from public high schools in Maine who plan to attend a 2- or 4-year college or university in any state; preference is given to applicants planning to attend college in Maine. The program includes the KeyBank Mitchell Scholarships, which give preference to first-generation college students. Students who attend high school in Maine but are not legal residents of Maine are not eligible. Selection is based on academic achievement and potential, financial need, and community service.

Financial data: The stipend is $1,250 per year. The KeyBank Mitchell Scholarships are $1,500 per year for students at 4-year institutions.

Duration: 2 years or 4 years (depending on whether the recipient attends a 2- or 4-year institution.

Number awarded: 130 each year: 1 to a graduating senior from each public high school in Maine. Recently, 116 of the scholarships were for students attending college in Maine and 14 for students at universities in other states. Included in those scholarships are 16 KeyBank Mitchell Scholarships (1 in each Maine county).

Deadline: March of each year.

901 SERTOMA SCHOLARSHIPS FOR HARD OF HEARING OR DEAF STUDENTS

Sertoma International
Attn: Director of Finance and Administration
1912 East Meyer Boulevard
Kansas City, MO 64132-1174
Phone: (816) 333-8300, ext. 214; Fax: (816) 333-4320; TDD: (816) 333-8300
Email: infosertoma@sertomahq.org
Web: www.sertoma.org/Scholarships

Summary: To provide financial assistance for college to hearing impaired students.

Eligibility: Open to students who have a minimum 40dB bilateral hearing loss and are interested in working full-time on a bachelor's degree at a 4-year college or university in the United States. Students working on a graduate degree, community college degree, associate degree, or vocational program degree are ineligible. Applicants must have a GPA of 3.2 or higher. Along with their application, they must submit a statement of purpose on how this scholarship will help them achieve their goals. U.S. citizenship is required. Selection is based on academic achievement, honors and awards received, community volunteer activities, interscholastic activities, extracurricular activities, and 2 letters of recommendation.

Financial data: The stipend is $1,000 per year.

Duration: 1 year; may be renewed up to 4 times.

Number awarded: 20 each year.

Deadline: April of each year.

902 SFM FOUNDATION SCHOLARSHIP

SFM Foundation
P.O. Box 582992
Minneapolis, MN 55458-2992
Phone: (952) 838-4200; Fax: (952) 838-2055
Email: foundation@sfmic.com
Web: www.sfmic.com/foundation/application_information.cfm

Summary: To provide financial assistance to residents of Minnesota and Wisconsin whose parent was injured or killed in a work-related accident and who are interested in attending college, preferably in those states.

Eligibility: Open to residents of Minnesota and Wisconsin between 16 and 25 years of age who are high school students, GED recipients, or high school graduates. Applicants must be the natural, adopted, or stepchild of a worker injured or killed in a work-related accident during the course and scope of employment with a Minnesota- or Wisconsin-based employer and entitled to receive benefits under the Minnesota Workers' Compensation Act or Worker's Compensation Act of Wisconsin. They must be planning to work on an associate or bachelor's degree or a certificate or license from any accredited school; preference is given to students attending institutions within the Minnesota State Colleges and Universities system or the University of Wisconsin Colleges system. Financial need is considered in the selection process.

Financial data: Stipends range from $1,000 to $5,000 per year. Funds are paid directly to the educational institution.

Duration: 1 year; may be renewed, provided the recipient maintains a GPA of 2.0 or higher.

Number awarded: Varies each year.

Deadline: March of each year.

903 SHERMAN AND NANCY REESE SCHOLARSHIPS

Epsilon Sigma Alpha International
Attn: ESA Foundation
P.O. Box 270517
Fort Collins, CO 80527
Phone: (970) 223-2824; Fax: (970) 223-4456
Email: esainfo@esaintl.com
Web: www.esaintl.com/esaf

Summary: To provide financial assistance to residents of South Carolina and Virginia who plan to attend college in any state.

Eligibility: Open to residents of South Carolina and Virginia who are enrolled at a college or university in any state and have a GPA of 3.0 or higher. Applicants may be majoring in any field. Selection is based on character (10%), leadership (10%), service (5%), financial need (50%), and scholastic ability (25%).

Financial data: The stipend is $3,000.

Duration: 1 year; may be renewed.

Number awarded: 2 each year: 1 to a student who graduated from high school in South Carolina and 1 who graduated from high school in Virginia.

Deadline: January of each year.

904 SHIRLEY A. DREYER MEMORIAL ENDOWMENT SCHOLARSHIP

Epsilon Sigma Alpha International
Attn: ESA Foundation
P.O. Box 270517
Fort Collins, CO 80527
Phone: (970) 223-2824; Fax: (970) 223-4456
Email: esainfo@esaintl.com
Web: www.esaintl.com/esaf

Summary: To provide financial assistance to residents of North Carolina who plan to attend college in any state.

Eligibility: Open to residents of North Carolina who are 1) graduating high school seniors with a GPA of 3.0 or higher or with minimum scores of 22 on the ACT or 1030 on the combined critical reading and mathematics SAT; 2) enrolled in college with a GPA of 3.0 or higher; 3) enrolled at a technical school or returning to school after an absence for retraining of job skills or obtaining a degree; or 4) engaged in online study through an accredited college, university, or vocational school. Applicants may be attending or planning to attend an accredited school in any state and major in any field. Selection is based on character (10%), leadership (20%), service (10%), financial need (30%), and scholastic ability (30%).

Financial data: The stipend is $1,500.

Duration: 1 year; may be renewed.

Number awarded: 1 each year.

Deadline: January of each year.

905 "SHOW ME STATE" ENDOWMENT SCHOLARSHIP

Epsilon Sigma Alpha International
Attn: ESA Foundation
P.O. Box 270517
Fort Collins, CO 80527
Phone: (970) 223-2824; Fax: (970) 223-4456
Email: esainfo@esaintl.com
Web: www.esaintl.com/esaf

Summary: To provide financial assistance to residents of Missouri who plan to attend college in any state.

Eligibility: Open to residents of Missouri who are 1) graduating high school seniors with a GPA of 3.0 to 3.5 or with minimum scores of 22 on the ACT or 1030 on the combined critical reading and mathematics SAT; 2) enrolled in college with a GPA of 3.0 to 3.5; 3) enrolled at a technical school or returning to school after an absence for retraining of job skills or obtaining a degree; or 4) engaged in online study through an accredited college, university, or vocational school. Applicants may be attending or planning to attend an accredited school anywhere in the United States and major in any field. Selection is based on character (10%), leadership (10%), service (5%), financial need (50%), and scholastic ability (25%).

Financial data: The stipend is $1,000.

Duration: 1 year; may be renewed.

Number awarded: 1 each year.

Deadline: January of each year.

906 SISTER ELIZABETH CANDON SCHOLARSHIP

Vermont Student Assistance Corporation
Attn: Scholarship Programs
10 East Allen Street
P.O. Box 2000
Winooski, VT 05404-2601
Phone: (802) 654-3798; (888) 253-4819; Fax: (802) 654-3765; TDD: (800) 281-3341 (within VT)
Email: info@vsac.org
Web: services.vsac.org/wps/wcm/connect/vsac/VSAC

Summary: To provide financial assistance to single mothers in Vermont who plan to attend college in any state.

Eligibility: Open to female residents of Vermont who are single parents with primary custody of at least 1 child 12 years of age or younger. Applicants must be enrolled at least half-time in an accredited undergraduate degree program in any state. Along with their application, they must submit 1) a 250-word essay on their short- and long-term academic, educational, career, vocational, and/or employment goals; 2) a 100-word essay on how the program in which they will be enrolled will enhance their career or vocation; and 3) a 250-word essay on what they believe distinguishes their application from others that may be submitted. Selection is based on those essays, a letter of recommendation, and financial need.

Financial data: The stipend is $1,000 per year.

Duration: 1 year; may be renewed up to 3 additional years.

Number awarded: 1 each year.

Deadline: March of each year.

907 SKANDALARIS FAMILY FOUNDATION SCHOLARSHIPS

Skandalaris Family Foundation
1030 Doris Road
Auburn Hills, MI 48326
Phone: (248) 292-5678; Fax: (248) 292-5697
Email: info@skandalaris.org
Web: www.skandalaris.org/college-scholarship.php

Summary: To provide financial assistance for college to high school seniors and current college students, especially those from Michigan.

Eligibility: Open to graduating high school seniors and students already enrolled in college. The majority of the scholarships are awarded to residents of Michigan. High school seniors must have a GPA of 3.5 or higher, minimum scores of 1800 on the SAT or 27 on the ACT, and a record of involvement in school, athletic, and community activities. College students must have a cumulative GPA of 3.4 or higher and a record of active involvement in university, athletic, or community services. All applicants must be U.S. citizens and able to demonstrate financial need.

Financial data: The stipend is at least $2,000 per year.

Duration: 1 year; may be renewed.

Number awarded: Varies each year; recently, 116 of these scholarships were awarded.

Deadline: April of each year.

908 SOCIETY OF DAUGHTERS OF THE UNITED STATES ARMY SCHOLARSHIPS

Society of Daughters of the United States Army
c/o Janet B. Otto, Scholarship Chair
7717 Rockledge Court
Springfield, VA 21152

Summary: To provide financial assistance for college to daughters and granddaughters of active, retired, or deceased career Army warrant and commissioned officers.

Eligibility: Open to the daughters, adopted daughters, stepdaughters, or granddaughters of career commissioned officers or warrant officers of the U.S. Army (active, regular, or Reserve) who 1) are currently on active duty; 2) retired after 20 years of active duty or were medically retired; or 3) died while on active duty or after retiring from active duty with 20 or more years of service. Applicants must have at least a 3.0 GPA and be studying or planning to study at the undergraduate level. Selection is based on depth of character, leadership, seriousness of purpose, academic achievement, and financial need.

Financial data: Scholarships, to a maximum of $1,000, are paid directly to the college or school for tuition, laboratory fees, books, or other expenses.

Duration: 1 year; may be renewed up to 4 additional years if the recipient maintains at least a 3.0 GPA.

Number awarded: Varies each year.

Deadline: February of each year.

909 SOCIETY OF MAYFLOWER DESCENDANTS IN THE STATE OF CONNECTICUT SCHOLARSHIPS

Society of Mayflower Descendants in the State of Connecticut
c/o Lois Johnson, Scholarship Chair
10 Holly Lane
Wallingford, CT 06492-4723
Web: www.ctmayflower.org/programs.php

Summary: To provide financial assistance to high school seniors in Connecticut who plan to attend college in any state.

Eligibility: Open to seniors graduating from high schools in Connecticut. Applicants must have confirmed plans to attend a college or university in any state. Selection is based on academic achievement, extracurricular involvement, community service, and financial need.

Financial data: The stipend is $1,250.

Duration: 1 year.

Number awarded: 3 each year.

Deadline: February of each year.

910 SODEXHO SCHOLARSHIP PROGRAM

Hispanic College Fund
Attn: Scholarship Processing
1301 K Street, N.W., Suite 450-A West
Washington, DC 20005
Phone: (202) 296-5400; (800) 644-4223; Fax: (202) 296-3774
Email: hcf-info@hispanicfund.org
Web: scholarships.hispanicfund.org/applications

Summary: To provide financial assistance for college to Hispanic American undergraduate students who are committed to alleviating hunger and poverty.

Eligibility: Open to U.S. citizens and permanent residents of Hispanic background (at least 1 grandparent must be 100% Hispanic) who are enrolled full-time at a college or university in the 50 states or Puerto Rico. Applicants may be studying any field, but they must be committed to alleviating hunger and poverty in the United States. They must have a GPA of 3.0 or higher and be able to demonstrate financial need.

Financial data: Stipends range from $500 to $5,000. Funds are paid directly to the recipient's college or university to help cover tuition and fees.

Duration: 1 year; may be renewed.

Number awarded: 18 each year.

Deadline: March of each year.

911 SOLVAYCARES SCHOLARSHIPS

Solvay Pharmaceuticals, Inc.
Attn: SolvayCARES Scholarship Program
901 Sawyer Road
Marietta, GA 30062
Phone: (770) 578-5898; (800) 354-0026, ext. 5898; Fax: (770) 578-5586
Email: SolvayCARES.Scholarship@solvay.com
Web: www.solvaycaresscholarship.com

Summary: To provide financial assistance for college or graduate school to students with cystic fibrosis (CF).

Eligibility: Open to high school seniors, vocational school students, college students, and graduate students with CF. U.S. citizenship is required. Applicants must submit 1) a 250-word essay on the topic, "My dream for the future is..."; 2) a creative presentation (e.g., written work, a piece of art, a craft, collage, photograph) on what sets them apart from their peers, what inspires them to live life to the fullest, or anything else that they think makes them unique; and 3) a photograph. Selection is based on academic excellence, creativity, community involvement, and ability to serve as a role model to others with CF. The program designates 1 applicant as the Thriving Student Achiever.

Financial data: The stipend is $2,500 per year. The Thriving Student Achiever receives an additional award (recently, $14,500 for a total award of $17,000 to honor the program's 17th year).

Duration: 1 year.

Number awarded: 40 each year, of whom 1 is designated the Thriving Student Achiever.

Deadline: April of each year.

912 SONS OF ITALY GENERAL STUDY SCHOLARSHIPS

Order Sons of Italy in America
Attn: Sons of Italy Foundation
219 E Street, N.E.
Washington, DC 20002
Phone: (202) 547-2900; (800) 552-OSIA; Fax: (202) 546-8168
Email: scholarships@osia.org
Web: www.osia.org/students/general-study-scholarships.php

Summary: To provide financial assistance to undergraduate and graduate students of Italian descent.

Eligibility: Open to U.S. citizens of Italian descent who are enrolled as full-time students in an undergraduate or graduate program at an accredited 4-year college or university. Both high school seniors and students already enrolled in college are eligible for the undergraduate awards. Applications must be accompanied by essays, from 500 to 750 words in length, on a personal experience that demonstrated or generated pride in their Italian heritage. These merit-based awards are presented to students who have demonstrated exceptional leadership qualities and distinguished scholastic abilities.

Financial data: Stipends range from $5,000 to $25,000.

Duration: 1 year; nonrenewable.

Number awarded: Varies each year; recently, 7 of these awards were presented.

Deadline: February of each year.

913 SOUTH CAROLINA ACCESS AND EQUITY UNDERGRADUATE SCHOLARS PROGRAM

South Carolina Commission on Higher Education
Attn: Director of Student Services
1333 Main Street, Suite 200
Columbia, SC 29201
Phone: (803) 737-2244; (877) 349-7183; Fax: (803) 737-2297
Email: kwoodfaulk@che.sc.gov
Web: www.che.sc.gov/New_Web/GoingToCollege/FinAsst.htm

Summary: To provide financial assistance to underrepresented students at public colleges or universities in South Carolina.

Eligibility: Open to residents of South Carolina who are members of a traditionally underrepresented group at the senior institution, regional campus of the University of South Carolina, or South Carolina technical college they are or will be attending. Full-time entering freshmen must have a high school GPA of at least 3.0 (or 2.5 for students entering a technical college); continuing full-time college students, continuing part-time college students, and those transferring to a 4-year institution must have a cumulative GPA of at least 2.0. Priority is given to full-time students. U.S. citizenship is required.

Financial data: Stipends of up to $2,000 per year are provided, funding permitting.

Duration: 1 year; may be renewed.

Number awarded: Varies each year, but no more than 20% of the grant funds at each institution may be used for entering freshmen.

Deadline: Deadline not specified.

914 SOUTH CAROLINA HOPE SCHOLARSHIPS

South Carolina Commission on Higher Education
Attn: Director of Student Services

1333 Main Street, Suite 200
Columbia, SC 29201
Phone: (803) 737-2244; (877) 349-7183; Fax: (803) 737-2297
Email: kwoodfaulk@che.sc.gov
Web: www.che.sc.gov/New_Web/GoingToCollege/HOPE_Hm.htm

Summary: To provide financial assistance to high school seniors in South Carolina who plan to attend a 4-year institution in the state.

Eligibility: Open to seniors graduating from high schools or completing a home school program in South Carolina who are planning to enroll full-time at a 4-year public or private college or university in the state, Applicants must have a GPA of 3.0 or higher. They cannot have been convicted of any felony or drug- or alcohol-related misdemeanor during the past academic year and cannot be eligible for the Palmetto Fellows or LIFE Scholarship Programs. U.S. citizenship or permanent resident status is required. Selection is based on merit.

Financial data: The maximum stipend is $2,800, including a $300 book allowance.

Duration: 1 year; nonrenewable.

Number awarded: Varies each year; recently, 2,556 students received support from this program.

Deadline: Deadline not specified.

915 SOUTH CAROLINA JUNIOR GOLF FOUNDATION SCHOLARSHIP PROGRAM

South Carolina Junior Golf Foundation
c/o Center for Scholarship Administration, Inc.
4320 Wade Hampton Boulevard, Suite G
P.O. Box 1465
Taylors, SC 29687-0031
Phone: (864) 268-3363; Fax: (864) 268-7160
Email: susanjlee@bellsouth.net
Web: www.scholarshipprograms.org/golf/index.htm

Summary: To provide financial assistance to residents of South Carolina who have a competitive or recreational interest in golf and are interested in attending college in the state.

Eligibility: Open to residents of South Carolina who are seniors in high school or already attending college in the state. Applicants must have a GPA of 2.75 or higher and a competitive or recreational interest in golf. Along with their application, they must submit a 1-page essay explaining why they believe they qualify for this scholarship, including their college and career plans. Selection is based on academic merit (SAT/ACT scores, rank in class, and GPA), community involvement, and financial need.

Financial data: The stipend is $2,500 per year. Funds are sent directly to the college, university, or technical college to be used for educational expenses, including tuition, fees, books, room, and board.

Duration: 1 year; may be renewed up to 3 additional years or until completion of a bachelor's degree, whichever is earlier, provided the recipient maintains a GPA of 2.75 or higher and remains enrolled at a college or university in South Carolina.

Number awarded: Varies each year; recently, 4 of these scholarships were awarded.

Deadline: January of each year.

916 SOUTH CAROLINA LOTTERY TUITION ASSISTANCE PROGRAM

South Carolina Commission on Higher Education
Attn: Lottery Tuition Assistance Program
1333 Main Street, Suite 200
Columbia, SC 29201
Phone: (803) 737-2262; (877) 349-7183; Fax: (803) 737-2297
Email: lmangwilliams@che.sc.gov
Web: www.che.sc.gov/New_Web/GoingToCollege/LTA_Hm.htm

Summary: To provide financial assistance to needy students at 2-year colleges in South Carolina.

Eligibility: Open to students at 2-year public and private colleges and technical schools in South Carolina who meet the qualifications of financial need as established by the financial aid office at the institution they are attending. Applicants must be U.S. citizens or permanent residents and residents of South Carolina. They may not be receiving other scholarship assistance from the South Carolina Commission on Higher Education.

Financial data: The amount of the assistance varies each year; recently, full-time students were eligible for up to $900 per semester and part-time students were eligible for up to $75 per credit hour.

Duration: 1 semester; may be renewed.

Number awarded: Varies each year; recently, 28,269 students received support from this program.

Deadline: Deadline not specified.

917 SOUTH CAROLINA NATIONAL GUARD COLLEGE ASSISTANCE PROGRAM

South Carolina Commission on Higher Education
Attn: Director of Student Services
1333 Main Street, Suite 200
Columbia, SC 29201
Phone: (803) 737-2144; (877) 349-7183; Fax: (803) 737-2297
Email: mbrown@che.sc.gov
Web: www.che.sc.gov/New_Web/GoingToCollege/FinAsst.htm

Summary: To provide financial assistance to members of the South Carolina National Guard who are interested in attending college in the state.

Eligibility: Open to members of the South Carolina National Guard who are in good standing and have not already received a bachelor's or graduate degree. Applicants must be admitted, enrolled, and classified as a degree-seeking full- or part-time student at an eligible institution in South Carolina. They may not be taking continuing education or graduate course work. U.S. citizenship or permanent resident status is required.

Financial data: This program provides full payment of the cost of attendance, including tuition, fees, and textbooks. The cumulative total of all benefits received from this program may not exceed $18,000.

Duration: Support is provided for up to 130 semester hours of study, provided the Guard member maintains satisfactory academic progress as defined by the institution.

Number awarded: Varies each year.

Deadline: Deadline not specified.

918 SOUTH CAROLINA NEED-BASED GRANTS PROGRAM

South Carolina Commission on Higher Education
Attn: Need-Based Grant Coordinator
1333 Main Street, Suite 200
Columbia, SC 29201
Phone: (803) 737-2262; (877) 349-7183; Fax: (803) 737-2297
Email: lmangwilliams@che.sc.gov
Web: www.che.sc.gov/New_Web/GoingToCollege/NBG_Hm.htm

Summary: To provide financial assistance to South Carolina residents who have financial need and plan to attend college in the state.

Eligibility: Open to residents of South Carolina who meet the qualifications of financial need as established by the financial aid office at the college or university in South Carolina that they are attending or planning to attend. Assistance is provided at participating South Carolina public or private 2- or 4-year colleges and universities. Applicants must be enrolled for their first 1-year program, first associate degree, first 2-year program leading to a bachelor's degree, first bachelor's degree, or first professional degree.

Financial data: Grants up to $2,500 per academic year are available to full-time students and up to $1,250 per academic year to part-time students.

Duration: 1 year; may be renewed for up to 8 full-time equivalent terms.

Number awarded: Varies each year; recently, 25,175 students received support from this program.

Deadline: Deadline not specified.

919 SOUTH CAROLINA STATE FAIR ACADEMIC SCHOLARSHIPS

South Carolina State Fair
Attn: Director of Entertainment and Commercial Exhibits
1200 Rosewood Drive
P.O. Box 393
Columbia, SC 29202
Phone: (803) 799-3387, ext. 15; (888) 444-3247; Fax: (803) 799-1760
Email: laurenf@scstatefair.org
Web: www.scstatefair.org/throughout-the-year/scholarships/index.php

Summary: To provide financial assistance to high school seniors in South Carolina who will be attending a college or university in the state.

Eligibility: Open to seniors at public and private high schools and at home schools in South Carolina. Applicants must be planning to attend a college, technical school, or university in South Carolina. Selection is based on financial need, academic and extracurricular achievement, and communication skills.

Financial data: The stipend is $2,000. Funds are paid directly to the recipient's college or university. Students who receive support for their sophomore year of college receive a stipend of $2,500.

Duration: 1 year; recipients may reapply for a second year of support as college sophomores.

Number awarded: 50 scholarships are awarded to high school seniors each year. An additional 10 scholarships are awarded to selected students entering their sophomore year of college.

Deadline: March of each year.

920 SOUTH CAROLINA TUITION GRANTS PROGRAM

South Carolina Higher Education Tuition Grants Commission
Attn: Executive Director
800 Dutch Square Boulevard, Suite 260A
Columbia, SC 29210-7317
Phone: (803) 896-1120; Fax: (803) 896-1126
Email: info@sctuitiongrants.org
Web: www.sctuitiongrants.com

Summary: To provide financial assistance to students at independent colleges and universities in South Carolina.

Eligibility: Open to residents of South Carolina who are attending or accepted for enrollment as full-time students at eligible private institutions in the state. Applicants must 1) graduate in the upper 75% of their high school class; 2) score 900 or above on the mathematics and critical reading SAT or 19 or above on the ACT; or 3) graduate with a high school GPA of 2.0 or higher. Selection is based on financial need.

Financial data: The amounts of the awards depend on the need of the recipient and the tuition and fees at the institution to be attended. Recently, the maximum grant was $3,200 and the average grant was approximately $2,900. Funds may not be used for part-time enrollment, room and board charges, summer school enrollment, or graduate school enrollment.

Duration: 1 year; may be renewed.

Number awarded: Varies each year; recently, 3,154 new scholarships were awarded through this program.

Deadline: June of each year.

921 SOUTH CAROLINA TUITION PROGRAM FOR CHILDREN OF CERTAIN WAR VETERANS

South Carolina Division of Veterans Affairs
c/o VA Regional Office Building
6437 Garners Ferry Road, Suite 1126
Columbia, SC 29209
Phone: (803) 647-2434; Fax: (803) 647-2312
Email: va@oepp.sc.gov
Web: www.govoepp.state.sc.us/va/benefits.html

Summary: To provide free college tuition to the children of disabled and other South Carolina veterans.

Eligibility: Open to the children of wartime veterans who were legal residents of South Carolina both at the time of entry into military or naval service and during service, or who have been residents of South Carolina for at least 1 year. Veteran parents must 1) be permanently and totally disabled as determined by the U.S. Department of Veterans Affairs; 2) have been a prisoner of war; 3) have been killed in action; 4) have died from other causes while in service; 5) have died of a disease or disability resulting from service; 6) be currently missing in action; 7) have received the Congressional Medal of Honor; 8) have received the Purple Heart Medal from wounds received in combat; or 9) now be deceased but qualified under categories 1 or 2 above. The veteran's child must be 26 years of age or younger and working on an undergraduate degree.

Financial data: Children who qualify are eligible for free tuition at any South Carolina state-supported college, university, or postsecondary technical education institution. The waiver applies to tuition only. The costs of room and board, certain fees, and books are not covered.

Duration: Students are eligible to receive this support as long as they are younger than 26 years of age and working on an undergraduate degree.

Number awarded: Varies each year.

Deadline: Deadline not specified.

922 SOUTH DAKOTA FREE TUITION FOR CHILDREN OF RESIDENTS WHO DIED DURING SERVICE IN THE ARMED FORCES

South Dakota Board of Regents
Attn: Scholarship Committee
306 East Capitol Avenue, Suite 200
Pierre, SD 57501-2545
Phone: (605) 773-3455; Fax: (605) 773-2422
Email: info@sdbor.edu
Web: www.sdbor.edu/student/prospective/Military.htm

Summary: To provide free tuition at South Dakota public colleges and universities to children of military personnel who died while in service.

Eligibility: Open to residents of South Dakota younger than 25 years of age. The applicant's parent must have been killed in action or died of other causes while on active duty and must have been a resident of South Dakota for at least 6 months immediately preceding entry into active service.

Financial data: Eligible children are entitled to attend any South Dakota state-supported institution of higher education or state-supported technical or vocational school free of tuition and mandatory fees.

Duration: 8 semesters or 12 quarters of either full- or part-time study.

Number awarded: Varies each year.

Deadline: Deadline not specified.

923 SOUTH DAKOTA FREE TUITION FOR DEPENDENTS OF PRISONERS OR MISSING IN ACTION

South Dakota Board of Regents
Attn: Scholarship Committee
306 East Capitol Avenue, Suite 200
Pierre, SD 57501-2545
Phone: (605) 773-3455; Fax: (605) 773-2422
Email: info@sdbor.edu
Web: www.sdbor.edu/student/prospective/Military.htm

Summary: To provide free tuition at South Dakota public colleges and universities to dependents of prisoners of war (POWs) and persons missing in action (MIAs).

Eligibility: Open to residents of South Dakota who are the spouses or children of POWs or of MIAs. Applicants may not be eligible for equal or greater benefits from any federal financial assistance program.

Financial data: Eligible dependents are entitled to attend any South Dakota state-supported institution of higher education or state-supported technical or vocational school free of tuition and mandatory fees.

Duration: 8 semesters or 12 quarters of either full- or part-time study.

Number awarded: Varies each year.

Deadline: Deadline not specified.

924 SOUTH DAKOTA FREE TUITION FOR SURVIVORS OF DECEASED FIRE FIGHTERS, CERTIFIED LAW ENFORCEMENT OFFICERS, AND EMERGENCY MEDICAL TECHNICIANS

South Dakota Board of Regents
Attn: Scholarship Committee
306 East Capitol Avenue, Suite 200
Pierre, SD 57501-2545
Phone: (605) 773-3455; Fax: (605) 773-2422
Email: info@sdbor.edu
Web: www.sdbor.edu

Summary: To provide free tuition at South Dakota public colleges and universities to children of deceased fire fighters, law enforcement officers, and emergency medical technicians.

Eligibility: Open to residents of South Dakota who are the survivor of a fire fighter, certified law enforcement officer, or emergency medical technician who died as a direct result of injuries received in performance of official duties. Applicants must have been accepted for enrollment at a state-supported institution of higher education or technical or vocational school.

Financial data: Eligible survivors are entitled to attend any South Dakota state-supported institution of higher education or state-supported technical or vocational school free of tuition.

Duration: Until completion of a bachelor's or vocational degree; the degree must be earned within 36 months or 8 semesters.

Number awarded: Varies each year.

Deadline: Deadline not specified.

925 SOUTH DAKOTA FREE TUITION FOR VETERANS AND OTHERS WHO PERFORMED WAR SERVICE

South Dakota Board of Regents
Attn: Scholarship Committee
306 East Capitol Avenue, Suite 200
Pierre, SD 57501-2545

Phone: (605) 773-3455; Fax: (605) 773-2422
Email: info@sdbor.edu
Web: http://mva.sd.gov/vet_benefits_info.html
Summary: To provide free tuition at South Dakota public colleges and universities to certain veterans.
Eligibility: Open to current residents of South Dakota who have been discharged from the military forces of the United States under honorable conditions. Applicants must meet 1 of the following criteria: 1) served on active duty at any time between August 2, 1990 and March 3, 1991; 2) received an Armed Forces Expeditionary Medal, Southwest Asia Service Medal, or other U.S. campaign or service medal for participation in combat operations against hostile forces outside the boundaries of the United States: or 3) have a service-connected disability rating of at least 10%. They may not be eligible for any other educational assistance from the U.S. government. Qualifying veterans must apply for this benefit within 20 years after the date proclaimed for the cassation of hostilities or within 6 years from and after the date of their discharge from military service, whichever is later.
Financial data: Eligible veterans are entitled to attend any South Dakota state-supported institution of higher education or state-supported technical or vocational school free of tuition and mandatory fees.
Duration: Eligible veterans are entitled to receive 1 month of free tuition for each month of qualifying service, from a minimum of 1 year to a maximum of 4 years.
Number awarded: Varies each year.
Deadline: Deadline not specified.

926 SOUTH DAKOTA OPPORTUNITY SCHOLARSHIP

South Dakota Board of Regents
Attn: Scholarship Committee
306 East Capitol Avenue, Suite 200
Pierre, SD 57501-2545
Phone: (605) 773-3455; Fax: (605) 773-2422
Email: info@sdbor.edu
Web: www.sdbor.edu/OpportunityScholarship/sdos.htm
Summary: To provide financial assistance to South Dakota high school seniors who plan to attend college in the state.
Eligibility: Open to seniors who are graduating from high schools in South Dakota and have completed the Distinguished Graduation Requirements. Applicants may have received no grade below a "C" and must have a cumulative high school GPA of 3.0 or higher as well as a score of at least 24 on the ACT or 1090 on the critical reading and mathematics portions of the SAT.
Financial data: The stipend is $1,000 per year for the first 3 years and $2,000 for the fourth year.
Duration: 4 years, provided recipients maintain a GPA of 3.0 or higher and full-time enrollment.
Number awarded: Varies each year.
Deadline: August of each year for fall term; January of each year for spring term.

927 SOVEREIGN NATIONS SCHOLARSHIP FUND FOR MAINSTREAM UNIVERSITIES

American Indian College Fund
Attn: Scholarship Department
8333 Greenwood Boulevard
Denver, CO 80221
Phone: (303) 426-8900; (800) 776-FUND; Fax: (303) 426-1200
Email: scholarships@collegefund.org
Web: www.collegefund.org/scholarships/schol_mainstream.html
Summary: To provide financial assistance to Native American students who are interested in attending a mainstream university and working for a tribe or Indian organization after graduation.
Eligibility: Open to American Indians and Alaska Natives who can document proof of enrollment or descendancy. Applicants must be planning to 1) enroll full-time in a bachelor's degree program at a mainstream institution; and 2) work for their tribe or an Indian organization after graduation. They must have a GPA of 3.0 or higher and be able to demonstrate exceptional academic achievement. Applications are available only online and include required essays on specified topics.
Financial data: The stipend is $2,000 per year.
Duration: 1 year; may be renewed.
Number awarded: Varies each year.
Deadline: May of each year.

928 SOVEREIGN NATIONS SCHOLARSHIP FUND FOR TRIBAL COLLEGES

American Indian College Fund
Attn: Scholarship Department
8333 Greenwood Boulevard
Denver, CO 80221
Phone: (303) 426-8900; (800) 776-FUND; Fax: (303) 426-1200
Email: scholarships@collegefund.org
Web: www.collegefund.org/scholarships/schol_tcu.html
Summary: To provide financial assistance for college to Native American students who are interested in attending a Tribal College or University (TCU) and working for a tribe or Indian organization after graduation.
Eligibility: Open to American Indians and Alaska Natives who can document proof of enrollment or descendancy. Applicants must be planning to 1) enroll full-time at a TCU; and 2) work for their tribe or an Indian organization after graduation. They must have a GPA of 3.0 or higher and be able to demonstrate exceptional academic achievement. Applications are available only online and include required essays on specified topics.
Financial data: The stipend is $2,000 per year.
Duration: 1 year; may be renewed.
Number awarded: Varies each year.
Deadline: May of each year.

929 SOWERS CLUB OF NEBRASKA CONTINUING EDUCATION SCHOLARSHIP

Sowers Club of Nebraska
Attn: Foundation
1701 South 17th Street, Suite 1H
Lincoln, NE 68502
Phone: (402) 438-2244; Fax: (402) 438-2426
Email: sowersclub@windstream.net
Web: www.thesowersclub.com/scholarshipinfo.htm
Summary: To provide financial assistance to residents of Nebraska currently enrolled in college in the state.
Eligibility: Open to residents of Nebraska currently enrolled at a college or university in the state. Applicants must be U.S. citizens and have a GPA of 3.0 or higher. Along with their application, they must submit high school transcripts, 3 to 5 letters of recommendation, information on their extracurricular activities, and documentation of financial need.
Financial data: The stipend is $1,000.
Duration: 1 year.
Number awarded: 1 or more each year.
Deadline: November of each year.

930 SOWERS CLUB OF NEBRASKA HIGH SCHOOL SENIOR SCHOLARSHIP

Sowers Club of Nebraska
Attn: Foundation
1701 South 17th Street, Suite 1H
Lincoln, NE 68502
Phone: (402) 438-2244; Fax: (402) 438-2426
Email: sowersclub@windstream.net
Web: www.thesowersclub.com/scholarshipinfo.htm
Summary: To provide financial assistance to high school seniors in Nebraska planning to attend college in the state.
Eligibility: Open to seniors graduating from high schools in Nebraska who have a GPA of 3.0 or higher. Applicants must be planning to attend a college or university in the state. They must be U.S. citizens. Along with their application, they must submit high school transcripts, 3 to 5 letters of recommendation, information on their extracurricular activities, and documentation of financial need.
Financial data: The stipend is $1,000.
Duration: 1 year.
Number awarded: 1 or more each year.
Deadline: November of each year.

931 SPORTSMANSHIP RECOGNITION PROGRAM SCHOLARSHIP

Kentucky High School Athletic Association
Attn: Assistant Commissioner
2280 Executive Drive

Lexington, KY 40505
Phone: (859) 299-5472; Fax: (859) 293-5999
Email: bcope@khsaa.org
Web: www.khsaa.org

Summary: To recognize and reward, with college scholarships, outstanding student-athletes (including cheerleaders) in Kentucky high schools.

Eligibility: Open to high school seniors in Kentucky who have participated in athletics or cheerleading. Applicants must have at least a 2.5 GPA, 3 letters of recommendation from coaches and administrators illustrating the student's traits of good sportsmanship, demonstrated leadership within the school and the community, and a 2-page response to a case study developed for each competition. They must be planning to attend a college or university in Kentucky. A male and a female are recognized from each school in the state. They are chosen on the basis of these traits: playing the game by the rules; treating game officials, coaches, and competitors with due respect; shaking hands with opponents at the end of each contest; taking victory and defeat without undue emotionalism; controlling their tempers; being positive with officials, coaches, and competitors who criticize them; cooperating with officials, coaches, and fellow players in trying to promote good sportsmanship; being positive with opponents; letting student and adult audiences know that inappropriate behavior reflects poorly on the team; and serving as a role model for future student-athletes. These students are awarded a certificate and are entered into a regional competition. Males and females continue to compete separately. The regional winners are given a plaque and are considered for the Sportsmanship Recognition Program Scholarship. Selection is based on GPA, recommendations, leadership roles and honors, and the case study essay.

Financial data: The stipend is $3,000.

Duration: 1 year.

Number awarded: 2 each year: 1 for a female and 1 for a male.

Deadline: Applications must be submitted to the school's athletic director in March.

932 SREB ACADEMIC COMMON MARKET

Southern Regional Education Board
592 10th Street, N.W.
Atlanta, GA 30318-5776
Phone: (404) 875-9211, ext. 261; Fax: (404) 872-1477
Email: acm-rcp@sreb.org
Web: www.sreb.org/programs/acm/acmindex.asp

Summary: To enable undergraduate and graduate students from southern states to attend a public college or university in another southern state at reduced tuition.

Eligibility: Open to residents of 16 southern states (Alabama, Arkansas, Delaware, Florida (graduate students only), Georgia, Kentucky, Louisiana, Maryland, Mississippi, North Carolina (graduate students only), Oklahoma, South Carolina, Tennessee, Texas (graduate students only), Virginia, and West Virginia) who wish to study in a program not available at any public institution of higher education in their home state. If their state has made arrangements to send students to another state, they may participate in this program.

Financial data: Participants pay only the in-state tuition at the institution outside their home state while they are studying in a program not available in their home state.

Duration: 1 year; may be renewed.

Number awarded: Varies each year; recently, more than 2,200 students participated in this program.

Deadline: Deadline not specified.

933 STANLEY O. MCNAUGHTON COMMUNITY SERVICE AWARD

Independent Colleges of Washington
600 Stewart Street, Suite 600
Seattle, WA 98101
Phone: (206) 623-4494; Fax: (206) 625-9621
Email: info@icwashington.org
Web: www.icwashington.org/scholarships/index.html

Summary: To provide financial assistance to upper-division students from any state enrolled at colleges and universities that are members of the Independent Colleges of Washington (ICW).

Eligibility: Open to residents of any state who are completing their sophomore or junior year at ICW-member colleges and universities. Applicants must submit a 1-page essay on their experience and views on volunteerism and community service. Selection is based on demonstrated commitment to volunteer community service both in high school and in college.

Financial data: The stipend is $2,500.

Duration: 1 year; nonrenewable.

Number awarded: 2 each year.

Deadline: March of each year.

934 STANLEY R. OSBORN SCHOLARSHIPS

Urban League of Nebraska, Inc.
Attn: Scholarships
3040 Lake Street
Omaha, NE 68111
Phone: (402) 451-1066
Web: www.urbanleagueneb.org/education_connection/scholarships.shtml

Summary: To provide financial assistance to residents of Nebraska who plan to attend college in any state.

Eligibility: Open to Nebraska residents who are seniors in high school or students currently enrolled in college. Applicants must be attending or planning to attend a college or university in any state. They must have a GPA of 2.5 or higher and be able to document financial need and at least 5 to 10 hours of community involvement. Along with their application, they must submit a 500-word essay on their goals and ambitions and the reasons they should receive this scholarship.

Financial data: A stipend is awarded (amount not specified).

Duration: 1 year.

Number awarded: Varies each year; recently, 7 of these scholarships were awarded.

Deadline: March of each year.

935 STANLEY Z. KOPLIK CERTIFICATE OF MASTERY TUITION WAIVER PROGRAM

Massachusetts Office of Student Financial Assistance
454 Broadway, Suite 200
Revere, MA 02151
Phone: (617) 727-9420; Fax: (617) 727-0667
Email: osfa@osfa.mass.edu
Web: www.osfa.mass.edu/default.asp?page=koplikWaiver

Summary: To provide financial assistance for college to Massachusetts residents who earn a Stanley Z. Koplik Certificate of Mastery while in high school.

Eligibility: Open to permanent Massachusetts residents who are U.S. citizens or permanent residents. In order to become a candidate for the Stanley Z. Koplik Certificate of Mastery, students must score "Advanced" on at least 1 grade 10 MCAS test subject and score "Proficient" on the remaining sections of the grade 10 MCAS. Once they become candidates, they must then fulfill additional requirements through 1 of the following combinations covering both arts/humanities and mathematics/science: 2 AP exams; 2 SAT II exams; 1 SAT II exam and 1 AP exam; 1 SAT II exam and 1 other achievement; or 1 AP exam and 1 other achievement. They must score at least 3 on any AP exam; if there are SAT II and AP exams in the same subject area, they must receive a score on the SAT II exam determined by the Department of Education to be comparable to a score of 3 on the AP exam. In subject areas where there are no corresponding AP exams, a student must achieve an SAT II score designated by the Department of Education.

Financial data: Recipients of Koplik Certificates are eligible for an award of a non-need-based tuition waiver for state-supported undergraduate courses in Massachusetts.

Duration: Up to 4 academic years, provided the student maintains a college GPA of 3.3 or higher.

Number awarded: Varies each year.

Deadline: April of each year.

936 STATE OF MAINE GRANT PROGRAM

Finance Authority of Maine
Attn: Education Finance Programs
5 Community Drive
P.O. Box 949
Augusta, ME 04332-0949
Phone: (207) 623-3263; (800) 228-3734; Fax: (207) 623-0095; TDD: (207) 626-2717
Email: education@famemaine.com
Web: www.famemaine.com/Education_Home.aspx

Summary: To provide financial assistance to Maine residents interested in working on a college degree.

Eligibility: Open to residents of Maine who have lived in the state for at least 1 year, have graduated from an approved secondary school, can demonstrate financial need, and are enrolled as full-time or part-time students in an approved institution for their first undergraduate degree. Approved schools include all accredited 2- and 4-year colleges, universities, and nursing programs in Maine, as well as regionally accredited 2- and 4-year colleges in states that have a reciprocity agreement with Maine (Connecticut, Massachusetts, New Hampshire, Pennsylvania, Rhode Island, Vermont, and Washington, D.C.).
Financial data: The maximum annual full-time stipend is $1,250 at private schools in Maine, $1,000 at public schools in Maine, $1,000 at private schools outside of Maine, or $500 at public schools outside of Maine.
Duration: 1 year; may be renewed up to 4 additional years if the recipient remains a Maine resident and maintains satisfactory academic progress.
Number awarded: Scholarships are presented to students who demonstrate the greatest financial need. The award process continues until all available funds have been exhausted.
Deadline: April of each year.

937 STATE VOCATIONAL REHABILITATION SERVICES PROGRAM

Department of Education
Office of Special Education and Rehabilitative Services
Attn: Rehabilitation Services Administration
500 12th Street, S.W., Room 503
Washington, DC 20202-2800
Phone: (202) 245-7325; Fax: (202) 245-7590
Email: Carol.Dobak@ed.gov
Web: www.ed.gov/programs/rsabvrs/index.html
Summary: To provide financial assistance to individuals with disabilities for undergraduate or graduate study pursued as part of their program of vocational rehabilitation.
Eligibility: Open to individuals who 1) have a physical or mental impairment that is a substantial impediment to employment; 2) are able to benefit in terms of employment from vocational rehabilitation services; and 3) require vocational rehabilitation services to prepare for, enter, engage in, or retain gainful employment. Priority is given to applicants with the most significant disabilities. Persons accepted for vocational rehabilitation develop an Individualized Written Rehabilitation Program (IWRP) in consultation with a counselor for the vocational rehabilitation agency in the state in which they live. The IWRP may include a program of postsecondary education, if the disabled person and counselor agree that such a program will fulfill the goals of vocational rehabilitation. In most cases, the IWRP will provide for postsecondary education only to a level at which the disabled person will become employable, but that may include graduate education if the approved occupation requires an advanced degree as a minimum condition of entry. Students accepted to a program of postsecondary education as part of their IWRP must apply for all available federal, state, and private financial aid.
Financial data: Funding for this program is provided by the federal government through grants to state vocational rehabilitation agencies. Grants under the basic support program currently total more than $3 billion per year. States must supplement federal funding with matching funds of 21.3%. Persons who are accepted for vocational rehabilitation by the appropriate state agency receive financial assistance based on the cost of their education and other funds available to them, including their own or family contribution and other sources of financial aid. Allowable costs in most states include tuition, fees, books, supplies, room, board, transportation, personal expenses, child care, and expenses related to disability (special equipment, readers, attendants, interpreters, or notetakers).
Duration: Assistance is provided until the disabled person achieves an educational level necessary for employment as provided in the IWRP.
Number awarded: Varies each year; recently, more than 1.2 million people (of whom more than 80% have significant disabilities) were participating in this program.
Deadline: Deadline not specified.

938 STEPHEN PHILLIPS MEMORIAL SCHOLARSHIP

Stephen Phillips Memorial Scholarship Fund
34 Chestnut Street
Salem, MA 01970
Phone: (978) 744-2111; Fax: (978) 744-0456
Email: info@spscholars.org
Web: www.phillips-scholarship.org
Summary: To provide financial assistance to residents of New England who are interested in attending college in any state.
Eligibility: Open to residents of the New England states (Connecticut, Maine, Massachusetts, New Hampshire, Rhode Island, or Vermont) who are entering or returning students at a college or university in any state. Preference is given to residents of Salem, Massachusetts and a few towns and cities north of Boston. Applicants must have a GPA of 3.0 or higher, be enrolled in a demanding course of study, demonstrate skilled writing ability, and be able to demonstrate substantial financial need. In addition, they should demonstrate a desire to make a meaningful contribution to society; be involved in a balance of community, school, and work activities; pursue goals and aspirations with integrity, resolution, self-discipline, and judgment; and earn money for college expenses through part-time work. U.S. citizenship or permanent resident status is required.
Financial data: Stipends generally range from $3,000 to $10,000 per year. Funds are paid in 2 equal installments to the recipient's school and must be used to pay for tuition and fees.
Duration: 1 year; may be renewed for up to 3 additional years, provided the recipient maintains a GPA of 2.5 or higher.
Number awarded: Varies each year; recently, 145 new and 390 renewal scholarships were awarded.
Deadline: March of each year.

939 STEVE SALLEE SCHOLARSHIP

Central Indiana Community Foundation
Attn: Scholarship Program
615 North Alabama Street, Suite 119
Indianapolis, IN 46204-1498
Phone: (317) 631-6542, ext. 279; Fax: (317) 684-0943
Email: scholarships@cicf.org
Web: www.cicf.org/page26452.cfm
Summary: To provide financial assistance to high school seniors in Indiana who have participated in go kart racing and are interested in attending college in any state.
Eligibility: Open to seniors graduating from high schools in Indiana who plan to attend a college, university, or postsecondary technical school in any state. Applicants must be a competitor for at least 50% of the go kart racing season at an Indiana go kart racing venue. They must have a GPA of 2.5 or higher and be able to exhibit qualities of exceptional sportsmanship on and off the track.
Financial data: A stipend is awarded (amount not specified).
Duration: 1 year.
Number awarded: 1 or more each year.
Deadline: March of each year.

940 STEVEN M. PEREZ FOUNDATION SCHOLARSHIPS

Steven M. Perez Foundation
P.O. Box 955
Melville, NY 11747
Phone: (631) 367-9016; Fax: (631) 367-3848
Email: info@smpfoundation.org
Web: www.smpfoundation.org
Summary: To provide financial assistance for college to high school seniors who have survived leukemia or lost a family member to cancer or a related disease.
Eligibility: Open to graduating high school seniors who have survived leukemia or who have lost a parent or sibling to cancer or a related disease. Applicants must be planning to attend a college or university in any state. Along with their application, they must submit medical certification, a recommendation from a counselor, and an essay that describes their connection to leukemia.
Financial data: Stipend amounts vary; recently, they averaged $1,450.
Duration: 1 year.
Number awarded: Varies each year; recently, 10 of these scholarships were awarded.
Deadline: April of each year.

941 STUCK AT PROM SCHOLARSHIP CONTEST

ShurTech Brancs, LLC
32150 Just Imagine Drive
Avon, OH 44011-1355
Phone: (800) 321-1733
Web: www.duckbrand.com/Home/Promotions/stuck-at-prom.aspx
Summary: To recognize and reward (with college scholarships) high school students who wear duct tape to their spring prom.

Eligibility: Open to residents of the United States and Canada who are 14 years of age or older. Applicants must enter as a couple who attend a high school (or home school association) spring prom wearing complete attire or accessories made from duct tape. They must submit a color photograph (professional or amateur) of themselves together in their prom attire. Judges select 10 finalists on the basis of workmanship (30%), originality (25%), use of color (15%), accessories (10%), and quantity of duct tape used (10%). Photographs are then posted on the sponsor's web site. Online votes determine the winners.
Financial data: Each member of the first-place couple receives a $3,000 cash scholarship, each member of the second-place couple receives a $2,000 cash scholarship, each member of the third-place couple receives a $1,000 cash scholarship, and each member of the runner-up couples receives a cash prize of $500. The schools that host the prize winners receive cash prizes of $3,000, $2,000, $1,000, and $500 respectively.
Duration: The competition is held annually.
Number awarded: 20 students receive cash scholarships each year: 1 first place, 1 second place, 1 third place, and 7 runners-up; 10 schools receive cash prizes.
Deadline: June of each year.

942 STUDENT OF INTEGRITY SCHOLARSHIP

Better Business Bureau of Wisconsin Foundation, Inc.
Attn: Scholarship Committee
10101 West Greenfield Avenue, Suite 125
Milwaukee, WI 53214
Phone: (414) 847-6016; (800) 273-1002
Email: scholarship@wisconsin.bbb.org
Web: Wisconsin.bbb.org/scholarship
Summary: To provide financial assistance to high school seniors in Wisconsin who have demonstrated integrity and plan to attend college in any state.
Eligibility: Open to seniors graduating from high schools in Wisconsin who plan to attend an accredited institution of higher education in any state. Applicants must have demonstrated character, leadership, and ethical values. They must have a GPA of 3.0 or higher. Along with their application, they must submit a 500-word essay that explains 1) why they consider themselves a passionate character-builder; and 2) how they have motivated others to join them as passionate character-builders and how they propose to do so in the future. Financial need is not considered in the selection process. U.S. citizenship is required.
Financial data: The stipend is $2,500.
Duration: 1 year.
Number awarded: 1 each year.
Deadline: February of each year.

943 STUDENTS WITH DISABILITIES ENDOWED SCHOLARSHIPS HONORING ELIZABETH DALEY JEFFORDS

Vermont Student Assistance Corporation
Attn: Scholarship Programs
10 East Allen Street
P.O. Box 2000
Winooski, VT 05404-2601
Phone: (802) 654-3798; (888) 253-4819; Fax: (802) 654-3765; TDD: (800) 281-3341 (within VT)
Email: info@vsac.org
Web: services.vsac.org/wps/wcm/connect/vsac/VSAC
Summary: To provide financial assistance to high school seniors with disabilities in Vermont who are interested in enrolling at a college in any state.
Eligibility: Open to graduating high school seniors in Vermont who have a documented disability. Applicants must be planning to attend a college or university in any state. Along with their application, they must submit a 250-word essay on what they believe distinguishes their application from others that may be submitted. Selection is based on that essay, a letter of recommendation, a personal interview, and financial need.
Financial data: The stipend is $1,500.
Duration: 1 year; nonrenewable.
Number awarded: 1 or more each year.
Deadline: March of each year.

944 SUBSIDIZED STAFFORD LOANS

Department of Education
Attn: Federal Student Aid Information Center
P.O. Box 84
Washington, DC 20044-0084
Phone: (319) 337-5665; (800) 4-FED-AID; TDD: (800) 730-8913
Web: www.FederalStudentAid.ed.gov
Summary: To provide loans, some of which may be forgiven, to college students in the United States who demonstrate financial need.
Eligibility: Open to U.S. citizens or eligible noncitizens who have or will have at least a high school diploma or GED certificate, are registered with the Selective Service if required, are enrolled as regular students working toward a degree or certificate in an eligible program, and have a valid Social Security number. This program is available to both dependent and independent students. Independent students are those who meet at least 1 of the following requirements: 1) are 22 years of age or older; 2) are married; 3) are enrolled in a master's or doctoral program; 4) have children for whom they provide more than half the support; 5) have dependents (other than their children or spouses) who live with them and for whom they provide more than half the support; 6) are orphans or wards of a court; or 7) are veterans of the U.S. armed forces. Students who meet none of those requirements are considered dependents. Financial need is required for this program. Students may apply for these loans either through the Federal Direct Loan Program (FDLP), in which loans are obtained directly from the federal government, or the Federal Family Education Loan (FFEL) Program, in which private lending agencies, such as banks, credit unions, or savings and loan associations, lend the money.
Financial data: Undergraduate students, both dependent and independent, may borrow subsidized loans up to $3,500 for the first full year of study, up to $4,500 for the second year, and up to $5,500 per year for the third and subsequent years. Graduate students may borrow up to $8,500 per academic year in subsidized loans. The total subsidized debt that may be incurred under this program is $23,000 for undergraduates or $65,500 for graduate students. A loan fee of 1.5% is deducted from each disbursement of the loan. The interest rate varies but never exceeds 8.25%. Recently, it was 5.6% for undergraduates or 6.8% for graduate students. For these loans, the federal government pays the interest while the student is enrolled in school at least half-time, during a grace period, or during authorized periods of deferment. Several repayment plans are available; exact details depend on the lender, but options include standard, extended, graduated, and income contingent repayment plans.
Duration: Up to 5 years of undergraduate study and up to 5 additional years of graduate or professional study.
Number awarded: Varies each year; in recent years, approximately 6 million new loans have been issued annually.
Deadline: June of each year.

945 SUNSTUDENTS SCHOLARSHIP PROGRAM

Phoenix Suns Charities
201 East Jefferson Street
P.O. Box 1369
Phoenix, AZ 85001-1369
Phone: (602) 379-7969; Fax: (602) 379-7922
Web: www.nba.com/suns/news/charities_index.html
Summary: To provide financial assistance to high school seniors in Arizona who are interested in attending college in any state.
Eligibility: Open to high school seniors in Arizona who have a cumulative GPA of 2.5 or higher and a record of involvement in charitable activities or volunteer service (in school, church, or community). Applicants must be interested in attending a college or university in any state. Along with their application, they must submit a 1-page essay on a topic that changes annually but relates to community service. Selection is based on community service (50 points), content and overall presentation of the essay (30 points), grades (15 points), and letters of recommendation (5 points). The applicant judged most outstanding is awarded the Kevin Johnson Scholarship.
Financial data: Stipends are $5,000 or $2,000.
Duration: The scholarship is offered annually.
Number awarded: 17 each year: 1 at $5,000 (the Kevin Johnson Scholarship) and 16 at $2,000.
Deadline: February of each year.

946 SUNYFAP STUDENT SCHOLARSHIPS

State University of New York Financial Aid Professionals, Inc.
c/o Sarah Izzo, Scholarship and Awards Committee Chair
Erie Community College
4041 Southwestern Boulevard
Orchard Park, NY 14127
Phone: (716) 851-1671
Email: izzo@ecc.edu
Web: www.sunyfap.org/scholarships_and_awards.html
Summary: To provide financial assistance to students enrolled at any of the branches of the State University of New York (SUNY).

Eligibility: Open to SUNY undergraduates. They must be nominated by a member of the State University of New York Financial Aid Professionals (SUNYFAP) at their institution. Nominees must be full-time students who have completed at least 1 year of study for a bachelor's degree or 12 credit hours toward an associate degree. They must submit an essay of up to 500 words on a topic that relates to the principle of equal access to higher education for all students. Selection is based on cumulative GPA (10%), content of the essay (10%), extracurricular activities and/or extenuating circumstances (10%), the student's educational indebtedness (20%), and financial need (50%).
Financial data: The stipend is $1,000.
Duration: 1 year; nonrenewable.
Number awarded: 4 each year: 2 for students working on a bachelor's degree and 2 for students working on an associate degree.
Deadline: March of each year.

947 SURVIVING DEPENDENTS OF MONTANA FIRE FIGHTERS/ PEACE OFFICERS WAIVER

Montana Guaranteed Student Loan Program
2500 Broadway
P.O. Box 203101
Helena, MT 59620-3101
Phone: (406) 444-0638; (800) 537-7508; Fax: (406) 444-1869
Email: scholarships@mgslp.state.mt.us
Web: www.mgslp.state.mt.us
Summary: To provide financial assistance for college to dependents of deceased fire fighters or peace officers in Montana.
Eligibility: Open to residents of Montana who are surviving spouses or children of Montana fire fighters or peace officers killed in the course and scope of employment. Financial need is considered.
Financial data: Students eligible for this benefit are entitled to attend any unit of the Montana University System without payment of undergraduate registration or incidental fees.
Duration: Undergraduate students are eligible for continued fee waiver as long as they maintain reasonable academic progress as full-time students.
Number awarded: Varies each year.
Deadline: Deadline not specified.

948 SURVIVING DEPENDENTS OF MONTANA NATIONAL GUARD MEMBER WAIVER

Montana Guaranteed Student Loan Program
2500 Broadway
P.O. Box 203101
Helena, MT 59620-3101
Phone: (406) 444-0638; (800) 537-7508; Fax: (406) 444-1869
Email: scholarships@mgslp.state.mt.us
Web: www.mgslp.state.mt.us
Summary: To provide financial assistance for undergraduate study to dependents of deceased National Guard members in Montana.
Eligibility: Open to residents of Montana who are surviving spouses or children of Montana National Guard members killed as a result of injury, disease, or other disability incurred in the line of duty while serving on state active duty. Financial need is considered.
Financial data: Students eligible for this benefit are entitled to attend any unit of the Montana University System without payment of undergraduate registration or incidental fees.
Duration: Undergraduate students are eligible for continued fee waiver as long as they maintain reasonable academic progress as full-time students.
Number awarded: Varies each year.
Deadline: Deadline not specified.

949 SURVIVORS' AND DEPENDENTS' EDUCATIONAL ASSISTANCE PROGRAM

Department of Veterans Affairs
Attn: Veterans Benefits Administration
810 Vermont Avenue, N.W.
Washington, DC 20420
Phone: (202) 418-4343; (888) GI-BILL1
Web: www.gibill.va.gov/GI_Bill_Info/benefits.htm
Summary: To provide financial assistance for undergraduate or graduate study to children and spouses of deceased and disabled veterans, MIAs, and POWs.
Eligibility: Open to spouses and children of 1) veterans who died or are permanently and totally disabled as the result of active service in the armed forces; 2) veterans who died from any cause while rated permanently and totally disabled from a service-connected disability; 3) servicemembers listed as missing in action or captured in the line of duty by a hostile force; 4) servicemembers listed as forcibly detained or interned by a foreign government or power; and 5) servicemembers who are hospitalized or receiving outpatient treatment for a service-connected permanent and total disability and are likely to be discharged for that disability. Children must be between 18 and 26 years of age, although extensions may be granted. Spouses and children over 14 years of age with physical or mental disabilities are also eligible.
Financial data: Monthly stipends from this program for study at an academic institution are $925 for full-time, $694 for three-quarter time, or $461 for half-time. For farm cooperative work, the monthly stipends are $745 for full-time, $559 for three-quarter time, or $372 for half-time. For an apprenticeship or on-the-job training, the monthly stipend is $674 for the first 6 months, $505 for the second 6 months, $333 for the third 6 months, and $168 for the remainder of the program. For special restorative training by beneficiaries with a physical or mental disability, the monthly stipend for full-time training is $925.
Duration: Up to 45 months (or the equivalent in part-time training). Spouses must complete their training within 10 years of the date they are first found eligible. For spouses of servicemembers who died on active duty, benefits end 20 years from the date of death.
Number awarded: Varies each year.
Deadline: Applications may be submitted at any time.

950 SUSAN THOMPSON BUFFETT FOUNDATION SCHOLARSHIP PROGRAM

Susan Thompson Buffett Foundation
Attn: Scholarship Office
222 Kiewit Plaza
Omaha, NE 68131
Phone: (402) 943-1383; Fax: (402) 943-1380
Email: scholarships@stbfoundation.org
Web: www.buffettscholarships.org/scholarships.shtml
Summary: To provide financial assistance to entering or currently-enrolled students at public colleges and universities in Nebraska.
Eligibility: Open to U.S. citizens who are Nebraska residents. Applicants must be entering or currently enrolled in a state public college, university, community college, or trade school in Nebraska. They must be in financial need, be the only family member presently receiving a grant from the foundation, have at least a 2.5 GPA, and have applied for federal financial aid. Selection is based primarily on financial need.
Financial data: The stipend is $3,200 per semester. A textbook allowance of $400 is also provided. Funds are sent directly to the recipient's school and must be used to pay tuition and fees; they may not be used to pay for books or other expenses.
Duration: Up to 5 years for a 4-year college, or up to 3 years for a 2-year school, provided the recipient maintains a GPA of 2.0 or higher. Students on scholarship may not drop out for a period of time and be reinstated as a scholarship recipient; they must reapply along with first-time students.
Deadline: February of each year.

951 T. ROWE PRICE FOUNDATION SCHOLARSHIPS

Independent College Fund of Maryland
Attn: Director of Programs and Scholarships
3225 Ellerslie Avenue, Suite C160
Baltimore, MD 21218-3519
Phone: (443) 997-5703; Fax: (443) 997-2740
Email: LSubot@jhmi.edu
Web: www.i-fundinfo.org/scholarships/business-scholarships.html
Summary: To provide financial assistance to students from Maryland at member institutions of the Independent College Fund of Maryland who have demonstrated outstanding leadership on campus or in the community.
Eligibility: Open to students from Maryland currently enrolled at member institutions. Applicants must have demonstrated outstanding leadership qualities on campus and/or in the community. They must have a GPA of 3.0 or higher and be able to demonstrate financial need.
Financial data: The stipend is $3,500.
Duration: 1 year.
Number awarded: 1 or more each year.
Deadline: Deadline not specified.

952 TAILHOOK EDUCATIONAL FOUNDATION SCHOLARSHIPS

Tailhook Educational Foundation
9696 Businesspark Avenue
P.O. Box 26626
San Diego, CA 92196-0626
Phone: (858) 689-9223; (800) 322-4665
Email: tag@tailhook.net
Web: www.tailhook.org/Foundation.html

Summary: To provide financial assistance for college to personnel associated with naval aviation and their children.

Eligibility: Open to 1) the children (natural, step, and adopted) of current or former U.S. Navy or Marine Corps personnel who served as an aviator, flight officer, or air crewman; or 2) personnel and children of personnel who are serving or have served on board a U.S. Navy aircraft carrier as a member of the ship's company or air wing. Applicants must be enrolled or accepted for enrollment at an accredited college or university. Selection is based on educational and extracurricular achievements, merit, and citizenship.

Financial data: The stipend ranges from $1,500 to $15,000.

Duration: 1 to 2 years.

Number awarded: Varies each year; recently, 85 of these scholarships were awarded.

Deadline: March of each year.

953 TELACU SCHOLARSHIPS

TELACU Education Foundation
Attn: Scholarship Program
5400 East Olympic Boulevard, Suite 300
Los Angeles, CA 90022
Phone: (323) 721-1655; Fax: (323) 724-3372
Email: info@telacu.com
Web: telacu.com/site/en/home/education/programs/college.html

Summary: To provide financial assistance to Latino students from New York and eligible communities in California, Texas, and Illinois who are interested in attending designated partner institutions.

Eligibility: Open to Latino students residing in New York and eligible communities in California, Texas, and Illinois. Applicants must 1) be a first-generation college student; 2) be from a low-income family; and 3) have a GPA of 2.5 or higher. They must be enrolled or planning to enroll full-time at a partner institution. Along with their application, they must submit brief essays on a dream they have, an event or experience in their life that inspired them to prepare for their intended career, how their extracurricular activities are helping them prepare for this career, and how they believe they can contribute to the sponsor's mission. Selection is based on extracurricular involvement demonstrating a commitment to the community and financial need.

Financial data: Stipends range from $500 to $5,000 per year.

Duration: Both 1-year and continuing scholarships are available. Continuing scholarships may be renewed for a total of 4 years, provided the recipient attends all sessions of the College Advisement and Leadership Program each year, maintains a GPA of 2.5 or higher, and volunteers 20 hours of service annually to the TELACU Education Foundation or other community organization.

Number awarded: Varies each year.

Deadline: March of each year.

954 TENNESSEE ASPIRE AWARDS

Tennessee Student Assistance Corporation
Parkway Towers
404 James Robertson Parkway, Suite 1510
Nashville, TN 37243-0820
Phone: (615) 741-1346; (800) 342-1663; Fax: (615) 741-6101
Email: TSAC.Aidinfo@tn.gov
Web: www.tn.gov/collegepays/mon_college/need_based_award.htm

Summary: To provide supplemental financial assistance to high school seniors in Tennessee who qualify for the Tennessee HOPE Scholarships and also demonstrate financial need.

Eligibility: Open to seniors graduating from public and private high schools in Tennessee and other residents of the state who qualify for a Tennessee HOPE Scholarship. Applicants must have an annual family income of $36,000 or less. They must be planning to attend an accredited public or private college or university in Tennessee.

Financial data: The stipend is an additional $1,500, so the total award is $5,500 per year for students at 4-year colleges and universities or $3,500 per year for students at 2-year schools.

Duration: 1 year; students may receive this supplemental funding only once.

Number awarded: Varies each year; recently, 11,625 students received more than $52.7 million in scholarships from this program.

Deadline: August of each year for fall semester; January of each year for spring and summer semesters.

955 TENNESSEE BURGLAR & FIRE ALARM ASSOCIATION YOUTH SCHOLARSHIP PROGRAM

Tennessee Burglar & Fire Alarm Association
Attn: Youth Scholarship Program
P.O. Box 150062
Nashville, TN 37215
Phone: (615) 791-9590; (800) 829-6465; Fax: (615) 791-1811
Email: tbfaaexdir@aol.com
Web: www.tbfaa.com

Summary: To provide financial assistance to high school seniors in Tennessee who are the children of active-duty law enforcement and fire service personnel and interested in attending college in any state.

Eligibility: Open to seniors graduating from high schools in Tennessee who have been accepted at an accredited college or university in any state. Applicants must have a father, mother, or legal guardian who is a full-time active employee (not on disability) of the police or sheriff's department or a paid employee or volunteer of a fire department in Tennessee. Along with their application, they must submit an essay of 500 to 700 words on how their parent or guardian helps us secure our community. Selection is based on that essay (15 points), grade average (25 points), class rank (25 points), SAT scores (20 points), and academic prizes, awards, school and outside extracurricular activities, and hobbies (15 points); financial need is not considered.

Financial data: The first-place winner receives a $1,000 scholarship and second a $500 scholarship.

Duration: The awards are presented annually.

Number awarded: 2 each year.

Deadline: February of each year.

956 TENNESSEE DEPENDENT CHILDREN SCHOLARSHIP

Tennessee Student Assistance Corporation
Parkway Towers
404 James Robertson Parkway, Suite 1510
Nashville, TN 37243-0820
Phone: (615) 741-1346; (800) 342-1663; Fax: (615) 741-6101
Email: TSAC.Aidinfo@tn.gov
Web: www.tn.gov/collegepays/mon_college/depend_child_scholar.htm

Summary: To provide financial assistance to the dependent children of disabled or deceased Tennessee law enforcement officers, fire fighters, or emergency medical service technicians who plan to attend college in the state.

Eligibility: Open to Tennessee residents who are the dependent children of a Tennessee law enforcement officer, fire fighter, or emergency medical service technician who was killed or totally and permanently disabled in the line of duty. Applicants must be enrolled or accepted for enrollment as a full-time undergraduate student at a college or university in Tennessee.

Financial data: The award covers tuition and fees, books, supplies, and room and board, minus any other financial aid for which the student is eligible.

Duration: 1 year; may be renewed for up to 3 additional years or until completion of a program of study.

Number awarded: Varies each year; recently, 19 students received $77,786 in support from this program.

Deadline: July of each year.

957 TENNESSEE GENERAL ASSEMBLY MERIT SCHOLARSHIPS

Tennessee Student Assistance Corporation
Parkway Towers
404 James Robertson Parkway, Suite 1510
Nashville, TN 37243-0820
Phone: (615) 741-1346; (800) 342-1663; Fax: (615) 741-6101
Email: TSAC.Aidinfo@tn.gov
Web: www.tn.gov/collegepays/mon_college/gams.htm

Summary: To provide supplemental financial assistance to high school seniors in Tennessee who meet academic requirements in excess of those for the Tennessee HOPE Scholarships and plan to attend college in the state.

Eligibility: Open to seniors graduating from public and private high schools in Tennessee and other residents of the state who qualify for a Tennessee HOPE Scholarship. Applicants for this supplemental funding must have higher levels of academic achievement: ACT scores of at least 29 (instead of 21), SAT scores of at least 1280 (instead of 980), and GPA of 3.75 or higher (instead of 3.0). The GPA may be weighted to include extra credit for AP or other advanced courses. They must be planning to attend an accredited public or private college or university in Tennessee.

Financial data: The stipend is an additional $1,000, so the total award is $5,000 per year for students at 4-year colleges and universities or $3,000 per year for students at 2-year schools.

Duration: 1 year; students may receive this supplemental funding only once.

Number awarded: Varies each year; recently, 3,915 students received more than $18.2 million in scholarships from this program.

Deadline: August of each year for fall semester; January of each year for spring and summer semesters.

958 TENNESSEE HELPING HEROES GRANTS

Tennessee Student Assistance Corporation
Parkway Towers
404 James Robertson Parkway, Suite 1510
Nashville, TN 37243-0820
Phone: (615) 741-1346; (800) 342-1663; Fax: (615) 741-6101
Email: TSAC.Aidinfo@tn.gov
Web: www.tn.gov/collegepays/mon_college/hh_grant.htm

Summary: To provide financial assistance to veterans and current Reservists or National Guard members who are residents of Tennessee and enrolled at a college or university in the state.

Eligibility: Open to residents of Tennessee who are veterans honorably discharged from the U.S. armed forces and former or current members of a Reserve or Tennessee National Guard unit who were called into active military service. Applicants must have been awarded, on or after September 11, 2001, the Iraq Campaign Medal, the Afghanistan Campaign Medal, or the Global War on Terrorism Expeditionary Medal. They must be enrolled at least half-time at an eligible college or university in Tennessee and receive no final failing grade in any course. No academic standard or financial need requirements apply.

Financial data: Grants are $1,000 per semester for full-time study or $500 per semester for part-time study. Funds are awarded after completion of each semester of work.

Duration: Grants are awarded until completion of the equivalent of 8 full semesters of work, completion of a baccalaureate degree, or the eighth anniversary of honorable discharge from military service, whichever comes first.

Number awarded: Varies each year.

Deadline: August of each year for fall enrollment, January of each year for spring, or April of each year for summer.

959 TENNESSEE HOPE ACCESS GRANTS

Tennessee Student Assistance Corporation
Parkway Towers
404 James Robertson Parkway, Suite 1510
Nashville, TN 37243-0820
Phone: (615) 741-1346; (800) 342-1663; Fax: (615) 741-6101
Email: TSAC.Aidinfo@tn.gov
Web: www.tn.gov/collegepays/mon_college/hope_grant.htm

Summary: To provide financial assistance to high school seniors in Tennessee who do not qualify for the Tennessee HOPE Scholarships but meet other academic and income requirements and plan to attend college in the state.

Eligibility: Open to seniors graduating from public and private high schools in Tennessee who have a weighted GPA of 2.75 to 2.99 and an ACT score from 18 to 21 or an SAT score from 860 to 970. Applicants must have an annual family income of $36,000 or less. They must be planning to attend an accredited public or private college or university in Tennessee.

Financial data: The stipend is $2,750 per year for students at 4-year colleges and universities or $1,750 per year for students at 2-year schools.

Duration: 1 year; this grant is nonrenewable but recipients may apply for a Tennessee HOPE Scholarship after 1 year of college if they have a cumulative GPA of 2.75 or higher.

Number awarded: Varies each year; recently, 314 of these grants, worth $639,716, were awarded.

Deadline: August of each year for fall semester; January of each year for spring and summer semesters.

960 TENNESSEE HOPE FOSTER CHILD TUITION GRANT

Tennessee Student Assistance Corporation
Parkway Towers
404 James Robertson Parkway, Suite 1510
Nashville, TN 37243-0820
Phone: (615) 741-1346; (800) 342-1663; Fax: (615) 741-6101
Email: TSAC.Aidinfo@tn.gov
Web: www.tn.gov/collegepays/mon_college/hope_foster_grant.html

Summary: To provide financial assistance to high school seniors in Tennessee who have been in foster care and are interested in attending college in the state.

Eligibility: Open to seniors graduating from public and private high schools in Tennessee who have been in the custody of the Tennessee Department of Children's Services 1) for at least 1 year after reaching 14 years of age; 2) for at least 1 year after reaching 14 years of age, were placed for adoption by the department or an adoption contract agency, and the adoption was finalized; or 3) for at least 1 year and were placed in permanent guardianship by the department after reaching 14 years of age. Applicants must qualify for either a Tennessee HOPE Scholarship (which requires a weighted GPA of 3.0 or higher and either an ACT score of at least 21 or an SAT score of at least 980) or a Tennessee HOPE Access Grant (which requires a weighted GPA of 2.75 or higher, an ACT score from 18 to 21 or an SAT score from 860 to 970, and an annual family income of $36,000 or less). They must be planning to attend an accredited public or private college or university in Tennessee.

Financial data: For students at public postsecondary institutions, awards cover all costs of tuition and associated fees remaining after applying all other student assistance from all sources towards the student's cost of attendance. For students at independent 2- and 4-year institutions, awards provide the cost of tuition and all associated fees remaining after applying all other student's financial assistance from all sources towards the student's cost of attendance, or the average of the sum of full tuition and associated fees charged at all 2- or 4-year public postsecondary institutions, whichever is less.

Duration: 1 year; may be renewed up to 3 additional years (or 5 additional years, provided the student maintains satisfactory academic progress as defined by their institution).

Number awarded: Varies each year; recently, 17 of these grants, worth $34,605, were awarded.

Deadline: August of each year for fall semester; January of each year for spring and summer semesters.

961 TENNESSEE HOPE SCHOLARSHIPS

Tennessee Student Assistance Corporation
Parkway Towers
404 James Robertson Parkway, Suite 1510
Nashville, TN 37243-0820
Phone: (615) 741-1346; (800) 342-1663; Fax: (615) 741-6101
Email: TSAC.Aidinfo@tn.gov
Web: www.tn.gov/collegepays/mon_college/hope_scholar.htm

Summary: To provide financial assistance to high school seniors in Tennessee who plan to attend college in the state.

Eligibility: Open to seniors graduating from public and private high schools in Tennessee, students in Tennessee who have completed a home school program, and residents of Tennessee who have attained a GED. High school seniors must have an ACT score of at least 21 (or SAT score of at least 980) or a weighted GPA of 3.0 or higher; home school students must have an ACT score of at least 21 (or SAT score of at least 980); and GED recipients must have a GED score of at least 525 and an ACT score of at least 21 (or SAT score of at least 980). Applicants must be planning to attend an accredited public or private college or university in Tennessee.

Financial data: The stipend is $4,000 per year for students at 4-year colleges and universities or $2,000 per year for students at 2-year schools.

Duration: 1 year; may be renewed up to 4 additional years if the recipient maintains a cumulative GPA of 2.75 or higher after 24 and 48 attempted semester hours and 3.0 or higher after 72 attempted semester hours and beyond.

Number awarded: Varies each year; recently, 33,120 students received more than $108.3 million in scholarships from this program.

Deadline: August of each year for fall semester; January of each year for spring and summer semesters.

962 TENNESSEE STUDENT ASSISTANCE AWARDS

Tennessee Student Assistance Corporation
Parkway Towers
404 James Robertson Parkway, Suite 1510
Nashville, TN 37243-0820
Phone: (615) 741-1346; (800) 342-1663; Fax: (615) 741-6101
Email: TSAC.Aidinfo@tn.gov
Web: www.tn.gov/collegepays/mon_college/tsa_award.htm

Summary: To provide financial assistance to students in Tennessee who have financial need.

Eligibility: Open to residents of Tennessee who are enrolled at least half-time at a public or eligible private college or university in the state and can demon-

strate financial need (expected family contribution of $2,100 or less). Awards are presented on a first-come, first-served basis; priority is given to U.S. citizens.
Financial data: Recently, the maximum annual award for full-time study was $4,000 at eligible Tennessee 2- and 4-year private institutions, $2,000 at public 4-year institutions, $1,300 at public 2-year institutions, or $1,000 at technology centers.
Duration: 1 year; nonrenewable.
Number awarded: Varies each year; recently, $3.2 million was available for this program.
Deadline: February of each year.

963 TERRITORIAL SCHOLARSHIP LOAN/GRANT PROGRAM

Virgin Islands Board of Education
Dronningen Gade 60B, 61, and 62
P.O. Box 11900
St. Thomas, VI 00801
Phone: (340) 774-4546; Fax: (340) 774-3384
Email: stt@myviboe.com
Web: myviboe.com
Summary: To provide financial assistance to residents of the Virgin Islands who are interested in attending college in the territory or on the mainland.
Eligibility: Open to residents of the Virgin Islands who are seniors or recent graduates of high schools in the territory. Applicants must have a GPA of 2.0 or higher and be attending or accepted for enrollment at an accredited institution of higher learning. Selection is based on the demand for the applicant's proposed major, financial need, GPA, and special circumstances. An effort is made to distribute awards equitably by island.
Financial data: Funding is provided in the form of loans and grants, to an annual maximum of $1,500 for students attending the University of the Virgin Islands on the undergraduate level, $2,500 for students attending off-island colleges and universities on the undergraduate level, and $3,000 for graduate students at both off-island and on-island institutions. The loan portions of the awards have a 6% interest rate.
Duration: 1 year; may be renewed 3 additional years.
Number awarded: Varies each year.
Deadline: April of each year.

964 TESA SCHOLARSHIP PROGRAM

Texas Elks State Association
c/o Robert R. Weems, Youth Activities Committee
4511 Goodnight Trail
Amarillo, TX 79109-5909
Email: Robert.weems@suddenlink.net
Web: www.texaselks.org/scholarships.htm
Summary: To provide financial assistance to high school seniors in Texas who are not at the top of their class and plan to attend college in the state.
Eligibility: Open to seniors at high schools in Texas who are not in the top 5% of their class. Candidates are nominated by their high school counselors; up to 3 boys and 3 girls may be nominated per school. Nominees must be U.S. citizens, residents of Texas, and planning to enroll full-time at an accredited junior college, college, or university in the state. The names of these nominees are submitted to the local lodge; each lodge then selects 1 boy and 1 girl and submits their applications to the state scholarship chair. Those students must submit 1) a 300-word statement on their professional goals and how their past, present, and future activities make attainment of those goals probable; 2) a transcript; 3) a 200-word parent statement on the family's financial situation; and 4) SAT and/or ACT scores. Females and males compete separately. Final selection at the state level is based on leadership and extracurricular activities (200 points), character (200 points), scholarship (300 points), and financial need (300 points).
Financial data: The stipend is $1,250 per year.
Duration: 4 years.
Number awarded: 6 each year: 3 boys and 3 girls.
Deadline: School nominations must be submitted to the local lodges by March of each year.

965 TESA TEENAGER OF THE YEAR CONTEST

Texas Elks State Association
c/o Charles S. Page, Youth Activities Committee
1911 Palo Duro Road
Austin, TX 78757
Email: charles@austinairbalancing.com
Web: www.texaselks.org/scholarships.htm
Summary: To provide financial assistance to seniors at high schools in Texas who plan to attend college in the state.
Eligibility: Open to seniors at high schools in Texas who are U.S. citizens. Applicants must be planning to enroll full-time an accredited college or university in the state. Each Elks lodge in the state may submit the application of 1 boy and 1 girl. Selection is based on SAT or ACT scores; participation, leadership, honors, and awards in academic organizations; participation, leadership, honors, and awards in extracurricular activities; participation, leadership, honors, and awards in civic organizations; part-time employment; future plans; and overall appearance of the application.
Financial data: Stipends are $1,500, $1,000, or $500.
Duration: 1 year.
Number awarded: 3 each year: 1 each at $1,500, $1,000, and $500.
Deadline: Students must submit applications to local lodges by February of each year.

966 TESA VOCATIONAL GRANT PROGRAM

Texas Elks State Association
c/o Laura W. Everington, Youth Activities Committee
2703 Oak Road
Pearland, TX 77584
Phone: (281) 997-2456
Email: leverinton@univ-wea.com
Web: www.texaselks.org/scholarships.htm
Summary: To provide financial assistance to residents of Texas who are interested in attending an eligible vocational/technical school in the state.
Eligibility: Open to Texas residents who are 18 years of age or older. Applicants must be attending or planning to attend a vocational/technical program in Texas that lasts 2 years or less and results in an associate degree, diploma, or certificate. Selection is based on motivation, financial need, skills, grades, and completeness of the application. U.S. citizenship is required.
Financial data: The stipend is $1,000 per year.
Duration: 1 year.
Number awarded: Up to 9 each year.
Deadline: Applications may be submitted at any time.

967 TEXAS B-ON-TIME LOAN PROGRAM

Texas Higher Education Coordinating Board
Attn: Hinson-Hazlewood College Student Loan Program
1200 East Anderson Lane
P.O. Box 12788, Capitol Station
Austin, TX 78711-2788
Phone: (512) 427-6340; (800) 242-3062; Fax: (512) 427-6423
Email: loaninfo@thecb.state.tx.us
Web: www.hhloans.com/borrowers/BOTfactsheet.cfm
Summary: To provide financial assistance to students in Texas who are residents of the state or entitled to pay resident tuition as a dependent child of a member of the U.S. armed forces.
Eligibility: Open to residents of Texas and residents of other states who are entitled to pay resident tuition as a dependent child of a member of the U.S. armed forces. Applicants must 1) have graduated from a public or accredited private high school in Texas or from a high school operated by the U.S. Department of Defense; or 2) earned an associate degree from an eligible Texas institution. They must be enrolled full-time in an undergraduate degree or certificate program at an eligible college, university, junior college, or public technical college in Texas.
Financial data: Eligible students may borrow up to $2,640 per semester ($5,280 per year) for a 4-year public or private institution, $865 per semester ($1,730 per year) for a 2-year public or private junior college, or $1,325 per semester ($2,650 per year) for a public technical college. A 3% origination fee is deducted from the loan proceeds. No interest is charged. Loans are forgiven if the students 1) graduate with a cumulative GPA of 3.0 or higher within 4 calendar years after they initially enroll; within 5 calendar years after they initially enroll in a degree program in architecture, engineering, or other field that normally requires more than 4 years for completion; or within 2 calendar years if they initially enroll in a public or private 2-year institution; or 2) graduate with a cumulative GPA of 3.0 or higher with a total number of credit hours that is no more than 6 hours beyond what is required to complete the degree or certificate.
Duration: 1 year. May be renewed after the first year if the recipient makes satisfactory academic progress toward a degree or certificate. May be renewed after the second and subsequent years if the recipient completes at least 75% of the semester credit hours attempted and has a cumulative GPA of 2.5 or higher on all course work. Loans are available for a maximum of 150 credit hours.

Number awarded: Varies each year.
Deadline: Deadline not specified.

968 TEXAS CHILDREN OF DISABLED OR DECEASED FIREMEN, PEACE OFFICERS, GAME WARDENS, AND EMPLOYEES OF CORRECTIONAL INSTITUTIONS EXEMPTION PROGRAM

Texas Higher Education Coordinating Board
Attn: Grants and Special Programs
1200 East Anderson Lane
P.O. Box 12788, Capitol Station
Austin, TX 78711-2788
Phone: (512) 427-6340; (800) 242-3062; Fax: (512) 427-6127
Email: grantinfo@thecb.state.tx.us
Web: www.collegeforalltexans.com/apps/financialaid/tofa2.cfm?ID=548

Summary: To provide educational assistance to the children of disabled or deceased Texas fire fighters, peace officers, game wardens, and employees of correctional institutions.
Eligibility: Open to children of Texas paid or volunteer fire fighters; paid municipal, county, or state peace officers; custodial employees of the Department of Corrections; or game wardens. The parent must have suffered an injury in the line of duty, resulting in disability or death. Applicants must be under 21 years of age.
Financial data: Eligible students are exempted from the payment of all dues, fees, and tuition charges at publicly-supported colleges and universities in Texas.
Duration: Support is provided for up to 120 semester credit hours of undergraduate study or until the recipient reaches 26 years of age, whichever comes first.
Number awarded: Varies each year; recently, 140 students received support through this program.
Deadline: Deadline not specified.

969 TEXAS CHILDREN OF U.S. MILITARY WHO ARE MISSING IN ACTION OR PRISONERS OF WAR EXEMPTION PROGRAM

Texas Higher Education Coordinating Board
Attn: Grants and Special Programs
1200 East Anderson Lane
P.O. Box 12788, Capitol Station
Austin, TX 78711-2788
Phone: (512) 427-6340; (800) 242-3062; Fax: (512) 427-6127
Email: grantinfo@thecb.state.tx.us
Web: www.collegeforalltexans.com/apps/financialaid/tofa2.cfm?ID=421

Summary: To provide educational assistance to the children of Texas military personnel declared prisoners of war or missing in action.
Eligibility: Open to dependent children of Texas residents who are either prisoners of war or missing in action. Applicants must be under 21 years of age, or under 25 if they receive the majority of support from their parent(s).
Financial data: Eligible students are exempted from the payment of all dues, fees, and tuition charges at publicly-supported colleges and universities in Texas.
Duration: Up to 8 semesters.
Number awarded: Varies each year; recently, 4 of these exemptions were granted.
Deadline: Deadline not specified.

970 TEXAS COMPETITIVE SCHOLARSHIP WAIVERS

Texas Higher Education Coordinating Board
Attn: Grants and Special Programs
1200 East Anderson Lane
P.O. Box 12788, Capitol Station
Austin, TX 78711-2788
Phone: (512) 427-6323; (800) 242-3062, ext. 6323; Fax: (512) 427-6127
Email: grantinfo@thecb.state.tx.us
Web: www.collegeforalltexans.com/apps/financialaid/tofa2.cfm?ID=435

Summary: To provide waivers of nonresident tuition at Texas public institutions to students from outside the state who receive other competitive scholarships.
Eligibility: Open to nonresident and foreign students who receive a competitive scholarship of at least $1,000 to attend a public institution in Texas. Applicants must have competed with other students, including Texas residents, for the award.
Financial data: Eligible students are able to attend Texas public institutions and pay the resident tuition rate.
Duration: 1 year; may be renewed.
Number awarded: Varies each year; recently, 13,417 of these waivers were awarded.
Deadline: Deadline not specified.

971 TEXAS EARLY HIGH SCHOOL GRADUATION SCHOLARSHIPS

Texas Higher Education Coordinating Board
Attn: Grants and Special Programs
1200 East Anderson Lane
P.O. Box 12788, Capitol Station
Austin, TX 78711-2788
Phone: (512) 427-6387; (800) 242-3062, ext. 6387; Fax: (512) 427-6127
Email: Earlygrad@thecb.state.tx.us
Web: www.collegeforalltexans.com/apps/financialaid/tofa2.cfm?ID=417

Summary: To provide financial assistance to students in Texas who are planning to attend college after completing high school in less than specified times.
Eligibility: Open to residents of Texas who are graduating from a public high school in the state and plan to attend a Texas public or private college or university. Applicants must have completed either the recommended high school curriculum or the distinguished achievement high school curriculum in no more than 36 consecutive months. They must be U.S. citizens or otherwise lawfully authorized to be in the United States. Smaller awards are available to applicants who complete the requirements for grades 9–12 within 41 months or within 46 months.
Financial data: Stipends are 1) $2,000 for students who complete the requirements within 36 months (an additional $1,000 is awarded if the student also graduates with at least 15 hours of college credit); 2) $500 for students who complete the requirements in more than 36 but less than 41 months (an additional $1,000 is awarded if the student also graduates with at least 30 hours of college credit); or 3) $1,000 for students who complete the requirements in more than 41 but less than 46 months and also have at least 30 hours of college credit. If the award is used at a private college or university, the school must provide a matching scholarship.
Duration: 1 year; nonrenewable.
Number awarded: Varies each year; recently, 5,959 of these scholarships were awarded.
Deadline: Deadline not specified.

972 TEXAS ECONOMIC DEVELOPMENT AND DIVERSIFICATION WAIVERS

Texas Higher Education Coordinating Board
Attn: Grants and Special Programs
1200 East Anderson Lane
P.O. Box 12788, Capitol Station
Austin, TX 78711-2788
Phone: (512) 427-6323; (800) 242-3062, ext. 6323; Fax: (512) 427-6127
Email: grantinfo@thecb.state.tx.us
Web: www.collegeforalltexans.com/apps/financialaid/tofa2.cfm?ID=567

Summary: To provide waivers of nonresident tuition at Texas public institutions to students from outside the state whose families come to the state as part of the promotional activities of the Economic Development and Tourism division of the Office of the Governor.
Eligibility: Open to students whose families move to Texas in response to the efforts of the Economic Development and Tourism division, which encourages businesses to relocate or expand their operations into the state. As an additional incentive to those businesses, employees and family members who move to Texas are entitled to attend public colleges and universities in the state before they have established residency. Applicants must be nonresidents of Texas but U.S. citizens, permanent residents, or eligible immigrants.
Financial data: Eligible students are able to attend Texas public institutions and pay the resident tuition rate.
Duration: 1 year; if the family is still residing in Texas, students may request a change in classification in order to pay resident tuition.
Number awarded: Varies each year; recently, 236 of these waivers were awarded.
Deadline: Deadline not specified.

973 TEXAS EDUCATION AND TRAINING VOUCHERS FOR YOUTHS AGING OUT OF FOSTER CARE

Texas Higher Education Coordinating Board
Attn: Grants and Special Programs
1200 East Anderson Lane
P.O. Box 12788, Capitol Station
Austin, TX 78711-2788
Phone: (512) 427-6340; (800) 242-3062; Fax: (512) 427-6127
Email: grantinfo@thecb.state.tx.us
Web: www.collegeforalltexans.com/apps/financialaid/tofa2.cfm?ID=480

Summary: To provide financial assistance for college to students in Texas who have been in foster care.

Eligibility: Open to residents of Texas who 1) are between 16 and 21 years of age, have a high school diploma or equivalent, and are attending a Texas public or private college that provides a bachelor's degree or not less than a 2-year program that provides credit toward an associate degree or certificate; 2) are beyond the age of compulsory school attendance (age 18) and are attending an accredited or preaccredited program that provides not less than 1 year of training toward gainful employment; 3) are in foster care of the Texas Department of Family and Protective Services (TDFPS), are at least 16 years of age, and are likely to remain in foster care until turning 18; 4) have aged out of TDFPS foster care but have not yet turned 21; or 5) are adopted from TDFPS foster care after turning 16 years of age but are not yet 21. Applicants must be attending or planning to attend a Texas public or private educational institution that is accredited or granted preaccredited status.

Financial data: Vouchers can be used to cover the cost of attendance (tuition and fees, books and supplies, room and board, transportation, child care, and some personal expenses) or $5,000 per year, whichever amount is less.

Duration: 1 year. Participants in the program remain eligible until age 23 as long as they are enrolled and making satisfactory progress toward completing their postsecondary education or training program.

Number awarded: Varies each year.

Deadline: Deadline not specified.

974 TEXAS EDUCATIONAL OPPORTUNITY GRANT PROGRAM

Texas Higher Education Coordinating Board
Attn: Grants and Special Programs
1200 East Anderson Lane
P.O. Box 12788, Capitol Station
Austin, TX 78711-2788
Phone: (512) 427-6340; (800) 242-3062; Fax: (512) 427-6127
Email: grantinfo@thecb.state.tx.us
Web: www.collegeforalltexans.com/apps/financialaid/tofa2.cfm?ID=529

Summary: To provide financial assistance to students entering a public 2-year college in Texas.

Eligibility: Open to residents of Texas enrolled at least half-time in the first 30 credit hours at a public community college, public technical college, or public state college in the state. Applicants must have an expected family contribution of no more than $2,000.

Financial data: Full-time stipends are approximately $2,585 per semester for public state college students, $865 per semester for community college students, or $1,325 per semester for technical college students.

Duration: 1 year. Students can receive awards for up to 75 semester credit hours, for 4 years, or until they receive an associate degree, whichever occurs first. Renewal requires completion of at least 75% of the hours taken in the prior year plus a cumulative college GPA of 2.5 or higher.

Number awarded: Varies each year; recently, 3,906 of these grants were awarded.

Deadline: Deadline not specified.

975 TEXAS ELKS STATE ASSOCIATION ANNUAL ESSAY CONTEST

Texas Elks State Association
c/o John Oswalt, Youth Activities Committee
312 East Carolanne
Marshall, TX 75672
Phone: (903) 407-2586
Email: joswalt980@aol.com
Web: www.texaselks.org/scholarships.htm

Summary: To recognize and reward high school students in Texas who submit outstanding essays on an assigned topic.

Eligibility: Open to all students at high schools in Texas. Applicants must submit an essay, from 1,000 to 1,500 words in length, on a topic that changes annually; recently, students were invited to write on "The American Dream—What Is It?" They must submit their entry to their local Elks lodge, which selects a winner and forwards it to the state competition.

Financial data: The award is $1,000 for first place, $800 for second, and $500 for third.

Duration: The competition is held annually.

Number awarded: 3 each year.

Deadline: Essay must be submitted to the local lodges by February of each year.

976 TEXAS EXEMPTION FOR HIGHEST RANKING HIGH SCHOOL GRADUATE PROGRAM

Texas Higher Education Coordinating Board
Attn: Grants and Special Programs
1200 East Anderson Lane
P.O. Box 12788, Capitol Station
Austin, TX 78711-2788
Phone: (512) 427-6340; (800) 242-3062; Fax: (512) 427-6127
Email: grantinfo@thecb.state.tx.us
Web: www.collegeforalltexans.com/apps/financialaid/tofa2.cfm?ID=431

Summary: To recognize and reward the top students in Texas high schools.

Eligibility: Open to the highest ranking graduate (i.e., valedictorians) of accredited high schools in Texas. Applicants may be Texas residents, nonresidents, or foreign students.

Financial data: Tuition is waived for award winners at any public college or university in Texas.

Duration: 1 year; nonrenewable.

Number awarded: Varies each year; recently, 1,014 of these exemptions were granted.

Deadline: Deadline not specified.

977 TEXAS EXEMPTION FOR SURVIVING SPOUSES AND DEPENDENT CHILDREN OF CERTAIN DECEASED PUBLIC SERVANTS

Texas Higher Education Coordinating Board
Attn: Grants and Special Programs
1200 East Anderson Lane
P.O. Box 12788, Capitol Station
Austin, TX 78711-2788
Phone: (512) 427-6340; (800) 242-3062; Fax: (512) 427-6127
Email: grantinfo@thecb.state.tx.us
Web: www.collegeforalltexans.com/apps/financialaid/tofa2.cfm?ID=476

Summary: To provide educational assistance to the children and spouses of certain deceased Texas public employees.

Eligibility: Open to residents of Texas whose parent or spouse was killed in the line of duty in certain public service positions after September 1, 2000. Eligible public service positions include peace officers, probation officers, parole officers, jailers, members of organized police reserve and auxiliary units, juvenile correctional employees, paid and volunteer fire fighters, and emergency medical service volunteers and paid personnel. Applicants must be enrolled or planning to enroll full-time at a Texas public college or university.

Financial data: Eligible students are exempted from the payment of all dues, fees, and tuition charges at publicly-supported colleges and universities in Texas. In addition, the institution provides them with an allowance for textbooks. If the student qualifies to live in the institution's housing, the institution must provide either free room and board or an equivalent room and board stipend.

Duration: 1 year; may be renewed.

Number awarded: Varies each year; recently, 167 students received support through this program.

Deadline: Deadline not specified.

978 TEXAS EXEMPTION PROGRAM FOR ADOPTED STUDENTS FORMERLY IN FOSTER OR OTHER RESIDENTIAL CARE

Texas Higher Education Coordinating Board
Attn: Grants and Special Programs
1200 East Anderson Lane
P.O. Box 12788, Capitol Station
Austin, TX 78711-2788
Phone: (512) 427-6340; (800) 242-3062; Fax: (512) 427-6127
Email: grantinfo@thecb.state.tx.us
Web: www.collegeforalltexans.com/apps/financialaid/tofa2.cfm?ID=551

Summary: To provide educational assistance to students in Texas who once were in foster or other residential care and have been adopted.

Eligibility: Open to students who have been in foster care or other residential care under the conservatorship of the Texas Department of Family and Protective Services and have been adopted. Applicants must be attending or planning to attend a public college or university in Texas.

Financial data: Eligible students are exempted from the payment of all dues, fees, and tuition charges at publicly-supported colleges and universities in Texas.

Duration: 1 year; may be renewed.

Number awarded: Varies each year; recently, 52 students received support through this program.

Deadline: Deadline not specified.

979 TEXAS FOSTER CARE STUDENT EXEMPTION PROGRAM

Texas Higher Education Coordinating Board
Attn: Grants and Special Programs
1200 East Anderson Lane
P.O. Box 12788, Capitol Station
Austin, TX 78711-2788
Phone: (512) 427-6340; (800) 242-3062; Fax: (512) 427-6127
Email: grantinfo@thecb.state.tx.us
Web: www.collegeforalltexans.com/apps/financialaid/tofa2.cfm?ID=429

Summary: To exempt students in Texas who were in foster care when they became 18 years of age from payment of tuition at public colleges and universities in the state.

Eligibility: Open to students who have been in the care or conservatorship of the Texas Department of Family and Protective Services 1) on the day before their 18th birthday, the day they graduated from high school, or the day they received a GED certificate; or 2) through their 14th birthday and were then adopted. Applicants must enroll as an undergraduate at a public college or university in Texas within 3 years of that relevant date, but no later than their 21st birthday.

Financial data: Eligible students are exempted from the payment of all dues, fees, and tuition charges at publicly-supported colleges and universities in Texas.

Duration: 1 year.

Number awarded: Varies each year; recently, 1,324 students received support through this program.

Deadline: Deadline not specified.

980 TEXAS GRANT

Texas Higher Education Coordinating Board
Attn: Grants and Special Programs
1200 East Anderson Lane
P.O. Box 12788, Capitol Station
Austin, TX 78711-2788
Phone: (512) 427-6340; (800) 242-3062; Fax: (512) 427-6127
Email: grantinfo@thecb.state.tx.us
Web: www.collegeforalltexans.com/apps/financialaid/tofa.cfm?Kind=GS

Summary: To provide financial assistance to undergraduate students entering college in Texas from high school or a community college.

Eligibility: Open to Texas residents who 1) graduated from a high school in the state no earlier than the 1998–99 school year, completed the recommended or distinguished achievement high school curriculum or its equivalent, enrolled at a public Texas college or university within 16 months of high school graduation, and have accumulated no more than 30 semester credit hours; or 2) earned an associate degree from a public technical, state, or community college in Texas and enrolled at a public university in Texas no more than 12 months after receiving their associate degree. Financial need is considered in the selection process.

Financial data: Full-time stipends are approximately $2,640 per semester for public university and state college students, $865 per semester for community college students, or $1,325 per semester for technical college students.

Duration: 1 year. Students who qualify on the basis of their high school curriculum can receive awards for up to 150 semester credit hours, for 6 years, or until their receive their bachelor's degree, whichever occurs first. Students who qualify on the basis of an associate degree can receive awards for up to 90 semester credit hours, for 4 years, or until they complete a baccalaureate degree, whichever occurs first. Renewal requires completion of at least 75% of the hours taken in the prior year plus a cumulative college GPA of 2.5 or higher.

Number awarded: Varies each year; recently, 61,086 of these grants were awarded.

Deadline: Deadline not specified.

981 TEXAS KNIGHTS TEMPLAR GRANTS

Texas Knights Templar Education Foundation
507 South Harwood Street
Dallas, TX 75201
Phone: (214) 651-6070; Fax: (214) 744-3622
Email: txgrandrecorder@att.net
Web: www.texasyorkrite.org/education.htm

Summary: To provide financial assistance to undergraduate and graduate students from Texas.

Eligibility: Open to students who have completed at least 30 college hours and are residents of Texas. They must be in school full-time and have at least 2 years to go before graduating. Selection is based on academic ability, character, responsibility, leadership, community service, and financial need.

Financial data: Grants range up to $3,000 per year although most are for $1,000. Funds must be used for tuition and living expenses.

Duration: 1 semester or year.

Number awarded: Varies each year.

Deadline: May for the fall semester; September for the spring semester.

982 TEXAS LYCEUM LEADERSHIP AWARDS

Texas Lyceum
Attn: Leadership Award Committee
7131 Lavendale Avenue
Dallas, TX 75230
Phone: (214) 891-0001
Email: administrator@texaslyceum.org
Web: www.texaslyceum.org/scholarships.aspx

Summary: To provide financial assistance to high school seniors in Texas who plan to attend college in the state.

Eligibility: Open to seniors graduating from high schools in Texas and planning to enroll, full- or part-time, at an accredited college or university in the state. Applicants must have a GPA of 3.0 or higher. Along with their application, they must submit 2 essays of 300 words each on 1) themselves and their potential to be a leader in Texas; and 2) their greatest challenge in a leadership role. Selection is based on academics (50 points, including 10 points for TAKS score, 10 points for SAT/ACT scores, 10 points for GPA, 10 points for class rank, and 10 points for honors and/or AP course work), and activities (350 points, including 10 points for employment, 90 points for volunteer activities, 200 points for leadership activities, 10 points for longevity of involvement, and 40 points for variety of involvement). U.S. citizenship or legal resident status is required.

Financial data: The stipend is $2,500. Funds are paid directly to the recipient's college or university.

Duration: 1 year.

Number awarded: 4 each year.

Deadline: February of each year.

983 TEXAS MUTUAL SCHOLARSHIP PROGRAM

Texas Mutual Insurance Company
Attn: Office of the President
6210 East Highway 290
Austin, TX 78723-1098
Phone: (512) 224-3820; (800) 859-5995, ext. 3820; Fax: (512) 224-3889; TDD: (800) 853-5339
Email: information@texasmutual.com
Web: www.texasmutual.com/workers/scholarship.shtm

Summary: To provide financial assistance for college to workers and their families covered by workers' compensation insurance in Texas.

Eligibility: Open to 1) employees who qualify for lifetime income benefits as a result of injuries suffered on the job as covered by the Texas Workers' Compensation Act; 2) children and spouses of injured workers; and 3) children and unremarried spouses of employees who died as a result of a work-related injury. Workers must be covered by the Texas Mutual Insurance Company, formerly the Texas Workers' Compensation Insurance Fund. Children must be between 16 and 25 years of age. Surviving spouses must still be eligible for workers' compensation benefits. Financial need is considered in the selection process.

Financial data: Scholarships are intended to cover normal undergraduate, technical, or vocational school tuition and fees, to a maximum of $4,000 per semester. Those funds are paid directly to the college or vocational school. The cost of course-related books and fees are also reimbursed, up to a maximum of $500 per semester. Those funds are paid directly to the student.

Duration: 1 year; may be renewed if the recipient maintains a GPA of 2.5 or higher.

Number awarded: Varies each year.
Deadline: Applications may be submitted at any time.

984 TEXAS PUBLIC EDUCATIONAL GRANT PROGRAM

Texas Higher Education Coordinating Board
Attn: Grants and Special Programs
1200 East Anderson Lane
P.O. Box 12788, Capitol Station
Austin, TX 78711-2788
Phone: (512) 427-6340; (800) 242-3062; Fax: (512) 427-6127
Email: grantinfo@thecb.state.tx.us
Web: www.collegeforalltexans.com/apps/financialaid/tofa2.cfm?ID=406

Summary: To provide financial assistance to undergraduate and graduate students in Texas.
Eligibility: Open to residents of Texas, nonresidents, and foreign students. Applicants may be undergraduate or graduate students. They must be attending a public college or university in Texas. Financial need is considered as part of the selection process.
Financial data: The amount awarded varies, depending upon the financial need of the recipient. No award may exceed the student's unmet financial need. Each institution sets its own maximum award amounts.
Duration: 1 year; may be renewed.
Number awarded: Varies each year; recently, 102,772 of these grants were awarded.
Deadline: Deadline not specified.

985 TEXAS STATE FIRE FIGHTERS COLLEGE SCHOLARSHIP FUND

Texas State Association of Fire Fighters
Attn: Emergency Relief and College Scholarship Fund
627 Radam Lane
Austin, TX 78745-1121
Phone: (512) 326-5050; Fax: (512) 326-5040
Web: www.tsaff.org

Summary: To provide financial assistance to dependent children of certified Texas fire fighters who plan to attend college in any state.
Eligibility: Open to dependents under 24 years of age of current, retired, or deceased certified fire fighters in Texas. Applicants must be first-time students enrolled full-time at an accredited college, university, or junior college in any state. Along with their application, they must submit a brief essay about their life and school years. Financial need is considered in the selection process. Males and females compete separately for scholarships.
Financial data: The stipend is at least $500 for the first 2 terms or semesters of college (a total of $1,000). Funds are paid directly to the recipient's school.
Duration: Freshman year.
Number awarded: At least 2 each year: 1 is set aside specifically for a female and 1 for a male. If additional funds are available, the program may award additional scholarships to equal numbers of female and male applicants.
Deadline: April of each year.

986 TEXAS TANF EXEMPTION PROGRAM

Texas Higher Education Coordinating Board
Attn: Grants and Special Programs
1200 East Anderson Lane
P.O. Box 12788, Capitol Station
Austin, TX 78711-2788
Phone: (512) 427-6340; (800) 242-3062; Fax: (512) 427-6127
Email: grantinfo@thecb.state.tx.us
Web: www.collegeforalltexans.com/apps/financialaid/tofa2.cfm?ID=559

Summary: To provide educational assistance to students in Texas whose families are receiving Temporary Assistance to Needy Families (TANF).
Eligibility: Open to students who graduated from a public high school in Texas and are dependent children whose parents received, during the year of their high school graduation, TANF for at least 6 months. Applicants must be younger than 22 years of age at the time of enrollment in college and must enroll in college within 24 months of high school graduation.
Financial data: Eligible students are exempt from the payment of all fees (other than building use fees) and tuition charges at publicly-supported colleges and universities in Texas.
Duration: 1 year; nonrenewable.
Number awarded: Varies each year; recently, 128 students received this assistance.
Deadline: Deadline not specified.

987 TEXAS TENNIS AND EDUCATION FOUNDATION SCHOLARSHIPS

Texas Tennis and Education Foundation
Attn: Executive Director
8105 Exchange Drive
Austin, TX 78754
Phone: (512) 443-1334, ext. 222; Fax: (512) 443-4748
Email: leichenbaum@texas.usta.com
Web: www.texastennisfoundation.com/web90/scholarships/default.asp

Summary: To provide financial assistance to residents of Texas who have an interest in tennis and are planning to attend college in any state.
Eligibility: Open to residents of Texas who have an interest in tennis. Applicants must be high school students who will be entering college or full-time college students who are in good standing at a college or university in any state. Along with their application, they must submit federal income tax returns from the previous 2 years, an academic transcript, a copy of their SAT or ACT test results, a list of extracurricular activities (including tennis activities), a personal statement (on their educational expectations and career goals), and 2 letters of recommendation. Selection is based on merit and financial need.
Financial data: The stipend is $1,000 per year.
Duration: 1 year; may be renewed.
Number awarded: Varies each year.
Deadline: April of each year.

988 TEXAS TOP 10% SCHOLARSHIP PROGRAM

Texas Higher Education Coordinating Board
Attn: Grants and Special Programs
1200 East Anderson Lane
P.O. Box 12788, Capitol Station
Austin, TX 78711-2788
Phone: (512) 427-6340; (800) 242-3062; Fax: (512) 427-6127
Email: grantinfo@thecb.state.tx.us
Web: www.collegeforalltexans.com/apps/financialaid/tofa2.cfm?ID=385

Summary: To provide financial assistance to residents of Texas who graduate in the top 10% of their high school class and plan to attend a public university in the state.
Eligibility: Open to seniors graduating from high schools in Texas who are ranked in the top 10% of their class and have completed the recommended or distinguished achievement high school curriculum. Applicants must be planning to enroll full-time at a public 2- or 4-year college or university in Texas. They must be able to demonstrate financial need.
Financial data: The stipend is $2,000 per year.
Duration: 1 year; may be renewed, provided the recipient completes at least 75% of the semester credit hours attempted, remains enrolled full-time, and maintains a cumulative GPA of 3.25 or higher.
Number awarded: Varies each year.
Deadline: Deadline not specified.

989 TEXAS TRIAL LAWYERS ASSOCIATION SCHOLARSHIP

Texas Trial Lawyers Association
Attn: Scholarship Program
1220 Colorado, Suite 500
P.O. Box 788
Austin, TX 78767
Phone: (512) 476-3852; Fax: (512) 473-2411
Email: mfults@ttla.com
Web: www.ttla.com/index.cfm?pg=scholarship%20information

Summary: To provide financial assistance to high school seniors in Texas who are interested in attending college in any state and can demonstrate financial need.
Eligibility: Open to seniors graduating from high schools in Texas who plan to attend a college or university in any state. Applicants must be able to demonstrate the ability to do college level work, and an inability to obtain financial aid through traditional sources. Along with their application, they must submit 1) an essay on why the jury is the cornerstone of the civil justice system; and 2) a personal statement of 1 to 2 pages explaining their career goals, why they wish to attend the college they have chosen, why they wish to receive this scholarship,

their financial support and need, and any unusual circumstances or other information relevant to this application.
Financial data: The stipend is $1,000.
Duration: 1 year.
Number awarded: 31 or more each year.
Deadline: March of each year.

990 TEXAS TUITION EQUALIZATION GRANT PROGRAM

Texas Higher Education Coordinating Board
Attn: Grants and Special Programs
1200 East Anderson Lane
P.O. Box 12788, Capitol Station
Austin, TX 78711-2788
Phone: (512) 427-6340; (800) 242-3062; Fax: (512) 427-6127
Email: grantinfo@thecb.state.tx.us
Web: www.collegeforalltexans.com/apps/financialaid/tofa2.cfm?ID=534
Summary: To provide financial assistance to undergraduate and graduate students attending private postsecondary schools in Texas.
Eligibility: Open to 1) residents of Texas; and 2) residents of other states who are National Merit Scholarship finalists. Applicants must be enrolled full-time as an undergraduate or graduate student at an eligible nonprofit independent college in the state. They may not be receiving an athletic scholarship. Financial need is considered in the selection process.
Financial data: The maximum awarded (currently $3,331 per academic year) may not exceed the student's financial need or the amount of tuition the student is paying in excess of what he or she would pay at a public institution. Students with exceptional financial need (those with an Expected Family Contribution of less than or equal to $1,000) may receive awards up to $4,966 per academic year.
Duration: 1 year; may be renewed, provided the recipient remains enrolled full-time and maintains a GPA of 2.5 or higher.
Number awarded: Varies each year; recently, 29,412 of these grants were awarded.
Deadline: Deadline not specified.

991 THE "DOC" AND CATHY HOLSTED HONORARIUM SCHOLARSHIP

Epsilon Sigma Alpha International
Attn: ESA Foundation
P.O. Box 270517
Fort Collins, CO 80527
Phone: (970) 223-2824; Fax: (970) 223-4456
Email: esainfo@esaintl.com
Web: www.esaintl.com/esaf
Summary: To provide financial assistance to residents of Oklahoma who plan to attend college in any state.
Eligibility: Open to residents of Oklahoma who are 1) graduating high school seniors with a GPA of 3.0 or higher or with minimum scores of 22 on the ACT or 1030 on the combined critical reading and mathematics SAT; 2) enrolled in college with a GPA of 3.0 or higher; 3) enrolled at a technical school or returning to school after an absence for retraining of job skills or obtaining a degree; or 4) engaged in online study through an accredited college, university, or vocational school. Applicants may be attending or planning to attend school in any state and major in any field. Selection is based on character (10%), leadership (20%), service (10%), financial need (30%), and scholastic ability (30%).
Financial data: The stipend is $1,000.
Duration: 1 year; may be renewed.
Number awarded: 1 each year.
Deadline: January of each year.

992 THE FUND FOR VETERANS' EDUCATION SCHOLARSHIP

The Fund for Veterans' Education
Attn: Program Director
111 Radio Circle
Mount Kisco, NY 10549
Phone: (914) 242-2377; Fax: (914) 241-7328
Email: scholarships@veteransfund.org
Web: www.veteransfund.org
Summary: To provide financial assistance for college to veterans who served in Afghanistan or Iraq.
Eligibility: Open to veterans of all branches of the armed forces (Army, Navy, Air Force, Marines), Coast Guard, National Guard, and Reserves who served at least 60 days in Afghanistan or Iraq (or less because of a service-connected injury of condition) after September 11, 2001. Applicants must be enrolled as a full-time or part-time undergraduate student at an accredited 2- or 4-year college, university, or technical school. They must have applied for and accepted all federal, state, and institutional need-based grants and all available military educational benefits. U.S. citizenship is not required as long as all other eligibility requirements, including military service, are met. Selection is based primarily on financial need, although length of military service is also considered.
Financial data: Awards are intended to cover any unmet financial need, according to standard federal procedures. Funds may be used for tuition, fees, books, supplies, and required equipment.
Duration: 1 year; recipients may reapply.
Number awarded: Up to 2 from each state, U.S. territory, and the District of Columbia. A total of $1 million is available for this program each year.
Deadline: October of each year.

993 THEODORE R. AND VIVIAN M. JOHNSON SCHOLARSHIP PROGRAM

State University System of Florida
Attn: Office of Academic and Student Affairs
325 West Gaines Street, Suite 1614
Tallahassee, FL 32399-0400
Phone: (850) 245-0466; Fax: (850) 245-9685
Web: www.flbog.org/forstudents/ati/johnsonscholarship.php
Summary: To provide financial assistance to Florida undergraduate students with disabilities.
Eligibility: Open to students with disabilities enrolled at a State University System of Florida institution. Applicants must submit an official transcript (with GPA of 2.0 or higher); documentation of the nature and/or extent of their disability, which may be in 1 or more of the following classifications: hearing impairment, physical impairment, specific learning disability, speech/language impairment, visual impairment, or other impairment; and documentation of financial need.
Financial data: The stipend depends on the availability of funds.
Duration: 1 year; may be renewed if recipient maintains a GPA of 2.0 or higher and enrolls in at least 18 credits each academic year.
Number awarded: Several each year.
Deadline: May of each year.

994 THOMAS M. HRICIK MEMORIAL SCHOLARSHIP AWARD FOR FEMALES

First Catholic Slovak Union of the United States and Canada
Jednota Benevolent Foundation, Inc.
Attn: Scholarship Program
6611 Rockside Road, Suite 300
Independence, OH 44131
Phone: (216) 642-9406; (800) JEDNOTA; Fax: (216) 642-4310
Email: FCSU@aol.com
Web: www.fcsu.com
Summary: To provide financial assistance for college to female high school seniors who are of Slovak descent and Catholic faith.
Eligibility: Open to women graduating from high schools in the United States and Canada and planning to attend an approved institution of higher education. Applicants must be of Slovak descent and Catholic faith. Along with their application, they must submit 1) a transcript of grades that includes ACT or SAT scores; 2) a list of volunteer community activities in which they have participated; 3) a list of awards received for academic excellence and leadership ability; 4) a description of their career objectives; 5) an essay on why they think they should receive this scholarship; and 6) information on their financial need.
Financial data: The stipend is $1,000. The winner also receives a $3,000 single premium life insurance policy upon proof of graduation from college.
Duration: 1 year; nonrenewable.
Number awarded: 1 each year.
Deadline: September of each year.

995 THOMAS M. HRICIK MEMORIAL SCHOLARSHIP AWARD FOR MALES

First Catholic Slovak Union of the United States and Canada
Jednota Benevolent Foundation, Inc.
Attn: Scholarship Program
6611 Rockside Road, Suite 300
Independence, OH 44131

Phone: (216) 642-9406; (800) JEDNOTA; Fax: (216) 642-4310
Email: FCSU@aol.com
Web: www.fcsu.com

Summary: To provide financial assistance for college to male high school seniors who are of Slovak descent and Catholic faith.

Eligibility: Open to men graduating from high schools in the United States and Canada and planning to attend an approved institution of higher education. Applicants must be of Slovak descent and Catholic faith. Along with their application, they must submit 1) a transcript of grades that includes ACT or SAT scores; 2) a list of volunteer community activities in which they have participated; 3) a list of awards received for academic excellence and leadership ability; 4) a description of their career objectives; 5) an essay on why they think they should receive this scholarship; and 6) information on their financial need.

Financial data: The stipend is $1,000. The winner also receives a $3,000 single premium life insurance policy upon proof of graduation from college.

Duration: 1 year; nonrenewable.

Number awarded: 1 each year.

Deadline: September of each year.

996 THROUGH THE LOOKING GLASS SCHOLARSHIPS

Through the Looking Glass
2198 Sixth Street, Suite 100
Berkeley, CA 94710-2204
Phone: (510) 848-1112; (800) 644-2666; Fax: (510) 848-4445; TDD: (510) 848-1005
Email: scholarships@lookingglass.org
Web: lookingglass.org/scholarships/index.php

Summary: To provide financial assistance for college to high school seniors who have a parent with a disability.

Eligibility: Open to graduating high school seniors and full-time college students who are 21 years of age or younger. Applicants must have at least 1 parent who has a disability. Along with their application, they must submit a 3-page essay describing the experience of growing up with a parent with a disability. Selection is based on that essay, academic performance, community service, and letters of recommendation; financial need is not considered.

Financial data: The stipend is $1,000.

Duration: 1 year.

Number awarded: 10 each year: 5 to high school seniors and 5 to college students.

Deadline: March of each year.

997 THURGOOD MARSHALL SCHOLARSHIPS

Thurgood Marshall College Fund
Attn: Scholarship Manager
80 Maiden Lane, Suite 2204
New York, NY 10038
Phone: (212) 573-8487; (877) 690-8673; Fax: (212) 573-8497
Email: srogers@tmcfund.org
Web: www.thurgoodmarshallfund.net

Summary: To provide financial assistance to African American high school seniors or graduates who are interested in working on a degree at colleges and universities that are members of the Thurgood Marshall College Fund (TMCF).

Eligibility: Open to full-time students enrolled or accepted at 1 of 47 designated TMCF institutions, most of which are Historically Black Colleges and Universities (HBCUs) or other schools with large African American enrollments. Applicants must be African Americans who are U.S. citizens, have a high school GPA of 3.0 or higher, have scored at least 1650 on the SAT or 25 on the ACT, are recommended by their high school as academically exceptional or outstanding in the creative and performing arts, and can demonstrate financial need. They must apply through the TMCF school they attend, and the institutions select the recipients. Along with their application, they must submit an essay of 500 to 1,000 words on what made them choose to attend an HBCU, how they have made a difference on their college campus, and what legacy will they leave behind once they have graduated.

Financial data: Stipends range up to $2,200 per semester, depending on the need of the recipient. Funds are awarded through the institution to be used for tuition, room, board, books, and fees.

Duration: 1 year; may be renewed for up to 3 additional years if the recipient maintains a GPA of 3.0 or higher in college.

Number awarded: Varies each year; recently, nearly 1,000 students were receiving support from this program.

Deadline: The online application process closes in August of each year.

998 TILF SCHOLARSHIPS

University Interscholastic League
Attn: Texas Interscholastic League Foundation
1701 Manor Road
P.O. Box 8028
Austin, TX 78713-8028
Phone: (512) 232-4937; Fax: (512) 232-7311
Email: bbaxendale@mail.utexas.edu
Web: www.uil.utexas.edu/tilf/scholarships.html

Summary: To provide financial assistance to high school seniors who participate in programs of the Texas Interscholastic League Foundation (TILF) and plan to attend college in the state.

Eligibility: Open to seniors graduating from high schools in Texas who have competed in a University Interscholastic League (UIL) academic state meet (participation in athletic or music contests does not qualify). Applicants must be planning to attend a college or university in the state and major in any field. Along with their application, they must submit high school transcripts that include SAT and/or ACT scores and documentation of financial need.

Financial data: Stipends range from $500 to $4,000 per year.

Duration: 1 year; some programs may be renewed up to 4 additional years.

Number awarded: Varies each year; recently, 354 new scholarships and 255 renewal scholarships were awarded.

Deadline: May of each year.

999 TOBY WRIGHT SCHOLARSHIP FUND

Workers' Compensation Association of New Mexico
Attn: Brock Carter
P.O. Box 35757, Station D
Albuquerque, NM 87176
Phone: (505) 881-1112; (800) 640-0724
Email: brock@safetycounseling.com
Web: www.wcaofnm.com/i6/Toby_Wright_Scholarship/information.html

Summary: To provide financial assistance for college to residents of New Mexico whose parent was permanently disabled or killed in an employment-related accident.

Eligibility: Open to residents of New Mexico between 16 and 25 years of age who are attending or planning to attend a college, university, or trade school in the state. Applicants must have a parent who was permanently or catastrophically injured or killed in an employment-related accident that resulted in a New Mexico workers' compensation claim. The parent's death or injury must have resulted in a substantial decline in the family income.

Financial data: A stipend is awarded (amount not specified). Funds may be used for tuition, books, housing, meals, and course fees.

Duration: 1 semester or quarter; may be renewed if the recipient maintains a GPA of 2.5 or higher and full-time enrollment.

Number awarded: Varies each year; recently, 8 of these scholarships were awarded.

Deadline: Deadline not specified.

1000 TOTEM OCEAN TRAILER EXPRESS SCHOLARSHIPS

Independent Colleges of Washington
600 Stewart Street, Suite 600
Seattle, WA 98101
Phone: (206) 623-4494; Fax: (206) 625-9621
Email: info@icwashington.org
Web: www.icwashington.org/scholarships/index.html

Summary: To provide financial assistance to residents of Alaska enrolled at colleges and universities that are members of the Independent Colleges of Washington (ICW).

Eligibility: Open to students enrolled at ICW-member colleges and universities who are residents of Alaska. Selection is based on academic merit. No application is required; each ICW institution makes a selection from all of its students.

Financial data: The stipend is $1,000.

Duration: 1 year; nonrenewable.

Number awarded: 10 each year: 1 at each of the 10 ICW colleges and universities.

Deadline: Each institution sets its own deadline.

1001 TOUCHSTONE ENERGY ALL "A" CLASSIC SCHOLARSHIPS

Touchstone Energy All "A" Classic
c/o Dave Cowden, Chair
Hancock County High School
80 State Route 271 South
Lewisport, KY 42351
Phone: (270) 927-6953; Fax: (270) 927-8677
Email: dcowden@hancock.k12.ky.us
Web: www.allaclassic.org

Summary: To provide financial assistance to seniors at small high schools in Kentucky who plan to attend college in the state.

Eligibility: Open to seniors graduating from high schools in Kentucky that are members or eligible to be a member of the All "A" Classic. Applicants must be planning to attend a public or private college or university, community college, or vocation and technical school in Kentucky. Along with their application, they must submit family financial information, transcripts, SAT and/or ACT scores, and a list of extracurricular activities, honors, awards, and community activities. They must be U.S. citizens or in the process of obtaining citizenship.

Financial data: The stipend is $1,000.

Duration: 1 year; nonrenewable.

Number awarded: Varies each year; recently, 62 of these scholarships were awarded.

Deadline: December of each year.

1002 TOWNSHIP OFFICIALS OF ILLINOIS SCHOLARSHIP FUND

Township Officials of Illinois
Attn: Scholarship Committee
408 South Fifth Street
Springfield, IL 62701-1804
Phone: (217) 744-2212; (866) 897-4688; Fax: (217) 744-7419
Web: www.toi.org

Summary: To provide financial assistance to high school seniors in Illinois who have a record of involvement in extracurricular activities and plan to attend college in the state.

Eligibility: Open to seniors graduating from high schools in Illinois who have a GPA of 3.0 or higher. Applicants must have demonstrated a history of involvement in extracurricular activities that demonstrates a willingness to accept leadership responsibilities or a commitment to civic responsibility, social consciousness, and a willingness to serve the community. They must be planning to attend a college or university in Illinois as a full-time undergraduate student working on a bachelor's degree. Along with their application, they must submit an essay (up to 500 words) on "The Role of Local Government in Today's Society and in the Future." Financial need is not considered in the selection process. U.S. citizenship is required.

Financial data: The stipend is $2,000.

Duration: 1 year.

Number awarded: Varies each year; recently, 7 of these scholarships were awarded.

Deadline: February of each year.

1003 TOYOTA COMMUNITY SCHOLARS PROGRAM

Toyota Motor Sales, U.S.A., Inc.
Attn: Toyota Community Scholars Program
19001 South Western Avenue
Department WC11
Torrance, CA 90501
Phone: (800) 331-4331; Fax: (301) 468-7814
Web: www.toyota.com/about/philanthropy/education/scholarships/tcs.html

Summary: To provide financial assistance to high school seniors who have outstanding records of academic performance and volunteerism.

Eligibility: Open to high school seniors. Each high school in the United States may nominate 1 graduating senior for these scholarships; schools with more than 600 graduating seniors may nominate 2 of them. Nominees must be U.S. citizens, nationals, or permanent residents who plan to work on an undergraduate degree at an accredited 4-year college or university in the United States. Selection is based on academic record (GPA of 3.0 or higher) and involvement in a service organization or project that has a positive impact on the school and/or community.

Financial data: The stipend is $5,000 or $2,500 per year. Winners also receive an all-expense paid trip to Louisville, Kentucky where they meet fellow awardees and are recognized for their achievements.

Duration: 4 years.

Number awarded: 100 each year: 12 national winners at $5,000 per year and 88 regional winners at $2,500 per year.

Deadline: December of each year.

1004 TRACK ATHLETE SCHOLARSHIP

Current Surfaces, Inc.
9600 Wilbur Lake Road
Hanover, MI 49241
Phone: (517) 524-6610; Fax: (517) 524-7250
Email: info@currentsurfaces.com
Web: www.currentsurfaces.com/scholarship.html

Summary: To provide financial assistance to high school seniors who have participated in track and field and are interested in attending college in any state.

Eligibility: Open to seniors graduating from high schools that have a running track surface installed by the sponsoring organization. Applicants must have participated in track and field for at least 3 years and be planning to enroll at an accredited college, university, or vocational/trade school in any state. They must have a GPA of 2.0 or higher and be able to demonstrate such qualities as initiative, honesty, integrity, community service, and a strong work ethic. Along with their application, they must submit an essay of 250 to 300 words on how they feel that running track has improved their life and what values they have learned. Financial need is not required but may be taken into consideration in the selection process.

Financial data: The stipend is $1,000. Funds may be used for school-related expenses, including (but not limited to) tuition, room and board, books, and laboratory fees.

Duration: 1 year; nonrenewable.

Number awarded: 1 each year.

Deadline: April of each year.

1005 TRANSPLANT SCHOLARS AWARDS

Astellas Pharma US, Inc.
Attn: Transplant Scholars Award
534 Fourth Street
San Francisco, CA 94107
Phone: (800) 888-7704
Web: astellastransplant.com/awards_scholar.php

Summary: To recognize and reward, with scholarships for college or graduate school, transplant recipients and donors who submit outstanding essays on their transplant experience.

Eligibility: Open to liver, kidney, or heart transplant recipients who are taking Prograf and to organ donors who have donated a portion of their liver or a kidney. Applicants must be beginning higher education, returning to school after their surgery, or working on an advanced degree. They must submit a 500-word essay that describes their transplant or donation experience, how the experience has changed their life, and how they would use the scholarship award to further their education and give back to the transplant community. Selection is based on the compelling nature of the story, the educational goals of the applicant and how those were affected by transplantation, and the applicant's intention to impact the transplant community positively.

Financial data: The award is a $5,000 scholarship to be used for educational expenses.

Duration: The awards are presented annually.

Number awarded: 5 each year.

Deadline: June of each year.

1006 TWO TEN FOOTWEAR FOUNDATION HIGHER EDUCATION SCHOLARSHIPS

Two Ten Footwear Foundation
Attn: Scholarship Director
1466 Main Street
Waltham, MA 02451
Phone: (781) 736-1500; (800) FIND-210, ext. 1512; Fax: (781) 736-1555
Email: scholarship@twoten.org
Web: www.twoten.org/Scholarships/Higher-Education-Scholarships

Summary: To provide financial assistance to undergraduate students who work, or whose parent works, in the footwear, leather, or allied industries.

Eligibility: Open to students attending or planning to attend a college, university, nursing school, or vocational/technical school to work on a 2- or 4-year undergraduate degree. Applicants must be affiliated with the footwear, leather, or allied industries in 1 of 2 ways: 1) the student must have been employed for

at least 500 hours in 1 of those industries during the preceding year; or 2) the student's parent (natural, step, or adopted) must have been employed in those industries for at least 2 years prior to applying. The employer must do 50% of its business in footwear, or the applicant or parent must work in a specific footwear division. U.S. citizenship or permanent resident status is required. Selection is based on academic record, personal promise, character, and financial need.
Financial data: Stipends range up to $3,000 per year, depending on the need of the recipient. The applicant who demonstrates the greatest financial need receives $15,000 per year. Funds are sent directly to the recipient's school.
Duration: 1 year; may be renewed up to 3 additional years.
Number awarded: Varies; generally, more than 200 new awards and 300 renewals are presented each year.
Deadline: January of each year.

1007 TY COBB UNDERGRADUATE SCHOLARSHIP PROGRAM

Ty Cobb Educational Foundation
P.O. Box 937
Sharpsburg, GA 30277
Email: tycobb@mindspring.com
Web: www.tycobbfoundation.com

Summary: To provide financial assistance to Georgia residents who need financial assistance and are attending college in any state.
Eligibility: Open to undergraduate students who are residents of Georgia, have demonstrated financial need, and have completed at least 45 quarter hours or 30 semester hours with a GPA of 3.0 or better at an accredited college or university in any state. Students with the highest academic averages and the greatest need are given priority.
Financial data: The amount awarded varies depending upon the needs of the recipient. Funds are paid directly to the recipient's school.
Duration: 1 academic year; may be renewed.
Number awarded: Varies each year.
Deadline: June of each year.

1008 UCB FAMILY EPILEPSY SCHOLARSHIP PROGRAM

UCB, Inc.
Family Scholarship Program
c/o Hudson Medical Communications
200 White Plains Road, Second Floor
Tarrytown, NY 10591
Phone: (866) 825-1920
Email: questions@hudsonmc.com
Web: www.ucbepilepsyscholarship.com/ProgramInformation.aspx

Summary: To provide financial assistance for college or graduate school to epilepsy patients and their family members and caregivers.
Eligibility: Open to epilepsy patients and their family members and caregivers. Applicants must be working on or planning to work on an undergraduate or graduate degree at an institution of higher education in the United States. They must be able to demonstrate academic achievement, a record of participation in activities outside of school, and service as a role model. Along with their application, they must submit a 1-page essay explaining why they should be selected for the scholarship, how epilepsy has impacted their life either as a patient or as a family member or caregiver, and how they will benefit from the scholarship. U.S. citizenship or permanent resident status is required.
Financial data: The stipend is $5,000.
Duration: 1 year; nonrenewable.
Number awarded: 40 each year.
Deadline: April of each year.

1009 UNITED CHURCH OF CHRIST UNDERGRADUATE SCHOLARSHIPS

United Church of Christ
Local Church Ministries
Attn: Parish Life and Leadership Team
700 Prospect Avenue East
Cleveland, OH 44115-1100
Phone: (216) 736-3839; (866) 822-8224, ext. 3839; Fax: (216) 736-3783
Email: scholars@ucc.org
Web: www.ucc.org/higher-education/scholarships

Summary: To provide financial assistance to undergraduate students who are affiliated with United Church of Christ (UCC) congregations.
Eligibility: Open to members of UCC congregations who are younger than 25 years of age. Applicants must be entering their sophomore, junior, or senior year at a 4-year accredited college of university in the United States. Entering sophomores must have a GPA of 2.0 or higher; entering juniors or seniors must have a GPA of 3.0 or higher. Financial need is considered in the selection process.
Financial data: Stipends range from $500 to $1,000. Funds are remitted to the recipient's college or university for tuition expenses.
Duration: 1 year; recipients may reapply.
Number awarded: Varies each year.
Deadline: May of each year.

1010 UNITED METHODIST ETHNIC MINORITY SCHOLARSHIPS

United Methodist Church
Attn: General Board of Higher Education and Ministry
Office of Loans and Scholarships
1001 19th Avenue South
P.O. Box 340007
Nashville, TN 37203-0007
Phone: (615) 340-7344; Fax: (615) 340-7367
Email: umscholar@gbhem.org
Web: www.gbhem.org/loansandscholarships

Summary: To provide financial assistance to undergraduate Methodist students who are of ethnic minority ancestry.
Eligibility: Open to full-time undergraduate students at accredited colleges and universities in the United States who have been active, full members of a United Methodist Church for at least 1 year prior to applying. Applicants must have at least 1 parent who is African American, Hispanic, Asian, Native American, Alaska Native, or Pacific Islander. They must have a GPA of 2.5 or higher and be able to demonstrate financial need. U.S. citizenship, permanent resident status, or membership in a central conference of the United Methodist Church is required. Selection is based on church membership, involvement in church and community activities, GPA, and financial need.
Financial data: A stipend is awarded (amount not specified).
Duration: 1 year; recipients may reapply.
Number awarded: Varies each year.
Deadline: April of each year.

1011 UNITED METHODIST FOUNDATION COLLEGE AND UNIVERSITY MERIT SCHOLARS PROGRAM

United Methodist Higher Education Foundation
Attn: Scholarships Administrator
1001 19th Avenue South
P.O. Box 340005
Nashville, TN 37203-0005
Phone: (615) 340-7385; (800) 811-8110; Fax: (615) 340-7330
Email: umhefscholarships@gbhem.org
Web: www.umhef.org/receive.php?id=foundation_merit

Summary: To provide financial assistance to undergraduate students attending colleges and universities affiliated with the United Methodist Church.
Eligibility: Open to freshmen, sophomores, juniors, and seniors at United Methodist–related 4-year colleges and universities and to freshmen and sophomores at 2-year colleges. Nominees must have been active members of the United Methodist Church for at least 1 year prior to application. They must be planning to enroll full-time and have a GPA of 3.0 or higher. Financial need is considered in the selection process. U.S. citizenship or permanent resident status is required.
Financial data: The stipend is $1,000.
Duration: 1 year; nonrenewable.
Number awarded: 420 each year: 1 to a member of each class at each school.
Deadline: Nominations from schools must be received by August of each year.

1012 UNITED METHODIST GENERAL SCHOLARSHIP PROGRAM

United Methodist Church
Attn: General Board of Higher Education and Ministry
Office of Loans and Scholarships
1001 19th Avenue South
P.O. Box 340007
Nashville, TN 37203-0007
Phone: (615) 340-7344; Fax: (615) 340-7367
Email: umscholar@gbhem.org
Web: www.gbhem.org/loansandscholarships

Summary: To provide financial assistance to undergraduate and graduate students who are members of United Methodist Church congregations.
Eligibility: Open to postsecondary students who are Methodists. This program includes a number of individual scholarships that were established by private donors through wills and annuities. The basic criteria for eligibility include 1) U.S. citizenship or permanent resident status; 2) active, full membership in a United Methodist Church for at least 1 year prior to applying (some scholarships require 3-years' membership); 3) GPA of 2.5 or higher (some scholarships require 3.0 or higher); 4) demonstrated financial need; and 5) full-time enrollment in an undergraduate or graduate degree program at an accredited educational institution in the United States. Students from the Central Conferences must be enrolled at a United Methodist–related institution. Most graduate scholarships are designated for persons working on a degree in theological studies (M.Div., D.Min., Ph.D.) or higher education administration. Some scholarships stipulate that the applicant meet more than the basic eligibility criteria (e.g., resident of specific conference, majoring in specified field).
Financial data: The funding is intended to supplement the student's own resources.
Duration: 1 year; renewal policies are set by participating universities.
Number awarded: Varies each year.
Deadline: May of each year.

1013 UNITED METHODIST LEADERSHIP SCHOLARS PROGRAM

United Methodist Higher Education Foundation
Attn: Scholarships Administrator
1001 19th Avenue South
P.O. Box 340005
Nashville, TN 37203-0005
Phone: (615) 340-7385; (800) 811-8110; Fax: (615) 340-7330
Email: umhefscholarships@gbhem.org
Web: umls.umc.org

Summary: To provide financial assistance to undergraduate Methodist students who are planning to enroll at a church-related institution in the Southeast.
Eligibility: Open to students entering 1 of 36 participating United Methodist–related colleges and universities in the southeastern states as a full-time first-year student. Applicants must have been an active member of a United Methodist Church in any state for at least 1 year. Their local church must agree to provide at least $1,000 for their support in college. Along with their application, they must submit a statement from their pastor, youth minister, or Sunday school teacher describing their leadership skills and potential.
Financial data: The local church must agree to provide a stipend of $1,000 and the participating college or university agrees to match that. In addition, the United Methodist Higher Education Foundation (UMHEF) has agreed to provide a limited number of $1,000 matching scholarships, so students may receive as much as $3,000.
Duration: 1 year; nonrenewable.
Number awarded: Varies each year; the UMHEF provides matching funds for up to 100 students.
Deadline: March of each year.

1014 UNITED SERVICES AUTOMOBILE ASSOCIATION SCHOLARSHIPS

U.S. Army
ROTC Cadet Command
Attn: ATCC-OP-I-S
55 Patch Road, Building 56
Fort Monroe, VA 23651-1052
Phone: (757) 788-3473; (800) USA-ROTC; Fax: (757) 788-4643
Email: atccps@usacc.army.mil
Web: www.goarmy.com/rotc/college_students.jsp

Summary: To provide financial assistance to Army ROTC non-scholarship cadets.
Eligibility: Open to students who are entering their senior year of the Army ROTC program. Applicants must be non-scholarship cadets.
Financial data: The national stipend is $1,500; regional stipends are $1,000.
Duration: 1 year.
Number awarded: 29 each year: 14 in the ROTC eastern region, 14 in the ROTC western region, and 1 awarded nationally.
Deadline: June of each year.

1015 UNITED STATES SENATE YOUTH PROGRAM SCHOLARSHIPS

William Randolph Hearst Foundation
90 New Montgomery Street, Suite 1212
San Francisco, CA 94105-4504
Phone: (415) 908-4540; (800) 841-7048, ext. 4540; Fax: (415) 243-0760
Email: ussyp@hearstfdn.org
Web: www.ussenateyouth.org

Summary: To recognize and reward, with a trip to Washington, D.C. and college scholarships, outstanding high school student leaders.
Eligibility: Open to high school juniors and seniors who are currently serving in 1 of the following student government offices: student body president, vice president, secretary, or treasurer; class president, vice president, secretary, or treasurer; student council representative; or student representative to a district, regional, or state-level civic or educational organization. Applications are available only through high school principals and state education administrators. Selection is based on ability and demonstrated leadership. Recipients must, within 2 years after high school graduation, enroll at an accredited U.S. college or university, pledging to include courses in government or related subjects in their undergraduate program.
Financial data: Winners receive an all-expense paid trip to Washington, D.C. for 1 week (to be introduced to the operation of the federal government and Congress) and are presented with a $5,000 college scholarship.
Duration: The awards are presented annually.
Number awarded: 104 each year: 2 from each state, Washington, D.C., and the Department of Defense Education Activity.
Deadline: September of each year.

1016 UNIVERSITY OF NORTH CAROLINA NEED-BASED GRANTS

North Carolina State Education Assistance Authority
Attn: Grants, Training, and Outreach Department
10 T.W. Alexander Drive
P.O. Box 13663
Research Triangle Park, NC 27709-3663
Phone: (919) 549-8614; (800) 700-1775; Fax: (919) 248-4687
Email: information@ncseaa.edu
Web: www.ncseaa.edu

Summary: To provide financial assistance to students enrolled at 1 of the more than 15 branches of the University of North Carolina.
Eligibility: Open to residents of North Carolina enrolled for at least 6 credit hours at any of the constituent institutions of the University of North Carolina. Applicants must be able to demonstrate financial need, based on data from the Free Application for Federal Student Aid (FAFSA).
Financial data: Stipends depend on the need of the recipient and the availability of funds; recently, they averaged more than $2,100.
Duration: 1 year.
Number awarded: Varies each year; recently, 43,975 students were receiving $95,304,710 in support through this program.
Deadline: Deadline not specified.

1017 UNSUBSIDIZED STAFFORD LOANS

Department of Education
Attn: Federal Student Aid Information Center
P.O. Box 84
Washington, DC 20044-0084
Phone: (319) 337-5665; (800) 4-FED-AID; TDD: (800) 730-8913
Web: www.FederalStudentAid.ed.gov

Summary: To provide loans, some of which may be forgiven, to college students in the United States who demonstrate financial need.
Eligibility: Open to U.S. citizens or eligible noncitizens who have or will have at least a high school diploma or GED certificate, are registered with the Selective Service if required, are enrolled as regular students working toward a degree or certificate in an eligible program, and have a valid Social Security number. This program is available to both dependent and independent students. Independent students are those who meet at least 1 of the following requirements: 1) are 22 years of age or older; 2) are married; 3) are enrolled in a master's or doctoral program; 4) have children for whom they provide more than half the support; 5) have dependents (other than their children or spouses) who live with them and for whom they provide more than half the support; 6) are orphans or wards of a court; or 7) are veterans of the U.S. armed forces. Students who meet none of those requirements are considered dependents. This program is available

to students who cannot demonstrate financial need. Students may apply for these loans either through the Federal Direct Loan Program (FDLP), in which loans are obtained directly from the federal government, or the Federal Family Education Loan (FFEL) Program, in which private lending agencies, such as banks, credit unions, or savings and loan associations, lend the money.

Financial data: Dependent undergraduate students may borrow up to $2,000 per year in unsubsidized loans, in addition to the subsidized loans for which they may be eligible (up to $3,500 for the first full year of study, up to $4,500 for the second year, and up to $5,500 per year for the third and subsequent years). Independent undergraduate students and those whose parents are unable to obtain a loan through the Federal PLUS Program may borrow unsubsidized loans up to $6,000 per year for the first and second full years of study and $7,000 per year for the third and subsequent years. Those amounts are in addition to the subsidized loans of $3,500 for the first year, $4,500 for the second year, and $5,500 per year for the third and subsequent years. Graduate students may borrow up to $12,000 per academic year in unsubsidized loans, in addition to the $8,500 in subsidized loans they may borrow. The total unsubsidized debt that may be incurred under this program is $8,000 for dependent undergraduate students (along with $23,000 in subsidized loans), $34,500 for independent undergraduate students (along with $23,000 in subsidized loans), or $73,00 for graduate or professional students (along with $65,500 in subsidized loans). A loan fee of 1.5% is deducted from each disbursement of the loan. The interest rate varies but never exceeds 8.25%. Recently, it was 6.8%. Interest is charged from the day the loan is disbursed, including in-school, grace, and deferment periods. Several repayment plans are available; exact details depend on the lender, but options include standard, extended, graduated, and income contingent repayment plans.

Duration: Up to 5 years of undergraduate study and up to 5 additional years of graduate or professional study.

Number awarded: Varies each year; in recent years, nearly 5 million new loans have been issued annually.

Deadline: June of each year.

1018 UPROMISE SCHOLARSHIPS

Upromise
95 Wells Avenue
Newton, MA 02459
Phone: (888) 434-9111; Fax: (617) 559-2426
Web: www.upromise.com/member/loans/scholarships.do

Summary: To provide financial assistance for college to parents who sign up for the Upromise service and their children.

Eligibility: Open to Upromise enrollees and their children who are high school seniors, high school graduates, or current full-time undergraduates at an accredited 2- or 4-year college, university, or vocational/technical school. Applicants must have a cumulative GPA of 3.0 or higher and a household income of $65,000 or less. They must be U.S. citizens or permanent residents.

Financial data: The stipend is $2,500.

Duration: 1 year.

Number awarded: 200 each year.

Deadline: February of each year.

1019 UPS SCHOLARSHIP PROGRAM

Association of Independent Colleges and Universities of Pennsylvania
101 North Front Street
Harrisburg, PA 17101-1405
Phone: (717) 232-8649; Fax: (717) 233-8574
Email: info@aicup.org
Web: www.aicup.org

Summary: To provide financial assistance to undergraduate students from any state enrolled at member institutions of the Association of Independent Colleges and Universities of Pennsylvania (AICUP).

Eligibility: Open to undergraduate students from any state enrolled full-time at AICUP colleges and universities. Each member institution establishes the specific criteria for selecting the recipient at that school.

Financial data: The AICUP provides each member college and university with $2,700 for this program. The school may distribute those funds to as many students as it desires.

Duration: 1 year.

Number awarded: At least 83 each year: 1 at each AICUP college and university.

Deadline: Each AICUP college and university sets its own deadline.

1020 URBAN LEAGUE OF NEBRASKA SCHOLARSHIPS

Urban League of Nebraska
Attn: Courtney Eugene Carter
3040 Lake Street
Omaha, NE 68111
Phone: (402) 451-1066, ext. 30
Email: ccarter@urbanleagueneb.org
Web: www.urbanleagueneb.org

Summary: To provide financial assistance to high school seniors in Nebraska who plan to attend college in any state.

Eligibility: Open to seniors graduating from high schools in Nebraska and planning to enroll at a college or university in any state. Applicants must have a GPA of 2.5 or higher and a record of at least 10 hours of documented community involvement. Along with their application, they must submit an essay of 250 to 500 words on their educational and career goals, ambitions, and reasons why they should receive this scholarship. Financial need is also considered in the selection process.

Financial data: A stipend is awarded (amount not specified).

Duration: 1 year.

Number awarded: 1 or more each year.

Deadline: March of each year.

1021 U.S. ARMY WOMEN'S FOUNDATION LEGACY SCHOLARSHIPS

U.S. Army Women's Foundation
Attn: Scholarship Committee
P.O. Box 5030
Fort Lee, VA 23801-0030
Phone: (804) 734-3078
Email: info@awfdn.org
Web: www.awfdn.org/programs/legacyscholarships.shtml

Summary: To provide financial assistance for college to 1) women who are serving or have served in the Army; and 2) their children.

Eligibility: Open to 1) women who have served or are serving honorably in the U.S. Army, U.S. Army Reserve, or Army National Guard; and 2) children of women who served honorably in the U.S. Army, U.S. Army Reserve, or Army National Guard. Applicants must be entering their junior or senior year at an accredited college or university and have a GPA of 3.0 or higher. Along with their application, they must submit a 2-page essay on why they should be considered for this scholarship, their future plans as related to their program of study, and information about their community service, activities, and work experience. Selection is based on merit, academic potential, community service, and financial need.

Financial data: The stipend is $2,500.

Duration: 1 year.

Number awarded: 5 to 10 each year.

Deadline: February of each year.

1022 U.S. JCI SENATE SCHOLARSHIP GRANTS

U.S. JCI Senate
Attn: Foundation
7447 South Lewis Avenue
P.O. Box 7
Tulsa, OK 74102-0007
Phone: (918) 584-2481; (800) JAYCEES; Fax: (918) 584-4422
Web: www.usjcisenate.org

Summary: To provide financial assistance for college to high school seniors in any state.

Eligibility: Open to graduating high school seniors who plan to continue their education at an accredited college, university, or vocational school as a full-time student. Applicants must submit information on leadership positions and offices in school, church, volunteer, and community activities; memberships and participation in school, church, volunteer, and community activities; honors and awards received during high school; employment experience; and family financial situation. They must also submit a personal statement of 100 to 300 words on their chosen field of college study, their reasons for this choice, and pertinent experiences, activities, and accomplishments. Applications are submitted to the JCI Senate in their state. Each state organization selects the 2 highest-ranked applications and forwards them to the national organization. U.S. citizenship is required.

Financial data: The stipend is $1,000.

Duration: 1 year; nonrenewable.
Number awarded: Varies each year; recently, 20 of these scholarships were awarded.
Deadline: Each state sets its own deadline; some are as early as November of each year.

1023 USA TODAY'S ALL-USA COLLEGE ACADEMIC TEAM

USA Today
Attn: Communications Director
7950 Jones Branch Drive
McLean, VA 22108-9995
Phone: (703) 854-5304
Email: hzimmerman@usatoday.com
Web: www.usatoday.com/marketing/academic_teams/index.html
Summary: To recognize and reward outstanding college students in the United States.
Eligibility: Open to full-time college or university students of at least junior standing at accredited 4-year institutions in the United States. Candidates must be nominated by college presidents or faculty members. U.S. citizenship is not required. Nominees submit a 500-word essay describing their most outstanding original academic or intellectual product. Selection is based primarily on the students' ability to describe their endeavor in their own words.
Financial data: Winners receive $2,500 in cash prizes and are guests of *USA Today* at a special awards luncheon.
Duration: This competition is held annually.
Number awarded: 60 students are chosen for the All-USA Academic Team and receive recognition in *USA Today;* of those, 20 are named to the first team and receive cash prizes.
Deadline: January of each year.

1024 USOC TUITION GRANTS

United States Olympic Committee
Attn: Athlete Support Department
One Olympic Plaza
Colorado Springs, CO 80909-5760
Phone: (719) 632-5551; (800) 933-4473; Fax: (719) 578-4654
Web: teamusa.org/content/index/894
Summary: To provide financial assistance to athletes who are currently in training for the Olympics and also enrolled in college.
Eligibility: Open to athletes who have demonstrated competitive excellence in important international competitions. Applicants must have been accepted to receive Elite Athlete Health Insurance and/or Direct Athlete Support from the United States Olympic Committee (USOC) and be endorsed by the National Governing Body (NGB) for their particular sport. They must be enrolled at an accredited college or university. Also eligible are retired athletes who participated in the Olympics Games or Pan American Games within the past 5 years; athletes with disabilities who are members of the current U.S. Paralympics Elite or National Team; and retired Paralympians who competed in a Paralympic Games within the past 5 years. Athletes currently in training at a U.S. Olympic Training Center are not eligible for these grants; they must apply for a B.J. Stupak Olympic Scholarship. Priority is given to applicants who have a current top 8 World Championships placement or world ranking. Financial need is considered in the selection process.
Financial data: Stipends range up to $5,000 per year for athletes who have an international rank of first through fourth in their sport or up to $2,500 for athletes who rank fifth through eighth. Stipends for retired athletes are limited to $2,500. Funds are available for tuition and mandatory fees only.
Duration: 1 year; may be renewed. Retired athletes are only eligible for 1 grant.
Number awarded: Varies each year; approximately $70,000 is available for this program annually.
Deadline: January, April, July, or October of each year.

1025 USTA DWIGHT F. DAVIS MEMORIAL SCHOLARSHIPS

United States Tennis Association
Attn: USTA Serves
70 West Red Oak Lane
White Plains, NY 10604
Phone: (914) 696-7223
Email: eliezer@usta.com
Web: www.usta.com/USTA/Home/AboutUs/USTAServes.aspx
Summary: To provide financial assistance for college to high school seniors who have participated in an organized community tennis program.
Eligibility: Open to high school seniors who have excelled academically, demonstrated achievements in leadership, and participated extensively in an organized community tennis program. Applicants must be planning to enroll as a full-time undergraduate student at a 4-year college or university. They must have a GPA of 3.0 or higher and be able to demonstrate financial need. Along with their application, they must submit an essay about themselves and how their participation in a tennis program has influenced their life.
Financial data: The stipend is $1,875 per year. Funds are paid directly to the recipient's college or university.
Duration: 4 years.
Number awarded: 2 each year.
Deadline: February of each year.

1026 USTA SERVES COLLEGE EDUCATION SCHOLARSHIPS

United States Tennis Association
Attn: USTA Serves
70 West Red Oak Lane
White Plains, NY 10604
Phone: (914) 696-7223
Email: eliezer@usta.com
Web: www.usta.com/USTA/Home/AboutUs/USTAServes.aspx
Summary: To provide financial assistance for college to high school seniors who have participated in an organized community tennis program.
Eligibility: Open to high school seniors who have excelled academically, demonstrated achievements in leadership, and participated extensively in an organized community tennis program. Applicants must be planning to enroll as a full-time undergraduate student at a 2- or 4-year college or university. They must have a GPA of 3.0 or higher and be able to demonstrate financial need. Along with their application, they must submit an essay about themselves and how their participation in a tennis program has influenced their life.
Financial data: The stipend is $1,500 per year. Funds are paid directly to the recipient's college or university.
Duration: 2 years for students at community colleges; 4 years for students at 4-year colleges and universities.
Number awarded: Varies each year; recently, 37 of these scholarships were awarded.
Deadline: February of each year.

1027 UTAH ALARM ASSOCIATION SCHOLARSHIPS

Utah Alarm Association
c/o Kent P. Griffith, Vice President
Northstar Alarm Services
1280 South 800 East, Suite 350
Orem, UT 84097
Phone: (801) 373-7827; Fax: (801) 373-4027
Email: kent@northstaralarm.com
Web: www.utahalarm.org/scholarships
Summary: To provide financial assistance to college-bound high school seniors in Utah who are the children of active-duty law enforcement and fire service personnel or of members of the Utah Alarm Association.
Eligibility: Open to seniors graduating from high schools in Utah who have been accepted at an accredited college or university in any state. Applicants must have a father, mother, or legal guardian who is 1) a full-time active employee (not on disability) of the police or sheriff's department; 2) a paid employee or volunteer of a fire department; or 3) an employee of a member company of the Utah Alarm Association. Along with their application, they must submit an essay of 500 to 1,000 words on what it means to them to have their parent or guardian involved in securing our community. Selection is based on that essay (25 points), grade average (25 points), SAT or ACT scores (30 points), and academic prizes, awards, school and outside extracurricular activities, and hobbies (20 points); financial need is not considered.
Financial data: The stipend is $1,000.
Duration: 1 year.
Number awarded: 3 each year: 1 to a student in each category.
Deadline: January of each year.

1028 UTAH CENTENNIAL OPPORTUNITY PROGRAM FOR EDUCATION

Utah Higher Education Assistance Authority
Board of Regents Building, The Gateway
60 South 400 West
P.O. Box 145110

Salt Lake City, UT 84114-5110
Phone: (801) 321-7294; (877) 336-7378; Fax: (801) 321-7299; TDD: (801) 321-7130
Email: uheaa@utahsbr.edu
Web: www.uheaa.org/parentStudent02b.html

Summary: To provide financial assistance and work-study to students at designated Utah institutions.

Eligibility: Open to students at participating colleges in Utah. They may request an application directly from their college's financial aid offices. The participating institutions in Utah are: Brigham Young University, College of Eastern Utah, Dixie State College, LDS Business College, Salt Lake Community College, Snow College, Southern Utah University, University of Utah, Utah State University, Utah Valley State College, Weber State University, and Westminster College. Applicants must meet the federal guidelines for financial need. They must also be willing to accept a work-study assignment in 1) an institutional job on campus; 2) school assistant jobs, as tutors, mentors, or teacher assistants, to work with educationally disadvantaged and high-risk school pupils, by contract, at individual schools or school districts; 3) community service jobs, with volunteer community service organizations; or 4) matching jobs, by contract with government agencies, private businesses, or nonprofit corporations.

Financial data: The maximum award to each eligible student is $5,000, of which no more than $2,500 may be a grant and the remainder provided in the form of a work-study award. For the work-study portion, students receive the current federal minimum wage.

Duration: 1 year; may be renewed.

Number awarded: Varies each year.

Deadline: Deadline not specified.

1029 UTAH CENTENNIAL SCHOLARSHIP FOR EARLY GRADUATION

Utah State Office of Education
Attn: Scholarship Specialist
251 East 500 South
P.O. Box 144200
Salt Lake City, UT 84114-4200
Phone: (801) 538-7884
Web: www.schools.utah.gov/curr/Early_College/Centennial.htm

Summary: To provide financial assistance to Utah residents who graduate from high school early and attend college in the state.

Eligibility: Open to public high school students in Utah who complete early graduation having completed all required courses and demonstrated mastery of required skills and competencies. Applicants must enroll full-time in an accredited Utah college or university within 1 calendar year of high school graduation.

Financial data: Stipends are $1,000 for students who graduate after their junior year, $750 after the first quarter of their senior year, $500 after the second quarter of their senior year, or $250 after the third quarter of their senior year. Funds are sent directly to the student's postsecondary institution.

Duration: These are 1-time awards.

Number awarded: Varies each year.

Deadline: Deadline not specified.

1030 UTAH LEGION AUXILIARY NATIONAL PRESIDENT'S SCHOLARSHIP

American Legion Auxiliary
Department of Utah
350 North State Street, Suite 80
P.O. Box 148000
Salt Lake City, UT 84114-8000
Phone: (801) 539-1015; (877) 345-6780; Fax: (801) 521-9191
Email: alaut@yahoo.com
Web: www.utlegion.org/Auxiliary/aux1.htm

Summary: To provide financial assistance to children of veterans in Utah who plan to attend college in any state.

Eligibility: Open to Utah residents who are the children of veterans who served during specified periods of war time. They must be high school seniors or graduates who have not yet attended an institution of higher learning. Selection is based on character, Americanism, leadership, scholarship, and financial need. The winners then compete for the American Legion Auxiliary National President's Scholarship. If the Utah winners are not awarded a national scholarship, then they receive this departmental scholarship.

Financial data: The stipend is $1,500.

Duration: 1 year.

Number awarded: 1 each year.

Deadline: February of each year.

1031 UTAH LEVERAGING EDUCATIONAL ASSISTANCE PARTNERSHIP PROGRAM

Utah Higher Education Assistance Authority
Board of Regents Building, The Gateway
60 South 400 West
P.O. Box 145110
Salt Lake City, UT 84114-5110
Phone: (801) 321-7294; (877) 336-7378; Fax: (801) 321-7299; TDD: (801) 321-7130
Email: uheaa@utahsbr.edu
Web: www.uheaa.org/parentStudent02b.html

Summary: To provide financial assistance for college to students in Utah with financial need.

Eligibility: Open to students at participating colleges in Utah. They may request an application directly from their college's financial aid offices. The participating colleges in Utah are: College of Eastern Utah, Dixie State College, Salt Lake Community College, Snow College, Southern Utah University, University of Utah, Utah State University, Utah Valley State College, Weber State University, and Westminster College. Applicants must have substantial financial need. Students taking correspondence courses are not eligible.

Financial data: The maximum stipend is $2,500.

Duration: 1 year; may be renewed.

Number awarded: Varies each year.

Deadline: Deadline not specified.

1032 UTAH NEW CENTURY SCHOLARSHIP PROGRAM

Utah System of Higher Education
State Board of Regents
Attn: New Century Scholarship Program
P.O. Box 145116
Salt Lake City, UT 84114-5116
Phone: (801) 321-7221; (800) 418-8757, ext. 7221; Fax: (801) 321-7168
Email: newcentury@utahsbr.edu
Web: www.utahsbr.edu/scholarships

Summary: To provide financial assistance to Utah residents who complete an associate degree while still enrolled in high school and plan to work on a bachelor's degree at a college or university in the state.

Eligibility: Open to high school students in Utah who take classes at a local community college and complete an associate degree by September of the year their class graduates from high school. Applicants must complete specified college courses while earning their associate degree and have a cumulative GPA of 3.0 or higher. They must be planning to enroll full-time at an accredited 4-year college or university in the state to work on a bachelor's degree. Financial need is not considered in the selection process.

Financial data: Stipends equal 75% of an eligible student's tuition cost at a Utah public institution of higher education that offers a bachelor's degree, or an equivalent amount at designated private institutions.

Duration: Up to 2 years, provided the student maintains at least a 3.0 GPA.

Number awarded: Varies each year.

Deadline: January of each year.

1033 UTAH REGENTS' SCHOLARSHIP PROGRAM

Utah System of Higher Education
State Board of Regents
Attn: Regents' Scholarship Program
P.O. Box 145114
Salt Lake City, UT 84114-5114
Phone: (801) 321-7294; (877) 336-7378; Fax: (801) 321-7168
Email: newcentury@utahsbr.edu
Web: www.utahsbr.edu/scholarships

Summary: To provide financial assistance to Utah residents who complete a core course of study in high school and plan to attend college in the state.

Eligibility: Open to seniors graduating from high schools in Utah who have completed the curriculum of the Utah Scholars Core Course of Study. Applicants must be planning to enroll full-time at an accredited 2- or 4-year college or university in the state. Students who have a cumulative weighted GPA of 3.0 or higher and no individual grade lower than a "C" in required core courses qualify for the Base Award. Students who have a weighted cumulative

GPA of 3.5 or higher, an ACT score of 26 or higher, and no individual grade lower than a "B" in required core courses qualify for the Exemplary Academic Achievement Award. Financial need is not considered in the selection process. U.S. citizenship or eligible noncitizen status is required.

Financial data: The Base Award is $1,000. The Exemplary Academic Achievement Award is $5,000.

Duration: The Base Award is a nonrenewable 1-time grant. The Exemplary Academic Achievement Award is paid over 2 years, provided the recipient verifies full-time enrollment and a GPA of 3.0 or higher each semester.

Number awarded: Varies each year.

Deadline: January of each year.

1034 VERIZON FUTURE LEADER SCHOLARSHIPS

Massachusetts Amateur Sports Foundation
55 Sixth Road
Woburn, MA 01801
Phone: (781) 932-6555; Fax: (781) 932-3441
Email: info@baystategames.org
Web: www.baystategames.org/html/bsgwww/scholarship/index.html

Summary: To provide financial assistance for college to high school juniors in Massachusetts who participate in the Bay State Games.

Eligibility: Open to juniors at high schools in Massachusetts who plan to attend college after graduation. Applicants must participate in either the winter or the summer Bay State Games. Selection is based on community service, academic excellence, and athletic achievement. Boys and girls are judged separately.

Financial data: The stipend is $2,000.

Duration: 1 year.

Number awarded: 6 each year: 1 boy and 1 girl in each of 3 regions (metro Boston/northeast, southeast/coastal, and central/west).

Deadline: Students must register in June to participate in the summer games or in December to participate in the winter games.

1035 VERMONT FOSTER/ADOPTIVE FAMILY ASSOCIATION SCHOLARSHIP

Vermont Student Assistance Corporation
Attn: Scholarship Programs
10 East Allen Street
P.O. Box 2000
Winooski, VT 05404-2601
Phone: (802) 654-3798; (888) 253-4819; Fax: (802) 654-3765; TDD: (800) 281-3341 (within VT)
Email: info@vsac.org
Web: services.vsac.org/wps/wcm/connect/vsac/VSAC

Summary: To provide financial assistance to residents of Vermont who are or have been under the custody of the Department for Children and Families (DCF) and wish to attend college in any state.

Eligibility: Open to residents of Vermont who are or have been under the custody of the DCF anytime after 13 years of age. Applicants must be attending or planning to attend college in any state. Along with their application, they must submit 1) a 100-word essay describing any significant barriers that limit their access to education; and 2) a 250-word essay on what they believe distinguishes their application from others that may be submitted. Selection is based on their essays, letters of recommendation, and financial need.

Financial data: Stipends range from $1,500 to $2,000.

Duration: 1 year.

Number awarded: Up to 2 each year.

Deadline: March of each year.

1036 VERMONT INCENTIVE GRANTS

Vermont Student Assistance Corporation
Attn: Scholarship Programs
10 East Allen Street
P.O. Box 2000
Winooski, VT 05404-2601
Phone: (802) 654-3798; (888) 253-4819; Fax: (802) 654-3765; TDD: (800) 281-3341 (within VT)
Email: info@vsac.org
Web: services.vsac.org/wps/wcm/connect/vsac/VSAC

Summary: To provide financial assistance for college to needy residents of Vermont.

Eligibility: Open to residents of Vermont who wish to attend college, either within or outside Vermont, as a full-time undergraduate student. U.S. citizenship or permanent resident status is required. Selection is based on financial need.

Financial data: Stipends depend on the need of the student and the cost of attendance at the school; recently, they ranged from $500 to $10,800 per year.

Duration: 1 year; may be renewed.

Number awarded: Varies each year.

Deadline: Applications are accepted on a first-come, first-served basis as long as funding is available.

1037 VERMONT JOHN H. CHAFEE EDUCATION AND TRAINING SCHOLARSHIP

Vermont Student Assistance Corporation
Attn: Scholarship Programs
10 East Allen Street
P.O. Box 2000
Winooski, VT 05404-2601
Phone: (802) 654-3798; (888) 253-4819; Fax: (802) 654-3765; TDD: (800) 281-3341 (within VT)
Email: info@vsac.org
Web: services.vsac.org/wps/wcm/connect/vsac/VSAC

Summary: To provide financial assistance to residents of Vermont who are or have been under the custody of the Commissioner of Children and Families (CCF) and wish to attend college in any state.

Eligibility: Open to residents of Vermont who are 21 years of age or younger. Applicants must have been under the custody of the CCF through their 18th birthday or have been adopted after age 16 but would have remained under the custody of CCF through their 18th birthday. They must be attending or planning to attend college in any state. Financial need is considered in the selection process.

Financial data: Stipends may range up to $5,000, but most range from $1,000 to $3,000.

Duration: 1 year.

Number awarded: Varies each year.

Deadline: March of each year.

1038 VERMONT KNIGHTS TEMPLAR EDUCATIONAL FOUNDATION SCHOLASTIC ACHIEVEMENT AWARDS

Knights Templar of Vermont
Attn: Grand Recorder Office
49 East Road-Berlin
Barre, VT 05641-5390
Phone: (802) 223-0411
Web: knightstemplar.org/gckt/vt

Summary: To provide financial assistance to residents of Vermont interested in working on an undergraduate or graduate degree at a school in any state.

Eligibility: Open to Vermont residents who have completed at least the freshman year of a 2- or 4-year degree, trade certificate, or graduate education program at a college, university, or trade school in any state. Applicants must be U.S. citizens and able to demonstrate financial need. Along with their application, they must submit an essay of 1 to 2 pages on either 1) why they chose their major and what they hope to gain from it; or 2) why they chose their college or university and what they hope to gain by attending there. In the selection process, no consideration is given to age, race, religion, national origin, gender, or Masonic ties or affiliation.

Financial data: Stipends range from $500 to $1,000.

Duration: 1 year.

Number awarded: 1 or 2 each year.

Deadline: February of each year.

1039 VERMONT PART-TIME GRANTS

Vermont Student Assistance Corporation
Attn: Scholarship Programs
10 East Allen Street
P.O. Box 2000
Winooski, VT 05404-2601
Phone: (802) 654-3798; (888) 253-4819; Fax: (802) 654-3765; TDD: (800) 281-3341 (within VT)
Email: info@vsac.org
Web: services.vsac.org/wps/wcm/connect/vsac/VSAC

Summary: To provide financial assistance to needy residents of Vermont who wish to attend college on a part-time basis.

Eligibility: Open to residents of Vermont who are enrolled or accepted for enrollment in an undergraduate degree, diploma, or certificate program. Applicants must be taking fewer than 12 credits per semester and not have received a baccalaureate degree. Financial need is considered in the selection process.
Financial data: The amounts of the awards depend on the number of credit hours and the need of the recipient.
Duration: 1 year; may be renewed.
Number awarded: Varies each year.
Deadline: Deadline not specified.

1040 VETERANS EDUCATIONAL ASSISTANCE PROGRAM (VEAP)

Department of Veterans Affairs
Attn: Veterans Benefits Administration
810 Vermont Avenue, N.W.
Washington, DC 20420
Phone: (202) 418-4343; (888) GI-BILL1
Web: www.gibill.va.gov/GI_Bill_Info/benefits.htm
Summary: To provide financial assistance for college to veterans who first entered active duty between January 1, 1977 and June 30, 1985.
Eligibility: Open to veterans who served and military servicemembers currently serving, if they 1) entered active duty between January 1, 1977 and June 30, 1985; 2) were released under conditions other than dishonorable or continue on active duty; 3) served for a continuous period of 181 days or more (or were discharged earlier for a service-connected disability); and 4) have satisfactorily contributed to the program. No individuals on active duty could enroll in this program after March 31, 1987. Veterans who enlisted for the first time after September 7, 1980 or entered active duty as an officer or enlistee after October 16, 1981 must have completed 24 continuous months of active duty. Benefits are available for the pursuit of an associate, bachelor, or graduate degree at a college or university; a certificate or diploma from a business, technical, or vocational school; apprenticeship or on-the-job training programs; cooperative courses; correspondence school courses; tutorial assistance; remedial, refresher, and deficiency training; flight training; study abroad programs leading to a college degree; nontraditional training away from school; and work-study for students enrolled at least three-quarter time.
Financial data: Participants contribute to the program, through monthly deductions from their military pay, from $25 to $100 monthly, up to a maximum of $2,700. They may also, while on active duty, make a lump sum contribution to the training fund. At the time the eligible participant elects to use the benefits to pursue an approved course of education or training, the Department of Veterans Affairs (VA) will match the contribution at the rate of $2 for every $1 made by the participant.
Duration: Participants receive monthly payments for the number of months they contributed or for 36 months, whichever is less. The amount of the payments is determined by dividing the number of months benefits will be paid into the participant's training fund total. Participants have 10 years from the date of last discharge or release from active duty within which to use these benefits.
Number awarded: Varies each year.
Deadline: Applications may be submitted at any time.

1041 VHSL-ALLSTATE ACHIEVEMENT AWARDS

Virginia High School League
1642 State Farm Boulevard
Charlottesville, VA 22911
Phone: (434) 977-8475; Fax: (434) 977-5943
Email: info@vhsl.org
Web: www.vhsl.org/about_vhsl/scholarships
Summary: To provide financial assistance to high school seniors who have participated in activities of the Virginia High School League (VHSL) and plan to attend college in any state.
Eligibility: Open to seniors graduating from high schools that are members of the VHSL and planning to attend a college or university in any state. Applicants must have participated in 1 or more VHSL athletic activities (baseball, basketball, cheer, cross country, field hockey, football, golf, gymnastics, soccer, softball, swimming, tennis, indoor and outdoor track, volleyball, wrestling) and/or academic activities (student publications, creative writing, theater, forensics, debate, scholastic bowl). They must have a GPA of 3.0 or higher. Each school may nominate up to 4 students: 1 female athlete, 1 male athlete, 1 academic participant, and 1 courageous achievement candidate. The courageous achievement category is reserved for students who have overcome serious obstacles to make significant contributions to athletic and/or academic activities. The obstacles may include a serious illness, injury, or disability; a challenging social or home situation; or another extraordinary situation where the student has displayed tremendous courage against overwhelming odds. Along with their application, students must submit a 500-word essay describing how extracurricular activities have enhanced their educational experience. Candidates are judged separately in the 3 VHSL groups (A, AA, and AAA). Selection is based on the essay; involvement in other school-sponsored activities; involvement in activities outside of school; and 2 letters of support.
Financial data: The stipend is $1,000.
Duration: 1 year.
Number awarded: 10 each year. For each of the 3 groups (A, AA, and AAA), 1 female athlete, 1 male athlete, and 1 academic participant are selected. In addition, 1 courageous achievement candidate is selected statewide.
Deadline: March of each year.

1042 VIETNAM VETERANS GROUP OF SAN QUENTIN SCHOLARSHIPS

Vietnam Veterans Group of San Quentin
c/o Education Department
San Quentin State Prison
San Quentin, CA 94964
Phone: (415) 454-1460, ext. 5148; Fax: (415) 455-5049
Web: vvgsq.tripod.com
Summary: To provide financial assistance to high school seniors in California who are interested in attending college in any state and are children of current or former members of the U.S. armed forces.
Eligibility: Open to graduating high school seniors in California who plan to attend a college or university in any state. Applicants must have a parent or legal guardian who is currently serving in the armed forces or has been honorably discharged. Along with their application, they must submit an essay, up to 250 words in length, on the effect their parent's military service has had on their life. The Mary Manley Inspirational Award may be presented for an exceptionally inspiring essay. Financial need is not considered in the selection process.
Financial data: The scholarship stipend is $1,500. The Mary Manley Inspirational Award, if presented, is an additional $750.
Duration: 1 year.
Number awarded: Up to 2 each year.
Deadline: May of each year.

1043 VII CORPS DESERT STORM VETERANS ASSOCIATION SCHOLARSHIP

VII Corps Desert Storm Veterans Association
Attn: Scholarship Committee
Army Historical Foundation
2425 Wilson Boulevard
Arlington, VA 22201
Phone: (703) 604-6565
Email: viicorpsdsva@aol.com
Web: www.desertstormvets.org/Scholarship/html
Summary: To provide financial assistance for college to students who served, or are the spouses or other family members of individuals who served, with VII Corps in Operations Desert Shield, Desert Storm, or related activities.
Eligibility: Open to applicants who have served, or are a family member of those who served, with VII Corps in Operations Desert Shield/Desert Storm, Provide Comfort, or 1 of the support base activities. Scholarships are limited to students entering or enrolled in accredited technical institutions (trade or specialty), 2-year colleges, and 4-year colleges or universities. Awards will not be made to individuals receiving military academy appointments or full 4-year scholarships. Letters of recommendation and a transcript are required. Selection is not based solely on academic standing; consideration is also given to extracurricular activities and other self-development skills and abilities obtained through on-the-job training or correspondence courses. Priority is given to survivors of VII Corps soldiers who died during Operations Desert Shield/Desert Storm or Provide Comfort, veterans who are also members of the VII Corps Desert Storm Veterans Association, and family members of veterans who are also members of the VII Corps Desert Storm Veterans Association.
Financial data: The stipend is $5,000 per year. Funds are paid to the recipients upon proof of admission or registration at an accredited institution, college, or university.
Duration: 1 year; recipients may reapply.
Number awarded: Approximately 3 each year.
Deadline: January of each year.

1044 VIRGIN ISLANDS NATIONAL GUARD GRANTS

Virgin Islands Board of Education
Dronningen Gade 60B, 61, and 62
P.O. Box 11900
St. Thomas, VI 00801
Phone: (340) 774-4546; Fax: (340) 774-3384
Email: stt@myviboe.com
Web: www.myviboe.com

Summary: To provide financial assistance to the children of deceased or disabled members of the Virgin Islands National Guard who wish to attend a college in the territory or on the mainland.

Eligibility: Open to children under 25 years of age of members of the National Guard of the Virgin Islands who have died or sustained permanent and total disability in the line of official duty while on territorial active military duty, federal active duty, or training duty. Applicants must have a GPA of 2.0 or higher and be attending or accepted for enrollment at an accredited institution of higher learning in the territory or on the mainland. They may be planning to major in any field. Financial need is considered in the selection process.

Financial data: The stipend is $2,000 per year.

Duration: 1 year; may be renewed up to 3 additional years.

Number awarded: 1 or more each year.

Deadline: April of each year.

1045 VIRGIN ISLANDS LEVERAGING EDUCATIONAL PARTNERSHIP (LEAP) PROGRAM GRANTS

Virgin Islands Board of Education
Dronningen Gade 60B, 61, and 62
P.O. Box 11900
St. Thomas, VI 00801
Phone: (340) 774-4546; Fax: (340) 774-3384
Email: stt@myviboe.com
Web: www.myviboe.com

Summary: To provide financial assistance to residents of the Virgin Islands who can demonstrate financial need and plan to attend college in the territory or on the mainland.

Eligibility: Open to residents of the Virgin Islands who are seniors or recent graduates of high schools in the territory. Applicants must have a GPA of 2.0 or higher and be attending or accepted for enrollment at an accredited institution of higher learning in the territory or on the mainland. They may be independent or dependent students and attending on a full-time or half-time basis. An unmet financial need of at least $500 must be demonstrated.

Financial data: Awards range up to $5,000.

Duration: 1 to 4 years.

Number awarded: 25 each year.

Deadline: Deadline not specified.

1046 VIRGIN ISLANDS VALEDICTORIAN/SALUTATORIAN AWARDS

Virgin Islands Board of Education
Dronningen Gade 60B, 61, and 62
P.O. Box 11900
St. Thomas, VI 00801
Phone: (340) 774-4546; Fax: (340) 774-3384
Email: stt@myviboe.com
Web: www.myviboe.com

Summary: To provide financial assistance to high school seniors in the Virgin Islands who graduate at the top of their class and wish to enroll at a college in the territory or on the mainland.

Eligibility: Open to seniors graduating from high schools in the Virgin Islands who rank as valedictorian or salutatorian of their class. Applicants must be accepted for enrollment at an accredited institution of higher learning in the territory or on the mainland.

Financial data: The stipend is $1,000 for the valedictorian or $700 for the salutatorian.

Duration: 1 year; nonrenewable.

Number awarded: 2 at each high school in the territory each year.

Deadline: April of each year.

1047 VIRGINIA COLLEGE SCHOLARSHIP ASSISTANCE PROGRAM

State Council of Higher Education for Virginia
Attn: Financial Aid Office
James Monroe Building
101 North 14th Street, Ninth Floor
Richmond, VA 23219-3659
Phone: (804) 225-2600; (877) 515-0138; Fax: (804) 225-2604; TDD: (804) 371-8017
Email: fainfo@schev.edu
Web: www.schev.edu/students/factsheetCSAP.asp?from=

Summary: To provide financial assistance to residents of Virginia who demonstrate extreme financial need and plan to attend college in the state.

Eligibility: Open to residents of Virginia who have been admitted into a Virginia public 2- or 4-year college or university or a participating Virginia private nonprofit 4-year college or university. Applicants must be enrolled or planning to enroll at least half-time, be a U.S. citizen or eligible noncitizen, and have a computed expected family contribution that is less than half the total cost of attendance.

Financial data: The amount awarded ranges from $400 to $5,000 per year, depending on the need of the recipient.

Duration: 1 year; may be renewed for up to 3 additional years if the recipient maintains at least half-time status and satisfactory academic progress.

Number awarded: Varies each year.

Deadline: Deadline not specified.

1048 VIRGINIA COMMONWEALTH AWARDS

State Council of Higher Education for Virginia
Attn: Financial Aid Office
James Monroe Building
101 North 14th Street, Ninth Floor
Richmond, VA 23219-3659
Phone: (804) 225-2600; (877) 515-0138; Fax: (804) 225-2604; TDD: (804) 371-8017
Email: fainfo@schev.edu
Web: www.schev.edu/students/factsheetCOMMA.asp?from=

Summary: To provide financial assistance to needy undergraduate students and some graduate students enrolled in Virginia colleges or universities.

Eligibility: Open to residents of Virginia who are undergraduate students enrolled at least half-time in Virginia's public colleges and universities. Applicants must be U.S. citizens or eligible noncitizens and able to demonstrate financial need. Some full-time graduate students, regardless of need or residency, are also eligible.

Financial data: Awards may be as much as full tuition and required fees.

Duration: 1 year; may be renewed if the recipient maintains satisfactory academic progress and continues to meet eligibility requirements.

Number awarded: Varies each year.

Deadline: Deadline dates vary by school.

1049 VIRGINIA DIVISION GIFT SCHOLARSHIPS

United Daughters of the Confederacy–Virginia Division
c/o Janice Busic, Education Committee Chair
P.O. Box 356
Honaker, VA 24260
Email: 2vp@vaudc.org
Web: vaudc.org/gift.html

Summary: To provide financial assistance for college to Confederate descendants from Virginia.

Eligibility: Open to residents of Virginia who are 1) lineal descendants of Confederates; or 2) collateral descendants and also members of the Children of the Confederacy or the United Daughters of the Confederacy. Applicants must submit proof of the Confederate military record of at least 1 ancestor, with the company and regiment in which he served. They must also submit a personal letter pledging to make the best possible use of the scholarship; describing their health, social, family, religious, and fraternal connections within the community; and reflecting on what a Southern heritage means to them (using the term "War Between the States" in lieu of "Civil War"). They must have a GPA of 3.0 or higher and be able to demonstrate financial need.

Financial data: The amount of the stipend depends on the availability of funds. Payment is made directly to the college or university the recipient attends.

Duration: 1 year; may be renewed up to 3 additional years if the recipient maintains a GPA of 3.0 or higher.
Number awarded: These scholarships are offered whenever a prior recipient graduates or is no longer eligible.
Deadline: April of years in which any of the scholarships are available.

1050 VIRGINIA ELECTRONIC SYSTEMS ASSOCIATION YOUTH SCHOLARSHIP PROGRAM

Virginia Electronic Systems Association
Attn: Youth Scholarship Program
225 North Washington Street, Suite 186
Ashland, VA 23005
Phone: (800) 538-2322
Web: www.vbfaa.org

Summary: To provide financial assistance to high school seniors in Virginia who are the children of active-duty law enforcement and fire service personnel and interested in attending college in any state.
Eligibility: Open to seniors graduating from high schools in Virginia who have been accepted at an accredited college or university in any state. Applicants must have a father, mother, or legal guardian who is a law enforcement employee (including emergency dispatchers and EMS personnel) or active-duty or volunteer fire service employee; children of those employees who were killed or disabled while on duty after at least 5 years of service or who are retired after at least 10 years of service are also eligible. Along with their application, they must submit an essay of 500 to 750 words on how their parent or guardian helps secure our community. Selection is based on that essay (25 points), grade average (25 points), SAT scores (25 points), and academic prizes, awards, school and outside extracurricular activities, and hobbies (25 points); financial need is not considered.
Financial data: The stipend is $500 for each regional winner. The state winner receives an additional $1,000.
Duration: The awards are presented annually.
Number awarded: 4 regional winners (1 in each region) are selected each year; of those, 1 is selected as the state winner.
Deadline: April of each year.

1051 VIRGINIA FOSTER CHILDREN GRANTS

State Council of Higher Education for Virginia
Attn: Financial Aid Office
James Monroe Building
101 North 14th Street, Ninth Floor
Richmond, VA 23219-3659
Phone: (804) 225-2600; (877) 515-0138; Fax: (804) 225-2604; TDD: (804) 371-8017
Email: fainfo@schev.edu
Web: www.vccs.edu/Students/TuitionGrant/tabid/413/Default.aspx

Summary: To provide financial assistance to community college students in Virginia who were in foster care.
Eligibility: Open to residents of Virginia who were in foster care, in the custody of the Department of Social Services, or considered a special needs adoption when their high school diploma or GED was awarded. Applicants may not have been previously enrolled in a postsecondary institution as a full-time student for more than 5 years, but they must be attending a community college in Virginia full-time in an eligible academic program of at least 1 academic year in length. Colleges rank eligible first-year applicants on the basis of when the college received the application for admission, federal financial aid data, and appropriate supporting documentation. Renewal applicants are given priority for selection.
Financial data: Awards up to full tuition and fees are provided to students who are not receiving other assistance.
Duration: 1 year; may be renewed.
Number awarded: Varies each year.
Deadline: Deadline not specified.

1052 VIRGINIA GUARANTEED ASSISTANCE PROGRAM

State Council of Higher Education for Virginia
Attn: Financial Aid Office
James Monroe Building
101 North 14th Street, Ninth Floor
Richmond, VA 23219-3659
Phone: (804) 225-2600; (877) 515-0138; Fax: (804) 225-2604; TDD: (804) 371-8017
Email: fainfo@schev.edu
Web: www.schev.edu/students/factsheetVGAP.asp?from=

Summary: To provide financial assistance to exceptionally needy students who plan to attend a public college or university in Virginia.
Eligibility: Open to residents of Virginia who are currently attending an elementary or secondary school in the state. Students are eligible to receive these awards if they graduate from a Virginia high school with a cumulative GPA of 2.5 or higher, are classified as a dependent, are a U.S. citizen or eligible noncitizen, are able to demonstrate financial need, and are admitted to a Virginia public 2- or 4-year college or university as a full-time student. Home-schooled students are eligible if they earn an SAT critical reading and mathematics combined score of 900 or higher or an ACT composite score of 19 or higher.
Financial data: Awards vary by institution but range up to the full cost of tuition, required fees, and an allowance for books. Students with the greatest need receive the largest awards.
Duration: 1 year; may be renewed as long as the recipient maintains full-time enrollment with at least a 2.0 GPA, demonstrated financial need, residency in Virginia, and satisfactory academic progress.
Number awarded: Varies each year.
Deadline: Deadline not specified.

1053 VIRGINIA LINQUIST WINKER SCHOLARSHIP

Tall Clubs International
Attn: Scholarship Committee
P.O. Box 441
Portland, OR 97207
Phone: (888) I-M-TALL-2
Email: tallwindmills@sbcglobal.net
Web: www.tall.org/scholarships.cfm?CFID=998394&CFTOKEN=81538320

Summary: To provide financial assistance for college to high school seniors and current college students who meet the minimum height requirements of the Tall Clubs International (TCI).
Eligibility: Open to 1) graduating high school seniors who will be attending a 2- or 4-year college or university; and 2) students currently attending a 2- or 4-year institution of higher learning who are younger than 21 years of age. Applicants must live within a geographic area served by a participating TCI and must meet the minimum TCI height requirements: 5'10" for females and 6'2" for males. Applications must be submitted to the local TCI club, which nominates the most outstanding applicant for the national competition. Selection is based on academic record and achievements, involvement in school clubs and activities, personal achievements, involvement in clubs and activities outside the school community, and an essay on "What being tall means to me."
Financial data: The stipend is $1,000.
Duration: 1 year.
Number awarded: 2 or 3 each year.
Deadline: Local clubs must submit their nominations by May of each year.

1054 VIRGINIA MILITARY SURVIVORS AND DEPENDENTS EDUCATION PROGRAM

Virginia Department of Veterans Services
270 Franklin Road, S.W., Room 503
Roanoke, VA 24011-2215
Phone: (540) 857-7101; Fax: (540) 857-7573
Web: www.dvs.virginia.gov/statebenefits.htm

Summary: To provide educational assistance to the children and spouses of disabled and other Virginia veterans or service personnel.
Eligibility: Open to residents of Virginia whose parent or spouse served in the U.S. armed forces (including the Reserves, the Virginia National Guard, or the Virginia National Guard Reserves) during any armed conflict subsequent to December 6, 1941, as a result of a terrorist act, during military operations against terrorism, or on a peacekeeping mission. The veterans must be at least 90% disabled due to an injury or disease incurred as a result of such service, have died, or be listed as a prisoner of war or missing in action. Applicants must have been accepted at a public college or university in Virginia as an undergraduate or graduate student. Children must be between 16 and 29 years of age; there are no age restrictions for spouses. The veteran must have been a resident of Virginia at the time of entry into active military service or for at least 5 consecutive years immediately prior to the date of application or death. The surviving spouse must have been a resident of Virginia for at least 5 years prior to marrying the veteran or for at least 5 years immediately prior to the date on which the application was submitted.

Financial data: The maximum allowable stipend is $1,500 per year, but current funding permits a maximum of $1,350, payable at the rate of $675 per term for full-time students, $450 per term for students enrolled at least half-time but less than full-time, or $225 per term for students enrolled less than half-time.
Duration: Entitlement extends to a maximum of 48 months.
Number awarded: Varies each year; recently, funding allowed for a total of 740 of these awards.
Deadline: Deadline not specified.

1055 VIRGINIA PART-TIME ASSISTANCE PROGRAM

State Council of Higher Education for Virginia
Attn: Financial Aid Office
James Monroe Building
101 North 14th Street, Ninth Floor
Richmond, VA 23219-3659
Phone: (804) 225-2600; (877) 515-0138; Fax: (804) 225-2604; TDD: (804) 371-8017
Email: fainfo@schev.edu
Web: www.schev.edu/students/undergrad/FinancialaidPrograms.asp
Summary: To provide financial assistance to community college students in Virginia who are attending part-time.
Eligibility: Open to residents of Virginia who are attending a community college in the state on a part-time basis. Applicants must be able to demonstrate financial need.
Financial data: Awards up to full tuition and fees are available.
Duration: 1 year; may be renewed.
Number awarded: Varies each year.
Deadline: Deadline not specified.

1056 VIRGINIA POLICE CHIEFS FOUNDATION COLLEGE SCHOLARSHIP PROGRAM

Virginia Police Chiefs Foundation
1606 Santa Rosa Road, Suite 134
Richmond, VA 23288
Phone: (804) 285-8227; Fax: (804) 285-3363
Email: info@vapolicefoundation.org
Web: www.vapolicefoundation.org/scholarships/index.html
Summary: To provide financial assistance to children of police officers in Virginia who are interested in attending college in any state.
Eligibility: Open to dependent children of active police officers employed in Virginia who are enrolled or planning to enroll full-time at a college or university in any state to work on their first undergraduate degree; children of sheriff's deputies, federal officers, or civilian personnel working in police agencies are not eligible. Applicants must submit an essay (up to 500 words) on a topic that changes annually; recently, students were asked to describe the most important quality a leader should possess and why. Selection is based on the essay, academic achievement, community and civic achievements, and financial need.
Financial data: A stipend is awarded (amount not specified).
Duration: 1 year.
Number awarded: 4 each year.
Deadline: March of each year.

1057 VIRGINIA TUITION ASSISTANCE GRANT PROGRAM

State Council of Higher Education for Virginia
Attn: Financial Aid Office
James Monroe Building
101 North 14th Street, Ninth Floor
Richmond, VA 23219-3659
Phone: (804) 225-2600; (877) 515-0138; Fax: (804) 225-2604; TDD: (804) 371-8017
Email: fainfo@schev.edu
Web: www.schev.edu/students/factsheetHETAP.asp?from=
Summary: To provide financial assistance to undergraduate and graduate students attending private colleges or universities in Virginia.
Eligibility: Open to undergraduate and graduate or professional students who are Virginia residents attending private colleges or universities in the state on a full-time basis in a degree program. Financial need is not considered in the selection process. Students pursuing religious training or theological education are not eligible.
Financial data: The amount awarded varies, depending on annual appropriations and number of applicants; recently, the maximum award was $3,000 for undergraduates or $1,300 for graduate students.
Duration: 1 year; may be renewed for 1 additional year for associate programs, 3 additional years for undergraduate study, 3 additional years for graduate study of medicine or pharmacy, or 2 additional years for all other graduate study.
Number awarded: Varies each year.
Deadline: The deadline for priority consideration for fall semester is July of each year. Applicants submitted through the end of November are considered only if funds are available.

1058 VIRGINIA TWO-YEAR COLLEGE TRANSFER GRANT PROGRAM

State Council of Higher Education for Virginia
Attn: Financial Aid Office
James Monroe Building
101 North 14th Street, Ninth Floor
Richmond, VA 23219-3659
Phone: (804) 225-2600; (877) 515-0138; Fax: (804) 225-2604; TDD: (804) 371-8017
Email: fainfo@schev.edu
Web: www.schev.edu/students/undergrad/FinancialaidPrograms.asp
Summary: To provide financial assistance to residents of Virginia who complete an associate degree at a 2-year public institution in the state and plan to transfer to a 4-year school.
Eligibility: Open to residents of Virginia who complete an associate degree at a 2-year public institution in the state with a GPA of 3.0 or higher. Applicants must be interested in transferring to a 4-year public or private college or university in the state and work on a degree in any field except religious training or theological education. They must be able to demonstrate financial need of a federally-calculated estimated family contribution of $8,000 or less. Additional funding is available to students planning to major in science, teaching, engineering, mathematics, or nursing.
Financial data: The maximum standard award is $1,000; the additional award for students majoring in designated fields is $1,000. Funds are disbursed directly to the recipient's 4-year institution.
Duration: 1 year; may be renewed up to 2 additional years, provided the recipient maintains a GPA of 3.0 or higher, satisfactory academic progress, and continued financial need.
Number awarded: Varies each year.
Deadline: Deadline not specified.

1059 VOCATIONAL REHABILITATION FOR DISABLED VETERANS

Department of Veterans Affairs
Attn: Veterans Benefits Administration
Vocational Rehabilitation and Employment Service
810 Vermont Avenue, N.W.
Washington, DC 20420
Phone: (202) 418-4343; (800) 827-1000
Web: www.vba.va.gov/bin/vre/index.htm
Summary: To provide vocational rehabilitation to certain categories of veterans with disabilities.
Eligibility: Open to veterans who have a service-connected disability of 1) at least 10% and a serious employment handicap; or 2) at least 20% and an employment handicap. They must have been discharged or released from military service under other than dishonorable conditions. The Department of Veterans Affairs (VA) must determine that they would benefit from a training program that would help them prepare for, find, and keep suitable employment. The program may be 1) institutional training at a certificate, 2-year college, 4-year college or university, or technical program; 2) unpaid on-the-job training in a federal, state, or local agency or a federally-recognized Indian tribal agency, training in a home, vocational course in a rehabilitation facility or sheltered workshop, independent instruction, or institutional non-farm cooperative; or 3) paid training through a farm cooperative, apprenticeship, on-the-job training, or on-the-job non-farm cooperative.
Financial data: While in training and for 2 months after, eligible disabled veterans may receive subsistence allowances in addition to their disability compensation or retirement pay. For most training programs, the current full-time monthly rate is $547.54 with no dependents, $679.18 with 1 dependent, $800.36 with 2 dependents, and $58.34 for each additional dependent; proportional rates apply for less than full-time training. The VA also pays the costs of tuition, books, fees, supplies, and equipment; it may also pay for special supportive services, such as tutorial assistance, prosthetic devices, lipreading training, and signing for the deaf. If during training or employment services the veteran's disabilities cause transportation expenses that would not be incurred by nondisabled persons, the VA will pay for at least a portion of those expenses. If the

veteran encounters financial difficulty during training, the VA may provide an advance against future benefit payments.

Duration: Up to 48 months of full-time training or its equivalent in part-time training. If a veteran with a serious disability receives services under an extended evaluation to improve training potential, the total of the extended evaluation and the training phases of the rehabilitation program may exceed 48 months. Usually, the veteran must complete a rehabilitation program within 12 years from the date of notification of entitlement to compensation by the VA. Following completion of the training portion of a rehabilitation program, a veteran may receive counseling and job search and adjustment services for 18 months.

Number awarded: Varies each year.

Deadline: Applications are accepted at any time.

1060 WAIVERS OF NONRESIDENT TUITION FOR DEPENDENTS OF MILITARY PERSONNEL MOVING TO TEXAS

Texas Higher Education Coordinating Board
Attn: Grants and Special Programs
1200 East Anderson Lane
P.O. Box 12788, Capitol Station
Austin, TX 78711-2788
Phone: (512) 427-6340; (800) 242-3062; Fax: (512) 427-6127
Email: grantinfo@thecb.state.tx.us
Web: www.collegeforalltexans.com/apps/financialaid/tofa2.cfm?ID=405

Summary: To exempt dependents of military personnel who move to Texas from the payment of nonresident tuition at public institutions of higher education in the state.

Eligibility: Open to the spouses and dependent children of members of the U.S. armed forces and commissioned officers of the Public Health Service who move to Texas while the servicemember remains assigned to another state. Applicants must be attending or planning to attend a public college or university in the state. They must indicate their intent to become a Texas resident. For dependent children to qualify, the spouse must also move to Texas.

Financial data: Although persons eligible under this program are still classified as nonresidents, they are entitled to pay the resident tuition at Texas institutions of higher education on an immediate basis.

Duration: 1 year.

Number awarded: Varies each year.

Deadline: Deadline not specified.

1061 WAIVERS OF NONRESIDENT TUITION FOR DEPENDENTS OF MILITARY PERSONNEL WHO PREVIOUSLY LIVED IN TEXAS

Texas Higher Education Coordinating Board
Attn: Grants and Special Programs
1200 East Anderson Lane
P.O. Box 12788, Capitol Station
Austin, TX 78711-2788
Phone: (512) 427-6340; (800) 242-3062; Fax: (512) 427-6127
Email: grantinfo@thecb.state.tx.us
Web: www.collegeforalltexans.com/apps/financialaid/tofa2.cfm?ID=536

Summary: To provide a partial tuition exemption to the spouses and dependent children of military personnel who are Texas residents but are not assigned to duty in the state.

Eligibility: Open to the spouses and dependent children of members of the U.S. armed forces who are not assigned to duty in Texas but have previously resided in the state for at least 6 months. Servicemembers must verify that they remain Texas residents by designating Texas as their place of legal residence for income tax purposes, registering to vote in the state, and doing 1 of the following: owning real property in Texas, registering an automobile in Texas, or executing a will indicating that they are a resident of the state. The spouse or dependent child must be attending or planning to attend a Texas public college or university.

Financial data: Although persons eligible under this program are classified as nonresidents, they are entitled to pay the resident tuition at Texas institutions of higher education, regardless of their length of residence in Texas.

Duration: 1 year.

Number awarded: Varies each year.

Deadline: Deadline not specified.

1062 WAL-MART SCHOLARSHIPS OF THE THURGOOD MARSHALL COLLEGE FUND

Thurgood Marshall College Fund
Attn: Scholarship Manager
80 Maiden Lane, Suite 2204
New York, NY 10038
Phone: (212) 573-8487; (877) 690-8673; Fax: (212) 573-8497
Email: srogers@tmcfund.org
Web: www.thurgoodmarshallfund.net

Summary: To provide financial assistance to African American males enrolled at colleges and universities that are members of the Thurgood Marshall College Fund (TMCF).

Eligibility: Open to African American males currently enrolled full-time at 1 of the 47 colleges and universities that are TMCF members. Applicants must have a GPA of 2.5 or higher and be able to demonstrate financial need. First-generation college students are strongly encouraged to apply. U.S. citizenship is required.

Financial data: The stipend is $2,200 per semester ($4,400 per year).

Duration: 1 year.

Number awarded: 66 each year.

Deadline: July of each year.

1063 WALTER H. MEYER–GARRY L. WHITE MEMORIAL EDUCATIONAL FUND

College Planning Network
Attn: Vicki Breithaupt
43 Bentley Place
Port Townsend, WA 98368
Phone: (206) 323-0624
Email: seacpn@collegeplan.org
Web: www.collegeplan.org/cpnow/pnwguide/onlineaps/mwonap.htm

Summary: To provide financial assistance for undergraduate or graduate study in the United States or other countries to mature residents of Washington state.

Eligibility: Open to residents of Washington who are attending or planning to attend a college or university in the United States, Canada, or Europe. Undergraduates must be older than 24 years of age; graduate students must be older than 30. Applicants must submit a 1-page personal essay explaining where they see their career and lifestyle in 10 years. Selection is based on the essay, 2 letters of recommendation, academic transcripts, and financial need.

Financial data: The stipend depends on the need of the recipient but is at least $5,000 per year.

Duration: 1 year.

Number awarded: 15 each year.

Deadline: March of each year.

1064 WARREN FENCL SCHOLARSHIP

Club 100 Veterans
Attn: Scholarship Committee
520 Kamoku Street
Honolulu, HI 96826-5120
Phone: (808) 946-0272
Email: daisyy@hgea.net

Summary: To provide financial assistance to high school seniors and college students who exemplify the sponsor's motto of "For Continuing Service."

Eligibility: Open to high school seniors planning to attend an institution of higher learning and full-time undergraduate students at community colleges, vocational/trade schools, 4-year colleges, and universities. Applicants must have a GPA of 2.5 or higher and be able to demonstrate civic responsibility and community service. Along with their application, they must submit an essay on a topic that changes annually but relates to challenges faced by Japanese Americans. Selection is based on that essay and the applicant's promotion of the legacy of the 100th Infantry Battalion and its motto of "For Continuing Service." Financial need is not considered.

Financial data: The stipend is $2,000.

Duration: 1 year; nonrenewable.

Number awarded: 1 each year.

Deadline: April of each year.

1065 WASHINGTON ADMIRAL'S FUND SCHOLARSHIP

National Naval Officers Association–Washington, D.C. Chapter
Attn: Scholarship Program
2701 Park Center Drive, A1108

Alexandria, VA 22302
Phone: (703) 566-3840; Fax: (703) 566-3813
Email: Stephen.Williams@Navy.mil
Web: dcnnoa.memberlodge.com/Default.aspx?pageId=309002

Summary: To provide financial assistance to minority high school seniors from the Washington, D.C. area who are interested in attending a college or university in any state and enrolling in the Navy Reserve Officers Training Corps (NROTC) program.

Eligibility: Open to minority seniors graduating from high schools in the Washington, D.C. metropolitan area who plan to enroll full-time at an accredited 2- or 4-year college or university in any state. Applicants must be planning to enroll in the NROTC program. They must have a GPA of 2.5 or higher and be U.S. citizens or permanent residents. Selection is based on academic achievement, community involvement, and financial need.

Financial data: The stipend is $1,000.

Duration: 1 year; nonrenewable.

Number awarded: 1 each year.

Deadline: March of each year.

1066 WASHINGTON AWARD FOR VOCATIONAL EXCELLENCE

Washington Higher Education Coordinating Board
917 Lakeridge Way
P.O. Box 43430
Olympia, WA 98504-3430
Phone: (360) 753-5680; (888) 535-0747; Fax: (360) 753-7808; TDD: (360) 753-7809
Email: finaid@hecb.wa.gov
Web: www.hecb.wa.gov/Paying/waaidprgm/wave.asp

Summary: To provide financial assistance to Washington residents who are attending vocational/technical schools.

Eligibility: Open to students at vocational/technical schools. They must be nominated. Nominees must 1) graduate from high school having completed at least 360 hours in a single, approved vocational program; or 2) be enrolled at a public community or technical college and complete at least 1 year (360 hours) in an approved vocational program. They may be planning to attend a public 2- or 4-year college or university or an accredited private college, university, or vocational school in Washington. Selection is based on financial need (25 points), leadership (20 points), community service (20 points), career and technical plans (30 points), other work experience (15 points), and a student narrative on what career and technical education has meant to them (30 points).

Financial data: Recently, maximum awards were $7,600 at Washington State University, independent colleges and universities, and private career colleges; $7,464 at the University of Washington; from $5,340 to $5,514 at the 4 regional universities in the state; from $2,925 to $3,288 at public technical colleges; and up to $2,925 at community colleges.

Duration: Up to 6 quarters or 4 semesters, provided the student maintains a GPA of 3.0 or higher.

Number awarded: 147 each year: 3 students (2 from high schools or skills centers and 1 from community or technical colleges) from each of the state's 49 legislative districts.

Deadline: February of each year.

1067 WASHINGTON BURGLAR & FIRE ALARM ASSOCIATION YOUTH SCHOLARSHIP PROGRAM

Washington Burglar & Fire Alarm Association
Attn: Executive Director
P.O. Box 1137
Duvall, WA 98019
Phone: (425) 788-3656; (800) 248-9272; Fax: (800) 248-9272
Email: Howard@washingtonbfaa.org
Web: www.washingtonbfaa.org/scholarships.html

Summary: To provide financial assistance to high school seniors in Washington who are the children of active-duty law enforcement and fire service personnel and interested in attending college in any state.

Eligibility: Open to seniors graduating from high schools in Washington who have been accepted at an accredited college or university in any state. Applicants must have a father, mother, or legal guardian who is a full-time active employee (not on disability) of the police or sheriff's department or a paid employee or volunteer of a fire department in Washington. Along with their application, they must submit an essay of 500 to 750 words on what it means to them to have their parent or guardian involved in securing our community. Selection is based on that essay (20 points), grade average (35 points), SAT scores (30 points), and academic prizes, awards, school and outside extracurricular activities, and hobbies (15 points); financial need is not considered. Children of law enforcement personnel and children of fire service personnel compete in separate categories; the category winner who has the highest score is designated the overall state winner.

Financial data: The winner in each category receives a $2,000 scholarship; the overall state winner receives an additional $500 scholarship.

Number awarded: 2 each year: 1 for the law enforcement category and 1 for the fire service category.

Deadline: March of each year.

1068 WASHINGTON GRAND LODGE SCHOLARSHIP PROGRAM

Most Worshipful Grand Lodge of Washington, F.&A.M.
Attn: Committee on Public Schools
47 St. Helens Avenue
Tacoma, WA 98402-2698
Phone: (253) 272-3263; (800) 628-4732; Fax: (253) 627-5369
Web: www.freemason-wa.org

Summary: To provide financial assistance to high school juniors and seniors in Washington who plan to attend college in any state.

Eligibility: Open to students currently enrolled as juniors or seniors at public high schools in Washington. Applicants must be planning to attend a college or university in any state. Along with their application, they must submit brief statements on the subject area they plan to study after high school, the ways in which they think their chosen field of study will influence their future and that of the community as a whole, their personal feelings on what they can do to meet the needs of their community, and their financial need. Selection is based on those statements, academic achievement, community service, and citizenship.

Financial data: The stipend is $1,000.

Duration: 1 year.

Number awarded: 10 each year.

Deadline: February.

1069 WASHINGTON PASSPORT FOR FOSTER YOUTH PROMISE SCHOLARSHIPS

Washington Higher Education Coordinating Board
917 Lakeridge Way
P.O. Box 43430
Olympia, WA 98504-3430
Phone: (360) 753-7846; (888) 535-0747; Fax: (360) 704-6246; TDD: (360) 753-7809
Email: passorttocollege@hecb.wa.gov
Web: www.hecb.wa.gov/Paying/waaidprgm/Passport.asp

Summary: To provide financial and other assistance to Washington residents who have been in foster care and plan to attend college in the state.

Eligibility: Open to residents of Washington who spent at least 1 year in foster care after their 16th birthday and emancipated from foster care on or after the beginning of the current year. Applicants must be enrolled at least half-time at an eligible college in Washington by the time they turn 21 years of age. They must be able to demonstrate financial need.

Financial data: Participants receive scholarships (up to $6,900 per year, depending on the college they attend), guidance from college academic and financial aid counselors, support finding housing during breaks and over the summer, special consideration for the State Need Grant and State Work Study, and help finding student employment.

Duration: 1 year; may be renewed up to 4 additional years.

Number awarded: Varies each year.

Deadline: Deadline not specified.

1070 WASHINGTON SCHOLARS PROGRAM

Washington Higher Education Coordinating Board
917 Lakeridge Way
P.O. Box 43430
Olympia, WA 98504-3430
Phone: (360) 753-7843; (888) 535-0747; Fax: (360) 704-6243; TDD: (360) 753-7809
Email: wascholars@hecb.wa.gov
Web: www.hecb.wa.gov/Paying/waaidprgm/wsp.asp

Summary: To provide financial assistance for education at colleges and universities in Washington to the top 1% of students who graduate from high schools in the state.

Eligibility: Open to graduating high school seniors in Washington who are in the top 1% of their program. They must be nominated by their high school principal. Nominees must be planning to attend a college or university in the state. Selection is based on academic accomplishments (75%), leadership (10%), community service (5%), honors and awards (5%), and overall excellence (5%).

Financial data: Awards provide payment of full-time undergraduate resident tuition and fees. Recently, maximum annual stipends were $6,840 at 4-year public research universities and independent colleges and universities, $4,963 at 4-year public comprehensive institutions, $2,959 at public technical colleges, or $2,633 at public community colleges.

Duration: Aid is provided for 12 quarters or 8 semesters of undergraduate study, provided the scholar maintains a GPA of 3.3 or higher.

Number awarded: 147 each year: 3 from each of the 49 legislative districts in the state.

Deadline: Deadline not specified.

1071 WASHINGTON STATE BUSINESS AND PROFESSIONAL WOMEN'S FOUNDATION MATURE WOMAN EDUCATIONAL SCHOLARSHIP

Washington State Business and Professional Women's Foundation
Attn: Virginia Murphy, Scholarship Committee Chair
P.O. Box 631
Chelan, WA 98816-0631
Phone: (509) 682-4747
Email: vamurf@nwi.net
Web: www.bpwwa.com/scholarships.htm

Summary: To provide financial assistance to mature women from Washington interested in attending postsecondary school in the state for retraining or continuing education.

Eligibility: Open to women over 35 years of age who have been residents of Washington for at least 2 years. Applicants must be planning to enroll at a college or university in the state for a program of retraining or continuing education. Along with their application, they must submit a 300-word essay on their specific short-term goals and how the proposed training will help them accomplish those goals and make a difference in their professional career. Financial need is considered in the selection process. U.S. citizenship is required.

Financial data: The stipend is $1,000.

Duration: 1 year.

Number awarded: 1 or more each year.

Deadline: March of each year.

1072 WASHINGTON STATE BUSINESS AND PROFESSIONAL WOMEN'S FOUNDATION SINGLE PARENT SCHOLARSHIP

Washington State Business and Professional Women's Foundation
Attn: Virginia Murphy, Scholarship Committee Chair
P.O. Box 631
Chelan, WA 98816-0631
Phone: (509) 682-4747
Email: vamurf@nwi.net
Web: www.bpwwa.com/scholarships.htm

Summary: To provide financial assistance to women from Washington who are single parents interested in returning to college to continue their education.

Eligibility: Open to women of any age who have been residents of Washington for at least 2 years. Applicants must have at least 1 dependent child, under 18 years of age, living at home. They must be interested in returning to school in the state to continue their education beyond the high school level. Along with their application, they must submit a 300-word essay on their specific short-term goals and how the proposed training will help them accomplish those goals and make a difference in their professional career. Financial need is considered in the selection process. U.S. citizenship is required.

Financial data: The stipend is $1,000.

Duration: 1 year.

Number awarded: 1 or more each year.

Deadline: March of each year.

1073 WASHINGTON STATE EDUCATION AND TRAINING VOUCHER PROGRAM

Washington State Department of Social and Health Services
Attn: ETV Program
1115 Washington Street, S.E.
P.O. Box 45710
Olympia, WA 98504-5710
Phone: (360) 902-8482; (877) 433-8388; Fax: (360) 902-7588
Email: ETVWASH@dshs.wa.gov
Web: independence.wa.gov/programs/etv.asp

Summary: To provide financial assistance to Washington residents who have been in foster care and are interested in attending college in any state.

Eligibility: Open to residents of Washington who are accepted into or enrolled in a degree, certificate, or other program at an accredited college, university, technical school, or vocational school in any state. Applicants must currently be a dependent youth in foster care or were a dependent of the state of Washington and aged out of foster care at 18 years of age, or emancipated or were adopted from foster care after their 16th birthday. They must not have reached their 21st birthday, or have received funds from this program as of their 21st birthday, and have not yet reached their 23rd birthday.

Financial data: The maximum stipend is $5,000 per year.

Duration: 1 year; may be renewed up to 4 additional years, provided the recipient maintains a GPA of 2.0 or higher.

Number awarded: Varies each year.

Deadline: Priority deadlines are July of each year for fall quarter, December of each year for winter quarter, February of each year for spring quarter, and May of each year for summer quarter.

1074 WASHINGTON STATE GOVERNOR'S SCHOLARSHIP FOR FOSTER YOUTH

College Success Foundation
1605 N.W. Sammamish Road, Suite 200
Issaquah, WA 98027
Phone: (425) 416-2000; (877) 655-4097; Fax: (425) 416-2001
Email: info@collegesuccessfoundation.org
Web: collegesuccessfoundation.org/Page.aspx?pid=417

Summary: To provide financial assistance to high school seniors in Washington who have been in foster, group, or kinship care and plan to attend college in the state.

Eligibility: Open to dependent youth who are, or have been until emancipation, in state, tribal, or federally-recognized foster, group, or kinship care in the state of Washington. Applicants must be high school seniors with a GPA of 2.0 or higher and planning to enroll full-time at a designated college or university in Washington. They must have resided in the state for at least 3 academic years prior to high school graduation. Selection is based on motivation and commitment to play a significant role in an activity, group, organization, or family; willingness to seek and use support from others when needed; ability to set educational and career goals; ability to persist toward goals in the face of obstacles or challenges; and financial need.

Financial data: Stipends range from $2,000 to $4,000 per year.

Duration: 1 year; may be renewed up to 4 additional years if the recipient continues to demonstrate financial need and satisfactory progress toward a degree.

Number awarded: Approximately 40 each year.

Deadline: March of each year.

1075 WASHINGTON STATE NEED GRANT

Washington Higher Education Coordinating Board
917 Lakeridge Way
P.O. Box 43430
Olympia, WA 98504-3430
Phone: (360) 753-7850; (888) 535-0747; Fax: (360) 753-7808; TDD: (360) 753-7809
Email: finaid@hecb.wa.gov
Web: www.hecb.wa.gov/Paying/waaidprgm/sng.asp

Summary: To provide financial assistance to Washington residents who come from a low-income or disadvantaged family and plan to attend college in the state.

Eligibility: Open to Washington residents. They can receive maximum grants if their family income is equal to or less than 50% of the state median (currently defined as $20,000 for a family of 1 ranging to $53,500 for a family of 8), 75% of maximum grants if their family income ranges from 51% to 65% of the state median (or $26,500 for a family of 1 ranging to $69,500 for a family of 8), or 50% of maximum grants if their family income ranges from 66% to 70% of the state median (or $28,500 for a family of 1 ranging to $75,000 for a family of 8). Applicants must be enrolled or planning to enroll at least half-time in an eligible certificate, first bachelor's degree, or first associate degree program at an academic institution in the state. They may not be working on a degree in theology. Consideration is automatic with the institution's receipt of the student's completed financial aid application.

Financial data: The maximum grant depends on the type of institution the recipient attends. Recently, it was $6,876 per year at public research universities or independent or private 4-year universities, $5,030 per year at public comprehensive universities, or $2,690 per year at community, technical, and private career colleges. Students whose family income falls between 51% and 65% of the state median are eligible for 75% of those maximums. Students who family income falls between 66% and 70% of the state median are eligible for 50% of those maximums.

Duration: 1 academic year; may be renewed up to 4 additional years or up to 125% or program length.

Number awarded: Varies each year; recently, more than 65,000 students received about $155 million in benefits from this program.

Deadline: Varies according to the participating institution; generally in October of each year.

1076 WASHINGTON STATE PTA SCHOLARSHIPS

Washington State PTA
Attn: Financial Grant Program
2003 65th Avenue West
Tacoma, WA 98466-6215
Phone: (253) 565-2153; (800) 562-3804; Fax: (253) 565-7753
Email: wapta@wastatepta.org
Web: www.wastatepta.org/programs/scholarship/index.html

Summary: To provide financial assistance to graduates of Washington public high schools who plan to attend college in any state.

Eligibility: Open to graduates of public high schools in Washington State who are entering postsecondary institutions in any state. Applicants may be current graduating seniors or graduates from prior years entering their freshman year. They must have a GPA of 3.0 or higher and an adjusted gross family income below specified levels; currently, the maximum is $44,250 for a family of 1, rising to $83,500 for a family of 8. Selection is based on financial need, academic performance, and community service.

Financial data: Stipends are $2,000 at 4-year colleges or universities or $1,000 at community colleges, vocational/technical schools, or other accredited institutions.

Duration: 1 year; nonrenewable.

Number awarded: Varies each year; recently, 30 of these scholarships were awarded.

Deadline: February of each year.

1077 WASHINGTON STATE SCHOLARSHIP FOUNDATION SCHOLARSHIPS

Washington State Scholarship Foundation
P.O. Box 53306
Bellevue, WA 98015
Phone: (206) 310-3851
Email: info@washingtonscholarships.org
Web: www.washingtonscholarships.org/apply.html

Summary: To provide financial assistance to high school seniors and GED recipients from Washington who demonstrate financial need and plan to attend college in any state.

Eligibility: Open to residents of Washington who have completed a public education in the state and are either high school seniors or GED recipients. Applicants may be of any age, but they must be entering a college or university in any state as an entering freshman. They must have a household income of less than $40,250 for a family of 1 ranging to less than $75,900 for a family of 8 or more. Along with their application, they must submit 1-page essays on 1) themselves, including community service, positions of leadership, involvement in school and community, work experience, and youth group activities; and 2) how this scholarship will be a bridge to their future. Selection is based primarily on financial need.

Financial data: Stipends are $5,000 for students at 4-year colleges and universities or $2,000 for students at community colleges, vocational/technical schools, or other accredited institutions.

Duration: 1 year.

Number awarded: A limited number are awarded each year. Since this foundation was established, it has awarded approximately $1 million to nearly 900 students.

Deadline: February of each year.

1078 WATSON-BROWN FOUNDATION SCHOLARSHIPS

Watson-Brown Foundation
Attn: Director of Scholarships and Alumni Relations
310 Tom Watson Way
Thomson, GA 30824
Phone: (706) 595-8886; (866) 923-6863; Fax: (706) 595-3948
Email: skmcneil@watson-brown.org
Web: www.watson-brown.org/scholarship

Summary: To provide financial assistance to residents of Georgia and South Carolina who are interested in attending college in any state.

Eligibility: Open to residents of Georgia and South Carolina who are attending or planning to attend a 4-year college or university in any state. Most recipients are from 10 counties in Georgia (Burke, Columbia, Glascock, Jefferson, Lincoln, McDuffie, Richmond, Taliferro, Warren, and Wilkes) or 6 counties in South Carolina (Abbeville, Aiken, Edgefield, Greenville, McCormick, and Spartanburg), but all high school seniors and current undergraduates from those 2 states are eligible. Applicants must be able to demonstrate financial need. Along with their application, they must submit a 500-word personal essay on an assigned topic.

Financial data: Stipends are $5,000 or $3,000 each year.

Duration: 1 year; may be renewed up to 3 additional years if the recipient maintains a GPA of 3.5 or higher (for the $5,000 scholarships) or 3.0 or higher (for the $3,000 scholarships) and remains enrolled full-time.

Number awarded: Approximately 200 new scholarships are awarded each year; more than 600 students are receiving support from this program each year.

Deadline: February of each year.

1079 W.C. AND PEARL CAMPBELL SCHOLARSHIP

Oregon Student Assistance Commission
Attn: Grants and Scholarships Division
1500 Valley River Drive, Suite 100
Eugene, OR 97401-2146
Phone: (541) 687-7395; (800) 452-8807, ext. 7395; Fax: (541) 687-7414; TDD: (800) 735-2900
Email: awardinfo@osac.state.or.us
Web: www.osac.state.or.us/osac_programs.html

Summary: To provide financial assistance to high school seniors in Oregon who have outstanding academic records and plan to attend college in the state.

Eligibility: Open to seniors graduating from high schools in Oregon who have a GPA of 3.85 or higher and test scores of at least 1220 on the combined mathematics and critical reading SAT or 27 on the ACT. Applicants must be planning to attend a college or university in the state.

Financial data: A stipend is awarded (amount not specified).

Duration: 1 year; nonrenewable.

Number awarded: Varies each year.

Deadline: February of each year.

1080 WEST VIRGINIA GOLF ASSOCIATION FUND SCHOLARSHIPS

Greater Kanawha Valley Foundation
Attn: Scholarship Coordinator
1600 Huntington Square
900 Lee Street, East
P.O. Box 3041
Charleston, WV 25331-3041
Phone: (304) 346-3620; (800) 467-5909; Fax: (304) 346-3640
Email: shoover@tgkvf.org
Web: www.tgkvf.org/scholar.htm

Summary: To provide financial assistance to residents of West Virginia who have been involved in golf and are interested in attending college in any state.

Eligibility: Open to residents of West Virginia who are students at a college or university anywhere in the country. Applicants must 1) have played golf in West Virginia as an amateur for recreation or competition; or 2) have been or are presently employed in West Virginia as a caddie, groundskeeper, bag boy, or in another golf-related job. Along with their application, they must include an essay explaining how the game of golf has made an impact on their life. They must have an ACT score of 20 or higher, be able to demonstrate good moral character, and have a GPA of 2.5 or higher. Selection is based on academic accomplishments, volunteer service, character, and level of exposure to the game of golf; skill level is not a major requirement.

Financial data: The stipend is $1,000 per year.

Duration: 1 year; may be renewed.

Number awarded: Varies each year; recently, 2 of these scholarships were awarded.

Deadline: January of each year.

1081 WEST VIRGINIA SCHOLARSHIP

Epsilon Sigma Alpha International
Attn: ESA Foundation
P.O. Box 270517
Fort Collins, CO 80527
Phone: (970) 223-2824; Fax: (970) 223-4456
Email: esainfo@esaintl.com
Web: www.esaintl.com/esaf

Summary: To provide financial assistance to residents of West Virginia who plan to attend college in any state.

Eligibility: Open to residents of West Virginia who are 1) graduating high school seniors with a GPA of 3.0 or higher or with minimum scores of 22 on the ACT or 1030 on the combined critical reading and mathematics SAT; 2) enrolled in college with a GPA of 3.0 or higher; 3) enrolled at a technical school or returning to school after an absence for retraining of job skills or obtaining a degree; or 4) engaged in online study through an accredited college, university, or vocational school. Applicants may be attending or planning to attend an accredited school in any state and major in any field. Selection is based on character (20%), leadership (20%), service (20%), financial need (20%), and scholastic ability (20%).

Financial data: The stipend is $1,000.

Duration: 1 year; may be renewed.

Number awarded: 1 each year.

Deadline: January of each year.

1082 WGAM JUNIOR SCHOLAR PROGRAM

Women's Golf Association of Massachusetts, Inc.
Attn: WGAM Junior Scholarship Fund, Inc.
William F. Connell Golf House & Museum
300 Arnold Palmer Boulevard
Norton, MA 02766
Phone: (774) 430-9010; Fax: (774) 430-9011
Email: info@wgam.org
Web: www.wgam.org/Pages/junior/jrscholarship.aspx

Summary: To provide financial assistance to female golfers from Massachusetts who plan to attend college in any state.

Eligibility: Open to female golfers who have participated in the Women's Golf Association of Massachusetts (WGAM) junior golf program. Applicants must be attending or planning to attend a college or university in any state. Selection is based on high school academic record and performance, leadership qualities, community and civic involvement, character, personality, and extent of participation in the WGAM junior golf program. Financial need may determine the size of the stipend, but it is not considered in the selection process. An interview is required.

Financial data: A stipend is awarded (amount not specified).

Duration: 1 year; may be renewed.

Number awarded: Varies each year; recently, 7 of these scholarships were awarded.

Deadline: May of each year.

1083 WHITE MEMORIAL SCHOLARSHIP

Lincoln Community Foundation
215 Centennial Mall South, Suite 100
Lincoln, NE 68508
Phone: (402) 474-2345; (888) 448-4668; Fax: (402) 476-8532
Email: lcf@lcf.org
Web: www.lcf.org/page29412.cfm

Summary: To provide financial assistance to high school seniors in Nebraska who plan to attend college in any state.

Eligibility: Open to seniors graduating from high schools in Nebraska and residents of the state who have a GED. Applicants must be planning to attend a qualified nonprofit 2- or 4-year college or university in any state. They must meet minimum standards for admission, but they are not required to have an exceptional academic record or a specified GPA. Preference is given to 1) first-generation college students; and 2) residents of Fairbury, Lincoln, and Lyons. Along with their application, they must submit an essay on how their choice of a trade or career will impact their life and contribute to their self-sufficiency. Financial need is also considered.

Financial data: Stipends provided by the foundation generally range from $500 to $2,000.

Duration: 1 year; may be renewed up to 3 additional years, provided the recipient continues to demonstrate satisfactory academic progress.

Number awarded: 1 or more each year.

Deadline: March of each year.

1084 WILBUR ELLIS SCHOLARSHIPS

Washington Apple Education Foundation
Attn: Scholarship Committee
2900 Euclid Avenue
Wenatchee, WA 98801
Phone: (509) 663-7713; Fax: (509) 663-7469
Email: waef@waef.org
Web: www.waef.org/index.php?page_id=238

Summary: To provide financial assistance to students in any state who are employed within the Washington apple industry or are the children of those employees.

Eligibility: Open to Washington residents. Applicants must be either employed or the children of employees in entry-level laborer or entry-level management positions at a commercial grower or packer in Washington's tree fruit, grape, or hop industries. They may be high school seniors or currently-enrolled students at a college or university in any state. Along with their application, they must submit an official transcript, their SAT or ACT scores, 2 letters of reference, and an essay on an assigned topic. Financial need is also considered in the selection process.

Financial data: The stipend is $1,000. The money may be used to pay for tuition, room, board, books, educational supplies, and miscellaneous institutional fees.

Duration: 1 year; recipients may reapply.

Number awarded: 10 each year.

Deadline: February of each year.

1085 WILDER-NAIFEH TECHNICAL SKILLS GRANTS

Tennessee Student Assistance Corporation
Parkway Towers
404 James Robertson Parkway, Suite 1510
Nashville, TN 37243-0820
Phone: (615) 741-1346; (800) 342-1663; Fax: (615) 741-6101
Email: TSAC.Aidinfo@tn.gov
Web: www.tn.gov/collegepays/mon_college/wilder_naifeh.htm

Summary: To provide financial assistance to students enrolled at Tennessee Technology Centers.

Eligibility: Open to students working on a certificate or diploma at a Tennessee Technology Center. Applicants must be enrolled full-time, but they are not required to meet any GPA or ACT minimum scores. They may not have previously received a Tennessee HOPE Scholarship.

Financial data: The stipend is $2,000 per year.

Duration: 1 year.

Number awarded: Varies each year; recently, 9,721 of these grants, worth more than $8 million, were awarded.

Deadline: August of each year for fall semester; January of each year for spring and summer semesters.

1086 WILLIAM AND SARA JENNE SCHOLARSHIP

Montana State Elks Association
c/o Robert J Byers
P.O. Box 1274
Polson, MT 59869
Phone: (406) 849-5276
Email: robert058@centurytel.net
Web: www.elks.org/states/?vhpID=8024

Summary: To provide financial assistance to second-year students at Montana colleges and universities.

Eligibility: Open to residents of Montana who have completed their first year of study at a university, college, vocational school, or community college in the state. Applicants must have a GPA of 2.0 or higher. Selection is based primarily on financial need, effort, activities, and community involvement (and less on academic achievement).

Financial data: A stipend is awarded (amount not specified).

Duration: 1 year.

Number awarded: Varies each year; recently, 5 of these scholarships were awarded.

Deadline: May of each year.

1087 WILLIAM C. DAVINI SCHOLARSHIP

UNICO National
Attn: UNICO Foundation, Inc.
271 U.S. Highway 46 West, Suite A-108

Fairfield, NJ 07004
Phone: (973) 808-0035; (800) 877-1492; Fax: (973) 808-0043
Email: unico.national@verizon.net
Web: www.unico.org/foundation.asp
Summary: To provide financial assistance for college to Italian American high school seniors.
Eligibility: Open to high school seniors of Italian origin (i.e., at least 1 parent or grandparent of Italian origin) who are planning to attend an accredited college or university. Applicants must have a GPA of 3.0 or higher and be able to demonstrate financial need, participation in extracurricular and community activities, character, and personality. Along with their application, they must submit SAT or ACT test scores and a letter of recommendation from a UNICO chapter in the city or town where they live.
Financial data: The stipend is $1,500 per year.
Duration: 4 years.
Number awarded: 1 each year.
Deadline: April of each year.

1088 WILLIAM E. DOCTER SCHOLARSHIPS

William E. Docter Educational Fund
c/o St. Mary Armenian Church
P.O. Box 39224
Washington, DC 20016
Phone: (202) 364-1440; Fax: (202) 364-1441
Email: WEDFund@aol.com
Web: wedfund.stmaryaac.org
Summary: To provide financial assistance to undergraduate or graduate students of Armenian ancestry.
Eligibility: Open to U.S. citizens of Armenian ancestry; preference is given to those with 2 parents of Armenian ancestry. Applicants must be working on undergraduate, graduate, or vocational study or training in the United States or Canada. Along with their application, they must submit a 1-page statement of their goals and what they plan to do after completing their education, 2 letters of recommendation, and evidence of financial need.
Financial data: The stipend is $5,000.
Duration: 1 year; may be renewed.
Number awarded: Varies each year; recently, 39 students received support from this fund.
Deadline: June of each year.

1089 WILLIAM F. GANDERT MEMORIAL SCHOLARSHIPS

National Leased Housing Association
Attn: NLHA Education Fund
1900 L Street, N.W., Suite 300
Washington, DC 20036
Phone: (202) 785-8888; Fax: (202) 785-2008
Email: info@hudnlha.com
Web: www.hudnlha.com/education_fund/index.asp
Summary: To provide financial assistance for trade school to residents of federally-assisted rental housing properties and members of families receiving rental subsidy through federal housing programs.
Eligibility: Open to U.S. citizens and permanent residents who reside in a federally-assisted rental housing property or whose families receive rental subsidy through a recognized federal housing program (e.g., Section 8, Rent Supplement, Rental Assistance Payments, Low Income Housing Tax Credit). Applicants must be graduating high school seniors, students currently enrolled in a certified training program for a specific trade, or GED recipients entering such a program. They must be able to demonstrate financial need and community leadership through volunteer work at school or in the community. Along with their application, they must submit a 1-page essay on their goals with respect to their education in the school they are interested in attending.
Financial data: A stipend is awarded (amount not specified). Funds are disbursed directly to an accredited trade school to be used for partial payment of tuition, books, equipment and tools, or other expenses directly related to the student's education.
Duration: 1 year.
Number awarded: Varies each year; recently, 2 of these scholarships were awarded.
Deadline: February of each year.

1090 WILLIAM F. MACKINTOSH MASONIC LEGACY SCHOLARSHIPS

Minnesota Masonic Charities
Attn: Scholarships
11501 Masonic Home Drive
Bloomington, MN 55437
Phone: (952) 948-6004; Fax: (952) 948-6210
Email: comments@mnmasonic.org
Web: mnmasoniccharities.org/content/signature-scholarships
Summary: To provide financial assistance to high school seniors in Minnesota who plan to attend college in any state or abroad.
Eligibility: Open to seniors graduating from high schools in Minnesota who have a GPA of 3.0 or higher. Applicants must be planning to attend a college or university in any geographic location, including outside of the United States. Along with their application, they must submit brief essays on 1) their accomplishments in classroom or extracurricular activities in which they took pride; 2) why they should receive this scholarship; and 3) the person after whom these scholarships are named with whom they most identify and why. They must also submit a long essay on the values of Masonry and the relationship of those to their own lives. In the selection process, no consideration is given to Masonic ties, age, gender, religion, national origin, or financial need.
Financial data: The stipend is $4,000 per year.
Duration: 1 year; may be renewed up to 3 additional years.
Number awarded: 2 each year.
Deadline: February of each year.

1091 WILLIAM L. BOYD, IV, FLORIDA RESIDENT ACCESS GRANTS

Florida Department of Education
Attn: Office of Student Financial Assistance
325 West Gaines Street
Tallahassee, FL 32399-0400
Phone: (850) 410-5160; (888) 827-2004; Fax: (850) 487-1809
Email: osfa@fldoe.org
Web: www.floridastudentfinancialaid.org/SSFAD/factsheets/FRAG.htm
Summary: To provide financial assistance to students at private colleges and universities in Florida.
Eligibility: Open to full-time undergraduate students who are attending any of 28 eligible private nonprofit colleges or universities in Florida and who have been Florida residents for at least 1 year. Applicants must be U.S. citizens or eligible noncitizens Financial need is not considered in the selection process.
Financial data: The amount of the award is specified by the state legislature annually; recently, the stipend was $2,529.
Duration: Up to 9 semesters or 14 quarters, provided the student maintains full-time enrollment and a GPA of 2.0 or higher.
Number awarded: Varies each year; recently, 15,286 new and 22,077 renewal grants were awarded.
Deadline: Deadline not specified.

1092 WILLIAM ORR DINGWALL FOUNDATION KOREAN ANCESTRY GRANTS

William Orr Dingwall Foundation
2201 N Street, N.W., Suite 117
Washington, DC 20037
Email: apply@dingwallfoundation.org
Web: www.dingwallfoundation.org/keligibility.htm
Summary: To provide financial assistance to undergraduates of Asian (preferably Korean) ancestry.
Eligibility: Open to graduating high school seniors and undergraduates currently enrolled at a college or university in the United States. Applicants should be of Korean ancestry, although exceptional students of other Asian ancestry may also be considered. They must have a GPA of 3.5 or higher but may be majoring in any field. Selection is based on academic record, written statements, and letters of recommendation.
Financial data: The stipend is $20,000 per year.
Duration: 1 year; may be renewed up to 3 additional years, provided the recipient maintains a GPA of 3.5 or higher.
Deadline: April of each year.

1093 WISCONSIN ACADEMIC EXCELLENCE SCHOLARSHIP PROGRAM

Wisconsin Higher Educational Aids Board
131 West Wilson Street, Suite 902
P.O. Box 7885
Madison, WI 53707-7885
Phone: (608) 267-2213; Fax: (608) 267-2808
Email: Nancy.Wilkison@wisconsin.gov
Web: heab.state.wi.us/programs.html

Summary: To provide financial assistance to Wisconsin high school seniors who have the highest GPAs in their schools and plan to attend college in the state.

Eligibility: Open to seniors at each public and private high school throughout Wisconsin who have the highest GPAs. Applicants must plan to attend a branch of the University of Wisconsin, a Wisconsin technical college, or an independent institution in the state as a full-time student in the following fall.

Financial data: The awards provide full tuition, up to $2,250 per year, during the first 3 years of undergraduate study; for subsequent years, the maximum award is equal to full tuition and fees at a campus of the University of Wisconsin.

Duration: Up to 10 semesters.

Number awarded: The number of scholarships allotted to each high school is based on total student enrollment, ranging from 1 scholarship for schools with enrollment of 80 to 499 up to 6 scholarships for schools with enrollment greater than 2,500. Students at schools with enrollment of less than 80 compete statewide for an additional 10 scholarships.

Deadline: Deadline not specified.

1094 WISCONSIN G.I. BILL TUITION REMISSION PROGRAM

Wisconsin Department of Veterans Affairs
30 West Mifflin Street
P.O. Box 7843
Madison, WI 53707-7843
Phone: (608) 266-1311; (800) WIS-VETS; Fax: (608) 267-0403
Email: WDVAInfo@dva.state.wi.us
Web: www.dva.state.wi.us/Ben_education.asp

Summary: To provide financial assistance for college or graduate school to Wisconsin veterans and their dependents.

Eligibility: Open to current residents of Wisconsin who 1) were residents of the state when they entered or reentered active duty in the U.S. armed forces; or 2) have moved to the state and have been residents for any consecutive 12-month period after entry or reentry into service. Applicants must have served on active duty for at least 2 continuous years or for at least 90 days during specified wartime periods. Also eligible are 1) qualifying children and unremarried surviving spouses of Wisconsin veterans who died in the line of duty or as the direct result of a service-connected disability; and 2) children and spouses of Wisconsin veterans who have a service-connected disability rated by the U.S. Department of Veterans Affairs as 30% or greater. Children must be between 17 and 25 years of age (regardless of the date of the veteran's death or initial disability rating) and be a Wisconsin resident for tuition purposes. Spouses remain eligible for 10 years following the date of the veteran's death or initial disability rating; they must be Wisconsin residents for tuition purposes but they may enroll full- or part-time. Students may attend any institution, center, or school within the University of Wisconsin (UW) System or the Wisconsin Technical College System (WCTS). There are no income limits, delimiting periods following military service during which the benefit must be used, or limits on the level of study (e.g., vocational, undergraduate, professional, or graduate).

Financial data: Veterans who qualify as a Wisconsin resident for tuition purposes are eligible for a remission of 100% of standard academic fees and segregated fees at a UW campus or 100% of program and material fees at a WCTS institution. Veterans who qualify as a Wisconsin veteran for purposes of this program but for other reasons fail to meet the definition of a Wisconsin resident for tuition purposes at the UW system are eligible for a remission of 100% of non-resident fees. Spouses and children of deceased or disabled veterans are entitled to a remission of 100% of tuition and fees at a UW or WCTS institution.

Duration: Up to 8 semesters or 128 credits, whichever is greater.

Number awarded: Varies each year.

Deadline: Applications must be submitted within 14 days from the office start of the academic term: in October for fall, March for spring, or June for summer.

1095 WISCONSIN HIGHER EDUCATION GRANT

Wisconsin Higher Educational Aids Board
131 West Wilson Street, Suite 902
P.O. Box 7885
Madison, WI 53707-7885
Phone: (608) 266-0888; Fax: (608) 267-2808
Email: Sandy.Thomas@wisconsin.gov
Web: heab.state.wi.us/programs.html

Summary: To provide financial assistance to financially needy undergraduate students attending public institutions of higher education in Wisconsin.

Eligibility: Open to Wisconsin residents enrolled at least half-time at any branch of the University of Wisconsin, at any Wisconsin technical college, or at any Tribal College or University (TCU) in the state. Selection is based on financial need.

Financial data: The stipend ranges from $250 to $3,000 per year.

Duration: Up to 10 semesters.

Number awarded: Varies each year.

Deadline: Deadline not specified.

1096 WISCONSIN JOB RETRAINING GRANTS

Wisconsin Department of Veterans Affairs
30 West Mifflin Street
P.O. Box 7843
Madison, WI 53707-7843
Phone: (608) 266-1311; (800) WIS-VETS; Fax: (608) 267-0403
Email: WDVAInfo@dva.state.wi.us
Web: www.dva.state.wi.us/Ben_retraininggrants.asp

Summary: To provide funds to recently unemployed Wisconsin veterans or their families who need financial assistance while being retrained for employment.

Eligibility: Open to current residents of Wisconsin who 1) were residents of the state when they entered or reentered active duty in the U.S. armed forces; or 2) have moved to the state and have been residents for any consecutive 12-month period after entry or reentry into service. Applicants must have served on active duty for at least 2 continuous years or for at least 90 days during specified wartime periods. Unremarried spouses and minor or dependent children of deceased veterans who would have been eligible for the grant if they were living today may also be eligible. The applicant must, within the year prior to the date of application, have become unemployed (involuntarily laid off or discharged, not due to willful misconduct) or underemployed (experienced an involuntary reduction of income). Underemployed applicants must have current annual income from employment that does not exceed federal poverty guidelines. All applicants must be retraining at accredited schools in Wisconsin or in a structured on-the-job program. Course work toward a college degree does not qualify. Training does not have to be full-time, but the program must be completed within 2 years and must reasonably be expected to lead to employment.

Financial data: The maximum grant is $3,000 per year; the actual amount varies, depending upon the amount of the applicant's unmet need. In addition to books, fees, and tuition, the funds may be used for living expenses.

Duration: 1 year; may be renewed 1 additional year.

Number awarded: Varies each year.

Deadline: Applications may be submitted at any time.

1097 WISCONSIN MINORITY UNDERGRADUATE RETENTION GRANTS

Wisconsin Higher Educational Aids Board
131 West Wilson Street, Suite 902
P.O. Box 7885
Madison, WI 53707-7885
Phone: (608) 267-2212; Fax: (608) 267-2808
Email: Mary.Kuzdas@wisconsin.gov
Web: heab.state.wi.us/programs.html

Summary: To provide financial assistance to minorities in Wisconsin who are currently enrolled at a college in the state.

Eligibility: Open to residents of Wisconsin who are African Americans, Hispanic Americans, American Indians, or southeast Asians (students who were admitted to the United States after December 31, 1975 and who are a former citizen of Laos, Vietnam, or Cambodia or whose ancestor was a citizen of 1 of those countries). Applicants must be enrolled at least half-time as sophomores, juniors, seniors, or fifth-year undergraduates at a Wisconsin technical college, tribal college, or independent college or university in the state. They must be nominated by their institution and be able to demonstrate financial need.

Financial data: Stipends range from $250 to $2,500 per year, depending on the need of the recipient.

Duration: Up to 4 years.

Number awarded: Varies each year.

Deadline: Deadline dates vary by institution; check with your school's financial aid office.

1098 WISCONSIN STATE TELECOMMUNICATIONS FOUNDATION SCHOLARSHIPS

Wisconsin State Telecommunications Association
Attn: Foundation
121 East Wilson Street, Suite 102
Madison, WI 53703
Phone: (608) 256-8866; Fax: (608) 256-2676
Email: info@wsta.info
Web: www.wsta.info/scholarships.htm

Summary: To provide financial assistance to high school seniors in Wisconsin who live in an area served by a local exchange telephone company and plan to attend college in any state.

Eligibility: Open to seniors graduating from high schools in Wisconsin where a local exchange company provides telephone service; AT&T (SBC/Ameritech, CenturyTel, Frontier Communications, Lakefield Telephone Company, and Verizon do not participate in the program. Applicants must be planning to attend a college or university in any state. Along with their application, they must submit a 500-word essay on their primary goal in life, why they chose that goal, how they expect to achieve that goal, and where they plan to be 5 years after college. Selection is based on the students' desire to continue their education, their academic ability (as measured by GPA and ACT/SAT test scores), and their financial need.

Financial data: The stipend is $1,500.

Duration: 1 year.

Number awarded: Varies each year; recently, 34 of these scholarships were awarded.

Deadline: February of each year.

1099 WISCONSIN TALENT INCENTIVE PROGRAM (TIP) GRANTS

Wisconsin Higher Educational Aids Board
131 West Wilson Street, Suite 902
P.O. Box 7885
Madison, WI 53707-7885
Phone: (608) 266-1665; Fax: (608) 267-2808
Email: colettem1.brown@wi.gov
Web: heab.state.wi.us/programs.html

Summary: To provide financial assistance for college to needy and educationally disadvantaged students in Wisconsin.

Eligibility: Open to residents of Wisconsin entering a college or university in the state who meet the requirements of both financial need and educational disadvantage. Financial need qualifications include 1) family contribution (a dependent student whose expected parent contribution is $200 or less, an independent student with dependents whose academic year contribution is $200 or less, or an independent student with no dependents whose maximum contribution is $200 or less); 2) Temporary Assistance to Needy Families (TANF) or Wisconsin Works (W2) benefits (a dependent student whose family is receiving TANF or W2 benefits or an independent student who is receiving TANF or W2 benefits); or 3) unemployment (a dependent student whose parents are ineligible for unemployment compensation and have no current income from employment, or an independent student and spouse, if married, who are ineligible for unemployment compensation and have no current income from employment). Educational disadvantage qualifications include students who are 1) minorities (African American, Native American, Hispanic, or southeast Asian); 2) enrolled in a special academic support program due to insufficient academic preparation; 3) a first-generation college student (neither parent graduated from a 4-year college or university); 4) disabled according to the Department of Workforce Development, the Division of Vocational Rehabilitation, or a Wisconsin college or university that uses the Americans with Disabilities Act definition; 5) currently or formerly incarcerated in a correctional institution; or 6) from an environmental and academic background that deters the pursuit of educational plans. Students already in college are not eligible.

Financial data: Stipends range up to $1,800 per year.

Duration: 1 year; may be renewed up to 4 additional years, provided the recipient continues to be a Wisconsin resident enrolled at least half-time in a degree or certificate program, makes satisfactory academic progress, demonstrates financial need, and remains enrolled continuously from semester to semester and from year to year. If recipients withdraw from school or cease to attend classes for any reason (other than medical necessity), they may not reapply.

Number awarded: Varies each year.

Deadline: Deadline not specified.

1100 WISCONSIN TUITION GRANT

Wisconsin Higher Educational Aids Board
131 West Wilson Street, Suite 902
P.O. Box 7885
Madison, WI 53707-7885
Phone: (608) 267-2212; Fax: (608) 267-2808
Email: Mary.Kuzdas@wisconsin.gov
Web: heab.state.wi.us/programs.html

Summary: To provide assistance to financially needy undergraduate students attending private institutions of higher education in Wisconsin or abroad.

Eligibility: Open to Wisconsin residents enrolled in independent nonprofit colleges and universities in the state. Students may study abroad if the tuition cost of the program is paid directly to the Wisconsin institution and the credits earned are acceptable by the institution as credit for the degree on which the student is working. Selection is based on financial need.

Financial data: Awards are based on financial need, but may not exceed tuition charged at the University of Wisconsin at Madison.

Duration: Up to 10 semesters.

Number awarded: Varies each year.

Deadline: Deadline not specified.

1101 WISCONSIN VETERANS EDUCATION (VETED) REIMBURSEMENT GRANTS

Wisconsin Department of Veterans Affairs
30 West Mifflin Street
P.O. Box 7843
Madison, WI 53707-7843
Phone: (608) 266-1311; (800) WIS-VETS; Fax: (608) 267-0403
Email: WDVAInfo@dva.state.wi.us
Web: www.dva.state.wi.us/Ben_VetEd.asp

Summary: To provide financial assistance for undergraduate education to Wisconsin veterans.

Eligibility: Open to current residents of Wisconsin who 1) were residents of the state when they entered or reentered active duty in the U.S. armed forces; or 2) have moved to the state and have been residents for any consecutive 12-month period after entry or reentry into service. Applicants must have served on active duty for at least 2 continuous years or for at least 90 days during specified wartime periods. They must be working full- or part-time on a degree, certificate of graduation, or course completion at an eligible campus of the University of Wisconsin, technical college, or approved private institution of higher education in Wisconsin or Minnesota. Their household income must be below $50,000 plus $1,000 for each dependent in excess of 2 dependents. Veterans seeking reimbursement through this program must first apply for Wisconsin G.I. Bill benefits. To qualify for reimbursement, they must achieve at least a 2.0 GPA or an average grade of "C" in the semester for which reimbursement is requested. Veterans may use this program up to 10 years after leaving active duty. Once a veteran reaches the 10-year delimiting date, he or she may "bank" up to 60 unused credits for part-time study.

Financial data: Eligible veterans are entitled to reimbursement of 100% of the costs of tuition and fees not covered by other grants, scholarships, or remissions, to a maximum of the UW-Madison rate for the same number of credits.

Duration: The amount of reimbursement depends on the time the veteran served on active duty: 30 credits or 2 semesters for 90 to 180 days of active service, 60 credits or 4 semesters for 181 to 730 days of active service, or 120 credits or 8 semesters for 731 days or more of active service.

Number awarded: Varies each year.

Deadline: Applications must be received within 60 days of the start of the course, semester, or term.

1102 WOMEN OF THE ELCA SCHOLARSHIP PROGRAM

Women of the Evangelical Lutheran Church in America
Attn: Scholarships
8765 West Higgins Road
Chicago, IL 60631-4101
Phone: (773) 380-2736; (800) 638-3522, ext. 2736; Fax: (773) 380-2419
Email: emily.hansen@elca.org
Web: www.elca.org/Growing-In-Faith/Ministry/Women-of-the-ELCA.aspx

Summary: To provide financial assistance to lay women affiliated with the Evangelical Lutheran Church of America (ELCA) congregations and who wish to take classes on the undergraduate, graduate, professional, or vocational school level.

Eligibility: Open to ELCA lay women who are at least 21 years of age and have experienced an interruption of at least 2 years in their education since high school. Applicants must have been admitted to an educational institution to

prepare for a career in other than the ordained ministry. They may be working on an undergraduate, graduate, professional, or vocational school degree. U.S. citizenship is required.
Financial data: The maximum stipend is $1,000.
Duration: Up to 2 years.
Number awarded: Varies each year, depending upon the funds available.
Deadline: February of each year.

1103 WOMEN'S ALABAMA GOLF ASSOCIATION SCHOLARSHIPS

Women's Alabama Golf Association
1025 Montgomery Highway, Suite 210
Birmingham, AL 35216
Phone: (205) 979-2550
Email: info@womensalabamagolf.com
Web: womensalabamagolf.com/scholarships/Scholarships.asp
Summary: To provide financial assistance for college to women in Alabama who can demonstrate an interest in golf.
Eligibility: Open to women graduating from high schools in Alabama who are planning to attend a college or university in the state. Applicants must be able to demonstrate an interest in the game of golf and financial need. They must have an ACT score of 22 or higher. Along with their application, they must submit a 200-word statement on why a college education is important to them. Selection is based on academic excellence, citizenship, sportsmanship, community involvement, and financial need.
Financial data: The stipend is $2,500 per year.
Duration: 1 year; may be renewed up to 3 additional years if the recipient maintains a GPA of 2.4 or higher during her freshman year and 2.8 or higher during subsequent years.
Number awarded: 1 each year.
Deadline: March of each year.

1104 WOMEN'S ARMY CORPS VETERANS' ASSOCIATION SCHOLARSHIP

Women's Army Corps Veterans' Association
P.O. Box 5577
Fort McClellan, AL 36205-5577
Email: info@armywomen.org
Web: www.armywomen.org
Summary: To provide financial assistance for college to the relatives of Army military women.
Eligibility: Open to high school seniors who are the children, grandchildren, nieces, or nephews of Army service women. Applicants must have a cumulative GPA of 3.5 or higher and be planning to enroll as a full-time student at an accredited college or university in the United States. They must submit a 500-word biographical sketch that includes their future goals and how the scholarship would be used. Selection is based on academic achievement, leadership ability as expressed through co-curricular activities and community involvement, the biographical sketch, and recommendations. Financial need is not considered. U.S. citizenship is required.
Financial data: The stipend is $1,500.
Duration: 1 year.
Number awarded: 1 or more each year.
Deadline: April of each year.

1105 WOMEN'S ITALIAN CLUB OF BOSTON SCHOLARSHIP

General Federation of Women's Clubs of Massachusetts
Attn: Scholarship Chair
245 Dutton Road
P.O. Box 679
Sudbury, MA 01776-0679
Phone: (781) 443-4569; Fax: (781) 443-1617
Email: Jwilchynski@aol.com
Web: www.gfwcma.org/scholarships.html
Summary: To provide financial assistance to high school seniors in Massachusetts who are of Italian heritage and interested in attending college in any state.
Eligibility: Open to seniors graduating from high schools or home schools in Massachusetts who are planning to attend a college or university in any state. Applicants must submit a high school transcript, letter of reference from a high school principal or counselor, and a 500-word essay on their goals, including their Italian heritage, work experience, and volunteer service.
Financial data: The stipend is $1,000. Funds are paid directly to the recipient's college or university for tuition only.
Duration: 1 year.
Number awarded: 1 or more each year.
Deadline: February of each year.

1106 WOMEN'S OVERSEAS SERVICE LEAGUE SCHOLARSHIPS FOR WOMEN

Women's Overseas Service League
Attn: Scholarship Committee
P.O. Box 7124
Washington, DC 20044-7124
Email: carolhabgood@sbcglobal.net
Web: www.wosl.org/scholarships.htm
Summary: To provide financial assistance for college to women who are committed to a military or other public service career.
Eligibility: Open to women who are committed to a military or other public service career. Applicants must have completed at least 12 semester or 18 quarter hours of postsecondary study with a GPA of 2.5 or higher. They must be working on an academic degree (the program may be professional or technical in nature) and must agree to enroll for at least 6 semester or 9 quarter hours of study each academic period. Along with their application, they must submit an official transcript, a 1-page essay on their career goals, 3 current letters of reference, and a brief statement describing sources of financial support and the need for scholarship assistance. They must also provide information on their educational background, employment experience, civic and volunteer activities, and expected degree completion date.
Financial data: Stipends range from $500 to $1,000 per year.
Duration: 1 year; may be renewed 1 additional year.
Deadline: February of each year.

1107 WOMEN'S SOUTHERN GOLF ASSOCIATION SCHOLARSHIP

Women's Southern Golf Association
c/o Lecia Alexander, Scholarship Committee Chair
12334 Meadow Ridge
Stafford, TX 77477
Phone: (281) 240-5485
Email: scholarship@womens-southerngolfassociation.org
Web: www.womens-southerngolfassociation.org/scholar.htm
Summary: To provide financial assistance to women golfers in the southern states who plan to attend college in any state.
Eligibility: Open to amateur female golfers who are residents of 1 of the 15 southern states (Alabama, Arkansas, Florida, Georgia, Kentucky, Louisiana, Maryland, Mississippi, North Carolina, Oklahoma, South Carolina, Tennessee, Texas, Virginia, and West Virginia) or the District of Columbia. Applicants must be graduating high school seniors planning to work on an undergraduate degree at an accredited institution of higher learning in any state. Along with their application, they must submit a 200-word personal statement on their goals for college and their future. Selection is based on academic excellence, citizenship, sportsmanship, and financial need.
Financial data: The stipend is $3,500 per year. Funds are paid directly to the recipient's college.
Duration: 1 year; may be renewed up to 3 additional years if the recipient maintains a GPA of 3.0 or higher.
Number awarded: 1 each year.
Deadline: April of each year.

1108 WOODMANSEE SCHOLARSHIP

Woodmansee Scholarship Fund
c/o Pioneer Trust Bank, N.A.
Attn: Trust Department
109 Commercial Street, N.E.
P.O. Box 2305
Salem, OR 97308-2305
Phone: (503) 363-3136, ext. 246
Summary: To provide financial assistance to graduating high school seniors in Oregon who plan to attend college in the state.
Eligibility: Open to seniors graduating from public or private high schools in Oregon. Applicants must be Oregon residents and planning to attend an institution of higher education in the state. Selection is based on financial need and academic ability.

Financial data: This scholarship covers up to one half the cost of the recipient's board, room, tuition, books, and fees.
Duration: 4 years, provided the recipient maintains satisfactory academic progress.
Number awarded: Varies each year.
Deadline: March of each year.

1109 WORLD WAR II ILLINOIS DESCENDANTS SCHOLARSHIP

Sangamon County Community Foundation
Attn: Scholarship Coordinator
205 South Fifth Street, Suite 930
Springfield, IL 62701
Phone: (217) 789-4431; Fax: (217) 789-4635
Email: scholarships@sccf.us
Web: www.sccf.us/scholarshipfunds.html
Summary: To provide financial assistance to high school seniors in Illinois who are the direct descendant of a veteran of World War II and plan to attend college in any state.
Eligibility: Open to seniors graduating from high schools in Illinois who are the direct descendant (i.e., grandchild or great-grandchild, but not a great niece or nephew) of an Illinois veteran of World War II. Applicants must be planning to enroll full-time at an accredited community college or 4-year college or university in any state. They must have an unweighted GPA of 4.0 or be projected to be the valedictorian or salutatorian of their class.
Financial data: The stipend is $2,000.
Duration: 1 year.
Number awarded: 2 each year.
Deadline: March of each year.

1110 W.P. BLACK FUND SCHOLARSHIPS

Greater Kanawha Valley Foundation
Attn: Scholarship Coordinator
1600 Huntington Square
900 Lee Street, East
P.O. Box 3041
Charleston, WV 25331-3041
Phone: (304) 346-3620; (800) 467-5909; Fax: (304) 346-3640
Email: shoover@tgkvf.org
Web: www.tgkvf.org/scholar.htm
Summary: To provide financial assistance to residents of West Virginia who are interested in attending college in any state.
Eligibility: Open to residents of West Virginia who are attending or planning to attend a college or university anywhere in the country. Applicants must have an ACT score of 20 or higher, be able to demonstrate good moral character and extreme financial need, and have a GPA of 2.5 or higher.
Financial data: The stipend is $1,000 per year.
Duration: 1 year; may be renewed.
Number awarded: Varies each year; recently, 126 of these scholarships were awarded.
Deadline: January of each year.

1111 WSAJ PRESIDENTS' SCHOLARSHIP

Washington State Association for Justice
1511 State Avenue, N.E.
Olympia, WA 98506-4552
Phone: (360) 786-9100; Fax: (360) 786-9103
Email: adrianne@wstlaoly.org
Web: www.wstla.org/AboutUs/Historical.aspx
Summary: To provide financial assistance for college to Washington residents who have a disability or have been a victim of injury.
Eligibility: Open to seniors at high schools in Washington who are planning to work on a bachelor's degree at an institution of higher education in the state. Applicants must be able to demonstrate 1) financial need; 2) a history of achievement despite having been a victim of injury or overcoming a disability, handicap, or similar challenge; 3) a record of serving others; and 4) a commitment to apply their education toward helping others.
Financial data: Stipends average $2,000. Funds are paid directly to the recipient's chosen institution of higher learning to be used for tuition, room, board, and fees.
Duration: 1 year.
Number awarded: 1 or more each year.
Deadline: March of each year.

1112 WSCA/TCF BANK SCHOLARSHIP

Wisconsin School Counselor Association
c/o Allison Ceponis, Scholarship Chair
1920 Lincoln Avenue
Stoughton, WI 53589
Phone: (608) 877-5415
Web: www.wscaweb.com
Summary: To provide financial assistance to high school seniors in Wisconsin who plan to attend college in any state.
Eligibility: Open to graduating seniors at public and private high schools in Wisconsin. Applicants must be planning to attend a 2- or 4-year college or university in any state. Along with their application, they must submit a 1-page essay describing how a school counselor or school counseling program has helped them plan, decide, resolve, or grow in some area of their life. Financial need is not considered in the selection process.
Financial data: The stipend is $1,000.
Duration: 1 year.
Number awarded: 4 each year.
Deadline: November of each year.

1113 WWGA FOUNDATION SCHOLARSHIP

Women's Western Golf Foundation
c/o Mrs. Richard Willis
393 Ramsay Road
Deerfield, IL 60015
Web: www.wwga.org/scholarship_info.htm
Summary: To provide financial assistance to high school senior girls who are interested in the sport of golf and plan to attend college.
Eligibility: Open to high school senior girls who intend to graduate in the year they submit their application. They must meet entrance requirements of, and plan to enroll at, an accredited college or university. Selection is based on academic achievement, financial need, excellence of character, and involvement with the sport of golf. Skill or excellence in the game is not a criterion. U.S. citizenship is required.
Financial data: The stipend is $2,000 per year. The funds are to be used to pay for room, board, tuition, and other university fees or charges.
Duration: 1 year; may be renewed up to 3 additional years if the recipient maintains a GPA of 3.0 or higher.
Number awarded: 15 each year.
Deadline: February of each year.

1114 WYOMING COMBAT VETERAN SURVIVING ORPHAN TUITION BENEFIT

Wyoming Veterans Commission
Attn: Executive Director
5500 Bishop Boulevard
Cheyenne, WY 82009
Phone: (307) 772-5145; (866) 992-7641, ext. 5145; Fax: (307) 772-5202
Email: lbartt@state.wy.us
Web: www.wy.ngb.army.mil/benefits
Summary: To provide financial assistance to children of deceased, POW, or MIA Wyoming veterans who are interested in attending college in the state.
Eligibility: Open to children of veterans whose parent had been a resident of Wyoming for at least 1 year at the time of entering service and received the armed forces expeditionary medal or a campaign medal for service in an armed conflict in a foreign country. The veteran parent must 1) have died during active service during armed conflict in a foreign country; 2) be listed officially as being a POW or MIA as a result of active service with the military forces of the United States; or 3) have been honorably discharged from the military and subsequently died of an injury or disease incurred while in service and was a Wyoming resident at the time of death. Applicants must have been younger than 21 years of age when the veteran died or was listed as POW or MIA and younger than 22 years of age when they enter college. They must be attending or planning to attend the University of Wyoming or a community college in the state.
Financial data: Qualifying veterans' children are eligible for free resident tuition at the University of Wyoming or at any of the state's community colleges.
Duration: Up to 10 semesters.
Number awarded: Varies each year.
Deadline: Applications may be submitted at any time, but they should be received 2 or 3 weeks before the beginning of the semester.

1115 WYOMING COMBAT VETERAN SURVIVING SPOUSE TUITION BENEFIT

Wyoming Veterans Commission
Attn: Executive Director
5500 Bishop Boulevard
Cheyenne, WY 82009
Phone: (307) 772-5145; (866) 992-7641, ext. 5145; Fax: (307) 772-5202
Email: lbartt@state.wy.us
Web: www.wy.ngb.army.mil/benefits

Summary: To provide financial assistance to surviving spouses of deceased, POW, or MIA Wyoming veterans who are interested in attending college in the state.

Eligibility: Open to spouses of veterans whose spouse had been a resident of Wyoming for at least 1 year at the time of entering service and received the armed forces expeditionary medal or a campaign medal for service in an armed conflict in a foreign country. The veteran spouse must 1) have died during active service during armed conflict in a foreign country; 2) be listed officially as being a POW or MIA as a result of active service with the military forces of the United States; or 3) have been honorably discharged from the military and subsequently died of an injury or disease incurred while in service and was a Wyoming resident at the time of death. Applicants must enroll at the University of Wyoming or a community college in the state within 10 years following the death of the combat veteran.

Financial data: Qualifying veterans' spouses are eligible for free resident tuition at the University of Wyoming or at any of the state's community colleges.

Duration: Up to 10 semesters.

Number awarded: Varies each year.

Deadline: Applications may be submitted at any time, but they should be received 2 or 3 weeks before the beginning of the semester.

1116 WYOMING GRAND LODGE SCHOLARSHIPS

Grand Lodge A.F. & A.M. of Wyoming
Attn: Grand Secretary
114 West Bridge Street
P.O. Box 646
Saratoga, WY 82331
Phone: (307) 326-8346
Email: grandsecretary@wyomingmasons.com
Web: www.wyomingmasons.com/scholarships.htm

Summary: To provide financial assistance to residents of Wyoming who plan to attend college in any state.

Eligibility: Open to Wyoming residents who are enrolled or planning to enroll at a college or university in any state. Applicants must have a GPA of 2.0 or higher. Along with their application, they must submit a 1-paragraph statement on their occupational and life goals. Selection is based on that statement, academic achievement, extracurricular activities, civic and community activities, outstanding achievements, work experience, and financial need. No connection to the Masonic family is required.

Financial data: The stipend is $1,000. Funds are paid to the financial office the recipient attends.

Duration: 1 year; recipients may reapply.

Number awarded: Approximately 25 each year.

Deadline: April of each year.

1117 WYOMING OVERSEAS COMBAT VETERAN TUITION BENEFIT

Wyoming Veterans Commission
Attn: Executive Director
5500 Bishop Boulevard
Cheyenne, WY 82009
Phone: (307) 772-5145; (866) 992-7641, ext. 5145; Fax: (307) 772-5202
Email: lbartt@state.wy.us
Web: www.wy.ngb.army.mil/benefits

Summary: To provide financial assistance to Wyoming veterans who served in overseas combat anytime except during the Vietnam era and are interested in attending college in the state.

Eligibility: Open to Wyoming veterans who served anytime except during the Vietnam era and were residents of Wyoming for at least 1 year before entering military service. Applicants must have received an honorable discharge and have been awarded the armed forces expeditionary medal or other authorized service or campaign medal indicating service to the United States in an armed conflict in a foreign country. They must enroll at the University of Wyoming or a community college in the state within 10 years following completion of military service.

Financial data: Qualifying veterans are eligible for free resident tuition at the University of Wyoming or at any of the state's community colleges.

Duration: Up to 10 semesters.

Number awarded: Varies each year.

Deadline: Applications may be submitted at any time, but they should be received 2 or 3 weeks before the beginning of the semester.

1118 WYOMING VIETNAM VETERAN SURVIVING CHILD TUITION BENEFIT

Wyoming Veterans Commission
Attn: Executive Director
5500 Bishop Boulevard
Cheyenne, WY 82009
Phone: (307) 772-5145; (866) 992-7641, ext. 5145; Fax: (307) 772-5202
Email: lbartt@state.wy.us
Web: www.wy.ngb.army.mil/benefits

Summary: To provide financial assistance to children of deceased, POW, or MIA Wyoming veterans of the Vietnam era who are interested in attending college in the state.

Eligibility: Open to children of veterans whose parent had been a resident of Wyoming for at least 1 year at the time of entering service, served some time between August 5, 1964 and May 7, 1975, and received the Vietnam service medal. The veteran parent must 1) have died as a result of service-connected causes; 2) be listed officially as being a POW or MIA as a result of active service with the military forces of the United States; or 3) have been honorably discharged from the military and subsequently died of an injury or disease incurred while in service and was a Wyoming resident at the time of death. Applicants must be attending or planning to attend the University of Wyoming or a community college in the state.

Financial data: Qualifying veterans' children are eligible for free resident tuition at the University of Wyoming or at any of the state's community colleges.

Duration: Up to 10 semesters.

Number awarded: Varies each year.

Deadline: Applications may be submitted at any time, but they should be received 2 or 3 weeks before the beginning of the semester.

1119 WYOMING VIETNAM VETERAN SURVIVING SPOUSE TUITION BENEFIT

Wyoming Veterans Commission
Attn: Executive Director
5500 Bishop Boulevard
Cheyenne, WY 82009
Phone: (307) 772-5145; (866) 992-7641, ext. 5145; Fax: (307) 772-5202
Email: lbartt@state.wy.us
Web: www.wy.ngb.army.mil/benefits

Summary: To provide financial assistance to surviving spouses of deceased, POW, or MIA Wyoming veterans of the Vietnam era who are interested in attending college in the state.

Eligibility: Open to spouses of veterans whose spouse had been a resident of Wyoming for at least 1 year at the time of entering service, served some time between August 5, 1964 and May 7, 1975, and received the Vietnam service medal. The veteran spouse must 1) have died as a result of service-connected causes; 2) be listed officially as being a POW or MIA as a result of active service with the military forces of the United States; or 3) have been honorably discharged from the military and subsequently died of an injury or disease incurred while in service and was a Wyoming resident at the time of death. Applicants must be attending or planning to attend the University of Wyoming or a community college in the state.

Financial data: Qualifying veterans' surviving spouses are eligible for free resident tuition at the University of Wyoming or at any of the state's community colleges.

Duration: Up to 10 semesters.

Number awarded: Varies each year.

Deadline: Applications may be submitted at any time, but they should be received 2 or 3 weeks before the beginning of the semester.

1120 WYOMING VIETNAM VETERAN TUITION BENEFIT

Wyoming Veterans Commission
Attn: Executive Director
5500 Bishop Boulevard
Cheyenne, WY 82009

Phone: (307) 772-5145; (866) 992-7641, ext. 5145; Fax: (307) 772-5202
Email: lbartt@state.wy.us
Web: www.wy.ngb.army.mil/benefits

Summary: To provide financial assistance to Wyoming veterans who served during the Vietnam era and are interested in attending college in the state.

Eligibility: Open to Wyoming veterans who 1) served on active duty with the U.S. armed forces between August 5, 1964 and May 7, 1975; 2) received a Vietnam service medal between those dates; 3) received an honorable discharge; 4) have lived in Wyoming for at least 1 year; and 5) have exhausted their veterans' benefits entitlement or for some other reason are no longer eligible for U.S. Department of Veterans Affairs benefits. Applicants must be attending or planning to attend the University of Wyoming or a community college in the state.

Financial data: Qualifying veterans are eligible for free resident tuition at the University of Wyoming or at any of the state's community colleges.

Duration: Up to 10 semesters.

Number awarded: Varies each year.

Deadline: Applications may be submitted at any time, but they should be received 2 or 3 weeks before the beginning of the semester.

1121 YASUKO ASADA MEMORIAL COLLEGE SCHOLARSHIP FUND

David S. Ishii Foundation
Attn: College Scholarship Committee Chair
P.O. Box 2927
Aiea, HI 96701
Phone: (808) 478-6440
Email: info@davidsishiifoundation.org
Web: www.davidsishiifoundation.org/scholarships

Summary: To provide financial assistance to high school seniors in Hawaii who have played on their school golf team and plan to attend college in any state.

Eligibility: Open to seniors graduating from high schools in Hawaii who have been active members of their high school golf team. Applicants must be planning to enroll full-time at an accredited 4-year college or university in any state. They must have a GPA of 2.0 or higher and be able to demonstrate financial need. Along with their application, they must submit a 250-word essay about the influence of golf in their life. Females and males are considered separately.

Financial data: The stipend is $2,500.

Duration: 1 year.

Number awarded: 4 each year: 2 to females and 2 to males.

Deadline: April of each year.

1122 YOSHIYAMA YOUNG ENTREPRENEUR AWARD

Hitachi Foundation
1215 17th Street, N.W.
Washington, DC 20036
Phone: (202) 457-0588; Fax: (202) 296-1098
Email: yoshiprogram@hitachifoundation.org
Web: www.hitachifoundation.org/yoshiyama/index.html

Summary: To recognize and reward high school seniors for outstanding community service.

Eligibility: Open to graduating high school seniors. Anyone other than a family member or relative may nominate the student. Nominees must have provided community service activities that have impacted a socially, economically, or culturally isolated area. Their activities must have 1) created longer-term, sustainable social change; 2) surpassed what is ordinarily expected of a socially responsible citizen; 3) demonstrated self-motivation, leadership, creativity, dedication, and commitment to pursuing service; and 4) made a conscious effort to involve and inspire others to participate in community action. Selection is based on the significance and extent of the candidate's community service and the relevance of those activities to solving serious community and societal problems; GPA, SAT scores, and school club memberships are not considered.

Financial data: The award is $2,500 per year.

Duration: Funds are dispersed over a 2-year period.

Number awarded: 10 each year.

Deadline: March of each year.

1123 YOUNG AMBASSADORS OF THE 21ST CENTURY SCHOLARSHIP PROGRAM

Oregon Lions Sight & Hearing Foundation
Attn: Multiple District 36
1010 N.W. 22nd Avenue, Suite N144
Portland, OR 97210
Phone: (503) 413-7399; (800) 635-4667, ext. 21; Fax: (503) 413-7522
Email: info@orlions.org
Web: www.orlions.org/foundation/index.html

Summary: To recognize and reward, with college scholarships, Oregon high school students who present outstanding speeches on topics related to community service.

Eligibility: Open to high school sophomores, juniors, and seniors between 15 and 19 years of age who live within participating Oregon districts of Lions International or Northwest Lions Auxiliaries. Applicants must be sponsored by a local Lions, Lioness, Leo, or Lions Auxiliary Club. They must prepare a speech, from 4 to 5 minutes in length, on an assigned topic. Students first compete to determine the nominee from their club, and those winners then participate in district contests. District winners then compete for state prizes. Selection is based on ideas and content, organization, language, delivery, and timing. Selection of scholarship winners is based on the speech (24 points), an interview (26 points), leadership accomplishments (20 points), and community service (30 points).

Financial data: At the state level, the winner receives $1,250 and the 3 other finalists each receive $300. At the district level, the winner receives $300, first runner-up $200, and third runner-up $150. All awards are in the form of scholarships to be used at the winner's college of choice.

Duration: The competition is held annually.

Number awarded: At the district level, 12 awards are presented (3 in each of the 4 Oregon Lions districts). The 4 district winners then compete for the state awards.

Deadline: January of each year.

1124 YOUNG HEROES SCHOLARSHIPS

Wipe Out Kids' Cancer
Attn: Young Heroes Scholarships
6350 LBJ Freeway, Suite 162
Dallas, TX 75240
Phone: (214) 987-4662; Fax: (214) 987-4668
Email: mail@wokc.org
Web: www.wokc.org/YoungHeroesScholarships_16.aspx

Summary: To provide financial assistance for college to pediatric cancer survivors.

Eligibility: Open to pediatric cancer survivors who are enrolled or planning to enroll at a college or university. Applicants must submit a 500-word essay on how their personal journey with cancer has prepared them for college. Selection is based on the content, originality, and overall impression of the essay (80%), and school and community recommendations (20%).

Financial data: Stipends are $2,500 or $1,000.

Duration: 1 year.

Number awarded: 10 each year.

Deadline: February of each year.

1125 YOUNG LADIES' RADIO LEAGUE SCHOLARSHIP

Foundation for Amateur Radio, Inc.
Attn: Scholarship Committee
P.O. Box 911
Columbia, MD 21044-0911
Phone: (410) 552-2652; Fax: (410) 981-5146
Email: dave.prestel@gmail.com
Web: www.farweb.org/scholarships

Summary: To provide funding to licensed radio amateurs (especially women) who are interested in earning a bachelor's or graduate degree in the United States.

Eligibility: Open to radio amateurs who have at least an FCC Technician Class license or equivalent foreign authorization. Applicants must intend to work full-time on a bachelor's or graduate degree at a college or university in the United States. There are no restrictions on the course of study or residency location. Non-U.S. amateurs are eligible. Preference is given to female applicants and to those studying communications, electronics, or related arts and sciences. Financial need is considered in the selection process.

Financial data: The stipend is $1,500.

Duration: 1 year.

Number awarded: 2 each year.

Deadline: March of each year.

1126 YOUNG SCHOLARS PROGRAM

Pauline C. Young Scholarship Foundation
115 West Short Street
Lexington, KY 40507
Phone: (859) 294-4284; Fax: (859) 294-4284
Email: Info@KyScholarships.org
Web: www.KyScholarships.org

Summary: To provide financial assistance to Kentucky high school seniors who plan to attend a college or university in the state.

Eligibility: Open to seniors graduating from high schools in Kentucky who are planning to attend a college or university in the state. Applicants must have a GPA of 3.5 or higher and an SAT or ACT score at least in the 70th percentile nationally. Selection is based primarily on financial need.

Financial data: The stipend is equivalent to the cost of attending the University of Kentucky (although recipients are not required to attend that university). Also provided are payment for all necessary books and supplies and an unrestricted grant of $500 per semester.

Duration: 1 year.

Number awarded: Varies each year; recently, 6 of these scholarships were awarded.

Deadline: March of each year.

1127 YOUR POINT OF VIEW STUDENT CONTEST

New Hope Charitable Foundation
1125 Linda Vista Drive, Suite 101
San Marcos, CA 92078-3819
Phone: (760) 591-0719
Web: www.t2ce.org/T2CE-Home/T2CE-Contests.aspx

Summary: To recognize and reward, with college scholarships, students who submit outstanding essays or videos on how they would change high school.

Eligibility: Open to students between 14 and 19 years of age. Applicants must submit an essay or video on how they would like high school to be more valuable to them. Their submission must clearly state the issues as they see them, briefly explain their solutions for fixing the issues, and explain a real life story to illustrate their perspective. Videos or essays may be of any length, but the maximum file size for videos is 100 MB.

Financial data: Prizes range from $300 to $1,000. Funds must be used for tuition, books, supplies, and other educational expenses.

Duration: The competition is held annually.

Number awarded: 3 cash prizes are awarded each year.

Deadline: September of each year.

1128 YOUTH EDUCATION SUMMIT SCHOLARSHIPS

National Rifle Association of America
Attn: Field Operations Division
11250 Waples Mill Road
Fairfax, VA 22030
Phone: (703) 267-1342; (800) 672-3888, ext. 1342; Fax: (703) 267-3743
Email: yes@nrahq.org
Web: www.friendsofnra.org/National.aspx?cid=580

Summary: To provide financial assistance for college to high school students who participate in the Youth Education Summit (Y.E.S.) of the National Rifle Association (NRA).

Eligibility: Open to high school sophomores and juniors who have a GPA of 3.0 or higher. Applicants must submit transcripts, information on their extracurricular and shooting sports activities, essays of 2 to 3 pages on the second amendment and gun control, recommendations, and a personal statement on why they are a good candidate for this program. Based on their applications, approximately 40 students each year are chosen to visit the Washington, D.C. area in June to spend 7 days touring the city and learning about American government and history, the U.S. constitution, the Bill of Rights, and the role and mission of the association. The participants in the program judged as most outstanding, based on their original applications and their work in Washington, are selected to receive these scholarships.

Financial data: A stipend is awarded (amount not specified). Funds are paid directly to the accredited college or technical school of the student's choice.

Duration: These scholarships are presented annually.

Number awarded: Varies each year; a total of $10,000 is available through this program annually.

Deadline: February of each year.

1129 YOUTHLAUNCH SCHOLARSHIP FOR OUTSTANDING SERVICE

YouthLaunch, Inc.
7756 Northcross Drive, Suite 203
Austin, TX 78757
Phone: (512) 342-0424; Fax: (512) 420-0058
Web: www.youthlaunch.org/programs/scholarship.php

Summary: To provide financial assistance to high school seniors and recent graduates in Texas who have an outstanding record of community service and plan to attend college in any state.

Eligibility: Open to residents of Texas who are high school seniors or recent graduates and planning to enter a postsecondary institution in any state. Applicants must have completed at least 50 hours of community service during their final year of high school and at least 400 hours during all years of high school. Selection is based on the impact of the student's area of service and how this service has changed the community, leadership (including service as a role model and encouragement to other young people to participate in service), personal growth, and perseverance (including challenges while serving the community and how those challenges were overcome). Financial need is not considered.

Financial data: The stipend is $3,000. Funds are paid directly to the recipient's college or university.

Duration: 1 year; nonrenewable.

Number awarded: 3 each year.

Deadline: February of each year.

1130 ZONTA CLUB OF BANGOR SCHOLARSHIPS

Zonta Club of Bangor
c/o Barbara A. Cardone
P.O. Box 1904
Bangor, ME 04402-1904
Web: www.zontaclubofbangor.org/?area=scholarship

Summary: To provide financial assistance to women attending or planning to attend college in Maine and major in any field.

Eligibility: Open to women who are attending or planning to attend an accredited 2- or 4-year college in Maine. Applicants may major in any field. Along with their application, they must submit brief essays on 1) their goals in seeking higher education and their plans for the future; and 2) any school and community activities that have been of particular importance to them and why they found them worthwhile. Financial need may be considered in the selection process.

Financial data: The stipend is $1,000.

Duration: 1 year.

Number awarded: 2 each year.

Deadline: March of each year.

1131 ZONTA CLUBS OF LOUISIANA WOMAN'S SCHOLARSHIP

Zonta Clubs of Louisiana
c/o Lisa LaBlanc
175 Antigua Drive
Lafayette, LA 70503
Phone: (337) 984-4197
Email: lebl3904@bellsouth.net
Web: www.zontalafayette.org/scholarships.htm

Summary: To provide financial assistance for college to female residents of Louisiana.

Eligibility: Open to female residents of Louisiana who are the major wage earner of their family. Applicants must have been accepted at a Louisiana university, college, or vocational/technical school in non-remedial courses and have satisfactory scores on the SAT, ACT, or entrance exam. U.S. citizenship and evidence of financial need are required.

Financial data: The stipend is $1,500.

Duration: 1 semester; may be renewed if the recipient enrolls in at least 6 hours per semester and maintains a GPA of 2.5 or higher.

Number awarded: 1 or more each year.

Deadline: June of each year.

1132 100 BLACK MEN OF AMERICA NATIONAL SCHOLARSHIP PROGRAM

100 Black Men of America, Inc.
Attn: Scholarship Administrator
141 Auburn Avenue

Atlanta, GA 30303
Phone: (404) 688-5100; (800) 598-3411; Fax: (404) 688-1028
Email: info@100bmoa.org
Web: www.100blackmen.org

Summary: To provide financial assistance for college to high school seniors and current undergraduates, particularly African American males, who submit essays on topics related to African Americans.

Eligibility: Open to high school seniors and undergraduates who are attending or planning to attend an accredited postsecondary institution as a full-time student. Applicants must have a GPA of 2.5 or higher and have completed at least 50 hours of active community service within the past 12 months. Along with their application, they must submit a 600-word essay on their choice of a topic that changes annually; recently, students were invited to write on 1 of the following: 1) Black male suicide; 2) the war in Iraq; 3) bailout for whom; 4) role of the Black church; or 5) the first African American president. Financial need is not considered in the selection process.

Financial data: Stipends range from $1,000 to $3,000 and are paid directly to the institution.

Duration: 1 year.

Number awarded: Varies each year.

Deadline: February of each year.

1133 100 MILE WAIVER FOR RESIDENTS OF ARKANSAS, LOUISIANA, NEW MEXICO OR OKLAHOMA ENROLLED IN TEXAS PUBLIC UNIVERSITIES

Texas Higher Education Coordinating Board
Attn: Grants and Special Programs
1200 East Anderson Lane
P.O. Box 12788, Capitol Station
Austin, TX 78711-2788
Phone: (512) 427-6323; (800) 242-3062, ext. 6323; Fax: (512) 427-6127
Email: grantinfo@thecb.state.tx.us
Web: www.collegeforalltexans.com/apps/financialaid/tofa2.cfm?ID=451

Summary: To enable residents of adjoining states to attend designated Texas public institutions at reduced rates.

Eligibility: Open to residents of Arkansas, Louisiana, New Mexico, and Oklahoma who are attending designated public institutions in Texas.

Financial data: Eligible students are able to attend Texas public institutions and pay a reduced tuition rate.

Duration: 1 year; may be renewed.

Number awarded: Varies each year; recently, 770 of these waivers were awarded.

Deadline: Deadline not specified.

Humanities

1134 AAF MINORITY/DISADVANTAGED SCHOLARSHIP PROGRAM

American Institute of Architects
Attn: American Architectural Foundation
1799 New York Avenue, N.W.
Washington, DC 20006-5292
Phone: (202) 626-7511; Fax: (202) 626-7420
Email: info@archfoundation.org
Web: www.archfoundation.org/aaf/aaf/Programs.Fellowships.htm

Summary: To provide financial assistance to high school and college students from minority and/or disadvantaged backgrounds who are interested in studying architecture in college.

Eligibility: Open to students from minority and/or disadvantaged backgrounds who are high school seniors, students in a community college or technical school transferring to an accredited architectural program, or college freshmen entering a professional degree program at an accredited program of architecture. Students who have completed 1 or more years of a 4-year college curriculum are not eligible. Initially, candidates must be nominated by 1 of the following organizations or persons: an individual architect or firm, a chapter of the American Institute of Architects (AIA), a community design center, a guidance counselor or teacher, the dean or professor at an accredited school of architecture, or the director of a community or civic organization. Nominees are reviewed and eligible candidates are invited to complete an application form in which they write an essay describing the reasons they are interested in becoming an architect and provide documentation of academic excellence and financial need. Selection is based primarily on financial need.

Financial data: Stipends range from $500 to $2,500 per year, depending upon individual need. Students must apply for supplementary funds from other sources.

Duration: 9 months; may be renewed for up to 2 additional years.

Number awarded: Up to 20 each year.

Deadline: Nominations are due by December of each year; final applications must be submitted in January.

1135 ABRUZZO AND MOLISE HERITAGE SOCIETY SCHOLARSHIP AWARDS

Abruzzo and Molise Heritage Society
Attn: Grant and Scholarship Fund, Inc.
c/o Romeo Sabatini, Scholarship Committee Chair
4218 Wicomico Avenue
Beltsville, MD 20705-2654
Phone: (301) 931-3340
Web: www.abruzzomoliseheritagesociety.org/scholarship.htm

Summary: To provide financial assistance to undergraduate students from the Washington, D.C. area who are interested in studying Italian culture and language.

Eligibility: Open to students who are enrolled or accepted for enrollment at a 4-year college or university to work on an undergraduate degree in Italian culture and language. Applicants must reside within 50 miles of Washington, D.C. or attend college in that region. Along with their application, they must submit a 400-word essay describing the reasons they believe they should be awarded this scholarship; their essay should reflect their interest in Italian culture and/or heritage. Financial need is not considered in the selection process.

Financial data: The stipend is $2,500.

Duration: 1 year.

Number awarded: 2 each year.

Deadline: March of each year.

1136 ACADEMY OF TELEVISION ARTS & SCIENCES COLLEGE TELEVISION AWARDS

Academy of Television Arts & Sciences Foundation
Attn: Education Department
5220 Lankershim Boulevard
North Hollywood, CA 91601-3109
Phone: (818) 754-2820; Fax: (818) 761-ATAS
Email: cta@emmys.org
Web: www.emmysfoundation.org/college-television-awards

Summary: To recognize and reward outstanding college student videos.

Eligibility: Open to undergraduate and graduate students currently enrolled at a college, university, or community college. U.S. citizenship is not required, but all applicants must be enrolled at schools in the United States. All entries must have been produced for school-related classes, groups, or projects. Competitions are held in the following categories: 1) animation (all forms); 2) children's; 3) comedy; 4) commercial; 5) documentary; 6) drama; 7) interactive media; 8) magazine; 9) music (best composition); 10) music (best use of music); 11) narrative series (comedy, drama, or webisodes); and 12) newscast. Entries in the comedy, documentary, drama, and narrative series category may not exceed 1 hour. Entries in the animation, music, children's, newscast, and magazine categories may not exceed 30 minutes. Commercial entries may not exceed 1 minute and must advertise a product or service. For the narrative series category, at least 6 episodes must have been produced and 2 episodes must be submitted. For the interactive media category, the video recording may not exceed 6 minutes in length. The children's category must be targeted for preschool through 15 years of age.

Financial data: In each category, first place is $2,000, second $1,000, and third $500. In addition, first-place winners in certain categories receive film stock from Kodak Entertainment Imaging. The Loreen Arbus Focus on Disability Scholarship of $10,000 is awarded to 1) a writer, producer, or director who has a disability; 2) a producer whose work focuses on people with disabilities; or 3) a piece that features a person with a disability as a main character. The Directing Award is $1,000 and the Seymour Bricker Family Humanitarian Award of $4,000 is presented to the first-place winner from any category whose work best represents a humanitarian concern.

Duration: The competition is held annually.

Number awarded: 39 each year: 1 first-place winner, 1 second-place winner, and 1 third-place winner in each category plus the 3 special awards.

Deadline: January of each year.

1137 ACL/NJCL NATIONAL GREEK EXAMINATION SCHOLARSHIP

American Classical League
Attn: National Greek Examination
Miami University
422 Wells Mill Drive
Oxford, OH 45056
Phone: (513) 529-7741; Fax: (513) 529-7742
Email: info@aclclassics.org
Web: nge.aclclassics.org

Summary: To recognize and reward students who achieve high scores on the National Greek Examination.

Eligibility: Open to students who take the National Green Examination. High school teachers and college instructors may order copies of the National Greek Examination for their students who are enrolled in first-year (elementary), second-year (intermediate), or third-year (advanced) Attic or Homeric Greek. The examinations consist of 40 multiple choice questions at 5 levels: beginning Attic (high school seniors only), intermediate Attic (first-year college and advanced high school students), Attic prose, Attic tragedy, and Homeric (*Odyssey*). The top scorers on each examination receive purple ribbons, followed by blue, red, and green ribbons. High school seniors who earn purple or blue ribbons are eligible to apply for this scholarship.

Financial data: The award is $1,000.

Duration: 1 year.

Number awarded: 1 each year.

Deadline: The examinations must be ordered by January of each year.

1138 ADCRAFT FOUNDATION SCHOLARSHIPS

Adcraft Club of Detroit
Attn: Foundation
3011 West Grand Boulevard, Suite 561
Detroit, MI 48202-3000
Phone: (313) 872-7850; Fax: (313) 872-7858
Email: adcraft@adcraft.org
Web: www.adcraft.org

Summary: To provide financial assistance to undergraduate and graduate students from any state majoring in advertising or marketing at colleges and universities in Michigan.

Eligibility: Open to undergraduate and graduate students from any state currently enrolled at colleges and universities in Michigan. Applicants must be working on a degree in advertising or marketing. Selection is based on academic achievement and potential.

Financial data: Stipends range from $1,000 to $5,500.

Duration: 1 year.

Number awarded: Varies each year; a total of $25,000 is available for this program annually.

Deadline: February of each year.

1139 ADVANCEMENT OF CONSTRUCTION TECHNOLOGY SCHOLARSHIP

Construction Specifications Institute–Maine Chapter
c/o Dick Eustis, Scholarship Committee Chair
35 Pride Street
Old Town, ME 04468-1925
Phone: (207) 827-2238
Web: www.mecsi.org/Scholarship-Honors/schsp-hnr.htm

Summary: To provide financial assistance to Maine residents preparing for a career in a field related to construction technology at a public college or university in the state.

Eligibility: Open to residents of Maine who have completed at least 1 year of study at a campus of the University of Maine system or at Central Maine Community College. Applicants must be preparing for a career in architectural or engineering technology, building construction, or mechanical drafting. They must be able to demonstrate active involvement in a career or industry organization or association.

Financial data: Stipends vary; recently, they were $2,000 for students in the University of Maine system and $600 for students at Central Maine Community College.

Duration: 1 year.

Number awarded: Varies each year; recently, 2 of these scholarships were awarded: 1 to a student in the University of Maine system and 1 to a student at Central Maine Community College.

Deadline: Each institution sets its own deadline.

1140 AFCEA UNDERGRADUATE INTELLIGENCE SCHOLARSHIPS

Armed Forces Communications and Electronics Association
Attn: AFCEA Educational Foundation
4400 Fair Lakes Court
Fairfax, VA 22033-3899
Phone: (703) 631-6149; (800) 336-4583, ext. 6149; Fax: (703) 631-4693
Email: scholarship@afcea.org
Web: www.afcea.org

Summary: To provide financial assistance to undergraduate students working on a degree in a field related to intelligence or homeland security.

Eligibility: Open to U.S. citizens entering their junior or senior year at an accredited 4-year college or university. Applicants must be working full-time on a degree in a field directly related to the support of U.S. intelligence or homeland security enterprises, such as global security, intelligence studies, and/or foreign languages. They must have a GPA of 3.0 or higher. Selection is based primarily on demonstrated academic excellence, leadership, and financial need.

Financial data: The stipend is $2,250.

Duration: 1 year.

Number awarded: 2 each year.

Deadline: November of each year.

1141 AFRO-ACADEMIC, CULTURAL, TECHNOLOGICAL AND SCIENTIFIC OLYMPICS (ACT-SO)

National Association for the Advancement of Colored People
Attn: ACT-SO Director
4805 Mt. Hope Drive
Baltimore, MD 21215
Phone: (410) 580-5650; (877) NAACP-98
Email: ACTSO@naacpnet.org
Web: www.naacp.org/programs/entry/act-so

Summary: To recognize and reward (with college scholarships) outstanding African American high school students who distinguish themselves in the Afro-Academic, Cultural, Technological and Scientific Olympics (ACT-SO) program.

Eligibility: Open to high school students (grades 9–12) of African descent who are U.S. citizens and amateurs in the category in which they wish to participate. Competitions are held in 26 categories in 5 general areas: humanities (music composition, original essay, playwriting, and poetry), sciences (biology and microbiology, biochemistry, computer science, earth and space science, engineering, mathematics, medicine and health, and physics), performing arts (dance, dramatics, music instrumental/classical, music instrumental/contemporary, music vocal/classical, music vocal/contemporary, and oratory), visual arts (architecture, drawing, filmmaking, painting, photography, and sculpture), and business (entrepreneurship). Competition is first conducted by local chapters of the NAACP; winners in each event at the local level then compete at the national level.

Financial data: In each category, the first-prize winner receives a gold medal and a $1,000 scholarship, the second-prize winner receives a silver medal and a $750 scholarship, and the third-prize winner receives a bronze medal and a $500 scholarship.

Duration: The competition is held annually.

Number awarded: 78 each year: 3 in each of 26 categories.

Deadline: Local competitions usually take place between February and April. The national finals are held each year in July.

1142 AGO/QUIMBY REGIONAL COMPETITIONS FOR YOUNG ORGANISTS

American Guild of Organists
475 Riverside Drive, Suite 1260
New York, NY 10115
Phone: (212) 870-2310; Fax: (212) 870-2163
Email: info@agohq.org
Web: www.agohq.org/competitions/index.html

Summary: To recognize and reward outstanding student organists.

Eligibility: Open to student organists 23 years of age or younger. Competitions are held in each of the 9 regions of the American Guild of Organists (AGO); contestants may enter the region either where they reside or where they attend school. Applicants must play an assigned repertoire with a total performance time up to 40 minutes. Students first compete in their local chapter; winners advance to the regional competitions.

Financial data: Each region awards a cash prize of $1,000 to the first-place winner and $500 to the second-place winner.

Duration: The competition is held biennially, in odd-numbered years.

Number awarded: 18 each year: a first and second prize in each AGO region.

Deadline: Competitors must register with their chapter by mid-January of each odd-numbered year.

1143 AIA/RHODE ISLAND ARCHITECTURAL FORUM SCHOLARSHIP AWARDS PROGRAM

AIA/Rhode Island
Attn: Architectural Forum
P.O. Box 6226
Providence, RI 02940
Phone: (401) 272-6418; Fax: (401) 228-6748
Email: info@aia-ri.org
Web: www.aia-ri.org/?section=aiari@page=4

Summary: To provide financial assistance to Rhode Island architecture students.

Eligibility: Open to students enrolled at a college or university in Rhode Island or residents of the state enrolled at an institution in any state. Applicants must be studying architecture, landscape architecture, interior architecture, or historical preservation. They must submit a 2-page application. The first page provides a biographical narrative describing their current academic status and a statement of how the award, if granted, would further their academic ambitions. The second page includes any illustrative material that is representative of their design experience and interests. Financial need is not considered in the selection process.

Financial data: The maximum stipend is $3,000. Funds are paid to the recipient's school for the payment of tuition costs, travel study expenses, research costs, or other costs incurred in other college-organized activities.

Duration: 1 year.

Number awarded: Several each year.

Deadline: April of each year.

1144 AIAC SCHOLARSHIP PROGRAM

American Indian Arts Council, Inc.
Attn: Scholarship Committee
725 Preston Forest Shopping Center, Suite B
Dallas, TX 75230
Phone: (214) 891-9640; Fax: (214) 891-0221
Email: aiac@flash.net

Summary: To provide financial assistance to American Indian undergraduates or graduate students planning a career in the arts or arts administration.

Eligibility: Open to American Indian undergraduate and graduate students who are preparing for a career in fine arts, visual and performing arts, communication arts, creative writing, or arts administration or management. Applicants must be currently enrolled in and attending a fully-accredited college or university. They must provide official tribal documentation verifying American Indian heritage and have a GPA of 2.5 or higher. Applicants majoring

in the visual or performing arts (including writing) must submit slides, photographs, videotapes, audio tapes, or other examples of their work. Letters of recommendation are required. Awards are based on either merit or merit and financial need. If the applicants wish to be considered for a need-based award, a letter from their financial aid office is required to verify financial need.
Financial data: Stipends range from $250 to $1,000 per semester.
Duration: 1 semester; may be renewed if the recipient maintains a GPA of 2.5 or higher.
Number awarded: Varies each year.
Deadline: September of each year for the fall semester; February of each year for the spring semester.

1145 AIR FORCE ROTC FOREIGN LANGUAGE MAJORS SCHOLARSHIPS

U.S. Air Force
Attn: Headquarters AFROTC/RRUC
551 East Maxwell Boulevard
Maxwell AFB, AL 36112-5917
Phone: (334) 953-2091; (866) 4-AFROTC; Fax: (334) 953-6167
Email: afrotc1@maxwell.af.mil
Web: afrotc.com/scholarships/in-college/foreign-language-majors
Summary: To provide financial assistance to students who are interested in joining Air Force ROTC and majoring in specified foreign languages of importance to the Air Force.
Eligibility: Open to U.S. citizens who are entering their junior or senior year of college and are working on a degree in foreign languages that may change annually but are of interest to the Air Force; currently, those are Arabic, Azeri, Bengali, Cambodian, Chinese, Hausa, Hindi, Indonesian, Japanese, Kazakh, Kurdish, Malay, Pashto, Persian-Iranian, Persian-Afghan, Russian, Serbo-Croatian, Swahili, Thai, Turkish, Uighar, Urdu/Punjabi, Uzbek, or Vietnamese. Applicants must have a GPA of 2.5 or higher and meet all other academic and physical requirements for participation in AFROTC. At the time of their Air Force commissioning, they may be no more than 31 years of age. They must be able to pass the Air Force Officer Qualifying Test (AFOQT) and the Air Force ROTC Physical Fitness Test.
Financial data: Awards are type 1 AFROTC scholarships that provide for full payment of tuition and fees plus an annual book allowance of $900. All recipients are also awarded a tax-free monthly subsistence allowance that is $450 for juniors and $500 for seniors.
Duration: 1 or 2 years, until completion of a bachelor's degree.
Deadline: Deadline not specified.

1146 AL MUAMMAR SCHOLARSHIPS FOR JOURNALISM

Arab American Institute Foundation
Attn: Scholarship Administrator
1600 K Street, N.W., Suite 601
Washington, DC 20006
Phone: (202) 429-9210; Fax: (202) 429-9214
Email: aaif@aaiusa.org
Web: www.aaiusa.org/foundation/33/scholarships
Summary: To provide financial assistance to Arab American students interested in working on an undergraduate or graduate degree in journalism.
Eligibility: Open to U.S. citizens and permanent residents of Arab descent who are enrolled full-time at an accredited college or university in the United States. Applicants must be undergraduates or college seniors admitted to a graduate program. They must have a GPA of 3.3 or higher and a demonstrated commitment to the field of print or broadcast journalism. Selection is based on sensitivity to Arab American issues, demonstrated community involvement, initiative in social advocacy and civic empowerment, journalistic ability, academic ability, commitment to the field of journalism, and financial need.
Financial data: The stipend is $5,000.
Duration: 1 year.
Number awarded: Up to 4 each year.
Deadline: February of each year.

1147 AL NEUHARTH FREE SPIRIT SCHOLARSHIP AND CONFERENCE PROGRAM

Freedom Forum
Attn: Manager, Free Spirit Program
555 Pennsylvania Avenue, N.W.
Washington, DC 20001
Phone: (202) 292-6261; Fax: (202) 292-6265
Email: freespirit@freedomforum.org
Web: www.freedomforum.org/freespirit
Summary: To provide financial assistance for college to high school journalists who demonstrate a "free spirit."
Eligibility: Open to high school seniors who are active in high school journalism. Applicants must be planning to attend college to prepare for a career in journalism. They must demonstrate qualities of a "free spirit" in their academic or personal life. A "free spirit" is defined as "a risk-taker, a visionary, an innovative leader, an entrepreneur, or a courageous achiever who accomplishes great things beyond his or her normal circumstances." Along with their application, they must submit 2 essays of 500 words each: 1) explaining why they want to prepare for a career in journalism; and 2) describing their specific qualities as a free spirit and their experiences and/or struggles that make them a free spirit. Men and women are judged separately. U.S. citizenship or permanent resident status is required. Financial need is not considered in the selection process.
Financial data: The stipend is $10,000 or $1,000.
Duration: 1 year.
Number awarded: 102 each year: a male and a female from each state and the District of Columbia. The recipients include 100 who receive $1,000 scholarships and 2 (a male and a female) who receive $10,000 scholarships.
Deadline: October of each year.

1148 AL SHACKLEFORD AND DAN MARTIN UNDERGRADUATE SCHOLARSHIP

Baptist Communicators Association
Attn: Scholarship Committee
1519 Menlo Drive
Kennesaw, GA 30152
Phone: (770) 425-3728
Email: office@baptistcommunicators.org
Web: www.baptistcommunicators.org/about/scholarship.cfm
Summary: To provide financial assistance to undergraduate students who are working on a college degree to prepare for a career in Baptist communications.
Eligibility: Open to undergraduate students who are majoring in communications, English, journalism, or public relations and have a GPA of 2.5 or higher. Their vocational objective must be in Baptist communications. Along with their application, they must submit a statement explaining why they desire to receive this scholarship.
Financial data: The stipend is $1,000.
Duration: 1 year; recipients may reapply.
Number awarded: 1 each year.
Deadline: December of each year.

1149 AL SPRAGUE MEMORIAL SCHOLARSHIP

Massachusetts Broadcasters Association
43 Riverside Avenue
PMB 401
Medford, MA 02155
Phone: (800) 471-1875; Fax: (800) 471-1876
Email: info@massbroadcasters.org
Web: www.massbroadcasters.org/students/index.cfm
Summary: To provide financial assistance to Massachusetts residents interested in attending college in any state to prepare for a career in broadcasting.
Eligibility: Open to residents of Massachusetts who are in the process of enrolling or are currently enrolled full-time at an accredited institution of higher learning in any state. Applicants must be preparing for a career in broadcasting. Along with their application, they must submit 150-word essays on 1) why they have chosen to prepare for a career in a broadcast-related field; and 2) why they believe they are a good candidate for this scholarship. The award is presented to the applicant who shows the most promise in industry advocacy, leadership, and entrepreneurship.
Financial data: The stipend is $2,500. Checks are made payable to the recipient and the recipient's school.
Duration: 1 year.
Number awarded: 1 each year.
Deadline: March of each year.

1150 ALABAMA JUNIOR AND COMMUNITY COLLEGE PERFORMING ARTS SCHOLARSHIPS

Alabama Commission on Higher Education
Attn: Grants Coordinator
100 North Union Street

P.O. Box 302000
Montgomery, AL 36130-2000
Phone: (334) 242-2273
Email: cheryl.newton@ache.alabama.gov
Web: www.ache.alabama.gov/StudentAsst/Programs.htm
Summary: To provide financial assistance to performing artists in Alabama interested in attending a junior or community college in the state.
Eligibility: Open to full-time students enrolled in public junior and community colleges in Alabama. Selection is based on artistic talent as determined through competitive auditions.
Financial data: Awards cover up to the cost of in-state tuition.
Number awarded: Varies each year.
Deadline: Deadline not specified.

1151 ALABAMA MEDIA PROFESSIONALS STUDENT SCHOLARSHIP

Alabama Media Professionals
c/o Lori Culpepper
112 Tocoa Circle
Helena, AL 35080-7129
Email: lori@alabamawriters.com
Web: alabamamediaprofessionals.com
Summary: To provide financial assistance to Alabama students interested in preparing for a career in journalism or a related field.
Eligibility: Open to seniors graduating from high schools in Alabama, students enrolled in a college or university in Alabama, and residents of Alabama attending college in other states. Applicants must be preparing for a career in journalism, communications, broadcasting, or other media fields. Along with their application, they must submit samples of their work, 2 letters of recommendation, and a brief statement telling why they are studying communications and describing their career plans.
Financial data: The stipend is $1,000.
Duration: 1 year.
Number awarded: 1 each year.
Deadline: March of each year.

1152 ALABAMA THESPIAN HIGH SCHOOL SENIOR SCHOLARSHIPS

Alabama Thespians
c/o Jamie Stephenson, Scholarship Director
Pelham High School
2500 Panther Circle
Pelham, AL 35124
Phone: (205) 682-5505
Email: jstephenson@shelbyed.k12.al.us
Web: www.alabamathespians.com/scholarships.html
Summary: To provide financial assistance to high school seniors in Alabama who have been active in theater and plan to major in theater education or a theater-related field at a college in any state.
Eligibility: Open to seniors graduating from high schools in Alabama who are thespians in good standing. Applicants must have a GPA of 2.5 or higher. They must be planning to attend a college or university in any state to major in a theater-related field, including theater education. At the Alabama State Thespian Festival, students must present a 3-minute audition. For students in performance and theater education, the audition consists of a song and/or monologue of their choice; theater education applicants are also required to show a portfolio supporting their theater experiences. Technical theater applicants must present a sampling of renderings and designs. In addition to the audition at the festival, applicants must submit a list of all thespian activities in grades 9 through 12; a resume that includes education, theatrical experiences, honors, and activities; and letters of recommendation. Selection is based on the audition (45%), thespian activities and resume (25%), an interview (15%), and recommendations (15%).
Financial data: The stipend is $1,500. Funds are sent directly to the recipient's college or university.
Duration: 1 year.
Number awarded: 4 each year.
Deadline: January of each year.

1153 ALAN COMPTON AND BOB STANLEY MINORITY AND INTERNATIONAL SCHOLARSHIP

Baptist Communicators Association
Attn: Scholarship Committee
1715-K South Rutherford Boulevard, Suite 295
Murfreesboro, TN 37130
Phone: (615) 904-0152
Email: bca.office@comcast.net
Web: www.baptistcommunicators.org/about/scholarship.cfm
Summary: To provide financial assistance to minority and international students who are working on an undergraduate degree to prepare for a career in Baptist communications.
Eligibility: Open to undergraduate students of minority or international origin. Applicants must be majoring in communications, English, journalism, or public relations with a GPA of 2.5 or higher. Their vocational objective must be in Baptist communications. Along with their application, they must submit a statement explaining why they want to receive this scholarship.
Financial data: The stipend is $1,000.
Duration: 1 year; recipients may reapply.
Number awarded: 1 each year.
Deadline: December of each year.

1154 ALASKA PROFESSIONAL COMMUNICATORS MEMORIAL SCHOLARSHIP

Alaska Professional Communicators
c/o Connie Huff, Scholarship Manager
644 East 79th Avenue
Anchorage, AK 99518
Phone: (907) 550-8464
Email: connie@kska.org
Web: www.akpresswomen.com/scholarships.php
Summary: To provide financial assistance to residents of Alaska enrolled as undergraduate students and majoring in journalism or public communications fields.
Eligibility: Open to residents of Alaska enrolled at 4-year colleges and universities as undergraduates. Applicants must be majoring in a phase of public communications, including advertising, public relations, print, radio-television, or video. Students with other majors may be eligible if they have a definite commitment to enter the media profession. Along with their application, they must submit a resume, a transcript covering all college work in Alaska or elsewhere, a statement of their career goals and why they desire the scholarship, at least 3 letters of recommendation, and up to 3 samples of their work. Selection is based on promise in the journalism or public communications fields and the likelihood that the applicant will enter those fields, financial need, and academic progress.
Financial data: The stipend is $1,000.
Duration: 1 year.
Number awarded: 2 each year.
Deadline: March of each year.

1155 ALFRED T. GRANGER STUDENT ART FUND

Vermont Student Assistance Corporation
Attn: Scholarship Programs
10 East Allen Street
P.O. Box 2000
Winooski, VT 05404-2601
Phone: (802) 654-3798; (888) 253-4819; Fax: (802) 654-3765; TDD: (800) 281-3341 (within VT)
Email: info@vsac.org
Web: services.vsac.org/wps/wcm/connect/vsac/VSAC
Summary: To provide financial assistance to residents of Vermont who are interested in working on an undergraduate or graduate degree in a field related to design at a school in any state.
Eligibility: Open to residents of Vermont who are graduating high school seniors, high school graduates, GED recipients, or current undergraduate or graduate students. Applicants must be interested in attending an accredited postsecondary institution in any state to work on a degree in architecture, interior design, fine arts, architectural engineering, mechanical drawing, or lighting design. Selection is based on academic achievement, a portfolio, letters of recommendation, and financial need.
Financial data: The stipend is $5,000 per year for graduate students or $2,500 per year for undergraduates.
Duration: 1 year; recipients may reapply.

Number awarded: 2 graduate scholarships and 4 undergraduate scholarships are awarded each year.
Deadline: March of each year.

1156 ALYCE SHEETZ OREGON HIGH SCHOOL JOURNALIST OF THE YEAR SCHOLARSHIP

Oregon Journalism Education Association
c/o Erin Simonsen, President
Lakeridge High School
1235 Overlook Drive
Lake Oswego, OR 97034-6998
Phone: (503) 534-2319
Email: simonsee@loswego.k12.or.us
Web: www.oregonjea.org/awards.html

Summary: To recognize and reward, with college scholarships, outstanding high school journalists in Oregon.
Eligibility: Open to seniors graduating from high schools in Oregon who have been involved in journalism for at least 2 years. Applicants must be planning to study journalism and/or mass communications at a college or university in any state and prepare for a career in that field. Along with their application, they must submit examples of their work that show the following 4 characteristics: 1) skilled and creative use of media content; 2) inquiring mind and investigative persistence resulting in an in-depth study of issues important to the local high school audience, high school students in general, or society; 3) courageous and responsible handling of controversial issues despite threat or imposition of censorship; and 4) variety of journalistic experiences, each handled in a quality manner, on a newspaper, yearbook, broadcast, or other medium.
Financial data: The winner receives a $1,000 scholarship and the runners-up receive $500 scholarships.
Duration: The competition is held annually.
Number awarded: 1 winner and 2 runners-up are selected each year.
Deadline: February of each year.

1157 AMEEN RIHANI SCHOLARSHIP

Ameen Rihani Organization
Attn: Scholarship Program
7979 Old Georgetown Road, Suite 700
Bethesda, MD 20814
Email: arorg@ameenrihani.org
Web: www.ameenrihani.org/index.php?page=scholarship

Summary: To provide financial assistance to Lebanese American and other Arab American high school seniors who plan to study any subject in college.
Eligibility: Open to Lebanese Americans and other Arab Americans who are high school seniors planning to enroll full-time in college, are U.S. citizens or permanent residents, have at least a 3.25 GPA, and have demonstrated leadership abilities through participation in community service, extracurricular activities, and other activities. They must be nominated by their teachers, counselors, or principals. Nominees may be interested in studying any subject, but preference is given to students who are interested in majoring in literature, philosophy, or political science. They must submit an essay of 250 to 300 words on their personal goals and aspirations for the next 10 to 15 years. Financial need is not considered in the selection process.
Financial data: This stipend is $1,500.
Duration: This is a 1-time award.
Number awarded: 1 each year.
Deadline: March of each year.

1158 AMERICAN ACADEMY OF CHEFS COLLEGE SCHOLARSHIPS

American Culinary Federation, Inc.
Attn: American Academy of Chefs
180 Center Place Way
St. Augustine, FL 32095
Phone: (904) 824-4468; (800) 624-9458, ext. 102; Fax: (904) 825-4758
Email: academy@acfchefs.net
Web: www.acfchefs.org

Summary: To provide financial assistance to students enrolled in a culinary program.
Eligibility: Open to students who are currently enrolled at an accredited college with a major in culinary or pastry arts. Applicants must have completed at least 1 grading or marking period. They must have a GPA of 2.5 or higher and be able to demonstrate financial need. Along with their application, they must submit 5 brief essays on: 1) their leadership ability and team building skills; 2) an example of when they have utilized their leadership skills in a culinary work environment; 3) where they see their professional career 5 years after graduation; 4) the importance and benefits of becoming a member of a professional organization; and 5) how important community service is to them. Selection is based on the essays (25 points), academic GPA (30 points), participation in culinary competitions (20 points), volunteer for school and industry activities (10 points), American Culinary Foundation involvement (10 points), and 2 letters of recommendation (5 points).
Financial data: The stipend is $1,000.
Duration: 1 year.
Number awarded: Varies each year; recently, 39 of these scholarships were awarded.
Deadline: April or August of each year.

1159 AMERICAN ACADEMY OF CHEFS HIGH SCHOOL STUDENT SCHOLARSHIPS

American Culinary Federation, Inc.
Attn: American Academy of Chefs
180 Center Place Way
St. Augustine, FL 32095
Phone: (904) 824-4468; (800) 624-9458, ext. 102; Fax: (904) 825-4758
Email: academy@acfchefs.net
Web: www.acfchefs.org

Summary: To provide financial assistance to high school seniors planning to attend college to prepare for a career as a chef or pastry chef.
Eligibility: Open to graduating high school seniors who plan to attend an accredited college and major in culinary or pastry arts. Applicants must have a GPA of 2.5 or higher and be able to demonstrate financial need. Along with their application, they must submit 5 brief essays on: 1) their leadership ability and teamwork building skills; 2) an example of when they have utilized their leadership skills in a culinary work environment; 3) where they see their professional career 5 years after graduation; 4) the importance and benefits of becoming a member of a professional organization; and 5) how important community service is to them. Selection is based on the essays (25 points), academic GPA (30 points), participation in culinary competitions (20 points), volunteer for school and industry activities (10 points), American Culinary Foundation involvement (10 points), and 2 letters of recommendation (5 points).
Financial data: A stipend is awarded (amount not specified).
Duration: 1 year.
Number awarded: Varies each year; recently, 4 of these scholarships were awarded.
Deadline: March of each year.

1160 AMERICAN ADVERTISING FEDERATION CLEVELAND EDUCATION FOUNDATION SCHOLARSHIPS

American Advertising Federation–Cleveland
Attn: Education Foundation
4700 Rockside Road, Suite 325
Independence, OH 44131
Phone: (216) 901-4000; Fax: (216) 901-4003
Email: adassoc@aafcleveland.com
Web: www.aafcleveland.com/education-foundation.html

Summary: To provide financial assistance to undergraduate students who are residents of Ohio majoring in a field related to advertising at a college or university in the state.
Eligibility: Open to residents of Ohio who are full-time seniors, juniors, or second-semester sophomores at colleges and universities in the state. Applicants must be majoring in a field related to communications or marketing (e.g., advertising, copywriting, graphic design, marketing, public relations, web design) and have a GPA of 3.0 or higher. They must submit transcripts, 2 letters of recommendation, and an essay describing their career goals. Some awards are based on merit and some on financial need.
Financial data: Stipends range from $500 to $2,500.
Duration: 1 year.
Number awarded: Varies each year; recently, 10 of these scholarships, with a value of $12,000, were awarded.
Deadline: October of each year.

1161 AMERICAN ADVERTISING FEDERATION FOURTH DISTRICT CLUB PRESIDENT'S SCHOLARSHIP

American Advertising Federation–District 4
c/o Tami L. Grimes, Education Chair
4712 Southwood Lane
Lakeland, FL 33813
Phone: (863) 648-5392
Email: tamilgrimes@yahoo.com
Web: www.4aaf.com/scholarships.cfm

Summary: To provide financial assistance to undergraduate and graduate students at colleges and universities in Florida who are residents of any state, interested in entering the field of advertising, and able to demonstrate outstanding service to the community.

Eligibility: Open to undergraduate and graduate students from any state currently enrolled at accredited colleges and universities in Florida. Applicants must be working on a bachelor's or master's degree in advertising, marketing, communications, public relations, art, graphic arts, or a related field. They must have a GPA of 3.0 or higher overall and 3.5 or higher in their major field. Along with their application, they must submit a 250-word essay on 1 of the following topics: 1) is advertising a profession, and why or why not; 2) if everyone should lead, then why learn to follow; or 3) if you were asked to serve your profession, what single thing would you do. Selection is based on academic excellence, leadership, and service to the community.

Financial data: The stipend is $1,000.

Duration: 1 year.

Number awarded: 1 each year.

Deadline: May of each year.

1162 ANA MULTICULTURAL EXCELLENCE SCHOLARSHIP

American Association of Advertising Agencies
Attn: AAAA Foundation
405 Lexington Avenue, 18th Floor
New York, NY 10174-1801
Phone: (212) 682-2500; (800) 676-9333; Fax: (212) 682-2028
Email: ameadows@aaaa.org
Web: www2.aaaa.org/careers/scholarships/Pages/scholar_ana.aspx

Summary: To provide financial assistance to multicultural students who are working on an undergraduate degree in advertising.

Eligibility: Open to undergraduate students who are U.S. citizens of proven multicultural heritage and have at least 1 grandparent of multicultural heritage. Applicants must be participating in the Multicultural Advertising Intern Program (MAIP). They must be entering their senior year at an accredited college or university in the United States and have a GPA of 3.0 or higher. Selection is based on academic ability.

Financial data: The stipend is $2,000.

Duration: 1 year.

Number awarded: 3 each year.

Deadline: Deadline not specified.

1163 ANGELUS AWARDS

Angelus Student Film Festival
c/o Family Theater Productions
7201 Sunset Boulevard
Hollywood, CA 90046
Phone: (323) 874-6633; (800) 874-0999
Email: info@angelus.org
Web: www.angelus.org

Summary: To recognize and reward outstanding student films on themes that "respect the dignity of the human person."

Eligibility: Open to undergraduate and graduate film and video students. Applicants must submit films that reflect such values as redemption, spirituality, dignity, tolerance, equality, diversity, hope, and the triumph of the human spirit. Acceptable genres include live action (drama, comedy, and narrative), animation, and documentary. Entries must 1) be in English, have English subtitles, or be dubbed in English; 2) be under 90 minutes in length; 3) have been completed during the previous 2 years while the filmmaker was a student at a recognized educational institute; and 4) be submitted on DVD for jury screening. Prizes include the Grand Prize (designated the Excellence in Filmmaking Award in Honor of Fr. Patrick Peyton, CSC) for the live action, documentary, or animation that best reflects the sponsor's theme through story, direction, and technical excellence; the Peter Glenville Foundation Triumph of the Spirit Award for the live action film whose theme best reflects the triumph of the human spirit; the Maryknoll Productions and FujiFilm Audience Impact Award for the live action film whose compelling story, imagery, content, and technical excellence delivers strong emotional audience impact; the Mole-Richardson Production Excellence Award for the live-action film with outstanding production design; the Priddy Brothers Outstanding Documentary Award for the documentary film whose characters best reflect a personal and moving reflection of the human spirit; and the Catholic Academy for Communication Arts Professionals Outstanding Animation Award for the animation film whose story both entertains and enlightens.

Financial data: The Excellence in Filmmaking Award in Honor of Fr. Patrick Peyton, CSC is $10,000; the Peter Glenville Foundation Triumph of the Spirit Award is $5,000; the Maryknoll Productions and FujiFilm Audience Impact Award is $2,500; the Mole-Richardson Production Excellence Award is $2,500; the Priddy Brothers Outstanding Documentary Award is $3,000; the Catholic Academy for Communication Arts Professionals Outstanding Animation Award is $2,000.

Duration: The festival is held annually.

Number awarded: Varies each year.

Deadline: May of each year.

1164 ANNUAL MUSIC STUDENT SCHOLARSHIPS

School Band and Orchestra Magazine
Attn: Student Scholarships
21 Highland Circle, Suite One
Needham, MA 02494
Phone: (781) 453-9310; (800) 964-5150; Fax: (781) 453-9389
Web: www.sbomagazine.com/Essay

Summary: To recognize and reward, with college scholarships, elementary and high school students who submit outstanding essays on playing a musical instrument.

Eligibility: Open to public and private school students in grades 4 through 12. Applicants must submit an essay of up to 250 words on a topic that changes annually but relates to music; recently, students were invited to write on the topic, "I believe music must remain a part of the school curriculum because. . . ."

Financial data: The award is a $1,000 college scholarship.

Duration: The competition is held annually.

Number awarded: 10 each year: 5 to students in grades 4–8 and 5 to students in grades 9–12.

Deadline: December of each year.

1165 APWA HORIZONS FRONT RANGE SCHOLARSHIP

American Public Works Association–Colorado Chapter
c/o Laura A. Kroeger, Scholarship Committee
Urban Drainage and Flood Control District
2480 West 26th Avenue, Suite 156-B
Denver, CO 80211
Phone: (303) 455-6277; Fax: (303) 455-7880
Email: lkroeger@udfcd.org
Web: colorado.apwa.net

Summary: To provide financial assistance to high school seniors in Colorado who plan to attend a college or university in the state to prepare for a career in public works.

Eligibility: Open to seniors graduating from high schools in Colorado who plan to attend a college, university, or junior college in the state. Applicants must be planning to major in accounting, architecture, biology, business, chemistry, construction management, engineering, finance, management, or other field associated with public works. Preference is given to applicants preparing for a career that promotes the public sector. Financial need is not considered in the selection process.

Financial data: The stipend is $1,500.

Duration: 1 year.

Number awarded: 1 or more each year.

Deadline: April of each year.

1166 ARCHIBALD RUTLEDGE SCHOLARSHIP PROGRAM

South Carolina State Department of Education
Attn: Office of Standards and Support
1429 Senate Street, Suite 802A
Columbia, SC 29201
Phone: (803) 734-0323; Fax: (803) 734-5953
Email: shockman@ed.sc.gov
Web: ed.sc.gov/agency/standards-and-learning/academic-standards

Summary: To recognize and reward, with scholarships for college in the state, high school seniors in South Carolina who participate in a competition in art, creative writing, dance, drama, or music.

Eligibility: Open to U.S. citizens who have attended South Carolina public high schools for at least 2 years, are currently seniors, and are planning to attend a South Carolina college or university. Applicants compete by submitting samples of their work in 1 of 4 areas: 1) visual arts, limited to 2-dimensional work such as drawing, painting, mixed media, printmaking, and collage; no 3-dimensional works, photographs, or computer-generated images are accepted; 2) creative writing, a sonnet, lyric, or narrative poem, up to 1 page; 3) theater, a 1-act play with a performing time of 20 to 45 minutes; 4) dance, an original short dance composition of 3 to 5 minutes composed for solo or ensemble dancers in any appropriate movement style; or 5) music, a composition of 3 to 5 minutes for solo or small ensemble, vocal or instrumental, in any appropriate style. In addition to the work, they must submit a process folio that contains documentation of the planning and development of the project and a 1-page reflection statement addressing the intent of the work and comparing the final product with the original concept. A panel of professionals in the field selects up to 10 finalists, based on originality, creativity, and the correlation and implications of the process folio for the final composition. Finalists must attend the scholarship competition, where they present a portfolio of a number of selected works as specified by the judges.

Financial data: The award consists of a $2,500 scholarship, to be used for tuition, room, board, and instructional resource expenses.

Duration: 1 year.

Number awarded: 4 each year: 1 in each of the 5 categories.

Deadline: February of each year.

1167 ARIZONA PRESS WOMEN ANNUAL JOURNALISM SCHOLARSHIP

Arizona Press Women
Attn: Joan Westlake, Scholarship Chair
736 East Loyola Drive
Tempe, AZ 85282
Phone: (480) 968-8902; Fax: (480) 262-8077
Email: jkwestlake@aol.com
Web: www.azpw.org/scholarship.html

Summary: To provide financial assistance to high school seniors in Arizona who plan to study journalism at a college or university in the state.

Eligibility: Open to seniors graduating from high schools in Arizona. Applicants must be planning to attend a college or university in the state to major in journalism. Along with their application, they must submit a letter of recommendation from a high school teacher, 2 samples of their writing, and a 1-page letter that includes information about their background and the reasons they want to study journalism in college. Financial need is also considered in the selection process.

Financial data: The stipend is $500.

Duration: 1 year.

Number awarded: 1 each year.

Deadline: April of each year.

1168 ARKANSAS POST SAME SCHOLARSHIPS

Society of American Military Engineers–Arkansas Post
c/o Craig Pierce, Scholarship and Camp Committee Chair
U.S. Army Corps of Engineers, Little Rock District
700 West Capitol Avenue
P.O. Box 867
Little Rock, AR 72203-0867
Phone: (501) 324-5842, ext. 1064; Fax: (501) 324-6518
Email: craig.pierce@usace.army.mil
Web: posts.same.org/Arkansas/scholarship

Summary: To provide financial assistance to Arkansas high school seniors interested in studying architecture or engineering at a college in any state.

Eligibility: Open to seniors graduating from high schools in Arkansas and planning to attend a college or university in any state. Applicants must be interested in studying architecture or a field of engineering related to construction (e.g., civil, electrical, environmental, geotechnical, mechanical, structural). Along with their application, they must submit a 200-word essay explaining why they want to study architecture or construction-related engineering and why receiving this scholarship is critical to achieving their continuing educational goals. Financial need is not considered in the selection process. U.S. citizenship or permanent resident status is required.

Financial data: The stipend is $1,000.

Duration: 1 year.

Number awarded: 2 each year.

Deadline: March of each year.

1169 ARKANSAS PRESS WOMEN SCHOLARSHIP

Arkansas Press Women
c/o Malea Hargett, Scholarship Chair
P.O. Box 7417
Little Rock, AR 72217
Phone: (501) 664-0125
Email: mhargett@doir.org
Web: www.arkansaspresswomen.org/profdev/school.htm

Summary: To provide financial assistance to upper-division students from any state preparing for a career in journalism or communications at a school in Arkansas.

Eligibility: Open to residents of any state entering their junior or senior year at a college or university in Arkansas and preparing for a career in journalism or mass communications. Applicants majoring in those fields are given preference. Along with their application, they must submit a copy of their college transcript, 3 letters of recommendation, 3 writing samples, and a 400-word statement of professional goals. Neither financial need nor gender is considered in the selection process.

Financial data: The stipend is $1,000 per year.

Duration: 1 year; recipients may reapply.

Number awarded: 1 each year.

Deadline: February of each year.

1170 ARKANSAS THESPIAN SCHOLARSHIPS

Arkansas State Thespian Society
c/o Gail Burns, College Auditions
Rector High School Drama
P.O. Box 367
Rector, AR 72461
Phone: (870) 595-1444
Email: gburns@hughes.net
Web: www.arkansasthespians.com

Summary: To provide financial assistance to high school seniors in Arkansas who plan to major in fields related to theater or theater education at a college in any state.

Eligibility: Open to seniors graduating from high schools in Arkansas who have been active in the thespian troupe. Applicants must be planning to attend college in any state and major or minor in the communication arts (theater, speech, radio, television, film, broadcasting, music, or dance) or in theater education. They must have a GPA of 2.7 or higher. Selection is based on auditions held at the Arkansas Thespian Festival. Auditions are held in the categories of performance, technical, theater education, and playwriting.

Financial data: Stipends are $1,200 or $500.

Duration: 1 year.

Number awarded: Varies each year; recently, 4 of these scholarships were awarded: 1 at $1,200 and 3 at $500.

Deadline: December of each year.

1171 ARMENIAN GENERAL BENEVOLENT UNION PERFORMING ARTS FELLOWSHIPS

Armenian General Benevolent Union
Attn: Scholarship Program
55 East 59th Street, Seventh Floor
New York, NY 10022-1112
Phone: (212) 319-6383; Fax: (212) 319-6507
Email: scholarship@agbu.org
Web: www.agbu.org/programs/projects.asp?program_id=14&parent_id=4

Summary: To provide financial assistance to undergraduate and graduate students of Armenian heritage worldwide working on a degree in performing arts at universities in any country.

Eligibility: Open to full-time undergraduate and graduate students of Armenian heritage from any country (except Armenians studying in Armenia). Applicants must be working on a degree in performing arts at a university in any country. They must have a GPA of 3.5 or higher, as measured by the U.S. grading system. Selection is based on academic excellence, public and community service (especially involvement in the Armenian community), and financial need.

Financial data: Stipends range from $1,000 to $5,000 per year.

Duration: Up to 5 years.

Number awarded: 1 or more each year.

Deadline: May of each year.

1172 ARTHUR N. TUTTLE, JR. GRADUATE FELLOWSHIP IN HEALTH FACILITY PLANNING AND DESIGN

American Institute of Architects
Attn: Academy of Architecture for Health
1735 New York Avenue, N.W.
Washington, DC 20006-5292
Phone: (202) 626-7366; (800) AIA-3837; Fax: (202) 626-7547
Email: aah@aia.org
Web: www.aia.org/practicing/groups/kc/AIAS074546

Summary: To provide financial assistance to upper-division and graduate students in architecture interested in studying health facility planning and design.

Eligibility: Open to 1) undergraduates entering the fifth year of a 5-year program leading to a professional degree in architecture with a program that focuses on health care design; 2) graduate students in the first year of a 2-year master of architecture program or the second year of a 3-year program with a plan listing courses that will permit them to concentrate on the planning and design of health care facilities; or 3) professional architects who have a bachelor's or master's of architecture degree and are working on a doctoral degree in the health facilities field or conducting an independent study that is near completion with the intent to present the results and publish in the *Academy Journal.* Undergraduates must demonstrate that resources are available, such as health care course work, an association with a health care organization, an association with a health care design firm, and/or a health care focused professional or instructor, that are adequate to supplement and support a program of study in health facility design. Graduate students must be at a site that is near health care organizations and resources that are adequate to supplement the prescribed graduate courses in health facilities design. All applicants must be enrolled at an accredited school of architecture in the United State, Mexico, or Canada. They must have a command of the English language and a record of past academic performance that strongly indicates an ability to complete the fellowship successfully. Selection is based on significance of the proposed research, qualifications of the applicant, content of the letters of recommendation, completeness and clarity of the application, and potential of the applicant to make significant future professional contributions.

Financial data: Stipends for undergraduate or graduate study range from $4,500 to $10,000. Stipends for doctoral-level graduate study in the health facilities field range from $3,000 to $5,000.

Duration: 1 year.

Number awarded: Normally, 2 or more each year.

Deadline: April of each year.

1173 ASCAP FOUNDATION YOUNG JAZZ COMPOSER AWARDS

American Society of Composers, Authors and Publishers
Attn: ASCAP Foundation
ASCAP Building
One Lincoln Plaza
New York, NY 10023-7142
Phone: (212) 621-6219; Fax: (212) 621-6236
Email: ascapfoundation@ascap.com
Web: www.ascapfoundation.org/awards.html

Summary: To recognize and reward outstanding jazz compositions.

Eligibility: Open to U.S. citizens and permanent residents who are younger than 30 years of age. Applicants may be students in grades K-12, college undergraduates, graduate students, or recipients of a D.M.A. or Ph.D. degree. They must submit completely original jazz compositions that have not previously earned awards or prizes in major national competitions. Arrangements are not eligible. Entries must include a completed application form; the notated score of 1 composition; a cassette or CD of the composition; and biographical information that includes prior music studies, background, and experience.

Financial data: Winners share $25,000 in prizes.

Duration: The prizes are presented annually.

Number awarded: Varies each year; recently, 22 composers shared these awards.

Deadline: November of each year.

1174 ASCAP/LOTTE LEHMANN FOUNDATION SONG CYCLE COMPETITION

Lotte Lehmann Foundation
545 Eighth Avenue, Suite 401
New York, NY 10018
Phone: (347) 684-1640
Email: daron@daronhagen.com
Web: www.lottelehmann.org/llf/programs

Summary: To recognize and reward, with commissions for further work, outstanding student and other composers of art songs.

Eligibility: Open to composers under 30 years of age who are U.S. citizens, permanent residents of the United States, or enrolled students with student visas. Applicants must submit an original art song with English text. Arrangements of pre-existing music are ineligible. They must submit a printed copy of the English text, a 200-word biography, and a CD or cassette recording of a live performance of the work.

Financial data: First prize is $3,500 and a commission to compose a song cycle for voice and piano, to be published by E.C. Schirmer and performed in 3 major American cities. Second prize is $1,000 and a commission to compose an art song for voice and piano. Third prize is $500 and a commission to compose an art song for voice and piano. Fourth prize is $500 and a commission to compose an art song for voice and piano on poetry by Andre Brunin and premiered at the Albert Roussel International Festival in France.

Duration: The competition is held biennially, in odd-numbered years.

Number awarded: 4 every other year.

Deadline: September of odd-numbered years.

1175 ASLA COUNCIL OF FELLOWS SCHOLARSHIPS

Landscape Architecture Foundation
Attn: Scholarship Program
818 18th Street, N.W., Suite 810
Washington, DC 20006-3520
Phone: (202) 331-7070; Fax: (202) 331-7079
Email: scholarships@lafoundation.org
Web: www.laprofession.org/financial/scholarships.htm

Summary: To provide financial assistance to upper-division students, especially those from disadvantaged and underrepresented groups, working on a degree in landscape architecture.

Eligibility: Open to landscape architecture students in the third, fourth, or fifth year of undergraduate work. Preference is given to, and 1 scholarship is reserved for, members of underrepresented ethnic or cultural groups. Applicants must submit a 300-word essay on how they envision themselves contributing to the profession of landscape architecture, 2 letters of recommendation, documentation of financial need, and (for students applying for the scholarship reserved for underrepresented groups) a statement identifying their association with a specific ethnic or cultural group. U.S. citizenship or permanent resident status is required.

Financial data: The stipend is $4,000. Students also receive a 1-year membership in the American Society of Landscape Architecture (ASLA), general registration fees for the ASLA annual meeting, and a travel stipend to attend the meeting.

Duration: 1 year.

Number awarded: 2 each year.

Deadline: February of each year.

1176 ASPIRING MUSIC TEACHER SCHOLARSHIP

Vermont Student Assistance Corporation
Attn: Scholarship Programs
10 East Allen Street
P.O. Box 2000
Winooski, VT 05404-2601
Phone: (802) 654-3798; (888) 253-4819; Fax: (802) 654-3765; TDD: (800) 281-3341 (within VT)
Email: info@vsac.org
Web: services.vsac.org/wps/wcm/connect/vsac/VSAC

Summary: To provide financial assistance to residents of Vermont who are interested in attending college in any state to study music education or piano pedagogy.

Eligibility: Open to residents of Vermont who are graduating high school seniors, high school graduates, or current college students. Applicants must be attending or planning to attend an accredited postsecondary institution in any state to study music education or piano pedagogy. Along with their application, they must submit 1) a 100-word essay on the school, church, and community activities in which they have participated; and 2) a 100-word essay on

their interest in and commitment to pursuing their chosen career or vocation. Selection is based on those essays, a letter of recommendation, and financial need.
Financial data: The stipend is $1,000.
Duration: 1 year.
Number awarded: 1 each year.
Deadline: March of each year.

1177 ASSOCIATED PRESS SPORTS EDITORS SCHOLARSHIPS

Associated Press Sports Editors
c/o Joe Sullivan
Boston Globe
135 Morrissey Boulevard
Boston, MA 02205-2845
Phone: (617) 929-2845
Email: jtsullivan@globe.com
Web: aspe.dallasnews.com
Summary: To provide financial assistance to college students interested in preparing for a career in sports journalism.
Eligibility: Open to students entering their sophomore, junior, or senior year at a college or university in the United States. Applicants must have indicated an interest in preparing for a career in sports journalism. Along with their application, they must submit a transcript, letters of recommendation, 5 examples of their sports journalism (usually stories but can be sections they have edited), and documentation of financial need.
Financial data: The stipend is $1,500.
Duration: 1 year.
Number awarded: 4 each year: 1 from each of 4 regions in the country.
Deadline: May of each year.

1178 ASTA NATIONAL SOLO COMPETITION–SENIOR DIVISION

American String Teachers Association
Attn: Competitions
4153 Chain Bridge Road
Fairfax, VA 22030
Phone: (703) 279-2113; Fax: (703) 279-2114
Email: asta@astaweb.com
Web: www.astaweb.com/AM/Template.cfm?Section=Competitions
Summary: To recognize and reward outstanding college-age performers on stringed instruments.
Eligibility: Open to students between 19 and 25 years of age who have graduated from high school. Competitions are held for violin, viola, cello, double bass, classical guitar, and harp. Candidates must be members of the American String Teachers Association (ASTA) or current students of ASTA members. They first enter their state competitions; they may enter either in their state of residency or the state in which they are studying. The state chairs then submit tapes or CDs of the winners in their state to the national chair. Musicians who live in states that do not have a state competition may submit recordings directly to the national chair. The repertoire must consist of a required work and a work of the competitor's choice; tapes of performances should run from 17 to 20 minutes. Based on those tapes or CDs, finalists are invited to the national competition, where the winners are selected.
Financial data: Prizes vary; recently, they were $7,000 for first place, $4,000 for second, $2,000 for third, and $1,000 for fourth.
Duration: The competition is held biennially, in odd-numbered years.
Number awarded: 4 each odd-numbered year.
Deadline: Each state sets the date of its competition, but all state competitions must be completed by October of even-numbered years so the winning tapes or CDs reach the national chair by the middle of November. The national competition is in March.

1179 ATLANTA PRESS CLUB JOURNALISM SCHOLARSHIP AWARD

Atlanta Press Club, Inc.
34 Broad Street, 18th Floor
Atlanta, GA 30303
Phone: (404) 57-PRESS; Fax: (404) 223-3706
Email: info@atlpressclub.org
Web: www.atlpressclub.org/scholarships
Summary: To provide financial assistance to college students majoring in journalism at a Georgia college or university.
Eligibility: Open to residents of Georgia currently majoring in journalism at a college or university in the state at the sophomore or junior level. Applicants must submit an essay of 250 to 500 words describing their career aspirations and how the scholarship would help them reach their goal. They must also submit samples of their work (published articles, audio, video, photos, and/or digital). Selection is based on skill, achievement, and commitment to journalism. Financial need is not considered in the selection process. A personal interview may be required.
Financial data: The stipend is $1,500.
Duration: 1 year; nonrenewable.
Number awarded: 4 each year: 2 to print journalism students and 2 to broadcast journalism students.
Deadline: February of each year.

1180 ATLAS SHRUGGED ESSAY CONTEST

Ayn Rand Institute
Attn: Essay Contests
2121 Alton Parkway, Suite 250
Irvine, CA 92606-4926
Phone: (949) 222-6550; Fax: (949) 222-6558
Email: essay@aynrand.org
Web: www.aynrand.org/site/PageServer?pagename=education_contests_atlas
Summary: To recognize and reward outstanding essays written by high school seniors, undergraduates, and graduate students on Ayn Rand's novel, *Atlas Shrugged.*
Eligibility: Open to high school seniors and part- or full-time undergraduate or graduate students. Applicants must submit an essay on questions selected each year from Ayn Rand's novel, *Atlas Shrugged.* The essay must be between 800 and 1,600 words. Selection is based on style and content. Judges look for writing that is clear, articulate, and logically organized. To win, an essay must demonstrate an outstanding grasp of the philosophic meaning of the novel.
Financial data: First prize is $10,000; second prizes are $2,000; third prizes are $1,000; finalist prizes are $100; and semifinalist prizes are $50.
Duration: The competition is held annually.
Number awarded: 84 each year: 1 first prize, 3 second prizes, 5 third prizes, 25 finalist prizes, and 50 semifinalist prizes.
Deadline: September of each year.

1181 B. PHINIZY SPALDING SCHOLARSHIP

Georgia Trust
Attn: Scholarship Committee
1516 Peachtree Street, N.W.
Atlanta, GA 30309
Phone: (404) 881-9980; Fax: (404) 875-2205
Email: info@georgiatrust.org
Web: www.georgiatrust.org/preservation/spalding_owens.php
Summary: To provide financial assistance to Georgia residents majoring in a field related to historical preservation at a college or university in the state.
Eligibility: Open to Georgia residents who are enrolled full-time in their first year of undergraduate study at a college or university in the state. Applicants must be working on a degree in historic preservation or a related field (e.g., archaeology, architecture, history, planning). U.S. citizenship is required. Selection is based on academic achievement and past and planned involvement within preservation-related fields.
Financial data: The stipend is $1,000.
Duration: 1 year.
Number awarded: 1 each year.
Deadline: February of each year.

1182 BARBARA L. FRYE SCHOLARSHIP

Capital Press Club of Florida
336 East College Avenue, Room 303
Tallahassee, FL 32301
Phone: (850) 224-7263
Email: barbarafryescholarship@gmail.com
Web: barbarafryescholarship.wordpress.com/about
Summary: To provide financial assistance to high school seniors and college students in Florida who are planning to prepare for a career in journalism.
Eligibility: Open to applicants who are 1) attending or expecting to attend a Florida college or university; or 2) a graduate or prospective graduate of a Florida high school attending or expecting to attend a college inside or outside of Florida. College seniors are not eligible to apply. Along with their application,

they must submit an essay (of 300 to 500 words) describing their reason for choosing a career in journalism, their experience in the field, and other factors that should be considered in the selection process; samples of their work (either clippings or tapes); and at least 1 letter of recommendation from a teacher, professor, or professional journalist. Selection is based on merit, dedication to journalism, and demonstrated aptitude for print or broadcast journalism. An applicant's racial minority status or financial need may be considered by the selection committee, but those are not required for eligibility.
Financial data: The stipend is $2,000.
Duration: 1 year; recipients may reapply.
Number awarded: 10 to 12 each year.
Deadline: June of each year.

1183 BAY AREA MEDIA NETWORK SCHOLARSHIPS

Bay Area Media Network
Attn: Jennifer Beaver
P.O. Box 20261
Tampa, FL 33622
Email: jennifer.beaver@mybrighthouse.com
Web: bayareamedianetwork.org/scholarships-inernships
Summary: To provide financial assistance to high school seniors in Florida who are interested in studying a field related to media at a college or university in the state.
Eligibility: Open to high school seniors who plan to attend a college or university in Florida. Applicants must have an interest in entering the field of media.
Financial data: The stipend is $1,000.
Duration: 1 year.
Number awarded: 2 each year.
Deadline: Deadline not specified.

1184 BEA 2-YEAR/COMMUNITY COLLEGE AWARD

Broadcast Education Association
Attn: Scholarships
1771 N Street, N.W.
Washington, DC 20036-2891
Phone: (202) 429-3935; (888) 380-7222
Email: BEAMemberServices@nab.org
Web: www.beaweb.org/AM/Template.cfm?Section=Home
Summary: To provide financial assistance to current or former community college students who are interested in preparing for a career in broadcasting.
Eligibility: Open to students who are either 1) enrolled full-time at a community college; or 2) graduates of a community college enrolled full-time at a 4-year college or university. Their current or former community college must be an institutional member of the Broadcast Education Association. Applicants must be studying for a career in broadcasting. Selection is based on evidence that the applicant possesses high integrity, superior academic ability, potential to be an outstanding electronic media professional, and a sense of personal and professional responsibility.
Financial data: The stipend is $1,500.
Duration: 1 year; may not be renewed.
Number awarded: 2 each year.
Deadline: October of each year.

1185 BEALL SCHOLARSHIP

Presbyterian Church (USA)
Attn: Office of Financial Aid for Studies
100 Witherspoon Street, Room M-052
Louisville, KY 40202-1396
Phone: (502) 569-5224; (888) 728-7228, ext. 5224; Fax: (502) 569-8766
Email: finaid@pcusa.org
Web: www.pcusa.org/financialaid/programs/beall.htm
Summary: To provide financial assistance to female Presbyterian residents of designated southeastern states who are interested in studying the arts at a school in any state.
Eligibility: Open to women who are members of the Presbyterian Church (USA) between 16 and 36 years of age. Applicants must be residents of Alabama, Florida, Georgia, Kentucky, Louisiana, Mississippi, North Carolina, South Carolina, Tennessee, or Virginia. They must be enrolled or planning to enroll full-time at a college or university in any state to major in the arts. Selection is based on academic standing (GPA of 2.5 or higher) and financial need.
Financial data: Stipends range up to $5,000 per year, depending upon the financial need of the recipient.
Duration: 1 year; may be renewed up to 3 additional years.
Number awarded: 1 or more each year.
Deadline: June of each year.

1186 BEN BERGER MEMORIAL SCHOLARSHIP

Oklahoma City Gridiron Foundation
330 North Country Club Terrace
Mustang, OK 73064
Web: www.okcgridiron.org
Summary: To provide financial assistance to high school seniors in Oklahoma planning to work on a degree in journalism at a college or university in the state.
Eligibility: Open to seniors graduating from high schools in Oklahoma and planning to enroll at a college or university in the state to work on a degree in journalism. Applicants must submit brief statements on what they hope to be doing 6 months after completing college, what they hope to be doing 10 years from today, why they have selected journalism as their profession, what they like most about working in journalism, and what they like least. They must also submit a copy of their transcript and samples of their work. Financial need is considered in the selection process.
Financial data: The stipend is $1,500.
Duration: 1 year.
Number awarded: 1 each year.
Deadline: March of each year.

1187 BERKELEY PRIZE ARCHITECTURAL DESIGN FELLOWSHIP

University of California at Berkeley
Department of Architecture
Attn: Raymond Lifchez
474 Wurster Hall
Berkeley, CA 94720
Phone: (510) 642-7585; Fax: (510) 643-5607
Email: info@berkeleyprize.org
Web: www.berkeleyprize.org
Summary: To recognize and reward undergraduate students from any country who submit outstanding essays describing an architectural design competition to be conducted at their own school.
Eligibility: Open to undergraduates currently enrolled at accredited schools of architecture worldwide. Applicants must submit a 1,250-word proposal for an architectural competition to be conducted at their school. The competition should relate to a theme selected annually; recently, the theme was historic preservation/heritage conservation. In their proposal, students should provide a complete description and rules of the competition, including its title, format (e.g., essay, sketch, design problem), time competitors have to complete it, publicity, members of the jury, criteria for evaluating the entries, schedule, and prizes. The competition must be endorsed by the applicant's academic institution; its winning design should be potentially built, assembled, and/or actually used by the public.
Financial data: The student who submits the most outstanding competition proposal receives a prize of $2,500. An additional $2,500 is awarded for use as prizes for the students who actually enter the competition at the winner's institution, to be distributed according to the rules described in the proposal.
Duration: The prize for the best proposal is awarded annually. The architectural competition described in the winning proposal must be organized and completed within the calendar year of the award.
Number awarded: 1 each year.
Deadline: March of each year.

1188 BERKELEY PRIZE ESSAY COMPETITION

University of California at Berkeley
Department of Architecture
Attn: Raymond Lifchez
474 Wurster Hall
Berkeley, CA 94720
Phone: (510) 642-7585; Fax: (510) 643-5607
Email: info@berkeleyprize.org
Web: www.berkeleyprize.org
Summary: To recognize and reward undergraduate students from any country who submit outstanding essays on architecture as a social art.
Eligibility: Open to undergraduates currently enrolled at accredited schools of architecture worldwide. An architecture student may team up with another undergraduate in architecture, urban studies, or the social sciences. Applicants must submit a 500-word proposal for an essay on a question that changes

annually but relates to architecture as a social art; recently, students were invited to write on sustainable architecture and traditional wisdom. On the basis of those proposals, semifinalists are invited to submit 2,500-word essays.
Financial data: A total of $9,500 is available for prizes each year; recently, the jury awarded $4,500 as first prize, $3,000 as second prize, and $2,000 as third prize. Additional funding permitted the award of honorable mentions at $500. For essays submitted by teams, the prize money is divided equally among the members.
Duration: The competition is held annually.
Number awarded: Varies each year; recently, 3 prizes and 2 honorable mentions were awarded.
Deadline: Initial proposals must be submitted by October of each year.

1189 BETTY ANN LIVINGSTON SCHOLARSHIP
United Methodist Higher Education Foundation
Attn: Scholarships Administrator
1001 19th Avenue South
P.O. Box 340005
Nashville, TN 37203-0005
Phone: (615) 340-7385; (800) 811-8110; Fax: (615) 340-7330
Email: umhefscholarships@gbhem.org
Web: www.umhef.org/receive.php?id=endowed_funds
Summary: To provide financial assistance to Methodist high school seniors who plan to study designated fields in college.
Eligibility: Open to graduating high school seniors who are planning to enroll full-time in a degree program at an accredited institution and major in pre-law, medicine, public policy, literature, or a related field. Applicants must have been active, full members of a United Methodist Church for at least 1 year prior to applying. They must have a GPA of 3.0 or higher and be able to demonstrate financial need. Along with their application, they must submit a 200-word essay on their involvement and/or leadership responsibilities in their church, school, and community within the last 3 years. Preference is given to members of Macedonia United Methodist Church in Macedonia, Ohio. U.S. citizenship or permanent resident status is required.
Financial data: A stipend is awarded (amount not specified).
Duration: 1 year; may be renewed.
Number awarded: Varies each year; recently, 3 of these scholarships were awarded.
Deadline: May of each year.

1190 BIG FISH IN A SMALL POND SCHOLARSHIP
Society of Professional Journalists–Kansas Professional Chapter
c/o Denise Neil, Scholarship Committee
Wichita Eagle
825 East Douglas Avenue
P.O. Box 820
Wichita, KS 67201-0820
Phone: (316) 268-6327
Email: dneil@wichitaeagle.com
Web: www.spjchapters.org/kansas/gridiron.html
Summary: To provide financial assistance to residents of any state enrolled at colleges and universities in Kansas (except the University of Kansas, Wichita State University, and Kansas State University) who are interested in a career in journalism.
Eligibility: Open to residents of any state entering their junior or senior year at colleges and universities in Kansas. Students at the University of Kansas, Wichita State University, and Kansas State University are not eligible, although they may transfer there in the fall following receipt of this award. Applicants do not have to be journalism or communication majors, but they must demonstrate a strong and sincere interest in print journalism, broadcast journalism, online journalism, or photojournalism. They must have a GPA of 2.5 or higher. Along with their application, they must submit a professional resume, 4 to 6 examples of their best work (clips or stories, copies of photographs, tapes or transcripts of broadcasts, printouts of web pages), and a 1-page cover letter about themselves, how they came to be interested in journalism, their professional goals, and (if appropriate) their financial need for this scholarship.
Financial data: The stipend is $1,000.
Duration: 1 year.
Number awarded: 1 each year.
Deadline: April of each year.

1191 BLANCHE PAYNE SCHOLARSHIP IN TEXTILE OR APPAREL DESIGN
International Textile and Apparel Association
Attn: Student Fellowship and Awards Committee
6060 Sunrise Vista Drive, Suite 1300
Citrus Heights, CA 95610
Phone: (916) 723-1628
Email: info@itaaonline.org
Web: www.itaaonline.org/template.asp?intPgeID=202
Summary: To provide financial assistance to students working on an undergraduate degree in a field related to design.
Eligibility: Open to undergraduate students who are working on a degree in a field that may include apparel, costume, textile, or accessory design; functional and technical design; apparel product development; or fashion illustration. Applicants must be sponsored by an active, reserve, or emeritus member of the International Textile and Apparel Association (ITAA). They must be planning to attend the ITAA annual meeting and present either 1) at least 1 design in the Design Exhibition; or 2) a research paper in the technical design/fashion illustration track. Selection is based on potential for future contributions to and leadership in the textiles and apparel profession; level of scholarship, with a balance of textiles and apparel and supporting disciplines; and aptitude for advanced study.
Financial data: The stipend is $5,000.
Duration: 1 year.
Number awarded: 1 each year.
Deadline: April of each year for students who plan to submit a research paper; May of each year for students who plan to enter the design competition.

1192 BLOUNT-SLAWSON YOUNG ARTISTS COMPETITION
Montgomery Symphony Orchestra
Attn: Young Artists Competition Committee
301 North Hull Street
P.O. Box 1864
Montgomery, AL 36102
Phone: (334) 240-4004
Email: msymphony@bellsouth.net
Web: www.montgomerysymphony.org/comp_Blount.htm
Summary: To recognize and reward talented young musicians who perform at a competition in Montgomery, Alabama.
Eligibility: Open to musicians in grades 7–12 who reside in and attend school in the United States. Students of strings, winds, brass, percussion, and piano are eligible to enter. Acceptable music for the competition includes 1 movement from any work in the standard concerto repertoire. Memorization is preferred but not required.
Financial data: First prize is $2,500 in cash, a $7,500 scholarship (to pay for music education at any institution of higher learning, summer music festival, seminar, etc.), and the opportunity to perform with the Montgomery Symphony Orchestra. Second prize is $4,000, third $1,000, fourth $500, and merit prizes are $250. The second- through fourth-place winners perform at the Young Artists recital.
Duration: The competition is held annually.
Number awarded: 9 cash prizes (including 5 merit prizes) and 1 scholarship are awarded each year.
Deadline: December of each year.

1193 BMI STUDENT COMPOSER AWARDS
Broadcast Music Inc.
Attn: BMI Foundation, Inc.
7 World Trade Center
250 Greenwich Street
New York, NY 10007-0030
Phone: (212) 220-3000
Email: info@bmifoundation.org
Web: www.bmifoundation.org/program/bmi_student_composer_awards
Summary: To recognize and reward outstanding student composers from the Western Hemisphere.
Eligibility: Open to citizens of countries in North, Central, or South America, the Caribbean Island nations, or the Hawaiian Islands who are younger than 28 years of age. Applicants must be 1) enrolled in accredited public, private, or parochial secondary schools; 2) enrolled in accredited colleges or conservatories of music; or 3) engaged in the private study of music with recognized and established teachers (other than a relative). Any composer having won the award 3

times previously is not eligible to enter the contest again. Compositions may be for vocal, instrumental, electronic, or any combination of those. There are no limitations on medium, instrumentation, or length of the work. Manuscripts may be submitted either on usual score paper or reproduced by a generally accepted reproduction process. Electronic music and recordings of graphic works that cannot adequately be presented in score may be submitted on cassette or CD. Selection is based on evidence of creative talent. Academic finesse is considered, but that is secondary to vital musicality and clarity of expression of the composer's work. Judges consider 1) formal content of the composition; 2) melodic, harmonic, and rhythmic idioms, but only in terms of their consistency and suitability for the intent of the particular composition; 3) suitability of the choice and use of instruments or voices to the ideas presented in the composition; and 4) age of the composer (if 2 compositions are of equal merit, preference is given to the younger contestant).

Financial data: Prizes range from $500 to $5,000.

Duration: The competition is held annually.

Number awarded: Varies each year; recently, 11 of these awards were presented. A total of $20,000 in prizes is awarded each year.

Deadline: February of each year.

1194 BOB EAST SCHOLARSHIP

National Press Photographers Foundation
3200 Croasdaile Drive, Suite 306
Durham, NC 27705-2586
Phone: (919) 383-7246; (800) 289-6772; Fax: (919) 383-7261
Email: info@nppa.org
Web: www.nppa.org

Summary: To provide financial assistance to college photojournalists who are interested in continuing college or going to graduate school.

Eligibility: Open to full-time undergraduates who are in the first 3 and a half years of college or planning to work on a graduate degree. Applicants must be preparing for a career in photojournalism. Along with their application, they must submit a list of the photographic and photojournalist activities they have undertaken in school, a list of photographic activities they have taken outside of school, information on their financial need, a statement of their philosophy and goals in photojournalism, and a portfolio that includes at least 5 single images in addition to a picture story. Selection is based primarily on the quality of the portfolio.

Financial data: The stipend is $2,000.

Duration: 1 year.

Number awarded: 1 each year.

Deadline: February of each year.

1195 BOB EDDY SCHOLARSHIP PROGRAM

Society of Professional Journalists–Connecticut Professional Chapter
Attn: Debra A. Estock, Scholarship Committee Chair
71 Kenwood Avenue
Fairfield, CT 06824
Phone: (203) 255-2127
Email: destock@ctspj.org
Web: www.ctspj.org/scholarship.html

Summary: To provide financial assistance to upper-division students residing or studying in Connecticut who are interested in preparing for a career in journalism.

Eligibility: Open to juniors or seniors who are either Connecticut residents (may attend school in any state) or from other states enrolled in a 4-year college or university in Connecticut. Applicants must be preparing for a career in journalism. Along with their application, they must submit 1) writing samples, tapes, or related work in any media that shows an interest and competency in journalism; and 2) a 500-word essay on why they want to become a journalist. Financial need must be demonstrated.

Financial data: Stipends are $2,000, $1,500, $1,000, or $250.

Duration: 1 year.

Number awarded: 5 each year: 1 at $2,000, 1 at $1,500, 1 at $1,000, and 2 at $250.

Deadline: April of each year.

1196 BOBBI MCCALLUM MEMORIAL SCHOLARSHIP

Seattle Foundation
Attn: Scholarship Administrator
1200 Fifth Avenue, Suite 1300
Seattle, WA 98101-3151
Phone: (206) 622-2294; Fax: (206) 622-7673
Email: scholarships@seattlefoundation.org
Web: www.seattlefoundation.org/page10004940.cfm

Summary: To provide financial assistance to women college students in Washington who are interested in preparing for a career in journalism.

Eligibility: Open to female residents of Washington who are entering their junior or senior year and studying print journalism at a 4-year public college or university in the state. Applicants must submit 5 samples of news writing (published or unpublished); brief essays on topics related to their interest in journalism; 2 letters of recommendation; and documentation of financial need. Selection is based on need, talent, and motivation to prepare for a career in print journalism.

Financial data: The stipend is $3,000 per year.

Duration: 1 year; may be renewed.

Number awarded: 2 each year.

Deadline: May of each year.

1197 BODIE MCDOWELL SCHOLARSHIPS

Outdoor Writers Association of America
121 Hickory Street, Suite 1
Missoula, MT 59801
Phone: (406) 728-7434; (800) 692-2477; Fax: (406) 728-7445
Web: www.owaa.org/scholarships.htm

Summary: To provide financial assistance for college or graduate school to students interested in a career in outdoor writing.

Eligibility: Open to undergraduates entering their junior or senior year of study and graduate students. Applicants must be majoring in a field related to outdoor communications, including print, photography, film, art, or broadcasting. Selection is based on 1) career goals in outdoor communications; 2) examples of work; and 3) letters of recommendation. Academic achievement is also considered but is not among the top 3 selection criteria.

Financial data: Stipends range from $1,000 to $5,000 per year.

Number awarded: 3 or more each year.

Deadline: February of each year.

1198 BRASLER PRIZE

National Scholastic Press Association
2221 University Avenue, S.E., Suite 121
Minneapolis, MN 55414
Phone: (612) 625-8335; Fax: (612) 626-0720
Email: info@studentpress.org
Web: www.studentpress.org/nspa/contests.html

Summary: To recognize and reward outstanding high school journalists.

Eligibility: Open to high school journalists who submit samples of stories that they have written in 5 categories: news, diversity, features, sports, and editorials. In each category, 1 student is selected as the author of the Story of the Year. Selection of those stories is based on quality of writing, sensitivity, and fairness. The first-place winners in each category then compete for this prize.

Financial data: The prize is $1,000.

Duration: The competition is held annually.

Number awarded: 1 each year.

Deadline: June of each year.

1199 BRIDGING THE GAP FOR HISPANIC SUCCESS AWARD

Hispanic Association of Colleges and Universities
Attn: National Scholarship Program
8415 Datapoint Drive, Suite 400
San Antonio, TX 78229
Phone: (210) 692-3805; Fax: (210) 692-0823; TDD: (800) 855-2880
Email: scholarships@hacu.net
Web: www.hacu.net/hacu/Scholarships_EN.asp?SnID=875148054

Summary: To provide financial assistance to undergraduate students at member institutions of the Hispanic Association of Colleges and Universities (HACU) who are majoring in fields related to the fashion retailing industry.

Eligibility: Open to undergraduate students at 2- and 4-year HACU member and partner colleges and universities. Applicants must be majoring in merchandise management, retail management, fashion design, or related fields. They must have a GPA of 3.0 or higher and be able to demonstrate financial need. Along with their application, they must submit an essay of 200 to 250 words that describes their academic and/or career goals, where they expect to be and what they expect to be doing 10 years from now, and what skills they can bring to an employer.

Financial data: The stipend is $1,000.
Duration: 1 year; may be renewed.
Number awarded: 1 or more each year.
Deadline: May of each year.

1200 BRONISLAW KAPER AWARDS FOR YOUNG ARTISTS

Los Angeles Philharmonic
Attn: Education Programs
151 South Grand Avenue
Los Angeles, CA 90012-3034
Phone: (213) 972-0704; Fax: (213) 972-7650
Email: education@laphil.org
Web: www.laphil.com/education/competition.cfm

Summary: To recognize and reward outstanding high school musicians in California.
Eligibility: Open to current residents of California who are no older than 17 years of age or seniors in high school. Applicants must be pianists (in even-numbered years) or string players (in odd-numbered years) who wish to enter a concerto competition at the Dorothy Chandler Pavilion in Los Angeles.
Financial data: First prize is $2,500, second prize is $2,000, and third prize is $1,000. In addition, a special prize of $500 is awarded to the student judged the most promising musician. Prize winners are also considered for solo opportunities with the Los Angeles Philharmonic.
Duration: The competition is held annually.
Number awarded: 4 each year.
Deadline: December of each year.

1201 BRUCE EAGLESON MEMORIAL SCHOLARSHIP AWARDS

Connecticut Association of Schools
Attn: Executive Director
30 Realty Drive
Cheshire, CT 06410
Phone: (203) 250-1111; Fax: (203) 250-1345
Email: msavage@casciac.org
Web: www.casciac.org

Summary: To provide financial assistance to high school seniors in Connecticut who plan to study the arts at a college in any state.
Eligibility: Open to seniors graduating from high schools in Connecticut who plan to enroll in college in any state to study the arts, including (but not limited to) visual arts, music, theater, dance, design, and architecture. Applicants must be able to demonstrate 1) considerable experience in the arts as evidenced by involvement in shows, exhibits, performances, video productions, or similar activities; 2) involvement in service to peers and/or community through artistic or other activities; and 3) financial need. Along with their application, they must submit a 250-word statement on what led them to their decision to prepare for a career in the arts.
Financial data: The stipend is $1,000.
Duration: 1 year.
Number awarded: 3 each year.
Deadline: March of each year.

1202 BURNHAM PRIZE OF THE CHICAGO ARCHITECTURAL CLUB

Chicago Architectural Club
c/o Chicago Gallery of the University of Illinois
230 West Superior Street, Second Floor
Chicago, IL 60610-3595
Phone: (312) 587-9976
Email: competition@chicagoarchitecturalclub.org
Web: www.chicagoarchitecturalclub.org/competitions/competitions.aspx

Summary: To recognize and reward professional and student architects who enter a competition on themes related to Chicago.
Eligibility: Open to professional and student architects internationally. Applicants are invited to submit entries in response to a theme for a project in Chicago; recently, entries were solicited for designs for the remodeling of Union Station.
Financial data: First prize is $10,000, second $3,000, and third $1,500.
Duration: The competition is held biennially, in even-numbered years.
Number awarded: 3 prizes are awarded each even-numbered year.
Deadline: October of each even-numbered year.

1203 CESAR E. CHAVEZ MEMORIAL EDUCATION AWARD

California Teachers Association
Attn: Human Rights Department
1705 Murchison Drive
P.O. Box 921
Burlingame, CA 94011-0921
Phone: (650) 552-5446; Fax: (650) 552-5002
Email: scholarships@cta.org
Web: www.cta.org/About-CTA/CTA-Foundation/Scholarships/index.aspx

Summary: To recognize and reward students in California who submit outstanding art work or essays on themes related to the legacy of Cesar Chavez.
Eligibility: Open to California students in grades preK through college sophomores. Applicants must submit 1) visual arts projects (paintings, drawings, collages, posters, original technologically generated art); or 2) written essays (no biographies). Essays must be of any age-appropriate length for grades preK–2, 200 to 300 words for grades 3–4, 400 to 600 words for grades 5–8, 800 to 1,100 words for grades 9–12, or 1,000 to 1,500 for college freshmen and sophomores. If written in a language other than English, an English translation is required. The theme of the artwork or essay must relate to a principle of Cesar Chavez's legacy: principles of non-violence; self-determination through unionization; social justice for farm workers; safe food, health, environmental issues; human and civil rights issues; teamwork, cooperation, collaboration, and service to others; empowerment of the disenfranchised; or innovation and education. A teacher or professor at the school or college who is a member of the California Teachers Association (CTA) must sponsor the work; each member may sponsor up to 5 entries.
Financial data: Awards are $1,000.
Duration: This competition is held annually.
Number awarded: Varies each year; recently, 63 of these awards were presented: 38 for visual arts and 25 for written essays.
Deadline: January of each year.

1204 CALIFORNIA RESTAURANT ASSOCIATION EDUCATIONAL FOUNDATION SCHOLARSHIPS FOR HIGH SCHOOL SENIORS

California Restaurant Association
Attn: CRAEF Scholarship Program
621 Capitol Mall, Suite 2000
Sacramento, CA 95814
Phone: (916) 447-5793; (800) 765-4842; Fax: (916) 447-6182
Email: craefinfo@calrest.org
Web: www.calrest.org/go/CRA/educational-foundation/scholarship-program

Summary: To provide financial assistance to California high school seniors planning to enroll in a postsecondary culinary program.
Eligibility: Open to high school seniors in California who have been accepted as a full-time student at a college or university (may be in any state) in a culinary program. Applicants must be U.S. citizens or permanent residents who have been employed at least 250 hours in a hospitality-related field. They must have a GPA of 2.75 or higher. Along with their application, they must submit essays on 1) why they think they should receive this scholarship; and 2) the experience or person that most influenced them in selecting restaurant and food service as their career. Selection is based on the essays, presentation of the application, GPA, industry-related work experience, and a personal interview.
Financial data: The stipend is $2,000.
Duration: 1 year.
Number awarded: Varies each year.
Deadline: April of each year.

1205 CALIFORNIA RESTAURANT ASSOCIATION EDUCATIONAL FOUNDATION SCHOLARSHIPS FOR UNDERGRADUATE STUDENTS

California Restaurant Association
Attn: CRAEF Scholarship Program
621 Capitol Mall, Suite 2000
Sacramento, CA 95814
Phone: (916) 447-5793; (800) 765-4842; Fax: (916) 447-6182
Email: craefinfo@calrest.org
Web: www.calrest.org/go/CRA/educational-foundation/scholarship-program

Summary: To provide financial assistance to California residents enrolled in a postsecondary culinary program at a school in any state.
Eligibility: Open to residents of California who are currently enrolled full-time in a college or university (may be in any state) in a culinary program. Applicants must have completed at least 1 academic term and have a GPA of 2.75 or higher. Freshmen entering their sophomore year must have been employed at least 400

hours in a hospitality-related field; students beyond the freshman year must have completed at least 550 hours of industry-related work experience. Along with their application, they must submit essays on 1) how their education will help them achieve their career objectives and future goals; and 2) a challenging situation or experience related to the restaurant and food service industry that demonstrates their ability to overcome adversity. Selection is based on the essays, presentation of the application, GPA, industry-related work experience, and a personal interview. U.S. citizenship or permanent resident status is required.

Financial data: The stipend is $2,000 per year.

Duration: 1 year; recipients may reapply.

Number awarded: Varies each year.

Deadline: April of each year.

1206 CALIFORNIA STATE FAIR ARTS SCHOLARSHIPS

California State Fair
Attn: Friends of the Fair Scholarship Program
1600 Exposition Boulevard
P.O. Box 15649
Sacramento, CA 95852
Phone: (916) 263-3149
Email: entryoffice@calexpo.com
Web: www.bigfun.org/competition-youth.php

Summary: To provide financial assistance to residents of California who are studying the arts at a college in the state.

Eligibility: Open to residents of California currently working on an undergraduate degree at a college or university in the state. Applicants must be studying the arts (e.g., visual arts, dance, music, film). They must have a GPA of 3.0 or higher. Along with their application, they must submit an essay of 2 to 3 pages indicating why they are pursuing their desired career and life goals and describing their involvement in community and volunteer service. Selection is based on personal commitment, goals established for their chosen field, leadership potential, and civic accomplishments.

Financial data: Stipends are $1,000 or $500.

Duration: 1 year.

Number awarded: 2 each year: 1 at $1,000 and 1 at $500.

Deadline: March of each year.

1207 CALIFORNIA STATE FAIR CULINARY COOKING AND HOSPITALITY MANAGEMENT SCHOLARSHIPS

California State Fair
Attn: Friends of the Fair Scholarship Program
1600 Exposition Boulevard
P.O. Box 15649
Sacramento, CA 95852
Phone: (916) 263-3149
Email: entryoffice@calexpo.com
Web: www.bigfun.org/competition-youth.php

Summary: To provide financial assistance to residents of California who are studying or planning to study culinary cooking or hospitality management at a college or university in the state.

Eligibility: Open to residents of California who are enrolled or planning to enroll in a culinary cooking or hospitality management program at a 4-year college or university, culinary specialty school, or community college in the state. Applicants must have a GPA of 3.0 or higher. Along with their application, they must submit an essay of 2 to 3 pages indicating why they are pursuing their desired career and life goals and describing their involvement in community and volunteer service. Selection is based on personal commitment, goals established for their chosen field, leadership potential, and civic accomplishments.

Financial data: Stipends are $1,250 or $750.

Duration: 1 year.

Number awarded: 2 each year: 1 at $1,250 and 1 at $750.

Deadline: March of each year.

1208 CALL TO SERVICE COLLEGIATE COMPETITION

National Association of Broadcasters
Attn: Education Foundation
1771 N Street, N.W.
Washington, DC 20036-2891
Phone: (202) 429-5424; Fax: (202) 429-4199
Email: rsultana@nab.org
Web: www.nabef.org/initiatives/callToService.asp

Summary: To recognize and reward, with scholarships for additional study, communications students who develop outstanding community service projects in partnership with a local charity.

Eligibility: Open to students enrolled at colleges and universities who have a major or minor in communications and at least 1 semester remaining before graduation. Applicants must submit a proposal describing a service project and execution plan that they have developed in partnership with a charity being served. They may work in pairs or in teams of up to 10 students. Along with their application, they must submit a description of the proposed service project and how it will serve their community, the charity with which they have chosen to work and why, the steps they have to take to complete the project in 45 days, a local television or radio station with which they might wish to partner, and what they hope to accomplish with their service project. Selection is based on creativity, community involvement, and use of technology and journalism to complete the project.

Financial data: Awards are a $10,000 scholarship for first place, a $5,000 scholarship for second, and a $2,000 scholarship for third. Funds are paid directly to the winners' institutions. Awards are divided among participants according to instructions given by a faculty sponsor. The charities with which the winning students participate receive donations of matching amounts.

Duration: The competition is held annually.

Number awarded: 3 winners are selected each year.

Deadline: February of each year.

1209 CANE CERTIFICATION SCHOLARSHIP

Classical Association of New England
c/o Katy Ganino Reddick, Chair, Committee on Scholarships
Strong Middle School
191 Main Street
Durham, CT 06422-2108
Phone: (860) 349-7222; Fax: (860) 349-7225
Email: kreddick@rsd13.org
Web: www.caneweb.org

Summary: To provide financial assistance to upper-division and graduate students in New England who are working on certification as a teacher of Latin or Greek.

Eligibility: Open to junior and senior undergraduates at colleges and universities in New England and to holders of master's degrees. Applicants must be preparing for secondary school certification as a teacher of Latin or Greek or both in a New England state. Full-time, part-time, and summer programs qualify. Along with their application, they must submit 2 letters of recommendation from college classicists, a letter attesting to their ability to communicate and work with young people and inspire them to high levels of achievement, a 1,000-word personal statement explaining why they are preparing for a career as a pre-collegiate classicist, college transcripts, and a description of their program and the expenses involved.

Financial data: The stipend is $1,500. Funds are intended to cover tuition and fees.

Duration: 1 year or summer session.

Number awarded: 1 each year.

Deadline: January of each year.

1210 CAP LATHROP ENDOWMENT SCHOLARSHIP FUND

Cook Inlet Region, Inc.
Attn: The CIRI Foundation
3600 San Jeronimo Drive, Suite 256
Anchorage, AK 99508-2870
Phone: (907) 793-3575; (800) 764-3382; Fax: (907) 793-3585
Email: tcf@thecirifoundation.org
Web: www.thecirifoundation.org/designated.htm

Summary: To provide financial assistance for undergraduate or graduate studies in media-related fields to Alaska Natives and their lineal descendants.

Eligibility: Open to Alaska Native enrollees under the Alaska Native Claims Settlement Act (ANCSA) of 1971 and their lineal descendants. Proof of eligibility must be submitted. Applicants may be enrollees of any of the 13 ANCSA regional corporations, but preference is given to original enrollees/descendants of Cook Inlet Region, Inc. (CIRI) who have a GPA of 3.0 or higher. There are no Alaska residency requirements or age limitations. Applicants must be accepted or enrolled full-time in a 2-year undergraduate, 4-year undergraduate, or graduate degree program. They must be majoring in a media-related field (e.g., telecommunications, broadcast, business, engineering, journalism) and planning to work in the telecommunications or broadcast industry in Alaska after graduation. Along with their application, they must submit a 500-word statement on their educational and career goals and how they are contributing, or planning

to contribute, to a positive Alaska Native community. Selection is based on that statement, academic achievement, rigor of course work or degree program, student financial contribution, financial need, grade level, previous work performance, community service, and relationship of degree program to career goals.
Financial data: The stipend is $3,500 per year. Funds must be used for tuition, university fees, books, required class supplies, and campus housing and meal plans for students who must live away from their permanent home to attend college. Checks are sent directly to the recipient's school.
Duration: 1 year (2 semesters).
Number awarded: 1 each year.
Deadline: May of each year.

1211 CAROLE SIMPSON RTDNF SCHOLARSHIP

Radio Television Digital News Foundation
Attn: RTDNF Fellowship Program
4121 Plank Road, Suite 512
Fredericksburg, VA 22407
Phone: (202) 467-5214; Fax: (202) 223-4007
Email: staceys@rtdna.org
Web: www.rtdna.org/pages/education/undergraduates.php
Summary: To provide financial assistance to minority undergraduate students who are interested in preparing for a career in electronic journalism.
Eligibility: Open to sophomore or more advanced minority undergraduate students enrolled in an electronic journalism sequence at an accredited or nationally-recognized college or university. Applicants must submit 1 to 3 examples of their journalistic skills on audio CD or DVD (no more than 15 minutes total, accompanied by scripts); a description of their role on each story and a list of who worked on each story and what they did; a 1-page statement explaining why they are preparing for a career in electronic journalism with reference to their specific career preference (radio, television, online, reporting, producing, or newsroom management); a resume; and a letter of reference from their dean or faculty sponsor explaining why they are a good candidate for the award and certifying that they have at least 1 year of school remaining.
Financial data: The stipend is $2,000, paid in semiannual installments of $1,000 each.
Duration: 1 year.
Number awarded: 1 each year.
Deadline: May of each year.

1212 CARY HERZ SCHOLARSHIP

New Mexico Press Women
c/o Laurie Mellas, Scholarship Chair
3939 Rio Grande Boulevard, N.W., Casita 53
Albuquerque, NM 87107
Phone: (505) 277-5915
Email: lmellas@unm.edu
Web: newmexicopresswomen.org
Summary: To provide financial assistance to residents of New Mexico who are majoring in photojournalism at a school in the state.
Eligibility: Open to residents of New Mexico who are majoring in photojournalism at a college or university in the state. Applicants must submit 3 samples of their work, a letter of recommendation, and a 500-word description of their career goals and plans and why they are applying for this scholarship. Selection is based primarily on career potential and financial need, although academic standing is also considered.
Financial data: The stipend is $2,000.
Duration: 1 year.
Number awarded: 1 each year.
Deadline: March of each year.

1213 CASE STUDY COMPETITION IN CORPORATE COMMUNICATIONS

Institute for Public Relations
c/o University of Florida
2096 Weimer Hall
P.O. Box 118400
Gainesville, FL 32611-8400
Phone: (352) 392-0280; Fax: (352) 846-1122
Web: www.instituteforpr.com/awards/case_study_competition
Summary: To recognize and reward undergraduate and graduate students in business, communications, or journalism who win a competition in public relations.
Eligibility: Open to undergraduate and graduate students enrolled at accredited schools of business, communications, or journalism. Students may participate as sole authors or members of a case-writing team (not to exceed 4 people). Each student author or case-writing team must be sponsored by a faculty member. Applicants must submit a case study on a topic within the field of corporate communication or public relations, including but not limited to communication strategy, crisis communication, issues management, government relations, integrated marketing communications, internal or employee communications, investor relations, media relations, issues involving use of technology, or reputation management. Cases should clearly describe a business problem, not the solutions to the problem. They must be accompanied by a teaching note. Selection is based on the significance of the business problem and the critical issues identified on the entry (20 points); factual and accurate nature of the entry (20 points); decisions and evaluations to be made (15 points); entry's style, tone, and quality of expression (15 points); balance, fairness, and absence of bias in the entry (15 points); and quality of the teaching note (15 points). Separate competitions are held for business schools and for communications and journalism schools.
Financial data: The prizes for submissions from business schools and from communications and journalism schools are $2,500 for first, $1,500 for second, and $800 for third. The faculty adviser for the first-place winners receives $650, for the second-place winners $350, and for the third-place winners $200. The grand prize is $5,000 for the student(s) and $1,500 for the faculty adviser.
Duration: The competition is held annually.
Number awarded: 6 winners are selected each year (3 from business schools and 3 from communications and journalism schools). From those, 1 is selected as the grand prize winner.
Deadline: Entries must be submitted by January of each year.

1214 CHAPEL OF FOUR CHAPLAINS NATIONAL ART SCHOLARSHIP CONTEST

Chapel of Four Chaplains
Naval Business Center, Building 649
1201 Constitution Avenue
Philadelphia, PA 19112-1307
Phone: (215) 218-1943; (866) 400-0975; Fax: (215) 218-1949
Email: chapel@fourchaplains.org
Web: www.fourchaplains.org/programs.html
Summary: To recognize and reward, with college scholarships, high school seniors who submit outstanding works of art on a topic related to public service.
Eligibility: Open to seniors at public and private high schools. Students are invited to submit any form of flat art (except photography) on a theme that changes annually; recently, students were invited to depict a compelling problem, need, or unresolved conflict (e.g., racial discrimination, religious intolerance, community injustice, public indifference, civic discord, societal ignorance) that, through caring intervention, demonstrates the high ideals of unity without uniformity. They are encouraged to capture the spirit of the theme in whatever manner they wish, through representational, stylized, or abstract means of expression. The medium may be watercolor, crayon, tempera, collage, pen and ink, or computer art. The maximum size is 24" x 30". The artwork should not contain any wording, including slogans, descriptions, narrative, or dialogue balloons. Selection is based on originality, meaning, and imaginative creativity.
Financial data: First prize is a $1,000 scholarship, second a $750 scholarship, and third a $500 scholarship.
Duration: The competition is held annually.
Number awarded: 3 each year.
Deadline: December of each year.

1215 CHARLES AND LUCILLE KING FAMILY FOUNDATION UNDERGRADUATE SCHOLARSHIPS

Charles and Lucille King Family Foundation, Inc.
c/o Charles Brucia & Co.
1212 Avenue of the Americas, Seventh Floor
New York, NY 10036
Phone: (212) 682-2913
Email: KingScholarships@aol.com
Web: www.kingfoundation.org
Summary: To provide financial assistance to undergraduate students who are majoring in television or film.
Eligibility: Open to full-time students who are entering their junior or senior year at a 4-year U.S. college or university and majoring in television or film. U.S. citizenship is not required. Applicants must submit a 2-page personal statement that describes their goals and why they feel that furthering their education will

help them accomplish those goals. Selection is based on academic excellence, professional potential, and financial need.
Financial data: Stipends range up to $3,500 per year.
Duration: 1 year; students who receive an award as a junior may renew the award in their senior year if they earn at least a 3.0 GPA.
Number awarded: Varies each year; recently, 14 of these scholarships were awarded.
Deadline: March of each year.

1216 CHARLES DUBOSE SCHOLARSHIP

Connecticut Architecture Foundation
Attn: Executive Vice President
370 James Street, Suite 402
New Haven, CT 06511
Phone: (203) 865-2195; Fax: (203) 562-5378
Email: aiainfo@aiact.org
Web: www.aiact.org/outreach/ctaf_scholarship.php
Summary: To provide financial assistance to Connecticut residents who are working on a bachelor's or master's degree in architecture at a school in any state.
Eligibility: Open to students who have completed at least 2 years of a bachelor of architecture program or have been accepted into an accredited graduate program. Connecticut residents are encouraged to apply. Applicants may be attending any college offering a 5-year accredited degree in architecture. Preference is given to students at the University of Pennsylvania, Georgia Institute of Technology, and the Fontainebleau summer program. Selection is based on academic record and financial need.
Financial data: Stipends range from $5,000 to $10,000.
Duration: 1 year; may be renewed.
Number awarded: 1 or 2 each year.
Deadline: April of each year.

1217 CHARLES M. SCHULZ AWARD FOR COLLEGE CARTOONISTS

Scripps Howard Foundation
Attn: Vice President, Programs
312 Walnut Street, 28th Floor
P.O. Box 5380
Cincinnati, OH 45201-5380
Phone: (513) 977-3030; (800) 888-3000, ext. 3030; Fax: (513) 977-3800
Email: sue.porter@scripps.com
Web: www.scripps.com/foundation/programs/nja/nja.html
Summary: To recognize and reward outstanding college cartoonists.
Eligibility: Open to student cartoonists at a college newspaper or magazine in the United States or its territories. Work must have been completed during the calendar year of the contest. Entries may be panels, strips, and/or editorial cartoons. Applicants must include a 250-word statement outlining their goals in cartooning.
Financial data: The award is $10,000 and a trophy.
Duration: The award is presented annually.
Number awarded: 1 each year.
Deadline: January of each year.

1218 CHOPIN FOUNDATION OF THE UNITED STATES SCHOLARSHIP PROGRAM FOR YOUNG PIANISTS

Chopin Foundation of the United States, Inc.
Attn: Scholarship Committee
1440 79th Street Causeway, Suite 117
Miami, FL 33141
Phone: (305) 868-0624; Fax: (305) 865-5150
Email: info@chopin.org
Web: www.chopin.org/ip.asp?op=Requirements&m=x0013000Scholarship
Summary: To recognize and reward (with scholarships) outstanding young American pianists who demonstrate "a special affinity for the interpretation of Chopin's music."
Eligibility: Open to any qualified American pianist (citizen or legal resident) between the ages of 14 and 17 whose field of study is music and whose major is piano. Enrollment at the secondary or undergraduate school level as a full-time student is required. Applicants must submit a formal application, along with a statement of career goals, a minimum of 2 references from piano teachers or performers, and a DVD of 20 to 30 minutes of Chopin's works. Each piece must be an unedited performance.
Financial data: The award is $1,000.
Duration: 1 year; renewable for up to 4 years, as long as the recipient continues to study piano, maintains satisfactory academic progress, and submits an annual audiocassette of unedited performances of designated works by Chopin for evaluation.
Number awarded: 8 each year.
Deadline: April of each year.

1219 CHRISTOPHER COLUMBUS ESSAY CONTEST

Daughters of the American Revolution–National Society
Attn: American History Committee
1776 D Street, N.W.
Washington, DC 20006-5303
Phone: (202) 628-1776
Email: historian@dar.org
Web: www.dar.org/natsociety/content.cfm?ID=320&FO=Y&hd=n
Summary: To recognize and reward high school students who submit essays on a topic related to Christopher Columbus.
Eligibility: Open to students in grades 9–12. Applicants must submit an essay, from 800 to 1,200 words, on a topic that changes annually but relates to Christopher Columbus. Recently, the topic was "What lessons from Christopher Columbus' life can we draw on today to bring clarity to our decisions in the face of an uncertain future?" Selection is based on historical accuracy, adherence to topic, organization of material, interest, originality, spelling, grammar, punctuation, and neatness. Competitions are held at the chapter, state, division, and then national level.
Financial data: The national winner receives an award of $1,200 and paid lodging and transportation for the winner and a parent to visit Washington, D.C. for the award ceremony. The national second-place winner receives $500 and the third-place winner receives $300.
Duration: The competition is held annually.
Number awarded: 3 national winners are selected each year.
Deadline: Each local chapter sets its own deadline; some are as early as November.

1220 CHRISTOPHERS POSTER CONTEST

The Christophers
Attn: Youth Department Coordinator
5 Hanover Square, 11th Floor
New York, NY 10004
Phone: (212) 759-4050; (888) 298-4050; Fax: (212) 838-5073
Email: youth@christophers.org
Web: www.christophers.org/Page.aspx?pid=274
Summary: To recognize and reward posters drawn by high school students that best illustrate the motto of The Christophers: "It's better to light one candle than to curse the darkness."
Eligibility: Open to all students in grades 9–12 who prepare posters on the theme: "You Can Make a Difference." The posters must be 15" x 20" and the original work of 1 student. Selection is based on overall impact, effectiveness in conveying the theme, originality, and artistic merit.
Financial data: First prize is $1,000, second prize is $500, third prize is $250, and honorable mentions are $100.
Duration: The competition is held annually.
Number awarded: 8 each year: 1 each for first, second, and third place plus 5 honorable mentions.
Deadline: January of each year.

1221 CHUCK FULGHAM SCHOLARSHIP

Dallas Foundation
Attn: Scholarship Administrator
900 Jackson Street, Suite 705
Dallas, TX 75202
Phone: (214) 741-9898; Fax: (214) 741-9848
Email: scholarships@dallasfoundation.org
Web: www.dallasfoundation.org/scholarship11.aspx?submenu=return
Summary: To provide financial assistance to adult students and high school seniors in Texas interested in studying the humanities at a college in any state.
Eligibility: Open to 1) adult graduates of a literacy program who need financial assistance to attend a regionally-accredited college or university; and 2) high school seniors who have not been successful in high school by traditional academic standards (must have a GPA below 3.0) but who have a genuine interest in literature and the humanities and show promise for achievement in college.

Applicants must be Texas residents and able to demonstrate financial need; preference is given to applicants from Dallas County and to those who have participated in sports.
Financial data: The maximum stipend is $2,500. Funds are paid directly to the recipient's school.
Duration: 1 year; nonrenewable.
Number awarded: 1 or more each year.
Deadline: March of each year.

1222 CHURCHILL FAMILY SCHOLARSHIP FUND

Maine Community Foundation
Attn: Program Director
245 Main Street
Ellsworth, ME 04605
Phone: (207) 667-9735; (877) 700-6800; Fax: (207) 667-0447
Email: info@mainecf.org
Web: www.mainecf.org/statewidescholars.aspx
Summary: To provide financial assistance to female high school seniors in Maine who are interested in studying music or music education at a college in any state.
Eligibility: Open to women graduating from high schools in Maine. Applicants must be planning to attend a college in any state to work on a degree in vocal music education or performance.
Financial data: A stipend is awarded (amount not specified).
Duration: 1 year.
Number awarded: 1 or more each year.
Deadline: April of each year.

1223 CLARE JOHNSON MARLEY–MARY EARLE BERGER FINE ARTS SCHOLARSHIP

Alpha Delta Kappa–North Carolina Chapter
c/o Rebecca R. Meyst, President
351 North Peace Haven Road
Winston-Salem, NC 27104-2536
Summary: To provide financial assistance to high school seniors in North Carolina who plan to attend college in any state to major in an area of the fine arts.
Eligibility: Open to seniors graduating from high schools in North Carolina and planning to enroll at a 4-year college or university in any state to major in an area of the fine arts. Applicants must rank in the top 20% of their class and have scores of at least 1344 on the SAT or 20 on the ACT. Along with their application, they must submit a letter on their plans, career goals, and reasons for wanting this scholarship. They must also submit samples of their work (a 4- to 10-minute performance tape for music, a 4- to 10-minute performance CD or DVD for dance, 4 to 10 examples in more than 1 medium for visual art, a 4- to 10-minute CD or DVD for drama in which other performers may appear but the applicant's role must be primary). Selection is based on character, ability or talent in the fine arts, and participation in extracurricular activities; financial need is not considered.
Financial data: The stipend is $2,000.
Duration: 1 year; nonrenewable.
Number awarded: 1 each year.
Deadline: January of each year.

1224 CLAY TRIPLETTE SCHOLARSHIPS

James Beard Foundation Scholarship Program
c/o Scholarship Management Services
One Scholarship Way
P.O. Box 297
St. Peter, MN 56082
Phone: (507) 931-1682; (800) 537-4180; Fax: (507) 931-9168
Email: jamesbeard@scholarshipamerica.org
Web: sms.scholarshipamerica.org/jamesbeard
Summary: To provide financial assistance to high school seniors and graduates interested in attending culinary school to study baking or pastry studies.
Eligibility: Open to high school seniors planning to enroll and students already enrolled at least part-time at a licensed or accredited culinary school. Applicants must be planning to work on a degree in baking or pastry studies. Along with their application, they must submit 1) a brief statement or summary of their plans as they relate to their culinary, educational, and career goals; and 2) a 250-word essay on what they find most inspiring, impressive, or notable about James Beard's life and work in American cuisine. Selection is based on those essays, academic record, leadership and participation in school and community activities, work experience, unusual personal or family circumstances, an outside appraisal, and financial need.
Financial data: The stipend is $4,250 per year.
Duration: 1 year; awards are not renewable, but recipients may reapply.
Number awarded: 4 each year.
Deadline: May of each year.

1225 CLETE ROBERTS MEMORIAL JOURNALISM SCHOLARSHIP AWARD

Associated Press Television and Radio Association
c/o Jeff Wilson
AP Los Angeles
221 South Figueroa Street, Suite 300
Los Angeles, CA 90012
Phone: (213) 626-1200
Email: jcwilson@ap.org
Web: www.aptra.com/scholarship.asp
Summary: To provide financial assistance to students from any state who are enrolled at colleges and universities in designated western states and are interested in broadcast journalism careers.
Eligibility: Open to residents of any state currently enrolled at colleges and universities in Alaska, Arizona, California, Colorado, Hawaii, Idaho, Montana, Nevada, New Mexico, Utah, Washington, and Wyoming. Applicants must have a broadcast journalism career objective. Selection is based on a 500-word essay on why the students wish to pursue broadcast journalism; another 500-word essay on their honors, awards, and broadcast experience; 3 letters of recommendation; and a statement of how they are financing their education.
Financial data: The stipend is $1,500.
Duration: 1 year.
Number awarded: 1 each year.
Deadline: December of each year.

1226 COLBURN-PLEDGE MUSIC SCHOLARSHIP

Colburn-Pledge Music Scholarship Foundation
Attn: Secretary
6322 Cornplanter
San Antonio, TX 78238-1514
Summary: To provide financial assistance to Texas residents who are interested in studying classical music at a school in any state.
Eligibility: Open to residents of Texas at the pre-high school, high school, or college level. Applicants must be interested in studying a string instrument (violin, viola, cello, bass) in classical music with the intention of becoming a professional musician. They must be attending or planning to attend a college, music school, or music camp in any state. Financial need must be demonstrated, but selection is based primarily on musical talent.
Financial data: Stipends range up to $3,000.
Duration: 1 year.
Deadline: April of each year.

1227 COLLEGE PHOTOGRAPHER OF THE YEAR

National Press Photographers Foundation
c/o University of Missouri at Columbia
Attn: CPOY Director
109 Lee Hills Hall
Columbia, MO 65211
Phone: (573) 882-4442; Fax: (573) 884-4999
Email: info@cpoy.org
Web: www.cpoy.org
Summary: To recognize and reward the outstanding photojournalism work of undergraduate and graduate students.
Eligibility: Open to students currently working on an undergraduate or graduate degree. Applicants may submit work completed during the previous academic year in up to 16 different categories. Single picture categories are: 1) spot news; 2) general news; 3) feature; 4) sports action; 5) sports feature; 6) portrait; 7) pictorial; and 8) illustration. Multiple picture categories are: 9) domestic picture story; 10) international picture story; and 11) documentary. Portfolio categories are 12) sports portfolio; and 13) portfolio. Multimedia categories are 14) individual still image/audio story or essay; 15) individual video or mixed media photo story or essay; and 16) multimedia project. Professional photographers who have worked 2 years or more are not eligible.

Financial data: In the portfolio competition, the first-place winner receives a 14-week internship at *National Geographic Magazine* and the Colonel William J. Lookadoo Award of $1,000. The second-place winner receives the Milton Freier Award of $500. Winners in other categories receive equipment and additional educational opportunities.
Duration: The competition is held annually, in the fall.
Deadline: September of each year.

1228 CONNECTICUT ARCHITECTURE FOUNDATION SCHOLARSHIPS

Connecticut Architecture Foundation
Attn: Executive Vice President
370 James Street, Suite 402
New Haven, CT 06511
Phone: (203) 865-2195; Fax: (203) 562-5378
Email: aiainfo@aiact.org
Web: www.aiact.org/outreach/ctaf_scholarship.php
Summary: To provide financial assistance to Connecticut residents who are working on a bachelor's or master's degree in architecture at a school in any state.
Eligibility: Open to Connecticut residents who 1) have completed at least 2 years of an accredited bachelor of architecture program; 2) have been accepted to an accredited master's degree program in architecture (may be enrolled in a non-accredited undergraduate program); or 3) are enrolled in an accredited master's degree program in architecture. Applicants must be enrolled as full-time students. They must submit a 1-page letter describing their accomplishments and goals; a 1- to 2-page resume of education, experience, honors, activities, and interests; documentation of financial need; 2 faculty letters of reference; and a favorite project with their rationale for their design.
Financial data: Stipends range from $500 to $1,000.
Duration: 1 year.
Number awarded: Varies each year.
Deadline: April of each year.

1229 CONNECTICUT BROADCASTERS ASSOCIATION SCHOLARSHIPS

Connecticut Broadcasters Association
Attn: Scholarships
90 South Park Street
Willimantic, CT 06226
Phone: (860) 633-5031; Fax: (860) 456-5688
Email: mcrice@prodigy.net
Web: www.ctba.org/page.cfm?page=17
Summary: To provide financial assistance to Connecticut residents who are interested in attending college in any state to prepare for a career in broadcasting.
Eligibility: Open to Connecticut residents who are entering their first, second, third, or fourth year at a 2- or 4-year college, university, or technical school in any state. Applicants must be majoring in broadcasting, communications, marketing, or a related field. Selection is based on academic achievement, community service, goals in the chosen field, and financial need.
Financial data: The stipend is $5,000.
Duration: 1 year.
Number awarded: Varies each year; recently, 7 of these scholarships were awarded.
Deadline: March of each year.

1230 COPY EDITING SCHOLARSHIPS

American Copy Editors Society
Attn: Carol DeMasters, ACES Administrator
7 Avenida Vista Grande, Suite B7 467
Santa Fe, MN 87508
Email: carolafj@execpc.com
Web: www.copydesk.org/edfund/index.php
Summary: To provide financial assistance to undergraduate and graduate students interested in becoming copy editors.
Eligibility: Open to college juniors, seniors, and graduate students who are interested in a career as a copy editor. Graduating students who will take full-time jobs or internships as copy editors are also eligible. Applicants must submit 1) a list of course work relevant to copy editing they have completed; 2) information on their copy editing experience, including work on student and professional newspapers; 3) an essay, up to 750 words, on what they think makes a good copy editor and why they want to prepare for that career; 4) 2 letters of recommendation; 5) 5 to 10 headlines they have written; and 6) a copy of a story they have edited, including an explanation of the changes they have made and the circumstances under which it was edited. Selection is based on commitment to copy editing as a career, work experience in copy editing, and abilities in copy editing. Financial need is not considered. The highest ranked applicant receives the Merv Aubespin Scholarship.
Financial data: Stipends are $2,500 (for the Merv Aubespin Scholarship) or $1,000.
Duration: 1 year.
Number awarded: 4 or 5 each year.
Deadline: November of each year.

1231 COURAGE IN STUDENT JOURNALISM AWARDS

Student Press Law Center
Attn: Executive Director
1101 Wilson Boulevard, Suite 1100
Arlington, VA 22209-2211
Phone: (703) 807-1904
Email: splc@splc.org
Web: www.splc.org/csjaward.asp
Summary: To recognize and reward secondary school student journalists and school officials who have supported the First Amendment.
Eligibility: Open to deserving middle school and high school student journalists and school officials who have stood up in support of the First Amendment. Student applicants must have shown determination, despite difficulty or resistance, in exercising their First Amendment press rights. School administrator applicants must have demonstrated support, under difficult circumstances, for the First Amendment press rights of their school's student media. Entrants should submit a written description (up to 600 words) of how their case meets the entry criteria, along with 2 letters of support and supporting materials or press clippings.
Financial data: The winners in each category (student and administrator) receive a $5,000 award.
Duration: The award is presented annually.
Number awarded: 2 each year: 1 student and 1 school official.
Deadline: June of each year.

1232 COURTLAND PAUL SCHOLARSHIP

Landscape Architecture Foundation
Attn: Scholarship Program
818 18th Street, N.W., Suite 810
Washington, DC 20006-3520
Phone: (202) 331-7070; Fax: (202) 331-7079
Email: scholarships@lafoundation.org
Web: www.laprofession.org/financial/scholarships.htm
Summary: To provide financial assistance to upper-division students working on a degree in landscape architecture.
Eligibility: Open to landscape architecture students in the final 2 years of undergraduate study. Applicants must be able to demonstrate financial need and a GPA of 2.0 or higher. Along with their application, they must submit a 500-word essay describing their aspirations, ability to surmount obstacles, high level of drive, and need for financial assistance. U.S. citizenship is required.
Financial data: The stipend is $5,000. Funds may be used only for tuition and books.
Duration: 1 year.
Number awarded: 1 each year.
Deadline: February of each year.

1233 CULINARY TRUST SCHOLARSHIPS

The Culinary Trust
P.O. Box 273
New York, NY 10013
Phone: (646) 224-6989; (888) 345-4666
Email: scholarships@theculinarytrust.com
Web: theculinarytrust.org/programs/scholarships-grants
Summary: To provide financial assistance to culinary professionals and students interested in pursuing additional training in the United States or abroad in the culinary arts.
Eligibility: Open to 1) culinary professionals who have at least 2 years of food service or related industry work experience; and 2) students who have a GPA of 3.0 or higher. Applicants may be from any country. They may apply in 1 or

more of 3 categories: 1) scholarships for culinary education; 2) scholarships for continuing education; or 3) grants for independent study and internships. Along with their application, they must submit a 2-page essay on their educational and career goals. Selection is based on that essay, awards and honors, volunteer activities and community service, 2 letters of recommendation, and financial need.
Financial data: Stipends range from $1,500 to $5,000.
Duration: 1 year.
Number awarded: Varies each year.
Deadline: February of each year.

1234 DAMARIS SMITH DESIMONE SCHOLARSHIP

Daughters of the American Revolution–New York State Organization
c/o Theresa Willemsen, Recording Secretary
1248 McKoons Road
Richfield Springs, NY 13438-4101
Email: sportster_harley@hotmail.com
Web: www.nydar.org/education.html
Summary: To provide financial assistance to high school seniors in New York who plan to study American history at a college in the state.
Eligibility: Open to seniors graduating from high schools in New York who plan to attend an accredited 4-year college or university in the state. Applicants must be intending to major in U.S. history. Selection is based on merit, including achievement in high school and the community and personal and academic interests.
Financial data: The stipend is $1,000.
Duration: 1 year; nonrenewable.
Number awarded: 1 each year.
Deadline: January of each year.

1235 DANCE SCHOLARSHIPS

Princess Grace Awards
Attn: Grants Coordinator
150 East 58th Street, 25th Floor
New York, NY 10155
Phone: (212) 317-1470; Fax: (212) 317-1473
Email: grants@pgfusa.com
Web: www.pgfusa.com
Summary: To provide financial support for college to students interested in dance.
Eligibility: Open to students who have completed at least 1 year of training at a professional, nonprofit school of dance in the United States and are seeking support for tuition. Candidates must be nominated by the dean or chair of the dance department; only 1 student may be nominated per institution. Individuals may not submit an application independently. Nominees are invited to send an application, an autobiography, an essay, a portfolio, and references. All nominees must be U.S. citizens or permanent residents. Students enrolled in dance education or a graduate program are not eligible. Selection is based on the candidates' past artistic merit, the significance of the award to their current artistic development, and the potential for future excellence and impact in the field.
Financial data: Stipends range from $5,000 to $25,000, depending upon tuition. No other expenses (e.g., room and board, materials, books, costumes) may be included.
Duration: Up to 1 year.
Number awarded: Varies each year; recently, 5 of these scholarships were awarded.
Deadline: April of each year.

1236 DAVID HAMILTON JACKSON GRANT

Virgin Islands Board of Education
Dronningen Gade 60B, 61, and 62
P.O. Box 11900
St. Thomas, VI 00801
Phone: (340) 774-4546; Fax: (340) 774-3384
Email: stt@myviboe.com
Web: www.myviboe.com
Summary: To provide financial assistance to residents of the Virgin Islands who wish to study labor relations or journalism at a college in the territory or on the mainland.
Eligibility: Open to residents of the Virgin Islands who are seniors or graduates of high schools in the territory. Applicants must have a GPA of 2.0 or higher and be attending or accepted for enrollment at an accredited institution of higher learning in the territory or on the mainland. They must be planning to major in labor relations or journalism. Financial need is considered in the selection process.
Financial data: The stipend is $1,000 per semester.
Duration: 1 semester; may be renewed up to 7 additional semesters.
Number awarded: 1 each year.
Deadline: April of each year.

1237 DAVID L. STASHOWER VISIONARY SCHOLARSHIPS

Liggett-Stashower, Inc.
Attn: Scholarship Award Committee
1240 Huron Road
Cleveland, OH 44115
Phone: (216) 348-8500
Email: bstolarski@liggett.com
Web: www.liggett.com/careers/dls-scholarship
Summary: To provide financial assistance to students at colleges and universities in Ohio who are majoring in fields related to communications.
Eligibility: Open to students entering their senior year at colleges and universities in Ohio. Applicants must be majoring in advertising, graphic design, public relations, or communications. Selection is based on academic achievement, faculty recommendations, and documentation of work (portfolio, writing samples, or other form of communication the applicant considers appropriate). Financial need is not considered.
Financial data: The stipend is $2,000.
Duration: 1 year; nonrenewable.
Number awarded: 2 each year.
Deadline: April of each year.

1238 DAVID L. WOLPER STUDENT DOCUMENTARY ACHIEVEMENT AWARD

International Documentary Association
1201 West Fifth Street, Suite M270
Los Angeles, CA 90017-2029
Phone: (213) 534-3600; Fax: (213) 534-3610
Email: programming@documentary.org
Web: www.documentary.org
Summary: To recognize and reward outstanding documentaries produced by college students.
Eligibility: Open to full-time college students. Applicants must submit (on 5 DVDs) a nonfiction film or video. Selection is based on overall creative excellence.
Financial data: The prize is a $1,000 honorarium, a $1,000 certificate toward the purchase of motion picture film (courtesy of the Eastman Kodak Company), and production of 1,000 DVDs (courtesy of Magic Rock Entertainment).
Duration: The competition is held annually, in the fall.
Deadline: The early, regular, and late deadlines are in June of each year. The final deadline is in July.

1239 DAVID S. BARR AWARDS

Newspaper Guild–CWA
501 Third Street, N.W., Sixth Floor
Washington, DC 20001-2797
Phone: (202) 434-7177; Fax: (202) 434-1472
Email: guild@cwa-union.org
Web: www.newsguild.org/index.php?ID=988
Summary: To recognize and reward student journalists whose work has helped to promote social justice.
Eligibility: Open to high school students (including those enrolled in vocational, technical, or special education programs) and part- and full-time college students (including those in community colleges and in graduate programs). Applicants must submit work published or broadcast during the preceding calendar year; entries should help to right a wrong, correct an injustice, or promote justice and fairness.
Financial data: The award is $1,500 for college students or $500 for high school students.
Duration: The awards are presented annually.
Number awarded: 2 each year.
Deadline: January of each year.

1240 DAVID W. MILLER AWARD FOR STUDENT JOURNALISTS

Chronicle of Higher Education
Attn: Deputy Managing Editor
1255 23rd Street, N.W.
Washington, DC 20037
Phone: (202) 466-1000; Fax: (202) 452-1033
Email: milleraward@chronicle.com
Web: http://chronicle.com/article/Stanford-Graduate-Wins/66269/

Summary: To recognize and reward college journalists who work as interns at *The Chronicle of Higher Education* and contribute outstanding articles to the journal.

Eligibility: Open to undergraduate students from any country who serve as interns at *The Chronicle of Higher Education* and submit 3 articles that they wrote and were published in the journal during their internship. Each piece should be journalistic, using expository, explanatory, narrative, or other techniques to report evenhandedly on a topic of intellectual interest.

Financial data: The award is $1,000.

Duration: The award is presented 3 times each year.

Number awarded: 3 each year.

Deadline: June of each year.

1241 DENDEL SCHOLARSHIPS

Handweavers Guild of America, Inc.
Attn: Scholarship Committee
1255 Buford Highway, Suite 211
Suwanee, GA 30024
Phone: (678) 730-0010; Fax: (678) 730-0836
Email: hga@weavespindye.org
Web: www.weavespindye.org/pages/?p=hgaschol.htm&loc=1-48-00

Summary: To provide financial assistance to undergraduate and graduate students working on a degree in the field of fiber arts.

Eligibility: Open to undergraduate and graduate students enrolled in accredited colleges and universities in the United States, its possessions, and Canada. Applicants must be working on a degree in the field of fiber arts, including training for research, textile history, and conservation. Along with their application, they must submit 1) a 50-word essay on their study goals and how those fit into their future plans; and 2) 5 to 16 slides of their work. Selection is based on artistic and technical merit; financial need is not considered.

Financial data: The stipend ranges up to $1,000. Recipients may use the funds for tuition, materials (e.g., film for photographs), or travel.

Duration: Funds must be spent within 1 year.

Number awarded: 1 each year.

Deadline: March of each year.

1242 DICK LARSEN SCHOLARSHIP

Washington News Council
Attn: Scholarship Committee
P.O. Box 3672
Seattle, WA 98124-3672
Phone: (206) 262-9793; Fax: (206) 464-7902
Email: info@wanewscouncil.org
Web: www.wanewscouncil.org

Summary: To provide financial assistance to Washington college students who are majoring in a communication-related field at an academic institution in the state.

Eligibility: Open to graduates of high schools in Washington who have a serious interest in communications, including journalism, politics, public relations, or related fields. Applicants must be enrolled at a 4-year public or private university in the state. Along with their application, they must submit a 750-word essay on a topic that changes annually; recently, students were asked to write on whether the expectations of journalists that other institutions should be transparent, accountable, and open also apply to them. Selection is based on that essay, academic achievement, and financial need.

Financial data: The stipend is $2,000.

Duration: 1 year.

Number awarded: 1 each year.

Deadline: April of each year.

1243 DONALD P. DUROCHER MEMORIAL SCHOLARSHIP

Public Relations Society of America–Detroit Chapter
Attn: Executive Secretary
1824 Grieg
Madison Heights, MI 48071
Phone: (248) 545-6499; Fax: (248) 545-4944
Email: nskidmore@earthlink.net
Web: www.prsadetroit.org/index.php?s=16

Summary: To provide financial assistance to students from any state majoring in fields related to public relations at universities in Michigan.

Eligibility: Open to residents of any state currently enrolled at universities in Michigan. Applicants must be majoring in public relations, journalism, communications, or a related field. They must submit written answers to 6 questions related to public relations and be available for an interview.

Financial data: The stipend is $2,000.

Duration: 1 year.

Number awarded: 2 each year.

Deadline: October of each year.

1244 DONG SUNG SUH SCHOLARSHIP

Philip Jaisohn Memorial Foundation
Attn: Education and Scholarship Committee
6705 Old York Road
Philadelphia, PA 19126
Phone: (215) 224-2000; Fax: (215) 224-9164
Email: jaisohnhouse@gmail.com or jaisohnfoundation@gmail.com
Web: www.jaisohn.org/

Summary: To provide financial assistance to Korean American undergraduate and graduate students who are working on a degree in journalism.

Eligibility: Open to Korean American undergraduate and graduate students who are currently enrolled at a college or university in the United States. Applicants must be working on a degree in journalism. They must be able to demonstrate academic excellence, leadership and service to their school and community, and financial need. Along with their application, they must submit an essay on either "Who is Dr. Jaisohn to Me" or "The Significance of Dr. Jaisohn's Ideal to Korean Americans." They must also submit a brief statement on how they can contribute to and be involved in the activities of the Philip Jaisohn Memorial Foundation.

Financial data: The stipend is $1,000.

Duration: 1 year.

Number awarded: 1 each year.

Deadline: November of each year.

1245 DOROTHY DYER VANEK ENDOWMENT SCHOLARSHIP

Epsilon Sigma Alpha International
Attn: ESA Foundation
P.O. Box 270517
Fort Collins, CO 80527
Phone: (970) 223-2824; Fax: (970) 223-4456
Email: esainfo@esaintl.com
Web: www.esaintl.com/esaf

Summary: To provide financial assistance to students from any state interested in majoring in architecture or interior design in college.

Eligibility: Open to students who are 1) graduating high school seniors with a GPA of 3.0 to 3.5 or with minimum scores of 22 on the ACT or 1030 on the combined critical reading and mathematics SAT; 2) enrolled in college with a GPA of 3.0 to 3.5; 3) enrolled at a technical school or returning to school after an absence for retraining of job skills or obtaining a degree; or 4) engaged in online study through an accredited college, university, or vocational school. Applicants may be attending or planning to attend an accredited school in any state and major in architecture or interior design. Selection is based on character (20%), leadership (20%), service (20%), financial need (20%), and scholastic ability (20%).

Financial data: The stipend is $1,000.

Duration: 1 year; may be renewed.

Number awarded: 1 each year.

Deadline: January of each year.

1246 DR. ALMA S. ADAMS SCHOLARSHIP

American Legacy Foundation
1724 Massachusetts Avenue, N.W.
Washington, DC 20036

Phone: (202) 454-5920; Fax: (202) 454-5775
Email: adamsscholarship@americanlegacy.org
Web: www.americanlegacy.org/adams-scholarship.aspx

Summary: To provide financial assistance to undergraduate or graduate students who have engaged in community service or visual arts activities to reduce smoking in communities designated as especially vulnerable to the tobacco industry.

Eligibility: Open to students entering or enrolled in college or graduate school and working on a degree in public health, education, social work, health communications, or other field related to reducing tobacco use. Applicants must be able to demonstrate experience working in an underserved community (Native American, Alaska Native, Hispanic, African American, Asian/Pacific Islander, low socioeconomic status, or lesbian, gay, bisexual, and transgender) that the sponsor has identified as disproportionately targeted by the tobacco industry or who often lack the tools and resources to combat smoking in their communities. Along with their application, they must submit 1) an essay of 500 to 600 words on their career aspirations, experience working in an underserved community to raise awareness of the harmful effects of commercial tobacco and other drug use, academic background, extracurricular activities, and leadership strengths; 2) a sample of their originally developed health communication material aimed at conveying a health message or raising community awareness of the harmful effects of tobacco or other drugs (e.g., poetry, essays, lyrics, scripts, sketches for murals or paintings, recordings for musical scores or dance performances); 3) copies of all college transcripts (or high school transcripts for high school seniors); 4) 2 letters of recommendation; and 5) information on financial need.

Financial data: A total of $10,000 is available for this program annually.

Duration: 1 year.

Number awarded: Up to 2 each year.

Deadline: April of each year.

1247 DR. AURA-LEE A. AND JAMES HOBBS PITTENGER AMERICAN HISTORY SCHOLARSHIP

Daughters of the American Revolution–National Society
Attn: Committee Services Office, Scholarships
1776 D Street, N.W.
Washington, DC 20006-5303
Phone: (202) 628-1776
Web: www.dar.org/natsociety/edout_scholar.cfm

Summary: To provide financial assistance to high school seniors planning to major in American history or government in college.

Eligibility: Open to graduating high school seniors who plan to major in American history or government. Applicants must be sponsored by a local chapter of the Daughters of the American Revolution (DAR). Judging first takes place at the state level; 2 state winners then enter the national competition. Selection is based on academic excellence, commitment to field of study, and financial need. U.S. citizenship is required.

Financial data: The stipend is $2,000 per year.

Duration: 4 years.

Number awarded: 1 each year.

Deadline: February of each year.

1248 DR. CHESTER A. MCPHEETERS SCHOLARSHIP

United Methodist Higher Education Foundation
Attn: Scholarships Administrator
1001 19th Avenue South
P.O. Box 340005
Nashville, TN 37203-0005
Phone: (615) 340-7385; (800) 811-8110; Fax: (615) 340-7330
Email: umhefscholarships@gbhem.org
Web: www.umhef.org/receive.php?id=endowed_funds

Summary: To provide financial assistance to undergraduate and graduate Methodist students who are preparing for ministry.

Eligibility: Open to full-time undergraduate and graduate students who are preparing for a career as a minister in the United Methodist Church. Applicants must have been active, full members of a United Methodist Church for at least 1 year prior to applying and be attending or planning to attend a seminary or theological school affiliated with that denomination. They must have a GPA of 3.0 or higher and be able to demonstrate financial need. Along with their application, they must submit a 200-word essay on their involvement and/or leadership responsibilities in their church, school, and community within the last 3 years. U.S. citizenship or permanent resident status is required.

Financial data: The stipend is at least $1,000 per year.

Duration: 1 year; recipients may reapply.

Number awarded: Varies each year; recently, 4 of these scholarships were awarded.

Deadline: May of each year.

1249 DR. JULIANNE MALVEAUX SCHOLARSHIP

National Association of Negro Business and Professional Women's Clubs
Attn: Scholarship Committee
1806 New Hampshire Avenue, N.W.
Washington, DC 20009-3206
Phone: (202) 483-4206; Fax: (202) 462-7253
Email: education@nanbpwc.org
Web: www.nanbpwc.org/ScholarshipApplications.asp

Summary: To provide financial assistance to African American women studying journalism, economics, or a related field in college.

Eligibility: Open to African American women enrolled at an accredited college or university as a sophomore or junior. Applicants must have a GPA of 3.0 or higher and be majoring in journalism, economics, or a related field. Along with their application, they must submit an essay, up to 1,000 words in length, on their career plans and their relevance to the theme of the program, "Black Women's Hands Can Rock the World." U.S. citizenship is required.

Financial data: The stipend is $1,000.

Duration: 1 year.

Number awarded: 1 or more each year.

Deadline: February of each year.

1250 DR. WALTER W. RISTOW PRIZE

Washington Map Society
c/o John Docktor
3100 North Highway A1A PHA 1
Fort Pierce, FL 34949-8831
Email: washmap@earthlink.net
Web: home.earthlink.net/~docktor/ristow.htm

Summary: To recognize and reward outstanding papers on cartographic history by students at all levels at universities in any country.

Eligibility: Open to full- and part-time undergraduate, graduate, and first-year postdoctoral students attending accredited colleges and universities anywhere in the world. Applicants must submit research papers that relate to the history of cartography. In the case of undergraduate and graduate students, the entries must have been completed in fulfillment of requirements for course work. A short edition of a longer paper is permitted, but the text may not exceed 7,500 words. All entries must be in English. Papers must be fully documented, in a style of the author's choice. Entries are judged on the importance of the research, the quality of the research, and the quality of writing.

Financial data: The prize is $1,000 and membership in the society.

Duration: The prize is offered annually.

Number awarded: 1 or 2 each year.

Deadline: May of each year.

1251 E. LANIER (LANNY) FINCH SCHOLARSHIP

Georgia Association of Broadcasters, Inc.
Attn: Scholarship Committee
8010 Roswell Road, Suite 150
Atlanta, GA 30350
Phone: (770) 395-7200; (877) 395-7200 (within GA); Fax: (770) 395-7235
Web: www.gab.org

Summary: To provide financial assistance to students in Georgia interested in preparing for a career in broadcasting.

Eligibility: Open to residents of Georgia who are full-time juniors or seniors studying broadcasting at a college, professional school, or university in the state. Applicants must submit brief essays on the specific area of broadcasting that interests them most and why, what they think is the broadcaster's primary responsibility, and the most important facts that the judges should know about them. Selection is based on academic records, extracurricular activities, community involvement, and leadership potential.

Financial data: The stipend is $1,500. Funds are paid directly to the recipient's institution.

Duration: 1 year.

Number awarded: 3 each year.

Deadline: April of each year.

1252 EASTMAN SCHOLARSHIP PROGRAM

University Film and Video Foundation
c/o Michele DeLano
343 State Street
Rochester, NY 14650-0315
Phone: (585) 724-6751
Email: michele.delano@kodak.com
Web: motion.kodak.com

Summary: To recognize and reward, with funding for payment of educational expenses and other products, undergraduate and graduate film students who submit outstanding samples of their work.

Eligibility: Open to students working on a bachelor's or master's degree in film, cinematography, or film production. Candidates must be enrolled full-time at a college or university in the United States, Canada, or a participating Latin American country. Each school may nominate up to 2 candidates. Nominees must submit samples of their work that communicate a story or theme in some fashion; clips or short vignettes are not acceptable. Selection is based on academic achievement, creative and technical ability, communications ability, and range of filmmaking experience.

Financial data: The Gold Prize includes $1,000 in cash (paid directly to the institution) and $5,000 in Kodak motion picture product; the Silver Prize is $4,000 in Kodak motion picture product; the Bronze Prize is $3,000 in Kodak motion picture product; and honorable mentions are $2,000 in Kodak motion picture product.

Duration: The competition is held annually.

Number awarded: 5 each year: 1 Gold Prize, 1 Silver Prize, 1 Bronze Prize, and 2 honorable mentions.

Deadline: Nominations must be submitted by June of each year.

1253 ED BRADLEY SCHOLARSHIP

Radio Television Digital News Foundation
Attn: RTDNF Fellowship Program
4121 Plank Road, Suite 512
Fredericksburg, VA 22407
Phone: (202) 467-5214; Fax: (202) 223-4007
Email: staceys@rtdna.org
Web: www.rtdna.org/pages/education/undergraduates.php

Summary: To provide financial assistance to minority undergraduate students who are preparing for a career in electronic journalism.

Eligibility: Open to sophomore or more advanced minority undergraduate students enrolled in an electronic journalism sequence at an accredited or nationally-recognized college or university. Applicants must submit 1 to 3 examples of their journalistic skills on audio CD or DVD (no more than 15 minutes total, accompanied by scripts); a description of their role on each story and a list of who worked on each story and what they did; a 1-page statement explaining why they are preparing for a career in electronic journalism with reference to their specific career preference (radio, television, online, reporting, producing, or newsroom management); a resume; and a letter of reference from their dean or faculty sponsor explaining why they are a good candidate for the award and certifying that they have at least 1 year of school remaining.

Financial data: The stipend is $10,000, paid in semiannual installments of $5,000 each.

Duration: 1 year.

Number awarded: 1 each year.

Deadline: May of each year.

1254 EDITH GAYLORD HARPER MEMORIAL SCHOLARSHIP

Oklahoma City Gridiron Foundation
330 North Country Club Terrace
Mustang, OK 73064
Web: www.okcgridiron.org

Summary: To provide financial assistance to journalism students in Oklahoma.

Eligibility: Open to residents of Oklahoma who are high school seniors or students already enrolled in college. Applicants must be working on or planning to work on a degree in journalism at a college or university in the state. Along with their application, they must submit brief statements on what they hope to be doing 6 months after completing college, what they hope to be doing 10 years from today, why they have selected journalism as their profession, what they like most about working in journalism, and what they like least. They must also submit a copy of their transcript and samples of their work. Financial need is considered in the selection process.

Financial data: The stipend is $2,000.

Duration: 1 year.

Number awarded: 1 each year.

Deadline: March of each year.

1255 EDSA MINORITY SCHOLARSHIP

Landscape Architecture Foundation
Attn: Scholarship Program
818 18th Street, N.W., Suite 810
Washington, DC 20006-3520
Phone: (202) 331-7070; Fax: (202) 331-7079
Email: scholarships@lafoundation.org
Web: www.laprofession.org/financial/scholarships.htm

Summary: To provide financial assistance to minority college students who are interested in studying landscape architecture.

Eligibility: Open to African American, Hispanic, Native American, and minority college students of other cultural and ethnic backgrounds. Applicants must be entering their final 2 years of undergraduate study in landscape architecture. Along with their application, they must submit a 500-word essay on a design or research effort they plan to pursue (explaining how it will contribute to the advancement of the profession and to their ethnic heritage), work samples, and 2 letters of recommendation. Selection is based on professional experience, community involvement, extracurricular activities, and financial need.

Financial data: The stipend is $3,500.

Number awarded: 1 each year.

Deadline: February of each year.

1256 EDSF BOARD OF DIRECTORS UPPER-DIVISION SCHOLARSHIPS

Electronic Document Systems Foundation
Attn: EDSF Scholarship Awards
1845 Precinct Line Road, Suite 212
Hurst, TX 76054
Phone: (817) 849-1145; Fax: (817) 849-1185
Email: info@edsf.org
Web: www.edsf.org/scholarships.cfm

Summary: To provide financial assistance to upper-division and graduate students interested in preparing for a career in document management and graphic communications.

Eligibility: Open to juniors, seniors, and graduate students who are committed to preparing for a career in document management and graphic communications, including marketing, graphic communications and arts, e-commerce, imaging science, printing, web authoring, electronic publishing, computer science, telecommunications, and/or business (e.g., sales, marketing). Applicants must be enrolled full-time at a college, university, or graduate school in the United States and have a GPA of 3.0 or higher. Along with their application, they must submit a statement of their career goals in the field of document management and graphic communications, an essay on a topic related to their view of the future of the document management and graphic communications industry, a list of current professional and college extracurricular activities and achievements, college transcripts, samples of their creative work, and 2 letters of recommendation. Financial need is not considered.

Financial data: The stipend ranges from $500 to $2,000.

Duration: 1 year.

Number awarded: Varies each year; recently, 34 of these scholarships were awarded: 1 at $2,000, 7 at $1,500, 25 at $1,000, and 1 at $500.

Deadline: April of each year.

1257 EDWARD J. NELL MEMORIAL SCHOLARSHIPS

Quill and Scroll
c/o University of Iowa
School of Journalism and Mass Communications
100 Adler Journalism Building, Room E346
Iowa City, IA 52242-2004
Phone: (319) 335-3457; Fax: (319) 335-3989
Email: quill-scroll@uiowa.edu
Web: www.uiowa.edu/~quill-sc/scholarships/nell.html

Summary: To provide financial assistance for college to high school journalists who are national winners of contests sponsored by Quill and Scroll (the international honor society for high school journalists).

Eligibility: Open to high school seniors who are winners in either of 2 contests conducted by Quill and Scroll for high school journalists: 1) the International Writing/Photography Contest, open to all high school students, with competitions in editorial, editorial cartoon, general columns, review columns, in-depth reporting (individual and team), news story, feature story, sports story, advertisement, and photography (news feature and sports); or 2) the Yearbook Excellence Contest, open to all Quill and Scroll charter high schools. In addition to being a winner of 1 of the contests, candidates for the scholarships must be planning to major in journalism or mass communications at a college or university in any state. Along with their application, they must submit 2 letters of recommendation, 3 examples of their journalistic work, and a 500-word personal statement on their journalistic experience, future plans, activities, honors, volunteer service, and how they plan to finance their college education.

Financial data: Stipends are either $1,500 or $500.

Duration: 1 year; nonrenewable.

Number awarded: 8 to 10 each year: 2 at $1,500 and 6 to 8 at $500.

Deadline: Entries in the International Writing/Photo Contest are due in February; entries in the Yearbook Excellence Contest must be submitted by the end of October. Scholarship applications must be submitted in May.

1258 ELECTRONIC DOCUMENT SYSTEMS FOUNDATION TECHNICAL AND COMMUNITY COLLEGE SCHOLARSHIP

Electronic Document Systems Foundation
Attn: EDSF Scholarship Awards
1845 Precinct Line Road, Suite 212
Hurst, TX 76054
Phone: (817) 849-1145; Fax: (817) 849-1185
Email: info@edsf.org
Web: www.edsf.org/scholarships.cfm

Summary: To provide financial assistance to students in technical schools and community colleges who are preparing for a career in the field of document management and graphic communications.

Eligibility: Open to first- and second-year students at technical and trade schools and community colleges. Applicants must be working on a degree in the field of electronic document communications, including graphic communications, computer science, and multimedia, and have a GPA of 3.0 or higher. Along with their application, they must submit a statement of their career goals in the field of document management and graphic communications, an essay on a topic related to their view of the future of the document management and graphic communications industry, a list of current professional and college extracurricular activities and achievements, college transcripts, samples of their creative work, and 2 letters of recommendation. Financial need is not considered.

Financial data: The stipend is $1,000 or $500.

Duration: 1 year.

Number awarded: Varies each year; recently, 4 of these scholarships were awarded: 1 at $1,000 and 3 at $500.

Deadline: April of each year.

1259 ELIE WIESEL PRIZE IN ETHICS

Elie Wiesel Foundation for Humanity
Attn: Prize in Ethics
555 Madison Avenue, 20th Floor
New York, NY 10022
Phone: (212) 490-7788; Fax: (212) 490-6006
Email: info@eliewieselfoundation.org
Web: www.eliewieselfoundation.org/prizeinethics.aspx

Summary: To recognize and reward upper-division students who submit outstanding essays on a topic related to ethics.

Eligibility: Open to full-time juniors and seniors at accredited colleges and universities in the United States. Students must submit an essay, between 3,000 and 4,000 words in length, on a theme of their choice that involves ethical choices. They must have a faculty sponsor review their essay and sign their entry form. Readers look for adherence to guidelines, carefully proofread essays, observance of rules for standard English usage, thoroughly thought-out essays that remain tightly focused, clear articulation and genuine grappling with a moral dilemma, originality and imagination, eloquence of writing style, and intensity and unity in the essay.

Financial data: First prize is $5,000, second prize is $2,500, third prize is $1,500, and each honorable mention is $500.

Duration: The competition is held annually.

Number awarded: 5 prizes each year: a first, second, and third prize as well as 2 honorable mentions.

Deadline: February of each year.

1260 ELIZABETH ANNE CARLSON MEMORIAL SCHOLARSHIP

Elizabeth Anne Carlson Memorial Scholarship Trust Fund
Bruce L. Carlson, Trustee
Attn: Selection Committee
31 Franklin Circle
Newington, CT 06111
Web: www.elizabethannecarlsonscholarship.com

Summary: To provide financial assistance to high school seniors in Connecticut who plan to major in performing arts at a college in any state.

Eligibility: Open to seniors graduating from high schools in Connecticut who plan to attend a 4-year college or university in any state. Applicants must be planning to major in the performing arts (dance, instrumental, vocal, drama). Along with their application, they must submit a 1-page essay on their reasons for pursuing a future in the performing arts, what they have learned about themselves through the performing arts, what they think they can contribute to the performing arts, and where they see themselves after completion of their college education. They must also submit a 2- to 5-minute DVD of their performance. Financial need is not considered in the selection process. Finalists are invited to audition before the selection committee.

Financial data: The stipend is $2,000 per year.

Duration: 1 year; may be renewed up to 3 additional years.

Number awarded: 1 or 2 each year.

Deadline: March of each year.

1261 ELLICE T. JOHNSTON SCHOLARSHIP FOR THE CERAMIC ARTS

Clayfolk
Attn: Scholarship Committee
P.O. Box 1334
Jacksonville, OR 97530
Email: scholarship@clayfolk.org
Web: www.clayfolk.org/scholarship.htm

Summary: To provide financial assistance to ceramic art students in California and Oregon who are interested in pursuing upper-division college courses, workshops at accredited institutions, or study at foreign institutions.

Eligibility: Open to residents or students in Oregon or northern California who have completed 2 years of college or the equivalent level of art education; this may include sculpture, drawing, design, and the study of aesthetics or technical ceramics. Applicants must be interested in furthering their education in upper-division college or art school courses, workshops at accredited institutions, or study abroad at accredited institutions. Along with their application, they must submit a portfolio of work (8 to 12 slides and/or photographs), a brief statement about their work and how they plan to use the award, 2 letters of recommendation, a recent academic transcript, and documentation of financial need.

Financial data: The stipend is $1,800. Funds are provided directly to the recipient.

Duration: 1 year; may be renewed.

Number awarded: 1 or 2 each year.

Deadline: June of each year.

1262 ERNEST I. AND EURICE MILLER BASS SCHOLARSHIP

United Methodist Higher Education Foundation
Attn: Scholarships Administrator
1001 19th Avenue South
P.O. Box 340005
Nashville, TN 37203-0005
Phone: (615) 340-7385; (800) 811-8110; Fax: (615) 340-7330
Email: umhefscholarships@gbhem.org
Web: www.umhef.org/receive.php?id=endowed_funds

Summary: To provide financial assistance to undergraduate Methodist students, especially those who are preparing for a career in ministry or other religious vocation.

Eligibility: Open to undergraduate students who are enrolled or planning to enroll full-time in a degree program at an accredited institution. Applicants must have been active, full members of a United Methodist Church for at least 1 year prior to applying. They must have a GPA of 2.5 or higher and be able to demonstrate financial need. Along with their application, they must submit a 200-word essay on their involvement and/or leadership responsibilities in their church, school, and community within the last 3 years. Preference is given to 1) students preparing for ministry or other religious vocations; and 2) students enrolled or planning to enroll at a United Methodist–related college or university. U.S. citizenship or permanent resident status is required.

Financial data: The stipend is at least $1,000 per year.

Duration: 1 year; recipients may reapply.

Number awarded: Varies each year; recently, 47 of these scholarships were awarded.

Deadline: May of each year.

1263 EVANGELICAL PRESS ASSOCIATION SCHOLARSHIPS

Evangelical Press Association
Attn: Scholarships
P.O. Box 28129
Crystal, MN 55428
Phone: (763) 535-4793; Fax: (763) 535-4794
Email: director@epassoc.org
Web: www.epassoc.org/index.php/scholarships.html

Summary: To provide financial assistance to upper-division and graduate students interested in preparing for a career in Christian journalism.

Eligibility: Open to entering juniors, seniors, and graduate students who have at least 1 year of full-time study remaining. Applicants must be majoring or minoring in journalism or communications, preferably with an interest in the field of Christian journalism. They must be enrolled at an accredited Christian or secular college or university in the United States or Canada and have a GPA of 3.0 or higher. Along with their application, they must submit a biographical sketch that includes their birth date, hometown, family, and something about the factors that shaped their interest in Christian journalism; a copy of their academic record; references from their pastor and from an instructor; samples of published writing from church or school publications; and an original essay (from 500 to 700 words) on the state of journalism today.

Financial data: Stipends range from $1,000 to $2,500.

Duration: 1 year.

Number awarded: Varies each year; recently, 4 of these scholarships were awarded.

Deadline: March of each year.

1264 FEDERAL COMMUNICATIONS BAR ASSOCIATION COLLEGE SCHOLARSHIP FUND

Federal Communications Bar Association
Attn: FCBA Foundation
1020 19th Street, N.W., Suite 325
Washington, DC 20036-6101
Phone: (202) 293-4000; Fax: (202) 293-4317
Email: fcba@fcba.org
Web: www.fcba.org/foundation/scholarship_fund.shtml

Summary: To provide financial assistance to high school seniors in Washington, D.C. who are interested in communications or information technology and plan to attend college in any state.

Eligibility: Open to seniors graduating from high schools in Washington, D.C. and planning to attend college in any state. Applicants should have demonstrated an interest and/or experience in communications and information technology (including journalism, radio and television broadcasting, cable television, satellites, computers, and the Internet), although all students are eligible to apply. Along with their application, they must submit a 250-word essay on 1 of the following topics: 1) the person or event that has most affected their life and how; 2) what they consider the most significant technological innovation in the last 20 years and why; or 3) why they want to prepare for their chosen career. Selection is based on academic achievement and honors, communication and presentation skills, motivation, attendance record, service to school, service to the community, interest in communications or information technology, and financial need.

Financial data: Stipends range up to $25,000, paid over 4 years.

Duration: 4 years.

Number awarded: Varies each year; recently, 9 of these scholarships were awarded.

Deadline: February of each year.

1265 FEDERAL JUNIOR DUCK STAMP PROGRAM AND SCHOLARSHIP COMPETITION

Fish and Wildlife Service
Attn: Federal Duck Stamp Office
4401 North Fairfax Drive
MBSP-4070
Arlington, VA 22203-1622
Phone: (703) 358-2000; Fax: (703) 358-2009
Email: duckstamps@fws.gov
Web: www.fws.gov/duckstamps/junior/junior.htm

Summary: To recognize and reward student artwork submitted to the Junior Duck Stamp Program.

Eligibility: Open to students in public or private kindergartens through high schools in the United States; home-schooled students are also eligible. U.S. citizenship or permanent resident status is required. Applicants must submit paintings of ducks as part of the federal government's Junior Duck Stamp program, which supports awards and scholarships for conservation education. Students are also encouraged to include a short conservation message that expresses the spirit of what they have learned through classroom discussions, research, and planning for their entries. They must submit their applications to a designated receiving site in their home state. Each state selects 12 first-place winners (3 in each of 4 grade level groups: K–3, 4–6, 7–9, and 10–12), and then designates 1 of those 12 as best of show to compete in the national competition. Artwork is judged on the basis of form, texture, line, colors, shape, clarity of visual symbol, and spatial divisions. The conservation messages are also judged for quality.

Financial data: First prize for artwork at the national level is $5,000. The winner also receives a free trip to Washington, D.C. in the fall to attend the (adult) Federal Duck Stamp Contest, along with an art teacher, a parent, and a state coordinator. Second prize is $3,000 and third prize is $2,000. In the judging for conservation message, first prize is $500, second $300, and third $200.

Duration: The competition is held annually.

Number awarded: 6 national prizes are awarded each year: 3 for artwork and 3 for conservation message.

Deadline: Applications must be submitted to the respective state receiving site by March of each year (or January for North or South Carolina, February for Ohio).

1266 FELLOWSHIP OF UNITED METHODISTS IN MUSIC AND WORSHIP ARTS SCHOLARSHIPS

The Fellowship of United Methodists in Music and Worship Arts
Attn: Executive Director
P.O. Box 24787
Nashville, TN 37202-4787
Phone: (615) 749-6875; (800) 952-8977; Fax: (615) 749-6874
Email: fummwa@aol.com
Web: fummwa.affiniscape.com/displaycommon.cfm?an=1&subarticlenbr=16

Summary: To provide financial assistance to Methodist students who are working on an academic degree in music or the worship arts.

Eligibility: Open to full-time students entering or enrolled at an accredited college, university, or school of theology. Applicants must be studying sacred music, worship, or the arts related to worship. They must have been members of the United Methodist Church (UMC) for at least 1 year immediately before applying. Members of other Christian denominations are also eligible if they have been employed in the UMC for at least 1 year. Applicants must be able to demonstrate exceptional artistic or musical talents, leadership abilities, and outstanding promise of future usefulness to the church in an area of worship and/or music.

Financial data: The stipend is $1,000.

Duration: 1 year.

Number awarded: 1 or more each year.

Deadline: February of each year.

1267 FFTA SCHOLARSHIP COMPETITION

Flexographic Technical Association
Attn: Foundation of Flexographic Technical Association
900 Marconi Avenue
Ronkonkoma, NY 11779-7212
Phone: (631) 737-6020; Fax: (631) 737-6813
Email: education@flexography.org
Web: www.flexography.org/edutrain/education/scholarship_info.cfm

Summary: To provide financial assistance for college to students interested in a career in flexography.

Eligibility: Open to 1) high school seniors enrolled in a Flexo in Education program and planning to attend a postsecondary school; and 2) students currently enrolled at a college offering a course of study in flexography. Applicants must demonstrate interest in a career in flexography, exhibit exemplary performance in their studies (particularly in the area of graphic communications), and have an overall GPA of 3.0 or higher. Along with their application, they must submit a 1-page essay providing personal information about themselves (including special circumstances, interests, and activities); career and/or educational goals and how those relate to the flexo industry; employment and internship experience; and reasons why they feel they should be selected for this scholarship. Financial need is not considered.

Financial data: Stipends are $2,000 per year.

Duration: 1 year; may be renewed.

Number awarded: Varies each year; recently, 14 of these scholarships were awarded.

Deadline: March of each year.

1268 FIRESIDE ESSAY SCHOLARSHIP

Fireside Catholic Publishing
Attn: Essay Scholarship
P.O. Box 780189
Wichita, KS 67278-0189
Phone: (800) 676-3264; Fax: (316) 267-1850
Email: scholarshipinfo@firesidecatholic.com
Web: www.firesidecatholic.com/essay.htm

Summary: To recognize and reward, with college scholarships, students at Catholic high schools who submit outstanding essays.

Eligibility: Open to seniors graduating from Catholic high schools. Applicants must first be nominated by their schools, after which they are invited to submit 750-word essays on a topic that changes annually but relates to religious education. Selection is based on that essay and leadership in embracing religious education. Financial need is not considered.

Financial data: The awards are $1,000 college scholarships.

Duration: The competition is held annually.

Number awarded: 5 each year.

Deadline: Nominations must be submitted by December of each year.

1269 FIRST FREEDOM STUDENT COMPETITION

First Freedom Center
Attn: Student Competition Coordinator
1301 East Main Street
Richmond, VA 23219-3629
Phone: (804) 643-1786; Fax: (804) 644-5024
Email: competition@firstfreedom.org
Web: firstfreedom.org/education/students.html

Summary: To recognize and reward high school students who submit outstanding essays or videos on religious freedom.

Eligibility: Open to students in grades 9–12 in public, private, parochial, and home schools in the United States and U.S. territories, along with U.S. students attending high schools overseas, students attending American high schools overseas, foreign exchange students in the United States, and legal aliens and visitors studying in the United States. GED students under 20 years of age are also eligible. Applicants must be interested in submitting an essay (from 750 to 1,450 words) or a video (from 3 to 5 minutes in play length on a topic that changes annually but relates to freedom of religion. Selection of the winning essay is based on knowledge of subject matter and historical accuracy (20 points), analysis and interpretation of the topic (15 points), use of supporting evidence (15 points), grammatical conventions (20 points), organization and clarity (15 points), and originality and creativity (15 points). Selection of the winning essay is based on knowledge of subject matter and historical accuracy (20 points), analysis and interpretation of the topic (15 points), use of supporting evidence (15 points), organization and clarity (15 points), originality and creativity (15 points), video quality (15 points), and video script (5 points).

Financial data: The prizes are $2,500.

Duration: The competition is held annually.

Number awarded: 2 each year: 1 for an essay and 1 for a video.

Deadline: November of each year.

1270 FIRST PERSON JOURNALISM SCHOLARSHIP FUND

MIGIZI Communications, Inc.
Attn: Scholarship Committee
3123 East Lake Street
Minneapolis, MN 55406
Phone: (612) 721-6631; Fax: (612) 721-3936
Web: migizi.org/mig/scholarships.html

Summary: To provide financial assistance to Native American students working on an undergraduate or graduate degree in journalism.

Eligibility: Open to Native American undergraduate and graduate students preparing for a career in journalism or mass communications. Applicants must be able to document financial need. Along with their application, they must submit a 500-word essay on 1) how and in what capacity they have been involved in journalism; 2) why journalism is important; and 3) their plans for the future and how they plan to use their studies to help the community.

Financial data: The stipend is $1,000.

Duration: 1 year; nonrenewable.

Number awarded: 1 each year.

Deadline: May of each year.

1271 FISHER COMMUNICATIONS SCHOLARSHIPS FOR MINORITIES

Fisher Communications
Attn: Minority Scholarship
100 Fourth Avenue North, Suite 510
Seattle, WA 98109
Phone: (206) 404-7000; Fax: (206) 404-6037
Email: Info@fsci.com
Web: www.fsci.com/scholarship.html

Summary: To provide financial assistance to minority college students in selected states who are interested in preparing for a career in broadcasting.

Eligibility: Open to U.S. citizens of non-white origin who have a GPA of 2.5 or higher and are at least sophomores enrolled in 1) a broadcasting curriculum (radio, television, marketing, or broadcast technology) leading to a bachelor's degree at an accredited 4-year college or university; 2) a broadcast curriculum at an accredited community college, transferable to a 4-year baccalaureate degree program; or 3) a broadcast curriculum at an accredited vocational/technical school. Applicants must be either 1) residents of California, Washington, Oregon, Idaho, or Montana; or 2) attending a school in those states. They must submit an essay that explains their financial need, educational and career goals, any experience or interest they have in broadcast communications that they feel qualifies them for this scholarship, and involvement in school activities. Selection is based on need, academic achievement, and personal qualities.

Financial data: A stipend is awarded (amount not specified).

Duration: 1 year; recipients may reapply.

Number awarded: Varies; a total of $10,000 is available for this program each year.

Deadline: May of each year.

1272 FOARE SCHOLARSHIP PROGRAM

Outdoor Advertising Association of America, Inc.
Attn: Foundation for Outdoor Advertising Research and Education
1850 M Street, N.W., Suite 1040
Washington, DC 20036
Phone: (202) 833-5566; Fax: (202) 833-1522
Email: mlaible@oaaa.org
Web: www.oaaaa.org/foundation/scholarship.aspx

Summary: To provide financial assistance to undergraduate and graduate students who are part of an outdoor advertising industry family or are interested in preparing for a career in the industry.

Eligibility: Open to graduating high school seniors, current undergraduates, and students entering or enrolled in a master's or doctoral program. Applicants must be able to demonstrate a relationship or connection to outdoor advertising; that may be a family or family friends who have ties to the industry or an interest in preparing for a career in the field. Along with their application, they must submit an essay of 1 to 2 pages on why they are applying for this scholarship, their career goals, their area of academic study, and/or what this scholarship would mean for them. High school seniors entering their first year of undergraduate study must include a copy of SAT/ACT scores; students entering their first year of a graduate program must include GRE or other graduate school admission tests. Selection is based on academic performance, career goals, relationship or connection to outdoor advertising, and financial need.

Financial data: The stipend is $3,000.

Duration: 1 year.

Number awarded: 6 each year.

Deadline: June of each year.

1273 FOOTWEAR DESIGN SCHOLARSHIPS

Two Ten Footwear Foundation
Attn: Scholarship Director
1466 Main Street
Waltham, MA 02451
Phone: (781) 736-1500; (800) FIND-210, ext. 1512; Fax: (781) 736-1555
Email: scholarship@twoten.org
Web: www.twoten.org/Scholarships/Footwear-Design-Scholarships

Summary: To provide financial assistance to undergraduate students working on a degree in a field related to footwear design.

Eligibility: Open to students attending or planning to attend an accredited college, university, or vocational/technical school. Applicants must be able to demonstrate an interest and commitment to footwear design. Along with their application, they must submit a motivational statement, footwear design portfolio, transcripts, a letter of recommendation, and documentation of financial need. They must be U.S. citizens or eligible noncitizens. Selection is based on design potential and financial need.

Financial data: Stipends range from $1,000 to $3,000 per year, depending on the need of the recipient. Funds are sent directly to the recipient's school.
Duration: 1 year; may be renewed up to 3 additional years.
Number awarded: 1 or more each year.
Deadline: January of each year.

1274 FORREST BASSFORD STUDENT AWARD

Livestock Publications Council
910 Currie Street
Fort Worth, TX 76107
Phone: (817) 336-1130; Fax: (817) 232-4820
Email: dianej@flash.net
Web: www.livestockpublications.com/awards.php
Summary: To provide financial assistance to students majoring in agricultural communications or related fields.
Eligibility: Open to college juniors and seniors majoring in agricultural journalism, agricultural communications, or agricultural public relations. Applicants must have at least 1 semester of school remaining at the time they receive the award. Along with their application, they must submit a 200-word essay on the future of agricultural communications and how they fit in that career. Selection is based on that essay, a transcript of college work completed and a list of courses in progress, scholarships and awards received, club and other organization memberships, extracurricular activities, employment record, a 1-page press release announcing that they have won this award, and 3 samples of communications work.
Financial data: The winner receives a $2,000 scholarship, plus a $750 travel scholarship (to attend the council's annual meeting). The runners-up receive $750 travel scholarships to attend the meeting.
Duration: 1 year.
Number awarded: 1 winner and up to 4 runners-up are selected each year.
Deadline: February of each year.

1275 FRANK WATTS SCHOLARSHIP

Watts Charity Association, Inc.
6245 Bristol Parkway, Suite 224
Culver City, CA 90230
Phone: (323) 671-0394; Fax: (323) 778-2613
Email: wattscharity@aol.com
Web: 4watts.tripod.com/id5.html
Summary: To provide financial assistance to upper-division African Americans interested in preparing for a career as a minister.
Eligibility: Open to U.S. citizens of African American descent who are enrolled full-time as a college or university junior. Applicants must be studying to become a minister. They must have a GPA of 3.0 or higher, be between 17 and 24 years of age, and be able to demonstrate that they intend to continue their education for at least 2 years. Along with their application, they must submit 1) a 1-paragraph statement on why they should be awarded a Watts Foundation scholarship; and 2) a 1- to 2-page essay on a specific type of cancer, based either on how it has impacted their life or on researched information.
Financial data: A stipend is awarded (amount not specified).
Duration: 1 year.
Number awarded: 1 each year.
Deadline: May of each year.

1276 FREEDOM FORUM–NCAA SPORTS JOURNALISM SCHOLARSHIPS

National Collegiate Athletic Association
Attn: Leadership Advisory Board
700 West Washington Avenue
P.O. Box 6222
Indianapolis, IN 46206-6222
Phone: (317) 917-6477; Fax: (317) 917-6888
Email: shays@ncaa.org
Web: www.ncaa.org/wps/ncaa?ContentID=465
Summary: To provide financial assistance to upper-division students interested in preparing for a career in sports journalism.
Eligibility: Open to college juniors who are planning a career in sports journalism and are either majoring in journalism or have experience in campus sports journalism. Along with their application, they must submit their official college transcript, 3 examples of sports journalism work, a letter of recommendation from a journalism professor, and (if they have had a professional internship) a letter of recommendation from their employer. They must also include a statement, 200 to 500 words in length, on assigned topics that change annually. Financial need is not considered.
Financial data: The stipend is $3,000.
Duration: 1 year; nonrenewable.
Number awarded: 8 each year: 1 in each of the geographical districts of the NCAA.
Deadline: December of each year.

1277 FREEDOM FROM RELIGION FOUNDATION HIGH SCHOOL ESSAY COMPETITION

Freedom from Religion Foundation
P.O. Box 750
Madison, WI 53701
Phone: (608) 256-8900; Fax: (608) 204-0422
Email: dbarker@ffrf.org
Web: www.ffrf.org/outreach/student-essay-contests
Summary: To recognize and reward outstanding essays written by high school students on freethought or state/church separation themes.
Eligibility: Open to college-bound high school seniors. They are invited to write an essay on a topic that changes annually but relates to freethinking and separation of church and state; recently, the topics were "The Harm of Religion" or "The Harm of Religion to Women." Essays should be from 1,100 to 1,300 words in length and deal with the harm of religion from an historic, psychological, or topical perspective. Students should include a paragraph biography, their hometown and high school, the name of the college they will be attending, their planned major, and their interests.
Financial data: First prize is $2,000, second $1,000, third $500, and honorable mentions $200.
Duration: The competition is held annually.
Number awarded: 3 prizes and a varying number of honorable mentions are awarded each year.
Deadline: May of each year.

1278 FREEDOM OF SPEECH PSA CONTEST

National Association of Broadcasters
Attn: Education Foundation
1771 N Street, N.W.
Washington, DC 20036-2891
Phone: (202) 429-5424; Fax: (202) 429-4199
Web: www.nabef.org/initiatives/FOS.asp
Summary: To recognize and reward, with scholarships for additional study, undergraduate and graduate communications students who create outstanding public service announcements (PSAs) for radio and television on the importance of free speech.
Eligibility: Open to undergraduate and graduate students enrolled at colleges, universities, and community/technical colleges who have a major or minor in a field related to communications. Applicants must create a 30-second PSA. They may work in pairs or in teams of up to 10 students. Along with their application, they must submit a description of the proposed service project over which they have significant control (producing, directing, writing, editing). The PSA must respond to the question, "what freedom of speech means to me," or otherwise highlight the importance of free speech. Entries may be for radio (2 CDs) or television (2 DVDs).
Financial data: For each category (radio and television), first prize is $3,000, second $2,000, and third $1,000. Prizes are in the form of scholarships made payable to the student's academic institution.
Duration: The competition is held annually.
Number awarded: 6 winners are selected each year (3 each for radio and television).
Deadline: April of each year.

1279 FREEDOM OF THE PRESS HIGH SCHOOL ESSAY CONTEST

Society of Professional Journalists
Attn: Awards and Fellowships Coordinator
3909 North Meridian Street
Indianapolis, IN 46208
Phone: (317) 927-8000; Fax: (317) 920-4789
Email: awards@spj.org
Web: www.spj.org/a-hs.asp
Summary: To recognize and reward, with college scholarships, high school students who write outstanding essays on the importance of a free press.

Eligibility: Open to students in grades 9–12 in the United States. Applicants must submit an essay (300 to 500 words) on "Why free news media are important" to their local chapter of the Society of Professional Journalists. Selection is based on material organization (40 points); vocabulary and style (30 points); grammar, punctuation, and spelling (20 points); neatness (5 points); and adherence to contest rules (5 points).
Financial data: Winners receive scholarships of $1,000 for first place, $500 for second place, and $300 for third place.
Duration: The competition is held annually.
Number awarded: 3 each year.
Deadline: March of each year.

1280 FRIENDS OF JAMES BEARD SCHOLARSHIPS

James Beard Foundation Scholarship Program
c/o Scholarship Management Services
One Scholarship Way
P.O. Box 297
St. Peter, MN 56082
Phone: (507) 931-1682; (800) 537-4180; Fax: (507) 931-9168
Email: jamesbeard@scholarshipamerica.org
Web: sms.scholarshipamerica.org/jamesbeard
Summary: To provide financial assistance to high school seniors and graduates interested in attending culinary school.
Eligibility: Open to high school seniors planning to enroll and students already enrolled at least part-time in a course of study leading to an associate or bachelor's degree at a licensed or accredited culinary school. Applicants must submit a brief statement or summary of their plans as they relate to their culinary, educational, and career goals. Selection is based on that statement, academic record, leadership and participation in school and community activities, work experience, unusual personal or family circumstances, an outside appraisal, and financial need.
Financial data: Stipends range from $1,750 to $4,340.
Duration: 1 year; awards are not renewable, but recipients may reapply.
Number awarded: Varies each year; recently 15 of these scholarships were awarded: 1 at $4,340, 1 at $4,000, 2 at $3,850, 2 at $3,750, 1 at $3,000, 7 at $2,500, and 1 at $1,750.
Deadline: May of each year.

1281 GARDEN CLUB COUNCIL OF WINSTON-SALEM AND FORSYTH COUNTY SCHOLARSHIP

Winston-Salem Foundation
Attn: Student Aid Department
860 West Fifth Street
Winston-Salem, NC 27101-2506
Phone: (336) 725-2382; (866) 227-1209; Fax: (336) 727-0581
Email: info@wsfoundation.org
Web: www.wsfoundation.org/students
Summary: To provide financial assistance to residents of North Carolina who are interested in working on an undergraduate degree in horticulture or landscape architecture at a school in the state.
Eligibility: Open to residents of North Carolina who are attending or planning to attend an accredited 2- or 4-year college or university in the state. Applicants must be planning to work full-time on an associate or bachelor's degree in horticulture technology or landscape architecture. They may be of traditional or nontraditional student age. Selection is based on academic potential and financial need. U.S. citizenship is required.
Financial data: A stipend is awarded (amount not specified).
Duration: 1 year; may be renewed 1 additional year if the recipient remains enrolled full-time with a GPA of 2.0 or higher.
Number awarded: 1 or more each year.
Deadline: April of each year.

1282 GARDEN WRITERS ASSOCIATION FOUNDATION GENERAL SCHOLARSHIPS

Garden Writers Association
Attn: Foundation
10210 Leatherleaf Court
Manassas, VA 20111
Phone: (703) 257-1032; Fax: (703) 257-0213
Email: info@gardenwriters.org
Web: www.gardenwriters.org
Summary: To provide financial assistance to upper-division students working on a degree in horticulture, plant science, or journalism.
Eligibility: Open to juniors and seniors enrolled full-time at a 4-year college or university. Applicants must be majoring in horticulture, plant science, or journalism, with an interest in garden communications (including garden photography). They must have a GPA of 3.0 or higher. Along with their application, they must submit 2 written compositions or photographs. Selection is based on academic record and writing or photographic skills.
Financial data: The stipend ranges from $250 to $2,000, depending on the availability of funds.
Duration: 1 year.
Number awarded: 2 to 6 each year.
Deadline: December of each year.

1283 GARIKIAN UNIVERSITY SCHOLARSHIP

Western Prelacy of the Armenian Apostolic Church of America
Attn: Garikian Scholarship Fund Coordinator
6252 Honolulu Avenue
La Crescenta, CA 91214
Phone: (818) 248-7737; Fax: (818) 248-7745
Email: info@WesternPrelacy.org
Web: www.westernprelacy.org
Summary: To provide money for college to students of Armenian heritage in California who have completed their freshman year in selected subject fields.
Eligibility: Open to students enrolled in a university in California who have completed their first academic year, are of Armenian heritage, and are studying in 1 of the following fields: Armenian studies or literature, political science, journalism, or education. Selection is based on academic merit, financial need, and community involvement.
Financial data: Stipends range from $850 to $1,000.
Duration: 1 year.
Number awarded: 4 to 5 each year.
Deadline: August of each year.

1284 GEORGE AND NAOUMA GIOLES SCHOLARSHIP

Greek Orthodox Archdiocese of America
Attn: Office of the Chancellor
8 East 79th Street
New York, NY 10075
Phone: (212) 774-0513; Fax: (212) 774-0251
Email: scholarships@goarch.org
Web: www.goarch.org/archdiocese/administration/chancellor/scholarships
Summary: To provide financial assistance to high school seniors and current undergraduates who are of the Greek Orthodox faith and plan to study the sciences, business, or the arts.
Eligibility: Open to high school seniors and current undergraduates who are enrolled or planning to enroll full-time at an accredited college or university in the United States. Applicants must be of the Greek Orthodox faith, preferably of Greek descent, and U.S. citizens or permanent residents. They must have a GPA of 3.0 or higher and an SAT score of at least 1500 (or an equivalent score on the ACT). Preference is given to applicants who are orphans and to those who are interested in studying the sciences, business, or the arts (with at least 1 scholarship reserved for a student majoring in journalism). Along with their application, they must submit a 500-word essay on 1 of the following topics: 1) how their background as an orphan, or as a person of Greek descent, or as a Greek Orthodox Christian, has affected their life; 2) how Hellenes abroad, or Greek Orthodox Christians in the United States, can retain their religious and ethnic identity for generations to come; or 3) how they will use their Hellenic culture, their Greek Orthodox faith, and their planned studies to contribute to the betterment of humanity. Financial need is considered in the selection process.
Financial data: The stipend is $1,500.
Duration: 1 year.
Number awarded: 5 each year, including 1 reserved for an applicant studying journalism.
Deadline: April of each year.

1285 GEORGE AND OPHELIA GALLUP SCHOLARSHIPS

Quill and Scroll
c/o University of Iowa
School of Journalism and Mass Communications
100 Adler Journalism Building, Room E346
Iowa City, IA 52242-2004

Phone: (319) 335-3457; Fax: (319) 335-3989
Email: quill-scroll@uiowa.edu
Web: www.uiowa.edu/~quill-sc/scholarships/nell.html

Summary: To provide financial assistance for college to high school journalists who are national winners of contests sponsored by Quill and Scroll (the international honor society for high school journalists).

Eligibility: Open to high school seniors who are winners in either of 2 contests conducted by Quill and Scroll for high school journalists: 1) the International Writing/Photography Contest, open to all high school students, with competitions in editorial, editorial cartoon, general columns, review columns, in-depth reporting (individual and team), news story, feature story, sports story, advertisement, and photography (news feature and sports); or 2) the Yearbook Excellence Contest, open to all Quill and Scroll charter high schools. In addition to being a winner of 1 of the contests, candidates for the scholarships must be planning to major in journalism or mass communications at a college or university in any state. Along with their application, they must submit 2 letters of recommendation, 3 examples of their journalistic work, and a 500-word personal statement on their journalistic experience, future plans, activities, honors, volunteer service, and how they plan to finance their college education.

Financial data: The stipend is $1,500.

Duration: 1 year; nonrenewable.

Number awarded: 2 each year.

Deadline: Entries in the International Writing/Photo Contest are due in February; entries in the Yearbook Excellence Contest must be submitted by the end of October. Scholarship applications must be submitted in May.

1286 GEORGE E. HADDAWAY SCHOLARSHIP

Communities Foundation of Texas
Attn: Scholarship Department
5500 Caruth Haven Lane
Dallas, TX 75225-8146
Phone: (214) 750-4222; Fax: (214) 750-4210
Email: scholarships@cftexas.org
Web: www.cftexas.org/NetCommunity/Page.aspx?pid=291

Summary: To provide financial assistance to upper-division and graduate students who are working on a degree in journalism and have an interest in aviation.

Eligibility: Open to college juniors, seniors, and graduate students who can demonstrate interest in aviation by such activities as 1) current or former membership in the aviation program of a college or university, the Boy or Girl Scouts of America, the Civil Air Patrol, or a similar organization; or 2) pursuit or completion of the requirements for an aircraft license. Applicants must be working on a baccalaureate or advanced degree in print or electronic journalism and have completed at least 52 hours of college course work with a GPA of 2.75 or higher. They must be able to demonstrate financial need. Along with their application, they must submit an essay (200 to 500 words) describing their interest in aviation and how they might combine that interest with a career in journalism. U.S. citizenship is required.

Financial data: The stipend is $2,500 per year.

Duration: 1 year; nonrenewable.

Number awarded: 1 each year.

Deadline: March of each year.

1287 GEORGE E. HOERTER SCHOLARSHIP AWARDS

Society for Technical Communication–Rocky Mountain Chapter
Attn: Scholarship Manager
820 South Monaco Parkway, Suite 286
Denver, CO 80224
Email: scholarships@stcrmc.org
Web: www.stcrmc.org/chapter/scholarships/scholar.htm

Summary: To provide financial assistance to undergraduate and graduate students working on a degree in technical communication at a college or university in Colorado.

Eligibility: Open to sophomores, juniors, seniors, and graduate students at Colorado colleges and universities within the geographic area of the Rocky Mountain chapter of the Society for Technical Communication (STC). Applicants must submit a 1- to 3-page letter describing their academic and career goals, a resume, an official transcript, and a letter of recommendation from a faculty member. Financial need is not considered in the selection process.

Financial data: The stipend is $1,000.

Duration: 1 year.

Number awarded: 2 each year.

Deadline: December of each year.

1288 GEORGE MONTGOMERY/NRA YOUTH WILDLIFE ART CONTEST

National Rifle Association of America
Attn: Youth Programs
11250 Waples Road
Fairfax, VA 22030-7400
Phone: (703) 267-1531; Fax: (703) 267-3993
Email: artcontest@nrahq.org
Web: www.nrahq.org/youth/wildlife.asp

Summary: To recognize and reward elementary and secondary school students who submit outstanding artwork of wild animals.

Eligibility: Open to children in public, private, or home school. Entries are accepted in 4 grade categories: grades 1 to 3, 4 to 6, 7 to 9, and 10 to 12. Participants submit original works of art portraying any North American game bird or animal that may be legally hunted or trapped. Endangered species, fish, and non-game animals are not eligible subjects. Artwork may be either color or black-and-white and done in a medium of the artist's choice (pencil, pen and ink, oil, water color, pastel, etc.).

Financial data: Prizes are $750 for first, $500 for second, and $250 for third. The entry judged Best In Show receives $1,000.

Duration: The contest is held annually.

Number awarded: 12 each year: 3 in each grade category.

Deadline: October of each year.

1289 GEORGE S. AND STELLA M. KNIGHT ESSAY CONTEST

National Society Sons of the American Revolution
Attn: Education Director
1000 South Fourth Street
Louisville, KY 40203-3208
Phone: (502) 589-1776, ext. 30; Fax: (502) 589-1671
Email: cwilson@sar.org
Web: www.sar.org/Youth/Knight_Essay

Summary: To recognize and reward outstanding high school essays on the American Revolution.

Eligibility: Open to juniors and seniors in all public, parochial, and private high schools in the United States who are U.S. citizens or legal residents. Applicants must write an essay of 800 to 1,200 words on an event, person, philosophy, or idea associated with the American Revolution, the Declaration of Independence, or the framing of the U.S. constitution. Selection is based on historical accuracy, clarity of thought, organization, grammar and spelling, and documentation. Winners at state and district levels advance to the national contest.

Financial data: At the national level, first prize is $2,000, a plaque, and airfare and hotel for 1 night to attend the sponsor's annual congress; second prize is $1,000; third prize is $500.

Duration: The competition is held annually.

Number awarded: 3 national scholarships are awarded each year.

Deadline: Deadline not specified.

1290 GEORGIA PRESS EDUCATIONAL FOUNDATION SCHOLARSHIPS

Georgia Press Association
Attn: Georgia Press Educational Foundation
3066 Mercer University Drive, Suite 200
Atlanta, GA 30341-4137
Phone: (770) 454-6776; Fax: (770) 454-6778
Email: mail@gapress.org
Web: www.gapress.org/scholarships.html

Summary: To provide financial assistance to high school seniors and college students in Georgia who are interested in preparing for a career in newspaper journalism.

Eligibility: Open to high school seniors and currently-enrolled college students who have been residents of Georgia for at least 3 years or whose parents have been residents of the state for at least 2 years. Applicants must be attending or planning to attend a college or university in Georgia to prepare for a career in newspaper journalism. They must be recommended by a high school counselor, principal, college professor, or member of the Georgia Press Association. Selection is based on academic record, standardized test scores, career plans, and financial need.

Financial data: Stipends range from $1,000 to $2,250.

Duration: 1 year.

Number awarded: Varies each year; recently, 12 of these scholarships were awarded: 1 at $2,250, 3 at $2,000, and 8 at $1,000.

Deadline: January of each year.

1291 GERALDO RIVERA SCHOLARSHIP

National Association of Hispanic Journalists
Attn: Scholarship Committee
1000 National Press Building
529 14th Street, N.W.
Washington, DC 20045-2001
Phone: (202) 662-7145; (888) 346-NAHJ; Fax: (202) 662-7144
Email: nahj@nahj.org
Web: www.nahj.org/educationalprograms/nahfscholarships.shtml

Summary: To provide financial assistance to Hispanic American college seniors and graduate students interested in preparing for a career in television broadcast journalism.

Eligibility: Open to Hispanic American college seniors and graduate students who are interested in preparing for a career in English- or Spanish-language television broadcast journalism. Applicants must be enrolled full-time at a college or university in the United States or Puerto Rico. Along with their application, they must submit transcripts, a 1-page resume, 2 letters of recommendation, work samples, and a 1,000-word autobiographical essay that includes why they are interested in a career in journalism, what inspired them to prepare for a career in the field, what hardships or obstacles they have experienced while trying to realize their goal of becoming a journalist, and the role Latino journalists play in the news industry. Selection is based on commitment to the field of journalism, academic achievement, awareness of the Latino community, and financial need.

Financial data: The stipend ranges up to $5,000.

Duration: 1 year.

Number awarded: 1 each year.

Deadline: April of each year.

1292 GLADYS C. ANDERSON MEMORIAL SCHOLARSHIP

American Foundation for the Blind
Attn: Scholarship Committee
11 Penn Plaza, Suite 300
New York, NY 10001
Phone: (212) 502-7661; (800) AFB-LINE; Fax: (212) 502-7771; TDD: (212) 502-7662
Email: afbinfo@afb.net
Web: www.afb.org/Section.asp?Documentid=2962

Summary: To provide financial assistance to legally blind undergraduate women who are studying classical or religious music.

Eligibility: Open to women who are legally blind, U.S. citizens, and enrolled in an undergraduate or graduate degree program in classical or religious music. Along with their application, they must submit a 200-word essay that includes their past and recent achievements and accomplishments; their intended field of study and why they have chosen it; and the role their visual impairment has played in shaping their life. They must also submit a sample performance tape or CD of up to 30 minutes. Financial need is considered in the selection process.

Financial data: The stipend is $1,000.

Duration: 1 academic year.

Number awarded: 1 each year.

Deadline: April of each year.

1293 GLENN MILLER SCHOLARSHIP COMPETITION

Glenn Miller Birthplace Society
Attn: Scholarship Program
107 East Main Street
P.O. Box 61
Clarinda, IA 51632
Phone: (712) 542-2461; Fax: (712) 542-2461
Email: gmbs@heartland.net
Web: www.glennmiller.org/scholarships.html

Summary: To recognize and reward, with college scholarships, present and prospective college music or music education majors.

Eligibility: Open to 1) graduating high school seniors planning to major in music in college; and 2) freshmen music majors at an accredited college, university, or school of music. Both instrumentalists and vocalists may compete. Those who entered as high school seniors and did not win first place are eligible to enter again as college freshmen. Each entrant must submit an audition tape or CD, from which 10 instrumentalist finalists and 10 vocalist finalists are selected. Finalists audition in person. They must perform a composition of concert quality, up to 5 minutes in length, sight read selections chosen by the judges, and perform technical exercises. They must also submit a statement that they intend to make music performance or teaching a central part of their future life. Selection is based on talent in any field of applied music; the competition is not intended to select Glenn Miller look-alikes or sound-alikes.

Financial data: Awards are $4,500 for first place, $2,000 for second, or $1,000 for third. The funds are to be used for any school-related expense.

Duration: The competition is held annually, in June.

Number awarded: 6 each year: 3 for instrumentalists and 3 for vocalists.

Deadline: March of each year.

1294 GRADUATE/MATURE STUDENT ESSAY COMPETITION

Freedom from Religion Foundation
P.O. Box 750
Madison, WI 53701
Phone: (608) 256-8900; Fax: (608) 204-0422
Email: dbarker@ffrf.org
Web: www.ffrf.org/outreach/student-essay-contests

Summary: To recognize and reward outstanding essays by mature undergraduates and graduate students on the separation of church and state.

Eligibility: Open to undergraduate students over 25 years of age and graduate students currently enrolled at colleges and universities in North America. Applicants write an essay on topics that change annually but involve rejecting religion; recently, students were asked to write on why we need to get "God Out of Government" and/or why we need to keep religion out of politics, including debunking the myth that the United States is "one nation under God." They may wish to use examples of the harm caused by acceptance of this myth, and by religion in government and politics from a legal, topical, and/or historical perspective. Essays should be from 1,400 to 1,600 words, accompanied by a paragraph biography identifying the student's college or university, year in school, major, and interests.

Financial data: First prize is $2,000, second $1,000, third $500, fourth $300, and honorable mentions $200.

Duration: The competition is held annually.

Number awarded: 4 prizes and a varying number of honorable mentions are awarded each year.

Deadline: June of each year.

1295 GRANDMA MOSES SCHOLARSHIP

Western Art Association
Attn: Foundation
13730 Loumont Street
Whittier, CA 90601

Summary: To provide financial assistance for art school to female high school seniors whose art demonstrates a "congruence with the art of Grandma Moses."

Eligibility: Open to female graduating high school seniors. Applicants must be planning to study art in a college, university, or specialized school of art. Preference is given to applicants from the western United States. Candidates must submit samples of their artwork; selection is based on the extent to which their work "manifests a congruence with the work of the famed folk artist, Grandma Moses." Financial need is not considered.

Financial data: The stipend is $3,000 per year.

Duration: 1 year; may be renewed up to 3 additional years.

Number awarded: 1 each year.

Deadline: March of each year.

1296 GREEN COMMUNITY INTERNATIONAL STUDENT DESIGN COMPETITION

Association of Collegiate Schools of Architecture
Attn: Project Manager
1735 New York Avenue, N.W.
Washington, DC 20006
Phone: (202) 785-2324, ext. 8; Fax: (202) 628-0448
Email: competitions@acsa-arch.org
Web: www.acsa-arch.org/competitions

Summary: To recognize and reward architecture and design students who submit outstanding entries in a design competition that focuses on issues of sustainable development in their communities.

Eligibility: Open to architecture students in their third year or higher, including graduate students, at colleges and universities in the United States, Canada, and Mexico that are members of the Association of Collegiate Schools of Architecture (ACSA). Participants are invited to locate a site in their local community or region, identify the barriers and strengths to living sustainable, and develop a proposal to create a flourishing and sustainable community, using the tools of the architectural design disciplines of architecture, landscape architecture, and urban planning. Submissions must be sponsored by a faculty member and are to be principally the product of design studio work. Both individual and team entries are eligible. Selection is based on awareness and innovative approach to environmental issues, mastery of formal concepts and aesthetic values, appreciation of human needs and social responsibilities, capability to integrate functional aspects of the problem, and capacity to derive the maximum potential afforded by the project.

Financial data: First prize is $2,500 for the student or team and $1,000 for the faculty sponsor, second prize is $1,500 for the student or team and $750 for the faculty sponsor, and third prize is $750 for the student or team and $500 for the faculty sponsor.

Duration: The competition is held annually.

Number awarded: 3 student prizes are awarded each year.

Deadline: Faculty who wish to enroll their studio classes must register by February of each year. Entries must be submitted by May.

1297 GREEN/SUSTAINABLE DESIGN SCHOLARSHIP

International Furnishings and Design Association
Attn: IFDA Educational Foundation
150 South Warner Road, Suite 156
King of Prussia, PA 19406
Phone: (610) 535-6422; Fax: (610) 535-6423
Email: info@ifda.com
Web: www.ifdaef.org/scholarships.html

Summary: To provide financial assistance to undergraduate students who are working on a degree in interior design with an emphasis on green or sustainable design.

Eligibility: Open to students enrolled at an accredited school, college, or university who are focusing on the green or sustainable field of study, defined as the development of innovative ways to create living spaces that are energy efficient and feature green or sustainable materials, fabrications, and products. Applicants must be able to demonstrate creative use of green products and eco friendly furnishings in class projects, familiarity with current information with the green/sustainable field, the application of this knowledge in class work, and a goal of seeking a Leadership in Energy and Environmental Design (LEED) accreditation. Along with their application, they must submit an essay of 200 to 400 words on their long- and short-term goals, extracurricular activities, and why they are interested in green or sustainable design; samples of their work featuring 1 or more aspects of green or sustainable design with detailed explanations; a transcript; and a letter of recommendation from a professor or instructor. Financial need is not considered.

Financial data: The stipend is $1,000.

Duration: 1 year.

Number awarded: At least 1 each year.

Deadline: March of each year.

1298 GUS SWANSON MEMORIAL COMMUNICATIONS SCHOLARSHIP PROGRAM FOR COLLEGE STUDENTS

Swanson Russell Associates
1222 P Street
Lincoln, NE 68508-1463
Phone: (402) 437-6400; Fax: (402) 437-6401
Email: daveh@swansonrussell.com
Web: swansonrussell.com/press/statewidescholarships.php

Summary: To provide financial assistance to residents of Nebraska who are studying a field related to communications at a college in the state.

Eligibility: Open to Nebraska residents who are enrolled at least part-time at a college or university in the state with at least sophomore standing. Applicants must be studying a field related to communications, including advertising, marketing, communications studies, mass communications, public relations, journalism, graphic design, desktop publishing, or associated areas. They must have a GPA of 3.25 or higher. Along with their application, they must submit a marketing strategy essay based on a current print, television, and/or radio advertising campaign. Financial need is not considered in the selection process.

Financial data: The stipend is $1,000.

Duration: 1 year.

Number awarded: 1 each year.

Deadline: April of each year.

1299 GUY P. GANNETT SCHOLARSHIP FUND

Maine Community Foundation
Attn: Program Director
245 Main Street
Ellsworth, ME 04605
Phone: (207) 667-9735; (877) 700-6800; Fax: (207) 667-0447
Email: info@mainecf.org
Web: www.mainecf.org/GraduateScholars.aspx

Summary: To provide financial assistance to Maine residents who are interested in studying journalism at a college or graduate school in any state.

Eligibility: Open to graduates of Maine high schools (public and private) and to Maine residents who were schooled at home during their last year of secondary education. Applicants must be attending either an undergraduate (including a trade school or a technical institute program) or a graduate program at an accredited postsecondary institution in the United States. They must be majoring in journalism or a related field, including all forms of print, broadcast, or electronic media. Selection is based on academic achievement, financial need, and a demonstrated interest in a career in a form of journalism. Preference is given to renewal applicants.

Financial data: A stipend is paid (amount not specified).

Duration: 1 year; may be renewed.

Number awarded: Varies each year; recently, 21 of these scholarships, with a total value of nearly $260,000, were awarded.

Deadline: April of each year.

1300 HANLON BROWN DESIGN SCHOLARSHIP

Oregon Student Assistance Commission
Attn: Grants and Scholarships Division
1500 Valley River Drive, Suite 100
Eugene, OR 97401-2146
Phone: (541) 687-7395; (800) 452-8807, ext. 7395; Fax: (541) 687-7414; TDD: (800) 735-2900
Email: awardinfo@osac.state.or.us
Web: www.osac.state.or.us/osac_programs.html

Summary: To provide financial assistance to residents of Oregon who are interested in working on an undergraduate or graduate degree related to graphic or web design at a school in any state.

Eligibility: Open to residents of Oregon who are enrolled as juniors, seniors, or graduate students at a college or university in any state. Applicants must be working on a degree in graphic design or interactive/web design. They must have a GPA of 3.0 or higher. Semifinalists are required to e-mail a design sample along with a 200-word description that includes the communication objective, intended audience, and the central idea behind the concept.

Financial data: A stipend is awarded (amount not specified).

Duration: 1 year; recipients may reapply.

Number awarded: Varies each year.

Deadline: February of each year.

1301 HARRIET IRSAY SCHOLARSHIP GRANT

American Institute of Polish Culture, Inc.
Attn: Scholarship Committee
1440 79th Street Causeway, Suite 117
Miami, FL 33141
Phone: (305) 864-2349; Fax: (305) 865-5150
Email: info@ampolinstitute.org
Web: www.ampolinstitute.org/ip.asp?op=Scholarship

Summary: To provide financial assistance to Polish American and other students interested in working on an undergraduate or graduate degree in selected fields.

Eligibility: Open to students working full-time on an undergraduate or graduate degree in the following fields: architecture, communications, education, film, history, international relations, journalism, liberal arts, Polish studies, or public relations. Also eligible are graduate students in business programs whose thesis is directly related to Poland and to graduate students in all majors whose thesis is on a Polish subject. U.S. citizenship or permanent resident status is required. Preference is given to applicants of Polish heritage. Along with their application, they must submit an essay of 200 to 400 words on why they should receive the scholarship, an article (up to 700 words) on any subject about Poland, transcripts, a detailed resume, and 3 letters of recommendation. Selection is based on merit.

Financial data: The stipend is $1,000.

Duration: 1 year.

Number awarded: 10 to 15 each year.

Deadline: May of each year.

1302 HARRY AND LORRAINE AUSPRICH ENDOWED SCHOLARSHIP FOR THE ARTS

Pennsylvania State System of Higher Education Foundation, Inc.
Attn: Director of Scholarship Programs
2986 North Second Street
Harrisburg, PA 17110
Phone: (717) 720-4065; Fax: (717) 720-7082
Email: eshowers@thePAfoundation.org
Web: www.thepafoundation.org/scholarships/index.asp

Summary: To provide financial assistance to upper-division students at institutions of the Pennsylvania State System of Higher Education (PASSHE) who are majoring in the visual or performing arts.
Eligibility: Open to full-time juniors and seniors enrolled at 1 of the 14 institutions within the PASSHE. Applicants must be majoring in the visual or performing arts (e.g., music, theater, fine arts, dance, pre-architecture) and must have a GPA of 3.0 or higher. Along with their application, they must submit an essay of 500 to 800 words explaining why they believe they are deserving of this scholarship. Financial need is not considered in the selection process.
Financial data: The stipend depends on the availability of funds.
Duration: 1 year; nonrenewable.
Number awarded: Varies each year, depending on the availability of funds.
Deadline: April of each year.

1303 HARRY BARFIELD SCHOLARSHIP

Kentucky Broadcasters Association
101 Enterprise Drive
Frankfort, KY 40601
Phone: (502) 848-0426; (888) THE-KBA1; Fax: (502) 848-5710
Email: kba@kba.org
Web: www.kba.org/Scholarship.htm

Summary: To provide financial assistance to residents of Kentucky who are majoring in broadcasting at a school in the state.
Eligibility: Open to Kentucky residents who are currently enrolled at a college or university in the state and majoring in broadcasting or telecommunications. Applicants must be preparing for a career in broadcasting. They must submit a college transcript, a list of extracurricular activities, and a faculty recommendation. Financial need is not considered in the selection process.
Financial data: The stipend is $2,500 per year.
Duration: 1 year; may be renewed for 1 additional year if the recipient maintains a GPA of 3.0 or higher.
Number awarded: Up to 4 each year.
Deadline: April of each year.

1304 HARVEY S. FRIEDMAN ANNUAL MEMORIAL GRANT

National Museum of American Jewish Military History
1811 R Street, N.W.
Washington, DC 20009-1659
Phone: (202) 265-6280; Fax: (202) 463-3192
Email: nmajmh@nmajmh.org
Web: www.nmajmh.org/educationAndEvents/scholarshipsAndGrants.php

Summary: To provide financial assistance to undergraduate and graduate students working on a degree in a field related to museums.
Eligibility: Open to students working on a bachelor's or master's degree or certificate in a museum-related field (e.g., museum studies, museum education, arts administration). Applicants must have a GPA of 3.0 or higher. Along with their application, they may submit a 250-word essay explaining any special circumstances they wish to have considered. Selection is based on academic achievement and extracurricular and community activities.
Financial data: The stipend is $1,000.
Duration: 1 year.
Number awarded: 1 each year.
Deadline: December of each year.

1305 HAWAII ASSOCIATION FOR HEALTH, PHYSICAL EDUCATION, RECREATION AND DANCE SCHOLARSHIPS

Hawaii Association for Health, Physical Education, Recreation and Dance
c/o Jewel Toyama, Scholarship Committee Chair
2583 Ahekolo Street
Honolulu, HI 96813
Phone: (808) 949-6461, ext. 232; Fax: (808) 941-2216
Email: jtoyama@hanahauoli.org
Web: www.hahperd.org

Summary: To provide financial assistance to high school seniors and graduates in Hawaii who are interested in attending college in any state to prepare for a career teaching health education, physical education, dance, or recreation.
Eligibility: Open to students who have been enrolled in a Hawaii high school for at least 2 years and are currently high school seniors or full-time undergraduate or graduate students. Applicants must have a GPA of 3.0 or higher and demonstrate evidence of leadership potential. They must be interested in preparing for a career as a teacher of health, physical education, dance, or recreation. Along with their application, they must submit a 2-page essay on why they want to be in the profession of teaching, how and why they believe they will be an effective educator in their chosen field, and their reaction to the proposal of the Hawaii Department of Education to reduce the high school physical education requirement.
Financial data: The stipend is $750 for high school seniors or $1,250 for undergraduate and graduate students.
Duration: 1 year; recipients may reapply.
Number awarded: 4 each year: 2 to graduating high school seniors and 2 to current undergraduate or graduate students.
Deadline: February of each year.

1306 HAWAII ASSOCIATION OF BROADCASTERS SCHOLARSHIP

Hawaii Association of Broadcasters, Inc.
Attn: Scholarship Committee
P.O. Box 61562
Honolulu, HI 96839
Email: stephanieuyeda@hawaii.rr.com
Web: www.hawaiibroadcasters.com/scholar.html

Summary: To provide financial assistance to high school seniors and current college students interested in preparing for a career in the broadcast industry in Hawaii.
Eligibility: Open to college-bound high school seniors and current students at 2- and 4-year colleges and universities and recognized broadcast schools in the United States. Applicants must have a GPA of 2.5 or higher and a stated intention to work in the broadcast industry in Hawaii upon completion of school. Financial need is considered in the selection process. Finalists are invited to an interview.
Financial data: The stipend is $3,500 per year.
Duration: 1 year.
Number awarded: 1 or more each year.
Deadline: April of each year.

1307 HAWAII CHAPTER/DAVID T. WOOLSEY SCHOLARSHIP

Landscape Architecture Foundation
Attn: Scholarship Program
818 18th Street, N.W., Suite 810
Washington, DC 20006-3520
Phone: (202) 331-7070; Fax: (202) 331-7079
Email: scholarships@lafoundation.org
Web: www.laprofession.org/financial/scholarships.htm

Summary: To provide financial assistance to residents of Hawaii who are working on an undergraduate or graduate degree in landscape architecture at a school in any state.
Eligibility: Open to third-, fourth-, or fifth-year undergraduate students and graduate students in landscape architecture who are residents of Hawaii enrolled at a college or university in any state. Applicants are required to submit 2 letters of recommendation (1 from a design instructor), a 500-word autobiographical essay that addresses personal and professional goals, and a sample of design work. Selection is based on professional experience, community involvement, extracurricular activities, and financial need.
Financial data: The stipend is $2,000.
Number awarded: 1 each year.
Deadline: February of each year.

1308 HEARST JOURNALISM AWARDS PROGRAM BROADCAST NEWS COMPETITIONS

William Randolph Hearst Foundation
90 New Montgomery Street, Suite 1212
San Francisco, CA 94105-4504
Phone: (415) 908-4560; (800) 841-7048, ext. 4560
Email: journalism@hearstfdn.org

Web: www.hearstfdn.org/hearst_journalism/index.php

Summary: To recognize and reward, with scholarships for additional study, outstanding college student broadcast news journalists.

Eligibility: Open to full-time undergraduate students majoring in journalism at 1 of the 110 accredited colleges and universities that are members of the Association of Schools of Journalism and Mass Communication (ASJMC). For each of the 2 semifinal competitions, each student submits either a CD (for radio) or a DVD (for television) originating with and produced by the undergraduate student with primary responsibility for the entry. Entries must have been "published" in the sense of having been made available to an anonymous audience of substantial size. The first competition of each year is for "features"; entries must be soft news: non-deadline reporting of personalities, events, or issues. They may be based on, but not limited to, public affairs, business, investigations, science, sports, or weather. The second competition of each year is for "news"; entries must be hard news, including enterprise reporting. They may be based on, but are not limited to, public affairs reporting, business reporting, investigative reporting, sports reporting, or weather reporting, as long as they have a hard news focus. All entries must have been produced since September of the previous year and must consist of at least 2 reports. Broadcast news CDs and DVDs are judged on the basis of writing quality, understandability, clarity, depth, focus, editing, knowledge of subject, broadcast skills, originality, visual story telling, graphics, human interest, design, reporting, and navigation and structure. Applicants submitting the 10 CDs and 10 DVDs selected by the judges as the best in the semifinals are then entered in the finals. The finalists submit new and different tapes, up to 10 minutes in length with a minimum of 3 reports, of which only 1 may have been submitted previously. The reports must include at least 1 news story and 1 feature. Judges select the top 5 CDs and the top 5 DVDs, and those 10 finalists go to San Francisco for an on-the-spot news assignment to rank the winners. Radio and television entries are judged separately.

Financial data: In each of the 2 semifinal competitions for both radio and television, each semifinalist receives a $1,000 scholarship. For the finals competitions for both radio and television, additional scholarships are awarded of $5,000 for first place, $4,000 for second, $3,000 for third, and $1,500 for each of the other 2 finalists; in addition, the students who make the best use of radio for news coverage and the best use of television for news coverage each receive another scholarship of $1,000. Scholarship funds are paid to the college or university and credited to the recipients' educational costs (tuition, matriculation and other fees, and room and board provided by or approved by the college or university). Schools receive points for their students who place in the top 20 places in the semifinals and in the finals; the school with the most points receives an additional cash prize of $10,000, second wins $5,000, and third wins $2,500. The total amount awarded in scholarships and grants in this and the writing and photojournalism competitions is nearly $500,000 per year.

Duration: The competition is held annually.

Number awarded: 20 semifinal (10 for radio and 10 for television) and 10 final (5 for radio and 5 for television) winners are chosen each year. In addition, 1 scholarship is awarded each year for best use of radio and 1 for best use of television.

Deadline: The deadline for the first competition is in November of each year and for the second competition in January of each year. Additional entries by finalists must be submitted by February of each year for the first competition or April of each year for the second competition. The competition among the top 10 finalists takes place in San Francisco in June.

1309 HEARST JOURNALISM AWARDS PROGRAM PHOTOJOURNALISM COMPETITIONS

William Randolph Hearst Foundation
90 New Montgomery Street, Suite 1212
San Francisco, CA 94105-4504
Phone: (415) 908-4560; (800) 841-7048, ext. 4560
Email: photos@hearstfdn.org
Web: www.hearstfdn.org/hearst_journalism/index.php

Summary: To recognize and reward, with scholarships for additional study, outstanding college student photojournalists.

Eligibility: Open to full-time undergraduate students enrolled at 1 of the 110 accredited colleges and universities that are members of the Association of Schools of Journalism and Mass Communication (ASJMC); they are not required to be majoring in journalism. For each of the 3 semifinal competitions, each student submits photographs from newspapers, magazines, online media, or web sites. For the first competition of each year, the categories are portrait/personality, feature, and "personal vision"; entries consist of 2 photographs in the portrait/personality category, 2 in the feature category, and 1 in the "personal vision" category (for a total of 5 photographs). For the second competition of each year, the categories are sports and news; entries consist of 2 photographs in each of those 2 categories. For the third competition of each year, the category is picture story/series; each entry must include 1 picture story/series, with at least 2 of the following additional components: audio, print, video, graphics. All photographs must have been taken since September of the previous year and may be color or black-and-white. Photography is judged on the basis of quality, visual story telling, versatility, consistency, human interest, news value, originality, editing, writing, reporting, audio and video (third competition only), graphics (third competition only), navigation and structure (third competition only), and design (third competition only). The judges select the top 10 entrants in each of the 3 competitions; of those 10, the 4 top scoring entrants qualify for the photojournalism finals. Those 12 finalists must submit a portfolio consisting of prints of the slides previously judged, plus 2 additional photographs (published or unpublished) from each of the other categories in the overall contest; complete portfolios must thus consist of 2 pictures each in news, features, sports, portrait/personality, plus a picture story/series. Based on those portfolios, judges select the top 6 finalists to go to San Francisco for on-the-spot assignments to rank the winners.

Financial data: In each of the 3 semifinal competitions, each semifinalist receives a $1,000 scholarship. For the finals competition, additional scholarships are awarded of $5,000 for first place, $4,000 for second, $3,000 for third, and $1,500 for each of the other 3 finalists. In addition, the photographers who submit the best single photo and the best picture story each receive another scholarship of $1,000. Scholarship funds are paid to the college or university and credited to the recipients' educational costs (tuition, matriculation and other fees, and room and board provided by or approved by the college or university). Schools receive points for their students who place in the top 20 places in the semifinals and in the finals; the school with the most points receives an additional cash prize of $10,000, second wins $5,000, and third wins $2,500. The total amount awarded in scholarships and grants in this and the writing and broadcast news competitions is nearly $500,000 per year.

Duration: The competition is held annually.

Number awarded: 30 semifinal and 6 final winners are chosen each year, and 2 additional scholarships are awarded each year for the best single photo and best picture story.

Deadline: The deadline for the first competition is in November of each year, for the second competition in January of each year, and for the third competition in March of each year. Additional entries by finalists must be submitted by April of each year. The competition among the top 6 finalists takes place in San Francisco in June.

1310 HEARST JOURNALISM AWARDS PROGRAM WRITING COMPETITIONS

William Randolph Hearst Foundation
90 New Montgomery Street, Suite 1212
San Francisco, CA 94105-4504
Phone: (415) 908-4560; (800) 841-7048, ext. 4560
Email: journalism@hearstfdn.org
Web: www.hearstfdn.org/hearst_journalism/index.php

Summary: To recognize and reward, with scholarships for additional study, outstanding college student journalists.

Eligibility: Open to full-time undergraduate students majoring in journalism at 1 of the 105 accredited colleges or universities that are members of the Association of Schools of Journalism and Mass Communication (ASJMC). Each entry consists of a single article written by the student with primary responsibility for the work and published in a campus or professional publication. Each month, a separate competition is held; October: feature writing—a background, color, or mood article as opposed to a conventional news story or personality profile; November: editorials or signed columns of opinion—must be well researched and express a clear and cogent viewpoint; December: in-depth writing—must illustrate the student's ability to handle a complex subject clearly, precisely, and with sufficient background; January: sports writing—relevant to an event or issue, not to a sports personality; February: personality profile—a personality sketch of someone on or off campus; and March: spot news writing—articles written about a breaking news event and against a deadline. The 6 monthly winners and the 2 finalists who place highest in their top 2 scores in the monthly competitions qualify for the national writing championship held in San Francisco in June; at that time, competition assignments consist of an on-the-spot assignment and a news story and personality profile from a press interview of a prominent individual in the San Francisco area. Writing is judged on the basis of knowledge of subject, understandability, clarity, color, reporting in depth, and construction. Additional awards are presented for article of the year and best reporting technique.

Financial data: In each of the 6 competitions, the first-place winner receives a $2,000 scholarship, second $1,500, third $1,000, fourth $750, fifth $600, and sixth through tenth $500; identical grants are awarded to the journalism schools attended by the students. For the finalists whose articles are judged best in the national writing championship, additional scholarships of $5,000 are

awarded for first place, $4,000 for second, $3,000 for third, and $1,500 for each of the other 5 finalists. The additional awards for article of the year and best reporting technique are each $1,000. Scholarship awards are paid to the college or university and credited to the recipients' educational costs (tuition, matriculation and other fees, and room and board provided by or approved by the college or university). Schools receive points for each of their students who place in the top 20 places in each monthly competition; the school with the most points receives an additional cash prize of $10,000, second wins $5,000, and third wins $2,500. The total amount awarded in scholarships and grants in this and the photojournalism and broadcast news competitions is nearly $500,000 per year.
Duration: The competition is held annually.
Number awarded: Each year, 60 scholarships are awarded to the monthly winners, and an additional 8 are presented to the national finalists.
Deadline: Articles for the monthly competitions must be submitted by the end of the respective month of each year. The championship is held in June of each year.

1311 HEATON-PERRY SCHOLARSHIP

Society of Professional Journalists–Kansas Professional Chapter
c/o Denise Neil, Scholarship Committee
Wichita Eagle
825 East Douglas Avenue
P.O. Box 820
Wichita, KS 67201-0820
Phone: (316) 268-6327
Email: dneil@wichitaeagle.com
Web: www.spjchapters.org/kansas/gridiron.html
Summary: To provide financial assistance to residents of any state enrolled at colleges and universities in Kansas who are interested in a career in journalism.
Eligibility: Open to residents of any state entering their junior or senior year at colleges and universities in Kansas. Applicants do not have to be journalism or communication majors, but they must demonstrate a strong and sincere interest in print journalism, broadcast journalism, online journalism, or photojournalism. They must have a GPA of 2.5 or higher. Along with their application, they must submit a professional resume, 4 to 6 examples of their best work (clips or stories, copies of photographs, tapes or transcripts of broadcasts, printouts of web pages) and a 1-page cover letter about themselves, how they came to be interested in journalism, their professional goals, and (if appropriate) their financial need for this scholarship.
Financial data: The stipend is $1,000.
Duration: 1 year.
Number awarded: 1 each year.
Deadline: April of each year.

1312 HELEN VERBA SCHOLARSHIPS

Society of Professional Journalists–Colorado Professional Chapter
c/o Robert Boczkiewicz, Scholarship Chair
1020 Pennsylvania Street, Apartment 207
Denver, CO 80203-5802
Phone: (303) 832-7472
Email: reb1den@aol.com
Web: www.coloradospjpro.com
Summary: To provide financial assistance to juniors from any state majoring in journalism at colleges and universities in Colorado.
Eligibility: Open to residents of any state entering their junior year at a college or university in Colorado. Applicants must be majoring in print or broadcast journalism. They must submit a resume, 2 references, at least 1 clip of a story or article published in a school or professional publication, and a 500-word essay illustrating their writing abilities and indicating their plans for a career in journalism.
Financial data: The stipend is $1,500.
Duration: 1 year.
Number awarded: 2 each year: 1 to a student in print journalism and 1 to a student in broadcast journalism.
Deadline: February of each year.

1313 HERB ROBINSON SCHOLARSHIP

Washington News Council
Attn: Scholarship Committee
P.O. Box 3672
Seattle, WA 98124-3672
Phone: (206) 262-9793; Fax: (206) 464-7902
Email: info@wanewscouncil.org
Web: www.wanewscouncil.org
Summary: To provide financial assistance to Washington high school seniors who are interested in majoring in a communication-related field at an academic institution in the state.
Eligibility: Open to seniors graduating from high schools in Washington who have a serious interest in communications, including journalism, politics, public relations, or related fields. Applicants must be accepted at a 4-year public or private university in the state. Along with their application, they must submit a 750-word essay on a topic that changes annually; recently, students were asked to write on whether the expectations of journalists that other institutions should be transparent, accountable, and open also apply to them. Selection is based on that essay, academic achievement, and financial need.
Financial data: The stipend is $2,000.
Duration: 1 year.
Number awarded: 1 each year.
Deadline: April of each year.

1314 HERFF JONES SCHOLARSHIP

University Interscholastic League
Attn: Interscholastic League Press Conference
1701 Manor Road
P.O. Box 8028
Austin, TX 78713-8028
Phone: (512) 232-4937; Fax: (512) 232-7311
Email: uilacad@uts.cc.utexas.edu
Web: www.uil.utexas.edu/academics/journalism/ilpc_forms.html
Summary: To provide financial assistance to high school seniors in Texas who plan to study communications in college.
Eligibility: Open to graduating seniors in Texas who have worked on their high school yearbook and plan to continue their education in a communications-related field (major or minor) in college. Applicants must have a GPA of "B" or higher. Along with their application, they must submit a statement on their involvement in journalism while in high school, a description of their college and potential career interests, a letter of recommendation, a list of journalism and other awards or honors they have received, and 3 to 5 samples of their work as a journalism student. Financial need is not considered in the selection process.
Financial data: The stipend is $1,200.
Duration: 1 year.
Number awarded: 1 each year.
Deadline: March of each year.

1315 HGA SCHOLARSHIPS

Handweavers Guild of America, Inc.
Attn: Scholarship Committee
1255 Buford Highway, Suite 211
Suwanee, GA 30024
Phone: (678) 730-0010; Fax: (678) 730-0836
Email: hga@weavespindye.org
Web: www.weavespindye.org/pages/?p=hgaschol.htm&loc=1-48-00
Summary: To provide financial assistance to undergraduate and graduate students working on a degree in the field of fiber arts.
Eligibility: Open to undergraduate and graduate students enrolled in accredited colleges and universities in the United States, its possessions, and Canada. Applicants must be working on a degree in the field of fiber arts, including training for research, textile history, and conservation. Along with their application, they must submit 1) a 50-word essay on their study goals and how those fit into their future plans; and 2) 5 to 16 slides of their work. Selection is based on artistic and technical merit; financial need is not considered.
Financial data: The stipend ranges up to $1,000. Use of funds is restricted to tuition.
Duration: Funds must be spent within 1 year.
Number awarded: 1 each year.
Deadline: March of each year.

1316 HOLOCAUST REMEMBRANCE PROJECT

Holland & Knight Charitable Foundation, Inc.
201 North Franklin Street, 11th Floor
P.O. Box 2877
Tampa, FL 33601-2877

Phone: (813) 227-8500; (866) HK-CARES
Email: holocaust@hklaw.com
Web: holocaust.hklaw.com

Summary: To recognize and reward high school students who submit outstanding essays on a topic related to the Holocaust.

Eligibility: Open to high school students in grades 9–12 (including graduating seniors) in the United States and Mexico. Applicants are expected to study the Holocaust and then, in a 1,200-word essay, analyze why it is vital to remember and pass to a new generation the history and lessons of the Holocaust, and suggest what they, as students, can do to combat and prevent prejudice, discrimination, and violence in our world today. In preparation for writing, students are encouraged to research their essay using a variety of sources, including historical and reference material, interviews, eyewitness accounts, oral testimonies, official documents and other primary sources, readings from diaries, letters, autobiographies, works of poetry, video or audio tapes, films, art, CD-ROMs, and Internet sources. Selection is based on 1) evidence of relevant reading and thoughtful use of resource materials; 2) treatment of the assigned theme; 3) clear and effective language, mechanics, and grammar; and 4) a coherent plan of organization.

Financial data: First-place winners receive a 5-day, all-expense-paid trip to Chicago to visit the new Illinois Holocaust Memorial Museum and other sites with teachers and Holocaust survivors (valued at more than $2,000), a gold medal, and a certificate of participation. They also receive scholarships that range from $2,500 to $10,000. These scholarships are paid to the recipients' colleges or universities, after they graduate from high school and upon receipt of proof of registration. Second-place winners receive $500, a silver medal, and a certificate of participation. Third-place winners receive $300, a bronze medal, and a certificate of participation.

Duration: The competition is held annually. Former first-place winners are not eligible to enter in subsequent years.

Number awarded: 30 each year: 10 first-place winners, 10 second-place winners, and 10 third-place winners.

Deadline: April of each year.

1317 HOME BUILDERS FOUNDATION BUILDING INDUSTRY SCHOLARSHIPS

Home Builders Association of Metropolitan Portland
Attn: Home Builders Foundation
15555 S.W. Bangy Road, Suite 301
Lake Oswego, OR 97035
Phone: (503) 684-1880; Fax: (503) 684-0588
Email: scholarships@hbapdx.org
Web: www.homebuildersportland.org/buildingindustryscholarships.htm

Summary: To provide financial assistance to residents of Oregon who are attending college in the state to prepare for a career in the home building industry.

Eligibility: Open to residents of Oregon who are currently enrolled full-time at a college or university in the state. Applicants must have completed at least 1 year of study in an approved home building or construction-related program (e.g., construction management, architectural design, architectural engineering technology, building inspection, building technology management) and have a GPA of 3.0 or higher. Along with their application, they must submit essays of 350 to 500 words on 2 of the following topics: 1) their career dreams and why they should receive this scholarship; 2) the experience or person that most influenced them in selecting the home building and construction industry as their career; 3) a specific event or program on which they worked that made a difference in their community; 4) the value of being paired with a career mentor; or 5) their work experience in construction or a related field. Selection is based on those essays, GPA, quality of the application, letters of recommendation, an interview, and financial need. Some scholarships are reserved for residents of the Portland Metropolitan area (Clackamas, Columbia, Multnomah, Washington, and Yamhill counties). U.S. citizenship or permanent resident status is required.

Financial data: Most stipends are $1,500 per year.

Duration: 1 year; recipients may reapply.

Number awarded: Varies each year; recently, 10 of these scholarships were awarded: 3 to students from the Portland Metropolitan area and 7 statewide.

Deadline: May of each year.

1318 HONORABLE ERNESTINE WASHINGTON LIBRARY SCIENCE/ENGLISH LANGUAGE ARTS SCHOLARSHIP

African-American/Caribbean Education Association, Inc.
P.O. Box 1224
Valley Stream, NY 11582-1224
Phone: (718) 949-6733
Email: aaceainc@yahoo.com
Web: www.aaceainc.com/Scholarships.html

Summary: To provide financial assistance to high school seniors of African American or Caribbean heritage who plan to study a field related to library science or English language arts in college.

Eligibility: Open to graduating high school seniors who are U.S. citizens of African American or Caribbean heritage. Applicants must be planning to attend a college or university and major in a field related to library science or English language arts. They must have completed 4 years of specified college preparatory courses with a grade of 90 or higher and have an SAT score of at least 1790. They must also have completed at least 200 hours of community service during their 4 years of high school, preferably in the field that they plan to study in college. Financial need is not considered in the selection process. New York residency is not required, but applicants must be available for an interviews in the Queens, New York area.

Financial data: The stipend ranges from $1,000 to $2,500. Funds are paid directly to the recipient.

Duration: 1 year.

Number awarded: 1 each year.

Deadline: April of each year.

1319 HONORARY STATE REGENTS' AMERICAN HISTORY SCHOLARSHIP

Daughters of the American Revolution–Colorado State Society
c/o Marcy Kimminau, State Scholarship Chair
17537 West 59th Place
Golden, CO 80403-2022
Email: marcyk12@aol.com
Web: www.coloradodar.org/scholarships.htm

Summary: To provide financial assistance to high school seniors in Colorado who are interested in majoring in American history and government at a college in any state.

Eligibility: Open to graduating high school seniors in Colorado who are 1) U.S. citizens; 2) in the upper fifth of their graduating class; 3) accepted at an accredited college or university (in any state); and 4) planning to major in American history and government. Interested students are invited to submit their complete application to the state scholarship chair (c/o the sponsor's address); they must include a statement of their career interest and goals (up to 500 words), 2 character references, their college transcripts, a letter of sponsorship from the Daughters of the American Revolution's Colorado chapter, and a list of their scholastic achievements, extracurricular activities, honors, and other significant accomplishments. Selection is based on academic excellence, commitment to field of study, and financial need.

Financial data: The maximum stipend is $2,500. Funds are paid directly to the students' school.

Duration: 1 year; nonrenewable.

Number awarded: 1 each year.

Deadline: January of each year.

1320 HOOSIER STATE PRESS ASSOCIATION FOUNDATION SCHOLARSHIP

Hoosier State Press Association Foundation
c/o Karen T. Braeckel, Director
41 East Washington Street, Suite 301
Indianapolis, IN 46204
Phone: (317) 624-4426; Fax: (317) 624-4428
Email: kbraeckel@hspa.com
Web: www.hspafoundation.org/scholarship.html

Summary: To provide financial assistance to high school seniors in Indiana who plan to attend college in any state and prepare for a career in newspapers.

Eligibility: Open to seniors graduating from high schools in Indiana who have a GPA of 3.0 or higher. Applicants must be planning to attend a college or university in any state and major in a field to prepare for a career in newspapers, including (but not limited to) reporting, photojournalism, graphic and page design, multimedia, and/or web design. Along with their application, they must submit 3 samples of their work, a letter of reference, and a 400-word personal statement explaining why they are interested in majoring in print journalism. Financial need is not considered in the selection process.

Financial data: The stipend is $1,000.

Duration: 1 year.

Number awarded: 1 each year.

Deadline: March of each year.

1321 HORACE AND SUSIE REVELS CAYTON SCHOLARSHIP

Public Relations Society of America–Puget Sound Chapter
c/o Diane Bevins
1006 Industry Drive
Seattle, WA 98188-4801
Phone: (206) 623-8632
Email: prsascholarship@asi-seattle.net
Web: www.prsapugetsound.org/scholars.html

Summary: To provide financial assistance to minority upper-classmen from Washington who are interested in preparing for a career in public relations.

Eligibility: Open to U.S. citizens who are members of minority groups, defined as African Americans, Asian Americans, Hispanic/Latino Americans, Native Americans, and Pacific Islanders. Applicants must be full-time juniors or seniors attending a college in Washington or Washington students (who graduated from a Washington high school or whose parents live in the state year-round) attending college elsewhere. They must be able to demonstrate aptitude in public relations and related courses, activities, and/or internships. Along with their application, they must submit a description of their career goals and the skills that are most important in general to a public relations career (15 points in the selection process); a description of their activities in communications in class, on campus, in the community, or during internships, including 3 samples of their work (15 points); a statement on the value of public relations to an organization (10 points); a description of any barriers, financial or otherwise, they have encountered in pursuing their academic or personal goals and how they have addressed them (15 points); a discussion of their heritage, and how their cultural background and/or the discrimination they may have experienced has impacted them (15 points); a certified transcript (15 points); and 2 or more letters of recommendation (15 points).

Financial data: The stipend is $2,500.

Duration: 1 year.

Number awarded: 1 each year.

Deadline: April of each year.

1322 HOUSTON SUN SCHOLARSHIP

National Association of Negro Business and Professional Women's Clubs
Attn: Scholarship Committee
1806 New Hampshire Avenue, N.W.
Washington, DC 20009-3206
Phone: (202) 483-4206; Fax: (202) 462-7253
Email: education@nanbpwc.org
Web: www.nanbpwc.org/ScholarshipApplications.asp

Summary: To provide financial assistance to African Americans from designated states studying journalism at a college in any state.

Eligibility: Open to African Americans (men or women) who are residents of Arkansas, Kansas, Louisiana, Missouri, New Mexico, Oklahoma, or Texas. Applicants must be enrolled at an accredited college or university in any state as a sophomore or junior. They must have a GPA of 3.0 or higher and be majoring in journalism. Along with their application, they must submit an essay, up to 750 words in length, on the topic, "Credo of the Black Press." U.S. citizenship is required.

Financial data: The stipend is $1,000.

Duration: 1 year.

Number awarded: 1 or more each year.

Deadline: February of each year.

1323 HOWARD BROWN RICKARD SCHOLARSHIP

National Federation of the Blind
Attn: Scholarship Committee
1800 Johnson Street
Baltimore, MD 21230
Phone: (410) 659-9314, ext. 2415; Fax: (410) 685-5653
Email: scholarships@nfb.org
Web: www.nfb.org/nfb/scholarship_program.asp

Summary: To provide financial assistance for college or graduate school to blind students studying or planning to study law, medicine, engineering, architecture, or the natural sciences.

Eligibility: Open to legally blind students who are enrolled in or planning to enroll in a full-time undergraduate or graduate course of study. Applicants must be studying or planning to study law, medicine, engineering, architecture, or the natural sciences. Along with their application, they must submit transcripts, standardized test scores, proof of legal blindness, 2 letters of recommendation, and a letter of endorsement from their National Federation of the Blind state president or designee. Selection is based on academic excellence, service to the community, and financial need.

Financial data: The stipend is $3,000.

Duration: 1 year; recipients may resubmit applications up to 2 additional years.

Number awarded: 1 each year.

Deadline: March of each year.

1324 HUBERT B. OWENS SCHOLARSHIP

Georgia Trust
Attn: Scholarship Committee
1516 Peachtree Street, N.W.
Atlanta, GA 30309
Phone: (404) 881-9980; Fax: (404) 875-2205
Email: info@georgiatrust.org
Web: www.georgiatrust.org/preservation/spalding_owens.php

Summary: To provide financial assistance to Georgia residents majoring in a field related to historical preservation at a college or university in the state.

Eligibility: Open to Georgia residents who are enrolled full-time in their first year of undergraduate study at a college or university in the state. Applicants must be working on a degree in historic preservation or a related field (e.g., archaeology, architecture, history, planning). U.S. citizenship is required. Selection is based on academic achievement and past and planned involvement within preservation-related fields.

Financial data: The stipend is $1,000.

Duration: 1 year.

Number awarded: 1 each year.

Deadline: February of each year.

1325 HUMANE STUDIES FELLOWSHIPS

Institute for Humane Studies at George Mason University
3301 North Fairfax Drive, Suite 440
Arlington, VA 22201-4432
Phone: (703) 993-4880; (800) 697-8799; Fax: (703) 993-4890
Email: ihs@gmu.edu
Web: www.theihs.org/ContentDetails.aspx?id=491

Summary: To provide financial assistance to undergraduate and graduate students in the United States or abroad who intend to pursue "intellectual careers" and have demonstrated an interest in classical liberal principles.

Eligibility: Open to students who will be full-time graduate students (including law, journalism, business, and other professional students) and undergraduate juniors and seniors. Applicants must be interested in "exploring the principles, practices, and institutions necessary for a free society." Along with their application, they must submit 1) an essay of 500 to 1,000 words on their interest in the intellectual and institutional foundations of a free society, how they expect to contribute to a better understanding of those foundations, and their career goals, especially where they expect to be in 5, 10, and 20 years; and 2) an essay of 1,000 to 2,000 words discussing a research paper, presentation, dissertation, or other intellectual project that they are working on now or have recently completed. Applications from students outside the United States or studying abroad receive equal consideration. Selection is based on academic or professional performance, relevance of work to the advancement of a free society, and potential for success.

Financial data: The maximum stipend is $12,000.

Duration: 1 year; may be renewed upon reapplication.

Number awarded: Approximately 120 each year.

Deadline: December of each year.

1326 IAN JAMES WALLACE SCHOLARSHIP

Ian James Wallace Scholarship Fund
16748-9C East Smoky Hill Road, Number 334
Centennial, CO 80015
Web: www.ianjameswallace.org

Summary: To provide financial assistance to high school seniors in Colorado who plan to study the arts or humanities at a college in any state.

Eligibility: Open to seniors graduating from high schools in Colorado and planning to enroll full-time at a college or university in any state. Applicants must be interested in studying the arts or humanities. They must have a high school GPA of 3.0 or higher. Along with their application, they must submit an essay of 500 to 750 words describing how they plan to apply their knowledge, skills, and values in order to contribute to building a more humane and just world. Selection is based on academic success, personal accomplishments (as in the arts, music, theater, technology, consumer and family studies, science, athletics, volunteer work), and community contributions. The program includes 1 scholarship reserved for a senior at Smoky Hill High School.

Financial data: The stipend is $1,500.

Duration: 1 year; nonrenewable.
Number awarded: 2 each year (including 1 reserved for a student at Smoky Hill High School).
Deadline: February of each year.

1327 IDAHO STATE BROADCASTERS ASSOCIATION SCHOLARSHIPS

Idaho State Broadcasters Association
270 North 27th Street, Suite B
Boise, ID 83702-4741
Phone: (208) 345-3072; Fax: (208) 343-8946
Email: isba@qwestoffice.net
Web: www.idahobroadcasters.org/scholarships.aspx

Summary: To provide financial assistance to students at Idaho colleges and universities who are preparing for a career in the broadcasting field (including the business side of broadcasting).
Eligibility: Open to full-time students at Idaho schools who are preparing for a career in broadcasting, including business administration, sales, journalism, or engineering. Applicants must have a GPA of at least 2.0 for the first 2 years of school or 2.5 for the last 2 years. Along with their application, they must submit a letter of recommendation from the general manager of a broadcasting station that is a member of the Idaho State Broadcasters Association and a 1-page essay describing their career plans and why they want the scholarship. Applications are encouraged from a wide and diverse student population. Financial need is not considered in the selection process.
Financial data: The stipend is $1,000.
Duration: 1 year.
Number awarded: 2 each year.
Deadline: March of each year.

1328 IDDBA SCHOLARSHIP

International Dairy-Deli-Bakery Association
Attn: Scholarship Committee
636 Science Drive
P.O. Box 5528
Madison, WI 53705-0528
Phone: (608) 310-5000; Fax: (608) 238-6330
Email: iddba@iddba.org
Web: www.iddba.org/scholarships.aspx

Summary: To provide financial assistance to high school seniors, undergraduates, or graduate students employed in a supermarket dairy, deli, or bakery department who are interested in working on a degree in a food-related field.
Eligibility: Open to high school seniors, college students, vocational/technical students, and graduate students. Applicants must be currently employed at least 13 hours per week in a supermarket dairy, deli, or bakery department or be employed by a company that services those departments (e.g., food manufacturers, brokers, or wholesalers). They must be working on a degree in a food-related field, including culinary arts, baking/pastry arts, food science, business, or marketing. Their employer must be a member of the International Dairy-Deli-Bakery Association (IDDBA). While a GPA of 2.5 or higher is required, this may be waived for first-time returning adult students. Selection is based on academic achievement, work experience, and a statement of career goals. Financial need is not considered.
Financial data: Stipends range from $250 to $1,000. Funds are paid jointly to the recipient and the recipient's school. If the award exceeds tuition fees, the excess may be used for other educational expenses.
Duration: 1 year; recipients may reapply.
Number awarded: Varies each year; a total of $75,000 is available for this program annually.
Deadline: Applications must be submitted prior to the end of March, June, September, or December of each year.

1329 I.F. STONE AWARD FOR EXCELLENCE IN STUDENT JOURNALISM

Nation Institute
Attn: Stone Award
116 East 16th Street, Eighth Floor
New York, NY 10003
Phone: (212) 822-0252; Fax: (212) 253-5356
Web: www.nationinstitute.org/p/stone

Summary: To recognize and reward outstanding college journalists.
Eligibility: Open to undergraduate students majoring in journalism at any college or university in the United States. Entrants may submit up to 3 articles, preferably published in student publications during the preceding year; unpublished articles will also be considered unless they were written as assignments for regular course work. Articles may be submitted by the writers themselves or nominated by editors of student publications or faculty members. Investigative articles are especially encouraged.
Financial data: The award is $1,000.
Duration: The award is presented annually.
Number awarded: 1 each year.
Deadline: June of each year.

1330 IFEC SCHOLARSHIPS

International Foodservice Editorial Council
27 Beadart Place
P.O. Box 491
Hyde Park, NY 12538
Phone: (845) 229-6973; Fax: (845) 229-6993
Email: ifec@ifenonline.com
Web: www.ifeconline.com/scholarship_info.cfm

Summary: To provide financial assistance to undergraduate or graduate students who are interested in preparing for a career in communications in the food service industry.
Eligibility: Open to currently-enrolled college students who are working on an associate, bachelor's, or master's degree. Applicants should be preparing for a career as a writer, editor, public relations and marketing communication practitioner, or closely-related area in the food service industry. They must be enrolled full-time with a combination of studies (and/or work experience) in both the food service and communication arts. Appropriate food service majors include culinary arts; hospitality management; hotel, restaurant, and institutional management; dietetics; food science and technology; and nutrition. Applicable communications areas include journalism, English, mass communications, public relations, marketing, broadcast journalism, graphic arts, and photography. Selection is based on academic record, character references, and demonstrated financial need.
Financial data: Stipends range from $500 to $4,000.
Duration: 1 year.
Number awarded: 4 to 6 each year.
Deadline: March of each year.

1331 IHA STUDENT DESIGN COMPETITION

International Housewares Association
Attn: Design Programs Coordinator
6400 Shafer Court, Suite 650
Rosemont, IL 60018
Phone: (847) 692-0136; Fax: (847) 292-4211
Email: vmatranga@nhma.com
Web: www.housewares.org/show/info/sdc

Summary: To recognize and reward outstanding young designers of housewares products.
Eligibility: Open to juniors, seniors, or graduate students at a school affiliated with the Industrial Designers Society of America (IDSA). They are invited to design a housewares product in any of the following categories: household small electric appliances; personal care and home health care products; tableware, serving products, and accessories; cook and bakeware; kitchenware; outdoor products and accessories; home organization; cleaning products; furniture; decorative accessories; and juvenile and pet products. Students may submit more than 1 entry, but they may not be awarded more than 1 prize. Selection is based on design research (40%), design (40%), and technical skills and presentation communication (20%).
Financial data: First place is $2,500, second place is $1,800, third place is $1,300, and honorable mentions are $250. Winners also receive transportation and lodging for the International Housewares Show.
Duration: The competition is held annually.
Number awarded: Each year, 1 first place, 2 second places, 3 third places, and a varying number of honorable mentions (recently, 8) are awarded.
Deadline: December of each year.

1332 IMA HOGG YOUNG ARTIST COMPETITION

Houston Symphony
Attn: Director of Education and Community Relations
Jones Hall
615 Louisiana Street, Suite 102

Houston, TX 77002-2798
Phone: (713) 238-1449; Fax: (713) 224-0453
Email: office@houstonsymphony.org
Web: www.houstonsymphony.org

Summary: To recognize and reward outstanding young musicians.

Eligibility: Open to citizens of the United States, Mexico, and Canada and to foreign students currently enrolled in a U.S. college, university, or conservatory. Applicants must be young adults between 16 and 29 years of age. They must submit a CD recording of a required solo work for their instrument as well as additional non-concerto solo works of their choice, representing a style and period different from the required work. The competition is open to the following orchestral instruments: piano, violin, viola, cello, bass, flute, oboe, clarinet, bassoon, horn, trumpet, trombone, tuba, harp, and marimba. Semifinalists are selected on the basis of the tapes and invited to Houston for further competition, where they perform the required solo work and either a required concerto or 1 of several optional concertos. The finals consist of the concerto not performed in the semifinals.

Financial data: The first-prize winner receives the Grace Woodson Memorial Award of $5,000 and a performance with the Houston Symphony; the second-prize winner receives the Houston Symphony League Jerry Priest Award of $2,500 and a performance with the Houston Symphony; the third-prize winner receives the Selma Neumann Memorial Award with a cash prize of $1,000; the fourth prize is $500.

Duration: The competition is held annually.

Number awarded: 4 cash prizes are awarded each year.

Deadline: Preliminary audition tapes must be received by February of each year.

1333 INDIANA BROADCASTERS ASSOCIATION COLLEGE SCHOLARSHIPS

Indiana Broadcasters Association
Attn: Scholarship Administrator
3003 East 98th Street, Suite 161
Indianapolis, IN 46280
Phone: (317) 573-0119; (800) 342-6276 (within IN); Fax: (317) 573-0895
Email: INDBA@aol.com
Web: www.indianabroadcasters.org/students/scholarships.php

Summary: To provide financial assistance to college students in Indiana who are interested in preparing for a career in a field related to broadcasting.

Eligibility: Open to residents of Indiana who are attending a college or university in the state that is a member of the Indiana Broadcasters Association (IBA) or that has a radio/TV facility on campus. Applicants must be majoring in telecommunications or broadcast journalism and have a GPA of 3.0 or higher. They must be actively participating on a college broadcast facility or working for a commercial broadcast facility while attending college. Along with their application, they must submit an essay on their interest in continuing their education in telecommunications or broadcast journalism. Financial need is not considered in the selection process.

Financial data: The stipend is $2,000.

Duration: 1 year.

Number awarded: Varies each year; recently, 6 of these scholarships were awarded.

Deadline: March of each year.

1334 INDIANA PROFESSIONAL CHAPTER SPJ SCHOLARSHIPS

Society of Professional Journalists–Indiana Professional Chapter
101 Branigin Boulevard
Franklin, IN 46131
Email: indyprospj@gmail.com
Web: indyprospj.org/?s=scholarship&x=21&y=8

Summary: To provide financial assistance to high school seniors in Indiana who plan to major in journalism at a college or university in the state.

Eligibility: Open to seniors graduating from high schools in Indiana who plan to major in journalism at a college or university in the state. Applicants must submit transcripts, ACT/SAT test scores, letters of recommendation, and an essay on how they think journalists can make a difference.

Financial data: The stipend is $2,500.

Duration: 1 year.

Number awarded: 2 each year.

Deadline: October of each year.

1335 INTERMARKETS-LUCIDO JOURNALISM SCHOLARSHIPS

Northern Virginia Community Foundation
Attn: Director of Grants
8283 Greensboro Drive
McLean, VA 22102
Phone: (703) 902-3158; Fax: (703) 902-3564
Email: MacDonald_Lesley@ne.bah.com
Web: www.novacf.org/page10003427.cfm

Summary: To provide financial assistance to high school seniors in Virginia who plan to attend college in any state to major in journalism.

Eligibility: Open to seniors graduating from public or private high schools in Virginia who plan to enroll at an accredited 4-year college or university in any state. Applicants must be planning to major in journalism. Along with their application, they must submit 1) a 200-word essay on 3 character traits that a journalist should have and why; 2) 2 published articles or graded essays that reflect their writing style; and 3) a 500-word essay that takes a current article from a major U.S. newspaper that the candidate views as biased, explains why it is biased, and describes how it should be changed. Selection is based on those submissions, extracurricular activities, and academic excellence. U.S. citizenship is required.

Financial data: The stipend is $5,000.

Duration: 1 year.

Number awarded: 1 each year.

Deadline: April of each year.

1336 INTERNATIONAL COMMUNICATIONS INDUSTRIES FOUNDATION AV SCHOLARSHIPS

InfoComm International
International Communications Industries Foundation
11242 Waples Mill Road, Suite 200
Fairfax, VA 22030
Phone: (703) 273-7200; (800) 659-7469; Fax: (703) 278-8082
Email: srieger@infocomm.org
Web: www.infocomm.org/cps/rde/xchg/infocomm/hs.xsl/7163.htm

Summary: To provide financial assistance to high school seniors and college students who are interested in preparing for a career in the audiovisual (AV) industry.

Eligibility: Open to high school seniors, undergraduates, and graduate students already enrolled in college. Applicants must have a GPA of 2.75 or higher and be majoring or planning to major in audiovisual subjects or related fields, including audio, video, electronics, telecommunications, technical aspects of the theater, data networking, software development, or information technology. Students in other programs, such as journalism, may be eligible if they can demonstrate a relationship to career goals in the AV industry. Along with their application, they must submit 1) an essay of 150 to 200 words on the career path they plan to pursue in the audiovisual industry in the next 5 years; and 2) an essay of 250 to 300 words on the experience or person that most influenced them in selecting the audiovisual industry as their career of choice. Minority and women candidates are especially encouraged to apply. Selection is based on the essays, presentation of the application, GPA, AV-related experience, work experience, and letters of recommendation.

Financial data: The stipend is $1,200 per year. Funds are sent directly to the school.

Duration: 1 year; recipients may reapply.

Number awarded: Varies each year; recently, 29 of these scholarships were awarded.

Deadline: May of each year.

1337 INTERNATIONAL FURNISHINGS AND DESIGN ASSOCIATION PART TIME STUDENT SCHOLARSHIP

International Furnishings and Design Association
Attn: IFDA Educational Foundation
150 South Warner Road, Suite 156
King of Prussia, PA 19406
Phone: (610) 535-6422; Fax: (610) 535-6423
Email: info@ifda.com
Web: www.ifdaef.org/scholarships.html

Summary: To provide financial assistance to undergraduate students working part-time on a degree in interior design.

Eligibility: Open to part-time undergraduates currently enrolled in at least 2 courses. Applicants must have completed at least 4 courses in interior design or a related field. Along with their application, they must submit an essay of 200 to 400 words on their long- and short-term goals, special interests, achievements, awards and accomplishments, volunteer and community service, and

what inspired them to prepare for a career in this field; samples of their design work; a transcript; and a letter of recommendation from a professor or instructor. Financial need is not considered.
Financial data: The stipend is $1,000.
Duration: 1 year.
Number awarded: At least 1 each year.
Deadline: March of each year.

1338 INTERNATIONAL SOLO COMPETITION

Walter W. Naumburg Foundation, Inc.
120 Claremont Avenue
New York, NY 10027-4698
Phone: (212) 362-9877
Web: www.naumburg.org
Summary: To recognize and reward outstanding young singers and instrumentalists of all nationalities.
Eligibility: Open to musicians who are at least 17 but not more than 33 years of age. Applicants must submit a tape recording of no less than 30 minutes of satisfactory listenable quality. Based on those tapes, judges select contestants for live preliminary auditions, followed by semifinals and finals. Musicians may be of any nationality.
Financial data: Prizes vary; recently, they were $10,000 for first, $4,000 for second, and $1,000 for honorable mention.
Duration: The competition is held annually.
Number awarded: Varies each year; recently, 1 first prize, 2 second prizes, and 1 honorable mention were awarded.
Deadline: February of each year.

1339 INTERNATIONAL STUDENT STORE DESIGN COMPETITION

Retail Design Institute
Attn: Student Competitions
25 North Broadway
Tarrytown, NY 10591-3221
Phone: (914) 332-1806; (800) 379-9912; Fax: (914) 332-1541
Email: info@retaildesigninstitute.org
Web: www.retaildesigninstitute.org/competitions.php
Summary: To recognize and reward outstanding student store designers.
Eligibility: Open to students presently enrolled in a recognized college-level architectural, interior design, or environmental design program. Each year, the sponsor defines a retail design problem, and students compete by submitting a front elevation, interior finishes, schematic backroom and service area layout, store layout and site plan, detailed departments (e.g., signage, fixture layout, fixture types), rendering of key areas, fixture design, and ceiling lighting plan and fixture types. Students may enter either as individuals or groups of 2 or more students.
Financial data: In the individual category, first prize is $4,000, second $2,000, and third $1,000. In addition, the school of the first-place winner receives $1,000. In the group category, no student cash prizes are awarded, but the school of the group selected as the first-prize winner receives $1,000.
Duration: The competition is held annually.
Number awarded: 3 winners each year.
Deadline: April of each year.

1340 IOWA SCHOLARSHIPS FOR THE ARTS

Iowa Arts Council
Attn: Iowa Scholarships for the Arts
600 East Locust
Des Moines, IA 50319-0290
Phone: (515) 281-3293; Fax: (515) 242-6498; TDD: (800) 735-2942
Email: Veronica.OHern@iowa.gov
Web: www.iowaartscouncil.org
Summary: To provide financial assistance to Iowa high school seniors who plan to study the arts at a college or university in the state.
Eligibility: Open to graduating seniors at high schools in Iowa who have been accepted as full-time undergraduate students at an accredited college or university in the state. Applicants must be planning to major in music, dance, visual arts, folk or traditional arts, theater, or literature. Along with their application, they must submit samples of their work and a 1-page essay on why their art form is significant, what they value about being an artist, and what they hope to gain from an education in their particular field. Selection is based on 1) proven artistic and academic abilities in the chosen artistic area; and 2) future goals and objectives relating to the intended field of study.
Financial data: The stipend is $1,000.
Duration: 1 year.
Number awarded: Varies each year; recently, 3 of these scholarships were awarded.
Deadline: January of each year.

1341 ITT AWARD FOR EXCELLENCE IN STUDENT WATER JOURNALISM

ITT Corporation
1133 Westchester Avenue
White Plains, NY 10604
Phone: (914) 641-2160; Fax: (914) 696-2950
Email: andy.hilton@itt.com
Web: www.itt.com/news/global-activities/water-journalism
Summary: To recognize and reward, with college scholarships, high school journalists who submit an article on a water-related environmental issue.
Eligibility: Open to high school journalism students who are invited to submit an editorial, feature, or commentary they have written for publication in a high school or professional newspaper, magazine, web site, or broadcast channel. Entries must focus on local, regional, national, or global topics of environmental, scientific, social, or technological importance as related to water. Applicants must also submit a 250-word statement indicating any sources used for background information, a list of individuals interviewed (including job title and why selected), and the environmental, social, scientific, or technological importance of the issue covered.
Financial data: The award is a $1,000 college scholarship.
Duration: The competition is held annually.
Number awarded: 1 each year.
Deadline: February of each year.

1342 J. NEEL REID PRIZE

Georgia Trust
Attn: Scholarship Committee
1516 Peachtree Street, N.W.
Atlanta, GA 30309
Phone: (404) 881-9980; Fax: (404) 875-2205
Email: info@georgiatrust.org
Web: www.georgiatrust.org/publications/neel_reid_prize.php
Summary: To recognize and reward architecture students and architects, especially those with a connection to Georgia, who are interested in a study travel program in the United States or abroad.
Eligibility: Open to architecture students, architect interns, and recently registered architects who are interested in a study travel program. The focus of the study travel should involve historic architecture (built prior to Neel Reid's death in 1926), historic preservation of classic architecture, or new construction that is classic and context-related. Applicants are encouraged to propose an independent study, but participation in an existing program is acceptable. Priority is given to applicants with a connection to Georgia (a resident of the state, a student in a Georgia academic institution, or an employee of a Georgia firm). The travel may be to any location in the world.
Financial data: The prize is $4,000.
Duration: The study travel should be completed within a year and a half of the announcement of the winner.
Number awarded: 1 each year.
Deadline: February of each year.

1343 J. WARREN MCCLURE SCHOLARSHIP

Vermont Student Assistance Corporation
Attn: Scholarship Programs
10 East Allen Street
P.O. Box 2000
Winooski, VT 05404-2601
Phone: (802) 654-3798; (888) 253-4819; Fax: (802) 654-3765; TDD: (800) 281-3341 (within VT)
Email: info@vsac.org
Web: services.vsac.org/wps/wcm/connect/vsac/VSAC
Summary: To provide financial assistance to residents of Vermont who are interested in majoring in journalism at a college in any state.
Eligibility: Open to high school seniors, high school graduates, and currently-enrolled college students who are residents of Vermont. Applicants must be

enrolled or planning to enroll in a journalism degree program at a college or university in any state. Along with their application, they must submit 1) a 100-word essay on their interest in and commitment to pursuing their chosen career or vocation; and 2) a 250-word essay on their short- and long-term academic, educational, career, vocational, and/or employment goals. Selection is based on those essays, financial need, academic achievement, and a letter of recommendation.
Financial data: The stipend is $5,000.
Duration: 1 year.
Number awarded: 1 each year.
Deadline: March of each year.

1344 JACK C. SHAHEEN MASS COMMUNICATIONS SCHOLARSHIP

American-Arab Anti-Discrimination Committee Research Institute
Attn: Scholarship
1732 Wisconsin Avenue, N.W.
Washington, DC 20007
Phone: (202) 244-2990; Fax: (202) 244-7968
Web: www.adc.org
Summary: To provide financial assistance to Arab American upper-division and graduate students working on a degree in media studies.
Eligibility: Open to U.S. citizens of Arab heritage who are enrolled as juniors, seniors, or graduate students. Applicants must be working on a degree in mass communications, journalism, radio, television, and/or film. They must have a GPA of 3.0 or higher. Along with their application, they must submit a 1-page explanation of their goals and why they merit the scholarship. Financial need is not considered in the selection process.
Financial data: The stipend is $2,000.
Duration: 1 year.
Number awarded: 1 or more each year.
Deadline: April of each year.

1345 JACK DYER MEMORIAL SCHOLARSHIP

Oklahoma City Gridiron Foundation
330 North Country Club Terrace
Mustang, OK 73064
Web: www.okcgridiron.org
Summary: To provide financial assistance to journalism students in Oklahoma.
Eligibility: Open to residents of Oklahoma who are high school seniors or students already enrolled in college. Applicants must be working on or planning to work on a degree in journalism at a college or university in the state. Along with their application, they must submit brief statements on what they hope to be doing 6 months after completing college, what they hope to be doing 10 years from today, why they have selected journalism as their profession, what they like most about working in journalism, and what they like least. They must also submit a copy of their transcript and samples of their work. Financial need is considered in the selection process.
Financial data: The stipend is $2,000.
Duration: 1 year.
Number awarded: 1 each year.
Deadline: March of each year.

1346 JACKSON FOUNDATION JOURNALISM SCHOLARSHIP

Oregon Student Assistance Commission
Attn: Grants and Scholarships Division
1500 Valley River Drive, Suite 100
Eugene, OR 97401-2146
Phone: (541) 687-7395; (800) 452-8807, ext. 7395; Fax: (541) 687-7414; TDD: (800) 735-2900
Email: awardinfo@osac.state.or.us
Web: www.osac.state.or.us/osac_programs.html
Summary: To provide financial assistance to students in Oregon interested in majoring in journalism.
Eligibility: Open to graduates of Oregon high schools who are studying or planning to study journalism at a college or university in the state. Preference is given to students who have taken the SAT examination and have good scores on the writing section.
Financial data: Stipend amounts vary; recently, they were at least $1,429.
Duration: 1 year; may be renewed.
Number awarded: Varies each year; recently, 7 of these scholarships were awarded.
Deadline: February of each year.

1347 JAMES ALAN COX FOUNDATION SCHOLARSHIPS

James Alan Cox Foundation for Student Photographers
P.O. Box 9158
Austin, TX 78766
Phone: (512) 459-8515
Web: www.jamesalancoxfoundation.org/application.php
Summary: To provide financial assistance to college students interested in photography or photojournalism.
Eligibility: Open to students who have completed at least 1 year at a recognized college, university, or professional school and have taken courses in photography or photojournalism. Applicants must have at least 1 semester of school remaining. They must submit either 5 images as digital still photography entries or 2 videos up to 3 minutes in length. Financial need is considered in the selection process. U.S. citizenship is required.
Financial data: The stipend is $2,000.
Duration: 1 year.
Number awarded: 5 each year: 4 for video work and 1 for still photography.
Deadline: October of each year.

1348 JAMES BEARD FOUNDATION HIGH SCHOOL SENIOR SCHOLARSHIP PROGRAM

James Beard Foundation Scholarship Program
c/o Scholarship Management Services
One Scholarship Way
P.O. Box 297
St. Peter, MN 56082
Phone: (507) 931-1682; (800) 537-4180; Fax: (507) 931-9168
Email: jamesbeard@scholarshipamerica.org
Web: sms.scholarshipamerica.org/jamesbeard
Summary: To provide financial assistance to high school seniors interested in attending culinary school.
Eligibility: Open to high school seniors planning to enroll at least part-time at a licensed or accredited culinary school. Applicants must have a GPA of 3.0 or higher. Along with their application, they must submit a brief statement or summary of their plans as they relate to their culinary, educational, and career goals. Selection is based on that statement, academic record, leadership and participation in school and community activities, work experience, unusual personal or family circumstances, an outside appraisal, and financial need.
Financial data: The stipend is $4,000 per year.
Duration: 1 year; awards are not renewable, but recipients may reapply.
Number awarded: Several named scholarships are awarded each year.
Deadline: May of each year.

1349 JAMES BEARD FOUNDATION SPECIFIC SCHOOL SCHOLARSHIPS

James Beard Foundation Scholarship Program
c/o Scholarship Management Services
One Scholarship Way
P.O. Box 297
St. Peter, MN 56082
Phone: (507) 931-1682; (800) 537-4180; Fax: (507) 931-9168
Email: jamesbeard@scholarshipamerica.org
Web: sms.scholarshipamerica.org/jamesbeard
Summary: To provide financial assistance to high school seniors and graduates interested in attending specified culinary institutes or restaurant management programs in the United States or abroad.
Eligibility: Open to students interested in attending 20 specified culinary institutes in the United States or in Australia, Canada, England, France, Italy, Japan, Mexico, or Turkey. Each participating institute offers specific programs, but most offer a certificate, associate degree, or bachelor's degree in culinary arts and/or restaurant management; a master's degree in hospitality management is available in some cases. Students may apply to this program if they have been accepted at the school of their choice and they meet additional requirements of that school. For a current list of participating institutes and further information on the program at each, contact the sponsor.
Financial data: Support is provided in the form of partial tuition waivers that range from $1,500 to $5,000 at schools in the United States or in foreign currencies at the schools located abroad.
Duration: Up to 1 year.
Number awarded: Varies each year; recently 44 of these tuition waivers were available.
Deadline: May of each year.

1350 JAMES J. WYCHOR SCHOLARSHIPS

Minnesota Broadcasters Association
Attn: Scholarship Program
3033 Excelsior Boulevard, Suite 440
Minneapolis, MN 55416
Phone: (612) 926-8123; (800) 245-5838; Fax: (612) 926-9761
Email: llasere@minnesotabroadcasters.com
Web: www.minnesotabroadcasters.com

Summary: To provide financial assistance to Minnesota residents interested in studying broadcasting at a college in any state.

Eligibility: Open to residents of Minnesota who are accepted or enrolled at an accredited postsecondary institution in any state offering a broadcast-related curriculum. Applicants must have a high school or college GPA of 3.0 or higher and must submit a 500-word essay on why they wish to prepare for a career in broadcasting or electronic media. Employment in the broadcasting industry is not required, but students who are employed must include a letter from their general manager describing the duties they have performed as a radio or television station employee and evaluating their potential for success in the industry. Financial need is not considered in the selection process. Some of the scholarships are awarded only to minority and women candidates.

Financial data: The stipend is $1,500.

Duration: 1 year; recipients who are college seniors may reapply for an additional 1-year renewal as a graduate student.

Number awarded: 10 each year, distributed as follows: 3 within the 7-county metro area, 5 allocated geographically throughout the state (northeast, northwest, central, southeast, southwest), and 2 reserved specifically for women and minority applicants.

Deadline: June of each year.

1351 JAMES JAMIESON MEMORIAL SCHOLARSHIP

Delaware Community Foundation
Attn: Executive Vice President
100 West 10th Street, Suite 115
P.O. Box 1636
Wilmington, DE 19899
Phone: (302) 571-8004; Fax: (302) 571-1553
Email: rgentsch@delcf.org
Web: www.delcf.org/scholarships_guidelines.html

Summary: To provide financial assistance to dance students who reside in or study dance in Delaware.

Eligibility: Open to dance students who reside in or study dance in Delaware. Applicants must be preparing for a professional career in ballet. They must submit a short essay on why they desire to undertake a career in ballet. Finalists must attend a personal interview and audition.

Financial data: A stipend is awarded (amount not specified).

Duration: 1 year.

Number awarded: 1 or more each year.

Deadline: March of each year.

1352 JAMES M. AND VIRGINIA M. SMYTH SCHOLARSHIP FUND

Community Foundation for Greater Atlanta, Inc.
50 Hurt Plaza, Suite 449
Atlanta, GA 30303
Phone: (404) 688-5525; Fax: (404) 688-3060
Email: scholarships@cfgreateratlanta.org
Web: www.cfgreateratlanta.org/Grants-Support/Scholarships.aspx

Summary: To provide financial assistance to high school seniors, especially those from designated states, who are interested in majoring in selected fields at colleges in any state.

Eligibility: Open to graduating high school seniors, with special consideration given to residents of Georgia, Illinois, Mississippi, Missouri, Oklahoma, Tennessee, and Texas. Applicants must have a GPA of 3.0 or higher and be interested in attending a college, university, or community college in any state to work on a degree in the arts and sciences, human services, music, or ministry. They must be able to demonstrate financial need and a commitment to community service through school, community, or religious organizations. Adults returning to school to increase employability are also eligible.

Financial data: The stipend is $2,000 per year.

Duration: 1 year; may be renewed up to 3 additional years.

Number awarded: 12 to 15 each year.

Deadline: March of each year.

1353 JAMES O. THOMASON SCHOLARSHIP

Harry Hampton Memorial Wildlife Fund, Inc.
P.O. Box 2641
Columbia, SC 29202
Phone: (803) 463-7387; Fax: (803) 749-9362
Email: mpugh@sc.rr.com
Web: www.hamptonwildlifefund.org/scholarship.html

Summary: To provide financial assistance to high school seniors in South Carolina who plan to major in a field related to journalism or communications at a college or university in the state.

Eligibility: Open to seniors graduating from high schools in South Carolina who plan to attend an institution of higher learning in the state. Applicants must be planning to major in electronic, print, or photo journalism; advertising; public relations; or mass communications. Along with their application, they must submit 1) a 1,200-word essay on a topic that changes annually; recently, students were asked to write on the costs of ethanol production to wildlife and natural resources; and 2) a 3-page autobiography that describes their career ambitions in the field of journalism, advertising, public relations, or mass communications and explains their interest in wildlife resources, the environment, coastal resources, or related topics and why they will be a good investment if they are awarded this scholarship. Financial need is also considered in the selection process.

Financial data: The stipend is $1,000 per year.

Duration: 1 year; may be renewed up to 3 additional years, provided the recipient maintains a GPA of 2.5 or higher.

Number awarded: 1 each year.

Deadline: January of each year.

1354 J.B. STEVENSON SCHOLARSHIP

Alabama Scholastic Press Association
c/o University of Alabama
490 Reese Phifer
P.O. Box 870172
Tuscaloosa, AL 35487-0172
Phone: (205) 348-ASPA; Fax: (205) 348-2780
Email: aspa@ua.edu
Web: aspa1.ua.edu

Summary: To provide financial assistance to high school seniors in Alabama who are interested in studying journalism in college.

Eligibility: Open to seniors graduating from high schools in Alabama who have been involved in journalism. Applicants must be interested in attending college to prepare for a career in print journalism. Along with their application, they must submit an official transcript, a self-analytical evaluation of their "journalistic life," letters of recommendation, a portfolio showing examples of their best published work, and an issue of their newspaper or magazine or photocopies of relevant yearbook spreads. Items to be covered in their self-analytical evaluation include how they feel about journalism, how they got started in the field, what they have had to go through to achieve, what they have contributed to journalism, and their journalism plans for the future.

Financial data: The stipend is $2,500.

Duration: 1 year.

Number awarded: 1 each year.

Deadline: December of each year.

1355 J.D. EDSAL ADVERTISING SCHOLARSHIP

Rhode Island Foundation
Attn: Funds Administrator
One Union Station
Providence, RI 02903
Phone: (401) 427-4017; Fax: (401) 331-8085
Email: lmonahan@rifoundation.org
Web: www.rifoundation.org

Summary: To provide financial assistance to residents of Rhode Island who are enrolled at a college in any state to prepare for a career in advertising.

Eligibility: Open to residents of Rhode Island who are enrolled full-time as undergraduates at the sophomore level or above at a college or university in any state. Applicants must be preparing for a career in advertising and majoring in a related field (e.g., broadcast production, graphic design, interactive film, marketing, public relations, television, or video). Along with their application, they must submit an essay (up to 300 words) on the impact they would like to have on the advertising industry. Financial need is also considered in the selection process.

Financial data: The stipend ranges from $500 to $1,000.

Duration: 1 year; nonrenewable.
Number awarded: 1 each year.
Deadline: April of each year.

1356 JEAN SIBELIUS MEMORIAL FUND

Finlandia Foundation–New York Metropolitan Chapter
Attn: Scholarships
P.O. Box 165, Bowling Green Station
New York, NY 10274-0165
Email: scholarships@finlandiafoundationny.org
Web: www.finlandiafoundationny.org/scholarships.html

Summary: To provide financial assistance to students interested in studying or conducting research on the Finnish arts in Finland or the United States.
Eligibility: Open to students at colleges and universities in the United States who are interested in studying or conducting research on the Finnish arts in Finland or the United States. Applicants must submit information on their language proficiency, work experience, memberships (academic, professional, and social), fellowships and scholarships, awards, publications, exhibitions, performances, and future goals and ambitions. Financial need is not considered in the selection process.
Financial data: Stipends range from $500 to $5,000 per year.
Duration: 1 year.
Number awarded: 1 or more each year.
Deadline: February of each year.

1357 JEFF HENDERSON SCHOLARSHIP FOR JOURNALISM EXCELLENCE

Texas Intercollegiate Press Association
c/o Texas A&M University at Commerce
2600 South Neal
Box 4104
Commerce, TX 75429
Phone: (903) 886-5231; Fax: (903) 468-3128
Web: www.texasipa.org/default.asp?pageName=scholarships

Summary: To provide financial assistance to journalism students at colleges and universities in Texas.
Eligibility: Open to students majoring in journalism at 2- and 4-year colleges and universities in Texas. Applicants must have a GPA of 3.0 or higher. Each school may nominate 1 student.
Financial data: The stipend is $1,000.
Duration: 1 year.
Number awarded: 1 each year.
Deadline: February of each year.

1358 JIM LANGE MEMORIAL SCHOLARSHIP

Oklahoma City Gridiron Foundation
330 North Country Club Terrace
Mustang, OK 73064
Web: www.okcgridiron.org

Summary: To provide financial assistance to journalism students in Oklahoma.
Eligibility: Open to residents of Oklahoma who are high school seniors or students already enrolled in college. Applicants must be working on or planning to work on a degree in journalism at a college or university in the state. Along with their application, they must submit brief statements on what they hope to be doing 6 months after completing college, what they hope to be doing 10 years from today, why they have selected journalism as their profession, what they like most about working in journalism, and what they like least. They must also submit a copy of their transcript and samples of their work. Financial need is considered in the selection process.
Financial data: The stipend is $1,000.
Duration: 1 year.
Number awarded: 1 each year.
Deadline: March of each year.

1359 JOANNE ROBINSON MEMORIAL SCHOLARSHIP

JoAnne Robinson Memorial Scholarship Fund
c/o WEWS
3001 Euclid Avenue
Cleveland, OH 44115
Phone: (216) 431-5555

Summary: To provide financial assistance to African American undergraduates who are majoring in broadcast journalism.
Eligibility: Open to full-time college students who are African American and majoring in broadcast journalism. Applicants must exemplify the following characteristics: hard working, detail oriented, outstanding communication and interpersonal skills, and dedication to excellence (personally and professionally). Along with their application, they must submit a statement on the goals, values, and characteristics that make them worthy of this scholarship. Financial need is not considered in the selection process.
Financial data: The stipend is $1,000. Funds may be used for tuition, books, and other educational expenses.
Duration: 1 year; nonrenewable.
Number awarded: 1 each year.
Deadline: February of each year.

1360 JOHANSEN INTERNATIONAL COMPETITION FOR YOUNG STRING PLAYERS

Friday Morning Music Club, Inc.
Attn: FMMC Foundation
801 K Street, N.W.
Washington, DC 20001
Phone: (202) 333-2075
Email: JohansenComp@fmmc.org
Web: www.fmmc.org

Summary: To recognize and reward outstanding young string players.
Eligibility: Open to young string players (13 through 17 years of age). Applicants must submit an audiocassette or CD with 1) 5 minutes or less of an unaccompanied sonata, partita, or suite of J.S. Bach; 2) 12 minutes or less of a sonata with piano from the classical, romantic, impressionist, or contemporary period; 3) 13 minutes or less of a concerto or major work for soloist or orchestra by a composer other than Bach; 4) a short work or a movement from a longer work that shows virtuosity; and 5) a new work commissioned for this competition. Based on those recordings, semifinalists are invited to compete in Washington, D.C. They must be prepared to play any selection from their preliminary repertoire as well as a new work commissioned for this competition and sent to them prior to the semifinals. Finalists are selected from those auditions and compete the following day. All repertoire must be performed from memory. Separate awards are presented for violin, viola, and cello.
Financial data: In each category, first prize is $10,000, second $7,000, and third $5,000. The prize for the best performance on the commissioned piece is $500.
Duration: The competition is held triennially (2012, 2015, etc.).
Number awarded: 3 first prizes (1 each for violin, viola, and cello) are awarded in each competition.
Deadline: November of the year prior to the competition.

1361 JOHN BAYLISS BROADCAST FOUNDATION SCHOLARSHIPS

John Bayliss Broadcast Foundation
Attn: Scholarship Chair
171 17th Street
P.O. Box 51126
Pacific Grove, CA 93950-6126
Phone: (831) 655-5229; Fax: (831) 655-5228
Email: info@baylissfoundation.org
Web: www.baylissfoundation.org/radio.html

Summary: To provide financial assistance to upper-division students who are preparing for a career in the radio industry.
Eligibility: Open to juniors and seniors who are preparing for a career in the radio industry, preferably commercial radio. Applicants must have a GPA of 3.0 or higher and a record of participation in radio-related activities. Along with their application, they must submit transcripts, 3 letters of recommendation, and a 2-page essay describing their broadcasting goals as they relate to radio and the ways in which they hope to achieve those goals. Although financial need is a consideration, students of merit with an extensive history of radio-related activities are given preference.
Financial data: The stipend is $5,000.
Duration: 1 year.
Number awarded: Up to 15 each year.
Deadline: April of each year.

1362 JOHN D. GRAHAM SCHOLARSHIP

Public Relations Student Society of America
Attn: Vice President of Member Services
33 Maiden Lane, 11th Floor
New York, NY 10038-5150
Phone: (212) 460-1474; Fax: (212) 995-0757
Email: prssa@prsa.org
Web: www.prssa.org/awards/awardJohnGraham.aspx

Summary: To provide financial assistance to upper-division students preparing for a career in public relations.

Eligibility: Open to college juniors and seniors who are enrolled in a program of journalism, public relations, or other field that will prepare them for a career in public relations. Applicants must submit a 1-page resume, letters of recommendation from faculty members, and a 300-word statement expressing their commitment to a public relations career and its ethical practice. Selection is based on writing skills as demonstrated by the statement; commitment to public relations, particularly as expressed in the statement; practical experience (e.g., internships, other work or service); demonstrated leadership; letters of recommendation; and academic achievement in public relations and overall studies.

Financial data: The stipend is $5,000.

Duration: 1 year.

Number awarded: 1 each year.

Deadline: October of each year.

1363 JOHN F. AND ANNA LEE STACEY SCHOLARSHIP FOR ART EDUCATION

National Cowboy and Western Heritage Museum
Attn: Art Director
1700 N.E. 63rd Street
Oklahoma City, OK 73111
Phone: (405) 478-2250; Fax: (405) 478-4714
Email: info@nationalcowboymuseum.org
Web: www.nationalcowboymuseum.org/education/staceyfund/default.aspx

Summary: To provide financial assistance to students of conservative or classical art interested in further education.

Eligibility: Open to U.S. citizens between 18 and 35 years of age. Applicants must be artists whose works (paintings and drawings) have their roots in the classical tradition of western culture and favor realism or naturalism. Artists working in related fields (e.g., sculpture, collage, fashion design, decoration) are ineligible. Applicants must submit up to 10 digital images of their best work in any of the following categories: painting from life, drawing from the figure (nude), composition, or landscape. Financial need is not considered in the selection process.

Financial data: Scholarships are $5,000; funds must be used to pursue art education along "conservative" lines.

Duration: 1 year.

Number awarded: 1 or more each year.

Deadline: January of each year.

1364 JOHN LENNON SCHOLARSHIP

Broadcast Music Inc.
Attn: BMI Foundation, Inc.
7 World Trade Center
250 Greenwich Street
New York, NY 10007-0030
Phone: (212) 220-3000
Email: LennonScholarship@bmifoundation.org
Web: www.bmifoundation.org/program/john_lennon_scholarships

Summary: To recognize and reward outstanding student composers attending designated institutions.

Eligibility: Open to musicians between 15 and 24 years of age who are 1) current students or graduates of 53 selected colleges, universities, or schools of music; or 2) participating through a local collegiate chapter of the National Association for Music Education at their school. Applicants may not have had any musical work commercially recorded or distributed or have been a prior winner in this competition. They must submit (on CD with a typed copy of the lyrics) an original song with lyrics and accompanied by any instrumentation. Both lyrics and music must be original and not based on any prior work.

Financial data: Prizes are $10,000 or $5,000.

Duration: The competition is held annually.

Number awarded: 3 each year: 1 at $10,000 and 2 at $5,000.

Deadline: January of each year.

1365 JOSEPH AND MARION GREENBAUM JUDAIC STUDIES SCHOLARSHIP

Jewish Federation of Delaware
Attn: Jewish Fund for the Future
100 West Tenth Street, Suite 301
Wilmington, DE 19801-1628
Phone: (302) 427-2100, ext. 19; Fax: (302) 427-2438
Email: karen.venezky@shalomdelaware.org
Web: www.shalomdelaware.org/page.aspx?ID=159112

Summary: To provide financial assistance to Jewish residents of Delaware and adjacent communities who are interested in taking courses in Jewish studies at a college or university in any state and to Jewish residents of other states interested in studying in Delaware.

Eligibility: Open to 1) Jewish residents of Delaware who wish to study at a college or university in any state; 2) Jewish residents of adjacent communities (including, but not limited to, Elkton, Maryland or the Pennsylvania towns of Avondale, Chadds Ford, Kennett Square, Landenberg, Lincoln University, or Westchester) who wish to study at a college or university in any state; and 3) Jewish residents of other states interested in studying at a college or university in Delaware. Applicants must be interested in taking courses in Judaic studies, preferably as part of a major or minor in the field. Along with their application, they must submit a brief essay on what they have learned or hope to learn during the proposed course of study and what they hope to be able to carry with them throughout their lifetime as a result of the courses they plan to take. Selection is based on the essay, GPA, references, volunteer and community activities, and information about the courses the applicant plans to take. Financial need is considered only if there are more applicants than available funds or if the applicant is seeking funds beyond the amount of the current guideline award; lack of financial need does not disqualify any applicant.

Financial data: The stipend is $83 per credit, based on the rate of $2,500 per year.

Duration: Funding is provided on a per credit basis for each course in Judaic studies the student completes as part of an undergraduate degree.

Number awarded: Varies each year.

Deadline: March of each year.

1366 JOSEPH S. RUMBAUGH HISTORICAL ORATION CONTEST

National Society Sons of the American Revolution
Attn: Education Director
1000 South Fourth Street
Louisville, KY 40203-3208
Phone: (502) 589-1776, ext. 30; Fax: (502) 589-1671
Email: cwilson@sar.org
Web: www.sar.org/Youth/Oration_Contest

Summary: To recognize and reward outstanding high school oratory on the American Revolution.

Eligibility: Open to freshmen, sophomore, junior, or senior class students in all public, parochial, private, and home high schools in the United States. Applicants must compose and present an original oration of 5 to 6 minutes on an event, a document, or a personality within the context of the Revolutionary War, showing the relationship it bears to America today. Winners are selected on the basis of composition, delivery, logic, significance, general excellence, and time allocated for delivery. Winners at state and district levels advance to the national contest.

Financial data: At the national level, first prize is a $3,000 scholarship, second prize is a $2,000 scholarship, and third prize is a $1,000 scholarship. All other finalists receive $300 and all other national contestants receive $200.

Duration: The competition is held annually.

Number awarded: 3 national scholarships are awarded each year.

Deadline: All local contests must by completed by June of each year to qualify winners for the national competition.

1367 JOSTENS SCHOLARSHIP

University Interscholastic League
Attn: Interscholastic League Press Conference
1701 Manor Road
P.O. Box 8028
Austin, TX 78713-8028
Phone: (512) 232-4937; Fax: (512) 232-7311
Email: uilacad@uts.cc.utexas.edu
Web: www.uil.utexas.edu/academics/journalism/ilpc_forms.html

Summary: To provide financial assistance to high school seniors in Texas who plan to study communications in college.

Eligibility: Open to seniors graduating from high schools in Texas who have been involved in journalism and plan to continue their education in a communications-related field (major or minor) in college. Applicants must have a GPA of "B" or higher. Along with their application, they must submit a statement on their involvement in journalism while in high school, a description of their college and future plans, a letter of recommendation, a list of journalism and other awards and honors they have received, and 3 to 5 samples of their work as a journalism student. Financial need is not considered in the selection process.
Financial data: The stipend is $1,000.
Duration: 1 year.
Number awarded: 1 each year.
Deadline: February of each year.

1368 JOURNALISM EDUCATION ASSOCIATION FUTURE TEACHER SCHOLARSHIP

Journalism Education Association
c/o Kansas State University
103 Kedzie Hall
Manhattan, KS 66506-1505
Phone: (785) 532-5532; (866) JEA-5JEA; Fax: (785) 532-5563
Email: jea@spub.ksu.edu
Web: www.jea.org/awards/futureteacher.html
Summary: To provide financial assistance to upper-division and master's degree students working on a degree in education who intend to teach journalism.
Eligibility: Open to upper-division undergraduates and master's degree students in a college program designed to prepare them for teaching journalism at the secondary school level. Current secondary school journalism teachers who are in a degree program to improve their journalism teaching skills are also eligible. Applicants must submit a 250-word essay explaining their desire to teach high school journalism, 2 letters of recommendation, and college transcripts. They must also provide information on the journalism courses they have completed, their high school journalism experience, and their experiences working with high school journalists since they graduated from high school.
Financial data: The stipend is $1,000.
Duration: 1 year.
Number awarded: Up to 3 each year.
Deadline: October of each year.

1369 JOYCE A. CHAFFER SCHOLARSHIP

Joyce A. Chaffer Trust
c/o Nadine M. Reece, Scholarship Chair
5834 North Arliss Avenue
Meridian, ID 83646
Phone: (208) 888-9092
Email: Nadine@technics.com
Summary: To provide financial assistance to students residing or attending college in Idaho and working on an undergraduate or graduate degree in music.
Eligibility: Open to college juniors, seniors, and graduate students who are residents of Idaho or attending college in the state. Applicants must be working full-time on a degree in music with an emphasis on (in order of preference) piano, harpsichord, or organ. Along with their application, they must submit a recording of 3 pieces from 3 different time periods.
Financial data: The maximum stipend is $4,800 per year.
Duration: 1 year; may be renewed 1 additional year.
Number awarded: Varies each year; recently, a total of $33,000 worth of these scholarships was awarded.
Deadline: April of each year.

1370 JULIUS & ESTHER STULBERG INTERNATIONAL STRING COMPETITION

Julius & Esther Stulberg Competition, Inc.
359 South Kalamazoo Mall, Suite 14
Kalamazoo, MI 49007
Phone: (269) 343-2776; Fax: (269) 343-2797
Email: Stulbergcomp@yahoo.com
Web: www.stulberg.org
Summary: To recognize and reward outstanding young string musicians.
Eligibility: Open to string players 19 years of age or younger who are studying violin, viola, cello, or double bass. Applicants must submit a CD of a performance from the standard solo repertoire (up to 20 minutes in length). If they wish to be considered for the Bach award, they must include required selections by Bach on their CD. On the basis of the CDs, judges select 12 finalists to come to Kalamazoo to compete.
Financial data: First place is the Stulberg Burdick-Thorne Gold Medal of $5,000 and an orchestral performance award. Second place is $4,000 and a return performance with the Western Michigan University Symphony Orchestra. Third place is $3,000 and a performance with the Kalamazoo Junior Symphony Society. The Bach Award is $500. Funds are to be used for the musical training and education of the winners.
Duration: The competition is held annually, in March.
Number awarded: 4 cash prizes are awarded each year.
Deadline: December of each year.

1371 KAB BROADCAST SCHOLARSHIP PROGRAM

Kansas Association of Broadcasters
Attn: Scholarship Committee
2709 S.W. 29th Street
Topeka, KS 66614
Phone: (785) 235-1307; Fax: (785) 233-3052
Email: info@kab.net
Web: www.kab.net/Programs/StudentServices/default.aspx
Summary: To provide financial assistance to residents of Kansas who are interested in attending college in the state to prepare for a career in broadcasting.
Eligibility: Open to residents of Kansas who are entering their junior year or above at a 4-year college or university in the state or their sophomore year at a 2-year college or vocational/technical trade school in the state. Applicants must be enrolled in a broadcast or related program as a full-time student. They must have a GPA of 2.5 or higher. Along with their application, they must submit a 3-page essay explaining why they selected broadcasting as a career, the specific area of broadcasting that most interests them and why, their eventual career goal, what they have learned during school that reinforced their decision to prepare for a career in broadcasting, their feeling about broadcast advertising and its importance to a station, whether the FCC's role in broadcasting has helped or hurt, how they think broadcasting could better serve society, the radio or television station they most admire, and their most rewarding broadcast-related experience. Selection is based on the depth of thought, clarity of expression, and commitment to broadcasting as revealed in the essay; extracurricular activities; community involvement; and financial need.
Financial data: The stipend is $2,000 per year.
Duration: 1 year; may be renewed.
Number awarded: 20 each year.
Deadline: April of each year.

1372 KANSAS AMERICAN LEGION MUSIC COMMITTEE SCHOLARSHIP

American Legion
Department of Kansas
1314 S.W. Topeka Boulevard
Topeka, KS 66612-1886
Phone: (785) 232-9315; Fax: (785) 232-1399
Web: www.ksamlegion.org/programs.htm
Summary: To provide financial assistance to students of music at institutions in Kansas.
Eligibility: Open to residents of Kansas who are high school seniors or college freshmen or sophomores. Applicants must be studying or planning to major or minor in music at an approved college, university, or community college in Kansas. They must have an average or better academic record. Financial need is considered in the selection process.
Financial data: The stipend is $1,000.
Duration: 1 year.
Number awarded: 1 each year.
Deadline: February of each year.

1373 KANSAS HIGH SCHOOL JOURNALIST OF THE YEAR SCHOLARSHIPS

Kansas Scholastic Press Association
Attn: Executive Director
University of Kansas–School of Journalism
317 Stauffer-Flint Hall
1435 Jayhawk Boulevard
Lawrence, KS 66045-7575
Phone: (785) 864-0605; Fax: (785) 864-5945
Email: staff@kspaonline.org

Web: www.kspaonline.org
Summary: To recognize and reward, with college scholarships, high school seniors in Kansas who demonstrate excellence as a journalist.
Eligibility: Open to seniors graduating from high schools in Kansas who have been involved in journalism for at least 2 years with an adviser who is a member of the Journalism Education Association (JEA). Applicants must be planning to study journalism and/or mass communications in college and to prepare for a career in those fields. They must have a GPA of 3.0 or higher. Along with their application, they must submit examples of their work that show the following 4 characteristics: 1) skilled and creative use of media content; 2) inquiring mind and investigative persistence resulting in an in-depth study of issues important to the local high school audience, high school students in general, or society; 3) courageous and responsible handling of controversial issues despite threat or imposition of censorship; and 4) variety of journalistic experiences, each handled in a quality manner, with a newspaper, yearbook, broadcast outlet, or other medium.
Financial data: The award is a $1,000 scholarship.
Duration: 1 year.
Number awarded: 1 each year.
Deadline: February of each year.

1374 KANSAS SPJ MINORITY STUDENT SCHOLARSHIP

Society of Professional Journalists–Kansas Professional Chapter
c/o Denise Neil, Scholarship Committee
Wichita Eagle
825 East Douglas Avenue
P.O. Box 820
Wichita, KS 67201-0820
Phone: (316) 268-6327
Email: dneil@wichitaeagle.com
Web: www.spjchapters.org/kansas/gridiron.html
Summary: To provide financial assistance to residents of any state enrolled at colleges and universities in Kansas who are members of a racial or ethnic minority group and interested in a career in journalism.
Eligibility: Open to residents of any state who are members of a racial or ethnic minority group and entering their junior or senior year at colleges and universities in Kansas. Applicants do not have to be journalism or communication majors, but they must demonstrate a strong and sincere interest in print journalism, broadcast journalism, online journalism, or photojournalism. They must have a GPA of 2.5 or higher. Along with their application, they must submit a professional resume, 4 to 6 examples of their best work (clips or stories, copies of photographs, tapes or transcripts of broadcasts, printouts of web pages) and a 1-page cover letter about themselves, how they came to be interested in journalism, their professional goals, and (if appropriate) their financial need for this scholarship.
Financial data: The stipend is $1,000.
Duration: 1 year.
Number awarded: 1 each year.
Deadline: April of each year.

1375 KANSAS SUNSHINE COALITION SCHOLARSHIP

Society of Professional Journalists–Kansas Professional Chapter
c/o Denise Neil, Scholarship Committee
Wichita Eagle
825 East Douglas Avenue
P.O. Box 820
Wichita, KS 67201-0820
Phone: (316) 268-6327
Email: dneil@wichitaeagle.com
Web: www.spjchapters.org/kansas/gridiron.html
Summary: To provide financial assistance to residents of any state enrolled at colleges and universities in Kansas who are preparing for a career in journalism and are interested in open government issues.
Eligibility: Open to residents of any state entering their junior or senior year at colleges and universities in Kansas. Applicants must have a commitment to a print or broadcast journalism major or a demonstrated special interest in open government issues. They must have a GPA of 2.5 or higher. Along with their application, they must submit a professional resume, 4 to 6 examples of their best work (clips or stories, tapes or transcripts of broadcasts) and a 1-page cover letter about themselves, how they came to be interested in journalism, their professional goals, and (if appropriate) their financial need for this scholarship.
Financial data: The stipend is $1,000.
Duration: 1 year.
Number awarded: 1 each year.
Deadline: April of each year.

1376 KATHRYN DETTMAN MEMORIAL JOURNALISM SCHOLARSHIP AWARD

Associated Press Television and Radio Association
c/o Jeff Wilson
AP Los Angeles
221 South Figueroa Street, Suite 300
Los Angeles, CA 90012
Phone: (213) 626-1200
Email: jcwilson@ap.org
Web: www.aptra.com/scholarship.asp
Summary: To provide financial assistance to students from any state who are enrolled at colleges and universities in designated western states and are interested in broadcast journalism careers.
Eligibility: Open to residents of any state currently enrolled at colleges and universities in Alaska, Arizona, California, Colorado, Hawaii, Idaho, Montana, Nevada, New Mexico, Utah, Washington, and Wyoming. Applicants must have a broadcast journalism career objective. Selection is based on a 500-word essay on why the students wish to pursue broadcast journalism; another 500-word essay on their honors, awards, and broadcast experience; 3 letters of recommendation; and a statement of how they are financing their education.
Financial data: The stipend is $1,500.
Duration: 1 year.
Number awarded: 1 each year.
Deadline: December of each year.

1377 KATINA JOHN MALTA SCHOLARSHIPS

Greek Orthodox Archdiocese of America
Attn: Office of the Chancellor
8 East 79th Street
New York, NY 10075
Phone: (212) 774-0513; Fax: (212) 774-0251
Email: scholarships@goarch.org
Web: www.goarch.org/archdiocese/administration/chancellor/scholarships
Summary: To provide financial assistance to high school seniors and current undergraduates who are of the Eastern Orthodox faith and plan to study the sciences, business, or the arts.
Eligibility: Open to high school seniors and current undergraduates who are enrolled or planning to enroll full-time at an accredited college or university in the United States. Applicants must be of the Eastern Orthodox faith (within a jurisdiction of the member churches of the Standing Conference of Canonical Orthodox Bishops in the Americas) and U.S. citizens or permanent residents. They must have an SAT score of at least 1500 (or an equivalent score on the ACT). Preference is given to applicants who are orphans and to those who are interested in studying the sciences, business, or the arts. Along with their application, they must submit a 1-page essay on their reasons for applying for this scholarship and how their planned studies will help them serve the Church and/or the community at large. Financial need is considered in the selection process.
Financial data: The stipend ranges from $1,000 to $3,000.
Duration: 1 year.
Number awarded: Varies each year; recently, 13 of these scholarships, with a value of $28,000, were awarded.
Deadline: April of each year.

1378 KATU THOMAS R. DARGAN SCHOLARSHIP

KATU-TV
Attn: Human Resources
2153 N.E. Sandy Boulevard
P.O. Box 2
Portland, OR 97207-0002
Phone: (503) 231-4222
Web: www.katu.com/about/scholarship
Summary: To provide financial assistance and work experience to minority students from Oregon and Washington who are studying broadcasting or communications in college.
Eligibility: Open to minority (Asian, Black/African American, Hispanic or Latino, Native Hawaiian or Pacific Islander, American Indian or Alaska Native) U.S. citizens, currently enrolled as a sophomore or higher at a 4-year college or university or an accredited community college in Oregon or Washington. Residents of Oregon or Washington enrolled at a school in any state are also eligible. Applicants must be majoring in broadcasting or communications and have a GPA of 3.0 or higher. Community college students must be enrolled in a broadcast curriculum that is transferable to a 4-year accredited university. Finalists will be interviewed. Selection is based on financial need, academic achievement, and an essay on personal and professional goals.

Financial data: The stipend is $6,000. Funds are sent directly to the recipient's school.
Duration: 1 year; recipients may reapply if they have maintained a GPA of 3.0 or higher.
Number awarded: 1 each year.
Deadline: April of each year.

1379 KAY LONGCOPE SCHOLARSHIP AWARD

National Lesbian & Gay Journalists Association
1420 K Street, N.W., Suite 910
Washington, DC 20005
Phone: (202) 588-9888; Fax: (202) 588-1818
Email: info@nlgfa.org
Web: www.nlgja.org/students/longcope.htm
Summary: To provide financial assistance to lesbian, gay, bisexual, and transgendered (LGBT) undergraduate and graduate students of color who are interested in preparing for a career in journalism.
Eligibility: Open to LGBT students of color who are 1) high school seniors accepted to a U.S. community college or 4-year university and planning to enroll full-time; 2) full-time undergraduate students at U.S. community colleges and 4-year universities; or 3) undergraduate students who have been accepted for their first year of a U.S. graduate school. Applicants must be planning a career in journalism and be committed to furthering the sponsoring organization's mission of fair and accurate coverage of the LGBT community. They must demonstrate an awareness of the issues facing the LGBT community and the importance of fair and accurate news coverage. For undergraduates, a declared major in journalism and/or communications is desirable but not required; non-journalism majors may demonstrate their commitment to a journalism career through work samples, internships, and work on a school news publication, online news service, or broadcast affiliate. Graduate students must be enrolled in a journalism program. Along with their application, they must submit a 1-page resume, 5 work samples, official transcripts, 3 letters of recommendation, and a 1,000-word autobiography written in the third person as a news story, describing the applicant's commitment and passion for journalism and career goals. U.S. citizenship or permanent resident status is required. Selection is based on journalistic and scholastic ability.
Financial data: A stipend is awarded (amount not specified).
Duration: 1 year.
Number awarded: 1 each year.
Deadline: Deadline not specified.

1380 KEN KASHIWAHARA SCHOLARSHIP

Radio Television Digital News Foundation
Attn: RTDNF Fellowship Program
4121 Plank Road, Suite 512
Fredericksburg, VA 22407
Phone: (202) 467-5214; Fax: (202) 223-4007
Email: staceys@rtdna.org
Web: www.rtdna.org/pages/education/undergraduates.php
Summary: To provide financial assistance to minority undergraduate students who are interested in preparing for a career in electronic journalism.
Eligibility: Open to sophomores or more advanced minority undergraduate students enrolled in an electronic journalism sequence at an accredited or nationally-recognized college or university. Applicants must submit 1 to 3 examples of their journalistic skills on audio CD or DVD (no more than 15 minutes total, accompanied by scripts); a description of their role on each story and a list of who worked on each story and what they did; a 1-page statement explaining why they are preparing for a career in electronic journalism with reference to their specific career preference (radio, television, online, reporting, producing, or newsroom management); a resume; and a letter of reference from their dean or faculty sponsor explaining why they are a good candidate for the award and certifying that they have at least 1 year of school remaining.
Financial data: The stipend is $2,500, paid in semiannual installments of $1,250 each.
Duration: 1 year.
Number awarded: 1 each year.
Deadline: May of each year.

1381 KENNETH E. BEHRING NATIONAL HISTORY DAY CONTEST

National History Day
Attn: Director
University of Maryland
0119 Cecil Hall
College Park, MD 20742
Phone: (301) 314-9739; Fax: (301) 314-9767
Email: info@nhd.org
Web: www.nationalhistoryday.org/KennethBehring.htm
Summary: To recognize and reward outstanding history papers, exhibits, performances, and media presentations prepared by middle and high school students around the country.
Eligibility: Open to middle and high school students in the United States. Contests are held in 2 divisions (junior, for grades 6–8, and senior, for grades 9–12) and, within each division, in 9 categories: paper, individual exhibit, group exhibit, individual performance, group performance, individual documentary, group documentary, individual web site, and group web site. The 3 group categories may include 2 to 5 students. Papers must be standard research essays from 1,500 to 2,500 words in length. Individual and group exhibits must be visual representations of research and interpretation, much like a small museum exhibit. Individual and group performances must be dramatic portrayals of an historical topic; they may not exceed 10 minutes in length. Individual and group documentaries must utilize photographs, film, video, audio tapes, and graphic presentations to communicate a topic's historical significance; they may not exceed 10 minutes in length. Individual and group web sites should be a collection of web pages, interconnected by hyperlinks, that presents primary and secondary sources, interactive multimedia, and historical analysis; it may contain no more than 1,200 visible, student-composed words and no more than 100MB of file space. Following local school and district contests, winners compete in state contests, where 2 entries in each category are selected to compete at the national level. Selection is based on historical quality (60%), relation to theme (20%), and clarity of presentation (20%). Special awards are presented to the best entries on designated topics. History Channel awards are presented to high school seniors who submit the best entries in the individual documentary and group documentary categories.
Financial data: At the national level, winners in each category of the 2 divisions receive prizes of $1,000 for first place, $500 for second place, and $250 for third place. The amounts of the special awards vary. The History Channel awards are $5,000.
Duration: The competition is held annually.
Number awarded: At the local level, more than 500,000 students and 50,000 teachers participate in the competition. Nearly 2,000 students each year advance to the national competition where 3 prizes are presented in each of the 2 divisions and 9 categories. The number of special awards varies. There are 2 History Channel awards.
Deadline: Each local contest sets its own deadline.

1382 KEVIN AND KELLY PERDUE MEMORIAL SCHOLARSHIP

Foundation for Amateur Radio, Inc.
Attn: Scholarship Committee
P.O. Box 911
Columbia, MD 21044-0911
Phone: (410) 552-2652; Fax: (410) 981-5146
Email: dave.prestel@gmail.com
Web: www.farweb.org/scholarships
Summary: To provide funding to licensed radio amateurs who are interested in studying humanities or the social sciences in college.
Eligibility: Open to licensed radio amateurs who are interested in working full-time on a bachelor's degree in the liberal arts, humanities, or social sciences. Financial need is considered in the selection process.
Financial data: The stipend is $2,000.
Duration: 1 year.
Number awarded: 1 each year.
Deadline: March of each year.

1383 KIMBALL OFFICE SCHOLARSHIP

International Interior Design Association
Attn: IIDA Foundation
222 Merchandise Mart, Suite 567
Chicago, IL 60654
Phone: (312) 467-1950; (888) 799-4432; Fax: (312) 467-0779
Email: iidahq@iida.org
Web: www.iida.org/i4a/pages/index.cfm?pageid=156
Summary: To provide financial assistance to minority students enrolled in the senior year of an interior design program.
Eligibility: Open to college seniors of African, Asian, Latino, or Native American heritage. Applicants must be working on a degree in interior design. Selection is based on excellence in academics and promising design talent.

Financial data: The stipend is $5,000.
Duration: 1 year.
Number awarded: 1 each year.
Deadline: Deadline not specified.

1384 KIRCHHOFF FAMILY FINE ARTS SCHOLARSHIP

Oregon Student Assistance Commission
Attn: Grants and Scholarships Division
1500 Valley River Drive, Suite 100
Eugene, OR 97401-2146
Phone: (541) 687-7395; (800) 452-8807, ext. 7395; Fax: (541) 687-7414; TDD: (800) 735-2900
Email: awardinfo@osac.state.or.us
Web: www.osac.state.or.us/osac_programs.html

Summary: To provide financial assistance to residents of Oregon who are enrolled as undergraduate or graduate students at a school in the state and working on a degree in a field related to fine arts.
Eligibility: Open to residents of Oregon who are enrolled at a 4-year college or university in the state. Applicants must be working on a degree in fine arts, graphic design, or art history. First preference is given to upper-division students, then to candidates for an M.F.A. degree. Semifinalists may be asked to submit non-returnable slides or photographs of their art samples. Financial need is not required, but it is considered in the selection process.
Financial data: A stipend is awarded (amount not specified).
Duration: 1 year; recipients may reapply.
Number awarded: Varies each year.
Deadline: February of each year.

1385 KITSAP QUILTERS' SCHOLARSHIP

Kitsap Quilters' Quilt Guild
c/o Eileen Veals
20343 N.W. Cedar Lane
Poulsbo, WA 98370
Email: toquilt@embarqmail.com
Web: www.kitsapquilters.com/scholarship.html

Summary: To provide financial assistance to residents of Washington working on an undergraduate degree in a field related to fiber art at a college in the state.
Eligibility: Open to residents of Washington who graduated from a high school in the state at least 4 years previously. Applicants must be enrolled at an accredited college, university, or technical institution in the state and have completed course work above the 100 level with a GPA of 2.0 or higher. They must be majoring in a field related to fiber arts, including (but not limited to) sewing, weaving, clothing design, quilting, dyeing, basketry, curatorship and preservation, or history and technical production of textiles; art courses that include design, composition, surface design, and art history are also considered. Financial need is not considered in the selection process.
Financial data: The stipend is $1,500.
Duration: 1 year.
Number awarded: 1 each year.
Deadline: May of each year.

1386 KNIGHTS OF PYTHIAS POSTER CONTEST

Knights of Pythias
Office of Supreme Lodge
25 South Morton Avenue
Morton, PA 19070
Phone: (610) 544-3500; Fax: (610) 328-6499
Web: www.pythias.org/poster/poster.html

Summary: To recognize and reward outstanding posters by high school students on topics that change periodically.
Eligibility: Open to any student enrolled in high school (grades 9 through 12) in the United States or Canada. Posters must be 14 by 22 inches. No collage, paste-on, or stencil lettering is allowed. Competitions are first held by each Knights of Pythias local lodge, with winners advancing to the Grand Domain (state or province) and from there to the national level. These winning entries are then submitted to the Supreme Lodge contest. Posters are evaluated on the basis of message, originality, effective display of message, and neatness. The topic changes periodically; recently, it was "Volunteer—Make a Difference in Your Community."
Financial data: Supreme Lodge prizes are $1,000 for first place, $500 for second place, $250 for third place, and $100 for fourth through eighth places. Grand Lodge prizes vary.
Duration: The contest is held annually.
Number awarded: 8 each year on the national level.
Deadline: Local lodges select their winners by the end of April of each year and submit them to the Grand Lodge in their Grand Domain (state or province) by the middle of May. Grand Domain winners must be submitted to the Supreme Lodge by the middle of June.

1387 L. PHIL WICKER SCHOLARSHIP

American Radio Relay League
Attn: ARRL Foundation
225 Main Street
Newington, CT 06111
Phone: (860) 594-0397; Fax: (860) 594-0259
Email: foundation@arrl.org
Web: www.arrlf.org/programs/scholarships

Summary: To provide financial assistance to licensed radio amateurs, especially those from designated states, who are interested in working on an undergraduate or graduate degree, preferably in electronics or communications.
Eligibility: Open to undergraduate or graduate students at accredited institutions who are licensed radio amateurs of general class. Preference is given to students who are 1) residents of North Carolina, South Carolina, Virginia, or West Virginia and attending school in those states; and 2) working on a degree in electronics, communications, or related fields. Applicants must submit an essay on the role amateur radio has played in their lives and provide documentation of financial need.
Financial data: The stipend is $1,000.
Duration: 1 year.
Number awarded: 1 each year.
Deadline: January of each year.

1388 LA TOQUE SCHOLARSHIPS IN WINE STUDIES

James Beard Foundation Scholarship Program
c/o Scholarship Management Services
One Scholarship Way
P.O. Box 297
St. Peter, MN 56082
Phone: (507) 931-1682; (800) 537-4180; Fax: (507) 931-9168
Email: jamesbeard@scholarshipamerica.org
Web: sms.scholarshipamerica.org/jamesbeard

Summary: To provide financial assistance to high school seniors and graduates interested in attending culinary school to work on a degree in wine studies.
Eligibility: Open to high school seniors planning to enroll and students already enrolled at least part-time at a licensed or accredited culinary school. Applicants must be planning to work on a degree in wine studies. Along with their application, they must submit a brief statement or summary of their plans as they relate to their culinary, educational, and career goals. Selection is based on that statement, academic record, leadership and participation in school and community activities, work experience, unusual personal or family circumstances, an outside appraisal, and financial need.
Financial data: The stipend is $3,000 per year.
Duration: 1 year; awards are not renewable, but recipients may reapply.
Number awarded: 2 each year.
Deadline: May of each year.

1389 LAGRANT FOUNDATION UNDERGRADUATE SCHOLARSHIPS

Lagrant Foundation
Attn: Programs Manager
626 Wilshire Boulevard, Suite 700
Los Angeles, CA 90071-2920
Phone: (323) 469-8680; Fax: (323) 469-8683
Email: erickaavila@lagrant.com
Web: www.lagrantfoundation.org/site/?page_id=3

Summary: To provide financial assistance to minority college students who are interested in majoring in advertising, public relations, or marketing.
Eligibility: Open to African Americans, Asian Pacific Americans, Hispanics/Latinos, and Native Americans/Alaska Natives who are full-time students at a 4-year accredited institution. Applicants must have a GPA of 2.75 or higher and be either majoring in advertising, marketing, or public relations or minoring in communications with plans to prepare for a career in advertising, marketing, or public relations. Along with their application, they must submit 1) a 1- to 2-page essay outlining their career goals; what steps they will take to increase

ethnic representation in the fields of advertising, marketing, and public relations; and the role of an advertising, marketing, or public relations practitioner; 2) a paragraph describing the college and/or community activities in which they are involved; 3) a brief paragraph describing any honors and awards they have received; 4) a letter of reference; 5) a resume; and 6) an official transcript. U.S. citizenship or permanent resident status is required.

Financial data: The stipend is $5,000.

Duration: 1 year.

Number awarded: 10 each year.

Deadline: February of each year.

1390 LANDMARK SCHOLARS PROGRAM

Landmark Media Enterprises LLC
c/o Ann Morris, Managing Editor
Greensboro News & Record
200 East Market Street
Greensboro, NC 27401
Phone: (540) 981-3211; (800) 346-1234
Email: amorris@news-record.com
Web: company.news-record.com/intern.htm

Summary: To provide work experience and financial aid to minority undergraduates who are interested in preparing for a career in journalism.

Eligibility: Open to minority (Asian, Hispanic, African American, Native American) college sophomores, preferably those with ties to the mid-Atlantic states (Delaware, Maryland, North Carolina, South Carolina, Virginia, and Washington, D.C.). Applicants must be full-time students with a GPA of 2.5 or higher in a 4-year degree program. They must be interested in preparing for a career in print journalism and participating in an internship in news, features, sports, copy editing, photography, or graphics/illustration. U.S. citizenship or permanent resident status is required. Selection is based on grades, work samples, recommendations, targeted selection interview skills, and financial need.

Financial data: The stipend is $5,000 per year. During the summers following their sophomore and junior years, recipients are provided with paid internships. Following graduation, they are offered a 1-year internship with full benefits and the possibility of continued employment.

Duration: 2 years (the junior and senior years of college).

Number awarded: 1 or more each year.

Deadline: December of each year.

1391 LANDSCAPE FORMS DESIGN FOR PEOPLE SCHOLARSHIP

Landscape Architecture Foundation
Attn: Scholarship Program
818 18th Street, N.W., Suite 810
Washington, DC 20006-3520
Phone: (202) 331-7070; Fax: (202) 331-7079
Email: scholarships@lafoundation.org
Web: www.laprofession.org/financial/scholarships.htm

Summary: To provide financial assistance to undergraduate landscape architecture students who demonstrate interest in design of public spaces.

Eligibility: Open to landscape architecture students entering the final year of full-time undergraduate study. Applicants must be able to demonstrate a proven contribution to the design of public spaces that integrates landscape design and the use of amenities to promote social interaction. Along with their application, they must submit 2 letters of recommendation, 3 academic or internship work samples, and a 300-word essay on the qualities essential to the creation of great and successful public spaces. Selection is based on financial need, creative ability, and academic accomplishment.

Financial data: The stipend is $3,000.

Duration: 1 year.

Number awarded: 1 each year.

Deadline: February of each year.

1392 LARRY W. MCCORMICK COMMUNICATIONS SCHOLARSHIP FOR UNDERREPRESENTED STUDENTS

The Lullaby Guild, Inc.
Attn: Scholarship Committee
6709 La Tijera, Suite 116
Los Angeles, CA 90045
Phone: (310) 335-5655
Email: mail@lullabyguild.org
Web: www.lullabyguild.org

Summary: To provide financial assistance to underrepresented upper-division students who are working on a degree in a field related to mass communications.

Eligibility: Open to underrepresented (e.g., African American, Hispanic American, Native American, Alaskan American, Pacific Islander, Asian) students entering their junior or senior year at an accredited college or university. Applicants must be working on a degree in a field related to mass communications, including audiovisual and electronic and print journalism. Along with their application, they must submit a personal statement regarding their volunteer services, official transcripts, 3 letters of recommendation, 3 samples of their journalistic work, and a 500-word personal statement about their interest in journalism or mass communication. Selection is based on academic achievement, letters of recommendation, journalistic experience and/or evidence of journalistic talent, clarity of purpose in plans and goals for a future in journalism or mass communications, and involvement in volunteer community service.

Financial data: The stipend is $2,500.

Duration: 1 year.

Number awarded: 1 each year.

Deadline: February of each year.

1393 LAVALLEE BRENSINGER ART SCHOLARSHIP AWARD

Lavallee Brensinger Architects
155 Dow Street, Suite 400
Manchester, NH 03101
Phone: (603) 622-5450; Fax: (603) 622-7908
Web: www.lbpa.com/flash.html

Summary: To provide financial assistance to high school seniors in New Hampshire who plan to study a field related to architecture at a college in any state.

Eligibility: Open to seniors graduating from high schools in New Hampshire and planning to attend an accredited 4-year college or university in any state. Applicants must be planning to major in architecture, graphic design, or interior design. Along with their application, they must submit 1 piece of art work, a description of that work, and a 350-word essay on their career goals, a transcript, and a list of all their high school's available art, media, and drafting courses or related extracurricular clubs (with a notation of those in which the applicant participated). Financial need is not considered in the selection process.

Financial data: The stipend is $2,000.

Duration: 1 year.

Number awarded: 1 each year.

Deadline: March of each year.

1394 LEADERS COMMEMORATIVE SCHOLARSHIP

International Furnishings and Design Association
Attn: IFDA Educational Foundation
150 South Warner Road, Suite 156
King of Prussia, PA 19406
Phone: (610) 535-6422; Fax: (610) 535-6423
Email: info@ifda.com
Web: www.ifdaef.org/scholarships.html

Summary: To provide financial assistance to undergraduate students who are working on a degree in interior design and have been involved in volunteer or community service.

Eligibility: Open to full-time undergraduates who have completed at least 4 courses in interior design or a related field. Applicants must have a record of involvement in volunteer or community service and have held leadership positions during the past 5 years. Along with their application, they must submit an essay of 300 to 400 words on their long- and short-term goals, extracurricular activities, volunteer work, and what led them to prepare for a career in this field; samples of their design work; a transcript; and a letter of recommendation from a professor or instructor. Financial need is not considered.

Financial data: The stipend is $1,000.

Duration: 1 year.

Number awarded: At least 1 each year.

Deadline: March of each year.

1395 LEE A. LYMAN MEMORIAL MUSIC SCHOLARSHIP

Vermont Student Assistance Corporation
Attn: Scholarship Programs
10 East Allen Street
P.O. Box 2000
Winooski, VT 05404-2601

Phone: (802) 654-3798; (888) 253-4819; Fax: (802) 654-3765; TDD: (800) 281-3341 (within VT)
Email: info@vsac.org
Web: services.vsac.org/wps/wcm/connect/vsac/VSAC

Summary: To provide financial assistance to residents of Vermont who are interested in working on a degree in music at a college in any state.

Eligibility: Open to the residents of Vermont who are seniors in high school, high school graduates, or currently enrolled in college. Applicants must be enrolled or planning to enroll at a college or university in any state and work on a degree in music. Along with their application, they must submit 100-word essays on 1) the school, church, and community activities in which they have participated; 2) their interest in and commitment to pursuing their chosen career or vocation; and 3) any significant barriers that limit their access to education. Selection is based on those essays; participation in music-related activities, performances, and/or groups; academic achievement; letters of recommendation; and financial need.

Financial data: The stipend is $1,000.

Duration: 1 year; recipients may reapply.

Number awarded: 4 each year.

Deadline: March of each year.

1396 LEE-JACKSON FOUNDATION SCHOLARSHIP

Lee-Jackson Foundation
P.O. Box 8121
Charlottesville, VA 22906
Phone: (434) 977-1861; Fax: (434) 977-6083
Web: www.lee-jackson.org

Summary: To recognize and reward high school students in Virginia who enter an historical essay contest and plan to attend a college or university in the United States.

Eligibility: Open to juniors and seniors at Virginia secondary schools who plan to attend a 4-year college or university in any state. Applicants must write an essay that demonstrates an appreciation of the character and virtues of Generals Robert E. Lee and Thomas J. "Stonewall" Jackson. The length of the papers is not specified, but most are between 7 and 10 pages. Selection is based on historical accuracy, quality of research, and clarity of written expression. Students first compete in the 8 high school regions in the state; winners are selected by a screening committee in their localities. In each region, a bonus scholarship is awarded to the paper judged the best; a grand prize is awarded to the author of the essay judged best of all the essays submitted.

Financial data: Total prizes are $10,000, $2,000, or $1,000. Each winner receives $1,000. The winners of bonus scholarships receive an additional $1,000 and the grand prize winner receives an additional $8,000. A $1,000 award is given to schools or home school regions that encourage the most participation. Funds are mailed to the financial aid director of the college the winner attends; they may be used only for payment of tuition and required fees.

Duration: The competition is held annually.

Number awarded: 27 each year: 3 winners in each of the 8 public high school regions of the state plus 3 to private and home school students. Bonus scholarships are awarded to 8 public school students (1 in each region) and 1 private or home-schooled student. The grand prize is awarded to the public school, private school, or home-schooled student whose essay is judged to be the best in the state. In addition, 9 schools (1 in each public school region plus 1 private/home school region) receive the awards for encouraging the most participation.

Deadline: January of each year.

1397 LEMUEL C. SUMMERS SCHOLARSHIP

United Methodist Higher Education Foundation
Attn: Scholarships Administrator
1001 19th Avenue South
P.O. Box 340005
Nashville, TN 37203-0005
Phone: (615) 340-7385; (800) 811-8110; Fax: (615) 340-7330
Email: umhefscholarships@gbhem.org
Web: www.umhef.org/receive.php?id=endowed_funds

Summary: To provide financial assistance to undergraduate and graduate Methodist students who are preparing for ministry.

Eligibility: Open to full-time undergraduate, graduate, and professional students at United Methodist–related colleges, universities, seminaries, and theological schools. Applicants must have been active, full members of a United Methodist Church for at least 1 year prior to applying and be preparing for Christian ministry. They must have a GPA of 3.0 or higher and be able to demonstrate financial need. Along with their application, they must submit a 200-word essay on their involvement and/or leadership responsibilities in their church, school, and community within the last 3 years. U.S. citizenship or permanent resident status is required.

Financial data: The stipend is at least $1,000 per year.

Duration: 1 year; recipients may reapply.

Number awarded: Varies each year; recently, 5 of these scholarships were awarded.

Deadline: May of each year.

1398 LEONARD M. PERRYMAN COMMUNICATIONS SCHOLARSHIP FOR ETHNIC MINORITY STUDENTS

United Methodist Communications
Attn: Communications Resourcing Team
810 12th Avenue South
P.O. Box 320
Nashville, TN 37202-0320
Phone: (615) 742-5481; (888) CRT-4UMC; Fax: (615) 742-5485
Email: scholarships@umcom.org
Web: crt.umc.org/interior.asp?ptid=44&mid=10270

Summary: To provide financial assistance to minority United Methodist college students who are interested in careers in religious communications.

Eligibility: Open to United Methodist ethnic minority students enrolled in accredited institutions of higher education as juniors or seniors. Applicants must be interested in preparing for a career in religious communications. For the purposes of this program, "communications" is meant to cover audiovisual, electronic, and print journalism. Selection is based on Christian commitment and involvement in the life of the United Methodist church, academic achievement, journalistic experience, clarity of purpose, and professional potential as a religion communicator.

Financial data: The stipend is $2,500 per year.

Duration: 1 year.

Number awarded: 1 each year.

Deadline: March of each year.

1399 LEONARDO WATTS SCHOLARSHIP

Watts Charity Association, Inc.
6245 Bristol Parkway, Suite 224
Culver City, CA 90230
Phone: (323) 671-0394; Fax: (323) 778-2613
Email: wattscharity@aol.com
Web: 4watts.tripod.com/id5.html

Summary: To provide financial assistance to upper-division African Americans working on a degree in classical music.

Eligibility: Open to U.S. citizens of African American descent who are enrolled full-time as a college or university junior. Applicants must be studying classical music, including voice and/or instrumental. They must have a GPA of 3.0 or higher, be between 17 and 24 years of age, and be able to demonstrate that they intend to continue their education for at least 2 years. Along with their application, they must submit 1) a 1-paragraph statement on why they should be awarded a Watts Foundation scholarship; and 2) a 1- to 2-page essay on a specific type of cancer, based either on how it has impacted their life or on researched information.

Financial data: A stipend is awarded (amount not specified).

Duration: 1 year.

Number awarded: 1 each year.

Deadline: May of each year.

1400 LEROY F. AARONS SCHOLARSHIP AWARD

National Lesbian & Gay Journalists Association
1420 K Street, N.W., Suite 910
Washington, DC 20005
Phone: (202) 588-9888; Fax: (202) 588-1818
Email: info@nlgfa.org
Web: www.nlgja.org/students/aarons.htm

Summary: To provide financial assistance to undergraduate and graduate students who are interested in serving the lesbian, gay, bisexual, and transgender (LGBT) community and are preparing for a career in journalism.

Eligibility: Open to 1) high school seniors who have been accepted to a U.S. community college or 4-year university and plan to enroll full-time; 2) full-time undergraduate students at U.S. community colleges and 4-year universities; and 3) undergraduate students who have been accepted for their first year of a U.S. graduate school. Applicants must be planning a career in journalism and be committed to furthering the sponsoring organization's mission of fair and

accurate coverage of the LGBT community. They must demonstrate an awareness of the issues facing the LGBT community and the importance of fair and accurate news coverage. For undergraduates, a declared major in journalism and/or communications is desirable but not required; non-journalism majors may demonstrate their commitment to a journalism career through work samples, internships, and work on a school news publication, online news service, or broadcast affiliate. Graduate students must be enrolled in a journalism program. Along with their application, they must submit a 1-page resume, 5 work samples, official transcripts, 3 letters of recommendation, and a 1,000-word autobiography written in the third person as a news story, describing the applicant's commitment and passion for journalism and career goals. U.S. citizenship or permanent resident status is required. Selection is based on journalistic and scholastic ability.
Financial data: The stipend is $5,000.
Duration: 1 year.
Number awarded: 1 each year.
Deadline: Deadline not specified.

1401 LINCOLN SCHOLARSHIPS

American Advertising Federation-Lincoln
Attn: Scholarship Chair
P.O. Box 80093
Lincoln, NE 68501-0093
Web: www.aaflincoln.org/resources/scholarships.htm
Summary: To provide financial assistance to residents of any state preparing for a career in a field related to advertising at a college in Nebraska.
Eligibility: Open to residents of any state currently enrolled full-time at an accredited college or university in Nebraska. Applicants must be working on a degree in advertising, marketing, public relations, communications, or commercial art. Along with their application, they must submit an essay describing their interest in receiving this scholarship and why they should be selected. They may also submit up to 3 samples of their work, although this is not required. Finalists are interviewed. Selection is based on ability, commitment and enthusiasm for the advertising profession, academic performance, participation in extracurricular activities, and career goals. U.S. citizenship is required.
Financial data: The stipend is $1,000. Awards are provided in the form of a credit at the recipient's institution.
Duration: 1 year.
Number awarded: 2 each year.
Deadline: October of each year.

1402 LINDA SIMMONS EDUCATIONAL SCHOLARSHIP

Alaska Broadcasters Association
700 West 41st Avenue, Suite 102
Anchorage, AK 99503
Phone: (907) 258-2424; Fax: (907) 258-2414
Email: akba@gci.net
Web: www.alaskabroadcasters.org/scholarship/info.html
Summary: To provide financial assistance to residents of Alaska who are attending college in any state to prepare for a career in broadcasting.
Eligibility: Open to Alaska residents who are working on an undergraduate degree or certified course of study at an accredited junior or community college, professional trade school, college, or university in any state. They must be majoring in radio and/or television broadcast communications or broadcast engineering; if there are no candidates in those fields, students majoring in advertising, journalism, or public relations are considered. Applicants must submit a resume that covers employment, school and community extracurricular activities, awards, and honors; 3 letters of reference; and a short essay on personal goals. Financial need is not considered.
Financial data: The stipend is $2,000. Funds are paid directly to the student's institution.
Duration: 1 year.
Number awarded: 1 each year.
Deadline: March of each year.

1403 LIVINGSTON SYMPHONY ORCHESTRA YOUNG ARTISTS' CONCERTO COMPETITION

Livingston Symphony Orchestra
P.O. Box 253
Livingston, NJ 07039
Web: lsonj.org/15.html
Summary: To recognize and reward outstanding young musicians (other than pianists) who reside in New Jersey.
Eligibility: Open to New Jersey residents between the ages of 14 and 21. Applicants may play any instrument other than the piano. Selecting the work to be performed for the competition is entirely the artist's choice. Any major work written for the solo instrument with orchestral accompaniment is acceptable, provided that the orchestral score is readily available for rent or purchase. All movements must be played from memory (although accompanists need not perform from memory). No performer will be heard without an accompanist.
Financial data: The winner receives a $1,000 scholarship.
Duration: The competition is held annually.
Number awarded: 1 each year.
Deadline: November of each year.

1404 LLEWELLYN L. CAYVAN STRING INSTRUMENT SCHOLARSHIP

Grand Rapids Community Foundation
Attn: Education Program Officer
185 Oakes Street, S.W.
Grand Rapids, MI 49503-4008
Phone: (616) 454-1751, ext. 103; Fax: (616) 454-6455
Email: rbishop@grfoundation.org
Web: www.grfoundation.org/scholarships
Summary: To provide financial assistance to undergraduate and graduate students working on a degree in string instruments at a college in any state.
Eligibility: Open to undergraduate and graduate students at a college or university in any state. Applicants must be working on a degree in violin, viola, violoncello, or bass viol. They must be U.S. citizens or permanent residents, but there are no residency or financial need requirements.
Financial data: The stipend depends on the need of the recipient and the availability of funds, but ranges from $500 to $5,000 and averages $1,000. Funds are paid directly to the recipient's institution.
Duration: 1 year.
Number awarded: 1 each year.
Deadline: March of each year.

1405 LOTTE LENYA COMPETITION FOR SINGERS

Kurt Weill Foundation for Music, Inc.
7 East 20th Street
New York, NY 10003-1106
Phone: (212) 505-5240; Fax: (212) 353-9663
Email: kwfinfo@kwf.org
Web: www.kwf.org/foundation/lotte-lenya-competition
Summary: To recognize and reward outstanding singers who reside in the United States or Canada.
Eligibility: Open to singers, including students, between 18 and 32 years of age who reside in the United States or Canada. Contestants must prepare 4 selections (at least 1 of which must be in a language other than English): 2 contrasting theatrical selections by Kurt Weill; an aria from the operatic or operetta repertoire (not by Kurt Weill); and a selection from the American musical theater repertoire (not by Kurt Weill). They must provide their own accompanist and perform the selections from memory. The competition begins at the regional level at 5 sites: Seattle, Washington; Rochester, New York; Lawrence, Kansas; Ann Arbor, Michigan; and New York, New York. Regional winners are then invited to the national finals at Rochester, New York.
Financial data: Finalists selected at the regional competitions each receive an award of $500 plus a stipend to help pay travel costs to compete in the national finals. In the national competition, first prize is $15,000, second $10,000, and third $5,000.
Duration: This competition is held annually.
Number awarded: 5 regional and 3 national winners are selected each year.
Deadline: January of each year.

1406 LOU AND CAROLE PRATO SPORTS REPORTING SCHOLARSHIP

Radio Television Digital News Foundation
Attn: RTDNF Fellowship Program
4121 Plank Road, Suite 512
Fredericksburg, VA 22407
Phone: (202) 467-5214; Fax: (202) 223-4007
Email: staceys@rtdna.org

Web: www.rtdna.org/pages/education/undergraduates.php
Summary: To provide financial assistance for undergraduate education to students whose career objective is radio or television sports reporting.
Eligibility: Open to sophomores, juniors, and seniors who are enrolled full-time in electronic journalism at a college or university where such a major is offered. Applicants must submit 1 to 3 examples of their journalistic skills on audio CD or DVD (no more than 15 minutes total, accompanied by scripts); a description of their role on each story and a list of who worked on each story and what they did; a 1-page statement explaining why they are preparing for a career as a sports reporter in television or radio; a resume; and a letter of reference from their dean or faculty sponsor explaining why they are a good candidate for the award and certifying that they have at least 1 year of school remaining.
Financial data: The stipend is $1,000.
Duration: 1 year.
Number awarded: 1 each year.
Deadline: May of each year.

1407 LOUISIANA WMU SCHOLARSHIP FOR AFRICAN-AMERICAN MISSION PASTORS

Louisiana Baptist Convention
Attn: Woman's Missionary Union
P.O. Box 311
Alexandria, LA 71309
Phone: (318) 448-3402; (800) 622-6549
Email: wmu@lbc.org
Web: www.lbc.org/Women/Interior.aspx?id=3400&terms=scholarship
Summary: To provide financial assistance to African American Southern Baptists from Louisiana who are enrolled at a seminary to prepare for a career as a missions pastor.
Eligibility: Open to African Americans who are endorsed by the director of missions and the pastor of a sponsoring Southern Baptist church in Louisiana. Applicants must be enrolled full-time at a seminary or a satellite campus to prepare for a career as a missions pastor and have a GPA of 2.5 or higher. They must be participating in a missions education organization of the church or on campus and must contribute to offerings of the church and other programs. Along with their application, they must submit a brief summary of their Christian walk in their life, including what they believe the Lord has called them to do in a church-related vocation.
Financial data: The stipend is $1,200 per year.
Duration: Up to 3 years.
Number awarded: 1 or more each year.
Deadline: June of each year.

1408 LUCINDA BENEVENTI FINDLEY HISTORY SCHOLARSHIP

Daughters of the American Revolution–National Society
Attn: Committee Services Office, Scholarships
1776 D Street, N.W.
Washington, DC 20006-5303
Phone: (202) 628-1776
Web: www.dar.org/natsociety/edout_scholar.cfm
Summary: To provide financial assistance to high school seniors who plan to major in history in college.
Eligibility: Open to graduating high school seniors who plan to enroll full-time at an accredited college or university in the United States and major in history. Applicants must be sponsored by a local chapter of the Daughters of the American Revolution (DAR). They must have a GPA of 3.25 or higher. Selection is based on academic excellence, commitment to the field of study, and financial need. U.S. citizenship is required.
Financial data: The stipend is $2,000.
Duration: 1 year; nonrenewable.
Number awarded: Varies each year.
Deadline: February of each year.

1409 LYNN DEAN FORD/INDIANAPOLIS ASSOCIATION OF BLACK JOURNALISTS SCHOLARSHIP

Indianapolis Association of Black Journalists
Attn: President
P.O. Box 441795
Indianapolis, IN 46244-1795
Phone: (317) 432-4469
Email: sjefferson@wthr.com
Web: www.iabj.org/contactiabj/scholarshipinformation.html
Summary: To provide financial assistance to African Americans from Indiana who are interested in studying journalism in college.
Eligibility: Open to African Americans who are either 1) graduates of an Indiana high school and enrolled in a school of communications or journalism in any state; or 2) current college students majoring in communications or journalism at a 4-year accredited college or university in Indiana. Applicants must submit 2 letters of recommendation, samples of their work in the media (newspaper or magazine clips, audition tapes), and an essay of 250 to 500 words on what attracted them to a career in journalism and their goals in their area of interest (print or broadcast).
Financial data: The stipend is $1,000.
Duration: 1 year.
Number awarded: 1 each year.
Deadline: Deadline not specified.

1410 M. JOSEPHINE O'NEIL ARTS AWARD

Delta Kappa Gamma Society International–Lambda State Organization
c/o Linda McDonnell
3201 Newell Drive
Granite City, IL 62040-5160
Phone: (618) 452-3201
Email: llmcdonnell@excite.com
Web: www.deltakappagamma.org/IL/WomenintheArts/index.html
Summary: To provide financial assistance to female residents of Illinois who are studying an arts-related field at a college in any state.
Eligibility: Open to female residents of Illinois who are in or approaching junior standing at an accredited college or university or in the sophomore year at an accredited community college. Applicants must be majoring in 1 or more areas of the arts, including music, visual arts, dance, theater, or the literary arts. Along with their application, they must submit 1) evidence of the quality and extent of accomplishment in the arts, such as programs of performances, catalogs, articles from the media, published reviews of their work, listings of awards and prizes, or other recognition; 2) samples of their work on 35mm slides, CD, videotapes, or audio tapes; 3) college transcripts; 4) letters of recommendation; and 5) a personal essay on their family, personal interests, awards, achievements, goals (short- and long-term), and philosophy. Selection is based on the essay, letters of recommendation, academic background, and evidence from all sources of potential for contribution to society.
Financial data: The stipend ranges up to $6,000.
Duration: 1 year.
Number awarded: 1 each year.
Deadline: January of each year.

1411 MAB SCHOLARSHIP PROGRAM

Mississippi Association of Broadcasters
Attn: Scholarship Committee
855 South Pear Orchard Road, Suite 403
Ridgeland, MS 39157
Phone: (601) 957-9121; Fax: (601) 957-9175
Email: email@msbroadcasters.org
Web: www.msbroadcasters.org/scholarship.html
Summary: To provide financial assistance to residents of Mississippi enrolled in broadcast programs at colleges and universities in the state.
Eligibility: Open to residents of Mississippi enrolled in accredited broadcast programs at 2- and 4-year colleges and universities in the state. Applicants must submit a 3-page statement that covers why they selected broadcasting as their career choice, the specific area of broadcasting that most interests them and why, their first job preference after college, their career goal 10 years after graduation, their eventual career goal, the broadcast activities in which they have participated, how they feel about broadcast advertising and its importance to a station, how they feel about broadcast advertising and its obligation to consumers, how they think broadcasting could better serve society, the radio or television station they respect most, how their college career could improve their value as a broadcaster, and their most rewarding broadcast-related experience. Selection is based on the essay, extracurricular activities, community involvement, commitment to broadcasting, 3 letters of recommendation, and financial need.
Financial data: Up to $4,000 is available for this program each year.
Duration: 1 year.
Number awarded: 1 or more each year.
Deadline: April of each year.

1412 MALCOLM HAYES AWARD FOR ARTISTS

David and Dovetta Wilson Scholarship Fund, Inc.
115-67 237th Street
Elmont, NY 11003-3926
Phone: (516) 285-4573
Email: DDWSF4@aol.com
Web: www.wilsonfund.org/Malcolm_Hayes.html

Summary: To provide financial assistance to high school seniors who are interested in going to college and majoring in an arts field.

Eligibility: Open to graduating high school seniors who plan to attend an accredited college or university and study the arts. Applicants must be U.S. citizens or permanent residents and have a GPA of 3.0 or higher. Along with their application, they must submit 3 letters of recommendation, high school transcripts, and an essay (up to 250 words) on "How My College Education Will Help Me Make a Positive Impact on My Community." Selection is based on community involvement, desire to prepare for a career in the arts, and financial need.

Financial data: The stipend is $1,000.

Duration: 1 year.

Number awarded: 1 each year.

Deadline: March of each year.

1413 MANAA MEDIA SCHOLARSHIPS

Media Action Network for Asian Americans
P.O. Box 11105
Burbank, CA 91510
Phone: (213) 486-4433; (888) 90-MANAA
Email: scholarship@manaa.org
Web: www.manaa.org

Summary: To provide financial assistance to Asian Pacific Islander undergraduate and graduate students interested in advancing a positive image of Asian Americans in the mainstream media.

Eligibility: Open to Asian Pacific Islander undergraduate and graduate students interested in preparing for careers in filmmaking and in television production (but not in broadcast journalism). Applicants must be interested in advancing a positive and enlightened understanding of the Asian American experience in the mainstream media. Along with their application, they must submit a 1,000-word essay on their involvement in the Asian Pacific Islander community, how that involvement influences their creative work, how their creative work will influence the Asian Pacific Islanders community, and how it is perceived in the next 5 to 10 years. Selection is based on academic and personal merit, a desire to uplift the image of Asian Americans in film and television (as demonstrated in the essay), potential, and financial need.

Financial data: The stipend is $1,000.

Duration: 1 year.

Number awarded: 1 each year.

Deadline: October of each year.

1414 MARGARET SLOGGETT FISHER SCHOLARSHIP

Waioli Corporation
Attn: Scholarship Committee
P.O. Box 1631
Lihue, HI 96766
Phone: (808) 245-3202; Fax: (808) 245-7988
Email: grovefarm@hawaiiantel.net

Summary: To provide financial assistance to upper-division and graduate students from Hawaii who are interested in working on a degree in historical preservation, history, or related subjects.

Eligibility: Open to graduate students and college juniors and seniors who are residents of Hawaii and are working on a degree (in Hawaii or the mainland) in historical preservation, museum studies, history, anthropology, Hawaiian studies, ethnic studies, or American studies. Preference is given to Kauai residents. Applicants must submit a short letter outlining their educational background and goals, college transcripts, and 2 letters of recommendation.

Financial data: The stipend is $1,000.

Duration: 1 year.

Number awarded: 1 each year.

Deadline: April of each year.

1415 MARIA ELENA SALINAS SCHOLARSHIP PROGRAM

National Association of Hispanic Journalists
Attn: Scholarship Committee
1000 National Press Building
529 14th Street, N.W.
Washington, DC 20045-2001
Phone: (202) 662-7145; (888) 346-NAHJ; Fax: (202) 662-7144
Email: nahj@nahj.org
Web: www.nahj.org/educationalprograms/nahfscholarships.shtml

Summary: To provide financial assistance and work experience to Hispanic American students interested in preparing for a career as a journalist in Spanish-language radio or television.

Eligibility: Open to undergraduates and first-year graduate students. Applicants must demonstrate a sincere desire to prepare for a career as a journalist in Spanish-language television or radio. They must be enrolled full-time at a college or university in the United States or Puerto Rico. Along with their application, they must submit 1) transcripts; 2) a 1-page resume; 3) 2 letters of recommendation; 4) work samples; 5) a 1,000-word autobiographical essay that includes why they are interested in a career in journalism, what inspired them to prepare for a career in the field, what hardships or obstacles they have experienced while trying to realize their goal of becoming a journalist, and the role Latino journalists play in the news industry; and 6) an essay written as a news story in Spanish. Selection is based on commitment to the field of journalism, academic achievement, awareness of the Latino community, and financial need.

Financial data: The stipend is $5,000 per year; the program also provides funding for an internship during the summer.

Duration: 2 years.

Number awarded: 2 each year.

Deadline: April of each year.

1416 MARION BARR STANFIELD ART SCHOLARSHIP

Unitarian Universalist Association
Attn: Unitarian Universalist Funding Program
P.O. Box 301149
Jamaica Plain, MA 02130
Phone: (617) 971-9600; Fax: (617) 971-0029
Email: uufp@aol.com
Web: www.uua.org/giving/awardsscholarships/stanfieldand/index.shtml

Summary: To provide financial assistance to Unitarian Universalist students working on an undergraduate or graduate degree in art.

Eligibility: Open to undergraduate and graduate students preparing for a career in fine arts (including painting, drawing, photography, and/or sculpture). Applicants must be active in a Unitarian Universalist congregation, active in community affairs, and able to demonstrate financial need. Performing arts majors are not eligible. The endowment that supports this scholarship stipulated that the committee selecting its recipient consider "not only the intellectual attainments and potentialities of the beneficiaries but that they consider whether in character and constructive spiritual philosophy the beneficiaries are most likely to use their training in art for the betterment of humankind." Applicants must include a 2-page essay explaining how their goals are consistent with those wishes.

Financial data: The amount of the award depends on the need of the recipient. Awards have recently ranged from $1,000 to $3,000 per year.

Duration: 1 year; recipients may reapply.

Number awarded: Varies each year; recently, 10 of these scholarships were awarded: 2 at $3,000, 4 at $2,500, 1 at $2,000, and 3 at $1,000.

Deadline: February of each year.

1417 MARSHALL E. MCCULLOUGH SCHOLARSHIPS

National Dairy Shrine
Attn: Executive Director
P.O. Box 1
Maribel, WI 54227
Phone: (920) 863-6333; Fax: (920) 863-8328
Email: info@dairyshrine.org
Web: www.dairyshrine.org/scholarships.php

Summary: To provide financial assistance to graduating high school students interested in a career in dairy journalism.

Eligibility: Open to high school seniors planning to enter a 4-year college or university and major in 1) dairy/animal science with a communications emphasis; or 2) agricultural journalism with a dairy/animal science emphasis. U.S. citizenship is required. Applicants must submit brief essays on their farm experiences, dairy-related participation, and communications-related experiences; how they would assure a concerned consumer that a carton of milk is safe to drink; and what they see as the future of the U.S. dairy industry and their role in it. Based on those written applications, 5 finalists are selected; they must submit a videotape, CD, or DVD on which they respond to specific questions about the dairy industry. Winners are selected from this group.

Financial data: Scholarships are $2,500 or $1,000.

Duration: 1 year.

Number awarded: 2 each year: 1 at $2,500 and 1 at $1,000.

Deadline: April of each year.

1418 MARTIN UMANSKY MEMORIAL SCHOLARSHIP

Society of Professional Journalists–Kansas Professional Chapter
c/o Denise Neil, Scholarship Committee
Wichita Eagle
825 East Douglas Avenue
P.O. Box 820
Wichita, KS 67201-0820
Phone: (316) 268-6327
Email: dneil@wichitaeagle.com
Web: www.spjchapters.org/kansas/gridiron.html

Summary: To provide financial assistance to residents of any state enrolled at colleges and universities in Kansas who are interested in a career in broadcast journalism or alternative media.

Eligibility: Open to residents of any state entering their junior or senior year at colleges and universities in Kansas. Applicants do not have to be journalism or communications majors, but they must demonstrate a strong and sincere interest in broadcast journalism or alternative media. They must have a GPA of 2.5 or higher. Along with their application, they must submit a professional resume, 4 to 6 examples of their best work (tapes or transcripts of broadcasts, printouts of web pages) and a 1-page cover letter about themselves, how they came to be interested in journalism, their professional goals, and (if appropriate) their financial need for this scholarship.

Financial data: The stipend is $1,000.

Duration: 1 year.

Number awarded: 1 each year.

Deadline: April of each year.

1419 MARY ANN TALLMAN SCHOLARSHIP ENDOWMENT

Daughters of the American Revolution–Arizona State Society
c/o Nancy Holcombe, Scholarship Chair
14091 South Palo Verde Trail
Arizona City, AZ 85223
Email: ranaholc@netzero.net
Web: www.rootsweb.ancestry.com/~azsodar/scholarships.html

Summary: To provide financial assistance to high school seniors in Arizona interested in studying U.S. history at a college in any state.

Eligibility: Open to seniors graduating from high schools in Arizona and preparing to enter an institution of higher learning in any state. Applicants must be planning to major or minor in American history. They must submit a letter describing their leadership experiences, evidence of patriotism, and plans for the future.

Financial data: A stipend is awarded (amount not specified).

Duration: 1 year.

Number awarded: 1 each year.

Deadline: January of each year.

1420 MARYLAND ASSOCIATION FOR HEALTH, PHYSICAL EDUCATION, RECREATION AND DANCE HIGH SCHOOL SCHOLARSHIPS

Maryland Association for Health, Physical Education, Recreation and Dance
Attn: Office Coordinator
828 Dulaney Valley Road, Suite 8
Towson, MD 21204
Phone: (410) 583-1370; Fax: (410) 583-1374
Email: mewilliams@mahperd.org
Web: www.mahperd.org/GrantsScholarships.aspx

Summary: To provide financial assistance to high school seniors in Maryland who plan to attend college in any state to prepare for a career as a teacher of health, physical education, recreation, or dance.

Eligibility: Open to seniors graduating from high schools in Maryland who plan to enroll full-time at a collegiate institution in any state in a teacher preparation program in dance, health, physical education, or recreation. Applicants must rank in the top half of their class and have a GPA of 2.5 or higher. They should be able to demonstrate leadership qualities in the community and extracurricular participation, especially those that may have an impact on the future career in teaching. Along with their application, they must submit a letter describing their plans for a career, community activities, awards, and other recognitions. Financial need is not considered in the selection process.

Financial data: The stipend is $1,000.

Duration: 1 year.

Number awarded: 2 each year.

Deadline: April of each year.

1421 MARYLAND ASSOCIATION FOR HEALTH, PHYSICAL EDUCATION, RECREATION AND DANCE UNDERGRADUATE SCHOLARSHIPS

Maryland Association for Health, Physical Education, Recreation and Dance
Attn: Office Coordinator
828 Dulaney Valley Road, Suite 8
Towson, MD 21204
Phone: (410) 583-1370; Fax: (410) 583-1374
Email: mewilliams@mahperd.org
Web: www.mahperd.org/GrantsScholarships.aspx

Summary: To provide financial assistance to upper-division students from any state who are enrolled at a school in Maryland and preparing for a career as a teacher of health, physical education, recreation, or dance.

Eligibility: Open to students from any state who are completing their sophomore or junior year at a college or university in Maryland and enrolled full-time in a teacher preparation program in dance, health, physical education, or recreation. Applicants must have a GPA of 3.0 or higher in their major and 2.5 or higher overall. They should be able to demonstrate leadership qualities in the community and extracurricular participation, especially those that may have an impact on their future career in teaching. Along with their application, they must submit a letter describing their plans for a career, community activities, awards, and other recognitions. Financial need is not considered in the selection process.

Financial data: The stipend is $1,000.

Duration: 1 year.

Number awarded: 2 each year.

Deadline: March of each year.

1422 MARYLAND LEGION AUXILIARY CHILDREN AND YOUTH FUND SCHOLARSHIP

American Legion Auxiliary
Department of Maryland
1589 Sulphur Spring Road, Suite 105
Baltimore, MD 21227
Phone: (410) 242-9519; Fax: (410) 242-9553
Email: hq@alamd.org
Web: www.alamd.org

Summary: To provide financial assistance for college to the daughters of veterans who are Maryland residents and wish to study arts, sciences, business, public administration, education, or a medical field at a school in the state.

Eligibility: Open to Maryland senior high school girls with a veteran parent who wish to study arts, sciences, business, public administration, education, or a medical field other than nursing at a college or university in the state. Preference is given to children of members of the American Legion or American Legion Auxiliary. Selection is based on character (30%), Americanism (20%), leadership (10%), scholarship (20%), and financial need (20%).

Financial data: The stipend is $2,000.

Duration: 1 year; may be renewed up to 3 additional years.

Number awarded: 1 each year.

Deadline: April of each year.

1423 MARYLAND SPJ PRO CHAPTER COLLEGE SCHOLARSHIP

Society of Professional Journalists–Maryland Professional Chapter
c/o Bryan Sears, President
Patuxent Publishing
10750 Little Patuxent Parkway
Columbia, MD 21044-3106
Phone: (410) 730-3620; Fax: (410) 997-4564
Email: bpsears@gmail.com
Web: www.spjchapters.org/mdpro/scholarship.html

Summary: To provide financial assistance to residents of Maryland working on an undergraduate degree in journalism at a school in the region.
Eligibility: Open to residents of Maryland who are full- or part-time students working on a bachelor's degree with an emphasis on or major in journalism. Applicants may be enrolled at a college or university in nearby Virginia, District of Columbia, or Pennsylvania. Along with their application, they must submit transcripts; a list of journalism activities, awards, or honors received; a list of special interests and skills; a brief essay on their plans for a journalism career; a statement of family income and financial need; and letters of recommendation.
Financial data: A stipend is awarded (amount not specified).
Duration: 1 year.
Number awarded: 1 or more each year.
Deadline: April of each year.

1424 MASSACHUSETTS STUDENT BROADCASTER SCHOLARSHIPS

Massachusetts Broadcasters Association
43 Riverside Avenue
PMB 401
Medford, MA 02155
Phone: (800) 471-1875; Fax: (800) 471-1876
Email: info@massbroadcasters.org
Web: www.massbroadcasters.org/students/index.cfm
Summary: To provide financial assistance to Massachusetts residents interested in attending college in any state to prepare for a career in broadcasting.
Eligibility: Open to residents of Massachusetts who are in the process of enrolling or are currently enrolled full-time at an accredited institution of higher learning in any state. Applicants must be preparing for a career in broadcasting. Along with their application, they must submit a 150-word essay on why they have chosen to prepare for a career in a broadcast-related field. Selection is based on financial need, academic merit, community service, extracurricular activities, and work experience. Highest priority is given to students with the most limited financial resources.
Financial data: The stipend is $2,000. Checks are made payable to the recipient and the recipient's school.
Duration: 1 year.
Number awarded: 1 or more each year.
Deadline: March of each year.

1425 MAURICE AND ROBERT EARLY SCHOLARSHIPS

Indianapolis Press Club Foundation Inc.
Attn: Scholarship Committee
P.O. Box 40923
Indianapolis, IN 46240-0923
Phone: (317) 701-1130; Fax: (317) 844-5805
Email: info@indypressfoundation.org
Web: www.indypressfoundation.org/52/70.html
Summary: To provide financial assistance to college students in Indiana who are interested in preparing for a career in journalism.
Eligibility: Open to students enrolled in an Indiana college or university who are interested in a career in the news business. Preference is given to students who are majoring in journalism or broadcast journalism. Along with their application, students must submit a 1-page essay in which they describe their career goals, how they plan to achieve those goals, why they are important to them, and how the scholarship will assist them in reaching their goal of a career in journalism. Financial need is considered, but career interest, writing ability, ethics, news judgment, and potential for success are the chief concerns in the selection process.
Financial data: The stipend is $1,750 or $1,000.
Duration: 1 year.
Number awarded: 2 each year: 1 at $1,750 and 1 at $1,000.
Deadline: April of each year.

1426 METROPOLITAN OPERA NATIONAL COUNCIL AUDITIONS

Metropolitan Opera
Attn: National Council Auditions
Lincoln Center
New York, NY 10023
Phone: (212) 870-4515; Fax: (212) 870-7648
Email: ncouncil@metopera.org
Web: www.metoperafamily.org/metopera/auditions/national
Summary: To recognize and reward singers who have the potential to appear in the Metropolitan Opera.
Eligibility: Open to singers between 20 and 30 years of age who have a voice with operatic potential (exceptional quality, range, projection, charisma, communication, and natural beauty) as well as musical training and background. They must be able to sing correctly in more than 1 language and show artistic aptitude. Applicants should be citizens of the United States or Canada; foreign applicants must show proof of a 1-year residency or full-time enrollment at a university or conservatory in the United States or Canada. Singers must present 5 arias of their choice and of no more than 8 minutes' duration, in contrasting languages and styles. The competition begins at the district level, with winners advancing to regional auditions. The winners from each of the 15 regions represent their region at the national semifinals in New York and then 10 of those singers are selected as national finalists. At the National Grand Finals concert, which is held exactly 1 week later, the 10 National Grand Finalists perform 2 arias each on the stage of the Metropolitan Opera accompanied by the MET Orchestra in a nationally-broadcast concert. The national winners are selected at that concert.
Financial data: At the regional level, each first-place winner receives the $800 Mrs. Edgar Tobin Award, each second-place winner receives $600, and each third-place winner receives $400; some regions award additional prizes or encouragement awards. At the national level, each winner receives $15,000, each finalist receives $5,000, and each semifinalist receives $1,500. Semifinalists, finalists, and winners are eligible to apply for educational grants up to $5,000 for continuation of their education.
Duration: The competition is held annually.
Number awarded: The country is divided into 15 regions, in each of which 3 prizes are awarded. The 15 regional winners are national semifinalists, from whom 10 national finalists are selected. From those finalists, up to 5 national winners are chosen.
Deadline: Deadlines are chosen by local districts and regions; most of them are in the fall of each year. District auditions usually occur in October or November, with the winners advancing to the regional auditions, usually in December or January. The national competition in New York usually takes place in late February.

1427 METZ SCHOLARSHIP

Alabama Press Association
Attn: Journalism Foundation
3324 Independence Drive, Suite 200
Birmingham, AL 35209
Phone: (205) 871-7737; (800) 264-7043; Fax: (205) 871-7740
Email: michelle@alabamapress.org
Web: www.alabamapress.org/jf/index.cfm?fuseaction=content&id=80
Summary: To provide financial assistance to journalism students in Alabama.
Eligibility: Open to students entering their senior year at a college or university in Alabama. They must be nominated by a faculty member who also submits a cover letter that serves as a letter of recommendation. Nominees must be majoring in journalism and have an interest in newspaper management. Applications must also include the student's resume, college transcript, and 1-page description of interest in newspaper management.
Financial data: The stipend is $2,500.
Duration: 1 year.
Number awarded: 1 each year.
Deadline: March of each year.

1428 MICHAEL BATES MEMORIAL SCHOLARSHIP

Society of Professional Journalists–Kansas Professional Chapter
c/o Denise Neil, Scholarship Committee
Wichita Eagle
825 East Douglas Avenue
P.O. Box 820
Wichita, KS 67201-0820
Phone: (316) 268-6327
Email: dneil@wichitaeagle.com
Web: www.spjchapters.org/kansas/gridiron.html
Summary: To provide financial assistance to residents of any state enrolled at colleges and universities in Kansas who have been involved in media-related activities and are interested in a career in journalism.
Eligibility: Open to residents of any state entering their junior or senior year at colleges and universities in Kansas. Applicants do not have to be journalism or communication majors, but they must demonstrate a strong and sincere interest in print journalism, broadcast journalism, online journalism, or photojournalism. They must have a GPA of 3.0 or higher and a record of involvement in student and/or professional news media. Along with their application, they must submit a professional resume, 4 to 6 examples of their best work (clips

or stories, copies of photographs, tapes or transcripts of broadcasts, printouts of web pages) and a 1-page cover letter about themselves, how they came to be interested in journalism, their professional goals, and (if appropriate) their financial need for this scholarship.

Financial data: The stipend is $1,500. The winner also receives an expense-paid trip to the national convention of the Society of Professional Journalists (SPJ).

Duration: 1 year.

Number awarded: 1 each year.

Deadline: April of each year.

1429 MICHAEL S. POWELL HIGH SCHOOL JOURNALIST OF THE YEAR AWARD

Maryland-Delaware-D.C. Press Association
Attn: MDDC Press Foundation
2191 Defense Highway, Suite 300
Crofton, MD 21114-2487
Phone: (410) 721-4000; Fax: (410) 721-4557
Email: service@mddcpress.com
Web: www.mddcpress.com/mc/page.do?sitePageID=77456

Summary: To recognize and reward, with a scholarship for study at a college in any state, outstanding high school senior journalists in Maryland, Delaware, or the District of Columbia.

Eligibility: Open to high school seniors working on a Maryland, Delaware, or District of Columbia high school newspaper. Applicants must submit 5 samples of their work, a letter of recommendation from their adviser, and an autobiographical statement. They must be interested in majoring in journalism at a college in any state.

Financial data: The award is a $1,500 scholarship.

Duration: The award is presented annually.

Number awarded: 1 each year.

Deadline: January of each year.

1430 MICHIGAN PRESS ASSOCIATION FOUNDATION COLLEGE SCHOLARSHIPS

Michigan Press Association
Attn: MPA Foundation
827 North Washington Avenue
Lansing, MI 48906-5199
Phone: (517) 372-2424; Fax: (517) 372-2429
Email: mpa@michiganpress.org
Web: www.michiganpress.org/index/39

Summary: To provide financial assistance to students majoring in journalism at colleges and universities in Michigan.

Eligibility: Open to residents of Michigan majoring in journalism at colleges and universities in the state. Candidates must be nominated by faculty members at their schools. They must demonstrate interest in community journalism and have journalistic potential. Selection is based on scholastic achievement and financial need.

Financial data: The stipend is $1,000.

Duration: 1 year.

Number awarded: Varies each year; recently, 9 of these scholarships were awarded.

Deadline: December of each year.

1431 MIKE REYNOLDS JOURNALISM SCHOLARSHIP

Radio Television Digital News Foundation
Attn: RTDNF Fellowship Program
4121 Plank Road, Suite 512
Fredericksburg, VA 22407
Phone: (202) 467-5214; Fax: (202) 223-4007
Email: staceys@rtdna.org
Web: www.rtdna.org/pages/education/undergraduates.php

Summary: To provide financial assistance for undergraduate education to students whose career objective is radio or television news.

Eligibility: Open to sophomores, juniors, and seniors who are enrolled full-time in electronic journalism at a college or university where such a major is offered. Applicants must submit 1 to 3 examples of their journalistic skills on audio CD or DVD (no more than 15 minutes total, accompanied by scripts); a description of their role on each story and a list of who worked on each story and what they did; a 1-page statement explaining why they are preparing for a career in electronic journalism with reference to their specific career preference (radio, television, online, reporting, producing, or newsroom management); a resume; and a letter of reference from their dean or faculty sponsor explaining why they are a good candidate for the award and certifying that they have at least 1 year of school remaining. Preference is given to undergraduate students who demonstrate need for financial assistance by indicating media-related jobs held and contributions made to funding their own education.

Financial data: The stipend is $1,000.

Duration: 1 year.

Number awarded: 1 each year.

Deadline: May of each year.

1432 MINISTERIAL EDUCATION FUND OF THE EVANGELICAL METHODIST CHURCH

Evangelical Methodist Church
Attn: General Board of Ministerial Education
P.O. Box 17070
Indianapolis, IN 46217
Phone: (317) 780-8017; Fax: (317) 780-8078
Email: hq@emchurch.org
Web: emchurch.org/general-boards/ministerial-education

Summary: To provide financial assistance to college, Bible school, and seminary students preparing for ministry service in the Evangelical Methodist Church.

Eligibility: Open to 1) undergraduate students enrolled in an accredited Christian college in the Wesleyan tradition who are majoring in Bible, pastoral ministry, Christian education, or missions; and 2) students enrolled in an accredited theological seminary in the Wesleyan tradition approved by the Board of Ministerial Education of the Evangelical Methodist Church. Applicants must be in process toward ordination as an Evangelical Methodist Elder as recommended by their home District Superintendent and Board of Ministerial Relations. They must be a member in good standing in an Evangelical Methodist Church. Students working on a degree beyond the M.Div. are not eligible.

Financial data: The maximum loan amount varies each year and is greater for seminary students than for undergraduates. Funds are disbursed jointly to the student and the school, for payment of tuition only. For each year of full-time ministry service while under a call to an Evangelical Methodist Church or the Board of World Missions, after being ordained an elder, one-sixth of the debt is cancelled. If the recipient does not complete the process of ordination as an Elder or drops out of school, the loan is repayable at an interest rate of 6%. Years of service as a Member on Trial do not qualify toward repaying the loan debt. If an Elder withdraws or is discontinued from ministerial service, the balance of the unpaid loan becomes due and is repayable at 6% interest.

Duration: 1 year; may be renewed, provided the recipient maintains a GPA of 2.0 or higher.

Number awarded: Varies each year.

Deadline: Deadline not specified.

1433 MINNESOTA PRO CHAPTER OF THE SOCIETY OF PROFESSIONAL JOURNALISTS SCHOLARSHIP

Society of Professional Journalists–Minnesota Professional Chapter
c/o Amanda Theisen
KSTP-TV
3415 University Avenue
St. Paul, MN 55114
Phone: (651) 642-4532
Email: minnesota.spj@gmail.com
Web: www.mnspj.org/category/scholarships

Summary: To provide financial assistance to undergraduate students from Minnesota interested in preparing for a career in journalism.

Eligibility: Open to undergraduate students who are enrolled at a postsecondary institution in Minnesota or graduates of high schools in the state who are enrolled in a postsecondary institution in any state. Applicants must be preparing for a career in journalism. Preference is given to members of the Society of Professional Journalists (SPJ). Along with their application, they must submit a resume, college transcript, 2 letters of recommendation, a 500-word essay on why they have chosen journalism as a career, and samples of their work (up to 2 clippings or articles for print journalism, 2 printed screen shots for web journalism, 2 radio or TV samples for broadcast journalism, or up to 5 photographs for photojournalism). Financial need is not considered in the selection process.

Financial data: The stipend is $1,000.

Duration: 1 year.

Number awarded: 2 each year.

Deadline: March of each year.

1434 MIRIAM HOFFMAN SCHOLARSHIPS

United Methodist Church
Attn: General Board of Higher Education and Ministry
Office of Loans and Scholarships
1001 19th Avenue South
P.O. Box 340007
Nashville, TN 37203-0007
Phone: (615) 340-7344; Fax: (615) 340-7367
Email: umscholar@gbhem.org
Web: www.gbhem.org/loansandscholarships

Summary: To provide financial assistance to undergraduate and graduate Methodist students who are preparing for a career in music or music education.

Eligibility: Open to undergraduate and graduate students who are enrolled full-time and preparing for a career in music. Applicants must have been active, full members of a United Methodist Church for at least 1 year prior to applying and have a GPA of 2.5 or higher. Preference is given to students interested in music education or music ministry. U.S. citizenship or permanent resident status is required.

Financial data: The stipend is $1,000.

Duration: 1 year; recipients may reapply.

Number awarded: Varies each year; recently, 12 of these scholarships were awarded.

Deadline: May of each year.

1435 MISSOURI BROADCASTERS ASSOCIATION SCHOLARSHIPS

Missouri Broadcasters Association
Attn: Scholarship Committee
1025 Northeast Drive
P.O. Box 104445
Jefferson City, MO 65110-4445
Phone: (573) 636-6692; Fax: (573) 634-8258
Email: mba@mbaweb.org
Web: www.mbaweb.org/mc/page.do?sitePageID=23560

Summary: To provide financial assistance to Missouri residents interested in studying broadcasting in college.

Eligibility: Open to Missouri residents who are currently attending a college, university, or accredited technical/trade school in the state or graduating high school seniors who have been admitted to a Missouri institution of higher education. Applicants must be enrolled or planning to enroll as a full-time student in a broadcast or related program that provides training and expertise applicable to broadcast operation. They must have a GPA of 3.0 or higher and submit their application to a radio or television station that is a member of the Missouri Broadcasters Association. Each station selects its top candidate to forward to the association for statewide consideration. Selection is based on curriculum and career goals, clarity of thought and expression, letters of recommendation, community involvement, extracurricular activities, and financial need. Finalists are invited for personal interviews.

Financial data: Stipends are $2,500 or $1,000 per year.

Duration: 1 year; may be renewed if the recipient continues to meet eligibility requirements.

Number awarded: Varies each year; recently, 7 of these scholarships were awarded: 1 at $2,500 (the Donald J. Hicks Scholarship) and 6 at $1,000.

Deadline: March of each year.

1436 MISSOURI STATE THESPIAN SCHOLARSHIPS

Missouri State Thespians
c/o Debbie Corbin, Director
1426 State Highway 176 East
Spokane, MO 65754
Phone: (417) 587-0506
Email: info@mo-thespians.com
Web: www.mo-thespians.com/mc/page.do?sitePageID=77835

Summary: To provide financial assistance to high school seniors in Missouri who have been active in theater and plan to attend college in any state to major in theater or theater education.

Eligibility: Open to seniors graduating from high schools in Missouri who have participated in activities of Missouri State Thespians. Applicants must be planning to enroll at a college or university in any state and major in theater, a related field, or theater education. They must attend the annual state conference and apply for scholarships in performance, technical, or theater education. Performance applicants must present a 2-minute audition that consists of 2 contrasting monologues or a monologue and a short segment of a song from a musical theater piece. Technical applicants must submit a portfolio with samples of their work. Theater education applicants must submit a 500-word essay on why they want to be a theater teacher and a portfolio that illustrates their dedication to that profession. Financial need is not considered in the selection process.

Financial data: The stipend is $1,000.

Duration: 1 year.

Number awarded: Varies each year; recently, 8 of these scholarships were awarded: 4 for performance, 2 for technical, and 2 for theater education.

Deadline: Students must register for the conference by November of each year.

1437 MISSOURI THESPIANS THEATRE FOR LIFE SCHOLARSHIP

Missouri State Thespians
c/o Debbie Corbin, Director
1426 State Highway 176 East
Spokane, MO 65754
Phone: (417) 587-0506
Email: info@mo-thespians.com
Web: www.mo-thespians.com/mc/page.do?sitePageID=77835

Summary: To provide financial assistance to high school seniors in Missouri who have supported theatrical activities and plan to attend college in any state.

Eligibility: Open to seniors graduating from high schools in Missouri who have been active in performances, projects, and/or advocacy of their thespian troupe. Applicants must be planning to enroll at a college or university in any state and major in theater or any other field. They may not apply for any other scholarship offered by Missouri State Thespians. Along with their application, they must submit a portfolio that contains photographs, news articles, letters of support, or other materials that demonstrate their participation in the life of the local troupe or other theater activities in their community. Portfolios are judged on breadth of activity in theater, depth of activity in theater, impact on the school at large by the student's theater activities, impact on the community at large by the student's theater activities, and style and presentation of the portfolio. Based on those portfolios, finalists are invited to the sponsor's annual state conference where they present additional multimedia supporting material to supplement their portfolio and talk with the judging committee. Financial need is not considered in the selection process.

Financial data: The stipend is $1,000 for the winning student. Other finalists receive $100 awards.

Duration: 1 year.

Number awarded: 1 winner and 5 other finalists are selected each year.

Deadline: November of each year.

1438 MJSA EDUCATION FOUNDATION JEWELRY SCHOLARSHIP

Rhode Island Foundation
Attn: Funds Administrator
One Union Station
Providence, RI 02903
Phone: (401) 427-4017; Fax: (401) 331-8085
Email: lmonahan@rifoundation.org
Web: www.rifoundation.org

Summary: To provide financial assistance to undergraduate and graduate students working on a degree in a field related to jewelry.

Eligibility: Open to undergraduate and students at colleges, universities, and postsecondary nonprofit technical schools in the United States. Applicants must be studying tool making, design, metals fabrication, or other field related to jewelry. Along with their application, they must submit an essay (up to 300 words), in which they describe their program of study, how far along they are towards completion, their reason for choosing the program, and their professional goal. Selection is based on course of study, career objectives, samples of work (if appropriate), jewelry industry experience, academic achievement, recommendations, and financial need.

Financial data: Stipends range from $500 to $2,000 per year.

Duration: 1 year; may be renewed for up to 3 additional years if the recipient maintains good academic standing.

Number awarded: Varies each year; recently, 5 of these scholarships were awarded.

Deadline: May of each year.

1439 MONTANA ASSOCIATION OF SYMPHONY ORCHESTRAS YOUNG ARTIST COMPETITION

Montana Association of Symphony Orchestras
P.O. Box 1872

Bozeman, MT 59715-1872
Phone: (406) 585-9551
Email: info@montanasymphonies.org
Web: www.montanasymphonies.org/competition.htm

Summary: To recognize and reward outstanding young musicians in Montana.

Eligibility: Open to students between the ages of 13 and 22 who play any of the standard orchestral instruments. Competitions are held in a junior division (ages 13 through 15), a senior division (age 16 through high school graduate), and a college division (post-high school through age 22). Students who are attending college out of Montana are eligible if they have retained their Montana resident status. Past winners are ineligible to compete in the same division in future competitions. Applicants must submit a CD (up to 15 minutes in length)of a concerto or work for solo instrument and orchestra. Pianists should perform without accompaniment; other instrumentalists should have a piano or orchestra accompaniment. On the basis of the CDs, finalists are invited to auditions on the campus of Montana State University in Bozeman where they perform from memory the same work as on the CD.

Financial data: Prizes are $450 for the junior division, $650 for the senior division, and $1,000 for the college division.

Duration: The competition is held biennially, in odd-numbered years.

Number awarded: 3 every other year: 1 in each of the divisions.

Deadline: October of even-numbered years.

1440 MONTANA STATE ELKS MUSIC SCHOLARSHIP

Montana State Elks Association
c/o John Morford, Music Scholarship Committee
604 Orion Way
Livingston, MT 59047
Phone: (406) 581-4182
Email: jmorford@bigskyracks.com
Web: www.elks.org/states/?vhpID=8024

Summary: To provide financial assistance to high school seniors in Montana who plan to study music or music education at a college or university in any state.

Eligibility: Open to seniors graduating from high schools in Montana and planning to enroll at a college or university in any state. Applicants must be planning to major or minor in music performance or education. Along with their application, they must submit a 300-word essay on their intentions to make music performance or teaching a central part of their life and how they plan to achieve their musical goals. They must also submit a 5-minute CD of a solo vocal or instrumental performance. Financial need is not considered in the selection process. U.S. citizenship is required.

Financial data: A stipend is awarded (amount not specified).

Duration: 1 year.

Number awarded: 1 or more each year.

Deadline: April of each year.

1441 MONTE ITO MEMORIAL SCHOLARSHIP

David S. Ishii Foundation
Attn: College Scholarship Committee Chair
P.O. Box 2927
Aiea, HI 96701
Phone: (808) 478-6440
Email: info@davidsishiifoundation.org
Web: www.davidsishiifoundation.org/scholarships/ito_gee

Summary: To provide financial assistance to residents of Hawaii who can demonstrate an interest in golf and journalism and are interested in attending college in any state.

Eligibility: Open to residents of Hawaii who are high school seniors or college students with at least 1 year of school remaining. Applicants must be enrolled or planning to enroll at an accredited college or university in any state. They must be able to demonstrate achievements or potential in journalism and golf and an appreciation of both, although they are not required to major in journalism. Along with their application, they must submit an essay of 1 to 2 pages illustrating their interest in journalism and golf. Selection is based on the essay; financial need is not considered. Up to 3 samples of published work may also be submitted to enhance an entry.

Financial data: The stipend is $1,500.

Duration: 1 year.

Number awarded: 1 each year.

Deadline: May of each year.

1442 MORRIS J. AND BETTY KAPLUN FOUNDATION ESSAY CONTEST

Morris J. and Betty Kaplun Foundation
Attn: Essay Contest Committee
P.O. Box 234428
Great Neck, NY 11023
Web: www.kaplunfoundation.org

Summary: To recognize and reward outstanding essays on topics related to being Jewish.

Eligibility: Open to junior high and high school students (grades 10–12). High school students must write an essay of 250 to 1,500 words on a topic that changes annually but is related to being Jewish. A recent topic was "Of all the aspects, tenets, and traditions of Judaism, which single one do you view as the most important for you to pass on to your children?" For students in junior high school (grades 7–9), the essay must be 250 to 1,000 words; a recent topic was "My favorite hero or heroine, Biblical, historical, or contemporary, and his or her influence on Jewish history and/or Jewish values."

Financial data: Prizes are $1,800 or $750.

Duration: The competition is held annually.

Number awarded: Each year, 1 prize of $1,800 and 5 prizes of $750 are awarded at both the high school and junior high levels.

Deadline: March of each year.

1443 MORTON GOULD YOUNG COMPOSER AWARDS

American Society of Composers, Authors and Publishers
Attn: ASCAP Foundation
ASCAP Building
One Lincoln Plaza
New York, NY 10023-7142
Phone: (212) 621-6320; Fax: (212) 621-6236
Email: ascapfoundation@ascap.com
Web: www.ascapfoundation.org/awards.html

Summary: To recognize and reward outstanding young American composers.

Eligibility: Open to U.S. citizens, permanent residents, or enrolled students with proper visas who are younger than 30 years of age, including students in grades K–12, undergraduates, graduate students, and recipients of a D.M.A. or Ph.D. degree. Original music of any style is considered. However, works that have earned awards or prizes in other national competitions are ineligible, as are arrangements. To compete, each applicant must submit a completed application form, 1 reproduction of a manuscript or score, biographical information, a list of compositions to date, and 2 professional recommendations. Only 1 composition per composer may be submitted. A cassette tape or CD of the composition may be included. So that music materials may be returned, each entry must be accompanied by a self-addressed envelope with sufficient postage.

Financial data: The winners share cash awards of more than $30,000.

Duration: The award is presented annually.

Number awarded: Varies each year; recently, 37 students received these awards.

Deadline: February of each year.

1444 NAHJ GENERAL SCHOLARSHIPS

National Association of Hispanic Journalists
Attn: Scholarship Committee
1000 National Press Building
529 14th Street, N.W.
Washington, DC 20045-2001
Phone: (202) 662-7145; (888) 346-NAHJ; Fax: (202) 662-7144
Email: nahj@nahj.org
Web: www.nahj.org/educationalprograms/nahfscholarships.shtml

Summary: To provide financial assistance to Hispanic American undergraduate and graduate students interested in preparing for careers in the media.

Eligibility: Open to Hispanic American high school seniors, undergraduates, and graduate students who are interested in preparing for a career in English- or Spanish-language print, broadcast (radio or television), online, or photojournalism; students majoring in other fields must be able to demonstrate a strong interest in preparing for a career in journalism. Applicants must be enrolled full-time at a college or university in the United States or Puerto Rico. Along with their application, they must submit transcripts, a 1-page resume, 2 letters of recommendation, work samples, and a 1,000-word autobiographical essay that includes why they are interested in a career in journalism, what inspired them to prepare for a career in the field, what hardships or obstacles they have experienced while trying to realize their goal of becoming a journalist, and the role Latino journalists play in the news industry. Selection is based on commitment to the field of journalism, academic achievement, awareness of the Latino community, and financial need.

Financial data: Stipends range from $1,000 to $2,000.
Duration: 1 year.
Number awarded: Varies each year; recently, 20 of these scholarships were awarded.
Deadline: April of each year.

1445 NAOMI BERBER MEMORIAL SCHOLARSHIP

Print and Graphics Scholarship Foundation
Attn: Scholarship Competition
200 Deer Run Road
Sewickley, PA 15143-2600
Phone: (412) 259-1740; (800) 910-GATF; Fax: (412) 741-2311
Email: pgsf@piagatf.org
Web: www.gain.net

Summary: To provide financial assistance for college to women who want to prepare for a career in the printing or publishing industry.
Eligibility: Open to women who are high school seniors or full-time college students. Applicants must be interested in preparing for a career in graphic communications or printing. This is a merit-based program; financial need is not considered.
Financial data: The stipend ranges from $1,000 to $5,000, depending upon the funds available each year.
Duration: 1 year; may be renewed for up to 3 additional years, provided the recipient maintains a GPA of 3.0 or higher.
Number awarded: 1 or more each year.
Deadline: February of each year for high school seniors; March of each year for students already in college.

1446 NATIONAL AD 2 STUDENT CREATIVE COMPETITION

National Ad 2
c/o Lindsay Ostrowski, Treasurer
Dean Foundation
2711 Allen Boulevard, Suite 300
Middleton, WI 53562
Phone: (608) 827-2300; (800) 844-6015; Fax: (608) 827-2399
Email: treasurer@ad2.org
Web: www.ad2.org/education/education.htm

Summary: To recognize and reward students who enter an advertising competition.
Eligibility: Open to students enrolled full- or part-time in an accredited U.S. college, university, or commercial art school. Applicants must be majoring in advertising or a closely-related field (e.g., art, communication, journalism, marketing, or public relations). They must submit a complete advertisement in 1 of the following categories: sales promotion, collateral material, direct marketing, newspaper, interactive media, editorial design, radio, television, campaigns, or elements of advertising. The work must be the student's own individual effort and developed specifically for this competition or submitted from previous projects or competitions. Work developed for paying clients is not accepted. Entries must be submitted through a local Ad 2 Club.
Financial data: The grand-prize winner receives $1,000, plus complimentary registration and travel vouchers for the sponsor's national conference.
Duration: The competition is held annually.
Number awarded: 1 each year.
Deadline: March of each year.

1447 NATIONAL ASSOCIATION OF FARM BROADCASTING SCHOLARSHIPS

National Association of Farm Broadcasting
Attn: NAFB Foundation
700 Branch Street, Suite 8
P.O. Box 500
Platte City, MO 64079
Phone: (816) 431-4032; Fax: (816) 431-4087
Email: info@nafb.com
Web: www.nafb.com/index.aspx?mid=9376

Summary: To provide financial assistance to upper-division and graduate students working on a degree in agricultural communications.
Eligibility: Open to college juniors and graduate students who are 1) working on a degree in agricultural journalism or agricultural communications; or 2) planning to transfer to a university that offers a professional program of study in agricultural radio and television broadcasting. Applicants must submit a 2-minute personal statement on audio cassette that includes a description of their communications experience, reasons for choosing agricultural broadcasting and how this training will be of value to their intended career, long-term career goals, and how they anticipate using electronic communications skills. Selection is based on agricultural communications aptitude and leadership achievements, academic record, and career plans.
Financial data: Stipends are $5,000 or $4,000. Expense-paid trips to the annual convention of the National Association of Farm Broadcasting are also provided.
Duration: 1 year.
Number awarded: 3 each year: 1 at $5,000 (the Glenn Kummerow Memorial Scholarship) and 2 at $4,000.
Deadline: May of each year.

1448 NATIONAL ASSOCIATION OF NEGRO MUSICIANS SCHOLARSHIP CONTEST

National Association of Negro Musicians, Inc.
Attn: National Scholarship Chair
11551 South Laflin Street
P.O. Box 43053
Chicago, IL 60643
Phone: (773) 568-3818; Fax: (773) 785-5388
Email: nanm@nanm.org
Web: www.nanm.org/Scholarship_competition.htm

Summary: To recognize and reward (with scholarships for additional study) young musicians who are sponsored by a branch of the National Association of Negro Musicians.
Eligibility: Open to musicians between 18 and 30 years of age. Contestants must be sponsored by a branch in good standing, although they do not need to be a member of a local branch or the national organization. For each category of the competition, they must select 2 compositions from assigned lists to perform, of which 1 list consists of works by African American composers. People ineligible to compete include former first-place winners of this competition; full-time public school teachers and college faculty (although graduate students holding teaching assistantships are still eligible if they receive less than 50% of their employment from that appointment); vocalists who have contracts as full-time solo performers in operatic, oratorio, or other types of professional singing organizations; instrumentalists with contractual full-time orchestral or ensemble jobs; and professional performers under management. Local branches nominate competitors for regional competitions. Regional winners advance to the national competition. Selection is based on musical accuracy (20 points), intonation (20 points), interpretation (20 points), tone quality (20 points), technical proficiency (10 points), and memorization (10 points). The category of the competition rotates on a 5-year schedule as follows: 2010: piano; 2011: voice; 2012: strings; 2013: organ; 2014: winds and percussion.
Financial data: In the national competition, first place is $1,500, second $1,000, third $750, fourth $500, and fifth $250. All funds are paid directly to the winner's teacher/coach or institution.
Duration: The competition is held annually.
Number awarded: 5 each year.
Deadline: Deadline not specified.

1449 NATIONAL GARDEN CLUBS SCHOLARSHIPS

National Garden Clubs, Inc.
4401 Magnolia Avenue
St. Louis, MO 63110-3492
Phone: (314) 776-7574; Fax: (314) 776-5108
Email: headquarters@gardenclub.org
Web: www.gardenclub.org/Youth/Scholarships.aspx

Summary: To provide financial assistance to upper-division and graduate students in horticulture, landscape design, and related disciplines.
Eligibility: Open to college juniors, seniors, and graduate students who are working on a degree in agricultural education, horticulture, floriculture, landscape design, city planning, botany, biology, plant pathology, forestry, agronomy, environmental science, economics, environmental engineering, environmental law, wildlife science, habitat or forest systems ecology, land management, or allied subjects. Applicants must have at least a 3.25 GPA and be able to demonstrate financial need. Along with their application, they must submit a personal letter discussing their background, future goals, financial need, and commitment to their chosen career. All applications must be submitted to the state garden club affiliate and are judged there first; then 1 from each state is submitted to the national competition. Selection is based on academic record (40%), applicant's letter (30%), listing of honors, extracurricular activities, and work experience (10%), financial need (15%), and recommendations (5%). U.S. citizenship or permanent resident status is required; international and foreign exchange students are not eligible.
Financial data: The stipend is $4,000.
Duration: 1 year.

Number awarded: 35 each year.
Deadline: Applications must be submitted to the appropriate state organization by February of each year.

1450 NATIONAL ITALIAN AMERICAN FOUNDATION GENERAL CATEGORY II SCHOLARSHIPS

National Italian American Foundation
Attn: Education Director
1860 19th Street, N.W.
Washington, DC 20009
Phone: (202) 387-0600; Fax: (202) 387-0800
Email: scholarships@niaf.org
Web: www.niaf.org/scholarships/about.asp

Summary: To provide financial assistance for college or graduate school to students interested in majoring in Italian language, Italian studies, or Italian American studies.

Eligibility: Open to students of any nationality who are currently enrolled at or entering an accredited college or university in the United States with a GPA of 3.5 or higher. Applicants must be majoring or planning to major in Italian language, Italian studies, Italian American studies, or a related field. They may be high school seniors, undergraduates, graduate students, or doctoral candidates. Selection is based on academic performance, field of study, career objectives, and the potential, commitment, and abilities applicants have demonstrated that would enable them to make significant contributions to their chosen field of study. Some scholarships also require financial need, but most do not.

Financial data: Stipends range from $2,000 to $12,000.
Duration: 1 year; recipients, are encouraged to reapply.
Number awarded: Varies each year.
Deadline: March of each year.

1451 NATIONAL LATIN EXAMINATION SCHOLARSHIPS

National Latin Examination
c/o University of Mary Washington
1301 College Avenue
Fredericksburg, VA 22401
Phone: (888) 378-7721; Fax: (540) 654-1567
Email: nle@umw.edu
Web: www.nle.org/awards.html

Summary: To recognize and reward, with college scholarships, high school seniors who achieve high scores on the National Latin Examination.

Eligibility: Open to high school students who are enrolled or have completed a Latin course during the current academic year. They must take the National Latin Examination. The examinations consist of 40 multiple choice questions on comprehension, grammar, historical background, classical literature, and literary devices. Different examinations are given for Introduction to Latin, Latin I, Latin II, Latin III-IV Prose, Latin III-IV Poetry, and Latin V-VI. The top scorers in each category receive gold medals; gold medal winners in Latin III-IV Prose, Latin III-IV Poetry, and Latin V-VI who are high school seniors are invited to apply for these scholarships.

Financial data: The award is a $1,000 scholarship.
Duration: 1 year; may be renewed if the recipient continues to study classical Greek or Latin in college.
Number awarded: 21 each year.
Deadline: The examinations must be ordered by January of each year.

1452 NATIONAL MAKE IT YOURSELF WITH WOOL CONTEST

American Sheep Industry Women
c/o Marie Lehfeldt
P.O. Box 175
Lavina, MT 59046
Phone: (406) 636-2036; Fax: (406) 636-2731
Email: levi@midrivers.com
Web: www.sheepusa.org

Summary: To recognize and reward, with college scholarships, students who sew, knit, or crochet fashionable wool garments.

Eligibility: Open to students in the United States. The junior division is open to all persons between 13 and 16 years of age, and the senior division is for 17 through 24 years of age; most states also have a pre-teen division for competitors 12 years of age and younger and an adult division for persons over 24 years of age. Competitors enter machine or hand-knitted, woven, or crocheted garments, or garments containing any part that has been knitted or crocheted; all entries must be made from loomed, knitted, or felted fabric or yarn with a minimum of 60% wool and no more than 40% synthetic fiber. All entrants must select, construct, and model the garment themselves. The garments in the junior, senior, and adult divisions may be 2-piece outfits (coat, jacket, blouse/shirt, vest or sweater with dress, skirt, pants, or shorts), ensembles (3 or more garments worn together at a time), or 1-piece garments (dresses, outerwear jackets, coats, capes, or jumpers). Preteens may enter a dress, jumper, skirt, pants, shorts, vest, sweater, blouse/shirt, or jacket. Selection is based on appropriateness of the garment to the contestant's lifestyle, coordination of fabric/yarn with garment style and design, contestant's presentation, creativity, and construction quality. Contestants must participate in the state where they live or attend school. State winners in the junior and senior divisions advance to the national competition. Scholarships are awarded to national junior and senior division winners.

Financial data: Scholarships awarded at the national level are $2,000 or $1,000, to be used for tuition, books, and fees; funds are paid directly to registrars of approved accredited colleges.
Duration: The competition is held annually.
Number awarded: 6 national scholarships are awarded each year: 2 at $2,000 (1 for the junior winner and 1 for the senior winner) and 4 at $1,000 (2 from the Mohair Council of America for the junior and senior winners of complete garments made of mohair, the Pendleton Woolen Mills award for the junior winner, and the American Wool Council Fashion/Apparel Design Award).
Deadline: November of each year.

1453 NATIONAL PRESS CLUB SCHOLARSHIP FOR JOURNALISM DIVERSITY

National Press Club
Attn: General Manager's Office
529 14th Street, N.W.
Washington, DC 20045
Phone: (202) 662-7599
Web: www.press.org/activities/aboutscholarship.cfm

Summary: To provide funding to high school seniors who are planning to major in journalism in college and who will bring diversity to the field.

Eligibility: Open to high school seniors who have been accepted to college and plan to prepare for a career in journalism. Applicants must submit 1) a 500-word essay explaining how they would add diversity to U.S. journalism; 2) up to 5 work samples demonstrating an ongoing interest in journalism through work on a high school newspaper or other media; 3) letters of recommendation from 3 people; 4) a copy of their high school transcript; 5) documentation of financial need; 6) a letter of acceptance from the college or university of their choice; and 7) a brief description of how they have pursued journalism in high school.

Financial data: The stipend is $2,000 for the first year and $2,500 for each subsequent year. The program also provides an additional $500 book stipend, designated the Ellen Masin Persina Scholarship, for the first year.
Duration: 4 years.
Number awarded: 1 each year.
Deadline: February of each year.

1454 NATIONAL SCHOOL TRAFFIC SAFETY POSTER PROGRAM

American Automobile Association
Attn: Poster Program Headquarters
1000 AAA Drive
Heathrow, FL 32746-5063
Phone: (407) 444-7916; Fax: (407) 444-7956
Web: www.aaaexchange.com

Summary: To recognize and reward outstanding elementary, middle, and high school artists in a highway safety poster competition.

Eligibility: Open to students enrolled in public, parochial, or private elementary, middle, and high schools in the United States or Canada. Competition is held in 4 geographic regions and 4 divisions: primary (grades K–2), elementary (grades 3–5), junior high (grades 6–8), and senior high (grades 9–12). Students select or create a slogan related to a traffic safety issue (pedestrian and child passenger safety for primary grades, getting to school safely for elementary grades, how to be a good passenger for junior high, and safe teen driving for senior high) and then prepare a poster illustrating that slogan. Senior high students may prepare a poster, graphic arts digitally enhanced submission, or an audio/visual public service announcement (PSA) between 1 and 2 minutes in length. Entries must be submitted to local AAA clubs. Selection is based on relationship of the poster design to traffic safety practices, originality of the poster and how the idea is expressed in the poster design, creativity and its execution, visual impact of the poster design, and relevance and creativity of slogan; for PSA entries in the high school division, selection is based on originality, creativity, and relationship to traffic safety.

Financial data: In each division, first-place awards are $300 Visa gift checks, second-place awards are $200 Visa gift checks, and third-place awards are $100 Visa gift checks. The grand award winners in the primary, elementary, and junior high divisions also receive a $1,000 Visa gift check and the grand award winners in each senior high category (poster, graphic arts, and PSA) receive $2,000 Visa gift checks.
Duration: The competition is held annually.
Number awarded: For each of the 4 grade-level divisions, 4 first-place, 4 second-place, and 4 third-place prizes are awarded: 1 for each geographic region. In addition, 6 grand awards (1 each for the primary, elementary, and junior high division plus 1 for each of the 3 categories in the senior high division) are presented.
Deadline: January of each year.

1455 NATIONAL SCULPTURE COMPETITION PRIZES

National Sculpture Society
Attn: National Sculpture Competition
237 Park Avenue, Ground Floor
New York, NY 10017
Phone: (212) 764-5645; Fax: (212) 764-5651
Email: nss1893@aol.com
Web: www.sculpturecompetition.info/competition/index.cfm
Summary: To recognize and reward outstanding creative work by students and other young sculptors.
Eligibility: Open to students and other young sculptors. This competition is a 2-part event; entrants may participate in either or both parts. The young sculptor awards are presented to sculptors under 40 years of age who are citizens or residents of the United States. They must submit slides of up to 5 different works of sculpture in bas-relief. The use of figurative or realist sculpture is preferred. Artists who wish to be considered for this part of the competition do not need to be present. The Dexter Jones Award is presented for the best work of sculpture in bas-relief, the Roger T. Williams Prize is awarded to the sculptor "who reaches for excellence in representational sculpture," and the Edward Fenno Hoffman Prize is awarded to the sculptor "who strives to uplift the human spirit through the medium of his/her art." For the second part of the competition, the jury invites 18 entrants to participate in a 5-day figure modeling contest. Selection of winners is based on the following criteria: mastery of the figure in sculptural form; comprehension of the action, unity, and rhythm of the pose; and how well the artist gives evidence of understanding proportion, stance, solidity, and continuity of line.
Financial data: The Dexter Jones Award is $1,000, the Roger T. Williams Prize is $750, and the Edward Fenno Hoffman Prize is $350. For sculptors who choose to enter the figure modeling contest, the first-place winner receives the Walker Hancock Prize of $1,000, the second-place winner receives the Walter and Michael Lantz Prize of $750, and the third-place winner receives the Elizabeth Gordon Chandler Prize of $300.
Duration: The competition is held annually.
Number awarded: Each year, 3 prizes are awarded on the basis of slides and 3 prizes are awarded to winners of the figure modeling contest.
Deadline: March of each year.

1456 NATIONAL SECURITY SCHOLARSHIPS OF THE INDEPENDENT COLLEGE FUND OF MARYLAND

Independent College Fund of Maryland
Attn: Director of Programs and Scholarships
3225 Ellerslie Avenue, Suite C160
Baltimore, MD 21218-3519
Phone: (443) 997-5703; Fax: (443) 997-2740
Email: LSubot@jhmi.edu
Web: www.i-fundinfo.org
Summary: To provide financial assistance to students from any state enrolled at member institutions of the Independent College Fund of Maryland and majoring in a field related to national security.
Eligibility: Open to students from any state who are enrolled as sophomores or juniors at member institutions. Applicants must be preparing for a career in the national security field by majoring in accounting, engineering, computer science, history, information systems, languages, mathematics, physics, or political science. They must be U.S. citizens and have a GPA of 3.0 or higher.
Financial data: The stipend is $20,000.
Duration: 1 year.
Number awarded: 1 or more each year.
Deadline: October of each year.

1457 NATIONAL SOCIETY OF NEWSPAPER COLUMNISTS SCHOLARSHIP CONTEST

National Society of Newspaper Columnists
Attn: Education Foundation
P.O. Box 411532
San Francisco, CA 94141-1532
Phone: (866) 440-NSNC; Fax: (866) 635-5759
Web: www.columnists.com
Summary: To recognize and reward, with college scholarships, undergraduate journalism students who write outstanding columns.
Eligibility: Open to undergraduates who write bylined general interest or editorial page columns for their college newspapers. It is not open to columnists writing on sports, arts, health, or other specialized topics. Candidates must submit 3 columns published during the 12-month period prior to the deadline. Columns published online are eligible if they also appeared in print editions.
Financial data: First prize is a $1,000 scholarship; second prize is a $500 scholarship; and third prize is a $250 scholarship.
Duration: The prizes are presented annually.
Number awarded: 3 each year.
Deadline: February of each year.

1458 NATIONAL SOCIETY OF THE COLONIAL DAMES OF AMERICA IN THE STATE OF GEORGIA SCHOLARSHIPS

Georgia Trust
Attn: Scholarship Committee
1516 Peachtree Street, N.W.
Atlanta, GA 30309
Phone: (404) 881-9980; Fax: (404) 875-2205
Email: info@georgiatrust.org
Web: www.georgiatrust.org/preservation/spalding_owens.php
Summary: To provide financial assistance to Georgia residents majoring in a field related to historical preservation at a college or university in the state.
Eligibility: Open to Georgia residents who are enrolled full-time in their first year of undergraduate study at a college or university in the state. Applicants must be working on a degree in historic preservation or a related field (e.g., archaeology, architecture, history, planning). They may not have a family affiliation to the National Society of the Colonial Dames of America. U.S. citizenship is required. Selection is based on academic achievement and past and planned involvement within preservation-related fields.
Financial data: The stipend is $1,500.
Duration: 1 year.
Number awarded: 2 each year.
Deadline: February of each year.

1459 NATIONAL STUDENT JOURNALIST OF THE YEAR SCHOLARSHIPS

Journalism Education Association
c/o Kansas State University
103 Kedzie Hall
Manhattan, KS 66506-1505
Phone: (785) 532-5532; (866) JEA-5JEA; Fax: (785) 532-5563
Email: jea@spub.ksu.edu
Web: www.jea.org/awards/journalist.html
Summary: To recognize and reward, with college scholarships, outstanding high school journalists.
Eligibility: Open to graduating high school seniors who are planning to study journalism and/or mass communications in college and prepare for a career in that field, have a GPA of 3.0 or higher, and have participated in high school journalism for at least 2 years. Applicants must submit examples of their work that show the following 4 characteristics: 1) skilled and creative use of media content; 2) inquiring mind and investigative persistence resulting in an in-depth study of issues important to the local high school audience, high school students in general, or society; 3) courageous and responsible handling of controversial issues despite threat or imposition of censorship; and 4) variety of journalistic experiences, each handled in a quality manner, on a newspaper, yearbook, broadcast, or other medium. Applications are to be sent to the applicant's state contest coordinator; winners from the state Journalist of the Year competitions are sent to the national level for judging.
Financial data: The award is $5,000 for the top winner and $2,000 for each runner-up. Funds are released when the recipient enrolls in a college journalism program.
Duration: The competition is held annually.

Number awarded: Approximately 7 each year: 1 top winner and approximately 6 runners-up.
Deadline: Applications must be submitted to state coordinators in February of each year.

1460 NATIONAL TRUMPET COMPETITION AWARDS

National Trumpet Competition
Attn: Director of Operations
3500 North Third Street
Arlington, VA 22201
Email: marvin@nationaltrumpetcomp.org
Web: www.nationaltrumpetcomp.org
Summary: To recognize and reward outstanding student trumpet players.
Eligibility: Open to student trumpet players in the following divisions: 1) the Noteworthy Tours junior solo division (through grade 9 or up to 15 years of age and enrolled full-time at a U.S. school or home-schooled in the United States); 2) the Schilke Music Products high school solo division (grades 10–12 or up to 19 years of age and enrolled full-time at a U.S. high school or home-schooled in the United States); 3) the Vincent Bach undergraduate solo division (up to 25 years of age and enrolled full-time in a U.S. undergraduate program); or 4) the Blackburn Trumpets graduate solo division (up to 28 years of age and enrolled full-time in a U.S. graduate program). In addition, the Dillon Music Jazz solo division and the Historic Trumpets division are open to all full-time students up to 28 years of age and the Southern Ohio Music Company Trumpet Ensemble Division is open to groups of 4 to 8 full-time students up to 28 years of age. Both U.S. and foreign students are eligible. Entrants submit CDs of their performances; times and repertoire vary according to division. Based on those CDs, semifinalists are selected and invited to the competitions at George Mason University in March.
Financial data: The following prizes are awarded: in the Noteworthy Tours junior solo division, first place is a Jupiter trumpet, second a Blessing trumpet, and third a cash award of $250; in the Schilke Music Products high school solo division, first place is full tuition to Interlochen Summer Camp, second a Schilke trumpet, and third a $500 GC Larson gift card plus $250 in cash; in the Vincent Bach undergraduate solo division, first place is a Bach trumpet plus $500 in cash, second $1,500 in cash, and third $750 in cash; in the Blackburn Trumpets graduate solo division, cash prizes are $3,000 for first, $1,500 for second, and $750 for third; in the Dillon Music Jazz solo division, cash prizes are $3,000 for first, $1,500 for second, and $750 for third; the Historic Trumpets division offers several non-cash prizes of trumpets, memberships in organizations, and tuition at performance institutes; In the Southern Ohio Music Company trumpet ensemble division, cash prizes (divided equally among all members) are $4,000 for first, $2,000 for second, $1,000 for third, and $500 for fourth.
Duration: The competition is held annually.
Number awarded: Varies each year.
Deadline: December of each year.

1461 NAUMBURG FOUNDATION COMPETITION FOR COMPOSERS

Walter W. Naumburg Foundation, Inc.
120 Claremont Avenue
New York, NY 10027-4698
Phone: (212) 362-9877
Web: www.naumburg.org
Summary: To recognize and reward outstanding young composers.
Eligibility: Open to U.S. citizens younger than 40 years of age. Applicants must submit 2 original compositions, 1 of which should be a chamber music work. Each work should be accompanied by a recording.
Financial data: The prize is a $5,000 commission to write a chamber music work that will be performed by a leading chamber music ensemble.
Duration: The competition is held annually.
Number awarded: 2 each year.
Deadline: September of each year.

1462 NAVY ADVANCED EDUCATION VOUCHER PROGRAM

U.S. Navy
Naval Education and Training Command
Center for Personal and Professional Development
Attn: AEV Program Office
6490 Saufley Field Road
Pensacola, FL 32509-5204
Phone: (850) 452-7271; Fax: (850) 452-1272
Email: rick.cusimano@navy.mil
Web: www.navycollege.navy.mil/aev/aev_home.cfm
Summary: To provide financial assistance to Navy enlisted personnel who are interested in earning an undergraduate or graduate degree in selected fields during off-duty hours.
Eligibility: Open to senior enlisted Navy personnel in ranks E-7 and E-8. Applicants should be transferring to, or currently on, shore duty with sufficient time ashore to complete a bachelor's or master's degree. Personnel at rank E-7 may have no more than 16 years in service and E-8 no more than 18 years. The area of study must be certified by the Naval Postgraduate School as Navy-relevant.
Financial data: This program covers 100% of education costs (tuition, books, and fees). For a bachelor's degree, the maximum is $6,700 per year or a total of $20,000 per participant. For a master's degree, the maximum is $20,000 per year or a total of $40,000 per participant.
Duration: Up to 36 months from the time of enrollment for a bachelor's degree; up to 24 months from the time of enrollment for a master's degree.
Number awarded: Varies each year; recently, 20 of these vouchers were awarded: 15 for bachelor's degrees and 5 for master's degrees.
Deadline: February of each year.

1463 NEBRASKA PRESS ASSOCIATION FOUNDATION SCHOLARSHIPS

Nebraska Press Association Foundation
845 S Street
Lincoln, NE 68508
Phone: (402) 476-2851; (800) 369-2850 (within NE); Fax: (402) 476-2942
Email: nebpress@nebpress.com
Web: www.nebpress.com
Summary: To provide financial assistance to high school seniors in Nebraska who are interested in preparing for a career in print journalism.
Eligibility: Open to high school seniors in Nebraska who are interested in attending a college or university in the state and majoring in print journalism. Preference is given to students with specific interests in news, editorial, photography, circulation, production, or advertising. Applicants must submit information on their academic accomplishments, reasons for applying for this scholarship (including their career plans), and family financial situation.
Financial data: The stipend is $2,000.
Duration: 1 year.
Deadline: February of each year.

1464 NELLIE LOVE BUTCHER MUSIC SCHOLARSHIP

Daughters of the American Revolution–National Society
Attn: Committee Services Office, Scholarships
1776 D Street, N.W.
Washington, DC 20006-5303
Phone: (202) 628-1776
Web: www.dar.org/natsociety/edout_scholar.cfm
Summary: To provide financial assistance to students working on an undergraduate degree in music.
Eligibility: Open to students who are working on or planning to work on a degree in piano or voice. Applicants must be sponsored by a local chapter of the Daughters of the American Revolution (DAR). Special consideration is given to students currently attending the Duke Ellington School of the Performing Arts in Washington, D.C. Selection is based on academic excellence, commitment to the field of study, and financial need. U.S. citizenship is required.
Financial data: The stipend is $5,000 per year.
Duration: 1 year; may be renewed up to 3 additional years, provided the recipient maintains a GPA of 3.0 or higher.
Number awarded: 1 each year.
Deadline: April of each year.

1465 NELSON BROWN AWARD

Connecticut Broadcasters Association
Attn: Scholarships
90 South Park Street
Willimantic, CT 06226
Phone: (860) 633-5031; Fax: (860) 456-5688
Email: mcrice@prodigy.net
Web: www.ctba.org/page.cfm?page=17

Summary: To provide financial assistance to Connecticut residents who are interested in attending college in any state to prepare for a career in broadcasting.
Eligibility: Open to Connecticut residents who are entering their first, second, third, or fourth year at a 2- or 4-year college, university, or technical school in any state. Applicants must be majoring in broadcasting, communications, marketing, or a related field. Selection is based on academic achievement, community service, goals in the chosen field, and financial need.
Financial data: The stipend is $5,000.
Duration: 1 year.
Number awarded: 1 each year.
Deadline: March of each year.

1466 NEW ENGLAND COX COMMUNICATIONS SCHOLARSHIPS

Cox Communications–New England
Attn: Community Relations Coordinator
9 JP Murphy Highway
West Warwick, RI 02893
Phone: (401) 383-2000
Email: rosie.fernandez@cox.com
Web: ww2.cox.com/myconnection/connecticut/community/editorial2.cox
Summary: To provide financial assistance to high school seniors in Connecticut and Rhode Island who plan to major in communications in college.
Eligibility: Open to seniors graduating from high schools in Rhode Island or in selected towns in Connecticut. Applicants must be planning to attend a college or university to major in communications or a communications-related field. Along with their application, they must submit an essay describing the greatest impact they have made on their community through a community service project. Selection is based on academic achievement, community involvement, and desire to prepare for a career in communications, telecommunications, engineering, or technology; financial need is not considered.
Financial data: The stipend is $2,000.
Duration: 1 year.
Number awarded: 16 each year: 8 for students from Rhode Island and 8 for students from Connecticut.
Deadline: March of each year.

1467 NEW ENGLAND GRAPHIC ARTS SCHOLARSHIP

Printing and Publishing Council of New England
c/o Jay Smith, Scholarship Chair
166 New Boston Street
Woburn, MA 01801
Email: jay@mhcp.com
Web: www.ppcne.org/scholarships.html
Summary: To provide financial assistance to high school seniors, graduates, and currently-enrolled college students from New England who are preparing for a career in printing or the graphic arts.
Eligibility: Open to residents of New England who are high school seniors or recent graduates. Applicants must be attending or planning to attend a 2- or 4-year college or university in any state that offers a certificate or degree related to printing or the graphic arts. Selection is based on academic achievement, extracurricular activities, personal qualifications, and financial need.
Financial data: The maximum stipend is $2,500. Funds are paid directly to the recipient's college or university.
Duration: Up to 4 years, provided the recipient maintains a GPA of 2.5 or higher.
Number awarded: 1 or more each year; nearly $100,000 in scholarships is awarded each year.
Deadline: May of each year.

1468 NEW ENGLAND PRESS EDUCATIONAL FOUNDATION SCHOLARSHIPS

New England Newspaper and Press Association
Attn: New England Press Educational Foundation
370 Common Street
Dedham, MA 02026
Phone: (781) 320-8050
Email: lywilliams@nenpa.com
Web: www.nenpa.com/Education
Summary: To provide financial assistance to residents of New England interested in studying print journalism at a college in any state.
Eligibility: Open to residents of New England who are high school seniors or college students. Applicants must demonstrate a serious interest in a career in print journalism through 1) a body of published work in a school newspaper, general circulation newspaper, or similar publication; 2) a body of work prepared for a journalism class; or 3) an essay of at least 1,000 words describing their journalistic interests and values. They must have a GPA of 2.3 or higher.
Financial data: The stipend is $1,000.
Duration: 1 year.
Number awarded: Several each year.
Deadline: April of each year.

1469 NEW JERSEY NEWSPAPER FOUNDATION INTERNSHIP/ SCHOLARSHIP PROGRAM FOR COLLEGE STUDENTS

New Jersey Press Association
Attn: New Jersey Newspaper Foundation
840 Bear Tavern Road, Suite 305
West Trenton, NJ 08628-1019
Phone: (609) 406-0600, ext. 19; Fax: (609) 406-0300
Email: foundationprograms@njpa.org
Web: www.njpa.org/foundation/internsnjpf.html
Summary: To provide financial assistance and internship opportunities to journalism majors in New Jersey.
Eligibility: Open to residents of New Jersey who are enrolled full-time at a college or university in the state. Applicants must be majoring in journalism and interested in participating in a summer internship at a daily, weekly, or other newspaper in New Jersey. Students who have worked as full-time or permanent part-time employees for a professional newspaper are ineligible. Along with their application, they must submit a resume, a 500-word autobiographical sketch, transcripts, 2 letters of recommendations, 3 work samples or clippings, and a statement of special financial or family circumstances (if appropriate).
Financial data: This program provides a $1,000 stipend and a paid internship (at least $325 per week) to each recipient. Approximately half of the internship salary is subsidized by the New Jersey Newspaper Foundation. Funds are paid directly to the recipient's school.
Duration: The scholarship covers 1 academic year; the internship lasts 8 weeks during the summer.
Number awarded: Varies each year; recently, 4 of these awards were presented.
Deadline: November of each year.

1470 NEW JERSEY POST SAME SCHOLARSHIP

Society of American Military Engineers–New Jersey Post
c/o John Booth
CTSC
P.O. Box 60
Fort Monmouth, NJ 07703
Phone: (732) 544-0995, ext. 102
Email: john.booth@ctsc.net
Web: posts.same.org/newjersey/scholarships.html
Summary: To provide financial assistance to students in New Jersey working on an undergraduate degree in architecture, engineering, or a related field.
Eligibility: Open to undergraduate students working on a degree in architecture, engineering, or a related field. Candidates must be nominated by a member of the New Jersey Post of the Society of American Military Engineers (SAME). Selection is based on school and community activities, educational goals, academics, recommendations, and employment experience.
Financial data: The stipend is $1,000.
Duration: 1 year; nonrenewable.
Number awarded: Varies each year; recently, 6 of these scholarships were awarded.
Deadline: March of each year.

1471 NEW JERSEY SPORTS WRITERS ASSOCIATION SCHOLARSHIP

New Jersey Sports Writers Association
Attn: Scholarship Committee
P.O. Box 2877
Hamilton Square, NJ 08690
Phone: (877) 257-0798
Email: njswa@njsportswriters.org
Web: www.njsportswriters.org/scholarship.html
Summary: To provide financial assistance to residents of New Jersey who are preparing for a career in sports reporting at a school in the state.

Eligibility: Open to residents of New Jersey majoring in journalism at a 4-year college or university in the state. Applicants must be interested in preparing for a career in sports reporting. Along with their application, they must submit a statement of interest in a sports writing career, a biographical sketch, a letter of recommendation, 3 or 4 samples of their work, and a statement of special financial or other family circumstances, if applicable. A transcript is optional. Financial need is considered in the selection process.
Financial data: The stipend is $1,000.
Duration: 1 year.
Number awarded: 1 each year.
Deadline: December of each year.

1472 NEW MEXICO BROADCASTERS ASSOCIATION SCHOLARSHIPS

New Mexico Broadcasters Association
Attn: Foundation
2333 Wisconsin Street, N.E.
Albuquerque, NM 87110-4654
Phone: (505) 881-4444; (800) 622-2414; Fax: (505) 881-5353
Web: www.nmbf.org/scholarship.php
Summary: To provide financial assistance to residents of New Mexico who are attending college in the state to prepare for a career in the broadcast industry.
Eligibility: Open to residents of New Mexico who are entering their sophomore, junior, or senior year at an accredited college, vocational institution, or university in the state. Applicants must be preparing for a career in the broadcast industry, including news, announcing, sales, accounting, management, engineering, traffic and billing, promotion, community affairs, programming, production, or other aspects of the industry. They must submit brief statements on their work experience at a broadcast facility and why they want to prepare for a career in the field. Race, gender, age, and financial need are not considered in the selection process. Nontraditional and reentry students are encouraged to apply.
Financial data: The stipend is $2,500 per year. Funds are sent directly to the student to help pay the cost of tuition, books, supplies and fees.
Duration: 1 year.
Number awarded: Up to 10 each year.
Deadline: April of each year.

1473 NHAB STUDENT BROADCASTER SCHOLARSHIP PROGRAM

New Hampshire Association of Broadcasters
707 Chestnut Street
Manchester, NH 03104
Phone: (603) 627-9600; Fax: (603) 627-9603
Email: info@nhab.org
Web: www.nhab.org/students/index.cfm
Summary: To provide financial assistance to New Hampshire residents interested in attending college in any state to prepare for a career in broadcasting or communications.
Eligibility: Open to residents of New Hampshire who are enrolled or planning to enroll full-time in a broadcast program at a 2- or 4-year college or university in any state. Applicants must submit a 150-word statement on why they have chosen to prepare for a career in a broadcast-related field. Selection is based on financial need, academic merit, community service, extracurricular activities, and work experience. Highest priority is given to students with the most limited financial resources.
Financial data: The stipend is $2,500.
Duration: 1 year.
Number awarded: At least 6 each year.
Deadline: March of each year.

1474 NICHOLAS DIERMANN MEMORIAL SCHOLARSHIP

Oregon Student Assistance Commission
Attn: Grants and Scholarships Division
1500 Valley River Drive, Suite 100
Eugene, OR 97401-2146
Phone: (541) 687-7395; (800) 452-8807, ext. 7395; Fax: (541) 687-7414; TDD: (800) 735-2900
Email: awardinfo@osac.state.or.us
Web: www.osac.state.or.us/osac_programs.html
Summary: To provide financial assistance to residents of Oregon who are interested in studying specified fields at colleges in any state.
Eligibility: Open to residents of Oregon who are currently enrolled or planning to enroll at a 4-year public college or university in any state. Applicants must be interested in working on a degree in music, performing arts, accounting, or sales (computer, software) operations. Along with their application, they must submit an essay of 250 to 350 words on what led to their career choice and what their participation in music or performing arts means to them; if technology has been an influence, they should include how it will affect their chosen profession.
Financial data: A stipend is awarded (amount not specified).
Duration: 1 year; recipients may reapply.
Number awarded: Varies each year.
Deadline: February of each year.

1475 NOLAN MOORE MEMORIAL EDUCATION FOUNDATION SCHOLARSHIP

Printing and Imaging Association of MidAmerica
Attn: Scholarship Administrator
8828 North Stemmons Freeway, Suite 505
Dallas, TX 75247
Phone: (214) 630-8871, ext. 205; (800) 788-2040
Email: dodier@piamidam.org
Web: www.piamidam.org/scholar.php
Summary: To provide financial assistance to residents of designated states who are attending college to prepare for a career in the printing industry.
Eligibility: Open to students enrolled or planning to enroll in an educational institution that offers a 2- or 4-year degree in printing technology, printing management, or related field. Applicants must be residents of Kansas, Missouri, Oklahoma, or Texas. They should be attending a school in those states, but they may go elsewhere if they can demonstrate the appropriate aptitude and industry interest. Along with their application, they must submit a 1-page statement outlining their career goals and a letter of endorsement from their faculty sponsor that reinforces their stated intention to prepare for a career in the graphic arts industry. Selection is based on interest in the industry and GPA; financial need is not considered.
Financial data: The stipend is $2,500 per year.
Duration: 1 year; may be renewed if the recipient remains enrolled full-time with a GPA of 2.5 or higher.
Number awarded: 1 or more each year.
Deadline: February of each year.

1476 NORMA ROSS WALTER SCHOLARSHIP PROGRAM

Willa Cather Pioneer Memorial and Educational Foundation
Attn: Scholarship Program
413 North Webster
Red Cloud, NE 68970
Phone: (402) 746-2653; (866) 731-7304; Fax: (402) 746-2652
Web: www.willacather.org/education/scholarships
Summary: To provide financial assistance to female graduates of Nebraska high schools who are or will be majoring in English at an accredited college or university in any state.
Eligibility: Open to women who have graduated or plan to graduate from a Nebraska high school and enter a college or university in any state as a first-year student. Applicants must plan to continue their education as English majors (journalism is not acceptable). Along with their application, they must submit a 1,500-word essay on several of the short stories or a novel written by Willa Cather. Selection is based on intellectual promise, creativity, and character.
Financial data: Stipends are $1,000, $750, or $500.
Duration: 1 year; nonrenewable.
Number awarded: 3 each year: 1 each at $1,000, $750, and $500.
Deadline: January of each year.

1477 NORTHWEST JOURNALISTS OF COLOR SCHOLARSHIP AWARDS

Northwest Journalists of Color
c/o Caroline Li
14601 Ninth Avenue, N.E.
Shoreline, WA 98155
Email: editor@earthwalkersmag.com
Web: www.aajaseattle.org
Summary: To provide financial assistance to minority students from Washington state who are interested in careers in journalism.

Eligibility: Open to members of minority groups (Asian American, African American, Native American, and Latino) who are 1) residents of Washington attending an accredited college or university in any state; 2) residents of any state attending a Washington college or university; or 3) seniors graduating from Washington high schools. Applicants must be planning a career in broadcast, photo, or print journalism. Along with their application, they must submit 1) a brief essay about themselves, including why they want to be a journalist, challenges they foresee, how they think they can contribute to the profession, and the influence their ethnic heritage might have on their perspective as a working journalist; 2) a current resume; 3) up to 3 work samples; 4) reference letters; and 5) documentation of financial need.
Financial data: Stipends range up to $2,500 per year.
Duration: 1 year; may be renewed.
Number awarded: Varies each year.
Deadline: April of each year.

1478 NPPA/BOB BAXTER SCHOLARSHIP

National Press Photographers Foundation
3200 Croasdaile Drive, Suite 306
Durham, NC 27705-2586
Phone: (919) 383-7246; (800) 289-6772; Fax: (919) 383-7261
Email: info@nppa.org
Web: www.nppa.org
Summary: To provide financial assistance to college students who are interested in preparing for a career in photojournalism.
Eligibility: Open to students enrolled full-time at a college or university in the United States. Applicants must be preparing for a career in photojournalism. Along with their application, they must submit a list of the photographic and photojournalist activities they have undertaken in school, a list of photographic activities they have taken outside of school, information on their financial need, and a statement of their philosophy and goals in photojournalism.
Financial data: The stipend is $1,000.
Duration: 1 year; nonrenewable.
Number awarded: 1 each year.
Deadline: February of each year.

1479 NSPA JOURNALISM HONOR ROLL AWARD

National Scholastic Press Association
2221 University Avenue, S.E., Suite 121
Minneapolis, MN 55414
Phone: (612) 625-8335; Fax: (612) 626-0720
Email: info@studentpress.org
Web: www.studentpress.org/nspa/contests.html
Summary: To recognize and reward outstanding high school journalists.
Eligibility: Open to high school seniors who have earned a GPA of 3.75 or higher and have worked in student media for 1 or more years. The publication on which the student works must have a current membership in the National Scholastic Press Association (NSPA). Candidates must be nominated by their teacher. The nominee judged most outstanding receives this award. Selection is based on cumulative GPA, publication experience (including years on staff, positions held, and workshops/conventions attended), college plans, and an essay of 500 words or less that explains "Why I'm choosing a career in journalism."
Financial data: The award is a $1,000 scholarship.
Duration: The competition is held annually.
Number awarded: 1 each year.
Deadline: February of each year.

1480 NSS SCHOLARSHIPS

National Sculpture Society
Attn: Scholarships
237 Park Avenue, Ground Floor
New York, NY 10017
Phone: (212) 764-5645; Fax: (212) 764-5651
Email: nss1893@aol.com
Web: www.nationalsculpture.org/nss/index.cfm/method/main.scholarships
Summary: To provide financial assistance for college to student sculpturers.
Eligibility: Open to students of figurative or representational sculpture. They must submit a letter of application that includes a brief biography and an explanation of their background in sculpture, 2 letters of recommendation, 8 to 10 images of at least 3 of their works (figurative, realist, or representational sculpture is preferred), and proof of financial need.
Financial data: The stipend is $2,000. Funds are paid directly to the academic institution through which the student applies, to be credited towards tuition.
Duration: 1 year.
Number awarded: At least 3 each year.
Deadline: May of each year.

1481 OH, THE PLACES YOU'LL GO COLLEGE SCHOLARSHIP PROGRAM

Random House Children's Books
Attn: College Scholarship Program
1745 Broadway, Mail-Drop 10-3
New York, NY 10019
Phone: (212) 782-9000
Web: origin-www.seussville.com/ohtheplaces
Summary: To recognize and reward, with college scholarships, high school seniors who submit outstanding essays on ideas presented in the book *Oh, the Places You'll Go* by Dr. Seuss.
Eligibility: Open to graduating high school seniors who are 21 years of age or younger. Applicants must submit a 500-word literary composition in the form of a personal essay or memoir. It should be based on the book and relate to the opportunities and challenges the student thinks their education will present in the future. Selection is based on technical merit of the essays, with writing that is original, creative, and clearly connected to the book.
Financial data: The prize is a $5,000 scholarship, paid directly to the postsecondary educational institution that the winner attends.
Duration: The prize is presented annually.
Number awarded: 1 each year.
Deadline: February of each year.

1482 OHIO CLASSICAL CONFERENCE SCHOLARSHIP FOR THE STUDY OF LATIN OR GREEK

Ohio Classical Conference
c/o Kelly Kusch, Scholarship Committee
Covington Latin School
21 East 11th Street
Covington, KY 41011
Phone: (513) 227-6847
Email: Kelly.kusch@covingtonlatin.org
Web: www.xavier.edu/occ/occ-scholarships.cfm
Summary: To provide financial assistance to Ohio high school seniors planning to study Latin or Greek at a college in any state.
Eligibility: Open to seniors graduating from high schools in Ohio and entering a college or university in any state. Applicants must be planning to study Latin or Greek. Their high school teacher must be a member of the Ohio Classical Conference. Along with their application, they must submit an official high school transcript, 2 letters of recommendation (including 1 from their high school Latin teacher), and a 1-page statement on their reasons for studying Latin or the classics.
Financial data: The stipend is $1,500 for the first year, $1,000 for the second year, and $500 for the third year.
Duration: Up to 3 years, provided the recipient maintains a GPA of 3.0 or higher.
Number awarded: 1 each year.
Deadline: March of each year.

1483 OHIO NEWSPAPER WOMEN'S SCHOLARSHIP

Ohio Newspapers Foundation
1335 Dublin Road, Suite 216-B
Columbus, OH 43215-7038
Phone: (614) 486-6677; Fax: (614) 486-4940
Email: ariggs@ohionews.org
Web: www.ohionews.org/students/scholarships
Summary: To provide financial assistance to women majoring in journalism at a college or university in Ohio.
Eligibility: Open to female juniors and seniors at Ohio colleges and universities who are majoring in journalism or an equivalent degree program. Applicants must be preparing for a career as a print journalist. Along with their application,

they must submit a 2-page essay that covers their inspiration to get involved in the field of journalism, why they selected print journalism as their area of interest, why they need a scholarship, what qualifies them for a scholarship, and what they hope to accomplish during their career as a professional journalist.
Financial data: The stipend is $1,500.
Duration: 1 year.
Number awarded: 1 each year.
Deadline: March of each year.

1484 OHIO NEWSPAPERS FOUNDATION MINORITY SCHOLARSHIPS

Ohio Newspapers Foundation
1335 Dublin Road, Suite 216-B
Columbus, OH 43215-7038
Phone: (614) 486-6677; Fax: (614) 486-4940
Email: ariggs@ohionews.org
Web: www.ohionews.org/students/scholarships
Summary: To provide financial assistance to minority high school seniors in Ohio planning to attend college in the state to prepare for a career in journalism.
Eligibility: Open to high school seniors in Ohio who are members of minority groups (African American, Hispanic, Asian American, or American Indian) and planning to prepare for a career in newspaper journalism. Applicants must have a high school GPA of 2.5 or higher and demonstrate writing ability in an autobiography of 750 to 1,000 words that describes their academic and career interests, awards, extracurricular activities, and journalism-related activities. They must be planning to attend a college or university in Ohio.
Financial data: The stipend is $1,500.
Duration: 1 year; nonrenewable.
Number awarded: 1 each year.
Deadline: March of each year.

1485 OHIO NEWSPAPERS FOUNDATION UNIVERSITY JOURNALISM SCHOLARSHIP

Ohio Newspapers Foundation
1335 Dublin Road, Suite 216-B
Columbus, OH 43215-7038
Phone: (614) 486-6677; Fax: (614) 486-4940
Email: ariggs@ohionews.org
Web: www.ohionews.org/students/scholarships
Summary: To provide financial assistance to students majoring in journalism at a college or university in Ohio.
Eligibility: Open to sophomores, juniors, and seniors at Ohio colleges and universities who are majoring in journalism and have a GPA of 2.5 or higher. Applicants must demonstrate the ability to write clearly in an autobiography of 750 to 1,000 words that describes their academic and career interests, awards, extracurricular activities, and journalism-related activities. Priority is given to students planning careers in newspaper or print journalism.
Financial data: The stipend is $1,500.
Duration: 1 year.
Number awarded: 3 each year.
Deadline: March of each year.

1486 OHIO SCHOLARSHIP IN TECHNICAL COMMUNICATION

Society for Technical Communication–Northeast Ohio Chapter
c/o Jeanette Evans, Scholarship Manager
5680 Hawthorne
Highland Heights, OH 44143
Email: jeanette.evans@sbcglobal.net
Web: www.neostc.org/scholarship
Summary: To provide financial assistance to undergraduate and graduate students from Ohio who are working on a degree or certificate in technical communication.
Eligibility: Open to residents of Ohio enrolled at a college, university, community college, or other postsecondary program in any state and to residents of other states enrolled at a school in Ohio. Applicants must be working on a certificate or an associate, bachelor's, master's, or doctoral degree in technical or scientific communication. Along with their application, they must submit a 1- to 3-page letter describing their career goals and significant achievements to date. Membership in the Society for Technical Communication (STC) is not required but is viewed favorable. Selection is based on academic performance, experience with technical communication, and participation in STC. Financial need is not considered.
Financial data: The stipend is $1,000.
Duration: 1 year; nonrenewable.
Number awarded: 1 each year.
Deadline: March of each year.

1487 OKC AD CLUB STUDENT SCHOLARSHIPS

Oklahoma City Advertising Club
Attn: Executive Secretary
P.O. Box 20408
Oklahoma City, OK 73156
Phone: (405) 728-3667
Email: debbieadclub@hotmail.com
Web: www.okcadclub.com/student-scholarships
Summary: To provide financial assistance to upper-division students from any state working on a degree in a field related to advertising at a college in Oklahoma.
Eligibility: Open to residents of any state who have completed at least 60 semester credit hours at a college or university in Oklahoma. Applicants must be enrolled in courses leading to a career in advertising, public relations, broadcast, visual communications, or other media. Along with their application, they must submit 3 graphic examples of their work or a 250-word essay on the effect online advertising will have on the media mix in the current and near future. Financial need is not considered in the selection process.
Financial data: The stipend is $2,000.
Duration: 1 year.
Number awarded: 3 each year.
Deadline: September of each year.

1488 OKLAHOMA ASSOCIATION OF BROADCASTERS SCHOLARSHIP AWARDS

Oklahoma Association of Broadcasters
Attn: OAB Education Foundation
6520 North Western, Suite 104
Oklahoma City, OK 73116
Phone: (405) 848-0771; Fax: (405) 848-0772
Email: info@oabok.org
Web: www.oabok.org/Careers/scholarships.html
Summary: To provide financial assistance to upper-division students majoring in broadcasting at a college in Oklahoma.
Eligibility: Open to residents of any state enrolled full-time at an Oklahoma college or university and majoring in broadcasting. Applicants must be entering their junior or senior year and have a GPA of 3.0 or higher. They must be planning to enter the broadcast industry upon graduation. Along with their application, they must submit a brief statement on why they desire a career in broadcasting and their goals. Selection is based on academic achievement, broadcast industry-related experience, career goals, extracurricular activities, and financial need.
Financial data: The stipend is $2,000.
Duration: 1 year.
Number awarded: 6 each year.
Deadline: March of each year.

1489 OKLAHOMA HERITAGE COUNTY SCHOLARSHIPS

Oklahoma Heritage Association
Attn: Scholarship Committee
1400 Classen Drive
Oklahoma City, OK 73106
Phone: (405) 523-3202; (888) 501-2059; Fax: (405) 235-2714
Email: gmc@oklahomaheritage.com
Web: oklahomaheritage.com
Summary: To recognize and reward, with college scholarships, high school students in Oklahoma who achieve high scores on a test about the state's history and geography.
Eligibility: Open to students in grades 9–12 at high schools in Oklahoma. Applicants take a 2-hour test on the state's history and geography at their choice of 12 sites around the state. Students in each county who achieve high scores on the test are awarded these scholarships for use at a college, university, community college, or vocational/technical school. Some scholarships may be used only at designated postsecondary institutions in Oklahoma; others may be used at any college or university in the country.

Financial data: Most awards are $1,000; a few are smaller. Funds are held in trust until the winner graduates from high school and enrolls at a postsecondary institution; then they are disbursed directly to that school.
Duration: The competition is held annually.
Number awarded: Varies each year; more than $400,000 in scholarships is awarded each year.
Deadline: March of each year.

1490 OKLAHOMA NEWSPAPER FOUNDATION SCHOLARSHIPS

Oklahoma Press Association
Attn: Oklahoma Newspaper Foundation
3601 North Lincoln Boulevard
Oklahoma City, OK 73105
Phone: (405) 499-0020; Fax: (405) 499-0048
Web: www.okpress.com/scholarships
Summary: To provide financial assistance to upper-division journalism students from any state enrolled at Oklahoma colleges and universities.
Eligibility: Open to residents of any state enrolled full-time at a college or university in Oklahoma and entering their junior or senior year. Applicants must be majoring in journalism or an equivalent field (e.g., advertising, communications, public relations); preference is given to students demonstrating a career commitment to newspaper journalism. Along with their application, they must submit a statement on their career goals within the journalism industry, how they plan to achieve those goals, and what they expect to be doing professionally 5 and 10 years after graduation. Financial need is not considered in the selection process.
Financial data: The stipend is $1,500.
Duration: 1 year.
Number awarded: 3 each year.
Deadline: February of each year.

1491 OLMSTED SCHOLARS PROGRAM

Landscape Architecture Foundation
Attn: Scholarship Program
818 18th Street, N.W., Suite 810
Washington, DC 20006-3520
Phone: (202) 331-7070; Fax: (202) 331-7079
Email: scholarships@lafoundation.org
Web: www.lafoundation.org/olmsted/olmsted.aspx
Summary: To provide financial assistance to upper-division and graduate students in landscape architecture who demonstrate outstanding potential for leadership.
Eligibility: Open to landscape architecture students from any country in the final 2 years of undergraduate study or in graduate school in an LAAB-accredited program. Each institution may nominate 1 student. Nominees must submit a 2-page essay describing their personal development and how it has influenced their direction and vision for the future, how they see their role in advancing sustainable planning and design and fostering human and societal health and well-being, and how they would use the funds to advance their leadership in their areas of interest. Selection is based on 1) the nominee's leadership potential in the areas covered in the essay; and 2) demonstration of leadership and vision, engagement with current issues, critical thinking, communication skill, and personal characteristics and values.
Financial data: The stipend is $25,000.
Duration: 1 year.
Number awarded: 1 each year.
Deadline: Nominations must be submitted by March of each year.

1492 OPERATION JUMP START III SCHOLARSHIPS

American Association of Advertising Agencies
Attn: AAAA Foundation
405 Lexington Avenue, 18th Floor
New York, NY 10174-1801
Phone: (212) 682-2500; (800) 676-9333; Fax: (212) 682-2028
Email: ameadows@aaaa.org
Web: www2.aaaa.org/careers/scholarships/Pages/scholar_jump.aspx
Summary: To provide financial assistance to multicultural art directors and copywriters interested in working on an undergraduate or graduate degree in advertising.
Eligibility: Open to African Americans, Asian Americans, Hispanic Americans, and Native Americans who are U.S. citizens or permanent residents. Applicants must be incoming graduate students at 1 of 6 designated portfolio schools or full-time juniors at 1 of 2 designated colleges. They must be able to demonstrate extreme financial need, creative talent, and promise. Along with their application, they must submit 10 samples of creative work in their respective field of expertise.
Financial data: The stipend is $5,000 per year.
Duration: Most awards are for 2 years.
Number awarded: 20 each year.
Deadline: Deadline not specified.

1493 OREGON ASSOCIATION OF BROADCASTERS SCHOLARSHIPS

Oregon Association of Broadcasters
Attn: OAB Foundation Scholarship Committee
7150 S.W. Hampton Street, Suite 240
Portland, OR 97223-8366
Phone: (503) 443-2299; Fax: (503) 443-2488
Email: theoab@theoab.org
Web: www.theoab.org/Foundation/Scholarships/tabid/424/Default.aspx
Summary: To provide financial assistance to residents of Oregon who are interested in majoring in broadcast-related fields at a college in the state.
Eligibility: Open to Oregon residents who are high school seniors, students in the first or second year at a 2-year college, or sophomores, juniors, or seniors at a 4-year college or university. Applicants must be enrolled or planning to enroll full-time at a college or university in Oregon and major in broadcast journalism, production, management, or other broadcast-related field. They must have a GPA of 3.25 or higher. Along with their application, they must submit an essay that explains their reasons for choosing a broadcast major and includes any broadcast activities in which they have participated, their first job preference after college, their 10-year goals, any other scholarships they have received, any academic honors they have received, and why they need this scholarship in order to continue their education.
Financial data: Stipends vary; recently, they were $3,500 or $2,500.
Duration: 1 year.
Number awarded: Varies each year; recently, 4 of these scholarships were awarded: 2 at $3,500 and 2 at $2,500.
Deadline: May of each year.

1494 OREGON BARBER AND HAIRDRESSER GRANT PROGRAM

Oregon Student Assistance Commission
Attn: Grants and Scholarships Division
1500 Valley River Drive, Suite 100
P.O. Box 40370
Eugene, OR 97404
Phone: (541) 687-7395; (800) 452-8807, ext. 7395; Fax: (541) 687-7414; TDD: (800) 735-2900
Email: awardinfo@osac.state.or.us
Web: www.getcollegefunds.org/barber_hairdresser.html
Summary: To provide financial assistance to Oregon residents who wish to prepare for a career as a barber or hairdresser.
Eligibility: Open to residents of Oregon who are attending or planning to attend a licensed school of barbering, hair design, cosmetology, or manicure in Oregon. Applicants must enroll full-time in a program that is at least 9 months long or 900 clock hours and must be able to demonstrate significant financial need. Students are not eligible if they are currently in prison, are concurrently enrolled in a high school beauty or barbering program, or are in default on any prior educational loan.
Financial data: The stipend is $1,000.
Duration: This is a 1-time award.
Number awarded: Approximately 30 to 40 each year.
Deadline: January of each year.

1495 OREGON MUSIC HALL OF FAME SCHOLARSHIPS

Oregon Music Hall of Fame
3158 East Burnside
Portland, OR 97214
Web: www.omhof.org/scholarships
Summary: To provide financial assistance to high school seniors in Oregon who plan to study music at a college in any state.

Eligibility: Open to seniors graduating from high schools in Oregon. Applicants must be planning to attend a college, university, or other institute in any state to study music.
Financial data: The stipend is $1,000.
Duration: 1 year.
Number awarded: 4 each year.
Deadline: March.

1496 OUTPUTLINKS WOMAN OF DISTINCTION AWARD

Electronic Document Systems Foundation
Attn: EDSF Scholarship Awards
1845 Precinct Line Road, Suite 212
Hurst, TX 76054
Phone: (817) 849-1145; Fax: (817) 849-1185
Email: info@edsf.org
Web: www.edsf.org/scholarships.cfm

Summary: To provide financial assistance to female upper-division and graduate students interested in preparing for a career in document management and graphic communications.
Eligibility: Open to female juniors, seniors, and graduate students who are committed to preparing for a career in document management and graphic communications, including marketing, graphic communications and arts, e-commerce, imaging science, printing, web authoring, electronic publishing, computer science, telecommunications, and/or business (e.g., sales, marketing). Applicants must be enrolled full-time at a college, university, or graduate school in the United States and have a GPA of 3.0 or higher. Along with their application, they must submit a statement of their career goals in the field of document management and graphic communications, an essay on a topic related to their view of the future of the document management and graphic communications industry, a list of current professional and college extracurricular activities and achievements, college transcripts, samples of their creative work, and 2 letters of recommendation. Financial need is not considered.
Financial data: The stipend is $5,000.
Duration: 1 year.
Number awarded: 1 each year.
Deadline: April of each year.

1497 OVERSEAS PRESS CLUB FOUNDATION SCHOLARSHIPS

Overseas Press Club
Attn: Director, Overseas Press Club Foundation
40 West 45th Street
New York, NY 10036
Phone: (212) 626-9220; Fax: (212) 626-9210
Email: foundation@opcofamerica.org
Web: www.opcofamerica.org

Summary: To provide financial assistance to undergraduate and graduate students who are preparing for a career as a foreign correspondent.
Eligibility: Open to undergraduate and graduate students who are studying in the United States and are interested in working as a foreign correspondent after graduation. Applicants are invited to submit an essay (up to 500 words) on an area of the world or an international topic that is in keeping with their interest. Also, they should attach a 1-page autobiographical letter that addresses such questions as how they developed their interest in that particular part of the world or issue and how they would use a scholarship to further their journalistic ambitions. U.S. citizenship is not required.
Financial data: The stipend is $2,000.
Duration: 1 year.
Number awarded: 12 each year.
Deadline: November of each year.

1498 P. BUCKLEY MOSS ENDOWED SCHOLARSHIP

P. Buckley Moss Society
20 Stoneridge Drive, Suite 102
Waynesboro, VA 22980
Phone: (540) 943-5678; Fax: (540) 949-8408
Email: society@mosssociety.org
Web: www.mosssociety.org/page.php?id=69

Summary: To provide financial assistance to high school seniors with language-related learning disabilities who plan to study visual arts in college.
Eligibility: Open to high school seniors with language-related learning disabilities and visual arts talent. They must be nominated; nominations must be submitted by a member of the P. Buckley Moss Society. Nominees must be planning to attend a 4-year college or university or a 2-year community college and prepare for a career in a visual art field. The nomination packets must include evidence of financial need, verification of a language-related learning disability from a counselor or case manager, a high school transcript, 2 letters of recommendation, and 3 essays by the nominees: 1) themselves; 2) their learning disability, how it has challenged them, specific strategies they have used to cope, and its effect on their lives; and 3) where they intend to go to school and why, how they plan to use their artistic talent, and what they see themselves doing with their art in 10 years.
Financial data: The stipend is $1,500. Funds are paid to the recipient's college or university.
Duration: 1 year; may be renewed for up to 3 additional years.
Number awarded: 1 each year.
Deadline: February of each year.

1499 PAGEL GRAPHIC ARTS SCHOLARSHIPS

Printing Industries of Wisconsin
Attn: PIW Educational Foundation
715 Main Street, Q Building
Pewaukee, WI 53072
Phone: (262) 695-6250; Fax: (262) 695-6254
Web: www.piw.org

Summary: To provide financial assistance to students working on a degree in print communications at a school in Wisconsin.
Eligibility: Open to students enrolled at colleges, universities, and technical schools in Wisconsin. Applicants must be preparing for a career in the print communications industry. Selection is based on academic performance, outside activities, and financial need.
Financial data: Stipends range from $500 to $1,000.
Duration: 1 year.
Number awarded: Varies each year; recently, 10 of these scholarships were awarded.
Deadline: March of each year.

1500 PAUL AND HELEN L. GRAUER SCHOLARSHIP

American Radio Relay League
Attn: ARRL Foundation
225 Main Street
Newington, CT 06111
Phone: (860) 594-0397; Fax: (860) 594-0259
Email: foundation@arrl.org
Web: www.arrlf.org/programs/scholarships

Summary: To provide financial assistance to licensed radio amateurs, especially those from designated midwestern states, who are interested in working on an undergraduate or graduate degree, preferably in electronics or communications.
Eligibility: Open to undergraduate or graduate students at accredited institutions who are licensed radio amateurs of the novice class or higher. Preference is given to students who are 1) residents of Iowa, Kansas, Missouri, or Nebraska and attending schools in those states; and 2) working on a degree in electronics, communications, or related fields. Applicants must submit an essay on the role amateur radio has played in their lives and provide documentation of financial need.
Financial data: The stipend is $1,000.
Duration: 1 year.
Number awarded: 1 each year.
Deadline: January of each year.

1501 PAUL K. TAFF SCHOLARSHIP AWARD

Connecticut Broadcasters Association
Attn: Scholarships
90 South Park Street
Willimantic, CT 06226
Phone: (860) 633-5031; Fax: (860) 456-5688
Email: mcrice@prodigy.net
Web: www.ctba.org/page.cfm?page=17

Summary: To provide financial assistance to Connecticut residents who are interested in attending college in any state to prepare for a career in broadcasting.
Eligibility: Open to Connecticut residents who are entering their first, second, third, or fourth year at a 2- or 4-year college, university, or technical school in any state. Applicants must be majoring in broadcasting, communications, mar-

keting, or a related field. Selection is based on academic achievement, community service, goals in the chosen field, and financial need.
Financial data: The stipend is $2,500.
Duration: 4 years.
Number awarded: 1 each year.
Deadline: March of each year.

1502 PAYNE COLLEGIATE AWARD FOR ETHICS IN JOURNALISM

University of Oregon
Attn: School of Journalism and Communication
1275 University of Oregon
Eugene, OR 97403-1275
Phone: (541) 346-2519; (888) 644-7989; Fax: (541) 346-0682
Email: payneawards@jcomm.uoregon.edu
Web: payneawards.uoregon.edu/index.html
Summary: To recognize and reward student journalists whose work has encouraged public trust in the media.
Eligibility: Open to student journalists enrolled in a 2- or 4-year college where the nominated work is published. Nominations are accepted from journalists, news organizations, and the public. Entries must have been published in a regularly distributed medium (a student or professional newspaper, magazine, broadcast, or cablecast news program or an edited Internet publication) during the previous calendar year. The award honors a student journalist "who reports with insight and clarity in the face of political or economic pressures."
Financial data: The award is $1,000.
Duration: The award is presented annually.
Number awarded: 1 each year.
Deadline: February of each year.

1503 PEERMUSIC LATIN SCHOLARSHIP

Broadcast Music Inc.
Attn: BMI Foundation, Inc.
7 World Trade Center
250 Greenwich Street
New York, NY 10007-0030
Phone: (212) 220-3000
Email: latinscholarship@bmifoundation.org
Web: www.bmifoundation.org/program/peermusic_latin_scholarship
Summary: To recognize and reward students at colleges and universities who submit outstanding songs or instrumental works in a Latin genre.
Eligibility: Open to students between 16 and 24 years of age enrolled at colleges and universities in the United States and Puerto Rico. Applicants may not have had any musical work commercially recorded or distributed. They must submit an original song or instrumental work in a Latin genre. The entry must be submitted on CD, accompanied by 3 typed copies of the lyric.
Financial data: The award is $5,000.
Duration: The award is presented annually.
Number awarded: 1 each year.
Deadline: February of each year.

1504 PENNSYLVANIA PUBLIC RELATIONS SOCIETY SCHOLARSHIPS

Pennsylvania Public Relations Society
c/o Leslie Suhr, Student Development Committee Chair
PA Partnerships for Children
116 Pine Street, Suite 430
Harrisburg, PA 17101
Phone: (717) 512-9615
Email: lsurh@papartnerships.org
Web: www.pprs-hbg.org
Summary: To provide financial assistance to upper-division students from Pennsylvania who are majoring in a communications-related field at a college or university in the state.
Eligibility: Open to full-time students entering their junior or senior year at a college or university in Pennsylvania who have a GPA of 2.75 or higher. Applicants must be residents of Pennsylvania majoring in a communications-related field of study (e.g., public relations, mass communications, journalism). Along with their application, they must submit a 300-word essay on why they are interested in a career in the communications field and their career goals and aspirations. Selection is based on that essay, grades, and participation in extracurricular activities related to the communications field. Financial need is not considered.
Financial data: The stipend is $1,000.
Duration: 1 year; recipients may reapply.
Number awarded: 1 each year.
Deadline: April of each year.

1505 PENNSYLVANIA WOMEN'S PRESS ASSOCIATION SCHOLARSHIP

Pennsylvania Women's Press Association
c/o Teresa Spatara
P.O. Box 152
Sharpsville, PA 16150
Phone: (724) 962-0990
Web: www.pwpa.us/pwpa_scholarship.htm
Summary: To provide financial assistance to residents of Pennsylvania working on an undergraduate or graduate degree in journalism at a school in the state.
Eligibility: Open to residents of Pennsylvania enrolled as juniors, seniors, or graduate students at a college or university in the state. Applicants must be working on a degree in print journalism. Both men and women are eligible. Along with their application, they must submit a 500-word essay summarizing their interest in journalism, career plans, and why they should receive this scholarship; they may also include information on their financial need. Selection is based on that information, proven journalistic merit, dedication to a newspaper career, and general merit.
Financial data: The stipend is $1,500.
Duration: 1 year.
Number awarded: 1 each year.
Deadline: April of each year.

1506 PERCUSSIVE ARTS SOCIETY DRUMSET COMPETITION

Percussive Arts Society
110 West Washington Street, Suite A
Indianapolis, IN 46204
Phone: (317) 974-4488; Fax: (317) 974-4499
Email: percarts@pas.org
Web: www.pas.org/experience/contests/drumsetcompetition.aspx
Summary: To recognize and reward outstanding young drumset instrumentalists.
Eligibility: Open to musical drumset artists in 2 age categories (14 to 17 years of age and 18 to 22 years of age) and 3 style categories (R&B/Funk/Gospel, jazz, and Brazilian/Afro-Cuban/African). Applicants must submit a live performance DVD, up to 6 minutes in length, that includes them and up to 8 other performers. For the jazz category, soloing must be trading 4's or 8's with band members (maximum 2 choruses); for the other style categories, the applicant must solo over an ensemble vamp (maximum of 64 measures). Based on the DVDs, 12 finalists are selected (2 from each age category in each style category) to compete at the Percussive Arts Society International Convention (PASIC), where winners are selected.
Financial data: Prizes are $1,000.
Duration: The competition is held annually.
Number awarded: 6 each year: 1 in each age category in each style category.
Deadline: May of each year.

1507 PERSIAN SCHOLARSHIP FOUNDATION UNDERGRADUATE RECOGNITION AWARD

Persian Scholarship Foundation
1434 Westwood Boulevard, Suite 5
Los Angeles, CA 90024
Email: info@persianscholarship.org
Web: www.persianscholarship.org/current_programs.htm
Summary: To recognize and reward, with scholarships for additional study, undergraduates who submit outstanding essays on contributions of Iran and Iranians to society and history.
Eligibility: Open to undergraduate students who are part of the Iranian-American community. Applicants must submit an essay or article that appeared in their school newspaper or a local or national newspaper in which they discuss themes relating to the history, culture, and/or heritage of the Iranian people or the achievements of scholars, scientists, and leaders of Iranian descent. The essay should aim to emphasize the positive achievements of Iran and Iranians and their contributions to society of enlightening aspects of history related to the Iranian-American community. Publications in Iranian-American journals

and newspapers do not qualify. In addition to the essay, applicants must also submit a cover letter about themselves, a copy of their student ID, and a copy of their official transcript indicating their GPA.
Financial data: The award is $1,000.
Duration: The award is presented annually.
Number awarded: 1 each year.
Deadline: December of each year.

1508 PETER AGRIS MEMORIAL SCHOLARSHIP

Alpha Omega Council
c/o Nancy Agris Savage
9 Nonesuch Drive
Natick, MA 01760
Fax: (508) 655-1402
Email: info@alphaomegacouncil.com
Web: www.alphaomegacouncil.com/scholarship.htm
Summary: To provide financial assistance to Greek American undergraduate and graduate students majoring in journalism or communications.
Eligibility: Open to undergraduate and graduate students of Greek American descent. Applicants must be enrolled full-time as a journalism or communications major at an accredited college or university in the United States. They must be able to demonstrate financial need, a GPA of 3.0 or higher, and active participation in school, community, and church organizations. Along with their application, they must submit an essay on the values from their Greek heritage they hope to carry with them into their career as a journalist.
Financial data: The stipend is $5,000.
Duration: 1 year; nonrenewable.
Number awarded: 6 each year.
Deadline: February of each year.

1509 PHOENIX POST SAME SCHOLARSHIPS

Society of American Military Engineers–Phoenix Post
c/o Michelle Obregon
The Durrant Group
410 North 44th Street, Suite 800
Phoenix, AZ 85008
Phone: (602) 275-6830; Fax: (602) 275-4331
Email: mobregon@durrant.com
Web: www.samephxaz.org/about-same/education-and-mentoring
Summary: To provide financial assistance to residents of Arizona who are interested in working on an undergraduate degree in a field related to the built environment at a college in the state.
Eligibility: Open to residents of Arizona who are either graduating high school seniors or college freshmen or sophomores enrolled or planning to enroll at an institution of higher learning in the state. Applicants must be working on or planning to work on a degree in engineering or a similar field related to the built environment (e.g., construction, architecture, civil engineering, electrical/mechanical/structural engineering for facilities). They must have a GPA of 3.0 or higher. Along with their application, they must submit brief essays on what distinguishes them from other candidates and why they are preparing for a career in engineering, architecture, or related sciences. Selection is based on those essays, academic achievement, leadership ability, and community service. U.S. citizenship is required.
Financial data: Stipends range from $1,500 to $5,000.
Duration: 1 year.
Number awarded: Varies each year; recently, 5 of these scholarships were awarded: 1 at $5,000, 1 at $4,000, and 3 at $1,500.
Deadline: May of each year.

1510 PIANO ARTS NORTH AMERICAN BIENNIAL COMPETITION

Piano Arts of Wisconsin
Attn: Sue Medford
2642 North Summit Avenue
Milwaukee, WI 53211-3849
Phone: (414) 962-3055; Fax: (414) 962-3211
Email: info@pianoarts.org
Web: www.pianoarts.org
Summary: To recognize and reward outstanding pianists between 15 and 20 years of age.
Eligibility: Open to pianists between the age of 15 and 20. In the preliminary round, contestants perform on DVD a solo of their choice and the first movement of a selected concerto. The 10 semifinalists are asked to come to Milwaukee where they perform solo recitals. Based on those recitals, 3 finalists are chosen to perform in the prize round. Those finalists perform concertos by Beethoven, Mendelssohn, Schumann, Chopin, or Mozart with the Milwaukee Chamber Orchestra to compete for prizes. Separate competitions for duos of piano and violin and for piano and cello are also conducted.
Financial data: Awards are $10,000 for first, $5,000 for second, and $3,000 for third. Winners have an opportunity to win a scholarship to attend the International Keyboard Institute and Festival. Other awards include $750 for the best contestant from Wisconsin, $500 for the best performance of a duo, and $500 for the audience communication prize.
Duration: The competition is held biennially, in even-numbered years.
Number awarded: 3 major prizes and at least 3 smaller prizes are awarded each year.
Deadline: Initial applications must be submitted by January of even-numbered years. Preliminary DVDs are due the following February. The semifinal round and finals take place in June.

1511 PLATT FAMILY SCHOLARSHIP PRIZE ESSAY CONTEST

Lincoln Forum
c/o Don McCue, Curator
Lincoln Memorial Shrine
125 West Vine Street
Redlands, CA 92373
Phone: (909) 798-7632
Email: archives@akspl.org
Web: www.thelincolnforum.org/scholarship-essay-contest.php
Summary: To recognize and reward college students who submit outstanding essays on topics related to Abraham Lincoln.
Eligibility: Open to all students, regardless of age or citizenship status, enrolled as a full-time undergraduate student at a U.S. college or university. Applicants must submit an essay, from 1,500 to 5,000 words, on a topic that changes annually but relates to Abraham Lincoln. Recently, the topic was "Lincoln and the Coming of the Civil War."
Financial data: Prizes are $1,000 for first, $500 for second, and $250 for third.
Duration: The competition is held annually.
Number awarded: 3 prizes are awarded each year.
Deadline: July of each year.

1512 PLAYBOY COLLEGE FICTION CONTEST

Playboy Magazine
Attn: Fiction Contest
730 Fifth Avenue
New York, NY 10019
Web: www.playboy.com/magazine/fiction.html
Summary: To recognize and reward outstanding fiction written by undergraduate or graduate students.
Eligibility: Open to undergraduate and graduate students. They are invited to submit a work of fiction no more than 25 pages in length.
Financial data: First prize is $3,000 and publication in *Playboy* magazine; second prize is $500 and a 1-year subscription to *Playboy;* third prize is $200 and a 1-year subscription to *Playboy.*
Duration: The competition is held annually.
Number awarded: 3 prizes are awarded each year.
Deadline: February of each year.

1513 POLISH ARTS CLUB OF BUFFALO SCHOLARSHIP

Polish Arts Club of Buffalo Inc.
Attn: Anne Flansburg, Scholarship Chair
20 South Woodside Lane
Williamsville, NY 14231-5949
Phone: (716) 626-9083
Email: anneflanswz@aol.com
Web: pacb.bfn.org/about/scholarship.html
Summary: To provide financial assistance to New York residents of Polish background who are majoring in the visual or performing arts at a college in any state.

Eligibility: Open to residents of New York who are of Polish background and enrolled as juniors, seniors, or graduate students at a college or university in any state. Applicants must be working on a degree in visual or performing arts. They must submit a 300-word essay on a Polish artist, composer, or musician who has contributed to their field of study. Letters of recommendation are also required. Finalists are interviewed. Financial need is not considered in the selection process.
Financial data: The stipend is $1,000.
Duration: 1 year.
Number awarded: 1 or 2 each year.
Deadline: May of each year.

1514 POWELL-DUFFELL SCHOLARSHIPS

Arkansas Baptist Foundation
10117 Kanis Road
Little Rock, AR 72205-6220
Phone: (501) 376-0732; (800) 798-0969; Fax: (501) 376-3831
Email: info@abf.org
Web: www.abf.org/individuals_scholarships.htm
Summary: To provide financial assistance to members of Southern Baptist churches in Arkansas who are attending colleges or universities in the state to prepare for vocational Christian ministry.
Eligibility: Open to members of churches affiliated with the Arkansas Baptist State Convention. Applicants must be entering their sophomore or junior year at an accredited Arkansas college or university. They must be preparing for vocational Christian ministry.
Financial data: The stipend is $1,500 per year. Funds are paid to the recipient's institution.
Duration: 1 year; sophomores may reapply.
Number awarded: Varies each year.
Deadline: February of each year.

1515 PRESS CLUB OF NEW ORLEANS JOURNALISM SCHOLARSHIP PROGRAM

Press Club of New Orleans
Attn: Scholarship Committee
846 Howard Avenue
New Orleans, LA 70113
Phone: (504) 679-0672
Email: pressclubneworleans@gmail.com
Web: www.pressclubneworleans.org
Summary: To provide financial assistance to residents of Louisiana who are majoring in journalism at a school in any state.
Eligibility: Open to Louisiana residents who are working on a degree in print or broadcast journalism at a college or university in any state. Applicants must submit 1) a brief written statement outlining their course of study, career goals, and financial need; 2) examples of their published or broadcast work, including newspaper stories, tapes, columns, and/or editorials; and 3) transcripts.
Financial data: A stipend is awarded (amount not specified).
Duration: 1 year.
Number awarded: 1 or more each year; a total of $5,000 is available for this program annually.
Deadline: June of each year.

1516 PRINCE KUHI'O HAWAIIAN CIVIC CLUB SCHOLARSHIP

Prince Kuhi'o Hawaiian Civic Club
Attn: Scholarship Chair
P.O. Box 4728
Honolulu, HI 96812
Email: pkhcc64@gmail.com
Web: www.pkhcc.com/scholarship.html
Summary: To provide financial assistance for undergraduate or graduate studies (particularly in education, journalism, or Hawaiian studies) to persons of Hawaiian descent.
Eligibility: Open to high school seniors and full-time undergraduate or graduate students who are of Hawaiian descent (descendants of the aboriginal inhabitants of the Hawaiian Islands prior to 1778). Graduating high school seniors and current undergraduate students must have a GPA of 2.5 or higher; graduate students must have at least a 3.3 GPA. Along with their application, they must submit an essay on how they will apply their education toward the well-being of the Hawaiian community. Special consideration is given to applicants majoring not only in Hawaiian studies or Hawaiian language, but also in educaton or journalism. Selection is based on academic achievement and leadership potential.
Financial data: Stipends range from $500 to $1,000 per year.
Duration: 1 year; may be renewed.
Number awarded: Varies each year.
Deadline: March of each year.

1517 PRINT AND GRAPHICS SCHOLARSHIP FOUNDATION SCHOLARSHIPS

Print and Graphics Scholarship Foundation
Attn: Scholarship Competition
200 Deer Run Road
Sewickley, PA 15143-2600
Phone: (412) 259-1740; (800) 910-GATF; Fax: (412) 741-2311
Email: pgsf@gatf.org
Web: www.gain.net
Summary: To provide financial assistance to college students interested in preparing for a career in the graphic communications industries.
Eligibility: Open to high school seniors, high school graduates who have not yet started college, and currently-enrolled college students. Applicants must be interested in a career in the graphic communications industry and be willing to attend school on a full-time basis (scholarships are not awarded for part-time study). High school students must take the SAT or ACT and arrange for their test scores to be sent to the Graphic Arts Technical Foundation. Current college students are requested to submit transcripts and a letter of recommendation from their major area adviser. College freshmen also need to submit a high school transcript. Semifinalists are interviewed. Selection is based on academic records and honors, extracurricular activities, and letters of recommendation.
Financial data: Stipends range from $1,000 to $5,000 per year. Funds are paid directly to the college selected by the award winner; the college will be authorized to draw upon the award to pay for tuition and other fees.
Duration: 1 year; may be renewed for up to 3 additional years if the recipient maintains a GPA of 3.0 or higher and full-time enrollment.
Number awarded: Approximately 300 per year.
Deadline: February of each year for high school seniors; March of each year for students already in college.

1518 PRINTING INDUSTRY OF MINNESOTA SCHOLARSHIPS

Printing Industry of Minnesota
Attn: Director of Education
1700 Highway 36 West, Suite 510
Roseville, MN 55113
Phone: (651) 789-5508; (800) 448-7566; Fax: (651) 789-5520
Email: kristinp@pimn.org
Web: www.pimn.org/scholar/scholarships.htm
Summary: To provide financial assistance to high school seniors and graduates in Minnesota who are interested in attending college to prepare for a career in the print communications industry.
Eligibility: Open to residents of Minnesota and children of individuals employed by Minnesota graphic arts firms. Applicants must be high school seniors or graduates (including GED recipients) who have a high school GPA of 3.0 or higher and scores of 970 or higher on the combined mathematics and critical reading SAT or 23 or higher on the ACT. They must have been admitted to a technical school, college, or university to work on a full-time degree or certificate in graphic arts. Along with their application, they must submit a career plan letter describing their personal aspirations and what they plan to do with their degree. Preference is given to children of employees of companies that are members of the Printing Industry of Minnesota. Financial need is also considered in the selection process.
Financial data: The stipend is at least $1,000 per year.
Duration: 1 year; may be renewed.
Number awarded: Varies each year; recently, 18 of these scholarships were awarded.
Deadline: March of each year.

1519 PROJECT 21 NEVADA SCHOLARSHIP PROGRAM

Nevada Council on Problem Gambling
Attn: Scholarship Program
4340 South Valley View Boulevard, Suite 220
Las Vegas, NV 89103
Phone: (702) 369-9740; Fax: (702) 369-9765
Email: contactus@nevadacouncil.org

Web: www.nevadacouncil.org/project_21.php

Summary: To recognize and reward high school and college students in Nevada who create original posters, essays, or public service announcements alerting their peers to the risks and consequences of underage gambling.

Eligibility: Open to Nevada students under 21 years of age who are enrolled in a high school, vocational or trade school, college, or university. Applicants must create an original work that educates their peers and discourages participation in gambling activities by persons under 21 years of age. They must disseminate their message to their peers prior to submitting it for the competition. Entries may be submitted in the following categories: 1) essays between 350 and 500 words and printed in the school newspaper or other authorized publication during the first 3 months of the year; 2) posters on standard-sized poster board (22"×28") and displayed in a public area of the student's school or other authorized public area for at least 1 week during the first 3 months of the year; 3) video public service announcement 30–seconds long in VHS format and viewed by at least 50 students in a public showing at the applicant's school or other authorized public forum during the first 3 months of the year; or 4) audio public service announcement 30–seconds long on audio cassette and heard by at least 50 students at an open announcement at the applicant's school or other authorized public forum during the first 3 months of the year. Selection is based on originality, content, style, and educational value. The applicant's economic status and academic GPA are not considered.

Financial data: The awards consist of $1,000 college scholarships.

Duration: The competition is held annually.

Number awarded: Varies each year; recently, 11 students received these awards.

Deadline: March of each year.

1520 PUBLIC RELATIONS SOCIETY OF AMERICA MULTICULTURAL AFFAIRS SCHOLARSHIPS

Public Relations Student Society of America
Attn: Vice President of Member Services
33 Maiden Lane, 11th Floor
New York, NY 10038-5150
Phone: (212) 460-1474; Fax: (212) 995-0757
Email: prssa@prsa.org
Web: www.prssa.org/awards/awardMulticultural.aspx

Summary: To provide financial assistance to minority college students who are interested in preparing for a career in public relations.

Eligibility: Open to minority (African American/Black, Hispanic/Latino, Asian, Native American, Alaskan Native, or Pacific Islander) students who are at least juniors at an accredited 4-year college or university. Applicants must be enrolled full-time, be able to demonstrate financial need, and have earned a GPA of 3.0 or higher. Membership in the Public Relations Student Society of America is preferred but not required. A major or minor in public relations is preferred; students who attend a school that does not offer a public relations degree or program must be enrolled in a communications degree program (e.g., journalism, mass communications).

Financial data: The stipend is $1,500.

Duration: 1 year.

Number awarded: 2 each year.

Deadline: April of each year.

1521 QUARTON-MCELROY/IOWA BROADCASTERS ASSOCIATION BROADCAST SCHOLARSHIPS

Iowa Broadcasters Association
P.O. Box 71186
Des Moines, IA 50325
Phone: (515) 224-7237; Fax: (515) 224-6560
Email: iowaiba@dwx.com
Web: www.iowabroadcasters.com/qmsch03.htm

Summary: To provide financial assistance to residents of Iowa who are interested in preparing for a career in broadcasting at a college in the state.

Eligibility: Open to residents of Iowa who are graduating or have graduated from a high school in the state. Applicants must be enrolled or planning to enroll full-time at a 2- or 4-year college or university in the state. They must be planning to prepare for a career in the broadcasting field, including electronic media, telecommunicative arts, broadcast production, or broadcast journalism. Along with their application, they must submit a 1- to 3-page letter on "Why I'm Interested in a Career in Broadcasting," including an analysis of their skills, interests, and work-related experiences that would contribute to a career in broadcasting; their thoughts about the need for a college education to help them reach their career goals; and the importance of receiving this scholarship. Selection is based on the essay, academic record (as indicated by their high school transcripts and ACT or SAT scores), honors and/or awards, extracurricular activities, work experience and/or internships, and financial need.

Financial data: The stipend is $3,000 per year.

Duration: 4 years.

Number awarded: 5 each year.

Deadline: March of each year.

1522 R. FRANK MUNDY SCHOLARSHIP

South Carolina Press Association
Attn: SCPA Foundation
106 Outlet Pointe Boulevard
P.O. Box 11429
Columbia, SC 29211
Phone: (803) 750-9561; (888) SC-PRESS; Fax: (803) 551-0903
Email: brogers@scpress.org
Web: www.scpress.org/scholar_intern.html

Summary: To provide financial assistance to upper-division students from any state majoring in journalism at a school in South Carolina.

Eligibility: Open to students from any state who are interested in newspaper careers and entering their junior year as full-time students at a South Carolina 4-year college or university. Applicants must submit brief statements on what they would like to do in the newspaper industry, the work they have done on student publications, the work they have done for newspapers, any scholarships or awards they have received, and their financial need. Selection is based on commitment to a newspaper career, participation in newspaper activities in college, recommendations of faculty members, grades, and financial need.

Financial data: The stipend is $3,500.

Duration: 1 year.

Number awarded: Up to 3 each year.

Deadline: March of each year.

1523 RADIO TELEVISION DIGITAL NEWS FOUNDATION PRESIDENTS' SCHOLARSHIPS

Radio Television Digital News Foundation
Attn: RTDNF Fellowship Program
4121 Plank Road, Suite 512
Fredericksburg, VA 22407
Phone: (202) 467-5214; Fax: (202) 223-4007
Email: staceys@rtdna.org
Web: www.rtdna.org/pages/education/undergraduates.php

Summary: To provide financial assistance to undergraduate students who are preparing for a career in electronic journalism.

Eligibility: Open to sophomores, juniors, and seniors who are enrolled full-time in electronic journalism at a college or university where such a major is offered. Applicants must submit 1 to 3 examples of their journalistic skills on audio CD or DVD (no more than 15 minutes total, accompanied by scripts); a description of their role on each story and a list of who worked on each story and what they did; a 1-page statement explaining why they are preparing for a career in electronic journalism with reference to their specific career preference (radio, television, online, reporting, producing, or newsroom management); a resume; and a letter of reference from their dean or faculty sponsor explaining why they are a good candidate for the award and certifying that they have at least 1 year of school remaining.

Financial data: The stipend is $2,500.

Duration: 1 year.

Number awarded: 2 each year.

Deadline: May of each year.

1524 RADIO-TELEVISION JOURNALISM DIVISION PRIZES

Association for Education in Journalism and Mass Communication
Attn: Radio-Television Journalism Division
234 Outlet Pointe Boulevard, Suite A
Columbia, SC 29210-5667
Phone: (803) 798-0271; Fax: (803) 772-3509
Email: aejmc@aejmc.org
Web: www.aejmc.org

Summary: To recognize and reward outstanding student and faculty papers on broadcast journalism.

Eligibility: Open to students and faculty members. They are invited to submit papers on an aspect of broadcast journalism or electronic communication with a journalism emphasis. A variety of methodological approaches are welcome. Papers are to be no more than 25 pages in length and must have been written during the past year.

Financial data: Cash prizes are awarded.

Duration: The competition is held annually.
Number awarded: 2 each year: 1 to a student and 1 to a faculty member.
Deadline: March of each year.

1525 RAIN BIRD INTELLIGENT USE OF WATER SCHOLARSHIP

Landscape Architecture Foundation
Attn: Scholarship Program
818 18th Street, N.W., Suite 810
Washington, DC 20006-3520
Phone: (202) 331-7070; Fax: (202) 331-7079
Email: scholarships@lafoundation.org
Web: www.laprofession.org
Summary: To provide financial assistance to landscape architecture students who are in need of financial assistance.
Eligibility: Open to landscape architecture, horticulture, and irrigation science students in the final 2 years of undergraduate study and in need of financial assistance. Applicants must submit a 300-word essay describing their career goals and explaining how they will contribute to the advancement of the profession of landscape architecture, horticulture, or irrigation science. Selection is based on demonstrated commitment to the profession, extracurricular activities, and scholastic record.
Financial data: The stipend is $2,500.
Number awarded: 1 each year.
Deadline: February of each year.

1526 RALPH FLAMMINIO MEMORIAL SCHOLARSHIP

Pennsylvania Associated Press Managing Editors
Attn: Scholarship Committee
3899 North Front Street
Harrisburg, PA 17110
Phone: (717) 703-3086; Fax: (717) 703-3001
Email: lholeva@citizensvoice.com
Web: www.papme.com/FlamminioScholarship.aspx
Summary: To provide financial assistance to residents of Pennsylvania who are attending college in any state to prepare for a career in newspaper journalism.
Eligibility: Open to Pennsylvania residents who are currently enrolled at a 4-year college or university in any state. Applicants must be preparing for a career in newspaper journalism and should be active on their campus newspaper or have print journalism experience, although they are not required to be a journalism major. Along with their application, they must submit a cover letter describing their experience in newspaper journalism, their interest in the field, and what they might contribute to the craft of journalism. Financial need is not considered in the selection process.
Financial data: The stipend is $3,000.
Duration: 1 year.
Number awarded: 1 each year.
Deadline: April of each year.

1527 RALPH V. "ANDY" ANDERSON-K0NL SCHOLARSHIP

Foundation for Amateur Radio, Inc.
Attn: Scholarship Committee
P.O. Box 911
Columbia, MD 21044-0911
Phone: (410) 552-2652; Fax: (410) 981-5146
Email: dave.prestel@gmail.com
Web: www.farweb.org/scholarships
Summary: To provide funding to licensed radio amateurs who are interested in earning a bachelor's degree, particularly in the field of journalism.
Eligibility: Open to residents of the United States and its territories who have an amateur radio license of at least general class. Applicants must be working full-time on a bachelor's degree. There is no restriction on the course of study, but preference is given to students majoring in journalism. Financial need is considered in the selection process.
Financial data: The stipend is $1,000.
Duration: 1 year.
Number awarded: 1 each year.
Deadline: March of each year.

1528 RALPH WALDO EMERSON PRIZES

Concord Review
Attn: Editor
730 Boston Post Road, Suite 24
Sudbury, MA 01776
Phone: (978) 443-0022; (800) 331-5007
Email: fitzhugh@tcr.org
Web: www.tcr.org/tcr/emerson.htm
Summary: To recognize and reward outstanding historical essays written by high school seniors in any country.
Eligibility: Open to high school students from any country. They are invited to submit historical essays to the *Concord Review,* the first and only quarterly journal in the world that publishes essays written by high school students from any country. Essays should be around 5,000 words, on any historical topic.
Financial data: The prize is $3,000.
Duration: The prizes are awarded annually.
Number awarded: 6 each year.
Deadline: Deadline not specified.

1529 RDW GROUP, INC. MINORITY SCHOLARSHIP FOR COMMUNICATIONS

Rhode Island Foundation
Attn: Funds Administrator
One Union Station
Providence, RI 02903
Phone: (401) 427-4017; Fax: (401) 331-8085
Email: lmonahan@rifoundation.org
Web: www.rifoundation.org
Summary: To provide financial assistance to Rhode Island undergraduate and graduate students of color interested in preparing for a career in communications at a school in any state.
Eligibility: Open to undergraduate and graduate students at colleges and universities in any state who are Rhode Island residents of color. Applicants must intend to work on a degree in communications (including computer graphics, art, cinematography, or other fields that would prepare them for a career in advertising). They must be able to demonstrate financial need and a commitment to a career in communications. Along with their application, they must submit an essay (up to 300 words) on the impact they would like to have on the communications field.
Financial data: The stipend ranges from $1,000 to $2,500 per year.
Duration: 1 year; recipients may reapply.
Number awarded: 1 each year.
Deadline: April of each year.

1530 REID BLACKBURN SCHOLARSHIP

National Press Photographers Foundation
3200 Croasdaile Drive, Suite 306
Durham, NC 27705-2586
Phone: (919) 383-7246; (800) 289-6772; Fax: (919) 383-7261
Email: info@nppa.org
Web: www.nppa.org
Summary: To provide financial assistance to college students who are interested in preparing for a career in photojournalism.
Eligibility: Open to students who have completed at least 1 year at a recognized 4-year college or university that offers courses in photojournalism, are working on a bachelor's degree, are intending to prepare for a career in journalism, and have at least half a year of undergraduate study remaining. A statement of philosophy and goals is especially important in the selection process, although financial need and academic achievement are also considered.
Financial data: The stipend is $1,000.
Duration: 1 year; nonrenewable.
Number awarded: 1 each year.
Deadline: February of each year.

1531 REPORTER OF THE YEAR AWARDS

Associated Collegiate Press
Attn: ACP Contest
2221 University Avenue, S.E., Suite 121
Minneapolis, MN 55414
Phone: (612) 625-8335; Fax: (612) 626-0720
Email: info@studentpress.org
Web: www.studentpress.org/acp/contests.html
Summary: To recognize and reward outstanding reporting by journalism students at college newspapers that are affiliated with the Associated Collegiate Press (ACP).

Eligibility: Open to reporters enrolled as full-time students and working on the staff of an ACP member publication. Applicants must submit copies of their 3 best single news or feature stories published during the preceding academic year. Stories must be the work of 1 reporter, although 1 of the 3 may have been published under a shared byline. The stories may be of any length. Only 1 student from each newspaper may enter the contest. Reporters compete in separate categories for 2-year colleges and 4-year colleges and universities.
Financial data: For each category, first prize is $1,000, second $500, and third $250.
Duration: The competition is held annually.
Number awarded: 6 each year: 3 in each category.
Deadline: June of each year.

1532 REV. CHARLES WILLIAMS MINORITY SCHOLARSHIP

Indiana Broadcasters Association
Attn: Scholarship Administrator
3003 East 98th Street, Suite 161
Indianapolis, IN 46280
Phone: (317) 573-0119; (800) 342-6276 (within IN); Fax: (317) 573-0895
Email: INDBA@aol.com
Web: www.indianabroadcasters.org/students/scholarships.php
Summary: To provide financial assistance to African American college students in Indiana who are interested in preparing for a career in a field related to broadcasting.
Eligibility: Open to African American residents of Indiana who are attending a college or university in the state that is a member of the Indiana Broadcasters Association (IBA) or that has a radio/TV facility on campus. Applicants must be majoring in telecommunications or broadcast journalism and have a GPA of 3.0 or higher. They must be actively participating on a college broadcast facility or working for a commercial broadcast facility while attending college. Along with their application, they must submit an essay on their interest in continuing an education in telecommunications or broadcast journalism. Financial need is not considered in the selection process.
Financial data: The stipend is $2,000.
Duration: 1 year.
Number awarded: 1 each year.
Deadline: March of each year.

1533 REV. CHUCK AND NANCY THOMAS SCHOLARSHIP

Unitarian Universalist Association
Attn: Ministerial Credentialing Office
25 Beacon Street
Boston, MA 02108-2800
Phone: (617) 948-6403; Fax: (617) 742-2875
Email: mco@uua.org
Web: www.uua.org/giving/awardsscholarships/thomasscholarships/index.shtml
Summary: To provide financial assistance to Unitarian Universalist (UU) lay leaders who are interested in entering a seminary to prepare for ministry.
Eligibility: Open to UU lay leaders who are planning to enroll in the first year at a seminary or pre-seminary work at the undergraduate level. Applicants must submit an essay of 2 to 3 pages that describes their path to seminary and highlights their work as a lay leader in their congregation and larger community. Selection is based on commitment to Unitarian Universalism as a lay leader.
Financial data: The stipend ranges from $1,000 to $11,000 per year.
Duration: 1 year.
Number awarded: 1 each year.
Deadline: March of each year.

1534 RICHARD G. ZIMMERMAN JOURNALISM SCHOLARSHIP

National Press Club
Attn: General Manager's Office
529 14th Street, N.W.
Washington, DC 20045
Phone: (202) 662-7599
Web: www.press.org/activities/aboutscholarship.cfm
Summary: To provide funding to high school seniors who are planning to major in journalism in college.
Eligibility: Open to high school seniors who have been accepted to college and plan to prepare for a career in journalism. Applicants must have a GPA of 3.0 or higher. Along with their application, they must submit 1) work samples that may be print articles or multimedia stories on a CD or DVD; 2) letters of recommendation from 3 people; 3) a copy of their high school transcript; 4) documentation of financial need; and 5) a letter of acceptance from the college or university of their choice.
Financial data: The stipend is $5,000.
Duration: 1 year; nonrenewable.
Number awarded: 1 each year.
Deadline: February of each year.

1535 RICHARD W. ELLIS ALL STATE SCHOLARSHIP

Vermont Music Educators Association
c/o Steffen C. Parker
141 Butternut Road
Williston, VT 05495
Phone: (802) 343-6282
Email: statemanager@vmea.org
Web: www.vmea.org/musicScholarships.php
Summary: To provide financial assistance to high school musicians in Vermont who participate in an ensemble at the Vermont All State Musical Festival and plan to study music at a college or university in any state.
Eligibility: Open to students attending a public or private high school in Vermont or a registered home school in the state. Applicants must compete in the Vermont All State Musical Festival in 1 of its 7 performance categories: brass, string, jazz, percussion, piano, voice, and woodwinds. Students who are selected to participate in 1 of the Vermont All State Music Festival Ensembles are eligible to compete for this scholarship. They must submit letters of reference, transcripts, documentation of financial need, and other material.
Financial data: The stipend is $1,000.
Duration: The competition is held annually.
Number awarded: 1 each year.
Deadline: April of each year.

1536 R.L. GILLETTE SCHOLARSHIPS

American Foundation for the Blind
Attn: Scholarship Committee
11 Penn Plaza, Suite 300
New York, NY 10001
Phone: (212) 502-7661; (800) AFB-LINE; Fax: (212) 502-7771; TDD: (212) 502-7662
Email: afbinfo@afb.net
Web: www.afb.org/Section.asp?Documentid=2962
Summary: To provide financial assistance to legally blind undergraduate women who are studying literature or music.
Eligibility: Open to women who are legally blind, U.S. citizens, and enrolled full-time in a 4-year baccalaureate degree program in literature or music. Along with their application, they must submit a 200-word essay that includes their past and recent achievements and accomplishments; their intended field of study and why they have chosen it; and the role their visual impairment has played in shaping their life. They must also submit a sample performance tape/CD (not to exceed 30 minutes) or a creative writing sample. Financial need is considered in the selection process.
Financial data: The stipend is $1,000.
Duration: 1 academic year.
Number awarded: 2 each year.
Deadline: April of each year.

1537 ROBERT E. LUCKIE, JR. MEMORIAL SCHOLARSHIP

American Advertising Federation–Birmingham
P.O. Box 530416
Birmingham, AL 35253
Email: student@aafbirmingham.com
Web: www.aafbirmingham.com/scholarships.php
Summary: To provide financial assistance to residents of Alabama who are attending college in the state to prepare for a career in a field related to creative writing.
Eligibility: Open to graduates of high schools in Alabama who are attending an accredited 4-year college or university in the state. Applicants must be preparing for a career in creative writing, copywriting, and/or advertising, with a major or minor in such fields as English, advertising, or journalism. Along with their application, they must submit an essay or video that illustrates their passion and interest in a career in the field. Financial need is considered in the selection process.
Financial data: The stipend is $2,500.

Duration: 1 year.
Number awarded: 1 or more each year.
Deadline: March of each year.

1538 ROBERT NOVAK COLLEGIATE JOURNALISM AWARDS

The Fund for American Studies
Attn: Collegiate Awards Committee
1706 New Hampshire Avenue, N.W.
Washington, DC 20009
Phone: (202) 986-0384; (800) 741-6964; Fax: (202) 986-0390
Email: jstarrs@tfas.org
Web: www.tfas.org/Page.aspx?pid=265

Summary: To recognize and reward college journalists who submit outstanding work that demonstrates an understanding of a free society.
Eligibility: Open to undergraduate students currently enrolled at a 4-year college or university in the United States. Applicants must submit a news story (not an editorial or commentary) that they have written for a school newspaper, publication, or online site. Work written for an internship or a class assignment is not eligible. Awards are presented for work that demonstrates an understanding of the basic ideas that support a free society, including freedom of the press, freedom of speech, and free market economic principles. Applicants should show initiative, original reporting, superior writing skills, an understanding of the principles of individual freedom, accuracy in reporting, and good use of sources.
Financial data: First prize is $5,000, second $2,500, and third $1,000.
Duration: The prizes are awarded annually.
Number awarded: 3 each year.
Deadline: March of each year.

1539 ROBERT SHERMAN SCHOLARSHIP

Broadcast Music Inc.
Attn: BMI Foundation, Inc.
7 World Trade Center
250 Greenwich Street
New York, NY 10007-0030
Phone: (212) 220-3000
Email: info@bmifoundation.org
Web: www.bmifoundation.org/program/robert_sherman_scholarship

Summary: To provide financial assistance to student composers interested in musical theater.
Eligibility: Open to students working on a degree in composition who are interested in musical composition. Candidates must be nominated; no applications are accepted.
Financial data: The stipend is $1,000.
Duration: 1 year.
Number awarded: 1 each year.
Deadline: Deadline not specified.

1540 ROBERT WALKER SCHOLARSHIPS IN CHRISTIAN JOURNALISM

Christian Life Missions
600 Rinehard Road
P.O. Box 952248
Lake Mary, FL 32795
Phone: (407) 333-0600
Email: Amy.condiff@strang.com
Web: www.christianlifemissions.com/scholarships/index.htm

Summary: To provide financial assistance to undergraduate and graduate students interested in preparing for a career in Christian journalism.
Eligibility: Open to undergraduate and graduate journalism students who have a GPA of 3.5 or higher. Applicants must submit a letter explaining their interest and commitment to Christian journalism, a current resume, an official transcript, and 5 published works.
Financial data: The stipend is $2,000 per year.
Duration: 1 year; recipients may reapply.
Number awarded: Up to 5 each year.
Deadline: April of each year.

1541 ROBERTA CAPPS SCHOLARSHIP

Daughters of the American Revolution–Missouri State Society
Attn: State Scholarship Chair
821 Main Street
Boonville, MO 65233-1657
Phone: (660) 882-5320
Email: hyhope@sbcglobal.net
Web: www.mssdar.org

Summary: To provide financial assistance to high school seniors in Missouri who plan to attend college in any state to study American history or government.
Eligibility: Open to seniors graduating from high schools in Missouri in the top 10% of their class. Applicants must be planning to attend an accredited college or university in any state to study American history or American government. They must be sponsored by a chapter of the Daughters of the American Revolution in Missouri and able to demonstrate financial need. U.S. citizenship is required.
Financial data: A stipend is awarded (amount not specified).
Duration: 1 year.
Number awarded: 1 or more each year.
Deadline: January of each year.

1542 ROSSINI FLEXOGRAPHIC SCHOLARSHIP COMPETITION

Flexographic Technical Association
Attn: Foundation of Flexographic Technical Association
900 Marconi Avenue
Ronkonkoma, NY 11779-7212
Phone: (631) 737-6020; Fax: (631) 737-6813
Email: education@flexography.org
Web: www.flexography.org/edutrain/education/rossini_info.cfm

Summary: To recognize and reward, with funding for research, undergraduate students who propose an outstanding project related to flexography.
Eligibility: Open to full-time sophomores and juniors at 4-year colleges and universities. Applicants must be majoring in graphic communications with a focus on flexography. They must submit a proposal for a research project in the field of flexography. The project must address an issue, topic, or problem facing the flexographic industry; the focus of the project must be directed at finding results that will benefit the flexographic industry; and the research must be conducted by an individual student. In addition to their research proposal, students must submit transcripts (GPA of 3.0 or higher), a statement of educational and personal goals, and 3 letters of recommendation.
Financial data: Awards are $10,000 for first place, $6,000 for second, and $4,000 for third. Winners also receive an all-expense-paid trip to the Foundation of Flexographic Technical Association (FFTA) annual forum where they will outline their projects. Funds are to be used to conduct the proposed research project.
Duration: The competition is held annually.
Number awarded: 3 each year.
Deadline: Applications must be submitted by January of each year. Progress reports are due in February, April, and July, and the research project must be completed by the end of August.

1543 RUTH CLARK FURNITURE DESIGN SCHOLARSHIP

International Furnishings and Design Association
Attn: IFDA Educational Foundation
150 South Warner Road, Suite 156
King of Prussia, PA 19406
Phone: (610) 535-6422; Fax: (610) 535-6423
Email: info@ifda.com
Web: www.ifdaef.org/scholarships.html

Summary: To provide financial assistance to undergraduate and graduate students working on a degree in residential furniture design.
Eligibility: Open to full-time undergraduate and graduate students enrolled in a design program at an accredited college or design school with a focus on residential upholstered and/or wood furniture design. Applicants must have completed at least 4 design courses. Along with their application, they must submit an essay of 200 to 400 words on their long- and short-term goals, special interests, achievements, awards and accomplishments, volunteer and community service, and what inspired them to prepare for a career in this field; 5 examples of their original residential furniture designs; a transcript; and a letter of recommendation from a professor or instructor. Financial need is not considered.
Financial data: The stipend is $2,500.
Duration: 1 year.
Number awarded: 1 each year.
Deadline: March of each year.

1544 RUTH JACOBS MEMORIAL SCHOLARSHIP

Choristers Guild
Attn: Memorial Scholarship Committee
12404 Park Central Drive, Suite 100
Dallas, TX 75251-1803
Phone: (469) 398-3606; (800) CHORISTER; Fax: (469) 398-3611
Email: Scholarships@mailcg.org
Web: www.choristersguild.org/rkj_scholarship.html

Summary: To provide financial assistance to upper-division and graduate students majoring in church music.

Eligibility: Open to juniors, seniors, and graduate students working full-time on a degree in church music. Applicants must submit a 2-page essay explaining why they have chosen to prepare for a career in choral church music, how children and youth choirs will be a part of their career, their choral experience as a singer and as a conductor, and their music background, both formal and informal. Selection is based on academic merit, interest in church music (especially children's and youth choirs), and interest in ministry of church music as a vocation.

Financial data: The stipend is $1,500 per year.

Duration: 1 year; recipients may reapply.

Number awarded: 1 or more each year.

Deadline: January of each year.

1545 SABIAN, LTD. LARRIE LONDIN MEMORIAL SCHOLARSHIP

Percussive Arts Society
110 West Washington Street, Suite A
Indianapolis, IN 46204
Phone: (317) 974-4488; Fax: (317) 974-4499
Email: percarts@pas.org
Web: www.pas.org/experience/grantsscholarships.aspx

Summary: To provide financial assistance to young drummers interested in furthering their drumset studies.

Eligibility: Open to drummers in 2 categories: those 17 years of age and under and those from 18 to 24 years of age. Applicants must submit 1) a DVD, up to 3 minutes in length, that demonstrates their ability to perform different drumming styles; 2) an essay (from 100 to 200 words in length) on why they feel they qualify for a scholarship and how the money would be used (e.g., college, summer camp, private teacher); and 3) a supporting letter of recommendation verifying their age and school attendance. Students in the age 18 to 24 category must be enrolled in, or apply funds to, an accredited, structured music education program. Financial need is not considered in the selection process.

Financial data: The stipend is $2,000 for students in the 18 to 24 age category or $1,000 for students under 17.

Duration: 1 year.

Number awarded: 2 each year: 1 in each age category.

Deadline: March of each year.

1546 SALLY HEET MEMORIAL SCHOLARSHIP

Public Relations Society of America–Puget Sound Chapter
c/o Diane Bevins
1006 Industry Drive
Seattle, WA 98188-4801
Phone: (206) 623-8632
Email: prsascholarship@asi-seattle.net
Web: www.prsapugetsound.org/scholars.html

Summary: To provide financial assistance to upper-division students in Washington who are interested in preparing for a career in public relations.

Eligibility: Open to U.S. citizens who are entering their junior or senior year of full-time study at colleges and universities in Washington. Applicants must be preparing for a career in public relations. They must be able to demonstrate aptitude in public relations and related courses, activities, and/or internships. Along with their application, they must submit a description of their career goals and the skills that are most important to a public relations career (20 points in the selection process); a description of their communications activities in class, on campus, in the community, or during internships, including 3 samples of their work (30 points); a statement on the value of public relations to an organization (10 points); a certified transcript (20 points); and 2 or more letters of recommendation (20 points).

Financial data: The stipend is $2,500.

Duration: 1 year.

Number awarded: 1 each year.

Deadline: April of each year.

1547 SAMUEL ROBINSON AWARD

Presbyterian Church (USA)
Attn: Office of Financial Aid for Studies
100 Witherspoon Street, Room M-052
Louisville, KY 40202-1396
Phone: (502) 569-5224; (888) 728-7228, ext. 5224; Fax: (502) 569-8766
Email: finaid@pcusa.org
Web: www.pcusa.org/financialaid/programs/samuelrobinson.htm

Summary: To recognize and reward students in Presbyterian colleges who write essays on religious topics.

Eligibility: Open to juniors and seniors enrolled full-time in 1 of the 65 colleges related to the Presbyterian Church (USA). Applicants must successfully recite the answers to the Westminster Shorter Catechism and write a 2,000-word original essay on an assigned topic related to the Shorter Catechism.

Financial data: Awards range from $200 to $1,000.

Duration: 1 year; nonrenewable.

Number awarded: 1 each year.

Deadline: March of each year.

1548 SARAH SOULE PATTON SCHOLARSHIP

Daughters of the American Revolution–Washington State Society
c/o Jackie Daniels, Scholarship Chair
11725 South Chalet Drive
Cheney, WA 99004-9018
Phone: (360) 838-0373
Web: www.rootsweb.ancestry.com/~wassdar/scholars.html

Summary: To provide financial assistance to American history majors entering their senior year at universities in Washington.

Eligibility: Open to students entering their senior year at Washington State University, Whitman College, St. Martin University, Pacific Lutheran University, University of Puget Sound, Gonzaga University, Whitworth College, Eastern Washington University, Seattle Pacific University, University of Washington, Western Washington University, Central Washington University, and Seattle University. Applicants must be majoring in American history, U.S. citizens, able to demonstrate financial need and good character, and recommended by the financial aid office at their college or university.

Financial data: The stipend is $1,100.

Duration: 1 year.

Number awarded: 1 each year.

Deadline: January of each year.

1549 SCHERING-PLOUGH "WILL TO WIN" SCHOLARSHIPS

Summary: To provide financial assistance for college to high school seniors with outstanding abilities in community service, athletics, art, or science who have asthma.

See Listing #887.

1550 SCHOLARSHIP IN BOOK PRODUCTION AND PUBLISHING

Bookbuilders West
Attn: Scholarships
9328 Elk Grove Boulevard, Suite 105-250
Elk Grove, CA 95624
Phone: (916) 320-0638
Email: scholarship@bookbuilders.org
Web: www.bookbuilders.org

Summary: To recognize and reward outstanding sample book projects created by students in the western states.

Eligibility: Open to students currently enrolled at a college, university, or technical school in the western states (Alaska, Arizona, California, Colorado, Hawaii, Idaho, Montana, Nevada, New Mexico, Oregon, Utah, Washington, and Wyoming). They must intend to prepare for a career in the field of book production or publishing, have at least a 2.0 GPA, and submit a sample book project (which usually comes from a course assignment). In addition to identifying and describing the subject book, the project submission should include the following items: a brief summary of the concept of the book selected for design and production; a definition of the design objective for the cover, interior, and any special features (e.g., slipcase); written design specifications for the cover, title page, table of contents, sample chapter opening, and interior text pages; a dummy that includes sample pages for the items listed above; and (optionally) a hand binding of the sample pages, slipcases, and other packaging. The project is judged in terms of creativity, meeting defined design objectives, and presentation of material.

Financial data: The stipend is $1,000.
Duration: 1 year.
Number awarded: Varies each year; recently, 5 of these scholarships were awarded.
Deadline: May of each year.

1551 SCHOLARSHIP OF THE ARTS

Boomer Esiason Foundation
c/o Jerry Cahill
483 Tenth Avenue, Suite 300
New York, NY 10018
Phone: (646) 292-7930; Fax: (646) 292-7945
Email: jcahillbef@aol.com
Web: www.cfscholarships.com/Arts/index.htm

Summary: To provide financial assistance to undergraduate and graduate students who have cystic fibrosis (CF) and are working on a degree in the arts.
Eligibility: Open to CF patients who are working on an undergraduate or graduate degree in the arts. Applicants must submit a picture of their work (painting, sketching, sculpture), a letter from their doctor confirming the diagnosis of CF and a list of daily medications, information on financial need, a detailed breakdown of tuition costs from their academic institution, transcripts, and a 2-page essay on 1) their post-graduation goals; and 2) the importance of compliance with CF therapies and what they practice on a daily basis to stay healthy. Selection is based on academic ability, character, leadership potential, service to the community, and financial need.
Financial data: Stipends range from $500 to $2,000. Funds are paid directly to the academic institution to assist in covering the cost of tuition and fees.
Duration: 1 year; nonrenewable.
Number awarded: 1 each year.
Deadline: May of each year.

1552 SCHOLASTIC ART AWARDS

Scholastic, Inc.
Attn: Alliance for Young Artists & Writers, Inc.
557 Broadway
New York, NY 10012
Phone: (212) 343-6730; Fax: (212) 389-3939
Email: info@artandwriting.org
Web: www.artandwriting.org

Summary: To recognize and reward outstanding middle school and high school artists and photographers.
Eligibility: Open to students in grades 7–12 who are currently enrolled in public and private schools in the United States, U.S. territories, Canada, or U.S.-sponsored schools abroad. Categories include architecture, comic art, ceramics and glass, digital art, design (commercial and applied arts), drawing, fashion, film and animation, jewelry, mixed media, painting, photography, printmaking, sculpture, and video games. Participants who are graduating seniors planning to attend college may submit an art portfolio of 8 works from any category or a photography portfolio of 8 works from any category.
Financial data: The Portfolio Gold Awards are $10,000 scholarships. In addition, teachers of the Portfolio Gold Award winners receive Portfolio Teacher Awards of $1,000. The teacher who submits the most outstanding group of entries in any category receives the Ovation Inspired Teaching Award of $1,000.
Number awarded: At the national level, 15 Portfolio Gold Awards are presented in the art, photography, general writing, and nonfiction categories. The teachers of those 15 winners receive Portfolio Teacher Awards. The Ovation Inspired Teaching Award is presented to 1 teacher.
Deadline: January of each year.

1553 SCHOLASTIC WRITING AWARDS

Scholastic, Inc.
Attn: Alliance for Young Artists & Writers, Inc.
557 Broadway
New York, NY 10012
Phone: (212) 343-6730; Fax: (212) 389-3939
Email: info@artandwriting.org
Web: www.artandwriting.org

Summary: To recognize and reward outstanding middle school and high school writers.
Eligibility: Open to all students in grades 7–12 who are currently enrolled in public and private schools in the United States, U.S. territories, U.S.-sponsored schools abroad, and Canada. Competitions are held in the following categories: dramatic script, humor, journalism, novel writing, personal essay/memoir, persuasive writing, poetry, science fiction/fantasy, short story, and short short story. A separate competition for graduating seniors consists of a minimum of 3 and maximum of 8 for the general writing portfolio (for writing from any of the categories) or the nonfiction portfolio (for writing from humor, journalism, personal essay/memoir, persuasive writing, or other nonfiction work). Entries may not have been submitted previously in this or any other competition and must be original. Each student may enter only 1 category.
Financial data: The Portfolio Gold Awards are $10,000 scholarships. In addition, teachers of the Portfolio Gold Award winners receive Portfolio Teacher Awards of $1,000. The teacher who submits the most outstanding group of entries in any category receives the Ovation Inspired Teaching Award of $1,000.
Number awarded: At the national level, 15 Portfolio Gold Awards are presented in the art, photography, general writing, and nonfiction categories. The teachers of those 15 winners receive Portfolio Teacher Awards. The Ovation Inspired Teaching Award is presented to 1 teacher.
Deadline: January of each year.

1554 SCRIPPS HOWARD TOP TEN SCHOLARSHIP PROGRAM

Scripps Howard Foundation
Attn: Vice President, Programs
312 Walnut Street, 28th Floor
P.O. Box 5380
Cincinnati, OH 45201-5380
Phone: (513) 977-3030; (800) 888-3000, ext. 3030; Fax: (513) 977-3800
Email: sue.porter@scripps.com
Web: www.scripps.com/foundation/programs/scholarships/topten.html

Summary: To provide financial assistance to college juniors and seniors interested in a career in journalism.
Eligibility: Open to full-time students entering their junior or senior year with a major in journalism. They must be nominated by the college or university they attend. Selection is based on academic achievement and a demonstrated interest in a career in journalism. Nominees also must submit a personal essay emphasizing their long-term goals.
Financial data: The stipend is $10,000.
Duration: 1 year; nonrenewable.
Number awarded: 10 each year.
Deadline: May of each year.

1555 SCUDDER ASSOCIATION EDUCATIONAL GRANTS

Scudder Association, Inc.
c/o Mrs. Cy Sherman, Secretary
33 Christian Avenue, Number 119
Concord, NH 03301-6128
Email: info@scudder.org
Web: www.scudder.org/philanthropy

Summary: To assist undergraduate and graduate students preparing for selected "careers as servants of God in various forms of ministry to men and women around the world."
Eligibility: Open to undergraduate and graduate students who are preparing for careers in the ministry, medicine, or social work. Applicants must be a Scudder family member or recommended by a member of the Scudder Association. Along with their application, they must submit an official transcript, 2 letters of recommendation from faculty members, a statement (up to 500 words) on their goals and objectives, and a verification of financial need from their school.
Financial data: Stipends range from $1,000 to $2,500.
Duration: Up to 4 years of undergraduate studies, graduate studies, or a combination of the two.
Number awarded: Up to 25 each year.
Deadline: April of each year.

1556 SDX FOUNDATION OF WASHINGTON, D.C. UNDERGRADUATE COLLEGE JOURNALISM SCHOLARSHIPS

Society of Professional Journalists-Washington, D.C. Professional Chapter
Attn: SDX Foundation of Washington, D.C.
Scholarship Committee
P.O. Box 19555
Washington, DC 20036
Phone: (202) 429-5361
Email: Sdxdc08Question@sdxdc.org
Web: www.sdxdc.org/SDX-Scholarship.htm

Summary: To provide financial assistance to upper-division students from any state at colleges and universities in the Washington, D.C. metropolitan area who are preparing for a career in journalism.
Eligibility: Open to residents of any state currently enrolled full-time as sophomores or juniors at colleges and universities in the Washington, D.C. metropolitan area. Applicants are not required to be majoring in journalism, but they must be able to demonstrate a sincere interest in preparing for a career in journalism, as through internships, work at campus news media outlets, or similar experiences. They must also be able to demonstrate financial need.
Financial data: The stipend is $4,000.
Duration: 1 year.
Number awarded: 5 each year.
Deadline: December of each year.

1557 SETC SECONDARY SCHOOL SCHOLARSHIP

Southeastern Theatre Conference, Inc.
1175 Revolution Mill Drive, Suite 14
P.O. Box 9868
Greensboro, NC 27429-0868
Phone: (336) 272-3645; Fax: (336) 272-8810
Email: setc@setc.org
Web: www.setc.org/scholarship/secondary.php
Summary: To provide financial assistance to high school seniors in the region of the Southeastern Theatre Conference (SETC) who plan to attend college in the area and major in theater arts.
Eligibility: Open to seniors graduating from high schools in the region served by the SETC. Applicants must be planning to attend an accredited college or university in the region and major in theater arts. Along with their application, they must submit an official transcript that includes their SAT or ACT scores and 3 letters of recommendation. Selection is based on aptitude in theatrical practices (e.g., playwriting, design, stage management, acting, directing) and potential for academic success in college.
Financial data: The stipend is $2,100. The winner also receives 1-year free student membership in SETC, complimentary convention registration, and 3 days' hotel accommodations to attend the annual awards banquet.
Duration: 1 year.
Number awarded: 1 each year.
Deadline: January of each year.

1558 SEVENTEEN MAGAZINE ANNUAL FICTION CONTEST

Seventeen Magazine
Attn: Fiction Contest
300 West 57th Street, 17th Floor
New York, NY 10019-1798
Phone: (212) 649-2000
Email: mail@seventeen.com
Web: www.seventeen.com/fun/articles/official-rules?click=main_sr
Summary: To recognize and reward female teenagers who write fiction that would interest the readers of *Seventeen* magazine.
Eligibility: Open to female residents of the United States and Canada who are between 13 and 21 years of age. Applicants must submit a fiction short story, up to 500 words in length, that has not been published previously in any form (except in school publications). Contestants may submit as many stories as they like. Selection is based on creativity (33%), originality (33%), and writing ability (34%).
Financial data: The prize is $5,000 and publication of the story in *Seventeen* magazine.
Duration: The competition is held annually.
Number awarded: 1 each year.
Deadline: December of each year.

1559 SHENG FUND SCHOLARSHIP

Connecticut Architecture Foundation
Attn: Executive Vice President
370 James Street, Suite 402
New Haven, CT 06511
Phone: (203) 865-2195; Fax: (203) 562-5378
Email: aiainfo@aiact.org
Web: www.aiact.org/outreach/ctaf_scholarship.php
Summary: To provide financial assistance to Connecticut residents who are working on a bachelor's or master's degree in architecture at a school in any state.
Eligibility: Open to students who have completed at least 2 years of a bachelor of architecture program or have been accepted into an accredited graduate program. Connecticut residents are encouraged to apply. Applicants may be attending any college offering a 5-year accredited degree in architecture. Preference is given to students at Cornell University. Selection is based on academic record and financial need.
Financial data: Stipends range from $1,200 to $5,000.
Duration: 1 year; may be renewed.
Number awarded: 1 each year.
Deadline: April of each year.

1560 SIGMA CORPORATION OF AMERICA SCHOLARSHIP CONTEST

Sigma Corporation of America
15 Fleetwood Court
Ronkonkoma, NY 11779
Phone: (631) 585-1144; (800) 896-6858; Fax: (631) 585-1895
Email: info@sigmaphoto.com
Web: scholarship.sigmaphoto.com
Summary: To recognize and reward high school seniors who are interested in preparing for a career in a photography-related field.
Eligibility: Open to high school seniors who are interested in working on a degree or certificate in a photography-related field (e.g., photojournalism, photography, graphic arts, design, art history, visual arts). Applicants must submit 1) 3 to 5 images of photographs that are thematically tied and that illustrate outstanding image quality; and 2) an 800-word essay that describes how the images are linked, how the images were captured, and the creative process the entrant used to obtain the images. The images and the essays are posted on the sponsor's web site and the public is invited to vote for their favorite. The top 3 vote-getters are then referred to executives of the sponsoring corporation and they select the winner.
Financial data: The winner receives a $5,000 cash award to be used for further study and $1,000 worth of products from the sponsor.
Duration: This competition is held annually.
Number awarded: 1 each year.
Deadline: February of each year.

1561 SIGNET CLASSICS STUDENT SCHOLARSHIP ESSAY CONTEST

Penguin Group (USA) Inc.
Attn: Academic Marketing Department
375 Hudson Street
New York, NY 10014-3657
Phone: (212) 366-2373; Fax: (212) 366-2933
Email: academic@us.penguingroup.com
Web: us.penguingroup.com/static/pages/services_academic/essayhome.html
Summary: To recognize and reward high school students who write essays on topics that relate to 1 of the books in the Signet Classic series (published by Penguin Group [USA], Inc.).
Eligibility: Open to high school juniors and seniors and to home-schooled students between 16 and 18 years of age. Applicants must submit essays, from 2 to 3 pages in length, on a topic that changes annually but relates to the books published in the Signet Classic series. Recently, the essay contest focused on *The Moonstone* by Wilkie Collins. Essays by high school students must be submitted by an English teacher. Essays by home-schooled students must be submitted by a parent or legal guardian. Submissions are judged on style, content, grammar, and originality. Judges look for clear, concise writing that is articulate, logically organized, and well supported.
Financial data: The grand-prize winners receive a $1,000 scholarship and a Signet Classic library for their school or public (for home school students) library (valued at $1,600).
Duration: The competition is held annually.
Number awarded: 5 grand-prize winners each year.
Deadline: April of each year.

1562 SISTER CITIES INTERNATIONAL YOUNG ARTISTS SHOWCASE

Sister Cities International
1301 Pennsylvania Avenue, N.W., Suite 850
Washington, DC 20004
Phone: (202) 347-8630; Fax: (202) 393-6524
Email: info@sister-cities.org

Web: www.sister-cities.org/programs/yap.cfm

Summary: To recognize and reward young artists who express, through original artwork, their concept of the Sister Cities' mission.

Eligibility: Open to student artists between 13 and 18 years of age who have the support of their local Sister Cities committee. Only U.S. cities that are members of Sister Cities International may submit entries. Acceptable media for entry are: watercolors, oils, pastels, pen and ink, charcoal, photography, computer-generated or mixed media (2 dimensional only). Artwork must be on paper, posterboard, or canvas, no larger than 24 × 30 inches, including the mat work. All entries must be the original design and artwork of the student. Parents, friends, teachers, or others may not assist the artist. The artwork must reflect the sponsor's annual theme (changes yearly); a recent theme was "Your World." Entries are submitted by the member cities to the national selection committee. Selection is based on originality, composition, and theme interpretation.

Financial data: Winners receive complimentary registration for the annual Youth Leadership Conference and $1,000, which may be used either to help pay airfare to the conference or taken as a cash prize.

Duration: The competition is held annually.

Number awarded: 2 each year: 1 for an American and 1 for a foreign artist.

Deadline: April of each year.

1563 SOCIETY OF MAYFLOWER DESCENDANTS IN THE STATE OF NEW JERSEY

Society of Mayflower Descendants in the State of New Jersey Scholarship
c/o Mark C. Fulcomer, Education Committee
48 Trainor Circle
Bordentown, NJ 08505
Email: eNJN@njmayflower.org

Summary: To provide financial assistance to high school seniors in New Jersey who plan to major in U.S. history at a college in the state.

Eligibility: Open to seniors graduating from high schools in New Jersey who rank in the top quarter or their class or have SAT or ACT scores at or above the 75th percentile. Applicants must be planning to enroll at a 4-year college or university in New Jersey and major in a field related to U.S. history. Each high school in the state may nominate 1 student for this award. Financial need is not considered in the selection process.

Financial data: The stipend is $1,500.

Duration: 1 year.

Number awarded: 3 each year.

Deadline: March of each year.

1564 SONS OF ITALY ITALIAN LANGUAGE SCHOLARSHIP

Order Sons of Italy in America
Attn: Sons of Italy Foundation
219 E Street, N.E.
Washington, DC 20002
Phone: (202) 547-2900; (800) 552-OSIA; Fax: (202) 546-8168
Email: scholarships@osia.org
Web: www.osia.org/students/study-abroad.php

Summary: To provide financial assistance to upper-division students majoring in Italian.

Eligibility: Open to U.S. citizens of Italian descent who are enrolled as full-time undergraduate juniors or seniors at an accredited 4-year college or university. Applicants must be majoring in the Italian language. They must submit an essay of 750 to 1,000 words in Italian on why learning Italian is important in today's world and how they plan to use their degree in Italian language in their career. Financial need is not considered in the selection process.

Financial data: Stipends range from $5,000 to $25,000.

Duration: 1 year; nonrenewable.

Number awarded: 1 each year.

Deadline: February of each year.

1565 SOUTH CAROLINA VOCATIONAL REHABILITATION DEPARTMENT JOURNALISM CONTEST

South Carolina Vocational Rehabilitation Department
Attn: Public Information Office
1410 Boston Avenue
P.O. Box 15
West Columbia, SC 29171-0015
Phone: (803) 896-6833; (866) 247-8354; TDD: (803) 896-6553
Email: info@scvrd.state.sc.us
Web: scvrd.net/g_journal_contest.html

Summary: To recognize and reward high school students in South Carolina who submit outstanding newspaper articles on topics related to the employment of people with disabilities.

Eligibility: Open to South Carolina residents between 16 and 19 years of age enrolled as juniors or seniors in high school or otherwise qualified to begin postsecondary education no later than 2 years after the contest. Applicants are not required to have a disability, but they must submit a newspaper article, up to 3 pages in length, on a topic that changes annually but relates to the employment of people with disabilities. A recent topic was "Expectation + opportunity = full participation!" Articles should use correct grammar and sentence structure and follow standard journalistic practice of the 5 Ws (who, what, where, when, and why).

Financial data: The winner receives full payment of tuition and fees at a South Carolina state-supported institution. Some schools include room and board as part of tuition and fees.

Duration: 4 years, provided the recipient meets general scholastic and conduct standards.

Number awarded: 1 each year.

Deadline: January of each year.

1566 SPRING MEADOW NURSERY SCHOLARSHIP

American Nursery and Landscape Association
Attn: Horticultural Research Institute
1000 Vermont Avenue, N.W., Suite 300
Washington, DC 20005-4914
Phone: (202) 741-4852; Fax: (202) 478-7288
Email: hriresearch@anla.org
Web: www.anla.org/research/scholarships/index.htm

Summary: To provide financial assistance to students working on an undergraduate or graduate degree in landscape architecture or horticulture.

Eligibility: Open to students enrolled or planning to enroll full-time in a landscape or horticulture undergraduate or graduate program at an accredited 2- or 4-year college or university. Students enrolled in a vocational agriculture program are also eligible. Applicants must have a minimum GPA of 2.25 overall and 2.7 in their major. Preference is given to applicants who plan to work within the nursery industry, including nursery operations; landscape architecture, design, construction, or maintenance; interiorscape; horticultural distribution; or retail garden center.

Financial data: The stipend is $2,500.

Duration: 1 year; may be renewed.

Number awarded: 1 each year.

Deadline: March of each year.

1567 STEPHEN G. KING PLAY ENVIRONMENTS SCHOLARSHIP

Landscape Architecture Foundation
Attn: Scholarship Program
818 18th Street, N.W., Suite 810
Washington, DC 20006-3520
Phone: (202) 331-7070; Fax: (202) 331-7079
Email: scholarships@lafoundation.org
Web: www.laprofession.org/financial/scholarships.htm

Summary: To provide financial assistance to upper-division and graduate students who wish to study landscape architecture with an emphasis on play environments.

Eligibility: Open to landscape architecture students in the final 2 years of undergraduate study or in graduate school. Applicants must have a demonstrated interest and aptitude in the design of play environments, including integrating playgrounds into parks, schools, and other play environments and understanding the significant social and educational value of play. Along with their application, they must submit 2 letters of recommendation, a plan and details of a play environment of their design, and an essay of 300 to 500 words on their views of the significant social and educational value of play and the value of integrating playgrounds into play and recreation environments. Selection is based on financial need, creativity, openness to innovation, and demonstrated interest in park and playground planning.

Financial data: The stipend is $5,000.

Duration: 1 year.

Number awarded: 1 each year.

Deadline: February of each year.

1568 STEVE HARPER MEMORIAL SCHOLARSHIP

Kansas Wildscape Foundation, Inc.
2500 West Sixth Street, Suite G

Lawrence, KS 66049
Phone: (785) 843-9453; (866) 655-6377; Fax: (785) 843-6379
Email: wildscape@sunflower.com
Web: www.kansaswildscape.org

Summary: To provide financial assistance to high school seniors in Kansas who plan to attend a college or university in the state to major in natural resources or photography.

Eligibility: Open to seniors graduating from high schools in Kansas and planning to attend a 4-year college or university in the state. Applicants must be planning to study photography or natural resources. Selection is based on past or current involvement in the natural resources or photography area, strength of application, academic performance, and financial need.

Financial data: The stipend is $1,000.

Duration: 1 year; nonrenewable.

Number awarded: 1 each year.

Deadline: April of each year.

1569 STILL PHOTOGRAPHER SCHOLARSHIP

National Press Photographers Foundation
3200 Croasdaile Drive, Suite 306
Durham, NC 27705-2586
Phone: (919) 383-7246; (800) 289-6772; Fax: (919) 383-7261
Email: info@nppa.org
Web: www.nppa.org

Summary: To provide financial assistance to outstanding photojournalism students.

Eligibility: Open to students who have completed at least 1 year at a recognized 4-year college or university that offers courses in photojournalism. They must be working on a bachelor's degree, be intending to prepare for a career in journalism, and have at least half a year of undergraduate study remaining. Along with their application, they must submit a list of the photographic and photojournalist activities they have undertaken in school, a list of photographic activities they have taken outside of school, information on their financial need, and a statement of their philosophy and goals in photojournalism. These awards are aimed at those with journalism potential but with little opportunity and great need.

Financial data: The stipend is $2,000.

Duration: 1 year.

Number awarded: 1 each year.

Deadline: February of each year.

1570 STOKES EDUCATIONAL SCHOLARSHIP PROGRAM

National Security Agency
Attn: Office of Recruitment and Hiring
9800 Savage Road, Suite 6779
P.O. Box 1661
Fort Meade, MD 20755-6779
Phone: (410) 854-4725; (866) NSA-HIRE
Web: www.nsa.gov

Summary: To provide minority and other high school seniors and college sophomores with financial assistance and work experience at the National Security Agency (NSA).

Eligibility: Open to 1) graduating high school seniors, particularly minorities, who are planning a college major in electrical or computer engineering or computer science; and 2) college sophomores who are majoring in mathematics, foreign language (currently, Russian or Farsi only), or fields related to intelligence analysis, such as regional studies (Middle East; south, east, or central Asia), topical studies (terrorism, proliferation, or related sciences), international banking and finance, telecommunications and information system networks, intelligence or information analysis, international relations, or security studies. High school seniors must have minimum scores of 1600 on the SAT (1100 on critical reading and mathematics, 500 in writing) or 25 on the ACT. All applicants must have a GPA of 3.0 or higher. Along with their application, they must submit a 1-page essay on why they want to have a career with the NSA. U.S. citizenship and eligibility to obtain a high-level security clearance are required.

Financial data: Participants receive college tuition for up to 4 years, reimbursement for books and certain fees, a year-round salary, and a housing allowance and travel reimbursement during summer employment if the distance between the agency and school exceeds 75 miles. Following graduation, participants must work for the agency for 1 and a half-times their length of study, usually 5 years. Students who leave agency employment earlier must repay the tuition cost.

Duration: Up to 4 years, followed by employment at the agency for 5 years.

Number awarded: Varies each year.

Deadline: November of each year.

1571 STUDENT ACADEMY AWARDS

Academy of Motion Picture Arts and Sciences
Attn: Academy Foundation
8949 Wilshire Boulevard
Beverly Hills, CA 90211-1972
Phone: (310) 247-3000, ext. 131; Fax: (310) 859-9619
Email: rmiller@oscars.org
Web: www.oscars.org/awards/saa/index.html

Summary: To recognize and reward student filmmakers who have no previous professional experience.

Eligibility: Open to student filmmakers who are enrolled in degree-granting programs at accredited colleges and universities as full-time students and have no previous professional experience. Applicants must submit films that they have completed within the past year as part of a teacher-student relationship within the curricular structure of their institution. There are 4 award categories: alternative, animation, narrative, and documentary. Entries must be submitted in DVD-R format and be no longer than 60 minutes. Selection is based on resourcefulness, originality, entertainment, and production quality, without regard to cost of production or subject matter.

Financial data: Gold, silver, and bronze awards in each category are $5,000, $3,000, and $2,000, respectively.

Duration: The awards are presented annually.

Number awarded: Up to 12 awards may be presented each year: 3 in each of the 4 categories.

Deadline: March of each year.

1572 STUDENT JOURNALIST INVESTIGATIVE REPORTING AWARD

Journalism Education Association
c/o Kansas State University
103 Kedzie Hall
Manhattan, KS 66506-1505
Phone: (785) 532-5532; (866) JEA-5JEA; Fax: (785) 532-5563
Email: jea@spub.ksu.edu
Web: www.jea.org/awards/investigativereport.html

Summary: To recognize and reward high school students who, through the practice of journalism, have made a significant difference in the lives of others.

Eligibility: Open to secondary school students (or teams of students who worked on the same entry) who, through the study and practice of journalism, have made a significant difference in their own life, the lives of others, or the students' school and/or community. Their entry should contain: 1) the article, series of articles, or mass communication media (radio, broadcast, video, etc.) that made the impact; 2) a narrative of at least 250 words explaining why the piece was produced and how the entry impacted the individual, others, the school, and/or the community; and 3) letters from the adviser, a school administrator, and a professional journalist describing the impact of the work. The entry must be original student work and must have been published within 2 years preceding the deadline. The applicant's teacher/adviser must be a member of the Journalism Education Association. In the selection process, the focus is on the impact of the work, not on the author(s).

Financial data: The award is $1,000.

Duration: The competition is held annually.

Number awarded: 1 each year.

Deadline: February of each year.

1573 STUDENT OPPORTUNITY SCHOLARSHIPS FOR ETHNIC MINORITY GROUPS

Presbyterian Church (USA)
Attn: Office of Financial Aid for Studies
100 Witherspoon Street, Room M-052
Louisville, KY 40202-1396
Phone: (502) 569-5224; (888) 728-7228, ext. 5224; Fax: (502) 569-8766
Email: finaid@pcusa.org
Web: www.pcusa.org/financialaid/programs/studentopportunities.htm

Summary: To provide financial assistance to upper-division college students who are Presbyterians, especially those of racial/ethnic minority heritage majoring in designated fields.

Eligibility: Open to members of the Presbyterian Church (USA), especially those from racial/ethnic minority groups (Asian American, African American, Hispanic American, Native American, Alaska Native). Applicants must be able to demonstrate financial need, be entering their junior or senior year of college as full-time students, and have a GPA of 2.5 or higher. Preference is given to applicants who are majoring in the following fields of interest to missions of the church: education, health services and sciences, religious studies, sacred music, social services, and social sciences.

Financial data: Stipends range up to $3,000 per year, depending upon the financial need of the recipient.

Duration: 1 year; may be renewed for up to 3 additional years if the recipient continues to need financial assistance and demonstrates satisfactory academic progress.

Number awarded: Varies each year.

Deadline: June of each year.

1574 SUSAN RICHMAN MUSIC SCHOLARSHIPS

From the Top Music Studio
47 Prospect Street
Midland Park, NJ 07432
Phone: (201) 445-8780
Email: info@fromthetopmusicstudio.com
Web: www.fromthetopmusicstudio.com/scholarship.htm

Summary: To provide financial assistance to high school seniors in New Jersey who plan to major in music at a college in any state.

Eligibility: Open to seniors graduating from high schools in New Jersey and planning to major in music at a college or university in any state. Applicants must submit a letter describing their musical experience, the name of the college or university they plan to attend, and the pieces they plan to perform at an audition.

Financial data: The stipend is $1,000.

Duration: 1 year.

Number awarded: 2 each year: 1 to an instrumentalist and 1 to a vocalist.

Deadline: January of each year.

1575 TADEUSZ SENDZIMIR FUND SCHOLARSHIPS

Connecticut Community Foundation
43 Field Street
Waterbury, CT 06702-1906
Phone: (203) 753-1315; Fax: (203) 756-3054
Email: jcarey@conncf.org
Web: www.conncf.org/scholarships

Summary: To provide financial assistance to Connecticut residents who are interested in studying Polish language, history, or culture in the United States or in Poland.

Eligibility: Open to Connecticut residents currently enrolled or planning to enroll at a 4-year college or university in Poland or the United States. Applicants may be 1) graduate students in Slavic studies with an emphasis on Polish culture; or 2) undergraduates taking courses in Polish language, history, or culture. Preference is given to applicants of Polish descent. Students may also apply to attend a summer school in Poland. Along with their application, they must submit a 2-page essay on how a higher education will help them make a contribution to their community. Selection is based on academic motivation, extracurricular activities, work experience, a letter of recommendation, financial need, and an essay. U.S. citizenship is required.

Financial data: Stipends are $5,000 for academic-year study in the United States or Poland or $3,000 for summer study in Poland.

Duration: 1 year or 1 summer; recipients may reapply, provided they maintain a GPA of 2.5 or higher.

Number awarded: Varies each year.

Deadline: March of each year.

1576 TAG AND LABEL MANUFACTURERS INSTITUTE SCHOLARSHIP GRANTS

Tag and Label Manufacturers Institute, Inc.
40 Shuman Boulevard, Suite 295
Naperville, IL 60563
Phone: (630) 357-9222; (800) 533-8564; Fax: (630) 357-0192
Email: office@tlmi.com
Web: www.tlmi.com/scholarships.php

Summary: To provide financial assistance and work experience to third- and fourth-year college students who are preparing for a career in the tag and label manufacturing industry.

Eligibility: Open to juniors and seniors who are attending school on a full-time basis and preparing for a career in the tag and label manufacturing industry. This includes students majoring in management, production, graphic arts, sales and marketing, and graphic design. Applicants must have a GPA of 3.0 or higher. They must submit references from 3 persons who are not members of their families and a 1-page personal statement describing their financial circumstances, career and/or educational goals, employment experience, and reasons why they should be selected for the award. A personal interview may be required. Selection is based on that statement, academic achievement, demonstrated interest in entering the industry, and an interview.

Financial data: The stipend is $5,000. Funds are sent to the recipient's school and paid in 2 equal installments.

Duration: 1 year; may be renewed for 1 additional year, provided the recipient maintains a GPA of 3.0 or higher.

Number awarded: 6 each year.

Deadline: March of each year.

1577 TCADVANCE SCHOLARSHIP FOR TURKISH AMERICAN STUDENTS

Turkish Coalition of America
1025 Connecticut Avenue, N.W., Suite 1000
Washington, DC 20036
Phone: (202) 370-1399; Fax: (202) 370-1398
Email: info@tc-america.org
Web: www.turkishcoalition.org/scholarship/scholar_tcadvance.html

Summary: To provide financial assistance to Turkish Americans entering or continuing an undergraduate or graduate program in fields related to public affairs.

Eligibility: Open to Turkish Americans who are graduating high school seniors, current undergraduates, or entering or continuing graduate students. Applicants must be enrolled or planning to enroll full-time to work on a degree in law, public policy, public affairs, political science, international relations, communications, journalism, or public relations. They must have a GPA of 3.3 or higher. Along with their application, they must submit an essay of 500 words or less on how they have been able to achieve success both academically and socially, the major obstacles they have faced, how they have been able to overcome those obstacles, and how they plan to contribute to the Turkish American community, to U.S.-Turkey relations, and to Turkey. Selection is based on academic achievement, interest in Turkish American issues as demonstrated by involvement in Turkish American community affairs, and individual leadership qualities conducive to preparing for a career in public affairs, media, or public relations. Financial need is not required, but special consideration is given to applicants who provide information about and prove financial need. Preference is given to students who are admitted to top national universities or liberal arts colleges. U.S. citizenship or permanent resident status is required.

Financial data: The stipend is $5,000 per year.

Duration: 1 year; may be renewed as long as the recipient maintains a GPA of 3.3 or higher.

Number awarded: Varies each year; recently, 12 of these scholarships were awarded.

Deadline: June of each year.

1578 TELACU ARTS AWARD

TELACU Education Foundation
Attn: Scholarship Program
5400 East Olympic Boulevard, Suite 300
Los Angeles, CA 90022
Phone: (323) 721-1655; Fax: (323) 724-3372
Email: info@telacu.com
Web: telacu.com/site/en/home/education/programs/college.html

Summary: To provide financial assistance to Latino students from eligible communities in California, Texas, Illinois, and New York who are interested in studying the arts at designated partner institutions.

Eligibility: Open to Latino students residing in eligible communities in California, Texas, Illinois, and New York. Applicants must 1) be a first-generation college student; 2) be from a low-income family; and 3) have a GPA of 2.5 or higher. They must be enrolled or planning to enroll full-time at a partner institution and major in fine arts, music, dance, drama, or theater. Along with their application, they must submit brief essays on a dream they have, an event or experience in their life that inspired them to prepare for their intended career, how their extracurricular activities are helping them prepare for this career, and how they believe they can contribute to the sponsor's mission. Selection is based on extracurricular involvement demonstrating a commitment to the community and financial need.

Financial data: The stipend is $1,000.

Duration: 1 year; renewable.

Number awarded: 1 each year.

Deadline: March of each year.

1579 TELEVISION NEWS SCHOLARSHIP

National Press Photographers Foundation
3200 Croasdaile Drive, Suite 306
Durham, NC 27705-2586
Phone: (919) 383-7246; (800) 289-6772; Fax: (919) 383-7261
Email: info@nppa.org
Web: www.nppa.org

Summary: To provide financial assistance to photojournalism students interested in a career in television news.

Eligibility: Open to students enrolled at a recognized 4-year college or university that offers courses in television news photojournalism. They must be working on a bachelor's degree as a junior or senior and intending to prepare for a career in television news photojournalism. As part of the selection process, they must submit a videotape containing examples of their work (including up to 3 complete stories with voice narration from their professor or adviser) and a 1-page biographical sketch that includes a personal statement on professional goals. Financial need and academic achievement are also considered.

Financial data: The stipend is $1,000.

Duration: 1 year.

Number awarded: 1 each year.

Deadline: February of each year.

1580 TEXAS ASSOCIATION OF JOURNALISM EDUCATORS SCHOLARSHIPS

Texas Association of Journalism Educators
Attn: Executive Director
P.O. Box 5554
Austin, TX 78763-5554
Phone: (512) 414-7539
Email: moore.rhonda@att.net
Web: taje.org

Summary: To provide financial assistance to high school seniors in Texas who are interested in journalism or journalism education.

Eligibility: Open to college-bound seniors graduating from high schools in Texas. Applicants must be 1) students planning to major in journalism; 2) student editors; 3) students who have made significant contributions to their high school journalism program even though they are not planning to major in journalism in college; or 4) students planning to become journalism teachers. They must have an overall "B" average and their adviser must be a member of the Texas Association of Journalism Educators (TAJE). Along with their application, they must submit a 1-page essay explaining their need and desire to be the recipient of this scholarship.

Financial data: Stipends are $1,500 or $1,000.

Duration: 1 year.

Number awarded: Up to 6 each year: 1 at $1,500 (the Bill Taylor Scholarship) and up to 5 at $1,000.

Deadline: February of each year.

1581 TEXAS BROADCAST EDUCATION FOUNDATION SCHOLARSHIPS

Texas Association of Broadcasters
Attn: Texas Broadcast Education Foundation
502 East 11th Street, Suite 200
Austin, TX 78701-2619
Phone: (512) 322-9944; Fax: (512) 322-0522
Email: tab@tab.org
Web: www.tab.org/scholarships

Summary: To provide financial assistance to undergraduates in Texas who are interested in preparing for a career in broadcasting.

Eligibility: Open to students enrolled in a fully-accredited program of instruction that emphasizes radio or television broadcasting or communications. Either the student or their school must be a member of the Texas Association of Broadcasters. Applicants must have a GPA of 3.0 or higher. Along with their application, they must submit a 3-page essay that covers why they selected broadcasting as their career choice, the specific area of broadcasting that most interests them and why, their first job preference after college, their career goal 10 years after graduation, their eventual career goal, the broadcast activities in which they have participated, how they feel about broadcast advertising and its importance to a station, how they feel about broadcast advertising and its obligation to consumers, the role they think government should play in a broadcast station's operations, how they think broadcasting could better serve society, the radio or television station they respect most, how their college career could improve their value as a broadcaster, and their most rewarding broadcast-related experience. Selection is based on the essay, commitment to broadcasting, extracurricular activities, community involvement, and financial need.

Financial data: The stipend is $2,000.

Duration: 1 year.

Number awarded: 8 each year.

Deadline: May of each year.

1582 TEXAS CONFERENCE FOR WOMEN SCHOLARSHIPS

Texas Conference for Women
Attn: Scholarship Program
98 San Jacinto Boulevard, Suite 1200
Austin, TX 78701
Phone: (866) 375-1785; Fax: (866) 747-2857
Email: info@txconferenceforwomen.org
Web: www.txconferenceforwomen.org/scholarships.htm

Summary: To provide financial assistance to women in Texas interested in studying specified areas at a college in the state.

Eligibility: Open to women who are residents of Texas and enrolled or accepted for enrollment at an institution of higher education in the state as a full- or part-time student. Applicants must be majoring or planning to major in the following 6 categories: the arts, business, education, nursing, mathematics and science, or public service. Along with their application, they must submit a 1,200-word autobiographical essay with information on their financial need, personal challenges they have experienced and how they have overcome or plan to overcome those, their plans for the future, and why they deserve this scholarship. Selection is based on that essay, academic record, volunteer community service, demonstrated leadership and participation in school and community activities, honors, work experience, and unusual personal or family circumstances and/or financial need. Top candidates may be asked to participate in a brief telephone interview.

Financial data: The stipend is $5,000.

Duration: 1 year.

Number awarded: 6 each year: 1 in each category.

Deadline: June of each year.

1583 TEXAS GRIDIRON SCHOLARSHIPS

Society of Professional Journalists–Fort Worth Professional Chapter
c/o Linda Campbell, Scholarships Coordinator
3558 Norfolk Road
Fort Worth, TX 76109
Email: lcampbell@star-telegram.com
Web: www.spjfw.org/pages/Scholarships.html

Summary: To provide financial assistance to students from Texas working on a degree in journalism.

Eligibility: Open to residents of Texas and students attending a college, university, or junior college in the state. Applicants must intend to obtain a degree and work in journalism. They must have a GPA of 2.25 or higher. Along with their application, they must submit a grade transcript, at least 3 work samples (e.g., writing, photography, news art, page design, video tape, audio tape), a 500-word essay on the reasons for choosing journalism as a career, and at least 2 letters of recommendation. Selection is based on ability, financial need, and perceived potential and dedication to a journalism career.

Financial data: Stipends range from $500 to $1,500.

Duration: 1 year.

Number awarded: Varies each year; recently, 13 of these scholarships were awarded.

Deadline: February of each year.

1584 THE CAR OF MY FUTURE STUDENT SCHOLARSHIP PROGRAM

College Planning Network
Attn: Vicki Breithaupt
43 Bentley Place
Port Townsend, WA 98368
Phone: (206) 323-0624
Email: seacpn@collegeplan.org
Web: www.collegeplan.org/cpnow/pnwguide/onlineaps/wsadaonap.htm

Summary: To recognize and reward, with college scholarships, high school seniors in Washington who submit essays or artwork on their vision of the car of the future.

Eligibility: Open to seniors graduating from public or private high schools, as well as home-schooled students, in Washington. Applicants must submit either

1) a 2-page essay explaining how their vision of the car of the future would support the career of their choice, lifestyle, or favorite hobby, and their advertising campaign for the vehicle, including their target purchaser; or 2) a 2-dimensional artwork (e.g., pen, ink, paint, collage) describing their perfect vehicle, along with brief statements on the same topics as students writing essays. All applicants must also submit 2 letters of recommendation, including 1 from a service or charitable organization that describes their community service work. For students entering the essay competition, selection is based on the vision, originality, and quality of the essay (80 points), and the letters of recommendation (20 points). For students entering the artwork competition, selection is based on the vision, originality, and quality of their artwork (50 points), their essays (30 points), and letters of recommendation (20 points).

Financial data: The grand prize is $4,000, first prize $2,500, second prize $2,000, and third prize $1,500. All prizes are in the form of scholarships that may be used at a college or university in any state. Renewals for up to 3 years of undergraduate study for $500 to $1,000 per year are available.

Duration: The competition is held annually.

Number awarded: 4 each year.

Deadline: March of each year.

1585 THE FOUNTAINHEAD ESSAY CONTEST

Ayn Rand Institute
Attn: Essay Contests
2121 Alton Parkway, Suite 250
Irvine, CA 92606-4926
Phone: (949) 222-6550; Fax: (949) 222-6558
Email: essay@aynrand.org
Web: www.aynrand.org/site/PageServer?pagename=education_contests_tf

Summary: To recognize and reward outstanding essays written by high school students on Ayn Rand's novel, *The Fountainhead.*

Eligibility: Open to juniors or seniors in high school. Applicants must submit an essay on questions selected each year from Ayn Rand's novel, *The Fountainhead.* The essay must be between 800 and 1,600 words. Selection is based on style and content. Judges look for writing that is clear, articulate, and logically organized. To win, an essay must demonstrate an outstanding grasp of the philosophical and psychological meaning of the novel.

Financial data: First prize is $10,000; second prizes are $2,000; third prizes are $1,000; finalist prizes are $100; and semifinalist prizes are $50.

Duration: The competition is held annually.

Number awarded: 236 each year: 1 first prize, 5 second prizes, 10 third prizes, 45 finalist prizes, and 175 semifinalist prizes.

Deadline: April of each year.

1586 THE HUMANIST ESSAY CONTEST

American Humanist Association
Attn: The Humanist Essay Contest
1777 T Street, N.W.
Washington, DC 20009-7125
Phone: (202) 238-9088; (800) 837-3792; Fax: (202) 238-9003
Email: contest@theHumanist.org
Web: www.thehumanist.org/essaycontest/essaycontest.html

Summary: To recognize and reward, with funding for additional study, high school students who submit outstanding essay on principles of humanism.

Eligibility: Open to students in grades 9–12 who submit essays of 1,500 to 2,500 words on any subject or field of endeavor that relates to humanism. Essays should be on topics suitable for publication. Selection is based on originality of thought, sense of emotional engagement, clarity and quality of presentation, amount of research evidenced, and future potential of the author.

Financial data: First prize is $1,000 to be used for further study, 3-year membership in the American Humanist Association (AHA), and an invitation to present the essay at the AHA annual conference; second prize is a humanist library and 3-year membership in the AHA; third prize is 3-year membership in the AHA.

Duration: The competition is held annually.

Number awarded: 1 cash prize and 2 other prizes are awarded annually.

Deadline: March of each year.

1587 THEATER AWARDS

Princess Grace Awards
Attn: Executive Director
150 East 58th Street, 25th Floor
New York, NY 10155
Phone: (212) 317-1470; Fax: (212) 317-1473
Email: grants@pgfusa.com
Web: www.pgfusa.com

Summary: To provide financial support to students and professionals interested in acting, directing, and scenic, lighting, sound, and costume design.

Eligibility: Open to actors, directors, or designers (costume, scenic, sound, and lighting). They must be nominated; these nominations must come from the artistic directors of theater companies and the deans and department chairs of professional schools of theater. Grants are available as 1) scholarships for tuition for the last year of professional training at a nonprofit school in the United States; 2) apprenticeships for salary assistance for individual artists who are "learning the trade" under the supervision of a skilled staff person or mentor; and 3) fellowships for salary assistance for individual artists who are "advanced" members of a company and are ready to assume significant production responsibilities on 1 or more mainstage production(s). Professional companies must employ professional artistic and management staff, have been in continuous operation as a professional company for at least 3 years, provide a total of 20 weeks of research and performance for the current and previous 3 years, and have demonstrated the ability to raise public and other private funds. Artists must have been with the company for less than 5 years. All nominees must be U.S. citizens or permanent residents. Individuals may not submit an application independently.

Financial data: Grants range from $5,000 to $25,000.

Duration: Up to 1 year.

Number awarded: Varies each year; recently, 10 of these grants were awarded: 6 as scholarships, 2 as apprenticeships, and 2 as fellowships.

Deadline: March of each year.

1588 THEODORE MAZZA SCHOLARSHIP

UNICO National
Attn: UNICO Foundation, Inc.
271 U.S. Highway 46 West, Suite A-108
Fairfield, NJ 07004
Phone: (973) 808-0035; (800) 877-1492; Fax: (973) 808-0043
Email: unico.national@verizon.net
Web: www.unico.org/foundation.asp

Summary: To provide financial assistance to high school seniors who may be of any nationality but are recommended by an Italian American service organization and are interested in studying the fine arts in college.

Eligibility: Open to high school seniors of any race, creed, or national origin who are planning to attend an accredited college or university and major in the fine arts (e.g., architecture, history of art, music, studio art, theater art). Applicants must have a GPA of 3.0 or higher and be able to demonstrate financial need, participation in extracurricular and community activities, character, and personality. Along with their application, they must submit SAT or ACT test scores and a letter of recommendation from a UNICO chapter in the city or town where they live.

Financial data: The stipend is $1,500 per year.

Duration: 4 years.

Number awarded: 1 each year.

Deadline: April of each year.

1589 THOMAS M. LEMONS SCHOLARSHIP

International Association of Lighting Designers
Attn: Education Trust Fund
The Merchandise Mart, Suite 9-104
200 World Trade Center
Chicago, IL 60654
Phone: (312) 527-3677; Fax: (312) 527-3680
Email: iald@iald.org
Web: www.iald.org/trust/programs.asp?altlink=152

Summary: To provide financial assistance to U.S. citizens working on an undergraduate degree in architectural lighting design.

Eligibility: Open to undergraduates who are pursuing architectural lighting design as a course of study. Applicants must be U.S. citizens enrolled at a college or university in the United States. Along with their application, they must submit 1) a 2-page resume; 2) an official transcript; 3) 2 letters of reference; 4) up to 10 images of their artwork that show their design ability; and 5) a personal statement, up to 2 pages, on their experience with lighting, why they want to study lighting, or why they should receive this scholarship. Selection is based on those submissions; financial need is not considered.

Financial data: The stipend is $4,000.

Duration: 1 year.

Number awarded: 1 each year.

Deadline: February of each year.

1590 THOMAS R. KEATING FEATURE WRITING COMPETITION

Indianapolis Press Club Foundation Inc.
Attn: Scholarship Committee
P.O. Box 40923
Indianapolis, IN 46240-0923
Phone: (317) 701-1130; Fax: (317) 844-5805
Email: info@indypressfoundation.org
Web: www.indypressfoundation.org/52/61.html

Summary: To recognize and reward journalism students in Indiana who submit outstanding entries in a writing competition.

Eligibility: Open to students enrolled at colleges and universities in Indiana. Applicants first submit 3 samples of their writing from which finalists are selected. They are invited to a newsroom in the state where they are given approximately 4 hours to develop a feature story under deadline pressure. Stories are judged the day of the competition and prizes are awarded at a banquet that evening.

Financial data: Prizes vary; recently, the first-place winner received $2,500, second $1,250, and third $750.

Duration: The competition is held annually.

Number awarded: 3 each year.

Deadline: Initial entries must be submitted in October of each year.

1591 TIMOTHY BIGELOW AND PALMER W. BIGELOW, JR. SCHOLARSHIPS

American Nursery and Landscape Association
Attn: Horticultural Research Institute
1000 Vermont Avenue, N.W., Suite 300
Washington, DC 20005-4914
Phone: (202) 741-4852; Fax: (202) 478-7288
Email: hriresearch@anla.org
Web: www.anla.org/research/scholarships/index.htm

Summary: To provide financial support to residents of New England interested in working on an undergraduate or graduate degree in landscape architecture or horticulture.

Eligibility: Open to full-time students enrolled in an accredited landscape or horticulture program in 1) the final year of a 2-year curriculum; 2) the third year of a 4-year curriculum; or 3) a graduate program. Applicants must have a minimum GPA of 2.25 as undergraduates or 3.0 as graduate students. They must be a resident of 1 of the 6 New England states, although attendance at an institution within those states is not required. Preference is given to applicants who plan to work in an aspect of the nursery industry, including a business of their own, and to applicants who demonstrate financial need.

Financial data: The stipend ranges from $2,500 to $3,500.

Duration: 1 year; nonrenewable.

Number awarded: Up to 3 each year.

Deadline: March of each year.

1592 TOCA PUBLISHERS SCHOLARSHIP PROGRAM

Turf and Ornamental Communicators Association
120 West Main Street, Suite 200
P.O. Box 156
New Prague, MN 56071
Phone: (952) 758-6340; Fax: (952) 758-5813
Email: toca@gardnerandgardnercommunications.com
Web: www.toca.org/awards.html

Summary: To provide financial assistance to undergraduate students preparing for a career in green industry communications.

Eligibility: Open to undergraduate students majoring or minoring in technical communications or in a green industry-related field (e.g., horticulture, plant sciences, botany, agronomy, plant pathology). Applicants must demonstrate an interest in using this course of study in the field of communications. They must have a GPA of 2.5 or higher overall and 3.0 or higher in their major field of study. Along with their application, they must submit 2 academic or professional references, a writing sample (a news article published or prepared for publication), a resume, their transcript, and an essay (500 words or less) that describes how they became interested in the turf and ornamental industry, their communications experience, and their professional goals.

Financial data: The stipend is $2,500. Funds are paid through the bursar's office at the recipient's college or university.

Duration: 1 year.

Number awarded: 1 each year.

Deadline: February of each year.

1593 TOMMY RAMEY SCHOLARSHIP

Tommy Ramey Foundation
Attn: Scholarship Committee
1052 Highland Colony Parkway, Suite 125
Ridgeland, MS 39157
Email: admin@tommyrameyscholarship.org
Web: www.tommyrameyscholarship.org

Summary: To provide financial assistance to college students who reside in Mississippi and are majoring in either 1) marketing or a related field; or 2) culinary arts or a related field.

Eligibility: Open to Mississippi residents who are full-time students at an accredited postsecondary institution in any state, have at least a 2.5 GPA, and are enrolled in either 1) marketing or a related field (business, advertising, communications, public relations, journalism, graphic design); or 2) culinary arts or a related field (travel or tourism, hotel or restaurant management, food production). Applicants must submit a list of student activities and a 500-word essay on either "My favorite TV commercial" (marketing students) or "My favorite meal" (culinary students). Selection is based more on personal merit than on academic record; financial need is not considered in the selection process.

Financial data: The stipend is either $5,000 or $2,500.

Duration: 1 year.

Number awarded: Up to 4 each year: either 1 at $5,000 or 2 at $2,500 for marketing students and either 1 at $5,000 or 2 at $2,500 for culinary students.

Deadline: October of each year.

1594 TONY TORRICE PROFESSIONAL DEVELOPMENT GRANT

International Furnishings and Design Association
Attn: IFDA Educational Foundation
150 South Warner Road, Suite 156
King of Prussia, PA 19406
Phone: (610) 535-6422; Fax: (610) 535-6423
Email: info@ifda.com
Web: www.ifdaef.org/grants.html

Summary: To provide funding to professionals working in the interior furnishing industry who are interested in advancing their career through independent or academic study.

Eligibility: Open to professionals working in the interior furnishing industry in the areas of design, marketing, education, writing and publishing, retailing, or manufacturing. Applicants must be interested in advancing their professional development and career through independent or academic study. Along with their application, they must submit an essay of 300 to 500 words explaining their reasons for wanting to pursue independent or academic study, how they will use the grant funds (a budget), and why they believe they are deserving of the award.

Financial data: The grant is $1,000.

Duration: 1 year.

Number awarded: 1 each year.

Deadline: June of each year.

1595 TOWN OF WILLISTON HISTORICAL SOCIETY SCHOLARSHIP

Vermont Student Assistance Corporation
Attn: Scholarship Programs
10 East Allen Street
P.O. Box 2000
Winooski, VT 05404-2601
Phone: (802) 654-3798; (888) 253-4819; Fax: (802) 654-3765; TDD: (800) 281-3341 (within VT)
Email: info@vsac.org
Web: services.vsac.org/wps/wcm/connect/vsac/VSAC

Summary: To provide financial assistance to residents of Vermont who are working on an undergraduate degree in history.

Eligibility: Open to residents of Vermont enrolled at an accredited postsecondary school. Applicants must be working on a bachelor's degree in history. Along with their application, they must submit 1) a 100-word essay on their interest in and commitment to pursuing their chosen career or vocation; 2) a 250-word essay on their short- and long-term academic, educational, career, vocational, and/or employment goals; and 3) a 250-word essay on what they believe distinguishes their application from others that may be submitted. Selection is based on those essays.

Financial data: The stipend is $1,000.

Duration: 1 year; nonrenewable.

Number awarded: 1 each year.

Deadline: March of each year.

1596 TRINITY VALLEY QUILTERS' GUILD FINE ARTS SCHOLARSHIP

Trinity Valley Quilters' Guild
Attn: Scholarship Committee
P.O. Box 122658
Fort Worth, TX 76121-2658
Phone: (817) 673-2106
Email: kapasitx@yahoo.com
Web: www.tvqg.org

Summary: To provide financial assistance to residents of Texas who are working on a bachelor's degree in fine arts at a college in the state.

Eligibility: Open to residents of Texas who are currently enrolled as undergraduates at a college or university in the state. Applicants must be working on a bachelor's degree in fine arts and have a GPA of at least 2.5 overall and 3.0 in their major. Along with their application, they must submit a 1-page letter describing an overall view of their field of study and the primary reason for applying for this scholarship. Selection is based on financial need and merit.

Financial data: The stipend is $2,500. Funds are sent directly to the recipient's institution.

Duration: 1 year.

Number awarded: 1 each year.

Deadline: June of each year.

1597 TWO-YEAR COLLEGE AND TECHNICAL SCHOOL SCHOLARSHIP PROGRAM

Tag and Label Manufacturers Institute, Inc.
40 Shuman Boulevard, Suite 295
Naperville, IL 60563
Phone: (630) 357-9222; (800) 533-8564; Fax: (630) 357-0192
Email: office@tlmi.com
Web: www.tlmi.com/scholarships.php

Summary: To provide financial assistance and work experience to students at 2-year and technical colleges who are preparing for a career in the tag and label manufacturing industry.

Eligibility: Open to students enrolled full-time in a flexographic printing program at a 2-year college or a technical school that grants degrees and preparing for a career in the tag and label manufacturing industry. Applicants must have a GPA of 3.0 or higher. Along with their application, they must submit a 1-page personal statement describing their financial circumstances, career and/or educational goals, employment experience, and reasons why they should be selected for the award. Selection is based on that statement, academic achievement, and demonstrated interest in entering the industry.

Financial data: The stipend is $1,000. Funds are sent to the recipient's school and paid in 2 equal installments.

Duration: 1 year.

Number awarded: 4 each year.

Deadline: March of each year.

1598 UNDERGRADUATES EXPLORING MINISTRY PROGRAM

The Fund for Theological Education, Inc.
Attn: Partnership for Excellence
825 Houston Mill Road, Suite 250
Atlanta, GA 30329
Phone: (404) 727-1450; Fax: (404) 727-1490
Email: fte@thefund.org
Web: www.thefund.org/programs/undergrads_fellowships.phtml

Summary: To provide financial assistance to undergraduate students who are considering the ministry as a career.

Eligibility: Open to rising juniors and seniors in accredited undergraduate programs at North American colleges and universities. Applicants must be considering ministry as a career. They must be nominated by a college faculty member, administrator, campus minister or chaplain, or current pastor. Nominees must demonstrate a GPA of 3.0 or higher, a love of God and church, imagination, creativity, compassion, a capacity for critical thinking, leadership skills, personal integrity, spiritual depth, dedication to a faith tradition, and an ability to understand and to serve the needs of others. U.S. or Canadian citizenship is required.

Financial data: The stipend is $2,000.

Duration: 1 year.

Number awarded: Up to 50 each year.

Deadline: Nominations must be submitted by January of each year.

1599 UNITED METHODIST GENERAL SCHOLARSHIP PROGRAM

Summary: To provide financial assistance to undergraduate and graduate students who are members of United Methodist Church congregations.

See Listing #1012.

1600 UNITED MUSLIM ASSOCIATION OF TOLEDO SCHOLARSHIP

Toledo Community Foundation, Inc.
Attn: Communications and Scholarship Officer
300 Madison Avenue, Suite 1300
Toledo, OH 43604-1583
Phone: (419) 241-5049; Fax: (419) 242-5549
Email: Joanne@toldeocf.org
Web: www.toledocf.org/main/scholarships

Summary: To provide financial assistance to Muslims, especially residents of southeastern Michigan and northwestern Ohio, who are interested in working on an undergraduate or graduate degree in journalism.

Eligibility: Open to U.S. citizens of the Islamic faith. Applicants must be working or planning to work full-time on an undergraduate or graduate degree in journalism or a related field. Along with their application, they must submit a 150-word essay on either 1) their most important achievements that they believe qualify them for this scholarship; or 2) their career goals and how their studies in the field of journalism will contribute to those goals. Selection is based on scholastic aptitude, academic achievement, and financial need. Priority consideration is given to applicants who have graduated from high schools in southeastern Michigan or northwestern Ohio.

Financial data: The stipend is $1,000.

Duration: 1 year; recipients may reapply.

Number awarded: 1 each year.

Deadline: February of each year.

1601 UNIVERSITY SALES SCHOLARSHIP

University Sales Education Foundation
3123 Research Boulevard, Suite 250
Dayton, OH 45420
Phone: (800) 776-4436
Email: martyholmes@saleseducationfoundation.org
Web: www.saleseducationfoundation.org

Summary: To provide financial assistance to university students taking classes in sales.

Eligibility: Open to students taking sales classes at the university level. Applicants must submit 250-word essays on 1) themselves; 2) either an experience in which they changed someone's mind or a person who has had a significant influence on them; and 3) either their vision of the media landscape in 2020 or an advertising campaign that sticks out to them and why. Financial need is not considered in the selection process.

Financial data: The stipend is $3,000.

Duration: 1 year.

Number awarded: 3 each year.

Deadline: June of each year.

1602 UPPER MIDWEST CHAPTER NATAS SCHOLARSHIPS

National Academy of Television Arts & Sciences–Upper Midwest Chapter
Attn: Scholarship Committee
4967 Kensington Gate
Shorewood, MN 55331
Phone: (952) 474-7126; Fax: (952) 474-7370
Email: info@midwestemmys.org
Web: midwestemmys.org/category/scholarship-recipients

Summary: To provide financial assistance to high school seniors in selected midwestern states who are planning to attend college in any state to major in a field related to television.

Eligibility: Open to seniors graduating from high schools in Iowa, Minnesota, North Dakota, South Dakota, or western Wisconsin. Applicants must be planning to attend a 4-year college or university in any state to prepare for a career in broadcasting, television, or electronic media. They should have, but are not required to have, a GPA of 3.0 or higher. Along with their application, they must submit an essay on how television can stay relevant as a source of news, information, and entertainment in the era of YouTube, MySpace, blogs, and mobile devices. Financial need is not considered in the selection process.

Financial data: The stipend is $2,000. Funds are issued directly to the recipient's college or university to be used for tuition and fees.
Duration: 1 year.
Number awarded: Varies each year; recently, 4 of these scholarships were awarded.
Deadline: February of each year.

1603 VERMONT AIWF CULINARY SCHOLARSHIP

Vermont Student Assistance Corporation
Attn: Scholarship Programs
10 East Allen Street
P.O. Box 2000
Winooski, VT 05404-2601
Phone: (802) 654-3798; (888) 253-4819; Fax: (802) 654-3765; TDD: (800) 281-3341 (within VT)
Email: info@vsac.org
Web: services.vsac.org/wps/wcm/connect/vsac/VSAC
Summary: To provide financial assistance to residents of Vermont who plan to study culinary arts at a school in any state.
Eligibility: Open to the residents of Vermont who are seniors in high school, high school graduates, or currently enrolled in college. Applicants must be working or planning to work on a degree in culinary arts in any state. Along with their application, they must submit 100-word essays on 1) their interest in and commitment to pursuing their chosen career or vocation; and 2) any significant barriers that limit their access to education. Selection is based on those essays, financial need, academic achievement, a letter of recommendation, and a personal interview.
Financial data: The stipend is $2,500.
Duration: 1 year; recipients may reapply.
Number awarded: 1 each year.
Deadline: March of each year.

1604 VIDEO CONTEST FOR COLLEGE STUDENTS

The Christophers
Attn: Youth Department Coordinator
5 Hanover Square, 11th Floor
New York, NY 10004
Phone: (212) 759-4050; (888) 298-4050; Fax: (212) 838-5073
Email: youth@christophers.org
Web: www.christophers.org/Page.aspx?pid=273
Summary: To recognize and reward videos produced by undergraduate and graduate students that best illustrate the motto of The Christophers, "It's better to light one candle than to curse the darkness."
Eligibility: Open to currently-enrolled undergraduate and graduate students. They are invited to submit films or videos on the theme: "One Person Can Make a Difference." They may use any style or format to express this theme in 5 minutes or less. Entries may be created using film or video, but they must be submitted as region 1 or regionless DVDs or on standard, full-sized VHS in NTSC format. Selection is based on overall impact, effectiveness in conveying the theme, artistic merit, and technical proficiency.
Financial data: First prize is $2,000, second $1,000, third $500, and honorable mentions $100.
Number awarded: 8 each year: 1 each for first, second, and third place plus 5 honorable mentions.
Deadline: June of each year.

1605 VIRGINIA SPJ/SDX EDUCATIONAL FOUNDATION SCHOLARSHIP

Society of Professional Journalists–Virginia Professional Chapter
c/o Brian Eckert, Scholarship Committee Coordinator
University of Richmond
Media and Public Relations Office
Maryland Hall, Suite 100
Richmond, VA 23173
Phone: (804) 287-6659
Email: beckert@richmond.edu
Web: spjchapters.org/virginia
Summary: To provide financial assistance to upper-division students from any state at colleges and universities in Virginia who are preparing for a career in journalism.
Eligibility: Open to residents of any state entering their junior or senior year at a college or university in Virginia. Applicants are not required to be journalism majors, but they must be able to demonstrate an intent to prepare for a journalism career in print, broadcast, or new media. Along with their application, they must submit a 2-page personal biography, an explanation of why they believe they are suited for a journalism career, 3 letters of recommendation, a resume, from 3 to 6 samples of their original journalism work that has been published or broadcast anywhere, and information on their financial need.
Financial data: The stipend is $2,000.
Duration: 1 year.
Number awarded: 2 each year.
Deadline: March.

1606 VOICE OF DEMOCRACY SCHOLARSHIP PROGRAM

Veterans of Foreign Wars of the United States
VFW Building
406 West 34th Street
Kansas City, MO 64111
Phone: (816) 968-1117; Fax: (816) 968-1149
Email: KHarmer@vfw.org
Web: www.vfw.org/index.cfm?fa=cmty.leveld&did=150
Summary: To recognize and reward, with college scholarships, outstanding high school students in a national broadcast scriptwriting competition dealing with freedom and democracy.
Eligibility: Open to students in grades 9–12 at high schools and home schools in the United States, its territories and possessions, and U.S. military and civilian dependent overseas schools. Contestants prepare a script, from 3 to 5 minutes in length, on a topic chosen annually but related to freedom and democracy; a recent theme was "Does My Generation Have a Role in America's Future?" Students record the script themselves on audiocassette and submit it for sponsorship by a local post or auxiliary of the Veterans of Foreign Wars (VFW). Scripts must reflect the entrant's own original thinking. Selection is based on delivery (35 points), content (35 points), and originality (30 points).
Financial data: A total of $149,000 in national scholarships is awarded each year; first place is $30,000, second $16,000, third $10,000, and fourth $7,000. Other state winners receive scholarships that may vary each year but range from $1,000 to $5,000. Winners in each state also receive an all-expense-paid trip to Washington, D.C. for the national competition.
Duration: The competition is held annually.
Number awarded: Recently, a total of 54 of these scholarships were awarded. In addition to the 4 top winners, other scholarships included 2 at $5,000, 1 at $4,000, 1 at $3,500, 2 at $3,000, 2 at $2,500, 12 at $2,000, 7 at $1,500, and 23 at $1,000.
Deadline: October of each year.

1607 VSA ARTS INTERNATIONAL YOUNG SOLOISTS AWARD

VSA arts
Attn: Education Office
818 Connecticut Avenue, N.W., Suite 600
Washington, DC 20006
Phone: (202) 628-2800; (800) 933-8721; Fax: (202) 429-0868; TDD: (202) 737-0645
Email: soloists@vsarts.org
Web: www.vsarts.org/x22.xml
Summary: To recognize and reward young musicians from any country who are physically or mentally challenged.
Eligibility: Open to vocalists or instrumentalists under 25 years of age (or under 30 if from outside the United States) who have a disability. Musical ensembles of 2 to 8 performers are also eligible. Applicants may be performers in any type of music, including country, classical, jazz, rap, rock, bluegrass, or ethnic. They are required to submit an audition tape and a 1-page biography that describes why they should be selected to receive this award. Tapes are evaluated on the basis of technique, tone, intonation, rhythm, and interpretation.
Financial data: The award is $5,000. Funds must be used to assist the recipients' music career.
Duration: The competition is held annually.
Number awarded: 4 each year: 2 from the United States and 2 from other countries.
Deadline: November of each year.

1608 WALFRID KUJALA PICCOLO ARTIST COMPETITION

Chicago Flute Club
c/o Jennifer Reiff, Competition Chair
1635 West Belmont Avenue, Number 205
Chicago, IL 60657

Phone: (630) 670-3375
Email: JJRflute@yahoo.com
Web: www.chicagofluteclub.org/competitions.html
Summary: To recognize and reward outstanding young piccolo players.
Eligibility: Open to piccolo players from any geographical area who are 18 years of age or older. Applicants must submit an audition CD that includes an assigned piece and 2 contrasting pieces of their choice. Based on those CDs, 4 finalists and 1 alternate are selected to appear at the final round performance in Chicago. Their performance there is limited to 20 minutes of playing time. Winners are selected on the basis of those performances.
Financial data: Prizes are $1,500 for first place, $750 for second place, and $500 for third place.
Duration: The competition is held annually.
Number awarded: 3 cash prizes are awarded each year.
Deadline: April of each year.

1609 WALLY WIKOFF SCHOLARSHIP FOR EDITORIAL LEADERSHIP

National Scholastic Press Association
2221 University Avenue, S.E., Suite 121
Minneapolis, MN 55414
Phone: (612) 625-8335; Fax: (612) 626-0720
Email: info@studentpress.org
Web: www.studentpress.org/nspa/contests.html
Summary: To provide financial assistance for college to high school journalists.
Eligibility: Open to high school seniors who have worked on the staff of a student newspaper that is a member of the National Scholastic Press Association (NSPA). Applicants must have a GPA of 3.5 or higher and must submit 3 published editorials and a brief recommendation from the program's adviser.
Financial data: The stipend is $1,000.
Duration: 1 year.
Number awarded: 1 each year.
Deadline: February of each year.

1610 WALSWORTH SCHOLARSHIP

University Interscholastic League
Attn: Interscholastic League Press Conference
1701 Manor Road
P.O. Box 8028
Austin, TX 78713-8028
Phone: (512) 232-4937; Fax: (512) 232-7311
Email: uilacad@uts.cc.utexas.edu
Web: www.uil.utexas.edu/academics/journalism/ilpc_forms.html
Summary: To provide financial assistance to high school seniors in Texas who plan to study communications in college.
Eligibility: Open to seniors graduating from high schools in Texas who have been involved in journalism and plan to continue their education in a communications-related field (major or minor) in college. Applicants must have a GPA of "B" or higher. Along with their application, they must submit a statement on their involvement in journalism while in high school, a list of journalism honors and awards they have received, a description of their college and future plans, a letter of recommendation, and 3 to 5 samples of their work as a journalism student. Financial need is not considered in the selection process.
Financial data: The stipend is $1,000.
Duration: 1 year.
Number awarded: 1 each year.
Deadline: March of each year.

1611 WASHINGTON FASHION GROUP INTERNATIONAL SCHOLARSHIP

Fashion Group International of Washington
c/o Myss Stephens, Scholarship Co-Chair
2206 Herring Creek Drive
Accokeek, MD 20607-3722
Email: missmyss@msn.com
Web: washingtondc.fgi.org/index.php?news=1715
Summary: To provide financial assistance for college or graduate school to residents of Maryland, Virginia, and Washington, D.C. interested in preparing for a career in fashion or a fashion-related field at a school in any state.
Eligibility: Open to residents of Washington, D.C. and all cities and counties in Maryland and Virginia. Applicants must be graduating high school seniors or current undergraduate or graduate students enrolled at a college or university in any state in a fashion or fashion-related degree program (e.g., fashion merchandising, fashion journalism, fashion photography, fashion illustration). They must submit a 200-word personal statement on their career goals and motivation for entering a fashion-related career. Selection is based on that statement, academic achievement, creative ability, related work activity (paid or unpaid), extracurricular activities and awards, and 3 letters of reference. Finalists are interviewed and asked to submit a portfolio of their work.
Financial data: The maximum stipend is $5,500.
Duration: 1 year; nonrenewable.
Number awarded: 1 or more each year.
Deadline: May of each year.

1612 WASHINGTON GRAND CHAPTER EASTERN STAR TRAINING AWARDS FOR RELIGIOUS LEADERSHIP

Order of the Eastern Star–Grand Chapter of Washington
c/o Kay Schroeder, ESTARL Committee
1500A East College Way, 466
Mount Vernon, WA 98273
Web: washingtoneos.org/Scholarships.htm
Summary: To provide financial assistance to residents of Washington who are attending college in any state to prepare for a career in Christian service.
Eligibility: Open to residents of Washington currently enrolled at a college or university in any state. Applicants must be preparing for a career in Christian service, including ministry, religious education, mission work, religious music, or youth work. Along with their application, they must submit an essay on their religious philosophy, including their ideas on the need for Christianity in present-day living, how the church can become more effective in the community, and how the church can be made to serve the needs of young people more effectively. Financial need is considered in the selection process.
Financial data: A stipend is awarded (amount not specified).
Duration: 1 year; recipients may reapply.
Number awarded: Varies each year.
Deadline: April of each year.

1613 WASHINGTON POST HIGH SCHOOL WRITING SEMINAR AND SCHOLARSHIP PROGRAM

Washington Post
Attn: Young Journalists Development Program
1150 15th Street, N.W.
Washington, DC 20071
Phone: (202) 334-7132; Fax: (202) 496-3516
Email: knighta@washpost.com
Web: washpost.com/community/education/yjdp/highschool.shtml
Summary: To provide financial assistance to high school seniors in the Washington, D.C. area who are interested in preparing for a career in newspaper journalism.
Eligibility: Open to high school seniors in 19 designated public school systems in the Washington, D.C. area. Applicants must have an interest in a print journalism career and a command of the English language. All students are eligible, but special emphasis is placed on participation by minority students. They must submit a 1-page autobiography and an essay of 250 to 500 words on why they want to be a journalist. From the original applicants, a group is selected to participate in a program of 4 Saturday seminars at *The Washington Post.* During those seminars, conducted by the newspaper's reporters and editors, students produce a newspaper or magazine story. Scholarship winners are selected on the basis of those stories, attendance and participation in the seminars, and financial need.
Financial data: The stipend is $2,500.
Duration: 1 year; nonrenewable.
Number awarded: Recently, 19 students were selected to participate in the seminar. From among those, 2 were chosen to receive scholarships.
Deadline: February of each year.

1614 WASHINGTON POST URBAN JOURNALISM WORKSHOP

Washington Post
Attn: Young Journalists Development Program
1150 15th Street, N.W.
Washington, DC 20071
Phone: (202) 334-7132; Fax: (202) 496-3516
Email: knighta@washpost.com
Web: washpost.com/community/education/yjdp/urban.shtml

Summary: To provide financial assistance to high school students in the Washington D.C. area who are interested in preparing for a career in journalism.

Eligibility: Open to high school seniors in 19 designated public school systems in the Washington, D.C. area. Applicants must have an interest in a journalism career and strong writing skills. The program is not limited to African Americans; all interested students are encouraged to apply. Along with their application, they must submit 1) an autobiography of 200 to 250 words, including what is important to them, why they want to participate in the program, and what they have to share with other students who will participate in the workshop; 2) a 1-page essay on the topic of what makes a good journalist; and 3) a news report based on a set of hypothetical facts. Students who are accepted to the program attend workshops on 8 consecutive Saturdays. They are assigned to 1 of 3 segments: newspaper, radio, or television. Scholarship recipients are selected on the basis of participation in those sessions and their application information.

Financial data: The stipend is $2,500.

Duration: 1 year; nonrenewable.

Number awarded: Recently, 32 students were selected to participate in the workshop. From among those, 3 were chosen to receive scholarships (1 each in the newspaper, radio, and television segments).

Deadline: January of each year.

1615 WASHINGTON STUDENT PHOTOGRAPHER OF THE YEAR AWARD

Professional Photographers of Washington
Attn: Executive Manager
5417 N.E. 200th Place
Lake Forest Park, WA 98155-1813
Phone: (206) 362-3015
Email: ppwoffice@gmail.com
Web: www.ppw.org/aspiring_studentofyear.asp

Summary: To provide financial assistance to high school seniors in Washington who plan to study photography at a school in any state.

Eligibility: Open to seniors graduating from high schools in Washington and planning to attend a college, university, or other postsecondary educational institution in any state. Applicants must submit 1) a portfolio of 4 of their photographic works (in any medium or format); and 2) a 1-page essay on their future plans for their photographic studies and/or degrees, what photography means to them, activities outside school, workshops, awards, and any volunteer work or job duties related to the photographic industry. Financial need is not considered in the selection process.

Financial data: The stipend is $2,000. Funds are paid directly to the recipient's school.

Duration: 1 year.

Number awarded: 1 each year.

Deadline: March of each year.

1616 WAYNE D. CORNILS SCHOLARSHIP

Idaho State Broadcasters Association
270 North 27th Street, Suite B
Boise, ID 83702-4741
Phone: (208) 345-3072; Fax: (208) 343-8946
Email: isba@qwestoffice.net
Web: www.idahobroadcasters.org/scholarships.aspx

Summary: To provide financial assistance to students at Idaho colleges and universities who are preparing for a career in the broadcasting field (including the business side) and can demonstrate financial need.

Eligibility: Open to full-time students at Idaho schools who are preparing for a career in broadcasting, including business administration, sales, journalism, or engineering. Applicants must have a GPA of at least 2.0 for the first 2 years of school or 2.5 for the last 2 years. Along with their application, they must submit a letter of recommendation from the general manager of a broadcasting station that is a member of the Idaho State Broadcasters Association and a 1-page essay describing their career plans and why they want the scholarship. Applications are encouraged from a wide and diverse student population. This scholarship is reserved for a less advantaged applicant.

Financial data: The stipend depends on the need of the recipient.

Duration: 1 year.

Number awarded: 1 each year.

Deadline: March of each year.

1617 WESTERN WASHINGTON CHAPTER JOURNALISM SCHOLARSHIP

Society of Professional Journalists–Western Washington Chapter
c/o Sharon Salyer, Scholarship Chair
The Herald
P.O. Box 930
Everett, WA 98203
Phone: (206) 545-7918
Email: spjscholarships@gmail.com
Web: www.spjwash.org/scholarships

Summary: To provide financial assistance to residents of any state who are majoring in journalism or communications at a college or university in Washington.

Eligibility: Open to undergraduates from any state currently enrolled at a 2- or 4-year college or university in Washington. Applicants are not required to be members of the Society of Professional Journalists (SPJ), but they must be preparing for a journalism career. Along with their application, they must submit a 500-word essay on why they have chosen a journalism career and what they hope to accomplish after graduation, a resume, a letter of recommendation, an official transcript of all college credits, and 3 work samples.

Financial data: The stipend is $2,000.

Duration: 1 year.

Number awarded: 4 each year.

Deadline: March of each year.

1618 WILLIAM B. RUGGLES RIGHT TO WORK SCHOLARSHIP

National Institute for Labor Relations Research
Attn: Scholarship Selection Committee
5211 Port Royal Road, Suite 510
Springfield, VA 22151
Phone: (703) 321-9606; Fax: (703) 321-7342
Email: research@nilrr.org
Web: www.nilrr.org/scholarships

Summary: To provide financial assistance for the undergraduate or graduate education of journalism students who are knowledgeable about the "Right to Work" principle.

Eligibility: Open to undergraduate and graduate students majoring in journalism at institutions of higher learning in the United States. Applicants must demonstrate the potential to complete the educational requirements of the degree program in journalism. Along with their application, they must submit an essay of approximately 500 words demonstrating an understanding of the principles of voluntary unionism and the economic and social problems of compulsory unionism. Selection is based on scholastic ability and a demonstrated interest in the work of the sponsoring organization to promote voluntary unionism.

Financial data: The stipend is $2,000.

Duration: 1 year.

Number awarded: 1 each year.

Deadline: December of each year.

1619 WILLIAM G. SALETIC SCHOLARSHIP

Independent Colleges of Washington
600 Stewart Street, Suite 600
Seattle, WA 98101
Phone: (206) 623-4494; Fax: (206) 625-9621
Email: info@icwashington.org
Web: www.icwashington.org/scholarships/index.html

Summary: To provide financial assistance to upper-division students from any state who are majoring in politics or history at colleges and universities that are members of the Independent Colleges of Washington (ICW).

Eligibility: Open to residents of any state who are completing their sophomore or junior year at ICW-member colleges and universities. Applicants must be studying or majoring in politics or history. They must submit a 1-page essay on why their special interest is in politics and/or history. Students with a GPA of 2.5 or higher are especially encouraged to apply.

Financial data: The stipend is $1,000.

Duration: 1 year; nonrenewable.

Number awarded: 1 each year.

Deadline: March of each year.

1620 WILLIAM P. FRANK PRIZE FOR EXCELLENCE IN COMMUNICATIONS

Delaware Community Foundation
Attn: Executive Vice President
100 West 10th Street, Suite 115
P.O. Box 1636
Wilmington, DE 19899
Phone: (302) 571-8004; Fax: (302) 571-1553
Email: rgentsch@delcf.org
Web: www.delcf.org/scholarships_guidelines.html

Summary: To provide financial assistance for college to high school seniors in Delaware who have been active in journalism and/or communications activities.
Eligibility: Open to Delaware high school seniors who have been active in journalism and/or communications, including school newspapers, magazines, and/or television and radio programs. Each school in the state may nominate 1 student.
Financial data: The stipend is $1,000 per year.
Duration: 1 year; nonrenewable.
Number awarded: 3 each year: 1 in each county of Delaware.
Deadline: February of each year.

1621 WISCONSIN BROADCASTERS ASSOCIATION FOUNDATION COLLEGE/UNIVERSITY STUDENT SCHOLARSHIP PROGRAM

Wisconsin Broadcasters Association
Attn: WBA Foundation
44 East Mifflin Street, Suite 900
Madison, WI 53703-2800
Phone: (608) 255-2600; Fax: (608) 256-3986
Email: contact@wi-broadcasters.org
Web: www.wbafoundation.org/scholarships/scholarships.htm

Summary: To provide financial assistance to students from Wisconsin who are preparing for a career in broadcasting.
Eligibility: Open to upper-division students majoring in broadcasting, communication, or a related field at a 4-year public or private college or university. Applicants must have graduated from a high school in Wisconsin or be attending a college or university in the state. They must be planning a career in radio or television broadcasting. Along with their application, they must submit an official transcript, 2 letters of recommendation, and an essay forecasting what the broadcasting industry will be like in 5 years and how they will contribute to radio or television during that time. Finalists may be asked to participate in a personal interview.
Financial data: The stipend is $2,000 or $1,000.
Duration: 1 year; nonrenewable.
Number awarded: 4 each year: 2 at $2,000 and 2 at $1,000.
Deadline: October of each year.

1622 WOMEN'S MUSIC COMMISSION

Broadcast Music Inc.
Attn: BMI Foundation, Inc.
7 World Trade Center
250 Greenwich Street
New York, NY 10007-0030
Phone: (212) 220-3000
Email: info@bmifoundation.org
Web: www.bmifoundation.org/program/womens_music_commission

Summary: To recognize and reward, with a commission for production of a new work, outstanding young female composers.
Eligibility: Open to women between 20 and 30 years of age who are citizens or permanent residents of the United States. Applicants must submit samples of their original compositions.
Financial data: The winner receives a $5,000 commission to create a new work.
Duration: The competition is held annually.
Number awarded: 1 each year.
Deadline: May of each year.

1623 WORLD WIDE BARACA PHILATHEA UNION SCHOLARSHIP

World Wide Baraca Philathea Union
610 South Harlem Avenue
Freeport, IL 61032-4833

Summary: To provide financial assistance to students preparing for Christian ministry, Christian missionary work, or Christian education.
Eligibility: Open to students enrolled in an accredited college or seminary who are majoring in Christian ministry, Christian missionary work, or Christian education (e.g., church youth pastor, writer of Sunday school curriculum).
Financial data: Stipends are paid directly to the recipient's school upon receipt of the first semester transcript and a letter confirming attendance.
Duration: 1 year; may be renewed.
Deadline: March of each year.

1624 WORLDFEST-HOUSTON STUDENT FILM AWARD

Houston International Film and Video Festival
9898 Bissonnet, Suite 650
P.O. Box 56566
Houston, TX 77256-6566
Phone: (713) 965-9955; (866) 965-9955; Fax: (713) 965-9960
Email: mail@worldfest.org
Web: www.worldfest.org

Summary: To recognize and reward outstanding independent films and videos, including those produced by students.
Eligibility: Open to independent filmmakers from any country. For the student film and video category, there are 5 sub-categories: graduate level productions, college level productions, high school level productions, middle and grade school (14 years of age and younger) productions, and student level screenplays. All films and videos must have been completed during the preceding 3 years. Entries must first be submitted on videotape; if a film is chosen to be screened during the festival, the entrant will be notified and a 16mm or 35mm print requested. The film chosen as the best in all of the student subcategories receives this award.
Financial data: The award includes $2,500 worth of Kodak raw film stock. The festival also sends information on all winning entries to the top 100 Hollywood studios, agencies, distributors, and development/production companies, as well as to other film festivals around the world.
Duration: The competition is held annually.
Deadline: The early deadline is in November of each year. The regular deadline is in December of each year. The late deadline is in January of each year.

1625 WORLDSTUDIO AIGA SCHOLARSHIPS

Worldstudio Foundation
Attn: Scholarships
164 Fifth Avenue
New York, NY 10010
Phone: (212) 807-1990; Fax: (212) 807-1799
Email: scholarship@aiga.org
Web: scholarships.worldstudioinc.com/worldstudio-foundation

Summary: To provide financial assistance to incoming and continuing undergraduate and graduate students, especially minorities, who wish to study fine or commercial arts, design, or architecture.
Eligibility: Open to undergraduate and graduate students who are currently enrolled or planning to enroll at an accredited college or university and major in 1 of the following areas: advertising (art direction only), animation, architecture, cartooning, crafts, environmental graphics, fashion design, film/video (direction or cinematography only), film/theater design (including set and costume design), fine arts, furniture design, graphic design, illustration, industrial/product design, interactive design, interior architecture, interior design, landscape architecture, motion graphics, photography, surface/textile design, or urban planning. Although not required, minority status is a significant factor in the selection process. U.S. citizenship or permanent resident status is required. Applicants must have a GPA of 2.0 or higher. Along with their application, they must submit a 600-word statement of purpose that includes a brief autobiography, an explanation of how their experiences have influenced their creative work and/or their career plans, and how they see themselves contributing to the community at large in the future. Selection is based on that statement, the quality of submitted work, financial need, minority status, recommendations, and academic record.
Financial data: Basic stipends range from $2,000 to $3,000, but awards up to $5,000 are also presented at the discretion of the jury. Honorable mentions are $500. Funds are paid directly to the recipient's school.
Duration: 1 academic year. Recipients may reapply.
Number awarded: Varies each year; recently, 22 scholarships and 9 honorable mentions were awarded.
Deadline: April of each year.

1626 WVHTA EDUCATIONAL FOUNDATION "CO-BRANDED" SCHOLARSHIP

West Virginia Hospitality and Travel Association
Attn: WVHTA Educational Foundation
P.O. Box 2391
Charleston, WV 25328-2391
Phone: (304) 342-6511; Fax: (304) 345-1538
Email: edfdn@wvhta.com
Web: www.wvhta.com/education-foundation.html

Summary: To provide financial assistance to high school seniors in West Virginia who are planning to enroll in a culinary or hospitality degree program in college.

Eligibility: Open to seniors graduating from high schools in West Virginia who have a GPA of 2.75 or higher. Applicants must have completed the ProStart program and have at least 250 hours of work experience related to the hospitality and travel industry. They must have applied to a culinary or hospitality degree program at a postsecondary institution anywhere in the country. Along with their application, they must submit an essay, from 250 to 350 words in length, on the experience that most influenced their decision to prepare for a career in hospitality, travel, and recreation management. Selection is based on the essay, academic performance, industry-related work experience, letters of recommendation, and presentation of the application.

Financial data: The stipend is $2,000.

Duration: 1 year.

Number awarded: 1 or more each year.

Deadline: March of each year.

1627 YOUBET.COM/TURF WRITERS' JOURNALISM SCHOLARSHIP

Race for Education
Attn: Student Services Manager
1818 Versailles Road
P.O. Box 11355
Lexington, KY 40575
Phone: (859) 252-8648; Fax: (859) 252-8030
Email: info@racingscholarships.com
Web: www.racingscholarships.com/page.php?page=programs

Summary: To provide financial assistance to undergraduate and graduate journalism students interested in covering the horse racing industry.

Eligibility: Open to undergraduate and graduate students with a major or minor in journalism at an accredited college or university in the United States. Applicants must be able to demonstrate the potential to make a contribution to the horse racing industry. They must have a GPA of 3.0 or higher. Along with their application, they must submit a 500-word essay on either why they decided to study journalism or the greatest obstacle the horse racing industry faces today and how it can be fixed. Financial need is also considered in the selection process.

Financial data: The stipend is $10,000 per year.

Duration: 1 year; may be renewed up to 3 additional years, provided the recipient maintains a GPA of 3.0 or higher.

Number awarded: 1 each year.

Deadline: March of each year.

1628 YOUNG AMERICAN CREATIVE PATRIOTIC ART AWARDS

Ladies Auxiliary to the Veterans of Foreign Wars
c/o National Headquarters
406 West 34th Street
Kansas City, MO 64111
Phone: (816) 561-8655; Fax: (816) 931-4753
Email: info@ladiesauxvfw.org
Web: www.ladiesauxvfw.org/html/scholarships.html

Summary: To recognize and reward high school students who submit outstanding works of art on patriotic themes.

Eligibility: Open to students in grades 9–12 at high schools in the United States. Home-schooled students are eligible; foreign exchange students are not. Entrants may submit art on paper or canvas using water color, pencil, pastel, charcoal, tempera, crayon, acrylic, pen-and-ink, or oil. Digital art may be submitted, but it must be on paper or canvas. Competitions are held in individual Veterans of Foreign Wars (VFW) Auxiliaries, then at the department level, and finally at the national level. Students must be sponsored by an Auxiliary; they must attend school in the same state as the sponsoring Auxiliary. Entries are judged on the originality of concept, presentation, and patriotism expressed; content, how it relates to patriotism, and clarity of ideas; design technique; total impact of work; and uniqueness.

Financial data: National awards are $10,000 for first prize, $5,000 for second, $2,500 for third, $1,500 for fourth, and $500 for fifth through eighth. Funds must be used for continued art education or for art supplies.

Number awarded: 8 national winners are selected each year.

Deadline: March of each year.

1629 YOUNG SOLOISTS' COMPETITION COLLEGE DIVISION

National Symphony Orchestra
Attn: Young Soloists' Competition
2700 F Street, N.W.
Washington, DC 20566
Phone: (202) 416-8820; (800) 444-1324; Fax: (202) 416-8853
Web: www.kennedy-center.org/nso/nsoed/youngsoloists.cfm

Summary: To recognize and reward outstanding college student performers in a musical competition in the Washington, D.C. area.

Eligibility: Open to high school graduates who are either 1) studying music in Delaware, the District of Columbia, Maryland, Virginia, or West Virginia; or 2) residents of metropolitan Washington (defined as the District of Columbia, the Maryland counties of Frederick, Montgomery, and Prince George's, the Virginia counties of Arlington, Fairfax, Loudoun, and Prince William, and the Virginia cities of Alexandria and Falls Church) currently studying elsewhere. Pianists and instrumentalists must be younger than 23 years of age and may not have completed an undergraduate degree. Singers must be younger than 26 years of age and may not have completed a doctorate. Former winners of this competition (either in the high school or college division) and performers under professional management are ineligible.

Financial data: The Bill Cerri Scholarship of $1,000, provided by WETA-FM90.9, is presented to 1 winner selected by the judges. All winners perform in a concert with the National Symphony Orchestra.

Duration: The competition is held annually.

Number awarded: 1 each year.

Deadline: January of each year.

1630 YOUNG SOLOISTS' COMPETITION HIGH SCHOOL DIVISION

National Symphony Orchestra
Attn: Young Soloists' Competition
2700 F Street, N.W.
Washington, DC 20566
Phone: (202) 416-8820; (800) 444-1324; Fax: (202) 416-8853
Web: www.kennedy-center.org/nso/nsoed/youngsoloists.cfm

Summary: To recognize and reward outstanding high school student performers in a musical competition in the Washington, D.C. area.

Eligibility: Open to students in grades 10–12 who are residents of metropolitan Washington or studying with an instrumental teacher in metropolitan Washington, defined as the District of Columbia, the Maryland counties of Frederick, Montgomery, and Prince George's, the Virginia counties of Arlington, Fairfax, Loudoun, and Prince William, and the Virginia cities of Alexandria and Falls Church. Former winners and performers under professional management are not eligible. Competitions are held in piano and instrumental.

Financial data: The Bill Cerri Scholarship of $1,000, provided by WETA-FM90.9, is presented to 1 winner selected by the judges. All winners perform in a concert with the National Symphony Orchestra.

Duration: The competition is held annually.

Number awarded: 1 each year.

Deadline: January of each year.

1631 YOUNGARTS COMPETITION AWARDS

National Foundation for Advancement in the Arts
Attn: YoungArts Program
444 Brickell Avenue, Suite 370
Miami, FL 33131
Phone: (305) 377-1140; (800) 970-ARTS; Fax: (305) 377-1149
Email: info@YoungArts.org
Web: www.youngarts.org/Programs/YoungArts%20Program

Summary: To recognize and reward outstanding high school students in the arts.

Eligibility: Open to U.S. citizens and permanent residents who are graduating high school seniors, or, if not enrolled in high school, are 17 or 18 years old. Applicants may enter competitions in cinematic arts, dance, jazz, music, photography, theater, visual arts, voice, or writing by submitting samples of their work as videotapes, DVDs, or portfolios. On the basis of the tapes or portfolios, award winners are invited to Miami for the final competitions.

Financial data: The gold award is $10,000, silver awards are $5,000, first level awards are $3,000 each, second level $1,500, and third level $1,000. Honorable mentions are $250 and merit awards are $100, but those winners are not invited to Miami.

Duration: The competition is held annually.

Number awarded: Up to 135 award candidates compete in Miami (5 in cinematic arts, 20 in dance, 20 in music, 5 in jazz, 5 in photography, 20 in theater, 25 in visual arts, 15 in voice, and 20 in writing); an unlimited number of honorable mention and merit awards are made to candidates who are not invited to Miami.

Deadline: October of each year.

1632 YOUTH COLLEGE ESSAY COMPETITION

Freedom from Religion Foundation
P.O. Box 750
Madison, WI 53701
Phone: (608) 256-8900; Fax: (608) 204-0422
Email: dbarker@ffrf.org
Web: www.ffrf.org/outreach/student-essay-contests

Summary: To recognize and reward outstanding college student essays on the separation of church and state.

Eligibility: Open to undergraduate students under 25 years of age currently enrolled at colleges and universities in North America. Applicants write an essay on topics that change annually but involve rejecting religion; recent topics were "Why I Reject Religion," "Growing Up a Freethinker," or "Why I Am an Atheist/Agnostic/Unbeliever." They may write about their own experiences in rejecting religion in a religious society or use a philosophical or historical approach. Essays should be from 1,400 to 1,600 words, accompanied by a paragraph biography identifying the student's college or university, year in school, major, and interests.

Financial data: First prize is $2,000, second $1,000, third $500, and honorable mentions $200.

Duration: The competition is held annually.

Number awarded: 3 prizes and a varying number of honorable mentions are awarded each year.

Deadline: June of each year.

1633 YOUTH FREE EXPRESSION PROJECT FILM CONTEST

National Coalition Against Censorship
Attn: Film Contest
275 Seventh Avenue, Suite 1504
New York, NY 10001
Phone: (212) 807-6222, ext. 17; Fax: (212) 807-6245
Email: yfen@ncac.org
Web: www.ncac.org/film-contest

Summary: To recognize and reward young filmmakers who create films on a topic related to free speech and democracy.

Eligibility: Open to U.S. residents (citizenship is not required) who are younger than 19 years of age. Applicants are invited to create a video in any category (e.g., documentary, animation, experimental, satire, fictional narrative) on a topic that changes annually but relates to freedom of expression; a recent topic was "I'm All for Free Speech, BUT" The video should be up to 4 minutes in length and submitted online (preferably) or in VHS or DVD format. It must be accompanied by a 250-word report that explains the intent in making the video, the creative process, and technical accomplishments. Selection is based on the video's content, artistic and technical merit, and creativity.

Financial data: First prize is $1,000, second $500, and third $250. All winners are invited to an all-expense-paid trip to New York City for the award ceremony.

Duration: The competition is held annually.

Number awarded: 3 each year.

Deadline: October of each year.

1634 YVAR MIKHASHOFF PIANIST/COMPOSER COMMISSIONING PROJECT

Yvar Mikhashoff Trust for New Music
152 Russell Street
Buffalo, NY 14214
Phone: (716) 474-1635
Email: info@mikhashofftrust.org
Web: www.mikhashofftrust.org

Summary: To recognize and reward young composers and pianists who collaborate on the performance of new works.

Eligibility: Open to teams consisting of a composer and a pianist, each of whom must be younger than 34 years of age. The composer must create a new work for piano solo (with or without electronics) of at least 12 minutes in duration; the pianist must perform the work. Pianists who are composers may not apply to commission themselves. Pianists may not apply to commission a work that is already in progress or has been publicly presented either in part or whole. Composers must submit a 1-page biography, a representative list of works and performances, a signed letter of commitment to the project, and a CD with 3 recent compositions. Pianists must submit a 1-page biography, a list of solo piano pieces and concertos in their repertoire composed since 1950, a demonstration CD with performances of a total of 3 pieces chosen from the repertoire list, copies of 3 programs of past solo piano recitals with at least 50% of the music composed since 1950, a CD or DVD documenting 1 of those recital programs, and a proposal for the premiere of the commissioned piece, including a letter of agreement with the presenting organization for a concert. The application for the competition must be submitted jointly by the pianist and composer.

Financial data: Each award is $3,000.

Duration: The competition is held annually.

Number awarded: 2 each year: 1 composer and 1 pianist.

Deadline: November of each year.

Sciences

1635 AAAS EDUCATIONAL FOUNDATION SCHOLARSHIPS

Automotive Aftermarket Association Southeast
Attn: AAAS Educational Foundation
11245 Chantilly Parkway Court
Montgomery, AL 36117-7585
Phone: (334) 834-1848; (800) 239-7779; Fax: (334) 834-1818
Email: kay@aaas.us
Web: www.aaas.us/benefitDetails.php?id=17

Summary: To provide financial assistance to residents of designated southeastern states interested in attending college or technical school in any state to prepare for a career in the automotive aftermarket industry.

Eligibility: Open to residents of Alabama, Florida, Georgia, and Mississippi who are graduating high school seniors, recent high school graduates, or holders of a GED certificate. Applicants must be enrolled or planning to enroll full-time at an accredited college, university, technical institute, or automotive technical program certified by the National Automotive Technicians Education Foundation-National Institute for Automotive Service Excellence (NATEF-ASE) in any state. They must be sponsored by a member of the Automotive Aftermarket Association Southeast (AAAS). Priority is given to 1) students planning to work on a degree or certificate in an automotive-related curriculum (e.g., engineering, computer science, accounting, marketing, business); and 2) AAAS members, employees of members, or family of members or employees. Along with their application, they must submit a 250-word essay on their career goals, how this scholarship will help them, and why they are considering a career in the automotive aftermarket. Financial need is not considered in the selection process.

Financial data: A stipend is awarded (amount not specified).

Duration: 1 year; recipients may reapply.

Number awarded: Varies each year; recently, 6 of these scholarships were awarded.

Deadline: March of each year.

1636 AABB-FENWAL SBB SCHOLARSHIP AWARDS

AABB
Attn: Scholarship Coordinator
8101 Glenbrook Road
Bethesda, MD 20814-2749
Phone: (301) 215-6482; Fax: (301) 907-6895
Email: education@aabb.org
Web: www.aabb.org/Content/Programs_and_Services/ps.htm

Summary: To recognize and reward essays by students enrolled in programs accredited by AABB (formerly the American Association of Blood Banks).

Eligibility: Open to students enrolled in an accredited program for the education of Specialists in Blood Banking (SBB). Applicants must submit 1 of the following types of entries: 1) a scientific paper reporting experimental work (the work may be an original concept, extension of a major concept, or application of a procedure in blood substitutes, IV immune globulin, hemophilia, or other transfusion medicine topics); 2) an analytical or interpretational review suitable for publication in a professional journal; or 3) an innovative educational syllabus using traditional or advanced technology modalities. The essays or scientific papers must be less than 3,000 words on a subject pertaining to blood banking or a related field. Scientific papers should describe materials and methods used, including experimental design, in sufficient detail to enable other scientists to evaluate or duplicate the work. Reviews should analyze or interpret the subject and not just restate the literature. Educational entries should include a brief summary covering the need for the program, how the program is innovative, and a list of references. A student may submit more than 1 entry; however, no student may receive more than 1 award.

Financial data: The award is $1,500.

Duration: The competition is held annually.

Number awarded: 1 each year.

Deadline: May of each year.

1637 AACE INTERNATIONAL COMPETITIVE SCHOLARSHIPS

AACE International
Attn: Staff Director-Education
209 Prairie Avenue, Suite 100
Morgantown, WV 26501-5934
Phone: (304) 296-8444; (800) 858-COST; Fax: (304) 291-5728
Email: info@aacei.org
Web: www.aacei.org/education/scholarship

Summary: To provide financial assistance to undergraduate and graduate students in the United States or Canada working on a degree related to total cost management (the effective application of professional and technical expertise to plan and control resources, costs, profitability, and risk).

Eligibility: Open to undergraduate students (second year standing or higher) or graduate students. They must be enrolled full-time in a degree program in the United States or Canada that is related to the field of cost management/cost engineering, including agricultural engineering, architectural engineering, building construction, business administration, chemical engineering, civil engineering, electrical engineering, industrial engineering, manufacturing engineering, mechanical engineering, mining engineering, or quantity surveying. Selection is based on academic performance (35%), extracurricular activities (35%), and an essay (30%) on the value of study in cost engineering or total cost management and why it is important to their academic objectives and career goals.

Financial data: Stipends range from $2,000 to $8,000 per year.

Duration: 1 year.

Number awarded: Varies each year; recently, 21 of these scholarships were awarded.

Deadline: February of each year.

1638 AAPA VETERAN'S CAUCUS SCHOLARSHIPS

American Academy of Physician Assistants–Veterans Caucus
Attn: Veterans Caucus
P.O. Box 362
Danville, PA 17821-0362
Phone: (570) 271-0292; Fax: (570) 271-5850
Email: admin@veteranscaucus.org
Web: www.veteranscaucus.org/displaycommon.cfm?an=1&subarticlenbr=37

Summary: To provide financial assistance to veterans and Reserve component personnel who are studying to become physician assistants.

Eligibility: Open to U.S. citizens who are currently enrolled in a physician assistant program. The program must be approved by the Commission on Accreditation of Allied Health Education. Applicants must be honorably discharged members of a uniformed service of the United States or an active member of the Guard or Reserve of a uniformed service of the United States. Selection is based on military honors and awards received, civic and college honors and awards received, professional memberships and activities, and GPA. An electronic copy of the applicant's DD Form 214 must accompany the application.

Financial data: The stipend is $2,000.

Duration: 1 year.

Number awarded: Varies each year; recently, 11 of these scholarships were awarded.

Deadline: February of each year.

1639 ABAK AGRICULTURE SCHOLARSHIP PROGRAM

AgriBusiness Association of Kentucky
Attn: Scholarship Program
512 Capitol Avenue
Frankfort, KY 40601
Phone: (502) 226-1122; Fax: (502) 875-1595
Email: info@kyagbusiness.org
Web: www.kyagbusiness.org

Summary: To provide financial assistance to Kentucky residents interested in working on an undergraduate degree in agriculture at a college in any state.

Eligibility: Open to residents of Kentucky enrolled or accepted for enrollment as an undergraduate at an institution of higher education in any state. Applicants must have a declared major in an agricultural-related field of study or be accepted into an agricultural study program. They must submit 2 essays of 500 words each: 1) why they decided to major in agriculture and what they plan on doing after graduation; 2) what they think the future holds for agriculture in the United States and the world; and 3) how this scholarship would impact them financially. Selection is based on commitment to agriculture and the quality of the application; financial need is not considered.

Financial data: The stipend is $1,000.

Duration: 1 year; nonrenewable.

Number awarded: 1 or more each year.

Deadline: May of each year.

1640 ABBOTT LABORATORIES/HENAAC SCHOLARS PROGRAM

Great Minds in STEM
Attn: HENAAC Scholars
3900 Whiteside Street
Los Angeles, CA 90063
Phone: (323) 262-0997; Fax: (323) 262-0946
Email: kbbarrera@greatmindsinstem.org
Web: www.greatmindsinstem.org/henaac/scholars

Summary: To provide financial assistance to Hispanic undergraduate students majoring in a field of science, technology, engineering, or mathematics (STEM).

Eligibility: Open to Hispanic students who are working on an undergraduate degree in a field of STEM. Applicants must be of Hispanic origin and/or must significantly participate in and promote organizations and activities in the Hispanic community. They must have a GPA of 3.0 or higher. Along with their application, they must submit a 700-word essay on a topic that changes annually; recently, students were asked to write on how they see their academic major contributing to global efforts and technology and how they, in their field of study, will contribute to global progress as well as actively contribute to their local communities. Selection is based on leadership through academic achievements and campus and community activities; financial need is not considered.

Financial data: Stipends range from $500 to $5,000.

Duration: 1 year; recipients may reapply.

Number awarded: Varies each year; recently, 2 of these scholarships were awarded.

Deadline: April of each year.

1641 ABRAHAM ANSON MEMORIAL SCHOLARSHIP

American Society for Photogrammetry and Remote Sensing
Attn: Scholarship Administrator
5410 Grosvenor Lane, Suite 210
Bethesda, MD 20814-2160
Phone: (301) 493-0290, ext. 101; Fax: (301) 493-0208
Email: scholarships@asprs.org
Web: www.asprs.org/membership/scholar.html

Summary: To provide financial assistance to undergraduate students interested in a program of study to prepare for a career related to geospatial science.

Eligibility: Open to students planning to enroll or currently enrolled as undergraduates at a college or university in the United States. Applicants must be interested in a program of study to prepare for a career in geospatial science or technology, surveying and mapping, photogrammetry, or remote sensing. Along with their application, they must submit a 2-page statement describing their plans for continuing studies towards becoming a professional in a field that uses photogrammetry, remote sensing, surveying and mapping, or land and/or geospatial information science or technology as a key part of its performance. Financial need is not considered in the selection process.

Financial data: The stipend is $1,000. A 1-year student membership in the American Society for Photogrammetry and Remote Sensing (ASPRS) is also provided.

Duration: 1 year.

Number awarded: 1 each year.

Deadline: October of each year.

1642 ACA NSF SCHOLARSHIPS FOR STEM MAJORS

Appalachian College Association
Attn: Director of Fellowships and Scholarships
210 Center Street
Berea, KY 40403
Phone: (859) 986-4584, ext. 1005; Fax: (859) 986-9549
Email: kimg@acaweb.org
Web: www.acaweb.org/programs-services/students/scholarship-funding

Summary: To provide financial assistance to students majoring in natural science, technology, engineering, or mathematics (STEM) disciplines at colleges and universities that are members of the Appalachian College Association (ACA).

Eligibility: Open to full-time students enrolled as sophomores, juniors, or seniors at ACA member institutions. Applicants must be majoring in a STEM discipline, have a GPA of 3.0 or higher, and be able to document financial need. They must be U.S. citizens, documented refugees, or permanent residents. Along with their application, they must submit a 500-word essay describing their career ambitions, their commitment to the Appalachian region, and the potential benefits to Appalachia of their degree choice. Preference is given to graduates of high schools in the Appalachian region.

Financial data: The stipend is $6,000 per year.

Duration: 1 year; may be renewed 1 additional year.

Number awarded: 30 each year.

Deadline: March of each year.

1643 ACCELERATOR APPLICATIONS DIVISION SCHOLARSHIP

American Nuclear Society
Attn: Scholarship Coordinator
555 North Kensington Avenue
La Grange Park, IL 60526-5592
Phone: (708) 352-6611; (800) 323-3044; Fax: (708) 352-0499
Email: outreach@ans.org
Web: www.ans.org/honors/scholarships/aad.html

Summary: To provide financial assistance to undergraduate students who are interested in preparing for a career dealing with accelerator applications aspects of nuclear science or nuclear engineering.

Eligibility: Open to students entering their junior year in physics, engineering, or materials science at an accredited institution in the United States. Applicants must submit a description of their long- and short-term professional objectives, including their research interests related to accelerator aspects of nuclear science and engineering. Selection is based on that statement, faculty recommendations, and academic performance. Special consideration is given to members of underrepresented groups (women and minorities), students who can demonstrate financial need, and applicants who have a record of service to the American Nuclear Society (ANS).

Financial data: The stipend is $1,000 per year.

Duration: 1 year (the junior year); may be renewed for the senior year.

Number awarded: 1 each year.

Deadline: January of each year.

1644 ACCENTURE UNDERGRADUATE SCHOLARSHIPS

American Indian Graduate Center
Attn: Executive Director
4520 Montgomery Boulevard, N.E., Suite 1-B
Albuquerque, NM 87109-1291
Phone: (505) 881-4584; (800) 628-1920; Fax: (505) 884-0427
Email: aigc@aigc.com
Web: www.aigc.com/02scholarships/accenture/accenture.htm

Summary: To provide financial assistance for college to Native American high school seniors interested in majoring in fields of business and technology.

Eligibility: Open to enrolled members of U.S. federally-recognized American Indian tribes and Alaska Native groups who can provide a Certificate of Indian Blood (CIB). Applicants must be entering freshmen at an accredited U.S. college or university, planning to work full-time on a bachelor's degree in engineering, computer science, operations management, finance, marketing, management, or other business-oriented fields. They must have a GPA of 3.0 or higher. Along with their application, they must submit an essay describing their character, personal merit, and commitment to community and American Indian or Alaska Native heritage. Financial need is also considered in the selection process.

Financial data: The stipend is $5,000 per year.

Duration: 4 years.

Number awarded: 3 each year.

Deadline: April of each year.

1645 ACCUWEATHER UNDERGRADUATE SCHOLARSHIP IN METEOROLOGY

National Weather Association
Attn: Executive Director
228 West Millbrook Road
Raleigh, NC 27609-4304
Phone: (919) 845-1546; Fax: (919) 845-2956
Email: exdir@nwas.org
Web: www.nwas.org/committees/ed_comm/application/AccuWeather.php

Summary: To provide financial assistance to undergraduate students working on a degree in operational meteorology.

Eligibility: Open to students who are entering their sophomore or higher year of undergraduate study. Applicants must be working on a degree in operational meteorology (forecasting, broadcasting, consulting). Along with their application, they must submit a 1-page statement explaining why they are applying for this scholarship. Selection is based on that statement, academic achievement, and 2 letters of recommendation.

Financial data: The stipend is $1,000.
Duration: 1 year.
Number awarded: 1 each year.
Deadline: May of each year.

1646 ACEC COLORADO SCHOLARSHIP PROGRAM

American Council of Engineering Companies of Colorado
Attn: Scholarship Coordinator
800 Grant Street, Suite 100
Denver, CO 80203
Phone: (303) 832-2200; Fax: (303) 832-0400
Email: acec@acec-co.org
Web: www.acec-co.org/education/scholarships.html

Summary: To provide financial assistance to students in Colorado currently working on a bachelor's degree in engineering.
Eligibility: Open to full-time students entering their junior, senior, or fifth year of an ABET-approved engineering program in Colorado. Applicants must be U.S. citizens. Along with their application, they must submit a 500-word essay on "What is the role or responsibility of the consulting engineer relative to shaping and protecting the natural environment?" Selection is based on the essay (25 points), cumulative GPA (28 points), work experience (20 points), a letter of recommendation (17 points), and extracurricular college activities (10 points).
Financial data: Stipends range from $1,500 to $6,000.
Duration: 1 year.
Number awarded: Varies each year; recently, 9 of these scholarships were awarded: 1 at $6,000, 1 at $5,000, 1 at $4,000, 1 at $3,500, 4 at $2,000, and 1 at $1,500.
Deadline: February of each year.

1647 ACEC INDIANA SCHOLARSHIP PROGRAM AWARDS

American Council of Engineering Companies of Indiana
Attn: Scholarship Coordinator
55 Monument Circle, Suite 819
Indianapolis, IN 46204
Phone: (317) 637-3563; Fax: (317) 637-9968
Email: staff@acecindiana.org
Web: www.acecindiana.org/content/education.htm

Summary: To provide financial assistance to residents of Indiana currently working on a bachelor's or master's degree in engineering or land surveying at a college or university in the state.
Eligibility: Open to Indiana residents who are working on a bachelor's or master's degree in an ABET-approved engineering program or in an accredited land surveying program. Applicants must be U.S. citizens entering their junior, senior, fifth, or graduate year at a college or university in Indiana. Along with their application, they must submit a 500-word essay on "What is the role or responsibility of the consulting engineer or land surveyor to shaping and protecting the natural environment?" Selection is based on the essay (25 points), cumulative GPA (24 points), work experience (24 points), a letter of recommendation (17 points), and extracurricular college activities (10 points).
Financial data: Recently, a total of $17,500 in scholarships was awarded by this program.
Duration: 1 year.
Number awarded: Varies each year; recently, 6 of these scholarships were awarded.
Deadline: February of each year.

1648 ACEC/MA PRESIDENTS' SCHOLARSHIP

American Council of Engineering Companies of Massachusetts
Attn: Scholarship Committee Chair
c/o The Engineering Center
One Walnut Street
Boston, MA 02108
Phone: (617) 227-5551; Fax: (617) 227-6783
Email: ndowney@engineers.org
Web: www.acecma.org

Summary: To provide financial assistance to residents of Massachusetts or Rhode Island working on an undergraduate degree in engineering or land surveying at a college in any state.
Eligibility: Open to residents of Massachusetts or Rhode Island who are working on a bachelor's degree at an ABET-approved engineering or accredited land surveying program in any state. Preference is given to children of employees of firms that are members of the American Council of Engineering Companies of Massachusetts (ACEC/MA). Applicants must have a GPA of 3.0 or higher. Along with their application, they must submit a 500-word essay on their career goals and why they think they deserve this scholarship. Selection is based on that essay (45%), relevance of course of study, voluntary effort, and extracurricular activities to engineering or land surveying (30%), GPA (15%), and a letter of recommendation (10%).
Financial data: The stipend is $1,500.
Duration: 1 year.
Number awarded: 1 or more each year.
Deadline: May of each year.

1649 ACEC NEW YORK SCHOLARSHIP PROGRAM

American Council of Engineering Companies of New York
Attn: President
6 Airline Drive
Albany, NY 12205-1022
Phone: (518) 452-8611; Fax: (518) 452-1710
Email: acecny@acecny.org
Web: www.acecny.org/scholar.html

Summary: To provide financial assistance to upper-division students in specified fields of engineering at colleges and universities in New York.
Eligibility: Open to students who have completed their junior year (or the fourth year of a 5-year program) at an approved college or university in New York. Applicants must intend to become a consulting engineer and must be majoring in an engineering field that makes up the primary practices of member firms of the American Council of Engineering Companies of New York (ACEC New York): chemical, civil, electrical, environmental, mechanical, structural engineering; surveying; or engineering technology. They must be U.S. citizens or permanent residents who intend to make New York their home and/or career area. Selection is based on work experience (25 points), college activities and recommendations (15 points), a 500-word essay on why they want to prepare for a career in consulting engineering (30 points), and cumulative GPA (30 points).
Financial data: Stipends are $5,000 or $2,500.
Duration: 1 year.
Number awarded: Varies each year; recently, 17 of these scholarships were awarded: 1 at $5,000 and 16 at $2,500. Since the program was established, it has awarded 114 scholarships worth $310,500.
Deadline: December of each year.

1650 ACEC OF MICHIGAN EDUCATION GRANT

American Council of Engineering Companies of Michigan, Inc.
215 North Walnut Street
P.O. Box 19189
Lansing, MI 48901-9189
Phone: (517) 332-2066; Fax: (517) 332-4333
Email: mail@acecmi.org
Web: www.acecmi.org/awards/scholarship.cfm

Summary: To provide financial assistance to undergraduate and graduate students in Michigan who are working on a degree in engineering or surveying.
Eligibility: Open to applicants who are enrolled full- or part-time as a sophomore, junior, senior, or graduate student working on a degree in an ABET-accredited engineering or surveying program in Michigan. They must have worked during the past 24 months for a consulting engineering, surveying, or architectural/engineering firm. Along with their application, they must submit an essay of 500 to 1,000 words on a topic that changes annually but relates to engineering and surveying; recently, applicants were invited to write on proposals to require a master's degree or 30 semester hours of equivalent course work as a prerequisite for professional engineering licensure. Selection is based on the essay, work experience, references, extracurricular and community activities, and GPA. Financial need is not considered in the selection process.
Financial data: A stipend is awarded (amount not specified).
Duration: 1 year; recipients may reapply for 1 more award.
Number awarded: Varies each year; a total of $8,000 is awarded annually.
Deadline: January of each year.

1651 ACIL ACADEMIC SCHOLARSHIPS

American Council of Independent Laboratories
Attn: ACIL Scholarship Alliance
1629 K Street, N.W., Suite 400
Washington, DC 20006-1633
Phone: (202) 887-5872; Fax: (202) 887-0021
Email: info@acil.org

Web: www.acil.org/displaycommon.cfm?an=13
Summary: To provide financial assistance to upper-division and graduate students working on a degree in the natural or physical sciences.
Eligibility: Open to college juniors, seniors, and graduate students majoring in physics, chemistry, engineering, geology, biology, or environmental sciences. Applicants must submit a brief resume or personal statement outlining their activities in college, including their field of study and future plans. Selection is based on academic achievement, career goals, leadership, and financial need. Children and grandchildren of employees of member companies of the American Council of Independent Laboratories (ACIL) who are planning scientific or engineering careers are especially encouraged to apply.
Financial data: Stipends range from $1,000 to $4,000.
Duration: 1 year.
Number awarded: Varies each year.
Deadline: April of each year.

1652 ADVANCEMENT OF CONSTRUCTION TECHNOLOGY SCHOLARSHIP

Summary: To provide financial assistance to Maine residents preparing for a career in a field related to construction technology at a public college or university in the state.
See Listing #1139.

1653 AESF UNDERGRADUATE SCHOLARSHIP PROGRAM

National Association for Surface Finishing
Attn: AESF Foundation
1155 15th Street, N.W., Suite 500
Washington, DC 20005
Phone: (202) 457-8401; Fax: (202) 530-0659
Email: cmariette@nasf.org
Web: www.nasf.org/Content/NavigationMenu/AESFFoundation/default.htm
Summary: To provide financial assistance to upper-division students who are interested in majoring in subjects related to plating and surface finishing technologies.
Eligibility: Open to juniors and seniors in college who are majoring in chemistry, chemical engineering, environmental engineering, metallurgy, materials science, or metallurgical engineering. Applicants must submit a 2-page statement describing their career objectives, intended plans for study in plating and surface finishing technologies, and long-range goals. Selection is based on academic history, extracurricular activities, and employment history. Financial need is not considered.
Financial data: The stipend is at least $1,500 per year. Funds are sent directly to the recipient's college or university. Schools are requested not to reduce federal, state, or institutional support for students who receive this scholarship.
Duration: 1 year; recipients may reapply for 1 additional year.
Number awarded: At least 1 each year.
Deadline: April of each year.

1654 AETNA NURSING SCHOLARSHIP

Hispanic Association of Colleges and Universities
Attn: National Scholarship Program
8415 Datapoint Drive, Suite 400
San Antonio, TX 78229
Phone: (210) 692-3805; Fax: (210) 692-0823; TDD: (800) 855-2880
Email: scholarships@hacu.net
Web: www.hacu.net/hacu/Scholarships_EN.asp?SnID=875148054
Summary: To provide financial assistance to undergraduate students who are preparing for a career in nursing at institutions that belong to the Hispanic Association of Colleges and Universities (HACU).
Eligibility: Open to full- or part-time undergraduate students who are enrolled at a 2- or 4-year HACU member institution. Applicants must be preparing for a career in nursing. They must have a GPA of 3.0 or higher and be able to demonstrate financial need. Along with their application, they must submit an essay of 200 to 250 words that describes their academic and/or career goals, where they expect to be and what they expect to be doing 10 years from now, and what skills they can bring to an employer.
Financial data: The stipend is $2,500.
Duration: 1 year; nonrenewable.
Number awarded: Varies each year.
Deadline: May of each year.

1655 AFCEA DISTANCE LEARNING/ONLINE SCHOLARSHIPS

Armed Forces Communications and Electronics Association
Attn: AFCEA Educational Foundation
4400 Fair Lakes Court
Fairfax, VA 22033-3899
Phone: (703) 631-6149; (800) 336-4583, ext. 6149; Fax: (703) 631-4693
Email: scholarship@afcea.org
Web: www.afcea.org/education/scholarships/undergraduate/pub1.asp
Summary: To provide financial assistance to undergraduate and graduate students who are working full-time on a degree in selected fields by means of a distance-learning or online program.
Eligibility: Open to U.S. citizens working full-time on a bachelor's or master's degree by means of a distance-learning or online program affiliated with a major accredited 4-year college or university in the United States. Applicants must have completed at least 1 year of course work based on a 30-semester hour equivalent; classes in progress at the time of application cannot be used toward the 1-year minimum completion requirement. Undergraduates must have completed at least 2 semesters of calculus (not pre-calculus). Graduate students must have completed at least 1 full semester of work and be enrolled full-time. Fields of study are limited to engineering (aerospace, chemical, electrical, or systems), mathematics, physics, science or mathematics education, technology management, or computer science. Selection is based primarily on academic excellence.
Financial data: The stipend is $2,000.
Duration: 1 year.
Number awarded: 1 or 2 each year.
Deadline: May of each year.

1656 AFCEA ROTC SCHOLARSHIPS

Armed Forces Communications and Electronics Association
Attn: AFCEA Educational Foundation
4400 Fair Lakes Court
Fairfax, VA 22033-3899
Phone: (703) 631-6149; (800) 336-4583, ext. 6149; Fax: (703) 631-4693
Email: scholarship@afcea.org
Web: www.afcea.org/education/scholarships/rotc/rotc1.asp
Summary: To provide financial assistance to ROTC cadets who are majoring in fields related to communications and electronics.
Eligibility: Open to ROTC cadets majoring in electronics, engineering (aerospace, chemical, computer, electrical, or systems), mathematics, computer science, physics, science or mathematics education, technology management, foreign languages, global security and intelligence studies, security and intelligence, international studies, or other fields directly related to the support of U.S. national security enterprises. Applicants must be nominated by their ROTC professor, be entering their junior or senior year, be U.S. citizens, be of good moral character, have demonstrated academic excellence, be motivated to complete a college education and serve as officers in the U.S. armed forces, and be able to demonstrate financial need.
Financial data: The stipend is $2,000.
Duration: 1 year; may be renewed.
Number awarded: 36 each year, divided equally among Army, Navy/Marine Corps, and Air Force ROTC programs; for each service, 6 are awarded to rising juniors, 6 to rising seniors.
Deadline: February of each year.

1657 AFCEA SCHOLARSHIP FOR WORKING PROFESSIONALS

Armed Forces Communications and Electronics Association
Attn: AFCEA Educational Foundation
4400 Fair Lakes Court
Fairfax, VA 22033-3899
Phone: (703) 631-6149; (800) 336-4583, ext. 6149; Fax: (703) 631-4693
Email: scholarship@afcea.org
Web: www.afcea.org/education/scholarships/workingstudents/ws1.asp
Summary: To provide financial assistance to undergraduate and graduate students who are working part-time on a degree in engineering or the sciences while already employed.
Eligibility: Open to part-time students at accredited 2- and 4-year colleges or universities in the United States while already employed in a science or technology field. Applicants must be U.S. citizens working toward a degree in engineering (aerospace, chemical, electrical, or systems), mathematics, physics, technical management, computer information systems, computer science, or a related field. Students enrolled in online or distance-learning programs are eligible. Undergraduates must be entering their sophomore, junior, or senior year and have a GPA of 3.0 or higher. Graduate students must have completed at

least 2 postgraduate-level courses and be enrolled in a master's degree program. Selection is based on academic achievement, patriotism, and potential to contribute to the American workforce.
Financial data: The stipend is $2,000.
Duration: 1 year; may be renewed.
Number awarded: 1 or more each year.
Deadline: August of each year.

1658 AFFIRM UNIVERSITY SCHOLARSHIPS

Association for Federal Information Resources Management
c/o CAPLEAD
428 Hume Avenue, Second Floor
P.O. Box 2848
Alexandria, VA 22301
Phone: (703) 549-1160; Fax: (703) 995-4890
Email: scholarships@affirm.org
Web: www.affirm.org/education/scholarships
Summary: To provide financial assistance to upper-division students at designated universities majoring in information technology.
Eligibility: Open to full-time juniors and seniors at designated partner universities (Syracuse, George Mason, George Washington, Carnegie Mellon, LaSalle, and Maryland University College). Applicants must be majoring in an aspect of information technology or a related field (e.g., computing, telecommunications, information management, software engineering, library science, records management). They must have a GPA of 3.0 or higher and be able to document financial need. Preference is given to U.S. citizens.
Financial data: A stipend is awarded (amount not specified).
Duration: 1 year; nonrenewable.
Number awarded: 1 or more each year.
Deadline: Each partner university sets its own application deadline.

1659 AFRO-ACADEMIC, CULTURAL, TECHNOLOGICAL AND SCIENTIFIC OLYMPICS (ACT-SO)

Summary: To recognize and reward (with college scholarships) outstanding African American high school students who distinguish themselves in the Afro-Academic, Cultural, Technological and Scientific Olympics (ACT-SO) program.
See Listing #1141.

1660 AFTERCOLLEGE/AACN NURSING SCHOLARSHIP FUND

American Association of Colleges of Nursing
One Dupont Circle, N.W., Suite 530
Washington, DC 20036
Phone: (202) 463-6930; Fax: (202) 785-8320
Email: scholarship@aacn.nche.edu
Web: www.aacn.nche.edu/Education/financialaid.htm
Summary: To provide financial assistance to students at institutions that are members of the American Association of Colleges of Nursing (AACN).
Eligibility: Open to students working on a baccalaureate, master's, or doctoral degree at an AACN member school. Special consideration is given to applicants who are 1) enrolled in a master's or doctoral program to prepare for a nursing faculty career; 2) completing an R.N. to baccalaureate (B.S.N.) or master's (M.S.N) program; or 3) enrolled in an accelerated baccalaureate or master's degree nursing program. Applicants must have a GPA of 3.25 or higher. Along with their application, they must submit an essay of 200 to 250 words on their goals and aspirations as related to their education, career, and future plans. They must also register and submit their resume to AfterCollege.com.
Financial data: The stipend is $2,500.
Duration: 1 year.
Number awarded: 8 each year: 2 for each application deadline.
Deadline: January, April, July, or October of each year.

1661 AGC ASSOCIATE DIVISION SCHOLARSHIP

Associated General Contractors of South Dakota
Attn: Highway-Heavy-Utilities Chapter
300 East Capitol Avenue, Suite 1
Pierre, SD 57501
Phone: (605) 224-8689; (800) 242-6373; Fax: (605) 224-9915
Web: www.sdagc.org
Summary: To provide financial assistance to residents of South Dakota who are interested in attending a college or university in any state to prepare for a career in a construction-related field.
Eligibility: Open to residents of South Dakota who are graduating high school seniors or students already enrolled at a college or university in any state. Applicants must be preparing for a career in a construction-related field. Along with their application, they must submit a brief essay that covers why they are interested in a career in the construction industry, the event or series of events that led them to that decision, and their career objectives. They must be sponsored by a member of the Associated General Contractors of South Dakota. Financial need is considered in the selection process.
Financial data: The stipend is $2,500.
Duration: 1 year.
Number awarded: 1 each year.
Deadline: April of each year.

1662 AGC OF NYS DIESEL TECHNOLOGY SCHOLARSHIP PROGRAM

Associated General Contractors of New York State
Attn: AGC Scholarship Fund
10 Airline Drive, Suite 203
Albany, NY 12205
Phone: (518) 456-1134; Fax: (518) 456-1198
Email: agcadmin@agcnys.org
Web: www.agcnys.org/programs/scholarship
Summary: To provide financial assistance to residents of New York who are working on a degree in diesel technology at a school in the state.
Eligibility: Open to residents of New York who are entering the second, third, or fourth year in a 2- or 4-year college in the state. Applicants must be interested in preparing for a career in the highway construction industry and be working on a degree in diesel technology. They must be enrolled full-time and have a GPA of 2.5 or higher. U.S. citizenship or permanent resident status is required. Selection is based on grades, interest in the highway construction industry, extracurricular activities, employment experience, evaluations, and financial need.
Financial data: The stipend is $1,500, payable in 2 equal installments.
Duration: 1 year.
Number awarded: 2 each year.
Deadline: May of each year.

1663 AGC OF OHIO SCHOLARSHIPS

Associated General Contractors of Ohio
Attn: AGC of Ohio Education Foundation
1755 Northwest Boulevard
Columbus, OH 43212
Phone: (614) 486-6446; (800) 557-OHIO; Fax: (614) 486-6498
Email: educationfoundation@agcohio.com
Web: www.agcohio.com/scholarships.html
Summary: To provide financial assistance to residents of Ohio and adjacent counties who are working on an undergraduate degree in a field related to the construction industry at a college or university in any state.
Eligibility: Open to residents of Ohio and adjacent counties who are undergraduates in at least the second year at a 2- or 4-year college or university in any state. Applicants must be enrolled in a construction degree program and be preparing for a career in construction. They must be U.S. citizens with a GPA of 2.5 or higher. Along with their application, they must submit a short statement on what they think is the most important issue currently facing the construction industry and 4 essays of 125 words each on 1) why they have decided to prepare for a career in construction; 2) the goals they hope to accomplish in their career; 3) how they plan to make a difference in the construction industry; and 4) anything else that might influence whether or not they receive this scholarship. Financial need is also considered in the selection process.
Financial data: The stipend is $1,000.
Duration: 1 year.
Number awarded: 4 each year.
Deadline: March of each year.

1664 AGC SCHOLARSHIP

Associated General Contractors of South Dakota
Attn: Highway-Heavy-Utilities Chapter
300 East Capitol Avenue, Suite 1
Pierre, SD 57501

Phone: (605) 224-8689; (800) 242-6373; Fax: (605) 224-9915
Web: www.sdagc.org
Summary: To provide financial assistance to residents of South Dakota who are interested in attending a college, university, or technical institute in any state to prepare for a career in a construction-related field.
Eligibility: Open to residents of South Dakota who are graduating high school seniors or students already enrolled at a college, university, or technical institute in any state. Applicants must be preparing for a career in a construction-related field. Along with their application, they must submit a brief essay that covers why they are interested in a career in the construction industry, the event or series of events that led them to that decision, and their career objectives. They must be sponsored by a member of the Associated General Contractors of South Dakota. Financial need is considered in the selection process.
Financial data: The stipend is $1,000.
Duration: 1 year.
Number awarded: 1 each year.
Deadline: April of each year.

1665 AGC UNDERGRADUATE SCHOLARSHIPS

Associated General Contractors of America
Attn: AGC Education and Research Foundation
2300 Wilson Boulevard, Suite 400
Arlington, VA 22201
Phone: (703) 837-5342; Fax: (703) 837-5451
Email: sladef@agc.org
Web: www.agcfoundation.org
Summary: To provide financial assistance to undergraduate students in a field related to construction.
Eligibility: Open to college sophomores and juniors who are enrolled or planning to enroll in a 4- or 5-year ABET- or ACCE-accredited construction management or construction-related engineering program. Beginning seniors in a 5-year program are also eligible. All applicants must be full-time students with at least 1 full academic year of course work remaining. They must be preparing for a career in construction. High school seniors and college freshmen are not eligible. Selection is based on academic performance, extracurricular activities, employment experience, financial status, and a demonstrated interest in a construction industry career. Finalists are interviewed. U.S. citizenship or permanent resident status is required.
Financial data: The stipend is $2,500 per year.
Duration: 1 year; may be renewed for up to 2 additional years.
Number awarded: More than 100 each year.
Deadline: October of each year.

1666 AGNES NAUGHTON RN-BSN FUND SCHOLARSHIP

Florida Nurses Association
Attn: Florida Nurses Foundation
1235 East Concord Street
P.O. Box 536985
Orlando, FL 32853-6985
Phone: (407) 896-3261; Fax: (407) 896-9042
Email: foundation@floridanurse.org
Web: www.floridanurse.org/foundationGrants/index.asp
Summary: To provide financial assistance to Florida residents who are interested in working on a bachelor's degree in nursing at a school in the state.
Eligibility: Open to registered nurses who have been Florida residents for at least 1 year and have completed at least 1 semester at an accredited nursing program in the state. They must be working on a baccalaureate degree and have a GPA of 2.5 or higher. Along with their application, they must submit 1-page essays on 1) why it is necessary for them to receive this scholarship; and 2) their goals and their assessment of their potential for making a contribution to nursing and society.
Financial data: A stipend is awarded (amount not specified).
Duration: 1 semester or year.
Number awarded: Varies each year.
Deadline: May of each year.

1667 AGRICULTURE FUTURE OF AMERICA LEADER AND ACADEMIC SCHOLARSHIPS

Agriculture Future of America
P.O. Box 414838
Kansas City, MO 64141
Phone: (816) 472-4232; (888) 472-4232; Fax: (816) 472-4239
Web: www.agfuture.org/students/scholar/index.html
Summary: To provide financial assistance to high school seniors who plan to study agriculture in college.
Eligibility: Open to graduating high school seniors who plan to attend a 4-year college or university and major in an agriculture-related field. Applicants must have a GPA of 3.0 or higher. Along with their application, they must submit an essay of 300 to 500 words on their personal vision for agriculture, including why they are interested in an agricultural career. Selection is based on that essay, leader and community involvement, and financial need.
Financial data: The stipend is $1,600. Funds are paid at the beginning of the second semester of the freshman year, provided the recipient attends the sponsor's Leaders Conference during the fall of the freshman year. The program provides a grant of $1,000 to help defray costs of attending the conference.
Duration: 1 year.
Number awarded: 20 each year.
Deadline: March of each year.

1668 AHETEMS NORTHROP GRUMMAN SCHOLARSHIPS

Advancing Hispanic Excellence in Technology, Engineering, Math and Science, Inc.
c/o University of Texas at Arlington
416 Yates Street, Room 609
Box 19019
Arlington, TX 76019-0019
Phone: (817) 272-1116; Fax: (817) 272-2548
Email: ahetems@shpe.org
Web: www.ahetems.org
Summary: To provide financial assistance to undergraduate students who are working on a degree in engineering or a related field at an Historically Black College or University (HBCU), an Hispanic Service Institution (HSI), or other specified universities.
Eligibility: Open to entering full-time sophomores, juniors, or seniors at an accredited university in the United States or Puerto Rico that is an HBCU, an HIS, or another designated institution. Applicants must be majoring in computer science, engineering (aerospace, computer, electrical, industrial, mechanical, or systems), mathematics, naval architecture, or physics. They must have a GPA of 3.0 or higher. Along with their application, they must submit a 500-word personal statement covering their community involvement, leadership, academic achievements, research internship and co-op experiences, and short-term and long-term goals and aspirations. Selection is based on merit. U.S. citizenship is required.
Financial data: The stipend is $5,000.
Duration: 1 year.
Number awarded: 1 or more each year.
Deadline: March of each year.

1669 AHETEMS U.S. STEEL CORPORATION SCHOLARSHIPS

Advancing Hispanic Excellence in Technology, Engineering, Math and Science, Inc.
c/o University of Texas at Arlington
416 Yates Street, Room 609
Box 19019
Arlington, TX 76019-0019
Phone: (817) 272-1116; Fax: (817) 272-2548
Email: ahetems@shpe.org
Web: www.ahetems.org/scholarships/ahetems-u-s-steel-corp-scholarships
Summary: To provide financial assistance to Latino undergraduate students who are working on a degree in engineering or a related field at specified universities.
Eligibility: Open to Latino students enrolled full-time at designated universities in the United States. Applicants must be majoring in applied physics, chemistry, computer science, engineering (chemical, civil, electrical, environmental industrial, manufacturing, materials, mechanical), engineering physics, engineering technology, materials science, or mathematics. They must have a GPA of 3.0 or higher. Along with their application, they must submit a 500-word personal statement covering their community involvement, leadership, academic achievements, research internship and co-op experiences, and short-term and long-term goals and aspirations. Selection is based on merit. U.S. citizenship or permission to work in the United States is required.
Financial data: The stipend is $5,000.
Duration: 1 year.
Number awarded: 1 or more each year.
Deadline: March of each year.

1670 AHETEMS VERIZON SCHOLARSHIPS

Advancing Hispanic Excellence in Technology, Engineering, Math and Science, Inc.
c/o University of Texas at Arlington
416 Yates Street, Room 609
Box 19019
Arlington, TX 76019-0019
Phone: (817) 272-1116; Fax: (817) 272-2548
Email: ahetems@shpe.org
Web: www.ahetems.org/scholarships/ahetems-verizon-scholarships

Summary: To provide financial assistance to Latino undergraduate students who are working on a degree in civil engineering or computer science or engineering at a college or university that has a student chapter of the Society of Hispanic Professional Engineers (SHPE).

Eligibility: Open to Latino students entering their junior year at a college or university in the United States that has a student chapter of SHPE. Applicants must be majoring in civil engineering, computer science, or computer engineering. They must have a GPA of 3.0 or higher. Along with their application, they must submit a 500-word personal statement covering their community involvement, leadership, academic achievements, research internship and co-op experiences, and short- and long-term goals and aspirations. Both merit and need-based scholarships are available.

Financial data: The stipend is $5,000.

Duration: 1 year.

Number awarded: 1 or more each year.

Deadline: March of each year.

1671 AIR FORCE ROTC BIOMEDICAL SCIENCES CORPS

U.S. Air Force
Attn: Headquarters AFROTC/RRUC
551 East Maxwell Boulevard
Maxwell AFB, AL 36112-5917
Phone: (334) 953-2091; (866) 4-AFROTC; Fax: (334) 953-6167
Email: afrotc1@maxwell.af.mil
Web: afrotc.com

Summary: To provide financial assistance to students who are interested in joining Air Force ROTC in college and preparing for a career as a physical therapist, optometrist, or pharmacist.

Eligibility: Open to U.S. citizens who are freshmen or sophomores in college and interested in a career as a physical therapist, optometrist, or pharmacist. Applicants must have a GPA of 2.0 or higher and meet all other academic and physical requirements for participation in AFROTC. At the time of their Air Force commissioning, they may be no more than 31 years of age. They must agree to serve for at least 4 years as nonline active-duty Air Force officers following graduation from college.

Financial data: Awards are type 2 AFROTC scholarships that provide for payment of tuition and fees, to a maximum of $18,000 per year, plus an annual book allowance of $900. All recipients are also awarded a tax-free subsistence allowance for 10 months of each year that is $350 per month during their sophomore year, $450 during their junior year, and $500 during their senior year.

Duration: 2 or 3 years, provided the recipient maintains a GPA of 2.0 or higher.

Deadline: June of each year.

1672 AIR FORCE ROTC EXPRESS SCHOLARSHIPS

U.S. Air Force
Attn: Headquarters AFROTC/RRUC
551 East Maxwell Boulevard
Maxwell AFB, AL 36112-5917
Phone: (334) 953-2091; (866) 4-AFROTC; Fax: (334) 953-6167
Email: afrotc1@maxwell.af.mil
Web: afrotc.com/scholarships/in-college/express-scholarships

Summary: To provide financial assistance to students who are interested in joining Air Force ROTC and majoring in critical Air Force officer technical fields in college.

Eligibility: Open to U.S. citizens who are entering their junior or senior year of college and are working on a degree in technical fields that may change annually but are of critical interest to the Air Force; currently, the eligible fields are computer, electrical, and environmental engineering. Applicants must have a GPA of 2.5 or higher and meet all other academic and physical requirements for participation in AFROTC. At the time of their Air Force commissioning, they may be no more than 31 years of age. They must be able to pass the Air Force Officer Qualifying Test (AFOQT) and the Air Force ROTC Physical Fitness Test.

Financial data: Awards are type 1 AFROTC scholarships that provide for full payment of tuition and fees plus an annual book allowance of $900. All recipients are also awarded a tax-free monthly subsistence allowance that is $450 for juniors and $500 for seniors.

Duration: 1 or 2 years, until completion of a bachelor's degree.

Deadline: Deadline not specified.

1673 AIR FORCE ROTC NURSING SCHOLARSHIPS

U.S. Air Force
Attn: Headquarters AFROTC/RRUC
551 East Maxwell Boulevard
Maxwell AFB, AL 36112-5917
Phone: (334) 953-2091; (866) 4-AFROTC; Fax: (334) 953-6167
Email: afrotc1@maxwell.af.mil
Web: afrotc.com/admissions/professional-programs/nursing

Summary: To provide financial assistance to college students who are interested in a career as a nurse, are interested in joining Air Force ROTC, and are willing to serve as Air Force officers following completion of their bachelor's degree.

Eligibility: Open to U.S. citizens who are freshmen or sophomores in college and interested in a career as a nurse. Applicants must have a cumulative GPA of 2.5 or higher at the end of their freshman year and meet all other academic and physical requirements for participation in AFROTC. They must be interested in working on a nursing degree from an accredited program. At the time of Air Force commissioning, they may be no more than 31 years of age. They must be able to pass the Air Force Officer Qualifying Test (AFOQT) and the Air Force ROTC Physical Fitness Test.

Financial data: Awards are type 1 AFROTC scholarships that provide for full payment of tuition and fees plus an annual book allowance of $900. All recipients are also awarded a tax-free subsistence allowance for 10 months of each year that is $350 per month during their sophomore year, $450 during their junior year, and $500 during their senior year.

Duration: 2 or 3 years, provided the recipient maintains a GPA of 2.5 or higher.

Deadline: June of each year.

1674 AIR PRODUCTS AND CHEMICALS SCHOLARSHIP FOR DIVERSITY IN ENGINEERING

Association of Independent Colleges and Universities of Pennsylvania
101 North Front Street
Harrisburg, PA 17101-1405
Phone: (717) 232-8649; Fax: (717) 233-8574
Email: info@aicup.org
Web: www.aicup.org

Summary: To provide financial assistance to women and minority students from any state who are enrolled at member institutions of the Association of Independent Colleges and Universities of Pennsylvania (AICUP) and majoring in designated fields of engineering.

Eligibility: Open to undergraduate students from any state enrolled full-time at AICUP colleges and universities. Applicants must be women and/or members of the following minority groups: American Indians, Alaska Natives, Asians, Blacks/African Americans, Hispanics/Latinos, Native Hawaiians, or Pacific Islanders. They must be juniors majoring in chemical or mechanical engineering with a GPA of 2.7 or higher. Along with their application, they must submit an essay on their characteristics, accomplishments, primary interests, plans, goals, and what sets them apart.

Financial data: The stipend is $7,500 per year.

Duration: 1 year; may be renewed 1 additional year if the recipient maintains appropriate academic standards.

Number awarded: 1 each year.

Deadline: April of each year.

1675 ALABAMA NURSES FOUNDATION SCHOLARSHIPS

Alabama State Nurses Association
Attn: Alabama Nurses Foundation
360 North Hull Street
Montgomery, AL 36104-3658
Phone: (334) 262-8321; Fax: (334) 262-8578
Email: alabamasna@mindspring.com
Web: www.alabamanurses.org

Summary: To provide financial assistance to residents of Alabama enrolled in an undergraduate or graduate program in nursing at a school in any state.

Eligibility: Open to residents of Alabama who are enrolled in an accredited associate, baccalaureate (either initial or R.N. to B.S.N.), master's, or doctoral program in nursing. Applicants may be attending school in any state, but they should be planning to remain employed in Alabama for at least 2 years after

graduation. Along with their application, they must submit a 100-word statement on their career goals. Financial need is not considered in the selection process. Priority is given to graduate students interested in teaching at a school of nursing.
Financial data: The stipend is $1,000 for undergraduates or $2,500 for graduate students.
Duration: 1 year.
Number awarded: 1 or more each year.
Deadline: June of each year.

1676 ALASKADVANTAGE EDUCATION GRANTS

Alaska Commission on Postsecondary Education
Attn: AlaskAdvantage Programs
3030 Vintage Boulevard
P.O. Box 110505
Juneau, AK 99811-0505
Phone: (907) 465-6779; (866) 427-5683; Fax: (907) 465-5316; TDD: (907) 465-3143
Email: customer_service@acpe.ak.us
Web: akadvantage.alaska.gov/page/276
Summary: To provide financial assistance to Alaska residents who attend college in the state to prepare for a career in designated fields with a workforce shortage.
Eligibility: Open to residents of Alaska who have been admitted to an undergraduate degree or vocational certificate program at a qualifying institution in the state. Applicants must be planning to work on a degree or certificate in a field that the state has designated as a workforce shortage area; currently, those are allied health sciences, community or social service, teaching, and process industries/natural resources extraction support. They must be able to demonstrate financial need and satisfactory academic progress. U.S. citizenship or permanent resident status is required.
Financial data: Grants range from $500 to $2,000 per year, depending on the need of the recipient.
Duration: 1 year; may be renewed as long as the recipient remains enrolled at least half-time, makes satisfactory academic progress, and continues to meet residency and financial need requirements.
Number awarded: Varies each year; students with the greatest financial need are awarded support until funds are exhausted.
Deadline: April of each year.

1677 ALBERT E. AND FLORENCE W. NEWTON NURSING SCHOLARSHIP

Rhode Island Foundation
Attn: Funds Administrator
One Union Station
Providence, RI 02903
Phone: (401) 427-4017; Fax: (401) 331-8085
Email: lmonahan@rifoundation.org
Web: www.rifoundation.org
Summary: To provide financial assistance to students, especially residents of Rhode Island, working on a degree in nursing.
Eligibility: Open to 1) students enrolled in a baccalaureate nursing program; 2) students in a diploma nursing program; 3) students in a 2-year associate degree nursing program; and 4) active practicing R.N.s working on a bachelor's degree in nursing. Applicants must be studying at a nursing school on a full- or part-time basis and able to demonstrate financial need. They may be enrolled at a school in any state, but preference is given to residents of Rhode Island. Along with their application, they must submit an essay, up to 300 words, on their career goals, particularly as they relate to practicing in or advancing the field of nursing in Rhode Island.
Financial data: The stipend ranges from $500 to $2,000.
Duration: 1 year; may be renewed.
Number awarded: Varies each year; recently, 8 of these scholarships were awarded: 3 new awards and 5 renewals.
Deadline: April of each year.

1678 ALBUQUERQUE POST SOCIETY OF AMERICAN MILITARY ENGINEERS SCHOLARSHIP

New Mexico Engineering Foundation
Attn: Scholarship Chair
P.O. Box 3828
Albuquerque, NM 87190-3828
Phone: (505) 615-1800
Email: info@nmef.net
Web: www.nmef.net/?section=scholarship
Summary: To provide financial assistance to high school seniors in New Mexico interested in studying engineering, mathematics, or science at a college in the state.
Eligibility: Open to seniors graduating from high schools in New Mexico who plan to work on an undergraduate degree in engineering, mathematics, or science at a college or university in the state. Applicants must have a GPA of 3.0 or higher and minimum scores of at least 29 on the ACT mathematics, 25 on the ACT English, 600 on the SAT mathematics, and 500 on the SAT critical reading. Along with their application, they must submit 12 brief statements related to their past activities and future plans. Selection is based on academic record, demonstrated school leadership positions, community involvement, and ability to earn partial tuition costs and fulfill financial needs.
Financial data: The stipend is $1,000.
Duration: 1 year; nonrenewable.
Number awarded: 2 each year.
Deadline: February of each year.

1679 ALICE GLAISYER WARFIELD MEMORIAL SCHOLARSHIP

Transportation Clubs International
P.O. Box 2223
Ocean Shores, WA 98569
Phone: (877) 858-8627
Email: info@transportationclubsinternational.com
Web: www.transportationclubsinternational.com/scholarships.html
Summary: To provide financial assistance to college students interested in preparing for a career in fields related to transportation.
Eligibility: Open to students enrolled at an academic institution (vocational or degree program) that offers courses in transportation, logistics, traffic management, or related fields. Applicants must intend to prepare for a career in those fields. Along with their application, they must submit a 200-word essay explaining why they have chosen transportation or an allied field as a career path and outlining their objectives. Selection is based on scholastic ability, character, potential, professional interest, and financial need.
Financial data: The stipend is $1,500.
Duration: 1 year.
Number awarded: 1 or more each year.
Deadline: May of each year.

1680 ALLEGHENY MOUNTAIN SECTION SCHOLARSHIPS

Air & Waste Management Association–Allegheny Mountain Section
c/o David Testa, Scholarship Chair
Equitable Resources, Inc.
225 North Shore Drive
Pittsburgh, PA 15212
Phone: (412) 787-6803
Email: dtesta@eqt.com
Web: www.ams-awma.org/ams_scholarship.htm
Summary: To provide financial assistance to undergraduate students in West Virginia and western Pennsylvania who are interested in preparing for a career in an environmental field.
Eligibility: Open to students currently enrolled and high school seniors accepted full-time in a 4- or 5-year college or university program that will lead to a career in the environmental field through environmental science, engineering, or law. Applicants must be attending or planning to attend a college or university in western Pennsylvania or West Virginia. They must have a GPA of 3.0 or higher. Along with their application, they must submit 1) transcripts; 2) a plan of study; 3) a letter of reference; 4) a 1-page essay on their interest in the fields of air, water, or waste management; and 5) a resume including work history, academic history, awards, hobbies, and volunteer work. Selection is based on academic record, plan of study, career goals, recommendations, and extracurricular activities; consideration is not given to sex, race, national origin, financial need, age, or physical disability.
Financial data: A total of $5,000 is available for this program each year.
Duration: 1 year.
Number awarded: 1 or more each year.
Deadline: March of each year.

1681 ALTRIA SCHOLARS

Virginia Foundation for Independent Colleges
Attn: Director of Development

8010 Ridge Road, Suite B
Richmond, VA 23229-7288
Phone: (804) 288-6609; (800) 230-6757; Fax: (804) 282-4635
Email: info@vfic.org
Web: www.vfic.org/scholarship/scholarships_vfic.html

Summary: To provide financial assistance to students majoring in designated fields at a college or university that is a member of the Virginia Foundation for Independent Colleges (VFIC).

Eligibility: Open to sophomores who are enrolled full-time at 1 of the 15 VFIC member institutions. Applicants must have a GPA of 3.0 or higher and a declared major in accounting, biology, business administration, chemistry, computer science, economics, engineering, finance, or physics. Selection is based on merit and financial need. Special consideration is given to underserved populations. U.S. citizenship is required.

Financial data: The stipend is $5,000 per year.

Duration: 1 year. May be renewed up to 3 additional years if the recipient maintains a GPA of 3.0 or higher and a record of good citizenship and conduct.

Number awarded: 20 each year.

Deadline: October of each year.

1682 AMADEO FRANCIS GRANT

Virgin Islands Board of Education
Dronningen Gade 60B, 61, and 62
P.O. Box 11900
St. Thomas, VI 00801
Phone: (340) 774-4546; Fax: (340) 774-3384
Email: stt@myviboe.com
Web: www.myviboe.com

Summary: To provide financial assistance to residents of the Virgin Islands who wish to study designated fields at a college in the territory or on the mainland.

Eligibility: Open to residents of the Virgin Islands who are seniors or graduates of high schools in the territory. Applicants must have a GPA of 2.0 or higher and be attending or accepted for enrollment at an accredited institution of higher learning in the territory or on the mainland. They must be planning to major in computer science, mathematics, or science. Financial need is considered in the selection process.

Financial data: The stipend is $2,500 per year.

Duration: 1 year; may be renewed up to 3 additional years.

Number awarded: 1 each year.

Deadline: April of each year.

1683 AMERICAN ASSEMBLY FOR MEN IN NURSING FOUNDATION/JOHNSON & JOHNSON SCHOLARSHIP FUND

American Assembly for Men in Nursing
AAMN Foundation
6700 Oporto-Madrid Boulevard
P.O. Box 130220
Birmingham, AL 35213
Phone: (205) 956-0146; Fax: (205) 956-0149
Email: aamn@aamn.org
Web: www.aamn.org

Summary: To provide financial assistance to men working on a pre-R.N. licensure or graduate degree in nursing.

Eligibility: Open to male students currently enrolled in an accredited pre-R.N. licensure or graduate degree program in nursing. Applicants must have a GPA of 2.75 or higher. Along with their application, they must submit an essay of 250 to 300 words that covers why they want to be a nurse, how they might contribute to the nursing profession, and their current career plans. Financial need is not considered in the selection process.

Financial data: The stipend is $1,000.

Duration: 1 year.

Number awarded: 20 each year: 16 for pre-R.N. licensure students and 4 for graduate students. Of the 20 scholarships, 4 are reserved for minority students.

Deadline: March of each year.

1684 AMERICAN ASSOCIATION OF OCCUPATIONAL HEALTH NURSES FOUNDATION ACADEMIC SCHOLARSHIP

American Association of Occupational Health Nurses, Inc.
Attn: AAOHN Foundation
7794 Grow Drive
Pensacola, FL 32514
Phone: (850) 474-6963; (800) 241-8014; Fax: (850) 484-8762
Email: aaohn@aaohn.org
Web: www.aaohn.org/scholarships/academic-study.html

Summary: To provide financial assistance to registered nurses who are working on a bachelor's or graduate degree to prepare for a career in occupational and environmental health.

Eligibility: Open to registered nurses who are enrolled in a baccalaureate or graduate degree program. Applicants must demonstrate an interest in, and commitment to, occupational and environmental health. Along with their application, they must submit a 500-word narrative on their professional goals as they relate to the academic activity and the field of occupational and environmental health. Selection is based on that essay (50%), impact of education on applicant's career (20%), and 2 letters of recommendation (30%).

Financial data: The stipend is $3,000.

Duration: 1 year; may be renewed up to 2 additional years.

Number awarded: 1 each year.

Deadline: January of each year.

1685 AMERICAN ASSOCIATION ON HEALTH AND DISABILITY SCHOLARSHIPS

American Association on Health and Disability
Attn: Executive Director
110 North Washington Street, Suite 328-J
Rockville, MD 20850
Phone: (301) 545-6140, ext. 206; Fax: (301) 545-6144
Email: contact@aahd,us
Web: www.aahd.us/page.php?pname=ScholarshipProgram

Summary: To provide financial assistance to undergraduate and graduate students who have a disability, especially those studying a field related to health and disability.

Eligibility: Open to high school graduates who have a documented disability and are enrolled in or accepted by an accredited U.S. 4-year university or graduate school on a full-time basis. Preference is given to students working on a degree in public health, disability studies, health promotion, or other field related to health and disability. Along with their application, they must submit a 3-page personal statement that includes a personal history, educational and career goals, extracurricular activities, and reasons why they should be selected to receive this scholarship. U.S. citizenship or permanent resident status is required.

Financial data: Stipends range up to $1,000.

Duration: 1 year.

Number awarded: 2 each year.

Deadline: November of each year.

1686 AMERICAN COUNCIL OF ENGINEERING COMPANIES GENERAL SCHOLARSHIPS

American Council of Engineering Companies
Attn: Awards Programs Director
1015 15th Street, N.W., Eighth Floor
Washington, DC 20005-2605
Phone: (202) 347-7474; Fax: (202) 898-0068
Email: acec@acec.org
Web: www.acec.org/awards/scholarships.cfm

Summary: To provide financial assistance to students currently working on an undergraduate or graduate degree in engineering or land surveying.

Eligibility: Open to students working on a bachelor's, master's, or Ph.D. degree in an ABET-approved engineering or accredited land surveying program. Applicants must be U.S. citizens entering their junior, senior, fifth, or graduate year. They must have received a scholarship from a participating state Member Organization (MO) of the American Council of Engineering Companies (ACEC). Along with their application, they must submit a 500-word essay on "What is the role or responsibility of the consulting engineer or land surveyor to shaping and protecting the natural environment?" Selection is based on the essay (25 points), cumulative GPA (24 points), work experience (24 points), a letter of recommendation (17 points), and extracurricular college activities (10 points).

Financial data: Stipends are $10,000, $7,500, or $5,000.

Duration: 1 year.

Number awarded: Varies each year; recently, 3 of these scholarships were awarded: the Scholar of the Year at $10,000, the Kennedy/Jenks Consultants Scholarship at $7,500, and the Small Firm Council Scholarship at $5,000.

Deadline: Participating MOs must forward applications by March of each year.

1687 AMERICAN COUNCIL OF ENGINEERING COMPANIES OF CALIFORNIA SCHOLARSHIPS

American Council of Engineering Companies of California
Attn: Communications and Membership Coordinator
1303 J Street, Suite 450
Sacramento, CA 95814
Phone: (916) 441-7991; Fax: (916) 441-6312
Email: staff@acec-ca.org
Web: www.acec-ca.org/?pid=19

Summary: To provide financial assistance to upper-division and graduate students working on a degree in engineering or land surveying at a college in California.

Eligibility: Open to students working on a bachelor's, master's, or Ph.D. degree in an ABET-approved engineering or accredited land surveying program in California. Applicants must be U.S. citizens entering their junior, senior, fifth, or graduate year. They must have a GPA of at least 3.2 in engineering and land surveying courses and at least 3.0 overall. Undergraduates must be enrolled full-time and graduate students at least half-time. Along with their application, they must submit a 500-word essay on "What is the role or responsibility of the consulting engineer or land surveyor to shaping and protecting the natural environment?" Selection is based on the essay (25 points), cumulative GPA (24 points), work experience (24 points), a letter of recommendation (17 points), and extracurricular college activities (10 points).

Financial data: Stipends range from $1,000 to $5,000 per year.

Duration: 1 year; recipients may reapply for 1 additional year.

Number awarded: Varies each year; recently, 7 of these scholarships were awarded: 1 at $5,000 for a graduate student, 1 at $5,000 for an undergraduate, 1 at $2,500 for a graduate student, 3 at $2,500 for undergraduates, and 1 at $1,000 for an undergraduate.

Deadline: February of each year.

1688 AMERICAN COUNCIL OF ENGINEERING COMPANIES OF IDAHO SCHOLARSHIPS

American Council of Engineering Companies of Idaho
Attn: Executive Director
5420 West Franklin Road, Suite B
P.O. Box 8224
Boise, ID 83707
Phone: (208) 321-1502; Fax: (208) 321-4819
Email: ams@cableone.net
Web: www.acecofidaho.org

Summary: To provide financial assistance to upper-division and graduate students working on a degree in engineering or land surveying at a college in Idaho.

Eligibility: Open to students working on a bachelor's, master's, or Ph.D. degree in an ABET-approved engineering or accredited land surveying program in Idaho. Applicants must be U.S. citizens entering their junior, senior, fifth, or graduate year. Along with their application, they must submit a 500-word essay on "What is the role or responsibility of the consulting engineer or land surveyor to shaping and protecting the natural environment?" Selection is based on the essay (25 points), cumulative GPA (24 points), work experience (24 points), a letter of recommendation (17 points), and extracurricular college activities (10 points).

Financial data: Stipends are $1,000 or $500.

Duration: 1 year.

Number awarded: 2 each year: 1 at $1,000 and 1 at $500.

Deadline: March of each year.

1689 AMERICAN COUNCIL OF ENGINEERING COMPANIES OF MISSISSIPPI SCHOLARSHIPS

American Council of Engineering Companies of Mississippi
Attn: Executive Director
3900 Lakeland Drive, Suite 201
Flowood, MS 39232
Phone: (601) 420-2002; Fax: (601) 420-2315
Email: acecms@bellsouth.net
Web: www.acecms.org/Scholarships

Summary: To provide financial assistance to upper-division and graduate students working on a degree in engineering or land surveying at a college in Mississippi.

Eligibility: Open to students working on a bachelor's, master's, or Ph.D. degree in an ABET-approved engineering or accredited land surveying program in Mississippi. Applicants must be U.S. citizens entering their junior, senior, fifth, or graduate year. Along with their application, they must submit a 500-word essay on "What is the role or responsibility of the consulting engineer or land surveyor to shaping and protecting the natural environment?" Selection is based on the essay (25 points), cumulative GPA (24 points), work experience (24 points), a letter of recommendation (17 points), and extracurricular college activities (10 points).

Financial data: The stipend is $1,000.

Duration: 1 year.

Number awarded: 1 or more each year.

Deadline: February of each year.

1690 AMERICAN COUNCIL OF ENGINEERING COMPANIES OF NEW JERSEY SCHOLARSHIPS

American Council of Engineering Companies of New Jersey
Attn: Executive Director
66 Morris Avenue, Suite 1A
Springfield, NJ 07081-1409
Phone: (973) 564-5848; Fax: (973) 564-7480
Email: barbara@acecnj.org
Web: www.acecnj.org/scholarships.html

Summary: To provide financial assistance to upper-division and graduate students working on a degree in engineering or land surveying at a college in New Jersey.

Eligibility: Open to students working on a bachelor's, master's, or Ph.D. degree in an ABET-approved engineering or accredited land surveying program in New Jersey. Applicants must be U.S. citizens entering their junior, senior, fifth, or graduate year. Along with their application, they must submit a 500-word essay on "What is the role or responsibility of the consulting engineer or land surveyor to shaping and protecting the natural environment?" Selection is based on the essay (25 points), cumulative GPA (24 points), work experience (24 points), a letter of recommendation (17 points), and extracurricular college activities (10 points).

Financial data: The award is $1,000, of which $500 is payable upon receipt of the award and $500 upon graduation.

Number awarded: Up to 5 each year.

Deadline: November of each year.

1691 AMERICAN COUNCIL OF ENGINEERING COMPANIES OF PENNSYLVANIA SCHOLARSHIP

American Council of Engineering Companies of Pennsylvania
Attn: Administrative Assistant
2040 Linglestown Road, Suite 200
Harrisburg, PA 17110
Phone: (717) 540-6811; Fax: (717) 540-6815
Email: laurie@acecpa.org
Web: www.acecpa.org/education

Summary: To provide financial assistance to engineering students who have a connection to Pennsylvania.

Eligibility: Open to U.S. citizens who are working full-time on a bachelor's degree in engineering at an accredited program. Applicants must meet 1 or more of the following criteria: 1) attend college in Pennsylvania; 2) be a Pennsylvania resident; or 3) serve or have served as an intern with a Pennsylvania office of a firm that is a member of the American Council of Engineering Companies of Pennsylvania (ACEC/PA). Along with their application, they must submit a 500-word essay on how they expect a career as a consulting engineer to benefit society. Financial need is not considered in the selection process.

Financial data: The stipend is $4,000.

Duration: 1 year.

Number awarded: 1 or more each year.

Deadline: December of each year.

1692 AMERICAN COUNCIL OF ENGINEERING COMPANIES OF SOUTH DAKOTA SCHOLARSHIP

American Council of Engineering Companies of South Dakota
Attn: Executive Director
P.O. Box 398
Rapid City, SD 57709-0398
Phone: (605) 394-6674; Fax: (605) 394-6674
Email: contact@cecsd.org
Web: www.cecsd.org/scholar.html

Summary: To provide financial assistance to students in South Dakota currently working on a bachelor's degree in specified engineering fields.

Eligibility: Open to students working on a bachelor's degree in an Accreditation Board for Engineering and Technology (ABET)-approved engineering program in South Dakota. Applicants must be U.S. citizens entering their junior, senior, or fifth year with a major in civil, electrical, or mechanical engineering. They must have expressed a desire to enter the field of consulting engineering after graduation. Along with their application, they must submit a 500-word essay on "What is a consulting engineer or land surveyor and why should you consider it as a career?" Selection is based on the essay (25 points), cumulative GPA (28 points), work experience (20 points), a letter of recommendation (17 points), and college activities (10 points).

Financial data: The stipend is $1,000 per year.

Duration: 1 year; may be renewed.

Number awarded: 1 each year.

Deadline: December of each year.

1693 AMERICAN COUNCIL OF ENGINEERING COMPANIES OF TENNESSEE SCHOLARSHIPS

American Council of Engineering Companies of Tennessee
c/o Tennessee Engineering Center
800 Fort Negley Boulevard
Nashville, TN 37203
Phone: (615) 242-2486; Fax: (615) 254-1923
Email: ctoler@tnec.org
Web: www.acectn.org/Scholar.htm

Summary: To provide financial assistance to upper-division and graduate students working on a degree in engineering or land surveying at a college in Tennessee.

Eligibility: Open to students working on a bachelor's, master's, or Ph.D. degree in an ABET-approved engineering or accredited land surveying program in Tennessee. Applicants must be U.S. citizens entering their junior, senior, fifth, or graduate year. Along with their application, they must submit a 500-word essay on "What is the role or responsibility of the consulting engineer or land surveyor to shaping and protecting the natural environment?" Selection is based on the essay (25 points), cumulative GPA (24 points), work experience (24 points), a letter of recommendation (17 points), and extracurricular college activities (10 points).

Financial data: The stipend is $1,000.

Duration: 1 year.

Number awarded: 1 each year.

Deadline: January of each year.

1694 AMERICAN METEOROLOGICAL SOCIETY UNDERGRADUATE NAMED SCHOLARSHIPS

American Meteorological Society
Attn: Fellowship/Scholarship Program
45 Beacon Street
Boston, MA 02108-3693
Phone: (617) 227-2426, ext. 246; Fax: (617) 742-8718
Email: scholar@ametsoc.org
Web: www.ametsoc.org

Summary: To provide financial assistance to undergraduates majoring in meteorology or an aspect of atmospheric sciences.

Eligibility: Open to full-time students entering their final year of undergraduate study and majoring in meteorology or an aspect of the atmospheric or related oceanic and hydrologic sciences. Applicants must intend to make atmospheric or related sciences their career. They must be U.S. citizens or permanent residents enrolled at a U.S. institution and have a cumulative GPA of 3.25 or higher. Along with their application, they must submit 200-word essays on 1) their most important attributes and achievements that qualify them for this scholarship; and 2) their career goals in the atmospheric or related sciences. Financial need is considered in the selection process. The sponsor specifically encourages applications from women, minorities, and students with disabilities who are traditionally underrepresented in the atmospheric and related oceanic sciences.

Financial data: Stipend amounts vary each year.

Duration: 1 year.

Number awarded: Varies each year; recently, 20 of these scholarships were awarded.

Deadline: February of each year.

1695 AMERICAN PUBLIC TRANSPORTATION FOUNDATION SCHOLARSHIP AWARDS PROGRAM

American Public Transportation Association
Attn: American Public Transportation Foundation
1666 K Street, N.W., Suite 1100
Washington, DC 20006
Phone: (202) 496-4803; Fax: (202) 496-4323
Email: yconley@apta.com
Web: www.aptfd.org

Summary: To provide financial assistance to undergraduate and graduate students who are preparing for a career in public transportation.

Eligibility: Open to college sophomores, juniors, seniors, and graduate students who are preparing for a career in the transit industry. Any member organization of the American Public Transportation Association (APTA) can nominate and sponsor candidates for this scholarship. Nominees must be enrolled in a fully-accredited institution, have and maintain at least a 3.0 GPA, and be either employed by or demonstrate a strong interest in entering the public transportation industry. They must submit a 1,000-word essay on "In what segment of the public transportation industry will you make a career and why?" Selection is based on demonstrated interest in the transit field as a career, need for financial assistance, academic achievement, essay content and quality, and involvement in extracurricular citizenship and leadership activities. The Donald C. Hyde Memorial Essay Award is presented to the Applicant who submits the best response to the required essay component of the program.

Financial data: The stipend is $2,500. The winner of the Donald C. Hyde Memorial Essay Award receives an additional $500.

Duration: 1 year; may be renewed.

Number awarded: At least 9 each year.

Deadline: June of each year.

1696 AMERICAN SOCIETY FOR ENOLOGY AND VITICULTURE SCHOLARSHIPS

American Society for Enology and Viticulture
Attn: Scholarship Committee
1784 Picasso Avenue, Suite D
P.O. Box 1855
Davis, CA 95617-1855
Phone: (530) 753-3142; Fax: (530) 753-3318
Email: society@asev.org
Web: www.asev.org/scholarship-program

Summary: To provide financial assistance to graduate and undergraduate students interested in working on a degree in enology, viticulture, or another area related to the wine and grape industry.

Eligibility: Open to upper-division and graduate students working on a degree in enology, viticulture, or another field emphasizing a science basic to the wine and grape industry. Applicants must be enrolled or accepted full-time at a 4-year accredited college or university. They must reside in North America (including Canada and Mexico) and have a GPA of 3.0 or higher as undergraduates or 3.2 as graduate students. Along with their application, they must supply a written statement of intent to prepare for a career in the wine or grape industry. Financial need is not considered in the selection process.

Financial data: The awards are not in predetermined amounts and may vary from year to year.

Duration: Students receive quarter or semester stipends. Recipients are eligible to reapply each year in open competition with new applicants.

Number awarded: Varies each year; recently, 17 of these scholarships were awarded.

Deadline: February of each year.

1697 AMERICAN SOCIETY OF CRIME LABORATORY DIRECTORS SCHOLARSHIP PROGRAM

American Society of Crime Laboratory Directors
Scholarship Application
139K Technology Drive
Garner, NC 27529
Phone: (919) 773-2044; Fax: (919) 773-2602
Web: www.ascld.org/content/student-resources

Summary: To provide financial assistance to students preparing for careers in forensic science.

Eligibility: Open to juniors, seniors, and graduate students who are working on a degree in forensic science, forensic chemistry, or physical or natural science. Current forensic science laboratory employees working on a graduate degree are not eligible. Applicants must submit a statement describing their motivation for applying for this award, including their interest in specific forensic disciplines, career goals, past projects, financial need, or any other topic that will help explain their situation. Selection is based on that statement, overall scholastic record, scholastic record in forensic science course work, motivation or commitment to a forensic science career, and recommendations.

Financial data: The stipend is $1,000.
Duration: 1 year.
Number awarded: 1 or more each year.
Deadline: April of each year.

1698 AMERICAN SOCIETY OF NAVAL ENGINEERS SCHOLARSHIP PROGRAM

American Society of Naval Engineers
Attn: Scholarship Committee
1452 Duke Street
Alexandria, VA 22314-3458
Phone: (703) 836-6727; Fax: (703) 836-7491
Email: asnehq@navalengineers.org
Web: www.navalengineers.org

Summary: To provide financial assistance to college and graduate students who are interested in the field of naval engineering.

Eligibility: Open to students entering the final year of a full-time or co-op undergraduate program or starting the first year of full-time graduate study at an accredited college or university. Scholarships are not available to doctoral candidates or to persons who already have an advanced degree. Applicants must be U.S. citizens who have demonstrated an interest in a career in naval engineering. Eligible programs of study include naval architecture; aeronautical, civil, electrical, electronic, environmental, marine, mechanical, nuclear, ocean, or structural engineering; or other relevant military and civilian fields. Graduate student candidates must be members of the American Society of Naval Engineers (ASNE). Selection is based on academic record, work history, professional promise and interest in naval engineering, extracurricular activities, and recommendations. Financial need may also be considered.

Financial data: The stipends are $3,000 per year for undergraduates or $4,000 per year for graduate students. Funds may be used for the payment of tuition, fees, and school-related expenses.

Duration: 1 year.

Number awarded: Varies each year; recently, 12 undergraduate and 9 graduate students received scholarships.

Deadline: February of each year.

1699 AMERICAN STANDARD SCHOLARSHIPS

Plumbing-Heating-Cooling Contractors–National Association
Attn: PHCC Educational Foundation
180 South Washington Street
P.O. Box 6808
Falls Church, VA 22040
Phone: (703) 237-8100, ext. 221; (800) 533-7694; Fax: (703) 237-7442
Email: scholarships@naphcc.org
Web: www.foundation.phccweb.org/Scholarships/ASScholarship.htm

Summary: To provide financial assistance to entering or continuing undergraduate students interested in the plumbing, heating, and cooling industry.

Eligibility: Open to 1) full-time undergraduate students (entering or continuing) who are majoring in a field related to plumbing, heating, and cooling (e.g., business management, construction management with a specialization in mechanical construction, mechanical engineering) at a 4-year college or university; 2) students enrolled full-time in an approved certificate or degree program at a 2-year technical college, community college, or trade school in business management, mechanical CAD design, construction management with a specialty in mechanical construction, or plumbing or HVACR installation, service, and repair; and 3) full-time employees of a licensed plumbing or HVAC contractor (must be a member of the Plumbing-Heating-Cooling Contractors [PHCC]–National Association) who are enrolled in an apprenticeship program in plumbing or HVACR installation, service, and repair. Students majoring in accounting, architecture, computer engineering, construction-related engineering, civil engineering, electrical engineering, or environmental engineering are not eligible. Applicants must have a GPA of 2.0 or higher. Along with their application, they must submit a letter of recommendation from a PHCC member; a copy of school transcripts; SAT and/or ACT scores; and a letter of recommendation from a school principal, counselor, or dean. U.S. or Canadian citizenship is required. Financial need is not considered in the selection process.

Financial data: The stipend is $2,500.

Duration: 1 year; nonrenewable.

Number awarded: Up to 4 each year.

Deadline: April of each year.

1700 AMS FRESHMAN UNDERGRADUATE SCHOLARSHIPS

American Meteorological Society
Attn: Fellowship/Scholarship Coordinator
45 Beacon Street
Boston, MA 02108-3693
Phone: (617) 227-2426, ext. 246; Fax: (617) 742-8718
Email: scholar@ametsoc.org
Web: www.ametsoc.org

Summary: To provide financial assistance to high school seniors planning to attend college to prepare for a career in the atmospheric or related oceanic or hydrologic sciences.

Eligibility: Open to high school seniors entering their freshman year of college to work on a bachelor's degree in the atmospheric or related oceanic or hydrologic sciences. Applicants must be U.S. citizens or permanent residents planning to enroll full-time. Along with their application, they must submit a 500-word essay on how they believe their college education, and what they learn in the atmospheric and related sciences, will help them to serve society during their professional career. Selection is based on performance in high school, including academic records, recommendations, scores from a national examination, and the essay. Financial need is not considered. The sponsor specifically encourages applications from women, minorities, and students with disabilities who are traditionally underrepresented in the atmospheric and related oceanic sciences.

Financial data: The stipend is $2,500 per academic year.

Duration: 1 year; may be renewed for the second year of college study.

Number awarded: Varies each year; recently, 14 of these scholarships were awarded.

Deadline: February of each year.

1701 AMTROL INC. SCHOLARSHIP

American Ground Water Trust
50 Pleasant Street
Concord, NH 03301
Phone: (603) 228-5444; Fax: (603) 228-6557
Email: trustinfo@agwt.org
Web: www.agwt.org/scholarships.htm

Summary: To provide financial assistance to high school seniors who are interested in preparing for a career in a ground water–related field.

Eligibility: Open to high school seniors who have a GPA of 3.0 or higher and are entering a 4-year college or university as a full-time student. Applicants must be planning a career in a ground water–related field and must have completed a science/environmental project in high school that directly involved ground water resources or have had vacation/out-of-school work experience that is directly related to the environment and natural resources. They must submit a 500-word essay on "Ground Water—An Important Environmental and Economic Resource for America" and a 300-word description of their high school ground water project and/or practical environmental work experience. Selection is based on the above criteria, and on the applicant's references and academic record. Financial need is not considered. U.S. citizenship or permanent resident status is required.

Financial data: The stipend is $1,000. Funds are paid directly to the recipient's college.

Duration: 1 year.

Number awarded: 1 or more each year.

Deadline: May of each year.

1702 ANAC STUDENT DIVERSITY MENTORSHIP SCHOLARSHIP

Association of Nurses in AIDS Care
Attn: Awards Committee
3538 Ridgewood Road
Akron, OH 44333-3122
Phone: (330) 670-0101; (800) 260-6780; Fax: (330) 670-0109
Email: anac@anacnet.org
Web: www.anacnet.org/i4a/pages/index.cfm?pageid=3321

Summary: To provide financial assistance to student nurses from minority groups who are interested in HIV/AIDS nursing and in attending the national conference of the Association of Nurses in AIDS Care (ANAC).

Eligibility: Open to student nurses from a diverse racial or ethnic background, defined to include African Americans, Hispanics/Latinos, Asians/Pacific Islanders, and American Indians/Alaskan Natives. Candidates must have a genuine interest in HIV/AIDS nursing, be interested in attending the ANAC national conference, and desire to develop a mentorship relationship with a member of the ANAC Diversity Specialty Committee. They must be currently enrolled in an accredited nursing program at any level (e.g., L.P.N., A.D.N., diploma, B.S.N., or graduate nursing). Nominees may be recommended by themselves, nursing faculty members, or ANAC members, but their nomination must be supported by an ANAC member. Along with their nomination form, they must submit a 500-word personal statement describing their interest or experience in HIV/AIDS care and why they want to attend the ANAC conference.

Financial data: Recipients are awarded a $1,000 scholarship (paid directly to the school), up to $599 in reimbursement of travel expenses to attend the ANAC annual conference, free conference registration, an award plaque, a free ticket to the awards ceremony at the conference, and a 1-year ANAC membership.

Duration: 1 year.

Number awarded: 1 each year.

Deadline: June of each year.

1703 ANNA N. DOSEN SERBIAN EDUCATIONAL FUND

Pittsburgh Foundation
Attn: Scholarship Coordinator
Five PPG Place, Suite 250
Pittsburgh, PA 15222-5414
Phone: (412) 394-2649; Fax: (412) 391-7259
Email: turnerd@pghfdn.org
Web: www.pittsburghfoundation.org

Summary: To provide financial assistance to undergraduate students of Serbian background interested in studying the health sciences or engineering in college.

Eligibility: Open to students of Serbian background who are attending or planning to attend a 2- or 4-year accredited college or university to major in health sciences or engineering. Applicants must submit a 1-page essay explaining why they chose their particular field of study and what accomplishments they hope to achieve in that field. Financial need is also considered in the selection process.

Financial data: Recently, the stipend was $4,500 per year.

Duration: 4 years.

Number awarded: 1 or more each year.

Deadline: March of each year.

1704 ANNIE'S SUSTAINABLE AGRICULTURE SCHOLARSHIPS

Annie's Homegrown, Inc.
Attn: Consumer Relations
564 Gateway Drive
Napa, CA 94558
Phone: (800) 288-1089
Email: cfc@annies.com
Web: www.annies.com/sustainable_agriculture_scholarship

Summary: To provide financial assistance to entering or enrolled undergraduate and graduate students working on a degree in sustainable agriculture.

Eligibility: Open to students beginning or returning to an accredited 2- or 4-year technical or college program and majoring in a field related to sustainable and organic agriculture. Graduate students are also eligible. Applicants must include a personal statement in which they answer 1 of 3 assigned questions that change annually. Selection is based on that statement, a transcript, 2 letters of recommendation, and a brief telephone interview. Financial need is not considered.

Financial data: Stipends are $10,000 or $2,500.

Duration: 1 year.

Number awarded: Varies each year; recently, 6 undergraduate scholarships (2 at $10,000 and 4 at $2,500) and 5 graduate scholarships (1 at $10,000 and 4 at $2,500) were awarded.

Deadline: August of each year.

1705 ANS INCOMING FRESHMAN SCHOLARSHIPS

American Nuclear Society
Attn: Scholarship Coordinator
555 North Kensington Avenue
La Grange Park, IL 60526-5592
Phone: (708) 352-6611; (800) 323-3044; Fax: (708) 352-0499
Email: outreach@ans.org
Web: www.ans.org/honors/scholarships

Summary: To provide financial assistance to students entering their freshman year of college and planning to prepare for a career in nuclear science or nuclear engineering.

Eligibility: Open to graduating high school seniors who have enrolled as a full-time college student. Applicants must be taking science, mathematics, or technical courses with an interest in working in nuclear science and technology. They must be U.S. citizens or permanent residents. Along with their application, they must submit a 500-word essay on their academic and career goals. Selection is based on that essay, high school academic achievement, freshmen college courses enrolled in, and letters of recommendation.

Financial data: The stipend is $1,000.

Duration: 1 year; nonrenewable.

Number awarded: 4 each year.

Deadline: March of each year.

1706 A.O. SMITH WATER HEATERS SCHOLARSHIP

Plumbing-Heating-Cooling Contractors–National Association
Attn: PHCC Educational Foundation
180 South Washington Street
P.O. Box 6808
Falls Church, VA 22040
Phone: (703) 237-8100, ext. 221; (800) 533-7694; Fax: (703) 237-7442
Email: scholarships@naphcc.org
Web: www.foundation.phccweb.org/Scholarships/AOSScholarship.htm

Summary: To provide financial assistance to entering or continuing undergraduate students interested in the plumbing, heating, and cooling industry.

Eligibility: Open to 1) full-time undergraduate students (entering or continuing) who are majoring in a field related to plumbing, heating, and cooling (e.g., business management, construction management with a specialization in mechanical construction, mechanical engineering) at a 4-year college or university; 2) students enrolled full-time in an approved certificate or degree program at a 2-year technical college, community college, or trade school in business management, mechanical CAD design, construction management with a specialty in mechanical construction, or plumbing or HVACR installation, service, and repair; and 3) full-time employees of a licensed plumbing or HVAC contractor (must be a member of the Plumbing-Heating-Cooling Contractors [PHCC]–National Association) who are enrolled in an apprenticeship program in plumbing or HVACR installation, service, and repair. Students majoring in accounting, architecture, computer engineering, construction-related engineering, civil engineering, electrical engineering, or environmental engineering are not eligible. Applicants must have a GPA of 2.0 or higher. Along with their application, they must submit a letter of recommendation from a PHCC member; a copy of school transcripts; SAT and/or ACT scores; and a letter of recommendation from a school principal, counselor, or dean. U.S. or Canadian citizenship is required. Financial need is not considered in the selection process.

Financial data: The stipend is $2,500.

Duration: 1 year; nonrenewable.

Number awarded: Up to 2 each year.

Deadline: April of each year.

1707 AORN FOUNDATION BACCALAUREATE DEGREE IN NURSING SCHOLARSHIP

Association of periOperative Registered Nurses
Attn: AORN Foundation
2170 South Parker Road, Suite 400
Denver, CO 80231-5711
Phone: (303) 755-6300, ext. 230; (800) 755-2676, ext. 230; Fax: (303) 755-4219
Email: foundation@aorn.org
Web: www.aorn.org/AORNFoundation/Scholarships

Summary: To provide financial assistance to students who wish to work on a baccalaureate degree in a field of interest to the Association of periOperative Registered Nurses (AORN).

Eligibility: Open to registered nurses who are committed to perioperative nursing and are currently enrolled in an accredited baccalaureate degree program. Along with their application, they must submit 4 essays: 1) their role as a perioperative nurse and why they chose that field; 2) their professional goals and what AORN does to support those goals; 3) how they will apply their degree to perioperative nursing; and 4) how they believe AORN promotes the specialty of perioperative nursing. Financial need is not considered in the selection process. Membership in AORN is not required, but applicants are encouraged to become members.

Financial data: A stipend is awarded (amount not specified); funds are intended to be used for payment of tuition, related fees, and books.

Duration: 1 year.

Number awarded: Varies each year; recently, 15 of these scholarships were awarded.

Deadline: June of each year.

1708 APS SCHOLARSHIPS FOR MINORITY UNDERGRADUATE PHYSICS MAJORS

American Physical Society
Attn: Committee on Minorities
One Physics Ellipse
College Park, MD 20740-3844
Phone: (301) 209-3232; Fax: (301) 209-0865
Web: www.aps.org/programs/minorities/honors/scholarship/index.cfm

Summary: To provide financial assistance to underrepresented minority students interested in studying physics on the undergraduate level.

Eligibility: Open to any African American, Hispanic American, or Native American who plans to major in physics and who is a high school senior or college freshman or sophomore. U.S. citizenship or permanent resident status is required. The selection committee especially encourages applications from students who are attending or planning to attend institutions with historically or predominantly Black, Hispanic, or Native American enrollment. Selection is based on commitment to the study of physics and plans to work on a physics baccalaureate degree.

Financial data: Stipends are $2,000 per year in the first year or $3,000 in the second year; funds must be used for tuition, room, and board. In addition, $500 is awarded to the host department.

Duration: 1 year; renewable for 1 additional year with the approval of the APS selection committee.

Number awarded: Varies each year; recently, 40 of these scholarships were awarded.

Deadline: February of each year.

1709 APWA HORIZONS FRONT RANGE SCHOLARSHIP

Summary: To provide financial assistance to high school seniors in Colorado who plan to attend a college or university in the state to prepare for a career in public works.

See Listing #1165.

1710 ARABIAN HORSE FOUNDATION GENERAL SCHOLARSHIPS

Arabian Horse Foundation
Attn: Scholarships
10805 East Bethany Drive
Aurora, CO 80014
Phone: (303) 696-4500; Fax: (303) 696-4599
Web: www.arabianhorsefoundation.org/scholarship.html

Summary: To provide financial assistance to undergraduate and graduate students in any field who have a record of equine involvement.

Eligibility: Open to students who have a record of involvement with horses. Applicants must be enrolled or planning to enroll as a full-time undergraduate or graduate student at an accredited college or university. High school seniors must have a GPA of "B" or higher; college and graduate students must have at least a 3.5 GPA. Along with their application, they must submit information on their financial need, honors or academic awards, extracurricular activities and offices, leadership role, career goal, and equine involvement for the past 2 years.

Financial data: A stipend is awarded (amount not specified).

Duration: 1 year; may be renewed if the recipient maintains a GPA of 2.5 or higher with no grade below a "D."

Number awarded: 1 or more each year.

Deadline: March of each year.

1711 ARC WELDING AWARDS—DIVISION I

James F. Lincoln Arc Welding Foundation
Attn: Secretary
22801 Saint Clair Avenue
P.O. Box 17188
Cleveland, OH 44117-1199
Phone: (216) 481-8100; Fax: (216) 486-1751
Email: innovate@lincolnelectric.com
Web: www.jflf.org/awards/division1.asp

Summary: To recognize and reward students younger than 18 years of age who submit outstanding arc welding projects.

Eligibility: Open to students 18 years of age or younger enrolled in a shop course at any time during their school or training program. Applicants must submit an arc welding project made by them or a problem concerned with the use and knowledge of arc welding. Entries must be submitted as a 3- to 25-page written description of the project or problem; drawings, photographs, and sketches are encouraged, but models or specimens may not be submitted. Written entries must have been completed during the previous 12-month period. Selection is based on the practicality or usefulness of the project or problem, how well the use or knowledge of arc welding was applied, the skill and ability with which the project or problem was completed, how clearly the project or problem is described, and how well the entry conforms to requirements.

Financial data: At the regional level, gold awards are $500, silver awards are $250, bronze awards are $100, and merit awards are $25. At the national level, the gold award is $1,000, the silver award is $750, and the bronze award is $500.

Duration: The competition is held annually.

Number awarded: In each of 4 geographic regions, 1 gold award, 2 silver awards, and 3 bronze awards are presented. A total of $8,000 is presented in merit awards regardless of region. At the national level, 3 students receive awards (1 each of gold, silver, and bronze).

Deadline: May of each year.

1712 ARC WELDING AWARDS—DIVISION II

James F. Lincoln Arc Welding Foundation
Attn: Secretary
22801 Saint Clair Avenue
P.O. Box 17188
Cleveland, OH 44117-1199
Phone: (216) 481-8100; Fax: (216) 486-1751
Email: innovate@lincolnelectric.com
Web: www.jflf.org/awards/division2.asp

Summary: To recognize and reward students 19 years of age and older who submit outstanding arc welding problems.

Eligibility: Open to students 19 years of age and older who are other than college students studying for a bachelor's or master's degree. Applicants may be enrolled in evening adult classes, high schools, vocational schools, private trade schools, in-plant training classes, technical institutes, apprenticeship programs, junior colleges, community colleges, or other 2-year college courses. They must submit a problem concerned with the use and knowledge of arc welding. It may involve the use of a welding technique, process or material, joint design, testing, welding procedure, tooling, or fixturing. Entries must be submitted as a 3- to 25-page written description of the problem; drawings, photographs, and sketches are encouraged, but models or specimens may not be submitted. Written entries must have been completed during the previous 12-month period. Selection is based on the practicality or usefulness of the problem, how well the use or knowledge of arc welding was applied, the skill and ability with which the problem was completed, how clearly the problem is described, and how well the entry conforms to requirements.

Financial data: The gold award is $1,000, the silver award is $500, the bronze award is $250, and merit awards are $25.

Duration: The competition is held annually.

Number awarded: 1 gold award, 2 silver awards, 3 bronze awards, and 40 merit awards are presented each year.

Deadline: May of each year.

1713 ARC WELDING AWARDS—DIVISION IV

James F. Lincoln Arc Welding Foundation
Attn: Secretary
22801 Saint Clair Avenue
P.O. Box 17188
Cleveland, OH 44117-1199
Phone: (216) 481-8100; Fax: (216) 486-1751
Email: innovate@lincolnelectric.com
Web: www.jflf.org/awards/division4.asp

Summary: To recognize and reward engineering and technology undergraduate and graduate students who submit outstanding papers involving the knowledge or application of arc welding.

Eligibility: Open to undergraduate and graduate students enrolled in a 4-year engineering or technology program at an accredited college or university in the United States. Participants must submit papers representing their work on design, engineering, or fabrication problems relating to 1) any type of building, bridge, structure machine, product, or mechanical apparatus; or 2) arc welding research, testing, procedure, or process development. Applicants may participate as individuals or in groups of up to 10 students. Reports prepared for course work, projects, or theses are eligible. Any number of entries may be submitted from 1 school, but no student may participate in more than 1 entry. Selection is based on originality or ingenuity, feasibility, results achieved or expected, engineering competence, and clarity of the presentation.

Financial data: Undergraduates qualify for awards of $1,000 for first place, $750 for second, $500 for third, or $250 for fourth. Graduate students qualify for a first prize of $1,000. All students qualify for the Chairman's Award of $1,000.

Duration: The competition is held annually.

Number awarded: The number of awards varies slightly. Recently, 5 undergraduate awards (1 each for first, second, and third, plus 2 fourth prizes), 1 graduate award, and 1 Chairman's Award were presented.

Deadline: June of each year.

1714 ARIZONA NURSES FOUNDATION ACADEMIC SCHOLARSHIP PROGRAM

Arizona Nurses Association
Attn: Arizona Nurses Foundation
1850 East Southern Avenue, Suite 1
Tempe, AZ 85282-5832
Phone: (480) 831-0404; Fax: (480) 839-4780
Email: info@aznurse.org
Web: www.aznurse.org/foundation/index.html

Summary: To provide financial assistance to undergraduate and graduate students from any state enrolled in or accepted to nursing programs in Arizona.

Eligibility: Open to undergraduate and graduate students from any state enrolled in, or accepted for enrollment in, an academic nursing education program in Arizona. Selection is based on potential for leadership in nursing, commitment to professional nursing in Arizona, and financial need. For graduate students, priority is given to applicants planning to teach nursing.

Financial data: Stipends are $500 per semester for associate degree students, $1,000 per semester for R.N. to B.S.N. students, $1,000 per semester for direct entry B.S.N. students, $1,000 per semester for master's degree students, and $2,500 per semester for doctoral students.

Duration: 1 semester; recipients may reapply.

Number awarded: 18 each semester: 4 for associate degree students, 4 for R.N. to B.S.N. students, 4 for direct entry B.S.N. students, 4 for master's degree students, and 2 for doctoral students.

Deadline: February or October of each year.

1715 ARIZONA SPECIAL LEVERAGING EDUCATIONAL ASSISTANCE PARTNERSHIP PROGRAM

Arizona Commission for Postsecondary Education
2020 North Central Avenue, Suite 550
Phoenix, AZ 85004-4503
Phone: (602) 258-2435; Fax: (602) 258-2483
Email: acpe@azhighered.gov
Web: www.azhighered.gov/SLEAP_Grant.html

Summary: To provide financial assistance to students at Arizona colleges and universities who are majoring in education or fields of science, technology, engineering, or mathematics (STEM) and can demonstrate substantial financial need.

Eligibility: Open to sophomores, juniors, and seniors at accredited postsecondary institutions in Arizona who have been residents of the state for at least the past 12 months. Applicants must be U.S. citizens or eligible noncitizens who can demonstrate substantial financial need. They must be majoring in education or designated STEM fields. Funds are awarded on a first-come, first-served basis.

Financial data: The maximum stipend is $2,000 per year for full-time students.

Duration: 1 year; recipients may reapply.

Number awarded: Varies each year.

Deadline: Deadline not specified.

1716 ARKANSAS POST SAME SCHOLARSHIPS

Summary: To provide financial assistance to Arkansas high school seniors interested in studying architecture or engineering at a college in any state.

See Listing #1168.

1717 ARKANSAS TECHNICAL CAREERS STUDENT LOAN FORGIVENESS PROGRAM

Arkansas Department of Career Education
Luther Hardin Building
Three Capitol Mall, Room 207
Little Rock, AR 72201-1083
Phone: (501) 682-1699; Fax: (501) 682-1509
Web: ace.arkansas.gov/LoanForgiveness/atcslfp.htm

Summary: To provide financial assistance to residents of Arkansas who are interested in pursuing technical education and working in the state.

Eligibility: Open to residents of Arkansas who are U.S. citizens or permanent residents admitted to an approved program resulting in a diploma, certificate, or degree in a high demand technical field. Applicants must indicate their intention to work in Arkansas in the field for which they receive the training.

Financial data: The maximum loan is $2,500 per year. Loans are forgiven if the recipient works full-time in the high demand technical field in Arkansas. Each year's loan may be forgiven with 1 year of full-time employment. Loan recipients who do not graduate from the program or work full-time in the field in Arkansas must repay the loan in full.

Duration: Up to 4 years.

Number awarded: Varies each year.

Deadline: Applications must be submitted within 6 months of the completion of the program of study.

1718 ARMED FORCES COMMUNICATIONS AND ELECTRONICS ASSOCIATION STEM TEACHER'S SCHOLARSHIP

Armed Forces Communications and Electronics Association
Attn: AFCEA Educational Foundation
4400 Fair Lakes Court
Fairfax, VA 22033-3899
Phone: (703) 631-6149; (800) 336-4583, ext. 6149; Fax: (703) 631-4693
Email: scholarship@afcea.org
Web: www.afcea.org

Summary: To provide financial assistance to undergraduate and graduate students who are preparing for a career as a teacher of science and mathematics.

Eligibility: Open to full-time juniors, seniors, and graduate students at accredited colleges and universities in the United States. Applicants must be U.S. citizens preparing for a career as a teacher of science, information technology, engineering, or mathematics (STEM) at a middle or secondary school. They must have a GPA of 3.0 or higher. Financial need is not considered in the selection process.

Financial data: The stipend is $2,500.

Duration: 1 year.

Number awarded: 2 each year.

Deadline: May of each year.

1719 ARMY NURSE CORPS ASSOCIATION SCHOLARSHIPS

Army Nurse Corps Association
Attn: Education Committee
P.O. Box 39235
San Antonio, TX 78218-1235
Phone: (210) 650-3534; Fax: (210) 650-3494
Email: education@e-anca.org
Web: e-anca.org/ANCAEduc.htm

Summary: To provide financial assistance to students who have a connection to the Army and are interested in working on an undergraduate or graduate degree in nursing.

Eligibility: Open to students attending colleges or universities that have accredited programs offering associate, bachelor's, master's, or doctoral degrees in nursing. Applicants must be 1) nursing students who plan to enter the active Army, Army National Guard, or Army Reserve and are not participating in a program funded by the active Army, Army National Guard, or Army Reserve; 2) nursing students who have previously served in the active Army, Army National Guard, or Army Reserve; 3) Army Nurse Corps officers enrolled in an undergraduate or graduate nursing program not funded by the active Army, Army National Guard, or Army Reserve; 4) Army enlisted soldiers in the active Army, Army National Guard, or Army Reserve who are working on a baccalaureate degree in nursing not funded by the active Army, Army National Guard, or Army Reserve; or 5) nursing students whose parent(s) or spouse is serving or has served in the active Army, Army National Guard, or Army Reserve. Along with their application, they must submit a personal statement on their professional career objectives, reasons for applying for this scholarship, financial need, special considerations, personal and academic interests, and why they are preparing for a nursing career.

Financial data: The stipend is $3,000. Funds are sent directly to the recipient's school.

Duration: 1 year.

Number awarded: 1 or more each year.

Deadline: March of each year.

1720 ARMY ROTC NURSE PROGRAM

U.S. Army
ROTC Cadet Command
Attn: ATCC-OP-I-S
55 Patch Road, Building 56
Fort Monroe, VA 23651-1052
Phone: (757) 788-4552; (800) USA-ROTC; Fax: (757) 788-4643
Email: atccps@usacc.army.mil
Web: www.goarmy.com/rotc/nurse_program.jsp

Summary: To provide financial assistance to high school seniors or graduates who are interested in enrolling in Army ROTC and majoring in nursing in college.

Eligibility: Open to applicants who 1) are U.S. citizens; 2) are at least 17 years of age by October of the year in which they are seeking a scholarship; 3) are no more than 27 years of age when they graduate from college after 4 years; 4) score at least 1050 on the combined mathematics and critical reading SAT or 21 on the ACT; 5) have a high school GPA of 3.0 or higher; and 6) meet medical and other regulatory requirements. They must wish to enroll in a nursing program at 1 of approximately 100 designated partner colleges and universities and become Army nurses after graduation.

Financial data: This scholarship provides financial assistance toward college tuition and educational fees up to an annual amount of $17,000. In addition, a flat rate of $1,000 is provided for the purchase of textbooks, classroom supplies, and equipment. Recipients are also awarded a stipend for up to 10 months of each year that is $300 per month during their freshman year, $350 per month during their sophomore year, $450 per month during their junior year, and $500 per month during their senior year.

Duration: 4 years, until completion of a baccalaureate degree. A limited number of 2- and 3-year scholarships are also available to students who are already attending an accredited B.S.N. program on a campus affiliated with ROTC.

Number awarded: A limited number each year.

Deadline: November of each year.

1721 ARNOLD SADLER MEMORIAL SCHOLARSHIP

American Council of the Blind
Attn: Coordinator, Scholarship Program
2200 Wilson Boulevard, Suite 650
Arlington, VA 22201
Phone: (202) 467-5081; (800) 424-8666; Fax: (703) 465-5085
Email: info@acb.org
Web: www.acb.org

Summary: To provide financial assistance to undergraduate or graduate students who are blind and are interested in studying in a field of service to persons with disabilities.

Eligibility: Open to undergraduate and graduate students in rehabilitation, education, law, or other fields of service to persons with disabilities. Applicants must be legally blind in both eyes. Along with their application, they must submit verification of legal blindness in both eyes; SAT, ACT, GRE, or similar scores; information on extracurricular activities (including membership in the American Council of the Blind); employment record; and an autobiographical sketch that includes their personal goals, strengths, weaknesses, hobbies, honors, achievements, and reasons for choice of field or courses of study. A cumulative GPA of 3.3 or higher is generally required. Financial need is not considered in the selection process.

Financial data: The stipend is $1,500. In addition, the winner receives a Kurzweil-1000 Reading System.

Duration: 1 year.

Number awarded: 1 each year.

Deadline: February of each year.

1722 ARTHUR C. PIKE SCHOLARSHIP IN METEOROLOGY

National Weather Association
Attn: Executive Director
228 West Millbrook Road
Raleigh, NC 27609-4304
Phone: (919) 845-1546; Fax: (919) 845-2956
Email: exdir@nwas.org
Web: www.nwas.org/committees/ed_comm/application/Pike.php

Summary: To provide financial assistance to students working on an undergraduate or graduate degree in meteorology.

Eligibility: Open to students who are either entering their junior or senior year of undergraduate study or enrolled as graduate students. Applicants must be working on a degree in meteorology. Along with their application, they must submit a 1-page statement explaining why they are applying for this scholarship. Selection is based on that statement, academic achievement, and 2 letters of recommendation.

Financial data: The stipend is $1,000.

Duration: 1 year.

Number awarded: 1 each year.

Deadline: April of each year.

1723 ARTHUR E. COTE SCHOLARSHIP

National Fire Protection Association
Attn: Fire Safety Educational Memorial Fund Committee
1 Batterymarch Park
Quincy, MA 02169-7471
Phone: (617) 984-7244; Fax: (617) 984-7222
Email: cellis@nfpa.org
Web: www.nfpa.org

Summary: To provide financial assistance to undergraduate students enrolled in fire protection engineering programs.

Eligibility: Open to undergraduate students enrolled in a fire protection engineering program. Colleges and universities in the United States and Canada are invited to nominate up to 2 students enrolled. Nominees must submit a letter describing their achievements, leadership abilities, volunteerism, interest in fire protection engineering, and specific long-range goals. Financial need is not considered in the selection process.

Financial data: The stipend is at least $5,000.

Duration: 1 year.

Number awarded: 1 each year.

Deadline: March of each year.

1724 ARTHUR H. GUENTHER PULSED POWER STUDENT AWARD

Institute of Electrical and Electronics Engineers
Nuclear and Plasma Sciences Society
c/o Bill Moses, NPSS Awards Committee
Lawrence Berkeley Laboratory
1 Cyclotron Road
Mailstop 55-121
Berkeley, CA 94720
Phone: (510) 486-4432; Fax: (510) 486-4768
Email: wwmoses@lbl.gov
Web: ewh.ieee.org/soc/nps/awards.htm

Summary: To recognize and reward outstanding student contributions to pulsed power engineering, science, and technology.

Eligibility: Open to full-time undergraduate and graduate students in pulsed power engineering or science. Nominees must be a student when nominated. Selection is based on quality of research contributions (40 points), quality of educational accomplishments (30 points), and quality and significance of publications and patents (20 points).

Financial data: The award consists of $1,000 and a certificate.

Duration: The award is presented annually.

Number awarded: 1 each year.

Deadline: January of each year.

1725 ARTHUR W. PENSE SCHOLARSHIP

NYSARC, Inc.
Attn: Scholarship and Awards Committee
393 Delaware Avenue
Delmar, NY 12054
Phone: (518) 439-8311; Fax: (518) 439-1893
Email: info@nysarc.org
Web: www.nysarc.org/family/nysarc-family-scholarships.asp

Summary: To provide financial assistance to college students in New York working on a degree in occupational or physical therapy.

Eligibility: Open to students enrolled at a college or university in New York in a 4- or 5-year degree program in occupational or physical therapy. Applicants must provide a list of work experience with people who have intellectual and other developmental disabilities and a 1-page autobiographical sketch indicating their interest in the field and their plans after graduation. Financial need is not considered in the selection process.

Financial data: The stipend is $1,500 per year.

Duration: 2 years (the final 2 years of study).

Number awarded: 1 each year.
Deadline: January of each year.

1726 ASCE MAINE SECTION SCHOLARSHIP

American Society of Civil Engineers–Maine Section
c/o Leslie L. Corrow, Scholarship Chair
Kleinschmidt Associates
75 Main Street
P.O. Box 576
Pittsfield, ME 04967
Phone: (207) 487-3328; Fax: (207) 487-3124
Email: scholarships@maineasce.org
Web: www.maineasce.org

Summary: To provide financial assistance to high school seniors in Maine who are interested in studying civil engineering in college.
Eligibility: Open to graduating high school seniors who are Maine residents and who intend to study civil engineering in college. Women and minorities are especially encouraged to apply. Applicants must submit a 200-word statement describing why they have chosen civil engineering as a career and what they hope to accomplish by being a civil engineer. Selection is based on the statement, academic performance, extracurricular activities, and letters of recommendation.
Financial data: The stipend is $2,000.
Duration: 1 year; nonrenewable.
Number awarded: 1 each year.
Deadline: January of each year.

1727 ASCO NUMATICS INDUSTRIAL AUTOMATION ENGINEERING COLLEGE SCHOLARSHIPS

ASCO Numatics
50 Hanover Road
Florham Park, NJ 07932
Phone: (973) 966-2000; (800) 972-ASCO; Fax: (973) 966-2448
Email: ascomarketing@asco.com
Web: www.asconumatics.com

Summary: To provide financial assistance to upper-division and graduate students interested in preparing for a career in fields related to industrial automation.
Eligibility: Open to U.S. citizens and permanent residents who have completed at least their sophomore year in an engineering bachelor's degree program or are attending graduate school. Applicants must be enrolled full-time in a program in an instrumentation, systems, electrical, mechanical, or automation discipline, particularly as those relate to the application of fluid control and fluid power technologies. They must have a GPA of 3.2 or higher. Financial need is not considered in the selection process.
Financial data: The stipend is $5,000. Funds are paid directly to the recipient's educational institution.
Duration: 1 year; nonrenewable.
Number awarded: 2 each year.
Deadline: June of each year.

1728 ASCP STUDENT SCHOLARSHIPS

American Society for Clinical Pathology
Attn: Membership Services
33 West Monroe Street, Suite 1600
Chicago, IL 60603
Phone: (312) 541-4999; (800) 267-2727; Fax: (312) 541-4998
Email: info@ascp.org
Web: www.ascp.org/scholarships

Summary: To provide funding to students enrolled in programs related to clinical laboratory science.
Eligibility: Open to students enrolled in an NAACLS- or CAAHEP-accredited college/university program as a cytotechnologist (CT), histologic technician (HT), histotechnologist (HTL), medical laboratory technician (MLT), medical technologist (MT), pathologist assistant (PA), or phlebotomy technician (PBT). Applicants must be in the final clinical year of education and either U.S. citizens or permanent residents. HT applicants have no minimum GPA requirement, but other applicants must have a GPA of 3.0 or higher. Selection is based on academic achievement, leadership abilities, professional goals, and community activities.
Financial data: The stipend is $1,000 for all fields except PBT, which is $500.
Duration: 1 year.
Number awarded: Varies each year; recently, 53 of these scholarships were awarded: 4 for CT students, 3 for HT students, 1 for an HTL student, 9 for MLT students, 31 for MT students, 1 for a PA student, and 4 for PBT students.
Deadline: November of each year.

1729 ASHADO SCHOLARSHIP

Race for Education
Attn: Student Services Manager
1818 Versailles Road
P.O. Box 11355
Lexington, KY 40575
Phone: (859) 252-8648; Fax: (859) 252-8030
Email: info@racingscholarships.com
Web: www.racingscholarships.com/page.php?page=programs

Summary: To provide financial assistance to female undergraduate students working on an equine-related degree.
Eligibility: Open to female undergraduate students under 24 years of age working on an equine-related degree, including (but not limited to) pre-veterinary medicine (equine practice only), equine science, equine business management, racetrack management, or other equine- or agriculture-related program. Applicants must have a GPA of 2.85 or higher and be a U.S. citizen or have a valid student visa. Their household income may not exceed $50,000 per year.
Financial data: The stipend covers payment of tuition, to a maximum of $6,000 per year. The student is responsible for all other fees.
Duration: 1 year; may be renewed up to 3 additional years, provided the recipient maintains a GPA of 3.0 or higher.
Number awarded: 1 or more each year.
Deadline: February of each year.

1730 ASHS SCHOLARS AWARD

American Society for Horticultural Science
113 South West Street, Suite 200
Alexandria, VA 22314-2851
Phone: (703) 836-4606; Fax: (703) 836-2024
Email: ashs@ashs.org
Web: www.ashs.org

Summary: To provide financial assistance to undergraduate students majoring in horticulture.
Eligibility: Open to full-time undergraduate students of any class standing who are actively working on a degree in horticulture at a 4-year college or university. Applicants must be nominated by the chair of the department in which they are majoring; each department may nominate only 1 student. They must submit transcripts, 3 letters of reference, a complete resume and/or vitae, and an essay of 250 to 500 words on their reasons for interest in horticulture and for selecting their intended field of work after graduation. Selection is based on academic excellence in the major and supporting areas of science; participation in extracurricular, leadership, and research activities relating to horticulture; participation in university and community service; demonstrated commitment to the horticultural science profession and related career fields; and related horticultural experiences. Financial need is not considered.
Financial data: The stipend is $1,500.
Duration: 1 year.
Number awarded: 2 each year.
Deadline: February of each year.

1731 ASIAN PACIFIC ISLANDER ORGANIZATION SCHOLARSHIP PROGRAM

Asian Pacific Islander Organization
P.O. Box 2391
Billings, MT 59103
Web: www.apio.org/scholarship.htm

Summary: To provide financial assistance to Asian and Pacific Islanders who are studying designated fields in college.
Eligibility: Open to Asian and Pacific Islander students who have completed at least 15 semester hours of credit at an accredited 2- or 4-year college or university. Applicants must be working on a degree in a field related to natural resources (e.g., agricultural business, agronomy, botany, environmental science, forestry, geology, horticulture, plant science, rangeland management, soil science, or agricultural, civil, or environmental engineering). Along with their application, they must submit a 1-page personal statement on their background, personal and career goals, and extracurricular activities. Selection is based on academic achievement, personal strengths, leadership abilities, career goals, and work experience. U.S. citizenship is required.

Financial data: The stipend is $1,000.
Duration: 1 year.
Number awarded: 3 each year.
Deadline: February of each year.

1732 ASLA COUNCIL OF FELLOWS SCHOLARSHIPS

Summary: To provide financial assistance to upper-division students, especially those from disadvantaged and underrepresented groups, working on a degree in landscape architecture.
See Listing #1175.

1733 ASSOCIATED GENERAL CONTRACTORS OF MAINE SCHOLARSHIPS

Associated General Contractors of Maine, Inc.
Attn: AGC of Maine Education Foundation
188 Whitten Road
P.O. Box 5519
Augusta, ME 04332-5519
Phone: (207) 622-4741; Fax: (207) 622-1625
Email: info@agcmaine.org
Web: agcmaine.org/training-development/education-foundation
Summary: To provide financial assistance to Maine residents interested in studying in a construction-related field at a college in the state.
Eligibility: Open to Maine residents who are entering their first, second, third, or fourth year at an accredited institution of higher education in the state. Applicants must be enrolled in a field of study related to construction. Along with their application, they must submit a 150-word essay on why they are preparing for a career in construction. Selection is based on academic record and financial need.
Financial data: Stipends range from $500 to $4,000.
Duration: 1 year.
Number awarded: Varies each year; recently, 12 of these scholarships were awarded.
Deadline: March of each year.

1734 ASSOCIATED GENERAL CONTRACTORS OF MINNESOTA SCHOLARSHIPS

Associated General Contractors of Minnesota
Capitol Office Building
525 Park Street, Suite 110
St. Paul, MN 55103-2186
Phone: (651) 632-8929; (800) 552-7670; Fax: (651) 632-8928
Email: info@agcmn.org
Web: www.agcmn.org
Summary: To provide financial assistance to students in Minnesota preparing for a career in the construction industry.
Eligibility: Open to residents of Minnesota enrolled in construction programs at colleges and universities in the state. Fields of study include, but are not limited to, architecture, civil engineering, construction management, electrical engineering, and HVAC systems services. Applicants must submit a personal statement that includes information on their work-related experience, involvement in student or community organizations, honors or awards they have received, their financial situation, and other appropriate information. Selection is based on academic standing (20%), career objectives (20%), financial need (20%), personal information (20%), and overall application clarity (20%).
Financial data: Stipends range from $750 to $2,000.
Duration: 1 year.
Number awarded: Varies each year; recently, 8 of these scholarships were awarded: 2 at $2,000, 4 at $1,000, and 2 at $750.
Deadline: May of each year.

1735 ASSOCIATED OREGON LOGGERS SCHOLARSHIPS

Associated Oregon Loggers, Inc.
1127 25th Street, S.E.
P.O. Box 12339
Salem, OR 97309-0339
Phone: (503) 364-1330; (800) 452-6023; Fax: (503) 364-0836
Email: aol@oregonloggers.org
Web: www.oregonloggers.org/scholarship.html
Summary: To provide financial assistance to high school seniors in Oregon who are planning to major in a forest resource production field of study at a school in any state.
Eligibility: Open to high school seniors in Oregon who will be attending a 4-year college or university in any state accredited by the Society of American Foresters. Applicants must be planning to major in a forest resource production field of study, including forest management, forest engineering, and forest products. They must submit high school transcripts, SAT or ACT scores, verification of college acceptance, and a 3-page essay on a topic that changes annually but relates to forestry; recently, students were asked to give their ideas on the forest values that are important to Oregon's economic, social, and environmental well being. Selection is based on academic record, SAT or ACT scores, relevant experiences, and thought process, grammatical usage, and expression in the required essay. Financial need is not considered. Finalists may be interviewed.
Financial data: The stipend is $1,500 per year.
Duration: 1 year; may be renewed for 3 additional years.
Number awarded: 1 or more each year.
Deadline: March of each year.

1736 ASSOCIATION FOR MANUFACTURING TECHNOLOGY 2-YEAR SCHOLARSHIP PROGRAM

Association for Manufacturing Technology
Attn: Scholarship Coordinator
7901 Westpark Drive
McLean, VA 22102-4206
Phone: (703) 827-5219; (800) 524-0475, ext. 5219; Fax: (703) 893-1151
Email: AMT@AMTonline.org
Web: www.amtonline.org/scholarship
Summary: To provide financial assistance and work experience to students interested in earning a 2-year degree in a manufacturing technology-related field or participating in a university cooperative program.
Eligibility: Open to students enrolled or planning to enroll in 1) a 2-year manufacturing technology-related degree program at an accredited junior, community, or technical college; or 2) a 4-year university that offers a cooperative education program in a field related to the business of a firm that is a member of the Association for Manufacturing Technology (AMT). Students must have demonstrated or expressed a specific interest in a manufacturing technology-related career and meet the admission requirements of their 2-year institution or the cooperative program of their university. They must meet the normal employment standards of a sponsoring AMT company and be employable in the industry. Eligible fields of study include engineering (computer, electrical, electronic, hydraulic, manufacturing, mechanical, metallurgical, quality) or sales and business (accounting, computer applications, finance, information services, management, production, purchasing). Along with their application, students must submit an essay of 250 to 500 words explaining why they would be the best candidate for this scholarship and how it would help them meet their career goals. Financial need is not considered in the selection process.
Financial data: The stipend is $4,000 per year, to cover tuition, books, and related academic fees. Funds are paid directly to the recipient's institution. Participants also receive the normal salary while working for the sponsoring company.
Duration: 1 year; may be renewed for 1 additional year provided the recipient remains in good academic standing, remains in the major curriculum area chosen at the time of enrollment in the scholarship program, and maintains an ongoing liaison with the sponsoring company that includes at least 375 hours of paid curriculum-related work assignments.
Number awarded: Between 10 to 20 companies sponsor scholarship students each year.
Deadline: Deadline not specified.

1737 ASSOCIATION FOR WOMEN GEOSCIENTISTS MINORITY SCHOLARSHIP

Association for Women Geoscientists
Attn: AWG Foundation
12000 North Washington Street, Suite 285
Thornton, CO 80241
Phone: (303) 412-6219; Fax: (303) 253-9220
Email: minorityscholarship@awg.org
Web: www.awg.org/EAS/scholarships.html
Summary: To provide financial assistance to underrepresented minority women who are interested in working on an undergraduate degree in the geosciences.
Eligibility: Open to women who are African American, Hispanic, or Native American (including Eskimo, Hawaiian, Samoan, or American Indian). Applicants must be full-time students working on, or planning to work on, an

undergraduate degree in the geosciences (including geology, geophysics, geochemistry, hydrology, meteorology, physical oceanography, planetary geology, or earth science education). They must submit a 500-word essay on their academic and career goals, 2 letters of recommendation, high school and/or college transcripts, and SAT or ACT scores. Financial need is not considered in the selection process.

Financial data: A total of $6,000 is available for this program each year.

Duration: 1 year; may be renewed.

Number awarded: 1 or more each year.

Deadline: June of each year.

1738 ASSOCIATION OF CALIFORNIA WATER AGENCIES SCHOLARSHIPS

Association of California Water Agencies
Attn: Scholarship Program
910 K Street, Suite 100
Sacramento, CA 95814-3514
Phone: (916) 441-4545; Fax: (916) 325-2316
Email: awards@acwa.com
Web: www.acwa.com/content/scholarships/scholarships

Summary: To provide financial assistance to upper-division students in California who are majoring in water resources–related fields of study.

Eligibility: Open to California residents attending selected colleges and universities in the state. Applicants must be full-time students in their junior or senior year at the time of the award and majoring in a field related to or identified with water resources, including engineering, agricultural and/or urban water supply, environmental sciences, or public administration. Along with their application, they must submit a 2-page essay on key water-related issues they would address if given the opportunity, why they have chosen a career in the water resources field, and how their educational and career goals relate to a future in California water resources. Selection is based on scholastic achievement, commitment to a career in the field of water resources, and financial need.

Financial data: The stipend is $3,000. Funds are paid directly to the recipient's school.

Duration: 1 year.

Number awarded: 2 each year.

Deadline: March of each year.

1739 ASSOCIATION OF ENERGY ENGINEERS SCHOLARSHIPS

Association of Energy Engineers
Attn: Foundation
4025 Pleasantdale Road, Suite 420
Atlanta, GA 30340
Phone: (770) 447-5083, ext. 221; Fax: (770) 446-3969
Email: info@aeecenter.org
Web: www.aeecenter.org

Summary: To provide financial assistance to undergraduate and graduate students interested in taking courses directly related to energy engineering or energy management.

Eligibility: Open to undergraduate and graduate students who are enrolled in engineering or management programs at accredited colleges and universities and who would be interested in taking courses directly related to energy engineering or energy management (preferably within a curriculum leading to a major or minor in energy engineering). Qualified students are invited to submit their applications to the association's local chapter, along with transcripts and letters of recommendation. Each chapter may then submit up to 6 nominees, no more than 2 of whom may be graduate students. Selection is based on scholarship, character, and need. In awarding scholarships, preference is given to candidates needing aid for their final year; second, to candidates needing aid for the last 2 years; third, to candidates needing aid for 3 years; and finally, to first-year students.

Financial data: Stipends are $1,000, $500, or $125. The 2 most outstanding candidates receive the Victor Ottaviano Scholarship and the Al Thumann Scholarship.

Duration: 1 year.

Number awarded: Varies each year; recently, 53 of these scholarships were awarded: 2 at $1,000, 46 at $500, and 5 at $125.

Deadline: April of each year.

1740 ASSOCIATION OF PERIOPERATIVE REGISTERED NURSES (AORN) FOUNDATION NURSING STUDENT SCHOLARSHIPS

Association of periOperative Registered Nurses
Attn: AORN Foundation
2170 South Parker Road, Suite 400
Denver, CO 80231-5711
Phone: (303) 755-6300, ext. 230; (800) 755-2676, ext. 230; Fax: (303) 755-4219
Email: foundation@aorn.org
Web: www.aorn.org/AORNFoundation/Scholarships

Summary: To provide financial assistance to students interested in preparing for a career in nursing, especially perioperative nursing.

Eligibility: Open to students currently enrolled in an accredited nursing program leading to initial licensure as an R.N. The program may be for a diploma or an A.D.N., B.S.N., master's entry, or accelerated second B.S.N. degree. Applicants must submit 3 essays: 1) why they have chosen to prepare for a career in nursing and their career goals; 2) their academic and/or clinical experience or exposure to the operating room/surgical field; and 3) how they believe the Association of periOperative Registered Nurses (AORN) promotes the specialty of perioperative nursing. Financial need is not considered in the selection process. Membership in AORN is not required, but applicants are encouraged to become members.

Financial data: A stipend is awarded (amount not specified); funds are intended to be used for payment of tuition, related fees, and books.

Duration: 1 year.

Number awarded: Varies each year; recently, 12 of these scholarships were awarded.

Deadline: June of each year.

1741 ASTRONAUT SCHOLARSHIP FOUNDATION SCHOLARSHIPS

Astronaut Scholarship Foundation
Attn: Executive Director
6225 Vectorspace Boulevard
Titusville, FL 32780
Phone: (321) 455-7011; Fax: (321) 264-9176
Email: Linn@astronautscholarship.org
Web: www.astronautscholarship.org

Summary: To provide financial assistance to upper-division and graduate students in science and engineering.

Eligibility: Open to juniors, seniors, and graduate students working on a bachelor's or master's degree in the natural or applied sciences (e.g., astronomy, biology, chemistry, computer science, earth science, mathematics, physics) or engineering fields. Candidates must be nominated by faculty or staff at 1 of 19 participating universities; each may nominate 2 students. Students intending to practice professional medicine are not eligible, but those intending to do biomedical research are considered. No special consideration is given to aeronautical or astronautical engineering students or those intending to prepare for a career as astronauts. Special consideration is given to applicants who have shown initiative, creativity, excellence, and/or resourcefulness in their field. U.S. citizenship is required.

Financial data: The stipend is $10,000.

Duration: 1 year.

Number awarded: Normally 19 each year: 1 at each of the participating universities.

Deadline: Deadline not specified.

1742 AUTO TECHNICIAN SCHOLARSHIP

California New Car Dealers Association
Attn: Scholarship Foundation
1415 L Street, Suite 700
Sacramento, CA 95814
Phone: (916) 441-2599; Fax: (916) 441-5612
Email: bsedlezky@cncda.org
Web: www.cncda.org/scholarship/scholarship.html

Summary: To provide financial assistance to California residents interested in attending an automotive technician training program in the state.

Eligibility: Open to residents of California who are enrolled or planning to enroll in a postsecondary mechanical automotive technician training program in the state. Applicants must be preparing for a career as an auto technician at a California franchised new car dealership. In the selection process, consideration is given to academic awards, recognitions, and honors; financial need; and diversity.

Financial data: A stipend is awarded (amount not specified); funds are paid directly to the recipient's institution to be used for tuition, fees, books, tools, and other eligible educational expenses.

Duration: 1 year; may be renewed, provided the recipient maintains a GPA of 2.5 or higher.

Number awarded: Varies each year.

Deadline: June of each year.

1743 AUTOMOTIVE EDUCATIONAL FUND UPPER-DIVISION SCHOLARSHIP PROGRAM

Automotive Hall of Fame
Attn: Scholarship Programs
21400 Oakwood Boulevard
Dearborn, MI 48124
Phone: (313) 240-4000; Fax: (313) 240-8641
Web: www.automotivehalloffame.org/scholarships.php

Summary: To provide funding to upper-division students who are preparing for an automotive career.

Eligibility: Open to upper-division students who have expressed a strong interest in an automotive career. Applicants must be enrolled full-time at an accredited college or university and able to demonstrate financial need. They must be a U.S. citizen or have a valid student visa. Along with their application, they must submit a brief explanation of their career goals and objectives for the next 5 years. Some programs specify a minimum GPA of 3.0, others require a GPA of 3.4 or higher.

Financial data: Stipends range from $250 to $2,000. Funds are sent to the recipient's institution.

Duration: 1 year; may be renewed.

Number awarded: 7 each year.

Deadline: May of each year.

1744 AVIATION INSURANCE ASSOCIATION SCHOLARSHIP

Aviation Insurance Association
Attn: AIA Education Foundation
400 Admiral Boulevard
Kansas City, MO 64106
Phone: (816) 221-8488; Fax: (816) 472-7765
Email: info@aiaweb.org
Web: www.aiaweb.org/Content.asp?CID=82

Summary: To provide financial assistance to college students preparing for a career in aviation.

Eligibility: Open to students enrolled in an undergraduate aviation degree program at a college or university that is a member of the University Aviation Association (UAA). Applicants must have completed at least 45 college credits, of which 15 must be in aviation, and have a GPA of 2.5 or higher. Along with their application, they must submit 1) a letter describing their activities, leadership qualities, goals, and reasons for applying for these funds; 2) at least 1 letter of recommendation from an employer or instructor; 3) an official transcript; and 4) any FAA certificates.

Financial data: The stipend is $5,000.

Duration: 1 year.

Number awarded: 1 each year.

Deadline: February of each year.

1745 A.W. BODINE-SUNKIST MEMORIAL SCHOLARSHIP

Sunkist Growers
Attn: Administrator
P.O. Box 7888
Van Nuys, CA 91409-7888
Phone: (818) 986-4800
Web: www.sunkist.com/about/bodine_scholarship.aspx

Summary: To provide financial assistance to undergraduate students in California and Arizona who have a farming background and are interested in attending college in any state.

Eligibility: Open to students entering or continuing an undergraduate program in any field at a college or university in any state. Applicants must have a background in California or Arizona agriculture (i.e., the student or someone in the student's immediate family must derive the majority of income from agriculture). They must have a GPA of 3.0 or higher and be able to demonstrate financial need. Along with their application, they must submit a 500-word essay on their agricultural background and goals. Selection is based on the essay, financial need, college board test scores, GPA, and recommendations.

Financial data: Stipends average $2,000 per year.

Duration: 1 year; may be renewed for up to 3 additional years, provided the recipients carry at least 12 units per term and earn a GPA of 2.7 or higher.

Number awarded: Varies each year; recently, 16 of these scholarships were awarded. Since the establishment of the program, more than 275 scholarships have been awarded.

Deadline: April of each year.

1746 BALL HORTICULTURAL COMPANY SCHOLARSHIP

American Floral Endowment
One Horticultural Lane
P.0. Box 945
Edwardsville, IL 62025
Phone: (618) 692-0045; Fax: (618) 692-4045
Email: afe@endowment.org
Web: endowment.org/education/afe

Summary: To provide financial assistance to undergraduates interested in a career in commercial floriculture.

Eligibility: Open to undergraduate students at 4-year colleges and universities who are entering their junior, senior, or fifth undergraduate year. Applicants must be horticulture majors who intend to prepare for a career in commercial floriculture. They must be U.S. or Canadian citizens or permanent residents and have a GPA of 3.0 or higher. Along with their application, they must submit a statement describing their career goals and the academic, work-related, and/or life experiences that support those goals. Financial need is considered in the selection process.

Financial data: The stipend ranges from $500 to $2,000.

Duration: 1 year.

Number awarded: 1 each year.

Deadline: April of each year.

1747 BANNER HEALTH SYSTEM NORTH COLORADO MEDICAL CENTER NIGHTINGALE SCHOLARSHIP

Colorado Nurses Foundation
7400 East Arapahoe Road, Suite 211
Centennial, CO 80112
Phone: (303) 694-4728; Fax: (303) 694-4869
Email: mail@cnfound.org
Web: www.cnfound.org/scholarships.html

Summary: To provide financial assistance to undergraduate and graduate nursing students in Colorado who are willing to work at a designated facility following graduation.

Eligibility: Open to Colorado residents who are enrolled in an approved nursing program in the state. Applicants may be 1) second-year students in an associate degree program; 2) junior or senior level B.S.N. undergraduate students; 3) R.N.s enrolled in a baccalaureate or higher degree program in a school of nursing; 4) R.N.s with a master's degree in nursing, currently practicing in Colorado and enrolled in a doctoral program; or 5) students in the second or third year of a Doctorate Nursing Practice (D.N.P.) program. They must be willing to work for a Banner Health Facility following graduation. Undergraduates must have a GPA of 3.25 or higher and graduate students must have a GPA of 3.5 or higher. Selection is based on professional philosophy and goals, dedication to the improvement of patient care in Colorado, demonstrated commitment to nursing, critical thinking skills, potential for leadership, involvement in community and professional organizations, recommendations, GPA, and financial need.

Financial data: The stipend is $1,000.

Duration: 1 year.

Number awarded: 1 each year.

Deadline: October of each year.

1748 BARBARA PALO FOSTER MEMORIAL SCHOLARSHIP

Ulman Cancer Fund for Young Adults
Attn: Scholarship Program Coordinator
10440 Little Patuxent Parkway, Suite 1G
Columbia, MD 21044
Phone: (410) 964-0202, ext. 106; (888) 393-FUND
Email: scholarship@ulmanfund.org
Web: www.ulmanfund.org/Scholarship.aspx

Summary: To provide financial assistance to undergraduate and graduate nursing students who have a parent with cancer.

Eligibility: Open to nursing students who have a parent with or have lost a parent to cancer. Applicants must be younger than 35 years of age and enrolled in, or planning to enroll in, an undergraduate or graduate program in nursing. They must demonstrate an interest in furthering patient education, focusing on persons from medically underserved communities and/or women's health issues. Along with their application, they must submit an essay of at least 1,000 words on the ways in which their experiences as a member of a marginalized group within the cancer community (i.e., young adults affected by cancer) have taught them lessons that inspire them to be of service to other socially, politically, and or economically marginalized people in the healthcare system. Selection is based on demonstrated dedication to community service, com-

mitment to educational and professional goals, use of their cancer experience to impact the lives of other young adults affected by cancer, medical hardship, and financial need.
Financial data: The stipend is $2,500. Funds are paid directly to the educational institution.
Duration: 1 year; nonrenewable.
Number awarded: 1 each year.
Deadline: April of each year.

1749 BAROID SCHOLARSHIP

American Ground Water Trust
50 Pleasant Street
Concord, NH 03301
Phone: (603) 228-5444; Fax: (603) 228-6557
Email: trustinfo@agwt.org
Web: www.agwt.org/scholarships.htm
Summary: To provide financial assistance to high school seniors who are interested in preparing for a career in a ground water–related field.
Eligibility: Open to high school seniors who have a GPA of 3.0 or higher and are entering a 4-year college or university as a full-time student. Applicants must be planning a career in a ground water–related field and must have completed a science/environmental project in high school that directly involved ground water resources or have had vacation/out-of-school work experience that is directly related to the environment and natural resources. They must submit a 500-word essay on "Ground Water—An Important Environmental and Economic Resource for America" and a 300-word description of their high school ground water project and/or practical environmental work experience. Selection is based on the above criteria, and on the applicant's references and academic record. Financial need is not considered. U.S. citizenship or permanent resident status is required.
Financial data: The stipend is $1,000. Funds are paid directly to the recipient's college.
Duration: 1 year.
Number awarded: 1 each year.
Deadline: May of each year.

1750 BARRY K. WENDT MEMORIAL SCHOLARSHIP

National Stone, Sand and Gravel Association
Attn: Human Resources Committee
1605 King Street
Arlington, VA 22314
Phone: (703) 525-8788; (800) 342-1415; Fax: (703) 525-7782
Email: info@nssga.org
Web: www.nssga.org/careerscholarships/scholarships.cfm
Summary: To provide financial assistance to engineering students intending to prepare for a career in the aggregates industry.
Eligibility: Open to engineering students who intend to prepare for a career in the crushed stone industry. Applicants must submit a letter of recommendation and a 300- to 500-word statement describing their career plans. Financial need is not considered in the selection process.
Financial data: The stipend is $2,500.
Duration: 1 year.
Number awarded: 1 each year.
Deadline: May of each year.

1751 BB&T CHARITABLE FOUNDATION SCHOLARSHIP PROGRAM OF THE HISPANIC SCHOLARSHIP FUND

Hispanic Scholarship Fund
Attn: Selection Committee
55 Second Street, Suite 1500
San Francisco, CA 94105
Phone: (415) 808-2365; (877) HSF-INFO; Fax: (415) 808-2302
Email: scholar1@hsf.net
Web: www.hsf.net/BBT.aspx
Summary: To provide financial assistance to Hispanic and African American upper-division students from selected states who are working on a degree related to business.
Eligibility: Open to U.S. citizens, permanent residents, and visitors with a passport stamped I-551 who are African American or of Hispanic heritage. Applicants must be residents of or attending school in Alabama, Florida, Georgia, Indiana, Kentucky, Maryland, North Carolina, Puerto Rico, South Carolina, Tennessee, Virginia, Washington, D.C., or West Virginia. They must be full-time juniors with a major in accounting, economics, or finance and a GPA of 3.0 or higher. Selection is based on academic achievement, personal strengths, leadership, and financial need.
Financial data: A stipend is awarded (amount not specified).
Duration: 1 year (the junior year of college).
Number awarded: 1 or more each year.
Deadline: February of each year.

1752 BECKY BURROWS SCHOLARSHIP PROGRAM

Pilot International
Attn: Foundation
102 Preston Court
P.O. Box 5600
Macon, GA 31208-5600
Phone: (478) 477-1208; Fax: (478) 477-6978
Email: pifinfo@pilothq.org
Web: www.pilotinternational.org/html/foundation/scholar.shtml
Summary: To provide financial assistance to adult students who are interested in working with people with brain-related disabilities or disorders.
Eligibility: Open to adult students who are reentering the job market, preparing for a second career, or improving their professional skills for an established career. They must be preparing for or already be involved in careers devoted to improving the quality of life for people who have brain-related disorders or disabilities. Applicants must have completed at least 1 semester at a college or university in the United States or Canada and have a GPA of 3.25 or higher. They must be sponsored by a Pilot Club in their hometown or in the city in which their college or university is located. Local Pilot Clubs are allowed to sponsor only 1 applicant per program.
Financial data: The stipend is $1,000 for full-time students or $500 for part-time students.
Duration: 1 year.
Number awarded: 1 each year.
Deadline: February of each year.

1753 BEEF INDUSTRY SCHOLARSHIP PROGRAM

National Cattlemen's Beef Association
Attn: National Cattlemen's Foundation
9110 East Nichols Avenue, Suite 300
Centennial, CO 80112
Phone: (303) 694-0305; Fax: (303) 770-7745
Email: ncf@beef.org
Web: www.nationalcattlemensfoundation.org
Summary: To provide financial assistance to students who are interested in preparing for a career in the beef industry.
Eligibility: Open to graduating high school seniors and full-time undergraduate students enrolled at a 2- or 4-year academic institution. Applicants must have demonstrated a commitment to a career in an area of the beef industry, through classes, internships, or life experiences. They must write a brief letter indicating what role they see themselves playing in the beef industry after graduation; write an essay (up to 750 words) on an issue confronting the beef industry and offering their solution; and submit 2 letters of reference. Essays are judged on the basis of clarity of expression, persuasiveness, originality, accuracy, relevance, and solutions offered. A career in the beef industry may include: education, communications, production, research, or other related areas. Financial need is not considered.
Financial data: The stipend is $1,500.
Duration: 1 year.
Number awarded: 10 each year.
Deadline: October of each year.

1754 BERNICE PICKENS PARSONS FUND SCHOLARSHIPS

Greater Kanawha Valley Foundation
Attn: Scholarship Coordinator
1600 Huntington Square
900 Lee Street, East
P.O. Box 3041
Charleston, WV 25331-3041
Phone: (304) 346-3620; (800) 467-5909; Fax: (304) 346-3640
Email: shoover@tgkvf.org
Web: www.tgkvf.org/scholar.htm
Summary: To provide financial assistance to residents of West Virginia who are interested in studying designated fields at a school in any state.

Eligibility: Open to residents of West Virginia who are working or planning to work full-time on a degree or certificate in the fields of library science, nursing, or paraprofessional legal work at a college or university in any state. Applicants must have an ACT score of 20 or higher, be able to demonstrate good moral character and financial need, and have a GPA of 2.5 or higher. Preference is given to residents of Jackson County.
Financial data: Stipends average $1,000 per year.
Duration: 1 year; may be renewed.
Number awarded: Varies each year; recently, 4 of these scholarships were awarded.
Deadline: January of each year.

1755 BERTHA P. SINGER SCHOLARSHIP

Oregon Student Assistance Commission
Attn: Grants and Scholarships Division
1500 Valley River Drive, Suite 100
Eugene, OR 97401-2146
Phone: (541) 687-7395; (800) 452-8807, ext. 7395; Fax: (541) 687-7414; TDD: (800) 735-2900
Email: awardinfo@osac.state.or.us
Web: www.osac.state.or.us/osac_programs.html

Summary: To provide financial assistance to residents of Oregon who are interested in studying nursing at a school in the state.
Eligibility: Open to residents of Oregon who are studying nursing at a college in the state and have a cumulative GPA of 3.0 or higher. Applicants must provide documentation of enrollment in the third year of a 4-year nursing degree program or the second year of a 2-year associate degree nursing program.
Financial data: Stipend amounts vary; recently, they were at least $1,087.
Duration: 1 year.
Number awarded: Varies each year; recently, 23 of these scholarships were awarded.
Deadline: February of each year.

1756 BETTY ANN LIVINGSTON SCHOLARSHIP

Summary: To provide financial assistance to Methodist high school seniors who plan to study designated fields in college.
See Listing #1189.

1757 BETTY MONTOYA GIFT OF LIFE SCHOLARSHIP

Organ Transplant Awareness Program of New Mexico
P.O. Box 37217
Albuquerque, NM 87176
Phone: (505) 867-0498
Email: otapscholarships@hotmail.com
Web: www.otapnm.org/scholarship.aspx

Summary: To provide financial assistance to high school seniors in New Mexico who plan to attend college in any state, especially those planning to major in a health-related field.
Eligibility: Open to seniors graduating from high schools in New Mexico who plan to enroll at an accredited 2- or 4-year college, university, or vocational/technical school in any state. Applicants may be planning to study any field, but preference is given to those preparing for a health-related career. They must have a GPA of 2.0 or higher. Along with their application, they must submit a 3-page essay about organ donation containing facts and/or myths or a personal story. Selection is based primarily on that essay; financial need is not considered.
Financial data: Stipends are $1,000 or $500. Funds are sent directly to the recipient's institution.
Duration: 1 year.
Number awarded: 4 each year: 2 at $1,000 and 2 at $500.
Deadline: February of each year.

1758 BG BENJAMIN B. TALLEY SCHOLARSHIP

Society of American Military Engineers–Anchorage Post
Attn: BG B.B. Talley Scholarship Endowment Fund
P.O. Box 6409
Anchorage, AK 99506-6409
Email: william_kontess@urscorp.com
Web: www.sameanchorage.org/h_about/scholinfo.html

Summary: To provide financial assistance to student members of the Society of American Military Engineers (SAME) from Alaska who are working on a bachelor's or master's degree in designated fields of engineering or the natural sciences.
Eligibility: Open to members of the Anchorage Post of SAME who are residents of Alaska, attending college in Alaska, an active-duty military member stationed in Alaska, or a dependent of an active-duty military member stationed in Alaska. Applicants must be 1) sophomores, juniors, or seniors majoring in engineering, architecture, construction or project management, natural sciences, physical sciences, applied sciences, or mathematics at an accredited college or university; or 2) students working on a master's degree in those fields. They must have a GPA of 2.5 or higher. U.S. citizenship is required. Along with their application, they must submit an essay of 250 to 500 words on their career goals. Selection is based on that essay, academic achievement, participation in school and community activities, and work/family activities; financial need is not considered.
Financial data: Stipends range up to $3,000.
Duration: 1 year.
Number awarded: Varies each year; at least 1 scholarship is reserved for a master's degree students.
Deadline: December of each year.

1759 BILL KANE UNDERGRADUATE SCHOLARSHIP

American Association for Health Education
Attn: Scholarship Committee
1900 Association Drive
Reston, VA 20191-1599
Phone: (703) 476-3437; (800) 213-7193, ext. 437; Fax: (703) 476-6638
Email: aahe@aahperd.org
Web: www.aahperd.org/aahe/events/Bill-Kane.cfm

Summary: To provide financial assistance to undergraduates who are currently enrolled in a health education program.
Eligibility: Open to undergraduate students who are enrolled full-time in a health education program at a 4-year college or university. Applicants must have a GPA of 3.25 or higher as a sophomore, junior, or senior. Along with their application, they must submit an essay of 400 to 450 words on what they hope to accomplish as a health educator (during training and in the future) and the attributes and aspirations they bring to the field of health education. Selection is based on evidence of leadership potential, academic talent, and activity in health education profession-related activities or organizations at the college, university, and/or community level.
Financial data: The stipend is $1,000 plus a 1-year complimentary student membership in the association.
Duration: 1 year; nonrenewable.
Number awarded: 1 each year.
Deadline: November of each year.

1760 BILL MARTIN MEMORIAL SCHOLARSHIP

Rocky Mountain Water Environment Association
c/o Ray Kemp, Scholarship Committee Drive
3036 Environmental Drive
Fort Collins, CO 80525
Phone: (970) 221-6900
Email: rkemp@fcgov.com
Web: www.rmwea.org

Summary: To provide financial assistance to high school seniors in Colorado, New Mexico, or Wyoming who plan to major in a field related to the water environment at a college in any state.
Eligibility: Open to seniors graduating from high schools in Colorado, New Mexico, or Wyoming and planning to attend a 2- or 4-year college or university in any state. Applicants must be planning to prepare for a career in the water environment profession. Along with their application, they must submit an essay of 200 to 300 words on their interest in the environment and how that interest influences their career goals. Financial need is not considered in the selection process.
Financial data: The stipend is $1,000.
Duration: 1 year.
Number awarded: 1 or more each year.
Deadline: April of each year.

1761 BILL WYCHE, JR. MEMORIAL SCHOLARSHIP

Society for Range Management–Texas Section
c/o Levi Tibbs, Scholarship Chair
39350 I10W, Suite 8
Boerne, TX 78006

Phone: (830) 249-2821
Email: levi.tibbs@tx.usda.gov
Web: www.rangelands.org/texas/awards.htm
Summary: To provide financial assistance to high school seniors interested in attending college to prepare for a career in range management.
Eligibility: Open to graduating high school seniors who plan to attend college to prepare for a career in range management. Applicants must be able to demonstrate academic achievement and financial need. Along with their application, they must submit a brief essay about their goals, interests and hobbies, and concerns for the future.
Financial data: The stipend is $1,000.
Duration: 1 year.
Number awarded: 1 or more each year.
Deadline: April of each year.

1762 BILLY D. YOUNG SCHOLARSHIP

National Safety Council
Attn: Utilities Division
1121 Spring Lake Drive
Itasca, IL 60143-3201
Phone: (630) 285-1121; Fax: (630) 285-1315
Email: info@nsc.org
Web: network.nsc.org/index.php/utilities
Summary: To provide financial assistance to undergraduate students working on a degree in safety or industrial hygiene.
Eligibility: Open to undergraduate students who are working on a degree in either safety or industrial hygiene and planning to go into the safety and/or health fields after graduation. Selection is based on safety and health-related work experience; activities, honors, and awards, especially those involving a safety or health organization; any unusual circumstances that have impacted their school activities, work experience, or achievements; and financial need.
Financial data: The stipend is $1,500.
Duration: 1 year.
Number awarded: 1 each year.
Deadline: May of each year.

1763 BIOOHIO ANNUAL SCHOLARSHIPS

BioOhio
Attn: Matt Schutte
1275 Kinnear Road
Columbus, OH 43212
Phone: (614) 675-3686, ext. 6; Fax: (614) 675-3687
Email: mschutte@BioOhio.com
Web: www.bioohio.com/working-learning/BioOhio-Scholarship.aspx
Summary: To provide financial assistance to high school seniors in Ohio who plan to study a bioscience field at a college in the state.
Eligibility: Open to seniors graduating from high schools in Ohio and planning to enroll at a 2- or 4-year college or university in the state. Applicants must be interested in working on a degree in a bioscience-related field. Along with their application, they must submit a 500-word essay on how they can contribute to the sponsor's mission to accelerate bioscience discovery, innovation, and commercialization of global value, driving economic growth and improved quality of life in Ohio. Selection is based on that essay (40%); a statement of activities, honors, and leadership (15%); letters of recommendation (25%); and other factors on the application (20%). Financial need is not considered.
Financial data: The stipend is $1,250.
Duration: 1 year; nonrenewable.
Number awarded: 4 each year.
Deadline: March of each year.

1764 BIOQUIP UNDERGRADUATE SCHOLARSHIP

Entomological Society of America
Attn: Entomological Foundation
9332 Annapolis Road, Suite 210
Lanham, MD 20706-3150
Phone: (301) 459-9082; Fax: (301) 459-9084
Email: melodie@entfdn.org
Web: www.entsoc.org/awards/student/bioquip.htm
Summary: To provide financial assistance to upper-division students working on a degree in entomology.
Eligibility: Open to undergraduate students majoring in entomology at a college or university in the United States, Canada, or Mexico; if their school does not offer a degree in entomology, they must be preparing for a career as an entomologist through their studies. Applicants must have accumulated at least 90 semester hours and have either completed 2 junior-level entomology courses or have a research project in entomology. Along with their application, they must submit a 2-page statement on their interest in entomology, career goals, financial need, and other pertinent factors that illustrate qualifications for the scholarship. Selection is based on that statement (10 points); academic credentials (10 points); extracurricular activities including research, meeting presentations, awards and honors, and professional memberships and affiliations (10 points); letters of recommendation (10 points); and enthusiasm for entomology (10 points).
Financial data: The stipend is $2,000.
Duration: 1 year.
Number awarded: 1 each year.
Deadline: June of each year.

1765 BIORX/HEMOPHILIA OF NORTH CAROLINA EDUCATIONAL SCHOLARSHIPS

BioRx
200 West Lexington Avenue, Suite 203
High Point, NC 27262
Phone: (919) 749-3196; (866) 44-BIORX
Email: cbarnes@biorx.net
Web: www.biorx.net/hemo_scholarships.php
Summary: To provide financial assistance for college to people with hemophilia, their caregivers, and their siblings, especially those who are interested in studying health care.
Eligibility: Open to caregivers of children affected with bleeding disorders, people who have been diagnosed with hemophilia, and siblings of people diagnosed with hemophilia. Applicants must submit an essay of 1 to 2 pages detailing their occupational goals and objectives in life and how the educational program they have chosen will meet those goals. Preference is given to applicants who are studying or planning to study a health care–related field at an accredited college, university, or certified training program. Residents of all states are eligible.
Financial data: The stipend is $2,000.
Duration: 1 year.
Number awarded: 3 each year.
Deadline: April of each year.

1766 BIOWORKS IPM/SUSTAINABLE PRACTICES SCHOLARSHIP

American Floral Endowment
One Horticultural Lane
P.O. Box 945
Edwardsville, IL 62025
Phone: (618) 692-0045; Fax: (618) 692-4045
Email: afe@endowment.org
Web: endowment.org/education/afe
Summary: To provide financial assistance to undergraduate students working on a degree in floriculture, especially those interested in the use of integrated pest management (IPM).
Eligibility: Open to undergraduate students who are working on a degree in horticulture and are interested in preparing for a career in floriculture. Preference is given to applicants who are interested in furthering the use of IPM or sustainable practices. They must be U.S. or Canadian citizens or permanent residents and have a GPA of 3.0 or higher. Along with their application, they must submit a statement describing their career goals and the academic, work-related, and/or life experiences that support those goals. Financial need is considered in the selection process.
Financial data: The stipend ranges from $500 to $2,000.
Duration: 1 year.
Number awarded: 1 each year.
Deadline: April of each year.

1767 BIRDSALL SERVICES GROUP SCHOLARSHIP FOR ENVIRONMENTAL SCIENCE AND ENGINEERING

Independent College Fund of New Jersey
797 Springfield Avenue

Summit, NJ 07901-1107
Phone: (908) 277-3424; Fax: (908) 277-0851
Email: scholarships@njcolleges.org
Web: www.njcolleges.org/i_about_schol_students.html

Summary: To provide financial assistance to students enrolled at selected member institutions of the Independent College Fund of New Jersey (ICFNJ) who are majoring in environmental science or engineering.

Eligibility: Open to students entering their junior or senior year at selected ICFNJ member institutions (Drew University, Fairleigh Dickinson University, Monmouth University, Princeton University, Rider University, or Stevens Institute of Technology). Applicants must be preparing for a career in environmental consulting and/or engineering. Along with their application, they must submit a 250-word personal statement on their academic and personal qualifications and their future academic and/or career plans. Financial need is not considered in the selection process.

Financial data: The amount of the stipend varies.

Duration: 1 year.

Number awarded: 2 each year.

Deadline: March of each year.

1768 BLADE YOUR RIDE SCHOLARSHIP

Sabertec, LLC
3801 North Capital of Texas Highway, E24D-87
Austin, TX 78746
Phone: (512) 703-8255; (877) 57-SABER
Email: byrschol@bladeyourride.com
Web: bladeyourride.com/byr-scholarship.html

Summary: To recognize and reward, with tuition scholarships, undergraduate and graduate students who design outstanding webcasts on reducing global climate change.

Eligibility: Open to students who are working or planning to work full-time on a bachelor's or master's degree at a college or university in the United States. Applicants may be citizens of any country. They may be majoring in any field, but they must have a GPA of 3.0 or higher. Selection is based primarily on the originality, creativity, and effectiveness of a webcast that students must produce and submit. The webcast must relate the environmental, economic, and human health issues of global climate change, including information on how the sponsor's products help reduce automotive emissions. It must run from 1 to 2 minutes, cannot exceed 100MB in size, and may be submitted in either AVI or MOV format. The webcasts of finalists selected by the sponsor are posted on its web site and the family, friends, and faculty of the students, along with the general public, are invited to vote online for the grand prize winner.

Financial data: The finalists selected by the sponsor receive $5,000 scholarships. Of those, the student whose entry is selected in the online voting as the grand prize winner receives an additional $10,000.

Duration: The competition is held annually.

Number awarded: 4 each year, of whom 1 is selected as the grand prize winner.

Deadline: June of each year.

1769 BOB AND ELEANOR GRANT TRUST SCHOLARSHIP

Bob and Eleanor Grant Trust
P.O. Box 75087
Seattle, WA 98175-0087
Web: www.bandegranttrust.org

Summary: To provide financial assistance to first-generation college students from Washington who are studying the natural, environmental, or social sciences at a college in any state.

Eligibility: Open to students enrolled in the second year at a 2-year college or as a junior at a 4-year college or university in any state who have been residents of Washington for at least 24 months. Applicants must be the first generation of their family to attend college. They must be majoring in the natural, environmental, or social sciences and preparing for a career in those fields with an environmental focus. Along with their application, they must submit 6 essays on assigned topics and documentation of financial need. Finalists are invited to an interview.

Financial data: Stipends range up to $15,000 per year.

Duration: 1 year; may be renewed, provided the recipient makes satisfactory progress.

Number awarded: 1 or more each year.

Deadline: March of each year.

1770 BOB GLAHN SCHOLARSHIP IN STATISTICAL METEOROLOGY

American Meteorological Society
Attn: Fellowship/Scholarship Program
45 Beacon Street
Boston, MA 02108-3693
Phone: (617) 227-2426, ext. 246; Fax: (617) 742-8718
Email: scholar@ametsoc.org
Web: www.ametsoc.org

Summary: To provide financial assistance to undergraduates majoring in meteorology or an aspect of atmospheric sciences with an interest in statistical meteorology.

Eligibility: Open to full-time students entering their final year of undergraduate study and majoring in meteorology or an aspect of the atmospheric or related oceanic and hydrologic sciences. Applicants must intend to make atmospheric or related sciences their career, with preference given to students who have demonstrated a strong interest in statistical meteorology. They must be U.S. citizens or permanent residents enrolled at a U.S. institution and have a cumulative GPA of 3.25 or higher. Along with their application, they must submit 200-word essays on 1) their studies in statistics and their career plans for the future; and 2) their career plans in the statistical meteorology field. Financial need is considered in the selection process. The sponsor specifically encourages applications from women, minorities, and students with disabilities who are traditionally underrepresented in the atmospheric and related oceanic sciences.

Financial data: The stipend is $2,500.

Duration: 1 year.

Number awarded: 1 each year.

Deadline: February of each year.

1771 BOB PIPER CONSTRUCTION EDUCATION SCHOLARSHIPS

Associated Builders and Contractors–Rocky Mountain Chapter
Attn: Scholarship Chair
2267 West Yale Avenue
Englewood, CO 80110
Phone: (303) 832-5812; Fax: (303) 832-5813
Email: info@abcrmc.org
Web: www.abcrmc.org/Education/Bob_Piper_Construction_Educati.aspx

Summary: To provide financial assistance to high school seniors in Colorado who plan to attend college in any state to study a construction-related field.

Eligibility: Open to seniors graduating from high schools in Colorado who plan to attend a college, university, or vocational school in any state. Applicants must be planning to work on a bachelor's degree or a certificate of completion in a construction-related field, including (but not limited to) electrical, plumbing, HVAC, masonry, painting, carpentry, architecture, or construction management. They must have a GPA of 2.0 or higher. Along with their application, they must submit brief statements on their educational plans, school projects or classes related to their field of study, how this scholarship would help them financially, and why they are preparing for a career in construction. U.S. citizenship is required.

Financial data: The stipend is $1,000. Funds are paid directly to the recipient's school for payment of tuition, books, room and board, and course-related materials and supplies.

Duration: 1 year.

Number awarded: Up to 4 each year.

Deadline: March of each year.

1772 BOOZ ALLEN HAMILTON/HENAAC SCHOLARS PROGRAM

Great Minds in STEM
Attn: HENAAC Scholars
3900 Whiteside Street
Los Angeles, CA 90063
Phone: (323) 262-0997; Fax: (323) 262-0946
Email: kbbarrera@greatmindsinstem.org
Web: www.greatmindsinstem.org/henaac/scholars

Summary: To provide financial assistance to Hispanic undergraduate students majoring in a field of science, technology, engineering, or mathematics (STEM).

Eligibility: Open to Hispanic students who are working on an undergraduate degree in a field of STEM. Applicants must be of Hispanic origin and/or must significantly participate in and promote organizations and activities in the Hispanic community. They must have a GPA of 3.0 or higher. Along with their application, they must submit a 700-word essay on a topic that changes

annually; recently, students were asked to write on how they see their academic major contributing to global efforts and technology and how they, in their field of study, will contribute to global progress as well as actively contribute to their local communities. Selection is based on leadership through academic achievements and campus and community activities; financial need is not considered.
Financial data: Stipends range from $500 to $5,000.
Duration: 1 year; recipients may reapply.
Number awarded: 1 or more each year.
Deadline: April of each year.

1773 BP/HENAAC SCHOLARS PROGRAM

Great Minds in STEM
Attn: HENAAC Scholars
3900 Whiteside Street
Los Angeles, CA 90063
Phone: (323) 262-0997; Fax: (323) 262-0946
Email: kbbarrera@greatmindsinstem.org
Web: www.greatmindsinstem.org/henaac/scholars

Summary: To provide financial assistance to Hispanic undergraduate students majoring in a field of engineering or science.
Eligibility: Open to Hispanic students who are working on an undergraduate degree in engineering or science. Applicants must be of Hispanic origin and/or must significantly participate in and promote organizations and activities in the Hispanic community. They must have a GPA of 3.0 or higher. Along with their application, they must submit a 700-word essay on a topic that changes annually; recently, students were asked to write on how they see their academic major contributing to global efforts and technology and how they, in their field of study, will contribute to global progress as well as actively contribute to their local communities. Selection is based on leadership through academic achievements and campus and community activities; financial need is not considered.
Financial data: Stipends range from $500 to $5,000.
Duration: 1 year; recipients may reapply.
Number awarded: Varies each year; recently, 4 of these scholarships were awarded.
Deadline: April of each year.

1774 BRADFORD WHITE SCHOLARSHIPS

Plumbing-Heating–Cooling Contractors–National Association
Attn: PHCC Educational Foundation
180 South Washington Street
P.O. Box 6808
Falls Church, VA 22040
Phone: (703) 237-8100, ext. 221; (800) 533-7694; Fax: (703) 237-7442
Email: scholarships@naphcc.org
Web: www.foundation.phccweb.org/Scholarships/BWScholarship.htm

Summary: To provide financial assistance to entering or continuing undergraduate students interested in the plumbing, heating, and cooling industry.
Eligibility: Open to 1) full-time undergraduate students (entering or continuing) who are majoring in a field related to plumbing, heating, and cooling (e.g., business management, construction management with a specialization in mechanical construction, mechanical engineering) at a 4-year college or university; 2) students enrolled full-time in an approved certificate or degree program at a 2-year technical college, community college, or trade school in business management, mechanical CAD design, construction management with a specialty in mechanical construction, or plumbing or HVACR installation, service, and repair; and 3) full-time employees of a licensed plumbing or HVAC contractor (must be a member of the Plumbing-Heating-Cooling Contractors [PHCC]–National Association) who are enrolled in an apprenticeship program in plumbing or HVACR installation, service, and repair. Students majoring in accounting, architecture, computer engineering, construction-related engineering, civil engineering, electrical engineering, or environmental engineering are not eligible. Applicants must have a GPA of 2.0 or higher. Along with their application, they must submit a letter of recommendation from a PHCC member; a copy of school transcripts; SAT and/or ACT scores; and a letter of recommendation from a school principal, counselor, or dean. U.S. or Canadian citizenship is required. Financial need is not considered in the selection process.
Financial data: The stipend is $2,500.
Duration: 1 year; nonrenewable.
Number awarded: Up to 3 each year.
Deadline: April of each year.

1775 BRAINTRACK COMPUTER SCIENCE SCHOLARSHIP

BrainTrack
c/o FutureMeld, LLC
221 Boston Post Road East
Marlborough, MA 01772
Phone: (978) 451-0471
Email: info@braintrack.com
Web: www.braintrack.com/about-braintrack-scholarships.htm

Summary: To provide financial assistance to students working on an undergraduate or graduate degree in a field related to computer science.
Eligibility: Open to students preparing for a career in such fields as programming, software engineering, systems analysis, database administration, network administration, systems administration, network analysis, and communications analysis. Applicants must be working on an associate, bachelor's, master's, or doctoral degree in computer science, information science, or information technology. They must have completed at least 1 semester of study as a full- or part-time student in an on-campus and/or online program. If they are not U.S. citizens or permanent residents, they must have an appropriate student visa. Along with their application, they must submit essays between 200 and 800 words each on 1) what led them to choose computer science as a career path; 2) what they have enjoyed most and least during their computer science degree program so far; 3) what they wish they had known about selecting and entering their computer science school that would be helpful to others going into the field. Selection is based entirely on the creativity, focus, overall thoughtfulness, accuracy, and practical value of their essays.
Financial data: Stipends are $1,000 or $500.
Duration: 1 year.
Number awarded: 4 each year: 2 at $1,000 and 2 at $500.
Deadline: October or February of each year.

1776 BRAINTRACK NURSING SCHOLARSHIP

BrainTrack
c/o FutureMeld, LLC
221 Boston Post Road East
Marlborough, MA 01772
Phone: (978) 451-0471
Email: info@braintrack.com
Web: www.braintrack.com/about-braintrack-scholarships.htm

Summary: To provide financial assistance to students and nurses working on an undergraduate or graduate degree in nursing.
Eligibility: Open to students preparing for a career in nursing as an L.P.N. or R.N. and to nurses advancing their education by working on an associate, bachelor's, master's, or doctoral degree. Applicants must have completed at least 1 semester of study as a full- or part-time student in an on-campus and/or online program. They must be a U.S. citizen, have permanent resident status, or have an appropriate student visa. Along with their application, they must submit essays between 200 and 800 words each on 1) what led them to choose nursing as a career path; 2) what they have enjoyed most and least during their nursing degree program so far; 3) what they wish they had known about selecting and entering their nursing school that would be helpful to others going into nursing. Selection is based entirely on the creativity, focus, overall thoughtfulness, accuracy, and practical value of their essays.
Financial data: Stipends are $1,000 or $500.
Duration: 1 year.
Number awarded: 4 each year: 2 at $1,000 and 2 at $500.
Deadline: October or February of each year.

1777 BREAKTHROUGH TO NURSING SCHOLARSHIPS

National Student Nurses' Association
Attn: Foundation
45 Main Street, Suite 606
Brooklyn, NY 11201
Phone: (718) 210-0705; Fax: (718) 797-1186
Email: nsna@nsna.org
Web: www.nsna.org/FoundationScholarships/FNSNAScholarships.aspx

Summary: To provide financial assistance to minority undergraduate and graduate students who wish to prepare for careers in nursing.
Eligibility: Open to students currently enrolled in state-approved schools of nursing or pre-nursing associate degree, baccalaureate, diploma, generic master's, generic doctoral, R.N. to B.S.N., R.N. to M.S.N., or L.P.N./L.V.N. to R.N. programs. Graduating high school seniors are not eligible. Support for graduate education is provided only for a first degree in nursing. Applicants must be members of a racial or ethnic minority underrepresented among registered nurses (American Indian or Alaska Native, Hispanic or Latino, Native

Hawaiian or other Pacific Islander, Black or African American, or Asian). They must be committed to providing quality health care services to underserved populations. Along with their application, they must submit a 200-word description of their professional and educational goals and how this scholarship will help them achieve those goals. Selection is based on academic achievement, financial need, and involvement in student nursing organizations and community health activities. U.S. citizenship or permanent resident status is required.
Financial data: Stipends range from $1,000 to $2,500. A total of approximately $155,000 is awarded each year by the foundation for all its scholarship programs.
Duration: 1 year.
Number awarded: Varies each year; recently, 5 of these scholarships were awarded: 2 sponsored by the American Association of Critical-Care Nurses and 3 sponsored by the Mayo Clinic.
Deadline: January of each year.

1778 BRIAN BENNETT SCHOLARSHIP

Professional Aviation Maintenance Association
Attn: PAMA Foundation
400 North Washington, Suite 300
Alexandria, VA 22314
Phone: (703) 778-4647
Email: hq@pama.org
Web: www.pama.org/content.asp?contentid=73
Summary: To provide financial assistance to students interested in studying aviation maintenance on the undergraduate level.
Eligibility: Open to students currently enrolled in an institution to obtain an airframe and powerplant (A&P) or avionics license. Applicants must have completed 25% of the required curriculum; have at least a 3.0 GPA; and need financial assistance. Selection is based on educational performance, work experience, participation in school and community activities, career commitment and future potential, financial need, and a recommendation by a counselor, adviser, aviation maintenance instructor, or current employer.
Financial data: The stipend is $2,000. Funds may be used for tuition, fees, books, or supplies.
Duration: 1 year; recipients may reapply.
Number awarded: 1 each year.
Deadline: November of each year.

1779 BROADCAST METEOROLOGY SCHOLARSHIP

National Weather Association
Attn: Executive Director
228 West Millbrook Road
Raleigh, NC 27609-4304
Phone: (919) 845-1546; Fax: (919) 845-2956
Email: exdir@nwas.org
Web: www.nwas.org/committees/ed_comm/application/Broadcast.php
Summary: To provide financial assistance to undergraduate students working on a degree in broadcast meteorology.
Eligibility: Open to students who are entering their sophomore or higher year of undergraduate study. Applicants must be working on a degree in broadcast meteorology. Along with their application, they must submit 1) a 1-page statement explaining why they want to be a broadcast meteorologist and their vision for the future; and 2) a DVD that includes 2 full on-camera weathercasts, with all graphics and show elements prepared by them. Selection is based on that statement, the DVD, academic achievement, and 2 letters of recommendation.
Financial data: The stipend is $1,000.
Duration: 1 year.
Number awarded: 1 each year.
Deadline: March of each year.

1780 BROTHER FRANCES SMITH SCHOLARSHIP

Connecticut Nurses' Association
Attn: Connecticut Nurses' Foundation
377 Research Parkway, Suite 2D
Meriden, CT 06450-7155
Phone: (203) 238-1207; Fax: (203) 238-3437
Email: info@ctnurses.org
Web: www.ctnurses.org/displaycommon.cfm?an=12
Summary: To provide financial assistance to Connecticut residents interested in preparing for a career as a licensed practical nurse (L.P.N.) or working on a degree in nursing at a school in any state.
Eligibility: Open to residents of Connecticut who are entering or enrolled at an accredited practical nurse education program in any state to earn a license as an L.P.N. or work on an associate, bachelor's, master's, or doctoral degree. Selection is based on employment experience; professional, community, and student activities; a statement of educational and practice goals; and financial need.
Financial data: The stipend depends on the qualifications of the recipient and the availability of funds.
Duration: 1 year.
Number awarded: 1 or more each year.
Deadline: June of each year.

1781 BRYCE ROWEN MEMORIAL SCHOLARSHIP

New Mexico Engineering Foundation
Attn: Scholarship Chair
P.O. Box 3828
Albuquerque, NM 87190-3828
Phone: (505) 615-1800
Email: info@nmef.net
Web: www.nmef.net/?section=scholarship
Summary: To provide financial assistance to residents of any state working on a degree in engineering at specified universities in New Mexico.
Eligibility: Open to juniors and seniors working on a degree in engineering at the University of New Mexico, New Mexico State University, or New Mexico Institute of Mining and Technology. Preference is given to non-scholarship ROTC students. Financial need is considered in the selection process.
Financial data: The stipend is $1,000.
Duration: 1 year; nonrenewable.
Number awarded: 1 or more each year.
Deadline: March of each year.

1782 BUILDING DIVISION ICA SCHOLARSHIP FUND

Central Indiana Community Foundation
Attn: Scholarship Program
615 North Alabama Street, Suite 119
Indianapolis, IN 46204-1498
Phone: (317) 631-6542, ext. 279; Fax: (317) 684-0943
Email: scholarships@cicf.org
Web: www.cicf.org/page26452.cfm
Summary: To provide financial assistance to residents of Indiana who are working on a degree in construction management at a college or university in the state.
Eligibility: Open to Indiana residents who have completed at least 60 credit hours in an ACCE- or ABET-accredited construction-related program at a 4-year college or university in the state. Applicants must have a GPA of 2.5 or higher, a record of demonstrated leadership skills on and off campus, and demonstrated professional aptitude through construction work experience. Preference is given to those who intend to work in Indiana. Financial need is not considered in the selection process.
Financial data: The stipend is $3,000.
Duration: 1 year.
Number awarded: 4 each year.
Deadline: March of each year.

1783 BURKE FUND TURFGRASS MANAGEMENT STUDY SCHOLARSHIP

Rhode Island Golf Association
Attn: John P. Burke Memorial Fund
One Button Hole Drive, Suite 2
Providence, RI 02909-5750
Phone: (401) 272-1350; Fax: (401) 331-3627
Email: burkefund@rigalinks.org
Web: burkefund.org/scholarships.html
Summary: To provide financial assistance to residents of Rhode Island who have worked at a golf course and are interested in studying turfgrass or agronomy at a college in any state.
Eligibility: Open to residents of Rhode Island who are graduating high school seniors or current college students. Applicants must have at least 2 years of successful employment as a caddie, golf shop operations worker, cart or bag room operations, practice range, golf course maintenance staff, or clubhouse staff at a member club of the Rhode Island Golf Association (RIGA). They must be attending or planning to attend an accredited college or university to study

turfgrass and agronomy. Along with their application, they must submit a high school or college transcript; 4 letters of recommendation (from a high school principal or guidance counselor, an officer or board member of the sponsoring club, a member of the sponsoring club who knows the student, and the golf professional of the sponsoring club); a list of school activities (e.g., academic and athletic interscholastic contests, editorships, entertainments, officer of student organizations, responsible positions in school functions); and documentation of financial need.
Financial data: A stipend is awarded (amount not specified); funds may be used only for tuition, room, board, and other costs billed by postsecondary schools.
Duration: 1 year; may be renewed for up to 3 additional years if the recipient maintains a GPA of 2.0 or higher.
Number awarded: 1 or more each year.
Deadline: April of each year.

1784 C. BERTRAND AND MARIAN OTHMER SCULTZ COLLEGIATE SCHOLARSHIP

Nebraska Academy of Sciences
c/o University of Nebraska
302 Morrill Hall
14th and U Streets
P.O. Box 880339
Lincoln, NE 68588-0339
Phone: (402) 472-2644
Email: nebacad@unl.edu
Web: www.neacadsci.org/Info/coll_scholarship.htm
Summary: To provide financial assistance to upper-division students from any state majoring in science at colleges and universities in Nebraska.
Eligibility: Open to students entering their junior or senior year at 4-year colleges and universities in Nebraska. Applicants must have a declared major in a natural science discipline (chemistry, physics, biology, or geology). They must be preparing for a career in a science-related industry, science teaching, or scientific research. A member of the Nebraska Academy of Sciences must provide a letter of nomination. Financial need is not considered in the selection process.
Financial data: The stipend is $3,000 per year.
Duration: 1 year; may be renewed 1 additional year.
Number awarded: 1 each year.
Deadline: January of each year.

1785 CABOT SUPERIOR MICROPOWDERS SCHOLARSHIPS

New Mexico Engineering Foundation
Attn: Scholarship Chair
P.O. Box 3828
Albuquerque, NM 87190-3828
Phone: (505) 615-1800
Email: info@nmef.net
Web: www.nmef.net/?section=scholarship
Summary: To provide financial assistance to engineering students from New Mexico.
Eligibility: Open to seniors graduating from high schools in New Mexico and students enrolled at colleges and universities in the state. Applicants must be enrolled or planning to enroll at a college or university with an ABET-accredited engineering program. They must be U.S. citizens with a GPA of 3.0 or higher. High school seniors must have minimum scores of 500 on the SAT critical reading examination and 600 on the SAT mathematics examination or 25 on the ACT English examination and 29 on the ACT mathematics examination. Along with their application, they must submit a 250-word essay on their interest in engineering, their major area of study and area of specialization, the occupation they propose to pursue after graduation, their long-term goals, and how they hope to achieve those. Selection is based on academic standing, participation in extracurricular activities, and evidence of leadership, character, and self-reliance.
Financial data: The stipend is $2,000.
Duration: 1 year.
Number awarded: 2 each year: 1 to a high school senior and 1 to a current college student.
Deadline: February of each year.

1786 CALIFORNIA FARM BUREAU SCHOLARSHIPS

California Farm Bureau Scholarship Foundation
Attn: Scholarship Foundation
2300 River Plaza Drive
Sacramento, CA 95833
Phone: (916) 561-5520; (800) 698-FARM (within CA); Fax: (916) 561-5699
Email: dlicciardo@cfbf.com
Web: www.cfbf.com/programs/scholar/index.cfm
Summary: To provide financial assistance for college to residents of California who are interested in preparing for a career in agriculture.
Eligibility: Open to students entering or attending a 4-year accredited college or university in California who are majoring or planning to major in an agriculture-related field. Students entering a junior college are not eligible. Applicants must submit an essay on the most important educational or personal experience that has led them to pursue a university education. Selection is based on academic achievement, career goals, extracurricular activities, leadership skills, determination, and commitment to study agriculture.
Financial data: The stipend ranges from $1,800 to $2,750 per year.
Duration: 1 year; recipients may reapply.
Number awarded: Approximately 30 each year.
Deadline: February of each year.

1787 CALIFORNIA GROUNDWATER ASSOCIATION WATER SCHOLARSHIP

California Groundwater Association
P.O. Box 14369
Santa Rosa, CA 95402
Phone: (707) 578-4408; Fax: (707) 546-4906
Email: wellguy@groundh2o.org
Web: www.groundh2o.org/programs/scholarship.html
Summary: To provide financial assistance to California residents who are interested in studying a field related to ground water at a college in the state.
Eligibility: Open to residents of California currently enrolled or accepted at a college or university in the state. Applicants must be interested in working on a degree in a field of study related to ground water. Along with their application, they must submit a 500-word essay demonstrating their interest in ground water technology. Financial need is not considered in the selection process.
Financial data: The stipend is $1,000.
Duration: 1 year.
Number awarded: 1 each year.
Deadline: March of each year.

1788 CALIFORNIA LEGION AUXILIARY PAST PRESIDENTS' PARLEY NURSING SCHOLARSHIPS

American Legion Auxiliary
Department of California
Veterans War Memorial Building
401 Van Ness Avenue, Room 113
San Francisco, CA 94102-4586
Phone: (415) 861-5092; Fax: (415) 861-8365
Email: calegionaux@calegionaux.org
Web: www.calegionaux.org/scholarships.htm
Summary: To provide financial assistance to California residents who are current military personnel, veterans, or members of their families and interested in studying nursing at a school in the state.
Eligibility: Open to California residents who are currently serving on active military duty, veterans who served during war time, or the spouse, widow(er), or child of such a veteran. Applicants must be entering or continuing students of nursing at an accredited institution of higher learning in California. Financial need is considered in the selection process.
Financial data: Stipends range up to $2,000.
Duration: 1 year.
Number awarded: Varies each year.
Deadline: April of each year.

1789 CALIFORNIA/NEVADA/ARIZONA AUTOMOTIVE WHOLESALERS' ASSOCIATION SCHOLARSHIPS

California/Nevada/Arizona Automotive Wholesalers' Association
Attn: Automotive Education Memorial Fund
11460 Sun Center Drive
Rancho Cordova, CA 95670
Phone: (916) 635-9774; (800) 332-2292; Fax: (916) 635-9995
Email: programs@cawa.org
Web: www.cawa.org/train.htm

Summary: To provide financial assistance to students from California, Nevada, and Arizona who are interested in preparing for a career in the automotive aftermarket.

Eligibility: Open to high school seniors and college undergraduates enrolled full-time in a college or vocational program and working on a degree or accreditation in the automotive aftermarket. Applicants must be residents of or attending school in California, Nevada, or Arizona. They must be sponsored by a member of the California/Nevada/Arizona Automotive Wholesalers' Association (CAWA). Along with their application, they must submit a 250-word essay on their career goals, how this scholarship will help them, and why they are considering a career in the automotive aftermarket. Financial need is not considered in the selection process.

Financial data: A stipend is awarded (amount not specified).

Duration: 1 year.

Number awarded: Varies each year; recently, 9 of these scholarships were awarded.

Deadline: March of each year.

1790 CALIFORNIA STATE FAIR HIGH SCHOOL AGRICULTURAL SCHOLARSHIPS

California State Fair
Attn: Friends of the Fair Scholarship Program
1600 Exposition Boulevard
P.O. Box 15649
Sacramento, CA 95852
Phone: (916) 263-3149
Email: entryoffice@calexpo.com
Web: www.bigfun.org/competition-youth.php

Summary: To provide financial assistance to high school students in California who plan to attend a college in the state to study agriculture.

Eligibility: Open to juniors and seniors currently enrolled at high schools in California. Applicants must be planning to attend a college, university, or community college in the state to major in agriculture. They must have a GPA of 3.0 or higher. Along with their application, they must submit an essay of 2 to 3 pages indicating why they are pursuing their desired career and life goals and describing their involvement in community and volunteer service. Selection is based on personal commitment, goals established for their chosen field, leadership potential, and civic accomplishments.

Financial data: Stipends are $1,500 or $750.

Duration: 1 year.

Number awarded: 2 each year: 1 at $1,500 and 1 at $750.

Deadline: March of each year.

1791 CALIFORNIA STATE FAIR UNIVERSITY SCHOLARSHIPS IN AGRICULTURE

California State Fair
Attn: Friends of the Fair Scholarship Program
1600 Exposition Boulevard
P.O. Box 15649
Sacramento, CA 95852
Phone: (916) 263-3149
Email: entryoffice@calexpo.com
Web: www.bigfun.org/competition-youth.php

Summary: To provide financial assistance to residents of California who are working on an undergraduate or graduate degree in agriculture at a university in the state.

Eligibility: Open to residents of California currently enrolled as undergraduate or graduate students at 4-year colleges and universities in the state. Applicants must be working on a degree in agriculture and have completed at least 12 units of course work. They must have a GPA of 3.0 or higher. Along with their application, they must submit an essay of 2 to 3 pages indicating why they are pursuing their desired career and life goals and describing their involvement in community and volunteer service. Selection is based on personal commitment, goals established for their chosen field, leadership potential, and civic accomplishments.

Financial data: Stipends are $1,500 or $750.

Duration: 1 year.

Number awarded: 2 each year: 1 at $1,500 and 1 at $750.

Deadline: March of each year.

1792 CALIFORNIA STATE FAIR VITICULTURE/ENOLOGY SCHOLARSHIPS

California State Fair
Attn: Friends of the Fair Scholarship Program
1600 Exposition Boulevard
P.O. Box 15649
Sacramento, CA 95852
Phone: (916) 263-3149
Email: entryoffice@calexpo.com
Web: www.bigfun.org/competition-youth.php

Summary: To provide financial assistance to residents of California who are working on an undergraduate or graduate degree in viticulture or enology at a college in the state.

Eligibility: Open to residents of California currently working on an undergraduate or graduate degree at a college or university in the state. Applicants must be studying or majoring in viticulture or enology. They must have a GPA of 3.0 or higher. Along with their application, they must submit an essay of 2 to 3 pages indicating why they are pursuing their desired career and life goals and describing their involvement in community and volunteer service. Selection is based on personal commitment, goals established for their chosen field, leadership potential, and civic accomplishments.

Financial data: Stipends are $1,000 or $500.

Duration: 1 year.

Number awarded: 2 each year: 1 at $1,000 and 1 at $500.

Deadline: March of each year.

1793 CAMPUS SAFETY, HEALTH, AND ENVIRONMENTAL MANAGEMENT ASSOCIATION SCHOLARSHIP AWARD PROGRAM

Campus Safety, Health, and Environmental Management Association
Attn: Scholarship Committee
120 West Seventh Street, Suite 204
Bloomington, IN 47404-3839
Phone: (812) 245-8084; Fax: (812) 245-0590
Email: info@cshema.org
Web: www.cshema.org/content.aspx?id=52

Summary: To provide financial assistance to undergraduate and graduate students working on a degree in a field related to the concerns of the Campus Safety, Health, and Environmental Management Association (CSHEMA).

Eligibility: Open to full-time undergraduate and graduate students who are majoring in any field but are interested in the study of environmental and occupational health, safety, or related disciplines. Applicants must have at least 1 year of study remaining in their degree program. Along with their application, they must submit a 1-page essay in which they describe a health, safety, or environmental issue relevant to their university or college and examine and discuss what actions and/or programs are needed to solve this issue. Financial need is not considered.

Financial data: The stipend is $2,000.

Duration: 1 year.

Number awarded: 1 each year.

Deadline: March of each year.

1794 CANERS COLLEGE SCHOLARSHIPS

California Association of Nurseries and Garden Centers
Attn: CANERS Foundation
1521 I Street
Sacramento, CA 95814
Phone: (916) 928-3900; (800) 748-6214; Fax: (916) 567-0505
Email: info@cangc.org
Web: www.cangc.org

Summary: To provide financial assistance to college students in California who are majoring in ornamental horticulture or related fields.

Eligibility: Open to residents of California at 2- and 4-year colleges and universities in the state who are currently enrolled in at least 6 credits and are majoring or planning to major in a field related to horticulture (e.g., agribusiness, viticulture, pomology). Applicants, must submit essays on their educational objectives and their occupational goals as they relate to horticulture. Selection is based on those essays, transcripts, high school and college activities related to horticulture, work experience, community activities related to horticulture, and 2 letters of reference. Financial need is not considered.

Financial data: Stipends range from $100 to $5,000.

Duration: 1 year.

Number awarded: 1 or more each year.
Deadline: June of each year.

1795 CANERS HIGH SCHOOL SCHOLARSHIPS

California Association of Nurseries and Garden Centers
Attn: CANERS Foundation
1521 I Street
Sacramento, CA 95814
Phone: (916) 928-3900; (800) 748-6214; Fax: (916) 567-0505
Email: info@cangc.org
Web: www.cangc.org

Summary: To provide financial assistance to high school seniors in California who are planning to major in horticulture at a college in the state.
Eligibility: Open to graduating high school seniors in California who are planning to attend a college or university in the state to major in a field related to horticulture (e.g., agribusiness, viticulture, pomology). Applicants must submit essays on their educational objectives and their occupational goals as they relate to the nursery industry or horticulture. Selection is based on those essays, transcripts, leadership activities and awards in FFA/ROP/4H, high school supervised occupational experience or industry work experience, community activities related to horticulture, other activities and offices held in high school, and 2 letters of reference. Financial need is not considered.
Financial data: Stipends range from $100 to $5,000.
Duration: 1 year.
Number awarded: 1 or more each year.
Deadline: June of each year.

1796 CAPTAIN JIM HICKERSON, USN (RET) AWARD FOR ACADEMIC ACHIEVEMENT

Armed Forces Communications and Electronics Association–Hawaii Chapter
Attn: Scholarship Committee
P.O. Box 31156
Honolulu, HI 96820
Phone: (808) 529-9501
Email: education.vp@afceahawaii.org
Web: www.afceahi.org/edu/default.htm

Summary: To provide financial assistance to high school seniors and undergraduate students from Hawaii who are interested in studying technical fields at a college in any state and have demonstrated outstanding academic achievement.
Eligibility: Open to residents of Hawaii who are either graduating high school seniors or undergraduates who have completed at least 1 year of college. Applicants must be majoring or planning to major in science, engineering, information technology, computer science, or a related technical field at a 4-year college or university in the United States. Along with their application, they must submit a 300-word personal statement on their career goals. Selection is based on academic standing (GPA, class standing, SAT or ACT scores), community involvement and volunteerism, demonstrated leadership, extracurricular activities, athletic achievement, and letters of recommendation. This award is reserved for an applicant who has consistently demonstrated high academic achievement.
Financial data: The stipend is $2,000.
Duration: 1 year.
Number awarded: 1 each year.
Deadline: March of each year.

1797 CAPTAIN KEN WIECKING, USN (RET) AWARD FOR COMMUNITY SERVICE

Armed Forces Communications and Electronics Association–Hawaii Chapter
Attn: Scholarship Committee
P.O. Box 31156
Honolulu, HI 96820
Phone: (808) 529-9501
Email: education.vp@afceahawaii.org
Web: www.afceahi.org/edu/default.htm

Summary: To provide financial assistance to high school seniors and undergraduate students from Hawaii who are interested in studying technical fields at a college in any state and have demonstrated outstanding volunteerism in school and community activities.
Eligibility: Open to residents of Hawaii who are either graduating high school seniors or undergraduates who have completed at least 1 year of college. Applicants must be majoring or planning to major in science, engineering, information technology, computer science, or a related technical field at a 4-year college or university in the United States. Along with their application, they must submit a 300-word personal statement on their career goals. Selection is based on academic standing (GPA, class standing, SAT or ACT scores), community involvement and volunteerism, demonstrated leadership, extracurricular activities, athletic achievement, and letters of recommendation. This award is reserved for an applicant who has most consistently demonstrated the highest ideals of volunteerism in school and community activities.
Financial data: The stipend is $2,000.
Duration: 1 year.
Number awarded: 1 each year.
Deadline: March of each year.

1798 CAPTAIN SALLY TOMPKINS NURSING AND APPLIED HEALTH SCIENCES SCHOLARSHIP

United Daughters of the Confederacy–Virginia Division
c/o Janice Busic, Education Committee Chair
P.O. Box 356
Honaker, VA 24260
Email: 2vp@vaudc.org
Web: vaudc.org/gift.html

Summary: To provide financial assistance for college to women who are Confederate descendants from Virginia and working on a degree in nursing.
Eligibility: Open to women residents of Virginia interested in working on a degree in nursing. Applicants must be 1) lineal descendants of Confederates; or 2) collateral descendants and also members of the Children of the Confederacy or the United Daughters of the Confederacy. They must submit proof of the Confederate military record of at least 1 ancestor, with the company and regiment in which he served. They must also submit a personal letter pledging to make the best possible use of the scholarship; describing their health, social, family, religious, and fraternal connections within the community; and reflecting on what a Southern heritage means to them (using the term "War Between the States" in lieu of "Civil War"). They must have a GPA of 3.0 or higher and be able to demonstrate financial need.
Financial data: The amount of the stipend depends on the availability of funds. Payment is made directly to the college or university the recipient attends.
Duration: 1 year; may be renewed up to 3 additional years if the recipient maintains a GPA of 3.0 or higher.
Number awarded: This scholarship is offered whenever a prior recipient graduates or is no longer eligible.
Deadline: April of the years in which a scholarship is available.

1799 CARDINAL HEALTH/HENAAC SCHOLARS PROGRAM

Great Minds in STEM
Attn: HENAAC Scholars
3900 Whiteside Street
Los Angeles, CA 90063
Phone: (323) 262-0997; Fax: (323) 262-0946
Email: kbbarrera@greatmindsinstem.org
Web: www.greatmindsinstem.org/henaac/scholars

Summary: To provide financial assistance to Hispanic undergraduate students majoring in a field of pharmaceutical or medical sciences.
Eligibility: Open to Hispanic students who are working on an undergraduate degree in pharmaceutical or medical sciences, including biology. Applicants must be of Hispanic origin and/or must significantly participate in and promote organizations and activities in the Hispanic community. They must have a GPA of 3.0 or higher. Along with their application, they must submit a 700-word essay on a topic that changes annually; recently, students were asked to write on how they see their academic major contributing to global efforts and technology and how they, in their field of study, will contribute to global progress as well as actively contribute to their local communities. Selection is based on leadership through academic achievements and campus and community activities; financial need is not considered.
Financial data: Stipends range from $500 to $5,000.
Duration: 1 year; recipients may reapply.
Number awarded: Varies each year; recently, 5 of these scholarships were awarded.
Deadline: April of each year.

1800 CAREERS IN AGRICULTURE SCHOLARSHIP PROGRAM

Agrisolutions
Attn: Careers in Agriculture, MS 5735
P.O. Box 64281

St. Paul, MN 55164-0281
Phone: (651) 765-5711; (800) 426-8109
Web: www.agrisolutionsinfo.com/Careers/Scholarships.aspx
Summary: To provide financial assistance to high school seniors interested in studying agriculture in college.
Eligibility: Open to high school seniors planning to work on a 2- or 4-year degree in crop production, agronomy, or a closely-related field. Applicants must submit essays describing 1) their career goals upon graduation; 2) the college or university they have selected and why; 3) any agriculture-related or leadership programs or projects in which they have been involved in high school or elsewhere; 4) why they are interested in agriculture as a career; and 5) why cooperatives are important to agriculture. Selection is based on academic achievement, leadership in agriculture, and perceived ability to contribute to agriculture in the future.
Financial data: The stipend is $1,000.
Duration: 1 year; nonrenewable.
Number awarded: 20 each year.
Deadline: January of each year.

1801 CAREFIRST BLUECROSS BLUESHIELD HEALTH AND LIFE SCIENCES SCHOLARS PROGRAM

Independent College Fund of Maryland
Attn: Director of Programs and Scholarships
3225 Ellerslie Avenue, Suite C160
Baltimore, MD 21218-3519
Phone: (443) 997-5703; Fax: (443) 997-2740
Email: LSubot@jhmi.edu
Web: www.i-fundinfo.org
Summary: To provide financial assistance to students from any state at member institutions of the Independent College Fund of Maryland who are majoring in designated fields of science.
Eligibility: Open to students from any state currently entering their sophomore, junior, or senior year at member institutions. Applicants must be majoring in or have demonstrated a career interest in the biological sciences, biochemistry, biophysics, microbiology, or related scientific fields, including chemistry, computer science, physics, or environmental health. They must have a GPA of 3.0 or higher.
Financial data: The stipend is $5,000.
Duration: 1 year.
Number awarded: 1 or more each year.
Deadline: Deadline not specified.

1802 CARGILL SCHOLARSHIP PROGRAM FOR TRIBAL COLLEGES

American Indian College Fund
Attn: Scholarship Department
8333 Greenwood Boulevard
Denver, CO 80221
Phone: (303) 426-8900; (800) 776-FUND; Fax: (303) 426-1200
Email: scholarships@collegefund.org
Web: www.collegefund.org/scholarships/schol_tcu.html
Summary: To provide financial assistance to Native American college students from any state who are working on a bachelor's degree in specified fields at Tribal Colleges and Universities (TCUs) in selected states.
Eligibility: Open to American Indians, Alaska Natives, and Hawaiian Natives who have proof of enrollment or descendancy. Applicants must be enrolled full-time at an eligible TCU in Kansas, Minnesota, North Dakota, South Dakota, or Wisconsin and be working on a bachelor's degree in agricultural studies, business, engineering, finance, mathematics, science, or technology. They must have a GPA of 3.0 or higher, be willing to commit to attend the "Backpacks to Briefcases" program, and have a record of leadership and service to the Native American community. Applications are available only online and include required essays on specified topics. Selection is based on exceptional academic achievement.
Financial data: The stipend is $2,500.
Duration: 1 year.
Number awarded: 1 or more each year.
Deadline: May of each year.

1803 CAROLINE ADAMS GRANT

Virgin Islands Board of Education
Dronningen Gade 60B, 61, and 62
P.O. Box 11900
St. Thomas, VI 00801
Phone: (340) 774-4546; Fax: (340) 774-3384
Email: stt@myviboe.com
Web: www.myviboe.com
Summary: To provide financial assistance to residents of the Virgin Islands who wish to study aviation at a college in the territory or on the mainland.
Eligibility: Open to residents of the Virgin Islands who are seniors or graduates of high schools in the territory. Applicants must have a GPA of 2.0 or higher and be attending or accepted for enrollment at an accredited institution of higher learning in the territory or on the mainland. They must be planning to major in aviation. Financial need is considered in the selection process.
Financial data: The stipend is $2,000 per semester.
Duration: 1 year; may be renewed up to 7 additional semesters.
Number awarded: 1 each year.
Deadline: April of each year.

1804 CAROLINE E. HOLT NURSING SCHOLARSHIP

Daughters of the American Revolution–National Society
Attn: Committee Services Office, Scholarships
1776 D Street, N.W.
Washington, DC 20006-5303
Phone: (202) 628-1776
Web: www.dar.org/natsociety/edout_scholar.cfm
Summary: To provide financial assistance to undergraduate nursing students.
Eligibility: Open to undergraduate students currently enrolled in accredited schools of nursing who have completed at least 1 year. Applicants must be sponsored by a local chapter of the Daughters of the American Revolution (DAR). Selection is based on academic excellence, commitment to field of study, and financial need. U.S. citizenship is required.
Financial data: The stipend is $1,000.
Duration: 1 year; nonrenewable.
Number awarded: Varies each year.
Deadline: February of each year.

1805 CAROLYN S. RICHARDSON MEMORIAL SCHOLARSHIP

California Farm Bureau Scholarship Foundation
Attn: Scholarship Foundation
2300 River Plaza Drive
Sacramento, CA 95833
Phone: (916) 561-5520; (800) 698-FARM (within CA); Fax: (916) 561-5699
Email: dlicciardo@cfbf.com
Web: www.cfbf.com/programs/scholar/index.cfm
Summary: To provide financial assistance for college to residents of California who are interested in preparing for a career in agriculture.
Eligibility: Open to students entering or attending a 4-year accredited college or university in California who are majoring or planning to major in an agriculture-related field. Students entering a junior college are not eligible. Applicants must be planning to specialize in agricultural resource issues. They must submit an essay on the most important educational or personal experience that has led them to pursue a university education. Selection is based on academic achievement, career goals, extracurricular activities, leadership skills, determination, and commitment to study agriculture.
Financial data: The stipend is $2,250 per year.
Duration: 1 year; recipients may reapply.
Number awarded: 1 each year.
Deadline: February of each year.

1806 CASSENS/PHILLIPS FAMILY UNDERGRADUATE SCHOLARSHIP FOR METEOROLOGY

National Weather Association
Attn: Executive Director
228 West Millbrook Road
Raleigh, NC 27609-4304
Phone: (919) 845-1546; Fax: (919) 845-2956
Email: exdir@nwas.org
Web: www.nwas.org/committees/ed_comm/application/AccuWeather.php
Summary: To provide financial assistance to undergraduate students working on a degree in operational meteorology.
Eligibility: Open to students who are enrolled in any year of undergraduate study. Applicants must be working on a degree in meteorology. Along with their application, they must submit a 1-page statement explaining why they are

applying for this scholarship. Selection is based on that statement, academic achievement, and 2 letters of recommendation.
Financial data: The stipend is $1,000.
Duration: 1 year.
Number awarded: 1 each year.
Deadline: October of each year.

1807 CENTRAL INDIANA SECTION SWE SCHOLARSHIPS

Society of Women Engineers–Central Indiana Section
Attn: Scholarship Coordinator
P.O. Box 44450
Indianapolis, IN 46244
Email: swe-ci_scholarship@swe.org
Web: www.swe-ci.com
Summary: To provide financial assistance to women who live or attend college in Indiana and are studying computer science or engineering.
Eligibility: Open to women who are residents of Indiana or attending a college or university in the state. Applicants must be sophomores, juniors, or seniors and working full-time on a bachelor's degree in an ABET/CSAB-accredited program in engineering or computer sciences. They must have a GPA of 3.0 or higher. Along with their application, they must submit a 500-word essay on the ways in which they are fulfilling the mission of the Society of Women Engineers (SWE): to stimulate women to achieve full potential in careers as engineers and leaders, expand the image of the engineering profession as a positive force in improving the quality of life, and demonstrate the value of diversity. Financial need may be considered in the selection process.
Financial data: Stipends are $1,000, $750, or $500.
Duration: 1 year.
Number awarded: 3 each year: 1 each at $1,000, $750, and $500.
Deadline: April of each year.

1808 CHARLES W. RILEY FIRE AND EMERGENCY MEDICAL SERVICES TUITION REIMBURSEMENT PROGRAM

Maryland Higher Education Commission
Attn: Office of Student Financial Assistance
839 Bestgate Road, Suite 400
Annapolis, MD 21401-3013
Phone: (410) 260-4545; (800) 974-1024, ext. 4545; Fax: (410) 260-3200; TDD: (800) 735-2258
Email: grogers@mhec.state.md.us
Web: www.mhec.state.md.us
Summary: To provide financial assistance for college and graduate school to fire fighters, ambulance, and rescue squad members in Maryland.
Eligibility: Open to fire fighters, ambulance, and rescue squad members who are enrolled as full-time or part-time undergraduate or graduate students at an accredited institution of higher education in Maryland in a degree or certificate program for fire service technology or emergency medical technology. Applicants must have received at least a grade of "C" in any course required for completion of their program. They must be serving a Maryland community while they are taking college courses.
Financial data: Awards provide full reimbursement of tuition charges the student has paid, up to the equivalent annual tuition of a resident undergraduate student at a 4-year public institution within the University System of Maryland.
Duration: 1 year; may be renewed if the recipient maintains satisfactory academic progress and remains enrolled in an eligible program.
Number awarded: Varies each year.
Deadline: June of each year.

1809 CHARLIE WELLS MEMORIAL AVIATION SCHOLARSHIPS

Charlie Wells Memorial Scholarship Fund
P.O. Box 262
Springfield, IL 62705-0262
Email: Rog@wellsscholarship.com
Web: www.wellsscholarship.com
Summary: To provide financial assistance to students preparing for an aviation-related program in college.
Eligibility: Open to students who are currently majoring full-time in an aviation-oriented curriculum at a college or university in the United States. Applicants must submit information on their career interests, 2 letters of reference, an essay on why they deserve the scholarship (including their past accomplishments, future goals, and financial need), and a list of their extracurricular activities.
Financial data: Stipends vary, depending on the availability of funds. Recently, they were $1,150. Funds are sent directly to the recipient's school to help pay the costs of tuition.
Duration: 1 year.
Number awarded: Varies each year; recently, 2 of these scholarships were awarded.
Deadline: April of each year.

1810 CHEMICAL AND PETROLEUM INDUSTRIES DIVISION SCHOLARSHIP

Instrumentation, Systems, and Automation Society
Attn: ISA Educational Foundation
67 Alexander Drive
Research Triangle Park, NC 27709
Phone: (919) 549-8411; Fax: (919) 549-8288
Email: info@isa.org
Web: www.isa.org
Summary: To provide financial assistance to undergraduate and graduate students majoring in fields related to instrumentation, systems, and automation.
Eligibility: Open to full-time undergraduate and graduate students enrolled in a program in instrumentation, systems, automation, or a closely-related field. Applicants must have a GPA of 3.0 or higher. They may be from any country but must be attending an institution in their own country. Applicants in a 2-year program must have completed at least 1 academic semester of 12 hours or its equivalent. Applicants in a 4-year program must be in their sophomore year or higher. Along with their application, they must submit an essay (up to 400 words) on their ambitions and qualifications as an innovator or future leader in a career in instrumentation, systems, or automation; they should describe their career objectives, how the award of this scholarship will help them attain their objectives, why they want to enter this particular field of engineering, what they have achieved and learned through their studies and activities, and what this indicates about their character and determination. Preference is given to applicants studying technology related to chemical and petroleum industries. Financial need is not considered in the selection process.
Financial data: The stipend is $2,000.
Duration: 1 year.
Number awarded: 1 each year.
Deadline: February of each year.

1811 CHEVRON/HENAAC SCHOLARS PROGRAM

Great Minds in STEM
Attn: HENAAC Scholars
3900 Whiteside Street
Los Angeles, CA 90063
Phone: (323) 262-0997; Fax: (323) 262-0946
Email: kbbarrera@greatmindsinstem.org
Web: www.greatmindsinstem.org/henaac/scholars
Summary: To provide financial assistance to Hispanic undergraduate students majoring in a field of science, technology, engineering, or mathematics (STEM).
Eligibility: Open to Hispanic students who are working on an undergraduate degree in a field of STEM. Applicants must be of Hispanic origin and/or must significantly participate in and promote organizations and activities in the Hispanic community. They must have a GPA of 3.0 or higher. Along with their application, they must submit a 700-word essay on a topic that changes annually; recently, students were asked to write on how they see their academic major contributing to global efforts and technology and how they, in their field of study, will contribute to global progress as well as actively contribute to their local communities. Selection is based on leadership through academic achievements and campus and community activities; financial need is not considered.
Financial data: Stipends range from $500 to $5,000.
Duration: 1 year; recipients may reapply.
Number awarded: 1 or more each year.
Deadline: April of each year.

1812 CHRYSLER FOUNDATION SCHOLARSHIP AWARD

Hispanic Association of Colleges and Universities
Attn: National Scholarship Program
8415 Datapoint Drive, Suite 400
San Antonio, TX 78229
Phone: (210) 692-3805; Fax: (210) 692-0823; TDD: (800) 855-2880
Email: scholarships@hacu.net

Web: www.hacu.net/hacu/Scholarships_EN.asp?SnID=875148054

Summary: To provide financial assistance to undergraduate students majoring in specified fields at institutions that are members of the Hispanic Association of Colleges and Universities (HACU).

Eligibility: Open to full-time undergraduate students at HACU member 2- and 4-year colleges and universities. Applicants must be majoring in accounting, automotive design, general business, electrical engineering, finance, information technology, marketing, mechanical engineering, or sales. They must have a GPA of 3.0 or higher and be able to demonstrate financial need. Along with their application, they must submit an essay of 200 to 250 words that describes their academic and/or career goals, where they expect to be and what they expect to be doing 10 years from now, and what skills they can bring to an employer.

Financial data: The stipend is $1,980 per year.

Duration: 1 year; may be renewed.

Number awarded: 1 or more each year.

Deadline: May of each year.

1813 CHRYSLER TECHNICAL SCHOLARSHIPS

Delaware Community Foundation
Attn: Executive Vice President
100 West 10th Street, Suite 115
P.O. Box 1636
Wilmington, DE 19899
Phone: (302) 571-8004; Fax: (302) 571-1553
Email: rgentsch@delcf.org
Web: www.delcf.org/scholarships_guidelines.html

Summary: To provide financial assistance to residents of Delaware who are working or planning to work on a college degree related to the automobile industry.

Eligibility: Open to Delaware residents who are enrolled or planning to enroll at a community college, trade school, or university. Applicants must be interested in working on a degree or certificate in a technical field related to the design, engineering, manufacturing, and repair of automotive products, including (but not limited to) automotive repair, skilled trades, and engineering. They must be younger than 23 years of age, have a GPA of 2.75 or higher, and be able to provide evidence of a commitment to leadership in the community. Selection is based on academic ability, leadership traits, and financial need.

Financial data: The stipend is $1,000 per year.

Duration: 1 year.

Number awarded: 20 each year.

Deadline: April of each year.

1814 CHS FOUNDATION HIGH SCHOOL SCHOLARSHIP PROGRAM

CHS Foundation
Attn: Scholarship Program
5500 Cenex Drive, MS 407
Inver Grove Heights, MN 55077
Phone: (651) 355-5129; (800) 814-0506; Fax: (651) 355-5073
Email: info@chsfoundation.org
Web: www.chsfoundation.org/scholarshipprog.html

Summary: To provide financial assistance to high school seniors planning to study a field related to agriculture at a college or university in any state.

Eligibility: Open to seniors who are graduating from high schools in the United States and planning to enroll at a 2- or 4-year college or university. Applicants must be planning to major in an agriculture-related field, including agribusiness and economics, agronomy, land use planning, agricultural communications, animal science, biotechnology, international agriculture, environmental science, or agricultural engineering. Along with their application, they must submit 500-word essays on 1) the role of the U.S. agricultural industry in a global economy; and 2) a leader whom they admire, the leadership qualities that he or she exhibits, and why they look up to him or her. Financial need is not considered in the selection process. U.S. citizenship is required.

Financial data: The stipend is $1,000.

Duration: 1 year; nonrenewable.

Number awarded: 25 each year.

Deadline: March of each year.

1815 CHS FOUNDATION TWO-YEAR SCHOLARSHIP PROGRAM

CHS Foundation
Attn: Scholarship Program
5500 Cenex Drive, MS 407
Inver Grove Heights, MN 55077
Phone: (651) 355-5129; (800) 814-0506; Fax: (651) 355-5073
Email: info@chsfoundation.org
Web: www.chsfoundation.org/scholarshipprog.html

Summary: To provide financial assistance to students enrolled at 2-year colleges who are interested in studying an agriculture-related program.

Eligibility: Open to students who are completing their first year at a 2-year college in the United States. Applicants must be studying an agriculture-related field. Along with their application, they must submit 1,000-word essays on 1) their career ambitions, why they chose that path, and how they are preparing for their career; and 2) their opinion on the value of cooperative-based business in the agricultural industry. Financial need is not considered in the selection process. U.S. citizenship is required.

Financial data: The stipend is $1,000.

Duration: 1 year; nonrenewable.

Number awarded: 50 each year.

Deadline: March of each year.

1816 CHS FOUNDATION UNIVERSITY SCHOLARSHIP PROGRAM

CHS Foundation
Attn: Scholarship Program
5500 Cenex Drive
Inver Grove Heights, MN 55077
Phone: (651) 355-5129; (800) 814-0506; Fax: (651) 355-5073
Email: info@chsfoundation.org
Web: www.chsfoundation.org/scholarshipprog.html

Summary: To provide financial assistance to students at 4-year universities throughout the country who are preparing for a career in agribusiness or production agriculture.

Eligibility: Open to students who are entering their sophomore, junior, or senior year at a participating university. Applicants must be working on an agriculture-related degree to prepare for a career in agribusiness or production agriculture. Preference is given to students with an interest in agricultural-based cooperatives. Students should apply through the financial aid, foundation, or college of agriculture at their university.

Financial data: The stipend is $1,000 per year.

Duration: 1 year; may be renewed.

Number awarded: Nearly 150 each year.

Deadline: Individual institutions administer this program; recipients are selected in the spring to receive the award in the fall.

1817 CHUCK REVILLE, K3FT, MEMORIAL SCHOLARSHIP

Foundation for Amateur Radio, Inc.
Attn: Scholarship Committee
P.O. Box 911
Columbia, MD 21044-0911
Phone: (410) 552-2652; Fax: (410) 981-5146
Email: dave.prestel@gmail.com
Web: www.farweb.org/scholarships

Summary: To provide funding to licensed radio amateurs who are interested in studying engineering or the physical sciences in college.

Eligibility: Open to radio amateurs who are interested in working full-time on a bachelor's degree in a branch of engineering or the physical sciences. There are no restrictions on license class or residence area. Financial need is considered in the selection process.

Financial data: The stipend is $1,000.

Duration: 1 year.

Number awarded: 1 each year.

Deadline: March of each year.

1818 CHURCHARMENIA.COM MEDICINE AND RESEARCH SCHOLARSHIP

Charles and Agnes Kazarian Eternal Foundation/ChurchArmenia.com
Attn: Educational Scholarships
30 Kennedy Plaza, Second Floor
Providence, RI 02903
Email: info@churcharmenia.com
Web: www.churcharmenia.com/scholarship1.html

Summary: To provide financial assistance to outstanding undergraduate or graduate students of Armenian descent who are interested in working on a degree in medicine or biological research.
Eligibility: Open to students of Armenian descent who are applying to or accepted by an undergraduate or graduate biological research program or an accredited medical program. Along with their application, they must submit 1) official academic transcripts; 2) a personal statement (2 to 3 pages) describing the program of study they are entering and their projected impact on the field of biological research or medicine and future returns to the Armenian community; 3) documentation of financial need; and 4) up to 3 letters of recommendation.
Financial data: The stipend is $5,000.
Duration: 1 year.
Number awarded: 1 or more each year.
Deadline: Applications may be submitted at any time.

1819 CLACKAMAS CHAPTER AWARD

Oregon Association of Nurseries
Attn: Oregon Nurseries Foundation
29751 S.W. Town Center Loop West
Wilsonville, OR 97070
Phone: (503) 682-5089; (800) 342-6401; Fax: (503) 682-5099
Email: info@oan.org
Web: www.oan.org/displaycommon.cfm?an=1&subarticlenbr=89
Summary: To provide financial assistance to high school seniors from Oregon and southwestern Washington who are interested in studying ornamental horticulture at a college in any state.
Eligibility: Open to seniors graduating from high schools in Oregon and southwestern Washington. Applicants must be interested in attending college in any state to major in ornamental horticulture. Along with their application, they must submit brief statements on 1) their activities, clubs, offices held, and awards; 2) how their college expenses will be financed; and 3) how they see their future involvement in the field of horticulture.
Financial data: The stipend is $1,000.
Duration: 1 year.
Number awarded: 1 each year.
Deadline: March of each year.

1820 CLACKAMAS CHAPTER ED WOOD MEMORIAL AWARD

Oregon Association of Nurseries
Attn: Oregon Nurseries Foundation
29751 S.W. Town Center Loop West
Wilsonville, OR 97070
Phone: (503) 682-5089; (800) 342-6401; Fax: (503) 682-5099
Email: info@oan.org
Web: www.oan.org/displaycommon.cfm?an=1&subarticlenbr=89
Summary: To provide financial assistance to students majoring in horticulture at colleges and universities in Oregon.
Eligibility: Open to students enrolled at colleges and universities in Oregon and majoring in horticulture. Applicants must submit brief statements on 1) their activities, clubs, offices held, and awards; 2) how their college expenses have been and will be financed; and 3) how they see their future involvement in the field of horticulture. Selection is based on letters of recommendation from nursery professionals or people affiliated with the nursery industry and the promise and commitment the applicants show toward making significant future contributions to the nursery industry.
Financial data: The stipend is $1,500.
Duration: 1 year.
Number awarded: 1 each year.
Deadline: March of each year.

1821 CLAIR A. HILL SCHOLARSHIP

Association of California Water Agencies
Attn: Scholarship Program
910 K Street, Suite 100
Sacramento, CA 95814-3514
Phone: (916) 441-4545; Fax: (916) 325-2316
Email: awards@acwa.com
Web: www.acwa.com/content/scholarships/scholarships
Summary: To provide financial assistance to upper-division students in California who are majoring in water resources–related fields of study.
Eligibility: Open to California residents attending colleges or universities in the state. They should 1) have completed their sophomore work; 2) be full-time students in their junior or senior year at the time of the award; and 3) be majoring in a field related to or identified with water resources, including engineering, agricultural sciences, urban water supply, environmental studies, or public administration. Along with their application, they must submit an essay of 1 to 2 pages that covers key water-related issues they would address, why they have chosen a career in the water resources field, and how their educational and career goals relate to a future in California water resources. Selection is based on scholastic achievement, career plans, and financial need.
Financial data: The stipend is $5,000. Funds are paid directly to the recipient's school.
Duration: 1 year.
Number awarded: 1 each year.
Deadline: January of each year.

1822 CLARK-PHELPS SCHOLARSHIP

Oregon Student Assistance Commission
Attn: Grants and Scholarships Division
1500 Valley River Drive, Suite 100
Eugene, OR 97401-2146
Phone: (541) 687-7395; (800) 452-8807, ext. 7395; Fax: (541) 687-7414; TDD: (800) 735-2900
Email: awardinfo@osac.state.or.us
Web: www.osac.state.or.us/osac_programs.html
Summary: To provide financial assistance to residents of Oregon and Alaska who are interested in studying nursing, dentistry, or medicine at schools in Oregon.
Eligibility: Open to residents of Oregon and Alaska who are currently enrolled or planning to enroll at a public college or university in Oregon. Applicants must be interested in working on a 4-year or graduate degree in nursing, a doctoral degree in dentistry, or a doctoral degree in medicine. Preference is given to applicants who are interested in studying at Oregon Health and Science University, including the nursing programs at Eastern Oregon University, Southern Oregon University, and Oregon Institute of Technology.
Financial data: A stipend is awarded (amount not specified).
Duration: 1 year; recipients may reapply.
Number awarded: Varies each year.
Deadline: February of each year.

1823 CLIFFORD H. "TED" REES, JR. SCHOLARSHIP

Air-Conditioning, Heating, and Refrigeration Institute
Attn: Clifford H. "Ted" Rees, Jr. Scholarship Foundation
2111 Wilson Boulevard, Suite 500
Arlington, VA 22201
Phone: (703) 524-8800; Fax: (703) 528-3816
Email: wlupson@ahrinet.org
Web: www.ahrinet.org/Content/ApplyforaScholarship_329.aspx
Summary: To provide financial assistance to students preparing for a career as a heating, ventilation, air-conditioning, and refrigeration (HVACR) technician.
Eligibility: Open to U.S. citizens, nationals, and permanent residents who are enrolled in a program for preparation for a career in residential air-conditioning and heating, light commercial air-conditioning and heating, or commercial refrigeration. They must be enrolled in a training program at an institutionally accredited school. Along with their application, they must submit an essay of 150 to 200 words on why this scholarship should be awarded to them.
Financial data: The stipend is $2,000.
Duration: 1 year; nonrenewable.
Number awarded: Up to 10 each year.
Deadline: June of each year.

1824 COASTAL NORTH CAROLINA AFCEA CHAPTER UNDERGRADUATE SCHOLARSHIPS

Armed Forces Communications and Electronics Association–Coastal North Carolina Chapter
c/o Daniel Egge, Secretary
201 South Shore Drive
Jacksonville, NC 28540-5633
Phone: (910) 451-8835
Email: daniel.egge@usmc.mil

Summary: To provide financial assistance to dependents and spouses of veterans and military personnel in North Carolina who are interested in studying a technical field at a college in any state.
Eligibility: Open to residents of North Carolina who are dependents or spouses of active-duty, retired, or honorably discharged military personnel. Applicants must be working on or planning to work on a technical degree at a school in any state in the following or related fields: electrical, chemical, systems, or aerospace engineering; mathematics; physics; science or mathematics education; computer science; or technology management. They must be U.S. citizens who can demonstrate academic excellence, moral character, dedication to completing their education, leadership abilities, and financial need.
Financial data: Stipends range from $500 to $2,000.
Duration: 1 year.
Number awarded: 1 or more each year.
Deadline: March of each year.

1825 COLLEEN CONLEY MEMORIAL SCHOLARSHIP

New Mexico Engineering Foundation
Attn: Scholarship Chair
P.O. Box 3828
Albuquerque, NM 87190-3828
Phone: (505) 615-1800
Email: info@nmef.net
Web: www.nmef.net/?section=scholarship
Summary: To provide financial assistance to female high school seniors in New Mexico who plan to study engineering at a college or university in any state.
Eligibility: Open to female seniors graduating from high schools in New Mexico who are planning to enroll at a college or university in any state and major in engineering, engineering technology, or a related field (including scientific disciplines). Applicants must have a GPA of 3.0 or higher. Along with their application, they must submit a 300-word letter discussing their interest in science or engineering and their future plans. Financial need is not considered in the selection process. Preference is given to applicants who are the first member of their family to attend college.
Financial data: The stipend is $1,000.
Duration: 1 year; may be renewed up to 3 additional years, provided the recipient remains enrolled at least half-time and maintains a GPA of 2.5 or higher.
Number awarded: 1 each year.
Deadline: February of each year.

1826 COLLEGIATE INVENTORS COMPETITION

National Inventors Hall of Fame
Attn: Collegiate Inventors Competition
221 South Broadway Street
Akron, OH 44308-1595
Phone: (330) 849-6887; (800) 968-4332
Email: collegiate@invent.org
Web: www.invent.org/collegiate
Summary: To recognize and reward outstanding inventions by college or graduate students in the fields of science, engineering, and technology.
Eligibility: Open to undergraduate and graduate students who are (or have been) enrolled full-time at least part of the 12-month period prior to entry in a college or university in the United States or Canada. Entries may also be submitted by teams, up to 4 members, of whom at least 1 must meet the full-time requirement and all others must have been enrolled at least half-time sometime during the preceding 24-month period. Applicants must submit a description of their invention, information on the faculty adviser, a letter of recommendation from the faculty adviser, a literature/patent search and summary, and relevant supporting or supplemental materials (e.g., charts, graphs, CDs or DVDs, slides, samples). Entries must be original ideas and the work of a student or team and a university adviser; the invention should be reproducible and may not have been 1) made available to the public as a commercial product or process; or 2) patented or published more than 1 year prior to the date of submission for this competition. Entries are first reviewed by a committee of judges that selects the finalists. Judges come from the fields of mathematics, engineering, biology, chemistry, physics, materials science, computer science, medicine, pharmacology, nanotechnology, and other disciplines related to invention and technology development. Selection is based on the degree of originality and inventiveness of the work presented; level of completeness or development of the invention; potential impact or benefit of the invention to society–economically, environmentally, and socially; and level of student initiative.
Financial data: Finalists receive an award of $2,000 and an all-expense-paid trip to Washington, D.C. to participate in a final round of judging and in the awards dinner and presentation. The Grand Prize winner or team receives $25,000. Other prizes are $15,000 for an undergraduate winner or team and $15,000 for a graduate winner or team. Academic advisers of the winning entries each receive a $3,000 cash prize. Awards are unrestricted cash gifts, not scholarships or grants.
Duration: The competition is held annually.
Number awarded: 15 semifinalists are selected each year; of those, 3 individuals or teams win prizes.
Deadline: May of each year.

1827 COLONEL BILL HANEY, USA (RET) AWARD FOR LEADERSHIP

Armed Forces Communications and Electronics Association–Hawaii Chapter
Attn: Scholarship Committee
P.O. Box 31156
Honolulu, HI 96820
Phone: (808) 529-9501
Email: education.vp@afceahawaii.org
Web: www.afceahi.org/edu/default.htm
Summary: To provide financial assistance to high school seniors and undergraduate students from Hawaii who are interested in studying technical fields at a college in any state and have demonstrated outstanding leadership.
Eligibility: Open to residents of Hawaii who are either graduating high school seniors or undergraduates who have completed at least 1 year of college. Applicants must be majoring or planning to major in science, engineering, information technology, computer science, or a related technical field at a 4-year college or university in the United States. Along with their application, they must submit a 300-word personal statement on their career goals. Selection is based on academic standing (GPA, class standing, SAT or ACT scores), community involvement and volunteerism, demonstrated leadership, extracurricular activities, athletic achievement, and letters of recommendation. This award is reserved for an applicant who has most consistently demonstrated outstanding leadership in school and community activities.
Financial data: The stipend is $2,000.
Duration: 1 year.
Number awarded: 1 each year.
Deadline: March of each year.

1828 COLORADO FLORICULTURE FOUNDATION COMMUNITY COLLEGE SCHOLARSHIP

Colorado Floriculture Foundation
6050 Greenwood Plaza Boulevard, Suite 130
Greenwood Village, CO 80111
Phone: (303) 996-0183
Email: Kathleen@hughesstuart.com
Web: www.coloradofloriculture.com
Summary: To provide financial assistance to residents of Colorado who are studying floriculture at a community college in the state.
Eligibility: Open to residents of Colorado who are attending a community college in the state. Applicants must be enrolled in an accredited horticulture program and be able to demonstrate a passion or interest in floriculture. They must have a GPA of 3.0 or higher. Selection is based on merit and an interview.
Financial data: The stipend is $1,000.
Duration: 1 year.
Number awarded: 1 each year.
Deadline: Deadline not specified.

1829 COLORADO FLORICULTURE FOUNDATION HIGH SCHOOL SCHOLARSHIP

Colorado Floriculture Foundation
6050 Greenwood Plaza Boulevard, Suite 130
Greenwood Village, CO 80111
Phone: (303) 996-0183
Email: Kathleen@hughesstuart.com
Web: www.coloradofloriculture.com
Summary: To provide financial assistance to high school seniors in Colorado who plan to study floriculture at a college in the state.
Eligibility: Open to seniors graduating from high schools in Colorado and planning to study floriculture at a college, university, or community college in the state. Applicants must have 1) enrolled in an FFA or vocational technical education program with a horticulture focus; 2) demonstrated a passion or interest in floriculture or other horticulture occupation; and 3) been a top performer in the floriculture division of the annual FFA Career Development Event. Selection is based on merit and an interview.

Financial data: The stipend is $1,000.
Duration: 1 year.
Number awarded: 1 each year.
Deadline: Deadline not specified.

1830 COLORADO FLORICULTURE FOUNDATION UNIVERSITY SCHOLARSHIP

Colorado Floriculture Foundation
6050 Greenwood Plaza Boulevard, Suite 130
Greenwood Village, CO 80111
Phone: (303) 996-0183
Email: Kathleen@hughesstuart.com
Web: www.coloradofloriculture.com
Summary: To provide financial assistance to residents of Colorado who are studying floriculture at a college or university in the state.
Eligibility: Open to residents of Colorado who are entering their junior or senior year at a college or university in the state. Applicants must be enrolled in a horticulture or landscape horticulture program with a concentration in floriculture, nursery and landscape management, or a related field of study. They must have a GPA of 3.0 or higher. Selection is based on merit and an interview.
Financial data: The stipend is $2,000.
Duration: 1 year.
Number awarded: 1 each year.
Deadline: Deadline not specified.

1831 COLORADO HIGH SCHOOL BRIDGE BUILDING CONTEST

Professional Engineers of Colorado
3030 West 81st Avenue
Westminster, CO 80031
Phone: (303) 480-1160; Fax: (303) 458-0002
Web: www.pec.org/BridgeBuilding.html
Summary: To recognize and reward, with college scholarships, high school students in Colorado who construct model bridges that meet technical specifications.
Eligibility: Open to students at high schools in Colorado. Entrants must construct a model bridge that conforms to the technical specifications of the contest. The bridges are then tested for efficiency and the highest scoring entries receive the prizes.
Financial data: Prizes include $1,000 college scholarships.
Duration: The competition is held annually.
Number awarded: Varies each year; recently, the prizes included 2 college scholarships.
Deadline: The testing takes place in February of each year. Students may either travel to the testing site in Denver or mail in their models.

1832 COLORADO LEGION AUXILIARY PAST PRESIDENT'S PARLEY NURSE'S SCHOLARSHIP

American Legion Auxiliary
Department of Colorado
7465 East First Avenue, Suite D
Denver, CO 80230
Phone: (303) 367-5388; Fax: (303) 367-5388
Email: ala@impactmail.net
Web: www.freewebs.com/ala-colorado
Summary: To provide financial assistance to wartime veterans and their descendants in Colorado who are interested in attending school in the state to prepare for a career in nursing.
Eligibility: Open to 1) daughters, sons, spouses, granddaughters, and great-granddaughters of veterans; and 2) veterans who served in the armed forces during eligibility dates for membership in the American Legion. Applicants must be Colorado residents who have been accepted by an accredited school of nursing in the state. Along with their application, they must submit a 500-word essay on the topic, "Americanism." Selection is based on scholastic ability (25%), financial need (25%), references (13%), a 500-word essay on Americanism (25%), and dedication to chosen field (12%).
Financial data: Stipends range from $500 to $1,000.
Duration: 1 year; nonrenewable.
Number awarded: Varies each year, depending on the availability of funds.
Deadline: April of each year.

1833 COLORADO NURSES FOUNDATION SCHOLARSHIPS

Colorado Nurses Foundation
7400 East Arapahoe Road, Suite 211
Centennial, CO 80112
Phone: (303) 694-4728; Fax: (303) 694-4869
Email: mail@cnfound.org
Web: www.cnfound.org/scholarships.html
Summary: To provide financial assistance to undergraduate and graduate nursing students in Colorado.
Eligibility: Open to Colorado residents who have been accepted as a student in an approved nursing program in the state. Applicants may be 1) second-year students in an associate degree program; 2) junior or senior level B.S.N. undergraduate students; 3) R.N.s enrolled in a baccalaureate or higher degree program in a school of nursing; 4) R.N.s with a master's degree in nursing, currently practicing in Colorado and enrolled in a doctoral program; or 5) students in the second or third year of a Doctorate Nursing Practice (D.N.P.) program. They must be committed to practicing nursing in Colorado. Undergraduates must have a GPA of 3.25 or higher and graduate students must have a GPA of 3.5 or higher. Selection is based on professional philosophy and goals, dedication to the improvement of patient care in Colorado, demonstrated commitment to nursing, critical thinking skills, potential for leadership, involvement in community and professional organizations, recommendations, GPA, and financial need.
Financial data: The stipend is $1,000.
Duration: 1 year.
Number awarded: Varies each year; recently, 15 of these scholarships were awarded.
Deadline: October of each year.

1834 COLORADO SECTION SCHOLARSHIPS

American Congress on Surveying and Mapping–Colorado Section
Attn: Kurt Ernstberger
Flatirons, Inc.
3825 Iris Avenue, Suite 100
Boulder, CO 80301
Phone: (303) 443-7001; Fax: (303) 443-9830
Email: kernstberger@flatsurv.com
Web: www.plsc.net/education/education.htm
Summary: To provide financial assistance to undergraduate and graduate students majoring in fields related to surveying and mapping at schools in Colorado.
Eligibility: Open to students enrolled at a Colorado university, college, community college, or technical school with a major in surveying, geography, remote sensing, geomatics, cartography, photogrammetry, geodesy, or GIS. Applicants must have a GPA of 2.5 or higher. Both undergraduate and graduate students are eligible, but preference is given to full-time students and members of the American Congress on Surveying and Mapping (ACSM). Applicants must submit an essay describing why they chose their field of study and their financial need, personal merit, career goals, academic honors, scholarships, community service, volunteer work, and awards.
Financial data: The stipend is $1,000.
Duration: 1 year.
Number awarded: 2 or more each year: 1 for each semester or term.
Deadline: May of each year for the fall semester or term; November of each year for the spring semester or term.

1835 COLVIN SCHOLARSHIP PROGRAM

Certified Angus Beef LLC
Attn: Trudi Hoyle
206 Riffel Road
Wooster, OH 44691-8588
Phone: (330) 345-2333; (800) 225-2333, ext. 211; Fax: (330) 345-0808
Email: thoyle@certifiedangusbeef.com
Web: www.certifiedangusbeef.com/corp/press/colvin/index.php
Summary: To provide financial assistance to upper-division students working on a degree related to the beef industry.
Eligibility: Open to students entering their junior or senior year of college. Applicants must have demonstrated a commitment to the beef industry through work on a degree in meat science, food science, animal science, marketing, business, communications, journalism, or other field related to the industry. Along with their application, they must submit a 1,000-word essay on a topic that changes annually but relates to the beef industry. They may also submit a statement of financial need. Selection is based on, in this order of

importance, activities and scholastic achievement, communication skills (both essay and verbal), and reference letters.
Financial data: Stipends are $3,500, $2,500, or $1,000.
Duration: 1 year.
Number awarded: 5 each year: 1 at $3,500, 1 at $2,500, and 3 at $1,000.
Deadline: November of each year.

1836 COMM1 AVIATION SCHOLARSHIP

E-Publishing Group, LLC
Attn: COMM1 Radio Simulators
P.O. Box 429
Jefferson, MD 21755
Phone: (301) 620-9500; (888) 333-2855; Fax: (301) 620-9501
Email: bbarkey@e-publishing.com
Web: www.comm1.com
Summary: To provide financial assistance to students attending college to prepare for a career in aviation.
Eligibility: Open to undergraduates working on a degree as preparation for a career in aviation. Applicants must complete the statement, "Proper pilot communications are essential to aviation safety because. ..." Selection is based on aviation career aspirations, academic and flight training records, recommendations from mentor, and financial need.
Financial data: The stipend is $1,000.
Duration: 1 year.
Number awarded: 1 each year.
Deadline: October of each year.

1837 COMMITMENT TO AGRICULTURE SCHOLARSHIP PROGRAM

National FFA Organization
Attn: Scholarship Office
6060 FFA Drive
P.O. Box 68960
Indianapolis, IN 46268-0960
Phone: (317) 802-4419; Fax: (317) 802-5419
Email: scholarships@ffa.org
Web: www.ffa.org/index.cfm?method=c_programs.Scholarships
Summary: To provide financial assistance to high school students from farm families who plan to study agriculture in college.
Eligibility: Open to high school seniors whose families are actively engaged in production agriculture. Applicants must be planning to study an agricultural field in college on a full-time basis and prepare for a career in agriculture. They must have an ACT composite score of 18 or higher or an SAT score of 1320 or higher. Along with their application, they must submit an essay on the importance of innovation to U.S. agriculture. If they are a member of FFA, they must also include a statement from their adviser evaluating their involvement in FFA activities and indicating special circumstances, such as financial need, that should be considered. If they are not FFA members, they must provide documentation of other school, community, leadership, and work activities.
Financial data: The stipend is $1,500.
Duration: 1 year; nonrenewable.
Number awarded: 100 each year.
Deadline: February of each year.

1838 CONNECTICUT ATHLETIC TRAINERS' ASSOCIATION UNDERGRADUATE SCHOLARSHIP

Connecticut Athletic Trainers' Association
P.O. Box 155
Durham, CT 06422-0155
Email: information@ctathletictrainers.org
Web: www.ctathletictrainers.org/Scholarships/Scholarships.htm
Summary: To provide financial assistance to upper-division students from any state preparing for a career as an athletic trainer at a college or university in Connecticut.
Eligibility: Open to students from any state enrolled full-time as juniors (or immediately prior to their final undergraduate year) at colleges and universities in Connecticut. Applicants must be able to confirm their intent to prepare for a career as an athletic trainer. They must have a distinguished record in academics and as a participant in their athletic training program. Financial need is not considered in the selection process.
Financial data: A stipend is awarded (amount not specified).
Duration: 1 year.
Number awarded: 1 each year.
Deadline: March of each year.

1839 CONNECTICUT BROADCASTERS ASSOCIATION ENGINEERING AWARD

Connecticut Broadcasters Association
Attn: Scholarships
90 South Park Street
Willimantic, CT 06226
Phone: (860) 633-5031; Fax: (860) 456-5688
Email: mcrice@prodigy.net
Web: www.ctba.org/page.cfm?page=17
Summary: To provide financial assistance to Connecticut residents who are interested in attending college in any state to prepare for a career in broadcast engineering.
Eligibility: Open to Connecticut residents who are entering their first, second, third, or fourth year at a 2- or 4-year college, university, or technical school in any state. Applicants must be majoring in electronics, engineering, or a related field. Selection is based on academic achievement, community service, goals in the chosen field, and financial need.
Financial data: The stipend is $2,500.
Duration: 1 year.
Number awarded: 1 each year.
Deadline: March of each year.

1840 CONNECTICUT BUILDING CONGRESS SCHOLARSHIPS

Connecticut Building Congress
Attn: Scholarship Fund
P.O. Box 743
Enfield, CT 06083
Phone: (860) 228-1387; Fax: (860) 741-8809
Email: cbc@cbc-ct.org
Web: www.cbc-ct.org/pages/scholarship.htm
Summary: To provide financial assistance to high school seniors in Connecticut who are interested in studying a field related to the construction industry at a college in any state.
Eligibility: Open to graduating seniors at high schools in Connecticut. Applicants must be interested in enrolling at a 2- or 4-year college or university in any state with the goal of completing an associate, bachelor's, or master's degree in a field related to construction (e.g., architecture, engineering, construction management, surveying, planning, drafting). They must submit an essay (up to 500 words) that explains how their planned studies will relate to a career in the construction industry. Selection is based on academic merit, extracurricular activities, potential, and financial need.
Financial data: Stipends range from $500 to $2,000 per year.
Duration: Up to 4 years.
Number awarded: Varies each year.
Deadline: March of each year.

1841 CONNECTICUT NURSES' FOUNDATION SCHOLARSHIPS

Connecticut Nurses' Association
Attn: Connecticut Nurses' Foundation
377 Research Parkway, Suite 2D
Meriden, CT 06450-7155
Phone: (203) 238-1207; Fax: (203) 238-3437
Email: info@ctnurses.org
Web: www.ctnurses.org/displaycommon.cfm?an=12
Summary: To provide financial assistance to Connecticut residents interested in preparing for a career as a registered nurse (R.N.) or working on a degree in nursing at a school in any state.
Eligibility: Open to residents of Connecticut who are entering or enrolled at an accredited school of nursing in any state to earn an R.N. certificate or work on an associate, bachelor's, master's, or doctoral degree. Selection is based on employment experience; professional, community, and student activities; a statement of educational and practice goals; and financial need.
Financial data: The stipend depends on the qualifications of the recipient and the availability of funds.
Duration: 1 year.
Number awarded: 1 or more each year.
Deadline: June of each year.

1842 CONNECTICUT TREE PROTECTIVE ASSOCIATION ARBORIST SCHOLARSHIPS

Connecticut Tree Protective Association, Inc.
58 Old Post Road
P.O. Box 356
Northford, CT 06472-0356
Phone: (203) 484-2512; (888) 919-2872 (within CT); Fax: (203) 484-2512
Web: www.ctpa.org/scholarship.htm

Summary: To provide financial assistance to residents of Connecticut who are attending college in any state to prepare for a career in tree care.

Eligibility: Open to Connecticut residents who are working full-time on a bachelor's or associate degree in urban forestry or arboriculture at a college or university in any state. Applicants must be preparing for a career in tree care; preference is given to students who plan to practice arboriculture in Connecticut. They must have a GPA of 2.0 or higher. Priority is given to applicants who demonstrate financial need.

Financial data: The stipend is $1,000 per year.

Duration: 1 year; may be renewed.

Number awarded: 2 each year.

Deadline: November of each year.

1843 CONSERVATION DISTRICTS OF IOWA SCHOLARSHIPS

Conservation Districts of Iowa
Attn: Executive Director
110 South Chestnut Street
P.O. Box 367
Earlham, IA 50072
Phone: (515) 758-3880; Fax: (515) 758-3881
Email: dweems@cdiowa.org
Web: www.cdiowa.org/education.html

Summary: To provide financial assistance to high school seniors in Iowa interested in studying a field related to natural resources or agriculture at a college in any state.

Eligibility: Open to Iowa high school seniors entering their first year at a college or university in any state. Applicants must be interested in working on a degree in a field related to agriculture or natural resources. Selection is based on 1) leadership, including service (20 points), character (20 points), and self-motivation (20 points); and 2) academic achievement (40 points).

Financial data: Stipends are $1,800, $1,200, $1,000 (paid directly to the recipients' school) or $300 (paid directly to the student).

Duration: 1 year; nonrenewable.

Number awarded: 9 each year: 1 at $1,800, 1 at $1,200, 1 at $1,000, and 6 (1 in each of the conservation regions in Iowa) at $300.

Deadline: Applications must be submitted to the local Soil and Water Conservation District office by February of each year.

1844 CONSTRUCTION MANAGEMENT ASSOCIATION OF AMERICA FOUNDATION SCHOLARSHIPS

Construction Management Association of America
Attn: CMAA Foundation
7926 Jones Branch Drive, Suite 800
McLean, VA 22101-3303
Phone: (703) 356-2622; Fax: (703) 356-6388
Email: CMAAFoundation@cmaanet.org
Web: www.cmaanet.org/cmaa-foundation-scholarships

Summary: To provide financial assistance to undergraduate and graduate students working on a degree in construction management.

Eligibility: Open to full-time undergraduate and graduate students who have completed at least 1 year of study and have at least 1 full year remaining. Applicants must be working on a bachelor's or master's degree in construction management or a related field. Along with their application, they must submit essays on why they are interested in a career in construction management and why they should be awarded this scholarship. Selection is based on academic objectives as they relate to the construction management profession, academic performance, relationship between the applicant's academic program and construction management as a professional field, and recommendations.

Financial data: The stipend is $3,000.

Duration: 1 year.

Number awarded: 3 undergraduates and 1 graduate student receive these scholarships each year.

Deadline: April of each year.

1845 CORRIE WHITLOCK MEMORIAL SCHOLARSHIP

National Garden Clubs, Inc.–South Atlantic Region
c/o Judy Ann Fray, Scholarship Committee Chair
1223 North Main Street
P.O. Box 255
Madison, VA 22727-0263
Phone: (540) 948-4220
Email: jafray@ns.gemlink.com
Web: www.southatlanticregiongardenclubs.org/scholarships.html

Summary: To provide financial assistance to residents of designated south Atlantic states who are working on an undergraduate degree in a field related to gardening at a college in any state.

Eligibility: Open to residents of Kentucky, North Carolina, South Carolina, Virginia, and West Virginia who are enrolled as sophomores or juniors at a college in any state. Applicants must be majoring in horticulture, floriculture, landscape design, botany, plant pathology, biology forestry, agronomy, environmental concerns, city planning, land management, or a related subject. Selection is based on academic record (50%), financial need (30%), character (10%), commitment to career (5%), and variety of avocation (5%).

Financial data: The stipend is $1,000.

Duration: 1 year; may be renewed 1 additional year if the recipient maintains a GPA of 3.0 or higher.

Number awarded: 1 each year.

Deadline: Applications must be received by the chair of the appropriate National Garden Club state scholarship committee by January of each year.

1846 COURTLAND PAUL SCHOLARSHIP

Summary: To provide financial assistance to upper-division students working on a degree in landscape architecture.

See Listing #1232.

1847 C.R. BARD FOUNDATION NURSING SCHOLARSHIP

Independent College Fund of New Jersey
797 Springfield Avenue
Summit, NJ 07901-1107
Phone: (908) 277-3424; Fax: (908) 277-0851
Email: scholarships@njcolleges.org
Web: www.njcolleges.org/i_about_schol_students.html

Summary: To provide financial assistance to students enrolled at member institutions of the Independent College Fund of New Jersey (ICFNJ) who are working on a bachelor's degree in nursing.

Eligibility: Open to students enrolled full-time at ICJNF member institutions that offer a program in nursing (Bloomfield College, Fairleigh Dickinson University, College of Saint Elizabeth, Felician College, Georgian Court University, Monmouth University, Saint Peter's College, or Seton Hall University). Applicants must be entering at least the second semester of their sophomore year or the second semester of the second year of their nursing program. They must have a GPA of 3.0 or higher, be a U.S. citizen or eligible to work in the United States, be able to demonstrate financial need, and be planning to prepare for a career in the health industry. Along with their application, they must submit a 200-word statement on why they want to prepare for the profession of nursing or a career in the health industry, what they hope to accomplish, and their qualifications for the award. Selection is based on the quality of that statement, academic performance, extracurricular activities, demonstrated leadership, and financial need.

Financial data: The stipend is $2,500 per year.

Duration: 1 year; may be renewed.

Number awarded: 8 each year.

Deadline: March of each year.

1848 CUMMINS/HENAAC SCHOLARS PROGRAM

Great Minds in STEM
Attn: HENAAC Scholars
3900 Whiteside Street
Los Angeles, CA 90063
Phone: (323) 262-0997; Fax: (323) 262-0946
Email: kbbarrera@greatmindsinstem.org
Web: www.greatmindsinstem.org/henaac/scholars

Summary: To provide financial assistance to Hispanic undergraduate students majoring in designated fields of engineering.

Eligibility: Open to Hispanic students who are working on an undergraduate degree in electrical, industrial, or mechanical engineering. Applicants must be of Hispanic origin and/or must significantly participate in and promote organizations and activities in the Hispanic community. They must have a GPA of 3.0 or higher. Along with their application, they must submit a 700-word essay on a topic that changes annually; recently, students were asked to write on how they see their academic major contributing to global efforts and technology and how they, in their field of study, will contribute to global progress as well as actively contribute to their local communities. Selection is based on leadership through academic achievements and campus and community activities; financial need is not considered. U.S. citizenship or permanent resident status is required.

Financial data: Stipends range from $500 to $5,000.

Duration: 1 year; recipients may reapply.

Number awarded: Varies each year; recently, 8 of these scholarships were awarded.

Deadline: April of each year.

1849 CYNTHIA E. MORGAN SCHOLARSHIPS

Cynthia E. Morgan Scholarship Fund
5516 Maudes Way
White Marsh, MD 21162
Email: administrator@cemsfund.com
Web: www.cemsfund.com

Summary: To provide financial assistance to residents of Maryland who are the first in their family to attend college and are interested in attending a school in the state to study a medical field.

Eligibility: Open to residents of Maryland who are high school juniors, high school seniors, or students already enrolled at an accredited college, university, trade school, or medical school in the state. Applicants must be preparing for a career in a medical field, including as a nurse, laboratory scientist, pharmacist, physiotherapist, speech therapist, occupational therapist, dietitian, or bioengineer. They must be the first member of their family to attend college. Along with their application, they must submit an essay of 350 to 500 words on their goals and aspiration as those relate to their education, career, and future plans. Financial need is not considered in the selection process.

Financial data: The stipend is $1,000.

Duration: 1 year.

Number awarded: 1 each year.

Deadline: February of each year.

1850 DAEDALIAN ACADEMIC MATCHING SCHOLARSHIP PROGRAM

Daedalian Foundation
Attn: Scholarship Committee
55 Main Circle (Building 676)
P.O. Box 249
Randolph AFB, TX 78148-0249
Phone: (210) 945-2113; Fax: (210) 945-2112
Email: icarus2@daedalians.org
Web: www.daedalians.org/foundation/scholarships.htm

Summary: To provide financial assistance to ROTC and other college students who wish to become military pilots.

Eligibility: Open to students who are attending or have been accepted at an accredited 4-year college or university and have demonstrated the desire and potential to become a commissioned military pilot. Usually, students in ROTC units of all services apply to local chapters (Flights) of Daedalian; if the Flight awards a scholarship, the application is forwarded to the Daedalian Foundation for one of these matching scholarships. College students not part of a ROTC program are eligible to apply directly to the Foundation if their undergraduate goals and performance are consistent with Daedalian criteria. Selection is based on intention to pursue a career as a military pilot, demonstrated moral character and patriotism, scholastic and military standing and aptitude, and physical condition and aptitude for flight. Financial need may also be considered. Additional eligibility criteria may be set by a Flight Scholarship Selection Board.

Financial data: The amount awarded varies but is intended to serve as matching funds for the Flight scholarship. Generally, the maximum awarded is $2,000.

Number awarded: Up to 99 each year.

Deadline: Students who are members of Daedalian Flights must submit their applications by November of each year; students who apply directly to the Daedalian Foundation must submit their applications by July of each year.

1851 DAIRY STUDENT RECOGNITION PROGRAM

National Dairy Shrine
Attn: Executive Director
P.O. Box 1
Maribel, WI 54227
Phone: (920) 863-6333; Fax: (920) 863-8328
Email: info@dairyshrine.org
Web: www.dairyshrine.org/scholarships.php

Summary: To recognize and reward outstanding college seniors who are planning a career related to dairy or production agriculture.

Eligibility: Open to graduating college seniors who are planning a career related to dairy (e.g., production agriculture, manufacturing, marketing, agricultural law, business, veterinary medicine, or environmental sciences). Each university may nominate 2 students for the awards. Selection is based on leadership ability and extracurricular activities (35 points), academic standing (10 points), interest and experience in the dairy industry (35 points), and plans for the future (20 points).

Financial data: First prize is $2,000, second $1,500, and third through seventh $1,000.

Duration: The awards are presented annually.

Number awarded: 7 each year.

Deadline: April of each year.

1852 DAKOTA CORPS SCHOLARSHIP PROGRAM

Education Assistance Corporation
115 First Avenue, S.W.
Aberdeen, SD 57401
Phone: (800) 874-9033
Email: eac@eac-easci.org
Web: www.state.sd.us/dakotacorps/default.html

Summary: To provide financial assistance to high school seniors in South Dakota who plan to attend a college or university in the state and work in the state in a critical need occupation following graduation.

Eligibility: Open to seniors graduating from high schools in South Dakota who are U.S. citizens or nationals. Applicants must plan to attend a participating college, university, technical college, or tribal college in the state and major in a field to prepare for a career in a critical need occupation; currently, those are 1) teaching K-12 music, special education, or foreign language in a public, private, or parochial school; 2) teaching high school mathematics or science in a public, private, or parochial school; or 3) working as a licensed practical nurse, registered nurse, or other allied health care provider. They must have a GPA of 2.8 or higher and an ACT score of at least 24 (or the SAT equivalent). Applications must be submitted within 1 year after high school graduation or release from active duty of a component of the U.S. armed forces. Along with their application, they must submit a short essay explaining what has attracted them to their profession and to remaining in South Dakota for employment. Selection is based on that essay, GPA, test scores, activities, honors, and community service.

Financial data: At public colleges, universities, and technical colleges, and at tribal colleges, awards provide full payment of tuition and generally-applicable fees up to 16 credit hours. At private colleges and universities, awards provide the same amount as at a public 4-year college; the remaining tuition and generally-applicable fees must be covered by the participating college through institutional scholarship or tuition waiver. This is a scholarship loan program; recipients must commit to work in a critical need occupation in South Dakota for a period of time equal to the number of years of scholarship support received plus 1 additional year. If recipients fail to complete their commitment, the scholarship converts to a low interest loan that must be repaid.

Duration: 1 year; may be renewed up to 3 additional years, provided the recipient maintains a GPA of 2.8 or higher and remains enrolled full-time.

Number awarded: A limited number each year.

Deadline: January of each year.

1853 DANIEL ALEX SCHOLARSHIP AND GRANT FUND

Cook Inlet Region, Inc.
Attn: The CIRI Foundation
3600 San Jeronimo Drive, Suite 256
Anchorage, AK 99508-2870
Phone: (907) 793-3575; (800) 764-3382; Fax: (907) 793-3585
Email: tcf@thecirifoundation.org
Web: www.thecirifoundation.org/designated.htm

Summary: To provide financial assistance for undergraduate or vocational studies in designated fields to Alaska Natives of certain communities and their lineal descendants.

Eligibility: Open to original enrollees and direct lineal descendants of the Cook Inlet Region, Inc. (CIRI), Eklutna, Inc., and/or the Native Village of Eklunta. There are no Alaska residency requirements or age limitations. Applicants must be accepted or enrolled full-time in a degree program or in a vocational training program. Preference is given to students majoring in physics, mathematics,

business management, or education. Along with their application, they must submit a 500-word statement on their educational and career goals and how they are contributing, or planning to contribute, to a positive Alaska Native community. Selection is based on that statement, academic achievement, rigor of course work or degree program, student financial contribution, financial need, grade level, previous work performance, community service, and relationship of degree program to career goals.
Financial data: A stipend is awarded (amount not specified). Funds must be used for tuition, university fees, books, required class supplies, and campus housing and meal plans for students who must live away from their permanent home to attend college. Checks are sent directly to the recipient's school.
Duration: 1 year (2 semesters).
Number awarded: 1 or more each year.
Deadline: May or December of each year for full-time degree-seeking students. June of each year for vocational training students.

1854 DAR OCCUPATIONAL/PHYSICAL THERAPY SCHOLARSHIP

Daughters of the American Revolution–National Society
Attn: Committee Services Office, Scholarships
1776 D Street, N.W.
Washington, DC 20006-5303
Phone: (202) 628-1776
Web: www.dar.org/natsociety/edout_scholar.cfm
Summary: To provide financial assistance to students working on an undergraduate degree in occupational, physical, art, music, or other therapy.
Eligibility: Open to students who are enrolled in an accredited program of occupational or physical therapy. Programs in art and music therapy also qualify. Applicants must be sponsored by a local chapter of the Daughters of the American Revolution (DAR). Selection is based on academic excellence, commitment to field of study, and financial need. U.S. citizenship is required.
Financial data: The stipend is $1,000 per year.
Duration: 1 year; may be renewed.
Number awarded: Varies each year.
Deadline: February of each year.

1855 DAVID E. KNOX MEMORIAL NURSING SCHOLARSHIP

Alaska Community Foundation
Attn: Scholarships
400 L Street, Suite 100
Anchorage, AK 99501
Phone: (907) 334-6700; Fax: (907) 334-5780
Email: info@alaskacf.org
Web: www.alaskacf.org
Summary: To provide grants-for-service to residents of Alaska who are interested in studying nursing at a school in any state and then practicing in a small community in Alaska.
Eligibility: Open to residents of Alaska who are graduating high school seniors or students already enrolled full-time at a college or university in any state. Applicants must be interested in working on a degree (R.N. or B.S.N.) in nursing and be willing to commit to a 1-year service obligation as a nurse in a small (less than 50,000 residents) community in Alaska. They must have a GPA of 3.0 or higher and be able to demonstrate financial need. Along with their application, they must submit a 1,000-word essay describing how their background is relevant to their interest in preparing for a nursing career, their educational goals and objectives, their plan and timeframe for meeting those goals, and their specific qualifications for this scholarship. Preference is given to applicants who wish to practice in operating rooms.
Financial data: The stipend is $2,500 per year. If recipients fail to honor their service commitment, they must repay all funds received.
Duration: 1 year; recipients may reapply.
Number awarded: 1 or more each year.
Deadline: January of each year.

1856 DAVID F. LUDOVICI SCHOLARSHIP

Florida Engineering Society
Attn: Scholarship Coordinator
125 South Gadsden Street
P.O. Box 750
Tallahassee, FL 32302-0750
Phone: (850) 224-7121; Fax: (850) 222-4349
Email: fes@fleng.org
Web: www.fleng.org/scholarships.cfm
Summary: To provide financial assistance to students working on a degree in designated engineering specialties at colleges and universities in Florida.
Eligibility: Open to residents of Florida entering their junior or senior year as a full-time student at an ABET-accredited engineering program at a college or university in the state. Applicants must be U.S. citizens with a GPA of 3.0 or higher and be recommended by a faculty member at their institution. They must be interested in civil, structural, or consulting engineering. Selection is based on academic performance, work experience, activities, honors, and letters of recommendation. Semifinalists are interviewed. Financial need is not considered in the selection process.
Financial data: The stipend is $1,000.
Duration: 1 year.
Number awarded: 1 each year.
Deadline: January of each year.

1857 DAVID MANN SCHOLARSHIP

American Mensa Education and Research Foundation
1229 Corporate Drive West
Arlington, TX 76006-6103
Phone: (817) 607-5577; (800) 66-MENSA; Fax: (817) 649-5232
Email: info@mensafoundation.org
Web: www.mensafoundation.org/AM/Template.cfm?Section=Scholarships1
Summary: To provide financial assistance for undergraduate or graduate study in aeronautical engineering or an aerospace field.
Eligibility: Open to students who are enrolled or planning to enroll in a degree program at an accredited American institution of postsecondary education with a major or career plans in aeronautical engineering or an aerospace field. Membership in Mensa is not required, but applicants must be U.S. citizens or permanent residents. There are no restrictions as to age, race, gender, level of postsecondary education, GPA, or financial need. Selection is based on a 550-word essay that describes the applicant's career, vocational, or academic goals.
Financial data: The stipend is $1,000.
Duration: 1 year; nonrenewable.
Number awarded: 1 each year.
Deadline: January of each year.

1858 DAVID SANKEY MINORITY SCHOLARSHIP IN METEOROLOGY

National Weather Association
Attn: Executive Director
228 West Millbrook Road
Raleigh, NC 27609-4304
Phone: (919) 845-1546; Fax: (919) 845-2956
Email: exdir@nwas.org
Web: www.nwas.org/committees/ed_comm/application/Sankey.php
Summary: To provide financial assistance to members of minority groups working on an undergraduate or graduate degree in meteorology.
Eligibility: Open to members of minority ethnic groups who are either entering their sophomore or higher year of undergraduate study or enrolled as graduate students. Applicants must be working on a degree in meteorology. Along with their application, they must submit a 1-page statement explaining why they are applying for this scholarship. Selection is based on that statement, academic achievement, and 2 letters of recommendation.
Financial data: The stipend is $1,000.
Duration: 1 year.
Number awarded: 1 each year.
Deadline: April of each year.

1859 DC-AMS SCHOLARSHIP

American Meteorological Society–District of Columbia Chapter
Attn: Chapter Scholarship Committee
P.O. Box 13557
Silver Spring, MD 20911-3557
Email: dc.ams.chapter@gmail.com
Web: www.dc-ams.org
Summary: To provide financial assistance to high school seniors in the Washington, D.C. area interested in studying a field related to meteorology at a college in any state.
Eligibility: Open to seniors graduating from high schools in Washington, D.C., Maryland, or Virginia. Applicants must have been accepted to an accredited college or university in any state intending to major in atmospheric science,

meteorology, or a closely-related field. They must have completed at least 3 years of science and 3 years of mathematics in high school. Along with their application, they must submit an essay describing why they feel they should be considered for this scholarship, including their academic goals, activities, achievements, and interests related to atmospheric science, meteorology, or a closely-related field. Financial need is not considered in the selection process.
Financial data: The stipend is $2,000.
Duration: 1 year.
Number awarded: 1 each year.
Deadline: May of each year.

1860 DECOMMISSIONING, DECONTAMINATION AND REUTILIZATION SCHOLARSHIP

American Nuclear Society
Attn: Scholarship Coordinator
555 North Kensington Avenue
La Grange Park, IL 60526-5592
Phone: (708) 352-6611; (800) 323-3044; Fax: (708) 352-0499
Email: outreach@ans.org
Web: www.ans.org/honors/scholarships/ddrd.html
Summary: To provide financial assistance to upper-division and graduate students who are working on a degree in engineering or science that is associated with decommissioning, decontamination, or environmental restoration aspects of nuclear power.
Eligibility: Open to juniors, seniors, and master's degree students in an engineering or science program at an accredited institution in the United States. The program must be associated with 1) decommissioning or decontamination of nuclear facilities; 2) management or characterization of nuclear waste; 3) restoration of the environment; or 4) nuclear engineering. Applicants must be U.S. citizens. Along with their application, they must submit a brief essay discussing the importance of an aspect of decommissioning, decontamination, and reutilization to the future of the nuclear field. Selection is based on that essay, academic achievement, and letters of recommendation.
Financial data: The stipend is $2,000 for undergraduates or $3,000 for graduate students.
Duration: 1 year; nonrenewable.
Number awarded: 2 each year: 1 undergraduate and 1 graduate student.
Deadline: January of each year.

1861 DEFENSE INTELLIGENCE AGENCY UNDERGRADUATE TRAINING ASSISTANCE PROGRAM

Defense Intelligence Agency
Attn: Human Resources, HCH-4
200 MacDill Boulevard, Building 6000
Bolling AFB, DC 20340-5100
Phone: (202) 231-8228; Fax: (202) 231-4889; TDD: (202) 231-5002
Email: staffing@dia.mil
Web: www.dia.mil/employment/student/index.htm
Summary: To provide financial assistance and work experience to high school seniors and lower-division students interested in majoring in specified fields and working for the U.S. Defense Intelligence Agency (DIA).
Eligibility: Open to graduating high school seniors and college freshmen and sophomores interested in working full-time on a baccalaureate degree in 1 of the following fields in college: biology, chemistry, computer science, engineering, foreign area studies, intelligence analysis, international relations, microbiology, pharmacology, physics, political science, or toxicology. High school seniors must have a GPA of 2.75 or higher and either 1) an SAT combined critical reading and mathematics score of 1000 or higher plus 500 or higher on the writing portion; or 2) an ACT score of 21 or higher. College freshmen and sophomores must have a GPA of 3.0 or higher. All applicants must be able to demonstrate financial need (household income ceiling of $70,000 for a family of 4 or $80,000 for a family of 5 or more) and leadership abilities through extracurricular activities, civic involvement, volunteer work, or part-time employment. Students and all members of their immediate family must be U.S. citizens. Minorities, women, and persons with disabilities are strongly encouraged to apply.
Financial data: Students accepted into this program receive tuition (up to $18,000 per year) at an accredited college or university selected by the student and endorsed by the sponsor; reimbursement for books and needed supplies; an annual salary to cover college room and board expenses and for summer employment; and a position at the sponsoring agency after graduation. Recipients must work for DIA after college graduation for at least 1 and a half times the length of study. For participants who leave DIA earlier than scheduled, the agency arranges for payments to reimburse DIA for the total cost of education (including the employee's pay and allowances).
Duration: 4 years, provided the recipient maintains a GPA of 2.75 during the freshman year and 3.0 or higher in subsequent semesters.
Number awarded: Only a few are awarded each year.
Deadline: November of each year.

1862 DELAWARE NURSING INCENTIVE PROGRAM

Delaware Higher Education Commission
Carvel State Office Building, Fifth Floor
820 North French Street
Wilmington, DE 19801-3509
Phone: (302) 577-5240; (800) 292-7935; Fax: (302) 577-6765
Email: dhec@doe.k12.de.us
Web: www.doe.k12.de.us/infosuites/students_family/dhec/default.shtml
Summary: To provide financial assistance to Delaware residents who are interested in studying nursing at a school in any state.
Eligibility: Open to residents of Delaware who are enrolled or planning to enroll full-time in an accredited program in any state leading to certification as an R.N. or L.P.N. High school seniors must rank in the upper half of their class and have a cumulative GPA of 2.5 or higher. Current undergraduate students must be enrolled full-time and have a GPA of 2.5 or higher. Also eligible are 1) current state employees (they are not required to be Delaware residents and may enroll part-time); and 2) registered nurses with 5 or more years of state service (they must be working on a bachelor of science in nursing degree, but they may enroll full- or part-time). U.S. citizenship or eligible noncitizen status is required.
Financial data: Awards up to the cost of tuition, fees, and other direct educational expenses are available. This is a scholarship/loan program; if the recipient performs required service at a state-owned hospital or clinic in Delaware, the loan is forgiven at the rate of 1 year of service for each year of assistance. Recipients who fail to perform the required service must repay the loan in full.
Duration: 1 year; may be renewed for up to 3 additional years, provided the recipient maintains a GPA of 2.75 or higher.
Number awarded: Up to 50 each year.
Deadline: March of each year.

1863 DELAWARE VALLEY CHAPTER AWMA UNDERGRADUATE SCHOLARSHIP

Air & Waste Management Association–Delaware Valley Chapter
c/o Marjorie J. Fitzpatrick
IES Engineers
1720 Walton Road
Blue Bell, PA 19422
Phone: (610) 828-3078; Fax: (610) 828-7842
Email: mfitzpatrick@iesengineers.com
Web: www.mass-awma.net/DVC/Scholarship.html
Summary: To provide financial assistance to undergraduate and graduate students from the area served by the Delaware Valley Chapter of the Air & Waste Management Association (AWMA) who are working on a degree in an environmental field.
Eligibility: Open to undergraduate and graduate students who are either attending school in Delaware, southern New Jersey, or Pennsylvania east of the Susquehanna River or residents of that area attending school in any state. Applicants must be preparing for a career in environmental sciences, environmental engineering, environmental management, or a related field. Selection is based on academic background related to the environmental field, interest in preparing for a career in the environmental field (as demonstrated through course work, extracurricular activities, volunteer activities, jobs, etc.), and a letter of recommendation.
Financial data: Stipends range from $500 to $2,000.
Duration: 1 year.
Number awarded: 1 or more each year.
Deadline: March of each year.

1864 DELMAR CENGAGE LEARNING SURGICAL TECHNOLOGY SCHOLARSHIP

Association of Surgical Technologists
Attn: Education Department
6 West Dry Creek Circle, Suite 200
Littleton, CO 80120-8031
Phone: (303) 694-9130; (800) 637-7433; Fax: (303) 694-9169
Email: ast@ast.org
Web: www.ast.org/educators/scholarships.aspx

Summary: To provide financial assistance to students enrolled in a surgical technology program.

Eligibility: Open to students enrolled or accepted in a surgical technology program accredited by the Commission on Accreditation of Allied Health Education Programs (CAAHEP). Applicants must have a GPA of 2.5 or higher. Along with their application, they must submit a 500-word statement on their professional goals, strengths as a student, and reasons for wanting to enter the surgical technology profession. Selection is based on academic achievement and progress and on the student's ability to communicate clearly and effectively through writing skills.

Financial data: The stipend is $1,500.

Duration: 1 year.

Number awarded: 1 each year.

Deadline: February of each year.

1865 DELTA FAUCET COMPANY SCHOLARSHIPS

Plumbing-Heating-Cooling Contractors–National Association
Attn: PHCC Educational Foundation
180 South Washington Street
P.O. Box 6808
Falls Church, VA 22040
Phone: (703) 237-8100, ext. 221; (800) 533-7694; Fax: (703) 237-7442
Email: scholarships@naphcc.org
Web: www.foundation.phccweb.org/Scholarships/DScholarship.htm

Summary: To provide financial assistance to entering or continuing undergraduate students interested in the plumbing, heating, and cooling industry.

Eligibility: Open to 1) full-time undergraduate students (entering or continuing) who are majoring in a field related to plumbing, heating, and cooling (e.g., business management, construction management with a specialization in mechanical construction, mechanical engineering) at a 4-year college or university; 2) students enrolled full-time in an approved certificate or degree program at a 2-year technical college, community college, or trade school in business management, mechanical CAD design, construction management with a specialty in mechanical construction, or plumbing or HVACR installation, service, and repair; and 3) full-time employees of a licensed plumbing or HVAC contractor (must be a member of the Plumbing-Heating-Cooling Contractors [PHCC]–National Association) who are enrolled in an apprenticeship program in plumbing or HVACR installation, service, and repair. Students majoring in accounting, architecture, computer engineering, construction-related engineering, civil engineering, electrical engineering, or environmental engineering are not eligible. Applicants must have a GPA of 2.0 or higher. Along with their application, they must submit a letter of recommendation from a PHCC member; a copy of school transcripts; SAT and/or ACT scores; and a letter of recommendation from a school principal, counselor, or dean. U.S. or Canadian citizenship is required. Financial need is not considered in the selection process.

Financial data: The stipend is $2,500.

Duration: 1 year; nonrenewable.

Number awarded: 6 each year: 4 to students at 4-year institutions and 2 to students at 2-year institutions or in apprenticeship programs.

Deadline: April of each year.

1866 DELTA GAMMA FOUNDATION FLORENCE MARGARET HARVEY MEMORIAL SCHOLARSHIP

American Foundation for the Blind
Attn: Scholarship Committee
11 Penn Plaza, Suite 300
New York, NY 10001
Phone: (212) 502-7661; (800) AFB-LINE; Fax: (212) 502-7771; TDD: (212) 502-7662
Email: afbinfo@afb.net
Web: www.afb.org/Section.asp?Documentid=2962

Summary: To provide financial assistance to blind undergraduate and graduate students who wish to study in the field of rehabilitation and/or education of the blind.

Eligibility: Open to legally blind juniors, seniors, or graduate students. U.S. citizenship is required. Applicants must be studying in the field of rehabilitation and/or education of visually impaired and blind persons. Along with their application, they must submit a 200-word essay that includes their past and recent achievements and accomplishments; their intended field of study and why they have chosen it; and the role their visual impairment has played in shaping their life. Financial need is considered in the selection process.

Financial data: The stipend is $1,000.

Duration: 1 year.

Number awarded: 1 each year.

Deadline: April of each year.

1867 DENISE SCHOLARSHIP FUND

New York State Grange
100 Grange Place
Cortland, NY 13045
Phone: (607) 756-7553; Fax: (607) 756-7757
Email: nysgrange@nysgrange.com
Web: www.nysgrange.com/educationalassistance.html

Summary: To provide financial assistance to undergraduate students from New York interested in majoring in agriculture at a school in any state.

Eligibility: Open to residents of New York enrolled or planning to enroll at a 2- or 4-year college or university in any state. Applicants must be interested in working on an undergraduate degree in the field of agriculture. They must be able to demonstrate financial need.

Financial data: A stipend is awarded (amount not specified).

Duration: 1 year.

Number awarded: 1 or more each year.

Deadline: April of each year.

1868 DENNY LYDIC SCHOLARSHIP

Transportation Clubs International
P.O. Box 2223
Ocean Shores, WA 98569
Phone: (877) 858-8627
Email: info@transportationclubsinternational.com
Web: www.transportationclubsinternational.com/scholarships.html

Summary: To provide financial assistance to college students interested in preparing for a career in fields related to transportation.

Eligibility: Open to students enrolled at an academic institution (vocational or degree program) that offers courses in transportation, logistics, traffic management, or related fields. Applicants must intend to prepare for a career in those fields. Along with their application, they must submit a 200-word essay explaining why they have chosen transportation or an allied field as a career path and outlining their objectives. Selection is based on scholastic ability, character, potential, professional interest, and financial need.

Financial data: The stipend is $1,000.

Duration: 1 year.

Number awarded: 1 or more each year.

Deadline: May of each year.

1869 DENTAL ASSISTING SCHOLARSHIPS

American Dental Association
Attn: ADA Foundation
211 East Chicago Avenue
Chicago, IL 60611
Phone: (312) 440-2547; Fax: (312) 440-3526
Email: adaf@ada.org
Web: www.ada.org/ada/adaf/grants/scholarships.asp

Summary: To provide financial assistance to currently-enrolled dental assisting students.

Eligibility: Open to full-time students entering a dental assisting program accredited by the Commission on Dental Accreditation. They must have a GPA of 3.0 or higher and be able to demonstrate financial need of at least $1,000. U.S. citizenship is required. Selection is based on academic achievement, a written summary of personal and professional goals, letters of reference, and financial need.

Financial data: Stipends range up to $1,000 per year. Funds are to be used to cover school expenses (tuition, fees, books, supplies, living expenses) and are paid in 2 equal installments to the recipient's school.

Duration: 1 year.

Number awarded: 10 each year.

Deadline: October of each year.

1870 DENTAL HYGIENE SCHOLARSHIPS

American Dental Association
Attn: ADA Foundation
211 East Chicago Avenue
Chicago, IL 60611
Phone: (312) 440-2547; Fax: (312) 440-3526
Email: adaf@ada.org
Web: www.ada.org/ada/adaf/grants/scholarships.asp

Summary: To provide financial assistance to currently-enrolled dental hygiene students.

Eligibility: Open to applicants who are entering their final year of full-time study at a dental hygiene program accredited by the Commission on Dental Accreditation. They must have a GPA of 3.0 or higher and be able to demonstrate financial need of at least $1,000. U.S. citizenship is required. Selection is based on academic achievement, a written summary of personal and professional goals, letters of reference, and financial need.
Financial data: Stipends range up to $1,000 per year. Funds are to be used to cover school expenses (tuition, fees, books, supplies, living expenses) and are paid in 2 equal installments to the recipient's school.
Duration: 1 year.
Number awarded: 15 each year.
Deadline: October of each year.

1871 DENTAL LABORATORY TECHNOLOGY SCHOLARSHIPS

American Dental Association
Attn: ADA Foundation
211 East Chicago Avenue
Chicago, IL 60611
Phone: (312) 440-2547; Fax: (312) 440-3526
Email: adaf@ada.org
Web: www.ada.org/ada/adaf/grants/scholarships.asp
Summary: To provide financial assistance to currently-enrolled dental laboratory technology students.
Eligibility: Open to applicants who are entering their final year of full-time study at a dental laboratory technology program accredited by the Commission on Dental Accreditation. They must have a GPA of 3.0 or higher and be able to demonstrate financial need of at least $1,000. U.S. citizenship is required. Selection is based on academic achievement, a written summary of personal and professional goals, letters of reference, and financial need.
Financial data: Stipends range up to $1,000 per year. Funds are to be used to cover school expenses (tuition, fees, books, supplies, living expenses) and are paid in 2 equal installments to the recipient's school.
Duration: 1 year.
Number awarded: 5 each year.
Deadline: October of each year.

1872 DEPARTMENT OF ENERGY/HENAAC SCHOLARS PROGRAM

Great Minds in STEM
Attn: HENAAC Scholars
3900 Whiteside Street
Los Angeles, CA 90063
Phone: (323) 262-0997; Fax: (323) 262-0946
Email: kbbarrera@greatmindsinstem.org
Web: www.greatmindsinstem.org/henaac/scholars
Summary: To provide financial assistance to Hispanic undergraduate students majoring in specified fields of science or engineering.
Eligibility: Open to Hispanic students who are working on an undergraduate degree in applied mathematics, chemistry, computer engineering, computer science, or physics. Applicants must be of Hispanic origin and/or must significantly participate in and promote organizations and activities in the Hispanic community. They must have a GPA of 3.0 or higher. Along with their application, they must submit a 700-word essay on a topic that changes annually; recently, students were asked to write on how they see their academic major contributing to global efforts and technology and how they, in their field of study, will contribute to global progress as well as actively contribute to their local communities. Selection is based on leadership through academic achievements and campus and community activities; financial need is not considered. U.S. citizenship or permanent resident status is required.
Financial data: Stipends range from $500 to $5,000.
Duration: 1 year; recipients may reapply.
Number awarded: Varies each year; recently, 5 of these scholarships were awarded.
Deadline: April of each year.

1873 DEPARTMENT OF ENERGY THURGOOD MARSHALL COLLEGE FUND SCHOLARSHIPS

Thurgood Marshall College Fund
Attn: Scholarship Manager
80 Maiden Lane, Suite 2204
New York, NY 10038
Phone: (212) 573-8487; (877) 690-8673; Fax: (212) 573-8497
Email: srogers@tmcfund.org
Web: www.thurgoodmarshallfund.net
Summary: To provide financial assistance and work experience to students majoring in science, technology, engineering, or mathematics (STEM) at colleges and universities that are members of the Thurgood Marshall College Fund (TMCF).
Eligibility: Open to full-time students majoring in STEM disciplines at 1 of the 47 colleges and universities that are TMCF members. Applicants must be available for an internship at a facility of the U.S. Department of Energy. They must have a GPA of 3.0 or higher and be able to demonstrate financial need. U.S. citizenship is required.
Financial data: The stipend is $2,200 per semester ($4,400 per year).
Duration: 1 year.
Number awarded: 10 each year.
Deadline: July of each year.

1874 DEPARTMENT OF HOMELAND SECURITY UNDERGRADUATE SCHOLARSHIPS

Oak Ridge Institute for Science and Education
Attn: Science and Engineering Education
P.O. Box 117
Oak Ridge, TN 37831-0117
Phone: (865) 576-8233; Fax: (865) 241-5219
Email: martha.payne@orau.gov
Web: see.orau.org/ProgramDescription.aspx?Program=10040
Summary: To provide financial assistance and summer research experience to undergraduate students who are working on a degree in a field of interest to the Department of Homeland Security (DHS).
Eligibility: Open to 1) full-time students who are in their second year of college as of the application deadline; and 2) part-time students who have completed at least 45 but no more than 60 semester hours as of the application deadline. Applicants must have a GPA of 3.3 or higher. Their field of study must be in science, technology, engineering, or mathematics related to homeland security (HS-STEM), including explosives detection, mitigation, and response; social, behavioral, and economic sciences; risk and decision sciences; human factors aspects of technology; chemical threats and countermeasures; biological threats and countermeasures; community, commerce, and infrastructure resilience; food and agricultural security; transportation security; border security; immigration studies; maritime and port security; infrastructure protection; natural disasters and related geophysical studies; emergency preparedness and response; communications and interoperability; or advanced data analysis and visualization. Along with their application, they must submit 2 statements on 1) relevant research experience they have already had or in which they are currently engaging; and 2) how this scholarship will influence their current research interests. Selection is based on those statements, academic record, references, and SAT or ACT scores, As part of their program, they must be interested in participating in summer research and development activities at a DHS-designated facility. U.S. citizenship is required.
Financial data: This program provides a stipend of $1,000 per month during the academic year and $5,000 for the internship plus full payment of tuition and mandatory fees.
Duration: 2 academic years plus 10 weeks during the intervening summer.
Number awarded: Approximately 30 each year.
Deadline: January of each year.

1875 DEW SUPERINTENDENTS SCHOLARSHIP

Vermont Student Assistance Corporation
Attn: Scholarship Programs
10 East Allen Street
P.O. Box 2000
Winooski, VT 05404-2601
Phone: (802) 654-3798; (888) 253-4819; Fax: (802) 654-3765; TDD: (800) 281-3341 (within VT)
Email: info@vsac.org
Web: services.vsac.org/wps/wcm/connect/vsac/VSAC
Summary: To provide financial assistance to high school seniors in Vermont who are interested in working on a degree in construction at a college or university in any state.
Eligibility: Open to residents of Vermont who are seniors in high school. Applicants must be planning to enroll at a 2- or 4-year college or university in any state and work on a degree in a field related to construction. Along with their application, they must submit 1) a 100-word essay on their interest in and

commitment to pursuing their chosen career or vocation; and 2) a 250-word essay on their beliefs related to the value of community service. Selection is based on those essays, letters of recommendation, academic achievement, and financial need.

Financial data: The stipend ranges from $1,000 to $2,000.

Duration: 1 year.

Number awarded: Up to 2 each year.

Deadline: March of each year.

1876 DISABLED WAR VETERANS SCHOLARSHIPS

Armed Forces Communications and Electronics Association
Attn: AFCEA Educational Foundation
4400 Fair Lakes Court
Fairfax, VA 22033-3899
Phone: (703) 631-6149; (800) 336-4583, ext. 6149; Fax: (703) 631-4693
Email: scholarship@afcea.org
Web: www.afcea.org

Summary: To provide financial assistance to disabled military personnel and veterans who are majoring in specified scientific fields in college.

Eligibility: Open to active-duty service personnel and honorably discharged U.S. military veterans, Reservists, and National Guard members who are disabled because of wounds received during service in Enduring Freedom (Afghanistan) or Iraqi Freedom operations. Applicants must be enrolled full- or part-time at an accredited 2- or 4-year college or university or in a distance learning or online degree program. They must be working toward a degree in engineering (aerospace, computer, electrical, or systems), computer science, computer engineering technology, computer network systems, computer information systems, electronics engineering technology, mathematics, physics, science or mathematics education, information systems management, information systems security, technology management, or other field directly related to the support of U.S. intelligence or national security enterprises. Selection is based on demonstrated academic excellence, leadership, and financial need.

Financial data: The stipend is $2,500.

Duration: 1 year.

Number awarded: 2 each year: 1 for spring and 1 for fall.

Deadline: March of each year for fall; November of each year for spring.

1877 DISTRICT 6 GENERIC SCHOLARSHIPS FOR FLORIDA

Florida Nurses Association
Attn: Florida Nurses Foundation
1235 East Concord Street
P.O. Box 536985
Orlando, FL 32853-6985
Phone: (407) 896-3261; Fax: (407) 896-9042
Email: foundation@floridanurse.org
Web: www.floridanurse.org/foundationGrants/index.asp

Summary: To provide financial assistance to residents of Florida who are interested in working on an undergraduate or graduate degree in nursing.

Eligibility: Open to residents of Florida (for at least 1 year) who have completed at least 1 semester at an accredited nursing program in the state. They may be working on an associate, baccalaureate, master's, or doctoral degree. Undergraduates must have a GPA of 2.5 or higher and graduate students a GPA of 3.0 or higher. Along with their application, they must submit 1-page essays on 1) why it is necessary for them to receive this scholarship; and 2) their goals and their assessment of their potential for making a contribution to nursing and society.

Financial data: A stipend is awarded (amount not specified).

Duration: 1 semester or year.

Number awarded: 4 each year.

Deadline: May of each year.

1878 DON MILLER MEMORIAL SCHOLARSHIP

The Arc of Texas
Attn: Scholarship
8001 Centre Park Drive, Suite 100
Austin, TX 78754-5107
Phone: (512) 454-6694; (800) 252-7929; Fax: (512) 454-4956
Email: secretary@thearcoftexas.org
Web: www.thearcoftexas.org/programs.dmms

Summary: To provide financial assistance to upper-division students in Texas who are preparing for a career serving people with developmental disabilities.

Eligibility: Open to juniors and seniors enrolled full-time at a state-supported college or university in Texas. Applicants must have a primary career interest in providing services and supports to people with intellectual or developmental disabilities. They must have a GPA of 2.5 or higher. Along with their application, they must submit an essay on how their career goals will advance the mission of the sponsoring organization to create opportunities for people with intellectual and developmental disabilities to be included in their communities and make the choices that affect their lives.

Financial data: The stipend is $1,000.

Duration: 1 year.

Number awarded: 1 each year.

Deadline: July of each year.

1879 DONALD BURNSIDE MEMORIAL SCHOLARSHIPS

Aircraft Owners and Pilots Association
Attn: AOPA Air Safety Foundation
421 Aviation Way
Frederick, MD 21701-4798
Phone: (301) 695-2084; (800) 638-3101; Fax: (301) 695-2375
Email: asf@aopa.org
Web: www.aopa.org/asf/scholarship/burnside.html

Summary: To provide funding to upper-division students who need financial assistance to continue their studies in the field of aviation.

Eligibility: Open to U.S. citizens who are interested in working on a bachelor's degree in the field of non-engineering aviation. Applicants must be juniors or seniors and have a GPA of 3.25 or higher. Along with their application, they must submit a 250-word essay on a topic that changes annually; recently, students were asked if flight simulators should play an increased role in primary flight instruction. Financial need is not considered in the selection process.

Financial data: The stipend is $1,000.

Duration: 1 year; nonrenewable.

Number awarded: 1 each year.

Deadline: March of each year.

1880 DONNIE ARTHUR MEMORIAL TURFGRASS SCHOLARSHIP

Alabama Golf Course Superintendents Association
Attn: Scholarship Committee
P.O. Box 661214
Birmingham, AL 35266-1214
Phone: (205) 967-0397; Fax: (205) 967-1466
Email: agcsa@charter.net
Web: www.agcsa.org/sites/courses/layout10.asp?id=665&page=36828

Summary: To provide financial assistance to students from Alabama who are majoring in turfgrass management in college.

Eligibility: Open to residents of Alabama who are currently enrolled full-time in an agricultural program emphasizing turfgrass management. Applicants must have a GPA of 2.0 or higher. Along with their application, they must submit a description of themselves that covers their academic ability, dependability, work habits, potential for leadership, and thoughts on what a superintendent needs in the 21st century to be successful.

Financial data: The stipend is $1,000. Funds are paid directly to the recipient.

Duration: 1 year.

Number awarded: 2 each year.

Deadline: October of each year.

1881 DOROTHY E. GENERAL SCHOLARSHIP

Seattle Foundation
Attn: African American Scholarship Program
1200 Fifth Avenue, Suite 1300
Seattle, WA 98101-3151
Phone: (206) 622-2294; Fax: (206) 622-7673
Email: scholarships@seattlefoundation.org
Web: www.seattlefoundation.org/page10004940.cfm

Summary: To provide financial assistance to African Americans from any state working on an undergraduate or graduate degree in a field related to health care.

Eligibility: Open to African American undergraduate and graduate students who are preparing for a career in a health care profession, including public health, medicine, nursing, or dentistry; pre-professional school students are also eligible. Applicants must be able to demonstrate financial need, academic competence, and leadership of African American students. They may be residents of any state attending school in any state. Along with their application,

they must submit a 2-page essay describing their future aspirations, including their career goals and how their study of health care will help them achieve those goals and contribute to the African American community.
Financial data: The stipend is $1,000 per year. Payments are made directly to the recipient's educational institution.
Duration: 1 year; may be renewed.
Number awarded: 1 or more each year.
Deadline: February of each year.

1882 DR. ALMA S. ADAMS SCHOLARSHIP

Summary: To provide financial assistance to undergraduate or graduate students who have engaged in community service or visual arts activities to reduce smoking in communities designated as especially vulnerable to the tobacco industry.
See Listing #1246.

1883 DR. HAROLD S. WOOD AWARD FOR EXCELLENCE

General Aviation Manufacturers Association
Attn: Director, Communications
1400 K Street, N.W., Suite 801
Washington, DC 20005-2485
Phone: (202) 393-1500; Fax: (202) 842-4063
Email: kpribyl@gama.aero
Web: www.gama.aero/advocacy/aviation-education/scholarships
Summary: To provide financial assistance to students at schools belonging to the National Intercollegiate Flying Association (NIFA).
Eligibility: Open to students who have completed at least 1 semester of college-level study at a NIFA member school. Applicants must have a GPA of 3.0 or higher. Along with their application, they must submit a 1-page statement on their future plans in aviation. There is no limit to the number of applications submitted by each school. Selection is based on academic record (30%), aviation-related extracurricular activities (50%), and service and contributions to school and community (20%).
Financial data: The winner is presented with an engraved propeller trophy and a $1,000 cash award.
Duration: 1 year; nonrenewable.
Number awarded: 1 each year.
Deadline: March of each year.

1884 DR. JON L. BOYES, VICE ADMIRAL, USN (RET.) MEMORIAL SCHOLARSHIP

Armed Forces Communications and Electronics Association
Attn: AFCEA Educational Foundation
4400 Fair Lakes Court
Fairfax, VA 22033-3899
Phone: (703) 631-6149; (800) 336-4583, ext. 6149; Fax: (703) 631-4693
Email: scholarship@afcea.org
Web: www.afcea.org/education/scholarships/rotc/Boyes.asp
Summary: To provide financial assistance to Navy ROTC midshipmen who are majoring in electrical engineering.
Eligibility: Open to Navy ROTC midshipmen enrolled full-time at an accredited degree-granting 4-year college or university in the United States. Applicants must be sophomores or juniors at the time of application and have a GPA of 3.0 or higher with a major in electrical engineering. Their application must be endorsed by the professor of naval science at their institution. Selection is based on demonstrated dedication, superior performance, and potential to serve as an officer in the United States Navy. Financial need is not considered in the selection process.
Financial data: The stipend is $3,000.
Duration: 1 year.
Number awarded: 1 each year.
Deadline: February of each year.

1885 DR. ROBERT H. GODDARD SCHOLARSHIP

National Space Club
2025 M Street, N.W., Suite 800
Washington, DC 20036
Phone: (202) 973-8661
Email: info@spaceclub.org
Web: www.spaceclub.org/goddard.html
Summary: To provide financial assistance to undergraduate and graduate students interested in preparing for a career in space research or exploration.
Eligibility: Open to U.S. citizens who are at least a junior in college and intending to pursue undergraduate or graduate studies in science or engineering. Selection is based on official college transcript, letters of recommendation from faculty, accomplishments demonstrating creativity and leadership, plans to prepare for a career in aerospace sciences or technology, and past research and participation in space-related science and engineering; financial need is considered but is not a primary factor.
Financial data: The stipend is $10,000. The winner's way is paid to the Goddard Memorial Dinner (usually held in March), where the winner is introduced to the nation's leaders in science, government, and industry.
Duration: 1 year.
Number awarded: 1 each year.
Deadline: January of each year.

1886 DR. ROBERT W. SIMS MEMORIAL SCHOLARSHIP

Florida Association of Educational Data Systems
c/o Stephen B. Muzzy, Scholarship Coordinator
Brevard County Public Schools
2700 Judge Fran Jamieson Way
Viera, FL 32940
Phone: (321) 633-1000, ext. 700
Email: muzzys@brevard.k12.fl.us
Web: www.faeds.org/school_DrRobertSims.cfm
Summary: To provide financial assistance to students attending a Florida college or university and majoring in computer science or information technology.
Eligibility: Open to residents of Florida enrolled full-time at a private or public college or university in the state. Applicants must have a GPA of 2.5 or higher and be majoring or planning to major in computer science or information technology. Along with their application, they must submit a 2-page autobiography that includes their academic success and course work in technology-related areas, why they selected their major, and how they intend to use it in the future. Financial need is not considered in the selection process. U.S. citizenship is required.
Financial data: The stipend is $3,000.
Duration: 1 year.
Number awarded: 1 or more each year.
Deadline: February of each year.

1887 DR. RODERICK A. SCOFIELD SCHOLARSHIP IN METEOROLOGY

National Weather Association
Attn: Executive Director
228 West Millbrook Road
Raleigh, NC 27609-4304
Phone: (919) 845-1546; Fax: (919) 845-2956
Email: exdir@nwas.org
Web: www.nwas.org/committees/ed_comm/application/Scofield.php
Summary: To provide financial assistance to students working on an undergraduate or graduate degree in meteorology.
Eligibility: Open to students who are either entering their junior or senior year of undergraduate study or enrolled as graduate students. Applicants must be working on a degree in meteorology or a related field. Along with their application, they must submit a 1-page statement explaining why they are applying for this scholarship. Selection is based on that statement, academic achievement, and 2 letters of recommendation.
Financial data: The stipend is $1,000.
Duration: 1 year.
Number awarded: 1 each year.
Deadline: May of each year.

1888 DR. ROE B. LEWIS MEMORIAL SCHOLARSHIPS

Southwest Indian Agricultural Association
P.O. Box 93524
Phoenix, AZ 85070-3524
Phone: (520) 562-6722; Fax: (520) 562-2840
Email: swiaa@att.net
Web: www.swindianag.com
Summary: To provide financial assistance to American Indians working on an undergraduate or graduate degree in a field related to agriculture or natural resources.

Eligibility: Open to American Indians enrolled in a federally-recognized band, nation, or tribe. Applicants must be working on an undergraduate or graduate degree in agriculture or natural resources at an accredited college, university, or vocational/technical school. Along with their application, they must submit an essay explaining how they plan to use their education to promote, educate, and/or improve agriculture on southwest reservations. First-year undergraduates must have a GPA of 2.5 or higher; all other students must have a GPA of 3.0 or higher. Financial need is not considered in the selection process.
Financial data: The stipend is $1,000.
Duration: 1 year.
Number awarded: 3 each year: 2 to undergraduates and 1 to a graduate student.
Deadline: November of each year.

1889 DR. S. BRADLEY BURSON MEMORIAL SCHOLARSHIP

American Council of the Blind
Attn: Coordinator, Scholarship Program
2200 Wilson Boulevard, Suite 650
Arlington, VA 22201
Phone: (202) 467-5081; (800) 424-8666; Fax: (703) 465-5085
Email: info@acb.org
Web: www.acb.org
Summary: To provide financial assistance to blind students who are working on an undergraduate or graduate degree in designated fields of science.
Eligibility: Open to undergraduate or graduate students working on a degree in the "hard" sciences (i.e., biology, chemistry, physics, and engineering, but not computer science). Applicants must be legally blind in both eyes. Along with their application, they must submit verification of legal blindness in both eyes; SAT, ACT, GRE, or similar scores; information on extracurricular activities (including membership in the American Council of the Blind); employment record; and an autobiographical sketch that includes their personal goals, strengths, weaknesses, hobbies, honors, achievements, and reasons for choice of field or courses of study. A cumulative GPA of 3.3 or higher is generally required. Financial need is not considered in the selection process.
Financial data: The stipend is $1,000. In addition, the winner receives a Kurzweil-1000 Reading System.
Duration: 1 year.
Number awarded: 1 each year.
Deadline: February of each year.

1890 DR. SCOTT HARKLEY MEMORIAL SCHOLARSHIP FOR HEAD START GRADUATES

National Head Start Association
Attn: Scholarships and Awards
1651 Prince Street
Alexandria, VA 22314
Phone: (703) 739-0875; Fax: (703) 739-0878
Email: yvinci@nhsa.org
Web: www.nhsa.org/services/programs/awards_and_scholarships
Summary: To provide financial assistance for college to students who were in the Head Start program and are planning to prepare for a medical career.
Eligibility: Open to former Head Start students who are enrolled or planning to enroll at a 4-year college or university, 2-year community college, or vocational/technical school. Applicants must be planning to prepare for a medical career. They must be an individual member of the National Head Start Association (NHSA) or their local program must be an NHSA member. Along with their application, they must submit a 300-word statement on their goals and aspirations for furthering their education and the role Head Start has played in their education. Selection is based on that statement (40 points), financial need (30 points), 3 letters of reference or recommendation (20 points), and completeness of information (10 points). Students submit their applications to their local program, which forwards 1 to the state association. Each state association forwards 1 application to the regional association, which selects 1 for nomination to the national headquarters.
Financial data: The stipend is $1,500 per year.
Duration: 4 years.
Number awarded: 1 each year.
Deadline: January of each year.

1891 DUPONT CHALLENGE

E.I. duPont de Nemours and Company, Inc.
Attn: DuPont Office of Education
P.O. Box 80357
Wilmington, DE 19880-0030
Email: TheChallenge@usa.dupont.com
Web: thechallenge.dupont.com
Summary: To recognize and reward outstanding essays written by junior and senior high school students on scientific subjects.
Eligibility: Open to students currently enrolled in grades 7–12 at a public, private, or home school in the United States, its territories, or Canada. Applicants must submit an essay between 700 and 1,000 words in length that deals with a scientific or technological development, event, or theory. Students compete in 2 divisions: senior, for grades 10 through 12, and junior, for grades 7 through 9. Selection is based on mechanics and conventions (25%), ideas and content (25%), organization (20%), style and creativity (20%), and voice (10%).
Financial data: In each division, the first-place winner receives a $5,000 U.S. savings bond, second a $3,000 U.S. savings bond, and third a $2,000 U.S. savings bond. All winners, along with a parent, also receive an all-expense-paid trip to Kennedy Space Center and Walt Disney World Resort. Honorable mentions receive $200 U.S. savings bonds. The teachers of the first-place winners receive an all-expense-paid trip to Kennedy Space Center and Walt Disney World Resort, an all-expense-paid trip to the annual conference of the National Science Teachers Association (NSTA), and a $500 grant. The teachers of the second-place winners receive an all-expense-paid trip to Kennedy Space Center and Walt Disney World Resort and a $500 grant. The teachers of the third-place winners receive an all-expense-paid trip to Kennedy Space Center and Walt Disney World Resort and a $250 grant.
Number awarded: 6 winners (3 in each division) and a varying number of honorable mentions (recently, 32 in the senior division and 22 in the junior division) are selected each year.
Deadline: January of each year.

1892 DWIGHT WELLER, KB3LA, MEMORIAL SCHOLARSHIP

Foundation for Amateur Radio, Inc.
Attn: Scholarship Committee
P.O. Box 911
Columbia, MD 21044-0911
Phone: (410) 552-2652; Fax: (410) 981-5146
Email: dave.prestel@gmail.com
Web: www.farweb.org/scholarships
Summary: To provide funding to licensed radio amateurs who are interested in studying engineering or the physical sciences in college.
Eligibility: Open to radio amateurs who are interested in working full-time on a bachelor's degree in a branch of engineering or the physical sciences. There are no restrictions on license class or residence area. Financial need is considered in the selection process.
Financial data: The stipend is $1,000.
Duration: 1 year.
Number awarded: 1 each year.
Deadline: March of each year.

1893 EAST MICHIGAN CHAPTER SCHOLARSHIPS

Air & Waste Management Association–East Michigan Chapter
c/o Sol P. Baltimore, Scholarship Committee Chair
28742 Blackstone Drive
Lathrup Village, MI 48076-2616
Phone: (248) 569-3633
Web: www.emawma.org
Summary: To provide financial assistance to undergraduate and graduate students in Michigan who are interested in preparing for a career in air and waste management.
Eligibility: Open to applicants who are enrolled in or entering their junior or senior year of undergraduate study or any year of graduate or professional school at a college or university in Michigan. They must be full-time students preparing for a career in air pollution control, toxic and/or hazardous waste management, or another environmental area. Preferred courses of study include engineering, physical or natural sciences, public health, law, and natural resources. Selection is based on academic achievement (at least a 3.0 GPA), a paper (between 500 and 600 words) on career interests and objectives, extracurricular activities, and financial need.
Financial data: The stipend is $1,500. Winners also receive a 1-year student membership in the Air & Waste Management Association (A&WMA).
Duration: 1 year; may be renewed.
Number awarded: Up to 4 each year.
Deadline: February of each year.

1894 ED AND CHARLOTTE RODGERS SCHOLARSHIPS

Alabama Road Builders Association
Attn: Scholarship Committee
630 Adams Avenue
Montgomery, AL 36104-4336
Phone: (334) 832-4331; (800) 239-5828; Fax: (334) 265-4931
Web: www.alrba.org/site/scholarship.html

Summary: To provide financial assistance to undergraduate and graduate students from Alabama working on a degree in civil engineering.

Eligibility: Open to full-time undergraduate and graduate students in civil engineering in Alabama. Applicants must have completed their freshman year, have a satisfactory GPA, be in good academic standing, and be able to demonstrate financial need. Selection is based on accomplishments in student, community, honorary, or service organizations; excellence in academics; and demonstrated leadership qualities.

Financial data: A stipend is awarded (amount not specified).

Duration: 1 year.

Number awarded: 3 to 5 each year.

Deadline: March of each year.

1895 EDDIE G. COLE MEMORIAL SCHOLARSHIPS

California State Fair
Attn: Friends of the Fair Scholarship Program
1600 Exposition Boulevard
P.O. Box 15649
Sacramento, CA 95852
Phone: (916) 263-3149
Email: entryoffice@calexpo.com
Web: www.bigfun.org/competition-youth.php

Summary: To provide financial assistance to residents of California who are attending college in the state and majoring in designated fields or preparing for a career in the Fair industry.

Eligibility: Open to residents of California currently working on an undergraduate degree at a college or university in the state. Applicants must 1) be majoring in physical education, agriculture, or equine studies; or 2) preparing for a career in the Fair industry. They must have a GPA of 3.0 or higher. Along with their application, they must submit an essay of 2 to 3 pages indicating why they are pursuing their desired career and life goals and describing their involvement in community and volunteer service. Selection is based on personal commitment, goals established for their chosen field, leadership potential, and civic accomplishments.

Financial data: Stipends are $1,000 or $250.

Duration: 1 year.

Number awarded: 2 each year: 1 at $1,000 and 1 at $250.

Deadline: March of each year.

1896 EDITH M. ALLEN SCHOLARSHIPS

United Methodist Church
Attn: General Board of Higher Education and Ministry
Office of Loans and Scholarships
1001 19th Avenue South
P.O. Box 340007
Nashville, TN 37203-0007
Phone: (615) 340-7344; Fax: (615) 340-7367
Email: umscholar@gbhem.org
Web: www.gbhem.org/loansandscholarships

Summary: To provide financial assistance to Methodist students who are African American and working on an undergraduate or graduate degree in specified fields.

Eligibility: Open to full-time undergraduate and graduate students at Methodist colleges and universities (preferably Historically Black United Methodist colleges) who have been active, full members of a United Methodist Church for at least 3 years prior to applying. Applicants must be African Americans working on a degree in education, social work, medicine, and/or other health professions. They must have at least a "B+" average and be recognized as a person whose academic and vocational contributions will help improve the quality of life for others.

Financial data: A stipend is awarded (amount not specified).

Duration: 1 year; recipients may reapply.

Number awarded: Varies each year.

Deadline: April of each year.

1897 EDSA MINORITY SCHOLARSHIP

Summary: To provide financial assistance to minority college students who are interested in studying landscape architecture.

See Listing #1255.

1898 EDSF BOARD OF DIRECTORS UPPER-DIVISION SCHOLARSHIPS

Summary: To provide financial assistance to upper-division and graduate students interested in preparing for a career in document management and graphic communications.

See Listing #1256.

1899 EDWARD J. AND VIRGINIA M. ROUTHIER NURSING SCHOLARSHIP

Rhode Island Foundation
Attn: Funds Administrator
One Union Station
Providence, RI 02903
Phone: (401) 427-4017; Fax: (401) 331-8085
Email: lmonahan@rifoundation.org
Web: www.rifoundation.org

Summary: To provide financial assistance to students enrolled in nursing programs in Rhode Island.

Eligibility: Open to students enrolled or accepted at an accredited nursing program in Rhode Island. Applicants must be 1) registered nurses (R.N.s) enrolled in a nursing baccalaureate degree program; 2) students enrolled in a baccalaureate nursing program; or 3) R.N.s working on a graduate degree (master's or Ph.D.). They must be able to demonstrate financial need and a commitment to practice in Rhode Island. Along with their application, they must submit an essay, up to 300 words, on their career goals, particularly as they relate to practicing in or advancing the field of nursing in Rhode Island.

Financial data: The stipend ranges from $500 to $3,000 per year.

Duration: 1 year; may be renewed.

Number awarded: Varies each year; recently, 11 of these scholarships were awarded: 6 new awards and 5 renewals.

Deadline: April of each year.

1900 EDWARDS-RIGDON SCHOLARSHIP

Hendricks County Community Foundation
Attn: Associate Director
5055 East Main Street, Suite A
Avon, IN 46123
Phone: (317) 718-1200; Fax: (317) 718-1033
Email: info@hendrickscountycf.org
Web: www.hendrickscountycf.org/scholarships

Summary: To provide financial assistance to high school seniors in Indiana who plan to major in a field related to construction at a college in any state.

Eligibility: Open to seniors graduating from high schools in Indiana and planning to enroll full-time at a 4-year college or university in any state. Applicants must be planning to major in a field related to construction (e.g., engineering, architecture, construction technology). They must be U.S. citizens. Financial need is considered in the selection process but is not required.

Financial data: The stipend is $1,000.

Duration: 1 year; nonrenewable.

Number awarded: 1 each year.

Deadline: February of each year.

1901 E.H. MARTH FOOD AND ENVIRONMENTAL SCIENCES SCHOLARSHIP

Wisconsin Association for Food Protection
P.O. Box 329
Sun Prairie, WI 53590
Phone: (608) 833-6181
Email: info@wafp-wi.org
Web: www.wafp-wi.org/scholarship.html

Summary: To provide financial assistance to residents of Wisconsin who are interested in attending college to prepare for a career in dairy, food, or environmental sanitation.

Eligibility: Open to residents of Wisconsin who are accepted or enrolled full-time at an accredited college, university, or technical institute in the state or an out-of-state school with a reciprocal enrollment agreement with Wisconsin.

Applicants must be interested in working on a degree or diploma that will lead to a career in dairy, food, or environmental sanitation. Along with their application, they must submit essays on 1) their career goals for the first 5 years after completing their academic program; and 2) why they should receive this scholarship. Selection is based on those essays, extracurricular activities, work experience, recommendations, academic achievement, and financial need.
Financial data: The stipend is $1,500.
Duration: 1 year; recipients may reapply.
Number awarded: 1 each year.
Deadline: June of each year.

1902 ELECTRONIC DOCUMENT SYSTEMS FOUNDATION TECHNICAL AND COMMUNITY COLLEGE SCHOLARSHIP

Summary: To provide financial assistance to students in technical schools and community colleges who are preparing for a career in the field of document management and graphic communications.
See Listing #1258.

1903 ELI LILLY AND COMPANY/BLACK DATA PROCESSING ASSOCIATES SCHOLARSHIP

Black Data Processing Associates
Attn: BDPA Education Technology Foundation
4423 Lehigh Road, Number 277
College Park, MD 20740
Phone: (513) 284-4968; Fax: (202) 318-2194
Email: scholarships@betf.org
Web: www.betf.org/scholarships/eli-lilly.shtml
Summary: To provide financial assistance to minority high school seniors and current college students who are interested in studying information technology at a college in any state.
Eligibility: Open to graduating high school seniors and current college undergraduates who are members of minority groups (African American, Hispanic, Asian, or Native American). Applicants must be enrolled or planning to enroll at an accredited 4-year college or university and work on a degree in information technology. They must have a GPA of 3.0 or higher. Along with their application, they must submit a 500-word essay on why information technology is important. Selection is based on that essay, academic achievement, leadership ability through academic or civic involvement, and participation in community service activities. U.S. citizenship or permanent resident status is required.
Financial data: The stipend is $2,500. Funds may be used to pay for tuition, fees, books, room and board, or other college-related expenses.
Duration: 1 year; nonrenewable.
Number awarded: 1 or more each year.
Deadline: July of each year.

1904 ELIZABETH AND SHERMAN ASCHE MEMORIAL SCHOLARSHIP

Association on American Indian Affairs, Inc.
Attn: Director of Scholarship Programs
966 Hungerford Drive, Suite 12-B
Rockville, MD 20850
Phone: (240) 314-7155; Fax: (240) 314-7159
Email: lw.aaia@verizon.net
Web: www.indian-affairs.org/scholarships/elizabeth_asche.htm
Summary: To provide financial assistance to Native Americans interested in working on an undergraduate or graduate degree in public health.
Eligibility: Open to American Indian and Alaskan Native full-time undergraduate and graduate students working on a degree in public health or science. Applicants must submit documentation of financial need, a Certificate of Indian Blood showing at least one-quarter Indian blood, proof of tribal enrollment, an essay on their educational goals, 2 letters of recommendation, and their most recent transcript. Selection is based on merit and need.
Financial data: The stipend is $1,500.
Duration: 1 year. Recipients may reapply.
Number awarded: Varies each year; recently, 6 of these scholarships were awarded.
Deadline: June of each year.

1905 ELIZABETH J. DAVIS SCHOLARSHIP

Vermont Student Assistance Corporation
Attn: Scholarship Programs
10 East Allen Street
P.O. Box 2000
Winooski, VT 05404-2601
Phone: (802) 654-3798; (888) 253-4819; Fax: (802) 654-3765; TDD: (800) 281-3341 (within VT)
Email: info@vsac.org
Web: services.vsac.org/wps/wcm/connect/vsac/VSAC
Summary: To provide financial assistance to residents of Vermont interested in obtaining an undergraduate degree, graduate degree, or certificate in a field related to home health care.
Eligibility: Open to residents of Vermont who are high school seniors, current undergraduate students, and home health care professionals. Applicants must be interested in obtaining a bachelor's degree in a health profession, certification as a home health aide, or (for home health care professionals) an advanced degree. They must be able to demonstrate interest in a career in the home health care field and an intent to work in Vermont for at least 2 years. Along with their application, they must submit 1) a 100-word essay on their interest in and commitment to pursuing their chosen career or vocation; 2) a 250-word essay on their short- and long-term academic, educational, career, vocational, and/or employment goals; and 3) a 100-word essay on how the program in which they will be enrolled will enhance their career or vocation. Selection is based on those essays, financial need, a letter of recommendation, and a personal interview (if necessary).
Financial data: Stipends range from $500 to $3,000 per year.
Duration: 1 year; may be renewed up to 3 additional years.
Number awarded: Varies each year; recently, 8 of these scholarships were awarded.
Deadline: March of each year.

1906 ELMER CARVEY MEMORIAL SCHOLARSHIP

AVS-Science and Technology of Materials, Interfaces, and Processing–Southern California Chapter
c/o Jeffrey Lince, Secretary
The Aerospace Corporation
P.O. Box 92957, Mail Stop M2-271
Los Angeles, CA 90009-2957
Web: sccavs.org/scholarship.htm
Summary: To provide financial assistance to students from any state majoring or planning to major in specified science and engineering fields at public 4-year universities in California.
Eligibility: Open to undergraduates at public 4-year universities in California. High school seniors are also eligible. Applicants must be majoring or planning to major in chemistry, engineering, materials science, or physics with a focus on topics of interest to the sponsor. Along with their application, they must submit a current transcript, 1 letter of recommendation (preferably from a science teacher), and a statement (up to 1 page) on their interest in science and plans for future studies or career goals. Selection is based on merit.
Financial data: The stipend is $1,500 per year. Funds may be used for payment of tuition.
Duration: 1 year; may be renewed.
Number awarded: 1 each year.
Deadline: May of each year.

1907 ENCOURAGE MINORITY PARTICIPATION IN OCCUPATIONS WITH EMPHASIS ON REHABILITATION

Courage Center
Attn: EMPOWER Scholarship Program
3915 Golden Valley Road
Minneapolis, MN 55422
Phone: (763) 520-0214; (888) 8-INTAKE; Fax: (763) 520-0562; TDD: (763) 520-0245
Email: empower@couragecenter.org
Web: www.couragecenter.org/ContentPages/empower.aspx
Summary: To provide financial assistance to students of color from Minnesota and western Wisconsin interested in attending college in any state to prepare for a career in the medical rehabilitation field.
Eligibility: Open to ethnically diverse students accepted at or enrolled in an institution of higher learning in any state. Applicants must be residents of Minnesota or western Wisconsin (Burnett, Pierce, Polk, and St. Croix counties). They must be able to demonstrate a career interest in the medical rehabilitation field by a record of volunteer involvement related to health care and must have a GPA of 2.0 or higher. Along with their application, they must submit a 1-page essay that covers their experiences and interactions to date with the area of volunteering, what they have accomplished and gained from those

experiences, how those experiences will assist them in their future endeavors, why education is important to them, how this scholarship will help them to address a financial need in pursuit of a position in the health care field, and their future career goals.

Financial data: The stipend is $1,500.

Duration: 1 year.

Number awarded: 2 each year.

Deadline: May of each year.

1908 ENERGY SOLUTIONS FOUNDATION SCHOLARSHIPS

Energy Solutions
Attn: Foundation
P.O. Box 510583
Salt Lake City, UT 84151
Phone: (801) 649-2286; Fax: (801) 413-5697
Email: pwright@energysolutionsfoundation.org
Web: www.energysolutions.foundation.org/scholar_info.php

Summary: To provide financial assistance to high school students in selected states who wish to attend college in any state and major in designated fields of science.

Eligibility: Open to sophomores at all high schools in Utah and at designated high schools in Georgia, Idaho, Illinois, New Mexico, Ohio, South Carolina, Tennessee, and Washington. Applicants must be planning to enter a bachelor's degree program in any state after graduating from high school and major in biochemistry, biology, chemistry, ecology, engineering, environmental sciences, geology, geophysics, mathematics, meteorology, or physics. They must have a GPA of 3.5 or higher and maintain that for the remainder of their high school years. Selection is based on participation and/or leadership in school, work, and/or extracurricular activities; financial need is not considered.

Financial data: Stipends are $25,000, $5,000, or $2,500. Funds are sent directly to the recipient's college or university upon verification of enrollment and declaration of a major in an approved field.

Duration: 1 year.

Number awarded: Varies each year; recently, 6 of these scholarships were awarded: 2 at $25,000, 2 at $5,000, and 2 at $2,500.

Deadline: January of each year.

1909 ERIC PRIMAVERA MEMORIAL SCHOLARSHIP

Florida Engineering Society
Attn: Scholarship Coordinator
125 South Gadsden Street
P.O. Box 750
Tallahassee, FL 32302-0750
Phone: (850) 224-7121; Fax: (850) 222-4349
Email: fes@fleng.org
Web: www.fleng.org/scholarships.cfm

Summary: To provide financial assistance to engineering students at colleges and universities in Florida, especially Florida Institute of Technology.

Eligibility: Open to residents of Florida entering their junior or senior year of an engineering program at a college or university in the state. Preference is given to full-time students at Florida Institute of Technology. Applicants must be U.S. citizens with a GPA of 3.0 or higher and be recommended by a faculty member at their institution. Selection is based on academic performance, work experience, activities, honors, and letters of recommendation. Semifinalists are interviewed. Financial need is not considered in the selection process.

Financial data: The stipend is $1,000.

Duration: 1 year.

Number awarded: 1 each year.

Deadline: January of each year.

1910 ERNEST F. HOLLINGS UNDERGRADUATE SCHOLARSHIP PROGRAM

National Oceanic and Atmospheric Administration
Attn: Office of Education
1315 East-West Highway
SSMC3, Room 10703
Silver Spring, MD 20910
Phone: (301) 713-9437, ext. 150; Fax: (301) 713-9465
Email: StudentScholarshipPrograms@noaa.gov
Web: www.oesd.noaa.gov/Hollings_info.html

Summary: To provide financial assistance and summer research experience to upper-division students who are working on a degree in a field of interest to the National Oceanic and Atmospheric Administration (NOAA).

Eligibility: Open to full-time students entering their junior year at an accredited college or university in the United States or its territories. Applicants must be majoring in a discipline related to oceanic and atmospheric science, research, technology, and education, and supportive of the purposes of NOAA's programs and mission, including (but not limited to) biological, social, and physical sciences; computer and information sciences; mathematics; engineering; or teacher education. They must have a GPA of 3.0 or higher. As part of their program, they must be interested in participating in summer research and development activities at NOAA headquarters (Silver Spring, Maryland) or field centers. U.S. citizenship is required.

Financial data: This program provides a stipend of $8,000 per academic year and $650 per week during the research internship, a housing subsidy and limited travel reimbursement for round-trip transportation to the internship site, and travel expenses to the scholarship program conference at the completion of the internship.

Duration: 2 academic years plus 10 weeks during the intervening summer.

Number awarded: Approximately 100 each year.

Deadline: January of each year.

1911 ETHAN AND ALLAN MURPHY ENDOWED MEMORIAL SCHOLARSHIP

American Meteorological Society
Attn: Fellowship/Scholarship Program
45 Beacon Street
Boston, MA 02108-3693
Phone: (617) 227-2426, ext. 246; Fax: (617) 742-8718
Email: scholar@ametsoc.org
Web: www.ametsoc.org

Summary: To provide financial assistance to undergraduates majoring in meteorology or an aspect of atmospheric sciences with an interest in weather forecasting.

Eligibility: Open to full-time students entering their final year of undergraduate study and majoring in meteorology or an aspect of the atmospheric or related oceanic and hydrologic sciences. Applicants must intend to make atmospheric or related sciences their career and be able to demonstrate, through curricular or extracurricular activities, an interest in weather forecasting or in the value and utilization of forecasts. They must be U.S. citizens or permanent residents enrolled at a U.S. institution and have a cumulative GPA of 3.25 or higher. Along with their application, they must submit 200-word essays on 1) their most important achievements that qualify them for this scholarship; and 2) their career goals in the atmospheric or related oceanic or hydrologic fields. Financial need is considered in the selection process. The sponsor specifically encourages applications from women, minorities, and students with disabilities who are traditionally underrepresented in the atmospheric and related oceanic sciences.

Financial data: The stipend is $2,000.

Duration: 1 year.

Number awarded: 1 each year.

Deadline: February of each year.

1912 EUGENE C. RENZI AWARD FOR ACADEMIC ACHIEVEMENT

Armed Forces Communications and Electronics Association–Hawaii Chapter
Attn: Scholarship Committee
P.O. Box 31156
Honolulu, HI 96820
Phone: (808) 529-9501
Email: education.vp@afceahawaii.org
Web: www.afceahi.org/edu/default.htm

Summary: To provide financial assistance to high school seniors and undergraduate students from Hawaii who are interested in studying technical fields at a college in any state and have demonstrated outstanding academic achievement.

Eligibility: Open to residents of Hawaii who are either graduating high school seniors or undergraduates who have completed at least 1 year of college. Applicants must be majoring or planning to major in science, engineering, information technology, computer science, or a related technical field at a 4-year college or university in the United States. Along with their application, they must submit a 300-word personal statement on their career goals. Selection is based on academic standing (GPA, class standing, SAT or ACT scores), community involvement and volunteerism, demonstrated leadership, extracurricular activities, athletic achievement, and letters of recommendation. This award

is reserved for an applicant who has consistently demonstrated high academic achievement.
Financial data: The stipend is $2,000.
Duration: 1 year.
Number awarded: 1 each year.
Deadline: March of each year.

1913 EUNICE FIORITO MEMORIAL SCHOLARSHIP

American Council of the Blind
Attn: Coordinator, Scholarship Program
2200 Wilson Boulevard, Suite 650
Arlington, VA 22201
Phone: (202) 467-5081; (800) 424-8666; Fax: (703) 465-5085
Email: info@acb.org
Web: www.acb.org
Summary: To provide financial assistance to undergraduate or graduate students who are blind and are interested in studying in a field of advocacy or service for persons with disabilities.
Eligibility: Open to undergraduate and graduate students in rehabilitation, education, law, or other fields of service or advocacy for persons with disabilities. Applicants must be legally blind in both eyes. Along with their application, they must submit verification of legal blindness in both eyes; SAT, ACT, GRE, or similar scores; information on extracurricular activities (including membership in the American Council of the Blind); employment record; and an autobiographical sketch that includes their personal goals, strengths, weaknesses, hobbies, honors, achievements, and reasons for choice of field or courses of study. A cumulative GPA of 3.3 or higher is generally required. Financial need is not considered in the selection process. Preference is given to students with little or no vision.
Financial data: The stipend is $2,000. In addition, the winner receives a Kurzweil-1000 Reading System.
Duration: 1 year.
Number awarded: 1 each year.
Deadline: February of each year.

1914 EVADNEY PETERSEN GRANT

Virgin Islands Board of Education
Dronningen Gade 60B, 61, and 62
P.O. Box 11900
St. Thomas, VI 00801
Phone: (340) 774-4546; Fax: (340) 774-3384
Email: stt@myviboe.com
Web: www.myviboe.com
Summary: To provide financial assistance to residents of the Virgin Islands who wish to study a health-related field at a college in the territory or on the mainland.
Eligibility: Open to residents of the Virgin Islands who are seniors or graduates of high schools in the territory. Applicants must have a GPA of 2.0 or higher and be attending or accepted for enrollment at an accredited institution of higher learning in the territory or on the mainland. They must be planning to major in a health-related field. Financial need is considered in the selection process.
Financial data: The stipend is $2,500 per semester.
Duration: 1 semester.
Number awarded: 1 each year.
Deadline: April of each year.

1915 EVELYN JOHNSON ENTREKIN SCHOLARSHIP

South Carolina Nurses Foundation, Inc.
Attn: Awards Committee Chair
1821 Gadsden Street
Columbia, SC 29201
Phone: (803) 252-4781; Fax: (803) 779-3870
Email: brownk1@aol.com
Web: www.scnursesfoundation.org/index_files/Page316.htm
Summary: To provide financial assistance to nursing students enrolled in a bachelor's degree program in South Carolina.
Eligibility: Open to residents of South Carolina who are entering their junior or senior year of a bachelor of science in nursing program in the state. Applicants must have a GPA of 3.0 or higher and be able to demonstrate financial need. They must intend to seek employment in South Carolina after graduation.
Financial data: The stipend is $1,500.
Duration: 1 year.
Number awarded: 1 or 2 each year.
Deadline: May of each year.

1916 "EVERY DROP COUNTS" EARTH SCIENCE SCHOLARSHIPS

Ozarka Spring Water
Attn: Scholarship Committee
3265 FM 2869
Hawkins, TX 75765
Email: edcfund@texas.net
Web: www.ozarkawater.com/DoingOurPart/Default.aspx
Summary: To provide financial assistance to residents of Texas who are working on an undergraduate degree in earth or environmental sciences at a college in any state.
Eligibility: Open to residents of Texas who are graduating high school seniors or students already enrolled at a 4-year college or university in any state. Applicants must be majoring in a field related to earth or environmental sciences, including geology, hydrogeology, environmental science, environmental law, environmental education, forestry, oceanography, or ecology. Along with their application, they must submit an essay of 1 or 2 pages describing why they are working on a degree in earth or environmental sciences and detailing their course of study. They must have a GPA of 3.0 or higher. Financial need is not considered in the selection process. U.S. citizenship is required.
Financial data: The stipend is $10,000. Funds are paid directly to the recipient's college or university.
Duration: 1 year.
Number awarded: 2 each year.
Deadline: March of each year.

1917 EXXONMOBIL BERNARD HARRIS MATH AND SCIENCE SCHOLARSHIPS

Council of the Great City Schools
1301 Pennsylvania Avenue, N.W., Suite 702
Washington, DC 20004
Phone: (202) 393-2427; Fax: (202) 393-2400
Web: www.cgcs.org/about/award_programs.aspx
Summary: To provide financial assistance to African American and Hispanic high school seniors interested in studying science, technology, engineering, or mathematics (STEM) in college.
Eligibility: Open to African American and Hispanic seniors graduating from high schools in a district that is a member of the Council of the Great City Schools, a coalition of 65 of the nation's largest urban public school systems. Applicants must be planning to enroll full-time at a 4-year college or university and major in a STEM field of study. They must have a GPA of 3.0 or higher. Along with their application, they must submit 1-page essays on 1) how mathematics and science education has impacted their lives so far; and 2) why they have chosen to prepare for a career in a STEM field. Selection is based on those essays; academic achievement; extracurricular activities, community service, or other experience that demonstrates commitment to a career in a STEM field; and 3 letters of recommendation. Financial need is not considered. Males and females are judged separately.
Financial data: The stipend is $5,000.
Duration: 1 year; nonrenewable.
Number awarded: 4 each year: an African American male and female and an Hispanic male and female.
Deadline: May of each year.

1918 FEDERAL COMMUNICATIONS BAR ASSOCIATION COLLEGE SCHOLARSHIP FUND

Summary: To provide financial assistance to high school seniors in Washington, D.C. who are interested in communications or information technology and plan to attend college in any state.
See Listing #1264.

1919 FEDERAL CYBER SERVICE: SCHOLARSHIP FOR SERVICE

Office of Personnel Management
Attn: Scholarship for Service Program Office

8610 Broadway, Suite 305
San Antonio, TX 78217-6352
Phone: (202) 369-1011
Email: sfs@opm.gov
Web: www.sfs.opm.gov

Summary: To provide financial assistance and summer work experience to upper-division undergraduates and graduate students who are majoring in information assurance at designated universities.

Eligibility: Open to rising juniors, seniors, and graduate students working full-time on a bachelor's, master's, or doctoral degree in a field related to information assurance at a participating university. Students must be nominated by the principal investigator at the university. They must be U.S. citizens, eligible for federal employment, and able to obtain a security clearance. Selection is based on merit, evidence of intensive academic training in the information assurance field, and indications that applicants can apply their education to real-world work experiences in the public sector.

Financial data: Scholarships pay tuition, room and board, books, travel costs related to attendance at a required summer symposium, and a stipend that is $8,000 per year for undergraduates or $12,000 per year for graduate students. Recipients must serve at a federal agency in an information assurance position for a period equivalent to the length of the scholarship or 1 year, whichever is longer. If they fail to complete that service obligation, they must repay a prorated amount of the assistance received.

Duration: Up to 2 years.

Number awarded: Varies each year.

Deadline: Deadline not specified.

1920 FFTA SCHOLARSHIP COMPETITION

Summary: To provide financial assistance for college to students interested in a career in flexography.

See Listing #1267.

1921 FLORIDA CHAPTER UNDERGRADUATE SCHOLARSHIPS

American Public Works Association–Florida West Coast Branch
c/o Keith Causey
Hillsborough County Brewster Technical Center
2222 North Tampa Street
Tampa, FL 33602
Phone: (813) 276-5448, ext. 367; Fax: (813) 276-5756
Email: keith.causey@sdhc.k12.fl.us

Summary: To provide financial assistance to undergraduate students in Florida who are working on a degree in civil engineering.

Eligibility: Open to students who have earned at least 60 units at an ABET-accredited school in Florida. Applicants must be working on a bachelor's degree in civil engineering or a related field. They must submit transcripts and information on their financial situation.

Financial data: The maximum stipend is $1,000.

Duration: 1 year.

Number awarded: 1 or more each year.

Deadline: February of each year.

1922 FLORIDA ENGINEERING HIGH SCHOOL GRADUATE SCHOLARSHIPS

Florida Engineering Society
Attn: Scholarship Coordinator
125 South Gadsden Street
P.O. Box 750
Tallahassee, FL 32302
Phone: (850) 224-7121; Fax: (850) 222-4349
Email: fes@fleng.org
Web: www.fleng.org/scholarships.cfm

Summary: To provide financial assistance to high school seniors in Florida who are interested in majoring in engineering at a college in any state.

Eligibility: Open to high school seniors in Florida who are interested in majoring in engineering in college and can document financial need. Applicants must be U.S. citizens, have a GPA of 3.5 or higher; have scores of at least 600 on SAT mathematics and 500 on SAT critical reading, or 26 on ACT mathematics and 21 ACT English; and be planning to enroll in an ABET-accredited engineering program in any state.

Financial data: The stipend is $2,000. Funds are paid directly to the recipient's school.

Duration: 1 year.

Number awarded: 6 each year.

Deadline: January of each year.

1923 FLORIDA ENGINEERING UNIVERSITY SCHOLARSHIPS

Florida Engineering Society
Attn: Scholarship Coordinator
125 South Gadsden Street
P.O. Box 750
Tallahassee, FL 32302-0750
Phone: (850) 224-7121; Fax: (850) 222-4349
Email: fes@fleng.org
Web: www.fleng.org/scholarships.cfm

Summary: To provide financial assistance to engineering students at colleges and universities in Florida.

Eligibility: Open to residents of Florida entering their junior or senior year of an engineering program at a college or university in the state. Applicants must be U.S. citizens with a GPA of 3.0 or higher and be recommended by a faculty member at their institution. Selection is based on academic performance, work experience, activities, honors, and letters of recommendation. Semifinalists are interviewed. Financial need is not considered in the selection process.

Financial data: The stipend is $2,500.

Duration: 1 year; nonrenewable.

Number awarded: 6 each year.

Deadline: January of each year.

1924 FLORIDA ENGINEERS IN CONSTRUCTION SCHOLARSHIP

Florida Engineers in Construction
Attn: Administrative Committee
125 South Gadsden Street
P.O. Box 750
Tallahassee, FL 32302-0750
Phone: (850) 224-7121; Fax: (850) 222-4349
Email: fes@fleng.org
Web: www.fleng.org/scholarships.cfm

Summary: To provide financial assistance to engineering students at colleges and universities in Florida.

Eligibility: Open to students entering their junior or senior year of an engineering program at a college or university in Florida. Applicants must have a GPA of 3.0 or higher and be recommended by a faculty member at their institution. They must be interested in preparing for a career in construction. Selection is based on academic performance, work experience, activities, honors, letters of recommendation, and an essay of 100 to 150 words on how they intend to use their engineering degree. Financial need is not considered in the selection process.

Financial data: The stipend is $1,000.

Duration: 1 year.

Number awarded: 1 each year.

Deadline: February of each year.

1925 FLORIDA INSTITUTE OF CONSULTING ENGINEERS SCHOLARSHIP

Florida Institute of Consulting Engineers
Attn: Scholarship Coordinator
125 South Gadsden Street
P.O. Box 750
Tallahassee, FL 32302-0750
Phone: (850) 224-7121
Email: fes@fleng.org
Web: www.fleng.org/scholarships.cfm

Summary: To provide financial assistance to students in Florida currently working on a bachelor's degree in engineering or land surveying.

Eligibility: Open to Florida students who are working on a bachelor's degree in an ABET-approved engineering program or in an accredited land surveying program. Applicants must be U.S. citizens entering their junior, senior, or fifth year. Along with their application, they must submit a 500-word essay on "What is the role or responsibility of the consulting engineer or land surveyor relative to shaping and protecting the natural environment." Selection is based on the essay (25 points), cumulative GPA (28 points), work experience (20 points), letter of recommendation (17 points), and college activities (10 points).

Financial data: The stipend is $5,000.

Duration: 1 year.

Number awarded: 1 each year.
Deadline: January of each year.

1926 FLORIDA NURSES FOUNDATION SCHOLARSHIPS

Florida Nurses Association
Attn: Florida Nurses Foundation
1235 East Concord Street
P.O. Box 536985
Orlando, FL 32853-6985
Phone: (407) 896-3261; Fax: (407) 896-9042
Email: foundation@floridanurse.org
Web: www.floridanurse.org/foundationGrants/index.asp

Summary: To provide financial assistance to Florida residents who are interested in working on an undergraduate or graduate degree in nursing.
Eligibility: Open to Florida residents (for at least 1 year) who have completed at least 1 semester at an accredited nursing program in the state. They may be working on an associate, baccalaureate, master's, or doctoral degree. Undergraduates must have a GPA of 2.5 or higher and graduate students a GPA of 3.0 or higher. Along with their application, they must submit 1-page essays on 1) why it is necessary for them to receive this scholarship; and 2) their goals and their assessment of their potential for making a contribution to nursing and society.
Financial data: A stipend is awarded (amount not specified).
Duration: 1 semester or year.
Number awarded: Varies each year.
Deadline: May of each year.

1927 FLORIDA SURVEYING AND MAPPING SOCIETY SCHOLARSHIPS

Florida Surveying and Mapping Society
Attn: Scholarship Foundation
1689-A Mahan Center Boulevard
Tallahassee, FL 32308-5454
Phone: (850) 942-1900; (800) 237-4384; Fax: (850) 877-4852
Email: fsms@fsms.org
Web: www.fsms.org/scholarships.cfm

Summary: To provide financial assistance to Florida residents interested in studying surveying in college.
Eligibility: Open to residents of Florida who are working on or planning to work on a degree in surveying. Applicants must submit an essay on their educational and career goals and factors that make them particularly deserving of support. U.S. citizenship or permanent resident status is required.
Financial data: A stipend is awarded (amount not specified).
Duration: 1 year.
Number awarded: 1 or more each year.
Deadline: February or August of each year.

1928 FLOYD KNIGHT MEMORIAL SCHOLARSHIP

Associated General Contractors of South Dakota
Attn: Highway-Heavy-Utilities Chapter
300 East Capitol Avenue, Suite 1
Pierre, SD 57501
Phone: (605) 224-8689; (800) 242-6373; Fax: (605) 224-9915
Web: www.sdagc.org

Summary: To provide financial assistance to residents of South Dakota who are interested in attending a technical institute in any state to prepare for a career in a construction-related field.
Eligibility: Open to residents of South Dakota who are graduating high school seniors or students already enrolled at a technical institute in any state. Applicants must be preparing for a career in a construction-related field. Along with their application, they must submit a brief essay that covers why they are interested in a career in the construction industry, the event or series of events that led them to that decision, and their career objectives. They must be sponsored by a member of the Associated General Contractors of South Dakota. Financial need is considered in the selection process.
Financial data: The stipend is $1,000.
Duration: 1 year.
Number awarded: 1 each year.
Deadline: April of each year.

1929 FNGLA ACTION CHAPTER SCHOLARSHIP

Florida Nurserymen, Growers and Landscape Association–Action Chapter
c/o Sarah Mazzie, Scholarship Committee Chair
P.O. Box 4384
Apopka, FL 32704-4384
Phone: (407) 302-9911; Fax: (321) 445-4199
Email: actionchapter@fngla.org
Web: www.fngla.org/chapters/action/default.html

Summary: To provide financial assistance to students in Florida interested in preparing for a career in horticulture.
Eligibility: Open to students who have been accepted by or are currently enrolled in a Florida junior college, college, or university. They may be attending school full- or part-time, but they must be majoring in 1 of the following subjects: environmental horticulture, landscaping, landscape architecture, turf management, or a related field. All applicants must have at least a 2.75 GPA. Selection is based on academic record, work experience, awards received, letters of recommendation, and an essay (300 words) on the applicant's career plans.
Financial data: Stipends range from $500 to $1,500.
Duration: 1 year.
Number awarded: 1 or more each year. A total of $3,000 is available through this program each year.
Deadline: June of each year.

1930 FORD MOTOR COMPANY SCHOLARSHIPS

American Indian College Fund
Attn: Scholarship Department
8333 Greenwood Boulevard
Denver, CO 80221
Phone: (303) 426-8900; (800) 776-FUND; Fax: (303) 426-1200
Email: scholarships@collegefund.org
Web: www.collegefund.org/scholarships/schol_mainstream.html

Summary: To provide financial assistance to Native American college students who are majoring in designated fields at mainstream colleges and universities.
Eligibility: Open to American Indians and Alaska Natives who have proof of enrollment or descendancy and are enrolled full-time in a bachelor's degree program at a mainstream institution. Applicants must have a GPA of 3.0 or higher and be able to demonstrate exceptional academic achievement or financial need. They must have declared a major in accounting, computer science, engineering, finance, marketing, or operations management. Applications are available only online and include required essays on specified topics.
Financial data: The stipend is $10,000 per year.
Duration: 1 year; may be renewed.
Number awarded: Varies each year.
Deadline: May of each year.

1931 FOUNDATION FOR SURGICAL TECHNOLOGY SCHOLARSHIP

Association of Surgical Technologists
Attn: Education Department
6 West Dry Creek Circle, Suite 200
Littleton, CO 80120-8031
Phone: (303) 694-9130; (800) 637-7433; Fax: (303) 694-9169
Email: ast@ast.org
Web: www.ast.org/educators/scholarships.aspx

Summary: To provide financial assistance to students who are preparing for a career in surgical technology.
Eligibility: Open to students currently enrolled in a surgical technology program accredited by the Commission on Accreditation of Allied Health Education Programs (CAAHEP). Applicants must have demonstrated superior academic ability and a need for financial assistance. Along with their application, they must submit a brief essay on why they want to become a surgical technologist, including their background and career goals. Selection is based on academic excellence and financial need.
Financial data: Stipends range from $500 to $2,000.
Duration: 1 year.
Number awarded: Varies each year; recently, 20 of these scholarships were awarded: 2 at $2,000, 3 at $1,500, 13 at $1,000, and 2 at $500.
Deadline: February of each year.

1932 FRAN JOHNSON NON-TRADITIONAL SCHOLARSHIP

American Floral Endowment
One Horticultural Lane

P.O. Box 945
Edwardsville, IL 62025
Phone: (618) 692-0045; Fax: (618) 692-4045
Email: afe@endowment.org
Web: endowment.org/education/afe

Summary: To provide financial assistance to nontraditional undergraduate students interested in studying horticulture.

Eligibility: Open to undergraduate students interested in working on a degree in horticulture (with a specific interest in bedding plants or other floral crops). Applicants must be reentering the academic setting after an absence of at least 5 years. They must be U.S. or Canadian citizens or permanent residents and have a GPA of 3.0 or higher. Along with their application, they must submit a statement describing their career goals and the academic, work-related, and/or life experiences that support those goals. Financial need is considered in the selection process.

Financial data: The stipend ranges from $500 to $2,000.

Duration: 1 year.

Number awarded: 1 each year.

Deadline: April of each year.

1933 FRANCES SYLVIA ZVERINA SCHOLARSHIPS

Western Reserve Herb Society
Attn: Scholarship Committee
11030 East Boulevard
Cleveland, OH 44106
Phone: (216) 721-1600; (888) 853-7091; Fax: (216) 721-2056
Email: scholarship@westernreserveherbsociety.org
Web: www.westernreserveherbsociety.org/scholarship.php

Summary: To provide financial assistance to college students interested in preparing for a career in a field related to horticulture.

Eligibility: Open to students who have completed their sophomore or junior year of college (or the senior year of a 5-year undergraduate program). Applicants may be residents of any state attending an accredited college or university anywhere in the United States. They must be planning a career in horticulture, landscape architecture, horticultural therapy, or a related field. U.S. citizenship is required. Preference is given to applicants whose horticultural career goals involve teaching or research or work in the public or nonprofit sector (such as public gardens, botanical gardens, parks, arboreta, city planning, or public education and awareness). Selection is based on an essay that includes a description of their interests, activities, and achievements; an account of their employment record on or off campus; a description of their career goals; and a discussion of their need for financial aid.

Financial data: The stipend is $2,000.

Duration: 1 year.

Number awarded: 1 each year.

Deadline: March of each year.

1934 FRANCES W. HARRIS SCHOLARSHIP

New England Regional Black Nurses Association, Inc.
P.O. Box 190690
Boston, MA 02119
Phone: (617) 524-1951
Web: www.nerbna.org/org/scholarships.html

Summary: To provide financial assistance to nursing students from New England who have contributed to the African American community.

Eligibility: Open to residents of the New England states who are enrolled full-time in a NLN-accredited generic diploma, associate, or bachelor's nursing program in any state. Applicants must have at least 1 full year of school remaining. Along with their application, they must submit a 3-page essay that covers their career aspirations in the nursing profession; how they have contributed to the African American or other communities of color in such areas as work, volunteering, church, or community outreach; an experience that has enhanced their personal and/or professional growth; and any financial hardships that may hinder them from completing their education.

Financial data: A stipend is awarded (amount not specified).

Duration: 1 year.

Number awarded: 1 or more each year.

Deadline: March of each year.

1935 FRANCIS M. KEVILLE MEMORIAL SCHOLARSHIP

Construction Management Association of America
Attn: CMAA Foundation
7926 Jones Branch Drive, Suite 800
McLean, VA 22101-3303
Phone: (703) 356-2622; Fax: (703) 356-6388
Email: CMAAFoundation@cmaanet.org
Web: www.cmaanet.org/cmaa-foundation-scholarships

Summary: To provide financial assistance to minority and female undergraduate and graduate students working on a degree in construction management.

Eligibility: Open to women and members of minority groups who are enrolled as full-time undergraduate or graduate students. Applicants must have completed at least 1 year of study and have at least 1 full year remaining for a bachelor's or master's degree in construction management or a related field. Along with their application, they must submit essays on why they are interested in a career in construction management and why they should be awarded this scholarship. Selection is based on academic objectives as they relate to the construction management profession, academic performance, relationship between the applicant's academic program and construction management as a professional field, and recommendations.

Financial data: The stipend is $3,000.

Duration: 1 year.

Number awarded: 1 each year.

Deadline: April of each year.

1936 FRANK LANZA MEMORIAL SCHOLARSHIPS

Phi Theta Kappa
Attn: Scholarship Programs Director
1625 Eastover Drive
P.O. Box 13729
Jackson, MS 39236-3729
Phone: (601) 984-3539; Fax: (601) 984-3546
Email: scholarship.programs@ptk.org
Web: www.ptk.org/scholarships/franklanza

Summary: To provide financial assistance to community college students who are working on an associate degree in registered nursing, respiratory care, or emergency medical services.

Eligibility: Open to full-time students, part-time students, and international students who have completed at least 50% of the course work for an associate degree in registered nursing, respiratory care, or emergency medical services at an accredited community college. Pre-major students, certificate students, and students who already have an associate or higher degree are not eligible. Applicants must have a GPA of 3.0 or higher and be able to demonstrate financial need.

Financial data: The stipend is $1,000.

Duration: 1 year.

Number awarded: Up to 25 each year.

Deadline: October of each year.

1937 FREDERICK J. HERINGER HONORARY AWARD

California Farm Bureau Scholarship Foundation
Attn: Scholarship Foundation
2300 River Plaza Drive
Sacramento, CA 95833
Phone: (916) 561-5520; (800) 698-FARM (within CA); Fax: (916) 561-5699
Email: dlicciardo@cfbf.com
Web: www.cfbf.com/programs/scholar/index.cfm

Summary: To provide financial assistance for college to residents of California who come from a farm family and are interested in preparing for a career in agriculture.

Eligibility: Open to students entering or attending a 4-year accredited college or university in California who are majoring or planning to major in an agriculture-related field. Students entering a junior college are not eligible. Applicants must come from a farm family (or have substantial farming experience). They must submit an essay on the most important educational or personal experience that has led them to pursue a university education. Selection is based on academic achievement, career goals, extracurricular activities, leadership skills, determination, and commitment to study agriculture.

Financial data: The stipend is $2,500 per year.

Duration: 1 year; recipients may reapply.

Number awarded: 1 each year.

Deadline: February of each year.

1938 FRIENDS OF NURSING SCHOLARSHIPS

Friends of Nursing
Attn: Scholarship Chair
P.O. Box 735

Englewood, CO 80151-0735
Phone: (303) 449-5318
Email: asmith2498@aol.com
Web: www.friendsofnursing.org/scholarships.htm

Summary: To provide financial assistance to residents of any state who are working on an undergraduate or graduate degree in nursing at a school in Colorado.

Eligibility: Open to registered nurses and nursing students who are residents of any state and working on a B.S.N. or higher degree at an NLN-accredited school of nursing in Colorado. Applicants must be enrolled at least as juniors and have a GPA of 3.0 or higher. Along with their application, they must submit a 3-page essay in which they identify a health care issue in Colorado that they believe will have a major impact on nursing in the future, a discussion of their professional nursing beliefs, and a description of their career goals (including how they anticipate their education or research will contribute or help them achieve those goals). Financial need is considered in the selection process.

Financial data: A stipend is awarded (amount not specified).

Duration: 1 year.

Number awarded: 1 or more each year.

Deadline: October of each year.

1939 GALLAGHER KOSTER HEALTH CAREERS SCHOLARSHIP PROGRAM

Gallagher Koster
Attn: Scholarship
500 Victory Road
Quincy, MA 02171
Phone: (617) 770-9889; (800) 457-5599; Fax: (617) 479-0860
Email: scholarship@gallagherkoster.com
Web: www.gallagherkoster.com/scholarship

Summary: To provide financial assistance to undergraduate students working on a degree in a health-related field.

Eligibility: Open to full-time undergraduates entering their second-to-last or final year of study in a health-related field, including (but not limited to) pre-medicine, nursing, public and community health, physical therapy, occupational therapy, pharmacy, biology, chemistry, physiology, social work, dentistry, or optometry. Applicants must have a GPA of 3.0 or higher and be able to demonstrate financial need. Along with their application, they must submit a 1-page essay describing their personal goals, including their reasons for preparing for a career in health care. Selection is based on motivation to pursue a career in health care, academic excellence, dedication to community service, and financial need.

Financial data: The stipend is $5,000 per year.

Duration: 1 year; may be renewed 1 additional year.

Number awarded: 5 each year.

Deadline: May of each year.

1940 GARDEN CLUB COUNCIL OF WINSTON-SALEM AND FORSYTH COUNTY SCHOLARSHIP

Summary: To provide financial assistance to residents of North Carolina who are interested in working on an undergraduate degree in horticulture or landscape architecture at a school in the state.

See Listing #1281.

1941 GARDEN WRITERS ASSOCIATION FOUNDATION GENERAL SCHOLARSHIPS

Summary: To provide financial assistance to upper-division students working on a degree in horticulture, plant science, or journalism.

See Listing #1282.

1942 GARMIN INTERNATIONAL SCHOLARSHIP

Women in Aviation, International
Attn: Scholarships
Morningstar Airport
3647 State Route 503 South
West Alexandria, OH 45381
Phone: (937) 839-4647; Fax: (937) 839-4645
Email: scholarships@wai.org
Web: www.wai.org/education/scholarships.cfm

Summary: To provide financial assistance to upper-division students working on a degree in computer or electrical engineering.

Eligibility: Open to full-time students who are expecting to graduate in either of the following 2 years. Applicants must have a cumulative GPA of 3.75 or higher and be working on a degree in computer or electrical engineering. Preference is given to applicants who have a pilot's license and to those with education, experience, and/or interest in 1 or more of the following fields: analog circuit design, digital system design, digital circuits, electronic devices and applications, computer architecture, embedded software engineering, RF/microwave circuit design, digital signal processing, or radar theory. Along with their application, they must submit 3 letters of recommendation, a 500-word essay on their aviation history and goals, a resume, copies of all aviation and medical certificates, and the last 3 pages of their pilot logbook (if applicable). Selection is based on achievements, attitude toward self and others, commitment to success, dedication to career, financial need, motivation, reliability, responsibility, and teamwork; no consideration is given to race, color, national origin, age, sex, or sexual orientation of the applicant.

Financial data: The stipend is $2,000. Funds may be used only for tuition and books.

Duration: 1 year.

Number awarded: 1 each year.

Deadline: November of each year.

1943 GARY WAGNER K3OMI SCHOLARSHIP

American Radio Relay League
Attn: ARRL Foundation
225 Main Street
Newington, CT 06111
Phone: (860) 594-0397; Fax: (860) 594-0259
Email: foundation@arrl.org
Web: www.arrlf.org/programs/scholarships

Summary: To provide financial assistance to licensed radio amateurs, particularly from selected states, who are interested in working on a bachelor's degree in engineering.

Eligibility: Open to ARRL members who are licensed radio amateurs of novice class or higher. Preference is given to residents of Maryland, North Carolina, Tennessee, Virginia, or West Virginia who are enrolled at a 4-year college or university in those states. Applicants must be working on a bachelor's degree in engineering. Along with their application, they must submit an essay on the role amateur radio has played in their lives and provide documentation of financial need.

Financial data: The stipend is $1,000.

Duration: 1 year.

Number awarded: 1 each year.

Deadline: January of each year.

1944 G.C. MORRIS/PAUL RUPP MEMORIAL EDUCATIONAL TRUST

Automotive Parts and Services Association
425 East McCarty
P.O. Box 1049
Jefferson City, MO 65102
Phone: (800) 375-2968; Fax: (573) 635-3215
Email: clrackers@suddenlink.net
Web: www.apsassociation.com/ll.html

Summary: To provide financial assistance to residents of designated states who are interested in attending college or technical school in any state to prepare for a career in the automotive aftermarket industry.

Eligibility: Open to residents of Arkansas, Colorado, Iowa, Kansas, Missouri, Nebraska, New Mexico, Oklahoma, Texas, and Wyoming who are graduating high school seniors, recent high school graduates, or holders of a GED certificate. Applicants must be enrolled or planning to enroll full-time at an accredited college, university, or technical institute in any state to work on a degree or certificate in an automotive-related curriculum (e.g., engineering, computer science, accounting, marketing, business). They must be recommended by a member of the Automotive Parts and Services Association (APSA). Along with their application, they must submit a 250-word essay on their career goals, how this scholarship will help them, and why they are considering a career in the automotive aftermarket. Financial need is not considered in the selection process.

Financial data: The stipend is $1,000.

Duration: 1 year; nonrenewable.

Number awarded: Varies each year.

Deadline: February of each year.

1945 GCA ZONE VI FELLOWSHIP IN URBAN FORESTRY

Garden Club of America
Attn: Scholarship Committee
14 East 60th Street, Third Floor
New York, NY 10022-1006
Phone: (212) 753-8287; Fax: (212) 753-0134
Email: scholarships@gcamerica.org
Web: www.gcamerica.org/scholarship/zone6_urban_forestry.pdf

Summary: To provide financial assistance to upper-division and graduate students interested in working on a degree in a field related to urban forestry.

Eligibility: Open to advanced undergraduates and graduate students working on a degree in urban forestry, environmental studies, horticulture, forestry, or related courses of study with an emphasis on the urban forest. Applicants must be enrolled at a 4-year college or university in the United States. Along with their application, they must submit brief statements on their career goals and how this fellowship will benefit them and help to further their academic and career goals. Financial need is not considered in the selection process.

Financial data: The stipend is $4,000.

Duration: 1 year; may be renewed 1 additional year.

Number awarded: 1 or more each year.

Deadline: January of each year.

1946 GENERAL EMMETT PAIGE SCHOLARSHIPS

Armed Forces Communications and Electronics Association
Attn: AFCEA Educational Foundation
4400 Fair Lakes Court
Fairfax, VA 22033-3899
Phone: (703) 631-6149; (800) 336-4583, ext. 6149; Fax: (703) 631-4693
Email: scholarship@afcea.org
Web: www.afcea.org/education/scholarships/undergraduate/genemm.asp

Summary: To provide financial assistance to veterans, military personnel, and their family members who are majoring in specified scientific fields in college.

Eligibility: Open to veterans, persons on active duty in the uniformed military services, and their spouses or dependents who are currently enrolled full-time in an accredited 4-year college or university in the United States. Graduating high school seniors are not eligible, but veterans entering college as freshmen may apply. Spouses or dependents must be sophomores or juniors. Applicants must be U.S. citizens, be of good moral character, have demonstrated academic excellence, be motivated to complete a college education, and be working toward a degree in engineering (aerospace, chemical, electrical, or systems), mathematics, physics, science or mathematics education, management information systems, technology management, computer science, or other field directly related to the support of U.S. intelligence enterprises or national security. They must have a GPA of 3.0 or higher. Along with their application, they must provide a copy of Discharge Form DD214, Certificate of Service, or facsimile of their current Department of Defense or Coast Guard Identification Card. Financial need is not considered in the selection process.

Financial data: The stipend is $2,000 per year.

Duration: 1 year; may be renewed.

Number awarded: Varies each year; recently, 9 of these scholarships were awarded.

Deadline: February of each year.

1947 GENERAL JAMES H. DOOLITTLE SCHOLARSHIP

Communities Foundation of Texas
Attn: Scholarship Department
5500 Caruth Haven Lane
Dallas, TX 75225-8146
Phone: (214) 750-4222; Fax: (214) 750-4210
Email: scholarships@cftexas.org
Web: www.cftexas.org/NetCommunity/Page.aspx?pid=291

Summary: To provide financial assistance to upper-division and graduate students who are working on a degree in aerospace science or aeronautical engineering.

Eligibility: Open to college juniors, college seniors, and graduate students who are working on a baccalaureate or advanced degree in aerospace science or aeronautical engineering. Applicants must have completed at least 52 hours of college course work and have a GPA of 2.75 or higher. They must be able to demonstrate financial need. Along with their application, they must submit an essay (up to 3 pages) describing their interest in the field of aerospace science or aeronautical engineering, how that interest began, the course of studies pursued as a result of the interest, any special projects or jobs they have held that are related to the field, and their career goals. U.S. citizenship is required.

Financial data: The stipend is $5,000.

Duration: 1 year; nonrenewable.

Number awarded: 1 or more each year.

Deadline: May of each year.

1948 GENERAL JOHN A. WICKHAM SCHOLARSHIPS

Armed Forces Communications and Electronics Association
Attn: AFCEA Educational Foundation
4400 Fair Lakes Court
Fairfax, VA 22033-3899
Phone: (703) 631-6149; (800) 336-4583, ext. 6149; Fax: (703) 631-4693
Email: scholarship@afcea.org
Web: www.afcea.org/education/scholarships/undergraduate/pub2.asp

Summary: To provide financial assistance to undergraduate students who are working full-time on a degree in engineering or the sciences.

Eligibility: Open to full-time students entering their junior or senior year at an accredited degree-granting 4-year college or university in the United States. Applicants must be U.S. citizens working toward a degree in engineering (aerospace, chemical, computer, electrical, or systems), mathematics, physics, science or mathematics education, management information systems, technology management, computer science, or other field directly related to the support of U.S. intelligence enterprises or national security. They must have a GPA of 3.5 or higher. Selection is based on academic achievement, patriotism, and potential to contribute to the American workforce. Financial need is not considered.

Financial data: The stipend is $2,000.

Duration: 1 year; may be renewed.

Number awarded: Varies each year; recently, 12 of these scholarships were awarded.

Deadline: April of each year.

1949 GENERAL MOTORS ENGINEERING EXCELLENCE AWARD

Hispanic Association of Colleges and Universities
Attn: National Scholarship Program
8415 Datapoint Drive, Suite 400
San Antonio, TX 78229
Phone: (210) 692-3805; Fax: (210) 692-0823; TDD: (800) 855-2880
Email: scholarships@hacu.net
Web: www.hacu.net/hacu/Scholarships_EN.asp?SnID=875148054

Summary: To provide financial assistance to undergraduate engineering students at institutions that are members of the Hispanic Association of Colleges and Universities (HACU).

Eligibility: Open to full-time undergraduate students at 4-year HACU member and partner colleges and universities who are working on an engineering degree. Applicants must submit an essay of 200 to 250 words that describes their academic and/or career goals, where they expect to be and what they expect to be doing 10 years from now, and what skills they can bring to an employer. They must be able to demonstrate financial need and have a GPA of 3.0 or higher.

Financial data: The stipend is $2,000 per year.

Duration: 1 year; may be renewed.

Number awarded: 1 or more each year.

Deadline: May of each year.

1950 GENERAL MOTORS SCHOLARSHIP PROGRAM OF THE HISPANIC SCHOLARSHIP FUND

Hispanic Scholarship Fund
Attn: Selection Committee
55 Second Street, Suite 1500
San Francisco, CA 94105
Phone: (415) 808-2376; (877) HSF-INFO; Fax: (415) 808-2302
Email: highschool@hsf.net
Web: www.hsf.net/scholarships.aspx?id=314

Summary: To provide financial assistance to Hispanic Americans who are interested in attending college to major in engineering, business, or human resources.

Eligibility: Open to U.S. citizens, permanent residents, and visitors with a passport stamped I-551 who are of Hispanic heritage. Applicants must have a GPA of 3.0 or higher and be enrolled or planning to enroll full-time at an accredited 4-year college or university in the United States, Puerto Rico, Guam, or the U.S. Virgin Islands. They must be planning to major in business (accounting, business administration, economics, or finance), engineering (electrical, industrial, manufacturing, or mechanical), or human resources. Selection is based on academic achievement, personal strengths, leadership, and financial need.

Financial data: The stipend is $2,500.

Duration: 1 year.
Number awarded: 1 or more each year.
Deadline: July of each year.

1951 GENEVIEVE CHRISTEN DISTINGUISHED UNDERGRADUATE STUDENT AWARD

American Dairy Science Association
Attn: Awards Coordinator
1111 North Dunlap Avenue
Savoy, IL 61874
Phone: (217) 356-5146; Fax: (217) 398-4119
Email: adsa@assochq.org
Web: www.adsa.org/awards/christen.html

Summary: To recognize and reward undergraduate students who have participated in dairy science activities.
Eligibility: Open to undergraduate students nominated by a faculty member at their institution; only 1 student may be nominated by a college or university each year. The nominator must be a member of the American Dairy Science Association (ADSA). Nominees must be residents of Canada, Mexico, or the United States. Selection is based on demonstrated leadership ability (25 points), academic standing (15 points), interest and experience in the dairy industry (20 points), participation in ADSA Student Affiliate Division and local club activities (30 points), and a statement of their plans for the future (10 points).
Financial data: The award consists of a plaque and a $1,000 honorarium.
Duration: The award is presented annually.
Number awarded: 1 each year.
Deadline: Nominations must be submitted by December of each year.

1952 GEOPHYSICAL SOCIETY OF ALASKA SCHOLARSHIP

Geophysical Society of Alaska
Attn: Scholarship Committee
P.O. Box 100196
Anchorage, AK 99510-0196
Phone: (907) 343-2134
Email: ak_gsa@yahoo.com
Web: gsa.seg.org/scholarships.html

Summary: To provide financial assistance to upper-division and graduate students from Alaska who are working on a degree in earth science.
Eligibility: Open to juniors, seniors, and graduate students at colleges and universities in Alaska and residents of Alaska studying outside the state. Applicants must be working full-time on a degree in earth science or a closely-related field to prepare for a career in geophysics. Along with their application, they must submit a letter describing their personal and educational career goals, their interest in the earth sciences, their financial need, and how they plan to use the scholarship funds. Graduate students must also submit a thesis proposal.
Financial data: The stipend ranges from $500 to $1,000.
Duration: 1 year.
Number awarded: 1 or more each year.
Deadline: December of each year.

1953 GEORGE AND LEOLA SMITH AWARD

David and Dovetta Wilson Scholarship Fund, Inc.
115-67 237th Street
Elmont, NY 11003-3926
Phone: (516) 285-4573
Email: DDWSF4@aol.com
Web: www.wilsonfund.org/GeorgeLeolaSmith.html

Summary: To provide financial assistance to high school seniors who are interested in studying nursing or business in college.
Eligibility: Open to graduating high school seniors who plan to attend an accredited college or university and study business or nursing. Applicants must be U.S. citizens or permanent residents and have a GPA of 3.0 or higher. Along with their application, they must submit 3 letters of recommendation, high school transcripts, and an essay (up to 250 words) on "How My College Education Will Help Me Make a Positive Impact on My Community." Selection is based on community involvement, desire to prepare for a career in the field of business or nursing, and financial need.
Financial data: The stipend is $1,000.
Duration: 1 year.
Number awarded: 1 each year.
Deadline: March of each year.

1954 GEORGE AND NAOUMA GIOLES SCHOLARSHIP

Summary: To provide financial assistance to high school seniors and current undergraduates who are of the Greek Orthodox faith and plan to study the sciences, business, or the arts.
See Listing #1284.

1955 GEORGE B. BOLAND NURSES TRAINING TRUST FUND

National Forty and Eight
Attn: Voiture Nationale
777 North Meridian Street
Indianapolis, IN 46204-1170
Phone: (317) 634-1804; Fax: (317) 632-9365
Email: voiturenationale@msn.com
Web: fortyandeight.org/40_8programs.htm

Summary: To provide financial assistance to students working on an undergraduate degree in nursing.
Eligibility: Open to students working full-time on an associate or bachelor's degree in nursing. Applications must be submitted to the local Voiture of the Forty and Eight in the county of the student's permanent residence; if the county organization has exhausted all of its nurses training funds, it will provide the student with an application for this scholarship. Students who are receiving assistance from the Forty and Eight Lung and Respiratory Disease Nursing Scholarship Program of the American Legion are not eligible. Financial need must be demonstrated.
Financial data: Grants may be used to cover tuition, required fees, room and board or similar living expenses, and other school-related expenses.
Number awarded: Varies each year; recently, 2,131 students received more than $1,100,000 in these scholarships.
Deadline: Deadline not specified.

1956 GEORGE D. MILLER SCHOLARSHIP

National Fire Protection Association
Attn: NFPA Fire Safety Educational Memorial Fund
1 Batterymarch Park
Quincy, MA 02169-7471
Phone: (617) 984-7244; Fax: (617) 984-7110
Email: cellis@nfpa.org
Web: www.nfpa.org

Summary: To provide financial assistance to undergraduate and graduate students enrolled in fire service or public administration programs.
Eligibility: Open to undergraduate or graduate students enrolled in a fire service or public administration program. Colleges may submit up to 2 student nominations. Nominees must submit a letter describing their achievements, leadership abilities, volunteerism, interest in fire service or public administration, and specific long-range goals. Financial need is not considered in the selection process.
Financial data: The stipend is at least $5,000.
Duration: 1 year.
Number awarded: 1 each year.
Deadline: March of each year.

1957 GEORGE EAGLE MEMORIAL UNDERGRADUATE SCHOLARSHIP

Ohio Environmental Health Association
Attn: Scholarship Committee Chair
P.O. Box 234
Columbus, OH 43216-0234
Web: oeha.tripod.com/awards.htm

Summary: To provide financial assistance to Ohio residents who are in college and preparing for a career in environmental health in the state.
Eligibility: Open to residents of Ohio enrolled at the sophomore level and above in a program leading to an undergraduate degree in environmental health or a related field. Applicants may be attending college in any state, but they must intend to become employed in environmental health in Ohio following graduation.
Financial data: The stipend is $3,000.
Duration: 1 year.
Number awarded: 2 each year.
Deadline: February of each year.

1958 GEORGE W. WILSON III AND KIAWA SCHOLARSHIP

Kentucky/Indiana Automotive Wholesalers Association
P.O. Box 68
Dublin, OH 43017-0068
Phone: (614) 889-1309; Fax: (614) 889-0463
Email: info@amgllcusa.com
Web: www.kiawa.org/scholarships307.cfm

Summary: To provide financial assistance to residents of Indiana and Kentucky who are interested in attending college or vocational school in any state to prepare for a career in the automotive aftermarket.

Eligibility: Open to residents of Indiana and Kentucky who either are graduating high school seniors or have graduated within the past 2 years. Applicants must be enrolled or planning to enroll full-time at a college, university, or automotive technical program certified by the National Automotive Technicians Education Foundation-National Institute for Automotive Service Excellence (NATEF-ASE) in any state. They must be preparing for a career in the automotive aftermarket. Along with their application, they must submit a 250-word essay on their career goals, how this scholarship will help them, and why they are considering a career in the automotive aftermarket. Priority is given to applicants who are 1) planning to become technicians in automotive, collision, or heavy duty fields; 2) planning to work for an automotive aftermarket company; or 3) children of families employed in the automotive aftermarket. Financial need is not considered in the selection process.

Financial data: The stipend is $1,000. Funds are paid directly to the recipient's school.

Duration: 1 year.

Number awarded: Normally, 2 of these scholarships are awarded each year: 1 to a resident of Indiana and 1 to a resident of Kentucky.

Deadline: March of each year.

1959 GEORGIA LEGION AUXILIARY PAST PRESIDENT PARLEY NURSING SCHOLARSHIP

American Legion Auxiliary
Department of Georgia
3035 Mt. Zion Road
Stockbridge, GA 30281-4101
Phone: (678) 289-8446
Email: amlegaux@bellsouth.net
Web: www.galegion.org/auxiliary.htm

Summary: To provide financial assistance to daughters of veterans in Georgia who are interested in attending college in any state to prepare for a career in nursing.

Eligibility: Open to George residents who are 1) interested in nursing education; and 2) the daughters of veterans. Applicants must be sponsored by a local unit of the American Legion Auxiliary. Selection is based on a statement explaining why they want to become a nurse and why they need a scholarship, a transcript of all high school or college grades, and 4 letters of recommendation (1 from a high school principal or superintendent, 1 from the sponsoring American Legion Auxiliary local unit, and 2 from other responsible people).

Financial data: The amount of the award depends on the availability of funds.

Number awarded: Varies, depending upon funds available.

Deadline: May of each year.

1960 GETCHELL AND ROTC SCHOLARSHIPS

Daedalian Foundation
Attn: Scholarship Committee
55 Main Circle (Building 676)
P.O. Box 249
Randolph AFB, TX 78148-0249
Phone: (210) 945-2113; Fax: (210) 945-2112
Email: icarus2@daedalians.org
Web: www.daedalians.org/foundation/scholarships.htm

Summary: To provide financial assistance to ROTC students who wish to become military pilots.

Eligibility: Open to students who are currently enrolled in an ROTC program at their college or university. Applicants must be interested in preparing for a career as a military pilot. They must apply through their ROTC detachment. Selection is based on intention to pursue a career as a military pilot, demonstrated moral character and patriotism, scholastic and military standing and aptitude, and physical condition and aptitude for flight. Financial need may also be considered.

Financial data: The stipend is $2,000.

Duration: 1 year.

Number awarded: 19 each year: 5 designated as Getchell Scholarships, 8 for Air Force ROTC cadets, 3 for Army ROTC cadets, and 3 for Navy/Marine ROTC midshipmen.

Deadline: November of each year.

1961 GLOBAL AUTOMOTIVE AFTERMARKET SYMPOSIUM SCHOLARSHIPS

Global Automotive Aftermarket Symposium
c/o Motor & Equipment Manufacturers Association
10 Laboratory Drive
P.O. Box 13966
Research Triangle Park, NC 27709-3966
Phone: (919) 549-4800; Fax: (919) 549-4824
Email: info@mema.org
Web: www.automotivescholarships.com

Summary: To provide financial assistance for college to students interested in preparing for a career in the automotive aftermarket.

Eligibility: Open to graduating high school seniors and to students who graduated from high school within the past 2 years. Applicants must be enrolled full-time in a college-level program or an automotive technician program in the United States or Canada accredited by the National Automotive Technician Education Foundation (NATEF). Along with their application, they must submit a 250-word essay on their career goals, how this scholarship will help them, and why they are considering a career in the automotive aftermarket. Preference is given to applicants who are preparing for a career in the automotive aftermarket and children of families employed in the automotive aftermarket. Financial need is not considered in the selection process.

Financial data: The stipend is $1,000 per year. Recipients who graduate from their program and show proof of employment in the automotive aftermarket for at least 12 months are awarded a further matching grant.

Duration: 1 year.

Number awarded: Varies each year; recently, 75 of these scholarships were awarded.

Deadline: March of each year.

1962 GOOD SAMARITAN FOUNDATION SCHOLARSHIPS

Good Samaritan Foundation
5615 Kirby Drive, Suite 308
Houston, TX 77005
Phone: (713) 529-4646; Fax: (713) 521-1169
Web: www.gsftx.org/scholarships

Summary: To provide financial assistance to student nurses enrolled in a program in nursing at an accredited university in Texas.

Eligibility: Open to residents of Texas who have attained the clinical level of their nursing education. Applicants must be enrolled at an institution in Texas in an accredited nursing program at the L.V.N., Diploma, A.D.N., B.S.N., M.S.N., Ph.D., D.S.N., or D.N.P. level. They must be U.S. citizens or eligible to work in the United States and be planning to work as a nurse in Texas after graduation. Financial need is considered in the selection process. A personal interview is required.

Financial data: Scholarship awards may be used for clinical education expenses: tuition, fees, books, and some copying and seminars. Undergraduate awards are based on the amount of the tuition fees of that school and its nursing program. Graduate awards are paid on a reimbursement basis up to a predetermined amount per semester.

Duration: 1 year.

Number awarded: Varies each year; since the program began, it has awarded more than 12,000 scholarships worth more than $14.6 million.

Deadline: There are no formal deadlines, but applications should be received at least 8 weeks before the start of the semester.

1963 GOOGLE LIME SCHOLARSHIPS FOR STUDENTS WITH DISABILITIES

Lime
590 Madison Avenue, 21st Floor
New York, NY 10022
Phone: (212) 521-4469; Fax: (212) 521-4099
Email: info@limeconnect.com
Web: www.limeconnect.com/google.html

Summary: To provide financial assistance to students with disabilities working on a bachelor's or graduate degree in a computer-related field at a college or university in Canada or the United States.

Eligibility: Open to students at colleges and universities in the United States or Canada who have a disability and are entering their junior or senior year of undergraduate study or are enrolled as graduate students. International students with disabilities enrolled at universities in the United States or Canada are also eligible. Applicants must be working full-time on a degree in computer science, computer engineering, or a closely-related technical field. Along with their application, they must submit 2 essays of 400 to 600 words each on 1) their academic accomplishments in terms of the technical projects on which they have worked; and 2) the issue about which they are passionate, what they have done to fulfill that passion, or what they dream of doing to fulfill it. Financial need is not considered in the selection process.
Financial data: The stipend is $10,000 for students at U.S. universities or $C5,000 for students at Canadian universities.
Duration: 1 year.
Number awarded: Varies each year.
Deadline: May of each year.

1964 GOOGLE SCHOLARSHIP PROGRAM

Hispanic College Fund
Attn: Scholarship Processing
1301 K Street, N.W., Suite 450-A West
Washington, DC 20005
Phone: (202) 296-5400; (800) 644-4223; Fax: (202) 296-3774
Email: hcf-info@hispanicfund.org
Web: scholarships.hispanicfund.org/applications
Summary: To provide financial assistance to Hispanic American upper-division and graduate students who are interested in preparing for a career in computer science or computer engineering.
Eligibility: Open to U.S. citizens and permanent residents of Hispanic background (at least 1 grandparent must be 100% Hispanic) who are entering their junior or senior year of college or who are enrolled in graduate school. Applicants must be working on a bachelor's, master's, or Ph.D. degree in computer science or computer engineering and have a cumulative GPA of 3.5 or higher. They must be enrolled at an accredited college or university in the 50 states or Puerto Rico as a full-time student. Financial need is considered in the selection process.
Financial data: This stipend is $10,000. Funds are paid directly to the recipient's college or university to help cover tuition and fees.
Duration: 1 year; recipients may reapply.
Number awarded: Varies each year.
Deadline: March of each year.

1965 GORGAS SCHOLARSHIP PROGRAM

Alabama Academy of Science
c/o Ellen B. Buckner, Gorgas Scholarship Program
University of South Alabama
College of Nursing
4064 HAHN Building
Mobile, AL 36688
Phone: (251) 445-9449
Email: ebuckner@usouthal.edu
Web: www.gorgasscholar.org
Summary: To recognize and reward, with scholarships for college in any state, high school seniors in Alabama who complete outstanding science projects.
Eligibility: Open to seniors graduating from high schools in Alabama and planning to attend a college or university in any state. Applicants must conduct a research project as part of the Intel National Science Talent Search or other similar competition and submit electronically the research report, up to 20 pages, to the chair of this program.
Financial data: Awards are a $4,000 tuition grant for first place, $3,000 tuition grant for first alternate, $2,000 tuition grant for second alternate, $1,500 tuition grant for third alternate, and $1,000 tuition grant for fourth alternate.
Duration: The competition is held annually. Tuition grants are for 1 year.
Number awarded: 5 each year.
Deadline: January of each year.

1966 GOVERNMENT INFORMATION TECHNOLOGY EXECUTIVE COUNCIL SCHOLARSHIP

Government Information Technology Executive Council
145 Fleet Street, Suite 165
National Harbor, MD 20745
Email: Gail.Scavongelli@ic.fbi.gov
Web: gitec.nctdnnhosting.com/NewsEvents/Scholarships.aspx
Summary: To provide financial assistance to high school seniors who plan to study a field related to information technology in college.
Eligibility: Open to graduating high school seniors who have a GPA of 2.75 or higher. Applicants must be planning to attend a college or university and major in information technology, computer science, computer information science, information technology management, information technology security management, or engineering. Along with their application, they must submit a 500-word essay on why they are interested in information technology and why they are a candidate for this scholarship. U.S. citizenship is required. Financial need is not considered in the selection process.
Financial data: A stipend is awarded (amount not specified); funds are to be used for such academic purposes as tuition, fees, room, board, and/or books.
Duration: 1 year.
Number awarded: 1 or more each year.
Deadline: January of each year.

1967 GRAND RAPIDS CHAPTER CSI SCHOLARSHIP

Construction Specifications Institute–Grand Rapids Chapter
c/o Bill Smith, Academic Affairs Committee Chair
P.O. Box 2826
Grand Rapids, MI 49501
Phone: (616) 456-4623; Fax: (616) 456-3828
Email: bsmith@ci.grand-rapids.mi.us
Web: www.csigrandrapids.org
Summary: To provide financial assistance to students from any state enrolled at colleges and universities in Michigan who are preparing for a career in the construction industry.
Eligibility: Open to residents of any state enrolled full-time at an accredited college, university, or trade school in Michigan with a GPA of 3.0 or higher. Applicants must be working on a degree in a field directly related to the construction industry, including architecture, engineering (electrical, mechanical, construction), management technology, or facilities maintenance. Along with their application, they must submit a 1-page essay about themselves, their future, and their need for financial assistance. Selection is based on scholastic ability, references, financial need, and how the applicant will benefit from receiving this scholarship. Preference is given to applicants who are members of the Construction Specifics Institute (CSI) or related to a member.
Financial data: Stipends up to $1,500 are available.
Duration: 1 year.
Number awarded: 1 or more each year.
Deadline: April of each year.

1968 GREATER KANAWHA VALLEY MATH AND SCIENCE SCHOLARSHIP

Greater Kanawha Valley Foundation
Attn: Scholarship Coordinator
1600 Huntington Square
900 Lee Street, East
P.O. Box 3041
Charleston, WV 25331-3041
Phone: (304) 346-3620; (800) 467-5909; Fax: (304) 346-3640
Email: shoover@tgkvf.org
Web: www.tgkvf.org/scholar.htm
Summary: To provide financial assistance to residents of West Virginia who are working on a degree in a mathematics or science field at a school in any state.
Eligibility: Open to residents of West Virginia who are working full-time on a degree in mathematics, science (chemistry, physics, or biology), or engineering at a college or university anywhere in the country. Applicants must have an ACT score of 20 or higher, be able to demonstrate good moral character, and have a GPA of 2.5 or higher.
Financial data: The stipend is $1,000 per year.
Duration: 1 year; may be renewed.
Number awarded: 1 each year.
Deadline: January of each year.

1969 GREEN MOUNTAIN WATER ENVIRONMENT ASSOCIATION SCHOLARSHIP

Vermont Student Assistance Corporation
Attn: Scholarship Programs
10 East Allen Street
P.O. Box 2000

Winooski, VT 05404-2601
Phone: (802) 654-3798; (888) 253-4819; Fax: (802) 654-3765; TDD: (800) 281-3341 (within VT)
Email: info@vsac.org
Web: services.vsac.org/wps/wcm/connect/vsac/VSAC

Summary: To provide financial assistance to Vermont residents who are interested in working on a degree in environmental studies at a college in any state.

Eligibility: Open to high school seniors, high school graduates, and currently-enrolled college students in Vermont who are enrolled or planning to enroll at a college or university in any state. Applicants must be interested in majoring in environmental studies, including (but not limited to) conservation, forestry, geology, natural resources management, renewable resources, water quality, or wildlife/wild lands management. They must have a GPA of 3.0 or higher. Along with their application, they must submit 1) a 100-word essay on their interest in and commitment to pursuing their chosen career or vocation; 2) a 250-word essay on their beliefs related to the value of community service; and 3) a 250-word essay on their short- and long-term academic, educational, career, vocational, and/or employment goals. Selection is based on those essays, academic achievement, community involvement and/or service, a letter of recommendation, and financial need.

Financial data: The stipend is $1,000.

Duration: 1 year; nonrenewable.

Number awarded: 1 each year.

Deadline: March of each year.

1970 GUS ARCHIE MEMORIAL SCHOLARSHIPS

Society of Petroleum Engineers
Attn: Student Activities Manager
222 Palisades Creek Drive
P.O. Box 833836
Richardson, TX 75083-3836
Phone: (972) 952-9452; (800) 456-6863; Fax: (972) 952-9435
Email: studentactivities@spe.org
Web: www.spe.org/spe-app/spe/about/foundation/gus_archie.htm

Summary: To provide financial assistance to high school seniors interested in preparing for a career in petroleum engineering.

Eligibility: Open to graduating high school seniors who have a score of at least 1800 on the SAT or 27 on the ACT and are planning to enroll in a petroleum engineering program at an accredited college or university. Selection is based on academic record, career plans, and financial need.

Financial data: The stipend is $6,000 per year.

Duration: 1 year; may be renewed for up to 3 additional years, provided the recipient maintains full-time enrollment and a GPA of 3.0 or higher both cumulatively and for the current semester.

Number awarded: 1 or more each year.

Deadline: April of each year.

1971 HANK EMERY SCHOLARSHIP

Geospatial Information & Technology Association–New England Chapter
c/o Michele N. Karas
Town of Winthrop
One Metcalf Square, Room 18
Winthrop, MA 02152
Phone: (617) 539-1100
Email: mkaras@town.winthrop.ma.us
Web: gita.org/chapters/new_england/nengland.asp

Summary: To provide financial assistance to students at universities in New England working on an undergraduate or graduate degree related to geospatial information systems (GIS).

Eligibility: Open to juniors, seniors, and graduate students at colleges and technical institutes in New England. Applicants must be working on a degree related to GIS. Along with their application, they must submit a statement of 300 to 500 words on their current educational goals and plans for their professional career, including how their professional aspirations relate to GIS. Financial need is not considered in the selection process.

Financial data: The stipend is $2,000.

Duration: 1 year.

Number awarded: 1 each year.

Deadline: February of each year.

1972 HARRINGTON/ARTHUR MEMORIAL SCHOLARSHIP

American Backflow Prevention Association
Attn: Scholarship
3016 Maloney Avenue
P.O. Box 3051
Bryan, TX 77805-3051
Phone: (979) 846-7606; Fax: (979) 846-7607
Email: Scholarship@abpa.org
Web: www.abpa.org/scholarship.htm

Summary: To recognize and reward, with funding for advanced education, high school students who submit outstanding essays on the protection of drinking water.

Eligibility: Open to residents of the United States and Canada who are of high school age (over 13 and under 20 years of age). Applicants must submit an essay, from 3 to 5 pages in length, on a topic that changes annually but relates to protection of drinking water supplies. Selection is based on how well the essay answers the question, the accuracy of the essay, citing of sources used, creativity, feasibility of proposal, vision, relevance to theme, spelling, grammar, and impact of content.

Financial data: The award is $1,000. Funds are deposited into a 529 Investment National College Savings Program account or sent directly to an accredited school in the name of the winner. The award may be used for any type of advanced education.

Duration: The competition is held annually.

Number awarded: 1 each year.

Deadline: February of each year.

1973 HARRY F. GAEKE MEMORIAL SCHOLARSHIP

Associated General Contractors of Ohio
Attn: AGC of Ohio Education Foundation
1755 Northwest Boulevard
Columbus, OH 43212
Phone: (614) 486-6446; (800) 557-OHIO; Fax: (614) 486-6498
Email: educationfoundation@agcohio.com
Web: www.agcohio.com/scholarships.html

Summary: To provide financial assistance to students from Indiana, Kentucky, or Ohio who are working on an undergraduate degree in a field related to construction or construction management.

Eligibility: Open to undergraduates who are residents of or attending school in Ohio, Indiana, or Kentucky and in at least the second year at a 2- or 4-year college or university. Applicants must be enrolled in a construction degree program and be preparing for a career in construction. They must be U.S. citizens with a GPA of 2.5 or higher. Along with their application, they must submit a short statement on what they think is the most important issue currently facing the construction industry and 4 essays of 125 words each on 1) why they have decided to prepare for a career in construction; 2) the goals they hope to accomplish in their career; 3) how they plan to make a difference in the construction industry; and 4) anything else that might influence whether or not they receive this scholarship. Financial need is also considered in the selection process.

Financial data: The stipend is $1,000.

Duration: 1 year.

Number awarded: 1 each year.

Deadline: March of each year.

1974 HARRY HAMPTON FUND SCHOLARSHIP

Harry Hampton Memorial Wildlife Fund, Inc.
P.O. Box 2641
Columbia, SC 29202
Phone: (803) 463-7387; Fax: (803) 749-9362
Email: mpugh@sc.rr.com
Web: www.hamptonwildlifefund.org/scholarship.html

Summary: To provide financial assistance to high school seniors in South Carolina who plan to major in a field related to natural resources at a college or university in the state.

Eligibility: Open to seniors graduating from high schools in South Carolina who plan to attend an institution of higher learning in the state. Applicants must be planning to major in a field related to natural resources, including wildlife, fisheries, biology, zoology, forestry, marine science, or environmental science. Along with their application, they must submit a 3-page autobiography that explains their interest in wildlife resources, the environment, coastal resources, or related topics and why they will be a good investment if they are awarded this scholarship. Financial need is also considered in the selection process.

Financial data: The stipend is $2,500 per year.

Duration: 1 year; may be renewed up to 3 additional years, provided the recipient maintains a GPA of 2.5 or higher.

Number awarded: 1 each year.

Deadline: January of each year.

1975 HARVEST SCHOLARSHIPS

Michigan Manufactured Housing, RV and Campground Association
Attn: HARVEST Education Foundation
2222 Association Drive
Okemos, MI 48864-5978
Phone: (517) 349-8881; (800) 422-6478
Email: marvac@marvac.org
Web: www.marvac.org/harvest.html

Summary: To provide financial assistance to Michigan residents interested in attending college in any state to prepare for a career in the manufactured homes, recreational vehicles, or campground industries.

Eligibility: Open to Michigan students enrolled or planning to enroll at an accredited college or university in any state to prepare for a career in the manufactured homes, recreational vehicles, or campground industries. Fields of study may include engineering, marketing, management, service, design, human resources, or any other discipline that will serve the needs of the industries. Applicants must submit an essay of 200 to 300 words on their career goals and why they feel they deserve this scholarship. Selection is based on merit and/or financial need.

Financial data: A stipend is awarded (amount not specified).

Duration: 1 year; may be renewed.

Number awarded: Varies each year; recently, 11 of these scholarships were awarded. Since the program was established, it has awarded $244,800 in scholarships to 463 students.

Deadline: March of each year.

1976 HAWAII CHAPTER AFCEA SCHOLARSHIPS

Armed Forces Communications and Electronics Association–Hawaii Chapter
Attn: Scholarship Committee
P.O. Box 31156
Honolulu, HI 96820
Phone: (808) 529-9501
Email: education.vp@afceahawaii.org
Web: www.afceahi.org/edu/default.htm

Summary: To provide financial assistance to high school seniors and undergraduate students from Hawaii who are interested in studying technical fields at a college in any state.

Eligibility: Open to residents of Hawaii who are either graduating high school seniors or undergraduates who have completed at least 1 year of college. Applicants must be majoring or planning to major in science, engineering, information technology, computer science, or a related technical field at a 4-year college or university in the United States. Along with their application, they must submit a 300-word personal statement on their career goals. Selection is based on academic standing (GPA, class standing, SAT or ACT scores), community involvement and volunteerism, demonstrated leadership, extracurricular activities, letters of recommendation, and financial need.

Financial data: The stipend is $2,000.

Duration: 1 year.

Number awarded: Varies each year; recently, 9 high school seniors and 3 college students received these scholarships.

Deadline: March of each year.

1977 HAWAII CHAPTER/DAVID T. WOOLSEY SCHOLARSHIP

Summary: To provide financial assistance to residents of Hawaii who are working on an undergraduate or graduate degree in landscape architecture at a school in any state.

See Listing #1307.

1978 HDR ENGINEERING SCHOLARSHIP FOR DIVERSITY IN ENGINEERING

Association of Independent Colleges and Universities of Pennsylvania
101 North Front Street
Harrisburg, PA 17101-1405
Phone: (717) 232-8649; Fax: (717) 233-8574
Email: info@aicup.org
Web: www.aicup.org

Summary: To provide financial assistance to women and minority students from any state who are enrolled at member institutions of the Association of Independent Colleges and Universities of Pennsylvania (AICUP) and majoring in designated fields of engineering.

Eligibility: Open to undergraduate students from any state enrolled full-time at AICUP colleges and universities. Applicants must be women and/or members of the following minority groups: American Indians, Alaska Natives, Asians, Blacks/African Americans, Hispanics/Latinos, Native Hawaiians, or Pacific Islanders. They must be juniors majoring in civil, geotechnical, or structural engineering with a GPA of 3.0 or higher. Along with their application, they must submit a 2-page essay on their characteristics, accomplishments, primary interests, plans, and goals.

Financial data: The stipend is $5,000 per year.

Duration: 1 year; may be renewed 1 additional year if the recipient maintains appropriate academic standards.

Number awarded: 1 each year.

Deadline: April of each year.

1979 HEALTH CARE FOR MONTANANS SCHOLARSHIP

New West Health Services
130 Neill Avenue
Helena, MT 59601
Phone: (406) 457-2200; (888) 500-3355; Fax: (406) 457-2299
Email: czipperian@nwhp.com
Web: www.newwesthealth.com/home/about/scholarships

Summary: To provide financial assistance to Montana residents who are working on an undergraduate or graduate degree in a field related to health care at designated institutions in the state.

Eligibility: Open to residents of Montana who are preparing for a career in health care at a designated institution within the state. Applicants must be enrolled in 1) their second year at a 2-year college; 2) their junior or senior year at a 4-year college or university; or 3) a graduate program in public health and/or nursing. They must have a GPA of 3.0 or higher and be able to demonstrate financial need (expected family financial contribution of $7,500 or less). Along with their application, they must submit a 250-word essay on their concept of an ideal health care job in 5 years and how that would fit their vision of what Montana's health care delivery should look like.

Financial data: The stipend for students working on a bachelor's or master's degree is $2,000. The stipend for students working on an associate degree is $1,000.

Duration: 1 year; nonrenewable.

Number awarded: Up to 9 each year.

Deadline: April of each year.

1980 HEALTH CAREERS SCHOLARSHIPS

International Order of the King's Daughters and Sons
Attn: Director, Health Careers Scholarship Department
34 Vincent Avenue
P.O. Box 1040
Chautauqua, NY 14722-1040
Phone: (716) 357-4951; Fax: (716) 357-3762
Email: iokds5@windstream.net
Web: www.iokds.org/scholarship.html

Summary: To provide financial assistance to Christian and other students preparing for careers in medicine, dentistry, pharmacy, physical and occupational therapy, and selected medical technologies.

Eligibility: Open to U.S. or Canadian citizens who are enrolled full-time at an accredited college or university and studying medicine, dentistry, nursing, pharmacy, physical or occupational therapy, or medical technology. Applicants in undergraduate programs must be in at least the third year of college. Nursing students must have completed their first year of schooling. Students seeking M.D. or D.D.S. degrees must be in at least the second year of medical or dental school. Pre-med students are not eligible. Preference is given to students of Christian background. Selection is based on personal statistics, educational background, financial statement, and a statement from the applicant describing the reason for choosing the field of training and future plans.

Financial data: The stipend is $1,000 per year.

Duration: 1 year; may be renewed up to 2 additional years.

Number awarded: Varies each year; recently, 43 of these scholarships were awarded.

Deadline: March of each year.

1981 HEALTH RESEARCH AND EDUCATIONAL TRUST SCHOLARSHIPS

New Jersey Hospital Association
Attn: Health Research and Educational Trust
760 Alexander Road
P.O. Box 1

Princeton, NJ 08543-0001
Phone: (609) 275-4224; Fax: (609) 452-8097
Web: www.njha.com/hret/scholarship.aspx

Summary: To provide financial assistance to New Jersey residents working on an undergraduate or graduate degree in a field related to health care administration at a school in any state.

Eligibility: Open to residents of New Jersey enrolled in an upper-division or graduate program in hospital or health care administration, public administration, nursing, or other allied health profession at a school in any state. Graduate students working on an advanced degree to prepare to teach nursing are also eligible. Applicants must have a GPA of 3.0 or higher and be able to demonstrate financial need. Along with their application, they must submit a 2-page essay (on which 50% of the selection is based) describing their academic plans for the future. Minorities and women are especially encouraged to apply.

Financial data: The stipend is $2,000.

Duration: 1 year.

Number awarded: Varies each year; recently, 3 of these scholarships were awarded.

Deadline: July of each year.

1982 HELEN K. AND ROBERT T. STAFFORD SCHOLARSHIP

Vermont Student Assistance Corporation
Attn: Scholarship Programs
10 East Allen Street
P.O. Box 2000
Winooski, VT 05404-2601
Phone: (802) 654-3798; (888) 253-4819; Fax: (802) 654-3765; TDD: (800) 281-3341 (within VT)
Email: info@vsac.org
Web: services.vsac.org/wps/wcm/connect/vsac/VSAC

Summary: To provide financial assistance to Vermont residents who are interested in working on a bachelor's degree in environmental studies or special education at a school in any state.

Eligibility: Open to high school seniors, high school graduates, and currently-enrolled college students in Vermont who are enrolled or planning to enroll in a bachelor's degree program at a college or university in any state. Applicants must be preparing for a career in environmental studies or special education. Along with their application, they must submit 1) a 100-word essay on their interest in and commitment to pursuing their chosen career or vocation; and 2) a 250-word essay on their beliefs related to the value of community service. Selection is based on those essays, community involvement and/or service, a letter of recommendation, and financial need.

Financial data: The stipend is $1,000.

Duration: 1 year; nonrenewable.

Number awarded: 1 each year.

Deadline: March of each year.

1983 HELEN ZIMMERMAN MEMORIAL SCHOLARSHIP

New Mexico Engineering Foundation
Attn: Scholarship Chair
P.O. Box 3828
Albuquerque, NM 87190-3828
Phone: (505) 615-1800
Email: info@nmef.net
Web: www.nmef.net/?section=scholarship

Summary: To provide financial assistance to women majoring in engineering at designated universities in New Mexico.

Eligibility: Open to women enrolled in the engineering program at the University of New Mexico, New Mexico State University, or New Mexico Institute of Mining and Technology. Applicants must be at least at the sophomore level. They must have demonstrated a commitment to furthering engineering education on campus and in the community. Selection is based on academic achievement and financial need.

Financial data: The stipend is $1,000.

Duration: 1 year.

Number awarded: 2 each year.

Deadline: February of each year.

1984 HENAAC HIGH SCHOOL SENIOR/COLLEGE FRESHMAN AWARDS

Great Minds in STEM
Attn: HENAAC Scholars
3900 Whiteside Street
Los Angeles, CA 90063
Phone: (323) 262-0997; Fax: (323) 262-0946
Email: kbbarrera@greatmindsinstem.org
Web: www.greatmindsinstem.org/henaac/scholars

Summary: To provide financial assistance to Hispanic high school seniors and college freshmen planning to major in fields of science, technology, engineering, and mathematics (STEM).

Eligibility: Open to Hispanic high school seniors and college freshmen who are enrolled or planning to enroll at a college or university and major in a STEM field. Applicants must be of Hispanic origin and/or must significantly participate in and promote organizations and activities in the Hispanic community. They must have a GPA of 3.0 or higher. Along with their application, they must submit a 700-word essay on a topic that changes annually; recently, students were asked to write on how they see their academic major contributing to global efforts and technology and how they, in their field of study, will contribute to global progress as well as actively contribute to their local communities. Selection is based on leadership through academic achievements and campus and community activities; financial need is not considered.

Financial data: Stipends range from $500 to $5,000.

Duration: 1 year; recipients may reapply.

Number awarded: Varies each year; recently, 5 of these scholarships were awarded.

Deadline: April of each year.

1985 HENAAC STUDENT LEADERSHIP AWARDS

Great Minds in STEM
Attn: HENAAC Scholars
3900 Whiteside Street
Los Angeles, CA 90063
Phone: (323) 262-0997; Fax: (323) 262-0946
Email: kbbarrera@greatmindsinstem.org
Web: www.greatmindsinstem.org/henaac/scholars

Summary: To provide financial assistance to Hispanic undergraduate and graduate students working on a degree in fields of science, technology, engineering, and mathematics (STEM).

Eligibility: Open to Hispanic undergraduate and graduate students who are enrolled at a college or university and working on a degree in a STEM field. Applicants must be of Hispanic origin and/or must significantly participate in and promote organizations and activities in the Hispanic community. They must have a GPA of 3.0 or higher. Along with their application, they must submit a 700-word essay on a topic that changes annually; recently, students were asked to write on how they see their academic major contributing to global efforts and technology and how they, in their field of study, will contribute to global progress as well as actively contribute to their local communities. Selection is based on leadership through academic achievements and campus and community activities; financial need is not considered.

Financial data: The stipend is $5,000.

Duration: 1 year.

Number awarded: 2 each year: 1 undergraduate and 1 graduate student.

Deadline: April of each year.

1986 HENRY DAVID THOREAU SCHOLARSHIPS

Henry David Thoreau Foundation
265 Medford Street, Suite 102
Somerville, MA 02143
Phone: (617) 666-6900; Fax: (617) 666-0345
Web: www.thoreauscholar.org/student/index.html

Summary: To provide financial assistance to Massachusetts high school seniors who plan to study an environmental field at a college in any state.

Eligibility: Open to seniors graduating from high schools in Massachusetts who plan to enroll at a college or university in any state. Applicants must be willing to commit to carry 25% of their undergraduate course work in subjects related to the environment. Selection is based on academic merit and commitment to the environmental field.

Financial data: The stipend is $5,000 per year.

Duration: 1 year; may be renewed up to 3 additional years, provided the recipient maintains a GPA of 2.5 or higher and submits an annual report of their activities in the environmental field, including academic courses.

Number awarded: Between 10 and 12 each year.

Deadline: January of each year.

1987 HERB SOCIETY OF NASHVILLE UNDERGRADUATE ACADEMIC SCHOLARSHIP AWARD

Herb Society of Nashville
P.O. Box 150711
Nashville, TN 37215
Phone: (614) 654-4819
Web: www.herbsocietynashville.org/Scholarship.htm

Summary: To provide financial assistance to residents of Tennessee who are working on an undergraduate degree in horticulture at a school in any state.

Eligibility: Open to residents of Tennessee who are entering their sophomore, junior, or senior year at a 4-year college or university in any state or their second year in a 2-year program. Applicants must be majoring in horticulture. Along with their application, they must submit a 2-page essay on their short- and long-range career goals, special interests, and contributions or projects in plants, herbs, gardening, and related areas. Financial need is not considered in the selection process. U.S. citizenship is required.

Financial data: The stipend is $2,500.

Duration: 1 year.

Number awarded: 1 each year.

Deadline: March of each year.

1988 H.H. HARRIS FOUNDATION SCHOLARSHIPS

H.H. Harris Foundation
Attn: Trustee
30 South Wacker Drive, Suite 2300
Chicago, IL 60606
Phone: (312) 346-7900; Fax: (312) 346-0904
Email: JohnHH@aol.com
Web: www.afsinc.org/content/view/664

Summary: To provide financial assistance to students and professionals in the metallurgical and metals casting fields.

Eligibility: Open to U.S. citizens who are enrolled in an undergraduate or graduate program in the metallurgical and casting of metals field. Preference is given to undergraduates. Along with their application, they must submit documentation of financial need and a statement of purpose that summarizes their career plans and goals with regard to the cast metal and/or metallurgical fields.

Financial data: Stipends are at least $1,000.

Duration: 1 year.

Number awarded: Varies each year.

Deadline: June of each year.

1989 HIGHMARK SCHOLARSHIP

Pennsylvania State System of Higher Education Foundation, Inc.
Attn: Director of Scholarship Programs
2986 North Second Street
Harrisburg, PA 17110
Phone: (717) 720-4065; Fax: (717) 720-7082
Email: eshowers@thePAfoundation.org
Web: www.thepafoundation.org/scholarships/index.asp

Summary: To provide financial assistance to freshmen entering institutions of the Pennsylvania State System of Higher Education (PASSHE) who plan to major in a health care–related field.

Eligibility: Open to freshmen entering 1 of the 14 institutions within the PASSHE. Applicants must be planning to major in a field of health care, including (but not limited to) nursing, pre-physician assistant, pre-medicine, biology, health science, audiology, speech pathology, health services administration, health education, medical imagery, or exercise science. Each PASSHE university establishes its own selection criteria.

Financial data: The stipend is $1,000.

Duration: 1 year; nonrenewable.

Number awarded: 140 each year: 10 at each PASSHE university.

Deadline: Each PASSHE university sets its own deadline.

1990 HIGHWAY, HEAVY AND UTILITY DIVISION ICA SCHOLARSHIP FUND

Central Indiana Community Foundation
Attn: Scholarship Program
615 North Alabama Street, Suite 119
Indianapolis, IN 46204-1498
Phone: (317) 631-6542, ext. 279; Fax: (317) 684-0943
Email: scholarships@cicf.org
Web: www.cicf.org/page26452.cfm

Summary: To provide financial assistance to high school seniors and current college students from Indiana who are interested in attending college in any state to prepare for a career in construction.

Eligibility: Open to residents of Indiana who are graduating high school students or already enrolled in college. Applicants must plan to work on or be currently working on a degree related to highway, bridge, and/or utility construction and plan to prepare for a career in the construction industry. They must be able to demonstrate academic achievement (GPA of 2.5 or higher), talent, and skill as shown through school, community, and work experiences. Current employees in the construction industry are also eligible. Along with their application, they must submit an essay on how they plan to contribution to the construction industry in Indiana after graduation. Preference is given to full-time students at accredited Indiana colleges and technical schools.

Financial data: The stipend is $2,000 per year.

Duration: 1 year; may be renewed up to 3 additional years.

Number awarded: Varies each year; recently, 6 of these scholarships were awarded.

Deadline: March of each year.

1991 HISPANIC IT EXECUTIVE COUNCIL/HENAAC SCHOLARS PROGRAM

Great Minds in STEM
Attn: HENAAC Scholars
3900 Whiteside Street
Los Angeles, CA 90063
Phone: (323) 262-0997; Fax: (323) 262-0946
Email: kbbarrera@greatmindsinstem.org
Web: www.greatmindsinstem.org/henaac/scholars

Summary: To provide financial assistance to Hispanic undergraduate students majoring in computer science or engineering.

Eligibility: Open to Hispanic students who are working on an undergraduate degree in computer science or engineering. Applicants must be of Hispanic origin and/or must significantly participate in and promote organizations and activities in the Hispanic community. They must have a GPA of 3.0 or higher. Along with their application, they must submit a 700-word essay on a topic that changes annually; recently, students were asked to write on how they see their academic major contributing to global efforts and technology and how they, in their field of study, will contribute to global progress as well as actively contribute to their local communities. Selection is based on leadership through academic achievements and campus and community activities; financial need is not considered. U.S. citizenship or permanent resident status is required.

Financial data: Stipends range from $500 to $5,000.

Duration: 1 year; recipients may reapply.

Number awarded: Varies each year; recently, 4 of these scholarships were awarded.

Deadline: April of each year.

1992 H.M. MUFFLY MEMORIAL SCHOLARSHIP

Colorado Nurses Foundation
7400 East Arapahoe Road, Suite 211
Centennial, CO 80112
Phone: (303) 694-4728; Fax: (303) 694-4869
Email: mail@cnfound.org
Web: www.cnfound.org/scholarships.html

Summary: To provide financial assistance to residents of Colorado who are working on a bachelor's or higher degree in nursing at a college or university in the state.

Eligibility: Open to Colorado residents who have been accepted as a student in an approved nursing program in the state. Applicants must be working on a bachelor's or higher degree. Undergraduates must have a GPA of 3.25 or higher and graduate students must have a GPA of 3.5 or higher. Selection is based on professional philosophy and goals, dedication to the improvement of patient care in Colorado, demonstrated commitment to nursing, critical thinking skills, potential for leadership, involvement in community and professional organizations, recommendations, GPA, and financial need.

Financial data: The stipend is $3,000.

Duration: 1 year.

Number awarded: 2 each year.

Deadline: October of each year.

1993 HOLLIS HANINGTON SCHOLARSHIP

Professional Logging Contractors of Maine
49 Pineland Drive, Suite 201A
New Gloucester, ME 04260
Phone: (207) 688-8195; Fax: (207) 688-8197
Email: wendy@tcnef.org
Web: www.maineloggers.com

Summary: To provide financial assistance to high school seniors in Maine who are interested in preparing for a career in the forest products industry.

Eligibility: Open to seniors in high school (and home-schooled students) who are residents of Maine. Applicants must be planning to enter college in any state to prepare for a career in the forest products industry.

Financial data: The stipend is $1,000. Funds are paid after successful completion of the first semester of college.

Duration: 1 year; nonrenewable.

Number awarded: 1 each year.

Deadline: May of each year.

1994 HOME BUILDERS FOUNDATION BUILDING INDUSTRY SCHOLARSHIPS

Summary: To provide financial assistance to residents of Oregon who are attending college in the state to prepare for a career in the home building industry.

See Listing #1317.

1995 HOOPER MEMORIAL SCHOLARSHIP

Transportation Clubs International
P.O. Box 2223
Ocean Shores, WA 98569
Phone: (877) 858-8627
Email: info@transportationclubsinternational.com
Web: www.transportationclubsinternational.com/scholarships.html

Summary: To provide financial assistance to college students interested in preparing for a career in fields related to transportation.

Eligibility: Open to students enrolled at an academic institution (vocational or degree program) that offers courses in transportation, logistics, traffic management, or related fields. Applicants must intend to prepare for a career in those fields. Along with their application, they must submit a 200-word essay explaining why they have chosen transportation or an allied field as a career path and outlining their objectives. Selection is based on scholastic ability, character, potential, professional interest, and financial need.

Financial data: The stipend is $2,000.

Duration: 1 year.

Number awarded: 1 or more each year.

Deadline: May of each year.

1996 HORIZONS FOUNDATION SCHOLARSHIP PROGRAM

Women in Defense
c/o National Defense Industrial Association
2111 Wilson Boulevard, Suite 400
Arlington, VA 22201-3061
Phone: (703) 247-2552; Fax: (703) 522-1885
Email: wid@ndia.org
Web: wid.ndia.org/horizons/Pages/default.aspx

Summary: To provide financial assistance to women who are upper-division or graduate students engaged in or planning careers related to the national security interests of the United States.

Eligibility: Open to women who are already working in national security fields as well as women planning such careers. Applicants must 1) be currently enrolled at an accredited college or university, either full-time or part-time, as graduate students or upper-division undergraduates; 2) demonstrate financial need; 3) be U.S. citizens; 4) have a GPA of 3.25 or higher; and 5) demonstrate interest in preparing for a career related to national security. The preferred fields of study include business (as it relates to national security or defense), computer science, economics, engineering, government relations, international relations, law (as it relates to national security or defense), mathematics, military history, political science, physics, and security studies; others are considered if the applicant can demonstrate relevance to a career in national security or defense. Selection is based on academic achievement, participation in defense and national security activities, field of study, work experience, statements of objectives, recommendations, and financial need.

Financial data: The stipend ranges up to $12,000.

Duration: 1 year; renewable.

Number awarded: Varies each year; recently, 3 of these scholarships were awarded: 1 at $12,000, 1 at $10,000, and 1 at $3,000. Since the program was established, 104 women have received more than $119,000 in support.

Deadline: June of each year.

1997 HORMEL SCHOLARSHIP PROGRAM OF THE HISPANIC SCHOLARSHIP FUND

Hispanic Scholarship Fund
Attn: Selection Committee
55 Second Street, Suite 1500
San Francisco, CA 94105
Phone: (415) 808-2365; (877) HSF-INFO; Fax: (415) 808-2302
Email: scholar1@hsf.net
Web: www.hsf.net/Hormel_Scholarship.aspx

Summary: To provide financial assistance to Hispanic upper-division students who are interested in a career in the food industry.

Eligibility: Open to U.S. citizens and permanent residents (must have a permanent resident card or a passport stamped I-551) who are of Hispanic heritage. Applicants must be full-time juniors at a college or university in the United States, Puerto Rico, Guam, or the U.S. Virgin Islands with a GPA of 3.0 or higher. They must be majoring in accounting, agriculture (including agribusiness, agricultural economics, agricultural engineering, agronomy, or food service), business administration (including operations), civil engineering, computer science, electrical engineering, engineering (including design and packaging engineering), finance, hospitality administration (including hotel and restaurant management), industrial engineering/technology (including industrial management), information technology (including management information systems and computer information systems), management, manufacturing engineering, marketing (including professional selling), mechanical engineering (including mechanical technology), or zoology (including animal science). Selection is based on academic achievement, personal strengths, leadership, and financial need.

Financial data: The stipend is $2,500.

Duration: 1 year.

Number awarded: 1 or more each year.

Deadline: December of each year.

1998 HOWARD BROWN RICKARD SCHOLARSHIP

Summary: To provide financial assistance for college or graduate school to blind students studying or planning to study law, medicine, engineering, architecture, or the natural sciences.

See Listing #1323.

1999 HOWARD P. WACKMAN II MEMORIAL AWARD

California Farm Bureau Scholarship Foundation
Attn: Scholarship Foundation
2300 River Plaza Drive
Sacramento, CA 95833
Phone: (916) 561-5520; (800) 698-FARM (within CA); Fax: (916) 561-5699
Email: dlicciardo@cfbf.com
Web: www.cfbf.com/programs/scholar/index.cfm

Summary: To provide financial assistance for college to residents of California who are interested in preparing for a career in agriculture.

Eligibility: Open to students entering or attending a 4-year accredited college or university in California who are majoring or planning to major in an agricultural-related field. Students entering a junior college are not eligible. Applicants must have a GPA of 3.0 or higher in high school or college. They must submit an essay on the most important educational or personal experience that has led them to pursue a university education. Selection is based on academic achievement, career goals, extracurricular activities, leadership skills, determination, and commitment to study agriculture.

Financial data: The stipend is $2,750 per year.

Duration: 1 year; recipients may reapply.

Number awarded: 1 each year.

Deadline: February of each year.

2000 HSBC-NORTH AMERICA SCHOLARSHIP PROGRAM OF THE HISPANIC SCHOLARSHIP FUND

Hispanic Scholarship Fund
Attn: Selection Committee

55 Second Street, Suite 1500
San Francisco, CA 94105
Phone: (415) 808-2365; (877) HSF-INFO; Fax: (415) 808-2302
Email: scholar1@hsf.net
Web: www.hsf.net/scholarships.aspx?id=856

Summary: To provide financial assistance to Hispanic upper-division students from selected states who are working on a degree related to business.

Eligibility: Open to U.S. citizens, permanent residents, and visitors with a passport stamped I-551 who are of Hispanic heritage and residents of California, Florida, Illinois, Nevada, New York, Texas, Virginia, or Washington, D.C. Applicants must be entering their junior year as continuing or transfer students at a 4-year college or university in the United States, Puerto Rico, Guam, or the U.S. Virgin Islands and have a GPA of 3.0 or higher. They must be majoring in accounting, business administration, economics, finance, or management. Selection is based on academic achievement, personal strengths, leadership, and financial need.

Financial data: The stipend is $2,500 per year.

Duration: 1 year (the junior year of college).

Number awarded: 1 or more each year.

Deadline: February of each year.

2001 HUBERTUS W.V. WILLEMS SCHOLARSHIP FOR MALE STUDENTS

National Association for the Advancement of Colored People
Attn: Education Department
4805 Mt. Hope Drive
Baltimore, MD 21215-3297
Phone: (410) 580-5760; (877) NAACP-98
Email: youth@naacpnet.org
Web: www.naacp.org/pages/naacp-scholarships

Summary: To provide funding to males, particularly male members of the National Association for the Advancement of Colored People (NAACP), who are interested in undergraduate or graduate education in selected scientific fields.

Eligibility: Open to males who are high school seniors, college students, or graduate students. Applicants must be majoring (or planning to major) in 1 of the following fields: engineering, chemistry, physics, or mathematics. Membership and participation in the NAACP are highly desirable. The required minimum GPA is 2.5 for graduating high school seniors and undergraduate students or 3.0 for graduate students. Applicants must be able to demonstrate financial need, defined as a family income of less than $16,245 for a family of 1 ranging to less than $49,905 for a family of 7. Along with their application, they must submit a 1-page essay on their interest in their major and a career, their life's ambition, what they hope to accomplish in their lifetime, and what position they hope to attain. Full-time enrollment is required for undergraduate students, although graduate students may be enrolled full- or part-time. U.S. citizenship is required.

Financial data: The stipend is $2,000 per year for undergraduate students or $3,000 per year for graduate students.

Duration: 1 year; may be renewed.

Number awarded: Varies each year; recently, 7 of these scholarships were awarded.

Deadline: March of each year.

2002 CIENCIA NATIONAL SCHOLARSHIPS

National Alliance for Hispanic Health
Alliance/Merck *Ciencia* Hispanic Scholars Program
1501 16th Street, N.W.
Washington, DC 20036
Phone: (202) 387-5000; (866) 783-2645
Web: alliancescholars.org/applications

Summary: To provide financial assistance to Hispanic college students who are majoring in a field of science, technology, engineering, or mathematics (STEM).

Eligibility: Open to students of Hispanic heritage enrolled full-time at an accredited college or university. Applicants must have a declared major in a STEM discipline and a GPA of 2.75 or higher. They must be working on a bachelor's degree, including a degree offered by a partnership between a community college and a 4-year institution.

Financial data: The stipend is $2,000.

Duration: 1 year; nonrenewable.

Number awarded: 25 each year.

Deadline: February of each year.

2003 IAGER DAIRY SCHOLARSHIP

National Dairy Shrine
Attn: Executive Director
P.O. Box 1
Maribel, WI 54227
Phone: (920) 863-6333; Fax: (920) 863-8328
Email: info@dairyshrine.org
Web: www.dairyshrine.org/scholarships.php

Summary: To provide financial assistance to 2-year college students majoring in animal or dairy science.

Eligibility: Open to students completing their first year at a 2-year agricultural school and preparing for a career in the dairy industry. Applicants must have a GPA of 2.5 or higher. Along with their application, they must submit a 500-word essay on why they are interested in the dairy industry and their plans for the future. Selection is based on that essay, academic standing, leadership ability and extracurricular activities, and interest in the dairy industry.

Financial data: The stipend is $1,000.

Duration: 1 year.

Number awarded: 1 each year.

Deadline: April of each year.

2004 IDAHO EDUCATION INCENTIVE LOAN FORGIVENESS

Idaho State Board of Education
Len B. Jordan Office Building
650 West State Street, Room 307
P.O. Box 83720
Boise, ID 83720-0037
Phone: (208) 332-1574; Fax: (208) 334-2632
Email: scholarshiphelp@osbe.idaho.gov
Web: www.boardofed.idaho.gov/scholarships/st_loan_forgive.asp

Summary: To provide financial assistance to Idaho students who wish to prepare for a teaching or nursing career in Idaho.

Eligibility: Open to students who have graduated from a secondary school in Idaho within the previous 2 years and rank within the upper 15% of their graduating high school class or have earned a cumulative GPA in college of 3.0 or higher. They must enroll as a full-time student at an Idaho public college or university, working on a degree that will qualify them to receive an Idaho teaching certificate or licensure by the Board of Nursing as a registered nurse.

Financial data: This is a scholarship/loan program. Loans are forgiven if the recipient pursues a teaching or nursing career within Idaho for at least 2 years.

Duration: 1 year; renewable.

Number awarded: Approximately 45 each year.

Deadline: Deadline not specified.

2005 IDAHO LEGION AUXILIARY NURSES SCHOLARSHIP

American Legion Auxiliary
Department of Idaho
905 Warren Street
Boise, ID 83706-3825
Phone: (208) 342-7066; Fax: (208) 342-7066
Email: idalegionaux@msn.com

Summary: To provide financial assistance to Idaho veterans and their children who are interested in studying nursing at a school in any state.

Eligibility: Open to student nurses who are veterans or the children or grandchildren of veterans and have resided in Idaho for 5 years prior to application. Applicants must be attending or planning to attend a school of nursing in any state. They must be between 17 and 35 years of age. Selection is based on financial need, scholarship, and deportment.

Financial data: The stipend is $1,000.

Duration: 1 year.

Number awarded: 1 each year.

Deadline: May of each year.

2006 IDDBA SCHOLARSHIP

Summary: To provide financial assistance to high school seniors, undergraduates, or graduate students employed in a supermarket dairy, deli, or bakery department who are interested in working on a degree in a food-related field.

See Listing #1328.

2007 ILLINOIS CONSERVATION ACHIEVEMENT SCHOLARSHIPS

Illinois Conservation Foundation
Attn: Executive Secretary
One Natural Resources Way
Springfield, IL 62702-1271
Phone: (217) 785-2003; Fax: (217) 785-8405; TDD: (217) 788-9175
Email: kwheeler@dnrmail.state.il.us
Web: www.ilcf.org/scholarships

Summary: To provide financial assistance to high school seniors in Illinois who have participated in natural resource activities and plan to attend college in any state.

Eligibility: Open to seniors graduating from high schools in Illinois who plan to enroll at a 2- or 4-year college or university in any state. Applicants must be able to document voluntary, effective contributions to Illinois' natural resources throughout their high school enrollment. They must have a GPA of 2.5 or higher. Along with their application, they must submit a 500-word essay giving specific examples of how their voluntary efforts have resulted in preservation, protection, enhancement, and/or promotion of Illinois' natural resources and how the efforts influenced people. Selection is based on that essay, a letter of support from their school, 3 additional letters of support, media documentation of their natural resource activities, and verification of academic achievement. Financial need is not considered in the selection process.

Financial data: Stipends are $5,000, $3,000, and $2,000.

Duration: 1 year; nonrenewable.

Number awarded: 3 each year: 1 each at $5,000, $3,000, and $2,000.

Deadline: November of each year.

2008 ILLINOIS EXCELLENCE IN AGRICULTURE SCHOLARSHIP

Office of the State Treasurer
Attn: Division of Economic Opportunity
400 West Monroe Street, Suite 401
Springfield, IL 62704
Phone: (217) 782-6540; Fax: (217) 524-3822
Web: www.treasurer.il.gov

Summary: To provide financial assistance to high school seniors in Illinois planning to study agriculture at a college or university in the state.

Eligibility: Open to seniors graduating from high schools in Illinois with a GPA of 2.75 or higher. Applicants must be planning to enroll at an accredited higher education institution in Illinois and major in agriculture or a related field (e.g., agribusiness, crop and livestock production, agricultural research, alternative agriculture). Along with their application, they must submit a 250-word essay on the reasons they want to prepare for a career in agriculture or a related field, an official high school transcript, 2 letters of recommendation, a list of extracurricular activities, and a statement of goals and future plans. Financial need is not considered in the selection process.

Financial data: The stipend is $2,000. Funds must be used for tuition, books, and/or room and board.

Duration: 1 year.

Number awarded: 10 each year.

Deadline: May of each year.

2009 ILLINOIS HEALTH IMPROVEMENT ASSOCIATION SCHOLARSHIPS

Illinois Community College System Foundation
401 East Capitol Avenue
Springfield, IL 62701
Phone: (217) 789-4230; Fax: (217) 492-5176
Email: iccsfoundation@sbcglobal.net
Web: www.iccsfoundation.com/Scholarships.htm

Summary: To provide financial assistance to students enrolled in a health care program at an Illinois community college.

Eligibility: Open to Illinois community college students enrolled in a health care program that provides direct medical care to individuals. Eligible areas of study may include certified nursing assistant, clinical laboratory technician, dental hygienist, electrocardiograph vascular technician, emergency medical technician, mental health associate, mortuary science, nephrology/renal technician, registered and practical nurse, occupational therapist assistant, paramedic, physician assistant, physical therapy aide, psychiatric rehabilitation, radiology technician, respiratory care, pharmacy technician, phlebotomy technician, or surgical technician. Applicants must be committed to practice in Illinois or a city adjacent to the Illinois border where state residents go for primary health care. They must have a GPA of 2.0 or higher and be able to demonstrate financial need.

Financial data: Stipends range up to $1,000.

Duration: 1 year.

Number awarded: Up to 2 each year at each participating Illinois community college.

Deadline: Each college sets its own deadline.

2010 ILLINOIS LUMBER AND MATERIAL DEALERS ASSOCIATION ACADEMIC SCHOLARSHIPS

Illinois Lumber and Material Dealers Association
Attn: Educational Foundation
932 South Spring Street
Springfield, IL 62704
Phone: (217) 544-5405; (800) 252-8641; Fax: (217) 544-4206
Email: ilmda@ilmda.com
Web: www.ilmda.com/Education.html

Summary: To provide financial assistance to residents of Illinois who are interested in attending college in any state to prepare for a career in the lumber and building materials industry or in allied fields.

Eligibility: Open to residents of Illinois who are enrolled or planning to enroll full-time at an accredited trade school, 2-year college, or 4-year college or university in any state. Applicants must be preparing for a career in lumber and building materials or an allied field (e.g., millwork, design). They must submit a statement of their activities and interests, record of military service (if any), an outline of their proposed program of study, a statement from a high school instructor, transcripts, and 2 letters of recommendation. Selection is based on academic achievement and financial need.

Financial data: Stipends range from $500 to $2,000.

Duration: 1 year; recipients may reapply.

Number awarded: 1 or more each year.

Deadline: March of each year.

2011 ILLINOIS NURSES ASSOCIATION CENTENNIAL SCHOLARSHIP

Illinois Nurses Association
Attn: Illinois Nurses Foundation
105 West Adams Street, Suite 2101
Chicago, IL 60603
Phone: (312) 419-2900; Fax: (312) 419-2920
Email: info@illinoisnurses.com
Web: www.illinoisnurses.com/displaycommon.cfm?an=1&subarticlenbr=274

Summary: To provide financial assistance to nursing undergraduate and graduate students who are members of underrepresented groups.

Eligibility: Open to students working on an associate, bachelor's, or master's degree at an accredited NLNAC or CCNE school of nursing. Applicants must be members of a group underrepresented in nursing (African Americans, Hispanics, American Indians, Asians, and males). Undergraduates must have earned a passing grade in all nursing courses taken to date and have a GPA of 2.85 or higher. Graduate students must have completed at least 12 semester hours of graduate work and have a GPA of 3.0 or higher. All applicants must be willing to 1) act as a spokesperson to other student groups on the value of the scholarship to continuing their nursing education; and 2) be profiled in any media or marketing materials developed by the Illinois Nurses Foundation. Along with their application, they must submit a narrative of 250 to 500 words on how they, as a nurse, plan to affect policy at either the state or national level that impacts on nursing or health care generally, or how they believe they will impact the nursing profession in general.

Financial data: A stipend is awarded (amount not specified).

Duration: 1 year.

Number awarded: 1 or more each year.

Deadline: March of each year.

2012 ILLINOIS PROFESSIONAL LAND SURVEYORS ASSOCIATION 24 SEMESTER HOUR SCHOLARSHIP AWARD

Illinois Professional Land Surveyors Association
521 East Washington Street
P.O. Box 5627
Springfield, IL 62705-5627
Phone: (217) 528-3053; Fax: (217) 528-3279
Email: info@iplsa.org

Web: www.iplsa.org/students.html

Summary: To provide financial assistance to Illinois residents working to complete the 24 semester hour requirement to earn a degree in land surveying at a college or university in the state.

Eligibility: Open to residents of Illinois enrolled at colleges and universities in the state and employed in the surveying and engineering field. Applicants must be working to complete the requirement of the Illinois Department of Professional Regulation Land Surveyors Licensing Board for at least 24 semester hours of approved land surveying courses. They may not be receiving financial aid from their employer. Along with their application, they must submit a statement of 1 to 5 pages that covers their work history; career goals in surveying; merit, as indicated by awards, GPA, honors society membership, or other performance; financial need; and extracurricular activities related to surveying.

Financial data: The stipend is $500 per semester.

Duration: 1 semester. Awardees can receive up to 3 semester stipends per year (spring, summer, and fall) and up to 2 annual awards in a lifetime.

Number awarded: 1 or more each year.

Deadline: November of each year.

2013 ILLINOIS PROFESSIONAL LAND SURVEYORS ASSOCIATION SCHOLARSHIP AWARD

Illinois Professional Land Surveyors Association
521 East Washington Street
P.O. Box 5627
Springfield, IL 62705-5627
Phone: (217) 528-3053; Fax: (217) 528-3279
Email: info@iplsa.org
Web: www.iplsa.org/students.html

Summary: To provide financial assistance to Illinois residents working on a degree in land surveying at a college or university in the state.

Eligibility: Open to residents of Illinois enrolled at colleges and universities in the state. Applicants must be working on a baccalaureate degree in surveying or in a related field that includes at least 24 semester hours of approved land surveying courses. Along with their application, they must submit a statement of 1 to 5 pages that covers their educational and career goals; merit, as indicated by awards, GPA, honors society membership, or other performance; financial need; and extracurricular activities related to surveying.

Financial data: The stipend is $1,000.

Duration: 1 year.

Number awarded: 5 each year.

Deadline: November of each year.

2014 INDEPENDENCE EXCAVATING 50TH ANNIVERSARY SCHOLARSHIP

Associated General Contractors of Ohio
Attn: AGC of Ohio Education Foundation
1755 Northwest Boulevard
Columbus, OH 43212
Phone: (614) 486-6446; (800) 557-OHIO; Fax: (614) 486-6498
Email: educationfoundation@agcohio.com
Web: www.agcohio.com/scholarships.html

Summary: To provide financial assistance to students from any state who are working on an undergraduate degree in a field related to construction at a college or university in Ohio, Pennsylvania, Michigan, or West Virginia.

Eligibility: Open to undergraduates who are residents of any state and attending school in Ohio, Pennsylvania, Michigan, or West Virginia in at least the second year at a 2- or 4-year college or university. Applicants must be enrolled in a construction degree program and be preparing for a career in construction. They must be U.S. citizens with a GPA of 2.5 or higher. Along with their application, they must submit a short statement on what they think is the most important issue currently facing the construction industry and 4 essays of 125 words each on 1) why they have decided to prepare for a career in construction; 2) the goals they hope to accomplish in their career; 3) how they plan to make a difference in the construction industry; and 4) anything else that might influence whether or not they receive this scholarship. Financial need is also considered in the selection process.

Financial data: The stipend is $1,000.

Duration: 1 year.

Number awarded: 1 each year.

Deadline: March of each year.

2015 INDIANA HEALTH CARE FOUNDATION SCHOLARSHIP

Indiana Health Care Foundation, Inc.
Attn: Scholarship Committee
One North Capitol Avenue, Suite 100
Indianapolis, IN 46204
Phone: (317) 636-6406; (800) 466-IHCA; Fax: (877) 298-3749
Email: dhenry@ihca.org
Web: www.ihca.org/pagesroot/pages/Education-Scholarships.aspx

Summary: To provide financial assistance to students in Indiana who are interested in working on a degree in long-term care nursing at a school in or near the state.

Eligibility: Open to residents of Indiana who have at least a high school degree or GED, have been accepted by a nursing degree program (R.N. or L.P.N.) in Indiana or a bordering state, and have a GPA of 2.5 or higher. Applicants must be preparing for a career working with the elderly in a long-term care environment. Along with their application, they must submit an essay (up to 750 words) on their reasons for applying for this scholarship, their interest in nursing, and their future professional plans and commitment to long-term care. Finalists are interviewed. Special consideration is given to applicants who show a dedication and commitment to working with the elderly in a long-term care environment (nursing homes and/or assisted living facilities). Financial need is not considered in the selection process.

Financial data: Stipends range from $750 to $1,500 per year. Funds are paid directly to the recipient's school and must be used for tuition, fees, or campus housing.

Duration: 1 year; recipients may reapply.

Deadline: May of each year.

2016 INDIANA MINORITY TEACHER/SPECIAL EDUCATION SERVICES SCHOLARSHIP

State Student Assistance Commission of Indiana
Attn: Director of Special Programs
150 West Market Street, Suite 500
Indianapolis, IN 46204-2811
Phone: (317) 232-2350; (888) 528-4719 (within IN); Fax: (317) 232-3260
Email: special@ssaci.state.in.us
Web: www.in.gov/ssaci/2342.htm

Summary: To provide financial assistance to Black and Hispanic undergraduate students in Indiana interested in preparing for a teaching career and to other residents of the state preparing for a career in special education, occupational therapy, or physical therapy.

Eligibility: Open to 1) Black and Hispanic students seeking teacher certification; 2) students seeking special education teaching certification; or 3) students seeking occupational or physical therapy certification. Applicants must be Indiana residents and U.S. citizens who are enrolled or accepted for enrollment as full-time students at an academic institution in Indiana. Students who are already enrolled in college must have a GPA of 2.0 or higher. Applicants must be preparing to teach in an accredited elementary or secondary school in Indiana or to work as an occupational or physical therapist at a school or rehabilitation facility. Financial need may be considered, but it is not a requirement. In the selection process, awards are presented in the following priority order: 1) minority students seeking a renewal scholarship; 2) newly enrolling minority students; 3) non-minority students seeking a renewal scholarship; and 4) newly enrolling non-minority students.

Financial data: Minority students demonstrating financial need may receive up to $4,000 per year. For non-minority students, the maximum award is $1,000. For 3 out of the 5 years following graduation, recipients must teach full-time in an elementary or secondary school in Indiana or practice as an occupational or physical therapist at a school or rehabilitation facility in the state. If they fail to meet that service requirement, they are required to reimburse the state of Indiana for all funds received.

Duration: 1 year; may be renewed up to 3 additional years if recipients maintain a 2.0 GPA. They may, however, take up to 6 years to complete the program from the start of receiving the first scholarship.

Number awarded: Varies each year.

Deadline: Each participating college or university establishes its own filing deadline for this program.

2017 INDIANA NURSING SCHOLARSHIP FUND PROGRAM

State Student Assistance Commission of Indiana
Attn: Director of Special Programs
150 West Market Street, Suite 500
Indianapolis, IN 46204-2811

Phone: (317) 232-2350; (888) 528-4719 (within IN); Fax: (317) 232-3260
Email: special@ssaci.state.in.us
Web: www.in.gov/ssaci/2343.htm

Summary: To provide financial assistance to Indiana residents who are interested in attending college in the state to prepare for a career as a nurse.

Eligibility: Open to Indiana residents who are admitted to an eligible Indiana school as a full- or part-time student to work on a certificate or bachelor's degree in nursing, are able to demonstrate financial need, are U.S. citizens, and have a GPA of 2.0 or higher. They must agree to work as a nurse in Indiana in 1 of the following locations: acute care or specialty hospital, long-term care facility, rehabilitation care facility, home health care entity, hospice program, mental health facility, or a facility located in a shortage area.

Financial data: The stipend is $5,000 per year. Funds may be used only for tuition and fees. Recipients agree in writing to work as a nurse in a health care setting in Indiana for at least the first 2 years after graduation. If they fail to fulfill that service obligation, they will be required to reimburse the state of Indiana.

Duration: 1 year; may be renewed up to 3 additional years, but recipients must complete the nursing program within 6 years from the time the first scholarship is awarded.

Number awarded: Varies each year.

Deadline: Deadline not specified.

2018 INDOT ENGINEERING SCHOLARSHIP

Indiana Department of Transportation
Attn: Human Resources
3650 South US Highway 41
Vincennes, IN 47591
Phone: (812) 895-7305
Email: BJittjumnongk@indot.IN.gov
Web: www.in.gov/indot/3278.htm

Summary: To provide financial assistance to undergraduate and graduate students who are enrolled in a civil engineering program at a college in Indiana and willing to work for the Indiana Department of Transportation (INDOT) following graduation.

Eligibility: Open to residents of any state who have completed at least 1 year of full-time study in an ABET-accredited undergraduate or graduate civil engineering program in Indiana. Applicants must have and maintain a GPA of 2.8 or higher. Along with their application, they must submit a brief statement covering their specific civil engineering goals, extracurricular activities, and leadership ability in and out of school. Selection is based on high school ranking and GPA, collegiate GPA, SAT and/or ACT scores, community or scholastic leadership activities, work experience, major accomplishments and achievements, and financial need.

Financial data: The stipend is $3,125 per semester. Funds are sent directly to the recipient to be used for tuition, fees, and books. This is a scholarship/loan program; recipients must agree to work for INDOT during summer breaks while in school and after graduation for 6 months per semester of support received. If they fail to complete that service obligation, they must repay all amounts received.

Duration: 1 year; may be renewed for up to an additional 4 years, including up to 2 years of graduate study.

Number awarded: A limited number are awarded each year.

Deadline: April of each year.

2019 INDUSTRY MINORITY SCHOLARSHIPS

American Meteorological Society
Attn: Fellowship/Scholarship Program
45 Beacon Street
Boston, MA 02108-3693
Phone: (617) 227-2426, ext. 246; Fax: (617) 742-8718
Email: scholar@ametsoc.org
Web: www.ametsoc.org/amsstudentinfo/scholfeldocs/index.html

Summary: To provide financial assistance to underrepresented minority students entering college and planning to major in meteorology or an aspect of atmospheric sciences.

Eligibility: Open to members of minority groups traditionally underrepresented in the sciences (especially Hispanics, Native Americans, and Blacks/African Americans) who are entering their freshman year at a college or university and planning to work on a degree in the atmospheric or related oceanic and hydrologic sciences. Applicants must submit an official high school transcript showing grades from the past 3 years, a letter of recommendation from a high school teacher or guidance counselor, a copy of scores from an SAT or similar national entrance exam, and a 500-word essay on a topic that changes annually; recently, applicants were invited to write on global change and how they would use their college education in atmospheric science (or a closely-related field) to make their community a better place in which to live. Selection is based on the essay and academic performance in high school.

Financial data: The stipend is $3,000 per year.

Duration: 1 year; may be renewed for the second year of college study.

Number awarded: Varies each year; recently, 5 of these scholarships were awarded.

Deadline: February of each year.

2020 INFORMATION ASSURANCE SCHOLARSHIP PROGRAM

National Security Agency
DoD Information Assurance Scholarship Program
Attn: I924
9800 Savage Road, Suite 6722
Fort Meade, MD 20755-6722
Phone: (410) 854-6206
Email: askiasp@nsa.gov
Web: www.nsa.gov

Summary: To provide financial assistance to undergraduate and graduate students interested in working on a degree in a field related to information assurance (IA) and then serving as a civilian or military employee of the Department of Defense.

Eligibility: Open to full-time college juniors, seniors, and graduate students working on a degree in a field related to IA, including biometrics, business management and administration, computer crime investigation, computer engineering, computer information science, computer network operations, computer programming, computer science, computer systems analysis, database administration, data management, digital and multimedia forensics, electrical and electronics engineering, information security, mathematics, network management, operations research, or software engineering. Applicants must be attending a designated National Center of Academic Excellence in Information Assurance Education or a National Center of Academic Excellence in Research (referred to as CAEs). They must be nominated by the CAE, which provides information on their academic major, GPA, projected degree and final graduation date, knowledge, skills, and attributes.

Financial data: Scholarships provide full payment of tuition and fees, an allowance for books, and a stipend to cover room and board expenses. Students incur a service commitment, either to work for a participating component of the Department of Defense as a civilian for 1 year for each year of scholarship support received or to serve on active duty as an officer or enlisted member of 1 of the military services for 4 years.

Duration: 1 year; may be renewed.

Number awarded: 25 to 30 each year.

Deadline: February of each year.

2021 INOVA NURSING EXCELLENCE SCHOLARSHIP PROGRAM

Inova Health System
Attn: Edelman Nursing Career Development Center
8110 Gatehouse Road, Suite 200 West
Falls Church, VA 22042
Phone: (703) 205-2142
Email: edelmannursingcareerdevelopmentcenter@inova.org
Web: www.inova.org/working-at-inova/for-nurses/index.jsp

Summary: To provide financial assistance to nursing students willing to work in facilities of the Inova Health System after graduation.

Eligibility: Open to nursing students enrolled full-time in the final year of a degree program (A.D.N. or B.S.N.). Applicants must have a GPA of 3.0 or higher and be able to complete their program on time. They must be willing to commit to working at a facility of Inova Health System in northern Virginia within 4 months of graduation. Along with their application, they must submit a 1-page narrative explaining their career goals as a registered nurse and why they should be considered for this scholarship. U.S. citizenship or permanent resident status is required.

Financial data: Stipends up to $5,000 are available. Recipients must commit to work full-time for at least 2 years within 4 months after graduation as a registered nurse. If they fail to complete the service obligation, they must repay all funds received.

Duration: 1 year.

Number awarded: 1 or more each year.

Deadline: April of each year.

2022 INSTITUTE OF FOOD TECHNOLOGISTS COLLEGE SCHOLARSHIPS

Institute of Food Technologists
Attn: Scholarship Department
525 West Van Buren, Suite 1000
Chicago, IL 60607
Phone: (312) 782-8424; Fax: (312) 782-8348
Email: info@ift.org
Web: www.ift.org/cms/?pid=1001271

Summary: To provide financial assistance to undergraduates interested in studying food science or food technology.

Eligibility: Open to sophomores, juniors, and seniors working on a bachelor's degree in food science or food technology at an educational institution in the United States or Canada. Applicants must have a GPA of 3.0 or higher. Along with their application, they must submit an essay on their career objectives; a list of awards, honors, and scholarships they have received; a list of extracurricular activities, community service, and leadership experience; and a summary of their past and current work experience and internships. Financial need is not considered in the selection process.

Financial data: Stipends are $2,000 or $1,000.

Duration: 1 year; recipients may reapply if they are members of the Institute of Food Technologists.

Number awarded: Varies each year; recently, 25 of these scholarships were awarded: 5 at $2,000 and 20 at $1,000.

Deadline: January of each year.

2023 INSTITUTE OF FOOD TECHNOLOGISTS HIGH SCHOOL SCHOLARSHIPS

Institute of Food Technologists
Attn: Scholarship Department
525 West Van Buren, Suite 1000
Chicago, IL 60607
Phone: (312) 782-8424; Fax: (312) 782-8348
Email: info@ift.org
Web: www.ift.org/cms/?pid=1000444

Summary: To provide financial assistance to high school seniors interested in studying food science or food technology in college.

Eligibility: Open to high school seniors planning to work on a bachelor's degree in food science or food technology at an educational institution in the United States or Canada. Applicants must have an outstanding academic record and a well-rounded personality. Along with their application, they must submit a brief biographical statement on why they would like to become a food scientist and/or food technologist. Financial need is not considered in the selection process.

Financial data: Stipends are $1,000.

Duration: 1 year; recipients may reapply if they are members of the Institute of Food Technologists.

Number awarded: Varies each year; recently, 15 of these scholarships were awarded.

Deadline: February of each year.

2024 INTEL INTERNATIONAL SCIENCE AND ENGINEERING FAIR

Society for Science & the Public
Attn: Director of Youth Programs
1719 N Street, N.W.
Washington, DC 20036
Phone: (202) 785-2255; Fax: (202) 785-1243
Email: isef@scienceforsociety.org
Web: www.societyforscience.org/isef

Summary: To recognize and reward outstanding high school students who enter a science and engineering competition.

Eligibility: Open to students in grades 9–12. First, they compete in approximately 540 affiliated fairs around the world. Each fair then sends 2 individuals and 1 team (up to 3 members) to compete in the ISEF in 1 of 19 categories: animal sciences, behavioral and social sciences, biochemistry, cellular and molecular biology, chemistry, computer science, earth and planetary sciences, electrical and mechanical engineering, environmental management, materials and bioengineering, energy and transportation, environmental science, mathematical sciences, medicine and health, microbiology, physics and astronomy, plant sciences, life sciences team projects, and physical sciences team projects. Each entry consists of a science project and a 250-word abstract that summarizes the project. Judging of individual projects is based on creative ability (30%), scientific thought or engineering goals (30%), thoroughness (15%), skill (15%), and clarity (10%).

Financial data: The student whose project is judged most outstanding receives the Gordon E. Moore Award of $75,000. The next 2 most outstanding projects receive Intel Foundation Young Scientist Awards of $50,000 each. In each of the categories, the first awards are $3,000, second awards $1,500, third awards $1,000, and fourth awards $500. The Intel Best of Category Awards, for the project that exemplifies the best in each scientific category that has also won a first-place in the category, are a $5,000 scholarship and a high-performance computer to the students, $1,000 to their schools, and $1,000 to their science fair. Winners also qualify for all-expense-paid trips to attend the Stockholm International Youth Science Seminar that includes the Nobel Prize Ceremony in Stockholm, Sweden, and the European Union Contest for Young Scientists. Special prizes, worth more than $1.5 million, include scholarships from individual colleges and universities, all-expense-paid trips to scientific and engineering installations or national conventions, summer jobs at research institutes, and laboratory equipment provided by Intel. Many professional organizations award prizes for projects that meet specified criteria.

Duration: The fair is held annually. The Intel Foundation Young Scientist Awards are paid in 8 equal installments. Most other awards are for 1 year.

Number awarded: 1 Gordon E. Moore Award and 2 Intel Foundation Young Scientist Awards are presented each year. The number of cash awards varies; recently, a total of 346 were presented, including 37 first awards, 70 second awards, 106 third awards, and 133 fourth awards. Other prizes include 19 Intel Best of Category Awards, other special awards, regional awards, and scholarships from individual colleges. A total of $4 million in scholarship and prizes is presented each year.

Deadline: The fair is always held in May.

2025 INTEL SCIENCE TALENT SEARCH SCHOLARSHIPS

Society for Science & the Public
Attn: Director of Youth Programs
1719 N Street, N.W.
Washington, DC 20036
Phone: (202) 785-2255; Fax: (202) 785-1243
Email: sts@societyforscience
Web: www.societyforscience.org/sts

Summary: To recognize and reward outstanding high school seniors who are interested in attending college to prepare for a career in mathematics, engineering, or any of the sciences.

Eligibility: Open to high school seniors in the United States and its territories, as well as U.S. citizens attending Department of Defense dependents schools and accredited overseas American and international schools. Applicants must complete an independent research project and submit a written report of up to 20 pages. The project may be in the following fields: animal sciences, behavioral and social sciences, biochemistry, bioinformatics and genomics, chemistry, computer science, earth and planetary science, engineering, environmental science, materials science, mathematics, medicine and health, microbiology, physics and space science, and plant sciences. Based on those reports, 300 students are designated as semifinalists, and from those 40 are chosen as finalists. Selection is based on individual research ability, scientific originality, and creative thinking.

Financial data: Semifinalists and their schools each receive $1,000 awards. Among the finalists, first place is a $100,000 scholarship, second place a $75,000 scholarship, third place a $50,000 scholarship, fourth place a $40,000 scholarship, fifth place a $30,000 scholarship, sixth and seventh places $25,000 scholarships, and eighth through tenth places $20,000 scholarships. In addition, 30 other finalists received at least $7,500 scholarships. The first 10 awards are paid in 8 equal installments.

Duration: The competition is held annually. Scholarships of the first 10 prize winners are for 4 years. The scholarships of the other 30 finalists are for 1 year.

Number awarded: Each year, 300 semifinalists are selected, and from those 40 are designated as finalists. Scholarships for finalists include 1 at $100,000, 1 at $75,000, 1 at $50,000, 3 at $25,000, 4 at $20,000, and 30 at $5,000.

Deadline: November of each year.

2026 INTERNATIONAL COMMUNICATIONS INDUSTRIES FOUNDATION AV SCHOLARSHIPS

Summary: To provide financial assistance to high school seniors and college students who are interested in preparing for a career in the audiovisual (AV) industry.

See Listing #1336.

2027 INTERNATIONAL COUNCIL OF AIR SHOWS FOUNDATION/GENERAL AVIATION MANUFACTURERS ASSOCIATION SCHOLARSHIP

International Council of Air Shows
Attn: ICAS Foundation, Inc.
751 Miller Drive, S.E., Suite F-4
Leesburg, VA 20175
Phone: (703) 779-8510; Fax: (703) 779-8511
Email: scholarships@icasfoundation.org
Web: www.icasfoundation.org/scholarships_ICASF-GAMA.htm

Summary: To provide financial assistance to students interested in working on an undergraduate degree in a field related to aviation.

Eligibility: Open to undergraduates who have completed at least 2 semesters of an aviation-related degree program. Applicants must be preparing for a career in an aspect of the aviation industry (e.g., professional pilot, maintenance/engineering, airport administrator). Along with their application, they must submit a 1-page essay on why they want to receive this scholarship, how the funds will be used, and their aviation career goals. Selection is based on academic record, extracurricular participation in school and community activities, approach toward aviation career goals, and other activities that distinguish the applicants from their peers.

Financial data: The stipend is $2,000.

Duration: 1 year.

Number awarded: 1 each year.

Deadline: December of each year.

2028 INVESTING IN THE FUTURE SCHOLARSHIP

Charles and Agnes Kazarian Eternal Foundation/ChurchArmenia.com
Attn: Educational Scholarships
30 Kennedy Plaza, Second Floor
Providence, RI 02903
Email: info@churcharmenia.com
Web: www.churcharmenia.com/scholarship1.html

Summary: To provide financial assistance to outstanding undergraduate or graduate students of Armenian descent who are preparing for a career in finance, business, medicine, or research.

Eligibility: Open to students of Armenian descent who are accepted to or qualified for highly competitive undergraduate or graduate degree programs focusing on finance, medicine, business, or research. Along with their application, they must submit 1) official academic transcripts; 2) a personal statement (2 to 3 pages) on their desired field of study, a brief history of their upbringing and values, and their goals in terms of future contributions to the Armenian community; 3) documentation of financial need; and 4) up to 3 letters of recommendation.

Financial data: The stipend is $10,000.

Duration: 1 year.

Number awarded: 1 or more each year.

Deadline: Applications may be submitted at any time.

2029 IOWA SCHOLARSHIPS FOR HEALTH CARE CAREERS

Iowa Hospital Association
Attn: Iowa Hospital Education and Research Foundation
100 East Grand Avenue, Suite 100
Des Moines, IA 50309-1835
Phone: (515) 288-1955; Fax: (515) 283-9366
Web: www.ihaonline.org/careers/iherfscholarship/scholarship.shtml

Summary: To provide financial assistance to students in Iowa working on a health care degree and willing to work for an Iowa hospital.

Eligibility: Open to students enrolled in an accredited program leading to licensure or a clinical laboratory degree in designated health care fields. Applicants must be within 2 years of completing their professional education. Nontraditional students are encouraged to apply. Eligible fields of study include clinical laboratory scientist/medical technician, clinical laboratory technician/medical laboratory technician, coding/medical records, nurse anesthetist, nursing (L.P.N., R.N., R.N. to B.S.N.), occupational therapist, pharmacist, physical therapist, physical therapy assistant, radiation therapist, respiratory therapist, surgery technician, or ultrasound technologist.

Financial data: The stipend is $3,000 per year. This is a scholarship/loan program. Recipients are required to repay the assistance with 1 year of work at an Iowa hospital for each year of support received.

Duration: 1 year; may be renewed 1 additional year.

Number awarded: Varies each year; recently, 31 of these scholarships were awarded.

Deadline: March of each year.

2030 IRVING PFLUG SCHOLARSHIP

Institute of Food Technologists
Attn: Scholarship Department
525 West Van Buren, Suite 1000
Chicago, IL 60607
Phone: (312) 782-8424; Fax: (312) 782-8348
Email: info@ift.org
Web: www.ift.org/cms/?pid=1001271

Summary: To provide financial assistance to undergraduates interested in studying food science, food engineering, or applied microbiology.

Eligibility: Open to sophomores, juniors, and seniors working on a bachelor's degree in food science, food engineering, or applied microbiology as it relates to food preservation at an educational institution in the United States or Canada. Applicants must have a GPA of 3.0 or higher. Along with their application, they must submit an essay on their career objectives; a list of awards, honors, and scholarships they have received; a list of extracurricular activities, community service, and leadership experience; and a summary of their past and current work experience and internships. Financial need is not considered in the selection process.

Financial data: The stipend is $1,500 per year.

Duration: 1 year; recipients may reapply if they are members of the Institute of Food Technologists.

Number awarded: 1 each year.

Deadline: January of each year.

2031 ISA EDUCATIONAL FOUNDATION SCHOLARSHIPS

Instrumentation, Systems, and Automation Society
Attn: ISA Educational Foundation
67 Alexander Drive
Research Triangle Park, NC 27709
Phone: (919) 549-8411; Fax: (919) 549-8288
Email: info@isa.org
Web: www.isa.org

Summary: To provide financial assistance to undergraduate and graduate students majoring in fields related to instrumentation, systems, and automation.

Eligibility: Open to full-time undergraduate and graduate students enrolled in a program in instrumentation, systems, automation, or a closely-related field. Applicants must have a GPA of 3.0 or higher. They may be from any country but must be attending an institution in their own country. Applicants in a 2-year program must have completed at least 1 academic semester of 12 hours or its equivalent. Applicants in a 4-year program must be in their sophomore year or higher. Along with their application, they must submit an essay (up to 400 words) on their ambitions and qualifications as an innovator or future leader in a career in instrumentation, systems, or automation; they should describe their career objectives, how the award of this scholarship will help them achieve their objectives, why they want to enter this particular field of engineering, what they have achieved and learned through their studies and activities, and what this indicates about their character and determination. Financial need is not considered in the selection process.

Financial data: Stipends have ranged from $500 to $3,500.

Duration: 1 year; may be renewed.

Number awarded: Varies each year; recently, 8 of these scholarships were awarded: 4 to undergraduates (2 at $500, 1 at $2,500, and 1 at $3,500) and 4 to graduate students (at $2,000 each).

Deadline: February of each year.

2032 ITW SCHOLARSHIPS

Society of Women Engineers
Attn: Scholarship Selection Committee
120 South LaSalle Street, Suite 1515
Chicago, IL 60603-3572
Phone: (312) 596-5223; (877) SWE-INFO; Fax: (312) 644-8557
Email: scholarshipapplication@swe.org
Web: societyofwomenengineers.swe.org

Summary: To provide financial assistance to undergraduate women majoring in designated engineering specialties.

Eligibility: Open to women who are entering their junior year at a 4-year ABET-accredited college or university. Applicants must be majoring in computer science, electrical or mechanical engineering, or polymer science. They must have a GPA of 3.0 or higher. Preference is given to members of groups underrepresented in engineering or computer science. Selection is based on merit. U.S. citizenship is required.

Financial data: The stipend is $2,500.

Duration: 1 year.

Number awarded: 2 each year.
Deadline: February of each year.

2033 J. EDGAR HOOVER FOUNDATION SCHOLARSHIPS

J. Edgar Hoover Foundation
Attn: Chairman
P.O. Box 5914
Hilton Head, SC 29938-5914
Email: mail@jedgarhooverfoundation.org
Web: www.jehooverfoundation.org/scholar/scholar.html

Summary: To provide financial assistance to undergraduate and graduate students working on a degree in law, enforcement studies, or forensic sciences.
Eligibility: Open to students working on or planning to work on an undergraduate or graduate degree in law, enforcement studies, or forensic sciences. Applicants must submit a brief essay on their educational and career plans. Financial need is considered in the selection process.
Financial data: Stipends range from $500 to $1,000.
Duration: 1 year.
Number awarded: Varies each year.
Deadline: March of each year.

2034 J. FIELDING REED SCHOLARSHIP

American Society of Agronomy
Attn: Scholarship Committee
677 South Segoe Road
Madison, WI 53711
Phone: (608) 273-8008; Fax: (608) 273-2021
Email: awards@agronomy.org
Web: www.agronomy.org/awards/award/detail/?a=6

Summary: To provide financial assistance to undergraduate students preparing for a career in soil or plant sciences.
Eligibility: Open to undergraduates who are preparing for a career in the plant or soil sciences. Applicants must have a GPA of 3.0 or higher and be able to document a history of community and campus leadership activities, particularly in agriculture.
Financial data: The stipend is $1,000.
Duration: 1 year.
Number awarded: 1 each year.
Deadline: March of each year.

2035 J. SPARGO AND ASSOCIATES TEACHER'S SCHOLARSHIP

Armed Forces Communications and Electronics Association
Attn: AFCEA Educational Foundation
4400 Fair Lakes Court
Fairfax, VA 22033-3899
Phone: (703) 631-6149; (800) 336-4583, ext. 6149; Fax: (703) 631-4693
Email: scholarship@afcea.org
Web: www.afcea.org

Summary: To provide financial assistance to undergraduate and graduate students who are preparing for a career as a teacher of science and mathematics.
Eligibility: Open to full-time juniors, seniors, and graduate students at accredited colleges and universities in the United States. Applicants must be U.S. citizens preparing for a career as a teacher of science, mathematics, or information technology at a middle or secondary school. They must have a GPA of 3.0 or higher. Financial need is not considered in the selection process.
Financial data: The stipend is $2,500.
Duration: 1 year.
Number awarded: 1 each year.
Deadline: May of each year.

2036 J.A. AND FLOSSIE MAE SMITH SCHOLARSHIP

J.A. and Flossie Mae Smith Scholarship Fund
c/o Raymond D. Taramasco
P.O. Box 1335
Rancho Santa Fe, CA 92067
Phone: (858) 756-4884; Fax: (858) 756-4886

Summary: To provide financial assistance to undergraduate or graduate students interested in majoring in agriculture.
Eligibility: Open to undergraduate or graduate students who are interested in pursuing a full-time academic program with an emphasis on agriculture. Applicants may be planning to attend an accredited college or university in any state. A personal interview is required. Selection is based on academic ability and financial need.
Financial data: The maximum stipend awarded is $2,500 per year. Funds may be paid either to the recipient or to the recipient's school.
Duration: 1 year; may be renewed up to a maximum of 6 years.
Number awarded: 1 or more each year.
Deadline: Deadline not specified.

2037 JACK BRUCE MEMORIAL SCHOLARSHIP

American Council of Engineering Companies of Colorado
Attn: Scholarship Coordinator
800 Grant Street, Suite 100
Denver, CO 80203
Phone: (303) 832-2200; Fax: (303) 832-0400
Email: acec@acec-co.org
Web: www.acec-co.org/education/scholarships.html

Summary: To provide financial assistance to students in Colorado currently working on a bachelor's degree in engineering.
Eligibility: Open to full-time students entering their junior, senior, or fifth year of an ABET-approved engineering program in Colorado. Applicants must be U.S. citizens. Along with their application, they must submit a 500-word essay on "What is the role or responsibility of the consulting engineer relative to shaping and protecting the natural environment?" Selection is based on the essay (25 points), cumulative GPA (28 points), work experience (20 points), a letter of recommendation (17 points), and college activities (10 points).
Financial data: The stipend is $2,000.
Duration: 1 year.
Number awarded: 1 each year.
Deadline: February of each year.

2038 JACK E. BARGER, SR. MEMORIAL NURSING SCHOLARSHIPS

Pennsylvania State Nurses Association
Attn: Nursing Foundation of Pennsylvania
2578 Interstate Drive, Suite 101
Harrisburg, PA 17110
Phone: (717) 692-0542; (888) 707-PSNA; Fax: (717) 692-4540
Email: nfp@panurses.org
Web: www.panurses.org/2008/section.cfm?SID=21&ID=4

Summary: To provide financial assistance to veterans, military personnel, and their dependents who are studying nursing in Pennsylvania.
Eligibility: Open to veterans, active-duty military personnel, and the children and spouses of veterans and active-duty military personnel. Applicants must be residents of Pennsylvania and currently enrolled in an undergraduate professional school of nursing in the state. Recipients are selected by lottery from among the qualified applicants.
Financial data: The stipend is $1,000.
Duration: 1 year.
Number awarded: 6 each year.
Deadline: April of each year.

2039 JAMES BRIDENBAUGH MEMORIAL SCHOLARSHIP

American Floral Endowment
One Horticultural Lane
P.0. Box 945
Edwardsville, IL 62025
Phone: (618) 692-0045; Fax: (618) 692-4045
Email: afe@endowment.org
Web: endowment.org/education/afe

Summary: To provide financial assistance to undergraduate students in horticulture interested in floral design and marketing.
Eligibility: Open to undergraduate students majoring in horticulture. Applicants must be interested in preparing for a career in floral design and marketing of fresh flowers and plants. They must be U.S. or Canadian citizens or permanent residents and have a GPA of 3.0 or higher. Along with their application, they must submit a statement describing their career goals and the academic, work-related, and/or life experiences that support those goals. Financial need is considered in the selection process.
Financial data: The stipend ranges from $500 to $2,000.
Duration: 1 year.
Number awarded: 1 each year.

Deadline: April of each year.

2040 JAMES F. REVILLE SCHOLARSHIP

NYSARC, Inc.
Attn: Scholarship and Awards Committee
393 Delaware Avenue
Delmar, NY 12054
Phone: (518) 439-8311; Fax: (518) 439-1893
Email: info@nysarc.org
Web: www.nysarc.org/family/nysarc-family-scholarships.asp

Summary: To provide financial assistance to college students in New York majoring in a field related to mental retardation.

Eligibility: Open to students enrolled full-time at a college or university in New York. Applicants must be working on a degree in a field related to mental retardation. Along with their application, they must submit brief statements on 1) how they became interested in becoming a professional in a field related to people who have intellectual and other developmental disabilities; 2) their experiences with people who have intellectual and other developmental disabilities; 3) any memberships in organizations concerned with people who have intellectual and other developmental disabilities; and 4) their career plans and how they relate to people who have intellectual and other developmental disabilities. Financial need is not considered in the selection process.

Financial data: The stipend is $1,500 per year.

Duration: 2 years.

Number awarded: 1 each year.

Deadline: January of each year.

2041 JAMES M. AND VIRGINIA M. SMYTH SCHOLARSHIP FUND

Summary: To provide financial assistance to high school seniors, especially those from designated states, who are interested in majoring in selected fields at colleges in any state.

See Listing #1352.

2042 JAMES R. VOGT RADIOCHEMISTRY SCHOLARSHIP

American Nuclear Society
Attn: Scholarship Coordinator
555 North Kensington Avenue
La Grange Park, IL 60526-5592
Phone: (708) 352-6611; (800) 323-3044; Fax: (708) 352-0499
Email: outreach@ans.org
Web: www.ans.org/honors/scholarships

Summary: To provide financial assistance to undergraduate and graduate students who are interested in preparing for a career in nuclear science as related to radiochemistry.

Eligibility: Open to juniors, seniors, and first-year graduate students who are enrolled in or proposing to undertake research in radio-analytical chemistry, analytical chemistry, or analytical applications of nuclear science at an accredited institution in the United States. Applicants must be members of the American Nuclear Society (ANS), but they may be citizens of any country. Selection is based on academic achievement.

Financial data: The stipend is $3,000.

Duration: 1 year; nonrenewable.

Number awarded: 1 each year.

Deadline: January of each year.

2043 JANET CULLEN TANAKA SCHOLARSHIP

Association for Women Geoscientists
Attn: AWG Foundation
12000 North Washington Street, Suite 285
Thornton, CO 80241
Phone: (303) 412-6219; Fax: (303) 253-9220
Email: office@awg.org
Web: www.awg.org/EAS/scholarships.html

Summary: To provide financial assistance to women from any state who are working on an undergraduate degree in geoscience at a college or university in Oregon or Washington.

Eligibility: Open to undergraduate women from any state who are working on a bachelor's degree and committed to preparing for a career or graduate work in the geosciences, including geology, environmental or engineering geology, geochemistry, geophysics, hydrogeology, or hydrology. Applicants must be currently enrolled in a 2- or 4-year college or university in Oregon or Washington and have a GPA of 3.2 or higher. Along with their application, they must submit a 1-page essay summarizing their commitment to a career in the geosciences. Selection is based on potential for professional success, academic achievements, and financial need.

Financial data: The stipend is $1,000. A second-place award of $500 may also be awarded, depending on the availability of funding.

Duration: 1 year.

Number awarded: 1 or 2 each year.

Deadline: November of each year.

2044 JEAN-GUY BELIVEAU, P.E. MATHCOUNTS SCHOLARSHIP

National Society of Professional Engineers
Attn: NSPE Educational Foundation
1420 King Street
Alexandria, VA 22314-2794
Phone: (703) 684-2833; (888) 285-NSPE; Fax: (703) 836-4875
Email: education@nspe.org
Web: www.nspe.org/Students/Scholarships/index.html

Summary: To provide financial assistance to high school seniors who have participated in the MATHCOUNTS program in middle school and are planning to study engineering in college.

Eligibility: Open to graduating high school seniors who participated in the MATHCOUNTS program when they were in middle school and have been accepted into an ABET-accredited engineering program at a 4-year college or university. Applicants must submit brief essays on 1) an experience from their life that they consider significant to their interest in engineering; and 2) how their participation in MATHCOUNTS influenced their decision to study engineering. Selection is based on those essays, GPA and SAT/ACT scores, internship and co-op experience, community involvement, extracurricular activities, 2 faculty recommendations, and honors and awards in high school.

Financial data: The stipend is $3,000; funds are paid directly to the recipient's institution.

Duration: 1 year.

Number awarded: 1 each year.

Deadline: February of each year.

2045 JERE W. THOMPSON, JR. SCHOLARSHIP

Dallas Foundation
Attn: Scholarship Administrator
900 Jackson Street, Suite 705
Dallas, TX 75202
Phone: (214) 741-9898; Fax: (214) 741-9848
Email: scholarships@dallasfoundation.org
Web: www.dallasfoundation.org/scholarship13.aspx?submenu=return

Summary: To provide financial assistance and work experience to students who are majoring in civil engineering at universities in Texas.

Eligibility: Open to students in civil engineering or construction engineering at colleges and universities in Texas; special consideration is given to residents of counties in the service area of the North Texas Tollway Authority: Collin, Dallas, Denton, or Tarrant. At the time of application, students must be full-time sophomores. Finalists may be interviewed. Financial need is considered in the selection process.

Financial data: Stipends range up to $2,000 per semester, beginning in the recipient's junior year; the maximum award is $8,000 over 4 semesters.

Duration: 1 semester; may be renewed for up to 3 additional semesters, provided the recipient remains a full-time student, maintains at least a 2.5 GPA, and submits a grade report within 45 days after the end of each semester.

Number awarded: 1 each year.

Deadline: March of each year.

2046 JIM MURRAY SCHOLARSHIPS

American Public Works Association–Colorado Chapter
c/o Laura A. Kroeger, Scholarship Committee
Urban Drainage and Flood Control District
2480 West 26th Avenue, Suite 156-B
Denver, CO 80211
Phone: (303) 455-6277; Fax: (303) 455-7880
Email: lkroeger@udfcd.org
Web: colorado.apwa.net

Summary: To provide financial assistance to civil engineering undergraduate students in Colorado.

Eligibility: Open to juniors, seniors, and fifth-year undergraduates at colleges and universities in Colorado that have an accredited program in civil engineering. Applicants must have a GPA of 2.5 or higher. Along with their application, they must submit a 300-word essay on an engineering problem over which a local, state, or federal government has jurisdiction, and how they would solve it. Financial need is not considered in the selection process.
Financial data: Stipends are $2,000 or $1,000.
Duration: 1 year.
Number awarded: 3 each year: 1 at $2,000 and 2 at $1,000.
Deadline: March of each year.

2047 JOE J. WELKER MEMORIAL SCHOLARSHIP

Delaware Engineering Society
c/o Stacy Ziegler
Duffield Associates, Inc.
5400 Limestone Road
Wilmington, DE 19808
Phone: (302) 239-6634; Fax: (302) 239-8485
Email: sziegler@duffnet.com
Web: www.desonline.us
Summary: To provide financial assistance to high school seniors in Delaware who are interested in majoring in engineering in college.
Eligibility: Open to graduating high school seniors in Delaware who are residents of the state and interested in majoring in engineering at an ABET-accredited college or university. Applicants must have SAT scores of 600 or higher in mathematics, 500 or higher in critical reading, and 500 or higher in writing (or ACT scores of 29 or higher in mathematics and 25 or higher in English). They must submit an essay (up to 500 words) on their interest in engineering, their major area of study and area of specialization, the occupation they propose to pursue after graduation, their long-term goals, and how they hope to achieve them. Selection is based on the essay, academic record, honors and scholarships, volunteer activities, work experience, and letters of recommendation. Financial need is not required.
Financial data: The stipend ranges from $1,500 to $2,000.
Duration: 1 year; nonrenewable.
Number awarded: Varies each year; recently, 3 of these scholarships were awarded.
Deadline: December of each year.

2048 JOHN AND ALICE EGAN MULTI-YEAR MENTORING SCHOLARSHIP PROGRAM

Daedalian Foundation
Attn: Scholarship Committee
55 Main Circle (Building 676)
P.O. Box 249
Randolph AFB, TX 78148-0249
Phone: (210) 945-2113; Fax: (210) 945-2112
Email: icarus2@daedalians.org
Web: www.daedalians.org/foundation/scholarships.htm
Summary: To provide financial assistance to college students who are participating in a ROTC program and wish to become military pilots.
Eligibility: Open to students who have completed at least the freshman year at an accredited 4-year college or university and have a GPA of 3.0 or higher. Applicants must be participating in an ROTC program and be medically qualified for flight training. They must plan to apply for and be awarded a military pilot training allocation at the appropriate juncture in their ROTC program. Selection is based on intention to prepare for a career as a military pilot, demonstrated moral character and patriotism, scholastic and military standing and aptitude, and physical condition and aptitude for flight. Financial need may also be considered.
Financial data: The stipend is $2,500 per year.
Duration: 1 year; may be renewed up to 2 or 3 additional years, provided the recipient maintains a GPA of 3.0 or higher and is enrolled in an undergraduate program.
Number awarded: Up to 11 each year.
Deadline: July of each year.

2049 JOHN AND MURIEL LANDIS SCHOLARSHIPS

American Nuclear Society
Attn: Scholarship Coordinator
555 North Kensington Avenue
La Grange Park, IL 60526-5592
Phone: (708) 352-6611; (800) 323-3044; Fax: (708) 352-0499
Email: outreach@ans.org
Web: www.ans.org/honors/scholarships
Summary: To provide financial assistance to undergraduate or graduate students who are interested in preparing for a career in nuclear-related fields.
Eligibility: Open to undergraduate and graduate students at colleges or universities located in the United States who are preparing for, or planning to prepare for, a career in nuclear science, nuclear engineering, or a nuclear-related field. Qualified high school seniors are also eligible. Applicants must have greater than average financial need and have experienced circumstances that render them disadvantaged. They must be sponsored by an organization (e.g., plant branch, local section, student section) within the American Nuclear Society (ANS). Along with their application, they must submit an essay on their academic and professional goals, experiences that have affected those goals, and other relevant information. Selection is based on that essay, academic achievement, letters of recommendation, and financial need. Women and members of minority groups are especially urged to apply. U.S. citizenship is not required.
Financial data: The stipend is $5,000, to be used to cover tuition, books, fees, room, and board.
Duration: 1 year; nonrenewable.
Number awarded: Up to 8 each year.
Deadline: January of each year.

2050 JOHN D. LORENZEN AND DEBBIE J. TRANELLO MEMORIAL SCHOLARSHIP FUND

New York State Automotive Aftermarket Association
Attn: Scholarship Funds
442 South Bay Road, Suite A
North Syracuse, NY 13212
Phone: (800) 888-6929
Email: dshea@nysaaa.net
Web: www.nysaaa.com/scholarship.html
Summary: To provide financial assistance to residents of New York who are interested in attending college or vocational school in any state to prepare for a career in the automotive aftermarket.
Eligibility: Open to residents of New York who are 1) high school seniors currently enrolled in a class related to the automotive industry; 2) students enrolled or planning to enroll full-time at an accredited college or university in any state to work on an associate or bachelor's degree; 3) high school graduates or GED recipients currently employed in the automotive aftermarket; or 4) high school graduates or GED recipients recommended by a member of the New York State Automotive Aftermarket Association (NYSAAA). Applicants must be committed to a career in the automotive aftermarket. Along with their application, they must submit a 250-word essay on their career goals, how this scholarship will help them, and why they are considering a career in the automotive aftermarket. Financial need is not considered in the selection process.
Financial data: Stipends are at least $1,000.
Duration: 1 year.
Number awarded: Up to 3 each year.
Deadline: March of each year.

2051 JOHN H. WIECHMAN MEMORIAL SCHOLARSHIP

California Farm Bureau Scholarship Foundation
Attn: Scholarship Foundation
2300 River Plaza Drive
Sacramento, CA 95833
Phone: (916) 561-5520; (800) 698-FARM (within CA); Fax: (916) 561-5699
Email: dlicciardo@cfbf.com
Web: www.cfbf.com/programs/scholar/index.cfm
Summary: To provide financial assistance for college to residents of California who are interested in preparing for a career in agriculture.
Eligibility: Open to students entering or attending a 4-year accredited college or university in California who are majoring or planning to major in an agriculture-related field. Students entering a junior college are not eligible. Applicants must submit an essay on the most important educational or personal experience that has led them to pursue a university education. Selection is based on academic achievement, career goals, extracurricular activities, leadership skills, determination, and commitment to study agriculture.
Financial data: The stipend is $2,250 per year.
Duration: 1 year; recipients may reapply.
Number awarded: 1 each year.
Deadline: February of each year.

2052 JOHN L. TOMASOVIC, SR. SCHOLARSHIP

American Floral Endowment

One Horticultural Lane
P.O. Box 945
Edwardsville, IL 62025
Phone: (618) 692-0045; Fax: (618) 692-4045
Email: afe@endowment.org
Web: endowment.org/education/afe

Summary: To provide financial assistance to undergraduate students in horticulture.

Eligibility: Open to sophomores, juniors, or seniors majoring in horticulture at 4-year colleges and universities. Applicants must be U.S. or Canadian citizens or permanent residents and have a GPA between 3.0 and 3.5. Along with their application, they must submit a statement describing their career goals and the academic, work-related, and/or life experiences that support those goals. Financial need is considered in the selection process.

Financial data: The stipend ranges from $500 to $2,000.

Duration: 1 year.

Number awarded: 1 each year.

Deadline: April of each year.

2053 JOHN O. BEHRENS INSTITUTE FOR LAND INFORMATION (ILI) MEMORIAL SCHOLARSHIP

American Society for Photogrammetry and Remote Sensing
Attn: Scholarship Administrator
5410 Grosvenor Lane, Suite 210
Bethesda, MD 20814-2160
Phone: (301) 493-0290, ext. 101; Fax: (301) 493-0208
Email: scholarships@asprs.org
Web: www.asprs.org/membership/scholar.html

Summary: To provide financial assistance to undergraduate students interested in a program of study to prepare for a career related to land information systems or records.

Eligibility: Open to students planning to enroll or currently enrolled as undergraduates at a college or university in the United States. Applicants must be interested in a program of study to prepare for a career in land information systems or records or in geospatial science or technology. Along with their application, they must submit a 2-page statement describing their plans for continuing studies towards becoming a professional in a field that uses land and/or geospatial information as a key part of its performance. Financial need is not considered in the selection process.

Financial data: The stipend is $1,000. A 1-year student membership in the American Society for Photogrammetry and Remote Sensing (ASPRS) is also provided.

Duration: 1 year.

Number awarded: 1 each year.

Deadline: October of each year.

2054 JOHN P. "PAT" HEALY SCHOLARSHIP

Delaware Higher Education Commission
Carvel State Office Building, Fifth Floor
820 North French Street
Wilmington, DE 19801-3509
Phone: (302) 577-5240; (800) 292-7935; Fax: (302) 577-6765
Email: dhec@doe.k12.de.us
Web: www.doe.k12.de.us/infosuites/students_family/dhec/default.shtml

Summary: To provide financial assistance to high school seniors and college students in Delaware who are interested in majoring in engineering or environmental sciences at a college in the state.

Eligibility: Open to high school seniors and full-time college students in their freshman or sophomore years who are Delaware residents and majoring in either environmental engineering or environmental sciences at a Delaware college. Applicants must submit a 500-word essay on "What would you do to protect the environment?" Selection is based on financial need, academic performance, community and school involvement, and leadership ability.

Financial data: The stipend is $2,000.

Duration: 1 year; automatically renewed for 3 additional years if a GPA of 3.0 or higher is maintained.

Number awarded: 1 or more each year.

Deadline: March of each year.

2055 JOSE F. SILVA MEMORIAL SCHOLARSHIPS

Great Minds in STEM
Attn: HENAAC Scholars
3900 Whiteside Street
Los Angeles, CA 90063
Phone: (323) 262-0997; Fax: (323) 262-0946
Email: kbbarrera@greatmindsinstem.org
Web: www.greatmindsinstem.org/henaac/scholars

Summary: To provide financial assistance to Hispanic undergraduate students from any state who are enrolled at universities in Texas or California and majoring in fields of science, technology, engineering, or mathematics (STEM).

Eligibility: Open to Hispanic undergraduate students from any state who are majoring in a field of STEM at a college or university in California or Texas. Applicants must be of Hispanic origin and/or must significantly participate in and promote organizations and activities in the Hispanic community. They must have a GPA of 3.0 or higher. Along with their application, they must submit a 700-word essay on a topic that changes annually; recently, students were asked to write on how they see their academic major contributing to global efforts and technology and how they, in their field of study, will contribute to global progress as well as actively contribute to their local communities. Selection is based on leadership through academic achievements and campus and community activities; financial need is not considered. U.S. citizenship is required.

Financial data: Stipends range from $500 to $5,000.

Duration: 1 year; recipients may reapply.

Number awarded: Varies each year; recently, 2 of these scholarships were awarded.

Deadline: April of each year.

2056 JOSEPH A. HOLMES SAFETY ASSOCIATION SCHOLARSHIP PROGRAM

Joseph A. Holmes Safety Association
P.O. Box 9375
Arlington, VA 22219
Phone: (703) 235-0249; Fax: (202) 693-9571
Email: mail@holmessafety.org
Web: holmessafety.org/scholarship

Summary: To provide financial assistance to undergraduate and graduate students preparing for a career in a field related to mine safety.

Eligibility: Open to graduating high school seniors, undergraduates, and graduate students. Applicants must be entering or enrolled at an accredited college or university in a degree program in mine safety, occupational or industrial health and safety, industrial hygiene, safety management, or other safety-related programs. Along with their application, they must submit a transcript, documentation of financial need, an essay of 100 to 300 words on why they are working on a degree in mining or in a mine safety and health-related field, and a list of extracurricular activities. U.S. citizenship or permanent resident status is required.

Financial data: A stipend is awarded (amount not specified).

Duration: 1 year.

Number awarded: 1 each year.

Deadline: January of each year.

2057 JOSEPH A. LEVENDUSKY MEMORIAL SCHOLARSHIP

Engineers' Society of Western Pennsylvania
Attn: Scholarship Committee
Pittsburgh Engineers' Building
337 Fourth Avenue
Pittsburgh, PA 15222
Phone: (412) 261-0710; Fax: (412) 261-1606
Email: eswp@eswp.com
Web: www.eswp.com/water/student_scholarships.htm

Summary: To provide financial assistance to undergraduate students majoring in chemical or mechanical engineering and committed to a career in the field of water technology.

Eligibility: Open to undergraduate students majoring in chemical or mechanical engineering who are preparing for a career in water technology. They must have been employed in the field of water technology (excluding environmental wastewater, water pollution control, and water resource management) for at least 1 year. Along with their application, they must submit a 250-word essay on the occupation they want to prepare for by attending college and the reasons they have decided on the field of water technology. Financial need is considered in the selection process.

Financial data: The stipend is $7,000.

Duration: 1 year.

Number awarded: 1 each year.

Deadline: August of each year.

2058 JOSEPH A. MCALINDEN DIVERS' SCHOLARSHIP

Navy-Marine Corps Relief Society
Attn: Education Division
875 North Randolph Street, Suite 225
Arlington, VA 22203-1757
Phone: (703) 696-4960; Fax: (703) 696-0144
Email: education@nmcrs.org
Web: www.nmcrs.org/education.html

Summary: To provide financial assistance to current and former Navy and Marine Corps divers and their families who are interested in working on an undergraduate or graduate degree in a field related to ocean agriculture.

Eligibility: Open to Navy and Marine Corps active-duty and retired divers and members of their families. Applicants must be enrolled full-time in an undergraduate or graduate program in oceanography, ocean agriculture, aquaculture, or a related field; they may also be engaged in advanced diver training, certification, or recertification. Financial need is considered in the selection process.

Financial data: The stipend ranges from $500 to $3,000, depending on the need of the recipient.

Duration: 1 year.

Number awarded: 1 or more each year.

Deadline: Applications may be submitted at any time.

2059 JOSEPH P. AND HELEN T. CRIBBINS SCHOLARSHIP

Association of the United States Army
Attn: National Secretary
2425 Wilson Boulevard
Arlington, VA 22201
Phone: (703) 841-4300, ext. 655; (800) 336-4570, ext. 655
Email: ausa-info@ausa.org
Web: www3.ausa.org/webpub/depthome.nsf/byid/kcat-6fcq8s

Summary: To provide financial assistance to active-duty and honorably-discharged soldiers interested in studying engineering in college.

Eligibility: Open to 1) soldiers currently serving in the active Army, Army Reserve, or Army National Guard of any rank; and 2) honorably-discharged soldiers from any component of the total Army. Applicants must have been accepted at an accredited college or university to work on a degree in engineering or a related field (e.g., computer science, biotechnology). Along with their application, they must submit a 1-page autobiography, 2 letters of recommendation, and a transcript of high school or college grades (depending on which they are currently attending). Selection is based on academic merit and personal achievement. Financial need is not normally a selection criterion but in some cases of extreme need it may be used as a factor; the lack of financial need, however, is never a cause for nonselection.

Financial data: The stipend is $2,000; funds are sent directly to the recipient's college or university.

Duration: 1 year.

Number awarded: 1 or more each year.

Deadline: June of each year.

2060 JOSHUA ESCH MITCHELL AVIATION SCHOLARSHIP

Grand Rapids Community Foundation
Attn: Education Program Officer
185 Oakes Street, S.W.
Grand Rapids, MI 49503-4008
Phone: (616) 454-1751, ext. 103; Fax: (616) 454-6455
Email: rbishop@grfoundation.org
Web: www.grfoundation.org/scholarships

Summary: To provide financial assistance to students working on a degree in a field related to aviation at a college in any state.

Eligibility: Open to U.S. citizens who are enrolled full- or part-time as sophomores or higher at a college or university in any state that provides an accredited flight science program. Applicants must have a current pilot's certificate and be studying a related field with an emphasis on aviation management, aviation safety, or general aviation. They must have a GPA of 2.75 or higher and be able to demonstrate financial need. A letter of recommendation from a professional in the aviation field is required.

Financial data: The stipend depends on the need of the recipient and the availability of funds, but ranges from $500 to $5,000 and averages $1,000. Funds are paid directly to the recipient's institution.

Duration: 1 year.

Number awarded: 1 each year.

Deadline: March of each year.

2061 J.R. HAINES MEMORIAL SCHOLARSHIP

Cumberland Valley Volunteer Firemen's Association
Attn: Home Office Manager
11018 Clinton Street
Hagerstown, MD 21740-7701
Phone: (301) 582-2345
Email: info@respondersafety.com
Web: cvvfa.org/scholarship.html

Summary: To provide financial assistance to residents of designated eastern states who are interested in working on a degree in fire science at a school in any state.

Eligibility: Open to residents of Delaware, Maryland, Pennsylvania, Virginia, and West Virginia. Applicants must be enrolled or planning to enroll at a 2- or 4-year accredited college or university in any state to work on a degree in fire science, including fire, fire investigation, and related subjects. Along with their application, they must submit a 250-word essay on why they are interested in a fire science–related career. Financial need is not considered in the selection process.

Financial data: The stipend is $1,000 per year.

Duration: 1 year.

Number awarded: 1 each year.

Deadline: February of each year.

2062 JUDY KNOX SCHOLARSHIP

North Carolina Nurses Association
Attn: North Carolina Foundation for Nursing
103 Enterprise Street
P.O. Box 12025
Raleigh, NC 27605-2025
Phone: (919) 821-4250; (800) 626-2153; Fax: (919) 829-5807
Email: rns@ncnurses.org
Web: www.ncnurses.org/ncfn.asp

Summary: To provide financial assistance to registered nurses in North Carolina who are interested in working on a bachelor's or master's degree.

Eligibility: Open to registered nurses in North Carolina who are working part-time on a bachelor's or master's degree at a school in the state. Applicants must have been North Carolina residents for at least 12 months prior to application and have a cumulative GPA of 3.0 or higher. Along with their application, they must submit a 500-word essay on their reasons for pursuing additional education and for doing so on a part-time basis. Selection is based on that essay (25 points), GPA (15 points), professional involvement (20 points), community involvement (5 points), honors (15 points), certifications (15 points), and letters of reference (5 points).

Financial data: The stipend is $1,000.

Duration: 1 year.

Number awarded: 1 or more each year.

Deadline: May of each year.

2063 JULIE EARLE SCHOLARSHIP

Oncology Nursing Society
Attn: ONS Foundation
125 Enterprise Drive
Pittsburgh, PA 15275-1214
Phone: (412) 859-6100; (866) 257-4ONS; Fax: (412) 859-6163
Email: foundation@ons.org
Web: www.ons.org/Awards/FoundationAwards/Bachelors

Summary: To provide financial assistance to nurses who are currently employed in radiation oncology and are interested in working on a bachelor's degree.

Eligibility: Open to nurses who already have a license to practice as a registered nurse (R.N.) and are accepted to or currently enrolled in a bachelor's degree program at an NLN- or CCNE-accredited school of nursing. Applicants must be currently working in radiation oncology. Along with their application, they must submit 1) an essay of 250 words or less on their current role in caring for persons with cancer; and 2) a statement of their professional goals and the relationship of those goals to the advancement of oncology nursing. Financial need is not considered in the selection process.

Financial data: The stipend is $2,000.

Duration: 1 year; nonrenewable.

Number awarded: 1 each year.

Deadline: January of each year.

2064 JUNIOR SCIENCE AND HUMANITIES SYMPOSIA SCHOLARSHIPS

Academy of Applied Science
Attn: JSHS National Office
24 Warren Street
Concord, NH 03301
Phone: (603) 228-4520; Fax: (603) 228-4730
Email: cousens@jshs.org
Web: www.jshs.org

Summary: To recognize and reward, with college scholarships, outstanding participants in the Army, Navy, and Air Force Junior Science and Humanities Symposia (JSHS).

Eligibility: Open to U.S. citizens and permanent residents enrolled in grades 9–12 at public, private, or home schools who have completed an original research investigation in a field of science, technology, engineering, or mathematics (STEM). Investigations reporting on experimental, field, observational, or applied research are eligible. Students present their findings at a regional symposium, held on a university campus in their area. At each regional symposium, selected paper presenters are chosen to receive scholarships. From each of the 48 regional symposia, 5 students are selected to attend the national JSHS, where 1 of them presents his or her research paper in competition for further awards.

Financial data: At each regional symposium, 5 finalists receive all-expense-paid trips to the national symposium, the first and second place winners are invited to present their research investigation at the national symposium, and scholarships of $2,000, $1,500, and $1,000, are awarded. In the national competition, first-place finalists receive $12,000 scholarships, second-place finalists receive $8,000 scholarships, and third-place finalists receive $4,000 scholarships (all national scholarships are in addition to the regional scholarships). Top finalists are also awarded an all-expense-paid trip to the International Youth Science Forum, held in London. The outstanding teacher in each region receives a $500 award.

Duration: This competition is held annually. National scholarships are paid over a period of 4 years, provided the recipients enroll full-time and maintain a GPA of at least 3.0.

Number awarded: Scholarships are awarded to 3 regional winners in each of the 48 regional symposia, to 6 first-place finalists in the national symposium, to 6 second-place national finalists, and to 6 third-place national finalists. Teacher awards are presented to 48 teachers, 1 in each of the regions.

Deadline: April of each year.

2065 KAISER PERMANENTE DENTAL ASSISTANT SCHOLARSHIP

Oregon Student Assistance Commission
Attn: Grants and Scholarships Division
1500 Valley River Drive, Suite 100
Eugene, OR 97401-2146
Phone: (541) 687-7395; (800) 452-8807, ext. 7395; Fax: (541) 687-7414; TDD: (800) 735-2900
Email: awardinfo@osac.state.or.us
Web: www.osac.state.or.us/osac_programs.html

Summary: To provide financial assistance to residents of Oregon or Washington who are enrolled or planning to enroll in a dental assistant program at designated colleges in Oregon.

Eligibility: Open to residents of Oregon or Washington who are enrolled or planning to enroll at Blue Mountain Community College (Pendleton), Central Oregon Community College (Bend), Chemeketa Community College (Salem), Lane Community College (Eugene), Linn-Benton Community College (Albany), Portland Community College (Portland), or Concorde Career Institute (Portland). Applicants must be majoring or planning to major in dental assisting.

Financial data: A stipend is awarded (amount not specified).

Duration: 1 year; nonrenewable.

Number awarded: 1 or more each year.

Deadline: February of each year.

2066 KAISER PERMANENTE DENTAL HYGIENIST SCHOLARSHIP

Oregon Student Assistance Commission
Attn: Grants and Scholarships Division
1500 Valley River Drive, Suite 100
Eugene, OR 97401-2146
Phone: (541) 687-7395; (800) 452-8807, ext. 7395; Fax: (541) 687-7414; TDD: (800) 735-2900
Email: awardinfo@osac.state.or.us
Web: www.osac.state.or.us/osac_programs.html

Summary: To provide financial assistance to residents of Oregon or Washington who are enrolled or planning to enroll in a dental hygiene program at designated colleges.

Eligibility: Open to residents of Oregon or Washington who are enrolled or planning to enroll at Lane Community College, Mt. Hood Community College, Portland Community College, Oregon Institute of Technology, Pacific University, or Clark College. Applicants must be majoring or planning to major in dental hygiene.

Financial data: A stipend is awarded (amount not specified).

Duration: 1 year; nonrenewable.

Number awarded: 1 or more each year.

Deadline: February of each year.

2067 KANSAS CITY ASSOCIATED EQUIPMENT DISTRIBUTORS SCHOLARSHIPS

Kansas City Associated Equipment Distributors
638 West 39th Street
P.O. Box 419264
Kansas City, MO 64141
Phone: (816) 561-5323

Summary: To provide financial assistance to students working on an associate degree or certification in diesel mechanics or large equipment repair.

Eligibility: Open to full-time students currently working on an associate degree or certification in diesel mechanics or large equipment repair. Applicants must have a high school GPA of 2.5 or higher or a GED minimum score of 260. Along with their application, they must submit an essay of 750 to 1,000 words in which they explain why they feel they should receive this scholarship and how they would use it if awarded. Selection is based on that essay (30%), interest in a career in diesel mechanics or heavy equipment repair (25%), attendance (15%), high school GPA (15%), and involvement and activities (15%).

Financial data: The stipend is $1,000 per year.

Duration: 1 year; may be renewed for 1 additional year, provided the recipient maintains a GPA of 3.0 or higher.

Number awarded: 4 each year.

Deadline: April of each year.

2068 KANSAS HOSPITAL EDUCATION AND RESEARCH FOUNDATION SCHOLARSHIPS

Kansas Hospital Association
Attn: Kansas Hospital Education and Research Foundation
215 S.E. Eighth Avenue
Topeka, KS 66603-3906
Phone: (785) 233-7436; Fax: (795) 233-6955
Web: www.kha-net.org

Summary: To provide financial assistance to employees of Kansas hospitals and other students in Kansas who are enrolled in a course of study leading to a certificate or degree in a health care program.

Eligibility: Open to students enrolled or planning to enroll full- or part-time at an area technical school, 2-year college, or 4-year college or university in Kansas. Applicants must be 1) employees of Kansas hospitals working on a certificate, degree, or credential in an allied health or nursing program that is accredited by its respective governing body; 2) employees of Kansas hospitals working on a master's or doctoral degree in a field of health care; 3) future nursing or allied health education faculty members working on a master's degree or certification; 4) undergraduate or graduate students working on a health care human resources degree; or 5) juniors, seniors, or graduate students working on a degree in health care administration. Priority is given to professions and geographic areas experiencing shortages in Kansas, applicants furthering their knowledge base in health care by working toward a degree or certificate not currently held, students working on a degree to enable them to teach in health care, applicants demonstrating leadership on a project or institutional level, and applicants committed to pursuing their health care career in Kansas.

Financial data: Stipends are $500 for undergraduate hospital employees, $1,000 for graduate hospital employees, $1,000 for students preparing to become a faculty member, $500 for health care human resources students, and $500 for health care administration students.

Duration: 1 year.

Number awarded: 16 each year: 6 for undergraduate and graduate students in fields of health care, 3 for students working on a master's degree or a final certification to enable them to teach in a health care field, 1 for a student working

on a degree in human resources in health care, and 6 for students working on a degree in health care administration.
Deadline: February of each year.

2069 KANSAS LEGION AUXILIARY L.P.N. SCHOLARSHIPS

American Legion Auxiliary
Department of Kansas
1314 S.W. Topeka Boulevard
Topeka, KS 66612-1886
Phone: (785) 232-1396; Fax: (785) 232-1008
Email: alakansas@sbcglobal.net
Web: www.kslegionaux.org/edcaschol.html

Summary: To provide financial assistance to veterans' dependents from Kansas who are attending a college or university in any state to prepare for a career as a Licensed Practical Nurse (L.P.N.).
Eligibility: Open to the children, spouses, and unremarried widows of veterans who are entering college for the first time. Applicants must be residents of Kansas attending a school in any state that offers certification as an L.P.N. Financial need is considered in the selection process.
Financial data: A stipend is awarded (amount not specified).
Duration: 1 year.
Number awarded: 1 or more each year.
Deadline: March of each year.

2070 KANSAS NURSING SERVICE SCHOLARSHIPS

Kansas Board of Regents
Attn: Student Financial Assistance
1000 S.W. Jackson Street, Suite 520
Topeka, KS 66612-1368
Phone: (785) 296-3517; Fax: (785) 296-0983
Email: dlindeman@ksbor.org
Web: www.kansasregents.org/financial_aid/nursing.html

Summary: To provide financial assistance to Kansas residents who are interested in preparing for a nursing career.
Eligibility: Open to students in Kansas who are committed to practicing nursing (L.P.N. or R.N.) in the state. Applicants must be accepted at a Kansas nursing program (pre-nursing students are ineligible). They must locate a sponsor (defined as a licensed adult care home, psychiatric hospital, medical care facility, home health agency, local health department, or state agency that employs L.P.N.s or R.N.s) that is willing to provide up to half of the scholarship and to provide full-time employment to the recipient after licensure. Financial need is considered if there are more applicants than available funding.
Financial data: Stipends are $2,500 per year for students in L.P.N. programs or $3,500 per year for students in R.N. (associate or bachelor's degree) programs. Sponsors pay from $1,000 to one half of the scholarship and the State of Kansas pays the remaining amount. This is a scholarship/loan program; recipients must work for the sponsor the equivalent of full-time for 1 year for each year of scholarship support received. If the recipient changes majors or decides not to work for the sponsor as a nurse, the scholarship becomes a loan, with interest at 5% above the federal PLUS loan rate.
Duration: 1 year; may be renewed.
Number awarded: Up to 50 for L.P.N. students; up to 200 for R.N. students, of which 100 are reserved for applicants whose sponsors are located in rural counties.
Deadline: April of each year.

2071 KAREN HAUSCHILD FRIDAY SCHOLARSHIP

American Meteorological Society
Attn: Fellowship/Scholarship Program
45 Beacon Street
Boston, MA 02108-3693
Phone: (617) 227-2426, ext. 246; Fax: (617) 742-8718
Email: scholar@ametsoc.org
Web: www.ametsoc.org

Summary: To provide financial assistance to female undergraduates majoring in meteorology or an aspect of atmospheric sciences.
Eligibility: Open to full-time female students entering their final year of undergraduate study and majoring in meteorology or an aspect of the atmospheric or related oceanic and hydrologic sciences. Applicants must intend to make atmospheric or related sciences their career. They must be U.S. citizens or permanent residents enrolled at a U.S. institution and have a cumulative GPA of 3.25 or higher. Along with their application, they must submit 200-word essays on 1) their most important achievements that qualify them for this scholarship; and 2) their career goals in the atmospheric or related oceanic or hydrologic fields. Financial need is considered in the selection process.
Financial data: The stipend is $2,500.
Duration: 1 year.
Number awarded: 1 each year.
Deadline: February of each year.

2072 KATE WARDER MEMORIAL SCHOLARSHIP

New Mexico Engineering Foundation
Attn: Scholarship Chair
P.O. Box 3828
Albuquerque, NM 87190-3828
Phone: (505) 615-1800
Email: info@nmef.net
Web: www.nmef.net/?section=scholarship

Summary: To provide financial assistance to residents of New Mexico majoring in engineering at designated universities in the state.
Eligibility: Open to residents of New Mexico enrolled as juniors or seniors in the engineering program at the University of New Mexico, New Mexico State University, or New Mexico Institute of Mining and Technology. Applicants must have a GPA of 3.0 or higher. They must be a member of the student chapter of their respective engineering society. Along with their application, they must submit a 1-page paper outlining their goals in engineering. Selection is based on academic achievement, participation in extracurricular activities, and financial need.
Financial data: The stipend is $1,000.
Duration: 1 year.
Number awarded: 2 each year.
Deadline: February of each year.

2073 KATHARINE M. GROSSCUP SCHOLARSHIP

Garden Club of America
Attn: Scholarship Committee
14 East 60th Street, Third Floor
New York, NY 10022-1006
Phone: (212) 753-8287; Fax: (212) 753-0134
Email: scholarships@gcamerica.org
Web: www.gcamerica.org/scholarship/grosscup.html

Summary: To provide financial assistance to undergraduate and graduate students working on a degree in horticulture or other field related to gardening.
Eligibility: Open to college sophomore, juniors, seniors, and master's degree students interested in working on a degree in horticulture or other subjects related to the field of gardening. Applicants must have a GPA of 3.0 or higher. Preference is given to students from Ohio, Pennsylvania, West Virginia, Michigan, Kentucky, and Indiana. A personal interview is required.
Financial data: The stipend is $3,000.
Duration: 1 year.
Number awarded: Several each year.
Deadline: January of each year.

2074 KATHERINE H. DILLEY SCHOLARSHIP FUND

Daughters of the American Revolution–Arizona State Society
c/o Nancy Holcombe, Scholarship Chair
14091 South Palo Verde Trail
Arizona City, AZ 85223
Email: ranaholc@netzero.net
Web: www.rootsweb.ancestry.com/~azsodar/scholarships.html

Summary: To provide financial assistance to residents of Arizona interested in studying physical or occupational therapy at a college in any state.
Eligibility: Open to residents of Arizona who are graduating high school seniors or current college students. Applicants must be attending or planning to attend a college or university in any state to work on a degree in occupational or physical therapy. Along with their application, they must submit 1) a letter describing their interests, goals, and extracurricular activities; 2) an explanation of how they would like to use the scholarship money; 3) a statement of why they are majoring in their field; 4) letters of recommendation; and 5) documentation of financial need.
Financial data: A stipend is awarded (amount not specified). Funds are paid directly to the recipient's educational institution.
Duration: 1 year; recipients may reapply.
Number awarded: 1 each year.
Deadline: January of each year.

2075 KATHY WELTER MEMORIAL SCHOLARSHIP

Wisconsin Paralyzed Veterans of America
Attn: Scholarship Committee
2311 South 108th Street
West Allis, WI 53227-1901
Phone: (414) 328-8910; (800) 875-WPVA; Fax: (414) 328-8948
Email: info@wisconsinpva.org
Web: www.wisconsinpva.org/scholarships.html

Summary: To provide financial assistance to nursing students in Wisconsin who are preparing for a career in a spinal cord injury unit or rehabilitation facility.

Eligibility: Open to 1) students enrolled in the final year of an NLN-accredited nursing program in Wisconsin; and 2) nurses (licensed practical nurses or certified nurse assistants) who have at least 2 years' employment on a spinal cord injury center or floor and are working on an R.N. degree. Applicants must be willing to seek employment in a spinal cord injury unit or rehabilitation facility after graduation. They must be able to demonstrate financial need.

Financial data: The stipend is $1,900.

Duration: 1 year.

Number awarded: 1 or 2 each year.

Deadline: March of each year.

2076 KATINA JOHN MALTA SCHOLARSHIPS

Summary: To provide financial assistance to high school seniors and current undergraduates who are of the Eastern Orthodox faith and plan to study the sciences, business, or the arts.

See Listing #1377.

2077 KELLIE CANNON MEMORIAL SCHOLARSHIP

American Council of the Blind
Attn: Coordinator, Scholarship Program
2200 Wilson Boulevard, Suite 650
Arlington, VA 22201
Phone: (202) 467-5081; (800) 424-8666; Fax: (703) 465-5085
Email: info@acb.org
Web: www.acb.org

Summary: To provide financial assistance to students who are blind and interested in preparing for a career in the computer field.

Eligibility: Open to high school seniors, high school graduates, and college students who are blind and interested in majoring in computer information systems or data processing. Applicants must submit verification of legal blindness in both eyes; SAT or ACT scores; information on extracurricular activities (including membership in the American Council of the Blind); employment record; and an autobiographical sketch that includes their personal goals, strengths, weaknesses, hobbies, honors, achievements, and reasons for choice of field or courses of study. A cumulative GPA of 3.3 or higher is generally required. Financial need is not considered in the selection process, but the severity of the applicant's visual impairment and his/her study methods are taken into account.

Financial data: The stipend is $1,000. In addition, the winner receives a Kurzweil-1000 Reading System.

Duration: 1 year.

Number awarded: 1 each year.

Deadline: February of each year.

2078 KENTUCKY ASSOCIATION OF PROFESSIONAL SURVEYORS SCHOLARSHIPS

Kentucky Association of Professional Surveyors
Attn: Scholarship Committee
124 Walnut Street
Frankfort, KY 40601
Phone: (502) 695-2349; (800) 866-3029; Fax: (502) 695-2667
Web: www.kapsl.com

Summary: To provide financial assistance to surveying and engineering students from Kentucky.

Eligibility: Open to students working on a degree in surveying, engineering, or related program to prepare for a career as a land surveyor. Preference is given, in order, to members of the Kentucky Association of Professional Surveyors (KAPS), immediate family of KAPS members, residents of the Capitol Chapter area, and residents of Kentucky. Residents of other areas and states and nonmembers of KAPS are considered in cases of financial need and hardship.

Financial data: The stipend is $2,000.

Duration: 1 year.

Number awarded: 2 each year.

Deadline: November of each year.

2079 KENTUCKY NURSING INCENTIVE SCHOLARSHIP FUND

Kentucky Board of Nursing
Attn: Nursing Incentive Scholarship Fund
312 Whittington Parkway, Suite 300
Louisville, KY 40222-5172
Phone: (502) 429-7180; (800) 305-2042, ext. 7180; Fax: (502) 429-7011
Web: kbn.ky.gov/education/nisf

Summary: To provide financial assistance to residents of Kentucky interested in preparing for a career as a nurse and working in the state.

Eligibility: Open to Kentucky residents who will be attending approved prelicensure nursing programs (registered nurse or practical nurse) or graduate nursing programs in any state. Applicants must be interested in working as a nurse in Kentucky following graduation. Preference is given to applicants with financial need, licensed practical nurses pursuing registered nursing education, and registered nurses pursuing graduate nursing education.

Financial data: The stipend is $3,000 per year. This is a scholarship/loan program. Recipients must work as a nurse in Kentucky for 1 year for each academic year funded. If a recipient does not complete the nursing program within the specified time period, or does not complete the required employment, then the recipient is required to repay any monies awarded plus accrued interest at 8%.

Duration: 1 year; may be renewed if the recipient maintains normal academic progress (15 credit hours per year for prelicensure and B.S.N. students; 9 credit hours per year for graduate nursing students).

Number awarded: Varies each year.

Deadline: May of each year.

2080 KENTUCKY TURFGRASS COUNCIL COLLEGE SCHOLARSHIPS

Kentucky Turfgrass Council
c/o David Williams, Executive Secretary
P.O. Box 701
Richmond, KY 40476-0701
Phone: (859) 484-3537; Fax: (859) 484-3537
Email: ktc@bellsouth.net
Web: www.uky.edu/Agriculture/ukturf/ktc_files/educscholarship.htm

Summary: To provide financial assistance to students from any state majoring in turfgrass science at colleges and universities in Kentucky.

Eligibility: Open to students from any state who are enrolled full-time at Kentucky universities and majoring in turfgrass science or horticulture. Applicants must submit 2 letters of recommendation, an official copy of their university transcripts, a copy of their resume, and 2 paragraphs on 1) their plans after graduation; and 2) why they believe they deserve this scholarship. All qualified candidates are interviewed.

Financial data: A stipend is awarded (amount not specified).

Duration: 1 year.

Number awarded: Varies each year; recently, 5 of these scholarships were awarded.

Deadline: September of each year.

2081 KILBOURN-SAWYER MEMORIAL SCHOLARSHIP

Vermont Student Assistance Corporation
Attn: Scholarship Programs
10 East Allen Street
P.O. Box 2000
Winooski, VT 05404-2601
Phone: (802) 654-3798; (888) 253-4819; Fax: (802) 654-3765; TDD: (800) 281-3341 (within VT)
Email: info@vsac.org
Web: services.vsac.org/wps/wcm/connect/vsac/VSAC

Summary: To provide financial assistance to high school seniors in Vermont who are interested in working on a degree in construction or engineering at a college or university in any state.

Eligibility: Open to the residents of Vermont who are seniors in high school. Applicants must be planning to enroll at a 2- or 4-year college or university in any state and work on a degree in engineering or construction. Along with their application, they must submit 1) a 100-word essay on their interest in and commitment to pursuing their chosen career or vocation; and 2) a 250-word essay on their short- and long-term academic, educational, career, vocational, and/or employment goals. Selection is based on those essays, letters of recommendation, academic achievement, and financial need.

Financial data: The stipend is $2,000.

Duration: 1 year; nonrenewable.

Number awarded: 1 each year.

Deadline: March of each year.

2082 KJ HENDERSHOTT MEMORIAL/CHELAN FRUIT SCHOLARSHIP

Washington Apple Education Foundation
Attn: Scholarship Committee
2900 Euclid Avenue
Wenatchee, WA 98801
Phone: (509) 663-7713; Fax: (509) 663-7469
Email: waef@waef.org
Web: www.waef.org/index.php?page_id=238

Summary: To provide financial assistance to residents of Washington who are interested in attending college in any state to prepare for a career in agribusiness.

Eligibility: Open to residents of Washington who are enrolled as juniors or seniors at a college or university in any state. Applicants must be preparing for a career directly related to agribusiness. Along with their application, they must submit an official transcript, their SAT or ACT scores, 2 letters of reference, and an essay on an assigned topic. Financial need is also considered in the selection process.

Financial data: The stipend is $1,000. The money may be used to pay for tuition, room, board, books, educational supplies, and miscellaneous institutional fees.

Duration: 1 year; recipients may reapply.

Number awarded: 1 each year.

Deadline: February of each year.

2083 KLUSSENDORF/MCKOWN SCHOLARSHIPS

National Dairy Shrine
Attn: Executive Director
P.O. Box 1
Maribel, WI 54227
Phone: (920) 863-6333; Fax: (920) 863-8328
Email: info@dairyshrine.org
Web: www.dairyshrine.org/scholarships.php

Summary: To provide financial assistance to college students majoring in dairy science or dairy business at a college or university in the United States or Canada.

Eligibility: Open to students who are completing their first, second, or third year at a 2- or 4-year college or university in the United States or Canada. Applicants must be majoring in dairy science, animal science, agribusiness, or other field that will help prepare them for a career in the dairy industry. They must submit essays on their dairy cattle experiences; their dairy-related participation in 4-H, FFA, judging, breed association, and other activities; and why they want to be part of the U.S. or Canadian dairy industry's future. Financial need is not considered in the selection process.

Financial data: The stipend is $2,000.

Duration: 1 year.

Number awarded: 6 each year.

Deadline: April of each year.

2084 L. PHIL WICKER SCHOLARSHIP

Summary: To provide financial assistance to licensed radio amateurs, especially those from designated states, who are interested in working on an undergraduate or graduate degree, preferably in electronics or communications.

See Listing #1387.

2085 LANDSCAPE FORMS DESIGN FOR PEOPLE SCHOLARSHIP

Summary: To provide financial assistance to undergraduate landscape architecture students who demonstrate interest in design of public spaces.

See Listing #1391.

2086 LAURENCE R. FOSTER MEMORIAL UNDERGRADUATE SCHOLARSHIPS

Oregon Student Assistance Commission
Attn: Grants and Scholarships Division
1500 Valley River Drive, Suite 100
Eugene, OR 97401-2146
Phone: (541) 687-7395; (800) 452-8807, ext. 7395; Fax: (541) 687-7414; TDD: (800) 735-2900
Email: awardinfo@osac.state.or.us
Web: www.osac.state.or.us/osac_programs.html

Summary: To provide financial assistance to undergraduate students from Oregon who are interested in enrolling at a school in any state to prepare for a public health career.

Eligibility: Open to residents of Oregon who are enrolled at least half-time at a 4-year college or university in any state to prepare for a career in public health (not private practice). Applicants must be entering the junior or senior year of a health program, including nursing, medical technology, and physician assistant. Preference is given to applicants from diverse environments. Along with their application, they must submit brief essays on 1) what public health means to them; 2) the public health aspect they intend to practice and the health and population issues impacted by that aspect; and 3) their experience living or working in diverse environments.

Financial data: Stipend amounts vary; recently, they were at least $4,167.

Duration: 1 year.

Number awarded: Varies each year; recently, 6 undergraduate and graduate scholarships were awarded.

Deadline: February of each year.

2087 LAWRENCE E. AND THELMA J. NORRIE MEMORIAL SCHOLARSHIP

Foundation for Amateur Radio, Inc.
Attn: Scholarship Committee
P.O. Box 911
Columbia, MD 21044-0911
Phone: (410) 552-2652; Fax: (410) 981-5146
Email: dave.prestel@gmail.com
Web: www.farweb.org/scholarships

Summary: To provide funding to licensed radio amateurs who are interested in working on an undergraduate or graduate degree in engineering or the sciences.

Eligibility: Open to licensed radio amateurs who are currently enrolled full-time as college juniors, seniors, or graduate students. Applicants may be working on a degree in science or engineering. They must have a GPA of 3.0 or higher. Financial need is considered in the selection process.

Financial data: The stipend is $2,500.

Duration: 1 year.

Number awarded: 1 each year.

Deadline: March of each year.

2088 LEGACY ENVIRONMENTAL SCHOLARSHIPS

Legacy, Inc.
P.O. Box 3813
Montgomery, AL 36109
Phone: (334) 270-5921; (800) 240-5115 (within AL); Fax: (334) 270-5527
Email: info@legacyenved.org
Web: www.legacyenved.org

Summary: To provide financial assistance to upper-division and graduate students in Alabama who are interested in preparing for an environmentally-related career.

Eligibility: Open to juniors, seniors, and graduate students who reside in Alabama, are enrolled at a college or university in the state, and are planning to prepare for an environmentally-related career. Because of the interdisciplinary nature of environmental education, it is not a requirement that all applicants have an environmental title attached to their major; some examples of career fields that have been funded in the past include: business, education, government, law, medicine, public relations, and geography. Applicants must submit a 100-word essay on how they feel they will contribute to environmental education in Alabama and a 250-word essay on their educational and career objectives as related to environmental issues and concerns. Finalists are interviewed. Financial need is not considered in the selection process.

Financial data: Stipends are $1,500 for undergraduates or $2,000 for graduate students.

Duration: 1 year.

Number awarded: Varies each year; a total of $20,000 is available for this program annually.
Deadline: May of each year.

2089 LEGACY OF LIFE SCHOLARSHIPS

Washington Regional Transplant Consortium
7619 Little River Turnpike, Suite 900
Annandale, VA 22003-2628
Phone: (703) 641-0100; (866) 232-3666; Fax: (703) 658-0711
Email: contactwrtc@wrtc.org
Web: www.beadonor.org

Summary: To recognize and reward, with college scholarships, high school seniors in the Washington, D.C. area who submit outstanding essays on organ, eye, and tissue donations.
Eligibility: Open to high school seniors in the District of Columbia; the Virginia counties of Arlington, Fairfax, Fauquier, Loudoun, Prince William, and Stafford; the Virginia cities of Alexandria, Falls Church, Fairfax, Manassas, and Manassas Park; and the Maryland counties of Charles, Montgomery, and Prince George's. Applicants must submit an essay, up to 1,000 words in length, on the theme, "Organ & Tissue Donation: Persuade Someone to Give the Gift of a Lifetime." Entries must be a persuasive argument in either fiction or nonfiction. Selection is based on originality, persuasiveness of the argument, proper grammar and spelling, adherence to the topic, and up-to-date citations.
Financial data: The first-place winner receives $5,000, the second-place winner receives $3,000 and each runner-up receives $1,000. All awards are in the form of college scholarships. Funds are paid directly to the college or university that the winner selects.
Duration: The competition is held annually.
Number awarded: 8 each year: 1 first-place winner, 1 second-place winner, and 6 runners-up.
Deadline: March of each year.

2090 LEOPOLD AND ELIZABETH MARMET SCHOLARSHIPS

Greater Kanawha Valley Foundation
Attn: Scholarship Coordinator
1600 Huntington Square
900 Lee Street, East
P.O. Box 3041
Charleston, WV 25331-3041
Phone: (304) 346-3620; (800) 467-5909; Fax: (304) 346-3640
Email: shoover@tgkvf.org
Web: www.tgkvf.org/scholar.htm

Summary: To provide financial assistance to residents of West Virginia who are interested in working on an undergraduate or graduate degree in science, energy, or natural resources.
Eligibility: Open to residents of West Virginia who are attending or planning to attend a college or university in any state. Applicants must be planning to study science, the production or conservation of energy, or natural resources. Both undergraduate and graduate students are eligible, but preference is given to graduate students. Financial need is not considered in the selection process.
Financial data: Recently, stipends averaged $3,150 per year.
Duration: 1 year; may be renewed.
Number awarded: Varies each year; recently, 42 of these scholarships were awarded.
Deadline: January of each year.

2091 LEROY APKER AWARD

American Physical Society
Attn: Honors Program
One Physics Ellipse
College Park, MD 20740-3844
Phone: (301) 209-3268; Fax: (301) 209-0865
Email: honors@aps.org
Web: www.aps.org/programs/honors/awards/apker.cfm

Summary: To recognize and reward undergraduate students for outstanding work in physics.
Eligibility: Open to undergraduate students at colleges and universities in the United States. Nominees should have completed or be completing the requirements for an undergraduate degree with an excellent academic record and should have demonstrated exceptional potential for scientific research by making an original contribution to physics. Each department of physics in the United States may nominate only 1 student. Each nomination packet should include the student's academic transcript, a description of the original contribution written by the student (such as a manuscript or reprint of a research publication or senior thesis), a 1,000-word summary, and 2 letters of recommendation.
Financial data: The award consists of a $5,000 honorarium for the student, a certificate citing the work and school of the recipient, and an allowance for travel expenses to the meeting of the American Physical Society (APS) at which the prize is presented. Each of the finalists receives an honorarium of $2,000 and a certificate. Each of the physics departments whose nominees are selected as recipients and finalists receives a certificate and an award; the departmental award is $5,000 for recipients and $1,000 for finalists.
Duration: The award is presented annually.
Number awarded: 2 recipients each year: 1 to a student at a Ph.D. granting institution and 1 at a non-Ph.D. granting institution.
Deadline: June of each year.

2092 L.G. WELLS SCHOLARSHIPS

Confederation of Oregon School Administrators
Attn: Youth Development Program
707 13th Street, S.E., Suite 100
Salem, OR 97301-4035
Phone: (503) 581-3141; Fax: (503) 581-9840
Web: www.cosa.k12.or.us

Summary: To provide financial assistance to high school seniors in Oregon who are interested in studying education or engineering at a community college, college, or university in the state.
Eligibility: Open to graduating high school seniors in Oregon. Applicants must be interested in attending a community college, college, or university in Oregon to study education or engineering. They must have been active in community and school affairs, have a GPA of 3.5 or higher, and be able to enroll in the fall term after graduating from high school. Along with their application, they must submit a 1-page autobiography (that includes their personal goals), the name of the school they plan to attend, and the endorsement of a member of the Confederation of Oregon School Administrators (COSA). Financial need is considered in the selection process.
Financial data: The stipend is $1,000. Funds are paid directly to the recipient.
Duration: 1 year; nonrenewable.
Number awarded: 3 each year.
Deadline: February of each year.

2093 LIEUTENANT GENERAL THOMAS M. RIENZI, USA (RET) MERIT SCHOLARSHIP

Armed Forces Communications and Electronics Association–Hawaii Chapter
Attn: Scholarship Committee
P.O. Box 31156
Honolulu, HI 96820
Phone: (808) 529-9501
Email: education.vp@afceahawaii.org
Web: www.afceahi.org/edu/default.htm

Summary: To provide financial assistance to high school seniors and undergraduate students from Hawaii who are interested in studying technical fields at a college in the state and have demonstrated outstanding academic achievement.
Eligibility: Open to residents of Hawaii who are either graduating high school seniors or undergraduates who have completed at least 1 year of college. Applicants must be majoring or planning to major in science, engineering, information technology, computer science, or a related technical field at a 4-year college or university in Hawaii. Along with their application, they must submit a 300-word personal statement on their career goals. Selection is based on academic standing (GPA, class standing, SAT or ACT scores), community involvement and volunteerism, demonstrated leadership, extracurricular activities, athletic achievement, and letters of recommendation. This award is reserved for an applicant who has consistently demonstrated high academic achievement.
Financial data: The stipend is $3,000.
Duration: 1 year.
Number awarded: 1 each year.
Deadline: March of each year.

2094 LILLIAN CAMPBELL MEDICAL SCHOLARSHIP

Wisconsin Veterans of Foreign Wars
214 North Hamilton Street
P.O. Box 1623
Madison, WI 53701-1623

Phone: (608) 255-6655; Fax: (608) 255-0652
Email: qm@wi.vfwwebmail.com
Web: vfwwebcom.org/wisconsin

Summary: To provide financial assistance to students working on a degree in a medical field in Wisconsin who served in the military or are related to a person who did.

Eligibility: Open to students who have completed at least 1 year of study in Wisconsin in a program in nursing, pharmacy, physician assistant, medical or surgical technology, physical or occupational therapy, dental assisting, radiology, or other related medical profession. Applicants or a member of their immediate family (parent, sibling, child, spouse, or grandparent) must have served in the military. They must have a high school diploma or GED but may be of any age. Along with their application, they must submit a 200-word essay on their goals for studying this medical profession. Financial need is considered in the selection process.

Financial data: The stipend is $1,000.

Duration: 1 year.

Number awarded: 1 or more each year.

Deadline: April of each year.

2095 LILLIE AND NOEL FITZGERALD MEMORIAL SCHOLARSHIP

New Jersey State Nurses Association
Attn: Institute for Nursing
1479 Pennington Road
Trenton, NJ 08618-2661
Phone: (609) 883-5335; (888) UR-NJSNA; Fax: (609) 883-5343
Email: institute@njsna.org
Web: www.njsna.org/displaycommon.cfm?an=5

Summary: To provide financial assistance to residents of New Jersey who are preparing for a career as a nurse at a school in the state.

Eligibility: Open to residents of New Jersey who are enrolled in an associate, baccalaureate, or diploma nursing program in the state. Applicants who are R.N.s working on a higher degree in nursing are also eligible if they are members of the New Jersey State Nurses Association. Both high school graduates and adults are eligible. Selection is based on financial need, GPA, and leadership potential.

Financial data: The stipend is $1,000.

Duration: 1 year.

Number awarded: 1 each year.

Deadline: January of each year.

2096 L.L. WATERS SCHOLARSHIP PROGRAM

American Society of Transportation and Logistics, Inc.
Attn: Scholarship Judging Panel
P.O. Box 3363
Warrenton, VA 20188
Phone: (202) 580-7270; Fax: (202) 962-3939
Email: info@astl.org
Web: www.astl.org/i4a/pages/index.cfm?pageid=3293

Summary: To provide financial assistance to advanced undergraduate and graduate students in the field of transportation.

Eligibility: Open to undergraduate students in their junior year at fully-accredited 4-year colleges or universities who are majoring in transportation, logistics, or physical distribution. Students in graduate school in the same areas are also eligible. Applicants must submit a letter explaining why they have chosen transportation, logistics, or physical distribution as their field of study and describing their professional objectives. Recipients are selected without regard to race, color, religion, sex, or national origin. Selection is based on scholastic performance and potential as well as commitment to a professional career in the field. Financial need is not considered.

Financial data: The stipend is $2,000.

Duration: 1 year; recipients may apply again but not in consecutive years.

Number awarded: 1 or more each year.

Deadline: September of each year.

2097 LOCKHEED MARTIN/HENAAC SCHOLARS PROGRAM

Great Minds in STEM
Attn: HENAAC Scholars
3900 Whiteside Street
Los Angeles, CA 90063
Phone: (323) 262-0997; Fax: (323) 262-0946
Email: kbbarrera@greatmindsinstem.org
Web: www.greatmindsinstem.org/henaac/scholars

Summary: To provide financial assistance to Hispanic undergraduate students majoring in designated fields of engineering or computer science.

Eligibility: Open to Hispanic students who are working on an undergraduate or master's degree in computer science, computer engineering, electrical engineering, or systems engineering. Applicants must be of Hispanic origin and/or must significantly participate in and promote organizations and activities in the Hispanic community. They must have a GPA of 3.0 or higher. Along with their application, they must submit a 700-word essay on a topic that changes annually; recently, students were asked to write on how they see their academic major contributing to global efforts and technology and how they, in their field of study, will contribute to global progress as well as actively contribute to their local communities. Selection is based on leadership through academic achievements and campus and community activities; financial need is not considered. U.S. citizenship or permanent resident status is required.

Financial data: Stipends range from $500 to $5,000.

Duration: 1 year; recipients may reapply.

Number awarded: Varies each year; recently, 7 of these scholarships were awarded.

Deadline: April of each year.

2098 LOCKHEED MARTIN SCHOLARSHIP AWARD

Hispanic Association of Colleges and Universities
Attn: National Scholarship Program
8415 Datapoint Drive, Suite 400
San Antonio, TX 78229
Phone: (210) 692-3805; Fax: (210) 692-0823; TDD: (800) 855-2880
Email: scholarships@hacu.net
Web: www.hacu.net/hacu/Scholarships_EN.asp?SnID=875148054

Summary: To provide financial assistance to undergraduate students who are majoring in fields related to engineering at institutions that are members of the Hispanic Association of Colleges and Universities (HACU).

Eligibility: Open to full-time undergraduate students at HACU member and partner 4-year colleges and universities who are majoring in electrical engineering, computer science, or computer engineering. Applicants must submit an essay of 200 to 250 words that describes their academic and/or career goals, where they expect to be and what they expect to be doing 10 years from now, and what skills they can bring to an employer. They must be able to demonstrate financial need, an interest in employment with Lockheed Martin, and a GPA of 3.0 or higher.

Financial data: The stipend is $2,800.

Duration: 1 year; nonrenewable.

Number awarded: 1 or more each year.

Deadline: May of each year.

2099 LOIS BRITT PORK INDUSTRY MEMORIAL SCHOLARSHIPS

National Pork Producers Council
P.O. Box 10383
Des Moines, IA 50306-9960
Phone: (515) 278-8012; Fax: (515) 278-8014
Email: pork@nppc.org
Web: www.nppc.org/producers/scholarships.html

Summary: To provide financial assistance to college students interested in preparing for a career in the pork industry.

Eligibility: Open to students who are currently enrolled in a 2-year swine program or 4-year undergraduate agricultural program. Applicants must submit a 750-word essay on an issue confronting the U.S. pork industry today, a letter indicating the role they see themselves playing in the pork industry upon graduation, and 2 letters of reference. Financial need is not considered in the selection process.

Financial data: The stipend is $2,500.

Duration: 1 year.

Number awarded: 4 each year.

Deadline: January of each year.

2100 LOREN W. CROW MEMORIAL SCHOLARSHIP

American Meteorological Society
Attn: Fellowship/Scholarship Program
45 Beacon Street

Boston, MA 02108-3693
Phone: (617) 227-2426, ext. 246; Fax: (617) 742-8718
Email: scholar@ametsoc.org
Web: www.ametsoc.org

Summary: To provide financial assistance to undergraduates majoring in meteorology or an aspect of atmospheric sciences with an interest in applied meteorology.

Eligibility: Open to full-time students entering their final year of undergraduate study and majoring in meteorology or an aspect of the atmospheric or related oceanic and hydrologic sciences. Applicants must intend to make atmospheric or related sciences their career; preference is given to students who have demonstrated a strong interest in applied meteorology. They must be U.S. citizens or permanent residents enrolled at a U.S. institution and have a cumulative GPA of 3.25 or higher. Along with their application, they must submit 200-word essays on 1) their most important achievements that qualify them for this scholarship; and 2) their career goals in the atmospheric or related oceanic or hydrologic fields. Financial need is considered in the selection process. The sponsor specifically encourages applications from women, minorities, and students with disabilities who are traditionally underrepresented in the atmospheric and related oceanic sciences.

Financial data: The stipend is $2,000.

Duration: 1 year.

Number awarded: 1 each year.

Deadline: February of each year.

2101 LOS HERMANOS MEMORIAL SCHOLARSHIP

Great Minds in STEM
Attn: HENAAC Scholars
3900 Whiteside Street
Los Angeles, CA 90063
Phone: (323) 262-0997; Fax: (323) 262-0946
Email: kbbarrera@greatmindsinstem.org
Web: www.greatmindsinstem.org/henaac/scholars

Summary: To provide financial assistance to Hispanic undergraduate students majoring in a field of science, technology, engineering, or mathematics (STEM).

Eligibility: Open to Hispanic students who are working on an undergraduate degree in a field of STEM. Applicants must be of Hispanic origin and/or must significantly participate in and promote organizations and activities in the Hispanic community. They must have a GPA of 3.0 or higher. Along with their application, they must submit a 700-word essay on a topic that changes annually; recently, students were asked to write on how they see their academic major contributing to global efforts and technology and how they, in their field of study, will contribute to global progress as well as actively contribute to their local communities. Selection is based on leadership through academic achievements and campus and community activities; financial need is not considered.

Financial data: Stipends range from $500 to $5,000.

Duration: 1 year; recipients may reapply.

Number awarded: 1 or more each year.

Deadline: April of each year.

2102 LOUIS T. KLAUDER SCHOLARSHIP

American Public Transportation Association
Attn: American Public Transportation Foundation
1666 K Street, N.W., Suite 1100
Washington, DC 20006
Phone: (202) 496-4803; Fax: (202) 496-4323
Email: yconley@apta.com
Web: www.aptfd.org

Summary: To provide financial assistance to undergraduate and graduate students who are preparing for a career in public transportation as an electrical or mechanical engineer.

Eligibility: Open to college sophomores, juniors, seniors, and graduate students who are preparing for a career in the transit industry as a mechanical or electrical engineer. Any member organization of the American Public Transportation Association (APTA) can nominate and sponsor candidates for this scholarship. Nominees must be enrolled in a fully-accredited institution, have and maintain at least a 3.0 GPA, and be either employed by or demonstrate a strong interest in entering the public transportation industry as an electrical or mechanical engineer. They must submit a 1,000-word essay on "In what segment of the public transportation industry will you make a career and why?" Selection is based on demonstrated interest in the transit field as a career, need for financial assistance, academic achievement, essay content and quality, and involvement in extracurricular citizenship and leadership activities.

Financial data: The stipend is $2,500.

Duration: 1 year; may be renewed.

Number awarded: 1 each year.

Deadline: June of each year.

2103 LOUISIANA SECTION AWMA SCHOLARSHIP AWARD

Air & Waste Management Association–Louisiana Section
c/o Karen J. Blakemore
Phelps Dunbar, LLP
445 North Boulevard, Suite 501
P.O. Box 4412
Baton Rouge, LA 70821-4412
Phone: (225) 346-0285; Fax: (225) 381-9197
Email: karen.blakemore@phelps.com
Web: la-awma.org/education/scholarships

Summary: To provide financial assistance to upper-division and master's degree students working on a degree in an environmental field at a university in the area served by the Louisiana Section of the Air & Waste Management Association (AWMA).

Eligibility: Open to juniors, seniors, and master's degree students at colleges and universities in Louisiana and the Sabine River Region of eastern Texas. Applicants must be working full-time on a degree in an environmental field, including engineering, physical or natural science, or public health and have a GPA of 3.0 or higher. They must be able to demonstrate through course work, projects, or personal interest a desire to promote air pollution control and/or solid or hazardous waste management. A personal interview is required. Selection is based on academic record, plan of study, career goals, recommendations, and financial status.

Financial data: The stipend is $1,000.

Duration: 1 year; nonrenewable.

Number awarded: 2 or more each year.

Deadline: March of each year.

2104 LUCY C. AYERS SCHOLARSHIPS

Lucy C. Ayers Foundation, Inc.
The Summit South
300 Centerville Road, Suite 300S
Warwick, RI 02886-0203

Summary: To provide financial assistance to nursing students in Rhode Island.

Eligibility: Open to students enrolled in an accredited Rhode Island nursing program leading to licensure as a registered nurse (R.N.). Applicants may be working on a diploma or an associate, bachelor's, master's, or doctoral degree. They must submit a brief statement describing their reasons for requesting financial aid.

Financial data: The stipend is $1,000.

Duration: 1 year.

Number awarded: 1 or more per year.

Deadline: Deadline not specified.

2105 MACKINAC SCHOLARSHIP

American Society of Civil Engineers–Michigan Section
Attn: Cindy Schmitz, Administrative Staff
P.O. Box 19189
Lansing, MI 48901
Phone: (517) 332-2066
Email: cschmitz@acecmi.org
Web: sections.asce.org/michigan

Summary: To provide financial assistance to Michigan residents who are entering the junior year of a civil engineering program at a school in the state.

Eligibility: Open to Michigan residents who are enrolled full-time in an ABET-accredited civil engineering program in the state. Applicants must be entering their junior year and have a GPA of 2.5 or higher. U.S. citizenship is required. Selection is based on academic record, participation in extracurricular activities, leadership, character, self-reliance, comments from employers and university officials, and financial need. Semifinalists may be contacted for an interview.

Financial data: The stipend is $5,000 per year.

Duration: 2 years.

Number awarded: 1 each year.

Deadline: May of each year.

2106 MADALENE HILL SCHOLARSHIP

Herb Society of America–South Texas Unit
Attn: Education Committee Chair
P.O. Box 6515
Houston, TX 77265-6515
Phone: (713) 513-7808
Web: www.herbsociety-stu.org/Scholarship.htm

Summary: To provide financial assistance to Texas students majoring in agronomy, horticulture, botany, or a related field.

Eligibility: Open to students who are studying agronomy, horticulture, botany, or a closely-related discipline at an accredited 4-year college or university. Applicants must be either a resident of Texas or attending an accredited college or university in Texas. They must have completed at least 2 full years of college and be entering their junior or senior year. Selection is based on academic achievement, letters of recommendation, and a 2- to 3-paragraph statement on their short- and long-term career goals, including examples of special interests or projects in plants, herbs, gardening, etc.

Financial data: The stipend is $1,000.

Duration: 1 year.

Number awarded: 1 each year.

Deadline: March of each year.

2107 MAINE METAL PRODUCTS ASSOCIATION SCHOLARSHIP

Maine Education Services
Attn: MES Foundation
One City Center, 11th Floor
Portland, ME 04101
Phone: (207) 791-3600; (800) 922-6352; Fax: (207) 791-3616
Email: info@mesfoundation.com
Web: www.mesfoundation.com

Summary: To provide financial assistance to students in Maine who are interested in furthering their education in the machine or related metal working trades.

Eligibility: Open to residents of Maine who have been accepted into a metal trade program at a college in the state. The field of specialization may be mechanical engineering, machine tool technology, sheet metal fabrication, welding, or CADCAM for metals industry. Applicants must submit an essay on their goals, aspirations, and accomplishments; why and how they decided on a career in metal working; and why they think they should receive this scholarship. They will be interviewed by a member of the association. Selection is based on aptitude or demonstrated ability in the metal working trades, high school scholastic and extracurricular records, and personal qualifications of attitude, initiative, seriousness of intent, and overall impression.

Financial data: A stipend is awarded (amount not specified); funds may be applied toward the costs of tuition and textbooks only.

Duration: 1 year; may be renewed, provided the recipient remains enrolled full-time and maintains a "C" average or higher.

Number awarded: Varies each year; recently, 9 of these scholarships were awarded.

Deadline: April of each year.

2108 MAJOR GENERAL ROCKLY TRIANTAFELLU, USAF (RET) AWARD FOR ACADEMIC ACHIEVEMENT

Armed Forces Communications and Electronics Association–Hawaii Chapter
Attn: Scholarship Committee
P.O. Box 31156
Honolulu, HI 96820
Phone: (808) 529-9501
Email: education.vp@afceahawaii.org
Web: www.afceahi.org/edu/default.htm

Summary: To provide financial assistance to high school seniors and undergraduate students from Hawaii who are interested in studying technical fields at a college in any state and have demonstrated outstanding academic achievement.

Eligibility: Open to residents of Hawaii who are either graduating high school seniors or undergraduates who have completed at least 1 year of college. Applicants must be majoring or planning to major in science, engineering, information technology, computer science, or a related technical field at a 4-year college or university in the United States. Along with their application, they must submit a 300-word personal statement on their career goals. Selection is based on academic standing (GPA, class standing, SAT or ACT scores), community involvement and volunteerism, demonstrated leadership, extracurricular activities, athletic achievement, and letters of recommendation. This award is reserved for an applicant who has consistently demonstrated high academic achievement.

Financial data: The stipend is $2,000.

Duration: 1 year.

Number awarded: 1 each year.

Deadline: March of each year.

2109 MALSCE SCHOLARSHIPS

Massachusetts Association of Land Surveyors and Civil Engineers, Inc.
c/o The Engineering Center
One Walnut Street
Boston, MA 02108-3616
Phone: (617) 227-5551; Fax: (617) 227-6783
Email: malsce@engineers.org
Web: www.malsce.org/index.cfm/page/Scholarship-Information/pid/10371

Summary: To provide financial assistance to Massachusetts residents who are studying surveying, civil engineering, or environmental engineering at a college in any state.

Eligibility: Open to Massachusetts residents enrolled full-time at a college, university, junior college, technical institute, or community college in any state. Applicants must be majoring in surveying, civil engineering, or environmental engineering.

Financial data: A stipend is awarded (amount not specified).

Duration: 1 year.

Number awarded: Varies each year.

Deadline: July of each year.

2110 MARATHON OIL CORPORATION COLLEGE SCHOLARSHIP PROGRAM OF THE HISPANIC SCHOLARSHIP FUND

Hispanic Scholarship Fund
Attn: Selection Committee
55 Second Street, Suite 1500
San Francisco, CA 94105
Phone: (415) 808-2365; (877) HSF-INFO; Fax: (415) 808-2302
Email: scholar1@hsf.net
Web: www.hsf.net/Scholarships.aspx?id=464

Summary: To provide financial assistance to minority upper-division and graduate students working on a degree in a field related to the oil and gas industry.

Eligibility: Open to U.S. citizens, permanent residents, and visitors with a passport stamped I-551 who are of Hispanic American, African American, Asian Pacific Islander American, or American Indian/Alaskan Native heritage. Applicants must be currently enrolled full-time at an accredited 4-year college or university in the United States, Puerto Rico, Guam, or the U.S. Virgin Islands with a GPA of 3.0 or higher. They must be 1) sophomores majoring in chemical engineering, civil engineering, electrical engineering, mechanical engineering, petroleum engineering, geology, geophysics, accounting, marketing, global procurement or supply chain management, environmental health and safety, energy management or petroleum land management, transportation and logistics, or geotechnical engineering; or 2) seniors planning to work on a master's degree in geology or geophysics. Selection is based on academic achievement, personal strengths, interest and commitment to a career in the oil and gas industry, leadership, and financial need.

Financial data: The stipend is $10,000 per year.

Duration: 2 years (the junior and senior undergraduate years or the first 2 years of a master's degree program).

Number awarded: 1 or more each year.

Deadline: November of each year.

2111 MARGARET A. STAFFORD NURSING SCHOLARSHIP

Delaware Community Foundation
Attn: Executive Vice President
100 West 10th Street, Suite 115
P.O. Box 1636
Wilmington, DE 19899
Phone: (302) 571-8004; Fax: (302) 571-1553
Email: rgentsch@delcf.org
Web: www.delcf.org/scholarships_guidelines.html

Summary: To provide financial assistance to residents of Delaware who are interested in attending college in any state to prepare for a career in nursing.

Eligibility: Open to Delaware residents who have been accepted into the nursing program at an accredited college or university in any state. Applicants must be beginning or furthering their nursing training. They should be seeking to improve the quality of health care in our society through nursing practices that ensure that patients' needs are a priority. Along with their application, they must submit a 1-page essay on why they desire to undertake a career in nursing. Selection is based on all facets of the applicant's education and activities that point to a successful college experience and nursing career. Preference is given to those students most in need of financial support.
Financial data: The stipend is $1,000.
Duration: 1 year; nonrenewable.
Number awarded: 1 each year.
Deadline: March of each year.

2112 MARILYN CASEY SCHOLARSHIP

Illinois Community College System Foundation
401 East Capitol Avenue
Springfield, IL 62701
Phone: (217) 789-4230; Fax: (217) 492-5176
Email: iccsfoundation@sbcglobal.net
Web: www.iccsfoundation.com/Scholarships.htm
Summary: To provide financial assistance to students enrolled in a nursing or other health care program at an Illinois community college.
Eligibility: Open to students at Illinois community colleges who are enrolled in a health care program, especially nursing. Preference is given to students in an A.D.N. program. Applicants must have a GPA of 3.0 or higher and be able to demonstrate financial need.
Financial data: Stipends range up to $2,000 per year.
Duration: 1 year; may be renewed 1 additional year.
Number awarded: 1 or 2 each year at each participating Illinois community college.
Deadline: Each college sets its own deadline.

2113 MARINE CORPS SGT. JEANNETTE L. WINTERS MEMORIAL SCHOLARSHIP

Armed Forces Communications and Electronics Association
Attn: AFCEA Educational Foundation
4400 Fair Lakes Court
Fairfax, VA 22033-3899
Phone: (703) 631-6149; (800) 336-4583, ext. 6149; Fax: (703) 631-4693
Email: scholarship@afcea.org
Web: www.afcea.org/education/scholarships/undergraduate/sgtjean.asp
Summary: To provide funding to members and veterans of the U.S. Marine Corps (USMC) who are majoring in specified fields in college.
Eligibility: Open to USMC personnel currently on active duty, in the Reserves, or honorably-discharged veterans who are enrolled full- or part-time in an accredited college or university in the United States. Applicants must be U.S. citizens, be of good moral character, have demonstrated academic excellence, be motivated to complete a college education, and be working on a bachelor's degree in engineering (aerospace, chemical, electrical, or systems), electronics, mathematics, physics, science or mathematics education, management information systems, technology management, computer science, or other field directly related to the support of U.S. intelligence enterprises or national security. They must provide a copy of Discharge Form DD214, Certificate of Service, or facsimile of their current Department of Defense Identification Card.
Financial data: The stipend is $2,000.
Duration: 1 year.
Number awarded: 1 each year.
Deadline: August of each year.

2114 MARY ANNE WILLIAMS SCHOLARSHIP

United Daughters of the Confederacy–Virginia Division
c/o Janice Busic, Education Committee Chair
P.O. Box 356
Honaker, VA 24260
Email: 2vp@vaudc.org
Web: vaudc.org/gift.html
Summary: To provide financial assistance for undergraduate or graduate study in medicine or engineering to Confederate descendants from Virginia.
Eligibility: Open to residents of Virginia who are 1) lineal descendants of Confederates; or 2) collateral descendants and also members of the Children of the Confederacy or the United Daughters of the Confederacy. Applicants must be interested in working on an undergraduate or graduate degree in medicine or engineering. They must submit proof of the Confederate military record of at least 1 ancestor, with the company and regiment in which he served. They must also submit a personal letter pledging to make the best possible use of the scholarship; describing their health, social, family, religious, and fraternal connections within the community; and reflecting on what a Southern heritage means to them (using the term "War Between the States" in lieu of "Civil War"). They must have a GPA of 3.0 or higher and be able to demonstrate financial need.
Financial data: The amount of the stipend depends on the availability of funds. Payment is made directly to the college or university the recipient attends.
Duration: 1 year; may be renewed up to 3 additional years if the recipient maintains a GPA of 3.0 or higher.
Number awarded: This scholarship is offered whenever a prior recipient graduates or is no longer eligible.
Deadline: April of the years in which the scholarship is available.

2115 MARYLAND LEGION AUXILIARY CHILDREN AND YOUTH FUND SCHOLARSHIP

Summary: To provide financial assistance for college to the daughters of veterans who are Maryland residents and wish to study arts, sciences, business, public administration, education, or a medical field at a school in the state.
See Listing #1422.

2116 MARYLAND LEGION AUXILIARY PAST PRESIDENTS' PARLEY NURSING SCHOLARSHIP

American Legion Auxiliary
Department of Maryland
1589 Sulphur Spring Road, Suite 105
Baltimore, MD 21227
Phone: (410) 242-9519; Fax: (410) 242-9553
Email: hq@alamd.org
Web: www.alamd.org
Summary: To provide financial assistance to the female descendants of Maryland veterans who wish to study nursing at a school in any state.
Eligibility: Open to Maryland residents who are the daughters, granddaughters, great-granddaughters, step-daughters, step-granddaughters, or step-great-granddaughters of ex-servicewomen (or of ex-servicemen, if there are no qualified descendants of ex-servicewomen). Applicants must be interested in attending a school in any state to become a registered nurse and be able to show financial need. They must submit a 300-word essay on the topic "What a Nursing Career Means to Me."
Financial data: The stipend is $2,000. Funds are sent directly to the recipient's school.
Duration: 1 year; may be renewed for up to 3 additional years if the recipient remains enrolled full-time.
Number awarded: 1 each year.
Deadline: April of each year.

2117 MARYLAND TUITION REDUCTION FOR NONRESIDENT NURSING STUDENTS

Maryland Higher Education Commission
Attn: Office of Student Financial Assistance
839 Bestgate Road, Suite 400
Annapolis, MD 21401-3013
Phone: (410) 260-4546; (800) 974-1024, ext. 4546; Fax: (410) 260-3200; TDD: (800) 735-2258
Email: tmckelvi@mhec.state.md.us
Web: www.mhec.state.md.us
Summary: To provide reduced tuition in exchange for service to residents of states other than Maryland interested in attending Maryland public nursing schools.
Eligibility: Open to nursing students at Maryland public colleges who are residents of states other than Maryland. Applicants must enroll for at least 6 credits per semester. They are not required to demonstrate financial need.
Financial data: Recipients are entitled to pay the same tuition as if they were Maryland residents. They must agree to work as a full-time nurse in Maryland in an eligible institution or in a home that provides domiciliary, personal, or nursing care for 2 or more unrelated individuals. They must work for 2 years if they attended a 2-year school, for 4 years if they attended a 4-year school, or repay the scholarship with interest. The service obligation must begin within 6 months of graduation.

Duration: 1 year; may be renewed for 1 additional year at a 2-year public institution or 3 additional years at a 4-year public institution.
Number awarded: Varies each year.
Deadline: Each participating Maryland school sets its own deadline.

2118 MARYLAND WORKFORCE SHORTAGE STUDENT ASSISTANCE GRANT PROGRAM

Maryland Higher Education Commission
Attn: Office of Student Financial Assistance
839 Bestgate Road, Suite 400
Annapolis, MD 21401-3013
Phone: (410) 260-4565; (800) 974-1024, ext. 4565; Fax: (410) 260-3200; TDD: (800) 735-2258
Email: osfamail@mhec.state.md.us
Web: www.mhec.state.md.us

Summary: To provide financial assistance to Maryland residents interested in a career in specified workforce shortage areas.
Eligibility: Open to residents of Maryland who are high school seniors, undergraduates, or graduate students. Applicants must be enrolled or planning to enroll at a 2- or 4-year Maryland college or university. They may major in the following service areas: 1) child development or early childhood education, for students who plan to become full-time employees as a director or senior staff member in a licensed Maryland child care center or as a licensed family day care provider in the state; 2) human services degree programs, for students who plan to become employees of Maryland community-based programs and are interested in working on a degree in aging services, counseling, disability services, mental health, nursing, occupational therapy, physical therapy, psychology, rehabilitation, social work, special education, supported employment, vocational rehabilitation, or other program providing support services to individuals with special needs; 3) education, for students who become teachers in the following areas of certification: technology education (secondary), chemistry (secondary), computer science (secondary), earth and space science (secondary), English for speakers of other languages (elementary and secondary), foreign languages (German, Italian, Japanese, Latin, or Spanish), mathematics [secondary], physical science [secondary], physics [secondary], or special education (infant/primary, elementary/middle, secondary/adult, severely and profoundly disabled, hearing impaired, or visually impaired); 4) nursing, for students who become employed as a nurse in a licensed hospital, adult day care center, nursing home, public health agency, home health agency, eligible institution of postsecondary education that awards nursing degrees or diplomas, or other approved organization; 5) physical therapy or occupational therapy, for students who plan to become employed as a therapist or therapy assistant to handicapped children in a public school in Maryland, in an approved nonpublic education program, or in a state therapeutic hospital; 6) law, for students interested in preparing for a career in providing legal services to low-income residents in the state; 7) social work; or 8) public service, for employment in services in the public or nonprofit sectors in which there is a shortage of qualified practitioners to low-income or underserved residents or areas of the state. Applicants are ranked by GPA and then by need within each occupational field. Students with the greatest need within each GPA range are awarded first.
Financial data: Awards are $4,000 per year for full-time undergraduate and graduate students at 4-year institutions, $2,000 per year for part-time undergraduate and graduate students at 4-year institutions, $2,000 per year for full-time students at community colleges, or $1,000 per year for part-time students at community colleges. Within 1 year of graduation, recipients must provide 1 year of service in Maryland in their field of study for each year of financial aid received under this program; failure to comply with that service obligation will require them to repay the scholarship money with interest.
Duration: 1 year; may be renewed up to 4 additional years, provided the recipient continues to meet eligibility requirements.
Number awarded: Varies each year.
Deadline: June of each year.

2119 MASONIC-RANGE SCIENCE SCHOLARSHIP

Society for Range Management
10030 West 27th Avenue
Wheat Ridge, CO 80215-6601
Phone: (303) 986-3309; Fax: (303) 986-3892
Email: info@rangelands.org
Web: www.rangelands.org/education_masonicscholarship.shtml

Summary: To provide financial assistance to students who are interested in majoring in range science in college.
Eligibility: Open to high school seniors and college freshmen and sophomores. Applicants must be interested in majoring in range science in college. They must be sponsored by a member of the Society for Range Management, the National Association of Conservation Districts, or the Soil and Water Conservation Society. Along with their application, they must submit an essay on why they are interested in a career in range science, including any experiences that have led them to choose a range science major. Selection is based on that essay, letters of reference, academic record, leadership experience, community service, and honors and awards.
Financial data: The amount awarded each year varies; recently, the stipend was $6,200.
Duration: 1 year; may be renewed provided the recipient maintains a GPA of 2.5 or higher.
Number awarded: 1 each year.
Deadline: January of each year.

2120 MASSACHUSETTS HIGH TECHNOLOGY SCHOLAR/INTERN TUITION WAIVER PROGRAM

Massachusetts Office of Student Financial Assistance
454 Broadway, Suite 200
Revere, MA 02151
Phone: (617) 727-9420; Fax: (617) 727-0667
Email: osfa@osfa.mass.edu
Web: www.osfa.mass.edu/default.asp?page=highTechWaiver

Summary: To provide financial assistance to students at Massachusetts public institutions of higher education who are participating in a high technology scholar/intern program.
Eligibility: Open to students at Massachusetts public institutions who are participating as interns in a computer, information technology, or engineering program approved by the Massachusetts Board of Higher Education. Applicants must be U.S. citizens or permanent residents who are residents of Massachusetts. Their institution must have obtained scholarship funding from business and industry.
Financial data: The awards match industry scholarships up to the resident undergraduate tuition rate at the participating institution.
Duration: Up to 4 academic years.
Number awarded: Varies each year.
Deadline: April of each year.

2121 MASSACHUSETTS MATHEMATICS AND SCIENCE TEACHERS SCHOLARSHIP PROGRAM

Massachusetts Office of Student Financial Assistance
454 Broadway, Suite 200
Revere, MA 02151
Phone: (617) 727-9420; Fax: (617) 727-0667
Email: osfa@osfa.mass.edu
Web: www.osfa.mass.edu/default.asp?page=mathScienceScholarship

Summary: To provide financial assistance to residents of Massachusetts who are interested in attending college to become certified as a mathematics or science teacher.
Eligibility: Open to Massachusetts residents who are currently employed, full- or part-time, as an educator at a Massachusetts public school. Applicants must be currently teaching mathematics or science (including technology and engineering) under a waiver from certificate regulations or as an out-of-field teacher. They must be enrolled in a degree-granting program at a public institution that leads to certification by the Massachusetts Department of Education for mathematics or science. U.S. citizenship or permanent resident status is required.
Financial data: Grants depend on the tuition and fees at their institution and the school district where they are currently employed. Teachers in high-need districts are eligible to receive 100% of the cost of tuition, fees, and related expenses. Teachers in non-high-need districts are eligible to receive 75% of the cost of tuition, fees, and related expenses. Awards cover up to 3 courses per semester. Recipients must agree to continue teaching mathematics or science at a Massachusetts public school after graduation. Teachers in high-need districts must continue teaching in such districts. If they fail to fulfill that obligation, they must repay all funds received.
Duration: Until completion of an undergraduate degree, provided the recipient maintains satisfactory academic progress.
Number awarded: Varies each year.
Deadline: October of each year.

2122 MASSACHUSETTS STEM SCHOLAR INTERNSHIP MATCH PROGRAM

Massachusetts Department of Higher Education
Attn: Coordinator for Workforce Development Initiatives

One Ashburton Place, Room 1401
Boston, MA 02108-1696
Phone: (617) 994-6950; Fax: (617) 727-0955
Email: emawm@bhe.mass.edu
Web: www.mass.edu

Summary: To provide supplemental funding to students who are enrolled in fields of science, technology, engineering, or mathematics (STEM) at public institutions in Massachusetts and who have also received a scholarship or internship from private sources.

Eligibility: Open to undergraduates currently enrolled full-time at public institutions of higher education in Massachusetts as sophomores or higher and majoring in an approved STEM field. Applicants must have been residents of Massachusetts for at least 1 year and be U.S. citizens or permanent residents. They must have obtained a scholarship or internship from a designated Massachusetts employer in an approved career-related field. Along with their application, they must submit a 2-page essay discussing the origins of their interest in their field of study, the responsibilities of their internship and how those relate to their academic course work, their personal and professional goals, and their extracurricular activities. Financial need is not considered in the selection process.

Financial data: The program matches the funding of the private scholarship or internship, to a maximum of $5,000 per year.

Duration: 1 year; may be renewed.

Number awarded: Varies each year.

Deadline: November of each year for fall term; March of each year for winter or spring term; July of each year for summer term.

2123 MATERIALS RESEARCH POSTER COMPETITION

American Association of Textile Chemists and Colorists
Attn: Technical Center
One Davis Drive
P.O. Box 12215
Research Triangle Park, NC 27709-2215
Phone: (919) 549-8141; Fax: (919) 549-8933
Email: holmes@aatcc.org
Web: www.aatcc.org/members/students/competitions.cfm

Summary: To recognize and reward undergraduate and graduate students who submit outstanding research posters on materials research.

Eligibility: Open to undergraduate and graduate students who work individually or in teams of up to 4 members. Applicants are invited to submit research posters in 3 areas: 1) industrial, technical, and sports materials, covering structures and materials for technical and engineering applications (e.g. advanced sporting equipment, aircraft or automotive components, architectural materials, composites, geo-synthetic materials, industrial filters, industrial and technical fabrics, or sports performance fabrics); 2) protective, medical, and biomedical materials and devices, explaining research in materials for use in hazardous or medical environments (e.g., artificial body implants, chemical or biological protective garments, protective medical gowns and masks, reactive barrier membranes, or self-detoxifying materials); and 3) smart, functional, and nano materials, communicating the creation of structures that incorporate smart functionality to polymers and fibers (e.g., anti-counterfeit materials, camouflage/electromagnetic management, conducting polymers, energy harvesting, functional nano-materials and nanofibers, integrated materials for multifunctional assemblies, novel energy storage, optical materials, or wearable electronic garments). Selection is based on concept originality; research quality; clarity; and results, discussions, and conclusions.

Financial data: For each area, first prize is $1,000 and second prize is $500. Winners also receive complimentary student registration for the international conference and exhibition of the American Association of Textile Chemists and Colorists (AATCC).

Duration: The competition is held annually.

Number awarded: 6 each year: 1 first prize and 1 second prize in each of the 3 areas.

Deadline: Online entries must be submitted by February of each year. Completed posters are due in March.

2124 MAURICE E. CORE SCHOLARSHIP

National Dairy Shrine
Attn: Executive Director
P.O. Box 1
Maribel, WI 54227
Phone: (920) 863-6333; Fax: (920) 863-8328
Email: info@dairyshrine.org
Web: www.dairyshrine.org/scholarships.php

Summary: To provide financial assistance to college freshmen working on a bachelor's degree in animal or dairy science.

Eligibility: Open to college freshmen working on a bachelor's degree in animal science, dairy science, or other field that will prepare them for a career in the dairy industry. Applicants must have a GPA of 2.5 or higher. Along with their application, they must submit a 300-word essay on their plans for the future and how this scholarship will assist them in meeting their goals. Selection is based on that essay, academic standing, high school leadership and activities, college and dairy club activities, awards and honors, and promotion and volunteer activities for the dairy industry.

Financial data: The stipend is $1,000.

Duration: 1 year.

Number awarded: 1 each year.

Deadline: April of each year.

2125 MAX MAYFIELD SCHOLARSHIP IN WEATHER FORECASTING

American Meteorological Society
Attn: Fellowship/Scholarship Program
45 Beacon Street
Boston, MA 02108-3693
Phone: (617) 227-2426, ext. 246; Fax: (617) 742-8718
Email: scholar@ametsoc.org
Web: www.ametsoc.org

Summary: To provide financial assistance to undergraduates majoring in meteorology or an aspect of atmospheric sciences with an interest in weather forecasting.

Eligibility: Open to full-time students entering their final year of undergraduate study and majoring in meteorology or an aspect of the atmospheric or related oceanic and hydrologic sciences. Applicants must have demonstrated a strong interest in weather forecasting. They must be U.S. citizens or permanent residents enrolled at a U.S. institution and have a cumulative GPA of 3.25 or higher. Along with their application, they must submit 200-word essays on 1) their most important achievements that qualify them for this scholarship; and 2) their career goals in the atmospheric or related oceanic or hydrologic fields. Financial need is considered in the selection process. The sponsor specifically encourages applications from women, minorities, and students with disabilities who are traditionally underrepresented in the atmospheric and related oceanic sciences.

Financial data: The stipend is $2,000.

Duration: 1 year.

Number awarded: 1 each year.

Deadline: February of each year.

2126 MAXINE V. FENNELL MEMORIAL SCHOLARSHIP

New England Regional Black Nurses Association, Inc.
P.O. Box 190690
Boston, MA 02119
Phone: (617) 524-1951
Web: www.nerbna.org/org/scholarships.html

Summary: To provide financial assistance to licensed practical nurses from New England who are studying to become a registered nurse (R.N.) and have contributed to the African American community.

Eligibility: Open to residents of the New England states who are licensed practical nurses and currently enrolled in an NLN-accredited R.N. program (diploma, associate, baccalaureate) at a school in any state. Applicants must have at least 1 full year of school remaining. Along with their application, they must submit a 3-page essay that covers their career aspirations in the nursing profession; how they have contributed to the African American or other communities of color in such areas as work, volunteering, church, or community outreach; an experience that has enhanced their personal and/or professional growth; and any financial hardships that may hinder them from completing their education.

Financial data: A stipend is awarded (amount not specified).

Duration: 1 year.

Number awarded: 1 or more each year.

Deadline: March of each year.

2127 MAXINE WILLIAMS SCHOLARSHIP PROGRAM

American Association of Medical Assistants
Attn: AAMA Endowment
20 North Wacker Drive, Suite 1575
Chicago, IL 60606-2903

Phone: (312) 899-1500; (800) 228-2262; Fax: (312) 899-1259
Email: boardservices@aama-ntl.org
Web: www.aama-ntl.org/endowment/scholarship/app.aspx

Summary: To provide financial assistance to high school graduates who are interested in becoming medical assistants.

Eligibility: Open to students who have completed at least 1 semester or 1 quarter in a postsecondary medical assisting program accredited by the Commission on Accreditation of Allied Health Education Programs (CAAHEP). Applications are only available from CAAHEP-accredited medical assisting program directors. Selection is based on academic ability (a GPA of 3.0 or higher) and financial need.

Financial data: The stipend is $1,000 per year.

Duration: 1 year; may be renewed for 1 additional year.

Number awarded: Varies each year; recently, 6 of these scholarships were awarded.

Deadline: February of each year.

2128 MCALLISTER MEMORIAL SCHOLARSHIPS

Aircraft Owners and Pilots Association
Attn: AOPA Air Safety Foundation
421 Aviation Way
Frederick, MD 21701-4798
Phone: (301) 695-2000; (800) 638-3101; Fax: (301) 695-2375
Email: asf@aopa.org
Web: www.aopa.org/asf/about/scholarship/mcallister.html

Summary: To provide funding to students who need financial assistance to continue their studies in the field of aviation.

Eligibility: Open to U.S. citizens who are interested in working on a bachelor's degree in the field of non-engineering aviation. Applicants must be juniors or seniors and have a GPA of 3.25 or higher. Along with their application, they must submit a 250-word essay on a topic that changes annually; recently, students were asked to write on whether they think voluntary operating guidelines for general aviation pilots would increase safety for that segment of aviation. Financial need is not considered in the selection process.

Financial data: The stipend is $1,000.

Duration: 1 year; nonrenewable.

Number awarded: 1 each year.

Deadline: March of each year.

2129 MCKESSON SCHOLARSHIPS

National Student Nurses' Association
Attn: Foundation
45 Main Street, Suite 606
Brooklyn, NY 11201
Phone: (718) 210-0705; Fax: (718) 797-1186
Email: nsna@nsna.org
Web: www.nsna.org/FoundationScholarships/FNSNAScholarships.aspx

Summary: To provide financial assistance to nursing students enrolled in programs leading to licensure as a registered nurse (R.N.).

Eligibility: Open to students currently enrolled in state-approved schools of nursing and working on an associate degree, baccalaureate degree, or diploma leading to licensure as an R.N. Graduating high school seniors are not eligible. Applicants must submit a 200-word description of their professional and educational goals and how this scholarship will help them achieve those goals. Selection is based on academic achievement, financial need, and involvement in student nursing organizations and community health activities. U.S. citizenship or permanent resident status is required.

Financial data: Stipends range from $1,000 to $2,500.

Duration: 1 year.

Number awarded: Varies each year; recently, 15 of these scholarships were awarded.

Deadline: January of each year.

2130 MCLEAN SCHOLARSHIP FOR NURSING AND PHYSICIAN ASSISTANT MAJORS

Association of Independent Colleges and Universities of Pennsylvania
101 North Front Street
Harrisburg, PA 17101-1405
Phone: (717) 232-8649; Fax: (717) 233-8574
Email: info@aicup.org
Web: www.aicup.org

Summary: To provide financial assistance to students from any state at member institutions of the Association of Independent Colleges and Universities of Pennsylvania (AICUP) who are enrolled in a nursing or physician assistant program.

Eligibility: Open to undergraduate students from any state enrolled full-time at AICUP colleges and universities. Applicants must be enrolled in a nursing or physician assistant program and have a GPA of 3.0 or higher. Along with their application, they must submit a 2-page essay on how they chose their major, the steps they are taking to ensure that they succeed in their major, what they plan to do after graduation, the volunteer and extracurricular activities in which they participate, and how those activities relate to their major. Selection is based on their GPA (30%), steps taken to ensure success in their major (10%), career goals (10%), volunteer work (25%), relationship of volunteer and extracurricular activities to major (10%), and extent of their leadership activities (15%). Applications must be submitted to the financial aid office at the AICUP college or university that the student attends.

Financial data: The stipend is $2,500.

Duration: 1 year.

Number awarded: Varies each year; recently, 7 of these scholarships were awarded.

Deadline: April of each year.

2131 MEMORIAL CONSERVATION SCHOLARSHIP

New Jersey Association of Conservation Districts
c/o New Jersey Department of Agriculture
P.O. Box 330, Room 204
Trenton, NJ 08625
Phone: (609) 292-5540; Fax: (609) 633-2550
Web: www.state.nj.us

Summary: To provide financial assistance to college students from New Jersey who are preparing for a career in a field related to the conservation and management of natural resources.

Eligibility: Open to New Jersey residents who are enrolled as full-time undergraduates at an accredited college or university in any state. Applicants must have successfully completed (or will have completed by the scholarship award date) at least 4 full semesters of study. They must be majoring in a field related to agriculture or natural resource conservation, including agronomy, soil science, plant science, forestry, geography, journalism, agricultural education, environmental science, wildlife or fisheries management, or environmental engineering. Selection is based on academic commitment to a field of conservation, demonstrated scholastic ability, involvement in extracurricular activities or volunteer projects related to conservation, and financial need.

Financial data: The stipend is $1,500.

Duration: 1 year.

Number awarded: 1 or 2 each year.

Deadline: June of each year.

2132 MESBEC PROGRAM

Catching the Dream
8200 Mountain Road, N.E., Suite 203
Albuquerque, NM 87110-7835
Phone: (505) 262-2351; Fax: (505) 262-0534
Email: NScholarsh@aol.com
Web: www.catchingthedream.org/Scholarship.htm

Summary: To provide financial assistance to American Indian students who are interested in working on an undergraduate or graduate degree in selected fields.

Eligibility: Open to American Indians who can provide proof that they have at least one-quarter Indian blood and are a member of a U.S. tribe that is federally-recognized, state-recognized, or terminated. Applicants must be enrolled or planning to enroll full-time and major in one of the following fields: mathematics, engineering, science (including medicine), business administration, education, or computer science. They may be entering freshmen, undergraduate students, graduate students, or Ph.D. candidates. Along with their application, they must submit documentation of financial need, 3 letters of recommendation, copies of applications and responses for all other sources of funding for which they are eligible, official transcripts, standardized test scores (ACT, SAT, GRE, MCAT, LSAT, etc.), and an essay explaining their goals in life, college plans, and career plans (especially how those plans include working with and benefiting Indians). Selection is based on merit and potential for improving the lives of Indian people.

Financial data: Stipends range from $500 to $5,000 per year.

Duration: 1 year; may be renewed.

Number awarded: Varies; generally, 30 to 35 each year.

Deadline: April of each year for fall term; September of each year for spring and winter terms; March of each year for summer school.

2133 METLIFE INTERNSHIP/SCHOLARSHIP

Thurgood Marshall College Fund
Attn: Scholarship Manager
80 Maiden Lane, Suite 2204
New York, NY 10038
Phone: (212) 573-8487; (877) 690-8673; Fax: (212) 573-8497
Email: srogers@tmcfund.org
Web: www.thurgoodmarshallfund.net

Summary: To provide financial assistance and work experience to students majoring in fields related to information technology at colleges and universities that are members of the Thurgood Marshall College Fund (TMCF).

Eligibility: Open to full-time students currently entering their senior year at 1 of the 47 colleges and universities that are TMCF members. Applicants must have a GPA of 3.0 or higher and be able to demonstrate financial need. They must be majoring in computer science, information technology (IT), or management information systems and have been accepted into the MetLife IT Internship Program.

Financial data: The stipend is $2,500 per semester ($5,000 per year).

Duration: 1 year.

Number awarded: 6 each year.

Deadline: July of each year.

2134 MG EUGENE C. RENZI, USA (RET.)/MANTECH INTERNATIONAL CORPORATION TEACHER'S SCHOLARSHIP

Armed Forces Communications and Electronics Association
Attn: AFCEA Educational Foundation
4400 Fair Lakes Court
Fairfax, VA 22033-3899
Phone: (703) 631-6149; (800) 336-4583, ext. 6149; Fax: (703) 631-4693
Email: scholarship@afcea.org
Web: www.afcea.org

Summary: To provide financial assistance to undergraduate and graduate students who are preparing for a career as a teacher of science and mathematics.

Eligibility: Open to full-time juniors, seniors, and graduate students at accredited colleges and universities in the United States. Applicants must be U.S. citizens preparing for a career as a teacher of science, mathematics, or information technology at a middle or secondary school. They must have a GPA of 3.0 or higher. In the selection process, first consideration is given to wounded or disabled veterans, then to honorably discharged veterans. Financial need is not considered.

Financial data: The stipend is $2,500.

Duration: 1 year.

Number awarded: 1 each year.

Deadline: May of each year.

2135 MHA ALLIED HEALTH PROFESSION SCHOLARSHIP

Massachusetts Hospital Association
Attn: Human Resources Manager
5 New England Executive Park
Burlington, MA 01803-5096
Phone: (781) 262-6000
Email: workforce@mhalink.org
Web: www.mhalink.org/public/education/scholarship.cfm

Summary: To provide financial assistance to health care professionals interested in working on an academic degree.

Eligibility: Open to health care professionals who have current or previous employment in the field. Applicants must have been accepted into an accredited degree program and be able to complete their degree requirements within 4 years. They must be able to demonstrate interest in clinical practice and health care delivery through documented clinical, community, and work experience; a commitment to get licensure upon graduation; and a commitment to practice in Massachusetts for at least 2 years after graduation. Selection is based on character, merit, references, and financial need.

Financial data: The stipend is $2,000.

Duration: 1 year.

Number awarded: 2 each year.

Deadline: April of each year.

2136 MHEFI SCHOLARSHIP PROGRAM

Material Handling Industry of America
Attn: Material Handling Education Foundation, Inc.
8720 Red Oak Boulevard, Suite 201
Charlotte, NC 28217-3992
Phone: (704) 676-1190; (800) 722-6832; Fax: (704) 676-1199
Email: vwheeler@mhia.org
Web: www.mhia.org/about/mhefi/scholarship

Summary: To provide financial assistance to undergraduate or graduate students who are studying material handling.

Eligibility: Open to 1) students at 4-year colleges and universities who have completed at least 2 years of undergraduate study; and 2) graduate students enrolled in a program leading to a master's or doctoral degree. Students from junior or community colleges are eligible if they have been accepted as a transfer student into a 4-year program. Applicants must be U.S. citizens; be attending an academic institution that has been prequalified for foundation funding; have earned a GPA of 3.0 or higher in college; and be enrolled full-time in a course of study relevant to the material handling industry, including engineering (civil, computer, industrial, electrical, or mechanical), engineering technology, computer science, or business administration with an emphasis on production management, industrial distribution, supply chain, and/or logistics. Along with their application, they must submit 3 letters of recommendation, official transcripts, documentation of financial need, and a 600-word essay on how their course of study, work experience, and career goals make them an appropriate candidate for this scholarship.

Financial data: Stipends range from $1,500 to $9,000.

Duration: 1 year.

Number awarded: Varies each year; recently, 31 of these scholarships, with a total value of $82,500, were awarded.

Deadline: February of each year.

2137 MICHAEL BAKER CORPORATION SCHOLARSHIP PROGRAM FOR DIVERSITY IN ENGINEERING

Association of Independent Colleges and Universities of Pennsylvania
101 North Front Street
Harrisburg, PA 17101-1405
Phone: (717) 232-8649; Fax: (717) 233-8574
Email: info@aicup.org
Web: www.aicup.org/fundraising

Summary: To provide financial assistance to women and minority students from any state enrolled at member institutions of the Association of Independent Colleges and Universities of Pennsylvania (AICUP) who are majoring in designated fields of engineering.

Eligibility: Open to full-time undergraduate students from any state enrolled at designated AICUP colleges and universities who are women and/or members of the following minority groups: American Indians, Alaska Natives, Asians, Blacks/African Americans, Hispanics/Latinos, Native Hawaiians, or Pacific Islanders. Applicants must be juniors majoring in architectural, civil, or environmental engineering with a GPA of 3.0 or higher. Along with their application, they must submit a 2-page essay on what they believe will be the greatest challenge facing the engineering profession over the next decade, and why.

Financial data: The stipend is $2,500 per year.

Duration: 1 year; may be renewed 1 additional year if the recipient maintains appropriate academic standards.

Number awarded: 1 each year.

Deadline: April of each year.

2138 MICHIGAN GREEN INDUSTRY ASSOCIATION SCHOLARSHIPS

Michigan Green Industry Association
Attn: Scholarship Committee
30600 Telegraph Road, Suite 3360
Bingham Farms, MI 48025
Phone: (248) 646-4992; Fax: (248) 646-4994
Web: www.landscape.org

Summary: To provide financial assistance to residents of Michigan interested in attending college in the state to prepare for a career in the "green industry."

Eligibility: Open to Michigan residents who are enrolled or planning to enroll at a college, university, or community college in the state. Applicants must be interested in preparing for a career in the "green industry," including horticulture, landscape, turf maintenance, and/or arboriculture. They must have a GPA of 2.5 or higher, a record of leadership in extracurricular activities, and a desire to pursue professional opportunities with a landscape management company or tree care company or agency in Michigan after graduation. Preference is given to students with financial need.

Financial data: The stipend is $1,000.

Duration: 1 year; nonrenewable.

Number awarded: 3 each year.
Deadline: April of each year.

2139 MICHIGAN SOCIETY OF PROFESSIONAL ENGINEERS SCHOLARSHIPS

Michigan Society of Professional Engineers
Attn: Scholarship Coordinator
215 North Walnut Street
P.O. Box 15276
Lansing, MI 48901-5276
Phone: (517) 487-9388; Fax: (517) 487-0635
Email: mspe@michiganspe.org
Web: www.michiganspe.org/scholarship.htm

Summary: To provide financial assistance to high school seniors in Michigan who are interested in working on a degree in engineering at a college in the state.
Eligibility: Open to graduating seniors at high schools in Michigan who have a GPA of 3.0 or higher and a composite ACT score of 26 or higher. U.S. citizenship and a demonstration of professional ethics are required. Applicants must have been accepted at an ABET-accredited college or university in the state. They must be planning to enroll in an engineering program and enter the practice of engineering after graduation. Along with their application, they must submit a 250-word essay on "How I Was Influenced to Pursue an Engineering Career." Selection is based on the essay; high school academic record; participation in extracurricular activities; evidence of leadership, character, and self-reliance; and comments from teachers and administrators. Financial need is not considered. Semifinalists are interviewed.
Financial data: The stipend is $1,000.
Duration: 1 year; nonrenewable.
Number awarded: 2 each year.
Deadline: February of each year.

2140 MILDRED COLLINS NURSING/HEALTH SCIENCE/ MEDICINE SCHOLARSHIP

African-American/Caribbean Education Association, Inc.
P.O. Box 1224
Valley Stream, NY 11582-1224
Phone: (718) 949-6733
Email: aaceainc@yahoo.com
Web: www.aaceainc.com/Scholarships.html

Summary: To provide financial assistance to high school seniors of African American or Caribbean heritage who plan to study a field related to nursing, health science, or medicine in college.
Eligibility: Open to graduating high school seniors who are U.S. citizens of African American or Caribbean heritage. Applicants must be planning to attend a college or university and major in a field related to a career in nursing, health science, or medicine. They must have completed 4 years of specified college preparatory courses with a grade of 90 or higher and have an SAT score of at least 1790. They must also have completed at least 200 hours of community service during their 4 years of high school, preferably in the field that they plan to study in college. Financial need is not considered in the selection process. New York residency is not required, but applicants must be available for an interviews in the Queens, New York area.
Financial data: The stipend ranges from $1,000 to $2,500. Funds are paid directly to the recipient.
Duration: 1 year.
Number awarded: 1 each year.
Deadline: April of each year.

2141 MILDRED NUTTING NURSING SCHOLARSHIP

Daughters of the American Revolution–National Society
Attn: Committee Services Office, Scholarships
1776 D Street, N.W.
Washington, DC 20006-5303
Phone: (202) 628-1776
Web: www.dar.org/natsociety/edout_scholar.cfm

Summary: To provide financial assistance to undergraduate students working on a degree in nursing.
Eligibility: Open to undergraduate students currently enrolled in accredited schools of nursing who have completed at least 1 year. Applicants must be sponsored by a local chapter of the Daughters of the American Revolution (DAR). Preference is given to applicants from the greater Lowell, Massachusetts area. Selection is based on academic excellence, commitment to field of study, and financial need. U.S. citizenship is required.
Financial data: The stipend is $1,000.
Duration: 1 year; nonrenewable.
Number awarded: Varies each year.
Deadline: February of each year.

2142 MINNESOTA SOYBEAN RESEARCH AND PROMOTION COUNCIL YOUTH SCHOLARSHIPS

Minnesota Soybean Research and Promotion Council
Attn: Youth Scholarship Program
151 Saint Andrews Court, Suite 710
Mankato, MN 56001
Phone: (507) 388-1635; (888) 896-9678; Fax: (507) 388-6751
Email: info@mnsoybean.com
Web: www.mnsoybean.org/msrpc

Summary: To provide financial assistance to upper-division students from Minnesota who are studying a field related to soybeans at a college in any state.
Eligibility: Open to residents of Minnesota whose family is active in agriculture and who have a record of activities in agriculture and their community. Applicants must be enrolled as a junior or senior at a college or university in any state. They must be working on a degree in soybean agronomy, soil science, or soybean genetics. Along with their application, they must submit a brief statement on how their proposed education will relate back to the soybean farmer or soybean industry. Selection is based on academic record, demonstrated leadership and participation in school and community activities, honors, work experience, goals and aspirations, and an outside appraisal.
Financial data: The stipend is $2,000.
Duration: 1 year; nonrenewable.
Number awarded: Up to 3 each year.
Deadline: February of each year.

2143 MINNESOTA SOYBEAN RESEARCH AND PROMOTION COUNCIL YOUTH SCHOLARSHIPS

Minnesota Soybean Research and Promotion Council
Attn: Youth Scholarship Program
151 Saint Andrews Court, Suite 710
Mankato, MN 56001
Phone: (507) 388-1635; (888) 896-9678; Fax: (507) 388-6751
Email: info@mnsoybean.com
Web: www.mnsoybean.org/checkoff-programs/education

Summary: To provide financial assistance to high school seniors in Minnesota who are planning to study a field related to agriculture at a college in any state.
Eligibility: Open to seniors graduating from high schools in Minnesota whose family is active in agriculture and who have a record of activities in agriculture and their community. Applicants must be planning to enroll at a 2- or 4-year college, university, or technical school in any state. They must be planning to major in agriculture, agribusiness, agricultural animal nutrition, or food science. Along with their application, they must submit a 500-word statement on how their proposed education will benefit the future of soybeans. Selection is based on academic record, demonstrated leadership and participation in school and community activities, honors, work experience, goals and aspirations, and an outside appraisal.
Financial data: The stipend is $1,000.
Duration: 1 year; nonrenewable.
Number awarded: Up to 4 each year.
Deadline: February of each year.

2144 MIRIAM SCHAEFER SCHOLARSHIP

Michigan Council of Teachers of Mathematics
Attn: Scholarship Committee
4767 Stadler Road
Monroe, MI 48162-9424
Phone: (734) 477-0421
Email: info@mictm.org
Web: www.mictm.org

Summary: To provide financial assistance to upper-division students who are enrolled in a teacher education program in Michigan with a mathematics specialty.
Eligibility: Open to Michigan residents who are currently enrolled as a junior or senior at a college or university in the state. Applicants must be majoring in

elementary or secondary education and have a GPA of 3.0 or higher. Secondary education students must be a mathematics major and have successfully completed the required calculus sequence. Elementary education students must have a major or minor in mathematics education. Along with their application, they must submit an essay of 2 to 4 pages on their interest in teaching mathematics, a personal history that led them to that field, why they wish to work with their selected level of student, their philosophy of teaching, and an example of a typical lesson in their classroom. Selection is based on that essay, a list of extracurricular and/or community activities and interests, transcripts, and 3 letters of recommendation.

Financial data: The stipend is $1,500. Funds are paid to the recipients, with their school as the second payee. The award is to be used for tuition, books, and fees.

Duration: 1 year; nonrenewable.

Number awarded: Varies each year; recently, 5 of these scholarships were awarded. Since the program began, a total of 121 scholarships, worth $147,000, have been presented.

Deadline: May of each year.

2145 MISSISSIPPI HEALTH CARE PROFESSIONS LOAN/SCHOLARSHIP PROGRAM

Mississippi Office of Student Financial Aid
3825 Ridgewood Road
Jackson, MS 39211-6453
Phone: (601) 432-6997; (800) 327-2980 (within MS); Fax: (601) 432-6527
Email: sfa@ihl.state.ms.us
Web: www.mississippi.edu/riseupms/financialaid-state.php

Summary: To provide financial assistance to Mississippi residents who are working on an undergraduate degree in speech pathology or psychology at a school in the state.

Eligibility: Open to Mississippi residents who are enrolled full-time as a junior or senior in an approved training program in speech pathology or psychology at a school in the state. Applicants must agree to provide service at a state-operated health institution in Mississippi. The highest priority is given to renewal students.

Financial data: The stipend is $1,500 per year. This is a scholarship/loan program. Obligation can be discharged on the basis of 1 year's service in the health profession at a state-operated health institution in Mississippi for 1 year's scholarship/loan award. In the event the recipient fails to fulfill the service obligation, repayment of principal and interest is required.

Duration: 1 year; may be renewed 1 additional year, provided the recipient maintains a GPA of 2.5 or higher.

Number awarded: Varies each year, depending on the availability of funds; awards are granted on a first-come, first-served basis.

Deadline: March of each year.

2146 MISSISSIPPI NURSING EDUCATION LOAN/SCHOLARSHIP PROGRAM–BSN

Mississippi Office of Student Financial Aid
3825 Ridgewood Road
Jackson, MS 39211-6453
Phone: (601) 432-6997; (800) 327-2980 (within MS); Fax: (601) 432-6527
Email: sfa@ihl.state.ms.us
Web: www.mississippi.edu/riseupms/financialaid-state.php

Summary: To provide financial assistance to Mississippi residents who are interested in working on a bachelor's degree in nursing.

Eligibility: Open to Mississippi residents working on a B.S.N. degree as a full- or part-time junior or senior at an accredited school of nursing in the state. Applicants must have earned a GPA of 2.5 or higher on all previous college work. They must agree to employment in professional nursing (patient care) in Mississippi.

Financial data: Scholarship/loans are $4,000 per academic year for up to 2 years or a total of $8,000 (prorated over 3 years for part-time participants). For each year of service in Mississippi as a professional nurse (patient care), 1 year's loan will be forgiven. For nurses who received prorated funding over 3 years, the time of service required is 2 years. In the event the recipient fails to fulfill the service obligation, repayment of principal and interest is required.

Duration: 1 year; may be renewed up to 1 additional year of full-time study or 2 years of part-time study provided the recipient maintains a GPA of 2.5 or higher each semester.

Number awarded: Varies each year, depending on the availability of funds; awards are granted on a first-come, first-served basis.

Deadline: March of each year.

2147 MISSISSIPPI NURSING EDUCATION LOAN/SCHOLARSHIP PROGRAM–RN TO BSN

Mississippi Office of Student Financial Aid
3825 Ridgewood Road
Jackson, MS 39211-6453
Phone: (601) 432-6997; (800) 327-2980 (within MS); Fax: (601) 432-6527
Email: sfa@ihl.state.ms.us
Web: www.mississippi.edu/riseupms/financialaid-state.php

Summary: To provide financial assistance to registered nurses in Mississippi who are interested in working on a bachelor's degree.

Eligibility: Open to residents of Mississippi who have a current nursing license (R.N.). Applicants must be working on a baccalaureate degree in nursing (B.S.N.) as a full- or part-time student at an accredited school of nursing in Mississippi and have earned a GPA of 2.5 or higher on all previous college work. They must agree to employment in professional nursing (patient care) in Mississippi or teaching at an accredited school of nursing in the state.

Financial data: Scholarship/loans are $4,000 per academic year for up to 2 years or a total of $8,000 (prorated over 3 years for part-time participants). For each year of service in Mississippi as a professional nurse (patient care) or teacher at an accredited school of nursing, 1 year's loan will be forgiven. For nurses who received prorated funding over 3 years, the time of service required is 2 years. In the event the recipient fails to fulfill the service obligation, repayment of principal and interest is required.

Duration: 1 year; may be renewed up to 1 additional year of full-time study or 2 years of part-time study provided the recipient maintains a GPA of 2.5 or higher each semester.

Number awarded: Varies each year, depending on the availability of funds; awards are granted on a first-come, first-served basis.

Deadline: March of each year.

2148 MISSOURI ASSOCIATION OF FAIRS & FESTIVALS PUBLIC SPEAKING CONTEST

Missouri Association of Fairs & Festivals
Attn: Executive Director
941 East Rodney
Cape Girardeau, MO 63701
Phone: (573) 270-0898
Web: www.missourifairsandfestivals.org/scholarships.htm

Summary: To recognize and reward, with college scholarships, high school students in Missouri who present outstanding speeches on fairs and agriculture.

Eligibility: Open to students enrolled in grades 9–12 at high schools in Missouri. Applicants must submit a copy of a speech, up to 4 pages in length, on an agricultural topic relating to county fairs and of general interest to the public. Based on those manuscripts, finalists are selected to present speeches, from 6 to 8 minutes in length, at the annual convention of the Missouri Association of Fairs & Festivals (MAFF). Following the speech, judges ask questions and speakers have 5 minutes for their answers.

Financial data: First prize is $1,000, second $600, and third $200. All prizes are scholarships that are presented to winners upon evidence of entrance into the college of their choice.

Duration: The competition is held annually.

Number awarded: 3 each year.

Deadline: December of each year.

2149 MISSOURI MINORITY TEACHER EDUCATION SCHOLARSHIP PROGRAM

Missouri Department of Higher Education
Attn: Student Financial Assistance
3515 Amazonas Drive
Jefferson City, MO 65109-5717
Phone: (573) 751-2361; (800) 473-6757; Fax: (573) 751-6635
Email: info@dhe.mo.gov
Web: www.dhe.mo.gov/minorityteaching.html

Summary: To provide financial assistance to minority high school seniors, high school graduates, and college students in Missouri who are interested in preparing for a teaching career in mathematics or science.

Eligibility: Open to Missouri residents who are African American, Asian American, Hispanic American, or Native American. Applicants must be 1) high school seniors, college students, or returning adults (without a degree) who rank in the top 25% of their high school class and scored at or above the 75th percentile on the ACT or SAT examination; 2) individuals who have completed 30 college hours and have a cumulative GPA of 3.0 or better; or 3) baccalaureate degree-holders who are returning to an approved mathematics or science teacher education program. They must be a U.S. citizen or permanent resident or otherwise lawfully present in the United States. All applicants must be enrolled full-time in an approved teacher education program at a community college, 4-year college, or university in Missouri. Selection is based on academic performance, the quantity and quality of school and community activities, range of interests and activities, leadership abilities, interpersonal skills, and desire to enter the field of education.

Financial data: The stipend is $3,000 per year, of which $2,000 is provided by the state as a forgivable loan and $1,000 is provided by the school as a scholarship. Recipients must commit to teaching in a Missouri public elementary or secondary school for 5 years following graduation. If they fail to fulfill that obligation, they must repay the state portion of the scholarship with interest at 9.5%.

Duration: Up to 4 years.

Number awarded: Up to 100 each year.

Deadline: February of each year.

2150 MLN/MCNEA NURSING STUDENT SCHOLARSHIP AWARDS

Michigan League for Nursing
Attn: Director
2410 Woodlake Drive
Okemos, MI 48864
Phone: (517) 347-8091; Fax: (517) 347-4096
Email: cstacy@mhc.org
Web: www.michleaguenursing.org/ViewPage.cfm?NavID=21

Summary: To provide financial assistance to undergraduate nursing students in Michigan.

Eligibility: Open to students who are currently enrolled in a licensed practical nurse, associate degree, or bachelor's degree nursing program in Michigan, have completed at least 1 nursing course with a clinical component, and have at least a 2.0 GPA. Applicants must submit a 500-word essay on a nursing-related topic. Selection is based on academic record, financial need, contributions, and quality of the essay.

Financial data: The stipend is $1,000.

Duration: 1 year.

Number awarded: Varies each year; recently, 7 of these scholarships were awarded.

Deadline: February of each year.

2151 MOLLIE C. AND LARENE B. WOODARD NURSING SCHOLARSHIP

Louisiana State Nurses Association
Attn: Louisiana Nurses Foundation
5713 Superior Drive, Suite A-6
Baton Rouge, LA 70816
Phone: (225) 201-0993; Fax: (225) 201-0971
Email: lsna@lsna.org
Web: www.lsna.org/Woodard-scholarship.html

Summary: To provide financial assistance to residents of Louisiana who are attending college in that state or a bordering state to prepare for a career as a registered nurse (R.N.).

Eligibility: Open to residents of Louisiana who are currently enrolled full-time in the clinical component of a program that prepares them for a career as an R.N. Applicants must be attending a school in Louisiana or a state that borders it (Arkansas, Mississippi, or Texas). They must have a GPA of 3.0 or higher and be able to demonstrate financial need. Along with their application, they must submit a 250-word statement describing their motivation for choosing nursing as a career.

Financial data: The stipend is $5,000 per year.

Duration: 1 year; may be renewed, provided the recipient maintains a GPA of 2.7 or higher.

Number awarded: 1 or more each year.

Deadline: June of each year.

2152 MONSANTO FUND SCHOLARSHIP PROGRAM OF THE HISPANIC SCHOLARSHIP FUND

Hispanic Scholarship Fund
Attn: Selection Committee
55 Second Street, Suite 1500
San Francisco, CA 94105
Phone: (415) 808-2365; (877) HSF-INFO; Fax: (415) 808-2302
Email: scholar1@hsf.net
Web: www.hsf.net/Monsanto_Fund.aspx

Summary: To provide financial assistance to Hispanic students who are working on an undergraduate degree in selected science, engineering, or business fields.

Eligibility: Open to U.S. citizens and permanent residents (must have a permanent resident card or a passport stamped I-551) who are of Hispanic heritage. Applicants must be enrolled as full-time sophomores at a 4-year college or university in the United States, Puerto Rico, Guam, or the U.S. Virgin Islands and have a GPA of 3.0 or higher. They must be majoring in accounting; agricultural science (includes agricultural engineering and agronomy); biology (includes molecular biology); biochemistry; bioinformatics; bioengineering/biotechnology; botany (includes crop science, horticulture, plant pathology, plant science); business administration (includes logistics, supply chain management, procurement); chemical engineering (includes process engineering); chemistry; civil engineering; computer engineering; computer science; electrical engineering; engineering; finance; industrial engineering; information technology/management information systems; mechanical engineering; or zoology (includes entomology). Selection is based on academic achievement, personal strengths, leadership, and financial need. Preference is given to students who participate in a College Assistance Migrant Program (CAMP).

Financial data: The stipend is $10,000 per year.

Duration: 1 year (the junior year); may be renewed for the senior year.

Number awarded: 1 or more each year.

Deadline: October of each year.

2153 MONSTER.COM NURSING DEGREE SCHOLARSHIP FOR EMERGENCY DEPARTMENT EMPLOYEES

Emergency Nurses Association
Attn: ENA Foundation
915 Lee Street
Des Plaines, IL 60016-6569
Phone: (847) 460-4100; (800) 900-9659, ext. 4100; Fax: (847) 460-4004
Email: foundation@ena.org
Web: www.ena.org/foundation/scholarships/Pages/Default.aspx

Summary: To provide financial assistance to emergency department personnel working on an undergraduate degree in nursing.

Eligibility: Open to hospital emergency department employees (e.g., emergency medical technicians, clerical coordinators, CNAs, registration clerks) who are working on an associate or baccalaureate degree in nursing. Applicants must submit a letter from their supervisor verifying their interest in emergency nursing and at least 1 year of emergency department employment. They are not required to be a member of the Emergency Nurses Association (ENA), but they must submit a letter of reference from an ENA member. Along with their application, they must submit a 1-page statement on their professional and educational goals and how this scholarship will help them attain those goals. Selection is based on content and clarity of the goal statement (45%), professional association involvement (35%), presentation of the application (10%), and letters of reference (10%).

Financial data: The stipend is $2,000.

Duration: 1 year.

Number awarded: 1 each year.

Deadline: May of each year.

2154 MONTANA GOVERNOR'S "BEST AND BRIGHTEST" NEED-BASED SCHOLARSHIPS

Summary: To provide financial assistance to Montana residents who are attending or planning to attend designated institutions in the state and can demonstrate financial need.

See Listing #633.

2155 MORRIS K. UDALL SCHOLARSHIPS

Morris K. Udall and Stewart L. Udall Foundation
Attn: Program Manager, Scholarship Program
130 South Scott Avenue
Tucson, AZ 85701-1922
Phone: (520) 901-8562; Fax: (520) 670-5530
Email: info@udall.gov
Web: www.udall.gov/OurPrograms/MKUScholarship/MKUScholarship.aspx

Summary: To provide financial assistance to 1) college sophomores and juniors who intend to prepare for a career in environmental public policy; and 2) Native American and Alaska Native students who intend to prepare for a career in health care or tribal public policy.

Eligibility: Open to undergraduate students. Each 2- and 4-year college and university in the United States and its possessions may nominate up to 6 sophomores or juniors for either or both categories of this program: 1) students who intend to prepare for a career in environmental public policy; and 2) Native American and Alaska Native students who intend to prepare for a career in health care or tribal public policy. For the first category, the program seeks future leaders across a wide spectrum of environmental fields, such as policy, engineering, science, education, urban planning and renewal, business, health, justice, and economics. For the second category, the program seeks future Native American and Alaska Native leaders in public and community health care, tribal government, and public policy affecting Native American communities, including land and resource management, economic development, and education. Nominees must be U.S. citizens, nationals, or permanent residents with a GPA of 3.0 or higher. Along with their application, they must submit an 800-word essay discussing a significant public speech, legislative act, or public policy statement by Congressman Morris K. Udall or Secretary of Interior Stewart L. Udall and its impact on their field of study, interests, and career goals. Selection is based on demonstrated commitment to 1) environmental issues through participation in 1 or more of the following: campus activities, research, community service, or public service; or 2) tribal public policy or Native American health through participation in 1 or more of the following: campus activities, tribal involvement, community or public service, or research; a course of study and proposed career likely to lead to positions where the nominee can make significant contributions to the shaping of environmental, tribal public policy, or Native American health care issues, whether through scientific advances, public or political service, or community action; and leadership, character, desire to make a difference, and general well-roundedness.

Financial data: The maximum stipend for scholarship winners is $5,000 per year. Funds are to be used for tuition, fees, books, and room and board. Honorable mention stipends are $350.

Duration: 1 year; recipients nominated as sophomores may be renominated in their junior year.

Number awarded: Approximately 80 scholarships and 50 honorable mentions are awarded each year.

Deadline: Faculty representatives must submit their nominations by early March of each year.

2156 MTS STUDENT SCHOLARSHIPS

Marine Technology Society
Attn: Student Scholarships
5565 Sterrett Place, Suite 108
Columbia, MD 21044
Phone: (410) 884-5330; Fax: (410) 884-9060
Email: scholarships@mtsociety.org
Web: www.mtsociety.org/education/scholarships.aspx

Summary: To provide financial assistance to entering or continuing undergraduate and graduate students working on a degree in a field related to marine science.

Eligibility: Open to high school seniors accepted into a full-time undergraduate program and current undergraduate and graduate students. Applicants must be planning to work on a degree in marine technology, marine engineering, or marine science. Along with their application, they must submit a 500-word essay on their interest in marine technology, how their interest in marine technology relates to their current field of study, and how they plan to use their degree. Selection is based on that essay, honors received, marine-oriented activities, extracurricular school activities, and community service activities. Membership in the Marine Technology Society (MTS) is not required.

Financial data: The stipend is $2,000. Funds are sent directly to the recipient's college bursar's office.

Duration: 1 year.

Number awarded: Varies each year; recently, 13 of these scholarships were awarded.

Deadline: April of each year.

2157 NAJERA CONSULTING GROUP/HENAAC SCHOLARS PROGRAM

Great Minds in STEM
Attn: HENAAC Scholars
3900 Whiteside Street
Los Angeles, CA 90063
Phone: (323) 262-0997; Fax: (323) 262-0946
Email: kbbarrera@greatmindsinstem.org
Web: www.greatmindsinstem.org/henaac/scholars

Summary: To provide financial assistance to Hispanic undergraduate students majoring in civil engineering.

Eligibility: Open to Hispanic students who are working on an undergraduate degree in civil engineering. Applicants must be of Hispanic origin and/or must significantly participate in and promote organizations and activities in the Hispanic community. They must have a GPA of 3.0 or higher. Along with their application, they must submit a 700-word essay on a topic that changes annually; recently, students were asked to write on how they see their academic major contributing to global efforts and technology and how they, in their field of study, will contribute to global progress as well as actively contribute to their local communities. Selection is based on leadership through academic achievements and campus and community activities; financial need is not considered.

Financial data: Stipends range from $500 to $5,000.

Duration: 1 year; recipients may reapply.

Number awarded: 1 or more each year.

Deadline: April of each year.

2158 NASA JOHNSON SPACE CENTER SCHOLARSHIPS

Great Minds in STEM
Attn: HENAAC Scholars
3900 Whiteside Street
Los Angeles, CA 90063
Phone: (323) 262-0997; Fax: (323) 262-0946
Email: kbbarrera@greatmindsinstem.org
Web: www.greatmindsinstem.org/henaac/scholars

Summary: To provide financial assistance to Hispanic undergraduate students from any state who are enrolled at universities in the service area of the Johnson Space Center of the National Aeronautics and Space Administration (NASA) and majoring in fields of science, technology, engineering, or mathematics (STEM).

Eligibility: Open to Hispanic undergraduate students from any state who are majoring in a field of STEM at a college or university in the service area of NASA's Johnson Space Center (Colorado, Kansas, Nebraska, New Mexico, North Dakota, Oklahoma, South Dakota, and Texas). Applicants must be of Hispanic origin and/or must significantly participate in and promote organizations and activities in the Hispanic community. They must have a GPA of 3.0 or higher. Along with their application, they must submit a 700-word essay on a topic that changes annually; recently, students were asked to write on how they see their academic major contributing to global efforts and technology and how they, in their field of study, will contribute to global progress as well as actively contribute to their local communities. Selection is based on leadership through academic achievements and campus and community activities; financial need is not considered.

Financial data: Stipends range from $500 to $5,000.

Duration: 1 year; recipients may reapply.

Number awarded: Varies each year; recently, 9 of these scholarships were awarded.

Deadline: April of each year.

2159 NASA MOTIVATING UNDERGRADUATES IN SCIENCE AND TECHNOLOGY (MUST) SCHOLARSHIP PROGRAM

Hispanic College Fund
Attn: Scholarship Processing
1301 K Street, N.W., Suite 450-A West
Washington, DC 20005
Phone: (202) 296-5400; (800) 644-4223; Fax: (202) 296-3774
Email: hcf-info@hispanicfund.org
Web: scholarships.hispanicfund.org/applications

Summary: To provide financial assistance to members of underrepresented groups who are working on an undergraduate degree in a field of science, technology, engineering, or mathematics (STEM).

Eligibility: Open to U.S. citizens from an underrepresented group, including women, African Americans, Hispanic Americans, Native Americans, and persons with disabilities. Applicants must be entering their freshman, sophomore, junior, or senior year at an accredited college or university in the 50 states or Puerto Rico as a full-time student. They must have a GPA of 3.0 or higher and a major in a STEM field of study.

Financial data: Stipends provide payment of 50% of the tuition and fees at the recipient's institution, to a maximum of $10,000. The stipend for the summer research experience is $5,000.

Duration: 1 year; recipients may reapply.

Number awarded: 100 each year.

Deadline: January of each year.

2160 NASA UNDERGRADUATE SCHOLARSHIP PROGRAM

American Society for Engineering Education
Attn: Projects Department
1818 N Street, N.W., Suite 600
Washington, DC 20036-2479
Phone: (202) 331-3546; Fax: (202) 265-8504
Email: nasa.asp@asee.org
Web: nasa.asee.org/undergraduate_program

Summary: To provide financial assistance and summer research experience at facilities of the National Aeronautics and Space Administration (NASA) to undergraduate students majoring in designated fields of science and engineering.

Eligibility: Open to U.S. citizens and nationals who are working on an undergraduate degree and have at least 2 years of full-time study remaining. Applicants must be majoring in computer sciences, mathematics, physics, or engineering (aeronautical and aerospace, chemical, civil, computer, electrical and electronic, energy, engineering mechanics, engineering science, industrial, materials, mechanical, metallurgical, polymer, or systems). They must be available for an internship at a NASA center performing aeronautical research during the summer between their junior and senior years. Along with their application, they must submit an essay describing what they think are the greatest technical challenges in aeronautics for the next 20 to 25 years and why. Financial need is not considered in the selection process.

Financial data: The academic stipend is $15,000 per year; funds must be used for educational related expenses. The salary for the summer internship is $10,000.

Duration: 2 years.

Number awarded: 20 each year.

Deadline: January of each year.

2161 NASCAR/WENDELL SCOTT AWARD

Hispanic Association of Colleges and Universities
Attn: National Scholarship Program
8415 Datapoint Drive, Suite 400
San Antonio, TX 78229
Phone: (210) 692-3805; Fax: (210) 692-0823; TDD: (800) 855-2880
Email: scholarships@hacu.net
Web: www.hacu.net/hacu/Scholarships_EN.asp?SnID=875148054

Summary: To provide financial assistance to undergraduate and graduate students majoring in specified fields at member institutions of the Hispanic Association of Colleges and Universities (HACU) in designated states.

Eligibility: Open to full-time undergraduate and graduate students at 4-year HACU member institutions in Florida, Georgia, and North Carolina. Applicants must be working on a degree in business, engineering, marketing, mass media, marketing management and technology, public relations, or sports marketing. They must have a GPA of 3.0 or higher and be able to demonstrate financial need. Along with their application, they must submit an essay of 200 to 250 words that describes their academic and/or career goals, where they expect to be and what they expect to be doing 10 years from now, and what skills they can bring to an employer.

Financial data: The stipend is $1,500 for undergraduates or $2,000 for graduate students.

Duration: 1 year.

Number awarded: 1 or more each year.

Deadline: May of each year.

2162 NATIONAL AMBUCS SCHOLARSHIP PROGRAM

National AMBUCS, Inc.
Attn: National Scholarship Committee
P.O. Box 5127
High Point, NC 27262
Phone: (800) 838-1845; Fax: (336) 852-6830
Email: ambucs@ambucs.org
Web: www.ambucs.com/scholarship-program-information

Summary: To provide financial assistance to upper-division and graduate students working on a degree in a therapy-related field.

Eligibility: Open to students in their junior or senior year of a bachelor's degree or a graduate program leading to a master's or doctoral degree. Applicants must be enrolled in an accredited program in physical therapy, occupational therapy, speech language pathology, or heating audiology. Assistant programs are not eligible. U.S. citizenship is required. Selection is based on academic accomplishment, character for compassion and integrity, career objectives, commitment to local community, and financial need.

Financial data: Stipends range from $500 to $1,500, although 1 scholarship is for $3,000 per year.

Duration: Up to 2 years.

Number awarded: Varies each year; approximately $150,000 is available for this program annually.

Deadline: April of each year.

2163 NATIONAL ASSOCIATION OF ABANDONED MINE LAND PROGRAMS SCHOLARSHIP

National Association of Abandoned Mine Land Programs
c/o Murray Balk, Section Chief
Kansas Department of Health and Environment
Surface Mining Section
4033 Parkview Drive
Frontenac, KS 66763-2302
Phone: (620) 231-8540; Fax: (620) 231-0753
Email: mbalk@kdheks.gov
Web: naamlp.net

Summary: To provide financial assistance to undergraduates preparing for a career as a scientist or technician in the field of mine land reclamation.

Eligibility: Open to undergraduates who can demonstrate a commitment to the reclamation and restoration of lands affected by abandoned mining. Applicants must be working on a degree in the field of mine land reclamation (e.g., biological, physical, or environmental science; mining, environmental, or civil engineering). Financial need is considered in the selection process.

Financial data: The stipend is $1,500. Funds are paid directly to the recipients' institutions.

Duration: 1 year.

Number awarded: 2 each year: 1 to a student in the Midwest or eastern United States; 1 to a student in the western United States.

Deadline: May of each year.

2164 NATIONAL DAIRY SHRINE/DMI MILK MARKETING SCHOLARSHIPS

National Dairy Shrine
Attn: Executive Director
P.O. Box 1
Maribel, WI 54227
Phone: (920) 863-6333; Fax: (920) 863-8328
Email: info@dairyshrine.org
Web: www.dairyshrine.org/scholarships.php

Summary: To provide financial assistance to college students enrolled in a dairy science program who are preparing for careers in the marketing of dairy products.

Eligibility: Open to college sophomores or juniors who have a cumulative GPA of 2.5 or higher. They must be majoring in dairy science, animal science, agricultural economics, agricultural communications, agricultural education, general agriculture, or food and nutrition. Selection is based on student organizational activities (15%), other organizational activities (10%), academic standing and course work associated with marketing (25%), honors and awards (10%), marketing experiences (10%), and a 500-word essay on why they are interested in dairy product marketing, including their plans for the future (30%).

Financial data: Stipends are $1,500 or $1,000.

Duration: 1 year.

Number awarded: 7 each year; 1 at $1,500 and 6 at $1,000.

Deadline: April of each year.

2165 NATIONAL FEDERATION OF THE BLIND COMPUTER SCIENCE SCHOLARSHIP

National Federation of the Blind
Attn: Scholarship Committee
1800 Johnson Street
Baltimore, MD 21230
Phone: (410) 659-9314, ext. 2415; Fax: (410) 685-5653
Email: scholarships@nfb.org
Web: www.nfb.org/nfb/scholarship_program.asp

Summary: To provide financial assistance to entering and continuing undergraduate and graduate students who are legally blind and working on a degree in computer science.

Eligibility: Open to legally blind students who are working on or planning to work full-time on an undergraduate or graduate degree in computer science. Along with their application, they must submit transcripts, standardized test scores, proof of legal blindness, 2 letters of recommendation, and a letter of endorsement from their National Federation of the Blind state president or designee. Selection is based on academic excellence, service to the community, and financial need.

Financial data: The stipend is $3,000.

Duration: 1 year; recipients may resubmit applications up to 2 additional years.

Number awarded: 1 each year.

Deadline: March of each year.

2166 NATIONAL GARDEN CLUBS HIGH SCHOOL ESSAY CONTEST

National Garden Clubs, Inc.
4401 Magnolia Avenue
St. Louis, MO 63110-3492
Phone: (314) 776-7574; Fax: (314) 776-5108
Email: headquarters@gardenclub.org
Web: www.gardenclub.org/Youth/Contests/EssayContest.aspx

Summary: To recognize and reward, with college scholarships, high school students who submit outstanding essays on a topic related to horticulture.

Eligibility: Open to high school students in grades 9–12. Each year, students are invited to submit an essay, between 500 to 600 words in length, on a topic that changes annually but relates to horticulture. Recently, the topic was "Nurture the Earth—Foster Our Environment." The contest must be sponsored by a garden club that is a member of National Garden Clubs, group of member clubs, council or district, or state garden club. State winners are forwarded to regional chairs; regional winners are then entered in the national competition. Selection is based on knowledge of subject (25 points), practicality of proposal (10 points), originality (15 points), clarity of presentation (15 points), vocabulary (15 points), conformance to length (10 points), and quality of manuscript (10 points).

Financial data: The national winner receives a $1,000 scholarship. Second prize is $100. If the national winner is an underclassman, the prize is held until the student graduates from high school. At that time, the funds are forwarded to the college that the student enters.

Duration: The contest is held annually.

Number awarded: 2 each year.

Deadline: Each state sets its own deadline; most are in October. State winners must be forwarded to the regional chair by December of each year.

2167 NATIONAL GARDEN CLUBS SCHOLARSHIPS

Summary: To provide financial assistance to upper-division and graduate students in horticulture, landscape design, and related disciplines.

See Listing #1449.

2168 NATIONAL HYDROPOWER ASSOCIATION PAST PRESIDENTS' LEGACY SCHOLARSHIP

National Hydropower Association
25 Massachusetts Avenue, N.W., Suite 450
Washington, DC 20001
Phone: (202) 682-1700; Fax: (202) 682-9478
Email: help@hydro.org
Web: www.hydro.org/news/scholarship.php

Summary: To provide financial assistance to undergraduate and graduate students working on a degree in a field related to the hydropower industry.

Eligibility: Open to juniors, seniors, and graduate students who are enrolled full-time at an accredited 4-year college or university or vocational/technical school. Applicants must be working on a degree in a program of study related to the hydropower industry: engineering (civil, earth sciences, electrical, mechanical, systems); science (biology, fisheries, hydrology); communications (public administration, public policy, public relations); or environmental (environmental studies, environmental management, renewable energy). They must have a cumulative GPA of 2.5 or higher. Along with their application, they must submit a brief statement on their plans as they relate to their education and career objectives and long-term goals, especially their desire and intent to work in the hydropower industry. U.S. citizenship or permanent resident status is required. Financial need is not considered in the selection process.

Financial data: The stipend is $2,000.

Duration: 1 year.

Number awarded: 1 or more each year.

Deadline: February of each year.

2169 NATIONAL MARKET NEWS ASSOCIATION SCHOLARSHIP PROGRAM

National Market News Association
c/o Sherry Warren
NCDA&CS, Market News
1020 Mail Service Center
Raleigh, NC 27699-1020
Phone: (919) 733-7252, ext. 312; Fax: (919) 715-6748
Email: Sherry.Warren@ncagr.gov
Web: www.ams.usda.gov/nmna

Summary: To provide financial assistance to undergraduate and graduate students working on a degree in an field related to agriculture or agribusiness.

Eligibility: Open to students working full-time on an undergraduate or graduate degree in agriculture, animal science, agricultural economics, agricultural marketing, plant science, or other agricultural field. Applicants must submit a 250-word essay on their past achievements, career goals after graduation, and why they should receive this scholarship. Selection is based on financial need, academic achievement, service activities, career goals, and potential for future leadership in the agricultural industry.

Financial data: Stipend amounts vary; recently, they were $1,500.

Duration: 1 year.

Number awarded: 1 or 2 each year.

Deadline: May of each year.

2170 NATIONAL SCIENCE AND MATHEMATICS ACCESS TO RETAIN TALENT (SMART) GRANTS

Department of Education
Attn: Federal Student Aid Information Center
P.O. Box 84
Washington, DC 20044-0084
Phone: (319) 337-5665; (800) 4-FED-AID; TDD: (800) 730-8913
Web: www.FederalStudentAid.ed.gov

Summary: To provide financial assistance to upper-division students in specified fields who can demonstrate financial need.

Eligibility: Open to U.S. citizens and eligible noncitizens who are entering their third or fourth year of a baccalaureate degree program and have a GPA of 3.0 or higher. Applicants must be majoring in computer sciences; engineering; foreign languages deemed critical to national security (currently, all languages are eligible); life sciences (including biology, biochemistry, biophysics, biotechnology, botany, cellular biology, ecology, genetics, microbiology, pharmacology and toxicology, physiology, and zoology); mathematics and statistics; natural resources and conservation (including agriculture, animal science, crop science and agronomy, fisheries science, food science and technology, forestry, horticulture, soil sciences, wildlife management), physical sciences (including astronomy and astrophysics, atmospheric sciences and meteorology, chemistry, geological and earth sciences, and physics); psychology; technology; and designated multidisciplinary studies (biological and physical sciences, systems science and theory, mathematics and computer science, accounting and computer sciences, natural sciences, neuroscience, and cognitive science). They must demonstrate financial need and qualify for a federal Pell Grant.

Financial data: The grant is $4,000 per year. Funding is in addition to that provided by the Pell Grant.

Duration: Up to 2 years.

Number awarded: Varies each year.

Deadline: Deadline not specified.

2171 NATIONAL SECURITY SCHOLARSHIPS OF THE INDEPENDENT COLLEGE FUND OF MARYLAND

Summary: To provide financial assistance to students from any state enrolled at member institutions of the Independent College Fund of Maryland and majoring in a field related to national security.

See Listing #1456.

2172 NATIONAL SPACE GRANT COLLEGE AND FELLOWSHIP PROGRAM

National Aeronautics and Space Administration
Attn: Office of Education
300 E Street, S.W.
Mail Suite 6M35
Washington, DC 20546-0001
Phone: (202) 358-1069; Fax: (202) 358-3048
Email: Diane.D.DeTroye@nasa.gov

Web: www.nasa.gov

Summary: To provide financial assistance to undergraduate and graduate students interested in preparing for a career in a space-related field.

Eligibility: Open to undergraduate and graduate students at colleges and universities that participate in the National Space Grant program of the U.S. National Aeronautics and Space Administration (NASA) through their state consortium. Applicants must be interested in a program of study and/or research in a field of science, technology, engineering, or mathematics (STEM) related to space. A specific goal of the program is to increase preparation by members of underrepresented groups (minorities, women, and persons with disabilities) for STEM space-related careers. Financial need is not considered in the selection process.

Financial data: Each consortium establishes the terms of the fellowship program in its state.

Number awarded: Varies each year.

Deadline: Each consortium sets its own deadlines.

2173 NATIONAL STUDENT NURSES' ASSOCIATION CAREER MOBILITY SCHOLARSHIPS

National Student Nurses' Association
Attn: Foundation
45 Main Street, Suite 606
Brooklyn, NY 11201
Phone: (718) 210-0705; Fax: (718) 797-1186
Email: nsna@nsna.org
Web: www.nsna.org/FoundationScholarships/FNSNAScholarships.aspx

Summary: To provide financial assistance to nurses interested in pursuing additional education.

Eligibility: Open to 1) registered nurses enrolled in programs leading to a baccalaureate or master's degree in nursing; or 2) licensed practical and vocational nurses enrolled in programs leading to licensure as a registered nurse. Graduating high school seniors are not eligible. Applicants must submit a 200-word description of their professional and educational goals and how this scholarship will help them achieve those goals. Selection is based on academic achievement, financial need, and involvement in student nursing organizations and community activities related to health care. U.S. citizenship or permanent resident status is required.

Financial data: Stipends range from $1,000 to $2,500. A total of approximately $155,000 is awarded each year by the foundation for all its scholarship programs.

Duration: 1 year.

Number awarded: Varies each year; recently, 2 of these scholarships were awarded, both sponsored by Anthony J. Jannetti, Inc.

Deadline: January of each year.

2174 NATIONAL STUDENT NURSES' ASSOCIATION GENERAL SCHOLARSHIPS

National Student Nurses' Association
Attn: Foundation
45 Main Street, Suite 606
Brooklyn, NY 11201
Phone: (718) 210-0705; Fax: (718) 797-1186
Email: nsna@nsna.org
Web: www.nsna.org/FoundationScholarships/FNSNAScholarships.aspx

Summary: To provide financial assistance to nursing or pre-nursing students.

Eligibility: Open to students currently enrolled in state-approved schools of nursing or pre-nursing associate degree, baccalaureate, diploma, generic master's, generic doctoral, R.N. to B.S.N., R.N. to M.S.N., or L.P.N./L.V.N. to R.N. programs. Graduating high school seniors are not eligible. Support for graduate education is provided only for a first degree in nursing. Applicants must submit a 200-word description of their professional and educational goals and how this scholarship will help them achieve those goals. Selection is based on academic achievement, financial need, and involvement in student nursing organizations and community health activities. U.S. citizenship or permanent resident status is required.

Financial data: Stipends range from $1,000 to $2,500. A total of approximately $125,000 is awarded each year by the foundation for all its scholarship programs.

Duration: 1 year.

Number awarded: Varies each year; recently, 63 of these scholarships were awarded.

Deadline: January of each year.

2175 NAVAL WEATHER SERVICE ASSOCIATION SCHOLARSHIP

Naval Weather Service Association
c/o Libby O'Brien, Secretary/Treasurer
515 Ashley Road
Cantonment, FL 32533-5610
Phone: (850) 968-0552
Email: nwsasectreas@panhandle.rr.com
Web: www.navalweather.org/NWSA_Scholarships.htm

Summary: To provide financial assistance to high school seniors and currently-enrolled undergraduates who plan to work on a degree in selected science or engineering fields.

Eligibility: Open to students who are enrolled or planning to enroll full-time in an undergraduate program in meteorology, oceanography, or aerospace engineering. Applicants must be U.S. citizens or permanent residents. Along with their application, they must submit a 250-word essay on their goals in attending college, their interests in the major they have selected, and their long-range career objectives. Selection is based on academic record; leadership skills; diverse interests and community involvement; commitment to a career in meteorology, oceanography, or aerospace engineering; and financial need.

Financial data: Stipends range from $1,000 to $3,000. Funds may be used to pay for tuition, fees, books, supplies, equipment, or any other educational expenses.

Duration: 1 year; recipients may reapply.

Number awarded: 1 or more each year.

Deadline: April of each year.

2176 NAVSEA/HENAAC SCHOLARS PROGRAM

Great Minds in STEM
Attn: HENAAC Scholars
3900 Whiteside Street
Los Angeles, CA 90063
Phone: (323) 262-0997; Fax: (323) 262-0946
Email: kbbarrera@greatmindsinstem.org
Web: www.greatmindsinstem.org/henaac/scholars

Summary: To provide financial assistance to Hispanic undergraduate students majoring in a field of science, technology, engineering, or mathematics (STEM) at a minority institution (MI).

Eligibility: Open to Hispanic students who are enrolled at an MI working on an undergraduate degree in a field of STEM. Applicants must be of Hispanic origin and/or must significantly participate in and promote organizations and activities in the Hispanic community. They must have a GPA of 3.0 or higher and a record of activity in school and community organizations. Along with their application, they must submit a 700-word essay on a topic that changes annually; recently, students were asked to write on how they see their academic major contributing to global efforts and technology and how they, in their field of study, will contribute to global progress as well as actively contribute to their local communities. Selection is based on leadership through academic achievements and campus and community activities and on financial need. U.S. citizenship is required.

Financial data: Stipends range from $500 to $5,000.

Duration: 1 year; recipients may reapply.

Number awarded: Varies each year; recently, 3 of these scholarships were awarded.

Deadline: April of each year.

2177 NAVY ADVANCED EDUCATION VOUCHER PROGRAM

Summary: To provide financial assistance to Navy enlisted personnel who are interested in earning an undergraduate or graduate degree in selected fields during off-duty hours.

See Listing #1462.

2178 NAVY COLLEGE ASSISTANCE/STUDENT HEADSTART (NAVY-CASH) PROGRAM

U.S. Navy
Attn: Navy Personnel Command
5722 Integrity Drive
Millington, TN 38054-5057
Phone: (901) 874-3070; (888) 633-9674; Fax: (901) 874-2651
Email: nukeprograms@cnrc.navy.mil
Web: www.cnrc.navy.mil/nucfield/college/enlisted_options.htm

Summary: To provide financial assistance to high school seniors and current college students interested in attending college for a year and then entering the Navy's nuclear program.
Eligibility: Open to applicants who are able to meet the specific requirements of the Navy's Enlisted Nuclear Field Program. They must be enrolled or accepted for enrollment at an accredited 2-year community or junior college or 4-year college or university.
Financial data: While they attend school, participants are paid a regular Navy salary at a pay grade up to E-3 (starting at $1,303.50 per month). They are also eligible for all of the Navy's enlistment incentives, including the Navy College Fund, the Loan Repayment Program, and an enlistment bonus up to $12,000.
Duration: 12 months.
Number awarded: Varies each year.
Deadline: Deadline not specified.

2179 NAVY NURSE CANDIDATE PROGRAM

U.S. Navy
Attn: Navy Medicine Manpower, Personnel, Education and Training Command Code OH
8901 Wisconsin Avenue, Building 1, Tower 13, Room 13132
Bethesda, MD 20889-5611
Phone: (301) 295-1217; (800) USA-NAVY; Fax: (301) 295-1811
Email: OH@med.navy.mil
Web: www.med.navy.mil
Summary: To provide financial assistance for nursing education to students interested in serving in the Navy.
Eligibility: Open to full-time students in a bachelor of science in nursing program who are U.S. citizens under 40 years of age. Prior to or during their junior year of college, applicants must enlist in the U.S. Navy Nurse Corps Reserve. Following receipt of their degree, they must be willing to serve on active duty as a nurse in the Navy.
Financial data: This program pays a $10,000 initial grant upon enlistment (paid in 2 installments of $5,000 each) and a stipend of $1,000 per month. Students are responsible for paying all school expenses.
Duration: Up to 24 months.
Number awarded: Varies each year.
Deadline: Deadline not specified.

2180 NAVY NURSE CORPS NROTC SCHOLARSHIP PROGRAM

U.S. Navy
Attn: Naval Education and Training Command
NSTC OD2
250 Dallas Street, Suite A
Pensacola, FL 32508-5268
Phone: (850) 452-4941, ext. 25166; (800) NAV-ROTC, ext. 25166; Fax: (850) 452-2486
Email: PNSC_NROTC.scholarship@navy.mil
Web: www.nrotc.navy.mil/nurse.aspx
Summary: To provide financial assistance to graduating high school seniors who are interested in joining Navy ROTC and majoring in nursing in college.
Eligibility: Open to graduating high school seniors who have been accepted at a college with a Navy ROTC unit on campus or a college with a cross-enrollment agreement with such a college. Applicants must be U.S. citizens between the ages of 17 and 23 who plan to study nursing in college and are willing to serve for 4 years as active-duty Navy officers in the Navy Nurse Corps following graduation from college. They must not have reached their 27th birthday by the time of college graduation and commissioning; applicants who have prior active-duty military service may be eligible for age adjustments for the amount of time equal to their prior service, up to a maximum of 36 months. They must have minimum SAT scores of 530 in critical reading and 520 in mathematics or minimum ACT scores of 22 in English and 21 in mathematics.
Financial data: This scholarship provides payment of full tuition and required educational fees, as well as $375 per semester for textbooks, supplies, and equipment. The program also provides a stipend for 10 months of the year that is $250 per month as a freshman, $300 per month as a sophomore, $350 per month as a junior, and $400 per month as a senior.
Duration: 4 years.
Number awarded: Varies each year.
Deadline: January of each year.

2181 NCA SCHOLARSHIP PROGRAM

Healthcare Information and Management Systems Society–National Capital Area Chapter
c/o Ann Kenny, Scholarship Chair
SRA International
4300 Fair Lakes Court
Fairfax, VA 22033
Phone: (703) 502-1119
Email: Ann_Kenny@sra.com
Web: www.himss-nca.org
Summary: To provide financial assistance to residents of any state enrolled at colleges and universities in the Washington, D.C. metropolitan area and working on an undergraduate or graduate degree in fields related to the health or management information systems industry.
Eligibility: Open to residents of any state enrolled at a college or university in the Washington, D.C. metropolitan area and working on an associate, bachelor's, master's, or Ph.D. degree. Applicants must be studying health management, health information, informatics, or a management systems-related field. They must have a GPA of 3.0 or higher. Membership in the National Capital Area (NCA) chapter of the Healthcare Information and Management Systems Society (HIMSS) is required, but that requirement may be waived upon request. Along with their application, they must submit a 500-word essay on why they have chosen the field of information management/information technology (IM/IT), why IM/IT is important to health care today, and a major issue facing the community today and how IM/IT can address that issue. Selection is based on that essay, academic achievement, demonstration of leadership potential, communication skills, and participation in such professional activities as HIMSS-NCA.
Financial data: The stipend is at least $3,000.
Duration: 1 year; nonrenewable.
Number awarded: 3 each year: 1 to an associate degree student, 1 to an undergraduate student, and 1 to a graduate student.
Deadline: April of each year.

2182 NCCE SCHOLARSHIPS

Summary: To provide financial assistance to students participating or planning to participate in cooperative education projects at designated colleges and universities.
See Listing #688.

2183 NDPRB UNDERGRADUATE SCHOLARSHIP PROGRAM

National Dairy Promotion and Research Board
c/o Dairy Management Inc.
10255 West Higgins Road, Suite 900
Rosemont, IL 60018-5615
Phone: (847) 627-3320; (800) 85-DAIRY; Fax: (847) 803-2077
Email: Jolene.griffin@rosedmi.com
Web: www.dairycheckoff.com
Summary: To provide financial assistance to undergraduate students in various fields related to the dairy industry.
Eligibility: Open to sophomores, juniors, and seniors enrolled in college and university programs that emphasize dairy. Eligible majors include agricultural education, business, communications and/or public relations, economics, food science, journalism, marketing, and nutrition. Fields related to production (e.g., animal science) are not eligible. Along with their application, they must submit a description of their career objectives, including what stimulated their interest in dairy. Selection is based on academic performance; courses related to dairy; commitment to a career in dairy; involvement in extracurricular activities, especially those relating to dairy; and evidence of leadership ability, initiative, character, and integrity. The applicant who is judged most outstanding is awarded the James H. Loper Jr. Memorial Scholarship.
Financial data: Stipends are $2,500 or $1,500.
Duration: 1 year; may be renewed.
Number awarded: 20 each year: the James H. Loper Jr. Memorial Scholarship at $2,500 and 19 other scholarships at $1,500.
Deadline: May of each year.

2184 NEHA/AAS SCHOLARSHIPS

National Environmental Health Association
Attn: Scholarship Coordinator
720 South Colorado Boulevard, Suite 1000-N
Denver, CO 80246-1926
Phone: (303) 756-9090, ext. 343; Fax: (303) 691-9490
Email: cdimmitt@neha.org
Web: www.neha.org/scholarship/scholarship.html
Summary: To provide financial assistance to upper-division and graduate students interested in preparing for a career in environmental health.

Eligibility: Open to undergraduate and graduate students preparing for a career in environmental health. Undergraduates must be entering their junior or senior year in an approved environmental health curriculum at a 4-year college or university accredited by the Environmental Health Accreditation Council (EHAC). Graduate applicants may be enrolled in a college or university with a program of studies in environmental health sciences and/or public health. Selection for both levels is based on academic record and letters of recommendation; at least 1 letter of recommendation must be from an active member of the National Environmental Health Association (NEHA). Some consideration is also given to financial need.
Financial data: Stipends range from $400 to $1,000.
Duration: 1 year; may be renewed.
Number awarded: Up to 3 each year.
Deadline: January of each year.

2185 NEIL HAMILTON MEMORIAL SCHOLARSHIP

Oregon Student Assistance Commission
Attn: Grants and Scholarships Division
1500 Valley River Drive, Suite 100
Eugene, OR 97401-2146
Phone: (541) 687-7395; (800) 452-8807, ext. 7395; Fax: (541) 687-7414; TDD: (800) 735-2900
Email: awardinfo@osac.state.or.us
Web: www.osac.state.or.us/osac_programs.html
Summary: To provide financial assistance to residents of Oregon who are interested in studying fire science at a community college in the state.
Eligibility: Open to graduates of high schools in Oregon, including GED recipients and home-schooled graduates. Applicants must be enrolled or planning to enroll at least half-time at a community college in the state and majoring in fire science or fire suppression/protection. They must have a GPA of 2.5 or higher or a GED score of at least 2500. Financial need is not required, but it is considered in the selection process.
Financial data: The stipend is $1,000.
Duration: 1 year; nonrenewable.
Number awarded: Varies each year.
Deadline: February of each year.

2186 NEW ENGLAND NAVY NURSE CORPS ASSOCIATION SCHOLARSHIP

New England Navy Nurse Corps Association
c/o Maria K. Carroll, Scholarship Committee
22 William Drive
Middletown, RI 02842-5266
Summary: To provide financial assistance to registered nurses (R.N.s) and nursing students working on a bachelor's or master's degree at a college or university in New England.
Eligibility: Open to R.N.s and nursing students in the New England states. Applicants must be working on a bachelor's or master's degree in nursing and have a GPA of 2.3 or higher. They must have completed at least 1 clinical nursing course. Along with their application, they must submit a 500-word essay on why they are qualified for this scholarship, their career goals, and their potential for contribution to the profession.
Financial data: The stipend is $1,000.
Duration: 1 year.
Number awarded: 2 each year.
Deadline: May of each year.

2187 NEW HAMPSHIRE ASCE HIGH SCHOOL SCHOLARSHIPS

American Society of Civil Engineers–New Hampshire Section
Attn: Scholarships
P.O. Box 4953
Manchester, NH 03108
Email: fdouglas@comcast.net
Web: ascenh.org/index.php?page=scholarship
Summary: To provide financial assistance to high school seniors in New Hampshire who plan to major in civil engineering at a college in any state.
Eligibility: Open to seniors graduating from high schools in New Hampshire and planning to enroll at a 4-year college or university in any state. Applicants must be planning to work on a bachelor's degree in civil engineering. Along with their application, they must submit a 2-page essay on a topic that changes annually but relates to civil engineering; recently, students were asked to write on how civil engineering impacts their daily life. Selection is based on that essay, completeness of the application materials, and letters of recommendation.
Financial data: The stipend is $1,000.
Duration: 1 year.
Number awarded: 4 each year.
Deadline: April of each year.

2188 NEW HAMPSHIRE TEACHERS OF MATHEMATICS PRE-SERVICE MATHEMATICS EDUCATION SCHOLARSHIP FOR COLLEGE STUDENTS

New Hampshire Teachers of Mathematics
c/o Judy Curran Black, President
5 Cole Road
Derry, NH 03038
Email: jcurranblack@aim.com
Web: sites.google.com/site/nhteachersofmathematics
Summary: To provide financial assistance to residents of New Hampshire who are attending college, preferably in the state, to prepare for a career as a teacher of mathematics.
Eligibility: Open to residents of New Hampshire who are entering their junior or senior year of a certification program for secondary, middle, or elementary mathematics education. Preference is given to students attending New Hampshire institutions of higher education. Applicants must submit a copy of all their transcripts, 2 letters of recommendation, documentation of financial need, and a brief essay on why they are interested in becoming a mathematics teacher. Selection is based on academic achievement, evidence of promise as a teacher of mathematics, and financial need.
Financial data: The stipend is $1,000.
Duration: 1 year.
Number awarded: 1 each year.
Deadline: May of each year.

2189 NEW HAMPSHIRE TEACHERS OF MATHEMATICS PRE-SERVICE MATHEMATICS EDUCATION SCHOLARSHIP FOR HIGH SCHOOL STUDENTS

New Hampshire Teachers of Mathematics
c/o Judy Curran Black, President
5 Cole Road
Derry, NH 03038
Email: jcurranblack@aim.com
Web: sites.google.com/site/nhteachersofmathematics
Summary: To provide financial assistance to high school students in New Hampshire who are planning to attend college in any state to prepare for a career as a teacher of mathematics.
Eligibility: Open to seniors graduating from high schools in New Hampshire and planning to enroll at an accredited college or university in any state. Applicants must be planning to major in mathematics or mathematics education with the intent of becoming a mathematics teacher. Along with their application, they must submit a copy of their transcripts (including GPA and Sat scores), 2 letters of recommendation, documentation of financial need, and a brief essay on why they selected their chosen career and the experiences or personal qualities that will help to enhance their career choice. Selection is based on academic achievement, involvement in extracurricular activities, involvement in school and community service, and financial need.
Financial data: The stipend is $1,000.
Duration: 1 year.
Number awarded: 1 each year.
Deadline: May of each year.

2190 NEW HAMPSHIRE WATER POLLUTION CONTROL ASSOCIATION STUDENT SCHOLARSHIP

New Hampshire Water Pollution Control Association
Attn: Scholarship Committee
P.O. Box 95
Concord, NH 03302-0095
Phone: (603) 929-5931
Email: mcarle@town.hampton.nh.us
Web: www.nhwpca.org/Scholarship%20Committee.htm
Summary: To provide financial assistance to high school seniors in New Hampshire who plan to attend college in any state to prepare for a career in a field related to the water environment.

Eligibility: Open to seniors who are graduating from high schools in New Hampshire and planning to attend a college or university in any state. Applicants must be planning to major in water pollution control, environmental science, engineering, chemistry, or other field to prepare for a career in a field directly related to the water environment. Along with their application, they must submit a 500-word essay on their career goals and how those relate to the water environment. Preference is given to vocational students and to members and families of the New Hampshire Water Pollution Control Association (NHWPCA). Financial need is not considered in the selection process.
Financial data: The stipend is $1,000.
Duration: 1 year.
Number awarded: 1 each year.
Deadline: March of each year.

2191 NEW HAMPSHIRE WORKFORCE INCENTIVE PROGRAM FORGIVABLE LOANS

New Hampshire Postsecondary Education Commission
Attn: Financial Aid Programs Coordinator
3 Barrell Court, Suite 300
Concord, NH 03301-8543
Phone: (603) 271-2555, ext. 360; Fax: (603) 271-2696; TDD: (800) 735-2964
Email: cynthia.capodestria@pec.state.nh.us
Web: www.nh.gov/postsecondary/financial/wip.html
Summary: To provide financial assistance to New Hampshire residents who are interested in attending college in the state to prepare for careers in designated professions.
Eligibility: Open to residents of New Hampshire who wish to prepare for careers in fields designated by the commission as shortage areas. Currently, the career shortage areas are education (chemistry, general science, mathematics, physical sciences, physics, special education, and world languages) and nursing (L.P.N. through graduate). Applicants must be enrolled as a junior, senior, or graduate student at a college in New Hampshire and able to demonstrate financial need.
Financial data: Stipends are determined by the institution; recently, they averaged $1,200 per year. This is a scholarship/loan program; recipients must agree to pursue, within New Hampshire, the professional career for which they receive training. Recipients of loans for 1 year have their notes cancelled upon completion of 1 year of full-time service; repayment by service must be completed within 3 years from the date of licensure, certification, or completion of the program. Recipients of loans for more than 1 year have their notes cancelled upon completion of 2 years of full-time service; repayment by service must be completed within 5 years from the date of licensure, certification, or completion of the program. If the note is not cancelled because of service, the recipient must repay the loan within 2 years.
Duration: 1 year; may be renewed.
Number awarded: Varies each year; recently, 45 of these loans were awarded.
Deadline: May of each year for fall semester; December of each year for spring semester.

2192 NEW JERSEY LEGION AUXILIARY PAST PRESIDENTS' PARLEY NURSES SCHOLARSHIPS

American Legion Auxiliary
Department of New Jersey
c/o Lucille M. Miller, Secretary/Treasurer
1540 Kuser Road, Suite A-8
Hamilton, NJ 08619
Phone: (609) 581-9580; Fax: (609) 581-8429
Email: newjerseyala@juno.com
Web: www.alanj.org
Summary: To provide financial assistance to New Jersey residents who are the descendants of veterans and interested in studying nursing at a school in any state.
Eligibility: Open to the children, grandchildren, and great-grandchildren of veterans who served in the U.S. armed forces during specified periods of war time. Applicants must be graduating high school seniors who have been residents of New Jersey for at least 2 years. They must be planning to study nursing at a school in any state. Along with their application, they must submit a 1,000-word essay on a topic that changes annually; recently, students were asked to write on the topic, "Honoring Our Promise Everyday—How I Can Serve My Country and Our Veterans." Selection is based on academic achievement (40%), character (15%), leadership (15%), Americanism (15%), and financial need (15%).
Financial data: A stipend is awarded (amount not specified).
Duration: 1 year.
Number awarded: 1 or more each year.
Deadline: April of each year.

2193 NEW JERSEY POST SAME SCHOLARSHIP

Summary: To provide financial assistance to students in New Jersey working on an undergraduate degree in architecture, engineering, or a related field.
See Listing #1470.

2194 NEW MEXICO ALLIED HEALTH STUDENT LOAN-FOR-SERVICE PROGRAM

New Mexico Higher Education Department
Attn: Financial Aid Division
2048 Galisteo Street
Santa Fe, NM 87505-2100
Phone: (505) 476-8411; (800) 279-9777; Fax: (505) 476-8454
Email: Theresa.acker@state.nm.us
Web: hed.state.nm.us
Summary: To provide financial assistance to health professions students willing to work in underserved areas of New Mexico.
Eligibility: Open to residents of New Mexico interested in preparing for a career as a health professional in the following fields: physical therapy, occupational therapy, speech-language pathology, audiology, pharmacy, nutrition, respiratory care, laboratory technology, mental health services, emergency medical services, or other licensed or certified health profession as defined by the commission. Applicants must be enrolled or accepted in an accredited program at a New Mexico public postsecondary institution. They must declare an intent to practice in a designated shortage area of New Mexico for at least 1 year after completing their education. Along with their application, they must submit a brief essay on why they want to enter their chosen health field and obligate themselves to a rural practice in New Mexico. U.S. citizenship or eligible noncitizen status is required.
Financial data: The award depends on the financial need of the recipient, to a total of $12,000 per year. This is a loan-for-service program; loans are forgiven if the student performs the required professional service as a health professional in a designated shortage area in New Mexico. For every year of service, a portion of the loan is forgiven. If the entire service agreement is fulfilled, 100% of the loan is eligible for forgiveness. Penalties may be assessed if the service agreement is not satisfied.
Duration: 1 year; may be renewed up to 3 additional years.
Number awarded: Varies each year, depending on the availability of funds.
Deadline: June of each year.

2195 NEW MEXICO BROADCASTERS ASSOCIATION SCHOLARSHIPS

Summary: To provide financial assistance to residents of New Mexico who are attending college in the state to prepare for a career in the broadcast industry.
See Listing #1472.

2196 NEW MEXICO LEGION AUXILIARY PAST PRESIDENTS PARLEY SCHOLARSHIPS

American Legion Auxiliary
Department of New Mexico
1215 Mountain Road, N.E.
Albuquerque, NM 87102
Phone: (505) 242-9918; Fax: (505) 247-0478
Email: alauxnm@netscape.com
Summary: To provide financial assistance to residents of New Mexico who are the children of veterans and studying nursing or a related field at a school in any state.
Eligibility: Open to New Mexico residents who are attending college in any state. Applicants must be the children of veterans who served during specified periods of war time. They must be studying nursing or a related medical field. Selection is based on scholarship, character, leadership, Americanism, and financial need.
Financial data: A stipend is awarded (amount not specified).
Deadline: April of each year.

2197 NEW MEXICO NURSE EDUCATOR LOAN-FOR-SERVICE PROGRAM

New Mexico Higher Education Department
Attn: Financial Aid Division
2048 Galisteo Street
Santa Fe, NM 87505-2100
Phone: (505) 476-8411; (800) 279-9777; Fax: (505) 476-8454
Email: Theresa.acker@state.nm.us
Web: hed.state.nm.us

Summary: To provide financial assistance to nursing education students from New Mexico who are willing to work in the state after graduation.

Eligibility: Open to residents of New Mexico interested in working on a bachelor's, master's, or doctoral degree to prepare for a career as a nursing educator. Applicants must have been accepted by a New Mexico public postsecondary institution in a program that will enable them to enhance or gain employment in a nursing faculty position at a public college or university in the state. Along with their application, they must submit an essay explaining their need for this assistance and why they are interested in becoming a nurse educator in New Mexico. U.S. citizenship or eligible noncitizen status is required.

Financial data: The loan is $5,000 per year for enrollment in 9 credit hours and above, $3,000 per year for enrollment in 6 to 8 credit hours, or $1,500 per year for enrollment in 5 credit hours or less. This is a loan-for-service program; for every year of service as a nursing faculty member in New Mexico, a portion of the loan is forgiven. If the entire service agreement is fulfilled, 100% of the loan is eligible for forgiveness. Penalties may be assessed if the service agreement is not satisfied.

Duration: 1 year; may be renewed.

Number awarded: Varies each year, depending on the availability of funds.

Deadline: June of each year.

2198 NEW MEXICO NURSING LOAN-FOR-SERVICE PROGRAM

New Mexico Higher Education Department
Attn: Financial Aid Division
2048 Galisteo Street
Santa Fe, NM 87505-2100
Phone: (505) 476-8411; (800) 279-9777; Fax: (505) 476-8454
Email: Theresa.acker@state.nm.us
Web: hed.state.nm.us

Summary: To provide financial assistance to nursing students from New Mexico willing to work in underserved areas of the state after graduation.

Eligibility: Open to residents of New Mexico interested in preparing for a career as a nurse (including a licensed practical nursing certificate, associate degree in nursing, bachelor of science in nursing, master of science in nursing, or advanced practice nurse). Applicants must be enrolled or accepted in an accredited program at a New Mexico public postsecondary institution. As a condition of the loan, they must declare an intent to practice in a designated shortage area of New Mexico for at least 1 year after completing their education. Along with their application, they must submit a brief essay on why they want to enter the field of nursing and obligate themselves to a rural practice in New Mexico. U.S. citizenship or eligible noncitizen status is required.

Financial data: The loan depends on the financial need of the recipient, to a total of $12,000 per year. This is a loan-for-service program; for every year of service as a nurse in New Mexico, a portion of the loan is forgiven. If the entire service agreement is fulfilled, 100% of the loan is eligible for forgiveness. Penalties may be assessed if the service agreement is not satisfied.

Duration: 1 year; may be renewed up to 3 additional years.

Number awarded: Varies each year, depending on the availability of funds.

Deadline: June of each year.

2199 NEW MEXICO PROFESSIONAL SURVEYORS SCHOLARSHIPS

New Mexico Professional Surveyors
Attn: NMPS Educational Foundation, Inc.
412 North Dal Paso
P.O. Box 2334
Hobbs, NM 88241-2334
Phone: (505) 393-1462; Fax: (505) 393-4836
Email: patty.nmps@gmail.com
Web: www.nmps.org

Summary: To provide financial assistance to students working on a degree in surveying at a college or university in New Mexico.

Eligibility: Open to students enrolled at a college or university in New Mexico in a program that will lead to a technical or professional degree in surveying. Applicants must submit an essay on 1) activities (community, school, surveying) that demonstrate their leadership and/or service abilities; and 2) their educational and career goals. Financial need is not considered in the selection process.

Financial data: A stipend is awarded (amount not specified).

Duration: 1 year.

Number awarded: 1 or more each year.

Deadline: Deadline not specified.

2200 NEW MEXICO SOCIETY OF PROFESSIONAL ENGINEERS SCHOLARSHIP

New Mexico Engineering Foundation
Attn: Scholarship Chair
P.O. Box 3828
Albuquerque, NM 87190-3828
Phone: (505) 615-1800
Email: info@nmef.net
Web: www.nmef.net/?section=scholarship

Summary: To provide financial assistance to high school seniors in New Mexico who plan to study engineering at a college or university in any state.

Eligibility: Open to seniors graduating from high schools in New Mexico who are or planning to enroll at a college or university in any state that has an ABET-accredited engineering program. Applicants must be U.S. citizens and have a GPA of 3.0 or higher. They must have minimum scores of 500 on the SAT critical reading examination and 600 on the SAT mathematics examination or 25 on the ACT English examination and 29 on the ACT mathematics examination. Along with their application, they must submit a 250-word essay on their interest in engineering, their major area of study and area of specialization, the occupation they propose to pursue after graduation, their long-term goals, and how they hope to achieve those. Selection is based on academic standing, participation in extracurricular activities, and evidence of leadership, character, and self-reliance.

Financial data: The stipend is $1,500.

Duration: 1 year.

Number awarded: 1 each year.

Deadline: February of each year.

2201 NEW YORK BEEF PRODUCERS' ASSOCIATION SCHOLARSHIP

New York Beef Producers' Association
Attn: Executive Secretary
4950 State Highway 51
West Burlington, NY 13482
Phone: (607) 965-8282
Email: nybpa2@aol.com
Web: www.nybpa.org

Summary: To provide financial assistance to residents of New York who are attending college in any state to prepare for a career in the cattle industry.

Eligibility: Open to residents of New York who are currently enrolled in an accredited 2- or 4-year agricultural college. Applicants must be majoring in a field of study related to agriculture (e.g., animal and/or crop science, business, economics, communications, agricultural engineering) and planning a career related to the beef industry. Along with their application, they must submit an essay that covers the following: 1) their experience and interest in the beef industry; 2) their involvement in agricultural-related activities, including organizations (community, school, 4-H), events, awards, and leadership positions; 3) their future intentions and career plans as they relate to the beef industry; and 4) how they view the future of the beef industry. Selection is based on interest in the beef industry, academic achievement, organizational involvement, and leadership. Financial need is not considered.

Financial data: The stipend is $1,000.

Duration: 1 year.

Number awarded: 1 each year.

Deadline: December of each year.

2202 NEW YORK LEGION AUXILIARY DISTRICT SCHOLARSHIPS

American Legion Auxiliary
Department of New York
112 State Street, Suite 1310
Albany, NY 12207

Phone: (518) 463-1162; (800) 421-6348; Fax: (518) 449-5406
Email: alanyterry@nycap.rr.com
Web: www.deptny.org/Scholarships.htm
Summary: To provide financial assistance to descendants of veterans in New York who are interested in attending college in any state to study a medical or teaching field.
Eligibility: Open to residents of New York who are high school seniors or graduates and attending or planning to attend an accredited college or university in any state to work on a degree in a medical or teaching field. Applicants must be the children, grandchildren, or great-grandchildren of veterans who served during specified periods of war time. Along with their application they must submit a 500-word essay on a subject of their choice. Selection is based on character (20%), Americanism (20%), leadership (20%), scholarship (15%), and financial need (25%). U.S. citizenship is required.
Financial data: The stipend is $1,000. Funds are paid directly to the recipient's school.
Duration: 1 year.
Number awarded: 10 each year: 1 in each of the 10 judicial districts in New York state.
Deadline: February of each year.

2203 NEW YORK LEGION AUXILIARY PAST PRESIDENTS PARLEY STUDENT SCHOLARSHIP IN MEDICAL FIELD

American Legion Auxiliary
Department of New York
112 State Street, Suite 1310
Albany, NY 12207
Phone: (518) 463-1162; (800) 421-6348; Fax: (518) 449-5406
Email: alanyterry@nycap.rr.com
Web: www.deptny.org/Scholarships.htm
Summary: To provide financial assistance to descendants of wartime veterans in New York who are interested in attending college in any state to prepare for a career in a medical field.
Eligibility: Open to residents of New York who are high school seniors or graduates and attending or planning to attend an accredited college or university in any state to prepare for a career in a medical field. Applicants must be the children, grandchildren, or great-grandchildren of veterans who served during specified periods of war time. Along with their application, they must submit a 500-word essay on why they selected the medical field. Selection is based on character (30%), Americanism (20%), leadership (10%), scholarship (20%), and financial need (20%). U.S. citizenship is required.
Financial data: The stipend is $1,500. Funds are paid directly to the recipient's school.
Duration: 1 year.
Number awarded: 3 each year.
Deadline: February of each year.

2204 NEW YORK STATE CHAPTER SCHOLARSHIP PROGRAM

Associated General Contractors of New York State
Attn: AGC Scholarship Fund
10 Airline Drive, Suite 203
Albany, NY 12205
Phone: (518) 456-1134; Fax: (518) 456-1198
Email: agcadmin@agcnys.org
Web: www.agcnys.org/programs/scholarship
Summary: To provide financial assistance to residents of New York who are working on a degree in construction or civil engineering at a school in any state.
Eligibility: Open to residents of New York who are entering the second, third, or fourth year in a 2- or 4-year school or the first year of graduate school at an institution of higher education in any state. Applicants must be interested in preparing for a career in the highway construction industry and be working on a degree in construction or civil engineering. They must be enrolled full-time and have a GPA of 2.5 or higher. U.S. citizenship or permanent resident status is required. Selection is based on academic achievement, extracurricular activities, employment experience, and financial need.
Financial data: The stipend is $2,500 per year, payable in 2 equal installments.
Duration: 1 year; undergraduates (but not graduate students) may reapply. A student may receive up to 4 awards: 3 as an undergraduate and 1 as a graduate student.
Number awarded: Up to 20 each year. Since the program was reestablished in 1988, more than 410 students have received more than $825,000 in scholarships.
Deadline: May of each year.

2205 NEW YORK STATE ENA SEPTEMBER 11 SCHOLARSHIP FUND

Emergency Nurses Association
Attn: ENA Foundation
915 Lee Street
Des Plaines, IL 60016-6569
Phone: (847) 460-4100; (800) 900-9659, ext. 4100; Fax: (847) 460-4004
Email: foundation@ena.org
Web: www.ena.org/foundation/scholarships/Pages/Default.aspx
Summary: To provide financial assistance to rescue workers working on an undergraduate degree in nursing.
Eligibility: Open to pre-hospital care providers, fire fighters, and police officers who are working on an associate or baccalaureate nursing degree. Rescue workers from all states are eligible. Applicants must have a GPA of 3.0 or higher and be a member of a state or national professional EMT, fire fighter, or police officer association. They are not required to be a member of the Emergency Nurses Association (ENA), but they must submit a letter of reference from an ENA member. Along with their application, they must submit a 1-page statement on their professional and educational goals and how this scholarship will help them attain those goals. Selection is based on content and clarity of the goal statement (45%), professional association involvement (35%), presentation of the application (10%), and letters of reference (10%).
Financial data: The stipend is $2,500.
Duration: 1 year.
Number awarded: 2 each year.
Deadline: May of each year.

2206 NEW YORK STATE GOLF ASSOCIATION SCHOLARSHIPS

New York State Golf Association
Attn: Executive Director
P.O. Box 15333
Syracuse, NY 13215-0333
Phone: (315) 471-6979; (888) NYSGA-23 (within NY); Fax: (315) 471-1372
Email: nysga@nysga.org
Web: www.nysga.org/scholarship-program.html
Summary: To provide financial assistance to residents of New York working on a degree in a field related to golf course management at a school in any state.
Eligibility: Open to New York residents enrolled full-time at a 2-or 4-year college or university in any state. Applicants must be studying agronomy, turfgrass management, professional golf and country club management, or a related field. Along with their application, they must submit an essay about themselves. Financial need is considered in the selection process.
Financial data: The stipend is $1,500.
Duration: 1 year.
Number awarded: Varies each year; recently, 10 of these scholarships, with a total value of $15,000, were awarded.
Deadline: April of each year.

2207 NEW YORK STATE MATH AND SCIENCE TEACHING INCENTIVE SCHOLARSHIPS

New York State Higher Education Services Corporation
Attn: Student Information
99 Washington Avenue
Albany, NY 12255
Phone: (518) 473-1574; (888) NYS-HESC; Fax: (518) 473-3749; TDD: (800) 445-5234
Email: webmail@hesc.com
Web: www.hesc.com/content.nsf/SFC/0/Grants_Scholarships_and_Awards
Summary: To provide financial assistance to undergraduate and graduate students in New York who agree to teach secondary science or mathematics in the state following graduation.
Eligibility: Open to residents of any state accepted or enrolled as a full-time undergraduate or graduate student at a college or university in New York. Applicants must be preparing for a career as a secondary education science or mathematics teacher in the state and have a cumulative GPA of 2.5 or higher. They are not required to be New York residents, but they must agree to a service contract of full-time employment for 5 years as a science or mathematics teacher at a secondary school (grades 7–12) in the state. U.S. citizenship or eligible noncitizen status is required. Financial need is not considered in the selection process.
Financial data: The maximum stipend is $4,995 per year or actual tuition, whichever is less. Funds are paid directly to the schools the recipients attend. If they fail to honor the service contract in any way, the award converts to a

10-year student loan and must be repaid with interest at the FFELP PLUS loan rate (currently, 8.5%).

Duration: This program is available for 4 years of undergraduate study or 1 year of graduate study, provided the recipient remains enrolled full-time and maintains a GPA of 2.5 or higher.

Number awarded: Varies each year.

Deadline: April of each year.

2208 NIGHTINGALE AWARDS OF PENNSYLVANIA SCHOLARSHIP

Nightingale Awards of Pennsylvania
2090 Linglestown Road, Suite 107
Harrisburg, PA 17110
Phone: (717) 909-0350
Email: nightingale@pronursingresources.com
Web: www.nightingaleawards.org/scholarships.htm

Summary: To provide financial assistance to residents of Pennsylvania who are interested in working on an undergraduate or graduate degree in nursing at an institution in the state.

Eligibility: Open to Pennsylvania residents who are enrolled in a program of basic (diploma, A.D., B.S.N., L.P.N.) or advanced (master's, doctoral) nursing at an educational institution in the state. Applicants must have a GPA of 3.0 or higher and have completed at least 1 course designated as "nursing." Along with their application, they must submit an essay on their reasons for preparing for a career in nursing. Students who have already completed a diploma or A.D. nursing program are not eligible. Selection is based on academic achievement, leadership potential, community service, and personal commitment to nursing.

Financial data: A stipend is awarded (amount not specified).

Duration: 1 year.

Number awarded: Varies each year; recently, 6 of these scholarships were awarded. Since the program was established, it has awarded 111 scholarships, worth a total of $203,000.

Deadline: January of each year.

2209 NISSAN COMMUNITY COLLEGE TRANSFER SCHOLARSHIP PROGRAM OF THE HISPANIC SCHOLARSHIP FUND

Hispanic Scholarship Fund
Attn: Selection Committee
55 Second Street, Suite 1500
San Francisco, CA 94105
Phone: (415) 808-2376; (877) HSF-INFO; Fax: (415) 808-2302
Email: cctransfer@hsf.net
Web: www.hsf.net/scholarships.aspx?id=452

Summary: To provide financial assistance to Hispanic American students who are attending a community college and interested in transferring to a 4-year institution in selected areas.

Eligibility: Open to U.S. citizens, permanent residents, and visitors with a passport stamped I-551. Applicants must be of Hispanic heritage and part-time or full-time community college students with a GPA of 3.0 or higher. They must reside in or transfer to and enroll full-time at an accredited 4-year college or university in 1 of the following locations: the Chicago, Illinois metropolitan area; Denver, Colorado; the Los Angeles, California metropolitan area; Miami/Fort Lauderdale, Florida; the San Antonio, Texas metropolitan area; or Washington, D.C. Their proposed major must be business, engineering, marketing, or public relations. Selection is based on academic achievement, personal strengths, leadership, and financial need.

Financial data: The stipend is $2,500.

Duration: 1 year.

Number awarded: 1 or more each year.

Deadline: July of each year.

2210 NMA UNDERGRADUATE SCHOLARSHIPS

National Meat Association
Attn: NMA Scholarship Foundation
1970 Broadway, Suite 825
Oakland, CA 94612
Phone: (510) 763-1533; Fax: (510) 763-6186
Email: staff@nmaonline.org
Web: www.nmascholars.org

Summary: To provide financial assistance to undergraduates working on a degree in the animal, meat, and food sciences.

Eligibility: Open to students entering their sophomore, junior, or senior year in an approved program in animal science, meat science, food science, or a related discipline. Applicants must be attending a 4-year college or university and have a GPA of 2.75 or higher. Along with their application, they must submit an essay of 300 to 350 words on their career goals and future endeavors, focusing on how those relate to post harvest and production of meat food products. Financial need, age, gender, race, religion, or national origin are not conditions for eligibility; essays that cite those as reasons for applying are marked down. Selection is based on the essay (25%), work experience (25%), awards and honors (5%), extracurricular activities (5%), a faculty letter of recommendation (10%), official transcript (20%), a list of completed and current courses (5%), and a list of pending courses (5%).

Financial data: Stipends are $2,500 or $2,000. Awardees who attend the annual convention of the National Meat Association (NMA) receive a $500 travel award and plaque.

Duration: 1 year; nonrenewable.

Number awarded: Varies each year: the 4 named scholarships plus several others at $2,000.

Deadline: April of each year.

2211 NORMAN F. JACOBS, JR. SCHOLARSHIP

Construction Specifications Institute–Richmond Chapter
Attn: Richmond CSI Scholarship Fund Foundation
9016 Peaks Road
Ashland, VA 23005
Phone: (804) 307-3282; Fax: (804) 752-2670
Email: csirichmond@comcast.net
Web: richmondcsi.org/scholarships

Summary: To provide financial assistance to residents of any state who are enrolled at a college in Virginia to prepare for a construction-related career.

Eligibility: Open to residents of any state who are enrolled full-time at an accredited Virginia college or university and majoring in architecture, construction, or a construction-related field of engineering (civil, structural, mechanical, electrical). Applicants must have completed 2 full years of a 4-year bachelor's degree program, have completed 3 full years of a 5-year bachelor's degree program, or be enrolled in a master's degree program. They must have a GPA of 2.5 or higher and be able to demonstrate financial need.

Financial data: The stipend is at least $1,000. Funds are sent directly to the recipient's institution.

Duration: 1 year.

Number awarded: Up to 2 each year.

Deadline: April of each year.

2212 NORTH CAROLINA NURSE EDUCATION SCHOLARSHIP LOAN PROGRAM

North Carolina State Education Assistance Authority
Attn: Nurse Education Scholarship Loan Program
10 T.W. Alexander Drive
P.O. Box 13663
Research Triangle Park, NC 27709-3663
Phone: (919) 549-8614; (800) 700-1775; Fax: (919) 248-4687
Email: information@ncseaa.edu
Web: www.ncseaa.edu/NESLP.htm

Summary: To provide financial assistance to residents of North Carolina enrolled at institutions in the state who wish to prepare for a career in nursing.

Eligibility: Open to students at any of the 56 North Carolina Community Colleges, the 11 constituent institutions of the University of North Carolina, or the 4 private colleges and universities in North Carolina that offer nursing education instruction. Applicants must be preparing for licensure in North Carolina as a Licensed Practical Nurse (L.P.N.) or a Registered Nurse (R.N.). U.S. citizenship and North Carolina residency are required. Selection is based on academic performance, student's willingness to practice full-time as an L.P.N. or R.N. in North Carolina following completion of the education program, student's willingness to comply with the rules and regulations of this program, and financial need.

Financial data: Scholarship/loans range from $2,000 to $5,000. The maximum for students enrolled in Associate Degree Nursing (A.D.N.) and practical nurse education (L.P.N.) programs is $3,000 per year; the maximum award for students enrolled in a baccalaureate (B.S.N.) program is $5,000 per year. This is a loan-for-service program; recipients are required to provide 1 year of service as a nurse in North Carolina for each year of support received. Loans not repaid in service must be repaid in cash plus 10% interest from the date of disbursement. Recipients have up to 7 years to repay loans with service or 10 years to repay in cash.

Duration: 1 year. Students in an A.D.N. program may renew the scholarship for 1 additional year. Students in a B.S.N. program may renew the scholarship for 3 additional years. Scholarships for L.P.N. programs are nonrenewable.

Number awarded: Varies each year; recently, a total of 484 students were receiving $1,041,569 in support through this program.

Deadline: Deadline not specified.

2213 NORTH CAROLINA UNDERGRADUATE NURSE SCHOLARS PROGRAM

North Carolina State Education Assistance Authority
Attn: Nurse Scholars Program
10 T.W. Alexander Drive
P.O. Box 13663
Research Triangle Park, NC 27709-3663
Phone: (919) 549-8614; (800) 700-1775; Fax: (919) 248-4687
Email: information@ncseaa.edu
Web: www.ncseaa.edu/NSP.htm

Summary: To provide financial assistance to residents of North Carolina who wish to attend school in the state to prepare for a career in nursing.

Eligibility: Open to high school seniors, high school graduates, or currently-enrolled college students who are U.S. citizens, North Carolina residents, and interested in becoming a nurse. Applicants must be enrolled or planning to enroll full-time at a North Carolina college, university, or hospital that prepares them for licensure as a registered nurse. They must have a GPA of 3.0 or higher. Selection is based on academic achievement, leadership potential, and the promise of service as a registered nurse in North Carolina; financial need is not considered.

Financial data: Annual stipends are $3,000 for candidates for an associate degree, $3,000 for candidates for a diploma in nursing, $5,000 for full-time students in a B.S.N. program, or $2,500 for part-time students in a B.S.N. program. This is a loan-for-service program; 1 year of full-time work as a nurse in North Carolina cancels 1 year of support under this program. Recipients who fail to honor the work obligation must repay the balance plus 10% interest. They have up to 7 years to repay the loan in service or 10 years to repay in cash.

Duration: 1 year; may be renewed 1 additional year by candidates for an associate degree, registered nurses completing a B.S.N. degree, and community college transfer students and juniors in a B.S.N. program, or for 3 additional years by freshmen and nontraditional students in a B.S.N. program.

Number awarded: Varies; generally, up to 450 new undergraduate degree awards are made each year; recently, a total of 679 students were receiving $3,061,750 through this program.

Deadline: February of each year for B.S.N. programs; May of each year for A.D.N. and diploma students.

2214 NORTH DAKOTA NURSING EDUCATION LOAN PROGRAM

North Dakota Board of Nursing
919 South Seventh Street, Suite 504
Bismarck, ND 58504-5881
Phone: (701) 328-9777; Fax: (701) 328-9785
Web: www.ndbon.org

Summary: To provide financial assistance to students in North Dakota who are working on an undergraduate degree, graduate degree, or continuing education program in nursing.

Eligibility: Open to 1) students enrolled in a North Dakota board-approved or recognized undergraduate nursing education program for practical nurses or registered nurses; 2) nurses who have a current North Dakota license and have been accepted into or are currently enrolled in a graduate program that is acceptable to the Board of Nursing; and 3) nurses who are residents of North Dakota and interested in taking refresher courses. All applicants must demonstrate financial need. Along with their application, they must submit official transcripts, co-signer information, 3 letters of reference, personal financial information, a financial aid inquiry form (except for graduate students), and a student status form verifying their acceptance and expected enrollment date in the nursing program or major.

Financial data: Students in a licensed practical nurse program who plan to complete studies for an associate degree in nursing may receive up to $1,000 per year. Students in a registered nurse program who plan to complete a baccalaureate degree in nursing may receive up to $1,500 per year. Graduate students may receive up to $2,500 to complete their master's degree in nursing. Graduate students working on a doctoral degree in nursing may receive up to $5,000. Licensed practical nurses or registered nurses may receive up to the cost of a continuing education/refresher course. This is a scholarship/loan program. Recipients must agree to work as a nurse in North Dakota after graduation; the repayment rate will be $1 for each hour of employment. If employment in North Dakota is terminated before the loan is canceled, or the recipient does not work in North Dakota, or the recipient does not pass the NCLEX examination within 180 days of graduation, the loan must be repaid. The interest rate charged is approximately 9%.

Duration: 2 years for students in a licensed practical nurse program; the last 2 years for students in a baccalaureate nursing degree program.

Number awarded: 30 to 35 each year.

Deadline: June of each year.

2215 NORTHROP GRUMMAN/HENAAC SCHOLARS PROGRAM

Great Minds in STEM
Attn: HENAAC Scholars
3900 Whiteside Street
Los Angeles, CA 90063
Phone: (323) 262-0997; Fax: (323) 262-0946
Email: kbbarrera@greatmindsinstem.org
Web: www.greatmindsinstem.org/henaac/scholars

Summary: To provide financial assistance to Hispanic undergraduate students majoring in engineering or related fields.

Eligibility: Open to Hispanic students who are majoring in computer engineering, computer science, electrical engineering, naval architecture, or systems engineering. Applicants must be of Hispanic origin and/or must significantly participate in and promote organizations and activities in the Hispanic community. They must have a GPA of 3.0 or higher, leadership experience, relevant internship or co-op experience, and an interest in working for Northrop Grumman. Along with their application, they must submit a 700-word essay on a topic that changes annually; recently, students were asked to write on how they see their academic major contributing to global efforts and technology and how they, in their field of study, will contribute to global progress as well as actively contribute to their local communities. Selection is based on leadership through academic achievements and campus and community activities; financial need is not considered. U.S. citizenship is required.

Financial data: Stipends range from $500 to $5,000.

Duration: 1 year; recipients may reapply.

Number awarded: Varies each year; recently, 5 of these scholarships were awarded.

Deadline: April of each year.

2216 NSCA HIGH SCHOOL SCHOLARSHIPS

National Strength and Conditioning Association
Attn: Grants and Scholarships Program
1885 Bob Johnson Drive
Colorado Springs, CO 80906
Phone: (719) 632-6722, ext. 105; (800) 815-6826; Fax: (719) 632-6367
Email: nsca@nsca-lift.org
Web: www.nsca-lift.org/NSCAFoundation/grants.shtml

Summary: To provide financial assistance for undergraduate study in strength training and conditioning to high school seniors.

Eligibility: Open to high school students preparing to enter college. Applicants must have a GPA of 3.0 or higher and be planning to major in a strength and conditioning field. Along with their application, they must submit a 500-word essay on their life ambitions, future in the strength and conditioning area, and financial need.

Financial data: The stipend is $1,000.

Duration: 1 year; nonrenewable.

Number awarded: 2 each year.

Deadline: March of each year.

2217 NSNA SPECIALTY SCHOLARSHIPS

National Student Nurses' Association
Attn: Foundation
45 Main Street, Suite 606
Brooklyn, NY 11201
Phone: (718) 210-0705; Fax: (718) 797-1186
Email: nsna@nsna.org
Web: www.nsna.org/FoundationScholarships/FNSNAScholarships.aspx

Summary: To provide financial assistance to nursing students in designated specialties.

Eligibility: Open to students currently enrolled in state-approved schools of nursing or pre-nursing associate degree, baccalaureate, diploma, generic master's, generic doctoral, R.N. to B.S.N., R.N. to M.S.N., or L.P.N./L.V.N. to R.N.

programs. Graduating high school seniors are not eligible. Support for graduate education is provided only for a first degree in nursing. Applicants must designate their intended specialty, which may be anesthesia nursing, critical care, emergency, gerontology, informatics, nephrology, nurse educator, oncology, orthopedic, or perioperative. Along with their application, they must submit a 200-word description of their professional and educational goals and how this scholarship will help them achieve those goals. Selection is based on academic achievement, financial need, and involvement in student nursing organizations and community activities related to health care. U.S. citizenship or permanent resident status is required.
Financial data: Stipends range from $1,000 to $2,500. A total of approximately $125,000 is awarded each year by the foundation for all its scholarship programs.
Duration: 1 year.
Number awarded: Varies each year; recently, 16 of these scholarships were awarded.
Deadline: January of each year.

2218 NUCLEAR PROPULSION OFFICER CANDIDATE (NUPOC) PROGRAM

U.S. Navy
Attn: Navy Personnel Command
5722 Integrity Drive
Millington, TN 38054-5057
Phone: (901) 874-3070; (888) 633-9674; Fax: (901) 874-2651
Email: nukeprograms@cnrc.navy.mil
Web: www.cnrc.navy.mil/nucfield/college/officer_options.htm
Summary: To provide financial assistance to college juniors and seniors who wish to serve in the Navy's nuclear propulsion training program following graduation.
Eligibility: Open to U.S. citizens who are entering their junior or senior year of college as a full-time student. Strong technical majors (mathematics, physics, chemistry, or an engineering field) are encouraged but not required. Applicants must have completed at least 1 year of calculus and 1 year of physics and must have earned a grade of "C" or better in all mathematics, science, and technical courses. Normally, they must be 26 years of age or younger at the expected date of commissioning, although applicants for the design and research specialty may be up to 29 years old.
Financial data: Participants become Active Reserve enlisted Navy personnel and receive a salary of up to $2,500 per month; the exact amount depends on the local cost of living and other factors. A bonus of $10,000 is also paid at the time of enlistment and another $2,000 upon completion of nuclear power training.
Duration: Up to 30 months, until completion of a bachelor's degree.
Number awarded: Varies each year.
Deadline: Deadline not specified.

2219 NURSERIES FOUNDATION AWARD

Oregon Association of Nurseries
Attn: Oregon Nurseries Foundation
29751 S.W. Town Center Loop West
Wilsonville, OR 97070
Phone: (503) 682-5089; (800) 342-6401; Fax: (503) 682-5099
Email: info@oan.org
Web: www.oan.org/displaycommon.cfm?an=1&subarticlenbr=89
Summary: To provide financial assistance to college students in Oregon and southwestern Washington who are majoring in horticulture.
Eligibility: Open to students at colleges and universities in Oregon and southwestern Washington who are majoring in horticulture. Applicants must submit brief statements on 1) their activities, clubs, offices held, and awards; 2) how their college expenses have been and will be financed; and 3) how they see their future involvement in the field of horticulture.
Financial data: The stipend is $1,000.
Duration: 1 year.
Number awarded: 1 each year.
Deadline: March of each year.

2220 NURSING EDUCATION ASSISTANCE LOAN PROGRAM

South Dakota Board of Nursing
4305 South Louise Avenue, Suite 201
Sioux Falls, SD 57106-3115
Phone: (605) 362-2760; Fax: (605) 362-2768
Web: doh.sd.gov/boards/nursing/loan.aspx
Summary: To provide financial assistance to South Dakota residents interested in preparing for a career as a nurse.
Eligibility: Open to South Dakota residents who have been accepted into an approved nursing education program (for licensed practical nurses, registered nurses, or advanced practice nurses). Applicants must be planning to work on a diploma, associate degree, baccalaureate, master's degree, or doctorate. They must be able to demonstrate financial need. U.S. citizenship is required.
Financial data: The amount of each loan is determined annually by the South Dakota Board of Nursing, up to a maximum of $1,000 per full academic year. Funds may be used only for direct educational expenses (e.g., tuition, books, and fees), not for room or board. Recipients may elect to repay the loan either in full (within 5 years) or by employment in nursing in the state at the conversion rate of $1 per hour.
Duration: 1 year; recipients may reapply. Loans must be repaid within 5 years (either in cash or by service as a nurse in South Dakota).
Number awarded: Varies each year.
Deadline: May of each year for students in registered nursing and advanced practice nursing programs; September of each year for students in licensed practical nursing programs.

2221 NURSING FOUNDATION OF RHODE ISLAND STUDENT SCHOLARSHIPS

Nursing Foundation of Rhode Island
Attn: Scholarship Committee
P.O. Box 41702
Providence, RI 02940
Phone: (401) 223-9680
Email: nfri@rinursingfoundation.org
Web: www.rinursingfoundation.org/scholarships.htm
Summary: To provide financial assistance to students currently enrolled in nursing schools in Rhode Island.
Eligibility: Open to students enrolled in a nursing program who have demonstrated financial need, have maintained at least a 3.0 GPA for registered nurses (R.N.s) or 2.0 for practical nurses, and have demonstrated clinical proficiency, enthusiasm, and motivation in their studies. Applicants must submit an essay of 2 to 3 paragraphs about the reasons why they need the scholarship to complete their nursing program. Preference is given to students who are in the latter half of their nursing program, full-time students, residents of Rhode Island, and students enrolled in a Rhode Island nursing program.
Financial data: The stipend ranges from $500 to $1,000. Checks are written jointly to the recipient and the recipient's school.
Duration: 1 year.
Number awarded: Varies each year; recently, 23 of these scholarships were awarded.
Deadline: April of each year for practical nursing students; May of each year for R.N. students.

2222 NUTS, BOLTS AND THINGAMAJIGS TRADE OR TECHNICAL SCHOOL SCHOLARSHIPS

Fabricators and Manufacturers Association, International
Attn: FMA Foundation
833 Featherstone Road
Rockford, IL 61107-6302
Phone: (815) 399-8700; (888) 394-4362; Fax: (815) 484-7767
Email: foundation@fmanet.org
Web: www.nutsandboltsfoundation.org/Scholarships.cfm
Summary: To provide financial assistance to students entering or continuing in a trade school or technical or community college to prepare for a career in manufacturing technology.
Eligibility: Open to students enrolled or planning to enroll full-time at a 2-year trade school or technical or community college to major in an engineering or related program that may lead to a career in manufacturing. Applicants must have a GPA of 2.5 or higher. They must become a student member of the Fabricators and Manufacturers Association, International (FMA), the Tube and Pipe Association, International (TPA), or OPC, unless they are already 1) a student or basic member; 2) the child of a basic member; 3) an employee of an Advantage-level member company; or 4) the child of an employee of an Advantage-level member company. Along with their application, they must submit information on their educational and career objectives, employment experience, extracurricular activities, and the experience that has influenced or confirmed their decision to prepare for a career in manufacturing. Financial need is not considered in the selection process.
Financial data: The stipend is $3,000 per year.

Duration: 1 year.
Number awarded: 1 or more each year.
Deadline: March of each year.

2223 NUTS, BOLTS AND THINGAMAJIGS UNIVERSITY SCHOLARSHIPS

Fabricators and Manufacturers Association, International
Attn: FMA Foundation
833 Featherstone Road
Rockford, IL 61107-6302
Phone: (815) 399-8700; (888) 394-4362; Fax: (815) 484-7767
Email: foundation@fmanet.org
Web: www.nutsandboltsfoundation.org/Scholarships.cfm

Summary: To provide financial assistance to students entering or continuing in a college or university to prepare for a career in manufacturing technology.

Eligibility: Open to students enrolled or planning to enroll full-time at a 4-year college or university to major in an engineering or related program that may lead to a career in manufacturing. Applicants must have a GPA of 3.0 or higher. They must become a student member of the Fabricators and Manufacturers Association, International (FMA), the Tube and Pipe Association, International (TPA), or OPC, unless they are already 1) a student or basic member; 2) the child of a basic member; 3) an employee of an Advantage-level member company; or 4) the child of an employee of an Advantage-level member company. Along with their application, they must submit information on their educational and career objectives, employment experience, extracurricular activities, and the experience that has influenced or confirmed their decision to prepare for a career in manufacturing. Financial need is not considered in the selection process.

Financial data: The stipends is $5,000 per year.
Duration: 1 year; may be renewed.
Number awarded: 1 or more each year.
Deadline: March of each year.

2224 NYWEA SCHOLARSHIPS

New York Water Environment Association
Attn: Executive Director
525 Plum Street, Suite 102
Syracuse, NY 13204
Phone: (315) 422-7811; Fax: (315) 422-3851
Email: pcr@nywea.org
Web: www.nywea.org/schol

Summary: To provide financial assistance to students who are enrolled or planning to enroll in an environmentally-related program in college.

Eligibility: Open to 3 categories of students: 1) children of members of the New York Water Environment Association (NYWEA) who are enrolled or planning to enroll full-time at a college or university in any state in a program that will prepare them for a professional career in the environmental field; 2) students enrolled full-time in a program that will prepare them for a professional career in the environmental field at a college or university that has an NYWEA student chapter; and 3) high school seniors who plan to enroll in an environmentally-related program at a 4-year college or university in any state. All applicants must submit essays, from 200 to 300 words in length, on 1) their interest in the environment and how that interest influences their career goals; and 2) a current environmental issue that impacts their life and their community and how it affects them. Selection is based on career objective, academic potential, other activities, character, and environmental interest.

Financial data: The stipend is $1,500.
Duration: 1 year.
Number awarded: 6 each year: 2 in each of the 3 categories.
Deadline: January of each year.

2225 OCCUPATIONAL THERAPY SCHOLARSHIP

Wisconsin Paralyzed Veterans of America
Attn: Scholarship Committee
2311 South 108th Street
West Allis, WI 53227-1901
Phone: (414) 328-8910; (800) 875-WPVA; Fax: (414) 328-8948
Email: info@wisconsinpva.org
Web: www.wisconsinpva.org/scholarships.html

Summary: To provide financial assistance to seniors in occupational therapy programs in Wisconsin who are interested in working in a spinal cord injury unit or rehabilitation facility after graduation.

Eligibility: Open to students enrolled in the final year of an accredited occupational therapy program in Wisconsin. Applicants must be willing to seek employment in a spinal cord injury unit or rehabilitation facility after graduation. They must be able to demonstrate financial need.

Financial data: The stipend is $1,000.
Duration: 1 year.
Number awarded: 1 each year.
Deadline: March of each year.

2226 OHIO ENVIRONMENTAL SCIENCE AND ENVIRONMENTAL ENGINEERING UNDERGRADUATE SCHOLARSHIP PROGRAM

Ohio Academy of Science
1500 West Third Avenue, Suite 228
Columbus, OH 43212-2817
Phone: (614) 488-2228; Fax: (614) 488-7629
Email: oas@iwaynet.net
Web: www.ohiosci.org/OESEESCHOLARSHIPS.htm

Summary: To provide financial assistance to students from any state who are majoring in environmental science or engineering at a college in Ohio.

Eligibility: Open to residents of any state who are entering the second year at a community or technical college in Ohio or the final year at a 4-year college or university in the state. Applicants must be majoring in environmental science or engineering. They must have a GPA of 3.0 or higher. Selection is based on academic record; education, employment and/or internships, honors and awards, professional memberships, publications, presentations given and professional meetings attended, and community service; reasons for choosing a career in environmental science or engineering and how the scholarship will help; original research, scholarship, employment and/or internships, or other unique contributions to environmental science or engineering; extracurricular activities and participation in organizations that demonstrate leadership, interpersonal skills, and social responsibility; and letters of recommendation.

Financial data: Stipends are $2,500 for students at 4-year colleges and universities or $1,250 for students at community and technical colleges.
Duration: 1 year; nonrenewable.
Number awarded: Up to 20 each year: 10 for students at 4-year institutions and 10 for students at community and technical colleges.
Deadline: May of each year.

2227 OHIO NURSE EDUCATION ASSISTANCE LOAN PROGRAM FOR NURSES

Ohio Board of Regents
Attn: State Grants and Scholarships
30 East Broad Street, 36th Floor
Columbus, OH 43215-3414
Phone: (614) 466-4818; (888) 833-1133; Fax: (614) 466-5866
Email: nealp_admin@regents.state.oh.us
Web: regents.ohio.gov/sgs/nealp/students.php

Summary: To provide financial assistance to students in Ohio who intend to study nursing.

Eligibility: Open to Ohio residents who are enrolled at least half-time in an approved nursing education program in Ohio. Applicants must demonstrate financial need and intend to engage in direct clinical practice as a registered nurse or licensed practical nurse following graduation. U.S. citizenship or permanent resident status is required.

Financial data: The maximum award is currently $1,500 per year. This is a scholarship/loan program; up to 100% of the loan may be forgiven at the rate of 20% per year if the recipient serves as a nurse under specified conditions for up to 5 years. If the loan is not repaid with service, it must be repaid in cash with interest at the rate of 8% per year.
Duration: 1 year; renewable for up to 3 additional years.
Number awarded: Varies each year; recently, 35 students received benefits through this program.
Deadline: July of each year.

2228 OKLAHOMA NURSING STUDENT ASSISTANCE PROGRAM

Physician Manpower Training Commission
Attn: Nursing Program Coordinator
5500 North Western Avenue, Suite 201
Oklahoma City, OK 73118

Phone: (405) 843-5667; Fax: (405) 843-5792
Email: michelle.cecil@pmtc.state.ok.us
Web: www.pmtc.state.ok.us/nsap.htm

Summary: To provide financial assistance to nursing students from Oklahoma who are interested in practicing in rural communities in the state.

Eligibility: Open to residents of Oklahoma who have been admitted to an accredited program of nursing in any state at the L.P.N., A.D.N., B.S.N., or M.S.N. level. Applicants must be interested in practicing nursing in Oklahoma communities, especially rural communities. They may apply either for direct funding from the state or with matching support from a health institution in the state, such as a hospital, nursing home, or other health care entity. Along with their application, they must submit ACT scores, high school and/or college GPA, and documentation of financial need. U.S. citizenship is required.

Financial data: The minimum scholarship/loan provided by the state for all levels is $500 per year. The maximum is $1,750 per year for L.P.N. students, $2,000 per year for A.D.N. students, or $2,500 per year for B.S.N. or M.S.N. students. The loan is forgiven if the nurse fulfills a work obligation at an approved health institution in Oklahoma of 1 year for each year of financial assistance received; participants in the matching program must work for their sponsor. Nurses who decide not to fulfill their work obligation are required to repay the principal amount plus 12% interest and a possible penalty of up to 98% of the principal.

Duration: Funding is available for completion of an L.P.N. program, for 2 years for an A.D.N. program, or the final 2 years of a B.S.N. or M.S.N. program.

Number awarded: Between 250 and 300 of these awards are granted each year. Since the program began, more than 5,250 nursing students have received support.

Deadline: June of each year.

2229 OKLAHOMA PHYSICIAN ASSISTANT SCHOLARSHIP PROGRAM

Physician Manpower Training Commission
Attn: Deputy Executive Director
5500 North Western Avenue, Suite 201
Oklahoma City, OK 73118
Phone: (405) 843-5667; Fax: (405) 843-5792
Email: PMTC@pmtc.ok.gov
Web: www.pmtc.state.ok.us/PA.htm

Summary: To provide financial assistance to physician assistant students who are willing to practice in rural Oklahoma.

Eligibility: Open to residents of Oklahoma who are currently enrolled in an accredited physician assistant program in any state and have no other conflicting service obligations. Applicants must be willing to begin practice in an approved Oklahoma rural community with a population of 20,000 or less within 90 days of completion of physician assistant training.

Financial data: The award is $1,000 per month. Loans are forgiven by each month of practice in a qualified Oklahoma rural community for each month of scholarship/loan. Physician assistants who decide not to repay the obligated scholarship/loan by practicing in rural Oklahoma are required to repay the principal amount, plus interest at the prime rate plus 1% and a penalty of up to 100% of the principal.

Duration: 1 month; may be renewed.

Number awarded: Varies each year; since the program began, 52 physician assistant students have received support from this program.

Deadline: Deadline not specified.

2230 OKLAHOMA READY MIXED CONCRETE ASSOCIATION ESSAY CONTEST

Oklahoma Ready Mixed Concrete Association
3535 N.W. 58th, Suite 770
Oklahoma City, OK 73112
Phone: (405) 840-2117; Fax: (405) 840-2474
Email: office@ormca.com
Web: www.ormca.com

Summary: To recognize and reward, with college scholarships, high school students in Oklahoma who submit outstanding essays on the benefits of concrete.

Eligibility: Open to high school students in Oklahoma who are between 16 and 18 years of age. Applicants must submit an essay, up to 600 words in length, on a topic that relates to concrete; examples include concrete's benefits to society, how concrete affects the environment, or using concrete to build homes, commercial buildings, bridges, and roads. Selection is based on the essay's content, creativity, and grammar. Special consideration is given to students who plan to attend a college with a concrete-related curriculum (e.g., Middle Tennessee State University, Alpena College in Michigan, or Rhodes State College in Ohio).

Financial data: The winner receives a $1,000 scholarship to attend a college with a concrete-related curriculum or $500 to attend a college with a non-concrete related curriculum.

Duration: 1 year.

Number awarded: 1 each year.

Deadline: November of each year.

2231 OLIVER JOEL AND ELLEN PELL DENNY HEALTHCARE SCHOLARSHIP FUND

Winston-Salem Foundation
Attn: Student Aid Department
860 West Fifth Street
Winston-Salem, NC 27101-2506
Phone: (336) 725-2382; (866) 227-1209; Fax: (336) 727-0581
Email: info@wsfoundation.org
Web: www.wsfoundation.org/students

Summary: To provide financial assistance to residents of North Carolina working on a degree or certificate in fields related to health care at a college or university in the state.

Eligibility: Open to North Carolina residents working on a certificate, diploma, or bachelor's or associate degree in health care fields, including (but not limited to) registered nursing, licensed practical nursing, nuclear medicine, radiography, and respiratory therapy. Applicants must be attending or planning to attend a 2- or 4-year college or university in North Carolina as a traditional or nontraditional student. They must have a cumulative GPA of 2.5 or higher in health care classes and be able to demonstrate financial need. Preference is given to residents of Davidson, Davie, Forsyth, Stokes, Surry, and Yadkin counties. Some of the scholarships are set aside for eligible noncitizens.

Financial data: The stipend is $1,200 per year.

Duration: 1 year; may be renewed.

Number awarded: 1 or more each year, including 5 scholarships set aside for eligible noncitizens.

Deadline: August of each year.

2232 OLMSTED SCHOLARS PROGRAM

Summary: To provide financial assistance to upper-division and graduate students in landscape architecture who demonstrate outstanding potential for leadership.

See Listing #1491.

2233 OMAHA VOLUNTEERS FOR HANDICAPPED CHILDREN SCHOLARSHIPS

Omaha Volunteers for Handicapped Children
c/o Lois Carlson
2010 Country Club Avenue
Omaha, NE 68104
Phone: (402) 553-0378

Summary: To provide financial assistance to Nebraska residents who have a physical disability or are preparing for a career related to people with orthopedic impairments or physical disabilities and are interested in attending college in any state.

Eligibility: Open to residents of Nebraska who are U.S. citizens. First priority applicants must have an orthopedic impairment or physical disability and be 1) high school seniors with a GPA of 2.25 or higher and accepted into the school of their choice; or 2) college students making satisfactory progress toward graduation. Second priority applicants must be enrolled in the college of their choice and preparing for a teaching or health-related career of service to people with orthopedic impairments or physical disabilities. All applicants must submit a 250-word essay on their future goals in relation to the orthopedically impaired and/or physically disabled and their need for the scholarship.

Financial data: The stipend is $1,000 per year.

Duration: 1 year; may be renewed.

Number awarded: 5 to 10 each year.

Deadline: July of each year.

2234 ONCOLOGY NURSING CERTIFICATION CORPORATION BACHELOR'S SCHOLARSHIPS

Oncology Nursing Society
Attn: ONS Foundation
125 Enterprise Drive
Pittsburgh, PA 15275-1214

Phone: (412) 859-6100; (866) 257-4ONS; Fax: (412) 859-6163
Email: foundation@ons.org
Web: www.ons.org/Awards/FoundationAwards/Bachelors

Summary: To provide financial assistance to nurses and other students who are interested in working on a bachelor's degree in oncology nursing.

Eligibility: Open to students who are accepted to or currently enrolled in a bachelor's degree program at an NLN- or CCNE-accredited school of nursing. Applicants must be able to demonstrate an interest in and commitment to oncology nursing. They may 1) already have a current license to practice as a registered nurse (R.N.); 2) currently have a postsecondary degree at some level but not be an R.N.; or 3) have only a high school diploma. Along with their application, they must submit 1) an essay of 250 words or less on their role or interest in caring for persons with cancer; and 2) a statement of their professional goals and the relationship of those goals to the advancement of oncology nursing. Non-R.N. applicants must be in the nursing component of the B.S.N. program. High school students and individuals in the liberal arts component of a B.S.N. program are not eligible. Financial need is not considered in the selection process.

Financial data: The stipend is $2,000.

Duration: 1 year; nonrenewable.

Number awarded: Varies each year; recently, 10 of these scholarships were awarded.

Deadline: January of each year.

2235 ONCOLOGY PRACTICE ALLIANCE SCHOLARSHIP

Oncology Nursing Society
Attn: ONS Foundation
125 Enterprise Drive
Pittsburgh, PA 15275-1214
Phone: (412) 859-6100; (866) 257-4ONS; Fax: (412) 859-6163
Email: foundation@ons.org
Web: www.ons.org/Awards/FoundationAwards/Bachelors

Summary: To provide financial assistance to residents of Ohio and West Virginia who are interested in working on a bachelor's degree in oncology nursing.

Eligibility: Open to residents of Ohio and West Virginia who are currently enrolled in the nursing component of a bachelor's degree program at an NLN-accredited school of nursing. Applicants must be able to demonstrate an interest in and commitment to oncology nursing. Along with their application, they must submit 1) an essay of 250 words or less on their interest in caring for persons with cancer; and 2) a statement of their professional goals and the relationship of those goals to the advancement of oncology nursing. High school students and individuals in the liberal arts component of a B.S.N. program are not eligible. Financial need is not considered in the selection process.

Financial data: The stipend is $2,000.

Duration: 1 year; nonrenewable.

Number awarded: 1 each year.

Deadline: January of each year.

2236 OREGON FARM BUREAU MEMORIAL SCHOLARSHIPS

Oregon Farm Bureau
Attn: Oregon Agricultural Education Foundation
3415 Commercial Street; S.E.
Salem, OR 97302-5169
Phone: (503) 399-1701, ext. 327; (800) 334-6323; Fax: (503) 399-8082
Email: andrea@oregonfb.org
Web: www.oregonfb.org/programs/scholarships.shtml

Summary: To provide financial assistance to Oregon residents interested in working on an undergraduate or graduate degree in agriculture or forestry at a school in any state.

Eligibility: Open to graduates of Oregon high schools who are new or continuing full-time undergraduate or graduate students at a college or university in any state. Applicants must be studying production agriculture or another field related to agriculture or forestry. Along with their application, they must submit 1) a brief description of their past agricultural experiences; and 2) a paper of 1 to 2 pages explaining how their course of study will impact Oregon agriculture or forestry. Financial need is not considered in the selection process.

Financial data: Stipends generally range up to $1,500.

Duration: 1 year; recipients may reapply.

Number awarded: 10 to 12 each year.

Deadline: February of each year.

2237 OREGON LEGION AUXILIARY DEPARTMENT NURSES SCHOLARSHIP

American Legion Auxiliary
Department of Oregon
30450 S.W. Parkway Avenue
P.O. Box 1730
Wilsonville, OR 97070-1730
Phone: (503) 682-3162; Fax: (503) 685-5008
Email: alaor@pcez.com

Summary: To provide financial assistance to the wives, widows, and children of Oregon veterans who are interested in studying nursing at a school in any state.

Eligibility: Open to Oregon residents who are the wives or children of veterans with disabilities or the widows of deceased veterans. Applicants must have been accepted by an accredited hospital or university school of nursing in any state. Selection is based on ability, aptitude, character, determination, seriousness of purpose, and financial need.

Financial data: The stipend is $1,500.

Duration: 1 year; may be renewed.

Number awarded: 1 each year.

Deadline: May of each year.

2238 OREGON NURSES FOUNDATION CENTENNIAL EDUCATION SCHOLARSHIP

Oregon Nurses Association
Attn: Oregon Nurses Foundation
18765 S.W. Boones Ferry Road, Suite 200
Tualatin, OR 97062-8498
Phone: (503) 293-0011; Fax: (503) 293-0013
Email: tangedal@oregonrn.org
Web: www.oregonrn.org/displaycommon.cfm?an=1&subarticlenbr=340

Summary: To provide financial assistance to students accepted to a nursing program in Oregon to work on an associate or bachelor's degree.

Eligibility: Open to students who are enrolled or planning to enroll in an accredited nursing program in Oregon. Applicants must have a GPA of 3.0 or higher and be planning to earn an associate or bachelor's degree in nursing. Selection is based on leadership abilities and experiences (35%); experiences with other cultures, minority groups, and underserved populations (30%); career plans in nursing (30%); and reasons for needing this funding (5%).

Financial data: The stipend is $1,000.

Duration: 1 year.

Number awarded: 1 or more each year.

Deadline: March, June, September, or December of each year.

2239 OUTPUTLINKS WOMAN OF DISTINCTION AWARD

Summary: To provide financial assistance to female upper-division and graduate students interested in preparing for a career in document management and graphic communications.

See Listing #1496.

2240 OUTSTANDING STUDENT IN PLASMA SCIENCE AWARD

Institute of Electrical and Electronics Engineers
Nuclear and Plasma Sciences Society
c/o Bill Moses, NPSS Awards Committee
Lawrence Berkeley Laboratory
1 Cyclotron Road
Mailstop 55-121
Berkeley, CA 94720
Phone: (510) 486-4432; Fax: (510) 486-4768
Email: wwmoses@lbl.gov
Web: ewh.ieee.org/soc/nps/awards.htm

Summary: To recognize and reward outstanding contributions to plasma science by undergraduate and graduate students.

Eligibility: Open to full-time undergraduate and graduate students at colleges and universities worldwide. Nominees must have made outstanding contributions to the field of plasma science and technology. Selection is based on quality of research contributions, quality of educational accomplishments, and quality and significance of publications and patents.

Financial data: The award consists of $1,000 and a certificate.

Duration: The award is presented annually.
Number awarded: 1 each year.
Deadline: October of each year.

2241 PACE INTERNATIONAL SCHOLARSHIPS

Washington Apple Education Foundation
Attn: Scholarship Committee
2900 Euclid Avenue
Wenatchee, WA 98801
Phone: (509) 663-7713; Fax: (509) 663-7469
Email: waef@waef.org
Web: www.waef.org/index.php?page_id=238

Summary: To provide financial assistance to residents of Washington whose family is involved in the tree fruit industry and who are interested in studying biology or chemistry at a college in any state.
Eligibility: Open to Washington residents who are graduating high school seniors or students currently enrolled at a college or university in any state. Applicants must have ties to the tree fruit industry. They must be interested in majoring in biology or chemistry to prepare for production-related careers in the tree fruit industry. Along with their application, they must submit an official transcript, their SAT or ACT scores, 2 letters of reference, and an essay on an assigned topic. Financial need is also considered in the selection process.
Financial data: The stipend is $1,000. The money may be used to pay for tuition, room, board, books, educational supplies, and miscellaneous institutional fees.
Duration: 1 year.
Number awarded: 2 each year.
Deadline: February of each year.

2242 PACIFIC NORTHWEST CHAPTER GITA SCHOLARSHIP

Geospatial Information & Technology Association–Pacific Northwest Chapter
c/o Nicole Lucas
6911 Southpoint Drive, Fifth Floor
Burnaby, BC V3N 4X8
Canada
Phone: (604) 528-2564; Fax: (604) 528-2172
Email: nicole.lucas@bchydro.com
Web: www.gita.org/chapters/pacific/pacific.asp

Summary: To provide financial assistance to upper-division and graduate students working on a degree related to geospatial information systems (GIS) at a university in the Pacific Northwest.
Eligibility: Open to juniors, seniors, and graduate students at postsecondary institutions in British Columbia, Idaho, Oregon, or Washington. Applicants are not required to be working on a degree specifically in GIS, but a focus within their degree program must include GIS. Along with their application, they must submit a statement of intent outlining the use of the scholarship funds and a description of their program's focus on GIS; technical papers, research reports, or other items demonstrating their GIS capabilities; at least 1 letter of recommendation from an instructor; and academic transcripts. Selection is based on the statement of intent, academic record, and letter of recommendation.
Financial data: The stipend is $1,000.
Duration: 1 year.
Number awarded: 1 or more each year.
Deadline: March of each year.

2243 PALMETTO GOLD SCHOLARSHIPS

South Carolina Nurses Foundation, Inc.
Attn: Palmetto Gold Committee
1821 Gadsden Street
Columbia, SC 29201
Phone: (803) 252-4781; Fax: (803) 779-3870
Email: info@scpalmettogold.org
Web: www.scpalmettogold.org

Summary: To provide financial assistance to students enrolled in a registered nurse training program in South Carolina.
Eligibility: Open to students who are nominated by the dean of a registered nurse program in South Carolina. Nominees must 1) display caring and commitment to patients, families, and colleagues; 2) demonstrate leadership and assistance to others to grow and develop; 3) promote the profession of nursing in a positive way; and 4) show promise of excellence by achieving a high level of academic success (at least a 3.0 GPA). They must submit a 200-word essay describing their career goals in nursing.
Financial data: The stipend is $1,000.
Duration: 1 year.
Number awarded: 23 each year: 1 at each registered nurse training program in South Carolina.
Deadline: Nominations must be submitted by October of each year.

2244 PAROS-DIGIQUARTZ SCHOLARSHIP

Marine Technology Society
Attn: Student Scholarships
5565 Sterrett Place, Suite 108
Columbia, MD 21044
Phone: (410) 884-5330; Fax: (410) 884-9060
Email: scholarships@mtsociety.org
Web: www.mtsociety.org/education/scholarships.aspx

Summary: To provide financial assistance to entering and continuing undergraduate and graduate students who are working on a degree in a field related to marine science and have shown an interest in marine instrumentation.
Eligibility: Open to high school seniors accepted into a full-time undergraduate program and current undergraduate and graduate students. Applicants must be planning to work on a degree in marine technology, marine engineering, or marine science. They must be able to demonstrate an interest in marine instrumentation. Along with their application, they must submit a 500-word essay on their interest in marine technology, how their interest in marine technology relates to their current field of study, and how they plan to use their degree. Selection is based on that essay, honors received, marine-oriented activities, extracurricular school activities, and community service activities. Membership in the Marine Technology Society (MTS) is not required.
Financial data: The stipend is $2,000. Funds are sent directly to the recipient's college bursar's office.
Duration: 1 year.
Number awarded: 1 each year.
Deadline: April of each year.

2245 PATRICK AND JUDITH MCHUGH SCHOLARSHIP

Vermont Student Assistance Corporation
Attn: Scholarship Programs
10 East Allen Street
P.O. Box 2000
Winooski, VT 05404-2601
Phone: (802) 654-3798; (888) 253-4819; Fax: (802) 654-3765; TDD: (800) 281-3341 (within VT)
Email: info@vsac.org
Web: services.vsac.org/wps/wcm/connect/vsac/VSAC

Summary: To provide financial assistance to Vermont residents who are working on an undergraduate or graduate degree in a health-related field at a college or university in any state.
Eligibility: Open to residents of Vermont who are enrolled at a college or university in any state. Applicants must be working on an undergraduate or graduate degree in a health care field, including (but not limited to) dentistry, medicine, nursing, pharmacy, psychiatry, or psychology. Along with their application, they must submit 1) a 100-word essay on their interest in and commitment to pursuing their chosen career or vocation; and 2) a 250-word essay on their short- and long-term academic, educational, career, vocational, and/or employment goals. Selection is based on those essays, financial need, and a letter of recommendation.
Financial data: The stipend is $1,000.
Duration: 1 year.
Number awarded: 1 each year.
Deadline: March of each year.

2246 PAUL AND ELLEN RUCKES SCHOLARSHIP

American Foundation for the Blind
Attn: Scholarship Committee
11 Penn Plaza, Suite 300
New York, NY 10001
Phone: (212) 502-7661; (800) AFB-LINE; Fax: (212) 502-7771; TDD: (212) 502-7662
Email: afbinfo@afb.net
Web: www.afb.org/Section.asp?Documentid=2962

Summary: To provide financial assistance to legally blind students who wish to work on a graduate or undergraduate degree in engineering or computer, physical, or life sciences.

Eligibility: Open to legally blind undergraduate or graduate students who are U.S. citizens working full-time on a degree in engineering or the computer, physical, or life sciences. Along with their application, they must submit a 200-word essay that includes their past and recent achievements and accomplishments; their intended field of study and why they have chosen it; and the role their visual impairment has played in shaping their life. Financial need is considered in the selection process.
Financial data: The stipend is $1,000.
Duration: 1 year.
Number awarded: 1 each year.
Deadline: April of each year.

2247 PAUL AND HELEN L. GRAUER SCHOLARSHIP

Summary: To provide financial assistance to licensed radio amateurs, especially those from designated midwestern states, who are interested in working on an undergraduate or graduate degree, preferably in electronics or communications.
See Listing #1500.

2248 PEGGY VATTER MEMORIAL SCHOLARSHIPS

Washington Science Teachers Association
c/o Patricia MacGowan, Washington MESA
University of Washington
P.O. Box 352181
Seattle, WA 98195-2181
Phone: (206) 543-0562; Fax: (206) 685-0666
Email: macgowan@engr.washington.edu
Web: www.wsta.net
Summary: To provide financial assistance to upper-division students and teachers in Washington interested in training in science education.
Eligibility: Open to 1) juniors and seniors at colleges and universities in Washington who are working on certification in science education or in elementary education with an emphasis on science; and 2) certified teachers in Washington interested in improving their skills in providing equitable science education through professional development. In the student category, preference is given to African Americans, Hispanics, Native Americans, and women. Applicants must submit a 1-page essay on why they are applying for this scholarship.
Financial data: The stipend is $1,500.
Duration: 1 year; nonrenewable.
Number awarded: 1 or more each year.
Deadline: April of each year.

2249 PENNSYLVANIA ASSOCIATION OF SCHOOL NURSES AND PRACTITIONERS CERTIFIED SCHOOL NURSE SCHOLARSHIP

Pennsylvania Association of School Nurses and Practitioners
c/o Michelle Ficca, Scholarship Chair
Bloomsburg University of Pennsylvania
3136 MCHS
Bloomsburg, PA 17815
Phone: (570) 389-4000
Email: pasnapweb@pasnap.org
Web: www.pasnap.org/education/scholarships.html
Summary: To provide financial assistance to students in Pennsylvania preparing for a career as a school nurse.
Eligibility: Open to 1) nursing and nurse practitioner students in Pennsylvania intending to practice school nursing and enrolled or accepted in a B.S.N. or school nurse certification program; and 2) certified school nurses working on a graduate degree in nursing in Pennsylvania. Applicants must submit a 1-page letter outlining their goals in school nursing, a copy of their acceptance letter or official transcript, a current resume, and a copy of their current nursing license. Selection is based on a random drawing from all qualified applications; financial need is not considered.
Financial data: The stipend is $1,000. Funds are paid directly to the financial aid office in the recipient's institution.
Duration: 1 year.
Number awarded: 2 each year.
Deadline: March of each year.

2250 PENNSYLVANIA ASSOCIATION OF SCHOOL NURSES AND PRACTITIONERS FUTURE NURSE SCHOLARSHIP

Pennsylvania Association of School Nurses and Practitioners
c/o Nancy Kaminski, Membership Chair
1300 Crest Lane
Oakdale, PA 15071
Phone: (412) 881-4940, ext. 2345
Email: pasnapweb@pasnap.org
Web: www.pasnap.org/education/scholarships.html
Summary: To provide financial assistance to high school seniors in Pennsylvania planning to attend college in any state to prepare for a career as a nurse.
Eligibility: Open to seniors graduating from high schools in Pennsylvania. Applicants must be planning to attend an institution of higher education in any state to work on a bachelor's degree in nursing. Along with their application, they must submit 1) a copy of their current high school transcript, including their SAT/ACT scores and class rank; 2) a list of their co-curricular and extracurricular activities; 3) a 1-page personal statement on why they are choosing nursing and what they think nursing will add to their life; and 4) 2 letters of reference. Financial need is not considered in the selection process.
Financial data: The stipend is $1,000. Funds are paid directly to the financial aid office in the recipient's institution.
Duration: 1 year.
Number awarded: 1 each year.
Deadline: April of each year.

2251 PENNSYLVANIA SCITECH SCHOLARSHIPS

Pennsylvania Higher Education Assistance Agency
Attn: State Grant and Special Programs
1200 North Seventh Street
P.O. Box 8114
Harrisburg, PA 17105-8114
Phone: (717) 720-2800; (800) 692-7392; TDD: (800) 654-5988
Email: nets@pheaa.org
Web: www.pheaa.org/specialprograms/nets/Sci_Tech_Scholarship.shtml
Summary: To provide financial assistance to residents of Pennsylvania who are interested in studying approved science or technology fields at a public or private college or university in the state and then working in the state after graduation.
Eligibility: Open to residents of Pennsylvania who graduated from a high school in the state and are currently enrolled full-time as at least a sophomore at an approved Pennsylvania public or private college or university. Applicants must be working on a bachelor's degree in an approved science or technology field and have a GPA of 3.0 or higher. They must apply for a federal Pell Grant and a Pennsylvania State Grant, but financial need is not considered in the selection process. Funds are awarded on a first-come, first-served basis.
Financial data: Scholarships provide up to $3,000 per year.
Duration: Up to 3 years, provided the recipient maintains a GPA of 3.0 or higher and full-time enrollment.
Number awarded: Varies each year.
Deadline: December of each year for first-time applicants; September of each year for renewal applicants.

2252 PERENNIAL PLANT ASSOCIATION SCHOLARSHIPS

Perennial Plant Association
Attn: Executive Director
3383 Schirtzinger Road
Hilliard, OH 43026
Phone: (614) 771-8431; Fax: (614) 876-5238
Email: ppa@perennialplant.org
Web: www.perennialplant.org/scholarship.asp
Summary: To provide financial assistance to college students majoring in horticulture or a related subject.
Eligibility: Open to college students in a 2- or 4-year program majoring in horticulture or a related subject. Applicants should have at least 1 quarter or semester remaining, should have at least a 3.0 GPA, and must be able to attend the annual perennial plant symposium. Along with their application, they must submit a statement of purpose, college transcript, and recommendation letters. An interest in perennials is preferred but not required. Financial need is not considered in the selection process.
Financial data: The stipend is $1,000 per year. Funds are sent directly to the recipient's school. Winners also receive complimentary registration and lodging to attend the symposium.

Duration: 1 year.
Number awarded: 5 each year.
Deadline: February of each year.

2253 PETER K. NEW STUDENT PRIZE COMPETITION

Society for Applied Anthropology
P.O. Box 2436
Oklahoma City, OK 73101-2436
Phone: (405) 843-5113; Fax: (405) 843-8553
Email: info@sfaa.net
Web: www.sfaa.net/pknew/pknew.html

Summary: To recognize and reward the best student research papers in applied social, health, or behavioral sciences.

Eligibility: Open to currently-enrolled undergraduate and graduate students in the applied social, health, and behavioral sciences. Applicants must not have already earned a doctoral degree (e.g., a person with an M.D. degree who is now registered as a student in a Ph.D. program is not eligible). Eligible students are invited to submit a manuscript that reports on research that, in large measure, has not been previously published. Research should be in the domain of health care or human services (broadly defined). The competition is limited to manuscripts that have a single author; multiple-authored papers are not eligible. The paper should be double spaced and must be less than 45 pages in length, including footnotes, tables, and appendices. Selection is based on originality, research design/method, clarity of analysis and presentation, and contribution to the social or behavioral sciences.

Financial data: The winner receives $2,000, a crystal trophy, and a travel allowance to partially offset the cost of transportation and lodging at the society's annual meeting.

Duration: The competition is held annually.
Number awarded: 1 each year.
Deadline: December of each year.

2254 PETROLEUM DIVISION HIGH SCHOOL SCHOLARSHIPS

International Petroleum Technology Institute
Attn: Student Scholarship Program
11757 Katy Freeway, Suite 865
Houston, TX 77079
Phone: (281) 493-3491; Fax: (281) 493-3493
Email: torkayc@asme.org
Web: www.asme-ipti.org/public/pagscholarshipprograms.aspx

Summary: To provide financial assistance to high school seniors planning to major in engineering in college and prepare for a career in the petroleum industry.

Eligibility: Open to high school seniors who have indicated a pre-declared major in the mechanical engineering field on their application to college. Applicants must have a GPA of 3.0 or higher. Along with their application, they must submit a 2-page essay on their interest in the petroleum industry, the challenges the industry offers them, and the value they may add to the industry. Financial need is not considered in the selection process.

Financial data: The stipend is $1,000.
Duration: 1 year.
Number awarded: 2 each year.
Deadline: May of each year.

2255 PHCC EDUCATIONAL FOUNDATION NEED-BASED SCHOLARSHIP

Plumbing-Heating-Cooling Contractors-National Association
Attn: PHCC Educational Foundation
180 South Washington Street
P.O. Box 6808
Falls Church, VA 22040
Phone: (703) 237-8100; (800) 533-7694; Fax: (703) 237-7442
Email: scholarships@naphcc.org
Web: www.foundation.phccweb.org/Scholarships/NeedScholarship.htm

Summary: To provide financial assistance to undergraduate students who are interested in the plumbing, heating, and cooling industry and can demonstrate financial need.

Eligibility: Open to 1) full-time undergraduate students (entering or continuing) who are majoring in a field related to plumbing, heating, and cooling (e.g., business management, construction management with a specialization in mechanical construction, mechanical engineering) at a 4-year college or university; 2) students enrolled full-time in an approved certificate or degree program at a 2-year technical college, community college, or trade school in business management, mechanical CAD design, construction management with a specialty in mechanical construction, or plumbing or HVACR installation, service, and repair; and 3) full-time employees of a licensed plumbing or HVAC contractor (must be a member of the Plumbing-Heating-Cooling Contractors [PHCC] National Association) who are enrolled in an apprenticeship program in plumbing or HVACR installation, service, and repair. Students majoring in accounting, architecture, computer engineering, construction-related engineering, civil engineering, electrical engineering, or environmental engineering are not eligible. Applicants must have a GPA of 2.0 or higher. Along with their application, they must submit a letter of recommendation from a PHCC member; a copy of school transcripts; SAT and/or ACT scores; documentation of financial need; and a letter of recommendation from a school principal, counselor, or dean. U.S. or Canadian citizenship is required.

Financial data: The stipend is $2,500.
Duration: 1 year.
Number awarded: 1 each year.
Deadline: April of each year.

2256 PHCC EDUCATIONAL FOUNDATION SCHOLARSHIP PROGRAM

Plumbing-Heating-Cooling Contractors–National Association
Attn: PHCC Educational Foundation
180 South Washington Street
P.O. Box 6808
Falls Church, VA 22040
Phone: (703) 237-8100; (800) 533-7694; Fax: (703) 237-7442
Email: scholarships@naphcc.org
Web: www.foundation.phccweb.org/Scholarships/EFScholarship.htm

Summary: To provide financial assistance to undergraduate students interested in the plumbing, heating, and cooling industry.

Eligibility: Open to 1) full-time undergraduate students (entering or continuing) who are majoring in a field related to plumbing, heating, and cooling (e.g., business management, construction management with a specialization in mechanical construction, mechanical engineering) at a 4-year college or university; 2) students enrolled full-time in an approved certificate or degree program at a 2-year technical college, community college, or trade school in business management, mechanical CAD design, construction management with a specialty in mechanical construction, or plumbing or HVACR installation, service, and repair; and 3) full-time employees of a licensed plumbing or HVAC contractor (must be a member of the Plumbing-Heating-Cooling Contractors [PHCC] National Association) who are enrolled in an apprenticeship program in plumbing or HVACR installation, service, and repair. Students majoring in accounting, architecture, computer engineering, construction-related engineering, civil engineering, electrical engineering, or environmental engineering are not eligible. Applicants must have a GPA of 2.0 or higher. Along with their application, they must submit a letter of recommendation from a PHCC member; a copy of school transcripts; SAT and/or ACT scores; and a letter of recommendation from a school principal, counselor, or dean. U.S. or Canadian citizenship is required. Financial need is not considered in the selection process.

Financial data: The stipend is $3,000 per year for students at a 4-year institution or $1,500 per year for students at a 2-year institution or in an apprenticeship program.

Duration: Up to 4 years for students at a 4-year college or university or 2 years for students at a 2-year technical college, community college, or trade school or enrolled in an apprenticeship program.

Number awarded: 5 each year: 3 to students at 4-year institutions and 2 to students at 2-year institutions or in apprenticeship programs.

Deadline: April of each year.

2257 PHOENIX POST SAME SCHOLARSHIPS

Summary: To provide financial assistance to residents of Arizona who are interested in working on an undergraduate degree in a field related to the built environment at a college in the state.

See Listing #1509.

2258 PHYSICAL THERAPY SCHOLARSHIP

Wisconsin Paralyzed Veterans of America
Attn: Scholarship Committee
2311 South 108th Street
West Allis, WI 53227-1901
Phone: (414) 328-8910; (800) 875-WPVA; Fax: (414) 328-8948
Email: info@wisconsinpva.org

Web: www.wisconsinpva.org/scholarships.html

Summary: To provide financial assistance to seniors in physical therapy programs in Wisconsin who are interested in working in a spinal cord injury unit or rehabilitation facility after graduation.

Eligibility: Open to students enrolled in the final year of an accredited physical therapy program in Wisconsin. Applicants must be willing to seek employment in a spinal cord injury unit or rehabilitation facility after graduation. They must be able to demonstrate financial need.

Financial data: The stipend is $1,000.

Duration: 1 year.

Number awarded: 1 each year.

Deadline: March of each year.

2259 PHYSIO-CONTROL ACADEMIC SCHOLARSHIP

American Association of Occupational Health Nurses, Inc.
Attn: AAOHN Foundation
7794 Grow Drive
Pensacola, FL 32514
Phone: (850) 474-6963; (800) 241-8014; Fax: (850) 484-8762
Email: aaohn@aaohn.org
Web: www.aaohn.org/scholarships/academic-study.html

Summary: To provide financial assistance to registered nurses who are working on a bachelor's or graduate degree to prepare for a career in occupational and environmental health.

Eligibility: Open to registered nurses who are enrolled in a baccalaureate or graduate degree program. Applicants must demonstrate an interest in, and commitment to, occupational and environmental health. Along with their application, they must submit a 500-word narrative on their professional goals as they relate to the academic activity and the field of occupational and environmental health. Selection is based on that essay (50%), impact of education on applicant's career (20%), and 2 letters of recommendation (30%).

Financial data: The stipend is $3,000.

Duration: 1 year; may be renewed up to 2 additional years.

Number awarded: 1 each year.

Deadline: January of each year.

2260 PIERRE H. GUILLEMETTE SCHOLARSHIP

Rhode Island Society of Professional Land Surveyors
Attn: Scholarship Committee
P.O. Box 544
East Greenwich, RI 02818
Phone: (401) 294-1262
Email: info@rispls.org
Web: www.rispls.org

Summary: To provide financial assistance to Rhode Island residents studying surveying at a school in any state.

Eligibility: Open to residents of Rhode Island who are enrolled in a course of study leading to a certificate program or degree in land surveying offered by a qualified institution of higher learning in any state. Applicants must submit brief essays on 1) any special skills or qualifications they have acquired from employment, previous volunteer work, or through other activities, including hobbies or sports; and 2) their previous surveying experience. Financial need is not considered in the selection process.

Financial data: The amount of the award depends on the availability of funds.

Duration: 1 year.

Number awarded: 1 or more each year.

Deadline: October of each year.

2261 PILOT INTERNATIONAL FOUNDATION SCHOLARSHIP PROGRAM

Pilot International
Attn: Foundation
102 Preston Court
P.O. Box 5600
Macon, GA 31208-5600
Phone: (478) 477-1208; Fax: (478) 477-6978
Email: pifinfo@pilothq.org
Web: www.pilotinternational.org/html/foundation/scholar.shtml

Summary: To provide financial assistance to undergraduate students who are interested in working with people who have brain-related disabilities or disorders.

Eligibility: Open to undergraduate students who are preparing for careers working with people who have brain-related disabilities or disorders or training those who will be working with them. Applicants must have completed at least 1 semester at a college or university in the United States or Canada and have a GPA of 3.25 or higher They must be sponsored by a Pilot Club in their hometown or in the city in which their college or university is located. Local Pilot Clubs are allowed to sponsor only 1 applicant per program.

Financial data: The stipend is $2,000 for seniors, $1,700 for juniors, $1,400 for sophomores, or $1,000 for freshmen.

Duration: 1 year; may be renewed up to 3 additional years.

Number awarded: 1 each year.

Deadline: February of each year.

2262 PIONEERS OF FLIGHT SCHOLARSHIP PROGRAM

National Air Transportation Foundation
Attn: Manager, Education and Training
4226 King Street
Alexandria, VA 22302
Phone: (703) 845-9000, ext. 125; (800) 808-6282; Fax: (703) 845-8176
Email: akoranda@nata.aero
Web: www.nata.aero

Summary: To provide financial assistance for college to students planning careers in general aviation.

Eligibility: Open to students intending to enroll full-time at an accredited 4-year college or university as a junior or senior. Applicants must demonstrate an interest in a career in general aviation (not the major commercial airlines) and have a GPA of 3.0 or higher. Along with their application, they must submit a 250-word essay on their goals in general aviation. Selection is based on that essay, academic record, and letter of recommendation.

Financial data: The stipend is $1,000.

Duration: 1 year; may be renewed 1 additional year if the recipient maintains a 3.0 GPA and full-time enrollment.

Number awarded: 1 each year.

Deadline: December of each year.

2263 PLANNING SYSTEMS INCORPORATED SCIENCE AND ENGINEERING SCHOLARSHIP

Navy League of the United States
Attn: Scholarships
2300 Wilson Boulevard, Suite 200
Arlington, VA 22201-5424
Phone: (703) 528-1775; (800) 356-5760; Fax: (703) 528-2333
Email: scholarships@navyleague.org
Web: www.navyleague.org/scholarship

Summary: To provide financial assistance to dependent children of sea service personnel or veterans who are interested in majoring in science or engineering in college.

Eligibility: Open to U.S. citizens who are dependent children of active or honorably discharged members of the U.S. sea service (including the Navy, Marine Corps, or Coast Guard). Applicants must be entering their freshman year at an accredited college or university and planning to major in science or engineering. They must have a GPA of 3.0 or higher. Along with their application, they must submit transcripts, 2 letters of recommendation, SAT/ACT scores, documentation of financial need, proof of qualifying sea service duty, and a 1-page personal statement on why they should be considered for this scholarship.

Financial data: The stipend is $2,500 per year.

Duration: 4 years, provided the recipient maintains a GPA of 3.0 or higher.

Number awarded: 1 each year.

Deadline: February of each year.

2264 P.O. PISTILLI SCHOLARSHIPS

Design Automation Conference
c/o Cherrice Traver
Union College
Steinmetz Hall, Room 202
Schenectady, NY 12308
Phone: (518) 388-6326; Fax: (518) 388-6789
Email: traverc@union.edu
Web: doc.union.edu/acsee.html

Summary: To provide financial assistance to female, minority, or disabled high school seniors who are interested in preparing for a career in computer science or electrical engineering.

Eligibility: Open to graduating high school seniors who are members of underrepresented groups: women, African Americans, Hispanics, Native Americans, and persons with disabilities. Applicants must be interested in preparing for a career in electrical engineering, computer engineering, or computer science. They must have at least a 3.0 GPA, have demonstrated high achievements in math and science courses, have demonstrated involvement in activities associated with the underrepresented group they represent, and be able to demonstrate significant financial need. U.S. citizenship is not required, but applicants must be U.S. residents when they apply and must plan to attend an accredited U.S. college or university. Along with their application, they must submit 3 letters of recommendation, official transcripts, ACT/SAT and/or PSAT scores, a personal statement outlining future goals and why they think they should receive this scholarship, and documentation of financial need.

Financial data: Stipends are $4,000 per year. Awards are paid each year in 2 equal installments.

Duration: 1 year; renewable for up to 4 additional years.

Number awarded: 2 to 7 each year.

Deadline: January of each year.

2265 PORK CHECKOFF PORK INDUSTRY SCHOLARSHIPS

National Pork Board
1776 N.W. 114th Street
Des Moines, IA 50325
Phone: (515) 223-2600; (800) 456-PORK; Fax: (515) 223-2646
Email: info@pork.org
Web: www.pork.org/porkscience/scholarship/default.aspx

Summary: To provide financial assistance to undergraduate students who are considering continuing on in a graduate program in a swine science discipline.

Eligibility: Open to students currently enrolled as college sophomores, juniors, and seniors and dedicated to a career in swine management or the pork industry. Applicants should be majoring in such fields as agriculture, agricultural business, agricultural engineering, agronomy, animal breeding/genetics/genomics, animal physiology, bioinformatics, environmental science, environmental physiology/behavior, food technology, meat science, nutrition, pork safety, reproductive physiology, or veterinary medicine. They must be planning to attend graduate school to continue their studies in a swine-related program. Preference is given to applicants affiliated with the pork industry as a member of a pork production family, as a member of a family associated with allied industry or the marketing segments of the pork industry, or active or past members of industry youth leadership development programs with emphasis on swine. Selection is based on academic record, youth and industry leadership activities, interest and involvement in the swine industry, and graduate degree selected and/or prospective career path.

Financial data: Stipends are $10,000, $5,000, or $2,500.

Duration: 1 year.

Number awarded: At least 16 each year, including 1 at $10,000, 1 at $5,000, and the remainder at $2,500.

Deadline: September of each year.

2266 POUDRE VALLEY HEALTH SYSTEM NIGHTINGALE SCHOLARSHIP

Colorado Nurses Foundation
7400 East Arapahoe Road, Suite 211
Centennial, CO 80112
Phone: (303) 694-4728; Fax: (303) 694-4869
Email: mail@cnfound.org
Web: www.cnfound.org/scholarships.html

Summary: To provide financial assistance to undergraduate and graduate nursing students in Colorado who are willing to work in designated communities following graduation.

Eligibility: Open to Colorado residents who are enrolled in an approved nursing program in the state. Applicants may be 1) second-year students in an associate degree program; 2) junior or senior level B.S.N. undergraduate students; 3) R.N.s enrolled in a baccalaureate or higher degree program in a school of nursing; 4) R.N.s with a master's degree in nursing, currently practicing in Colorado and enrolled in a doctoral program; or 5) students in the second or third year of a Doctorate Nursing Practice (D.N.P.) program. They must be willing to work in Fort Collins, Loveland, or Estes Park, Colorado following graduation. Undergraduates must have a GPA of 3.25 or higher and graduate students must have a GPA of 3.5 or higher. Selection is based on professional philosophy and goals, dedication to the improvement of patient care in Colorado, demonstrated commitment to nursing, critical thinking skills, potential for leadership, involvement in community and professional organizations, recommendations, GPA, and financial need.

Financial data: The stipend is $1,000.

Duration: 1 year.

Number awarded: 2 each year.

Deadline: October of each year.

2267 POWDER RIVER BASIN SECTION ANNUAL SCHOLARSHIP AWARDS

Society of Petroleum Engineers–Powder River Basin Section
Attn: Bob Christofferson, Scholarships
P.O. Box 3977
Gillette, WY 82717-3977
Phone: (307) 682-4853
Email: bchristofferson@cogc.com

Summary: To provide financial assistance to Wyoming residents interested in attending college in any state to prepare for a career in the oil and gas industry.

Eligibility: Open to Wyoming residents preparing for a career in the oil and gas industry at a college or university in any state. Applicants should be majoring in engineering (especially petroleum engineering), although some of the scholarships may go to non-engineering students. They must be enrolled full-time as entering freshmen, sophomores, juniors, or seniors in a 4-year program or freshmen or sophomores in a 2-year program. Along with their application, they must submit a letter that covers their academic qualifications, primary career interests, extracurricular activities, and names of 2 references. Financial need is not considered in the selection process.

Financial data: Stipends range from $500 to $2,000.

Duration: 1 year.

Number awarded: 5 to 15 each year.

Deadline: March of each year.

2268 PPQ WILLIAM F. HELMS STUDENT SCHOLARSHIP PROGRAM

Department of Agriculture
Animal and Plant Health Inspection Service
Attn: Human Resources/Recruitment
1400 Independence Avenue, S.W., Room 1710
Washington, DC 20250
Phone: (202) 690-4759
Web: www.aphis.usda.gov/plant_health/helms/index.shtml

Summary: To provide financial assistance and work experience to college students majoring in the agricultural or biological sciences.

Eligibility: Open to college sophomores and juniors who are attending an accredited college or university, are majoring in an agricultural or biological science (such as biology, plant pathology, entomology, virology, bacteriology, mycology, or ecology), are interested in a career in plant protection and quarantine, and are U.S. citizens. Applicants must submit a personal letter that describes their interests, goals, and chosen career plans; explains how they envision their ability to contribute to the sponsor's mission; and outlines why they should be selected over other candidates for this program. A preference is given to veterans of the U.S. armed forces.

Financial data: The stipend is $5,000 per year.

Duration: 1 year; may be renewed if the recipient maintains a GPA of 2.5 or higher.

Number awarded: Several each year.

Deadline: February of each year.

2269 PRESIDENT OBAMA/HISPANIC SCHOLARSHIP FUND/ STEM TEACHER SCHOLARSHIP PROGRAM

Hispanic Scholarship Fund
Attn: Selection Committee
55 Second Street, Suite 1500
San Francisco, CA 94105
Phone: (415) 808-2365; (877) HSF-INFO; Fax: (415) 808-2302
Email: scholar1@hsf.net
Web: www.hsf.net/STEM_Teacher.aspx

Summary: To provide financial assistance to Hispanic college juniors who are majoring in a field of science, technology, engineering, or mathematics (STEM) with plans to become a teacher.

Eligibility: Open to U.S. citizens and permanent residents (must have a permanent resident card or a passport stamped I-551) who are of Hispanic heritage. Applicants must be full-time juniors at a college or university in the United States with a GPA of 3.0 or higher. They must be majoring in a field of STEM with the intent to become a teacher. Selection is based on academic achievement, personal strengths, leadership, and financial need.

Financial data: The stipend is $2,500 per year.
Duration: 2 years.
Number awarded: 1 or more each year.
Deadline: December of each year.

2270 PRISCILLA CARNEY JONES SCHOLARSHIP

American Chemical Society
Attn: Department of Diversity Programs
1155 16th Street, N.W.
Washington, DC 20036
Phone: (202) 872-6334; (800) 227-5558, ext. 6334; Fax: (202) 776-8003
Email: diversity@acs.org
Web: womenchemists.sites.acs.org/attracting.htm

Summary: To provide financial assistance to female upper-division students majoring in chemistry.

Eligibility: Open to women entering their junior or senior year of full-time study with a major in chemistry or chemistry-related science. Students in pre-med programs who intend to go to medical school are not eligible. Applicants must have a GPA of 3.25 or higher and be able to demonstrate financial need. They must have completed research or plan to conduct research during their undergraduate years. Along with their application, they must submit brief statements on why they are a good candidate to receive this scholarship, their community service activities and related responsibilities, the key leadership roles they have fulfilled, any research presentations or publications, and their future plans and goals. U.S. citizenship or permanent resident status is required.

Financial data: The stipend is at least $1,500.
Duration: 1 year.
Number awarded: 1 each year.
Deadline: April of each year.

2271 PROCTER & GAMBLE COMPANY SCHOLARSHIP PROGRAM OF THE HISPANIC SCHOLARSHIP FUND

Hispanic Scholarship Fund
Attn: Selection Committee
55 Second Street, Suite 1500
San Francisco, CA 94105
Phone: (415) 808-2365; (877) HSF-INFO; Fax: (415) 808-2302
Email: scholar1@hsf.net
Web: www.hsf.net/scholarships.aspx?id=470

Summary: To provide financial assistance to Hispanic high school seniors and college students from selected areas who are working on an undergraduate degree in fields of science, technology, engineering, or mathematics (STEM).

Eligibility: Open to U.S. citizens, permanent residents, and visitors with a passport stamped I-551 who are of Hispanic heritage. Applicants must be enrolled or planning to enroll full-time at a 4-year college or university in the United States, Puerto Rico, Guam, or the U.S. Virgin Islands and have a GPA of 3.0 or higher. They must be majoring or planning to major in a STEM field. The program is restricted to the metropolitan area of Los Angeles; the cities of Chicago, Dallas, Houston, McAllen (Texas), Miami, or San Antonio; or the states of Georgia, Indiana, Kentucky, New York, North Carolina, or Ohio. Selection is based on academic achievement, personal strengths, leadership, and financial need.

Financial data: The stipend is $2,500.
Duration: 1 year.
Number awarded: 1 or more each year.
Deadline: February of each year.

2272 PROFESSIONAL AVIATION MAINTENANCE ASSOCIATION STUDENT SCHOLARSHIP PROGRAM

Professional Aviation Maintenance Association
Attn: PAMA Foundation
400 North Washington, Suite 300
Alexandria, VA 22314
Phone: (703) 778-4647
Email: hq@pama.org
Web: www.pama.org/content.asp?contentid=73

Summary: To provide financial assistance to students interested in studying aviation maintenance on the undergraduate level.

Eligibility: Open to students currently enrolled in an institution to obtain an airframe and powerplant (A&P) or avionics license. Applicants must have completed 25% of the required curriculum; have at least a 3.0 GPA; and need financial assistance. Selection is based on educational performance, work experience, participation in school and community activities, career commitment and future potential, financial need, and a recommendation by a counselor, adviser, aviation maintenance instructor, or current employer.

Financial data: The stipend is $1,000. Funds may be used for tuition, fees, books, or supplies.
Duration: 1 year; recipients may reapply.
Number awarded: Varies each year; recently, 5 of these scholarships were awarded.
Deadline: November of each year.

2273 PROFESSIONAL LAND SURVEYORS OF OREGON SCHOLARSHIP

Oregon Student Assistance Commission
Attn: Grants and Scholarships Division
1500 Valley River Drive, Suite 100
Eugene, OR 97401-2146
Phone: (541) 687-7395; (800) 452-8807, ext. 7395; Fax: (541) 687-7414; TDD: (800) 735-2900
Email: awardinfo@osac.state.or.us
Web: www.osac.state.or.us/osac_programs.html

Summary: To provide financial assistance to students in Oregon interested in a career in land surveying.

Eligibility: Open to residents of Oregon enrolled at colleges and universities in the state. Applicants must be enrolled in a program leading to a career as a land surveyor, including community college applicants who intend to transfer to eligible 4-year schools or complete a degree in land surveying at the community college level. They must intend to take the Fundamentals of Land Surveying (FLS) examination. Along with their application, they must submit a brief essay on what led them to prepare for a land surveying career and what surveying means to them.

Financial data: The stipend is at least $1,600 per year.
Duration: 1 year.
Number awarded: Varies each year; recently, 5 of these scholarships were awarded.
Deadline: February of each year.

2274 PROMISE OF NURSING SCHOLARSHIPS

National Student Nurses' Association
Attn: Foundation
45 Main Street, Suite 606
Brooklyn, NY 11201
Phone: (718) 210-0705; Fax: (718) 797-1186
Email: nsna@nsna.org
Web: www.nsna.org/FoundationScholarships/FNSNAScholarships.aspx

Summary: To provide financial assistance to nursing or pre-nursing students at schools in selected geographic locations.

Eligibility: Open to students currently enrolled in state-approved schools of nursing or pre-nursing associate degree, baccalaureate, diploma, generic master's, generic doctoral, R.N. to B.S.N., R.N. to M.S.N., or L.P.N./L.V.N. to R.N. programs. Graduating high school seniors are not eligible. Support for graduate education is provided only for a first degree in nursing. Applicants must be attending school in the Dallas/Fort Worth area of Texas, the Houston/Galveston area of Texas (Austin, Brazoria, Chambers, Colorado, Fort Bend, Galveston, Harris, Liberty, Matagorda, Montgomery, Walker, Waller, and Wharton counties), central Florida, southern Florida, southern California (Los Angeles, Orange, Riverside, San Bernardino, Santa Barbara, and Ventura counties), or the states of Georgia (graduate students only), Louisiana, Maryland, Massachusetts, Mississippi, New Jersey (graduate students only), Oregon, Pennsylvania, Tennessee, or Washington. Selection is based on academic achievement, financial need, and involvement in student nursing organizations and community health activities.

Financial data: Stipends range from $1,000 to $2,500.
Duration: 1 year.
Number awarded: Varies each year; recently, 57 of these scholarships were awarded: 2 in Dallas/Fort Worth, Texas; 1 in Houston/Galveston, Texas; 2 in central Florida, 9 in southern California; 9 in Maryland; 11 in Massachusetts; 4 in New Jersey; 5 in Pennsylvania; 3 in Tennessee; and 11 in Washington.
Deadline: January of each year.

2275 PROTON ENERGY SCHOLARSHIP

Proton Energy Systems
Attn: Hydrogen Education Foundation
1211 Connecticut Avenue, N.W., Suite 600

Washington, DC 20036-2701
Phone: (202) 223-5547
Email: info@protonenergyscholarship.org
Web: www.protonenergyscholarship.otg

Summary: To provide financial assistance to high school seniors interested in studying science and technology in college.

Eligibility: Open to U.S. citizens and permanent residents who are graduating high school seniors and planning to enroll full-time at a college or university. Applicants must have a GPA of 3.0 or higher. Their proposed major must be in the area of science and technology, including engineering, physics, computer science, earth and life sciences, nursing and health sciences, and psychology. Selection is based on academic performance, ability, and promise; commitment to further education and a career in a field of science or technology; strength of application; demonstrated leadership, work ethic, and community involvement; and financial need.

Financial data: The stipend is $25,000 per year for the winner and $500 for honorable mentions.

Duration: The winner's scholarship may be renewed for up to 3 additional years.

Number awarded: 1 winner and a varying number of honorable mentions are selected each year.

Deadline: February of each year.

2276 QUALCOMM Q AWARDS SCHOLARSHIPS OF THE HISPANIC SCHOLARSHIP FUND

Hispanic Scholarship Fund
Attn: Selection Committee
55 Second Street, Suite 1500
San Francisco, CA 94105
Phone: (415) 808-2365; (877) HSF-INFO; Fax: (415) 808-2302
Email: scholar1@hsf.net
Web: www.hsf.net/STEM_Teacher.aspx

Summary: To provide financial assistance to Hispanic undergraduate and graduate students who are working on a degree in computers or electrical engineering.

Eligibility: Open to U.S. citizens and permanent residents (must have a permanent resident card or a passport stamped I-551) who are of Hispanic heritage. Applicants must be full-time sophomores, juniors, seniors, or graduate students at a 4-year college or university in the United States with a GPA of 3.0 or higher. They must be working on a degree in computer engineering, computer science, or electrical engineering. Preference is given to students at the University of California campuses in Berkeley and San Diego, but students at all U.S. institutions are eligible. Selection is based on academic achievement, personal strengths, leadership, and financial need.

Financial data: The stipend is $5,000.

Duration: 1 year.

Number awarded: 1 or more each year.

Deadline: December of each year.

2277 RACE FOR EDUCATION FLORIDA RESIDENT SCHOLARSHIP

Race for Education
Attn: Student Services Manager
1818 Versailles Road
P.O. Box 11355
Lexington, KY 40575
Phone: (859) 252-8648; Fax: (859) 252-8030
Email: info@racingscholarships.com
Web: www.racingscholarships.com/page.php?page=programs

Summary: To provide financial assistance to residents of Florida attending college in any state to prepare for a career in the equine industry.

Eligibility: Open to undergraduate students under 24 years of age who are residents of Florida. Applicants must be attending a college or university in any state to prepare for a career in the equine industry. Fields of study may include (but are not limited to) equine science, racetrack management, equine business management, pasture management as it relates to horse farms, or other equine-related fields. They must have a GPA of 2.85 or higher and be U.S. citizens or have a valid student visa. Financial need is also considered in the selection process.

Financial data: The stipend covers payment of tuition, to a maximum of $7,500 per year. The student is responsible for all other fees. Students who meet certain financial need requirements may be eligible for up to $4,000 in additional funding.

Duration: 1 year; may be renewed up to 3 additional years, provided the recipient maintains a GPA of 3.0 or higher.

Number awarded: 1 each year.

Deadline: February of each year.

2278 RACE FOR EDUCATION THOROUGHBRED SCHOLARSHIPS

Race for Education
Attn: Student Services Manager
1818 Versailles Road
P.O. Box 11355
Lexington, KY 40575
Phone: (859) 252-8648; Fax: (859) 252-8030
Email: info@racingscholarships.com
Web: www.racingscholarships.com/page.php?page=programs

Summary: To provide financial assistance to undergraduate students working on an equine-related degree.

Eligibility: Open to undergraduate students under 24 years of age working on an equine-related degree, including (but not limited to) pre-veterinary medicine (equine practice only), equine science, equine business management, racetrack management, or other equine- or agriculture-related program. Applicants must have a GPA of 2.85 or higher and be a U.S. citizen or have a valid student visa. Their household income may not exceed $50,000 per year.

Financial data: The stipend covers payment of tuition, to a maximum of $6,000 per year. The student is responsible for all other fees.

Duration: 1 year; may be renewed up to 3 additional years, provided the recipient maintains a GPA of 3.0 or higher.

Number awarded: 1 or more each year.

Deadline: February of each year.

2279 RADIO CLUB OF AMERICA SCHOLARSHIPS

Foundation for Amateur Radio, Inc.
Attn: Scholarship Committee
P.O. Box 911
Columbia, MD 21044-0911
Phone: (410) 552-2652; Fax: (410) 981-5146
Email: dave.prestel@gmail.com
Web: www.farweb.org/scholarships

Summary: To provide funding to licensed radio amateurs who are interested in studying electrical engineering in college.

Eligibility: Open to college juniors and seniors who have a general class amateur radio license and are working full-time on a bachelor's degree. Applicants must be majoring in electrical engineering; preference is given to students taking courses in wireless communications. U.S. citizenship is required. Financial need is considered in the selection process.

Financial data: The stipend is $1,000.

Duration: 1 year.

Number awarded: 3 each year.

Deadline: March of each year.

2280 RAIN BIRD INTELLIGENT USE OF WATER SCHOLARSHIP

Summary: To provide financial assistance to landscape architecture students who are in need of financial assistance.

See Listing #1525.

2281 RAYMOND DAVIS SCHOLARSHIP

Society for Imaging Science and Technology
Attn: Membership Office
7003 Kilworth Lane
Springfield, VA 22151
Phone: (703) 642-9090; Fax: (703) 642-9094
Email: info@imaging.org
Web: www.imaging.org

Summary: To provide financial assistance to undergraduate and graduate students interested in studying or conducting research on photographic or imaging science or technology.

Eligibility: Open to full-time undergraduate or graduate students who have completed or will complete 2 academic years at an accredited institution before the term of the scholarship begins. Support is provided for academic study or research in photographic or imaging science or engineering. Graduate students

must provide an abstract of their plan for advanced study, research, and thesis. All applicants must outline their career objectives and indicate how the academic work they propose to undertake will further their objectives. Financial need is not considered.
Financial data: Grants are $1,000 or more.
Number awarded: 1 or more each year.
Deadline: December of each year.

2282 RAYMOND R. MOONEY SCHOLARSHIP

Vermont Student Assistance Corporation
Attn: Scholarship Programs
10 East Allen Street
P.O. Box 2000
Winooski, VT 05404-2601
Phone: (802) 654-3798; (888) 253-4819; Fax: (802) 654-3765; TDD: (800) 281-3341 (within VT)
Email: info@vsac.org
Web: services.vsac.org/wps/wcm/connect/vsac/VSAC
Summary: To provide financial assistance to high school seniors in Vermont who plan to study a field related to emergency services at a college in any state.
Eligibility: Open to high school seniors in Vermont who are enrolled or planning to enroll in an academic, vocational, or technical program in a field related to emergency services at a school in any state. Applicants must submit 1) a 100-word essay on their interest in and commitment to pursuing their chosen career or vocation; 2) a 100-word essay on any significant barriers that limit their access to education; and 3) a 250-word essay on their short- and long-term academic, educational, career, vocational, and/or employment goals. Selection is based on those essays and financial need.
Financial data: The stipend is $1,000.
Duration: 1 year; recipients may reapply.
Number awarded: 1 each year.
Deadline: June of each year.

2283 RAYMOND W. MILLER, PE AND ALICE E. MILLER SCHOLARSHIP

Florida Engineering Society
Attn: Scholarship Coordinator
125 South Gadsden Street
P.O. Box 750
Tallahassee, FL 32302-0750
Phone: (850) 224-7121; Fax: (850) 222-4349
Email: fes@fleng.org
Web: www.fleng.org/scholarships.cfm
Summary: To provide financial assistance to engineering students at colleges and universities in Florida, especially the University of Florida.
Eligibility: Open to residents of Florida entering their junior or senior year of an engineering program at a college or university in the state. Preference is given to full-time students at the University of Florida. Applicants must be U.S. citizens with a GPA of 3.0 or higher and be recommended by a faculty member at their institution. Selection is based on academic performance, work experience, activities, honors, and letters of recommendation. Semifinalists are interviewed. Financial need is not considered in the selection process.
Financial data: The stipend is $1,000.
Duration: 1 year.
Number awarded: 1 each year.
Deadline: January of each year.

2284 RED BOUCHER SCHOLARSHIP

Alaska Community Foundation
Attn: Scholarships
400 L Street, Suite 100
Anchorage, AK 99501
Phone: (907) 334-6700; Fax: (907) 334-5780
Email: info@alaskacf.org
Web: www.alaskacf.org
Summary: To provide financial assistance to residents of Alaska who are interested in studying a field related to technology at a college in any state.
Eligibility: Open to residents of Alaska who are graduating high school seniors or students already enrolled full-time at a college or university in any state. Applicants must be interested in studying a field related to technology and preparing for a career in a technology-related field. They must have a GPA of 3.0 or higher and be able to demonstrate financial need. Along with their application, they must submit a 1,000-word essay describing how their background is relevant to their interest in preparing for a technology career, their educational goals and objectives, their plan and timeframe for meeting those goals, and their specific qualifications for this scholarship.
Financial data: The stipend is $1,000.
Duration: 1 year.
Number awarded: 1 or more each year.
Deadline: January of each year.

2285 RHODE ISLAND PILOTS ASSOCIATION SCHOLARSHIP

Rhode Island Pilots Association
Attn: Scholarship Chair
644 Airport Road, Hangar One
Warwick, RI 02886
Phone: (401) 568-3497; Fax: (401) 568-5392
Email: ripaemail@aol.com
Web: www.ripilots.com/Scholarships.htm
Summary: To provide financial assistance to Rhode Island residents interested in obtaining pilot flight training or a college degree in an aviation-related field.
Eligibility: Open to residents of Rhode Island who are at least 16 years of age. Applicants must be interested in a program of pilot flight training or a college degree program in a field that is related to aviation and approved by the sponsoring organization. Flight training candidates must be able to pass the FAA Class III physical. Along with their application, they must submit a 2-page personal letter describing how scholarship funds would be used to pursue goals in aviation or related areas; a list of extracurricular activities, hobbies, and personal interests; 2 letters of recommendation; details of school record; and documentation of financial need.
Financial data: The stipend is $1,000.
Duration: 1 year.
Number awarded: 2 each year.
Deadline: February of each year.

2286 RICHARD A. HERBERT MEMORIAL UNDERGRADUATE SCHOLARSHIP

American Water Resources Association
Attn: Scholarship Coordinator
4 West Federal Street
P.O. Box 1626
Middleburg, VA 20118-1626
Phone: (540) 687-8390; Fax: (540) 687-8395
Email: info@awra.org
Web: www.awra.org
Summary: To provide financial assistance to undergraduate students enrolled in a program related to water resources.
Eligibility: Open to full-time undergraduate students enrolled in a program related to water resources. Applicants must submit a 2-page summary of their academic interests and achievements, extracurricular activities, and career goals. Selection is based on that statement, cumulative GPA, relevance of the student's curriculum to water resources, and leadership in extracurricular activities related to water resources.
Financial data: The stipend is $2,000.
Duration: 1 year.
Number awarded: 1 each year.
Deadline: April of each year.

2287 RICHARD DANIEL MEMORIAL SCHOLARSHIP

Illinois Trappers Association
c/o Paul Kelley
412 North Broadway
Box 75
Hudson, IL 61748
Phone: (309) 726-1443
Email: pkelleyp@aol.com
Web: illinoistrappersassociation.com
Summary: To provide financial assistance to Illinois residents who are interested in majoring in fields related to natural resources at a college in any state.
Eligibility: Open to Illinois residents who are outdoorsmen: fishermen, hunters, trappers, and conservationists. Applicants must be attending or planning to attend a college or university in any state. Along with their application, they

must submit a transcript of all high school and college grades, a list of their leadership and community service activities, 2 letters of recommendation, and a personal letter stating their reasons for seeking the scholarship.
Financial data: The stipend is $1,000.
Duration: 1 year.
Number awarded: 1 each year.
Deadline: May of each year.

2288 RICHARD E. LOMAX NATIONAL TRIG-STAR SCHOLARSHIPS

National Society of Professional Surveyors
Attn: Trig-Star Program
6 Montgomery Village Avenue, Suite 403
Gaithersburg, MD 20879
Phone: (240) 632-9716, ext. 105; Fax: (240) 632-1321
Email: trisha.milburn@acsm.net
Web: www.nspsmo.org/index.cfm?fuseaction=Page.viewPage&pageId=522
Summary: To recognize and reward (with college scholarships) high school students who participate in a trigonometry contest.
Eligibility: Open to high school students who participate at their school in a timed exercise in solving trigonometry problems that incorporate the use of right triangle formulas and the laws of sines and cosines. Contestants have up to 1 hour to complete the test, and the student who achieves the highest score in the shortest amount of time is the winner. School winners then compete in a state test, and state winners compete in the national test.
Financial data: At the national level, the first-place winner receives a $2,000 scholarship, second a $1,000 scholarship, and third a $500 scholarship. The teachers of the 3 winners receive awards of $1,000, $500, and $250, respectively. Local and state awards may also be provided by the local chapter or sponsor.
Duration: The competition is held annually.
Number awarded: 3 students win national awards each year.
Deadline: Deadline not specified.

2289 RICHARD GROENDYKE SCHOLARSHIPS

American Council of Engineering Companies of Alabama
Attn: Scholarship Coordinator
531 Herron Street
Montgomery, AL 36104
Phone: (334) 264-1500; Fax: (334) 264-0099
Email: chall@aceca.org
Web: www.aceca.org/Awards.htm
Summary: To provide financial assistance to upper-division and graduate students working on a degree in engineering or land surveying at a college in Alabama.
Eligibility: Open to students working on a bachelor's, master's, or Ph.D. degree in an ABET-approved engineering or accredited land surveying program in Alabama. Applicants must be U.S. citizens entering their junior, senior, fifth, or graduate year. Along with their application, they must submit a 500-word essay on "What is the role or responsibility of the consulting engineer or land surveyor to shaping and protecting the natural environment?" Selection is based on the essay (25 points), cumulative GPA (24 points), work experience (24 points), a letter of recommendation (17 points), and extracurricular college activities (10 points).
Financial data: The stipend is $3,000.
Duration: 1 year.
Number awarded: 2 each year.
Deadline: January.

2290 RICHARD J. SCHNELL MEMORIAL SCHOLARSHIPS

Community Foundation of Northern Illinois
Attn: Program and Scholarship Officer
946 North Second Street
Rockford, IL 61107
Phone: (815) 962-2110, ext. 11; Fax: (815) 962-2116
Email: jpatterson@cfnil.org
Web: www.cfnil.org/Scholarships/scholarships.asp
Summary: To provide financial assistance to residents of any state who are entering or enrolled in a dental, dental hygiene, or dental postdoctoral program in any state.
Eligibility: Open to residents of any state who have been accepted into or are enrolled in a dental, dental hygiene, or dental graduate postdoctoral program in any state. Applicants must be able to demonstrate financial need. Their program must be accredited by the American Dental Association.
Financial data: The stipend is $1,000.
Duration: 1 year.
Number awarded: Varies each year; recently, 5 of these scholarships were awarded.
Deadline: February of each year.

2291 RICHARD MARKS EDUCATIONAL FUND

Ke Ali'i Pauahi Foundation
Attn: Financial Aid & Scholarship Services
567 South King Street, Suite 160
Honolulu, HI 96813
Phone: (808) 534-3966; (800) 842-4682, ext. 43966; Fax: (808) 534-3890
Email: scholarships@pauahi.org
Web: www.pauahi.org/scholarships
Summary: To provide financial assistance to students, especially Native Hawaiians, who are interested in working on an undergraduate degree in a medical field at a school in Hawaii.
Eligibility: Open to students working full-time on a 4-year undergraduate degree in a medical field at a college or university in Hawaii. preference is given to Native Hawaiians (descendants of the aboriginal inhabitants of the Hawaiian Islands prior to 1778).
Financial data: The stipend is $1,000.
Duration: 1 year.
Number awarded: 1 each year.
Deadline: March of each year.

2292 RITA LOWE COLLEGE SCHOLARSHIPS

Washington State Mathematics Council
c/o Pat Reistroffer, Scholarship Chair
146 Scenic View Drive
Longview, WA 98632
Phone: (360) 636-5125
Email: preistrof@aol.com
Web: www.wsmc.net/scholarship
Summary: To provide financial assistance to students from any state majoring in mathematics education at colleges and universities in Washington.
Eligibility: Open to residents of any state currently attending a college or university in Washington and majoring in mathematics education. Applicants must be preparing for teaching certification in order to become a professional educator teaching mathematics at the elementary or secondary level. They must submit a transcript (from the ninth grade to the date of application), a 300-word statement on their experience with and interest in mathematics, and 2 letters of recommendation. Selection is based on academic achievement, demonstrated intent to become a mathematics educator, character, academic potential, and leadership potential.
Financial data: The stipend is $1,000.
Duration: 1 year.
Number awarded: 2 each year.
Deadline: May of each year.

2293 RITA LOWE HIGH SCHOOL SCHOLARSHIP

Washington State Mathematics Council
c/o Pat Reistroffer, Scholarship Chair
146 Scenic View Drive
Longview, WA 98632
Phone: (360) 636-5125
Email: preistrof@aol.com
Web: www.wsmc.net/scholarship
Summary: To provide financial assistance to high school seniors in Washington planning to major in mathematics education at a college or university in the state.
Eligibility: Open to seniors graduating from high schools in Washington and planning to attend a college or university in the state to major in mathematics education. Applicants must be preparing for teaching certification in order to become a professional educator teaching mathematics at the elementary or secondary level. They must submit a transcript (from the ninth grade to the date of application), a 300-word statement on their experience with and interest in mathematics, and 2 letters of recommendation. Selection is based on academic achievement, demonstrated intent to become a mathematics educator, character, academic potential, and leadership potential.

Financial data: The stipend is $1,000.
Duration: 1 year.
Number awarded: 1 each year.
Deadline: May of each year.

2294 RN GENERAL EDUCATION SCHOLARSHIP

Society of Gastroenterology Nurses and Associates, Inc.
Attn: Awards Committee
401 North Michigan Avenue
Chicago, IL 60611-4267
Phone: (312) 321-5165; (800) 245-SGNA; Fax: (312) 673-6694
Email: sgna@smithbucklin.com
Web: www.sgna.org/Education/scholarships.cfm
Summary: To provide financial assistance to full-time students working toward licensure as a registered nurse (R.N.).
Eligibility: Open to students currently enrolled full-time in an accredited nursing program with a GPA of 3.0 or higher. Applicants must be studying to become an R.N. Along with their application, they must submit a 2-page essay on a challenging situation they see in the health care environment today and how they, as an R.N., would best address and meet that challenge. Financial need is not considered in the selection process.
Financial data: The stipend is $2,500. Funds are issued as reimbursement after the recipient has completed the proposed course work with a GPA of 3.0 or higher.
Duration: 1 year.
Number awarded: 1 or more each year.
Deadline: July of each year.

2295 ROBERT H. WEITBRECHT SCHOLARSHIP

Alexander Graham Bell Association for the Deaf and Hard of Hearing
Attn: Financial Aid Coordinator
3417 Volta Place, N.W.
Washington, DC 20007-2778
Phone: (202) 337-5220; Fax: (202) 337-8314; TDD: (202) 337-5221
Email: financialaid@agbell.org
Web: nc.agbell.org/NetCommunity/Page.aspx?pid=493
Summary: To provide financial assistance to undergraduate and graduate students with moderate to profound hearing loss, especially those working on a degree in engineering or science.
Eligibility: Open to undergraduate and graduate students who have been diagnosed with a moderate to profound hearing loss prior to acquiring spoken language (hearing loss averages 60dB or greater in the better ear in the speech frequencies of 500, 1000, and 2000 Hz). Applicants must be able to demonstrate leadership potential and be committed to using spoken language as their primary mode of communication. They must be accepted or enrolled at a mainstream college or university as a full-time student. Along with their application, they must submit a 1-page essay discussing their career goals and how spoken communication is helping them to reach those goals as a person with a hearing loss. Financial need is considered in the selection process. Priority for this scholarship is given to applicants studying engineering or science.
Financial data: The stipend is $2,500 per year.
Duration: 1 year; may be renewed 1 additional year.
Number awarded: 1 each year.
Deadline: February of each year.

2296 ROBERT N. HUBBY ACADEMIC SCHOLARSHIP

Instrumentation, Systems, and Automation Society
Attn: Power Industry Division
c/o Michael J. Skoncey, Honors and Awards Chair
First Energy Generation Corporation, W.H. Sammis Plant
P.O. Box 176
Stratton, OH 43961
Phone: (740) 537-6324; Fax: (740) 537-6320
Email: mskoncey@firstenergycorp.com
Web: www.isa.org/MSTemplate.cfm?MicrositeID=538&CommitteeID=5230
Summary: To provide financial assistance to undergraduate students working on a degree in a field related to the power industry.
Eligibility: Open to full-time students in the sophomore year or higher of an undergraduate program in a field related to the power industry (e.g., computer science, electrical engineering, mechanical engineering). Applicants must have a GPA of 3.0 or higher. Along with their application, they must submit a resume that includes career-related extracurricular activities in which they have participated; non-career related activities; academic honors, civic honors, or awards; any professional and honorary society memberships; and jobs they have held. Financial need is not considered in the selection process.
Financial data: The stipend is $4,000.
Duration: 1 year.
Number awarded: 1 each year.
Deadline: January of each year.

2297 ROBERT NOYCE SCHOLARSHIPS OF PENNSYLVANIA

Pennsylvania State System of Higher Education Foundation, Inc.
Attn: Director of Scholarship Programs
2986 North Second Street
Harrisburg, PA 17110
Phone: (717) 720-4065; Fax: (717) 720-7082
Email: eshowers@thePAfoundation.org
Web: www.thepafoundation.org/scholarships/index.asp
Summary: To provide financial assistance to upper-division students and professionals at institutions of the Pennsylvania State System of Higher Education (PASSHE) who are majoring in a discipline of science, technology, engineering, or mathematics (STEM) and planning to become a high school science and mathematics teacher in Pennsylvania.
Eligibility: Open to 1) juniors and seniors enrolled at 1 of the 14 institutions within the PASSHE and majoring in a STEM discipline; and 2) post-baccalaureate students who have a bachelor's degree in science or mathematics and have returned to college to receive additional training. Applicants must be interested in completing certification requirements for secondary science and mathematics education and be willing to commit to teaching at a high school in Pennsylvania. They must have a GPA of 3.0 or higher (preferably 3.5 or higher); transfer students and post-baccalaureates must complete a semester or more of course work at a State System university to establish the 3.0 qualifying GPA. Along with their application, they must submit a 2-page essay on their personal and professional goals, commitment to teaching, and personal philosophy of teaching. Selection is based on that essay (20 points), GPA (30 points for 3.0 or higher; 40 points for 3.5 or higher), letters of recommendation (15 points), resume quality (15 points), evidence of leadership experiences and/or abilities (15 points), and professionally prepared application packet (10 points).
Financial data: Stipends range from $7,500 to $10,000 per year; funds are paid directly to the recipient's university account for payment of educational expenses.
Duration: 1 semester; may be renewed up to 3 additional semesters, provided the recipient remains enrolled full-time, maintains a GPA of 3.0 or higher, and provides specified services for the program.
Number awarded: Varies each year, depending on the availability of funds.
Deadline: April of each year for fall awards; October of each year for spring awards.

2298 ROBERT V. PIRRIE MEMORIAL SCHOLARSHIP

Missouri Society of Professional Surveyors
722 East Capitol Avenue
P.O. Box 1342
Jefferson City, MO 65102
Phone: (573) 635-9446; Fax: (573) 635-7823
Web: www.missourisurveyor.org/forms/rvp.asp
Summary: To provide financial assistance to high school seniors in Missouri who plan to attend college in any state to study land surveying or a related field.
Eligibility: Open to seniors graduating from high schools in Missouri and planning to enroll at a college, university, or community college in any state. Applicants must be planning to major in land surveying or a related field. Selection is based on academic promise and potential for completion of college studies, enrollment in classes or participation in activities related to the land surveying field, and financial need.
Financial data: The stipend is $1,500.
Duration: 1 year; nonrenewable.
Number awarded: 1 or more each year.
Deadline: March of each year.

2299 ROBERTA PIERCE SCOFIELD BACHELOR'S SCHOLARSHIPS

Oncology Nursing Society
Attn: ONS Foundation
125 Enterprise Drive
Pittsburgh, PA 15275-1214

Phone: (412) 859-6100; (866) 257-4ONS; Fax: (412) 859-6163
Email: foundation@ons.org
Web: www.ons.org/Awards/FoundationAwards/Bachelors

Summary: To provide financial assistance to nurses and other students who are interested in working on a bachelor's degree in oncology nursing.

Eligibility: Open to students who are accepted to or currently enrolled in a bachelor's degree program at an NLN- or CCNE-accredited school of nursing. Applicants must be able to demonstrate an interest in and commitment to oncology nursing. They may 1) already have a current license to practice as a registered nurse (R.N.); 2) currently have a postsecondary degree at some level but not be an R.N.; or 3) have only a high school diploma. Along with their application, they must submit 1) an essay of 250 words or less on their role or interest in caring for persons with cancer; and 2) a statement of their professional goals and the relationship of those goals to the advancement of oncology nursing. Non-R.N. applicants must be in the nursing component of the B.S.N. program. High school students and individuals in the liberal arts component of a B.S.N. program are not eligible. Financial need is not considered in the selection process.

Financial data: The stipend is $2,000.

Duration: 1 year; nonrenewable.

Number awarded: Varies each year; recently, 7 of these scholarships were awarded.

Deadline: January of each year.

2300 ROCKEFELLER STATE WILDLIFE SCHOLARSHIP

Louisiana Office of Student Financial Assistance
1885 Wooddale Boulevard
P.O. Box 91202
Baton Rouge, LA 70821-9202
Phone: (225) 922-3258; (800) 259-LOAN, ext. 1012; Fax: (225) 922-0790
Email: custserv@osfa.state.la.us
Web: www.osfa.state.la.us

Summary: To provide financial assistance to high school seniors, college undergraduates, and graduate students in Louisiana who are interested in working on a degree in forestry, wildlife, or marine science.

Eligibility: Open to U.S. citizens and eligible noncitizens who have been residents of Louisiana for at least 1 year. Applicants must be enrolled or planning to enroll full-time at a public or private university in Louisiana to work on 1) a bachelor's degree in forestry or forestry management, natural resource ecology or management, or wildlife conservation or management; 2) a master's degree in fisheries, forestry, marine and environmental science, or wildlife; or 3) a doctoral degree in forestry or wildlife and fisheries science. Students majoring in biology, biostatics, coastal science and coastal environmental science, oceanography, or urban forestry may be considered on a case by case basis. Applicants must 1) have graduated from high school with a GPA of 2.5 or higher and have an ACT score of 20 or higher; 2) have completed the 12th grade of an approved home study program and have an ACT score of 22 or higher: 3) have completed at least 24 college credit hours with a GPA of 2.5 or higher; or 4) be a graduate student with a GPA of 3.0 or higher. This is a merit-based award; financial need is not considered.

Financial data: The stipend is $1,000 per year.

Duration: Support is provided for up to 5 years of undergraduate and 2 years of graduate study, provided the recipient remains enrolled full-time with a GPA of 2.5 or higher.

Number awarded: Varies; generally, 60 students (30 new and 30 continuing) receive awards each year.

Deadline: July of each year.

2301 ROCKWELL COLLINS/HENAAC SCHOLARS PROGRAM

Great Minds in STEM
Attn: HENAAC Scholars
3900 Whiteside Street
Los Angeles, CA 90063
Phone: (323) 262-0997; Fax: (323) 262-0946
Email: kbbarrera@greatmindsinstem.org
Web: www.greatmindsinstem.org/henaac/scholars

Summary: To provide financial assistance to Hispanic undergraduate students majoring in designated fields related to engineering.

Eligibility: Open to college sophomores and juniors who are majoring in computer engineering, computer science, or electrical engineering. Applicants must be of Hispanic origin and/or must significantly participate in and promote organizations and activities in the Hispanic community. They must have a GPA of 3.0 or higher and be available to accept, if offered, a co-op or internship with Rockwell Collins. Along with their application, they must submit a 700-word essay on a topic that changes annually; recently, students were asked to write on how they see their academic major contributing to global efforts and technology and how they, in their field of study, will contribute to global progress as well as actively contribute to their local communities. Selection is based on leadership through academic achievements and campus and community activities; financial need is not considered.

Financial data: Stipends range from $500 to $5,000.

Duration: 1 year; recipients may reapply.

Number awarded: Varies each year; recently, 3 of these scholarships were awarded.

Deadline: April of each year.

2302 ROCKY MOUNTAIN COAL MINING INSTITUTE ENGINEERING SCHOLARSHIPS

Rocky Mountain Coal Mining Institute
Attn: Executive Director
8057 South Yukon Way
Littleton, CO 80128-5510
Phone: (303) 948-3300; Fax: (303) 948-1132
Email: mail@rmcmi.org
Web: www.rmcmi.org/index.cfm/ID/13/Apply-for-Scholarships

Summary: To provide financial assistance to college students from Rocky Mountain states who are preparing for a career in the mining industry.

Eligibility: Open to full-time sophomores or juniors in college who are U.S. citizens and residents of Arizona, Colorado, Montana, New Mexico, North Dakota, Texas, Utah, or Wyoming. Applicants must be working on a degree in engineering (e.g., electrical, environmental, geological, mechanical, metallurgical, mining) or in a mining-related field (e.g., geology, mineral processing, metallurgy). They may be attending school in one of those states or another school approved by the sponsor (e.g., Missouri University of Science and Technology, South Dakota School of Mines). Along with their application, they must submit a 150-word autobiography that covers any academic or athletic honors, extracurricular activities, and why they feel they deserve this scholarship. Financial need is not considered. Preference is given to students who are particularly interested in western coal as a career. Interviews are required.

Financial data: The stipend is $2,500 per year. Funds are disbursed to the recipient's institution to be used as a tuition credit.

Duration: 2 years.

Number awarded: 8 each year (1 from each of the participating states).

Deadline: January of each year.

2303 ROCKY MOUNTAIN COAL MINING INSTITUTE TECHNICAL SCHOLARSHIPS

Rocky Mountain Coal Mining Institute
Attn: Executive Director
8057 South Yukon Way
Littleton, CO 80128-5510
Phone: (303) 948-3300; Fax: (303) 948-1132
Email: mail@rmcmi.org
Web: www.rmcmi.org/index.cfm/ID/13/Apply-for-Scholarships

Summary: To provide financial assistance to technical school students from Rocky Mountain states who are preparing for a career in the mining industry.

Eligibility: Open to residents of Arizona, Colorado, Montana, New Mexico, North Dakota, Texas, Utah, or Wyoming who are completing the first year at a 2-year technical/trade school in those states. Applicants must be studying a technical field to prepare for a career in the coal industry. They must be U.S. citizens. Along with their application, they must submit 100-word statements on their choice of a job and why, their plans after graduating, why they are working on their present degree, and why they are applying for this scholarship. Financial need is not considered in the selection process. Interviews are required.

Financial data: The stipend is $1,000. Funds are disbursed to the recipient's institution to be used as a tuition credit.

Duration: 1 year; nonrenewable.

Number awarded: 8 each year (1 from each of the participating states).

Deadline: January of each year.

2304 ROSSINI FLEXOGRAPHIC SCHOLARSHIP COMPETITION

Summary: To recognize and reward, with funding for research, undergraduate students who propose an outstanding project related to flexography.

See Listing #1542.

2305 ROY ANDERSON MEMORIAL SCHOLARSHIP

Colorado Nurses Foundation
7400 East Arapahoe Road, Suite 211
Centennial, CO 80112
Phone: (303) 694-4728; Fax: (303) 694-4869
Email: mail@cnfound.org
Web: www.cnfound.org/scholarships.html

Summary: To provide financial assistance to residents of Colorado who are working on a bachelor's or higher degree in nursing at a college or university in the state.

Eligibility: Open to Colorado residents who have been accepted as a student in an approved nursing program in the state. Applicants must be working on a bachelor's or higher degree. Undergraduates must have a GPA of 3.25 or higher and graduate students must have a GPA of 3.5 or higher. Selection is based on professional philosophy and goals, dedication to the improvement of patient care in Colorado, demonstrated commitment to nursing, critical thinking skills, potential for leadership, involvement in community and professional organizations, recommendations, GPA, and financial need.

Financial data: The stipend is $5,000.

Duration: 1 year.

Number awarded: 2 each year.

Deadline: October of each year.

2306 ROYCE OSBORN MINORITY STUDENT SCHOLARSHIPS

American Society of Radiologic Technologists
Attn: ASRT Education and Research Foundation
15000 Central Avenue, S.E.
Albuquerque, NM 87123-3909
Phone: (505) 298-4500, ext. 2541; (800) 444-2778, ext. 2541; Fax: (505) 298-5063
Email: foundation@asrt.org
Web: www.asrt.org/content/asrtfoundation/scholarships/royceosborn.aspx

Summary: To provide financial assistance to minority students enrolled in entry-level radiologic sciences programs.

Eligibility: Open to African Americans, Native Americans (including American Indians, Eskimos, Hawaiians, and Samoans), Hispanic Americans, Asian Americans, and Pacific Islanders who are enrolled in an entry-level radiologic sciences program. Applicants must have a GPA in radiologic sciences core courses of 3.0 or higher and be able to demonstrate financial need. They may not have a previous degree or certificate in the radiologic sciences. Along with their application, they must submit 150-word essays on 1) their reason for entering the radiologic sciences; 2) their career goals; 3) their financial need; and 4) why they should receive this scholarship. Only U.S. citizens, nationals, and permanent residents are eligible.

Financial data: The stipend is $4,000.

Duration: 1 year; may be renewed for 1 additional year.

Number awarded: 5 each year.

Deadline: January of each year.

2307 ROYCE R. WATTS SR. SCHOLARSHIP

Watts Charity Association, Inc.
6245 Bristol Parkway, Suite 224
Culver City, CA 90230
Phone: (323) 671-0394; Fax: (323) 778-2613
Email: wattscharity@aol.com
Web: 4watts.tripod.com/id5.html

Summary: To provide financial assistance to upper-division African American college students interested in health, civil rights, or administration.

Eligibility: Open to U.S. citizens of African American descent who are enrolled full-time as a college or university junior. Applicants must have an interest in health and pre-medicine, community activities and civil rights, or administration. They must have a GPA of 3.0 or higher, be between 17 and 24 years of age, and be able to demonstrate that they intend to continue their education for at least 2 years. Along with their application, they must submit 1) a 1-paragraph statement on why they should be awarded a Watts Foundation scholarship; and 2) a 1- to 2-page essay on a specific type of cancer, based either on how it has impacted their life or on researched information.

Financial data: A stipend is awarded (amount not specified).

Duration: 1 year.

Number awarded: 1 each year.

Deadline: May of each year.

2308 RUDOLPH DILLMAN MEMORIAL SCHOLARSHIP

American Foundation for the Blind
Attn: Scholarship Committee
11 Penn Plaza, Suite 300
New York, NY 10001
Phone: (212) 502-7661; (800) AFB-LINE; Fax: (212) 502-7771; TDD: (212) 502-7662
Email: afbinfo@afb.net
Web: www.afb.org/Section.asp?Documentid=2962

Summary: To provide financial assistance to legally blind undergraduate or graduate students studying in the field of rehabilitation and/or education of visually impaired and blind persons.

Eligibility: Open to legally-blind U.S. citizens who have been accepted to an accredited undergraduate or graduate training program within the broad field of rehabilitation and/or education of blind and visually impaired persons. Along with their application, they must submit a 200-word essay that includes their past and recent achievements and accomplishments; their intended field of study and why they have chosen it; and the role their visual impairment has played in shaping their life. Financial need is considered for 1 of the scholarships.

Financial data: The stipend is $2,500 per year.

Duration: 1 academic year; previous recipients may not reapply.

Number awarded: 4 each year: 3 without consideration to financial need and 1 based on financial need.

Deadline: April of each year.

2309 RUSSELL A. COOKINGHAM SCHOLARSHIP

The Wildlife Society–New Jersey Chapter
c/o Eric Schrading, Vice-President
U.S. Fish and Wildlife Service
927 North Main Street, Building D
Pleasantville, NJ 08232
Phone: (609) 383-33938, ext. 46
Email: Eric_Schrading@fws.gov
Web: joomla.wildlife.org/NJ

Summary: To provide financial assistance to New Jersey residents enrolled in college in any state and working on a degree in wildlife and fisheries or conservation education and communications.

Eligibility: Open to residents of New Jersey currently enrolled at a college or university in any state. Applicants must have completed at least half the degree requirements for a major in wildlife and fisheries or conservation education and communications. Conservation education and communications majors must also have completed at least 15 credits in the biological sciences.

Financial data: The stipend is $1,000.

Duration: 1 year.

Number awarded: 1 each year.

Deadline: March of each year.

2310 RUSSELL W. MYERS SCHOLARSHIP

The Land Conservancy of New Jersey
Attn: Scholarship Program
19 Boonton Avenue
Boonton, NJ 07005
Phone: (973) 541-1010; Fax: (973) 541-1131
Email: info@morrislandconservancy.org
Web: www.morrislandconservancy.org/scholarship.html

Summary: To provide financial assistance to undergraduate and graduate students from New Jersey who are working on a degree in an environmental field at a school in any state.

Eligibility: Open to New Jersey residents who have completed at least 15 credits at a college or university in any state offering a degree in environmental science, natural resource management, conservation, horticulture, park administration, or a related field. Applicants must have a cumulative GPA of 3.0 or higher. They must be considering a career in New Jersey in an environmental field. Along with their application, they must submit a 500-word essay on their career goals and how those will advance the effort of land conservation. Financial need is not considered in the selection process.

Financial data: The stipend is $5,500.

Duration: 1 year.

Number awarded: 1 each year.

Deadline: March of each year.

2311 RUSTICI LIVESTOCK AND RANGELAND SCHOLARSHIP

California Farm Bureau Scholarship Foundation
Attn: Scholarship Foundation
2300 River Plaza Drive
Sacramento, CA 95833
Phone: (916) 561-5520; (800) 698-FARM (within CA); Fax: (916) 561-5699
Email: dlicciardo@cfbf.com
Web: www.cfbf.com/programs/scholar/rustici.cfm

Summary: To provide financial assistance for college to residents of California who are interested in preparing for a career in rangeland management.

Eligibility: Open to students entering or attending a California 4-year accredited college or university or a 2-year community college. Applicants must be planning to prepare for a career that benefits the beef cattle or sheep industry by studying a field with a focus on rangeland management. Preference is given to students who plan to return to the family ranch. They must have a GPA of 2.0 or higher, although grades are not a primary factor in the selection process. Along with their application, they must submit a 500-word essay on why they have chosen the field of beef cattle or sheep ranching or range management, their goals, and how their past, present, and future activities make the accomplishment of those goals possible. Financial need is not considered in the selection process.

Financial data: The stipend is $5,000 per year for students at 4-year colleges or universities or $2,500 per year for students at 2-year community colleges.

Duration: 1 year; may be renewed, provided the recipient remains enrolled full-time and maintains a GPA of 2.0 or higher.

Number awarded: 1 each year.

Deadline: February of each year.

2312 RUTH LUTES BACHMANN SCHOLARSHIP

Grand Lodge of Missouri, A.F. & A.M.
Attn: Masonic Scholarship Fund of Missouri
6033 Masonic Drive, Suite B
Columbia, MO 65202-6535
Phone: (573) 474-8561
Web: www.momason.org/programs.asp

Summary: To provide financial assistance to Missouri residents interested in attending college to prepare for a career as a teacher or a nurse.

Eligibility: Open to residents of Missouri who are graduating from or have graduated from a public high school in the state. Applicants must be attending or planning to attend an accredited college or university in the United States as a full-time student with a major in education or nursing. They must have a GPA of 3.0 or higher and be able to demonstrate financial need. Along with their application, they must submit an essay of 300 to 500 words on why they are applying for this scholarship.

Financial data: The stipend is $1,000.

Duration: 1 year; may be renewed if the recipient remains enrolled full-time with a GPA of 3.0 or higher.

Number awarded: Several each year.

Deadline: March of each year.

2313 SAN ANTONIO POST SAME SCHOLARSHIPS

Society of American Military Engineers–San Antonio Post
P.O. Box 353586
Brooks City Base, TX 78235-0386
Web: www.same-satx.org

Summary: To provide financial assistance to ROTC students majoring in designated fields at colleges and universities in Texas.

Eligibility: Open to full-time students participating in an ROTC program at a college or university in Texas. Applicants must be majoring in architecture, construction science or management, engineering, physical science, or a related program. Preference is given to students planning a career in the U.S. Army, Navy, Marine Corps, Coast Guard, or Air Force. Selection is based on academic achievement, leadership, professionalism, participation in extracurricular activities, and service to university and/or local community. Financial need is not considered, but students receiving a full scholarship from another source are not eligible.

Financial data: Stipends range from $1,000 to $5,000.

Duration: 1 year; nonrenewable.

Number awarded: 15 each year: 6 at $5,000 and 9 ranging from $1,000 to $3,000.

Deadline: October of each year.

2314 SANDRA R. SPAULDING MEMORIAL SCHOLARSHIPS

California Nurses Association
Attn: Scholarship Fund
2000 Franklin Street, Suite 300
Oakland, CA 94612
Phone: (510) 273-2200, ext. 344; Fax: (510) 663-1625
Email: membershipbenefits@calnurses.org
Web: www.calnurses.org/membership

Summary: To provide financial assistance to students from diverse ethnic backgrounds who are enrolled in an associate degree in nursing (A.D.N.) program in California.

Eligibility: Open to students who have been admitted to a second-year accredited A.D.N. program in California and plan to complete the degree within 2 years. Along with their application, they must submit a 1-page essay describing their personal and professional goals. Selection is based on that essay, commitment and active participation in nursing and health-related organizations, professional vision and direction, and financial need. A goal of this scholarship program is to encourage ethnic and socioeconomic diversity in nursing.

Financial data: A stipend is awarded (amount not specified).

Duration: 1 year; nonrenewable.

Number awarded: 1 or more each year.

Deadline: June of each year.

2315 SAUL T. WILSON, JR. SCHOLARSHIP

Department of Agriculture
Animal and Plant Health Inspection Service
Attn: Human Resources/Recruitment
1400 Independence Avenue, S.W., Room 1710
Washington, DC 20250
Phone: (202) 690-4759
Web: www.aphis.usda.gov

Summary: To provide financial assistance and work experience to undergraduate and graduate students interested in preparing for a career in veterinary medicine and biomedical sciences.

Eligibility: Open to U.S. citizens enrolled in an accredited college or university in the United States as a full-time student. Undergraduates must have completed at least 2 years of a 4-year preveterinary medicine or other biomedical science program. Graduate students must have completed not more than 1 year of study in veterinary medicine. All applicants must submit a 500-word essay on why they should receive this scholarship and what contributions they would make to veterinary services of the Animal and Plant Health Inspection Service (APHIS). Preference is given to veterans of the U.S. armed forces. Financial need is not considered in the selection process.

Financial data: The maximum stipend is $5,000 per year for undergraduates or $10,000 per year for graduate students. Funds must be used for tuition, books, tutors, and laboratory fees. During summers and school breaks, scholars receive paid employment as a veterinary student trainee with APHIS at a salary that ranges from $9 to $13 per hour, depending on the student's qualifications. After 640 hours of study-related work with APHIS in the career experience program and graduation with a D.V.M. degree, and at the option of APHIS, the student must become a full-time employee for at least 1 calendar year for each school year of support from this scholarship. If scholarship recipients refuse to accept an APHIS offer of employment, they must reimburse the agency for all financial assistance received. If recipients fail to serve the entire length of the mandatory APHIS employment period, they must reimburse APHIS a prorated share of scholarship funds used.

Duration: 1 year; may be renewed.

Number awarded: 1 or more each year.

Deadline: February of each year.

2316 S.C. INTERNATIONAL ACTUARIAL SCIENCE SCHOLARSHIPS

S.C. International, Ltd.
1315 Butterfield Road, Suite 224
Downers Grove, IL 60515
Phone: (630) 963-3033; (800) 543-2553; Fax: (630) 963-3170
Email: search@scinternational.com
Web: www.scinternational.com/scholarship_application.asp

Summary: To provide financial assistance to college seniors majoring in actuarial science or mathematics.

Eligibility: Open to students who are entering their senior year of undergraduate study in actuarial science or mathematics. Applicants must have a GPA of 3.0 or higher both overall and in their major, have passed at least 1 actuarial examination, and be eligible to work in the United States. Along with their application, they must submit 1) a list of activities and honors; and 2) an essay on why they want to be an actuary and their short- and long-term career goals. Financial need is not considered in the selection process.

Financial data: The stipend is either $1,000 or $500 per semester.

Duration: 1 semester; nonrenewable.

Number awarded: 4 each year (2 per semester: 1 at $1,000 and 1 at $500).

Deadline: May of each year for the fall scholarship; December of each year for the spring scholarship.

2317 SCHERING-PLOUGH "WILL TO WIN" SCHOLARSHIPS

Summary: To provide financial assistance for college to high school seniors with outstanding abilities in community service, athletics, art, or science who have asthma.

See Listing #887.

2318 SCHOLARSHIP AWARD IN VISION AND MEDICINE

University of Missouri at Columbia
Mason Eye Institute
Attn: Ophthalmology Residency Program Director
1 Hospital Drive
Columbia, MO 65212
Phone: (573) 449-5656
Email: SAVM@health.missouri.edu
Web: som.missouri.edu/Ophthalmology/SAVM

Summary: To provide financial assistance to high school seniors who are members of underrepresented minority groups and planning to attend college to prepare for a career in visual sciences and medicine.

Eligibility: Open to graduating high school seniors who are members of underrepresented minority groups (American Indian, African American, Mexican American, or mainland Puerto Rican). Applicants must be planning to attend an accredited 4-year college or university in the United States to study a field that will prepare them for a career in visual sciences and medicine. They must have a GPA of 3.0 or higher and a score of 1500 or higher on the SAT or 21 or higher on the ACT. Along with their application, they must submit an essay on "The Influence of the History of African Americans in Ophthalmology on My Role in Improving Healthcare for African Americans and Others." Selection is based on that essay (300 points), academic achievement (200 points), leadership (200 points), letters of recommendation (200 points), and financial need (100 points). U.S. citizenship or permanent resident status is required.

Financial data: Stipends range from $2,500 to $5,000. Funds are disbursed to the recipients' institutions to supplement any other benefits that the students receive for tuition, fees, books, room and board, computers, health insurance, general living expenses, and other college-related expenses. The high schools that nominate the winning students receive $500 for use in their science departments.

Duration: 1 year.

Number awarded: 7 each year.

Deadline: March of each year.

2319 SCHOLARSHIP FOR RNS MAJORING IN NURSING

Ohio Nurses Association
Attn: Ohio Nurses Foundation
4000 East Main Street
Columbus, OH 43213-2983
Phone: (614) 237-5414; Fax: (614) 237-6074
Email: gharsheymeade@ohnurses.org
Web: www.ohnurses.org/AM/Template.cfm?Section=Foundation

Summary: To provide financial assistance to registered nurses in Ohio who are working on a nursing degree at a school in any state.

Eligibility: Open to Ohio residents who have a valid Ohio nursing license. Applicants must have a GPA of 2.5 or higher as an undergraduate or 3.5 or higher if working on a graduate degree. They must be planning to enroll full-time in a nursing degree program at a school in any state. Along with their application, they must submit a 100-word personal statement on how they will advance the profession of nursing in Ohio. Selection is based on that statement, college academic records, school activities, and community services.

Financial data: The stipend is $1,000 per year.

Duration: 1 year; recipients may reapply for 1 additional year if they maintain a cumulative GPA of 2.5 or higher.

Number awarded: 1 or more each year.

Deadline: January of each year.

2320 SCHOLARSHIP FOR STUDENTS RETURNING TO SCHOOL TO MAJOR IN NURSING

Ohio Nurses Association
Attn: Ohio Nurses Foundation
4000 East Main Street
Columbus, OH 43213-2983
Phone: (614) 237-5414; Fax: (614) 237-6074
Email: gharsheymeade@ohnurses.org
Web: www.ohnurses.org/AM/Template.cfm?Section=Foundation

Summary: To provide financial assistance to residents of Ohio who are interested in returning to school in any state to work on a degree in nursing.

Eligibility: Open to Ohio residents who are not R.N.s and have been out of school for 2 or more years. Applicants must be interested in returning to school in any state to enroll full-time in a nursing degree program. Along with their application, they must submit a 100-word personal statement on how they will advance the profession of nursing in Ohio. Selection is based on that statement, college academic records, school activities, and community services.

Financial data: The stipend is $1,000 per year.

Duration: 1 year; recipients may reapply for 1 additional year if they maintain a cumulative GPA of 2.5 or higher.

Number awarded: 1 or more each year.

Deadline: January of each year.

2321 SCHOLARSHIPS FOR ELCA SERVICE ABROAD

Summary: To provide financial assistance to lay women who are affiliated with the Evangelical Lutheran Church of America (ELCA) congregations and who wish to pursue postsecondary education to prepare for service abroad, either in general or in health fields.

See Listing #889.

2322 SCHOLARSHIPS IN MATHEMATICS EDUCATION

Illinois Council of Teachers of Mathematics
c/o Sue and Randy Pippen, ICTM Scholarship
24807 Winterberry Lane
Plainfield, IL 60585
Web: www.ictm.org/scholarship.html

Summary: To provide financial assistance to undergraduate students in Illinois who are interested in preparing for a career as a mathematics teacher.

Eligibility: Open to juniors and seniors at accredited colleges and universities in Illinois. Applicants must have a GPA of 3.0 or higher and a mathematics education major, a mathematics major with an education minor, or an education major with an official mathematics concentration. Along with their application, they must submit an essay of 200 to 300 words on why they wish to teach mathematics and what they see as their contribution to the profession. Selection is based on the essay, a lesson plan, transcripts from all colleges attended, and letters of recommendation from 2 mathematics teachers (high school or college).

Financial data: The stipend is $1,500.

Duration: 1 year.

Number awarded: 2 to 5 each year.

Deadline: March of each year.

2323 SCHUBMEHL-PREIN PRIZE

University of Notre Dame
Attn: Department of Computer Science and Engineering
384 Fitzpatrick Hall
Notre Dame, IN 46556
Phone: (574) 631-8320; Fax: (574) 631-9260
Email: essay@cse.nd.edu
Web: www.cse.nd.edu/EssayContest

Summary: To recognize and reward high school juniors who submit outstanding essays on the social impact of computing technology.

Eligibility: Open to students currently enrolled as juniors in high school and in the top fifth of their class. Applicants must submit an essay, approximately 2,500 words in length, on a topic that changes annually but relates to the social impact of computing technology; recently, students were invited to present their ideas on individual privacy rights with respect to such services as "Street View." Selection is based on accuracy of technical concepts, quality and clarity of expression, logic of argument, originality of ideas, and conformance to the entry guidelines.

Financial data: Prizes are $1,000 for first, $500 for second, and $250 for third.

Duration: The competition is held annually.

Number awarded: 3 each year.

Deadline: May of each year.

2324 SCHWEIGER MEMORIAL SCHOLARSHIP FUND

Advanced American Construction, Inc.
Attn: Schweiger Memorial Scholarship Fund
8444 N.W. St. Helens Road
P.O. Box 83599
Portland, OR 97283
Phone: (503) 445-9000; Fax: (503) 546-3031
Web: www.callaac.com/Scholarships/Scholarships.html

Summary: To provide financial assistance to high school seniors and current college students interested in preparing for a career in construction or construction management.

Eligibility: Open to high school seniors and college undergraduates working on or planning to work on a degree in a field related to construction. Applicants must have a GPA of 2.5 or higher. Along with their application, they must submit brief statements on their awards and/or significant academic achievements, extracurricular activities, anticipated degree or certification, career goals and their relationship to construction, and how receipt of this scholarship will benefit their education and a career in construction. Financial need is not considered in the selection process.

Financial data: Stipends range from $1,000 to $5,000.

Duration: 1 year; may be renewed.

Number awarded: Approximately 10 each year; since the program was established, it has awarded 131 scholarships worth $310,000.

Deadline: February of each year.

2325 SCIENCE APPLICATIONS INTERNATIONAL CORPORATION ENGINEERING SCHOLARSHIP

National Naval Officers Association-Washington, D.C. Chapter
Attn: Scholarship Program
2701 Park Center Drive, A1108
Alexandria, VA 22302
Phone: (703) 566-3840; Fax: (703) 566-3813
Email: Stephen.Williams@Navy.mil
Web: dcnnoa.memberlodge.com/Default.aspx?pageId=309002

Summary: To provide financial assistance to minority high school seniors from the Washington, D.C. area who are interested in majoring in engineering at a college in any state.

Eligibility: Open to minority seniors graduating from high schools in the Washington, D.C. metropolitan area who plan to enroll full-time in an engineering program at an accredited 2- or 4-year college or university in any state. Applicants must have a GPA of 2.5 or higher and be U.S. citizens or permanent residents. Selection is based on academic achievement, community involvement, and financial need.

Financial data: The stipend is $4,500.

Duration: 1 year; nonrenewable.

Number awarded: 1 each year.

Deadline: March of each year.

2326 SCIENCE APPLICATIONS INTERNATIONAL CORPORATION SCIENCE AND MATHEMATICS SCHOLARSHIP

National Naval Officers Association-Washington, D.C. Chapter
Attn: Scholarship Program
2701 Park Center Drive, A1108
Alexandria, VA 22302
Phone: (703) 566-3840; Fax: (703) 566-3813
Email: Stephen.Williams@Navy.mil
Web: dcnnoa.memberlodge.com/Default.aspx?pageId=309002

Summary: To provide financial assistance to minority high school seniors from the Washington, D.C. area who are interested in majoring in science or mathematics at a college in any state.

Eligibility: Open to minority seniors graduating from high schools in the Washington, D.C. metropolitan area who plan to enroll full-time at an accredited 2- or 4-year college or university in any state and major in science or mathematics. Applicants must have a GPA of 2.5 or higher and be U.S. citizens or permanent residents. Selection is based on academic achievement, community involvement, and financial need.

Financial data: The stipend is $4,500.

Duration: 1 year; nonrenewable.

Number awarded: 1 each year.

Deadline: March of each year.

2327 SCIENCE, MATHEMATICS, AND RESEARCH FOR TRANSFORMATION (SMART) DEFENSE SCHOLARSHIP FOR SERVICE PROGRAM

American Society for Engineering Education
Attn: SMART Defense Scholarship Program
1818 N Street, N.W., Suite 600
Washington, DC 20036-2479
Phone: (202) 331-3544; Fax: (202) 265-8504
Email: smart@asee.org
Web: www.asee.org/fellowships/smart

Summary: To provide financial assistance and work experience to undergraduate and graduate students in designated science, technology, engineering, or mathematics (STEM) disciplines that are of interest to the U.S. Department of Defense (DoD).

Eligibility: Open to full-time undergraduate and graduate students working on a degree in any of the following fields: aeronautical and astronautical engineering; biosciences; chemical engineering; chemistry; civil engineering; cognitive, neural, and behavioral sciences; computer and computational sciences; electrical engineering; geosciences, including terrain, water, and air; industrial and systems engineering (technical tracks only); information sciences; materials science and engineering; mathematics; mechanical engineering; naval architecture and ocean engineering; nuclear engineering, oceanography; operations research (technical tracks only); or physics. Applicants must be U.S. citizens or nationals who have a GPA of 3.0 or higher. They must be available to work as interns at DoD laboratories during the summer months. Selection is based on academic records, personal statements, letters of recommendation, and ACT/SAT or GRE scores.

Financial data: The program provides 1) full payment of tuition and related educational fees at the recipient's institution; 2) a stipend ranging from $25,000 to $41,000 per year, depending on prior educational experience, for the academic year and summer internship; 3) a book allowance of $1,000 per year; and 4) health insurance reimbursement up to $1,200 per calendar year. This is a scholarship/loan program; recipients must agree to serve for 1 year per year of support received as a civilian employee of the DoD in a science and engineering position. If they fail to fulfill that service obligation, they must reimburse the federal government for all funds they received.

Duration: Until completion of a degree (to a maximum of 4 years for a bachelor's, 2 years for a master's, or 5 years for a Ph.D.).

Number awarded: Varies each year; recently, 30 of these scholarships were awarded.

Deadline: December of each year.

2328 SCOTT TARBELL SCHOLARSHIP

Accredo's Hemophilia Health Services
Attn: Scholarship Committee
201 Great Circle Road
Nashville, TN 37228
Phone: (615) 850-5212; (800) 800-6606; Fax: (615) 261-6730
Email: Shayne.harris@accredo.com
Web: www.hemophiliahealth.com/Scholarships.html

Summary: To provide financial assistance to high school seniors and current college students who have hemophilia and are interested in working on a degree or certification in computer science and/or mathematics.

Eligibility: Open to high school seniors and college freshmen, sophomores, and juniors who have hemophilia A or B severe. Applicants must be enrolled or planning to enroll full-time at an accredited nonprofit college, university, or vocational/technical school in the United States or Puerto Rico. They must be interested in working on a degree or certification in computer science and/or mathematics. Along with their application, they must submit an essay, up to 250 words, on the following topic: "Upon receiving your education in math and/or computer science, how will you use the new technologies (e.g., computer, internet) to better mankind, and what ethical issues will you need to address?" U.S. citizenship is required. Selection is based on the essay, academic achievements and records, community involvement, and financial need.

Financial data: The stipend is at least $1,500. Funds are issued payable to the recipient's school.

Duration: 1 year; recipients may reapply.

Number awarded: 1 or more each year, depending on the availability of funds.

Deadline: April of each year.

2329 SCOTTS COMPANY SCHOLARS PROGRAM

Golf Course Superintendents Association of America
Attn: Environmental Institute for Golf

1421 Research Park Drive
Lawrence, KS 66049-3859
Phone: (785) 832-4445; (800) 472-7878, ext. 4445; Fax: (785) 832-4448
Email: mwright@gcsaa.org
Web: www.gcsaa.org/students/Scholarships.aspx

Summary: To provide financial assistance and summer work experience to high school seniors and college students, particularly those from diverse backgrounds, who are preparing for a career in golf management.

Eligibility: Open to high school seniors and college students (freshmen, sophomores, and juniors) who are interested in preparing for a career in golf management (the "green industry"). Applicants should come from diverse ethnic, cultural, and socioeconomic backgrounds, defined to include women, minorities, and people with disabilities. Selection is based on cultural diversity, academic achievement, extracurricular activities, leadership, employment potential, essay responses, and letters of recommendation. Financial need is not considered. Finalists are selected for summer internships and then compete for scholarships.

Financial data: The finalists receive a $500 award to supplement their summer internship income. Scholarship stipends are $2,500.

Duration: 1 year.

Number awarded: 5 finalists, of whom 2 receive scholarships, are selected each year.

Deadline: February of each year.

2330 SCUDDER ASSOCIATION EDUCATIONAL GRANTS

Summary: To assist undergraduate and graduate students preparing for selected "careers as servants of God in various forms of ministry to men and women around the world."

See Listing #1555.

2331 SDMS PRESIDENTIAL SCHOLARSHIP

Society of Diagnostic Medical Sonography
Attn: SDMS Educational Foundation
2745 North Dallas Parkway, Suite 350
Plano, TX 75093-8730
Phone: (214) 473-8057; (800) 229-9506; Fax: (214) 473-8563
Email: foundation@sdms.org
Web: www.sdms.org/foundation/presidential.asp

Summary: To provide financial assistance to students enrolled in a diagnostic medical sonography (ultrasound) program.

Eligibility: Open to students enrolled in diagnostic medical sonography programs accredited by the Commission on Accreditation of Allied Health Education Programs (CAAHEP) or the Canadian Medical Association (CMA). Applicants who graduated from high school within the past 2 years must have an ACT score of at least 22 or an SAT critical reading and mathematics score of at least 950. Applicants who graduated from high school more than 2 years ago must submit transcripts of all postsecondary education. All applicants must submit 100-word essays on why they chose sonography as a career, the contribution they would make to the ultrasound profession, and why they should receive this scholarship. Financial need is also considered in the selection process.

Financial data: The stipend is $1,500.

Duration: 1 year.

Number awarded: 1 each year.

Deadline: July of each year.

2332 SEASPACE SCHOLARSHIP PROGRAM

Seaspace, Inc.
Attn: Scholarship Committee
c/o Houston Underwater Club, Inc.
P.O. Box 3753
Houston, TX 77253-3753
Phone: (713) 467-6675
Email: j.cancelmo@sbcglobal.net
Web: www.seaspace.org/schship.htm

Summary: To provide financial assistance to upper-division and graduate students interested in preparing for a marine-related career.

Eligibility: Open to full-time juniors, seniors, and graduate students who are interested in preparing for a marine-related career. They should be majoring in marine science, marine biology, wildlife and fisheries, environmental toxicology, biological oceanography, genetics, ocean engineering, aquaculture, or zoology with marine mammal applications. Preference is given to graduate students. Selection is based on academic excellence (minimum GPA of 3.3), demonstrated course direction, and financial need.

Financial data: The amount awarded varies each year; recently, awards averaged approximately $1,666.

Duration: 1 year.

Number awarded: Varies each year; recently, 11 students received scholarships, including 4 undergraduates and 7 graduate students. To date, financial assistance has been provided to more than 324 students.

Deadline: January of each year.

2333 SEMA MEMORIAL SCHOLARSHIP FUND AWARDS

Specialty Equipment Market Association
Attn: Education Director
1575 South Valley Vista Drive
Diamond Bar, CA 91765-3914
Phone: (909) 396-0289, ext. 125; Fax: (909) 860-0184
Email: member@sema.org
Web: www.sema.org/scholarships

Summary: To provide financial assistance for college to students interested in preparing for a career in the automotive aftermarket.

Eligibility: Open to students who are currently enrolled full-time in 1) a graduate program at an accredited college or university; 2) a 4-year degree program at an accredited college or university, have completed at least 50 hours of credit, and are classified as a junior or senior; or 3) a 2-year community college or proprietary vocational/technical program, have completed at least 25 hours of credit, and are classified as a sophomore. The school must be located in the continental United States or Canada. Applicants must be working on a degree or certificate that will lead to a career in the automotive aftermarket or related field. They must have a GPA of 2.5 or higher and be able to demonstrate financial need.

Financial data: The stipend for 4-year and graduate students is $4,000 for the top-ranked applicant in each category or $2,000 for all other recipients. The stipend for community college and vocational/technical students is $1,000.

Duration: 1 year.

Number awarded: Varies each year; recently, 72 of these scholarships were awarded. Up to 20% of all scholarships are awarded to dependents and/or employees of member companies of the Specialty Equipment Market Association (SEMA).

Deadline: April of each year.

2334 SHAW INDUSTRIES/HENAAC SCHOLARS PROGRAM

Great Minds in STEM
Attn: HENAAC Scholars
3900 Whiteside Street
Los Angeles, CA 90063
Phone: (323) 262-0997; Fax: (323) 262-0946
Email: kbbarrera@greatmindsinstem.org
Web: www.greatmindsinstem.org/henaac/scholars

Summary: To provide financial assistance to Hispanic undergraduate students majoring in designated fields of engineering.

Eligibility: Open to college sophomores and juniors who are majoring in engineering (chemical, electrical, industrial, mechanical, or textile). Applicants must be of Hispanic origin and/or must significantly participate in and promote organizations and activities in the Hispanic community. They must have a GPA of 3.0 or higher. Along with their application, they must submit a 700-word essay on a topic that changes annually; recently, students were asked to write on how they see their academic major contributing to global efforts and technology and how they, in their field of study, will contribute to global progress as well as actively contribute to their local communities. Selection is based on leadership through academic achievements and campus and community activities; financial need is not considered. U.S. citizenship or permanent resident status is required.

Financial data: Stipends range from $500 to $5,000.

Duration: 1 year; recipients may reapply.

Number awarded: Varies each year; recently, 4 of these scholarships were awarded.

Deadline: April of each year.

2335 SHAW-WORTH MEMORIAL SCHOLARSHIP

Humane Society of the United States
Attn: Humane Society Youth
67 Norwich Essex Turnpike

East Haddam, CT 06423-1726
Phone: (860) 434-8666
Email: teens@humanesociety.org
Web: www.humanesociety.org

Summary: To provide financial assistance to New England high school seniors who have contributed to animal protection and plan to attend college in any state.

Eligibility: Open to seniors graduating from public, parochial, and independent high schools in New England and planning to attend a college or university in any state. Applicants must have made a meaningful contribution to animal protection over a significant period of time. The contribution may have taken the form of long-term direct work on behalf of animals; inspiring leadership in animal protection organizations; papers, speeches, or presentations on humane topics; or heroic rescues of animals in danger. A humane attitude, understanding of humane ethics, and past academic performance on behalf of animals are essential. A passive liking for animals or a desire to enter an animal care field is not adequate justification for the award. High scholastic standing is not required and financial need is not considered.

Financial data: The stipend is $2,500. Funds are paid directly to the college of the recipient's choice.

Duration: 1 year.

Number awarded: 1 each year.

Deadline: March of each year.

2336 SHELL OIL COMPANY PROCESS TECHNOLOGY SCHOLARSHIP

Center for the Advancement of Process Technology
Attn: CAPT Scholarships
1200 Amburn Road
Texas City, TX 77591
Phone: (409) 938-1211, ext. 163; Fax: (409) 938-1285
Email: info@captech.org
Web: www.captech.org/careers/scholarships.php

Summary: To provide financial assistance to students interested in a college degree in process technology.

Eligibility: Open to students currently enrolled or planning to enroll in a 2-year degree program in process/production technology, petroleum technology, compressor/compression technology, electrical/electronics technology, industrial maintenance technology, instrumentation/analyzer technology, or machinist/mechanical technology. Applicants must have a GPA of 2.5 or higher. Along with their application, they must submit a 1-page essay on why they should be considered for this scholarship and selected over other qualified, worthy applicants. Selection is based on scholastic performance; financial need is not considered.

Financial data: Stipends are $750 per semester for full-time students or $500 per semester for part-time students. Eligible expenses are limited to tuition, books, fees, and educational supplies.

Duration: Recipients have up to 3 years to complete the 2-year process technology degree program. The maximum amount of support they may receive is $2,200.

Number awarded: 1 or more each year.

Deadline: May of each year.

2337 SHELL OIL COMPANY TECHNICAL SCHOLARSHIP PROGRAM FOR COLLEGE STUDENTS

Shell Oil Company
Attn: Scholarship Administrator
910 Louisiana, Suite 4476C
Houston, TX 77002
Phone: (713) 241-0514
Web: www.shell.com.sg/home/content/usa/aboutshell/careers

Summary: To provide financial assistance to undergraduate students majoring in specified engineering and geosciences fields at designated universities.

Eligibility: Open to students enrolled full-time as sophomores, juniors, or seniors at 21 participating universities. Applicants must have a GPA of 3.2 or higher with a major in engineering (chemical, civil, electrical, geological, geophysical, mechanical, or petroleum) or geosciences (geology, geophysics, or physics). They must be U.S. citizens or authorized to work in the United States. Along with their application, they must submit a 100-word essay on the kind of work they plan to be doing in 10 years, both in their career and in their community. Financial need is not considered in the selection process.

Financial data: The stipend is $5,000 per year.

Duration: 1 year; may be renewed up to 3 additional years, provided the recipient remains qualified and accepts a Shell Oil Company internship (if offered).

Number awarded: Approximately 20 each year.

Deadline: February of each year.

2338 SHELL OIL COMPANY TECHNICAL SCHOLARSHIP PROGRAM FOR HIGH SCHOOL SENIORS

Shell Oil Company
Attn: Scholarship Administrator
910 Louisiana, Suite 4476C
Houston, TX 77002
Phone: (713) 241-0514
Web: www.shell.com.sg/home/content/usa/aboutshell/careers

Summary: To provide financial assistance to high school seniors planning to major in specified engineering and geosciences fields at designated universities.

Eligibility: Open to graduating high school seniors planning to enroll full-time at 22 participating universities. Applicants must be planning to major in engineering (chemical, civil, electrical, geological, geophysical, mechanical, or petroleum) or geosciences (geology, geophysics, or physics). They must be U.S. citizens or authorized to work in the United States. Along with their application, they must submit a 100-word essay on the kind of work they plan to be doing in 10 years, both in their career and in their community; they should comment specifically on how they could potentially contribute to the petrochemical industry. Financial need is not considered in the selection process.

Financial data: The stipend is $2,500.

Duration: 1 year; nonrenewable, although recipients may apply to the Shell Oil Company Technical Scholarship Program for College Students to cover the remaining years of their undergraduate program.

Number awarded: Approximately 20 each year.

Deadline: February of each year.

2339 SHERYL KRATZ MEMORIAL SCHOLARSHIP

California Groundwater Association
P.O. Box 14369
Santa Rosa, CA 95402
Phone: (707) 578-4408; Fax: (707) 546-4906
Email: wellguy@groundh2o.org
Web: www.groundh2o.org/programs/scholarship.html

Summary: To provide financial assistance to women in California who are interested in attending college in the state and either have a relationship to the California Groundwater Association (CGA) or plan to major in a field related to ground water.

Eligibility: Open to female residents of California currently enrolled or accepted at a college or university in the state. Applicants must either 1) have a family affiliation with a CGA member (including employees of business members) and be interested in working on a degree in any field; or 2) be interested in working on a degree in a field of study related to ground water. Along with their application, they must submit a 500-word essay demonstrating their interest in either their chosen field of interest or in ground water technology. Financial need is not considered in the selection process.

Financial data: The stipend is $1,000.

Duration: 1 year.

Number awarded: 1 each year.

Deadline: March of each year.

2340 SIEMENS AWARDS FOR ADVANCED PLACEMENT

Siemens Foundation
170 Wood Avenue South
Iselin, NJ 08830
Phone: (877) 822-5233; Fax: (732) 603-5890
Email: foundation.us@siemens.com
Web: www.siemens-foundation.org/en/advanced_placement.htm

Summary: To recognize and reward high school students with exceptional scores on the Advanced Placement (AP) examinations in mathematics and the sciences.

Eligibility: Open to all high school students in the United States (including home-schooled students and those in U.S. territories). Each fall, the College Board identifies the male and female seniors in each state who have earned the highest number of scores of 5 on 8 AP exams: biology, calculus BC, chemistry, computer science A, environmental science, physics C mechanics, physics C electricity and magnetism, and statistics. Males and females are considered separately. Students with the highest scores nationally receive separate awards. The program also provides awards to teachers who demonstrate excellence in teaching AP mathematics and science.

Financial data: State scholarships are $2,000; in addition, national winners receive $5,000 scholarships. State awards for high schools teachers are $1,000; the National AP Teacher of the Year receives $5,000.
Duration: The awards are presented annually.
Number awarded: 100 state scholarships (1 female and 1 male from each state) and 2 national scholarships (1 female and 1 male) are awarded each year. In addition, 50 teachers (1 from each state) receive awards and 1 of those is designated the National AP Teacher of the Year.
Deadline: There is no application or nomination process for these awards. The College Board identifies the students and teachers for the Siemens Foundation.

2341 SIEMENS COMPETITION IN MATH, SCIENCE AND TECHNOLOGY AWARDS

Siemens Foundation
170 Wood Avenue South
Iselin, NJ 08830
Phone: (877) 822-5233; Fax: (732) 603-5890
Email: foundation.us@siemens.com
Web: www.siemens-foundation.org/en/competition.htm

Summary: To recognize and reward outstanding high school seniors who have undertaken individual or team research projects in science, mathematics, and technology (or in combinations of those disciplines).
Eligibility: Open to high school seniors who are legal or permanent U.S. residents. They must be enrolled in a high school in the United States, Puerto Rico, Guam, Virgin Islands, American Samoa, Wake and Midway Islands, or the Marianas. U.S. high school students enrolled in a Department of Defense dependents school, an accredited overseas American or international school, a foreign school as an exchange student, or a foreign school because their parent(s) live and work abroad are also eligible. Students being home-schooled qualify if they obtain the endorsement of the school district official responsible for such programs. Research projects may be submitted in mathematics, engineering, or the biological or physical sciences, or involve combinations of disciplines, such as astrophysics, biochemistry, bioengineering, biology, biophysics, botany, chemical engineering, chemistry, computer science, civil engineering, earth and atmospheric science, electrical engineering, environmental science and engineering, genetics, geology, materials science, mathematics, mechanical engineering, microbiology, nutritional science, physics, or toxicology. Both individual and team projects (2 or 3 members) may be entered. All team members must meet the eligibility requirements. Team projects may include seniors, but that is not a requirement. Competition entrants must submit a detailed report on their research project, including a description of the purpose of the research, rationale for the research, pertinent scientific literature, methodology, results, discussion, and conclusion. All projects must be endorsed by a sponsoring high school (except home-schooled students, who obtain their endorsement from the district or state home school official). Each project must have a project adviser or mentor who is a member of the instructional staff or a person approved by the endorsing high school. There are 3 judging phases to the competition. An initial review panel selects outstanding research projects from 6 different regions of the country. The students submitting these projects are identified as regional semifinalists. Out of those, the highest-rated projects from each region are selected and the students who submitted them are recognized as regional finalists. For the next phase, the regional finalists are offered all-expense-paid trips to the regional competition on the campus of a regional university partner, where their projects are reviewed by a panel of judges appointed by the host institution. Regional finalists are required to prepare a poster display of their research project, make an oral presentation about the research and research findings, and respond to questions from the judges. The top-rated individual and the top-rated team project in each region are selected as regional winners to represent the region in the national competition as national finalists. At that competition, the national finalists again display their projects, make oral presentations, and respond to judges' questions. At each phase, selection is based on clarity of expression, comprehensiveness, creativity, field knowledge, future work, interpretation, literature review, presentation, scientific importance, and validity.
Financial data: At the regional level, finalists receive $1,000 scholarships, both as individuals and members of teams. Individual regional winners receive $3,000 scholarships. Winning regional teams receive $6,000 scholarships to be divided among the team members. Those regional winners then receive additional scholarships as national finalists. In the national competition, first-place winners receive an additional $100,000 scholarship, second $50,000, third $40,000, fourth $30,000, fifth $20,000, and sixth $10,000. Those national awards are provided both to individuals and to teams to be divided equally among team members. Scholarship money is sent directly to the recipient's college or university to cover undergraduate and/or graduate educational expenses.
Duration: The competition is held annually.
Number awarded: In the initial round of judging, up to 300 regional semifinalists (up to 50 in each region) are selected. Of those, 60 are chosen as regional finalists (5 individuals and 5 teams in each of the 6 regions). Then 12 regional winners (1 individual and 1 team) are selected in each regional competition, and they become the national finalists.
Deadline: September of each year.

2342 SIEMENS HEALTHCARE DIAGNOSTICS MEDICAL TECHNICIAN SCHOLARSHIPS

American Society for Clinical Laboratory Science
Attn: Coordinating Council on the Clinical Laboratory Workforce
6701 Democracy Boulevard, Suite 300
Bethesda, MD 20817
Phone: (301) 657-2768; Fax: (301) 657-2909
Email: ascls@ascls.org
Web: www.ascls.org/ssclp/index.asp

Summary: To provide financial assistance to students enrolled in an associate degree program in clinical laboratory technology.
Eligibility: Open to students entering the second year of an NAACLS-accredited associate degree program in clinical laboratory technology or medical laboratory technology. Applicants must have a GPA of 2.5 or higher. Along with their application, they must submit a transcript of grades, 2 letters of recommendation, a statement explaining why they chose this field, and documentation of financial need.
Financial data: The stipend is $1,000.
Duration: 1 year.
Number awarded: 50 each year.
Deadline: October of each year.

2343 SIEMENS HEALTHCARE DIAGNOSTICS SCHOLARSHIPS

American Society for Clinical Pathology
Attn: Membership Services
33 West Monroe Street, Suite 1600
Chicago, IL 60603
Phone: (312) 541-4999; (800) 267-2727; Fax: (312) 541-4998
Email: info@ascp.org
Web: www.ascp.org/scholarships

Summary: To provide funding to students enrolled in a medical technologist program.
Eligibility: Open to students enrolled in the fourth or final year of an NAACLS-accredited medical technologist/clinical laboratory scientist program. Applicants must be U.S. citizens or permanent residents and have a GPA of 2.8 or higher. Along with their application, they must submit a 500-word essay on their professional goals and what makes them among the best students in the nation. Selection is based on academic achievement, professional goals, leadership abilities, and community activities.
Financial data: The stipend is $2,500.
Duration: 1 year.
Number awarded: 34 each year.
Deadline: October of each year.

2344 SIEMENS HEALTHCARE DIAGNOSTICS-LEGACY SCHOLARSHIPS

American Society for Clinical Pathology
Attn: Membership Services
33 West Monroe Street, Suite 1600
Chicago, IL 60603
Phone: (312) 541-4999; (800) 267-2727; Fax: (312) 541-4998
Email: info@ascp.org
Web: www.ascp.org/scholarships

Summary: To provide funding to students enrolled in a medical technologist program who are relatives of clinical laboratory professionals.
Eligibility: Open to students who are the children, grandchildren, or siblings of clinical laboratory professionals. Applicants must be enrolled at an NAACLS-accredited institution in the final year of a medical laboratory technician/clinical laboratory technician program or the fourth or final year of a medical technologist/clinical laboratory scientist program. They must be U.S. citizens or permanent residents and have a GPA of 2.8 or higher. Along with their application, they must submit a 500-word essay on the role their family played in their laboratory career choice and why they chose their profession. Selection is based on academic achievement, professional goals, leadership abilities, and community activities.

Financial data: The stipend is $5,000.
Duration: 1 year.
Number awarded: 5 each year.
Deadline: October of each year.

2345 SIOUX FALLS CONTRACTORS ASSOCIATION SCHOLARSHIP

Associated General Contractors of South Dakota
Attn: Highway-Heavy–Utilities Chapter
300 East Capitol Avenue, Suite 1
Pierre, SD 57501
Phone: (605) 224-8689; (800) 242-6373; Fax: (605) 224-9915
Web: www.sdagc.org

Summary: To provide financial assistance to residents of South Dakota who are interested in attending a college, university, or technical institute in any state to prepare for a career in a construction-related field.
Eligibility: Open to residents of South Dakota who are graduating high school seniors or students already enrolled at a college, university, or technical institute in any state. Applicants must be preparing for a career in a construction-related field. Along with their application, they must submit a brief essay that covers why they are interested in a career in the construction industry, the event or series of events that led them to that decision, and their career objectives. They must be sponsored by a member of the Associated General Contractors of South Dakota and by a member of the Sioux Falls Contractors Association. Financial need is considered in the selection process.
Financial data: The stipend is $2,000.
Duration: 1 year.
Number awarded: 1 each year.
Deadline: April of each year.

2346 SOCIETY OF PETROPHYSICISTS AND WELL LOG ANALYSTS SCHOLARSHIPS

Society of Petrophysicists and Well Log Analysts Foundation
Attn: Scholarship and Grant Committee
8866 Gulf Freeway, Suite 320
Houston, TX 77017
Phone: (713) 947-8727; Fax: (713) 947-7181
Web: www.spwla.org/spwla_foundation/foundation.html

Summary: To provide financial assistance to upper-division and graduate students working on a degree in a field related to the science of oil, gas, or other mineral formation evaluation.
Eligibility: Open to college juniors, seniors, and graduate students enrolled full-time at a college or university in Canada or the United States in a program directly related to or bearing a reasonable relationship to the science of oil, gas, or other mineral formation evaluation. Graduate students must have a GPA of 3.0 or higher. Applicants must submit a narrative discussion of their career objectives and expectations and the ways in which those may involve other or further the technical and professional objectives of the sponsoring organization. Selection is based on that narrative, academic achievement, honors and activities, letters of recommendation, and financial need.
Financial data: Stipends are either $1,500 or $1,000.
Duration: 1 year; may be renewed.
Number awarded: Varies each year; recently, 11 of these scholarships were awarded: 7 at $1,500 and 4 at $1,000.
Deadline: Deadline not specified.

2347 SOCIETY OF WOMEN ENGINEERS–DELMAR SECTION SCHOLARSHIP AWARD

Delaware Engineering Society
c/o Stacy Ziegler
Duffield Associates, Inc.
5400 Limestone Road
Wilmington, DE 19808
Phone: (302) 239-6634; Fax: (302) 239-8485
Email: sziegler@duffnet.com
Web: www.desonline.us

Summary: To provide financial assistance to female high school seniors in the DelMar area who are interested in majoring in engineering in college.
Eligibility: Open to female high school seniors in Delaware and Maryland who will be enrolling in an engineering program at an ABET-accredited college or university. Applicants must have SAT scores of 600 or higher in mathematics, 500 or higher in critical reading, and 500 or higher in writing (or ACT scores of 29 or higher in mathematics and 25 or higher in English). They must submit an essay (up to 500 words) on their interest in engineering, their major area of study and area of specialization, the occupation they propose to pursue after graduation, their long-term goals, and how they hope to achieve them. Selection is based on the essay, academic record, honors and scholarships, volunteer activities, work experience, and letters of recommendation. Financial need is not required.
Financial data: A stipend is awarded (amount not specified).
Duration: 1 year (freshman year); nonrenewable.
Number awarded: Varies each year.
Deadline: December of each year.

2348 SOL J. BARER SCHOLARSHIP IN LIFE SCIENCES

Independent College Fund of New Jersey
797 Springfield Avenue
Summit, NJ 07901-1107
Phone: (908) 277-3424; Fax: (908) 277-0851
Email: scholarships@njcolleges.org
Web: www.njcolleges.org/i_about_schol_students.html

Summary: To provide financial assistance to students enrolled at member institutions of the Independent College Fund of New Jersey (ICFNJ) who are preparing for a career in the life sciences.
Eligibility: Open to students entering their junior or senior year at an ICNJ member institution. Applicants must be majoring in a life science and have a cumulative GPA of 3.25 or higher. Along with their application, they must submit a 250-word personal statement on their academic and personal qualifications and their future academic and/or career plans. Financial need is not considered in the selection process.
Financial data: The stipend is $2,500 per year.
Duration: 1 year; may be renewed.
Number awarded: 1 or more each year.
Deadline: March of each year.

2349 SOLAR TURBINES SCHOLARSHIP

Society of Women Engineers
Attn: Scholarship Selection Committee
120 South LaSalle Street, Suite 1515
Chicago, IL 60603-3572
Phone: (312) 596-5223; (877) SWE-INFO; Fax: (312) 644-8557
Email: scholarshipapplication@swe.org
Web: societyofwomenengineers.swe.org

Summary: To provide financial assistance to women who will be entering college as freshmen and are interested in studying computer science or specified fields of engineering.
Eligibility: Open to women who are entering college as freshmen with a GPA of 3.5 or higher. Applicants must be planning to enroll full-time at an ABET-accredited 4-year college or university and major in computer science or aeronautical, computer, electrical, manufacturing, materials, or mechanical engineering. Selection is based on merit.
Financial data: The stipend is $1,000. The award also includes a travel grant for the recipient to attend the national conference of the Society of Women Engineers.
Duration: 1 year.
Number awarded: 1 each year.
Deadline: May of each year.

2350 SOLE SCHOLARSHIP

SOLE—The International Society of Logistics
Attn: Logistics Education Foundation
8100 Professional Place, Suite 111
Hyattsville, MD 20785-2229
Phone: (301) 459-8446; Fax: (301) 459-1522
Email: solehq@erols.com
Web: www.sole.org/lef.asp

Summary: To provide financial assistance to students working on an undergraduate or graduate degree in logistics.
Eligibility: Open to students working full-time on a bachelor's or master's degree in logistics or a related major. Applicants must submit brief essays on their career interests and objectives, their scholastic and/or extracurricular activities related to logistics, and the topic of a student paper they will submit if they receive a scholarship. Financial need is not considered in the selection process.

Financial data: The stipend is $1,000.
Duration: 1 year.
Number awarded: 1 or more each year.
Deadline: May of each year.

2351 SOUTH CAROLINA NURSES CARE SCHOLARSHIPS

South Carolina Nurses Foundation, Inc.
Attn: Awards Committee Chair
1821 Gadsden Street
Columbia, SC 29201
Phone: (803) 252-4781; Fax: (803) 779-3870
Email: brownk1@aol.com
Web: www.scnursesfoundation.org/index_files/Page316.htm

Summary: To provide financial assistance to students enrolled in an undergraduate or graduate nursing degree program in South Carolina.
Eligibility: Open to students currently enrolled in an undergraduate or graduate nursing degree program in South Carolina. Applicants must submit documentation of financial need and brief statements of their career goals, both upon graduation and in 5 years.
Financial data: The stipend is $1,500.
Duration: 1 year.
Number awarded: 4 each year: 2 to undergraduates and 2 to graduate students.
Deadline: May of each year.

2352 SOUTH CAROLINA SWCS CHAPTER SCHOLARSHIP

Soil and Water Conservation Society–South Carolina Chapter
c/o Hugh Caldwell, Secretary/Treasurer
400 Mill Creek Road
Lexington, SC 29072
Phone: (803) 576-2082
Email: caldwellh@rcgov.us
Web: www.swcssc.org/scholarship.htm

Summary: To provide financial assistance to South Carolina residents working on an undergraduate degree in a field related to natural resources at a college in any state.
Eligibility: Open to residents of South Carolina who are enrolled or planning to enroll at a college or university in any state. Applicants must be interested in working on an undergraduate degree in a field of conservation or natural resources. They must submit a 300-word essay on "The Value of This Scholarship to Me." Selection is based on that essay, GPA, community involvement, career goals, and financial need.
Financial data: The stipend is $1,000.
Duration: 1 year; recipients may not receive the scholarship for any 2 consecutive years.
Number awarded: 1 each year.
Deadline: March of each year.

2353 SOUTHWEST CHAPTER ACADEMIC SCHOLARSHIPS

American Association of Airport Executives-Southwest Chapter
P.O. Box 4228
Sparks, NV 89432
Phone: (775) 353-2080
Email: swaaae@sbcglobal.net
Web: www.swaaae.org/scholarships.html

Summary: To provide financial assistance to residents of any state working on an undergraduate or graduate degree in airport management at a college or university in the Southwest.
Eligibility: Open to residents of any state working on an undergraduate or graduate degree in airport management at colleges and universities in Arizona, California, Hawaii, Nevada, or Utah. Applicants must submit an autobiography (not to exceed 1 page) and a statement of their interest in aviation and airport management (not to exceed 1 page). Selection is based on academic record, extracurricular activities, and financial need.
Financial data: The stipend is $1,500; the sponsor also provides a $1,000 travel allowance for recipients to attend the awards ceremony.
Duration: 1 year.
Number awarded: 2 each year.
Deadline: October of each year.

2354 SPENCE REESE SCHOLARSHIPS

Boys & Girls Clubs of Greater San Diego
Attn: Greater San Diego Boys & Girls Clubs Foundation
115 West Woodward Avenue
Escondido, CA 92025
Phone: (760) 746-3315; (866) SD-YOUTH
Web: www.sdyouth.org/scholarships.htm

Summary: To provide financial assistance to graduating male high school seniors who plan to study designated fields in college.
Eligibility: Open to graduating male high school seniors planning to study law, medicine, engineering, or political science in college. They may live anywhere in the United States, but they must attend an interview in San Diego, California. Selection is based on academic standing, potential for good citizenship, academic ability, and financial need.
Financial data: The stipend is $4,000 per year.
Duration: 4 years.
Number awarded: 4 each year: 1 in each of the designated fields.
Deadline: April of each year.

2355 SPIRIT OF SOVEREIGNTY FOUNDATION TRIBAL SCHOLARS PROGRAM

American Indian College Fund
Attn: Scholarship Department
8333 Greenwood Boulevard
Denver, CO 80221
Phone: (303) 426-8900; (800) 776-FUND; Fax: (303) 426-1200
Email: scholarships@collegefund.org
Web: www.collegefund.org/scholarships/schol_tcu.html

Summary: To provide financial assistance to Native American students enrolled at a Tribal College or University (TCU), especially those majoring in designated fields.
Eligibility: Open to American Indians and Alaska Natives who are enrolled full-time at an eligible TCU. Applicants may be majoring in any field, but preference is given to business, hospitality, information technology, or marketing. They must have a GPA of 3.0 or higher. Applications are available only online and include required essays on specified topics.
Financial data: The stipend is $2,000.
Duration: 1 year.
Number awarded: 1 or more each year.
Deadline: May of each year.

2356 SPIROL SCHOLARSHIPS

SPIROL International Corporation
30 Rock Avenue
Danielson, CT 06239-1434
Phone: (860) 774-8571, ext. 4328
Web: www.spirol.com/company/news/scholarships.php

Summary: To provide financial assistance to high school seniors in California, Connecticut, Ohio, and Vermont who plan to major in designated fields at a college in any state.
Eligibility: Open to seniors graduating from 4 designated high schools in California, 8 public schools or a local private school in Connecticut, 4 high schools in Ohio, or 7 high schools in Vermont. Applicants must be planning to enroll full-time at an accredited 2- or 4-year college or university in any state. They must have a GPA of 2.5 or higher and be planning to prepare for a career in business, engineering, accounting, computer science, sales or marketing, a business/manufacturing/technical field, or human resources. Along with their application, they must submit a personal essay that covers what this scholarship would mean to them, their personal goals, and their educational and career goals. Financial need is not considered in the selection process.
Financial data: The stipend is $5,000 per year.
Duration: 4 years.
Number awarded: Varies each year.
Deadline: April of each year.

2357 SPRING MEADOW NURSERY SCHOLARSHIP

Summary: To provide financial assistance to students working on an undergraduate or graduate degree in landscape architecture or horticulture.
See Listing #1566.

2358 SSGT ROBERT V. MILNER MEMORIAL SCHOLARSHIP

American Academy of Physician Assistants–Veterans Caucus
Attn: Veterans Caucus
P.O. Box 362
Danville, PA 17821-0362
Phone: (570) 271-0292; Fax: (570) 271-5850
Email: admin@veteranscaucus.org
Web: www.veteranscaucus.org/displaycommon.cfm?an=1&subarticlenbr=37

Summary: To provide financial assistance to children of past or present members of the Air Force who are studying to become physician assistants.

Eligibility: Open to U.S. citizens who are currently enrolled in a physician assistant program. The program must be approved by the Commission on Accreditation of Allied Health Education. Applicants must be children of current members or honorably discharged members of the U.S. Air Force. Selection is based on military honors and awards received, civic and college honors and awards received, professional memberships and activities, and GPA. For children of veterans, an electronic copy of the sponsor's DD Form 214 must accompany the application.

Financial data: The stipend is $2,000.

Duration: 1 year.

Number awarded: 1 each year.

Deadline: February of each year.

2359 ST. FRANCIS SCHOOL OF NURSING ALUMNI OF PITTSBURGH, PA SCHOLARSHIP FUND

Pittsburgh Foundation
Attn: Scholarship Coordinator
Five PPG Place, Suite 250
Pittsburgh, PA 15222-5414
Phone: (412) 394-2649; Fax: (412) 391-7259
Email: turnerd@pghfdn.org
Web: www.pittsburghfoundation.org

Summary: To provide financial assistance to students working on an undergraduate or graduate degree in nursing.

Eligibility: Open to 1) students working on their first academic degree or diploma that leads to professional licensure as a registered nurse; and 2) licensed registered nurses working on an advanced degree in nursing. Applicants must have a GPA of 3.0 or higher and be able to demonstrate financial need. Along with their application, they must submit brief essays on their prior work experience, prior education, financial obligations, extracurricular activities and volunteer work, past achievements related to nursing, and career goals. U.S. citizenship is required.

Financial data: A stipend is awarded (amount not specified).

Duration: 1 year.

Number awarded: 1 or more each year.

Deadline: December of each year.

2360 STAN BECK FELLOWSHIP

Entomological Society of America
Attn: Entomological Foundation
9332 Annapolis Road, Suite 210
Lanham, MD 20706-3150
Phone: (301) 459-9082; Fax: (301) 459-9084
Email: melodie@entfdn.org
Web: www.entsoc.org/awards/student/beck.htm

Summary: To assist "needy" students working on an undergraduate or graduate degree in entomology who are nominated by members of the Entomological Society of America (ESA).

Eligibility: Open to students working on an undergraduate or graduate degree in entomology at a college or university in Canada, Mexico, or the United States. Candidates must be nominated by members of the society. They must be "needy" students; for the purposes of this program, need may be based on physical limitations or economic, minority, or environmental conditions.

Financial data: The stipend is $2,000 per year.

Duration: 1 year; may be renewed up to 3 additional years.

Number awarded: 1 each year.

Deadline: June of each year.

2361 STEPHANIE CARROLL SCHOLARSHIP

National Association Directors of Nursing Administration in Long Term Care
Attn: Education/Scholarship Committee
11353 Reed Hartman Highway, Suite 210
Cincinnati, OH 45241
Phone: (513) 791-3679; (800) 222-0539; Fax: (513) 791-3699
Email: info@nadona.org
Web: www.nadona.org/wysiwyg.php?wID=6

Summary: To provide financial assistance to nursing undergraduate and graduate students who plan to practice in long-term care or geriatrics.

Eligibility: Open to students entering or continuing in an accredited undergraduate or graduate nursing program. Applicants must indicate an intent to practice in long-term care or geriatrics for at least 2 years after graduation. Along with their application, they must submit an essay of at least 100 words on why they have chosen nursing as a career, why they are seeking this degree and how it will impact their nursing practice, and their commitment to the nursing profession, including their goals for their nursing career after graduation. Financial need is considered in the selection process.

Financial data: The stipend is $5,000.

Duration: 1 year.

Number awarded: At least 1 each year.

Deadline: June of each year.

2362 STEPHEN AND SANDY SHELLER SCHOLARSHIP

Pennsylvania State System of Higher Education Foundation, Inc.
Attn: Director of Scholarship Programs
2986 North Second Street
Harrisburg, PA 17110
Phone: (717) 720-4065; Fax: (717) 720-7082
Email: eshowers@thePAfoundation.org
Web: www.thepafoundation.org/scholarships/index.asp

Summary: To provide financial assistance to upper-division students at institutions of the Pennsylvania State System of Higher Education (PASSHE) who are preparing for a career in law or art therapy.

Eligibility: Open to full-time students currently working on an undergraduate degree leading to a career in law or in art therapy at 1 of the 14 institutions within the PASSHE. Applicants must have completed at least 60 credits with a GPA of 3.5 or higher. Along with their application, they must submit an essay of 500 to 800 words on a quotation from Winston Churchill regarding the importance of giving. Financial need is considered in the selection process.

Financial data: The stipend is $1,000.

Duration: 1 year; nonrenewable.

Number awarded: 5 each year.

Deadline: July of each year.

2363 STEPHEN G. KING PLAY ENVIRONMENTS SCHOLARSHIP

Summary: To provide financial assistance to upper-division and graduate students who wish to study landscape architecture with an emphasis on play environments.

See Listing #1567.

2364 STEVE DEARDUFF SCHOLARSHIP

Community Foundation for Greater Atlanta, Inc.
50 Hurt Plaza, Suite 449
Atlanta, GA 30303
Phone: (404) 688-5525; Fax: (404) 688-3060
Email: scholarships@cfgreateratlanta.org
Web: www.cfgreateratlanta.org/Grants-Support/Scholarships.aspx

Summary: To provide financial assistance to Georgia residents who are working on an undergraduate or graduate degree in medicine or social work at a school in any state.

Eligibility: Open to legal residents of Georgia who are enrolled in or accepted at an accredited institution of higher learning in any state to work on an undergraduate or graduate degree in medicine or social work. Applicants must be able to demonstrate a history of outstanding community service and potential for success in their chosen field. They must have a GPA of 2.0 or higher and be able to demonstrate financial need.

Financial data: Stipends range up to $2,500 per year.

Duration: 1 year; recipients may reapply.

Number awarded: 3 each year.

Deadline: March of each year.

2365 STEVE HARPER MEMORIAL SCHOLARSHIP

Summary: To provide financial assistance to high school seniors in Kansas who plan to attend a college or university in the state to major in natural resources or photography.

See Listing #1568.

2366 STEVE WAGNER SCHOLARSHIP

Saginaw Community Foundation
100 South Jefferson, Suite 201
Saginaw, MI 48607
Phone: (989) 755-0545; Fax: (989) 755-6524
Email: info@saginawfoundation.org
Web: www.saginawfoundation.org/grants_and_scholarships/scholarships

Summary: To provide financial assistance to high school seniors in Michigan who plan to work on an undergraduate degree in civil engineering or land surveying at a school in any state.

Eligibility: Open to seniors graduating from high schools in Michigan who have a GPA of 3.0 or higher. Applicants must be planning to work full-time on an undergraduate degree in civil engineering or land surveying in an ABET-accredited program in any state. Along with their application, they must submit an essay describing their personal and educational goals, including their plans for a major, why they have chosen that field, and what they plan to do with their degree. Selection is based on academic record (10 points), community service (40 points), recommendations (20 points), and overall involvement in community, school, and work activities (30 points). Special consideration is given to students who have worked for a firm that is a member of the American Council of Engineering Companies (ACEC) in the last 24 months.

Financial data: A stipend is awarded (amount not specified).

Duration: 1 year.

Number awarded: 1 or more each year.

Deadline: February of each year.

2367 STEW TWEED FISHERIES AND AQUACULTURE SCHOLARSHIP FUND

New Jersey Marine Sciences Consortium/New Jersey Sea Grant
Attn: Scholarship Fund
22 Magruder Road
Fort Hancock, NJ 07732
Phone: (732) 872-1300
Email: msamuel@njmsc.org
Web: www.njmsc.org/Scholarships/Stew_Tweed.html

Summary: To provide financial assistance to residents of New Jersey who are interested in preparing for a career in fisheries or aquaculture at a school in any state.

Eligibility: Open to residents of New Jersey who are high school students or undergraduate or graduate students enrolled at a college or university in any state. Applicants must be working on or planning to work on a degree in a field that will prepare them for a career in fisheries or aquaculture. They must be U.S. citizens and have a GPA of 3.0 or higher. Along with their application, they must submit an essay of 250 to 500 words on their interest in fisheries or aquaculture and the contributions they hope to make to the field. Financial need is not considered in the selection process.

Financial data: The stipend is $1,000 for a high school senior or $1,500 for a current undergraduate or graduate student.

Duration: 1 year.

Number awarded: 2 each year: 1 to a high school senior and 1 to a current undergraduate or graduate student.

Deadline: March of each year.

2368 STOKES EDUCATIONAL SCHOLARSHIP PROGRAM

Summary: To provide minority and other high school seniors and college sophomores with financial assistance and work experience at the National Security Agency (NSA).

See Listing #1570.

2369 STUDENT OPPORTUNITY SCHOLARSHIPS FOR ETHNIC MINORITY GROUPS

Summary: To provide financial assistance to upper-division college students who are Presbyterians, especially those of racial/ethnic minority heritage majoring in designated fields.

See Listing #1573.

2370 SYMANTEC SCHOLARSHIPS

Society of Women Engineers
Attn: Scholarship Selection Committee
120 South LaSalle Street, Suite 1515
Chicago, IL 60603-3572
Phone: (312) 596-5223; (877) SWE-INFO; Fax: (312) 644-8557
Email: scholarshipapplication@swe.org
Web: societyofwomenengineers.swe.org

Summary: To provide financial assistance to undergraduate women majoring in computer science or designated engineering specialties.

Eligibility: Open to women who are entering their junior or senior year at a 4-year ABET-accredited college or university. Applicants must be majoring in computer science or computer or electrical engineering. They must have a GPA of 3.0 or higher. Preference is given to members of groups underrepresented in engineering or computer science. Selection is based on merit.

Financial data: The stipend is $5,000.

Duration: 1 year.

Number awarded: 3 each year.

Deadline: February of each year.

2371 TECH HIGH SCHOOL ALUMNI ASSOCIATION/W.O. CHENEY MERIT SCHOLARSHIP

Community Foundation for Greater Atlanta, Inc.
50 Hurt Plaza, Suite 449
Atlanta, GA 30303
Phone: (404) 688-5525; Fax: (404) 688-3060
Email: scholarships@cfgreateratlanta.org
Web: www.cfgreateratlanta.org/Grants-Support/Scholarships.aspx

Summary: To provide financial assistance to high school seniors in Georgia who are working on an undergraduate degree in engineering, mathematics, or physical science at a school in any state.

Eligibility: Open to graduating high school seniors who have been residents of Georgia for at least 3 years. Applicants must have a cumulative GPA of 3.7 or higher or a rank in the top 10% of their class and an SAT mathematics and critical reading score of 1300 or higher. They must have been accepted as a full-time student at an accredited 4-year college or university in any state to work on a degree in engineering, mathematics, or the physical sciences. They must be able to demonstrate commitment to community service, but financial need is not considered. U.S. citizenship is required.

Financial data: The stipend is $5,000 per year.

Duration: 1 year; may be renewed up to 3 additional years.

Number awarded: 4 each year.

Deadline: March of each year.

2372 TED G. WILSON MEMORIAL SCHOLARSHIP

Professional Construction Estimators Association
Attn: Wilson Memorial Scholarship Foundation
P.O. Box 680336
Charlotte, NC 28216-0336
Phone: (704) 489-1494; (877) 521-7232
Email: pcea@pcea.org
Web: www.pcea.org/scholarships.cfm

Summary: To provide financial assistance to high school seniors and currently-enrolled college students in selected states interested in working on a degree in construction or engineering.

Eligibility: Open to high school seniors and college freshmen, sophomores, and juniors who are attending or planning to attend a college or university full-time and work on a bachelor's degree in construction or engineering (to prepare for a career in the construction industry). Applicants must reside or attend school in a state where the Professional Construction Estimators Association (PCEA) has an established chapter; currently, those are limited to Florida, Georgia, North Carolina, South Carolina, and Virginia. Along with their application, they must submit 2 recommendations and an official transcript. Finalists may be interviewed. Selection is based on academic ability, financial need, and desire to enter the construction industry.

Financial data: The stipend is $1,500.

Duration: 1 year.

Number awarded: 5 each year: 1 from each of the states with a PCEA chapter.

Deadline: March of each year.

2373 TELACU ENGINEERING AWARD

TELACU Education Foundation
Attn: Scholarship Program
5400 East Olympic Boulevard, Suite 300
Los Angeles, CA 90022
Phone: (323) 721-1655; Fax: (323) 724-3372
Email: info@telacu.com
Web: telacu.com/site/en/home/education/programs/college.html

Summary: To provide financial assistance to Latino students from eligible communities in California, Texas, Illinois, and New York who are interested in studying engineering at designated partner institutions.

Eligibility: Open to Latino students residing in eligible communities in California, Texas, Illinois, and New York. Applicants must 1) be a first-generation college student; 2) be from a low-income family; and 3) have a GPA of 3.0 or higher. They must be enrolled full-time at a partner institution and have completed at least 12 units of course work in engineering. Along with their application, they must submit brief essays on a dream they have, an event or experience in their life that inspired them to prepare for their intended career, how their extracurricular activities are helping them prepare for this career, and how they believe they can contribute to the sponsor's mission. Selection is based on extracurricular involvement demonstrating a commitment to the community and financial need.

Financial data: The stipend is $10,000 per year.

Duration: 1 year.

Number awarded: 1 each year.

Deadline: March of each year.

2374 TENNESSEE ELKS BENEVOLENT TRUST SCHOLARSHIP IN NURSING

Tennessee Elks Association
Attn: Tennessee Elks Benevolent Trust
c/o Jim Birdsong, Scholarship Chair
503 Dogwood Street
Pulaski, TN 38478-4537
Email: bird@energize.net
Web: www.tnelks.org/scholarship/nursing.php

Summary: To provide financial assistance to residents of Tennessee who are interested in studying nursing at a school in the state.

Eligibility: Open to Tennessee residents who are high school seniors, high school graduates, or GED recipients. Applicants must be attending or planning to attend a school of nursing in the state. Along with their application, they must submit 1) a letter giving their reasons for wishing to become a nurse; and 2) a letter from their parents describing their need for financial support. Selection is based on academic achievements (based on GPA, SAT and/or ACT scores, proficiency in subjects essential to nursing), desire and interest (based on volunteer service, employment, motivation), completeness and neatness of the application, and financial need. U.S. citizenship is required.

Financial data: Stipends are $1,500 per year or $2,000.

Duration: 1 year. The $1,500 award may be renewed up to 3 additional years, provided the recipient maintains a GPA of 3.0 or higher. The $2,000 awards are nonrenewable.

Number awarded: 5 each year; 1 at $1,500 per year and 4 at $2,000.

Deadline: January of each year.

2375 TEXAS AMERICAN LEGION AUXILIARY PAST PRESIDENT'S PARLEY SCHOLARSHIPS

American Legion Auxiliary
Department of Texas
P.O. Box 140407
Austin, TX 78714-0407
Phone: (512) 476-7278; Fax: (512) 482-8391
Email: alatexas@txlegion.org
Web: alatexas.org/scholarship/ppp.html

Summary: To provide financial assistance to the children and grandchildren of Texas veterans who wish to study a field related to medicine at a school in any state.

Eligibility: Open to the children and grandchildren of veterans who served during specified periods of war time. Applicants must be residents of Texas studying or planning to study a medical field at a postsecondary institution in any state. Selection is based on need, goals, character, citizenship, and objectives.

Financial data: The stipend is $1,000.

Duration: 1 year.

Number awarded: 1 or more each year.

Deadline: May of each year.

2376 TEXAS CONFERENCE FOR WOMEN SCHOLARSHIPS

Summary: To provide financial assistance to women in Texas interested in studying specified areas at a college in the state.

See Listing #1582.

2377 TEXAS COUNCIL OF CHAPTERS SCHOLARSHIPS

Soil and Water Conservation Society–Texas Council of Chapters
c/o Robert Knight, Scholarship Committee Chair
Texas A&M University
Department of Rangeland Ecology and Management
Animal Industries Building, Room 322
College Station, TX 77843-2138
Phone: (979) 845-5557; Fax: (979) 845-6430
Email: bob.knight@tamu.edu
Web: www.tx-swcs.org

Summary: To provide financial assistance to upper-division students working in conservation-related fields at colleges and universities in Texas.

Eligibility: Open to students who have completed at least 2 years of undergraduate work at a Texas college or university. Applicants must plan to continue their education by working on a degree in conservation or a related field. They must submit a 1-page letter describing their study plans (including subject matter area), attitude toward conservation, career plans, and financial need.

Financial data: Stipends are $1,000 or $500.

Duration: 1 year; nonrenewable.

Number awarded: 3 each year: 1 at $1,000 and 2 at $500.

Deadline: May of each year.

2378 TEXAS OUTSTANDING RURAL SCHOLAR RECOGNITION PROGRAM

Office of Rural Community Affairs
Attn: Rural Health Unit
1700 North Congress Street, Suite 220
P.O. Box 12877
Austin, TX 78711-2877
Phone: (512) 936-6701; (800) 544-2042; Fax: (512) 936-6776
Email: agrant@orca.state.tx.us
Web: www.orca.state.tx.us/index.php/Home/Grants

Summary: To provide financial assistance to outstanding Texas students who are interested in preparing for a career in health care in rural areas.

Eligibility: Open to Texas residents who are either high school seniors in the top quarter of their graduating class or college students who have earned a GPA of 3.0 or higher. Applicants must be enrolled or intend to enroll in an eligible academic institution in Texas to become a health care professional and arrange to be sponsored by an organization in 1 of the 177 rural counties in the state. Eligible health care professions include medicine (with a residency in family practice, emergency medicine, general internal medicine, general pediatrics, general surgery, or general obstetrics and gynecology), dentistry, optometry, nursing, pharmacy, chiropractic, behavioral health, and allied health (rehabilitative services, radiology technician, medical laboratory technician, health systems management, and dietary and nutritional services). Eligible sponsoring organizations include local hospitals, rural health clinics, and community organizations. Funds are awarded on a competitive basis. Selection is based on academic achievements, essay content, sponsor's financial commitment, community statement of need, and overall quality of the nominee.

Financial data: The amount of the award is based on the cost of attendance at the recipient's academic institution. Sponsoring communities pledge to cover half the student's educational expenses; the state covers the other half. Students must pledge to provide 1 year of work in the sponsoring community for each year of support they receive while in college.

Duration: 1 year; may be renewed.

Number awarded: Varies each year.

Deadline: May of each year for fall semester; September of each year for spring semester; January of each year for summer semesters.

2379 TEXAS SURVEYORS FOUNDATION SCHOLARSHIPS

Texas Society of Professional Surveyors
Attn: Texas Surveyors Foundation, Inc.
2525 Wallingwood Drive, Suite 300

Austin, TX 78746
Phone: (512) 327-7871; Fax: (512) 327-7872
Email: DougL@tsps.org
Web: www.tsps.org/Education/TSFI.htm
Summary: To provide financial assistance to Texas residents interested in working on an undergraduate degree in surveying.
Eligibility: Open to residents of Texas who are enrolled, or accepted for enrollment, in a college or university surveying program or surveying-related course of study. Applicants must submit a 2-page essay that includes a brief autobiography, career plans, reason for applying for this scholarship, and reason for choosing land surveying as a career. Selection is based on academic achievement and financial need.
Financial data: A stipend is awarded (amount not specified).
Duration: 1 year; may be renewed.
Number awarded: Varies each year.
Deadline: January of each year for spring semester; April of each year for summer semester; September of each year for fall semester.

2380 TEXAS TRANSPORTATION SCHOLARSHIP

Transportation Clubs International
P.O. Box 2223
Ocean Shores, WA 98569
Phone: (877) 858-8627
Email: info@transportationclubsinternational.com
Web: www.transportationclubsinternational.com/scholarships.html
Summary: To provide financial assistance to college students from Texas interested in preparing for a career in fields related to transportation.
Eligibility: Open to students enrolled in an academic institution (vocational or degree program) that offers courses in transportation, logistics, traffic management, or related fields. Applicants must intend to prepare for a career in those fields. They must have been enrolled in a school in Texas during some phase of their education (elementary or secondary). Along with their application, they must submit a 200-word essay explaining why they have chosen transportation or an allied field as a career path and outlining their objectives. Selection is based on scholastic ability character, potential, professional interest, and financial need.
Financial data: The stipend is $1,500.
Duration: 1 year.
Number awarded: 1 each year.
Deadline: May of each year.

2381 TEXAS VEGETATION MANAGEMENT ASSOCIATION SCHOLARSHIPS

Texas Vegetation Management Association
c/o Stan Jones, Scholarship Chair
P.O. Box 1053
Pasadena, TX 77501
Phone: (713) 924-6929; Fax: (713) 921-0074
Email: stan.jones@rrsi.com
Web: www.tvma.net/scholarship.htm
Summary: To provide financial assistance to residents of Texas who are interested in attending college in the state to work on an undergraduate degree in a field of vegetation management.
Eligibility: Open to residents of Texas who are attending or planning to attend an accredited college or university in the state. Applicants must be interested in working on an undergraduate degree in the field of or directly related to vegetation management. Along with their application, they must submit a 1-page resume that addresses their academic record (diversity and difficulty of course work taken, GPA, significant honors and awards, and membership in honor societies); leadership and extracurricular activities (participation in recognized clubs and organizations, elected offices, committees, projects, and honors and awards for leadership and extracurricular activities); and personal traits (character, ethics, dependability, innovation, work ethic, and communication skills). Selection is based on academic record (50%), leadership and extracurricular activities (25%), and personal traits (25%).
Financial data: The stipend is $2,000.
Duration: 1 year.
Number awarded: 3 each year.
Deadline: March of each year.

2382 THACHER ENVIRONMENTAL RESEARCH CONTEST

Institute for Global Environmental Strategies
Attn: Thacher Contest
1600 Wilson Boulevard, Suite 901
Arlington, VA 22209
Phone: (703) 312-0823; Fax: (703) 312-8657
Email: ThacherContest@strategies.org
Web: www.strategies.org
Summary: To recognize and reward high school students who conduct outstanding projects using satellites and other geospatial technologies or data to study Earth.
Eligibility: Open to students in grades 9–12 at public, private, parochial, or home schools in the United States or U.S. territories and to U.S. citizens enrolled in overseas schools (e.g., Department of Defense Overseas School, as an exchange student, parents are temporarily living abroad). Entries may be submitted by individuals or teams. Students must submit a report, up to 20 pages in length, on a project that demonstrates the best use of satellites and other geospatial technologies or data to study Earth. Eligible tools and data include satellite remote sensing, aerial photography, geographic information systems (GIS), and global positioning systems (GPS). The main focus of the project must be on the application of the geospatial tool or data to study a problem related to Earth's environment. Selection is based on scientific and technical accuracy; creativity and originality; quality of presentation; thoroughness of research, methods, and procedures; quality of conclusions; and demonstration of knowledge gained.
Financial data: Awards are $2,000 for first place, $1,000 for second, and $500 for third. If winners are a team, the awards are split equally among team members. The teacher of each winner receives a $200 gift card for Amazon.com.
Duration: The competition is held annually.
Number awarded: 3 each year.
Deadline: April of each year.

2383 THE CAR OF MY FUTURE STUDENT SCHOLARSHIP PROGRAM

Summary: To recognize and reward, with college scholarships, high school seniors in Washington who submit essays or artwork on their vision of the car of the future.
See Listing #1584.

2384 THE MIKKELSON FOUNDATION STUDENT SCHOLARSHIP PROGRAM

The Mikkelson Foundation
P.O. Box 768
Monument, CO 80132
Web: www.mikkelson.com/foundation/students.html
Summary: To provide financial assistance to high school seniors in Colorado who plan to study engineering, mathematics, or science at a college in any state.
Eligibility: Open to seniors graduating from high schools in Colorado who plan to attend an accredited 4-year college or university in any state. Applicants must be planning to major in engineering, mathematics, or science (biology, chemistry, or physical sciences). They must have an unweighted GPA of 3.7 or higher and a cumulative SAT score of at least 1800 or a composite ACT score of at least 28. Along with their application, they must submit a 2-page personal essay on their strengths, accomplishments, and interests; why they have chosen their projected course of study; what motivated their interest in that area; their plans following college graduation; and how they plan to finance their education. They may add additional information on any special financial hardships they are facing.
Financial data: The stipend is $3,000 per year.
Duration: 4 years, provided the recipient remains in good standing at their university.
Number awarded: 2 each year.
Deadline: April of each year.

2385 THOMAS C. GRIFFIN MEMORIAL SCHOLARSHIP

California Association of Pest Control Advisers–Kern County Chapter
c/o Roger Williams, President
7908 Selkirk Drive
Bakersfield, CA 93309-4225

Phone: (661) 747-9243
Email: capca@capca.com
Web: www.capca.com/general_information/scholorships

Summary: To provide financial assistance to high school seniors, high school graduates, and currently-enrolled college students in California who are majoring in agriculture or horticulture and planning to prepare for a career in pest management.

Eligibility: Open to California students who are currently attending, entering, or returning to college. Applicants must be enrolled or planning to enroll in an agricultural or horticultural program to prepare for a career in pest management. They must have a GPA of 2.5 or higher. Selection is based on academic record (25%), extracurricular activities (15%), pest management experience (20%), professional and career goals (20%), financial need (10%), and class standing (10%). Students working on a bachelor's degree are given priority.

Financial data: The stipend is $2,000.

Duration: 1 year.

Number awarded: 1 each year.

Deadline: May of each year.

2386 THOMAS K. MATHISON MEMORIAL SCHOLARSHIP

Washington Apple Education Foundation
Attn: Scholarship Committee
2900 Euclid Avenue
Wenatchee, WA 98801
Phone: (509) 663-7713; Fax: (509) 663-7469
Email: waef@waef.org
Web: www.waef.org/index.php?page_id=238

Summary: To provide financial assistance to Washington residents who are involved in the tree fruit industry and interested in attending college in any state.

Eligibility: Open to Washington residents who are either graduating high school seniors or current students at a college or university in any state. Applicants must be involved in the Washington tree fruit industry, either preparing for a career in the industry or having been raised in a family involved in the industry. Along with their application, they must submit an official transcript, their SAT or ACT scores, 2 letters of reference, and an essay on an assigned topic. Financial need is also considered in the selection process.

Financial data: The stipend is $5,000. Funds may be used to pay for tuition, room, board, books, educational supplies, and miscellaneous institutional fees.

Duration: 1 year; recipients may reapply.

Number awarded: 1 each year.

Deadline: February of each year.

2387 THOMSEN/BP NORTH AMERICA SCHOLARSHIP

Society of Exploration Geophysicists
Attn: SEG Foundation
8801 South Yale, Suite 500
P.O. Box 702740
Tulsa, OK 74170-2740
Phone: (918) 497-5500; Fax: (918) 497-5557
Email: scholarships@seg.org
Web: www.seg.org/web/foundation/programs/scholarship

Summary: To provide financial assistance to entering or continuing undergraduate and graduate students at universities in North America who are interested in studying exploration geophysics.

Eligibility: Open to 1) high school students planning to enter college in the fall; and 2) undergraduate or graduate students whose grades are above average. Applicants must intend to work full-time on a degree directed toward a career in exploration geophysics at a university in North America. Along with their application, they must submit a 150-word essay on how they plan to use geophysics in their future. Financial need is not considered in the selection process.

Financial data: Stipends provided by this sponsor average $2,500 per year.

Duration: 1 academic year; nonrenewable.

Number awarded: 1 each year.

Deadline: February of each year.

2388 THROLSON AMERICAN BISON FOUNDATION SCHOLARSHIPS

National Bison Association
Attn: Throlson American Bison Foundation
8690 Wolff Court, Suite 200
Westminster, CO 80031
Phone: (303) 292-2833; Fax: (303) 845-9081
Email: info@bisoncentral.com
Web: www.bisoncentral.com

Summary: To provide financial assistance to upper-division and graduate students studying bison or fields related to the bison industry.

Eligibility: Open to full-time college juniors, seniors, and graduate students in a recognized livestock, animal science, veterinary, agriculture, or human nutrition program in the United States or Canada. Applicants must be preparing for a career related to the bison or bison industry. Selection is based on essays on the following topics: how they may play a role in the growth of the bison industry in the next 15 years (30 points); community and professional organizations to which they belong and their involvement with them (10 points); their livestock, veterinary, biological, zoological, human nutrition, agribusiness, or agricultural work experience (10 points); their hobbies and leisure activities (5 points); their philosophy of bison in today's environment (10 points); what they believe to be the most critical issue affecting their field of study during the next 10 years (10 points); and their career goals and objectives (25 points).

Financial data: The stipend is either $2,000 or $1,000.

Duration: 1 year; nonrenewable.

Number awarded: 3 each year: 1 at $2,000 and 2 at $1,000.

Deadline: September of each year.

2389 TIMOTHY BIGELOW AND PALMER W. BIGELOW, JR. SCHOLARSHIPS

Summary: To provide financial support to residents of New England interested in working on an undergraduate or graduate degree in landscape architecture or horticulture.

See Listing #1591.

2390 TINY RAUCH SCHOLARSHIP

Associated General Contractors of Ohio
Attn: AGC of Ohio Education Foundation
1755 Northwest Boulevard
Columbus, OH 43212
Phone: (614) 486-6446; (800) 557-OHIO; Fax: (614) 486-6498
Email: educationfoundation@agcohio.com
Web: www.agcohio.com/scholarships.html

Summary: To provide financial assistance to residents of Ohio and adjacent counties who are working on an undergraduate degree in a field related to the construction industry at a college or university in any state.

Eligibility: Open to residents of Ohio and adjacent counties who are undergraduates in at least the second year at a 2- or 4-year college or university in any state. Applicants must be enrolled in a construction degree program and be preparing for a career in construction. They must be U.S. citizens with a GPA of 2.5 or higher. Along with their application, they must submit a short statement on what they think is the most important issue currently facing the construction industry and 4 essays of 125 words each on 1) why they have decided to prepare for a career in construction; 2) the goals they hope to accomplish in their career; 3) how they plan to make a difference in the construction industry; and 4) anything else that might influence whether or not they receive this scholarship. Financial need is also considered in the selection process.

Financial data: The stipend is $1,000.

Duration: 1 year.

Number awarded: 1 each year.

Deadline: March of each year.

2391 TMCF SIEMENS TEACHER SCHOLARSHIPS

Thurgood Marshall College Fund
Attn: Scholarship Manager
80 Maiden Lane, Suite 2204
New York, NY 10038
Phone: (212) 573-8487; (877) 690-8673; Fax: (212) 573-8497
Email: srogers@tmcfund.org
Web: www.thurgoodmarshallfund.net

Summary: To provide financial assistance to upper-division students at colleges and universities that are members of the Thurgood Marshall College Fund (TMCF) and who are preparing for a career as a science or mathematics teacher.

Eligibility: Open to full-time students entering their junior or senior year at 1 of the 47 colleges and universities that are TMCF members. Applicants must be majoring in education or a field of science or mathematics and preparing for a career as a teacher of science or mathematics at the elementary or secondary level. They must have a GPA of 2.75 or higher and be able to demonstrate financial need. U.S. citizenship is required.

Financial data: The stipend is $2,200 per semester ($4,400 per year).

Duration: 1 year.

Number awarded: 20 each year.

Deadline: September of each year.

2392 TNLA SCHOLARSHIP PROGRAM

Texas Nursery and Landscape Association
Attn: Education and Research Foundation
7730 South IH-35
Austin, TX 78745-6698
Phone: (512) 280-5182; (800) 880-0343; Fax: (512) 280-3012
Email: info@tnlaonline.org
Web: www.tnlaonline.org/education/ed-foundation.html

Summary: To provide financial assistance to high school seniors and returning undergraduate and graduate students in Texas who are majoring in horticulture.

Eligibility: Open to Texas residents who are either high school seniors or returning undergraduate or graduate students. Applicants must be majoring or planning to major in horticulture at an approved college in Texas; currently, these include: Central Texas College, Houston Community College, Northeast Texas Community College, North Central Texas College, Palo Alto College, Richland College, Prairie View A&M University, Sam Houston State, Texas State University, Stephen F. Austin State University, Tarleton University, Tarrant County College, Texas A&M University (College Station, Commerce, and Kingsville campuses), Texas State Technical College, Texas Tech University, Trinity Valley College, Tyler Junior College, University of Texas (Arlington and Austin campuses), Wharton County Junior College, and Western Texas College. Along with their application, they must submit a statement on why they are applying for the scholarships and their career objectives as they relate to the field of horticulture and the nursery and landscape industry. Financial need is not considered in the selection process.

Financial data: The standard award is $1,000, divided into a $500 payment per semester. Other scholarships, ranging from $500 to $2,000, are also available.

Duration: The standard award is for 1 year.

Number awarded: Varies each year; recently, 18 of these scholarships were awarded.

Deadline: May of each year.

2393 TOCA PUBLISHERS SCHOLARSHIP PROGRAM

Summary: To provide financial assistance to undergraduate students preparing for a career in green industry communications.

See Listing #1592.

2394 TONY CAMPMAN SCHOLARSHIP

Rocky Mountain Water Environment Association
c/o Ray Kemp, Scholarship Committee Drive
3036 Environmental Drive
Fort Collins, CO 80525
Phone: (970) 221-6900
Email: rkemp@fcgov.com
Web: www.rmwea.org

Summary: To provide financial assistance to undergraduates from Colorado, New Mexico, or Wyoming who are majoring in a field related to the water environment.

Eligibility: Open to undergraduates who reside or attend a 2- or 4-year college or university in Colorado, New Mexico, or Wyoming. Applicants must be majoring in a field related to the water environment profession (e.g., biology, environmental science, engineering with a strong emphasis in wastewater treatment, water pollution control, environmental protection). Along with their application, they must submit an essay of 200 to 300 words on their interest in the environment and how that interest influences their career goals. Financial need is not considered in the selection process.

Financial data: The stipend is $1,000.

Duration: 1 year.

Number awarded: 1 or more each year.

Deadline: April of each year.

2395 TRADITIONAL NURSING STUDENT SCHOLARSHIP

Ohio Nurses Association
Attn: Ohio Nurses Foundation
4000 East Main Street
Columbus, OH 43213-2983
Phone: (614) 237-5414; Fax: (614) 237-6074
Email: gharsheymeade@ohnurses.org
Web: www.ohnurses.org/AM/Template.cfm?Section=Foundation

Summary: To provide financial assistance to residents of Ohio who are interested in working on a degree in nursing at a school in any state.

Eligibility: Open to residents of Ohio interested in attending college in any state to prepare for a career as a nurse. Applicants must be attending or have attended a high school in the state. If still in high school, they must have a cumulative GPA of 3.5 or higher at the end of their junior year. If out of high school, they may not have had a break of more than 2 years between high school and enrollment in a nursing program. Along with their application, they must submit a 100-word personal statement on how they will advance the profession of nursing in Ohio. Selection is based on that statement, high school or college academic records, school activities, and community services.

Financial data: The stipend is $1,000 per year.

Duration: 1 year; recipients may reapply for 1 additional year if they remain enrolled full-time and maintain a cumulative GPA of 2.5 or higher.

Number awarded: 1 or more each year.

Deadline: January of each year.

2396 TRANSPORTATION ENGINEERING SCHOLARSHIP

Virginia Transportation Construction Alliance
620 Moorefield Park Drive, Suite 120
Richmond, VA 23236-3692
Phone: (804) 330-3312; Fax: (804) 330-3850
Email: stephanie@vtca.org
Web: www.vtca.org/about_vtca/vtca_programs_and_scholarships

Summary: To provide financial assistance to currently-enrolled college students in Virginia who are majoring in an engineering or technical field.

Eligibility: Open to freshmen, sophomores, or juniors from any state working full-time on a degree in an undergraduate engineering or technical field at a 4-year institution in Virginia. Applicants must have a GPA of 2.0 or higher and a demonstrated interest in preparing for a career in the transportation design and building industry. Along with their application, they must submit a statement explaining their interest in a career in the transportation design and construction industry and how their previous work experience may relate to a construction industry career. Selection is based on academic performance, employment experience, extracurricular and leadership activities, and demonstrated interest in the transportation industries. U.S. citizenship is required.

Financial data: The stipend is $2,000 per year.

Duration: 1 year; recipients may reapply.

Number awarded: 2 each year.

Deadline: May of each year.

2397 TRUDY DUBINSKY MEMORIAL SCHOLARSHIP

Society of Diagnostic Medical Sonography
Attn: SDMS Educational Foundation
2745 North Dallas Parkway, Suite 350
Plano, TX 75093-8730
Phone: (214) 473-8057; (800) 229-9506; Fax: (214) 473-8563
Email: foundation@sdms.org
Web: www.sdms.org/foundation/dubinsky.asp

Summary: To provide financial assistance to students enrolled in a diagnostic medical sonography (ultrasound) program.

Eligibility: Open to students enrolled in diagnostic medical sonography programs accredited by the Commission on Accreditation of Allied Health Education Programs (CAAHEP) or the Canadian Medical Association (CMA). Applicants who graduated from high school within the past 2 years must have an ACT score of at least 22 or an SAT critical reading and mathematics score of at least 950. Applicants who graduated from high school more than 2 years ago must submit transcripts of all postsecondary education. All applicants must submit 100-word essays on why they chose sonography as a career, the contribution they would make to the ultrasound profession, and why they should receive this scholarship. Financial need is also considered in the selection process.

Financial data: The stipend ranges from $500 to $1,000.

Duration: 1 year.

Number awarded: 1 each year.
Deadline: July of each year.

2398 TRUMAN D. PICARD SCHOLARSHIP PROGRAM

Intertribal Timber Council
Attn: Education Committee
1112 N.E. 21st Avenue, Suite 4
Portland, OR 97232-2114
Phone: (503) 282-4296; Fax: (503) 282-1274
Email: itc1@teleport.com
Web: www.itcnet.org/about_us/scholarships.html

Summary: To provide financial assistance to American Indians or Alaskan Natives who are interested in studying natural resources in college.
Eligibility: Open to 1) graduating high school seniors; and 2) currently-enrolled college students. Applicants must be enrolled in a federally-recognized tribe or Native Alaska corporation. They must be majoring or planning to major in natural resources. Selection is based on interest in natural resources; commitment to education, community, and culture; academic merit; and financial need.
Financial data: The stipend is $1,500 for high school seniors entering college or $2,000 for students already enrolled in college.
Duration: 1 year.
Number awarded: Varies each year; recently, 21 of these scholarships were awarded.
Deadline: January of each year.

2399 TWEEDALE SCHOLARSHIPS

U.S. Navy
Attn: Naval Education and Training Command
NSTC OD2
250 Dallas Street, Suite A
Pensacola, FL 32508-5268
Phone: (850) 452-4941, ext. 25166; (800) NAV-ROTC, ext. 25166; Fax: (850) 452-2486
Email: PNSC_NROTC.scholarship@navy.mil
Web: www.nrotc.navy.mil/tweedale.aspx

Summary: To provide financial assistance to currently-enrolled college students who are interested in joining Navy ROTC and majoring in a technical field in college.
Eligibility: Open to students who have completed at least 1 but not more than 4 academic terms with a cumulative GPA that places them above their peer mean or 3.0, whichever is higher, and a grade of "C" or better in all classes attempted. They must have a strong mathematics and science background in high school (with a grade of "B" or higher in calculus, if taken) and completed at least 1 academic term of college-level mathematics or science. They must be majoring in specified technical fields (recently, those were chemistry, computer science, engineering, mathematics, and physics). Students must be interviewed by the professor of naval science (PNS) at their college or university and must comply with standards of leadership potential and military/physical fitness. They must submit a plan indicating that they will complete the introductory naval science course as soon as possible and be able to complete all naval science requirements and graduate on time with their class.
Financial data: These scholarships provide payment of full tuition and required educational fees, as well as a specified amount for textbooks, supplies, and equipment. The program also provides a stipend for 10 months of the year that is $300 per month as a sophomore, $350 per month as a junior, and $400 per month as a senior.
Duration: 2 or 3 years, until the recipient completes the bachelor's degree.
Number awarded: Approximately 140 each year: 2 at each college and university with a Navy ROTC unit.
Deadline: March of each year.

2400 TYLENOL SCHOLARSHIPS

McNeil Consumer and Specialty Pharmaceuticals
c/o International Scholarship and Tuition Services, Inc.
200 Crutchfield Avenue
Nashville, TN 37210
Phone: (615) 320-3149; (866) 851-4275; Fax: (615) 320-3151
Email: contactus@applyists.com
Web: www.tylenol.com/page.jhtml?id=tylenol/news/subptyschol.inc

Summary: To provide financial assistance for college or graduate school to students intending to prepare for a career in a health-related field.
Eligibility: Open to students who have completed at least 1 year of an undergraduate or graduate course of study at an accredited 2- or 4-year college, university, or vocational/technical school. Applicants must be working on a degree in health education, medicine, nursing, pharmacy, or public health. Along with their application, they must submit 1) a 500-word essay on the experiences or persons that have contributed to their plans to prepare for a career in a health-related field; and 2) a 100-word summary of their professional plans. Selection is based on the essays, academic record, community involvement, and college GPA.
Financial data: Stipends are $10,000 or $5,000.
Duration: 1 year.
Number awarded: 40 each year: 10 at $10,000 and 30 at $5,000.
Deadline: May of each year.

2401 UNITED HEALTH FOUNDATION LATINO HEALTH SCHOLARS PROGRAM

Hispanic College Fund
Attn: Scholarship Processing
1301 K Street, N.W., Suite 450-A West
Washington, DC 20005
Phone: (202) 296-5400; (800) 644-4223; Fax: (202) 296-3774
Email: hcf-info@hispanicfund.org
Web: scholarships.hispanicfund.org/applications

Summary: To provide financial assistance to Hispanic American undergraduate and graduate students who are interested in preparing for a career in the health field.
Eligibility: Open to U.S. citizens and permanent residents of Hispanic background (at least 1 grandparent must be 100% Hispanic) who are high school seniors or graduates. Applicants must be enrolled or planning to enroll full-time at an accredited 2- or 4-year college, university, or vocational/technical school to work on an undergraduate or graduate degree in a health-related field. They must have a GPA of 3.0 or higher, be able to demonstrate financial need, and be able to demonstrate a commitment to working in underserved communities, including community health centers. Relevant fields of study include medicine, nursing, mental health, pharmacy, public health, allied health, and health sciences.
Financial data: Stipends range from $2,500 to $5,000 per year, depending on the need of the recipient. Funds are paid directly to the student's college or university to help cover tuition and fees.
Duration: 1 year; recipients may reapply.
Number awarded: Varies each year; recently, a total of $42,500 was available for this program.
Deadline: March of each year.

2402 UNITED HEALTH FOUNDATION SCHOLARSHIP

Hispanic Association of Colleges and Universities
Attn: National Scholarship Program
8415 Datapoint Drive, Suite 400
San Antonio, TX 78229
Phone: (210) 692-3805; Fax: (210) 692-0823; TDD: (800) 855-2880
Email: scholarships@hacu.net
Web: www.hacu.net/hacu/Scholarships_EN.asp?SnID=875148054

Summary: To provide financial assistance to undergraduate and graduate students who are working on a degree in a health-related field at institutions that belong to the Hispanic Association of Colleges and Universities (HACU).
Eligibility: Open to full-time undergraduate and graduate students who are enrolled at a 2- or 4-year HACU member institution. Applicants must be working on a degree in health sciences or allied health. They must have a GPA of 3.0 or higher and be able to demonstrate financial need. Along with their application, they must submit an essay of 200 to 250 words that describes their academic and/or career goals, where they expect to be and what they expect to be doing 10 years from now, and what skills they can bring to an employer.
Financial data: The stipend is $2,000.
Duration: 1 year; nonrenewable.
Number awarded: Varies each year.
Deadline: May of each year.

2403 UNITED HOSPICE FOUNDATION SCHOLARSHIP PROGRAM

United Hospice Foundation
Attn: Executive Director
1626 Jeurgens Court
Norcross, GA 30093
Phone: (678) 533-6462; (800) 956-5354; Fax: (678) 533-6463
Email: fpoole@unitedhospicefoundation.org
Web: www.unitedhospicefoundation.org/scholarships.html

Summary: To provide financial assistance to residents of designated southeastern states who are working on a degree in nursing, pharmacy, or therapy to prepare for a career working in hospice or long-term care.

Eligibility: Open to residents of Florida, Georgia, North Carolina, or South Carolina who are enrolled at an educational institution in any state. Applicants must be accepted or enrolled in 1) a nursing program and working on a diploma, associate, bachelor's, or master's degree as a registered nurse (R.N.) or licensed practical nurse (L.P.N.); 2) a school of pharmacy and working on a Pharm.D. degree; or 3) a school of rehabilitation working on a degree in physical therapy, occupational therapy, or speech therapy. They must be able to demonstrate financial need and a strong commitment to hospice nursing, long-term care, and/or pain management.

Financial data: The stipend is $1,000 per year.

Duration: 1 year; recipients may reapply, provided they maintain a "B" average.

Number awarded: 1 or more each year.

Deadline: June of each year.

2404 UPS FOUNDATION ACADEMIC SCHOLARSHIPS

American Association of Occupational Health Nurses, Inc.
Attn: AAOHN Foundation
7794 Grow Drive
Pensacola, FL 32514
Phone: (850) 474-6963; (800) 241-8014; Fax: (850) 484-8762
Email: aaohn@aaohn.org
Web: www.aaohn.org/scholarships/academic-study.html

Summary: To provide financial assistance to registered nurses who are working on a bachelor's or graduate degree to prepare for a career in occupational and environmental health.

Eligibility: Open to registered nurses who are enrolled in a baccalaureate or graduate degree program. Applicants must demonstrate an interest in, and commitment to, occupational and environmental health. Along with their application, they must submit a 500-word narrative on their professional goals as they relate to the academic activity and the field of occupational and environmental health. Selection is based on that essay (50%), impact of education on applicant's career (20%), and 2 letters of recommendation (30%).

Financial data: The stipend is $2,500.

Duration: 1 year; may be renewed up to 2 additional years.

Number awarded: 2 each year.

Deadline: January of each year.

2405 URBAN WATERSHED RESEARCH INSTITUTE SCHOLARSHIP

American Council of Engineering Companies of Colorado
Attn: Scholarship Coordinator
800 Grant Street, Suite 100
Denver, CO 80203
Phone: (303) 832-2200; Fax: (303) 832-0400
Email: acec@acec-co.org
Web: www.acec-co.org/education/scholarships.html

Summary: To provide financial assistance to students in Colorado currently working on a bachelor's degree in engineering.

Eligibility: Open to full-time students entering their junior, senior, or fifth year of an ABET-approved engineering program in Colorado. Applicants must be U.S. citizens. Along with their application, they must submit a 500-word essay on "What is the role or responsibility of the consulting engineer relative to shaping and protecting the natural environment?" Selection is based on the essay (25 points), cumulative GPA (28 points), work experience (20 points), a letter of recommendation (17 points), and college activities (10 points).

Financial data: The stipend is $2,500.

Duration: 1 year.

Number awarded: 1 each year.

Deadline: February of each year.

2406 URBAN WATERSHEDS SCHOLARSHIPS

American Public Works Association–Colorado Chapter
c/o Laura A. Kroeger, Scholarship Committee
Urban Drainage and Flood Control District
2480 West 26th Avenue, Suite 156-B
Denver, CO 80211
Phone: (303) 455-6277; Fax: (303) 455-7880
Email: lkroeger@udfcd.org
Web: colorado.apwa.net

Summary: To provide financial assistance to civil engineering undergraduate students in Colorado.

Eligibility: Open to sophomores and juniors majoring in civil engineering at colleges and universities in Colorado. Applicants must submit brief essays on their biggest challenge as a student, who or what influenced them to go into engineering, and how they like to spend their free time. They must be recommended by a faculty member. Financial need is not considered in the selection process.

Financial data: The stipend is $2,000.

Duration: 1 year.

Number awarded: 1 each year.

Deadline: March of each year.

2407 USDA PUBLIC SERVICE LEADERS SCHOLARSHIP PROGRAM

Department of Agriculture
Hispanic-Serving Institutions National Program
Attn: Sandra Cortez
P.O. Box 44083
Washington, DC 20026-4083
Phone: (210) 486-3959
Email: sandra.cortez@ars.usda.gov
Web: www.usdascholarships.com/applications

Summary: To provide financial assistance and work experience to undergraduate and graduate students interested in a preparing for a career with the U.S. Department of Agriculture (USDA).

Eligibility: Open to undergraduate and graduate students who are U.S. citizens or in the final stages of obtaining U.S. citizenship. Applicants must be majoring in a field of interest to USDA and have a strong interest in a career in public service with that agency. They must have a GPA of 2.75 or higher and a major in a field of current interest to USDA for which internships are available. Recently, those included mathematics, statistics, agriculture, agribusiness, agricultural economics, management, marketing, accounting, finance, business agricultural production and technology, agronomy, animal science, and related fields. Applicants may be enrolled anywhere in the country, but they must meet the class level and academic field requirements for an available internship. Along with their application, they must submit 4 essays of 400 to 500 words each related to their interest in the program.

Financial data: Scholars receive full payment of tuition at their college or university, mandatory university fees, and books. Funds are sent directly to the school. During the summers, they receive a salary for their internship. Following graduation, they are guaranteed employment with USDA, and they are required to work 1 year for each year of financial assistance they receive.

Duration: 2 or 3 years.

Number awarded: Varies each year; recently, 7 of these scholarships were available.

Deadline: April of each year.

2408 USRA SCHOLARSHIPS

Universities Space Research Association
Attn: Scholarship Program
10227 Wincopin Circle, Suite 500
Columbia, MD 21044-3432
Phone: (410) 730-2656; Fax: (410) 730-3496
Email: info@hq.usra.edu
Web: www.usra.edu/cs/usra_scholarship_program

Summary: To provide financial assistance to upper-division students interested in preparing for a career in a space-related field.

Eligibility: Open to full-time undergraduate students who have shown a career interest in the physical sciences or engineering with an emphasis on space research or space science education. Applicants must be U.S. citizens who have completed at least 2 years at a 4-year accredited college or university that offers

courses leading to a degree in physical sciences or engineering (including, but not limited to, aerospace engineering, astronomy, biophysics, chemistry, chemical engineering, computer science, electrical engineering, geophysics, geology, mathematics, mechanical engineering, physics, and space science education). Selection is based on 2 letters of recommendation, a college transcript showing GPA of 3.5 or higher, and a 1-page statement of the applicant's qualifications and educational and career goals; financial need is not considered.
Financial data: The stipend is $1,000. Funds are paid directly to the recipient.
Duration: 1 year; recipients may reapply.
Number awarded: Varies each year; recently, 4 of these scholarships were awarded.
Deadline: April of each year.

2409 UTAH COUNCIL OF LAND SURVEYORS SCHOLARSHIP

Utah Council of Land Surveyors
P.O. Box 1032
Salt Lake City, UT 84110
Phone: (801) 964-6192; Fax: (801) 964-6192
Web: www.ucls.org/mc/page.do?sitePageId=29686&orgId=ucls
Summary: To provide financial assistance to residents of Utah who are preparing for a career in land surveying at a college in the state.
Eligibility: Open to Utah residents currently enrolled at a college or university in the state that offers a curriculum approved by the Utah Council of Land Surveyors Education Committee. Applicants must intend to take the Fundamentals of Surveying (FS), Principles and Practice of Surveying (PS), and the state final examination for licensure in Utah as a professional land surveyor. Selection is based on academic achievement, employment within a company that is presently engaged in the practice of land surveying, letters of recommendation, a statement of education and career goals, and financial need.
Financial data: The stipend is $2,200 per year.
Duration: 1 year; may be renewed.
Number awarded: 1 or more each year.
Deadline: May of each year.

2410 VADM SAMUEL L. GRAVELY, JR., USN (RET.) MEMORIAL SCHOLARSHIPS

Armed Forces Communications and Electronics Association
Attn: AFCEA Educational Foundation
4400 Fair Lakes Court
Fairfax, VA 22033-3899
Phone: (703) 631-6149; (800) 336-4583, ext. 6149; Fax: (703) 631-4693
Email: scholarship@afcea.org
Web: www.afcea.org/education/scholarships/undergraduate/Gravely.asp
Summary: To provide funding to students majoring in specified scientific fields at an Historically Black College or University (HBCU).
Eligibility: Open to sophomores and juniors enrolled full-or part-time at an accredited 2- or 4-year HBCU or in a distance learning or online degree program affiliated with those institutions. They must be working toward a degree in engineering (aerospace, computer, electrical, or systems), computer science, computer engineering technology, computer information systems, mathematics, physics, information systems management, or other field directly related to the support of U.S. intelligence or homeland security enterprises. Special consideration is given to military enlisted personnel and veterans.
Financial data: The stipend is $5,000.
Duration: 1 year; may be renewed.
Number awarded: At least 2 each year.
Deadline: October of each year.

2411 VANGUARD WOMEN IN INFORMATION TECHNOLOGY SCHOLARSHIP PROGRAM

Scholarship America
Attn: Scholarship Management Services
One Scholarship Way
P.O. Box 297
St. Peter, MN 56082
Phone: (507) 931-1682; (800) 537-4180; Fax: (507) 931-9168
Web: www.sms.scholarshipamerica.org/vanguardwomenintechnology
Summary: To provide financial assistance to women working on an undergraduate degree in fields related to information technology.
Eligibility: Open to women who are U.S. citizens or permanent residents. Applicants must be entering their senior year as a full-time student at an accredited 4-year college or university in the United States and have a GPA of 3.0 or higher. They must be working on a degree in computer science, computer engineering, web design, or other field related to information technology. Selection is based on academic record, demonstrated leadership and participation in school and community activities, honors, work experience, a statement of goals and aspirations, unusual personal or family circumstances, recommendations, and a resume; financial need is not considered.
Financial data: The stipend is $8,000.
Duration: 1 year; nonrenewable.
Number awarded: Up to 6 each year.
Deadline: November of each year.

2412 VARIAN RADIATION THERAPY STUDENT SCHOLARSHIPS

American Society of Radiologic Technologists
Attn: ASRT Education and Research Foundation
15000 Central Avenue, S.E.
Albuquerque, NM 87123-3909
Phone: (505) 298-4500, ext. 2541; (800) 444-2778, ext. 2541; Fax: (505) 298-5063
Email: foundation@asrt.org
Web: www.asrt.org/content/asrtfoundation/scholarships/varian.aspx
Summary: To provide financial assistance to students enrolled in entry-level radiation therapy programs.
Eligibility: Open to U.S. citizens, nationals, and permanent residents who are enrolled in an entry-level radiation therapy program. Applicants must have a GPA in radiologic sciences core courses of 3.0 or higher and be able to demonstrate financial need. They may not have a previous degree or certificate in radiation therapy. Along with their application, they must submit 150-word essays on 1) their reason for entering the radiologic sciences; 2) their career goals; 3) their financial need; and 4) why they should receive this scholarship.
Financial data: The stipend is $5,000.
Duration: 1 year; may be renewed for 1 additional year.
Number awarded: Varies each year; recently, 19 of these scholarships were awarded.
Deadline: January of each year.

2413 VERIZON FOUNDATION SCHOLARSHIP PROGRAM OF THE HISPANIC SCHOLARSHIP FUND

Hispanic Scholarship Fund
Attn: Selection Committee
55 Second Street, Suite 1500
San Francisco, CA 94105
Phone: (415) 808-2365; (877) HSF-INFO; Fax: (415) 808-2302
Email: scholar1@hsf.net
Web: www.hsf.net/Scholarships.aspx?id=796
Summary: To provide financial assistance to Hispanic students from selected areas who are working on an undergraduate degree in selected engineering or business fields.
Eligibility: Open to U.S. citizens, permanent residents, and visitors with a passport stamped I-551 who are of Hispanic heritage. Applicants must be enrolled full-time at a 4-year college or university in the United States, Puerto Rico, Guam, or the U.S. Virgin Islands and have a GPA of 3.0 or higher. They must be majoring in accounting, business, computer engineering, computer science, electrical engineering, finance, human resource management, industrial engineering, information technology, marketing, or mechanical engineering. The program is restricted to residents of New York City, Washington, D.C., and the states of California, Florida, Illinois, Maine, Massachusetts, New Hampshire, New Jersey, Pennsylvania, Texas, Virginia, and Washington. Selection is based on academic achievement, personal strengths, leadership, and financial need.
Financial data: The stipend ranges from $2,500 to $5,000.
Duration: 1 year.
Number awarded: 1 or more each year.
Deadline: July of each year.

2414 VERIZON/HENAAC SCHOLARS PROGRAM

Great Minds in STEM
Attn: HENAAC Scholars
3900 Whiteside Street

Los Angeles, CA 90063
Phone: (323) 262-0997; Fax: (323) 262-0946
Email: kbbarrera@greatmindsinstem.org
Web: www.greatmindsinstem.org/henaac/scholars

Summary: To provide financial assistance to Hispanic undergraduate students from any state who are enrolled at universities in designated states and majoring in selected fields of science or engineering.

Eligibility: Open to Hispanic undergraduate students from any state who are enrolled at a college or university in California, Florida, Illinois, New Jersey, New York, North Carolina, Pennsylvania, or Texas. Applicants must be of Hispanic origin and/or must significantly participate in and promote organizations and activities in the Hispanic community. They must have a GPA of 3.0 or higher and be majoring in computer information systems, computer programming, computer science, electrical engineering, industrial engineering, information technology, management information systems, or mechanical engineering. Along with their application, they must submit a 700-word essay on a topic that changes annually; recently, students were asked to write on how they see their academic major contributing to global efforts and technology and how they, in their field of study, will contribute to global progress as well as actively contribute to their local communities. Selection is based on leadership through academic achievements and campus and community activities; financial need is not considered. U.S. citizenship is required.

Financial data: Stipends range from $500 to $5,000.

Duration: 1 year; recipients may reapply.

Number awarded: Varies each year; recently, 5 of these scholarships were awarded.

Deadline: April of each year.

2415 VERIZON SCHOLARSHIP PROGRAM OF THE HISPANIC COLLEGE FUND

Hispanic College Fund
Attn: Scholarship Processing
1301 K Street, N.W., Suite 450-A West
Washington, DC 20005
Phone: (202) 296-5400; (800) 644-4223; Fax: (202) 296-3774
Email: hcf-info@hispanicfund.org
Web: scholarships.hispanicfund.org/applications

Summary: To provide financial assistance to Hispanic American undergraduate students who are working on a degree in specified fields.

Eligibility: Open to U.S. citizens and permanent residents of Hispanic background (at least 1 grandparent must be 100% Hispanic) who are working full-time on a degree in accounting, business administration, computer engineering, computer science, finance, or information technology. Applicants must have a cumulative GPA of 3.0 or higher and be able to demonstrate financial need. They must be enrolled or planning to enroll at an accredited college or university in the 50 states or Puerto Rico.

Financial data: Stipends range from $500 to $5,000, depending on the need of the recipient. Funds are paid directly to the recipient's college or university to help cover tuition and fees.

Duration: 1 year; recipients may reapply.

Number awarded: Varies each year.

Deadline: March of each year.

2416 VERMONT DENTAL HYGIENE SCHOLARSHIP

Vermont Student Assistance Corporation
Attn: Scholarship Programs
10 East Allen Street
P.O. Box 2000
Winooski, VT 05404-2601
Phone: (802) 654-3798; (888) 253-4819; Fax: (802) 654-3765; TDD: (800) 281-3341 (within VT)
Email: info@vsac.org
Web: services.vsac.org/wps/wcm/connect/vsac/VSAC

Summary: To provide financial assistance to Vermont residents who are studying dental hygiene at a school in any state.

Eligibility: Open to residents of Vermont who are currently enrolled in the second year of a dental hygiene program. Applicants must submit 1) a 100-word essay on their interest in and commitment to pursuing their chosen career or vocation; 2) a 250-word essay on their short- and long-term academic, educational, career, vocational, and/or employment goals; and 3) a 250-word essay on what they believe distinguishes their application from others that may be submitted. Selection is based on those essays, academic achievement, letters of recommendation, and financial need.

Financial data: Stipends range up to $8,000 (for scholarships sponsored by the Hill family) or up to $4,000 (for students at Vermont Technical College).

Duration: 1 year; nonrenewable.

Number awarded: Varies each year; recently, 5 of these scholarships were awarded.

Deadline: March of each year.

2417 VERMONT FEED DEALERS AND MANUFACTURERS ASSOCIATION SCHOLARSHIP

Vermont Student Assistance Corporation
Attn: Scholarship Programs
10 East Allen Street
P.O. Box 2000
Winooski, VT 05404-2601
Phone: (802) 654-3798; (888) 253-4819; Fax: (802) 654-3765; TDD: (800) 281-3341 (within VT)
Email: info@vsac.org
Web: services.vsac.org/wps/wcm/connect/vsac/VSAC

Summary: To provide financial assistance to residents of Vermont who are interested in majoring in an agriculture-related field at a college in any state.

Eligibility: Open to high school seniors, high school graduates, and currently-enrolled college students in Vermont who are enrolled or planning to enroll in a postsecondary degree program in any state. Applicants must be interested in majoring in a field related to agriculture, including (but not limited to) animal sciences, equine studies, agribusiness, plant and soil science, forestry, horticulture, or veterinary medicine or technology. Along with their application, they must submit 1) a 100-word essay on their interest in and commitment to pursuing their chosen career or vocation; 2) a 250-word essay on their short- and long-term academic, educational, career, vocational, and/or employment goals; and 3) a 250-word essay on what they believe distinguishes their application from others that may be submitted. Selection is based on those essays and a letter of recommendation.

Financial data: The maximum stipend is $3,000.

Duration: 1 year; recipients may reapply.

Number awarded: Varies each year; recently, 6 of these scholarships were awarded.

Deadline: March of each year.

2418 VERMONT HEALTHCARE HUMAN RESOURCES ASSOCIATION SCHOLARSHIP

Vermont Student Assistance Corporation
Attn: Scholarship Programs
10 East Allen Street
P.O. Box 2000
Winooski, VT 05404-2601
Phone: (802) 654-3798; (888) 253-4819; Fax: (802) 654-3765; TDD: (800) 281-3341 (within VT)
Email: info@vsac.org
Web: services.vsac.org/wps/wcm/connect/vsac/VSAC

Summary: To provide financial assistance to nontraditional students in Vermont who are interested in majoring in a health-related field or human resources at a college in any state.

Eligibility: Open to nontraditional students who reside in Vermont and have been accepted to attend an accredited postsecondary school in any state to work on a degree in a health care field and/or human resources. Applicants must intend to work in Vermont for at least 1 year. Along with their application, they must submit 1) a 100-word essay on their interest in and commitment to pursuing their chosen career or vocation; and 2) a 250-word essay on their short- and long-term academic, educational, career, vocational, and/or employment goals. Selection is based on those essays, commitment to employment in Vermont, financial need, a letter of recommendation, and a resume.

Financial data: The stipend is $1,000.

Duration: 1 year.

Number awarded: 1 or 2 each year.

Deadline: April of each year.

2419 VERMONT STATE DENTAL HYGIENIST INCENTIVE LOAN PROGRAM

Vermont Student Assistance Corporation
Attn: Scholarship Programs
10 East Allen Street

P.O. Box 2000
Winooski, VT 05404-2601
Phone: (802) 654-3798; (888) 253-4819; Fax: (802) 654-3765; TDD: (800) 281-3341 (within VT)
Email: info@vsac.org
Web: services.vsac.org/wps/wcm/connect/vsac/VSAC

Summary: To provide financial assistance to residents of Vermont who are studying dental hygiene at a school in any state.

Eligibility: Open to residents of Vermont who have completed the first year of a dental hygiene program at a school in any state. Applicants must intend to complete the program and work as a dental hygienist in Vermont for at least 1 year following licensure. Along with their application, they must submit 1) a 100-word essay on their interest in and commitment to pursuing their chosen career or vocation; and 2) a 250-word essay on their short- and long-term academic, educational, career, vocational, and/or employment goals. Selection is based on those essays, financial need, and a letter of recommendation.

Financial data: The loan is $5,000. If the recipient passes the NDHBE, NERB, and state licensing examinations and completes 1 year of employment as a dental hygienist in Vermont, the loan is forgiven.

Duration: 1 year.

Number awarded: Varies each year; recently, 4 of these loans were granted.

Deadline: March of each year.

2420 VERMONT STATE NURSE INCENTIVE LOAN PROGRAM

Vermont Student Assistance Corporation
Attn: Scholarship Programs
10 East Allen Street
P.O. Box 2000
Winooski, VT 05404-2601
Phone: (802) 654-3798; (888) 253-4819; Fax: (802) 654-3765; TDD: (800) 281-3341 (within VT)
Email: info@vsac.org
Web: services.vsac.org/wps/wcm/connect/vsac/VSAC

Summary: To provide financial assistance to Vermont residents who are interested in earning a nursing degree and then working within the state.

Eligibility: Open to high school seniors, high school graduates, and currently-enrolled college students in Vermont. Applicants must be enrolled or planning to enroll in 1) an accredited licensed practical nursing (L.P.N.) degree program; 2) the final year of an accredited associate in nursing (A.S., R.N.) degree program; 3) the final 2 years of an accredited bachelor of science in nursing (B.S.N., R.N.) degree program; or 4) the master's entry program in nursing (M.E.P.N.). They must intend to work in Vermont or within 10 miles of the Vermont border for at least 1 year following licensure as an L.P.N. or R.N. Along with their application, they must submit 1) a 100-word essay on their interest in and commitment to pursuing their chosen career or vocation; and 2) a 250-word essay on their short- and long-term academic, educational, career, vocational, and/or employment goals. Selection is based on those essays, financial need, and a letter of recommendation.

Financial data: The maximum award is $6,000 per year. This is a scholarship/loan program. Funds are provided as an interest-free loan, but the debt is cancelled if the recipient successfully graduates from the L.P.N. or R.N. degree program and completes 1 year of employment in Vermont or within 10 miles of the Vermont border.

Duration: 1 year.

Number awarded: Approximately 13 each year.

Deadline: March of each year.

2421 VERTICAL FLIGHT FOUNDATION ENGINEERING SCHOLARSHIPS

Vertical Flight Foundation
Attn: Scholarship Coordinator
217 North Washington Street
Alexandria, VA 22314-2538
Phone: (703) 684-6777; Fax: (703) 739-9279
Email: Staff@vtol.org
Web: www.vtol.org/vff.html

Summary: To provide financial assistance to undergraduate and graduate students interested in preparing for a career in rotorcraft and vertical-takeoff-and-landing (VTOL) aircraft engineering.

Eligibility: Open to full-time students in the final 2 years of undergraduate study or the first year of graduate study at an accredited school of engineering. They need not be a member or relative of a member of the American Helicopter Society. Along with their application, they must submit a narrative that covers their past and future academic interests, future career interest in the rotorcraft or VTOL engineering field, past work or research experience related to rotorcraft or VTOL aircraft, and other reasons for consideration. Selection is based on academic record, letters of recommendation, and career plans.

Financial data: Stipends range from $1,000 to $4,000 per year, depending on the availability of funds.

Duration: Students are eligible to receive a scholarship once as an undergraduate, once as a master's student, and once as a doctoral student.

Number awarded: Varies each year; recently, 16 of these scholarships were awarded.

Deadline: January of each year.

2422 VETERANS OF ENDURING FREEDOM (AFGHANISTAN) AND IRAQI FREEDOM SCHOLARSHIP

Armed Forces Communications and Electronics Association
Attn: AFCEA Educational Foundation
4400 Fair Lakes Court
Fairfax, VA 22033-3899
Phone: (703) 631-6149; (800) 336-4583, ext. 6149; Fax: (703) 631-4693
Email: scholarship@afcea.org
Web: www.afcea.org/education/scholarships/undergraduate/veteran.asp

Summary: To provide financial assistance to veterans and military personnel who served in Afghanistan or Iraq and are working on an undergraduate degree in fields related to the support of U.S. intelligence enterprises.

Eligibility: Open to active-duty and honorably discharged U.S. military members (including Reservists and National Guard personnel) who served in Enduring Freedom (Afghanistan) or Iraqi Freedom operations. Applicants must be enrolled at a 2- or 4-year institution in the United States and working on an undergraduate degree in computer engineering technology, computer information systems, computer network systems, computer science, electronics engineering technology, engineering (aerospace, computer, electrical, or systems), information systems management, information systems security, mathematics, physics, science or mathematics education, technology management, or other field directly related to the support of U.S. intelligence enterprises or national security. Along with their application, they must submit an essay that includes a brief synopsis of relevant work experience (including military assignments), a brief statement of career goals after graduation, and an explanation of how their academic and career goals will contribute to the areas related to communications, intelligence and/or information systems, and the mission of the Armed Forces Communications and Electronics Association (AFCEA). Financial need is also considered in the selection process.

Financial data: The stipend is $2,500.

Duration: 1 year.

Number awarded: 6 each year: 3 for the fall semester and 3 for the spring semester.

Deadline: March of each year for fall semester; October of each year for spring semester.

2423 VIOLET E. MACLAREN CONSERVATION SCHOLARSHIP

Garden Club Federation of Massachusetts, Inc.
c/o Katherine Jones, Scholarship Secretary
40 Berkshire Drive
Williamstown, MA 01267-2518
Email: gcfmscholarship@aol.com
Web: gardencentral.org/gcfm/scholarships

Summary: To provide financial assistance to residents of Massachusetts interested in working on an undergraduate or graduate degree in a field related to conservation at a college in any state.

Eligibility: Open to high school seniors, undergraduates, and graduate students who have been residents of Massachusetts for at least 1 year. Applicants must be working on or planning to work on a degree in a field related to conservation, including floriculture, landscape design, horticulture, forestry, agronomy, city planning, environmental studies, land management, botany, or biology. They must have a GPA of 3.0 or higher. Along with their application, they must submit official transcripts; a brief essay about their goals, aspirations, and career plans; a list of their activities, including special honors and/or leadership positions; 3 letters of recommendation; and documentation of financial need.

Financial data: The stipend is $1,000.

Duration: 1 year.

Number awarded: Varies each year.

Deadline: February of each year.

2424 VIRGINIA ASSOCIATION OF SOIL AND WATER CONSERVATION DISTRICTS SCHOLARSHIPS

Virginia Association of Soil and Water Conservation Districts
Attn: VASWCD Educational Foundation, Inc.
7308 Hanover Green Drive, Suite 100
Mechanicsville, VA 23111
Phone: (804) 559-0324; Fax: (804) 559-0325
Web: www.vaswcd.org/scholarship.htm

Summary: To provide financial assistance to residents of Virginia interested in majoring in natural resource conservation and/or environmental studies at a college in any state.

Eligibility: Open to seniors graduating from high schools in Virginia who plan to enroll full-time at a college or university in any state to study natural resource conservation and/or environmental studies. Applicants must rank in the top 20% of their class or have a GPA of 3.0 or higher. They must be nominated by the local Virginia Soil and Water Conservation District within which they reside. Each district may nominate only 1 student. Selection is based on academic record and interest in conservation; financial need may also be considered.

Financial data: The stipend is $1,000.

Duration: 1 year.

Number awarded: Varies each year; recently, 11 of those scholarships were awarded.

Deadline: Applications must be submitted to a local Soil and Water Conservation District office by March of each year.

2425 VIRGINIA ATHLETIC TRAINERS ASSOCIATION SCHOLARSHIP AWARD

Virginia Athletic Trainers Association
c/o Terry Zablocki, Scholarship Committee Chair
Maury High School
322 Shirley Avenue
Norfolk, VA 23517
Phone: (757) 628-9189
Email: tzablocki@nps.k12.va.us
Web: www.vata.us/scholarship/index.htm

Summary: To provide financial assistance to high school seniors in Virginia who are interested in attending college in any state to prepare for a career as an athletic trainer.

Eligibility: Open to seniors graduating from high schools in Virginia who intend to study athletic training at a college or university in any state. Applicants must provide evidence of interest in athletic training through experience as a high school student athletic trainer and/or attendance at an athletic training seminar or workshop. Along with their application, they must submit an essay of 250 to 500 words on their interest in a career in the allied health profession of athletic training. Selection is based on academic ability, leadership ability, responsible citizenship, and dedication and interest in athletic training.

Financial data: Stipends are $1,000 or $500.

Duration: 1 year.

Number awarded: 2 each year: 1 at $1,000 and 1 at $500.

Deadline: March of each year.

2426 VIRGINIA "BEA" ROOT NURSING SCHOLARSHIP

Wisconsin Paralyzed Veterans of America
Attn: Scholarship Committee
2311 South 108th Street
West Allis, WI 53227-1901
Phone: (414) 328-8910; (800) 875-WPVA; Fax: (414) 328-8948
Email: info@wisconsinpva.org
Web: www.wisconsinpva.org/scholarships.html

Summary: To provide financial assistance to seniors in nursing programs in Wisconsin who are interested in working in a spinal cord injury unit or rehabilitation facility after graduation.

Eligibility: Open to students enrolled in the final year of an NLN-accredited nursing program in Wisconsin. Applicants must be willing to seek employment in a spinal cord injury unit or rehabilitation facility after graduation. They must be able to demonstrate financial need.

Financial data: The stipend is $1,000 or $500.

Duration: 1 year.

Number awarded: 2 each year: 1 at $1,000 and 1 at $500.

Deadline: March of each year.

2427 VIRGINIA C. PHILLIPS UNDERGRADUATE SCHOLARSHIP AWARD

South Carolina Nurses Foundation, Inc.
Attn: Virginia C. Phillips Scholarship Fund
1821 Gadsden Street
Columbia, SC 29201
Phone: (803) 252-4781; Fax: (803) 779-3870
Email: brownk1@aol.com
Web: www.scnursesfoundation.org

Summary: To provide financial assistance to nurses in South Carolina who are enrolled in a bachelor's degree program in public health nursing.

Eligibility: Open to nurses who are currently employed with at least 2 years' experience in public health nursing in South Carolina. Applicants must be enrolled in a bachelor's of science in nursing program and have successfully completed 10 hours of course work. Along with their application, they must submit a 1-page narrative that describes their contributions to public/community health nursing and future career goals in public health nursing. Financial need is not considered in the selection process.

Financial data: The stipend is $1,500.

Duration: 1 year.

Number awarded: 1 each year.

Deadline: July of each year.

2428 VIRGINIA ELIZABETH AND ALMA VANE TAYLOR NURSING SCHOLARSHIP

Winston-Salem Foundation
Attn: Student Aid Department
860 West Fifth Street
Winston-Salem, NC 27101-2506
Phone: (336) 725-2382; (866) 227-1209; Fax: (336) 727-0581
Email: info@wsfoundation.org
Web: www.wsfoundation.org/students

Summary: To provide financial assistance to residents of North Carolina interested in studying nursing at a school in the state.

Eligibility: Open to traditional and nontraditional students in North Carolina who are interested in working on an associate or baccalaureate degree in nursing at a school in the state. Applicants must have a high school or college cumulative GPA of 2.5 or higher and be able to demonstrate financial need. Preference is given to residents of Davidson, Davie, Forsyth, Stokes, Surry, and Yadkin counties. Some of the scholarships are set aside for eligible noncitizens.

Financial data: The stipend is $1,200 per year.

Duration: 1 year; may be renewed.

Number awarded: 1 or more each year, including 5 scholarships set aside for eligible noncitizens.

Deadline: August of each year.

2429 VIRGINIA ENGINEER SCHOLARSHIP PROGRAM

Virginia Department of Transportation
Attn: Scholarship Coordinator
VDOT Learning Center
1401 East Broad Street, 10th Floor
Richmond, VA 23219-1939
Phone: (804) 786-3875; Fax: (804) 786-4290
Email: scholarship@VirginiaDOT.org
Web: www.VirginiaDOT.org/jobs/engscholprog.asp

Summary: To provide financial assistance and work experience to college students working on a degree in civil engineering or civil engineering technology in Virginia.

Eligibility: Open to students who are entering their junior or senior year in a bachelor's degree program in civil engineering or civil engineering technology. Applicants must have a GPA of 2.5 or higher, be interested in a career with the Virginia Department of Transportation, take at least 12 credit hours per semester, be residents of Virginia or attending a school in Virginia, and be U.S. citizens or permanent residents. Selection is based on scholastic record, interest in the field of civil engineering (specifically highway engineering), participation in extracurricular activities, volunteer experiences, employment history, and recommendations.

Financial data: Students receive a stipend of $3,500 per semester. Funds can be spent on any educational expense, including fees, tuition, books, and housing. This is a scholarship/loan program. Immediately following satisfactory completion of the required civil engineering degree, the recipient agrees to continue employment with the Virginia Department of Transportation as an engi-

neering trainee. Recipients must work 6 months for each academic semester of course work funded by the program. Funds must be repaid with interest if the recipient fails to remain in school full-time and work on a degree in civil engineering, fails to maintain a GPA of 2.5 or higher, or fails to accept employment with the Virginia Department of Transportation immediately after graduation.
Duration: 1 year; may be renewed up to 3 additional years, provided the recipient maintains full-time enrollment and a GPA of 2.5 or higher.
Number awarded: 40 each year.
Deadline: January of each year.

2430 VIRGINIA LEYDA ROBERTS NURSING SCHOLARSHIP

Daughters of the American Revolution–Colorado State Society
c/o Marcy Kimminau, State Scholarship Chair
17537 West 59th Place
Golden, CO 80403-2022
Email: marcyk12@aol.com
Web: www.coloradodar.org/scholarships.htm
Summary: To provide financial assistance to high school seniors in Colorado who are interested in studying nursing at a school in any state.
Eligibility: Open to graduating high school seniors in Colorado who are 1) U.S. citizens; 2) in the top third of their graduating class; and 3) accepted at an accredited school of nursing in any state. Applications must include a statement of career interest and goals (up to 500 words), 2 character references, college transcripts, a letter of sponsorship from the Daughters of the American Revolution's Colorado chapter, and a list of scholastic achievements, extracurricular activities, honors, and other significant accomplishments. Selection is based on academic excellence, commitment to field of study, and financial need.
Financial data: The stipend is $1,000. Funds are paid directly to the student's school.
Duration: 1 year; nonrenewable.
Number awarded: 1 each year.
Deadline: January of each year.

2431 VIRGINIA NURSES FOUNDATION SCHOLARSHIP

Virginia Nurses Association
Attn: Virginia Nurses Foundation
7113 Three Chopt Road, Suite 204
Richmond, VA 23226
Phone: (804) 282-1808; (800) 868-6877; Fax: (804) 282-4916
Email: admin@virginianurses.com
Web: www.virginianurses.com/displaycommon.cfm?an=9
Summary: To provide financial assistance to registered nurses in Virginia working on a bachelor's degree at a school in any state.
Eligibility: Open to registered nurses who are residents of Virginia. Applicants must be enrolled in an R.N. to B.S.N. program at a school in any state and have a GPA of 3.0 or higher. They must intend to practice in Virginia. Selection is based on academic achievement, commitment to nursing, and clinical and leadership abilities.
Financial data: The stipend is $2,000.
Duration: 1 year.
Number awarded: 1 each year.
Deadline: September of each year.

2432 VIVA TECHNOLOGY/HENAAC SCHOLARS PROGRAM

Great Minds in STEM
Attn: HENAAC Scholars
3900 Whiteside Street
Los Angeles, CA 90063
Phone: (323) 262-0997; Fax: (323) 262-0946
Email: kbbarrera@greatmindsinstem.org
Web: www.greatmindsinstem.org/henaac/scholars
Summary: To provide financial assistance to Hispanic undergraduate students majoring in fields of science, technology, engineering, or mathematics (STEM).
Eligibility: Open to Hispanic undergraduate students who are working on a degree in a field of STEM. Applicants must be of Hispanic origin and/or must significantly participate in and promote organizations and activities in the Hispanic community. They must have participated as a college captain at a Viva Technology Program and have a GPA of 3.0 or higher. Along with their application, they must submit a 700-word essay on a topic that changes annually; recently, students were asked to write on how they see their academic major contributing to global efforts and technology and how they, in their field of study, will contribute to global progress as well as actively contribute to their local communities. Selection is based on leadership through academic achievements and campus and community activities; financial need is not considered.
Financial data: Stipends range from $500 to $5,000.
Duration: 1 year; recipients may reapply.
Number awarded: Varies each year; recently, 4 of these scholarships were awarded.
Deadline: April of each year.

2433 VTCA AGGREGATE PRODUCER SCHOLARSHIP

Virginia Transportation Construction Alliance
620 Moorefield Park Drive, Suite 120
Richmond, VA 23236-3692
Phone: (804) 330-3312; Fax: (804) 330-3850
Email: stephanie@vtca.org
Web: www.vtca.org/about_vtca/vtca_programs_and_scholarships
Summary: To provide financial assistance to currently-enrolled college students in Virginia who are majoring in designated fields related to the aggregates industry.
Eligibility: Open to freshmen, sophomores, or juniors from any state working full-time on a degree at a 4-year institution in Virginia. Applicants must be majoring in civil engineering, construction management, geology, or mining and mineral engineering. Along with their application, they must submit an essay of 250 to 500 words on 1) why they are interested in preparing for a career in the aggregates industries; and 2) their interest in interning with a member firm of the Virginia Transportation Construction Alliance (VTCA). Selection is based on academic performance, employment experience, extracurricular and leadership activities, and demonstrated interest in the aggregates industries. U.S. citizenship is required.
Financial data: The stipend is $1,500 per year.
Duration: 1 year; recipients may reapply.
Number awarded: 1 each year.
Deadline: April of each year.

2434 W. REESE HARRIS AGRICULTURAL SCHOLARSHIP

Florida Federation of Garden Clubs, Inc.
Attn: Scholarship Chair
1400 South Denning Drive
Winter Park, FL 32789-5662
Phone: (407) 647-7016; Fax: (407) 647-5479
Email: ffgc@earthlink.net
Web: www.ffgc.org/education/ffgc_scholarships.html
Summary: To provide financial aid to Florida residents working on an undergraduate or graduate degree in a field related to agriculture at a school in the state.
Eligibility: Open to Florida residents who are enrolled as full-time sophomores, juniors, seniors, or graduate students at a college or university in the state. Applicants must be enrolled in a college of agriculture to major in agronomy, horticulture, environmental science, or a related field. They must have a GPA of 3.0 or higher and be able to demonstrate financial need. U.S. citizenship is required.
Financial data: The stipend is $2,500. The funds are sent directly to the recipient's school and distributed semiannually.
Duration: 1 year.
Number awarded: 1 each year.
Deadline: April of each year.

2435 WAAIME SCHOLARSHIPS

Woman's Auxiliary to the American Institute of Mining, Metallurgical and Petroleum Engineers
c/o Society for Mining, Metallurgy, and Exploration, Inc.
Student Center
8307 Shaffer Parkway
Littleton, CO 80127-4102
Phone: (303) 948-4208; (800) 763-3132; Fax: (303) 948-4265
Email: estrada@smenet.org
Web: www.smenet.org/scholarships

Summary: To provide financial assistance to upper-division and graduate students working on a degree in earth sciences as related to the minerals industry.
Eligibility: Open to full-time upper-division students (juniors or seniors) or graduate students (program space permitting) who are working on a degree in earth sciences as related to and supporting the efforts of the minerals industry. Acceptable areas of study include chemical engineering, geological sciences, materials science and engineering, metallurgy, mineral sciences, mining economics, petroleum engineering, and other related fields. Preference is given to undergraduate applicants. Selection is based on character, academic standing, and financial need.
Financial data: Recently, stipends averaged $3,000.
Duration: 1 year; may be renewed.
Number awarded: Varies each year; recently, more than 50 students received support from this program.
Deadline: January of each year.

2436 WALLACE F. PATE SCHOLARSHIP

Harry Hampton Memorial Wildlife Fund, Inc.
P.O. Box 2641
Columbia, SC 29202
Phone: (803) 463-7387; Fax: (803) 749-9362
Email: mpugh@sc.rr.com
Web: www.hamptonwildlifefund.org/scholarship.html
Summary: To provide financial assistance to high school seniors in South Carolina who plan to major in a field related to natural resources at a college or university in the state.
Eligibility: Open to seniors graduating from high schools in South Carolina who plan to attend an institution of higher learning in the state. Applicants must be planning to major in a field related to natural resources, including wildlife, fisheries, biology, zoology, forestry, marine science, or environmental science. Along with their application, they must submit a 3-page autobiography that explains their interest in wildlife resources, the environment, coastal resources, or related topics and why they will be a good investment if they are awarded this scholarship. Financial need is also considered in the selection process.
Financial data: The stipend is $1,500.
Duration: 1 year; nonrenewable.
Number awarded: 1 each year.
Deadline: January of each year.

2437 WALMAN OPTICAL COMPANY SCHOLARSHIP

Walman Optical Company
c/o Scholarship America
Attn: Scholarship Management Services
One Scholarship Way
P.O. Box 297
St. Peter, MN 56082
Phone: (507) 931-1682; (800) 537-4180; Fax: (507) 931-9168
Email: smsinfo@csfa.org
Web: www.walman.com/default.aspx?File=scholarship.htm&Section=100
Summary: To provide financial assistance to students enrolled at schools and colleges of optometry throughout the country.
Eligibility: Open to students currently enrolled in the second or third year of a full-time 4-year program leading to a Doctor of Optometry degree at a school selected by Walman Optical Company. Selection is based on academic record, demonstrated leadership and participation in school and community activities, honors, work experience, a statement of goals and aspirations, unusual personal or family circumstances, and an outside appraisal.
Financial data: The stipend ranges from $500 to $3,000 per year, depending on the need of the recipient.
Duration: 1 year; nonrenewable, although recipients may reapply.
Number awarded: Varies each year.
Deadline: April of each year.

2438 WALTER I.M. HODGE GRANT

Virgin Islands Board of Education
Dronningen Gade 60B, 61, and 62
P.O. Box 11900
St. Thomas, VI 00801
Phone: (340) 774-4546; Fax: (340) 774-3384
Email: stt@myviboe.com
Web: www.myviboe.com
Summary: To provide financial assistance to residents of the Virgin Islands who wish to study designated fields at a college in the territory or on the mainland.
Eligibility: Open to residents of the Virgin Islands who are seniors or graduates of high schools in the territory. Applicants must have a GPA of 2.0 or higher and be attending or accepted for enrollment at an accredited institution of higher learning in the territory or on the mainland. They must be planning to major in agriculture, animal husbandry, political science, veterinary science, or zoology. Financial need is considered in the selection process.
Financial data: The stipend is $5,000 per year.
Duration: 1 year.
Number awarded: 1 each year.
Deadline: April of each year.

2439 WALTER "PORKY" WHITE SCHOLARSHIP FUND

MIGIZI Communications, Inc.
Attn: Scholarship Committee
3123 East Lake Street
Minneapolis, MN 55406
Phone: (612) 721-6631; Fax: (612) 721-3936
Web: migizi.org/mig/scholarships.html
Summary: To provide financial assistance to Native American students working on an undergraduate or graduate degree in natural resources or an environmental field.
Eligibility: Open to Native American undergraduate and graduate students enrolled at an accredited 4-year college or university. Applicants must be working on a degree in environmental science, natural resource management, biology, marine biology, or a related discipline. Along with their application, they must submit documentation of financial need and a 500-word essay on 1) their current involvement in protecting and working with the environment and natural resources; 2) why it is important to protect and study our environment and natural resources; and 3) their plans for the future and how they plan to use their studies to help the community.
Financial data: The stipend is $1,000.
Duration: 1 year; nonrenewable.
Number awarded: 1 each year.
Deadline: May of each year.

2440 WALTER SAMUEL MCAFEE SCHOLARSHIP IN SPACE PHYSICS

National Society of Black Physicists
Attn: Scholarship Committee Chair
1100 North Glebe Road, Suite 1010
Arlington, VA 22201
Phone: (703) 536-4207; Fax: (703) 536-4203
Email: scholarship@nsbp.org
Web: www.nsbp.org/scholarships
Summary: To provide financial assistance to African American students majoring in space physics in college.
Eligibility: Open to African American students who are entering their junior or senior year of college and majoring in space physics. Applicants must submit an essay on their academic and career objectives, information on their participation in extracurricular activities, a description of any awards and honors they have received, and 3 letters of recommendation. Financial need is not considered.
Financial data: The stipend is $1,000.
Duration: 1 year; nonrenewable.
Number awarded: 1 each year.
Deadline: January of each year.

2441 WASHINGTON APPLE EDUCATION FOUNDATION SCHOLARSHIPS

Washington Apple Education Foundation
Attn: Scholarship Committee
2900 Euclid Avenue
Wenatchee, WA 98801
Phone: (509) 663-7713; Fax: (509) 663-7469
Email: waef@waef.org
Web: www.waef.org/index.php?page_id=238
Summary: To provide financial assistance to Washington residents who are involved in the tree fruit industry and interested in attending college in any state.

Eligibility: Open to Washington residents who are either graduating high school seniors or current students at a college or university in any state. Applicants must be involved in the Washington tree fruit industry, either preparing for a career in the industry or having been raised in a family involved in the industry. Along with their application, they must submit an official transcript, their SAT or ACT scores, 2 letters of reference, and an essay on an assigned topic. Financial need is also considered in the selection process.

Financial data: The stipend is $2,500. Funds may be used to pay for tuition, room, board, books, educational supplies, and miscellaneous institutional fees.

Duration: 1 year; recipients may reapply.

Number awarded: 5 each year.

Deadline: February of each year.

2442 WASHINGTON CATTLE FEEDERS ASSOCIATION SCHOLARSHIPS

Washington Cattle Feeders Association
P.O. Box 1256
Quincy, WA 98848
Phone: (509) 787-2921; Fax: (801) 751-2921
Email: ed@wafeeders.org
Web: wafeeders.org/page.php?showarticle=46b5b113bd801

Summary: To provide financial assistance to residents of Washington who have a connection to the beef industry and are interested in attending college in the state.

Eligibility: Open to residents of Washington who are high school seniors or students already enrolled at a college or university in the state. Applicants must have a family history in the beef industry and/or be planning a field of study pertaining to the beef cattle industry. Along with their application, they must submit a summary of their experience with feedlots, livestock, and/or agriculture; a statement of their future goals and how this scholarship will help them achieve those; and a resume showing their in-school and out-of school activities, awards or honors they have received, and any work experience. Financial need is not considered in the selection process.

Financial data: Stipends are $1,500 or $1,000.

Duration: 1 year.

Number awarded: Varies each year; recently, 5 of these scholarships were awarded.

Deadline: March of each year.

2443 WASHINGTON ENGINEERING EDUCATION INCENTIVE AWARDS

Washington Society of Professional Engineers
P.O. Box 1206
Sumas, WA 98295-1390
Phone: (866) 296-4324; Fax: (866) 296-4324
Email: wspe@washingtonengineer.org
Web: www.washingtonengineer.org/service_to_students.shtml

Summary: To provide financial assistance to community college students in Washington who plan to transfer to a 4-year engineering program in the state.

Eligibility: Open to students currently enrolled at a community college in Washington who are nominated by a faculty member at their college. Nominees must be planning to transfer to a 4-year university in the state with an engineering program that is accredited by the Engineering Accreditation Commission of the Accreditation Board for Engineering and Technology (EAC-ABET). Letters of nomination must be accompanied by the nominee's transcripts and a statement of interest in an engineering career. Selection is based on academic accomplishment and interest in preparing for a career in engineering.

Financial data: The stipend is $1,000.

Duration: 1 year; nonrenewable.

Number awarded: 2 to 4 each year.

Deadline: March of each year.

2444 WASHINGTON GET READY FOR MATH AND SCIENCE CONDITIONAL SCHOLARSHIP PROGRAM

Washington Higher Education Coordinating Board
917 Lakeridge Way
P.O. Box 43430
Olympia, WA 98504-3430
Phone: (360) 753-7845; (888) 535-0747; Fax: (360) 753-7808; TDD: (360) 753-7809
Email: futureteachers@hecb.wa.gov
Web: www.hecb.wa.gov/Paying/waaidprgm/GETREADYformathscience.asp

Summary: To provide financial assistance to high school students in Washington who are interested in attending college to prepare for a career in a mathematics or science program.

Eligibility: Open to students at high schools in Washington who participate as early as their sophomore year. Applicants must have a family income at or below 125% of the state median (currently, $97,095 or less for a family of 4) at the time of application and for the 2 preceding years. They must also 1) achieve a level 4 on the mathematics or science portion of the tenth-grade WASL; or 2) score above the 95th percentile on the mathematics section of either the SAT or ACT. Within 1 year of high school graduation, they must enroll at a college or university in Washington and major in a qualified mathematics or science program. Following graduation from college, they must work full-time in Washington in a qualified mathematics or science field, including computer sciences and mathematics, engineering, physical sciences (e.g., atmospheric and space science, chemistry, environmental science, materials science, physics), life sciences (e.g., agricultural and food science, biological technology), health professions (e.g., physician, physician assistant, nursing, veterinary science), or teaching, for at least 3 years.

Financial data: The maximum stipend is equal to resident undergraduate tuition and required state fees at the University of Washington. Students who fail to fulfill the mathematics or science service requirement must repay all funds received.

Duration: 1 year; may be renewed up to 4 additional years or until completion of 180 quarter credits (or semester equivalent), whichever comes first.

Number awarded: Varies each year.

Deadline: January of each year.

2445 WASHINGTON STATE HEALTH PROFESSIONAL SCHOLARSHIP PROGRAM

Washington Higher Education Coordinating Board
917 Lakeridge Way
P.O. Box 43430
Olympia, WA 98504-3430
Phone: (360) 596-4817; (888) 535-0747; Fax: (360) 664-9273; TDD: (360) 753-7809
Email: health@hecb.wa.gov
Web: www.hecb.wa.gov/Paying/waaidprgm/HPScholarshipPage.asp

Summary: To provide financial assistance for primary care health professional education to students who agree to work in designated areas of Washington after graduation.

Eligibility: Open to students enrolled or accepted for enrollment in an accredited program leading to eligibility for licensure in Washington State as a physician, osteopathic physician and surgeon, pharmacist, licensed midwife or certified nurse-midwife, physician assistant, nurse practitioner, nurse faculty, dentist, dental hygienist, registered nurse, or practical nurse. They must be U.S. citizens, but Washington residency is not required. Selection is based on prior experience in a rural or shortage area, academic and humanitarian achievements, letters of recommendation, academic standing, and commitment and experience in serving the medically underserved or shortage areas. Preference is given to applicants with community sponsorship and support. The community sponsor may be a rural hospital, a rural health care facility, a community clinic, or a local health care provider that can provide training or employment opportunities. Support should be a financial commitment that may include educational and living stipends, matching funds, or employment and training opportunities.

Financial data: The stipend is intended to cover eligible expenses: tuition, books, equipment, fees, and room and board. This is a scholarship/loan program. Recipients who fail to complete the course of study are required to repay the amount received, plus a penalty and interest. Scholars who fail to serve in a designated rural, underserved urban, or other health professional shortage area in Washington are required to repay the scholarship, with penalty plus interest.

Duration: Up to 5 years.

Number awarded: Varies each year.

Deadline: April of each year.

2446 WASHINGTON STATE NURSES FOUNDATION SCHOLARSHIPS

Washington State Nurses Association
Attn: Washington State Nurses Foundation
575 Andover Park West, Suite 101
Seattle, WA 98188-9961
Phone: (206) 575-7979; Fax: (206) 575-1908
Email: wsnf@wsna.org
Web: www.wsna.org/WSNF/Scholarship

Summary: To provide financial assistance to students in Washington preparing for a career as a registered nurse in the state.

Eligibility: Open to nursing students who are residents of Washington or attending a college or university in the state. Applicants must have a GPA of 3.0 or higher in a program leading to an associate, baccalaureate, or graduate degree. They must submit essays on the following topics: 1) their participation in school and volunteer activities, including offices and positions of leadership; 2) honors and awards they have received and the relevance of those to nursing; 3) special or unusual life experiences or activities that have made an impact on their nursing career or that assisted them to decide on nursing as a profession; 4) their long- and short-term goals for their nursing career; 5) what they anticipate their role in the Washington State Nurses Association (WSNA) will be, why it is important to them, and (if they are already an R.N.) their involvement in the organization and reasons for participation; and 6) their past work experience (both paid and volunteer) and why this may or may not impact their career in nursing. Undergraduate students must have completed at least 12 nursing credits in the R.N. program. Applicants who are already R.N.s must be members of the WSNA. Financial need is not considered in the selection process.

Financial data: The stipend is $1,000.

Duration: 1 year.

Number awarded: Varies each year; recently, 5 of these scholarships were awarded.

Deadline: February of each year.

2447 WASHINGTON STATE THOROUGHBRED FOUNDATION SCHOLARSHIP

Race for Education
Attn: Student Services Manager
1818 Versailles Road
P.O. Box 11355
Lexington, KY 40575
Phone: (859) 252-8648; Fax: (859) 252-8030
Email: info@racingscholarships.com
Web: www.racingscholarships.com/page.php?page=programs

Summary: To provide financial assistance to residents of Washington attending college in any state to prepare for a career in the equine industry.

Eligibility: Open to undergraduate students under 24 years of age who are residents of Washington. Applicants must be attending a college or university in any state to prepare for a career in the equine industry. Fields of study may include (but are not limited to) equine science, pre-veterinary medicine (equine practice only), equine business management, racetrack management, pasture management as it relates to horse farms, or other related field. They must have a GPA of 2.85 or higher and be U.S. citizens or have a valid student visa. Financial need is also considered in the selection process.

Financial data: A stipend is awarded (amount not specified).

Duration: 1 year.

Number awarded: 1 each year.

Deadline: February of each year.

2448 WASTE MANAGEMENT CHARITABLE FOUNDATION SCHOLARSHIP

Possible Woman Foundation International
1054 Redwood Drive
Norcross, GA 30093
Fax: (770) 381-9616
Email: info@possiblewomanfoundation
Web: www.possiblewomanfoundation.org/scholarships.html

Summary: To provide financial assistance for college or graduate school to women who are returning to school to work on a degree in an environmental field.

Eligibility: Open to women who are returning to school after a hiatus, changing careers, seeking advancement in their career or work life, or stay-at-home mothers entering the workplace and in need of additional education or training. Applicants must be at least 25 years of age and may be at any level of education (high school graduate, some college, 4-year college graduate, graduate school, doctoral). They must be working on a degree in an environmental services field, including (but not limited to) environmental engineering, health care waste management, environmental horticulture, chemical waste management, renewable fuels or energy, or another area that will positively impact our environment. Along with their application, they must submit a 2-page essay on the topic, "How Having the Opportunity for Beginning or Continuing My Academic Education Will Positively Impact My Life." Selection is based on the essay, career and life goals, leadership and participation in community activities, honors and awards received, and financial need. U.S. citizenship or permanent resident status is required and study must be conducted in the United States.

Financial data: The stipend ranges from $2,000 to $5,000. Funds are paid directly to the recipient's institution.

Duration: 1 year; nonrenewable.

Number awarded: 1 each year.

Deadline: January of each year.

2449 WATDA TECHNICIAN SCHOLARSHIPS

Wisconsin Automobile and Truck Dealers Association
Attn: Foundation
150 East Gilman, Suite A
P.O. Box 5345
Madison, WI 53705-0345
Phone: (608) 251-5577; Fax: (608) 251-4379
Email: watda-info@watda.org
Web: www.watda.org/WATDA/Public/Foundation/fdn_scholarship.asp

Summary: To provide financial assistance to students attending or planning to attend an automotive, diesel, or auto collision technician program in Wisconsin.

Eligibility: Open to Wisconsin residents enrolled or planning to enroll as an automotive, auto collision, or diesel technician student at a certified Wisconsin technical college. Applicants must be planning to prepare for a career in the automotive, diesel, or auto collision industry. They must have completed a series of assessment evaluations relevant to their field of interest. Finalists must participate in a personal interview.

Financial data: Stipends average $1,250 per year. Snap-On Corporation of Kenosha, Wisconsin also provides tools valued from $1,200 to $2,875 to scholarship recipients.

Duration: 1 semester; may be renewed up to 3 additional semesters provided the recipient remains enrolled full-time with a GPA of 2.8 or higher.

Number awarded: 1 or more each year.

Deadline: December of each year.

2450 WAYNE D. CORNILS SCHOLARSHIP

Summary: To provide financial assistance to students at Idaho colleges and universities who are preparing for a career in the broadcasting field (including the business side) and can demonstrate financial need.

See Listing #1616.

2451 WAYNE V. BLACK SCHOLARSHIP AWARD

Energy Telecommunications and Electrical Association
Attn: Sales/Operations Coordinator
5005 Royal Lane, Suite 116
Irving, TX 75063
Phone: (888) 503-8700, ext. 205; Fax: (972) 915-6040
Email: tiffany@entelec.org
Web: www.entelec.org/resources/scholarship

Summary: To provide financial assistance to undergraduates working on a degree in a field related to telecommunications.

Eligibility: Open to full-time undergraduates at accredited colleges and universities in the United States and Canada. Applicants must be working on a bachelor's degree in engineering or engineering technology, computer science or management information systems, pre-law, political science, or telecommunications or information technology. They must be citizens or permanent residents of the United States or citizens of Canada. Along with their application, they must submit a 1-page autobiography and a 5-page essay on a topic that changes annually but relates to telecommunications and similar technologies. Financial need is not considered in the selection process.

Financial data: The stipend is $5,000.

Duration: 1 year.

Number awarded: 1 each year.

Deadline: March of each year.

2452 WEISMAN SCHOLARSHIPS

Connecticut Department of Higher Education
Attn: Office of Student Financial Aid
61 Woodland Street
Hartford, CT 06105-2326

Phone: (860) 947-1857; Fax: (860) 947-1838
Email: mtip@ctdhe.org
Web: www.ctdhe.org/SFA/default.htm

Summary: To provide financial assistance to minority upper-division college students from any state who are enrolled at a college in Connecticut and interested in teaching mathematics or science at public middle and high schools in the state.

Eligibility: Open to residents of any state who are enrolled full-time as juniors or seniors at Connecticut colleges and universities and preparing to become a mathematics or science teacher at the middle or high school level. Applicants must be members of a minority group, defined as African American, Hispanic/Latino, Asian American, or Native American. They must be nominated by the education dean at their institution.

Financial data: The maximum stipend is $5,000 per year. In addition, if recipients complete a credential and begin teaching at a public school in Connecticut within 16 months of graduation, they may receive up to $2,500 per year, for up to 4 years, to help pay off college loans.

Number awarded: Varies each year.

Deadline: September of each year.

2453 WELLS FARGO SCHOLARSHIP PROGRAM OF THE HISPANIC SCHOLARSHIP FUND

Hispanic Scholarship Fund
Attn: Selection Committee
55 Second Street, Suite 1500
San Francisco, CA 94105
Phone: (415) 808-2365; (877) HSF-INFO; Fax: (415) 808-2302
Email: scholar1@hsf.net
Web: www.hsf.net/scholarships.aspx?id=468

Summary: To provide financial assistance to Hispanic upper-division students from selected states working on a degree related to business at designated universities.

Eligibility: Open to U.S. citizens, permanent residents, and visitors with a passport stamped I-551 who are of Hispanic heritage. Applicants must be currently enrolled full-time as sophomores at a 4-year college or university with a major in business, economics, finance, accounting, or information technology (including CIS, MIS, and computer engineering). They must have a GPA of 3.0 or higher. First priority is given to students who are enrolled at the following institutions: Arizona State University, Fresno State University, San Francisco State University, California State University at Fullerton, Columbia University, Iowa State University, San Jose State University, Santa Clara University, Stanford University, Texas A&M University, University of Arizona, University of California at Berkeley, University of California at Davis, University of California at Los Angeles, University of California at San Diego, University of Minnesota, University of Southern California, University of Texas at Austin, or University of Washington. Second priority is given to residents of the following states: Alaska, Arizona, Arkansas, California, Colorado, Idaho, Illinois, Indiana, Iowa, Michigan, Minnesota, Montana, Nebraska, Nevada, New Mexico, North Dakota, Ohio, Oregon, South Dakota, Texas, Utah, Washington, Wisconsin, or Wyoming. Selection is based on academic achievement, personal strengths, leadership, and financial need.

Financial data: The stipend is $2,000.

Duration: 1 year (the junior year of college).

Number awarded: 1 or more each year.

Deadline: February of each year.

2454 WEST MICHIGAN CHAPTER AWMA SCHOLARSHIPS

Air & Waste Management Association–West Michigan Chapter
c/o Jim Enright, Scholarship Chair
Miller Johnson
Calder Plaza Building
250 Monroe Avenue, N.W., Suite 800
Grand Rapids, MI 49503-2250
Phone: (616) 831-1700; Fax: (616) 831-1701
Email: enrightj@millerjohnson.com
Web: www.wmawma.org

Summary: To provide financial assistance to upper-division and master's degree students in Michigan who are interested in preparing for a career in an environmental field.

Eligibility: Open to 1) students currently enrolled at an accredited college or university in Michigan; and 2) members of the West Michigan Chapter of the Air & Waste Management Association (AWMA) and their children who are attending an accredited college or university in any state. Applicants must be entering their junior or senior year of undergraduate studies or enrolled in a master's degree program and preparing for a career in air pollution control, hazardous waste management, or other environmental area. Preferred courses of study include environmental engineering, physical or natural sciences, or natural resources. Selection is based on academic achievement (GPA of 3.0 or higher), an essay of 500 to 600 words on interests and objectives, and participation in extracurricular activities.

Financial data: The stipend is $1,500.

Duration: 1 year; recipients may reapply.

Number awarded: Up to 3 each year.

Deadline: November of each year.

2455 WESTERN FEDERATION OF PROFESSIONAL SURVEYORS SCHOLARSHIPS

Western Federation of Professional Surveyors
Attn: Executive Director
P.O. Box 2722
Santa Rosa, CA 95405
Phone: (707) 578-1130; Fax: (707) 578-4406
Email: admin@wfps.org
Web: www.wfps.org/files/scholarsh.html

Summary: To provide financial assistance to upper-division students majoring in surveying at colleges and universities in 13 designated western states.

Eligibility: Open to students attending accredited private and public colleges that 1) offer a program leading to a 4-year bachelor's degree with a land surveying major; and 2) are in the states of Alaska, Arizona, California, Colorado, Hawaii, Idaho, Montana, Nevada, New Mexico, Oregon, Utah, Washington, or Wyoming. Applicants must have completed at least 2 years of study. Community college students must be planning to transfer to an eligible 4-year school. Along with their application, they must submit a 1-page essay on their educational goals, career goals, and why their qualifications justify their receiving this scholarship. Selection is based on the quality and neatness of the essay, academic achievement, professional qualifications, college activities, community activities, work experience, and letters of recommendation.

Financial data: The stipend is $1,200.

Duration: 1 year; recipients may reapply.

Number awarded: Varies each year; recently, 4 of these scholarships were awarded.

Deadline: March of each year.

2456 WESTERN POULTRY SCHOLARSHIPS

Pacific Egg and Poultry Association
Attn: Western Poultry Scholarship and Research Foundation
1521 "I" Street
Sacramento, CA 95814
Phone: (916) 441-0801; Fax: (916) 446-1063
Email: info@pacificegg.org
Web: www.pacificegg.org/scholarship.html

Summary: To provide financial assistance to undergraduate and graduate students at institutions in western states and Canadian provinces who are interested in preparing for a career in the poultry industry.

Eligibility: Open to high school seniors, undergraduates, and graduate students (including veterinary students) who are enrolled or planning to enroll full-time at a college or university in the 11 western states (Alaska, Arizona, California, Colorado, Hawaii, Idaho, Montana, Nevada, Oregon, Utah, and Washington) or the western provinces of Canada that offer a poultry curriculum. Selection is based on academic achievement, financial need, and interest (current and future) in the poultry industry.

Financial data: The stipend is $1,000 for high school seniors or $1,350 for students currently enrolled at a college or university.

Duration: 1 year.

Number awarded: Varies each year; recently, 26 of these scholarships were awarded.

Deadline: January of each year.

2457 WESTERN RESERVE HERB SOCIETY SCHOLARSHIPS

Western Reserve Herb Society
Attn: Scholarship Committee
11030 East Boulevard
Cleveland, OH 44106

Phone: (216) 721-1600; (888) 853-7091; Fax: (216) 721-2056
Email: scholarship@westernreserveherbsociety.org
Web: www.westernreserveherbsociety.org/scholarship.php

Summary: To provide financial assistance to college students from Ohio interested in preparing for a career in a field related to horticulture.

Eligibility: Open to residents of Ohio who have completed at least 1 year of college. Applicants may be attending an accredited college or university anywhere in the United States. They must be planning a career in horticulture, landscape architecture, horticultural therapy, or a related field. U.S. citizenship is required. Preference is given to applicants whose horticultural career goals involve teaching or research or work in the public or nonprofit sector (such as public gardens, botanical gardens, parks, arboreta, city planning, or public education and awareness). Selection is based on an essay that includes a description of their interests, activities, and achievements; an account of their employment record on or off campus; a description of their career goals; and a discussion of their need for financial aid.

Financial data: The stipend is $2,000.

Duration: 1 year.

Number awarded: 1 each year.

Deadline: March of each year.

2458 WILD BILL FOGLE MEMORIAL SCHOLARSHIP

Oregon Student Assistance Commission
Attn: Grants and Scholarships Division
1500 Valley River Drive, Suite 100
Eugene, OR 97401-2146
Phone: (541) 687-7395; (800) 452-8807, ext. 7395; Fax: (541) 687-7414; TDD: (800) 735-2900
Email: awardinfo@osac.state.or.us
Web: www.osac.state.or.us/osac_programs.html

Summary: To provide financial assistance to residents of any state who are interested in studying veterinary science at schools in the Northwest, especially designated institutions in Oregon.

Eligibility: Open to residents of any state who are currently enrolled or planning to enroll at a college or university in Idaho, Montana, Oregon, or Washington; preference is given to students at Oregon State University and Linn-Benton Community College. Applicants must be interested in working on a degree in veterinary science or pre-veterinary studies. Preference is given to applicants with a GPA of 3.2 or higher. Financial need is not required, but it is considered in the selection process.

Financial data: A stipend is awarded (amount not specified).

Duration: 1 year; recipients may reapply.

Number awarded: Varies each year.

Deadline: February of each year.

2459 WILLAMETTE VALLEY AGRICULTURE ASSOCIATION SCHOLARSHIPS

Oregon Student Assistance Commission
Attn: Grants and Scholarships Division
1500 Valley River Drive, Suite 100
Eugene, OR 97401-2146
Phone: (541) 687-7395; (800) 452-8807, ext. 7395; Fax: (541) 687-7414; TDD: (800) 735-2900
Email: awardinfo@osac.state.or.us
Web: www.osac.state.or.us/osac_programs.html

Summary: To provide financial assistance to residents of Oregon working on an undergraduate or graduate degree related to agriculture at a college or university in the state.

Eligibility: Open to graduates of Oregon high schools who are 1) entering or continuing undergraduates in production agriculture, animal science, or other agriculture-related field; or 2) graduate students in a teaching degree program. Preference is given to students who have a GPA of 3.5 or higher or a GED score of 2950 or higher. Applicants must be enrolled full-time at a 4-year public college or university in Oregon. Along with their application, they must submit a paper of 1 to 2 pages explaining how their course of study will impact Oregon agriculture. Financial need is not considered in the selection process.

Financial data: The stipend is $1,000.

Duration: 1 year; recipients may reapply.

Number awarded: Varies each year; recently, 7 of these scholarships were awarded.

Deadline: February of each year.

2460 WILLIAM J. ENGLISH MEMORIAL SCHOLARSHIP

Florida Association of Educational Data Systems
c/o Stephen B. Muzzy, Scholarship Coordinator
Brevard County Public Schools
2700 Judge Fran Jamieson Way
Viera, FL 32940
Phone: (321) 633-1000, ext. 700
Email: muzzys@brevard.k12.fl.us
Web: www.faeds.org/schol_WilliamEnglish.cfm

Summary: To provide financial assistance to high school seniors in Florida planning to attend a college or university in the state and major in computer science or information technology.

Eligibility: Open to high school and vocational school seniors in Florida who have a GPA of 2.5 or higher. Applicants must be planning to enroll full-time at a Florida private or public college and major in computer science or information technology. Along with their application, they must submit a 2-page autobiography that includes their academic success and course work in technology-related areas, why they selected their major, and how they intend to use it in the future. Financial need is not considered in the selection process. U.S. citizenship is required.

Financial data: The stipend is $3,000.

Duration: 1 year.

Number awarded: 1 or more each year.

Deadline: February of each year.

2461 WILLIAM M. OLSON/WARREN E. TAYLOR SCIENCE AND ENGINEERING SCHOLARSHIPS

AVS-Science and Technology of Materials, Interfaces, and Processing–New Mexico Chapter
c/o Jonathan Custer, Scholarship and Awards Chair
Sandia National Laboratories
MS 0889
P.O. Box 5800
Albuquerque, NM 87185-0889
Phone: (505) 845-8594; Fax: (505) 844-7910
Email: tklits@sandia.gov
Web: www-chne.unm.edu/avs/avsinformation.htm

Summary: To provide financial assistance to high school seniors in Arizona, New Mexico, Oklahoma, and parts of Texas who are interested in majoring in physical science or engineering at a college in any state.

Eligibility: Open to seniors graduating from high schools in Arizona, New Mexico, Oklahoma, and the part of Texas that is in the mountain time zone. Applicants must have completed at least 1 additional science course beyond that required for graduation and be planning to major in physical science or engineering at a college or university in any state. Along with their application, they must submit an official copy of their grades, SAT and/or ACT scores, letters of endorsement from 2 high school teachers, and a 1-page statement describing their short-term goals for college and long-term goals. Selection is based on performance and achievement.

Financial data: The stipend is $2,500.

Duration: 1 year.

Number awarded: 1 or more each year.

Deadline: April of each year.

2462 WILLIAM R. GOLDFARB MEMORIAL SCHOLARSHIP

American Radio Relay League
Attn: ARRL Foundation
225 Main Street
Newington, CT 06111
Phone: (860) 594-0397; Fax: (860) 594-0259
Email: foundation@arrl.org
Web: www.arrlf.org/programs/scholarships

Summary: To provide financial assistance to high school seniors who are licensed radio amateurs and interested in working on an undergraduate degree in selected fields.

Eligibility: Open to licensed radio amateurs of any class who are graduating high school seniors planning to attend an accredited institution of higher education. Preference is given to students planning to major in computers, medicine, nursing, engineering, science, or a business-related field. Applicants must submit an essay on the role amateur radio has played in their lives and provide documentation of financial need.

Financial data: The stipend is at least $10,000.

Duration: 1 year.
Number awarded: 1 each year.
Deadline: January of each year.

2463 WILLIAM RUCKER GREENWOOD SCHOLARSHIP

Association for Women Geoscientists
Attn: AWG Foundation
12000 North Washington Street, Suite 285
Thornton, CO 80241
Phone: (303) 412-6219; Fax: (303) 253-9220
Email: office@awg.org
Web: www.awg.org/EAS/scholarships.html

Summary: To provide financial assistance to minority women from any state working on an undergraduate or graduate degree in the geosciences at a college in the Potomac Bay region.

Eligibility: Open to minority women who are residents of any state and currently enrolled as full-time undergraduate or graduate geoscience majors at an accredited, degree-granting college or university in Delaware, the District of Columbia, Maryland, Virginia, or West Virginia. Selection is based on the applicant's 1) participation in geoscience or earth science educational activities; and 2) potential for leadership as a future geoscience professional.

Financial data: The stipend is $1,000. The recipient also is granted a 1-year membership in the Association for Women Geoscientists (AWG).

Duration: 1 year.
Number awarded: 1 each year.
Deadline: April of each year.

2464 WILLIAM SAMBER SR. AVIATION/MATH AND SCIENCE SCHOLARSHIP

African-American/Caribbean Education Association, Inc.
P.O. Box 1224
Valley Stream, NY 11582-1224
Phone: (718) 949-6733
Email: aaceainc@yahoo.com
Web: www.aaceainc.com/Scholarships.html

Summary: To provide financial assistance to high school seniors of African American or Caribbean heritage who plan to study a field related to aviation, mathematics, or science in college.

Eligibility: Open to graduating high school seniors who are U.S. citizens of African American or Caribbean heritage. Applicants must be planning to attend a college or university and major in a field related to a career in aviation, mathematics, or science. They must have completed 4 years of specified college preparatory courses with a grade of 90 or higher and have an SAT score of at least 1790. They must also have completed at least 200 hours of community service during their 4 years of high school, preferably in the field that they plan to study in college. Financial need is not considered in the selection process. New York residency is not required, but applicants must be available for an interview in the Queens, New York area.

Financial data: The stipend ranges from $1,000 to $2,500. Funds are paid directly to the recipient.

Duration: 1 year.
Number awarded: 2 each year.
Deadline: April of each year.

2465 WISCONSIN ASSOCIATION OF PROFESSIONAL AGRICULTURAL CONSULTANTS SCHOLARSHIPS

Wisconsin Association of Professional Agricultural Consultants
Attn: Executive Secretary
7310 Farmington Way
Madison, WI 53717
Phone: (608) 833-7989; Fax: (608) 833-1965
Email: wapac@itis.com
Web: www.wapac.info/Scholarships.htm

Summary: To provide financial assistance to college students in Wisconsin who are preparing for a career in production agriculture or applied research.

Eligibility: Open to undergraduate students enrolled at colleges and universities in Wisconsin. Applicants must be preparing for a career in production agriculture or applied crop or livestock research. They must have been enrolled the previous summer in an internship that was production-related. Selection is based on merit; financial need is not considered.

Financial data: The stipend is $1,500.
Duration: 1 year.
Number awarded: 1 or more each year.
Deadline: November of each year.

2466 WISCONSIN DIETETIC ASSOCIATION SCHOLARSHIPS

Wisconsin Dietetic Association
Attn: Executive Coordinator
1411 West Montgomery Street
Sparta, WI 54656-1003
Phone: (608) 269-0042; (888) 232-8631; Fax: (608) 269-0043
Email: wda@centurytel.net
Web: www.eatrightwisc.org

Summary: To provide financial assistance to undergraduate and graduate students in dietetics programs at colleges and universities in Wisconsin.

Eligibility: Open to students at colleges, universities, and technical schools in Wisconsin who are working on an undergraduate or graduate degree in dietetics or a certificate as a dietetic technician. Applicants must submit a brief summary of their professional and career goals and what they hope to bring to the profession of dietetics, 3 letters of reference, official transcripts, and a financial statement.

Financial data: Stipends are $1,000 for undergraduates and full-time graduate students or $500 for part-time graduate students and dietetic technician students.

Duration: 1 year.
Number awarded: Generally, 5 each year: 2 for undergraduates, 1 for a full-time graduate student, 1 for a part-time graduate student, and 1 for a dietetic technician student.
Deadline: February of each year.

2467 WISCONSIN ENVIRONMENTAL HEALTH ASSOCIATION ACADEMIC SCHOLARSHIP

Wisconsin Environmental Health Association, Inc.
Attn: Awards Committee
P.O. Box 8365
Madison, WI 53708-8565
Email: questions@weha.net
Web: www.weha.net/home/whatWeDo/scholarship.htm

Summary: To provide financial assistance to undergraduates from any state working on a degree in environmental health at a university in Wisconsin.

Eligibility: Open to residents of any state currently enrolled at a college or university in Wisconsin. Applicants must be working on a degree in the field of environmental health. They must have demonstrated a commitment to the pursuit of academic excellence and service to the community.

Financial data: The stipend is $1,500.
Duration: 1 year.
Number awarded: 1 each year.
Deadline: March of each year.

2468 WISCONSIN LEGION AUXILIARY PAST PRESIDENTS PARLEY HEALTH CAREER SCHOLARSHIPS

American Legion Auxiliary
Department of Wisconsin
Attn: Education Chair
2930 American Legion Drive
P.O. Box 140
Portage, WI 53901-0140
Phone: (608) 745-0124; (866) 664-3863; Fax: (608) 745-1947
Email: alawi@amlegionauxwi.org
Web: www.amlegionauxwi.org/Scholarships.htm

Summary: To provide financial assistance for health-related education at a school in any state to the dependents and descendants of veterans in Wisconsin.

Eligibility: Open to the children, wives, and widows of veterans who are attending or entering a hospital, university, or technical school in any state to prepare for a health-related career. Grandchildren and great-grandchildren of veterans are eligible if they are members of the American Legion Auxiliary. Applicants must be residents of Wisconsin and have a GPA of 3.5 or higher. Along with their application, they must submit a 300-word essay on "The Importance of Health Careers Today." Financial need is considered in the selection process.

Financial data: The stipend is $1,200.

Duration: 1 year; nonrenewable.
Number awarded: 2 each year.
Deadline: March of each year.

2469 WISCONSIN LEGION AUXILIARY PAST PRESIDENTS PARLEY REGISTERED NURSE SCHOLARSHIPS

American Legion Auxiliary
Department of Wisconsin
Attn: Education Chair
2930 American Legion Drive
P.O. Box 140
Portage, WI 53901-0140
Phone: (608) 745-0124; (866) 664-3863; Fax: (608) 745-1947
Email: alawi@amlegionauxwi.org
Web: www.amlegionauxwi.org/Scholarships.htm

Summary: To provide financial assistance to the dependents and descendants of Wisconsin veterans who are interested in studying nursing at a school in any state.
Eligibility: Open to the wives, widows, and children of Wisconsin veterans who are enrolled or have been accepted in an accredited school of nursing in any state to prepare for a career as a registered nurse. Grandchildren and great-grandchildren of veterans are also eligible if they are American Legion Auxiliary members. Applicants must be Wisconsin residents and have a GPA of 3.5 or higher. Along with their application, they must submit a 300-word essay on "The Need for Trained Nurses Today." Financial need is considered in the selection process.
Financial data: The stipend is $1,200.
Duration: 1 year.
Number awarded: 3 each year.
Deadline: March of each year.

2470 WISCONSIN ORGANIZATION OF NURSE EXECUTIVES BACHELOR'S DEGREE EDUCATIONAL STIPEND PROGRAM

Wisconsin Organization of Nurse Executives, Inc.
c/o Kathryn Olson, Professional Development Committee
Saint Joseph's Hospital, Patient Care Services
611 St. Joseph Avenue
Marshfield, WI 54449
Phone: (715) 387-7592; Fax: (715) 387-7616
Email: kathryn.olson@ministryhealth.org
Web: www.w-one.org/display.aspx?page=/professionaldev.aspx

Summary: To provide financial assistance to nurses in Wisconsin who are interested in working on a bachelor's degree in nursing at a school in any state.
Eligibility: Open to Wisconsin nurses working on a bachelor's (B.S.N.) degree in nursing. Applicants must have a GPA of 3.0 or higher. Along with their application, they must submit a letter identifying their professional goals and how they plan to attain them, the way they plan to affect nursing and patient care in Wisconsin, areas of interest, memberships in professional and community organizations and any related activities, and how they perceive their role as a nursing leader in the future.
Financial data: The stipend is $1,000.
Duration: 1 year; nonrenewable.
Number awarded: 1 or more each year.
Deadline: July of each year.

2471 WISCONSIN READY MIXED CONCRETE ASSOCIATION ESSAY CONTEST

Wisconsin Ready Mixed Concrete Association
Attn: Scholarship Committee
16 North Carroll Street, Suite 925
Madison, WI 53703
Phone: (608) 250-6304; (800) 242-6298; Fax: (608) 250-6306
Email: info@wrmca.com
Web: www.wrmca.com/cmt_scholarship.htm

Summary: To recognize and reward, with scholarships to specified institutions, high school seniors in Wisconsin and the upper peninsula of Michigan who submit outstanding essays on the concrete industry.
Eligibility: Open to seniors graduating from high schools in Wisconsin and the upper peninsula of Michigan. Applicants must submit an essay, up to 600 words in length, on a topic related to the concrete industry (e.g., concrete's benefits to society; how concrete affects the environment; using concrete to build homes, commercial buildings, bridges, or roads). They should be planning to enroll in a concrete-related program at Middle Tennessee State University, New Jersey Institute of Technology, California State University at Chico, or Arizona State University. Other eligible programs include those at Alpena College in Michigan or Rhodes State College in Ohio. Selection is based on the essay's content and the author's writing ability.
Financial data: The winner receives a $5,000 scholarship for use at Middle Tennessee State University, New Jersey Institute of Technology, California State University at Chico, or Arizona State University; if he or she enrolls at Alpena College or Rhodes State College, the award is a $2,000 scholarship. At any other college or university of the winner's choice, the award is a $1,000 scholarship.
Duration: 1 year; nonrenewable.
Number awarded: 1 each year.
Deadline: November of each year.

2472 WOCN SOCIETY ACCREDITED NURSING EDUCATION SCHOLARSHIP PROGRAM

Wound, Ostomy and Continence Nurses Society
Attn: Scholarship Committee
15000 Commerce Parkway, Suite C
Mt. Laurel, NJ 08054
Phone: (888) 224-WOCN
Email: info@wocn.org
Web: www.wocn.org/Education/Scholarships

Summary: To provide financial assistance to students interested in preparing for a career in wound, ostomy, and continence nursing care.
Eligibility: Open to students seeking education in wound, ostomy, and continence nursing care. Applicants must provide evidence of 1 of the following: 1) acceptance in a wound, ostomy, and continence education program accredited by the Wound, Ostomy and Continence Nurses (WOCN) Society; 2) current enrollment in a WOCN-accredited wound, ostomy, and continence education program; or 3) certificate of completion from a WOCN-accredited wound, ostomy, and continence education program within 3 months of completion. Selection is based on motivation to be an ET nurse and financial need.
Financial data: Stipends range from $1,000 to $3,500 per year.
Duration: 1 year.
Number awarded: Approximately 20 each year.
Deadline: April or October of each year.

2473 WOMEN'S WILDLIFE MANAGEMENT/CONSERVATION SCHOLARSHIP

National Rifle Association of America
Attn: Women's Program Department
11250 Waples Mill Road
Fairfax, VA 22030-7400
Phone: (703) 267-1399; (800) 861-1166
Email: rherr@nrahq.org
Web: www.nrahq.org/women/awards/wmc-scholarship.asp

Summary: To provide financial assistance to women who are upper-division students working on a degree in wildlife management or conservation.
Eligibility: Open to women currently enrolled full-time as college juniors or seniors. Applicants must be working on a degree in wildlife management or conservation. They must have a GPA of 3.0 or higher. Financial need is not considered in the selection process.
Financial data: The stipend is $1,000 per year.
Duration: 1 year; may be renewed 1 additional year.
Number awarded: 1 each year.
Deadline: November of each year.

2474 WYOMING TRUCKING ASSOCIATION SCHOLARSHIPS

Wyoming Trucking Association, Inc.
Attn: WTA Scholarship Trust Fund
555 North Poplar
P.O. Box 1909
Casper, WY 82602
Phone: (307) 234-1579; Fax: (307) 234-7082
Email: wytruck@aol.com
Web: wytruck.org

Summary: To provide financial assistance to high school seniors and currently-enrolled college students in Wyoming who are interested in preparing for a career in the highway transportation industry.

Eligibility: Open to high school seniors and graduates in Wyoming who are enrolled or planning to enroll at a community college in Wyoming, a trade school in the state, or the University of Wyoming. Applicants must be majoring or planning to major in a course of study that could lead to a career in the highway transportation industry, including (but not limited to) business management, computer skills, accounting, office procedures and management, safety, diesel mechanics, and truck driving. Along with their application, they must submit a 1-page essay on "How is the trucking industry important to you and the State of Wyoming." Financial need is considered in the selection process.
Financial data: Stipends range from $500 to $1,000.
Duration: 1 year.
Number awarded: Up to 10 each year.
Deadline: February of each year.

2475 XEROX TECHNICAL MINORITY SCHOLARSHIP PROGRAM

Xerox Corporation
Attn: Technical Minority Scholarship Program
150 State Street, Fourth Floor
Rochester, NY 14614
Phone: (585) 422-7689
Email: xtmsp@rballiance.com
Web: www.xeroxstudentcareers.com/why-xerox/scholarship.aspx
Summary: To provide financial assistance to minorities interested in undergraduate or graduate education in the sciences and/or engineering.
Eligibility: Open to minorities (people of African American, Asian, Pacific Islander, Native American, Native Alaskan, or Hispanic descent) working full-time on a bachelor's, master's, or doctoral degree in chemistry, computing and software systems, engineering (chemical, computer, electrical, imaging, manufacturing, mechanical, optical, or software), information management, laser optics, materials science, physics, or printing management science. Applicants must be U.S. citizens or permanent residents with a GPA of 3.0 or higher and attending a 4-year college or university.
Financial data: Stipends range from $1,000 to $10,000.
Duration: 1 year.
Number awarded: Varies each year; recently, 125 of these scholarships were awarded.
Deadline: September of each year.

2476 YASME FOUNDATION SCHOLARSHIPS

American Radio Relay League
Attn: ARRL Foundation
225 Main Street
Newington, CT 06111
Phone: (860) 594-0397; Fax: (860) 594-0259
Email: foundation@arrl.org
Web: www.arrlf.org/programs/scholarships
Summary: To provide financial assistance to licensed radio amateurs who are interested in working on an undergraduate degree in science or engineering.
Eligibility: Open to undergraduate students who are licensed radio amateurs of any active class. Applicants must be enrolled or planning to enroll at an accredited 4-year college or university. They must submit an essay on the role amateur radio has played in their lives and provide documentation of financial need. Preference is given to 1) students majoring in science or engineering; 2) high school seniors ranked in the top 5% to 10% of their class; 3) college students ranked in the top 10% of their class; and 4) students who have participated in a local amateur radio club and community service activities.
Financial data: The stipend is $2,000 per year.
Duration: 1 year; the program includes 2 awards that may be renewed for up to 3 additional years or until successful completion of undergraduate study.
Number awarded: 5 each year.
Deadline: January of each year.

2477 YOUNG EPIDEMIOLOGY SCHOLARS STUDENT COMPETITION

College Board
11911 Freedom Drive, Suite 300
Reston, VA 20190
Phone: (800) 626-9795, ext. 5849; Fax: (703) 707-5599
Email: yes@collegeboard.org
Web: www.collegeboard.com/yes/fs/atc.html
Summary: To recognize and reward, with college scholarships, high school juniors and seniors who conduct outstanding research projects that apply epidemiological methods of analysis to a health-related issue.
Eligibility: Open to high school juniors and seniors who have conducted original research that applies epidemiological methods of analysis to a health-related issue. Epidemiology is the science of exploring patterns of disease, illness, and injury within populations, with the goal of developing methods of prevention, control, and treatment to improve health. Applicants must be U.S. citizens or permanent residents and enrolled in high school in the United States, Puerto Rico, Guam, U.S. Virgin Islands, American Samoa, Midway, or the Mariana Islands. Home-schooled students are also eligible. Only 1 project per student may be submitted. To apply, students must register on the College Board's web site. The judging and awards process takes place in 3 rounds: 1) the semifinal round, where 120 semifinalists are selected based on the quality of a written summary of their work; of those, 60 (10 from each of 6 regions) advance to compete in the next round; 2) the regional finalist round, where students are judged on their summaries, an oral presentation, and a question-and-answer session; 12 of those students (2 from each region) advance to the next level; and 3) the national finalist round, where, based on their summary reports, oral presentations, and question-and-answer sessions, 10 are selected as national finalists and 2 are selected as national winners.
Financial data: A total of $456,000 in college scholarships is awarded each year: $1,000 scholarships to semifinalists, $2,000 scholarship awards to regional finalists, scholarship awards to national finalists that range from $15,000 to $35,000, and $50,000 scholarship awards to national winners.
Duration: The competition is held annually.
Number awarded: 120 of these scholarships are awarded each year: 60 students who are selected as semifinalists but do not advance to the regional finalist round receive scholarships of $1,000 each; the 48 students who are selected as regional finalists but do not advance to the national finalist round receive scholarships of $2,000 each; of the 12 national finalists, 6 receive scholarships of $15,000 each, 2 receive scholarships of $20,000 each, 2 receive scholarships of $35,000 each, and 2 (the national winners) receive scholarships of $50,000 each.
Deadline: January of each year.

2478 YOUNG NATURALIST AWARDS

American Museum of Natural History
Attn: National Center for Science Literacy, Education, and Technology
Central Park West at 79th Street
New York, NY 10024-5192
Phone: (212) 496-3498
Email: yna@amnh.org
Web: www.amnh.org/nationalcenter/youngnaturalistawards
Summary: To recognize and reward high school students who develop outstanding science projects.
Eligibility: Open to students in grades 7–12 currently enrolled in a public, private, parochial, or home school in the United States, Canada, the U.S. territories, or U.S.-sponsored schools abroad. Applicants are invited to submit reports of observation-based projects on a scientific topic of their own selection. Entries must be between 500 and 2,000 words for grades 7 and 8, between 750 and 2,500 words for grades 9 and 10, or between 1,000 and 3,000 words for grades 11 and 12. Students may include writing. Entries are judged by grade level. Selection is based on focus of investigation, procedure, analysis and interpretation, documentation of research materials, personal voice, clarity and style, and use of visuals.
Financial data: This program provides scholarships of $2,500 for grade 12, $2,000 for grade 11, $1,500 for grade 10, $1,000 for grade 9, $750 for grade 8, or $500 for grade 7.
Duration: Awards are presented annually.
Number awarded: 12 awards are presented each year: 2 for each grade level.
Deadline: February of each year.

2479 ZIEGLER/CATERPILLAR DIESEL SCHOLARSHIP

Iowa Motor Truck Association
Attn: Iowa Motor Carriers Foundation
717 East Court Avenue
Des Moines, IA 50309
Phone: (515) 244-5193; Fax: (515) 244-2204
Email: imta@iowamotortruck.com
Web: www.iowamotortruck.com/Scholarships/Foundation.asp
Summary: To provide financial assistance to residents of Iowa majoring in diesel technology at a college or university in the state.
Eligibility: Open to Iowa residents attending or planning to attend a college, university, trade school, or community college in the state. Applicants must be

interested in studying diesel technology. Along with their application, they must submit a brief letter describing why they are applying for this scholarship, their intended career goal, its estimated cost, and their choices of educational institutions. Selection is based on academic record, outside activities that pertain to school and community citizenship, and financial need.

Financial data: The stipend is $1,000.

Duration: 1 year.

Number awarded: 1 each year.

Deadline: March of each year.

2480 ZONTA CLUB OF MILWAUKEE TECHNICAL SPECIALTY SCHOLARSHIP AWARD

Zonta Club of Milwaukee
Attn: Scholarship Team
P.O. Box 1494
Milwaukee, WI 53201
Email: zcscholarship@zontamilwaukee.org
Web: www.zontamilwaukee.org/OurScholarships.htm

Summary: To provide financial assistance to women, especially residents of Wisconsin, who are interested in working on an associate degree or certificate at a technical college or institute in any state.

Eligibility: Open to women who are interested in working on an associate degree or certificate in a nontraditional technical field, including (but not limited to) health occupations, computer, electronic, mechanical, or other technological fields. Preference is given to residents of Wisconsin and to low income or otherwise disadvantaged women. Applicants must be currently enrolled at an accredited technical college or institute in any state. They must have a GPA of 2.5 or higher. Along with their application, they must submit a description of their anticipated course of study and current career interests, including how they plan to continue to advance the status of women through their career.

Financial data: The stipend is $1,000.

Duration: 1 year.

Number awarded: 1 or more each year.

Deadline: May of each year.

2481 ZONTA CLUB OF MILWAUKEE WOMEN IN SCIENCE SCHOLARSHIP

Zonta Club of Milwaukee
Attn: Scholarship Team
P.O. Box 1494
Milwaukee, WI 53201
Email: zcscholarship@zontamilwaukee.org
Web: www.zontamilwaukee.org/OurScholarships.htm

Summary: To provide financial assistance to women, especially residents of Wisconsin, who are upper-division students working on a degree in a field of science, technology, engineering, or mathematics (STEM) at a college in any state.

Eligibility: Open to women who are entering the third or fourth year of an undergraduate degree program in a STEM-related field at a college, university, or institute in any state. Preference is given to residents of Wisconsin. Applicants must submit a 300-word essay that describes their academic and professional goals, the relevance of their program of study to STEM, and how the scholarship will assist them in reaching their goals. Financial need is not considered in the selection process.

Financial data: The stipend is $1,000.

Duration: 1 year.

Number awarded: 1 each year.

Deadline: May of each year.

Social Sciences

2482 A LEGACY OF LEADERSHIP: THE RONALD REAGAN ESSAY CONTEST

Freedom Foundation of Minnesota
900 Second Avenue South, Suite 570
Minneapolis, MN 55402
Phone: (612) 354-2192
Email: Info@freedomfoundationofminnesota.com
Web: freedomfoundationofminnesota.com/Reagan

Summary: To recognize and reward, with college scholarships, high school students in Minnesota who submit outstanding essays on a topic related to former President Ronald Reagan.

Eligibility: Open to students enrolled in public, private, home school, or charter high schools in Minnesota. Applicants must submit an essay on a topic related to the leadership, legacies, and values of Ronald Reagan. Recently, students were invited to describe his most important public policy achievement. Essays must be shorter than 1,200 words in length and submitted in English. Selection is based on intellectual cogency of original argumentation, imagination, quality of writing, and relevance of the thesis to contemporary political concerns.

Financial data: First prize is $5,000, second $1,000, and third $500. All prizes are in the form of scholarships payable to and accredited college or university in the United States. No cash awards are presented.

Duration: The competition is held annually.

Number awarded: 3 each year.

Deadline: January of each year.

2483 AAAS EDUCATIONAL FOUNDATION SCHOLARSHIPS

Summary: To provide financial assistance to residents of designated southeastern states interested in attending college or technical school in any state to prepare for a career in the automotive aftermarket industry.

See Listing #1635.

2484 AACE INTERNATIONAL COMPETITIVE SCHOLARSHIPS

Summary: To provide financial assistance to undergraduate and graduate students in the United States or Canada working on a degree related to total cost management (the effective application of professional and technical expertise to plan and control resources, costs, profitability, and risk).

See Listing #1637.

2485 ACADEMIC SCHOLARSHIPS FOR HIGH SCHOOL SENIORS AND GED GRADUATES

National Restaurant Association Educational Foundation
Attn: Scholarships Program
175 West Jackson Boulevard, Suite 1500
Chicago, IL 60604-2702
Phone: (312) 715-1010, ext. 738; (800) 765-2122, ext. 6738; Fax: (312) 566-9733
Email: scholars@nraef.org
Web: www.nraef.org/scholarships

Summary: To provide financial assistance to high school seniors and GED graduates who are interested in preparing for a career in the hospitality industry.

Eligibility: Open to graduating high school seniors, GED graduates enrolling in college for the first time, and high school graduates enrolling in college for the first time. Applicants must be planning to enroll either full-time or substantial part-time at an accredited culinary school, college, or university to major in culinary, restaurant management, or other food service–related field of study. They must be U.S. citizens or permanent residents. Along with their application, they must submit 1) an essay of 150 to 200 words on their career goals in the restaurant/food service industry; and 2) an essay of 450 to 500 words on the experience or person that most influenced them to select restaurant and food service as their career. Selection is based on the essays, presentation of the application, industry-related work experience, and letters of recommendation.

Financial data: The stipend is $2,500.

Duration: 1 year.

Number awarded: Approximately 150 each year.

Deadline: May of each year.

2486 ACCENTURE UNDERGRADUATE SCHOLARSHIPS

Summary: To provide financial assistance for college to Native American high school seniors interested in majoring in fields of business and technology.

See Listing #1644.

2487 ACI-NA COMMISSIONERS COMMITTEE SCHOLARSHIP

Airports Council International-North America
1775 K Street, N.W., Suite 500
Washington, DC 20006
Phone: (202) 293-8500; (888) 424-7767; Fax: (202) 331-1362
Web: www.aci-na.org/about/scholarships

Summary: To provide financial support for college or graduate school to students preparing for a career in airport management or airport operations.

Eligibility: Open to students enrolled in an undergraduate or graduate program that focuses on airport management or airport operations at an accredited college or university in the United States or Canada. Students in flight-related majors are not eligible. Applicants must have a GPA of 3.0 or higher. Along with their application, they must submit a personal statement (from 350 to 500 words) on their interest in airport management or airport operations. Selection is based on academic excellence, leadership, expected impact on the airport industry, and financial need.

Financial data: The stipend is $2,500.

Duration: 1 year; recipients may reapply.

Number awarded: Up to 6 each year.

Deadline: April or December of each year.

2488 ACTUARIAL DIVERSITY SCHOLARSHIPS

Actuarial Foundation
Attn: Actuarial Education and Research Fund Committee
475 North Martingale Road, Suite 600
Schaumburg, IL 60173-2226
Phone: (847) 706-3535; Fax: (847) 706-3599
Email: scholarships@actfnd.org
Web: www.aerf.org/programs/actuarial/scholarships.shtml

Summary: To provide financial assistance to minority undergraduate and graduate students who are preparing for a career in actuarial science.

Eligibility: Open to members of minority groups, defined as having at least 1 birth parent who is Black/African American, Hispanic, or Native American Indian. Applicants must be graduating high school seniors or current full-time undergraduate or graduate students working on or planning to work on a degree at an accredited 2- or 4-year college or university that may lead to a career in the actuarial profession. They must have a GPA of 3.0 or higher; high school seniors must also have a minimum score of 28 on the ACT mathematics examination or 600 on the SAT mathematics examination. Along with their application, they must submit a 1- or 2-page personal statement that covers why they are interested in becoming an actuary, the steps they are taking to enter the actuarial profession, participation in actuarial internships, and participation in extracurricular activities. Financial need is not considered in the selection process.

Financial data: Annual stipends are $1,000 for high school seniors applying for freshman year or college freshmen applying for sophomore year, $2,000 for college sophomores applying for junior year, $4,000 for college juniors applying for senior year, or $5,000 for college seniors applying for graduate school or continuing graduate students.

Duration: 1 year; may be renewed, provided the recipient remains enrolled full-time, in good academic standing, in a course of study that may lead to a career in the actuarial profession, and (for college juniors and higher) passes actuarial examinations.

Number awarded: Varies each year; recently, 12 of these scholarships were awarded.

Deadline: May of each year.

2489 ADCRAFT FOUNDATION SCHOLARSHIPS

Summary: To provide financial assistance to undergraduate and graduate students from any state majoring in advertising or marketing at colleges and universities in Michigan.

See Listing #1138.

2490 AERO PERSONNEL PREPARATION SCHOLARSHIPS

Association for Education and Rehabilitation of the Blind and Visually Impaired of Ohio
c/o Mrs. Jan Jasko
7012 Beresford Avenue
Parma Heights, OH 44130-5050
Phone: (440) 888-6236
Web: www.aerohio.org/ScholarshipsGrants.html

Summary: To provide financial assistance to Ohio residents who are working on an undergraduate or graduate degree in a field related to rehabilitation of the blind.

Eligibility: Open to undergraduate and graduate students in rehabilitation counseling, rehabilitation teaching, orientation and mobility, or education of students with visual disabilities. Applicants must be residents of Ohio, although they may be studying in any state. Undergraduates must have at least junior standing. All applicants must have a GPA of 3.0 or higher. Along with their application, they must submit 1) a short essay explaining why they have chosen their specific field as their profession and what they would like to contribute to the field; 2) a short description of volunteer or paid involvement with individuals with visual disabilities or any other disability; 3) transcripts; and 4) 3 letters of recommendation.

Financial data: The stipend is $1,000.

Duration: 1 year; nonrenewable.

Number awarded: 1 each year.

Deadline: August of each year.

2491 AFCEA UNDERGRADUATE INTELLIGENCE SCHOLARSHIPS

Summary: To provide financial assistance to undergraduate students working on a degree in a field related to intelligence or homeland security.

See Listing #1140.

2492 AGATHA PRATOR SCHOLARSHIP

Delta Kappa Gamma Society International–Kappa State Organization
c/o Susan Riggs, Professional Affairs Committee
1847 Wheeler Avenue
Fayetteville, AR 72703
Email: sriggs@uark.edu
Web: www.deltakappagamma.org/AR/forms.html

Summary: To provide financial assistance to residents of Arkansas who are enrolled in a pre-service teaching program at a school in any state.

Eligibility: Open to residents of Arkansas (and Texarkana, Texas) who are enrolled as a student teacher, either as a senior or as an intern. The student's school may be in any state, but it must be NCATE-approved. Along with their application, they must submit a 1-page narrative on how they will use this educational experience and how it will benefit them. Selection is based on academic record, leadership, and potential for future service to the field of education.

Financial data: The stipend is $2,500.

Duration: 1 semester.

Number awarded: 1 each year.

Deadline: March of each year for fall semester; November of each year for spring semester.

2493 AH&LEF INCOMING FRESHMAN SCHOLARSHIPS

American Hotel & Lodging Educational Foundation
Attn: Manager of Foundation Programs
1201 New York Avenue, N.W., Suite 600
Washington, DC 20005-3931
Phone: (202) 289-3181; Fax: (202) 289-3199
Email: ahlef@ahlef.org
Web: www.ahlef.org/content.aspx?id=19836

Summary: To provide financial assistance to students entering college as a freshman and planning to work on a degree in hospitality management.

Eligibility: Open to U.S. citizens and permanent residents who are entering freshmen at a college or university. Applicants must be planning to work full-time on an associate or baccalaureate degree in hospitality management. They must have a GPA of 2.0 or higher. Preference is given to graduates of the Lodging Management Program of the American Hotel & Lodging Educational Foundation (AH&LEF). Along with their application, they must submit a 500-word essay on their personal background, including when they became interested in the hospitality field, what traits they possess or will need to succeed in the industry, and their plans as related to their educational and career objectives and future goals. Selection is based on industry-related work experience; financial need; academic record and educational qualifications; professional, community, and extracurricular activities; personal attributes, including career goals; the essay; and neatness and completeness of the application.

Financial data: The stipend is $2,000 for students in 4-year baccalaureate programs or $1,000 for students in 2-year associate programs. Funds are distributed in 2 equal installments (in August and December). Checks are made out jointly to the recipient and the recipient's academic institution. Funds may be used only for tuition, fees, and books.

Duration: 1 year.

Number awarded: Varies each year; recently, 8 of these scholarships were awarded.

Deadline: April of each year.

2494 A.J. (ANDY) SPIELMAN SCHOLARSHIPS

Tourism Cares
Attn: American Society of Travel Agents Scholarship Fund
275 Turnpike Street, Suite 307
Canton, MA 02021
Phone: (781) 821-5990; Fax: (781) 821-8949
Email: info@tourismcares.org
Web: www.tourismcares.org/scholarships/asta-scholarships

Summary: To provide financial assistance to reentry students who are interested in preparing for a career in the travel/tourism industry.

Eligibility: Open to students who are enrolled or preparing to enroll at a recognized proprietary travel school as reentry students. Applicants must have a GPA of 2.5 or higher, be citizens or permanent residents of the United States or Canada, and write a 500-word essay on "Why I Have Chosen the Travel Profession for My Re-Entry into the Work Force."

Financial data: The stipend is $2,500.

Duration: 1 year.

Number awarded: Up to 2 each year.

Deadline: Applications may be submitted at any time.

2495 AL SCHUMAN ECOLAB UNDERGRADUATE ENTREPRENEURIAL SCHOLARSHIPS

National Restaurant Association Educational Foundation
Attn: Scholarships Program
175 West Jackson Boulevard, Suite 1500
Chicago, IL 60604-2702
Phone: (312) 715-1010, ext. 738; (800) 765-2122, ext. 6738; Fax: (312) 566-9733
Email: scholars@nraef.org
Web: www.nraef.org/scholarships

Summary: To provide financial assistance to entering or currently-enrolled students at selected universities who have demonstrated entrepreneurship relevant to the food service industry.

Eligibility: Open to students entering their freshman, sophomore, or junior year at any of 10 designated universities. Applicants must be enrolled or planning to enroll full-time in a restaurant and/or food service program and have a GPA of 3.0 or higher. Along with their application, they must submit an entrepreneurial project that they have completed. Selection is based on that project, presentation of the application, GPA, strength of letters of recommendation, and academic honors and achievements.

Financial data: The stipend ranges from $3,500 to $7,500.

Duration: 1 year.

Number awarded: 1 or more each year.

Deadline: March of each year.

2496 ALABAMA THESPIAN HIGH SCHOOL SENIOR SCHOLARSHIPS

Summary: To provide financial assistance to high school seniors in Alabama who have been active in theater and plan to major in theater education or a theater-related field at a college in any state.

See Listing #1152.

2497 ALASKA TEACHER EDUCATION LOAN PROGRAM

Alaska Commission on Postsecondary Education
Attn: AlaskAdvantage Programs
3030 Vintage Boulevard
P.O. Box 110505

Juneau, AK 99811-0505
Phone: (907) 465-2962; (800) 441-2962; Fax: (907) 465-5316; TDD: (907) 465-3143
Email: customer_service@acpe.ak.us
Web: akadvantage.alaska.gov/page/254
Summary: To provide financial assistance to Alaska high school graduates who wish to prepare for a teaching career in a rural elementary or secondary school in the state.
Eligibility: Open to Alaska high school graduates who are enrolled or intend to enroll in a 4-year bachelor's degree program in elementary or secondary teacher education or a fifth-year teacher certification program. They may be nominated by a rural school district for receipt of this funding. Nominees must meet all the eligibility criteria of the AlaskAdvantage Education Loan Programs. Currently, only rural school districts may nominate loan recipients. Rural is defined as communities with a population of 5,500 or less that are not on road or rail to Anchorage or Fairbanks or with a population of 1,500 or less that are on road or rail to Anchorage or Fairbanks.
Financial data: This is a scholarship/loan program. Students may borrow up to $7,500 per year for in-state or out-of-state study. Loans may be used for tuition, room and board, books and supplies, and transportation costs (up to 2 round trips between the student's home community and the school of attendance). An origination fee of 5% of the amount loaned is added to the principal balance to be repaid. No interest is charged while the borrower is in school; subsequently, the rate is 7.6%. If the borrower is employed after graduation as a teacher in a rural elementary or secondary school in Alaska, he or she may be eligible for up to 100% forgiveness of the total loan.
Duration: Loans may be awarded for up to a maximum of 5 years of undergraduate study. Repayment must begin no later than 12 months from the time the borrower terminates full-time student status. The loan must be repaid within 15 years.
Number awarded: Varies each year; recently, 187 of these scholarship/loans were issued.
Deadline: June of each year.

2498 ALASKA TRAVEL ADVENTURES SCHOLARSHIP

Alaska Travel Industry Association
Attn: ATIA Education Foundation
2600 Cordova Street, Suite 201
Anchorage, AK 99503
Phone: (907) 929-2842; Fax: (907) 561-5727
Email: ATIA@alaskatia.org
Web: www.alaskatia.org/scholarship/default.asp
Summary: To provide financial assistance to Alaska residents interested in attending college in any state, preferably Alaska, to prepare for a career in tourism.
Eligibility: Open to residents of Alaska who are enrolled or planning to enroll full-time at a college or university in any state. Applicants must be interested in studying a field that will prepare them for a career in tourism. Along with their application, they must submit a 500-word essay that covers their career goals and objectives and how they plan to achieve those, why they want to be involved in the travel and visitor industry, and what they consider the major challenges facing the visitor industry today. Selection is based on GPA, demonstrated tourism initiative, and financial need; special consideration is given to applicants attending an educational institution in Alaska.
Financial data: The stipend is $1,000.
Duration: 1 year.
Number awarded: 1 each year.
Deadline: March of each year.

2499 ALASKA TRAVEL INDUSTRY ASSOCIATION CONTINUING EDUCATION SCHOLARSHIP

Alaska Travel Industry Association
Attn: ATIA Education Foundation
2600 Cordova Street, Suite 201
Anchorage, AK 99503
Phone: (907) 929-2842; Fax: (907) 561-5727
Email: ATIA@alaskatia.org
Web: www.alaskatia.org/scholarship/default.asp
Summary: To provide financial assistance to adult Alaska residents interested in attending college in any state, preferably Alaska, to work on an undergraduate or graduate degree or certificate in tourism.
Eligibility: Open to residents of Alaska who are enrolled or planning to enroll full- or part-time at a college or university in any state. Applicants must be interested in preparing for a career in tourism. Preference is given to students returning to school for degree or certificate completion or for graduate study. Along with their application, they must submit a 500-word essay that covers their career goals and objectives and how they plan to achieve those, why they want to be involved in the travel and visitor industry, and what they consider the major challenges facing the visitor industry today. Selection is based on GPA, demonstrated tourism initiative, and financial need; special consideration is given to applicants attending an educational institution in Alaska.
Financial data: The stipend is $2,500.
Duration: 1 year.
Number awarded: 1 each year.
Deadline: March of each year.

2500 ALASKADVANTAGE EDUCATION GRANTS

Summary: To provide financial assistance to Alaska residents who attend college in the state to prepare for a career in designated fields with a workforce shortage.
See Listing #1676.

2501 ALICE GLAISYER WARFIELD MEMORIAL SCHOLARSHIP

Summary: To provide financial assistance to college students interested in preparing for a career in fields related to transportation.
See Listing #1679.

2502 ALICIA SHANKS MEMORIAL SCHOLARSHIP

Vermont Student Assistance Corporation
Attn: Scholarship Programs
10 East Allen Street
P.O. Box 2000
Winooski, VT 05404-2601
Phone: (802) 654-3798; (888) 253-4819; Fax: (802) 654-3765; TDD: (800) 281-3341 (within VT)
Email: info@vsac.org
Web: services.vsac.org/wps/wcm/connect/vsac/VSAC
Summary: To provide financial assistance to residents of Vermont who are interested in working on a bachelor's degree in elementary education at a college in any state.
Eligibility: Open to residents of Vermont who are entering their junior or senior year of a bachelor's degree program in elementary education at a college or university in any state. Applicants must have a GPA of 3.0 or higher. Along with their application, they must submit 1) a 100-word essay on their interest in and commitment to pursuing their chosen career or vocation; and 2) a 250-word essay on their short- and long-term academic, educational, career, vocational, and/or employment goals. Selection is based on those essays, academic achievement, and a letter of recommendation.
Financial data: The stipend is $1,000.
Duration: 1 year.
Number awarded: 1 or more each year.
Deadline: March of each year.

2503 ALMA EXLEY SCHOLARSHIP

Community Foundation of Greater New Britain
Attn: Scholarship Manager
74A Vine Street
New Britain, CT 06052-1431
Phone: (860) 229-6018, ext. 305; Fax: (860) 225-2666
Email: cfarmer@cfgnb.org
Web: www.cfgnb.org
Summary: To provide financial assistance to minority college students in Connecticut who are interested in preparing for a teaching career.
Eligibility: Open to students of color (African Americans, Asian Americans, Hispanic Americans, and Native Americans) enrolled in a teacher preparation program in Connecticut. Applicant must 1) have been admitted to a traditional teacher preparation program at an accredited 4-year college or university in the state; or 2) be participating in the Alternate Route to Certification (ARC) program sponsored by the Connecticut Department of Higher Education.
Financial data: The stipend is $1,500 per year for students at a 4-year college or university or $500 for a student in the ARC program.
Duration: 2 years for students at 4-year colleges or universities; 1 year for students in the ARC program.
Number awarded: 2 each year: 1 to a 4-year student and 1 to an ARC student.
Deadline: October of each year.

2504 ALPHA GAMMA CHAPTER RECRUITMENT GRANT

Delta Kappa Gamma Society International–Mississippi Alpha Gamma Chapter
c/o Donna Matthews
910 South 34th Avenue
Hattiesburg, MS 39402
Phone: (601) 268-6987
Email: donnamatthews527@gmail.com
Web: www.alphagammachapter.com/scholarship.htm

Summary: To provide financial assistance to women enrolled at colleges in Mississippi and majoring in education, library science, or a related field.

Eligibility: Open to women currently enrolled as juniors at colleges and universities in Mississippi. Applicants must be majoring in education, library science, or a related field. Along with their application, they must submit a brief autobiography that includes career plans and any unique financial needs. Preference is given to applicants planning to teach in Lamar, Forrest, Covington, or Perry counties of Mississippi.

Financial data: The stipend is $1,000.

Duration: 1 year.

Number awarded: 1 each year.

Deadline: December.

2505 ALTRIA SCHOLARS

Summary: To provide financial assistance to students majoring in designated fields at a college or university that is a member of the Virginia Foundation for Independent Colleges (VFIC).

See Listing #1681.

2506 AMERICAN EXPRESS SCHOLARSHIP COMPETITION

American Hotel & Lodging Educational Foundation
Attn: Manager of Foundation Programs
1201 New York Avenue, N.W., Suite 600
Washington, DC 20005-3931
Phone: (202) 289-3188; Fax: (202) 289-3199
Email: ahlef@ahlef.org
Web: www.ahlef.org/content.aspx?id=19832

Summary: To provide financial assistance to undergraduate students who have a connection to the hotel and motel industry and are interested in majoring in hospitality management in college.

Eligibility: Open to applicants who are 1) employed (at least 20 hours per week) at a hotel or motel that is a member of the American Hotel & Lodging Association (AH&LA) and have been employed at least 12 months by a hotel, or 2) the dependent of an employee who meets those requirements and has been employed in the hospitality industry in some capacity in the past. In addition, applicants must be enrolled or planning to enroll as an undergraduate student in a hospitality management program offered by a university or college. Along with their application, they must submit a 500-word essay on their personal background, including when they became interested in the hospitality field, what traits they possess or will need to succeed in the industry, and their plans as related to their educational and career objectives and future goals. Selection is based on financial need, industry-related work experience, academic record, extracurricular activities, career goals, the essay, and neatness and completeness of the application.

Financial data: Full-time students at 4-year institutions receive $2,000; part-time students at 4-year institutions receive $1,000; full-time students at 2-year institutions receive $1,000; part-time students at 2-year institutions receive $500. Funds are paid in 2 equal installments. Checks are made out jointly to the recipient and the academic institution and must be endorsed by both. Funds may be used only for tuition, fees, and books.

Duration: 1 year.

Number awarded: Varies each year; recently, this program awarded 6 scholarships. Since it was founded, it has awarded 204 scholarships worth more than $248,000.

Deadline: April of each year.

2507 AMERICAN FOREIGN SERVICE ASSOCIATION NATIONAL HIGH SCHOOL ESSAY CONTEST

American Foreign Service Association
Attn: National High School Essay Contest
2101 E Street, N.W.
Washington, DC 20037
Phone: (202) 338-4045; (800) 704-AFSA; Fax: (202) 338-6820
Email: perigreen@aol.com
Web: www.afsa.org/essaycontest

Summary: To recognize and reward high school students who submit essays on a topic related to U.S. foreign relations.

Eligibility: Open to students in grades 9–12 attending a public, private, parochial, or home school or participating in a high school correspondence program in any of the 50 states, the District of Columbia, or the U.S. territories. U.S. citizens attending schools overseas are also eligible. Students whose parents are members of the U.S. Foreign Service or have served on the Advisory Committees are not eligible. Applicants must submit an essay of 750 to 1,000 words on a topic that changes annually. Recently, participants were invited to write on the challenges facing the American Foreign Service in the 21st century. Selection is based on the quality of research, quality of analysis, and style and mechanics.

Financial data: The winner receives $2,500 and an all-expense paid trip to Washington, D.C. for the awards ceremony. The winner's school or sponsoring organization receives $500.

Duration: The competition is held annually.

Number awarded: 1 each year.

Deadline: April of each year.

2508 AMERICAN HOTEL & LODGING EDUCATIONAL FOUNDATION ANNUAL SCHOLARSHIP GRANT PROGRAM

American Hotel & Lodging Educational Foundation
Attn: Manager of Foundation Programs
1201 New York Avenue, N.W., Suite 600
Washington, DC 20005-3931
Phone: (202) 289-3181; Fax: (202) 289-3199
Email: ahlef@ahlef.org
Web: www.ahlef.org/content.aspx?id=19818

Summary: To provide financial assistance to students working on an undergraduate degree in hospitality management at participating schools.

Eligibility: Open to sophomores in baccalaureate programs and freshmen in associate programs at a college or university in the United States that is preapproved and participating in the foundation's scholarship program (for a list of schools, write to the foundation). Applicants must be majoring in hospitality management (including hotel and restaurant management) as full-time students and have a GPA of 3.0 or higher. Individual schools select the final recipients. U.S. citizenship or permanent resident status is required.

Financial data: Stipends range up to $3,000 for students at 4-year institutions or up to $1,500 for students at 2-year institutions.

Duration: 1 year.

Number awarded: Varies each year; recently, a total of $234,000 was allocated for this program.

Deadline: Schools must submit their nominations by April of each year.

2509 AMERICAN INDIAN FELLOWSHIP IN BUSINESS SCHOLARSHIP

National Center for American Indian Enterprise Development
Attn: Scholarship Committee
953 East Juanita Avenue
Mesa, AZ 85204
Phone: (480) 545-1298, ext. 243; (800) 4-NCAIED, ext. 243; Fax: (480) 545-4208
Email: events@ncaied.org
Web: www.ncaied.org/scholarships.php

Summary: To provide financial assistance to American Indian upper-division and graduate students working on a business degree.

Eligibility: Open to American Indians who are currently enrolled full-time in college at the upper-division or graduate school level and working on a business degree. Applicants must submit a letter on their reasons for pursuing higher education and their plans following completion of their degree. Selection is based on grades (30%), an essay on their community involvement (30%), an essay on personal challenges they have faced (25%), an essay on their paid or volunteer business experience (10%), and the quality of those essays (5%).

Financial data: A stipend is awarded (amount not specified).

Duration: 1 year.

Number awarded: Up to 5 each year.

Deadline: July of each year.

2510 AMERICAN INSTITUTE OF WINE & FOOD COLORADO CHAPTER SCHOLARSHIP AWARDS

Colorado Restaurant Association
Attn: CRA Education Foundation
430 East Seventh Avenue

Denver, CO 80203
Phone: (303) 830-2972; (800) 522-2972; Fax: (303) 830-2973
Email: info@coloradorestaurant.com
Web: www.coloradorestaurant.com

Summary: To provide financial assistance to residents of Colorado who are working on an associate or bachelor's degree at a college in any state to prepare for a career in the food service or hospitality industry.

Eligibility: Open to residents of Colorado who are enrolled full-or part-time in an accredited food service program at a college or university in any state. Applicants must be in the second half of an approved associate degree program or juniors or seniors in a bachelor's degree program. They must have a GPA of 2.75 or higher and at least 6 months of industry-related work experience. Along with their application, they must submit brief essays on their career objectives, their skills and personal characteristics that will contribute to the food service or hospitality industry, special recognition or honors they have received, their extracurricular and community service activities, their interests or hobbies, the 2 major advantages of a career in the food service or hospitality industry, the 2 major disadvantages (aside from an irregular work schedule) of a career in the food service or hospitality industry, why they have chosen the food service or hospitality industry, and why they feel they are qualified to receive this scholarship. Financial need is also considered in the selection process.

Financial data: The stipend is $1,000.

Duration: 1 year.

Number awarded: 2 each year.

Deadline: April of each year.

2511 AMERICAN LEGION NATIONAL HIGH SCHOOL ORATORICAL CONTEST

American Legion
Attn: Americanism and Children & Youth Division
700 North Pennsylvania Street
P.O. Box 1055
Indianapolis, IN 46206-1055
Phone: (317) 630-1202; Fax: (317) 630-1223
Email: acy@legion.org
Web: www.legion.org/programs/youthprograms/oratorical

Summary: To recognize and reward, with college scholarships, high school students who participate in an oratorical contest on a theme related to the U.S. Constitution.

Eligibility: Open to U.S. citizens and permanent residents under 20 years of age who are currently enrolled in junior high or high school (grades 9–12). Students enter the contest through their Department (state) American Legion. Each department chooses 1 contestant to enter the regional contest. Regional winners compete in sectional contests; sectional winners compete on the national level. In all competitions, participants are evaluated on both the content and presentation of their prepared and extemporaneous speeches, which must deal with an aspect of the American Constitution or principles of government under the Constitution.

Financial data: Scholarship awards are presented to the 3 finalists in the national contest: $18,000 to the first-place winner; $16,000 to the second-place winner; and $14,000 to the third-place winner. Each Department (state) winner who participates in the first round of the national contest receives a $1,500 scholarship; each first-round winner who advances to and participates in the second round, but does not advance to the final round, receives an additional $1,500 scholarship.

Duration: The competition is held annually.

Number awarded: 3 national winners; hundreds of sectional, regional, and departmental winners.

Deadline: The dates of departmental competitions vary; check with your local American Legion post. The national competition is generally held in April.

2512 AMERICAN PUBLIC TRANSPORTATION FOUNDATION SCHOLARSHIP AWARDS PROGRAM

Summary: To provide financial assistance to undergraduate and graduate students who are preparing for a career in public transportation.

See Listing #1695.

2513 AMERICAN SOCIETY OF TRAVEL AGENTS SCHOLARSHIP FUND

Tourism Cares
275 Turnpike Street, Suite 307
Canton, MA 02021
Phone: (781) 821-5990; Fax: (781) 821-8949
Email: info@tourismcares.org
Web: www.tourismcares.org/scholarships/asta-scholarships

Summary: To provide financial assistance to students preparing for a career in the travel industry at a 2-year college, 4-year college or university, or proprietary travel school.

Eligibility: Open to students who are enrolled or able to provide proof of acceptance at a proprietary travel school or a 2- or 4-year college in the United States or Canada that offers a travel and tourism program. Applicants must have a GPA of 2.5 or higher, be residents of the United States or Canada, and write a 500-word essay on their plans in travel and tourism and their view of the travel industry's future. Selection is based on academic record, work performance, potential, and plans for a career in the travel/tourism industry.

Financial data: Stipends are at least $1,000.

Duration: 1 year.

Number awarded: Several each year.

Deadline: June of each year.

2514 AMERISTAR CARES SCHOLARSHIPS

Colorado Restaurant Association
Attn: CRA Education Foundation
430 East Seventh Avenue
Denver, CO 80203
Phone: (303) 830-2972; (800) 522-2972; Fax: (303) 830-2973
Email: info@coloradorestaurant.com
Web: www.coloradorestaurant.com

Summary: To provide financial assistance to residents of Colorado who are working on an associate or bachelor's degree at a college in any state to prepare for a career in the food service or hospitality industry.

Eligibility: Open to residents of Colorado who are enrolled full- or part-time in an accredited food service program at a college or university in any state. Applicants must be in the second half of an approved associate degree program or juniors or seniors in a bachelor's degree program. They must have a GPA of 2.75 or higher and at least 6 months of industry-related work experience. Along with their application, they must submit brief essays on their career objectives, their skills and personal characteristics that will contribute to the food service or hospitality industry, special recognition or honors they have received, their extracurricular and community service activities, their interests or hobbies, the 2 major advantages of a career in the food service or hospitality industry, the 2 major disadvantages (aside from an irregular work schedule) of a career in the food service or hospitality industry, why they have chosen the food service or hospitality industry, and why they feel they are qualified to receive this scholarship. Financial need is also considered in the selection process.

Financial data: The stipend is $1,000.

Duration: 1 year.

Number awarded: 2 each year.

Deadline: April of each year.

2515 ANCHORAGE CHAPTER SCHOLARSHIP

Alaska Travel Industry Association
Attn: ATIA Education Foundation
2600 Cordova Street, Suite 201
Anchorage, AK 99503
Phone: (907) 929-2842; Fax: (907) 561-5727
Email: ATIA@alaskatia.org
Web: www.alaskatia.org/scholarship/default.asp

Summary: To provide financial assistance to Alaska residents, especially high school seniors, who are interested in attending college in any state, preferably Alaska, to prepare for a career in tourism.

Eligibility: Open to residents of Alaska who are enrolled or planning to enroll full-time at a college or university in any state. Preference is given to graduating high school seniors. Applicants must be interested in studying a field that will prepare them for a career in tourism. Along with their application, they must submit a 500-word essay that covers their career goals and objectives and how they plan to achieve those, why they want to be involved in the travel and visitor industry, and what they consider the major challenges facing the visitor industry today. Selection is based on GPA, demonstrated tourism initiative, and financial need; special consideration is given to applicants attending an educational institution in Alaska.

Financial data: The stipend is $3,000.

Duration: 1 year.

Number awarded: 1 each year.

Deadline: March of each year.

2516 ANNIS IRENE FOWLER/KADEN SCHOLARSHIP

South Dakota Board of Regents
Attn: Scholarship Committee
306 East Capitol Avenue, Suite 200
Pierre, SD 57501-2545
Phone: (605) 773-3455; Fax: (605) 773-5320
Email: info@sdbor.edu
Web: www.sdbor.edu/administration/academics/Scholarships.htm

Summary: To provide financial assistance to high school seniors planning to attend a public university in South Dakota and major in elementary education.

Eligibility: Open to first-time entering freshmen at public universities in South Dakota. Applicants must have a GPA of 3.0 or higher and an intent to major in elementary education. They must submit an essay (from 1,000 to 1,500 words) on a topic that changes annually; recently, the topic related to the challenges South Dakota elementary teachers face because of the increasing number of minority students in the state's classrooms. Selection is based on the essay, GPA, high school courses, and letters of recommendation; financial need is not considered. Special consideration is given to students who demonstrate motivational ability, who have a disability, or who are self-supporting.

Financial data: The stipend is $1,000; funds are allocated to the institution for distribution to the student.

Duration: 1 year; nonrenewable.

Number awarded: 2 each year.

Deadline: February of each year.

2517 APPLEGATE/JACKSON/PARKS FUTURE TEACHER SCHOLARSHIP

National Institute for Labor Relations Research
Attn: Future Teacher Scholarships
5211 Port Royal Road, Suite 510
Springfield, VA 22151
Phone: (703) 321-9606; Fax: (703) 321-7342
Email: research@nilrr.org
Web: www.nilrr.org/scholarships

Summary: To provide financial assistance to students majoring in education who oppose compulsory unionism in the education community.

Eligibility: Open to undergraduate and graduate students majoring in education at institutions of higher learning in the United States. Applicants must demonstrate the potential to complete a degree program in education and receive a teaching license. Along with their application, they must submit an essay of approximately 500 words demonstrating an understanding of the principles of voluntary unionism and the problems of compulsory unionism in relation to education. Selection is based on scholastic ability and a demonstrated interest in the work of the sponsoring organization to promote voluntary unionism.

Financial data: The stipend is $1,000.

Duration: 1 year.

Number awarded: 1 each year.

Deadline: December of each year.

2518 APWA HORIZONS FRONT RANGE SCHOLARSHIP

Summary: To provide financial assistance to high school seniors in Colorado who plan to attend a college or university in the state to prepare for a career in public works.

See Listing #1165.

2519 ARIZONA SPECIAL LEVERAGING EDUCATIONAL ASSISTANCE PARTNERSHIP PROGRAM

Summary: To provide financial assistance to students at Arizona colleges and universities who are majoring in education or fields of science, technology, engineering, or mathematics (STEM) and can demonstrate substantial financial need.

See Listing #1715.

2520 ARKANSAS MINORITY TEACHERS SCHOLARSHIPS

Arkansas Department of Higher Education
Attn: Financial Aid Division
114 East Capitol Avenue
Little Rock, AR 72201-3818
Phone: (501) 371-2050; (800) 54-STUDY; Fax: (501) 371-2001
Email: finaid@adhe.edu
Web: www.adhe.edu/divisions/financialaid/Pages/fa_mtsp.aspx

Summary: To provide financial assistance to minority undergraduates in Arkansas who want to become teachers in the state.

Eligibility: Open to minority (African American, Native American, Hispanic, or Asian American) residents of Arkansas who are U.S. citizens or permanent residents and enrolled full-time as juniors or seniors in an approved teacher certification program at an Arkansas public or independent 4-year institution. Applicants must have a cumulative GPA of 2.5 or higher and be willing to teach in an Arkansas public school for at least 5 years after completion of their teaching certificate (3 years if the teaching is in 1 of the 42 counties of Arkansas designated as the Delta Region, or if the teaching is in a critical subject shortage area, or if the recipient is an African American male teaching at the elementary level).

Financial data: Loans up to $5,000 per year are available. The loan will be forgiven at the rate of 20% for each year the recipient teaches full-time in an Arkansas public school (or 33% per year if the obligation is fulfilled in 3 years). If the loan is not forgiven by service, it must be repaid with interest at 10%.

Duration: 1 year; may be renewed for 1 additional year if the recipient remains enrolled full-time with a GPA of 2.5 or higher.

Number awarded: Varies each year; recently, 97 of these forgivable loans were approved.

Deadline: May of each year.

2521 ARKANSAS THESPIAN SCHOLARSHIPS

Summary: To provide financial assistance to high school seniors in Arkansas who plan to major in fields related to theater or theater education at a college in any state.

See Listing #1170.

2522 ARMED FORCES COMMUNICATIONS AND ELECTRONICS ASSOCIATION STEM TEACHER'S SCHOLARSHIP

Summary: To provide financial assistance to undergraduate and graduate students who are preparing for a career as a teacher of science and mathematics.

See Listing #1718.

2523 ARNOLD SADLER MEMORIAL SCHOLARSHIP

Summary: To provide financial assistance to undergraduate or graduate students who are blind and are interested in studying in a field of service to persons with disabilities.

See Listing #1721.

2524 ART PFAFF SCHOLARSHIP PROGRAM

Missouri Middle School Association
c/o Bob Stewart
12836 Sycamore
Grandview, MO 64030
Phone: (816) 885-7052
Email: rstewart4@kc.rr.com
Web: www.mmsa-mo.org/pfaff_scholarship.html

Summary: To provide financial assistance to students in Missouri who are working on a degree to receive entry-level certification for teaching at the middle school level.

Eligibility: Open to students currently enrolled in an education program that will qualify them for entry-level middle school certification in Missouri. Applicants must be classified as a sophomore or higher by their college or university and have a cumulative GPA of 2.5 or higher. They must have made a commitment to be trained as a middle level teacher and to teach at that level after completing their degree. Along with their application, they must submit a brief autobiographical sketch and essays on why they have chosen to become a middle school teacher, how they think they can make a difference as a middle school teacher, the activities during high school and/or college in which they have been involved with middle school age children, what someone would expect to see if they came into their middle school classroom, why a middle school should be different from a typical junior high school, and how this scholarship will help them attain their career goals. Financial need is not considered.

Financial data: The stipend is $1,000.

Duration: 1 year.

Number awarded: 1 or more each year.

Deadline: February of each year.

2525 ARTHUR J. PACKARD MEMORIAL SCHOLARSHIP COMPETITION

American Hotel & Lodging Educational Foundation
Attn: Manager of Foundation Programs
1201 New York Avenue, N.W., Suite 600
Washington, DC 20005-3931
Phone: (202) 289-3181; Fax: (202) 289-3199
Email: ahlef@ahlef.org
Web: www.ahlef.org/content.aspx?id=19822

Summary: To recognize and reward outstanding students working on an undergraduate degree in lodging management at participating universities.

Eligibility: Open to applicants who are attending a 4-year college or university that is preapproved and participating in the foundation's scholarship program (for a list of schools, write to the foundation). They must be enrolled full-time in a hospitality-related degree-granting program, be a sophomore or junior at the time of application, have a GPA of 3.5 or higher, be a U.S. citizen or permanent resident, and be nominated by their school. Selection is based on academic performance, hospitality work experience, financial need, extracurricular involvement (activities and honors), and personal attributes.

Financial data: The national winner receives $5,000, the second-place runner-up receives $3,000, and the third-place runner-up receives $2,000.

Duration: The competition is held annually.

Number awarded: 1 winner and 2 runners-up each year.

Deadline: April of each year.

2526 ASHRM FOUNDATION SCHOLARSHIPS

American Society for Healthcare Risk Management
Attn: ASHRM Foundation
One North Franklin, Suite 2800
Chicago, IL 60606
Phone: (312) 422-3980; Fax: (312) 422-4580
Email: jciatto@aha.org
Web: www.ashrm.org/ashrm/about/foundation/index.shtml

Summary: To provide financial assistance to students working on an undergraduate or graduate degree in fields related to health care risk management.

Eligibility: Open to undergraduate and graduate students working on a degree in health care management, clinical areas, insurance, risk management, or finance. Applicants must have a GPA of 3.0 or higher and be able to document financial need. Along with their application, they must submit a narrative that includes information on their work experience; academic and career goals; professional experience, activities, and accomplishments; potential impact in field of study; and academic and/or employer recommendations. An interview, either by telephone or onsite, may be required.

Financial data: The stipend is $2,500.

Duration: 1 year.

Number awarded: Varies each year; recently, 7 of these scholarships were awarded.

Deadline: February, June, or September of each year.

2527 ASPARAGUS CLUB SCHOLARSHIPS

Baton Rouge Area Foundation
Attn: Scholarship Program Officer
402 North Fourth Street
Baton Rouge, LA 70802
Phone: (225) 381-7084; (877) 387-6126; Fax: (225) 387-6153
Email: moecker@braf.org
Web: www.braf.org/site/c.jfISK0OxFkG/b.2713895/k.91CD/Scholarships.htm

Summary: To provide financial assistance to undergraduate and graduate students interested in preparing for a career in the grocery industry.

Eligibility: Open to upper-division and graduate students who are working on a degree in an academic discipline relevant to the grocery industry. Their field of study may relate to retailing (including supermarket management, convenience store management, produce management, advertising, accounts management, marketing, public relations), processing and manufacturing (including food plant management, personnel management, purchasing management, sales management, packaging, new product development), or wholesaling (including merchandising, marketing, accounting, store construction and remodeling, computer applications). Applicants must submit a letter of recommendation from a professor in the food management and/or business school, a statement of 250 to 500 words on why they are preparing for a career in the grocery industry, transcripts, ACT and/or SAT scores, and documentation of financial need.

Financial data: Stipends range up to $3,000 per year. Funds are sent directly to the recipients with a check payable to them and their universities to be used for tuition and fees.

Duration: 1 year; may be renewed if the recipient maintains a GPA of 2.5 or higher.

Number awarded: Varies each year.

Deadline: June of each year.

2528 ASPIRING MUSIC TEACHER SCHOLARSHIP

Summary: To provide financial assistance to residents of Vermont who are interested in attending college in any state to study music education or piano pedagogy.

See Listing #1176.

2529 ASSOCIATION FOR MANUFACTURING TECHNOLOGY 2-YEAR SCHOLARSHIP PROGRAM

Summary: To provide financial assistance and work experience to students interested in earning a 2-year degree in a manufacturing technology-related field or participating in a university cooperative program.

See Listing #1736.

2530 ASSOCIATION OF CALIFORNIA WATER AGENCIES SCHOLARSHIPS

Summary: To provide financial assistance to upper-division students in California who are majoring in water resources–related fields of study.

See Listing #1738.

2531 ASSOCIATION OF ENERGY ENGINEERS SCHOLARSHIPS

Summary: To provide financial assistance to undergraduate and graduate students interested in taking courses directly related to energy engineering or energy management.

See Listing #1739.

2532 ASSOCIATION OF LATINO PROFESSIONALS IN FINANCE AND ACCOUNTING SCHOLARSHIP PROGRAM

Hispanic College Fund
Attn: Scholarship Processing
1301 K Street, N.W., Suite 450-A West
Washington, DC 20005
Phone: (202) 296-5400; (800) 644-4223; Fax: (202) 296-3774
Email: hcf-info@hispanicfund.org
Web: scholarships.hispanicfund.org/applications

Summary: To provide financial assistance to Hispanic American undergraduate or graduate students who are interested in preparing for a career in accounting or a related field.

Eligibility: Open to U.S. citizens and permanent residents of Hispanic background (at least 1 grandparent must be 100% Hispanic) who are interested in working on an undergraduate or master's degree in business, accounting, or finance. Applicants must have a GPA of 3.0 or higher and be able to demonstrate financial need. They must be enrolled at an accredited college or university in the 50 states or Puerto Rico as a full-time student.

Financial data: Stipends normally range from $1,250 to $1,500, depending on the need of the recipient. In exceptional cases, stipends up to $10,000 are available. Funds are paid directly to the recipient's college or university to help cover tuition and fees.

Duration: 1 year; recipients may reapply.

Number awarded: Varies each year; recently, a total of $150,000 was available for these scholarships.

Deadline: April of each year.

2533 ATIA ONE-YEAR SCHOLARSHIP

Alaska Travel Industry Association
Attn: ATIA Education Foundation
2600 Cordova Street, Suite 201
Anchorage, AK 99503
Phone: (907) 929-2842; Fax: (907) 561-5727
Email: ATIA@alaskatia.org
Web: www.alaskatia.org/scholarship/default.asp

Summary: To provide financial assistance to Alaska residents interested in attending college in any state, preferably Alaska, to prepare for a career in tourism.

Eligibility: Open to residents of Alaska who are enrolled or planning to enroll full-time at a college or university in any state. Applicants must be interested in studying a field that will prepare them for a career in tourism. Along with their application, they must submit a 500-word essay that covers their career goals and objectives and how they plan to achieve those, why they want to be involved in the travel and visitor industry, and what they consider the major challenges facing the visitor industry today. Selection is based on GPA, demonstrated tourism initiative, and financial need; special consideration is given to applicants attending an educational institution in Alaska.
Financial data: The stipend is $1,000.
Duration: 1 year.
Number awarded: 1 each year.
Deadline: March of each year.

2534 ATIA TWO-YEAR SCHOLARSHIP

Alaska Travel Industry Association
Attn: ATIA Education Foundation
2600 Cordova Street, Suite 201
Anchorage, AK 99503
Phone: (907) 929-2842; Fax: (907) 561-5727
Email: ATIA@alaskatia.org
Web: www.alaskatia.org/scholarship/default.asp
Summary: To provide financial assistance to Alaska residents interested in attending college in any state, preferably Alaska, to prepare for a career in tourism.
Eligibility: Open to residents of Alaska who are enrolled or planning to enroll full-time at a college or university in any state. Applicants must be interested in studying a field that will prepare them for a career in tourism. Along with their application, they must submit a 500-word essay that covers their career goals and objectives and how they plan to achieve those, why they want to be involved in the travel and visitor industry, and what they consider the major challenges facing the visitor industry today. Selection is based on GPA, demonstrated tourism initiative, and financial need; special consideration is given to applicants attending an educational institution in Alaska.
Financial data: The stipend is $2,500 per year.
Duration: 2 years.
Number awarded: 1 each year.
Deadline: March of each year.

2535 AUTOMOTIVE EDUCATIONAL FUND UPPER-DIVISION SCHOLARSHIP PROGRAM

Summary: To provide funding to upper-division students who are preparing for an automotive career.
See Listing #1743.

2536 B. JUNE WEST RECRUITMENT GRANT

Delta Kappa Gamma Society International–Theta State Organization
c/o Megan Savage, Committee on Professional Affairs Chair
1101 West Third Street
Roswell, NM 88201-3031
Email: meganandjames@cableone.net
Web: deltakappagamma.org/NM
Summary: To provide financial assistance to women in New Mexico who are interested in preparing for a career as a teacher.
Eligibility: Open to women residents of New Mexico who are 1) graduating high school seniors planning to go into education; 2) college students majoring in education; or 3) teachers needing educational assistance. Applicants must submit a list of activities in which they are involved, 3 letters of recommendation, a list of achievements and awards, and a statement of their educational goal and how this grant would be of assistance to them. Financial need is not considered in the selection process.
Financial data: A stipend is awarded (amount not specified).
Duration: 1 year.
Number awarded: 1 or more each year.
Deadline: February of each year.

2537 BACHELOR'S DEGREE SCHOLARSHIPS OF THE NEBRASKA LIBRARY COMMISSION

Nebraska Library Commission
Attn: Communications Coordinator
1200 N Street, Suite 120
Lincoln, NE 68508-2023
Phone: (402) 471-3434; (800) 307-2665 (within NE); Fax: (402) 471-2083
Email: maryjo.ryan@nebraska.gov
Web: www.nlc.state.ne.us/NowHiring/ScholarshipsBSBA.asp
Summary: To provide financial assistance to residents of Nebraska interested in working on a bachelor's degree in a library-related field at a school in any state.
Eligibility: Open to Nebraska residents who are interested in working on a bachelor's degree in library science, in general studies with a major in library science, or in education in school library media. Applicants must be planning to enroll at least half-time at an accredited university in any state. They must agree to seek employment in a Nebraska public, school, institutional, tribal, or special library after completing their degree. Along with their application, they must submit a statement of 500 to 750 words on their professional experiences, aspirations, and goals. Financial need is not considered in the selection process. An interview may be required.
Financial data: The stipend is $1,000 per year. Funds may be used for tuition, course-related materials, and fees associated with courses.
Duration: 1 year; may be renewed 1 additional year.
Number awarded: Varies each year; recently, 4 of these scholarships were awarded.
Deadline: January, June, or October of each year.

2538 BATYA LEWTON AWARD OF INSPIRATION

David and Dovetta Wilson Scholarship Fund, Inc.
115-67 237th Street
Elmont, NY 11003-3926
Phone: (516) 285-4573
Email: DDWSF4@aol.com
Web: www.wilsonfund.org/BatyaLewton.html
Summary: To provide financial assistance to high school seniors who are interested in studying education in college.
Eligibility: Open to graduating high school seniors who plan to attend an accredited college or university and major in education. Applicants must be U.S. citizens or permanent residents and have a GPA of 3.0 or higher. Along with their application, they must submit 3 letters of recommendation, high school transcripts, and an essay (up to 250 words) on "How My College Education Will Help Me Make a Positive Impact on My Community." Selection is based on community involvement, desire to prepare for a career in the field of education, and financial need.
Financial data: The stipend is $1,000.
Duration: 1 year.
Number awarded: 1 each year.
Deadline: March of each year.

2539 BB&T CHARITABLE FOUNDATION SCHOLARSHIP PROGRAM OF THE HISPANIC SCHOLARSHIP FUND

Summary: To provide financial assistance to Hispanic and African American upper-division students from selected states who are working on a degree related to business.
See Listing #1751.

2540 BB&T SCHOLARSHIPS

Independent College Fund of Maryland
Attn: Director of Programs and Scholarships
3225 Ellerslie Avenue, Suite C160
Baltimore, MD 21218-3519
Phone: (443) 997-5703; Fax: (443) 997-2740
Email: LSubot@jhmi.edu
Web: www.i-fundinfo.org/scholarships/business-scholarships.html
Summary: To provide financial assistance to upper-division students from any state at member institutions of the Independent College Fund of Maryland who are majoring in business.
Eligibility: Open to students from any state currently entering their junior or senior year at member institutions. Applicants must 1) be majoring in a business-related field; 2) have a demonstrated interest in a business-related career; or 3) have 6 credit hours of accounting plus a demonstrated interest in financial accounting. They must have a GPA of 3.0 or higher.
Financial data: The stipend is $2,500.
Duration: 1 year.
Number awarded: 1 or more each year.
Deadline: Deadline not specified.

2541 BERNICE PICKENS PARSONS FUND SCHOLARSHIPS

Summary: To provide financial assistance to residents of West Virginia who are interested in studying designated fields at a school in any state.
See Listing #1754.

2542 BETTY ANN LIVINGSTON SCHOLARSHIP

Summary: To provide financial assistance to Methodist high school seniors who plan to study designated fields in college.
See Listing #1189.

2543 BEV AND WES STOCK SCHOLARSHIP

Seattle Mariners Women's Club
Attn: Scholarship Committee
P.O. Box 4100
Seattle, WA 98194-0100
Phone: (206) 628-3555

Summary: To provide financial assistance to high school athletes in Washington state who are interested in attending college in any state to prepare for an athletic-related career.
Eligibility: Open to athletes graduating from high schools in Washington who display good character both on and off the playing field. They must be planning to attend a college or university in any state to prepare for an athletic-related career. There is no application form. Applicants must submit an essay outlining why they are applying for the scholarship, their extracurricular activities, their goals for college and beyond, and how receiving the scholarship will benefit them in their pursuit of their goals. Also required are a transcript and 3 letters of recommendation. Selection is based on merit.
Financial data: The stipend is $1,500.
Duration: 1 year; nonrenewable.
Number awarded: 1 each year.
Deadline: May of each year.

2544 BILL KANE UNDERGRADUATE SCHOLARSHIP

Summary: To provide financial assistance to undergraduates who are currently enrolled in a health education program.
See Listing #1759.

2545 BILLY DON SIMS SCHOLARSHIP

Association for Education and Rehabilitation of the Blind and Visually Impaired–Alabama Chapter
c/o Julie Brock, Scholarship Chair
P.O. Box 19888
Birmingham, AL 35219-0888
Phone: (205) 290-4451
Email: julie.brock@rehab.alabama.gov
Web: www.alabamaaer.com/Scholarship.html

Summary: To provide financial assistance to residents of Alabama who are working on a degree in a field related to education and rehabilitation of the blind and visually impaired at a school in any state.
Eligibility: Open to residents of Alabama who are currently enrolled at a college or university in any state. Applicants must be working on a degree in one of the following fields: rehabilitation teaching, orientation and mobility, teacher of the visually impaired; or rehabilitation counseling. They must submit a brief statement of their purpose for applying for this scholarship.
Financial data: The stipend is $1,000.
Duration: 1 year.
Number awarded: 1 each year.
Deadline: June of each year.

2546 BOB AND ELEANOR GRANT TRUST SCHOLARSHIP

Summary: To provide financial assistance to first-generation college students from Washington who are studying the natural, environmental, or social sciences at a college in any state.
See Listing #1769.

2547 BOB HERSH MEMORIAL SCHOLARSHIP

Mary M. Gooley Hemophilia Center
Attn: Scholarship Selection Committee
1415 Portland Avenue, Suite 500
Rochester, NY 14621
Phone: (585) 922-5700; Fax: (585) 922-5775
Email: Tricia.oppelt@rochestergeneral.org
Web: www.hemocenter.org/Scholarship%20Info.asp

Summary: To provide financial assistance to people with a bleeding disorder and their families who plan to attend college to prepare for a career in a teaching or helping profession.
Eligibility: Open to people who are affected directly or indirectly by hemophilia, von Willebrand Disease, hereditary bleeding disorder, or hemochromatosis. Applicants must be enrolled or planning to enroll at an accredited 2- or 4-year college or university, vocational/technical school, or certified training program. They must be preparing for a career in a teaching or helping profession. Along with their application, they must submit 1) a 1,000-word essay on their goals and aspirations, their biggest challenge and how they met it, and anything else they want the selection committee to know about them; and 2) a 250-word essay on any unusual family or personal circumstances that have affected their achievement in school, work, or participation in school and community activities, including how the bleeding disorder of themselves or their family member has affected their life. Selection is based on the essays, academic performance, participation in school and community activities, work or volunteer experience, personal or family circumstances, recommendations, and financial need.
Financial data: The stipend is $1,000.
Duration: 1 year.
Number awarded: 1 each year.
Deadline: April of each year.

2548 BRAINTRACK BUSINESS SCHOLARSHIP

BrainTrack
c/o FutureMeld, LLC
221 Boston Post Road East
Marlborough, MA 01772
Phone: (978) 451-0471
Email: info@braintrack.com
Web: www.braintrack.com/about-braintrack-scholarships.htm

Summary: To provide financial assistance to students working on an undergraduate or graduate degree in a field related to business.
Eligibility: Open to students preparing for a career in such fields as general management, marketing, advertising, sales, accounting, finance, management analysis, or consulting. Applicants must be working on an associate, bachelor's, master's, or higher degree in business administration or a related field. They must have completed at least 1 semester of study as a full- or part-time student in an on-campus and/or online program. If they are not U.S. citizens or permanent residents, they must have an appropriate student visa. Along with their application, they must submit essays between 200 and 800 words each on 1) what led them to choose business as a career path; 2) what they have enjoyed most and least during their business degree program so far; 3) what they wish they had known about selecting and entering their business school that would be helpful to others going into business. Selection is based entirely on the creativity, focus, overall thoughtfulness, accuracy, and practical value of their essays.
Financial data: Stipends are $1,000 or $500.
Duration: 1 year.
Number awarded: 4 each year: 2 at $1,000 and 2 at $500.
Deadline: October or February of each year.

2549 BRAINTRACK TEACHING SCHOLARSHIP

BrainTrack
c/o FutureMeld, LLC
221 Boston Post Road East
Marlborough, MA 01772
Phone: (978) 451-0471
Email: info@braintrack.com
Web: www.braintrack.com/about-braintrack-scholarships.htm

Summary: To provide financial assistance to students working on an undergraduate degree in education.
Eligibility: Open to students preparing for a career in teaching at any level from kindergarten through grade 12. Applicants must have completed at least 1 semester of study as a full- or part-time student in an on-campus and/or online program. They must be a U.S. citizen, have permanent resident status, or have an appropriate student visa. Along with their application, they must submit essays between 200 and 800 words each on 1) what led them to choose teaching as a career path; 2) what they have enjoyed most and least during their teaching degree program so far; 3) what they wish they had known about selecting and

entering their teaching school that would be helpful to others going into teaching. Selection is based entirely on the creativity, focus, overall thoughtfulness, accuracy, and practical value of their essays.
Financial data: Stipends are $1,000 or $500.
Duration: 1 year.
Number awarded: 4 each year: 2 at $1,000 and 2 at $500.
Deadline: October or February of each year.

2550 BRIAN CUMMINS MEMORIAL SCHOLARSHIP

National Federation of the Blind of Connecticut
477 Connecticut Boulevard, Suite 217
East Hartford, CT 06108
Phone: (860) 289-1971
Email: info@nfbct.org
Web: www.nfbct.org/html/bcmsch.htm
Summary: To provide financial assistance to residents of Connecticut who plan to become a teacher of the blind and visually impaired.
Eligibility: Open to graduate and undergraduate students enrolled full-time at colleges and universities in Connecticut who are preparing for a career in the state as a certified teacher of the blind and visually impaired. Along with their application, they must submit a letter on their career goals and how the scholarship might help them achieve those. Applicants do not need to be blind or members of the National Federation of the Blind of Connecticut. Selection is based on academic quality, service to the community, and financial need.
Financial data: The stipend is $5,000.
Duration: 1 year.
Number awarded: 1 each year.
Deadline: September of each year.

2551 BRIDGING THE GAP FOR HISPANIC SUCCESS AWARD

Summary: To provide financial assistance to undergraduate students at member institutions of the Hispanic Association of Colleges and Universities (HACU) who are majoring in fields related to the fashion retailing industry.
See Listing #1199.

2552 BRODART UNDERGRADUATE SCHOLARSHIPS

Pennsylvania Library Association
Attn: Administrative Assistant
220 Cumberland Parkway, Suite 10
Mechanicsburg, PA 17055
Phone: (717) 766-7663; (800) 622-3308 (within PA); Fax: (717) 766-5440
Email: ellen@palibraries.org
Web: www.palibraries.org/displaycommon.cfm?an=1&subarticlenbr=57
Summary: To provide financial assistance to residents of Pennsylvania who are working on an undergraduate degree in library science.
Eligibility: Open to residents of Pennsylvania who are enrolled in a state-certified institution and have completed at least 3 credits in library science courses leading to state certification. Preference is given to members of the Pennsylvania Library Association (PaLA). Selection is based on scholarship, motivation, previous library experience, civic activities, PaLA activities, and financial need.
Financial data: The maximum stipend is $2,000.
Duration: 1 year.
Number awarded: 1 or more each year.
Deadline: May of each year.

2553 BROOKMIRE-HASTINGS SCHOLARSHIPS

Wisconsin Congress of Parents and Teachers, Inc.
4797 Hayes Road, Suite 102
Madison, WI 53704-3256
Phone: (608) 244-1455; Fax: (608) 244-4785
Email: wi_office@pta.org
Web: www.wisconsinpta.org/pages/brookmire.cfm
Summary: To provide financial assistance to high school seniors in Wisconsin who are interested in attending college in any state to prepare for a teaching career.
Eligibility: Open to seniors graduating from high schools in Wisconsin that have a PTA/PTSA chapter. Applicants must be planning to attend a 4-year college or university in any state to prepare for a career in the field of education. Along with their application, they must submit a 2-page essay on "What I Would Accomplish as a Teacher." Finalists are interviewed.
Financial data: The stipend is $1,000.
Duration: 1 year.
Number awarded: 2 each year.
Deadline: February of each year.

2554 BROWN FOUNDATION TEACHER QUEST SCHOLARSHIP

Brown Foundation for Educational Equity, Excellence and Research
Attn: Scholarship Committee
1515 S.E. Monroe
Topeka, KS 66615
Phone: (785) 235-3939; Fax: (785) 235-1001
Email: brownfound@juno.com
Web: brownvboard.org/foundation/scholarships/teacherquest/index.php
Summary: To provide financial assistance to undergraduate and graduate students of color who are interested in preparing for a teaching career.
Eligibility: Open to members of minority groups who are enrolled at least half-time at an institution of higher education with an accredited teacher education program. Applicants must be enrolled at the undergraduate, graduate, or post-baccalaureate level and have a GPA of 3.0 or higher. Along with their application, they must submit brief essays on 1) their involvement in school, community, and/or other activities and how those activities have prepared them to be an educator; 2) why they aspire to a career in education, their goals, and the level at which they plan to teach; and 3) how they think *Brown v. Board of Education* has influenced their own life experiences. Selection is based on the essays; GPA; school, community, and leisure activities; career plans and goals in education; and recommendations.
Financial data: The stipend is $1,000 per year.
Duration: 2 years.
Number awarded: Varies each year; recently, 5 of these scholarships were awarded.
Deadline: March of each year.

2555 BUILDING DIVISION ICA SCHOLARSHIP FUND

Summary: To provide financial assistance to residents of Indiana who are working on a degree in construction management at a college or university in the state.
See Listing #1782.

2556 BURKE FUND PROFESSIONAL GOLF MANAGEMENT STUDIES SCHOLARSHIP

Rhode Island Golf Association
Attn: John P. Burke Memorial Fund
One Button Hole Drive, Suite 2
Providence, RI 02909-5750
Phone: (401) 272-1350; Fax: (401) 331-3627
Email: burkefund@rigalinks.org
Web: burkefund.org/scholarships.html
Summary: To provide financial assistance to residents of Rhode Island who have worked at a golf course and are interested in attending college in any state to prepare for a career in golf.
Eligibility: Open to residents of Rhode Island who are graduating high school seniors or current college students. Applicants must have at least 2 years of successful employment as a caddie or in golf shop operations, the cart or bag room, golf course maintenance, or the clubhouse at a member club of the Rhode Island Golf Association (RIGA). They must be attending or planning to attend an accredited college or university to prepare for a career in golf business fields. Along with their application, they must submit a high school or college transcript; 4 letters of recommendation (from a high school principal or guidance counselor, an officer or board member of the sponsoring club, a member of the sponsoring club who knows the student, and the golf professional of the sponsoring club); a list of school activities (e.g., academic and athletic interscholastic contests, editorships, entertainments, officer of student organizations, responsible positions in school functions); and documentation of financial need.
Financial data: A stipend is awarded (amount not specified); funds may be used only for tuition, room, board, and other costs billed by postsecondary schools.
Duration: 1 year; may be renewed for up to 3 additional years if the recipient maintains a GPA of 2.0 or higher.
Number awarded: 1 or more each year.
Deadline: April of each year.

2557 CALIFORNIA CHAPTER OUTSTANDING DIVERSITY AWARD

American Planning Association–California Chapter
Attn: California Planning Foundation
c/o Paul Wack
P.O. Box 1086
Morro Bay, CA 93443-1086
Phone: (805) 756-6331; Fax: (805) 756-1340
Email: pwack@calpoly.edu
Web: www.californiaplanningfoundation.org/scholarships.html

Summary: To provide financial assistance to undergraduate and graduate students in accredited planning programs at California universities who will increase diversity in the profession.

Eligibility: Open to students entering their final year for an undergraduate or master's degree in an accredited planning program at a university in California. Applicants must be students who will increase diversity in the planning profession. Selection is based on academic performance, professional promise, and financial need.

Financial data: The stipend is $3,000. The award includes a 1-year student membership in the American Planning Association (APA) and payment of registration for the APA California Conference.

Duration: 1 year.

Number awarded: 1 each year.

Deadline: March of each year.

2558 CALIFORNIA FOUNDATION FOR PARKS AND RECREATION SCHOLARSHIPS

California Park and Recreation Society
Attn: California Foundation for Parks and Recreation
7971 Freeport Boulevard
Sacramento, CA 95832-9701
Phone: (916) 665-2777; Fax: (916) 665-9149
Web: www.cprs.org

Summary: To provide financial assistance to upper-division and graduate students majoring in fields related to recreation, parks, and leisure studies at colleges and universities in California.

Eligibility: Open to juniors, seniors, and graduate students majoring in aspects of recreation, parks, and leisure studies, including parks operations, natural resource management, recreation therapy, commercial recreation, tourism, community recreation, recreation aquatic management, recreational sports management, and recreation leadership. Applicants must be enrolled at a 4-year college or university in California. Undergraduates must have a GPA of 3.0 or higher in their major and 2.5 or higher overall. Graduate students must have a GPA of 3.5 or higher overall and in their major. Along with their application, they must submit an essay on a topic that changes periodically but relates to the work of the sponsoring agency. Selection is based on academic achievement, paid and/or volunteer experience in recreation and park agencies, involvement in campus organizations and leadership activities, community and professional organization membership activity, professional and faculty references, and career orientation and objectives.

Financial data: Stipends range from $1,000 to $2,000.

Duration: 1 year.

Number awarded: Approximately 20 each year.

Deadline: October of each year.

2559 CALIFORNIA HOTEL & LODGING ASSOCIATION GENERAL SCHOLARSHIPS

California Hotel & Lodging Association
Attn: CH&LA Educational Foundation
414 29th Street
Sacramento, CA 95816-3211
Phone: (916) 444-5780; Fax: (916) 444-5848
Email: tiffany@calodging.com
Web: www.calodging.com/events/scholarship.shtml

Summary: To provide financial assistance to residents of California who are interested in attending college in any state to prepare for a career in the lodging industry.

Eligibility: Open to residents of California who graduated from high school with a GPA of 2.7 or higher and are currently enrolled or planning to enroll at an accredited college or university in any state. California residents who are not high school graduates but who have lodging work experience are also eligible. Applicants must be preparing for a career in the lodging industry. Students working on a culinary degree are not eligible, although they may be considered if they are interested in hotel-related food and beverage operations. Selection is based on merit; submission of financial information is optional. If 2 or more students are otherwise ranked equally, preference may be given to an applicant who includes documentation of financial need.

Financial data: Stipends range from $500 to $1,500 per year. Funds are paid directly to the student.

Duration: 1 year; may be renewed.

Number awarded: Several each year.

Deadline: March of each year.

2560 CALIFORNIA/NEVADA/ARIZONA AUTOMOTIVE WHOLESALERS' ASSOCIATION SCHOLARSHIPS

Summary: To provide financial assistance to students from California, Nevada, and Arizona who are interested in preparing for a career in the automotive aftermarket.

See Listing #1789.

2561 CALIFORNIA PLANNING FOUNDATION CONTINUING STUDENT SCHOLARSHIPS

American Planning Association–California Chapter
Attn: California Planning Foundation
c/o Paul Wack
P.O. Box 1086
Morro Bay, CA 93443-1086
Phone: (805) 756-6331; Fax: (805) 756-1340
Email: pwack@calpoly.edu
Web: www.californiaplanningfoundation.org/scholarships.html

Summary: To provide financial assistance to undergraduate and graduate students in accredited planning programs at California universities.

Eligibility: Open to undergraduate and master's degree students who will be continuing in accredited planning programs at universities in California. Selection is based on academic performance and financial need.

Financial data: Stipends are $1,000. A 1-year student membership in the American Planning Association is also provided.

Duration: 1 year.

Number awarded: 9 each year: 2 at each Cal Poly campus and 1 at each of the other accredited programs.

Deadline: March of each year.

2562 CALIFORNIA PLANNING FOUNDATION OUTSTANDING STUDENT SCHOLARSHIPS

American Planning Association–California Chapter
Attn: California Planning Foundation
c/o Paul Wack
P.O. Box 1086
Morro Bay, CA 93443-1086
Phone: (805) 756-6331; Fax: (805) 756-1340
Email: pwack@calpoly.edu
Web: www.californiaplanningfoundation.org/scholarships.html

Summary: To provide financial assistance to undergraduate and graduate students in accredited planning programs at California universities.

Eligibility: Open to students entering their final year for an undergraduate or master's degree in an accredited planning program at a university in California. Selection is based on academic performance, professional promise, and financial need.

Financial data: Stipends are $5,000 or $3,000. The award includes a 1-year student membership in the American Planning Association (APA) and payment of registration for the APA California Conference.

Duration: 1 year.

Number awarded: 4 each year: 1 at $5,000 and 3 at $3,000.

Deadline: March of each year.

2563 CALIFORNIA STATE FAIR CULINARY COOKING AND HOSPITALITY MANAGEMENT SCHOLARSHIPS

Summary: To provide financial assistance to residents of California who are studying or planning to study culinary cooking or hospitality management at a college or university in the state.

See Listing #1207.

2564 CALIFORNIA STATE FAIR INTERNATIONAL STUDIES SCHOLARSHIPS

California State Fair
Attn: Friends of the Fair Scholarship Program
1600 Exposition Boulevard
P.O. Box 15649
Sacramento, CA 95852
Phone: (916) 263-3149
Email: entryoffice@calexpo.com
Web: www.bigfun.org/competition-youth.php

Summary: To provide financial assistance to residents of California working on an undergraduate or graduate degree in international studies at a college or university in the state.

Eligibility: Open to residents of California who are enrolled as undergraduate or graduate students at a college or university in the state. Applicants must be studying or majoring in international studies. They must have a GPA of 3.0 or higher. Along with their application, they must submit an essay of 2 to 3 pages indicating why they are pursuing their desired career and life goals and describing their involvement in community and volunteer service. Selection is based on personal commitment, goals established for their chosen field, leadership potential, and civic accomplishments.

Financial data: Stipends are $1,500 or $750.

Duration: 1 year.

Number awarded: 2 each year: 1 at $1,500 and 1 at $750.

Deadline: March of each year.

2565 CALIFORNIA STATE FAIR TEACHER CREDENTIAL SCHOLARSHIPS

California State Fair
Attn: Friends of the Fair Scholarship Program
1600 Exposition Boulevard
P.O. Box 15649
Sacramento, CA 95852
Phone: (916) 263-3149
Email: entryoffice@calexpo.com
Web: www.bigfun.org/competition-youth.php

Summary: To provide financial assistance to residents of California who are working on a teacher credential at a college in the state.

Eligibility: Open to residents of California currently working on a teacher credential at a college or university in the state. Reentry professionals are also eligible. Applicants must have a GPA of 3.0 or higher. Along with their application, they must submit an essay of 2 to 3 pages indicating why they are pursuing their desired career and life goals and describing their involvement in community and volunteer service. Selection is based on personal commitment, goals established for their chosen field, leadership potential, and civic accomplishments.

Financial data: Stipends are $1,000 or $500.

Duration: 1 year.

Number awarded: 2 each year: 1 at $1,000 and 1 at $500.

Deadline: March of each year.

2566 CALVIN COOLIDGE MEMORIAL FOUNDATION SCHOLARSHIP

Vermont Student Assistance Corporation
Attn: Scholarship Programs
10 East Allen Street
P.O. Box 2000
Winooski, VT 05404-2601
Phone: (802) 654-3798; (888) 253-4819; Fax: (802) 654-3765; TDD: (800) 281-3341 (within VT)
Email: info@vsac.org
Web: services.vsac.org/wps/wcm/connect/vsac/VSAC

Summary: To provide financial assistance to high school seniors in Vermont who are interested in working on a degree in the social sciences at a college in any state.

Eligibility: Open to seniors graduating from high schools in Vermont. Applicants must be planning to enroll at a college or university in any state to work on a degree in the social sciences, including (but not limited to) anthropology, archaeology, criminology, economics, geography, history, international relations, philosophy, political science, psychology, social work, sociology, or urban studies. Along with their application, they must submit 1) a 100-word essay on their interest in and commitment to pursuing their chosen career or vocation; and 2) a 250-word essay on their beliefs related to the value of community service. Selection is based on those essays, financial need, academic achievement, and a letter of recommendation.

Financial data: The stipend is $1,000.

Duration: 1 year.

Number awarded: 1 each year.

Deadline: March of each year.

2567 CAMERON E. WILLIAMS MEMORIAL SCHOLARSHIP

Griffith Insurance Education Foundation
623 High Street
Worthington, OH 43085
Phone: (614) 880-9870; Fax: (614) 880-9872
Email: info@griffithfoundation.org
Web: www.griffithfoundation.org/higher-ed/scholarships

Summary: To provide financial assistance to students working on an undergraduate degree in a field related to insurance.

Eligibility: Open to U.S. citizens enrolled full-time at a college or university in the United States with a GPA of 3.0 or higher. Applicants must be at least sophomores and enrolled in an insurance, risk management, actuarial science, business, computer science, finance, or other insurance-related program. They must be planning to enter an insurance-related field after graduation. Preference is given to 1) children, stepchildren, or legally adopted children of The Motorists Insurance Group employees and agents; and 2) students recommended by a Motorists employee or retiree. Selection is based on academic achievement, extracurricular activities and honors, work experience, 3 letters of recommendation, and financial need.

Financial data: The stipend is $2,000.

Duration: 1 year.

Number awarded: 1 each year.

Deadline: March of each year.

2568 CAMPUS SAFETY, HEALTH, AND ENVIRONMENTAL MANAGEMENT ASSOCIATION SCHOLARSHIP AWARD PROGRAM

Summary: To provide financial assistance to undergraduate and graduate students working on a degree in a field related to the concerns of the Campus Safety, Health, and Environmental Management Association (CSHEMA).

See Listing #1793.

2569 CANE CERTIFICATION SCHOLARSHIP

Summary: To provide financial assistance to upper-division and graduate students in New England who are working on certification as a teacher of Latin or Greek.

See Listing #1209.

2570 CAP LATHROP ENDOWMENT SCHOLARSHIP FUND

Summary: To provide financial assistance for undergraduate or graduate studies in media-related fields to Alaska Natives and their lineal descendants.

See Listing #1210.

2571 CAREFIRST BLUECROSS BLUESHIELD BUSINESS SCHOLARSHIPS

Independent College Fund of Maryland
Attn: Director of Programs and Scholarships
3225 Ellerslie Avenue, Suite C160
Baltimore, MD 21218-3519
Phone: (443) 997-5703; Fax: (443) 997-2740
Email: LSubot@jhmi.edu
Web: www.i-fundinfo.org/scholarships/business-scholarships.html

Summary: To provide financial assistance to upper-division students from any state at member institutions of the Independent College Fund of Maryland who are majoring in business.

Eligibility: Open to students from any state currently entering their junior or senior year at member institutions. Applicants must be (1 majoring in a business-related field; and 2) have a demonstrated interest in statistics, business, medical accounting, or finance. They must have a GPA of 3.0 or higher.

Financial data: The stipend is $2,500.

Duration: 1 year.

Number awarded: 1 or more each year.
Deadline: Deadline not specified.

2572 CARGILL SCHOLARSHIP PROGRAM FOR TRIBAL COLLEGES

Summary: To provide financial assistance to Native American college students from any state who are working on a bachelor's degree in specified fields at Tribal Colleges and Universities (TCUs) in selected states.
See Listing #1802.

2573 CARL E. JORGENSEN AND WOODIE L. TUCKER SCHOLARSHIPS

Virginia Business Education Association
c/o Beth Downey, Student Scholarships
Fairfax County Public Schools
Third Floor CTE
3877 Fairfax Ridge Road
Fairfax, VA 22030
Phone: (571) 423-4523; Fax: (571) 423-4597
Email: Beth.Downey@fcps.edu
Web: vbea.net/awards.html
Summary: To provide financial assistance to upper-division and graduate students from any state enrolled in a business education program at colleges and universities in Virginia.
Eligibility: Open to residents of any state who are 1) undergraduate juniors; or 2) graduate students with at least 1 semester of courses remaining. Applicants must be enrolled full-time at a 4-year college or university in Virginia in a program leading to the teaching of business or a business-related major. Along with their application, they must submit a 2-page essay on how they plan to contribute to the world by choosing business as a major. Financial need is not considered in the selection process.
Financial data: A stipend is awarded (amount not specified).
Duration: 1 year.
Number awarded: 1 or more each year.
Deadline: February of each year.

2574 CARLSTROM FAMILY SCHOLARSHIP

Carlstrom Family Scholarship and Literacy Fund
c/o Otis Federal Credit Union
170 Main Street
P.O. Box 27
Jay, ME 04239
Phone: (207) 897-0900
Email: info@carlstromfund.org
Web: www.carlstromfund.org
Summary: To provide financial assistance to high school seniors in Maine who plan to study education at a college in any state.
Eligibility: Open to seniors graduating from high schools in Maine and planning to enroll full-time at an accredited college or university in any state. Applicants must be planning to major in education. Along with their application, they must submit a 500-word essay on a topic that changes annually but relates to education; recently, students were asked to give their answer to the question, "What role should the Internet and computers play in modern K-12 education?" Selection is based on the essay and educational merit; financial need is not considered.
Financial data: The stipend is $1,000.
Duration: 1 year.
Number awarded: 1 each year.
Deadline: May.

2575 CARROLL R. GIBSON SCHOLARSHIP AWARD

National Association of Black Narcotic Agents
Attn: Scholarship Award Committee
P.O. Box 6467
Fredericksburg, VA 22403
Email: nabna1@verizon.net
Web: www.nabna.org/scholarship.htm
Summary: To provide financial assistance to undergraduates working on a degree in criminal justice at an Historically Black College or University (HBCU).
Eligibility: Open to full-time students currently enrolled at an HBCU and working on a degree in criminal justice. Applicants must have a GPA of 2.5 or higher and a record of school and community involvement. A personal interview is required. Selection is based on merit; financial need is not considered.
Financial data: Stipends range from $500 to $5,000.
Duration: 1 year.
Number awarded: 1 or more each year.
Deadline: Deadline not specified.

2576 CAS TRUST SCHOLARSHIP PROGRAM

Casualty Actuarial Society
Attn: CAS Trust Scholarship Coordinator
4350 North Fairfax Drive, Suite 250
Arlington, VA 22203
Phone: (703) 276-3100; Fax: (703) 276-3108
Email: mthurgood@casact.org
Web: www.casact.org/academic/index.cfm?fa=scholarship
Summary: To provide financial assistance to U.S. and Canadian students who are preparing for a career in the property and casualty actuarial profession.
Eligibility: Open to U.S. and Canadian citizens and permanent residents who are enrolled full-time at a college or university in the United States or Canada. Incoming freshmen and first-year students are not eligible. Applicants must be preparing for a career in the property and casualty actuarial profession and pursuit of the Casualty Actuarial Society (CAS) designations. They must have demonstrated high scholastic achievement and strong interest in mathematics or a mathematics-related field. Preference is given to students who have passed an actuarial examination and who have not yet won this or another scholarship from this sponsor or the Society of Actuaries. Selection is based on individual merit.
Financial data: The stipend is $2,000.
Duration: 1 year.
Number awarded: Up to 3 each year.
Deadline: April of each year.

2577 CASE STUDY COMPETITION IN CORPORATE COMMUNICATIONS

Summary: To recognize and reward undergraduate and graduate students in business, communications, or journalism who win a competition in public relations.
See Listing #1213.

2578 CASUALTY ACTUARIES OF GREATER NEW YORK SCHOLARSHIP

Casualty Actuaries of Greater New York
c/o Michael Dubin, Education Chair
Casualty Actuarial Society
4350 North Fairfax Drive, Suite 250
Arlington, VA 22203
Phone: (609) 575-9797
Email: CAGNY@casact.org
Web: www.casact.org/affiliates/cagny
Summary: To provide financial assistance to students at colleges and universities in the United States or Canada who are preparing for an actuarial career in the property/casualty insurance industry.
Eligibility: Open to U.S. and Canadian citizens and permanent residents who are enrolled or planning to enroll full-time at a college or university in the United States or Canada. Preference is given to residents of the greater New York area and those attending school in that area. Applicants must be able to demonstrate academic achievement and a strong interest in preparing for an actuarial career in the property/casualty insurance industry. Selection is based on merit.
Financial data: The stipend is $2,500.
Duration: 1 year.
Number awarded: 1 or more each year.
Deadline: April of each year.

2579 CENTRAL OHIO INSURANCE EDUCATION DAY SCHOLARSHIPS

Griffith Insurance Education Foundation
623 High Street
Worthington, OH 43085

Phone: (614) 880-9870; Fax: (614) 880-9872
Email: info@griffithfoundation.org
Web: www.griffithfoundation.org/higher-ed/scholarships
Summary: To provide financial assistance to undergraduate students from Ohio who are preparing for a career in a field related to insurance.
Eligibility: Open to U.S. citizens from Ohio who are attending a college or university anywhere in the United States. Applicants must be studying actuarial science, business, computer science, finance, risk management, or other insurance-related area and be planning to enter an insurance-related field upon graduation. They must have a GPA of 3.5 or higher. Selection is based on academic achievement, extracurricular activities and honors, work experience, 3 letters of recommendation, and financial need.
Financial data: The stipend is $1,500.
Duration: 1 year.
Number awarded: 2 each year.
Deadline: March or December of each year.

2580 CENTRAL OHIO RIMS CHAPTER SCHOLARSHIPS

Griffith Insurance Education Foundation
623 High Street
Worthington, OH 43085
Phone: (614) 880-9870; Fax: (614) 880-9872
Email: info@griffithfoundation.org
Web: www.griffithfoundation.org/higher-ed/scholarships
Summary: To provide financial assistance to residents of Ohio, especially central Ohio, who are working on an undergraduate degree in a field related to insurance.
Eligibility: Open to Ohio residents attending a college or university in any state. Applicants must be enrolled in an insurance, risk management, actuarial science, business, computer science, finance, or other insurance-related program. They must be planning to enter an insurance-related field after graduation. Preference is given to central Ohio residents and students. Selection is based on academic achievement, extracurricular activities and honors, work experience, 3 letters of recommendation, and financial need.
Financial data: The stipend is $1,000.
Duration: 1 year.
Number awarded: Several each year.
Deadline: December of each year.

2581 CHARLES H. SELMAN MEMORIAL SCHOLARSHIPS

Alaska Cabaret, Hotel, Restaurant & Retailers Association
Attn: Alaska CHARR Education Fund
1503 West 31st Avenue, Suite 102
Anchorage, AK 99503
Phone: (907) 274-8133; (800) 478-2427; Fax: (907) 274-8640
Email: info@alaskacharr.com
Web: www.alaskacharr.com/scholarships.html
Summary: To provide financial assistance to residents of Alaska interested in attending college in any state to prepare for a career in the hospitality industry.
Eligibility: Open to graduating high school seniors and graduates who have been residents of Alaska for at least 2 years. Applicants must be attending or planning to attend an accredited college, university, or postsecondary school in any state to prepare for a career in the Alaska hospitality industry. Along with their application, they must submit brief statements about 1) their career goals and reasons for their career choice; 2) themselves, their history, and their community activities; and 3) why they should be awarded this scholarship above all other applicants. Financial need is not considered in the selection process.
Financial data: The highest-ranked applicant receives a $5,000 scholarship. Other stipends average $1,000.
Duration: 1 year; the $5,000 scholarship may be renewed up to 3 additional years; other awards are nonrenewable.
Number awarded: Varies each year; recently, 17 of these scholarships were awarded.
Deadline: May of each year.

2582 CHARLES MCDANIEL TEACHER SCHOLARSHIPS

Georgia Student Finance Commission
Attn: Scholarships and Grants Division
2082 East Exchange Place, Suite 200
Tucker, GA 30084-5305
Phone: (770) 724-9000; (800) 505-GSFC; Fax: (770) 724-9089
Email: gsfcinfo@gsfc.org
Web: www.gacollege411.org
Summary: To provide financial assistance to Georgia residents who wish to prepare for a career as a teacher.
Eligibility: Open to residents of Georgia who graduated from a public high school in the state and are currently enrolled as full-time juniors or seniors in a college or department of education within an approved Georgia public institution. Each of the public colleges in Georgia that offers a teaching degree may nominate 1 student for these scholarships. Nominees must be working toward an initial baccalaureate degree, have a GPA of 3.25 or higher, and indicate a strong desire to prepare for a career as an elementary or secondary school teacher. They must submit an essay discussing their professional goals, reasons for pursuing a teaching career at the elementary or secondary level, and accomplishments, experiences, and honors that relate to teaching. Selection is based on merit.
Financial data: The stipend is $1,000 per year.
Duration: 1 year.
Number awarded: Normally, 3 each year.
Deadline: July of each year.

2583 CHARLOTTE CHAPTER NBMBAA UNDERGRADUATE SCHOLARSHIP

National Black MBA Association–Charlotte Chapter
Attn: Scholarship Program
P.O. Box 34613
Charlotte, NC 28234
Phone: (877) 732-0314
Email: info@nbmbaacharlotte.org
Web: nbmbaacharlotte.org/Education.aspx
Summary: To provide financial assistance to minority residents of North and South Carolina who are working on a bachelor's degree at a business school in any state.
Eligibility: Open to minority residents of North and South Carolina who are currently enrolled full-time at a college or university in any state. Applicants must be working on a bachelor's degree in business or management and have a GPA of 3.0 or higher. Selection is based primarily on a 2-page essay on a topic that changes annually but relates to African Americans and business.
Financial data: Stipends are $1,000 or $500.
Duration: 1 year.
Number awarded: Varies each year; recently, 6 of these scholarships were awarded: 5 at $1,000 and 1 at $500.
Deadline: August of each year.

2584 CHARLOTTE MOTTER CETA THEATRE EDUCATION SCHOLARSHIP

California Educational Theatre Association
c/o Gai Jones
1410 White Oak Circle
Ojai, CA 93023-1932
Email: gjones@ceta.org
Web: www.cetoweb.org/ceta_pages/sch_opp.html
Summary: To provide financial assistance to high school seniors in California who plan to attend college in any state to prepare for a career as a theater educator.
Eligibility: Open to seniors graduating from high schools that are institutional members of the California Educational Theatre Association (CETA). Applicants must be planning to attend a college, university, or conservatory in any state to study theater education as preparation for a career in the field. They may have received no grade lower than "B" in any theater class and no grade lower than "C" in any high school class. Along with their application, they must submit a 1-page resume, a 1-page essay on why they want to become a theater educator, and a letter of recommendation. Financial need is not considered in the selection process.
Financial data: A stipend is awarded (amount not specified).
Duration: 1 year.
Number awarded: Varies each year.
Deadline: April of each year.

2585 CHEVY CHASE BANK SCHOLARSHIPS

Independent College Fund of Maryland
Attn: Director of Programs and Scholarships
3225 Ellerslie Avenue, Suite C160
Baltimore, MD 21218-3519

Phone: (443) 997-5703; Fax: (443) 997-2740
Email: LSubot@jhmi.edu
Web: www.i-fundinfo.org/scholarships/business-scholarships.html
Summary: To provide financial assistance to students from any state at member institutions of the Independent College Fund of Maryland who are majoring in business.
Eligibility: Open to students from any state currently entering their sophomore, junior, or senior year at member institutions. Applicants must be majoring in or have demonstrated a career interest in business management, finance, sales, or accounting. They must have a GPA of 3.0 or higher.
Financial data: The stipend is $2,500.
Duration: 1 year.
Number awarded: 1 or more each year.
Deadline: Deadline not specified.

2586 CHILD DEVELOPMENT DIVISION COLLEGE COURSEWORK SCHOLARSHIP

Vermont Student Assistance Corporation
Attn: Scholarship Programs
10 East Allen Street
P.O. Box 2000
Winooski, VT 05404-2601
Phone: (802) 654-3798; (888) 253-4819; Fax: (802) 654-3765; TDD: (800) 281-3341 (within VT)
Email: info@vsac.org
Web: services.vsac.org/wps/wcm/connect/vsac/VSAC
Summary: To provide financial assistance to residents of Vermont who are working at child care facilities and interested in obtaining additional education.
Eligibility: Open to residents of Vermont who have been employed for at least 6 months 1) by a state-regulated child care facility not operated by a public school; or 2) in the field of early intervention providing services in settings that include child care facilities. Applicants must be interested in attending college to take courses related to 1 or more of the following areas: child development (including special needs), family and community teaching and learning, professionalism and program organization, and health and safety (including mental health). They must be able to demonstrate a commitment to remaining in the child care field for at least 1 year following completion of the courses. Along with their application, they must submit 1) a 100-word essay on their interest in and commitment to pursuing their chosen career or vocation; and 2) a 250-word essay on their short- and long-term academic, educational, career, vocational, and/or employment goals. Selection is based on those essays, academic achievement, a letter of recommendation, and financial need.
Financial data: The stipend is $1,000.
Duration: 1 year.
Number awarded: Varies each year; a total of $30,000 is available for this program annually.
Deadline: June of each year.

2587 CH&LA WORKING PROFESSIONALS SCHOLARSHIPS

California Hotel & Lodging Association
Attn: CH&LA Educational Foundation
414 29th Street
Sacramento, CA 95816-3211
Phone: (916) 444-5780; Fax: (916) 444-5848
Email: tiffany@calodging.com
Web: www.calodging.com/events/scholarship.shtml
Summary: To provide financial assistance to employees of the lodging industry in California who are interested in attending college in any state to improve their career opportunities in the industry.
Eligibility: Open to residents of California who graduated from high school with a GPA of 2.7 or higher and are currently employed in the lodging industry. Applicants must be enrolled or planning to enroll at an accredited college or university in any state in order to 1) expand their education and knowledge in their current job positions; or 2) expand their education and knowledge in order to obtain a different or better job in the lodging industry. Students working on a culinary degree are not eligible, although they may be considered if they are interested in hotel-related food and beverage operations. Selection is based on merit; submission of financial information is optional. If 2 or more students are otherwise ranked equally, preference may be given to an applicant who includes documentation of financial need.
Financial data: Stipends range from $500 to $1,500 per year.
Duration: 1 year; may be renewed.
Number awarded: Several each year.
Deadline: March of each year.

2588 CHRISTA MCAULIFFE FIELD OF EDUCATION SCHOLARSHIP

American Legion
Department of New Hampshire
State House Annex
25 Capitol Street, Room 431
Concord, NH 03301-6312
Phone: (603) 271-2211; (800) 778-3816; Fax: (603) 271-5352
Email: adjutantnh@amlegion.state.nh.us
Web: www.nhlegion.org/Legion%20Scholarships/Index%20Page.htm
Summary: To provide financial assistance to high school seniors in New Hampshire who are interested in getting a degree in education at a college in any state.
Eligibility: Open to seniors graduating from high schools in New Hampshire who have been residents of the state for at least 3 years. Applicants must be entering their first year at an accredited 4-year college or university in any state to work on a bachelor's degree in the field of education. They must have a GPA of 3.0 or higher in their junior and senior high school years. Financial need is considered in the selection process.
Financial data: The stipend is $1,000.
Duration: 1 year.
Number awarded: 1 each year.
Deadline: April of each year.

2589 CHRISTA MCAULIFFE SCHOLARSHIP

Baltimore Community Foundation
Attn: Grants Administrator
2 East Read Street, Ninth Floor
Baltimore, MD 21202
Phone: (410) 332-4171; Fax: (410) 837-4701
Email: aknoeller@bcf.org
Web: www.bcf.org/scholarships/default.aspx
Summary: To provide financial assistance to residents of Maryland who are interested in attending a college or university in the state to prepare for a career as a teacher.
Eligibility: Open to high school seniors and currently-enrolled college students who have been residents of Maryland for at least 6 months. Applicants must be attending or planning to attend a college or university in Maryland to prepare for a career as a teacher in the state. They must have a GPA of 3.0 or higher. Along with their application, they must submit 300-word essays on 1) why they want to be a teacher; and 2) the special talents and abilities they possess that will be helpful in a teaching career. Financial need is considered in the selection process.
Financial data: The stipend is at least $1,000 per year.
Duration: 1 year; recipients may reapply.
Number awarded: Varies each year; recently, 4 of these scholarships were awarded.
Deadline: February of each year for early applications; March of each year for standard applications.

2590 CHRISTA MCAULIFFE TEACHER INCENTIVE PROGRAM

Delaware Higher Education Commission
Carvel State Office Building, Fifth Floor
820 North French Street
Wilmington, DE 19801-3509
Phone: (302) 577-5240; (800) 292-7935; Fax: (302) 577-6765
Email: dhec@doe.k12.de.us
Web: www.doe.k12.de.us/infosuites/students_family/dhec/default.shtml
Summary: To provide financial assistance for teacher training to Delaware residents with outstanding academic records.
Eligibility: Open to Delaware residents who are enrolled or accepted for enrollment at a Delaware college or university in a program leading to teacher qualification. Preference is given to applicants planning to teach in an area of critical need. High school seniors must rank in the top half of their class and have a combined score of at least 1570 on the SAT; applicants who are already enrolled in college must have a cumulative GPA of 2.75 or higher. Selection is based on academic achievement. U.S. citizenship or eligible noncitizen status is required.
Financial data: Funds up to the cost of tuition, fees, and other direct educational expenses are provided. This is a scholarship/loan program; if the recipient performs required service at a school in Delaware, the loan is forgiven at the rate of 1 year of assistance for each year of service.
Duration: 1 year; may be renewed for up to 3 additional years, provided the recipient maintains a GPA of 2.75 or higher.
Number awarded: Up to 50 each year.
Deadline: March of each year.

2591 CHRISTINE O. GREGOIRE YOUTH/YOUNG ADULT AWARD

American Legacy Foundation
1724 Massachusetts Avenue, N.W.
Washington, DC 20036
Phone: (202) 454-5555; Fax: (202) 454-5999
Email: awards@americanlegacy.org
Web: www.americanlegacy.org/awards

Summary: To recognize and reward young people who contribute to the health of the public through use of tobacco documents.

Eligibility: Open to people under 24 years of age who use documents provided by the tobacco industry to further the goals of tobacco prevention and control. Nominees should have made a notable impact through innovative use of tobacco industry documents as applied to research, policy, or advocacy. Letters of nomination should be accompanied by 250-word statements on 1) the nominee's involvement with the tobacco control field; 2) what makes their use of tobacco industry documents unique and innovative for policy, advocacy, or research; 3) how their work has raised awareness or demonstrated leadership among their peer group; 4) any lessons that are applicable to other potential uses of documents in research, policy, or advocacy; and 5) how the challenges faced by the nominee relate to advancing or promoting the use of tobacco industry documents.

Financial data: The award is $7,500.

Duration: The award is presented annually.

Number awarded: 1 each year.

Deadline: February of each year.

2592 CHRISTOPHER K. SMITH FUTURE TEACHER SCHOLARSHIP

Delaware State Education Association
Attn: Scholarship Task Force
136 East Water Street
Dover, DE 19901
Phone: (302) 734-5834; (866) 734-5834; Fax: (302) 674-8499
Email: info@dsea.org
Web: www.dsea.org/AboutDSEA/Scholarship.html

Summary: To provide financial assistance to high school seniors in Delaware who are interested in attending college in any state to prepare for a teaching career.

Eligibility: Open to seniors graduating from public high schools in Delaware who are interested in preparing for a career in teaching. Applicants must be planning to enroll at a college or university in any state. Selection is based on class rank, GPA, SAT scores, school activities, awards and honors, career plans, and letters of reference.

Financial data: The stipend is $1,000 per year. Funds are paid directly to the recipient.

Duration: 4 years, provided the recipient maintains a GPA of 3.0 or higher and a major in education.

Number awarded: 1 each year.

Deadline: March of each year.

2593 CHRYSLER FOUNDATION SCHOLARSHIP AWARD

Summary: To provide financial assistance to undergraduate students majoring in specified fields at institutions that are members of the Hispanic Association of Colleges and Universities (HACU).

See Listing #1812.

2594 CHS FOUNDATION UNIVERSITY SCHOLARSHIP PROGRAM

Summary: To provide financial assistance to students at 4-year universities throughout the country who are preparing for a career in agribusiness or production agriculture.

See Listing #1816.

2595 CHURCHARMENIA.COM FINANCE AND BUSINESS SCHOLARSHIP

Charles and Agnes Kazarian Eternal Foundation/ChurchArmenia.com
Attn: Educational Scholarships
30 Kennedy Plaza, Second Floor
Providence, RI 02903
Email: info@churcharmenia.com
Web: www.churcharmenia.com/scholarship1.html

Summary: To provide financial assistance to outstanding undergraduate or graduate students of Armenian descent who are working on a degree in business or finance.

Eligibility: Open to applicants of Armenian descent who are applying to or accepted by a highly competitive undergraduate or graduate degree (including M.B.A.) program in economics, finance, or other similar field. Along with their application, they must submit 1) official academic transcripts; 2) an essay (2 to 3 pages) describing their previous business endeavors or community service in relation to business, finance, or economics; 3) documentation of financial need; and 4) up to 3 letters of recommendation.

Financial data: The stipend is $5,000.

Duration: 1 year.

Number awarded: 1 or more each year.

Deadline: Applications may be submitted at any time.

2596 CHURCHILL FAMILY SCHOLARSHIP FUND

Summary: To provide financial assistance to female high school seniors in Maine who are interested in studying music or music education at a college in any state.

See Listing #1222.

2597 C.J. DAVIDSON COLLEGE SCHOLARSHIP

Family, Career and Community Leaders of America–Texas Association
Attn: Scholarship Coordinator
6513 Circle S Road
Austin, TX 78745
Phone: (512) 306-0099; Fax: (512) 442-7100
Email: fccla@texasfccla.org
Web: www.texasfccla.org/Scholarships/scholarships2%20Home%20Page.htm

Summary: To provide financial assistance to college students in Texas who are working on a degree in family and consumer sciences education.

Eligibility: Open to students currently enrolled at colleges and universities in Texas who completed at least 1 year of family and consumer sciences while in high school in the state. Applicants must be majoring in an area of family and consumer sciences and planning to receive a teaching certificate. They must have a GPA of 2.5 or higher and may not be married. Along with their application, they must submit their ACT or SAT score and a 200-word essay on the importance of family and consumer sciences education. Financial need is also considered.

Financial data: The stipend is paid at the rate of $2,000 per semester ($4,000 per year).

Duration: 1 year; may be renewed until completion of a bachelor's degree, provided the recipient maintains a GPA of 2.5 or higher and remains enrolled full-time.

Number awarded: 1 each year.

Deadline: February of each year.

2598 CLAIR A. HILL SCHOLARSHIP

Summary: To provide financial assistance to upper-division students in California who are majoring in water resources–related fields of study.

See Listing #1821.

2599 CLARK E. DEHAVEN SCHOLARSHIPS

National Association of Colleges and University Food Services
2525 Jolly Road, Suite 280
Okemos, MI 48864-3680
Phone: (517) 332-2494; Fax: (517) 332-8144
Web: www.nacufs.org/i4a/pages/index.cfm?pageid=3334

Summary: To provide financial assistance to college students preparing for a career in the food service industry.

Eligibility: Open to U.S. or Canadian citizens currently enrolled full-time as sophomores, juniors, or seniors in an accredited program that will lead to an undergraduate degree in food service or a related field. Applicants must be enrolled at institutions that are members of the National Association of Colleges and University Food Services. They must have a GPA of 2.75 or higher. Along with their application, they must submit an official transcript, 2 letters of recommendation, a letter of personal evaluation, and a resume. Selection is based on academic record, financial need, commitment to a career in food service

professions, character, campus citizenship, volunteer activities, and campus involvement.
Financial data: The stipend is $5,000.
Duration: 1 year.
Number awarded: Varies each year; recently, 10 of these scholarships were awarded.
Deadline: February of each year.

2600 CLAUDE O. MARKOE GRANT

Virgin Islands Board of Education
Dronningen Gade 60B, 61, and 62
P.O. Box 11900
St. Thomas, VI 00801
Phone: (340) 774-4546; Fax: (340) 774-3384
Email: stt@myviboe.com
Web: myviboe.com
Summary: To provide financial assistance to residents of the Virgin Islands who wish to study education at a college in the territory or on the mainland.
Eligibility: Open to residents of the Virgin Islands who are seniors or graduates of high schools in the territory. Applicants must have a GPA of 2.0 or higher and be attending or accepted for enrollment at an accredited institution of higher learning in the territory or on the mainland. They must be planning to major in elementary, secondary, or vocational education. Financial need is considered in the selection process.
Financial data: The stipend is $1,000 per semester.
Duration: 1 semester; may be renewed up to 7 additional semesters.
Number awarded: 1 each year.
Deadline: April of each year.

2601 CLEM JUDD, JR. MEMORIAL SCHOLARSHIP

Hawai'i Hotel & Lodging Association
Attn: Hawaii Hotel Industry Foundation
2270 Kalakaua Avenue, Suite 1506
Honolulu, HI 96815
Phone: (808) 923-0407; Fax: (808) 924-3843
Email: hhla@hawaiihotels.org
Web: www.hawaiihotels.org/displaycommon.cfm?an=6
Summary: To provide financial assistance to Native Hawaiians who are upper-division students working on a degree in hotel management at a school in any state.
Eligibility: Open to Hawaii residents who can provide proof of their Hawaiian ancestry through birth certificates of their parents or grandparents. Applicants must be a junior or senior at an accredited college or university (in any state) and majoring in hotel management. They must have a GPA of 2.8 or higher. Financial need is not considered in the selection process.
Financial data: The stipend ranges from $1,000 to $2,500.
Duration: 1 year.
Number awarded: 1 each year.
Deadline: June of each year.

2602 COCA-COLA SALUTE TO EXCELLENCE SCHOLARSHIP AWARD

National Restaurant Association Educational Foundation
Attn: Scholarships Program
175 West Jackson Boulevard, Suite 1500
Chicago, IL 60604-2702
Phone: (312) 715-1010, ext. 738; (800) 765-2122, ext. 6738; Fax: (312) 566-9733
Email: scholars@nraef.org
Web: www.nraef.org/scholarships
Summary: To provide financial assistance to undergraduate students who are interested in preparing for a career in the hospitality industry.
Eligibility: Open to full-time and substantial part-time college students who have completed at least 1 term of a food service–related program at an accredited culinary school, college, or university. Applicants must be U.S. citizens or permanent residents. Along with their application, they must submit 1) an essay of 150 to 200 words on their career goals in the restaurant/food service industry; and 2) an essay of 450 to 500 words on 1 of the following issues that affects the restaurant industry: sustainability, food safety, or nutrition. Selection is based on the essays, presentation of the application, industry-related work experience, and letters of recommendation.
Financial data: The stipend is $5,000.
Duration: 1 year.
Number awarded: 1 or more each year.
Deadline: March of each year.

2603 COLLEGE FED CHALLENGE

Federal Reserve Bank of New York
Attn: Director of School Programs
33 Liberty Street
New York, NY 10045-0001
Phone: (212) 720-7966; (877) FED-CHLG
Email: lloyd.bromberg@ny.frb.org
Web: www.ny.frb.org/education/fedchallenge_college.html
Summary: To recognize and reward outstanding students who participate in the College Fed Challenge economics competition.
Eligibility: Open to students at colleges and community colleges in participating Federal Reserve Districts. Currently, 3 of the 12 Federal Reserve Banks participate in the competition: Boston (which serves the New England states), New York (which serves New York, northern New Jersey, and southwestern Connecticut), and Richmond (which serves Maryland, North Carolina, South Carolina, Virginia, Washington, D.C., and West Virginia). Teams of 3 to 5 undergraduates make a 20-minute presentation followed by a 15-minute question-and-answer session with a panel of judges. Presentations should include discussion of current economic and financial conditions; near-term forecast of economic and financial conditions that affect monetary policy; identification of risks that threaten the economic well-being of the country; and recommendation as to the action the Federal Reserve System should take with regard to short-term interest rates. Selection is based on 1) knowledge about the Federal Reserve's role in developing and implementing monetary policy; 2) responses to judges' questions; 3) presentation skills; 4) quality of research and analysis; and 5) evidence of teamwork and cooperation. Competitions are held in each district and then at the interdistrict level.
Financial data: In the interdistrict competition, the first-place team wins $15,000 and its department receives $10,000, the second-place team wins $10,000 and its department receives $5,000, the third-place team wins $5,000 and its department receives $2,500, and the honorable mention team wins $3,000 and its department receives $1,500. In the community college competition, the first-place team wins $3,000 and its department receives $2,000 and the second-place team wins $1,500 and its department receives $1,000.
Duration: The competition is held annually.
Number awarded: 6 teams (including 2 from community colleges) win interdistrict prizes. Additional prizes are awarded by the 3 participating Federal Reserve Banks within their Districts.
Deadline: Each of the 3 participating Federal Reserve Banks sets its own deadlines.

2604 COLLEGE SCHOLARSHIPS FOUNDATION LIBRARY AND INFORMATION SCIENCE SCHOLARSHIP

College Scholarships Foundation
5506 Red Robin Road
Raleigh, NC 27613
Phone: (919) 630-4895; (888) 501-9050
Email: info@collegescholarships.org
Web: www.collegescholarships.org/our-scholarships/library-science.htm
Summary: To provide financial assistance to undergraduate and graduate students working on a degree in library and information science.
Eligibility: Open to U.S. citizens currently working on an undergraduate or graduate degree in library and information science. Applicants must have a GPA of 3.0 or higher. Along with their application, they must submit a 300-word essay on how libraries will stay relevant in the future, how they see information retrieval changing, and where they see themselves in 10 years.
Financial data: The stipend is $1,000.
Duration: 1 year.
Number awarded: 1 each year.
Deadline: December of each year.

2605 COLORADO RESTAURANT ASSOCIATION EDUCATION FOUNDATION UNDERGRADUATE SCHOLARSHIPS

Colorado Restaurant Association
Attn: CRA Education Foundation

430 East Seventh Avenue
Denver, CO 80203
Phone: (303) 830-2972; (800) 522-2972; Fax: (303) 830-2973
Email: info@coloradorestaurant.com
Web: www.coloradorestaurant.com

Summary: To provide financial assistance to residents of Colorado who are working on an associate or bachelor's degree at a college in any state to prepare for a career in the food service or hospitality industry.

Eligibility: Open to residents of Colorado who are enrolled full-or part-time in an accredited food service program at a college or university in any state. Applicants must be in the second half of an approved associate degree program or juniors or seniors in a bachelor's degree program. They must have a GPA of 2.75 or higher and at least 6 months of industry-related work experience. Along with their application, they must submit brief essays on their career objectives, their skills and personal characteristics that will contribute to the food service or hospitality industry, special recognition or honors they have received, their extracurricular and community service activities, their interests or hobbies, the 2 major advantages of a career in the food service or hospitality industry, the 2 major disadvantages (aside from an irregular work schedule) of a career in the food service or hospitality industry, why they have chosen the food service or hospitality industry, and why they feel they are qualified to receive this scholarship. Financial need is also considered in the selection process.

Financial data: Stipends range from $1,000 to $2,000.

Duration: 1 year.

Number awarded: Varies each year.

Deadline: April of each year.

2606 COLORADO SUPPLEMENTAL LEVERAGING EDUCATIONAL ASSISTANCE PARTNERSHIP (SLEAP)

Colorado Commission on Higher Education
1560 Broadway, Suite 1600
Denver, CO 80202
Phone: (303) 866-2723; Fax: (303) 866-4266
Email: cche@state.co.us
Web: highered.colorado.gov

Summary: To provide funding to Colorado undergraduate education students who need assistance in paying for college while they are working as student teachers.

Eligibility: Open to residents of Colorado who are enrolled in an undergraduate or postbaccalaureate teacher education program in the states. Applicants must be engaged full-time in a student teaching assignment as preparation for teacher education licensure. They must be able to demonstrate substantial financial need. U.S. citizenship or permanent resident status is required.

Financial data: The amount of assistance varies, to a maximum of $5,000 per year.

Duration: 1 year.

Number awarded: Varies each year.

Deadline: Each participating institution sets its own deadlines.

2607 COMMUNITY SERVICE SCHOLARSHIPS

Association of Government Accountants
Attn: National Awards Committee
2208 Mount Vernon Avenue
Alexandria, VA 22301-1314
Phone: (703) 684-6931; (800) AGA-7211, ext. 321; Fax: (703) 548-9367
Email: mwheeler@agacgfm.org
Web: www.agacgfm.org/membership/awards

Summary: To provide financial assistance to high school seniors, undergraduates, and graduate students who are interested in majoring in financial management and are involved in community service.

Eligibility: Open to graduating high school seniors, high school graduates, college and university undergraduates, and graduate students. Applicants must be working on or planning to work on a degree in a financial management discipline, including accounting, auditing, budgeting, economics, finance, electronic data processing, information resources management, or public administration. They must have a GPA of 2.5 or higher and be actively involved in community service projects. Along with their application, they must submit a 2-page essay on "My community service accomplishments," high school or college transcripts, and a reference letter from a community service organization. Selection is based on community service involvement and accomplishments; financial need is not considered.

Financial data: The stipend is $3,000 per year.

Duration: 1 year; renewable.

Number awarded: 2 each year: 1 to a high school senior or graduate and 1 to an undergraduate or graduate student.

Deadline: March of each year.

2608 CONNECTICUT ASSOCIATION OF WOMEN POLICE SCHOLARSHIPS

Connecticut Association of Women Police
P.O. Box 1653
Hartford, CT 06144-1653
Email: admin@cawp.net
Web: www.cawp.net/scholarship_aca.html

Summary: To provide financial assistance to high school seniors in Connecticut who are interested in studying criminal justice at a college in any state.

Eligibility: Open to seniors graduating from high schools in Connecticut who are interested in attending a 4-year college or university in any state to prepare for a career in criminal justice. Applicants must submit a personal essay of 200 to 250 words on their personal goals and why they should be selected for this scholarship. Selection is based on the essay and financial need.

Financial data: A stipend is awarded (amount not specified).

Duration: 1 year.

Number awarded: Varies each year; recently, 5 of these scholarships were awarded.

Deadline: April of each year.

2609 CONNECTICUT MINORITY TEACHER INCENTIVE PROGRAM

Connecticut Department of Higher Education
Attn: Office of Student Financial Aid
61 Woodland Street
Hartford, CT 06105-2326
Phone: (860) 947-1857; Fax: (860) 947-1838
Email: mtip@ctdhe.org
Web: www.ctdhe.org/SFA/default.htm

Summary: To provide financial assistance and loan repayment to minority upper-division college students in Connecticut who are interested in teaching at public schools in the state.

Eligibility: Open to juniors and seniors enrolled full-time in Connecticut college and university teacher preparation programs. Applicants must be members of a minority group, defined as African American, Hispanic/Latino, Asian American, or Native American. They must be nominated by the education dean at their institution.

Financial data: The maximum stipend is $5,000 per year. In addition, if recipients complete a credential and begin teaching at a public school in Connecticut within 16 months of graduation, they may receive up to $2,500 per year, for up to 4 years, to help pay off college loans.

Duration: Up to 2 years.

Number awarded: Varies each year.

Deadline: September of each year.

2610 CONSTRUCTION MANAGEMENT ASSOCIATION OF AMERICA FOUNDATION SCHOLARSHIPS

Summary: To provide financial assistance to undergraduate and graduate students working on a degree in construction management.

See Listing #1844.

2611 CONTINENTAL SOCIETY, DAUGHTERS OF INDIAN WARS SCHOLARSHIP

Continental Society, Daughters of Indian Wars
c/o Julia A. Farrigan, Scholarship Chair
326 South Oak Street
Jackson, GA 30233
Email: farrigan@bellsouth.net
Web: www.rootsweb.ancestry.com/~azcsdiw/Scholarships.htm

Summary: To provide financial assistance to Native American college students who are interested in preparing for a career in education or social service.

Eligibility: Open to enrolled tribal members of a federally-recognized tribe who are accepted at or already attending an accredited college or university. Applicants must be planning to work with a tribe or nation in the field of education or social service. They must have a GPA of 3.0 or higher and be carry-

ing at least 10 quarter hours or 8 semester hours. Preference is given to students entering their junior year. Financial need is considered in the selection process.
Financial data: The stipend is $5,000 per year.
Duration: 1 year; may be renewed.
Number awarded: 1 each year.
Deadline: June of each year.

2612 CRACKER BARREL-MINORITY TEACHER EDUCATION SCHOLARSHIPS

Florida Fund for Minority Teachers, Inc.
Attn: Executive Director
G415 Norman Hall
P.O. Box 117045
Gainesville, FL 32611-7045
Phone: (352) 392-9196, ext. 21; Fax: (352) 846-3011
Email: info@ffmt.org
Web: www.ffmt.org
Summary: To provide financial assistance to Florida residents who are members of minority groups preparing for a career as a teacher.
Eligibility: Open to Florida residents who are African American/Black, Hispanic/Latino, Asian American/Pacific Islander, or American Indian/Alaskan Native. Applicants must be entering their junior year in a teacher education program at a participating college or university in Florida. Special consideration is given to community college graduates. Selection is based on writing ability, communication skills, overall academic performance, and evidence of commitment to the youth of America (preferably demonstrated through volunteer activities).
Financial data: The stipend is $2,000 per year. Recipients are required to teach 1 year in a Florida public school for each year they receive the scholarship. If they fail to teach in a public school, they are required to repay the total amount of support received at an annual interest rate of 8%.
Duration: Up to 2 consecutive years, provided the recipient remains enrolled full-time with a GPA of 2.5 or higher.
Number awarded: Varies each year.
Deadline: July of each year for fall semester; November of each year for spring semester.

2613 CRITICAL NEED TEACHER SCHOLARSHIP

Mid-Atlantic Association for Employment in Education
c/o Kerri G. Gardi
Kutztown University
Director, Career Development Center
P.O. Box 730
Kutztown, PA 19530
Phone: (610) 683-4647
Email: gardi@kutztown.edu
Web: www.maeeonline.org/pages/scholarships_jump.aspx
Summary: To provide financial assistance to upper-division students at universities in the Mid-Atlantic region who are preparing for a career as a teacher of designated areas of critical need.
Eligibility: Open to full-time students who have completed between 48 and 90 credits at a college or university in Delaware, Maryland, New Jersey, New York, Pennsylvania, Virginia, Washington, D.C., or West Virginia. Applicants must be preparing for a career as a teacher of designated areas of critical need (currently, business education, computer science, consumer and family studies, foreign languages [including ESL and bilingual], library science or media specialist, mathematics, sciences [all fields], special education [all categories, including speech pathology], and technology education and industrial arts). Along with their application, they must submit a 1-page essay on why they have chosen to become a teacher and what they hope to accomplish as an educator. Selection is based on academic success, service to college and/or community, and potential to achieve excellence as a teacher. U.S. citizenship is required.
Financial data: The stipend is $1,000.
Duration: 1 year; nonrenewable.
Number awarded: 1 each year.
Deadline: November of each year.

2614 DAGMAR JEPPESON GRANT

Delta Kappa Gamma Society International–Alpha Rho State Organization
c/o Alyce Sandusky, State Scholarship Chair
7619 Highway 66
Klamath Falls, OR 97601-9538
Phone: (541) 884-0524
Email: terryandalyce@charter.net
Web: www.deltakappagamma.org/OR/scholarships/index.htm
Summary: To provide financial assistance to women from Oregon who are enrolled as upper-division students at a college in any state and preparing for a career in elementary education.
Eligibility: Open to female residents of Oregon who are at least juniors at a college in any state and interested in preparing for a career in elementary education. Applicants may not be members of Delta Kappa Gamma (an honorary society of women educators), but they must be sponsored by a local chapter of the society. Along with their application, they must submit a summary of their education from high school through the present, high school and college activities and achievements, community service, employment history, career goals, and financial need.
Financial data: A stipend is awarded (amount not specified).
Duration: 1 year.
Number awarded: 1 or more each year.
Deadline: February of each year.

2615 DAKOTA CORPS SCHOLARSHIP PROGRAM

Summary: To provide financial assistance to high school seniors in South Dakota who plan to attend a college or university in the state and work in the state in a critical need occupation following graduation.
See Listing #1852.

2616 DAMON P. MOORE SCHOLARSHIP

Indiana State Teachers Association
Attn: Scholarships
150 West Market Street, Suite 900
Indianapolis, IN 46204-2875
Phone: (317) 263-3400; (800) 382-4037; Fax: (317) 655-3700
Email: mshoup@ista-in.org
Web: www.ista-in.org/dynamic.aspx?id=1212
Summary: To provide financial assistance to ethnic minority high school seniors in Indiana who are interested in studying education in college.
Eligibility: Open to ethnic minority public high school seniors in Indiana who are interested in studying education in college. Selection is based on academic achievement, leadership ability as expressed through co-curricular activities and community involvement, recommendations, and a 300-word essay on their educational goals and how they plan to use this scholarship.
Financial data: The stipend is $1,000.
Duration: 1 year; may be renewed for 2 additional years if the recipient maintains at least a "C+" GPA.
Number awarded: 1 each year.
Deadline: February of each year.

2617 DANIEL ALEX SCHOLARSHIP AND GRANT FUND

Summary: To provide financial assistance for undergraduate or vocational studies in designated fields to Alaska Natives of certain communities and their lineal descendants.
See Listing #1853.

2618 DARREL HESS COMMUNITY COLLEGE GEOGRAPHY SCHOLARSHIP

Association of American Geographers
Attn: Grants and Awards
1710 16th Street, N.W.
Washington, DC 20009-3198
Phone: (202) 234-1450; Fax: (202) 234-2744
Email: grantsawards@aag.org
Web: www.aag.org/cs/grants/hess
Summary: To provide financial assistance to community college students interested in transferring to a 4-year college or university and majoring in geography.
Eligibility: Open to students currently enrolled at a community college, junior college, city college, or similar 2-year educational institution. Applicants must have completed at least 2 transfer courses in geography and plan to transfer to a

4-year university as a geography major. Selection is based on the overall quality of the application, scholastic excellence, academic promise, and financial need.
Financial data: The stipend is $1,000.
Duration: 1 year.
Number awarded: 2 each year.
Deadline: December of each year.

2619 DAVID HAMILTON JACKSON GRANT

Summary: To provide financial assistance to residents of the Virgin Islands who wish to study labor relations or journalism at a college in the territory or on the mainland.
See Listing #1236.

2620 DEALER DEVELOPMENT SCHOLARSHIP PROGRAM

General Motors Corporation
Women's Retail Network
Attn: GM Scholarship Administration Center
700 West Fifth Avenue
Mail Code 2001
Naperville, IL 60563
Phone: (888) 377-5233
Email: wrnscholarshipinfo@gmsac.com
Web: www.gmsac.com
Summary: To provide financial assistance to women attending college or graduate school to prepare for a retail automotive career.
Eligibility: Open to women who are enrolled full-time in undergraduate, graduate, and nontraditional continuing education institutions that offer degrees in the automotive retail field. Applicants must be interested in preparing for a career in automotive retail and/or service management. They must be citizens of the United States or have the ability to accept permanent employment in the United States without the need for visa sponsorship now or in the future. Current and former enrollees in the General Motors National Candidate Program are not eligible, but applications are accepted from female employees and female employee dependents working at GM dealerships. Selection is based on academic performance, community service and volunteerism, work experience, and a personal statement. Financial need is not considered.
Financial data: The stipend is $5,000 per year.
Duration: 1 year; recipients may reapply.
Number awarded: Several each year.
Deadline: April of each year.

2621 DEFENSE INTELLIGENCE AGENCY UNDERGRADUATE TRAINING ASSISTANCE PROGRAM

Summary: To provide financial assistance and work experience to high school seniors and lower-division students interested in majoring in specified fields and working for the U.S. Defense Intelligence Agency (DIA).
See Listing #1861.

2622 DEFENSE OF ACADEMIC FREEDOM AWARD

National Council for the Social Studies
Attn: Program Manager, External Relations
8555 16th Street, Suite 500
Silver Spring, MD 20910-2844
Phone: (301) 588-1800, ext. 106; Fax: (301) 588-2049
Email: excellence@ncss.org
Web: www.socialstudies.org/awards/academicfreedom
Summary: To recognize and reward individuals who contributed significantly to the preservation of academic freedom in the area of social studies education.
Eligibility: Open to students, teachers, administrators, professionals, and parents. They are eligible to be nominated for the award or may nominate themselves. Nominees must 1) have engaged in or be currently engaged in activities that support academic freedom in the face of personal challenge or promote awareness of and support for academic freedom; 2) have personal involvement in a particular controversy, the use of controversial issues or materials, defense of the presentation of divergent materials and views, and/or the preparation of materials involving controversy and divergent views; and 3) have personal involvement in activities that highlight issues surrounding censorship and academic freedom through writings, speeches, or other advocacy. The defense or advocacy of academic freedom must have been related to the teaching of social studies.
Financial data: The amount awarded is $1,500.
Duration: This award is presented annually.
Number awarded: 1 each year.
Deadline: May of each year.

2623 DELAWARE ASSOCIATION OF SCHOOL ADMINISTRATORS ESSAY CONTEST

Delaware Association of School Administrators
860 Silver Lake Boulevard, Suite 150
Dover, DE 19904-2402
Phone: (302) 674-0630; Fax: (302) 674-8305
Web: www.edasa.org
Summary: To recognize and reward, with college scholarships, high school seniors in Delaware who submit outstanding essays on their plans to become a teacher.
Eligibility: Open to seniors graduating from high schools in Delaware where at least 1 administrator is a member of the Delaware Association of School Administrators. Applicants must submit an essay (from 300 to 500 words) on "Why I Chose Education as My Career Field." They must be planning to major in education at a college or university in any state.
Financial data: The award is $1,000; funds are paid directly to the recipient's college as a scholarship.
Duration: 1 year.
Number awarded: 2 each year.
Deadline: March of each year.

2624 DELAWARE TEACHER CORPS PROGRAM

Delaware Higher Education Commission
Carvel State Office Building, Fifth Floor
820 North French Street
Wilmington, DE 19801-3509
Phone: (302) 577-5240; (800) 292-7935; Fax: (302) 577-6765
Email: dhec@doe.k12.de.us
Web: www.doe.k12.de.us/infosuites/students_family/dhec/default.shtml
Summary: To provide funding for teacher training to Delaware residents at public institutions in the state.
Eligibility: Open to Delaware residents who are enrolled or accepted for enrollment in an undergraduate or graduate program leading to teacher qualification at a public college or university in the state. Applicants must be planning to teach in an area of critical need, currently defined to include bilingual education, business education, English, foreign languages, English to speakers of other languages, mathematics, music, reading, science, school librarianship, special education, and technology education. First priority is given to students who intend to teach middle and high school mathematics and science; second priority is given to students who intend to teach special education in a content area. High school seniors must rank in the top half of their class and have a combined score of at least 1570 on the SAT; undergraduates must have a cumulative GPA of 2.75 or higher. Selection is based on academic achievement. U.S. citizenship or eligible noncitizen status is required.
Financial data: The maximum loan is equal to the cost of tuition at a public college or university in Delaware. This is a scholarship/loan program; if the recipient performs required service at a school in Delaware, the loan is forgiven at the rate of 1 year of assistance for each year of service.
Duration: 1 year; may be renewed for up to 3 additional years, provided the recipient maintains a GPA of 2.75 or higher.
Number awarded: Varies each year.
Deadline: March of each year.

2625 DELTA GAMMA FOUNDATION FLORENCE MARGARET HARVEY MEMORIAL SCHOLARSHIP

Summary: To provide financial assistance to blind undergraduate and graduate students who wish to study in the field of rehabilitation and/or education of the blind.
See Listing #1866.

2626 DENNY LYDIC SCHOLARSHIP

Summary: To provide financial assistance to college students interested in preparing for a career in fields related to transportation.
See Listing #1868.

2627 DEPARTMENT OF HOMELAND SECURITY UNDERGRADUATE SCHOLARSHIPS

Summary: To provide financial assistance and summer research experience to undergraduate students who are working on a degree in a field of interest to the Department of Homeland Security (DHS).
See Listing #1874.

2628 DEREK HUGHES/NAPSLO EDUCATIONAL FOUNDATION SCHOLARSHIPS

National Association of Professional Surplus Lines Offices, Ltd.
Attn: Derek Hughes/NAPSLO Educational Foundation
200 N.E. 54th Street, Suite 200
Kansas City, MO 64118
Phone: (816) 741-3910; Fax: (816) 741-5409
Email: foundation@napslo.org
Web: www.napslo.org/imispublic/AM/Template.cfm?Section=Foundation

Summary: To provide financial assistance to undergraduate and graduate students working on a degree in a field of importance to the insurance industry.

Eligibility: Open to students who are enrolled or accepted for enrollment in an undergraduate or graduate program, working on a degree in actuarial science, business, economics, insurance, finance, management, risk management, statistics, or any field that relates to a career in insurance. Applicants must have a GPA of 3.0 or higher (entering freshmen must also rank in the top 25% of their high school class). Along with their application, they must submit a 1- or 2-page essay summarizing their career objectives, academic accomplishments, work experience, pertinent extracurricular activities, and (if appropriate) their financial need.

Financial data: The stipend is $5,000.

Duration: 1 year; recipients may reapply.

Number awarded: Varies each year; recently, 12 of these scholarships were awarded.

Deadline: May of each year.

2629 DETROIT CHAPTER ARMA SCHOLARSHIP

ARMA International–Detroit Chapter
c/o Cheryl Brunette, Scholarship Chair
GMAC Company Records and Information Management
300 Galleria Officentre, Suite 210
MC 482-300-210
Southfield, MI 48034
Phone: (248) 263-3063
Email: Cheryl.brunette@gmacfs.com
Web: www.armadetroit.org/view_announcement.php?ID=22

Summary: To provide financial assistance to upper-division and graduate students from any state working on a degree in records and information management at a college or university in Michigan.

Eligibility: Open to juniors, seniors, and graduate students at accredited 4-year colleges and universities in Michigan that offer a program or courses in records and information management. Applicants must have completed at least 12 credit hours in records and management courses with a GPA of 3.0 or higher. Selection is based on academic achievement, career commitment, and financial need.

Financial data: The stipend is $1,200 for full-time students or $600 for part-time students.

Duration: 1 year.

Number awarded: 1 or more each year.

Deadline: November of each year.

2630 DEVELOPMENTAL DISABILITIES SCHOLASTIC EXCELLENCE AWARD FOR LUTHERAN STUDENTS IN COLLEGE OR UNIVERSITY

Bethesda Lutheran Communities
Attn: Coordinator, Bethesda Institute
600 Hoffmann Drive
Watertown, WI 53094
Phone: (920) 261-3050; (800) 369-4636, ext. 4449; Fax: (920) 262-6513
Email: Bethesda.institute@mailblc.org
Web: bethesdalutherancommunities.org/youth/scholarships

Summary: To provide financial assistance to undergraduates who are Lutherans and interested in preparing for a career in an area of service to people with developmental disabilities.

Eligibility: Open to applicants who are active communicant members of a Lutheran congregation; are classified as a sophomore or junior at a college or university (not necessarily a Lutheran college); have an overall GPA of 3.0 or higher; and are interested in preparing for a career in the field of developmental disabilities. Along with their application, they must submit 1) an essay of 250 to 300 words on the career they are planning in the field of developmental disabilities and how that career choice would impact the lives of people with developmental disabilities; 2) 4 letters of recommendation; 3) an official college transcript; and 4) documentation that they have completed at least 100 hours of volunteer and/or paid service to people who are developmentally disabled within the past 2 calendar years. Financial need is not considered in the selection process.

Financial data: The stipend is $3,000.

Duration: 1 year.

Number awarded: 2 each year.

Deadline: April of each year.

2631 DISABLED WAR VETERANS SCHOLARSHIPS

Summary: To provide financial assistance to disabled military personnel and veterans who are majoring in specified scientific fields in college.
See Listing #1876.

2632 DON SAHLI–KATHY WOODALL FUTURE TEACHERS OF AMERICA SCHOLARSHIP

Tennessee Education Association
801 Second Avenue North
Nashville, TN 37201-1099
Phone: (615) 242-8392; (800) 342-8367; Fax: (615) 259-4581
Email: wdickens@tea.nea.org
Web: www.teateachers.org

Summary: To provide financial assistance to high school seniors in Tennessee who are interested in attending a college or university in the state to major in education.

Eligibility: Open to high school seniors in Tennessee who are planning to major in education at a college or university in the state. Application must be made through a Future Teachers of America chapter affiliated with the Tennessee Education Association. Selection is based on academic excellence, demonstrated leadership abilities, financial need, and demonstrated interest in becoming a teacher.

Financial data: The stipend is $1,000.

Duration: 1 year.

Number awarded: 1 each year.

Deadline: February of each year.

2633 DON SAHLI–KATHY WOODALL MINORITY STUDENT SCHOLARSHIP

Tennessee Education Association
801 Second Avenue North
Nashville, TN 37201-1099
Phone: (615) 242-8392; (800) 342-8367; Fax: (615) 259-4581
Email: wdickens@tea.nea.org
Web: www.teateachers.org

Summary: To provide financial assistance to minority high school seniors in Tennessee who are interested in majoring in education at a college or university in the state.

Eligibility: Open to minority high school seniors in Tennessee who are planning to attend a college or university in the state and major in education. Application must be made either by a Future Teachers of America chapter affiliated with the Tennessee Education Association (TEA) or by the student with the recommendation of an active TEA member. Selection is based on academic record, leadership ability, financial need, and demonstrated interest in becoming a teacher.

Financial data: The stipend is $1,000.

Duration: 1 year.

Number awarded: 1 each year.

Deadline: February of each year.

2634 DOROTHEA DEITZ MEMORIAL SCHOLARSHIPS

New York State Association for Health, Physical Education, Recreation and Dance
77 North Ann Street

Little Falls, NY 13365
Phone: (315) 823-1015; Fax: (315) 823-1012
Email: ccorsi@nysahperd.org
Web: www.nysahperd.org/deitz_scholarship.htm
Summary: To provide financial assistance to women in New York who plan to major in physical education in college.
Eligibility: Open to women graduating from high schools in New York who plan to attend a 4-year college or university, preferably in New York. Applicants must be planning to major in physical education. Along with their application, they must submit an essay about themselves, including their interests, significant occurrences in their lives, and their reasons for attending college. Selection is based on academic achievement, character, physical education competence, participation in athletics, qualities of leadership, and financial need.
Financial data: Stipends are $7,500, $6,500, or $5,000.
Duration: 1 year (the freshman year in college). Loans are available to students after their freshman year.
Number awarded: 3 each year.
Deadline: February of each year.

2635 DOROTHY E. SCHOELZEL MEMORIAL SCHOLARSHIP

General Federation of Women's Clubs of Connecticut
c/o JoAnn Calnen, President
74 Spruceland Road
Enfield, CT 06082-2359
Email: gfwcct@yahoo.com
Web: www.gfwcct.org
Summary: To provide financial assistance to women in Connecticut who are working on an undergraduate or graduate degree in education.
Eligibility: Open to female residents of Connecticut who have completed at least 3 years of college. Applicants must have a GPA of 3.0 or higher and be working on a bachelor's or master's degree in education. Selection is based on academic ability, future promise, and financial need.
Financial data: The stipend is $2,000.
Duration: 1 year.
Number awarded: 1 each year.
Deadline: February of each year.

2636 DR. ALMA S. ADAMS SCHOLARSHIP

Summary: To provide financial assistance to undergraduate or graduate students who have engaged in community service or visual arts activities to reduce smoking in communities designated as especially vulnerable to the tobacco industry.
See Listing #1246.

2637 DR. AURA-LEE A. AND JAMES HOBBS PITTENGER AMERICAN HISTORY SCHOLARSHIP

Summary: To provide financial assistance to high school seniors planning to major in American history or government in college.
See Listing #1247.

2638 DR. JULIANNE MALVEAUX SCHOLARSHIP

Summary: To provide financial assistance to African American women studying journalism, economics, or a related field in college.
See Listing #1249.

2639 DR. WALTER W. RISTOW PRIZE

Summary: To recognize and reward outstanding papers on cartographic history by students at all levels at universities in any country.
See Listing #1250.

2640 D.W. SIMPSON & COMPANY ACTUARIAL SCIENCE SCHOLARSHIPS

D.W. Simpson & Company
1800 West Larchmont Avenue
Chicago, IL 60613
Phone: (312) 867-2300; (800) 837-8338; Fax: (312) 951-8386
Email: scholarship@dwsimpson.com
Web: www.dwsimpson.com/scholar.html
Summary: To provide financial assistance to college seniors majoring in actuarial science.
Eligibility: Open to students who are entering their senior year of undergraduate study in actuarial science. Applicants must have a GPA of 3.0 or higher overall and 3.2 or higher in their major, have passed at least 1 actuarial examination, and be eligible to work in the United States. Along with their application, they must submit 1) a list of internships, scholarships, honors, and extracurricular activities; and 2) an essay on their long-term career goals. Financial need is not considered in the selection process.
Financial data: The stipend is $1,000 per semester.
Duration: 1 semester; nonrenewable.
Number awarded: 2 each year (1 per semester).
Deadline: April of each year for the fall scholarship; October of each year for the spring scholarship.

2641 EARL E. AND MILDRED L. BLESS HUDSON SCHOLARSHIP FOR EDUCATION

Heritage Fund–The Community Foundation for Bartholomew County
Attn: Educational Scholarships
538 Franklin Street
P.O. Box 1547
Columbus, IN 47202-1547
Phone: (812) 376-7772; Fax: (812) 376-0051
Email: info@heritagefundbc.org
Web: www.heritagefundbc.org/scholarships
Summary: To provide financial assistance to residents of Indiana who are working on an undergraduate or graduate degree in education at a school in any state.
Eligibility: Open to Indiana residents enrolled at an accredited postsecondary institution in any state. Applicants must be working on an undergraduate or graduate degree in education. Along with their application, they must submit a 1-page essay on how they have been influenced by an individual or an event and how they believe it will shape their future. Financial need is also considered in the selection process.
Financial data: The stipend is $1,400.
Duration: 1 year.
Number awarded: 1 or more each year.
Deadline: February of each year.

2642 EARL G. GRAVES SCHOLARSHIP

National Association for the Advancement of Colored People
Attn: Education Department
4805 Mt. Hope Drive
Baltimore, MD 21215-3297
Phone: (410) 580-5760; (877) NAACP-98
Email: youth@naacpnet.org
Web: www.naacp.org/pages/naacp-scholarships
Summary: To provide financial assistance to upper-division and graduate students majoring in business.
Eligibility: Open to full-time juniors, seniors, and graduate students working on a degree in business. Applicants must be currently in good academic standing, making satisfactory progress toward an undergraduate or graduate degree, and in the top 20% of their class. Along with their application, they must submit a 1-page essay on their interest in their major and a career, their life's ambition, what they hope to accomplish in their lifetime, and what position they hope to attain. Financial need is not considered in the selection process.
Financial data: The stipend is $5,000.
Duration: 1 year.
Number awarded: Varies each year; recently, 12 of these scholarships were awarded.
Deadline: March of each year.

2643 EAST MICHIGAN CHAPTER SCHOLARSHIPS

Summary: To provide financial assistance to undergraduate and graduate students in Michigan who are interested in preparing for a career in air and waste management.
See Listing #1893.

2644 ECOLAB SCHOLARSHIP COMPETITION

American Hotel & Lodging Educational Foundation
Attn: Manager of Foundation Programs

1201 New York Avenue, N.W., Suite 600
Washington, DC 20005-3931
Phone: (202) 289-3181; Fax: (202) 289-3199
Email: ahlef@ahlef.org
Web: www.ahlef.org/content.aspx?id=19830

Summary: To provide financial assistance to students interested working on a college degree in hospitality management.

Eligibility: Open to students interested in working on an associate or baccalaureate degree in hospitality management. Applicants must be enrolled or planning to enroll full-time. Along with their application, they must submit a 500-word essay on their personal background, including when they became interested in the hospitality field, what traits they possess or will need to succeed in the industry, and their plans as related to their educational and career objectives and future goals. Selection is based on industry-related work experience; financial need; academic record and educational qualifications; professional, community, and extracurricular activities; personal attributes, including career goals; the essay; and neatness and completeness of the application.

Financial data: The stipend is $2,000 for students in 4-year baccalaureate programs or $1,000 for students in 2-year associate programs. Funds are distributed in 2 equal installments (in August and December). Checks are made out jointly to the recipient and the recipient's academic institution. Funds may be used only for tuition, fees, and books.

Duration: 1 year.

Number awarded: Varies each year; recently, 11 of these scholarships were awarded. Since the establishment of the program, it has awarded 182 hospitality students more than $265,000 in support.

Deadline: April of each year.

2645 EDDIE G. COLE MEMORIAL SCHOLARSHIPS

Summary: To provide financial assistance to residents of California who are attending college in the state and majoring in designated fields or preparing for a career in the Fair industry.

See Listing #1895.

2646 EDEN INSTITUTE FOUNDATION SCHOLARSHIP AWARDS

Eden Autism Services
2031 Old Trenton Road
West Windsor, NJ 08550
Phone: (609) 426-8658
Email: aileen.kornblatt@edenservices.org
Web: www.edenautismservices.org/index.php/resources/scholarship

Summary: To provide financial assistance for college to high school seniors who are interested in preparing for a career in special education, especially as it relates to autism.

Eligibility: Open to high school seniors who plan to attend college and major in special education or a related discipline. Applicants must indicate how their proposed major relates to autism or the disability field. Although the program encourages students to prepare for a career focusing on autism, its goal is "to generate, through education and support, a respect for the rights and interests of individuals with disabilities in general, and those with autism in particular." Along with their application, they must submit an essay that explains why they feel they are a qualified applicant for this scholarship and how their career objective relates to the autism or disability field. Selection is based on that essay, academic achievement, school activities, employment history, hobbies or special talents, and service activities.

Financial data: The stipend is $1,000.

Duration: 1 year.

Number awarded: 1 or more each year.

Deadline: April of each year.

2647 EDITH GREEN GRANT

Delta Kappa Gamma Society International–Alpha Rho State Organization
c/o Alyce Sandusky, State Scholarship Chair
7619 Highway 66
Klamath Falls, OR 97601-9538
Phone: (541) 884-0524
Email: terryandalyce@charter.net
Web: www.deltakappagamma.org/OR/scholarships/index.htm

Summary: To provide financial assistance to women from Oregon who are enrolled as upper-division students at a college in any state and preparing for a career in secondary education.

Eligibility: Open to female residents of Oregon who are at least juniors at a college in any state and interested in preparing for a career in secondary education. Applicants may not be members of Delta Kappa Gamma (an honorary society of women educators), but they must be sponsored by a local chapter of the society. Along with their application, they must submit a summary of their education from high school through the present, high school and college activities and achievements, community service, employment history, career goals, and financial need.

Financial data: A stipend is awarded (amount not specified).

Duration: 1 year.

Number awarded: 1 or more each year.

Deadline: February of each year.

2648 EDITH M. ALLEN SCHOLARSHIPS

Summary: To provide financial assistance to Methodist students who are African American and working on an undergraduate or graduate degree in specified fields.

See Listing #1896.

2649 EDSF BOARD OF DIRECTORS UPPER-DIVISION SCHOLARSHIPS

Summary: To provide financial assistance to upper-division and graduate students interested in preparing for a career in document management and graphic communications.

See Listing #1256.

2650 EDUCATOR OF TOMORROW AWARD

National Federation of the Blind
Attn: Scholarship Committee
1800 Johnson Street
Baltimore, MD 21230
Phone: (410) 659-9314, ext. 2415; Fax: (410) 685-5653
Email: scholarships@nfb.org
Web: www.nfb.org/nfb/scholarship_program.asp

Summary: To provide financial assistance to entering or continuing blind undergraduate or graduate students who wish to prepare for a career as a teacher.

Eligibility: Open to legally blind students who are working on or planning to work full-time on an undergraduate or graduate degree. Applicants must be preparing for a career in elementary, secondary, or postsecondary teaching. Along with their application, they must submit transcripts, standardized test scores, proof of legal blindness, 2 letters of recommendation, and a letter of endorsement from their National Federation of the Blind state president or designee. Selection is based on academic excellence, service to the community, and financial need.

Financial data: The stipend is $3,000.

Duration: 1 year; recipients may resubmit applications up to 2 additional years.

Number awarded: 1 each year.

Deadline: March of each year.

2651 EDUCATORS FOR MAINE PROGRAM

Finance Authority of Maine
Attn: Education Finance Programs
5 Community Drive
P.O. Box 949
Augusta, ME 04332-0949
Phone: (207) 623-3263; (800) 228-3734; Fax: (207) 623-0095; TDD: (207) 626-2717
Email: education@famemaine.com
Web: www.famemaine.com/Education_Home.aspx

Summary: To provide financial assistance to residents of Maine who are interested in attending college in any state to prepare for a career as a teacher.

Eligibility: Open to residents of Maine who are graduating high school seniors, currently-enrolled college students, or students accepted into a post-baccalaureate program. Applicants must be enrolled or planning to enroll at a college or university in any state in a program leading to certification as a teacher, including speech pathology or child care. Applicants must have a GPA of 3.0 or higher. Selection is based on academic performance, relevant activities, awards and special honors, and an essay; financial need is not considered. Preference is given to applicants planning to teach an underserved subject area.

Financial data: Full-time undergraduate students receive $3,000 per academic year; post-baccalaureate students receive $2,000 per academic year. This is a scholarship/loan program. Recipients may receive 1 year of loan forgiveness by completing 1 year of full-time teaching in a Maine public or private elementary or secondary school or child care center. The repayment option can be accelerated to 2 years of loan forgiveness for each year of teaching if the service is conducted in an educator shortage area or underserved subject area. If the loan recipient does not meet the service obligation, the total amount borrowed must be repaid with interest.

Duration: 1 year; may be renewed up to 3 additional years if the recipient remains a Maine resident and maintains a cumulative GPA of 2.5 or higher.

Deadline: May of each year.

2652 EDWARD G. AND HELEN A. BORGENS ELEMENTARY AND SECONDARY TEACHER EDUCATION SCHOLARSHIP

Daughters of the American Revolution–National Society
Attn: Committee Services Office, Scholarships
1776 D Street, N.W.
Washington, DC 20006-5303
Phone: (202) 628-1776
Web: www.dar.org/natsociety/edout_scholar.cfm

Summary: To provide financial assistance to mature students preparing for a career as an elementary or secondary school teacher.

Eligibility: Open to students who are 25 years of age or older and enrolled in at least their sophomore year of college. Applicants must be preparing for a career as a teacher at the elementary or secondary level and have a GPA of 3.5 or higher. They must be sponsored by a local chapter of the Daughters of the American Revolution (DAR). Selection is based on academic excellence, commitment to the field of study, and financial need. U.S. citizenship is required.

Financial data: The stipend is $1,500 per year.

Duration: 1 year; recipients may reapply.

Number awarded: 2 each year: 1 for a student of elementary education and 1 for a student of secondary education.

Deadline: April of each year.

2653 EDWARD W. O'CONNELL MEMORIAL SCHOLARSHIP FUND

WISS & Company, LLP
Attn: Francine Henry
354 Eisenhower Parkway
Livingston, NJ 07039
Phone: (973) 994-9400, ext. 215; Fax: (973) 992-6760
Email: fhenry@wiss.com
Web: www.wiss.com

Summary: To provide financial assistance to residents of New Jersey who are majoring or planning to major in accounting at a college in the state.

Eligibility: Open to seniors graduating from high schools in New Jersey and students already enrolled in college. Applicants must be attending or planning to attend a college or university in New Jersey and major in accounting. Selection is based on academic achievement, high school and/or community activities, work history, an essay on an assigned topic, and 2 letters of recommendation; financial need is not considered.

Financial data: The stipend is $2,500.

Duration: 1 year.

Number awarded: Varies each year; recently, 8 of these scholarships were awarded: 6 to high school seniors and 2 to college students.

Deadline: March of each year.

2654 EFWA WOMEN IN NEED SCHOLARSHIP

Educational Foundation for Women in Accounting
Attn: Foundation Administrator
136 South Keowee Street
Dayton, OH 45402
Phone: (937) 424-3391; Fax: (937) 222-5749
Email: info@efwa.org
Web: www.efwa.org/witwin.htm

Summary: To provide financial support to women who are the sole source of support for themselves and their families and are in the junior year of an accounting degree program.

Eligibility: Open to women who, either through divorce or death of a spouse, have become the sole source of support for themselves and their families. Women who are single parents as a result of other circumstances are also considered. Applicants must be working on a degree in accounting as incoming, current, or reentry juniors. Selection is based on aptitude for accounting and business, commitment to the goal of working on a degree in accounting (including evidence of continued commitment after receiving this award), clear evidence that the candidate has established goals and a plan for achieving those goals (both personal and professional), and financial need.

Financial data: The stipend is $2,000 per year.

Duration: 1 year; may be renewed 1 additional year if the recipient completes at least 12 hours each semester.

Number awarded: 4 each year (of which 3 are supported by KPMG).

Deadline: April of each year.

2655 EILEEN J. GARRETT SCHOLARSHIP FOR PARAPSYCHOLOGICAL RESEARCH

Parapsychology Foundation, Inc.
Attn: Executive Director
P.O. Box 1562
New York, NY 10021-0043
Phone: (212) 628-1550; Fax: (212) 628-1559
Email: info@parapsychology.org
Web: www.parapsychology.org

Summary: To provide financial assistance to undergraduate or graduate students interested in studying or conducting research in parapsychology.

Eligibility: Open to undergraduate and graduate students attending accredited colleges and universities who plan to pursue parapsychological studies or research. Funding is restricted to study, research, and experimentation in the field of parapsychology; it is not for general study, nor is it for those with merely a general interest in the subject matter. Applicants must demonstrate a previous academic interest in parapsychology by including, with the application form, a sample of writings on the subject. Letters of reference are also required from 3 individuals who are familiar with the applicant's work and/or studies in parapsychology.

Financial data: The stipend is $3,000.

Duration: 1 year.

Number awarded: 1 each year.

Deadline: July of each year.

2656 ELECTRONIC DOCUMENT SYSTEMS FOUNDATION TECHNICAL AND COMMUNITY COLLEGE SCHOLARSHIP

Summary: To provide financial assistance to students in technical schools and community colleges who are preparing for a career in the field of document management and graphic communications.

See Listing #1258.

2657 EMILIE HESEMEYER MEMORIAL SCHOLARSHIP

Association on American Indian Affairs, Inc.
Attn: Director of Scholarship Programs
966 Hungerford Drive, Suite 12-B
Rockville, MD 20850
Phone: (240) 314-7155; Fax: (240) 314-7159
Email: lw.aaia@verizon.net
Web: www.indian-affairs.org/scholarships/emilie_hesemeyer.htm

Summary: To provide financial assistance for college to Native American students, especially those interested in majoring in education.

Eligibility: Open to American Indian and Native Alaskan full-time undergraduate students. Preference is given to students working on a degree in education. Applicants must submit documentation of financial need, a Certificate of Indian Blood showing at least one-quarter Indian blood, proof of tribal enrollment, an essay on their educational goals, 2 letters of recommendation, and their most recent transcript.

Financial data: The stipend is $1,500 per year.

Duration: 1 year; may be renewed up to 3 additional years or until completion of a degree, provided the recipient maintains satisfactory progress.

Number awarded: Varies each year; recently, 3 new and 16 renewal scholarships were awarded.

Deadline: June of each year.

2658 ENID HALL GRISWOLD MEMORIAL SCHOLARSHIP

Daughters of the American Revolution–National Society
Attn: Committee Services Office, Scholarships
1776 D Street, N.W.
Washington, DC 20006-5303
Phone: (202) 628-1776

Web: www.dar.org/natsociety/edout_scholar.cfm
Summary: To provide financial assistance to upper-division college students majoring in selected social science fields.
Eligibility: Open to undergraduate students entering their junior or senior year with a major in political science, history, government, or economics. Applicants must be sponsored by a local chapter of the Daughters of the American Revolution (DAR). Selection is based on academic excellence, commitment to the field of study, and financial need. U.S. citizenship is required.
Financial data: The stipend is $1,000.
Duration: 1 year; nonrenewable.
Number awarded: Varies each year.
Deadline: February of each year.

2659 ERNEST F. HOLLINGS UNDERGRADUATE SCHOLARSHIP PROGRAM

Summary: To provide financial assistance and summer research experience to upper-division students who are working on a degree in a field of interest to the National Oceanic and Atmospheric Administration (NOAA).
See Listing #1910.

2660 ERWIN BUGBEE MEMORIAL SCHOLARSHIP

Vermont Student Assistance Corporation
Attn: Scholarship Programs
10 East Allen Street
P.O. Box 2000
Winooski, VT 05404-2601
Phone: (802) 654-3798; (888) 253-4819; Fax: (802) 654-3765; TDD: (800) 281-3341 (within VT)
Email: info@vsac.org
Web: services.vsac.org/wps/wcm/connect/vsac/VSAC
Summary: To provide financial assistance to high school seniors in Vermont who are interested in majoring in law enforcement at a college in any state.
Eligibility: Open to high school seniors in Vermont who are interested in working on a degree in law enforcement at a college or university in any state. Applicants must submit 1) a 100-word essay on their interest in and commitment to pursuing their chosen career or vocation; 2) a 100-word essay on any significant barriers that limit their access to education; and 3) a 250-word essay on their short- and long-term academic, educational, career, vocational, and/or employment goals. Selection is based on those essays and financial need.
Financial data: The stipend is $1,000.
Duration: 1 year.
Number awarded: 1 each year.
Deadline: March of each year.

2661 ETHEL LEE HOOVER ELLIS SCHOLARSHIP

National Association of Negro Business and Professional Women's Clubs
Attn: Scholarship Committee
1806 New Hampshire Avenue, N.W.
Washington, DC 20009-3206
Phone: (202) 483-4206; Fax: (202) 462-7253
Email: education@nanbpwc.org
Web: www.nanbpwc.org/ScholarshipApplications.asp
Summary: To provide financial assistance to African American women from designated southern states studying business at a college in any state.
Eligibility: Open to African Americans women who are residents of Alabama, Florida, Georgia, Mississippi, North Carolina, South Carolina, Tennessee, or West Virginia. Applicants must be enrolled at an accredited college or university in any state as a sophomore or junior. They must have a GPA of 3.0 or higher and be majoring in business. Along with their application, they must submit an essay, up to 750 words in length, on the topic, "Business and Community United: How the Two Can Work Together for Success." U.S. citizenship is required.
Financial data: A stipend is awarded (amount not specified).
Duration: 1 year.
Number awarded: 1 or more each year.
Deadline: February of each year.

2662 ETHEL O. WASHINGTON MEMORIAL SCHOLARSHIP

Michigan Association of Family and Consumer Sciences
c/o Joy Jacobs, President
Michigan State University
14 Human Ecology Building
East Lansing, MI 48824-1030
Phone: (517) 432-9225
Email: jacobsj@msu.edu
Web: www.msu.edu/~mafcs
Summary: To provide financial assistance to students from Michigan interested in working on an undergraduate degree in a field related to family and consumer sciences.
Eligibility: Open to students enrolled at 2- and 4-year colleges and universities in Michigan who are majoring in family and consumer sciences, home economics, human ecology, or a related program (e.g., child development, interior design, nutrition, human services). High school seniors who have been accepted into such a program are also eligible.
Financial data: The stipend is $1,000.
Duration: 1 year.
Number awarded: 1 each year.
Deadline: April of each year.

2663 EUNICE FIORITO MEMORIAL SCHOLARSHIP

Summary: To provide financial assistance to undergraduate or graduate students who are blind and are interested in studying in a field of advocacy or service for persons with disabilities.
See Listing #1913.

2664 EXECUTIVE WOMEN INTERNATIONAL SCHOLARSHIP PROGRAM

Summary: To provide financial assistance for college to high school juniors with outstanding business and leadership potential.
See Listing #261.

2665 EXTENDED EDUCATION FUND OF THE CALIFORNIA ASSOCIATION OF FAMILY AND CONSUMER SCIENCES

American Association of Family and Consumer Sciences–California Affiliate
c/o Kay M. Wilder
Point Loma Nazarene University
Department of Family and Consumer Sciences
3900 Lomaland Drive
San Diego, CA 92106
Phone: (619) 849-2270; Fax: (619) 226-7341
Email: kwilder@pointloma.edu
Web: www.aafcs-ca.org/ca/scholarships-grants/scholarships
Summary: To provide financial assistance to undergraduate and graduate students from any state working on a degree in family and consumer sciences at a college in California.
Eligibility: Open to residents of any state currently enrolled in an undergraduate or graduate program at a college or university in California. Applicants must be working on a degree in the field of family and consumer sciences, including nutrition and food, fashion and apparel, child and family development, interior design, family financial management, consumer economics, or family and consumer sciences education. Along with their application, they must submit 150-word essays on 1) their professional aims and goals; 2) the leadership roles they have held professionally or as a community citizen, and 3) the experiences or responsibilities that especially qualify them for this scholarship. Financial need is not considered in the selection process.
Financial data: The stipend is $1,000.
Duration: 1 year.
Number awarded: 5 each year.
Deadline: February of each year.

2666 FEDERAL PLANNING DIVISION ANNUAL STUDENT SCHOLARSHIP

American Planning Association
Attn: Federal Planning Division
205 North Michigan Avenue, Suite 1200
Chicago, IL 60601
Phone: (312) 431-9100; Fax: (312) 786-6700
Email: fpd-info@list.planning.org
Web: www.federalplanning.org/scholarships.htm

Summary: To provide financial assistance to undergraduate and graduate students preparing for a career in planning, especially as it relates to activities of the federal government.

Eligibility: Open to juniors, seniors, and graduate students at U.S. and Canadian accredited colleges and universities. Each year, the sponsor selects a university that nominates students for these awards. Nominees must be preparing for a career in public service, especially at the federal level, as a planner. They must have a GPA of 3.0 or higher. Along with their application, they must submit an essay that addresses the federal government's role in managing its lands and resources in the best interests of the United States. Selection is based primarily on the essay, which is judged on clarity of message, freshness of ideas, and potential for implementation.

Financial data: The stipend is $2,000.

Duration: 1 year.

Number awarded: 3 each year.

Deadline: November of each year.

2667 FEDERAL RESERVE BANK OF DALLAS ECONOMIC ESSAY CONTEST

Federal Reserve Bank of Dallas
Attn: Senior Economic Education Specialist
2200 North Pearl Street
Dallas, TX 75201-2272
Phone: (214) 922-6826; (800) 333-4460, ext. 6826
Email: princeton.williams@dal.frb.org
Web: dallasfed.org/educate/essay/index.html

Summary: To recognize and reward outstanding essays on economics written by high school students in the Eleventh Federal Reserve District.

Eligibility: Open to all students in grades 11–12 in the Eleventh Federal Reserve District (Texas, northern Louisiana, and southern New Mexico). Applicants must submit an essay, up to 5 pages in length, on a topic that changes annually but relates to economics and the work of the Federal Reserve System. They must have a supervising teacher, who will verify that each essay represents the student's own thoughts and writing. Competitions are first held in each of the 4 branch offices of the District (in Dallas, El Paso, Houston, and San Antonio); those winners advance to the District finals. Selection is based on the author's understanding of the topic, conclusions, creativity, organization, and writing style.

Financial data: Each finalist receives a $100 savings bond. In the District finals, the first-place winner receives an additional $1,000 savings bond, the second-place winner receives an additional $500 savings bond, and the third-place winner receives an additional $200 savings bond.

Duration: The competition is held annually.

Number awarded: 12 finalists (3 from each office) are selected each year; of those, 3 are selected to receive additional savings bonds.

Deadline: March of each year.

2668 FEDERAL RESERVE BANK OF KANSAS CITY ESSAY CONTEST

Federal Reserve Bank of Kansas City
Attn: Education
1 Memorial Drive
Kansas City, MO 64198-0001
Phone: (816) 881-2736; (800) 333-1010, ext. 2736
Email: essaycontest@kc.frb.org
Web: www.kansascityfed.org/essaycontest

Summary: To recognize and reward high school students in the Kansas City Federal Reserve District who submit outstanding essays on topics related to economics.

Eligibility: Open to students in grades 9–12 at high schools in the Kansas City Federal Reserve District (Colorado, Kansas, western Missouri, Nebraska, northern New Mexico, Oklahoma, and Wyoming). Applicants must submit an essay, up to 4 pages in length, on a topic that changes annually but relates to economics; recently, students were invited to write on the economic impact of natural disasters. Competitions are held at regional offices in Kansas City, Denver, Oklahoma City, and Omaha. Each regional first-place winner is entered into a competition for the grand prize. Selection is based on comprehension (how well the essay reflects a thorough understanding of the topic), organization (how well the argument follows a logical and easily understood progression), creativity (use of diverse resources and ideas), writing style (grammar, spelling, and punctuation), and conclusions (how well the conclusions follow from the argument).

Financial data: In each regional competition, first prize is $1,000, second $500, and third $250. The grand prize is an additional $1,000. All prizes are in the form of U.S. savings bonds.

Duration: The competition is held annually.

Number awarded: 12 each year: 3 in each region, of whom 1 is awarded the grand prize.

Deadline: April of each year.

2669 FIRESIDE ESSAY SCHOLARSHIP

Summary: To recognize and reward, with college scholarships, students at Catholic high schools who submit outstanding essays.

See Listing #1268.

2670 FLEET RESERVE ASSOCIATION AMERICANISM ESSAY CONTEST

Fleet Reserve Association
Attn: National Committee on Americanism-Patriotism
125 North West Street
Alexandria, VA 22314-2754
Phone: (703) 683-1400; (800) FRA-1924; Fax: (703) 549-6610
Email: fra@fra.org
Web: www.fra.org/Content/fra/AboutFRA/EssayContest/default.cfm

Summary: To recognize and reward outstanding high school student essays on Americanism.

Eligibility: Open to students in grades 7–12. The contest is not restricted to children of the Fleet Reserve Association (FRA) or its Ladies Auxiliary. However, each entrant must be sponsored by an FRA member, branch, or Ladies Auxiliary unit. Essays must be on the annual theme (recently: "What Memorial Day Means to Me") and cannot exceed 350 words. Students may submit only 1 entry per year. Essays are first graded on the FRA branch level and the top essays from each branch are forwarded to the regional level. From there, the top essays in each region are sent to the national level to be graded.

Financial data: The Grand National Prize is a $10,000 U.S. savings bond. For each grade level, first place is a $5,000 U.S. savings bond, second place is a $3,000 U.S. savings bond, and third place is a $2,000 U.S. savings bond. Additional prizes are awarded to students winning at local branch and regional levels of competition.

Duration: The competition is held annually.

Number awarded: 1 Grand Prize and 18 grade-level prizes (3 for each grade from 7 through 12) are offered on the national level. Many smaller prizes are awarded on the local and regional levels.

Deadline: November of each year.

2671 FLORIDA ALPHA DELTA KAPPA PAST STATE PRESIDENTS' SCHOLARSHIP AWARD

Alpha Delta Kappa-Florida Chapter
c/o Deborah King
1198 Three Meadows Drive
Rockledge, FL 32955
Web: www.flalphadeltakappa.org

Summary: To provide financial assistance to female residents of Florida attending college in the state, especially those majoring in education.

Eligibility: Open to women attending 1) a 4-year university in Florida and working on an undergraduate degree; or 2) a community college in Florida and planning to transfer to a 4-year university in the state to work on an undergraduate degree. Applicants must have maintained an unweighted GPA of 3.3 or higher in high school and 3.0 or higher in college. Preference is given to students majoring in education. In the selection process, some consideration is given to financial need.

Financial data: The stipend is $1,000.

Duration: 1 year.

Number awarded: 1 each year.

Deadline: December of each year.

2672 FLORIDA ASSOCIATION OF CONVENTION AND VISITORS BUREAUS SCHOLARSHIP

Community Foundation of Sarasota County
Attn: Scholarship Manager
2635 Fruitville Road
P.O. Box 49587
Sarasota, FL 34230-6587
Phone: (941) 556-7156; Fax: (941) 556-7157
Email: mimi@cfsarasota.org

Web: www.cfsarasota.org/Default.aspx?tabid=264

Summary: To provide financial assistance to residents of any state who are enrolled at designated colleges in Florida to prepare for a career in the hospitality industry in the state.

Eligibility: Open to students currently enrolled as juniors in the hospitality and tourism management program at Florida Gulf Coast University, Florida International University, Florida State University, University of Central Florida, University of South Florida (Sarasota campus), University of Florida, University of West Florida, Bethune Cookman, or St. Petersburg College. Applicants must be preparing for a career in the hospitality industry in Florida. Along with their application, they must submit an essay on the importance of the hospitality and tourism industry in Florida and their goals on participating in that industry. Selection is based on that essay, community involvement, and financial need.

Financial data: The stipend is $5,000. Funds are paid directly to the student's law school.

Duration: 1 year.

Number awarded: 1 or more each year.

Deadline: March of each year.

2673 FLORIDA BANKERS EDUCATIONAL FOUNDATION GRANTS

Florida Bankers Association
Attn: Florida Bankers Educational Foundation
1001 Thomasville Road, Suite 201
P.O. Box 1360
Tallahassee, FL 32302-1360
Phone: (850) 224-2265, ext. 139; Fax: (850) 224-2423
Email: lnewton@flbankers.net
Web: www.floridabankers.com

Summary: To provide financial assistance to undergraduate and graduate students who are interested in preparing for a career in Florida banking and have experience working in that field.

Eligibility: Open to undergraduate and graduate students who are interested in preparing for a career in Florida banking and have at least 5 years of full-time experience working in Florida banking. Applicants must be Florida residents, registered at 1 of 26 participating 4-year colleges or universities in the state or at a community college and taking banking-related classes. They must have a GPA of 2.5 or higher. Along with their application, they must submit 2 letters of recommendation from their place of employment: 1 from the bank president or other high-level employee and 1 from an immediate supervisor. Selection is based on interest in Florida banking, scholastic achievement, aptitude, ability, leadership, and character.

Financial data: The amount of assistance is based on the number of semester hours the student has remaining until graduation. The maximum award is $1,500 per year for the freshman and sophomore years, $2,000 per year for the junior and senior years, and $5,000 for graduate studies.

Duration: Up to 4 years as an undergraduate and another 2 years as a graduate student.

Number awarded: Several each year.

Deadline: February, May, August, or November of each year.

2674 FLORIDA BANKERS EDUCATIONAL FOUNDATION SCHOLARSHIP/LOANS

Florida Bankers Association
Attn: Florida Bankers Educational Foundation
1001 Thomasville Road, Suite 201
P.O. Box 1360
Tallahassee, FL 32302-1360
Phone: (850) 224-2265, ext. 139; Fax: (850) 224-2423
Email: lnewton@flbankers.net
Web: www.floridabankers.com

Summary: To provide financial assistance to upper-division and graduate students who are interested in preparing for a career in Florida banking.

Eligibility: Open to college juniors, seniors, and graduate students who are interested in preparing for a career in Florida banking. Applicants must be Florida residents, registered at 1 of 26 participating colleges or universities in the state, and taking banking-related classes. They must have a GPA of 2.5 or higher. Along with their application, they must submit a report signed by an authorized banker in the state who interviewed the applicant. Selection is based on interest in Florida banking, scholastic achievement, aptitude, ability, leadership, personality, and character.

Financial data: The amount of assistance is based on the number of semester hours the student has remaining until graduation. The maximum award is $1,500 per year or a total of $3,000 as an undergraduate and $3,000 as a graduate student. This is a loan forgiveness program. When recipients complete 1 year of continuous full-time employment in Florida banking, they are released from their financial obligation to repay the loan. Students who do not work for a Florida bank must repay the loan.

Duration: Up to 2 years as an undergraduate and another 2 years as a graduate student.

Number awarded: Several each year.

Deadline: February, May, August, or November of each year.

2675 FLORIDA FUND FOR MINORITY TEACHERS SCHOLARSHIPS

Florida Fund for Minority Teachers, Inc.
Attn: Executive Director
G415 Norman Hall
P.O. Box 117045
Gainesville, FL 32611-7045
Phone: (352) 392-9196, ext. 21; Fax: (352) 846-3011
Email: info@ffmt.org
Web: www.ffmt.org

Summary: To provide financial assistance to Florida residents who are members of minority groups preparing for a career as a teacher.

Eligibility: Open to Florida residents who are African American/Black, Hispanic/Latino, Asian American/Pacific Islander, or American Indian/Alaskan Native. Applicants must be entering their junior year in a teacher education program at a participating college or university in Florida. Special consideration is given to community college graduates. Selection is based on writing ability, communication skills, overall academic performance, and evidence of commitment to the youth of America (preferably demonstrated through volunteer activities).

Financial data: The stipend is $4,000 per year. Recipients are required to teach 1 year in a Florida public school for each year they receive the scholarship. If they fail to teach in a public school, they are required to repay the total amount of support received at an annual interest rate of 8%.

Duration: Up to 2 consecutive years, provided the recipient remains enrolled full-time with a GPA of 2.5 or higher.

Number awarded: Varies each year.

Deadline: July of each year for fall semester; November of each year for spring semester.

2676 FORD MOTOR COMPANY SCHOLARSHIPS

Summary: To provide financial assistance to Native American college students who are majoring in designated fields at mainstream colleges and universities.

See Listing #1930.

2677 FRANCIS A. HERZOG SCHOLARSHIP

Griffith Insurance Education Foundation
623 High Street
Worthington, OH 43085
Phone: (614) 880-9870; Fax: (614) 880-9872
Email: info@griffithfoundation.org
Web: www.griffithfoundation.org/higher-ed/scholarships

Summary: To provide financial assistance to students from Ohio working on an undergraduate degree in a field related to insurance.

Eligibility: Open to U.S. citizens who are either Ohio residents attending a college or university in any state or residents of other states attending a college or university in Ohio. Applicants must be full-time juniors or seniors with a GPA of 2.5 or higher and enrolled in an insurance, risk management, actuarial science, business, computer science, finance, or other insurance-related program. They must be planning to enter an insurance-related field after graduation. Preference is given to 1) children, stepchildren, or legally adopted children of members of Independent Insurance Agents of Ohio (Ohio Big I); and 2) students recommended by an Ohio Big I member or retiree. Selection is based on academic achievement, extracurricular activities and honors, work experience, 3 letters of recommendation, and financial need.

Financial data: The stipend is $1,000.

Duration: 1 year.

Number awarded: 1 each year.

Deadline: March of each year.

2678 FRANCIS M. KEVILLE MEMORIAL SCHOLARSHIP

Summary: To provide financial assistance to minority and female undergraduate and graduate students working on a degree in construction management.
See Listing #1935.

2679 FRANCIS PITKIN FUND SCHOLARSHIPS

American Planning Association–Pennsylvania Chapter
587 James Drive
Harrisburg, PA 17112-2273
Phone: (717) 671-4510; Fax: (717) 545-9247
Email: info@planningpa.org
Web: www.planningpa.org/education_scholarships.shtml

Summary: To provide financial assistance to undergraduate and graduate students from Pennsylvania who are working on a degree in planning.

Eligibility: Open to residents of Pennsylvania who are enrolled as juniors, seniors, or graduate students in a planning curriculum that has a demonstrated record of preparing students to become planners at a school in the state. Applicants must have a GPA of 3.0 or higher and be able to demonstrate financial need. Along with their application, they must submit a 900-word statement on the intended use of the funds and their desire to enter or continue in the field of planning.

Financial data: A stipend is awarded (amount not specified).

Duration: 1 year.

Number awarded: 1 or more each year.

Deadline: June of each year.

2680 FRED WIESNER EDUCATIONAL EXCELLENCE SCHOLARSHIP

Association of Texas Professional Educators
Attn: ATPE Foundation
305 East Huntland Drive, Suite 300
Austin, TX 78752-3792
Phone: (512) 467-0071; (800) 777-ATPE; Fax: (512) 467-2203
Email: admin@atpefoundation.org
Web: www.atpefoundation.org/scholarships.asp

Summary: To provide financial assistance to upper-division and graduate students from any state who are enrolled in educator preparation programs at institutions in Texas.

Eligibility: Open to juniors, seniors, and graduate students from any state who are enrolled in educator preparation programs at colleges and universities in Texas. Applicants must submit a 2-page essay on their personal educational philosophy, why they want to become an educator, who influenced them the most in making their career decision, and why they are applying for the scholarship. Financial need is not considered in the selection process.

Financial data: The stipend is $1,500 per year.

Duration: 1 year.

Number awarded: 4 each year: 3 to undergraduates and 1 to a graduate student.

Deadline: May of each year.

2681 FRIENDS OF OREGON STUDENTS PROGRAM

Oregon Student Assistance Commission
Attn: Grants and Scholarships Division
1500 Valley River Drive, Suite 100
Eugene, OR 97401-2146
Phone: (541) 687-7395; (800) 452-8807, ext. 7395; Fax: (541) 687-7414; TDD: (800) 735-2900
Email: awardinfo@osac.state.or.us
Web: www.osac.state.or.us/osac_programs.html

Summary: To provide financial assistance to students in Oregon who are employed while working on an undergraduate or graduate degree in teaching at a school in any state.

Eligibility: Open to residents of Oregon who are working and will continue to work at least 20 hours per week while attending college or graduate school in any state at least three-quarter time. Applicants must be interested in preparing for a career in teaching. They must be able to demonstrate a cumulative GPA of 2.5 or higher and volunteer or work experience relevant to their chosen profession. Preference is given to applicants who 1) are nontraditional students (e.g., older, returning, single parents); 2) have overcome significant personal obstacles; or 3) graduated from an alternative high school, obtained a GED, or are transferring from an Oregon community college to a 4-year college. Along with their application, they must submit essays and letters of reference on how they balance school, work, and personal life as well as their experiences in overcoming obstacles. Selection is based on work experience, community service and volunteer activities, responses to essay questions, letters of reference, and financial need; academic promise (as indicated by GPA and SAT/ACT scores) is also considered.

Financial data: Stipends range from $3,000 to $5,000 per year.

Duration: 1 year; may be renewed.

Number awarded: Varies each year; recently, 28 of these scholarships were awarded.

Deadline: February of each year.

2682 FUTURE ENTREPRENEUR OF THE YEAR AWARD

National Association for the Self-Employed
P.O. Box 612067
DFW Airport
Dallas, TX 75261-2067
Phone: (800) 232-NASE; Fax: (800) 551-4446
Web: www.nase.org

Summary: To provide financial assistance to high school seniors and college undergraduates interested in studying entrepreneurship.

Eligibility: Open to high school seniors and college undergraduates who demonstrate leadership, academic excellence, ingenuity, and entrepreneurial spirit. Applicants must be interested in a program that stresses the philosophy of entrepreneurship rather than a specific field of study.

Financial data: The stipend is $12,000 for the first year and $4,000 for each subsequent year.

Duration: 1 year; may be renewed up to 3 additional years.

Number awarded: 1 each year.

Deadline: April of each year.

2683 FUTURE TEACHERS OF NORTH CAROLINA SCHOLARSHIP/LOAN PROGRAM

North Carolina State Education Assistance Authority
Attn: Future Teachers Scholarship Loan Program
10 Alexander Drive
P.O. Box 13663
Research Triangle Park, NC 27709-3663
Phone: (919) 549-8614; (800) 700-1775; Fax: (919) 248-4687
Email: information@ncseaa.edu
Web: www.ncseaa.edu/FTNC.htm

Summary: To provide financial assistance to upper-division students in North Carolina seeking teacher licensure in designated areas.

Eligibility: Open to residents of North Carolina enrolled as juniors or seniors at a college or university in the state. Applicants must be seeking licensure to teach mathematics, science, special education, or English as a second language in North Carolina's public schools. They must be enrolled full-time and have a GPA of 3.0 or higher.

Financial data: The maximum stipend is $6,500 per year. This is a loan for service program. Recipients are obligated to teach 1 year in a North Carolina public school for each year of assistance they receive. Service repayment must be completed within 5 years from graduation. If they fail to meet that service obligation, cash repayment must be completed within 10 years with interest at 10%.

Duration: 1 year; may be renewed.

Number awarded: Up to 100 each year; recently, 64 students received $373,750 through this program.

Deadline: May of each year.

2684 GAIL BURNS-SMITH "DARE TO DREAM" FUND

Connecticut Sexual Assault Crisis Services, Inc.
Attn: Special Projects Coordinator
96 Pitkin Street
East Hartford, CT
Phone: (860) 282-9881; Fax: (860) 291-9335
Email: ayana@connsacs.org
Web: www.connsacs.org/GailBurns-SmithDaretoDreamFund.htm

Summary: To provide financial assistance to students from Connecticut interested in preparing for a career in the field of women's issues or sexual violence prevention.

Eligibility: Open to students who are residents of Connecticut or currently enrolled at a college or university in the state. Applicants must have paid or volunteer work experience in the field of women's issues or sexual violence prevention and advocacy. They must be committed to continuing work in those fields. Along with their application, they must submit essays on 1) their experience

working in the field of sexual violence prevention and/or advocating on behalf of sexual assault victims; and 2) their plans for future work in that field and how they feel they can make a difference.
Financial data: The stipend is $1,000.
Duration: 1 year.
Number awarded: 1 each year.
Deadline: February of each year.

2685 GARIKIAN UNIVERSITY SCHOLARSHIP

Summary: To provide money for college to students of Armenian heritage in California who have completed their freshman year in selected subject fields.
See Listing #1283.

2686 G.C. MORRIS/PAUL RUPP MEMORIAL EDUCATIONAL TRUST

Summary: To provide financial assistance to residents of designated states who are interested in attending college or technical school in any state to prepare for a career in the automotive aftermarket industry.
See Listing #1944.

2687 GENE CERGE GRANT

Virgin Islands Board of Education
Dronningen Gade 60B, 61, and 62
P.O. Box 11900
St. Thomas, VI 00801
Phone: (340) 774-4546; Fax: (340) 774-3384
Email: stt@myviboe.com
Web: www.myviboe.com

Summary: To provide financial assistance to residents of the Virgin Islands who wish to study physical education at a college in the territory or on the mainland.
Eligibility: Open to residents of the Virgin Islands who are seniors or graduates of high schools in the territory. Applicants must have a GPA of 2.0 or higher and be attending or accepted for enrollment at an accredited institution of higher learning in the territory or on the mainland. They must be planning to major in physical education. Financial need is considered in the selection process.
Financial data: The stipend is $1,000 per year.
Duration: 1 year; nonrenewable.
Number awarded: 1 each year.
Deadline: April of each year.

2688 GENERAL EMMETT PAIGE SCHOLARSHIPS

Summary: To provide financial assistance to veterans, military personnel, and their family members who are majoring in specified scientific fields in college.
See Listing #1946.

2689 GENERAL MOTORS SCHOLARSHIP PROGRAM OF THE HISPANIC SCHOLARSHIP FUND

Summary: To provide financial assistance to Hispanic Americans who are interested in attending college to major in engineering, business, or human resources.
See Listing #1950.

2690 GEORGE AND DONNA NIGH PUBLIC SERVICE SCHOLARSHIP

Oklahoma State Regents for Higher Education
Attn: Director of Scholarship and Grant Programs
655 Research Parkway, Suite 200
P.O. Box 108850
Oklahoma City, OK 73101-8850
Phone: (405) 225-9239; (800) 858-1840; Fax: (405) 225-9230
Email: studentinfo@osrhe.edu
Web: www.okhighered.org/student-center/financial-aid/nigh.shtml

Summary: To provide financial assistance to residents in Oklahoma who are interested in attending college in the state to prepare for a career in public service.
Eligibility: Open to residents of Oklahoma who are enrolled full-time in an undergraduate program at a public or private college or university in the state. Applicants must be enrolled in a degree program leading to a career in public service (as determined by the institution). Selection is based on academic achievement, including GPA, class rank, national awards, honors, teachers' recommendations, and participation in extracurricular activities. Each participating college or university may nominate 1 student each year.
Financial data: The stipend is $1,000.
Duration: 1 year; nonrenewable.
Number awarded: Varies each year.
Deadline: Deadline not specified.

2691 GEORGE AND LEOLA SMITH AWARD

Summary: To provide financial assistance to high school seniors who are interested in studying nursing or business in college.
See Listing #1953.

2692 GEORGE AND NAOUMA GIOLES SCHOLARSHIP

Summary: To provide financial assistance to high school seniors and current undergraduates who are of the Greek Orthodox faith and plan to study the sciences, business, or the arts.
See Listing #1284.

2693 GEORGE D. MILLER SCHOLARSHIP

Summary: To provide financial assistance to undergraduate and graduate students enrolled in fire service or public administration programs.
See Listing #1956.

2694 GEORGE REINKE SCHOLARSHIPS

Tourism Cares
Attn: American Society of Travel Agents Scholarship Fund
275 Turnpike Street, Suite 307
Canton, MA 02021
Phone: (781) 821-5990; Fax: (781) 821-8949
Email: info@tourismcares.org
Web: www.tourismcares.org/scholarships/asta-scholarships

Summary: To provide financial assistance to vocational or junior college students who are interested in preparing for a career in the travel/tourism industry.
Eligibility: Open to students who are registered at a recognized proprietary travel school or 2-year junior college that specializes in travel or tourism studies. Applicants must have a GPA of 2.5 or higher, write a 500-word essay on "My Objectives in the Travel Agency Industry," and explain why they need the scholarship. They must be U.S. citizens studying in the United States.
Financial data: The award is $2,000. A copy of the tuition bill is required.
Duration: 1 year.
Number awarded: Up to 6 each year.
Deadline: Applications may be submitted at any time.

2695 GEORGE W. WILSON III AND KIAWA SCHOLARSHIP

Summary: To provide financial assistance to residents of Indiana and Kentucky who are interested in attending college or vocational school in any state to prepare for a career in the automotive aftermarket.
See Listing #1958.

2696 GLADYS L. MERSEREAU GRANTS-IN-AID

Delta Kappa Gamma Society International–Pi State Organization
c/o Joan Slagle
1524 Amsterdam Road
Balston Spa, NY 12020-3318
Phone: (518) 885-7215
Email: jns172@yahoo.com
Web: www.deltakappagamma.org/NY/ASaGiA.html

Summary: To provide financial assistance to women in New York whose education was interrupted and who now need help to become teachers.
Eligibility: Open to women in New York who are interested in completing teacher certification requirements but whose education has been interrupted. Along with their application, they must submit a statement on their educational

philosophy, documentation of their financial need, and 3 letters of recommendation (including at least 1 from a member of the sponsoring organization). Members of that organization are not eligible.
Financial data: The amounts of the grants depend on the availability of funds.
Duration: 1 year.
Number awarded: Varies each year; recently, 5 of these grants were awarded.
Deadline: January of each year.

2697 GLENN MILLER SCHOLARSHIP COMPETITION

Summary: To recognize and reward, with college scholarships, present and prospective college music or music education majors.
See Listing #1293.

2698 GLENN MOON SCHOLARSHIPS

Association of Retired Teachers of Connecticut
Attn: Executive Director
68 Loomis Street
Manchester, CT 06042
Phone: (866) 343-2782
Email: wpw@artct.org
Web: artct.org/Scholarship.html
Summary: To provide financial assistance to high school seniors in Connecticut who are interested in majoring in education at a college in any state.
Eligibility: Open to seniors graduating from high schools in Connecticut who plan to attend a 4-year college or university in any state to prepare for a career as a teacher. Applicants must submit an autobiographical essay that includes their personal history, special interests, ambitions, community service, educational goals, teaching or tutoring experience, reasons for wishing to teach, experiences that influenced their selection of teaching as a career, desired teaching level, and desired subject area. Selection is based on the essay, academic record (GPA, class rank, SAT scores), financial need, and character references.
Financial data: Stipends are $2,000 or $1,500.
Duration: 1 year; the $2,000 award may be renewed up to 3 additional years; the $1,500 awards are nonrenewable.
Number awarded: 4 each year: 1 at $2,000 and 3 at $1,500.
Deadline: March of each year.

2699 GLOBAL AUTOMOTIVE AFTERMARKET SYMPOSIUM SCHOLARSHIPS

Summary: To provide financial assistance for college to students interested in preparing for a career in the automotive aftermarket.
See Listing #1961.

2700 GOLDMAN SACHS 10,000 WOMEN BUSINESS LEADERSHIP AWARD

Hispanic Scholarship Fund
Attn: Selection Committee
55 Second Street, Suite 1500
San Francisco, CA 94105
Phone: (415) 808-2376; (877) HSF-INFO; Fax: (415) 808-2302
Email: scholar1@hsf.net
Web: www.hsf.net/Scholarships.aspx?id=2674
Summary: To provide financial assistance to Hispanic American women who are attending specified universities to prepare for a career in business.
Eligibility: Open to Hispanic American women entering their junior year at Baruch College (CUNY), Barnard College, Fordham University, Rutgers University, Columbia University, New York University, the University of California at Berkeley, or the University of Texas at Austin. Applicants must be enrolled full-time and have a GPA of 3.0 or higher. They must be able to demonstrate an interest in entrepreneurship or a business career. Along with their application, they must submit a personal statement, resume, and letter of recommendation that attest to their leadership, entrepreneurial and business activities, and how participation in the Goldman Sachs 10,000 Women scholarship and mentoring program would advance those interests. An interview may be included as part of the selection process. U.S. citizenship or permanent resident status is required.
Financial data: The stipend is $5,000 per year.
Duration: 2 years (the junior and senior years of college).
Number awarded: 1 or more each year.
Deadline: May of each year.

2701 HAINES MEMORIAL SCHOLARSHIP

South Dakota Board of Regents
Attn: Scholarship Committee
306 East Capitol Avenue, Suite 200
Pierre, SD 57501-2545
Phone: (605) 773-3455; Fax: (605) 773-5320
Email: info@sdbor.edu
Web: www.sdbor.edu/administration/academics/Scholarships.htm
Summary: To provide financial assistance to students at public universities in South Dakota who are enrolled in a teacher education program.
Eligibility: Open to sophomores, juniors, and seniors at public universities in South Dakota. Applicants must have a GPA of 2.5 or higher and a declared major in a teacher preparation program. They must submit 2 statements of 2 pages each that describe 1) their personal philosophy; and 2) their philosophy of education.
Financial data: The stipend is $2,150; funds are allocated to the institution for distribution to the student.
Duration: 1 year; nonrenewable.
Number awarded: 1 each year.
Deadline: February of each year.

2702 HARDWOOD FOREST FOUNDATION EDUCATOR SCHOLARSHIP

National Hardwood Lumber Association
Attn: Hardwood Forest Foundation
P.O. Box 34518
Memphis, TN 38184-0518
Phone: (901) 507-0312; Fax: (901) 377-9169
Email: c.oldham@hardwoodforest.org
Web: www.hardwoodforest.org
Summary: To provide financial assistance to college seniors and graduate students completing a degree in education.
Eligibility: Open to college seniors completing a degree in education and graduate students working on a master's or doctoral degree in education. Applicants must be sponsored by a member company of the Hardwood Forest Foundation and have an expressed interest in incorporating knowledge and teaching tools concerning the forest and forest industry into their work. Financial need is not considered in the selection process.
Financial data: The stipend is $1,500 or $1,000.
Duration: 1 year.
Number awarded: Varies each year; recently, 15 of these scholarships were awarded: 1 at $1,500 and 14 at $1,000.
Deadline: January of each year.

2703 HAROLD AND MARIA RANSBURG AMERICAN PATRIOT SCHOLARSHIPS

Association for Intelligence Officers
Attn: Scholarships Committee
6723 Whittier Avenue, Suite 303A
McLean, VA 22101-4533
Phone: (703) 790-0320; Fax: (703) 991-1278
Email: afio@afio.com
Web: www.afio.com/13_scholarships.htm
Summary: To provide financial assistance to undergraduate and graduate students who have a career interest in intelligence and national security.
Eligibility: Open to undergraduates who are entering their sophomore or junior year and graduate students who apply in their senior undergraduate year or first graduate year. Applicants must share the sponsor's educational mission on behalf of "national security, patriotism, and loyalty to the constitution." They must be working on a degree in intelligence, foreign affairs, and/or national security. Along with their application, they must submit a cover letter that explains their need for assistance, their career goals and dreams, and their views of U.S. world standing and its intelligence community. Selection is based on merit, character, estimated future potential, background, and relevance of their studies to the full spectrum of national security interests and career ambitions. U.S. citizenship is required.
Financial data: The stipend is $2,000.
Duration: 1 year.
Number awarded: 10 each year.
Deadline: June of each year.

2704 HARRIET IRSAY SCHOLARSHIP GRANT

Summary: To provide financial assistance to Polish American and other students interested in working on an undergraduate or graduate degree in selected fields.

See Listing #1301.

2705 HARRY F. GAEKE MEMORIAL SCHOLARSHIP

Summary: To provide financial assistance to students from Indiana, Kentucky, or Ohio who are working on an undergraduate degree in a field related to construction or construction management.

See Listing #1973.

2706 HARVEST SCHOLARSHIPS

Summary: To provide financial assistance to Michigan residents interested in attending college in any state to prepare for a career in the manufactured homes, recreational vehicles, or campground industries.

See Listing #1975.

2707 HARVEY S. FRIEDMAN ANNUAL MEMORIAL GRANT

Summary: To provide financial assistance to undergraduate and graduate students working on a degree in a field related to museums.

See Listing #1304.

2708 HASSON/NEWMAN MEMORIAL ESSAY CONTEST

Oregon Student Assistance Commission
Attn: Grants and Scholarships Division
1500 Valley River Drive, Suite 100
Eugene, OR 97401-2146
Phone: (541) 687-7395; (800) 452-8807, ext. 7395; Fax: (541) 687-7414; TDD: (800) 735-2900
Email: awardinfo@osac.state.or.us
Web: www.osac.state.or.us/osac_programs.html

Summary: To recognize and reward, with scholarships for college study in Oregon, high school seniors in the state who submit essays on the proper use of credit.

Eligibility: Open to seniors graduating from high schools in Oregon who submit a 3- to 4-page essay entitled "Credit in the 21st Century." Children and grandchildren of owners and officers of collection agencies registered in Oregon are not eligible. Applicants must be planning to enroll at a college or vocational school in Oregon.

Financial data: Awards are $3,000 for first place, $2,000 for second, or $1,000 for third. Funds must be used for tuition and other educational expenses at a college or vocational school in Oregon.

Duration: The award, presented annually, may not be renewed.

Number awarded: 3 each year.

Deadline: February of each year.

2709 HAWAII ASSOCIATION FOR HEALTH, PHYSICAL EDUCATION, RECREATION AND DANCE SCHOLARSHIPS

Summary: To provide financial assistance to high school seniors and graduates in Hawaii who are interested in attending college in any state to prepare for a career teaching health education, physical education, dance, or recreation.

See Listing #1305.

2710 HEALTH RESEARCH AND EDUCATIONAL TRUST SCHOLARSHIPS

Summary: To provide financial assistance to New Jersey residents working on an undergraduate or graduate degree in a field related to health care administration at a school in any state.

See Listing #1981.

2711 HEARLD AND MARGE AMBLER SCHOLARSHIP

Community Foundation of the Ozarks
Attn: Scholarship Coordinator
421 East Trafficway
Springfield, MO 65806
Phone: (417) 864-6199; (888) 266-6815; Fax: (417) 864-8344
Email: jbillings@cfozarks.org
Web: www.cfozarks.org/cfo-grantmaking-programs/scholarship-programs

Summary: To provide financial assistance to residents of Missouri and contiguous states who are upper-division students majoring in business at a college in their state.

Eligibility: Open to residents of Missouri and contiguous states (Arkansas, Illinois, Iowa, Kansas, Kentucky, Nebraska, Oklahoma, and Tennessee) who are enrolled full-time in the third, fourth, or fifth year of undergraduate study at a college in those states. Applicants must be majoring in business; preference is given to accounting majors. They must have a GPA of 3.0 or higher and be able to demonstrate financial need. Along with their application, they must submit a 1-page essay describing their college activities, work experience, and personal and career goals. The program is limited to students who are employed while attending college.

Financial data: The stipend is $3,600.

Duration: 1 year.

Number awarded: 1 each year.

Deadline: March of each year.

2712 HELEN HOPPER SCHOLARSHIP

Virginia Association for Teachers of Family and Consumer Sciences
c/o Kelly M. Thompson, Past President
209 Crawford Drive
Churchville, VA 24421
Phone: (540) 292-5307
Email: teachinfacs@aol.com
Web: vatfacs.com/scholarships

Summary: To provide financial assistance to undergraduate and graduate students in Virginia who are interested in studying family and consumer sciences.

Eligibility: Open to 1) Virginia high school seniors who plan to attend college in any state and major in family life education; 2) college students who graduated from a high school in Virginia and are currently enrolled in a family life program in any state; and 3) students working on a master's degree in a family life program in Virginia and planning to teach the subject. Applicants must submit a letter explaining why they wish to major in family life education and describing their general career goals, a transcript, 2 letters of recommendation, and documentation of financial need.

Financial data: The stipend is $1,000.

Duration: 1 year.

Number awarded: 1 or more each year.

Deadline: April of each year.

2713 HELEN K. AND ROBERT T. STAFFORD SCHOLARSHIP

Summary: To provide financial assistance to Vermont residents who are interested in working on a bachelor's degree in environmental studies or special education at a school in any state.

See Listing #1982.

2714 HENRY H. WELCH SCHOLARSHIP

Colorado Gerontological Society
3006 East Colfax Avenue
Denver, CO 80206
Phone: (303) 333-3482; Fax: (303) 333-9112
Email: cogs@senioranswers.org
Web: www.senioranswers.org/Pages/hhwapplication.htm

Summary: To provide financial assistance to undergraduate and graduate students in Colorado who are preparing for work in the field of aging.

Eligibility: Open to undergraduate and graduate students who may be residents of any state but must be enrolled at a college or university in Colorado. Only students who need financial assistance to prepare for work in the field of aging are eligible. Applicants are asked to describe their previous experience with geriatrics/gerontology, their leadership qualities, their interest in working with the elderly, their previous involvement in school and community activities, and their plans for the future.

Financial data: The stipend is $1,000.

Duration: 1 year.

Number awarded: 2 each year.

Deadline: October of each year.

2715 HENRY SALVATORI SCHOLARSHIP

Order Sons of Italy in America
Attn: Sons of Italy Foundation
219 E Street, N.E.
Washington, DC 20002
Phone: (202) 547-2900; (800) 552-OSIA; Fax: (202) 546-8168
Email: scholarships@osia.org
Web: www.osia.org/students/general-study-scholarships.php

Summary: To provide financial assistance for college to high school seniors of Italian descent who write about the principles of liberty, freedom, and equality in the United States.

Eligibility: Open to U.S. citizens of Italian descent who are high school seniors planning to enroll as full-time students in an undergraduate program at an accredited 4-year college or university. Applicants must submit essays, from 750 to 1,000 words, on the Declaration of Independence, the Constitution, or the Bill of Rights and the meaning of those documents to the principles of liberty, freedom, and equality in the United States today. The scholarship is presented to a student who has demonstrated exceptional leadership, distinguished scholarship, and an understanding of the principles for which the country was founded.

Financial data: The stipend is $25,000.

Duration: 1 year; nonrenewable.

Number awarded: 1 each year.

Deadline: February of each year.

2716 HIGH SCHOOL SCHOLARSHIP FOR FUTURE BILINGUAL EDUCATORS

Texas Association for Bilingual Education
110 Broadway, Suite 480
San Antonio, TX 78205
Phone: (210) 979-6390; (800) TABE-930; Fax: (210) 979-6485
Web: www.tabe.org

Summary: To provide financial assistance to high school seniors who are interested in attending a college or university in Texas to prepare for a career as a bilingual educator.

Eligibility: Open to high school seniors who have applied to an accredited Texas college or university, including 2-year colleges, and have a grade average of 75 or higher. Applicants must 1) declare a specialization in bilingual education; and 2) be bilingual and biliterate in English and another language. They must submit a completed application, official transcripts, and 3 letters of recommendation.

Financial data: The stipend is $1,000.

Duration: 1 year.

Number awarded: Varies each year; recently, 5 of these scholarships were awarded.

Deadline: March of each year.

2717 HILDA BASTIAN ENGLAND GRANT

Virgin Islands Board of Education
Dronningen Gade 60B, 61, and 62
P.O. Box 11900
St. Thomas, VI 00801
Phone: (340) 774-4546; Fax: (340) 774-3384
Email: stt@myviboe.com
Web: www.myviboe.com

Summary: To provide financial assistance to residents of the Virgin Islands who wish to study guidance counseling at a college in the territory or on the mainland.

Eligibility: Open to residents of the Virgin Islands who are seniors or graduates of high schools in the territory. Applicants must have a GPA of 2.0 or higher and be attending or accepted for enrollment at an accredited institution of higher learning in the territory or on the mainland. They must be planning to major in guidance counseling. Financial need is considered in the selection process.

Financial data: The stipend is $5,000 per year.

Duration: 1 year.

Number awarded: 1 each year.

Deadline: April of each year.

2718 HISPANIC SCHOLARSHIP FUND/ASSOCIATION OF LATINO PROFESSIONALS IN FINANCE AND ACCOUNTING SCHOLARSHIPS

Hispanic Scholarship Fund
Attn: Selection Committee
55 Second Street, Suite 1500
San Francisco, CA 94105
Phone: (415) 808-2365; (877) HSF-INFO; Fax: (415) 808-2302
Email: scholar1@hsf.net
Web: www.hsf.net/ALPFA.aspx

Summary: To provide financial assistance to Hispanic students working on a bachelor's or master's degree in a business-related field.

Eligibility: Open to U.S. citizens and permanent residents (must have a permanent resident card or a passport stamped I-551) who are of Hispanic heritage. Applicants must be currently enrolled full-time and entering their sophomore, junior, or senior year or enrolling in a master's degree program at an accredited 4-year college or university in the United States, Puerto Rico, Guam, or the U.S. Virgin Islands (including community college students transferring to a 4-year institution). They must be working on a degree in accounting, business administration, economics, finance, or management and have a GPA of 3.0 or higher.

Financial data: The stipend ranges from $1,500 to $10,000.

Duration: 1 year.

Number awarded: 1 or more each year.

Deadline: January of each year.

2719 HOME DEPOT SCHOLARSHIP AWARD

Hispanic Association of Colleges and Universities
Attn: National Scholarship Program
8415 Datapoint Drive, Suite 400
San Antonio, TX 78229
Phone: (210) 692-3805; Fax: (210) 692-0823; TDD: (800) 855-2880
Email: scholarships@hacu.net
Web: www.hacu.net/hacu/Scholarships_EN.asp?SnID=875148054

Summary: To provide financial assistance to undergraduate students majoring in finance and related fields at institutions that are members of the Hispanic Association of Colleges and Universities (HACU).

Eligibility: Open to full-time undergraduate students at 4-year HACU member and partner colleges and universities. Applicants must be majoring in supply chain and logistics, finance, or information systems. They must have a GPA of 3.0 or higher and be able to demonstrate financial need. Along with their application, they must submit an essay of 200 to 250 words that describes their academic and/or career goals, where they expect to be and what they expect to be doing 10 years from now, and what skills they can bring to an employer.

Financial data: The stipend is $3,520 per year.

Duration: 1 year; nonrenewable.

Number awarded: 1 or more each year.

Deadline: May of each year.

2720 HONORABLE ERNESTINE WASHINGTON LIBRARY SCIENCE/ENGLISH LANGUAGE ARTS SCHOLARSHIP

Summary: To provide financial assistance to high school seniors of African American or Caribbean heritage who plan to study a field related to library science or English language arts in college.

See Listing #1318.

2721 HONORARY STATE REGENTS' AMERICAN HISTORY SCHOLARSHIP

Summary: To provide financial assistance to high school seniors in Colorado who are interested in majoring in American history and government at a college in any state.

See Listing #1319.

2722 HOOPER MEMORIAL SCHOLARSHIP

Summary: To provide financial assistance to college students interested in preparing for a career in fields related to transportation.

See Listing #1995.

2723 HORIZONS FOUNDATION SCHOLARSHIP PROGRAM

Summary: To provide financial assistance to women who are upper-division or graduate students engaged in or planning careers related to the national security interests of the United States.

See Listing #1996.

2724 HORMEL SCHOLARSHIP PROGRAM OF THE HISPANIC SCHOLARSHIP FUND

Summary: To provide financial assistance to Hispanic upper-division students who are interested in a career in the food industry.
See Listing #1997.

2725 HSBC-NORTH AMERICA SCHOLARSHIP PROGRAM OF THE HISPANIC SCHOLARSHIP FUND

Summary: To provide financial assistance to Hispanic upper-division students from selected states who are working on a degree related to business.
See Listing #2000.

2726 HSMAI FOUNDATION SCHOLARSHIPS

Hospitality Sales and Marketing Association International
Attn: HSMAI Foundation
1760 Old Meadow Road, Suite 500
McLean, VA 22102
Phone: (703) 506-3280; Fax: (703) 506-3266
Email: info@hsmai.org
Web: www.hsmai.org/Resources/Scholarships.cfm

Summary: To provide financial assistance to undergraduate and graduate students who are preparing for a career in hospitality sales and marketing.

Eligibility: Open to students working full- or part-time on an associate, bachelor's, or graduate degree in hospitality management or a related field. Applicants must be preparing for a career in hospitality sales and marketing. Along with their application, they must submit 3 essays: their interest in the hospitality industry and their career goals, the personal characteristics that will enable them to succeed in reaching those goals, and a situation in which they faced a challenge or were in a leadership role and how they dealt with the situation. Selection is based on the essays, industry-related work experience, GPA, extracurricular involvement, 2 letters of recommendation, involvement in the Hospitality Sales and Marketing Association International (HSMAI), and presentation of the application.

Financial data: The stipend is $2,000 for bachelor's/graduate degree students or $500 for associate degree students.

Duration: 1 year.

Number awarded: Varies each year; recently, 5 of these scholarships were awarded.

Deadline: June of each year.

2727 HUMANE STUDIES FELLOWSHIPS

Summary: To provide financial assistance to undergraduate and graduate students in the United States or abroad who intend to pursue "intellectual careers" and have demonstrated an interest in classical liberal principles.
See Listing #1325.

2728 HYATT HOTELS FUND FOR MINORITY LODGING MANAGEMENT STUDENTS

American Hotel & Lodging Educational Foundation
Attn: Manager of Foundation Programs
1201 New York Avenue, N.W., Suite 600
Washington, DC 20005-3931
Phone: (202) 289-3181; Fax: (202) 289-3199
Email: ahlef@ahlef.org
Web: www.ahlef.org/content.aspx?id=19828

Summary: To provide financial assistance to minority college students working on a degree in hotel management.

Eligibility: Open to students majoring in hospitality management at a 4-year college or university as at least a sophomore. Applicants must be members of a minority group (African American, Hispanic, American Indian, Alaskan Native, Asian, or Pacific Islander). They must be enrolled full-time. Along with their application, they must submit a 500-word essay on their personal background, including when they became interested in the hospitality field, what traits they possess or will need to succeed in the industry, and their plans as related to their educational and career objectives and future goals. Selection is based on industry-related work experience; financial need; academic record and educational qualifications; professional, community, and extracurricular activities; personal attributes, including career goals; the essay; and neatness and completeness of the application. U.S. citizenship or permanent resident status is required.

Financial data: The stipend is $2,000.

Duration: 1 year.

Number awarded: Varies each year; recently, 10 of these scholarships were awarded. Since this program was established, it has awarded scholarships worth $508,000 to approximately 254 minority students.

Deadline: April of each year.

2729 IDAHO EDUCATION INCENTIVE LOAN FORGIVENESS

Summary: To provide financial assistance to Idaho students who wish to prepare for a teaching or nursing career in Idaho.
See Listing #2004.

2730 IDAHO STATE BROADCASTERS ASSOCIATION SCHOLARSHIPS

Summary: To provide financial assistance to students at Idaho colleges and universities who are preparing for a career in the broadcasting field (including the business side of broadcasting).
See Listing #1327.

2731 IDDBA SCHOLARSHIP

Summary: To provide financial assistance to high school seniors, undergraduates, or graduate students employed in a supermarket dairy, deli, or bakery department who are interested in working on a degree in a food-related field.
See Listing #1328.

2732 ILLINOIS COMMUNITY COLLEGE STATE FARM INSURANCE TEACHER EDUCATION SCHOLARSHIP

Illinois Community College System Foundation
401 East Capitol Avenue
Springfield, IL 62701
Phone: (217) 789-4230; Fax: (217) 492-5176
Email: iccsfoundation@sbcglobal.net
Web: www.iccsfoundation.com/Scholarships.htm

Summary: To provide financial assistance to students attending an Illinois community college and preparing for a career as a teacher.

Eligibility: Open to full-time students at Illinois community colleges who have a high school GPA of 2.5 or higher or an equivalent GED score. Applicants must be enrolled in an approved course of study that leads to admission to a teacher education program or an associate in teacher education program at an Illinois community college, leading to transfer to an approved university offering a baccalaureate degree in teacher education. They must be planning to become a public school teacher in a low-income area of Illinois with traditionally high concentrations of minorities.

Financial data: The stipend is $1,666 per semester ($3,333 per year).

Duration: 1 semester; may be renewed 3 additional semesters, provided the recipient remains enrolled full-time and maintains a GPA of 3.0 or higher.

Number awarded: 1 or more each year.

Deadline: Deadline not specified.

2733 ILLINOIS FUTURE TEACHER CORPS PROGRAM

Illinois Student Assistance Commission
Attn: Scholarship and Grant Services
1755 Lake Cook Road
Deerfield, IL 60015-5209
Phone: (847) 948-8550; (800) 899-ISAC; Fax: (847) 831-8549; TDD: (800) 526-0844
Email: collegezone@isac.org
Web: www.collegezone.com/studentzone/407_660.htm

Summary: To provide financial assistance to college students in Illinois who are interested in training or retraining for a teaching career in academic shortage areas.

Eligibility: Open to Illinois residents who are enrolled at the junior level or higher at an institution of higher education in the state. Applicants must be planning to prepare for a career as a preschool, elementary, or secondary school teacher. They must have a cumulative GPA of 2.5 or higher. Priority is given to 1) minority students; 2) students with financial need; and 3) applicants working on a degree in designated teacher shortage disciplines or making a commitment to teach at a hard-to-staff school. Recently, the teacher shortage disciplines included early childhood education, special education (speech and language impaired, learning behavior specialist), and regular education (bilingual education, mathematics, physical education [K–8], reading, and science). U.S. citizenship or eligible noncitizen status is required.

Financial data: Stipends are $5,000 per year for students who agree to teach in a teacher shortage discipline, $5,000 per year for students who agree to teach at a hard-to-staff school, or $10,000 for students who agree to teach in a teacher shortage discipline at a hard-to-staff school. Funds are paid directly to the school. This is a scholarship/loan program. Recipients must agree to teach in an Illinois public, private, or parochial preschool, elementary school, or secondary school for 1 year for each full year of assistance received. The teaching obligation must be completed within 5 years of completion of the degree or certificate program for which the scholarship was awarded. That time period may be extended if the recipient serves in the U.S. armed forces, enrolls full-time in a graduate program related to teaching, becomes temporarily disabled, is unable to find employment as a teacher, or takes additional courses on at least a half-time basis to teach in a specialized teacher shortage discipline. Recipients who fail to honor this work obligation must repay the award with interest.

Duration: 1 year; may be renewed.

Number awarded: Varies each year, depending on the availability of funds.

Deadline: Priority consideration is given to applications submitted by February of each year.

2734 ILLINOIS LEGION AUXILIARY SPECIAL EDUCATION TEACHER SCHOLARSHIP

American Legion Auxiliary
Department of Illinois
2720 East Lincoln Street
P.O. Box 1426
Bloomington, IL 61702-1426
Phone: (309) 663-9366; Fax: (309) 663-5827
Email: staff@ilala.org
Web: ilala.org/scholar.html

Summary: To provide financial assistance to Illinois veterans and their descendants who are attending college in any state to prepare for a career as a special education teacher.

Eligibility: Open to veterans who served during designated periods of war time and their children, grandchildren, and great-grandchildren. Applicants must be currently enrolled in their second or third year at a college or university in any state and studying teaching physically and mentally disabled children. They must be residents of Illinois or members of the American Legion Family, Department of Illinois. Along with their application, they must submit a 1,000-word essay on "What my education will do for me." Selection is based on that essay (25%) character and leadership (25%), scholarship (25%), and financial need (25%).

Financial data: The stipend is $1,000.

Duration: 1 year.

Number awarded: 1 or more each year.

Deadline: March of each year.

2735 ILLINOIS RESTAURANT ASSOCIATION GENERAL SCHOLARSHIPS

Illinois Restaurant Association
Attn: Educational Foundation
30 West Monroe Street, Suite 250
Chicago, IL 60603
Phone: (312) 787-4000, ext. 117; (800) 572-1086, ext. 117 (within IL); Fax: (312) 787-4792
Email: prostart@illinoisrestaurants.org
Web: www.illinoisrestaurants.org/displaycommon.cfm?an=4

Summary: To provide financial assistance to Illinois residents interested in attending college in any state to prepare for a career in the food service industry.

Eligibility: Open to permanent residents of Illinois who are high school seniors, GED graduates, or college students enrolled or planning to enroll full-time in an accredited program in the food service and hospitality industry in any state. Applicants must submit 3 essays: 1) the experience or individual that influenced them to prepare for a career in the food service or hospitality industry; 2) their career goal in the restaurant or food service industry; and 3) how receiving this scholarship will affect their ability to further their education and career in the food service and hospitality industry. Selection is based on the essays, presentation of the application (spelling, grammar, etc.), industry-related work experience (both paid and volunteer), honors and achievements, transcripts, and letters of recommendation.

Financial data: Stipends are $2,000 or $1,500.

Duration: 1 year; may be renewed upon reapplication.

Number awarded: Varies each year.

Deadline: May of each year.

2736 ILLINOIS SPECIAL EDUCATION TEACHER TUITION WAIVER PROGRAM

Illinois Student Assistance Commission
Attn: Scholarship and Grant Services
1755 Lake Cook Road
Deerfield, IL 60015-5209
Phone: (847) 948-8550; (800) 899-ISAC; Fax: (847) 831-8549; TDD: (800) 526-0844
Email: collegezone@isac.org
Web: www.collegezone.com/studentzone/407_677.htm

Summary: To provide financial assistance to students in Illinois who are interested in training or retraining for a career in special education.

Eligibility: Open to Illinois residents who are enrolled or planning to enroll at an Illinois public institution of higher education to prepare for a career as a public, private, or parochial elementary or secondary school teacher in the state. Applicants must be undergraduate or graduate students seeking certification in an area of special education. They must rank in the upper half of their Illinois high school graduating class. Current teachers who have a valid teaching certificate that is not in the discipline of special education are also eligible. Selection of high school seniors is based on ACT or SAT scores; selection of current college students and teachers returning to school to study special education is determined in a lottery. U.S. citizenship or eligible noncitizenship status is required.

Financial data: This program waives tuition and fees at 12 participating Illinois public 4-year universities. Recipients must agree to teach full-time in a special education discipline at an Illinois public, private, or parochial school for 2 of the 5 years immediately following graduation or termination of enrollment. That teaching requirement may be postponed if the recipient serves in the U.S. armed forces, enrolls full-time in a graduate or postgraduate program, becomes temporarily disabled, is unable to find employment as a teacher, or withdraws from a course of study leading to a teacher certification in special education but remains enrolled full-time in another academic discipline. Participants who fail to fulfill that teaching requirement must repay the entire amount of the tuition waiver prorated to the fraction of the teaching requirement not completed, plus interest at a rate of 5% per year.

Duration: Up to 4 continuous calendar years.

Number awarded: 250 each year: 105 graduating high school seniors, 105 current college students, and 40 teachers returning to school to study special education.

Deadline: February of each year.

2737 INDEPENDENT INSURANCE AGENTS OF ILLINOIS COLLEGE SCHOLARSHIP

Independent Insurance Agents of Illinois
Attn: Scholarship Committee
4360 Wabash Avenue
Springfield, IL 62711-7009
Phone: (217) 793-6660; (800) 628-6436, ext. 3004; Fax: (217) 793-6744
Email: schurchill@iiaofillinois.org
Web: www.iiaofillinois.org/YoungAgents/CollegeScholarship.html

Summary: To provide financial assistance to upper-division students from Illinois who are majoring in business and have an interest in insurance.

Eligibility: Open to residents of Illinois who are full-time juniors or seniors at a college or university in the state. Applicants must be enrolled in a business degree program with an interest in insurance. They must have a letter of recommendation from a current or retired member of the Independent Insurance Agents of Illinois. Along with their application, they must submit an essay (1 or 2 pages in length) on their career objectives, academic accomplishments, work experience, pertinent extracurricular activities, and reasons for applying for this scholarship. Financial need is not considered in the selection process.

Financial data: Stipends range up to $5,000. Funds are paid directly to the recipient's school.

Duration: 1 year.

Number awarded: 1 each year.

Deadline: June of each year.

2738 INDIANA AMERICAN LEGION AMERICANISM AND GOVERNMENT TEST

American Legion
Department of Indiana
777 North Meridian Street
Indianapolis, IN 46204
Phone: (317) 630-1200; Fax: (317) 630-1277
Web: www.indlegion.org/A&G%20Program.htm

Summary: To recognize and reward high school students in Indiana who score highest on a test on Americanism.
Eligibility: Open to all Indiana students in grades 10–12. They are eligible to take a written test on Americanism and government. Scholarships are awarded to the students with the highest scores. Girls and boys compete separately.
Financial data: The award is a $1,000 scholarship.
Duration: The awards are presented annually.
Number awarded: 6 each year: 3 are set aside for girls in grades 10, 11, and 12, respectively, and 3 to a boy in each of the participating grades.
Deadline: Schools that wish to have their students participate must order the tests by October of each year.

2739 INDIANA MINORITY TEACHER/SPECIAL EDUCATION SERVICES SCHOLARSHIP

Summary: To provide financial assistance to Black and Hispanic undergraduate students in Indiana interested in preparing for a teaching career and to other residents of the state preparing for a career in special education, occupational therapy, or physical therapy.
See Listing #2016.

2740 INDIANA MORTGAGE BROKERS EDUCATION SCHOLARSHIP

Central Indiana Community Foundation
Attn: Scholarship Program
615 North Alabama Street, Suite 119
Indianapolis, IN 46204-1498
Phone: (317) 631-6542, ext. 279; Fax: (317) 684-0943
Email: scholarships@cicf.org
Web: www.cicf.org/page26452.cfm
Summary: To provide financial assistance to residents of Indiana who are interested in attending college in the state to prepare for a career in real estate or real estate finance.
Eligibility: Open to residents of Indiana who are graduating high school seniors or students currently attending a college or university in the state. Applicants must be interested in working on a degree in the area of real estate and/or real estate finance. They must have a GPA of 3.0 or higher. Selection is based on community involvement and financial need.
Financial data: A stipend is awarded (amount not specified).
Duration: 1 year.
Number awarded: 1 or more each year.
Deadline: March of each year.

2741 INFORMATION ASSURANCE SCHOLARSHIP PROGRAM

Summary: To provide financial assistance to undergraduate and graduate students interested in working on a degree in a field related to information assurance (IA) and then serving as a civilian or military employee of the Department of Defense.
See Listing #2020.

2742 INTEL INTERNATIONAL SCIENCE AND ENGINEERING FAIR

Summary: To recognize and reward outstanding high school students who enter a science and engineering competition.
See Listing #2024.

2743 INTEL SCIENCE TALENT SEARCH SCHOLARSHIPS

Summary: To recognize and reward outstanding high school seniors who are interested in attending college to prepare for a career in mathematics, engineering, or any of the sciences.
See Listing #2025.

2744 INTERNATIONAL ASSOCIATION OF BLACK ACTUARIES SCHOLARSHIPS

International Association of Black Actuaries
Attn: IABA Foundation Scholarship Committee
c/o Mosher and Associates
19 South LaSalle Street, Suite 1400
Chicago, IL 60603
Phone: (215) 392-4598; Fax: (215) 395-6400
Email: iabafdvp@blackactuaries.org
Web: blackactuaries.org/actuary/scholarships.php
Summary: To provide financial assistance to Black upper-division and graduate students preparing for an actuarial career.
Eligibility: Open to full-time juniors, seniors, and graduate students who are of African descent, originating from the United States, Canada, Caribbean, or African nations. Applicants must have been admitted to a college or university offering either a program in actuarial science or courses that will prepare them for an actuarial career. They must be citizens or permanent residents of the United States or Canada or eligible to study in those countries under a U.S. student visa or Canadian student authorization. Other requirements include a GPA of 3.0 or higher, a mathematics SAT score of at least 600 or a mathematics ACT score of at least 28, completion of probability and calculus courses, attempting or passing an actuarial examination, completion of Validation by Educational Experience (VEE) requirements, and familiarity with actuarial profession demands. Selection is based on merit and financial need.
Financial data: A stipend is awarded (amount not specified).
Duration: 1 year; may be renewed.
Number awarded: 1 or more each year.
Deadline: May of each year.

2745 INVESTING IN THE FUTURE SCHOLARSHIP

Summary: To provide financial assistance to outstanding undergraduate or graduate students of Armenian descent who are preparing for a career in finance, business, medicine, or research.
See Listing #2028.

2746 IOWA NARCOTICS OFFICERS ASSOCIATION YOUTH SCHOLARSHIPS

Iowa Narcotics Officers Association
c/o J. Douglas Hurley, Secretary
Division of Narcotics Enforcement
P.O. Box 756
Centerville, IA 52544
Phone: (641) 437-4443
Email: hurley@dps.state.ia.us
Web: www.iowanarcs.com/scholarship.asp
Summary: To provide financial assistance to high school seniors in Iowa who submit outstanding essays on the legalization of drugs and plan to attend college in any state.
Eligibility: Open to seniors graduating from high schools in Iowa and planning to attend a college or university in any state. Applicants must submit letters of recommendation from a teacher, community leader, and member (for at least 2 years) of the Iowa Narcotics Officers Association (INOA). Selection is based primarily on an original essay, up to 300 words in length, on why or why not drugs should be legalized.
Financial data: The stipend is $1,000.
Duration: 1 year.
Number awarded: 2 each year.
Deadline: February of each year.

2747 IRENE AND LEETA WAGY MEMORIAL SCHOLARSHIP

Daughters of the American Revolution–Missouri State Society
Attn: State Scholarship Chair
821 Main Street
Boonville, MO 65233-1657
Phone: (660) 882-5320
Email: hyhope@sbcglobal.net
Web: www.mssdar.org
Summary: To provide financial assistance to female high school seniors in Missouri who plan to study education at a college or university in the state.
Eligibility: Open to female seniors graduating from high schools in Missouri in the top 10% of their class. Applicants must be planning to attend an accredited college or university in Missouri to major in education. They must be sponsored by a chapter of the Daughters of the American Revolution in Missouri and able to demonstrate financial need. U.S. citizenship is required.
Financial data: A stipend is awarded (amount not specified).
Duration: 1 year.
Number awarded: 1 or more each year.
Deadline: January of each year.

2748 ISFA COLLEGE SCHOLARSHIPS

National Association of Insurance Women
Attn: Insurance Scholarship Foundation of America
P.O. Box 866
Hendersonville, NC 28793-0866
Phone: (828) 890-3328; Fax: (828) 891-2667
Email: foundation@inssfa.org
Web: www.inssfa.org/college.html

Summary: To provide financial assistance to college and graduate students working on a degree in insurance and risk management.

Eligibility: Open to candidates for a bachelor's degree or higher with a major or minor in insurance, risk management, or actuarial science. Applicants must 1) be completing or have completed their second year of college; 2) have an overall GPA of 3.0 or higher; 3) have successfully completed at least 2 insurance, risk management, or actuarial science courses; and 4) not be receiving full reimbursement for the cost of tuition, books, or other educational expenses from their employer or any other outside source. Selection is based on academic record and honors, extracurricular and personal activities, work experience, 3 letters of recommendation, and a 500-word essay on career path and goals.

Financial data: Stipends range from $500 to $2,500 per year; funds are paid jointly to the institution and to the student.

Duration: 1 year.

Number awarded: Varies each year; recently, 4 of these scholarships were awarded.

Deadline: January or July of each year.

2749 J. EDGAR HOOVER FOUNDATION SCHOLARSHIPS

Summary: To provide financial assistance to undergraduate and graduate students working on a degree in law, enforcement studies, or forensic sciences.

See Listing #2033.

2750 J. SPARGO AND ASSOCIATES TEACHER'S SCHOLARSHIP

Summary: To provide financial assistance to undergraduate and graduate students who are preparing for a career as a teacher of science and mathematics.

See Listing #2035.

2751 JACK J. ISGUR SCHOLARSHIPS

Jack J. Isgur Foundation
c/o Stinson Morrison Hecker LLP
Attn: Charles F. Jensen
1201 Walnut Street, Suite 2800
Kansas City, MO 64106-2150
Phone: (816) 691-2760; Fax: (816) 691-3495
Email: cjensen@stinson.com

Summary: To provide financial assistance to Missouri residents majoring in education and planning to teach humanities in elementary and middle schools in the state after graduation.

Eligibility: Open to residents of Missouri who are enrolled at a 4-year college or university. Applicants must be majoring in education with the goal of teaching the humanities (e.g., literature, dance, fine arts, music, art, and poetry) at the elementary or middle school level following graduation. Preference is given to students entering their junior year of college and planning to teach in rural school districts in Missouri, rather than metropolitan districts. The application process includes brief essays on the following topics: 1) work and life experiences indicating an interest in teaching subjects in the humanities to grade school and middle school students in Missouri upon graduation; 2) other activities (organizations to which they belong, hobbies, volunteer work) and their interest in them; 3) the 3 books that have most influenced them and why; and 4) their employment experiences.

Financial data: A stipend is awarded (amount not specified).

Duration: 1 year; recipients may reapply.

Number awarded: 20 each year.

Deadline: April of each year.

2752 JAMES BEARD FOUNDATION SPECIFIC SCHOOL SCHOLARSHIPS

Summary: To provide financial assistance to high school seniors and graduates interested in attending specified culinary institutes or restaurant management programs in the United States or abroad.

See Listing #1349.

2753 JAMES CARLSON MEMORIAL SCHOLARSHIP

Oregon Student Assistance Commission
Attn: Grants and Scholarships Division
1500 Valley River Drive, Suite 100
Eugene, OR 97401-2146
Phone: (541) 687-7395; (800) 452-8807, ext. 7395; Fax: (541) 687-7414; TDD: (800) 735-2900
Email: awardinfo@osac.state.or.us
Web: www.osac.state.or.us/osac_programs.html

Summary: To provide financial assistance to Oregon residents majoring in education on the undergraduate or graduate school level at a school in any state.

Eligibility: Open to residents of Oregon who are U.S. citizens or permanent residents and enrolled at a college or university in any state. Applicants must be either 1) college seniors or fifth-year students majoring in elementary or secondary education; or 2) graduate students working on an elementary or secondary certificate. Full-time enrollment and financial need are required. Priority is given to 1) students who come from diverse environments and submit an essay of 250 to 350 words on their experience living or working in diverse environments; 2) dependents of members of the Oregon Education Association; and 3) applicants committed to teaching autistic children.

Financial data: Stipend amounts vary; recently, they were at least $1,300.

Duration: 1 year.

Number awarded: Varies each year; recently, 3 of these scholarships were awarded.

Deadline: February of each year.

2754 JAMES M. AND VIRGINIA M. SMYTH SCHOLARSHIP FUND

Summary: To provide financial assistance to high school seniors, especially those from designated states, who are interested in majoring in selected fields at colleges in any state.

See Listing #1352.

2755 JANE M. KLAUSMAN WOMEN IN BUSINESS SCHOLARSHIPS

Zonta International
Attn: Foundation
1211 West 22nd Street, Suite 900
Oak Brook, IL 60523-3384
Phone: (630) 928-1400; Fax: (630) 928-1559
Email: programs@zonta.org
Web: www.zonta.org/WhatWeDo/InternationalPrograms.aspx

Summary: To provide financial assistance to women working on an undergraduate or master's degree in business at a school in any country.

Eligibility: Open to women who are working on a business-related degree at a college or university anywhere in the world at the level of the second year of an undergraduate program through the final year of a master's degree program. Applicants first compete at the club level, and then advance to district and international levels. Along with their application, they must submit a 500-word essay that describes their academic and professional goals, the relevance of their program to the business field, and how this scholarship will assist them in reaching their goals. Selection is based on that essay, academic record, demonstrated intent to complete a program in business, achievement in business-related subjects, and 2 letters of recommendation.

Financial data: District winners receive a $1,000 scholarship; the international winners receive a $5,000 scholarship.

Duration: 1 year.

Number awarded: The number of district winners varies each year; recently, 12 international winners (including 6 from the United States) were selected. Since this program was established, it has awarded nearly 200 of these scholarships to women from 34 countries.

Deadline: Clubs set their own deadlines but must submit their winners to the district governor by May of each year.

2756 JEDIDIAH ZABROSKY SCHOLARSHIP

Vermont Student Assistance Corporation
Attn: Scholarship Programs
10 East Allen Street
P.O. Box 2000
Winooski, VT 05404-2601

Phone: (802) 654-3798; (888) 253-4819; Fax: (802) 654-3765; TDD: (800) 281-3341 (within VT)
Email: info@vsac.org
Web: services.vsac.org/wps/wcm/connect/vsac/VSAC
Summary: To provide financial assistance to Vermont residents who are studying business or education at a college in the state.
Eligibility: Open to residents of Vermont who currently attend a public college in the state. Applicants must be working on a 2- or 4-year degree in business or education and be employed at least 10 hours per week. They must have a GPA of 2.5 or higher. Along with their application, they must submit 1) a 250-word essay on their beliefs related to the value of community service; and 2) a 250-word essay on what they believe distinguishes their application from others that may be submitted. Selection is based on those essays, academic achievement, school and community involvement, letters of recommendation, and financial need.
Financial data: The stipend is $2,000.
Duration: 1 year.
Number awarded: 1 each year.
Deadline: March of each year.

2757 JEFFREY WHITEHEAD MEMORIAL AWARD

David and Dovetta Wilson Scholarship Fund, Inc.
115-67 237th Street
Elmont, NY 11003-3926
Phone: (516) 285-4573
Email: DDWSF4@aol.com
Web: www.wilsonfund.org/Jeffrey_Whitehead.html
Summary: To provide financial assistance to high school seniors who are interested in going to college to prepare for a career in social service.
Eligibility: Open to graduating high school seniors who plan to attend an accredited college or university to prepare for a career in social service. Applicants must be U.S. citizens or permanent residents and have a GPA of 3.0 or higher. Along with their application, they must submit 3 letters of recommendation, high school transcripts, and an essay (up to 250 words) on "How My College Education Will Help Me Make a Positive Impact on My Community." Selection is based on community involvement, desire to prepare for a career in the field of social service, and financial need.
Financial data: The stipend is $1,000.
Duration: 1 year.
Number awarded: 1 each year.
Deadline: March of each year.

2758 JEWELL L. TAYLOR NATIONAL UNDERGRADUATE SCHOLARSHIPS

American Association of Family and Consumer Sciences
Attn: Manager of Awards and Grants
400 North Columbus Street, Suite 202
Alexandria, VA 22314
Phone: (703) 706-4600; (800) 424-8080, ext. 119; Fax: (703) 706-4663
Email: staff@aafcs.org
Web: www.aafcs.org/Recognition/Scholarships.asp
Summary: To provide financial assistance to undergraduate students in the field of family and consumer affairs.
Eligibility: Open to U.S. citizens and permanent residents working on an undergraduate degree in an area of family and consumer sciences. Selection is based on ability to pursue undergraduate study (10 points); enrollment in undergraduate study in family and consumer sciences (10 points); experience in relation to preparation for study in proposed field (10 points); special recognition and awards (5 points); voluntary participation in professional and community organizations and activities (10 points); evidence (or degree) of professional commitment and leadership (10 points); significance of proposed area of study to families and individuals (15 points); professional goals (10 points); written communication (5 points); and recommendations (15 points). Special consideration is given to applicants who have been members of the American Association of Family and Consumer Sciences (AAFCS) for up to 2 years (3 points) or for 2 or more years (5 points).
Financial data: The award provides a stipend of $5,000 and financial support of up to $1,000 for 1 year of AAFCS membership and participation in its annual conference and exposition.
Duration: 1 year; recipients may reapply.
Number awarded: 1 each year.
Deadline: January of each year.

2759 JOE PERDUE SCHOLARSHIPS

Club Foundation
Attn: Scholarship Coordinator
1733 King Street
Alexandria, VA 22314-2720
Phone: (703) 739-9500; Fax: (703) 739-0124
Email: joeperduescholarship@clubfoundation.org
Web: www.clubfoundation.org/stuscholar.html
Summary: To provide financial assistance for college to students planning a career in private club management.
Eligibility: Open to students who are currently attending an accredited 4-year college or university and are actively preparing for a managerial career in the private club industry. Applicants must have completed their freshman year with a GPA of 2.5 or higher. Along with their application, they must submit an essay of 500 to 1,000 words on their career objectives and goals, the characteristics they possess that will allow them to succeed as a club manager, their perception of the Club Management Association of America (CMAA) and the private club industry, their specific interests within the private club management field, and why they feel the Club Foundation should select them as a scholarship recipient. Selection is based on academic record (20 points), extracurricular activities (15 points), the essay (20 points), and employment record (15 points). Additional points are awarded for CMAA student chapter members.
Financial data: The stipend is $2,500 per year. Funds are paid directly to the recipient's college or university.
Duration: 1 year.
Number awarded: Varies each year; recently, 7 of these scholarships were awarded.
Deadline: April of each year.

2760 JOHN CULVER WOODDY SCHOLARSHIPS

Actuarial Foundation
Attn: Actuarial Education and Research Fund Committee
475 North Martingale Road, Suite 600
Schaumburg, IL 60173-2226
Phone: (847) 706-3535; Fax: (847) 706-3599
Email: scholarships@actfnd.org
Web: www.aerf.org/programs/actuarial/scholarships.shtml
Summary: To provide financial assistance to undergraduate students who are preparing for a career in actuarial science.
Eligibility: Open to undergraduate students who will have senior standing in the semester after receiving the scholarship. They must be nominated; nominees must rank in the top quartile of their class and have successfully completed 1 actuarial examination. Each university may nominate only 1 student. Preference is given to candidates who have demonstrated leadership potential by participating in extracurricular activities. Financial need is not considered in the selection process.
Financial data: The stipend is $2,000 per academic year.
Duration: 1 year.
Number awarded: Varies each year; recently, 12 of these scholarships were awarded.
Deadline: June of each year.

2761 JOHN D. LORENZEN AND DEBBIE J. TRANELLO MEMORIAL SCHOLARSHIP FUND

Summary: To provide financial assistance to residents of New York who are interested in attending college or vocational school in any state to prepare for a career in the automotive aftermarket.
See Listing #2050.

2762 JOHN DENNIS SCHOLARSHIP

Missouri Sheriff's Association
6605 Business Highway 50 West
Jefferson City, MO 65109
Phone: (573) 635-5925; Fax: (573) 635-2128
Web: www.mosheriffs.com/scholarship_info.php?id=12
Summary: To provide financial assistance to high school seniors in Missouri who are interested in majoring in criminal justice at a college in the state.
Eligibility: Open to seniors graduating from high schools in Missouri who plan to major in criminal justice at a college or university in the state. Applicants must have a GPA of 2.0 or higher and be able to demonstrate financial need and participation in extracurricular activities.
Financial data: The stipend is $1,000 per year.

Duration: 1 year.
Number awarded: 16 each year.
Deadline: January of each year.

2763 JOHN M. BUNCH STUDENT SCHOLARSHIP

North Carolina Business Education Association
c/o Lisa Gueldenzoph Snyder, Past President
500 Curbside Court
Whitsett, NC 27377
Phone: (336) 337-4983
Email: gueldenzoph@att.net
Web: www.ncbea.org/bunch.htm

Summary: To provide financial assistance to high school seniors in North Carolina who plan to study business or business education in college.
Eligibility: Open to seniors graduating from high schools in North Carolina who have taken 1 or more business education courses. Applicants must be planning to attend a technical school, community college, college, or university in North Carolina to prepare for a career in business and/or business education. Along with their application, they must submit a 500-word essay on their future goals or aspirations and how college can help them achieve those goals. Financial need is not considered in the selection process.
Financial data: Stipends are $1,000 or $500. Funds are disbursed through the financial aid office at the recipient's college.
Duration: 1 year.
Number awarded: 1 or more each year.
Deadline: May of each year.

2764 JOHN SWAIN MEMORIAL SCHOLARSHIP

Direct Marketing Association of Washington
Attn: Educational Foundation
11709 Bowman Green Drive
Reston, VA 20190
Phone: (703) 689-DMAW; Fax: (703) 481-DMAW
Email: info@dmaw.org
Web: www.dmaw.org/educational-foundation/awards.aspx

Summary: To provide financial assistance to residents of any state who are enrolled as upper-division students at colleges and universities in the mid-Atlantic region and have an interest in direct marketing.
Eligibility: Open to juniors and seniors from any state enrolled at a college or university in Maryland, Virginia, or Washington, D.C. Applicants must have a GPA of 3.0 or higher and an interest in direct marketing.
Financial data: The stipend is $2,000.
Duration: 1 year.
Number awarded: 1 each year.
Deadline: April of each year.

2765 JOSEPH AND MARION GREENBAUM JUDAIC STUDIES SCHOLARSHIP

Summary: To provide financial assistance to Jewish residents of Delaware and adjacent communities who are interested in taking courses in Jewish studies at a college or university in any state and to Jewish residents of other states interested in studying in Delaware.
See Listing #1365.

2766 JOSEPH BRACONE MEMORIAL SCHOLARSHIP

Order Sons of Italy in America
Attn: Sons of Italy Foundation
219 E Street, N.E.
Washington, DC 20002
Phone: (202) 547-2900; (800) 552-OSIA; Fax: (202) 546-8168
Email: scholarships@osia.org
Web: www.osia.org/students/study-abroad.php

Summary: To provide financial assistance for college or graduate school to students of Italian descent, particularly those working on a degree in business, finance, or pre-law.
Eligibility: Open to U.S. citizens of Italian descent who are entering or enrolled in an undergraduate or graduate program at a 4-year college or university. Both high school seniors and students already enrolled in college are eligible for the undergraduate awards. Applicants may be working on or planning to work on a degree in any liberal arts field, but preference is given to those studying business, finance, or pre-law. Along with their application, they must submit essays, from 500 to 750 words in length, on a personal experience that demonstrated or generated pride in their Italian heritage. These merit-based awards are presented to students who have demonstrated exceptional leadership qualities and distinguished scholastic abilities.
Financial data: Stipends range from $5,000 to $25,000.
Duration: 1 year; nonrenewable.
Number awarded: 1 each year.
Deadline: February of each year.

2767 JOSEPH G. PEARSON BOOK STIPEND

Connecticut PTA
60 Connolly Parkway, Building 12, Suite 103
Hamden, CT 06514
Phone: (203) 281-6617; Fax: (203) 281-6749
Email: connecticutpta@snet.net
Web: www.ctpta.org/NSPTA-History/NSPTA-Scholarship.html

Summary: To provide financial assistance to seniors at high schools in Connecticut with a PTA unit who are planning to attend college in any state to prepare for a career working with children.
Eligibility: Open to seniors graduating from Connecticut high schools that have a PTA unit in good standing. Applicants must be planning to attend a 4-year college or university in any state to prepare for a career in service to children. Along with their application, they must submit a 1-page essay on how they expect to be serving children 10 years after college graduation. Selection is based on the essay (5 points), class rank (3 points), and school and community involvement (2 points). Each school may submit only 1 application.
Financial data: The stipend is $1,000. Funds are intended for the purchase of books.
Duration: 1 year.
Number awarded: 1 each year.
Deadline: February of each year.

2768 JOSEPH T. WEINGOLD SCHOLARSHIP

NYSARC, Inc.
Attn: Scholarship and Awards Committee
393 Delaware Avenue
Delmar, NY 12054
Phone: (518) 439-8311; Fax: (518) 439-1893
Email: info@nysarc.org
Web: www.nysarc.org/family/nysarc-family-scholarships.asp

Summary: To provide financial assistance to college students in New York majoring in special education.
Eligibility: Open to sophomores enrolled at colleges and universities in New York and working on certification in special education. Applicants must provide a list of work experience with people who have intellectual and other developmental disabilities and a 1-page autobiographical sketch indicating their interest in the field and their plans after graduation. Financial need is not considered in the selection process.
Financial data: The stipend is $1,500 per year.
Duration: 2 years.
Number awarded: 1 each year.
Deadline: January of each year.

2769 JOSEPHINE AND BENJAMIN WEBBER TRUST SCHOLARSHIPS

Arizona Association of Family and Consumer Sciences
Attn: Webber Educational Grant Committee
Kathryn L. Hatch
4843 North Via Sonrisa
Tucson, AZ 85718-5724
Phone: (502) 577-6109
Email: klhatch@u.arizona.edu
Web: ag.arizona.edu/webbertrusts

Summary: To provide financial assistance to Hispanic women from mining towns in Arizona who are interested in working on an undergraduate or graduate degree in a field related to family and consumer sciences at a school in the state.
Eligibility: Open to Hispanic women who reside in the following Arizona mining towns: Ajo, Arizona City, Bisbee, Clifton, Douglas, Duncan, Globe, Green Valley, Hayden, Kearny, Kingman, Mammoth, Morenci, Prescott, Safford, Sahuarita, San Manuel, Seligman, Superior, or Winkelman. If too few female

Hispanic residents of those towns apply, the program may be open to 1) non-Hispanic women who live in those towns; and/or 2) Hispanic women who currently live elsewhere in Arizona and whose parents or grandparents had lived or continue to live in those communities. Applicants must be enrolled or planning to enroll at a college or university in Arizona to work on an undergraduate or graduate degree. Eligible fields of study include those in the following categories: foods, nutrition, and/or dietetics; restaurant and food service management; culinary arts; family studies; interior design; family and consumer science education; dietetic education; early childhood education; or apparel and clothing. Along with their application, they must submit a 4-page essay that includes information on 1) why they have chosen to work on a degree in family and consumer sciences; 2) what they think will be the major obstacles to the successful completion of their first year as a Webber scholar; and 3) what do they think their personal and professional life will be like following completion of their postsecondary education. Financial need is also considered in the selection process.

Financial data: Funding at public colleges and universities provides for payment of tuition and fees, books, educational supplies, housing, food, and transportation to and from campus. At private institutions, stipend amounts are equivalent to those at public schools.

Duration: 1 year; may be renewed for a total of 8 semesters and 2 summers of undergraduate study or 4 semesters and 2 summers of graduate study.

Number awarded: Varies each year; recently, 5 of these scholarships were awarded.

Deadline: March of each year.

2770 JOURNALISM EDUCATION ASSOCIATION FUTURE TEACHER SCHOLARSHIP

Summary: To provide financial assistance to upper-division and master's degree students working on a degree in education who intend to teach journalism.

See Listing #1368.

2771 JOYCE WASHINGTON SCHOLARSHIP

Watts Charity Association, Inc.
6245 Bristol Parkway, Suite 224
Culver City, CA 90230
Phone: (323) 671-0394; Fax: (323) 778-2613
Email: wattscharity@aol.com
Web: 4watts.tripod.com/id5.html

Summary: To provide financial assistance to upper-division African Americans majoring in child development, teaching, or social services.

Eligibility: Open to U.S. citizens of African American descent who are enrolled full-time as a college or university junior. Applicants must be majoring in child development, teaching, or the study of social services. They must have a GPA of 3.0 or higher, be between 17 and 24 years of age, and be able to demonstrate that they intend to continue their education for at least 2 years. Along with their application, they must submit 1) a 1-paragraph statement on why they should be awarded a Watts Foundation scholarship, and 2) a 1- to 2-page essay on a specific type of cancer, based either on how it has impacted their life or on researched information.

Financial data: A stipend is awarded (amount not specified).

Duration: 1 year.

Number awarded: 1 each year.

Deadline: May of each year.

2772 JUDITH CARY MEMORIAL SCHOLARSHIP

P. Buckley Moss Society
20 Stoneridge Drive, Suite 102
Waynesboro, VA 22980
Phone: (540) 943-5678; Fax: (540) 949-8408
Email: society@mosssociety.org
Web: www.mosssociety.org/page.php?id=29

Summary: To provide financial assistance to students working on a bachelor's or master's degree in special education.

Eligibility: Open to students who have completed at least 2 years of undergraduate study and are working on a bachelor's or master's degree in special education. They must be nominated; nominations must be submitted by a member of the P. Buckley Moss Society. The nomination packet must include proof of acceptance into a specific program to teach special needs students, 2 letters of recommendation, a short essay on school and community work activities and achievements, and an essay of 250 to 500 words on their career goals, teaching philosophies, reasons for choosing this career, and ways in which they plan to make a difference in the lives of special needs students. Financial need is not considered in the selection process.

Financial data: The stipend is $1,000. Funds are paid to the recipient's college or university.

Duration: 1 year.

Number awarded: 1 each year.

Deadline: March of each year.

2773 JUDITH MCMANUS PRICE SCHOLARSHIPS

American Planning Association
Attn: Leadership Affairs Associate
205 North Michigan Avenue, Suite 1200
Chicago, IL 60601
Phone: (312) 431-9100; Fax: (312) 786-6700
Email: fellowship@planning.org
Web: www.planning.org/scholarships/apa

Summary: To provide financial assistance to women and underrepresented minority students enrolled in undergraduate or graduate degree programs at recognized planning schools.

Eligibility: Open to undergraduate and graduate students in urban and regional planning who are women or members of the following minority groups: African American, Hispanic American, or Native American. Applicants must be citizens of the United States and able to document financial need. They must intend to work as practicing planners in the public sector. Along with their application, they must submit a 2-page personal and background statement describing how their education will be applied to career goals and why they chose planning as a career path. Selection is based (in order of importance) on: 1) commitment to planning as reflected in their personal statement and on their resume; 2) academic achievement and/or improvement during the past 2 years; 3) letters of recommendation; 4) financial need; and 5) professional presentation.

Financial data: Stipends range from $2,000 to $4,000 per year. The money may be applied to tuition and living expenses only. Payment is made to the recipient's university and divided by terms in the school year.

Duration: 1 year; recipients may reapply.

Number awarded: Varies each year; recently, 3 of these scholarships were awarded.

Deadline: April of each year.

2774 JULIAN AND JAN HESTER MEMORIAL SCHOLARSHIPS

Community Bankers Association of Georgia
1900 The Exchange, Suite 600
Atlanta, GA 30339-2022
Phone: (770) 541-4490; Fax: (770) 541-4496
Email: info@cbaofga.com
Web: www.cbaofga.com/?page=Scholarship

Summary: To provide financial assistance to high school seniors in Georgia who are interested in attending college in the state to prepare for a career in banking.

Eligibility: Open to high school seniors in Georgia who are planning to attend a college, university, or technical institute in the state. Applicants must be interested in preparing for a career in community banking. Along with their application, they must submit a 500-word essay on community banking. Selection is based solely on merit; family financial need is not considered.

Financial data: The stipend is $1,000. Funds are paid directly to the student's institution.

Duration: 1 year; nonrenewable.

Number awarded: At least 4 each year.

Deadline: Students must submit an application to their local community bank by March of each year.

2775 KANSAS RESTAURANT AND HOSPITALITY ASSOCIATION EDUCATION FOUNDATION SCHOLARSHIPS

Kansas Restaurant and Hospitality Association
Attn: KHRA Education Foundation
3500 North Rock Road, Building 1300
Wichita, KS 67226
Phone: (316) 267-8383; (800) 369-6787 (within KS); Fax: (316) 267-8400
Email: ncarlson@krha.org
Web: www.krha.org/displaycommon.cfm?an=1&subarticlenbr=257

Summary: To provide financial assistance to Kansas residents interested in preparing for a career in the restaurant and food service industry.

Eligibility: Open to 1) high school seniors in Kansas who have been accepted at an accredited college as a full-time student; and 2) undergraduate full-time students at colleges in Kansas who have completed at least 1 academic term. Applicants must be interested in preparing for a career in the restaurant and food service industry. They must be able to demonstrate a GPA of 2.75 or higher, previous or current employment in the restaurant or hospitality industry, and financial need. Along with their application, they must submit 2 essays of 150 to 200 words each: 1) how their education will help them achieve their career objectives and future goals; and 2) the career path they see themselves pursuing in the food service and/or hospitality industry in the next 5 years. U.S. citizenship or permanent resident status is required.
Financial data: The stipend is $2,000. Funds are sent directly to the school to be used for tuition, room and board, or any other school-related expenses.
Duration: 1 year.
Number awarded: Varies each year; recently, 5 of these scholarships were awarded.
Deadline: May of each year.

2776 KANSAS TEACHER SERVICE SCHOLARSHIPS

Kansas Board of Regents
Attn: Student Financial Assistance
1000 S.W. Jackson Street, Suite 520
Topeka, KS 66612-1368
Phone: (785) 296-3517; Fax: (785) 296-0983
Email: dlindeman@ksbor.org
Web: www.kansasregents.org/financial_aid/awards.html
Summary: To provide financial assistance to high school seniors, current undergraduates, licensed teachers, and selected graduate students who are interested in teaching specified disciplines or in designated areas of Kansas.
Eligibility: Open to Kansas residents who are attending a postsecondary institution in the state. Applicants must be 1) accepted for admission to, or currently enrolled in, a course of instruction leading to licensure as a teacher in a hard-to-fill discipline (recently defined as special education, mathematics, science, foreign language, and English as a Second Language) or an underserved geographic area of Kansas (recently defined as Topeka, Kansas City, Wichita, and the western third of the state); 2) currently licensed as a teacher and enrolled in a course of instruction leading to endorsement in a hard-to-fill discipline or teaching in an underserved geographic area of Kansas; or 3) currently licensed as a teacher and accepted for admission or enrolled in a course of instruction leading to a master's degree in a field of education as a teacher in a hard-to-fill discipline or in an underserved geographic area of the state. They must submit evidence of completion of the Kansas Scholars Curriculum (4 years of English, 4 years of mathematics, 3 years of science, 3 years of social studies, 2 years of foreign language, and 1 year of computer technology), ACT or SAT scores, high school GPA, high school class rank, and (if relevant) college transcripts and letters of recommendation from a college or university official.
Financial data: The stipend is $5,100 per year for full-time students or prorated amounts for part-time students. This is a scholarship/loan program. Recipients must teach a hard-to-fill discipline or in an underserved geographic area of Kansas for the period of time they received support, or they must repay the amount received with interest (currently, 12.9%).
Duration: 1 year; may be renewed for up to 3 additional years or up to 4 additional years for designated 5-year courses of study requiring graduate work.
Number awarded: Approximately 100 each year.
Deadline: April of each year.

2777 KATINA JOHN MALTA SCHOLARSHIPS

Summary: To provide financial assistance to high school seniors and current undergraduates who are of the Eastern Orthodox faith and plan to study the sciences, business, or the arts.
See Listing #1377.

2778 KEMPER SCHOLARS GRANT PROGRAM

James S. Kemper Foundation
20 North Wacker Drive, Suite 1823
Chicago, IL 60606
Phone: (312) 332-3114
Email: dmattison@jskemper.org
Web: www.jskemper.org/kemper_scholar_pgm.htm
Summary: To provide financial assistance and work experience to freshmen at selected colleges and universities who are interested in preparing for a career in business and/or administration.
Eligibility: Open to students enrolled as full-time freshmen at 1 of 15 participating colleges and universities. Applicants must be interested in preparing for a career in administration and/or business and must have a record of academic achievement, extracurricular activity, community service, and leadership ability. They must be willing to participate in community service by engaging in campus activities, exploring their vocational calling outside the classroom, participating in a full-time work program with a nonprofit organization in Chicago for 1 summer, and conducting an independent project during the next summer.
Financial data: The stipend for the school year ranges from $3,000 to $8,000 per year, depending on the need of the recipient. For the summer following their sophomore year, scholars receive a stipend of $6,000 for their work with a major nonprofit organization in Chicago. For the summer following their junior year, they receive a grant for an independent project that ranges from $2,000 to $6,000, depending on the expenses associated with the project.
Duration: 3 years, as long as the scholar maintains a GPA of 3.0 or higher each academic term.
Number awarded: Varies each year; recently, 19 of these grants were awarded.
Deadline: Deadlines vary at each institution.

2779 KEN MILAM SCHOLARSHIP

American Planning Association–California Chapter
Attn: California Planning Foundation
c/o Paul Wack
P.O. Box 1086
Morro Bay, CA 93443-1086
Phone: (805) 756-6331; Fax: (805) 756-1340
Email: pwack@calpoly.edu
Web: www.californiaplanningfoundation.org/scholarships.html
Summary: To provide financial assistance to undergraduate and graduate students in accredited planning programs at California universities.
Eligibility: Open to students entering their final year for an undergraduate or master's degree in an accredited planning program at a university in California. Applicants must be interested in preparing for a career in public planning in California. Selection is based on academic excellence, financial need, and commitment to serve the planning profession in California.
Financial data: The stipend is $1,000. A 1-year student membership in the American Planning Association is also provided.
Duration: 1 year.
Number awarded: 1 each year.
Deadline: March of each year.

2780 KENNETH HARRIGAN GRANT

Virgin Islands Board of Education
Dronningen Gade 60B, 61, and 62
P.O. Box 11900
St. Thomas, VI 00801
Phone: (340) 774-4546; Fax: (340) 774-3384
Email: stt@myviboe.com
Web: www.myviboe.com
Summary: To provide financial assistance to male residents of the Virgin Islands who wish to study education at a college in the territory or on the mainland.
Eligibility: Open to male residents of the Virgin Islands who are seniors or graduates of high schools in the territory. Applicants must have a GPA of 2.0 or higher and be attending or accepted for enrollment at an accredited institution of higher learning in the territory or on the mainland. They must be planning to major in elementary, secondary, or vocational education. Financial need is considered in the selection process.
Financial data: The stipend is $7,000 per year.
Duration: 1 year; may be renewed up to 3 additional years.
Number awarded: 1 each year.
Deadline: April of each year.

2781 KEVIN AND KELLY PERDUE MEMORIAL SCHOLARSHIP

Summary: To provide funding to licensed radio amateurs who are interested in studying humanities or the social sciences in college.
See Listing #1382.

2782 KEVIN JOHNSON MEMORIAL SCHOLARSHIP

California Hotel & Lodging Association
Attn: CH&LA Educational Foundation
414 29th Street
Sacramento, CA 95816-3211
Phone: (916) 444-5780; Fax: (916) 444-5848
Email: tiffany@calodging.com
Web: www.calodging.com/events/scholarship.shtml

Summary: To provide financial assistance to high school seniors in California who have participated in a lodging management program and plan to attend college in any state to continue their education in that field.

Eligibility: Open to seniors graduating from high schools in California who have participated in a lodging management program at their school. Applicants must be planning to enroll full-time at a college or university in any state to prepare for a career in the lodging industry. They must have a GPA of 2.7 or higher. Along with their application, they must submit brief essays on why they think they deserve this scholarship and their 5-year career plan. Selection is based on merit; submission of financial information is optional. If 2 or more students are otherwise ranked equally, preference may be given to an applicant who includes documentation of financial need.

Financial data: The stipend is $1,500 per year.

Duration: 1 year; may be renewed up to 3 additional years.

Number awarded: 1 or more each year.

Deadline: March of each year.

2783 KJ HENDERSHOTT MEMORIAL/CHELAN FRUIT SCHOLARSHIP

Summary: To provide financial assistance to residents of Washington who are interested in attending college in any state to prepare for a career in agribusiness.

See Listing #2082.

2784 KLUSSENDORF/MCKOWN SCHOLARSHIPS

Summary: To provide financial assistance to college students majoring in dairy science or dairy business at a college or university in the United States or Canada.

See Listing #2083.

2785 KRIS GELDAKER MEMORIAL SCHOLARSHIP

Alaska Travel Industry Association
Attn: ATIA Education Foundation
2600 Cordova Street, Suite 201
Anchorage, AK 99503
Phone: (907) 929-2842; Fax: (907) 561-5727
Email: ATIA@alaskatia.org
Web: www.alaskatia.org/scholarship/default.asp

Summary: To provide financial assistance to Alaska residents interested in attending college in any state, preferably Alaska, to prepare for a career in tourism or a maritime-related field.

Eligibility: Open to residents of Alaska who are enrolled or planning to enroll full-time at a college or university in any state. Applicants must be interested in preparing for a career in tourism or a maritime-related field. Preference is given to applicants who are 1) intending to work in Alaska; or 2) the child of a current employee in the tourism industry. Along with their application, they must submit a 500-word essay that covers their career goals and objectives and how they plan to achieve those, why they want to be involved in the travel and visitor industry, and what they consider the major challenges facing the visitor industry today. Selection is based on GPA, demonstrated tourism initiative, and financial need; special consideration is given to applicants attending an educational institution in Alaska.

Financial data: The stipend is $2,500 per year.

Duration: 1 year; may be renewed up to 3 additional years.

Number awarded: 1 each year.

Deadline: March of each year.

2786 KRISTEN SCHROEDER MEMORIAL SCHOLARSHIP

Minnesota Association of Administrators of State and Federal Education Programs
c/o Matthew Mohs, Treasurer
2140 Timmy Street
St. Paul, MN 55120
Phone: (651) 632-3787
Email: matthew.mohs@spps.org
Web: www.maasfep.org/scholarships.shtml

Summary: To provide financial assistance to high school seniors in Minnesota who have participated in a Title I program and plan to major in education or criminal justice at a college in any state.

Eligibility: Open to seniors graduating from high schools in Minnesota who have participated in a Title I program while in high school. Applicants must be planning to attend a 4-year college or university in any state and major in education or criminal justice. They must have a GPA of 2.5 or higher for their junior and senior years of high school. Along with their application, they must submit 1) a 100-word essay on how the Title I program helped them with their education; 2) a 100-word essay on their plans for the future; and 3) a 250-word essay on a challenging experience they have had in their life and how they overcame it. Selection is based on those essays, desire for education beyond high school, study habits, positive attitude, and interest in school, community, and/or work-related activities.

Financial data: The stipend is $2,000.

Duration: 1 year.

Number awarded: 1 each year.

Deadline: January of each year.

2787 LAGRANT FOUNDATION UNDERGRADUATE SCHOLARSHIPS

Summary: To provide financial assistance to minority college students who are interested in majoring in advertising, public relations, or marketing.

See Listing #1389.

2788 LAUNCHING LEADERS UNDERGRADUATE SCHOLARSHIP

JPMorgan Chase
Campus Recruiting
Attn: Launching Leaders
277 Park Avenue, Second Floor
New York, NY 10172
Phone: (212) 270-6000
Email: bronwen.x.baumgardner@jpmorgan.com
Web: www.jpmorgan.com

Summary: To provide financial assistance and work experience to underrepresented minority undergraduate students interested in a career in financial services.

Eligibility: Open to Black, Hispanic, and Native American students enrolled as sophomores or juniors and interested in financial services. Applicants must have a GPA of 3.5 or higher. Along with their application, they must submit 500-word essays on 1) why they should be considered potential candidates for CEO of the sponsoring bank in 2020; and 2) the special background and attributes they would contribute to the sponsor's diversity agenda. They must be interested in a summer associate position in the sponsor's investment banking, sales and trading, or research divisions.

Financial data: The stipend is $5,000 for recipients accepted as sophomores or $10,000 for recipients accepted as juniors. For students accepted as sophomores and whose scholarship is renewed for a second year, the stipend is $15,000. The summer internship is a paid position.

Duration: 1 year; may be renewed 1 additional year if the recipient successfully completes the 10-week summer intern program and maintains a GPA of 3.5 or higher.

Number awarded: Approximately 12 each year.

Deadline: October of each year.

2789 LAW ENFORCEMENT EDUCATION PROGRAM DREAM SCHOLARSHIP

Law Enforcement Education Program
Attn: Scholarship Committee
667 East Big Beaver Road, Suite 205
Troy, MI 48083
Phone: (800) 451-1220; Fax: (248) 524-2752
Email: info@leepusa.com
Web: www.leepusa.com/scholarships.html

Summary: To provide financial assistance to high school seniors who are interested in preparing for a career in a field related to public safety.

Eligibility: Open to graduating high school seniors who are interested in preparing for a career as a law enforcement officer, police-fire dispatcher, corrections officer, fire fighter, or emergency medical technician. Applicants must be planning to attend a college, university, community college, or vocational training institution that grants a degree, certificate, or license in public safety or a related field. Selection is based on academic achievement, school activities and service, community involvement, work experience, and a brief essay on why they feel they should receive this scholarship.

Financial data: The stipend is $1,000.

Duration: 1 year.

Number awarded: Varies each year; recently, 16 of these scholarships were awarded.

Deadline: April of each year.

2790 LEGACY ENVIRONMENTAL SCHOLARSHIPS

Summary: To provide financial assistance to upper-division and graduate students in Alabama who are interested in preparing for an environmentally-related career.

See Listing #2088.

2791 LEGAL ASSISTANTS SECTION SCHOLARSHIPS

State Bar of Michigan
Attn: Paralegal/Legal Assistant Section
306 Townsend Street
Lansing, MI 48933-2012
Phone: (517) 346-6300; (800) 968-1442; Fax: (517) 482-6248
Web: www.michbar.org/paralegal/scholarship.cfm

Summary: To provide financial assistance to Michigan residents who are enrolled or planning to enroll in a paralegal/legal assistant program in the state.

Eligibility: Open to residents of Michigan who are high school seniors planning to enroll or students currently enrolled in a paralegal/legal assistant degree/certificate program at a college or university in the state. Applicants must have a GPA of 2.0 or higher (or at least 70%). Along with their application, they must submit 2 letters of recommendation, transcripts, a 1-page autobiographical statement, and an essay of 250 to 1,000 words on their career goals and desires. Selection is based on academic achievement, career goals, and financial need.

Financial data: Stipends range from $250 to $1,000.

Duration: 1 year; nonrenewable.

Number awarded: At least 2 each year.

Deadline: May of each year.

2792 LEGG MASON SCHOLARSHIPS

Independent College Fund of Maryland
Attn: Director of Programs and Scholarships
3225 Ellerslie Avenue, Suite C160
Baltimore, MD 21218-3519
Phone: (443) 997-5703; Fax: (443) 997-2740
Email: LSubot@jhmi.edu
Web: www.i-fundinfo.org/scholarships/business-scholarships.html

Summary: To provide financial assistance to upper-division students from any state at member institutions of the Independent College Fund of Maryland who are majoring in business.

Eligibility: Open to students from any state currently entering their junior or senior year at member institutions. Applicants must be majoring in business or have a demonstrated interest in financial services. They must have a GPA of 3.0 or higher.

Financial data: The stipend is $2,500.

Duration: 1 year.

Number awarded: 1 or more each year.

Deadline: Deadline not specified.

2793 LEO H. GRETHER MEMORIAL SCHOLARSHIP

Iowa High School Music Association
Attn: Executive Director
P.O. Box 10
Boone, IA 50036-0010
Phone: (515) 432-2013; Fax: (515) 432-2961
Email: alan@ihsma.org
Web: www.ihsma.org/association.shtml

Summary: To provide financial assistance for college to high school seniors in Iowa who are interested in attending college in any state to prepare for a career in choral music education.

Eligibility: Open to seniors graduating from high schools in Iowa. Applicants must be planning to enroll at a college or university in any state and major in choral music education. Along with their application, they must submit 1) a tape containing 2 selections of a contrasting nature; 2) a listing of school music participation and accomplishments; 3) a letter listing music involvement in church and/or community cosigned by the pastor or civic leader; and 4) a 1-page essay on why they have chosen choral music education as a career. Financial need is not considered in the selection process.

Financial data: The stipend is $1,000.

Duration: 1 year.

Number awarded: 1 each year.

Deadline: April of each year.

2794 LESLIE AND GRETA SPAULDING EDUCATION FUND SCHOLARSHIPS

American Planning Association-Pennsylvania Chapter
587 James Drive
Harrisburg, PA 17112-2273
Phone: (717) 671-4510; Fax: (717) 545-9247
Email: info@planningpa.org
Web: www.planningpa.org/education_scholarships.shtml

Summary: To provide financial assistance to undergraduate and graduate students at schools in Pennsylvania who are working on a degree in planning.

Eligibility: Open to students enrolled as juniors, seniors, or graduate students in a planning curriculum that has a demonstrated record of preparing students to become planners at a college or university in Pennsylvania. Preference is given to residents of Pennsylvania, but residency in that state is not required. Applicants must have a GPA of 3.0 or higher and be able to demonstrate financial need. Along with their application, they must submit a 900-word statement on the intended use of the funds and their desire to enter or continue in the field of planning.

Financial data: A stipend is awarded (amount not specified).

Duration: 1 year.

Number awarded: 1 or more each year.

Deadline: June of each year.

2795 L.G. WELLS SCHOLARSHIPS

Summary: To provide financial assistance to high school seniors in Oregon who are interested in studying education or engineering at a community college, college, or university in the state.

See Listing #2092.

2796 LILLIAN E. GLOVER SCHOLARSHIPS

Illinois PTA
P.O. Box 907
Springfield, IL 62705-0907
Phone: (217) 528-9617; (800) 877-9617; Fax: (217) 528-9490
Email: ilpta@ameritech.net
Web: www.illinoispta.org/scholarship.html

Summary: To provide financial assistance to high school seniors in Illinois who plan to major in education or a related field at a college in any state.

Eligibility: Open to public high school seniors in Illinois who are graduating in the top 33% of their class. Applicants must be interested in attending college in any state to prepare for a career in education or in an educationally-related field (school librarian, instructional media specialist, school nurse, school psychologist, or social worker, provided the position requires certification from a state board of education). Along with their application, they must submit statements on 1) why they want to enter the field of education; and 2) how parent involvement enhances educational growth. Selection is based on that statement, academic ability, leadership qualities, school activities, and out-of-school activities. Financial need is not considered.

Financial data: Stipends are $2,500 or $1,500.

Duration: 1 year; nonrenewable.

Number awarded: 10 each year: 2 in each Illinois PTA field service area (1 at $2,500 and 1 at $1,500).

Deadline: February of each year.

2797 LILLIAN WALL SCHOLARSHIP

Zonta Club of Bangor
c/o Barbara A. Cardone
P.O. Box 1904

Bangor, ME 04402-1904
Web: www.zontaclubofbangor.org/?area=scholarship

Summary: To provide financial assistance to women attending or planning to attend college in Maine and major in special education or a related field.

Eligibility: Open to women who are attending or planning to attend an accredited 2- or 4-year college in Maine. Applicants must major in special education or a related field. Along with their application, they must submit brief essays on 1) their goals in seeking higher education and their plans for the future; and 2) any school and community activities that have been of particular importance to them and why they found them worthwhile. Financial need may be considered in the selection process.

Financial data: The stipend is $1,000.

Duration: 1 year.

Number awarded: 1 each year.

Deadline: March of each year.

2798 L.L. WATERS SCHOLARSHIP PROGRAM

Summary: To provide financial assistance to advanced undergraduate and graduate students in the field of transportation.

See Listing #2096.

2799 MAINE QUALITY CHILD CARE EDUCATION SCHOLARSHIP PROGRAM

Finance Authority of Maine
Attn: Education Finance Programs
5 Community Drive
P.O. Box 949
Augusta, ME 04332-0949
Phone: (207) 623-3263; (800) 228-3734; Fax: (207) 623-0095; TDD: (207) 626-2717
Email: education@famemaine.com
Web: www.famemaine.com/Education_Home.aspx

Summary: To provide financial assistance to Maine residents interested in working on a degree in child development or early childhood education at a school in the state.

Eligibility: Open to residents of Maine who are current or future child care professionals. Applicants must be enrolled or planning to enroll at a participating college or university in Maine to work on a degree in child development or early childhood education. They must be able to demonstrate financial need (maximum Expected Family Contribution of $6,600).

Financial data: The stipend is $500 per course or $2,000 per year.

Duration: 1 semester or 1 year.

Number awarded: Varies each year.

Deadline: Applications may be submitted at any time; scholarships are awarded on a first-come, first-served basis.

2800 MAJOR JAMES W. LOVELL SCHOLARSHIP

Club 100 Veterans
Attn: Scholarship Committee
520 Kamoku Street
Honolulu, HI 96826-5120
Phone: (808) 946-0272
Email: daisyy@hgea.net

Summary: To provide financial assistance to high school seniors and college students who major in education and exemplify the sponsor's motto of "For Continuing Service."

Eligibility: Open to high school seniors planning to attend an institution of higher learning and full-time undergraduate students at community colleges, vocational/trade schools, 4-year colleges, and universities. Applicants must have a GPA of 2.5 or higher and be able to demonstrate civic responsibility and community service. They must be majoring or planning to major in education. Along with their application, they must submit an essay on why education appeals to them as the focus of their postsecondary degree and their long-term goals. Selection is based on that essay and the applicant's promotion of the legacy of the 100th Infantry Battalion and its motto of "For Continuing Service." Financial need is not considered.

Financial data: The stipend is $1,000.

Duration: 1 year; nonrenewable.

Number awarded: 1 each year.

Deadline: April of each year.

2801 MALCOLM BALDRIGE SCHOLARSHIPS

Connecticut Community Foundation
43 Field Street
Waterbury, CT 06702-1906
Phone: (203) 753-1315; Fax: (203) 756-3054
Email: jcarey@conncf.org
Web: www.conncf.org/scholarships

Summary: To provide financial assistance to residents of Connecticut interested in attending college in the state to prepare for a career in foreign trade or manufacturing.

Eligibility: Open to residents of Connecticut who are attending or entering their freshmen year at a college or university in the state. Applicants must be interested in majoring in international business or manufacturing. U.S. citizenship is required. Along with their application, they must submit essays on 1) why they believe they are a qualified candidate for this scholarship; and 2) how they will incorporate Malcolm Baldrige's perspective on international trade into their studies and future career. Selection is based on academic achievement, financial need, and (for students studying international business) accomplishment in foreign language study.

Financial data: Stipends range from $2,000 to $4,000 per year.

Duration: 1 year; renewable.

Number awarded: 1 to 3 each year.

Deadline: March of each year.

2802 MARATHON OIL CORPORATION COLLEGE SCHOLARSHIP PROGRAM OF THE HISPANIC SCHOLARSHIP FUND

Summary: To provide financial assistance to minority upper-division and graduate students working on a degree in a field related to the oil and gas industry.

See Listing #2110.

2803 MARIEL C. NEWTON GRANT

Virgin Islands Board of Education
Dronningen Gade 60B, 61, and 62
P.O. Box 11900
St. Thomas, VI 00801
Phone: (340) 774-4546; Fax: (340) 774-3384
Email: stt@myviboe.com
Web: www.myviboe.com

Summary: To provide financial assistance to residents of the Virgin Islands who wish to study police science at a college in the territory or on the mainland.

Eligibility: Open to residents of the Virgin Islands who are seniors or graduates of high schools in the territory. Applicants must have a GPA of 2.0 or higher and be attending or accepted for enrollment at an accredited institution of higher learning in the territory or on the mainland. They must be planning to major in police science. Financial need is considered in the selection process.

Financial data: The stipend is $3,000 per year.

Duration: 1 year.

Number awarded: 1 each year.

Deadline: April of each year.

2804 MARINE CORPS SGT. JEANNETTE L. WINTERS MEMORIAL SCHOLARSHIP

Summary: To provide funding to members and veterans of the U.S. Marine Corps (USMC) who are majoring in specified fields in college.

See Listing #2113.

2805 MARRIOTT SCHOLARS PROGRAM

Hispanic College Fund
Attn: Scholarship Processing
1301 K Street, N.W., Suite 450-A West
Washington, DC 20005
Phone: (202) 296-5400; (800) 644-4223; Fax: (202) 296-3774
Email: hcf-info@hispanicfund.org
Web: scholarships.hispanicfund.org/applications

Summary: To provide financial assistance to Hispanic American undergraduate students who are interested in preparing for a career in the hospitality industry.

Eligibility: Open to U.S. citizens and permanent residents of Hispanic background (at least 1 grandparent must be 100% Hispanic) who are enrolled full-time at an accredited 4-year college or university in the 50 states or Puerto Rico. Applicants must be entering their freshman or sophomore year and working on or planning to work on a degree within the hospitality management, hotel management, culinary, or food and beverage field. They must have a GPA of 3.0 or higher and be able to demonstrate financial need.
Financial data: Stipends provide for full payment of tuition, to a maximum of $9,000 per year.
Duration: 4 years.
Number awarded: Varies each year.
Deadline: February of each year.

2806 MARSH COLLEGE SCHOLARSHIPS

National Association of Insurance Women
Attn: Insurance Scholarship Foundation of America
P.O. Box 866
Hendersonville, NC 28793-0866
Phone: (828) 890-3328; Fax: (828) 891-2667
Email: foundation@inssfa.org
Web: www.inssfa.org/college.html
Summary: To provide financial assistance to college and graduate students working on a degree in insurance and risk management.
Eligibility: Open to candidates for a bachelor's degree or higher with a major or minor in insurance, risk management, or actuarial science. Applicants must 1) be completing or have completed their second year of college; 2) have an overall GPA of 3.0 or higher; 3) have successfully completed at least 2 insurance, risk management, or actuarial science courses; and 4) not be receiving full reimbursement for the cost of tuition, books, or other educational expenses from their employer or any other outside source. Selection is based on academic record and honors, extracurricular and personal activities, work experience, 3 letters of recommendation, and a 500-word essay on career path and goals.
Financial data: Stipends range from $500 to $2,500 per year; funds are paid jointly to the institution and to the student.
Duration: 1 year.
Number awarded: Varies each year; recently, 17 of these scholarships were awarded.
Deadline: January or July of each year.

2807 MARTHA CREIGHTON SCHOLARSHIP

Virginia Association for Teachers of Family and Consumer Sciences
c/o Kelly M. Thompson, Past President
209 Crawford Drive
Churchville, VA 24421
Phone: (540) 292-5307
Email: teachinfacs@aol.com
Web: vatfacs.com/scholarships
Summary: To provide financial assistance to graduates of Virginia high schools who are studying family and consumer sciences education at a college in any state.
Eligibility: Open to graduates of Virginia high schools who are working on a bachelor's degree in family and consumer sciences education or a related field at a college or university in any state. Applicants must submit a letter explaining why they wish to major in family and consumer sciences education and describing their general career goals, a transcript, 2 letters of recommendation, and documentation of financial need.
Financial data: The stipend is $1,000.
Duration: 1 year.
Number awarded: 1 or more each year.
Deadline: April of each year.

2808 MARTIN R. SULLIVAN MEMORIAL/ PRICEWATERHOUSECOOPERS SCHOLARSHIP

Independent College Fund of New Jersey
797 Springfield Avenue
Summit, NJ 07901-1107
Phone: (908) 277-3424; Fax: (908) 277-0851
Email: scholarships@njcolleges.org
Web: www.njcolleges.org/i_about_schol_students.html
Summary: To provide financial assistance to students enrolled at selected member institutions of the Independent College Fund of New Jersey (ICFNJ) who are majoring in accounting.
Eligibility: Open to students entering their junior or senior year at selected ICFNJ member institutions (Fairleigh Dickinson University, Monmouth University, and Seton Hall University). Applicants must be majoring in accounting and have a cumulative GPA of 3.3 or higher. Along with their application, they must submit a 250-word personal statement on their academic and personal qualifications, their future academic and/or career plans, and their plans for attaining the 150 credit hour requirement. Financial need is not considered in the selection process.
Financial data: The stipend is typically $2,500.
Duration: 1 year.
Number awarded: 1 or more each year.
Deadline: March of each year.

2809 MARY FAULKNER SCHOLARSHIP

Maryland Association of Family and Consumer Sciences
c/o Cheryl Doughty
5202 Sanborn Terrace
Salisbury, MD 21801
Email: cdoughty76@gmail.com
Web: sites.google.com
Summary: To provide financial assistance to undergraduate and graduate students from Maryland working on a degree in a field of family and consumer sciences at a school in any state.
Eligibility: Open to residents of Maryland who are working on an undergraduate or graduate degree in a field of family and consumer sciences, including family and consumer sciences education, foods and nutrition, clothing and textiles, child development, family relations, fashion merchandising, or consumer economics. Applicants must have a GPA of 3.0 or higher. They may be attending school in any state, but students who are enrolled at an institution outside of Maryland must plan to return to the state after graduation. Financial need is considered in the selection process.
Financial data: The stipend is $1,000.
Duration: 1 year.
Number awarded: 1 each year.
Deadline: January of each year.

2810 MARYLAND ASSOCIATION FOR HEALTH, PHYSICAL EDUCATION, RECREATION AND DANCE HIGH SCHOOL SCHOLARSHIPS

Summary: To provide financial assistance to high school seniors in Maryland who plan to attend college in any state to prepare for a career as a teacher of health, physical education, recreation, or dance.
See Listing #1420.

2811 MARYLAND ASSOCIATION FOR HEALTH, PHYSICAL EDUCATION, RECREATION AND DANCE UNDERGRADUATE SCHOLARSHIPS

Summary: To provide financial assistance to upper-division students from any state who are enrolled at a school in Maryland and preparing for a career as a teacher of health, physical education, recreation, or dance.
See Listing #1421.

2812 MARYLAND LEGION AUXILIARY CHILDREN AND YOUTH FUND SCHOLARSHIP

Summary: To provide financial assistance for college to the daughters of veterans who are Maryland residents and wish to study arts, sciences, business, public administration, education, or a medical field at a school in the state.
See Listing #1422.

2813 MARYLAND WORKFORCE SHORTAGE STUDENT ASSISTANCE GRANT PROGRAM

Summary: To provide financial assistance to Maryland residents interested in a career in specified workforce shortage areas.
See Listing #2118.

2814 MASSACHUSETTS AFL-CIO SCHOLARSHIP AWARDS

Massachusetts AFL-CIO
Attn: Scholarship Coordinator

389 Main Street, Suite 101
Malden, MA 02148
Phone: (781) 324-8230; Fax: (781) 324-8225
Email: mconnolly@massaflcio.org
Web: www.massaflcio.org/scholarship-program

Summary: To recognize and reward the high school seniors in Massachusetts receiving the highest scores on a statewide labor history written examination.

Eligibility: Open to high school seniors in Massachusetts. They may apply to their guidance office, social studies teacher, or principal to take a competitive examination that deals with the history and structure of the labor movement in America, legislation affecting American workers, child labor laws, minimum wages, civil rights, safety in the workplace, old age and health insurance, unemployment compensation, workers' compensation, and past and current labor events. The students with the highest scores on the examination receive these scholarships to attend the college or university of their choice.

Financial data: The first-place winner receives the John F. Kennedy Memorial Scholarship of $3,000. The second-place winner receives the Francis E. Lavigne Memorial Scholarship of $2,000. The third-place winner receives the Arthur R. Osborn Scholarship of $1,000. The fourth-place winner receives the Joseph C. Faherty Award of $1,000. The fifth-place winner receives the Massachusetts AFL-CIO Scholarship Award of $1,000. The sixth-place winners (1 female and 1 male) each receive a Union City Press Award of $1,000. The seventh-place winner receives the Salvatore Camelio Memorial Award of $1,000. The eighth-place winner receives the James W. DeBow Memorial Award of $1,000. The Massachusetts AFL-CIO Vocational Award of $1,000 is presented to the vocational education student who scores highest on the examination. The Henry and Julie Khoury Memorial Award of $500 is presented to a child of a member of the Massachusetts AFL-CIO. In addition, prizes are awarded to students who are children of members of many central labor councils or locals throughout the state and score highest from among the children of members of that council or local who take the examination; these additional awards range in value from $100 to $3,000; the total value of scholarships provided by the Massachusetts AFL-CIO, its locals, central labor councils, and other affiliates exceeds $1,085,000 each year.

Duration: Most scholarships are for 1 year.

Number awarded: More than 300 scholarships are awarded each year, of which 10 are awarded to the students with the highest scores in the state regardless of union affiliation and most of the others to children of various councils or locals.

Deadline: Applications to take the examination must be submitted by December of each year.

2815 MASSACHUSETTS EARLY CHILDHOOD EDUCATORS SCHOLARSHIP PROGRAM

Massachusetts Office of Student Financial Assistance
454 Broadway, Suite 200
Revere, MA 02151
Phone: (617) 727-9420; Fax: (617) 727-0667
Email: osfa@osfa.mass.edu
Web: www.osfa.mass.edu/default.asp?page=eceScholarship

Summary: To provide financial assistance to early childhood employees in Massachusetts who are interested in completing a college degree and becoming certified as early childhood educators.

Eligibility: Open to Massachusetts residents who 1) have been employed as an educator or provider at an early education or care program in the state for at least 1 year; and 2) are enrolled in an eligible undergraduate program of study that meets the standards of the Department of Early Education and Care. Applicants must agree to remain employed in an early childhood education and care program in Massachusetts while completing the requirements for their degree program. U.S. citizenship or permanent resident status is required.

Financial data: Grants depend on the type of institution attended. At public universities, the maximum award is $400 per credit, to a total of $3,600 per semester. At state colleges, the maximum award is $300 per credit, to a total of $2,700 per semester. At community colleges, the maximum award is $150 per credit, to a total of $1,350 per semester. At private universities and colleges, the maximum award is $400 per credit, to a total of $3,600 per semester. This is a scholarship/loan program. Recipients must agree to continue employment as an early childhood educator or provider in Massachusetts after graduation. If they fail to fulfill that obligation, they must repay all funds received.

Duration: Until completion of an undergraduate degree, provided the recipient maintains satisfactory academic progress.

Number awarded: Varies each year.

Deadline: The priority deadline is June of each year.

2816 MASSACHUSETTS INCENTIVE PROGRAM FOR ASPIRING TEACHERS

Massachusetts Office of Student Financial Assistance
454 Broadway, Suite 200
Revere, MA 02151
Phone: (617) 727-9420; Fax: (617) 727-0667
Email: osfa@osfa.mass.edu
Web: www.osfa.mass.edu/default.asp?page=aspireTeachersWaiver

Summary: To provide financial assistance to students at colleges and universities in Massachusetts who are interested in becoming teachers in the state following graduation.

Eligibility: Open to students enrolled in their third or fourth year of a Massachusetts state-approved teacher certification program field with teacher shortages. Applicants must 1) have been residents of Massachusetts for at least 1 year; and 2) be U.S. citizens or permanent residents. They must be attending 1 of the 9 Massachusetts state colleges or the 4 campuses of the University of Massachusetts and have a cumulative GPA of 3.0 or higher. A condition of the program is that they must commit to teaching for 2 years in a public school in Massachusetts upon successful completion of a bachelor's degree.

Financial data: Eligible students are entitled to a tuition waiver equal to the resident tuition rate at the state college or university campus where they are enrolled. If they do not complete their college education within 4 years of entering the program, or if they fail to complete their 2-year teaching commitment within 4 years following graduation from college, they must pay the state the full amount of the tuition waivers granted, with interest.

Duration: 2 years, provided the recipient maintains a GPA of 3.0 or higher.

Number awarded: Varies each year.

Deadline: April of each year.

2817 MASSACHUSETTS MATHEMATICS AND SCIENCE TEACHERS SCHOLARSHIP PROGRAM

Summary: To provide financial assistance to residents of Massachusetts who are interested in attending college to become certified as a mathematics or science teacher.

See Listing #2121.

2818 MASSACHUSETTS PARAPROFESSIONAL TEACHER PREPARATION GRANT PROGRAM

Massachusetts Office of Student Financial Assistance
454 Broadway, Suite 200
Revere, MA 02151
Phone: (617) 727-9420; Fax: (617) 727-0667
Email: osfa@osfa.mass.edu
Web: www.osfa.mass.edu/default.asp?page=paraprofessional

Summary: To provide financial assistance to educational paraprofessionals in Massachusetts who are interested in completing a college degree and becoming certified as teachers.

Eligibility: Open to Massachusetts residents who 1) have been employed as paraprofessionals in public schools in the state for at least 2 years; or 2) are working on a degree in an area of high need (recently defined as bilingual education, foreign languages, mathematics, science, and special education). Applicants must be enrolled full-time in an undergraduate degree program leading to teacher certification at a Massachusetts public institution. U.S. citizenship or permanent resident status is required. Applicants must submit a Free Application for Federal Student Aid (FAFSA), but financial need is not required.

Financial data: Grants depend on the type of institution attended. At public universities, the maximum award is $625 per credit, to a total of $7,500 per academic year. At state colleges, the maximum award is $450 per credit, to a total of $6,000 per academic year. At community colleges, the maximum award is $250 per credit, to a total of $4,000 per academic year. At private universities and colleges, the maximum award is $625 per credit, to a total of $7,500 per academic year. This is a scholarship/loan program. Recipients must agree to teach in a Massachusetts public school 1 year for each year of full- or partial grant received. If they fail to complete that teaching obligation, they must repay the amount of the grant received.

Duration: Until completion of an undergraduate degree, provided the recipient maintains satisfactory academic progress.

Number awarded: Varies each year.

Deadline: The priority deadline is July of each year.

2819 MATT MARVIN SCHOLARSHIP

USA Boxing, Inc.
Attn: Foundation
One Olympic Plaza
Colorado Springs, CO 80909
Phone: (719) 866-2315
Email: dsprowls@usaboxing.org
Web: www.usaboxing.org/content/index/4752

Summary: To provide financial assistance to athletes registered with USA Boxing who are working on a college degree in business.

Eligibility: Open to students currently enrolled at a college or university and working on a degree in business. Applicants must have been registered USA Boxing athletes for at least 3 consecutive years with at least 2 bouts at sanctioned events each year. They must be recommended by the chair of the Local Boxing Committee (LBC). Selection is based on information in the application (including financial need), not on boxing achievement.

Financial data: The stipend is at least $1,000.

Duration: 1 year; may be renewed.

Number awarded: 1 each year.

Deadline: July of each year.

2820 MERCER DIVERSITY SCHOLARSHIP PROGRAM

Mercer LLC
1166 Avenue of the Americas
New York, NY 10036
Phone: (212) 345-7000; Fax: (212) 345-7414
Web: www.mercer.com/summary.htm?idContent=1315000

Summary: To provide financial assistance and work experience to minority students preparing for a career in the human resource consulting industry.

Eligibility: Open to college sophomores and juniors who identify as Hispanic or Latino, Black or African American, Native Hawaiian or other Pacific Islander, American Indian or Alaska Native, or Asian. Applicants must be working on a degree in actuarial sciences, business, economics, finance, human resources management, mathematics, organizational psychology, or statistics. They must have a GPA of 3.25 or higher or a rank in the top 5% of their class. An interview is required. Selection is based on academic achievement, campus and community involvement, leadership potential, and ability to take initiative.

Financial data: Participants receive a paid internship at a Mercer office and a stipend (paid directly to their college or university) of $5,000.

Duration: 1 year; may be renewed, provided the recipient accepts an internship at a Mercer office and maintains a GPA of 3.25 or higher and/or a class rank in the top 5%.

Number awarded: Up to 9 each year.

Deadline: March of each year.

2821 MESBEC PROGRAM

Summary: To provide financial assistance to American Indian students who are interested in working on an undergraduate or graduate degree in selected fields.

See Listing #2132.

2822 METLIFE INTERNSHIP/SCHOLARSHIP

Summary: To provide financial assistance and work experience to students majoring in fields related to information technology at colleges and universities that are members of the Thurgood Marshall College Fund (TMCF).

See Listing #2133.

2823 METRO DENVER HOTEL ASSOCIATION SCHOLARSHIPS

Colorado Restaurant Association
Attn: CRA Education Foundation
430 East Seventh Avenue
Denver, CO 80203
Phone: (303) 830-2972; (800) 522-2972; Fax: (303) 830-2973
Email: info@coloradorestaurant.com
Web: www.coloradorestaurant.com

Summary: To provide financial assistance to high school seniors in Colorado who have participated in the ProStart Program and are interested in attending college in any state to prepare for a career in the hotel or hospitality management industry.

Eligibility: Open to seniors graduating from high schools in Colorado who are enrolled in the ProStart program of the Colorado Restaurant Association (CRA). Applicants must be interested in attending an approved postsecondary institution in any state to prepare for a career in a hotel or hospitality-related field. They must have a GPA of 2.75 or higher, a demonstrated interest in the lodging industry, and at least 250 hours of industry-related work experience. Along with their application, they must submit brief essays on their career objectives, their skills and personal characteristics that will contribute to the lodging or hospitality industry, special recognition or honors they have received, their extracurricular and community service activities, their interests or hobbies, the 2 major advantages of a career in the lodging or hospitality industry, the 2 major disadvantages (aside from an irregular work schedule) of a career in the lodging or hospitality industry, why they have chosen the lodging or hospitality industry, and why they feel they are qualified to receive this scholarship. Financial need is also considered in the selection process.

Financial data: The stipend is $1,000.

Duration: 1 year.

Number awarded: 2 each year.

Deadline: April of each year.

2824 MG EUGENE C. RENZI, USA (RET.)/MANTECH INTERNATIONAL CORPORATION TEACHER'S SCHOLARSHIP

Summary: To provide financial assistance to undergraduate and graduate students who are preparing for a career as a teacher of science and mathematics.

See Listing #2134.

2825 MHEFI SCHOLARSHIP PROGRAM

Summary: To provide financial assistance to undergraduate or graduate students who are studying material handling.

See Listing #2136.

2826 MICHAEL MURPHY MEMORIAL EDUCATION LOAN

Alaska Commission on Postsecondary Education
Attn: AlaskAdvantage Programs
3030 Vintage Boulevard
P.O. Box 110505
Juneau, AK 99811-0505
Phone: (907) 465-2962; (800) 441-2962; Fax: (907) 465-5316; TDD: (907) 465-3143
Email: customer_service@acpe.ak.us
Web: akadvantage.alaska.gov/page/255

Summary: To provide financial assistance to Alaska residents who are interested in working on an undergraduate degree in law enforcement at a school in any state.

Eligibility: Open to full-time undergraduates working on a degree in law enforcement, probation and parole, penology, or other closely-related field anywhere in the United States. Applicants must have been residents of Alaska for at least 2 years, be high school graduates or the equivalent, and demonstrate financial need.

Financial data: Loans up to $1,000 per year are available. No interest is charged. An origination fee of 3% of the amount disbursed is added to the principal balance to be repaid. This is a scholarship/loan program. Recipients are forgiven 20% of the total loan for each 1-year period they are employed full-time in Alaska law enforcement or related fields, up to 5 years.

Duration: 1 year; may be renewed.

Number awarded: Varies each year.

Deadline: March of each year.

2827 MICHAEL NUNNALLY SCHOLARSHIP

USA Boxing, Inc.
Attn: Foundation
One Olympic Plaza
Colorado Springs, CO 80909
Phone: (719) 866-2315
Email: dsprowls@usaboxing.org
Web: www.usaboxing.org/content/index/4752

Summary: To provide financial assistance to athletes registered with USA Boxing who are working on a college degree in education.

Eligibility: Open to students currently enrolled at a college or university and working on a degree in elementary or secondary education. Applicants must have been registered USA Boxing athletes for at least 3 consecutive years with

at least 2 bouts at sanctioned events each year. They must be recommended by the chair of the Local Boxing Committee (LBC). Selection is based on information in the application (including financial need), not on boxing achievement.
Financial data: The stipend is at least $1,000.
Duration: 1 year; may be renewed.
Number awarded: 1 each year.
Deadline: July of each year.

2828 MICHAEL T. AND MARY L. CLOYD SCHOLARSHIP

Daughters of the American Revolution–National Society
Attn: Committee Services Office, Scholarships
1776 D Street, N.W.
Washington, DC 20006-5303
Phone: (202) 628-1776
Web: www.dar.org/natsociety/edout_scholar.cfm
Summary: To provide financial assistance to upper-division and graduate students working on a degree in library science.
Eligibility: Open to students who are 1) undergraduates at the junior level or higher; or 2) graduate students. Applicants must be working on a degree in library science and have a GPA of 3.0 or higher. They must be sponsored by a local chapter of the Daughters of the American Revolution (DAR). Selection is based on academic excellence, commitment to the field of study, and financial need. U.S. citizenship is required.
Financial data: The stipend is $3,000.
Duration: 1 year; nonrenewable.
Number awarded: 1 each year.
Deadline: February of each year.

2829 MICHELLE L. MCDONALD SCHOLARSHIP

Educational Foundation for Women in Accounting
Attn: Foundation Administrator
136 South Keowee Street
Dayton, OH 45402
Phone: (937) 424-3391; Fax: (937) 222-5749
Email: info@efwa.org
Web: www.efwa.org/mcdonald.htm
Summary: To provide financial support to women who are returning to college from the workforce or after raising their family to work on a degree in accounting.
Eligibility: Open to women who are returning to college from the workforce or after raising children. Applicants must be planning to begin a program of study for a college degree in accounting. Selection is based on aptitude for accounting and business, commitment to the goal of working on a degree in accounting (including evidence of continued commitment after receiving this award), clear evidence that the candidate has established goals and a plan for achieving those goals (both personal and professional), and financial need.
Financial data: The stipend is $1,000 per year.
Duration: 1 year; may be renewed 1 additional year if the recipient completes at least 12 hours each semester.
Number awarded: 1 each year.
Deadline: April of each year.

2830 MICHIGAN ASSOCIATION FOR THE EDUCATION OF YOUNG CHILDREN STUDENT LEADERSHIP AWARD

Michigan Association for the Education of Young Children
Beacon Place
4572 South Hagadorn Road, Suite 1D
East Lansing, MI 48823-5385
Phone: (517) 336-9700; (800) 336-6424; Fax: (517) 336-9790
Email: MiAEYC@miaeyc.org
Web: www.miaeyc.org/programs/studentleadership.htm
Summary: To provide financial assistance to students at colleges and universities in Michigan who are working on a degree in a field related to early childhood education.
Eligibility: Open to students who have completed at least 60 credit hours at a 4-year college or university in Michigan. Applicants must be enrolled in a teacher education program with a major or minor in early childhood education, child development, or a related field. They must have a GPA of 2.75 or higher.
Financial data: The stipend is $1,000. The winner also receives a 1-year membership in the Michigan Association for the Education of Young Children (MiAEYC), complimentary registration to the association's annual early childhood conference, and 1 night of lodging at the conference.
Duration: 1 year.
Number awarded: 1 each year.
Deadline: Deadline not specified.

2831 MINORITIES IN HOSPITALITY SCHOLARS PROGRAM

International Franchise Association
Attn: IFA Educational Foundation
1501 K Street, N.W., Suite 350
Washington, DC 20005
Phone: (202) 662-0784; Fax: (202) 628-0812
Email: mbrewer@franchise.org
Web: www.franchise.org/Scholarships.aspx
Summary: To provide financial assistance to minority students working on an undergraduate degree related to hospitality.
Eligibility: Open to college sophomores, juniors, and seniors who are U.S. citizens and members of a minority group (defined as African Americans, American Indians, Hispanic Americans, and Asian Americans). Applicants must be working on a degree in a field related to the hospitality industry. Along with their application, they must submit a 500-word essay on why they should be selected to receive this scholarship. Financial need is not considered in the selection process.
Financial data: The stipend is $2,000.
Duration: 1 year.
Number awarded: 1 or more each year.
Deadline: January of each year.

2832 MINORITY ENTREPRENEURS SCHOLARSHIP PROGRAM

International Franchise Association
Attn: IFA Educational Foundation
1501 K Street, N.W., Suite 350
Washington, DC 20005
Phone: (202) 662-0784; Fax: (202) 628-0812
Email: mbrewer@franchise.org
Web: www.franchise.org/Scholarships.aspx
Summary: To provide financial assistance to minority students and adult entrepreneurs enrolled in academic or professional development programs related to franchising.
Eligibility: Open to 1) college students enrolled at an accredited college or university; and 2) adult entrepreneurs who have at least 5 years of business ownership or managerial experience. Applicants must be U.S. citizens and members of a minority group (defined as African Americans, American Indians, Hispanic Americans, and Asian Americans). Students should be enrolled in courses or programs relating to business, finance, marketing, hospitality, franchising, or entrepreneurship. Adult entrepreneurs should be enrolled in professional development courses related to franchising, such as those recognized by the Institute of Certified Franchise Executives (ICFE). All applicants must submit a 500-word essay on why they want the scholarship and their career goals. Financial need is not considered in the selection process.
Financial data: The stipend is $3,000.
Duration: 1 year.
Number awarded: 5 each year.
Deadline: June of each year.

2833 MINORITY TEACHERS OF ILLINOIS SCHOLARSHIP PROGRAM

Illinois Student Assistance Commission
Attn: Scholarship and Grant Services
1755 Lake Cook Road
Deerfield, IL 60015-5209
Phone: (847) 948-8550; (800) 899-ISAC; Fax: (847) 831-8549; TDD: (800) 526-0844
Email: collegezone@isac.org
Web: www.collegezone.com/studentzone/407_655.htm
Summary: To provide financial assistance to minority students in Illinois who plan to become teachers at the preschool, elementary, or secondary level.
Eligibility: Open to Illinois residents who are U.S. citizens or eligible noncitizens, members of a minority group (African American/Black, Hispanic American, Asian American, or Native American), and high school graduates or holders of a General Educational Development (GED) certificate. They must be enrolled in college full-time at the sophomore level or above, have a GPA of 2.5 or higher, not be in default on any student loan, and be enrolled or accepted for enrollment in a teacher education program. U.S. citizenship or eligible noncitizenship status is required.

Financial data: Grants up to $5,000 per year are awarded. This is a scholarship/loan program. Recipients must agree to teach full-time 1 year for each year of support received. The teaching agreement may be fulfilled at a public, private, or parochial preschool, elementary school, or secondary school in Illinois; at least 30% of the student body at those schools must be minority. It must be fulfilled within the 5-year period following the completion of the undergraduate program for which the scholarship was awarded. The time period may be extended if the recipient serves in the U.S. armed forces, enrolls full-time in a graduate program related to teaching, becomes temporarily disabled, is unable to find employment as a teacher at a qualifying school, or takes additional courses on at least a half-time basis to obtain certification as a teacher in Illinois. Recipients who fail to honor this work obligation must repay the award with 5% interest.

Duration: 1 year; may be renewed for a total of 8 semesters or 12 quarters.

Number awarded: Varies each year.

Deadline: Priority consideration is given to applications received by February of each year.

2834 MIRIAM HOFFMAN SCHOLARSHIPS

Summary: To provide financial assistance to undergraduate and graduate Methodist students who are preparing for a career in music or music education.

See Listing #1434.

2835 MIRIAM SCHAEFER SCHOLARSHIP

Summary: To provide financial assistance to upper-division students who are enrolled in a teacher education program in Michigan with a mathematics specialty.

See Listing #2144.

2836 MISSISSIPPI CRITICAL NEEDS ALTERNATE ROUTE TEACHER LOAN/SCHOLARSHIP PROGRAM

Mississippi Office of Student Financial Aid
3825 Ridgewood Road
Jackson, MS 39211-6453
Phone: (601) 432-6997; (800) 327-2980 (within MS); Fax: (601) 432-6527
Email: sfa@ihl.state.ms.us
Web: www.mississippi.edu/riseupms/financialaid-state.php

Summary: To provide financial assistance to students in Mississippi interested in preparing for a career as a teacher and willing to work in selected areas of the state or teach in specified subject areas.

Eligibility: Open to juniors and seniors at Mississippi 4-year colleges and universities. Mississippi residency is not required. Applicants must be working on their first bachelor's degree and planning to enroll in a program of study leading to an Alternate Route teacher license. They must have passed Praxis I; agree to employment immediately after completing their degree as a full-time classroom teacher in a Mississippi public school located in a critical teacher shortage area of the state or in a subject shortage area; participate in entrance counseling; and have a cumulative GPA of 2.5 or higher.

Financial data: The program provides payment of tuition and required fees (at the in-state rate only), an allowance for room and board equal to the state average for a Mississippi resident, and an allowance for books. This is a scholarship/loan program; recipients must sign a contract agreeing to teach 1 year for each year the award is received in an accredited public school or public school district in a critical teacher geographic shortage area of Mississippi as defined at the time of graduation. If the recipient fails to remain enrolled in a teacher education program or fails to fulfill the service obligation, repayment of principal and interest is required.

Duration: 1 year; may be renewed 1 additional year if the recipient maintains a GPA of 2.5 or higher, meets the satisfactory academic progress standards of their institution, and remains enrolled in a program of study leading to an Alternate Route teacher license.

Number awarded: Varies each year, depending on the availability of funds; awards are granted on a first-come, first-served basis.

Deadline: March of each year.

2837 MISSISSIPPI CRITICAL NEEDS TEACHER LOAN/SCHOLARSHIP PROGRAM

Mississippi Office of Student Financial Aid
3825 Ridgewood Road
Jackson, MS 39211-6453
Phone: (601) 432-6997; (800) 327-2980 (within MS); Fax: (601) 432-6527
Email: sfa@ihl.state.ms.us
Web: www.mississippi.edu/riseupms/financialaid-state.php

Summary: To provide financial assistance to students in Mississippi interested in preparing for a career as a teacher and willing to work in selected areas of the state or teach in specified subject areas.

Eligibility: Open to juniors and seniors at Mississippi 4-year colleges and universities. Mississippi residency is not required. Applicants must have passed Praxis I or had an ACT score of 21 or higher with a minimum of 18 on all subscores. They must enroll in a program of study leading to a bachelor's degree and a Class "A" teacher educator license; agree to employment immediately after completing their degree as a full-time classroom teacher in a Mississippi public school located in a critical teacher shortage area of the state or in a subject shortage area; and have a cumulative GPA of 2.5 or higher.

Financial data: Full-time students receive an award equal to the highest cost of tuition, room, and board at a public institution in the state; part-time students receive a prorated amount. This is a scholarship/loan program; recipients must sign a contract agreeing to teach 1 year for each year the award is received in an accredited public school or public school district in a critical teacher geographic shortage area of Mississippi as defined at the time of graduation. If the recipient fails to remain enrolled in a teacher education program or fails to fulfill the service obligation, repayment of principal and interest is required.

Duration: 1 year; may be renewed 1 additional year if the recipient maintains a GPA of 2.5 or higher, meets the satisfactory academic progress standards of their institution, and remains enrolled in a program of study leading to a Class "A" teacher educator license.

Number awarded: Varies each year, depending on the availability of funds; awards are granted on a first-come, first-served basis.

Deadline: March of each year.

2838 MISSISSIPPI MUNICIPAL LEAGUE GENERAL SCHOLARSHIP

Mississippi Municipal League
Attn: Scholarship
600 East Amite Street, Suite 104
Jackson, MS 39201
Phone: (601) 353-5854; (800) 325-7641; Fax: (601) 353-6980
Email: info@mmlonline.com
Web: www.mmlonline.com/services.aspx

Summary: To provide financial assistance to high school seniors in Mississippi who are interested in attending college in the state to prepare for a career in municipal government.

Eligibility: Open to seniors graduating from high schools in Mississippi who plan to attend an accredited college, university, or community college in the state. Applicants must submit an essay, up to 2,000 words in length, on why they should consider a career in municipal government. Selection is based primarily on that essay; financial need is not considered.

Financial data: The stipend is $2,000.

Duration: 1 year.

Number awarded: 1 each year.

Deadline: April of each year.

2839 MISSOURI ASSOCIATION OF RURAL EDUCATION SCHOLARSHIPS

Missouri Association of Rural Education
Attn: Scholarship Fund
201 South Holden Street, Suite 202
Warrensburg, MO 64093-3400
Phone: (660) 747-8050; Fax: (660) 747-8160
Email: rpatrick@moare.com
Web: www.moare.com/vnews/display.v/SEC/Services%7CScholarships

Summary: To provide financial assistance to upper-division education students at colleges and universities in Missouri who are interested in teaching at a rural school in the state.

Eligibility: Open to juniors and seniors at colleges and universities in Missouri who have declared a major in education. Applicants must have a GPA of 2.5 or higher and be able to demonstrate financial need. Along with their application, they must submit a 2-page essay on their connection and interest in rural Missouri and why they want to teach in a rural community. Selection is based on leadership ability, academic achievement, dependability, ability to relate to students and faculty, and potential for success as a rural teacher.

Financial data: The stipend is $1,000 per year.

Duration: 1 year; may be renewed.

Number awarded: 5 each year.

Deadline: April of each year.

2840 MISSOURI MINORITY TEACHER EDUCATION SCHOLARSHIP PROGRAM

Summary: To provide financial assistance to minority high school seniors, high school graduates, and college students in Missouri who are interested in preparing for a teaching career in mathematics or science.

See Listing #2149.

2841 MISSOURI PERSONAL FINANCE CHALLENGE

Missouri Council on Economic Education
c/o University of Missouri at Kansas City
Manheim Hall 104H
5100 Rockhill Road
Kansas City, MO 64110
Phone: (816) 235-2653; (800) 746-7432; Fax: (816) 235-2651
Email: gravensteinm@umkc.edu
Web: cas.umkc.edu/mcee/MPFC/MPFC_Index.htm

Summary: To recognize and reward high school students in Missouri who achieve outstanding scores in an examination on personal finance.

Eligibility: Open to students in grades 9–12 at high schools in Missouri. In teams of 4 students each, they take an online examination on material covered in the state's required personal finance curriculum. The top 20 teams in each of 4 districts advance to a regional city (Kansas City, Springfield, Columbia, and St. Louis) for an on-site competition with questions on income, money management, spending and credit, and saving and investment. The 2 teams in each regional competition advance to the state finals in Jefferson City. The format in both the regional competitions and the state finals includes a written (multiple choice) examination followed by a "quiz bowl" with verbal responses to questions.

Financial data: In the regional competitions, each member of the winning team and its teacher receive a $500 U.S. Savings Bond and each member of the second-place team and its teacher receive a $250 U.S. Savings Bond. All members of the winning and second-place teams receive financial support to attend the state finals. Each member of the state winning team and its teacher receive an additional $1,000 U.S. Savings Bond and each member of the second-place team and its teacher receive an additional $500 U.S. Savings Bond.

Duration: The competition is held annually.

Number awarded: 8 teams receive regional awards and 2 teams receive state awards.

Deadline: The online competition is in March, the regional competitions in April, and the state competition in May.

2842 MISSOURI STATE THESPIAN SCHOLARSHIPS

Summary: To provide financial assistance to high school seniors in Missouri who have been active in theater and plan to attend college in any state to major in theater or theater education.

See Listing #1436.

2843 MISSOURI TEACHER EDUCATION SCHOLARSHIP PROGRAM

Missouri Department of Elementary and Secondary Education
Attn: Educator Recruitment and Retention
205 Jefferson Street
P.O. Box 480
Jefferson City, MO 65102-0480
Phone: (573) 751-1668; Fax: (573) 526-3580
Email: Laura.Harrison@dese.mo.gov
Web: dese.mo.gov/divteachqual/scholarships

Summary: To provide financial assistance to high school seniors, high school graduates, and college students in Missouri who are interested in preparing for a teaching career.

Eligibility: Open to Missouri residents who are high school students or already enrolled full-time at a community or 4-year college or university in the state. Applicants must rank in the top 15% of their high school class or score in the top 15% on the ACT or SAT. They must be entering or already enrolled at a teacher education program in a 4-year college or university in Missouri. Selection is based on academic performance, the quantity and quality of school and community activities, range of interests and activities, employment experience, leadership abilities, interpersonal skills, and desire to enter the field of education.

Financial data: The stipend is $2,000 (half of the award is paid by the state of Missouri and the other half is paid by the participating college or university). This is a scholarship/loan program. Recipients must commit to teaching in a Missouri public elementary or secondary school for 5 years following graduation. If they fail to fulfill that obligation, they must repay the state portion of the scholarship.

Duration: 1 year; nonrenewable.

Number awarded: Approximately 240 each year.

Deadline: February of each year.

2844 MISSOURI URBAN FLIGHT AND RURAL NEEDS SCHOLARSHIP PROGRAM

Missouri Department of Elementary and Secondary Education
Attn: Teacher Quality and Urban Education
205 Jefferson Street
P.O. Box 480
Jefferson City, MO 65102-0480
Phone: (573) 751-1191; Fax: (573) 526-3580
Email: Rosalyn.Wieberg@dese.mo.gov
Web: dese.mo.gov/divteachqual/scholarships

Summary: To provide financial assistance to residents of Missouri who are interested in preparing for a teaching career and working at a school with a large "at-risk" student population.

Eligibility: Open to Missouri residents who are 1) high school seniors, college freshmen or sophomores, or returning adults at a community college or 4-year college or university in the state; 2) graduates of a Missouri high school who have a cumulative GPA of 2.5 or higher; 3) individuals who have completed 30 college hours and have a cumulative GPA of 2.5 or higher; or 4) holders of a baccalaureate degree with a cumulative GPA of 2.5 or higher who are returning to an approved teacher education program. Applicants must be entering or enrolled in an approved teacher education program in Missouri as a full-time student. U.S. citizenship is required. Selection is based on academic performance and financial need.

Financial data: The program covers the total cost of tuition and fees at the appropriate undergraduate rate for the attending institution, up to a maximum of the rate at the University of Missouri. Recipients must commit to teaching for 8 years at a public school in Missouri that is defined as having a higher than average "at-risk" student population. If they fail to fulfill that requirement, the scholarship converts to a loan and must be repaid.

Duration: Up to 4 years.

Number awarded: Varies each year; recently, 25 of these scholarships were awarded.

Deadline: April of each year.

2845 MONSANTO FUND SCHOLARSHIP PROGRAM OF THE HISPANIC SCHOLARSHIP FUND

Summary: To provide financial assistance to Hispanic students who are working on an undergraduate degree in selected science, engineering, or business fields.

See Listing #2152.

2846 MONTANA STATE ELKS MUSIC SCHOLARSHIP

Summary: To provide financial assistance to high school seniors in Montana who plan to study music or music education at a college or university in any state.

See Listing #1440.

2847 MORGAN STANLEY SCHOLARS PROGRAM

American Indian College Fund
Attn: Scholarship Department
8333 Greenwood Boulevard
Denver, CO 80221
Phone: (303) 426-8900; (800) 776-FUND; Fax: (303) 426-1200
Email: scholarships@collegefund.org
Web: www.collegefund.org/scholarships/schol_mainstream.html

Summary: To provide financial assistance to American Indian students at mainstream 4-year institutions who are preparing for a career in the business and financial services industry.

Eligibility: Open to American Indians or Alaska Natives who are currently enrolled full-time in a bachelor's degree program at a mainstream institution in the United States. Applicants must be interested in preparing for a career in the financial services industry (e.g., information technology, investment banking, investment management, marketing, branch operations, financial advising, financial accounting, credit card services). They must have a GPA of 3.0 or higher. Applications are available only online and include required essays on specified topics. Selection is based on exceptional academic achievement.
Financial data: The stipend is $10,000.
Duration: 1 year.
Number awarded: 5 each year.
Deadline: May of each year.

2848 MORGAN STANLEY TRIBAL SCHOLARS PROGRAM

American Indian College Fund
Attn: Scholarship Department
8333 Greenwood Boulevard
Denver, CO 80221
Phone: (303) 426-8900; (800) 776-FUND; Fax: (303) 426-1200
Email: scholarships@collegefund.org
Web: www.collegefund.org/scholarships/schol_tcu.html
Summary: To provide financial assistance to Native American students currently enrolled full-time at a Tribal College or University (TCU) to prepare for a career in business and the financial services industry.
Eligibility: Open to American Indians and Alaska Natives who are enrolled full-time at an eligible TCU. Applicants must have declared a major in business or a related field and have a GPA of 3.0 or higher. Applications are available only online and include required essays on specified topics. Selection is based on exceptional academic achievement.
Financial data: The stipend is $2,500.
Duration: 1 year.
Number awarded: 10 each year.
Deadline: May of each year.

2849 MORRIS K. UDALL SCHOLARSHIPS

Summary: To provide financial assistance to 1) college sophomores and juniors who intend to prepare for a career in environmental public policy; and 2) Native American and Alaska Native students who intend to prepare for a career in health care or tribal public policy.
See Listing #2155.

2850 MRCA FOUNDATION SCHOLARSHIP AWARD

Midwest Roofing Contractors Association
Attn: MRCA Foundation
4840 Bob Billings Parkway, Suite 1000
Lawrence, KS 66049-3862
Phone: (785) 843-4888; (800) 497-6722; Fax: (785) 843-7555
Email: mrca@mrca.org
Web: www.mrca.org/i4a/pages/index.cfm?pageid=3576
Summary: To provide financial assistance to students from midwestern states who are interested in preparing for a career in the construction industry.
Eligibility: Open to undergraduate and graduate students who are enrolled or planning to enroll at an accredited college, community college, vocational school, or trade school that offers a program of preparation for a career in the construction industry. Selection is based on the applicant's academic performance, employment experience, financial need, and demonstrated desire to prepare for a career in the construction industry.
Financial data: Stipends are awarded (amount not specified).
Duration: 1 year.
Number awarded: 1 or more each year.
Deadline: June of each year.

2851 MYRT WILLEY SCHOLARSHIP

Zonta Club of Bangor
c/o Barbara A. Cardone
P.O. Box 1904
Bangor, ME 04402-1904
Web: www.zontaclubofbangor.org/?area=scholarship
Summary: To provide financial assistance to women attending or planning to attend college in Maine and major in a business-related field.
Eligibility: Open to women who are attending or planning to attend an accredited 2- or 4-year college in Maine. Applicants must major in a business-related field. Along with their application, they must submit brief essays on 1) their goals in seeking higher education and their plans for the future; and 2) any school and community activities that have been of particular importance to them and why they found them worthwhile. Financial need may be considered in the selection process.
Financial data: The stipend is $1,000.
Duration: 1 year.
Number awarded: 1 each year.
Deadline: March of each year.

2852 NAFOA STUDENT SCHOLARSHIP FUND

Native American Finance Officers Association
Attn: Christina Morbelli, Program Coordinator
P.O. Box 50637
Phoenix, AZ 85076-0637
Phone: (602) 466-8697; Fax: (201) 447-0945
Email: christina@nafoa.org
Web: www.nafoa.org/education.html
Summary: To provide financial assistance to Native Americans who are studying a business-related field in college or graduate school.
Eligibility: Open to enrolled members of a federally-recognized tribe who are currently a junior or senior in college or studying for an M.B.A. Applicants must be majoring in finance, accounting, business administration, or management and must maintain a GPA of 2.8 or higher. Along with their application, they must submit an essay of 200 to 400 words that includes information on their connection to their Native community, their history in the finance profession, and their future goals in finance.
Financial data: A stipend is awarded (amount not specified).
Duration: 1 year.
Number awarded: Varies each year; recently, 3 of these scholarships were awarded.
Deadline: October of each year.

2853 NANCY LARSON FOUNDATION COLLEGE SCHOLARSHIPS

Nancy Larson Foundation, Inc.
P.O. Box 6
Old Lyme, CT 06371
Phone: (803) 547-6913
Web: www.nancylarsonfoundation.org/scholarship.php
Summary: To provide financial assistance to upper-division and graduate students working on a degree in elementary education.
Eligibility: Open to juniors, seniors, and graduate students working on a degree in elementary education. Applicants must submit an essay, up to 500 words in length, describing 3 traits they possess that will make them a successful teacher. Selection is based on that essay, transcripts, a resume that includes employment history, activities, and community service.
Financial data: The stipend is $1,000.
Duration: 1 year.
Number awarded: At least 5 each year.
Deadline: November of each year.

2854 NAOMI BERBER MEMORIAL SCHOLARSHIP

Summary: To provide financial assistance for college to women who want to prepare for a career in the printing or publishing industry.
See Listing #1445.

2855 NASCAR/WENDELL SCOTT AWARD

Summary: To provide financial assistance to undergraduate and graduate students majoring in specified fields at member institutions of the Hispanic Association of Colleges and Universities (HACU) in designated states.
See Listing #2161.

2856 NATIONAL ECONOMICS CHALLENGE

Council for Economic Education
122 East 42nd Street, Suite 2600
New York, NY 10168

Phone: (212) 730-1064; (800) 338-1192; Fax: (212) 730-1793
Email: nelyasi@councilforeconed.org
Web: economicschallengecouncilforeconed.org

Summary: To recognize and reward high school students who demonstrate excellence on an examination in economics.

Eligibility: Open to teams of 4 students enrolled at a public, private, or home-based high school. Each team may compete in either a division for students enrolled in Advanced Placement (AP Micro, AP Macro, AP Micro and Macro), International Baccalaureate (pre-IB and IB), honors, 2-semester, or other advanced economics courses (designated the Adam Smith division) or a division for students enrolled in 1-semester (or less) economics courses or other courses that include introductory economics concepts (e.g., social studies, business, personal finance) and taught by a secondary teacher (designated the David Ricardo division). Students first participate at the state level in 3 rounds of written competitions: round 1 on microeconomics, round 2 on macroeconomics, and round 3 on international economics and current events. For rounds 1 and 2, students answer individually and their scores are totaled; for round 3, they collaborate and answer as a team. The 2 highest scoring teams in each division after those 3 rounds then advance to round 4, where they compete against each other in a quiz bowl format. Winners of the state competitions then advance to 1 of 4 regional competitions, where the same format is followed. Regional winners advance to the national competition, where the same format is followed again.

Financial data: Regional winners and their teachers each receive $1,000 U.S. Savings Bonds; regional runner-up teams and their teachers each receive $500 U.S. Savings Bonds. In the national finals, each member of the winning team and its teacher receive an additional $3,000 U.S. Savings Bond and each member of the runner-up team and its teacher receive an additional $1,500 U.S. Savings bond. Regional winners also receive an all-expense-paid trip to New York City to participate in the national finals.

Duration: The competition is held annually.

Number awarded: 8 regional winners (1 in each division in each of 4 regions), 8 regional runners-up, 2 national winners (1 in each division), and 2 national runners-up are selected each year.

Deadline: Each state schedules its own competition, beginning in February. The regional competitions are in April and the national competition is in New York City in May.

2857 NATIONAL HYDROPOWER ASSOCIATION PAST PRESIDENTS' LEGACY SCHOLARSHIP

Summary: To provide financial assistance to undergraduate and graduate students working on a degree in a field related to the hydropower industry.

See Listing #2168.

2858 NATIONAL ITALIAN AMERICAN FOUNDATION GENERAL CATEGORY II SCHOLARSHIPS

Summary: To provide financial assistance for college or graduate school to students interested in majoring in Italian language, Italian studies, or Italian American studies.

See Listing #1450.

2859 NATIONAL MANAGEMENT ASSOCIATION LEADERSHIP SPEECH CONTEST

National Management Association
Attn: Leadership Speech Contest
2210 Arbor Boulevard
Dayton, OH 45439-1580
Phone: (937) 294-0421; Fax: (937) 294-2374
Email: nma@nma1.org
Web: nma1.us/aespeech/index.htm

Summary: To recognize and reward high school students who deliver outstanding speeches on leadership.

Eligibility: Open to students in grades 9–12 in a high school within an area of a sponsoring chapter of the National Management Association (NMA). Contestants prepare speeches of 4 to 6 minutes on a topic related to leadership. Non-leadership issues (e.g., social, medical, environmental, political) should not be used unless integrated into how leadership plays a role. No audio/visual aids are allowed with the presentations, and speeches may not be read verbatim, although notes are allowed. Winners of the chapter contests advance to council competition, from which winners proceed to compete at either the East or the West Leadership Development (LDC) of the NMA. The first- and second-place LDC winners then compete in the national contest. Speeches are judged on the basis of content (50%), delivery (30%), and language (20%).

Financial data: Chapter awards are determined by each chapter, up to a maximum of $300 for the first-place winner; each council also determines its own awards, to a maximum of $500 for the first-place winner. At each LDC, first prize is $1,000 and second is $500. In the national contest, first prize is $4,000, second $1,000, third $500, and fourth $500.

Number awarded: 4 LDC winners are selected each year and compete for the national prizes; the number of chapter and council prizes awarded varies.

Deadline: Chapter contests are held in January or early February of each year, council contests in February or March, LDC contests in April or May, and the national contest in September or October.

2860 NATIONAL MARKET NEWS ASSOCIATION SCHOLARSHIP PROGRAM

Summary: To provide financial assistance to undergraduate and graduate students working on a degree in a field related to agriculture or agribusiness.

See Listing #2169.

2861 NATIONAL PEACE ESSAY CONTEST

United States Institute of Peace
Attn: National Peace Essay Contest Project Officer
1200 17th Street, N.W., Suite 200
Washington, DC 20036-3011
Phone: (202) 429-7178; Fax: (202) 429-6063; TDD: (202) 457-1719
Email: essay_contest@usip.org
Web: www.usip.org/programs/initiatives/national-peace-essay-contest

Summary: To recognize and reward, with college scholarships, high school seniors who submit outstanding entries in the National Peace Essay Contest.

Eligibility: Open to students in grades 9–12 at a public, private, parochial, or home school in the United States or its territories. U.S. citizens studying in other countries are also eligible. Contestants must prepare a 1,500-word essay on a topic that changes each year; recently, the topic was "Governance, Corruption, and Conflict." Selection is based on the essay's focus, organization, analysis, conclusions and recommendations, originality, voice, and style and mechanics.

Financial data: Each state-level winner receives a $1,000 scholarship. National-level scholarships are $10,000 for first place, $5,000 for second place, and $2,500 for third place.

Duration: The competition is held annually.

Number awarded: Each year, 53 state winners (1 in each state, the District of Columbia, U.S. territories, and American students abroad) are selected; of those, 3 receive national scholarships.

Deadline: January of each year.

2862 NATIONAL RESTAURANT ASSOCIATION EDUCATIONAL FOUNDATION ACADEMIC SCHOLARSHIPS FOR UNDERGRADUATE STUDENTS

National Restaurant Association Educational Foundation
Attn: Scholarships Program
175 West Jackson Boulevard, Suite 1500
Chicago, IL 60604-2702
Phone: (312) 715-1010, ext. 738; (800) 765-2122, ext. 6738; Fax: (312) 566-9733
Email: scholars@nraef.org
Web: www.nraef.org/scholarships

Summary: To provide financial assistance to undergraduate students who are interested in preparing for a career in the hospitality industry.

Eligibility: Open to full-time and substantial part-time college students who have completed at least 1 term of a food service–related program at an accredited culinary school, college, or university. Applicants must be U.S. citizens or permanent residents. Along with their application, they must submit 1) an essay of 150 to 200 words on their career goals in the restaurant/food service industry; and 2) an essay of 450 to 500 words on 1 of the following issues that affects the restaurant industry: sustainability, food safety, or nutrition. Selection is based on the essays, presentation of the application, industry-related work experience, and letters of recommendation.

Financial data: The stipend is $2,500.

Duration: 1 year.

Number awarded: Approximately 200 each year.

Deadline: March or July of each year.

2863 NATIONAL SECURITY SCHOLARSHIPS OF THE INDEPENDENT COLLEGE FUND OF MARYLAND

Summary: To provide financial assistance to students from any state enrolled at member institutions of the Independent College Fund of Maryland and majoring in a field related to national security.
See Listing #1456.

2864 NATIONAL TOUR ASSOCIATION STATE SCHOLARSHIPS

Tourism Cares
Attn: National Tour Association Scholarship Fund
275 Turnpike Street, Suite 307
Canton, MA 02021
Phone: (781) 821-5990; Fax: (781) 821-8949
Email: info@tourismcares.org
Web: www.tourismcares.org/scholarships/nta-scholarships
Summary: To provide financial assistance to upper-division and graduate students who are majoring in tourism.
Eligibility: Open to 1) students entering their junior or senior year; and 2) entering and continuing graduate students. Applicants must be enrolled at an accredited 4-year college or university in the United States or Canada. They must be working on a degree in a travel and tourism-related program and have a GPA of 3.0 or higher. Along with their application, they must submit a 2-page essay on why they have chosen to prepare for a career in the hospitality and tourism industry. Financial need is not considered in the selection process. U.S. or Canadian citizenship or permanent resident status is required.
Financial data: The stipend is $1,000.
Duration: 1 year.
Number awarded: 13 each year.
Deadline: March of each year.

2865 NATIONWIDE HISPANIC SCHOLARSHIPS OF THE INDEPENDENT COLLEGE FUND OF MARYLAND

Independent College Fund of Maryland
Attn: Director of Programs and Scholarships
3225 Ellerslie Avenue, Suite C160
Baltimore, MD 21218-3519
Phone: (443) 997-5703; Fax: (443) 997-2740
Email: LSubot@jhmi.edu
Web: www.i-fundinfo.org/scholarships/minority-scholarships.html
Summary: To provide financial assistance to upper-division Hispanic students from any state at member institutions of the Independent College Fund of Maryland who are majoring in business.
Eligibility: Open to Hispanic students from any state currently entering their junior, or senior year at member institutions. Applicants must be enrolled full-time and majoring in or have demonstrated a career interest in business, particularly financial services. They must have a GPA of 3.0 or higher.
Financial data: The stipend is $2,000.
Duration: 1 year.
Number awarded: 1 or more each year.
Deadline: Deadline not specified.

2866 NATIVE AMERICAN LEADERSHIP IN EDUCATION (NALE) PROGRAM

Catching the Dream
8200 Mountain Road, N.E., Suite 203
Albuquerque, NM 87110-7835
Phone: (505) 262-2351; Fax: (505) 262-0534
Email: NScholarsh@aol.com
Web: www.catchingthedream.org/Scholarship.htm
Summary: To provide financial assistance to American Indian paraprofessionals in the education field who wish to return to college or graduate school.
Eligibility: Open to paraprofessionals who are working in Indian schools and who plan to return to college or graduate school to complete their degree in education, counseling, or school administration. Applicants must be able to provide proof that they are at least one-quarter Indian blood and a member of a U.S. tribe that is federally-recognized, state-recognized, or terminated. Along with their application, they must submit documentation of financial need, 3 letters of recommendation, copies of applications and responses from all other sources of funding for which they are eligible, official transcripts, standardized test scores (ACT, SAT, GRE, MCAT, LSAT, etc.), and an essay explaining their goals in life, college plans, and career plans (especially how those plans include working with and benefiting Indians). Selection is based on merit and potential for improving the lives of Indian people.
Financial data: Stipends range from $500 to $5,000 per year.
Duration: 1 year; may be renewed.
Number awarded: Varies; generally, 15 or more each year.
Deadline: April of each year for fall term; September of each year for spring and winter terms; March of each year for summer school.

2867 NAVY ADVANCED EDUCATION VOUCHER PROGRAM

Summary: To provide financial assistance to Navy enlisted personnel who are interested in earning an undergraduate or graduate degree in selected fields during off-duty hours.
See Listing #1462.

2868 NCA SCHOLARSHIP PROGRAM

Summary: To provide financial assistance to residents of any state enrolled at colleges and universities in the Washington, D.C. metropolitan area and working on an undergraduate or graduate degree in fields related to the health or management information systems industry.
See Listing #2181.

2869 NDPRB UNDERGRADUATE SCHOLARSHIP PROGRAM

Summary: To provide financial assistance to undergraduate students in various fields related to the dairy industry.
See Listing #2183.

2870 NEBRASKA LEGAL PROFESSIONALS SCHOLARSHIP

Nebraska Legal Professionals Association
c/o Mary Nuss, Scholarship Chair
1323 Central Avenue
P.O. Box 10
Kearney, NE 68848
Phone: (308) 236-6441; Fax: (308) 234-3747
Summary: To provide financial assistance to residents of Nebraska enrolled in a law-related program.
Eligibility: Open to residents of Nebraska enrolled full-time in a pre-law, paralegal, legal secretary, or other law-related program. Applicants must submit a certified copy of their latest transcript; a resume covering their educational history, school and community activities, and work history for the last 5 years; a 1-page personal statement on why they wish to become a legal secretary/paralegal or why they wish to continue their formal legal secretarial/paralegal education; and a copy of their acceptance to the school of their choice.
Financial data: The stipend is $1,250 for first place and $750 for second.
Duration: 1 year.
Number awarded: 2 each year.
Deadline: March of each year.

2871 NEBRASKA LIBRARY AND INFORMATION SERVICES SCHOLARSHIPS

Nebraska Library Commission
Attn: Communications Coordinator
1200 N Street, Suite 120
Lincoln, NE 68508-2023
Phone: (402) 471-3434; (800) 307-2665 (within NE); Fax: (402) 471-2083
Email: maryjo.ryan@nebraska.gov
Web: www.nlc.state.ne.us/NowHiring/ScholarshipsLTA.asp
Summary: To provide financial assistance to residents of Nebraska interested in working on a library technical assistant associate degree at a community college in the state.
Eligibility: Open to Nebraska residents who are interested in working on a library technical assistant associate degree. Applicants must be planning to enroll in at least 1 library science course at a Nebraska community college. They must agree to seek employment in a Nebraska public, school, institutional, tribal, or special library after completing their degree. Along with their application, they must submit a statement of 500 to 750 words on their professional experiences, aspirations, and goals. Financial need is not considered in the selection process. An interview may be required.
Financial data: The stipend is $1,000 per year. Funds may be used for tuition, course-related materials, and fees associated with courses. Recipients may also

use scholarship funds for other non-educational expenses incurred to attend courses, such as travel expenses and child care.
Duration: 1 year; may be renewed 1 additional year.
Number awarded: Varies each year; recently, 3 of these scholarships were awarded.
Deadline: January, June, or October of each year.

2872 NEHRA FUTURE STARS IN HR SCHOLARSHIPS

Northeast Human Resources Association
Attn: Scholarship Awards
303 Wyman Street, Suite 285
Waltham, MA 02451-1253
Phone: (781) 235-2900; Fax: (781) 237-8745
Email: info@nehra.com
Web: www.nehra.com
Summary: To provide financial assistance to undergraduate and graduate students at colleges and universities in New England who are preparing for a career in human resources.
Eligibility: Open to full-time undergraduate and graduate students at accredited colleges and universities in New England. Applicants must have completed at least 1 course related to human resources and have a GPA of 3.0 or higher. Along with their application, they must submit 2 essays: 1) why they are interested in becoming a human resources professional, the qualities they currently possess, the qualities they need to acquire, and how they intend to do that; and 2) the most important contribution human resources can make to the success of an organization. Selection is based on interest in becoming a human resources professional, academic success, leadership skills, and participation in non-academic activities. The applicant who is judged most outstanding receives the John D. Erdlen Scholarship Award.
Financial data: Stipends are $3,000 or $2,500 per year.
Duration: 1 year; may be renewed.
Number awarded: 2 each year: 1 at $3,000 (the John D. Erdlen Scholarship Award) and 1 at $2,500.
Deadline: March of each year.

2873 NEW HAMPSHIRE DUNKIN' DONUTS SCHOLARSHIPS

New Hampshire Charitable Foundation
37 Pleasant Street
Concord, NH 03301-4005
Phone: (603) 225-6641; (800) 464-6641; Fax: (603) 225-1700
Email: info@nhcf.org
Web: www.nhcf.org/page16960.cfm
Summary: To provide financial assistance to high school seniors in New Hampshire who plan to attend college in any state, especially those interested in preparing for a career related to the food service industry.
Eligibility: Open to seniors graduating from high schools in New Hampshire who are planning to attend a 2- or 4-year college, university, or technical school in any state. Applicants must have a GPA of 3.25 or higher. Preference is given to students preparing for a career in business, hospitality, or the food service industries. Selection is based on academic merit, involvement in school activities, volunteer or community service, paid work experience, and financial need.
Financial data: The stipend is $2,000.
Duration: 1 year.
Number awarded: 10 each year.
Deadline: April of each year.

2874 NEW HAMPSHIRE EDUCATIONAL MEDIA ASSOCIATION SCHOLARSHIP

New Hampshire Educational Media Association
P.O. Box 418
Concord, NH 03302-0418
Web: www.nhema.net/awards.htm
Summary: To provide financial assistance to residents of New Hampshire who are interested in taking courses related to school librarianship.
Eligibility: Open to New Hampshire residents who are interested in taking undergraduate, graduate, postgraduate, techniques, or continuing education courses related to school librarianship. Applicants must submit a statement outlining their professional and educational goals.
Financial data: A stipend is awarded (amount not specified).
Duration: 1 year.
Number awarded: 1 each year.
Deadline: February of each year.

2875 NEW HAMPSHIRE TEACHERS OF MATHEMATICS PRE-SERVICE MATHEMATICS EDUCATION SCHOLARSHIP FOR COLLEGE STUDENTS

Summary: To provide financial assistance to residents of New Hampshire who are attending college, preferably in the state, to prepare for a career as a teacher of mathematics.
See Listing #2188.

2876 NEW HAMPSHIRE TEACHERS OF MATHEMATICS PRE-SERVICE MATHEMATICS EDUCATION SCHOLARSHIP FOR HIGH SCHOOL STUDENTS

Summary: To provide financial assistance to high school students in New Hampshire who are planning to attend college in any state to prepare for a career as a teacher of mathematics.
See Listing #2189.

2877 NEW HAMPSHIRE WORKFORCE INCENTIVE PROGRAM FORGIVABLE LOANS

Summary: To provide financial assistance to New Hampshire residents who are interested in attending college in the state to prepare for careers in designated professions.
See Listing #2191.

2878 NEW MEXICO BROADCASTERS ASSOCIATION SCHOLARSHIPS

Summary: To provide financial assistance to residents of New Mexico who are attending college in the state to prepare for a career in the broadcast industry.
See Listing #1472.

2879 NEW MEXICO LIBRARY ASSOCIATION COLLEGE SCHOLARSHIP

New Mexico Library Association
P.O. Box 26074
Albuquerque, NM 87125
Phone: (505) 400-7309; Fax: (505) 891-5171
Email: admin@nmla.org
Web: www.nmla.org/scholarships-grants
Summary: To provide financial assistance to residents of New Mexico who are working on an associate degree in library science to prepare for a career as a school librarian.
Eligibility: Open to residents of New Mexico who are working on 1) an associate degree in library science that leads to certification; or 2) undergraduate or graduate study toward school librarian endorsement. Applicants must submit a resume, 3 letters of reference, transcripts, and a 1-page statement of professional needs, goals, and intent to serve New Mexico's libraries. Financial need is not considered in the selection process. Preference is given to applicants currently employed in a New Mexico library and to members of the New Mexico Library Association (NMLA).
Financial data: The stipend is $1,500.
Duration: 1 year.
Number awarded: Varies each year.
Deadline: January of each year.

2880 NEW MEXICO TEACHER LOAN-FOR-SERVICE PROGRAM

New Mexico Higher Education Department
Attn: Financial Aid Division
2048 Galisteo Street
Santa Fe, NM 87505-2100
Phone: (505) 476-8411; (800) 279-9777; Fax: (505) 476-8454
Email: Theresa.acker@state.nm.us
Web: hed.state.nm.us
Summary: To provide financial assistance to residents of New Mexico who are interested in becoming teachers in the state.
Eligibility: Open to residents of New Mexico who are enrolled at least half-time in an undergraduate, graduate, or alternative licensure teacher preparation program at an approved college or university in the state. Applicants must intend to practice as a teacher at a public school in a designated shortage area in New Mexico. They must be able to demonstrate financial need. Along with their application, they must submit an essay on why they want to become a teacher

and obligate themselves to teach in a shortage area in New Mexico. U.S. citizenship or eligible noncitizenship status is required.

Financial data: Loans range up to $4,000 per year, depending on financial need. This is a loan-for-service program; for every year of service as a teacher in New Mexico, a portion of the loan is forgiven. If the entire service agreement is fulfilled, 100% of the loan is eligible for forgiveness. Penalties may be assessed if the service agreement is not satisfied.

Duration: 1 year; may be renewed up to 4 additional consecutive years.

Number awarded: Varies each year.

Deadline: June of each year.

2881 NEW YORK LEGION AUXILIARY DISTRICT SCHOLARSHIPS

Summary: To provide financial assistance to descendants of veterans in New York who are interested in attending college in any state to study a medical or teaching field.

See Listing #2202.

2882 NEW YORK STATE GOLF ASSOCIATION SCHOLARSHIPS

Summary: To provide financial assistance to residents of New York working on a degree in a field related to golf course management at a school in any state.

See Listing #2206.

2883 NEW YORK STATE MATH AND SCIENCE TEACHING INCENTIVE SCHOLARSHIPS

Summary: To provide financial assistance to undergraduate and graduate students in New York who agree to teach secondary science or mathematics in the state following graduation.

See Listing #2207.

2884 NFIB YOUNG ENTREPRENEUR AWARDS

National Federation of Independent Business
Attn: NFIB Young Entrepreneur Foundation
1201 F Street, N.W., Suite 200
Washington, DC 20004
Phone: (202) 314-2055; (800) NFIB-NOW
Email: hank.kopcial@nfib.org
Web: www.nfib.com/tabid/347/Default.aspx

Summary: To provide financial assistance for college to high school seniors who are interested in private enterprise and entrepreneurship.

Eligibility: Open to graduating high school seniors who plan to enter their freshman year at an accredited 2-year college, 4-year college or university, or vocational/technical institute. Students must be nominated by a member of the National Federation of Independent Business (NFIB). Nominees must meet or exceed academic standards, using standardized test scores (ACT/SAT), class rank, and GPA as indicators. They must answer a short, personal question defining their entrepreneurial efforts and compose another essay of 500 words or less about the importance of free enterprise. Selection is based on those essays, involvement in extracurricular and/or community activities, and special recognition or honors.

Financial data: The highest-ranked applicant receives $10,000 and 5 other finalists receive $5,000. Another 25 awards, sponsored by the McKelvey Foundation, are $2,000. Other stipends are $1,000.

Duration: 1 year; most are nonrenewable, but some of the $1,000 awards may be renewed up to 3 additional years.

Number awarded: Varies each year; recently, a total of 166 of these scholarships was awarded: 1 at $10,000, 5 at $5,000, and 160 at $1,000. Since the program began, it has awarded more than $2 million in scholarships to nearly 2,000 students.

Deadline: December of each year.

2885 NIB GRANT M. MACK MEMORIAL SCHOLARSHIP

American Council of the Blind
Attn: Coordinator, Scholarship Program
2200 Wilson Boulevard, Suite 650
Arlington, VA 22201
Phone: (202) 467-5081; (800) 424-8666; Fax: (703) 465-5085
Email: info@acb.org
Web: www.acb.org

Summary: To provide financial assistance to blind students who are working on an undergraduate or graduate degree in business or management.

Eligibility: Open to undergraduate and graduate students working on a degree in business or management. Applicants must submit verification of legal blindness in both eyes; SAT, ACT, GMAT, or similar scores; information on extracurricular activities (including membership in the American Council of the Blind); employment record; and an autobiographical sketch that includes their personal goals, strengths, weaknesses, hobbies, honors, achievements, and reasons for choice of field or courses of study. A cumulative GPA of 3.3 or higher is generally required. Financial need is not considered in the selection process. U.S. citizenship or permanent resident status is required.

Financial data: The stipend is $2,000. In addition, the winner receives a Kurzweil-1000 Reading System.

Duration: 1 year.

Number awarded: 1 each year.

Deadline: February of each year.

2886 NICHOLAS DIERMANN MEMORIAL SCHOLARSHIP

Summary: To provide financial assistance to residents of Oregon who are interested in studying specified fields at colleges in any state.

See Listing #1474.

2887 NISSAN COMMUNITY COLLEGE TRANSFER SCHOLARSHIP PROGRAM OF THE HISPANIC SCHOLARSHIP FUND

Summary: To provide financial assistance to Hispanic American students who are attending a community college and interested in transferring to a 4-year institution in selected areas.

See Listing #2209.

2888 NMIA/NMIF SCHOLARSHIP PROGRAM

National Military Intelligence Association
Attn: Scholarship Committee
256 Morris Creek Road
Cullen, VA 23934
Phone: (434) 542-5929; Fax: (703) 738-7487
Email: admin@nmia.org
Web: www.nmia.org/about/scholarshipprogram.html

Summary: To provide financial assistance to undergraduate and graduate students majoring in a field of interest to the intelligence community.

Eligibility: Open to full- and part-time juniors, seniors, and graduate students who are preparing for a career in a field related to the intelligence community. Applicants must list special activities, internships, prior or current military service, or other activities that provide tangible evidence of career aspirations to serve as a member of the intelligence community. Along with their application, they must submit a 1,000-word essay that covers 1) their intelligence community career goals and objectives; 2) the relationship between courses completed, courses planned, extracurricular activities, and prior work experience (including military service) to identified career goals and objectives; and 3) how this scholarship will make a difference to their efforts to realize their career goals and aspirations. Selection is based primarily on past academic success; financial need is not considered.

Financial data: The stipend is $3,000 for full-time students or $2,000 for part-time students.

Duration: 1 year; nonrenewable.

Number awarded: 6 each year: 3 for full-time students and 3 for part-time students.

Deadline: November each year.

2889 NOLAN MOORE MEMORIAL EDUCATION FOUNDATION SCHOLARSHIP

Summary: To provide financial assistance to residents of designated states who are attending college to prepare for a career in the printing industry.

See Listing #1475.

2890 NORFOLK SOUTHERN SCHOLARS

Virginia Foundation for Independent Colleges
Attn: Director of Development
8010 Ridge Road, Suite B
Richmond, VA 23229-7288

Phone: (804) 288-6609; (800) 230-6757; Fax: (804) 282-4635
Email: info@vfic.org
Web: www.vfic.org/scholarship/scholarships_vfic.html

Summary: To provide financial assistance to students majoring in business-related fields at a college or university that is a member of the Virginia Foundation for Independent Colleges (VFIC).

Eligibility: Open to students who are enrolled full-time at 1 of the 15 VFIC member institutions. Applicants must be majoring in accounting, business administration, economics, or finance. Selection is based on merit and financial need. U.S. citizenship is required.

Financial data: The stipend is $5,000 per year.

Duration: 1 year. May be renewed up to 3 additional years if the recipient maintains a GPA of 3.0 or higher and a record of good citizenship and conduct.

Number awarded: 3 each year.

Deadline: October of each year.

2891 NORTH CAROLINA SHERIFFS' ASSOCIATION UNDERGRADUATE CRIMINAL JUSTICE SCHOLARSHIPS

North Carolina State Education Assistance Authority
Attn: Grants, Training, and Outreach Department
10 T.W. Alexander Drive
P.O. Box 13663
Research Triangle Park, NC 27709-3663
Phone: (919) 549-8614; (800) 700-1775; Fax: (919) 248-4687
Email: information@ncseaa.edu
Web: www.ncseaa.edu/Ncsheriffs.htm

Summary: To provide financial assistance to residents of North Carolina, especially children of deceased or disabled law enforcement officers, who are majoring in criminal justice at a college in the state.

Eligibility: Open to North Carolina residents enrolled full-time in a criminal justice program at any of the 10 state institutions offering that major: Appalachian State University, East Carolina University, Elizabeth City State University, Fayetteville State University, North Carolina Central University, North Carolina State University, the University of North Carolina at Charlotte, the University of North Carolina at Pembroke, the University of North Carolina at Wilmington, and Western Carolina University. First priority in selection is given to children of law enforcement officers killed in the line of duty; second priority is given to children of sheriffs or deputy sheriffs who are deceased, retired (regular or disability), or currently active in law enforcement in North Carolina; third priority is given to other resident criminal justice students meeting their institution's academic and financial need criteria.

Financial data: The stipend is $2,000 per year.

Duration: 1 year; nonrenewable.

Number awarded: Up to 10 each year: 1 at each of the participating universities.

Deadline: Deadline not specified.

2892 NORTH CAROLINA TEACHER ASSISTANT SCHOLARSHIP FUND

North Carolina State Education Assistance Authority
Attn: Teacher Assistant Scholarship Fund
P.O. Box 13663
Research Triangle Park, NC 27709-3663
Phone: (919) 549-8614; (800) 700-1775; Fax: (919) 248-4687
Email: ralbritton@ncseaa.edu
Web: www.ncseaa.edu/TASF.htm

Summary: To provide financial assistance to public school teacher assistants in North Carolina who are interested in working on a college degree to become a teacher.

Eligibility: Open to teacher assistants employed full-time in North Carolina public schools. Applicants must be enrolled in at least 6 semester hours pursuing teacher licensure at an accredited 2- or 4-year college in North Carolina with a teacher education program. They must have a GPA of 3.0 or higher and remain employed as a teacher assistant while attending college part-time.

Financial data: Students at 4-year institutions receive $1,200 per term, up to an annual maximum of $3,600. Students at 2-year institutions receive $600 per term, up to an annual maximum of $1,800. The maximum amount that a student can receive over time through this program is $25,200.

Duration: 1 year; may be renewed if the recipient completes at least 12 semester hours with a GPA of 3.0 or higher.

Number awarded: Varies each year; recently, a total of 470 students were receiving $1,222,910 in support through this program.

Deadline: April of each year.

2893 NORTH CAROLINA TEACHING FELLOWS SCHOLARSHIP PROGRAM

North Carolina Teaching Fellows Commission
Koger Center, Cumberland Building
3739 National Drive, Suite 100
Raleigh, NC 27612
Phone: (919) 781-6833; Fax: (919) 781-6527
Email: tfellows@ncforum.org
Web: www.teachingfellows.org

Summary: To provide financial assistance to high school seniors in North Carolina who wish to prepare for a career in teaching.

Eligibility: Open to seniors at high schools in North Carolina who are interested in preparing for a career as a teacher and have been accepted for enrollment at a participating school in the state. Applicants must demonstrate superior achievement on the basis of high school grades, class standing, SAT scores, writing samples, community service, extracurricular activities, and references from teachers and members of the community. U.S. citizenship is required. A particular goal of the program is to recruit and retain greater numbers of male and minority teacher education candidates in North Carolina. Financial need is not considered in the selection process.

Financial data: The maximum stipend is $6,500 per year. This is a scholarship/loan program; recipients must teach in a North Carolina public school 1 year for each year of support received. If they cannot fulfill the service requirement, they must repay the loan with 10% interest.

Duration: 1 year; renewable for up to 3 additional years if the recipient maintains full-time enrollment and a GPA of 2.25 or higher for the freshman year and 2.50 or higher in the sophomore year.

Number awarded: Up to 500 each year. Approximately 20% of the program's recipients are minority and 30% are male.

Deadline: October of each year.

2894 NORTHWEST WOMEN IN EDUCATIONAL ADMINISTRATION SCHOLARSHIP

Confederation of Oregon School Administrators
Attn: Youth Development Program
707 13th Street, S.E., Suite 100
Salem, OR 97301-4035
Phone: (503) 581-3141; Fax: (503) 581-9840
Web: www.cosa.k12.or.us

Summary: To provide financial assistance to women who are high school seniors in Oregon and interested in preparing for a teaching career at a community college, college, or university in the state.

Eligibility: Open to women who are graduating from high schools in Oregon. Applicants must be interested in attending a community college, college, or university in the state to major in education. They must have been active in community and school affairs, have a GPA of 3.5 or higher, and be able to enroll in the fall term after graduating from high school. Along with their application, they must submit a 1-page autobiography (that includes their personal goals), the name of the school they plan to attend, and the endorsement of a member of the Confederation of Oregon School Administrators (COSA). Financial need is not considered in the selection process.

Financial data: The stipend is $1,000. Funds are paid directly to the recipient.

Duration: 1 year; nonrenewable.

Number awarded: 2 each year.

Deadline: February of each year.

2895 NRA CIVIL RIGHTS DEFENSE FUND YOUTH ESSAY CONTEST

National Rifle Association of America
Attn: NRA Civil Rights Defense Fund
11250 Waples Road
Fairfax, VA 22030-9400
Phone: (703) 267-1250; Fax: (703) 267-3985
Email: nracrdf@nrahq.org
Web: www.nradefensefund.org/writingcontest.aspx

Summary: To recognize and reward outstanding papers written by elementary and secondary school students on the constitutional right to keep and bear arms.

Eligibility: Open to students in elementary, junior high, and high school. Students must submit an essay, about 1,000 words in length, on "The Second Amendment to the Constitution: Why It Is Important to Our Nation." Essays are judged in 2 categories: senior, for grades 10 through 12, and junior, for grades 9 and below. Selection is based on originality, scholarship, and presentation.

Financial data: In each division, first prize is $1,000, second $600, third $200, and honorable mention $100. All prizes are in the form of U.S. savings bonds.
Duration: The program is held annually.
Number awarded: 8 each year: 4 in each of the 2 grade-level categories.
Deadline: November of each year.

2896 NRAEF/MFHA DIVERSITY SCHOLARSHIPS

National Restaurant Association Educational Foundation
Attn: Scholarships Program
175 West Jackson Boulevard, Suite 1500
Chicago, IL 60604-2702
Phone: (312) 715-1010, ext. 738; (800) 765-2122, ext. 6738; Fax: (312) 566-9733
Email: scholars@nraef.org
Web: www.nraef.org/scholarships

Summary: To provide financial assistance to minority undergraduate students who are interested in preparing for a career in the hospitality industry.
Eligibility: Open to Hispanic, African American, Asian American, and Native American students preparing for a career in the restaurant and food service industry. Applicants must be U.S. citizens or permanent residents who have completed at least 1 term of their college program. They must be enrolled full-time or substantial part-time and have a GPA of 2.75 or higher or a GED score of 470 or higher. Along with their application, they must submit 1) an essay of 200 to 250 words that provides a description of their current educational and work experience and their goals in the industry; and 2) an essay of 300 to 400 words on what diversity and inclusion mean to them, why they are important for a successful business, and how they plan to give back to the industry or community once they have reached their career goals. Selection is based on the essay, presentation of the application, GPA or GED scores, industry-related experience, and strength of letters of recommendation.
Financial data: The stipend is $2,500.
Duration: 1 year.
Number awarded: 5 each year.
Deadline: March of each year.

2897 NSA ANNUAL SCHOLARSHIP AWARDS

National Society of Accountants
Attn: NSA Scholarship Foundation
1010 North Fairfax Street
Alexandria, VA 22314-1574
Phone: (703) 549-6400, ext. 1312; (800) 966-6679, ext. 1312; Fax: (703) 549-2984
Email: gsesse@nsacct.org
Web: www.nsacct.org/foundation.asp

Summary: To provide financial assistance to undergraduate students majoring in accounting.
Eligibility: Open to undergraduate students enrolled full-time in an accounting degree program at an accredited 2- or 4-year college or university with a GPA of 3.0 or better. Students in 2-year colleges may apply during their first year or during their second year if transferring to a 4-year institution, provided they have committed themselves to a major in accounting throughout the remainder of their college career; students in 4-year colleges may apply for a scholarship for their second, third, or fourth year of studies, provided they have committed themselves to a major in accounting through the remainder of their college career. Only U.S. or Canadian citizens attending a U.S. accredited business school, college, or university may apply. Selection is based on academic attainment, demonstrated leadership ability, and financial need.
Financial data: The stipend is approximately $500 per year for students entering their second year of studies or approximately $1,000 per year for students entering their third or fourth year.
Duration: 1 year.
Number awarded: Approximately 32 each year.
Deadline: March of each year.

2898 NUTMEG STATEWIDE PTA SCHOLARSHIP

Connecticut PTA
60 Connolly Parkway, Building 12, Suite 103
Hamden, CT 06514
Phone: (203) 281-6617; Fax: (203) 281-6749
Email: connecticutpta@snet.net
Web: www.ctpta.org/NSPTA-History/NSPTA-Scholarship.html

Summary: To provide financial assistance to seniors at high schools in Connecticut with a PTA unit who are planning to attend college in any state to prepare for a career working with children.
Eligibility: Open to seniors graduating from Connecticut high schools that have a PTA unit in good standing. Applicants must be planning to attend a 4-year college or university in any state to prepare for a career in service to children. Along with their application, they must submit a 1-page essay on how they expect to be serving children 10 years after college graduation. Selection is based on the essay (5 points), class rank (3 points), and school and community involvement (2 points). Each school may submit only 1 application.
Financial data: The stipend is $2,000.
Duration: 1 year.
Number awarded: 1 each year.
Deadline: February of each year.

2899 OELMA SCHOLARSHIP

Ohio Educational Library Media Association
17 South High Street, Suite 200
Columbus, OH 43215
Phone: (614) 221-1900; Fax: (614) 221-1989
Email: oelma@assnoffices.com
Web: www.oelma.org/awards.htm

Summary: To provide financial assistance to residents of Ohio who are preparing for a career as a school library media specialist.
Eligibility: Open to Ohio residents who are currently enrolled as a college junior, senior, or graduate student. Applicants must be interested in preparing for a career as a school library media specialist at the K–12 or higher education level. They must be able to demonstrate financial need. Membership in the Ohio Educational Library Media Association (OELMA) is preferred but not required.
Financial data: The stipend is $1,000.
Duration: 1 year.
Number awarded: 1 each year.
Deadline: April of each year.

2900 OFFICE DEPOT SCHOLARSHIP

Hispanic Association of Colleges and Universities
Attn: National Scholarship Program
8415 Datapoint Drive, Suite 400
San Antonio, TX 78229
Phone: (210) 692-3805; Fax: (210) 692-0823; TDD: (800) 855-2880
Email: scholarships@hacu.net
Web: www.hacu.net/hacu/Scholarships_EN.asp?SnID=875148054

Summary: To provide financial assistance to undergraduate students at member institutions of the Hispanic Association of Colleges and Universities (HACU) who are majoring in fields related to business.
Eligibility: Open to undergraduate students at HACU member and partner 4-year colleges and universities who have a declared major in business administration, information systems, international business, marketing, or merchandising. Applicants must have a GPA of 3.0 or higher and be able to demonstrate financial need. They must submit an essay of 200 to 250 words that describes their academic and/or career goals, where they expect to be and what they expect to be doing 10 years from now, and what skills they can bring to an employer.
Financial data: The stipend is $1,000.
Duration: 1 year.
Number awarded: 1 or more each year.
Deadline: May of each year.

2901 OHIO ASSOCIATION OF FAMILY AND CONSUMER SCIENCES SCHOLARSHIPS

Ohio Association of Family and Consumer Sciences
c/o Donna Green, Scholarship Chair
OSU Extension
2900 South Columbus Avenue
Sandusky, OH 44870
Email: green.308@osu.edu
Web: www.oafcs.org/students.html

Summary: To provide financial assistance to residents of Ohio who are working on an undergraduate or graduate degree in family and consumer sciences at a school in the state.
Eligibility: Open to residents of Ohio who are enrolled full-time as sophomores, juniors, seniors, or graduate students in a family and consumer science program at a college or university in the state. Fields of study include housing and furnishing, family economics, home management, family relations, child

development, food and nutrition, institutional administration, family and consumer sciences education, or apparel and textiles. Applicants must have a GPA of 3.0 or higher. Along with their application, they must submit a resume that includes their work experience, career plans, community service, school activities, future educational objectives, why they are interested in family and consumer science, and their current college financing plans.
Financial data: The stipend is $1,000; funds are paid directly to the college or university.
Duration: 1 year.
Number awarded: 3 each year.
Deadline: January of each year.

2902 OHIO BUSINESS TEACHERS ASSOCIATION SCHOLARSHIPS

Ohio Business Teachers Association
c/o Matthew White, President
ITT Technical Institute
3781 Park Mill Run Drive, Suite 1
Hilliard, OH 43026
Phone: (614) 771-4888; Fax: (614) 921-4179
Email: mcwhite@itt-tech.edu
Web: www.obta-ohio.org/scholarships.html
Summary: To provide financial assistance to upper-division and graduate students in Ohio who are interested in business education.
Eligibility: Open to juniors, seniors, and graduate students enrolled full-time at colleges and universities in Ohio. Applicants must be working on a degree in business education and have a GPA of 3.0 or higher. Along with their application, they must submit an essay of 300 to 500 words on why they are entering the business education field. Selection is based on that essay, skills related to business education, community activities, educational achievements, and work experience.
Financial data: The stipend is $1,000.
Duration: 1 year.
Number awarded: 1 each year.
Deadline: July of each year.

2903 OHIO CLASSICAL CONFERENCE SCHOLARSHIP FOR PROSPECTIVE LATIN TEACHERS

Ohio Classical Conference
c/o Kelly Kusch, Scholarship Committee
Covington Latin School
21 East 11th Street
Covington, KY 41011
Phone: (513) 227-6847
Email: Kelly.kusch@covingtonlatin.org
Web: www.xavier.edu/occ/occ-scholarships.cfm
Summary: To provide financial assistance to Ohio residents preparing for a career as a Latin teacher.
Eligibility: Open to college students at least at the sophomore level who are either residents of Ohio enrolled at a college or university in any state or residents of other states enrolled at a college or university in Ohio. Applicants must be taking courses leading to a career in the teaching of Latin at the K–12 level in a public, private, or parochial school. They must submit college transcripts, 2 letters of recommendation (including 1 from a member of their classics department), a prospectus of courses completed and to be taken as part of the program, and a 1-page statement of their academic goals and reasons for applying for the scholarship. Nontraditional students (e.g., those returning to college for teacher training or a second career) are not eligible.
Financial data: The stipend is $1,500.
Duration: 1 year; nonrenewable.
Number awarded: 1 each year.
Deadline: March of each year.

2904 OKLAHOMA COUNCIL OF PUBLIC AFFAIRS CITIZENSHIP ESSAY CONTEST

Oklahoma Council of Public Affairs
1401 North Lincoln Boulevard
Oklahoma City, OK 73104
Phone: (405) 602-1667; Fax: (405) 602-1238
Email: ocpa@ocpathink.org
Web: www.ocpathink.org/events/essay-contest
Summary: To recognize and reward, with college scholarships, high school seniors in Oklahoma who submit essays on topics related to public affairs.
Eligibility: Open to seniors graduating from public, private, or home-school high schools in Oklahoma. Applicants must submit an essay, from 1,000 to 1,250 words in length, on a topic that changes annually but relates to public affairs and politics. Recently, students were invited to write on the 3 issues they would consider high priority if they were to become President of the United States.
Financial data: Prizes are $5,000 for first place, $2,500 for second, $2,000 for third, $1,500 for fourth, and $1,000 for fifth. Funds must be used for payment of tuition at a college or university in any state.
Duration: The competition is held annually.
Number awarded: 5 each year.
Deadline: February of each year.

2905 OKLAHOMA FUTURE TEACHERS SCHOLARSHIP PROGRAM

Oklahoma State Regents for Higher Education
Attn: Director of Scholarship and Grant Programs
655 Research Parkway, Suite 200
P.O. Box 108850
Oklahoma City, OK 73101-8850
Phone: (405) 225-9239; (800) 858-1840; Fax: (405) 225-9230
Email: studentinfo@osrhe.edu
Web: www.okhighered.org
Summary: To provide financial assistance to Oklahoma residents who are interested in teaching in designated shortage fields in the state.
Eligibility: Open to high school seniors, high school graduates, or currently-enrolled undergraduate or graduate students who are nominated by their institution. They must 1) rank in the top 15% of their high school graduating class; 2) have an ACT or SAT score ranking in the top 15% for high school graduates of the same year; 3) have been admitted into a professional education program at an accredited Oklahoma institution of higher education; or 4) have achieved an undergraduate record of outstanding success as defined by the institution. Both part-time and full-time students are eligible, but preference is given to full-time students. Applicants must be interested in teaching in critical shortage areas in the state upon graduation. These areas change periodically but recently have included mathematics, science, English, foreign language, early childhood education, counselor, library media specialist, and speech language pathologist.
Financial data: Full-time students receive up to $1,500 per year if they have completed 60 hours or more or up to $1,000 if they have completed fewer than 60 hours; part-time students receive up to $750 per year if they have completed 60 hours or more or up to $500 per year if they have completed fewer than 60 hours. Funds are paid directly to the institution on the student's behalf. This is a forgivable loan program; recipients must agree to teach in Oklahoma public schools for 3 years following graduation and licensure.
Duration: 1 year; may be renewable for up to 3 additional years, provided the recipient maintains a GPA of 2.5 or higher.
Number awarded: Varies each year; recently, 136 students received support through this program.
Deadline: Each eligible institution establishes its own deadline.

2906 OKLAHOMA HERITAGE COUNTY SCHOLARSHIPS

Summary: To recognize and reward, with college scholarships, high school students in Oklahoma who achieve high scores on a test about the state's history and geography.
See Listing #1489.

2907 OMAHA VOLUNTEERS FOR HANDICAPPED CHILDREN SCHOLARSHIPS

Summary: To provide financial assistance to Nebraska residents who have a physical disability or are preparing for a career related to people with orthopedic impairments or physical disabilities and are interested in attending college in any state.
See Listing #2233.

2908 OREGON AFL-CIO SCHOLARSHIPS

Oregon Student Assistance Commission
Attn: Grants and Scholarships Division
1500 Valley River Drive, Suite 100
Eugene, OR 97401-2146
Phone: (541) 687-7395; (800) 452-8807, ext. 7395; Fax: (541) 687-7414; TDD: (800) 735-2900
Email: awardinfo@osac.state.or.us
Web: www.osac.state.or.us/osac_programs.html

Summary: To provide financial assistance for college to graduating high school seniors in Oregon who submit an essay on a labor-related topic.

Eligibility: Open to seniors graduating from high schools in Oregon who submit an essay of 500 words or less on either 1) their own experience as an employee and why it leads them to believe that workers do (or do not) need a union on the job; or 2) why many people who work full-time cannot provide a decent standard of living for their families and what they believe should be done about it. Selection is based on the essay, financial need, GPA, and an interview by a panel of individuals with expertise in labor history and labor affairs. Preference is given to applicants from union families.

Financial data: The stipends are $3,000, $1,200, $1,000, or $850.

Duration: 1 year; nonrenewable.

Number awarded: 4 each year.

Deadline: February of each year.

2909 OUTPUTLINKS WOMAN OF DISTINCTION AWARD

Summary: To provide financial assistance to female upper-division and graduate students interested in preparing for a career in document management and graphic communications.

See Listing #1496.

2910 PACIFIC TEACHER SCHOLARSHIP

Pacific Resources for Education and Learning
Attn: Pacific Teacher Scholarship
900 Fort Street Mall, Suite 1300
Honolulu, HI 96813-3718
Phone: (808) 441-1300; (800) 377-4773; Fax: (808) 441-1416
Email: scholarships@prel.org
Web: www.prel.org/opportunities/pacific-teacher-scholarship.aspx

Summary: To provide financial assistance to residents of the U.S.-affiliated Pacific Islands who are enrolled in a teacher preparation program and plan to teach at a school in the region following graduation.

Eligibility: Open to residents of American Samoa, the Commonwealth of the Northern Mariana Islands, the Federated States of Micronesia, Guam, the Republic of Palau, and the Republic of the Marshall Islands. Applicants must be enrolled in the second, third, or fourth year of an accredited teacher preparation program at a college or university in any state. They must have a GPA of 2.5 or higher and plans to teach in a school in the U.S.-affiliated Pacific following graduation. Along with their application, they must submit a personal statement that covers why they chose to be a teacher, their experience working in schools, where in the U.S.-affiliated Pacific they intend to work, the grade level and subject area in which they plan to concentrate, and relevant financial information.

Financial data: The stipend ranges from $750 to $1,000. Funds are disbursed directly to the recipient's college or university.

Duration: 1 year.

Number awarded: Varies each year; recently, 6 of these scholarships were awarded.

Deadline: March of each year.

2911 PAGEL GRAPHIC ARTS SCHOLARSHIPS

Summary: To provide financial assistance to students working on a degree in print communications at a school in Wisconsin.

See Listing #1499.

2912 PATRICIA SONNTAG MEMORIAL SCHOLARSHIP

California Association for Postsecondary Education and Disability
Attn: Executive Assistant
71423 Biskra Road
Rancho Mirage, CA 92270
Phone: (760) 346-8206; Fax: (760) 340-5275; TDD: (760) 341-4084
Email: caped2000@aol.com
Web: www.caped.net/scholarships.html

Summary: To provide financial assistance to students enrolled at 4-year college and universities in California who have a disability and are involved in activities or classes related to providing services to people with disabilities.

Eligibility: Open to students at 4-year colleges and universities in California who have a disability. Applicants must have completed at least 6 semester credits with a GPA of 2.5 or higher. They must be majoring in a field related to policy formulation or service delivery to students with disabilities or be actively engaged in advocacy or leadership in campus, community, or governmental organizations that benefit individuals with disabilities, regardless of their major. Along with their application, they must submit a 1-page personal letter that demonstrates their writing skills, progress towards meeting their educational and vocational goals, management of their disability, and involvement in community activities. They must also submit a letter of recommendation from a faculty member, verification of disability, official transcripts, proof of current enrollment, and documentation of financial need.

Financial data: The stipend is $1,000.

Duration: 1 year.

Number awarded: 1 each year.

Deadline: September of each year.

2913 PATRIOT EDUCATION SCHOLARSHIP

Maine Community Foundation
Attn: Program Director
245 Main Street
Ellsworth, ME 04605
Phone: (207) 667-9735; (877) 700-6800; Fax: (207) 667-0447
Email: info@mainecf.org
Web: www.mainecf.org/statewidescholars.aspx

Summary: To provide financial assistance to residents of Maine who are working on an undergraduate degree in business at a school in the state.

Eligibility: Open to graduates of high schools in Maine who are currently enrolled full-time at a college or university in the state. Applicants must be working on a degree in business. Preference is given to students who have a demonstrated interest in personal and commercial insurance professions.

Financial data: A stipend is awarded (amount not specified).

Duration: 1 year.

Number awarded: 1 or more each year.

Deadline: May of each year.

2914 PAUL CRAWFORD SCHOLARSHIP

American Planning Association–California Chapter
Attn: California Planning Foundation
c/o Paul Wack
P.O. Box 1086
Morro Bay, CA 93443-1086
Phone: (805) 756-6331; Fax: (805) 756-1340
Email: pwack@calpoly.edu
Web: www.californiaplanningfoundation.org/scholarships.html

Summary: To provide financial assistance to undergraduate and graduate students in accredited planning programs at California universities.

Eligibility: Open to students entering their final year for an undergraduate or master's degree in an accredited planning program at a university in California. Applicants must be interested in preparing for a career in public planning in California. Selection is based on academic excellence, financial need, and commitment to serve the planning profession in California.

Financial data: The stipend is $2,000. A 1-year student membership in the American Planning Association is also provided.

Duration: 1 year.

Number awarded: 1 each year.

Deadline: March of each year.

2915 PEGGY VATTER MEMORIAL SCHOLARSHIPS

Summary: To provide financial assistance to upper-division students and teachers in Washington interested in training in science education.

See Listing #2248.

2916 PENNSYLVANIA AFL-CIO SCHOLARSHIP ESSAY CONTEST

Pennsylvania AFL-CIO
Attn: Director of Education

319 Market Street, Third Floor
Harrisburg, PA 17101-2207
Phone: (717) 231-2843; (800) 242-3770; Fax: (717) 238-8541
Web: www.paaflcio.org

Summary: To recognize and reward high school and college students in Pennsylvania who submit outstanding essays on a labor topic.

Eligibility: Open to 1) graduating seniors at high schools in Pennsylvania; 2) students currently enrolled in accredited postsecondary school programs in the state; and 3) affiliated union members attending an accredited institution. Applicants must submit essays on topics that change annually but relate to labor unions. Recently, high school seniors were to write on why we should vote as union members, as workers, and as a community. College students were to write on the health care crisis in the United States. Union members were to write on what a true Voice@Work means to them. In each competition, all essays must be 1,500 words in length and include 3 references, of which at least 1 must be a labor organization.

Financial data: In each category, first prize is $2,000, second $1,000, and third $500.

Duration: The competition is held annually.

Number awarded: 9 each year: 3 in each of the 3 categories.

Deadline: January of each year.

2917 PENNSYLVANIA AMERICAN LEGION HIGH SCHOOL ESSAY CONTEST

American Legion
Department of Pennsylvania
Attn: Scholarship Secretary
P.O. Box 2324
Harrisburg, PA 17105-2324
Phone: (717) 730-9100; Fax: (717) 975-2836
Email: hq@pa-legion.com
Web: www.pa-legion.com/programs/student-programs/essay

Summary: To recognize and reward high school students in Pennsylvania who submit outstanding essays on a patriotic topic.

Eligibility: Open to students who are currently enrolled in grades 9–12 in a Pennsylvania public, parochial, private, or home school. Applicants must submit an essay, from 500 to 1,000 words, on a topic that changes annually but relates to a patriotic theme; a recent topic was "Is the Stimulus Package Worthwhile?" Competitions are held at the level of local American Legion post, county, district, inter-district, sectional, and then state. Selection is based on proper English structure, accuracy, extent of information, and originality.

Financial data: At the state level, the first-place winner receives a $3,500 scholarship, second a $3,000 scholarship, and third a $2,500 scholarship. If winners choose not to attend college, prizes are $300 for first place, $200 for second, and $200 for third. Local posts, counties, districts, and sections also offer awards.

Duration: The competition is held annually.

Number awarded: 3 state winners are selected each year.

Deadline: Applications must be submitted to the local American Legion post by February of each year.

2918 PENNSYLVANIA BUSINESS EDUCATION ASSOCIATION SCHOLARSHIP AWARD

Pennsylvania Business Education Association
c/o Sharon Diggans, Scholarships and Awards
Neshaminy High School
2001 Old Lincoln Highway
Langhorne, PA 19047
Phone: (215) 809-6677
Email: sdiggans@neshaminy.k12.pa.us
Web: www.pbea.info/winners.html

Summary: To provide financial assistance to undergraduate and graduate students from any state working on a business teacher education degree or certificate in Pennsylvania.

Eligibility: Open to residents of any state enrolled in undergraduate, master's, or teacher certification programs at a business teacher education program in Pennsylvania. Applicants must have completed at least 90 semester hours and have a GPA of 3.0 or higher. Along with their application, they must submit 3 letters of recommendation and a 1-page formal business letter that includes a statement of intent to enter business education and at least 2 reasons for preparing for a career in teaching. Financial need is not considered in the selection process.

Financial data: The stipend is $1,000.

Duration: 1 year.

Number awarded: 1 each year.

Deadline: April of each year.

2919 PERSIAN SCHOLARSHIP FOUNDATION UNDERGRADUATE RECOGNITION AWARD

Summary: To recognize and reward, with scholarships for additional study, undergraduates who submit outstanding essays on the contributions of Iran and Iranians to society and history.

See Listing #1507.

2920 PETER K. NEW STUDENT PRIZE COMPETITION

Summary: To recognize and reward the best student research papers in applied social, health, or behavioral sciences.

See Listing #2253.

2921 PETER W. JASIN SCHOLARSHIPS

Association for Intelligence Officers
Attn: Scholarships Committee
6723 Whittier Avenue, Suite 303A
McLean, VA 22101-4533
Phone: (703) 790-0320; Fax: (703) 991-1278
Email: afio@afio.com
Web: www.afio.com/13_scholarships.htm

Summary: To provide financial assistance to undergraduate and graduate students who are preparing for a career in the U.S. intelligence community.

Eligibility: Open to undergraduates who are entering their sophomore or junior year and graduate students who apply in their senior undergraduate year or first graduate year. Applicants must be able to demonstrate a goal of serving in the U.S. intelligence community following graduation. They must be working on a degree in counterterrorism, homeland security, intelligence, counterintelligence, or other intelligence-related discipline. Along with their application, they must submit a cover letter that explains their need for assistance, their career goals and dreams, and their views of U.S. world standing and its intelligence community. Selection is based on merit, character, estimated future potential, background, and relevance of their studies to the full spectrum of national security interests and career ambitions. U.S. citizenship is required.

Financial data: The stipend is $4,000.

Duration: 1 year.

Number awarded: 6 each year.

Deadline: June of each year.

2922 POLITICAL BLOGGING SCHOLARSHIP

College Scholarships Foundation
5506 Red Robin Road
Raleigh, NC 27613
Phone: (919) 630-4895; (888) 501-9050
Email: info@collegescholarships.org
Web: www.collegescholarships.org

Summary: To recognize and reward, with college scholarships, students who maintain a political weblog.

Eligibility: Open to U.S. citizens currently enrolled full-time at a postsecondary institution in the United States. Applicants must be maintaining a political weblog that contains unique and interesting information about political issues, current events, opinions, etc. They must have a GPA of 3.0 or higher and identify themselves as Republican, Democratic, or other. Their blog will be posted online and the public will elect the winner.

Financial data: The prize is a $2,000 scholarship.

Duration: The prize is awarded annually.

Number awarded: 1 each year.

Deadline: February of each year.

2923 PRESIDENT OBAMA/HISPANIC SCHOLARSHIP FUND/ STEM TEACHER SCHOLARSHIP PROGRAM

Summary: To provide financial assistance to Hispanic college juniors who are majoring in a field of science, technology, engineering, or mathematics (STEM) with plans to become a teacher.

See Listing #2269.

2924 PREZELL R. ROBINSON SCHOLARS PROGRAM

North Carolina Department of Public Instruction
Attn: Educator Recruitment and Development
6330 Mail Service Center
Raleigh, NC 27699-6330
Phone: (919) 807-3371; Fax: (919) 807-3362
Email: scholars@dpi.state.nc.us
Web: www.ncpublicschools.org/recruitment/scholarships/robinson

Summary: To provide an incentive to high school students in "low-wealth" school systems of North Carolina to choose teaching as a career objective.

Eligibility: Open to students in grades 9–11 attending schools in "low-wealth" North Carolina school systems or systems documenting extreme difficulty in recruiting qualified teachers. Each participating local educational agency (LEA) is invited to nominate 1 candidate per year from the designated grade levels. Each nominee must have at least a 3.0 cumulative GPA, a desire to pursue teaching as a career objective, and a willingness to participate in programs designed to prepare them for college and a career in teaching. Robinson Scholars are eligible to receive a college scholarship if they 1) maintain a GPA of 3.0 or higher throughout their remaining high school years; 2) pursue a program of study throughout high school to prepare them for admission to an institution of higher education; 3) achieve a score of at least 900 on the SAT critical reading and mathematics tests; and 4) pursue a course of study for licensure to teach in the public schools of North Carolina.

Financial data: Each Robinson Scholar receives a scholarship to be used to pursue teacher licensure; the amount of the scholarship is the same as awarded to recipients of North Carolina's Prospective Teacher Scholarship Loan (currently up to $2,500 per year).

Duration: Up to 4 years (or the minimum number of years required to earn licensure based on the entry-level degree).

Number awarded: Varies each year; recently, 56 of these scholarships were awarded.

Deadline: June of each year.

2925 PRINCE KUHI'O HAWAIIAN CIVIC CLUB SCHOLARSHIP

Summary: To provide financial assistance for undergraduate or graduate studies (particularly in education, journalism, or Hawaiian studies) to persons of Hawaiian descent.

See Listing #1516.

2926 PRINCESS CRUISES & TOURS SCHOLARSHIP

Alaska Travel Industry Association
Attn: ATIA Education Foundation
2600 Cordova Street, Suite 201
Anchorage, AK 99503
Phone: (907) 929-2842; Fax: (907) 561-5727
Email: ATIA@alaskatia.org
Web: www.alaskatia.org/scholarship/default.asp

Summary: To provide financial assistance to Alaska residents interested in attending college in any state, preferably Alaska, to prepare for a career in tourism.

Eligibility: Open to residents of Alaska who are enrolled or planning to enroll full-time at a college or university in any state. Applicants must be interested in studying a field that will prepare them for a career in tourism. Along with their application, they must submit a 500-word essay that covers their career goals and objectives and how they plan to achieve those, why they want to be involved in the travel and visitor industry, and what they consider the major challenges facing the visitor industry today. Selection is based on GPA, demonstrated tourism initiative, and financial need; special consideration is given to applicants attending an educational institution in Alaska.

Financial data: The stipend is $1,000.

Duration: 1 year.

Number awarded: 1 each year.

Deadline: March of each year.

2927 PROFESSIONAL GOLF MANAGEMENT DIVERSITY SCHOLARSHIP

Professional Golfers' Association of America
Attn: PGA Foundation
100 Avenue of the Champions
Palm Beach Gardens, FL 33418
Phone: (888) 532-6661
Web: www.pgafoundation.com/sortpage.cfm?id=scholarships

Summary: To provide financial assistance to women and minorities interested in attending a designated college or university to prepare for a career as a golf professional.

Eligibility: Open to women and minorities interested in becoming a licensed PGA Professional. Applicants must be interested in attending 1 of 20 colleges and universities that offer the Professional Golf Management (PGM) curriculum sanctioned by the PGA.

Financial data: The stipend is $3,000 per year.

Duration: 1 year; may be renewed.

Number awarded: Varies each year; recently, 20 of these scholarships were awarded.

Deadline: Deadline not specified.

2928 PROFILES IN COURAGE ESSAY CONTEST

John F. Kennedy Library Foundation
Attn: Profile in Courage Essay Contest
Columbia Point
Boston, MA 02125-3313
Phone: (617) 514-1550; Fax: (617) 436-3395
Email: profiles@nara.gov
Web: www.jfklibrary.org

Summary: To recognize and reward high school authors of essays on public officials who have demonstrated political courage.

Eligibility: Open to 1) U.S. students in grades 9–12 attending public, private, parochial, or home schools; 2) U.S. students under 20 years of age enrolled in a high school correspondence course or GED program in any of the 50 states, the District of Columbia, or the U.S. territories; and 3) U.S. citizens attending schools overseas. Applicants must submit an essay, up to 1,000 words, that identifies an elected public official in the United States, either serving currently or since 1956, who is acting or has acted courageously to address a political issue at the local, state, national, or international level. Selection is based on overall originality of the topic and clear communication of ideas through language.

Financial data: The first-place winner receives $10,000 ($5,000 in cash and $5,000 in a John Hancock Freedom 529 College Savings Plan), the second-place winner receives $1,000, and the other finalists receive $500. The nominating teacher of the first-place winner receives $500 for school projects encouraging student leadership and civic engagement.

Duration: The awards are presented annually.

Number awarded: 7 each year: 1 first place, 1 second place, and 5 other finalists.

Deadline: January of each year.

2929 PROMISE TEACHER SCHOLARSHIP LOAN

Georgia Student Finance Commission
Attn: Scholarships and Grants Division
2082 East Exchange Place, Suite 200
Tucker, GA 30084-5305
Phone: (770) 724-9000; (800) 505-GSFC; Fax: (770) 724-9089
Email: gsfcinfo@gsfc.org
Web: www.gacollege411.org/default.aspx

Summary: To provide financial assistance to students in Georgia who are preparing for a career as a teacher.

Eligibility: Open to students entering their junior year in a teacher education program at an approved college or university in Georgia. Applicants must have a cumulative GPA of 3.0 or higher and be certified by the college of education teacher certification official at their institution. They do not need to be residents of Georgia but must be U.S. citizens or permanent residents.

Financial data: Full-time students may borrow up to a maximum of $3,000 per year and part-time students up to $1,500; loan funds may be used for tuition and fees, room and board, and any other part of the student's cost of attendance budget. Loans are forgiven at the rate of $1,500 for each year that the recipient teaches in a Georgia public school system at the preschool, elementary, middle, or secondary level. Otherwise, all money received must be repaid with interest at a rate up to 10%.

Duration: 1 year; may be renewed 1 additional year if the recipient maintains satisfactory academic progress (a continuing 3.0 GPA is not required).

Number awarded: 600 each year.

Deadline: Applications must be submitted on or before the last day of the academic term.

2930 PROSPECTIVE TEACHER SCHOLARSHIP LOAN PROGRAM

North Carolina State Education Assistance Authority
Attn: Grants, Training, and Outreach Department

10 Alexander Drive
P.O. Box 13663
Research Triangle Park, NC 27709-3663
Phone: (919) 549-8614; (800) 700-1775; Fax: (919) 248-4687
Email: information@ncseaa.edu
Web: www.ncseaa.edu/PTSL.htm

Summary: To provide financial assistance to undergraduate students in North Carolina preparing for a career as a public school teacher in the state.

Eligibility: Open to high school seniors and college students in North Carolina who are enrolled or planning to enroll full-time in a teacher preparation program at a college or university in the state. High school seniors must have an ACT score of 19 or higher or a combined mathematics and critical reading SAT score of 900 or higher. All applicants must have a GPA of 2.5 or higher. Selection is based on merit.

Financial data: The stipend is $4,000 per year for juniors and seniors or $2,500 per year for freshmen, sophomores, and students at community colleges. This is a loan for service program. Recipients are obligated to teach 1 year in a North Carolina public school for each year of assistance they receive. Service repayment must be completed within 7 years from graduation. If they fail to meet that service obligation, cash repayment must be completed within 10 years with interest at 10%.

Duration: 1 year; may be renewed up to 3 additional years.

Number awarded: Varies each year; recently, a total of 1,182 students were receiving $3,604,871 in support through this program.

Deadline: April of each year.

2931 PWC EXCEED SCHOLARSHIP PROGRAM

PricewaterhouseCoopers LLP
Attn: Campus Recruiting Manager
125 High Street
Boston, MA 02110
Phone: (617) 530-5349; Fax: (813) 741-8595
Email: ann.ulett@us.pwc.clom
Web: www.pwc.com/us/en/careers/pwctv/about-pwctv.jhtml

Summary: To provide financial assistance to underrepresented minority undergraduate students interested in preparing for a career in public accounting.

Eligibility: Open to African American, Native American, and Hispanic American students entering their sophomore or junior year of college. Applicants must have a GPA of 3.2 or higher, be able to demonstrate interpersonal skills and leadership ability, and intend to prepare for a career in accounting, management information systems, or computer science. Along with their application, they must submit a 300-word essay on how they have demonstrated the core values of PricewaterhouseCoopers (PwC) of achieving excellence, developing teamwork, and inspiring leadership in their academic and/or professional career.

Financial data: The stipend is $3,000.

Duration: 1 year; nonrenewable.

Number awarded: 60 each year.

Deadline: December of each year.

2932 R. GENE RICHTER SCHOLARSHIP

Institute for Supply Management
Attn: Senior Vice President
2055 East Centennial Circle
P.O. Box 22160
Tempe, AZ 85285-2160
Phone: (480) 752-6276, ext. 3029; (800) 888-6276, ext. 3029; Fax: (480) 752-7890
Email: jcavinato@ism.ws
Web: www.ism.ws/education/content.cfm?ItemNumber=18640

Summary: To provide financial support to college seniors working on a degree in supply management.

Eligibility: Open to undergraduates entering their senior year of a full-time program in supply management or a related field (e.g., supply chain management, purchasing, procurement). Applicants must be U.S. or Canadian citizens or possess a valid green card. Selection is based on academic achievement, leadership ability, ethical standards, and commitment to preparing for a career in the field of supply management.

Financial data: The stipend is $5,000.

Duration: 1 year.

Number awarded: 1 or more each year.

Deadline: February of each year.

2933 RACHEL RAY'S YUM-O! ORGANIZATION SCHOLARSHIPS

National Restaurant Association Educational Foundation
Attn: Scholarships Program
175 West Jackson Boulevard, Suite 1500
Chicago, IL 60604-2702
Phone: (312) 715-1010, ext. 738; (800) 765-2122, ext. 6738; Fax: (312) 566-9733
Email: scholars@nraef.org
Web: www.nraef.org/scholarships

Summary: To provide financial assistance to high school seniors and GED graduates who are interested in preparing for a career in the hospitality industry.

Eligibility: Open to graduating high school seniors, GED graduates enrolling in college for the first time, and high school graduates enrolling in college for the first time. Applicants must be planning to enroll either full-time or substantial part-time at an accredited culinary school, college, or university to major in culinary, restaurant management, or other food service–related field of study. They must be U.S. citizens or permanent residents. Along with their application, they must submit 1) an essay of 150 to 200 words on their career goals in the restaurant/food service industry; and 2) an essay of 450 to 500 words on the experience or person that most influenced them to select restaurant and food service as their career. Selection is based on the essays, presentation of the application, industry-related work experience, and letters of recommendation.

Financial data: The stipend is $2,500.

Duration: 1 year.

Number awarded: 1 or more each year.

Deadline: May of each year.

2934 RALEIGH-DURHAM CHAPTER NBMBAA UNDERGRADUATE SCHOLARSHIPS

National Black MBA Association-Raleigh–Durham Chapter
Attn: Scholarship Program
P.O. Box 13614
Research Triangle Park, NC 27709
Phone: (919) 990-2351
Email: rdumba@gmail.com
Web: www.rdumba.org/?page_id=25

Summary: To provide financial assistance to minority students who have ties to North Carolina and are working on an undergraduate degree in business.

Eligibility: Open to minority students who are enrolled full-time in a business or management bachelor's degree program at a college or university in any state. Applicants must have some ties to North Carolina, either through residence or college attendance there. Along with their application, they must submit a 2-page essay on a topic that changes annually but relates to African Americans and business. Selection is based on that essay, transcripts, a resume, and extracurricular activities.

Financial data: The stipend is $1,000.

Duration: 1 year.

Number awarded: 1 or more each year.

Deadline: October of each year.

2935 RAMA SCHOLARSHIP FOR THE AMERICAN DREAM

American Hotel & Lodging Educational Foundation
Attn: Manager of Foundation Programs
1201 New York Avenue, N.W., Suite 600
Washington, DC 20005-3931
Phone: (202) 289-3181; Fax: (202) 289-3199
Email: ahlef@ahlef.org
Web: www.ahlef.org/content.aspx?id=19820

Summary: To provide financial assistance to minority undergraduate and graduate students working on a degree in hotel management at designated schools.

Eligibility: Open to U.S. citizens and permanent residents enrolled as full-time undergraduate or graduate students with a GPA of 2.5 or higher. Applicants must be attending 1 of 13 designated hospitality management schools, which select the recipients. Preference is given to students of Asian-Indian descent and other minority groups and to JHM Hotel employees and their dependents.

Financial data: The stipend varies at each of the participating schools, but ranges from $1,000 to $3,000.

Duration: 1 year.

Number awarded: Varies each year; recently, 20 of these scholarships were awarded. Since the program was established, it has awarded more than $491,000 to 287 recipients.

Deadline: April of each year.

2936 REGION 8 LABOR ESSAY CONTEST

United Automobile, Aerospace and Agricultural Implement Workers of America
United Region 8 Community Action Program
Attn: Essay Contest
1005 North Point Boulevard, Suite 701
Baltimore, MD 21224-3402
Phone: (410) 284-1500
Web: www.uawregion8.net/region-news.htm

Summary: To recognize and reward outstanding essays written on labor-related topics by high school seniors.

Eligibility: Open to graduating high school seniors who plan to enroll full-time at an accredited college or university. Applicants must write an essay (up to 4 pages) on 1 of the following labor-related topics: a great labor leader of the past, history of a specific international union (e.g., United Auto Workers, Steel Workers), women's role in labor's past, labor history of a specific era, history of labor's role in education, or history of labor's role in politics.

Financial data: First place is $2,000, second $1,500, third $1,000, and fourth $500.

Duration: The competition is held annually.

Number awarded: 4 each year.

Deadline: March of each year.

2937 RICHARD A. BROWN MEMORIAL SCHOLARSHIPS FOR STUDENTS

Texas Computer Education Association
8134 Exchange Drive
P.O. Box 141759
Austin, TX 78714-1759
Phone: (512) 476-8500; (800) 282-8232; Fax: (512) 476-8574
Email: tceaoffice@tcea.org
Web: www.tcea.org

Summary: To provide financial assistance to undergraduate students in Texas who are interested in preparing for a career in education with an emphasis on technology.

Eligibility: Open to full-time students who have completed at least 24 hours at a college or university in Texas and have a GPA of 2.75 or higher. Applicants must be interested in preparing for a career in education. Along with their application, they must submit personal and family information, including a statement of financial need; 3 letters of recommendation; a college transcript; and a 1-page personal profile on their philosophy of the importance of technology in education and their goals in the field of education.

Financial data: The stipend is $1,000.

Duration: 1 year; nonrenewable.

Number awarded: Varies each year; recently, 3 of these scholarships were awarded.

Deadline: November of each year.

2938 RICHARD E. BANGERT BUSINESS AWARD

Independent Colleges of Washington
600 Stewart Street, Suite 600
Seattle, WA 98101
Phone: (206) 623-4494; Fax: (206) 625-9621
Email: info@icwashington.org
Web: www.icwashington.org/scholarships/index.html

Summary: To provide financial assistance to upper-division students from any state who are majoring in business at colleges and universities that are members of the Independent Colleges of Washington (ICW).

Eligibility: Open to residents of any state who are completing their sophomore or junior year and majoring in business or a business-related field at ICW-member colleges and universities. Applicants must be able to demonstrate financial need and an understanding of the role of a business leader in our society. Along with their application, they must submit a 1-page essay on how their education at this college will impact their career choice.

Financial data: The stipend is $1,000.

Duration: 1 year; nonrenewable.

Number awarded: 1 each year.

Deadline: March of each year.

2939 RICHARD G. MUNSELL/CPR SCHOLARSHIP-ACCREDITED

American Planning Association–California Chapter
Attn: California Planning Foundation
c/o Paul Wack
P.O. Box 1086
Morro Bay, CA 93443-1086
Phone: (805) 756-6331; Fax: (805) 756-1340
Email: pwack@calpoly.edu
Web: www.californiaplanningfoundation.org/scholarships.html

Summary: To provide financial assistance to undergraduate and graduate students in accredited planning programs at California universities.

Eligibility: Open to students entering their final year for an undergraduate or master's degree in an accredited planning program at a university in California. Applicants must be interested in preparing for a career in public planning in California. Selection is based on academic excellence, financial need, and commitment to serve the planning profession in California.

Financial data: The stipend is $2,000. A 1-year student membership in the American Planning Association is also provided.

Duration: 1 year.

Number awarded: 1 each year.

Deadline: March of each year.

2940 RITA LOWE COLLEGE SCHOLARSHIPS

Summary: To provide financial assistance to students from any state majoring in mathematics education at colleges and universities in Washington.

See Listing #2292.

2941 RITA LOWE HIGH SCHOOL SCHOLARSHIP

Summary: To provide financial assistance to high school seniors in Washington planning to major in mathematics education at a college or university in the state.

See Listing #2293.

2942 ROBERT NOYCE SCHOLARSHIPS OF PENNSYLVANIA

Summary: To provide financial assistance to upper-division students and professionals at institutions of the Pennsylvania State System of Higher Education (PASSHE) who are majoring in a discipline of science, technology, engineering, or mathematics (STEM) and planning to become a high school science and mathematics teacher in Pennsylvania.

See Listing #2297.

2943 ROBERT R. COLY PRIZE

Parapsychology Foundation, Inc.
Attn: Executive Director
P.O. Box 1562
New York, NY 10021-0043
Phone: (212) 628-1550; Fax: (212) 628-1559
Email: info@parapsychology.org
Web: www.parapsychology.org

Summary: To recognize and reward undergraduate or graduate students who submit outstanding papers on parapsychology.

Eligibility: Open to undergraduate and graduate students who submit an essay of 1,000 to 1,500 words on the topic, "The Challenge of Parapsychology." Applicants may be studying in any field, but they must have sufficient interest in the field of parapsychology to understand its complexities and to demonstrate a desire to help conceptualize its future. They may be attending school in any country, but the essay, application form, and letters of reference must be written in English.

Financial data: The award is $1,000.

Duration: 1 year.

Number awarded: 1 each year.

Deadline: October of each year.

2944 ROBERTA CAPPS SCHOLARSHIP

Summary: To provide financial assistance to high school seniors in Missouri who plan to attend college in any state to study American history or government.

See Listing #1541.

2945 ROLLIE HOPGOOD FUTURE TEACHERS HIGH SCHOOL SENIOR SCHOLARSHIPS

AFT Michigan
Attn: Scholarship Committee
2661 East Jefferson Avenue
Detroit, MI 48207
Phone: (313) 393-2200; (800) MFT-8868; Fax: (313) 393-2236
Web: aftmichigan.org/members/scholarships.html

Summary: To provide financial assistance to high school seniors in Michigan who are interested in attending college in any state to prepare for a career as a teacher.

Eligibility: Open to seniors graduating from high schools that are represented by AFT Michigan. Applicants must be planning to attend a college or university in any state to prepare for a career as a teacher. Along with their application, they must submit a 500-word essay on why they want to become a teacher, why they should be considered for this scholarship, and the correlation between education and politics. Selection is based on the essay, GPA, extracurricular activities, community-related activities, and financial need. Female and male applicants compete separately.

Financial data: The stipend is $1,000.

Duration: 1 year.

Number awarded: 2 each year: 1 female and 1 male.

Deadline: May of each year.

2946 ROSS N. AND PATRICIA PANGERE FOUNDATION SCHOLARSHIPS

American Council of the Blind
Attn: Coordinator, Scholarship Program
2200 Wilson Boulevard, Suite 650
Arlington, VA 22201
Phone: (202) 467-5081; (800) 424-8666; Fax: (703) 465-5085
Email: info@acb.org
Web: www.acb.org

Summary: To provide financial assistance to blind students working on an undergraduate or graduate degree in business.

Eligibility: Open to undergraduate and graduate students working on a degree in business. Applicants must submit verification of legal blindness in both eyes; SAT, ACT, GMAT, or similar scores; information on extracurricular activities (including membership in the American Council of the Blind); employment record; and an autobiographical sketch that includes their personal goals, strengths, weaknesses, hobbies, honors, achievements, and reasons for choice of field or courses of study. A cumulative GPA of 3.3 or higher is generally required. Financial need is not considered in the selection process.

Financial data: The stipend is $2,500. In addition, the winner receives a Kurzweil-1000 Reading System.

Duration: 1 year.

Number awarded: 2 each year.

Deadline: February of each year.

2947 ROWLING, DOLD & ASSOCIATES LLP SCHOLARSHIP

Educational Foundation for Women in Accounting
Attn: Foundation Administrator
136 South Keowee Street
Dayton, OH 45402
Phone: (937) 424-3391; Fax: (937) 222-5749
Email: info@efwa.org
Web: www.efwa.org/seattle.htm

Summary: To provide financial support to women, including minority women, who are working on an accounting degree.

Eligibility: Open to women who are enrolled full-time in an accounting degree program at an accredited college or university. Applicants must meet 1 of the following criteria: 1) returning to school as an undergraduate; 2) incoming, current, or reentry juniors or seniors; or 3) minority women. Selection is based on aptitude for accounting and business, commitment to the goal of working on a degree in accounting (including evidence of continued commitment after receiving this award), clear evidence that the candidate has established goals and a plan for achieving those goals (both personal and professional), financial need, and a demonstration of how the scholarship will affect her life.

Financial data: The stipend is $1,000.

Duration: 1 year.

Number awarded: 1 each year.

Deadline: April of each year.

2948 ROYCE R. WATTS SR. SCHOLARSHIP

Summary: To provide financial assistance to upper-division African American college students interested in health, civil rights, or administration.
See Listing #2307.

2949 RUDOLPH DILLMAN MEMORIAL SCHOLARSHIP

Summary: To provide financial assistance to legally blind undergraduate or graduate students studying in the field of rehabilitation and/or education of visually impaired and blind persons.
See Listing #2308.

2950 RURAL SCHOLARSHIP

Alaska Travel Industry Association
Attn: ATIA Education Foundation
2600 Cordova Street, Suite 201
Anchorage, AK 99503
Phone: (907) 929-2842; Fax: (907) 561-5727
Email: ATIA@alaskatia.org
Web: www.alaskatia.org/scholarship/default.asp

Summary: To provide financial assistance to Alaska residents, especially those who live in rural areas, and are interested in attending college in any state, preferably Alaska, to prepare for a career in tourism.

Eligibility: Open to residents of Alaska who are enrolled or planning to enroll full-time at a college or university in any state. Preference is given to students from rural Alaska, outside of the road network. Applicants must be interested in studying a field that will prepare them for a career in tourism. Along with their application, they must submit a 500-word essay that covers their career goals and objectives and how they plan to achieve those, why they want to be involved in the travel and visitor industry, and what they consider the major challenges facing the visitor industry today. Selection is based on GPA, demonstrated tourism initiative, and financial need; special consideration is given to applicants attending an educational institution in Alaska.

Financial data: The stipend is $2,500.

Duration: 1 year.

Number awarded: 1 each year.

Deadline: March of each year.

2951 RUSSELL A. COOKINGHAM SCHOLARSHIP

Summary: To provide financial assistance to New Jersey residents enrolled in college in any state and working on a degree in wildlife and fisheries or conservation education and communications.
See Listing #2309.

2952 RUTH LUTES BACHMANN SCHOLARSHIP

Summary: To provide financial assistance to Missouri residents interested in attending college to prepare for a career as a teacher or a nurse.
See Listing #2312.

2953 RUTH SEGAL SCHOLARSHIP

Outdoor Advertising Association of America, Inc.
Attn: Foundation for Outdoor Advertising Research and Education
1850 M Street, N.W., Suite 1040
Washington, DC 20036
Phone: (202) 833-5566; Fax: (202) 833-1522
Email: mlaible@oaaa.org
Web: www.oaaaa.org/foundation/scholarship.aspx

Summary: To provide financial assistance to undergraduate and graduate students who are part of an outdoor advertising industry family or interested in working on a degree in a field related to public affairs.

Eligibility: Open to graduating high school seniors, current undergraduates, and students entering or enrolled in a master's or doctoral program. Applicants must be able to demonstrate a relationship or connection to outdoor advertising; that may be a family member or family friend who has ties to the industry or only an interest in preparing for a career related to the field. They must be interested in working on a degree in government affairs, urban affairs, public affairs, political science, or other field involving the study of issues specifically related to outdoor advertising and public affairs. Along with their application, they must submit an essay of 1 to 2 pages on why they are applying for this scholarship, their career goals, their area of academic study, and/or what this scholarship would mean for them. High school seniors entering their first

year of undergraduate study must include a copy of SAT/ACT scores; students entering their first year of a graduate program must include GRE or other graduate school admission tests. Selection is based on academic performance, career goals, relationship or connection to outdoor advertising, and financial need.
Financial data: The stipend is $4,500.
Duration: 1 year.
Number awarded: 1 each year.
Deadline: June of each year.

2954 SAKAE TAKAHASHI SCHOLARSHIP

Club 100 Veterans
Attn: Scholarship Committee
520 Kamoku Street
Honolulu, HI 96826-5120
Phone: (808) 946-0272
Email: daisyy@hgea.net
Summary: To provide financial assistance to high school seniors and college students who major in business, political science, or law and exemplify the sponsor's motto of "For Continuing Service."
Eligibility: Open to high school seniors planning to attend an institution of higher learning and full-time undergraduate students at community colleges, vocational/trade schools, 4-year colleges, and universities. Applicants must have a GPA of 2.5 or higher and be able to demonstrate civic responsibility and community service. They must be majoring or planning to major in business, political science, or law. Along with their application, they must submit an essay on a topic that changes annually but relates to Asian Americans who served in the military. Selection is based on that essay and the applicant's promotion of the legacy of the 100th Infantry Battalion and its motto of "For Continuing Service." Financial need is not considered.
Financial data: The stipend is $1,000.
Duration: 1 year; nonrenewable.
Number awarded: 1 each year.
Deadline: April of each year.

2955 SARAH KLENKE MEMORIAL TEACHING SCHOLARSHIP

Sarah Klenke Memorial
c/o Aaron Klenke
3131 Glade Springs
Kingwood, TX 77339
Phone: (281) 358-7933
Email: aaron.klenke@gmail.com
Summary: To provide financial assistance to high school seniors and graduates who have participated in JROTC or a team sport and are interested in majoring in education in college.
Eligibility: Open to high school seniors and graduates or those who are already enrolled in college. Applicants must plan to major in education. They must have a GPA of 2.0 or higher and have participated in a team sport or JROTC. Along with their application, they must submit a handwritten essay on why they are interested in education as a major or career.
Financial data: The stipend is $1,000.
Duration: 1 year.
Number awarded: 1 or 2 each year.
Deadline: April of each year.

2956 S.C. INTERNATIONAL ACTUARIAL SCIENCE SCHOLARSHIPS

Summary: To provide financial assistance to college seniors majoring in actuarial science or mathematics.
See Listing #2316.

2957 SCHOLARS FOR EXCELLENCE IN CHILD CARE PROGRAM

Oklahoma State Regents for Higher Education
Attn: Director of Scholarship and Grant Programs
655 Research Parkway, Suite 200
P.O. Box 108850
Oklahoma City, OK 73101-8850
Phone: (405) 225-9397; (866) 343-3881; Fax: (405) 225-9230
Email: kmcwilliams@osrhe.edu
Web: www.okhighered.org/scholars
Summary: To provide financial assistance to child care professionals in Oklahoma who wish to obtain additional education at a community college or career technology center in the state.
Eligibility: Open to child care professionals in Oklahoma who 1) work in an approved child care facility with a minimum of 10% subsidy children; 2) work at least 30 hours per week earning $15.50 or less per hour as a teacher, family child care provider, or director; and 3) have been employed at least 3 months. Employees from federally-funded child care programs and from school-age programs are not eligible. Applicants must be interested in 1) taking courses at a community college in Oklahoma for a CDA credential, certificate of mastery, director's certificate of mastery, director's certificate of completion, or associate degree in child development or early childhood education; or 2) taking Pathway to CDA course work at a career technology center in the state.
Financial data: Awards provide payment of 80% of tuition and fees and 100% of books for required courses.
Duration: Until completion of the degree or certificate.
Number awarded: Varies each year.
Deadline: Deadline not specified.

2958 SCHOLARSHIP FOR DIVERSITY IN TEACHING

Mid-Atlantic Association for Employment in Education
c/o Kerri G. Gardi
Kutztown University
Director, Career Development Center
P.O. Box 730
Kutztown, PA 19530
Phone: (610) 683-4647
Email: gardi@kutztown.edu
Web: www.maeeonline.org/pages/scholarships_jump.aspx
Summary: To provide financial assistance to minority upper-division students at universities in the Mid-Atlantic region who are preparing for a career as a teacher.
Eligibility: Open to members of racial and ethnic minority groups who have completed between 48 and 90 credits at a college or university in Delaware, Maryland, New Jersey, New York, Pennsylvania, Virginia, Washington, D.C., or West Virginia. Applicants must be enrolled full-time majoring in a field to prepare for a career in teaching. Along with their application, they must submit a 1-page essay on why they have chosen to become a teacher and what they hope to accomplish as an educator. Selection is based on academic success, service to college and/or community, and potential to achieve excellence as a teacher. U.S. citizenship is required.
Financial data: The stipend is $1,000.
Duration: 1 year; nonrenewable.
Number awarded: 1 each year.
Deadline: November of each year.

2959 SCHOLARSHIPS IN MATHEMATICS EDUCATION

Summary: To provide financial assistance to undergraduate students in Illinois who are interested in preparing for a career as a mathematics teacher.
See Listing #2322.

2960 SCHWEIGER MEMORIAL SCHOLARSHIP FUND

Summary: To provide financial assistance to high school seniors and current college students interested in preparing for a career in construction or construction management.
See Listing #2324.

2961 SCIENCE TEACHER PREPARATION PROGRAM

Alabama Alliance for Science, Engineering, Mathematics, and Science Education
Attn: Project Director
University of Alabama at Birmingham
Campbell Hall, Room 401
1300 University Boulevard
Birmingham, AL 35294-1170
Phone: (205) 934-8762; Fax: (205) 934-1650
Email: LDale@uab.edu
Web: www.uab.edu/istp/alabama.html
Summary: To provide financial assistance to underrepresented minority students at designated institutions in Alabama who are interested in preparing for a career as a science teacher.

Eligibility: Open to members of underrepresented minority groups who have been unconditionally admitted to a participating Alabama college or university. Applicants must be interested in becoming certified to teach science and mathematics in K-12 schools. They may be 1) entering freshmen enrolling in a science education program leading to a bachelor's degree and certification; 2) students transferring from a community college and enrolling in a science education program leading to a bachelor's degree and certification; 3) students with a bachelor's degree in mathematics, science, or education and enrolling in a certification program; or 4) students with a bachelor's degree in mathematics, science, or education and enrolling in a fifth-year program leading to a master's degree and certification.
Financial data: The stipend is $1,000 per year.
Duration: 1 year; may be renewed.
Number awarded: Varies each year.
Deadline: Deadline not specified.

2962 SCUDDER ASSOCIATION EDUCATIONAL GRANTS

Summary: To assist undergraduate and graduate students preparing for selected "careers as servants of God in various forms of ministry to men and women around the world."
See Listing #1555.

2963 SEMA MEMORIAL SCHOLARSHIP FUND AWARDS

Summary: To provide financial assistance for college to students interested in preparing for a career in the automotive aftermarket.
See Listing #2333.

2964 SOCIETY OF AUTOMOTIVE ANALYSTS SCHOLARSHIP

Society of Automotive Analysts
Attn: Scholarships
3300 Washtenaw Avenue, Suite 220
Ann Arbor, MI 48104-4200
Phone: (734) 677-3518; Fax: (734) 677-2407
Email: cybersaa@cybersaa.org
Web: www.cybersaa.org/scholarship_info.html
Summary: To provide financial assistance to undergraduate students preparing for a career in an analytic field related to the automotive industry.
Eligibility: Open to full-time undergraduate students who are majoring in business, economics, finance, marketing, or management. Applicants must have at least a 3.0 GPA and demonstrate interest in automotive analysis. Along with their application, they must submit a 1-page essay explaining their interest in the automotive industry and their future career ambitions.
Financial data: The stipend is $1,500. Funds are paid to the recipient's school.
Duration: 1 year; nonrenewable.
Number awarded: 1 or more each year.
Deadline: May of each year.

2965 SOCIETY OF SPONSORS OF THE UNITED STATES NAVY CENTENNIAL SCHOLARSHIP

Navy-Marine Corps Relief Society
Attn: Education Division
875 North Randolph Street, Suite 225
Arlington, VA 22203-1757
Phone: (703) 696-4960; Fax: (703) 696-0144
Email: education@nmcrs.org
Web: www.nmcrs.org/education.html
Summary: To provide financial assistance to wounded Navy and Marine Corps veterans of Operation Iraqi Freedom (OIF) and Operation Enduring Freedom (OEF) who are interested in preparing to become a teacher.
Eligibility: Open to Navy and Marine Corps veterans who were injured in combat in Iraq or Afghanistan. Applicants must have at least an associate degree or equivalent and be enrolled full-time in an undergraduate program leading to a bachelor's degree and teacher licensure. They must have a GPA of 2.0 or higher. Financial need is considered in the selection process.
Financial data: The stipend is $3,000 per year.
Duration: 1 year; may be renewed 1 additional year.
Number awarded: 5 each year.
Deadline: Applications may be submitted at any time.

2966 SOUTH DAKOTA EXCELLENCE IN ACCOUNTING SCHOLARSHIPS

South Dakota CPA Society
Attn: Executive Director
1000 North West Avenue, Suite 100
P.O. Box 2080
Sioux Falls, SD 57101-2080
Phone: (605) 334-3848; Fax: (605) 334-8595
Email: lcoome@iw.net
Web: www.sdcpa.org/displaycommon.cfm?an=1&subarticlenbr=43
Summary: To provide financial assistance to college seniors and fifth-year students in South Dakota who are majoring in accounting.
Eligibility: Open to accounting majors in South Dakota who have completed at least 90 credit hours with a demonstrated excellence in academics, leadership potential, and an interest in the profession of public accountancy. Applicants must submit information on their extracurricular activities, civic activities, awards, job experience, and career goals and objectives. Financial need is not considered in the selection process.
Financial data: The stipend ranges from $500 to $1,000.
Duration: 1 year; recipients may reapply.
Number awarded: Varies each year; recently, 10 accounting students received $7,000 in these scholarships.
Deadline: November of each year.

2967 SOUTHWEST CHAPTER ACADEMIC SCHOLARSHIPS

Summary: To provide financial assistance to residents of any state working on an undergraduate or graduate degree in airport management at a college or university in the Southwest.
See Listing #2353.

2968 SPENCE REESE SCHOLARSHIPS

Summary: To provide financial assistance to graduating male high school seniors who plan to study designated fields in college.
See Listing #2354.

2969 SPIRIT OF SOVEREIGNTY FOUNDATION TRIBAL SCHOLARS PROGRAM

Summary: To provide financial assistance to Native American students enrolled at a Tribal College or University (TCU), especially those majoring in designated fields.
See Listing #2355.

2970 SPIROL SCHOLARSHIPS

Summary: To provide financial assistance to high school seniors in California, Connecticut, Ohio, and Vermont who plan to major in designated fields at a college in any state.
See Listing #2356.

2971 STAN AND LEONE POLLARD SCHOLARSHIPS

Tourism Cares
Attn: American Society of Travel Agents Scholarship Fund
275 Turnpike Street, Suite 307
Canton, MA 02021
Phone: (781) 821-5990; Fax: (781) 821-8949
Email: info@tourismcares.org
Web: www.tourismcares.org/scholarships/asta-scholarships
Summary: To provide financial assistance to individuals attempting to reenter the job market by enrolling in a travel and tourism program at a junior college or travel school.
Eligibility: Open to students who are registered at a recognized proprietary travel school or 2-year junior college that specializes in travel or tourism studies. Applicants must be reentering the job market, have been out of high school for at least 5 years, have a GPA of 2.5 or higher, and write a 500-word essay on their objectives in the travel and tourism industry.
Financial data: The stipend is $2,000. A copy of the tuition bill is required.
Duration: 1 year.
Number awarded: 2 each year.
Deadline: June of each year.

2972 STANLEY LESSOFF MEMORIAL SCHOLARSHIP

Connecticut Business Educators Association
c/o Lisa Ann Fioravanti
Lincoln College of New England
2279 Mount Vernon Road
Southington, CT 06489
Phone: (860) 628-4751; (800) 825-0087
Email: lfioravanti@lincolncollegene.edu
Web: www.cbea.biz/scholarships.html

Summary: To provide financial assistance to high school seniors in Connecticut who plan to major in accounting at a college in any state.

Eligibility: Open to seniors graduating from high schools in Connecticut who have taken at least 1 credit in accounting and at least 1 additional credit in a business-related course. Applicants must be planning to major in accounting at a college or university in any state. They must have at least a "B" grade average. Along with their application, they must submit a letter of recommendation from a member of the Connecticut Business Educators Association (CBEA) and a transcript. Financial need is not considered in the selection process.

Financial data: A stipend is awarded (amount not specified).

Duration: 1 year.

Number awarded: 1 each year.

Deadline: April of each year.

2973 STANLEY MCFARLAND SCHOLARSHIP

National Association of Federal Education Program Administrators
c/o Rick Carder, President
125 David Drive
Sutter Creek, CA 95685
Phone: (916) 669-5102; Fax: (888) 487-6441
Email: rickc@sia-us.com
Web: www.nafepa.org

Summary: To provide financial assistance to high school seniors and college freshmen who are interested in working on a degree in education.

Eligibility: Open to graduating high school seniors and graduates already enrolled in the first year of college. Applicants must be working on or planning to work on a degree in education. They must be nominated by their state affiliate of the sponsoring organization. Along with their application, they must submit a 300-word personal narrative explaining why they are applying for this scholarship, including their awards, interests, leadership activities within the community, and future goals. Selection is based on that essay (20 points), a high school or college transcript from the current semester (20 points), extracurricular and leadership activities within the community or church (20 points), 3 letters of recommendation (20 points), and financial need (20 points).

Financial data: The stipend is $2,500.

Duration: 1 year.

Number awarded: 1 each year.

Deadline: Each state affiliate sets its own deadline; for a list of those, contact the sponsor.

2974 STEVE DEARDUFF SCHOLARSHIP

Summary: To provide financial assistance to Georgia residents who are working on an undergraduate or graduate degree in medicine or social work at a school in any state.

See Listing #2364.

2975 STOKES EDUCATIONAL SCHOLARSHIP PROGRAM

Summary: To provide minority and other high school seniors and college sophomores with financial assistance and work experience at the National Security Agency (NSA).

See Listing #1570.

2976 STUDENT OPPORTUNITY SCHOLARSHIPS FOR ETHNIC MINORITY GROUPS

Summary: To provide financial assistance to upper-division college students who are Presbyterians, especially those of racial/ethnic minority heritage, majoring in designated fields.

See Listing #1573.

2977 SURETY INDUSTRY SCHOLARSHIP PROGRAM

The Surety Foundation
Attn: Scholarship Program for Minority Students
1101 Connecticut Avenue, N.W., Suite 800
Washington, DC 20036
Phone: (202) 778-3638; Fax: (202) 463-0606
Email: scarradine@surety.org
Web: www.thesuretyfoundation.org/scholarshipprogram.html

Summary: To provide financial assistance to minority undergraduates working on a degree in a field related to insurance.

Eligibility: Open to full-time undergraduates who are U.S. citizens and members of a minority group (Black, Native American/Alaskan Native, Asian/Pacific Islander, Hispanic). Applicants must have completed at least 30 semester hours of study at an accredited 4-year college or university and have a declared major in insurance/risk management, accounting, business, or finance. They must have a GPA of 3.0 or higher and be able to demonstrate financial need. Along with their application, they must submit an essay of 500 to 1,000 words on the role of surety bonding and the surety industry in public sector construction.

Financial data: The stipend is $2,500 per year.

Duration: 1 year; recipients may reapply.

Number awarded: Varies each year.

Deadline: April of each year.

2978 TAER PROFESSIONAL PREPARATION SCHOLARSHIP

Texas Association for Education and Rehabilitation of the Blind and Visually Impaired
c/o Olivia Chavez
Education Service Center-Region 19
6611 Boeing Drive
El Paso, TX 79925
Phone: (915) 780-5344; Fax: (915) 780-6537
Email: ochavez@esc19.net
Web: www.txaer.org/Scholarships_Awards/scholaraward.htm

Summary: To provide financial assistance to residents of Texas who are interested in attending college in any state to prepare for a career in rehabilitation or education of people with visual impairments.

Eligibility: Open to residents of Texas who are attending or planning to attend a college or university in any state. Applicants must be interested in studying a field related to rehabilitation or education of people with visual impairments. They must be able to demonstrate financial need. Along with their application, they must submit a letter regarding the goal of their education.

Financial data: The stipend is $1,000.

Duration: 1 year.

Number awarded: 1 or more each year.

Deadline: February.

2979 TAG AND LABEL MANUFACTURERS INSTITUTE SCHOLARSHIP GRANTS

Summary: To provide financial assistance and work experience to third- and fourth-year college students who are preparing for a career in the tag and label manufacturing industry.

See Listing #1576.

2980 TCADVANCE SCHOLARSHIP FOR TURKISH AMERICAN STUDENTS

Summary: To provide financial assistance to Turkish-Americans entering or continuing an undergraduate or graduate program in fields related to public affairs.

See Listing #1577.

2981 TEACHER EDUCATION ASSISTANCE FOR COLLEGE AND HIGHER EDUCATION (TEACH) GRANTS

Department of Education
Attn: Federal Student Aid Information Center
P.O. Box 84
Washington, DC 20044-0084
Phone: (319) 337-5665; (800) 4-FED-AID; TDD: (800) 730-8913
Web: www.FederalStudentAid.ed.gov

Summary: To provide financial assistance to undergraduate and graduate students interested in completing a degree in education and teaching in a high-need field at a school that serves low-income students.

Eligibility: Open to U.S. citizens and eligible noncitizens who are enrolled as an undergraduate, post-baccalaureate, or graduate student at a postsecondary educational institution that has chosen to participate in this program. Applicants must be enrolled in course work that will prepare them for a career in teaching. They must meet certain academic achievement requirements (scoring above the 75th percentile on a college admissions test or maintaining a cumulative GPA of 3.25 or higher). The program requires that they sign an agreement to provide service as a teacher in 1) designated high-need fields, currently defined as bilingual education and English language acquisition, foreign language, mathematics, reading specialist, science, or special education; and 2) at a school serving low-income students at the elementary or secondary level.

Financial data: The grant is $4,000 per year. This is a scholarship/loan program; recipients must teach a high-need field at a school serving low-income students for at least 4 academic years per year of grant support they receive. If they fail to complete the service obligation, the grant is converted to a Federal Direct Unsubsidized Stafford Loan and must be repaid with interest from the date the grant was disbursed.

Duration: Up to 2 years.

Number awarded: Varies each year.

Deadline: Deadline not specified.

2982 TELACU TEACHING AWARD

TELACU Education Foundation
Attn: Scholarship Program
5400 East Olympic Boulevard, Suite 300
Los Angeles, CA 90022
Phone: (323) 721-1655; Fax: (323) 724-3372
Email: info@telacu.com
Web: telacu.com/site/en/home/education/programs/college.html

Summary: To provide financial assistance to Latino students from eligible communities in California, Texas, Illinois, and New York who are interested in attending designated partner institutions to prepare for a career as a teacher.

Eligibility: Open to Latino students residing in eligible communities in California, Texas, Illinois, and New York. Applicants must 1) be a first-generation college student; 2) be from a low-income family; and 3) have a GPA of 2.5 or higher. They must be enrolled or planning to enroll full-time at a partner institution and preparing for a career as a teacher. Along with their application, they must submit brief essays on a dream they have, an event or experience in their life that inspired them to prepare for their intended career, how their extracurricular activities are helping them prepare for this career, and how they believe they can contribute to the sponsor's mission. Selection is based on extracurricular involvement demonstrating a commitment to the community and financial need.

Financial data: The stipend is $1,000 per year.

Duration: Up to 4 years.

Number awarded: 1 each year.

Deadline: March of each year.

2983 TENNESSEE MINORITY TEACHING FELLOWS PROGRAM

Tennessee Student Assistance Corporation
Parkway Towers
404 James Robertson Parkway, Suite 1510
Nashville, TN 37243-0820
Phone: (615) 741-1346; (800) 342-1663; Fax: (615) 741-6101
Email: TSAC.Aidinfo@tn.gov
Web: www.tn.gov/collegepays/mon_college/minority_teach.htm

Summary: To provide financial assistance to minority residents of Tennessee who wish to attend college in the state to prepare for a career in the teaching field.

Eligibility: Open to minority residents of Tennessee who are either high school seniors planning to enroll full-time at a college or university in the state or continuing college students at a Tennessee college or university. High school seniors must have a GPA of 2.75 or higher and an ACT score of at least 18, a combined mathematics and critical reading SAT score of at least 860, or a rank in the top 25% of their high school class. Continuing college students must have a college GPA of 2.5 or higher. All applicants must agree to teach at the K–12 level in a Tennessee public school following graduation from college. Along with their application, they must submit a 250-word essay on why they chose teaching as a profession. U.S. citizenship is required.

Financial data: The scholarship/loan is $5,000 per year. Recipients incur an obligation to teach at the preK–12 level in a Tennessee public school 1 year for each year the award is received.

Duration: 1 year; may be renewed for up to 3 additional years, provided the recipient maintains full-time enrollment and a cumulative GPA of 2.5 or higher.

Number awarded: 20 new awards are granted each year.

Deadline: April of each year.

2984 TENNESSEE TEACHING SCHOLARS PROGRAM

Tennessee Student Assistance Corporation
Parkway Towers
404 James Robertson Parkway, Suite 1510
Nashville, TN 37243-0820
Phone: (615) 741-1346; (800) 342-1663; Fax: (615) 741-6101
Email: TSAC.Aidinfo@tn.gov
Web: www.tn.gov/collegepays/mon_college/tn_teach_sch.htm

Summary: To provide financial assistance to residents of Tennessee who are interested in attending college in the state to prepare for a teaching career.

Eligibility: Open to college juniors, seniors, and postbaccalaureate students in approved teacher education programs in Tennessee. Applicants must be U.S. citizens, be Tennessee residents, have a GPA of 2.75 or higher, and agree to teach at the public preschool, elementary, or secondary level in Tennessee. Undergraduates must be enrolled full-time; graduate students must be enrolled at least half-time.

Financial data: Loans up to $4,500 per year are available. For each year of teaching in Tennessee, 1 year of the loan is forgiven.

Duration: 1 year; may be renewed for up to 3 additional years, provided the recipient maintains a GPA of 2.75 or higher.

Number awarded: 185 each year.

Deadline: April of each year.

2985 TERRENCE TODMAN GRANT

Virgin Islands Board of Education
Dronningen Gade 60B, 61, and 62
P.O. Box 11900
St. Thomas, VI 00801
Phone: (340) 774-4546; Fax: (340) 774-3384
Email: stt@myviboe.com
Web: www.myviboe.com

Summary: To provide financial assistance to residents of the Virgin Islands who wish to study international affairs at a college in the territory or on the mainland.

Eligibility: Open to residents of the Virgin Islands who are seniors or graduates of high schools in the territory. Applicants must have a GPA of 2.0 or higher and be attending or accepted for enrollment at an accredited institution of higher learning in the territory or on the mainland. They must be planning to major in international affairs. Financial need is considered in the selection process.

Financial data: The stipend is $5,000 per year.

Duration: 1 year; may be renewed 1 additional year.

Number awarded: 1 each year.

Deadline: April of each year.

2986 TEXAS ASSOCIATION OF JOURNALISM EDUCATORS SCHOLARSHIPS

Summary: To provide financial assistance to high school seniors in Texas who are interested in journalism or journalism education.

See Listing #1580.

2987 TEXAS CONFERENCE FOR WOMEN SCHOLARSHIPS

Summary: To provide financial assistance to women in Texas interested in studying specified areas at a college in the state.

See Listing #1582.

2988 TEXAS TRANSPORTATION SCHOLARSHIP

Summary: To provide financial assistance to college students from Texas interested in preparing for a career in fields related to transportation.

See Listing #2380.

2989 TEXAS YOUTH ENTREPRENEUR OF THE YEAR AWARD

Texas Christian University
Steve and Sarah Smith Entrepreneurs Hall
2805 West Lowden, Suite 309
TCU Box 298530
Fort Worth, Texas 76129
Phone: (817) 257-6544; Fax: (817) 257-5775
Email: s.doll@tcu.edu
Web: www.tcuyeya.org

Summary: To recognize and reward outstanding high school entrepreneurs in Texas who have achieved success in their own business.

Eligibility: Open to high school students in Texas who have started and managed a business that has been in operation for at least 1 year. An application may be submitted by the student entrepreneur, family member, friend, teacher, or mentor. Finalists are interviewed.

Financial data: The top winner receives a $5,000 award; the other winners receive $1,000 each. Funds may be used to offset tuition at any school of the student's choice. If the student attends Texas Christian University (TCU), the award is doubled.

Duration: The competition is held annually.

Number awarded: 6 each year: 1 top winner and 5 other winners.

Deadline: October of each year.

2990 THE CAR OF MY FUTURE STUDENT SCHOLARSHIP PROGRAM

Summary: To recognize and reward, with college scholarships, high school seniors in Washington who submit essays or artwork on their vision of the car of the future.

See Listing #1584.

2991 THOMAS R. PICKERING UNDERGRADUATE FOREIGN AFFAIRS FELLOWSHIPS

Woodrow Wilson National Fellowship Foundation
Attn: Foreign Affairs Fellowship Program
5 Vaughn Drive, Suite 300
P.O. Box 2437
Princeton, NJ 08543-2437
Phone: (609) 452-7007; Fax: (609) 452-0066
Email: pickeringfaf@woodrow.org
Web: www.woodrow.org

Summary: To provide financial assistance and work experience to undergraduate students interested in preparing for a career with the Department of State's Foreign Service.

Eligibility: Open to U.S. citizens in the sophomore year of undergraduate study at an accredited college or university who have a cumulative GPA of 3.2 or higher. Applicants must plan to work on a graduate degree in the field of international affairs and prepare for a career in the Foreign Service. Selection is based on strength of undergraduate course work, financial need, college honors and awards, and participation and leadership in extracurricular and community activities. Women, members of minority groups historically underrepresented in the Foreign Service, and students with financial need are encouraged to apply.

Financial data: The award includes tuition, room, board, and mandatory fees during the final 2 years of undergraduate study and the first year of graduate work. The cost of books and 1 round trip are reimbursed. The graduate institution provides similar support during the second year of graduate study, depending upon financial need. For the summer institute and the internships, travel expenses and stipends are paid.

Duration: 3 years: the final 2 years of undergraduate study and the first year of graduate work (provided the student maintains a GPA of 3.2 or higher).

Number awarded: Approximately 20 each year.

Deadline: February of each year.

2992 TIM SMITH MEMORIAL SCHOLARSHIP

Colorado Fiscal Managers Association
c/o Tom Kingsolver, Scholarship Committee Chair
Colorado Department of Revenue
1375 Sherman Street, Room 336
Denver, CO 80261
Phone: (303) 492-9714
Email: roger.cusworth@cusys.edu
Web: www.colorado.gov/cfma

Summary: To provide financial assistance to Colorado students majoring in accounting, finance, or related fields.

Eligibility: Open to residents of Colorado entering their sophomore, junior, or senior year at an accredited state-supported higher education institution in the state. Applicants must be enrolled in a degree program with a declared major in accounting, finance, or other financial management study. Selection is based on academic achievement, involvement in extracurricular organizations and/or activities, work experience, and community involvement.

Financial data: The stipend is $1,500.

Duration: 1 year.

Number awarded: 4 each year.

Deadline: March of each year.

2993 TINY RAUCH SCHOLARSHIP

Summary: To provide financial assistance to residents of Ohio and adjacent counties who are working on an undergraduate degree in a field related to the construction industry at a college or university in any state.

See Listing #2390.

2994 TMCF COCA-COLA FOUNDATION SCHOLARSHIPS

Thurgood Marshall College Fund
Attn: Scholarship Manager
80 Maiden Lane, Suite 2204
New York, NY 10038
Phone: (212) 573-8487; (877) 690-8673; Fax: (212) 573-8497
Email: srogers@tmcfund.org
Web: www.thurgoodmarshallfund.net

Summary: To provide financial assistance to students majoring in finance at colleges and universities that are members of the Thurgood Marshall College Fund (TMCF) and who are the first member of their family to attend college.

Eligibility: Open to full-time students majoring in finance at 1 of the 47 colleges and universities that are TMCF members. Applicants must be the first member of their family to attend college. They must have a GPA of 3.0 or higher and be able to demonstrate financial need. U.S. citizenship is required.

Financial data: The stipend is $1,100 per semester ($2,200 per year).

Duration: 1 year.

Number awarded: 47 each year: 1 at each participating institution.

Deadline: July of each year.

2995 TMCF SIEMENS TEACHER SCHOLARSHIPS

Summary: To provide financial assistance to upper-division students at colleges and universities that are members of the Thurgood Marshall College Fund (TMCF) and who are preparing for a career as a science or mathematics teacher.

See Listing #2391.

2996 TOBIN SORENSON PHYSICAL EDUCATION SCHOLARSHIP

Pi Lambda Theta
Attn: Scholarships Committee
4101 East Third Street
P.O. Box 6626
Bloomington, IN 47407-6626
Phone: (812) 339-3411; (800) 487-3411; Fax: (812) 339-3462
Email: office@pilambda.org
Web: www.pilambda.org/benefits/awards/ScholarshipsAwards.html

Summary: To provide financial assistance to students preparing for careers as a teacher of physical education or a related field.

Eligibility: Open to students preparing for careers at the K–12 level. Applicants must be interested in becoming a physical education teacher, adaptive physical education teacher, coach, recreational therapist, dance therapist, or similar professional teaching the knowledge and use of the human body. They must be sophomores or above and have a GPA of 3.5 or higher. Selection is based on academic achievement, potential for leadership, and extracurricular involvement in physical/sports education, recreation therapy, or similar activities (e.g., coaching, tutoring, volunteer work for appropriate organizations on or off campus).

Financial data: The stipend is $1,000.

Duration: 1 year.

Number awarded: 1 every other year.

Deadline: February of each odd-numbered year.

2997 TOMMY RAMEY SCHOLARSHIP

Summary: To provide financial assistance to college students who reside in Mississippi and are majoring in either 1) marketing or a related field; or 2) culinary arts or a related field.

See Listing #1593.

2998 TONY TORRICE PROFESSIONAL DEVELOPMENT GRANT

Summary: To provide funding to professionals working in the interior furnishing industry who are interested in advancing their career through independent or academic study.

See Listing #1594.

2999 TRANSPORTATION PLANNING DIVISION STUDENT PAPER COMPETITION

American Planning Association
Attn: Transportation Planning Division
205 North Michigan Avenue, Suite 1200
Chicago, IL 60601
Phone: (312) 431-9100; Fax: (312) 786-6700
Web: www.apa-tpd.org/competition.html

Summary: To recognize and reward outstanding papers written by planning students on transportation planning.

Eligibility: Open to students in accredited undergraduate and master's degree planning programs at U.S. colleges and universities; doctoral students are not eligible. Applicants must submit a paper, up to 25 pages in length, written as a course requirement in an undergraduate or graduate degree program. Entries must relate to current transportation planning or policy issues. Selection is based on 1) relevance to a major current issue in transportation planning or policy; 2) insight and significance of discussion; and 3) quality of the writing, documentation, and argument.

Financial data: Prizes are $1,000 for first place and $500 for second place.

Duration: The competition is held annually.

Number awarded: 2 each year.

Deadline: February of each year.

3000 TRIBAL BUSINESS MANAGEMENT (TBM) PROGRAM

Catching the Dream
8200 Mountain Road, N.E., Suite 203
Albuquerque, NM 87110-7835
Phone: (505) 262-2351; Fax: (505) 262-0534
Email: NScholarsh@aol.com
Web: www.catchingthedream.org/Scholarship.htm

Summary: To provide financial assistance for college to American Indian students interested in studying a field related to economic development for tribes.

Eligibility: Open to American Indians who can provide proof that they are at least one-quarter Indian blood and a member of a U.S. tribe that is federally-recognized, state-recognized, or terminated. Applicants must be enrolled or planning to enroll full-time and major in the 1 of the following fields: business administration, finance, management, economics, banking, hotel management, or other fields related to economic development for tribes. They may be entering freshmen, undergraduate students, graduate students, or Ph.D. candidates. Along with their application, they must submit documentation of financial need, 3 letters of recommendation, copies of applications and responses for all other sources of funding for which they are eligible, official transcripts, standardized test scores (ACT, SAT, GRE, MCAT, LSAT, etc.), and an essay explaining their goals in life, college plans, and career plans (especially how those plans include working with and benefiting Indians). Selection is based on merit and potential for improving the lives of Indian people.

Financial data: Stipends range from $500 to $5,000 per year.

Duration: 1 year.

Number awarded: Varies; generally, 30 to 35 each year.

Deadline: April of each year for fall term; September of each year for spring and winter terms; March of each year for summer school.

3001 TROY DOUGLASS CARR CRIMINAL JUSTICE SCHOLARSHIP

Troy Douglass Carr Criminal Justice Scholarship Fund
Attn: Tom Carr
611 Broken Ridge Trail
West End, NC 27376
Phone: (910) 673-4951
Web: www.troycarr.org

Summary: To provide financial assistance to criminal justice students who are recommended by law enforcement officers in North Carolina.

Eligibility: Open to students enrolled or accepted for enrollment at an accredited college or university in any state with a major in criminal justice. Applicants must be recommended by a law enforcement officer presently serving or retired from service in North Carolina. They must be able to demonstrate the potential, character, and professionalism to serve the people of North Carolina in a law enforcement career. Along with their application, they must submit a brief biographical sketch describing their interests, accomplishments, future plans, and how they would benefit from the scholarship. They should also describe any special or unusual financial circumstances affecting their family.

Financial data: A stipend is awarded (amount not specified).

Duration: 1 year.

Number awarded: 1 or 2 each year.

Deadline: April of each year.

3002 UCT SCHOLARSHIP PROGRAM

United Commercial Travelers of America
Attn: UCT Charities Trust Fund
1801 Watermark Drive, Suite 100
P.O. Box 159019
Columbus, OH 43215-8619
Phone: (614) 487-9680; (800) 848-0123, ext. 126; Fax: (614) 487-9688
Email: info@uct.org
Web: www.uct.org/UCT-CTF/apply_ctf.html

Summary: To provide financial assistance to those who wish to teach people with intellectual disabilities.

Eligibility: Open to those who are teaching or planning to teach people with intellectual disabilities; teaching in areas of special education other than intellectual disabilities is not covered. Applicants may be 1) current teachers of people with intellectual disabilities who need additional course work to be certified or to retain certification; 2) experienced teachers who wish to become certified to teach people with intellectual disabilities; 3) holders of bachelor's or master's degrees who wish to pursue graduate work in the field of special education with an emphasis on teaching people with intellectual disabilities; 4) college juniors or seniors whose course of study is special education focusing on people with intellectual disabilities; and 5) anyone who has plans to become an instructor under a structured trade, vocational, or recreation program at a facility for people with intellectual disabilities. All applicants must plan to serve people with intellectual disabilities in the United States or Canada. Financial need is considered in the selection process.

Financial data: The stipend is $2,500 per year. Funds are to be used for registration fees, tuition, and textbooks only.

Duration: 1 year; may be renewed for up to 3 additional years.

Number awarded: Varies each year.

Deadline: Applications may be submitted at any time.

3003 UNIVERSITY SALES SCHOLARSHIP

Summary: To provide financial assistance to university students taking classes in sales.

See Listing #1601.

3004 USDA PUBLIC SERVICE LEADERS SCHOLARSHIP PROGRAM

Summary: To provide financial assistance and work experience to undergraduate and graduate students interested in a preparing for a career with the U.S. Department of Agriculture (USDA).

See Listing #2407.

3005 UTAH SHERIFF'S ASSOCIATION SCHOLARSHIPS

Utah Sheriff's Association
Attn: Executive Director
P.O. Box 489
Santa Clara, UT 84765
Email: ki-ho-alu@hotmail.com
Web: www.utahsheriffs.org/scholarships/scholarships.html

Summary: To provide financial assistance to residents of Utah interested in attending college in any state to prepare for a career in law enforcement.

Eligibility: Open to residents of Utah who are peace officers, family members of peace officers, or other students. Applicants must be interested in attending or planning to attend a college or university in any state to prepare for a career in law enforcement.

Financial data: The stipend is $1,000.

Duration: 1 year.

Number awarded: Varies each year; recently, 44 of these scholarships were awarded.

Deadline: March of each year.

3006 VANGUARD SCHOLARSHIP PROGRAM

Scholarship America
Attn: Scholarship Management Services
One Scholarship Way
P.O. Box 297
St. Peter, MN 56082
Phone: (507) 931-1682; (800) 537-4180; Fax: (507) 931-9168
Web: www.sms.scholarshipamerica.org/vanguard

Summary: To provide financial assistance to minority students working on an undergraduate degree in specified social science and professional fields.

Eligibility: Open to U.S. citizens and permanent residents who are members of racial minorities. Applicants must be entering their senior year as a full-time student at an accredited 4-year college or university in the United States and have a GPA of 3.0 or higher. They must be working on a degree in accounting, business, economics, finance, information technology, or liberal arts. Selection is based on academic record, demonstrated leadership and participation in school and community activities, honors, work experience, a statement of goals and aspirations, unusual personal or family circumstances, recommendations, and a resume; financial need is not considered.

Financial data: The stipend is $10,000.

Duration: 1 year; nonrenewable.

Number awarded: Up to 10 each year.

Deadline: November of each year.

3007 VERDE DICKEY MEMORIAL SCHOLARSHIP

United Methodist Higher Education Foundation
Attn: Scholarships Administrator
1001 19th Avenue South
P.O. Box 340005
Nashville, TN 37203-0005
Phone: (615) 340-7385; (800) 811-8110; Fax: (615) 340-7330
Email: umhefscholarships@gbhem.org
Web: www.umhef.org/receive.php?id=endowed_funds

Summary: To provide financial assistance to upper-division students at schools affiliated with the United Methodist Church who are preparing for a career as a teacher or coach.

Eligibility: Open to full-time students entering their junior or senior year at a United Methodist–related college or university. Applicants must have been active, full members of a United Methodist Church for at least 1 year prior to applying. They must 1) be majoring in education or physical education; 2) be planning to become teachers or coaches; 3) have a GPA of 3.0 or higher; 4) be able to demonstrate financial need; and 5) be a citizen or permanent resident of the United States.

Financial data: The stipend is $7,500.

Duration: 1 year.

Number awarded: 2 each year.

Deadline: May of each year.

3008 VERIZON FOUNDATION SCHOLARSHIP PROGRAM OF THE HISPANIC SCHOLARSHIP FUND

Summary: To provide financial assistance to Hispanic students from selected areas who are working on an undergraduate degree in selected engineering or business fields.

See Listing #2413.

3009 VERIZON SCHOLARSHIP PROGRAM OF THE HISPANIC COLLEGE FUND

Summary: To provide financial assistance to Hispanic American undergraduate students who are working on a degree in specified fields.

See Listing #2415.

3010 VERMONT HEALTHCARE HUMAN RESOURCES ASSOCIATION SCHOLARSHIP

Summary: To provide financial assistance to nontraditional students in Vermont who are interested in majoring in a health-related field or human resources at a college in any state.

See Listing #2418.

3011 VERMONT/NEW HAMPSHIRE DIRECT MARKETING GROUP SCHOLARSHIP

Vermont Student Assistance Corporation
Attn: Scholarship Programs
10 East Allen Street
P.O. Box 2000
Winooski, VT 05404-2601
Phone: (802) 654-3798; (888) 253-4819; Fax: (802) 654-3765; TDD: (800) 281-3341 (within VT)
Email: info@vsac.org
Web: services.vsac.org/wps/wcm/connect/vsac/VSAC

Summary: To provide financial assistance to residents of Vermont and New Hampshire who are interested in working on a degree in direct marketing.

Eligibility: Open to high school seniors, high school graduates, and currently-enrolled college students in New Hampshire and Vermont. Applicants must be enrolled or planning to enroll in an education or training program in any state in a field related to direct marketing or business. Along with their application, they must submit 1) a 100-word essay on their interest in and commitment to pursuing their chosen career or vocation; and 2) a 250-word essay on what they believe distinguishes their application from others that may be submitted. Selection is based on those essays, academic achievement, financial need, and a letter of recommendation.

Financial data: The maximum stipend is $1,000.

Duration: 1 year; recipients may reapply.

Number awarded: 1 or more each year.

Deadline: March of each year.

3012 VERMONT SHERIFFS' ASSOCIATION SCHOLARSHIP

Vermont Student Assistance Corporation
Attn: Scholarship Programs
10 East Allen Street
P.O. Box 2000
Winooski, VT 05404-2601
Phone: (802) 654-3798; (888) 253-4819; Fax: (802) 654-3765; TDD: (800) 281-3341 (within VT)
Email: info@vsac.org
Web: services.vsac.org/wps/wcm/connect/vsac/VSAC

Summary: To provide financial assistance to residents of Vermont who are interested in majoring in law enforcement at a college in any state.

Eligibility: Open to residents of Vermont who are graduating high school seniors, high school graduates, or current college students. Applicants must be interested in working on a degree in law enforcement at a college or university in any state. Along with their application, they must submit 1) a 100-word essay on their commitment to pursing their chosen career or vocation; 2) a 100-word essay on any significant barriers that limit their access to education; and 3) a 250-word essay on their short- and long-term academic, educational, career, vocational, and/or employment goals. Selection is based on those essays, academic achievement, and financial need.

Financial data: The stipend is $1,000.

Duration: 1 year.

Number awarded: 1 each year.

Deadline: March of each year.

3013 VERMONT TRAVEL INDUSTRY CONFERENCE SCHOLARSHIPS

Vermont Travel Industry Conference
Attn: Conference Coordinator
One Mill Street, Suite 301
Burlington, VT 05401
Phone: (802) 865-5202
Email: cindy@delaneymeetingevent.com
Web: www.vtic.org/html/scholarship.shtml

Summary: To provide financial assistance to students from any state who are working on a degree related to the travel industry at a college in Vermont.

Eligibility: Open to residents of any state who are currently enrolled full-time at an accredited 2- or 4-year college or university in Vermont. Applicants must be working on a degree in a field related to the travel industry, including (but not limited to) hotel management, restaurant management, tourism, ski area management, or recreation management. They must have a GPA of 3.0 or higher. Along with their application, they must submit 2 letters of recommendation; a resume; transcripts; a description of paid, volunteer, or academic-credit work or internship experiences in the tourism industry; a list of extracurricular activities in which they are involved; a summary of tourism-related projects or research they have completed; a list of memberships they hold in professional organizations; a description, in 25 words or less, of their future plans or aspirations in the tourism industry; and a 2-page essay on a strategic issue relating to the tourism industry in Vermont. Financial need is not considered in the selection process.
Financial data: The stipend is $2,000.
Duration: 1 year.
Number awarded: 1 or more each year.
Deadline: February of each year.

3014 VETERANS OF ENDURING FREEDOM (AFGHANISTAN) AND IRAQI FREEDOM SCHOLARSHIP

Summary: To provide financial assistance to veterans and military personnel who served in Afghanistan or Iraq and are working on an undergraduate degree in fields related to the support of U.S. intelligence enterprises.
See Listing #2422.

3015 VICKIE CLARK-FLAHERTY SCHOLARSHIP

North Carolina Restaurant and Lodging Association
Attn: NC Hospitality Education Foundation
6036 Six Forks Road
Raleigh, NC 27609
Phone: (919) 844-0098; (800) 582-8750; Fax: (919) 844-0190
Email: alyssab@ncrla.biz
Web: www.ncra.org/displaycommon.cfm?an=1&subarticlenbr=95

Summary: To provide financial assistance to female residents of North Carolina who are interested in attending college in any state to major in a hospitality-related field.
Eligibility: Open to female residents of North Carolina who are high school seniors, high school graduates, or undergraduates attending or planning to attend an accredited 2- or 4-year college, university, or vocational/technical school in the United States as a full-time student. Preference is given to students majoring in a hospitality-related field. Selection is based on academic achievement, community involvement, student leadership, extracurricular activities, employment and/or school references, and financial need.
Financial data: The stipend ranges from $1,500 to $2,500 per year.
Duration: 1 year; recipients may reapply.
Number awarded: 1 or more each year.
Deadline: January of each year.

3016 VIRGINIA ASSOCIATION FOR CAREER AND TECHNICAL EDUCATION HIGH SCHOOL SCHOLARSHIP

Virginia Association for Career and Technical Education
c/o Sandy Jones, Awards Chair
Fairfax County Public Schools
Third Floor CTE
3877 Fairfax Ridge Road
Fairfax, VA 22030
Phone: (571) 423-4528
Email: srjones@fcps.edu
Web: www.vacte.net/scholarship.html

Summary: To provide financial assistance to high school seniors in Virginia planning to attend college in any state to prepare for a career as a teacher in the career and technical education field.
Eligibility: Open to seniors graduating from high schools in Virginia and planning to attend college in any state to prepare to teach career and technical education. Applicants must submit a statement explaining why they feel they should receive this scholarship and describing their educational and career plans. Financial need is considered in the selection process.
Financial data: The stipend is $1,000.
Duration: 1 year.
Number awarded: 1 each year.
Deadline: March of each year.

3017 VIRGINIA BUSINESS EDUCATION ASSOCIATION HIGH SCHOOL SENIOR SCHOLARSHIPS

Virginia Business Education Association
c/o Beth Downey, Student Scholarships
Fairfax County Public Schools
Third Floor CTE
3877 Fairfax Ridge Road
Fairfax, VA 22030
Phone: (571) 423-4523; Fax: (571) 423-4597
Email: Beth.Downey@fcps.edu
Web: vbea.net/awards.html

Summary: To provide financial assistance to high school seniors in Virginia who plan to major in business or information technology at a college in any state.
Eligibility: Open to seniors graduating from high schools in Virginia and planning to enroll full-time at a college or university in any state. Applicants must intend to major in business or information technology. Along with their application, they must submit a 2-page essay on how they plan to contribute to the world by choosing business as a major. Financial need is not considered in the selection process.
Financial data: A stipend is awarded (amount not specified).
Duration: 1 year.
Number awarded: 1 or more each year.
Deadline: February of each year.

3018 VIRGINIA CHILD CARE PROVIDER SCHOLARSHIP

Virginia Department of Social Services
Attn: Office of Early Childhood Development
Division of Child Care and Development
7 North Eighth Street, Sixth Floor
Richmond, VA 23219
Phone: (804) 726-7000; (866) 636-1608
Email: childcare.scholarship@dss.virginia.gov
Web: www.dss.virginia.gov/family/cc/scholarship.cgi

Summary: To provide financial assistance to Virginia residents who are interested in working on a degree or certificate in preschool education.
Eligibility: Open to current and future child care providers. Applicants must 1) already be providing child care in a program located in Virginia; 2) live in Virginia but be employed in a child care program outside of the state; or 3) live in Virginia and be planning to become employed in child care. They must be interested in taking courses at approved colleges and universities in Virginia that will provide them with additional training for a career in child care.
Financial data: The scholarship award pays the tuition and technology fee for each qualifying course, up to a lifetime maximum of $2,068. Funds are paid to the recipient's school. These funds may not be used to pay for books.
Duration: 2 courses per semester, up to a total of 8 courses.
Number awarded: Varies each year.
Deadline: November of each year for the spring semester; April of each year for the summer semester; July of each year for the fall semester.

3019 VIRGINIA HIGHER EDUCATION TEACHER ASSISTANCE PROGRAM

State Council of Higher Education for Virginia
Attn: Financial Aid Office
James Monroe Building
101 North 14th Street, Ninth Floor
Richmond, VA 23219-3659
Phone: (804) 225-2600; (877) 515-0138; Fax: (804) 225-2604; TDD: (804) 371-8017
Email: fainfo@schev.edu
Web: www.schev.edu/students/factsheetHETAP.asp?from=

Summary: To provide financial assistance to residents of Virginia who are enrolled or interested in enrolling in a K–12 teacher preparation program in college.
Eligibility: Open to residents of Virginia who are enrolled, or intend to enroll, full-time in an eligible K–12 teacher preparation program at a public or private Virginia college or university. Applicants must 1) be U.S. citizens or eligible noncitizens; 2) demonstrate financial need; 3) have a cumulative college GPA of 2.5 or higher; and 4) be nominated by a faculty member. Preference is given to applicants enrolled in a teacher shortage content area. Recently, those included special education, mathematics, science (earth science, grades 6–8, and biology), reading specialist, career and technical education (technology education and family and consumer sciences), foreign languages (Spanish preK–12), English as a second language, middle grades (all subjects), library media, and English (grades 6–12).

Financial data: Stipends are $2,000 per year for students at 4-year institutions or $1,000 per year for students at 2-year institutions.
Duration: 1 year; may be renewed if funds are available and the recipient maintains satisfactory academic progress.
Number awarded: Varies each year.
Deadline: Deadline not specified.

3020 VIRGINIA SOCIETY FOR HEALTHCARE HUMAN RESOURCES ADMINISTRATION SCHOLARSHIP

Virginia Society for Healthcare Human Resources Administration
c/o Cindi Derricott, Scholarship Chair
Bon Secours Richmond Health System
8580 Magellan Parkway
Richmond, VA 23227
Phone: (540) 627-5003
Email: info@vashhra.org
Web: www.vashhra.org
Summary: To provide financial assistance to undergraduate and graduate students in Virginia working on a degree in human relations and interested in a career in a health care setting.
Eligibility: Open to residents of Virginia currently enrolled in an accredited college or university in the state and working on an undergraduate or graduate degree in human resources administration or a related field. Applicants must be at least a second-semester sophomore when the application is submitted and have a demonstrated interest in working in a health care setting. Along with their application, they must submit a 1-page statement on their contribution to the human resources profession to date, their future goals as a human resources professional, and how this scholarship would help them to achieve those goals. Selection is based on that statement, work experience, 2 letters of recommendation from faculty members, and financial need.
Financial data: The stipend is $1,000.
Duration: 1 year; nonrenewable.
Number awarded: 1 each year.
Deadline: October of each year.

3021 VIRGINIA TEACHING SCHOLARSHIP LOAN PROGRAM

Virginia Department of Education
Division of Teacher Education and Licensure
Attn: Director of Teacher Education
P.O. Box 2120
Richmond, VA 23218-2120
Phone: (804) 371-2475; (800) 292-3820; Fax: (804) 786-6759
Email: JoAnne.Carver@doe.virginia.gov
Web: www.doe.virginia.gov/teaching/financial_support/index.shtml
Summary: To provide financial assistance to upper-division and graduate students in Virginia who are interested in a career in teaching.
Eligibility: Open to Virginia residents who are enrolled full- or part-time as a sophomore, junior, senior, or graduate student in a state-approved teacher preparation program in Virginia with a GPA of 2.7 or higher. Applicants must agree to engage in full-time teaching following graduation in 1) designated teacher shortage areas within Virginia; 2) a school with a high concentration of students eligible for free or reduced lunch; 3) within a school division with a shortage of teachers; 4) in a rural or urban region of the state with a teacher shortage; or 5) in a career and technical education discipline. Males interested in teaching in the elementary grades and people of color in all teaching areas also qualify.
Financial data: The scholarship/loan is $3,720 per year. Loans are forgiven at the rate of $1,000 for each semester the recipient teaches in designated teacher shortage areas. If the recipient fails to fulfill the teaching service requirement, the loan must be repaid with interest.
Duration: 1 year; may be renewed 1 additional year.
Number awarded: Varies each year; recently, 265 of these scholarship/loans were granted, including 111 in elementary education, 14 in English, 8 in foreign languages, 2 in history and social science, 18 in mathematics, 22 in middle grades, 2 in science, 30 in special education, 20 for males in elementary grades, 4 for males in middle grades, and 34 for people of color.
Deadline: Deadline not specified.

3022 VOICE OF DEMOCRACY SCHOLARSHIP PROGRAM

Summary: To recognize and reward, with college scholarships, outstanding high school students in a national broadcast scriptwriting competition dealing with freedom and democracy.
See Listing #1606.

3023 W. PRICE, JR. MEMORIAL SCHOLARSHIP

Texas Restaurant Association
Attn: Education Foundation
1400 Lavaca
P.O. Box 1429
Austin, TX 78767-1429
Phone: (512) 457-4100; (800) 395-2872; Fax: (512) 472-2777
Email: foundinfo@tramail.org
Web: www.restaurantville.com/6636050_65221.htm
Summary: To provide financial assistance to Texas residents who are interested in working on an undergraduate or graduate degree in restaurant or food service at a school in any state.
Eligibility: Open to Texas residents who are enrolled or planning to enroll full-time as undergraduate or graduate students in a food service or hospitality program at a college, culinary academy, or university in any state. Applicants must have a GPA of 2.75 or higher and (for students already in college) 3.25 or higher in courses in their major. They must be able to demonstrate the ability to become an asset to the food service industry. Along with their application, they must submit 500-word essays on 1) why they are applying for this scholarship and its effect on their education and career, including their philosophy of the food service industry and their career goals; and 2) how they plan to contribute to their local community during their career as a restaurant and food service professional. Selection is based on those essays, GPA and SAT/ACT scores, class ranking (high school seniors only), honors and community service, letters of reference, and industry-related work experience.
Financial data: The stipend is $5,000 for students attending a 4-year university, culinary academy, or graduate program or $2,000 for students attending a 2-year college.
Duration: 1 year.
Number awarded: Varies each year; recently, 4 of these scholarships were awarded.
Deadline: January of each year.

3024 WACHOVIA SCHOLARS PROGRAM

Hispanic Association of Colleges and Universities
Attn: National Scholarship Program
8415 Datapoint Drive, Suite 400
San Antonio, TX 78229
Phone: (210) 692-3805; Fax: (210) 692-0823; TDD: (800) 855-2880
Email: scholarships@hacu.net
Web: www.hacu.net/hacu/Scholarships_EN.asp?SnID=875148054
Summary: To provide financial assistance to undergraduate students who are majoring in business-related fields at institutions that belong to the Hispanic Association of Colleges and Universities (HACU).
Eligibility: Open to full- and part-time undergraduate students who are enrolled at a 2- or 4-year HACU member institution. Applicants must be majoring in accounting, finance, or business administration. They must have a GPA of 3.0 or higher and be able to demonstrate financial need. Along with their application, they must submit an essay of 200 to 250 words that describes their academic and/or career goals, where they expect to be and what they expect to be doing 10 years from now, and what skills they can bring to an employer.
Financial data: The stipend is $1,000.
Duration: 1 year; nonrenewable.
Number awarded: Varies each year.
Deadline: May of each year.

3025 WACHOVIA SCHOLARSHIPS OF THE THURGOOD MARSHALL COLLEGE FUND

Thurgood Marshall College Fund
Attn: Scholarship Manager
80 Maiden Lane, Suite 2204
New York, NY 10038
Phone: (212) 573-8487; (877) 690-8673; Fax: (212) 573-8497
Email: srogers@tmcfund.org
Web: www.thurgoodmarshallfund.net
Summary: To provide financial assistance to students enrolled at colleges and universities that are members of the Thurgood Marshall College Fund (TMCF), especially those majoring in business or finance.
Eligibility: Open to full-time students currently enrolled as sophomores at 1 of the 47 colleges and universities that are TMCF members. Applicants must have a GPA of 3.0 or higher and be able to demonstrate financial need. Special consideration is given to students majoring in business or finance. First-generation college students are strongly encouraged to apply. U.S. citizenship is required.

Financial data: The stipend is $2,200 per semester ($4,400 per year).
Duration: 1 year.
Number awarded: 35 each year; approximately 25% of the scholarships are reserved for students majoring in business or finance and the other 75% are open to students with any major.
Deadline: July of each year.

3026 WAL-MART ACHIEVERS SCHOLARSHIP

Hispanic Association of Colleges and Universities
Attn: National Scholarship Program
8415 Datapoint Drive, Suite 400
San Antonio, TX 78229
Phone: (210) 692-3805; Fax: (210) 692-0823; TDD: (800) 855-2880
Email: scholarships@hacu.net
Web: www.hacu.net/hacu/Scholarships_EN.asp?SnID=875148054
Summary: To provide financial assistance to undergraduate students who are majoring in business-related fields at institutions that belong to the Hispanic Association of Colleges and Universities (HACU).
Eligibility: Open to full-time undergraduate students who are enrolled at a 2- or 4-year HACU member institution. Applicants must be majoring in business administration, general management, food merchandising, or retail management. They must have a GPA of 3.0 or higher and be able to demonstrate financial need. Preference is given to students who have an interest in retail and are working while attending school. Along with their application, they must submit an essay of 200 to 250 words that describes their academic and/or career goals, where they expect to be and what they expect to be doing 10 years from now, and what skills they can bring to an employer.
Financial data: The stipend is $1,000.
Duration: 1 year; nonrenewable.
Number awarded: Varies each year.
Deadline: May of each year.

3027 WALTER I.M. HODGE GRANT

Summary: To provide financial assistance to residents of the Virgin Islands who wish to study designated fields at a college in the territory or on the mainland.
See Listing #2438.

3028 WALTER VAUGHN EXCELLENCE IN HUMAN RESOURCES SCHOLARSHIP

National Forum for Black Public Administrators
Attn: Scholarship Program
777 North Capitol Street, N.E., Suite 807
Washington, DC 20002
Phone: (202) 408-9300, ext. 112; Fax: (202) 408-8558
Email: vreed@nfbpa.org
Web: www.nfbpa.org/i4a/pages/index.cfm?pageid=3630
Summary: To provide financial assistance to African Americans working on an undergraduate or graduate degree in public administration with an emphasis on human resource management.
Eligibility: Open to African American undergraduate and graduate students preparing for a career in public service. Applicants must be working full-time on a degree in public administration, human resource management, or a related field. They must have a GPA of 3.0 or higher, a record of involvement in extracurricular activities (excluding athletics), excellent interpersonal and leadership abilities, and strong oral and written communication skills. Along with their application, they must submit a 3-page autobiographical essay that includes their academic and career goals and objectives. Although this is not a need-based program, first consideration is given to applicants who are not currently receiving other financial aid.
Financial data: The stipend is $2,500.
Duration: 1 year.
Number awarded: 1 each year.
Deadline: February of each year.

3029 WARNER NORCROSS & JUDD PARALEGAL ASSISTANT SCHOLARSHIP

Grand Rapids Community Foundation
Attn: Education Program Officer
185 Oakes Street S.W.
Grand Rapids, MI 49503-4008
Phone: (616) 454-1751, ext. 103; Fax: (616) 454-6455
Email: rbishop@grfoundation.org
Web: www.grfoundation.org/scholarships
Summary: To provide financial assistance to minority residents of Michigan who are interested in working on a paralegal studies degree at an institution in the state.
Eligibility: Open to residents of Michigan who are students of color attending or planning to attend an accredited public or private 2- or 4-year college or university in the state. Applicants must have a declared major in paralegal/legal assistant studies. They must be U.S. citizens or permanent residents and have a GPA of 2.5 or higher. Financial need is considered in the selection process.
Financial data: The stipend is $2,000. Funds are paid directly to the recipient's institution.
Duration: 1 year.
Number awarded: 1 each year.
Deadline: March of each year.

3030 WASHINGTON CROSSING FOUNDATION SCHOLARSHIPS

Washington Crossing Foundation
Attn: Vice Chairman
P.O. Box 503
Levittown, PA 19058-0503
Phone: (215) 949-8841
Email: info@gwcf.org
Web: www.gwcf.org
Summary: To provide financial assistance for college to high school seniors planning careers in government service.
Eligibility: Open to high school seniors who are U.S. citizens planning careers of service in local, state, or federal government. Applicants must submit a 1-page essay describing why they plan a career in government service, including any inspiration derived from the leadership of George Washington in his famous crossing of the Delaware. Selection is based on understanding of career requirements, purpose in choice of a career, preparation for their career, leadership, sincerity, and historical perspective.
Financial data: Stipends range from $500 to $5,000 per year.
Duration: 4 years, provided the recipients maintain a suitable scholastic level, meet the requirements of their college, and continue their career objective.
Number awarded: Varies each year; recently, 34 of these scholarships were awarded.
Deadline: January of each year.

3031 WASHINGTON FUTURE TEACHERS CONDITIONAL SCHOLARSHIP AND LOAN REPAYMENT PROGRAM

Washington Higher Education Coordinating Board
917 Lakeridge Way
P.O. Box 43430
Olympia, WA 98504-3430
Phone: (360) 753-7845; (888) 535-0747; Fax: (360) 753-7808; TDD: (360) 753-7809
Email: futureteachers@hecb.wa.gov
Web: www.hecb.wa.gov/Paying/waaidprgm/future.asp
Summary: To provide financial assistance and repayment of existing federal loans to students, paraprofessionals, and teachers in Washington who are interested in becoming a teacher or obtaining additional training.
Eligibility: Open to Washington residents who are either 1) students enrolled or planning to enroll in an approved program leading to a residency teacher certificate; or 2) current teachers and paraprofessionals interested in obtaining additional endorsements in teacher shortage subjects. Applicants must plan to be employed as a certificated classroom teacher in a Washington K–12 public school and to attend an eligible college at least half-time. Priority is given to applicants who are seeking additional endorsements in mathematics, science, special education, agricultural education, business and marketing education, family and consumer science education, or technology education. Selection is based on academic ability, bilingual ability, contributions to school systems, potential to serve as a positive role model for students, length of time until completion of the educational program, and commitment to serve as a Washington classroom teacher.
Financial data: The award for full-time study is $7,440 per academic year at the University of Washington, Washington State University, or private 4-year colleges and universities; $5,340 per academic year at the 4 regional universities; or

$2,880 per academic year at community and technical colleges. Recipients may use the funds for payment of tuition and fees or for repayment of existing federal loans. They must commit to provide 2 years of eligible teaching service for each year of support. If they fail to complete that service obligation, they must repay all funds received with interest and fees.
Duration: 1 year; may be renewed up to 4 additional years.
Number awarded: Approximately 100 each year.
Deadline: October of each year.

3032 WASHINGTON GRAND CHAPTER EASTERN STAR TRAINING AWARDS FOR RELIGIOUS LEADERSHIP

Summary: To provide financial assistance to residents of Washington who are attending college in any state to prepare for a career in Christian service.
See Listing #1612.

3033 WAYNE D. CORNILS SCHOLARSHIP

Summary: To provide financial assistance to students at Idaho colleges and universities who are preparing for a career in the broadcasting field (including the business side) and can demonstrate financial need.
See Listing #1616.

3034 WAYNE V. BLACK SCHOLARSHIP AWARD

Summary: To provide financial assistance to undergraduates working on a degree in a field related to telecommunications.
See Listing #2451.

3035 WEISMAN SCHOLARSHIPS

Summary: To provide financial assistance to minority upper-division college students from any state who are enrolled at a college in Connecticut and interested in teaching mathematics or science at public middle and high schools in the state.
See Listing #2452.

3036 WELLS FARGO SCHOLARSHIP PROGRAM OF THE HISPANIC SCHOLARSHIP FUND

Summary: To provide financial assistance to Hispanic upper-division students from selected states working on a degree related to business at designated universities.
See Listing #2453.

3037 WELLS FARGO UNDERGRADUATE SCHOLARSHIPS

American Indian Graduate Center
Attn: Executive Director
4520 Montgomery Boulevard, N.E., Suite 1-B
Albuquerque, NM 87109-1291
Phone: (505) 881-4584; (800) 628-1920; Fax: (505) 884-0427
Email: aigc@aigc.com
Web: www.aigc.com/02scholarships/wellsfargo/wellsfargo.htm
Summary: To provide financial assistance to Native American upper-division students working on a business-related degree.
Eligibility: Open to enrolled members of U.S. federally-recognized American Indian tribes and Alaska Native groups who can provide a Certificate of Indian Blood (CIB). Applicants must be entering their junior or senior year as a full-time student and working on a degree to prepare for a career in banking, resort management, gaming operations, or management and administration, including accounting, finance, human resources, and information systems. They must have a GPA of 3.0 or higher. Along with their application, they must submit an essay on their personal, educational, and professional goals. Financial need is also considered in the selection process.
Financial data: A stipend is awarded (amount not specified).
Duration: 1 year.
Number awarded: 1 or more each year.
Deadline: April of each year.

3038 WEST VIRGINIA ELKS ASSOCIATION SCHOLARSHIPS

West Virginia Elks Association
c/o Jeffrey R. Miller, Scholarship Committee Chair
Wheeling Elks Lodge 28
P.O. Box 351
Wheeling, WV 26003
Phone: (304) 233-3511; Fax: (304) 233-3199
Email: jmiller@bhbglaw.com
Web: www.wvelks.org
Summary: To provide financial assistance to high school seniors in West Virginia who plan to attend college in any state and study special education.
Eligibility: Open to seniors graduating from high schools in West Virginia. Applicants must be planning to attend a college or university in any state to prepare for a career as a teacher of special education.
Financial data: The stipend is $1,000.
Duration: 1 year; nonrenewable.
Number awarded: Varies each year; recently, 16 of these scholarships were awarded.
Deadline: Deadline not specified.

3039 WILBURN SMITH GRANT

Virgin Islands Board of Education
Dronningen Gade 60B, 61, and 62
P.O. Box 11900
St. Thomas, VI 00801
Phone; (340) 774-4546; Fax: (340) 774-3384
Email: stt@myviboe.com
Web: myviboe.com
Summary: To provide financial assistance to residents of the Virgin Islands who wish to study education at a college in the territory or on the mainland.
Eligibility: Open to residents of the Virgin Islands who are seniors or graduates of high schools in the territory. Applicants must have a GPA of 2.0 or higher and be attending or accepted for enrollment at an accredited institution of higher learning in the territory or on the mainland. They must be planning to major in elementary, secondary, or vocational education. Financial need is considered in the selection process.
Financial data: The stipend is $2,000.
Duration: 1 year; nonrenewable.
Number awarded: 1 each year.
Deadline: April of each year.

3040 WILLARD H. ERWIN, JR. SCHOLARSHIP

Greater Kanawha Valley Foundation
Attn: Scholarship Coordinator
1600 Huntington Square
900 Lee Street, East
P.O. Box 3041
Charleston, WV 25331-3041
Phone: (304) 346-3620; (800) 467-5909; Fax: (304) 346-3640
Email: shoover@tgkvf.org
Web: www.tgkvf.org/scholar.htm
Summary: To provide financial assistance to students in West Virginia who are working on an undergraduate or graduate degree in a field related to health care finance at a public institution in the state.
Eligibility: Open to residents of West Virginia who are entering their junior, senior, or graduate year of study at a public college or university in the state. Applicants must have at least a 2.5 GPA and demonstrate good moral character. Preference is given to students working on a degree in business or a phase of health care finance. Selection is based on financial need, academic performance, leadership abilities, and contributions to school and community.
Financial data: The stipend is $1,000 per year.
Duration: Normally, 2 years.
Number awarded: 1 each year.
Deadline: January of each year.

3041 WILLIAM B. BRANDT MEMORIAL SCHOLARSHIPS

Nebraska Bankers Association
Attn: Educational Foundation
233 South 13th Street, Suite 700
P.O. Box 80008
Lincoln, NE 68501-0008
Phone: (402) 474-1555; Fax: (402) 474-2946
Email: karen.miller@nebankers.org
Web: www.nebankers.org/public/consumer.html

Summary: To provide financial assistance to Nebraska residents working on a degree in business at a college or university in the state.
Eligibility: Open to residents of Nebraska who are enrolled as full-time juniors or seniors at a college or university in the state (except for the University of Nebraska). Applicants must be working on a bachelor of science in business administration with an emphasis on finance, accounting, or economics and have a GPA of 3.0 or higher. Along with their application, they must submit an essay of 100 to 200 words on how the banking industry has impacted their community or the role they expect the banking industry to play in their future. Financial need is not considered in the selection process.
Financial data: The stipend is $1,000.
Duration: 1 year.
Number awarded: Up to 12 each year.
Deadline: January of each year.

3042 WILLIAM F. CARL SCHOLARSHIP

North Carolina Restaurant and Lodging Association
Attn: NC Hospitality Education Foundation
6036 Six Forks Road
Raleigh, NC 27609
Phone: (919) 844-0098; (800) 582-8750; Fax: (919) 844-0190
Email: alyssab@ncrla.biz
Web: www.ncra.org/displaycommon.cfm?an=1&subarticlenbr=95
Summary: To provide financial assistance to residents of North Carolina who are children of restaurant employees and interested in attending college in any state, especially if they are planning to major in a hospitality-related field.
Eligibility: Open to residents of North Carolina who are younger than 24 years of age and children of a restaurant employee. Applicants may be high school seniors, high school graduates, or undergraduates attending or planning to attend an accredited 2- or 4-year college, university, or vocational/technical school in the United States as a full-time student. Legal U.S. resident status is required. Preference is given to students majoring in a hospitality-related field. Selection is based on academic success, community involvement, and recommendations.
Financial data: The stipend ranges from $500 to $5,000 per year.
Duration: 1 year; may be renewed if the recipient maintains a GPA of 3.0 or higher.
Number awarded: 1 or more each year.
Deadline: January of each year.

3043 WILLIAM G. SALETIC SCHOLARSHIP

Summary: To provide financial assistance to upper-division students from any state who are majoring in politics or history at colleges and universities that are members of the Independent Colleges of Washington (ICW).
See Listing #1619.

3044 WILLIAM R. GOLDFARB MEMORIAL SCHOLARSHIP

Summary: To provide financial assistance to high school seniors who are licensed radio amateurs and interested in working on an undergraduate degree in selected fields.
See Listing #2462.

3045 WILLIAM WINTER TEACHER SCHOLAR LOAN PROGRAM

Mississippi Office of Student Financial Aid
3825 Ridgewood Road
Jackson, MS 39211-6453
Phone: (601) 432-6997; (800) 327-2980 (within MS); Fax: (601) 432-6527
Email: sfa@ihl.state.ms.us
Web: www.mississippi.edu/riseupms/financialaid-state.php
Summary: To provide financial assistance to Mississippi residents working on a Class "A" teacher educator license.
Eligibility: Open to Mississippi residents who are enrolled full-time as juniors or seniors at an accredited Mississippi 4-year public or private college or university. Applicants must be working on a bachelor's degree in a program of study leading to a Class "A" teacher educator license and have a cumulative GPA of 2.5 or higher. They must be able to document that they have passed Praxis I or have an ACT score of 21 or higher with a minimum of 18 on all sub-scores. Programs of study that do not qualify include, but are not limited to, speech and language pathology, psychological and counseling services, and recreational therapy.
Financial data: Loans are provided up to $4,000 per academic year. For each year of service as a full-time classroom teacher in an accredited public school or public school district in Mississippi, 1 year's loan will be forgiven.
Duration: 1 year; may be renewed 1 additional year if the recipient maintains a GPA of 2.5 or higher, remains enrolled full-time in a program of study leading to a Class "A" teacher educator license, exhibits satisfactory academic progress, and documents that Praxis II has been passed after no more than 3 semesters of participation in this program.
Number awarded: Varies each year, depending on the availability of funds; awards are granted on a first-come, first-served basis.
Deadline: March of each year.

3046 WILMA D. HOYAL/MAXINE CHILTON SCHOLARSHIPS

American Legion Auxiliary
Department of Arizona
4701 North 19th Avenue, Suite 100
Phoenix, AZ 85015-3727
Phone: (602) 241-1080; Fax: (602) 604-9640
Email: amlegauxaz@mcleodusa.net
Web: www.azlegion.org/scholar3.txt
Summary: To provide financial assistance to veterans, the dependents of veterans, and other students who are majoring in selected social science fields at Arizona public universities.
Eligibility: Open to second-year or upper-division full-time students majoring in political science, public programs, or special education at public universities in Arizona (the University of Arizona, Northern Arizona University, or Arizona State University). Applicants must have been Arizona residents for at least 1 year. They must have a GPA of 3.0 or higher. U.S. citizenship is required. Honorably-discharged veterans and immediate family members of veterans receive preference. Selection is based on scholarship (20%), financial need (40%), character (25%), and initiative (15%).
Financial data: The stipend is $1,000.
Duration: 1 year; renewable.
Number awarded: 3 each year: 1 to each of the 3 universities.
Deadline: May of each year.

3047 WINNERS' CLUB SCHOLARSHIPS

Winners' Club
P.O. Box 148
Louisville, OH 44641
Web: winnersclubscholarship.visioncomm.net
Summary: To provide financial assistance to high school seniors in Ohio who plan to attend a college or university in the state to prepare for a career as a teacher.
Eligibility: Open to seniors graduating from high schools in Ohio with a GPA of 3.5 or higher. Applicants must be planning to attend a state-supported college or university in Ohio to work on a degree in elementary or secondary education. Along with their application, they must submit a short essay describing why they want to pursue further education, why they desire a career in education, and how this scholarship could affect their plans. Selection is based on academic merit, extracurricular activities, and financial need.
Financial data: The stipend is $1,500.
Duration: 1 year; nonrenewable.
Number awarded: 3 each year.
Deadline: April of each year.

3048 WISCONSIN MINORITY TEACHER LOANS

Wisconsin Higher Educational Aids Board
131 West Wilson Street, Suite 902
P.O. Box 7885
Madison, WI 53707-7885
Phone: (608) 267-2212; Fax: (608) 267-2808
Email: Mary.Kuzdas@wisconsin.gov
Web: heab.state.wi.us/programs.html
Summary: To provide funding to minorities in Wisconsin who are interested in teaching in Wisconsin school districts with large minority enrollments.
Eligibility: Open to residents of Wisconsin who are African Americans, Hispanic Americans, American Indians, or southeast Asians (students who were admitted to the United States after December 31, 1975 and who are a former citizen of Laos, Vietnam, or Cambodia or whose ancestor was a citizen of one of those countries). Applicants must be enrolled at least half-time as juniors, seniors, or graduate students at an independent or public institution in the state in a program leading to teaching licensure and have a GPA of 2.5 or

higher. They must agree to teach in a Wisconsin school district in which minority students constitute at least 29% of total enrollment or in a school district participating in the inter-district pupil transfer program. Financial need is not considered in the selection process.
Financial data: Loans are provided up to $2,500 per year. For each year the student teaches in an eligible school district, 25% of the loan is forgiven; if the student does not teach in an eligible district, the loan must be repaid at an interest rate of 5%.
Duration: 1 year; may be renewed 1 additional year.
Number awarded: Varies each year.
Deadline: Deadline dates vary by institution; check with your school's financial aid office.

3049 WISCONSIN PROFESSIONAL POLICE ASSOCIATION SCHOLARSHIP PROGRAM

Wisconsin Professional Police Association
Attn: Scholarship Committee
340 Coyier Lane
Madison, WI 53713
Phone: (608) 273-3840; (800) 362-8838; Fax: (608) 273-3904
Email: bahr@wppa.com
Web: www.wppa.com/resources/scholarship_program.htm
Summary: To provide financial assistance to residents of Wisconsin and the upper peninsula of Michigan who are entering or attending a program in law enforcement.
Eligibility: Open to residents of Wisconsin and the upper peninsula of Michigan who are enrolled or planning to enroll in a 2- or 4-year program in police science, criminal justice, or a related field of law enforcement. Applicants must submit a 200-word essay on why they have chosen a career in law enforcement, including any special projects relating to their interest in the field. Financial need is not considered in the selection process.
Financial data: Stipends range from $500 to $1,000; funds are sent directly to the recipient.
Duration: 1 year.
Number awarded: Approximately 10 each year.
Deadline: January of each year.

3050 WISCONSIN TEACHER OF THE VISUALLY IMPAIRED LOANS

Wisconsin Higher Educational Aids Board
131 West Wilson Street, Suite 902
P.O. Box 7885
Madison, WI 53707-7885
Phone: (608) 266-1665; Fax: (608) 267-2808
Email: colettem1.brown@wi.gov
Web: heab.state.wi.us/programs.html
Summary: To provide financial assistance to residents of Wisconsin who are interested in teaching the visually impaired at a school in Wisconsin or an adjacent state.
Eligibility: Open to residents of Wisconsin who are enrolled at least half-time in a program that prepares them to be licensed as teachers of the visually impaired or as orientation and mobility instructors. Applicants must be attending an institution that offers such a program in Wisconsin or in an adjacent state (Illinois, Iowa, Michigan, or Minnesota). They must agree to be a licensed teacher or an orientation and mobility instructor in a Wisconsin school district, the Wisconsin Center for the Blind and Visually Impaired, or a cooperative educational service agency. Financial need is considered in the selection process.
Financial data: Scholarship/loans are provided up to $10,000 per year, or a lifetime maximum of $40,000. For each of the first 2 years the student teaches and meets the eligibility criteria, 25% of the loan is forgiven; for the third year, 50% of the loan is forgiven. If the student does not teach and meet the eligibility criteria, the loan must be repaid at an interest rate of 5%.
Duration: 1 year; may be renewed up to 3 additional years.
Number awarded: Varies each year.
Deadline: Deadline dates vary by institution; check with your school's financial aid office.

3051 WLMA STUDENT GRANT-IN-AID

Washington Library Media Association
c/o Jeanne Staley
711 Scenic Bluff
Yakima, WA 98908
Phone: (509) 972-5899
Email: scholarships@wlma.org
Web: www.wlma.org/scholarships
Summary: To provide financial assistance to college students in Washington who are interested in library media training.
Eligibility: Open to undergraduates in Washington who are enrolled in a degree program and are interested in library media training. Applicants must be planning to work in a school following graduation. Along with their application, they must submit a brief description of their reasons for applying, goals as a teacher librarian, plans for the future, interest in librarianship, plans for further education, and interest in this award. Financial need is considered in the selection process.
Financial data: The stipend is $1,000.
Duration: 1 year.
Number awarded: 1 each year.
Deadline: March of each year.

3052 WOMEN IN TRANSITION ACCOUNTING SCHOLARSHIP

Educational Foundation for Women in Accounting
Attn: Foundation Administrator
136 South Keowee Street
Dayton, OH 45402
Phone: (937) 424-3391; Fax: (937) 222-5749
Email: info@efwa.org
Web: www.efwa.org/witwin.htm
Summary: To provide financial support to women who have become the sole support of their family and wish to begin work on an undergraduate accounting degree.
Eligibility: Open to women who, either through divorce or death of a spouse, have become the sole source of support for themselves and their family. Women who are single parents as a result of other circumstances are also considered. Applicants should be incoming or current freshmen, or they may be returning to school with sufficient credits to qualify for freshman status. Selection is based on aptitude for accounting, commitment to the goal of working on a degree in accounting (including evidence of continued commitment after receiving this award), clear evidence that the candidate has established goals and a plan for achieving those goals (both personal and professional), and financial need.
Financial data: The stipend is $4,000 per year.
Duration: 1 year; may be renewed 3 additional years if the recipient completes at least 12 hours each semester.
Number awarded: 1 each year.
Deadline: April of each year.

3053 WOMEN'S BUSINESS ALLIANCE SCHOLARSHIP PROGRAM

Choice Hotels International
Attn: Foundation
4225 East Windrose Drive
Phoenix, AZ 85032
Phone: (602) 953-4478
Web: www.choicehotels.com/ires/en-us/html/WBA
Summary: To provide financial assistance to women interested in preparing for a career in the hospitality industry.
Eligibility: Open to female high school seniors, undergraduates, and graduate students. Applicants must be U.S. citizens or permanent residents interested in preparing for a career in the hospitality industry. They must submit an essay of 500 words or less on why they are interested in a career in the hospitality industry, the area of the industry that appeals to them the most, and some of their major accomplishments and/or personal characteristics that will benefit their work in the hospitality industry. Financial need is not considered in the selection process.
Financial data: The stipend is $2,000.
Duration: 1 year; recipients may reapply.
Number awarded: 2 or more each year.
Deadline: January of each year.

3054 WORDA RUSSELL MEMORIAL ENDOWMENT SCHOLARSHIPS

Epsilon Sigma Alpha International
Attn: ESA Foundation
P.O. Box 270517
Fort Collins, CO 80527

Phone: (970) 223-2824; Fax: (970) 223-4456
Email: esainfo@esaintl.com
Web: www.esaintl.com/esaf

Summary: To provide financial assistance to students from any state planning to attend college to prepare for a teaching career.

Eligibility: Open to students who are 1) graduating high school seniors with a GPA of 3.0 or higher or with minimum scores of 22 on the ACT or 1030 on the combined critical reading and mathematics SAT; 2) enrolled in college with a GPA of 3.0 or higher; 3) enrolled at a technical school or returning to school after an absence for retraining of job skills or obtaining a degree; or 4) engaged in online study through an accredited college, university, or vocational school. Applicants must be planning to prepare for a teaching career. They may attend school in any state. Selection is based on character (10%), leadership (20%), service (10%), financial need (30%), and scholastic ability (30%).

Financial data: The stipend is $1,000.

Duration: 1 year; may be renewed.

Number awarded: 1 each year.

Deadline: January of each year.

3055 WORLD WIDE BARACA PHILATHEA UNION SCHOLARSHIP

Summary: To provide financial assistance to students preparing for Christian ministry, Christian missionary work, or Christian education.

See Listing #1623.

3056 WSAJ AMERICAN JUSTICE ESSAY SCHOLARSHIP CONTEST

Washington State Association for Justice
1511 State Avenue, N.E.
Olympia, WA 98506-4552
Phone: (360) 786-9100; Fax: (360) 786-9103
Email: adrianne@wstlaoly.org
Web: www.wstla.org/AboutUs/Historical.aspx

Summary: To recognize and reward, with scholarships for college in any state, high school students in Washington who submit an essay on a topic related to the role of the civil justice system in our society.

Eligibility: Open to students attending high school in the state of Washington. Applicants must submit an essay, from 4 to 5 pages in length, on a topic that changes annually; recently, students were invited to write on how the civil justice system improves American society. They must be interested in attending college in any state.

Financial data: Awards range from $1,000 to $3,000, to be used when the recipient attends college. Funds are paid directly to the winners' institutions, to be used for tuition, room, board, or fees.

Duration: The competition is held annually.

Number awarded: Up to 3 each year.

Deadline: March of each year.

3057 WVHTA EDUCATIONAL FOUNDATION "CO-BRANDED" SCHOLARSHIP

Summary: To provide financial assistance to high school seniors in West Virginia who are planning to enroll in a culinary or hospitality degree program in college.

See Listing #1626.

3058 WVHTA EDUCATIONAL FOUNDATION GENERAL SCHOLARSHIP

West Virginia Hospitality and Travel Association
Attn: WVHTA Educational Foundation
P.O. Box 2391
Charleston, WV 25328-2391
Phone: (304) 342-6511; Fax: (304) 345-1538
Email: edfdn@wvhta.com
Web: www.wvhta.com/education-foundation.html

Summary: To provide financial assistance to high school seniors in West Virginia who are planning to enroll in a hospitality degree program in college.

Eligibility: Open to seniors graduating from high schools in West Virginia who have a GPA of 2.75 or higher. Applicants must have at least 250 hours of work experience related to the hospitality and travel industry. They must have applied to a hospitality degree program at a postsecondary institution anywhere in the country. Along with their application, they must submit an essay, from 250 to 350 words in length, on the experience that most influenced their decision to prepare for a career in hospitality, travel, and recreation management. Selection is based on the essay, academic performance, industry-related work experience, letters of recommendation, and presentation of the application.

Financial data: The stipend is $1,000.

Duration: 1 year.

Number awarded: 1 or more each year.

Deadline: March of each year.

3059 WYOMING ASSOCIATION OF PUBLIC ACCOUNTANTS SCHOLARSHIP

Wyoming Association of Public Accountants
c/o Jarvis Windom, Scholarship Chair
1064 Gilchrist Street
Wheatland, WY 82201
Phone: (307) 322-3433
Email: jarvis@windom.org
Web: www.wyopa.com/scholarship.htm

Summary: To provide financial assistance to residents of Wyoming interested in working on a degree in business or accounting at a school in the state.

Eligibility: Open to residents of Wyoming who are enrolled or planning to enroll full-time at an accredited college or university in the state. Applicants must be majoring or planning to major in accounting or business. Along with their application, they must submit a brief paragraph on their reasons for wishing to study in the professional field of accounting. Financial need is considered in the selection process.

Financial data: A stipend is awarded (amount not specified).

Duration: 1 year.

Number awarded: 1 each year.

Deadline: Deadline not specified.

3060 WYOMING SUPERIOR STUDENT IN EDUCATION SCHOLARSHIP

University of Wyoming
Attn: Office of Teacher Education
100 East University Avenue, Department 3374
McWhinnie Hall, Room 100
Laramie, WY 82071
Phone: (307) 766-2230
Email: edquest@uwyo.edu

Summary: To provide financial assistance to residents of Wyoming who are attending college in the state to prepare for a career in teaching.

Eligibility: Open to graduates of Wyoming high schools who are currently enrolled in the teacher preparation program at the University of Wyoming or a community college in the state. Applicants or their parent or legal guardian must currently be and have been a resident of Wyoming for at least 5 years. They must have a GPA of 3.5 or higher in high school or 3.25 or higher at the university or community college and either an SAT score (critical reading and mathematics) of 1120 or higher or an ACT score of 25 or higher. Selection is based on academic record, courses completed, extracurricular activities, and the student's responses to prepared questions.

Financial data: The stipend is $500 per semester ($1,000 per year).

Duration: 1 year; may be renewed if the recipient maintains full-time enrollment and a GPA of 2.75 or higher. Support may be provided for up to 10 semesters, of which no more than 5 semesters may be at a community college.

Number awarded: Up to 16 each year: up to 2 at the University of Wyoming and each of the 7 community colleges in the state.

Deadline: March of each year.

3061 WYOMING TEACHER SHORTAGE LOAN REPAYMENT PROGRAM

Align
1401 Airport Parkway, Suite 300
Cheyenne, WY 82001-1543
Phone: (307) 638-0800; (800) 999-6541; Fax: (307) 778-3943
Web: www.mystudentloanalign.org/tslr.asp

Summary: To provide financial assistance to education students interested in working in Wyoming after graduation.

Eligibility: Open to education students who have educational loans from WyoLoan, First Education FCU, Trona Valley FCU, or UniWyo FCU. Applicants must be preparing for a career as a teacher of mathematics, science, special education, foreign language, English as a second language, or reading education. They must agree to acquire a teaching certificate within 180 days after graduation and seek employment at a public school in Wyoming within 240 days after receipt of their certificate.

Financial data: Repayment of loans is provided for the full amount or $12,000 per year, whichever is less.

Duration: Loans that can be repaid with work of 2 years or less must be repaid within 3 years; loans that can be repaid with work of greater than 2 but no more than 4 years must be repaid within 5 years; loans that can be repaid with work of greater than 4 years must be repaid within the amount of time the loan could be repaid plus 2 years.

Number awarded: Varies each year.

Deadline: Applications may be submitted at any time.

3062 WYOMING TRUCKING ASSOCIATION SCHOLARSHIPS

Summary: To provide financial assistance to high school seniors and currently-enrolled college students in Wyoming who are interested in preparing for a career in the highway transportation industry.

See Listing #2474.

3063 YELLOW RIBBON SCHOLARSHIP

Tourism Cares
Attn: National Tour Association Scholarship Fund
275 Turnpike Street, Suite 307
Canton, MA 02021
Phone: (781) 821-5990; Fax: (781) 821-8949
Email: info@tourismcares.org
Web: www.tourismcares.org/scholarships/nta-scholarships

Summary: To provide financial assistance for college or graduate school to students with disabilities who are planning a career in the travel and tourism industry.

Eligibility: Open to citizens and permanent residents of the United States and Canada who have a physical or sensory disability. Applicants must be entering or attending an accredited 2- or 4-year college or university in the United States or Canada. They must be working on or planning to work on an undergraduate or graduate degree in a field related to travel and tourism and have a GPA of 2.5 or higher. Along with their application, they must submit a 2-page essay on contributions they feel they might make in the travel, tourism, and hospitality industry. Financial need is not considered in the selection process.

Financial data: The stipend is $5,000.

Duration: 1 year.

Number awarded: 1 each year.

Deadline: March of each year.

3064 YOUNG ENTREPRENEURS ESSAY CONTEST

Skandalaris Family Foundation
1030 Doris Road
Auburn Hills, MI 48326
Phone: (248) 292-5678; Fax: (248) 292-5697
Email: info@skandalaris.org
Web: www.skandalaris.org/young-entrepreneurs.php

Summary: To recognize and reward, with college scholarships, high school seniors who submit outstanding essays based on the *The Entrepreneur's Game* books.

Eligibility: Open to graduating high school seniors who are U.S. citizens and planning to attend a college or university in any state that offers a bachelor's degree. Applicants must purchase a copy of either *The Entrepreneur's Game: Logan's Story* or *The Entrepreneur's Game: Adrienne's Story,* and write an essay, from 3 to 5 pages, on the actions of the main character in the story. The essay should use examples from the book and the student's own understanding of business and entrepreneurship to critique what the character did wrong and right. Selection is based on that essay, personal information, and other short essays on the student's planned career path, how the concepts of innovation and risk-taking relate to their chosen career, and 3 lessons they learned from the book and how they can apply those lessons to their life. Neither academic achievement nor financial need are considered in the selection process.

Financial data: Awards range from $1,000 to $5,000. Funds must be used as partial payment of college tuition in the year following the competition.

Duration: The competition is held annually.

Number awarded: 27 each year.

Deadline: Books must be purchased by January of each year. Essays must be submitted prior to the end of February.

3065 ZONTA INTERNATIONAL YOUNG WOMEN IN PUBLIC AFFAIRS AWARDS

Zonta International
Attn: Foundation
1211 West 22nd Street, Suite 900
Oak Brook, IL 60523-3384
Phone: (630) 928-1400; Fax: (630) 928-1559
Email: programs@zonta.org
Web: www.zonta.org/WhatWeDo/InternationalPrograms.aspx

Summary: To recognize and reward women in secondary schools who are interested in a career in public policy, government, or volunteer organizations.

Eligibility: Open to young women, 16 to 19 years of age, who are currently living or studying in a district or region of Zonta International. Applicants must be interested in preparing for a career in public affairs, public policy, or community organization. Along with their application, they must submit essays on their student activities and leadership roles (200 words), their community service activities (200 words), their efforts to understand other countries (150 words), and the status of women in their country and worldwide (300 words). Selection is based on commitment to volunteerism, experience in local or student government, volunteer leadership achievements, knowledge of Zonta International and its programs, and advocating in Zonta International's mission of advancing the status of women worldwide. Winners are selected at the club level and forwarded for a district competition; district winners are entered in the international competition.

Financial data: District awardees receive $1,000 and international awardees receive $3,000.

Duration: The competition is held annually.

Number awarded: Varies each year; recently, 24 district winners and 5 international winners were selected. Since the program began, it has presented 565 awards to 503 young women from 49 countries.

Deadline: Clubs set their own deadlines but must submit their winners to the district governor by March of each year.

Subject Index

Use this index when you want to identify funding programs by subject. To help you pinpoint your search, we've also included hundreds of "see" and "see also" references. In addition to looking for terms that represent your specific subject interests, be sure to check the "General programs" entry; hundred of programs are listed there that can be used to support study in any subject area (although the programs may be restricted in other ways). Remember: The numbers cited in this index refer to book entry numbers, not page numbers in the book.

A.V.. *See* Audiovisual materials and equipment

Accounting: 1165, 1472, 1474, 1635, 1681, 1709, 1736, 1751, 1812, 1930, 1944, 1950, 1997, 2000, 2110, 2152, 2170, 2195, 2356, 2407, 2413, 2415, 2453, 2474, 2483, 2505, 2518, 2527, 2529, 2532, 2539–2540, 2548, 2571, 2585, 2593, 2607, 2653–2654, 2676, 2686, 2689, 2711, 2718, 2724–2725, 2802, 2808, 2829, 2845, 2847, 2852, 2878, 2886, 2890, 2897, 2931, 2947, 2966, 2970, 2972, 2977, 2992, 3004, 3006, 3008–3009, 3024, 3036–3037, 3041, 3052, 3059, 3062. *See also* Finance; General programs

Acquired Immunodeficiency Syndrome. *See* AIDS

Acting. *See* Performing arts

Actuarial sciences: 2316, 2488, 2526, 2567, 2576, 2578–2580, 2628, 2640, 2677, 2737, 2744, 2748, 2760, 2806, 2820, 2913, 2956, 2977. *See also* General programs; Statistics

Administration. *See* Business administration; Education, administration; Management; Nurses and nursing, administration; Personnel administration; Public administration

Advertising: 1138, 1154, 1160–1162, 1237, 1272, 1298, 1353, 1355, 1389, 1401–1402, 1446, 1463, 1487, 1490, 1492, 1529, 1537, 1593, 1625, 2489, 2527, 2548, 2787, 2953, 2997. *See also* Communications; General programs; Marketing; Public relations

Aeronautical engineering. *See* Engineering, aeronautical

Aerospace engineering. *See* Engineering, aerospace

Aerospace sciences. *See* Space sciences

Aged and aging: 2118, 2714, 2813. *See also* General programs; Social sciences

Agribusiness: 1731, 1794–1795, 1814, 1816, 1997, 2008, 2082–2083, 2143, 2169, 2201, 2265, 2407, 2417, 2594, 2724, 2783–2784, 2860, 3004. *See also* Agriculture and agricultural sciences; Business administration; General programs

Agricultural communications: 1274, 1417, 1447, 1592, 1814, 2131, 2164, 2201, 2393. *See also* Agriculture and agricultural sciences; Communications; General programs

Agricultural economics. *See* Economics, agricultural

Agricultural education. *See* Education, agricultural

Agricultural engineering. *See* Engineering, agricultural

Agricultural technology: 2407, 3004. *See also* Agriculture and agricultural sciences; General programs; Technology

Agriculture and agricultural sciences: 79, 1566, 1639, 1667, 1704, 1729, 1738, 1786, 1790–1791, 1800, 1802, 1805, 1814–1816, 1821, 1837, 1843, 1851, 1867, 1874, 1888, 1895, 1937, 1997, 1999, 2008, 2036, 2051, 2143, 2148, 2152, 2164, 2169–2170, 2201, 2236, 2265, 2268, 2277–2278, 2357, 2381, 2385–2386, 2388, 2407, 2417, 2434, 2438, 2441, 2444, 2459, 2465, 2530, 2572, 2594, 2598, 2627, 2645, 2724, 2845, 2860, 3004, 3027. *See also* Biological sciences; General programs

Agrimarketing and sales. *See* Agribusiness

Agronomy: 1449, 1592, 1731, 1783, 1800, 1814, 1845, 1997, 2034, 2106, 2131, 2142, 2152, 2167, 2170, 2206, 2265, 2393, 2407, 2423, 2434, 2724, 2845, 2882, 3004. *See also* Agriculture and agricultural sciences; General programs

AIDS: 1702. *See also* Disabilities; General programs; Medical sciences

Air conditioning industry. *See* Cooling industry

American history. *See* History, American

American Indian studies. *See* Native American studies

American literature. *See* Literature, American

American studies: 1414. *See also* General programs; Humanities

Anesthetic nurses and nursing. *See* Nurses and nursing, anesthesiology

Animal rights: 2335. *See also* General programs; Veterinary sciences

Animal science: 1417, 1814, 1835, 1997, 2003, 2024–2025, 2083, 2124, 2164, 2169–2170, 2201, 2210, 2265, 2388, 2407, 2417, 2438, 2459, 2724, 2742–2743, 2784, 2860, 3004, 3027. *See also* General programs; Sciences; names of specific animal sciences

Animation: 1136, 1625. *See also* Cartoonists and cartoons; Filmmaking; General programs

Anthropology: 1414, 2566. *See also* General programs; Social sciences

Applied arts. *See* Arts and crafts

Aquaculture: 2058, 2332, 2367. *See also* Agriculture and agricultural sciences; General programs

Aquatic sciences. *See* Oceanography

Arabic language. *See* Language, Arabic

Arboriculture: 1842, 2138. *See also* General programs; Horticulture

Archaeology: 1181, 1324, 1458, 2566. *See also* General programs; History; Social sciences

Architectural engineering. *See* Engineering, architectural

Architecture: 8, 1134, 1139, 1141, 1143, 1155, 1165, 1168, 1172, 1181, 1187–1188, 1201–1202, 1216, 1228, 1245, 1296, 1301–1302, 1317, 1323–1324, 1339, 1342, 1393, 1458, 1470, 1509, 1552, 1559, 1588, 1625, 1652, 1659, 1709, 1716, 1734, 1758, 1771, 1840, 1900, 1967, 1994, 1998, 2193, 2211, 2257, 2313, 2518, 2704. *See also* Fine arts; General programs; Historical preservation

Architecture, naval. *See* Naval architecture

Arithmetic. *See* Mathematics

Armed services. *See* Military affairs

Armenian studies: 1283, 2685. *See also* General programs; Humanities

Art: 79, 1141, 1144, 1161, 1166, 1197, 1214, 1261, 1288, 1295, 1363, 1385, 1401, 1422, 1446, 1513, 1529, 1551–1552, 1562, 1625, 1628, 1659, 2115, 2751, 2812. *See also* Education, art; Fine arts; General programs; Illustrators and illustrations; names of specific art forms

Art conservation: 1241, 1315, 1385. *See also* Art; General programs

Art education. *See* Education, art

Art history. *See* History, art

Art therapy: 1854, 2362. *See also* General programs

Arts administration: 1144, 1304, 2707. *See also* Fine arts; General programs; Management

Arts and crafts: 1625. *See also* Art; General programs; names of specific crafts

Asian studies: 1570, 2368, 2975. *See also* General programs; Humanities

Astronomy: 1741, 2024, 2170, 2408, 2742. *See also* General programs; Physical sciences

Astrophysics: 2170, 2341. *See also* Astronomy; General programs

Athletic training: 1838, 1989, 2216, 2425. *See also* Athletics; General programs

Athletics: 2161, 2543, 2558, 2855, 2996. *See also* Athletic training; Education, physical; General programs; Sports medicine; names of specific sports

Atmospheric sciences: 1694, 1700, 1770, 1859, 1910–1911, 2019, 2071, 2100, 2125, 2170, 2341, 2444, 2659. *See also* General programs; Physical sciences

Attorneys. *See* Law, general

Audiology: 1989, 2162, 2194. *See also* General programs; Health and health care; Medical sciences

Audiovisual materials and equipment: 1336, 1392, 2026. *See also* General programs; names of specific types of media

Autism: 2646. *See also* Disabilities; General programs

Automation. *See* Computer sciences; Information science; Technology

Automobile industry: 1635, 1743, 1789, 1813, 1944, 1958, 1961, 2050, 2333, 2483, 2535, 2560, 2620, 2686, 2695, 2699, 2761, 2963–2964. *See also* General programs

Automotive engineering. *See* Engineering, automotive

Automotive repair: 552, 1813, 2067, 2449. *See also* General programs

Automotive technology: 552, 1635, 1662, 1742, 1789, 1813, 1944, 1958, 1961, 2050, 2067, 2333, 2449, 2474, 2479, 2483, 2560, 2686, 2695, 2699, 2761, 2963, 3062. *See also* Engineering, automotive; General programs; Transportation

Aviation: 1286, 1744, 1778, 1803, 1809, 1836, 1850, 1879, 1883, 1960, 2027, 2048, 2060, 2128, 2262, 2272, 2285, 2353, 2464, 2967. *See also* General programs; Space sciences; Transportation

Azerbaijani language. *See* Language, Azeri

Azeri language. *See* Language, Azeri

Ballet. *See* Dance

Banking: 1570, 2368, 2667, 2673–2674, 2774, 2788, 2847, 2975, 3000, 3037. *See also* Finance; General programs

Barbering. *See* Hair design

Basketry: 1385. *See also* Arts and crafts; General programs

Beef industry: 1753, 1835, 2201, 2311, 2442. *See also* General programs; Ranching

Behavioral sciences: 1874, 2024–2025, 2253, 2327, 2627, 2742–2743, 2920. *See also* General programs; Social sciences; names of special behavioral sciences

Bengali language. *See* Language, Bengali

Bilingualism: 2716. *See also* Education, bilingual; English as a foreign language; English as a second language; General programs; Language and linguistics

Biochemistry: 1141, 1659, 1801, 1908, 2024–2025, 2170, 2341, 2742–2743. *See also* Biological sciences; Chemistry; General programs

Biological sciences: 200, 1141, 1165, 1449, 1592, 1651, 1659, 1681, 1709, 1717, 1741, 1763–1764, 1784, 1799, 1801, 1818, 1826, 1845, 1861, 1874, 1889, 1908, 1910, 1939, 1968, 1974, 1989, 2152, 2163, 2167–2168, 2170, 2241, 2246, 2268, 2275, 2300, 2327, 2332, 2340–2341, 2348, 2384, 2393–2394, 2423, 2436, 2439, 2444, 2505, 2518, 2621, 2627, 2659, 2845, 2857, 3019. *See also* General programs; Sciences; names of specific biological sciences

Biomedical engineering. *See* Engineering, biomedical

Biomedical sciences: 2170, 2315. *See also* Biological sciences; General programs; Medical sciences

Biometrics: 2020, 2741. *See also* Biological sciences; Statistics

Biophysics: 1801, 2170, 2341, 2408. *See also* Biological sciences; Chemistry; Computer sciences; General programs; Mathematics; Physics
Biotechnology: 1717, 1814, 2059, 2152, 2170, 2845. *See also* Biological sciences; General programs; Technology
Blindness. *See* Visual impairments
Botany: 1282, 1449, 1592, 1731, 1845, 1941, 2024–2025, 2034, 2106, 2131, 2152, 2167, 2170, 2268, 2341, 2381, 2393, 2417, 2423, 2742–2743, 2845. *See also* Biological sciences; General programs
Brain research. *See* Neuroscience
Broadcast engineering. *See* Engineering, broadcast
Broadcast journalism. *See* Journalism, broadcast
Broadcasting: 552, 1149, 1151, 1170, 1183–1184, 1197, 1210, 1229, 1251, 1264, 1271, 1303, 1306, 1327, 1330, 1333, 1350, 1355, 1361, 1371, 1378, 1402, 1411, 1424, 1435, 1465, 1472–1473, 1487–1488, 1493, 1501, 1521, 1532, 1581, 1602, 1616, 1621, 1918, 2195, 2450, 2521, 2570, 2730, 2878, 3033. *See also* Communications; Radio; Television
Building trades: 552, 1139, 1317, 1652, 1771, 1994, 2010. *See also* General programs
Business administration: 79, 261, 508, 1165, 1210, 1213, 1256, 1284, 1301, 1325, 1327–1328, 1377, 1422, 1462, 1496, 1576, 1582, 1593, 1616, 1635, 1637, 1644, 1681, 1699, 1706, 1709, 1774, 1802, 1812, 1835, 1851, 1853, 1865, 1898, 1944, 1950, 1953–1954, 1996–1997, 2000, 2006, 2020, 2028, 2076, 2088, 2115, 2132, 2136, 2152, 2155, 2161, 2177, 2183, 2209, 2239, 2255–2256, 2307, 2355–2356, 2376, 2407, 2413, 2415, 2450, 2453, 2462, 2474, 2483–2484, 2486, 2505, 2509, 2518, 2532, 2540, 2548, 2556, 2567, 2570–2573, 2577, 2579–2580, 2583, 2585, 2593, 2595, 2617, 2628, 2642, 2649, 2661, 2664, 2677, 2686, 2689, 2691–2692, 2700, 2704, 2711, 2718, 2723–2725, 2727, 2730–2731, 2737, 2741, 2745, 2755–2756, 2763, 2766, 2777–2778, 2788, 2790, 2792, 2801, 2812, 2819–2821, 2825, 2832, 2845, 2848–2849, 2851–2852, 2855, 2865, 2867, 2869, 2873, 2885, 2887, 2890, 2900, 2909, 2913, 2932, 2934, 2938, 2946, 2948, 2954, 2964, 2969–2970, 2977, 2979, 2987, 2997, 3000, 3004, 3006, 3008–3009, 3017, 3024–3026, 3033, 3036–3037, 3040–3041, 3044, 3059, 3062. *See also* Entrepreneurship; General programs; Management
Business education. *See* Education, business
Business enterprises. *See* Entrepreneurship
Cable TV industry: 1264, 1918. *See also* General programs; Television
Cable TV journalism. *See* Journalism, cable
Cambodian Language. *See* Language, Cambodian
Cancer: 2063, 2234–2235, 2299. *See also* Disabilities; General programs; Health and health care; Medical sciences
Cars. *See* Automobile industry; Engineering, automotive
Cartography: 1250, 1641, 1834, 2639. *See also* General programs; Geography
Cartoonists and cartoons: 1217, 1625. *See also* Art; General programs; Illustrators and illustrations
Cast metal industry: 1988. *See also* General programs
Cataloging. *See* Libraries and librarianship, technical services
Cattle ranching. *See* Ranching
Cell biology: 2024, 2170, 2742. *See also* Biological sciences; General programs
Censorship: 1633. *See also* Civil liberties; General programs; Intellectual freedom
Ceramics: 1261, 1552. *See also* Arts and crafts; General programs
Chemical engineering. *See* Engineering, chemical
Chemistry: 8, 200, 1165, 1651, 1653, 1669, 1681, 1697, 1709, 1737, 1741, 1784, 1801, 1826, 1861, 1872, 1874, 1889, 1906, 1908, 1939, 1968, 2001, 2024–2025, 2042–2043, 2118, 2152, 2170, 2190–2191, 2218, 2241, 2270, 2327, 2340–2341, 2384, 2399, 2408, 2444, 2475, 2505, 2518, 2621, 2627, 2742–2743, 2813, 2845, 2877. *See also* Engineering, chemical; General programs; Physical sciences
Child care. *See* Day care
Child development: 2118, 2586, 2651, 2662, 2665, 2767, 2771, 2799, 2809, 2813, 2815, 2830, 2898, 2901, 2957. *See also* General programs
Chinese language. *See* Language, Chinese
Chiropractic: 2378. *See also* General programs; Medical sciences
Choreography: 1166, 1631. *See also* Dance; General programs; Performing arts
Choruses. *See* Voice
Church music. *See* Music, church
Cinema: 1206, 1301, 2704. *See also* Filmmaking; General programs; Literature
City and regional planning: 1181, 1296, 1324, 1449, 1458, 1625, 1840, 1845, 2155, 2167, 2423, 2557, 2561–2562, 2666, 2679, 2773, 2779, 2794, 2849, 2914, 2939, 2999. *See also* General programs; Urban affairs
Civil engineering. *See* Engineering, civil
Civil liberties: 1269. *See also* Civil rights; General programs; Political science and politics
Civil rights: 2307, 2895, 2948. *See also* General programs; Political science and politics
Clairvoyance. *See* Parapsychology
Classical music. *See* Music, classical
Clerical skills. *See* Secretarial sciences
Clothing: 1191, 1385, 2769, 2809. *See also* Fashion design; General programs; Home economics
Colleges and universities. *See* Education, higher
Commerce. *See* Business administration
Communications: 79, 487, 1125, 1148, 1151, 1153–1154, 1160–1161, 1169–1170, 1197, 1208, 1210, 1213, 1229, 1237, 1242–1243, 1246, 1256–1258, 1263–1264, 1270, 1278, 1285, 1287, 1298, 1301, 1313–1314, 1330, 1344, 1353, 1367, 1378, 1387, 1392, 1398, 1401–1402, 1446, 1465–1466, 1486–1487, 1490, 1496, 1500–1501, 1504, 1508, 1517, 1520, 1529, 1577, 1581, 1593, 1610, 1617, 1620–1621, 1835, 1874, 1882, 1898, 1902, 1918, 2084, 2183, 2239, 2247, 2309, 2521, 2570, 2577, 2627, 2636, 2649, 2656, 2704, 2869, 2909, 2951, 2980, 2997. *See also* General programs; Humanities
Communications, agricultural. *See* Agricultural communications
Community colleges. *See* Education, higher
Community services. *See* Social services
Composers and compositions: 200, 1166, 1173–1174, 1193, 1364, 1443, 1461, 1503, 1539, 1622, 1631, 1634. *See also* General programs; Music; Musicals
Computer engineering. *See* Engineering, computer
Computer sciences: 8, 79, 200, 310, 552, 1141, 1256, 1258, 1264, 1496, 1570, 1635, 1644, 1655–1659, 1668–1670, 1681–1682, 1717, 1736, 1741, 1775, 1796–1797, 1801, 1807, 1824, 1826–1827, 1861, 1872, 1874, 1876, 1886, 1898, 1902, 1910, 1912, 1918, 1930, 1944, 1946, 1948, 1963–1964, 1966, 1976, 1991, 1996–1997, 2020, 2024–2025, 2032, 2059, 2077, 2093, 2097–2098, 2108, 2113, 2118, 2120, 2132–2133, 2136, 2152, 2160, 2165, 2170, 2215, 2239, 2246, 2251, 2264, 2275–2276, 2296, 2301, 2323, 2327–2328, 2340–2341, 2349, 2356, 2368, 2370, 2399, 2408, 2410–2411, 2413–2415, 2422, 2444, 2451, 2460, 2462, 2474–2475, 2480, 2483, 2486, 2505, 2529, 2567, 2579–2580, 2621, 2627, 2631, 2649, 2656, 2659, 2676–2677, 2686, 2688, 2723–2724, 2741–2743, 2804, 2813, 2821–2822, 2825, 2845, 2909, 2931, 2970, 2975, 3008–3009, 3014, 3034, 3044, 3062. *See also* General programs; Mathematics; Technology
Computers. *See* Computer sciences
Concrete industry: 2471. *See also* Building trades; General programs
Conflict resolution. *See* Peace studies
Conservation. *See* Art conservation; Environmental sciences
Construction. *See* Building trades; Housing
Construction engineering. *See* Engineering, construction
Construction industry: 1139, 1165, 1317, 1462, 1509, 1637, 1652, 1661, 1663–1665, 1699, 1706, 1709, 1733–1734, 1758, 1771, 1774, 1782, 1840, 1844, 1865, 1875, 1900, 1924, 1928, 1935, 1967, 1973, 1990, 1994, 2010, 2014, 2081, 2177, 2204, 2211, 2255–2257, 2313, 2324, 2345, 2372, 2390, 2396, 2433, 2484, 2518, 2555, 2610, 2678, 2705, 2850, 2867, 2960, 2993. *See also* Building trades; General programs
Consumer and family studies education. *See* Education, family and consumer studies
Consumer law. *See* Nurses and nursing, wound, ostomy and continence
Cooking. *See* Culinary arts
Cooling industry: 1699, 1706, 1734, 1771, 1774, 1823, 1865, 2255–2256. *See also* General programs
Cosmetology. *See* Hair design
Costume: 1191, 1587, 1625. *See also* Art; Fashion design; General programs
Counseling: 2118, 2490, 2813. *See also* Behavioral sciences; General programs; Psychiatry; Psychology
Counselors and counseling, school: 2717, 2796, 2866, 2905, 3021. *See also* Counseling; Education; General programs
Counter-intelligence service. *See* Intelligence service
Crafts. *See* Arts and crafts
Creative writing: 597, 1144, 1166, 1537, 1631. *See also* Fine arts; General programs; Literature
Criminal justice: 2033, 2566, 2575, 2608, 2660, 2749, 2762, 2786, 2789, 2803, 2826, 2891, 3001, 3005, 3012, 3049. *See also* General programs; Law, general
Critical care nurses and nursing. *See* Nurses and nursing, critical care
Culinary arts: 1158–1159, 1204–1205, 1207, 1224, 1233, 1280, 1328, 1330, 1348–1349, 1388, 1593, 1603, 1626, 2006, 2563, 2731, 2752, 2769, 2805, 2997, 3015, 3042, 3057–3058. *See also* Food service industry; General programs; Home economics
Dairy science: 1417, 1851, 1901, 1951, 2003, 2083, 2124, 2164, 2183, 2784, 2869. *See also* Agriculture and agricultural sciences; General programs
Dance: 541, 887, 1141, 1170, 1201, 1206, 1223, 1235, 1260, 1302, 1305, 1340, 1351, 1410, 1420–1421, 1549, 1578, 1631, 1659, 2317, 2521, 2709, 2751, 2810–2811, 2996. *See also* Choreography; General programs; Performing arts
Data entry. *See* Computer sciences; Secretarial sciences
Day care: 2118, 2813, 2957. *See also* Education, preschool; General programs
Deafness. *See* Hearing impairments
Defense. *See* Military affairs
Dental assisting: 1869, 2065. *See also* Dentistry; General programs

Dental hygiene: 552, 1870, 2009, 2066, 2094, 2290, 2416, 2419, 2445. *See also* Dentistry; General programs
Dental laboratory technology: 1871. *See also* Dental hygiene; General programs
Dentistry: 1822, 1881, 1939, 1980, 2245, 2290, 2378, 2445. *See also* General programs; Health and health care; Medical sciences
Design: 1191, 1201, 1261, 1273, 1297, 1331, 1337, 1339, 1385, 1394, 1543, 1552, 1594, 1625, 1713, 1975, 2010, 2706, 2998. *See also* Art; General programs
Developmental disabilities. *See* Disabilities, developmental
Die-casting industry. *See* Cast metal industry
Dietetics. *See* Nutrition
Disabilities: 1685, 1721, 1752, 1913, 2118, 2233, 2261, 2523, 2663, 2736, 2813, 2907, 2912, 3021. *See also* General programs; Rehabilitation; names of specific disabilities
Disabilities, developmental: 1878, 2040, 2630, 3002, 3021. *See also* Disabilities; General programs
Disabilities, learning: 2736, 3021. *See also* Disabilities; General programs
Disabilities, hearing. *See* Hearing impairments
Disabilities, visual. *See* Visual impairments
Disability law: 1721, 1913, 2523, 2663. *See also* General programs; Law, general
Divinity. *See* Religion and religious activities
Documentaries. *See* Filmmaking
Domestic science. *See* Home economics
Drafting: 552, 1139, 1652. *See also* General programs
Early childhood education. *See* Education, preschool
Earth sciences: 200, 1141, 1659, 1737, 1741, 1916, 1952, 2024–2025, 2043, 2118, 2170, 2275, 2327, 2341, 2435, 2463, 2742–2743, 2813, 3019. *See also* General programs; Natural sciences; names of specific earth sciences
Ecology. *See* Environmental sciences
Economic development: 2155, 2849. *See also* Economics; General programs
Economic planning. *See* Economics
Economics: 1249, 1681, 1751, 1874, 1950, 1996, 2000, 2155, 2183, 2453, 2505, 2539, 2566, 2595, 2603, 2607, 2627–2628, 2638, 2658, 2667–2668, 2689, 2718, 2723, 2725, 2820, 2849, 2856, 2869, 2890, 2964, 3000, 3006, 3036, 3041. *See also* General programs; Social sciences
Economics, agricultural: 1814, 1997, 2164, 2169, 2201, 2407, 2724, 2860, 3004. *See also* Agriculture and agricultural sciences; Economics; General programs
Education: 310, 406, 508, 751, 872, 1058, 1246, 1283, 1301, 1422, 1516, 1573, 1582, 1594, 1676, 1715, 1853, 1882, 1896, 2004, 2088, 2092, 2115, 2132, 2149, 2155, 2202, 2312, 2369, 2376, 2492, 2500, 2503–2504, 2517, 2519, 2536, 2538, 2547, 2553–2554, 2565, 2574, 2588–2590, 2592, 2606, 2609, 2611–2612, 2616–2617, 2622–2624, 2632–2633, 2635–2636, 2641, 2648, 2657, 2671, 2675, 2680–2681, 2685, 2696, 2698, 2701–2702, 2704, 2729, 2732, 2747, 2756, 2767, 2771, 2786, 2790, 2795–2796, 2800, 2812, 2818, 2821, 2836–2837, 2839–2840, 2843–2844, 2849, 2866, 2880–2881, 2892–2894, 2898, 2910, 2924–2925, 2930, 2937, 2945, 2952, 2955, 2958, 2965, 2973, 2976, 2982–2983, 2987, 2998, 3007, 3045, 3048, 3054, 3060. *See also* General programs; Social sciences; names of specific types and levels of education
Education, administration: 1462, 2177, 2866–2867. *See also* Education; General programs; Management
Education, agricultural: 1449, 2131, 2164, 2167, 2183, 2459, 2869, 3031. *See also* Agriculture and agricultural sciences; Education; General programs
Education, art: 2520. *See also* Art; Education; General programs
Education, bilingual: 2590, 2613, 2624, 2716, 2733, 2818, 2981. *See also* Bilingualism; Education; English as a second language; General programs
Education, business: 2573, 2590, 2613, 2624, 2763, 2902, 2918, 3021, 3031. *See also* Education; General programs
Education, elementary: 944, 1017, 2016, 2118, 2248, 2292–2293, 2391, 2497, 2502, 2516, 2520, 2549, 2582, 2600, 2614, 2650, 2652, 2733, 2739, 2751, 2753, 2780, 2813, 2816, 2827, 2833, 2853, 2903, 2915, 2929, 2940–2941, 2961, 2981, 2984, 2995–2996, 3019, 3021, 3039, 3047. *See also* Education; General programs
Education, English and language arts: 2520, 2590, 2613, 2624, 2683, 2776, 2905, 3019, 3021, 3061. *See also* Education; General programs; Language, English
Education, environmental: 1910, 1916, 2088, 2309, 2659, 2790, 2951. *See also* Education; Environmental sciences; General programs
Education, family and consumer studies: 2597, 2613, 2665, 2712, 2769, 2807, 2809, 2901, 3019, 3021, 3031. *See also* Education; Family and consumer studies; General programs
Education, foreign languages: 1209, 1852, 2118, 2191, 2520, 2569, 2590, 2613, 2615, 2624, 2651, 2733, 2776, 2813, 2818, 2836–2837, 2877, 2905, 2981, 3019, 3021, 3061. *See also* Education; General programs; Language and linguistics
Education, gifted and talented: 2651. *See also* Education; General programs
Education, health: 1759, 1989, 2400, 2544. *See also* Education; General programs; Health and health care
Education, higher: 1012, 1599, 2650. *See also* Education; General programs
Education, journalism: 1368, 1580, 2770, 2986. *See also* Education; General programs; Journalism
Education, music: 1176, 1222, 1293, 1434, 1440, 1852, 2528, 2590, 2596, 2615, 2624, 2697, 2793, 2834, 2846. *See also* Education; General programs; Music
Education, physical: 1305, 1420–1421, 1895, 2216, 2543, 2634, 2645, 2687, 2709, 2733, 2810–2811, 2996, 3007, 3021. *See also* Athletics; Education; General programs
Education, preschool: 2118, 2586, 2733, 2769, 2799, 2813, 2815, 2830, 2833, 2905, 2929, 2957, 2984, 3018. *See also* Day care; Education; General programs
Education, religious: 432, 1432, 1612, 1623, 3032, 3055. *See also* Education; General programs; Religion and religious activities
Education, science and mathematics: 1655–1656, 1718, 1737, 1784, 1824, 1852, 1876, 1946, 1948, 2035, 2113, 2121, 2134, 2144, 2149, 2188–2189, 2191, 2207, 2248, 2269, 2292–2293, 2297, 2322, 2391, 2408, 2422, 2444, 2452, 2520, 2522, 2590, 2613, 2615, 2624, 2631, 2651, 2683, 2688, 2733, 2750, 2776, 2804, 2817–2818, 2824, 2835–2837, 2840, 2875–2877, 2883, 2905, 2915, 2923, 2940–2942, 2959, 2961, 2981, 2995, 3014, 3019, 3021, 3031, 3035, 3061. *See also* Education; General programs; Sciences
Education, secondary: 944, 1017, 1209, 1368, 2016, 2118, 2207, 2292–2293, 2297, 2391, 2452, 2497, 2520, 2524, 2549, 2569, 2582, 2600, 2647, 2650, 2652, 2733, 2739, 2753, 2770, 2780, 2813, 2816, 2827, 2833, 2883, 2903, 2929, 2940–2942, 2961, 2981, 2984, 2995–2996, 3019, 3021, 3035, 3039, 3047. *See also* Education; General programs
Education, special: 681, 1721, 1852, 1866, 1913, 1982, 2016, 2118, 2191, 2233, 2308, 2490, 2520, 2523, 2545, 2550, 2590, 2613, 2615, 2624–2625, 2630, 2646, 2651, 2663, 2683, 2713, 2733–2734, 2736, 2739, 2753, 2768, 2772, 2776, 2797, 2813, 2818, 2836–2837, 2877, 2907, 2949, 2978, 2981, 3002, 3019, 3021, 3031, 3038, 3046, 3050, 3061. *See also* Disabilities; Education; General programs
Education, technology: 2121, 2590, 2613, 2624, 2651, 2817, 2937, 3019, 3021, 3031. *See also* Education; General programs; Technology
Education, theater: 1152, 1170, 1436, 2496, 2521, 2584, 2842. *See also* Education; General programs; Performing arts
Education, vocational: 495, 2118, 2600, 2613, 2651, 2780, 2813, 3016, 3019, 3039. *See also* Education; General programs
Electrical engineering. *See* Engineering, electrical
Electronic engineering. *See* Engineering, electronic
Electronic journalism. *See* Journalism, broadcast
Electronics: 1125, 1336, 1387, 1500, 1656, 1839, 2026, 2084, 2113, 2247, 2336, 2480, 2804. *See also* Engineering, electronic; General programs; Physics
Elementary education. *See* Education, elementary
Elementary school librarians. *See* Libraries and librarianship, school
Emergency medical technology: 1936, 2009, 2194, 2789. *See also* General programs; Health and health care
Emergency nurses and nursing. *See* Nurses and nursing, emergency
Emotional disabilities. *See* Mental health
Employment: 1059, 1618. *See also* General programs; Occupational therapy
Energy: 1739, 2024, 2090, 2110, 2346, 2448, 2531, 2742, 2802. *See also* Environmental sciences; General programs; Natural resources
Energy engineering. *See* Engineering, energy
Engineering: 200, 310, 688, 1058, 1165, 1210, 1323, 1462, 1470, 1635, 1640, 1642, 1644, 1646–1648, 1650–1651, 1678, 1681, 1686–1691, 1693, 1703, 1709, 1713, 1715, 1738–1739, 1741, 1750, 1758, 1772–1773, 1781, 1785, 1796–1797, 1802, 1807, 1810–1811, 1817, 1821, 1825–1827, 1861, 1873–1874, 1885, 1889, 1892, 1906, 1908–1910, 1912, 1917, 1922–1925, 1930, 1943–1944, 1949, 1968, 1975–1976, 1983–1985, 1996, 1998, 2001–2002, 2025, 2031, 2037, 2044, 2047, 2055, 2059, 2064, 2072, 2078, 2081, 2087, 2092–2093, 2101, 2103, 2108, 2114, 2122, 2132, 2139, 2158–2159, 2161, 2170, 2176–2177, 2182, 2193, 2200, 2209, 2218, 2246, 2254, 2263, 2269, 2271, 2275, 2281, 2283, 2289, 2295, 2297, 2313, 2325, 2347, 2354, 2356, 2371, 2373, 2384, 2399, 2405, 2432, 2443–2444, 2451, 2461–2462, 2476, 2481, 2483, 2486, 2505, 2518–2519, 2530–2531, 2570, 2572, 2598, 2621, 2627, 2659, 2676, 2686, 2706, 2723, 2743, 2795, 2821, 2855, 2867, 2887, 2923, 2942, 2968, 2970, 3034, 3044. *See also* General programs; Physical sciences; names of specific types of engineering
Engineering, aeronautical: 8, 1698, 1857, 1947, 2160, 2327, 2349, 2421. *See also* Engineering; General programs
Engineering, aerospace: 8, 1655–1657, 1668, 1824, 1876, 1946, 1948, 2113, 2160, 2172, 2175, 2408, 2410, 2422, 2631, 2688, 2804, 3014. *See also* Engineering; General programs; Space sciences
Engineering, agricultural: 1637, 1731, 1814, 1997, 2152, 2201, 2265, 2484, 2724, 2845. *See also* Agriculture and agricultural sciences; Engineering; General programs
Engineering, architectural: 8, 1155, 1317, 1637, 1994, 2137, 2484. *See also* Architecture; Engineering; General programs
Engineering, automotive: 1813. *See also* Engineering; General programs
Engineering, biomedical: 1717, 1849, 2024, 2742. *See also* Biomedical sciences; Engineering; General programs
Engineering, broadcast: 1327, 1402, 1466, 1472, 1616, 1839, 2195, 2450, 2730, 2878, 3033. *See also* Engineering; General programs; Radio; Television
Engineering, chemical: 1637, 1649, 1653, 1655–1657, 1669, 1674, 1810, 1824, 1946, 1948, 2057, 2110, 2113, 2160, 2327, 2334, 2337–2338, 2341, 2408, 2435,

2475, 2484, 2688, 2802, 2804. *See also* Chemistry; Engineering; General programs

Engineering, civil: 8, 1168, 1509, 1637, 1649, 1669–1670, 1692, 1698, 1716, 1726, 1731, 1734, 1831, 1856, 1894, 1921, 1978, 1997, 2018, 2045–2046, 2105, 2109–2110, 2136–2137, 2152, 2157, 2160, 2163, 2168, 2187, 2204, 2211, 2257, 2327, 2337–2338, 2341, 2366, 2406, 2429, 2433, 2484, 2724, 2802, 2825, 2845, 2857. *See also* Engineering; General programs

Engineering, computer: 8, 1256, 1496, 1570, 1656, 1658, 1668, 1670, 1672, 1717, 1736, 1775, 1872, 1876, 1898, 1942, 1948, 1963–1964, 1966, 1991, 2020, 2097–2098, 2120, 2136, 2152, 2160, 2215, 2239, 2264, 2276, 2301, 2349, 2368, 2370, 2410–2411, 2413, 2415, 2422, 2453, 2475, 2529, 2631, 2649, 2741, 2825, 2845, 2909, 2975, 3008–3009, 3014, 3036. *See also* Computer sciences; Engineering; General programs

Engineering, construction: 1168, 1663, 1665, 1716, 1840, 1900, 1967, 1973, 2014, 2045, 2204, 2211, 2372, 2390, 2396, 2705, 2993. *See also* Engineering; General programs

Engineering, electrical: 8, 1168, 1509, 1570, 1637, 1649, 1655–1657, 1668–1669, 1672, 1692, 1698, 1716–1717, 1724, 1727, 1734, 1736, 1812, 1824, 1848, 1876, 1884, 1942, 1946, 1948, 1950, 1967, 1997, 2020, 2024, 2032, 2097–2098, 2102, 2110, 2113, 2136, 2152, 2160, 2168, 2211, 2215, 2257, 2264, 2276, 2279, 2296, 2301–2302, 2327, 2334, 2337–2338, 2341, 2349, 2368, 2370, 2408, 2410, 2413–2414, 2422, 2475, 2484, 2529, 2593, 2631, 2688–2689, 2724, 2741–2742, 2802, 2804, 2825, 2845, 2857, 2975, 3008, 3014. *See also* Engineering; General programs

Engineering, electronic: 1698, 1717, 1736, 1876, 2020, 2160, 2529, 2631, 2741. *See also* Electronics; Engineering; General programs

Engineering, energy: 2160. *See also* Energy; Engineering; Environmental sciences

Engineering, environmental: 8, 1168, 1449, 1649, 1653, 1669, 1672, 1680, 1698, 1716, 1731, 1767, 1863, 1893, 2054, 2109, 2131, 2137, 2155, 2163, 2167, 2190, 2226, 2302, 2341, 2394, 2448, 2454, 2643, 2849. *See also* Engineering; Environmental sciences; General programs

Engineering, fire protection: 1723. *See also* Engineering; Fire science; General programs

Engineering, food: 2030. *See also* Agriculture and agricultural sciences; Engineering; General programs

Engineering, forestry: 1735. *See also* Engineering; General programs

Engineering, geological: 1978, 2110, 2168, 2302, 2337–2338, 2802, 2857. *See also* Engineering; General programs; Geology

Engineering, hydraulic: 1736, 2529. *See also* Engineering; General programs

Engineering, industrial: 1637, 1668–1669, 1727, 1848, 1950, 1997, 2136, 2152, 2160, 2327, 2334, 2413–2414, 2484, 2689, 2724, 2825, 2845, 3008. *See also* Engineering; General programs

Engineering, manufacturing: 1637, 1669, 1717, 1736, 1950, 1997, 2222–2223, 2349, 2475, 2484, 2529, 2689, 2724. *See also* Engineering; General programs

Engineering, materials: 1669, 2024, 2160, 2327, 2349, 2435, 2742. *See also* Engineering; General programs; Materials sciences

Engineering, mechanical: 8, 1168, 1509, 1637, 1649, 1668–1669, 1674, 1692, 1698–1699, 1706, 1716, 1727, 1736, 1774, 1812, 1848, 1865, 1950, 1967, 1997, 2024, 2032, 2057, 2102, 2107, 2110, 2136, 2152, 2160, 2168, 2211, 2255–2257, 2296, 2302, 2327, 2334, 2337–2338, 2341, 2349, 2408, 2413–2414, 2475, 2484, 2529, 2593, 2689, 2724, 2742, 2802, 2825, 2845, 2857, 3008. *See also* Engineering; General programs

Engineering, metallurgical: 1653, 1736, 2160, 2302, 2435, 2529. *See also* Engineering; General programs; Metallurgy

Engineering, mining: 1637, 2163, 2302, 2433, 2484. *See also* Engineering; General programs; Mining industry

Engineering, naval: 1698. *See also* Engineering; General programs

Engineering, nuclear: 1643, 1698, 1705, 1860, 2049, 2178, 2240, 2251, 2327. *See also* Engineering; General programs; Nuclear science

Engineering, ocean: 1698, 2156, 2244, 2327. *See also* Engineering; General programs; Oceanography

Engineering, optical: 2475. *See also* Engineering; General programs; Optics

Engineering, packaging: 1997, 2724. *See also* Engineering; General programs; Packaging

Engineering, petroleum: 1810, 1970, 2110, 2267, 2337–2338, 2435, 2802. *See also* Engineering; General programs; Petroleum industry

Engineering, structural: 1168, 1509, 1649, 1698, 1716, 1856, 1978, 2211, 2257. *See also* Engineering; General programs

Engineering, surveying: 2012. *See also* Engineering; General programs; Surveying

Engineering, systems: 1462, 1655–1657, 1668, 1727, 1824, 1876, 1946, 1948, 2097, 2113, 2160, 2168, 2177, 2215, 2327, 2410, 2422, 2631, 2688, 2804, 2857, 2867, 3014. *See also* Engineering; General programs

Engineering technology: 552, 1139, 1462, 1649, 1652, 1669, 1717, 1825, 1876, 1997, 2136, 2177, 2336, 2422, 2429, 2451, 2631, 2724, 2825, 2867, 3014, 3034. *See also* Engineering; General programs

Engineering, textile: 2334. *See also* Engineering; General programs

Engineering, transportation: 2396. *See also* Engineering; General programs; Transportation

English as a foreign language: 2118, 2813. *See also* Bilingualism; Education, bilingual; English as a second language; General programs; Language and linguistics

English as a second language: 79, 2590, 2624, 2651, 2776, 3019, 3021. *See also* Bilingualism; Education, bilingual; English as a foreign language; General programs; Language and linguistics

English language. *See* Language, English

English literature. *See* Literature, English

Enology and viticulture: 1388, 1696, 1792, 1794–1795. *See also* Agriculture and agricultural sciences; General programs

Enterostomal therapy nurses and nursing. *See* Nurses and nursing, wound, ostomy and continence

Entomology: 1764, 2152, 2268, 2360, 2845. *See also* General programs; Zoology

Entrepreneurship: 1141, 1659, 2495, 2682, 2700, 2832, 2884, 2989, 3064. *See also* Business administration; General programs

Environmental engineering. *See* Engineering, environmental

Environmental health: 1684, 1793, 1801, 1957, 2110, 2184, 2259, 2404, 2467, 2568, 2802. *See also* General programs; Public health

Environmental law: 1449, 1680, 1851, 1893, 1916, 2088, 2167, 2643, 2790. *See also* General programs; Law, general

Environmental sciences: 200, 552, 1265, 1341, 1449, 1651, 1680, 1701, 1731, 1738, 1749, 1760, 1767, 1769, 1814, 1821, 1845, 1851, 1860, 1863, 1893, 1901, 1908, 1916, 1945, 1969, 1974, 1982, 1986, 2024–2025, 2043, 2054, 2088, 2103, 2119, 2131, 2155, 2163, 2167–2168, 2170, 2190, 2224, 2226, 2265, 2268, 2287, 2300, 2309–2310, 2332, 2340–2341, 2352, 2377, 2394, 2423–2424, 2434, 2436, 2439, 2444, 2448, 2454, 2473, 2530, 2546, 2598, 2643, 2713, 2742–2743, 2790, 2849, 2857, 2951. *See also* General programs; Sciences

Epidemiology: 2477. *See also* General programs; Medical sciences

Equine science: 1729, 1895, 2277–2278, 2417, 2447, 2645. *See also* Agriculture and agricultural sciences; Animal science; General programs

Ethics: 1259, 2335. *See also* General programs; Humanities

Ethnic studies. *See* Minority studies

Exercise science. *See* Athletic training

Extrasensory perception. *See* Parapsychology

Eye doctors. *See* Ophthalmology; Optometry

Eye problems. *See* Visual impairments

Fabric. *See* Clothing

Family and consumer studies: 2597, 2662, 2665, 2712, 2758, 2769, 2809, 2901, 3021. *See also* General programs; Social sciences

Family and consumer studies education. *See* Education, family and consumer studies

Family relations: 2769, 2809. *See also* General programs; Sociology

Farming. *See* Agriculture and agricultural sciences

Farsi language. *See* Language, Farsi

Fashion design: 941, 1191, 1199, 1552, 1611, 1625, 2551, 2665, 2809. *See also* Clothing; Costume; Design; General programs; Home economics

Feminist movement. *See* Women's studies and programs

Fiber. *See* Textiles

Film as a literary art. *See* Cinema

Filmmaking: 887, 1136, 1141, 1163, 1170, 1197, 1206, 1215, 1238, 1252, 1344, 1355, 1413, 1529, 1549, 1552, 1571, 1624–1625, 1631, 1633, 1659, 2317, 2521. *See also* Audiovisual materials and equipment; General programs; Television

Finance: 1165, 1462, 1570, 1644, 1681, 1709, 1751, 1802, 1812, 1930, 1950, 2000, 2028, 2152, 2177, 2368, 2407, 2413, 2415, 2453, 2486, 2505, 2518, 2526, 2532, 2539–2540, 2548, 2567, 2571–2572, 2579–2580, 2585, 2593, 2595, 2607, 2628, 2676–2677, 2689, 2708, 2718–2719, 2725, 2740, 2745, 2766, 2788, 2792, 2820, 2832, 2841, 2845, 2847, 2852, 2865, 2867, 2890, 2964, 2975, 2977, 2992, 2994, 3000, 3004, 3006, 3008–3009, 3024–3025, 3036–3037, 3040–3041. *See also* Accounting; Banking; Economics; General programs

Fine arts: 597, 1144, 1155, 1185, 1223, 1284, 1302, 1326, 1377, 1384, 1412, 1416, 1578, 1582, 1588, 1596, 1625, 1954, 2076, 2376, 2692, 2751, 2777, 2987. *See also* General programs; Humanities; names of specific fine arts

Finnish studies: 1356. *See also* General programs; Humanities

Fire protection engineering. *See* Engineering, fire protection

Fire science: 1808, 1956, 2061, 2185, 2693, 2789. *See also* General programs; Sciences

Fisheries science: 1974, 2131, 2168, 2170, 2300, 2309, 2367, 2436, 2857, 2951. *See also* General programs; Zoology

Flight science. *See* Aviation

Floriculture. *See* Horticulture

Flying. *See* Aviation

Food. *See* Culinary arts; Nutrition

Food science: 1328, 1330, 1835, 1874, 1901, 2006, 2022–2023, 2030, 2143, 2170, 2183, 2210, 2265, 2444, 2627, 2665, 2731, 2769, 2809, 2869. *See also* Food service industry; General programs; Nutrition
Food service industry: 1204–1205, 1207, 1330, 1349, 1593, 1626, 1997, 2206, 2355, 2485, 2493, 2495, 2506, 2508, 2510, 2514, 2525, 2563, 2581, 2599, 2602, 2605, 2644, 2724, 2735, 2752, 2759, 2769, 2775, 2805, 2831, 2862, 2864, 2873, 2882, 2896, 2933, 2969, 2997, 3013, 3015, 3023, 3026, 3037, 3042, 3053, 3057–3058, 3063. *See also* General programs
Food technology. *See* Food science
Foreign affairs. *See* International affairs
Foreign language. *See* Language and linguistics
Foreign language education. *See* Education, foreign languages
Forensic science: 1697, 2033, 2749. *See also* Criminal justice; General programs
Forestry engineering. *See* Engineering, forestry
Forestry management: 1449, 1731, 1735, 1842, 1845, 1916, 1945, 1969, 1974, 1993, 2131, 2167, 2170, 2236, 2300, 2417, 2423, 2436, 2702. *See also* General programs; Management; Wood industry
French language. *See* Language, French
Funerals. *See* Mortuary science
Gaming industry: 3037. *See also* General programs
Gardening. *See* Horticulture
Gastroenterology, nurses and nursing. *See* Nurses and nursing, gastroenterology
Gender. *See* Women's studies and programs
General programs: 1–78, 80–245, 247–551, 553–596, 598–1133, 1203, 1220, 1238, 1264, 1268, 1277, 1279, 1288–1289, 1294, 1325, 1366, 1386, 1437, 1442, 1454, 1456, 1481, 1489, 1507, 1512, 1519, 1549, 1553, 1558, 1584–1586, 1599, 1604, 1606, 1632, 1710, 1745, 1768, 1918, 1972, 2069, 2089, 2154, 2171, 2182, 2230, 2233, 2317, 2321, 2339, 2383, 2482, 2511, 2657, 2664, 2669, 2715, 2727, 2738, 2746, 2814, 2861, 2863, 2895, 2906–2908, 2912, 2916–2917, 2919, 2922, 2990, 3006, 3022, 3025, 3042, 3056
Genetics: 2170, 2265, 2332, 2341. *See also* General programs; Medical sciences
Geography: 1834, 2088, 2131, 2566, 2618, 2790. *See also* General programs; Social sciences
Geological engineering. *See* Engineering, geological
Geology: 1651, 1731, 1737, 1784, 1908, 1916, 1969, 2043, 2110, 2170, 2302, 2337–2338, 2341, 2408, 2433, 2435, 2463, 2802. *See also* Earth sciences; General programs; Physical sciences
Geophysics: 1737, 1874, 1908, 1952, 2043, 2110, 2337–2338, 2346, 2387, 2408, 2627, 2802. *See also* General programs; Meteorology; Oceanography; Physics
Geosciences. *See* Earth sciences
Geospatial information technology: 1641, 1971, 2053, 2242, 2382. *See also* General programs; Geography
Geriatric nurses and nursing. *See* Nurses and nursing, geriatrics
Geriatrics. *See* Aged and aging
German language. *See* Language, German
Gerontology. *See* Aged and aging
Gifted and talented. *See* Education, gifted and talented
Golf course management. *See* Turfgrass science
Golf industry: 1783, 1880, 2206, 2329, 2556, 2882, 2927. *See also* Athletics; Business administration; General programs
Government. *See* Political science and politics; Public administration
Grade school. *See* Education, elementary
Graphic arts: 1155, 1161, 1166, 1256, 1258, 1267, 1467, 1475, 1496, 1499, 1517–1518, 1529, 1542, 1552, 1560, 1576, 1597, 1625, 1898, 1902, 1920, 2239, 2304, 2649, 2656, 2889, 2909, 2911, 2979. *See also* Art; General programs
Graphic design: 1160, 1237, 1298, 1300, 1320, 1330, 1355, 1373, 1384, 1390, 1393, 1550, 1560, 1576, 1583, 1593, 1597, 2979, 2997. *See also* Design; General programs; Graphic arts
Greek language. *See* Language, Greek
Grocery industry: 2527. *See also* General programs
Guidance. *See* Counseling
Gynecology: 2378. *See also* General programs; Medical sciences; Obstetrics
Hair design: 552, 1494. *See also* General programs
Handicapped. *See* Disabilities
Hausa language. *See* Language, Hausa
Hawaiian language. *See* Language, Hawaiian
Hawaiian studies: 1414, 1516, 2925. *See also* General programs; Native American studies
Health and health care: 633, 889, 1141, 1305, 1420–1421, 1573, 1659, 1676, 1685, 1703, 1717, 1757, 1762, 1765, 1849, 1852, 1881, 1896, 1905, 1914, 1939, 1979–1981, 1989, 2009, 2024–2025, 2068, 2112, 2118, 2127, 2135, 2140, 2154–2155, 2194, 2231, 2233, 2253, 2275, 2307, 2321, 2369, 2378, 2401–2402, 2418, 2444, 2468, 2477, 2480, 2500, 2526, 2615, 2648, 2709–2710, 2742–2743, 2810–2811, 2813, 2849, 2907, 2920, 2948, 2976, 3010. *See also* General programs; Medical sciences
Health and health care, administration: 1981, 1989, 2068, 2181, 2526, 2710, 2868, 3020. *See also* Business administration; General programs; Health and health care
Health and health care, informatics: 2181, 2868. *See also* General programs; Health and health care
Health education. *See* Education, health
Health information. *See* Health and health care, informatics
Health information administration. *See* Health and health care, informatics
Hearing impairments: 2118, 2733, 2813, 3021. *See also* Disabilities; General programs; Rehabilitation
Heating industry: 1699, 1706, 1734, 1771, 1774, 1823, 1865, 2255–2256. *See also* Building trades; General programs
High school librarians. *See* Libraries and librarianship, school
High schools. *See* Education, secondary
Higher education. *See* Education, higher
Hindi language. *See* Language, Hindi
Historical preservation: 1143, 1181, 1324, 1342, 1414, 1458. *See also* General programs; History
History: 79, 1181, 1241, 1250, 1301, 1315, 1324, 1381, 1396, 1408, 1414, 1458, 1528, 1595, 1619, 2566, 2639, 2658, 2704, 3043. *See also* Archaeology; General programs; Humanities; Social sciences; names of specific types of history
History, American: 1219, 1234, 1247, 1289, 1319, 1366, 1419, 1511, 1541, 1548, 1563, 2637, 2721, 2944. *See also* American studies; General programs; History
History, art: 1384–1385, 1560, 1588. *See also* Art; General programs; History
History, Jewish: 1316. *See also* General programs; History; Jewish studies
History, military: 1996, 2723. *See also* History; Military affairs
History, Polish: 1575. *See also* General programs; Polish studies
Home economics: 79, 2662. *See also* Family and consumer studies; General programs
Homeland security. *See* Security, national
Horses. *See* Equine science
Horticulture: 1281–1282, 1449, 1525, 1566, 1591–1592, 1730–1731, 1746, 1766, 1794–1795, 1819–1820, 1828–1830, 1845, 1929, 1932–1933, 1940–1941, 1945, 1987, 2039, 2052, 2073, 2080, 2106, 2138, 2152, 2166–2167, 2219, 2252, 2280, 2310, 2357, 2385, 2389, 2392–2393, 2417, 2423, 2434, 2448, 2457, 2845. *See also* Agriculture and agricultural sciences; General programs; Landscape architecture; Sciences
Hospitality industry. *See* Hotel and motel industry
Hospitals. *See* Health and health care
Hotel and motel industry: 1207, 1330, 1593, 1626, 1997, 2355, 2493, 2506, 2508, 2525, 2559, 2563, 2581, 2587, 2601, 2644, 2672, 2724, 2726, 2728, 2759, 2775, 2782, 2805, 2823, 2831–2832, 2864, 2935, 2969, 2997, 3000, 3013, 3015, 3037, 3042, 3053, 3057–3058, 3063. *See also* General programs
Housing: 2901. *See also* Family and consumer studies; General programs
Human resources. *See* Personnel administration
Human rights. *See* Civil rights
Human services. *See* Social services
Humanities: 1141, 1221, 1326, 1352, 1382, 1659, 2041, 2751, 2754, 2781. *See also* General programs; names of specific humanities
Hydraulic engineering. *See* Engineering, hydraulic
Hydrology: 1694, 1700, 1737, 1770, 1911, 1916, 2019, 2043, 2071, 2100, 2125, 2168, 2857. *See also* Earth sciences; General programs
Illustrators and illustrations: 1191, 1611, 1625. *See also* Art; General programs; Graphic arts
Imaging science: 1256, 1496, 1898, 1989, 2239, 2281, 2649, 2909. *See also* General programs; Physics
Immigration: 1874, 2627. *See also* General programs
Indonesian language. *See* Language, Indonesian
Industrial engineering. *See* Engineering, industrial
Industrial hygiene: 1762, 2056. *See also* General programs; Health and health care; Safety studies
Information science: 1736, 1775, 1910, 2025, 2453, 2529, 2659, 2743, 3036. *See also* General programs; Library and information services, general
Information systems: 1876, 1919, 1946, 1948, 1997, 2113, 2133, 2152, 2410, 2414, 2422, 2451, 2607, 2631, 2688, 2719, 2724, 2804, 2822, 2845, 2900, 2931, 3014, 3034, 3037. *See also* Business administration; General programs
Information technology: 1264, 1336, 1462, 1570, 1657–1658, 1717, 1775, 1796–1797, 1812, 1827, 1876, 1886, 1903, 1912, 1918, 1966, 1976, 1997, 2026, 2093, 2108, 2120, 2133, 2177, 2181, 2327, 2355, 2368, 2410–2411, 2413–2415, 2451, 2460, 2475, 2593, 2631, 2724, 2822, 2847, 2867–2868, 2969, 2975, 3006, 3008–3009, 3017, 3034. *See also* Computer sciences; General programs
Insurance. *See* Actuarial sciences
Intellectual freedom: 283, 1231, 1278, 2622. *See also* Censorship; Civil liberties; General programs

Intelligence service: 1140, 1656, 1861, 1876, 1946, 1948, 2113, 2410, 2422, 2491, 2621, 2631, 2688, 2703, 2804, 2888, 2921, 3014. *See also* General programs; International affairs; Military affairs
Interior design: 1155, 1245, 1297, 1337, 1339, 1383, 1393–1394, 1594, 1625, 2662, 2665, 2769, 2809, 2998. *See also* Architecture; Design; General programs; Home economics
International affairs: 1301, 1497, 1570, 1577, 1656, 1861, 1996, 2368, 2507, 2564, 2566, 2621, 2703–2704, 2723, 2801, 2975, 2980, 2985, 2991. *See also* General programs; Political science and politics
International relations. *See* International affairs
Internet design and development: 90, 1160, 1256, 1300, 1320, 1496, 1898, 2239, 2411, 2649, 2909, 2922. *See also* General programs; Graphic arts; Technology
Internet journalism. *See* Journalism, online
Inventors and inventions: 1826. *See also* Entrepreneurship; General programs; Technology
Italian American studies: 1450, 2858. *See also* American studies; General programs; History, American; Literature, American
Italian language. *See* Language, Italian
Italian studies: 1135, 1450, 2858. *See also* General programs; Humanities
Japanese language. *See* Language, Japanese
Jazz. *See* Music, jazz
Jewelry: 1438, 1552. *See also* Arts and crafts; General programs
Jewish affairs: 1316. *See also* General programs; History, Jewish
Jewish history. *See* History, Jewish
Jewish studies: 1365, 1442, 2765. *See also* General programs; Middle Eastern studies; Religion and religious activities
Jobs. *See* Employment
Journalism: 1146–1148, 1151, 1153–1154, 1156, 1167, 1169, 1179, 1182, 1186, 1190, 1195–1198, 1208, 1210, 1213, 1217, 1230–1231, 1236, 1239–1240, 1242–1244, 1249, 1254, 1257, 1263–1264, 1270, 1274, 1276, 1279, 1282–1286, 1290, 1298–1299, 1301, 1310–1314, 1320, 1322, 1325, 1329–1330, 1334–1336, 1341, 1343–1346, 1353–1354, 1357–1358, 1367, 1373–1375, 1379, 1390, 1392, 1398, 1400, 1402, 1409, 1417, 1423, 1425, 1427–1430, 1433, 1441, 1444, 1446, 1453, 1457, 1459, 1463, 1468–1469, 1477, 1479, 1483–1485, 1490, 1497, 1502, 1504–1505, 1508, 1515–1516, 1520, 1522, 1526–1527, 1531, 1534, 1537–1538, 1540, 1553–1554, 1556, 1565, 1572, 1577, 1580, 1583, 1590, 1593, 1600, 1605, 1609–1611, 1613–1614, 1617–1618, 1620, 1627, 1835, 1918, 1941, 1954, 2026, 2131, 2183, 2570, 2577, 2619, 2638, 2685, 2692, 2704, 2727, 2869, 2925, 2980, 2986, 2997. *See also* Broadcasting; Communications; General programs; names of specific types of journalism
Journalism, broadcast: 1136, 1146, 1154, 1179, 1183, 1190, 1211, 1225, 1239, 1253, 1278, 1286, 1291, 1299, 1308, 1311–1312, 1327, 1330, 1333–1334, 1341, 1350, 1353, 1359, 1373–1376, 1379–1380, 1392, 1398, 1400, 1406, 1409, 1415, 1418, 1425, 1428, 1431, 1433, 1444, 1447, 1459, 1472, 1477, 1493, 1502, 1515, 1521, 1523–1524, 1532, 1572, 1579, 1583, 1602, 1605, 1614, 1616, 1620, 1779, 2195, 2450, 2730, 2878, 3033. *See also* Communications; General programs; Radio; Television
Journalism, cable: 1211, 1253, 1380, 1406, 1431, 1502, 1523. *See also* Cable TV industry; General programs; Journalism, broadcast
Journalism, online: 1190, 1211, 1253, 1299, 1311, 1341, 1353, 1374, 1379–1380, 1398, 1400, 1418, 1428, 1431, 1433, 1444, 1502, 1523, 1605. *See also* General programs; Journalism
Journalism, agriculture. *See* Agricultural communications
Journalism, education. *See* Education, journalism
Journalism, medical. *See* Science reporting
Journalism, religion. *See* Religious reporting
Journalism, science. *See* Science reporting
Journalism, sports. *See* Sports reporting
Junior colleges. *See* Education, higher
Jurisprudence. *See* Law, general
Kazakh language. *See* Language, Kazakh
Kurdish language. *See* Language, Kurdish
Labor unions and members: 1236, 2619, 2814, 2908, 2916, 2936. *See also* General programs
Land management: 1845, 2423. *See also* Environmental sciences; General programs
Landscape architecture: 1143, 1175, 1232, 1255, 1281, 1296, 1307, 1391, 1449, 1491, 1525, 1566–1567, 1591, 1625, 1732, 1845–1846, 1897, 1929, 1933, 1940, 1977, 2085, 2138, 2167, 2232, 2280, 2357, 2363, 2389, 2423, 2457. *See also* Botany; General programs; Horticulture
Language and linguistics: 79, 597, 1140, 1462, 1656, 2170, 2177, 2191, 2491, 2590, 2624, 2776, 2818, 2867, 2877, 3019. *See also* General programs; Humanities; names of specific languages
Language, Arabic: 8, 1145. *See also* General programs; Language and linguistics
Language, Azeri: 8, 1145. *See also* General programs; Language and linguistics
Language, Bengali: 8, 1145. *See also* General programs; Language and linguistics
Language, Cambodian: 8, 1145. *See also* General programs; Language and linguistics
Language, Chinese: 8, 1145, 2651. *See also* General programs; Language and linguistics
Language, English: 79, 597, 1148, 1153, 1318, 1330, 1476, 1537, 2590, 2624, 2720. *See also* English as a foreign language; English as a second language; General programs; Language and linguistics
Language, Farsi: 8, 1145, 1570, 2368, 2975. *See also* General programs; Language and linguistics
Language, French: 2651. *See also* General programs; Language and linguistics
Language, German: 2118, 2651, 2813. *See also* General programs; Language and linguistics
Language, Greek: 1137, 1209, 1482, 2569. *See also* General programs; Language and linguistics
Language, Hausa: 8, 1145. *See also* General programs; Language and linguistics
Language, Hawaiian: 1516, 2925. *See also* General programs; Language and linguistics
Language, Hindi: 8, 1145. *See also* General programs; Language and linguistics
Language, Indonesian: 8, 1145. *See also* General programs; Language and linguistics
Language, Italian: 1135, 1450, 1564, 2118, 2813, 2858. *See also* General programs; Language and linguistics
Language, Japanese: 8, 1145, 2118, 2651, 2813. *See also* General programs; Language and linguistics
Language, Kazakh: 8, 1145. *See also* General programs; Language and linguistics
Language, Kurdish: 8, 1145. *See also* General programs; Language and linguistics
Language, Latin: 1209, 1451, 1482, 2118, 2569, 2651, 2813, 2903. *See also* General programs; Language and linguistics
Language, Malay: 8, 1145, *See also* General programs; Language and linguistics
Language, Pashto: 8, 1145. *See also* General programs; Language and linguistics
Language, Polish: 1575. *See also* General programs; Language and linguistics
Language, Russian: 8, 1145, 1570, 2368, 2651, 2975. *See also* General programs; Language and linguistics
Language, Serbo-Croatian: 8, 1145. *See also* General programs; Language and linguistics
Language, Spanish: 2118, 2651, 2813. *See also* General programs; Language and linguistics
Language, Swahili: 8, 1145. *See also* General programs; Language and linguistics
Language, Thai: 8, 1145. *See also* General programs; Language and linguistics
Language, Turkish: 8, 1145. *See also* General programs; Language and linguistics
Language, Uighar: 8, 1145. *See also* General programs; Language and linguistics
Language, Urdu: 8, 1145. *See also* General programs; Language and linguistics
Language, Uzbek: 8, 1145. *See also* General programs; Language and linguistics
Language, Vietnamese: 8, 1145. *See also* General programs; Language and linguistics
Language, Yugoslavian. *See* Language, Serbo-Croatian
Laser science: 2475. *See also* General programs; Physical sciences
Latin. *See* Language, Latin
Law enforcement. *See* Criminal justice
Law, general: 246, 411, 666, 831, 1189, 1323, 1325, 1577, 1756, 1996, 1998, 2033, 2354, 2362, 2451, 2542, 2723, 2727, 2749, 2766, 2870, 2954, 2968, 2980, 3034, 3056. *See also* Criminal justice; General programs; Paralegal studies; Social sciences; names of legal specialties
Lawyers. *See* Law, general
Leadership: 1015, 1462, 2177, 2859, 2867. *See also* General programs; Management
Learning disabilities. *See* Disabilities, learning
Legal assistants. *See* Paralegal studies
Legal studies and services. *See* Law, general
Leisure studies: 2558. *See also* General programs; Recreation
Librarians. *See* Library and information services, general
Libraries and librarianship, school: 2537, 2590, 2613, 2624, 2651, 2796, 2874, 2879, 2899, 2905, 3019, 3051. *See also* General programs; Library and information services, general
Libraries and librarianship, technical services: 2871. *See also* General programs; Library and information services, general
Libraries and librarianship, technology: 1658. *See also* General programs; Information science; Library and information services, general; Technology
Library and information services, general: 310, 1318, 1754, 2504, 2537, 2541, 2552, 2604, 2720, 2828. *See also* General programs; Information science; Social sciences; names of specific types of librarianship
Life insurance. *See* Actuarial sciences
Life sciences. *See* Biological sciences
Lighting: 1155, 1587, 1589. *See also* Architecture; General programs
Linguistics. *See* Language and linguistics

Literature: 1157, 1189, 1340, 1410, 1476, 1536, 1561, 1756, 2542, 2751. *See also* General programs; Humanities; names of specific types of literature
Literature, American: 1180. *See also* American studies; General programs; Literature
Literature, English: 79, 2590, 2624. *See also* General programs; Literature
Literature, Middle Eastern: 1283, 2685. *See also* General programs; Literature; Middle Eastern studies
Logistics: 1679, 1868, 1995, 2096, 2110, 2136, 2152, 2350, 2380, 2501, 2626, 2719, 2722, 2798, 2802, 2825, 2845, 2932, 2988. *See also* General programs; Transportation
Long-term care nurses and nursing. *See* Nurses and nursing, long-term care
Machine trades: 2107. *See also* General programs
Magazines. *See* Journalism; Literature
Malay language. *See* Language, Malay
Management: 1144, 1165, 1199, 1330, 1462, 1472, 1475, 1644, 1709, 1729, 1736, 1739, 1840, 1853, 1975, 1997, 2000, 2020, 2133, 2136, 2161, 2177, 2181, 2195, 2206, 2277–2278, 2353, 2407, 2447, 2474, 2486–2487, 2518, 2527, 2529, 2531, 2548, 2551, 2583, 2607, 2617, 2628, 2706, 2718, 2724–2725, 2741, 2759, 2822, 2825, 2852, 2855, 2867–2868, 2878, 2882, 2885, 2889, 2932, 2934, 2964, 2967, 3000, 3004, 3026, 3062. *See also* General programs; Social sciences
Management, nurses and nursing. *See* Nurses and nursing, administration
Manufacturing engineering. *See* Engineering, manufacturing
Maps and mapmaking. *See* Cartography
Marine sciences: 1974, 2156, 2244, 2300, 2332, 2436, 2439. *See also* General programs; Sciences; names of specific marine sciences
Marketing: 1138, 1160–1161, 1229, 1256, 1271, 1298, 1328, 1330, 1355, 1389, 1401, 1446, 1465, 1496, 1501, 1576, 1593–1594, 1635, 1644, 1812, 1835, 1851, 1898, 1930, 1944, 1975, 1997, 2006, 2039, 2110, 2161, 2164, 2183, 2209, 2239, 2355–2356, 2407, 2413, 2483, 2486, 2489, 2527, 2548, 2593, 2649, 2676, 2686, 2706, 2724, 2726, 2731, 2764, 2787, 2802, 2832, 2847, 2855, 2869, 2887, 2900, 2909, 2964, 2969–2970, 2979, 2997–2998, 3004, 3008, 3011. *See also* Advertising; General programs; Public relations; Sales
Marketing education. *See* Education, business
Marriage. *See* Family relations
Mass communications. *See* Communications
Materials engineering. *See* Engineering, materials
Materials sciences: 1643, 1653, 1669, 1826, 1906, 2025, 2123, 2327, 2341, 2435, 2444, 2475, 2743. *See also* General programs; Physical sciences
Mathematics: 8, 79, 200, 310, 597, 688, 1058, 1141, 1570, 1582, 1640, 1642, 1655–1657, 1659, 1668–1669, 1678, 1682, 1715, 1741, 1758, 1772, 1802, 1811, 1824, 1826, 1853, 1872–1874, 1876, 1908, 1910, 1917, 1946, 1948, 1968, 1984–1985, 1996, 2001–2002, 2020, 2024–2025, 2055, 2064, 2101, 2113, 2118, 2122, 2132, 2144, 2149, 2158–2160, 2170, 2172, 2176, 2182, 2191, 2218, 2269, 2271, 2288, 2292–2293, 2297, 2316, 2322, 2326–2328, 2340–2341, 2368, 2371, 2376, 2384, 2399, 2408, 2410, 2422, 2432, 2444, 2464, 2481, 2519, 2572, 2576, 2590, 2617, 2624, 2627, 2631, 2659, 2688, 2723, 2741–2743, 2804, 2813, 2818, 2820–2821, 2835, 2840, 2877, 2923, 2940–2942, 2956, 2959, 2975, 2987, 3014, 3019, 3021. *See also* Computer sciences; General programs; Physical sciences; Statistics
Mechanical engineering. *See* Engineering, mechanical
Media. *See* Broadcasting; Communications
Media specialists. *See* Libraries and librarianship, school; Library and information services, general
Medical journalism. *See* Science reporting
Medical sciences: 200, 681, 1141, 1189, 1323, 1422, 1555, 1636, 1659, 1756, 1799, 1818, 1822, 1826, 1881, 1890, 1896, 1980, 1989, 1998, 2024–2025, 2028, 2088, 2114–2115, 2127, 2140, 2196, 2202–2203, 2245, 2251, 2282, 2291, 2307, 2318, 2330, 2354, 2364, 2375, 2378, 2400–2401, 2444–2445, 2462, 2542, 2648, 2742–2743, 2745, 2790, 2812, 2881, 2948, 2962, 2968, 2974, 3044. *See also* General programs; Health and health care; Sciences; names of medical specialties; names of specific diseases
Medical technology: 552, 1728, 1808, 1849, 1864, 1931, 2009, 2029, 2086, 2094, 2331, 2342–2344, 2378, 2397. *See also* General programs; Medical sciences; Technology
Mental health: 2118, 2194, 2401, 2813. *See also* General programs; Health and health care; Psychiatry
Mental retardation: 2040, 3002. *See also* Disabilities, developmental; General programs; Medical sciences
Merchandising. *See* Sales
Metal trades. *See* Machine trades
Metallurgical engineering. *See* Engineering, metallurgical
Metallurgy: 1653, 1988, 2302, 2435. *See also* Engineering, metallurgical; General programs; Sciences
Meteorology: 8, 1645, 1694, 1700, 1722, 1737, 1770, 1779, 1806, 1858–1859, 1887, 1908, 1911, 2019, 2071, 2100, 2125, 2170, 2175. *See also* Atmospheric sciences; General programs
Microbiology: 1141, 1659, 1801, 1861, 2024–2025, 2030, 2170, 2341, 2621, 2742–2743. *See also* Biological sciences; General programs
Microcomputers. *See* Computer sciences
Microscopy. *See* Medical technology
Middle Eastern literature. *See* Literature, Middle Eastern
Middle Eastern studies: 1570, 2368, 2975. *See also* General programs; Humanities
Midwifery. *See* Nurses and nursing, midwifery
Military affairs: 1996, 2723, 2888. *See also* General programs
Military history. *See* History, military
Mineral law. *See* Environmental law
Mining engineering. *See* Engineering, mining
Mining industry: 2056, 2302–2303, 2435. *See also* General programs
Minority studies: 1414. *See also* General programs; names of specific ethnic minority studies
Missionary work. *See* Religion and religious activities
Molecular biology: 2024, 2152, 2742, 2845. *See also* Biological sciences; General programs
Mortuary science: 2009. *See also* General programs
Motel industry. *See* Hotel and motel industry
Museum studies: 1304, 1414, 2707. *See also* General programs; Library and information services, general
Music: 79, 541, 887, 1141–1142, 1164, 1170, 1192–1193, 1201, 1206, 1222–1223, 1260, 1293, 1302, 1332, 1338, 1340, 1352, 1369, 1372, 1395, 1403, 1410, 1434, 1439–1440, 1448, 1460, 1474, 1495, 1506, 1535–1536, 1545, 1549, 1574, 1578, 1588, 1607–1608, 1629–1631, 1659, 2041, 2317, 2521, 2590, 2596, 2624, 2697, 2751, 2754, 2834, 2846, 2886. *See also* Education, music; Fine arts; General programs; Humanities; Performing arts
Music, church: 1266, 1292, 1434, 1544, 1573, 1612, 2369, 2834, 2976, 3032. *See also* General programs; Music; Performing arts; Religion and religious activities
Music, classical: 200, 1141, 1226, 1292, 1399, 1607, 1659. *See also* General programs; Music
Music education. *See* Education, music
Music, jazz: 200, 1506, 1535, 1607, 1631. *See also* General programs; Music
Music, piano: 1176, 1192, 1200, 1218, 1369, 1439, 1464, 1510, 1535, 1630, 1634, 2528. *See also* General programs; Music
Music, strings: 1178, 1192, 1200, 1226, 1360, 1370, 1404, 1535. *See also* General programs; Music
Music therapy: 1854. *See also* General programs; Music
Musicals: 1539. *See also* Composers and compositions; General programs; Music
Mycology: 2268. *See also* Botany; General programs
National security. *See* Security, national
Native American studies: 2155, 2849. *See also* General programs; Minority studies
Natural resources: 1568, 1676, 1731, 1843, 1888, 1893, 1969, 1974, 2007, 2090, 2155, 2287, 2310, 2352, 2365, 2377, 2398, 2424, 2436, 2439, 2454, 2500, 2643, 2849. *See also* General programs; names of specific resources
Natural resources law. *See* Environmental law
Natural sciences: 1323, 1642, 1697, 1758, 1769, 1893, 1998, 2103, 2454, 2546, 2643. *See also* General programs; Sciences; names of specific sciences
Naval architecture: 1668, 1698, 2215, 2327. *See also* Architecture; General programs; Naval science
Naval engineering. *See* Engineering, naval
Naval science: 682–684. *See also* General programs
Nephrology nurses and nursing. *See* Nurses and nursing, nephrology
Neuroscience: 2170. *See also* General programs; Medical sciences
Newspapers. *See* Journalism; Newsroom management
Newsroom management: 1427. *See also* Broadcasting; General programs
Nonprofit sector: 3065. *See also* General programs; Public administration
Nuclear engineering. *See* Engineering, nuclear
Nuclear science: 1643, 1705, 1860, 2042, 2049. *See also* General programs; Physical sciences
Nurses and nursing, administration: 2470. *See also* General programs; Management; Nurses and nursing, general
Nurses and nursing, anesthesiology: 2029, 2217. *See also* General programs; Nurses and nursing, general
Nurses and nursing, critical care: 2017, 2217. *See also* General programs; Nurses and nursing, general
Nurses and nursing, educator: 1981, 2068, 2197, 2217, 2445, 2710. *See also* General programs; Nurses and nursing, general
Nurses and nursing, emergency: 2153, 2205, 2217, 2282. *See also* General programs; Nurses and nursing, general
Nurses and nursing, gastroenterology: 2294. *See also* General programs; Nurses and nursing, general
Nurses and nursing, general: 552, 751, 1058, 1462, 1582, 1654, 1660, 1666, 1673, 1675, 1677, 1683, 1702, 1714, 1719–1720, 1747–1748, 1754–1755, 1776–1777, 1780, 1788, 1798, 1804, 1822, 1832–1833, 1841, 1847, 1849, 1852, 1855, 1862,

1877, 1881, 1899, 1915, 1926, 1934, 1936, 1938–1939, 1953, 1955, 1959, 1962, 1979, 1981, 1989, 1992, 2004–2005, 2009, 2011, 2017, 2021, 2029, 2038, 2062, 2068, 2070, 2079, 2086, 2094–2095, 2104, 2111–2112, 2116–2118, 2126, 2129–2130, 2140–2141, 2146–2147, 2150–2151, 2173–2174, 2177, 2179–2180, 2186, 2191–2192, 2196, 2198, 2208, 2212–2214, 2220–2221, 2227–2228, 2231, 2237–2238, 2243, 2245, 2250–2251, 2266, 2274–2275, 2305, 2312, 2314, 2319–2320, 2351, 2359, 2374, 2376, 2378, 2395, 2400–2401, 2420, 2428, 2430–2431, 2444–2446, 2462, 2469, 2541, 2615, 2691, 2710, 2729, 2813, 2867, 2877, 2952, 2987, 3044. *See also* General programs; Health and health care; Medical sciences; names of specific nursing specialties

Nurses and nursing, geriatrics: 2217, 2361. *See also* Aged and aging; General programs; Nurses and nursing, general

Nurses and nursing, informatics: 2217. *See also* General programs; Health and health care, informatics; Nurses and nursing, general

Nurses and nursing, long-term care: 2015, 2017, 2070, 2361, 2403. *See also* General programs; Nurses and nursing, general

Nurses and nursing, midwifery: 2445. *See also* General programs; Nurses and nursing, general

Nurses and nursing, nephrology: 2217. *See also* General programs; Nurses and nursing, general

Nurses and nursing, occupational health: 1684, 2259, 2404. *See also* General programs; Nurses and nursing, general

Nurses and nursing, oncology: 2063, 2217, 2234–2235, 2299. *See also* Cancer; General programs; Nurses and nursing, general

Nurses and nursing, operating room: 1707, 1740, 2217. *See also* General programs; Nurses and nursing, general; Surgery

Nurses and nursing, orthopedics: 2217. *See also* General programs; Nurses and nursing, general

Nurses and nursing, palliative care: 2017. *See also* General programs; Nurses and nursing, general

Nurses and nursing, public health: 2427. *See also* General programs; Nurses and nursing, general; Public health

Nurses and nursing, rehabilitation: 2017, 2075, 2426. *See also* General programs; Nurses and nursing, general; Rehabilitation

Nurses and nursing, school health: 2249, 2796. *See also* General programs; Nurses and nursing, general

Nurses and nursing, wound, ostomy and continence: 2472. *See also* General programs; Nurses and nursing, general

Nutrition: 1330, 1849, 2164, 2183, 2194, 2251, 2265, 2341, 2378, 2388, 2466, 2662, 2665, 2769, 2809, 2869, 2901. *See also* General programs; Home economics; Medical sciences

Obstetrics: 2378. *See also* General programs; Gynecology; Medical sciences

Occupational health nurses and nursing. *See* Nurses and nursing, occupational health

Occupational safety: 1793, 2056, 2568. *See also* Employment; General programs; Health and health care

Occupational therapy: 552, 1725, 1849, 1854, 1939, 1980, 2009, 2016, 2029, 2074, 2094, 2118, 2162, 2194, 2225, 2403, 2739, 2813. *See also* Counseling; Employment; General programs

Ocean engineering. *See* Engineering, ocean

Oceanography: 1694, 1700, 1737, 1770, 1910–1911, 1916, 2019, 2058, 2071, 2100, 2125, 2175, 2300, 2327, 2332, 2659. *See also* General programs; Marine sciences

Office skills. *See* Secretarial sciences

Oil industry. *See* Petroleum industry

Oncology. *See* Cancer

Oncology nurses and nursing. *See* Nurses and nursing, oncology

Online journalism. *See* Journalism, online

Opera. *See* Music; Voice

Operations research: 8, 1644, 1930, 2020, 2327, 2486, 2676, 2741. *See also* General programs; Mathematics; Sciences

Ophthalmology: 2318. *See also* General programs; Medical sciences

Optical engineering. *See* Engineering, optical

Optics: 2475. *See also* General programs; Physics

Optometry: 1671, 1939, 2378, 2437. *See also* General programs; Medical sciences

Oratory: 1141, 1170, 1659, 2521. *See also* General programs

Orthopedic nurses and nursing. *See* Nurses and nursing, orthopedics

Osteopathy: 2445. *See also* General programs; Medical sciences

Ostomy. *See* Nurses and nursing, wound, ostomy and continence

Packaging: 1517. *See also* Engineering, packaging; General programs

Packaging engineering. *See* Engineering, packaging

Painting: 887, 1141, 1166, 1265, 1363, 1416, 1549, 1551–1552, 1659, 2317. *See also* Art; General programs

Paralegal studies: 552, 1462, 1754, 2177, 2541, 2791, 2867, 2870, 3029. *See also* General programs; Social sciences

Parapsychology: 2655, 2943. *See also* General programs; Psychology

Pashto language. *See* Language, Pashto

Pathology: 2170. *See also* General programs; Medical sciences

Patriotism: 1628, 2670. *See also* General programs

Peace studies: 2861. *See also* General programs; Political science and politics

Pediatrics: 2378. *See also* General programs; Medical sciences

Performing arts: 612, 887, 1141, 1144, 1150, 1152, 1170–1171, 1201, 1206, 1223, 1260, 1302, 1340, 1436, 1474, 1513, 1549, 1557, 1578, 1587–1588, 1631, 1659, 2317, 2496, 2521, 2842, 2886. *See also* Fine arts; General programs; names of specific performing arts

Personnel administration: 1462, 1950, 1975, 2068, 2177, 2356, 2413, 2418, 2527, 2689, 2706, 2820, 2867, 2872, 2970, 3008, 3010, 3020, 3028, 3037. *See also* General programs; Management

Pest management: 1766, 2385. *See also* Biological sciences; General programs

Petroleum engineering. *See* Engineering, petroleum

Petroleum industry: 2254, 2267, 2336. *See also* General programs

Pharmaceutical sciences: 1671, 1799, 1826, 1849, 1861, 1939, 1980, 2009, 2029, 2094, 2170, 2194, 2245, 2251, 2378, 2400–2401, 2403, 2445, 2621. *See also* General programs; Medical sciences

Philology. *See* Language and linguistics

Philosophy: 200, 1157, 2566. *See also* General programs; Humanities

Photogrammetry: 1641, 1834. *See also* Cartography; General programs; Photography

Photography: 887, 1141, 1197, 1282, 1330, 1347, 1416, 1549, 1552, 1560, 1568, 1611, 1615, 1625, 1631, 1659, 1941, 2317, 2365. *See also* Fine arts; General programs

Photojournalism: 1179, 1190, 1194, 1197, 1212, 1227, 1309, 1311, 1320, 1330, 1347, 1373–1374, 1390, 1428, 1433, 1444, 1463, 1477–1478, 1530, 1560, 1569, 1579, 1583. *See also* General programs; Journalism; Photography

Physical education. *See* Education, physical

Physical sciences: 1697, 1717, 1741, 1758, 1817, 1892–1893, 1910, 2103, 2118, 2163, 2170, 2191, 2246, 2313, 2371, 2384, 2444, 2454, 2461, 2643, 2659, 2813, 2877. *See also* General programs; Sciences; names of specific physical sciences

Physical therapy: 552, 1671, 1725, 1854, 1939, 1980, 2009, 2016, 2029, 2074, 2094, 2118, 2162, 2194, 2216, 2258, 2403, 2739, 2813. *See also* Disabilities; General programs; Health and health care; Rehabilitation

Physician assistant: 1638, 1989, 2009, 2086, 2094, 2130, 2229, 2251, 2358, 2444–2445. *See also* General programs; Health and health care; Medical sciences

Physics: 8, 200, 1141, 1643, 1651, 1655–1657, 1659, 1668–1669, 1681, 1708, 1741, 1784, 1801, 1824, 1826, 1853, 1861, 1872, 1876, 1889, 1906, 1908, 1946, 1948, 1968, 1996, 2001, 2024–2025, 2091, 2113, 2118, 2160, 2170, 2191, 2218, 2240, 2327, 2337–2338, 2340–2341, 2399, 2408, 2410, 2422, 2440, 2444, 2475, 2505, 2617, 2621, 2631, 2688, 2723, 2742–2743, 2804, 2813, 2877, 3014. *See also* General programs; Mathematics; Physical sciences

Physiology: 1939, 2170. *See also* General programs; Medical sciences

Piano. *See* Music, piano

Plant pathology: 1449, 1592, 1845, 2152, 2167, 2268, 2381, 2393, 2845. *See also* Agriculture and agricultural sciences; Botany; General programs

Plumbing industry: 1699, 1706, 1771, 1774, 1865, 2255–2256. *See also* Building trades; General programs

Poisons. *See* Toxicology

Police science. *See* Criminal justice

Polish history. *See* History, Polish

Polish language. *See* Language, Polish

Polish studies: 1301, 1575, 2704. *See also* General programs; Humanities

Political science and politics: 347, 487, 1015, 1157, 1242, 1247, 1283, 1313, 1319, 1541, 1577, 1606, 1619, 1861, 1996, 2155, 2354, 2438, 2451, 2511, 2566, 2621, 2637, 2658, 2685, 2721, 2723, 2838, 2849, 2904, 2917, 2922, 2928, 2944, 2953–2954, 2968, 2980, 3022, 3027, 3034, 3043, 3046, 3065. *See also* General programs; Public administration; Social sciences

Pollution: 1893, 2454, 2643. *See also* Environmental sciences; General programs

Polymer science: 2032. *See also* Chemistry; General programs

Pomology: 1794–1795, 2386, 2441. *See also* General programs; Horticulture

Pork industry: 2099, 2265. *See also* Agriculture and agricultural sciences; General programs

Posters. *See* Graphic arts

Poultry science: 2456. *See also* Agriculture and agricultural sciences; Animal science; General programs

Preschool education. *See* Education, preschool

Preservation, historical. *See* Historical preservation

Presidents, U.S. *See* History, American

Press. *See* Journalism

Print journalism. *See* Journalism

Printing industry: 1256, 1258, 1267, 1445, 1467, 1475, 1496, 1499, 1518, 1542, 1597, 1898, 1902, 1920, 2239, 2304, 2649, 2656, 2854, 2889, 2909, 2911. *See also* General programs

Prints. *See* Art; Graphic arts

Psychiatry: 2245. *See also* Behavioral sciences; Counseling; General programs; Medical sciences; Psychology
Psychology: 2118, 2145, 2170, 2245, 2275, 2378, 2566, 2630, 2796, 2813, 2820. *See also* Behavioral sciences; Counseling; General programs; Psychiatry; Social sciences
Public administration: 347, 1189, 1325, 1422, 1577, 1738, 1756, 1821, 1956, 1981, 2088, 2115, 2118, 2168, 2307, 2530, 2542, 2598, 2607, 2693, 2710, 2727, 2778, 2790, 2812–2813, 2838, 2857, 2928, 2948, 2953, 2980, 3028, 3030, 3046, 3065. *See also* General programs; Management; Political science and politics; Social sciences
Public affairs. *See* Public administration
Public health: 310, 1246, 1685, 1881–1882, 1893, 1904, 1939, 1979, 2086, 2103, 2155, 2184, 2400–2401, 2636, 2643, 2849. *See also* General programs; Health and health care; Nurses and nursing, public health
Public interest law: 2118, 2813. *See also* General programs; Law, general
Public policy. *See* Public administration
Public relations: 1148, 1153–1154, 1160–1161, 1213, 1237, 1242–1243, 1274, 1298, 1301, 1313, 1321, 1330, 1353, 1355, 1362, 1389, 1401–1402, 1446, 1487, 1490, 1504, 1520, 1546, 1577, 1593, 2088, 2161, 2168, 2183, 2209, 2527, 2577, 2704, 2787, 2790, 2855, 2857, 2869, 2887, 2980, 2997. *See also* General programs; Marketing
Public sector. *See* Public administration
Public service: 1106, 1582, 2155, 2376, 2666, 2690, 2849, 2987. *See also* General programs; Public administration; Social services
Public speaking. *See* Oratory
Publicity. *See* Public relations
Publishers and publishing: 552, 1298, 1517, 1550. *See also* General programs
Radio: 1154, 1170, 1251, 1264, 1271, 1278, 1308, 1336, 1344, 1361, 1371, 1402, 1581, 1620–1621, 1918, 2026, 2521. *See also* Communications; General programs
Radiology: 2009, 2029, 2094, 2231, 2306, 2378, 2412. *See also* General programs; Medical sciences
Ranching: 1761, 2119, 2311, 2388. *See also* Agriculture and agricultural sciences; General programs
Rape: 2684. *See also* General programs; Women's studies and programs
Reading: 2590, 2624, 2981, 3019, 3061. *See also* Education; General programs
Real estate: 2740. *See also* General programs
Records and information management: 1658, 2629. *See also* General programs; Library and information services, general
Recreation: 1305, 1420–1421, 1567, 1626, 2310, 2363, 2558, 2709, 2810–2811, 2996, 3013, 3057–3058. *See also* General programs; Leisure studies; names of specific recreational activities
Refrigeration industry. *See* Cooling industry
Regional planning. *See* City and regional planning
Rehabilitation: 1721, 1866, 1907, 1913, 2118, 2308, 2378, 2490, 2523, 2545, 2625, 2630, 2663, 2813, 2949, 2978. *See also* General programs; Health and health care; names of specific types of therapy
Religion and religious activities: 79, 218, 432, 1012, 1248, 1262, 1266, 1275, 1352, 1397, 1407, 1432, 1514, 1533, 1547, 1555, 1573, 1598–1599, 1612, 1623, 2041, 2330, 2369, 2754, 2962, 2976, 3032, 3055. *See also* General programs; Humanities; Philosophy
Religious education. *See* Education, religious
Religious reporting: 1263, 1398. *See also* Broadcasting; General programs; Journalism; Religion and religious activities
Resource management: 2057, 2155, 2300, 2310, 2439, 2558, 2849. *See also* Environmental sciences; General programs; Management
Respiratory therapy: 1936, 2009, 2029, 2194, 2231. *See also* General programs; Health and health care
Restaurants. *See* Food service industry
Retailing. *See* Sales
Retardation. *See* Mental retardation
Risk management: 1874, 2526, 2567, 2579–2580, 2627–2628, 2677, 2748, 2806, 2977. *See also* Actuarial sciences; Business administration; Finance; General programs
Russian language. *See* Language, Russian
Safety studies: 253, 1762, 2056. *See also* Engineering; General programs
Sales: 1199, 1256, 1327, 1472, 1474, 1496, 1576, 1594, 1601, 1611, 1616, 1736, 1812, 1898, 1997, 2195, 2239, 2356, 2450, 2527, 2529, 2548, 2551, 2585, 2593, 2649, 2724, 2726, 2730, 2878, 2886, 2900, 2909, 2970, 2979, 2998, 3003, 3026, 3033. *See also* General programs; Marketing
School counselors. *See* Counselors and counseling, school
School health nurses and nursing. *See* Nurses and nursing, school health
School libraries and librarians. *See* Libraries and librarianship, school
Schools. *See* Education
Science education. *See* Education, science and mathematics
Science reporting: 1197, 1308, 1417, 1592, 2393. *See also* Broadcasting; General programs; Journalism; Sciences
Sciences: 79, 310, 597, 688, 887, 1058, 1141, 1284, 1352, 1377, 1422, 1549, 1582, 1640, 1659, 1678, 1682, 1715, 1764, 1772–1773, 1796–1797, 1802, 1811, 1825, 1827, 1873, 1885, 1891, 1912, 1917, 1954, 1965, 1976, 1984–1985, 2002, 2041, 2055, 2064, 2076, 2087, 2090, 2093, 2101, 2108, 2115, 2122, 2132, 2149, 2158–2159, 2176, 2182, 2191, 2263, 2269, 2271, 2275, 2295, 2297, 2317, 2326, 2376, 2432, 2462, 2464, 2476, 2478, 2481, 2519, 2572, 2692, 2754, 2776–2777, 2812, 2818, 2821, 2840, 2877, 2923, 2942, 2987, 3044. *See also* General programs; names of specific sciences
Sculpture: 887, 1141, 1261, 1416, 1455, 1480, 1549, 1551–1552, 1659, 2317. *See also* Fine arts; General programs
Secondary education. *See* Education, secondary
Secret service. *See* Intelligence service
Secretarial sciences: 552, 2474, 2870, 3062. *See also* General programs
Security, national: 1140, 1570, 1656, 1876, 1946, 1948, 1996, 2113, 2368, 2410, 2422, 2491, 2631, 2688, 2703, 2723, 2804, 2921, 2975, 3014. *See also* General programs; Military affairs
Serbo-Croatian language. *See* Language, Serbo-Croatian
Sewing: 1385, 1452. *See also* Arts and crafts; General programs
Sexual abuse. *See* Rape
Sight impairments. *See* Visual impairments
Singing. *See* Voice
Slavic studies: 1575. *See also* General programs; Humanities
Smoking. *See* Tobacco consumption
Social sciences: 79, 597, 1188, 1325, 1382, 1573, 1769, 1874, 1910, 2024–2025, 2253, 2369, 2546, 2566, 2627, 2659, 2727, 2742–2743, 2781, 2920, 2976. *See also* General programs; names of specific social sciences
Social services: 1352, 1573, 1676, 2041, 2253, 2369, 2500, 2611, 2662, 2754, 2757, 2771, 2920, 2976. *See also* General programs; Public service; Social work
Social studies: 2622. *See also* General programs; Social sciences
Social work: 1246, 1555, 1882, 1896, 1939, 2118, 2330, 2364, 2566, 2630, 2636, 2648, 2796, 2813, 2962, 2974. *See also* General programs; Social sciences
Sociology: 2566. *See also* General programs; Social sciences
Soils science: 1731, 2034, 2131, 2142, 2170, 2417. *See also* Agriculture and agricultural sciences; General programs; Horticulture
Songs. *See* Music
South Asian studies: 1570, 2368, 2975. *See also* Asian studies; General programs; Humanities
Space sciences: 10, 200, 1141, 1659, 1857, 1885, 1947, 2025, 2118, 2172, 2382, 2408, 2440, 2444, 2743, 2813. *See also* General programs; Physical sciences
Spanish language. *See* Language, Spanish
Special education. *See* Education, special
Speech pathology: 1989, 2118, 2145, 2162, 2194, 2613, 2651, 2813, 2905, 3021. *See also* General programs; Medical sciences; Speech therapy
Speech therapy: 1849, 2403. *See also* General programs; Health and health care
Speeches. *See* Oratory
Sports. *See* Athletics
Sports medicine: 2216. *See also* General programs; Medical sciences
Sports reporting: 1177, 1198, 1276, 1308, 1390, 1406, 1471. *See also* Broadcasting; General programs; Journalism
Spying. *See* Intelligence service
Stage design. *See* Performing arts
Statistics: 1770, 2170, 2340, 2571, 2628, 2820. *See also* General programs; Mathematics
Stone industry: 1750. *See also* Building trades; General programs
Structural engineering. *See* Engineering, structural
Surgery: 1864, 1931, 2094, 2378. *See also* General programs; Medical sciences
Surveying: 1637, 1641, 1647–1650, 1686–1687, 1689–1690, 1693, 1834, 1840, 1925, 1927, 2012–2013, 2053, 2078, 2109, 2199, 2260, 2273, 2289, 2298, 2366, 2379, 2409, 2455, 2484. *See also* Engineering, surveying; General programs
Surveying engineering. *See* Engineering, surveying
Swahili language. *See* Language, Swahili
Swine industry. *See* Pork industry
Systems engineering. *See* Engineering, systems
Teaching. *See* Education
Technology: 200, 633, 688, 1287, 1462, 1466, 1486, 1640, 1642, 1655–1656, 1713, 1715, 1772, 1796–1797, 1802, 1811, 1824, 1826–1827, 1873–1874, 1876, 1912, 1917, 1946, 1948, 1976, 1984–1985, 2002, 2055, 2064, 2093, 2101, 2108, 2113, 2120, 2122, 2154, 2158–2159, 2170, 2172, 2176–2177, 2182, 2251, 2269, 2271, 2275, 2284, 2297, 2336, 2396, 2422, 2432, 2480–2481, 2519, 2572, 2627, 2631, 2688, 2804, 2867, 2923, 2942, 3014. *See also* Computer sciences; General programs; Sciences
Telecommunications: 552, 1210, 1256, 1303, 1333, 1336, 1466, 1496, 1532, 1570, 1658, 1898, 2026, 2239, 2368, 2451, 2570, 2649, 2909, 2975, 3034. *See also* Communications; General programs; Radio; Television
Telepathy. *See* Parapsychology

Television: 1136, 1154, 1170, 1215, 1251, 1264, 1271, 1278, 1308, 1336, 1344, 1355, 1371, 1402, 1413, 1579, 1581, 1602, 1620–1621, 1624, 1918, 2026, 2521. *See also* Communications; Filmmaking; General programs
Textile engineering. *See* Engineering, textile
Textiles: 1191, 1241, 1315, 1385, 2809, 2901. *See also* Arts and crafts; General programs; Home economics
Thai language. *See* Language, Thai
Theater. *See* Performing arts
Theater education. *See* Education, theater
Theology. *See* Religion and religious activities
Tobacco consumption: 1246, 1882, 2591, 2636. *See also* General programs; Medical sciences
Tourism: 552, 1593, 1626, 2355, 2494, 2498–2499, 2513, 2515, 2533–2534, 2558, 2581, 2672, 2694, 2785, 2831, 2864, 2926, 2950, 2969, 2971, 2997, 3013, 3037, 3057–3058, 3063. *See also* General programs
Toxicology: 1861, 2170, 2332, 2341, 2621. *See also* General programs; Medical sciences
Trade unions. *See* Labor unions and members
Transportation: 1679, 1695, 1868, 1874, 1995, 2024, 2096, 2102, 2110, 2380, 2474, 2487, 2501, 2512, 2626–2627, 2722, 2742, 2798, 2802, 2988, 2999, 3062. *See also* Automobile industry; Aviation; Engineering, transportation; General programs; Space sciences
Transportation engineering. *See* Engineering, transportation
Travel and tourism. *See* Tourism
Turfgrass science: 1592, 1783, 1880, 1929, 2080, 2138, 2206, 2329, 2393, 2882. *See also* Biological sciences; General programs; Management
Turkish language. *See* Language, Turkish
TV. *See* Television
Typing. *See* Secretarial sciences
Uighar language. *See* Language, Uighar
Unions and unionization. *See* Labor unions and members
Universities. *See* Education, higher
Unrestricted programs. *See* General programs
Urban affairs: 2953. *See also* City and regional planning; General programs
Urban planning. *See* City and regional planning
Urban studies: 1188, 2566. *See also* General programs; Urban affairs
Urdu language. *See* Language, Urdu
Uzbek language. *See* Language, Uzbek
Vacuum sciences: 1906. *See also* General programs; Sciences
Veterans. *See* Military affairs
Veterinary sciences: 1729, 1851, 2251, 2265, 2278, 2315, 2388, 2417, 2438, 2444, 2447, 2456, 2458, 3027. *See also* Animal science; General programs; Sciences
Video. *See* Filmmaking; Television
Vietnamese language. *See* Language, Vietnamese
Virology: 2268. *See also* General programs; Medical sciences
Visual arts: 541, 887, 1141, 1144, 1166, 1201, 1206, 1223, 1302, 1340, 1410, 1498, 1549, 1560, 1631, 1659, 2317. *See also* General programs; Humanities; names of specific visual arts
Visual impairments: 1866, 2118, 2308, 2490, 2545, 2550, 2625, 2733, 2813, 2949, 2978, 3021. *See also* Disabilities; General programs; Health and health care
Viticulture. *See* Enology and viticulture
Vocational education. *See* Education, vocational
Voice: 200, 541, 1260, 1293, 1338, 1399, 1405, 1410, 1426, 1440, 1448, 1464, 1535, 1574, 1607, 1629, 1631, 2697, 2846. *See also* General programs; Music; Performing arts
Water resources: 1341, 1701, 1738, 1749, 1760, 1787, 1821, 1969, 2057, 2190, 2286, 2339, 2394, 2530, 2598. *See also* Environmental sciences; General programs; Natural resources
Weaving: 1385. *See also* Arts and crafts; General programs
Web design. *See* Internet design and development
Web journalism. *See* Journalism, online
Welding: 1711–1713, 2107. *See also* Building trades; General programs
Welfare. *See* Social services
Wildlife management: 1449, 1969, 1974, 2131, 2167, 2170, 2300, 2309, 2332, 2436, 2473, 2951. *See also* Environmental sciences; General programs
Wine making. *See* Enology and viticulture
Women's studies and programs: 2684. *See also* General programs
Wood industry: 1993, 2702. *See also* Forestry management; General programs
Work. *See* Employment
World literature. *See* Literature
Wound, ostomy and continence nurses and nursing. *See* Nurses and nursing, wound, ostomy and continence
Youth. *See* Child development
Yugoslavian language. *See* Language, Serbo-Croatian
Yugoslavian studies. *See* Slavic studies
Zoology: 1974, 1997, 2024–2025, 2152, 2170, 2332, 2436, 2438, 2724, 2742–2743, 2845, 3027. *See also* Biological Sciences; General programs; names of specific zoological subfields

Residency Index

Some programs listed in this book are restricted to residents of a particular state, region, or other geographic location. Others are open to students wherever they live. The Residency Index will help you pinpoint programs available only to residents in your area as well as programs that have no residency restrictions (these are listed under the term "United States"). To use this index, look up the geographic areas that apply to you (always check the listings under "United States"), jot down the entry numbers listed after the subject areas that interest you, and use those numbers to find the program descriptions in the directory. To help you in your search, we've provided some "see also" references in each index entry. Remember: The numbers cited here refer to program entry numbers, not to page numbers in the book.

Alabama: **Unrestricted by Subject Area** 14–18, 83, 215–216, 440, 1103, 1107. **Humanities** 1150–1152, 1185, 1354, 1537. **Sciences** 1635, 1675, 1751, 1880, 1894, 1965, 2088. **Social Sciences** 2483, 2496, 2539, 2545, 2661, 2790. *See also* Southern states; United States

Alaska: **Unrestricted by Subject Area** 19–22, 76, 439, 1000. **Humanities** 1154, 1402. **Sciences** 1676, 1758, 1822, 1855, 1952, 2284, 2453. **Social Sciences** 2497–2500, 2515, 2533–2534, 2581, 2785, 2826, 2926, 2950, 3036. *See also* United States

American Samoa: **Sciences** 2477. **Social Sciences** 2910. *See also* United States

Arizona: **Unrestricted by Subject Area** 28, 44, 46–52, 253, 945. **Humanities** 1167, 1419, 1509. **Sciences** 1714–1715, 1745, 1789, 2074, 2257, 2302–2303, 2453, 2461. **Social Sciences** 2519, 2560, 2769, 3036, 3046. *See also* United States; Western states

Arkansas: **Unrestricted by Subject Area** 30, 45, 53–61, 83, 215–216, 846, 875, 1107, 1133. **Humanities** 1168, 1170, 1322, 1514. **Sciences** 1716–1717, 1944, 2453. **Social Sciences** 2492, 2520–2521, 2686, 2711, 3036. *See also* Southern states; United States

California: **Unrestricted by Subject Area** 44, 76, 79, 102–111, 115, 137–139, 217, 253, 294–295, 420, 504, 953, 1042. **Humanities** 1200, 1203–1207, 1261, 1271, 1283, 1578. **Sciences** 1738, 1742, 1745, 1786–1792, 1794–1795, 1805, 1821, 1895, 1937, 1999–2000, 2051, 2209, 2271, 2311, 2314, 2339, 2354, 2356, 2373, 2385, 2413, 2453. **Social Sciences** 2530, 2557–2565, 2584, 2587, 2598, 2645, 2685, 2725, 2779, 2782, 2887, 2912, 2914, 2939, 2968, 2970, 2982, 3008, 3036. *See also* United States; Western states

Canada: **Unrestricted by Subject Area** 43, 100, 309, 354–355, 362–363, 430, 493, 763, 785–787, 799, 941, 994–995. **Humanities** 1172, 1193, 1241, 1252, 1263, 1294, 1296, 1315, 1332, 1386, 1426, 1454, 1552–1553, 1558, 1598, 1632. **Sciences** 1637, 1696, 1699, 1706, 1723, 1746, 1752, 1764, 1766, 1774, 1826, 1865, 1891, 1932, 1951, 1956, 1961, 1963, 1972, 1980, 2022–2023, 2030, 2039, 2052, 2063, 2083, 2234, 2242, 2255–2256, 2261, 2299, 2331, 2333, 2346, 2360, 2387–2388, 2397, 2437, 2451, 2456, 2478. **Social Sciences** 2484, 2487, 2494, 2513, 2576, 2578, 2599, 2666, 2693, 2699, 2744, 2784, 2864, 2897, 2932, 2963, 3002, 3034, 3063

Colorado: **Unrestricted by Subject Area** 30, 44, 93, 161–162, 166–173, 197, 470, 880. **Humanities** 1165, 1287, 1319, 1326. **Sciences** 1709, 1747, 1760, 1771, 1828–1833, 1944, 1992, 2046, 2209, 2266, 2302–2303, 2305, 2384, 2394, 2406, 2430, 2453. **Social Sciences** 2510, 2514, 2518, 2605–2606, 2668, 2686, 2721, 2823, 2887, 2992, 3036. *See also* United States; Western states

Connecticut: **Unrestricted by Subject Area** 69, 96–97, 117, 177–182, 212, 229, 343, 348, 352, 432, 532, 596, 804, 823, 836, 872, 909, 938. **Humanities** 1195, 1201, 1216, 1228–1229, 1260, 1465–1466, 1501, 1559, 1575. **Sciences** 1780, 1839–1842, 2356. **Social Sciences** 2503, 2550, 2608, 2635, 2684, 2698, 2767, 2801, 2898, 2970, 2972. *See also* New England states; Northeastern states; United States

Delaware: **Unrestricted by Subject Area** 87, 203–207, 210, 277, 358, 539, 569, 872. **Humanities** 1351, 1365, 1390, 1429, 1620. **Sciences** 1813, 1862–1863, 2047, 2054, 2061, 2111, 2347. **Social Sciences** 2590, 2592, 2623–2624, 2765. *See also* Northeastern states; Southeastern states; Southern states; United States

District of Columbia. *See* Washington, D.C.

Florida: **Unrestricted by Subject Area** 83, 215–216, 237, 269, 281–291, 346, 841, 993, 1091, 1107. **Humanities** 1182–1183, 1185. **Sciences** 1635, 1666, 1751, 1856, 1877, 1886, 1909, 1921–1923, 1925–1927, 1929, 2000, 2209, 2271, 2277, 2283, 2372, 2403, 2413, 2434, 2460. **Social Sciences** 2483, 2539, 2612, 2661, 2671, 2673–2675, 2725, 2887, 3008. *See also* Southeastern states; Southern states; United States

Georgia: **Unrestricted by Subject Area** 44, 83, 122, 215–216, 268, 323–329, 373–374, 655, 1007, 1078, 1107. **Humanities** 1179, 1181, 1185, 1251, 1290, 1324, 1342, 1352, 1458. **Sciences** 1635, 1751, 1908, 1959, 2041, 2271, 2364, 2371–2372, 2403. **Social Sciences** 2483, 2539, 2582, 2661, 2754, 2774, 2974. *See also* Southeastern states; Southern states; United States

Guam: **Unrestricted by Subject Area** 128, 154, 158, 293, 351. **Sciences** 1950, 1997, 2110, 2152, 2477. **Social Sciences** 2689, 2718, 2724, 2802, 2845, 2910. *See also* United States

Hawaii: **Unrestricted by Subject Area** 76, 95, 110–111, 350, 650, 1121. **Humanities** 1305–1307, 1414, 1441, 1516. **Sciences** 1796–1797, 1827, 1912, 1976–1977, 2093, 2108, 2291. **Social Sciences** 2601, 2709, 2925. *See also* United States; Western states

Idaho: **Unrestricted by Subject Area** 383–384, 386–388, 867. **Humanities** 1271, 1327, 1369, 1616. **Sciences** 1908, 2004–2005, 2450, 2453. **Social Sciences** 2729–2730, 3033, 3036. *See also* United States; Western states

Illinois: **Unrestricted by Subject Area** 129, 360, 389–396, 581, 585, 802, 868, 899, 953, 1002, 1109. **Humanities** 1352, 1410, 1578. **Sciences** 1908, 2000, 2007–2010, 2012–2013, 2041, 2112, 2209, 2271, 2287, 2373, 2413, 2453. **Social Sciences** 2711, 2725, 2732–2737, 2754, 2796, 2833, 2887, 2982, 3008, 3036. *See also* Midwestern states; United States

Indiana: **Unrestricted by Subject Area** 220, 239, 301, 381, 400–401, 407, 468, 472, 495, 581–582, 802, 868, 939. **Humanities** 1320, 1333–1334, 1409, 1532. **Sciences** 1647, 1663, 1751, 1782, 1807, 1900, 1958, 1973, 1990, 2015–2017, 2073, 2271, 2390, 2453. **Social Sciences** 2539, 2555, 2616, 2641, 2695, 2705, 2738–2740, 2993, 3036. *See also* Midwestern states; United States

Iowa: **Unrestricted by Subject Area** 121, 129, 194, 232, 336, 403–404, 411, 581, 802, 865, 869, 894. **Humanities** 1340, 1500, 1521, 1602. **Sciences** 1843, 1944, 2029, 2247, 2453, 2479. **Social Sciences** 2686, 2711, 2746, 2793, 3036. *See also* Midwestern states; United States

Kansas: **Unrestricted by Subject Area** 444–453, 582. **Humanities** 1322, 1371–1373, 1475, 1500, 1568. **Sciences** 1944, 2068–2070, 2247, 2365. **Social Sciences** 2668, 2686, 2711, 2775–2776, 2889. *See also* Midwestern states; United States

Kentucky: **Unrestricted by Subject Area** 265, 458–462, 481, 531, 828, 931, 1001, 1004, 1107, 1126. **Humanities** 1185, 1303. **Sciences** 1639, 1642, 1663, 1751, 1845, 1958, 1973, 2073, 2078–2079, 2271, 2390. **Social Sciences** 2539, 2695, 2705, 2711, 2993. *See also* Southern states; United States

Louisiana: **Unrestricted by Subject Area** 30, 83, 215–216, 498–503, 875, 1107, 1131, 1133. **Humanities** 1185, 1322, 1407, 1515. **Sciences** 2151, 2300. **Social Sciences** 2667. *See also* Southern states; United States

Maine: **Unrestricted by Subject Area** 80, 143, 196, 208, 432, 479, 507–515, 735–736, 872, 900, 936, 938, 1130. **Humanities** 1139, 1222, 1299. **Sciences** 1652, 1726, 1733, 1993, 2107, 2413. **Social Sciences** 2574, 2596, 2651, 2797, 2799, 2851, 2913, 3008. *See also* New England states; Northeastern states; United States

Maryland: **Unrestricted by Subject Area** 82, 112, 118, 148, 152, 175, 188, 376–377, 424, 478, 506, 539–546, 645, 663, 678, 872, 951, 1065, 1107. **Humanities** 1135, 1365, 1390, 1420–1423, 1429, 1611, 1613–1614, 1629–1630. **Sciences** 1751, 1808, 1849, 1859, 1943, 2061, 2089, 2115–2116, 2118, 2325–2326, 2347. **Social Sciences** 2539, 2589, 2765, 2809–2813. *See also* Northeastern states; Southeastern states; Southern states; United States

Massachusetts: **Unrestricted by Subject Area** 229, 300, 330, 427, 432, 548–562, 781, 807, 872, 935, 938, 1034, 1082, 1105. **Humanities** 1149, 1424. **Sciences** 1648, 1986, 2109, 2120–2122, 2141, 2413, 2423. **Social Sciences** 2814–2818, 3008. *See also* New England states; Northeastern states; United States

Michigan: **Unrestricted by Subject Area** 44, 259, 487, 547, 571–582, 685, 802, 868, 873–874, 907, 1004. **Humanities** 1430, 1600. **Sciences** 1663, 1893, 1975, 2073, 2105, 2138–2139, 2144, 2150, 2366, 2390, 2453–2454, 2471. **Social Sciences** 2643, 2662, 2706, 2791, 2835, 2945, 2993, 3029, 3036, 3049. *See also* Midwestern states; United States

Midwestern states: **Social Sciences** 2850. *See also* United States

Minnesota: **Unrestricted by Subject Area** 187, 314, 505, 581–582, 597–610, 802, 863, 885, 902, 1090. **Humanities** 1350, 1433, 1518, 1602. **Sciences** 1734, 1907, 2142–2143, 2453. **Social Sciences** 2482, 2786, 3036. *See also* Midwestern states; United States

Mississippi: **Unrestricted by Subject Area** 30, 83, 215–216, 615–619, 737, 1107. **Humanities** 1185, 1352, 1411, 1593. **Sciences** 1635, 2041, 2145–2147. **Social Sciences** 2483, 2661, 2754, 2836–2838, 2997, 3045. *See also* Southern states; United States

Missouri: **Unrestricted by Subject Area** 3, 246, 518, 563, 581–582, 620–627, 651, 802, 884, 905. **Humanities** 1322, 1352, 1435–1437, 1475, 1500, 1541. **Sciences** 1944, 2041, 2148–2149, 2247, 2298, 2312. **Social Sciences** 2524, 2668, 2686, 2711, 2747, 2751, 2754, 2762, 2840–2844, 2889, 2944, 2952. *See also* Midwestern states; United States

Montana: **Unrestricted by Subject Area** 629–640, 947–948, 1086. **Humanities** 1271, 1439–1440. **Sciences** 1979, 2154, 2302–2303, 2453. **Social Sciences** 2846, 3036. *See also* United States; Western states

Nebraska: **Unrestricted by Subject Area** 127, 581–582, 690–691, 743, 802, 894, 929–930, 934, 950, 1020, 1083. **Humanities** 1298, 1463, 1476, 1500. **Sciences** 1784, 1944, 2233, 2247, 2453. **Social Sciences** 2537, 2668, 2686, 2711, 2870–2871, 2907, 3036, 3041. *See also* Midwestern states; United States

Nevada: **Unrestricted by Subject Area** 253, 694. **Humanities** 1519. **Sciences** 1789, 2000, 2453. **Social Sciences** 2560, 2725, 3036. *See also* United States; Western states

New England states: **Unrestricted by Subject Area** 320, 372, 697. **Humanities** 1209, 1467–1468, 1591. **Sciences** 1934, 2126, 2186, 2335, 2389. **Social Sciences** 2569, 2872. *See also* Northeastern states; United States

New Hampshire: **Unrestricted by Subject Area** 119, 278, 432, 526, 565, 698–704, 872, 938. **Humanities** 1393, 1473. **Sciences** 2187–2191, 2413. **Social Sciences** 2588, 2873–2877, 3008, 3011. *See also* New England states; Northeastern states; United States

New Jersey: **Unrestricted by Subject Area** 44, 114, 141, 223, 242, 258, 343, 352, 417, 432, 705–713, 739, 872. **Humanities** 1403, 1469–1471, 1563, 1574. **Sciences** 1863, 1981, 2095, 2131, 2192–2193, 2309–2310, 2367, 2413. **Social Sciences** 2653, 2710, 2951, 3008. *See also* Northeastern states; United States

New Mexico: **Unrestricted by Subject Area** 195, 197, 202, 238, 714–716, 718–724, 740, 842, 847, 875, 999, 1133. **Humanities** 1212, 1322, 1472. **Sciences** 1678, 1757, 1760, 1785, 1825, 1908, 1944, 2072, 2194–2198, 2200, 2302–2303, 2394, 2453, 2461. **Social Sciences** 2536, 2667–2668, 2686, 2878–2880, 3036. *See also* United States; Western states

New York: **Unrestricted by Subject Area** 343, 352, 357, 432, 538, 596, 725–727, 729–734, 849, 872, 946, 953, 1004. **Humanities** 1234, 1513, 1578. **Sciences** 1662, 1867, 2000, 2050, 2201–2204, 2206, 2224, 2271, 2373, 2413. **Social Sciences** 2578, 2634, 2696, 2725, 2761, 2881–2882, 2982, 3008. *See also* Northeastern states; United States

North Carolina: **Unrestricted by Subject Area** 83, 189, 215–216, 255, 413, 416, 529, 537, 686–687, 744–751, 872, 904, 1016, 1107. **Humanities** 1185, 1223, 1281, 1387, 1390. **Sciences** 1642, 1751, 1824, 1845, 1940, 1943, 2062, 2084, 2212–2213, 2231, 2271, 2372, 2403, 2428. **Social Sciences** 2539, 2583, 2661, 2683, 2763, 2891–2893, 2924, 2930, 2934, 3001, 3015, 3042. *See also* Southeastern states; Southern states; United States

North Dakota: **Unrestricted by Subject Area** 260, 339, 349, 582, 752–758. **Humanities** 1602. **Sciences** 2214, 2302–2303, 2453. **Social Sciences** 3036. *See also* Midwestern states; United States

Northeastern states: **Unrestricted by Subject Area** 99. *See also* United States

Northern Marianas: **Sciences** 2477. **Social Sciences** 2910. *See also* United States

Ohio: **Unrestricted by Subject Area** 250, 337, 581, 764–770, 802, 831, 868, 872, 1004. **Humanities** 1160, 1189, 1482, 1484, 1486, 1600. **Sciences** 1663, 1756, 1763, 1908, 1957, 1973, 2073, 2227, 2235, 2271, 2319–2320, 2356, 2390, 2395, 2453, 2457. **Social Sciences** 2490, 2542, 2579–2580, 2677, 2705, 2899, 2901–2903, 2970, 2993, 3036, 3047. *See also* Midwestern states; United States

Oklahoma: **Unrestricted by Subject Area** 30, 86, 89, 380, 441, 771–780, 852, 875, 991, 1107, 1133. **Humanities** 1186, 1254, 1322, 1345, 1352, 1358, 1475, 1489. **Sciences** 1944, 2041, 2228–2230, 2461. **Social Sciences** 2668, 2686, 2690, 2711, 2754, 2889, 2904–2906, 2957. *See also* Southern states; United States

Oregon: **Unrestricted by Subject Area** 76, 81, 137, 185, 198, 209, 222, 294–295, 353, 519, 788–798, 820, 832, 1079, 1108, 1123. **Humanities** 1156, 1261, 1271, 1300, 1317, 1346, 1378, 1384, 1474, 1493–1495. **Sciences** 1735, 1755, 1819, 1822, 1994, 2065–2066, 2086, 2092, 2185, 2219, 2236–2238, 2273, 2453, 2459. **Social Sciences** 2614, 2647, 2681, 2708, 2753, 2795, 2886, 2894, 2908, 3036. *See also* United States; Western states

Pennsylvania: **Unrestricted by Subject Area** 803, 809–818, 872, 1004. **Humanities** 1302, 1365, 1504–1505, 1526. **Sciences** 1663, 1680, 1691, 1863, 1989, 2038, 2061, 2073, 2208, 2249–2251, 2297, 2362, 2390, 2413. **Social Sciences** 2552, 2679, 2765, 2794, 2916–2918, 2942, 2993, 3008. *See also* Northeastern states; United States

Puerto Rico: **Unrestricted by Subject Area** 77, 100, 128, 154, 158, 293, 351, 370, 375, 845. **Humanities** 1291, 1415, 1444, 1503. **Sciences** 1668, 1751, 1950, 1964, 1997, 2110, 2152, 2159, 2328, 2401, 2415, 2437, 2477. **Social Sciences** 2532, 2539, 2689, 2718, 2724, 2802, 2805, 2845, 3009. *See also* United States

Rhode Island: **Unrestricted by Subject Area** 160, 219, 229, 432, 434, 806, 859–860, 872, 938. **Humanities** 1143, 1355, 1466, 1529. **Sciences** 1648, 1677, 1783, 1899, 2104, 2221, 2260, 2285. **Social Sciences** 2556. *See also* New England states; Northeastern states; United States

Samoa. *See* American Samoa

South Carolina: **Unrestricted by Subject Area** 83, 189, 215–216, 233, 412, 416, 471, 489, 527, 800, 893, 903, 913–921, 1078, 1107. **Humanities** 1166, 1185, 1353, 1387, 1390, 1565. **Sciences** 1751, 1845, 1908, 1915, 1974, 2084, 2243, 2351–2352, 2372, 2403, 2427, 2436. **Social Sciences** 2539, 2583, 2661. *See also* Southeastern states; Southern states; United States

South Dakota: **Unrestricted by Subject Area** 305, 528, 581, 802, 894, 896, 922–926. **Humanities** 1602. **Sciences** 1661, 1664, 1852, 1928, 2220, 2345, 2453. **Social Sciences** 2516, 2615, 2701, 3036. *See also* Midwestern states; United States

Southeastern states: **Unrestricted by Subject Area** 99. **Humanities** 1557. *See also* Southern states; United States

Southern states: **Unrestricted by Subject Area** 932. *See also* United States

Tennessee: **Unrestricted by Subject Area** 83, 215–216, 692, 954–962, 1085, 1107. **Humanities** 1185, 1352. **Sciences** 1642, 1751, 1908, 1943, 1987, 2041, 2374. **Social Sciences** 2539, 2632–2633, 2661, 2711, 2754, 2983–2984. *See also* Southern states; United States

Texas: **Unrestricted by Subject Area** 30, 44, 73, 83, 120, 128, 215–216, 262–264, 405, 421, 533, 588–590, 649, 722, 741, 875, 953, 964–969, 971, 973–990, 998, 1060–1061, 1107, 1129. **Humanities** 1221, 1226, 1314, 1322, 1352, 1367, 1475, 1578, 1580–1583, 1596, 1610. **Sciences** 1916, 1944, 1962, 2000, 2041, 2045, 2106, 2209, 2271, 2302–2303, 2373, 2375–2376, 2378–2381, 2392, 2413, 2453, 2461. **Social Sciences** 2597, 2667, 2686, 2725, 2754, 2887, 2889, 2937, 2978, 2982, 2986–2989, 3008, 3023, 3036. *See also* Southern states; United States; Western states

United States: **Unrestricted by Subject Area** 1–2, 4–13, 18, 24–27, 29, 31–43, 62–68, 70–72, 74–75, 77–78, 84–85, 88, 90–92, 94, 98, 100, 113, 116, 123–126, 128, 131–135, 140, 142, 144–147, 149–151, 153–158, 163–165, 174, 176, 183–184, 186, 190–193, 199–201, 211, 213–214, 218, 221, 225–228, 230–231, 234–235, 240–241, 244–245, 247–252, 254, 257, 261, 266–267, 270–276, 279, 292–293, 296–299, 302–303, 306–313, 315–319, 321, 331–335, 338, 340–342, 344–345, 347, 351, 354–356, 359, 361–364, 366–371, 375, 382, 385, 397–399, 402, 406, 408–410, 415, 418–419, 422–423, 425–426, 428–431, 433, 435–436, 438, 442–443, 455–457, 463–464, 466–467, 473–477, 480, 483–484, 486, 490, 492–494, 496–497, 516, 520–525, 530, 533–534, 536, 564, 566–567, 570, 584, 586–587, 589, 591–595, 611–614, 628, 641–644, 646–648, 652–654, 656–662, 664–677, 679–684, 688–689, 693, 695–696, 717, 728, 738, 742, 761–763, 775, 782, 784–787, 799, 801, 805, 808, 819–822, 824–825, 827, 829–830, 833–835, 837–840, 843–845, 851, 853–854, 856–858, 862, 864, 866, 870–871, 876, 878–879, 881–883, 886–892, 897–898, 901, 908, 910–912, 927–928, 933, 937, 940–941, 944, 949, 952, 967, 970, 972, 984, 990, 992, 994–997, 1003, 1005–1006, 1008–1015, 1017–1019, 1021–1026, 1040, 1043, 1048, 1053, 1059, 1062, 1064, 1087–1089, 1092, 1102, 1104, 1106, 1113, 1122, 1124–1125, 1127–1128, 1132. **Humanities** 1134, 1136–1138, 1140–1142, 1144–1148, 1153, 1157–1159, 1161–1164, 1169, 1171–1175, 1177–1178, 1180, 1184, 1187–1195, 1197–1199, 1202, 1208, 1210–1211, 1213–1215, 1217–1220, 1224–1225, 1227, 1230–1233, 1235, 1237–1241, 1243–1250, 1252–1253, 1255–1259, 1262–1263, 1265–1270, 1272–1280, 1282, 1284–1286, 1288–1289, 1291–1297, 1301, 1304, 1308–1312, 1315–1316, 1318, 1323, 1325, 1328–1332, 1336–1339, 1341, 1344, 1347–1349, 1356–1357, 1359–1364, 1366, 1368, 1370, 1374–1383, 1386, 1388–1392, 1394, 1397–1401, 1404–1406, 1408, 1412–1413, 1415–1418, 1425–1428, 1431–1432, 1434, 1438, 1442–1457, 1459–1462, 1464, 1478–1481, 1483, 1485, 1487–1488, 1490–1492, 1496–1499, 1502–1503, 1506–1508, 1510–1512, 1516–1517, 1520, 1522–1525, 1527–1528, 1530–1531, 1533–1534, 1536, 1538–1540, 1542–1545, 1547, 1549–1556, 1558, 1560–1562, 1564, 1566–1567, 1569–1573, 1576–1577, 1579, 1585–1590, 1592, 1594, 1597–1601, 1604–1609, 1617–1619, 1622–1625, 1627–1629, 1631–1634. **Sciences** 1636–1638, 1640–1641, 1643–1646, 1649–1651, 1653–1660, 1665, 1667–1674, 1677, 1679, 1681, 1683–1690, 1692–1708, 1710–1713, 1718–1725, 1727–1732, 1736–1737, 1739–1741, 1743–1744, 1746, 1748–1750, 1752–1753, 1756, 1759, 1761–1762, 1764–1768, 1770, 1772–1779, 1781, 1793, 1799–1802, 1804, 1806, 1809–1812, 1814–1818, 1820, 1823, 1826, 1834–1838, 1844, 1846–1848, 1850–1851, 1853–1854, 1857–1858, 1860–1861, 1864–1866, 1868–1874, 1876, 1878–1879, 1881–1885, 1887–1892, 1896–1898, 1902–1904, 1906, 1910–1911, 1913, 1917, 1919–1920, 1924, 1930–1933, 1935–1936, 1938–1939, 1941–1942, 1945–1951, 1953–1956, 1960–1961, 1963–1964, 1966–1967, 1970–1972, 1978, 1980, 1983–1985, 1988, 1991, 1995–1998, 2001–2003, 2006, 2011, 2014, 2018–2028, 2030–2037, 2039–2040, 2042–2045, 2048–2049, 2052–2053, 2055–2060, 2063–2064, 2067, 2071, 2073, 2076–2077, 2080, 2083, 2085, 2087, 2091, 2096–2103, 2110, 2113, 2117, 2119, 2123–2125, 2127–2130, 2132–2137, 2140–2141, 2152–2153, 2155–2184, 2199, 2205, 2207, 2210–2211, 2215–2218, 2222–2223, 2225–2226, 2232, 2234, 2239–2240, 2242, 2244, 2246, 2248, 2252–2256, 2258–2259, 2261–2265, 2268–2270, 2272, 2274–2276, 2278–2281, 2286, 2288–2290, 2292, 2294–2296, 2299, 2301, 2304, 2306–2308, 2313, 2315–2318, 2321–2324, 2327–2334, 2336–2338, 2340–2344, 2346, 2348–2350, 2353–2355, 2357–2361, 2363, 2368–2370, 2377, 2380, 2382, 2387–2388, 2391, 2393, 2396–2400, 2402, 2404–2405, 2407–2408, 2410–2412, 2414–2415, 2421–2422, 2426, 2432–2433, 2435, 2437, 2439–2440, 2445–2446, 2448, 2451–2452, 2455–2456, 2458, 2462–2465, 2467, 2472–2473, 2475–2478. **Social Sciences** 2484–2489, 2491, 2493–2495, 2501, 2504–2509, 2511–2513, 2517, 2522–2523, 2525–2527, 2529, 2531–2532, 2535, 2538, 2540, 2542, 2544, 2547–2549, 2551, 2554, 2567–2568, 2570–2573, 2575–2578, 2585, 2591, 2593–2595, 2599, 2602–2604, 2607, 2609–2611, 2613, 2617–2618, 2620–2622, 2625–2631, 2636–2640, 2642, 2644, 2646, 2648–2650, 2652, 2654–2659, 2663–2666, 2669–2670, 2672, 2676, 2678, 2680, 2682, 2688–2689, 2691–2694, 2697, 2699–2700, 2702–2704, 2707, 2714–2716, 2718–2720, 2722–2724, 2726–2728, 2731, 2741–2745, 2748–2750, 2752, 2755, 2757–2760, 2764, 2766, 2768, 2770–2773, 2777–2778, 2781, 2784, 2787–2789, 2792, 2794, 2798, 2800, 2802, 2804–2806, 2808, 2819–2822, 2824–2825, 2827–2832, 2834, 2836–2837, 2839, 2845, 2847–2849, 2852–2869, 2883–2885, 2888, 2890, 2895–2897, 2900, 2909, 2911, 2915, 2919–2923, 2925, 2927–2929, 2931–2933, 2935–2936, 2938, 2940, 2943, 2946–2949, 2953–2956, 2958–2969, 2971, 2973, 2975–2977, 2979–2981, 2988, 2991, 2994–2996, 2998–3000, 3002–3004, 3006–3007, 3009, 3013–3014, 3022, 3024–3026, 3028, 3030, 3034–3035, 3037, 3043–3044, 3052–3055, 3063–3065

Utah: **Unrestricted by Subject Area** 197, 488, 850, 1027–1033. **Sciences** 1908, 2302–2303, 2409, 2453. **Social Sciences** 3005, 3036. *See also* United States; Western states

Vermont: **Unrestricted by Subject Area** 136, 243, 278, 365, 432, 568, 760, 783, 848, 855, 872, 906, 938, 943, 1035–1039. **Humanities** 1155, 1176, 1343, 1395, 1535, 1595, 1603. **Sciences** 1875, 1905, 1969, 1982, 2081, 2245, 2282, 2356, 2416–2420. **Social Sciences** 2502, 2528, 2566, 2586, 2660, 2713, 2756, 2970, 3010–3012. *See also* New England states; Northeastern states; United States

Virgin Islands: **Unrestricted by Subject Area** 128, 154, 158, 236, 293, 351, 491, 963, 1044–1046. **Humanities** 1236. **Sciences** 1682, 1803, 1914, 1950, 1997, 2110, 2152, 2438, 2477. **Social Sciences** 2600, 2619, 2687, 2689, 2717–2718, 2724, 2780, 2802–2803, 2845, 2985, 3027, 3039. *See also* United States

Virginia: **Unrestricted by Subject Area** 82–83, 112, 118, 148, 152, 215–216, 280, 378, 414, 424, 478, 506, 527, 535, 645, 647, 663, 678, 872, 903, 1041, 1047–1052, 1054–1058, 1065, 1107. **Humanities** 1135, 1185, 1335, 1387, 1390, 1396, 1611, 1613–1614, 1629–1630. **Sciences** 1642, 1751, 1798, 1845, 1859, 1943, 2000, 2061, 2084, 2089, 2114, 2325–2326, 2372, 2413, 2424–2425, 2429, 2431. **Social Sciences** 2539, 2712, 2725, 2807, 3008, 3016–3021. *See also* Southeastern states; Southern states; United States

Washington: **Unrestricted by Subject Area** 76, 130, 137, 224, 322, 437, 465, 485, 517, 583, 759, 826, 895, 1063, 1066–1077, 1084, 1111. **Humanities** 1196, 1242, 1271, 1313, 1321, 1378, 1385, 1477, 1546, 1548, 1584, 1612, 1615. **Sciences** 1769, 1819, 1908, 2065–2066, 2082, 2219, 2241, 2248, 2293, 2383, 2386, 2413, 2441–2444, 2446–2447, 2453. **Social Sciences** 2543, 2546, 2783, 2915, 2941, 2990, 3008, 3031–3032, 3036, 3051, 3056. *See also* United States; Western states

Washington, D.C.: **Unrestricted by Subject Area** 44, 82, 112, 118, 148, 152, 159, 188, 304, 424, 454, 478, 506, 539, 645, 647, 663, 678, 872, 1065, 1107. **Humanities** 1135, 1264, 1429, 1611, 1613–1614, 1629–1630. **Sciences** 1751, 1859, 1918, 2000, 2089, 2209, 2325–2326, 2413. **Social Sciences** 2539, 2725, 2887, 3008. *See also* Northeastern states; Southeastern states; Southern states; United States

West Virginia: **Unrestricted by Subject Area** 23, 101, 256, 469, 482, 872, 877, 1004, 1080–1081, 1107, 1110. **Humanities** 1387, 1626. **Sciences** 1642, 1663, 1680, 1751, 1754, 1845, 1943, 1968, 2061, 2073, 2084, 2090, 2235, 2390. **Social Sciences** 2539, 2541, 2661, 2993, 3038, 3040, 3057–3058. *See also* Southern states; United States

Western states: **Humanities** 1295. *See also* United States

Wisconsin: **Unrestricted by Subject Area** 379, 581–582, 802, 861, 902, 942, 1093–1101, 1112. **Humanities** 1602, 1621. **Sciences** 1901, 1907, 2075, 2094, 2449, 2453, 2466, 2468–2471, 2480–2481. **Social Sciences** 2553, 3036, 3048–3050. *See also* Midwestern states; United States

Wyoming: **Unrestricted by Subject Area** 30, 197, 1114–1120. **Sciences** 1760, 1944, 2267, 2302–2303, 2394, 2453, 2474. **Social Sciences** 2668, 2686, 3036, 3059–3062. *See also* United States; Western states

Tenability Index

Some programs listed in this book can be used only in specific cities, counties, states, or regions. Others may be used anywhere in the United States (or even abroad). The Tenability Index will help you locate funding that is restricted to a specific area as well as funding that has no tenability restrictions (these are listed under the term "United States"). To use this index, look up the geographic areas where you'd like to go (always check the listings under "United States"), jot down the entry numbers listed under the subject areas that interest you, and use those numbers to find the program descriptions in the directory. To help you in your search, we've provided some "see also" references in each index entry. Remember: The numbers cited here refer to program entry numbers, not to page numbers in the book.

Alabama: **Unrestricted by Subject Area** 14–18, 440, 1103. **Humanities** 1150–1151, 1427, 1537. **Sciences** 1751, 1894, 2088, 2289. **Social Sciences** 2539, 2790, 2961. *See also* Southern states; United States; names of specific cities and counties

Alaska: **Unrestricted by Subject Area** 19–20. **Humanities** 1225, 1376, 1550. **Sciences** 1758, 1952, 2455–2456. **Social Sciences** 2497–2499, 2515, 2533–2534, 2785, 2926, 2950. *See also* Northwestern states; United States; names of specific cities

Alberta (Canada): **Unrestricted by Subject Area** 695. *See also* Canada

Albuquerque, New Mexico: **Sciences** 1781, 1983, 2072. *See also* New Mexico

Alexandria, Virginia: **Humanities** 1630. *See also* Virginia

Alpena, Michigan: **Sciences** 2230, 2471. *See also* Michigan

American Samoa: **Sciences** 2477. *See also* United States

Ames, Iowa: **Sciences** 1816, 1919, 2453. **Social Sciences** 2594, 3036. *See also* Iowa

Amherst, Massachusetts: **Social Sciences** 2495. *See also* Massachusetts

Ann Arbor, Michigan: **Sciences** 1741. *See also* Michigan

Arizona: **Unrestricted by Subject Area** 46–52. **Humanities** 1167, 1225, 1376, 1509, 1550. **Sciences** 1714–1715, 1789, 2257, 2302–2303, 2353, 2455–2456. **Social Sciences** 2519, 2560, 2769, 2967, 3046. *See also* United States; names of specific cities and counties

Arkansas: **Unrestricted by Subject Area** 45, 53, 55–61, 846, 875. **Humanities** 1169, 1514. **Sciences** 1717, 2151. **Social Sciences** 2520, 2711. *See also* Southern states; United States; names of specific cities and counties

Arlington County, Virginia: **Humanities** 1630. *See also* Virginia

Arlington, Virginia: **Sciences** 1919. *See also* Virginia

Atlanta, Georgia: **Humanities** 1216, 1492. **Sciences** 1741, 1919. **Social Sciences** 2935. *See also* Georgia

Auburn, Alabama: **Sciences** 1919. *See also* Alabama

Austin County, Texas: **Sciences** 2274. *See also* Texas

Austin, Texas: **Humanities** 1492. **Sciences** 2453. **Social Sciences** 2700, 3036. *See also* Texas

Australia: **Unrestricted by Subject Area** 43. **Humanities** 1233, 1349. **Social Sciences** 2752. *See also* Foreign countries

Baltimore, Maryland: **Sciences** 1919. *See also* Maryland

Beloit, Wisconsin: **Social Sciences** 2778. *See also* Wisconsin

Berkeley, California: **Sciences** 2453. **Social Sciences** 2700, 3036. *See also* California

Big Rapids, Michigan: **Social Sciences** 2927. *See also* Michigan

Blacksburg, Virginia: **Social Sciences** 2935. *See also* Virginia

Boston, Massachusetts: **Unrestricted by Subject Area** 688. **Sciences** 1919, 2182. *See also* Massachusetts

Boulder, Colorado: **Sciences** 1741. *See also* Colorado

Bozeman, Montana: **Sciences** 1816. **Social Sciences** 2594. *See also* Montana

Brazoria County, Texas: **Sciences** 2274. *See also* Texas

Brookings, South Dakota: **Sciences** 1816. **Social Sciences** 2594. *See also* South Dakota

Brookville, New York: **Unrestricted by Subject Area** 688. **Sciences** 2182. *See also* New York

Buffalo, New York: **Sciences** 1919. *See also* New York

Buies Creek, North Carolina: **Social Sciences** 2927. *See also* North Carolina

California: **Unrestricted by Subject Area** 103–104, 106–109, 115, 137, 139, 294–295, 504, 953. **Humanities** 1200, 1203, 1206–1207, 1225, 1271, 1283, 1376, 1550, 1578. **Sciences** 1687, 1738, 1742, 1786–1792, 1794–1795, 1805, 1821, 1895, 1906, 1937, 1999, 2051, 2055, 2311, 2314, 2339, 2353, 2373, 2414, 2455–2456. **Social Sciences** 2530, 2557–2558, 2560–2565, 2598, 2645, 2665, 2685, 2779, 2912, 2914, 2939, 2967, 2982. *See also* United States; names of specific cities and counties

California, northern: **Humanities** 1261. *See also* California

Canada: **Unrestricted by Subject Area** 43, 100, 309, 354–355, 362–363, 430, 493, 763, 785–787, 941, 994–995, 1063, 1088. **Humanities** 1172, 1193, 1233, 1241, 1252, 1263, 1294, 1296, 1315, 1332, 1349, 1386, 1426, 1454, 1552–1553, 1558, 1598, 1632. **Sciences** 1637, 1696, 1699, 1706, 1723, 1746, 1752, 1764, 1766, 1774, 1826, 1865, 1891, 1932, 1951, 1956, 1961, 1963, 1972, 1980, 2022–2023, 2030, 2039, 2052, 2063, 2083, 2234, 2242, 2255–2256, 2261, 2299, 2331, 2333, 2346, 2360, 2387–2388, 2397, 2437, 2451, 2456, 2478. **Social Sciences** 2484, 2487, 2494, 2513, 2576, 2578, 2599, 2666, 2693, 2699, 2744, 2752, 2784, 2864, 2932, 2963, 3002, 3034, 3063. *See also* Foreign countries

Caribbean: **Unrestricted by Subject Area** 785–787. **Humanities** 1193, 1252. *See also* Foreign countries; names of specific countries

Central America: **Humanities** 1193, 1252. *See also* Foreign countries; names of specific countries

Chambers County, Texas: **Sciences** 2274. *See also* Texas

Champaign, Illinois: **Sciences** 1816, 1919. **Social Sciences** 2594. *See also* Illinois

Charleston, South Carolina: **Unrestricted by Subject Area** 688. **Sciences** 2182. *See also* South Carolina

Charlotte, North Carolina: **Unrestricted by Subject Area** 688. **Sciences** 1919, 2182. *See also* North Carolina

Chicago, Illinois: **Unrestricted by Subject Area** 953. **Humanities** 1578. **Sciences** 2209, 2373. **Social Sciences** 2778, 2887, 2982. *See also* Illinois

Chico, California: **Sciences** 2471. *See also* California

Cincinnati, Ohio: **Unrestricted by Subject Area** 688. **Sciences** 2182. *See also* Ohio

Claremont, California: **Sciences** 1741. **Social Sciences** 2778. *See also* California

Clemson, South Carolina: **Social Sciences** 2927. *See also* South Carolina

College Station, Texas: **Sciences** 1741, 1816, 2453. **Social Sciences** 2594, 3036. *See also* Texas

Collegeville, Pennsylvania: **Social Sciences** 2778. *See also* Pennsylvania

Colorado: **Unrestricted by Subject Area** 93, 161–162, 166–170, 172–173, 880. **Humanities** 1165, 1225, 1287, 1312, 1376, 1550. **Sciences** 1646, 1709, 1747, 1828–1834, 1938, 1992, 2037, 2046, 2158, 2266, 2302–2303, 2305, 2394, 2405–2406, 2455–2456. **Social Sciences** 2518, 2606, 2668, 2714, 2992. *See also* United States; names of specific cities and counties

Colorado County, Texas: **Sciences** 2274. *See also* Texas

Colorado Springs, Colorado: **Social Sciences** 2927. *See also* Colorado

Columbia, Missouri: **Sciences** 1816. **Social Sciences** 2594. *See also* Missouri

Columbia, South Carolina: **Social Sciences** 2935. *See also* South Carolina

Columbus, Ohio: **Sciences** 1816. **Social Sciences** 2594. *See also* Ohio

Connecticut: **Unrestricted by Subject Area** 39, 96–97, 117, 177, 179, 182, 343, 352, 562, 596, 735–736, 823, 936. **Humanities** 1195. **Sciences** 1838, 2452. **Social Sciences** 2503, 2550, 2609, 2635, 2801, 3035. *See also* New England states; United States; names of specific cities and counties

Conway, South Carolina: **Social Sciences** 2927. *See also* South Carolina

Corvallis, Oregon: **Sciences** 1816. **Social Sciences** 2594. *See also* Oregon

Crookston, Minnesota: **Sciences** 1816. **Social Sciences** 2594. *See also* Minnesota

Dallas, Texas: **Sciences** 2274. *See also* Texas

Davis, California: **Sciences** 2453. **Social Sciences** 3036. *See also* California

Daytona Beach, Florida: **Social Sciences** 2935. *See also* Florida

Decatur, Georgia: **Social Sciences** 2778. *See also* Georgia

Decatur, Illinois: **Social Sciences** 2778. *See also* Illinois

Delaware: **Unrestricted by Subject Area** 203–207, 735. **Humanities** 1351, 1365, 1629. **Sciences** 1863, 2054, 2463. **Social Sciences** 2590, 2613, 2624, 2765, 2958. *See also* Southeastern states; Southern states; United States; names of specific cities and counties

Denver, Colorado: **Unrestricted by Subject Area** 36, 688. **Humanities** 1233. **Sciences** 2182, 2209. **Social Sciences** 2495, 2887. *See also* Colorado

Dickinson, North Dakota: **Sciences** 1816. **Social Sciences** 2594. *See also* North Dakota

District of Columbia. *See* Washington, D.C.

East Lansing, Michigan: **Sciences** 1816. **Social Sciences** 2495, 2594. *See also* Michigan

Edmond, Oklahoma: **Social Sciences** 2927. *See also* Oklahoma

England: **Humanities** 1233, 1349. **Sciences** 2064. **Social Sciences** 2752. *See also* Foreign countries; United Kingdom

Europe: **Unrestricted by Subject Area** 1063. **Sciences** 2024. **Social Sciences** 2742. *See also* Foreign countries; names of specific countries

Fairfax County, Virginia: **Humanities** 1630. *See also* Virginia

Falls Church, Virginia: **Humanities** 1630. *See also* Virginia

Fargo, North Dakota: **Sciences** 1741, 1816. **Social Sciences** 2594. *See also* North Dakota

Fayetteville, North Carolina: **Unrestricted by Subject Area** 245. **Social Sciences** 2927. *See also* North Carolina

Finland: **Humanities** 1356. *See also* Europe; Foreign countries

Flint, Michigan: **Unrestricted by Subject Area** 688. **Sciences** 2182. *See also* Michigan

Florida: **Unrestricted by Subject Area** 237, 281–282, 284–289, 291, 841, 993, 1091. **Humanities** 1161, 1182–1183. **Sciences** 1666, 1751, 1856, 1877, 1886, 1909, 1921, 1923–1926, 1929, 2161, 2283, 2372, 2414, 2434, 2460. **Social Sciences** 2539, 2612, 2671–2675, 2855. *See also* Southeastern states; Southern states; United States; names of specific cities and counties

Florida, central: **Sciences** 2274. *See also* Florida

Florida, southern: **Sciences** 2274. *See also* Florida
Foreign countries: **Unrestricted by Subject Area** 93, 298, 389, 409, 604, 695, 863, 866, 890, 949, 1040, 1090, 1125. **Humanities** 1171, 1187–1188, 1202, 1240, 1250, 1325, 1338, 1342, 1363, 1528, 1562, 1607, 1624. **Sciences** 1810, 2031, 2240. **Social Sciences** 2639, 2727, 2755, 2861, 2943, 2991, 3065. *See also* names of specific continents; names of specific countries
Fort Bend County, Texas: **Sciences** 2274. *See also* Texas
Fort Collins, Colorado: **Sciences** 1816. **Social Sciences** 2594. *See also* Colorado
Fort Lauderdale, Florida: **Sciences** 2209. **Social Sciences** 2887. *See also* Florida
Fort Meade, Maryland: **Humanities** 1570. **Sciences** 2368. **Social Sciences** 2975. *See also* Maryland
Fort Myers, Florida: **Social Sciences** 2927. *See also* Florida
Fort Worth, Texas: **Sciences** 2274. *See also* Texas
France: **Humanities** 1233, 1349. **Social Sciences** 2752. *See also* Europe; Foreign countries
Frederick County, Maryland: **Humanities** 1630. *See also* Maryland
Fresno, California: **Sciences** 2453. **Social Sciences** 3036. *See also* California
Fullerton, California: **Sciences** 2453. **Social Sciences** 3036. *See also* California
Gainesville, Florida: **Sciences** 2283. *See also* Florida
Gaithersburg, Maryland: **Humanities** 1233. *See also* Maryland
Galesburg, Illinois: **Social Sciences** 2778. *See also* Illinois
Galveston County, Texas: **Sciences** 2274. *See also* Texas
Georgetown, Texas: **Social Sciences** 2778. *See also* Texas
Georgia: **Unrestricted by Subject Area** 323, 325–326, 328–329, 373–374. **Humanities** 1179, 1181, 1251, 1290, 1324, 1342, 1458. **Sciences** 1751, 1959, 2161, 2274, 2372. **Social Sciences** 2539, 2582, 2774, 2855, 2929. *See also* Southeastern states; Southern states; United States; names of specific cities and counties
Greensboro, North Carolina: **Unrestricted by Subject Area** 245. **Humanities** 1390. **Sciences** 1741, 1919. *See also* North Carolina
Greenville, South Carolina: **Social Sciences** 2935. *See also* South Carolina
Guam: **Unrestricted by Subject Area** 128, 154, 158, 293, 351. **Sciences** 1950, 1997, 2000, 2110, 2152, 2271, 2413, 2477. **Social Sciences** 2689, 2718, 2724–2725, 2802, 2845, 3008. *See also* United States
Harris County, Texas: **Sciences** 2274. *See also* Texas
Hawaii: **Unrestricted by Subject Area** 350. **Humanities** 1225, 1376, 1414, 1516, 1550. **Sciences** 2093, 2291, 2353, 2455–2456. **Social Sciences** 2925, 2967. *See also* United States; names of specific cities and counties
Hoboken, New Jersey: **Sciences** 1919. *See also* New Jersey
Houston, Texas: **Humanities** 1624. **Social Sciences** 2495, 2935. *See also* Texas
Huntsville, Texas: **Social Sciences** 2927. *See also* Texas
Hyde Park, New York: **Humanities** 1233. **Social Sciences** 2495. *See also* New York
Idaho: **Unrestricted by Subject Area** 383–388, 867. **Humanities** 1225, 1271, 1327, 1369, 1376, 1550, 1616. **Sciences** 1688, 2004, 2242, 2450, 2455–2456, 2458. **Social Sciences** 2729–2730, 3033. *See also* Northwestern states; United States; names of specific cities and counties
Illinois: **Unrestricted by Subject Area** 390–396, 530, 1002. **Sciences** 2008–2009, 2012–2013, 2015, 2112, 2322, 2414. **Social Sciences** 2711, 2732–2733, 2736–2737, 2833, 2959, 3050. *See also* United States; names of specific cities and counties
India: **Unrestricted by Subject Area** 43. *See also* Foreign countries
Indiana: **Unrestricted by Subject Area** 301, 400–401, 530, 582. **Humanities** 1333–1334, 1409, 1425, 1532, 1590. **Sciences** 1647, 1751, 1782, 1807, 1973, 2015–2018. **Social Sciences** 2539, 2555, 2705, 2738–2740. *See also* United States; names of specific cities and counties
Iowa: **Unrestricted by Subject Area** 121, 194, 232, 403, 411, 865, 869. **Humanities** 1340, 1500, 1521. **Sciences** 2029, 2247, 2479. **Social Sciences** 2711, 3050. *See also* United States; names of specific cities and counties
Iran: **Unrestricted by Subject Area** 628. *See also* Foreign countries
Ireland: **Unrestricted by Subject Area** 43. *See also* Europe; Foreign countries
Irvine, California: **Sciences** 1919. *See also* California
Italy: **Humanities** 1233, 1349. **Social Sciences** 2752. *See also* Europe; Foreign countries
Ithaca, New York: **Humanities** 1559. **Social Sciences** 2935. *See also* New York
Jackson, Mississippi: **Unrestricted by Subject Area** 245. *See also* Mississippi
Japan: **Humanities** 1233, 1349. **Social Sciences** 2752. *See also* Foreign countries
Kansas: **Unrestricted by Subject Area** 444–445, 447–448, 450–453, 582. **Humanities** 1190, 1311, 1371–1372, 1374–1375, 1418, 1428, 1475, 1500, 1568. **Sciences** 1802, 2068–2070, 2158, 2247, 2365. **Social Sciences** 2572, 2668, 2711, 2775–2776, 2889. *See also* United States; names of specific cities and counties
Kentucky: **Unrestricted by Subject Area** 265, 460, 462, 530–531, 931, 1001, 1126. **Humanities** 1303. **Sciences** 1642, 1751, 1973, 2015, 2078, 2080. **Social Sciences** 2539, 2705, 2711. *See also* Southern states; United States; names of specific cities and counties
Lake Forest, Illinois: **Social Sciences** 2778. *See also* Illinois
Laramie, Wyoming: **Sciences** 1816. **Social Sciences** 2594. *See also* Wyoming
Las Cruces, New Mexico: **Unrestricted by Subject Area** 244. **Sciences** 1781, 1983, 2072. **Social Sciences** 2927. *See also* New Mexico
Las Vegas, Nevada: **Social Sciences** 2495, 2927. *See also* Nevada
Lexington, Kentucky: **Sciences** 1741. *See also* Kentucky
Lexington, Virginia: **Social Sciences** 2778. *See also* Virginia
Liberty County, Texas: **Sciences** 2274. *See also* Texas
Lima, Ohio: **Sciences** 2230, 2471. *See also* Ohio
Lincoln, Nebraska: **Sciences** 1816. **Social Sciences** 2594, 2927. *See also* Nebraska
Logan, Utah: **Sciences** 1816. **Social Sciences** 2594. *See also* Utah
Los Angeles, California: **Sciences** 2209, 2453. **Social Sciences** 2887, 3036. *See also* California
Los Angeles County, California: **Sciences** 2274. *See also* California
Loudoun County, Virginia: **Humanities** 1630. *See also* Virginia
Louisiana: **Unrestricted by Subject Area** 498–500, 502–503, 875, 1131. **Sciences** 2103, 2151, 2274, 2300. *See also* Southern states; United States; names of specific cities and parishes
Louisiana, northern: **Social Sciences** 2667. *See also* Louisiana
Lubbock, Texas: **Sciences** 1816. **Social Sciences** 2594. *See also* Texas
Madison, Wisconsin: **Sciences** 1816. **Social Sciences** 2594. *See also* Wisconsin
Maine: **Unrestricted by Subject Area** 117, 479, 507–508, 510–513, 562, 735–736, 900, 936, 1130. **Humanities** 1139. **Sciences** 1652, 1726, 1733, 2107. **Social Sciences** 2797, 2799, 2851, 2913. *See also* New England states; United States; names of specific cities and counties
Manhattan, Kansas: **Sciences** 1816. **Social Sciences** 2594. *See also* Kansas
Maryland: **Unrestricted by Subject Area** 41, 112, 175, 376–377, 399, 540–546, 951. **Humanities** 1421–1423, 1456, 1556, 1629. **Sciences** 1751, 1801, 1808, 1849, 1943, 2115, 2117–2118, 2171, 2274, 2463. **Social Sciences** 2539–2540, 2571, 2585, 2589, 2603, 2613, 2764, 2792, 2811–2813, 2863, 2865, 2958. *See also* Southeastern states; Southern states; United States; names of specific cities and counties
Maryland, southern: **Humanities** 1135. **Sciences** 2181. **Social Sciences** 2868. *See also* Maryland
Maryville, Missouri: **Sciences** 1816. **Social Sciences** 2594. *See also* Missouri
Massachusetts: **Unrestricted by Subject Area** 117, 330, 427, 549–552, 556–562, 735–736, 781, 807, 935–936. **Sciences** 2120–2122, 2274. **Social Sciences** 2815–2818. *See also* New England states; United States; names of specific cities and counties
Matagorda County, Texas: **Sciences** 2274. *See also* Texas
Medford, Massachusetts: **Sciences** 1741. *See also* Massachusetts
Melbourne, Florida: **Sciences** 1909. *See also* Florida
Mesa, Arizona: **Social Sciences** 2927. *See also* Arizona
Mexico: **Unrestricted by Subject Area** 363. **Humanities** 1172, 1193, 1252, 1296, 1316, 1332, 1349. **Sciences** 1696, 1764, 1951, 2360. **Social Sciences** 2752. *See also* Foreign countries
Miami, Florida: **Humanities** 1492. **Sciences** 2209. **Social Sciences** 2887. *See also* Florida
Michigan: **Unrestricted by Subject Area** 259, 530, 571–572, 575, 579–580, 582, 874. **Humanities** 1138, 1243, 1430. **Sciences** 1650, 1893, 1967, 2014–2015, 2105, 2138–2139, 2144, 2150, 2454. **Social Sciences** 2489, 2629, 2643, 2662, 2791, 2830, 2835, 3029, 3050. *See also* United States; names of specific cities and counties
Minneapolis, Minnesota: **Humanities** 1492. **Sciences** 1741, 2453. **Social Sciences** 3036. *See also* Minnesota
Minnesota: **Unrestricted by Subject Area** 582, 597–598, 600–603, 606, 608, 610, 902, 1101. **Humanities** 1433. **Sciences** 1734, 1802. **Social Sciences** 2572, 3050. *See also* United States; names of specific cities and counties
Mississippi: **Unrestricted by Subject Area** 615–619, 737. **Humanities** 1411. **Sciences** 1689, 2145–2147, 2151, 2274. **Social Sciences** 2504, 2836–2838, 3045. *See also* Southern states; United States; names of specific cities and counties
Mississippi State, Mississippi: **Sciences** 1919. **Social Sciences** 2927. *See also* Mississippi
Missouri: **Unrestricted by Subject Area** 3, 518, 582, 620, 622–623, 625–627, 651. **Humanities** 1435, 1475, 1500. **Sciences** 2149, 2247. **Social Sciences** 2524, 2711, 2747, 2751, 2762, 2839–2841, 2843–2844, 2889. *See also* United States; names of specific cities and counties
Missouri, western: **Social Sciences** 2668. *See also* Missouri
Montana: **Unrestricted by Subject Area** 629–640, 947–948, 1086. **Humanities** 1225, 1271, 1376, 1439, 1550. **Sciences** 1979, 2154, 2302–2303, 2455–2456, 2458. *See also* United States; names of specific cities and counties
Monterey, California: **Sciences** 1919. *See also* California
Montgomery, Alabama: **Unrestricted by Subject Area** 245. **Sciences** 1919. *See also* Alabama
Montgomery County, Maryland: **Humanities** 1630. *See also* Maryland
Montgomery County, Texas: **Sciences** 2274. *See also* Texas
Moscow, Idaho: **Sciences** 1816, 1919. **Social Sciences** 2594, 2927. *See also* Idaho
Murfreesboro, Tennessee: **Sciences** 2230, 2471. *See also* Tennessee
Nashville, Tennessee: **Unrestricted by Subject Area** 245. *See also* Tennessee

Nebraska: **Unrestricted by Subject Area** 582, 690–691, 743, 929–930, 950. **Humanities** 1298, 1401, 1463, 1500. **Sciences** 1784, 2158, 2247. **Social Sciences** 2668, 2711, 2871, 3041. *See also* United States; names of specific cities and counties

Nevada: **Humanities** 1225, 1376, 1519, 1550. **Sciences** 1789, 2353, 2455–2456. **Social Sciences** 2560, 2967. *See also* United States; names of specific cities

New Brunswick, New Jersey: **Social Sciences** 2700. *See also* New Jersey

New England states: **Unrestricted by Subject Area** 320, 700. **Humanities** 1209. **Sciences** 1971, 2186. **Social Sciences** 2569, 2603, 2872. *See also* United States; names of specific states

New Hampshire: **Unrestricted by Subject Area** 117, 119, 562, 565, 698–699, 703–704, 735–736, 936. **Sciences** 2188–2189, 2191. **Social Sciences** 2875–2877. *See also* New England states; United States; names of specific cities and counties

New Jersey: **Unrestricted by Subject Area** 39, 343, 352, 709–710. **Humanities** 1403, 1469–1471, 1563. **Sciences** 1690, 1767, 1847, 2095, 2193, 2274, 2348, 2414. **Social Sciences** 2613, 2653, 2808, 2958. *See also* United States; names of specific cities and counties

New Jersey, northern: **Social Sciences** 2603. *See also* New Jersey

New Jersey, southern: **Sciences** 1863. *See also* New Jersey

New Mexico: **Unrestricted by Subject Area** 202, 716–717, 719–721, 723–724, 740, 847, 875, 999. **Humanities** 1212, 1225, 1376, 1472, 1550. **Sciences** 1678, 1785, 2158, 2194–2195, 2197–2199, 2302–2303, 2394, 2455. **Social Sciences** 2536, 2878, 2880. *See also* United States; names of specific cities and counties

New Mexico, northern: **Social Sciences** 2668. *See also* New Mexico

New Mexico, southern: **Social Sciences** 2667. *See also* New Mexico

New Orleans, Louisiana: **Social Sciences** 2778. *See also* Louisiana

New York: **Unrestricted by Subject Area** 39, 343, 352, 725, 727, 729–734, 946. **Humanities** 1234. **Sciences** 1649, 1725, 2040, 2207, 2224, 2414. **Social Sciences** 2603, 2613, 2634, 2768, 2883, 2958. *See also* United States; names of specific cities and counties

New York, New York: **Unrestricted by Subject Area** 596, 688. **Humanities** 1233, 1426, 1492. **Sciences** 1919, 2182, 2453. **Social Sciences** 2578, 2700, 2935, 3036. *See also* New York

New Zealand: **Unrestricted by Subject Area** 43. *See also* Foreign countries

Newark, New Jersey: **Sciences** 2471. *See also* New Jersey

Norfolk, Virginia: **Unrestricted by Subject Area** 688. **Humanities** 1390. **Sciences** 2182. *See also* Virginia

Norman, Oklahoma: **Sciences** 1741. *See also* Oklahoma

North Carolina: **Unrestricted by Subject Area** 150, 255, 413, 537, 686–687, 747, 749–751, 1016. **Humanities** 1223, 1281, 1387. **Sciences** 1642, 1751, 1940, 1943, 2062, 2084, 2161, 2212–2213, 2231, 2372, 2414, 2428. **Social Sciences** 2539, 2603, 2683, 2763, 2855, 2891–2893, 2924, 2930, 2934. *See also* Southeastern states; Southern states; United States; names of specific cities and counties

North Dakota: **Unrestricted by Subject Area** 582, 752–758. **Sciences** 1802, 2158, 2214, 2302–2303. **Social Sciences** 2572. *See also* United States; names of specific cities

North Miami, Florida: **Unrestricted by Subject Area** 688. **Sciences** 2182. **Social Sciences** 2935. *See also* Florida

Northern Marianas: **Sciences** 2477. *See also* United States

Northwestern states: **Unrestricted by Subject Area** 876. *See also* United States; names of specific states

Ohio: **Unrestricted by Subject Area** 250, 530, 765, 769–770. **Humanities** 1160, 1237, 1483–1486. **Sciences** 1763, 1973, 2014–2015, 2226–2227. **Social Sciences** 2677, 2705, 2901–2903, 3047. *See also* United States; names of specific cities and counties

Ohio, central: **Social Sciences** 2580. *See also* Ohio

Oklahoma: **Unrestricted by Subject Area** 86, 771, 773–779, 852, 875. **Humanities** 1186, 1254, 1345, 1358, 1475, 1487–1490. **Sciences** 2158, 2228. **Social Sciences** 2668, 2690, 2711, 2889, 2905–2906, 2957. *See also* Southern states; United States; names of specific cities and counties

Omaha, Nebraska: **Sciences** 1919. *See also* Nebraska

Orange County, California: **Sciences** 2274. *See also* California

Oregon: **Unrestricted by Subject Area** 137, 185, 198, 209, 222, 294–295, 519, 788, 791–793, 796, 1079, 1108. **Humanities** 1261, 1271, 1317, 1346, 1378, 1384, 1493–1494, 1550. **Sciences** 1755, 1820, 1822, 1994, 2043, 2065–2066, 2092, 2185, 2219, 2238, 2242, 2273–2274, 2455–2456, 2458–2459. **Social Sciences** 2708, 2795, 2894. *See also* Northwestern states; United States; names of specific cities and counties

Orlando, Florida: **Sciences** 1741. **Social Sciences** 2935. *See also* Florida

Oxford, Ohio: **Sciences** 1741. *See also* Ohio

Pasadena, California: **Humanities** 1492. *See also* California

Pennsylvania: **Unrestricted by Subject Area** 117, 206, 562, 735–736, 803, 810–811, 813–817, 844, 936, 1019. **Humanities** 1302, 1423, 1504–1505. **Sciences** 1674, 1691, 1978, 1989, 2014, 2038, 2130, 2137, 2208, 2249, 2251, 2274, 2297, 2362, 2414. **Social Sciences** 2552, 2613, 2679, 2794, 2917–2918, 2942, 2958. *See also* United States; names of specific cities and counties

Pennsylvania, eastern: **Sciences** 1863. *See also* Pennsylvania

Pennsylvania, western: **Sciences** 1680. *See also* Pennsylvania

Perry Point, Maryland: **Unrestricted by Subject Area** 36. *See also* Maryland

Philadelphia, Pennsylvania: **Unrestricted by Subject Area** 688. **Humanities** 1216. **Sciences** 2182. **Social Sciences** 2778. *See also* Pennsylvania

Phoenix, Arizona: **Sciences** 2471. *See also* Arizona

Pittsburgh, Pennsylvania: **Sciences** 1919. *See also* Pennsylvania

Platteville, Wisconsin: **Sciences** 1816. **Social Sciences** 2594. *See also* Wisconsin

Pleasantville, New York: **Unrestricted by Subject Area** 688. **Sciences** 2182. *See also* New York

Pocantico Hills, New York: **Humanities** 1233. *See also* New York

Pocatello, Idaho: **Sciences** 1919. *See also* Idaho

Poland: **Humanities** 1575. *See also* Europe; Foreign countries

Pomona, California: **Social Sciences** 2495, 2935. *See also* California

Portland, Oregon: **Humanities** 1378. *See also* Oregon

Prince George's County, Maryland: **Humanities** 1630. *See also* Maryland

Prince William County, Virginia: **Humanities** 1630. *See also* Virginia

Princess Anne, Maryland: **Social Sciences** 2927. *See also* Maryland

Providence, Rhode Island: **Unrestricted by Subject Area** 688. **Sciences** 2182. **Social Sciences** 2495, 2935. *See also* Rhode Island

Puerto Rico: **Unrestricted by Subject Area** 38, 77, 100, 128, 154, 158, 244, 293, 351, 370, 375, 845, 879, 910. **Humanities** 1291, 1415, 1444, 1503. **Sciences** 1668, 1751, 1950, 1964, 1997, 2000, 2110, 2152, 2159, 2271, 2328, 2401, 2413, 2415, 2437, 2477. **Social Sciences** 2532, 2539, 2689, 2718, 2724–2725, 2802, 2805, 2845, 3008–3009. *See also* Caribbean; United States

Pullman, Washington: **Sciences** 1816. **Social Sciences** 2594. *See also* Washington

Raleigh, North Carolina: **Sciences** 1741. **Social Sciences** 2927. *See also* North Carolina

Rapid City, South Dakota: **Sciences** 2302. *See also* South Dakota

Rhode Island: **Unrestricted by Subject Area** 117, 562, 735, 860, 936. **Humanities** 1143. **Sciences** 1899, 2104, 2221. *See also* New England states; United States; names of specific cities

Richmond, Kentucky: **Social Sciences** 2927. *See also* Kentucky

Richmond, Virginia: **Humanities** 1492. *See also* Virginia

River Falls, Wisconsin: **Sciences** 1816. **Social Sciences** 2594. *See also* Wisconsin

Riverside County, California: **Sciences** 2274. *See also* California

Roanoke, Virginia: **Humanities** 1390. *See also* Virginia

Rochester, New York: **Unrestricted by Subject Area** 688. **Sciences** 2182. *See also* New York

Rolla, Missouri: **Sciences** 2302. *See also* Missouri

Sacramento, California: **Unrestricted by Subject Area** 36. *See also* California

St. Helena, California: **Humanities** 1233. *See also* California

St. Louis, Missouri: **Sciences** 1741. *See also* Missouri

St. Paul, Minnesota: **Sciences** 1816. **Social Sciences** 2594. *See also* Minnesota

Salem, Oregon: **Social Sciences** 2778. *See also* Oregon

Samoa. *See* American Samoa

San Antonio, Texas: **Unrestricted by Subject Area** 244. **Sciences** 2209. **Social Sciences** 2778, 2887. *See also* Texas

San Bernardino, California: **Unrestricted by Subject Area** 244. **Sciences** 1919. *See also* California

San Bernardino County, California: **Sciences** 2274. *See also* California

San Diego, California: **Sciences** 2453. **Social Sciences** 3036. *See also* California

San Francisco, California: **Sciences** 2453. **Social Sciences** 3036. *See also* California

San Jose, California: **Sciences** 2453. **Social Sciences** 3036. *See also* California

Santa Barbara County, California: **Sciences** 2274. *See also* California

Santa Clara, California: **Sciences** 2453. **Social Sciences** 3036. *See also* California

Seattle, Washington: **Sciences** 1741, 2453. **Social Sciences** 3036. *See also* Washington

Silver Spring, Maryland: **Sciences** 1910. **Social Sciences** 2659. *See also* Maryland

Socorro, New Mexico: **Sciences** 1781, 1919, 1983, 2072. *See also* New Mexico

South America: **Humanities** 1193, 1252. *See also* Foreign countries; names of specific countries

South Carolina: **Unrestricted by Subject Area** 233, 471, 489, 800, 893, 913–921. **Humanities** 1166, 1353, 1387, 1522, 1565. **Sciences** 1751, 1915, 1974, 2084, 2243, 2351, 2372, 2427, 2436. **Social Sciences** 2539, 2603. *See also* Southeastern states; Southern states; United States; names of specific cities and counties

South Dakota: **Unrestricted by Subject Area** 305, 528, 896, 922–926. **Sciences** 1692, 1802, 1852, 2158. **Social Sciences** 2516, 2572, 2615, 2701, 2966. *See also* United States; names of specific cities and counties

Southeastern states: **Unrestricted by Subject Area** 1013. **Humanities** 1557. *See also* Southern states; United States; names of specific states

Southern states: **Unrestricted by Subject Area** 932. *See also* United States; names of specific states

Springfield, Missouri: **Sciences** 1816. **Social Sciences** 2594. *See also* Missouri

Stanford, California: **Sciences** 2453. **Social Sciences** 3036. *See also* California

Stony Brook, New York: **Sciences** 1919. *See also* New York

Sweden: **Sciences** 2024. **Social Sciences** 2742. *See also* Europe; Foreign countries

Syracuse, New York: **Sciences** 1741, 1919. *See also* New York

Tallahassee, Florida: **Social Sciences** 2927. *See also* Florida

Tempe, Arizona: **Sciences** 2453. **Social Sciences** 3036. *See also* Arizona

Tennessee: **Unrestricted by Subject Area** 692, 954, 956–962, 1085. **Sciences** 1642, 1693, 1751, 1943, 2274, 2374. **Social Sciences** 2539, 2632–2633, 2711, 2983–2984. *See also* Southern states; United States; names of specific cities and counties

Texas: **Unrestricted by Subject Area** 120, 262–264, 361, 405, 588–590, 741, 875, 964–980, 982, 984, 986, 988, 990, 998, 1060–1061, 1133. **Humanities** 1357, 1475, 1581–1583, 1596. **Sciences** 1878, 1962, 2045, 2055, 2106, 2151, 2158, 2302–2303, 2313, 2375–2378, 2381, 2392, 2414. **Social Sciences** 2597, 2667, 2680, 2716, 2889, 2937, 2987. *See also* Southern states; United States; names of specific cities and counties

Texas, eastern: **Sciences** 2103. *See also* Texas

Toledo, Ohio: **Unrestricted by Subject Area** 688. **Sciences** 2182. *See also* Ohio

Tucson, Arizona: **Sciences** 2453. **Social Sciences** 3036. *See also* Arizona

Tulsa, Oklahoma: **Sciences** 1919. *See also* Oklahoma

Turkey: **Humanities** 1349. **Social Sciences** 2752. *See also* Europe; Foreign countries

Tuskegee, Alabama: **Unrestricted by Subject Area** 245. **Sciences** 1919. *See also* Alabama

United Kingdom: **Unrestricted by Subject Area** 43. *See also* Europe; Foreign countries; names of specific countries

United States: **Unrestricted by Subject Area** 1–2, 4–13, 21–35, 37–38, 40, 42–44, 54, 62–85, 87–91, 94–95, 97–102, 105, 110–114, 116, 118, 122–129, 131–138, 140–149, 151–160, 163–165, 171, 174, 176, 178, 180–181, 183–184, 187–193, 195–197, 199–201, 203, 206, 208, 210–221, 223–231, 233–236, 238–243, 246–249, 251–254, 257–258, 260–261, 266–280, 283, 290, 292–293, 296–300, 302–304, 306–319, 321, 324, 327, 331–342, 344–351, 353–360, 362–372, 375, 378–381, 389, 397–398, 402, 404, 406–412, 414–426, 428–439, 441–443, 446, 449, 454–459, 461, 463–470, 472–478, 480–484, 486–488, 490–497, 501, 505–506, 508–509, 513–517, 520–527, 529, 532–534, 536, 538–540, 545, 547–548, 553–555, 563–564, 566–570, 573–574, 576–578, 581, 583–587, 591–596, 599, 604–605, 607, 609, 611–614, 621, 624, 628, 641–650, 652–685, 689, 693–697, 699, 701–702, 705–708, 711–715, 718, 722, 726, 728, 738–739, 742, 744–746, 748, 759–764, 766–768, 772, 780, 782–787, 789–790, 794–795, 797–799, 801–806, 808–809, 812–814, 817–822, 824–840, 842–843, 845–846, 849, 851, 853–859, 861–864, 866, 868, 870–873, 877–879, 881–892, 894, 897–901, 903–912, 927–928, 934, 937–945, 949, 952, 955, 963, 981, 983, 985, 987, 989, 991–992, 994–997, 1003–1012, 1014–1015, 1017–1018, 1020–1027, 1030, 1034–1038, 1040–1046, 1049–1050, 1053, 1056, 1059, 1062–1065, 1067–1068, 1073, 1076–1078, 1080–1084, 1087–1090, 1092, 1098, 1102, 1104–1107, 1109–1110, 1112–1113, 1116, 1121–1125, 1127–1129, 1132. **Humanities** 1134–1137, 1140–1149, 1151–1159, 1162–1164, 1168, 1170–1178, 1180, 1182, 1184–1185, 1187–1189, 1191–1195, 1197–1199, 1201–1202, 1204–1205, 1208, 1210–1211, 1213–1222, 1224, 1226–1233, 1235–1236, 1238–1241, 1244–1250, 1252–1253, 1255–1260, 1262–1280, 1282, 1284–1286, 1288–1289, 1291–1297, 1299–1301, 1304–1310, 1314–1316, 1318–1323, 1325–1326, 1328–1332, 1335–1339, 1341–1344, 1347–1352, 1354–1356, 1359–1370, 1373, 1377–1383, 1386, 1388–1400, 1402, 1404–1410, 1412–1417, 1419–1420, 1424, 1426, 1429, 1431–1434, 1436–1455, 1457, 1459–1462, 1464–1468, 1473–1482, 1486, 1489, 1491, 1495–1498, 1501–1503, 1506–1508, 1510–1513, 1515–1520, 1523–1531, 1533–1536, 1538–1545, 1547, 1549, 1551–1555, 1558–1562, 1564, 1566–1567, 1569–1577, 1579–1580, 1583–1589, 1591–1594, 1597–1604, 1606–1615, 1618, 1620–1629, 1631–1634. **Sciences** 1635–1641, 1643–1645, 1648, 1651, 1653–1665, 1667–1673, 1675–1677, 1679, 1682–1686, 1691, 1694–1708, 1710–1713, 1716, 1718–1724, 1726–1732, 1735–1737, 1739–1740, 1743–1746, 1748–1754, 1756–1762, 1764–1766, 1768–1780, 1783, 1785, 1789, 1793, 1796–1800, 1803–1804, 1806–1807, 1809–1815, 1817–1819, 1823–1827, 1835–1837, 1839–1846, 1848, 1850–1851, 1853–1855, 1857–1876, 1879–1885, 1887–1892, 1896–1898, 1900, 1902–1905, 1907–1908, 1910–1914, 1916–1918, 1920, 1922, 1927–1928, 1930–1936, 1939, 1941–1942, 1944–1958, 1960–1961, 1963–1966, 1968–1970, 1972–1973, 1975–1977, 1980–1982, 1984–1988, 1990–1991, 1993, 1995–1998, 2000–2003, 2005–2007, 2010–2011, 2019–2036, 2039, 2041–2042, 2044, 2047–2050, 2052–2053, 2056–2061, 2063–2064, 2067, 2071, 2073–2074, 2076–2079, 2081–2083, 2085–2087, 2089–2091, 2096–2102, 2106, 2108–2111, 2113–2114, 2116, 2119, 2123–2129, 2131–2136, 2140–2143, 2148, 2152–2153, 2155–2157, 2159–2160, 2162–2170, 2172–2180, 2183–2184, 2187, 2190, 2192, 2194, 2196, 2198, 2200–2206, 2209–2210, 2215–2218, 2220, 2222–2224, 2228–2230, 2232–2237, 2239–2241, 2244–2246, 2250, 2252–2256, 2259–2265, 2267–2272, 2275–2282, 2284–2288, 2290, 2294–2296, 2298–2299, 2301, 2304, 2306–2310, 2312, 2315–2321, 2323–2338, 2340–2347, 2349–2350, 2352, 2354–2361, 2363–2364, 2366–2372, 2379–2380, 2382–2391, 2393–2395, 2397–2404, 2407–2408, 2410–2413, 2415–2419, 2421–2425, 2430–2432, 2435, 2437–2441, 2443, 2445–2448, 2451, 2454, 2457, 2461–2462, 2464, 2468–2473, 2475–2478, 2480–2481. **Social Sciences** 2482–2488, 2490–2494, 2496–2502, 2506–2515, 2517, 2521–2523, 2525–2529, 2531–2539, 2541–2549, 2551, 2553–2554, 2556, 2559–2560, 2566–2568, 2570, 2574–2581, 2583–2584, 2587–2588, 2591–2593, 2595–2596, 2599–2602, 2604–2605, 2607–2608, 2610–2611, 2614, 2616–2623, 2625–2628, 2630–2631, 2636–2642, 2644, 2646–2652, 2654–2661, 2663–2664, 2666, 2669–2670, 2676–2678, 2681–2682, 2684, 2686–2689, 2691–2699, 2702–2707, 2709–2710, 2712–2713, 2715, 2717–2728, 2731, 2734–2735, 2741–2746, 2748–2750, 2752–2755, 2757–2761, 2765–2767, 2770–2773, 2777, 2780–2789, 2793, 2796, 2798, 2800, 2802–2807, 2809–2810, 2814, 2819–2829, 2831–2832, 2834, 2842, 2845–2850, 2852–2854, 2856–2862, 2864, 2866–2867, 2869–2870, 2873–2874, 2879, 2881–2882, 2884–2889, 2895–2900, 2903–2904, 2906–2910, 2916, 2919–2923, 2925–2926, 2928, 2931–2934, 2936, 2943–2956, 2960, 2962–2965, 2968–2981, 2985–2986, 2988–2991, 2993–3012, 3014–3017, 3022–3028, 3030, 3032, 3034, 3037–3039, 3042, 3044, 3049, 3052–3058, 3061, 3063–3065. *See also* names of specific cities, counties, states, and regions

University Park, Pennsylvania: **Sciences** 1741. **Social Sciences** 2495, 2927. *See also* Pennsylvania

Utah: **Unrestricted by Subject Area** 850, 1028–1029, 1031–1033. **Humanities** 1225, 1376, 1550. **Sciences** 2302–2303, 2353, 2409, 2455–2456. **Social Sciences** 2967. *See also* United States; names of specific cities and counties

Valparaiso, Indiana: **Social Sciences** 2778. *See also* Indiana

Vancouver, Washington: **Sciences** 2066. *See also* Washington

Ventura County, California: **Sciences** 2274. *See also* California

Vermont: **Unrestricted by Subject Area** 117, 562, 735–736, 848, 936, 1039. **Humanities** 1595. **Sciences** 2420. **Social Sciences** 2586, 2756, 3013. *See also* New England states; United States; names of specific cities and counties

Vicksburg, Mississippi: **Unrestricted by Subject Area** 36. *See also* Mississippi

Vinton, Iowa: **Unrestricted by Subject Area** 36. *See also* Iowa

Virgin Islands: **Unrestricted by Subject Area** 38, 128, 154, 158, 236, 293, 351, 491, 963, 1044–1046. **Humanities** 1236. **Sciences** 1682, 1803, 1914, 1950, 1997, 2000, 2110, 2152, 2271, 2413, 2438, 2477. **Social Sciences** 2600, 2619, 2687, 2689, 2717–2718, 2724–2725, 2780, 2802–2803, 2845, 2985, 3008, 3027, 3039. *See also* Caribbean; United States

Virginia: **Unrestricted by Subject Area** 112, 535, 1047–1048, 1051–1052, 1054–1055, 1057–1058. **Humanities** 1387, 1423, 1605, 1629. **Sciences** 1642, 1681, 1751, 1943, 2084, 2211, 2372, 2396, 2429, 2433, 2463. **Social Sciences** 2505, 2539, 2573, 2603, 2613, 2712, 2764, 2890, 2958, 3018–3021. *See also* Southeastern states; Southern states; United States; names of specific cities and counties

Virginia, northern: **Humanities** 1135, 1556. **Sciences** 2181. **Social Sciences** 2868. *See also* Virginia

Walker County, Texas: **Sciences** 2274. *See also* Texas

Waller County, Texas: **Sciences** 2274. *See also* Texas

Washington: **Unrestricted by Subject Area** 92, 130, 137, 186, 322, 382, 485, 895, 933, 1000, 1066, 1069–1072, 1074–1075, 1111. **Humanities** 1196, 1225, 1242, 1271, 1313, 1321, 1376, 1378, 1385, 1477, 1546, 1548, 1550, 1617, 1619. **Sciences** 2043, 2242, 2248, 2274, 2292–2293, 2442, 2444, 2446, 2455–2456, 2458. **Social Sciences** 2915, 2938, 2940–2941, 3031, 3043, 3051. *See also* Northwestern states; United States; names of specific cities and counties

Washington, D.C.: **Unrestricted by Subject Area** 112, 117, 245, 562, 735–736, 936. **Humanities** 1135, 1423, 1464, 1556, 1629–1630. **Sciences** 1751, 1919, 2181, 2209, 2463. **Social Sciences** 2539, 2603, 2613, 2764, 2868, 2887, 2935, 2958, 2991. *See also* Southeastern states; Southern states; United States

Washington, southwestern: **Sciences** 2219. *See also* Washington

West Lafayette, Indiana: **Sciences** 1741, 1816. **Social Sciences** 2495, 2594. *See also* Indiana

West Virginia: **Unrestricted by Subject Area** 256. **Humanities** 1387, 1629. **Sciences** 1642, 1680, 1751, 1943, 2014, 2084, 2463. **Social Sciences** 2539, 2603, 2613, 2958, 3040. *See also* Southern states; United States; names of specific cities

Wharton County, Texas: **Sciences** 2274. *See also* Texas

White Plains, New York: **Unrestricted by Subject Area** 688. **Sciences** 2182. *See also* New York

Winston–Salem, North Carolina: **Social Sciences** 2778. *See also* North Carolina

Wisconsin: **Unrestricted by Subject Area** 582, 902, 1093–1097, 1099–1101. **Humanities** 1499, 1621. **Sciences** 1802, 1901, 2075, 2094, 2225, 2258, 2426, 2449, 2465–2467. **Social Sciences** 2572, 2911, 3048, 3050. *See also* United States; names of specific cities and counties

Wright–Patterson AFB, Ohio: **Sciences** 1919. *See also* Ohio

Wyoming: **Unrestricted by Subject Area** 1114–1115, 1117–1120. **Humanities** 1225, 1376, 1550. **Sciences** 2302–2303, 2394, 2455, 2474. **Social Sciences** 2668, 3059–3060, 3062. *See also* United States; names of specific cities and counties

Sponsoring Organization Index

The Sponsoring Organization Index makes it easy to identify agencies that offer college funding. In this index, sponsoring organizations are listed alphabetically, word by word. In addition, we've used a code (within parentheses) to help you identify which programs sponsored by these organizations fall within your scope of interest: U = Unrestricted by Subject Area; H = Humanities; S = Sciences; SS = Social Sciences. Here's how the codes work: if an organization's name is followed by (U) 41, the program sponsored by that organization is described in entry 41, in the Unrestricted by Subject Area section. If that sponsoring organization's name is followed by another entry number—for example, (SS) 2649—the same or a different program is described in entry 2649, in the Social Sciences section. Remember: the numbers cited here refer to program entry numbers, not to page numbers in the book.

A+ Media, (S) 1891
AAA Michigan, (U) 576
AABB, (S) 1636
AACE International, (S) 1637, (SS) 2484
Abbott Fund, (S) 1826
Abbott Laboratories, (S) 1640
Abramson Scholarship Foundation, (U) 304
Abruzzo and Molise Heritage Society, (H) 1135
Academy of Applied Science, (S) 2064
Academy of Motion Picture Arts and Sciences, (H) 1571
Academy of Television Arts & Sciences Foundation, (H) 1136
Accenture LLP, (S) 1644, (SS) 2486
AccuWeather, Inc., (S) 1645
ACT Scholarship and Recognition Services, (U) 665
Acton Foundation for Entrepreneurial Excellence, (SS) 2884
Actuarial Foundation, (SS) 2488, 2760
Adcraft Club of Detroit, (H) 1138, (SS) 2489
Adirondack Spintacular, (U) 483
Advanced American Construction, Inc., (S) 2324, (SS) 2960
Advancing Hispanic Excellence in Technology, Engineering, Math and Science, Inc., (S) 1668–1670, 2159
Aetna, Inc., (S) 1654
African–American/Caribbean Education Association, Inc., (H) 1318, (S) 2140, 2464, (SS) 2720
AFT Michigan, (SS) 2945
AfterCollege, (S) 1660
AgriBusiness Association of Kentucky, (S) 1639
Agricultural History Society, (H) 1381
Agriculture Future of America, (S) 1667
Agrisolutions, (S) 1800
Agronomic Science Foundation, (S) 2034
AIA/Rhode Island, (H) 1143
AIGA, (H) 1625
Air Force Aid Society, (U) 315
Air Force Sergeants Association, (U) 12, 134
Air Products and Chemicals, Inc., (S) 1674
Air & Waste Management Association. Allegheny Mountain Section, (S) 1680
Air & Waste Management Association. Delaware Valley Chapter, (S) 1863
Air & Waste Management Association. Louisiana Section, (S) 2103
Air & Waste Management Association. West Michigan Chapter, (S) 2454
Air & Waste Management Association–East Michigan Chapter, (S) 1893, (SS) 2643
Air–Conditioning, Heating, and Refrigeration Institute, (S) 1823
Airmen Memorial Foundation, (U) 12, 134
Airports Council International–North America, (SS) 2487
Akash Kuruvilla Memorial Scholarship Fund, (U) 13
Alabama Academy of Science, (S) 1965
Alabama Alliance for Science, Engineering, Mathematics, and Science Education, (SS) 2961
Alabama Commission on Higher Education, (U) 15–18, 440, (H) 1150
Alabama Department of Veterans Affairs, (U) 14
Alabama Golf Course Superintendents Association, (S) 1880
Alabama Media Professionals, (H) 1151
Alabama Power Foundation., (S) 1965
Alabama Press Association, (H) 1427
Alabama Press Association Journalism Foundation, (H) 1354
Alabama Road Builders Association, (S) 1894
Alabama Scholastic Press Association, (H) 1354
Alabama State Nurses Association, (S) 1675
Alabama Thespians, (H) 1152, (SS) 2496
Alabama–West Florida United Methodist Foundation, (U) 218
Alan Mascord Design Associates, (H) 1317, (S) 1994
Alaska Broadcasters Association, (H) 1402
Alaska Cabaret, Hotel, Restaurant & Retailers Association, (SS) 2581
Alaska Commission on Postsecondary Education, (S) 1676, (SS) 2497, 2500, 2826
Alaska Community Foundation, (S) 1855, 2284
Alaska Housing Finance Corporation, (U) 20
Alaska. Office of Veterans Affairs, (U) 19
Alaska Professional Communicators, (H) 1154
Alaska Travel Adventures, (SS) 2498
Alaska Travel Industry Association, (SS) 2498–2499, 2515, 2533–2534, 2785, 2926, 2950
Alcoa Foundation, (S) 2478
Alexander Graham Bell Association for the Deaf and Hard of Hearing, (S) 2295
Align, (SS) 3061
Alliance of State Automotive Aftermarket Associations, (S) 1961, (SS) 2699
Allianz Global Investors Distributors LLC, (S) 1852, (SS) 2615
All–Ink.com, (U) 26
Allstate Foundation, (U) 1041
Alpha Delta Kappa. Florida Chapter, (SS) 2671
Alpha Delta Kappa. North Carolina Chapter, (U) 255, 537, 744, (H) 1223
Alpha Omega Council, (H) 1508
Alpha Research & Development, (U) 39
Alpine Mortgage Planning, (H) 1317, (S) 1994
Altria Group, (S) 1681, (SS) 2505
Ameen Rihani Organization, (H) 1157
American Academy of Chefs, (H) 1158–1159
American Academy of Physician Assistants–Veterans Caucus, (S) 1638, 2358
American Advertising Federation, (H) 1446
American Advertising Federation. Birmingham, (H) 1537
American Advertising Federation. Cleveland, (H) 1160
American Advertising Federation. District 4, (H) 1161
American Advertising Federation. Lincoln, (H) 1401
American Airlines, (U) 84
American Architectural Foundation, (H) 1134
American Assembly for Men in Nursing, (S) 1683
American Association for Health Education, (S) 1759, (SS) 2544
American Association of Advertising Agencies, (H) 1162, 1492
American Association of Airport Executives. Southwest Chapter, (S) 2353, (SS) 2967
American Association of Colleges for Teacher Education, (U) 1023
American Association of Colleges of Nursing, (S) 1660
American Association of Community Colleges, (U) 149, 695, 822, (S) 1936
American Association of Critical–Care Nurses, (S) 1777, 2217
American Association of Family and Consumer Sciences, (SS) 2758
American Association of Family and Consumer Sciences. California Affiliate, (SS) 2665
American Association of Medical Assistants, (S) 2127
American Association of Nurse Anesthetists, (S) 2217
American Association of Occupational Health Nurses, Inc., (S) 1684, 2259, 2404
American Association of Retired Persons, (U) 1
American Association of State Colleges and Universities, (U) 997
American Association of Textile Chemists and Colorists, (S) 2123
American Association on Health and Disability, (S) 1685
American Astronomical Society, (S) 2440
American Automobile Association, (H) 1454
American Backflow Prevention Association, (S) 1972
American Chemical Society. Department of Diversity Programs, (S) 2270
American Classical League, (H) 1137
American Congress on Surveying and Mapping. Colorado Section, (S) 1834
American Copy Editors Society, (H) 1230
American Council of Engineering Companies, (S) 1686
American Council of Engineering Companies of Alabama, (S) 2289
American Council of Engineering Companies of California, (S) 1687
American Council of Engineering Companies of Colorado, (S) 1646, 1831, 2037, 2405
American Council of Engineering Companies of Idaho, (S) 1688
American Council of Engineering Companies of Indiana, (S) 1647
American Council of Engineering Companies of Massachusetts, (S) 1648
American Council of Engineering Companies of Michigan, Inc., (S) 1650, 2366
American Council of Engineering Companies of Mississippi, (S) 1689
American Council of Engineering Companies of New Jersey, (S) 1690
American Council of Engineering Companies of New York, (S) 1649

American Council of Engineering Companies of Pennsylvania, (S) 1691
American Council of Engineering Companies of South Dakota, (S) 1692
American Council of Engineering Companies of Tennessee, (S) 1693
American Council of Independent Laboratories, (S) 1651
American Council of the Blind, (U) 225–226, 228, 292, 415, (S) 1721, 1889, 1913, 2077, (SS) 2523, 2663, 2885, 2946
American Council on Education, (U) 1023
American Culinary Federation, Inc., (H) 1158–1159
American Dairy Science Association, (S) 1951
American Deficit Disorder Association, (U) 762
American Dental Association, (S) 1869–1871
American Diabetes Association, (U) 761
American Express, (SS) 2506
American Ex–prisoners of War, Inc. Columbia River Chapter, (U) 820
American Federation of Police and Concerned Citizens, (U) 829
American Federation of Teachers, (H) 1381
American Floral Endowment, (S) 1766, 1932, 2039, 2052
American Foreign Service Association, (SS) 2507
American Foundation for the Blind, (H) 1292, 1536, (S) 1866, 2246, 2308, (SS) 2625, 2949
American Ground Water Trust, (S) 1701, 1749
American Guild of Organists, (H) 1142
American Helicopter Society, (S) 2421
American Hospital Association, (SS) 2526
American Hospital Association. American Society for Hospital Engineering, (H) 1172
American Hotel & Lodging Educational Foundation, (SS) 2493, 2506, 2508, 2525, 2644, 2728, 2935
American Humanist Association, (H) 1586
American Indian Arts Council, Inc., (H) 1144
American Indian College Fund, (U) 738, 927–928, (S) 1802, 1930, 2355, (SS) 2572, 2676, 2847–2848, 2969
American Indian Graduate Center, (U) 24, 310, (S) 1644, (SS) 2486, 3037
American Institute of Architects, (H) 1134
American Institute of Architects. Academy of Architecture for Health, (H) 1172
American Institute of Polish Culture, Inc., (H) 1301, (SS) 2704
American Institute of Wine and Food. Vermont Chapter, (H) 1603
American Institute of Wine & Food. Colorado Chapter, (SS) 2510
American Legacy Foundation, (H) 1246, (S) 1882, (SS) 2591, 2636
American Legion. Alaska Auxiliary, (U) 21
American Legion. Americanism and Children & Youth Division, (U) 11, 34, 883, (SS) 2511
American Legion. Arizona Auxiliary, (SS) 3046
American Legion Auxiliary, (U) 668, 883
American Legion Baseball, (U) 33, 851
American Legion. California Auxiliary, (U) 106–107, (S) 1788
American Legion. Colorado Auxiliary, (U) 169, (S) 1832
American Legion. Florida Auxiliary, (U) 285
American Legion. Georgia Auxiliary, (U) 327, (S) 1959
American Legion. Idaho Auxiliary, (S) 2005
American Legion. Illinois Auxiliary, (U) 585, (SS) 2734
American Legion. Indiana Department, (SS) 2738
American Legion. Kansas Auxiliary, (S) 2069
American Legion. Kansas Department, (H) 1372
American Legion. Kentucky Auxiliary, (U) 481, 531
American Legion. Maine Department, (U) 196
American Legion. Maryland Auxiliary, (H) 1422, (S) 2115–2116, (SS) 2812
American Legion. Michigan Auxiliary, (U) 574
American Legion. Minnesota Auxiliary, (U) 603
American Legion. Missouri Department, (U) 620
American Legion. New Hampshire Auxiliary, (U) 526
American Legion. New Hampshire Department, (U) 701–702, (SS) 2588
American Legion. New Jersey Auxiliary, (U) 114, 141, 223, 242, 708, (S) 2192
American Legion. New Mexico Auxiliary, (S) 2196
American Legion. New York Auxiliary, (U) 357, 538, 726, 849, (S) 2202–2203, (SS) 2881
American Legion. North Dakota Department, (U) 349
American Legion. Ohio Auxiliary, (U) 767
American Legion. Ohio Department, (U) 768
American Legion. Oregon Auxiliary, (U) 793–794, (S) 2237
American Legion. Pennsylvania Department, (SS) 2917
American Legion. Texas Auxiliary, (S) 2375
American Legion. Utah Auxiliary, (U) 1030
American Legion. Wisconsin Auxiliary, (U) 379, (S) 2468–2469
American Mensa Education and Research Foundation, (U) 425, (S) 1857
American Meteorological Society, (S) 1694, 1700, 1770, 1911, 2019, 2071, 2100, 2125
American Meteorological Society. District of Columbia Chapter, (S) 1859
American Mideast Leadership Network, (U) 39
American Museum of Natural History, (S) 2478
American Nephrology Nurses' Association, (S) 2217
American Nuclear Society, (S) 1643, 1705, 1860, 2042, 2049
American Nursery and Landscape Association, (H) 1566, 1591, (S) 2357, 2389
American Organization of Nurse Executives, (S) 2217
American Physical Society, (S) 1708, 2091
American Planning Association, (SS) 2666, 2773, 2999
American Planning Association. California Chapter, (SS) 2557, 2561–2562, 2779, 2914, 2939
American Planning Association. Pennsylvania Chapter, (SS) 2679, 2794
American Public Transportation Association, (S) 1695, 2102, (SS) 2512
American Public Works Association. Colorado Chapter, (H) 1165, (S) 1709, 2037, 2046, 2406, (SS) 2518
American Public Works Association. Florida West Coast Branch, (S) 1921
American Radio Relay League, (U) 70, 442, 484, 689, 697, 862, 888, (H) 1387, 1500, (S) 1943, 2084, 2247, 2462, 2476, (SS) 3044
American Road and Transportation Builders Association, (U) 480
American Sheep Industry Women, (H) 1452
American Society for Clinical Laboratory Science, (S) 2342
American Society for Clinical Pathology, (S) 1728, 2343–2344
American Society for Engineering Education, (S) 2160, 2327
American Society for Enology and Viticulture, (S) 1696
American Society for Healthcare Risk Management, (SS) 2526
American Society for Horticultural Science, (S) 1730
American Society for Photogrammetry and Remote Sensing, (S) 1641, 2053
American Society of Agronomy, (S) 2034
American Society of Civil Engineers. Maine Section, (S) 1726
American Society of Civil Engineers. Michigan Section, (S) 2105
American Society of Civil Engineers. New Hampshire Section, (S) 2187
American Society of Composers, Authors and Publishers, (H) 1173–1174, 1443
American Society of Crime Laboratory Directors, (S) 1697
American Society of Landscape Architecture, (H) 1175, (S) 1732
American Society of Naval Engineers, (S) 1698
American Society of Newspaper Editors, (H) 1198
American Society of Radiologic Technologists, (S) 2306, 2412
American Society of Transportation and Logistics, Inc., (S) 2096, (SS) 2798
American Society of Women Accountants. Albuquerque Chapter, (SS) 2829
American Standard Companies, (S) 1699
American String Teachers Association, (H) 1178
American Student Financial Aid, (U) 302
American Systems, (S) 2410
American Water Resources Association, (S) 2286
American Wool Council, (H) 1452
American–Arab Anti–Discrimination Committee Research Institute, (H) 1344
Ameristar Cares, (SS) 2514
AMTROL Inc., (S) 1701
Ancient Order of Hibernians, (H) 1381
Andre Sobel River of Life Foundation, (U) 40
Angelus Student Film Festival, (H) 1163
Angie M. Houtz Memorial Fund, (U) 41
Annie's Homegrown, Inc., (S) 1704
Answers Corporation, (U) 43
Anthony J. Jannetti, Inc., (S) 2173
A.O. Smith Water Heaters, (S) 1706
AOPA Air Safety Foundation, (S) 1879, 2128
Apartment Investment and Management Company, (U) 784
Appalachian College Association, (S) 1642
Arab American Institute Foundation, (U) 356, (H) 1146
Arabian Horse Foundation, (S) 1710
The Arc of Texas, (S) 1878
Arizona Association of Family and Consumer Sciences, (SS) 2769
Arizona Commission for Postsecondary Education, (U) 46–50, (S) 1715, (SS) 2519
Arizona Newspapers Foundation, (H) 1167
Arizona Nurses Association, (S) 1714
Arizona Press Women, (H) 1167
Arizona Private School Association, (U) 51
Arizona PTA, (U) 52

Arkansas Baptist Foundation, (H) 1514
Arkansas Community Foundation, (U) 45
Arkansas Department of Career Education, (S) 1717
Arkansas Department of Higher Education, (U) 53, 55–61, (SS) 2520
Arkansas Governor's Commission on People with Disabilities, (U) 54
Arkansas Press Women, (H) 1169
Arkansas State Thespian Society, (H) 1170, (SS) 2521
Arkansas Student Loan Authority, (U) 846
ARMA International. Detroit Chapter, (SS) 2629
Armed Forces Communications and Electronics Association, (U) 564, (H) 1140, (S) 1655–1657, 1718, 1876, 1884, 1946, 1948, 2035, 2113, 2134, 2410, 2422, (SS) 2491, 2522, 2631, 2688, 2750, 2804, 2824, 3014
Armed Forces Communications and Electronics Association. Coastal North Carolina Chapter, (S) 1824
Armed Forces Communications and Electronics Association. Hawaii Chapter, (S) 1796–1797, 1827, 1912, 1976, 2093, 2108
Armed Forces Communications and Electronics Association. Northern Virginia Chapter, (S) 2422, (SS) 3014
Armed Forces Insurance Company, (U) 316
Armed Services YMCA, (U) 62
Armenian General Benevolent Union, (H) 1171
Armenian Students' Association, (U) 63
Armenian Youth Federation, (U) 656
Army and Air Force Mutual Aid Association, (U) 64
Army Emergency Relief, (U) 5, 567
Army Nurse Corps Association, (S) 1719
Arthur B. Klussendorf Memorial Association, (S) 2083, (SS) 2784
Arthur W. Page Society, (H) 1213, (SS) 2577
ASCO Numatics, (S) 1727
Asian American Journalists Association, (H) 1613
Asian American Journalists Association. Seattle Chapter, (H) 1477
Asian & Pacific Islander American Scholarship Fund, (U) 310
Asian Pacific Islander Organization, (S) 1731
Asian Pacific Islanders for Professional and Community Advancement, (U) 44
Associate Jobbers Warehouse, Inc., (S) 1635, (SS) 2483
Associated Builders and Contractors. Rocky Mountain Chapter, (S) 1771
Associated Collegiate Press, (H) 1531
Associated General Contractors of America, (S) 1665
Associated General Contractors of Maine, Inc., (S) 1733
Associated General Contractors of Minnesota, (S) 1734
Associated General Contractors of New York State, (S) 1662, 2204
Associated General Contractors of Ohio, (S) 1663, 1973, 2014, 2390, (SS) 2705, 2993
Associated General Contractors of South Dakota, (S) 1661, 1664, 1928, 2345
Associated Oregon Loggers, Inc., (S) 1735
Associated Press Sports Editors, (H) 1177
Associated Press Television and Radio Association, (H) 1225, 1376
Association for Compensatory Educators of Texas, (U) 73
Association for Computing Machinery, (S) 2264
Association for Education and Rehabilitation of the Blind and Visually Impaired. Alabama Chapter, (SS) 2545
Association for Education and Rehabilitation of the Blind and Visually Impaired. Ohio Chapter, (SS) 2490
Association for Education in Journalism and Mass Communication, (H) 1524
Association for Federal Information Resources Management, (S) 1658
Association for Intelligence Officers, (SS) 2703, 2921
Association for Manufacturing Technology, (S) 1736, (SS) 2529
Association for Women Geoscientists, (S) 1737, 2043, 2463
Association of Alaska School Boards, (U) 439
Association of American Geographers, (SS) 2618
Association of Blind Citizens, (U) 74
Association of California Water Agencies, (S) 1738, 1821, (SS) 2530, 2598
Association of Collegiate Schools of Architecture, (H) 1296
Association of Energy Engineers, (S) 1739, (SS) 2531
Association of Government Accountants, (SS) 2607
Association of Independent Colleges and Universities of Pennsylvania, (U) 844, 1019, (S) 1674, 1978, 2130, 2137
Association of Latino Professionals in Finance and Accounting, (SS) 2532, 2718
Association of National Advertisers, (H) 1162
Association of Nurses in AIDS Care, (S) 1702
Association of periOperative Registered Nurses, (S) 1707, 1740
Association of Retired Teachers of Connecticut, (SS) 2698
Association of Schools of Journalism and Mass Communication, (H) 1308–1310
Association of Surgical Technologists, (S) 1864, 1931
Association of Texas Professional Educators, (SS) 2680
Association of the United States Army, (S) 2059
Association on American Indian Affairs, Inc., (U) 27, 75, (S) 1904, (SS) 2657
Astellas Pharma US, Inc., (U) 1005
Astronaut Scholarship Foundation, (S) 1741
Atlanta Press Club, Inc., (H) 1179
AT&T, (H) 1456, (S) 2171, (SS) 2863
Autism Society of America, (U) 190
Automotive Aftermarket Association Southeast, (S) 1635, (SS) 2483
Automotive Aftermarket Industry Association, (S) 1961, (SS) 2699
Automotive Aftermarket Suppliers Association, (S) 1961, (SS) 2699
Automotive Hall of Fame, (S) 1743, (SS) 2535
Automotive Industries Association of Canada, (S) 1961, (SS) 2699
Automotive Parts and Services Association, (S) 1944, (SS) 2686
Automotive Parts Remanufacturers Association, (S) 1961, (SS) 2699
Automotive Service Association, (S) 1961, (SS) 2699
Automotive Warehouse Distributors Association, (S) 1961, (SS) 2699
Available Light, (H) 1589
Avera Health, (S) 1852, (SS) 2615
Aviation Insurance Association, (S) 1744
AVS–Science and Technology of Materials, Interfaces, and Processing. New Mexico Chapter, (S) 2461
AVS–Science and Technology of Materials, Interfaces, and Processing. Southern California Chapter, (S) 1906
AXA Foundation, (U) 77
Ayn Rand Institute, (H) 1180, 1585
Azarian Group, LLC, (U) 433
Babe Ruth League, Inc., (U) 98, 410
Ball Horticultural Company, (S) 1746
Baltimore Community Foundation, (SS) 2589
Bank of America, (U) 1018, (S) 2174
Bank of America. Fort Sam Houston Branch, (U) 313
Bank of America Foundation, (U) 79, 997
Baptist Communicators Association, (H) 1148, 1153
Barking Foundation, (U) 80
Baroid, (S) 1749
Barrington Engineering Consultants, Ltd., (S) 2013
Baton Rouge Area Foundation, (SS) 2527
Baxter Healthcare Corporation, (U) 235, 248
Bay Area Media Network, (H) 1183
BB&T Charitable Foundation, (S) 1751, (SS) 2539–2540
Bed Bath & Beyond, (U) 1018
Best Buy Children's Foundation, (U) 85
Bethesda Lutheran Communities, (SS) 2630
Better Business Bureau of Delaware, (U) 87
Better Business Bureau of Nebraska, South Dakota, and Southwest Iowa, (U) 894
Better Business Bureau of Wisconsin Foundation, Inc., (U) 942
Better Business Bureau Serving Denver/Boulder, (U) 173
Bill and Melinda Gates Foundation, (U) 310
Bill of Rights Institute, (H) 1381
Billie Jean King WTT Charities, Inc., (U) 761
BioOhio, (S) 1763
BioQuip Products, (S) 1764
BioRx, (S) 1765
Birdsall Services Group, (S) 1767
Black Data Processing Associates, (S) 1903
Black Mesa Foundation, Inc., (U) 89
Blackburn Trumpets, (H) 1460
Blacks in Government. Benjamin Banneker Chapter, (U) 82
Blacks in Government. Coast Guard Headquarters Chapter, (U) 148
Blacks in Government. National Maritime Intelligence Center Chapter, (U) 663
Blind Information Technology Specialist, Inc., (S) 2077
Blind Mice Mart, (U) 648
Blinded Veterans Association, (U) 455
Blinded Veterans Association Auxiliary, (U) 856
Blount Foundation, (H) 1192
Bob and Eleanor Grant Trust, (S) 1769, (SS) 2546
Boeing Company, (U) 92, (S) 2432
Boettcher Foundation, (U) 93
Boise Tuesday Musicale, (H) 1369
Bookbuilders West, (H) 1550

Boomer Esiason Foundation, (U) 94, 266, (H) 1551
Booz Allen Hamilton, (H) 1456, (S) 1772, 2171, (SS) 2863
Boys & Girls Clubs of Greater San Diego, (S) 2354, (SS) 2968
Bradford White Corporation, (S) 1774
BrainTrack, (S) 1775–1776, (SS) 2548–2549
British Petroleum, (S) 1773, 2387
Broadcast Education Association, (H) 1184, 1278
Broadcast Music Inc., (H) 1193, 1364, 1503, 1539, 1622
Brodart, (SS) 2552
Brookgreen Gardens, (H) 1455
Brown and Root Services, (S) 2045
Brown Foundation for Educational Equity, Excellence and Research, (SS) 2554
Buddy Pelletier Surfing Foundation, (U) 99
Burger King Corporation, (U) 100
Burkart Flutes and Piccolos, (H) 1608
Burlington Northern Santa Fe Foundation, (U) 370
Cabot Corporation, (S) 1785
California Alarm Association, (U) 102
California Association for Postsecondary Education and Disability, (U) 115, 139, 504, (SS) 2912
California Association for the Gifted, (U) 105
California Association of Nurseries and Garden Centers, (S) 1794–1795
California Association of Pest Control Advisers. Kern County Chapter, (S) 2385
California Association of Winegrape Growers, (U) 109
California Department of Veterans Affairs, (U) 103–104
California Educational Theatre Association, (SS) 2584
California Farm Bureau Scholarship Foundation, (S) 1786, 1805, 1937, 1999, 2051, 2311
California Groundwater Association, (S) 1787, 2339
California Hotel & Lodging Association, (SS) 2559, 2587, 2782
California Interscholastic Federation, (U) 138
California/Nevada/Arizona Automotive Wholesalers' Association, (S) 1789, (SS) 2560
California New Car Dealers Association, (S) 1742
California Nurses Association, (S) 2314
California Park and Recreation Society, (SS) 2558
California Planning Director's Association, (SS) 2779
California Planning Roundtable, (SS) 2914, 2939
California Restaurant Association, (H) 1204–1205
California State Fair, (U) 108, (H) 1206–1207, (S) 1790–1792, 1895, (SS) 2563–2565, 2645
California Teachers Association, (H) 1203
California–Hawaii Elks Association, (U) 110–111
Calvary United Methodist Church, (U) 112
Campus Safety, Health, and Environmental Management Association, (S) 1793, (SS) 2568
CampusDiscovery.com, (U) 113
Canon U.S.A., Inc., (U) 1018
Capital Press Club of Florida, (H) 1182
Cappex.com, LLC, (U) 116
Capstone Corporation, (U) 118
Cardinal Health, (S) 1799
Career College Association, (U) 4, 397
Career Colleges & Schools of Texas, (U) 120
CareFirst BlueCross BlueShield, (S) 1801, (SS) 2571
Cargill, Inc., (S) 1802, (SS) 2572
Carlstrom Family Scholarship and Literacy Fund, (SS) 2574
Carter & Burgess, Inc., (S) 2045
Carter Mario Injury Lawyers, (U) 69
Casualty Actuarial Society, (SS) 2576
Casualty Actuaries of Greater New York, (SS) 2578
Catching the Dream, (U) 276, (S) 2132, (SS) 2821, 2866, 3000
Catholic Healthcare West, (S) 2174
Celgene Corporation, (S) 2348
Center for Education Solutions, (U) 123
Center for Scholarship Administration, Inc., (U) 43, 237, 268, 471, 915
Center for the Advancement of Process Technology, (S) 2336
Central Indiana Community Foundation, (U) 939, (S) 1782, 1990, (SS) 2555, 2740
Certified Angus Beef LLC, (S) 1835
CH2M Hill, (S) 1821, (SS) 2598
ChairScholars Foundation, Inc., (U) 124
Chapel of Four Chaplains, (U) 125, (H) 1214
Charles and Agnes Kazarian Eternal Foundation/ChurchArmenia.com, (S) 1818, 2028, (SS) 2595, 2745
Charles and Lucille King Family Foundation, Inc., (H) 1215
Charlie Trotter Culinary Education Foundation, (H) 1233
Charlie Wells Memorial Scholarship Fund, (S) 1809
Chartered Property Casualty Underwriters Society. Columbus Chapter, (SS) 2579
Chevron Corporation, (S) 1811
Chevy Chase Bank, (SS) 2585
Chi Eta Phi Sorority, Inc., (S) 2174
Chicago Architectural Club, (H) 1202
Chicago Flute Club, (H) 1608
Chicago Lighthouse for People who are Blind or Visually Impaired, (U) 131
Chicago Mercantile Exchange, (H) 1274
Chicano Organizing & Research in Education, (U) 845
Children of Deaf Adults Inc., (U) 594
Chinese American Citizens Alliance, (U) 135
Choice Hotels International, (SS) 2831, 3053
Chopin Foundation of the United States, Inc., (H) 1218
Choristers Guild, (H) 1544
Christian Church (Disciples of Christ), (U) 362
Christian Life Missions, (H) 1540
The Christophers, (H) 1220, 1604
Chronicle of Higher Education, (H) 1240
Chrysler Corporation, (S) 1813
Chrysler Foundation, (S) 1812, (SS) 2593
CHS Foundation, (S) 1814–1816, (SS) 2594
Chuck Levin's Washington Music Center, (H) 1460
Civil Service Employees Insurance Group, (U) 253
Civil War Preservation Trust, (H) 1381
Clarke Sinclair Memorial Archery Scholarship Corporation, (U) 142
Classical Association of New England, (H) 1209, (SS) 2569
Clayfolk, (H) 1261
Club 100 Veterans, (U) 650, 782, 1064, (SS) 2800, 2954
Club Foundation, (SS) 2759
Clyde Russell Scholarship Fund, (U) 143
CME Group, (S) 1753, 2099
CoaguLife, (U) 144
Coast Guard Exchange System, (U) 145
Coast Guard Foundation, (U) 146–147
Coca–Cola Company, (U) 150, 381
Coca–Cola Foundation, (U) 149, 695, (SS) 2602, 2994
Coca–Cola Scholars Foundation, Inc., (U) 151
Cochlear Americas, (U) 335
Colburn–Pledge Music Scholarship Foundation, (H) 1226
Colgate–Palmolive Company, (U) 351
Colin Higgins Foundation, (U) 153
College Assist, (U) 167
College Board, (S) 2340–2341, 2477
College in Colorado, (U) 167
College Planning Network, (U) 1063, (H) 1584, (S) 2383, (SS) 2990
College Scholarships Foundation, (U) 90, 155–157, (SS) 2604, 2922
College Success Foundation, (U) 130, 159, 485, 1074
CollegeNET, (U) 163
Colonial Williamsburg Foundation, (H) 1381
Colorado Commission on Higher Education, (U) 166–168, 170, 172, (SS) 2606
Colorado Department of Higher Education. CollegeInvest, (U) 161–162
Colorado Fiscal Managers Association, (SS) 2992
Colorado Floriculture Foundation, (S) 1828–1830
Colorado Gerontological Society, (SS) 2714
Colorado Nurses Foundation, (S) 1747, 1833, 1992, 2266, 2305
Colorado Restaurant Association, (SS) 2510, 2514, 2605, 2823
Columbus Foundation, (U) 250
Commander William S. Stuhr Scholarship Fund, (U) 174
Commissioned Officers Association of the USPHS Inc., (U) 891
Communities Foundation of Texas, (H) 1286, (S) 1947
Community Bankers Association of Georgia, (SS) 2774
Community Foundation for Greater Atlanta, Inc., (U) 227, 655, (H) 1352, (S) 2041, 2364, 2371, (SS) 2754, 2974
Community Foundation for Greater New Haven, (U) 596
Community Foundation of Gaston County, (U) 416
Community Foundation of Greater New Britain, (SS) 2503
Community Foundation of Muncie and Delaware County, Inc., (U) 220

Community Foundation of Northern Illinois, (S) 2290
Community Foundation of Sarasota County, (SS) 2672
Community Foundation of the Ozarks, (SS) 2711
Concord Review, (H) 1528
Confederation of Oregon School Administrators, (U) 185, 788, (S) 2092, (SS) 2795, 2894
Congressional Medal of Honor Foundation, (U) 564
Congressional Medal of Honor Society, (U) 176
Connecticut Alarm & Systems Integrators Association, (U) 178
Connecticut Architecture Foundation, (H) 1216, 1228, 1559
Connecticut Association of Affirmative Action Professionals, (U) 532
Connecticut Association of Schools, (H) 1201
Connecticut Association of Women Police, (SS) 2608
Connecticut Athletic Trainers' Association, (S) 1838
Connecticut Broadcasters Association, (H) 1229, 1465, 1501, (S) 1839
Connecticut Building Congress, (S) 1840
Connecticut Business Educators Association, (SS) 2972
Connecticut Community Foundation, (H) 1575, (SS) 2801
Connecticut Department of Higher Education, (U) 117, 177, 179, 182, (S) 2452, (SS) 2609, 3035
Connecticut Junior Soccer Association, (U) 180
Connecticut National Guard Foundation, Inc., (U) 181
Connecticut Nurses' Association, (S) 1780, 1841
Connecticut PTA, (SS) 2767, 2898
Connecticut Sexual Assault Crisis Services, Inc., (SS) 2684
Connecticut Sun Foundation, (U) 96
Connecticut Tree Protective Association, Inc., (S) 1842
Connecticut Women's Golf Association, (U) 804, 836
Conservation Districts of Iowa, (S) 1843
Construction Management Association of America, (S) 1844, 1935, (SS) 2610, 2678
Construction Specifications Institute. Grand Rapids Chapter, (S) 1967
Construction Specifications Institute. Maine Chapter, (H) 1139, (S) 1652
Construction Specifications Institute. Richmond Chapter, (S) 2211
Continental Society, Daughters of Indian Wars, (SS) 2611
ConvaTec, (U) 398
Cook Inlet Region, Inc., (H) 1210, (S) 1853, (SS) 2570, 2617
Coordinating Council for Women in History, (H) 1381
Corporation for the Promotion of Rifle Practice and Firearms Safety, Inc., (U) 140
Costco Wholesale, (U) 186, 997
Council for Advancement and Support of Education, (U) 1023
Council for Economic Education, (SS) 2856
Council of Citizens with Low Vision International, (U) 303
Council of the Great City Schools, (S) 1917
Courage Center, (U) 187, (S) 1907
Cox Communications. New England, (H) 1466
CPS Human Resource Services, (SS) 3028
C.R. Bard, Inc., (S) 1847
Credit Union Foundation of Maryland and the District of Columbia, (U) 188
Crohn's and Colitis Foundation of America, (U) 398
Croplan Genetics, (S) 1800
Crumley Roberts Attorneys at Law, (U) 189
CSL Behring, (U) 248, 839
The Culinary Trust, (H) 1233
Cumberland Valley Volunteer Firemen's Association, (S) 2061
Cummins, Inc., (S) 1848
Current Surfaces, Inc., (U) 1004
CVS Caremark, (U) 191
CVS/Pharmacy Charitable Trust, (U) 190
Cynthia E. Morgan Scholarship Fund, (S) 1849
Cystic Fibrosis Scholarship Foundation, (U) 192
Czech Center Museum Houston, (U) 533
Daedalian Foundation, (S) 1850, 1960, 2048
Dairy Management Inc., (U) 882, (S) 1851, 2164, 2183, (SS) 2869
Dale Schroeder Charitable Trust, (U) 194
Dallas Foundation, (H) 1221, (S) 2045
Daniels Fund, (U) 197
Daughters of the American Revolution. Arizona State Society, (H) 1419, (S) 2074
Daughters of the American Revolution. Colorado State Society, (H) 1319, (S) 2430, (SS) 2721
Daughters of the American Revolution. Michigan State Society, (U) 874
Daughters of the American Revolution. Missouri State Society, (U) 651, (H) 1541, (SS) 2747, 2944
Daughters of the American Revolution. National Society, (U) 32, (H) 1219, 1247, 1408, 1464, (S) 1804, 1854, 2141, (SS) 2637, 2652, 2658, 2828
Daughters of the American Revolution. New York State Organization, (H) 1234
Daughters of the American Revolution. Washington State Society, (H) 1548
Daughters of the Cincinnati, (U) 199
David and Dovetta Wilson Scholarship Fund, Inc., (U) 646, (H) 1412, (S) 1953, (SS) 2538, 2691, 2757
David S. Ishii Foundation, (U) 1121, (H) 1441
Davidson Institute for Talent Development, (U) 200
Davis–Putter Scholarship Fund, (U) 201
Decision Critical, Inc., (S) 2217
Delaware Association of School Administrators, (SS) 2623
Delaware Community Foundation, (U) 358, (H) 1351, 1620, (S) 1813, 2111
Delaware Engineering Society, (S) 2047, 2347
Delaware Higher Education Commission, (U) 203–207, 210, 277, 569, (S) 1862, 2054, (SS) 2590, 2624
Delaware Solid Waste Authority, (S) 2054
Delaware State Education Association, (SS) 2592
Delmar Cengage Learning, (S) 1864, 2174
Delta Dental Foundation of Vermont, (S) 2416
Delta Faucet Company, (S) 1865
Delta Gamma Foundation, (S) 1866, (SS) 2625
Delta Kappa Gamma Society International. Alpha Rho State Organization, (SS) 2614, 2647
Delta Kappa Gamma Society International. Kappa State Organization, (SS) 2492
Delta Kappa Gamma Society International. Lambda State Organization, (H) 1410
Delta Kappa Gamma Society International. Mississippi Alpha Gamma Chapter, (SS) 2504
Delta Kappa Gamma Society International. Pi State Organization, (SS) 2696
Delta Kappa Gamma Society International. Theta State Organization, (SS) 2536
DeMolay and Pine Tree Youth Foundation, (U) 208
Denny's, (U) 370
Design Automation Conference, (S) 2264
DEW Construction Corporation, (S) 1875
Dillon Music, Inc., (H) 1460
Direct Marketing Association of Washington, (SS) 2764
Disabled American Veterans, (U) 422
Disabled Workers Committee, (U) 212
Dixie Boys Baseball, Inc., (U) 83
Dixie Softball, Inc., (U) 215
Dixie Youth Baseball, Inc., (U) 216
DKF Veterans Assistance Foundation, (U) 217
Dow Jones & Company, (H) 1601, (SS) 3003
D.P. Associates Inc., (U) 673
DuBose Associates, Inc., (H) 1216
Dunkin' Brands, Inc., (U) 229, (SS) 2873
D.W. Simpson & Company, (SS) 2640
Easter Seals South Carolina, (U) 233
Eastman Kodak Company, (H) 1238, 1252
Ecolab, (SS) 2644
Eden Autism Services, (SS) 2646
Education Assistance Corporation, (S) 1852, (SS) 2615
Educational Foundation for Women in Accounting, (SS) 2654, 2829, 2947, 3052
Educational Research Center of America, Inc., (U) 247
Educational Testing Service, (U) 1003, (S) 2337–2338
E.I. duPont de Nemours and Company, Inc., (S) 1891
El Pomar Foundation, (SS) 2884
Electronic Document Systems Foundation, (H) 1256, 1258, 1496, (S) 1898, 1902, 2239, (SS) 2649, 2656, 2909
Electronic Security Association, (U) 240
Electronic Security Association of Indiana, (U) 239
Eli Lilly and Company, (S) 1903
Elie Wiesel Foundation for Humanity, (H) 1259
Elizabeth Anne Carlson Memorial Scholarship Trust Fund, (H) 1260
Elizabeth Nash Foundation, (U) 241
Ellis Music Company, (H) 1535
Elsevier Science Ltd., (S) 2174
Emergency Nurses Association, (S) 2153, 2205, 2217
Emergency Nurses Association. New York State Council, (S) 2205
Energy Solutions, (S) 1908

Energy Telecommunications and Electrical Association, (S) 2451, (SS) 3034
Engineers' Society of Western Pennsylvania, (S) 2057
Entomological Society of America, (S) 1764, 2360
Epsilon Sigma Alpha International, (U) 28, 86, 91, 202, 251, 280, 353, 414, 421, 441, 449, 461, 517, 527, 581, 609, 624, 637, 722, 771, 797, 802, 847, 885, 899, 903–905, 991, 1081, (H) 1245, (SS) 3054
E–Publishing Group, LLC, (S) 1836
Ernst & Young LLP, (U) 370
Evangelical Methodist Church, (H) 1432
Evangelical Press Association, (H) 1263
Everly Scholarship Fund, Inc., (U) 258
Executive Women International, (U) 261, (SS) 2664
Explosive Ordnance Disposal Memorial, (U) 267
ExxonMobil Corporation, (S) 1917
ExxonMobil Foundation, (S) 1737
Fabricators and Manufacturers Association, International, (S) 2222–2223
Factor Support Network Pharmacy, (U) 584, 595
Family, Career and Community Leaders of America. Texas Association, (SS) 2597
Farmers Insurance, (U) 138
Fashion Group International of Washington, (H) 1611
Federal Communications Bar Association, (H) 1264, (S) 1918
Federal Employee Education and Assistance Fund, (U) 270
Federal Reserve Bank of Boston, (SS) 2603
Federal Reserve Bank of Dallas, (SS) 2667
Federal Reserve Bank of Kansas City, (SS) 2668, 2841
Federal Reserve Bank of New York, (SS) 2603
Federal Reserve Bank of Richmond, (SS) 2603
Federal Reserve Bank of St. Louis, (SS) 2841
The Fellowship of United Methodists in Music and Worship Arts, (H) 1266
Fenwal Inc., (S) 1636
Finlandia Foundation. New York Metropolitan Chapter, (U) 728, (H) 1356
Fireside Catholic Publishing, (H) 1268, (SS) 2669
First Catholic Slovak Union of the United States and Canada, (U) 994–995
First Cavalry Division Association, (U) 273
First Command Educational Foundation, (U) 221, 274
First Freedom Center, (H) 1269
First Interstate Bank, (SS) 2938
First Marine Division Association, (U) 275
Fisher Communications, (H) 1271
Fisher House Foundation, (U) 890
Fleet Reserve Association, (SS) 2670
Fleishman–Hillard International Communications, (H) 1362
Fletcher "Buster" Brush Memorial Scholarship Fund, (U) 278
Flexographic Technical Association, (H) 1267, 1542, (S) 1920, 2304
Flicker of Hope Foundation, (U) 279
Floriculture Industry Research and Scholarship Trust, (S) 1746
Florida Association for Media in Education, (U) 283
Florida Association of Educational Data Systems, (S) 1886, 2460
Florida Association of State and Federal Educational Program Administrators, (U) 269
Florida Bankers Association, (SS) 2673–2674
Florida Department of Education, (U) 281–282, 284, 286–289, 291, 1091
Florida Engineering Society, (S) 1856, 1909, 1922–1923, 2283
Florida Engineers in Construction, (S) 1924
Florida Federation of Garden Clubs, Inc., (S) 2434
Florida Fund for Minority Teachers, Inc., (SS) 2612, 2675
Florida Institute of Consulting Engineers, (S) 1925
Florida Nurserymen, Growers and Landscape Association. Action Chapter, (S) 1929
Florida Nurses Association, (S) 1666, 1877, 1926
Florida State Elks Association, (U) 290
Florida Surveying and Mapping Society, (S) 1927
Forcht Group of Kentucky, (U) 931
Ford Family Foundation, (U) 294–295
Ford Motor Company, (U) 293, (S) 1930, (SS) 2676
Formal Specialists, Ltd., (U) 30
Forward Face, (U) 297
Foundation for Amateur Radio, Inc., (U) 298, 1125, (H) 1382, 1527, (S) 1817, 1892, 2087, 2279, (SS) 2781
Foundation for Ashley's Dream, (U) 71
Foundation for College Christian Leaders, (U) 137
The Foundation for Enhancing Communities, (U) 815
Foundation for Individual Rights in Education, (U) 307
Foundation for Rural Service, (U) 299
Francis Ouimet Scholarship Fund, (U) 300
Frankenmuth Mutual Insurance Company, (SS) 2913
Franklin and Eleanor Roosevelt Institute, (H) 1381
Freedom Alliance, (U) 306
Freedom Forum, (H) 1147, 1276
Freedom Foundation of Minnesota, (SS) 2482
Freedom from Religion Foundation, (H) 1277, 1294, 1632
Friday Morning Music Club, Inc., (H) 1360
Friends of Nursing, (S) 1938
Friends of Oregon Students Fund, (SS) 2681
From the Top Music Studio, (H) 1574
The Fund for American Studies, (H) 1538
The Fund for Theological Education, Inc., (H) 1598
The Fund for Veterans' Education, (U) 992
Gallagher Koster, (S) 1939
Gamewardens of Vietnam Association, Inc., (U) 308
Gap, Inc., (H) 1199, (SS) 2551
Garden Club Federation of Massachusetts, Inc., (S) 2423
Garden Club of America, (S) 1945, 2073
Garden Writers Association, (H) 1282, (S) 1941
Garmin International, (S) 1942
Gay, Lesbian and Allies at Dow Employee Network, (U) 332
Gen and Kelly Tanabe, (U) 311
General Aviation Manufacturers Association, (S) 1883, 2027
General Dynamics, (U) 370, (H) 1456, (S) 2171, (SS) 2863
General Federation of Women's Clubs of Connecticut, (U) 823, (SS) 2635
General Federation of Women's Clubs of Massachusetts, (U) 1105
General Federation of Women's Clubs of Virginia, (U) 535
General Mills Foundation, (U) 997
General Motors Corporation, (S) 1949–1950, (SS) 2689
General Motors Corporation. Women's Retail Network, (SS) 2620
Geoffrey Foundation, (U) 318
Geophysical Society of Alaska, (S) 1952
George and Donna Nigh Institute, (SS) 2690
George Bartol Memorial Scholarship Fund, (U) 319
George C. Marshall Foundation, (H) 1381
George Mason University. Department of Music, (H) 1460
George Washington Foundation, (U) 322
Georgia Association of Broadcasters, Inc., (H) 1251
Georgia Association of Homes and Services for Children, (U) 122
Georgia Electronic Life Safety & Systems Association, (U) 324
Georgia Press Association, (H) 1290
Georgia Student Finance Commission, (U) 323, 325–326, 328–329, 373–374, (SS) 2582, 2929
Georgia Trust, (H) 1181, 1324, 1342, 1458
Geospatial Information & Technology Association. New England Chapter, (S) 1971
Geospatial Information & Technology Association. Pacific Northwest Chapter, (S) 2242
Gibson Foundation, (H) 1173
Glenn Miller Birthplace Society, (H) 1293, (SS) 2697
Global Automotive Aftermarket Symposium, (S) 1961, (SS) 2699
Goldman Sachs, (SS) 2700
Goldman Sachs Foundation, (SS) 2856
Golf Course Superintendents Association of America, (S) 2329
Good Samaritan Foundation, (S) 1962
Google Inc., (S) 1963–1964
Government Information Technology Executive Council, (S) 1966
Governor's Coalition for Youth with Disabilities, (U) 97
Grand Lodge A.F. & A.M. of Wyoming, (U) 1116
Grand Lodge of Free & Accepted Masons of the State of Florida, (U) 841
Grand Lodge of Iowa, A.F. & A.M., (U) 336
Grand Lodge of Minnesota, A.F. & A.M., (U) 314, 605
Grand Lodge of Missouri, A.F. & A.M., (U) 884, (S) 2312, (SS) 2952
Grand Lodge of Ohio, Free & Accepted Masons, (U) 337
Grand Rapids Community Foundation, (H) 1404, (S) 2060, (SS) 3029
Great Comebacks Award Program, (U) 398
Great Minds in STEM, (S) 1640, 1772–1773, 1799, 1811, 1848, 1872, 1984–1985, 1991, 2055, 2097, 2101, 2157–2158, 2176, 2215, 2301, 2334, 2414, 2432
Great Plains Education Foundation, (S) 1852, (SS) 2615
Great Western Bank, (S) 1852, (SS) 2615
Greater Cedar Rapids Community Foundation, (U) 496

Greater Kanawha Valley Foundation, (U) 101, 256, 469, 482, 877, 1080, 1110, (S) 1754, 1968, 2090, (SS) 2541, 3040
Greater Kansas City Community Foundation, (U) 246, 446
Greek Orthodox Archdiocese of America, (H) 1284, 1377, (S) 1954, 2076, (SS) 2692, 2777
Green Mountain Water Environment Association, (S) 1969
Griffith Insurance Education Foundation, (SS) 2567, 2579–2580, 2677
Grifols, (U) 248
Group Photographers Association, (U) 338
Guardian Life Insurance Company of America, (U) 331
Guide Dogs for the Blind, (U) 225
Gulfstream Park, (S) 2277
Handler Manufacturing, Inc., (S) 1871
Handweavers Guild of America, Inc., (H) 1241, 1315
The Harris Foundation, (S) 1917
Harry Hampton Memorial Wildlife Fund, Inc., (H) 1353, (S) 1974, 2436
Hartford Foundation for Public Giving, (U) 348, 532, (SS) 2684
Hartford Whalers Booster Club, (U) 348
Hawaii Association for Health, Physical Education, Recreation and Dance, (H) 1305, (SS) 2709
Hawaii Association of Broadcasters, Inc., (H) 1306
Hawai'i Hotel & Lodging Association, (SS) 2601
Hawaiian Civic Club of Honolulu, (U) 350
HDR Engineering, Inc., (S) 1978
Health Foundation for the Americas, (S) 2002
Healthcare Financial Management Association. West Virginia Chapter, (SS) 3040
Healthcare Information and Management Systems Society. National Capital Area Chapter, (S) 2181, (SS) 2868
Hearing Bridges, (U) 611
Hellenic Professional Society of Illinois, (U) 360
Hellenic Professional Society of Texas, (U) 361
Helping Hands Foundation, (U) 363
Hemophilia Federation of America, (U) 364
Hemophilia Health Services, (S) 2328
Hemophilia of North Carolina, (S) 1765
Hendricks County Community Foundation, (S) 1900
Henry David Thoreau Foundation, (S) 1986
Herb Society of America. South Texas Unit, (S) 2106
Herb Society of Nashville, (S) 1987
Herff Jones, Inc., (U) 835, (H) 1314
Heritage Fund–The Community Foundation for Bartholomew County, (U) 530, (SS) 2641
H.H. Harris Foundation, (S) 1988
Highmark Inc., (S) 1989
Hispanic Association of Colleges and Universities, (H) 1199, (S) 1654, 1812, 1949, 2098, 2161, 2402, (SS) 2551, 2593, 2719, 2855, 2900, 3024, 3026
Hispanic College Fund, (U) 370, 879, 910, (S) 1964, 2159, 2401, 2415, (SS) 2532, 2805, 3009
Hispanic IT Executive Council, (S) 1991
Hispanic Scholarship Fund, (U) 154, 293, 310, 351, (S) 1751, 1950, 1997, 2000, 2110, 2152, 2209, 2269, 2271, 2276, 2413, 2453, (SS) 2539, 2689, 2700, 2718, 2724–2725, 2802, 2845, 2887, 2923, 3008, 3036
History Channel, (H) 1381
Hitachi Foundation, (U) 1122
H–Mart, (U) 371
HNTB Companies, (S) 2045
Hoehl Family Foundation, (U) 783
Holland & Knight Charitable Foundation, Inc., (H) 1316
Home Builders Association of Metropolitan Portland, (H) 1317, (S) 1994
Home Depot, (SS) 2719
Honolulu Star–Advertiser, (H) 1441
Hoosier State Press Association Foundation, (H) 1320
Hoover Presidential Library Association, Inc., (U) 404
Horatio Alger Association of Distinguished Americans, Inc., (U) 375
Hormel Foods Corporation, (S) 1997, (SS) 2724
Hospitality Sales and Marketing Association International, (SS) 2726
Houston International Film and Video Festival, (H) 1624
Houston Symphony, (H) 1332
Houston Underwater Club, Inc., (S) 2332
HP Hood LLC, (U) 372
HSBC Bank USA, (S) 2174
HSBC–North America, (U) 997, (S) 2000, (SS) 2725
Humane Society of the United States, (S) 2335
Hyatt Hotels & Resorts, (SS) 2728
Ian James Wallace Scholarship Fund, (H) 1326
Idaho State Board of Education, (U) 383–388, 867, (S) 2004, (SS) 2729
Idaho State Broadcasters Association, (H) 1327, 1616, (S) 2450, (SS) 2730, 3033
Illinois Community College System Foundation, (S) 2009, 2112, (SS) 2732
Illinois Conservation Foundation, (S) 2007
Illinois Council of Teachers of Mathematics, (S) 2322, (SS) 2959
Illinois Department of Veterans' Affairs, (U) 393
Illinois Lumber and Material Dealers Association, (S) 2010
Illinois Nurses Association, (S) 2011
Illinois. Office of the State Treasurer, (U) 389, (S) 2008
Illinois Professional Land Surveyors Association, (S) 2012–2013
Illinois PTA, (SS) 2796
Illinois Restaurant Association, (SS) 2735
Illinois Sheriffs' Association, (U) 395
Illinois State Board of Education, (U) 390
Illinois Student Assistance Commission, (U) 391–392, 394, 396, (SS) 2733, 2736, 2833
Illinois Tool Works, Inc., (S) 2032
Illinois Trappers Association, (S) 2287
Immune Deficiency Foundation, (U) 248
Independence Excavating, (S) 2014
Independent College Fund of Maryland, (U) 175, 399, 951, (H) 1456, (S) 1801, 2171, (SS) 2540, 2571, 2585, 2792, 2863, 2865
Independent College Fund of New Jersey, (S) 1767, 1847, 2348, (SS) 2808
Independent Colleges of Washington, (U) 92, 186, 382, 933, 1000, (H) 1619, (SS) 2938, 3043
Independent Insurance Agents of Illinois, (SS) 2737
Independent Insurance Agents of Ohio, (SS) 2579, 2677
Indiana Black Expo, Inc., (U) 381
Indiana Broadcasters Association, (H) 1333, 1532
Indiana Construction Association, (S) 1782, 1990, (SS) 2555
Indiana Department of Transportation, (S) 2018
Indiana Health Care Foundation, Inc., (S) 2015
Indiana State Teachers Association, (U) 495, (SS) 2616
Indianapolis Association of Black Journalists, (H) 1409
Indianapolis Press Club Foundation Inc., (H) 1425, 1590
InfoComm International, (H) 1336, (S) 2026
Infusion Nurses Society, (S) 2217
Inova Health System, (S) 2021
Institute for Global Environmental Strategies, (S) 2382
Institute for Humane Studies at George Mason University, (H) 1325, (SS) 2727
Institute for Land Information, (S) 2053
Institute for Public Relations, (H) 1213, (SS) 2577
Institute for Supply Management, (SS) 2932
Institute for Thermal Processing Specialists, (S) 2030
Institute of Electrical and Electronics Engineers. Nuclear and Plasma Physics Society, (S) 1724, 2240
Institute of Food Technologists, (S) 2022–2023
Instrumentation, Systems, and Automation Society, (S) 1810, 2031, 2296
Insurance Professionals of Columbus Ohio, (SS) 2579
Intel Corporation, (S) 2024–2025, (SS) 2742–2743
Interlochen Arts Camp, (H) 1460
Intermarkets, Inc., (H) 1335
International Association of Black Actuaries, (SS) 2744
International Association of Fire Chiefs, (U) 309, 355
International Association of Lighting Designers, (H) 1589
International Council of Air Shows, (S) 2027
International Council of Community Churches, (U) 436
International Dairy–Deli–Bakery Association, (H) 1328, (S) 2006, (SS) 2731
International Documentary Association, (H) 1238
International Foodservice Editorial Council, (H) 1330
International Franchise Association, (SS) 2831–2832
International Furnishings and Design Association, (H) 1297, 1337, 1394, 1543, 1594, (SS) 2998
International Housewares Association, (H) 1331
International Interior Design Association, (H) 1383
International Order of the King's Daughters and Sons, (S) 1980
International Petroleum Technology Institute, (S) 2254
International Scholarship and Tuition Services, Inc., (U) 6, 72, 100, 369, 870, 881, (S) 2328, 2400
International Textile and Apparel Association, (H) 1191
International Trumpet Guild, (H) 1460
Inter–Tribal Council of AT&T Employees, (U) 402

Intertribal Timber Council, (S) 2398
Iowa Arts Council, (H) 1340
Iowa Broadcasters Association, (H) 1521
Iowa Girls High School Athletic Union, (U) 232, 869
Iowa High School Music Association, (SS) 2793
Iowa Hospital Association, (S) 2029
Iowa Motor Truck Association, (U) 403, (S) 2479
Iowa Narcotics Officers Association, (SS) 2746
Iowa Section PGA of America, (U) 129
Iowa. Treasurer of State, (U) 865
ITT Corporation, (H) 1341
J. Edgar Hoover Foundation, (S) 2033, (SS) 2749
J. Spargo and Associates, (S) 2035, (SS) 2750
J. Willard and Alice S. Marriott Foundation, (U) 370, (SS) 2805
J.A. and Flossie Mae Smith Scholarship Fund, (S) 2036
J.A. Henckels International, (H) 1233
Jack and Jill Foundation of America, (U) 408
Jack J. Isgur Foundation, (SS) 2751
Jack Kent Cooke Foundation, (U) 409
James Alan Cox Foundation for Student Photographers, (H) 1347
James B. Morris Scholarship Fund, (U) 411
James Beard Foundation Scholarship Program, (H) 1224, 1280, 1348–1349, 1388, (SS) 2752
James F. Byrnes Foundation, (U) 412
James F. Lincoln Arc Welding Foundation, (S) 1711–1713
James S. Kemper Foundation, (SS) 2778
Janus Foundation, (U) 470
Jeff Krosnoff Scholarship Fund, (U) 420
Jewish Federation of Delaware, (H) 1365, (SS) 2765
Jewish Federation of Greater Washington, (U) 645
Jewish Guild for the Blind, (U) 341
Jewish Social Service Agency of Metropolitan Washington, (U) 424, 645
Jewish War Veterans of the U.S.A., (U) 234
JHM Hotels, Inc., (SS) 2935
JoAnne Robinson Memorial Scholarship Fund, (H) 1359
John Bayliss Broadcast Foundation, (H) 1361
John Edgar Thomson Foundation, (U) 429
John F. Kennedy Library Foundation, (SS) 2928
John Gyles Education Center, (U) 430
John I. Haas, Inc., (U) 431
Johns Hopkins University. Center for American Indian Health, (U) 672
Johnson & Johnson Medical, Inc., (S) 1683, 2174, 2274
Jon C. Ladda Memorial Foundation, (U) 435
Joseph A. Holmes Safety Association, (S) 2056
Joshua David Gardner Memorial Scholarship Endowment, Inc., (U) 438
Jostens Publishing Company, (H) 1367
Journal of Women's History, (H) 1381
Journalism Education Association, (H) 1368, 1373, 1459, 1572, (SS) 2770
Joyce A. Chaffer Trust, (H) 1369
JPMorgan Chase, (SS) 2788
Julia Child Fund, (H) 1233
Julius & Esther Stulberg Competition, Inc., (H) 1370
Kaiser Permanente, (S) 2174
Kalos Kagathos Foundation, (H) 1572
Kansas Association of Broadcasters, (H) 1371
Kansas Association of Health Care Executives, (S) 2068
Kansas Board of Regents, (U) 444–445, 447–448, 450–453, (S) 2070, (SS) 2776
Kansas City Associated Equipment Distributors, (S) 2067
Kansas Department of Social and Rehabilitation Services, (U) 447
Kansas Hospital Association, (S) 2068
Kansas Hospital Human Resources' Association, (S) 2068
Kansas Restaurant and Hospitality Association, (SS) 2775
Kansas Scholastic Press Association, (H) 1373
Kansas Sunshine Coalition for Open Government, (H) 1375
Kansas Wildscape Foundation, Inc., (H) 1568, (S) 2365
Kaplan, Inc., (U) 1018
Kappa Alpha Mu, (H) 1227
Kappa Alpha Psi Fraternity. Washington (DC) Alumni Chapter, (U) 454
KATU–TV, (H) 1378
Ke Ali'i Pauahi Foundation, (U) 350, 653, (S) 2291
Kentucky Association for Pupil Transportation, (U) 458
Kentucky Association of Professional Surveyors, (S) 2078
Kentucky Board of Nursing, (S) 2079
Kentucky Broadcasters Association, (H) 1303
Kentucky Burglar & Fire Alarm Association, (U) 459
Kentucky Department of Veterans Affairs, (U) 265, 462
Kentucky Fire Commission, (U) 460
Kentucky High School Athletic Association, (U) 828, 931
Kentucky/Indiana Automotive Wholesalers Association, (S) 1958, (SS) 2695
Kentucky National Insurance Company, (U) 931
Kentucky Turfgrass Council, (S) 2080
KFC Corporation, (U) 466
Kidney & Urology Foundation of America, (U) 467, 696
Kids' Chance of Indiana, Inc., (U) 468
Kids' Chance of West Virginia, Inc., (U) 469
Kimball International, Inc., (H) 1383
Kit Faragher Foundation, (U) 470
Kitsap Quilters' Quilt Guild, (H) 1385
Knights of Pythias, (H) 1386
Knights of Pythias of Indiana, (U) 472
Knights Templar of Vermont, (U) 1038
Kohl's Department Stores, Inc., (U) 473
KPMG Foundation, (SS) 2654
Kraft Foods, Inc., (U) 211
Kurt Weill Foundation for Music, Inc., (H) 1405
Kurzweil Foundation, (U) 225–226, 228, 292, 415, (S) 1721, 1889, 1913, 2077, (SS) 2523, 2663, 2885, 2946
Kyle Lee Foundation, Inc., (U) 475
L3 Communications, (U) 673, (S) 1936
Ladies Auxiliary of the Fleet Reserve Association, (U) 476–477
Ladies of Imani, (U) 478
Ladies Professional Golf Association, (U) 211, 521, 824
Lagrant Foundation, (H) 1389, (SS) 2787
Lamey–Wellehan Shoes, (U) 479
The Land Conservancy of New Jersey, (S) 2310
Landau Uniforms, (S) 2174
Landmark Media Enterprises LLC, (H) 1390
Landscape Architecture Foundation, (H) 1232, 1255, 1307, 1391, 1491, 1525, 1567, (S) 1846, 1897, 1977, 2085, 2232, 2280, 2363
Latino Media Association. Seattle Chapter, (H) 1477
Lavallee Brensinger Architects, (H) 1393
Law Enforcement Education Program, (SS) 2789
Lebanese American Heritage Club, (U) 487
Lee–Jackson Foundation, (H) 1396
Legacy, Inc., (S) 2088, (SS) 2790
Legg Mason, Inc., (SS) 2792
Lesbian, Bisexual, Gay and Transgendered United Employees (LEAGUE) at AT&T Foundation, (U) 486
Liggett–Stashower, Inc., (H) 1237
Lime, (S) 1963
Lincoln Community Foundation, (U) 743, 1083
Lincoln Forum, (H) 1511
Linda Lael Miller Scholarships, (U) 493
Little People of America, Inc., (U) 494
Livestock Publications Council, (H) 1274
Livingston Symphony Orchestra, (H) 1403
Lockheed Martin Corporation, (U) 62, 370, (H) 1456, (S) 2097–2098, 2171, (SS) 2863
Los Angeles Philharmonic, (H) 1200
Lotte Lehmann Foundation, (H) 1174
Louise Tumarkin Zazove Foundation, (U) 497
Louisiana Baptist Convention, (H) 1407
Louisiana Department of Veterans Affairs, (U) 498
Louisiana Life Safety & Security Association, (U) 501
Louisiana Office of Student Financial Assistance, (U) 499–500, 502–503, (S) 2300
Louisiana State Nurses Association, (S) 2151
Lucy C. Ayers Foundation, Inc., (S) 2104
The Lullaby Guild, Inc., (H) 1392
Lyme Academy College of Fine Arts, (H) 1455
Magic Rock Entertainment, (H) 1238
Maine. Bureau of Veterans' Services, (U) 513
Maine Community Foundation, (U) 514, (H) 1222, 1299, (SS) 2596, 2913
Maine Education Services, (U) 507–508, (S) 2107
Maine. Finance Authority, (U) 510–512, 735–736, 936, (SS) 2651, 2799
Maine. Legislative Information Office, (U) 507

Maine Metal Products Association, (S) 2107
Maine State Golf Association, (U) 509
Mainely Character, (U) 515
ManTech International Corporation, (S) 2134, (SS) 2824
Manufacturing Jewelers and Suppliers of America, Inc., (H) 1438
Marathon Oil Corporation, (S) 2110, (SS) 2802
Marine Corps Heritage Foundation, (H) 1381
Marine Corps League, (U) 522
Marine Corps Scholarship Foundation, Inc., (U) 368, 523
Marine Corps Tankers Association, (U) 428
Marine Technology Society, (S) 2156, 2244
Marriott International, Inc., (SS) 2832
Marsh & McLellan, (SS) 2806
Mary M. Gooley Hemophilia Center, (SS) 2547
Maryland Association for Health, Physical Education, Recreation and Dance, (H) 1420–1421, (SS) 2810–2811
Maryland Association of Family and Consumer Sciences, (SS) 2809
Maryland, Delaware, and District of Columbia Elks Association, (U) 539
Maryland Higher Education Commission, (U) 376–377, 540–546, (S) 1808, 2117–2118, (SS) 2813
Maryland–Delaware–D.C. Press Association, (H) 1429
Massachusetts AFL–CIO, (SS) 2814
Massachusetts Amateur Sports Foundation, (U) 1034
Massachusetts Association of Land Surveyors and Civil Engineers, Inc., (S) 2109
Massachusetts Broadcasters Association, (H) 1149, 1424
Massachusetts Department of Higher Education, (S) 2122
Massachusetts Elks Association, (U) 553–554
Massachusetts Healthcare Human Resources Association, (S) 2135
Massachusetts Hospital Association, (S) 2135
Massachusetts Office of Student Financial Assistance, (U) 330, 427, 549–552, 555–562, 807, 935, (S) 2120–2121, (SS) 2815–2818
MasterCard, (U) 370
Material Handling Industry of America, (S) 2136, (SS) 2825
Mayo Clinic, (S) 1777
McCormick Foundation, (H) 1208, 1278
McKelvey Foundation, (SS) 2884
McKesson Foundation, (S) 2129
McLean Contributionship, (S) 2130
McNeil Consumer and Specialty Pharmaceuticals, (S) 2400
MCT Campus, (H) 1531
Media Action Network for Asian Americans, (H) 1413
Medical Education Technologies, Inc., (S) 1936
Mercer LLC, (SS) 2820
Merck Company Foundation, (S) 2002
Merck Institute for Science Education, (S) 2002
MetLife Corporation, (S) 2133, (SS) 2822
Metropolitan Opera, (H) 1426
Michael Baker Corporation, (S) 2137
Michigan Association for the Education of Young Children, (SS) 2830
Michigan Association of Family and Consumer Sciences, (SS) 2662
Michigan Association of Recreation Vehicles and Campgrounds, (S) 1975, (SS) 2706
Michigan Association of State and Federal Program Specialists, (U) 547
Michigan Commission on Law Enforcement Standards, (U) 575
Michigan Council of Nursing Education Administrators, (S) 2150
Michigan Council of Teachers of Mathematics, (S) 2144, (SS) 2835
Michigan Department of Treasury, (U) 571–572, 579–580
Michigan Elks Association, (U) 573
Michigan Green Industry Association, (S) 2138
Michigan League for Nursing, (S) 2150
Michigan Manufactured Housing Association, (S) 1975, (SS) 2706
Michigan Press Association, (H) 1430
Michigan Society of Professional Engineers, (S) 2139
Michigan State Troopers Assistance Fund, (U) 577
Michigan State Youth Soccer Association, (U) 578
Mid–Atlantic Association for Employment in Education, (SS) 2613, 2958
Midwest Roofing Contractors Association, (SS) 2850
Midwestern Higher Education Commission, (U) 582
MIGIZI Communications, Inc., (H) 1270, (S) 2439
The Mikkelson Foundation, (S) 2384
Military Family Support Trust, (U) 587
Military Officers Association of America, (U) 35
Milk Processor Education Program, (U) 882
Miller Brewing Company, (U) 652, 997
Minnesota Association of Administrators of State and Federal Education Programs, (U) 505, (SS) 2786
Minnesota Association of Townships, (U) 599
Minnesota Broadcasters Association, (H) 1350
Minnesota Department of Human Services, (U) 601
Minnesota Masonic Charities, (U) 604, 863, 1090
Minnesota Office of Higher Education, (U) 597–598, 600, 602, 606, 608, 610
Minnesota Soybean Research and Promotion Council, (S) 2142–2143
Miss America Pageant, (U) 612–613, 843
Mississippi Association of Broadcasters, (H) 1411
Mississippi Municipal League, (SS) 2838
Mississippi Office of Student Financial Aid, (U) 616–619, 737, (S) 2145–2147, (SS) 2836–2837, 3045
Mississippi Power Company, (SS) 2838
Mississippi State Veterans Affairs Board, (U) 615
Mississippi United Methodist Foundation, (U) 218
Missouri Association of Fairs & Festivals, (S) 2148
Missouri Association of Rural Education, (SS) 2839
Missouri Broadcasters Association, (H) 1435
Missouri Business and Professional Women's Foundation, Inc., (U) 621
Missouri Cheerleading Coaches Association, (U) 563
Missouri Council on Economic Education, (SS) 2841
Missouri Department of Elementary and Secondary Education, (U) 627, (SS) 2843–2844
Missouri Department of Higher Education, (U) 3, 518, 622–623, 625–626, (S) 2149, (SS) 2840
Missouri Middle School Association, (SS) 2524
Missouri Photo Workshop, (H) 1227
Missouri School of Journalism, (H) 1227
Missouri Sheriff's Association, (SS) 2762
Missouri Society of Professional Surveyors, (S) 2298
Missouri State Thespians, (H) 1436–1437, (SS) 2842
Missouri United Methodist Foundation, (U) 218
The Mitchell Institute, (U) 900
Mohair Council of America, (H) 1452
Momeni Foundation, (U) 628
Monsanto Company, (S) 1837, 2152, (SS) 2845
Monster.com, (S) 2153
Montana Association of Symphony Orchestras, (H) 1439
Montana Guaranteed Student Loan Program, (U) 629, 631–635, 638–640, 947–948, (S) 2154
Montana National Guard, (U) 636
Montana. Office of the Commissioner of Higher Education, (U) 630
Montana State Elks Association, (U) 1086, (H) 1440, (SS) 2846
Montgomery Symphony Orchestra, (H) 1192
Moody's Foundation, (SS) 2603
Moose International, Inc., (U) 644
Morgan Stanley, (SS) 2847–2848
Morris J. and Betty Kaplun Foundation, (H) 1442
Morris K. Udall and Stewart L. Udall Foundation, (S) 2155, (SS) 2849
Most Worshipful Grand Lodge of Washington, F.&A.M., (U) 1068
Motor & Equipment Manufacturers Association, (S) 1961, (SS) 2699
Motorist Assurance Program, (S) 1961, (SS) 2699
The Motorists Insurance Group, (SS) 2567
Motorola Foundation, (U) 309, 886, (S) 2432
Mount Olivet United Methodist Church, (U) 647
Multicultural Foodservice & Hospitality Alliance, (SS) 2896
Musica de Filia Girlchoir, (H) 1222, (SS) 2596
MYI Consulting, (S) 2432
NAACP Legal Defense and Educational Fund, (U) 366
Najera Consulting Group, Inc., (S) 2157
Nancy Larson Foundation, Inc., (SS) 2853
NASCAR, (S) 2161, (SS) 2855
Nashville Area United Methodist Foundation, (U) 218
Nation Institute, (H) 1329
National Academy of Television Arts & Sciences. Upper Midwest Chapter, (H) 1602
National Ad 2, (H) 1446
National Air Transportation Foundation, (S) 2262
National Alliance for Hispanic Health, (S) 2002
National AMBUCS, Inc., (S) 2162

National Association Directors of Nursing Administration in Long Term Care, (S) 2361
National Association for Campus Activities, (U) 654
National Association for Surface Finishing, (S) 1653
National Association for the Advancement of Colored People, (H) 1141, (S) 1659, 2001, (SS) 2642
National Association for the Education of Homeless Children and Youth, (U) 490
National Association for the Self–Employed, (SS) 2682
National Association of Abandoned Mine Land Programs, (S) 2163
National Association of Black Journalists. Seattle Chapter, (H) 1477
National Association of Black Narcotic Agents, (SS) 2575
National Association of Broadcasters, (H) 1208, 1278
National Association of Colleges and University Food Services, (SS) 2599
National Association of Farm Broadcasters, (S) 1837
National Association of Farm Broadcasting, (H) 1447
National Association of Federal Education Program Administrators, (U) 406, 426, (SS) 2973
National Association of Hispanic Journalists, (H) 1291, 1415, 1444, 1613
National Association of Independent Colleges and Universities, (U) 1023
National Association of Insurance Women, (SS) 2748, 2806
National Association of Negro Business and Professional Women's Clubs, (U) 658, (H) 1249, 1322, (SS) 2638, 2661
National Association of Negro Musicians, Inc., (H) 1448
National Association of Professional Surplus Lines Offices, Ltd., (SS) 2628
National Association of Secondary School Principals, (U) 835, 840
National Association of State Universities and Land–Grant Colleges, (U) 997, 1023
National Association of the Deaf, (U) 614
National Bison Association, (S) 2388
National Black MBA Association. Charlotte Chapter, (SS) 2583
National Black MBA Association. Raleigh–Durham Chapter, (SS) 2934
National Cattlemen's Foundation, (S) 1753
National Center for American Indian Enterprise Development, (SS) 2509
National Center for Learning Disabilities, (U) 296
National Coalition Against Censorship, (H) 1633
National Collegiate Athletic Association, (U) 213–214, (H) 1276
National Collegiate Cancer Foundation, (U) 659
National Commission for Cooperative Education, (U) 688, (S) 2182
National Council for the Social Studies, (SS) 2622
National Council of Jewish Women. Colorado Section, (U) 171
National Cowboy and Western Heritage Museum, (H) 1363
National Dairy Promotion and Research Board, (S) 2183, (SS) 2869
National Dairy Shrine, (H) 1417, (S) 1851, 2003, 2083, 2124, 2164, (SS) 2784
National Environmental Health Association, (S) 2184
National Fallen Firefighters Foundation, (U) 886
National Federation of Independent Business, (SS) 2884
National Federation of the Blind, (U) 126, 254, 340, 345, 367, 419, 457, 474, 660, (H) 1323, (S) 1998, 2165, (SS) 2650
National Federation of the Blind of Connecticut, (SS) 2550
National FFA Organization, (S) 1837
National Fire Protection Association, (S) 1723, 1956, (SS) 2693
National Football League Players Association, (U) 672
National Forty and Eight, (S) 1955
National Forum for Black Public Administrators, (SS) 3028
National Foundation for Advancement in the Arts, (H) 1631
National Garden Clubs, Inc., (H) 1449, (S) 2166–2167
National Garden Clubs, Inc. South Atlantic Region, (S) 1845
National Geographic Society, (H) 1227
National Hardwood Lumber Association, (SS) 2702
National Head Start Association, (U) 825, (S) 1890
National Hemophilia Foundation, (U) 464, 839
National History Day, (H) 1381
National Hydropower Association, (S) 2168, (SS) 2857
National Independent Automobile Dealers Association, (U) 661
National Indian Gaming Association, (S) 2355, (SS) 2969
National Industries for the Blind, (SS) 2885
National Institute for Labor Relations Research, (H) 1618, (SS) 2517
National Intercollegiate Flying Association, (S) 1883
National Inventors Hall of Fame, (S) 1826
National Italian American Foundation, (U) 662, (H) 1135, 1219, 1450, (SS) 2858
National Junior Classical League, (H) 1137
National Latin Examination, (H) 1451
National Leased Housing Association, (U) 534, 693, 784, 1089
National Lesbian & Gay Journalists Association, (H) 1379, 1400
National Management Association, (SS) 2859
National Market News Association, (S) 2169, (SS) 2860
National Meat Association, (S) 2210
National Merit Scholarship Corporation, (U) 164–165, 183–184, 657, 664
National Military Family Association, Inc., (U) 591–593
National Military Intelligence Association, (SS) 2888
National Military Intelligence Foundation, (SS) 2888
National Multiple Sclerosis Society, (U) 665
National Museum of American Jewish Military History, (H) 1304, (SS) 2707
National Naval Officers Association. Washington, D.C. Chapter, (U) 118, 152, 506, 678, 1065, (S) 2325–2326
National Organization of Black County Officials, (U) 347
National Organization of Italian American Women, (U) 666
National PKU News, (U) 866
National Pork Board, (S) 2265
National Pork Producers Council, (S) 2099
National Press Club, (H) 1453, 1534
National Press Photographers Foundation, (H) 1194, 1227, 1478, 1530, 1569, 1579
National Ready Mixed Concrete Association, (S) 2471
National Restaurant Association Educational Foundation, (H) 1626, (SS) 2485, 2495, 2602, 2862, 2896, 2933, 3057
National Rifle Association of America, (U) 1128, (H) 1288, (S) 2473, (SS) 2895
National Safety Council, (S) 1762
National Scholastic Press Association, (H) 1198, 1231, 1479, 1609
National Science Foundation, (S) 1642, 1919, 2297, (SS) 2942, 2961
National Science Teachers Association, (S) 1891
National Sculpture Society, (H) 1455, 1480
National Society of Accountants, (SS) 2897
National Society of Black Physicists, (S) 2440
National Society of Newspaper Columnists, (H) 1457
National Society of Professional Engineers, (S) 2044
National Society of Professional Surveyors, (S) 2288
National Society Sons of the American Revolution, (H) 1289, 1366
National Space Club, (S) 1885
National Stone, Sand and Gravel Association, (S) 1750
National Strength and Conditioning Association, (S) 2216
National Student Nurses' Association, (S) 1777, 2129, 2173–2174, 2217, 2274
National Symphony Orchestra, (H) 1629–1630
National Telecommunications Cooperative Association, (U) 299
National Tour Association, (SS) 2864
National Trumpet Competition, (H) 1460
National Turf Writers Association, (H) 1627
National Weather Association, (S) 1645, 1722, 1779, 1806, 1858, 1887
National Wild Turkey Federation, (U) 763
National World War II Museum, (H) 1381
Native American Community Board. Native American Women's Health Education Resource Center, (U) 671
Native American Finance Officers Association, (SS) 2852
Native American Journalists Association. Seattle Chapter, (H) 1477
Native Vision, (U) 672
Naumann Trumpets, (H) 1460
Naval Helicopter Association, (U) 673
Naval Historical Foundation, (H) 1381
Naval Special Warfare Foundation, (U) 674
Naval Weather Service Association, (S) 2175
Navy League of the United States, (U) 22, 423, 676, (S) 2263
Navy Supply Corps Foundation, (U) 679–680
Navy Wives Clubs of America, (U) 677, 681
Navy–Marine Corps Relief Society, (U) 333–334, 342, 819, (S) 2058, (SS) 2965
Nazareth Association, (U) 685
NC Reach, (U) 686
Nebraska Academy of Sciences, (S) 1784
Nebraska Bankers Association, (SS) 3041
Nebraska. Department of Veterans' Affairs, (U) 691
Nebraska Elks Association, (U) 690
Nebraska Legal Professionals Association, (SS) 2870
Nebraska Library Commission, (SS) 2537, 2871
Nebraska Press Association Foundation, (H) 1463
Nevada Council on Problem Gambling, (H) 1519
Nevada State Elks Association, (U) 694

New England Association of Collegiate Registrars and Admissions Officers, (U) 320
New England Navy Nurse Corps Association, (S) 2186
New England Newspaper and Press Association, (H) 1468
New England Regional Black Nurses Association, Inc., (S) 1934, 2126
New Hampshire Association of Broadcasters, (H) 1473
New Hampshire Charitable Foundation, (U) 119, 565, 698–699, (SS) 2873
New Hampshire Educational Media Association, (SS) 2874
New Hampshire Postsecondary Education Commission, (U) 700, 703–704, (S) 2191, (SS) 2877
New Hampshire Teachers of Mathematics, (S) 2188–2189, (SS) 2875–2876
New Hampshire Water Pollution Control Association, (S) 2190
New Hope Charitable Foundation, (U) 1127
New Jersey Association for College Admission Counseling, (U) 705
New Jersey Association of Conservation Districts, (S) 2131
New Jersey Bankers Association, (U) 706
New Jersey Burglar & Fire Alarm Association, (U) 707
New Jersey Cheerleading & Dance Coaches Association, (U) 739
New Jersey Department of Environmental Protection. Division of Fish and Wildlife, (S) 2309, (SS) 2951
New Jersey Department of Military and Veterans Affairs, (U) 710
New Jersey Hospital Association, (S) 1981, (SS) 2710
New Jersey Marine Sciences Consortium/New Jersey Sea Grant, (S) 2367
New Jersey Nets and Devils Foundation, (U) 709
New Jersey Press Association, (H) 1469
New Jersey Sports Writers Association, (H) 1471
New Jersey State Elks, (U) 711
New Jersey State Nurses Association, (S) 2095
New Jersey Utilities Association, (U) 712
New Jersey Vietnam Veterans' Memorial, (U) 713
New Jersey Youth Soccer, (U) 417
New Mexico Activities Association, (U) 195, 238, 714–715, 842
New Mexico Association of School Business Officials, (U) 740
New Mexico Broadcasters Association, (H) 1472, (S) 2195, (SS) 2878
New Mexico Department of Veterans' Services, (U) 716, 724
New Mexico Elks Association, (U) 718
New Mexico Engineering Foundation, (S) 1678, 1781, 1785, 1825, 1983, 2072, 2200
New Mexico Higher Education Department, (U) 717, 719–721, 723, (S) 2194, 2197–2198, (SS) 2880
New Mexico Library Association, (SS) 2879
New Mexico Press Women, (H) 1212
New Mexico Professional Surveyors, (S) 2199
New Mexico Society of Professional Engineers, (S) 2200
New West Health Services, (S) 1979
New York Academy of Art, (H) 1455
New York Beef Producers' Association, (S) 2201
New York Community Trust, (U) 343, 352
New York Lottery, (U) 730
New York State Association for Health, Physical Education, Recreation and Dance, (SS) 2634
New York State Automotive Aftermarket Association, (S) 2050, (SS) 2761
New York State Golf Association, (S) 2206, (SS) 2882
New York State Grange, (S) 1867
New York State Higher Education Services Corporation, (U) 725, 727, 729, 731–734, (S) 2207, (SS) 2883
New York Water Environment Association, (S) 2224
The Newseum, (H) 1231
Newspaper Guild–CWA, (H) 1239
Nightingale Awards of Pennsylvania, (S) 2208
Nikon Camera, (H) 1227
Nissan North America, Inc., (U) 737–738, (S) 2209, (SS) 2887
Norfolk Southern Corporation, (SS) 2890
North Carolina Alliance for Athletics, Health, Physical Education, Recreation and Dance, (U) 687
North Carolina Association of Educational Office Professionals, Inc., (U) 745
North Carolina Association of Educators, Inc., (U) 529
North Carolina Business Education Association, (SS) 2763
North Carolina Community Foundation, (U) 744
North Carolina Department of Public Instruction, (SS) 2924
North Carolina. Division of Veterans Affairs, (U) 750
North Carolina Education and Training Voucher Program, (U) 746
North Carolina Electronic Security Association, (U) 748
North Carolina Independent Colleges and Universities, (U) 150
North Carolina Nurses Association, (S) 2062
North Carolina Restaurant and Lodging Association, (SS) 3015, 3042
North Carolina Sheriffs' Association, (SS) 2891
North Carolina State Education Assistance Authority, (U) 413, 747, 749, 751, 1016, (S) 2212–2213, (SS) 2683, 2891–2892, 2930
North Carolina Teaching Fellows Commission, (SS) 2893
North Carolina United Methodist Foundation, (U) 218
North Dakota Board of Nursing, (S) 2214
North Dakota Department of Career and Technical Education, (U) 752–753
North Dakota Department of Public Instruction, (U) 752–753
North Dakota. Department of Veterans Affairs, (U) 754
North Dakota University System, (U) 752–753, 755–758
North Georgia United Methodist Foundation, (U) 218
North Texas Tollway Authority, (S) 2045
Northeast Bank, (U) 515
Northeast Human Resources Association, (SS) 2872
Northern California DX Foundation, Inc., (U) 689
Northern Indiana Community Foundation, (U) 407
Northern Virginia Community Foundation, (H) 1335
Northrop Grumman Corporation, (H) 1456, (S) 1668, 2171, 2215, (SS) 2863
Northwest Journalists of Color, (H) 1477
Northwest Scholastic Press, (H) 1156
Northwest Women in Educational Administration, (SS) 2894
Northwestern Vermont Vietnam Veterans of America, (U) 760
Novo Nordisk Inc., (U) 838
Novo Nordisk Pharmaceuticals, Inc., (U) 761
NuFACTOR Specialty Pharmacy, (U) 249
Nursing Foundation of Pennsylvania, (S) 2038
Nursing Foundation of Rhode Island, (S) 2221
NYSARC, Inc., (S) 1725, 2040, (SS) 2768
Oak Ridge Institute for Science and Education, (S) 1874, (SS) 2627
Octapharma, (U) 248
Office Depot, (SS) 2900
Ohio Academy of Science, (S) 2226
Ohio Association of Family and Consumer Sciences, (SS) 2901
Ohio Board of Nursing, (S) 2227
Ohio Board of Regents, (U) 765, 769–770, (S) 2227
Ohio Burglar & Fire Alarm Association, (U) 764
Ohio Business Teachers Association, (SS) 2902
Ohio Classical Conference, (H) 1482, (SS) 2903
Ohio Educational Library Media Association, (SS) 2899
Ohio Elks Association, (U) 766
Ohio Environmental Education Fund, (S) 2226
Ohio Environmental Health Association, (S) 1957
Ohio Insurance Institute, (SS) 2579
Ohio Newspapers Foundation, (H) 1483–1485
Ohio Nurses Association, (S) 2319–2320, 2395
Oklahoma Association of Broadcasters, (H) 1488
Oklahoma City Advertising Club, (H) 1487
Oklahoma City Community Foundation, (U) 89, 380, 780
Oklahoma City Gridiron Foundation, (H) 1186, 1254, 1345, 1358
Oklahoma Council of Public Affairs, (SS) 2904
Oklahoma Foundation for Excellence, (U) 772
Oklahoma Heritage Association, (H) 1489, (SS) 2906
Oklahoma. Physician Manpower Training Commission, (S) 2228–2229
Oklahoma Press Association, (H) 1490
Oklahoma Ready Mixed Concrete Association, (S) 2230
Oklahoma State Regents for Higher Education, (U) 773–779, 852, (SS) 2690, 2905, 2957
Oklahoma United Methodist Foundation, (U) 218
Omaha Volunteers for Handicapped Children, (S) 2233, (SS) 2907
Oncology Nursing Certification Corporation, (S) 2234
Oncology Nursing Society, (S) 2063, 2217, 2234–2235, 2299
Oncology Practice Alliance, Inc., (S) 2235
One Family, Inc., (U) 781
Optimist International, (U) 785–787
Order of the Eastern Star. Grand Chapter of Washington, (H) 1612, (SS) 3032
Order Sons of Italy in America, (U) 912, (H) 1564, (SS) 2715, 2766
Oregon AFL–CIO, (SS) 2908
Oregon Association of Broadcasters, (H) 1493
Oregon Association of Nurseries, (S) 1819–1820, 2219
Oregon Association of Student Councils, (U) 788
Oregon Collectors Association, (SS) 2708

Oregon Community Foundation, (U) 198, 222, 820, (H) 1346, 1384, (S) 1822, 2086, 2273, (SS) 2753
Oregon Dairy Women, (U) 790
Oregon Department of Human Services. Children, Adult and Families Division, (U) 209, 789
Oregon Department of Veterans' Affairs, (U) 792
Oregon Farm Bureau, (S) 2236
Oregon Fire Marshal's Association, (S) 2185
Oregon Journalism Education Association, (H) 1156
Oregon Lions Sight & Hearing Foundation, (U) 1123
Oregon Music Hall of Fame, (H) 1495
Oregon Nurses Association, (S) 2238
Oregon State Elks Association, (U) 798
Oregon Student Assistance Commission, (U) 81, 198, 209, 222, 294–295, 519, 789, 791, 795–796, 820, 832, 1079, (H) 1300, 1346, 1384, 1474, 1494, (S) 1755, 1822, 2065–2066, 2086, 2185, 2273, 2458–2459, (SS) 2681, 2708, 2753, 2886, 2908
Organ Transplant Awareness Program of New Mexico, (S) 1757
Organization for Autism Research, (U) 892
Orphan Foundation of America, (U) 686
Orphan Foundation of America Scholarships, (U) 746
Oscar P. Stone Research Trust Fund, (S) 1842
Oticon, Inc., (U) 901
Outdoor Advertising Association of America, Inc., (H) 1272, (SS) 2953
Outdoor Writers Association of America, (H) 1197
OutputLinks, (H) 1496, (S) 2239, (SS) 2909
Overseas Press Club, (H) 1497
Ozarka Spring Water, (S) 1916
P. Buckley Moss Society, (U) 42, (H) 1498, (SS) 2772
Pacific Egg and Poultry Association, (S) 2456
Pacific Resources for Education and Learning, (SS) 2910
Papa John's International, Inc., (U) 801
Parapsychology Foundation, Inc., (SS) 2655, 2943
Parents, Families and Friends of Lesbians and Gays, (U) 252, 332, 418
Patsy Takemoto Mink Education Foundation for Low–Income Women and Children, (U) 805
Paul and Phyllis Fireman Charitable Foundation, (U) 781
Pauline C. Young Scholarship Foundation, (U) 1126
Pearl Harbor Submarine Officers' Wives' Club, (U) 95
peermusic Companies, (H) 1503
Pendleton Woolen Mills, (H) 1452
Penguin Group (USA) Inc., (H) 1561
Pennsylvania AFL–CIO, (SS) 2916
Pennsylvania Associated Press Managing Editors, (H) 1526
Pennsylvania Association of School Nurses and Practitioners, (S) 2249–2250
Pennsylvania Burglar & Fire Alarm Association, (U) 809
Pennsylvania Business Education Association, (SS) 2918
Pennsylvania Department of Education, (S) 2251
Pennsylvania Department of Public Welfare, (U) 810
Pennsylvania Federation of Democratic Women, (U) 812
Pennsylvania Higher Education Assistance Agency, (U) 803, 810, 813–814, 816–817, (S) 2251
Pennsylvania Library Association, (SS) 2552
Pennsylvania. Office of the Deputy Adjutant General for Veterans Affairs, (U) 811
Pennsylvania Public Relations Society, (H) 1504
Pennsylvania State System of Higher Education Foundation, Inc., (H) 1302, (S) 1989, 2297, 2362, (SS) 2942
Pennsylvania Women's Press Association, (H) 1505
Pennsylvania Wrestling Coaches Association, (U) 818
Percussive Arts Society, (H) 1506, 1545
Perennial Plant Association, (S) 2252
Persian Scholarship Foundation, (H) 1507, (SS) 2919
Pfizer Inc., (U) 821, (S) 2174
Phi Theta Kappa, (U) 149, 695, 822, (S) 1936
Philip Jaisohn Memorial Foundation, (U) 359, 371, (H) 1244
Phillips Foundation, (U) 871
Phoenix Suns Charities, (U) 945
Physio–Control, Inc., (S) 2259
Pi Lambda Theta, (SS) 2996
Piano Arts of Wisconsin, (H) 1510
Pilot International, (S) 1752, 2261
PinkRose Foundation, Inc., (U) 827
Pittsburgh Foundation, (S) 1703, 2359
Pizzagalli Construction Company, (S) 2081
Playboy Magazine, (H) 1512
Plumbing–Heating–Cooling Contractors–National Association, (U) 548, (S) 1699, 1706, 1774, 1865, 2255–2256
PNC Bank, (U) 828
Polish Arts Club of Buffalo Inc., (H) 1513
Polish Roman Catholic Union of America, (U) 830
Polonia Foundation of Ohio, Inc., (U) 831
Possible Woman Foundation International, (U) 833, (S) 2448
Poynter Institute for Media Studies, (H) 1227
Presbyterian Church (USA), (U) 667, 670, (H) 1185, 1547, 1573, (S) 2369, (SS) 2976
Presbyterian Church (USA). Synod of the Northeast, (U) 432
Press Club of New Orleans, (H) 1515
PricewaterhouseCoopers LLP, (SS) 2808, 2931
Prince Kuhi'o Hawaiian Civic Club, (H) 1516, (SS) 2925
Princess Cruises & Tours, (SS) 2785, 2926
Princess Grace Awards, (H) 1235, 1587
Print and Graphics Scholarship Foundation, (H) 1445, 1517, (SS) 2854
Printing and Imaging Association of MidAmerica, (H) 1475, (SS) 2889
Printing and Publishing Council of New England, (H) 1467
Printing Industries of Wisconsin, (H) 1499, (SS) 2911
Printing Industry of Minnesota, (H) 1518
Procter & Gamble Company, (S) 2271
Professional Aviation Maintenance Association, (S) 1778, 2272
Professional Bowlers Association, (U) 88
Professional Construction Estimators Association, (S) 2372
Professional Engineers of Colorado, (S) 1831
Professional Golfers' Association. Minnesota Section, (U) 607
Professional Golfers' Association of America, (SS) 2927
Professional Insurance Agents Association of Ohio, (SS) 2579
Professional Logging Contractors of Maine, (S) 1993
Professional Photographers of Washington, (H) 1615
Proton Energy Systems, (S) 2275
Prudential Insurance Company of America, (U) 840
Public Relations Society of America. Detroit Chapter, (H) 1243
Public Relations Society of America. Puget Sound Chapter, (H) 1321, 1546
Public Relations Student Society of America, (H) 1362, 1520
Putnam Investments, (U) 781
Quaker Oats, (U) 851
Qualcomm Incorporated, (S) 2276
Quill and Scroll, (H) 1257, 1285, 1341
Quimby Pipe Organs, Inc., (H) 1142
Race for Education, (H) 1627, (S) 1729, 2277–2278, 2447
Radio Club of America, Inc., (S) 2279
Radio Television Digital News Foundation, (H) 1211, 1253, 1380, 1406, 1431, 1523
Rain Bird Corporation, (H) 1525, (S) 2280
Random House Children's Books, (H) 1481
The RARE Foundation, (U) 259
Raytheon Corporation, (U) 673, (H) 1456, (S) 2055, 2171, (SS) 2863
RDW Group, Inc., (H) 1529
Rebekah Assembly of Texas, (U) 405
Recording for the Blind and Dyslexic, (U) 525, 536
Renee B. Fisher Foundation, (U) 596
Retail Design Institute, (H) 1339
Rhode Island. Division of Veterans Affairs, (U) 860
Rhode Island Foundation, (U) 806, 859, (H) 1355, 1438, 1529, (S) 1677, 1899
Rhode Island Golf Association, (U) 434, (S) 1783, (SS) 2556
Rhode Island High School Hockey Coaches Association, (U) 219
Rhode Island Higher Education Assistance Authority, (U) 160
Rhode Island Pilots Association, (S) 2285
Rhode Island Society of Professional Land Surveyors, (S) 2260
Richard and Susan Smith Foundation, (U) 781
Risk & Insurance Management Society. Central Ohio Chapter, (SS) 2579–2580
Robert S. Shumake Family Foundation, (U) 868
Robert Wood Johnson Foundation, (S) 2477
Rockwell Collins, Inc., (S) 2301
Rocky Mountain Coal Mining Institute, (S) 2302–2303
Rocky Mountain Water Environment Association, (S) 1760, 2394
Rolls–Royce Corporation, (S) 1807
Ronald McDonald House Charities, (U) 6, 72, 369, 870
Roothbert Fund, Inc., (U) 872

Rosa L. Parks Scholarship Foundation, (U) 873
Rotary District 5520, (S) 1757
Rowling, Dold & Associates LLP, (SS) 2947
Roy J. Carver Charitable Trust, (U) 121
Rural American Scholarship Fund, (U) 876
Ryan Mullaly Second Chance Fund, (U) 878
Sabertec, LLC, (S) 1768
Sabian, Ltd., (H) 1545
Saginaw Community Foundation, (S) 2366
Sallie Mae Fund, (U) 879, 1018
Salvatore Taddonio Family Foundation, (U) 880
Sam's Club, (SS) 2884
San Antonio Area Foundation, (U) 649
Sanford Health, (S) 1852, (SS) 2615
Sangamon County Community Foundation, (U) 1109
Sarah Klenke Memorial, (SS) 2955
S.C. International, Ltd., (S) 2316, (SS) 2956
Schering–Plough Corporation, (U) 887, (H) 1549, (S) 2317
Schilke Music Products, (H) 1460
Scholarship America, (U) 77, 85, 128, 191, 229, 235, 473, 613, 699, 992, 1018, (H) 1224, 1280, 1348–1349, 1388, (S) 2168, 2411, 2437, (SS) 2752, 2857, 3006
Scholastic, Inc., (H) 1552–1553
School Band and Orchestra Magazine, (H) 1164
Science Applications International Corporation, (S) 2325–2326
Scottish Rite Foundation of Washington, (U) 895
Scotts Company, (S) 2329
Scripps Howard Foundation, (H) 1217, 1359, 1554
Scudder Association, Inc., (H) 1555, (S) 2330, (SS) 2962
Seabee Memorial Scholarship Association, (U) 897
Seaspace, Inc., (S) 2332
Seattle Foundation, (U) 76, 742, (H) 1196, (S) 1881
Seattle Mariners Women's Club, (SS) 2543
Seattle Post–Intelligencer, (H) 1196
Sertoma International, (U) 901
Seventeen Magazine, (H) 1558
SFM Foundation, (U) 902
Shaw Industries, (S) 2334
Shell Oil Company, (S) 2336–2338, 2432
Shook Construction, (S) 1973, (SS) 2705
ShurTech Brancs, LLC, (U) 941
Sickle Cell Disease Association of America, (U) 463
Siemens Foundation, (S) 2340–2341, 2391, (SS) 2995
Siemens Healthcare Diagnostics, (S) 2342–2344
Sigma Corporation of America, (H) 1560
Sigma Theta Tau International, (S) 2174
SIRS Mandarin, (SS) 2622
Sister Cities International, (H) 1562
Skandalaris Family Foundation, (U) 907, (SS) 3064
Society for American Baseball Research, (H) 1381
Society for Applied Anthropology, (S) 2253, (SS) 2920
Society for History in the Federal Government, (H) 1381
Society for Imaging Science and Technology, (S) 2281
Society for Range Management, (S) 2119
Society for Range Management. Texas Section, (S) 1761
Society for Science & the Public, (S) 2024–2025, (SS) 2742–2743
Society for Technical Communication. Northeast Ohio Chapter, (H) 1486
Society for Technical Communication. Rocky Mountain Chapter, (H) 1287
Society for Technical Communication. Southwestern Ohio Chapter, (H) 1486
Society of American Military Engineers. Albuquerque Post, (S) 1678, 1781
Society of American Military Engineers. Anchorage Post, (S) 1758
Society of American Military Engineers. Arkansas Post, (H) 1168, (S) 1716
Society of American Military Engineers. New Jersey Post, (H) 1470, (S) 2193
Society of American Military Engineers. Phoenix Post, (H) 1509, (S) 2257
Society of American Military Engineers. San Antonio Post, (S) 2313
Society of Automotive Analysts, (SS) 2964
Society of Daughters of the United States Army, (U) 908
Society of Diagnostic Medical Sonography, (S) 2331, 2397
Society of Exploration Geophysicists, (S) 2387
Society of Gastroenterology Nurses and Associates, Inc., (S) 2294
Society of Mayflower Descendants in the State of Connecticut, (U) 909
Society of Mayflower Descendants in the State of New Jersey Scholarship, (H) 1563
Society of Petroleum Engineers, (S) 1970
Society of Petroleum Engineers. Powder River Basin Section, (S) 2267
Society of Petrophysicists and Well Log Analysts Foundation, (S) 2346
Society of Professional Journalists, (H) 1279
Society of Professional Journalists. Colorado Professional Chapter, (H) 1312
Society of Professional Journalists. Connecticut Professional Chapter, (H) 1195
Society of Professional Journalists. Fort Worth Professional Chapter, (H) 1583
Society of Professional Journalists. Indiana Professional Chapter, (H) 1334
Society of Professional Journalists. Kansas Professional Chapter, (H) 1190, 1311, 1374–1375, 1418, 1428
Society of Professional Journalists. Maryland Professional Chapter, (H) 1423
Society of Professional Journalists. Minnesota Professional Chapter, (H) 1433
Society of Professional Journalists. Virginia Professional Chapter, (H) 1605
Society of Professional Journalists. Washington, D.C. Professional Chapter, (H) 1556
Society of Professional Journalists. Western Washington Chapter, (H) 1477, 1617
Society of Sponsors of the United States Navy, (SS) 2965
Society of the First Infantry Division, (U) 317, 492
Society of Women Engineers, (S) 2032, 2349, 2370
Society of Women Engineers. Central Indiana Section, (S) 1807
Society of Women Engineers. Central New Mexico Section, (S) 1825
Society of Women Engineers. DelMar Section, (S) 2347
Sodexho Foundation, (U) 910
Soil and Water Conservation Society. South Carolina Chapter, (S) 2352
Soil and Water Conservation Society. Texas Council of Chapters, (S) 2377
Soil and Water Conservation Society. Virginia Chapter, (S) 2424
SOLE–The International Society of Logistics, (S) 2350
Solvay Pharmaceuticals, Inc., (U) 911
Sonare Winds, (H) 1460
South Carolina Commission on Higher Education, (U) 489, 800, 913–914, 916–918
South Carolina Department of Health and Environmental Control, (S) 2427
South Carolina Department of Natural Resources, (S) 1974
South Carolina Division of Veterans Affairs, (U) 921
South Carolina Governor's Committee on Employment of People with Disabilities, (H) 1565
South Carolina Governor's Cup Billfishing Series, (S) 2436
South Carolina Higher Education Tuition Grants Commission, (U) 920
South Carolina Junior Golf Foundation, (U) 915
South Carolina Law Enforcement Officers' Association, (U) 893
South Carolina Nurses Foundation, Inc., (S) 1915, 2243, 2351, 2427
South Carolina. Office of the Adjutant General, (U) 917
South Carolina Press Association, (H) 1522
South Carolina State Department of Education, (H) 1166
South Carolina State Fair, (U) 919
South Carolina Vocational Rehabilitation Department, (H) 1565
South Dakota Association of Towns and Townships, (U) 896
South Dakota Board of Nursing, (S) 2220
South Dakota Board of Regents, (U) 305, 528, 922–926, (SS) 2516, 2701
South Dakota CPA Society, (SS) 2966
South Dakota Department of Labor, (S) 1852, (SS) 2615
Southeastern Theatre Conference, Inc., (H) 1557
Southern Ohio Music Company, (H) 1460
Southern Regional Education Board, (U) 932
Southwest Indian Agricultural Association, (S) 1888
Sowers Club of Nebraska, (U) 929–930
Specialty Equipment Market Association, (S) 1961, 2333, (SS) 2699, 2963
SPIROL International Corporation, (S) 2356, (SS) 2970
State Bar of Michigan, (SS) 2791
State Farm Insurance Companies, (SS) 2732
State Student Assistance Commission of Indiana, (U) 301, 400–401, (S) 2016–2017, (SS) 2739
State University of New York Financial Aid Professionals, Inc., (U) 946
State University System of Florida, (U) 993
Stay Fit, (U) 354
Stephen Phillips Memorial Scholarship Fund, (U) 938
STERIS Corporation, (H) 1172
Steven M. Perez Foundation, (U) 940
StraightForward Media, (U) 193
Student Press Law Center, (H) 1231
Stu's Music Shop, (H) 1460
Stuttgart Chamber of Commerce, (U) 132
Sunkist Growers, (S) 1745
The Surety Foundation, (SS) 2977

Susan Thompson Buffett Foundation, (U) 950
Swanson Russell Associates, (H) 1298
Symantec Corporation, (S) 2370
T. Rowe Price Foundation, (U) 951
Tag and Label Manufacturers Institute, Inc., (H) 1576, 1597, (SS) 2979
Tailhook Educational Foundation, (U) 952
Talecris Biotherapeutics, (U) 248
Tall Clubs International, (U) 443, 1053
TCF Bank, (U) 1112
TELACU Education Foundation, (U) 953, (H) 1578, (S) 2373, (SS) 2982
Tennessee Burglar & Fire Alarm Association, (U) 955
Tennessee Education Association, (SS) 2632–2633
Tennessee Elks Association, (S) 2374
Tennessee Student Assistance Corporation, (U) 692, 954, 956–962, 1085, (SS) 2983–2984
Terremark Worldwide, Inc., (H) 1140, (SS) 2491
Texas Association for Bilingual Education, (SS) 2716
Texas Association for Education and Rehabilitation of the Blind and Visually Impaired, (SS) 2978
Texas Association of Broadcasters, (H) 1581
Texas Association of Journalism Educators, (H) 1580, (SS) 2986
Texas Christian University. M.J. Neeley School of Business, (SS) 2989
Texas Computer Education Association, (SS) 2937
Texas Conference for Women, (H) 1582, (S) 2376, (SS) 2987
Texas Elks State Association, (U) 964–966, 975
Texas Guaranteed Student Loan Corporation, (U) 128
Texas Higher Education Coordinating Board, (U) 262–264, 588–590, 741, 967–974, 976–980, 984, 986, 988, 990, 1060–1061, 1133
Texas Intercollegiate Press Association, (H) 1357
Texas Knights Templar Education Foundation, (U) 981
Texas Lyceum, (U) 982
Texas Mutual Insurance Company, (U) 983
Texas Nursery and Landscape Association, (S) 2392
Texas. Office of Rural Community Affairs, (S) 2378
Texas Rangers Foundation, (U) 1124
Texas Restaurant Association, (SS) 3023
Texas Society of Professional Surveyors, (S) 2379
Texas State Association of Fire Fighters, (U) 985
Texas Tennis and Education Foundation, (U) 987
Texas Trial Lawyers Association, (U) 989
Texas Vegetation Management Association, (S) 2381
Theodore R. and Vivian M. Johnson Foundation, (U) 993
Through the Looking Glass, (U) 996
Thurgood Marshall College Fund, (U) 868
Thurgood Marshall Scholarship Fund, (U) 652, 997, 1062, (S) 1873, 2133, 2391, (SS) 2822, 2994–2995, 3025
Time Warner Cable, (U) 515
Tire Industry Association, (S) 1961, (SS) 2699
Toledo Community Foundation, Inc., (H) 1600
Tommy Hilfiger Corporate Foundation, (U) 24
Tommy Ramey Foundation, (H) 1593, (SS) 2997
Totem Ocean Trailer Express, (U) 1000
Touchstone Energy All "A" Classic, (U) 1001
Tourism Cares, (SS) 2494, 2513, 2694, 2971, 3063
Tourism Cares for Tomorrow, (SS) 2864
Town of Williston Historical Society, (H) 1595
Township Officials of Illinois, (U) 1002
Toyota Motor Sales, U.S.A., Inc., (U) 523
Toyota USA Foundation, (U) 1003
Transportation Clubs International, (S) 1679, 1868, 1995, 2380, (SS) 2501, 2626, 2722, 2988
Trinity Valley Quilters' Guild, (H) 1596
Troy Douglass Carr Criminal Justice Scholarship Fund, (SS) 3001
Turf and Ornamental Communicators Association, (H) 1592, (S) 2393
Turkish Coalition of America, (H) 1577, (SS) 2980
Tuttle Construction, Inc., (S) 2390, (SS) 2993
Two Ten Footwear Foundation, (U) 1006, (H) 1273
Ty Cobb Educational Foundation, (U) 1007
UCB, Inc., (U) 1008
Ulman Cancer Fund for Young Adults, (U) 898, (S) 1748
UNICO National, (U) 29, 516, 1087, (H) 1588
Unitarian Universalist Association, (H) 1416, 1533
United Automobile, Aerospace and Agricultural Implement Workers of America. Region 8, (SS) 2936
United Church of Christ, (U) 1009
United Commercial Travelers of America, (SS) 3002
United Daughters of the Confederacy. Virginia Division, (U) 378, 1049, (S) 1798, 2114
United Health Foundation, (S) 2401–2402
United Healthcare, (S) 2174
United Hospice Foundation, (S) 2403
United Methodist Church. General Board of Higher Education and Ministry, (U) 25, 231, 344, 858, 1010, 1012–1013, (H) 1434, 1599, (S) 1896, (SS) 2648, 2834
United Methodist Communications, (H) 1398
United Methodist Foundation of Arkansas, (U) 218
United Methodist Foundation of South Indiana, (U) 218
United Methodist Foundation of Western North Carolina, (U) 218
United Methodist Higher Education Foundation, (U) 218, 456, 566, 669, 808, 837, 1011, 1013, (H) 1189, 1248, 1262, 1397, (S) 1756, (SS) 2542, 3007
United Negro College Fund, (U) 310
United Negro College Fund Special Programs Corporation, (S) 2159
United States Institute of Peace, (SS) 2861
United States Olympic Committee, (U) 1024
United States Patent and Trademark Office, (S) 1826
United States Steel Corporation, (S) 1669
United States Tennis Association, (U) 230, 257, 520, 1025–1026
Universities Space Research Association, (S) 2408
University Aviation Association, (S) 1879, 2128, 2262
University Film and Video Foundation, (H) 1252
University Interscholastic League, (U) 998, (H) 1314, 1367, 1610
University of California at Berkeley. Department of Architecture, (H) 1187–1188
University of Missouri at Columbia. Mason Eye Institute, (S) 2318
University of Notre Dame. Department of Computer Science and Engineering, (S) 2323
University of Oregon. School of Journalism and Communication, (H) 1502
University of the Aftermarket, (S) 1961, (SS) 2699
University of Wyoming. Office of Teacher Preparation, (SS) 3060
University Sales Education Foundation, (H) 1601, (SS) 3003
Univision Network, (H) 1415
Upromise, (U) 1018
UPS Foundation, (U) 382, 1019, (S) 2404
Urban League of Nebraska, (U) 1020
Urban League of Nebraska, Inc., (U) 127, 934
Urban Watershed Research Institute, (S) 2405
Urban Watersheds Research Institute, (S) 2406
U.S. Air Force. Office of Scientific Research, (S) 2064
U.S. Air Force. Reserve Officers' Training Corps, (U) 7–10, 140, 244–245, 853–854, (H) 1145, (S) 1671–1673
U.S. Army, (S) 2432
U.S. Army. Corps of Engineers, (S) 2432
U.S. Army. Human Resources Command, (U) 65
U.S. Army. Research Office, (S) 2064
U.S. Army. Reserve Officers' Training Corps, (U) 64, 66–68, 140, 274, 313, 316, 1014, (S) 1720
U.S. Army Women's Foundation, (U) 1021
U.S. Bureau of Reclamation, (S) 1831
U.S. Centers for Disease Control and Prevention, (U) 839
U.S. Central Intelligence Agency, (S) 2432
U.S. Coast Guard, (U) 158, (S) 2432
U.S. Corporation for National and Community Service, (U) 36–38
U.S. Defense Commissary Agency, (U) 890
U.S. Defense Intelligence Agency, (S) 1861, (SS) 2621
U.S. Department of Agriculture, (S) 2407, (SS) 3004
U.S. Department of Agriculture. Animal and Plant Health Inspection Service, (S) 2268, 2315
U.S. Department of Commerce. National Oceanic and Atmospheric Administration, (S) 1910, (SS) 2659
U.S. Department of Defense, (S) 2020, 2327, (SS) 2741
U.S. Department of Education, (U) 61
U.S. Department of Education. Office of Postsecondary Education, (U) 2, 271–272, 864, 944, 1017, (S) 2170, (SS) 2981
U.S. Department of Education. Office of Special Education and Rehabilitative Services, (U) 937
U.S. Department of Energy, (S) 1872–1873
U.S. Department of Homeland Security, (S) 1874, (SS) 2627
U.S. Department of State, (SS) 2991
U.S. Department of Veterans Affairs, (U) 524, 641–643, 834, 857, 949, 1040, 1059

U.S. Fish and Wildlife Service, (H) 1265
U.S. JCI Senate, (U) 1022
U.S. Marine Corps, (U) 140
U.S. National Aeronautics and Space Administration, (S) 1891, 2158–2160, 2172, 2432
U.S. National Archives and Records Administration, (H) 1381
U.S. National Security Agency, (H) 1456, 1570, (S) 2020, 2171, 2368, (SS) 2741, 2863, 2975
U.S. Navy. Naval Education and Training Command, (U) 682–684, (H) 1462, (S) 2177, 2180, 2399, (SS) 2867
U.S. Navy. Naval Personnel Command, (U) 675, (S) 2178, 2218
U.S. Navy. Naval Sea Systems Command, (S) 2176
U.S. Navy. Naval Service Training Command, (U) 140
U.S. Navy. Navy Medicine Manpower, Personnel, Education and Training Command, (S) 2179
U.S. Navy. Office of Naval Research, (S) 2064
U.S. News and World Report, (U) 77
U.S. Office of Personnel Management, (S) 1919
USA Boxing, Inc., (U) 312, (SS) 2819, 2827
USA Funds, (U) 997
USA Today, (U) 822, 882, 1023
USAA Insurance Corporation, (U) 12, 1014
Utah Alarm Association, (U) 1027
Utah Council of Land Surveyors, (S) 2409
Utah Higher Education Assistance Authority, (U) 1028, 1031
Utah Sheriff's Association, (SS) 3005
Utah Sports Hall of Fame Foundation, (U) 850
Utah State Office of Education, (U) 1029
Utah System of Higher Education, (U) 1032–1033
VA Mortgage Center.com, (U) 586
Vanguard Group, Inc., (S) 2411, (SS) 3006
Varian Medical Systems, (S) 2412
Vasa Order of America, (U) 799
Verizon, (U) 175, 1034, (S) 1670, 2414–2415, (SS) 3009
Verizon Federal Network Systems, (H) 1456, (S) 2171, (SS) 2863
Verizon Foundation, (S) 2413, (SS) 3008
Vermont. Child Development Division, (SS) 2586
Vermont Department of Health, (S) 2419–2420
Vermont Foster/Adoptive Family Association, (U) 1035
Vermont Healthcare Human Resources Association, (S) 2418, (SS) 3010
Vermont Music Educators Association, (H) 1535
Vermont/New Hampshire Direct Marketing Group, (SS) 3011
Vermont Police Association, (U) 365, (S) 2282, (SS) 2660
Vermont Principals' Association, (U) 848
Vermont Sheriffs' Association, (SS) 3012
Vermont State Dental Society, (S) 2416
Vermont Student Assistance Corporation, (U) 136, 243, 365, 568, 783, 855, 906, 943, 1035–1037, 1039, (H) 1155, 1176, 1343, 1395, 1595, 1603, (S) 1875, 1905, 1969, 1982, 2081, 2245, 2282, 2416–2420, (SS) 2502, 2528, 2566, 2586, 2660, 2713, 2756, 3010–3012
Vermont Travel Industry Conference, (SS) 3013
Vertical Flight Foundation, (S) 2421
Veterans of Foreign Wars. Ladies Auxiliary, (H) 1628
Veterans of Foreign Wars of the United States, (H) 1606, (SS) 3022
Veterans of Foreign Wars of the United States. Pennsylvania Department, (S) 2038
Vietnam Veterans Group of San Quentin, (U) 1042
Vietnam Veterans of America. Chapter 522, (U) 346
Vietnam Veterans of America. Chapter 753, (U) 760
Vietnam Veterans of America. Wisconsin State Council, (U) 861
VII Corps Desert Storm Veterans Association, (U) 1043
Vincent Bach Brass, (H) 1460
Virgin Islands Board of Education, (U) 236, 491, 963, 1044–1046, (H) 1236, (S) 1682, 1803, 1914, 2438, (SS) 2600, 2619, 2687, 2717, 2780, 2803, 2985, 3027, 3039
Virginia Association for Career and Technical Education, (SS) 3016
Virginia Association for Teachers of Family and Consumer Sciences, (SS) 2712, 2807
Virginia Association of Soil and Water Conservation Districts, (S) 2424
Virginia Athletic Trainers Association, (S) 2425
Virginia Business Education Association, (SS) 2573, 3017
Virginia Department of Education, (SS) 3021
Virginia Department of Social Services, (SS) 3018
Virginia Department of Transportation, (S) 2429
Virginia Department of Veterans Services, (U) 1054
Virginia Electronic Systems Association, (U) 1050
Virginia Foundation for Independent Colleges, (S) 1681, (SS) 2505, 2890
Virginia High School League, (U) 1041
Virginia Nurses Association, (S) 2431
Virginia Police Chiefs Foundation, (U) 1056
Virginia Polytechnic Institute and State University. Department of Forestry, (S) 1945
Virginia Society for Healthcare Human Resources Administration, (SS) 3020
Virginia. State Council of Higher Education, (U) 1047–1048, 1051–1052, 1055, 1057–1058, (SS) 3019
Virginia Transportation Construction Alliance, (S) 2396, 2433
Visa, (SS) 2884
VSA arts, (H) 1607
Wachovia Bank, (SS) 3024
Wachovia Foundation, (SS) 3025
Waioli Corporation, (H) 1414
Walman Optical Company, (S) 2437
Wal–Mart Foundation, (U) 1, 881
Wal–Mart Stores, Inc., (U) 1062, (SS) 3026
Walsworth Publishing Company, (H) 1610
Walt Disney Company, (S) 1891
Walter W. Naumburg Foundation, Inc., (H) 1338, 1461
Warner Norcross & Judd LLP, (SS) 3029
Washington Apple Education Foundation, (U) 465, 583, 759, 1084, (S) 2082, 2241, 2386, 2441, (SS) 2783
Washington Association of Black Journalists, (H) 1614
Washington Association of Vocational Administrators, (U) 826
Washington Burglar & Fire Alarm Association, (U) 1067
Washington Cattle Feeders Association, (S) 2442
Washington Crossing Foundation, (SS) 3030
Washington Higher Education Coordinating Board, (U) 1066, 1069–1070, 1075, (S) 2444–2445, (SS) 3031
Washington Library Media Association, (SS) 3051
Washington Map Society, (H) 1250, (SS) 2639
Washington News Council, (H) 1242, 1313
Washington Post, (H) 1613–1614
Washington Regional Transplant Consortium, (S) 2089
Washington Science Teachers Association, (S) 2248, (SS) 2915
Washington Society of Professional Engineers, (S) 2443
Washington State Association for Justice, (U) 1111, (SS) 3056
Washington State Auto Dealers Association, (H) 1584, (S) 2383, (SS) 2990
Washington State Business and Professional Women's Foundation, (U) 1071–1072
Washington State Department of Health, (S) 2445
Washington State Department of Social and Health Services, (U) 1073
Washington State Elks Association, (U) 224, 437
Washington State Mathematics Council, (S) 2292–2293, (SS) 2940–2941
Washington State Nurses Association, (S) 2446
Washington State PTA, (U) 1076
Washington State Scholarship Foundation, (U) 1077
Washington Workforce Training and Education Coordinating Board, (U) 1066
Waste Management Charitable Foundation, (S) 2448
Watson–Brown Foundation, (U) 1078
Watts Charity Association, Inc., (H) 1275, 1399, (S) 2307, (SS) 2771, 2948
The Weekly, (U) 84
Wells Fargo Bank, (H) 1369, (S) 2453, (SS) 3036–3037
West Virginia Department of Education, (U) 23
West Virginia Elks Association, (SS) 3038
West Virginia Golf Association, (U) 1080
West Virginia Hospitality and Travel Association, (H) 1626, (SS) 3057–3058
Western Art Association, (H) 1295
Western Athletic Scholarship Association, (U) 78, 321, 570
Western Federation of Professional Surveyors, (S) 2455
Western Golf Association, (U) 133
Western Prelacy of the Armenian Apostolic Church of America, (H) 1283, (SS) 2685
Western Reserve Herb Society, (S) 1933, 2457
Westfield Corporation, (H) 1201
WETA–FM90.9, (H) 1629–1630
Wilbur Ellis Company, (U) 1084
The Wildlife Society. New Jersey Chapter, (S) 2309, (SS) 2951
Willa Cather Pioneer Memorial and Educational Foundation, (H) 1476
Willamette Valley Agriculture Association, (S) 2459
William E. Docter Educational Fund, (U) 1088

William Orr Dingwall Foundation, (U) 1092
William Randolph Hearst Foundation, (U) 1015, (H) 1308–1310
Winners' Club, (SS) 3047
Winston–Salem Foundation, (H) 1281, (S) 1940, 2231, 2428
Wipe Out Kids' Cancer, (U) 1124
Wisconsin Association for Food Protection, (S) 1901
Wisconsin Association of Professional Agricultural Consultants, (S) 2465
Wisconsin Auto Collision Technicians Association, Ltd., (S) 2449
Wisconsin Automobile and Truck Dealers Association, (S) 2449
Wisconsin Broadcasters Association, (H) 1621
Wisconsin Congress of Parents and Teachers, Inc., (SS) 2553
Wisconsin Department of Veterans Affairs, (U) 1094, 1096, 1101
Wisconsin Dietetic Association, (S) 2466
Wisconsin Environmental Health Association, Inc., (S) 2467
Wisconsin Higher Educational Aids Board, (U) 1093, 1095, 1097, 1099–1100, (SS) 3048, 3050
Wisconsin Organization of Nurse Executives, Inc., (S) 2470
Wisconsin Paralyzed Veterans of America, (S) 2075, 2225, 2258, 2426
Wisconsin Professional Police Association, (SS) 3049
Wisconsin Ready Mixed Concrete Association, (S) 2471
Wisconsin School Counselor Association, (U) 1112
Wisconsin State Telecommunications Association, (U) 1098
Wisconsin Veterans of Foreign Wars, (S) 2094
WISS & Company, LLP, (SS) 2653
Woman's Auxiliary to the American Institute of Mining, Metallurgical and Petroleum Engineers, (S) 2435
Women in Aviation, International, (S) 1942
Women in Defense, (S) 1996, (SS) 2723
Women of the Evangelical Lutheran Church in America, (U) 31, 889, 1102, (S) 2321
Women's Alabama Golf Association, (U) 1103
Women's Army Corps Veterans' Association, (U) 1104
Women's Golf Association of Massachusetts, Inc., (U) 1082
Women's Overseas Service League, (U) 1106
Women's Southern Golf Association, (U) 1107
Women's Western Golf Foundation, (U) 1113
Woodmansee Scholarship Fund, (U) 1108
Woodrow Wilson National Fellowship Foundation, (SS) 2991
Workers' Compensation Association of New Mexico, (U) 999
Workers Compensation Fund, (U) 488
Workforce Safety & Insurance, (U) 260, 339
World Team Tennis, Inc., (U) 761
World Wide Baraca Philathea Union, (H) 1623, (SS) 3055
Worldstudio Foundation, (H) 1625
Wound, Ostomy and Continence Nurses Society, (S) 2472
Wyoming Association of Public Accountants, (SS) 3059
Wyoming Trucking Association, Inc., (S) 2474, (SS) 3062
Wyoming Veterans Commission, (U) 1114–1115, 1117–1120
Xerox Corporation, (S) 2475
YASME Foundation, (S) 2476
Youbet.com, (H) 1627
Young Ladies' Radio League, (U) 1125
YouthLaunch, Inc., (U) 1129
Yum–o! Organization, (SS) 2933
Yvar Mikhashoff Trust for New Music, (H) 1634
Zonta Club of Bangor, (U) 1130, (SS) 2797, 2851
Zonta Club of Milwaukee, (S) 2480–2481
Zonta Clubs of Louisiana, (U) 1131
Zonta International, (SS) 2755, 3065
Zonta International District 10 Foundation, (U) 875
100 Black Men of America, Inc., (U) 1132
10–10 International Net, Inc., (U) 298
3M Health Care, (S) 2174

Calendar Index

Since most financial aid programs have specific deadline dates, some may have already closed by the time you begin to look for funding. You can use the Calendar Index to identify which programs are still open. To do that, look at the subject categories that interest you, think about when you'll be able to complete your application forms, go to the appropriate months, jot down the entry numbers listed there, and use those numbers to find the program descriptions in the directory. Keep in mind that the numbers cited here refer to program entry numbers, not to page numbers in the book. Note: not all sponsoring organizations supplied deadline information to us, so not all programs are listed in this index.

Unrestricted by Subject Area

January: 25, 28, 55–56, 70, 73, 79, 82, 86–87, 91, 100–101, 113, 143, 193, 200, 202, 251, 255–256, 280, 285, 297, 310, 336, 353, 384, 409, 414, 420–421, 425, 441–442, 449, 461, 469, 471–472, 482, 484, 505, 517, 527, 529, 537, 547, 554, 563, 578, 581, 591–593, 609, 624, 637, 651, 665, 667, 673, 683, 689–690, 697, 722, 744, 766, 771, 797, 802, 825, 833, 847, 861–862, 867, 871–872, 877, 881, 885, 888, 899, 903–905, 915, 926, 954, 957–961, 991, 1006, 1023–1024, 1027, 1032–1033, 1043, 1080–1081, 1085, 1110, 1123

February: 5–6, 9, 22, 31, 35, 52, 54, 72, 76, 78, 80–81, 85, 89, 95, 97, 105, 117, 124, 135, 138, 145, 153–154, 158, 160, 174, 185, 195, 198, 200, 209, 215–216, 219, 222, 224–226, 228, 230–231, 238, 249, 257, 259, 269, 292–295, 299, 303, 321–322, 331, 333–334, 337, 342, 348, 357, 369, 376–377, 380, 387, 391–392, 412–413, 415–416, 422–423, 437, 458, 465–466, 495, 515, 519–520, 528, 530, 534, 538, 540–546, 553, 564, 567, 570, 572, 574, 579, 583, 587, 604, 631–633, 639, 658, 666, 668, 676, 688, 692–694, 705, 710, 714–715, 726, 728, 737, 750, 759, 767, 784, 786, 788–789, 794–795, 799, 819–820, 823, 828, 832, 841–842, 845, 849, 863, 870, 873, 876, 889–890, 893, 908–909, 912, 942, 945, 950, 955, 962, 965, 975, 982, 1002, 1018, 1021, 1025–1026, 1030, 1038, 1066, 1068, 1073, 1076–1079, 1084, 1089–1090, 1098, 1102, 1105–1106, 1113, 1124, 1128–1129, 1132

March: 1, 3, 12, 21, 23, 32, 36, 38, 40, 42–43, 62–63, 69, 71, 83, 92, 94, 106–109, 111, 118, 121, 123, 126–127, 134, 136, 140, 146–148, 152, 161–162, 169, 171, 178, 180–181, 188–190, 192, 199, 201, 208, 210, 218, 220, 227, 229, 234, 237, 239, 243, 248, 252, 254, 261, 267, 270, 281–284, 286, 289, 298, 301, 315, 318, 320, 332, 338, 340, 344–346, 356, 358, 362, 365–368, 370, 372, 379, 395, 403–404, 407–408, 411, 418–419, 424, 428, 431–432, 435, 439, 444, 454, 457, 459, 473–474, 478, 480–481, 496, 501, 506, 509, 518, 523, 531–533, 535, 539, 568, 576–577, 585, 594, 603, 607, 611, 617, 645–647, 649, 653, 656, 660–663, 671, 674, 678–680, 682, 684–685, 707, 712, 718, 739–740, 742, 748, 757, 760, 762, 764, 781, 783, 790, 793, 798, 809, 815–816, 818, 846, 850, 855, 864, 868–869, 874–875, 882, 884, 886, 894–896, 900, 902, 906, 910, 919, 931, 933–934, 938–939, 943, 946, 952–953, 964, 989, 996, 1013, 1020, 1035, 1037, 1041, 1056, 1063, 1065, 1067, 1071–1072, 1074, 1083, 1094, 1103, 1108–1109, 1111, 1122, 1125–1126, 1130

April: 20, 24, 29, 34, 41, 44–45, 58–59, 74, 102, 112, 114, 122, 131, 141–142, 193–194, 196, 206–207, 212, 214, 223, 235–236, 241–242, 250, 253, 258, 268, 276–278, 304, 308, 324, 343, 349, 352, 364, 378, 381, 402, 427, 434, 438, 445, 448, 450, 455, 476–477, 486–487, 491, 494, 507–508, 514, 516, 525–526, 536, 541, 548, 550–551, 555–557, 559, 562, 575, 584, 586, 595–596, 599, 620, 650, 654–655, 699–702, 708, 711, 713, 727, 730–736, 743, 761, 768, 782, 804, 807, 810, 812–814, 817, 826, 836, 838, 844, 848, 856, 858, 879, 887, 892, 897–898, 901, 907, 911, 935–936, 940, 958, 963, 985, 987, 1004, 1008, 1010, 1024, 1044, 1046, 1049–1050, 1064, 1087, 1092, 1104, 1107, 1116, 1121

May: 13, 30, 53, 88, 96, 99, 128, 130, 137, 144, 187, 211, 213, 218, 279, 309, 327, 350, 355, 360, 430, 443, 456, 463–464, 467, 470, 475, 479, 483, 485, 492, 497, 521, 648, 659, 669, 672, 677, 681, 696, 698, 738, 780, 806, 808, 824, 830–831, 837, 839, 859, 865, 878, 891, 927–928, 981, 993, 998, 1009, 1012, 1042, 1053, 1073, 1082, 1086

June: 4, 27, 58–59, 64, 75, 94, 98, 119, 129, 191, 233, 246, 266, 271, 273–274, 313, 316, 329, 341, 347, 391–392, 433, 502–503, 522, 601, 608, 628, 647, 670, 687, 706, 752–753, 770, 773, 776, 785, 787, 800, 805, 821, 920, 941, 944, 1005, 1007, 1014, 1017, 1034, 1088, 1094, 1131

July: 33, 36, 58–59, 116, 193, 247, 311–312, 325, 328, 335, 363, 398, 622, 652, 813–814, 817, 880, 956, 1024, 1057, 1062, 1073

August: 57, 176, 306, 410, 493, 698, 796, 827, 926, 954, 957–961, 997, 1011, 1085

September: 94, 115, 133, 139, 173, 276, 314, 319, 391–392, 402, 490, 504, 552, 616, 618–619, 647, 710, 765, 775, 981, 994–995, 1015, 1127

October: 38, 90, 93, 151, 156, 164, 183–184, 193, 375, 586, 644, 657, 664, 742, 840, 866, 992, 1024, 1075, 1094

November: 8, 58–59, 66, 125, 132, 149, 290, 300, 307, 359, 371, 573, 630, 695, 745, 772, 822, 929–930, 1022, 1057, 1112

December: 26, 39, 68, 77, 84, 94, 155, 157, 176, 197, 232, 296, 302, 351, 354, 361, 363, 397, 405, 417, 621, 647, 698, 763, 800, 835, 1001, 1003, 1034, 1073

Any time: 14, 48–50, 65, 110, 203–205, 244–245, 396, 446, 510–512, 565–566, 623, 642, 675, 750, 853–854, 857, 949, 966, 983, 1036, 1040, 1059, 1096, 1101, 1114–1115, 1117–1120

Humanities

January: 1136–1137, 1142, 1152, 1203, 1209, 1213, 1217, 1220, 1223, 1234, 1239, 1245, 1273, 1290, 1308–1310, 1319, 1340, 1353, 1363–1364, 1387, 1396, 1405, 1410, 1419, 1429, 1451, 1454, 1476, 1494, 1500, 1510, 1514, 1541–1542, 1544, 1548, 1552–1553, 1557, 1565, 1574, 1598, 1614, 1624, 1629–1630

February: 1138, 1144, 1146, 1156, 1166, 1169, 1175, 1179, 1181, 1193–1194, 1197, 1208, 1232–1233, 1246–1247, 1249, 1255, 1257, 1259, 1264, 1266, 1274, 1285, 1296, 1300, 1305, 1307, 1310, 1312, 1322, 1324, 1326, 1332, 1338, 1341–1342, 1346, 1356–1357, 1359, 1367, 1372–1373, 1384, 1389, 1391–1392, 1408, 1416, 1443, 1445, 1449, 1453, 1457–1459, 1462–1463, 1474–1475, 1478–1479, 1481, 1490, 1498, 1502–1503, 1508, 1512, 1517, 1525, 1530, 1534, 1560, 1564, 1567, 1569, 1572, 1579–1580, 1583, 1589, 1592, 1600, 1602, 1609, 1611, 1613, 1620

March: 1135, 1149, 1151, 1154–1155, 1157, 1159, 1168, 1176, 1186–1187, 1201, 1206–1207, 1212, 1215, 1221, 1229, 1241, 1254, 1260, 1263, 1265, 1267, 1279, 1286, 1293, 1295, 1297, 1309–1310, 1314–1315, 1320, 1323, 1327–1328, 1330, 1333, 1337, 1343, 1345, 1351–1352, 1358, 1365, 1382, 1393–1395, 1398, 1402, 1404, 1412, 1421, 1424, 1427, 1433, 1435, 1442, 1445–1446, 1450, 1455, 1465–1466, 1470, 1473, 1482–1486, 1488–1489, 1491, 1495, 1499, 1501, 1516–1519, 1521–1522, 1524, 1527, 1532–1533, 1537–1538, 1543, 1545, 1547, 1563, 1566, 1571, 1575–1576, 1578, 1584, 1586–1587, 1591, 1595, 1597, 1603, 1605, 1610, 1615–1617, 1619, 1623, 1626–1628

April: 1143, 1158, 1165, 1167, 1172, 1190–1191, 1195, 1204–1205, 1216, 1218, 1222, 1226, 1228, 1235–1237, 1242, 1251, 1256, 1258, 1278, 1281, 1284, 1291–1292, 1298–1299, 1302–1303, 1306, 1311, 1313, 1316, 1318, 1321, 1335, 1339, 1344, 1355, 1361, 1369, 1371, 1374–1375, 1377–1378, 1386, 1411, 1414–1415, 1417–1418, 1420, 1422–1423, 1425, 1428, 1440, 1444, 1464, 1468, 1472, 1477, 1496, 1504–1505, 1520, 1526, 1529, 1535–1536, 1540, 1546, 1555, 1559, 1561–1562, 1568, 1585, 1588, 1608, 1612, 1625

May: 1139, 1161, 1163, 1171, 1177, 1189, 1191, 1196, 1199, 1210–1211, 1224, 1248, 1250, 1253, 1262, 1270–1271, 1275, 1277, 1280, 1301, 1317, 1336, 1348–1349, 1380, 1385, 1388, 1397, 1399, 1406, 1431, 1434, 1438, 1441, 1447, 1467, 1480, 1493, 1506, 1509, 1513, 1523, 1550–1551, 1554, 1581, 1622

June: 1182, 1185, 1198, 1231, 1238, 1240, 1252, 1261, 1272, 1294, 1328–1329, 1350, 1366, 1407, 1515, 1531, 1573, 1577, 1582, 1594, 1596, 1601, 1604, 1632

July: 1141, 1238, 1511

August: 1158, 1283

September: 1144, 1174, 1180, 1227, 1328, 1461, 1487

October: 1147, 1160, 1184, 1188, 1202, 1243, 1257, 1285, 1288, 1310, 1334, 1347, 1362, 1368, 1401, 1413, 1439, 1456, 1590, 1593, 1606, 1621, 1631, 1633

November: 1140, 1173, 1219, 1230, 1244, 1269, 1308–1310, 1360, 1403, 1436–1437, 1452, 1469, 1497, 1570, 1607, 1624, 1634

December: 1134, 1148, 1153, 1164, 1170, 1192, 1200, 1214, 1225, 1268, 1276, 1282, 1287, 1304, 1310, 1325, 1328, 1331, 1354, 1370, 1376, 1390, 1430, 1460, 1471, 1507, 1556, 1558, 1618, 1624

Sciences

January: 1643, 1650, 1660, 1684, 1693, 1724–1726, 1754, 1777, 1784, 1800, 1821, 1845, 1852, 1855–1857, 1860, 1874, 1885, 1890–1891, 1908–1910, 1922–1923, 1925, 1943, 1945, 1965–1966, 1968, 1974, 1986, 2022, 2030, 2040, 2042, 2049, 2056, 2063, 2073–2074, 2090, 2095, 2099, 2119, 2129, 2159–2160, 2173–2174, 2180, 2184, 2208, 2217, 2224, 2234–2235, 2259, 2264, 2274, 2283–2284, 2289, 2296, 2299, 2302–2303, 2306, 2319–2320, 2332, 2374, 2378–2379, 2395, 2398, 2404, 2412, 2421, 2429–2430, 2435–2436, 2440, 2444, 2448, 2456, 2462, 2476–2477

February: 1637–1638, 1646–1647, 1656, 1678, 1687, 1689, 1694, 1696, 1698, 1700, 1708, 1714, 1721, 1729–1731, 1744, 1751–1752, 1755, 1757, 1770, 1775–1776, 1785–1786, 1804–1805, 1810, 1822, 1825, 1831, 1837, 1843, 1849, 1854, 1864, 1881, 1884, 1886, 1889, 1893, 1900, 1911, 1913, 1921, 1924, 1927, 1931, 1937, 1944, 1946, 1957, 1971–1972, 1983, 1999–2000, 2002, 2019–2020, 2023, 2031–2032, 2037, 2044, 2051, 2061, 2065–2066, 2068, 2071–2072, 2077, 2082, 2086, 2092, 2100, 2123, 2125, 2127, 2136, 2139, 2141–2143, 2149–2150, 2168, 2185, 2200, 2202–2203, 2213, 2236, 2241, 2252, 2261, 2263, 2268, 2271, 2273, 2275, 2277–2278, 2285, 2290, 2295, 2311, 2315, 2324, 2329, 2337–2338, 2358, 2366, 2370, 2386–2387, 2405, 2423, 2441, 2446–2447, 2453, 2458–2460, 2466, 2474, 2478

March: 1635, 1642, 1663, 1667–1670, 1680, 1683, 1686, 1688, 1703, 1705, 1710, 1719, 1723, 1733, 1735, 1738, 1763, 1767, 1769, 1771, 1779, 1781–1782, 1787, 1789–1793, 1796–1797, 1814–1815, 1817, 1819–1820, 1824, 1827, 1838–1840, 1847, 1862–1863, 1875–1876, 1879, 1883, 1892, 1894–1895, 1905, 1912, 1916, 1933–1934, 1953, 1956, 1958, 1961, 1964, 1969, 1973, 1975–1976, 1980, 1982, 1987, 1990, 2001, 2010–2011, 2014, 2029, 2033–2034, 2045–2046, 2050, 2054, 2060, 2069, 2075, 2081, 2087, 2089, 2093, 2103, 2106, 2108, 2111, 2122, 2126, 2128, 2132, 2145–2147, 2155, 2165, 2190, 2216, 2219, 2222–2223, 2225, 2238, 2242, 2245, 2249, 2258, 2267, 2279, 2291, 2298, 2309–2310, 2312, 2318, 2322, 2325–2326, 2335, 2339, 2348, 2352, 2364, 2367, 2371–2373, 2381, 2390, 2399, 2401, 2406, 2415–2417, 2419–2420, 2422, 2424–2426, 2442–2443, 2451, 2455, 2457, 2467–2469, 2479

April: 1640, 1644, 1651, 1653, 1660–1661, 1664, 1674, 1676–1677, 1682, 1697, 1699, 1706, 1722, 1739, 1745–1746, 1748, 1760–1761, 1765–1766, 1772–1774, 1783, 1788, 1798–1799, 1803, 1807, 1809, 1811, 1813, 1832, 1844, 1848, 1851, 1858, 1865–1867, 1872, 1896, 1899, 1914, 1928, 1932, 1935, 1948, 1967, 1970, 1978–1979, 1984–1985, 1991, 2003, 2018, 2021, 2038–2039, 2052, 2055, 2064, 2067, 2070, 2083, 2094, 2097, 2101, 2107, 2114, 2116, 2120, 2124, 2130, 2132, 2135, 2137–2138, 2140, 2156–2158, 2162, 2164, 2175–2176, 2181, 2187, 2192, 2196, 2206–2207, 2210–2211, 2215, 2221, 2244, 2246, 2248, 2250, 2255–2256, 2270, 2286, 2297, 2301, 2308, 2328, 2333–2334, 2345, 2354, 2356, 2379, 2382, 2384, 2394, 2407–2408, 2414, 2418, 2432–2434, 2437–2438, 2445, 2461, 2463–2464, 2472

May: 1636, 1639, 1645, 1648, 1654–1655, 1662, 1666, 1679, 1701, 1711–1712, 1718, 1734, 1743, 1749–1750, 1762, 1802, 1812, 1826, 1834, 1853, 1859, 1868, 1877, 1887, 1906–1907, 1915, 1917, 1926, 1930, 1939, 1947, 1949, 1959, 1963, 1993, 1995, 2005, 2008–2009, 2015, 2024, 2035, 2062, 2079, 2088, 2098, 2105, 2134, 2144, 2153, 2161, 2163, 2169, 2183, 2186, 2188–2189, 2191, 2204–2205, 2213, 2220–2221, 2226, 2237, 2254, 2287, 2292–2293, 2307, 2316, 2323, 2336, 2349–2351, 2355, 2375, 2377–2378, 2380, 2385, 2392, 2396, 2400, 2402, 2409, 2439, 2480–2481

June: 1671, 1673, 1675, 1695, 1702, 1707, 1713, 1727, 1737, 1740, 1742, 1764, 1768, 1780, 1794–1795, 1808, 1823, 1841, 1853, 1901, 1904, 1929, 1988, 1996, 2059, 2091, 2102, 2118, 2131, 2151, 2194, 2197–2198, 2214, 2228, 2238, 2282, 2314, 2360–2361, 2403

July: 1660, 1850, 1873, 1878, 1903, 1950, 1981, 2048, 2109, 2122, 2133, 2209, 2227, 2233, 2294, 2300, 2331, 2362, 2397, 2413, 2427, 2470

August: 1657, 1704, 1927, 2057, 2113, 2231, 2428

September: 2080, 2096, 2132, 2220, 2238, 2251, 2265, 2341, 2378–2379, 2388, 2391, 2431, 2452, 2475

October: 1641, 1660, 1665, 1681, 1714, 1747, 1753, 1775–1776, 1806, 1833, 1836, 1869–1871, 1880, 1936, 1938, 1992, 2053, 2121, 2152, 2166, 2240, 2243, 2260, 2266, 2297, 2305, 2313, 2342–2344, 2410, 2422, 2472

November: 1685, 1690, 1720, 1728, 1759, 1778, 1834–1835, 1842, 1850, 1861, 1876, 1888, 1942, 1960, 2007, 2012–2013, 2025, 2043, 2078, 2110, 2122, 2230, 2272, 2411, 2454, 2465, 2471, 2473

December: 1649, 1691–1692, 1758, 1853, 1951–1952, 1997, 2027, 2047, 2148, 2191, 2201, 2238, 2251, 2253, 2262, 2269, 2276, 2281, 2316, 2327, 2347, 2353, 2359, 2449

Any time: 1818, 1962, 2028, 2058

Social Sciences

January: 2482, 2537, 2696, 2702, 2718, 2747–2748, 2758, 2762, 2768, 2786, 2806, 2809, 2831, 2859, 2861, 2871, 2879, 2901, 2916, 2928, 3015, 3023, 3030, 3040–3042, 3049, 3053–3054, 3064

February: 2516, 2524, 2526, 2536, 2548–2549, 2553, 2573, 2589, 2591, 2597, 2599, 2614, 2616, 2632–2635, 2641, 2647, 2658, 2661, 2665, 2673–2674, 2681, 2684, 2701, 2708, 2715, 2733, 2736, 2746, 2753, 2766–2767, 2796, 2805, 2828, 2833, 2843, 2856, 2874, 2885, 2894, 2898, 2904, 2908, 2917, 2922, 2932, 2946, 2978, 2991, 2996, 2999, 3013, 3017, 3028

March: 2492, 2495, 2498–2499, 2502, 2515, 2533–2534, 2538, 2554, 2557, 2559, 2561–2562, 2564–2567, 2579, 2587, 2589–2590, 2592, 2602, 2607, 2623–2624, 2642, 2650, 2653, 2660, 2667, 2672, 2677, 2698, 2711, 2716, 2734, 2740, 2756–2757, 2769, 2772, 2774, 2776, 2779, 2782, 2785, 2797, 2801, 2808, 2820, 2826, 2836–2837, 2841, 2851, 2862, 2864, 2866, 2870, 2872, 2896–2897, 2903, 2910, 2914, 2926, 2936, 2938–2939, 2950, 2982, 2992, 3000, 3005, 3011–3012, 3016, 3029, 3045, 3051, 3056, 3058, 3060, 3063, 3065

April: 2487, 2493, 2506–2508, 2510, 2514, 2525, 2532, 2547, 2556, 2576, 2578, 2584, 2588, 2600, 2605, 2608, 2620, 2630, 2640, 2644, 2646, 2652, 2654, 2662, 2668, 2682, 2687, 2712, 2717, 2728, 2751, 2759, 2764, 2773, 2780, 2789, 2793, 2800, 2803, 2807, 2816, 2823, 2829, 2838–2839, 2844, 2866, 2873, 2892, 2899, 2918, 2930, 2935, 2947, 2954–2955, 2972, 2977, 2983–2985, 3000–3001, 3018, 3037, 3039, 3047, 3052

May: 2485, 2488, 2520, 2543, 2552, 2574, 2581, 2622, 2628, 2651, 2673–2674, 2680, 2683, 2700, 2719, 2735, 2744, 2755, 2763, 2771, 2775, 2791, 2847–2848, 2900, 2913, 2933, 2945, 2964, 3007, 3024, 3026, 3046

June: 2497, 2513, 2526–2527, 2537, 2545, 2586, 2601, 2611, 2657, 2679, 2703, 2726, 2737, 2760, 2794, 2815, 2832, 2850, 2871, 2880, 2921, 2924, 2953, 2971

July: 2509, 2582, 2612, 2655, 2675, 2748, 2806, 2818–2819, 2827, 2862, 2902, 2994, 3018, 3025

August: 2490, 2583, 2673–2674

September: 2526, 2550, 2609, 2866, 2912, 3000

October: 2503, 2537, 2548–2549, 2558, 2640, 2714, 2738, 2788, 2852, 2871, 2890, 2893, 2934, 2943, 2989, 3020, 3031

November: 2492, 2612–2613, 2629, 2666, 2670, 2673–2675, 2853, 2888, 2895, 2937, 2958, 2966, 3006, 3018

December: 2487, 2504, 2517, 2579–2580, 2604, 2618, 2671, 2814, 2884, 2931

Any time: 2494, 2595, 2694, 2799, 2965, 3002, 3061

NOTES